Presented to:

Marcus Henderson
Presented to

A new relationship with God
On the occasion of

_12-15-02_
Date

Tanya Kelly-Boye (My Aunt)
By

And what does the Lord require of you?
To act justly and to love mercy and to walk
humbly with your God. Micah 6:8

Youthwalk Devotional Bible

Hot Topic

As Christians, we look to the Bible for wisdom to face all the hot topics of life. But is the Bible really all that reliable? Yes! Here are five reasons:

It says so.
The Scriptures claim to be "the very words of God" (Romans 3:2), written by men who were guided by the Holy Spirit (2 Peter 1:21). The human authors of the Bible regarded their writings as revelations from God (Exodus 24:3-4; Galatians 1:12) and took great care in recording the words of God (Luke 1:1-4; John 21:24).

Jesus said so.
Jesus constantly defended the authority and reliability of Scripture, and he promised the supernatural completion of the New Testament (John 10:35; 14:26).

Manuscript evidence says so.
Even though we don't have the original Biblical manuscripts, we can trust our modern-day Bibles. The Dead Sea Scrolls date back to the first century A.D. and verify that the Old Testament was handed down through the years with great care. The New Testament is authenticated by thousands of Greek manuscripts, some as early as the second and third century A.D.—very near the time of the original documents. No wonder the New Testament is considered the most attested ancient document of its kind!

Prophecy says so.
The Bible is packed with prophecies that have been fulfilled with incredible accuracy (Daniel 2,7). Many were written hundreds of years before their fulfillment!

Archaeology says so.
Excavations in this century have constantly confirmed—rather than contradicted—the accuracy of Scripture.

Despite the doubts of some, it is clear that the Bible is the reliable Word of God, "useful for teaching, rebuking, correcting and training in righteousness, so that the man of God may be thoroughly equipped for every good work" (2 Timothy 3:16-17).

why the Bible is Reliable

Hot Topic

Plane crashes. Car wrecks. Murder. Rape. Cancer. Horrible things happen daily all around us (and sometimes to us and to those we love).

It's pretty hard to fit some of the events and circumstances of our lives into an overall scheme of the goodness of God. The Bible says that God is both all-powerful and all-good. That may seem to contradict reality. The argument goes like this: An all-powerful God *could* prevent suffering, and an all-good God *would* prevent suffering.

The Reality of Suffering

There *is* suffering in the world. That's something we can't get away from. The basic question then becomes: Who's in charge? Does God send suffering? Or does all suffering come from Satan, and God just isn't quite powerful enough to stop him?

The best answer is that God *allows* or *permits* suffering. Satan is the originator of all suffering and evil. But he is allowed by God only to go so far. He is, so to speak, on a divine tether or chain (see Job 1:12; 2:6). God's control is the ultimate factor, not Satan's ability to produce suffering.

God has never guaranteed that suffering will not be a part of our lives as believers. He only guarantees that we will not suffer alone.

The Reality of God's Goodness

God's goodness is very real. The fact that we suffer in no way makes God any less good.

Paul suffered more than most. You can read his list of sufferings in 2 Corinthians 11:16-33. But in his suffering he was overwhelmed by the reality of God's love and nearness (2 Corinthians 4:16-18; 2 Corinthians 12:7-10).

The evil and suffering in our world are confusing and depressing. There are no easy answers, and sometimes we just plain don't know why we suffer. But God is in control, and he can and will bring good out of the suffering in our lives. Just think: The best example that good *can* come from evil is the death of Christ. From an unjust Roman crucifixion came salvation for the world.

And remember. All these circumstances are only temporary. Our God will one day defeat all forms of evil (Revelation 20—22). In the end God's goodness and power will conquer—and there will be no more suffering.

Suffering

Hot Topic

What is hell like?

Tormented sinners burning in fiery flames? Little red devils running around, poking and jabbing their screaming victims with pitchforks? For accurate answers we need to go to the source of truth—God's Word.

Jesus clearly taught about a real place called hell (Matthew 5:22-30; Luke 6:19-31). Therefore, the issue isn't, "Does hell exist?" but, "What is hell like?"

The Bible tells us three main things about hell:

- It will last forever (Matthew 25:46).

- It will be punishment for sin and unbelief (2 Thessalonians 1:8).

- It will be separation from God (2 Thessalonians 1:9).

The Bible also describes hell as "the second death" (Revelation 21:8). In the Bible death always refers to physical or spiritual separation (not nothingness). So, while the first death will be the physical separation from life, the second death will be separation from the source of life—God. In short, heaven will be eternal life for the believer. Hell will be eternal death for the unbeliever.

C.S. Lewis probably summed it up best when he said that sin is a person saying to God, "Go away and leave me alone." Hell is God finally saying to that person, "You may have your wish," and leaving him or her alone for eternity.

How should we as believers respond to the Biblical truth of hell?

First, we need to take life, and death, more seriously.

Second, we need to share our faith with unbelievers. People around us are sick with sin, and we have the cure for their spiritual disease.

Third, we should be grateful to a loving God for delivering us from hell.

Hot Topic

How would you describe heaven? Streets of gold? Worshiping God forever? Mansions? Are you anxious to go there? Or does it honestly sound just a bit boring? Like an eternal church service? Do you sort of feel like it would be okay to go, but not today? You want to graduate, get married, have a career, have a few kids.

Never fear. Those feelings are perfectly normal.

A Hunger for Heaven

You may think you don't have a hunger for heaven, but have you ever wished for a life without conflict or trouble, a life of peace? That's a hunger for heaven. Ecclesiastes 3:11 tells us that God has "set eternity in the hearts of men." We long for a perfect place because we were made to live in just such a place. We were created for eternity.

The Presence of God

So what is heaven all about? Will heaven be like going to church for eternity? Will we sit around playing harps? The Bible says that heaven is the place where God lives (Matthew 6:9). Even more than being a *place*, heaven is the very *presence of God*. The most important thing about heaven is that we will spend eternity in God's presence.

Heavenly Citizens

We Christians need to remember that our true citizenship is in heaven (Philippians 3:20-21). This world is just our temporary residence. Our real home is the place for which we long—heaven.

Absolute Fulfillment

Heaven will be the fulfillment of the deepest longings of our hearts. Once and for all, we will experience ultimate satisfaction and joy and peace in the presence of the one we were created to enjoy forever—our Father in heaven—God.

Heaven

God.

Is He a Real Being?

Or is he someone people have conjured up in their minds? For all of recorded history, humans have thought about, written about and talked about God. Though the term *God* has been understood in many ways, to most people it implies an intelligent creator. Such discussion raises life's most serious and important question: Does such a being *really* exist?

All Effects Have Causes

Science (as well as everyday experience) tells us that every effect must have a cause. Things don't create themselves. They are brought into existence by someone or something else. Cars don't just pop out of thin air. Auto parts are first designed by engineers, then produced by manufacturers, then put together on an assembly line. The result—or effect—is a car.

The Universe Is an Effect

Like a huge wind-up clock, the universe now seems to be running down. Scientists see this as evidence that the universe had a beginning. If that is the case, the universe is an effect that requires a cause. But what kind of cause?

Consider the obvious complexity in the universe. The simplest one-celled organism contains enough complex information to fill one complete volume of an encyclopedia. Intricate, exquisitely designed organisms could not have been caused by blind chance or an unintelligent force. No, the complexity of the universe demands an intelligent cause.

God Must Exist

Since the universe is an effect, it must have an adequate cause for its existence. Since the universe displays incredible complexity and design, the cause of the universe must be intelligent. Therefore, an intelligent creator of the universe must exist. This is the one we know as God.

God Reveals Himself

God has revealed his intelligence and power through the created universe (Psalm 19:1-4) . . . and even more of himself through the person of Jesus Christ. Jesus came to earth so that we could more fully know our God, the intelligent creator of the universe (John 1:1-14).

God: Fact or Fiction

Hot Topic

The Case of the Empty Tomb
Almost 2,000 years ago, Jesus Christ died and was buried. Three days later, his grave was mysteriously empty!

What Happened?
The Bible says Jesus supernaturally rose from the dead. Some disputers have claimed that Jesus didn't die but fainted, revived in the tomb and then escaped; others have said that Jesus' disciples stole his body.

Did Jesus Merely Faint?
Matthew and John were eyewitnesses to Christ's death and resurrection (Matthew 28; John 20). The testimony of an eyewitness has more validity than the testimony of anyone else. It makes sense to believe the record John and Matthew left of the event.

John 19:33 records that the soldiers who crucified Jesus recognized he was, in fact, dead. Who is in a better position to judge Jesus' condition: the professionals who executed him or modern doubters?

Was Jesus' Body Stolen?
Is it reasonable to believe that the same disciples who had scattered in terror at Jesus' capture mustered up the courage and strength to overpower a detachment of battle-hardened Roman soldiers and then steal the body?

Think about it: Would the disciples and many others commit their lives—even to the point of death—to a resurrection they knew to be a hoax? The answer: The earliest Christians had proof of the resurrection. They saw with their own eyes an empty tomb and the living Son of God.

The resurrection is absolutely essential to Christianity: "If Christ has not been raised, your faith is futile; you are still in your sins" (1 Corinthians 15:17).

Do you believe Christ rose from the dead as Lord of lords?

If so, here's good news: You'll rise too. Hallelujah!

Resurrection

⧓ Hot Topic

Quick!

When I say "Christmas," what is the first word that comes to your mind? Parties? Presents? Snow? Incarnation?

Incarnation? It probably isn't the first word that comes to your mind. But when you celebrate Christmas each year, you are actually celebrating the incarnation of Christ.

Jesus is God incarnate, God made into human flesh. Jesus is called "Immanuel," which in Hebrew means "God with us." Jesus inherited his humanity from his earthly mother, Mary. Because she was a virgin, overshadowed by "the power of the Most High" (Luke 1:35), Jesus was born as the Son of God. Jesus inherited God the Father's divinity.

Jesus is fully human. He had a birth, was raised in a family and learned how to be a carpenter. He got hungry, got dirty and went to sleep at night. He felt great love for his friends and great pain when he was betrayed by them. Hebrews 2:18 tells us that Jesus understands and identifies with all of our difficulties in living a life pleasing to God:

"Because he himself suffered when he was tempted, he is able to help those who are being tempted."

Jesus is fully divine. He is fully God. He never left anyone in doubt about this: "I came from the Father and entered the world" (John 16:28). His purpose on earth was to give his life as a payment for our sins so we could be forgiven. If his life was to be an acceptable payment, it had to be totally free of sin. God knew that no man's life was, or ever would be, free or sin. The only possible way he could save us was to give his own life.

We can put our full trust in everything Jesus taught or did because we know he is God. We can know and love him personally as our friend and brother because he is a man.

What fantastic news! Have you told anyone lately what the incarnation means to you?

Incarnation

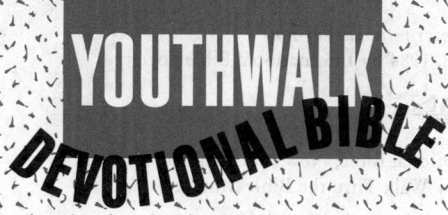

YOUTHWALK DEVOTIONAL BIBLE

Dr. Bruce H. Wilkinson
EXECUTIVE EDITOR

Calvin W. Edwards
SENIOR EDITOR

Len Woods
EDITOR

Paula A. Kirk
GENERAL EDITOR

Jean E. Syswerda
PROJECT EDITOR

Walk Thru the Bible Ministries
ATLANTA, GEORGIA

ZONDERVAN™

GRAND RAPIDS, MICHIGAN 49530

CONTENTS

THE BOOKS OF THE OLD TESTAMENT

THE BOOKS OF THE NEW TESTAMENT

ACKNOWLEDGMENTS

The *Youthwalk Devotional Bible* is based on topical studies taken from *Youthwalk*, a magazine for teens published monthly by Walk Thru the Bible Ministries. We thank the many folks who have helped us out over the years, especially all the teens and youth leaders who made up our focus groups, posed for photos, and wrote articles and letters that kept us on track. And we're especially grateful to all the people in Walk Thru the Bible's Specialized Publishing Group, from the leadership team to the staff in production.

Special thanks to Tim Walker, Michelle Strickland, Kyle Henderson, Helen Ryser and Robyn Holmes, our *Youthwalk* design and production team. Also the creative contributions of Cary McNeal are much appreciated. All invested their time and talents with the prayer that their work will make a lasting difference in the lives of young people.

WALK THRU THE BIBLE MINISTRIES

Walk Thru the Bible Ministries (WTB) began in the early 1970s in Portland, Oregon. A young teacher named Bruce Wilkinson developed an innovative way of teaching Old and New Testament surveys of the Bible. By enabling people to actively participate in the learning process through memorable hand signs, the Word of God came alive for them and lives were changed.

From these small beginnings emerged the multifaceted Bible-teaching outreach that Dr. Wilkinson officially founded as a nonprofit ministry in 1976. In 1978 WTB moved to its current home in Atlanta, Georgia. Since then, WTB has grown into one of the leading Christian organizations in America with an international ministry extending to thirty countries representing twenty-two languages. International branch offices are located in Australia, Brazil, Great Britain, Singapore and New Zealand.

By focusing on the central themes of Scripture and their practical application, WTB has been able to develop and maintain wide acceptance in denominations and fellowships around the world. In addition, it has carefully initiated strategic ministry alliances with over one hundred Christian organizations and missions of wide diversity and background.

WTB has four major outreach ministries: seminars, publishing, leadership training, and video training curricula.

Seminars

Since it began its seminar ministry two decades ago, WTB has instructed more than one million people worldwide through seminars taught by more than two hundred certified teachers. People of all ages and religious persuasions have developed a deeper understanding of the Bible through these unique Old and New Testament surveys, and many have come to know Christ in a new and more personal way.

Publishing

WTB's publishing ministry began in 1978 with the launching of *The Daily Walk* magazine. Since then, WTB Publishing has continued to develop additional publications that enable individuals and families to maintain a regular, meaningful habit of daily devotional time in the Word of God. The publications include *Closer Walk, Family Walk, LifeWalk, Quiet Walk* and *Youthwalk*. WTB is one of the largest publishers of devotional magazines in the Christian community.

Leadership Training

The third strategic ministry of WTB is the training of Christian leaders and communicators. Launched in the late 1980s, the Applied Principles of Learning (APL) training conference for teachers, pastors and parents has rapidly become the most widely used interdenominational teacher training program in North America. Dozens of certified WTB instructors regularly conduct this life-changing course in schools, churches, businesses and colleges. In addition, WTB's Leadership

Training curriculum is an integral part of the regular and ongoing discipleship training in hundreds of churches.

Video Training Curriculum

The newest ministry of WTB is the video training curriculum. In just a few short years, the WTB creative team has developed a number of leading video courses that have enjoyed widespread distribution. *The Seven Laws of the Learner,* featuring Dr. Bruce H. Wilkinson, focuses on the needs of the student and helps teachers learn to communicate in the most effective and compelling manner possible. *The Seven Laws of the Teacher,* featuring Dr. Howard G. Hendricks, equips church school teachers, parents and others to effectively prepare and teach Bible lessons that capture attention and change lives. *Master Your Money,* a six-part presentation by Christian financial planner Ron Blue, trains people to maximize their effectiveness as stewards of God's resources. Thousands of churches use these and other WTB videos with their congregations each year.

WTB has had a consistent history of strategic ministry from the beginning. The organization strives to help fulfill the Great Commission in obedience to the Lord's call. With this mission in mind, WTB lives out its commitment to excellence with the highest standards of ethical conduct and integrity, not only in ministry but also in its internal operational policies and procedures. No matter what the ministry, no matter where the ministry, WTB focuses on the Word of God and encourages people of all nations to grow in their knowledge of him and in their unreserved obedience and service to him.

For more information about Walk Thru the Bible's publications, videos, or seminars in your area, write to Walk Thru the Bible Ministries, P.O. Box 80587, Atlanta, GA 30366 or call (770) 458-9300.

HOW TO USE YOUR *NIV YOUTHWALK DEVOTIONAL BIBLE*

The Bible you hold in your hands can provide an extraordinary avenue of growth for you as a Christian teenager. God's Word has incredible value. It isn't just a bunch of silly stories about people who lived in the stone ages . . . it is God's message of love and hope to people of all ages, including you, the teenager of the nineties.

The *NIV Youthwalk Devotional Bible* has been carefully designed to help you discover how God relates to the world you live in today. Do you ever feel like there are just no answers to the hassles in your life? Do you ever wonder if God really cares about the decisions you have to make? The *NIV Youthwalk Devotional Bible* will help you discover answers to those and many other questions you face.

God's Word

This Bible contains the complete text of the New International Version of the Bible, today's most popular modern translation. It is well known for its accuracy, and you'll find that it is easy to read and understand.

Devotions

Your *NIV Youthwalk Devotional Bible* contains devotions for Monday through Friday, plus special, shorter devotions for Saturday and Sunday. There are 365 devotions—one for every day of the year. Each devotion is placed close to the Scripture reading for that day, encouraging you to read the devotion *and* the related Bible verses. You don't have to start using your new Bible on January 1—you can start anytime—right now!

Daily Use

You can use the devotions in this Bible in two ways. The first (and probably most obvious) way is simply to start on a Monday with the first devotion in Genesis (page 2). At the bottom of the page, you'll find directions for where to find the devotion for Tuesday. Tuesday's devotion will direct you to the reading for Wednesday, and so on. You could read all the way through your *NIV Youthwalk Devotional Bible* in this manner.

Topical Use

Another way to read the *NIV Youthwalk Devotional Bible* is by topic. You'll notice that each devotion includes a topic, listed at the bottom of the page within a color block. In paging through this Bible, you may discover a topic that particularly interests you. After reading the devotion on this topic, look at the bottom of the page to find where other devotions on this same topic are located.

If you wonder whether a particular topic is covered in the devotional material, refer to the subject index found on page 1417 at the back of the Bible. The index lists several hundred subjects covered in the daily and weekend devotions as well as in the "Hot Topics."

Introductions

At the beginning of each book of the Bible, you'll find an interesting and informative introduction, as well as a concise outline of the book's contents.

Hot Topics

Seven colorful "Hot Topics" can be found at the front and eight at the back of your *NIV Youthwalk Devotional Bible.* Do you ever wonder what heaven will be like? Have you ever struggled with the issues of homosexuality or abortion? Then be sure to check the "Hot Topics" on those subjects. The "Hot Topics" will give you Biblical insight into current issues and will challenge you to think them through yourself.

WWJD

Interspersed within the text of your *NIV Youthwalk Devotional Bible* are eight pages asking "What Would Jesus Do?" on topics ranging from racism to temptation to kindness. These pages will challenge you to take a closer look at the example Christ gave while here on earth and to ask yourself "What would Jesus do?" when faced with a tough decision or awkward situation.

Index

At the back of your *NIV Youthwalk Devotional Bible,* on page 1417, you'll find a guide for locating information within this Bible. If you're looking for Biblical perspectives on sexuality or contentment or wealth or any of several hundred other topics, this is the place to find help.

Reading Plans

Do you need a structure to follow for reading your Bible in a disciplined way? Several reading plans (see page 1414) should provide just what you need, including ways to read the *whole* Bible!

Your *NIV Youthwalk Devotional Bible.* Open it and use it every day. You'll never be sorry you took the time.

PREFACE

THE NEW INTERNATIONAL VERSION is a completely new translation of the Holy Bible made by over a hundred scholars working directly from the best available Hebrew, Aramaic and Greek texts. It had its beginning in 1965 when, after several years of exploratory study by committees from the Christian Reformed Church and the National Association of Evangelicals, a group of scholars met at Palos Heights, Illinois, and concurred in the need for a new translation of the Bible in contemporary English. This group, though not made up of official church representatives, was transdenominational. Its conclusion was endorsed by a large number of leaders from many denominations who met in Chicago in 1966.

Responsibility for the new version was delegated by the Palos Heights group to a self-governing body of fifteen, the Committee on Bible Translation, composed for the most part of biblical scholars from colleges, universities and seminaries. In 1967 the New York Bible Society (now the International Bible Society) generously undertook the financial sponsorship of the project—a sponsorship that made it possible to enlist the help of many distinguished scholars. The fact that participants from the United States, Great Britain, Canada, Australia and New Zealand worked together gave the project its international scope. That they were from many denominations—including Anglican, Assemblies of God, Baptist, Brethren, Christian Reformed, Church of Christ, Evangelical Free, Lutheran, Mennonite, Methodist, Nazarene, Presbyterian, Wesleyan and other churches—helped to safeguard the translation from sectarian bias.

How it was made helps to give the New International Version its distinctiveness. The translation of each book was assigned to a team of scholars. Next, one of the Intermediate Editorial Committees revised the initial translation, with constant reference to the Hebrew, Aramaic or Greek. Their work then went to one of the General Editorial Committees, which checked it in detail and made another thorough revision. This revision in turn was carefully reviewed by the Committee on Bible Translation, which made further changes and then released the final version for publication. In this way the entire Bible underwent three revisions, during each of which the translation was examined for its faithfulness to the original languages and for its English style.

All this involved many thousands of hours of research and discussion regarding the meaning of the texts and the precise way of putting them into English. It may well be that no other translation has been made by a more thorough process of review and revision from committee to committee than this one.

From the beginning of the project, the Committee on Bible Translation held to certain goals for the New International Version: that it would be an accurate translation and one that would have clarity and literary quality and so prove suitable for public and private reading, teaching, preaching, memorizing and liturgical use. The Committee also sought to preserve some measure of continuity with the long tradition of translating the Scriptures into English.

In working toward these goals, the translators were united in their commitment to the authority and infallibility of the Bible as God's Word in written form. They believe that it contains the divine answer to the deepest needs of humanity, that it sheds unique light on our path in a dark world, and that it sets forth the way to our eternal well-being.

The first concern of the translators has been the accuracy of the translation and its fidelity to the thought of the biblical writers. They have weighed the significance of the lexical and grammatical details of the Hebrew, Aramaic and Greek texts. At the same time, they have striven for more than a word-for-word translation. Because thought patterns and syntax differ from language to language, faithful communication of the meaning of the writers of the Bible demands frequent modifications in sentence structure and constant regard for the contextual meanings of words.

A sensitive feeling for style does not always accompany scholarship. Accordingly the Committee on Bible Translation submitted the developing version to a number of stylistic consultants. Two of them read every book of both Old and New Testaments twice—once before and once after the last major revision—and made invaluable suggestions. Samples of the translation were tested for clarity and ease of reading by various kinds of people—young and old, highly educated and less well educated, ministers and laymen.

Concern for clear and natural English—that the New International Version should be idiomatic but not idiosyncratic, contemporary but not dated—motivated the translators and consultants. At the same time, they tried to reflect the differing styles of the biblical writers. In view of the international use of English, the translators sought to avoid obvious Americanisms on the one hand and obvious Anglicisms on the other. A British edition reflects the comparatively few differences of significant idiom and of spelling.

As for the traditional pronouns "thou," "thee" and "thine" in reference to the Deity, the translators judged that to use these archaisms (along with the old verb forms such as "doest," "wouldest" and "hadst") would violate accuracy in translation. Neither Hebrew, Aramaic nor Greek uses special pronouns for the persons of the Godhead. A present-day translation is not enhanced by forms that in the time of the King James Version were used in everyday speech, whether referring to God or man.

For the Old Testament the standard Hebrew text, the Masoretic Text as published in the latest editions of *Biblia Hebraica,* was used throughout. The Dead Sea Scrolls contain material bearing on an earlier stage of the Hebrew text. They were consulted, as were the Samaritan Pentateuch and the ancient scribal traditions relating to textual changes. Sometimes a variant Hebrew reading in the margin of the Masoretic Text was followed instead of the text itself. Such instances, being variants within the Masoretic tradition, are not specified by footnotes. In rare cases, words in the consonantal text were divided differently from the way they appear in the Masoretic Text. Footnotes indicate this. The translators also consulted the more important early versions—the Septuagint; Aquila, Symmachus and Theodotion; the Vulgate; the Syriac Peshitta; the Targums; and for the Psalms the *Juxta Hebraica* of Jerome. Readings from these versions were occasionally followed where the Masoretic Text seemed doubtful and where accepted principles of textual criticism showed that one or more of these textual witnesses appeared to provide the correct reading. Such instances are footnoted. Sometimes vowel letters and vowel signs did not, in the judgment of the translators, represent the correct vowels for the original consonantal text. Accordingly some words were read with a different set of vowels. These instances are usually not indicated by footnotes.

The Greek text used in translating the New Testament was an eclectic one. No other piece of ancient literature has such an abundance of manuscript witnesses as does the New Testament. Where existing manuscripts differ, the translators made their choice of readings according to accepted principles of New Testament textual criticism. Footnotes call attention to places where there was uncertainty about what the original text was. The best current printed texts of the Greek New Testament were used.

There is a sense in which the work of translation is never wholly finished. This applies to all great literature and uniquely so to the Bible. In 1973 the New Testament in the New International Version was published. Since then, suggestions for corrections and revisions have been received from various sources. The Committee on Bible Translation carefully considered the suggestions and adopted a number of them. These were incorporated in the first printing of the entire Bible in 1978. Additional revisions were made by the Committee on Bible Translation in 1983 and appear in printings after that date.

As in other ancient documents, the precise meaning of the biblical texts is sometimes uncertain. This is more often the case with the Hebrew and Aramaic texts than with the Greek text. Although archaeological and linguistic discoveries in this century aid in understanding difficult passages, some uncertainties remain. The more significant of these have been called to the reader's attention in the footnotes.

In regard to the divine name *YHWH,* commonly referred to as the *Tetragrammaton,* the translators adopted the device used in most English versions of rendering that name as "Lord" in capital letters to distinguish it from *Adonai,* another Hebrew word rendered "Lord," for which small letters are used. Wherever the two names stand together in the Old Testament as a compound name of God, they are rendered "Sovereign Lord."

Because for most readers today the phrases "the Lord of hosts" and "God of hosts" have little meaning, this version renders them "the Lord Almighty" and "God Almighty." These renderings convey the sense of the Hebrew, namely, "he who is sovereign over all the 'hosts' (powers) in heaven and on earth, especially over the 'hosts' (armies) of Israel." For readers unacquainted with Hebrew this does not make clear the distinction between *Sabaoth* ("hosts" or "Almighty") and *Shaddai* (which can also be translated "Almighty"), but the latter occurs infrequently and is always footnoted. When *Adonai* and *YHWH Sabaoth* occur together, they are rendered "the Lord, the Lord Almighty."

As for other proper nouns, the familiar spellings of the King James Version are generally retained. Names traditionally spelled with "ch," except where it is final, are usually spelled in this translation with "k" or "c," since the biblical languages do not have the sound that "ch" frequently indicates in English—for example, in *chant.* For well-known names such as Zechariah, however, the traditional spelling has been retained. Variation in the spelling of names in the original languages has usually not been indicated. Where a person or place has two or more different names in the Hebrew, Aramaic or Greek texts, the more familiar one has generally been used, with footnotes where needed.

To achieve clarity the translators sometimes supplied words not in the original texts but required by the context. If there was uncertainty about such material, it is enclosed in brackets. Also for the sake of clarity or style, nouns, including some proper nouns, are sometimes substituted for pronouns, and vice versa. And though the Hebrew writers often shifted back and forth between first, second and third personal pronouns without change of antecedent, this translation often makes them uniform, in accordance with English style and without the use of footnotes.

Poetical passages are printed as poetry, that is, with indentation of lines and with separate stanzas. These are generally designed to reflect the structure of Hebrew poetry. This poetry is normally characterized by parallelism in balanced lines. Most of the poetry in the Bible is in the Old Testament, and scholars differ regarding the scansion of Hebrew lines. The translators determined the stanza divisions for the most part by analysis of the subject matter. The stanzas therefore serve as poetic paragraphs.

As an aid to the reader, italicized sectional headings are inserted in most of the books. They are not to be regarded as part of the NIV text, are not for oral reading, and are not intended to dictate the interpretation of the sections they head.

The footnotes in this version are of several kinds, most of which need no explanation. Those giving alternative translations begin with "Or" and generally introduce the alternative with the last word preceding it in the text, except when it is a single-word alternative; in poetry quoted in a footnote a slant mark indicates a line division. Footnotes introduced by "Or" do not have uniform significance. In some cases two possible translations were considered to have about equal validity. In other cases, though the translators were convinced that the translation in the text was correct, they judged that another interpretation was possible and of sufficient importance to be represented in a footnote.

In the New Testament, footnotes that refer to uncertainty regarding the original text are introduced by "Some manuscripts" or similar expressions. In the Old Testament, evidence for the reading chosen is given first and evidence for the alternative is added after a semicolon (for example: Septuagint; Hebrew *father*). In such notes the term "Hebrew" refers to the Masoretic Text.

It should be noted that minerals, flora and fauna, architectural details, articles of clothing and jewelry, musical instruments and other articles cannot always be identified with precision. Also measures of capacity in the biblical period are particularly uncertain (see the table of weights and measures following the text).

Like all translations of the Bible, made as they are by imperfect man, this one undoubtedly falls short of its goals. Yet we are grateful to God for the extent to which he has enabled us to realize these goals and for the strength he has given us and our colleagues to complete our task. We offer this version of the Bible to him in whose name and for whose glory it has been made. We pray that it will lead many into a better understanding of the Holy Scriptures and a fuller knowledge of Jesus Christ the incarnate Word, of whom the Scriptures so faithfully testify.

The Committee on Bible Translation

June 1978
(Revised August 1983)

Names of the translators and editors may be secured
from the International Bible Society
translation sponsors of the New International Version,
1820 Jet Stream Drive, Colorado Springs, Colorado
80921-3696 U.S.A.

OLD TESTAMENT

GENESIS

TO know God's Word, you have to begin at the beginning, the book of Genesis. The universe, the human race, marriage, sin—Genesis records the beginning of these and more. God's dealings with Adam, Noah, Abraham, Isaac, Jacob and Joseph make crystal clear that God loves and leads his people—even though they still sin. As you read Genesis, remember: From the beginning God has always wanted his people to return his love by obeying him. He still wants the same from you.

Outline of Contents

The Beginning

1 In the beginning God created the heavens and the earth. ²Now the earth was^a formless and empty, darkness was over the surface of the deep, and the Spirit of God was hovering over the waters.

³And God said, "Let there be light," and there was light. ⁴God saw that the light was good, and he separated the light from the darkness. ⁵God called the light "day," and the darkness he called "night." And there was evening, and there was morning—the first day.

⁶And God said, "Let there be an expanse between the waters to separate water from water." ⁷So God made the expanse and separated the water under the expanse from the water above it. And it was so. ⁸God called the expanse "sky." And there was evening, and there was morning—the second day.

⁹And God said, "Let the water under the sky

^{a}2 Or possibly *became*

WAS THERE A BEGINNING IN THE BEGINNING?

In science class, Alene is being exposed to the latest theories about the origin of the universe.

"Students, some scientists believe the big bang theory that the cosmos suddenly exploded into existence by chance about 15 billion years ago. Others think the universe has always existed. Those are probably the two best theories."

Look It Up
• • • •

Without chemical details, mentions of atomic theory, descriptions of pulsars or precise dates, the Bible asserts: "In the beginning God created the heavens and the earth" (Genesis 1:1).

Someone has suggested that the reason for this lack of technical information is that the Bible wasn't written as a science textbook. It's primarily a revelation from God about how we can know him.

So while it doesn't answer every little question about origins, the Bible does answer the big one: The universe is not the product of blind chance, and it hasn't always existed. It was specially created by God.

Think It Through
• • • •

Follow this reasoning:
• Anything that comes into existence must have a cause. (The scientific principle of causality.)
• The universe came into existence.
(The second law of thermodynamics, or the fact that the universe is running out of energy and moving toward disorder, plus the rapid expansion of the universe and the discovery of a universal radiation "echo" all suggest an initial point of beginning. Noted scientists agree with this conclusion.)
• Therefore, the universe must have a cause.

Work It Out
• • • •

Is the debate over origins important? Most definitely. Is it hard to comprehend? You bet.

All the more reason to pray: "Father, I probably will never understand all the technical arguments on the subject of origins. But at least give me a good general grasp of the main issues so that I can stand against the attacks on my faith that are sure to come. Amen."

Nail It Down
• • • •

Read the story of beginnings in Genesis 1.

Turn to pages 529, 621, 1188 and 1348 for other readings on origins.
Turn to page 5 for Tuesday's reading.

Topic
• • • •

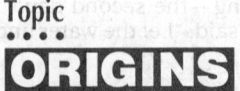

be gathered to one place, and let dry ground appear." And it was so. ¹⁰God called the dry ground "land," and the gathered waters he called "seas." And God saw that it was good.

¹¹Then God said, "Let the land produce vegetation: seed-bearing plants and trees on the land that bear fruit with seed in it, according to their various kinds." And it was so. ¹²The land produced vegetation: plants bearing seed according to their kinds and trees bearing fruit with seed in it according to their kinds. And God saw that it was good. ¹³And there was evening, and there was morning—the third day.

¹⁴And God said, "Let there be lights in the expanse of the sky to separate the day from the night, and let them serve as signs to mark seasons and days and years, ¹⁵and let them be lights in the expanse of the sky to give light on the earth." And it was so. ¹⁶God made two great lights—the greater light to govern the day and the lesser light to govern the night. He also made the stars. ¹⁷God set them in the expanse of the sky to give light on the earth, ¹⁸to govern the day and the night, and to separate light from darkness. And God saw that it was good. ¹⁹And there was evening, and there was morning—the fourth day.

²⁰And God said, "Let the water teem with living creatures, and let birds fly above the earth across the expanse of the sky." ²¹So God created the great creatures of the sea and every living and moving thing with which the water teems, according to their kinds, and every winged bird according to its kind. And God saw that it was good. ²²God blessed them and said, "Be fruitful and increase in number and fill the water in the seas, and let the birds increase on the earth." ²³And there was evening, and there was morning—the fifth day.

²⁴And God said, "Let the land produce living creatures according to their kinds: livestock, creatures that move along the ground, and wild animals, each according to its kind." And it was so. ²⁵God made the wild animals according to their kinds, the livestock according to their kinds, and all the creatures that move along the ground according to

their kinds. And God saw that it was good.

²⁶Then God said, "Let us make man in our image, in our likeness, and let them rule over the fish of the sea and the birds of the air, over the livestock, over all the earth,ᵃ and over all the creatures that move along the ground."

²⁷So God created man in his own image,
    in the image of God he created him;
    male and female he created them.

²⁸God blessed them and said to them, "Be fruitful and increase in number; fill the earth and subdue it. Rule over the fish of the sea and the birds of the air and over every living creature that moves on the ground."

²⁹Then God said, "I give you every seed-bearing plant on the face of the whole earth and every tree that has fruit with seed in it. They will be yours for food. ³⁰And to all the beasts of the earth and all the birds of the air and all the creatures that move on the ground—everything that has the breath of life in it—I give every green plant for food." And it was so.

³¹God saw all that he had made, and it was very good. And there was evening, and there was morning—the sixth day.

2 Thus the heavens and the earth were completed in all their vast array.

²By the seventh day God had finished the work he had been doing; so on the seventh day he restedᵇ from all his work. ³And God blessed the seventh day and made it holy, because on it he rested from all the work of creating that he had done.

Adam and Eve

⁴This is the account of the heavens and the earth when they were created.

When the LORD God made the earth and the heavens— ⁵and no shrub of the field had yet appeared on the earthᶜ and no plant of the field had yet sprung up, for the LORD God had not sent rain on the earthᶜ and there was no man to work the ground, ⁶but streamsᵈ came up from the earth and watered the whole surface of the ground— ⁷the LORD God formed the manᵉ from the

---

ᵃ26 Hebrew; Syriac *all the wild animals*   ᵇ2 Or *ceased*; also in verse 3   ᶜ5 Or *land*; also in verse 6
ᵈ6 Or *mist*   ᵉ7 The Hebrew for *man (adam)* sounds like and may be related to the Hebrew for *ground (adamah)*; it is also the name *Adam* (see Gen. 2:20).

dust of the ground and breathed into his nostrils the breath of life, and the man became a living being.

[8]Now the LORD God had planted a garden in the east, in Eden; and there he put the man he had formed. [9]And the LORD God made all kinds of trees grow out of the ground—trees that were pleasing to the eye and good for food. In the middle of the garden were the tree of life and the tree of the knowledge of good and evil.

[10]A river watering the garden flowed from Eden; from there it was separated into four headwaters. [11]The name of the first is the Pishon; it winds through the entire land of Havilah, where there is gold. [12](The gold of that land is good; aromatic resin[a] and onyx are also there.) [13]The name of the second river is the Gihon; it winds through the entire land of Cush.[b] [14]The name of the third river is the Tigris; it runs along the east side of Asshur. And the fourth river is the Euphrates.

[15]The LORD God took the man and put him in the Garden of Eden to work it and take care of it. [16]And the LORD God commanded the man, "You are free to eat from any tree in the garden; [17]but you must not eat from the tree of the knowledge of good and evil, for when you eat of it you will surely die."

[18]The LORD God said, "It is not good for the man to be alone. I will make a helper suitable for him."

[19]Now the LORD God had formed out of the ground all the beasts of the field and all the birds of the air. He brought them to the man to see what he would name them; and whatever the man called each living creature, that was its name. [20]So the man gave names to all the livestock, the birds of the air and all the beasts of the field.

But for Adam[c] no suitable helper was found. [21]So the LORD God caused the man to fall into a deep sleep; and while he was sleeping, he took one of the man's ribs[d] and closed up the place with flesh. [22]Then the LORD God made a woman from the rib[e] he had taken out of the man, and he brought her to the man.

[23]The man said,

"This is now bone of my bones
　　and flesh of my flesh;
she shall be called 'woman,'[f]
　　for she was taken out of man."

[24]For this reason a man will leave his father and mother and be united to his wife, and they will become one flesh.

[25]The man and his wife were both naked, and they felt no shame.

The Fall of Man

3 Now the serpent was more crafty than any of the wild animals the LORD God had made. He said to the woman, "Did God really say, 'You must not eat from any tree in the garden'?"

[2]The woman said to the serpent, "We may eat fruit from the trees in the garden, [3]but God did say, 'You must not eat fruit from the tree that is in the middle of the garden, and you must not touch it, or you will die.' "

[4]"You will not surely die," the serpent said to the woman. [5]"For God knows that when you eat of it your eyes will be opened, and you will be like God, knowing good and evil."

[6]When the woman saw that the fruit of the tree was good for food and pleasing to the eye, and also desirable for gaining wisdom, she took some and ate it. She also gave some to her husband, who was with her, and he ate it. [7]Then the eyes of both of them were opened, and they realized they were naked; so they sewed fig leaves together and made coverings for themselves.

[8]Then the man and his wife heard the sound of the LORD God as he was walking in the garden in the cool of the day, and they hid from the LORD God among the trees of the garden. [9]But the LORD God called to the man, "Where are you?"

[10]He answered, "I heard you in the garden, and I was afraid because I was naked; so I hid."

[11]And he said, "Who told you that you were naked? Have you eaten from the tree that I commanded you not to eat from?"

[12]The man said, "The woman you put here with me—she gave me some fruit from the tree, and I ate it."

[13]Then the LORD God said to the woman, "What is this you have done?"

The woman said, "The serpent deceived me, and I ate."

[14]So the LORD God said to the serpent, "Because you have done this,

"Cursed are you above all the livestock
　　and all the wild animals!
You will crawl on your belly
　　and you will eat dust

---

[a]12 Or good; pearls　　[b]13 Possibly southeast Mesopotamia　　[c]20 Or the man　　[d]21 Or took part of the man's side　　[e]22 Or part　　[f]23 The Hebrew for woman sounds like the Hebrew for man.

LOOK AT ALL THE LONELY PEOPLE

R on is about to begin his last year at Murphy High. He's a starter on the football team. He has a bunch of friends—even a girlfriend. On top of everything, he's a Christian. But believe it or not, Ron still feels lonely sometimes:

"I don't know . . . it's hard to explain. I mean, I can find people to do stuff with, but nobody is willing to take the time to listen to what I think. Nobody really understands me. I guess you could say I just don't feel very important."

Look It Up
• • • •

Loneliness is something all people feel some of the time, and some people feel all of the time. Even some prominent Bible characters wrestled with that awful dilemma of feeling cut off and isolated.

King David:

> Because of all my enemies,
>   I am the utter contempt of my neighbors;
> I am a dread to my friends—
>   those who see me on the street flee from me.
> I am forgotten by them as though I were dead;
>   I have become like broken pottery
>   (Psalm 31:11–12).

Job: Job 19:13–14.

The apostle Paul: "At my first defense, no one came to my support, but everyone deserted me" (2 Timothy 4:16).

Think It Through
• • • •

Let's correct a common misconception: It isn't just homeless people or society's outcasts who feel the sting of loneliness. Albert Einstein reportedly once told a friend, "It is strange to be known so universally and yet be so lonely." And despite being one of the richest men in America, Howard Hughes spent the last 20 years of his life in almost total seclusion.

Work It Out
• • • •

You live in a world filled with lonely people (you may even be one yourself). If you're lonely, here's a prayer you can pray right now:

"Father in heaven, I need you right now. Give me insight as I read your Word. Fill my loneliness with your life. Then use me to bring comfort to other people who face lives of 'solitary confinement.' "

Nail It Down
• • • •

Read and think about the implications of Genesis 2:18.

Turn to pages 816, 1047 and 1222 for other readings on loneliness.
Turn to page 6 for Wednesday's reading.

Topic
• • • •

LONELINESS

GUILT BEGAN IN THE GARDEN

Jenny wakes up on Sunday morning feeling especially guilty. She and her boyfriend got way too physical last night. They didn't go all the way, but they went much further than Jenny ever intended.

In the evening, Jenny calls a friend and explains the situation. What advice does she get?

"Forget about it, Jen! You were a saint not to go all the way! If anyone is guilty, it's that super-strict church of yours for making you feel so bad!"

Look It Up
• • • •

Though the world declares guilt to be an obsolete remnant of our "religious past," the Bible insists that people *feel* guilty because they *are* guilty!

"Everyone has turned away, they have together become corrupt; there is no one who does good, not even one" (Psalm 53:3).

"All of us have become like one who is unclean, and all our righteous acts are like filthy rags; we all shrivel up like a leaf, and like the wind our sins sweep us away" (Isaiah 64:6).

"If we claim to be without sin, we deceive ourselves and the truth is not in us" (1 John 1:8).

Think It Through
• • • •

Suppose a ruthless criminal guns down an elderly lady in cold blood . . . and then laughs. Is the man guilty? Of course! Does he feel guilty? No. In his own perverted way, he feels good—even glad—about what he did.

The point? Guilt is more than a feeling. In fact, it is best defined as the condition of being in violation of moral and/or civil laws. Guilt may be accompanied by feelings of remorse or sorrow, but it doesn't have to be. A person can *be* guilty without *feeling* guilty.

Work It Out
• • • •

Discuss these questions/statements with a close Christian friend:
1. What would make you feel more guilty than anything else?
2. What advice would you give to a friend like Jenny?
3. The way to overcome guilt is to _____.
4. I am guilty right now of _____.
5. If I could erase one guilty memory from my past, it would be the time I _____.

Nail It Down
• • • •

See where guilt began by reading Genesis 3:1–10 (especially verse 10).

Turn to pages 565, 957 and 1213 for other readings on guilt.
Turn to page 9 for Thursday's reading.

Topic
• • • •

all the days of your life.
15And I will put enmity
    between you and the woman,
    and between your offspring*a* and
        hers;
    he will crush*b* your head,
    and you will strike his heel."

  16To the woman he said,

"I will greatly increase your pains in
    childbearing;
  with pain you will give birth to
    children.
Your desire will be for your husband,
  and he will rule over you."

  17To Adam he said, "Because you listened to your wife and ate from the tree about which I commanded you, 'You must not eat of it,'

"Cursed is the ground because of you;
  through painful toil you will eat of it
  all the days of your life.
18It will produce thorns and thistles for
    you,
  and you will eat the plants of the
    field.
19By the sweat of your brow
  you will eat your food
until you return to the ground,
  since from it you were taken;
for dust you are
  and to dust you will return."

  20Adam*c* named his wife Eve,*d* because she would become the mother of all the living.
  21The LORD God made garments of skin for Adam and his wife and clothed them. **22**And the LORD God said, "The man has now become like one of us, knowing good and evil. He must not be allowed to reach out his hand and take also from the tree of life and eat, and live forever." **23**So the LORD God banished him from the Garden of Eden to work the ground from which he had been taken. **24**After he drove the man out, he placed on the east side*e* of the Garden of Eden cherubim and a flaming sword flashing back and forth to guard the way to the tree of life.

Cain and Abel

4 Adam*c* lay with his wife Eve, and she became pregnant and gave birth to Cain.*f* She said, "With the help of the LORD I have brought forth*g* a man." **2**Later she gave birth to his brother Abel.

  Now Abel kept flocks, and Cain worked the soil. **3**In the course of time Cain brought some of the fruits of the soil as an offering to the LORD. **4**But Abel brought fat portions from some of the firstborn of his flock. The LORD looked with favor on Abel and his offering, **5**but on Cain and his offering he did not look with favor. So Cain was very angry, and his face was downcast.

  6Then the LORD said to Cain, "Why are you angry? Why is your face downcast? **7**If you do what is right, will you not be accepted? But if you do not do what is right, sin is crouching at your door; it desires to have you, but you must master it."

  8Now Cain said to his brother Abel, "Let's go out to the field."*h* And while they were in the field, Cain attacked his brother Abel and killed him.

  9Then the LORD said to Cain, "Where is your brother Abel?"

  "I don't know," he replied. "Am I my brother's keeper?"

  10The LORD said, "What have you done? Listen! Your brother's blood cries out to me from the ground. **11**Now you are under a curse and driven from the ground, which opened its mouth to receive your brother's blood from your hand. **12**When you work the ground, it will no longer yield its crops for you. You will be a restless wanderer on the earth."

  13Cain said to the LORD, "My punishment is more than I can bear. **14**Today you are driving me from the land, and I will be hidden from your presence; I will be a restless wanderer on the earth, and whoever finds me will kill me."

  15But the LORD said to him, "Not so*i*; if anyone kills Cain, he will suffer vengeance seven times over." Then the LORD put a mark on Cain so that no one who found him would kill him. **16**So Cain went out from the LORD's presence and lived in the land of Nod,*j* east of Eden.

  17Cain lay with his wife, and she became pregnant and gave birth to Enoch. Cain was then building a city, and he named it after his son Enoch. **18**To Enoch was born Irad, and Irad was the father of Mehujael, and Mehujael was the father of Methushael, and Methushael was the father of Lamech.

---

a15 Or seed   b15 Or strike   c20,1 Or The man   d20 Eve probably means living.   e24 Or placed in front
f1 Cain sounds like the Hebrew for brought forth or acquired.   g1 Or have acquired   h8 Samaritan
Pentateuch, Septuagint, Vulgate and Syriac; Masoretic Text does not have "Let's go out to the field."
i15 Septuagint, Vulgate and Syriac; Hebrew Very well   j16 Nod means wandering (see verses 12 and 14).

[19]Lamech married two women, one named Adah and the other Zillah. [20]Adah gave birth to Jabal; he was the father of those who live in tents and raise livestock. [21]His brother's name was Jubal; he was the father of all who play the harp and flute. [22]Zillah also had a son, Tubal-Cain, who forged all kinds of tools out of[a] bronze and iron. Tubal-Cain's sister was Naamah. [23]Lamech said to his wives,

"Adah and Zillah, listen to me;
    wives of Lamech, hear my words.
I have killed[b] a man for wounding me,
    a young man for injuring me.
[24]If Cain is avenged seven times,
    then Lamech seventy-seven times."

[25]Adam lay with his wife again, and she gave birth to a son and named him Seth,[c] saying, "God has granted me another child in place of Abel, since Cain killed him." [26]Seth also had a son, and he named him Enosh.

At that time men began to call on[d] the name of the Lord.

From Adam to Noah

5 This is the written account of Adam's line.

When God created man, he made him in the likeness of God. [2]He created them male and female and blessed them. And when they were created, he called them "man.[e]"

[3]When Adam had lived 130 years, he had a son in his own likeness, in his own image; and he named him Seth. [4]After Seth was born, Adam lived 800 years and had other sons and daughters. [5]Altogether, Adam lived 930 years, and then he died.

[6]When Seth had lived 105 years, he became the father[f] of Enosh. [7]And after he became the father of Enosh, Seth lived 807 years and had other sons and daughters. [8]Altogether, Seth lived 912 years, and then he died.

[9]When Enosh had lived 90 years, he became the father of Kenan. [10]And after he became the father of Kenan, Enosh lived 815 years and had other sons and daughters. [11]Altogether, Enosh lived 905 years, and then he died.

[12]When Kenan had lived 70 years, he became the father of Mahalalel. [13]And after he became the father of Mahalalel, Kenan lived 840 years and had other sons and daugh-

ters. [14]Altogether, Kenan lived 910 years, and then he died.

[15]When Mahalalel had lived 65 years, he became the father of Jared. [16]And after he became the father of Jared, Mahalalel lived 830 years and had other sons and daughters. [17]Altogether, Mahalalel lived 895 years, and then he died.

[18]When Jared had lived 162 years, he became the father of Enoch. [19]And after he became the father of Enoch, Jared lived 800 years and had other sons and daughters. [20]Altogether, Jared lived 962 years, and then he died.

[21]When Enoch had lived 65 years, he became the father of Methuselah. [22]And after he became the father of Methuselah, Enoch walked with God 300 years and had other sons and daughters. [23]Altogether, Enoch lived 365 years. [24]Enoch walked with God; then he was no more, because God took him away.

[25]When Methuselah had lived 187 years, he became the father of Lamech. [26]And after he became the father of Lamech, Methuselah lived 782 years and had other sons and daughters. [27]Altogether, Methuselah lived 969 years, and then he died.

[28]When Lamech had lived 182 years, he had a son. [29]He named him Noah[g] and said, "He will comfort us in the labor and painful toil of our hands caused by the ground the Lord has cursed." [30]After Noah was born, Lamech lived 595 years and had other sons and daughters. [31]Altogether, Lamech lived 777 years, and then he died.

[32]After Noah was 500 years old, he became the father of Shem, Ham and Japheth.

The Flood

6 When men began to increase in number on the earth and daughters were born to them, [2]the sons of God saw that the daughters of men were beautiful, and they married any of them they chose. [3]Then the Lord said, "My Spirit will not contend with[h] man forever, for he is mortal[i]; his days will be a hundred and twenty years."

[4]The Nephilim were on the earth in those days—and also afterward—when the sons of God went to the daughters of men and had children by them. They were the heroes of old, men of renown.

[5]The Lord saw how great man's wickedness on the earth had become, and that ev-

---

[a]22 Or *who instructed all who work in*   [b]23 Or *I will kill*   [c]25 *Seth* probably means *granted.*   [d]26 Or *to proclaim*   [e]2 Hebrew *adam*   [f]6 *Father* may mean *ancestor*; also in verses 7-26.   [g]29 *Noah* sounds like the Hebrew for *comfort.*   [h]3 Or *My spirit will not remain in*   [i]3 Or *corrupt*

LOOKING FOR A GOOD VALUE?

Lugging two huge suitcases, Dave trudges up the steps. His family has just driven six hundred miles. Aunt Bonnie meets them at the door with tears in her eyes.

The living room is crammed with older people, many of them sniffling. About a million dishes of food sit on the table in the kitchen. Dave has one goal in mind—to grab some of that food and head for the TV set in the basement.

A white-haired woman approaches him in the kitchen. "I'm sorry about your Uncle Pete. He was a really godly man."

Look It Up
••••

Dave nods, grabs his food and rushes downstairs. Under his breath, he says in a mocking voice, " 'He was a really godly man.' Big deal! He was also sick all the time, he was little, he never finished high school, and he never had a decent job. What's so great about being godly?"

Hey, Dave, glad you asked. Check out this verse: "For physical training is of some value, but godliness has value for all things, holding promise for both the present life and the life to come" (1 Timothy 4:8).

"Value for all things" makes godliness the best value in the world (and in the *next* world)!

Think It Through
••••

Two jobs are available. One offers big bucks, but only until the summer ends. The other pays well now, and it promises millions in the future. Which will you take?

The point? Godliness pays temporal *and* eternal dividends! What are some of the present blessings of a godly life? Are you enjoying these benefits? Right now in your life, are you devoted to God? Are you living a life that is pleasing to him? Put more simply, are you a godly person?

Work It Out
••••

List some of the things the world values. How many of these things will be valuable in the life to come?

You might want to pray this: "Lord, help me to realize that godliness has value not just now but forever. Teach me what it means to be godly. Deepen my devotion to you. Amen."

Nail It Down
••••

Read about Enoch, a godly man, in Genesis 5:24.

Turn to pages 864 and 1372 for other readings on godliness.
Turn to page 12 for Friday's reading.

Topic
••••

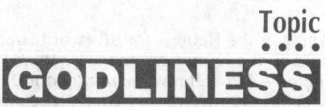

GODLINESS

ery inclination of the thoughts of his heart was only evil all the time. **6**The LORD was grieved that he had made man on the earth, and his heart was filled with pain. **7**So the LORD said, "I will wipe mankind, whom I have created, from the face of the earth — men and animals, and creatures that move along the ground, and birds of the air — for I am grieved that I have made them." **8**But Noah found favor in the eyes of the LORD.

9This is the account of Noah.

Noah was a righteous man, blameless among the people of his time, and he walked with God. **10**Noah had three sons: Shem, Ham and Japheth.

11Now the earth was corrupt in God's sight and was full of violence. **12**God saw how corrupt the earth had become, for all the people on earth had corrupted their ways. **13**So God said to Noah, "I am going to put an end to all people, for the earth is filled with violence because of them. I am surely going to destroy both them and the earth. **14**So make yourself an ark of cypress*a* wood; make rooms in it and coat it with pitch inside and out. **15**This is how you are to build it: The ark is to be 450 feet long, 75 feet wide and 45 feet high.*b* **16**Make a roof for it and finish*c* the ark to within 18 inches*d* of the top. Put a door in the side of the ark and make lower, middle and upper decks. **17**I am going to bring floodwaters on the earth to destroy all life under the heavens, every creature that has the breath of life in it. Everything on earth will perish. **18**But I will establish my covenant with you, and you will enter the ark — you and your sons and your wife and your sons' wives with you. **19**You are to bring into the ark two of all living creatures, male and female, to keep them alive with you. **20**Two of every kind of bird, of every kind of animal and of every kind of creature that moves along the ground will come to you to be kept alive. **21**You are to take every kind of food that is to be eaten and store it away as food for you and for them."

22Noah did everything just as God commanded him.

7 The LORD then said to Noah, "Go into the ark, you and your whole family, because I have found you righteous in this generation. **2**Take with you seven*e* of every kind of clean animal, a male and its mate,

and two of every kind of unclean animal, a male and its mate, **3**and also seven of every kind of bird, male and female, to keep their various kinds alive throughout the earth. **4**Seven days from now I will send rain on the earth for forty days and forty nights, and I will wipe from the face of the earth every living creature I have made."

5And Noah did all that the LORD commanded him.

6Noah was six hundred years old when the floodwaters came on the earth. **7**And Noah and his sons and his wife and his sons' wives entered the ark to escape the waters of the flood. **8**Pairs of clean and unclean animals, of birds and of all creatures that move along the ground, **9**male and female, came to Noah and entered the ark, as God had commanded Noah. **10**And after the seven days the floodwaters came on the earth.

11In the six hundredth year of Noah's life, on the seventeenth day of the second month — on that day all the springs of the great deep burst forth, and the floodgates of the heavens were opened. **12**And rain fell on the earth forty days and forty nights.

13On that very day Noah and his sons, Shem, Ham and Japheth, together with his wife and the wives of his three sons, entered the ark. **14**They had with them every wild animal according to its kind, all livestock according to their kinds, every creature that moves along the ground according to its kind and every bird according to its kind, everything with wings. **15**Pairs of all creatures that have the breath of life in them came to Noah and entered the ark. **16**The animals going in were male and female of every living thing, as God had commanded Noah. Then the LORD shut him in.

17For forty days the flood kept coming on the earth, and as the waters increased they lifted the ark high above the earth. **18**The waters rose and increased greatly on the earth, and the ark floated on the surface of the water. **19**They rose greatly on the earth, and all the high mountains under the entire heavens were covered. **20**The waters rose and covered the mountains to a depth of more than twenty feet.*f,g* **21**Every living thing that moved on the earth perished — birds, livestock, wild animals, all the creatures that swarm over the earth, and all mankind. **22**Everything on dry land that had

---

the breath of life in its nostrils died. ²³Every living thing on the face of the earth was wiped out; men and animals and the creatures that move along the ground and the birds of the air were wiped from the earth. Only Noah was left, and those with him in the ark.

²⁴The waters flooded the earth for a hundred and fifty days.

8 But God remembered Noah and all the wild animals and the livestock that were with him in the ark, and he sent a wind over the earth, and the waters receded. ²Now the springs of the deep and the floodgates of the heavens had been closed, and the rain had stopped falling from the sky. ³The water receded steadily from the earth. At the end of the hundred and fifty days the water had gone down, ⁴and on the seventeenth day of the seventh month the ark came to rest on the mountains of Ararat. ⁵The waters continued to recede until the tenth month, and on the first day of the tenth month the tops of the mountains became visible.

⁶After forty days Noah opened the window he had made in the ark ⁷and sent out a raven, and it kept flying back and forth until the water had dried up from the earth. ⁸Then he sent out a dove to see if the water had receded from the surface of the ground. ⁹But the dove could find no place to set its feet because there was water over all the surface of the earth; so it returned to Noah in the ark. He reached out his hand and took the dove and brought it back to himself in the ark. ¹⁰He waited seven more days and again sent out the dove from the ark. ¹¹When the dove returned to him in the evening, there in its beak was a freshly plucked olive leaf! Then Noah knew that the water had receded from the earth. ¹²He waited seven more days and sent the dove out again, but this time it did not return to him.

¹³By the first day of the first month of Noah's six hundred and first year, the water had dried up from the earth. Noah then removed the covering from the ark and saw that the surface of the ground was dry. ¹⁴By the twenty-seventh day of the second month the earth was completely dry.

¹⁵Then God said to Noah, ¹⁶"Come out of the ark, you and your wife and your sons and their wives. ¹⁷Bring out every kind of living creature that is with you—the birds, the animals, and all the creatures that move along the ground—so they can multiply on the earth and be fruitful and increase in number upon it."

¹⁸So Noah came out, together with his sons and his wife and his sons' wives. ¹⁹All the animals and all the creatures that move along the ground and all the birds—everything that moves on the earth—came out of the ark, one kind after another.

²⁰Then Noah built an altar to the Lord and, taking some of all the clean animals and clean birds, he sacrificed burnt offerings on it. ²¹The Lord smelled the pleasing aroma and said in his heart: "Never again will I curse the ground because of man, even though*a* every inclination of his heart is evil from childhood. And never again will I destroy all living creatures, as I have done.

²²"As long as the earth endures,
    seedtime and harvest,
    cold and heat,
    summer and winter,
    day and night
    will never cease."

God's Covenant With Noah

9 Then God blessed Noah and his sons, saying to them, "Be fruitful and increase in number and fill the earth. ²The fear and dread of you will fall upon all the beasts of the earth and all the birds of the air, upon every creature that moves along the ground, and upon all the fish of the sea; they are given into your hands. ³Everything that lives and moves will be food for you. Just as I gave you the green plants, I now give you everything.

⁴"But you must not eat meat that has its lifeblood still in it. ⁵And for your lifeblood I will surely demand an accounting. I will demand an accounting from every animal. And from each man, too, I will demand an accounting for the life of his fellow man.

⁶"Whoever sheds the blood of man,
    by man shall his blood be shed;
for in the image of God
    has God made man.

⁷As for you, be fruitful and increase in number; multiply on the earth and increase upon it."

⁸Then God said to Noah and to his sons with him: ⁹"I now establish my covenant with you and with your descendants after you ¹⁰and with every living creature that was with you—the birds, the livestock and all the wild animals, all those that came out

GOD'S PATIENCE WITH HUMAN REBELLION

After watching a news report about a homosexual minister, Lou Ann is disgusted.

"That is so gross! How can he be like that? More than that, how can he stand there and say that God is happy about what he's doing?"

Later Lou Ann is even more appalled by a documentary featuring several prominent scientists. In the program the scholars ridicule belief in a Supreme Being and attack the accuracy of the Bible.

"Why does God let them get away with that?"

Look It Up
••••

The answer is simple—God is patient!

He is patient when his own children slip into sin. "Or do you show contempt for the riches of his kindness, tolerance and patience, not realizing that God's kindness leads you toward repentance?" (Romans 2:4).

He also demonstrates patience toward unbelieving sinners. "The Lord is not slow in keeping his promise, as some understand slowness. He is patient with you, not wanting anyone to perish, but everyone to come to repentance" (2 Peter 3:9).

Think It Through
••••

The Bible says that God is "slow to anger" (Exodus 34:6; Nahum 1:3). That phrase shows God's incredible patience. But it also hints at another truth: We can, humanly speaking, exhaust God's patience and make him angry. (Definitely not a wise move!)

Are you involved in sinful behavior that may be testing God's patience?

Work It Out
••••

Let God's patience motivate you today.

1. Pray for the salvation of the wildest, most rebellious person you know.

2. Eliminate a habit that you know is wrong.

3. Spend a few minutes thanking God for putting up with your foolish mistakes and repeated sins.

4. Reread the story of the lost son and patient father in Luke 15:11–32.

5. Forgive that person who hurt your feelings this week. In other words, be as patient with others as God has been with you.

Nail It Down
••••

Consider the patience Noah must have had during those last weeks on the ark as recorded in Genesis 8:3–17.

Turn to pages 58, 85 and 1227 for other readings on patience.
Turn to page 15 for the weekend reading.

Topic
••••

of the ark with you—every living creature on earth. **11**I establish my covenant with you: Never again will all life be cut off by the waters of a flood; never again will there be a flood to destroy the earth."

12And God said, "This is the sign of the covenant I am making between me and you and every living creature with you, a covenant for all generations to come: **13**I have set my rainbow in the clouds, and it will be the sign of the covenant between me and the earth. **14**Whenever I bring clouds over the earth and the rainbow appears in the clouds, **15**I will remember my covenant between me and you and all living creatures of every kind. Never again will the waters become a flood to destroy all life. **16**Whenever the rainbow appears in the clouds, I will see it and remember the everlasting covenant between God and all living creatures of every kind on the earth."

17So God said to Noah, "This is the sign of the covenant I have established between me and all life on the earth."

The Sons of Noah

18The sons of Noah who came out of the ark were Shem, Ham and Japheth. (Ham was the father of Canaan.) **19**These were the three sons of Noah, and from them came the people who were scattered over the earth.

20Noah, a man of the soil, proceeded*a* to plant a vineyard. **21**When he drank some of its wine, he became drunk and lay uncovered inside his tent. **22**Ham, the father of Canaan, saw his father's nakedness and told his two brothers outside. **23**But Shem and Japheth took a garment and laid it across their shoulders; then they walked in backward and covered their father's nakedness. Their faces were turned the other way so that they would not see their father's nakedness.

24When Noah awoke from his wine and found out what his youngest son had done to him, **25**he said,

"Cursed be Canaan!
    The lowest of slaves
    will he be to his brothers."

26He also said,

"Blessed be the LORD, the God of Shem!
    May Canaan be the slave of Shem.*b*

27May God extend the territory of Japheth*c*;
    may Japheth live in the tents of Shem,
    and may Canaan be his*d* slave."

28After the flood Noah lived 350 years. **29**Altogether, Noah lived 950 years, and then he died.

The Table of Nations

10 This is the account of Shem, Ham and Japheth, Noah's sons, who themselves had sons after the flood.

The Japhethites

2The sons*e* of Japheth:
    Gomer, Magog, Madai, Javan, Tubal, Meshech and Tiras.
3The sons of Gomer:
    Ashkenaz, Riphath and Togarmah.
4The sons of Javan:
    Elishah, Tarshish, the Kittim and the Rodanim.*f* **5**(From these the maritime peoples spread out into their territories by their clans within their nations, each with its own language.)

The Hamites

6The sons of Ham:
    Cush, Mizraim,*g* Put and Canaan.
7The sons of Cush:
    Seba, Havilah, Sabtah, Raamah and Sabteca.
    The sons of Raamah:
    Sheba and Dedan.

8Cush was the father*h* of Nimrod, who grew to be a mighty warrior on the earth. **9**He was a mighty hunter before the LORD; that is why it is said, "Like Nimrod, a mighty hunter before the LORD." **10**The first centers of his kingdom were Babylon, Erech, Akkad and Calneh, in*i* Shinar.*j* **11**From that land he went to Assyria, where he built Nineveh, Rehoboth Ir,*k* Calah **12**and Resen, which is between Nineveh and Calah; that is the great city.

13Mizraim was the father of
    the Ludites, Anamites, Lehabites, Naphtuhites, **14**Pathrusites, Caslu-

---

a20 Or *soil, was the first*   *b26* Or *be his slave*   *c27* *Japheth* sounds like the Hebrew for *extend.*   *d27* Or *their*   *e2* *Sons* may mean *descendants* or *successors* or *nations;* also in verses 3, 4, 6, 7, 20-23, 29 and 31.
f4 Some manuscripts of the Masoretic Text and Samaritan Pentateuch (see also Septuagint and 1 Chron. 1:7); most manuscripts of the Masoretic Text *Dodanim*   *g6* That is, Egypt; also in verse 13   *h8* *Father* may mean *ancestor* or *predecessor* or *founder;* also in verses 13, 15, 24 and 26.   *i10* Or *Erech and Akkad—all of them in*
j10 That is, Babylonia   *k11* Or *Nineveh with its city squares*

hites (from whom the Philistines came) and Caphtorites. ¹⁵Canaan was the father of

¹⁵Canaan was the father of
Sidon his firstborn,^a and of the Hittites, ¹⁶Jebusites, Amorites, Girgashites, ¹⁷Hivites, Arkites, Sinites, ¹⁸Arvadites, Zemarites and Hamathites.

Later the Canaanite clans scattered ¹⁹and the borders of Canaan reached from Sidon toward Gerar as far as Gaza, and then toward Sodom, Gomorrah, Admah and Zeboiim, as far as Lasha.
²⁰These are the sons of Ham by their clans and languages, in their territories and nations.

The Semites

²¹Sons were also born to Shem, whose older brother was^b Japheth; Shem was the ancestor of all the sons of Eber.

²²The sons of Shem:
Elam, Asshur, Arphaxad, Lud and Aram.
²³The sons of Aram:
Uz, Hul, Gether and Meshech.^c
²⁴Arphaxad was the father of^d Shelah, and Shelah the father of Eber.
²⁵Two sons were born to Eber:
One was named Peleg,^e because in his time the earth was divided; his brother was named Joktan.
²⁶Joktan was the father of
Almodad, Sheleph, Hazarmaveth, Jerah, ²⁷Hadoram, Uzal, Diklah, ²⁸Obal, Abimael, Sheba, ²⁹Ophir, Havilah and Jobab. All these were sons of Joktan.

³⁰The region where they lived stretched from Mesha toward Sephar, in the eastern hill country.
³¹These are the sons of Shem by their clans and languages, in their territories and nations.

³²These are the clans of Noah's sons, according to their lines of descent, within their nations. From these the nations spread out over the earth after the flood.

The Tower of Babel

11 Now the whole world had one language and a common speech. ²As men moved eastward,^f they found a plain in Shinar^g and settled there.

³They said to each other, "Come, let's make bricks and bake them thoroughly." They used brick instead of stone, and tar for mortar. ⁴Then they said, "Come, let us build ourselves a city, with a tower that reaches to the heavens, so that we may make a name for ourselves and not be scattered over the face of the whole earth."

⁵But the Lord came down to see the city and the tower that the men were building. ⁶The Lord said, "If as one people speaking the same language they have begun to do this, then nothing they plan to do will be impossible for them. ⁷Come, let us go down and confuse their language so they will not understand each other."

⁸So the Lord scattered them from there over all the earth, and they stopped building the city. ⁹That is why it was called Babel^h— because there the Lord confused the language of the whole world. From there the Lord scattered them over the face of the whole earth.

From Shem to Abram

¹⁰This is the account of Shem.

Two years after the flood, when Shem was 100 years old, he became the fatherⁱ of Arphaxad. ¹¹And after he became the father of Arphaxad, Shem lived 500 years and had other sons and daughters.

¹²When Arphaxad had lived 35 years, he became the father of Shelah. ¹³And after he became the father of Shelah, Arphaxad lived 403 years and had other sons and daughters.^j

¹⁴When Shelah had lived 30 years, he became the father of Eber. ¹⁵And after he became the father of Eber, Shelah lived 403 years and had other sons and daughters.

¹⁶When Eber had lived 34 years, he became the father of Peleg. ¹⁷And after he became the father of Peleg, Eber lived 430 years and had other sons and daughters.

¹⁸When Peleg had lived 30 years, he be-

---

^a15 Or of the Sidonians, the foremost   ^b21 Or Shem, the older brother of   ^c23 See Septuagint and 1 Chron. 1:17; Hebrew Mash   ^d24 Hebrew; Septuagint father of Cainan, and Cainan was the father of   ^e25 Peleg means division.   ^f2 Or from the east; or in the east   ^g2 That is, Babylonia   ^h9 That is, Babylon; Babel sounds like the Hebrew for confused.   ⁱ10 Father may mean ancestor; also in verses 11-25.
^j12,13 Hebrew; Septuagint (see also Luke 3:35, 36 and note at Gen. 10:24) 35 years, he became the father of Cainan. ¹³And after he became the father of Cainan, Arphaxad lived 430 years and had other sons and daughters, and then he died. When Cainan had lived 130 years, he became the father of Shelah. And after he became the father of Shelah, Cainan lived 330 years and had other sons and daughters

MAKE YOUR WORDS COUNT

Work It Out • • • •

Listen to yourself and your friends for one full day. Make a mental list of all the words you use that adults don't usually say—words like *geek, nerd, rad, awesome.* The words themselves change so quickly that even making a list is difficult. What words would be on your list?

Many teenagers have their own language, one that adults don't understand. Along with other problems, language can cause conflict between adults and teens. When people can't or don't or won't understand each other, conflict is inevitable.

Which of the following is most likely to cause conflict?

• "Yo! Mom! Me and the guys are cruising into the city tonight. I need the car by six!" Or, "Mom, can I borrow the car tonight?"

• "You be in this house by 11 o'clock tonight, or you'll be in big trouble!" Or, "You should be home by 11 o'clock tonight, okay?"

Not too difficult to figure out, is it? The language used by both adults and teens, as well as how the words are spoken, can be a big source of conflict. You may have to be an interpreter of "teen-ese" for the adults in your life. Be willing to do what you can to avoid conflict in this area.

Nail It Down • • • •

Read Genesis 11:1–9 for the story of a time when language confused a whole bunch of people.

Think It Through • • • •

Sometimes the solutions to problems are more simple than you think. When parents and their kids don't communicate, it may be as simple as the language each uses. Or it may be as subtle as *how* things are said.

You and only you are responsible for what you say and how you say it. Think about it the next time you talk to an adult.

Nail It Down • • • •

Reread Genesis 11:1–9. For further insight read Proverbs 18:4–8.

Turn to pages 178 and 1327 for other readings on conflict.
Turn to page 18 for Monday's reading.

Topic
• • • •

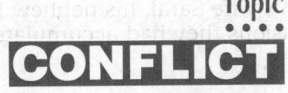

CONFLICT

came the father of Reu. ¹⁹And after he became the father of Reu, Peleg lived 209 years and had other sons and daughters.

²⁰When Reu had lived 32 years, he became the father of Serug. ²¹And after he became the father of Serug, Reu lived 207 years and had other sons and daughters.

²²When Serug had lived 30 years, he became the father of Nahor. ²³And after he became the father of Nahor, Serug lived 200 years and had other sons and daughters.

²⁴When Nahor had lived 29 years, he became the father of Terah. ²⁵And after he became the father of Terah, Nahor lived 119 years and had other sons and daughters.

²⁶After Terah had lived 70 years, he became the father of Abram, Nahor and Haran.

²⁷This is the account of Terah.

Terah became the father of Abram, Nahor and Haran. And Haran became the father of Lot. ²⁸While his father Terah was still alive, Haran died in Ur of the Chaldeans, in the land of his birth. ²⁹Abram and Nahor both married. The name of Abram's wife was Sarai, and the name of Nahor's wife was Milcah; she was the daughter of Haran, the father of both Milcah and Iscah. ³⁰Now Sarai was barren; she had no children.

³¹Terah took his son Abram, his grandson Lot son of Haran, and his daughter-in-law Sarai, the wife of his son Abram, and together they set out from Ur of the Chaldeans to go to Canaan. But when they came to Haran, they settled there.

³²Terah lived 205 years, and he died in Haran.

The Call of Abram

12 The LORD had said to Abram, "Leave your country, your people and your father's household and go to the land I will show you.

²"I will make you into a great nation
    and I will bless you;
 I will make your name great,
    and you will be a blessing.
³I will bless those who bless you,
    and whoever curses you I will curse;
 and all peoples on earth
    will be blessed through you."

⁴So Abram left, as the LORD had told him; and Lot went with him. Abram was seventy-five years old when he set out from Haran. ⁵He took his wife Sarai, his nephew Lot, all the possessions they had accumulated and the people they had acquired in Haran, and they set out for the land of Canaan, and they arrived there.

⁶Abram traveled through the land as far as the site of the great tree of Moreh at Shechem. At that time the Canaanites were in the land. ⁷The LORD appeared to Abram and said, "To your offspring*a* I will give this land." So he built an altar there to the LORD, who had appeared to him.

⁸From there he went on toward the hills east of Bethel and pitched his tent, with Bethel on the west and Ai on the east. There he built an altar to the LORD and called on the name of the LORD. ⁹Then Abram set out and continued toward the Negev.

Abram in Egypt

¹⁰Now there was a famine in the land, and Abram went down to Egypt to live there for a while because the famine was severe. ¹¹As he was about to enter Egypt, he said to his wife Sarai, "I know what a beautiful woman you are. ¹²When the Egyptians see you, they will say, 'This is his wife.' Then they will kill me but will let you live. ¹³Say you are my sister, so that I will be treated well for your sake and my life will be spared because of you."

¹⁴When Abram came to Egypt, the Egyptians saw that she was a very beautiful woman. ¹⁵And when Pharaoh's officials saw her, they praised her to Pharaoh, and she was taken into his palace. ¹⁶He treated Abram well for her sake, and Abram acquired sheep and cattle, male and female donkeys, menservants and maidservants, and camels.

¹⁷But the LORD inflicted serious diseases on Pharaoh and his household because of Abram's wife Sarai. ¹⁸So Pharaoh summoned Abram. "What have you done to me?" he said. "Why didn't you tell me she was your wife? ¹⁹Why did you say, 'She is my sister,' so that I took her to be my wife? Now then, here is your wife. Take her and go!" ²⁰Then Pharaoh gave orders about Abram to his men, and they sent him on his way, with his wife and everything he had.

Abram and Lot Separate

13 So Abram went up from Egypt to the Negev, with his wife and everything he had, and Lot went with him. ²Abram had become very wealthy in livestock and in silver and gold.

³From the Negev he went from place to

a7 Or seed

place until he came to Bethel, to the place between Bethel and Ai where his tent had been earlier ⁴and where he had first built an altar. There Abram called on the name of the Lord.

⁵Now Lot, who was moving about with Abram, also had flocks and herds and tents. ⁶But the land could not support them while they stayed together, for their possessions were so great that they were not able to stay together. ⁷And quarreling arose between Abram's herdsmen and the herdsmen of Lot. The Canaanites and Perizzites were also living in the land at that time.

⁸So Abram said to Lot, "Let's not have any quarreling between you and me, or between your herdsmen and mine, for we are brothers. ⁹Is not the whole land before you? Let's part company. If you go to the left, I'll go to the right; if you go to the right, I'll go to the left."

¹⁰Lot looked up and saw that the whole plain of the Jordan was well watered, like the garden of the Lord, like the land of Egypt, toward Zoar. (This was before the Lord destroyed Sodom and Gomorrah.) ¹¹So Lot chose for himself the whole plain of the Jordan and set out toward the east. The two men parted company: ¹²Abram lived in the land of Canaan, while Lot lived among the cities of the plain and pitched his tents near Sodom. ¹³Now the men of Sodom were wicked and were sinning greatly against the Lord.

¹⁴The Lord said to Abram after Lot had parted from him, "Lift up your eyes from where you are and look north and south, east and west. ¹⁵All the land that you see I will give to you and your offspring*a* forever. ¹⁶I will make your offspring like the dust of the earth, so that if anyone could count the dust, then your offspring could be counted. ¹⁷Go, walk through the length and breadth of the land, for I am giving it to you."

¹⁸So Abram moved his tents and went to live near the great trees of Mamre at Hebron, where he built an altar to the Lord.

Abram Rescues Lot

14 At this time Amraphel king of Shinar,*b* Arioch king of Ellasar, Kedorlaomer king of Elam and Tidal king of Goiim ²went to war against Bera king of Sodom, Birsha king of Gomorrah, Shinab king of Admah, Shemeber king of Zeboiim, and the king of Bela (that is, Zoar). ³All these latter kings joined forces in the Valley of Siddim (the Salt Sea*c*). ⁴For twelve years they had been subject to Kedorlaomer, but in the thirteenth year they rebelled.

⁵In the fourteenth year, Kedorlaomer and the kings allied with him went out and defeated the Rephaites in Ashteroth Karnaim, the Zuzites in Ham, the Emites in Shaveh Kiriathaim ⁶and the Horites in the hill country of Seir, as far as El Paran near the desert. ⁷Then they turned back and went to En Mishpat (that is, Kadesh), and they conquered the whole territory of the Amalekites, as well as the Amorites who were living in Hazazon Tamar.

⁸Then the king of Sodom, the king of Gomorrah, the king of Admah, the king of Zeboiim and the king of Bela (that is, Zoar) marched out and drew up their battle lines in the Valley of Siddim ⁹against Kedorlaomer king of Elam, Tidal king of Goiim, Amraphel king of Shinar and Arioch king of Ellasar—four kings against five. ¹⁰Now the Valley of Siddim was full of tar pits, and when the kings of Sodom and Gomorrah fled, some of the men fell into them and the rest fled to the hills. ¹¹The four kings seized all the goods of Sodom and Gomorrah and all their food; then they went away. ¹²They also carried off Abram's nephew Lot and his possessions, since he was living in Sodom.

¹³One who had escaped came and reported this to Abram the Hebrew. Now Abram was living near the great trees of Mamre the Amorite, a brother*d* of Eshcol and Aner, all of whom were allied with Abram. ¹⁴When Abram heard that his relative had been taken captive, he called out the 318 trained men born in his household and went in pursuit as far as Dan. ¹⁵During the night Abram divided his men to attack them and he routed them, pursuing them as far as Hobah, north of Damascus. ¹⁶He recovered all the goods and brought back his relative Lot and his possessions, together with the women and the other people.

¹⁷After Abram returned from defeating Kedorlaomer and the kings allied with him, the king of Sodom came out to meet him in the Valley of Shaveh (that is, the King's Valley).

¹⁸Then Melchizedek king of Salem*e* brought out bread and wine. He was priest of God Most High, ¹⁹and he blessed Abram, saying,

---

*a*15 Or *seed*; also in verse 16   *b*1 That is, Babylonia; also in verse 9   *c*3 That is, the Dead Sea   *d*13 Or *a relative*; or *an ally*   *e*18 That is, Jerusalem

WITH FRIENDS LIKE THESE...

Mark is in shock. Here's the reason:
Two weeks ago he met Heather, a new girl at church. Though he talked to her for only about five minutes, he was hooked big time! Naturally, he immediately found his best friend Terry and told him everything. "You've got to see her, Terry. She's awesome! I'm calling her tonight for next weekend."

Sure enough, Mark called. Heather was interested but had to go out of town.

Mark called again the following week and asked Heather out for Saturday. Heather's reply? "Oh, I'd love to Mark, but I'm already planning to go snowboarding with Terry."

Now do you see why Mark is so hurt and angry?

Look It Up
••••

Take a look at a few rules that can help reduce the competition between friends:

The Golden Rule—"Do to others as you would have them do to you" (Luke 6:31).

The Love Rule—"Love does no harm to its neighbor. Therefore love is the fulfillment of the law" (Romans 13:10).

The Rule of Unselfishness—"Nobody should seek his own good, but the good of others" (1 Corinthians 10:24).

Follow those rules and your friendships can't help but get better!

Think It Through
••••

Have you ever pulled a stunt like the one Terry pulled on Mark? What happened?

How would you feel if you were in Mark's place? What should Mark do in response?

Work It Out
••••

List the competitive situations you face with your closest friends (trying for the same honor, award, position on the team, elective office, boyfriend/girlfriend, etc.). You can either let those things come between you . . . or you can apply the friendship rules just listed.

Try filling in the blank in this sentence: "The Golden Rule demands that I _____ in this situation." (Be specific!) Do this with each rule and for each potential problem area.

Nail It Down
••••

Read Genesis 13:5–12 for how Abraham avoided competing with Lot.

Turn to pages 43, 1230 and 1360 for other readings on competition.
Turn to page 21 for Tuesday's reading.

Topic
••••

COMPETITION

"Blessed be Abram by God Most High,
   Creator^a of heaven and earth.
²⁰And blessed be^b God Most High,
   who delivered your enemies into your
      hand."

Then Abram gave him a tenth of everything.
   ²¹The king of Sodom said to Abram, "Give
me the people and keep the goods for yourself."

   ²²But Abram said to the king of Sodom, "I
have raised my hand to the LORD, God Most
High, Creator of heaven and earth, and have
taken an oath ²³that I will accept nothing belonging to you, not even a thread or the
thong of a sandal, so that you will never be
able to say, 'I made Abram rich.' ²⁴I will accept nothing but what my men have eaten
and the share that belongs to the men who
went with me — to Aner, Eshcol and Mamre.
Let them have their share."

God's Covenant With Abram

15 After this, the word of the LORD came
to Abram in a vision:

"Do not be afraid, Abram.
   I am your shield,^c
   your very great reward.^d"

   ²But Abram said, "O Sovereign LORD, what
can you give me since I remain childless and
the one who will inherit^e my estate is Eliezer of Damascus?" ³And Abram said, "You
have given me no children; so a servant in
my household will be my heir." ⁴Then the word of the LORD came to him:
"This man will not be your heir, but a son
coming from your own body will be your
heir." ⁵He took him outside and said, "Look
up at the heavens and count the stars — if
indeed you can count them." Then he said
to him, "So shall your offspring be."

   ⁶Abram believed the LORD, and he credited
it to him as righteousness.

   ⁷He also said to him, "I am the LORD, who
brought you out of Ur of the Chaldeans to
give you this land to take possession of it."

   ⁸But Abram said, "O Sovereign LORD, how
can I know that I will gain possession of it?"

   ⁹So the LORD said to him, "Bring me a heifer, a goat and a ram, each three years old,
along with a dove and a young pigeon."

   ¹⁰Abram brought all these to him, cut
them in two and arranged the halves opposite each other; the birds, however, he did
not cut in half. ¹¹Then birds of prey came
down on the carcasses, but Abram drove
them away.

   ¹²As the sun was setting, Abram fell into
a deep sleep, and a thick and dreadful darkness came over him. ¹³Then the LORD said to
him, "Know for certain that your descendants will be strangers in a country not their
own, and they will be enslaved and mistreated four hundred years. ¹⁴But I will punish the nation they serve as slaves, and
afterward they will come out with great
possessions. ¹⁵You, however, will go to your
fathers in peace and be buried at a good old
age. ¹⁶In the fourth generation your descendants will come back here, for the sin of the
Amorites has not yet reached its full measure."

   ¹⁷When the sun had set and darkness had
fallen, a smoking firepot with a blazing torch
appeared and passed between the pieces.
¹⁸On that day the LORD made a covenant
with Abram and said, "To your descendants
I give this land, from the river^f of Egypt to
the great river, the Euphrates — ¹⁹the land
of the Kenites, Kenizzites, Kadmonites,
²⁰Hittites, Perizzites, Rephaites, ²¹Amorites,
Canaanites, Girgashites and Jebusites."

Hagar and Ishmael

16 Now Sarai, Abram's wife, had borne
him no children. But she had an
Egyptian maidservant named Hagar; ²so she
said to Abram, "The LORD has kept me from
having children. Go, sleep with my maidservant; perhaps I can build a family through
her."

   Abram agreed to what Sarai said. ³So after
Abram had been living in Canaan ten years,
Sarai his wife took her Egyptian maidservant Hagar and gave her to her husband to
be his wife. ⁴He slept with Hagar, and she
conceived.

   When she knew she was pregnant, she
began to despise her mistress. ⁵Then Sarai
said to Abram, "You are responsible for the
wrong I am suffering. I put my servant in
your arms, and now that she knows she is
pregnant, she despises me. May the LORD
judge between you and me."

   ⁶"Your servant is in your hands," Abram
said. "Do with her whatever you think best."
Then Sarai mistreated Hagar; so she fled
from her.

   ⁷The angel of the LORD found Hagar near
a spring in the desert; it was the spring that
is beside the road to Shur. ⁸And he said,

---

^a19 Or *Possessor*; also in verse 22   ^b20 Or *And praise be to*   ^c1 Or *sovereign*   ^d1 Or *shield; / your
reward will be very great*   ^e2 The meaning of the Hebrew for this phrase is uncertain.   ^f18 Or *Wadi*

"Hagar, servant of Sarai, where have you come from, and where are you going?"

"I'm running away from my mistress Sarai," she answered.

⁹Then the angel of the LORD told her, "Go back to your mistress and submit to her." ¹⁰The angel added, "I will so increase your descendants that they will be too numerous to count."

¹¹The angel of the LORD also said to her:

"You are now with child
    and you will have a son.
You shall name him Ishmael,ᵃ
    for the LORD has heard of your misery.
¹²He will be a wild donkey of a man;
    his hand will be against everyone
    and everyone's hand against him,
and he will live in hostility
    towardᵇ all his brothers."

¹³She gave this name to the LORD who spoke to her: "You are the God who sees me," for she said, "I have now seenᶜ the One who sees me." ¹⁴That is why the well was called Beer Lahai Roiᵈ; it is still there, between Kadesh and Bered.

¹⁵So Hagar bore Abram a son, and Abram gave the name Ishmael to the son she had borne. ¹⁶Abram was eighty-six years old when Hagar bore him Ishmael.

The Covenant of Circumcision

17 When Abram was ninety-nine years old, the LORD appeared to him and said, "I am God Almightyᵉ; walk before me and be blameless. ²I will confirm my covenant between me and you and will greatly increase your numbers."

³Abram fell facedown, and God said to him, ⁴"As for me, this is my covenant with you: You will be the father of many nations. ⁵No longer will you be called Abramᶠ; your name will be Abraham,ᵍ for I have made you a father of many nations. ⁶I will make you very fruitful; I will make nations of you, and kings will come from you. ⁷I will establish my covenant as an everlasting covenant between me and you and your descendants after you for the generations to come, to be your God and the God of your descendants after you. ⁸The whole land of Canaan, where you are now an alien, I will give as an everlasting possession to you and your descendants after you; and I will be their God."

⁹Then God said to Abraham, "As for you, you must keep my covenant, you and your descendants after you for the generations to come. ¹⁰This is my covenant with you and your descendants after you, the covenant you are to keep: Every male among you shall be circumcised. ¹¹You are to undergo circumcision, and it will be the sign of the covenant between me and you. ¹²For the generations to come every male among you who is eight days old must be circumcised, including those born in your household or bought with money from a foreigner—those who are not your offspring. ¹³Whether born in your household or bought with your money, they must be circumcised. My covenant in your flesh is to be an everlasting covenant. ¹⁴Any uncircumcised male, who has not been circumcised in the flesh, will be cut off from his people; he has broken my covenant."

¹⁵God also said to Abraham, "As for Sarai your wife, you are no longer to call her Sarai; her name will be Sarah. ¹⁶I will bless her and will surely give you a son by her. I will bless her so that she will be the mother of nations; kings of peoples will come from her."

¹⁷Abraham fell facedown; he laughed and said to himself, "Will a son be born to a man a hundred years old? Will Sarah bear a child at the age of ninety?" ¹⁸And Abraham said to God, "If only Ishmael might live under your blessing!"

¹⁹Then God said, "Yes, but your wife Sarah will bear you a son, and you will call him Isaac.ʰ I will establish my covenant with him as an everlasting covenant for his descendants after him. ²⁰And as for Ishmael, I have heard you: I will surely bless him; I will make him fruitful and will greatly increase his numbers. He will be the father of twelve rulers, and I will make him into a great nation. ²¹But my covenant I will establish with Isaac, whom Sarah will bear to you by this time next year." ²²When he had finished speaking with Abraham, God went up from him.

²³On that very day Abraham took his son Ishmael and all those born in his household or bought with his money, every male in his household, and circumcised them, as God told him. ²⁴Abraham was ninety-nine years old when he was circumcised, ²⁵and his son Ishmael was thirteen; ²⁶Abraham and his son Ishmael were both circumcised on that same day. ²⁷And every male in Abraham's

ᵃ11 Ishmael means God hears.   ᵇ12 Or live to the east / of   ᶜ13 Or seen the back of   ᵈ14 Beer Lahai Roi
means well of the Living One who sees me.   ᵉ1 Hebrew El-Shaddai   ᶠ5 Abram means exalted father.
ᵍ5 Abraham means father of many.   ʰ19 Isaac means he laughs.

SOME DIVINE ALIASES

• •

Brent is extremely nervous about pitching in an important baseball game tomorrow afternoon.

Gretchen feels sure that she is supposed to go on the youth retreat next weekend, but she doesn't have the $35 registration fee. The deadline is tonight.

Thomas dreads visiting his dad tonight. "He always makes fun of my faith. I never know what to say."

Look It Up
••••

Those anxious, hurting individuals could find real encouragement by studying some of the names by which God has revealed himself in the Bible.

1. Variations of Elohim:
• El Shaddai ("God Almighty")—"When Abram was ninety-nine years old, the LORD appeared to him and said, 'I am God Almighty'" (Genesis 17:1). Other instances of this name (Genesis 28:3–4; Psalm 91:1–2) indicate that it implies not only power but provision and protection as well.
• El Elyon ("God Most High")—Genesis 14:19.
• El Olam ("Eternal God")—Genesis 21:33.
2. Variations of Yahweh (or Jehovah):
• Yahweh-jireh ("the LORD will provide")—"So Abraham called that place The LORD Will Provide" (Genesis 22:14).
• Yahweh-rapha ("the LORD who heals")—Exodus 15:26.
• Yahweh-nissi ("The LORD is my Banner," that is, he is the one who fights my battles)—Exodus 17:15.
• Yahweh-shalom ("The LORD is Peace")—Judges 6:23–24.

Think It Through
••••

Which aspect of God just revealed means the most to you right now? Which aspect of God's character does your best friend need to hear about today?

Work It Out
••••

What is it that you need most right now? Peace? Strength? Healing? Help? Call God by his appropriate name and trust him to meet that need.

Don't end your devotional time until you've read all the passages just cited. Pick out one of the verses and memorize it for future reference.

Nail It Down
••••

Read about another name for God (El Roi—the God who sees our trouble and pain)—Genesis 16:13.

Turn to pages 96, 185 and 192 for other readings on God's names.
Turn to page 23 for Wednesday's reading.

Topic
••••

GOD'S NAMES

household, including those born in his household or bought from a foreigner, was circumcised with him.

The Three Visitors

18 The LORD appeared to Abraham near the great trees of Mamre while he was sitting at the entrance to his tent in the heat of the day. ²Abraham looked up and saw three men standing nearby. When he saw them, he hurried from the entrance of his tent to meet them and bowed low to the ground.

³He said, "If I have found favor in your eyes, my lord,ᵃ do not pass your servant by. ⁴Let a little water be brought, and then you may all wash your feet and rest under this tree. ⁵Let me get you something to eat, so you can be refreshed and then go on your way—now that you have come to your servant."

"Very well," they answered, "do as you say."

⁶So Abraham hurried into the tent to Sarah. "Quick," he said, "get three seahsᵇ of fine flour and knead it and bake some bread."

⁷Then he ran to the herd and selected a choice, tender calf and gave it to a servant, who hurried to prepare it. ⁸He then brought some curds and milk and the calf that had been prepared, and set these before them. While they ate, he stood near them under a tree.

⁹"Where is your wife Sarah?" they asked him.

"There, in the tent," he said.

¹⁰Then the LORDᶜ said, "I will surely return to you about this time next year, and Sarah your wife will have a son."

Now Sarah was listening at the entrance to the tent, which was behind him. ¹¹Abraham and Sarah were already old and well advanced in years, and Sarah was past the age of childbearing. ¹²So Sarah laughed to herself as she thought, "After I am worn out and my masterᵈ is old, will I now have this pleasure?"

¹³Then the LORD said to Abraham, "Why did Sarah laugh and say, 'Will I really have a child, now that I am old?' ¹⁴Is anything too hard for the LORD? I will return to you at the appointed time next year and Sarah will have a son."

¹⁵Sarah was afraid, so she lied and said, "I did not laugh."

But he said, "Yes, you did laugh."

Abraham Pleads for Sodom

¹⁶When the men got up to leave, they looked down toward Sodom, and Abraham walked along with them to see them on their way. ¹⁷Then the LORD said, "Shall I hide from Abraham what I am about to do? ¹⁸Abraham will surely become a great and powerful nation, and all nations on earth will be blessed through him. ¹⁹For I have chosen him, so that he will direct his children and his household after him to keep the way of the LORD by doing what is right and just, so that the LORD will bring about for Abraham what he has promised him."

²⁰Then the LORD said, "The outcry against Sodom and Gomorrah is so great and their sin so grievous ²¹that I will go down and see if what they have done is as bad as the outcry that has reached me. If not, I will know."

²²The men turned away and went toward Sodom, but Abraham remained standing before the LORD.ᵉ ²³Then Abraham approached him and said: "Will you sweep away the righteous with the wicked? ²⁴What if there are fifty righteous people in the city? Will you really sweep it away and not spareᶠ the place for the sake of the fifty righteous people in it? ²⁵Far be it from you to do such a thing—to kill the righteous with the wicked, treating the righteous and the wicked alike. Far be it from you! Will not the Judgeᵍ of all the earth do right?"

²⁶The LORD said, "If I find fifty righteous people in the city of Sodom, I will spare the whole place for their sake."

²⁷Then Abraham spoke up again: "Now that I have been so bold as to speak to the Lord, though I am nothing but dust and ashes, ²⁸what if the number of the righteous is five less than fifty? Will you destroy the whole city because of five people?"

"If I find forty-five there," he said, "I will not destroy it."

²⁹Once again he spoke to him, "What if only forty are found there?"

He said, "For the sake of forty, I will not do it."

³⁰Then he said, "May the Lord not be angry, but let me speak. What if only thirty can be found there?"

ᵃ3 Or O Lord   ᵇ6 That is, probably about 20 quarts (about 22 liters)   ᶜ10 Hebrew *Then he*   ᵈ12 Or *husband*   ᵉ22 Masoretic Text; an ancient Hebrew scribal tradition *but the* LORD *remained standing before Abraham*   ᶠ24 Or *forgive*; also in verse 26   ᵍ25 Or *Ruler*

IT'S TIME WE SAID, "ENOUGH!"

After reading an article on all the wrongs in our society, Shelly is suffering from 3-D disease: discouragement, depression and deflation. She laments, "Our nation really is going down the tubes! And it sounds like it may be too late to do anything now. Besides, I'm just one person. In fact, I'm only fourteen. What can I do?"

Look It Up

Consider these thoughts:
Your age isn't the issue! "Don't let anyone look down on you because you are young, but set an example for the believers in speech, in life, in love, in faith and in purity" (1 Timothy 4:12).

The size of your God is the real issue. When King Saul told David, "You can't fight Goliath . . . you're only a kid!" David responded, "The LORD who delivered me from the paw of the lion and the paw of the bear will deliver me from the hand of this Philistine" (1 Samuel 17:37).

David got the job . . . and he won the battle!

Think It Through

This is not a time simply for thinking. It's time for action! Read on!

Work It Out

Pick a project or two and go for it.
1. Join your school newspaper staff and speak out on moral issues from a Biblical perspective.
2. Work at local and national levels to elect candidates who share your views.
3. When TV stations show trashy movies, voice your disapproval in letters to the station manager and to the program's sponsors.
4. Join a pro-life group that is active in your area.
5. Call your elected officials and urge them to stand for morality.
6. Petition local video stores, urging them to refuse to rent pornographic videos.
7. Inform your parents and/or pastor if your school textbooks contain antireligious or immoral material.
8. Start a social-action committee in your youth group. Make each other aware of issues that need to be faced, and as a group decide exactly what you're going to do.

Nail It Down

When you get discouraged about the condition of society, recite the first part of Genesis 18:14.

Turn to pages 949 and 1017 for other readings on society.
Turn to page 43 for Thursday's reading.

Topic
SOCIETY

He answered, "I will not do it if I find thirty there."

31Abraham said, "Now that I have been so bold as to speak to the Lord, what if only twenty can be found there?"

He said, "For the sake of twenty, I will not destroy it."

32Then he said, "May the Lord not be angry, but let me speak just once more. What if only ten can be found there?"

He answered, "For the sake of ten, I will not destroy it."

33When the LORD had finished speaking with Abraham, he left, and Abraham returned home.

Sodom and Gomorrah Destroyed

19 The two angels arrived at Sodom in the evening, and Lot was sitting in the gateway of the city. When he saw them, he got up to meet them and bowed down with his face to the ground. **2**"My lords," he said, "please turn aside to your servant's house. You can wash your feet and spend the night and then go on your way early in the morning."

"No," they answered, "we will spend the night in the square."

3But he insisted so strongly that they did go with him and entered his house. He prepared a meal for them, baking bread without yeast, and they ate. **4**Before they had gone to bed, all the men from every part of the city of Sodom—both young and old—surrounded the house. **5**They called to Lot, "Where are the men who came to you tonight? Bring them out to us so that we can have sex with them."

6Lot went outside to meet them and shut the door behind him **7**and said, "No, my friends. Don't do this wicked thing. **8**Look, I have two daughters who have never slept with a man. Let me bring them out to you, and you can do what you like with them. But don't do anything to these men, for they have come under the protection of my roof."

9"Get out of our way," they replied. And they said, "This fellow came here as an alien, and now he wants to play the judge! We'll treat you worse than them." They kept bringing pressure on Lot and moved forward to break down the door.

10But the men inside reached out and pulled Lot back into the house and shut the door. **11**Then they struck the men who were at the door of the house, young and old, with

blindness so that they could not find the door.

12The two men said to Lot, "Do you have anyone else here—sons-in-law, sons or daughters, or anyone else in the city who belongs to you? Get them out of here, **13**because we are going to destroy this place. The outcry to the LORD against its people is so great that he has sent us to destroy it."

14So Lot went out and spoke to his sons-in-law, who were pledged to marry*a* his daughters. He said, "Hurry and get out of this place, because the LORD is about to destroy the city!" But his sons-in-law thought he was joking.

15With the coming of dawn, the angels urged Lot, saying, "Hurry! Take your wife and your two daughters who are here, or you will be swept away when the city is punished."

16When he hesitated, the men grasped his hand and the hands of his wife and of his two daughters and led them safely out of the city, for the LORD was merciful to them. **17**As soon as they had brought them out, one of them said, "Flee for your lives! Don't look back, and don't stop anywhere in the plain! Flee to the mountains or you will be swept away!"

18But Lot said to them, "No, my lords,*b* please! **19**Your*c* servant has found favor in your*c* eyes, and you*c* have shown great kindness to me in sparing my life. But I can't flee to the mountains; this disaster will overtake me, and I'll die. **20**Look, here is a town near enough to run to, and it is small. Let me flee to it—it is very small, isn't it? Then my life will be spared."

21He said to him, "Very well, I will grant this request too; I will not overthrow the town you speak of. **22**But flee there quickly, because I cannot do anything until you reach it." (That is why the town was called Zoar.*d*)

23By the time Lot reached Zoar, the sun had risen over the land. **24**Then the LORD rained down burning sulfur on Sodom and Gomorrah—from the LORD out of the heavens. **25**Thus he overthrew those cities and the entire plain, including all those living in the cities—and also the vegetation in the land. **26**But Lot's wife looked back, and she became a pillar of salt.

27Early the next morning Abraham got up and returned to the place where he had stood before the LORD. **28**He looked down to-

---

*a*14 Or *were married to*　　*b*18 Or *No, Lord*; or *No, my lord* *c*19 The Hebrew is singular.　　*d*22 *Zoar* means *small*.

ward Sodom and Gomorrah, toward all the land of the plain, and he saw dense smoke rising from the land, like smoke from a furnace. **29**So when God destroyed the cities of the plain, he remembered Abraham, and he brought Lot out of the catastrophe that overthrew the cities where Lot had lived.

Lot and His Daughters

30Lot and his two daughters left Zoar and settled in the mountains, for he was afraid to stay in Zoar. He and his two daughters lived in a cave. **31**One day the older daughter said to the younger, "Our father is old, and there is no man around here to lie with us, as is the custom all over the earth. **32**Let's get our father to drink wine and then lie with him and preserve our family line through our father."

33That night they got their father to drink wine, and the older daughter went in and lay with him. He was not aware of it when she lay down or when she got up.

34The next day the older daughter said to the younger, "Last night I lay with my father. Let's get him to drink wine again tonight, and you go in and lie with him so we can preserve our family line through our father." **35**So they got their father to drink wine that night also, and the younger daughter went and lay with him. Again he was not aware of it when she lay down or when she got up.

36So both of Lot's daughters became pregnant by their father. **37**The older daughter had a son, and she named him Moab*a*; he is the father of the Moabites of today. **38**The younger daughter also had a son, and she named him Ben-Ammi*b*; he is the father of the Ammonites of today.

Abraham and Abimelech

20 Now Abraham moved on from there into the region of the Negev and lived between Kadesh and Shur. For a while he stayed in Gerar, **2**and there Abraham said of his wife Sarah, "She is my sister." Then Abimelech king of Gerar sent for Sarah and took her.

3But God came to Abimelech in a dream one night and said to him, "You are as good as dead because of the woman you have taken; she is a married woman."

4Now Abimelech had not gone near her, so he said, "Lord, will you destroy an innocent nation? **5**Did he not say to me, 'She is

my sister,' and didn't she also say, 'He is my brother'? I have done this with a clear conscience and clean hands."

6Then God said to him in the dream, "Yes, I know you did this with a clear conscience, and so I have kept you from sinning against me. That is why I did not let you touch her. **7**Now return the man's wife, for he is a prophet, and he will pray for you and you will live. But if you do not return her, you may be sure that you and all yours will die."

8Early the next morning Abimelech summoned all his officials, and when he told them all that had happened, they were very much afraid. **9**Then Abimelech called Abraham in and said, "What have you done to us? How have I wronged you that you have brought such great guilt upon me and my kingdom? You have done things to me that should not be done." **10**And Abimelech asked Abraham, "What was your reason for doing this?"

11Abraham replied, "I said to myself, 'There is surely no fear of God in this place, and they will kill me because of my wife.' **12**Besides, she really is my sister, the daughter of my father though not of my mother; and she became my wife. **13**And when God had me wander from my father's household, I said to her, 'This is how you can show your love to me: Everywhere we go, say of me, "He is my brother." ' "

14Then Abimelech brought sheep and cattle and male and female slaves and gave them to Abraham, and he returned Sarah his wife to him. **15**And Abimelech said, "My land is before you; live wherever you like."

16To Sarah he said, "I am giving your brother a thousand shekels*c* of silver. This is to cover the offense against you before all who are with you; you are completely vindicated."

17Then Abraham prayed to God, and God healed Abimelech, his wife and his slave girls so they could have children again, **18**for the Lᴏʀᴅ had closed up every womb in Abimelech's household because of Abraham's wife Sarah.

The Birth of Isaac

21 Now the Lᴏʀᴅ was gracious to Sarah as he had said, and the Lᴏʀᴅ did for Sarah what he had promised. **2**Sarah became pregnant and bore a son to Abraham in his old age, at the very time God had promised him. **3**Abraham gave the name

a37 Moab sounds like the Hebrew for *from father.*   *b38 Ben-Ammi* means *son of my people.*   *c16* That is, about 25 pounds (about 11.5 kilograms)

Isaac[a] to the son Sarah bore him. [4]When his son Isaac was eight days old, Abraham circumcised him, as God commanded him. [5]Abraham was a hundred years old when his son Isaac was born to him.

[6]Sarah said, "God has brought me laughter, and everyone who hears about this will laugh with me." [7]And she added, "Who would have said to Abraham that Sarah would nurse children? Yet I have borne him a son in his old age."

Hagar and Ishmael Sent Away

[8]The child grew and was weaned, and on the day Isaac was weaned Abraham held a great feast. [9]But Sarah saw that the son whom Hagar the Egyptian had borne to Abraham was mocking, [10]and she said to Abraham, "Get rid of that slave woman and her son, for that slave woman's son will never share in the inheritance with my son Isaac."

[11]The matter distressed Abraham greatly because it concerned his son. [12]But God said to him, "Do not be so distressed about the boy and your maidservant. Listen to whatever Sarah tells you, because it is through Isaac that your offspring[b] will be reckoned. [13]I will make the son of the maidservant into a nation also, because he is your offspring."

[14]Early the next morning Abraham took some food and a skin of water and gave them to Hagar. He set them on her shoulders and then sent her off with the boy. She went on her way and wandered in the desert of Beersheba.

[15]When the water in the skin was gone, she put the boy under one of the bushes. [16]Then she went off and sat down nearby, about a bowshot away, for she thought, "I cannot watch the boy die." And as she sat there nearby, she[c] began to sob.

[17]God heard the boy crying, and the angel of God called to Hagar from heaven and said to her, "What is the matter, Hagar? Do not be afraid; God has heard the boy crying as he lies there. [18]Lift the boy up and take him by the hand, for I will make him into a great nation."

[19]Then God opened her eyes and she saw a well of water. So she went and filled the skin with water and gave the boy a drink. [20]God was with the boy as he grew up. He lived in the desert and became an archer. [21]While he was living in the Desert of Paran, his mother got a wife for him from Egypt.

The Treaty at Beersheba

[22]At that time Abimelech and Phicol the commander of his forces said to Abraham, "God is with you in everything you do. [23]Now swear to me here before God that you will not deal falsely with me or my children or my descendants. Show to me and the country where you are living as an alien the same kindness I have shown to you."

[24]Abraham said, "I swear it."

[25]Then Abraham complained to Abimelech about a well of water that Abimelech's servants had seized. [26]But Abimelech said, "I don't know who has done this. You did not tell me, and I heard about it only today."

[27]So Abraham brought sheep and cattle and gave them to Abimelech, and the two men made a treaty. [28]Abraham set apart seven ewe lambs from the flock, [29]and Abimelech asked Abraham, "What is the meaning of these seven ewe lambs you have set apart by themselves?"

[30]He replied, "Accept these seven lambs from my hand as a witness that I dug this well."

[31]So that place was called Beersheba,[d] because the two men swore an oath there.

[32]After the treaty had been made at Beersheba, Abimelech and Phicol the commander of his forces returned to the land of the Philistines. [33]Abraham planted a tamarisk tree in Beersheba, and there he called upon the name of the LORD, the Eternal God. [34]And Abraham stayed in the land of the Philistines for a long time.

Abraham Tested

22 Some time later God tested Abraham. He said to him, "Abraham!"

"Here I am," he replied.

[2]Then God said, "Take your son, your only son, Isaac, whom you love, and go to the region of Moriah. Sacrifice him there as a burnt offering on one of the mountains I will tell you about."

[3]Early the next morning Abraham got up and saddled his donkey. He took with him two of his servants and his son Isaac. When he had cut enough wood for the burnt offering, he set out for the place God had told him about. [4]On the third day Abraham looked up and saw the place in the distance. [5]He said to his servants, "Stay here with the donkey while I and the boy go over there. We will

---

[a]3 *Isaac* means *he laughs*.   [b]12 Or *seed*   [c]16 Hebrew; Septuagint *the child*   [d]31 *Beersheba* can mean *well of seven* or *well of the oath*.

worship and then we will come back to you."

6Abraham took the wood for the burnt offering and placed it on his son Isaac, and he himself carried the fire and the knife. As the two of them went on together, **7**Isaac spoke up and said to his father Abraham, "Father?"

"Yes, my son?" Abraham replied.

"The fire and wood are here," Isaac said, "but where is the lamb for the burnt offering?"

8Abraham answered, "God himself will provide the lamb for the burnt offering, my son." And the two of them went on together. **9**When they reached the place God had told him about, Abraham built an altar there and arranged the wood on it. He bound his son Isaac and laid him on the altar, on top of the wood. **10**Then he reached out his hand and took the knife to slay his son. **11**But the angel of the LORD called out to him from heaven, "Abraham! Abraham!"

"Here I am," he replied.

12"Do not lay a hand on the boy," he said. "Do not do anything to him. Now I know that you fear God, because you have not withheld from me your son, your only son."

13Abraham looked up and there in a thicket he saw a ram[a] caught by its horns. He went over and took the ram and sacrificed it as a burnt offering instead of his son. **14**So Abraham called that place The LORD Will Provide. And to this day it is said, "On the mountain of the LORD it will be provided."

15The angel of the LORD called to Abraham from heaven a second time **16**and said, "I swear by myself, declares the LORD, that because you have done this and have not withheld your son, your only son, **17**I will surely bless you and make your descendants as numerous as the stars in the sky and as the sand on the seashore. Your descendants will take possession of the cities of their enemies, **18**and through your offspring[b] all nations on earth will be blessed, because you have obeyed me."

19Then Abraham returned to his servants, and they set off together for Beersheba. And Abraham stayed in Beersheba.

Nahor's Sons

20Some time later Abraham was told, "Milcah is also a mother; she has borne sons to your brother Nahor: **21**Uz the firstborn, Buz his brother, Kemuel (the father of

Aram), **22**Kesed, Hazo, Pildash, Jidlaph and Bethuel." **23**Bethuel became the father of Rebekah. Milcah bore these eight sons to Abraham's brother Nahor. **24**His concubine, whose name was Reumah, also had sons: Tebah, Gaham, Tahash and Maacah.

The Death of Sarah

23 Sarah lived to be a hundred and twenty-seven years old. **2**She died at Kiriath Arba (that is, Hebron) in the land of Canaan, and Abraham went to mourn for Sarah and to weep over her.

3Then Abraham rose from beside his dead wife and spoke to the Hittites.[c] He said, **4**"I am an alien and a stranger among you. Sell me some property for a burial site here so I can bury my dead."

5The Hittites replied to Abraham, **6**"Sir, listen to us. You are a mighty prince among us. Bury your dead in the choicest of our tombs. None of us will refuse you his tomb for burying your dead."

7Then Abraham rose and bowed down before the people of the land, the Hittites. **8**He said to them, "If you are willing to let me bury my dead, then listen to me and intercede with Ephron son of Zohar on my behalf **9**so he will sell me the cave of Machpelah, which belongs to him and is at the end of his field. Ask him to sell it to me for the full price as a burial site among you."

10Ephron the Hittite was sitting among his people and he replied to Abraham in the hearing of all the Hittites who had come to the gate of his city. **11**"No, my lord," he said. "Listen to me; I give[d] you the field, and I give[d] you the cave that is in it. I give[d] it to you in the presence of my people. Bury your dead."

12Again Abraham bowed down before the people of the land **13**and he said to Ephron in their hearing, "Listen to me, if you will. I will pay the price of the field. Accept it from me so I can bury my dead there."

14Ephron answered Abraham, **15**"Listen to me, my lord; the land is worth four hundred shekels[e] of silver, but what is that between me and you? Bury your dead."

16Abraham agreed to Ephron's terms and weighed out for him the price he had named in the hearing of the Hittites: four hundred shekels of silver, according to the weight current among the merchants.

17So Ephron's field in Machpelah near

---

a13 Many manuscripts of the Masoretic Text, Samaritan Pentateuch, Septuagint and Syriac; most manuscripts of the Masoretic Text *a ram behind him.*   *b18* Or *seed*   *c3* Or *the sons of Heth*; also in verses 5, 7, 10, 16, 18 and 20   *d11* Or *sell*   *e15* That is, about 10 pounds (about 4.5 kilograms)

Mamre—both the field and the cave in it, and all the trees within the borders of the field—was deeded **18**to Abraham as his property in the presence of all the Hittites who had come to the gate of the city. **19**Afterward Abraham buried his wife Sarah in the cave in the field of Machpelah near Mamre (which is at Hebron) in the land of Canaan. **20**So the field and the cave in it were deeded to Abraham by the Hittites as a burial site.

Isaac and Rebekah

24 Abraham was now old and well advanced in years, and the Lord had blessed him in every way. **2**He said to the chief[a] servant in his household, the one in charge of all that he had, "Put your hand under my thigh. **3**I want you to swear by the Lord, the God of heaven and the God of earth, that you will not get a wife for my son from the daughters of the Canaanites, among whom I am living, **4**but will go to my country and my own relatives and get a wife for my son Isaac."

5The servant asked him, "What if the woman is unwilling to come back with me to this land? Shall I then take your son back to the country you came from?"

6"Make sure that you do not take my son back there," Abraham said. **7**"The Lord, the God of heaven, who brought me out of my father's household and my native land and who spoke to me and promised me on oath, saying, 'To your offspring[b] I will give this land'—he will send his angel before you so that you can get a wife for my son from there. **8**If the woman is unwilling to come back with you, then you will be released from this oath of mine. Only do not take my son back there." **9**So the servant put his hand under the thigh of his master Abraham and swore an oath to him concerning this matter.

10Then the servant took ten of his master's camels and left, taking with him all kinds of good things from his master. He set out for Aram Naharaim[c] and made his way to the town of Nahor. **11**He had the camels kneel down near the well outside the town; it was toward evening, the time the women go out to draw water.

12Then he prayed, "O Lord, God of my master Abraham, give me success today, and show kindness to my master Abraham. **13**See, I am standing beside this spring, and the daughters of the townspeople are coming out to draw water. **14**May it be that when I say to a girl, 'Please let down your jar that I may have a drink,' and she says, 'Drink, and I'll water your camels too'—let her be the one you have chosen for your servant Isaac. By this I will know that you have shown kindness to my master."

15Before he had finished praying, Rebekah came out with her jar on her shoulder. She was the daughter of Bethuel son of Milcah, who was the wife of Abraham's brother Nahor. **16**The girl was very beautiful, a virgin; no man had ever lain with her. She went down to the spring, filled her jar and came up again.

17The servant hurried to meet her and said, "Please give me a little water from your jar."

18"Drink, my lord," she said, and quickly lowered the jar to her hands and gave him a drink.

19After she had given him a drink, she said, "I'll draw water for your camels too, until they have finished drinking." **20**So she quickly emptied her jar into the trough, ran back to the well to draw more water, and drew enough for all his camels. **21**Without saying a word, the man watched her closely to learn whether or not the Lord had made his journey successful.

22When the camels had finished drinking, the man took out a gold nose ring weighing a beka[d] and two gold bracelets weighing ten shekels.[e] **23**Then he asked, "Whose daughter are you? Please tell me, is there room in your father's house for us to spend the night?"

24She answered him, "I am the daughter of Bethuel, the son that Milcah bore to Nahor." **25**And she added, "We have plenty of straw and fodder, as well as room for you to spend the night."

26Then the man bowed down and worshiped the Lord, **27**saying, "Praise be to the Lord, the God of my master Abraham, who has not abandoned his kindness and faithfulness to my master. As for me, the Lord has led me on the journey to the house of my master's relatives."

28The girl ran and told her mother's household about these things. **29**Now Rebekah had a brother named Laban, and he hurried out to the man at the spring. **30**As soon as he had seen the nose ring, and the bracelets on his sister's arms, and had heard Rebekah tell what the man said to her, he

---

a2 Or *oldest*   *b7* Or *seed*   *c10* That is, Northwest Mesopotamia   *d22* That is, about 1/5 ounce (about 5.5 grams)   *e22* That is, about 4 ounces (about 110 grams) went out to the man and found him standing by the camels near the spring. **31**"Come, you who are blessed by the LORD," he said. "Why are you standing out here? I have prepared the house and a place for the camels."

32So the man went to the house, and the camels were unloaded. Straw and fodder were brought for the camels, and water for him and his men to wash their feet. **33**Then food was set before him, but he said, "I will not eat until I have told you what I have to say."

"Then tell us," ⌊Laban⌋ said.

34So he said, "I am Abraham's servant. **35**The LORD has blessed my master abundantly, and he has become wealthy. He has given him sheep and cattle, silver and gold, menservants and maidservants, and camels and donkeys. **36**My master's wife Sarah has borne him a son in her[a] old age, and he has given him everything he owns. **37**And my master made me swear an oath, and said, 'You must not get a wife for my son from the daughters of the Canaanites, in whose land I live, **38**but go to my father's family and to my own clan, and get a wife for my son.'

39"Then I asked my master, 'What if the woman will not come back with me?'

40"He replied, 'The LORD, before whom I have walked, will send his angel with you and make your journey a success, so that you can get a wife for my son from my own clan and from my father's family. **41**Then, when you go to my clan, you will be released from my oath even if they refuse to give her to you — you will be released from my oath.'

42"When I came to the spring today, I said, 'O LORD, God of my master Abraham, if you will, please grant success to the journey on which I have come. **43**See, I am standing beside this spring; if a maiden comes out to draw water and I say to her, "Please let me drink a little water from your jar," **44**and if she says to me, "Drink, and I'll draw water for your camels too," let her be the one the LORD has chosen for my master's son.'

45"Before I finished praying in my heart, Rebekah came out, with her jar on her shoulder. She went down to the spring and drew water, and I said to her, 'Please give me a drink.'

46"She quickly lowered her jar from her shoulder and said, 'Drink, and I'll water your camels too.' So I drank, and she watered the camels also.

47"I asked her, 'Whose daughter are you?'

"She said, 'The daughter of Bethuel son of Nahor, whom Milcah bore to him.'

"Then I put the ring in her nose and the bracelets on her arms, **48**and I bowed down and worshiped the LORD. I praised the LORD, the God of my master Abraham, who had led me on the right road to get the granddaughter of my master's brother for his son. **49**Now if you will show kindness and faithfulness to my master, tell me; and if not, tell me, so I may know which way to turn."

50Laban and Bethuel answered, "This is from the LORD; we can say nothing to you one way or the other. **51**Here is Rebekah; take her and go, and let her become the wife of your master's son, as the LORD has directed."

52When Abraham's servant heard what they said, he bowed down to the ground before the LORD. **53**Then the servant brought out gold and silver jewelry and articles of clothing and gave them to Rebekah; he also gave costly gifts to her brother and to her mother. **54**Then he and the men who were with him ate and drank and spent the night there.

When they got up the next morning, he said, "Send me on my way to my master."

55But her brother and her mother replied, "Let the girl remain with us ten days or so; then you[b] may go."

56But he said to them, "Do not detain me, now that the LORD has granted success to my journey. Send me on my way so I may go to my master."

57Then they said, "Let's call the girl and ask her about it." **58**So they called Rebekah and asked her, "Will you go with this man?"

"I will go," she said.

59So they sent their sister Rebekah on her way, along with her nurse and Abraham's servant and his men. **60**And they blessed Rebekah and said to her,

"Our sister, may you increase
    to thousands upon thousands;
may your offspring possess
    the gates of their enemies."

61Then Rebekah and her maids got ready and mounted their camels and went back with the man. So the servant took Rebekah and left.

62Now Isaac had come from Beer Lahai Roi, for he was living in the Negev. **63**He went out to the field one evening to meditate,[c] and as he looked up, he saw camels approaching. **64**Rebekah also looked up and saw Isaac. She got down from her camel ⁶⁵and asked the servant, "Who is that man in the field coming to meet us?"

"He is my master," the servant answered. So she took her veil and covered herself. ⁶⁶Then the servant told Isaac all he had done. ⁶⁷Isaac brought her into the tent of his mother Sarah, and he married Rebekah. So she became his wife, and he loved her; and Isaac was comforted after his mother's death.

The Death of Abraham

25 Abraham took^a another wife, whose name was Keturah. ²She bore him Zimran, Jokshan, Medan, Midian, Ishbak and Shuah. ³Jokshan was the father of Sheba and Dedan; the descendants of Dedan were the Asshurites, the Letushites and the Leummites. ⁴The sons of Midian were Ephah, Epher, Hanoch, Abida and Eldaah. All these were descendants of Keturah.

⁵Abraham left everything he owned to Isaac. ⁶But while he was still living, he gave gifts to the sons of his concubines and sent them away from his son Isaac to the land of the east.

⁷Altogether, Abraham lived a hundred and seventy-five years. ⁸Then Abraham breathed his last and died at a good old age, an old man and full of years; and he was gathered to his people. ⁹His sons Isaac and Ishmael buried him in the cave of Machpelah near Mamre, in the field of Ephron son of Zohar the Hittite, ¹⁰the field Abraham had bought from the Hittites.^b There Abraham was buried with his wife Sarah. ¹¹After Abraham's death, God blessed his son Isaac, who then lived near Beer Lahai Roi.

Ishmael's Sons

¹²This is the account of Abraham's son Ishmael, whom Sarah's maidservant, Hagar the Egyptian, bore to Abraham.

¹³These are the names of the sons of Ishmael, listed in the order of their birth: Nebaioth the firstborn of Ishmael, Kedar, Adbeel, Mibsam, ¹⁴Mishma, Dumah, Massa, ¹⁵Hadad, Tema, Jetur, Naphish and Kedemah. ¹⁶These were the sons of Ishmael, and these are the names of the twelve tribal rulers according to their settlements and camps. ¹⁷Altogether, Ishmael lived a hundred and thirty-seven years. He breathed his last and

died, and he was gathered to his people. ¹⁸His descendants settled in the area from Havilah to Shur, near the border of Egypt, as you go toward Asshur. And they lived in hostility toward^c all their brothers.

Jacob and Esau

¹⁹This is the account of Abraham's son Isaac.

Abraham became the father of Isaac, ²⁰and Isaac was forty years old when he married Rebekah daughter of Bethuel the Aramean from Paddan Aram^d and sister of Laban the Aramean.

²¹Isaac prayed to the LORD on behalf of his wife, because she was barren. The LORD answered his prayer, and his wife Rebekah became pregnant. ²²The babies jostled each other within her, and she said, "Why is this happening to me?" So she went to inquire of the LORD.

²³The LORD said to her,

"Two nations are in your womb,
    and two peoples from within you will
        be separated;
one people will be stronger than the
        other,
    and the older will serve the younger."

²⁴When the time came for her to give birth, there were twin boys in her womb. ²⁵The first to come out was red, and his whole body was like a hairy garment; so they named him Esau.^e ²⁶After this, his brother came out, with his hand grasping Esau's heel; so he was named Jacob.^f Isaac was sixty years old when Rebekah gave birth to them.

²⁷The boys grew up, and Esau became a skillful hunter, a man of the open country, while Jacob was a quiet man, staying among the tents. ²⁸Isaac, who had a taste for wild game, loved Esau, but Rebekah loved Jacob.

²⁹Once when Jacob was cooking some stew, Esau came in from the open country, famished. ³⁰He said to Jacob, "Quick, let me have some of that red stew! I'm famished!" (That is why he was also called Edom.^g)

³¹Jacob replied, "First sell me your birthright."

³²"Look, I am about to die," Esau said. "What good is the birthright to me?"

³³But Jacob said, "Swear to me first." So he swore an oath to him, selling his birthright to Jacob.

---

^a1 Or had taken   ^b10 Or the sons of Heth   ^c18 Or lived to the east of   ^d20 That is, Northwest Mesopotamia   ^e25 Esau may mean hairy; he was also called Edom, which means red.   ^f26 Jacob means he grasps the heel (figuratively, he deceives).   ^g30 Edom means red.

34Then Jacob gave Esau some bread and some lentil stew. He ate and drank, and then got up and left.

So Esau despised his birthright.

Isaac and Abimelech

26 Now there was a famine in the land—besides the earlier famine of Abraham's time—and Isaac went to Abimelech king of the Philistines in Gerar. **2**The LORD appeared to Isaac and said, "Do not go down to Egypt; live in the land where I tell you to live. **3**Stay in this land for a while, and I will be with you and will bless you. For to you and your descendants I will give all these lands and will confirm the oath I swore to your father Abraham. **4**I will make your descendants as numerous as the stars in the sky and will give them all these lands, and through your offspring*a* all nations on earth will be blessed, **5**because Abraham obeyed me and kept my requirements, my commands, my decrees and my laws." **6**So Isaac stayed in Gerar.

7When the men of that place asked him about his wife, he said, "She is my sister," because he was afraid to say, "She is my wife." He thought, "The men of this place might kill me on account of Rebekah, because she is beautiful."

8When Isaac had been there a long time, Abimelech king of the Philistines looked down from a window and saw Isaac caressing his wife Rebekah. **9**So Abimelech summoned Isaac and said, "She is really your wife! Why did you say, 'She is my sister'?"

Isaac answered him, "Because I thought I might lose my life on account of her."

10Then Abimelech said, "What is this you have done to us? One of the men might well have slept with your wife, and you would have brought guilt upon us."

11So Abimelech gave orders to all the people: "Anyone who molests this man or his wife shall surely be put to death."

12Isaac planted crops in that land and the same year reaped a hundredfold, because the LORD blessed him. **13**The man became rich, and his wealth continued to grow until he became very wealthy. **14**He had so many flocks and herds and servants that the Philistines envied him. **15**So all the wells that his father's servants had dug in the time of his father Abraham, the Philistines stopped up, filling them with earth.

16Then Abimelech said to Isaac, "Move away from us; you have become too powerful for us."

17So Isaac moved away from there and encamped in the Valley of Gerar and settled there. **18**Isaac reopened the wells that had been dug in the time of his father Abraham, which the Philistines had stopped up after Abraham died, and he gave them the same names his father had given them.

19Isaac's servants dug in the valley and discovered a well of fresh water there. **20**But the herdsmen of Gerar quarreled with Isaac's herdsmen and said, "The water is ours!" So he named the well Esek,*b* because they disputed with him. **21**Then they dug another well, but they quarreled over that one also; so he named it Sitnah.*c* **22**He moved on from there and dug another well, and no one quarreled over it. He named it Rehoboth,*d* saying, "Now the LORD has given us room and we will flourish in the land."

23From there he went up to Beersheba. **24**That night the LORD appeared to him and said, "I am the God of your father Abraham. Do not be afraid, for I am with you; I will bless you and will increase the number of your descendants for the sake of my servant Abraham."

25Isaac built an altar there and called on the name of the LORD. There he pitched his tent, and there his servants dug a well.

26Meanwhile, Abimelech had come to him from Gerar, with Ahuzzath his personal adviser and Phicol the commander of his forces. **27**Isaac asked them, "Why have you come to me, since you were hostile to me and sent me away?"

28They answered, "We saw clearly that the LORD was with you; so we said, 'There ought to be a sworn agreement between us'—between us and you. Let us make a treaty with you **29**that you will do us no harm, just as we did not molest you but always treated you well and sent you away in peace. And now you are blessed by the LORD."

30Isaac then made a feast for them, and they ate and drank. **31**Early the next morning the men swore an oath to each other. Then Isaac sent them on their way, and they left him in peace.

32That day Isaac's servants came and told him about the well they had dug. They said, "We've found water!" **33**He called it Shibah,*e* and to this day the name of the town has been Beersheba.*f*

---

a4 Or *seed*   *b20 Esek* means *dispute.*   *c21 Sitnah* means *opposition.*   *d22 Rehoboth* means *room.*
e33 Shibah can mean *oath* or *seven.*   *f33 Beersheba* can mean *well of the oath* or *well of seven.*

34When Esau was forty years old, he married Judith daughter of Beeri the Hittite, and also Basemath daughter of Elon the Hittite. **35**They were a source of grief to Isaac and Rebekah.

Jacob Gets Isaac's Blessing

27 When Isaac was old and his eyes were so weak that he could no longer see, he called for Esau his older son and said to him, "My son."

"Here I am," he answered.

2Isaac said, "I am now an old man and don't know the day of my death. **3**Now then, get your weapons—your quiver and bow—and go out to the open country to hunt some wild game for me. **4**Prepare me the kind of tasty food I like and bring it to me to eat, so that I may give you my blessing before I die."

5Now Rebekah was listening as Isaac spoke to his son Esau. When Esau left for the open country to hunt game and bring it back, **6**Rebekah said to her son Jacob, "Look, I overheard your father say to your brother Esau, **7**'Bring me some game and prepare me some tasty food to eat, so that I may give you my blessing in the presence of the LORD before I die.' **8**Now, my son, listen carefully and do what I tell you: **9**Go out to the flock and bring me two choice young goats, so I can prepare some tasty food for your father, just the way he likes it. **10**Then take it to your father to eat, so that he may give you his blessing before he dies."

11Jacob said to Rebekah his mother, "But my brother Esau is a hairy man, and I'm a man with smooth skin. **12**What if my father touches me? I would appear to be tricking him and would bring down a curse on myself rather than a blessing."

13His mother said to him, "My son, let the curse fall on me. Just do what I say; go and get them for me."

14So he went and got them and brought them to his mother, and she prepared some tasty food, just the way his father liked it. **15**Then Rebekah took the best clothes of Esau her older son, which she had in the house, and put them on her younger son Jacob. **16**She also covered his hands and the smooth part of his neck with the goatskins. **17**Then she handed to her son Jacob the tasty food and the bread she had made.

18He went to his father and said, "My father."

"Yes, my son," he answered. "Who is it?"

19Jacob said to his father, "I am Esau your firstborn. I have done as you told me. Please sit up and eat some of my game so that you may give me your blessing."

20Isaac asked his son, "How did you find it so quickly, my son?"

"The LORD your God gave me success," he replied.

21Then Isaac said to Jacob, "Come near so I can touch you, my son, to know whether you really are my son Esau or not."

22Jacob went close to his father Isaac, who touched him and said, "The voice is the voice of Jacob, but the hands are the hands of Esau." **23**He did not recognize him, for his hands were hairy like those of his brother Esau; so he blessed him. **24**"Are you really my son Esau?" he asked.

"I am," he replied.

25Then he said, "My son, bring me some of your game to eat, so that I may give you my blessing."

Jacob brought it to him and he ate; and he brought some wine and he drank. **26**Then his father Isaac said to him, "Come here, my son, and kiss me."

27So he went to him and kissed him. When Isaac caught the smell of his clothes, he blessed him and said,

"Ah, the smell of my son
   is like the smell of a field
   that the LORD has blessed.
28May God give you of heaven's dew
   and of earth's richness—
   an abundance of grain and new wine.
29May nations serve you
   and peoples bow down to you.
Be lord over your brothers,
   and may the sons of your mother
   bow down to you.
May those who curse you be cursed
   and those who bless you be blessed."

30After Isaac finished blessing him and Jacob had scarcely left his father's presence, his brother Esau came in from hunting. **31**He too prepared some tasty food and brought it to his father. Then he said to him, "My father, sit up and eat some of my game, so that you may give me your blessing."

32His father Isaac asked him, "Who are you?"

"I am your son," he answered, "your firstborn, Esau."

33Isaac trembled violently and said, "Who was it, then, that hunted game and brought it to me? I ate it just before you came and I blessed him—and indeed he will be blessed!"

34When Esau heard his father's words, he burst out with a loud and bitter cry and said to his father, "Bless me — me too, my father!"

35But he said, "Your brother came deceitfully and took your blessing."

36Esau said, "Isn't he rightly named Jacob[a]? He has deceived me these two times: He took my birthright, and now he's taken my blessing!" Then he asked, "Haven't you reserved any blessing for me?"

37Isaac answered Esau, "I have made him lord over you and have made all his relatives his servants, and I have sustained him with grain and new wine. So what can I possibly do for you, my son?"

38Esau said to his father, "Do you have only one blessing, my father? Bless me too, my father!" Then Esau wept aloud.

39His father Isaac answered him,

"Your dwelling will be
    away from the earth's richness,
    away from the dew of heaven above.
40You will live by the sword
    and you will serve your brother.
But when you grow restless,
    you will throw his yoke
    from off your neck."

Jacob Flees to Laban

41Esau held a grudge against Jacob because of the blessing his father had given him. He said to himself, "The days of mourning for my father are near; then I will kill my brother Jacob."

42When Rebekah was told what her older son Esau had said, she sent for her younger son Jacob and said to him, "Your brother Esau is consoling himself with the thought of killing you. **43**Now then, my son, do what I say: Flee at once to my brother Laban in Haran. **44**Stay with him for a while until your brother's fury subsides. **45**When your brother is no longer angry with you and forgets what you did to him, I'll send word for you to come back from there. Why should I lose both of you in one day?"

46Then Rebekah said to Isaac, "I'm disgusted with living because of these Hittite women. If Jacob takes a wife from among the women of this land, from Hittite women like these, my life will not be worth living."

28 So Isaac called for Jacob and blessed[b] him and commanded him: "Do not marry a Canaanite woman. **2**Go at once to Paddan Aram,[c] to the house of your mother's father Bethuel. Take a wife for yourself there, from among the daughters of Laban, your mother's brother. **3**May God Almighty[d] bless you and make you fruitful and increase your numbers until you become a community of peoples. **4**May he give you and your descendants the blessing given to Abraham, so that you may take possession of the land where you now live as an alien, the land God gave to Abraham." **5**Then Isaac sent Jacob on his way, and he went to Paddan Aram, to Laban son of Bethuel the Aramean, the brother of Rebekah, who was the mother of Jacob and Esau.

6Now Esau learned that Isaac had blessed Jacob and had sent him to Paddan Aram to take a wife from there, and that when he blessed him he commanded him, "Do not marry a Canaanite woman," **7**and that Jacob had obeyed his father and mother and had gone to Paddan Aram. **8**Esau then realized how displeasing the Canaanite women were to his father Isaac; **9**so he went to Ishmael and married Mahalath, the sister of Nebaioth and daughter of Ishmael son of Abraham, in addition to the wives he already had.

Jacob's Dream at Bethel

10Jacob left Beersheba and set out for Haran. **11**When he reached a certain place, he stopped for the night because the sun had set. Taking one of the stones there, he put it under his head and lay down to sleep. **12**He had a dream in which he saw a stairway[e] resting on the earth, with its top reaching to heaven, and the angels of God were ascending and descending on it. **13**There above it[f] stood the LORD, and he said: "I am the LORD, the God of your father Abraham and the God of Isaac. I will give you and your descendants the land on which you are lying. **14**Your descendants will be like the dust of the earth, and you will spread out to the west and to the east, to the north and to the south. All peoples on earth will be blessed through you and your offspring. **15**I am with you and will watch over you wherever you go, and I will bring you back to this land. I will not leave you until I have done what I have promised you."

16When Jacob awoke from his sleep, he thought, "Surely the LORD is in this place, and I was not aware of it." **17**He was afraid and said, "How awesome is this place! This is none other than the house of God; this is the gate of heaven."

---

a36 Jacob means *he grasps the heel* (figuratively, *he deceives*).   *b1* Or *greeted*   *c2* That is, Northwest Mesopotamia; also in verses 5, 6 and 7   *d3* Hebrew *El-Shaddai*   *e12* Or *ladder*   *f13* Or *There beside him*

[18]Early the next morning Jacob took the stone he had placed under his head and set it up as a pillar and poured oil on top of it. [19]He called that place Bethel,[a] though the city used to be called Luz.

[20]Then Jacob made a vow, saying, "If God will be with me and will watch over me on this journey I am taking and will give me food to eat and clothes to wear [21]so that I return safely to my father's house, then the Lord[b] will be my God [22]and[c] this stone that I have set up as a pillar will be God's house, and of all that you give me I will give you a tenth."

Jacob Arrives in Paddan Aram

29 Then Jacob continued on his journey and came to the land of the eastern peoples. [2]There he saw a well in the field, with three flocks of sheep lying near it because the flocks were watered from that well. The stone over the mouth of the well was large. [3]When all the flocks were gathered there, the shepherds would roll the stone away from the well's mouth and water the sheep. Then they would return the stone to its place over the mouth of the well.

[4]Jacob asked the shepherds, "My brothers, where are you from?"

"We're from Haran," they replied.

[5]He said to them, "Do you know Laban, Nahor's grandson?"

"Yes, we know him," they answered.

[6]Then Jacob asked them, "Is he well?"

"Yes, he is," they said, "and here comes his daughter Rachel with the sheep."

[7]"Look," he said, "the sun is still high; it is not time for the flocks to be gathered. Water the sheep and take them back to pasture."

[8]"We can't," they replied, "until all the flocks are gathered and the stone has been rolled away from the mouth of the well. Then we will water the sheep."

[9]While he was still talking with them, Rachel came with her father's sheep, for she was a shepherdess. [10]When Jacob saw Rachel daughter of Laban, his mother's brother, and Laban's sheep, he went over and rolled the stone away from the mouth of the well and watered his uncle's sheep. [11]Then Jacob kissed Rachel and began to weep aloud. [12]He had told Rachel that he was a relative of her father and a son of Rebekah. So she ran and told her father.

[13]As soon as Laban heard the news about Jacob, his sister's son, he hurried to meet him. He embraced him and kissed him and brought him to his home, and there Jacob told him all these things. [14]Then Laban said to him, "You are my own flesh and blood."

Jacob Marries Leah and Rachel

After Jacob had stayed with him for a whole month, [15]Laban said to him, "Just because you are a relative of mine, should you work for me for nothing? Tell me what your wages should be."

[16]Now Laban had two daughters; the name of the older was Leah, and the name of the younger was Rachel. [17]Leah had weak[d] eyes, but Rachel was lovely in form, and beautiful. [18]Jacob was in love with Rachel and said, "I'll work for you seven years in return for your younger daughter Rachel."

[19]Laban said, "It's better that I give her to you than to some other man. Stay here with me." [20]So Jacob served seven years to get Rachel, but they seemed like only a few days to him because of his love for her.

[21]Then Jacob said to Laban, "Give me my wife. My time is completed, and I want to lie with her."

[22]So Laban brought together all the people of the place and gave a feast. [23]But when evening came, he took his daughter Leah and gave her to Jacob, and Jacob lay with her. [24]And Laban gave his servant girl Zilpah to his daughter as her maidservant.

[25]When morning came, there was Leah! So Jacob said to Laban, "What is this you have done to me? I served you for Rachel, didn't I? Why have you deceived me?"

[26]Laban replied, "It is not our custom here to give the younger daughter in marriage before the older one. [27]Finish this daughter's bridal week; then we will give you the younger one also, in return for another seven years of work."

[28]And Jacob did so. He finished the week with Leah, and then Laban gave him his daughter Rachel to be his wife. [29]Laban gave his servant girl Bilhah to his daughter Rachel as her maidservant. [30]Jacob lay with Rachel also, and he loved Rachel more than Leah. And he worked for Laban another seven years.

Jacob's Children

[31]When the Lord saw that Leah was not loved, he opened her womb, but Rachel was barren. [32]Leah became pregnant and gave

---

[a]19 Bethel means house of God.   [b]20,21 Or Since God . . . father's house, the Lord   [c]21,22 Or house, and the Lord will be my God, [22]then   [d]17 Or delicate

birth to a son. She named him Reuben,[a] for she said, "It is because the LORD has seen my misery. Surely my husband will love me now."

[33]She conceived again, and when she gave birth to a son she said, "Because the LORD heard that I am not loved, he gave me this one too." So she named him Simeon.[b]

[34]Again she conceived, and when she gave birth to a son she said, "Now at last my husband will become attached to me, because I have borne him three sons." So he was named Levi.[c]

[35]She conceived again, and when she gave birth to a son she said, "This time I will praise the LORD." So she named him Judah.[d] Then she stopped having children.

30 When Rachel saw that she was not bearing Jacob any children, she became jealous of her sister. So she said to Jacob, "Give me children, or I'll die!"

[2]Jacob became angry with her and said, "Am I in the place of God, who has kept you from having children?"

[3]Then she said, "Here is Bilhah, my maidservant. Sleep with her so that she can bear children for me and that through her I too can build a family."

[4]So she gave him her servant Bilhah as a wife. Jacob slept with her, [5]and she became pregnant and bore him a son. [6]Then Rachel said, "God has vindicated me; he has listened to my plea and given me a son." Because of this she named him Dan.[e]

[7]Rachel's servant Bilhah conceived again and bore Jacob a second son. [8]Then Rachel said, "I have had a great struggle with my sister, and I have won." So she named him Naphtali.[f]

[9]When Leah saw that she had stopped having children, she took her maidservant Zilpah and gave her to Jacob as a wife. [10]Leah's servant Zilpah bore Jacob a son. [11]Then Leah said, "What good fortune!"[g] So she named him Gad.[h]

[12]Leah's servant Zilpah bore Jacob a second son. [13]Then Leah said, "How happy I am! The women will call me happy." So she named him Asher.[i]

[14]During wheat harvest, Reuben went out into the fields and found some mandrake plants, which he brought to his mother

Leah. Rachel said to Leah, "Please give me some of your son's mandrakes."

[15]But she said to her, "Wasn't it enough that you took away my husband? Will you take my son's mandrakes too?"

"Very well," Rachel said, "he can sleep with you tonight in return for your son's mandrakes."

[16]So when Jacob came in from the fields that evening, Leah went out to meet him. "You must sleep with me," she said. "I have hired you with my son's mandrakes." So he slept with her that night.

[17]God listened to Leah, and she became pregnant and bore Jacob a fifth son. [18]Then Leah said, "God has rewarded me for giving my maidservant to my husband." So she named him Issachar.[j]

[19]Leah conceived again and bore Jacob a sixth son. [20]Then Leah said, "God has presented me with a precious gift. This time my husband will treat me with honor, because I have borne him six sons." So she named him Zebulun.[k]

[21]Some time later she gave birth to a daughter and named her Dinah.

[22]Then God remembered Rachel; he listened to her and opened her womb. [23]She became pregnant and gave birth to a son and said, "God has taken away my disgrace." [24]She named him Joseph,[l] and said, "May the LORD add to me another son."

Jacob's Flocks Increase

[25]After Rachel gave birth to Joseph, Jacob said to Laban, "Send me on my way so I can go back to my own homeland. [26]Give me my wives and children, for whom I have served you, and I will be on my way. You know how much work I've done for you."

[27]But Laban said to him, "If I have found favor in your eyes, please stay. I have learned by divination that[m] the LORD has blessed me because of you." [28]He added, "Name your wages, and I will pay them."

[29]Jacob said to him, "You know how I have worked for you and how your livestock has fared under my care. [30]The little you had before I came has increased greatly, and the LORD has blessed you wherever I have been. But now, when may I do something for my own household?"

---

[a]32 *Reuben* sounds like the Hebrew for *he has seen my misery*; the name means *see, a son*.   [b]33 *Simeon* probably means *one who hears*.   [c]34 *Levi* sounds like and may be derived from the Hebrew for *attached*.   [d]35 *Judah* sounds like and may be derived from the Hebrew for *praise*.   [e]6 *Dan* here means *he has vindicated*.   [f]8 *Naphtali* means *my struggle*.   [g]11 Or *"A troop is coming!"*   [h]11 *Gad* can mean *good fortune* or *a troop*.   [i]13 *Asher* means *happy*.   [j]18 *Issachar* sounds like the Hebrew for *reward*.   [k]20 *Zebulun* probably means *honor*.   [l]24 *Joseph* means *may he add*.   [m]27 Or possibly *have become rich and*

31"What shall I give you?" he asked.

"Don't give me anything," Jacob replied. "But if you will do this one thing for me, I will go on tending your flocks and watching over them: **32**Let me go through all your flocks today and remove from them every speckled or spotted sheep, every dark-colored lamb and every spotted or speckled goat. They will be my wages. **33**And my honesty will testify for me in the future, whenever you check on the wages you have paid me. Any goat in my possession that is not speckled or spotted, or any lamb that is not dark-colored, will be considered stolen."

34"Agreed," said Laban. "Let it be as you have said." **35**That same day he removed all the male goats that were streaked or spotted, and all the speckled or spotted female goats (all that had white on them) and all the dark-colored lambs, and he placed them in the care of his sons. **36**Then he put a three-day journey between himself and Jacob, while Jacob continued to tend the rest of Laban's flocks.

37Jacob, however, took fresh-cut branches from poplar, almond and plane trees and made white stripes on them by peeling the bark and exposing the white inner wood of the branches. **38**Then he placed the peeled branches in all the watering troughs, so that they would be directly in front of the flocks when they came to drink. When the flocks were in heat and came to drink, **39**they mated in front of the branches. And they bore young that were streaked or speckled or spotted. **40**Jacob set apart the young of the flock by themselves, but made the rest face the streaked and dark-colored animals that belonged to Laban. Thus he made separate flocks for himself and did not put them with Laban's animals. **41**Whenever the stronger females were in heat, Jacob would place the branches in the troughs in front of the animals so they would mate near the branches, **42**but if the animals were weak, he would not place them there. So the weak animals went to Laban and the strong ones to Jacob. **43**In this way the man grew exceedingly prosperous and came to own large flocks, and maidservants and menservants, and camels and donkeys.

Jacob Flees From Laban

31 Jacob heard that Laban's sons were saying, "Jacob has taken everything our father owned and has gained all this wealth from what belonged to our father." **2**And Jacob noticed that Laban's attitude toward him was not what it had been.

3Then the LORD said to Jacob, "Go back to the land of your fathers and to your relatives, and I will be with you."

4So Jacob sent word to Rachel and Leah to come out to the fields where his flocks were. **5**He said to them, "I see that your father's attitude toward me is not what it was before, but the God of my father has been with me. **6**You know that I've worked for your father with all my strength, **7**yet your father has cheated me by changing my wages ten times. However, God has not allowed him to harm me. **8**If he said, 'The speckled ones will be your wages,' then all the flocks gave birth to speckled young; and if he said, 'The streaked ones will be your wages,' then all the flocks bore streaked young. **9**So God has taken away your father's livestock and has given them to me.

10"In breeding season I once had a dream in which I looked up and saw that the male goats mating with the flock were streaked, speckled or spotted. **11**The angel of God said to me in the dream, 'Jacob.' I answered, 'Here I am.' **12**And he said, 'Look up and see that all the male goats mating with the flock are streaked, speckled or spotted, for I have seen all that Laban has been doing to you. **13**I am the God of Bethel, where you anointed a pillar and where you made a vow to me. Now leave this land at once and go back to your native land.' "

14Then Rachel and Leah replied, "Do we still have any share in the inheritance of our father's estate? **15**Does he not regard us as foreigners? Not only has he sold us, but he has used up what was paid for us. **16**Surely all the wealth that God took away from our father belongs to us and our children. So do whatever God has told you."

17Then Jacob put his children and his wives on camels, **18**and he drove all his livestock ahead of him, along with all the goods he had accumulated in Paddan Aram,^{a} to go to his father Isaac in the land of Canaan.

19When Laban had gone to shear his sheep, Rachel stole her father's household gods. **20**Moreover, Jacob deceived Laban the Aramean by not telling him he was running away. **21**So he fled with all he had, and crossing the River,^{b} he headed for the hill country of Gilead.

Laban Pursues Jacob

22On the third day Laban was told that Jacob had fled. **23**Taking his relatives with him, he pursued Jacob for seven days and caught up with him in the hill country of Gilead. **24**Then God came to Laban the Aramean in a dream at night and said to him, "Be careful not to say anything to Jacob, either good or bad."

25Jacob had pitched his tent in the hill country of Gilead when Laban overtook him, and Laban and his relatives camped there too. **26**Then Laban said to Jacob, "What have you done? You've deceived me, and you've carried off my daughters like captives in war. **27**Why did you run off secretly and deceive me? Why didn't you tell me, so I could send you away with joy and singing to the music of tambourines and harps? **28**You didn't even let me kiss my grandchildren and my daughters good-by. You have done a foolish thing. **29**I have the power to harm you; but last night the God of your father said to me, 'Be careful not to say anything to Jacob, either good or bad.' **30**Now you have gone off because you longed to return to your father's house. But why did you steal my gods?"

31Jacob answered Laban, "I was afraid, because I thought you would take your daughters away from me by force. **32**But if you find anyone who has your gods, he shall not live. In the presence of our relatives, see for yourself whether there is anything of yours here with me; and if so, take it." Now Jacob did not know that Rachel had stolen the gods.

33So Laban went into Jacob's tent and into Leah's tent and into the tent of the two maidservants, but he found nothing. After he came out of Leah's tent, he entered Rachel's tent. **34**Now Rachel had taken the household gods and put them inside her camel's saddle and was sitting on them. Laban searched through everything in the tent but found nothing.

35Rachel said to her father, "Don't be angry, my lord, that I cannot stand up in your presence; I'm having my period." So he searched but could not find the household gods.

36Jacob was angry and took Laban to task. "What is my crime?" he asked Laban. "What sin have I committed that you hunt me down? **37**Now that you have searched through all my goods, what have you found that belongs to your household? Put it here

in front of your relatives and mine, and let them judge between the two of us.

38"I have been with you for twenty years now. Your sheep and goats have not miscarried, nor have I eaten rams from your flocks. **39**I did not bring you animals torn by wild beasts; I bore the loss myself. And you demanded payment from me for whatever was stolen by day or night. **40**This was my situation: The heat consumed me in the daytime and the cold at night, and sleep fled from my eyes. **41**It was like this for the twenty years I was in your household. I worked for you fourteen years for your two daughters and six years for your flocks, and you changed my wages ten times. **42**If the God of my father, the God of Abraham and the Fear of Isaac, had not been with me, you would surely have sent me away empty-handed. But God has seen my hardship and the toil of my hands, and last night he rebuked you."

43Laban answered Jacob, "The women are my daughters, the children are my children, and the flocks are my flocks. All you see is mine. Yet what can I do today about these daughters of mine, or about the children they have borne? **44**Come now, let's make a covenant, you and I, and let it serve as a witness between us."

45So Jacob took a stone and set it up as a pillar. **46**He said to his relatives, "Gather some stones." So they took stones and piled them in a heap, and they ate there by the heap. **47**Laban called it Jegar Sahadutha,*a* and Jacob called it Galeed.*b*

48Laban said, "This heap is a witness between you and me today." That is why it was called Galeed. **49**It was also called Mizpah,*c* because he said, "May the LORD keep watch between you and me when we are away from each other. **50**If you mistreat my daughters or if you take any wives besides my daughters, even though no one is with us, remember that God is a witness between you and me."

51Laban also said to Jacob, "Here is this heap, and here is this pillar I have set up between you and me. **52**This heap is a witness, and this pillar is a witness, that I will not go past this heap to your side to harm you and that you will not go past this heap and pillar to my side to harm me. **53**May the God of Abraham and the God of Nahor, the God of their father, judge between us."

So Jacob took an oath in the name of the

*a*47 The Aramaic *Jegar Sahadutha* means *witness heap.*
*c*49 *Mizpah* means *watchtower.*
*b*47 The Hebrew *Galeed* means *witness heap.*

Fear of his father Isaac. **54**He offered a sacrifice there in the hill country and invited his relatives to a meal. After they had eaten, they spent the night there.

55Early the next morning Laban kissed his grandchildren and his daughters and blessed them. Then he left and returned home.

Jacob Prepares to Meet Esau

32 Jacob also went on his way, and the angels of God met him. **2**When Jacob saw them, he said, "This is the camp of God!" So he named that place Mahanaim.*a*

3Jacob sent messengers ahead of him to his brother Esau in the land of Seir, the country of Edom. **4**He instructed them: "This is what you are to say to my master Esau: 'Your servant Jacob says, I have been staying with Laban and have remained there till now. **5**I have cattle and donkeys, sheep and goats, menservants and maidservants. Now I am sending this message to my lord, that I may find favor in your eyes.'"

6When the messengers returned to Jacob, they said, "We went to your brother Esau, and now he is coming to meet you, and four hundred men are with him."

7In great fear and distress Jacob divided the people who were with him into two groups,*b* and the flocks and herds and camels as well. **8**He thought, "If Esau comes and attacks one group,*c* the group*c* that is left may escape."

9Then Jacob prayed, "O God of my father Abraham, God of my father Isaac, O Lord, who said to me, 'Go back to your country and your relatives, and I will make you prosper,' **10**I am unworthy of all the kindness and faithfulness you have shown your servant. I had only my staff when I crossed this Jordan, but now I have become two groups. **11**Save me, I pray, from the hand of my brother Esau, for I am afraid he will come and attack me, and also the mothers with their children. **12**But you have said, 'I will surely make you prosper and will make your descendants like the sand of the sea, which cannot be counted.'"

13He spent the night there, and from what he had with him he selected a gift for his brother Esau: **14**two hundred female goats and twenty male goats, two hundred ewes and twenty rams, **15**thirty female camels with their young, forty cows and ten bulls, and twenty female donkeys and ten male

donkeys. **16**He put them in the care of his servants, each herd by itself, and said to his servants, "Go ahead of me, and keep some space between the herds."

17He instructed the one in the lead: "When my brother Esau meets you and asks, 'To whom do you belong, and where are you going, and who owns all these animals in front of you?' **18**then you are to say, 'They belong to your servant Jacob. They are a gift sent to my lord Esau, and he is coming behind us.'"

19He also instructed the second, the third and all the others who followed the herds: "You are to say the same thing to Esau when you meet him. **20**And be sure to say, 'Your servant Jacob is coming behind us.'" For he thought, "I will pacify him with these gifts I am sending on ahead; later, when I see him, perhaps he will receive me." **21**So Jacob's gifts went on ahead of him, but he himself spent the night in the camp.

Jacob Wrestles With God

22That night Jacob got up and took his two wives, his two maidservants and his eleven sons and crossed the ford of the Jabbok. **23**After he had sent them across the stream, he sent over all his possessions. **24**So Jacob was left alone, and a man wrestled with him till daybreak. **25**When the man saw that he could not overpower him, he touched the socket of Jacob's hip so that his hip was wrenched as he wrestled with the man. **26**Then the man said, "Let me go, for it is daybreak."

But Jacob replied, "I will not let you go unless you bless me."

27The man asked him, "What is your name?"

"Jacob," he answered.

28Then the man said, "Your name will no longer be Jacob, but Israel,*d* because you have struggled with God and with men and have overcome."

29Jacob said, "Please tell me your name." But he replied, "Why do you ask my name?" Then he blessed him there.

30So Jacob called the place Peniel,*e* saying, "It is because I saw God face to face, and yet my life was spared."

31The sun rose above him as he passed Peniel,*f* and he was limping because of his hip. **32**Therefore to this day the Israelites do not eat the tendon attached to the socket of

---

a2 Mahanaim means *two camps.*   *b7* Or *camps;* also in verse 10   *c8* Or *camp*   *d28 Israel* means *he struggles with God.*   *e30 Peniel* means *face of God.*   *f31* Hebrew *Penuel,* a variant of *Peniel* the hip, because the socket of Jacob's hip was touched near the tendon.

Jacob Meets Esau

33 Jacob looked up and there was Esau, coming with his four hundred men; so he divided the children among Leah, Rachel and the two maidservants. ²He put the maidservants and their children in front, Leah and her children next, and Rachel and Joseph in the rear. ³He himself went on ahead and bowed down to the ground seven times as he approached his brother.

⁴But Esau ran to meet Jacob and embraced him; he threw his arms around his neck and kissed him. And they wept. ⁵Then Esau looked up and saw the women and children. "Who are these with you?" he asked.

Jacob answered, "They are the children God has graciously given your servant."

⁶Then the maidservants and their children approached and bowed down. ⁷Next, Leah and her children came and bowed down. Last of all came Joseph and Rachel, and they too bowed down.

⁸Esau asked, "What do you mean by all these droves I met?"

"To find favor in your eyes, my lord," he said.

⁹But Esau said, "I already have plenty, my brother. Keep what you have for yourself."

¹⁰"No, please!" said Jacob. "If I have found favor in your eyes, accept this gift from me. For to see your face is like seeing the face of God, now that you have received me favorably. ¹¹Please accept the present that was brought to you, for God has been gracious to me and I have all I need." And because Jacob insisted, Esau accepted it.

¹²Then Esau said, "Let us be on our way; I'll accompany you."

¹³But Jacob said to him, "My lord knows that the children are tender and that I must care for the ewes and cows that are nursing their young. If they are driven hard just one day, all the animals will die. ¹⁴So let my lord go on ahead of his servant, while I move along slowly at the pace of the droves before me and that of the children, until I come to my lord in Seir."

¹⁵Esau said, "Then let me leave some of my men with you."

"But why do that?" Jacob asked. "Just let me find favor in the eyes of my lord."

¹⁶So that day Esau started on his way back to Seir. ¹⁷Jacob, however, went to Succoth, where he built a place for himself and made shelters for his livestock. That is why the place is called Succoth.ᵃ

¹⁸After Jacob came from Paddan Aram,ᵇ he arrived safely at theᶜ city of Shechem in Canaan and camped within sight of the city. ¹⁹For a hundred pieces of silver,ᵈ he bought from the sons of Hamor, the father of Shechem, the plot of ground where he pitched his tent. ²⁰There he set up an altar and called it El Elohe Israel.ᵉ

Dinah and the Shechemites

34 Now Dinah, the daughter Leah had borne to Jacob, went out to visit the women of the land. ²When Shechem son of Hamor the Hivite, the ruler of that area, saw her, he took her and violated her. ³His heart was drawn to Dinah daughter of Jacob, and he loved the girl and spoke tenderly to her. ⁴And Shechem said to his father Hamor, "Get me this girl as my wife."

⁵When Jacob heard that his daughter Dinah had been defiled, his sons were in the fields with his livestock; so he kept quiet about it until they came home.

⁶Then Shechem's father Hamor went out to talk with Jacob. ⁷Now Jacob's sons had come in from the fields as soon as they heard what had happened. They were filled with grief and fury, because Shechem had done a disgraceful thing inᶠ Israel by lying with Jacob's daughter—a thing that should not be done.

⁸But Hamor said to them, "My son Shechem has his heart set on your daughter. Please give her to him as his wife. ⁹Intermarry with us; give us your daughters and take our daughters for yourselves. ¹⁰You can settle among us; the land is open to you. Live in it, tradeᵍ in it, and acquire property in it."

¹¹Then Shechem said to Dinah's father and brothers, "Let me find favor in your eyes, and I will give you whatever you ask. ¹²Make the price for the bride and the gift I am to bring as great as you like, and I'll pay whatever you ask me. Only give me the girl as my wife."

¹³Because their sister Dinah had been de-

ᵃ17 Succoth means shelters.   ᵇ18 That is, Northwest Mesopotamia   ᶜ18 Or arrived at Shalem, a
ᵈ19 Hebrew hundred kesitahs; a kesitah was a unit of money of unknown weight and value.   ᵉ20 El Elohe Israel can mean God, the God of Israel or mighty is the God of Israel.   ᶠ7 Or against   ᵍ10 Or move about freely; also in verse 21

filed, Jacob's sons replied deceitfully as they spoke to Shechem and his father Hamor. [14]They said to them, "We can't do such a thing; we can't give our sister to a man who is not circumcised. That would be a disgrace to us. [15]We will give our consent to you on one condition only: that you become like us by circumcising all your males. [16]Then we will give you our daughters and take your daughters for ourselves. We'll settle among you and become one people with you. [17]But if you will not agree to be circumcised, we'll take our sister[a] and go."

[18]Their proposal seemed good to Hamor and his son Shechem. [19]The young man, who was the most honored of all his father's household, lost no time in doing what they said, because he was delighted with Jacob's daughter. [20]So Hamor and his son Shechem went to the gate of their city to speak to their fellow townsmen. [21]"These men are friendly toward us," they said. "Let them live in our land and trade in it; the land has plenty of room for them. We can marry their daughters and they can marry ours. [22]But the men will consent to live with us as one people only on the condition that our males be circumcised, as they themselves are. [23]Won't their livestock, their property and all their other animals become ours? So let us give our consent to them, and they will settle among us."

[24]All the men who went out of the city gate agreed with Hamor and his son Shechem, and every male in the city was circumcised.

[25]Three days later, while all of them were still in pain, two of Jacob's sons, Simeon and Levi, Dinah's brothers, took their swords and attacked the unsuspecting city, killing every male. [26]They put Hamor and his son Shechem to the sword and took Dinah from Shechem's house and left. [27]The sons of Jacob came upon the dead bodies and looted the city where[b] their sister had been defiled. [28]They seized their flocks and herds and donkeys and everything else of theirs in the city and out in the fields. [29]They carried off all their wealth and all their women and children, taking as plunder everything in the houses.

[30]Then Jacob said to Simeon and Levi, "You have brought trouble on me by making me a stench to the Canaanites and Periz-zites, the people living in this land. We are few in number, and if they join forces against me and attack me, I and my household will be destroyed."

[31]But they replied, "Should he have treated our sister like a prostitute?"

Jacob Returns to Bethel

35 Then God said to Jacob, "Go up to Bethel and settle there, and build an altar there to God, who appeared to you when you were fleeing from your brother Esau."

[2]So Jacob said to his household and to all who were with him, "Get rid of the foreign gods you have with you, and purify yourselves and change your clothes. [3]Then come, let us go up to Bethel, where I will build an altar to God, who answered me in the day of my distress and who has been with me wherever I have gone." [4]So they gave Jacob all the foreign gods they had and the rings in their ears, and Jacob buried them under the oak at Shechem. [5]Then they set out, and the terror of God fell upon the towns all around them so that no one pursued them.

[6]Jacob and all the people with him came to Luz (that is, Bethel) in the land of Canaan. [7]There he built an altar, and he called the place El Bethel,[c] because it was there that God revealed himself to him when he was fleeing from his brother.

[8]Now Deborah, Rebekah's nurse, died and was buried under the oak below Bethel. So it was named Allon Bacuth.[d]

[9]After Jacob returned from Paddan Aram,[e] God appeared to him again and blessed him. [10]God said to him, "Your name is Jacob,[f] but you will no longer be called Jacob; your name will be Israel.[g]" So he named him Israel.

[11]And God said to him, "I am God Almighty[h]; be fruitful and increase in number. A nation and a community of nations will come from you, and kings will come from your body. [12]The land I gave to Abraham and Isaac I also give to you, and I will give this land to your descendants after you." [13]Then God went up from him at the place where he had talked with him.

[14]Jacob set up a stone pillar at the place where God had talked with him, and he poured out a drink offering on it; he also

poured oil on it. **15**Jacob called the place where God had talked with him Bethel.*a*

The Deaths of Rachel and Isaac

16Then they moved on from Bethel. While they were still some distance from Ephrath, Rachel began to give birth and had great difficulty. **17**And as she was having great difficulty in childbirth, the midwife said to her, "Don't be afraid, for you have another son." **18**As she breathed her last—for she was dying—she named her son Ben-Oni.*b* But his father named him Benjamin.*c*

19So Rachel died and was buried on the way to Ephrath (that is, Bethlehem). **20**Over her tomb Jacob set up a pillar, and to this day that pillar marks Rachel's tomb.

21Israel moved on again and pitched his tent beyond Migdal Eder. **22**While Israel was living in that region, Reuben went in and slept with his father's concubine Bilhah, and Israel heard of it.

Jacob had twelve sons:
23The sons of Leah:
Reuben the firstborn of Jacob,
Simeon, Levi, Judah, Issachar and Zebulun.
24The sons of Rachel:
Joseph and Benjamin.
25The sons of Rachel's maidservant Bilhah:
Dan and Naphtali.
26The sons of Leah's maidservant Zilpah:
Gad and Asher.
These were the sons of Jacob, who were born to him in Paddan Aram.

27Jacob came home to his father Isaac in Mamre, near Kiriath Arba (that is, Hebron), where Abraham and Isaac had stayed. **28**Isaac lived a hundred and eighty years. **29**Then he breathed his last and died and was gathered to his people, old and full of years. And his sons Esau and Jacob buried him.

Esau's Descendants

36 This is the account of Esau (that is, Edom).

2Esau took his wives from the women of Canaan: Adah daughter of Elon the Hittite, and Oholibamah daughter of Anah and granddaughter of Zibeon the Hivite— **3**also Basemath daughter of Ishmael and sister of Nebaioth.

4Adah bore Eliphaz to Esau, Basemath bore Reuel, **5**and Oholibamah bore Jeush, Jalam and Korah. These were the sons of Esau, who were born to him in Canaan.

6Esau took his wives and sons and daughters and all the members of his household, as well as his livestock and all his other animals and all the goods he had acquired in Canaan, and moved to a land some distance from his brother Jacob. **7**Their possessions were too great for them to remain together; the land where they were staying could not support them both because of their livestock. **8**So Esau (that is, Edom) settled in the hill country of Seir.

9This is the account of Esau the father of the Edomites in the hill country of Seir.

10These are the names of Esau's sons:
Eliphaz, the son of Esau's wife Adah, and Reuel, the son of Esau's wife Basemath.
11The sons of Eliphaz:
Teman, Omar, Zepho, Gatam and Kenaz.
12Esau's son Eliphaz also had a concubine named Timna, who bore him Amalek. These were grandsons of Esau's wife Adah.
13The sons of Reuel:
Nahath, Zerah, Shammah and Mizzah. These were grandsons of Esau's wife Basemath.
14The sons of Esau's wife Oholibamah daughter of Anah and granddaughter of Zibeon, whom she bore to Esau:
Jeush, Jalam and Korah.

15These were the chiefs among Esau's descendants:
The sons of Eliphaz the firstborn of Esau:
Chiefs Teman, Omar, Zepho, Kenaz, **16**Korah,*d* Gatam and Amalek. These were the chiefs descended from Eliphaz in Edom; they were grandsons of Adah.
17The sons of Esau's son Reuel:
Chiefs Nahath, Zerah, Shammah and Mizzah. These were the chiefs descended from Reuel in Edom; they were grandsons of Esau's wife Basemath.
18The sons of Esau's wife Oholibamah:

---

a15 Bethel means *house of God.*   *b18 Ben-Oni* means *son of my trouble.*   *c18 Benjamin* means *son of my right hand.*   *d16* Masoretic Text; Samaritan Pentateuch (see also Gen. 36:11 and 1 Chron. 1:36) does not have *Korah.*

Chiefs Jeush, Jalam and Korah. These were the chiefs descended from Esau's wife Oholibamah daughter of Anah.

¹⁹These were the sons of Esau (that is, Edom), and these were their chiefs.

²⁰These were the sons of Seir the Horite, who were living in the region:

Lotan, Shobal, Zibeon, Anah, ²¹Dishon, Ezer and Dishan. These sons of Seir in Edom were Horite chiefs.

²²The sons of Lotan:

Hori and Homam.ᵃ Timna was Lotan's sister.

²³The sons of Shobal:

Alvan, Manahath, Ebal, Shepho and Onam.

²⁴The sons of Zibeon:

Aiah and Anah. This is the Anah who discovered the hot springsᵇ in the desert while he was grazing the donkeys of his father Zibeon.

²⁵The children of Anah:

Dishon and Oholibamah daughter of Anah.

²⁶The sons of Dishonᶜ:

Hemdan, Eshban, Ithran and Keran.

²⁷The sons of Ezer:

Bilhan, Zaavan and Akan.

²⁸The sons of Dishan:

Uz and Aran.

²⁹These were the Horite chiefs:

Lotan, Shobal, Zibeon, Anah, ³⁰Dishon, Ezer and Dishan. These were the Horite chiefs, according to their divisions, in the land of Seir.

The Rulers of Edom

³¹These were the kings who reigned in Edom before any Israelite king reignedᵈ:

³²Bela son of Beor became king of Edom. His city was named Dinhabah.

³³When Bela died, Jobab son of Zerah from Bozrah succeeded him as king.

³⁴When Jobab died, Husham from the land of the Temanites succeeded him as king.

³⁵When Husham died, Hadad son of Bedad, who defeated Midian in the country of Moab, succeeded him as king. His city was named Avith.

³⁶When Hadad died, Samlah from Masrekah succeeded him as king.

³⁷When Samlah died, Shaul from Rehoboth on the riverᵉ succeeded him as king.

³⁸When Shaul died, Baal-Hanan son of Acbor succeeded him as king.

³⁹When Baal-Hanan son of Acbor died, Hadadᶠ succeeded him as king. His city was named Pau, and his wife's name was Mehetabel daughter of Matred, the daughter of Me-Zahab.

⁴⁰These were the chiefs descended from Esau, by name, according to their clans and regions:

Timna, Alvah, Jetheth, ⁴¹Oholibamah, Elah, Pinon, ⁴²Kenaz, Teman, Mibzar, ⁴³Magdiel and Iram. These were the chiefs of Edom, according to their settlements in the land they occupied.

This was Esau the father of the Edomites.

Joseph's Dreams

37 Jacob lived in the land where his father had stayed, the land of Canaan.

²This is the account of Jacob.

Joseph, a young man of seventeen, was tending the flocks with his brothers, the sons of Bilhah and the sons of Zilpah, his father's wives, and he brought their father a bad report about them.

³Now Israel loved Joseph more than any of his other sons, because he had been born to him in his old age; and he made a richly ornamentedᵍ robe for him. ⁴When his brothers saw that their father loved him more than any of them, they hated him and could not speak a kind word to him.

⁵Joseph had a dream, and when he told it to his brothers, they hated him all the more. ⁶He said to them, "Listen to this dream I had: ⁷We were binding sheaves of grain out in the field when suddenly my sheaf rose and stood upright, while your sheaves gathered around mine and bowed down to it."

⁸His brothers said to him, "Do you intend to reign over us? Will you actually rule us?" And they hated him all the more because of his dream and what he had said.

⁹Then he had another dream, and he told

ᵃ22 Hebrew *Hemam*, a variant of *Homam* (see 1 Chron. 1:39)   ᵇ24 Vulgate; Syriac *discovered water*; the meaning of the Hebrew for this word is uncertain.   ᶜ26 Hebrew *Dishan*, a variant of *Dishon*   ᵈ31 Or *before an Israelite king reigned over them*   ᵉ37 Possibly the Euphrates   ᶠ39 Many manuscripts of the Masoretic Text, Samaritan Pentateuch and Syriac (see also 1 Chron. 1:50); most manuscripts of the Masoretic Text *Hadar*   ᵍ3 The meaning of the Hebrew for *richly ornamented* is uncertain; also in verses 23 and 32.

COMPETITION... RELATIVELY SPEAKING

A s Kent, seventeen, walks past his younger brother's room, he hears the sounds of muffled sobs.

After ten minutes of banging on the door and ten more minutes of "C'mon, Scooter, what's wrong?" he finally gets this confession:

"Mom and Dad never jump on your case. Everything you do is 'perfect' and 'wonderful.' But I can't do anything right! I bet Dad asks me fifty times a week, 'Why can't you be more like Kent?' "

Look It Up
••••

Competing for love and approval. Many of us do it—consciously or unconsciously—all the time. Here are two examples:

1. The story of the brothers Jacob and Esau:
"When Esau heard his father's words [that Jacob had been given a special blessing], he burst out with a loud and bitter cry and said to his father, 'Bless me—me too, my father! . . . Haven't you reserved any blessing for me?' . . . Then Esau wept aloud" (Genesis 27:34,36,38).

2. The story of the lost son (Luke 15:11–32).

Think It Through
••••

Do you compete with your brother(s) and/or sister(s) for your parents' love and favor? What strategies do you use to try to get attention and approval? Are you winning?

Is it right for parents to play favorites? Why or why not? How does it make you feel? Would your family be better if this competition ended?

Work It Out
••••

The problem with competition (especially between brothers and sisters) is that it results in winners and losers. If you lose, you feel awful. If you win, others feel awful. So no matter what, someone ends up hurt.

Stop the hurt today.

If your parents give you more attention than your brothers and sisters, deflect some of that attention to your siblings. Brag about them to your parents. Point out the good things they have done. If the special treatment continues, talk to your parents and express your concern.

If you are the one who feels overshadowed and forgotten, tell God and another friend about your hurt feelings. Then prayerfully approach your parents about the issue.

Nail It Down
••••

Read another account of sibling rivalry in Genesis 37:1–4.

Turn to pages 18, 1230 and 1360 for other readings on competition.
Turn to page 52 for Friday's reading.

Topic
••••

COMPETITION

it to his brothers. "Listen," he said, "I had another dream, and this time the sun and moon and eleven stars were bowing down to me."

[10]When he told his father as well as his brothers, his father rebuked him and said, "What is this dream you had? Will your mother and I and your brothers actually come and bow down to the ground before you?" [11]His brothers were jealous of him, but his father kept the matter in mind.

Joseph Sold by His Brothers

[12]Now his brothers had gone to graze their father's flocks near Shechem, [13]and Israel said to Joseph, "As you know, your brothers are grazing the flocks near Shechem. Come, I am going to send you to them."

"Very well," he replied.

[14]So he said to him, "Go and see if all is well with your brothers and with the flocks, and bring word back to me." Then he sent him off from the Valley of Hebron.

When Joseph arrived at Shechem, [15]a man found him wandering around in the fields and asked him, "What are you looking for?"

[16]He replied, "I'm looking for my brothers. Can you tell me where they are grazing their flocks?"

[17]"They have moved on from here," the man answered. "I heard them say, 'Let's go to Dothan.' "

So Joseph went after his brothers and found them near Dothan. [18]But they saw him in the distance, and before he reached them, they plotted to kill him.

[19]"Here comes that dreamer!" they said to each other. [20]"Come now, let's kill him and throw him into one of these cisterns and say that a ferocious animal devoured him. Then we'll see what comes of his dreams."

[21]When Reuben heard this, he tried to rescue him from their hands. "Let's not take his life," he said. [22]"Don't shed any blood. Throw him into this cistern here in the desert, but don't lay a hand on him." Reuben said this to rescue him from them and take him back to his father.

[23]So when Joseph came to his brothers, they stripped him of his robe — the richly ornamented robe he was wearing — [24]and they took him and threw him into the cistern. Now the cistern was empty; there was no water in it.

[25]As they sat down to eat their meal, they looked up and saw a caravan of Ishmaelites coming from Gilead. Their camels were loaded with spices, balm and myrrh, and they were on their way to take them down to Egypt.

[26]Judah said to his brothers, "What will we gain if we kill our brother and cover up his blood? [27]Come, let's sell him to the Ishmaelites and not lay our hands on him; after all, he is our brother, our own flesh and blood." His brothers agreed.

[28]So when the Midianite merchants came by, his brothers pulled Joseph up out of the cistern and sold him for twenty shekels[a] of silver to the Ishmaelites, who took him to Egypt.

[29]When Reuben returned to the cistern and saw that Joseph was not there, he tore his clothes. [30]He went back to his brothers and said, "The boy isn't there! Where can I turn now?"

[31]Then they got Joseph's robe, slaughtered a goat and dipped the robe in the blood. [32]They took the ornamented robe back to their father and said, "We found this. Examine it to see whether it is your son's robe."

[33]He recognized it and said, "It is my son's robe! Some ferocious animal has devoured him. Joseph has surely been torn to pieces."

[34]Then Jacob tore his clothes, put on sackcloth and mourned for his son many days. [35]All his sons and daughters came to comfort him, but he refused to be comforted. "No," he said, "in mourning will I go down to the grave[b] to my son." So his father wept for him.

[36]Meanwhile, the Midianites[c] sold Joseph in Egypt to Potiphar, one of Pharaoh's officials, the captain of the guard.

Judah and Tamar

38 At that time, Judah left his brothers and went down to stay with a man of Adullam named Hirah. [2]There Judah met the daughter of a Canaanite man named Shua. He married her and lay with her; [3]she became pregnant and gave birth to a son, who was named Er. [4]She conceived again and gave birth to a son and named him Onan. [5]She gave birth to still another son and named him Shelah. It was at Kezib that she gave birth to him.

[6]Judah got a wife for Er, his firstborn, and her name was Tamar. [7]But Er, Judah's first-

---

[a]28 That is, about 8 ounces (about 0.2 kilogram)   [b]35 Hebrew *Sheol*   [c]36 Samaritan Pentateuch, Septuagint, Vulgate and Syriac (see also verse 28); Masoretic Text *Medanites*

born, was wicked in the Lord's sight; so the Lord put him to death.

8Then Judah said to Onan, "Lie with your brother's wife and fulfill your duty to her as a brother-in-law to produce offspring for your brother." 9But Onan knew that the offspring would not be his; so whenever he lay with his brother's wife, he spilled his semen on the ground to keep from producing offspring for his brother. 10What he did was wicked in the Lord's sight; so he put him to death also.

11Judah then said to his daughter-in-law Tamar, "Live as a widow in your father's house until my son Shelah grows up." For he thought, "He may die too, just like his brothers." So Tamar went to live in her father's house.

12After a long time Judah's wife, the daughter of Shua, died. When Judah had recovered from his grief, he went up to Timnah, to the men who were shearing his sheep, and his friend Hirah the Adullamite went with him.

13When Tamar was told, "Your father-in-law is on his way to Timnah to shear his sheep," 14she took off her widow's clothes, covered herself with a veil to disguise herself, and then sat down at the entrance to Enaim, which is on the road to Timnah. For she saw that, though Shelah had now grown up, she had not been given to him as his wife.

15When Judah saw her, he thought she was a prostitute, for she had covered her face. 16Not realizing that she was his daughter-in-law, he went over to her by the roadside and said, "Come now, let me sleep with you."

"And what will you give me to sleep with you?" she asked.

17"I'll send you a young goat from my flock," he said.

"Will you give me something as a pledge until you send it?" she asked.

18He said, "What pledge should I give you?"

"Your seal and its cord, and the staff in your hand," she answered. So he gave them to her and slept with her, and she became pregnant by him. 19After she left, she took off her veil and put on her widow's clothes again.

20Meanwhile Judah sent the young goat by his friend the Adullamite in order to get his pledge back from the woman, but he did not find her. 21He asked the men who lived there, "Where is the shrine prostitute who was beside the road at Enaim?"

"There hasn't been any shrine prostitute here," they said.

22So he went back to Judah and said, "I didn't find her. Besides, the men who lived there said, 'There hasn't been any shrine prostitute here.' "

23Then Judah said, "Let her keep what she has, or we will become a laughingstock. After all, I did send her this young goat, but you didn't find her."

24About three months later Judah was told, "Your daughter-in-law Tamar is guilty of prostitution, and as a result she is now pregnant."

Judah said, "Bring her out and have her burned to death!"

25As she was being brought out, she sent a message to her father-in-law. "I am pregnant by the man who owns these," she said. And she added, "See if you recognize whose seal and cord and staff these are."

26Judah recognized them and said, "She is more righteous than I, since I wouldn't give her to my son Shelah." And he did not sleep with her again.

27When the time came for her to give birth, there were twin boys in her womb. 28As she was giving birth, one of them put out his hand; so the midwife took a scarlet thread and tied it on his wrist and said, "This one came out first." 29But when he drew back his hand, his brother came out, and she said, "So this is how you have broken out!" And he was named Perez.a 30Then his brother, who had the scarlet thread on his wrist, came out and he was given the name Zerah.b

Joseph and Potiphar's Wife

39 Now Joseph had been taken down to Egypt. Potiphar, an Egyptian who was one of Pharaoh's officials, the captain of the guard, bought him from the Ishmaelites who had taken him there.

2The Lord was with Joseph and he prospered, and he lived in the house of his Egyptian master. 3When his master saw that the Lord was with him and that the Lord gave him success in everything he did, 4Joseph found favor in his eyes and became his attendant. Potiphar put him in charge of his household, and he entrusted to his care everything he owned. 5From the time he put him in charge of his household and of all that he owned, the Lord blessed the house-

---

a29 Perez means breaking out.   b30 Zerah can mean scarlet or brightness.

hold of the Egyptian because of Joseph. The blessing of the Lord was on everything Potiphar had, both in the house and in the field. [6]So he left in Joseph's care everything he had; with Joseph in charge, he did not concern himself with anything except the food he ate.

Now Joseph was well-built and handsome, [7]and after a while his master's wife took notice of Joseph and said, "Come to bed with me!"

[8]But he refused. "With me in charge," he told her, "my master does not concern himself with anything in the house; everything he owns he has entrusted to my care. [9]No one is greater in this house than I am. My master has withheld nothing from me except you, because you are his wife. How then could I do such a wicked thing and sin against God?" [10]And though she spoke to Joseph day after day, he refused to go to bed with her or even be with her.

[11]One day he went into the house to attend to his duties, and none of the household servants was inside. [12]She caught him by his cloak and said, "Come to bed with me!" But he left his cloak in her hand and ran out of the house.

[13]When she saw that he had left his cloak in her hand and had run out of the house, [14]she called her household servants. "Look," she said to them, "this Hebrew has been brought to us to make sport of us! He came in here to sleep with me, but I screamed. [15]When he heard me scream for help, he left his cloak beside me and ran out of the house."

[16]She kept his cloak beside her until his master came home. [17]Then she told him this story: "That Hebrew slave you brought us came to me to make sport of me. [18]But as soon as I screamed for help, he left his cloak beside me and ran out of the house."

[19]When his master heard the story his wife told him, saying, "This is how your slave treated me," he burned with anger. [20]Joseph's master took him and put him in prison, the place where the king's prisoners were confined.

But while Joseph was there in the prison, [21]the Lord was with him; he showed him kindness and granted him favor in the eyes of the prison warden. [22]So the warden put Joseph in charge of all those held in the prison, and he was made responsible for all that was done there. [23]The warden paid no attention to anything under Joseph's care, because the Lord was with Joseph and gave him success in whatever he did.

The Cupbearer and the Baker

40 Some time later, the cupbearer and the baker of the king of Egypt offended their master, the king of Egypt. [2]Pharaoh was angry with his two officials, the chief cupbearer and the chief baker, [3]and put them in custody in the house of the captain of the guard, in the same prison where Joseph was confined. [4]The captain of the guard assigned them to Joseph, and he attended them.

After they had been in custody for some time, [5]each of the two men — the cupbearer and the baker of the king of Egypt, who were being held in prison — had a dream the same night, and each dream had a meaning of its own.

[6]When Joseph came to them the next morning, he saw that they were dejected. [7]So he asked Pharaoh's officials who were in custody with him in his master's house, "Why are your faces so sad today?"

[8]"We both had dreams," they answered, "but there is no one to interpret them."

Then Joseph said to them, "Do not interpretations belong to God? Tell me your dreams."

[9]So the chief cupbearer told Joseph his dream. He said to him, "In my dream I saw a vine in front of me, [10]and on the vine were three branches. As soon as it budded, it blossomed, and its clusters ripened into grapes. [11]Pharaoh's cup was in my hand, and I took the grapes, squeezed them into Pharaoh's cup and put the cup in his hand."

[12]"This is what it means," Joseph said to him. "The three branches are three days. [13]Within three days Pharaoh will lift up your head and restore you to your position, and you will put Pharaoh's cup in his hand, just as you used to do when you were his cupbearer. [14]But when all goes well with you, remember me and show me kindness; mention me to Pharaoh and get me out of this prison. [15]For I was forcibly carried off from the land of the Hebrews, and even here I have done nothing to deserve being put in a dungeon."

[16]When the chief baker saw that Joseph had given a favorable interpretation, he said to Joseph, "I too had a dream: On my head were three baskets of bread.[a] [17]In the top basket were all kinds of baked goods for

---

Pharaoh, but the birds were eating them out of the basket on my head."

[18]"This is what it means," Joseph said. "The three baskets are three days. [19]Within three days Pharaoh will lift off your head and hang you on a tree.[a] And the birds will eat away your flesh."

[20]Now the third day was Pharaoh's birthday, and he gave a feast for all his officials. He lifted up the heads of the chief cupbearer and the chief baker in the presence of his officials: [21]He restored the chief cupbearer to his position, so that he once again put the cup into Pharaoh's hand, [22]but he hanged[b] the chief baker, just as Joseph had said to them in his interpretation.

[23]The chief cupbearer, however, did not remember Joseph; he forgot him.

Pharaoh's Dreams

41 When two full years had passed, Pharaoh had a dream: He was standing by the Nile, [2]when out of the river there came up seven cows, sleek and fat, and they grazed among the reeds. [3]After them, seven other cows, ugly and gaunt, came up out of the Nile and stood beside those on the riverbank. [4]And the cows that were ugly and gaunt ate up the seven sleek, fat cows. Then Pharaoh woke up.

[5]He fell asleep again and had a second dream: Seven heads of grain, healthy and good, were growing on a single stalk. [6]After them, seven other heads of grain sprouted — thin and scorched by the east wind. [7]The thin heads of grain swallowed up the seven healthy, full heads. Then Pharaoh woke up; it had been a dream.

[8]In the morning his mind was troubled, so he sent for all the magicians and wise men of Egypt. Pharaoh told them his dreams, but no one could interpret them for him.

[9]Then the chief cupbearer said to Pharaoh, "Today I am reminded of my shortcomings. [10]Pharaoh was once angry with his servants, and he imprisoned me and the chief baker in the house of the captain of the guard. [11]Each of us had a dream the same night, and each dream had a meaning of its own. [12]Now a young Hebrew was there with us, a servant of the captain of the guard. We told him our dreams, and he interpreted them for us, giving each man the interpretation of his dream. [13]And things turned out exactly as he interpreted them to us: I was restored to my position, and the other man was hanged.[b]"

[14]So Pharaoh sent for Joseph, and he was quickly brought from the dungeon. When he had shaved and changed his clothes, he came before Pharaoh.

[15]Pharaoh said to Joseph, "I had a dream, and no one can interpret it. But I have heard it said of you that when you hear a dream you can interpret it."

[16]"I cannot do it," Joseph replied to Pharaoh, "but God will give Pharaoh the answer he desires."

[17]Then Pharaoh said to Joseph, "In my dream I was standing on the bank of the Nile, [18]when out of the river there came up seven cows, fat and sleek, and they grazed among the reeds. [19]After them, seven other cows came up — scrawny and very ugly and lean. I had never seen such ugly cows in all the land of Egypt. [20]The lean, ugly cows ate up the seven fat cows that came up first. [21]But even after they ate them, no one could tell that they had done so; they looked just as ugly as before. Then I woke up.

[22]"In my dreams I also saw seven heads of grain, full and good, growing on a single stalk. [23]After them, seven other heads sprouted — withered and thin and scorched by the east wind. [24]The thin heads of grain swallowed up the seven good heads. I told this to the magicians, but none could explain it to me."

[25]Then Joseph said to Pharaoh, "The dreams of Pharaoh are one and the same. God has revealed to Pharaoh what he is about to do. [26]The seven good cows are seven years, and the seven good heads of grain are seven years; it is one and the same dream. [27]The seven lean, ugly cows that came up afterward are seven years, and so are the seven worthless heads of grain scorched by the east wind: They are seven years of famine.

[28]"It is just as I said to Pharaoh: God has shown Pharaoh what he is about to do. [29]Seven years of great abundance are coming throughout the land of Egypt, [30]but seven years of famine will follow them. Then all the abundance in Egypt will be forgotten, and the famine will ravage the land. [31]The abundance in the land will not be remembered, because the famine that follows it will be so severe. [32]The reason the dream was given to Pharaoh in two forms is that the matter has been firmly decided by God, and God will do it soon.

[33]"And now let Pharaoh look for a discerning and wise man and put him in charge of

the land of Egypt. **34**Let Pharaoh appoint commissioners over the land to take a fifth of the harvest of Egypt during the seven years of abundance. **35**They should collect all the food of these good years that are coming and store up the grain under the authority of Pharaoh, to be kept in the cities for food. **36**This food should be held in reserve for the country, to be used during the seven years of famine that will come upon Egypt, so that the country may not be ruined by the famine."

37The plan seemed good to Pharaoh and to all his officials. **38**So Pharaoh asked them, "Can we find anyone like this man, one in whom is the spirit of God*a*?"

39Then Pharaoh said to Joseph, "Since God has made all this known to you, there is no one so discerning and wise as you. **40**You shall be in charge of my palace, and all my people are to submit to your orders. Only with respect to the throne will I be greater than you."

Joseph in Charge of Egypt

41So Pharaoh said to Joseph, "I hereby put you in charge of the whole land of Egypt." **42**Then Pharaoh took his signet ring from his finger and put it on Joseph's finger. He dressed him in robes of fine linen and put a gold chain around his neck. **43**He had him ride in a chariot as his second-in-command,*b* and men shouted before him, "Make way*c*!" Thus he put him in charge of the whole land of Egypt.

44Then Pharaoh said to Joseph, "I am Pharaoh, but without your word no one will lift hand or foot in all Egypt." **45**Pharaoh gave Joseph the name Zaphenath-Paneah and gave him Asenath daughter of Potiphera, priest of On,*d* to be his wife. And Joseph went throughout the land of Egypt.

46Joseph was thirty years old when he entered the service of Pharaoh king of Egypt. And Joseph went out from Pharaoh's presence and traveled throughout Egypt. **47**During the seven years of abundance the land produced plentifully. **48**Joseph collected all the food produced in those seven years of abundance in Egypt and stored it in the cities. In each city he put the food grown in the fields surrounding it. **49**Joseph stored up huge quantities of grain, like the sand of the sea; it was so much that he stopped keeping records because it was beyond measure.

50Before the years of famine came, two sons were born to Joseph by Asenath daughter of Potiphera, priest of On. **51**Joseph named his firstborn Manasseh*e* and said, "It is because God has made me forget all my trouble and all my father's household." **52**The second son he named Ephraim*f* and said, "It is because God has made me fruitful in the land of my suffering."

53The seven years of abundance in Egypt came to an end, **54**and the seven years of famine began, just as Joseph had said. There was famine in all the other lands, but in the whole land of Egypt there was food. **55**When all Egypt began to feel the famine, the people cried to Pharaoh for food. Then Pharaoh told all the Egyptians, "Go to Joseph and do what he tells you."

56When the famine had spread over the whole country, Joseph opened the storehouses and sold grain to the Egyptians, for the famine was severe throughout Egypt. **57**And all the countries came to Egypt to buy grain from Joseph, because the famine was severe in all the world.

Joseph's Brothers Go to Egypt

42 When Jacob learned that there was grain in Egypt, he said to his sons, "Why do you just keep looking at each other?" **2**He continued, "I have heard that there is grain in Egypt. Go down there and buy some for us, so that we may live and not die."

3Then ten of Joseph's brothers went down to buy grain from Egypt. **4**But Jacob did not send Benjamin, Joseph's brother, with the others, because he was afraid that harm might come to him. **5**So Israel's sons were among those who went to buy grain, for the famine was in the land of Canaan also.

6Now Joseph was the governor of the land, the one who sold grain to all its people. So when Joseph's brothers arrived, they bowed down to him with their faces to the ground. **7**As soon as Joseph saw his brothers, he recognized them, but he pretended to be a stranger and spoke harshly to them. "Where do you come from?" he asked.

"From the land of Canaan," they replied, "to buy food."

8Although Joseph recognized his brothers, they did not recognize him. **9**Then he remembered his dreams about them and

---

a38 Or of the gods   *b43 Or in the chariot of his second-in-command; or in his second chariot*   *c43 Or Bow down*   *d45 That is, Heliopolis; also in verse 50*   *e51 Manasseh sounds like and may be derived from the Hebrew for forget.*   *f52 Ephraim sounds like the Hebrew for twice fruitful.*

said to them, "You are spies! You have come to see where our land is unprotected."

¹⁰"No, my lord," they answered. "Your servants have come to buy food. ¹¹We are all the sons of one man. Your servants are honest men, not spies."

¹²"No!" he said to them. "You have come to see where our land is unprotected."

¹³But they replied, "Your servants were twelve brothers, the sons of one man, who lives in the land of Canaan. The youngest is now with our father, and one is no more."

¹⁴Joseph said to them, "It is just as I told you: You are spies! ¹⁵And this is how you will be tested: As surely as Pharaoh lives, you will not leave this place unless your youngest brother comes here. ¹⁶Send one of your number to get your brother; the rest of you will be kept in prison, so that your words may be tested to see if you are telling the truth. If you are not, then as surely as Pharaoh lives, you are spies!" ¹⁷And he put them all in custody for three days.

¹⁸On the third day, Joseph said to them, "Do this and you will live, for I fear God: ¹⁹If you are honest men, let one of your brothers stay here in prison, while the rest of you go and take grain back for your starving households. ²⁰But you must bring your youngest brother to me, so that your words may be verified and that you may not die." This they proceeded to do.

²¹They said to one another, "Surely we are being punished because of our brother. We saw how distressed he was when he pleaded with us for his life, but we would not listen; that's why this distress has come upon us."

²²Reuben replied, "Didn't I tell you not to sin against the boy? But you wouldn't listen! Now we must give an accounting for his blood." ²³They did not realize that Joseph could understand them, since he was using an interpreter.

²⁴He turned away from them and began to weep, but then turned back and spoke to them again. He had Simeon taken from them and bound before their eyes.

²⁵Joseph gave orders to fill their bags with grain, to put each man's silver back in his sack, and to give them provisions for their journey. After this was done for them, ²⁶they loaded their grain on their donkeys and left.

²⁷At the place where they stopped for the night one of them opened his sack to get feed for his donkey, and he saw his silver in the mouth of his sack. ²⁸"My silver has been

returned," he said to his brothers. "Here it is in my sack."

Their hearts sank and they turned to each other trembling and said, "What is this that God has done to us?"

²⁹When they came to their father Jacob in the land of Canaan, they told him all that had happened to them. They said, ³⁰"The man who is lord over the land spoke harshly to us and treated us as though we were spying on the land. ³¹But we said to him, 'We are honest men; we are not spies. ³²We were twelve brothers, sons of one father. One is no more, and the youngest is now with our father in Canaan.'

³³"Then the man who is lord over the land said to us, 'This is how I will know whether you are honest men: Leave one of your brothers here with me, and take food for your starving households and go. ³⁴But bring your youngest brother to me so I will know that you are not spies but honest men. Then I will give your brother back to you, and you can trade*a* in the land.'"

³⁵As they were emptying their sacks, there in each man's sack was his pouch of silver! When they and their father saw the money pouches, they were frightened. ³⁶Their father Jacob said to them, "You have deprived me of my children. Joseph is no more and Simeon is no more, and now you want to take Benjamin. Everything is against me!"

³⁷Then Reuben said to his father, "You may put both of my sons to death if I do not bring him back to you. Entrust him to my care, and I will bring him back."

³⁸But Jacob said, "My son will not go down there with you; his brother is dead and he is the only one left. If harm comes to him on the journey you are taking, you will bring my gray head down to the grave*b* in sorrow."

The Second Journey to Egypt

43 Now the famine was still severe in the land. ²So when they had eaten all the grain they had brought from Egypt, their father said to them, "Go back and buy us a little more food."

³But Judah said to him, "The man warned us solemnly, 'You will not see my face again unless your brother is with you.' ⁴If you will send our brother along with us, we will go down and buy food for you. ⁵But if you will not send him, we will not go down, because

---

a34 Or *move about freely*   *b38* Hebrew *Sheol*

the man said to us, 'You will not see my face again unless your brother is with you.' "

⁶Israel asked, "Why did you bring this trouble on me by telling the man you had another brother?"

⁷They replied, "The man questioned us closely about ourselves and our family. 'Is your father still living?' he asked us. 'Do you have another brother?' We simply answered his questions. How were we to know he would say, 'Bring your brother down here'?"

⁸Then Judah said to Israel his father, "Send the boy along with me and we will go at once, so that we and you and our children may live and not die. ⁹I myself will guarantee his safety; you can hold me personally responsible for him. If I do not bring him back to you and set him here before you, I will bear the blame before you all my life. ¹⁰As it is, if we had not delayed, we could have gone and returned twice."

¹¹Then their father Israel said to them, "If it must be, then do this: Put some of the best products of the land in your bags and take them down to the man as a gift—a little balm and a little honey, some spices and myrrh, some pistachio nuts and almonds. ¹²Take double the amount of silver with you, for you must return the silver that was put back into the mouths of your sacks. Perhaps it was a mistake. ¹³Take your brother also and go back to the man at once. ¹⁴And may God Almighty*ᵃ* grant you mercy before the man so that he will let your other brother and Benjamin come back with you. As for me, if I am bereaved, I am bereaved."

¹⁵So the men took the gifts and double the amount of silver, and Benjamin also. They hurried down to Egypt and presented themselves to Joseph. ¹⁶When Joseph saw Benjamin with them, he said to the steward of his house, "Take these men to my house, slaughter an animal and prepare dinner; they are to eat with me at noon."

¹⁷The man did as Joseph told him and took the men to Joseph's house. ¹⁸Now the men were frightened when they were taken to his house. They thought, "We were brought here because of the silver that was put back into our sacks the first time. He wants to attack us and overpower us and seize us as slaves and take our donkeys."

¹⁹So they went up to Joseph's steward and spoke to him at the entrance to the house. ²⁰"Please, sir," they said, "we came down here the first time to buy food. ²¹But at the place where we stopped for the night we opened our sacks and each of us found his silver—the exact weight—in the mouth of his sack. So we have brought it back with us. ²²We have also brought additional silver with us to buy food. We don't know who put our silver in our sacks."

²³"It's all right," he said. "Don't be afraid. Your God, the God of your father, has given you treasure in your sacks; I received your silver." Then he brought Simeon out to them.

²⁴The steward took the men into Joseph's house, gave them water to wash their feet and provided fodder for their donkeys. ²⁵They prepared their gifts for Joseph's arrival at noon, because they had heard that they were to eat there.

²⁶When Joseph came home, they presented to him the gifts they had brought into the house, and they bowed down before him to the ground. ²⁷He asked them how they were, and then he said, "How is your aged father you told me about? Is he still living?"

²⁸They replied, "Your servant our father is still alive and well." And they bowed low to pay him honor.

²⁹As he looked about and saw his brother Benjamin, his own mother's son, he asked, "Is this your youngest brother, the one you told me about?" And he said, "God be gracious to you, my son." ³⁰Deeply moved at the sight of his brother, Joseph hurried out and looked for a place to weep. He went into his private room and wept there.

³¹After he had washed his face, he came out and, controlling himself, said, "Serve the food."

³²They served him by himself, the brothers by themselves, and the Egyptians who ate with him by themselves, because Egyptians could not eat with Hebrews, for that is detestable to Egyptians. ³³The men had been seated before him in the order of their ages, from the firstborn to the youngest; and they looked at each other in astonishment. ³⁴When portions were served to them from Joseph's table, Benjamin's portion was five times as much as anyone else's. So they feasted and drank freely with him.

A Silver Cup in a Sack

44 Now Joseph gave these instructions to the steward of his house: "Fill the men's sacks with as much food as they can carry, and put each man's silver in the mouth of his sack. ²Then put my cup, the silver one, in the mouth of the youngest

---

*ᵃ*14 Hebrew *El-Shaddai*

one's sack, along with the silver for his grain." And he did as Joseph said.

[3]As morning dawned, the men were sent on their way with their donkeys. [4]They had not gone far from the city when Joseph said to his steward, "Go after those men at once, and when you catch up with them, say to them, 'Why have you repaid good with evil? [5]Isn't this the cup my master drinks from and also uses for divination? This is a wicked thing you have done.' "

[6]When he caught up with them, he repeated these words to them. [7]But they said to him, "Why does my lord say such things? Far be it from your servants to do anything like that! [8]We even brought back to you from the land of Canaan the silver we found inside the mouths of our sacks. So why would we steal silver or gold from your master's house? [9]If any of your servants is found to have it, he will die; and the rest of us will become my lord's slaves."

[10]"Very well, then," he said, "let it be as you say. Whoever is found to have it will become my slave; the rest of you will be free from blame."

[11]Each of them quickly lowered his sack to the ground and opened it. [12]Then the steward proceeded to search, beginning with the oldest and ending with the youngest. And the cup was found in Benjamin's sack. [13]At this, they tore their clothes. Then they all loaded their donkeys and returned to the city.

[14]Joseph was still in the house when Judah and his brothers came in, and they threw themselves to the ground before him. [15]Joseph said to them, "What is this you have done? Don't you know that a man like me can find things out by divination?"

[16]"What can we say to my lord?" Judah replied. "What can we say? How can we prove our innocence? God has uncovered your servants' guilt. We are now my lord's slaves—we ourselves and the one who was found to have the cup."

[17]But Joseph said, "Far be it from me to do such a thing! Only the man who was found to have the cup will become my slave. The rest of you, go back to your father in peace."

[18]Then Judah went up to him and said: "Please, my lord, let your servant speak a word to my lord. Do not be angry with your servant, though you are equal to Pharaoh himself. [19]My lord asked his servants, 'Do you have a father or a brother?' [20]And we answered, 'We have an aged father, and there is a young son born to him in his old age. His brother is dead, and he is the only one of his mother's sons left, and his father loves him.'

[21]"Then you said to your servants, 'Bring him down to me so I can see him for myself.' [22]And we said to my lord, 'The boy cannot leave his father; if he leaves him, his father will die.' [23]But you told your servants, 'Unless your youngest brother comes down with you, you will not see my face again.' [24]When we went back to your servant my father, we told him what my lord had said.

[25]"Then our father said, 'Go back and buy a little more food.' [26]But we said, 'We cannot go down. Only if our youngest brother is with us will we go. We cannot see the man's face unless our youngest brother is with us.'

[27]"Your servant my father said to us, 'You know that my wife bore me two sons. [28]One of them went away from me, and I said, "He has surely been torn to pieces." And I have not seen him since. [29]If you take this one from me too and harm comes to him, you will bring my gray head down to the grave[a] in misery.'

[30]"So now, if the boy is not with us when I go back to your servant my father and if my father, whose life is closely bound up with the boy's life, [31]sees that the boy isn't there, he will die. Your servants will bring the gray head of our father down to the grave in sorrow. [32]Your servant guaranteed the boy's safety to my father. I said, 'If I do not bring him back to you, I will bear the blame before you, my father, all my life!'

[33]"Now then, please let your servant remain here as my lord's slave in place of the boy, and let the boy return with his brothers. [34]How can I go back to my father if the boy is not with me? No! Do not let me see the misery that would come upon my father."

Joseph Makes Himself Known

45 Then Joseph could no longer control himself before all his attendants, and he cried out, "Have everyone leave my presence!" So there was no one with Joseph when he made himself known to his brothers. [2]And he wept so loudly that the Egyptians heard him, and Pharaoh's household heard about it.

[3]Joseph said to his brothers, "I am Joseph! Is my father still living?" But his brothers were not able to answer him, because they were terrified at his presence.

[4]Then Joseph said to his brothers, "Come

a29 Hebrew *Sheol*; also in verse 31

YOU'LL KNOW IT WHEN YOU BLOW IT!

T heresa and Elise head for the rest room right after English class. There Theresa begins to talk and joke about Becky, a fellow student.

Elise joins in. The remarks get louder and more obnoxious. ("Did you see that excuse for a dress she's wearing?" "It would help if she would wash her hair at least once a month.")

This goes on nonstop for five minutes. Suddenly the girls realize that Becky is sitting in one of the stalls!

Look It Up
••••

Sometimes embarrassment comes from sin. You do something wrong, and you get caught. It's that simple. The Bible gives a crystal-clear example of this sort of embarrassment—the story of Adam and Eve.

When the first couple disobeyed God and ate from the tree of the knowledge of good and evil, "The eyes of both of them were opened, and they realized they were naked; so they sewed fig leaves together and made coverings for themselves.

"Then the man and his wife heard the sound of the LORD God as he was walking in the garden in the cool of the day, and they hid from the LORD God among the trees of the garden. But the LORD God called to the man, 'Where are you?'

"He answered, 'I heard you in the garden, and I was afraid because I was naked; so I hid' " (Genesis 3:7–10).

Think It Through
••••

Have you ever been in a situation like the one involving Becky? Put yourself in Elise's shoes. How would you feel? What would you do? How might Elise have stopped the situation before it got out of hand?

Work It Out
••••

List all the possible embarrassing consequences of:
• Throwing a party while your parents are gone.
• Cheating on tests or assignments at school.
• Lying to your parents.
• Driving recklessly.
• Getting sexually involved.
• Shoplifting.

If you regularly do one (or more) of these things and you think you'll never get caught, ask yourself, "Suppose my luck runs out. Is this really worth the potential embarrassment?"

Nail It Down
••••

Read in Genesis 45:1–5 how Joseph avoided possible embarrassment by asking certain people to leave the room.

Turn to pages 1063 and 1272 for other readings on embarrassment.
Turn to page 58 for the weekend reading.

Topic
••••
EMBARRASSMENT

close to me." When they had done so, he said, "I am your brother Joseph, the one you sold into Egypt! 5And now, do not be distressed and do not be angry with yourselves for selling me here, because it was to save lives that God sent me ahead of you. 6For two years now there has been famine in the land, and for the next five years there will not be plowing and reaping. 7But God sent me ahead of you to preserve for you a remnant on earth and to save your lives by a great deliverance.*

8"So then, it was not you who sent me here, but God. He made me father to Pharaoh, lord of his entire household and ruler of all Egypt. 9Now hurry back to my father and say to him, 'This is what your son Joseph says: God has made me lord of all Egypt. Come down to me; don't delay. 10You shall live in the region of Goshen and be near me — you, your children and grandchildren, your flocks and herds, and all you have. 11I will provide for you there, because five years of famine are still to come. Otherwise you and your household and all who belong to you will become destitute.'

12"You can see for yourselves, and so can my brother Benjamin, that it is really I who am speaking to you. 13Tell my father about all the honor accorded me in Egypt and about everything you have seen. And bring my father down here quickly."

14Then he threw his arms around his brother Benjamin and wept, and Benjamin embraced him, weeping. 15And he kissed all his brothers and wept over them. Afterward his brothers talked with him.

16When the news reached Pharaoh's palace that Joseph's brothers had come, Pharaoh and all his officials were pleased. 17Pharaoh said to Joseph, "Tell your brothers, 'Do this: Load your animals and return to the land of Canaan, 18and bring your father and your families back to me. I will give you the best of the land of Egypt and you can enjoy the fat of the land.'

19"You are also directed to tell them, 'Do this: Take some carts from Egypt for your children and your wives, and get your father and come. 20Never mind about your belongings, because the best of all Egypt will be yours.' "

21So the sons of Israel did this. Joseph gave them carts, as Pharaoh had commanded, and he also gave them provisions for their journey. 22To each of them he gave new clothing, but to Benjamin he gave three hundred shekels*b* of silver and five sets of clothes. 23And this is what he sent to his father: ten donkeys loaded with the best things of Egypt, and ten female donkeys loaded with grain and bread and other provisions for his journey. 24Then he sent his brothers away, and as they were leaving he said to them, "Don't quarrel on the way!"

25So they went up out of Egypt and came to their father Jacob in the land of Canaan. 26They told him, "Joseph is still alive! In fact, he is ruler of all Egypt." Jacob was stunned; he did not believe them. 27But when they told him everything Joseph had said to them, and when he saw the carts Joseph had sent to carry him back, the spirit of their father Jacob revived. 28And Israel said, "I'm convinced! My son Joseph is still alive. I will go and see him before I die."

Jacob Goes to Egypt

46 So Israel set out with all that was his, and when he reached Beersheba, he offered sacrifices to the God of his father Isaac.

2And God spoke to Israel in a vision at night and said, "Jacob! Jacob!"

"Here I am," he replied.

3"I am God, the God of your father," he said. "Do not be afraid to go down to Egypt, for I will make you into a great nation there. 4I will go down to Egypt with you, and I will surely bring you back again. And Joseph's own hand will close your eyes."

5Then Jacob left Beersheba, and Israel's sons took their father Jacob and their children and their wives in the carts that Pharaoh had sent to transport him. 6They also took with them their livestock and the possessions they had acquired in Canaan, and Jacob and all his offspring went to Egypt. 7He took with him to Egypt his sons and grandsons and his daughters and granddaughters — all his offspring.

8These are the names of the sons of Israel (Jacob and his descendants) who went to Egypt:

Reuben the firstborn of Jacob.
9The sons of Reuben:
Hanoch, Pallu, Hezron and Carmi.
10The sons of Simeon:
Jemuel, Jamin, Ohad, Jakin, Zohar and Shaul the son of a Canaanite woman.
11The sons of Levi:
Gershon, Kohath and Merari.

*a*7 Or *save you as a great band of survivors*   *b*22 That is, about 7 1/2 pounds (about 3.5 kilograms)

¹²The sons of Judah:

Er, Onan, Shelah, Perez and Zerah (but Er and Onan had died in the land of Canaan).

The sons of Perez:

Hezron and Hamul.

¹³The sons of Issachar:

Tola, Puah,ᵃ Jashubᵇ and Shimron.

¹⁴The sons of Zebulun:

Sered, Elon and Jahleel.

¹⁵These were the sons Leah bore to Jacob in Paddan Aram,ᶜ besides his daughter Dinah. These sons and daughters of his were thirty-three in all.

¹⁶The sons of Gad:

Zephon,ᵈ Haggi, Shuni, Ezbon, Eri, Arodi and Areli.

¹⁷The sons of Asher:

Imnah, Ishvah, Ishvi and Beriah.

Their sister was Serah.

The sons of Beriah:

Heber and Malkiel.

¹⁸These were the children born to Jacob by Zilpah, whom Laban had given to his daughter Leah — sixteen in all.

¹⁹The sons of Jacob's wife Rachel:

Joseph and Benjamin. ²⁰In Egypt, Manasseh and Ephraim were born to Joseph by Asenath daughter of Potiphera, priest of On.ᵉ

²¹The sons of Benjamin:

Bela, Beker, Ashbel, Gera, Naaman, Ehi, Rosh, Muppim, Huppim and Ard.

²²These were the sons of Rachel who were born to Jacob — fourteen in all.

²³The son of Dan:

Hushim.

²⁴The sons of Naphtali:

Jahziel, Guni, Jezer and Shillem.

²⁵These were the sons born to Jacob by Bilhah, whom Laban had given to his daughter Rachel — seven in all.

²⁶All those who went to Egypt with Jacob — those who were his direct descendants, not counting his sons' wives — numbered sixty-six persons. ²⁷With the two sonsᶠ who had been born to Joseph in Egypt, the members of Jacob's family, which went to Egypt, were seventyᵍ in all.

²⁸Now Jacob sent Judah ahead of him to Joseph to get directions to Goshen. When they arrived in the region of Goshen, ²⁹Joseph had his chariot made ready and went to Goshen to meet his father Israel. As soon as Joseph appeared before him, he threw his arms around his fatherʰ and wept for a long time.

³⁰Israel said to Joseph, "Now I am ready to die, since I have seen for myself that you are still alive."

³¹Then Joseph said to his brothers and to his father's household, "I will go up and speak to Pharaoh and will say to him, 'My brothers and my father's household, who were living in the land of Canaan, have come to me. ³²The men are shepherds; they tend livestock, and they have brought along their flocks and herds and everything they own.' ³³When Pharaoh calls you in and asks, 'What is your occupation?' ³⁴you should answer, 'Your servants have tended livestock from our boyhood on, just as our fathers did.' Then you will be allowed to settle in the region of Goshen, for all shepherds are detestable to the Egyptians."

47 Joseph went and told Pharaoh, "My father and brothers, with their flocks and herds and everything they own, have come from the land of Canaan and are now in Goshen." ²He chose five of his brothers and presented them before Pharaoh.

³Pharaoh asked the brothers, "What is your occupation?"

"Your servants are shepherds," they replied to Pharaoh, "just as our fathers were." ⁴They also said to him, "We have come to live here awhile, because the famine is severe in Canaan and your servants' flocks have no pasture. So now, please let your servants settle in Goshen."

⁵Pharaoh said to Joseph, "Your father and your brothers have come to you, ⁶and the land of Egypt is before you; settle your father and your brothers in the best part of the land. Let them live in Goshen. And if you know of any among them with special ability, put them in charge of my own livestock."

⁷Then Joseph brought his father Jacob in and presented him before Pharaoh. After Ja-

---

ᵃ13 Samaritan Pentateuch and Syriac (see also 1 Chron. 7:1); Masoretic Text *Puvah*　　ᵇ13 Samaritan Pentateuch and some Septuagint manuscripts (see also Num. 26:24 and 1 Chron. 7:1); Masoretic Text *Iob*　　ᶜ15 That is, Northwest Mesopotamia　　ᵈ16 Samaritan Pentateuch and Septuagint (see also Num. 26:15); Masoretic Text *Ziphion*　　ᵉ20 That is, Heliopolis　　ᶠ27 Hebrew; Septuagint *the nine children*　　ᵍ27 Hebrew (see also Exodus 1:5 and footnote); Septuagint (see also Acts 7:14) *seventy-five*　　ʰ29 Hebrew *around him* cob blessed[a] Pharaoh, **8**Pharaoh asked him, "How old are you?"

9And Jacob said to Pharaoh, "The years of my pilgrimage are a hundred and thirty. My years have been few and difficult, and they do not equal the years of the pilgrimage of my fathers." **10**Then Jacob blessed[b] Pharaoh and went out from his presence.

11So Joseph settled his father and his brothers in Egypt and gave them property in the best part of the land, the district of Rameses, as Pharaoh directed. **12**Joseph also provided his father and his brothers and all his father's household with food, according to the number of their children.

Joseph and the Famine

13There was no food, however, in the whole region because the famine was severe; both Egypt and Canaan wasted away because of the famine. **14**Joseph collected all the money that was to be found in Egypt and Canaan in payment for the grain they were buying, and he brought it to Pharaoh's palace. **15**When the money of the people of Egypt and Canaan was gone, all Egypt came to Joseph and said, "Give us food. Why should we die before your eyes? Our money is used up."

16"Then bring your livestock," said Joseph. "I will sell you food in exchange for your livestock, since your money is gone." **17**So they brought their livestock to Joseph, and he gave them food in exchange for their horses, their sheep and goats, their cattle and donkeys. And he brought them through that year with food in exchange for all their livestock.

18When that year was over, they came to him the following year and said, "We cannot hide from our lord the fact that since our money is gone and our livestock belongs to you, there is nothing left for our lord except our bodies and our land. **19**Why should we perish before your eyes—we and our land as well? Buy us and our land in exchange for food, and we with our land will be in bondage to Pharaoh. Give us seed so that we may live and not die, and that the land may not become desolate."

20So Joseph bought all the land in Egypt for Pharaoh. The Egyptians, one and all, sold their fields, because the famine was too severe for them. The land became Pharaoh's, **21**and Joseph reduced the people to servitude,[c] from one end of Egypt to the other. **22**However, he did not buy the land of the priests, because they received a regular allotment from Pharaoh and had food enough from the allotment Pharaoh gave them. That is why they did not sell their land.

23Joseph said to the people, "Now that I have bought you and your land today for Pharaoh, here is seed for you so you can plant the ground. **24**But when the crop comes in, give a fifth of it to Pharaoh. The other four-fifths you may keep as seed for the fields and as food for yourselves and your households and your children."

25"You have saved our lives," they said. "May we find favor in the eyes of our lord; we will be in bondage to Pharaoh."

26So Joseph established it as a law concerning land in Egypt—still in force today—that a fifth of the produce belongs to Pharaoh. It was only the land of the priests that did not become Pharaoh's.

27Now the Israelites settled in Egypt in the region of Goshen. They acquired property there and were fruitful and increased greatly in number.

28Jacob lived in Egypt seventeen years, and the years of his life were a hundred and forty-seven. **29**When the time drew near for Israel to die, he called for his son Joseph and said to him, "If I have found favor in your eyes, put your hand under my thigh and promise that you will show me kindness and faithfulness. Do not bury me in Egypt, **30**but when I rest with my fathers, carry me out of Egypt and bury me where they are buried."

"I will do as you say," he said.

31"Swear to me," he said. Then Joseph swore to him, and Israel worshiped as he leaned on the top of his staff.[d]

Manasseh and Ephraim

48 Some time later Joseph was told, "Your father is ill." So he took his two sons Manasseh and Ephraim along with him. **2**When Jacob was told, "Your son Joseph has come to you," Israel rallied his strength and sat up on the bed.

3Jacob said to Joseph, "God Almighty[e] appeared to me at Luz in the land of Canaan, and there he blessed me **4**and said to me, 'I am going to make you fruitful and will increase your numbers. I will make you a

---

a7 Or *greeted*   *b10* Or *said farewell to*   *c21* Samaritan Pentateuch and Septuagint (see also Vulgate); Masoretic Text *and he moved the people into the cities*   *d31* Or *Israel bowed down at the head of his bed*
e3 Hebrew *El-Shaddai*

community of peoples, and I will give this land as an everlasting possession to your descendants after you.'

5"Now then, your two sons born to you in Egypt before I came to you here will be reckoned as mine; Ephraim and Manasseh will be mine, just as Reuben and Simeon are mine. 6Any children born to you after them will be yours; in the territory they inherit they will be reckoned under the names of their brothers. 7As I was returning from Paddan,*a* to my sorrow Rachel died in the land of Canaan while we were still on the way, a little distance from Ephrath. So I buried her there beside the road to Ephrath" (that is, Bethlehem).

8When Israel saw the sons of Joseph, he asked, "Who are these?"

9"They are the sons God has given me here," Joseph said to his father.

Then Israel said, "Bring them to me so I may bless them."

10Now Israel's eyes were failing because of old age, and he could hardly see. So Joseph brought his sons close to him, and his father kissed them and embraced them.

11Israel said to Joseph, "I never expected to see your face again, and now God has allowed me to see your children too."

12Then Joseph removed them from Israel's knees and bowed down with his face to the ground. 13And Joseph took both of them, Ephraim on his right toward Israel's left hand and Manasseh on his left toward Israel's right hand, and brought them close to him. 14But Israel reached out his right hand and put it on Ephraim's head, though he was the younger, and crossing his arms, he put his left hand on Manasseh's head, even though Manasseh was the firstborn.

15Then he blessed Joseph and said,

"May the God before whom my fathers
    Abraham and Isaac walked,
the God who has been my shepherd
    all my life to this day,
16the Angel who has delivered me from
        all harm
    —may he bless these boys.
May they be called by my name
    and the names of my fathers
        Abraham and Isaac,
and may they increase greatly
    upon the earth."

17When Joseph saw his father placing his right hand on Ephraim's head he was displeased; so he took hold of his father's hand to move it from Ephraim's head to Manasseh's head. 18Joseph said to him, "No, my father, this one is the firstborn; put your right hand on his head."

19But his father refused and said, "I know, my son, I know. He too will become a people, and he too will become great. Nevertheless, his younger brother will be greater than he, and his descendants will become a group of nations." 20He blessed them that day and said,

"In your*b* name will Israel pronounce
        this blessing:
    'May God make you like Ephraim and
        Manasseh.' "

So he put Ephraim ahead of Manasseh.

21Then Israel said to Joseph, "I am about to die, but God will be with you*c* and take you*c* back to the land of your*c* fathers. 22And to you, as one who is over your brothers, I give the ridge of land*d* I took from the Amorites with my sword and my bow."

Jacob Blesses His Sons

49 Then Jacob called for his sons and said: "Gather around so I can tell you what will happen to you in days to come.

2"Assemble and listen, sons of Jacob;
    listen to your father Israel.

3"Reuben, you are my firstborn,
    my might, the first sign of my
        strength,
    excelling in honor, excelling in power.
4Turbulent as the waters, you will no
        longer excel,
    for you went up onto your father's
        bed,
    onto my couch and defiled it.

5"Simeon and Levi are brothers—
    their swords*e* are weapons of
        violence.
6Let me not enter their council,
    let me not join their assembly,
for they have killed men in their anger
    and hamstrung oxen as they pleased.
7Cursed be their anger, so fierce,
    and their fury, so cruel!
I will scatter them in Jacob
    and disperse them in Israel.

8"Judah,*f* your brothers will praise you;

---

a7 That is, Northwest Mesopotamia   *b20* The Hebrew is singular.   *c21* The Hebrew is plural.   *d22* Or
And to you I give one portion more than to your brothers—the portion   *e5* The meaning of the Hebrew for
this word is uncertain.   *f8* Judah sounds like and may be derived from the Hebrew for *praise*.

your hand will be on the neck of your
    enemies;
your father's sons will bow down to
    you.
  9You are a lion's cub, O Judah;
    you return from the prey, my son.
Like a lion he crouches and lies down,
    like a lioness — who dares to rouse
    him?
10The scepter will not depart from Judah,
    nor the ruler's staff from between his
    feet,
until he comes to whom it belongs*a*
    and the obedience of the nations is
    his.
11He will tether his donkey to a vine,
    his colt to the choicest branch;
he will wash his garments in wine,
    his robes in the blood of grapes.
12His eyes will be darker than wine,
    his teeth whiter than milk.*b*

13"Zebulun will live by the seashore
    and become a haven for ships;
    his border will extend toward Sidon.

14"Issachar is a rawboned*c* donkey
    lying down between two saddlebags.*d*
15When he sees how good is his resting
    place
    and how pleasant is his land,
he will bend his shoulder to the burden
    and submit to forced labor.

16"Dan*e* will provide justice for his
    people
    as one of the tribes of Israel.
17Dan will be a serpent by the roadside,
    a viper along the path,
that bites the horse's heels
    so that its rider tumbles backward.

18"I look for your deliverance, O Lord.

19"Gad*f* will be attacked by a band of
    raiders,
    but he will attack them at their heels.

20"Asher's food will be rich;
    he will provide delicacies fit for a
    king.

21"Naphtali is a doe set free
    that bears beautiful fawns.*g*

22"Joseph is a fruitful vine,
    a fruitful vine near a spring,

    whose branches climb over a wall.*h*
23With bitterness archers attacked him;
    they shot at him with hostility.
24But his bow remained steady,
    his strong arms stayed*i* limber,
because of the hand of the Mighty One
    of Jacob,
because of the Shepherd, the Rock of
    Israel,
25because of your father's God, who helps
    you,
because of the Almighty,*j* who
    blesses you
with blessings of the heavens above,
    blessings of the deep that lies below,
    blessings of the breast and womb.
26Your father's blessings are greater
    than the blessings of the ancient
    mountains,
than*k* the bounty of the age-old hills.
Let all these rest on the head of Joseph,
    on the brow of the prince among*l*
    his brothers.

27"Benjamin is a ravenous wolf;
    in the morning he devours the prey,
    in the evening he divides the
    plunder."

28All these are the twelve tribes of Israel,
and this is what their father said to them
when he blessed them, giving each the
blessing appropriate to him.

The Death of Jacob

29Then he gave them these instructions: "I
am about to be gathered to my people. Bury
me with my fathers in the cave in the field
of Ephron the Hittite, **30**the cave in the field
of Machpelah, near Mamre in Canaan,
which Abraham bought as a burial place
from Ephron the Hittite, along with the field.
31There Abraham and his wife Sarah were
buried, there Isaac and his wife Rebekah
were buried, and there I buried Leah. **32**The
field and the cave in it were bought from the
Hittites.*m*"

33When Jacob had finished giving instructions to his sons, he drew his feet up into the
bed, breathed his last and was gathered to
his people.

50 Joseph threw himself upon his father and wept over him and kissed

*a*10 Or until Shiloh comes; or until he comes to whom tribute belongs   *b*12 Or will be dull from wine, / his
teeth white from milk   *c*14 Or strong   *d*14 Or campfires   *e*16 Dan here means he provides justice.
*f*19 Gad can mean attack and band of raiders.   *g*21 Or free; / he utters beautiful words   *h*22 Or Joseph is a
wild colt, / a wild colt near a spring, / a wild donkey on a terraced hill   *i*23,24 Or archers will attack . . . will
shoot . . . will remain . . . will stay   *j*25 Hebrew Shaddai   *k*26 Or of my progenitors, / as great as   *l*26 Or
the one separated from   *m*32 Or the sons of Heth

GOOD THINGS COME TO THOSE WHO WAIT

Work It Out
••••

Try this: Next time you get your allowance or a paycheck, make yourself wait seven full days before you spend even one cent of it.

Or try this: Next time you go shopping and you see a sweater or a CD or something else you want, wait a week before you make your purchase. You'll probably be surprised at how often your decisions will change if you are patient and wait a bit.

The Bible is filled with stories of people who had to wait a long time for good things to finally happen. If they could communicate with you today, Abraham (Hebrews 6:15) and Isaac (Genesis 29:15–30) would both tell you that the end result was well worth the wait.

Nail It Down
••••

Read Genesis 50:19–20 for Joseph's reaction to waiting for good things to happen to him.

Think It Through
••••

We live in a "can't-wait" society. Charge cards, easy credit, fax machines, microwave ovens, instant this and instant that all make us impatient when we have to wait. We want what we want and we want it *right now*. We're impatient when we wait for the microwave to pop popcorn in half the time it took to pop it on the stove. We're impatient when we wait in line at the grocery store while tellers whisk items across a scanner in half the time it used to take to punch the right keys. No doubt about it, waiting is not something most of us are good at.

What are you waiting for? A girlfriend or boyfriend to enter your life? Better grades? Graduation? A new outfit? The world says, "Go for it!" But God says, "No. Come to me to fulfill all your desires in *my* time. You may have to wait, but it will be worth it. I promise."

Nail It Down
••••

Read about Joseph again in Genesis 50:19–20. For further insight read Psalm 37:3–6.

Turn to pages 12, 85 and 1227 for other readings on patience.
Turn to page 62 for Monday's reading.

Topic
••••

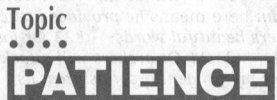
PATIENCE

him. [2]Then Joseph directed the physicians in his service to embalm his father Israel. So the physicians embalmed him, [3]taking a full forty days, for that was the time required for embalming. And the Egyptians mourned for him seventy days.

[4]When the days of mourning had passed, Joseph said to Pharaoh's court, "If I have found favor in your eyes, speak to Pharaoh for me. Tell him, [5]'My father made me swear an oath and said, "I am about to die; bury me in the tomb I dug for myself in the land of Canaan." Now let me go up and bury my father; then I will return.'"

[6]Pharaoh said, "Go up and bury your father, as he made you swear to do."

[7]So Joseph went up to bury his father. All Pharaoh's officials accompanied him — the dignitaries of his court and all the dignitaries of Egypt — [8]besides all the members of Joseph's household and his brothers and those belonging to his father's household. Only their children and their flocks and herds were left in Goshen. [9]Chariots and horsemen[a] also went up with him. It was a very large company.

[10]When they reached the threshing floor of Atad, near the Jordan, they lamented loudly and bitterly; and there Joseph observed a seven-day period of mourning for his father. [11]When the Canaanites who lived there saw the mourning at the threshing floor of Atad, they said, "The Egyptians are holding a solemn ceremony of mourning." That is why that place near the Jordan is called Abel Mizraim.[b]

[12]So Jacob's sons did as he had commanded them: [13]They carried him to the land of Canaan and buried him in the cave in the field of Machpelah, near Mamre, which Abraham had bought as a burial place from Ephron the Hittite, along with the field. [14]After burying his father, Joseph returned to Egypt, together with his brothers and all the others who had gone with him to bury his father.

Joseph Reassures His Brothers

[15]When Joseph's brothers saw that their father was dead, they said, "What if Joseph holds a grudge against us and pays us back for all the wrongs we did to him?" [16]So they sent word to Joseph, saying, "Your father left these instructions before he died: [17]'This is what you are to say to Joseph: I ask you to forgive your brothers the sins and the wrongs they committed in treating you so badly.' Now please forgive the sins of the servants of the God of your father." When their message came to him, Joseph wept.

[18]His brothers then came and threw themselves down before him. "We are your slaves," they said.

[19]But Joseph said to them, "Don't be afraid. Am I in the place of God? [20]You intended to harm me, but God intended it for good to accomplish what is now being done, the saving of many lives. [21]So then, don't be afraid. I will provide for you and your children." And he reassured them and spoke kindly to them.

The Death of Joseph

[22]Joseph stayed in Egypt, along with all his father's family. He lived a hundred and ten years [23]and saw the third generation of Ephraim's children. Also the children of Makir son of Manasseh were placed at birth on Joseph's knees.[c]

[24]Then Joseph said to his brothers, "I am about to die. But God will surely come to your aid and take you up out of this land to the land he promised on oath to Abraham, Isaac and Jacob." [25]And Joseph made the sons of Israel swear an oath and said, "God will surely come to your aid, and then you must carry my bones up from this place."

[26]So Joseph died at the age of a hundred and ten. And after they embalmed him, he was placed in a coffin in Egypt.

---

[a]9 Or charioteers   [b]11 Abel Mizraim means mourning of the Egyptians.   [c]23 That is, were counted as his

EXODUS

NEARLY four hundred years after Joseph dies, God's people are slaves in Egypt. Then Moses enters the scene. The result? God performs miracles to set them free. They leave Egypt, cross the Red Sea and set up camp at Mount Sinai. There they receive God's law and build the tabernacle. God thunders: "I love you. Obey me and worship me, and I will bless you." Keep in mind as you read that sin still enslaves, God still sets free, and he still wants his people to obey and worship him.

Outline of Contents

The Israelites Oppressed

1 These are the names of the sons of Israel who went to Egypt with Jacob, each with his family: **2**Reuben, Simeon, Levi and Judah; **3**Issachar, Zebulun and Benjamin; **4**Dan and Naphtali; Gad and Asher. **5**The descendants of Jacob numbered seventy[a] in all; Joseph was already in Egypt.

6Now Joseph and all his brothers and all that generation died, **7**but the Israelites were fruitful and multiplied greatly and became exceedingly numerous, so that the land was filled with them.

8Then a new king, who did not know about Joseph, came to power in Egypt.

9"Look," he said to his people, "the Israelites have become much too numerous for us. **10**Come, we must deal shrewdly with them or they will become even more numerous and, if war breaks out, will join our enemies, fight against us and leave the country."

11So they put slave masters over them to oppress them with forced labor, and they built Pithom and Rameses as store cities for Pharaoh. **12**But the more they were oppressed, the more they multiplied and spread; so the Egyptians came to dread the Israelites **13**and worked them ruthlessly. **14**They made their lives bitter with hard labor in brick and mortar and with all kinds of

---

[a]5 Masoretic Text (see also Gen. 46:27); Dead Sea Scrolls and Septuagint (see also Acts 7:14 and note at Gen. 46:27) *seventy-five*

work in the fields; in all their hard labor the Egyptians used them ruthlessly.

¹⁵The king of Egypt said to the Hebrew midwives, whose names were Shiphrah and Puah, ¹⁶"When you help the Hebrew women in childbirth and observe them on the delivery stool, if it is a boy, kill him; but if it is a girl, let her live." ¹⁷The midwives, however, feared God and did not do what the king of Egypt had told them to do; they let the boys live. ¹⁸Then the king of Egypt summoned the midwives and asked them, "Why have you done this? Why have you let the boys live?"

¹⁹The midwives answered Pharaoh, "Hebrew women are not like Egyptian women; they are vigorous and give birth before the midwives arrive."

²⁰So God was kind to the midwives and the people increased and became even more numerous. ²¹And because the midwives feared God, he gave them families of their own.

²²Then Pharaoh gave this order to all his people: "Every boy that is born*a* you must throw into the Nile, but let every girl live."

The Birth of Moses

2 Now a man of the house of Levi married a Levite woman, ²and she became pregnant and gave birth to a son. When she saw that he was a fine child, she hid him for three months. ³But when she could hide him no longer, she got a papyrus basket for him and coated it with tar and pitch. Then she placed the child in it and put it among the reeds along the bank of the Nile. ⁴His sister stood at a distance to see what would happen to him.

⁵Then Pharaoh's daughter went down to the Nile to bathe, and her attendants were walking along the river bank. She saw the basket among the reeds and sent her slave girl to get it. ⁶She opened it and saw the baby. He was crying, and she felt sorry for him. "This is one of the Hebrew babies," she said.

⁷Then his sister asked Pharaoh's daughter, "Shall I go and get one of the Hebrew women to nurse the baby for you?"

⁸"Yes, go," she answered. And the girl went and got the baby's mother. ⁹Pharaoh's daughter said to her, "Take this baby and nurse him for me, and I will pay you." So the woman took the baby and nursed him. ¹⁰When the child grew older, she took him to Pharaoh's daughter and he became her son. She named him Moses,*b* saying, "I drew him out of the water."

Moses Flees to Midian

¹¹One day, after Moses had grown up, he went out to where his own people were and watched them at their hard labor. He saw an Egyptian beating a Hebrew, one of his own people. ¹²Glancing this way and that and seeing no one, he killed the Egyptian and hid him in the sand. ¹³The next day he went out and saw two Hebrews fighting. He asked the one in the wrong, "Why are you hitting your fellow Hebrew?"

¹⁴The man said, "Who made you ruler and judge over us? Are you thinking of killing me as you killed the Egyptian?" Then Moses was afraid and thought, "What I did must have become known."

¹⁵When Pharaoh heard of this, he tried to kill Moses, but Moses fled from Pharaoh and went to live in Midian, where he sat down by a well. ¹⁶Now a priest of Midian had seven daughters, and they came to draw water and fill the troughs to water their father's flock. ¹⁷Some shepherds came along and drove them away, but Moses got up and came to their rescue and watered their flock.

¹⁸When the girls returned to Reuel their father, he asked them, "Why have you returned so early today?"

¹⁹They answered, "An Egyptian rescued us from the shepherds. He even drew water for us and watered the flock."

²⁰"And where is he?" he asked his daughters. "Why did you leave him? Invite him to have something to eat."

²¹Moses agreed to stay with the man, who gave his daughter Zipporah to Moses in marriage. ²²Zipporah gave birth to a son, and Moses named him Gershom,*c* saying, "I have become an alien in a foreign land."

²³During that long period, the king of Egypt died. The Israelites groaned in their slavery and cried out, and their cry for help because of their slavery went up to God. ²⁴God heard their groaning and he remembered his covenant with Abraham, with Isaac and with Jacob. ²⁵So God looked on the Israelites and was concerned about them.

Moses and the Burning Bush

3 Now Moses was tending the flock of Jethro his father-in-law, the priest of

---

a22 Masoretic Text; Samaritan Pentateuch, Septuagint and Targums born to the Hebrews　　*b10 Moses sounds like the Hebrew for draw out.*　　*c22 Gershom sounds like the Hebrew for an alien there.*

WHEN PARENTS HURT YOU

• •

Parent-child relationships can produce a lot of pain.

Larry's stepdad is verbally abusive. The daily name-calling and cruel remarks are destroying Larry's self-image.

Audrey's mom is physically abusive. She slaps five-foot Audrey all over the house. Last spring Audrey wore sunglasses for two weeks to hide a black eye.

Shelly's dad is sexually abusive. He's been molesting Shelly for more than two years now.

Darren's parents are emotionally abusive. They constantly buy Darren stuff, but they never get involved in his life. Darren feels totally ignored.

Look It Up
• • • •

Question: What can you do when an earthly parent hurts you?
Answer: Remember the love of your heavenly Father.

• He sees. "The eyes of the LORD are everywhere, keeping watch on the wicked and the good" (Proverbs 15:3).

• He cares (1 Peter 5:7).

• He comforts (Psalm 86:17).

• He heals. "He heals the brokenhearted and binds up their wounds" (Psalm 147:3).

• He promises justice. "The LORD works righteousness and justice for all the oppressed" (Psalm 103:6).

Think It Through
• • • •

Parents can also hurt their children by deserting them. Few things are as painful as being abandoned or watching your parents separate and divorce or having a parent commit suicide. It's even common to feel rejected when a parent dies.

Can you relate to any of those situations? Do you have friends who are experiencing similar pain?

Work It Out
• • • •

If you are hurting because of parental abuse (no matter what kind), seek some help—today. Call your youth leader, or make an appointment with your favorite teacher or a Christian counselor. You don't have to continue to live with all that hurt. You can find hope and healing . . . beginning with a simple phone call.

If you have friends who are the victims of parental abuse, be supportive and loving. Offer to go with them to get help. (And pray as you've never prayed before!)

Nail It Down
• • • •

Reflect on God's care for his children as demonstrated in Exodus 2:23—3:4.

Turn to pages 122, 680 and 1384 for other readings on parents.
Turn to page 65 for Tuesday's reading.

Topic
• • • •

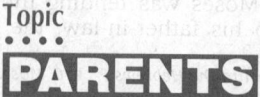

Midian, and he led the flock to the far side of the desert and came to Horeb, the mountain of God. **2**There the angel of the Lord appeared to him in flames of fire from within a bush. Moses saw that though the bush was on fire it did not burn up. **3**So Moses thought, "I will go over and see this strange sight—why the bush does not burn up."

4When the Lord saw that he had gone over to look, God called to him from within the bush, "Moses! Moses!"

And Moses said, "Here I am."

5"Do not come any closer," God said. "Take off your sandals, for the place where you are standing is holy ground." **6**Then he said, "I am the God of your father, the God of Abraham, the God of Isaac and the God of Jacob." At this, Moses hid his face, because he was afraid to look at God.

7The Lord said, "I have indeed seen the misery of my people in Egypt. I have heard them crying out because of their slave drivers, and I am concerned about their suffering. **8**So I have come down to rescue them from the hand of the Egyptians and to bring them up out of that land into a good and spacious land, a land flowing with milk and honey—the home of the Canaanites, Hittites, Amorites, Perizzites, Hivites and Jebusites. **9**And now the cry of the Israelites has reached me, and I have seen the way the Egyptians are oppressing them. **10**So now, go. I am sending you to Pharaoh to bring my people the Israelites out of Egypt."

11But Moses said to God, "Who am I, that I should go to Pharaoh and bring the Israelites out of Egypt?"

12And God said, "I will be with you. And this will be the sign to you that it is I who have sent you: When you have brought the people out of Egypt, you*a* will worship God on this mountain."

13Moses said to God, "Suppose I go to the Israelites and say to them, 'The God of your fathers has sent me to you,' and they ask me, 'What is his name?' Then what shall I tell them?"

14God said to Moses, "I AM WHO I AM.*b* This is what you are to say to the Israelites: 'I AM has sent me to you.'"

15God also said to Moses, "Say to the Israelites, 'The Lord,*c* the God of your fathers—the God of Abraham, the God of Isaac and the God of Jacob—has sent me to you.' This is my name forever, the name by which I am

to be remembered from generation to generation.

16"Go, assemble the elders of Israel and say to them, 'The Lord, the God of your fathers—the God of Abraham, Isaac and Jacob—appeared to me and said: I have watched over you and have seen what has been done to you in Egypt. **17**And I have promised to bring you up out of your misery in Egypt into the land of the Canaanites, Hittites, Amorites, Perizzites, Hivites and Jebusites—a land flowing with milk and honey.'

18"The elders of Israel will listen to you. Then you and the elders are to go to the king of Egypt and say to him, 'The Lord, the God of the Hebrews, has met with us. Let us take a three-day journey into the desert to offer sacrifices to the Lord our God.' **19**But I know that the king of Egypt will not let you go unless a mighty hand compels him. **20**So I will stretch out my hand and strike the Egyptians with all the wonders that I will perform among them. After that, he will let you go.

21"And I will make the Egyptians favorably disposed toward this people, so that when you leave you will not go empty-handed. **22**Every woman is to ask her neighbor and any woman living in her house for articles of silver and gold and for clothing, which you will put on your sons and daughters. And so you will plunder the Egyptians."

Signs for Moses

4 Moses answered, "What if they do not believe me or listen to me and say, 'The Lord did not appear to you'?"

2Then the Lord said to him, "What is that in your hand?"

"A staff," he replied.

3The Lord said, "Throw it on the ground." Moses threw it on the ground and it became a snake, and he ran from it. **4**Then the Lord said to him, "Reach out your hand and take it by the tail." So Moses reached out and took hold of the snake and it turned back into a staff in his hand. **5**"This," said the Lord, "is so that they may believe that the Lord, the God of their fathers—the God of Abraham, the God of Isaac and the God of Jacob—has appeared to you."

6Then the Lord said, "Put your hand inside your cloak." So Moses put his hand into his cloak, and when he took it out, it was leprous,*d* like snow.

7"Now put it back into your cloak," he

---

a 12 The Hebrew is plural.   *b 14* Or *I will be what I will be*   *c 15* The Hebrew for Lord sounds like and may be derived from the Hebrew for *I am* in verse 14.   *d 6* The Hebrew word was used for various diseases affecting the skin—not necessarily leprosy.

said. So Moses put his hand back into his cloak, and when he took it out, it was restored, like the rest of his flesh.

8Then the LORD said, "If they do not believe you or pay attention to the first miraculous sign, they may believe the second. **9**But if they do not believe these two signs or listen to you, take some water from the Nile and pour it on the dry ground. The water you take from the river will become blood on the ground."

10Moses said to the LORD, "O Lord, I have never been eloquent, neither in the past nor since you have spoken to your servant. I am slow of speech and tongue."

11The LORD said to him, "Who gave man his mouth? Who makes him deaf or mute? Who gives him sight or makes him blind? Is it not I, the LORD? **12**Now go; I will help you speak and will teach you what to say."

13But Moses said, "O Lord, please send someone else to do it."

14Then the LORD's anger burned against Moses and he said, "What about your brother, Aaron the Levite? I know he can speak well. He is already on his way to meet you, and his heart will be glad when he sees you. **15**You shall speak to him and put words in his mouth; I will help both of you speak and will teach you what to do. **16**He will speak to the people for you, and it will be as if he were your mouth and as if you were God to him. **17**But take this staff in your hand so you can perform miraculous signs with it."

Moses Returns to Egypt

18Then Moses went back to Jethro his father-in-law and said to him, "Let me go back to my own people in Egypt to see if any of them are still alive."

Jethro said, "Go, and I wish you well."

19Now the LORD had said to Moses in Midian, "Go back to Egypt, for all the men who wanted to kill you are dead." **20**So Moses took his wife and sons, put them on a donkey and started back to Egypt. And he took the staff of God in his hand.

21The LORD said to Moses, "When you return to Egypt, see that you perform before Pharaoh all the wonders I have given you the power to do. But I will harden his heart so that he will not let the people go. **22**Then say to Pharaoh, 'This is what the LORD says: Israel is my firstborn son, **23**and I told you, "Let my son go, so he may worship me." But you refused to let him go; so I will kill your firstborn son.' "

24At a lodging place on the way, the LORD met ˌMosesˌ[a] and was about to kill him. **25**But Zipporah took a flint knife, cut off her son's foreskin and touched ˌMoses'ˌ feet with it.[b] "Surely you are a bridegroom of blood to me," she said. **26**So the LORD let him alone. (At that time she said "bridegroom of blood," referring to circumcision.)

27The LORD said to Aaron, "Go into the desert to meet Moses." So he met Moses at the mountain of God and kissed him. **28**Then Moses told Aaron everything the LORD had sent him to say, and also about all the miraculous signs he had commanded him to perform.

29Moses and Aaron brought together all the elders of the Israelites, **30**and Aaron told them everything the LORD had said to Moses. He also performed the signs before the people, **31**and they believed. And when they heard that the LORD was concerned about them and had seen their misery, they bowed down and worshiped.

Bricks Without Straw

5 Afterward Moses and Aaron went to Pharaoh and said, "This is what the LORD, the God of Israel, says: 'Let my people go, so that they may hold a festival to me in the desert.' "

2Pharaoh said, "Who is the LORD, that I should obey him and let Israel go? I do not know the LORD and I will not let Israel go."

3Then they said, "The God of the Hebrews has met with us. Now let us take a three-day journey into the desert to offer sacrifices to the LORD our God, or he may strike us with plagues or with the sword."

4But the king of Egypt said, "Moses and Aaron, why are you taking the people away from their labor? Get back to your work!" **5**Then Pharaoh said, "Look, the people of the land are now numerous, and you are stopping them from working."

6That same day Pharaoh gave this order to the slave drivers and foremen in charge of the people: **7**"You are no longer to supply the people with straw for making bricks; let them go and gather their own straw. **8**But require them to make the same number of bricks as before; don't reduce the quota. They are lazy; that is why they are crying out, 'Let us go and sacrifice to our God.' **9**Make the work harder for the men so that they keep working and pay no attention to lies."

10Then the slave drivers and the foremen

---

*a*24 Or ˌMoses' sonˌ; Hebrew *him*   *b*25 Or *and drew near ˌMoses'ˌ feet*

THE PERSISTENT PROBLEM OF PRIDE

Anita and Ellen are whispering in the corner.

"So, anyway, I—oh wow! Look who just walked in!"

The girls watch handsome Sherman pull up a chair on the other side of the room.

Suddenly, Anita turns into a pit bull: "I can't stand him. He thinks he's God. Like everyone is supposed to bow to him or something."

Meanwhile Ellen wonders which is worse—Sherman's cocky attitude or Anita's wounded pride. (Sherman dumped her for Molly last weekend!)

Look It Up
• • • •

Where did pride originate? Many Bible scholars point to the rebellion of Lucifer (that is, Satan) against God before the world was created.

> You said in your heart,
> "I will ascend to heaven;
> I will raise my throne
>   above the stars of God;
> I will sit enthroned on the mount of assembly,
>   on the utmost heights of the sacred mountain.
> I will ascend above the tops of the clouds;
>   I will make myself like the Most High."
> But you are brought down to the grave,
>   to the depths of the pit (Isaiah 14:13–15).

Notice Lucifer's five "I will" declarations. Pride is that self-centeredness that is at the heart of sin.

Think It Through
• • • •

Reflect back over the last few days. What are some of the things that you have done or said that reflect a prideful attitude? Have others acted proudly toward you? In what ways?

Work It Out
• • • •

Take this pride quiz. Answer each question with a yes or no.
1. I talk a lot about myself.
2. I find it hard to laugh at myself.
3. I get jealous of others easily.
4. I am very competitive.
5. I sometimes enjoy watching others fail.
6. I hate to admit it when I'm wrong.
7. I think I am better than most people.
8. I brag a lot.
9. I like to look good in front of others.
10. I like to be the center of attention.

Even just one "yes" answer means your attitude of pride could use some work!

Nail It Down
• • •

See Pharaoh's prideful remark in Exodus 5:2.

Turn to pages 371, 462 and 1113 for other readings on pride.
Turn to page 78 for Wednesday's reading.

Topic
• • • •

went out and said to the people, "This is what Pharaoh says: 'I will not give you any more straw. **11**Go and get your own straw wherever you can find it, but your work will not be reduced at all.' " **12**So the people scattered all over Egypt to gather stubble to use for straw. **13**The slave drivers kept pressing them, saying, "Complete the work required of you for each day, just as when you had straw." **14**The Israelite foremen appointed by Pharaoh's slave drivers were beaten and were asked, "Why didn't you meet your quota of bricks yesterday or today, as before?"

15Then the Israelite foremen went and appealed to Pharaoh: "Why have you treated your servants this way? **16**Your servants are given no straw, yet we are told, 'Make bricks!' Your servants are being beaten, but the fault is with your own people."

17Pharaoh said, "Lazy, that's what you are — lazy! That is why you keep saying, 'Let us go and sacrifice to the Lord.' **18**Now get to work. You will not be given any straw, yet you must produce your full quota of bricks."

19The Israelite foremen realized they were in trouble when they were told, "You are not to reduce the number of bricks required of you for each day." **20**When they left Pharaoh, they found Moses and Aaron waiting to meet them, **21**and they said, "May the Lord look upon you and judge you! You have made us a stench to Pharaoh and his officials and have put a sword in their hand to kill us."

God Promises Deliverance

22Moses returned to the Lord and said, "O Lord, why have you brought trouble upon this people? Is this why you sent me? **23**Ever since I went to Pharaoh to speak in your name, he has brought trouble upon this people, and you have not rescued your people at all."

6 Then the Lord said to Moses, "Now you will see what I will do to Pharaoh: Because of my mighty hand he will let them go; because of my mighty hand he will drive them out of his country."

2God also said to Moses, "I am the Lord. **3**I appeared to Abraham, to Isaac and to Jacob as God Almighty,*a* but by my name the Lord*b* I did not make myself known to them.*c* **4**I also established my covenant with them to give them the land of Canaan, where they lived as aliens. **5**Moreover, I have heard the groaning of the Israelites, whom the Egyptians are enslaving, and I have remembered my covenant.

6"Therefore, say to the Israelites: 'I am the Lord, and I will bring you out from under the yoke of the Egyptians. I will free you from being slaves to them, and I will redeem you with an outstretched arm and with mighty acts of judgment. **7**I will take you as my own people, and I will be your God. Then you will know that I am the Lord your God, who brought you out from under the yoke of the Egyptians. **8**And I will bring you to the land I swore with uplifted hand to give to Abraham, to Isaac and to Jacob. I will give it to you as a possession. I am the Lord.' "

9Moses reported this to the Israelites, but they did not listen to him because of their discouragement and cruel bondage.

10Then the Lord said to Moses, **11**"Go, tell Pharaoh king of Egypt to let the Israelites go out of his country."

12But Moses said to the Lord, "If the Israelites will not listen to me, why would Pharaoh listen to me, since I speak with faltering lips*d*?"

Family Record of Moses and Aaron

13Now the Lord spoke to Moses and Aaron about the Israelites and Pharaoh king of Egypt, and he commanded them to bring the Israelites out of Egypt.

14These were the heads of their families*e*:

The sons of Reuben the firstborn son of Israel were Hanoch and Pallu, Hezron and Carmi. These were the clans of Reuben.

15The sons of Simeon were Jemuel, Jamin, Ohad, Jakin, Zohar and Shaul the son of a Canaanite woman. These were the clans of Simeon.

16These were the names of the sons of Levi according to their records: Gershon, Kohath and Merari. Levi lived 137 years.

17The sons of Gershon, by clans, were Libni and Shimei.

18The sons of Kohath were Amram, Izhar, Hebron and Uzziel. Kohath lived 133 years.

19The sons of Merari were Mahli and Mushi.

---

a3 Hebrew *El-Shaddai*   *b3* See note at Exodus 3:15.   *c3* Or *Almighty, and by my name the Lord did I not let myself be known to them?*   *d12* Hebrew *I am uncircumcised of lips*; also in verse 30   *e14* The Hebrew for *families* here and in verse 25 refers to units larger than clans.

These were the clans of Levi according to their records.

20Amram married his father's sister Jochebed, who bore him Aaron and Moses. Amram lived 137 years. **21**The sons of Izhar were Korah, Nepheg and Zicri. **22**The sons of Uzziel were Mishael, Elzaphan and Sithri. **23**Aaron married Elisheba, daughter of Amminadab and sister of Nahshon, and she bore him Nadab and Abihu, Eleazar and Ithamar. **24**The sons of Korah were Assir, Elkanah and Abiasaph. These were the Korahite clans.

25Eleazar son of Aaron married one of the daughters of Putiel, and she bore him Phinehas.

These were the heads of the Levite families, clan by clan.

26It was this same Aaron and Moses to whom the LORD said, "Bring the Israelites out of Egypt by their divisions." **27**They were the ones who spoke to Pharaoh king of Egypt about bringing the Israelites out of Egypt. It was the same Moses and Aaron.

Aaron to Speak for Moses

28Now when the LORD spoke to Moses in Egypt, **29**he said to him, "I am the LORD. Tell Pharaoh king of Egypt everything I tell you."

30But Moses said to the LORD, "Since I speak with faltering lips, why would Pharaoh listen to me?"

7 Then the LORD said to Moses, "See, I have made you like God to Pharaoh, and your brother Aaron will be your prophet. **2**You are to say everything I command you, and your brother Aaron is to tell Pharaoh to let the Israelites go out of his country. **3**But I will harden Pharaoh's heart, and though I multiply my miraculous signs and wonders in Egypt, **4**he will not listen to you. Then I will lay my hand on Egypt and with mighty acts of judgment I will bring out my divisions, my people the Israelites. **5**And the Egyptians will know that I am the LORD when I stretch out my hand against Egypt and bring the Israelites out of it."

6Moses and Aaron did just as the LORD commanded them. **7**Moses was eighty years old and Aaron eighty-three when they spoke to Pharaoh.

Aaron's Staff Becomes a Snake

8The LORD said to Moses and Aaron, **9**"When Pharaoh says to you, 'Perform a miracle,' then say to Aaron, 'Take your staff and throw it down before Pharaoh,' and it will become a snake."

10So Moses and Aaron went to Pharaoh and did just as the LORD commanded. Aaron threw his staff down in front of Pharaoh and his officials, and it became a snake. **11**Pharaoh then summoned wise men and sorcerers, and the Egyptian magicians also did the same things by their secret arts: **12**Each one threw down his staff and it became a snake. But Aaron's staff swallowed up their staffs. **13**Yet Pharaoh's heart became hard and he would not listen to them, just as the LORD had said.

The Plague of Blood

14Then the LORD said to Moses, "Pharaoh's heart is unyielding; he refuses to let the people go. **15**Go to Pharaoh in the morning as he goes out to the water. Wait on the bank of the Nile to meet him, and take in your hand the staff that was changed into a snake. **16**Then say to him, 'The LORD, the God of the Hebrews, has sent me to say to you: Let my people go, so that they may worship me in the desert. But until now you have not listened. **17**This is what the LORD says: By this you will know that I am the LORD: With the staff that is in my hand I will strike the water of the Nile, and it will be changed into blood. **18**The fish in the Nile will die, and the river will stink; the Egyptians will not be able to drink its water.' "

19The LORD said to Moses, "Tell Aaron, 'Take your staff and stretch out your hand over the waters of Egypt — over the streams and canals, over the ponds and all the reservoirs' — and they will turn to blood. Blood will be everywhere in Egypt, even in the wooden buckets and stone jars."

20Moses and Aaron did just as the LORD had commanded. He raised his staff in the presence of Pharaoh and his officials and struck the water of the Nile, and all the water was changed into blood. **21**The fish in the Nile died, and the river smelled so bad that the Egyptians could not drink its water. Blood was everywhere in Egypt.

22But the Egyptian magicians did the same things by their secret arts, and Pharaoh's heart became hard; he would not listen to Moses and Aaron, just as the LORD had said. **23**Instead, he turned and went into his palace, and did not take even this to heart. **24**And all the Egyptians dug along the Nile to get drinking water, because they could not drink the water of the river.

The Plague of Frogs

25Seven days passed after the LORD struck the Nile. **8** **1**Then the LORD said to Moses, "Go to Pharaoh and say to him, 'This is what the LORD says: Let my people go, so that they may worship me. **2**If you refuse to let them go, I will plague your whole country with frogs. **3**The Nile will teem with frogs. They will come up into your palace and your bedroom and onto your bed, into the houses of your officials and on your people, and into your ovens and kneading troughs. **4**The frogs will go up on you and your people and all your officials.' "

5Then the LORD said to Moses, "Tell Aaron, 'Stretch out your hand with your staff over the streams and canals and ponds, and make frogs come up on the land of Egypt.' "

6So Aaron stretched out his hand over the waters of Egypt, and the frogs came up and covered the land. **7**But the magicians did the same things by their secret arts; they also made frogs come up on the land of Egypt.

8Pharaoh summoned Moses and Aaron and said, "Pray to the LORD to take the frogs away from me and my people, and I will let your people go to offer sacrifices to the LORD."

9Moses said to Pharaoh, "I leave to you the honor of setting the time for me to pray for you and your officials and your people that you and your houses may be rid of the frogs, except for those that remain in the Nile."

10"Tomorrow," Pharaoh said.

Moses replied, "It will be as you say, so that you may know there is no one like the LORD our God. **11**The frogs will leave you and your houses, your officials and your people; they will remain only in the Nile."

12After Moses and Aaron left Pharaoh, Moses cried out to the LORD about the frogs he had brought on Pharaoh. **13**And the LORD did what Moses asked. The frogs died in the houses, in the courtyards and in the fields. **14**They were piled into heaps, and the land reeked of them. **15**But when Pharaoh saw that there was relief, he hardened his heart and would not listen to Moses and Aaron, just as the LORD had said.

The Plague of Gnats

16Then the LORD said to Moses, "Tell Aaron, 'Stretch out your staff and strike the dust of the ground,' and throughout the land of Egypt the dust will become gnats." **17**They did this, and when Aaron stretched out his hand with the staff and struck the dust of the ground, gnats came upon men and animals. All the dust throughout the land of Egypt became gnats. **18**But when the magicians tried to produce gnats by their secret arts, they could not. And the gnats were on men and animals.

19The magicians said to Pharaoh, "This is the finger of God." But Pharaoh's heart was hard and he would not listen, just as the LORD had said.

The Plague of Flies

20Then the LORD said to Moses, "Get up early in the morning and confront Pharaoh as he goes to the water and say to him, 'This is what the LORD says: Let my people go, so that they may worship me. **21**If you do not let my people go, I will send swarms of flies on you and your officials, on your people and into your houses. The houses of the Egyptians will be full of flies, and even the ground where they are.

22" 'But on that day I will deal differently with the land of Goshen, where my people live; no swarms of flies will be there, so that you will know that I, the LORD, am in this land. **23**I will make a distinction*a* between my people and your people. This miraculous sign will occur tomorrow.' "

24And the LORD did this. Dense swarms of flies poured into Pharaoh's palace and into the houses of his officials, and throughout Egypt the land was ruined by the flies.

25Then Pharaoh summoned Moses and Aaron and said, "Go, sacrifice to your God here in the land."

26But Moses said, "That would not be right. The sacrifices we offer the LORD our God would be detestable to the Egyptians. And if we offer sacrifices that are detestable in their eyes, will they not stone us? **27**We must take a three-day journey into the desert to offer sacrifices to the LORD our God, as he commands us."

28Pharaoh said, "I will let you go to offer sacrifices to the LORD your God in the desert, but you must not go very far. Now pray for me."

29Moses answered, "As soon as I leave you, I will pray to the LORD, and tomorrow the flies will leave Pharaoh and his officials and his people. Only be sure that Pharaoh does not act deceitfully again by not letting the people go to offer sacrifices to the LORD."

30Then Moses left Pharaoh and prayed to

a23 Septuagint and Vulgate; Hebrew *will put a deliverance* the LORD, **31**and the LORD did what Moses asked: The flies left Pharaoh and his officials and his people; not a fly remained. **32**But this time also Pharaoh hardened his heart and would not let the people go.

The Plague on Livestock

9 Then the LORD said to Moses, "Go to Pharaoh and say to him, 'This is what the LORD, the God of the Hebrews, says: "Let my people go, so that they may worship me." **2**If you refuse to let them go and continue to hold them back, **3**the hand of the LORD will bring a terrible plague on your livestock in the field — on your horses and donkeys and camels and on your cattle and sheep and goats. **4**But the LORD will make a distinction between the livestock of Israel and that of Egypt, so that no animal belonging to the Israelites will die.' "

5The LORD set a time and said, "Tomorrow the LORD will do this in the land." **6**And the next day the LORD did it: All the livestock of the Egyptians died, but not one animal belonging to the Israelites died. **7**Pharaoh sent men to investigate and found that not even one of the animals of the Israelites had died. Yet his heart was unyielding and he would not let the people go.

The Plague of Boils

8Then the LORD said to Moses and Aaron, "Take handfuls of soot from a furnace and have Moses toss it into the air in the presence of Pharaoh. **9**It will become fine dust over the whole land of Egypt, and festering boils will break out on men and animals throughout the land."

10So they took soot from a furnace and stood before Pharaoh. Moses tossed it into the air, and festering boils broke out on men and animals. **11**The magicians could not stand before Moses because of the boils that were on them and on all the Egyptians. **12**But the LORD hardened Pharaoh's heart and he would not listen to Moses and Aaron, just as the LORD had said to Moses.

The Plague of Hail

13Then the LORD said to Moses, "Get up early in the morning, confront Pharaoh and say to him, 'This is what the LORD, the God of the Hebrews, says: Let my people go, so that they may worship me, **14**or this time I will send the full force of my plagues against you and against your officials and your people, so you may know that there is no one

like me in all the earth. **15**For by now I could have stretched out my hand and struck you and your people with a plague that would have wiped you off the earth. **16**But I have raised you up*a* for this very purpose, that I might show you my power and that my name might be proclaimed in all the earth. **17**You still set yourself against my people and will not let them go. **18**Therefore, at this time tomorrow I will send the worst hailstorm that has ever fallen on Egypt, from the day it was founded till now. **19**Give an order now to bring your livestock and everything you have in the field to a place of shelter, because the hail will fall on every man and animal that has not been brought in and is still out in the field, and they will die.' "

20Those officials of Pharaoh who feared the word of the LORD hurried to bring their slaves and their livestock inside. **21**But those who ignored the word of the LORD left their slaves and livestock in the field.

22Then the LORD said to Moses, "Stretch out your hand toward the sky so that hail will fall all over Egypt — on men and animals and on everything growing in the fields of Egypt." **23**When Moses stretched out his staff toward the sky, the LORD sent thunder and hail, and lightning flashed down to the ground. So the LORD rained hail on the land of Egypt; **24**hail fell and lightning flashed back and forth. It was the worst storm in all the land of Egypt since it had become a nation. **25**Throughout Egypt hail struck everything in the fields — both men and animals; it beat down everything growing in the fields and stripped every tree. **26**The only place it did not hail was the land of Goshen, where the Israelites were.

27Then Pharaoh summoned Moses and Aaron. "This time I have sinned," he said to them. "The LORD is in the right, and I and my people are in the wrong. **28**Pray to the LORD, for we have had enough thunder and hail. I will let you go; you don't have to stay any longer."

29Moses replied, "When I have gone out of the city, I will spread out my hands in prayer to the LORD. The thunder will stop and there will be no more hail, so you may know that the earth is the LORD's. **30**But I know that you and your officials still do not fear the LORD God."

31(The flax and barley were destroyed, since the barley had headed and the flax was in bloom. **32**The wheat and spelt, how-

---

*a*16 Or *have spared you*

ever, were not destroyed, because they ripen later.) ³³Then Moses left Pharaoh and went out of the city. He spread out his hands toward the LORD; the thunder and hail stopped, and the rain no longer poured down on the land. ³⁴When Pharaoh saw that the rain and hail and thunder had stopped, he sinned again: He and his officials hardened their hearts. ³⁵So Pharaoh's heart was hard and he would not let the Israelites go, just as the LORD had said through Moses.

The Plague of Locusts

10 Then the LORD said to Moses, "Go to Pharaoh, for I have hardened his heart and the hearts of his officials so that I may perform these miraculous signs of mine among them ²that you may tell your children and grandchildren how I dealt harshly with the Egyptians and how I performed my signs among them, and that you may know that I am the LORD."

³So Moses and Aaron went to Pharaoh and said to him, "This is what the LORD, the God of the Hebrews, says: 'How long will you refuse to humble yourself before me? Let my people go, so that they may worship me. ⁴If you refuse to let them go, I will bring locusts into your country tomorrow. ⁵They will cover the face of the ground so that it cannot be seen. They will devour what little you have left after the hail, including every tree that is growing in your fields. ⁶They will fill your houses and those of all your officials and all the Egyptians — something neither your fathers nor your forefathers have ever seen from the day they settled in this land till now.' " Then Moses turned and left Pharaoh.

⁷Pharaoh's officials said to him, "How long will this man be a snare to us? Let the people go, so that they may worship the LORD their God. Do you not yet realize that Egypt is ruined?"

⁸Then Moses and Aaron were brought back to Pharaoh. "Go, worship the LORD your God," he said. "But just who will be going?"

⁹Moses answered, "We will go with our young and old, with our sons and daughters, and with our flocks and herds, because we are to celebrate a festival to the LORD."

¹⁰Pharaoh said, "The LORD be with you — if I let you go, along with your women and children! Clearly you are bent on evil.ᵃ ¹¹No! Have only the men go; and worship the LORD, since that's what you have been

asking for." Then Moses and Aaron were driven out of Pharaoh's presence.

¹²And the LORD said to Moses, "Stretch out your hand over Egypt so that locusts will swarm over the land and devour everything growing in the fields, everything left by the hail."

¹³So Moses stretched out his staff over Egypt, and the LORD made an east wind blow across the land all that day and all that night. By morning the wind had brought the locusts; ¹⁴they invaded all Egypt and settled down in every area of the country in great numbers. Never before had there been such a plague of locusts, nor will there ever be again. ¹⁵They covered all the ground until it was black. They devoured all that was left after the hail — everything growing in the fields and the fruit on the trees. Nothing green remained on tree or plant in all the land of Egypt.

¹⁶Pharaoh quickly summoned Moses and Aaron and said, "I have sinned against the LORD your God and against you. ¹⁷Now forgive my sin once more and pray to the LORD your God to take this deadly plague away from me."

¹⁸Moses then left Pharaoh and prayed to the LORD. ¹⁹And the LORD changed the wind to a very strong west wind, which caught up the locusts and carried them into the Red Sea.ᵇ Not a locust was left anywhere in Egypt. ²⁰But the LORD hardened Pharaoh's heart, and he would not let the Israelites go.

The Plague of Darkness

²¹Then the LORD said to Moses, "Stretch out your hand toward the sky so that darkness will spread over Egypt — darkness that can be felt." ²²So Moses stretched out his hand toward the sky, and total darkness covered all Egypt for three days. ²³No one could see anyone else or leave his place for three days. Yet all the Israelites had light in the places where they lived.

²⁴Then Pharaoh summoned Moses and said, "Go, worship the LORD. Even your women and children may go with you; only leave your flocks and herds behind."

²⁵But Moses said, "You must allow us to have sacrifices and burnt offerings to present to the LORD our God. ²⁶Our livestock too must go with us; not a hoof is to be left behind. We have to use some of them in worshiping the LORD our God, and until we get there we will not know what we are to use to worship the LORD."

ᵃ10 Or *Be careful, trouble is in store for you!*   ᵇ19 Hebrew *Yam Suph*; that is, Sea of Reeds

[27]But the Lord hardened Pharaoh's heart, and he was not willing to let them go. [28]Pharaoh said to Moses, "Get out of my sight! Make sure you do not appear before me again! The day you see my face you will die."

[29]"Just as you say," Moses replied, "I will never appear before you again."

The Plague on the Firstborn

11 Now the Lord had said to Moses, "I will bring one more plague on Pharaoh and on Egypt. After that, he will let you go from here, and when he does, he will drive you out completely. [2]Tell the people that men and women alike are to ask their neighbors for articles of silver and gold." [3](The Lord made the Egyptians favorably disposed toward the people, and Moses himself was highly regarded in Egypt by Pharaoh's officials and by the people.)

[4]So Moses said, "This is what the Lord says: 'About midnight I will go throughout Egypt. [5]Every firstborn son in Egypt will die, from the firstborn son of Pharaoh, who sits on the throne, to the firstborn son of the slave girl, who is at her hand mill, and all the firstborn of the cattle as well. [6]There will be loud wailing throughout Egypt — worse than there has ever been or ever will be again. [7]But among the Israelites not a dog will bark at any man or animal.' Then you will know that the Lord makes a distinction between Egypt and Israel. [8]All these officials of yours will come to me, bowing down before me and saying, 'Go, you and all the people who follow you!' After that I will leave." Then Moses, hot with anger, left Pharaoh.

[9]The Lord had said to Moses, "Pharaoh will refuse to listen to you — so that my wonders may be multiplied in Egypt." [10]Moses and Aaron performed all these wonders before Pharaoh, but the Lord hardened Pharaoh's heart, and he would not let the Israelites go out of his country.

The Passover

12 The Lord said to Moses and Aaron in Egypt, [2]"This month is to be for you the first month, the first month of your year. [3]Tell the whole community of Israel that on the tenth day of this month each man is to take a lamb[a] for his family, one for each household. [4]If any household is too small for a whole lamb, they must share one with their nearest neighbor, having taken into account the number of people there are. You

are to determine the amount of lamb needed in accordance with what each person will eat. [5]The animals you choose must be year-old males without defect, and you may take them from the sheep or the goats. [6]Take care of them until the fourteenth day of the month, when all the people of the community of Israel must slaughter them at twilight. [7]Then they are to take some of the blood and put it on the sides and tops of the doorframes of the houses where they eat the lambs. [8]That same night they are to eat the meat roasted over the fire, along with bitter herbs, and bread made without yeast. [9]Do not eat the meat raw or cooked in water, but roast it over the fire — head, legs and inner parts. [10]Do not leave any of it till morning; if some is left till morning, you must burn it. [11]This is how you are to eat it: with your cloak tucked into your belt, your sandals on your feet and your staff in your hand. Eat it in haste; it is the Lord's Passover.

[12]"On that same night I will pass through Egypt and strike down every firstborn — both men and animals — and I will bring judgment on all the gods of Egypt. I am the Lord. [13]The blood will be a sign for you on the houses where you are; and when I see the blood, I will pass over you. No destructive plague will touch you when I strike Egypt.

[14]"This is a day you are to commemorate; for the generations to come you shall celebrate it as a festival to the Lord — a lasting ordinance. [15]For seven days you are to eat bread made without yeast. On the first day remove the yeast from your houses, for whoever eats anything with yeast in it from the first day through the seventh must be cut off from Israel. [16]On the first day hold a sacred assembly, and another one on the seventh day. Do no work at all on these days, except to prepare food for everyone to eat — that is all you may do.

[17]"Celebrate the Feast of Unleavened Bread, because it was on this very day that I brought your divisions out of Egypt. Celebrate this day as a lasting ordinance for the generations to come. [18]In the first month you are to eat bread made without yeast, from the evening of the fourteenth day until the evening of the twenty-first day. [19]For seven days no yeast is to be found in your houses. And whoever eats anything with yeast in it must be cut off from the community of Israel, whether he is an alien or native-born. [20]Eat nothing made with yeast.

---

[a]3 The Hebrew word can mean *lamb* or *kid*; also in verse 4.

Wherever you live, you must eat unleavened bread."

²¹Then Moses summoned all the elders of Israel and said to them, "Go at once and select the animals for your families and slaughter the Passover lamb. ²²Take a bunch of hyssop, dip it into the blood in the basin and put some of the blood on the top and on both sides of the doorframe. Not one of you shall go out the door of his house until morning. ²³When the LORD goes through the land to strike down the Egyptians, he will see the blood on the top and sides of the doorframe and will pass over that doorway, and he will not permit the destroyer to enter your houses and strike you down.

²⁴"Obey these instructions as a lasting ordinance for you and your descendants. ²⁵When you enter the land that the LORD will give you as he promised, observe this ceremony. ²⁶And when your children ask you, 'What does this ceremony mean to you?' ²⁷then tell them, 'It is the Passover sacrifice to the LORD, who passed over the houses of the Israelites in Egypt and spared our homes when he struck down the Egyptians.' " Then the people bowed down and worshiped. ²⁸The Israelites did just what the LORD commanded Moses and Aaron.

²⁹At midnight the LORD struck down all the firstborn in Egypt, from the firstborn of Pharaoh, who sat on the throne, to the firstborn of the prisoner, who was in the dungeon, and the firstborn of all the livestock as well. ³⁰Pharaoh and all his officials and all the Egyptians got up during the night, and there was loud wailing in Egypt, for there was not a house without someone dead.

The Exodus

³¹During the night Pharaoh summoned Moses and Aaron and said, "Up! Leave my people, you and the Israelites! Go, worship the LORD as you have requested. ³²Take your flocks and herds, as you have said, and go. And also bless me."

³³The Egyptians urged the people to hurry and leave the country. "For otherwise," they said, "we will all die!" ³⁴So the people took their dough before the yeast was added, and carried it on their shoulders in kneading troughs wrapped in clothing. ³⁵The Israelites did as Moses instructed and asked the Egyptians for articles of silver and gold and for clothing. ³⁶The LORD had made the Egyptians favorably disposed toward the people,

and they gave them what they asked for; so they plundered the Egyptians.

³⁷The Israelites journeyed from Rameses to Succoth. There were about six hundred thousand men on foot, besides women and children. ³⁸Many other people went up with them, as well as large droves of livestock, both flocks and herds. ³⁹With the dough they had brought from Egypt, they baked cakes of unleavened bread. The dough was without yeast because they had been driven out of Egypt and did not have time to prepare food for themselves.

⁴⁰Now the length of time the Israelite people lived in Egyptᵃ was 430 years. ⁴¹At the end of the 430 years, to the very day, all the LORD's divisions left Egypt. ⁴²Because the LORD kept vigil that night to bring them out of Egypt, on this night all the Israelites are to keep vigil to honor the LORD for the generations to come.

Passover Restrictions

⁴³The LORD said to Moses and Aaron, "These are the regulations for the Passover:

"No foreigner is to eat of it. ⁴⁴Any slave you have bought may eat of it after you have circumcised him, ⁴⁵but a temporary resident and a hired worker may not eat of it.

⁴⁶"It must be eaten inside one house; take none of the meat outside the house. Do not break any of the bones. ⁴⁷The whole community of Israel must celebrate it.

⁴⁸"An alien living among you who wants to celebrate the LORD's Passover must have all the males in his household circumcised; then he may take part like one born in the land. No uncircumcised male may eat of it. ⁴⁹The same law applies to the native-born and to the alien living among you."

⁵⁰All the Israelites did just what the LORD had commanded Moses and Aaron. ⁵¹And on that very day the LORD brought the Israelites out of Egypt by their divisions.

Consecration of the Firstborn

13 The LORD said to Moses, ²"Consecrate to me every firstborn male. The first offspring of every womb among the Israelites belongs to me, whether man or animal."

³Then Moses said to the people, "Commemorate this day, the day you came out of Egypt, out of the land of slavery, because the LORD brought you out of it with a mighty hand. Eat nothing containing yeast. ⁴Today,

---

ᵃ40 Masoretic Text; Samaritan Pentateuch and Septuagint *Egypt and Canaan* in the month of Abib, you are leaving. [5]When the Lord brings you into the land of the Canaanites, Hittites, Amorites, Hivites and Jebusites—the land he swore to your forefathers to give you, a land flowing with milk and honey—you are to observe this ceremony in this month: [6]For seven days eat bread made without yeast and on the seventh day hold a festival to the Lord. [7]Eat unleavened bread during those seven days; nothing with yeast in it is to be seen among you, nor shall any yeast be seen anywhere within your borders. [8]On that day tell your son, 'I do this because of what the Lord did for me when I came out of Egypt.' [9]This observance will be for you like a sign on your hand and a reminder on your forehead that the law of the Lord is to be on your lips. For the Lord brought you out of Egypt with his mighty hand. [10]You must keep this ordinance at the appointed time year after year.

[11]"After the Lord brings you into the land of the Canaanites and gives it to you, as he promised on oath to you and your forefathers, [12]you are to give over to the Lord the first offspring of every womb. All the firstborn males of your livestock belong to the Lord. [13]Redeem with a lamb every firstborn donkey, but if you do not redeem it, break its neck. Redeem every firstborn among your sons.

[14]"In days to come, when your son asks you, 'What does this mean?' say to him, 'With a mighty hand the Lord brought us out of Egypt, out of the land of slavery. [15]When Pharaoh stubbornly refused to let us go, the Lord killed every firstborn in Egypt, both man and animal. This is why I sacrifice to the Lord the first male offspring of every womb and redeem each of my firstborn sons.' [16]And it will be like a sign on your hand and a symbol on your forehead that the Lord brought us out of Egypt with his mighty hand."

Crossing the Sea

[17]When Pharaoh let the people go, God did not lead them on the road through the Philistine country, though that was shorter. For God said, "If they face war, they might change their minds and return to Egypt." [18]So God led the people around by the desert road toward the Red Sea.[a] The Israelites went up out of Egypt armed for battle.

[19]Moses took the bones of Joseph with him because Joseph had made the sons of Israel swear an oath. He had said, "God will surely come to your aid, and then you must carry my bones up with you from this place."[b]

[20]After leaving Succoth they camped at Etham on the edge of the desert. [21]By day the Lord went ahead of them in a pillar of cloud to guide them on their way and by night in a pillar of fire to give them light, so that they could travel by day or night. [22]Neither the pillar of cloud by day nor the pillar of fire by night left its place in front of the people.

14 Then the Lord said to Moses, [2]"Tell the Israelites to turn back and encamp near Pi Hahiroth, between Migdol and the sea. They are to encamp by the sea, directly opposite Baal Zephon. [3]Pharaoh will think, 'The Israelites are wandering around the land in confusion, hemmed in by the desert.' [4]And I will harden Pharaoh's heart, and he will pursue them. But I will gain glory for myself through Pharaoh and all his army, and the Egyptians will know that I am the Lord." So the Israelites did this.

[5]When the king of Egypt was told that the people had fled, Pharaoh and his officials changed their minds about them and said, "What have we done? We have let the Israelites go and have lost their services!" [6]So he had his chariot made ready and took his army with him. [7]He took six hundred of the best chariots, along with all the other chariots of Egypt, with officers over all of them. [8]The Lord hardened the heart of Pharaoh king of Egypt, so that he pursued the Israelites, who were marching out boldly. [9]The Egyptians—all Pharaoh's horses and chariots, horsemen[c] and troops—pursued the Israelites and overtook them as they camped by the sea near Pi Hahiroth, opposite Baal Zephon.

[10]As Pharaoh approached, the Israelites looked up, and there were the Egyptians, marching after them. They were terrified and cried out to the Lord. [11]They said to Moses, "Was it because there were no graves in Egypt that you brought us to the desert to die? What have you done to us by bringing us out of Egypt? [12]Didn't we say to you in Egypt, 'Leave us alone; let us serve the Egyptians'? It would have been better for us to serve the Egyptians than to die in the desert!"

[13]Moses answered the people, "Do not be afraid. Stand firm and you will see the deliv-

---

[a]18 Hebrew *Yam Suph*; that is, Sea of Reeds   [b]19 See Gen. 50:25.   [c]9 Or *charioteers*; also in verses 17, 18, 23, 26 and 28

erance the LORD will bring you today. The Egyptians you see today you will never see again. [14]The LORD will fight for you; you need only to be still."

[15]Then the LORD said to Moses, "Why are you crying out to me? Tell the Israelites to move on. [16]Raise your staff and stretch out your hand over the sea to divide the water so that the Israelites can go through the sea on dry ground. [17]I will harden the hearts of the Egyptians so that they will go in after them. And I will gain glory through Pharaoh and all his army, through his chariots and his horsemen. [18]The Egyptians will know that I am the LORD when I gain glory through Pharaoh, his chariots and his horsemen."

[19]Then the angel of God, who had been traveling in front of Israel's army, withdrew and went behind them. The pillar of cloud also moved from in front and stood behind them, [20]coming between the armies of Egypt and Israel. Throughout the night the cloud brought darkness to the one side and light to the other side; so neither went near the other all night long.

[21]Then Moses stretched out his hand over the sea, and all that night the LORD drove the sea back with a strong east wind and turned it into dry land. The waters were divided, [22]and the Israelites went through the sea on dry ground, with a wall of water on their right and on their left.

[23]The Egyptians pursued them, and all Pharaoh's horses and chariots and horsemen followed them into the sea. [24]During the last watch of the night the LORD looked down from the pillar of fire and cloud at the Egyptian army and threw it into confusion. [25]He made the wheels of their chariots come off[a] so that they had difficulty driving. And the Egyptians said, "Let's get away from the Israelites! The LORD is fighting for them against Egypt."

[26]Then the LORD said to Moses, "Stretch out your hand over the sea so that the waters may flow back over the Egyptians and their chariots and horsemen." [27]Moses stretched out his hand over the sea, and at daybreak the sea went back to its place. The Egyptians were fleeing toward[b] it, and the LORD swept them into the sea. [28]The water flowed back and covered the chariots and horsemen — the entire army of Pharaoh that had followed the Israelites into the sea. Not one of them survived.

[29]But the Israelites went through the sea on dry ground, with a wall of water on their right and on their left. [30]That day the LORD saved Israel from the hands of the Egyptians, and Israel saw the Egyptians lying dead on the shore. [31]And when the Israelites saw the great power the LORD displayed against the Egyptians, the people feared the LORD and put their trust in him and in Moses his servant.

The Song of Moses and Miriam

15 Then Moses and the Israelites sang this song to the LORD:

"I will sing to the LORD,
  for he is highly exalted.
The horse and its rider
  he has hurled into the sea.
[2]The LORD is my strength and my song;
  he has become my salvation.
He is my God, and I will praise him,
  my father's God, and I will exalt him.
[3]The LORD is a warrior;
  the LORD is his name.
[4]Pharaoh's chariots and his army
  he has hurled into the sea.
The best of Pharaoh's officers
  are drowned in the Red Sea.[c]
[5]The deep waters have covered them;
  they sank to the depths like a stone.

[6]"Your right hand, O LORD,
  was majestic in power.
Your right hand, O LORD,
  shattered the enemy.
[7]In the greatness of your majesty
  you threw down those who opposed
    you.
You unleashed your burning anger;
  it consumed them like stubble.
[8]By the blast of your nostrils
  the waters piled up.
The surging waters stood firm like a
    wall;
  the deep waters congealed in the
    heart of the sea.

[9]"The enemy boasted,
  'I will pursue, I will overtake them.
I will divide the spoils;
  I will gorge myself on them.
I will draw my sword
  and my hand will destroy them.'
[10]But you blew with your breath,
  and the sea covered them.
They sank like lead
  in the mighty waters.

---

[a]25 Or *He jammed the wheels of their chariots* (see Samaritan Pentateuch, Septuagint and Syriac)
[b]27 Or *from*   [c]4 Hebrew *Yam Suph*; that is, Sea of Reeds; also in verse 22

11"Who among the gods is like you,
    O Lord?
  Who is like you—
      majestic in holiness,
      awesome in glory,
      working wonders?
12You stretched out your right hand
    and the earth swallowed them.

13"In your unfailing love you will lead
    the people you have redeemed.
  In your strength you will guide them
    to your holy dwelling.
14The nations will hear and tremble;
    anguish will grip the people of
      Philistia.
15The chiefs of Edom will be terrified,
    the leaders of Moab will be seized
      with trembling,
  the people*a* of Canaan will melt away;
16   terror and dread will fall upon them.
  By the power of your arm
    they will be as still as a stone—
  until your people pass by, O Lord,
    until the people you bought*b* pass
      by.
17You will bring them in and plant them
    on the mountain of your
      inheritance—
  the place, O Lord, you made for your
      dwelling,
  the sanctuary, O Lord, your hands
      established.
18The Lord will reign
    for ever and ever."

19When Pharaoh's horses, chariots and horsemen*c* went into the sea, the Lord brought the waters of the sea back over them, but the Israelites walked through the sea on dry ground. 20Then Miriam the prophetess, Aaron's sister, took a tambourine in her hand, and all the women followed her, with tambourines and dancing. 21Miriam sang to them:

  "Sing to the Lord,
    for he is highly exalted.
  The horse and its rider
    he has hurled into the sea."

The Waters of Marah and Elim

22Then Moses led Israel from the Red Sea and they went into the Desert of Shur. For three days they traveled in the desert without finding water. 23When they came to Marah, they could not drink its water because it was bitter. (That is why the place is called

Marah.*d*) 24So the people grumbled against Moses, saying, "What are we to drink?"

25Then Moses cried out to the Lord, and the Lord showed him a piece of wood. He threw it into the water, and the water became sweet.

There the Lord made a decree and a law for them, and there he tested them. 26He said, "If you listen carefully to the voice of the Lord your God and do what is right in his eyes, if you pay attention to his commands and keep all his decrees, I will not bring on you any of the diseases I brought on the Egyptians, for I am the Lord, who heals you." 27Then they came to Elim, where there were twelve springs and seventy palm trees, and they camped there near the water.

Manna and Quail

16 The whole Israelite community set out from Elim and came to the Desert of Sin, which is between Elim and Sinai, on the fifteenth day of the second month after they had come out of Egypt. 2In the desert the whole community grumbled against Moses and Aaron. 3The Israelites said to them, "If only we had died by the Lord's hand in Egypt! There we sat around pots of meat and ate all the food we wanted, but you have brought us out into this desert to starve this entire assembly to death."

4Then the Lord said to Moses, "I will rain down bread from heaven for you. The people are to go out each day and gather enough for that day. In this way I will test them and see whether they will follow my instructions. 5On the sixth day they are to prepare what they bring in, and that is to be twice as much as they gather on the other days."

6So Moses and Aaron said to all the Israelites, "In the evening you will know that it was the Lord who brought you out of Egypt, 7and in the morning you will see the glory of the Lord, because he has heard your grumbling against him. Who are we, that you should grumble against us?" 8Moses also said, "You will know that it was the Lord when he gives you meat to eat in the evening and all the bread you want in the morning, because he has heard your grumbling against him. Who are we? You are not grumbling against us, but against the Lord."

9Then Moses told Aaron, "Say to the entire Israelite community, 'Come before the Lord, for he has heard your grumbling.' " 10While Aaron was speaking to the whole

---

*a*15 Or *rulers*   *b*16 Or *created*   *c*19 Or *charioteers*   *d*23 *Marah* means *bitter.*

Israelite community, they looked toward the desert, and there was the glory of the LORD appearing in the cloud.

11The LORD said to Moses, **12**"I have heard the grumbling of the Israelites. Tell them, 'At twilight you will eat meat, and in the morning you will be filled with bread. Then you will know that I am the LORD your God.' "

13That evening quail came and covered the camp, and in the morning there was a layer of dew around the camp. **14**When the dew was gone, thin flakes like frost on the ground appeared on the desert floor. **15**When the Israelites saw it, they said to each other, "What is it?" For they did not know what it was.

Moses said to them, "It is the bread the LORD has given you to eat. **16**This is what the LORD has commanded: 'Each one is to gather as much as he needs. Take an omer*a* for each person you have in your tent.' "

17The Israelites did as they were told; some gathered much, some little. **18**And when they measured it by the omer, he who gathered much did not have too much, and he who gathered little did not have too little. Each one gathered as much as he needed.

19Then Moses said to them, "No one is to keep any of it until morning."

20However, some of them paid no attention to Moses; they kept part of it until morning, but it was full of maggots and began to smell. So Moses was angry with them.

21Each morning everyone gathered as much as he needed, and when the sun grew hot, it melted away. **22**On the sixth day, they gathered twice as much — two omers*b* for each person — and the leaders of the community came and reported this to Moses. **23**He said to them, "This is what the LORD commanded: 'Tomorrow is to be a day of rest, a holy Sabbath to the LORD. So bake what you want to bake and boil what you want to boil. Save whatever is left and keep it until morning.' "

24So they saved it until morning, as Moses commanded, and it did not stink or get maggots in it. **25**"Eat it today," Moses said, "because today is a Sabbath to the LORD. You will not find any of it on the ground today. **26**Six days you are to gather it, but on the seventh day, the Sabbath, there will not be any."

27Nevertheless, some of the people went out on the seventh day to gather it, but they found none. **28**Then the LORD said to Moses,

"How long will you*c* refuse to keep my commands and my instructions? **29**Bear in mind that the LORD has given you the Sabbath; that is why on the sixth day he gives you bread for two days. Everyone is to stay where he is on the seventh day; no one is to go out." **30**So the people rested on the seventh day.

31The people of Israel called the bread manna.*d* It was white like coriander seed and tasted like wafers made with honey. **32**Moses said, "This is what the LORD has commanded: 'Take an omer of manna and keep it for the generations to come, so they can see the bread I gave you to eat in the desert when I brought you out of Egypt.' "

33So Moses said to Aaron, "Take a jar and put an omer of manna in it. Then place it before the LORD to be kept for the generations to come."

34As the LORD commanded Moses, Aaron put the manna in front of the Testimony, that it might be kept. **35**The Israelites ate manna forty years, until they came to a land that was settled; they ate manna until they reached the border of Canaan. **36**(An omer is one tenth of an ephah.)

Water From the Rock

17 The whole Israelite community set out from the Desert of Sin, traveling from place to place as the LORD commanded. They camped at Rephidim, but there was no water for the people to drink. **2**So they quarreled with Moses and said, "Give us water to drink."

Moses replied, "Why do you quarrel with me? Why do you put the LORD to the test?"

3But the people were thirsty for water there, and they grumbled against Moses. They said, "Why did you bring us up out of Egypt to make us and our children and livestock die of thirst?"

4Then Moses cried out to the LORD, "What am I to do with these people? They are almost ready to stone me."

5The LORD answered Moses, "Walk on ahead of the people. Take with you some of the elders of Israel and take in your hand the staff with which you struck the Nile, and go. **6**I will stand there before you by the rock at Horeb. Strike the rock, and water will come out of it for the people to drink." So Moses did this in the sight of the elders of Israel.

---

a16 That is, probably about 2 quarts (about 2 liters); also in verses 18, 32, 33 and 36   *b22* That is, probably about 4 quarts (about 4.5 liters)   *c28* The Hebrew is plural.   *d31* *Manna* means *What is it?* (see verse 15).

7And he called the place Massah*a* and Meribah*b* because the Israelites quarreled and because they tested the LORD saying, "Is the LORD among us or not?"

The Amalekites Defeated

8The Amalekites came and attacked the Israelites at Rephidim. **9**Moses said to Joshua, "Choose some of our men and go out to fight the Amalekites. Tomorrow I will stand on top of the hill with the staff of God in my hands."

10So Joshua fought the Amalekites as Moses had ordered, and Moses, Aaron and Hur went to the top of the hill. **11**As long as Moses held up his hands, the Israelites were winning, but whenever he lowered his hands, the Amalekites were winning. **12**When Moses' hands grew tired, they took a stone and put it under him and he sat on it. Aaron and Hur held his hands up — one on one side, one on the other — so that his hands remained steady till sunset. **13**So Joshua overcame the Amalekite army with the sword.

14Then the LORD said to Moses, "Write this on a scroll as something to be remembered and make sure that Joshua hears it, because I will completely blot out the memory of Amalek from under heaven."

15Moses built an altar and called it The LORD is my Banner. **16**He said, "For hands were lifted up to the throne of the LORD. The*c* LORD will be at war against the Amalekites from generation to generation."

Jethro Visits Moses

18 Now Jethro, the priest of Midian and father-in-law of Moses, heard of everything God had done for Moses and for his people Israel, and how the LORD had brought Israel out of Egypt.

2After Moses had sent away his wife Zipporah, his father-in-law Jethro received her **3**and her two sons. One son was named Gershom,*d* for Moses said, "I have become an alien in a foreign land"; **4**and the other was named Eliezer,*e* for he said, "My father's God was my helper; he saved me from the sword of Pharaoh."

5Jethro, Moses' father-in-law, together with Moses' sons and wife, came to him in the desert, where he was camped near the mountain of God. **6**Jethro had sent word to him, "I, your father-in-law Jethro, am coming to you with your wife and her two sons."

7So Moses went out to meet his father-in-law and bowed down and kissed him. They greeted each other and then went into the tent. **8**Moses told his father-in-law about everything the LORD had done to Pharaoh and the Egyptians for Israel's sake and about all the hardships they had met along the way and how the LORD had saved them.

9Jethro was delighted to hear about all the good things the LORD had done for Israel in rescuing them from the hand of the Egyptians. **10**He said, "Praise be to the LORD, who rescued you from the hand of the Egyptians and of Pharaoh, and who rescued the people from the hand of the Egyptians. **11**Now I know that the LORD is greater than all other gods, for he did this to those who had treated Israel arrogantly." **12**Then Jethro, Moses' father-in-law, brought a burnt offering and other sacrifices to God, and Aaron came with all the elders of Israel to eat bread with Moses' father-in-law in the presence of God.

13The next day Moses took his seat to serve as judge for the people, and they stood around him from morning till evening. **14**When his father-in-law saw all that Moses was doing for the people, he said, "What is this you are doing for the people? Why do you alone sit as judge, while all these people stand around you from morning till evening?"

15Moses answered him, "Because the people come to me to seek God's will. **16**Whenever they have a dispute, it is brought to me, and I decide between the parties and inform them of God's decrees and laws."

17Moses' father-in-law replied, "What you are doing is not good. **18**You and these people who come to you will only wear yourselves out. The work is too heavy for you; you cannot handle it alone. **19**Listen now to me and I will give you some advice, and may God be with you. You must be the people's representative before God and bring their disputes to him. **20**Teach them the decrees and laws, and show them the way to live and the duties they are to perform. **21**But select capable men from all the people — men who fear God, trustworthy men who hate dishonest gain — and appoint them as officials over thousands, hundreds, fifties and tens. **22**Have them serve as judges for the people at all times, but have them bring every diffi-

---

a7 Massah means *testing.*   *b7 Meribah* means *quarreling.*   *c16* Or *"Because a hand was against the throne of the LORD, the*   *d3 Gershom* sounds like the Hebrew for *an alien there.*   *e4 Eliezer* means *my God is helper.*

TWO C'S FOR CHARTING YOUR COURSE

Jill has basically two goals in life: to develop her God-given artistic abilities and to reach people for Christ. Now, however, she's being forced to choose between two good opportunities.

She's been offered a job at one of the leading art galleries in her city—a chance to learn new things and meet some talented, influential people. She's also just been given the opportunity to travel with a missionary team to Mexico. She'd love to do both, but if she goes to Mexico for three weeks, someone else will get the job in the gallery.

Jill has three days to decide!

Look It Up

Choosing between several good options is extremely tough. But you can discover the best option by evaluating these two C's:

Circumstances. Realize that there are no coincidences. God is in control of your life and uses every incident to direct your steps. Investigate the various circumstances—spiritual, financial, emotional, social, physical—surrounding each option before deciding.

Counsel. Don't neglect the wisdom of older, more mature Christians—your parents, pastor, teachers, youth workers. "Plans fail for lack of counsel, but with many advisers they succeed" (Proverbs 15:22).

Think It Through

If your goal is to be a great drummer, but you have neither rhythm nor a drum set, your circumstances might be God's way of telling you that he has something else for you. If your minister or youth pastor keeps telling you, "God has given you some real gifts. Have you ever considered being a missionary or a pastor?" maybe God is using such counsel to guide you.

But be careful! Circumstances can also make wrong choices look good. And some counsel, though meant for good, can be totally off base. Use these C's cautiously and only after much prayer.

Work It Out

On an index card, write down tough choices you face today as well as "biggies" that loom on the horizon.

Under them write in big letters "Circumstances" and "Counsel." The point is to develop a simple tool that you can carry around with you to help you make good decisions in tough situations.

Nail It Down

Read Exodus 18:13–27 for the story of a tough decision Moses had to make and the advice he got from his father-in-law.

Turn to pages 644, 1286 and 1298 for other readings on God's will.
Turn to page 81 for Thursday's reading.

Topic

GOD'S WILL

cult case to you; the simple cases they can decide themselves. That will make your load lighter, because they will share it with you. **23**If you do this and God so commands, you will be able to stand the strain, and all these people will go home satisfied."

24Moses listened to his father-in-law and did everything he said. **25**He chose capable men from all Israel and made them leaders of the people, officials over thousands, hundreds, fifties and tens. **26**They served as judges for the people at all times. The difficult cases they brought to Moses, but the simple ones they decided themselves.

27Then Moses sent his father-in-law on his way, and Jethro returned to his own country.

At Mount Sinai

19 In the third month after the Israelites left Egypt—on the very day—they came to the Desert of Sinai. **2**After they set out from Rephidim, they entered the Desert of Sinai, and Israel camped there in the desert in front of the mountain.

3Then Moses went up to God, and the Lord called to him from the mountain and said, "This is what you are to say to the house of Jacob and what you are to tell the people of Israel: **4**'You yourselves have seen what I did to Egypt, and how I carried you on eagles' wings and brought you to myself. **5**Now if you obey me fully and keep my covenant, then out of all nations you will be my treasured possession. Although the whole earth is mine, **6**you*a* will be for me a kingdom of priests and a holy nation.' These are the words you are to speak to the Israelites."

7So Moses went back and summoned the elders of the people and set before them all the words the Lord had commanded him to speak. **8**The people all responded together, "We will do everything the Lord has said." So Moses brought their answer back to the Lord.

9The Lord said to Moses, "I am going to come to you in a dense cloud, so that the people will hear me speaking with you and will always put their trust in you." Then Moses told the Lord what the people had said.

10And the Lord said to Moses, "Go to the people and consecrate them today and tomorrow. Have them wash their clothes **11**and be ready by the third day, because on that day the Lord will come down on Mount Sinai in the sight of all the people. **12**Put limits for the people around the mountain and tell them, 'Be careful that you do not go up the mountain or touch the foot of it. Whoever touches the mountain shall surely be put to death. **13**He shall surely be stoned or shot with arrows; not a hand is to be laid on him. Whether man or animal, he shall not be permitted to live.' Only when the ram's horn sounds a long blast may they go up to the mountain."

14After Moses had gone down the mountain to the people, he consecrated them, and they washed their clothes. **15**Then he said to the people, "Prepare yourselves for the third day. Abstain from sexual relations."

16On the morning of the third day there was thunder and lightning, with a thick cloud over the mountain, and a very loud trumpet blast. Everyone in the camp trembled. **17**Then Moses led the people out of the camp to meet with God, and they stood at the foot of the mountain. **18**Mount Sinai was covered with smoke, because the Lord descended on it in fire. The smoke billowed up from it like smoke from a furnace, the whole mountain*b* trembled violently, **19**and the sound of the trumpet grew louder and louder. Then Moses spoke and the voice of God answered him.*c*

20The Lord descended to the top of Mount Sinai and called Moses to the top of the mountain. So Moses went up **21**and the Lord said to him, "Go down and warn the people so they do not force their way through to see the Lord and many of them perish. **22**Even the priests, who approach the Lord, must consecrate themselves, or the Lord will break out against them."

23Moses said to the Lord, "The people cannot come up Mount Sinai, because you yourself warned us, 'Put limits around the mountain and set it apart as holy.'"

24The Lord replied, "Go down and bring Aaron up with you. But the priests and the people must not force their way through to come up to the Lord, or he will break out against them."

25So Moses went down to the people and told them.

The Ten Commandments

20 And God spoke all these words:

2"I am the Lord your God, who

---

brought you out of Egypt, out of the land of slavery.

³"You shall have no other gods before[a] me.

⁴"You shall not make for yourself an idol in the form of anything in heaven above or on the earth beneath or in the waters below. ⁵You shall not bow down to them or worship them; for I, the Lord your God, am a jealous God, punishing the children for the sin of the fathers to the third and fourth generation of those who hate me, ⁶but showing love to a thousand ˌgenerationsˌ of those who love me and keep my commandments.

⁷"You shall not misuse the name of the Lord your God, for the Lord will not hold anyone guiltless who misuses his name.

⁸"Remember the Sabbath day by keeping it holy. ⁹Six days you shall labor and do all your work, ¹⁰but the seventh day is a Sabbath to the Lord your God. On it you shall not do any work, neither you, nor your son or daughter, nor your manservant or maidservant, nor your animals, nor the alien within your gates. ¹¹For in six days the Lord made the heavens and the earth, the sea, and all that is in them, but he rested on the seventh day. Therefore the Lord blessed the Sabbath day and made it holy.

¹²"Honor your father and your mother, so that you may live long in the land the Lord your God is giving you.

¹³"You shall not murder.

¹⁴"You shall not commit adultery.

¹⁵"You shall not steal.

¹⁶"You shall not give false testimony against your neighbor.

¹⁷"You shall not covet your neighbor's house. You shall not covet your neighbor's wife, or his manservant or maidservant, his ox or donkey, or anything that belongs to your neighbor."

¹⁸When the people saw the thunder and lightning and heard the trumpet and saw the mountain in smoke, they trembled with fear. They stayed at a distance ¹⁹and said to Moses, "Speak to us yourself and we will listen. But do not have God speak to us or we will die."

²⁰Moses said to the people, "Do not be afraid. God has come to test you, so that the fear of God will be with you to keep you from sinning."

²¹The people remained at a distance, while Moses approached the thick darkness where God was.

Idols and Altars

²²Then the Lord said to Moses, "Tell the Israelites this: 'You have seen for yourselves that I have spoken to you from heaven: ²³Do not make any gods to be alongside me; do not make for yourselves gods of silver or gods of gold.

²⁴" 'Make an altar of earth for me and sacrifice on it your burnt offerings and fellowship offerings,[b] your sheep and goats and your cattle. Wherever I cause my name to be honored, I will come to you and bless you. ²⁵If you make an altar of stones for me, do not build it with dressed stones, for you will defile it if you use a tool on it. ²⁶And do not go up to my altar on steps, lest your nakedness be exposed on it.'

21 "These are the laws you are to set before them:

Hebrew Servants

²"If you buy a Hebrew servant, he is to serve you for six years. But in the seventh year, he shall go free, without paying anything. ³If he comes alone, he is to go free alone; but if he has a wife when he comes, she is to go with him. ⁴If his master gives him a wife and she bears him sons or daughters, the woman and her children shall belong to her master, and only the man shall go free.

⁵"But if the servant declares, 'I love my master and my wife and children and do not want to go free,' ⁶then his master must take him before the judges.[c] He shall take him to the door or the doorpost and pierce his ear with an awl. Then he will be his servant for life.

⁷"If a man sells his daughter as a servant, she is not to go free as menservants do. ⁸If she does not please the master who has selected her for himself,[d] he must let her be redeemed. He has no right to sell her to for-

---

a3 Or besides   b24 Traditionally peace offerings   c6 Or before God   d8 Or master so that he does not choose her

MORE THAN A HECTIC VACATION

"Think of it," Mr. Morrow would say almost every night at supper. "A solid week of leisure. No work and no homework. Just our family together . . . relaxing and having fun at DisneyWorld!"

Uh, not quite. The Morrows drove 1,200 miles in two days. They rushed about frantically—maps, cameras and souvenirs flapping in the wind—desperately trying to do it all. While the parents complained about the high prices, the kids argued constantly about which attraction to see next.

The Morrows arrived home last night from their "dream vacation," disappointed, sunburned and totally exhausted.

Look It Up

Does the Bible offer a solution to "vacation burnout"? Does it even discuss leisure? Well, it doesn't use that exact word, but look:

"By the seventh day God had finished the work he had been doing; so on the seventh day he rested from all his work. And God blessed the seventh day and made it holy, because on it he rested from all the work of creating that he had done" (Genesis 2:2–3).

God wasn't tired. He didn't need to rest. But in ceasing from work one day out of seven, he was establishing a pattern to follow.

Life that is fulfilling includes both work and leisure!

Think It Through

Ask one hundred people what leisure is, and you'll get one hundred different answers.

The word actually comes from the Latin *licere*, which means "to be allowed," that is, free to do something. The Greeks used the word *schole*, which originally meant "to halt or cease," and later came to include the idea of developing as a person. (It's the term from which we derive our word *school.*)

For our purposes, we'll define leisure as "pausing from the pressures and responsibilities of life to pursue activities that will refresh us."

Work It Out

What are your attitudes and behavior when it comes to leisure? Ask God to help you gain a more proper perspective on what leisure should mean in your life.

Nail It Down

Read the commandment that covers the issue of leisure in Exodus 20:8–11.

Turn to pages 339, 553, 609 and 692 for other readings on leisure.
Turn to page 85 for Friday's reading.

Topic
••••
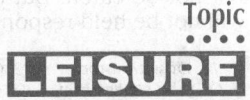

eigners, because he has broken faith with her. **9**If he selects her for his son, he must grant her the rights of a daughter. **10**If he marries another woman, he must not deprive the first one of her food, clothing and marital rights. **11**If he does not provide her with these three things, she is to go free, without any payment of money.

Personal Injuries

12"Anyone who strikes a man and kills him shall surely be put to death. **13**However, if he does not do it intentionally, but God lets it happen, he is to flee to a place I will designate. **14**But if a man schemes and kills another man deliberately, take him away from my altar and put him to death.

15"Anyone who attacks*a* his father or his mother must be put to death.

16"Anyone who kidnaps another and either sells him or still has him when he is caught must be put to death.

17"Anyone who curses his father or mother must be put to death.

18"If men quarrel and one hits the other with a stone or with his fist*b* and he does not die but is confined to bed, **19**the one who struck the blow will not be held responsible if the other gets up and walks around outside with his staff; however, he must pay the injured man for the loss of his time and see that he is completely healed.

20"If a man beats his male or female slave with a rod and the slave dies as a direct result, he must be punished, **21**but he is not to be punished if the slave gets up after a day or two, since the slave is his property.

22"If men who are fighting hit a pregnant woman and she gives birth prematurely*c* but there is no serious injury, the offender must be fined whatever the woman's husband demands and the court allows. **23**But if there is serious injury, you are to take life for life, **24**eye for eye, tooth for tooth, hand for hand, foot for foot, **25**burn for burn, wound for wound, bruise for bruise.

26"If a man hits a manservant or maidservant in the eye and destroys it, he must let the servant go free to compensate for the eye. **27**And if he knocks out the tooth of a manservant or maidservant, he must let the servant go free to compensate for the tooth.

28"If a bull gores a man or a woman to death, the bull must be stoned to death, and its meat must not be eaten. But the owner of the bull will not be held responsible. **29**If,

however, the bull has had the habit of goring and the owner has been warned but has not kept it penned up and it kills a man or woman, the bull must be stoned and the owner also must be put to death. **30**However, if payment is demanded of him, he may redeem his life by paying whatever is demanded. **31**This law also applies if the bull gores a son or daughter. **32**If the bull gores a male or female slave, the owner must pay thirty shekels*d* of silver to the master of the slave, and the bull must be stoned.

33"If a man uncovers a pit or digs one and fails to cover it and an ox or a donkey falls into it, **34**the owner of the pit must pay for the loss; he must pay its owner, and the dead animal will be his.

35"If a man's bull injures the bull of another and it dies, they are to sell the live one and divide both the money and the dead animal equally. **36**However, if it was known that the bull had the habit of goring, yet the owner did not keep it penned up, the owner must pay, animal for animal, and the dead animal will be his.

Protection of Property

22 "If a man steals an ox or a sheep and slaughters it or sells it, he must pay back five head of cattle for the ox and four sheep for the sheep.

2"If a thief is caught breaking in and is struck so that he dies, the defender is not guilty of bloodshed; **3**but if it happens*e* after sunrise, he is guilty of bloodshed.

"A thief must certainly make restitution, but if he has nothing, he must be sold to pay for his theft.

4"If the stolen animal is found alive in his possession—whether ox or donkey or sheep—he must pay back double.

5"If a man grazes his livestock in a field or vineyard and lets them stray and they graze in another man's field, he must make restitution from the best of his own field or vineyard.

6"If a fire breaks out and spreads into thornbushes so that it burns shocks of grain or standing grain or the whole field, the one who started the fire must make restitution.

7"If a man gives his neighbor silver or goods for safekeeping and they are stolen from the neighbor's house, the thief, if he is caught, must pay back double. **8**But if the thief is not found, the owner of the house must appear before the judges*f* to deter-

---

a15 Or *kills*   *b18* Or *with a tool*   *c22* Or *she has a miscarriage*   *d32* That is, about 12 ounces (about 0.3 kilogram)   *e3* Or *if he strikes him*   *f8* Or *before God*; also in verse 9 mine whether he has laid his hands on the other man's property. [9]In all cases of illegal possession of an ox, a donkey, a sheep, a garment, or any other lost property about which somebody says, 'This is mine,' both parties are to bring their cases before the judges. The one whom the judges declare[a] guilty must pay back double to his neighbor.

[10]"If a man gives a donkey, an ox, a sheep or any other animal to his neighbor for safekeeping and it dies or is injured or is taken away while no one is looking, [11]the issue between them will be settled by the taking of an oath before the LORD that the neighbor did not lay hands on the other person's property. The owner is to accept this, and no restitution is required. [12]But if the animal was stolen from the neighbor, he must make restitution to the owner. [13]If it was torn to pieces by a wild animal, he shall bring in the remains as evidence and he will not be required to pay for the torn animal.

[14]"If a man borrows an animal from his neighbor and it is injured or dies while the owner is not present, he must make restitution. [15]But if the owner is with the animal, the borrower will not have to pay. If the animal was hired, the money paid for the hire covers the loss.

Social Responsibility

[16]"If a man seduces a virgin who is not pledged to be married and sleeps with her, he must pay the bride-price, and she shall be his wife. [17]If her father absolutely refuses to give her to him, he must still pay the bride-price for virgins.

[18]"Do not allow a sorceress to live.

[19]"Anyone who has sexual relations with an animal must be put to death.

[20]"Whoever sacrifices to any god other than the LORD must be destroyed.[b]

[21]"Do not mistreat an alien or oppress him, for you were aliens in Egypt.

[22]"Do not take advantage of a widow or an orphan. [23]If you do and they cry out to me, I will certainly hear their cry. [24]My anger will be aroused, and I will kill you with the sword; your wives will become widows and your children fatherless.

[25]"If you lend money to one of my people among you who is needy, do not be like a moneylender; charge him no interest.[c] [26]If you take your neighbor's cloak as a pledge, return it to him by sunset, [27]because his cloak is the only covering he has for his body. What else will he sleep in? When he cries out to me, I will hear, for I am compassionate.

[28]"Do not blaspheme God[d] or curse the ruler of your people.

[29]"Do not hold back offerings from your granaries or your vats.[e]

"You must give me the firstborn of your sons. [30]Do the same with your cattle and your sheep. Let them stay with their mothers for seven days, but give them to me on the eighth day.

[31]"You are to be my holy people. So do not eat the meat of an animal torn by wild beasts; throw it to the dogs.

Laws of Justice and Mercy

23 "Do not spread false reports. Do not help a wicked man by being a malicious witness.

[2]"Do not follow the crowd in doing wrong. When you give testimony in a lawsuit, do not pervert justice by siding with the crowd, [3]and do not show favoritism to a poor man in his lawsuit.

[4]"If you come across your enemy's ox or donkey wandering off, be sure to take it back to him. [5]If you see the donkey of someone who hates you fallen down under its load, do not leave it there; be sure you help him with it.

[6]"Do not deny justice to your poor people in their lawsuits. [7]Have nothing to do with a false charge and do not put an innocent or honest person to death, for I will not acquit the guilty.

[8]"Do not accept a bribe, for a bribe blinds those who see and twists the words of the righteous.

[9]"Do not oppress an alien; you yourselves know how it feels to be aliens, because you were aliens in Egypt.

Sabbath Laws

[10]"For six years you are to sow your fields and harvest the crops, [11]but during the seventh year let the land lie unplowed and unused. Then the poor among your people may get food from it, and the wild animals may eat what they leave. Do the same with your vineyard and your olive grove.

[12]"Six days do your work, but on the seventh day do not work, so that your ox and your donkey may rest and the slave born in

---

[a]9 Or *whom God declares*   [b]20 The Hebrew term refers to the irrevocable giving over of things or persons to the LORD, often by totally destroying them.   [c]25 Or *excessive interest*   [d]28 Or *Do not revile the judges*
[e]29 The meaning of the Hebrew for this phrase is uncertain.

your household, and the alien as well, may be refreshed.

¹³"Be careful to do everything I have said to you. Do not invoke the names of other gods; do not let them be heard on your lips.

The Three Annual Festivals

¹⁴"Three times a year you are to celebrate a festival to me.

¹⁵"Celebrate the Feast of Unleavened Bread; for seven days eat bread made without yeast, as I commanded you. Do this at the appointed time in the month of Abib, for in that month you came out of Egypt.

"No one is to appear before me empty-handed.

¹⁶"Celebrate the Feast of Harvest with the firstfruits of the crops you sow in your field.

"Celebrate the Feast of Ingathering at the end of the year, when you gather in your crops from the field.

¹⁷"Three times a year all the men are to appear before the Sovereign Lord.

¹⁸"Do not offer the blood of a sacrifice to me along with anything containing yeast.

"The fat of my festival offerings must not be kept until morning.

¹⁹"Bring the best of the firstfruits of your soil to the house of the Lord your God.

"Do not cook a young goat in its mother's milk.

God's Angel to Prepare the Way

²⁰"See, I am sending an angel ahead of you to guard you along the way and to bring you to the place I have prepared. ²¹Pay attention to him and listen to what he says. Do not rebel against him; he will not forgive your rebellion, since my Name is in him. ²²If you listen carefully to what he says and do all that I say, I will be an enemy to your enemies and will oppose those who oppose you. ²³My angel will go ahead of you and bring you into the land of the Amorites, Hittites, Perizzites, Canaanites, Hivites and Jebusites, and I will wipe them out. ²⁴Do not bow down before their gods or worship them or follow their practices. You must demolish them and break their sacred stones to pieces. ²⁵Worship the Lord your God, and his blessing will be on your food and water. I will take away sickness from among you, ²⁶and none will miscarry or be barren in your land. I will give you a full life span.

²⁷"I will send my terror ahead of you and throw into confusion every nation you en-

counter. I will make all your enemies turn their backs and run. ²⁸I will send the hornet ahead of you to drive the Hivites, Canaanites and Hittites out of your way. ²⁹But I will not drive them out in a single year, because the land would become desolate and the wild animals too numerous for you. ³⁰Little by little I will drive them out before you, until you have increased enough to take possession of the land.

³¹"I will establish your borders from the Red Sea^a to the Sea of the Philistines,^{b} and from the desert to the River.^{c} I will hand over to you the people who live in the land and you will drive them out before you. ³²Do not make a covenant with them or with their gods. ³³Do not let them live in your land, or they will cause you to sin against me, because the worship of their gods will certainly be a snare to you."

The Covenant Confirmed

24 Then he said to Moses, "Come up to the Lord, you and Aaron, Nadab and Abihu, and seventy of the elders of Israel. You are to worship at a distance, ²but Moses alone is to approach the Lord; the others must not come near. And the people may not come up with him."

³When Moses went and told the people all the Lord's words and laws, they responded with one voice, "Everything the Lord has said we will do." ⁴Moses then wrote down everything the Lord had said.

He got up early the next morning and built an altar at the foot of the mountain and set up twelve stone pillars representing the twelve tribes of Israel. ⁵Then he sent young Israelite men, and they offered burnt offerings and sacrificed young bulls as fellowship offerings^d to the Lord. ⁶Moses took half of the blood and put it in bowls, and the other half he sprinkled on the altar. ⁷Then he took the Book of the Covenant and read it to the people. They responded, "We will do everything the Lord has said; we will obey."

⁸Moses then took the blood, sprinkled it on the people and said, "This is the blood of the covenant that the Lord has made with you in accordance with all these words."

⁹Moses and Aaron, Nadab and Abihu, and the seventy elders of Israel went up ¹⁰and saw the God of Israel. Under his feet was something like a pavement made of sapphire,^{e} clear as the sky itself. ¹¹But God did

---

^{a}31 Hebrew *Yam Suph*; that is, Sea of Reeds ^{b}31 That is, the Mediterranean ^{c}31 That is, the Euphrates
^{d}5 Traditionally *peace offerings* ^{e}10 Or *lapis lazuli*

GROWTH TAKES A LOT OF TIME!

Bill, a college freshman, trusted Christ as his Savior about a year ago; and his life has definitely changed for the better. His relationship with God is getting deeper all the time. So why is he frustrated?

"I just want to see more growth in my life. I still don't know the Bible very well, and I get mad at myself when I lose my temper or do other things that I know I shouldn't do. I want to be more like the Christians at my church. Most of them really have it all together."

Look It Up ● ● ● ●

Bill, you've got it all wrong.

1. Your friends don't have it all together. If the apostle Paul didn't have it all together (Philippians 3:12–14), then you can bet your friends don't!

2. God is working in your life right now—even if you can't see it. "For it is God who works in you to will and to act according to his good purpose" (Philippians 2:13).

3. God won't be finished working in your life until you see Christ face to face. "He who began a good work in you will carry it on to completion until the day of Christ Jesus" (Philippians 1:6).

In other words, relax! Growth takes time.

Think It Through ● ● ● ●

The story is told of a college student who wasn't exactly thrilled at the thought of spending a long time in school. In an interview with the college president the student asked if there were any shortcuts to a particular degree.

"Of course! But it all depends on what you want to be. When God wants to make an oak, he takes a hundred years. When he wants to make a squash, he takes six months!"

Work It Out ● ● ● ●

How can you avoid impatience in your spiritual life?

Don't fret that some believers are more mature than you. Every mature Christian was once a new Christian.

Focus as much on the changes God has already made in your life as on the changes still needed.

Remember that growth isn't easy—it's hard work. Farmers work all year long, but the actual harvest is brief. If you don't see growth in a "thorny" area of your spiritual life, just keep working at it. If you have to work extra hard, you'll feel really great when the success comes (Psalm 126:5–6).

Nail It Down ● ● ● ●

Notice God's gradual method of dealing with his children in Exodus 23:29–30.

Turn to pages 12, 58 and 1227 for other readings on patience.
Turn to page 93 for the weekend reading.

Topic
● ● ● ●
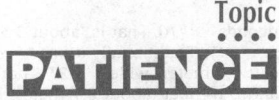

not raise his hand against these leaders of the Israelites; they saw God, and they ate and drank.

¹²The Lᴏʀᴅ said to Moses, "Come up to me on the mountain and stay here, and I will give you the tablets of stone, with the law and commands I have written for their instruction."

¹³Then Moses set out with Joshua his aide, and Moses went up on the mountain of God. ¹⁴He said to the elders, "Wait here for us until we come back to you. Aaron and Hur are with you, and anyone involved in a dispute can go to them."

¹⁵When Moses went up on the mountain, the cloud covered it, ¹⁶and the glory of the Lᴏʀᴅ settled on Mount Sinai. For six days the cloud covered the mountain, and on the seventh day the Lᴏʀᴅ called to Moses from within the cloud. ¹⁷To the Israelites the glory of the Lᴏʀᴅ looked like a consuming fire on top of the mountain. ¹⁸Then Moses entered the cloud as he went on up the mountain. And he stayed on the mountain forty days and forty nights.

Offerings for the Tabernacle

25 The Lᴏʀᴅ said to Moses, ²"Tell the Israelites to bring me an offering. You are to receive the offering for me from each man whose heart prompts him to give. ³These are the offerings you are to receive from them: gold, silver and bronze; ⁴blue, purple and scarlet yarn and fine linen; goat hair; ⁵ram skins dyed red and hides of sea cows[a]; acacia wood; ⁶olive oil for the light; spices for the anointing oil and for the fragrant incense; ⁷and onyx stones and other gems to be mounted on the ephod and breastpiece.

⁸"Then have them make a sanctuary for me, and I will dwell among them. ⁹Make this tabernacle and all its furnishings exactly like the pattern I will show you.

The Ark

¹⁰"Have them make a chest of acacia wood—two and a half cubits long, a cubit and a half wide, and a cubit and a half high.[b] ¹¹Overlay it with pure gold, both inside and out, and make a gold molding around it. ¹²Cast four gold rings for it and fasten them to its four feet, with two rings on one side and two rings on the other. ¹³Then

make poles of acacia wood and overlay them with gold. ¹⁴Insert the poles into the rings on the sides of the chest to carry it. ¹⁵The poles are to remain in the rings of this ark; they are not to be removed. ¹⁶Then put in the ark the Testimony, which I will give you.

¹⁷"Make an atonement cover[c] of pure gold—two and a half cubits long and a cubit and a half wide.[d] ¹⁸And make two cherubim out of hammered gold at the ends of the cover. ¹⁹Make one cherub on one end and the second cherub on the other; make the cherubim of one piece with the cover, at the two ends. ²⁰The cherubim are to have their wings spread upward, overshadowing the cover with them. The cherubim are to face each other, looking toward the cover. ²¹Place the cover on top of the ark and put in the ark the Testimony, which I will give you. ²²There, above the cover between the two cherubim that are over the ark of the Testimony, I will meet with you and give you all my commands for the Israelites.

The Table

²³"Make a table of acacia wood—two cubits long, a cubit wide and a cubit and a half high.[e] ²⁴Overlay it with pure gold and make a gold molding around it. ²⁵Also make around it a rim a handbreadth[f] wide and put a gold molding on the rim. ²⁶Make four gold rings for the table and fasten them to the four corners, where the four legs are. ²⁷The rings are to be close to the rim to hold the poles used in carrying the table. ²⁸Make the poles of acacia wood, overlay them with gold and carry the table with them. ²⁹And make its plates and dishes of pure gold, as well as its pitchers and bowls for the pouring out of offerings. ³⁰Put the bread of the Presence on this table to be before me at all times.

The Lampstand

³¹"Make a lampstand of pure gold and hammer it out, base and shaft; its flowerlike cups, buds and blossoms shall be of one piece with it. ³²Six branches are to extend from the sides of the lampstand—three on one side and three on the other. ³³Three cups shaped like almond flowers with buds and blossoms are to be on one branch, three on the next branch, and the same for all six

---

a5 That is, dugongs   *b10* That is, about 3 3/4 feet (about 1.1 meters) long and 2 1/4 feet (about 0.7 meter) wide and high   *c17* Traditionally *a mercy seat*   *d17* That is, about 3 3/4 feet (about 1.1 meters) long and 2 1/4 feet (about 0.7 meter) wide   *e23* That is, about 3 feet (about 0.9 meter) long and 1 1/2 feet (about 0.5 meter) wide and 2 1/4 feet (about 0.7 meter) high   *f25* That is, about 3 inches (about 8 centimeters) branches extending from the lampstand. [34]And on the lampstand there are to be four cups shaped like almond flowers with buds and blossoms. [35]One bud shall be under the first pair of branches extending from the lampstand, a second bud under the second pair, and a third bud under the third pair — six branches in all. [36]The buds and branches shall all be of one piece with the lampstand, hammered out of pure gold.

[37]"Then make its seven lamps and set them up on it so that they light the space in front of it. [38]Its wick trimmers and trays are to be of pure gold. [39]A talent[a] of pure gold is to be used for the lampstand and all these accessories. [40]See that you make them according to the pattern shown you on the mountain.

The Tabernacle

26 "Make the tabernacle with ten curtains of finely twisted linen and blue, purple and scarlet yarn, with cherubim worked into them by a skilled craftsman. [2]All the curtains are to be the same size — twenty-eight cubits long and four cubits wide.[b] [3]Join five of the curtains together, and do the same with the other five. [4]Make loops of blue material along the edge of the end curtain in one set, and do the same with the end curtain in the other set. [5]Make fifty loops on one curtain and fifty loops on the end curtain of the other set, with the loops opposite each other. [6]Then make fifty gold clasps and use them to fasten the curtains together so that the tabernacle is a unit.

[7]"Make curtains of goat hair for the tent over the tabernacle — eleven altogether. [8]All eleven curtains are to be the same size — thirty cubits long and four cubits wide.[c] [9]Join five of the curtains together into one set and the other six into another set. Fold the sixth curtain double at the front of the tent. [10]Make fifty loops along the edge of the end curtain in one set and also along the edge of the end curtain in the other set. [11]Then make fifty bronze clasps and put them in the loops to fasten the tent together as a unit. [12]As for the additional length of the tent curtains, the half curtain that is left over is to hang down at the rear of the tabernacle. [13]The tent curtains will be a cubit[d] longer on both sides; what is left will hang over the

sides of the tabernacle so as to cover it. [14]Make for the tent a covering of ram skins dyed red, and over that a covering of hides of sea cows.[e]

[15]"Make upright frames of acacia wood for the tabernacle. [16]Each frame is to be ten cubits long and a cubit and a half wide,[f] [17]with two projections set parallel to each other. Make all the frames of the tabernacle in this way. [18]Make twenty frames for the south side of the tabernacle [19]and make forty silver bases to go under them — two bases for each frame, one under each projection. [20]For the other side, the north side of the tabernacle, make twenty frames [21]and forty silver bases — two under each frame. [22]Make six frames for the far end, that is, the west end of the tabernacle, [23]and make two frames for the corners at the far end. [24]At these two corners they must be double from the bottom all the way to the top, and fitted into a single ring; both shall be like that. [25]So there will be eight frames and sixteen silver bases — two under each frame.

[26]"Also make crossbars of acacia wood: five for the frames on one side of the tabernacle, [27]five for those on the other side, and five for the frames on the west, at the far end of the tabernacle. [28]The center crossbar is to extend from end to end at the middle of the frames. [29]Overlay the frames with gold and make gold rings to hold the crossbars. Also overlay the crossbars with gold.

[30]"Set up the tabernacle according to the plan shown you on the mountain.

[31]"Make a curtain of blue, purple and scarlet yarn and finely twisted linen, with cherubim worked into it by a skilled craftsman. [32]Hang it with gold hooks on four posts of acacia wood overlaid with gold and standing on four silver bases. [33]Hang the curtain from the clasps and place the ark of the Testimony behind the curtain. The curtain will separate the Holy Place from the Most Holy Place. [34]Put the atonement cover on the ark of the Testimony in the Most Holy Place. [35]Place the table outside the curtain on the north side of the tabernacle and put the lampstand opposite it on the south side.

[36]"For the entrance to the tent make a curtain of blue, purple and scarlet yarn and finely twisted linen — the work of an embroiderer. [37]Make gold hooks for this curtain

---

[a]39 That is, about 75 pounds (about 34 kilograms)   [b]2 That is, about 42 feet (about 12.5 meters) long and 6 feet (about 1.8 meters) wide   [c]8 That is, about 45 feet (about 13.5 meters) long and 6 feet (about 1.8 meters) wide   [d]13 That is, about 1 1/2 feet (about 0.5 meter)   [e]14 That is, dugongs   [f]16 That is, about 15 feet (about 4.5 meters) long and 2 1/4 feet (about 0.7 meter) wide

and five posts of acacia wood overlaid with gold. And cast five bronze bases for them.

The Altar of Burnt Offering

27 "Build an altar of acacia wood, three cubits[a] high; it is to be square, five cubits long and five cubits wide.[b] ²Make a horn at each of the four corners, so that the horns and the altar are of one piece, and overlay the altar with bronze. ³Make all its utensils of bronze — its pots to remove the ashes, and its shovels, sprinkling bowls, meat forks and firepans. ⁴Make a grating for it, a bronze network, and make a bronze ring at each of the four corners of the network. ⁵Put it under the ledge of the altar so that it is halfway up the altar. ⁶Make poles of acacia wood for the altar and overlay them with bronze. ⁷The poles are to be inserted into the rings so they will be on two sides of the altar when it is carried. ⁸Make the altar hollow, out of boards. It is to be made just as you were shown on the mountain.

The Courtyard

⁹"Make a courtyard for the tabernacle. The south side shall be a hundred cubits[c] long and is to have curtains of finely twisted linen, ¹⁰with twenty posts and twenty bronze bases and with silver hooks and bands on the posts. ¹¹The north side shall also be a hundred cubits long and is to have curtains, with twenty posts and twenty bronze bases and with silver hooks and bands on the posts.

¹²"The west end of the courtyard shall be fifty cubits[d] wide and have curtains, with ten posts and ten bases. ¹³On the east end, toward the sunrise, the courtyard shall also be fifty cubits wide. ¹⁴Curtains fifteen cubits[e] long are to be on one side of the entrance, with three posts and three bases, ¹⁵and curtains fifteen cubits long are to be on the other side, with three posts and three bases.

¹⁶"For the entrance to the courtyard, provide a curtain twenty cubits[f] long, of blue, purple and scarlet yarn and finely twisted linen — the work of an embroiderer — with four posts and four bases. ¹⁷All the posts around the courtyard are to have silver bands and hooks, and bronze bases. ¹⁸The courtyard shall be a hundred cubits long

and fifty cubits wide,[g] with curtains of finely twisted linen five cubits[h] high, and with bronze bases. ¹⁹All the other articles used in the service of the tabernacle, whatever their function, including all the tent pegs for it and those for the courtyard, are to be of bronze.

Oil for the Lampstand

²⁰"Command the Israelites to bring you clear oil of pressed olives for the light so that the lamps may be kept burning. ²¹In the Tent of Meeting, outside the curtain that is in front of the Testimony, Aaron and his sons are to keep the lamps burning before the LORD from evening till morning. This is to be a lasting ordinance among the Israelites for the generations to come.

The Priestly Garments

28 "Have Aaron your brother brought to you from among the Israelites, along with his sons Nadab and Abihu, Eleazar and Ithamar, so they may serve me as priests. ²Make sacred garments for your brother Aaron, to give him dignity and honor. ³Tell all the skilled men to whom I have given wisdom in such matters that they are to make garments for Aaron, for his consecration, so he may serve me as priest. ⁴These are the garments they are to make: a breastpiece, an ephod, a robe, a woven tunic, a turban and a sash. They are to make these sacred garments for your brother Aaron and his sons, so they may serve me as priests. ⁵Have them use gold, and blue, purple and scarlet yarn, and fine linen.

The Ephod

⁶"Make the ephod of gold, and of blue, purple and scarlet yarn, and of finely twisted linen — the work of a skilled craftsman. ⁷It is to have two shoulder pieces attached to two of its corners, so it can be fastened. ⁸Its skillfully woven waistband is to be like it — of one piece with the ephod and made with gold, and with blue, purple and scarlet yarn, and with finely twisted linen.

⁹"Take two onyx stones and engrave on them the names of the sons of Israel ¹⁰in the order of their birth — six names on one stone and the remaining six on the other. ¹¹Engrave the names of the sons of Israel on the

---

a1 That is, about 4 1/2 feet (about 1.3 meters)   *b1* That is, about 7 1/2 feet (about 2.3 meters) long and wide   *c9* That is, about 150 feet (about 46 meters); also in verse 11   *d12* That is, about 75 feet (about 23 meters); also in verse 13   *e14* That is, about 22 1/2 feet (about 6.9 meters); also in verse 15   *f16* That is, about 30 feet (about 9 meters)   *g18* That is, about 150 feet (about 46 meters) long and 75 feet (about 23 meters) wide   *h18* That is, about 7 1/2 feet (about 2.3 meters) two stones the way a gem cutter engraves a seal. Then mount the stones in gold filigree settings [12]and fasten them on the shoulder pieces of the ephod as memorial stones for the sons of Israel. Aaron is to bear the names on his shoulders as a memorial before the LORD. [13]Make gold filigree settings [14]and two braided chains of pure gold, like a rope, and attach the chains to the settings.

The Breastpiece

[15]"Fashion a breastpiece for making decisions—the work of a skilled craftsman. Make it like the ephod: of gold, and of blue, purple and scarlet yarn, and of finely twisted linen. [16]It is to be square—a span[a] long and a span wide—and folded double. [17]Then mount four rows of precious stones on it. In the first row there shall be a ruby, a topaz and a beryl; [18]in the second row a turquoise, a sapphire[b] and an emerald; [19]in the third row a jacinth, an agate and an amethyst; [20]in the fourth row a chrysolite, an onyx and a jasper.[c] Mount them in gold filigree settings. [21]There are to be twelve stones, one for each of the names of the sons of Israel, each engraved like a seal with the name of one of the twelve tribes.

[22]"For the breastpiece make braided chains of pure gold, like a rope. [23]Make two gold rings for it and fasten them to two corners of the breastpiece. [24]Fasten the two gold chains to the rings at the corners of the breastpiece, [25]and the other ends of the chains to the two settings, attaching them to the shoulder pieces of the ephod at the front. [26]Make two gold rings and attach them to the other two corners of the breastpiece on the inside edge next to the ephod. [27]Make two more gold rings and attach them to the bottom of the shoulder pieces on the front of the ephod, close to the seam just above the waistband of the ephod. [28]The rings of the breastpiece are to be tied to the rings of the ephod with blue cord, connecting it to the waistband, so that the breastpiece will not swing out from the ephod.

[29]"Whenever Aaron enters the Holy Place, he will bear the names of the sons of Israel over his heart on the breastpiece of decision as a continuing memorial before the LORD. [30]Also put the Urim and the Thummim in the breastpiece, so they may be over Aaron's heart whenever he enters the presence of the LORD. Thus Aaron will always bear the means of making decisions for the Israelites over his heart before the LORD.

Other Priestly Garments

[31]"Make the robe of the ephod entirely of blue cloth, [32]with an opening for the head in its center. There shall be a woven edge like a collar[d] around this opening, so that it will not tear. [33]Make pomegranates of blue, purple and scarlet yarn around the hem of the robe, with gold bells between them. [34]The gold bells and the pomegranates are to alternate around the hem of the robe. [35]Aaron must wear it when he ministers. The sound of the bells will be heard when he enters the Holy Place before the LORD and when he comes out, so that he will not die.

[36]"Make a plate of pure gold and engrave on it as on a seal: HOLY TO THE LORD. [37]Fasten a blue cord to it to attach it to the turban; it is to be on the front of the turban. [38]It will be on Aaron's forehead, and he will bear the guilt involved in the sacred gifts the Israelites consecrate, whatever their gifts may be. It will be on Aaron's forehead continually so that they will be acceptable to the LORD.

[39]"Weave the tunic of fine linen and make the turban of fine linen. The sash is to be the work of an embroiderer. [40]Make tunics, sashes and headbands for Aaron's sons, to give them dignity and honor. [41]After you put these clothes on your brother Aaron and his sons, anoint and ordain them. Consecrate them so they may serve me as priests.

[42]"Make linen undergarments as a covering for the body, reaching from the waist to the thigh. [43]Aaron and his sons must wear them whenever they enter the Tent of Meeting or approach the altar to minister in the Holy Place, so that they will not incur guilt and die.

"This is to be a lasting ordinance for Aaron and his descendants.

Consecration of the Priests

29 "This is what you are to do to consecrate them, so they may serve me as priests: Take a young bull and two rams without defect. [2]And from fine wheat flour, without yeast, make bread, and cakes mixed with oil, and wafers spread with oil. [3]Put them in a basket and present them in it—along with the bull and the two rams. [4]Then bring Aaron and his sons to the entrance to the Tent of Meeting and wash them with water. [5]Take the garments and

---

[a]16 That is, about 9 inches (about 22 centimeters)   [b]18 Or lapis lazuli   [c]20 The precise identification of some of these precious stones is uncertain.   [d]32 The meaning of the Hebrew for this word is uncertain.

dress Aaron with the tunic, the robe of the ephod, the ephod itself and the breastpiece. Fasten the ephod on him by its skillfully woven waistband. **6**Put the turban on his head and attach the sacred diadem to the turban. **7**Take the anointing oil and anoint him by pouring it on his head. **8**Bring his sons and dress them in tunics **9**and put headbands on them. Then tie sashes on Aaron and his sons.*a* The priesthood is theirs by a lasting ordinance. In this way you shall ordain Aaron and his sons.

10"Bring the bull to the front of the Tent of Meeting, and Aaron and his sons shall lay their hands on its head. **11**Slaughter it in the LORD's presence at the entrance to the Tent of Meeting. **12**Take some of the bull's blood and put it on the horns of the altar with your finger, and pour out the rest of it at the base of the altar. **13**Then take all the fat around the inner parts, the covering of the liver, and both kidneys with the fat on them, and burn them on the altar. **14**But burn the bull's flesh and its hide and its offal outside the camp. It is a sin offering.

15"Take one of the rams, and Aaron and his sons shall lay their hands on its head. **16**Slaughter it and take the blood and sprinkle it against the altar on all sides. **17**Cut the ram into pieces and wash the inner parts and the legs, putting them with the head and the other pieces. **18**Then burn the entire ram on the altar. It is a burnt offering to the LORD, a pleasing aroma, an offering made to the LORD by fire.

19"Take the other ram, and Aaron and his sons shall lay their hands on its head. **20**Slaughter it, take some of its blood and put it on the lobes of the right ears of Aaron and his sons, on the thumbs of their right hands, and on the big toes of their right feet. Then sprinkle blood against the altar on all sides. **21**And take some of the blood on the altar and some of the anointing oil and sprinkle it on Aaron and his garments and on his sons and their garments. Then he and his sons and their garments will be consecrated.

22"Take from this ram the fat, the fat tail, the fat around the inner parts, the covering of the liver, both kidneys with the fat on them, and the right thigh. (This is the ram for the ordination.) **23**From the basket of bread made without yeast, which is before the LORD, take a loaf, and a cake made with oil, and a wafer. **24**Put all these in the hands of Aaron and his sons and wave them before the LORD as a wave offering. **25**Then take them from their hands and burn them on the altar along with the burnt offering for a pleasing aroma to the LORD, an offering made to the LORD by fire. **26**After you take the breast of the ram for Aaron's ordination, wave it before the LORD as a wave offering, and it will be your share.

27"Consecrate those parts of the ordination ram that belong to Aaron and his sons: the breast that was waved and the thigh that was presented. **28**This is always to be the regular share from the Israelites for Aaron and his sons. It is the contribution the Israelites are to make to the LORD from their fellowship offerings.*b*

29"Aaron's sacred garments will belong to his descendants so that they can be anointed and ordained in them. **30**The son who succeeds him as priest and comes to the Tent of Meeting to minister in the Holy Place is to wear them seven days.

31"Take the ram for the ordination and cook the meat in a sacred place. **32**At the entrance to the Tent of Meeting, Aaron and his sons are to eat the meat of the ram and the bread that is in the basket. **33**They are to eat these offerings by which atonement was made for their ordination and consecration. But no one else may eat them, because they are sacred. **34**And if any of the meat of the ordination ram or any bread is left over till morning, burn it up. It must not be eaten, because it is sacred.

35"Do for Aaron and his sons everything I have commanded you, taking seven days to ordain them. **36**Sacrifice a bull each day as a sin offering to make atonement. Purify the altar by making atonement for it, and anoint it to consecrate it. **37**For seven days make atonement for the altar and consecrate it. Then the altar will be most holy, and whatever touches it will be holy.

38"This is what you are to offer on the altar regularly each day: two lambs a year old. **39**Offer one in the morning and the other at twilight. **40**With the first lamb offer a tenth of an ephah*c* of fine flour mixed with a quarter of a hin*d* of oil from pressed olives, and a quarter of a hin of wine as a drink offering. **41**Sacrifice the other lamb at twilight with the same grain offering and its drink offering as in the morning — a pleasing aroma, an offering made to the LORD by fire.

42"For the generations to come this burnt

---

a9 Hebrew; Septuagint *on them* *b28* Traditionally *peace offerings* *c40* That is, probably about 2 quarts (about 2 liters) *d40* That is, probably about 1 quart (about 1 liter) offering is to be made regularly at the entrance to the Tent of Meeting before the Lord. There I will meet you and speak to you; [43]there also I will meet with the Israelites, and the place will be consecrated by my glory.

[44]"So I will consecrate the Tent of Meeting and the altar and will consecrate Aaron and his sons to serve me as priests. [45]Then I will dwell among the Israelites and be their God. [46]They will know that I am the Lord their God, who brought them out of Egypt so that I might dwell among them. I am the Lord their God.

The Altar of Incense

30 "Make an altar of acacia wood for burning incense. [2]It is to be square, a cubit long and a cubit wide, and two cubits high[a] — its horns of one piece with it. [3]Overlay the top and all the sides and the horns with pure gold, and make a gold molding around it. [4]Make two gold rings for the altar below the molding — two on opposite sides — to hold the poles used to carry it. [5]Make the poles of acacia wood and overlay them with gold. [6]Put the altar in front of the curtain that is before the ark of the Testimony — before the atonement cover that is over the Testimony — where I will meet with you.

[7]"Aaron must burn fragrant incense on the altar every morning when he tends the lamps. [8]He must burn incense again when he lights the lamps at twilight so incense will burn regularly before the Lord for the generations to come. [9]Do not offer on this altar any other incense or any burnt offering or grain offering, and do not pour a drink offering on it. [10]Once a year Aaron shall make atonement on its horns. This annual atonement must be made with the blood of the atoning sin offering for the generations to come. It is most holy to the Lord."

Atonement Money

[11]Then the Lord said to Moses, [12]"When you take a census of the Israelites to count them, each one must pay the Lord a ransom for his life at the time he is counted. Then no plague will come on them when you number them. [13]Each one who crosses over to those already counted is to give a half shekel,[b] according to the sanctuary shekel, which weighs twenty gerahs. This half shekel is an offering to the Lord. [14]All who cross

over, those twenty years old or more, are to give an offering to the Lord. [15]The rich are not to give more than a half shekel and the poor are not to give less when you make the offering to the Lord to atone for your lives. [16]Receive the atonement money from the Israelites and use it for the service of the Tent of Meeting. It will be a memorial for the Israelites before the Lord, making atonement for your lives."

Basin for Washing

[17]Then the Lord said to Moses, [18]"Make a bronze basin, with its bronze stand, for washing. Place it between the Tent of Meeting and the altar, and put water in it. [19]Aaron and his sons are to wash their hands and feet with water from it. [20]Whenever they enter the Tent of Meeting, they shall wash with water so that they will not die. Also, when they approach the altar to minister by presenting an offering made to the Lord by fire, [21]they shall wash their hands and feet so that they will not die. This is to be a lasting ordinance for Aaron and his descendants for the generations to come."

Anointing Oil

[22]Then the Lord said to Moses, [23]"Take the following fine spices: 500 shekels[c] of liquid myrrh, half as much (that is, 250 shekels) of fragrant cinnamon, 250 shekels of fragrant cane, [24]500 shekels of cassia — all according to the sanctuary shekel — and a hin[d] of olive oil. [25]Make these into a sacred anointing oil, a fragrant blend, the work of a perfumer. It will be the sacred anointing oil. [26]Then use it to anoint the Tent of Meeting, the ark of the Testimony, [27]the table and all its articles, the lampstand and its accessories, the altar of incense, [28]the altar of burnt offering and all its utensils, and the basin with its stand. [29]You shall consecrate them so they will be most holy, and whatever touches them will be holy.

[30]"Anoint Aaron and his sons and consecrate them so they may serve me as priests. [31]Say to the Israelites, 'This is to be my sacred anointing oil for the generations to come. [32]Do not pour it on men's bodies and do not make any oil with the same formula. It is sacred, and you are to consider it sacred. [33]Whoever makes perfume like it and whoever puts it on anyone other than a priest must be cut off from his people.' "

---

[a]2 That is, about 1 1/2 feet (about 0.5 meter) long and wide and about 3 feet (about 0.9 meter) high
[b]13 That is, about 1/5 ounce (about 6 grams); also in verse 15   [c]23 That is, about 12 1/2 pounds (about 6 kilograms)   [d]24 That is, probably about 4 quarts (about 4 liters)

Incense

34Then the LORD said to Moses, "Take fragrant spices — gum resin, onycha and galbanum — and pure frankincense, all in equal amounts, **35**and make a fragrant blend of incense, the work of a perfumer. It is to be salted and pure and sacred. **36**Grind some of it to powder and place it in front of the Testimony in the Tent of Meeting, where I will meet with you. It shall be most holy to you. **37**Do not make any incense with this formula for yourselves; consider it holy to the LORD. **38**Whoever makes any like it to enjoy its fragrance must be cut off from his people."

Bezalel and Oholiab

31 Then the LORD said to Moses, **2**"See, I have chosen Bezalel son of Uri, the son of Hur, of the tribe of Judah, **3**and I have filled him with the Spirit of God, with skill, ability and knowledge in all kinds of crafts — **4**to make artistic designs for work in gold, silver and bronze, **5**to cut and set stones, to work in wood, and to engage in all kinds of craftsmanship. **6**Moreover, I have appointed Oholiab son of Ahisamach, of the tribe of Dan, to help him. Also I have given skill to all the craftsmen to make everything I have commanded you: **7**the Tent of Meeting, the ark of the Testimony with the atonement cover on it, and all the other furnishings of the tent — **8**the table and its articles, the pure gold lampstand and all its accessories, the altar of incense, **9**the altar of burnt offering and all its utensils, the basin with its stand — **10**and also the woven garments, both the sacred garments for Aaron the priest and the garments for his sons when they serve as priests, **11**and the anointing oil and fragrant incense for the Holy Place. They are to make them just as I commanded you."

The Sabbath

12Then the LORD said to Moses, **13**"Say to the Israelites, 'You must observe my Sabbaths. This will be a sign between me and you for the generations to come, so you may know that I am the LORD, who makes you holy.*a*

14" 'Observe the Sabbath, because it is holy to you. Anyone who desecrates it must be put to death; whoever does any work on that day must be cut off from his people.

15For six days, work is to be done, but the seventh day is a Sabbath of rest, holy to the LORD. Whoever does any work on the Sabbath day must be put to death. **16**The Israelites are to observe the Sabbath, celebrating it for the generations to come as a lasting covenant. **17**It will be a sign between me and the Israelites forever, for in six days the LORD made the heavens and the earth, and on the seventh day he abstained from work and rested.' "

18When the LORD finished speaking to Moses on Mount Sinai, he gave him the two tablets of the Testimony, the tablets of stone inscribed by the finger of God.

The Golden Calf

32 When the people saw that Moses was so long in coming down from the mountain, they gathered around Aaron and said, "Come, make us gods*b* who will go before us. As for this fellow Moses who brought us up out of Egypt, we don't know what has happened to him."

2Aaron answered them, "Take off the gold earrings that your wives, your sons and your daughters are wearing, and bring them to me." **3**So all the people took off their earrings and brought them to Aaron. **4**He took what they handed him and made it into an idol cast in the shape of a calf, fashioning it with a tool. Then they said, "These are your gods,*c* O Israel, who brought you up out of Egypt."

5When Aaron saw this, he built an altar in front of the calf and announced, "Tomorrow there will be a festival to the LORD." **6**So the next day the people rose early and sacrificed burnt offerings and presented fellowship offerings.*d* Afterward they sat down to eat and drink and got up to indulge in revelry.

7Then the LORD said to Moses, "Go down, because your people, whom you brought up out of Egypt, have become corrupt. **8**They have been quick to turn away from what I commanded them and have made themselves an idol cast in the shape of a calf. They have bowed down to it and sacrificed to it and have said, 'These are your gods, O Israel, who brought you up out of Egypt.'

9"I have seen these people," the LORD said to Moses, "and they are a stiff-necked people. **10**Now leave me alone so that my anger may burn against them and that I may destroy them. Then I will make you into a great nation."

---

*a*13 Or *who sanctifies you*; or *who sets you apart as holy*   *b*1 Or *a god*; also in verses 23 and 31   *c*4 Or *This is your god*; also in verse 8   *d*6 Traditionally *peace offerings*

USING YOUR EXCELLENT ABILITIES
☐ SATURDAY

Work It Out
••••

Think about the person you know personally who is best at each of the following:

- singing
- throwing a football
- sewing
- golfing
- drawing
- leading a group
- cooking

Your talents and abilities were given to you by God to use for your own benefit, for the benefit of others, and to bring praise and glory to God (1 Corinthians 10:31; 1 Peter 4:10–11). So whatever you do, whether it's baby-sitting the neighbor kids or helping your dad with the car, do your very best at it—for yourself, for others and for God.

Nail It Down
••••

In Exodus 31:1–11 read how Bezalel and Oholiab used the talents God had given them.

☐ SUNDAY

Think It Through
••••

Some of you are now thinking, "Count me out. God must have! I don't have any special talent or ability." Sorry, but you don't get off the hook that easily. God has given everyone some gift (1 Corinthians 12:7). And that includes you.

Take a good look at yourself. Be honest. What do you do well? What do you enjoy doing? Is there something you have never tried but that you think you would be good at?

Pick one activity and work at it until you're the best you can be at it. If you bake, bake the best muffins or cakes you can, and then share them with a friend or neighbor. If you are successful in the classroom, do the best you can and then offer to help someone who doesn't do as well. If you sing, practice and practice and then use your talent whenever you have the opportunity.

The point is to do your best. That doesn't mean you have to be better at what you do than everyone else. It just means that you are doing your very best to use and develop the gifts God has given you.

Nail It Down
••••

Read the story of Bezalel and Oholiab again in Exodus 31:1–11. For further insight read Proverbs 16:3.

Turn to pages 212, 1296, 1332 and 1334 for other readings on excellence.
Turn to page 96 for Monday's reading.

Topic
••••
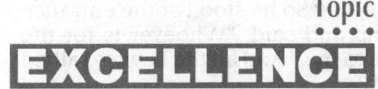

[11]But Moses sought the favor of the Lord his God. "O Lord," he said, "why should your anger burn against your people, whom you brought out of Egypt with great power and a mighty hand? [12]Why should the Egyptians say, 'It was with evil intent that he brought them out, to kill them in the mountains and to wipe them off the face of the earth'? Turn from your fierce anger; relent and do not bring disaster on your people. [13]Remember your servants Abraham, Isaac and Israel, to whom you swore by your own self: 'I will make your descendants as numerous as the stars in the sky and I will give your descendants all this land I promised them, and it will be their inheritance forever.'" [14]Then the Lord relented and did not bring on his people the disaster he had threatened.

[15]Moses turned and went down the mountain with the two tablets of the Testimony in his hands. They were inscribed on both sides, front and back. [16]The tablets were the work of God; the writing was the writing of God, engraved on the tablets.

[17]When Joshua heard the noise of the people shouting, he said to Moses, "There is the sound of war in the camp."

[18]Moses replied:

"It is not the sound of victory,
    it is not the sound of defeat;
    it is the sound of singing that I hear."

[19]When Moses approached the camp and saw the calf and the dancing, his anger burned and he threw the tablets out of his hands, breaking them to pieces at the foot of the mountain. [20]And he took the calf they had made and burned it in the fire; then he ground it to powder, scattered it on the water and made the Israelites drink it.

[21]He said to Aaron, "What did these people do to you, that you led them into such great sin?"

[22]"Do not be angry, my lord," Aaron answered. "You know how prone these people are to evil. [23]They said to me, 'Make us gods who will go before us. As for this fellow Moses who brought us up out of Egypt, we don't know what has happened to him.' [24]So I told them, 'Whoever has any gold jewelry, take it off.' Then they gave me the gold, and I threw it into the fire, and out came this calf!"

[25]Moses saw that the people were running wild and that Aaron had let them get out of control and so become a laughingstock to their enemies. [26]So he stood at the entrance to the camp and said, "Whoever is for the Lord, come to me." And all the Levites rallied to him.

[27]Then he said to them, "This is what the Lord, the God of Israel, says: 'Each man strap a sword to his side. Go back and forth through the camp from one end to the other, each killing his brother and friend and neighbor.'" [28]The Levites did as Moses commanded, and that day about three thousand of the people died. [29]Then Moses said, "You have been set apart to the Lord today, for you were against your own sons and brothers, and he has blessed you this day."

[30]The next day Moses said to the people, "You have committed a great sin. But now I will go up to the Lord; perhaps I can make atonement for your sin."

[31]So Moses went back to the Lord and said, "Oh, what a great sin these people have committed! They have made themselves gods of gold. [32]But now, please forgive their sin — but if not, then blot me out of the book you have written."

[33]The Lord replied to Moses, "Whoever has sinned against me I will blot out of my book. [34]Now go, lead the people to the place I spoke of, and my angel will go before you. However, when the time comes for me to punish, I will punish them for their sin."

[35]And the Lord struck the people with a plague because of what they did with the calf Aaron had made.

33 Then the Lord said to Moses, "Leave this place, you and the people you brought up out of Egypt, and go up to the land I promised on oath to Abraham, Isaac and Jacob, saying, 'I will give it to your descendants.' [2]I will send an angel before you and drive out the Canaanites, Amorites, Hittites, Perizzites, Hivites and Jebusites. [3]Go up to the land flowing with milk and honey. But I will not go with you, because you are a stiff-necked people and I might destroy you on the way."

[4]When the people heard these distressing words, they began to mourn and no one put on any ornaments. [5]For the Lord had said to Moses, "Tell the Israelites, 'You are a stiff-necked people. If I were to go with you even for a moment, I might destroy you. Now take off your ornaments and I will decide what to do with you.'" [6]So the Israelites stripped off their ornaments at Mount Horeb.

The Tent of Meeting

[7]Now Moses used to take a tent and pitch it outside the camp some distance away, calling it the "tent of meeting." Anyone inquiring of the Lord would go to the tent of meeting outside the camp. [8]And whenever Moses went out to the tent, all the people

rose and stood at the entrances to their tents, watching Moses until he entered the tent. **9**As Moses went into the tent, the pillar of cloud would come down and stay at the entrance, while the Lord spoke with Moses. **10**Whenever the people saw the pillar of cloud standing at the entrance to the tent, they all stood and worshiped, each at the entrance to his tent. **11**The Lord would speak to Moses face to face, as a man speaks with his friend. Then Moses would return to the camp, but his young aide Joshua son of Nun did not leave the tent.

Moses and the Glory of the Lord

12Moses said to the Lord, "You have been telling me, 'Lead these people,' but you have not let me know whom you will send with me. You have said, 'I know you by name and you have found favor with me.' **13**If you are pleased with me, teach me your ways so I may know you and continue to find favor with you. Remember that this nation is your people."

14The Lord replied, "My Presence will go with you, and I will give you rest."

15Then Moses said to him, "If your Presence does not go with us, do not send us up from here. **16**How will anyone know that you are pleased with me and with your people unless you go with us? What else will distinguish me and your people from all the other people on the face of the earth?"

17And the Lord said to Moses, "I will do the very thing you have asked, because I am pleased with you and I know you by name."

18Then Moses said, "Now show me your glory."

19And the Lord said, "I will cause all my goodness to pass in front of you, and I will proclaim my name, the Lord, in your presence. I will have mercy on whom I will have mercy, and I will have compassion on whom I will have compassion. **20**But," he said, "you cannot see my face, for no one may see me and live."

21Then the Lord said, "There is a place near me where you may stand on a rock. **22**When my glory passes by, I will put you in a cleft in the rock and cover you with my hand until I have passed by. **23**Then I will remove my hand and you will see my back; but my face must not be seen."

The New Stone Tablets

34 The Lord said to Moses, "Chisel out two stone tablets like the first ones,

and I will write on them the words that were on the first tablets, which you broke. **2**Be ready in the morning, and then come up on Mount Sinai. Present yourself to me there on top of the mountain. **3**No one is to come with you or be seen anywhere on the mountain; not even the flocks and herds may graze in front of the mountain."

4So Moses chiseled out two stone tablets like the first ones and went up Mount Sinai early in the morning, as the Lord had commanded him; and he carried the two stone tablets in his hands. **5**Then the Lord came down in the cloud and stood there with him and proclaimed his name, the Lord. **6**And he passed in front of Moses, proclaiming, "The Lord, the Lord, the compassionate and gracious God, slow to anger, abounding in love and faithfulness, **7**maintaining love to thousands, and forgiving wickedness, rebellion and sin. Yet he does not leave the guilty unpunished; he punishes the children and their children for the sin of the fathers to the third and fourth generation."

8Moses bowed to the ground at once and worshiped. **9**"O Lord, if I have found favor in your eyes," he said, "then let the Lord go with us. Although this is a stiff-necked people, forgive our wickedness and our sin, and take us as your inheritance."

10Then the Lord said: "I am making a covenant with you. Before all your people I will do wonders never before done in any nation in all the world. The people you live among will see how awesome is the work that I, the Lord, will do for you. **11**Obey what I command you today. I will drive out before you the Amorites, Canaanites, Hittites, Perizzites, Hivites and Jebusites. **12**Be careful not to make a treaty with those who live in the land where you are going, or they will be a snare among you. **13**Break down their altars, smash their sacred stones and cut down their Asherah poles.[a] **14**Do not worship any other god, for the Lord, whose name is Jealous, is a jealous God.

15"Be careful not to make a treaty with those who live in the land; for when they prostitute themselves to their gods and sacrifice to them, they will invite you and you will eat their sacrifices. **16**And when you choose some of their daughters as wives for your sons and those daughters prostitute themselves to their gods, they will lead your sons to do the same.

17"Do not make cast idols.

18"Celebrate the Feast of Unleavened

---

*a*13 That is, symbols of the goddess Asherah

MORE NAMES THAN A BIG CITY PHONE BOOK

Davil is like a lot of people. He tends to think that God is just a heavenly version of his earthly dad. Consequently, David imagines God to be an excellent provider, someone who is distant, stern, demanding and impatient—not someone he can be really close to.

Meanwhile, Serina also bases her concept of God on her father, so she lives with the constant fear that something awful is about to happen to her.

Look It Up A study of the names of God can do wonders for our wrong attitudes and scared feelings. Other devotions on this topic will give you information about God as *Elohim, Adonai, El Shaddai.* And if you think that covers all the Biblical names for God, well, think again! He is also called:

- King (Psalm 47:7).
- Rock (this means that God is strong and unchanging; see Deuteronomy 32:3–4).
- Fortress—"Turn your ear to me, come quickly to my rescue; be my rock of refuge, a strong fortress to save me" (Psalm 31:2).
- Husband (this refers to his faithful love for his people; see Isaiah 54:5; Jeremiah 3:14).
- Shepherd (Psalm 23:1).
- Father—"If you, then, though you are evil, know how to give good gifts to your children, how much more will your Father in heaven give good gifts to those who ask him!" (Matthew 7:11).

Think It Through Think of the best earthly dad you know. Now realize this: Our heavenly Father is infinitely better than that! He cares for us, loves us and wants only the very best for us.

Work It Out For a month, keep a "God" journal. Write down every reference to God you come across in your Bible reading. Jot down your thoughts and feelings. Record prayers to God . . . and his answers to prayer. Include any other good quotes or insights you come across. (Warning: You may find keeping a journal so rewarding that you can't stop at the end of the month!)

Nail It Down Consider the intriguing name of God found in Exodus 34:14.

Turn to pages 21, 185 and 192 for other readings on God's names.
Turn to page 122 for Tuesday's reading.

Topic
•••

GOD'S NAMES

Bread. For seven days eat bread made without yeast, as I commanded you. Do this at the appointed time in the month of Abib, for in that month you came out of Egypt.

19"The first offspring of every womb belongs to me, including all the firstborn males of your livestock, whether from herd or flock. **20**Redeem the firstborn donkey with a lamb, but if you do not redeem it, break its neck. Redeem all your firstborn sons.

"No one is to appear before me empty-handed.

21"Six days you shall labor, but on the seventh day you shall rest; even during the plowing season and harvest you must rest.

22"Celebrate the Feast of Weeks with the firstfruits of the wheat harvest, and the Feast of Ingathering at the turn of the year.*a* **23**Three times a year all your men are to appear before the Sovereign Lord, the God of Israel. **24**I will drive out nations before you and enlarge your territory, and no one will covet your land when you go up three times each year to appear before the Lord your God.

25"Do not offer the blood of a sacrifice to me along with anything containing yeast, and do not let any of the sacrifice from the Passover Feast remain until morning.

26"Bring the best of the firstfruits of your soil to the house of the Lord your God.

"Do not cook a young goat in its mother's milk."

27Then the Lord said to Moses, "Write down these words, for in accordance with these words I have made a covenant with you and with Israel." **28**Moses was there with the Lord forty days and forty nights without eating bread or drinking water. And he wrote on the tablets the words of the covenant—the Ten Commandments.

The Radiant Face of Moses

29When Moses came down from Mount Sinai with the two tablets of the Testimony in his hands, he was not aware that his face was radiant because he had spoken with the Lord. **30**When Aaron and all the Israelites saw Moses, his face was radiant, and they were afraid to come near him. **31**But Moses called to them; so Aaron and all the leaders of the community came back to him, and he spoke to them. **32**Afterward all the Israelites came near him, and he gave them all the commands the Lord had given him on Mount Sinai.

33When Moses finished speaking to them, he put a veil over his face. **34**But whenever he entered the Lord's presence to speak with him, he removed the veil until he came out. And when he came out and told the Israelites what he had been commanded, **35**they saw that his face was radiant. Then Moses would put the veil back over his face until he went in to speak with the Lord.

Sabbath Regulations

35 Moses assembled the whole Israelite community and said to them, "These are the things the Lord has commanded you to do: **2**For six days, work is to be done, but the seventh day shall be your holy day, a Sabbath of rest to the Lord. Whoever does any work on it must be put to death. **3**Do not light a fire in any of your dwellings on the Sabbath day."

Materials for the Tabernacle

4Moses said to the whole Israelite community, "This is what the Lord has commanded: **5**From what you have, take an offering for the Lord. Everyone who is willing is to bring to the Lord an offering of gold, silver and bronze; **6**blue, purple and scarlet yarn and fine linen; goat hair; **7**ram skins dyed red and hides of sea cows*b*; acacia wood; **8**olive oil for the light; spices for the anointing oil and for the fragrant incense; **9**and onyx stones and other gems to be mounted on the ephod and breastpiece.

10"All who are skilled among you are to come and make everything the Lord has commanded: **11**the tabernacle with its tent and its covering, clasps, frames, crossbars, posts and bases; **12**the ark with its poles and the atonement cover and the curtain that shields it; **13**the table with its poles and all its articles and the bread of the Presence; **14**the lampstand that is for light with its accessories, lamps and oil for the light; **15**the altar of incense with its poles, the anointing oil and the fragrant incense; the curtain for the doorway at the entrance to the tabernacle; **16**the altar of burnt offering with its bronze grating, its poles and all its utensils; the bronze basin with its stand; **17**the curtains of the courtyard with its posts and bases, and the curtain for the entrance to the courtyard; **18**the tent pegs for the tabernacle and for the courtyard, and their ropes; **19**the woven garments worn for ministering in the sanctuary—both the sacred garments for

a22 That is, in the fall   b7 That is, dugongs; also in verse 23

Aaron the priest and the garments for his sons when they serve as priests."

²⁰Then the whole Israelite community withdrew from Moses' presence, ²¹and everyone who was willing and whose heart moved him came and brought an offering to the Lᴏʀᴅ for the work on the Tent of Meeting, for all its service, and for the sacred garments. ²²All who were willing, men and women alike, came and brought gold jewelry of all kinds: brooches, earrings, rings and ornaments. They all presented their gold as a wave offering to the Lᴏʀᴅ. ²³Everyone who had blue, purple or scarlet yarn or fine linen, or goat hair, ram skins dyed red or hides of sea cows brought them. ²⁴Those presenting an offering of silver or bronze brought it as an offering to the Lᴏʀᴅ, and everyone who had acacia wood for any part of the work brought it. ²⁵Every skilled woman spun with her hands and brought what she had spun — blue, purple or scarlet yarn or fine linen. ²⁶And all the women who were willing and had the skill spun the goat hair. ²⁷The leaders brought onyx stones and other gems to be mounted on the ephod and breastpiece. ²⁸They also brought spices and olive oil for the light and for the anointing oil and for the fragrant incense. ²⁹All the Israelite men and women who were willing brought to the Lᴏʀᴅ freewill offerings for all the work the Lᴏʀᴅ through Moses had commanded them to do.

Bezalel and Oholiab

³⁰Then Moses said to the Israelites, "See, the Lᴏʀᴅ has chosen Bezalel son of Uri, the son of Hur, of the tribe of Judah, ³¹and he has filled him with the Spirit of God, with skill, ability and knowledge in all kinds of crafts — ³²to make artistic designs for work in gold, silver and bronze, ³³to cut and set stones, to work in wood and to engage in all kinds of artistic craftsmanship. ³⁴And he has given both him and Oholiab son of Ahisamach, of the tribe of Dan, the ability to teach others. ³⁵He has filled them with skill to do all kinds of work as craftsmen, designers, embroiderers in blue, purple and scarlet yarn and fine linen, and weavers — all of them master craftsmen and designers.

36 ¹So Bezalel, Oholiab and every skilled person to whom the Lᴏʀᴅ has given skill and ability to know how to carry out all the work of constructing the sanctu-

ary are to do the work just as the Lord has commanded."

²Then Moses summoned Bezalel and Oholiab and every skilled person to whom the Lᴏʀᴅ had given ability and who was willing to come and do the work. ³They received from Moses all the offerings the Israelites had brought to carry out the work of constructing the sanctuary. And the people continued to bring freewill offerings morning after morning. ⁴So all the skilled craftsmen who were doing all the work on the sanctuary left their work ⁵and said to Moses, "The people are bringing more than enough for doing the work the Lᴏʀᴅ commanded to be done."

⁶Then Moses gave an order and they sent this word throughout the camp: "No man or woman is to make anything else as an offering for the sanctuary." And so the people were restrained from bringing more, ⁷because what they already had was more than enough to do all the work.

The Tabernacle

⁸All the skilled men among the workmen made the tabernacle with ten curtains of finely twisted linen and blue, purple and scarlet yarn, with cherubim worked into them by a skilled craftsman. ⁹All the curtains were the same size — twenty-eight cubits long and four cubits wide.ᵃ ¹⁰They joined five of the curtains together and did the same with the other five. ¹¹Then they made loops of blue material along the edge of the end curtain in one set, and the same was done with the end curtain in the other set. ¹²They also made fifty loops on one curtain and fifty loops on the end curtain of the other set, with the loops opposite each other. ¹³Then they made fifty gold clasps and used them to fasten the two sets of curtains together so that the tabernacle was a unit.

¹⁴They made curtains of goat hair for the tent over the tabernacle — eleven altogether. ¹⁵All eleven curtains were the same size — thirty cubits long and four cubits wide.ᵇ ¹⁶They joined five of the curtains into one set and the other six into another set. ¹⁷Then they made fifty loops along the edge of the end curtain in one set and also along the edge of the end curtain in the other set. ¹⁸They made fifty bronze clasps to fasten the tent together as a unit. ¹⁹Then they made for the tent a covering of ram skins

ᵃ9 That is, about 42 feet (about 12.5 meters) long and 6 feet (about 1.8 meters) wide   ᵇ15 That is, about 45 feet (about 13.5 meters) long and 6 feet (about 1.8 meters) wide dyed red, and over that a covering of hides of sea cows.[a]

20They made upright frames of acacia wood for the tabernacle. 21Each frame was ten cubits long and a cubit and a half wide,[b] 22with two projections set parallel to each other. They made all the frames of the tabernacle in this way. 23They made twenty frames for the south side of the tabernacle 24and made forty silver bases to go under them — two bases for each frame, one under each projection. 25For the other side, the north side of the tabernacle, they made twenty frames 26and forty silver bases — two under each frame. 27They made six frames for the far end, that is, the west end of the tabernacle, 28and two frames were made for the corners of the tabernacle at the far end. 29At these two corners the frames were double from the bottom all the way to the top and fitted into a single ring; both were made alike. 30So there were eight frames and sixteen silver bases — two under each frame.

31They also made crossbars of acacia wood: five for the frames on one side of the tabernacle, 32five for those on the other side, and five for the frames on the west, at the far end of the tabernacle. 33They made the center crossbar so that it extended from end to end at the middle of the frames. 34They overlaid the frames with gold and made gold rings to hold the crossbars. They also overlaid the crossbars with gold.

35They made the curtain of blue, purple and scarlet yarn and finely twisted linen, with cherubim worked into it by a skilled craftsman. 36They made four posts of acacia wood for it and overlaid them with gold. They made gold hooks for them and cast their four silver bases. 37For the entrance to the tent they made a curtain of blue, purple and scarlet yarn and finely twisted linen — the work of an embroiderer; 38and they made five posts with hooks for them. They overlaid the tops of the posts and their bands with gold and made their five bases of bronze.

The Ark

37 Bezalel made the ark of acacia wood — two and a half cubits long, a cubit and a half wide, and a cubit and a half high.[c] 2He overlaid it with pure gold, both inside and out, and made a gold molding around it. 3He cast four gold rings for it and fastened them to its four feet, with two rings on one side and two rings on the other. 4Then he made poles of acacia wood and overlaid them with gold. 5And he inserted the poles into the rings on the sides of the ark to carry it.

6He made the atonement cover of pure gold — two and a half cubits long and a cubit and a half wide.[d] 7Then he made two cherubim out of hammered gold at the ends of the cover. 8He made one cherub on one end and the second cherub on the other; at the two ends he made them of one piece with the cover. 9The cherubim had their wings spread upward, overshadowing the cover with them. The cherubim faced each other, looking toward the cover.

The Table

10They[e] made the table of acacia wood — two cubits long, a cubit wide, and a cubit and a half high.[f] 11Then they overlaid it with pure gold and made a gold molding around it. 12They also made around it a rim a handbreadth[g] wide and put a gold molding on the rim. 13They cast four gold rings for the table and fastened them to the four corners, where the four legs were. 14The rings were put close to the rim to hold the poles used in carrying the table. 15The poles for carrying the table were made of acacia wood and were overlaid with gold. 16And they made from pure gold the articles for the table — its plates and dishes and bowls and its pitchers for the pouring out of drink offerings.

The Lampstand

17They made the lampstand of pure gold and hammered it out, base and shaft; its flowerlike cups, buds and blossoms were of one piece with it. 18Six branches extended from the sides of the lampstand — three on one side and three on the other. 19Three cups shaped like almond flowers with buds and blossoms were on one branch, three on the next branch and the same for all six branches extending from the lampstand. 20And on the lampstand were four cups shaped like almond flowers with buds and blossoms. 21One bud was under the first

---

[a]19 That is, dugongs   [b]21 That is, about 15 feet (about 4.5 meters) long and 2 1/4 feet (about 0.7 meter) wide   [c]1 That is, about 3 3/4 feet (about 1.1 meters) long and 2 1/4 feet (about 0.7 meter) wide and high   [d]6 That is, about 3 3/4 feet (about 1.1 meters) long and 2 1/4 feet (about 0.7 meter) wide   [e]10 Or He; also in verses 11-29   [f]10 That is, about 3 feet (about 0.9 meter) long, 1 1/2 feet (about 0.5 meter) wide, and 2 1/4 feet (about 0.7 meter) high   [g]12 That is, about 3 inches (about 8 centimeters)

pair of branches extending from the lampstand, a second bud under the second pair, and a third bud under the third pair — six branches in all. **22**The buds and the branches were all of one piece with the lampstand, hammered out of pure gold.

23They made its seven lamps, as well as its wick trimmers and trays, of pure gold. **24**They made the lampstand and all its accessories from one talent*a* of pure gold.

The Altar of Incense

25They made the altar of incense out of acacia wood. It was square, a cubit long and a cubit wide, and two cubits high*b* — its horns of one piece with it. **26**They overlaid the top and all the sides and the horns with pure gold, and made a gold molding around it. **27**They made two gold rings below the molding — two on opposite sides — to hold the poles used to carry it. **28**They made the poles of acacia wood and overlaid them with gold.

29They also made the sacred anointing oil and the pure, fragrant incense — the work of a perfumer.

The Altar of Burnt Offering

38 They*c* built the altar of burnt offering of acacia wood, three cubits*d* high; it was square, five cubits long and five cubits wide.*e* **2**They made a horn at each of the four corners, so that the horns and the altar were of one piece, and they overlaid the altar with bronze. **3**They made all its utensils of bronze — its pots, shovels, sprinkling bowls, meat forks and firepans. **4**They made a grating for the altar, a bronze network, to be under its ledge, halfway up the altar. **5**They cast bronze rings to hold the poles for the four corners of the bronze grating. **6**They made the poles of acacia wood and overlaid them with bronze. **7**They inserted the poles into the rings so they would be on the sides of the altar for carrying it. They made it hollow, out of boards.

Basin for Washing

8They made the bronze basin and its bronze stand from the mirrors of the women who served at the entrance to the Tent of Meeting.

The Courtyard

9Next they made the courtyard. The south side was a hundred cubits*f* long and had curtains of finely twisted linen, **10**with twenty posts and twenty bronze bases, and with silver hooks and bands on the posts. **11**The north side was also a hundred cubits long and had twenty posts and twenty bronze bases, with silver hooks and bands on the posts.

12The west end was fifty cubits*g* wide and had curtains, with ten posts and ten bases, with silver hooks and bands on the posts. **13**The east end, toward the sunrise, was also fifty cubits wide. **14**Curtains fifteen cubits*h* long were on one side of the entrance, with three posts and three bases, **15**and curtains fifteen cubits long were on the other side of the entrance to the courtyard, with three posts and three bases. **16**All the curtains around the courtyard were of finely twisted linen. **17**The bases for the posts were bronze. The hooks and bands on the posts were silver, and their tops were overlaid with silver; so all the posts of the courtyard had silver bands.

18The curtain for the entrance to the courtyard was of blue, purple and scarlet yarn and finely twisted linen — the work of an embroiderer. It was twenty cubits*i* long and, like the curtains of the courtyard, five cubits*j* high, **19**with four posts and four bronze bases. Their hooks and bands were silver, and their tops were overlaid with silver. **20**All the tent pegs of the tabernacle and of the surrounding courtyard were bronze.

The Materials Used

21These are the amounts of the materials used for the tabernacle, the tabernacle of the Testimony, which were recorded at Moses' command by the Levites under the direction of Ithamar son of Aaron, the priest. **22**(Bezalel son of Uri, the son of Hur, of the tribe of Judah, made everything the Lord commanded Moses; **23**with him was Oholiab son of Ahisamach, of the tribe of Dan — a craftsman and designer, and an embroiderer in blue, purple and scarlet yarn and fine linen.) **24**The total amount of the gold from the wave offering used for all the work on the sanctuary was 29 talents and 730

---

a24 That is, about 75 pounds (about 34 kilograms)   *b25* That is, about 1 1/2 feet (about 0.5 meter) long and wide, and about 3 feet (about 0.9 meter) high   *c1* Or *He*; also in verses 2-9   *d1* That is, about 4 1/2 feet (about 1.3 meters)   *e1* That is, about 7 1/2 feet (about 2.3 meters) long and wide   *f9* That is, about 150 feet (about 46 meters)   *g12* That is, about 75 feet (about 23 meters)   *h14* That is, about 22 1/2 feet (about 6.9 meters)   *i18* That is, about 30 feet (about 9 meters)   *j18* That is, about 7 1/2 feet (about 2.3 meters) shekels,[a] according to the sanctuary shekel.

25The silver obtained from those of the community who were counted in the census was 100 talents and 1,775 shekels,[b] according to the sanctuary shekel— **26**one beka per person, that is, half a shekel,[c] according to the sanctuary shekel, from everyone who had crossed over to those counted, twenty years old or more, a total of 603,550 men. **27**The 100 talents[d] of silver were used to cast the bases for the sanctuary and for the curtain—100 bases from the 100 talents, one talent for each base. **28**They used the 1,775 shekels[e] to make the hooks for the posts, to overlay the tops of the posts, and to make their bands.

29The bronze from the wave offering was 70 talents and 2,400 shekels.[f] **30**They used it to make the bases for the entrance to the Tent of Meeting, the bronze altar with its bronze grating and all its utensils, **31**the bases for the surrounding courtyard and those for its entrance and all the tent pegs for the tabernacle and those for the surrounding courtyard.

The Priestly Garments

39 From the blue, purple and scarlet yarn they made woven garments for ministering in the sanctuary. They also made sacred garments for Aaron, as the LORD commanded Moses.

The Ephod

2They[g] made the ephod of gold, and of blue, purple and scarlet yarn, and of finely twisted linen. **3**They hammered out thin sheets of gold and cut strands to be worked into the blue, purple and scarlet yarn and fine linen—the work of a skilled craftsman. **4**They made shoulder pieces for the ephod, which were attached to two of its corners, so it could be fastened. **5**Its skillfully woven waistband was like it—of one piece with the ephod and made with gold, and with blue, purple and scarlet yarn, and with finely twisted linen, as the LORD commanded Moses.

6They mounted the onyx stones in gold filigree settings and engraved them like a seal with the names of the sons of Israel. **7**Then they fastened them on the shoulder pieces of the ephod as memorial stones for the sons of Israel, as the LORD commanded Moses.

The Breastpiece

8They fashioned the breastpiece—the work of a skilled craftsman. They made it like the ephod: of gold, and of blue, purple and scarlet yarn, and of finely twisted linen. **9**It was square—a span[h] long and a span wide—and folded double. **10**Then they mounted four rows of precious stones on it. In the first row there was a ruby, a topaz and a beryl; **11**in the second row a turquoise, a sapphire[i] and an emerald; **12**in the third row a jacinth, an agate and an amethyst; **13**in the fourth row a chrysolite, an onyx and a jasper.[j] They were mounted in gold filigree settings. **14**There were twelve stones, one for each of the names of the sons of Israel, each engraved like a seal with the name of one of the twelve tribes.

15For the breastpiece they made braided chains of pure gold, like a rope. **16**They made two gold filigree settings and two gold rings, and fastened the rings to two of the corners of the breastpiece. **17**They fastened the two gold chains to the rings at the corners of the breastpiece, **18**and the other ends of the chains to the two settings, attaching them to the shoulder pieces of the ephod at the front. **19**They made two gold rings and attached them to the other two corners of the breastpiece on the inside edge next to the ephod. **20**Then they made two more gold rings and attached them to the bottom of the shoulder pieces on the front of the ephod, close to the seam just above the waistband of the ephod. **21**They tied the rings of the breastpiece to the rings of the ephod with blue cord, connecting it to the waistband so that the breastpiece would not swing out from the ephod—as the LORD commanded Moses.

Other Priestly Garments

22They made the robe of the ephod entirely of blue cloth—the work of a weaver— **23**with an opening in the center of the robe like the opening of a collar,[k] and a band around this opening, so that it would not

---

[a]24 The weight of the gold was a little over one ton (about 1 metric ton).   [b]25 The weight of the silver was a little over 3 3/4 tons (about 3.4 metric tons).   [c]26 That is, about 1/5 ounce (about 5.5 grams)   [d]27 That is, about 3 3/4 tons (about 3.4 metric tons)   [e]28 That is, about 45 pounds (about 20 kilograms)   [f]29 The weight of the bronze was about 2 1/2 tons (about 2.4 metric tons).   [g]2 Or He; also in verses 7, 8 and 22   [h]9 That is, about 9 inches (about 22 centimeters)   [i]11 Or lapis lazuli   [j]13 The precise identification of some of these precious stones is uncertain.   [k]23 The meaning of the Hebrew for this word is uncertain.

tear. **24**They made pomegranates of blue, purple and scarlet yarn and finely twisted linen around the hem of the robe. **25**And they made bells of pure gold and attached them around the hem between the pomegranates. **26**The bells and pomegranates alternated around the hem of the robe to be worn for ministering, as the LORD commanded Moses.

27For Aaron and his sons, they made tunics of fine linen — the work of a weaver — **28**and the turban of fine linen, the linen headbands and the undergarments of finely twisted linen. **29**The sash was of finely twisted linen and blue, purple and scarlet yarn — the work of an embroiderer — as the LORD commanded Moses.

30They made the plate, the sacred diadem, out of pure gold and engraved on it, like an inscription on a seal: HOLY TO THE LORD. **31**Then they fastened a blue cord to it to attach it to the turban, as the LORD commanded Moses.

Moses Inspects the Tabernacle

32So all the work on the tabernacle, the Tent of Meeting, was completed. The Israelites did everything just as the LORD commanded Moses. **33**Then they brought the tabernacle to Moses: the tent and all its furnishings, its clasps, frames, crossbars, posts and bases; **34**the covering of ram skins dyed red, the covering of hides of sea cows[a] and the shielding curtain; **35**the ark of the Testimony with its poles and the atonement cover; **36**the table with all its articles and the bread of the Presence; **37**the pure gold lampstand with its row of lamps and all its accessories, and the oil for the light; **38**the gold altar, the anointing oil, the fragrant incense, and the curtain for the entrance to the tent; **39**the bronze altar with its bronze grating, its poles and all its utensils; the basin with its stand; **40**the curtains of the courtyard with its posts and bases, and the curtain for the entrance to the courtyard; the ropes and tent pegs for the courtyard; all the furnishings for the tabernacle, the Tent of Meeting; **41**and the woven garments worn for ministering in the sanctuary, both the sacred garments for Aaron the priest and the garments for his sons when serving as priests.

42The Israelites had done all the work just as the LORD had commanded Moses. **43**Moses inspected the work and saw that they had done it just as the LORD had commanded. So Moses blessed them.

Setting Up the Tabernacle

40 Then the LORD said to Moses: **2**"Set up the tabernacle, the Tent of Meeting, on the first day of the first month. **3**Place the ark of the Testimony in it and shield the ark with the curtain. **4**Bring in the table and set out what belongs on it. Then bring in the lampstand and set up its lamps. **5**Place the gold altar of incense in front of the ark of the Testimony and put the curtain at the entrance to the tabernacle.

6"Place the altar of burnt offering in front of the entrance to the tabernacle, the Tent of Meeting; **7**place the basin between the Tent of Meeting and the altar and put water in it. **8**Set up the courtyard around it and put the curtain at the entrance to the courtyard.

9"Take the anointing oil and anoint the tabernacle and everything in it; consecrate it and all its furnishings, and it will be holy. **10**Then anoint the altar of burnt offering and all its utensils; consecrate the altar, and it will be most holy. **11**Anoint the basin and its stand and consecrate them.

12"Bring Aaron and his sons to the entrance to the Tent of Meeting and wash them with water. **13**Then dress Aaron in the sacred garments, anoint him and consecrate him so he may serve me as priest. **14**Bring his sons and dress them in tunics. **15**Anoint them just as you anointed their father, so they may serve me as priests. Their anointing will be to a priesthood that will continue for all generations to come." **16**Moses did everything just as the LORD commanded him.

17So the tabernacle was set up on the first day of the first month in the second year. **18**When Moses set up the tabernacle, he put the bases in place, erected the frames, inserted the crossbars and set up the posts. **19**Then he spread the tent over the tabernacle and put the covering over the tent, as the LORD commanded him.

20He took the Testimony and placed it in the ark, attached the poles to the ark and put the atonement cover over it. **21**Then he brought the ark into the tabernacle and hung the shielding curtain and shielded the ark of the Testimony, as the LORD commanded him.

22Moses placed the table in the Tent of Meeting on the north side of the tabernacle outside the curtain **23**and set out the bread on it before the LORD, as the LORD commanded him.

---

a34 That is, dugongs

²⁴He placed the lampstand in the Tent of Meeting opposite the table on the south side of the tabernacle ²⁵and set up the lamps before the Lord, as the Lord commanded him.

²⁶Moses placed the gold altar in the Tent of Meeting in front of the curtain ²⁷and burned fragrant incense on it, as the Lord commanded him. ²⁸Then he put up the curtain at the entrance to the tabernacle.

²⁹He set the altar of burnt offering near the entrance to the tabernacle, the Tent of Meeting, and offered on it burnt offerings and grain offerings, as the Lord commanded him.

³⁰He placed the basin between the Tent of Meeting and the altar and put water in it for washing, ³¹and Moses and Aaron and his sons used it to wash their hands and feet. ³²They washed whenever they entered the Tent of Meeting or approached the altar, as the Lord commanded Moses.

³³Then Moses set up the courtyard around the tabernacle and altar and put up the curtain at the entrance to the courtyard. And so Moses finished the work.

The Glory of the Lord

³⁴Then the cloud covered the Tent of Meeting, and the glory of the Lord filled the tabernacle. ³⁵Moses could not enter the Tent of Meeting because the cloud had settled upon it, and the glory of the Lord filled the tabernacle.

³⁶In all the travels of the Israelites, whenever the cloud lifted from above the tabernacle, they would set out; ³⁷but if the cloud did not lift, they did not set out—until the day it lifted. ³⁸So the cloud of the Lord was over the tabernacle by day, and fire was in the cloud by night, in the sight of all the house of Israel during all their travels.

LEVITICUS

LEVITICUS. Is it dull? Is it boring? It may seem so, but this book has an exciting message: God's holiness affects every area of life. Named for the priestly tribe of Levi, Leviticus reveals how God wants ancient Israel governed. And through the offerings and feasts, God paints a picture of the way Christ would reconcile sinners by his death on the cross. You live in a different world, but remember when you read that God still wants his holiness to be your guide. And he still provides a way of forgiveness when you fail.

Outline of Contents

The Burnt Offering

1 The LORD called to Moses and spoke to him from the Tent of Meeting. He said, ²"Speak to the Israelites and say to them: 'When any of you brings an offering to the LORD, bring as your offering an animal from either the herd or the flock.

³" 'If the offering is a burnt offering from the herd, he is to offer a male without defect. He must present it at the entrance to the Tent of Meeting so that it*a* will be accept-able to the LORD. ⁴He is to lay his hand on the head of the burnt offering, and it will be accepted on his behalf to make atonement for him. ⁵He is to slaughter the young bull before the LORD, and then Aaron's sons the priests shall bring the blood and sprinkle it against the altar on all sides at the entrance to the Tent of Meeting. ⁶He is to skin the burnt offering and cut it into pieces. ⁷The sons of Aaron the priest are to put fire on the altar and arrange wood on the fire. ⁸Then Aaron's sons the priests shall arrange the

*a*3 Or *he*

pieces, including the head and the fat, on the burning wood that is on the altar. **9**He is to wash the inner parts and the legs with water, and the priest is to burn all of it on the altar. It is a burnt offering, an offering made by fire, an aroma pleasing to the LORD.

10" 'If the offering is a burnt offering from the flock, from either the sheep or the goats, he is to offer a male without defect. **11**He is to slaughter it at the north side of the altar before the LORD, and Aaron's sons the priests shall sprinkle its blood against the altar on all sides. **12**He is to cut it into pieces, and the priest shall arrange them, including the head and the fat, on the burning wood that is on the altar. **13**He is to wash the inner parts and the legs with water, and the priest is to bring all of it and burn it on the altar. It is a burnt offering, an offering made by fire, an aroma pleasing to the LORD.

14" 'If the offering to the LORD is a burnt offering of birds, he is to offer a dove or a young pigeon. **15**The priest shall bring it to the altar, wring off the head and burn it on the altar; its blood shall be drained out on the side of the altar. **16**He is to remove the crop with its contents*a* and throw it to the east side of the altar, where the ashes are. **17**He shall tear it open by the wings, not severing it completely, and then the priest shall burn it on the wood that is on the fire on the altar. It is a burnt offering, an offering made by fire, an aroma pleasing to the LORD.

The Grain Offering

2 " 'When someone brings a grain offering to the LORD, his offering is to be of fine flour. He is to pour oil on it, put incense on it **2**and take it to Aaron's sons the priests. The priest shall take a handful of the fine flour and oil, together with all the incense, and burn this as a memorial portion on the altar, an offering made by fire, an aroma pleasing to the LORD. **3**The rest of the grain offering belongs to Aaron and his sons; it is a most holy part of the offerings made to the LORD by fire.

4" 'If you bring a grain offering baked in an oven, it is to consist of fine flour: cakes made without yeast and mixed with oil, or*b* wafers made without yeast and spread with oil. **5**If your grain offering is prepared on a griddle, it is to be made of fine flour mixed with oil, and without yeast. **6**Crumble it and pour oil on it; it is a grain offering. **7**If your grain offering is cooked in a pan, it is to be

made of fine flour and oil. **8**Bring the grain offering made of these things to the LORD; present it to the priest, who shall take it to the altar. **9**He shall take out the memorial portion from the grain offering and burn it on the altar as an offering made by fire, an aroma pleasing to the LORD. **10**The rest of the grain offering belongs to Aaron and his sons; it is a most holy part of the offerings made to the LORD by fire.

11" 'Every grain offering you bring to the LORD must be made without yeast, for you are not to burn any yeast or honey in an offering made to the LORD by fire. **12**You may bring them to the LORD as an offering of the firstfruits, but they are not to be offered on the altar as a pleasing aroma. **13**Season all your grain offerings with salt. Do not leave the salt of the covenant of your God out of your grain offerings; add salt to all your offerings.

14" 'If you bring a grain offering of firstfruits to the LORD, offer crushed heads of new grain roasted in the fire. **15**Put oil and incense on it; it is a grain offering. **16**The priest shall burn the memorial portion of the crushed grain and the oil, together with all the incense, as an offering made to the LORD by fire.

The Fellowship Offering

3 " 'If someone's offering is a fellowship offering,*c* and he offers an animal from the herd, whether male or female, he is to present before the LORD an animal without defect. **2**He is to lay his hand on the head of his offering and slaughter it at the entrance to the Tent of Meeting. Then Aaron's sons the priests shall sprinkle the blood against the altar on all sides. **3**From the fellowship offering he is to bring a sacrifice made to the LORD by fire: all the fat that covers the inner parts or is connected to them, **4**both kidneys with the fat on them near the loins, and the covering of the liver, which he will remove with the kidneys. **5**Then Aaron's sons are to burn it on the altar on top of the burnt offering that is on the burning wood, as an offering made by fire, an aroma pleasing to the LORD.

6" 'If he offers an animal from the flock as a fellowship offering to the LORD, he is to offer a male or female without defect. **7**If he offers a lamb, he is to present it before the LORD. **8**He is to lay his hand on the head of his offering and slaughter it in front of the

---

a16 Or *crop and the feathers*; the meaning of the Hebrew for this word is uncertain.   *b4* Or *and*
c1 Traditionally *peace offering*; also in verses 3, 6 and 9

Tent of Meeting. Then Aaron's sons shall sprinkle its blood against the altar on all sides. [9]From the fellowship offering he is to bring a sacrifice made to the LORD by fire: its fat, the entire fat tail cut off close to the backbone, all the fat that covers the inner parts or is connected to them, [10]both kidneys with the fat on them near the loins, and the covering of the liver, which he will remove with the kidneys. [11]The priest shall burn them on the altar as food, an offering made to the LORD by fire.

[12]"'If his offering is a goat, he is to present it before the LORD. [13]He is to lay his hand on its head and slaughter it in front of the Tent of Meeting. Then Aaron's sons shall sprinkle its blood against the altar on all sides. [14]From what he offers he is to make this offering to the LORD by fire: all the fat that covers the inner parts or is connected to them, [15]both kidneys with the fat on them near the loins, and the covering of the liver, which he will remove with the kidneys. [16]The priest shall burn them on the altar as food, an offering made by fire, a pleasing aroma. All the fat is the LORD's.

[17]"'This is a lasting ordinance for the generations to come, wherever you live: You must not eat any fat or any blood.'"

The Sin Offering

4 The LORD said to Moses, [2]"Say to the Israelites: 'When anyone sins unintentionally and does what is forbidden in any of the LORD's commands—

[3]"'If the anointed priest sins, bringing guilt on the people, he must bring to the LORD a young bull without defect as a sin offering for the sin he has committed. [4]He is to present the bull at the entrance to the Tent of Meeting before the LORD. He is to lay his hand on its head and slaughter it before the LORD. [5]Then the anointed priest shall take some of the bull's blood and carry it into the Tent of Meeting. [6]He is to dip his finger into the blood and sprinkle some of it seven times before the LORD, in front of the curtain of the sanctuary. [7]The priest shall then put some of the blood on the horns of the altar of fragrant incense that is before the LORD in the Tent of Meeting. The rest of the bull's blood he shall pour out at the base of the altar of burnt offering at the entrance to the Tent of Meeting. [8]He shall remove all the fat from the bull of the sin offering—the

fat that covers the inner parts or is connected to them, [9]both kidneys with the fat on them near the loins, and the covering of the liver, which he will remove with the kidneys— [10]just as the fat is removed from the ox[a] sacrificed as a fellowship offering.[b] Then the priest shall burn them on the altar of burnt offering. [11]But the hide of the bull and all its flesh, as well as the head and legs, the inner parts and offal— [12]that is, all the rest of the bull—he must take outside the camp to a place ceremonially clean, where the ashes are thrown, and burn it in a wood fire on the ash heap.

[13]"'If the whole Israelite community sins unintentionally and does what is forbidden in any of the LORD's commands, even though the community is unaware of the matter, they are guilty. [14]When they become aware of the sin they committed, the assembly must bring a young bull as a sin offering and present it before the Tent of Meeting. [15]The elders of the community are to lay their hands on the bull's head before the LORD, and the bull shall be slaughtered before the LORD. [16]Then the anointed priest is to take some of the bull's blood into the Tent of Meeting. [17]He shall dip his finger into the blood and sprinkle it before the LORD seven times in front of the curtain. [18]He is to put some of the blood on the horns of the altar that is before the LORD in the Tent of Meeting. The rest of the blood he shall pour out at the base of the altar of burnt offering at the entrance to the Tent of Meeting. [19]He shall remove all the fat from it and burn it on the altar, [20]and do with this bull just as he did with the bull for the sin offering. In this way the priest will make atonement for them, and they will be forgiven. [21]Then he shall take the bull outside the camp and burn it as he burned the first bull. This is the sin offering for the community.

[22]"'When a leader sins unintentionally and does what is forbidden in any of the commands of the LORD his God, he is guilty. [23]When he is made aware of the sin he committed, he must bring as his offering a male goat without defect. [24]He is to lay his hand on the goat's head and slaughter it at the place where the burnt offering is slaughtered before the LORD. It is a sin offering. [25]Then the priest shall take some of the blood of the sin offering with his finger and put it on the horns of the altar of burnt offer-

---

[a]10 The Hebrew word can include both male and female. 31 and 35   [b]10 Traditionally *peace offering*; also in verses 26,

ing and pour out the rest of the blood at the base of the altar. **26**He shall burn all the fat on the altar as he burned the fat of the fellowship offering. In this way the priest will make atonement for the man's sin, and he will be forgiven.

27" 'If a member of the community sins unintentionally and does what is forbidden in any of the LORD's commands, he is guilty. **28**When he is made aware of the sin he committed, he must bring as his offering for the sin he committed a female goat without defect. **29**He is to lay his hand on the head of the sin offering and slaughter it at the place of the burnt offering. **30**Then the priest is to take some of the blood with his finger and put it on the horns of the altar of burnt offering and pour out the rest of the blood at the base of the altar. **31**He shall remove all the fat, just as the fat is removed from the fellowship offering, and the priest shall burn it on the altar as an aroma pleasing to the LORD. In this way the priest will make atonement for him, and he will be forgiven.

32" 'If he brings a lamb as his sin offering, he is to bring a female without defect. **33**He is to lay his hand on its head and slaughter it for a sin offering at the place where the burnt offering is slaughtered. **34**Then the priest shall take some of the blood of the sin offering with his finger and put it on the horns of the altar of burnt offering and pour out the rest of the blood at the base of the altar. **35**He shall remove all the fat, just as the fat is removed from the lamb of the fellowship offering, and the priest shall burn it on the altar on top of the offerings made to the LORD by fire. In this way the priest will make atonement for him for the sin he has committed, and he will be forgiven.

5 " 'If a person sins because he does not speak up when he hears a public charge to testify regarding something he has seen or learned about, he will be held responsible.

2" 'Or if a person touches anything ceremonially unclean — whether the carcasses of unclean wild animals or of unclean livestock or of unclean creatures that move along the ground — even though he is unaware of it, he has become unclean and is guilty.

3" 'Or if he touches human uncleanness — anything that would make him unclean — even though he is unaware of it, when he learns of it he will be guilty.

4" 'Or if a person thoughtlessly takes an oath to do anything, whether good or evil — in any matter one might carelessly swear about — even though he is unaware of it, in any case when he learns of it he will be guilty.

5" 'When anyone is guilty in any of these ways, he must confess in what way he has sinned **6**and, as a penalty for the sin he has committed, he must bring to the LORD a female lamb or goat from the flock as a sin offering; and the priest shall make atonement for him for his sin.

7" 'If he cannot afford a lamb, he is to bring two doves or two young pigeons to the LORD as a penalty for his sin — one for a sin offering and the other for a burnt offering. **8**He is to bring them to the priest, who shall first offer the one for the sin offering. He is to wring its head from its neck, not severing it completely, **9**and is to sprinkle some of the blood of the sin offering against the side of the altar; the rest of the blood must be drained out at the base of the altar. It is a sin offering. **10**The priest shall then offer the other as a burnt offering in the prescribed way and make atonement for him for the sin he has committed, and he will be forgiven.

11" 'If, however, he cannot afford two doves or two young pigeons, he is to bring as an offering for his sin a tenth of an ephah*a* of fine flour for a sin offering. He must not put oil or incense on it, because it is a sin offering. **12**He is to bring it to the priest, who shall take a handful of it as a memorial portion and burn it on the altar on top of the offerings made to the LORD by fire. It is a sin offering. **13**In this way the priest will make atonement for him for any of these sins he has committed, and he will be forgiven. The rest of the offering will belong to the priest, as in the case of the grain offering.' "

The Guilt Offering

14The LORD said to Moses: **15**"When a person commits a violation and sins unintentionally in regard to any of the LORD's holy things, he is to bring to the LORD as a penalty a ram from the flock, one without defect and of the proper value in silver, according to the sanctuary shekel.*b* It is a guilt offering. **16**He must make restitution for what he has failed to do in regard to the holy things, add a fifth of the value to that and give it all to the priest, who will make atonement for him

---

a11 That is, probably about 2 quarts (about 2 liters)   *b15* That is, about 2/5 ounce (about 11.5 grams) with the ram as a guilt offering, and he will be forgiven.

17"If a person sins and does what is forbidden in any of the LORD's commands, even though he does not know it, he is guilty and will be held responsible. **18**He is to bring to the priest as a guilt offering a ram from the flock, one without defect and of the proper value. In this way the priest will make atonement for him for the wrong he has committed unintentionally, and he will be forgiven. **19**It is a guilt offering; he has been guilty of *a* wrongdoing against the LORD."

6 The LORD said to Moses: **2**"If anyone sins and is unfaithful to the LORD by deceiving his neighbor about something entrusted to him or left in his care or stolen, or if he cheats him, **3**or if he finds lost property and lies about it, or if he swears falsely, or if he commits any such sin that people may do— **4**when he thus sins and becomes guilty, he must return what he has stolen or taken by extortion, or what was entrusted to him, or the lost property he found, **5**or whatever it was he swore falsely about. He must make restitution in full, add a fifth of the value to it and give it all to the owner on the day he presents his guilt offering. **6**And as a penalty he must bring to the priest, that is, to the LORD, his guilt offering, a ram from the flock, one without defect and of the proper value. **7**In this way the priest will make atonement for him before the LORD, and he will be forgiven for any of these things he did that made him guilty."

The Burnt Offering

8The LORD said to Moses: **9**"Give Aaron and his sons this command: 'These are the regulations for the burnt offering: The burnt offering is to remain on the altar hearth throughout the night, till morning, and the fire must be kept burning on the altar. **10**The priest shall then put on his linen clothes, with linen undergarments next to his body, and shall remove the ashes of the burnt offering that the fire has consumed on the altar and place them beside the altar. **11**Then he is to take off these clothes and put on others, and carry the ashes outside the camp to a place that is ceremonially clean. **12**The fire on the altar must be kept burning; it must not go out. Every morning the priest is to add firewood and arrange the burnt offering on the fire and burn the fat of the fel-

lowship offerings*b* on it. **13**The fire must be kept burning on the altar continuously; it must not go out.

The Grain Offering

14" 'These are the regulations for the grain offering: Aaron's sons are to bring it before the LORD, in front of the altar. **15**The priest is to take a handful of fine flour and oil, together with all the incense on the grain offering, and burn the memorial portion on the altar as an aroma pleasing to the LORD. **16**Aaron and his sons shall eat the rest of it, but it is to be eaten without yeast in a holy place; they are to eat it in the courtyard of the Tent of Meeting. **17**It must not be baked with yeast; I have given it as their share of the offerings made to me by fire. Like the sin offering and the guilt offering, it is most holy. **18**Any male descendant of Aaron may eat it. It is his regular share of the offerings made to the LORD by fire for the generations to come. Whatever touches them will become holy.*c*' "

19The LORD also said to Moses, **20**"This is the offering Aaron and his sons are to bring to the LORD on the day he*d* is anointed: a tenth of an ephah*e* of fine flour as a regular grain offering, half of it in the morning and half in the evening. **21**Prepare it with oil on a griddle; bring it well-mixed and present the grain offering broken*f* in pieces as an aroma pleasing to the LORD. **22**The son who is to succeed him as anointed priest shall prepare it. It is the LORD's regular share and is to be burned completely. **23**Every grain offering of a priest shall be burned completely; it must not be eaten."

The Sin Offering

24The LORD said to Moses, **25**"Say to Aaron and his sons: 'These are the regulations for the sin offering: The sin offering is to be slaughtered before the LORD in the place the burnt offering is slaughtered; it is most holy. **26**The priest who offers it shall eat it; it is to be eaten in a holy place, in the courtyard of the Tent of Meeting. **27**Whatever touches any of the flesh will become holy, and if any of the blood is spattered on a garment, you must wash it in a holy place. **28**The clay pot the meat is cooked in must be broken; but if it is cooked in a bronze pot, the pot is to be scoured and rinsed with water. **29**Any male in a priest's family may eat it; it is most

---

a 19 Or *has made full expiation for his*   *b 12* Traditionally *peace offerings*   *c 18* Or *Whoever touches them must be holy*; similarly in verse 27   *d 20* Or *each*   *e 20* That is, probably about 2 quarts (about 2 liters) *f 21* The meaning of the Hebrew for this word is uncertain.

holy. ³⁰But any sin offering whose blood is brought into the Tent of Meeting to make atonement in the Holy Place must not be eaten; it must be burned.

The Guilt Offering

7 " 'These are the regulations for the guilt offering, which is most holy: ²The guilt offering is to be slaughtered in the place where the burnt offering is slaughtered, and its blood is to be sprinkled against the altar on all sides. ³All its fat shall be offered: the fat tail and the fat that covers the inner parts, ⁴both kidneys with the fat on them near the loins, and the covering of the liver, which is to be removed with the kidneys. ⁵The priest shall burn them on the altar as an offering made to the LORD by fire. It is a guilt offering. ⁶Any male in a priest's family may eat it, but it must be eaten in a holy place; it is most holy.

⁷" 'The same law applies to both the sin offering and the guilt offering: They belong to the priest who makes atonement with them. ⁸The priest who offers a burnt offering for anyone may keep its hide for himself. ⁹Every grain offering baked in an oven or cooked in a pan or on a griddle belongs to the priest who offers it, ¹⁰and every grain offering, whether mixed with oil or dry, belongs equally to all the sons of Aaron.

The Fellowship Offering

¹¹" 'These are the regulations for the fellowship offering[a] a person may present to the LORD:

¹²" 'If he offers it as an expression of thankfulness, then along with this thank offering he is to offer cakes of bread made without yeast and mixed with oil, wafers made without yeast and spread with oil, and cakes of fine flour well-kneaded and mixed with oil. ¹³Along with his fellowship offering of thanksgiving he is to present an offering with cakes of bread made with yeast. ¹⁴He is to bring one of each kind as an offering, a contribution to the LORD; it belongs to the priest who sprinkles the blood of the fellowship offerings. ¹⁵The meat of his fellowship offering of thanksgiving must be eaten on the day it is offered; he must leave none of it till morning.

¹⁶" 'If, however, his offering is the result of a vow or is a freewill offering, the sacrifice shall be eaten on the day he offers it, but anything left over may be eaten on the next day. ¹⁷Any meat of the sacrifice left over till the third day must be burned up. ¹⁸If any meat of the fellowship offering is eaten on the third day, it will not be accepted. It will not be credited to the one who offered it, for it is impure; the person who eats any of it will be held responsible.

¹⁹" 'Meat that touches anything ceremonially unclean must not be eaten; it must be burned up. As for other meat, anyone ceremonially clean may eat it. ²⁰But if anyone who is unclean eats any meat of the fellowship offering belonging to the LORD, that person must be cut off from his people. ²¹If anyone touches something unclean — whether human uncleanness or an unclean animal or any unclean, detestable thing — and then eats any of the meat of the fellowship offering belonging to the LORD, that person must be cut off from his people.' "

Eating Fat and Blood Forbidden

²²The LORD said to Moses, ²³"Say to the Israelites: 'Do not eat any of the fat of cattle, sheep or goats. ²⁴The fat of an animal found dead or torn by wild animals may be used for any other purpose, but you must not eat it. ²⁵Anyone who eats the fat of an animal from which an offering by fire may be[b] made to the LORD must be cut off from his people. ²⁶And wherever you live, you must not eat the blood of any bird or animal. ²⁷If anyone eats blood, that person must be cut off from his people.' "

The Priests' Share

²⁸The LORD said to Moses, ²⁹"Say to the Israelites: 'Anyone who brings a fellowship offering to the LORD is to bring part of it as his sacrifice to the LORD. ³⁰With his own hands he is to bring the offering made to the LORD by fire; he is to bring the fat, together with the breast, and wave the breast before the LORD as a wave offering. ³¹The priest shall burn the fat on the altar, but the breast belongs to Aaron and his sons. ³²You are to give the right thigh of your fellowship offerings to the priest as a contribution. ³³The son of Aaron who offers the blood and the fat of the fellowship offering shall have the right thigh as his share. ³⁴From the fellowship offerings of the Israelites, I have taken the breast that is waved and the thigh that is presented and have given them to Aaron the priest and his sons as their regular share from the Israelites.' "

³⁵This is the portion of the offerings made to the LORD by fire that were allotted to Aaron

---

a11 Traditionally *peace offering*; also in verses 13-37   b25 Or *fire is* and his sons on the day they were presented to serve the Lord as priests. **36**On the day they were anointed, the Lord commanded that the Israelites give this to them as their regular share for the generations to come.

37These, then, are the regulations for the burnt offering, the grain offering, the sin offering, the guilt offering, the ordination offering and the fellowship offering, **38**which the Lord gave Moses on Mount Sinai on the day he commanded the Israelites to bring their offerings to the Lord, in the Desert of Sinai.

The Ordination of Aaron and His Sons

8 The Lord said to Moses, **2**"Bring Aaron and his sons, their garments, the anointing oil, the bull for the sin offering, the two rams and the basket containing bread made without yeast, **3**and gather the entire assembly at the entrance to the Tent of Meeting." **4**Moses did as the Lord commanded him, and the assembly gathered at the entrance to the Tent of Meeting.

5Moses said to the assembly, "This is what the Lord has commanded to be done." **6**Then Moses brought Aaron and his sons forward and washed them with water. **7**He put the tunic on Aaron, tied the sash around him, clothed him with the robe and put the ephod on him. He also tied the ephod to him by its skillfully woven waistband; so it was fastened on him. **8**He placed the breastpiece on him and put the Urim and Thummim in the breastpiece. **9**Then he placed the turban on Aaron's head and set the gold plate, the sacred diadem, on the front of it, as the Lord commanded Moses.

10Then Moses took the anointing oil and anointed the tabernacle and everything in it, and so consecrated them. **11**He sprinkled some of the oil on the altar seven times, anointing the altar and all its utensils and the basin with its stand, to consecrate them. **12**He poured some of the anointing oil on Aaron's head and anointed him to consecrate him. **13**Then he brought Aaron's sons forward, put tunics on them, tied sashes around them and put headbands on them, as the Lord commanded Moses.

14He then presented the bull for the sin offering, and Aaron and his sons laid their hands on its head. **15**Moses slaughtered the bull and took some of the blood, and with his finger he put it on all the horns of the altar to purify the altar. He poured out the rest of the blood at the base of the altar. So

he consecrated it to make atonement for it. **16**Moses also took all the fat around the inner parts, the covering of the liver, and both kidneys and their fat, and burned it on the altar. **17**But the bull with its hide and its flesh and its offal he burned up outside the camp, as the Lord commanded Moses.

18He then presented the ram for the burnt offering, and Aaron and his sons laid their hands on its head. **19**Then Moses slaughtered the ram and sprinkled the blood against the altar on all sides. **20**He cut the ram into pieces and burned the head, the pieces and the fat. **21**He washed the inner parts and the legs with water and burned the whole ram on the altar as a burnt offering, a pleasing aroma, an offering made to the Lord by fire, as the Lord commanded Moses.

22He then presented the other ram, the ram for the ordination, and Aaron and his sons laid their hands on its head. **23**Moses slaughtered the ram and took some of its blood and put it on the lobe of Aaron's right ear, on the thumb of his right hand and on the big toe of his right foot. **24**Moses also brought Aaron's sons forward and put some of the blood on the lobes of their right ears, on the thumbs of their right hands and on the big toes of their right feet. Then he sprinkled blood against the altar on all sides. **25**He took the fat, the fat tail, all the fat around the inner parts, the covering of the liver, both kidneys and their fat and the right thigh. **26**Then from the basket of bread made without yeast, which was before the Lord, he took a cake of bread, and one made with oil, and a wafer; he put these on the fat portions and on the right thigh. **27**He put all these in the hands of Aaron and his sons and waved them before the Lord as a wave offering. **28**Then Moses took them from their hands and burned them on the altar on top of the burnt offering as an ordination offering, a pleasing aroma, an offering made to the Lord by fire. **29**He also took the breast—Moses' share of the ordination ram—and waved it before the Lord as a wave offering, as the Lord commanded Moses.

30Then Moses took some of the anointing oil and some of the blood from the altar and sprinkled them on Aaron and his garments and on his sons and their garments. So he consecrated Aaron and his garments and his sons and their garments.

31Moses then said to Aaron and his sons, "Cook the meat at the entrance to the Tent of Meeting and eat it there with the bread from the basket of ordination offerings, as I commanded, saying,[a] 'Aaron and his sons are to eat it.' [32]Then burn up the rest of the meat and the bread. [33]Do not leave the entrance to the Tent of Meeting for seven days, until the days of your ordination are completed, for your ordination will last seven days. [34]What has been done today was commanded by the Lord to make atonement for you. [35]You must stay at the entrance to the Tent of Meeting day and night for seven days and do what the Lord requires, so you will not die; for that is what I have been commanded." [36]So Aaron and his sons did everything the Lord commanded through Moses.

The Priests Begin Their Ministry

9 On the eighth day Moses summoned Aaron and his sons and the elders of Israel. [2]He said to Aaron, "Take a bull calf for your sin offering and a ram for your burnt offering, both without defect, and present them before the Lord. [3]Then say to the Israelites: 'Take a male goat for a sin offering, a calf and a lamb—both a year old and without defect—for a burnt offering, [4]and an ox[b] and a ram for a fellowship offering[c] to sacrifice before the Lord, together with a grain offering mixed with oil. For today the Lord will appear to you.'"

[5]They took the things Moses commanded to the front of the Tent of Meeting, and the entire assembly came near and stood before the Lord. [6]Then Moses said, "This is what the Lord has commanded you to do, so that the glory of the Lord may appear to you."

[7]Moses said to Aaron, "Come to the altar and sacrifice your sin offering and your burnt offering and make atonement for yourself and the people; sacrifice the offering that is for the people and make atonement for them, as the Lord has commanded."

[8]So Aaron came to the altar and slaughtered the calf as a sin offering for himself. [9]His sons brought the blood to him, and he dipped his finger into the blood and put it on the horns of the altar; the rest of the blood he poured out at the base of the altar. [10]On the altar he burned the fat, the kidneys and the covering of the liver from the sin offering, as the Lord commanded Moses; [11]the flesh and the hide he burned up outside the camp.

[12]Then he slaughtered the burnt offering. His sons handed him the blood, and he sprinkled it against the altar on all sides.

[13]They handed him the burnt offering piece by piece, including the head, and he burned them on the altar. [14]He washed the inner parts and the legs and burned them on top of the burnt offering on the altar.

[15]Aaron then brought the offering that was for the people. He took the goat for the people's sin offering and slaughtered it and offered it for a sin offering as he did with the first one.

[16]He brought the burnt offering and offered it in the prescribed way. [17]He also brought the grain offering, took a handful of it and burned it on the altar in addition to the morning's burnt offering.

[18]He slaughtered the ox and the ram as the fellowship offering for the people. His sons handed him the blood, and he sprinkled it against the altar on all sides. [19]But the fat portions of the ox and the ram—the fat tail, the layer of fat, the kidneys and the covering of the liver— [20]these they laid on the breasts, and then Aaron burned the fat on the altar. [21]Aaron waved the breasts and the right thigh before the Lord as a wave offering, as Moses commanded.

[22]Then Aaron lifted his hands toward the people and blessed them. And having sacrificed the sin offering, the burnt offering and the fellowship offering, he stepped down.

[23]Moses and Aaron then went into the Tent of Meeting. When they came out, they blessed the people; and the glory of the Lord appeared to all the people. [24]Fire came out from the presence of the Lord and consumed the burnt offering and the fat portions on the altar. And when all the people saw it, they shouted for joy and fell facedown.

The Death of Nadab and Abihu

10 Aaron's sons Nadab and Abihu took their censers, put fire in them and added incense; and they offered unauthorized fire before the Lord, contrary to his command. [2]So fire came out from the presence of the Lord and consumed them, and they died before the Lord. [3]Moses then said to Aaron, "This is what the Lord spoke of when he said:

> " 'Among those who approach me
>   I will show myself holy;
> in the sight of all the people
>   I will be honored.' "

Aaron remained silent.

---

[a]31 Or I was commanded: [b]4 The Hebrew word can include both male and female; also in verses 18 and 19.   [c]4 Traditionally peace offering; also in verses 18 and 22

⁴Moses summoned Mishael and Elzaphan, sons of Aaron's uncle Uzziel, and said to them, "Come here; carry your cousins outside the camp, away from the front of the sanctuary." ⁵So they came and carried them, still in their tunics, outside the camp, as Moses ordered.

⁶Then Moses said to Aaron and his sons Eleazar and Ithamar, "Do not let your hair become unkempt,ᵃ and do not tear your clothes, or you will die and the LORD will be angry with the whole community. But your relatives, all the house of Israel, may mourn for those the LORD has destroyed by fire. ⁷Do not leave the entrance to the Tent of Meeting or you will die, because the LORD's anointing oil is on you." So they did as Moses said.

⁸Then the LORD said to Aaron, ⁹"You and your sons are not to drink wine or other fermented drink whenever you go into the Tent of Meeting, or you will die. This is a lasting ordinance for the generations to come. ¹⁰You must distinguish between the holy and the common, between the unclean and the clean, ¹¹and you must teach the Israelites all the decrees the LORD has given them through Moses."

¹²Moses said to Aaron and his remaining sons, Eleazar and Ithamar, "Take the grain offering left over from the offerings made to the LORD by fire and eat it prepared without yeast beside the altar, for it is most holy. ¹³Eat it in a holy place, because it is your share and your sons' share of the offerings made to the LORD by fire; for so I have been commanded. ¹⁴But you and your sons and your daughters may eat the breast that was waved and the thigh that was presented. Eat them in a ceremonially clean place; they have been given to you and your children as your share of the Israelites' fellowship offerings.ᵇ ¹⁵The thigh that was presented and the breast that was waved must be brought with the fat portions of the offerings made by fire, to be waved before the LORD as a wave offering. This will be the regular share for you and your children, as the LORD has commanded."

¹⁶When Moses inquired about the goat of the sin offering and found that it had been burned up, he was angry with Eleazar and Ithamar, Aaron's remaining sons, and asked, ¹⁷"Why didn't you eat the sin offering in the sanctuary area? It is most holy; it was given to you to take away the guilt of the community by making atonement for them before the LORD. ¹⁸Since its blood was not taken into the Holy Place, you should have eaten the goat in the sanctuary area, as I commanded."

¹⁹Aaron replied to Moses, "Today they sacrificed their sin offering and their burnt offering before the LORD, but such things as this have happened to me. Would the LORD have been pleased if I had eaten the sin offering today?" ²⁰When Moses heard this, he was satisfied.

Clean and Unclean Food

11 The LORD said to Moses and Aaron, ²"Say to the Israelites: 'Of all the animals that live on land, these are the ones you may eat: ³You may eat any animal that has a split hoof completely divided and that chews the cud.

⁴" 'There are some that only chew the cud or only have a split hoof, but you must not eat them. The camel, though it chews the cud, does not have a split hoof; it is ceremonially unclean for you. ⁵The coney,ᶜ though it chews the cud, does not have a split hoof; it is unclean for you. ⁶The rabbit, though it chews the cud, does not have a split hoof; it is unclean for you. ⁷And the pig, though it has a split hoof completely divided, does not chew the cud; it is unclean for you. ⁸You must not eat their meat or touch their carcasses; they are unclean for you.

⁹" 'Of all the creatures living in the water of the seas and the streams, you may eat any that have fins and scales. ¹⁰But all creatures in the seas or streams that do not have fins and scales—whether among all the swarming things or among all the other living creatures in the water—you are to detest. ¹¹And since you are to detest them, you must not eat their meat and you must detest their carcasses. ¹²Anything living in the water that does not have fins and scales is to be detestable to you.

¹³" 'These are the birds you are to detest and not eat because they are detestable: the eagle, the vulture, the black vulture, ¹⁴the red kite, any kind of black kite, ¹⁵any kind of raven, ¹⁶the horned owl, the screech owl, the gull, any kind of hawk, ¹⁷the little owl, the cormorant, the great owl, ¹⁸the white owl, the desert owl, the osprey, ¹⁹the stork, any kind of heron, the hoopoe and the bat.ᵈ

²⁰" 'All flying insects that walk on all fours

ᵃ6 Or *Do not uncover your heads*   ᵇ14 Traditionally *peace offerings*   ᶜ5 That is, the hyrax or rock badger
ᵈ19 The precise identification of some of the birds, insects and animals in this chapter is uncertain.

are to be detestable to you. ²¹There are, however, some winged creatures that walk on all fours that you may eat: those that have jointed legs for hopping on the ground. ²²Of these you may eat any kind of locust, katydid, cricket or grasshopper. ²³But all other winged creatures that have four legs you are to detest.

²⁴" 'You will make yourselves unclean by these; whoever touches their carcasses will be unclean till evening. ²⁵Whoever picks up one of their carcasses must wash his clothes, and he will be unclean till evening.

²⁶" 'Every animal that has a split hoof not completely divided or that does not chew the cud is unclean for you; whoever touches ₗthe carcass ofↄ any of them will be unclean. ²⁷Of all the animals that walk on all fours, those that walk on their paws are unclean for you; whoever touches their carcasses will be unclean till evening. ²⁸Anyone who picks up their carcasses must wash his clothes, and he will be unclean till evening. They are unclean for you.

²⁹" 'Of the animals that move about on the ground, these are unclean for you: the weasel, the rat, any kind of great lizard, ³⁰the gecko, the monitor lizard, the wall lizard, the skink and the chameleon. ³¹Of all those that move along the ground, these are unclean for you. Whoever touches them when they are dead will be unclean till evening. ³²When one of them dies and falls on something, that article, whatever its use, will be unclean, whether it is made of wood, cloth, hide or sackcloth. Put it in water; it will be unclean till evening, and then it will be clean. ³³If one of them falls into a clay pot, everything in it will be unclean, and you must break the pot. ³⁴Any food that could be eaten but has water on it from such a pot is unclean, and any liquid that could be drunk from it is unclean. ³⁵Anything that one of their carcasses falls on becomes unclean; an oven or cooking pot must be broken up. They are unclean, and you are to regard them as unclean. ³⁶A spring, however, or a cistern for collecting water remains clean, but anyone who touches one of these carcasses is unclean. ³⁷If a carcass falls on any seeds that are to be planted, they remain clean. ³⁸But if water has been put on the seed and a carcass falls on it, it is unclean for you.

³⁹" 'If an animal that you are allowed to eat dies, anyone who touches the carcass will be unclean till evening. ⁴⁰Anyone who eats some of the carcass must wash his clothes, and he will be unclean till evening.

Anyone who picks up the carcass must wash his clothes, and he will be unclean till evening.

⁴¹" 'Every creature that moves about on the ground is detestable; it is not to be eaten. ⁴²You are not to eat any creature that moves about on the ground, whether it moves on its belly or walks on all fours or on many feet; it is detestable. ⁴³Do not defile yourselves by any of these creatures. Do not make yourselves unclean by means of them or be made unclean by them. ⁴⁴I am the LORD your God; consecrate yourselves and be holy, because I am holy. Do not make yourselves unclean by any creature that moves about on the ground. ⁴⁵I am the LORD who brought you up out of Egypt to be your God; therefore be holy, because I am holy.

⁴⁶" 'These are the regulations concerning animals, birds, every living thing that moves in the water and every creature that moves about on the ground. ⁴⁷You must distinguish between the unclean and the clean, between living creatures that may be eaten and those that may not be eaten.' "

Purification After Childbirth

12 The LORD said to Moses, ²"Say to the Israelites: 'A woman who becomes pregnant and gives birth to a son will be ceremonially unclean for seven days, just as she is unclean during her monthly period. ³On the eighth day the boy is to be circumcised. ⁴Then the woman must wait thirty-three days to be purified from her bleeding. She must not touch anything sacred or go to the sanctuary until the days of her purification are over. ⁵If she gives birth to a daughter, for two weeks the woman will be unclean, as during her period. Then she must wait sixty-six days to be purified from her bleeding.

⁶" 'When the days of her purification for a son or daughter are over, she is to bring to the priest at the entrance to the Tent of Meeting a year-old lamb for a burnt offering and a young pigeon or a dove for a sin offering. ⁷He shall offer them before the LORD to make atonement for her, and then she will be ceremonially clean from her flow of blood.

" 'These are the regulations for the woman who gives birth to a boy or a girl. ⁸If she cannot afford a lamb, she is to bring two doves or two young pigeons, one for a burnt offering and the other for a sin offering. In this way the priest will make atonement for her, and she will be clean.' "

Regulations About Infectious Skin Diseases

13 The LORD said to Moses and Aaron, 2"When anyone has a swelling or a rash or a bright spot on his skin that may become an infectious skin disease,[a] he must be brought to Aaron the priest or to one of his sons[b] who is a priest. 3The priest is to examine the sore on his skin, and if the hair in the sore has turned white and the sore appears to be more than skin deep,[c] it is an infectious skin disease. When the priest examines him, he shall pronounce him ceremonially unclean. 4If the spot on his skin is white but does not appear to be more than skin deep and the hair in it has not turned white, the priest is to put the infected person in isolation for seven days. 5On the seventh day the priest is to examine him, and if he sees that the sore is unchanged and has not spread in the skin, he is to keep him in isolation another seven days. 6On the seventh day the priest is to examine him again, and if the sore has faded and has not spread in the skin, the priest shall pronounce him clean; it is only a rash. The man must wash his clothes, and he will be clean. 7But if the rash does spread in his skin after he has shown himself to the priest to be pronounced clean, he must appear before the priest again. 8The priest is to examine him, and if the rash has spread in the skin, he shall pronounce him unclean; it is an infectious disease.

9"When anyone has an infectious skin disease, he must be brought to the priest. 10The priest is to examine him, and if there is a white swelling in the skin that has turned the hair white and if there is raw flesh in the swelling, 11it is a chronic skin disease and the priest shall pronounce him unclean. He is not to put him in isolation, because he is already unclean.

12"If the disease breaks out all over his skin and, so far as the priest can see, it covers all the skin of the infected person from head to foot, 13the priest is to examine him, and if the disease has covered his whole body, he shall pronounce that person clean. Since it has all turned white, he is clean. 14But whenever raw flesh appears on him, he will be unclean. 15When the priest sees the raw flesh, he shall pronounce him unclean. The raw flesh is unclean; he has an infectious disease. 16Should the raw flesh change and turn white, he must go to the priest. 17The priest is to examine him, and if the sores have turned white, the priest shall pronounce the infected person clean; then he will be clean.

18"When someone has a boil on his skin and it heals, 19and in the place where the boil was, a white swelling or reddish-white spot appears, he must present himself to the priest. 20The priest is to examine it, and if it appears to be more than skin deep and the hair in it has turned white, the priest shall pronounce him unclean. It is an infectious skin disease that has broken out where the boil was. 21But if, when the priest examines it, there is no white hair in it and it is not more than skin deep and has faded, then the priest is to put him in isolation for seven days. 22If it is spreading in the skin, the priest shall pronounce him unclean; it is infectious. 23But if the spot is unchanged and has not spread, it is only a scar from the boil, and the priest shall pronounce him clean.

24"When someone has a burn on his skin and a reddish-white or white spot appears in the raw flesh of the burn, 25the priest is to examine the spot, and if the hair in it has turned white, and it appears to be more than skin deep, it is an infectious disease that has broken out in the burn. The priest shall pronounce him unclean; it is an infectious skin disease. 26But if the priest examines it and there is no white hair in the spot and if it is not more than skin deep and has faded, then the priest is to put him in isolation for seven days. 27On the seventh day the priest is to examine him, and if it is spreading in the skin, the priest shall pronounce him unclean; it is an infectious skin disease. 28If, however, the spot is unchanged and has not spread in the skin but has faded, it is a swelling from the burn, and the priest shall pronounce him clean; it is only a scar from the burn.

29"If a man or woman has a sore on the head or on the chin, 30the priest is to examine the sore, and if it appears to be more than skin deep and the hair in it is yellow and thin, the priest shall pronounce that person unclean; it is an itch, an infectious disease of the head or chin. 31But if, when the priest examines this kind of sore, it does not seem to be more than skin deep and there is no black hair in it, then the priest is to put the infected person in isolation for

---

a2 Traditionally *leprosy*; the Hebrew word was used for various diseases affecting the skin—not necessarily leprosy; also elsewhere in this chapter.   b2 Or *descendants*   c3 Or *be lower than the rest of the skin*; also elsewhere in this chapter seven days. **32**On the seventh day the priest is to examine the sore, and if the itch has not spread and there is no yellow hair in it and it does not appear to be more than skin deep, **33**he must be shaved except for the diseased area, and the priest is to keep him in isolation another seven days. **34**On the seventh day the priest is to examine the itch, and if it has not spread in the skin and appears to be no more than skin deep, the priest shall pronounce him clean. He must wash his clothes, and he will be clean. **35**But if the itch does spread in the skin after he is pronounced clean, **36**the priest is to examine him, and if the itch has spread in the skin, the priest does not need to look for yellow hair; the person is unclean. **37**If, however, in his judgment it is unchanged and black hair has grown in it, the itch is healed. He is clean, and the priest shall pronounce him clean.

38"When a man or woman has white spots on the skin, **39**the priest is to examine them, and if the spots are dull white, it is a harmless rash that has broken out on the skin; that person is clean.

40"When a man has lost his hair and is bald, he is clean. **41**If he has lost his hair from the front of his scalp and has a bald forehead, he is clean. **42**But if he has a reddish-white sore on his bald head or forehead, it is an infectious disease breaking out on his head or forehead. **43**The priest is to examine him, and if the swollen sore on his head or forehead is reddish-white like an infectious skin disease, **44**the man is diseased and is unclean. The priest shall pronounce him unclean because of the sore on his head.

45"The person with such an infectious disease must wear torn clothes, let his hair be unkempt,*a* cover the lower part of his face and cry out, 'Unclean! Unclean!' **46**As long as he has the infection he remains unclean. He must live alone; he must live outside the camp.

Regulations About Mildew

47"If any clothing is contaminated with mildew—any woolen or linen clothing, **48**any woven or knitted material of linen or wool, any leather or anything made of leather— **49**and if the contamination in the clothing, or leather, or woven or knitted material, or any leather article, is greenish or reddish, it is a spreading mildew and must be shown

to the priest. **50**The priest is to examine the mildew and isolate the affected article for seven days. **51**On the seventh day he is to examine it, and if the mildew has spread in the clothing, or the woven or knitted material, or the leather, whatever its use, it is a destructive mildew; the article is unclean. **52**He must burn up the clothing, or the woven or knitted material of wool or linen, or any leather article that has the contamination in it, because the mildew is destructive; the article must be burned up.

53"But if, when the priest examines it, the mildew has not spread in the clothing, or the woven or knitted material, or the leather article, **54**he shall order that the contaminated article be washed. Then he is to isolate it for another seven days. **55**After the affected article has been washed, the priest is to examine it, and if the mildew has not changed its appearance, even though it has not spread, it is unclean. Burn it with fire, whether the mildew has affected one side or the other. **56**If, when the priest examines it, the mildew has faded after the article has been washed, he is to tear the contaminated part out of the clothing, or the leather, or the woven or knitted material. **57**But if it reappears in the clothing, or in the woven or knitted material, or in the leather article, it is spreading, and whatever has the mildew must be burned with fire. **58**The clothing, or the woven or knitted material, or any leather article that has been washed and is rid of the mildew, must be washed again, and it will be clean."

59These are the regulations concerning contamination by mildew in woolen or linen clothing, woven or knitted material, or any leather article, for pronouncing them clean or unclean.

Cleansing From Infectious Skin Diseases

14 The LORD said to Moses, **2**"These are the regulations for the diseased person at the time of his ceremonial cleansing, when he is brought to the priest: **3**The priest is to go outside the camp and examine him. If the person has been healed of his infectious skin disease,*b* **4**the priest shall order that two live clean birds and some cedar wood, scarlet yarn and hyssop be brought for the one to be cleansed. **5**Then the priest shall order that one of the birds be killed over fresh water in a clay pot. **6**He is then to take the live bird and dip it, together with the cedar wood, the scarlet yarn and the

---

a45 Or *clothes, uncover his head*   *b3* Traditionally *leprosy*; the Hebrew word was used for various diseases affecting the skin—not necessarily leprosy; also elsewhere in this chapter.

hyssop, into the blood of the bird that was killed over the fresh water. **7**Seven times he shall sprinkle the one to be cleansed of the infectious disease and pronounce him clean. Then he is to release the live bird in the open fields.

8"The person to be cleansed must wash his clothes, shave off all his hair and bathe with water; then he will be ceremonially clean. After this he may come into the camp, but he must stay outside his tent for seven days. **9**On the seventh day he must shave off all his hair; he must shave his head, his beard, his eyebrows and the rest of his hair. He must wash his clothes and bathe himself with water, and he will be clean.

10"On the eighth day he must bring two male lambs and one ewe lamb a year old, each without defect, along with three-tenths of an ephah*a* of fine flour mixed with oil for a grain offering, and one log*b* of oil. **11**The priest who pronounces him clean shall present both the one to be cleansed and his offerings before the LORD at the entrance to the Tent of Meeting.

12"Then the priest is to take one of the male lambs and offer it as a guilt offering, along with the log of oil; he shall wave them before the LORD as a wave offering. **13**He is to slaughter the lamb in the holy place where the sin offering and the burnt offering are slaughtered. Like the sin offering, the guilt offering belongs to the priest; it is most holy. **14**The priest is to take some of the blood of the guilt offering and put it on the lobe of the right ear of the one to be cleansed, on the thumb of his right hand and on the big toe of his right foot. **15**The priest shall then take some of the log of oil, pour it in the palm of his own left hand, **16**dip his right forefinger into the oil in his palm, and with his finger sprinkle some of it before the LORD seven times. **17**The priest is to put some of the oil remaining in his palm on the lobe of the right ear of the one to be cleansed, on the thumb of his right hand and on the big toe of his right foot, on top of the blood of the guilt offering. **18**The rest of the oil in his palm the priest shall put on the head of the one to be cleansed and make atonement for him before the LORD.

19"Then the priest is to sacrifice the sin offering and make atonement for the one to be cleansed from his uncleanness. After that, the priest shall slaughter the burnt offering

20and offer it on the altar, together with the grain offering, and make atonement for him, and he will be clean.

21"If, however, he is poor and cannot afford these, he must take one male lamb as a guilt offering to be waved to make atonement for him, together with a tenth of an ephah*c* of fine flour mixed with oil for a grain offering, a log of oil, **22**and two doves or two young pigeons, which he can afford, one for a sin offering and the other for a burnt offering.

23"On the eighth day he must bring them for his cleansing to the priest at the entrance to the Tent of Meeting, before the LORD. **24**The priest is to take the lamb for the guilt offering, together with the log of oil, and wave them before the LORD as a wave offering. **25**He shall slaughter the lamb for the guilt offering and take some of its blood and put it on the lobe of the right ear of the one to be cleansed, on the thumb of his right hand and on the big toe of his right foot. **26**The priest is to pour some of the oil into the palm of his own left hand, **27**and with his right forefinger sprinkle some of the oil from his palm seven times before the LORD. **28**Some of the oil in his palm he is to put on the same places he put the blood of the guilt offering—on the lobe of the right ear of the one to be cleansed, on the thumb of his right hand and on the big toe of his right foot. **29**The rest of the oil in his palm the priest shall put on the head of the one to be cleansed, to make atonement for him before the LORD. **30**Then he shall sacrifice the doves or the young pigeons, which the person can afford, **31**one*d* as a sin offering and the other as a burnt offering, together with the grain offering. In this way the priest will make atonement before the LORD on behalf of the one to be cleansed."

32These are the regulations for anyone who has an infectious skin disease and who cannot afford the regular offerings for his cleansing.

Cleansing From Mildew

33The LORD said to Moses and Aaron, **34**"When you enter the land of Canaan, which I am giving you as your possession, and I put a spreading mildew in a house in that land, **35**the owner of the house must go and tell the priest, 'I have seen something that looks like mildew in my house.' **36**The

---

*a10 That is, probably about 6 quarts (about 6.5 liters) also in verses 12, 15, 21 and 24   *c21 That is, probably about 2 quarts (about 2 liters)   *b10 That is, probably about 2/3 pint (about 0.3 liter);   *d31 Septuagint and Syriac; Hebrew *31such as the person can afford, one* priest is to order the house to be emptied before he goes in to examine the mildew, so that nothing in the house will be pronounced unclean. After this the priest is to go in and inspect the house. **37**He is to examine the mildew on the walls, and if it has greenish or reddish depressions that appear to be deeper than the surface of the wall, **38**the priest shall go out the doorway of the house and close it up for seven days. **39**On the seventh day the priest shall return to inspect the house. If the mildew has spread on the walls, **40**he is to order that the contaminated stones be torn out and thrown into an unclean place outside the town. **41**He must have all the inside walls of the house scraped and the material that is scraped off dumped into an unclean place outside the town. **42**Then they are to take other stones to replace these and take new clay and plaster the house.

43"If the mildew reappears in the house after the stones have been torn out and the house scraped and plastered, **44**the priest is to go and examine it and, if the mildew has spread in the house, it is a destructive mildew; the house is unclean. **45**It must be torn down — its stones, timbers and all the plaster — and taken out of the town to an unclean place.

46"Anyone who goes into the house while it is closed up will be unclean till evening. **47**Anyone who sleeps or eats in the house must wash his clothes.

48"But if the priest comes to examine it and the mildew has not spread after the house has been plastered, he shall pronounce the house clean, because the mildew is gone. **49**To purify the house he is to take two birds and some cedar wood, scarlet yarn and hyssop. **50**He shall kill one of the birds over fresh water in a clay pot. **51**Then he is to take the cedar wood, the hyssop, the scarlet yarn and the live bird, dip them into the blood of the dead bird and the fresh water, and sprinkle the house seven times. **52**He shall purify the house with the bird's blood, the fresh water, the live bird, the cedar wood, the hyssop and the scarlet yarn. **53**Then he is to release the live bird in the open fields outside the town. In this way he will make atonement for the house, and it will be clean."

54These are the regulations for any infectious skin disease, for an itch, **55**for mildew in clothing or in a house, **56**and for a swelling, a rash or a bright spot, **57**to determine when something is clean or unclean.

These are the regulations for infectious skin diseases and mildew.

Discharges Causing Uncleanness

15 The LORD said to Moses and Aaron, **2**"Speak to the Israelites and say to them: 'When any man has a bodily discharge, the discharge is unclean. **3**Whether it continues flowing from his body or is blocked, it will make him unclean. This is how his discharge will bring about uncleanness:

4" 'Any bed the man with a discharge lies on will be unclean, and anything he sits on will be unclean. **5**Anyone who touches his bed must wash his clothes and bathe with water, and he will be unclean till evening. **6**Whoever sits on anything that the man with a discharge sat on must wash his clothes and bathe with water, and he will be unclean till evening.

7" 'Whoever touches the man who has a discharge must wash his clothes and bathe with water, and he will be unclean till evening.

8" 'If the man with the discharge spits on someone who is clean, that person must wash his clothes and bathe with water, and he will be unclean till evening.

9" 'Everything the man sits on when riding will be unclean, **10**and whoever touches any of the things that were under him will be unclean till evening; whoever picks up those things must wash his clothes and bathe with water, and he will be unclean till evening.

11" 'Anyone the man with a discharge touches without rinsing his hands with water must wash his clothes and bathe with water, and he will be unclean till evening.

12" 'A clay pot that the man touches must be broken, and any wooden article is to be rinsed with water.

13" 'When a man is cleansed from his discharge, he is to count off seven days for his ceremonial cleansing; he must wash his clothes and bathe himself with fresh water, and he will be clean. **14**On the eighth day he must take two doves or two young pigeons and come before the LORD to the entrance to the Tent of Meeting and give them to the priest. **15**The priest is to sacrifice them, the one for a sin offering and the other for a burnt offering. In this way he will make atonement before the LORD for the man because of his discharge.

16" 'When a man has an emission of semen, he must bathe his whole body with water, and he will be unclean till evening. **17**Any clothing or leather that has semen on it must be washed with water, and it will be unclean till evening. **18**When a man lies with a woman and there is an emission of semen, both must bathe with water, and they will be unclean till evening.

19" 'When a woman has her regular flow of blood, the impurity of her monthly period will last seven days, and anyone who touches her will be unclean till evening. **20**" 'Anything she lies on during her period will be unclean, and anything she sits on will be unclean. **21**Whoever touches her bed must wash his clothes and bathe with water, and he will be unclean till evening. **22**Whoever touches anything she sits on must wash his clothes and bathe with water, and he will be unclean till evening. **23**Whether it is the bed or anything she was sitting on, when anyone touches it, he will be unclean till evening.

24" 'If a man lies with her and her monthly flow touches him, he will be unclean for seven days; any bed he lies on will be unclean.

25" 'When a woman has a discharge of blood for many days at a time other than her monthly period or has a discharge that continues beyond her period, she will be unclean as long as she has the discharge, just as in the days of her period. **26**Any bed she lies on while her discharge continues will be unclean, as is her bed during her monthly period, and anything she sits on will be unclean, as during her period. **27**Whoever touches them will be unclean; he must wash his clothes and bathe with water, and he will be unclean till evening.

28" 'When she is cleansed from her discharge, she must count off seven days, and after that she will be ceremonially clean. **29**On the eighth day she must take two doves or two young pigeons and bring them to the priest at the entrance to the Tent of Meeting. **30**The priest is to sacrifice one for a sin offering and the other for a burnt offering. In this way he will make atonement for her before the LORD for the uncleanness of her discharge.

31" 'You must keep the Israelites separate from things that make them unclean, so they will not die in their uncleanness for defiling my dwelling place,*a* which is among them.' "

32These are the regulations for a man with a discharge, for anyone made unclean by an emission of semen, **33**for a woman in her monthly period, for a man or a woman with

a discharge, and for a man who lies with a woman who is ceremonially unclean.

The Day of Atonement

16 The LORD spoke to Moses after the death of the two sons of Aaron who died when they approached the LORD. **2**The LORD said to Moses: "Tell your brother Aaron not to come whenever he chooses into the Most Holy Place behind the curtain in front of the atonement cover on the ark, or else he will die, because I appear in the cloud over the atonement cover.

3"This is how Aaron is to enter the sanctuary area: with a young bull for a sin offering and a ram for a burnt offering. **4**He is to put on the sacred linen tunic, with linen undergarments next to his body; he is to tie the linen sash around him and put on the linen turban. These are sacred garments; so he must bathe himself with water before he puts them on. **5**From the Israelite community he is to take two male goats for a sin offering and a ram for a burnt offering.

6"Aaron is to offer the bull for his own sin offering to make atonement for himself and his household. **7**Then he is to take the two goats and present them before the LORD at the entrance to the Tent of Meeting. **8**He is to cast lots for the two goats — one lot for the LORD and the other for the scapegoat.*b* **9**Aaron shall bring the goat whose lot falls to the LORD and sacrifice it for a sin offering. **10**But the goat chosen by lot as the scapegoat shall be presented alive before the LORD to be used for making atonement by sending it into the desert as a scapegoat.

11"Aaron shall bring the bull for his own sin offering to make atonement for himself and his household, and he is to slaughter the bull for his own sin offering. **12**He is to take a censer full of burning coals from the altar before the LORD and two handfuls of finely ground fragrant incense and take them behind the curtain. **13**He is to put the incense on the fire before the LORD, and the smoke of the incense will conceal the atonement cover above the Testimony, so that he will not die. **14**He is to take some of the bull's blood and with his finger sprinkle it on the front of the atonement cover; then he shall sprinkle some of it with his finger seven times before the atonement cover.

15"He shall then slaughter the goat for the sin offering for the people and take its blood behind the curtain and do with it as he did with the bull's blood: He shall sprinkle it on

---

*a*31 Or *my tabernacle*   *b*8 That is, the goat of removal; Hebrew *azazel*; also in verses 10 and 26 the atonement cover and in front of it. **16**In this way he will make atonement for the Most Holy Place because of the uncleanness and rebellion of the Israelites, whatever their sins have been. He is to do the same for the Tent of Meeting, which is among them in the midst of their uncleanness. **17**No one is to be in the Tent of Meeting from the time Aaron goes in to make atonement in the Most Holy Place until he comes out, having made atonement for himself, his household and the whole community of Israel.

18"Then he shall come out to the altar that is before the Lord and make atonement for it. He shall take some of the bull's blood and some of the goat's blood and put it on all the horns of the altar. **19**He shall sprinkle some of the blood on it with his finger seven times to cleanse it and to consecrate it from the uncleanness of the Israelites.

20"When Aaron has finished making atonement for the Most Holy Place, the Tent of Meeting and the altar, he shall bring forward the live goat. **21**He is to lay both hands on the head of the live goat and confess over it all the wickedness and rebellion of the Israelites — all their sins — and put them on the goat's head. He shall send the goat away into the desert in the care of a man appointed for the task. **22**The goat will carry on itself all their sins to a solitary place; and the man shall release it in the desert.

23"Then Aaron is to go into the Tent of Meeting and take off the linen garments he put on before he entered the Most Holy Place, and he is to leave them there. **24**He shall bathe himself with water in a holy place and put on his regular garments. Then he shall come out and sacrifice the burnt offering for himself and the burnt offering for the people, to make atonement for himself and for the people. **25**He shall also burn the fat of the sin offering on the altar.

26"The man who releases the goat as a scapegoat must wash his clothes and bathe himself with water; afterward he may come into the camp. **27**The bull and the goat for the sin offerings, whose blood was brought into the Most Holy Place to make atonement, must be taken outside the camp; their hides, flesh and offal are to be burned up. **28**The man who burns them must wash his clothes and bathe himself with water; afterward he may come into the camp.

29"This is to be a lasting ordinance for you: On the tenth day of the seventh month you must deny yourselves[a] and not do any work — whether native-born or an alien living among you — **30**because on this day atonement will be made for you, to cleanse you. Then, before the Lord, you will be clean from all your sins. **31**It is a sabbath of rest, and you must deny yourselves; it is a lasting ordinance. **32**The priest who is anointed and ordained to succeed his father as high priest is to make atonement. He is to put on the sacred linen garments **33**and make atonement for the Most Holy Place, for the Tent of Meeting and the altar, and for the priests and all the people of the community.

34"This is to be a lasting ordinance for you: Atonement is to be made once a year for all the sins of the Israelites."

And it was done, as the Lord commanded Moses.

Eating Blood Forbidden

17 The Lord said to Moses, **2**"Speak to Aaron and his sons and to all the Israelites and say to them: 'This is what the Lord has commanded: **3**Any Israelite who sacrifices an ox,[b] a lamb or a goat in the camp or outside of it **4**instead of bringing it to the entrance to the Tent of Meeting to present it as an offering to the Lord in front of the tabernacle of the Lord — that man shall be considered guilty of bloodshed; he has shed blood and must be cut off from his people. **5**This is so the Israelites will bring to the Lord the sacrifices they are now making in the open fields. They must bring them to the priest, that is, to the Lord, at the entrance to the Tent of Meeting and sacrifice them as fellowship offerings.[c] **6**The priest is to sprinkle the blood against the altar of the Lord at the entrance to the Tent of Meeting and burn the fat as an aroma pleasing to the Lord. **7**They must no longer offer any of their sacrifices to the goat idols[d] to whom they prostitute themselves. This is to be a lasting ordinance for them and for the generations to come.'

8"Say to them: 'Any Israelite or any alien living among them who offers a burnt offering or sacrifice **9**and does not bring it to the entrance to the Tent of Meeting to sacrifice it to the Lord — that man must be cut off from his people.

10" 'Any Israelite or any alien living among them who eats any blood — I will set my face against that person who eats blood and will cut him off from his people. **11**For the life of

---

a29 Or *must fast*; also in verse 31   *b3* The Hebrew word can include both male and female.
c5 Traditionally *peace offerings*   *d7* Or *demons*

a creature is in the blood, and I have given it to you to make atonement for yourselves on the altar; it is the blood that makes atonement for one's life. [12]Therefore I say to the Israelites, "None of you may eat blood, nor may an alien living among you eat blood."

[13] 'Any Israelite or any alien living among you who hunts any animal or bird that may be eaten must drain out the blood and cover it with earth, [14]because the life of every creature is its blood. That is why I have said to the Israelites, "You must not eat the blood of any creature, because the life of every creature is its blood; anyone who eats it must be cut off."

[15] 'Anyone, whether native-born or alien, who eats anything found dead or torn by wild animals must wash his clothes and bathe with water, and he will be ceremonially unclean till evening; then he will be clean. [16]But if he does not wash his clothes and bathe himself, he will be held responsible.' "

Unlawful Sexual Relations

18 The LORD said to Moses, [2]"Speak to the Israelites and say to them: 'I am the LORD your God. [3]You must not do as they do in Egypt, where you used to live, and you must not do as they do in the land of Canaan, where I am bringing you. Do not follow their practices. [4]You must obey my laws and be careful to follow my decrees. I am the LORD your God. [5]Keep my decrees and laws, for the man who obeys them will live by them. I am the LORD.

[6] 'No one is to approach any close relative to have sexual relations. I am the LORD.

[7] 'Do not dishonor your father by having sexual relations with your mother. She is your mother; do not have relations with her.

[8] 'Do not have sexual relations with your father's wife; that would dishonor your father.

[9] 'Do not have sexual relations with your sister, either your father's daughter or your mother's daughter, whether she was born in the same home or elsewhere.

[10] 'Do not have sexual relations with your son's daughter or your daughter's daughter; that would dishonor you.

[11] 'Do not have sexual relations with the daughter of your father's wife, born to your father; she is your sister.

[12] 'Do not have sexual relations with your father's sister; she is your father's close relative.

[13] 'Do not have sexual relations with your mother's sister, because she is your mother's close relative.

[14] 'Do not dishonor your father's brother by approaching his wife to have sexual relations; she is your aunt.

[15] 'Do not have sexual relations with your daughter-in-law. She is your son's wife; do not have relations with her.

[16] 'Do not have sexual relations with your brother's wife; that would dishonor your brother.

[17] 'Do not have sexual relations with both a woman and her daughter. Do not have sexual relations with either her son's daughter or her daughter's daughter; they are her close relatives. That is wickedness.

[18] 'Do not take your wife's sister as a rival wife and have sexual relations with her while your wife is living.

[19] 'Do not approach a woman to have sexual relations during the uncleanness of her monthly period.

[20] 'Do not have sexual relations with your neighbor's wife and defile yourself with her.

[21] 'Do not give any of your children to be sacrificed[a] to Molech, for you must not profane the name of your God. I am the LORD.

[22] 'Do not lie with a man as one lies with a woman; that is detestable.

[23] 'Do not have sexual relations with an animal and defile yourself with it. A woman must not present herself to an animal to have sexual relations with it; that is a perversion.

[24] 'Do not defile yourselves in any of these ways, because this is how the nations that I am going to drive out before you became defiled. [25]Even the land was defiled; so I punished it for its sin, and the land vomited out its inhabitants. [26]But you must keep my decrees and my laws. The native-born and the aliens living among you must not do any of these detestable things, [27]for all these things were done by the people who lived in the land before you, and the land became defiled. [28]And if you defile the land, it will vomit you out as it vomited out the nations that were before you.

[29] 'Everyone who does any of these detestable things—such persons must be cut off from their people. [30]Keep my requirements and do not follow any of the detestable customs that were practiced before you came and do not defile yourselves with them. I am the LORD your God.' "

---

a21 Or to be passed through ⌊the fire⌋

Various Laws

19 The LORD said to Moses, [2]"Speak to the entire assembly of Israel and say to them: 'Be holy because I, the LORD your God, am holy.

[3]" 'Each of you must respect his mother and father, and you must observe my Sabbaths. I am the LORD your God.

[4]" 'Do not turn to idols or make gods of cast metal for yourselves. I am the LORD your God.

[5]" 'When you sacrifice a fellowship offering[a] to the LORD, sacrifice it in such a way that it will be accepted on your behalf. [6]It shall be eaten on the day you sacrifice it or on the next day; anything left over until the third day must be burned up. [7]If any of it is eaten on the third day, it is impure and will not be accepted. [8]Whoever eats it will be held responsible because he has desecrated what is holy to the LORD; that person must be cut off from his people.

[9]" 'When you reap the harvest of your land, do not reap to the very edges of your field or gather the gleanings of your harvest. [10]Do not go over your vineyard a second time or pick up the grapes that have fallen. Leave them for the poor and the alien. I am the LORD your God.

[11]" 'Do not steal.

" 'Do not lie.

" 'Do not deceive one another.

[12]" 'Do not swear falsely by my name and so profane the name of your God. I am the LORD.

[13]" 'Do not defraud your neighbor or rob him.

" 'Do not hold back the wages of a hired man overnight.

[14]" 'Do not curse the deaf or put a stumbling block in front of the blind, but fear your God. I am the LORD.

[15]" 'Do not pervert justice; do not show partiality to the poor or favoritism to the great, but judge your neighbor fairly.

[16]" 'Do not go about spreading slander among your people.

" 'Do not do anything that endangers your neighbor's life. I am the LORD.

[17]" 'Do not hate your brother in your heart. Rebuke your neighbor frankly so you will not share in his guilt.

[18]" 'Do not seek revenge or bear a grudge against one of your people, but love your neighbor as yourself. I am the LORD.

[19]" 'Keep my decrees.

" 'Do not mate different kinds of animals.

" 'Do not plant your field with two kinds of seed.

" 'Do not wear clothing woven of two kinds of material.

[20]" 'If a man sleeps with a woman who is a slave girl promised to another man but who has not been ransomed or given her freedom, there must be due punishment. Yet they are not to be put to death, because she had not been freed. [21]The man, however, must bring a ram to the entrance to the Tent of Meeting for a guilt offering to the LORD. [22]With the ram of the guilt offering the priest is to make atonement for him before the LORD for the sin he has committed, and his sin will be forgiven.

[23]" 'When you enter the land and plant any kind of fruit tree, regard its fruit as forbidden.[b] For three years you are to consider it forbidden[b]; it must not be eaten. [24]In the fourth year all its fruit will be holy, an offering of praise to the LORD. [25]But in the fifth year you may eat its fruit. In this way your harvest will be increased. I am the LORD your God.

[26]" 'Do not eat any meat with the blood still in it.

" 'Do not practice divination or sorcery.

[27]" 'Do not cut the hair at the sides of your head or clip off the edges of your beard.

[28]" 'Do not cut your bodies for the dead or put tattoo marks on yourselves. I am the LORD.

[29]" 'Do not degrade your daughter by making her a prostitute, or the land will turn to prostitution and be filled with wickedness.

[30]" 'Observe my Sabbaths and have reverence for my sanctuary. I am the LORD.

[31]" 'Do not turn to mediums or seek out spiritists, for you will be defiled by them. I am the LORD your God.

[32]" 'Rise in the presence of the aged, show respect for the elderly and revere your God. I am the LORD.

[33]" 'When an alien lives with you in your land, do not mistreat him. [34]The alien living with you must be treated as one of your native-born. Love him as yourself, for you were aliens in Egypt. I am the LORD your God.

[35]" 'Do not use dishonest standards when measuring length, weight or quantity. [36]Use honest scales and honest weights, an honest

---

a5 Traditionally *peace offering*   *b23* Hebrew *uncircumcised*

WHEN PARENTS NEED YOU

●●●

Sally's parents divorced a few months ago. Since then, the fifteen-year-old, soon-to-be sophomore has been through the wringer.

Her mom cries all the time and seems barely able to function. Her dad keeps calling and asking Sally silly questions like, "Sweetie, do you still love me?" and "Honey, can you come show me how to iron a shirt?"

Sally feels pulled in two directions. How strange! Her parents are suddenly like two helpless little kids!

Look It Up
●●●●

Believe it or not, moms and dads need their teenage children. Not just parents with shaky marriages, but even those in strong relationships.

Can you really make a difference and be a help? Absolutely!

You can pray. "Pray in the Spirit on all occasions with all kinds of prayers and requests. With this in mind, be alert and always keep on praying for all the saints" (Ephesians 6:18).

You can listen. "My dear brothers, take note of this: Everyone should be quick to listen, slow to speak and slow to become angry" (James 1:19).

You can help. "Carry each other's burdens, and in this way you will fulfill the law of Christ" (Galatians 6:2).

Think It Through
●●●●

Are your parents facing any of the following:
• Unexpected pressures at work?
• A career change or even the loss of a job?
• Health problems?
• The illness or loss of their own parents?
• Added responsibilities at church or around the house?
• Depression or other emotional difficulties?
If so, you can step into their lives and assist in a major way.

Work It Out
●●●●

Here are some ideas for those times when your parents need you:
1. Do a task your dad hates.
2. Run an errand for your mom.
3. Volunteer to clear the table and do the dishes.
4. Offer to fix dinner.
5. Vacuum the house.
6. Wash the car.
7. Say, "I love you."
8. Give a hug and/or a kiss.
9. Write an encouraging note and leave it under your mom or dad's pillow.
10. Do the laundry.

Nail It Down
●●●●

Consider Leviticus 19:3.

Turn to pages 62, 680 and 1384 for other readings on parents.
Turn to page 124 for Wednesday's reading.

Topic
●●●●
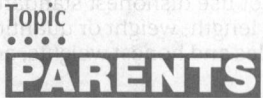
PARENTS

ephah*a* and an honest hin.*b* I am the Lord your God, who brought you out of Egypt.

37" 'Keep all my decrees and all my laws and follow them. I am the Lord.' "

Punishments for Sin

20 The Lord said to Moses, **2**"Say to the Israelites: 'Any Israelite or any alien living in Israel who gives*c* any of his children to Molech must be put to death. The people of the community are to stone him. **3**I will set my face against that man and I will cut him off from his people; for by giving his children to Molech, he has defiled my sanctuary and profaned my holy name. **4**If the people of the community close their eyes when that man gives one of his children to Molech and they fail to put him to death, **5**I will set my face against that man and his family and will cut off from their people both him and all who follow him in prostituting themselves to Molech.

6" 'I will set my face against the person who turns to mediums and spiritists to prostitute himself by following them, and I will cut him off from his people.

7" 'Consecrate yourselves and be holy, because I am the Lord your God. **8**Keep my decrees and follow them. I am the Lord, who makes you holy.*d*

9" 'If anyone curses his father or mother, he must be put to death. He has cursed his father or his mother, and his blood will be on his own head.

10" 'If a man commits adultery with another man's wife — with the wife of his neighbor — both the adulterer and the adulteress must be put to death.

11" 'If a man sleeps with his father's wife, he has dishonored his father. Both the man and the woman must be put to death; their blood will be on their own heads.

12" 'If a man sleeps with his daughter-in-law, both of them must be put to death. What they have done is a perversion; their blood will be on their own heads.

13" 'If a man lies with a man as one lies with a woman, both of them have done what is detestable. They must be put to death; their blood will be on their own heads.

14" 'If a man marries both a woman and her mother, it is wicked. Both he and they must be burned in the fire, so that no wickedness will be among you.

15" 'If a man has sexual relations with an animal, he must be put to death, and you must kill the animal.

16" 'If a woman approaches an animal to have sexual relations with it, kill both the woman and the animal. They must be put to death; their blood will be on their own heads.

17" 'If a man marries his sister, the daughter of either his father or his mother, and they have sexual relations, it is a disgrace. They must be cut off before the eyes of their people. He has dishonored his sister and will be held responsible.

18" 'If a man lies with a woman during her monthly period and has sexual relations with her, he has exposed the source of her flow, and she has also uncovered it. Both of them must be cut off from their people.

19" 'Do not have sexual relations with the sister of either your mother or your father, for that would dishonor a close relative; both of you would be held responsible.

20" 'If a man sleeps with his aunt, he has dishonored his uncle. They will be held responsible; they will die childless.

21" 'If a man marries his brother's wife, it is an act of impurity; he has dishonored his brother. They will be childless.

22" 'Keep all my decrees and laws and follow them, so that the land where I am bringing you to live may not vomit you out. **23**You must not live according to the customs of the nations I am going to drive out before you. Because they did all these things, I abhorred them. **24**But I said to you, "You will possess their land; I will give it to you as an inheritance, a land flowing with milk and honey." I am the Lord your God, who has set you apart from the nations.

25" 'You must therefore make a distinction between clean and unclean animals and between unclean and clean birds. Do not defile yourselves by any animal or bird or anything that moves along the ground — those which I have set apart as unclean for you. **26**You are to be holy to me*e* because I, the Lord, am holy, and I have set you apart from the nations to be my own.

27" 'A man or woman who is a medium or spiritist among you must be put to death. You are to stone them; their blood will be on their own heads.' "

Rules for Priests

21 The Lord said to Moses, "Speak to the priests, the sons of Aaron, and

---

a36 An ephah was a dry measure.   *b36* A hin was a liquid measure.   *c2* Or *sacrifices*; also in verses 3 and 4   *d8* Or *who sanctifies you*; or *who sets you apart as holy*   *e26* Or *be my holy ones*

PURITY IN A POLLUTED WORLD

Johnny and Angie just ended their relationship. After a year together, their break-up is sad, but not nearly as difficult as it would be if the Central High juniors had been sexually involved.

See, that was a commitment they made from the very start—no messing around! And because they worked hard to keep their relationship pure, they're able to be friends.

Look It Up

How can you be pure in a polluted world?
1. Fill your mind with pure thoughts (Philippians 4:8), not media garbage.
2. Find pure friends who can encourage you to walk with God (1 Corinthians 5:11; 15:33).
3. Reject the philosophy that says, "Live for the moment!" Remember that today's pleasure very often leads to tomorrow's pain. "Do not be deceived: God cannot be mocked. A man reaps what he sows" (Galatians 6:7).

Think It Through

Which of the following items would encourage sexual purity? Which activities might be dangerous?
• time alone
• praying together
• suggestive clothing
• unplanned dates
• watching sexy videos
• setting standards
• being accountable to someone

Work It Out

Come up with a good response for each of the following stupid lines (we've given you a hint in each case):
"Real men are sexually active." (So is my real dog.)
"If you loved me, you'd let me." (If you loved me, you wouldn't ask.)
"But I want to." (Well, I don't.)
"Everybody's doing it." (Not true. I'm somebody, and I'm not doing it.)
"Have you ever done it?" (Have you ever made the wonderful discovery of knowing Jesus Christ?)
"Don't you love me?" (Yeah, but I love God more.)
"I won't get you pregnant." (That's right, because you're not going to touch me.)
"If you won't let me, I'll find someone who will." (It was nice knowing you.)
"But you owe me!" (Okay, I'll get you a key chain or something.)

Nail It Down

Read God's response to impure sexual acts in Leviticus 20:10–21.

Turn to pages 654, 705 and 1237 for other readings on sex.
Turn to page 146 for Thursday's reading.

Topic

SEX

say to them: 'A priest must not make himself ceremonially unclean for any of his people who die, **2**except for a close relative, such as his mother or father, his son or daughter, his brother, **3**or an unmarried sister who is dependent on him since she has no husband — for her he may make himself unclean. **4**He must not make himself unclean for people related to him by marriage,*a* and so defile himself.

5" 'Priests must not shave their heads or shave off the edges of their beards or cut their bodies. **6**They must be holy to their God and must not profane the name of their God. Because they present the offerings made to the Lord by fire, the food of their God, they are to be holy.

7" 'They must not marry women defiled by prostitution or divorced from their husbands, because priests are holy to their God. **8**Regard them as holy, because they offer up the food of your God. Consider them holy, because I the Lord am holy — I who make you holy.*b*

9" 'If a priest's daughter defiles herself by becoming a prostitute, she disgraces her father; she must be burned in the fire.

10" 'The high priest, the one among his brothers who has had the anointing oil poured on his head and who has been ordained to wear the priestly garments, must not let his hair become unkempt*c* or tear his clothes. **11**He must not enter a place where there is a dead body. He must not make himself unclean, even for his father or mother, **12**nor leave the sanctuary of his God or desecrate it, because he has been dedicated by the anointing oil of his God. I am the Lord.

13" 'The woman he marries must be a virgin. **14**He must not marry a widow, a divorced woman, or a woman defiled by prostitution, but only a virgin from his own people, **15**so he will not defile his offspring among his people. I am the Lord, who makes him holy.*d*' "

16The Lord said to Moses, **17**"Say to Aaron: 'For the generations to come none of your descendants who has a defect may come near to offer the food of his God. **18**No man who has any defect may come near: no man who is blind or lame, disfigured or deformed; **19**no man with a crippled foot or

hand, **20**or who is hunchbacked or dwarfed, or who has any eye defect, or who has festering or running sores or damaged testicles. **21**No descendant of Aaron the priest who has any defect is to come near to present the offerings made to the Lord by fire. He has a defect; he must not come near to offer the food of his God. **22**He may eat the most holy food of his God, as well as the holy food; **23**yet because of his defect, he must not go near the curtain or approach the altar, and so desecrate my sanctuary. I am the Lord, who makes them holy.*e*' "

24So Moses told this to Aaron and his sons and to all the Israelites.

22 The Lord said to Moses, **2**"Tell Aaron and his sons to treat with respect the sacred offerings the Israelites consecrate to me, so they will not profane my holy name. I am the Lord.

3"Say to them: 'For the generations to come, if any of your descendants is ceremonially unclean and yet comes near the sacred offerings that the Israelites consecrate to the Lord, that person must be cut off from my presence. I am the Lord.

4" 'If a descendant of Aaron has an infectious skin disease*f* or a bodily discharge, he may not eat the sacred offerings until he is cleansed. He will also be unclean if he touches something defiled by a corpse or by anyone who has an emission of semen, **5**or if he touches any crawling thing that makes him unclean, or any person who makes him unclean, whatever the uncleanness may be. **6**The one who touches any such thing will be unclean till evening. He must not eat any of the sacred offerings unless he has bathed himself with water. **7**When the sun goes down, he will be clean, and after that he may eat the sacred offerings, for they are his food. **8**He must not eat anything found dead or torn by wild animals, and so become unclean through it. I am the Lord.

9" 'The priests are to keep my requirements so that they do not become guilty and die for treating them with contempt. I am the Lord, who makes them holy.*g*

10" 'No one outside a priest's family may eat the sacred offering, nor may the guest of a priest or his hired worker eat it. **11**But if a priest buys a slave with money, or if a slave is born in his household, that slave may eat

---

a4 Or *unclean as a leader among his people*   *b8* Or *who sanctify you;* or *who set you apart as holy*   *c10* Or *not uncover his head*   *d15* Or *who sanctifies him;* or *who sets him apart as holy*   *e23* Or *who sanctifies them;* or *who sets them apart as holy*   *f4* Traditionally *leprosy;* the Hebrew word was used for various diseases affecting the skin — not necessarily leprosy.   *g9* Or *who sanctifies them;* or *who sets them apart as holy;* also in verse 16 his food. **12**If a priest's daughter marries anyone other than a priest, she may not eat any of the sacred contributions. **13**But if a priest's daughter becomes a widow or is divorced, yet has no children, and she returns to live in her father's house as in her youth, she may eat of her father's food. No unauthorized person, however, may eat any of it.

14" 'If anyone eats a sacred offering by mistake, he must make restitution to the priest for the offering and add a fifth of the value to it. **15**The priests must not desecrate the sacred offerings the Israelites present to the LORD **16**by allowing them to eat the sacred offerings and so bring upon them guilt requiring payment. I am the LORD, who makes them holy.' "

Unacceptable Sacrifices

17The LORD said to Moses, **18**"Speak to Aaron and his sons and to all the Israelites and say to them: 'If any of you — either an Israelite or an alien living in Israel — presents a gift for a burnt offering to the LORD, either to fulfill a vow or as a freewill offering, **19**you must present a male without defect from the cattle, sheep or goats in order that it may be accepted on your behalf. **20**Do not bring anything with a defect, because it will not be accepted on your behalf. **21**When anyone brings from the herd or flock a fellowship offering*a* to the LORD to fulfill a special vow or as a freewill offering, it must be without defect or blemish to be acceptable. **22**Do not offer to the LORD the blind, the injured or the maimed, or anything with warts or festering or running sores. Do not place any of these on the altar as an offering made to the LORD by fire. **23**You may, however, present as a freewill offering an ox*b* or a sheep that is deformed or stunted, but it will not be accepted in fulfillment of a vow. **24**You must not offer to the LORD an animal whose testicles are bruised, crushed, torn or cut. You must not do this in your own land, **25**and you must not accept such animals from the hand of a foreigner and offer them as the food of your God. They will not be accepted on your behalf, because they are deformed and have defects.' "

26The LORD said to Moses, **27**"When a calf, a lamb or a goat is born, it is to remain with its mother for seven days. From the eighth day on, it will be acceptable as an offering made to the LORD by fire. **28**Do not slaughter a cow or a sheep and its young on the same day.

29"When you sacrifice a thank offering to the LORD, sacrifice it in such a way that it will be accepted on your behalf. **30**It must be eaten that same day; leave none of it till morning. I am the LORD.

31"Keep my commands and follow them. I am the LORD. **32**Do not profane my holy name. I must be acknowledged as holy by the Israelites. I am the LORD, who makes*c* you holy*d* **33**and who brought you out of Egypt to be your God. I am the LORD."

23 The LORD said to Moses, **2**"Speak to the Israelites and say to them: 'These are my appointed feasts, the appointed feasts of the LORD, which you are to proclaim as sacred assemblies.

The Sabbath

3" 'There are six days when you may work, but the seventh day is a Sabbath of rest, a day of sacred assembly. You are not to do any work; wherever you live, it is a Sabbath to the LORD.

The Passover and Unleavened Bread

4" 'These are the LORD's appointed feasts, the sacred assemblies you are to proclaim at their appointed times: **5**The LORD's Passover begins at twilight on the fourteenth day of the first month. **6**On the fifteenth day of that month the LORD's Feast of Unleavened Bread begins; for seven days you must eat bread made without yeast. **7**On the first day hold a sacred assembly and do no regular work. **8**For seven days present an offering made to the LORD by fire. And on the seventh day hold a sacred assembly and do no regular work.' "

Firstfruits

9The LORD said to Moses, **10**"Speak to the Israelites and say to them: 'When you enter the land I am going to give you and you reap its harvest, bring to the priest a sheaf of the first grain you harvest. **11**He is to wave the sheaf before the LORD so it will be accepted on your behalf; the priest is to wave it on the day after the Sabbath. **12**On the day you wave the sheaf, you must sacrifice as a burnt offering to the LORD a lamb a year old without defect, **13**together with its grain offering of two-tenths of an ephah*e* of fine

---

a21 Traditionally *peace offering*   *b23* The Hebrew word can include both male and female.   *c32* Or *made*
d32 Or *who sanctifies you*; or *who sets you apart as holy*   *e13* That is, probably about 4 quarts (about 4.5 liters); also in verse 17

flour mixed with oil—an offering made to the Lord by fire, a pleasing aroma—and its drink offering of a quarter of a hin[a] of wine. [14]You must not eat any bread, or roasted or new grain, until the very day you bring this offering to your God. This is to be a lasting ordinance for the generations to come, wherever you live.

Feast of Weeks

[15]" 'From the day after the Sabbath, the day you brought the sheaf of the wave offering, count off seven full weeks. [16]Count off fifty days up to the day after the seventh Sabbath, and then present an offering of new grain to the Lord. [17]From wherever you live, bring two loaves made of two-tenths of an ephah of fine flour, baked with yeast, as a wave offering of firstfruits to the Lord. [18]Present with this bread seven male lambs, each a year old and without defect, one young bull and two rams. They will be a burnt offering to the Lord, together with their grain offerings and drink offerings—an offering made by fire, an aroma pleasing to the Lord. [19]Then sacrifice one male goat for a sin offering and two lambs, each a year old, for a fellowship offering.[b] [20]The priest is to wave the two lambs before the Lord as a wave offering, together with the bread of the firstfruits. They are a sacred offering to the Lord for the priest. [21]On that same day you are to proclaim a sacred assembly and do no regular work. This is to be a lasting ordinance for the generations to come, wherever you live.

[22]" 'When you reap the harvest of your land, do not reap to the very edges of your field or gather the gleanings of your harvest. Leave them for the poor and the alien. I am the Lord your God.' "

Feast of Trumpets

[23]The Lord said to Moses, [24]"Say to the Israelites: 'On the first day of the seventh month you are to have a day of rest, a sacred assembly commemorated with trumpet blasts. [25]Do no regular work, but present an offering made to the Lord by fire.' "

Day of Atonement

[26]The Lord said to Moses, [27]"The tenth day of this seventh month is the Day of Atonement. Hold a sacred assembly and deny yourselves,[c] and present an offering made to the Lord by fire. [28]Do no work on that day, because it is the Day of Atonement, when atonement is made for you before the Lord your God. [29]Anyone who does not deny himself on that day must be cut off from his people. [30]I will destroy from among his people anyone who does any work on that day. [31]You shall do no work at all. This is to be a lasting ordinance for the generations to come, wherever you live. [32]It is a sabbath of rest for you, and you must deny yourselves. From the evening of the ninth day of the month until the following evening you are to observe your sabbath."

Feast of Tabernacles

[33]The Lord said to Moses, [34]"Say to the Israelites: 'On the fifteenth day of the seventh month the Lord's Feast of Tabernacles begins, and it lasts for seven days. [35]The first day is a sacred assembly; do no regular work. [36]For seven days present offerings made to the Lord by fire, and on the eighth day hold a sacred assembly and present an offering made to the Lord by fire. It is the closing assembly; do no regular work.

[37](" 'These are the Lord's appointed feasts, which you are to proclaim as sacred assemblies for bringing offerings made to the Lord by fire—the burnt offerings and grain offerings, sacrifices and drink offerings required for each day. [38]These offerings are in addition to those for the Lord's Sabbaths and[d] in addition to your gifts and whatever you have vowed and all the freewill offerings you give to the Lord.)

[39]" 'So beginning with the fifteenth day of the seventh month, after you have gathered the crops of the land, celebrate the festival to the Lord for seven days; the first day is a day of rest, and the eighth day also is a day of rest. [40]On the first day you are to take choice fruit from the trees, and palm fronds, leafy branches and poplars, and rejoice before the Lord your God for seven days. [41]Celebrate this as a festival to the Lord for seven days each year. This is to be a lasting ordinance for the generations to come; celebrate it in the seventh month. [42]Live in booths for seven days: All native-born Israelites are to live in booths [43]so your descendants will know that I had the Israelites live in booths when I brought them out of Egypt. I am the Lord your God.' "

[44]So Moses announced to the Israelites the appointed feasts of the Lord.

---

[a]13 That is, probably about 1 quart (about 1 liter)   [b]19 Traditionally *peace offering*   [c]27 Or *and fast*; also in verses 29 and 32   [d]38 Or *These feasts are in addition to the Lord's Sabbaths, and these offerings are*

Oil and Bread Set Before the LORD

24 The LORD said to Moses, [2]"Command the Israelites to bring you clear oil of pressed olives for the light so that the lamps may be kept burning continually. [3]Outside the curtain of the Testimony in the Tent of Meeting, Aaron is to tend the lamps before the LORD from evening till morning, continually. This is to be a lasting ordinance for the generations to come. [4]The lamps on the pure gold lampstand before the LORD must be tended continually.

[5]"Take fine flour and bake twelve loaves of bread, using two-tenths of an ephah[a] for each loaf. [6]Set them in two rows, six in each row, on the table of pure gold before the LORD. [7]Along each row put some pure incense as a memorial portion to represent the bread and to be an offering made to the LORD by fire. [8]This bread is to be set out before the LORD regularly, Sabbath after Sabbath, on behalf of the Israelites, as a lasting covenant. [9]It belongs to Aaron and his sons, who are to eat it in a holy place, because it is a most holy part of their regular share of the offerings made to the LORD by fire."

A Blasphemer Stoned

[10]Now the son of an Israelite mother and an Egyptian father went out among the Israelites, and a fight broke out in the camp between him and an Israelite. [11]The son of the Israelite woman blasphemed the Name with a curse; so they brought him to Moses. (His mother's name was Shelomith, the daughter of Dibri the Danite.) [12]They put him in custody until the will of the LORD should be made clear to them.

[13]Then the LORD said to Moses: [14]"Take the blasphemer outside the camp. All those who heard him are to lay their hands on his head, and the entire assembly is to stone him. [15]Say to the Israelites: 'If anyone curses his God, he will be held responsible; [16]anyone who blasphemes the name of the LORD must be put to death. The entire assembly must stone him. Whether an alien or native-born, when he blasphemes the Name, he must be put to death.

[17]"'If anyone takes the life of a human being, he must be put to death. [18]Anyone who takes the life of someone's animal must make restitution—life for life. [19]If anyone injures his neighbor, whatever he has done must be done to him: [20]fracture for fracture, eye for eye, tooth for tooth. As he has in-

jured the other, so he is to be injured. [21]Whoever kills an animal must make restitution, but whoever kills a man must be put to death. [22]You are to have the same law for the alien and the native-born. I am the LORD your God.'"

[23]Then Moses spoke to the Israelites, and they took the blasphemer outside the camp and stoned him. The Israelites did as the LORD commanded Moses.

The Sabbath Year

25 The LORD said to Moses on Mount Sinai, [2]"Speak to the Israelites and say to them: 'When you enter the land I am going to give you, the land itself must observe a sabbath to the LORD. [3]For six years sow your fields, and for six years prune your vineyards and gather their crops. [4]But in the seventh year the land is to have a sabbath of rest, a sabbath to the LORD. Do not sow your fields or prune your vineyards. [5]Do not reap what grows of itself or harvest the grapes of your untended vines. The land is to have a year of rest. [6]Whatever the land yields during the sabbath year will be food for you—for yourself, your manservant and maidservant, and the hired worker and temporary resident who live among you, [7]as well as for your livestock and the wild animals in your land. Whatever the land produces may be eaten.

The Year of Jubilee

[8]"'Count off seven sabbaths of years—seven times seven years—so that the seven sabbaths of years amount to a period of forty-nine years. [9]Then have the trumpet sounded everywhere on the tenth day of the seventh month; on the Day of Atonement sound the trumpet throughout your land. [10]Consecrate the fiftieth year and proclaim liberty throughout the land to all its inhabitants. It shall be a jubilee for you; each one of you is to return to his family property and each to his own clan. [11]The fiftieth year shall be a jubilee for you; do not sow and do not reap what grows of itself or harvest the untended vines. [12]For it is a jubilee and is to be holy for you; eat only what is taken directly from the fields.

[13]"'In this Year of Jubilee everyone is to return to his own property.

[14]"'If you sell land to one of your countrymen or buy any from him, do not take advantage of each other. [15]You are to buy from your countryman on the basis of the num-

---

[a]5 That is, probably about 4 quarts (about 4.5 liters)

ber of years since the Jubilee. And he is to sell to you on the basis of the number of years left for harvesting crops. ¹⁶When the years are many, you are to increase the price, and when the years are few, you are to decrease the price, because what he is really selling you is the number of crops. ¹⁷Do not take advantage of each other, but fear your God. I am the LORD your God.

¹⁸" 'Follow my decrees and be careful to obey my laws, and you will live safely in the land. ¹⁹Then the land will yield its fruit, and you will eat your fill and live there in safety. ²⁰You may ask, "What will we eat in the seventh year if we do not plant or harvest our crops?" ²¹I will send you such a blessing in the sixth year that the land will yield enough for three years. ²²While you plant during the eighth year, you will eat from the old crop and will continue to eat from it until the harvest of the ninth year comes in.

²³" 'The land must not be sold permanently, because the land is mine and you are but aliens and my tenants. ²⁴Throughout the country that you hold as a possession, you must provide for the redemption of the land.

²⁵" 'If one of your countrymen becomes poor and sells some of his property, his nearest relative is to come and redeem what his countryman has sold. ²⁶If, however, a man has no one to redeem it for him but he himself prospers and acquires sufficient means to redeem it, ²⁷he is to determine the value for the years since he sold it and refund the balance to the man to whom he sold it; he can then go back to his own property. ²⁸But if he does not acquire the means to repay him, what he sold will remain in the possession of the buyer until the Year of Jubilee. It will be returned in the Jubilee, and he can then go back to his property.

²⁹" 'If a man sells a house in a walled city, he retains the right of redemption a full year after its sale. During that time he may redeem it. ³⁰If it is not redeemed before a full year has passed, the house in the walled city shall belong permanently to the buyer and his descendants. It is not to be returned in the Jubilee. ³¹But houses in villages without walls around them are to be considered as open country. They can be redeemed, and they are to be returned in the Jubilee.

³²" 'The Levites always have the right to redeem their houses in the Levitical towns, which they possess. ³³So the property of the Levites is redeemable — that is, a house sold in any town they hold — and is to be re-

turned in the Jubilee, because the houses in the towns of the Levites are their property among the Israelites. ³⁴But the pastureland belonging to their towns must not be sold; it is their permanent possession.

³⁵" 'If one of your countrymen becomes poor and is unable to support himself among you, help him as you would an alien or a temporary resident, so he can continue to live among you. ³⁶Do not take interest of any kind*a* from him, but fear your God, so that your countryman may continue to live among you. ³⁷You must not lend him money at interest or sell him food at a profit. ³⁸I am the LORD your God, who brought you out of Egypt to give you the land of Canaan and to be your God.

³⁹" 'If one of your countrymen becomes poor among you and sells himself to you, do not make him work as a slave. ⁴⁰He is to be treated as a hired worker or a temporary resident among you; he is to work for you until the Year of Jubilee. ⁴¹Then he and his children are to be released, and he will go back to his own clan and to the property of his forefathers. ⁴²Because the Israelites are my servants, whom I brought out of Egypt, they must not be sold as slaves. ⁴³Do not rule over them ruthlessly, but fear your God.

⁴⁴" 'Your male and female slaves are to come from the nations around you; from them you may buy slaves. ⁴⁵You may also buy some of the temporary residents living among you and members of their clans born in your country, and they will become your property. ⁴⁶You can will them to your children as inherited property and can make them slaves for life, but you must not rule over your fellow Israelites ruthlessly.

⁴⁷" 'If an alien or a temporary resident among you becomes rich and one of your countrymen becomes poor and sells himself to the alien living among you or to a member of the alien's clan, ⁴⁸he retains the right of redemption after he has sold himself. One of his relatives may redeem him: ⁴⁹An uncle or a cousin or any blood relative in his clan may redeem him. Or if he prospers, he may redeem himself. ⁵⁰He and his buyer are to count the time from the year he sold himself up to the Year of Jubilee. The price for his release is to be based on the rate paid to a hired man for that number of years. ⁵¹If many years remain, he must pay for his redemption a larger share of the price paid for him. ⁵²If only a few years remain until the Year of Jubilee, he is to compute

---

a36 Or take excessive interest; similarly in verse 37

that and pay for his redemption accordingly. ⁵³He is to be treated as a man hired from year to year; you must see to it that his owner does not rule over him ruthlessly.

⁵⁴" 'Even if he is not redeemed in any of these ways, he and his children are to be released in the Year of Jubilee, ⁵⁵for the Israelites belong to me as servants. They are my servants, whom I brought out of Egypt. I am the LORD your God.

Reward for Obedience

26 " 'Do not make idols or set up an image or a sacred stone for yourselves, and do not place a carved stone in your land to bow down before it. I am the LORD your God.

²" 'Observe my Sabbaths and have reverence for my sanctuary. I am the LORD.

³" 'If you follow my decrees and are careful to obey my commands, ⁴I will send you rain in its season, and the ground will yield its crops and the trees of the field their fruit. ⁵Your threshing will continue until grape harvest and the grape harvest will continue until planting, and you will eat all the food you want and live in safety in your land.

⁶" 'I will grant peace in the land, and you will lie down and no one will make you afraid. I will remove savage beasts from the land, and the sword will not pass through your country. ⁷You will pursue your enemies, and they will fall by the sword before you. ⁸Five of you will chase a hundred, and a hundred of you will chase ten thousand, and your enemies will fall by the sword before you.

⁹" 'I will look on you with favor and make you fruitful and increase your numbers, and I will keep my covenant with you. ¹⁰You will still be eating last year's harvest when you will have to move it out to make room for the new. ¹¹I will put my dwelling place*a* among you, and I will not abhor you. ¹²I will walk among you and be your God, and you will be my people. ¹³I am the LORD your God, who brought you out of Egypt so that you would no longer be slaves to the Egyptians; I broke the bars of your yoke and enabled you to walk with heads held high.

Punishment for Disobedience

¹⁴" 'But if you will not listen to me and carry out all these commands, ¹⁵and if you reject my decrees and abhor my laws and fail to carry out all my commands and so violate my covenant, ¹⁶then I will do this to you: I will bring upon you sudden terror, wasting diseases and fever that will destroy your sight and drain away your life. You will plant seed in vain, because your enemies will eat it. ¹⁷I will set my face against you so that you will be defeated by your enemies; those who hate you will rule over you, and you will flee even when no one is pursuing you.

¹⁸" 'If after all this you will not listen to me, I will punish you for your sins seven times over. ¹⁹I will break down your stubborn pride and make the sky above you like iron and the ground beneath you like bronze. ²⁰Your strength will be spent in vain, because your soil will not yield its crops, nor will the trees of the land yield their fruit.

²¹" 'If you remain hostile toward me and refuse to listen to me, I will multiply your afflictions seven times over, as your sins deserve. ²²I will send wild animals against you, and they will rob you of your children, destroy your cattle and make you so few in number that your roads will be deserted.

²³" 'If in spite of these things you do not accept my correction but continue to be hostile toward me, ²⁴I myself will be hostile toward you and will afflict you for your sins seven times over. ²⁵And I will bring the sword upon you to avenge the breaking of the covenant. When you withdraw into your cities, I will send a plague among you, and you will be given into enemy hands. ²⁶When I cut off your supply of bread, ten women will be able to bake your bread in one oven, and they will dole out the bread by weight. You will eat, but you will not be satisfied.

²⁷" 'If in spite of this you still do not listen to me but continue to be hostile toward me, ²⁸then in my anger I will be hostile toward you, and I myself will punish you for your sins seven times over. ²⁹You will eat the flesh of your sons and the flesh of your daughters. ³⁰I will destroy your high places, cut down your incense altars and pile your dead bodies on the lifeless forms of your idols, and I will abhor you. ³¹I will turn your cities into ruins and lay waste your sanctuaries, and I will take no delight in the pleasing aroma of your offerings. ³²I will lay waste the land, so that your enemies who live there will be appalled. ³³I will scatter you among the nations and will draw out my sword and pursue you. Your land will be laid waste, and your cities will lie in ruins. ³⁴Then the land will enjoy its sabbath years all the time that it lies desolate and you are

---

a 11 Or *my tabernacle*

in the country of your enemies; then the land will rest and enjoy its sabbaths. **35**All the time that it lies desolate, the land will have the rest it did not have during the sabbaths you lived in it.

36" 'As for those of you who are left, I will make their hearts so fearful in the lands of their enemies that the sound of a wind-blown leaf will put them to flight. They will run as though fleeing from the sword, and they will fall, even though no one is pursuing them. **37**They will stumble over one another as though fleeing from the sword, even though no one is pursuing them. So you will not be able to stand before your enemies. **38**You will perish among the nations; the land of your enemies will devour you. **39**Those of you who are left will waste away in the lands of their enemies because of their sins; also because of their fathers' sins they will waste away.

40" 'But if they will confess their sins and the sins of their fathers — their treachery against me and their hostility toward me, **41**which made me hostile toward them so that I sent them into the land of their enemies — then when their uncircumcised hearts are humbled and they pay for their sin, **42**I will remember my covenant with Jacob and my covenant with Isaac and my covenant with Abraham, and I will remember the land. **43**For the land will be deserted by them and will enjoy its sabbaths while it lies desolate without them. They will pay for their sins because they rejected my laws and abhorred my decrees. **44**Yet in spite of this, when they are in the land of their enemies, I will not reject them or abhor them so as to destroy them completely, breaking my covenant with them. I am the LORD their God. **45**But for their sake I will remember the covenant with their ancestors whom I brought out of Egypt in the sight of the nations to be their God. I am the LORD.' "

46These are the decrees, the laws and the regulations that the LORD established on Mount Sinai between himself and the Israelites through Moses.

Redeeming What Is the LORD's

27 The LORD said to Moses, **2**"Speak to the Israelites and say to them: 'If anyone makes a special vow to dedicate persons to the LORD by giving equivalent values, **3**set the value of a male between the ages of twenty and sixty at fifty shekels*a* of silver, according to the sanctuary shekel*b*; **4**and if it is a female, set her value at thirty shekels.*c* **5**If it is a person between the ages of five and twenty, set the value of a male at twenty shekels*d* and of a female at ten shekels.*e* **6**If it is a person between one month and five years, set the value of a male at five shekels*f* of silver and that of a female at three shekels*g* of silver. **7**If it is a person sixty years old or more, set the value of a male at fifteen shekels*h* and of a female at ten shekels. **8**If anyone making the vow is too poor to pay the specified amount, he is to present the person to the priest, who will set the value for him according to what the man making the vow can afford.

9" 'If what he vowed is an animal that is acceptable as an offering to the LORD, such an animal given to the LORD becomes holy. **10**He must not exchange it or substitute a good one for a bad one, or a bad one for a good one; if he should substitute one animal for another, both it and the substitute become holy. **11**If what he vowed is a ceremonially unclean animal — one that is not acceptable as an offering to the LORD — the animal must be presented to the priest, **12**who will judge its quality as good or bad. Whatever value the priest then sets, that is what it will be. **13**If the owner wishes to redeem the animal, he must add a fifth to its value.

14" 'If a man dedicates his house as something holy to the LORD, the priest will judge its quality as good or bad. Whatever value the priest then sets, so it will remain. **15**If the man who dedicates his house redeems it, he must add a fifth to its value, and the house will again become his.

16" 'If a man dedicates to the LORD part of his family land, its value is to be set according to the amount of seed required for it — fifty shekels of silver to a homer*i* of barley seed. **17**If he dedicates his field during the Year of Jubilee, the value that has been set remains. **18**But if he dedicates his field after the Jubilee, the priest will determine the value according to the number of years that remain until the next Year of Jubilee, and its set value will be reduced. **19**If the man who

---

a3 That is, about 1 1/4 pounds (about 0.6 kilogram); also in verse 16   *b3* That is, about 2/5 ounce (about 11.5 grams); also in verse 25   *c4* That is, about 12 ounces (about 0.3 kilogram)   *d5* That is, about 8 ounces (about 0.2 kilogram)   *e5* That is, about 4 ounces (about 110 grams); also in verse 7   *f6* That is, about 2 ounces (about 55 grams)   *g6* That is, about 1 1/4 ounces (about 35 grams)   *h7* That is, about 6 ounces (about 170 grams)   *i16* That is, probably about 6 bushels (about 220 liters) dedicates the field wishes to redeem it, he must add a fifth to its value, and the field will again become his. **20**If, however, he does not redeem the field, or if he has sold it to someone else, it can never be redeemed. **21**When the field is released in the Jubilee, it will become holy, like a field devoted to the LORD; it will become the property of the priests.*a*

22" 'If a man dedicates to the LORD a field he has bought, which is not part of his family land, **23**the priest will determine its value up to the Year of Jubilee, and the man must pay its value on that day as something holy to the LORD. **24**In the Year of Jubilee the field will revert to the person from whom he bought it, the one whose land it was. **25**Every value is to be set according to the sanctuary shekel, twenty gerahs to the shekel.

26" 'No one, however, may dedicate the firstborn of an animal, since the firstborn already belongs to the LORD; whether an ox*b* or a sheep, it is the LORD's. **27**If it is one of the unclean animals, he may buy it back at its set value, adding a fifth of the value to it. If

he does not redeem it, it is to be sold at its set value.

28" 'But nothing that a man owns and devotes*c* to the LORD — whether man or animal or family land — may be sold or redeemed; everything so devoted is most holy to the LORD.

29" 'No person devoted to destruction*d* may be ransomed; he must be put to death.

30" 'A tithe of everything from the land, whether grain from the soil or fruit from the trees, belongs to the LORD; it is holy to the LORD. **31**If a man redeems any of his tithe, he must add a fifth of the value to it. **32**The entire tithe of the herd and flock — every tenth animal that passes under the shepherd's rod — will be holy to the LORD. **33**He must not pick out the good from the bad or make any substitution. If he does make a substitution, both the animal and its substitute become holy and cannot be redeemed.' "

34These are the commands the LORD gave Moses on Mount Sinai for the Israelites.

---

a21 Or *priest*   *b26* The Hebrew word can include both male and female.   *c28* The Hebrew term refers to the irrevocable giving over of things or persons to the LORD.   *d29* The Hebrew term refers to the irrevocable giving over of things or persons to the LORD, often by totally destroying them.

NUMBERS

THE book of Numbers could be called the "book of censuses," for that's how it begins and ends. But between those two numberings it depicts a downward spiral. The Israelites disobey God, refusing to trust him. He judges them unworthy of entering the promised land. They tragically wander for forty years in the desert, where almost the entire generation dies. But the lives of Moses, Caleb and Joshua show that God rewards those who obey his Word. As you read Numbers commit yourself to trusting God and staying on the path of obedience.

Outline of Contents

The Census

1 The LORD spoke to Moses in the Tent of Meeting in the Desert of Sinai on the first day of the second month of the second year after the Israelites came out of Egypt. He said: 2"Take a census of the whole Israelite community by their clans and families, listing every man by name, one by one. 3You and Aaron are to number by their divisions all the men in Israel twenty years old or more who are able to serve in the army. 4One man from each tribe, each the head of his family, is to help you. 5These are the names of the men who are to assist you:

from Reuben, Elizur son of Shedeur;
6from Simeon, Shelumiel son of Zurishaddai;

7from Judah, Nahshon son of Amminadab;
8from Issachar, Nethanel son of Zuar;
9from Zebulun, Eliab son of Helon;
10from the sons of Joseph:
from Ephraim, Elishama son of Ammihud;
from Manasseh, Gamaliel son of Pedahzur;
11from Benjamin, Abidan son of Gideoni;
12from Dan, Ahiezer son of Ammishaddai;
13from Asher, Pagiel son of Ocran;
14from Gad, Eliasaph son of Deuel;
15from Naphtali, Ahira son of Enan."

16These were the men appointed from the community, the leaders of their ancestral tribes. They were the heads of the clans of Israel.

¹⁷Moses and Aaron took these men whose names had been given, ¹⁸and they called the whole community together on the first day of the second month. The people indicated their ancestry by their clans and families, and the men twenty years old or more were listed by name, one by one, ¹⁹as the LORD commanded Moses. And so he counted them in the Desert of Sinai:

²⁰From the descendants of Reuben the first-born son of Israel:

All the men twenty years old or more who were able to serve in the army were listed by name, one by one, according to the records of their clans and families. ²¹The number from the tribe of Reuben was 46,500.

²²From the descendants of Simeon:

All the men twenty years old or more who were able to serve in the army were counted and listed by name, one by one, according to the records of their clans and families. ²³The number from the tribe of Simeon was 59,300.

²⁴From the descendants of Gad:

All the men twenty years old or more who were able to serve in the army were listed by name, according to the records of their clans and families. ²⁵The number from the tribe of Gad was 45,650.

²⁶From the descendants of Judah:

All the men twenty years old or more who were able to serve in the army were listed by name, according to the records of their clans and families. ²⁷The number from the tribe of Judah was 74,600.

²⁸From the descendants of Issachar:

All the men twenty years old or more who were able to serve in the army were listed by name, according to the records of their clans and families. ²⁹The number from the tribe of Issachar was 54,400.

³⁰From the descendants of Zebulun:

All the men twenty years old or more who were able to serve in the army were listed by name, according to the records of their clans and families. ³¹The number from the tribe of Zebulun was 57,400.

³²From the sons of Joseph:

From the descendants of Ephraim:

All the men twenty years old or more who were able to serve in the army were listed by name, according to the records of their clans and families. ³³The number from the tribe of Ephraim was 40,500.

³⁴From the descendants of Manasseh:

All the men twenty years old or more who were able to serve in the army were listed by name, according to the records of their clans and families. ³⁵The number from the tribe of Manasseh was 32,200.

³⁶From the descendants of Benjamin:

All the men twenty years old or more who were able to serve in the army were listed by name, according to the records of their clans and families. ³⁷The number from the tribe of Benjamin was 35,400.

³⁸From the descendants of Dan:

All the men twenty years old or more who were able to serve in the army were listed by name, according to the records of their clans and families. ³⁹The number from the tribe of Dan was 62,700.

⁴⁰From the descendants of Asher:

All the men twenty years old or more who were able to serve in the army were listed by name, according to the records of their clans and families. ⁴¹The number from the tribe of Asher was 41,500.

⁴²From the descendants of Naphtali:

All the men twenty years old or more who were able to serve in the army were listed by name, according to the records of their clans and families. ⁴³The number from the tribe of Naphtali was 53,400.

⁴⁴These were the men counted by Moses and Aaron and the twelve leaders of Israel, each one representing his family. ⁴⁵All the Israelites twenty years old or more who were able to serve in Israel's army were counted according to their families. ⁴⁶The total number was 603,550.

⁴⁷The families of the tribe of Levi, however, were not counted along with the others. ⁴⁸The LORD had said to Moses: ⁴⁹"You must not count the tribe of Levi or include them in the census of the other Israelites. ⁵⁰Instead, appoint the Levites to be in charge of

the tabernacle of the Testimony — over all its furnishings and everything belonging to it. They are to carry the tabernacle and all its furnishings; they are to take care of it and encamp around it. ⁵¹Whenever the tabernacle is to move, the Levites are to take it down, and whenever the tabernacle is to be set up, the Levites shall do it. Anyone else who goes near it shall be put to death. ⁵²The Israelites are to set up their tents by divisions, each man in his own camp under his own standard. ⁵³The Levites, however, are to set up their tents around the tabernacle of the Testimony so that wrath will not fall on the Israelite community. The Levites are to be responsible for the care of the tabernacle of the Testimony."

⁵⁴The Israelites did all this just as the Lᴏʀᴅ commanded Moses.

The Arrangement of the Tribal Camps

2 The Lᴏʀᴅ said to Moses and Aaron: ²"The Israelites are to camp around the Tent of Meeting some distance from it, each man under his standard with the banners of his family."

³On the east, toward the sunrise, the divisions of the camp of Judah are to encamp under their standard. The leader of the people of Judah is Nahshon son of Amminadab. ⁴His division numbers 74,600.

⁵The tribe of Issachar will camp next to them. The leader of the people of Issachar is Nethanel son of Zuar. ⁶His division numbers 54,400.

⁷The tribe of Zebulun will be next. The leader of the people of Zebulun is Eliab son of Helon. ⁸His division numbers 57,400.

⁹All the men assigned to the camp of Judah, according to their divisions, number 186,400. They will set out first.

¹⁰On the south will be the divisions of the camp of Reuben under their standard. The leader of the people of Reuben is Elizur son of Shedeur. ¹¹His division numbers 46,500.

¹²The tribe of Simeon will camp next to them. The leader of the people of Simeon is Shelumiel son of Zurishaddai. ¹³His division numbers 59,300.

¹⁴The tribe of Gad will be next. The leader of the people of Gad is Eliasaph son of Deuel.ᵃ ¹⁵His division numbers 45,650.

¹⁶All the men assigned to the camp of Reuben, according to their divisions, number 151,450. They will set out second.

¹⁷Then the Tent of Meeting and the camp of the Levites will set out in the middle of the camps. They will set out in the same order as they encamp, each in his own place under his standard.

¹⁸On the west will be the divisions of the camp of Ephraim under their standard. The leader of the people of Ephraim is Elishama son of Ammihud. ¹⁹His division numbers 40,500.

²⁰The tribe of Manasseh will be next to them. The leader of the people of Manasseh is Gamaliel son of Pedahzur. ²¹His division numbers 32,200.

²²The tribe of Benjamin will be next. The leader of the people of Benjamin is Abidan son of Gideoni. ²³His division numbers 35,400.

²⁴All the men assigned to the camp of Ephraim, according to their divisions, number 108,100. They will set out third.

²⁵On the north will be the divisions of the camp of Dan, under their standard. The leader of the people of Dan is Ahiezer son of Ammishaddai. ²⁶His division numbers 62,700.

²⁷The tribe of Asher will camp next to them. The leader of the people of Asher is Pagiel son of Ocran. ²⁸His division numbers 41,500.

²⁹The tribe of Naphtali will be next. The leader of the people of Naphtali is Ahira son of Enan. ³⁰His division numbers 53,400.

³¹All the men assigned to the camp of Dan number 157,600. They will set out last, under their standards.

³²These are the Israelites, counted according to their families. All those in the camps, by their divisions, number 603,550. ³³The Levites, however, were not counted along with the other Israelites, as the Lᴏʀᴅ commanded Moses.

³⁴So the Israelites did everything the Lᴏʀᴅ commanded Moses; that is the way they encamped under their standards, and that is

---

ᵃ14 Many manuscripts of the Masoretic Text, Samaritan Pentateuch and Vulgate (see also Num. 1:14); most manuscripts of the Masoretic Text *Reuel* the way they set out, each with his clan and family.

The Levites

3 This is the account of the family of Aaron and Moses at the time the LORD talked with Moses on Mount Sinai.

²The names of the sons of Aaron were Nadab the firstborn and Abihu, Eleazar and Ithamar. ³Those were the names of Aaron's sons, the anointed priests, who were ordained to serve as priests. ⁴Nadab and Abihu, however, fell dead before the LORD when they made an offering with unauthorized fire before him in the Desert of Sinai. They had no sons; so only Eleazar and Ithamar served as priests during the lifetime of their father Aaron.

⁵The LORD said to Moses, ⁶"Bring the tribe of Levi and present them to Aaron the priest to assist him. ⁷They are to perform duties for him and for the whole community at the Tent of Meeting by doing the work of the tabernacle. ⁸They are to take care of all the furnishings of the Tent of Meeting, fulfilling the obligations of the Israelites by doing the work of the tabernacle. ⁹Give the Levites to Aaron and his sons; they are the Israelites who are to be given wholly to him.ᵃ ¹⁰Appoint Aaron and his sons to serve as priests; anyone else who approaches the sanctuary must be put to death."

¹¹The LORD also said to Moses, ¹²"I have taken the Levites from among the Israelites in place of the first male offspring of every Israelite woman. The Levites are mine, ¹³for all the firstborn are mine. When I struck down all the firstborn in Egypt, I set apart for myself every firstborn in Israel, whether man or animal. They are to be mine. I am the LORD."

¹⁴The LORD said to Moses in the Desert of Sinai, ¹⁵"Count the Levites by their families and clans. Count every male a month old or more." ¹⁶So Moses counted them, as he was commanded by the word of the LORD.

¹⁷These were the names of the sons of Levi:
Gershon, Kohath and Merari.
¹⁸These were the names of the Gershonite clans:
Libni and Shimei.
¹⁹The Kohathite clans:
Amram, Izhar, Hebron and Uzziel.
²⁰The Merarite clans:
Mahli and Mushi.

These were the Levite clans, according to their families.

²¹To Gershon belonged the clans of the Libnites and Shimeites; these were the Gershonite clans. ²²The number of all the males a month old or more who were counted was 7,500. ²³The Gershonite clans were to camp on the west, behind the tabernacle. ²⁴The leader of the families of the Gershonites was Eliasaph son of Lael. ²⁵At the Tent of Meeting the Gershonites were responsible for the care of the tabernacle and tent, its coverings, the curtain at the entrance to the Tent of Meeting, ²⁶the curtains of the courtyard, the curtain at the entrance to the courtyard surrounding the tabernacle and altar, and the ropes—and everything related to their use.

²⁷To Kohath belonged the clans of the Amramites, Izharites, Hebronites and Uzzielites; these were the Kohathite clans. ²⁸The number of all the males a month old or more was 8,600.ᵇ The Kohathites were responsible for the care of the sanctuary. ²⁹The Kohathite clans were to camp on the south side of the tabernacle. ³⁰The leader of the families of the Kohathite clans was Elizaphan son of Uzziel. ³¹They were responsible for the care of the ark, the table, the lampstand, the altars, the articles of the sanctuary used in ministering, the curtain, and everything related to their use. ³²The chief leader of the Levites was Eleazar son of Aaron, the priest. He was appointed over those who were responsible for the care of the sanctuary.

³³To Merari belonged the clans of the Mahlites and the Mushites; these were the Merarite clans. ³⁴The number of all the males a month old or more who were counted was 6,200. ³⁵The leader of the families of the Merarite clans was Zuriel son of Abihail; they were to camp on the north side of the tabernacle. ³⁶The Merarites were appointed to take care of the frames of the tabernacle, its crossbars, posts, bases, all its equipment, and everything related to their use, ³⁷as well as the posts of the surrounding courtyard with their bases, tent pegs and ropes.

³⁸Moses and Aaron and his sons were to camp to the east of the tabernacle, toward the sunrise, in front of the Tent of Meeting.

ᵃ9 Most manuscripts of the Masoretic Text; some manuscripts of the Masoretic Text, Samaritan Pentateuch and Septuagint (see also Num. 8:16) *to me*   ᵇ28 Hebrew; some Septuagint manuscripts *8,300*

They were responsible for the care of the sanctuary on behalf of the Israelites. Anyone else who approached the sanctuary was to be put to death.

[39]The total number of Levites counted at the Lord's command by Moses and Aaron according to their clans, including every male a month old or more, was 22,000.

[40]The Lord said to Moses, "Count all the firstborn Israelite males who are a month old or more and make a list of their names. [41]Take the Levites for me in place of all the firstborn of the Israelites, and the livestock of the Levites in place of all the firstborn of the livestock of the Israelites. I am the Lord." [42]So Moses counted all the firstborn of the Israelites, as the Lord commanded him. [43]The total number of firstborn males a month old or more, listed by name, was 22,273.

[44]The Lord also said to Moses, [45]"Take the Levites in place of all the firstborn of Israel, and the livestock of the Levites in place of their livestock. The Levites are to be mine. I am the Lord. [46]To redeem the 273 firstborn Israelites who exceed the number of the Levites, [47]collect five shekels[a] for each one, according to the sanctuary shekel, which weighs twenty gerahs. [48]Give the money for the redemption of the additional Israelites to Aaron and his sons."

[49]So Moses collected the redemption money from those who exceeded the number redeemed by the Levites. [50]From the firstborn of the Israelites he collected silver weighing 1,365 shekels,[b] according to the sanctuary shekel. [51]Moses gave the redemption money to Aaron and his sons, as he was commanded by the word of the Lord.

The Kohathites

4 The Lord said to Moses and Aaron: [2]"Take a census of the Kohathite branch of the Levites by their clans and families. [3]Count all the men from thirty to fifty years of age who come to serve in the work in the Tent of Meeting.

[4]"This is the work of the Kohathites in the Tent of Meeting: the care of the most holy things. [5]When the camp is to move, Aaron and his sons are to go in and take down the shielding curtain and cover the ark of the Testimony with it. [6]Then they are to cover this with hides of sea cows,[c] spread a cloth of solid blue over that and put the poles in place.

[7]"Over the table of the Presence they are to spread a blue cloth and put on it the plates, dishes and bowls, and the jars for drink offerings; the bread that is continually there is to remain on it. [8]Over these they are to spread a scarlet cloth, cover that with hides of sea cows and put its poles in place. [9]They are to take a blue cloth and cover the lampstand that is for light, together with its lamps, its wick trimmers and trays, and all its jars for the oil used to supply it. [10]Then they are to wrap it and all its accessories in a covering of hides of sea cows and put it on a carrying frame.

[11]"Over the gold altar they are to spread a blue cloth and cover that with hides of sea cows and put its poles in place. [12]"They are to take all the articles used for ministering in the sanctuary, wrap them in a blue cloth, cover that with hides of sea cows and put them on a carrying frame. [13]"They are to remove the ashes from the bronze altar and spread a purple cloth over it. [14]Then they are to place on it all the utensils used for ministering at the altar, including the firepans, meat forks, shovels and sprinkling bowls. Over it they are to spread a covering of hides of sea cows and put its poles in place.

[15]"After Aaron and his sons have finished covering the holy furnishings and all the holy articles, and when the camp is ready to move, the Kohathites are to come to do the carrying. But they must not touch the holy things or they will die. The Kohathites are to carry those things that are in the Tent of Meeting.

[16]"Eleazar son of Aaron, the priest, is to have charge of the oil for the light, the fragrant incense, the regular grain offering and the anointing oil. He is to be in charge of the entire tabernacle and everything in it, including its holy furnishings and articles."

[17]The Lord said to Moses and Aaron, [18]"See that the Kohathite tribal clans are not cut off from the Levites. [19]So that they may live and not die when they come near the most holy things, do this for them: Aaron and his sons are to go into the sanctuary and assign to each man his work and what he is to carry. [20]But the Kohathites must not go in to look at the holy things, even for a moment, or they will die."

---

[a]47 That is, about 2 ounces (about 55 grams)   [b]50 That is, about 35 pounds (about 15.5 kilograms)
[c]6 That is, dugongs; also in verses 8, 10, 11, 12, 14 and 25

The Gershonites

21The LORD said to Moses, **22**"Take a census also of the Gershonites by their families and clans. **23**Count all the men from thirty to fifty years of age who come to serve in the work at the Tent of Meeting.

24"This is the service of the Gershonite clans as they work and carry burdens: **25**They are to carry the curtains of the tabernacle, the Tent of Meeting, its covering and the outer covering of hides of sea cows, the curtains for the entrance to the Tent of Meeting, **26**the curtains of the courtyard surrounding the tabernacle and altar, the curtain for the entrance, the ropes and all the equipment used in its service. The Gershonites are to do all that needs to be done with these things. **27**All their service, whether carrying or doing other work, is to be done under the direction of Aaron and his sons. You shall assign to them as their responsibility all they are to carry. **28**This is the service of the Gershonite clans at the Tent of Meeting. Their duties are to be under the direction of Ithamar son of Aaron, the priest.

The Merarites

29"Count the Merarites by their clans and families. **30**Count all the men from thirty to fifty years of age who come to serve in the work at the Tent of Meeting. **31**This is their duty as they perform service at the Tent of Meeting: to carry the frames of the tabernacle, its crossbars, posts and bases, **32**as well as the posts of the surrounding courtyard with their bases, tent pegs, ropes, all their equipment and everything related to their use. Assign to each man the specific things he is to carry. **33**This is the service of the Merarite clans as they work at the Tent of Meeting under the direction of Ithamar son of Aaron, the priest."

The Numbering of the Levite Clans

34Moses, Aaron and the leaders of the community counted the Kohathites by their clans and families. **35**All the men from thirty to fifty years of age who came to serve in the work in the Tent of Meeting, **36**counted by clans, were 2,750. **37**This was the total of all those in the Kohathite clans who served in the Tent of Meeting. Moses and Aaron counted them according to the LORD's command through Moses.

38The Gershonites were counted by their clans and families. **39**All the men from thirty to fifty years of age who came to serve in the work at the Tent of Meeting, **40**counted by their clans and families, were 2,630. **41**This was the total of those in the Gershonite clans who served at the Tent of Meeting. Moses and Aaron counted them according to the LORD's command.

42The Merarites were counted by their clans and families. **43**All the men from thirty to fifty years of age who came to serve in the work at the Tent of Meeting, **44**counted by their clans, were 3,200. **45**This was the total of those in the Merarite clans. Moses and Aaron counted them according to the LORD's command through Moses.

46So Moses, Aaron and the leaders of Israel counted all the Levites by their clans and families. **47**All the men from thirty to fifty years of age who came to do the work of serving and carrying the Tent of Meeting **48**numbered 8,580. **49**At the LORD's command through Moses, each was assigned his work and told what to carry.

Thus they were counted, as the LORD commanded Moses.

The Purity of the Camp

5 The LORD said to Moses, **2**"Command the Israelites to send away from the camp anyone who has an infectious skin disease*a* or a discharge of any kind, or who is ceremonially unclean because of a dead body. **3**Send away male and female alike; send them outside the camp so they will not defile their camp, where I dwell among them." **4**The Israelites did this; they sent them outside the camp. They did just as the LORD had instructed Moses.

Restitution for Wrongs

5The LORD said to Moses, **6**"Say to the Israelites: 'When a man or woman wrongs another in any way*b* and so is unfaithful to the LORD, that person is guilty **7**and must confess the sin he has committed. He must make full restitution for his wrong, add one fifth to it and give it all to the person he has wronged. **8**But if that person has no close relative to whom restitution can be made for the wrong, the restitution belongs to the LORD and must be given to the priest, along with the ram with which atonement is made for him. **9**All the sacred contributions the Israelites bring to a priest will belong to him. **10**Each man's sacred gifts are his own, but

---

*a*2 Traditionally *leprosy*; the Hebrew word was used for various diseases affecting the skin—not necessarily leprosy.   *b*6 Or *woman commits any wrong common to mankind* what he gives to the priest will belong to the priest.'"

The Test for an Unfaithful Wife

[11]Then the LORD said to Moses, [12]"Speak to the Israelites and say to them: 'If a man's wife goes astray and is unfaithful to him [13]by sleeping with another man, and this is hidden from her husband and her impurity is undetected (since there is no witness against her and she has not been caught in the act), [14]and if feelings of jealousy come over her husband and he suspects his wife and she is impure — or if he is jealous and suspects her even though she is not impure — [15]then he is to take his wife to the priest. He must also take an offering of a tenth of an ephah[a] of barley flour on her behalf. He must not pour oil on it or put incense on it, because it is a grain offering for jealousy, a reminder offering to draw attention to guilt.

[16]"'The priest shall bring her and have her stand before the LORD. [17]Then he shall take some holy water in a clay jar and put some dust from the tabernacle floor into the water. [18]After the priest has had the woman stand before the LORD, he shall loosen her hair and place in her hands the reminder offering, the grain offering for jealousy, while he himself holds the bitter water that brings a curse. [19]Then the priest shall put the woman under oath and say to her, "If no other man has slept with you and you have not gone astray and become impure while married to your husband, may this bitter water that brings a curse not harm you. [20]But if you have gone astray while married to your husband and you have defiled yourself by sleeping with a man other than your husband" — [21]here the priest is to put the woman under this curse of the oath — "may the LORD cause your people to curse and denounce you when he causes your thigh to waste away and your abdomen to swell.[b] [22]May this water that brings a curse enter your body so that your abdomen swells and your thigh wastes away.[c]"

"'Then the woman is to say, "Amen. So be it."

[23]"'The priest is to write these curses on a scroll and then wash them off into the bitter water. [24]He shall have the woman drink the bitter water that brings a curse, and this water will enter her and cause bitter suffering. [25]The priest is to take from her hands the grain offering for jealousy, wave it before the LORD and bring it to the altar. [26]The priest is then to take a handful of the grain offering as a memorial offering and burn it on the altar; after that, he is to have the woman drink the water. [27]If she has defiled herself and been unfaithful to her husband, then when she is made to drink the water that brings a curse, it will go into her and cause bitter suffering; her abdomen will swell and her thigh waste away,[d] and she will become accursed among her people. [28]If, however, the woman has not defiled herself and is free from impurity, she will be cleared of guilt and will be able to have children.

[29]"'This, then, is the law of jealousy when a woman goes astray and defiles herself while married to her husband, [30]or when feelings of jealousy come over a man because he suspects his wife. The priest is to have her stand before the LORD and is to apply this entire law to her. [31]The husband will be innocent of any wrongdoing, but the woman will bear the consequences of her sin.'"

The Nazirite

6 The LORD said to Moses, [2]"Speak to the Israelites and say to them: 'If a man or woman wants to make a special vow, a vow of separation to the LORD as a Nazirite, [3]he must abstain from wine and other fermented drink and must not drink vinegar made from wine or from other fermented drink. He must not drink grape juice or eat grapes or raisins. [4]As long as he is a Nazirite, he must not eat anything that comes from the grapevine, not even the seeds or skins.

[5]"'During the entire period of his vow of separation no razor may be used on his head. He must be holy until the period of his separation to the LORD is over; he must let the hair of his head grow long. [6]Throughout the period of his separation to the LORD he must not go near a dead body. [7]Even if his own father or mother or brother or sister dies, he must not make himself ceremonially unclean on account of them, because the symbol of his separation to God is on his head. [8]Throughout the period of his separation he is consecrated to the LORD.

[9]"'If someone dies suddenly in his presence, thus defiling the hair he has dedicat-

---

[a]15 That is, probably about 2 quarts (about 2 liters)   [b]21 Or causes you to have a miscarrying womb and barrenness   [c]22 Or body and cause you to be barren and have a miscarrying womb   [d]27 Or suffering; she will have barrenness and a miscarrying womb

ed, he must shave his head on the day of his cleansing — the seventh day. ¹⁰Then on the eighth day he must bring two doves or two young pigeons to the priest at the entrance to the Tent of Meeting. ¹¹The priest is to offer one as a sin offering and the other as a burnt offering to make atonement for him because he sinned by being in the presence of the dead body. That same day he is to consecrate his head. ¹²He must dedicate himself to the LORD for the period of his separation and must bring a year-old male lamb as a guilt offering. The previous days do not count, because he became defiled during his separation.

¹³" 'Now this is the law for the Nazirite when the period of his separation is over. He is to be brought to the entrance to the Tent of Meeting. ¹⁴There he is to present his offerings to the LORD: a year-old male lamb without defect for a burnt offering, a year-old ewe lamb without defect for a sin offering, a ram without defect for a fellowship offering,ᵃ ¹⁵together with their grain offerings and drink offerings, and a basket of bread made without yeast — cakes made of fine flour mixed with oil, and wafers spread with oil.

¹⁶" 'The priest is to present them before the LORD and make the sin offering and the burnt offering. ¹⁷He is to present the basket of unleavened bread and is to sacrifice the ram as a fellowship offering to the LORD, together with its grain offering and drink offering.

¹⁸" 'Then at the entrance to the Tent of Meeting, the Nazirite must shave off the hair that he dedicated. He is to take the hair and put it in the fire that is under the sacrifice of the fellowship offering.

¹⁹" 'After the Nazirite has shaved off the hair of his dedication, the priest is to place in his hands a boiled shoulder of the ram, and a cake and a wafer from the basket, both made without yeast. ²⁰The priest shall then wave them before the LORD as a wave offering; they are holy and belong to the priest, together with the breast that was waved and the thigh that was presented. After that, the Nazirite may drink wine.

²¹" 'This is the law of the Nazirite who vows his offering to the LORD in accordance with his separation, in addition to whatever else he can afford. He must fulfill the vow he has made, according to the law of the Nazirite.' "

The Priestly Blessing

²²The LORD said to Moses, ²³"Tell Aaron and his sons, 'This is how you are to bless the Israelites. Say to them:

²⁴" ' "The LORD bless you
    and keep you;
²⁵the LORD make his face shine upon you
    and be gracious to you;
²⁶the LORD turn his face toward you
    and give you peace." '

²⁷"So they will put my name on the Israelites, and I will bless them."

Offerings at the Dedication of the Tabernacle

7 When Moses finished setting up the tabernacle, he anointed it and consecrated it and all its furnishings. He also anointed and consecrated the altar and all its utensils. ²Then the leaders of Israel, the heads of families who were the tribal leaders in charge of those who were counted, made offerings. ³They brought as their gifts before the LORD six covered carts and twelve oxen — an ox from each leader and a cart from every two. These they presented before the tabernacle.

⁴The LORD said to Moses, ⁵"Accept these from them, that they may be used in the work at the Tent of Meeting. Give them to the Levites as each man's work requires."

⁶So Moses took the carts and oxen and gave them to the Levites. ⁷He gave two carts and four oxen to the Gershonites, as their work required, ⁸and he gave four carts and eight oxen to the Merarites, as their work required. They were all under the direction of Ithamar son of Aaron, the priest. ⁹But Moses did not give any to the Kohathites, because they were to carry on their shoulders the holy things, for which they were responsible.

¹⁰When the altar was anointed, the leaders brought their offerings for its dedication and presented them before the altar. ¹¹For the LORD had said to Moses, "Each day one leader is to bring his offering for the dedication of the altar."

¹²The one who brought his offering on the first day was Nahshon son of Amminadab of the tribe of Judah.

¹³His offering was one silver plate weighing a hundred and thirty shekels,ᵇ and one silver sprinkling bowl

---

ᵃ14 Traditionally *peace offering*; also in verses 17 and 18 kilograms); also elsewhere in this chapter

ᵇ13 That is, about 3 1/4 pounds (about 1.5

weighing seventy shekels,[a] both according to the sanctuary shekel, each filled with fine flour mixed with oil as a grain offering; [14]one gold dish weighing ten shekels,[b] filled with incense; [15]one young bull, one ram and one male lamb a year old, for a burnt offering; [16]one male goat for a sin offering; [17]and two oxen, five rams, five male goats and five male lambs a year old, to be sacrificed as a fellowship offering.[c] This was the offering of Nahshon son of Amminadab.

[18]On the second day Nethanel son of Zuar, the leader of Issachar, brought his offering. [19]The offering he brought was one silver plate weighing a hundred and thirty shekels, and one silver sprinkling bowl weighing seventy shekels, both according to the sanctuary shekel, each filled with fine flour mixed with oil as a grain offering; [20]one gold dish weighing ten shekels, filled with incense; [21]one young bull, one ram and one male lamb a year old, for a burnt offering; [22]one male goat for a sin offering; [23]and two oxen, five rams, five male goats and five male lambs a year old, to be sacrificed as a fellowship offering. This was the offering of Nethanel son of Zuar.

[24]On the third day, Eliab son of Helon, the leader of the people of Zebulun, brought his offering. [25]His offering was one silver plate weighing a hundred and thirty shekels, and one silver sprinkling bowl weighing seventy shekels, both according to the sanctuary shekel, each filled with fine flour mixed with oil as a grain offering; [26]one gold dish weighing ten shekels, filled with incense; [27]one young bull, one ram and one male lamb a year old, for a burnt offering; [28]one male goat for a sin offering; [29]and two oxen, five rams, five male goats and five male lambs a year old, to be sacrificed as a fellowship offering. This was the offering of Eliab son of Helon.

[30]On the fourth day Elizur son of Shedeur, the leader of the people of Reuben, brought his offering. [31]His offering was one silver plate weighing a hundred and thirty shekels,

and one silver sprinkling bowl weighing seventy shekels, both according to the sanctuary shekel, each filled with fine flour mixed with oil as a grain offering; [32]one gold dish weighing ten shekels, filled with incense; [33]one young bull, one ram and one male lamb a year old, for a burnt offering; [34]one male goat for a sin offering; [35]and two oxen, five rams, five male goats and five male lambs a year old, to be sacrificed as a fellowship offering. This was the offering of Elizur son of Shedeur.

[36]On the fifth day Shelumiel son of Zurishaddai, the leader of the people of Simeon, brought his offering. [37]His offering was one silver plate weighing a hundred and thirty shekels, and one silver sprinkling bowl weighing seventy shekels, both according to the sanctuary shekel, each filled with fine flour mixed with oil as a grain offering; [38]one gold dish weighing ten shekels, filled with incense; [39]one young bull, one ram and one male lamb a year old, for a burnt offering; [40]one male goat for a sin offering; [41]and two oxen, five rams, five male goats and five male lambs a year old, to be sacrificed as a fellowship offering. This was the offering of Shelumiel son of Zurishaddai.

[42]On the sixth day Eliasaph son of Deuel, the leader of the people of Gad, brought his offering. [43]His offering was one silver plate weighing a hundred and thirty shekels, and one silver sprinkling bowl weighing seventy shekels, both according to the sanctuary shekel, each filled with fine flour mixed with oil as a grain offering; [44]one gold dish weighing ten shekels, filled with incense; [45]one young bull, one ram and one male lamb a year old, for a burnt offering; [46]one male goat for a sin offering; [47]and two oxen, five rams, five male goats and five male lambs a year old, to be sacrificed as a fellowship offering. This was the offering of Eliasaph son of Deuel.

[48]On the seventh day Elishama son of Ammihud, the leader of the people of Ephraim, brought his offering. [49]His offering was one silver plate

---

[a]13 That is, about 1 3/4 pounds (about 0.8 kilogram); also elsewhere in this chapter   [b]14 That is, about 4 ounces (about 110 grams); also elsewhere in this chapter   [c]17 Traditionally *peace offering*; also elsewhere in this chapter

weighing a hundred and thirty shekels, and one silver sprinkling bowl weighing seventy shekels, both according to the sanctuary shekel, each filled with fine flour mixed with oil as a grain offering; ⁵⁰one gold dish weighing ten shekels, filled with incense; ⁵¹one young bull, one ram and one male lamb a year old, for a burnt offering; ⁵²one male goat for a sin offering; ⁵³and two oxen, five rams, five male goats and five male lambs a year old, to be sacrificed as a fellowship offering. This was the offering of Elishama son of Ammihud.

⁵⁴On the eighth day Gamaliel son of Pedahzur, the leader of the people of Manasseh, brought his offering.

⁵⁵His offering was one silver plate weighing a hundred and thirty shekels, and one silver sprinkling bowl weighing seventy shekels, both according to the sanctuary shekel, each filled with fine flour mixed with oil as a grain offering; ⁵⁶one gold dish weighing ten shekels, filled with incense; ⁵⁷one young bull, one ram and one male lamb a year old, for a burnt offering; ⁵⁸one male goat for a sin offering; ⁵⁹and two oxen, five rams, five male goats and five male lambs a year old, to be sacrificed as a fellowship offering. This was the offering of Gamaliel son of Pedahzur.

⁶⁰On the ninth day Abidan son of Gideoni, the leader of the people of Benjamin, brought his offering.

⁶¹His offering was one silver plate weighing a hundred and thirty shekels, and one silver sprinkling bowl weighing seventy shekels, both according to the sanctuary shekel, each filled with fine flour mixed with oil as a grain offering; ⁶²one gold dish weighing ten shekels, filled with incense; ⁶³one young bull, one ram and one male lamb a year old, for a burnt offering; ⁶⁴one male goat for a sin offering; ⁶⁵and two oxen, five rams, five male goats and five male lambs a year old, to be sacrificed as a fellowship offering. This was the offering of Abidan son of Gideoni.

⁶⁶On the tenth day Ahiezer son of Ammishaddai, the leader of the people of Dan, brought his offering.

⁶⁷His offering was one silver plate weighing a hundred and thirty shekels, and one silver sprinkling bowl weighing

seventy shekels, both according to the sanctuary shekel, each filled with fine flour mixed with oil as a grain offering; ⁶⁸one gold dish weighing ten shekels, filled with incense; ⁶⁹one young bull, one ram and one male lamb a year old, for a burnt offering; ⁷⁰one male goat for a sin offering; ⁷¹and two oxen, five rams, five male goats and five male lambs a year old, to be sacrificed as a fellowship offering. This was the offering of Ahiezer son of Ammishaddai.

⁷²On the eleventh day Pagiel son of Ocran, the leader of the people of Asher, brought his offering.

⁷³His offering was one silver plate weighing a hundred and thirty shekels, and one silver sprinkling bowl weighing seventy shekels, both according to the sanctuary shekel, each filled with fine flour mixed with oil as a grain offering; ⁷⁴one gold dish weighing ten shekels, filled with incense; ⁷⁵one young bull, one ram and one male lamb a year old, for a burnt offering; ⁷⁶one male goat for a sin offering; ⁷⁷and two oxen, five rams, five male goats and five male lambs a year old, to be sacrificed as a fellowship offering. This was the offering of Pagiel son of Ocran.

⁷⁸On the twelfth day Ahira son of Enan, the leader of the people of Naphtali, brought his offering.

⁷⁹His offering was one silver plate weighing a hundred and thirty shekels, and one silver sprinkling bowl weighing seventy shekels, both according to the sanctuary shekel, each filled with fine flour mixed with oil as a grain offering; ⁸⁰one gold dish weighing ten shekels, filled with incense; ⁸¹one young bull, one ram and one male lamb a year old, for a burnt offering; ⁸²one male goat for a sin offering; ⁸³and two oxen, five rams, five male goats and five male lambs a year old, to be sacrificed as a fellowship offering. This was the offering of Ahira son of Enan.

⁸⁴These were the offerings of the Israelite leaders for the dedication of the altar when it was anointed: twelve silver plates, twelve silver sprinkling bowls and twelve gold dishes. ⁸⁵Each silver plate weighed a hundred and thirty shekels, and each sprinkling bowl seventy shekels. Altogether, the silver dishes weighed two thousand four hundred

shekels,ᵃ according to the sanctuary shekel. **86**The twelve gold dishes filled with incense weighed ten shekels each, according to the sanctuary shekel. Altogether, the gold dishes weighed a hundred and twenty shekels.ᵇ **87**The total number of animals for the burnt offering came to twelve young bulls, twelve rams and twelve male lambs a year old, together with their grain offering. Twelve male goats were used for the sin offering. **88**The total number of animals for the sacrifice of the fellowship offering came to twenty-four oxen, sixty rams, sixty male goats and sixty male lambs a year old. These were the offerings for the dedication of the altar after it was anointed.

89When Moses entered the Tent of Meeting to speak with the LORD, he heard the voice speaking to him from between the two cherubim above the atonement cover on the ark of the Testimony. And he spoke with him.

Setting Up the Lamps

8 The LORD said to Moses, **2**"Speak to Aaron and say to him, 'When you set up the seven lamps, they are to light the area in front of the lampstand.'"

3Aaron did so; he set up the lamps so that they faced forward on the lampstand, just as the LORD commanded Moses. **4**This is how the lampstand was made: It was made of hammered gold—from its base to its blossoms. The lampstand was made exactly like the pattern the LORD had shown Moses.

The Setting Apart of the Levites

5The LORD said to Moses: **6**"Take the Levites from among the other Israelites and make them ceremonially clean. **7**To purify them, do this: Sprinkle the water of cleansing on them; then have them shave their whole bodies and wash their clothes, and so purify themselves. **8**Have them take a young bull with its grain offering of fine flour mixed with oil; then you are to take a second young bull for a sin offering. **9**Bring the Levites to the front of the Tent of Meeting and assemble the whole Israelite community. **10**You are to bring the Levites before the LORD, and the Israelites are to lay their hands on them. **11**Aaron is to present the Levites before the LORD as a wave offering from the Israelites, so that they may be ready to do the work of the LORD.

12"After the Levites lay their hands on the heads of the bulls, use the one for a sin offering to the LORD and the other for a burnt offering, to make atonement for the Levites. **13**Have the Levites stand in front of Aaron and his sons and then present them as a wave offering to the LORD. **14**In this way you are to set the Levites apart from the other Israelites, and the Levites will be mine.

15"After you have purified the Levites and presented them as a wave offering, they are to come to do their work at the Tent of Meeting. **16**They are the Israelites who are to be given wholly to me. I have taken them as my own in place of the firstborn, the first male offspring from every Israelite woman. **17**Every firstborn male in Israel, whether man or animal, is mine. When I struck down all the firstborn in Egypt, I set them apart for myself. **18**And I have taken the Levites in place of all the firstborn sons in Israel. **19**Of all the Israelites, I have given the Levites as gifts to Aaron and his sons to do the work at the Tent of Meeting on behalf of the Israelites and to make atonement for them so that no plague will strike the Israelites when they go near the sanctuary."

20Moses, Aaron and the whole Israelite community did with the Levites just as the LORD commanded Moses. **21**The Levites purified themselves and washed their clothes. Then Aaron presented them as a wave offering before the LORD and made atonement for them to purify them. **22**After that, the Levites came to do their work at the Tent of Meeting under the supervision of Aaron and his sons. They did with the Levites just as the LORD commanded Moses.

23The LORD said to Moses, **24**"This applies to the Levites: Men twenty-five years old or more shall come to take part in the work at the Tent of Meeting, **25**but at the age of fifty, they must retire from their regular service and work no longer. **26**They may assist their brothers in performing their duties at the Tent of Meeting, but they themselves must not do the work. This, then, is how you are to assign the responsibilities of the Levites."

The Passover

9 The LORD spoke to Moses in the Desert of Sinai in the first month of the second year after they came out of Egypt. He said, **2**"Have the Israelites celebrate the Passover at the appointed time. **3**Celebrate it at the appointed time, at twilight on the fourteenth day of this month, in accordance with all its rules and regulations."

4So Moses told the Israelites to celebrate

ᵃ85 That is, about 60 pounds (about 28 kilograms)   ᵇ86 That is, about 3 pounds (about 1.4 kilograms) the Passover, **5**and they did so in the Desert of Sinai at twilight on the fourteenth day of the first month. The Israelites did everything just as the Lord commanded Moses.

6But some of them could not celebrate the Passover on that day because they were ceremonially unclean on account of a dead body. So they came to Moses and Aaron that same day **7**and said to Moses, "We have become unclean because of a dead body, but why should we be kept from presenting the Lord's offering with the other Israelites at the appointed time?"

8Moses answered them, "Wait until I find out what the Lord commands concerning you."

9Then the Lord said to Moses, **10**"Tell the Israelites: 'When any of you or your descendants are unclean because of a dead body or are away on a journey, they may still celebrate the Lord's Passover. **11**They are to celebrate it on the fourteenth day of the second month at twilight. They are to eat the lamb, together with unleavened bread and bitter herbs. **12**They must not leave any of it till morning or break any of its bones. When they celebrate the Passover, they must follow all the regulations. **13**But if a man who is ceremonially clean and not on a journey fails to celebrate the Passover, that person must be cut off from his people because he did not present the Lord's offering at the appointed time. That man will bear the consequences of his sin.

14" 'An alien living among you who wants to celebrate the Lord's Passover must do so in accordance with its rules and regulations. You must have the same regulations for the alien and the native-born.' "

The Cloud Above the Tabernacle

15On the day the tabernacle, the Tent of the Testimony, was set up, the cloud covered it. From evening till morning the cloud above the tabernacle looked like fire. **16**That is how it continued to be; the cloud covered it, and at night it looked like fire. **17**Whenever the cloud lifted from above the Tent, the Israelites set out; wherever the cloud settled, the Israelites encamped. **18**At the Lord's command the Israelites set out, and at his command they encamped. As long as the cloud stayed over the tabernacle, they remained in camp. **19**When the cloud remained over the tabernacle a long time, the Israelites obeyed the Lord's order and did not set out. **20**Sometimes the cloud was over the tabernacle only a few days; at the Lord's command they would encamp, and then at his command they would set out. **21**Sometimes the cloud stayed only from evening till morning, and when it lifted in the morning, they set out. Whether by day or by night, whenever the cloud lifted, they set out. **22**Whether the cloud stayed over the tabernacle for two days or a month or a year, the Israelites would remain in camp and not set out; but when it lifted, they would set out. **23**At the Lord's command they encamped, and at the Lord's command they set out. They obeyed the Lord's order, in accordance with his command through Moses.

The Silver Trumpets

10 The Lord said to Moses: **2**"Make two trumpets of hammered silver, and use them for calling the community together and for having the camps set out. **3**When both are sounded, the whole community is to assemble before you at the entrance to the Tent of Meeting. **4**If only one is sounded, the leaders — the heads of the clans of Israel — are to assemble before you. **5**When a trumpet blast is sounded, the tribes camping on the east are to set out. **6**At the sounding of a second blast, the camps on the south are to set out. The blast will be the signal for setting out. **7**To gather the assembly, blow the trumpets, but not with the same signal.

8"The sons of Aaron, the priests, are to blow the trumpets. This is to be a lasting ordinance for you and the generations to come. **9**When you go into battle in your own land against an enemy who is oppressing you, sound a blast on the trumpets. Then you will be remembered by the Lord your God and rescued from your enemies. **10**Also at your times of rejoicing — your appointed feasts and New Moon festivals — you are to sound the trumpets over your burnt offerings and fellowship offerings,*a* and they will be a memorial for you before your God. I am the Lord your God."

The Israelites Leave Sinai

11On the twentieth day of the second month of the second year, the cloud lifted from above the tabernacle of the Testimony. **12**Then the Israelites set out from the Desert of Sinai and traveled from place to place until the cloud came to rest in the Desert of Paran. **13**They set out, this first time, at the Lord's command through Moses.

a 10 Traditionally *peace offerings*

¹⁴The divisions of the camp of Judah went first, under their standard. Nahshon son of Amminadab was in command. ¹⁵Nethanel son of Zuar was over the division of the tribe of Issachar, ¹⁶and Eliab son of Helon was over the division of the tribe of Zebulun. ¹⁷Then the tabernacle was taken down, and the Gershonites and Merarites, who carried it, set out.

¹⁸The divisions of the camp of Reuben went next, under their standard. Elizur son of Shedeur was in command. ¹⁹Shelumiel son of Zurishaddai was over the division of the tribe of Simeon, ²⁰and Eliasaph son of Deuel was over the division of the tribe of Gad. ²¹Then the Kohathites set out, carrying the holy things. The tabernacle was to be set up before they arrived.

²²The divisions of the camp of Ephraim went next, under their standard. Elishama son of Ammihud was in command. ²³Gamaliel son of Pedahzur was over the division of the tribe of Manasseh, ²⁴and Abidan son of Gideoni was over the division of the tribe of Benjamin.

²⁵Finally, as the rear guard for all the units, the divisions of the camp of Dan set out, under their standard. Ahiezer son of Ammishaddai was in command. ²⁶Pagiel son of Ocran was over the division of the tribe of Asher, ²⁷and Ahira son of Enan was over the division of the tribe of Naphtali. ²⁸This was the order of march for the Israelite divisions as they set out.

²⁹Now Moses said to Hobab son of Reuel the Midianite, Moses' father-in-law, "We are setting out for the place about which the LORD said, 'I will give it to you.' Come with us and we will treat you well, for the LORD has promised good things to Israel."

³⁰He answered, "No, I will not go; I am going back to my own land and my own people."

³¹But Moses said, "Please do not leave us. You know where we should camp in the desert, and you can be our eyes. ³²If you come with us, we will share with you whatever good things the LORD gives us."

³³So they set out from the mountain of the LORD and traveled for three days. The ark of the covenant of the LORD went before them during those three days to find them a place to rest. ³⁴The cloud of the LORD was over them by day when they set out from the camp.

³⁵Whenever the ark set out, Moses said,

"Rise up, O LORD!
    May your enemies be scattered;
    may your foes flee before you."

³⁶Whenever it came to rest, he said,

"Return, O LORD,
    to the countless thousands of Israel."

Fire From the LORD

11 Now the people complained about their hardships in the hearing of the LORD, and when he heard them his anger was aroused. Then fire from the LORD burned among them and consumed some of the outskirts of the camp. ²When the people cried out to Moses, he prayed to the LORD and the fire died down. ³So that place was called Taberah,ᵃ because fire from the LORD had burned among them.

Quail From the LORD

⁴The rabble with them began to crave other food, and again the Israelites started wailing and said, "If only we had meat to eat! ⁵We remember the fish we ate in Egypt at no cost—also the cucumbers, melons, leeks, onions and garlic. ⁶But now we have lost our appetite; we never see anything but this manna!"

⁷The manna was like coriander seed and looked like resin. ⁸The people went around gathering it, and then ground it in a handmill or crushed it in a mortar. They cooked it in a pot or made it into cakes. And it tasted like something made with olive oil. ⁹When the dew settled on the camp at night, the manna also came down.

¹⁰Moses heard the people of every family wailing, each at the entrance to his tent. The LORD became exceedingly angry, and Moses was troubled. ¹¹He asked the LORD, "Why have you brought this trouble on your servant? What have I done to displease you that you put the burden of all these people on me? ¹²Did I conceive all these people? Did I give them birth? Why do you tell me to carry them in my arms, as a nurse carries an infant, to the land you promised on oath to their forefathers? ¹³Where can I get meat for all these people? They keep wailing to me, 'Give us meat to eat!' ¹⁴I cannot carry all these people by myself; the burden is too heavy for me. ¹⁵If this is how you are going to treat me, put me to death right now—if I have found favor in your eyes—and do not let me face my own ruin."

¹⁶The LORD said to Moses: "Bring me sev-

ᵃ3 Taberah means burning.

WHAT ABOUT GLUTTONY?

It's Saturday night and six friends are eating out together at their favorite spot, McMurphy's. With the dinner winding down, the topic of conversation turns to a girl from Larry's church, a senior who just found out she's pregnant.

"Are you serious?" Caroline inquires.

"As a heart attack," replies Larry, who's polishing off the last of his two (giant) cheeseburgers and the rest of Caroline's salad.

The waiter walks up. "Would anyone like to order dessert?"

With his mouth full, Larry blurts, "Yeah, I'll take a chocolate sundae."

Look It Up
• • • •

Christians are curious creatures. We express shock and/or outrage when another Christian commits sexual sin. But we think nothing about the believer who makes a pig of himself at the table.

Make no mistake about it—gluttony is wrong!

Solomon urged: "Do not join those who drink too much wine or gorge themselves on meat, for drunkards and gluttons become poor, and drowsiness clothes them in rags" (Proverbs 23:20–21).

And Paul, noting that "Cretans are always . . . lazy gluttons" (Titus 1:12), preached self-control to the church at Crete: to the leaders (Titus 1:7–8), to the older men (Titus 2:2), to the women (Titus 2:4), to the younger men (Titus 2:6)—in short, to everyone (Titus 2:12).

Think It Through
• • • •

Is it hard for you to push away from the table? Do you continue to eat even after you've had enough?

Why do you think some people have a harder time exercising self-control in this area than in others?

Work It Out
• • • •

If overeating is a problem for you:

1. Put signs that say "No snacking!" or "Are you really hungry?" on the refrigerator and/or pantry door.

2. Ask a friend to hold you accountable.

3. Eat off of a plate instead of out of a package. (You'll eat a lot less!)

4. Eat slowly and put your fork down between bites (you'll fill up faster).

5. Drink lots of water (it gives you a full feeling).

6. Remember that God has already given you self-discipline (2 Timothy 1:7). You just need to exercise this quality.

Nail It Down
• • • •

Read in Numbers 11:4–34 about the Israelites, who got too carried away with themselves at a God-sponsored, all-you-can-eat quail dinner.

Turn to pages 188 and 1225 for other readings on food.
Turn to page 150 for Friday's reading.

Topic
• • • •

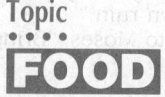

enty of Israel's elders who are known to you as leaders and officials among the people. Have them come to the Tent of Meeting, that they may stand there with you. **17**I will come down and speak with you there, and I will take of the Spirit that is on you and put the Spirit on them. They will help you carry the burden of the people so that you will not have to carry it alone.

18"Tell the people: 'Consecrate yourselves in preparation for tomorrow, when you will eat meat. The LORD heard you when you wailed, "If only we had meat to eat! We were better off in Egypt!" Now the LORD will give you meat, and you will eat it. **19**You will not eat it for just one day, or two days, or five, ten or twenty days, **20**but for a whole month—until it comes out of your nostrils and you loathe it—because you have rejected the LORD, who is among you, and have wailed before him, saying, "Why did we ever leave Egypt?"'"

21But Moses said, "Here I am among six hundred thousand men on foot, and you say, 'I will give them meat to eat for a whole month!' **22**Would they have enough if flocks and herds were slaughtered for them? Would they have enough if all the fish in the sea were caught for them?"

23The LORD answered Moses, "Is the LORD's arm too short? You will now see whether or not what I say will come true for you."

24So Moses went out and told the people what the LORD had said. He brought together seventy of their elders and had them stand around the Tent. **25**Then the LORD came down in the cloud and spoke with him, and he took of the Spirit that was on him and put the Spirit on the seventy elders. When the Spirit rested on them, they prophesied, but they did not do so again.[a]

26However, two men, whose names were Eldad and Medad, had remained in the camp. They were listed among the elders, but did not go out to the Tent. Yet the Spirit also rested on them, and they prophesied in the camp. **27**A young man ran and told Moses, "Eldad and Medad are prophesying in the camp."

28Joshua son of Nun, who had been Moses' aide since youth, spoke up and said, "Moses, my lord, stop them!"

29But Moses replied, "Are you jealous for my sake? I wish that all the LORD's people were prophets and that the LORD would put

his Spirit on them!" **30**Then Moses and the elders of Israel returned to the camp.

31Now a wind went out from the LORD and drove quail in from the sea. It brought them[b] down all around the camp to about three feet[c] above the ground, as far as a day's walk in any direction. **32**All that day and night and all the next day the people went out and gathered quail. No one gathered less than ten homers.[d] Then they spread them out all around the camp. **33**But while the meat was still between their teeth and before it could be consumed, the anger of the LORD burned against the people, and he struck them with a severe plague. **34**Therefore the place was named Kibroth Hattaavah,[e] because there they buried the people who had craved other food.

35From Kibroth Hattaavah the people traveled to Hazeroth and stayed there.

Miriam and Aaron Oppose Moses

12 Miriam and Aaron began to talk against Moses because of his Cushite wife, for he had married a Cushite. **2**"Has the LORD spoken only through Moses?" they asked. "Hasn't he also spoken through us?" And the LORD heard this.

3(Now Moses was a very humble man, more humble than anyone else on the face of the earth.)

4At once the LORD said to Moses, Aaron and Miriam, "Come out to the Tent of Meeting, all three of you." So the three of them came out. **5**Then the LORD came down in a pillar of cloud; he stood at the entrance to the Tent and summoned Aaron and Miriam. When both of them stepped forward, **6**he said, "Listen to my words:

"When a prophet of the LORD is among
      you,
   I reveal myself to him in visions,
   I speak to him in dreams.
7But this is not true of my servant Moses;
   he is faithful in all my house.
8With him I speak face to face,
   clearly and not in riddles;
   he sees the form of the LORD.
Why then were you not afraid
   to speak against my servant Moses?"

9The anger of the LORD burned against them, and he left them.

10When the cloud lifted from above the Tent, there stood Miriam—leprous,[f] like

---

[a]25 Or *prophesied and continued to do so*   [b]31 Or *They flew*   [c]31 Hebrew *two cubits* (about 1 meter)
[d]32 That is, probably about 60 bushels (about 2.2 kiloliters)   [e]34 *Kibroth Hattaavah* means *graves of craving*.
[f]10 The Hebrew word was used for various diseases affecting the skin—not necessarily leprosy.

snow. Aaron turned toward her and saw that she had leprosy; [11]and he said to Moses, "Please, my lord, do not hold against us the sin we have so foolishly committed. [12]Do not let her be like a stillborn infant coming from its mother's womb with its flesh half eaten away."

[13]So Moses cried out to the LORD, "O God, please heal her!"

[14]The LORD replied to Moses, "If her father had spit in her face, would she not have been in disgrace for seven days? Confine her outside the camp for seven days; after that she can be brought back." [15]So Miriam was confined outside the camp for seven days, and the people did not move on till she was brought back.

[16]After that, the people left Hazeroth and encamped in the Desert of Paran.

Exploring Canaan

13 The LORD said to Moses, [2]"Send some men to explore the land of Canaan, which I am giving to the Israelites. From each ancestral tribe send one of its leaders."

[3]So at the LORD's command Moses sent them out from the Desert of Paran. All of them were leaders of the Israelites. [4]These are their names:

from the tribe of Reuben, Shammua son of Zaccur;
[5]from the tribe of Simeon, Shaphat son of Hori;
[6]from the tribe of Judah, Caleb son of Jephunneh;
[7]from the tribe of Issachar, Igal son of Joseph;
[8]from the tribe of Ephraim, Hoshea son of Nun;
[9]from the tribe of Benjamin, Palti son of Raphu;
[10]from the tribe of Zebulun, Gaddiel son of Sodi;
[11]from the tribe of Manasseh (a tribe of Joseph), Gaddi son of Susi;
[12]from the tribe of Dan, Ammiel son of Gemalli;
[13]from the tribe of Asher, Sethur son of Michael;
[14]from the tribe of Naphtali, Nahbi son of Vophsi;
[15]from the tribe of Gad, Geuel son of Maki.

[16]These are the names of the men Moses sent to explore the land. (Moses gave Hoshea son of Nun the name Joshua.)

[17]When Moses sent them to explore Canaan, he said, "Go up through the Negev and on into the hill country. [18]See what the land is like and whether the people who live there are strong or weak, few or many. [19]What kind of land do they live in? Is it good or bad? What kind of towns do they live in? Are they unwalled or fortified? [20]How is the soil? Is it fertile or poor? Are there trees on it or not? Do your best to bring back some of the fruit of the land." (It was the season for the first ripe grapes.)

[21]So they went up and explored the land from the Desert of Zin as far as Rehob, toward Lebo[a] Hamath. [22]They went up through the Negev and came to Hebron, where Ahiman, Sheshai and Talmai, the descendants of Anak, lived. (Hebron had been built seven years before Zoan in Egypt.) [23]When they reached the Valley of Eshcol,[b] they cut off a branch bearing a single cluster of grapes. Two of them carried it on a pole between them, along with some pomegranates and figs. [24]That place was called the Valley of Eshcol because of the cluster of grapes the Israelites cut off there. [25]At the end of forty days they returned from exploring the land.

Report on the Exploration

[26]They came back to Moses and Aaron and the whole Israelite community at Kadesh in the Desert of Paran. There they reported to them and to the whole assembly and showed them the fruit of the land. [27]They gave Moses this account: "We went into the land to which you sent us, and it does flow with milk and honey! Here is its fruit. [28]But the people who live there are powerful, and the cities are fortified and very large. We even saw descendants of Anak there. [29]The Amalekites live in the Negev; the Hittites, Jebusites and Amorites live in the hill country; and the Canaanites live near the sea and along the Jordan."

[30]Then Caleb silenced the people before Moses and said, "We should go up and take possession of the land, for we can certainly do it."

[31]But the men who had gone up with him said, "We can't attack those people; they are stronger than we are." [32]And they spread among the Israelites a bad report about the land they had explored. They said, "The land we explored devours those living in it.

---

[a]21 Or toward the entrance to   [b]23 Eshcol means cluster; also in verse 24.

All the people we saw there are of great size. 33We saw the Nephilim there (the descendants of Anak come from the Nephilim). We seemed like grasshoppers in our own eyes, and we looked the same to them."

The People Rebel

14 That night all the people of the community raised their voices and wept aloud. 2All the Israelites grumbled against Moses and Aaron, and the whole assembly said to them, "If only we had died in Egypt! Or in this desert! 3Why is the Lord bringing us to this land only to let us fall by the sword? Our wives and children will be taken as plunder. Wouldn't it be better for us to go back to Egypt?" 4And they said to each other, "We should choose a leader and go back to Egypt."

5Then Moses and Aaron fell facedown in front of the whole Israelite assembly gathered there. 6Joshua son of Nun and Caleb son of Jephunneh, who were among those who had explored the land, tore their clothes 7and said to the entire Israelite assembly, "The land we passed through and explored is exceedingly good. 8If the Lord is pleased with us, he will lead us into that land, a land flowing with milk and honey, and will give it to us. 9Only do not rebel against the Lord. And do not be afraid of the people of the land, because we will swallow them up. Their protection is gone, but the Lord is with us. Do not be afraid of them."

10But the whole assembly talked about stoning them. Then the glory of the Lord appeared at the Tent of Meeting to all the Israelites. 11The Lord said to Moses, "How long will these people treat me with contempt? How long will they refuse to believe in me, in spite of all the miraculous signs I have performed among them? 12I will strike them down with a plague and destroy them, but I will make you into a nation greater and stronger than they."

13Moses said to the Lord, "Then the Egyptians will hear about it! By your power you brought these people up from among them. 14And they will tell the inhabitants of this land about it. They have already heard that you, O Lord, are with these people and that you, O Lord, have been seen face to face, that your cloud stays over them, and that you go before them in a pillar of cloud by day and a pillar of fire by night. 15If you put these people to death all at one time, the nations who have heard this report about

you will say, 16'The Lord was not able to bring these people into the land he promised them on oath; so he slaughtered them in the desert.'

17"Now may the Lord's strength be displayed, just as you have declared: 18'The Lord is slow to anger, abounding in love and forgiving sin and rebellion. Yet he does not leave the guilty unpunished; he punishes the children for the sin of the fathers to the third and fourth generation.' 19In accordance with your great love, forgive the sin of these people, just as you have pardoned them from the time they left Egypt until now."

20The Lord replied, "I have forgiven them, as you asked. 21Nevertheless, as surely as I live and as surely as the glory of the Lord fills the whole earth, 22not one of the men who saw my glory and the miraculous signs I performed in Egypt and in the desert but who disobeyed me and tested me ten times— 23not one of them will ever see the land I promised on oath to their forefathers. No one who has treated me with contempt will ever see it. 24But because my servant Caleb has a different spirit and follows me wholeheartedly, I will bring him into the land he went to, and his descendants will inherit it. 25Since the Amalekites and Canaanites are living in the valleys, turn back tomorrow and set out toward the desert along the route to the Red Sea.*a*"

26The Lord said to Moses and Aaron: 27"How long will this wicked community grumble against me? I have heard the complaints of these grumbling Israelites. 28So tell them, 'As surely as I live, declares the Lord, I will do to you the very things I heard you say: 29In this desert your bodies will fall—every one of you twenty years old or more who was counted in the census and who has grumbled against me. 30Not one of you will enter the land I swore with uplifted hand to make your home, except Caleb son of Jephunneh and Joshua son of Nun. 31As for your children that you said would be taken as plunder, I will bring them in to enjoy the land you have rejected. 32But you—your bodies will fall in this desert. 33Your children will be shepherds here for forty years, suffering for your unfaithfulness, until the last of your bodies lies in the desert. 34For forty years—one year for each of the forty days you explored the land—you will suffer for your sins and know what it is like to have me against you.' 35I, the Lord, have spoken,

a25 Hebrew Yam Suph; that is, Sea of Reeds

ARE YOU TARNISHING GOD'S IMAGE?

Frank could probably do the cause of Christ a lot of good these days by not telling people he's a Christian.

See, he's hanging out with a group of students who aren't exactly angelic in their behavior. As a result, Frank has developed some new habits—drinking, smoking, watching X-rated videos, shoplifting—all while continuing to go to church and youth group.

**Look
It Up**
• • • •

Throughout the Bible, different individuals were disciplined for dishonoring God's name.

"And wherever they went among the nations they profaned my holy name, for it was said of them, 'These are the LORD's people, and yet they had to leave his land.' I [the Lord] had concern for my holy name, which the house of Israel profaned among the nations where they had gone" (Ezekiel 36:20–21).

"As it is written: 'God's name is blasphemed among the Gentiles because of you' " (Romans 2:24).

"They claim to know God, but by their actions they deny him. They are detestable, disobedient and unfit for doing anything good" (Titus 1:16).

**Think It
Through**
• • • •

It's bad enough to have a rotten reputation. It's even worse to do rotten things and—at the same time—claim to be a Christian.

How do you feel when you see someone who professes to be a believer in Christ doing outrageous or even sinful things? How do you think God feels when individuals drag his name through the mud?

Is there anything about your life that is presently dishonoring God's name?

**Work It
Out**
• • • •

Look up the word *hypocrite* in the dictionary. Does that word describe you right now? If so, tell God that you want to change. Apologize for disgracing his name, and ask him for the strength to be a better ambassador (2 Corinthians 5:20).

Remember: God isn't looking for perfect people, but he does expect you to live according to his standards. Why? Because the way you live affects others. Your behavior can make people hungry to know God . . . or it can leave a bad taste in their mouths!

**Nail It
Down**
• • • •

Notice how concerned Moses was about God's reputation in Numbers 14:13–16.

Turn to pages 674, 1074, 1078 and 1306 for other readings on reputation.
Turn to page 159 for the weekend reading.

Topic
• • • •

REPUTATION

and I will surely do these things to this whole wicked community, which has banded together against me. They will meet their end in this desert; here they will die."

³⁶So the men Moses had sent to explore the land, who returned and made the whole community grumble against him by spreading a bad report about it— ³⁷these men responsible for spreading the bad report about the land were struck down and died of a plague before the LORD. ³⁸Of the men who went to explore the land, only Joshua son of Nun and Caleb son of Jephunneh survived.

³⁹When Moses reported this to all the Israelites, they mourned bitterly. ⁴⁰Early the next morning they went up toward the high hill country. "We have sinned," they said. "We will go up to the place the LORD promised."

⁴¹But Moses said, "Why are you disobeying the LORD's command? This will not succeed! ⁴²Do not go up, because the LORD is not with you. You will be defeated by your enemies, ⁴³for the Amalekites and Canaanites will face you there. Because you have turned away from the LORD, he will not be with you and you will fall by the sword."

⁴⁴Nevertheless, in their presumption they went up toward the high hill country, though neither Moses nor the ark of the LORD's covenant moved from the camp. ⁴⁵Then the Amalekites and Canaanites who lived in that hill country came down and attacked them and beat them down all the way to Hormah.

Supplementary Offerings

15 The LORD said to Moses, ²"Speak to the Israelites and say to them: 'After you enter the land I am giving you as a home ³and you present to the LORD offerings made by fire, from the herd or the flock, as an aroma pleasing to the LORD—whether burnt offerings or sacrifices, for special vows or freewill offerings or festival offerings— ⁴then the one who brings his offering shall present to the LORD a grain offering of a tenth of an ephah^a of fine flour mixed with a quarter of a hin^b of oil. ⁵With each lamb for the burnt offering or the sacrifice, prepare a quarter of a hin of wine as a drink offering.

⁶"With a ram prepare a grain offering of two-tenths of an ephah^c of fine flour mixed with a third of a hin^d of oil, ⁷and a third of a hin of wine as a drink offering. Offer it as an aroma pleasing to the LORD.

⁸"'When you prepare a young bull as a burnt offering or sacrifice, for a special vow or a fellowship offering^e to the LORD, ⁹bring with the bull a grain offering of three-tenths of an ephah^f of fine flour mixed with half a hin^g of oil. ¹⁰Also bring half a hin of wine as a drink offering. It will be an offering made by fire, an aroma pleasing to the LORD. ¹¹Each bull or ram, each lamb or young goat, is to be prepared in this manner. ¹²Do this for each one, for as many as you prepare.

¹³"'Everyone who is native-born must do these things in this way when he brings an offering made by fire as an aroma pleasing to the LORD. ¹⁴For the generations to come, whenever an alien or anyone else living among you presents an offering made by fire as an aroma pleasing to the LORD, he must do exactly as you do. ¹⁵The community is to have the same rules for you and for the alien living among you; this is a lasting ordinance for the generations to come. You and the alien shall be the same before the LORD: ¹⁶The same laws and regulations will apply both to you and to the alien living among you.'"

¹⁷The LORD said to Moses, ¹⁸"Speak to the Israelites and say to them: 'When you enter the land to which I am taking you ¹⁹and you eat the food of the land, present a portion as an offering to the LORD. ²⁰Present a cake from the first of your ground meal and present it as an offering from the threshing floor. ²¹Throughout the generations to come you are to give this offering to the LORD from the first of your ground meal.

Offerings for Unintentional Sins

²²"'Now if you unintentionally fail to keep any of these commands the LORD gave Moses— ²³any of the LORD's commands to you through him, from the day the LORD gave them and continuing through the generations to come— ²⁴and if this is done unintentionally without the community being aware of it, then the whole community is to offer a young bull for a burnt offering as an aroma pleasing to the LORD, along with its prescribed grain offering and drink offering, and a male goat for a sin offering. ²⁵The

---

^a4 That is, probably about 2 quarts (about 2 liters) ^b4 That is, probably about 1 quart (about 1 liter); also in verse 5 ^c6 That is, probably about 4 quarts (about 4.5 liters) ^d6 That is, probably about 1 1/4 quarts (about 1.2 liters); also in verse 7 ^e8 Traditionally *peace offering* ^f9 That is, probably about 6 quarts (about 6.5 liters) ^g9 That is, probably about 2 quarts (about 2 liters); also in verse 10

priest is to make atonement for the whole Israelite community, and they will be forgiven, for it was not intentional and they have brought to the LORD for their wrong an offering made by fire and a sin offering. **26**The whole Israelite community and the aliens living among them will be forgiven, because all the people were involved in the unintentional wrong.

27" 'But if just one person sins unintentionally, he must bring a year-old female goat for a sin offering. **28**The priest is to make atonement before the LORD for the one who erred by sinning unintentionally, and when atonement has been made for him, he will be forgiven. **29**One and the same law applies to everyone who sins unintentionally, whether he is a native-born Israelite or an alien.

30" 'But anyone who sins defiantly, whether native-born or alien, blasphemes the LORD, and that person must be cut off from his people. **31**Because he has despised the LORD's word and broken his commands, that person must surely be cut off; his guilt remains on him.' "

The Sabbath-Breaker Put to Death

32While the Israelites were in the desert, a man was found gathering wood on the Sabbath day. **33**Those who found him gathering wood brought him to Moses and Aaron and the whole assembly, **34**and they kept him in custody, because it was not clear what should be done to him. **35**Then the LORD said to Moses, "The man must die. The whole assembly must stone him outside the camp." **36**So the assembly took him outside the camp and stoned him to death, as the LORD commanded Moses.

Tassels on Garments

37The LORD said to Moses, **38**"Speak to the Israelites and say to them: 'Throughout the generations to come you are to make tassels on the corners of your garments, with a blue cord on each tassel. **39**You will have these tassels to look at and so you will remember all the commands of the LORD, that you may obey them and not prostitute yourselves by going after the lusts of your own hearts and eyes. **40**Then you will remember to obey all my commands and will be consecrated to your God. **41**I am the LORD your God, who brought you out of Egypt to be your God. I am the LORD your God.' "

Korah, Dathan and Abiram

16 Korah son of Izhar, the son of Kohath, the son of Levi, and certain Reubenites—Dathan and Abiram, sons of Eliab, and On son of Peleth—became insolent[a] **2**and rose up against Moses. With them were 250 Israelite men, well-known community leaders who had been appointed members of the council. **3**They came as a group to oppose Moses and Aaron and said to them, "You have gone too far! The whole community is holy, every one of them, and the LORD is with them. Why then do you set yourselves above the LORD's assembly?"

4When Moses heard this, he fell facedown. **5**Then he said to Korah and all his followers: "In the morning the LORD will show who belongs to him and who is holy, and he will have that person come near him. The man he chooses he will cause to come near him. **6**You, Korah, and all your followers are to do this: Take censers **7**and tomorrow put fire and incense in them before the LORD. The man the LORD chooses will be the one who is holy. You Levites have gone too far!"

8Moses also said to Korah, "Now listen, you Levites! **9**Isn't it enough for you that the God of Israel has separated you from the rest of the Israelite community and brought you near himself to do the work at the LORD's tabernacle and to stand before the community and minister to them? **10**He has brought you and all your fellow Levites near himself, but now you are trying to get the priesthood too. **11**It is against the LORD that you and all your followers have banded together. Who is Aaron that you should grumble against him?"

12Then Moses summoned Dathan and Abiram, the sons of Eliab. But they said, "We will not come! **13**Isn't it enough that you have brought us up out of a land flowing with milk and honey to kill us in the desert? And now you also want to lord it over us? **14**Moreover, you haven't brought us into a land flowing with milk and honey or given us an inheritance of fields and vineyards. Will you gouge out the eyes of[b] these men? No, we will not come!"

15Then Moses became very angry and said to the LORD, "Do not accept their offering. I have not taken so much as a donkey from them, nor have I wronged any of them."

16Moses said to Korah, "You and all your

---

a 1 Or Peleth—took ₍men₎   b 14 Or you make slaves of; or you deceive followers are to appear before the LORD tomorrow—you and they and Aaron. **17**Each man is to take his censer and put incense in it—250 censers in all—and present it before the LORD. You and Aaron are to present your censers also." **18**So each man took his censer, put fire and incense in it, and stood with Moses and Aaron at the entrance to the Tent of Meeting. **19**When Korah had gathered all his followers in opposition to them at the entrance to the Tent of Meeting, the glory of the LORD appeared to the entire assembly. **20**The LORD said to Moses and Aaron, **21**"Separate yourselves from this assembly so I can put an end to them at once."

22But Moses and Aaron fell facedown and cried out, "O God, God of the spirits of all mankind, will you be angry with the entire assembly when only one man sins?"

23Then the LORD said to Moses, **24**"Say to the assembly, 'Move away from the tents of Korah, Dathan and Abiram.'"

25Moses got up and went to Dathan and Abiram, and the elders of Israel followed him. **26**He warned the assembly, "Move back from the tents of these wicked men! Do not touch anything belonging to them, or you will be swept away because of all their sins." **27**So they moved away from the tents of Korah, Dathan and Abiram. Dathan and Abiram had come out and were standing with their wives, children and little ones at the entrances to their tents.

28Then Moses said, "This is how you will know that the LORD has sent me to do all these things and that it was not my idea: **29**If these men die a natural death and experience only what usually happens to men, then the LORD has not sent me. **30**But if the LORD brings about something totally new, and the earth opens its mouth and swallows them, with everything that belongs to them, and they go down alive into the grave,^{a} then you will know that these men have treated the LORD with contempt."

31As soon as he finished saying all this, the ground under them split apart **32**and the earth opened its mouth and swallowed them, with their households and all Korah's men and all their possessions. **33**They went down alive into the grave, with everything they owned; the earth closed over them, and they perished and were gone from the community. **34**At their cries, all the Israelites around them fled, shouting, "The earth is going to swallow us too!"

35And fire came out from the LORD and consumed the 250 men who were offering the incense.

36The LORD said to Moses, **37**"Tell Eleazar son of Aaron, the priest, to take the censers out of the smoldering remains and scatter the coals some distance away, for the censers are holy— **38**the censers of the men who sinned at the cost of their lives. Hammer the censers into sheets to overlay the altar, for they were presented before the LORD and have become holy. Let them be a sign to the Israelites."

39So Eleazar the priest collected the bronze censers brought by those who had been burned up, and he had them hammered out to overlay the altar, **40**as the LORD directed him through Moses. This was to remind the Israelites that no one except a descendant of Aaron should come to burn incense before the LORD, or he would become like Korah and his followers.

41The next day the whole Israelite community grumbled against Moses and Aaron. "You have killed the LORD's people," they said.

42But when the assembly gathered in opposition to Moses and Aaron and turned toward the Tent of Meeting, suddenly the cloud covered it and the glory of the LORD appeared. **43**Then Moses and Aaron went to the front of the Tent of Meeting, **44**and the LORD said to Moses, **45**"Get away from this assembly so I can put an end to them at once." And they fell facedown.

46Then Moses said to Aaron, "Take your censer and put incense in it, along with fire from the altar, and hurry to the assembly to make atonement for them. Wrath has come out from the LORD; the plague has started." **47**So Aaron did as Moses said, and ran into the midst of the assembly. The plague had already started among the people, but Aaron offered the incense and made atonement for them. **48**He stood between the living and the dead, and the plague stopped. **49**But 14,700 people died from the plague, in addition to those who had died because of Korah. **50**Then Aaron returned to Moses at the entrance to the Tent of Meeting, for the plague had stopped.

The Budding of Aaron's Staff

17 The LORD said to Moses, **2**"Speak to the Israelites and get twelve staffs from them, one from the leader of each of their ancestral tribes. Write the name of each man on his staff. **3**On the staff of Levi

---

^{a}30 Hebrew *Sheol*; also in verse 33

write Aaron's name, for there must be one staff for the head of each ancestral tribe. [4]Place them in the Tent of Meeting in front of the Testimony, where I meet with you. [5]The staff belonging to the man I choose will sprout, and I will rid myself of this constant grumbling against you by the Israelites."

[6]So Moses spoke to the Israelites, and their leaders gave him twelve staffs, one for the leader of each of their ancestral tribes, and Aaron's staff was among them. [7]Moses placed the staffs before the LORD in the Tent of the Testimony.

[8]The next day Moses entered the Tent of the Testimony and saw that Aaron's staff, which represented the house of Levi, had not only sprouted but had budded, blossomed and produced almonds. [9]Then Moses brought out all the staffs from the LORD's presence to all the Israelites. They looked at them, and each man took his own staff.

[10]The LORD said to Moses, "Put back Aaron's staff in front of the Testimony, to be kept as a sign to the rebellious. This will put an end to their grumbling against me, so that they will not die." [11]Moses did just as the LORD commanded him.

[12]The Israelites said to Moses, "We will die! We are lost, we are all lost! [13]Anyone who even comes near the tabernacle of the LORD will die. Are we all going to die?"

Duties of Priests and Levites

18 The LORD said to Aaron, "You, your sons and your father's family are to bear the responsibility for offenses against the sanctuary, and you and your sons alone are to bear the responsibility for offenses against the priesthood. [2]Bring your fellow Levites from your ancestral tribe to join you and assist you when you and your sons minister before the Tent of the Testimony. [3]They are to be responsible to you and are to perform all the duties of the Tent, but they must not go near the furnishings of the sanctuary or the altar, or both they and you will die. [4]They are to join you and be responsible for the care of the Tent of Meeting — all the work at the Tent — and no one else may come near where you are.

[5]"You are to be responsible for the care of the sanctuary and the altar, so that wrath will not fall on the Israelites again. [6]I myself have selected your fellow Levites from among the Israelites as a gift to you, dedicated to the LORD to do the work at the Tent of

Meeting. [7]But only you and your sons may serve as priests in connection with everything at the altar and inside the curtain. I am giving you the service of the priesthood as a gift. Anyone else who comes near the sanctuary must be put to death."

Offerings for Priests and Levites

[8]Then the LORD said to Aaron, "I myself have put you in charge of the offerings presented to me; all the holy offerings the Israelites give me I give to you and your sons as your portion and regular share. [9]You are to have the part of the most holy offerings that is kept from the fire. From all the gifts they bring me as most holy offerings, whether grain or sin or guilt offerings, that part belongs to you and your sons. [10]Eat it as something most holy; every male shall eat it. You must regard it as holy.

[11]"This also is yours: whatever is set aside from the gifts of all the wave offerings of the Israelites. I give this to you and your sons and daughters as your regular share. Everyone in your household who is ceremonially clean may eat it.

[12]"I give you all the finest olive oil and all the finest new wine and grain they give the LORD as the firstfruits of their harvest. [13]All the land's firstfruits that they bring to the LORD will be yours. Everyone in your household who is ceremonially clean may eat it.

[14]"Everything in Israel that is devoted[a] to the LORD is yours. [15]The first offspring of every womb, both man and animal, that is offered to the LORD is yours. But you must redeem every firstborn son and every firstborn male of unclean animals. [16]When they are a month old, you must redeem them at the redemption price set at five shekels[b] of silver, according to the sanctuary shekel, which weighs twenty gerahs.

[17]"But you must not redeem the firstborn of an ox, a sheep or a goat; they are holy. Sprinkle their blood on the altar and burn their fat as an offering made by fire, an aroma pleasing to the LORD. [18]Their meat is to be yours, just as the breast of the wave offering and the right thigh are yours. [19]Whatever is set aside from the holy offerings the Israelites present to the LORD I give to you and your sons and daughters as your regular share. It is an everlasting covenant of salt before the LORD for both you and your offspring."

[20]The LORD said to Aaron, "You will have

---

[a]14 The Hebrew term refers to the irrevocable giving over of things or persons to the LORD.   [b]16 That is, about 2 ounces (about 55 grams)

no inheritance in their land, nor will you have any share among them; I am your share and your inheritance among the Israelites.

21"I give to the Levites all the tithes in Israel as their inheritance in return for the work they do while serving at the Tent of Meeting. 22From now on the Israelites must not go near the Tent of Meeting, or they will bear the consequences of their sin and will die. 23It is the Levites who are to do the work at the Tent of Meeting and bear the responsibility for offenses against it. This is a lasting ordinance for the generations to come. They will receive no inheritance among the Israelites. 24Instead, I give to the Levites as their inheritance the tithes that the Israelites present as an offering to the LORD. That is why I said concerning them: 'They will have no inheritance among the Israelites.' "

25The LORD said to Moses, 26"Speak to the Levites and say to them: 'When you receive from the Israelites the tithe I give you as your inheritance, you must present a tenth of that tithe as the LORD's offering. 27Your offering will be reckoned to you as grain from the threshing floor or juice from the winepress. 28In this way you also will present an offering to the LORD from all the tithes you receive from the Israelites. From these tithes you must give the LORD's portion to Aaron the priest. 29You must present as the LORD's portion the best and holiest part of everything given to you.'

30"Say to the Levites: 'When you present the best part, it will be reckoned to you as the product of the threshing floor or the winepress. 31You and your households may eat the rest of it anywhere, for it is your wages for your work at the Tent of Meeting. 32By presenting the best part of it you will not be guilty in this matter; then you will not defile the holy offerings of the Israelites, and you will not die.' "

The Water of Cleansing

19 The LORD said to Moses and Aaron: 2"This is a requirement of the law that the LORD has commanded: Tell the Israelites to bring you a red heifer without defect or blemish and that has never been under a yoke. 3Give it to Eleazar the priest; it is to be taken outside the camp and slaughtered in his presence. 4Then Eleazar the priest is to take some of its blood on his finger and sprinkle it seven times toward the front of the Tent of Meeting. 5While he watches, the heifer is to be burned — its hide, flesh, blood and offal. 6The priest is to

take some cedar wood, hyssop and scarlet wool and throw them onto the burning heifer. 7After that, the priest must wash his clothes and bathe himself with water. He may then come into the camp, but he will be ceremonially unclean till evening. 8The man who burns it must also wash his clothes and bathe with water, and he too will be unclean till evening.

9"A man who is clean shall gather up the ashes of the heifer and put them in a ceremonially clean place outside the camp. They shall be kept by the Israelite community for use in the water of cleansing; it is for purification from sin. 10The man who gathers up the ashes of the heifer must also wash his clothes, and he too will be unclean till evening. This will be a lasting ordinance both for the Israelites and for the aliens living among them.

11"Whoever touches the dead body of anyone will be unclean for seven days. 12He must purify himself with the water on the third day and on the seventh day; then he will be clean. But if he does not purify himself on the third and seventh days, he will not be clean. 13Whoever touches the dead body of anyone and fails to purify himself defiles the LORD's tabernacle. That person must be cut off from Israel. Because the water of cleansing has not been sprinkled on him, he is unclean; his uncleanness remains on him.

14"This is the law that applies when a person dies in a tent: Anyone who enters the tent and anyone who is in it will be unclean for seven days, 15and every open container without a lid fastened on it will be unclean.

16"Anyone out in the open who touches someone who has been killed with a sword or someone who has died a natural death, or anyone who touches a human bone or a grave, will be unclean for seven days.

17"For the unclean person, put some ashes from the burned purification offering into a jar and pour fresh water over them. 18Then a man who is ceremonially clean is to take some hyssop, dip it in the water and sprinkle the tent and all the furnishings and the people who were there. He must also sprinkle anyone who has touched a human bone or a grave or someone who has been killed or someone who has died a natural death. 19The man who is clean is to sprinkle the unclean person on the third and seventh days, and on the seventh day he is to purify him. The person being cleansed must wash his clothes and bathe with water, and that evening he will be clean. 20But if a person who is unclean does not purify himself, he must be cut off from the community, because he has defiled the sanctuary of the LORD. The water of cleansing has not been sprinkled on him, and he is unclean. **21**This is a lasting ordinance for them.

"The man who sprinkles the water of cleansing must also wash his clothes, and anyone who touches the water of cleansing will be unclean till evening. **22**Anything that an unclean person touches becomes unclean, and anyone who touches it becomes unclean till evening."

Water From the Rock

20 In the first month the whole Israelite community arrived at the Desert of Zin, and they stayed at Kadesh. There Miriam died and was buried.

2Now there was no water for the community, and the people gathered in opposition to Moses and Aaron. **3**They quarreled with Moses and said, "If only we had died when our brothers fell dead before the LORD! **4**Why did you bring the LORD's community into this desert, that we and our livestock should die here? **5**Why did you bring us up out of Egypt to this terrible place? It has no grain or figs, grapevines or pomegranates. And there is no water to drink!"

6Moses and Aaron went from the assembly to the entrance to the Tent of Meeting and fell facedown, and the glory of the LORD appeared to them. **7**The LORD said to Moses, **8**"Take the staff, and you and your brother Aaron gather the assembly together. Speak to that rock before their eyes and it will pour out its water. You will bring water out of the rock for the community so they and their livestock can drink."

9So Moses took the staff from the LORD's presence, just as he commanded him. **10**He and Aaron gathered the assembly together in front of the rock and Moses said to them, "Listen, you rebels, must we bring you water out of this rock?" **11**Then Moses raised his arm and struck the rock twice with his staff. Water gushed out, and the community and their livestock drank.

12But the LORD said to Moses and Aaron, "Because you did not trust in me enough to honor me as holy in the sight of the Israelites, you will not bring this community into the land I give them."

13These were the waters of Meribah,*a* where the Israelites quarreled with the LORD

and where he showed himself holy among them.

Edom Denies Israel Passage

14Moses sent messengers from Kadesh to the king of Edom, saying:

"This is what your brother Israel says: You know about all the hardships that have come upon us. **15**Our forefathers went down into Egypt, and we lived there many years. The Egyptians mistreated us and our fathers, **16**but when we cried out to the LORD, he heard our cry and sent an angel and brought us out of Egypt.

"Now we are here at Kadesh, a town on the edge of your territory. **17**Please let us pass through your country. We will not go through any field or vineyard, or drink water from any well. We will travel along the king's highway and not turn to the right or to the left until we have passed through your territory."

18But Edom answered:

"You may not pass through here; if you try, we will march out and attack you with the sword."

19The Israelites replied:

"We will go along the main road, and if we or our livestock drink any of your water, we will pay for it. We only want to pass through on foot — nothing else."

20Again they answered:

"You may not pass through."

Then Edom came out against them with a large and powerful army. **21**Since Edom refused to let them go through their territory, Israel turned away from them.

The Death of Aaron

22The whole Israelite community set out from Kadesh and came to Mount Hor. **23**At Mount Hor, near the border of Edom, the LORD said to Moses and Aaron, **24**"Aaron will be gathered to his people. He will not enter the land I give the Israelites, because both of you rebelled against my command at the waters of Meribah. **25**Get Aaron and his son Eleazar and take them up Mount Hor. **26**Remove Aaron's garments and put them on his son Eleazar, for Aaron will be gathered to his people; he will die there."

27Moses did as the LORD commanded:

---

a13 Meribah means *quarreling.*

They went up Mount Hor in the sight of the whole community. **28**Moses removed Aaron's garments and put them on his son Eleazar. And Aaron died there on top of the mountain. Then Moses and Eleazar came down from the mountain, **29**and when the whole community learned that Aaron had died, the entire house of Israel mourned for him thirty days.

Arad Destroyed

21 When the Canaanite king of Arad, who lived in the Negev, heard that Israel was coming along the road to Atharim, he attacked the Israelites and captured some of them. **2**Then Israel made this vow to the Lord: "If you will deliver these people into our hands, we will totally destroy*a* their cities." **3**The Lord listened to Israel's plea and gave the Canaanites over to them. They completely destroyed them and their towns; so the place was named Hormah.*b*

The Bronze Snake

4They traveled from Mount Hor along the route to the Red Sea,*c* to go around Edom. But the people grew impatient on the way; **5**they spoke against God and against Moses, and said, "Why have you brought us up out of Egypt to die in the desert? There is no bread! There is no water! And we detest this miserable food!"

6Then the Lord sent venomous snakes among them; they bit the people and many Israelites died. **7**The people came to Moses and said, "We sinned when we spoke against the Lord and against you. Pray that the Lord will take the snakes away from us." So Moses prayed for the people.

8The Lord said to Moses, "Make a snake and put it up on a pole; anyone who is bitten can look at it and live." **9**So Moses made a bronze snake and put it up on a pole. Then when anyone was bitten by a snake and looked at the bronze snake, he lived.

The Journey to Moab

10The Israelites moved on and camped at Oboth. **11**Then they set out from Oboth and camped in Iye Abarim, in the desert that faces Moab toward the sunrise. **12**From there they moved on and camped in the Zered Valley. **13**They set out from there and camped alongside the Arnon, which is in the

desert extending into Amorite territory. The Arnon is the border of Moab, between Moab and the Amorites. **14**That is why the Book of the Wars of the Lord says:

> ". . . Waheb in Suphah*d* and the ravines,
> the Arnon **15**and*e* the slopes of the ravines
> that lead to the site of Ar
> and lie along the border of Moab."

16From there they continued on to Beer, the well where the Lord said to Moses, "Gather the people together and I will give them water." **17**Then Israel sang this song:

> "Spring up, O well!
> Sing about it,
> **18**about the well that the princes dug,
> that the nobles of the people sank —
> the nobles with scepters and staffs."

Then they went from the desert to Mattanah, **19**from Mattanah to Nahaliel, from Nahaliel to Bamoth, **20**and from Bamoth to the valley in Moab where the top of Pisgah overlooks the wasteland.

Defeat of Sihon and Og

21Israel sent messengers to say to Sihon king of the Amorites:

> **22**"Let us pass through your country. We will not turn aside into any field or vineyard, or drink water from any well. We will travel along the king's highway until we have passed through your territory."

23But Sihon would not let Israel pass through his territory. He mustered his entire army and marched out into the desert against Israel. When he reached Jahaz, he fought with Israel. **24**Israel, however, put him to the sword and took over his land from the Arnon to the Jabbok, but only as far as the Ammonites, because their border was fortified. **25**Israel captured all the cities of the Amorites and occupied them, including Heshbon and all its surrounding settlements. **26**Heshbon was the city of Sihon king of the Amorites, who had fought against the former king of Moab and had taken from him all his land as far as the Arnon. **27**That is why the poets say:

---

a2 The Hebrew term refers to the irrevocable giving over of things or persons to the Lord, often by totally destroying them; also in verse 3.   *b3* *Hormah* means *destruction.*   *c4* Hebrew *Yam Suph*; that is, Sea of Reeds   *d14* The meaning of the Hebrew for this phrase is uncertain.   *e14,15* Or *"I have been given from Suphah and the ravines / of the Arnon 15to*

"Come to Heshbon and let it be rebuilt;
let Sihon's city be restored.

28"Fire went out from Heshbon,
a blaze from the city of Sihon.
It consumed Ar of Moab,
the citizens of Arnon's heights.
29Woe to you, O Moab!
You are destroyed, O people of
Chemosh!
He has given up his sons as fugitives
and his daughters as captives
to Sihon king of the Amorites.

30"But we have overthrown them;
Heshbon is destroyed all the way to
Dibon.
We have demolished them as far as
Nophah,
which extends to Medeba."

31So Israel settled in the land of the Amorites. 32After Moses had sent spies to Jazer, the Israelites captured its surrounding settlements and drove out the Amorites who were there. 33Then they turned and went up along the road toward Bashan, and Og king of Bashan and his whole army marched out to meet them in battle at Edrei.

34The LORD said to Moses, "Do not be afraid of him, for I have handed him over to you, with his whole army and his land. Do to him what you did to Sihon king of the Amorites, who reigned in Heshbon."

35So they struck him down, together with his sons and his whole army, leaving them no survivors. And they took possession of his land.

Balak Summons Balaam

22 Then the Israelites traveled to the plains of Moab and camped along the Jordan across from Jericho.ᵃ

2Now Balak son of Zippor saw all that Israel had done to the Amorites, 3and Moab was terrified because there were so many people. Indeed, Moab was filled with dread because of the Israelites.

4The Moabites said to the elders of Midian, "This horde is going to lick up everything around us, as an ox licks up the grass of the field."

So Balak son of Zippor, who was king of Moab at that time, 5sent messengers to summon Balaam son of Beor, who was at Pethor, near the River,ᵇ in his native land. Balak said:

"A people has come out of Egypt; they cover the face of the land and have settled next to me. 6Now come and put a curse on these people, because they are too powerful for me. Perhaps then I will be able to defeat them and drive them out of the country. For I know that those you bless are blessed, and those you curse are cursed."

7The elders of Moab and Midian left, taking with them the fee for divination. When they came to Balaam, they told him what Balak had said.

8"Spend the night here," Balaam said to them, "and I will bring you back the answer the LORD gives me." So the Moabite princes stayed with him.

9God came to Balaam and asked, "Who are these men with you?"

10Balaam said to God, "Balak son of Zippor, king of Moab, sent me this message: 11'A people that has come out of Egypt covers the face of the land. Now come and put a curse on them for me. Perhaps then I will be able to fight them and drive them away.' "

12But God said to Balaam, "Do not go with them. You must not put a curse on those people, because they are blessed."

13The next morning Balaam got up and said to Balak's princes, "Go back to your own country, for the LORD has refused to let me go with you."

14So the Moabite princes returned to Balak and said, "Balaam refused to come with us."

15Then Balak sent other princes, more numerous and more distinguished than the first. 16They came to Balaam and said:

"This is what Balak son of Zippor says: Do not let anything keep you from coming to me, 17because I will reward you handsomely and do whatever you say. Come and put a curse on these people for me."

18But Balaam answered them, "Even if Balak gave me his palace filled with silver and gold, I could not do anything great or small to go beyond the command of the LORD my God. 19Now stay here tonight as the others did, and I will find out what else the LORD will tell me."

20That night God came to Balaam and said, "Since these men have come to summon you, go with them, but do only what I tell you."

ᵃ1 Hebrew *Jordan of Jericho*; possibly an ancient name for the Jordan River   ᵇ5 That is, the Euphrates

WANTING TO OBEY

Work It Out

Make a list of all the people in your life who have a "right" to tell you what to do:

- parents
- teachers
- principal
- youth pastor
- God

Parents want you in by your curfew; teachers want assignments done; the principal wants you to obey school rules; your youth pastor wants you at youth meetings; God want you to follow him, to spend time with him, to stay pure. And the list goes on.

How do you feel about obeying all the "have to's" in your life? Read on to find out what God had to do to get the attention of some people who didn't want to obey.

Nail It Down

Read Numbers 22:21–35 for the story of how God got Balaam's attention when he disobeyed.

Think It Through

Obedience. Obey. Must. Should. Have to. The very words make some teens run the other way. And some adults as well.

Does being told you *must* do something automatically make you not want to do it? It's a pretty universal problem. You're far from alone.

For some of you obedience comes easy. You do as you're told without much fuss. Be thankful God has given you a willing spirit. But for others of you obedience is a problem. Just knowing you have to do something or should do something makes you not want to do it.

It may sometimes take a wild experience (like Balaam and his talking donkey), but God is there, willing and ready not only to help you obey, but willing and ready to make you *want* to obey.

Nail It Down

Read about Balaam's unique experience again in Numbers 22:21–35. For further insight read Psalm 119:33–40.

Turn to pages 281, 892, 1013, 1082 and 1156 for other readings on obedience.
Turn to page 163 for Monday's reading.

Topic

OBEDIENCE

Balaam's Donkey

21Balaam got up in the morning, saddled his donkey and went with the princes of Moab. **22**But God was very angry when he went, and the angel of the LORD stood in the road to oppose him. Balaam was riding on his donkey, and his two servants were with him. **23**When the donkey saw the angel of the LORD standing in the road with a drawn sword in his hand, she turned off the road into a field. Balaam beat her to get her back on the road.

24Then the angel of the LORD stood in a narrow path between two vineyards, with walls on both sides. **25**When the donkey saw the angel of the LORD, she pressed close to the wall, crushing Balaam's foot against it. So he beat her again.

26Then the angel of the LORD moved on ahead and stood in a narrow place where there was no room to turn, either to the right or to the left. **27**When the donkey saw the angel of the LORD, she lay down under Balaam, and he was angry and beat her with his staff. **28**Then the LORD opened the donkey's mouth, and she said to Balaam, "What have I done to you to make you beat me these three times?"

29Balaam answered the donkey, "You have made a fool of me! If I had a sword in my hand, I would kill you right now."

30The donkey said to Balaam, "Am I not your own donkey, which you have always ridden, to this day? Have I been in the habit of doing this to you?"

"No," he said.

31Then the LORD opened Balaam's eyes, and he saw the angel of the LORD standing in the road with his sword drawn. So he bowed low and fell facedown.

32The angel of the LORD asked him, "Why have you beaten your donkey these three times? I have come here to oppose you because your path is a reckless one before me.[a] **33**The donkey saw me and turned away from me these three times. If she had not turned away, I would certainly have killed you by now, but I would have spared her."

34Balaam said to the angel of the LORD, "I have sinned. I did not realize you were standing in the road to oppose me. Now if you are displeased, I will go back."

35The angel of the LORD said to Balaam, "Go with the men, but speak only what I tell you." So Balaam went with the princes of Balak.

36When Balak heard that Balaam was coming, he went out to meet him at the Moabite town on the Arnon border, at the edge of his territory. **37**Balak said to Balaam, "Did I not send you an urgent summons? Why didn't you come to me? Am I really not able to reward you?"

38"Well, I have come to you now," Balaam replied. "But can I say just anything? I must speak only what God puts in my mouth."

39Then Balaam went with Balak to Kiriath Huzoth. **40**Balak sacrificed cattle and sheep, and gave some to Balaam and the princes who were with him. **41**The next morning Balak took Balaam up to Bamoth Baal, and from there he saw part of the people.

Balaam's First Oracle

23 Balaam said, "Build me seven altars here, and prepare seven bulls and seven rams for me." **2**Balak did as Balaam said, and the two of them offered a bull and a ram on each altar.

3Then Balaam said to Balak, "Stay here beside your offering while I go aside. Perhaps the LORD will come to meet with me. Whatever he reveals to me I will tell you." Then he went off to a barren height.

4God met with him, and Balaam said, "I have prepared seven altars, and on each altar I have offered a bull and a ram."

5The LORD put a message in Balaam's mouth and said, "Go back to Balak and give him this message."

6So he went back to him and found him standing beside his offering, with all the princes of Moab. **7**Then Balaam uttered his oracle:

"Balak brought me from Aram,
    the king of Moab from the eastern
        mountains.
'Come,' he said, 'curse Jacob for me;
    come, denounce Israel.'
8How can I curse
    those whom God has not cursed?
How can I denounce
    those whom the LORD has not
        denounced?
9From the rocky peaks I see them,
    from the heights I view them.
I see a people who live apart
    and do not consider themselves one
        of the nations.
10Who can count the dust of Jacob

---

*a*32 The meaning of the Hebrew for this clause is uncertain.

or number the fourth part of Israel?
Let me die the death of the righteous,
and may my end be like theirs!"

11Balak said to Balaam, "What have you done to me? I brought you to curse my enemies, but you have done nothing but bless them!"

12He answered, "Must I not speak what the LORD puts in my mouth?"

Balaam's Second Oracle

13Then Balak said to him, "Come with me to another place where you can see them; you will see only a part but not all of them. And from there, curse them for me." **14**So he took him to the field of Zophim on the top of Pisgah, and there he built seven altars and offered a bull and a ram on each altar.

15Balaam said to Balak, "Stay here beside your offering while I meet with him over there."

16The LORD met with Balaam and put a message in his mouth and said, "Go back to Balak and give him this message."

17So he went to him and found him standing beside his offering, with the princes of Moab. Balak asked him, "What did the LORD say?"

18Then he uttered his oracle:

"Arise, Balak, and listen;
hear me, son of Zippor.
19God is not a man, that he should lie,
nor a son of man, that he should
change his mind.
Does he speak and then not act?
Does he promise and not fulfill?
20I have received a command to bless;
he has blessed, and I cannot change
it.

21"No misfortune is seen in Jacob,
no misery observed in Israel.[a]
The LORD their God is with them;
the shout of the King is among them.
22God brought them out of Egypt;
they have the strength of a wild ox.
23There is no sorcery against Jacob,
no divination against Israel.
It will now be said of Jacob
and of Israel, 'See what God has
done!'
24The people rise like a lioness;
they rouse themselves like a lion
that does not rest till he devours his
prey

and drinks the blood of his victims."

25Then Balak said to Balaam, "Neither curse them at all nor bless them at all!"
26Balaam answered, "Did I not tell you I must do whatever the LORD says?"

Balaam's Third Oracle

27Then Balak said to Balaam, "Come, let me take you to another place. Perhaps it will please God to let you curse them for me from there." **28**And Balak took Balaam to the top of Peor, overlooking the wasteland.
29Balaam said, "Build me seven altars here, and prepare seven bulls and seven rams for me." **30**Balak did as Balaam had said, and offered a bull and a ram on each altar.

24 Now when Balaam saw that it pleased the LORD to bless Israel, he did not resort to sorcery as at other times, but turned his face toward the desert. **2**When Balaam looked out and saw Israel encamped tribe by tribe, the Spirit of God came upon him **3**and he uttered his oracle:

"The oracle of Balaam son of Beor,
the oracle of one whose eye sees
clearly,
4the oracle of one who hears the words
of God,
who sees a vision from the
Almighty,[b]
who falls prostrate, and whose eyes
are opened:

5"How beautiful are your tents, O Jacob,
your dwelling places, O Israel!

6"Like valleys they spread out,
like gardens beside a river,
like aloes planted by the LORD,
like cedars beside the waters.
7Water will flow from their buckets;
their seed will have abundant water.

"Their king will be greater than Agag;
their kingdom will be exalted.

8"God brought them out of Egypt;
they have the strength of a wild ox.
They devour hostile nations
and break their bones in pieces;
with their arrows they pierce them.
9Like a lion they crouch and lie down,
like a lioness — who dares to rouse
them?

"May those who bless you be blessed

---

a21 Or *He has not looked on Jacob's offenses / or on the wrongs found in Israel.*   b4 Hebrew *Shaddai*; also in verse 16 and those who curse you be cursed!"

¹⁰Then Balak's anger burned against Balaam. He struck his hands together and said to him, "I summoned you to curse my enemies, but you have blessed them these three times. ¹¹Now leave at once and go home! I said I would reward you handsomely, but the Lord has kept you from being rewarded."

¹²Balaam answered Balak, "Did I not tell the messengers you sent me, ¹³'Even if Balak gave me his palace filled with silver and gold, I could not do anything of my own accord, good or bad, to go beyond the command of the Lord — and I must say only what the Lord says'? ¹⁴Now I am going back to my people, but come, let me warn you of what this people will do to your people in days to come."

Balaam's Fourth Oracle

¹⁵Then he uttered his oracle:

"The oracle of Balaam son of Beor,
    the oracle of one whose eye sees
        clearly,
¹⁶the oracle of one who hears the words
        of God,
    who has knowledge from the Most
        High,
who sees a vision from the Almighty,
    who falls prostrate, and whose eyes
        are opened:

¹⁷"I see him, but not now;
    I behold him, but not near.
A star will come out of Jacob;
    a scepter will rise out of Israel.
He will crush the foreheads of Moab,
    the skulls*a* of*b* all the sons of
        Seth.*c*
¹⁸Edom will be conquered;
    Seir, his enemy, will be conquered,
    but Israel will grow strong.
¹⁹A ruler will come out of Jacob
    and destroy the survivors of the city."

Balaam's Final Oracles

²⁰Then Balaam saw Amalek and uttered his oracle:

"Amalek was first among the nations,
    but he will come to ruin at last."

²¹Then he saw the Kenites and uttered his oracle:

"Your dwelling place is secure,
    your nest is set in a rock;
²²yet you Kenites will be destroyed
    when Asshur takes you captive."

²³Then he uttered his oracle:

"Ah, who can live when God does
        this?*d*
²⁴   Ships will come from the shores of
        Kittim;
they will subdue Asshur and Eber,
    but they too will come to ruin."

²⁵Then Balaam got up and returned home and Balak went his own way.

Moab Seduces Israel

25 While Israel was staying in Shittim, the men began to indulge in sexual immorality with Moabite women, ²who invited them to the sacrifices to their gods. The people ate and bowed down before these gods. ³So Israel joined in worshiping the Baal of Peor. And the Lord's anger burned against them.

⁴The Lord said to Moses, "Take all the leaders of these people, kill them and expose them in broad daylight before the Lord, so that the Lord's fierce anger may turn away from Israel."

⁵So Moses said to Israel's judges, "Each of you must put to death those of your men who have joined in worshiping the Baal of Peor."

⁶Then an Israelite man brought to his family a Midianite woman right before the eyes of Moses and the whole assembly of Israel while they were weeping at the entrance to the Tent of Meeting. ⁷When Phinehas son of Eleazar, the son of Aaron, the priest, saw this, he left the assembly, took a spear in his hand ⁸and followed the Israelite into the tent. He drove the spear through both of them — through the Israelite and into the woman's body. Then the plague against the Israelites was stopped; ⁹but those who died in the plague numbered 24,000.

¹⁰The Lord said to Moses, ¹¹"Phinehas son of Eleazar, the son of Aaron, the priest, has turned my anger away from the Israelites; for he was as zealous as I am for my honor among them, so that in my zeal I did not put an end to them. ¹²Therefore tell him I am making my covenant of peace with him. ¹³He and his descendants will have a covenant of a lasting priesthood, because he

---

a17 Samaritan Pentateuch (see also Jer. 48:45); the meaning of the word in the Masoretic Text is uncertain.
b17 Or possibly *Moab, / batter*   *c17* Or *all the noisy boasters*   *d23* Masoretic Text; with a different word division of the Hebrew *A people will gather from the north.*

NEGATIVE FORCES CAN NUKE YOUR FAITH!

☐ **MONDAY**

Last weekend, Matt didn't speak up when his friends decided to head into the city, a seventy-mile trip! He was more than two hours late getting home.

After his weekend adventure, Matt was threatened with almost every form of punishment ever devised. Now three days into a judgment of "three weeks with no privileges," Matt is quite sure he'll speak up next time the gang suggests a night on the town. "I was pretty stupid," he admits.

Look It Up
••••

Negative peer pressure prompts poor decisions.

"Wanting to release Jesus, Pilate appealed to them again. But they kept shouting, 'Crucify him! Crucify him!'

"For the third time he spoke to them: 'Why? What crime has this man committed? I have found in him no grounds for the death penalty. Therefore I will have him punished and then release him.'

"But with loud shouts they insistently demanded that he be crucified, and their shouts prevailed. So Pilate decided to grant their demand" (Luke 23:20–24).

Negative peer pressure also harms one's relationship with God.

"Then the Israelites did evil in the eyes of the LORD and served the Baals. They forsook the LORD, the God of their fathers, who had brought them out of Egypt. They followed and worshiped various gods of the peoples around them. They provoked the LORD to anger" (Judges 2:11–12).

Think It Through
••••

Have you let others pressure you into bad decisions? Are certain friends and/or activities pulling you away from God?

Work It Out
••••

Here are some tips for saying no:

1. Set some standards now—before friends start applying the pressure. If you mark out firmly in your own mind what you will and won't do, you stand a much better chance of resisting.

2. Be firm. The crowd can be like a school of sharks. If they sense any hesitation, they'll go for the kill.

3. Let people know that though you like them, you can't participate in certain activities.

4. Say, "Look, stop pressuring me! I don't ask you to do things you don't believe in. Would you please give me the same courtesy?"

Nail It Down
••••

Read Numbers 25:1–3 for how peer pressure can damage your faith.

Turn to pages 683, 1174 and 1386 for other readings on peer pressure.
Turn to page 178 for Tuesday's reading.

Topic
••••

PEER PRESSURE

was zealous for the honor of his God and made atonement for the Israelites."

14The name of the Israelite who was killed with the Midianite woman was Zimri son of Salu, the leader of a Simeonite family. **15**And the name of the Midianite woman who was put to death was Cozbi daughter of Zur, a tribal chief of a Midianite family.

16The LORD said to Moses, **17**"Treat the Midianites as enemies and kill them, **18**because they treated you as enemies when they deceived you in the affair of Peor and their sister Cozbi, the daughter of a Midianite leader, the woman who was killed when the plague came as a result of Peor."

The Second Census

26 After the plague the LORD said to Moses and Eleazar son of Aaron, the priest, **2**"Take a census of the whole Israelite community by families — all those twenty years old or more who are able to serve in the army of Israel." **3**So on the plains of Moab by the Jordan across from Jericho,*a* Moses and Eleazar the priest spoke with them and said, **4**"Take a census of the men twenty years old or more, as the LORD commanded Moses."

These were the Israelites who came out of Egypt:

5The descendants of Reuben, the firstborn son of Israel, were:

through Hanoch, the Hanochite clan;
through Pallu, the Palluite clan;
6through Hezron, the Hezronite clan;
through Carmi, the Carmite clan.
7These were the clans of Reuben; those numbered were 43,730.

8The son of Pallu was Eliab, **9**and the sons of Eliab were Nemuel, Dathan and Abiram. The same Dathan and Abiram were the community officials who rebelled against Moses and Aaron and were among Korah's followers when they rebelled against the LORD. **10**The earth opened its mouth and swallowed them along with Korah, whose followers died when the fire devoured the 250 men. And they served as a warning sign. **11**The line of Korah, however, did not die out.

12The descendants of Simeon by their clans were:

through Nemuel, the Nemuelite clan;
through Jamin, the Jaminite clan;
through Jakin, the Jakinite clan;
13through Zerah, the Zerahite clan;
through Shaul, the Shaulite clan.
14These were the clans of Simeon; there were 22,200 men.

15The descendants of Gad by their clans were:

through Zephon, the Zephonite clan;
through Haggi, the Haggite clan;
through Shuni, the Shunite clan;
16through Ozni, the Oznite clan;
through Eri, the Erite clan;
17through Arodi,*b* the Arodite clan;
through Areli, the Arelite clan.
18These were the clans of Gad; those numbered were 40,500.

19Er and Onan were sons of Judah, but they died in Canaan. **20**The descendants of Judah by their clans were:

through Shelah, the Shelanite clan;
through Perez, the Perezite clan;
through Zerah, the Zerahite clan.
21The descendants of Perez were:
through Hezron, the Hezronite clan;
through Hamul, the Hamulite clan.
22These were the clans of Judah; those numbered were 76,500.

23The descendants of Issachar by their clans were:

through Tola, the Tolaite clan;
through Puah, the Puite*c* clan;
24through Jashub, the Jashubite clan;
through Shimron, the Shimronite clan.
25These were the clans of Issachar; those numbered were 64,300.

26The descendants of Zebulun by their clans were:

through Sered, the Seredite clan;
through Elon, the Elonite clan;
through Jahleel, the Jahleelite clan.
27These were the clans of Zebulun; those numbered were 60,500.

28The descendants of Joseph by their clans through Manasseh and Ephraim were:

29The descendants of Manasseh:
through Makir, the Makirite clan (Makir was the father of Gilead);
through Gilead, the Gileadite clan.
30These were the descendants of Gilead:
through Iezer, the Iezerite clan;
through Helek, the Helekite clan;

31through Asriel, the Asrielite clan;
through Shechem, the Shechemite clan;
32through Shemida, the Shemidaite clan;
through Hepher, the Hepherite clan.
33(Zelophehad son of Hepher had no sons; he had only daughters, whose names were Mahlah, Noah, Hoglah, Milcah and Tirzah.)
34These were the clans of Manasseh; those numbered were 52,700.

35These were the descendants of Ephraim by their clans:
through Shuthelah, the Shuthelahite clan;
through Beker, the Bekerite clan;
through Tahan, the Tahanite clan.
36These were the descendants of Shuthelah:
through Eran, the Eranite clan.
37These were the clans of Ephraim; those numbered were 32,500.

These were the descendants of Joseph by their clans.

38The descendants of Benjamin by their clans were:
through Bela, the Belaite clan;
through Ashbel, the Ashbelite clan;
through Ahiram, the Ahiramite clan;
39through Shupham,*a* the Shuphamite clan;
through Hupham, the Huphamite clan.
40The descendants of Bela through Ard and Naaman were:
through Ard,*b* the Ardite clan;
through Naaman, the Naamite clan.
41These were the clans of Benjamin; those numbered were 45,600.

42These were the descendants of Dan by their clans:
through Shuham, the Shuhamite clan.
These were the clans of Dan: **43**All of them were Shuhamite clans; and those numbered were 64,400.

44The descendants of Asher by their clans were:
through Imnah, the Imnite clan;
through Ishvi, the Ishvite clan;
through Beriah, the Beriite clan;
45and through the descendants of Beriah:

through Heber, the Heberite clan;
through Malkiel, the Malkielite clan.
46(Asher had a daughter named Serah.)
47These were the clans of Asher; those numbered were 53,400.

48The descendants of Naphtali by their clans were:
through Jahzeel, the Jahzeelite clan;
through Guni, the Gunite clan;
49through Jezer, the Jezerite clan;
through Shillem, the Shillemite clan.
50These were the clans of Naphtali; those numbered were 45,400.

51The total number of the men of Israel was 601,730.

52The LORD said to Moses, **53**"The land is to be allotted to them as an inheritance based on the number of names. **54**To a larger group give a larger inheritance, and to a smaller group a smaller one; each is to receive its inheritance according to the number of those listed. **55**Be sure that the land is distributed by lot. What each group inherits will be according to the names for its ancestral tribe. **56**Each inheritance is to be distributed by lot among the larger and smaller groups."

57These were the Levites who were counted by their clans:
through Gershon, the Gershonite clan;
through Kohath, the Kohathite clan;
through Merari, the Merarite clan.
58These also were Levite clans:
the Libnite clan,
the Hebronite clan,
the Mahlite clan,
the Mushite clan,
the Korahite clan.
(Kohath was the forefather of Amram; **59**the name of Amram's wife was Jochebed, a descendant of Levi, who was born to the Levites*c* in Egypt. To Amram she bore Aaron, Moses and their sister Miriam. **60**Aaron was the father of Nadab and Abihu, Eleazar and Ithamar. **61**But Nadab and Abihu died when they made an offering before the LORD with unauthorized fire.)

62All the male Levites a month old or more numbered 23,000. They were not counted

---

a39 A few manuscripts of the Masoretic Text, Samaritan Pentateuch, Vulgate and Syriac (see also Septuagint); most manuscripts of the Masoretic Text *Shephupham* *b40* Samaritan Pentateuch and Vulgate (see also Septuagint); Masoretic Text does not have *through Ard*. *c59* Or *Jochebed, a daughter of Levi, who was born to Levi* along with the other Israelites because they received no inheritance among them.

63These are the ones counted by Moses and Eleazar the priest when they counted the Israelites on the plains of Moab by the Jordan across from Jericho. **64**Not one of them was among those counted by Moses and Aaron the priest when they counted the Israelites in the Desert of Sinai. **65**For the LORD had told those Israelites they would surely die in the desert, and not one of them was left except Caleb son of Jephunneh and Joshua son of Nun.

Zelophehad's Daughters

27 The daughters of Zelophehad son of Hepher, the son of Gilead, the son of Makir, the son of Manasseh, belonged to the clans of Manasseh son of Joseph. The names of the daughters were Mahlah, Noah, Hoglah, Milcah and Tirzah. They approached **2**the entrance to the Tent of Meeting and stood before Moses, Eleazar the priest, the leaders and the whole assembly, and said, **3**"Our father died in the desert. He was not among Korah's followers, who banded together against the LORD, but he died for his own sin and left no sons. **4**Why should our father's name disappear from his clan because he had no son? Give us property among our father's relatives."

5So Moses brought their case before the LORD **6**and the LORD said to him, **7**"What Zelophehad's daughters are saying is right. You must certainly give them property as an inheritance among their father's relatives and turn their father's inheritance over to them.

8"Say to the Israelites, 'If a man dies and leaves no son, turn his inheritance over to his daughter. **9**If he has no daughter, give his inheritance to his brothers. **10**If he has no brothers, give his inheritance to his father's brothers. **11**If his father had no brothers, give his inheritance to the nearest relative in his clan, that he may possess it. This is to be a legal requirement for the Israelites, as the LORD commanded Moses.' "

Joshua to Succeed Moses

12Then the LORD said to Moses, "Go up this mountain in the Abarim range and see the land I have given the Israelites. **13**After you have seen it, you too will be gathered to your people, as your brother Aaron was, **14**for when the community rebelled at the waters in the Desert of Zin, both of you disobeyed my command to honor me as holy before their eyes." (These were the waters of Meribah Kadesh, in the Desert of Zin.)

15Moses said to the LORD, **16**"May the LORD, the God of the spirits of all mankind, appoint a man over this community **17**to go out and come in before them, one who will lead them out and bring them in, so the LORD's people will not be like sheep without a shepherd."

18So the LORD said to Moses, "Take Joshua son of Nun, a man in whom is the spirit,*a* and lay your hand on him. **19**Have him stand before Eleazar the priest and the entire assembly and commission him in their presence. **20**Give him some of your authority so the whole Israelite community will obey him. **21**He is to stand before Eleazar the priest, who will obtain decisions for him by inquiring of the Urim before the LORD. At his command he and the entire community of the Israelites will go out, and at his command they will come in."

22Moses did as the LORD commanded him. He took Joshua and had him stand before Eleazar the priest and the whole assembly. **23**Then he laid his hands on him and commissioned him, as the LORD instructed through Moses.

Daily Offerings

28 The LORD said to Moses, **2**"Give this command to the Israelites and say to them: 'See that you present to me at the appointed time the food for my offerings made by fire, as an aroma pleasing to me.' **3**Say to them: 'This is the offering made by fire that you are to present to the LORD: two lambs a year old without defect, as a regular burnt offering each day. **4**Prepare one lamb in the morning and the other at twilight, **5**together with a grain offering of a tenth of an ephah*b* of fine flour mixed with a quarter of a hin*c* of oil from pressed olives. **6**This is the regular burnt offering instituted at Mount Sinai as a pleasing aroma, an offering made to the LORD by fire. **7**The accompanying drink offering is to be a quarter of a hin of fermented drink with each lamb. Pour out the drink offering to the LORD at the sanctuary. **8**Prepare the second lamb at twilight, along with the same kind of grain offering and drink offering that you prepare in the morning. This is an offering made by fire, an aroma pleasing to the LORD.

---

a18 Or *Spirit*   *b5* That is, probably about 2 quarts (about 2 liters); also in verses 13, 21 and 29   *c5* That is, probably about 1 quart (about 1 liter); also in verses 7 and 14

Sabbath Offerings

9" 'On the Sabbath day, make an offering of two lambs a year old without defect, together with its drink offering and a grain offering of two-tenths of an ephah*a* of fine flour mixed with oil. **10**This is the burnt offering for every Sabbath, in addition to the regular burnt offering and its drink offering.

Monthly Offerings

11" 'On the first of every month, present to the LORD a burnt offering of two young bulls, one ram and seven male lambs a year old, all without defect. **12**With each bull there is to be a grain offering of three-tenths of an ephah*b* of fine flour mixed with oil; with the ram, a grain offering of two-tenths of an ephah of fine flour mixed with oil; **13**and with each lamb, a grain offering of a tenth of an ephah of fine flour mixed with oil. This is for a burnt offering, a pleasing aroma, an offering made to the LORD by fire. **14**With each bull there is to be a drink offering of half a hin*c* of wine; with the ram, a third of a hin*d*; and with each lamb, a quarter of a hin. This is the monthly burnt offering to be made at each new moon during the year. **15**Besides the regular burnt offering with its drink offering, one male goat is to be presented to the LORD as a sin offering.

The Passover

16" 'On the fourteenth day of the first month the LORD's Passover is to be held. **17**On the fifteenth day of this month there is to be a festival; for seven days eat bread made without yeast. **18**On the first day hold a sacred assembly and do no regular work. **19**Present to the LORD an offering made by fire, a burnt offering of two young bulls, one ram and seven male lambs a year old, all without defect. **20**With each bull prepare a grain offering of three-tenths of an ephah of fine flour mixed with oil; with the ram, two-tenths; **21**and with each of the seven lambs, one-tenth. **22**Include one male goat as a sin offering to make atonement for you. **23**Prepare these in addition to the regular morning burnt offering. **24**In this way prepare the food for the offering made by fire every day for seven days as an aroma pleasing to the LORD; it is to be prepared in addition to the regular burnt offering and its drink offering.

25On the seventh day hold a sacred assembly and do no regular work.

Feast of Weeks

26" 'On the day of firstfruits, when you present to the LORD an offering of new grain during the Feast of Weeks, hold a sacred assembly and do no regular work. **27**Present a burnt offering of two young bulls, one ram and seven male lambs a year old as an aroma pleasing to the LORD. **28**With each bull there is to be a grain offering of three-tenths of an ephah of fine flour mixed with oil; with the ram, two-tenths; **29**and with each of the seven lambs, one-tenth. **30**Include one male goat to make atonement for you. **31**Prepare these together with their drink offerings, in addition to the regular burnt offering and its grain offering. Be sure the animals are without defect.

Feast of Trumpets

29 " 'On the first day of the seventh month hold a sacred assembly and do no regular work. It is a day for you to sound the trumpets. **2**As an aroma pleasing to the LORD, prepare a burnt offering of one young bull, one ram and seven male lambs a year old, all without defect. **3**With the bull prepare a grain offering of three-tenths of an ephah*e* of fine flour mixed with oil; with the ram, two-tenths*f*; **4**and with each of the seven lambs, one-tenth.*g* **5**Include one male goat as a sin offering to make atonement for you. **6**These are in addition to the monthly and daily burnt offerings with their grain offerings and drink offerings as specified. They are offerings made to the LORD by fire—a pleasing aroma.

Day of Atonement

7" 'On the tenth day of this seventh month hold a sacred assembly. You must deny yourselves*h* and do no work. **8**Present as an aroma pleasing to the LORD a burnt offering of one young bull, one ram and seven male lambs a year old, all without defect. **9**With the bull prepare a grain offering of three-tenths of an ephah of fine flour mixed with oil; with the ram, two-tenths; **10**and with each of the seven lambs, one-tenth. **11**Include one male goat as a sin offering, in addition to the sin offering for atonement and

---

a9 That is, probably about 4 quarts (about 4.5 liters); also in verses 12, 20 and 28   *b12* That is, probably about 6 quarts (about 6.5 liters); also in verses 20 and 28   *c14* That is, probably about 2 quarts (about 2 liters)   *d14* That is, probably about 1 1/4 quarts (about 1.2 liters)   *e3* That is, probably about 6 quarts (about 6.5 liters); also in verses 9 and 14   *f3* That is, probably about 4 quarts (about 4.5 liters); also in verses 9 and 14   *g4* That is, probably about 2 quarts (about 2 liters); also in verses 10 and 15   *h7* Or *must fast* the regular burnt offering with its grain offering, and their drink offerings.

Feast of Tabernacles

12 " 'On the fifteenth day of the seventh month, hold a sacred assembly and do no regular work. Celebrate a festival to the LORD for seven days. 13Present an offering made by fire as an aroma pleasing to the LORD, a burnt offering of thirteen young bulls, two rams and fourteen male lambs a year old, all without defect. 14With each of the thirteen bulls prepare a grain offering of three-tenths of an ephah of fine flour mixed with oil; with each of the two rams, two-tenths; 15and with each of the fourteen lambs, one-tenth. 16Include one male goat as a sin offering, in addition to the regular burnt offering with its grain offering and drink offering.

17 " 'On the second day prepare twelve young bulls, two rams and fourteen male lambs a year old, all without defect. 18With the bulls, rams and lambs, prepare their grain offerings and drink offerings according to the number specified. 19Include one male goat as a sin offering, in addition to the regular burnt offering with its grain offering, and their drink offerings.

20 " 'On the third day prepare eleven bulls, two rams and fourteen male lambs a year old, all without defect. 21With the bulls, rams and lambs, prepare their grain offerings and drink offerings according to the number specified. 22Include one male goat as a sin offering, in addition to the regular burnt offering with its grain offering and drink offering.

23 " 'On the fourth day prepare ten bulls, two rams and fourteen male lambs a year old, all without defect. 24With the bulls, rams and lambs, prepare their grain offerings and drink offerings according to the number specified. 25Include one male goat as a sin offering, in addition to the regular burnt offering with its grain offering and drink offering.

26 " 'On the fifth day prepare nine bulls, two rams and fourteen male lambs a year old, all without defect. 27With the bulls, rams and lambs, prepare their grain offerings and drink offerings according to the number specified. 28Include one male goat as a sin offering, in addition to the regular burnt offering with its grain offering and drink offering.

29 " 'On the sixth day prepare eight bulls, two rams and fourteen male lambs a year

old, all without defect. 30With the bulls, rams and lambs, prepare their grain offerings and drink offerings according to the number specified. 31Include one male goat as a sin offering, in addition to the regular burnt offering with its grain offering and drink offering.

32 " 'On the seventh day prepare seven bulls, two rams and fourteen male lambs a year old, all without defect. 33With the bulls, rams and lambs, prepare their grain offerings and drink offerings according to the number specified. 34Include one male goat as a sin offering, in addition to the regular burnt offering with its grain offering and drink offering.

35 " 'On the eighth day hold an assembly and do no regular work. 36Present an offering made by fire as an aroma pleasing to the LORD, a burnt offering of one bull, one ram and seven male lambs a year old, all without defect. 37With the bull, the ram and the lambs, prepare their grain offerings and drink offerings according to the number specified. 38Include one male goat as a sin offering, in addition to the regular burnt offering with its grain offering and drink offering.

39 " 'In addition to what you vow and your freewill offerings, prepare these for the LORD at your appointed feasts: your burnt offerings, grain offerings, drink offerings and fellowship offerings.*a* ' "

40Moses told the Israelites all that the LORD commanded him.

Vows

30 Moses said to the heads of the tribes of Israel: "This is what the LORD commands: 2When a man makes a vow to the LORD or takes an oath to obligate himself by a pledge, he must not break his word but must do everything he said.

3"When a young woman still living in her father's house makes a vow to the LORD or obligates herself by a pledge 4and her father hears about her vow or pledge but says nothing to her, then all her vows and every pledge by which she obligated herself will stand. 5But if her father forbids her when he hears about it, none of her vows or the pledges by which she obligated herself will stand; the LORD will release her because her father has forbidden her.

6"If she marries after she makes a vow or after her lips utter a rash promise by which she obligates herself 7and her husband hears about it but says nothing to her, then her vows or the pledges by which she obligated herself will stand. **8**But if her husband forbids her when he hears about it, he nullifies the vow that obligates her or the rash promise by which she obligates herself, and the LORD will release her.

9"Any vow or obligation taken by a widow or divorced woman will be binding on her.

10"If a woman living with her husband makes a vow or obligates herself by a pledge under oath **11**and her husband hears about it but says nothing to her and does not forbid her, then all her vows or the pledges by which she obligated herself will stand. **12**But if her husband nullifies them when he hears about them, then none of the vows or pledges that came from her lips will stand. Her husband has nullified them, and the LORD will release her. **13**Her husband may confirm or nullify any vow she makes or any sworn pledge to deny herself. **14**But if her husband says nothing to her about it from day to day, then he confirms all her vows or the pledges binding on her. He confirms them by saying nothing to her when he hears about them. **15**If, however, he nullifies them some time after he hears about them, then he is responsible for her guilt."

16These are the regulations the LORD gave Moses concerning relationships between a man and his wife, and between a father and his young daughter still living in his house.

Vengeance on the Midianites

31 The LORD said to Moses, **2**"Take vengeance on the Midianites for the Israelites. After that, you will be gathered to your people."

3So Moses said to the people, "Arm some of your men to go to war against the Midianites and to carry out the LORD's vengeance on them. **4**Send into battle a thousand men from each of the tribes of Israel." **5**So twelve thousand men armed for battle, a thousand from each tribe, were supplied from the clans of Israel. **6**Moses sent them into battle, a thousand from each tribe, along with Phinehas son of Eleazar, the priest, who took with him articles from the sanctuary and the trumpets for signaling.

7They fought against Midian, as the LORD commanded Moses, and killed every man. **8**Among their victims were Evi, Rekem, Zur, Hur and Reba—the five kings of Midian. They also killed Balaam son of Beor with the sword. **9**The Israelites captured the Midianite women and children and took all the Midianite herds, flocks and goods as plunder. **10**They burned all the towns where the Midianites had settled, as well as all their camps. **11**They took all the plunder and spoils, including the people and animals, **12**and brought the captives, spoils and plunder to Moses and Eleazar the priest and the Israelite assembly at their camp on the plains of Moab, by the Jordan across from Jericho. *a*

13Moses, Eleazar the priest and all the leaders of the community went to meet them outside the camp. **14**Moses was angry with the officers of the army—the commanders of thousands and commanders of hundreds—who returned from the battle. **15**"Have you allowed all the women to live?" he asked them. **16**"They were the ones who followed Balaam's advice and were the means of turning the Israelites away from the LORD in what happened at Peor, so that a plague struck the LORD's people. **17**Now kill all the boys. And kill every woman who has slept with a man, **18**but save for yourselves every girl who has never slept with a man.

19"All of you who have killed anyone or touched anyone who was killed must stay outside the camp seven days. On the third and seventh days you must purify yourselves and your captives. **20**Purify every garment as well as everything made of leather, goat hair or wood."

21Then Eleazar the priest said to the soldiers who had gone into battle, "This is the requirement of the law that the LORD gave Moses: **22**Gold, silver, bronze, iron, tin, lead **23**and anything else that can withstand fire must be put through the fire, and then it will be clean. But it must also be purified with the water of cleansing. And whatever cannot withstand fire must be put through that water. **24**On the seventh day wash your clothes and you will be clean. Then you may come into the camp."

Dividing the Spoils

25The LORD said to Moses, **26**"You and Eleazar the priest and the family heads of the community are to count all the people and animals that were captured. **27**Divide the spoils between the soldiers who took part in the battle and the rest of the community. **28**From the soldiers who fought in the battle, set apart as tribute for the LORD one out of every five hundred, whether persons, cattle, donkeys, sheep or goats. **29**Take this tribute

---

a12 Hebrew *Jordan of Jericho*; possibly an ancient name for the Jordan River from their half share and give it to Eleazar the priest as the LORD's part. [30]From the Israelites' half, select one out of every fifty, whether persons, cattle, donkeys, sheep, goats or other animals. Give them to the Levites, who are responsible for the care of the LORD's tabernacle." [31]So Moses and Eleazar the priest did as the LORD commanded Moses.

[32]The plunder remaining from the spoils that the soldiers took was 675,000 sheep, [33]72,000 cattle, [34]61,000 donkeys [35]and 32,000 women who had never slept with a man.

[36]The half share of those who fought in the battle was:

337,500 sheep, [37]of which the tribute for the LORD was 675;
[38]36,000 cattle, of which the tribute for the LORD was 72;
[39]30,500 donkeys, of which the tribute for the LORD was 61;
[40]16,000 people, of which the tribute for the LORD was 32.

[41]Moses gave the tribute to Eleazar the priest as the LORD's part, as the LORD commanded Moses.

[42]The half belonging to the Israelites, which Moses set apart from that of the fighting men— [43]the community's half—was 337,500 sheep, [44]36,000 cattle, [45]30,500 donkeys [46]and 16,000 people. [47]From the Israelites' half, Moses selected one out of every fifty persons and animals, as the LORD commanded him, and gave them to the Levites, who were responsible for the care of the LORD's tabernacle.

[48]Then the officers who were over the units of the army—the commanders of thousands and commanders of hundreds— went to Moses [49]and said to him, "Your servants have counted the soldiers under our command, and not one is missing. [50]So we have brought as an offering to the LORD the gold articles each of us acquired—armlets, bracelets, signet rings, earrings and necklaces—to make atonement for ourselves before the LORD."

[51]Moses and Eleazar the priest accepted from them the gold—all the crafted articles. [52]All the gold from the commanders of thousands and commanders of hundreds that Moses and Eleazar presented as a gift to the LORD weighed 16,750 shekels.[a] [53]Each soldier had taken plunder for himself. [54]Moses and Eleazar the priest accepted the gold

from the commanders of thousands and commanders of hundreds and brought it into the Tent of Meeting as a memorial for the Israelites before the LORD.

The Transjordan Tribes

32 The Reubenites and Gadites, who had very large herds and flocks, saw that the lands of Jazer and Gilead were suitable for livestock. [2]So they came to Moses and Eleazar the priest and to the leaders of the community, and said, [3]"Ataroth, Dibon, Jazer, Nimrah, Heshbon, Elealeh, Sebam, Nebo and Beon— [4]the land the LORD subdued before the people of Israel—are suitable for livestock, and your servants have livestock. [5]If we have found favor in your eyes," they said, "let this land be given to your servants as our possession. Do not make us cross the Jordan."

[6]Moses said to the Gadites and Reubenites, "Shall your countrymen go to war while you sit here? [7]Why do you discourage the Israelites from going over into the land the LORD has given them? [8]This is what your fathers did when I sent them from Kadesh Barnea to look over the land. [9]After they went up to the Valley of Eshcol and viewed the land, they discouraged the Israelites from entering the land the LORD had given them. [10]The LORD's anger was aroused that day and he swore this oath: [11]'Because they have not followed me wholeheartedly, not one of the men twenty years old or more who came up out of Egypt will see the land I promised on oath to Abraham, Isaac and Jacob— [12]not one except Caleb son of Jephunneh the Kenizzite and Joshua son of Nun, for they followed the LORD wholeheartedly.' [13]The LORD's anger burned against Israel and he made them wander in the desert forty years, until the whole generation of those who had done evil in his sight was gone.

[14]"And here you are, a brood of sinners, standing in the place of your fathers and making the LORD even more angry with Israel. [15]If you turn away from following him, he will again leave all this people in the desert, and you will be the cause of their destruction."

[16]Then they came up to him and said, "We would like to build pens here for our livestock and cities for our women and children. [17]But we are ready to arm ourselves and go ahead of the Israelites until we have brought them to their place. Meanwhile our

---

[a]52 That is, about 420 pounds (about 190 kilograms)

women and children will live in fortified cities, for protection from the inhabitants of the land. **18**We will not return to our homes until every Israelite has received his inheritance. **19**We will not receive any inheritance with them on the other side of the Jordan, because our inheritance has come to us on the east side of the Jordan."

20Then Moses said to them, "If you will do this — if you will arm yourselves before the LORD for battle, **21**and if all of you will go armed over the Jordan before the LORD until he has driven his enemies out before him — **22**then when the land is subdued before the LORD, you may return and be free from your obligation to the LORD and to Israel. And this land will be your possession before the LORD.

23"But if you fail to do this, you will be sinning against the LORD; and you may be sure that your sin will find you out. **24**Build cities for your women and children, and pens for your flocks, but do what you have promised."

25The Gadites and Reubenites said to Moses, "We your servants will do as our lord commands. **26**Our children and wives, our flocks and herds will remain here in the cities of Gilead. **27**But your servants, every man armed for battle, will cross over to fight before the LORD, just as our lord says."

28Then Moses gave orders about them to Eleazar the priest and Joshua son of Nun and to the family heads of the Israelite tribes. **29**He said to them, "If the Gadites and Reubenites, every man armed for battle, cross over the Jordan with you before the LORD, then when the land is subdued before you, give them the land of Gilead as their possession. **30**But if they do not cross over with you armed, they must accept their possession with you in Canaan."

31The Gadites and Reubenites answered, "Your servants will do what the LORD has said. **32**We will cross over before the LORD into Canaan armed, but the property we inherit will be on this side of the Jordan."

33Then Moses gave to the Gadites, the Reubenites and the half-tribe of Manasseh son of Joseph the kingdom of Sihon king of the Amorites and the kingdom of Og king of Bashan — the whole land with its cities and the territory around them. **34**The Gadites built up Dibon, Ataroth,

Aroer, **35**Atroth Shophan, Jazer, Jogbehah, **36**Beth Nimrah and Beth Haran as fortified cities, and built pens for their flocks. **37**And the Reubenites rebuilt Heshbon, Elealeh and Kiriathaim, **38**as well as Nebo and Baal Meon (these names were changed) and Sibmah. They gave names to the cities they rebuilt.

39The descendants of Makir son of Manasseh went to Gilead, captured it and drove out the Amorites who were there. **40**So Moses gave Gilead to the Makirites, the descendants of Manasseh, and they settled there. **41**Jair, a descendant of Manasseh, captured their settlements and called them Havvoth Jair.[a] **42**And Nobah captured Kenath and its surrounding settlements and called it Nobah after himself.

Stages in Israel's Journey

33 Here are the stages in the journey of the Israelites when they came out of Egypt by divisions under the leadership of Moses and Aaron. **2**At the LORD's command Moses recorded the stages in their journey. This is their journey by stages:

3The Israelites set out from Rameses on the fifteenth day of the first month, the day after the Passover. They marched out boldly in full view of all the Egyptians, **4**who were burying all their firstborn, whom the LORD had struck down among them; for the LORD had brought judgment on their gods.

5The Israelites left Rameses and camped at Succoth.

6They left Succoth and camped at Etham, on the edge of the desert.

7They left Etham, turned back to Pi Hahiroth, to the east of Baal Zephon, and camped near Migdol.

8They left Pi Hahiroth[b] and passed through the sea into the desert, and when they had traveled for three days in the Desert of Etham, they camped at Marah.

9They left Marah and went to Elim, where there were twelve springs and seventy palm trees, and they camped there.

10They left Elim and camped by the Red Sea.[c]

11They left the Red Sea and camped in the Desert of Sin.

---

a41 Or *them the settlements of Jair*   *b8* Many manuscripts of the Masoretic Text, Samaritan Pentateuch and Vulgate; most manuscripts of the Masoretic Text *left from before Hahiroth*   *c10* Hebrew *Yam Suph*; that is, Sea of Reeds; also in verse 11

¹²They left the Desert of Sin and camped at Dophkah.

¹³They left Dophkah and camped at Alush.

¹⁴They left Alush and camped at Rephidim, where there was no water for the people to drink.

¹⁵They left Rephidim and camped in the Desert of Sinai.

¹⁶They left the Desert of Sinai and camped at Kibroth Hattaavah.

¹⁷They left Kibroth Hattaavah and camped at Hazeroth.

¹⁸They left Hazeroth and camped at Rithmah.

¹⁹They left Rithmah and camped at Rimmon Perez.

²⁰They left Rimmon Perez and camped at Libnah.

²¹They left Libnah and camped at Rissah.

²²They left Rissah and camped at Kehelathah.

²³They left Kehelathah and camped at Mount Shepher.

²⁴They left Mount Shepher and camped at Haradah.

²⁵They left Haradah and camped at Makheloth.

²⁶They left Makheloth and camped at Tahath.

²⁷They left Tahath and camped at Terah.

²⁸They left Terah and camped at Mithcah.

²⁹They left Mithcah and camped at Hashmonah.

³⁰They left Hashmonah and camped at Moseroth.

³¹They left Moseroth and camped at Bene Jaakan.

³²They left Bene Jaakan and camped at Hor Haggidgad.

³³They left Hor Haggidgad and camped at Jotbathah.

³⁴They left Jotbathah and camped at Abronah.

³⁵They left Abronah and camped at Ezion Geber.

³⁶They left Ezion Geber and camped at Kadesh, in the Desert of Zin.

³⁷They left Kadesh and camped at Mount Hor, on the border of Edom. ³⁸At the Lord's command Aaron the priest went up Mount Hor, where he died on the first day of the fifth month of the fortieth year after the Israelites came out of Egypt. ³⁹Aaron was a hundred and twenty-three years old when he died on Mount Hor.

⁴⁰The Canaanite king of Arad, who lived in the Negev of Canaan, heard that the Israelites were coming.

⁴¹They left Mount Hor and camped at Zalmonah.

⁴²They left Zalmonah and camped at Punon.

⁴³They left Punon and camped at Oboth.

⁴⁴They left Oboth and camped at Iye Abarim, on the border of Moab.

⁴⁵They left Iyim*ᵃ* and camped at Dibon Gad.

⁴⁶They left Dibon Gad and camped at Almon Diblathaim.

⁴⁷They left Almon Diblathaim and camped in the mountains of Abarim, near Nebo.

⁴⁸They left the mountains of Abarim and camped on the plains of Moab by the Jordan across from Jericho.*ᵇ* ⁴⁹There on the plains of Moab they camped along the Jordan from Beth Jeshimoth to Abel Shittim.

⁵⁰On the plains of Moab by the Jordan across from Jericho the Lord said to Moses, ⁵¹"Speak to the Israelites and say to them: 'When you cross the Jordan into Canaan, ⁵²drive out all the inhabitants of the land before you. Destroy all their carved images and their cast idols, and demolish all their high places. ⁵³Take possession of the land and settle in it, for I have given you the land to possess. ⁵⁴Distribute the land by lot, according to your clans. To a larger group give a larger inheritance, and to a smaller group a smaller one. Whatever falls to them by lot will be theirs. Distribute it according to your ancestral tribes.

⁵⁵" 'But if you do not drive out the inhabitants of the land, those you allow to remain will become barbs in your eyes and thorns in your sides. They will give you trouble in the land where you will live. ⁵⁶And then I will do to you what I plan to do to them.' "

Boundaries of Canaan

34 The Lord said to Moses, ²"Command the Israelites and say to them: 'When you enter Canaan, the land that will

---

ᵃ45 That is, Iye Abarim   *ᵇ48* Hebrew *Jordan of Jericho*; possibly an ancient name for the Jordan River; also in verse 50 be allotted to you as an inheritance will have these boundaries:

3" 'Your southern side will include some of the Desert of Zin along the border of Edom. On the east, your southern boundary will start from the end of the Salt Sea,*a* **4**cross south of Scorpion*b* Pass, continue on to Zin and go south of Kadesh Barnea. Then it will go to Hazar Addar and over to Azmon, **5**where it will turn, join the Wadi of Egypt and end at the Sea.*c*

6" 'Your western boundary will be the coast of the Great Sea. This will be your boundary on the west.

7" 'For your northern boundary, run a line from the Great Sea to Mount Hor **8**and from Mount Hor to Lebo*d* Hamath. Then the boundary will go to Zedad, **9**continue to Ziphron and end at Hazar Enan. This will be your boundary on the north.

10" 'For your eastern boundary, run a line from Hazar Enan to Shepham. **11**The boundary will go down from Shepham to Riblah on the east side of Ain and continue along the slopes east of the Sea of Kinnereth.*e* **12**Then the boundary will go down along the Jordan and end at the Salt Sea.

" 'This will be your land, with its boundaries on every side.' "

13Moses commanded the Israelites: "Assign this land by lot as an inheritance. The LORD has ordered that it be given to the nine and a half tribes, **14**because the families of the tribe of Reuben, the tribe of Gad and the half-tribe of Manasseh have received their inheritance. **15**These two and a half tribes have received their inheritance on the east side of the Jordan of Jericho,*f* toward the sunrise."

16The LORD said to Moses, **17**"These are the names of the men who are to assign the land for you as an inheritance: Eleazar the priest and Joshua son of Nun. **18**And appoint one leader from each tribe to help assign the land. **19**These are their names:

Caleb son of Jephunneh,
    from the tribe of Judah;
20Shemuel son of Ammihud,
    from the tribe of Simeon;
21Elidad son of Kislon,
    from the tribe of Benjamin;
22Bukki son of Jogli,

    the leader from the tribe of Dan;
23Hanniel son of Ephod,
    the leader from the tribe of Manasseh son of Joseph;
24Kemuel son of Shiphtan,
    the leader from the tribe of Ephraim son of Joseph;
25Elizaphan son of Parnach,
    the leader from the tribe of Zebulun;
26Paltiel son of Azzan,
    the leader from the tribe of Issachar;
27Ahihud son of Shelomi,
    the leader from the tribe of Asher;
28Pedahel son of Ammihud,
    the leader from the tribe of Naphtali."

29These are the men the LORD commanded to assign the inheritance to the Israelites in the land of Canaan.

Towns for the Levites

35 On the plains of Moab by the Jordan across from Jericho,*g* the LORD said to Moses, **2**"Command the Israelites to give the Levites towns to live in from the inheritance the Israelites will possess. And give them pasturelands around the towns. **3**Then they will have towns to live in and pasturelands for their cattle, flocks and all their other livestock.

4"The pasturelands around the towns that you give the Levites will extend out fifteen hundred feet*h* from the town wall. **5**Outside the town, measure three thousand feet*i* on the east side, three thousand on the south side, three thousand on the west and three thousand on the north, with the town in the center. They will have this area as pastureland for the towns.

Cities of Refuge

6"Six of the towns you give the Levites will be cities of refuge, to which a person who has killed someone may flee. In addition, give them forty-two other towns. **7**In all you must give the Levites forty-eight towns, together with their pasturelands. **8**The towns you give the Levites from the land the Israelites possess are to be given in proportion to the inheritance of each tribe: Take many towns from a tribe that has many, but few from one that has few."

9Then the LORD said to Moses: **10**"Speak to

---

a3 That is, the Dead Sea; also in verse 12   *b4* Hebrew *Akrabbim*   *c5* That is, the Mediterranean; also in verses 6 and 7   *d8* Or *to the entrance to*   *e11* That is, Galilee   *f15* *Jordan of Jericho* was possibly an ancient name for the Jordan River.   *g1* Hebrew *Jordan of Jericho*; possibly an ancient name for the Jordan River   *h4* Hebrew *a thousand cubits* (about 450 meters)   *i5* Hebrew *two thousand cubits* (about 900 meters) the Israelites and say to them: 'When you cross the Jordan into Canaan, ¹¹select some towns to be your cities of refuge, to which a person who has killed someone accidentally may flee. ¹²They will be places of refuge from the avenger, so that a person accused of murder may not die before he stands trial before the assembly. ¹³These six towns you give will be your cities of refuge. ¹⁴Give three on this side of the Jordan and three in Canaan as cities of refuge. ¹⁵These six towns will be a place of refuge for Israelites, aliens and any other people living among them, so that anyone who has killed another accidentally can flee there.

¹⁶" 'If a man strikes someone with an iron object so that he dies, he is a murderer; the murderer shall be put to death. ¹⁷Or if anyone has a stone in his hand that could kill, and he strikes someone so that he dies, he is a murderer; the murderer shall be put to death. ¹⁸Or if anyone has a wooden object in his hand that could kill, and he hits someone so that he dies, he is a murderer; the murderer shall be put to death. ¹⁹The avenger of blood shall put the murderer to death; when he meets him, he shall put him to death. ²⁰If anyone with malice aforethought shoves another or throws something at him intentionally so that he dies ²¹or if in hostility he hits him with his fist so that he dies, that person shall be put to death; he is a murderer. The avenger of blood shall put the murderer to death when he meets him.

²²" 'But if without hostility someone suddenly shoves another or throws something at him unintentionally ²³or, without seeing him, drops a stone on him that could kill him, and he dies, then since he was not his enemy and he did not intend to harm him, ²⁴the assembly must judge between him and the avenger of blood according to these regulations. ²⁵The assembly must protect the one accused of murder from the avenger of blood and send him back to the city of refuge to which he fled. He must stay there until the death of the high priest, who was anointed with the holy oil.

²⁶" 'But if the accused ever goes outside the limits of the city of refuge to which he has fled ²⁷and the avenger of blood finds him outside the city, the avenger of blood may kill the accused without being guilty of murder. ²⁸The accused must stay in his city of refuge until the death of the high priest; only after the death of the high priest may he return to his own property.

²⁹" 'These are to be legal requirements for you throughout the generations to come, wherever you live.

³⁰" 'Anyone who kills a person is to be put to death as a murderer only on the testimony of witnesses. But no one is to be put to death on the testimony of only one witness.

³¹" 'Do not accept a ransom for the life of a murderer, who deserves to die. He must surely be put to death.

³²" 'Do not accept a ransom for anyone who has fled to a city of refuge and so allow him to go back and live on his own land before the death of the high priest.

³³" 'Do not pollute the land where you are. Bloodshed pollutes the land, and atonement cannot be made for the land on which blood has been shed, except by the blood of the one who shed it. ³⁴Do not defile the land where you live and where I dwell, for I, the LORD, dwell among the Israelites.' "

Inheritance of Zelophehad's Daughters

36 The family heads of the clan of Gilead son of Makir, the son of Manasseh, who were from the clans of the descendants of Joseph, came and spoke before Moses and the leaders, the heads of the Israelite families. ²They said, "When the LORD commanded my lord to give the land as an inheritance to the Israelites by lot, he ordered you to give the inheritance of our brother Zelophehad to his daughters. ³Now suppose they marry men from other Israelite tribes; then their inheritance will be taken from our ancestral inheritance and added to that of the tribe they marry into. And so part of the inheritance allotted to us will be taken away. ⁴When the Year of Jubilee for the Israelites comes, their inheritance will be added to that of the tribe into which they marry, and their property will be taken from the tribal inheritance of our forefathers."

⁵Then at the LORD's command Moses gave this order to the Israelites: "What the tribe of the descendants of Joseph is saying is right. ⁶This is what the LORD commands for Zelophehad's daughters: They may marry anyone they please as long as they marry within the tribal clan of their father. ⁷No inheritance in Israel is to pass from tribe to tribe, for every Israelite shall keep the tribal land inherited from his forefathers. ⁸Every daughter who inherits land in any Israelite tribe must marry someone in her father's tribal clan, so that every Israelite will possess the inheritance of his fathers. ⁹No inheritance may pass from tribe to tribe, for each Israelite tribe is to keep the land it inherits."

[10]So Zelophehad's daughters did as the LORD commanded Moses. [11]Zelophehad's daughters — Mahlah, Tirzah, Hoglah, Milcah and Noah — married their cousins on their father's side. [12]They married within the clans of the descendants of Manasseh son of Joseph, and their inheritance remained in their father's clan and tribe.

[13]These are the commands and regulations the LORD gave through Moses to the Israelites on the plains of Moab by the Jordan across from Jericho.[a]

[a]13 Hebrew Jordan of Jericho; possibly an ancient name for the Jordan River

DEUTERONOMY

PICTURE this scenario: Moses and the Israelites are poised on the banks of the Jordan River, ready to cross over and conquer the land of Canaan. But Moses is not allowed to go because of an earlier act of disobedience to God. So he delivers his farewell speech, challenging the nation to remember God's love and obey God's laws. That speech is this book, a repetition of the law God gave forty years before. As you read it, remember what God has done for you in the past and dedicate yourself to serving him.

Outline of Contents

Moses reviews Israel's history (1:1–4:43)
Moses reviews the law (4:44–11:32)
Rules for daily living (12:1–28:68)
The renewal of the covenant (29:1–30:20)
Moses' blessing on Israel and his death (31:1–34:12)

The Command to Leave Horeb

1 These are the words Moses spoke to all Israel in the desert east of the Jordan — that is, in the Arabah — opposite Suph, between Paran and Tophel, Laban, Hazeroth and Dizahab. ²(It takes eleven days to go from Horeb to Kadesh Barnea by the Mount Seir road.)

³In the fortieth year, on the first day of the eleventh month, Moses proclaimed to the Israelites all that the LORD had commanded him concerning them. ⁴This was after he had defeated Sihon king of the Amorites, who reigned in Heshbon, and at Edrei had defeated Og king of Bashan, who reigned in Ashtaroth.

⁵East of the Jordan in the territory of Moab, Moses began to expound this law, saying:

⁶The LORD our God said to us at Horeb, "You have stayed long enough at this mountain. ⁷Break camp and advance into the hill country of the Amorites; go to all the neighboring peoples in the Arabah, in the mountains, in the western foothills, in the Negev and along the coast, to the land of the Canaanites and to Lebanon, as far as the great river, the Euphrates. ⁸See, I have given you this land. Go in and take possession of the land that the LORD swore he would give to your fathers — to Abraham, Isaac and Jacob — and to their descendants after them."

The Appointment of Leaders

9At that time I said to you, "You are too heavy a burden for me to carry alone. **10**The LORD your God has increased your numbers so that today you are as many as the stars in the sky. **11**May the LORD, the God of your fathers, increase you a thousand times and bless you as he has promised! **12**But how can I bear your problems and your burdens and your disputes all by myself? **13**Choose some wise, understanding and respected men from each of your tribes, and I will set them over you."

14You answered me, "What you propose to do is good."

15So I took the leading men of your tribes, wise and respected men, and appointed them to have authority over you — as commanders of thousands, of hundreds, of fifties and of tens and as tribal officials. **16**And I charged your judges at that time: Hear the disputes between your brothers and judge fairly, whether the case is between brother Israelites or between one of them and an alien. **17**Do not show partiality in judging; hear both small and great alike. Do not be afraid of any man, for judgment belongs to God. Bring me any case too hard for you, and I will hear it. **18**And at that time I told you everything you were to do.

Spies Sent Out

19Then, as the LORD our God commanded us, we set out from Horeb and went toward the hill country of the Amorites through all that vast and dreadful desert that you have seen, and so we reached Kadesh Barnea. **20**Then I said to you, "You have reached the hill country of the Amorites, which the LORD our God is giving us. **21**See, the LORD your God has given you the land. Go up and take possession of it as the LORD, the God of your fathers, told you. Do not be afraid; do not be discouraged."

22Then all of you came to me and said, "Let us send men ahead to spy out the land for us and bring back a report about the route we are to take and the towns we will come to."

23The idea seemed good to me; so I selected twelve of you, one man from each tribe. **24**They left and went up into the hill country, and came to the Valley of Eshcol and explored it. **25**Taking with them some of the fruit of the land, they brought it down to us and reported, "It is a good land that the LORD our God is giving us."

Rebellion Against the LORD

26But you were unwilling to go up; you rebelled against the command of the LORD your God. **27**You grumbled in your tents and said, "The LORD hates us; so he brought us out of Egypt to deliver us into the hands of the Amorites to destroy us. **28**Where can we go? Our brothers have made us lose heart. They say, 'The people are stronger and taller than we are; the cities are large, with walls up to the sky. We even saw the Anakites there.' "

29Then I said to you, "Do not be terrified; do not be afraid of them. **30**The LORD your God, who is going before you, will fight for you, as he did for you in Egypt, before your very eyes, **31**and in the desert. There you saw how the LORD your God carried you, as a father carries his son, all the way you went until you reached this place."

32In spite of this, you did not trust in the LORD your God, **33**who went ahead of you on your journey, in fire by night and in a cloud by day, to search out places for you to camp and to show you the way you should go.

34When the LORD heard what you said, he was angry and solemnly swore: **35**"Not a man of this evil generation shall see the good land I swore to give your forefathers, **36**except Caleb son of Jephunneh. He will see it, and I will give him and his descendants the land he set his feet on, because he followed the LORD wholeheartedly."

37Because of you the LORD became angry with me also and said, "You shall not enter it, either. **38**But your assistant, Joshua son of Nun, will enter it. Encourage him, because he will lead Israel to inherit it. **39**And the little ones that you said would be taken captive, your children who do not yet know good from bad — they will enter the land. I will give it to them and they will take possession of it. **40**But as for you, turn around and set out toward the desert along the route to the Red Sea. *a*"

41Then you replied, "We have sinned against the LORD. We will go up and fight, as the LORD our God commanded us." So every one of you put on his weapons, thinking it easy to go up into the hill country.

42But the LORD said to me, "Tell them, 'Do not go up and fight, because I will not be with you. You will be defeated by your enemies.' "

---

*a*40 Hebrew *Yam Suph*; that is, Sea of Reeds

DIGGING A GRAVE FOR OUR DISPUTES

TUESDAY □

Darrell is angry at his mom because she won't let him use all of his savings to buy a new keyboard. And his anger has lasted for over a week. During that time he has tried to get back at her: leaving his room and the kitchen in a mess, ignoring her, talking back to her.

One evening at supper (after he said that the mashed potatoes tasted like cement) Mrs. Burns finally said, "Okay, Darrell, let's go."

"Where?"

"Just grab your jacket!"

Mrs. Burns and Darrell got in the car and drove around for about an hour and a half. The conversation was pretty intense at first. But finally they got to the root of the conflict. After a lot of discussion, they reached an agreement. Then, to celebrate the end of their fight, they stopped and got ice cream sundaes.

Look It Up

Just a nice story? No! According to the Bible, conflict resolution really is possible! Consider these verses:

"Make every effort to live in peace with all men" (Hebrews 12:14).

"But the wisdom that comes from heaven is first of all pure; then peace-loving . . . . Peacemakers who sow in peace raise a harvest of righteousness" (James 3:17–18).

See? God not only tells us to pursue peace, he promises us his wisdom to accomplish the task!

Think It Through

What might happen if Darrell tried to resolve the other conflicts in his life? With his little sister? With his English teacher Mrs. Mitchell? With his classmate Walker?

Are you making every effort to live in peace with all people? If not, why not?

Work It Out

Do you want to end a conflict in your life?

1. Cool down first.
2. Define the disagreement (talk about one issue at a time).
3. Admit where you have been wrong.
4. Communicate carefully. (Watch your tone of voice and the words you choose. Avoid personal attacks, blame laying, and phrases like "you always" or "you never.")
5. Make every effort to understand the other person's point of view.
6. List your options and spend time thinking through them.
7. See the conflict as a problem to be solved, not a war to be won.

Nail It Down

Read about the need for mediators in more complex arguments in Deuteronomy 1:12–17.

Turn to pages 15 and 1327 for other readings on conflict.
Turn to page 182 for Wednesday's reading.

Topic

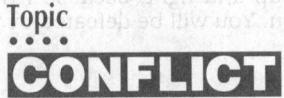

CONFLICT

43So I told you, but you would not listen. You rebelled against the Lord's command and in your arrogance you marched up into the hill country. **44**The Amorites who lived in those hills came out against you; they chased you like a swarm of bees and beat you down from Seir all the way to Hormah. **45**You came back and wept before the Lord, but he paid no attention to your weeping and turned a deaf ear to you. **46**And so you stayed in Kadesh many days—all the time you spent there.

Wanderings in the Desert

2 Then we turned back and set out toward the desert along the route to the Red Sea,*a* as the Lord had directed me. For a long time we made our way around the hill country of Seir.

2Then the Lord said to me, **3**"You have made your way around this hill country long enough; now turn north. **4**Give the people these orders: 'You are about to pass through the territory of your brothers the descendants of Esau, who live in Seir. They will be afraid of you, but be very careful. **5**Do not provoke them to war, for I will not give you any of their land, not even enough to put your foot on. I have given Esau the hill country of Seir as his own. **6**You are to pay them in silver for the food you eat and the water you drink.' "

7The Lord your God has blessed you in all the work of your hands. He has watched over your journey through this vast desert. These forty years the Lord your God has been with you, and you have not lacked anything.

8So we went on past our brothers the descendants of Esau, who live in Seir. We turned from the Arabah road, which comes up from Elath and Ezion Geber, and traveled along the desert road of Moab.

9Then the Lord said to me, "Do not harass the Moabites or provoke them to war, for I will not give you any part of their land. I have given Ar to the descendants of Lot as a possession."

10(The Emites used to live there—a people strong and numerous, and as tall as the Anakites. **11**Like the Anakites, they too were considered Rephaites, but the Moabites called them Emites. **12**Horites used to live in Seir, but the descendants of Esau drove them out. They destroyed the Horites from before them and settled in their place, just as Israel did in the land the Lord gave them as their possession.)

13And the Lord said, "Now get up and cross the Zered Valley." So we crossed the valley.

14Thirty-eight years passed from the time we left Kadesh Barnea until we crossed the Zered Valley. By then, that entire generation of fighting men had perished from the camp, as the Lord had sworn to them. **15**The Lord's hand was against them until he had completely eliminated them from the camp.

16Now when the last of these fighting men among the people had died, **17**the Lord said to me, **18**"Today you are to pass by the region of Moab at Ar. **19**When you come to the Ammonites, do not harass them or provoke them to war, for I will not give you possession of any land belonging to the Ammonites. I have given it as a possession to the descendants of Lot."

20(That too was considered a land of the Rephaites, who used to live there; but the Ammonites called them Zamzummites. **21**They were a people strong and numerous, and as tall as the Anakites. The Lord destroyed them from before the Ammonites, who drove them out and settled in their place. **22**The Lord had done the same for the descendants of Esau, who lived in Seir, when he destroyed the Horites from before them. They drove them out and have lived in their place to this day. **23**And as for the Avvites who lived in villages as far as Gaza, the Caphtorites coming out from Caphtor*b* destroyed them and settled in their place.)

Defeat of Sihon King of Heshbon

24"Set out now and cross the Arnon Gorge. See, I have given into your hand Sihon the Amorite, king of Heshbon, and his country. Begin to take possession of it and engage him in battle. **25**This very day I will begin to put the terror and fear of you on all the nations under heaven. They will hear reports of you and will tremble and be in anguish because of you."

26From the desert of Kedemoth I sent messengers to Sihon king of Heshbon offering peace and saying, **27**"Let us pass through your country. We will stay on the main road; we will not turn aside to the right or to the left. **28**Sell us food to eat and water to drink for their price in silver. Only let us pass through on foot— **29**as the descendants of Esau, who live in Seir, and the Moabites, who live in Ar, did for us—until we cross the

---

a1 Hebrew *Yam Suph*; that is, Sea of Reeds   *b23* That is, Crete

Jordan into the land the LORD our God is giving us." ³⁰But Sihon king of Heshbon refused to let us pass through. For the LORD your God had made his spirit stubborn and his heart obstinate in order to give him into your hands, as he has now done.

³¹The LORD said to me, "See, I have begun to deliver Sihon and his country over to you. Now begin to conquer and possess his land."

³²When Sihon and all his army came out to meet us in battle at Jahaz, ³³the LORD our God delivered him over to us and we struck him down, together with his sons and his whole army. ³⁴At that time we took all his towns and completely destroyed[a] them — men, women and children. We left no survivors. ³⁵But the livestock and the plunder from the towns we had captured we carried off for ourselves. ³⁶From Aroer on the rim of the Arnon Gorge, and from the town in the gorge, even as far as Gilead, not one town was too strong for us. The LORD our God gave us all of them. ³⁷But in accordance with the command of the LORD our God, you did not encroach on any of the land of the Ammonites, neither the land along the course of the Jabbok nor that around the towns in the hills.

Defeat of Og King of Bashan

3 Next we turned and went up along the road toward Bashan, and Og king of Bashan with his whole army marched out to meet us in battle at Edrei. ²The LORD said to me, "Do not be afraid of him, for I have handed him over to you with his whole army and his land. Do to him what you did to Sihon king of the Amorites, who reigned in Heshbon."

³So the LORD our God also gave into our hands Og king of Bashan and all his army. We struck them down, leaving no survivors. ⁴At that time we took all his cities. There was not one of the sixty cities that we did not take from them — the whole region of Argob, Og's kingdom in Bashan. ⁵All these cities were fortified with high walls and with gates and bars, and there were also a great many unwalled villages. ⁶We completely destroyed[a] them, as we had done with Sihon king of Heshbon, destroying[a] every city — men, women and children. ⁷But all the livestock and the plunder from their cities we carried off for ourselves.

⁸So at that time we took from these two kings of the Amorites the territory east of the Jordan, from the Arnon Gorge as far as Mount Hermon. ⁹(Hermon is called Sirion by the Sidonians; the Amorites call it Senir.) ¹⁰We took all the towns on the plateau, and all Gilead, and all Bashan as far as Salecah and Edrei, towns of Og's kingdom in Bashan. ¹¹(Only Og king of Bashan was left of the remnant of the Rephaites. His bed[b] was made of iron and was more than thirteen feet long and six feet wide.[c] It is still in Rabbah of the Ammonites.)

Division of the Land

¹²Of the land that we took over at that time, I gave the Reubenites and the Gadites the territory north of Aroer by the Arnon Gorge, including half the hill country of Gilead, together with its towns. ¹³The rest of Gilead and also all of Bashan, the kingdom of Og, I gave to the half tribe of Manasseh. (The whole region of Argob in Bashan used to be known as a land of the Rephaites. ¹⁴Jair, a descendant of Manasseh, took the whole region of Argob as far as the border of the Geshurites and the Maacathites; it was named after him, so that to this day Bashan is called Havvoth Jair.[d] ¹⁵And I gave Gilead to Makir. ¹⁶But to the Reubenites and the Gadites I gave the territory extending from Gilead down to the Arnon Gorge (the middle of the gorge being the border) and out to the Jabbok River, which is the border of the Ammonites. ¹⁷Its western border was the Jordan in the Arabah, from Kinnereth to the Sea of the Arabah (the Salt Sea[e]), below the slopes of Pisgah.

¹⁸I commanded you at that time: "The LORD your God has given you this land to take possession of it. But all your able-bodied men, armed for battle, must cross over ahead of your brother Israelites. ¹⁹However, your wives, your children and your livestock (I know you have much livestock) may stay in the towns I have given you, ²⁰until the LORD gives rest to your brothers as he has to you, and they too have taken over the land that the LORD your God is giving them, across the Jordan. After that, each of you may go back to the possession I have given you."

Moses Forbidden to Cross the Jordan

²¹At that time I commanded Joshua: "You have seen with your own eyes all that the

a34,6 The Hebrew term refers to the irrevocable giving over of things or persons to the LORD, often by totally destroying them.   b11 Or sarcophagus   c11 Hebrew nine cubits long and four cubits wide (about 4 meters long and 1.8 meters wide)   d14 Or called the settlements of Jair   e17 That is, the Dead Sea

LORD your God has done to these two kings. The LORD will do the same to all the kingdoms over there where you are going. 22Do not be afraid of them; the LORD your God himself will fight for you."

23At that time I pleaded with the LORD: 24"O Sovereign LORD, you have begun to show to your servant your greatness and your strong hand. For what god is there in heaven or on earth who can do the deeds and mighty works you do? 25Let me go over and see the good land beyond the Jordan—that fine hill country and Lebanon."

26But because of you the LORD was angry with me and would not listen to me. "That is enough," the LORD said. "Do not speak to me anymore about this matter. 27Go up to the top of Pisgah and look west and north and south and east. Look at the land with your own eyes, since you are not going to cross this Jordan. 28But commission Joshua, and encourage and strengthen him, for he will lead this people across and will cause them to inherit the land that you will see." 29So we stayed in the valley near Beth Peor.

Obedience Commanded

4 Hear now, O Israel, the decrees and laws I am about to teach you. Follow them so that you may live and may go in and take possession of the land that the LORD, the God of your fathers, is giving you. 2Do not add to what I command you and do not subtract from it, but keep the commands of the LORD your God that I give you.

3You saw with your own eyes what the LORD did at Baal Peor. The LORD your God destroyed from among you everyone who followed the Baal of Peor, 4but all of you who held fast to the LORD your God are still alive today.

5See, I have taught you decrees and laws as the LORD my God commanded me, so that you may follow them in the land you are entering to take possession of it. 6Observe them carefully, for this will show your wisdom and understanding to the nations, who will hear about all these decrees and say, "Surely this great nation is a wise and understanding people." 7What other nation is so great as to have their gods near them the way the LORD our God is near us whenever we pray to him? 8And what other nation is so great as to have such righteous decrees and laws as this body of laws I am setting before you today?

9Only be careful, and watch yourselves closely so that you do not forget the things your eyes have seen or let them slip from your heart as long as you live. Teach them to your children and to their children after them. 10Remember the day you stood before the LORD your God at Horeb, when he said to me, "Assemble the people before me to hear my words so that they may learn to revere me as long as they live in the land and may teach them to their children." 11You came near and stood at the foot of the mountain while it blazed with fire to the very heavens, with black clouds and deep darkness. 12Then the LORD spoke to you out of the fire. You heard the sound of words but saw no form; there was only a voice. 13He declared to you his covenant, the Ten Commandments, which he commanded you to follow and then wrote them on two stone tablets. 14And the LORD directed me at that time to teach you the decrees and laws you are to follow in the land that you are crossing the Jordan to possess.

Idolatry Forbidden

15You saw no form of any kind the day the LORD spoke to you at Horeb out of the fire. Therefore watch yourselves very carefully, 16so that you do not become corrupt and make for yourselves an idol, an image of any shape, whether formed like a man or a woman, 17or like any animal on earth or any bird that flies in the air, 18or like any creature that moves along the ground or any fish in the waters below. 19And when you look up to the sky and see the sun, the moon and the stars—all the heavenly array—do not be enticed into bowing down to them and worshiping things the LORD your God has apportioned to all the nations under heaven. 20But as for you, the LORD took you and brought you out of the iron-smelting furnace, out of Egypt, to be the people of his inheritance, as you now are.

21The LORD was angry with me because of you, and he solemnly swore that I would not cross the Jordan and enter the good land the LORD your God is giving you as your inheritance. 22I will die in this land; I will not cross the Jordan; but you are about to cross over and take possession of that good land. 23Be careful not to forget the covenant of the LORD your God that he made with you; do not make for yourselves an idol in the form of anything the LORD your God has forbidden. 24For the LORD your God is a consuming fire, a jealous God.

25After you have had children and grandchildren and have lived in the land a long time—if you then become corrupt and make any kind of idol, doing evil in the eyes

THE DANGER OF DRIFTING

Last year at this time Lisbeth was fired up for God. She was involved in her youth group, talking to all her friends about Christ, and serious about renewing her mind (she had quit seeing R-rated movies and had begun a Bible memory plan).

Now look at her. Oh, she's not doing anything outrageous — robbing banks or shooting drugs into her eyeballs — but she's not doing much positive either. She makes it to youth group maybe twice a month, she rarely talks about her faith and she doesn't even know where her Bible is!

What happened?

Look It Up
• • • •

The Bible warns us not to drift away from God.

"We must pay more careful attention, therefore, to what we have heard, so that we do not drift away" (Hebrews 2:1).

You need to understand that the phrase "drift away" doesn't refer to active rebellion. It's not talking about a person who suddenly decides, "I don't want to be committed to God anymore."

No, it refers to a gradual process. Imagine the boater who carelessly forgets to drop anchor at bedtime. By morning the boat has drifted out to sea . . . and into trouble!

That's what the drifting Christian is like.

Think It Through
• • • •

This question may sting, but here goes: If every other Christian in the world was as committed to Christ as you are right now, how much impact would the church be having?

Here are some other questions to consider: Have you floated away from God? Is your life like a boat purposely piloted by Christ? Or is it more like a piece of driftwood aimlessly bobbing in the surf?

Work It Out
• • • •

First, with Colossians 3 as your map/compass, chart out your present position. (This will help you see if you are drifting.)

Second, send out an "SOS signal." (This means asking God in prayer to either rescue you from your drifting or keep you from drifting.)

Third, look for a new crew of "sailors" (that is, a group of committed Christians) nearby who can help you keep your life shipshape.

Remember: Commitment means fighting against the tide, not going with the flow!

Nail It Down
• • • •

Read the warning in Deuteronomy 4:9.

Turn to pages 358, 445 and 699 for other readings on commitment.
Turn to page 185 for Thursday's reading.

Topic
• • • •

COMMITMENT

of the LORD your God and provoking him to anger, **26**I call heaven and earth as witnesses against you this day that you will quickly perish from the land that you are crossing the Jordan to possess. You will not live there long but will certainly be destroyed. **27**The LORD will scatter you among the peoples, and only a few of you will survive among the nations to which the LORD will drive you. **28**There you will worship man-made gods of wood and stone, which cannot see or hear or eat or smell. **29**But if from there you seek the LORD your God, you will find him if you look for him with all your heart and with all your soul. **30**When you are in distress and all these things have happened to you, then in later days you will return to the LORD your God and obey him. **31**For the LORD your God is a merciful God; he will not abandon or destroy you or forget the covenant with your forefathers, which he confirmed to them by oath.

The LORD Is God

32Ask now about the former days, long before your time, from the day God created man on the earth; ask from one end of the heavens to the other. Has anything so great as this ever happened, or has anything like it ever been heard of? **33**Has any other people heard the voice of God[a] speaking out of fire, as you have, and lived? **34**Has any god ever tried to take for himself one nation out of another nation, by testings, by miraculous signs and wonders, by war, by a mighty hand and an outstretched arm, or by great and awesome deeds, like all the things the LORD your God did for you in Egypt before your very eyes?

35You were shown these things so that you might know that the LORD is God; besides him there is no other. **36**From heaven he made you hear his voice to discipline you. On earth he showed you his great fire, and you heard his words from out of the fire. **37**Because he loved your forefathers and chose their descendants after them, he brought you out of Egypt by his Presence and his great strength, **38**to drive out before you nations greater and stronger than you and to bring you into their land to give it to you for your inheritance, as it is today.

39Acknowledge and take to heart this day that the LORD is God in heaven above and on the earth below. There is no other. **40**Keep his decrees and commands, which I am giv-

ing you today, so that it may go well with you and your children after you and that you may live long in the land the LORD your God gives you for all time.

Cities of Refuge

41Then Moses set aside three cities east of the Jordan, **42**to which anyone who had killed a person could flee if he had unintentionally killed his neighbor without malice aforethought. He could flee into one of these cities and save his life. **43**The cities were these: Bezer in the desert plateau, for the Reubenites; Ramoth in Gilead, for the Gadites; and Golan in Bashan, for the Manassites.

Introduction to the Law

44This is the law Moses set before the Israelites. **45**These are the stipulations, decrees and laws Moses gave them when they came out of Egypt **46**and were in the valley near Beth Peor east of the Jordan, in the land of Sihon king of the Amorites, who reigned in Heshbon and was defeated by Moses and the Israelites as they came out of Egypt. **47**They took possession of his land and the land of Og king of Bashan, the two Amorite kings east of the Jordan. **48**This land extended from Aroer on the rim of the Arnon Gorge to Mount Siyon[b] (that is, Hermon), **49**and included all the Arabah east of the Jordan, as far as the Sea of the Arabah,[c] below the slopes of Pisgah.

The Ten Commandments

5 Moses summoned all Israel and said:
Hear, O Israel, the decrees and laws I declare in your hearing today. Learn them and be sure to follow them. **2**The LORD our God made a covenant with us at Horeb. **3**It was not with our fathers that the LORD made this covenant, but with us, with all of us who are alive here today. **4**The LORD spoke to you face to face out of the fire on the mountain. **5**(At that time I stood between the LORD and you to declare to you the word of the LORD, because you were afraid of the fire and did not go up the mountain.) And he said:

> **6**"I am the LORD your God, who brought you out of Egypt, out of the land of slavery.
> **7**"You shall have no other gods before[d] me.

---

*a*33 Or *of a god*   *b*48 Hebrew; Syriac (see also Deut. 3:9) *Sirion*   *c*49 That is, the Dead Sea
*d*7 Or *besides*

8"You shall not make for yourself an idol in the form of anything in heaven above or on the earth beneath or in the waters below. 9You shall not bow down to them or worship them; for I, the LORD your God, am a jealous God, punishing the children for the sin of the fathers to the third and fourth generation of those who hate me, 10but showing love to a thousand ₎generations₎ of those who love me and keep my commandments.

11"You shall not misuse the name of the LORD your God, for the LORD will not hold anyone guiltless who misuses his name.

12"Observe the Sabbath day by keeping it holy, as the LORD your God has commanded you. 13Six days you shall labor and do all your work, 14but the seventh day is a Sabbath to the LORD your God. On it you shall not do any work, neither you, nor your son or daughter, nor your manservant or maidservant, nor your ox, your donkey or any of your animals, nor the alien within your gates, so that your manservant and maidservant may rest, as you do. 15Remember that you were slaves in Egypt and that the LORD your God brought you out of there with a mighty hand and an outstretched arm. Therefore the LORD your God has commanded you to observe the Sabbath day.

16"Honor your father and your mother, as the LORD your God has commanded you, so that you may live long and that it may go well with you in the land the LORD your God is giving you.

17"You shall not murder.

18"You shall not commit adultery.

19"You shall not steal.

20"You shall not give false testimony against your neighbor.

21"You shall not covet your neighbor's wife. You shall not set your desire on your neighbor's house or land, his manservant or maidservant, his ox or donkey, or anything that belongs to your neighbor."

22These are the commandments the LORD proclaimed in a loud voice to your whole assembly there on the mountain from out of the fire, the cloud and the deep darkness; and he added nothing more. Then he wrote them on two stone tablets and gave them to me.

23When you heard the voice out of the darkness, while the mountain was ablaze with fire, all the leading men of your tribes and your elders came to me. 24And you said, "The LORD our God has shown us his glory and his majesty, and we have heard his voice from the fire. Today we have seen that a man can live even if God speaks with him. 25But now, why should we die? This great fire will consume us, and we will die if we hear the voice of the LORD our God any longer. 26For what mortal man has ever heard the voice of the living God speaking out of fire, as we have, and survived? 27Go near and listen to all that the LORD our God says. Then tell us whatever the LORD our God tells you. We will listen and obey."

28The LORD heard you when you spoke to me and the LORD said to me, "I have heard what this people said to you. Everything they said was good. 29Oh, that their hearts would be inclined to fear me and keep all my commands always, so that it might go well with them and their children forever!

30"Go, tell them to return to their tents. 31But you stay here with me so that I may give you all the commands, decrees and laws you are to teach them to follow in the land I am giving them to possess."

32So be careful to do what the LORD your God has commanded you; do not turn aside to the right or to the left. 33Walk in all the way that the LORD your God has commanded you, so that you may live and prosper and prolong your days in the land that you will possess.

Love the LORD Your God

6 These are the commands, decrees and laws the LORD your God directed me to teach you to observe in the land that you are crossing the Jordan to possess, 2so that you, your children and their children after them may fear the LORD your God as long as you live by keeping all his decrees and commands that I give you, and so that you may enjoy long life. 3Hear, O Israel, and be careful to obey so that it may go well with you and that you may increase greatly in a land flowing with milk and honey, just as the LORD, the God of your fathers, promised you.

4Hear, O Israel: The LORD our God, the

ELOHIM—OUR CREATIVE, TRIUNE GOD!

Kirsten and Alex are walking out of the movie theater . . . and the film is only half over!

"Alex, why do they do that? Why can't anyone seem to make a movie without taking God's name in vain every two seconds? I mean, I can handle some things, but that really gets me."

"I know. As often as they mention God, you'd think they really liked him or something. But they don't even know what they're saying! God is just a four-letter word to them."

Kirsten smiles, "God only has three letters."

"Okay, smarty!"

Look It Up
• • • •

The first name used for God in the Bible is the Hebrew title *Elohim*: "In the beginning God [*Elohim*] created the heavens and the earth" (Genesis 1:1).

A few paragraphs later the creation account adds these verses: "Then God [*Elohim*] said, 'Let us make man in our image, in our likeness. . . .' So God [*Elohim*] created man in his own image" (Genesis 1:26–27).

Based on these (and more than 2,500 other) usages, the name *Elohim* indicates the power and creative activity of God. The name may stem from either a Hebrew word meaning "the strong one" or from a similar root word meaning "fear."

So what's the point? Simply this: Such an awesome Creator deserves our respect, not our scorn!

Think It Through
• • • •

The term *Elohim* is plural in form. Some scholars believe the plural form is an attempt to express in grammatical fashion the truth that God's greatness and majesty put him in a class all by himself. Others argue that the plural form implies the Trinity—that God is three persons in one.

Question: Which view is correct? Answer: Both viewpoints are credible. *Elohim* is used in passages that suggest God's singular essence. It is also used in passages that hint at the truth of the Trinity.

Work It Out
• • • •

Hop on your bike and take a slow spin around the block. Observe with your eyes, your ears, your nose, your sense of touch. What makes more sense to you—that the world around you happened by accidental evolution or that it was specially created by our creative and powerful *Elohim*?

Do you use the name of God as a swear word? Determine, in his power, to stop today.

Nail It Down
• • • •

Read the description of God in Deuteronomy 6:4.

Turn to pages 21, 96 and 192 for other readings on God's names.
Turn to page 188 for Friday's reading.

Topic
• • • •

GOD'S NAMES

LORD is one.*a* **5**Love the LORD your God with all your heart and with all your soul and with all your strength. **6**These commandments that I give you today are to be upon your hearts. **7**Impress them on your children. Talk about them when you sit at home and when you walk along the road, when you lie down and when you get up. **8**Tie them as symbols on your hands and bind them on your foreheads. **9**Write them on the doorframes of your houses and on your gates.

10When the LORD your God brings you into the land he swore to your fathers, to Abraham, Isaac and Jacob, to give you — a land with large, flourishing cities you did not build, **11**houses filled with all kinds of good things you did not provide, wells you did not dig, and vineyards and olive groves you did not plant — then when you eat and are satisfied, **12**be careful that you do not forget the LORD, who brought you out of Egypt, out of the land of slavery.

13Fear the LORD your God, serve him only and take your oaths in his name. **14**Do not follow other gods, the gods of the peoples around you; **15**for the LORD your God, who is among you, is a jealous God and his anger will burn against you, and he will destroy you from the face of the land. **16**Do not test the LORD your God as you did at Massah. **17**Be sure to keep the commands of the LORD your God and the stipulations and decrees he has given you. **18**Do what is right and good in the LORD's sight, so that it may go well with you and you may go in and take over the good land that the LORD promised on oath to your forefathers, **19**thrusting out all your enemies before you, as the LORD said.

20In the future, when your son asks you, "What is the meaning of the stipulations, decrees and laws the LORD our God has commanded you?" **21**tell him: "We were slaves of Pharaoh in Egypt, but the LORD brought us out of Egypt with a mighty hand. **22**Before our eyes the LORD sent miraculous signs and wonders — great and terrible — upon Egypt and Pharaoh and his whole household. **23**But he brought us out from there to bring us in and give us the land that he promised on oath to our forefathers. **24**The LORD commanded us to obey all these decrees and to fear the LORD our God, so that we might always prosper and be kept alive, as is the case today. **25**And if we are careful to obey all this law before the LORD our God, as he has commanded us, that will be our righteousness."

Driving Out the Nations

7 When the LORD your God brings you into the land you are entering to possess and drives out before you many nations — the Hittites, Girgashites, Amorites, Canaanites, Perizzites, Hivites and Jebusites, seven nations larger and stronger than you — **2**and when the LORD your God has delivered them over to you and you have defeated them, then you must destroy them totally.*b* Make no treaty with them, and show them no mercy. **3**Do not intermarry with them. Do not give your daughters to their sons or take their daughters for your sons, **4**for they will turn your sons away from following me to serve other gods, and the LORD's anger will burn against you and will quickly destroy you. **5**This is what you are to do to them: Break down their altars, smash their sacred stones, cut down their Asherah poles*c* and burn their idols in the fire. **6**For you are a people holy to the LORD your God. The LORD your God has chosen you out of all the peoples on the face of the earth to be his people, his treasured possession.

7The LORD did not set his affection on you and choose you because you were more numerous than other peoples, for you were the fewest of all peoples. **8**But it was because the LORD loved you and kept the oath he swore to your forefathers that he brought you out with a mighty hand and redeemed you from the land of slavery, from the power of Pharaoh king of Egypt. **9**Know therefore that the LORD your God is God; he is the faithful God, keeping his covenant of love to a thousand generations of those who love him and keep his commands. **10**But

those who hate him he will repay to
their face by destruction;
he will not be slow to repay to their
face those who hate him.

11Therefore, take care to follow the commands, decrees and laws I give you today. **12**If you pay attention to these laws and are careful to follow them, then the LORD your God will keep his covenant of love with you, as he swore to your forefathers. **13**He

---

a4 Or *The LORD our God is one LORD*; or *The LORD is our God, the LORD is one*; or *The LORD is our God, the LORD alone*   *b2* The Hebrew term refers to the irrevocable giving over of things or persons to the LORD, often by totally destroying them; also in verse 26.   *c5* That is, symbols of the goddess Asherah; here and elsewhere in Deuteronomy will love you and bless you and increase your numbers. He will bless the fruit of your womb, the crops of your land — your grain, new wine and oil — the calves of your herds and the lambs of your flocks in the land that he swore to your forefathers to give you. [14]You will be blessed more than any other people; none of your men or women will be childless, nor any of your livestock without young. [15]The LORD will keep you free from every disease. He will not inflict on you the horrible diseases you knew in Egypt, but he will inflict them on all who hate you. [16]You must destroy all the peoples the LORD your God gives over to you. Do not look on them with pity and do not serve their gods, for that will be a snare to you.

[17]You may say to yourselves, "These nations are stronger than we are. How can we drive them out?" [18]But do not be afraid of them; remember well what the LORD your God did to Pharaoh and to all Egypt. [19]You saw with your own eyes the great trials, the miraculous signs and wonders, the mighty hand and outstretched arm, with which the LORD your God brought you out. The LORD your God will do the same to all the peoples you now fear. [20]Moreover, the LORD your God will send the hornet among them until even the survivors who hide from you have perished. [21]Do not be terrified by them, for the LORD your God, who is among you, is a great and awesome God. [22]The LORD your God will drive out those nations before you, little by little. You will not be allowed to eliminate them all at once, or the wild animals will multiply around you. [23]But the LORD your God will deliver them over to you, throwing them into great confusion until they are destroyed. [24]He will give their kings into your hand, and you will wipe out their names from under heaven. No one will be able to stand up against you; you will destroy them. [25]The images of their gods you are to burn in the fire. Do not covet the silver and gold on them, and do not take it for yourselves, or you will be ensnared by it, for it is detestable to the LORD your God. [26]Do not bring a detestable thing into your house or you, like it, will be set apart for destruction. Utterly abhor and detest it, for it is set apart for destruction.

Do Not Forget the LORD

8 Be careful to follow every command I am giving you today, so that you may live and increase and may enter and possess the land that the LORD promised on oath to your forefathers. [2]Remember how the LORD your God led you all the way in the desert these forty years, to humble you and to test you in order to know what was in your heart, whether or not you would keep his commands. [3]He humbled you, causing you to hunger and then feeding you with manna, which neither you nor your fathers had known, to teach you that man does not live on bread alone but on every word that comes from the mouth of the LORD. [4]Your clothes did not wear out and your feet did not swell during these forty years. [5]Know then in your heart that as a man disciplines his son, so the LORD your God disciplines you.

[6]Observe the commands of the LORD your God, walking in his ways and revering him. [7]For the LORD your God is bringing you into a good land — a land with streams and pools of water, with springs flowing in the valleys and hills; [8]a land with wheat and barley, vines and fig trees, pomegranates, olive oil and honey; [9]a land where bread will not be scarce and you will lack nothing; a land where the rocks are iron and you can dig copper out of the hills.

[10]When you have eaten and are satisfied, praise the LORD your God for the good land he has given you. [11]Be careful that you do not forget the LORD your God, failing to observe his commands, his laws and his decrees that I am giving you this day. [12]Otherwise, when you eat and are satisfied, when you build fine houses and settle down, [13]and when your herds and flocks grow large and your silver and gold increase and all you have is multiplied, [14]then your heart will become proud and you will forget the LORD your God, who brought you out of Egypt, out of the land of slavery. [15]He led you through the vast and dreadful desert, that thirsty and waterless land, with its venomous snakes and scorpions. He brought you water out of hard rock. [16]He gave you manna to eat in the desert, something your fathers had never known, to humble and to test you so that in the end it might go well with you. [17]You may say to yourself, "My power and the strength of my hands have produced this wealth for me." [18]But remember the LORD your God, for it is he who gives you the ability to produce wealth, and so confirms his covenant, which he swore to your forefathers, as it is today.

[19]If you ever forget the LORD your God and follow other gods and worship and bow down to them, I testify against you today that you will surely be destroyed. [20]Like the nations the LORD destroyed before you, so

ARE YOU STARVING YOURSELF SPIRITUALLY?

Late Saturday night, a group of friends leaves McMurphy's Restaurant and says good night in the parking lot. Frances turns to Rita, "Do you want me to pick you up for church in the morning?"

"Uh, I don't think I'm gonna go. I'm really tired. I've been so busy lately, I think I'll sleep in."

"Rita! That's three weeks in a row!"

"Frances, lighten up! It's just church. I won't die or anything."

As Frances gets in her car, she feels sad. She knows that Rita isn't getting any solid spiritual input.

Look It Up
• • • •

The topic for today is *spiritual* food (and about how important it is for you to eat daily at God's "restaurant")!

"Would you like something to drink?"—"Like newborn babies, crave pure spiritual milk, so that by it you may grow up in your salvation" (1 Peter 2:2).

"May I suggest an entree?" (John 6:51).

"And for dessert . . ."—"How sweet are your words to my taste, sweeter than honey to my mouth!" (Psalm 119:103).

The message is clear: Without food for the soul, Christians become spiritually malnourished! (Plus, they miss out on some delicious treats.)

Think It Through
• • • •

What if your physical intake of food was tied to your spiritual diet? In other words, suppose you were permitted to eat one calorie of physical food for each word of Scripture you presently read per day? Would you enjoy a feast (because you have a healthy appetite for God's Word) or would you experience famine?

Work It Out
• • • •

Try this three-step experiment.

First, ask God to give you a greater hunger for his Word.

Second, before today is over, call a Christian friend and agree together to read Galatians, Ephesians, Philippians and Colossians during the next week. Have daily discussions together. Pick out one verse from each book to memorize. Each day think of a specific way you can practice a command that you have read.

Third, when the week is over, get together and evaluate the success of your experiment.

Nail It Down
• • • •

Contemplate Deuteronomy 8:3.

Turn to pages 146 and 1225 for other readings on food.
Turn to page 190 for the weekend reading.

Topic
• • • •

you will be destroyed for not obeying the LORD your God.

Not Because of Israel's Righteousness

9 Hear, O Israel. You are now about to cross the Jordan to go in and dispossess nations greater and stronger than you, with large cities that have walls up to the sky. ²The people are strong and tall—Anakites! You know about them and have heard it said: "Who can stand up against the Anakites?" ³But be assured today that the LORD your God is the one who goes across ahead of you like a devouring fire. He will destroy them; he will subdue them before you. And you will drive them out and annihilate them quickly, as the LORD has promised you.

⁴After the LORD your God has driven them out before you, do not say to yourself, "The LORD has brought me here to take possession of this land because of my righteousness." No, it is on account of the wickedness of these nations that the LORD is going to drive them out before you. ⁵It is not because of your righteousness or your integrity that you are going in to take possession of their land; but on account of the wickedness of these nations, the LORD your God will drive them out before you, to accomplish what he swore to your fathers, to Abraham, Isaac and Jacob. ⁶Understand, then, that it is not because of your righteousness that the LORD your God is giving you this good land to possess, for you are a stiff-necked people.

The Golden Calf

⁷Remember this and never forget how you provoked the LORD your God to anger in the desert. From the day you left Egypt until you arrived here, you have been rebellious against the LORD. ⁸At Horeb you aroused the LORD's wrath so that he was angry enough to destroy you. ⁹When I went up on the mountain to receive the tablets of stone, the tablets of the covenant that the LORD had made with you, I stayed on the mountain forty days and forty nights; I ate no bread and drank no water. ¹⁰The LORD gave me two stone tablets inscribed by the finger of God. On them were all the commandments the LORD proclaimed to you on the mountain out of the fire, on the day of the assembly.

¹¹At the end of the forty days and forty nights, the LORD gave me the two stone tablets, the tablets of the covenant. ¹²Then the LORD told me, "Go down from here at once, because your people whom you brought out of Egypt have become corrupt. They have turned away quickly from what I commanded them and have made a cast idol for themselves."

¹³And the LORD said to me, "I have seen this people, and they are a stiff-necked people indeed! ¹⁴Let me alone, so that I may destroy them and blot out their name from under heaven. And I will make you into a nation stronger and more numerous than they."

¹⁵So I turned and went down from the mountain while it was ablaze with fire. And the two tablets of the covenant were in my hands.ᵃ ¹⁶When I looked, I saw that you had sinned against the LORD your God; you had made for yourselves an idol cast in the shape of a calf. You had turned aside quickly from the way that the LORD had commanded you. ¹⁷So I took the two tablets and threw them out of my hands, breaking them to pieces before your eyes.

¹⁸Then once again I fell prostrate before the LORD for forty days and forty nights; I ate no bread and drank no water, because of all the sin you had committed, doing what was evil in the LORD's sight and so provoking him to anger. ¹⁹I feared the anger and wrath of the LORD, for he was angry enough with you to destroy you. But again the LORD listened to me. ²⁰And the LORD was angry enough with Aaron to destroy him, but at that time I prayed for Aaron too. ²¹Also I took that sinful thing of yours, the calf you had made, and burned it in the fire. Then I crushed it and ground it to powder as fine as dust and threw the dust into a stream that flowed down the mountain.

²²You also made the LORD angry at Taberah, at Massah and at Kibroth Hattaavah.

²³And when the LORD sent you out from Kadesh Barnea, he said, "Go up and take possession of the land I have given you." But you rebelled against the command of the LORD your God. You did not trust him or obey him. ²⁴You have been rebellious against the LORD ever since I have known you.

²⁵I lay prostrate before the LORD those forty days and forty nights because the LORD had said he would destroy you. ²⁶I prayed to the LORD and said, "O Sovereign LORD, do not destroy your people, your own inheritance that you redeemed by your great power and brought out of Egypt with a mighty hand. ²⁷Remember your servants Abraham, Isaac and Jacob. Overlook the stubbornness of this people, their wickedness and their sin.

ᵃ 15 Or And I had the two tablets of the covenant with me, one in each hand

THE PLACE GOD WANTS

Work It Out
• • • •

Look around your room. Pick up something that's important to you, something you value. Maybe it's a new shirt or a video game you enjoy playing. Maybe it's an old stuffed animal or your favorite basketball.

Now imagine worshiping that item. Imagine bowing down and praying to it. Pretty weird, huh?

But that's exactly what idolatry is. You probably don't bow down and pray, but you put more importance on one thing or another than on God. In this modern world, it's easy to do. You get caught up in needing this and wanting that; you have to do this and you want to go there. Gradually, almost without realizing it, God is pushed and squeezed out of your life.

Make no mistake. The only place God wants in your life is first place. It takes hard work and commitment to keep him there, but it's worth it.

Nail It Down
• • • •

Read about Israel's dash into idolatry in Deuteronomy 9:11–17.

Think It Through
• • • •

Anything in your life that is more important to you than God is an idol. Friends, cars, sports, music, clothes, dating, food—all can become idols if you treat them like they are more important than God.

There is nothing wrong with any of these things. Friends make life enjoyable; cars get you where you need to go (some more quickly than others, of course); sports provide exercise and competition; music provides a way to express and release emotion; clothes cover your body; dating provides a way to find a mate; food gives nourishment. But any one of these things can become an idol if you put it before God in your life. So enjoy your car, your friends, your dates, your new clothes . . . but enjoy God more.

Nail It Down
• • • •

Remind yourself of what idolatry is by reading Deuteronomy 9:11–17. For further insight read Psalm 17:14–15.

Turn to pages 348, 483 and 713 for other readings on idols.
Turn to page 192 for Monday's reading.

Topic
• • • •

28Otherwise, the country from which you brought us will say, 'Because the LORD was not able to take them into the land he had promised them, and because he hated them, he brought them out to put them to death in the desert.' 29But they are your people, your inheritance that you brought out by your great power and your outstretched arm."

Tablets Like the First Ones

10 At that time the LORD said to me, "Chisel out two stone tablets like the first ones and come up to me on the mountain. Also make a wooden chest.*a* 2I will write on the tablets the words that were on the first tablets, which you broke. Then you are to put them in the chest."

3So I made the ark out of acacia wood and chiseled out two stone tablets like the first ones, and I went up on the mountain with the two tablets in my hands. 4The LORD wrote on these tablets what he had written before, the Ten Commandments he had proclaimed to you on the mountain, out of the fire, on the day of the assembly. And the LORD gave them to me. 5Then I came back down the mountain and put the tablets in the ark I had made, as the LORD commanded me, and they are there now.

6(The Israelites traveled from the wells of the Jaakanites to Moserah. There Aaron died and was buried, and Eleazar his son succeeded him as priest. 7From there they traveled to Gudgodah and on to Jotbathah, a land with streams of water. 8At that time the LORD set apart the tribe of Levi to carry the ark of the covenant of the LORD, to stand before the LORD to minister and to pronounce blessings in his name, as they still do today. 9That is why the Levites have no share or inheritance among their brothers; the LORD is their inheritance, as the LORD your God told them.)

10Now I had stayed on the mountain forty days and nights, as I did the first time, and the LORD listened to me at this time also. It was not his will to destroy you. 11"Go," the LORD said to me, "and lead the people on their way, so that they may enter and possess the land that I swore to their fathers to give them."

Fear the LORD

12And now, O Israel, what does the LORD your God ask of you but to fear the LORD your God, to walk in all his ways, to love him, to serve the LORD your God with all your heart and with all your soul, 13and to observe the LORD's commands and decrees that I am giving you today for your own good?

14To the LORD your God belong the heavens, even the highest heavens, the earth and everything in it. 15Yet the LORD set his affection on your forefathers and loved them, and he chose you, their descendants, above all the nations, as it is today. 16Circumcise your hearts, therefore, and do not be stiff-necked any longer. 17For the LORD your God is God of gods and Lord of lords, the great God, mighty and awesome, who shows no partiality and accepts no bribes. 18He defends the cause of the fatherless and the widow, and loves the alien, giving him food and clothing. 19And you are to love those who are aliens, for you yourselves were aliens in Egypt. 20Fear the LORD your God and serve him. Hold fast to him and take your oaths in his name. 21He is your praise; he is your God, who performed for you those great and awesome wonders you saw with your own eyes. 22Your forefathers who went down into Egypt were seventy in all, and now the LORD your God has made you as numerous as the stars in the sky.

Love and Obey the LORD

11 Love the LORD your God and keep his requirements, his decrees, his laws and his commands always. 2Remember today that your children were not the ones who saw and experienced the discipline of the LORD your God: his majesty, his mighty hand, his outstretched arm; 3the signs he performed and the things he did in the heart of Egypt, both to Pharaoh king of Egypt and to his whole country; 4what he did to the Egyptian army, to its horses and chariots, how he overwhelmed them with the waters of the Red Sea*b* as they were pursuing you, and how the LORD brought lasting ruin on them. 5It was not your children who saw what he did for you in the desert until you arrived at this place, 6and what he did to Dathan and Abiram, sons of Eliab the Reubenite, when the earth opened its mouth right in the middle of all Israel and swallowed them up with their households, their tents and every living thing that belonged to them. 7But it was your own eyes that saw all these great things the LORD has done.

8Observe therefore all the commands I am giving you today, so that you may have the strength to go in and take over the land

---

a1 That is, an ark   *b4* Hebrew *Yam Suph*; that is, Sea of Reeds

ADONAI—OUR LORD AND MASTER

In various passages in Scripture," Pastor Vern pronounced, "God is called *Yahweh,* which means he's our personal, eternal God. In other passages he's called *Elohim,* which means he's our creative, triune God. Now the question for today. Who is your *Adonai?* Who is your *Kurios?"*

"My what?" asked Larry.

"Your *Adonai,* your *Kurios,"* repeated Pastor Vern.

"I have absolutely no idea what you're talking about."

Look It Up
••••

Adonai is the Hebrew word for Lord. *Kurios* is Lord in the Greek of New Testament times. That title—Lord—is used of God hundreds of times in the Bible:

"Moses said to the Lord, 'O Lord, I have never been eloquent' " (Exodus 4:10).

"I will praise you, O Lord my God, with all my heart; I will glorify your name forever" (Psalm 86:12).

"At that time Jesus said, 'I praise you, Father, Lord of heaven and earth, because you have hidden these things from the wise and learned, and revealed them to little children' " (Matthew 11:25).

Think It Through
••••

The title *Lord* implies control or possession. It is often applied to human beings by their servants or slaves (Numbers 12:11; 2 Samuel 10:3; 1 Kings 1:43). Used of God, the meaning is much more profound. As your sovereign Lord, God expects obedience from you. As your perfect, good Master, he also provides for all your needs.

Work It Out
••••

Examine the following areas of your life. Who or what is lord over your thoughts, words and behavior in each area? In other words, who or what determines how you function in each situation?
1. School
2. Dating life
3. Work
4. Relationships at home
5. Time with friends
6. Athletics
7. Religious activities

Discuss your findings with a Christian friend, and pray together that you will surrender more of yourself to the Lord.

Nail It Down
••••

See Lord, God and Lord all used in the same verse— Deuteronomy 10:17!

Turn to pages 21, 96 and 185 for other readings on God's names.
Turn to page 195 for Tuesday's reading.

Topic
••••

GOD'S NAMES

that you are crossing the Jordan to possess, ⁹and so that you may live long in the land that the Lord swore to your forefathers to give to them and their descendants, a land flowing with milk and honey. ¹⁰The land you are entering to take over is not like the land of Egypt, from which you have come, where you planted your seed and irrigated it by foot as in a vegetable garden. ¹¹But the land you are crossing the Jordan to take possession of is a land of mountains and valleys that drinks rain from heaven. ¹²It is a land the Lord your God cares for; the eyes of the Lord your God are continually on it from the beginning of the year to its end.

¹³So if you faithfully obey the commands I am giving you today — to love the Lord your God and to serve him with all your heart and with all your soul — ¹⁴then I will send rain on your land in its season, both autumn and spring rains, so that you may gather in your grain, new wine and oil. ¹⁵I will provide grass in the fields for your cattle, and you will eat and be satisfied.

¹⁶Be careful, or you will be enticed to turn away and worship other gods and bow down to them. ¹⁷Then the Lord's anger will burn against you, and he will shut the heavens so that it will not rain and the ground will yield no produce, and you will soon perish from the good land the Lord is giving you. ¹⁸Fix these words of mine in your hearts and minds; tie them as symbols on your hands and bind them on your foreheads. ¹⁹Teach them to your children, talking about them when you sit at home and when you walk along the road, when you lie down and when you get up. ²⁰Write them on the doorframes of your houses and on your gates, ²¹so that your days and the days of your children may be many in the land that the Lord swore to give your forefathers, as many as the days that the heavens are above the earth.

²²If you carefully observe all these commands I am giving you to follow — to love the Lord your God, to walk in all his ways and to hold fast to him — ²³then the Lord will drive out all these nations before you, and you will dispossess nations larger and stronger than you. ²⁴Every place where you set your foot will be yours: Your territory will extend from the desert to Lebanon, and from the Euphrates River to the western sea.^a ²⁵No man will be able to stand against you. The Lord your God, as he promised you, will put the terror and fear of you on the whole land, wherever you go.

²⁶See, I am setting before you today a blessing and a curse — ²⁷the blessing if you obey the commands of the Lord your God that I am giving you today; ²⁸the curse if you disobey the commands of the Lord your God and turn from the way that I command you today by following other gods, which you have not known. ²⁹When the Lord your God has brought you into the land you are entering to possess, you are to proclaim on Mount Gerizim the blessings, and on Mount Ebal the curses. ³⁰As you know, these mountains are across the Jordan, west of the road,^b toward the setting sun, near the great trees of Moreh, in the territory of those Canaanites living in the Arabah in the vicinity of Gilgal. ³¹You are about to cross the Jordan to enter and take possession of the land the Lord your God is giving you. When you have taken it over and are living there, ³²be sure that you obey all the decrees and laws I am setting before you today.

The One Place of Worship

12 These are the decrees and laws you must be careful to follow in the land that the Lord, the God of your fathers, has given you to possess — as long as you live in the land. ²Destroy completely all the places on the high mountains and on the hills and under every spreading tree where the nations you are dispossessing worship their gods. ³Break down their altars, smash their sacred stones and burn their Asherah poles in the fire; cut down the idols of their gods and wipe out their names from those places.

⁴You must not worship the Lord your God in their way. ⁵But you are to seek the place the Lord your God will choose from among all your tribes to put his Name there for his dwelling. To that place you must go; ⁶there bring your burnt offerings and sacrifices, your tithes and special gifts, what you have vowed to give and your freewill offerings, and the firstborn of your herds and flocks. ⁷There, in the presence of the Lord your God, you and your families shall eat and shall rejoice in everything you have put your hand to, because the Lord your God has blessed you.

⁸You are not to do as we do here today, everyone as he sees fit, ⁹since you have not yet reached the resting place and the inheritance the Lord your God is giving you. ¹⁰But you will cross the Jordan and settle in the

^a24 That is, the Mediterranean   ^b30 Or Jordan, westward

land the LORD your God is giving you as an inheritance, and he will give you rest from all your enemies around you so that you will live in safety. **11**Then to the place the LORD your God will choose as a dwelling for his Name — there you are to bring everything I command you: your burnt offerings and sacrifices, your tithes and special gifts, and all the choice possessions you have vowed to the LORD. **12**And there rejoice before the LORD your God, you, your sons and daughters, your menservants and maidservants, and the Levites from your towns, who have no allotment or inheritance of their own. **13**Be careful not to sacrifice your burnt offerings anywhere you please. **14**Offer them only at the place the LORD will choose in one of your tribes, and there observe everything I command you.

15Nevertheless, you may slaughter your animals in any of your towns and eat as much of the meat as you want, as if it were gazelle or deer, according to the blessing the LORD your God gives you. Both the ceremonially unclean and the clean may eat it. **16**But you must not eat the blood; pour it out on the ground like water. **17**You must not eat in your own towns the tithe of your grain and new wine and oil, or the firstborn of your herds and flocks, or whatever you have vowed to give, or your freewill offerings or special gifts. **18**Instead, you are to eat them in the presence of the LORD your God at the place the LORD your God will choose — you, your sons and daughters, your menservants and maidservants, and the Levites from your towns — and you are to rejoice before the LORD your God in everything you put your hand to. **19**Be careful not to neglect the Levites as long as you live in your land.

20When the LORD your God has enlarged your territory as he promised you, and you crave meat and say, "I would like some meat," then you may eat as much of it as you want. **21**If the place where the LORD your God chooses to put his Name is too far away from you, you may slaughter animals from the herds and flocks the LORD has given you, as I have commanded you, and in your own towns you may eat as much of them as you want. **22**Eat them as you would gazelle or deer. Both the ceremonially unclean and the clean may eat. **23**But be sure you do not eat the blood, because the blood is the life, and you must not eat the life with the meat. **24**You must not eat the blood; pour it out on the ground like water. **25**Do not eat it, so that it may go well with you and your children

after you, because you will be doing what is right in the eyes of the LORD.

26But take your consecrated things and whatever you have vowed to give, and go to the place the LORD will choose. **27**Present your burnt offerings on the altar of the LORD your God, both the meat and the blood. The blood of your sacrifices must be poured beside the altar of the LORD your God, but you may eat the meat. **28**Be careful to obey all these regulations I am giving you, so that it may always go well with you and your children after you, because you will be doing what is good and right in the eyes of the LORD your God.

29The LORD your God will cut off before you the nations you are about to invade and dispossess. But when you have driven them out and settled in their land, **30**and after they have been destroyed before you, be careful not to be ensnared by inquiring about their gods, saying, "How do these nations serve their gods? We will do the same." **31**You must not worship the LORD your God in their way, because in worshiping their gods, they do all kinds of detestable things the LORD hates. They even burn their sons and daughters in the fire as sacrifices to their gods.

32See that you do all I command you; do not add to it or take away from it.

Worshiping Other Gods

13 If a prophet, or one who foretells by dreams, appears among you and announces to you a miraculous sign or wonder, **2**and if the sign or wonder of which he has spoken takes place, and he says, "Let us follow other gods" (gods you have not known) "and let us worship them," **3**you must not listen to the words of that prophet or dreamer. The LORD your God is testing you to find out whether you love him with all your heart and with all your soul. **4**It is the LORD your God you must follow, and him you must revere. Keep his commands and obey him; serve him and hold fast to him. **5**That prophet or dreamer must be put to death, because he preached rebellion against the LORD your God, who brought you out of Egypt and redeemed you from the land of slavery; he has tried to turn you from the way the LORD your God commanded you to follow. You must purge the evil from among you.

6If your very own brother, or your son or daughter, or the wife you love, or your closest friend secretly entices you, saying, "Let us go and worship other gods" (gods that neither you nor your fathers have known,

USE YOUR HEAD TO CHOOSE YOUR FRIENDS

The Wagners moved to Denver almost eight months ago. Karen, fourteen, has yet to make a friend. She sits around watching television and listening to music. She's bored out of her mind.

Sixteen-year-old Helen, on the other hand, has made friends with almost everybody in town. She's always doing stuff, going to parties and getting asked out. Problem is, she's hanging out with a crowd that is definitely on the wild side. It's to the point where she's seriously hurting her walk with God.

Which of the Wagner girls is in worse shape?

Look It Up
••••

Friendship is more than just finding a group of people to run around with. In fact, by picking your pals too quickly and without much thought, it's possible to end up with "friends" who really aren't friends after all. This is why the Bible warns you to choose your friends wisely:

"A righteous man is cautious in friendship, but the way of the wicked leads them astray" (Proverbs 12:26).

Another verse points out that "a man of many companions may come to ruin, but there is a friend who sticks closer than a brother" (Proverbs 18:24).

Finally, Proverbs urges you to watch out for people who just want to use you (Proverbs 19:6–7).

Think It Through
••••

Think about your circle of friends. (Maybe it's a lot of people, or maybe your circle is really small.) How many of those people genuinely care about you? How many of them would stick closer to you than a brother during a crisis? Are any of them using you because of your popularity, wit, money, looks or abilities?

Work It Out
••••

As a Christian, you should have relationships with people who don't know Christ. How else can you be a witness for him? The problem comes when you let those friendships pull you away from the truth.

If you're involved in a close friendship that's hurting your walk with God, rearrange your priorities. Don't completely walk away from the friendship, but be more cautious. If you're trying to be the best friend to everyone in your whole school, stop and evaluate. Two or three quality friendships are much more valuable than knowing the names of a thousand people.

Here's a prayer for the week: "Lord, I want to learn how to be the best friend I can be. Change me as I study what your Word says. Amen."

Nail It Down
••••

Read Deuteronomy 13:6–11 for the radical treatment in the Old Testament of friends who tried to lead someone away from God.

**Turn to pages 291, 509, 670 and 1346 for other readings on friendship.
Turn to page 212 for Wednesday's reading.**

Topic
••••

FRIENDSHIP

7gods of the peoples around you, whether near or far, from one end of the land to the other), 8do not yield to him or listen to him. Show him no pity. Do not spare him or shield him. 9You must certainly put him to death. Your hand must be the first in putting him to death, and then the hands of all the people. 10Stone him to death, because he tried to turn you away from the LORD your God, who brought you out of Egypt, out of the land of slavery. 11Then all Israel will hear and be afraid, and no one among you will do such an evil thing again.

12If you hear it said about one of the towns the LORD your God is giving you to live in 13that wicked men have arisen among you and have led the people of their town astray, saying, "Let us go and worship other gods" (gods you have not known), 14then you must inquire, probe and investigate it thoroughly. And if it is true and it has been proved that this detestable thing has been done among you, 15you must certainly put to the sword all who live in that town. Destroy it completely,a both its people and its livestock. 16Gather all the plunder of the town into the middle of the public square and completely burn the town and all its plunder as a whole burnt offering to the LORD your God. It is to remain a ruin forever, never to be rebuilt. 17None of those condemned thingsa shall be found in your hands, so that the LORD will turn from his fierce anger; he will show you mercy, have compassion on you, and increase your numbers, as he promised on oath to your forefathers, 18because you obey the LORD your God, keeping all his commands that I am giving you today and doing what is right in his eyes.

Clean and Unclean Food

14 You are the children of the LORD your God. Do not cut yourselves or shave the front of your heads for the dead, 2for you are a people holy to the LORD your God. Out of all the peoples on the face of the earth, the LORD has chosen you to be his treasured possession.

3Do not eat any detestable thing. 4These are the animals you may eat: the ox, the sheep, the goat, 5the deer, the gazelle, the roe deer, the wild goat, the ibex, the antelope and the mountain sheep.b 6You may eat any animal that has a split hoof divided in two and that chews the cud. 7However, of those that chew the cud or that have a split hoof completely divided you may not eat the camel, the rabbit or the coney.c Although they chew the cud, they do not have a split hoof; they are ceremonially unclean for you. 8The pig is also unclean; although it has a split hoof, it does not chew the cud. You are not to eat their meat or touch their carcasses.

9Of all the creatures living in the water, you may eat any that has fins and scales. 10But anything that does not have fins and scales you may not eat; for you it is unclean.

11You may eat any clean bird. 12But these you may not eat: the eagle, the vulture, the black vulture, 13the red kite, the black kite, any kind of falcon, 14any kind of raven, 15the horned owl, the screech owl, the gull, any kind of hawk, 16the little owl, the great owl, the white owl, 17the desert owl, the osprey, the cormorant, 18the stork, any kind of heron, the hoopoe and the bat.

19All flying insects that swarm are unclean to you; do not eat them. 20But any winged creature that is clean you may eat.

21Do not eat anything you find already dead. You may give it to an alien living in any of your towns, and he may eat it, or you may sell it to a foreigner. But you are a people holy to the LORD your God.

Do not cook a young goat in its mother's milk.

Tithes

22Be sure to set aside a tenth of all that your fields produce each year. 23Eat the tithe of your grain, new wine and oil, and the firstborn of your herds and flocks in the presence of the LORD your God at the place he will choose as a dwelling for his Name, so that you may learn to revere the LORD your God always. 24But if that place is too distant and you have been blessed by the LORD your God and cannot carry your tithe (because the place where the LORD will choose to put his Name is so far away), 25then exchange your tithe for silver, and take the silver with you and go to the place the LORD your God will choose. 26Use the silver to buy whatever you like: cattle, sheep, wine or other fermented drink, or anything you wish. Then you and your household shall eat there in the presence of the LORD your God and rejoice. 27And do not neglect the Levites living in your towns, for they

---

a15,17 The Hebrew term refers to the irrevocable giving over of things or persons to the LORD, often by totally destroying them.　　b5 The precise identification of some of the birds and animals in this chapter is uncertain.　　c7 That is, the hyrax or rock badger have no allotment or inheritance of their own.

28At the end of every three years, bring all the tithes of that year's produce and store it in your towns, **29**so that the Levites (who have no allotment or inheritance of their own) and the aliens, the fatherless and the widows who live in your towns may come and eat and be satisfied, and so that the Lord your God may bless you in all the work of your hands.

The Year for Canceling Debts

15 At the end of every seven years you must cancel debts. **2**This is how it is to be done: Every creditor shall cancel the loan he has made to his fellow Israelite. He shall not require payment from his fellow Israelite or brother, because the Lord's time for canceling debts has been proclaimed. **3**You may require payment from a foreigner, but you must cancel any debt your brother owes you. **4**However, there should be no poor among you, for in the land the Lord your God is giving you to possess as your inheritance, he will richly bless you, **5**if only you fully obey the Lord your God and are careful to follow all these commands I am giving you today. **6**For the Lord your God will bless you as he has promised, and you will lend to many nations but will borrow from none. You will rule over many nations but none will rule over you.

7If there is a poor man among your brothers in any of the towns of the land that the Lord your God is giving you, do not be hardhearted or tightfisted toward your poor brother. **8**Rather be openhanded and freely lend him whatever he needs. **9**Be careful not to harbor this wicked thought: "The seventh year, the year for canceling debts, is near," so that you do not show ill will toward your needy brother and give him nothing. He may then appeal to the Lord against you, and you will be found guilty of sin. **10**Give generously to him and do so without a grudging heart; then because of this the Lord your God will bless you in all your work and in everything you put your hand to. **11**There will always be poor people in the land. Therefore I command you to be openhanded toward your brothers and toward the poor and needy in your land.

Freeing Servants

12If a fellow Hebrew, a man or a woman, sells himself to you and serves you six years, in the seventh year you must let him go free. **13**And when you release him, do not send him away empty-handed. **14**Supply him liberally from your flock, your threshing floor and your winepress. Give to him as the Lord your God has blessed you. **15**Remember that you were slaves in Egypt and the Lord your God redeemed you. That is why I give you this command today.

16But if your servant says to you, "I do not want to leave you," because he loves you and your family and is well off with you, **17**then take an awl and push it through his ear lobe into the door, and he will become your servant for life. Do the same for your maidservant.

18Do not consider it a hardship to set your servant free, because his service to you these six years has been worth twice as much as that of a hired hand. And the Lord your God will bless you in everything you do.

The Firstborn Animals

19Set apart for the Lord your God every firstborn male of your herds and flocks. Do not put the firstborn of your oxen to work, and do not shear the firstborn of your sheep. **20**Each year you and your family are to eat them in the presence of the Lord your God at the place he will choose. **21**If an animal has a defect, is lame or blind, or has any serious flaw, you must not sacrifice it to the Lord your God. **22**You are to eat it in your own towns. Both the ceremonially unclean and the clean may eat it, as if it were gazelle or deer. **23**But you must not eat the blood; pour it out on the ground like water.

Passover

16 Observe the month of Abib and celebrate the Passover of the Lord your God, because in the month of Abib he brought you out of Egypt by night. **2**Sacrifice as the Passover to the Lord your God an animal from your flock or herd at the place the Lord will choose as a dwelling for his Name. **3**Do not eat it with bread made with yeast, but for seven days eat unleavened bread, the bread of affliction, because you left Egypt in haste — so that all the days of your life you may remember the time of your departure from Egypt. **4**Let no yeast be found in your possession in all your land for seven days. Do not let any of the meat you sacrifice on the evening of the first day remain until morning.

5You must not sacrifice the Passover in any town the Lord your God gives you **6**except in the place he will choose as a dwelling for his Name. There you must sacrifice the

Passover in the evening, when the sun goes down, on the anniversary[a] of your departure from Egypt. [7]Roast it and eat it at the place the LORD your God will choose. Then in the morning return to your tents. [8]For six days eat unleavened bread and on the seventh day hold an assembly to the LORD your God and do no work.

Feast of Weeks

[9]Count off seven weeks from the time you begin to put the sickle to the standing grain. [10]Then celebrate the Feast of Weeks to the LORD your God by giving a freewill offering in proportion to the blessings the LORD your God has given you. [11]And rejoice before the LORD your God at the place he will choose as a dwelling for his Name — you, your sons and daughters, your menservants and maidservants, the Levites in your towns, and the aliens, the fatherless and the widows living among you. [12]Remember that you were slaves in Egypt, and follow carefully these decrees.

Feast of Tabernacles

[13]Celebrate the Feast of Tabernacles for seven days after you have gathered the produce of your threshing floor and your winepress. [14]Be joyful at your Feast — you, your sons and daughters, your menservants and maidservants, and the Levites, the aliens, the fatherless and the widows who live in your towns. [15]For seven days celebrate the Feast to the LORD your God at the place the LORD will choose. For the LORD your God will bless you in all your harvest and in all the work of your hands, and your joy will be complete.

[16]Three times a year all your men must appear before the LORD your God at the place he will choose: at the Feast of Unleavened Bread, the Feast of Weeks and the Feast of Tabernacles. No man should appear before the LORD empty-handed: [17]Each of you must bring a gift in proportion to the way the LORD your God has blessed you.

Judges

[18]Appoint judges and officials for each of your tribes in every town the LORD your God is giving you, and they shall judge the people fairly. [19]Do not pervert justice or show partiality. Do not accept a bribe, for a bribe blinds the eyes of the wise and twists the words of the righteous. [20]Follow justice and justice alone, so that you may live and possess the land the LORD your God is giving you.

Worshiping Other Gods

[21]Do not set up any wooden Asherah pole[b] beside the altar you build to the LORD your God, [22]and do not erect a sacred stone, for these the LORD your God hates.

17 Do not sacrifice to the LORD your God an ox or a sheep that has any defect or flaw in it, for that would be detestable to him.

[2]If a man or woman living among you in one of the towns the LORD gives you is found doing evil in the eyes of the LORD your God in violation of his covenant, [3]and contrary to my command has worshiped other gods, bowing down to them or to the sun or the moon or the stars of the sky, [4]and this has been brought to your attention, then you must investigate it thoroughly. If it is true and it has been proved that this detestable thing has been done in Israel, [5]take the man or woman who has done this evil deed to your city gate and stone that person to death. [6]On the testimony of two or three witnesses a man shall be put to death, but no one shall be put to death on the testimony of only one witness. [7]The hands of the witnesses must be the first in putting him to death, and then the hands of all the people. You must purge the evil from among you.

Law Courts

[8]If cases come before your courts that are too difficult for you to judge — whether bloodshed, lawsuits or assaults — take them to the place the LORD your God will choose. [9]Go to the priests, who are Levites, and to the judge who is in office at that time. Inquire of them and they will give you the verdict. [10]You must act according to the decisions they give you at the place the LORD will choose. Be careful to do everything they direct you to do. [11]Act according to the law they teach you and the decisions they give you. Do not turn aside from what they tell you, to the right or to the left. [12]The man who shows contempt for the judge or for the priest who stands ministering there to the LORD your God must be put to death. You must purge the evil from Israel. [13]All the people will hear and be afraid, and will not be contemptuous again.

The King

[14]When you enter the land the LORD your

God is giving you and have taken possession of it and settled in it, and you say, "Let us set a king over us like all the nations around us," **15**be sure to appoint over you the king the LORD your God chooses. He must be from among your own brothers. Do not place a foreigner over you, one who is not a brother Israelite. **16**The king, moreover, must not acquire great numbers of horses for himself or make the people return to Egypt to get more of them, for the LORD has told you, "You are not to go back that way again." **17**He must not take many wives, or his heart will be led astray. He must not accumulate large amounts of silver and gold.

18When he takes the throne of his kingdom, he is to write for himself on a scroll a copy of this law, taken from that of the priests, who are Levites. **19**It is to be with him, and he is to read it all the days of his life so that he may learn to revere the LORD his God and follow carefully all the words of this law and these decrees **20**and not consider himself better than his brothers and turn from the law to the right or to the left. Then he and his descendants will reign a long time over his kingdom in Israel.

Offerings for Priests and Levites

18 The priests, who are Levites—indeed the whole tribe of Levi—are to have no allotment or inheritance with Israel. They shall live on the offerings made to the LORD by fire, for that is their inheritance. **2**They shall have no inheritance among their brothers; the LORD is their inheritance, as he promised them.

3This is the share due the priests from the people who sacrifice a bull or a sheep: the shoulder, the jowls and the inner parts. **4**You are to give them the firstfruits of your grain, new wine and oil, and the first wool from the shearing of your sheep, **5**for the LORD your God has chosen them and their descendants out of all your tribes to stand and minister in the LORD's name always.

6If a Levite moves from one of your towns anywhere in Israel where he is living, and comes in all earnestness to the place the LORD will choose, **7**he may minister in the name of the LORD his God like all his fellow Levites who serve there in the presence of the LORD. **8**He is to share equally in their benefits, even though he has received money from the sale of family possessions.

Detestable Practices

9When you enter the land the LORD your God is giving you, do not learn to imitate the detestable ways of the nations there. **10**Let no one be found among you who sacrifices his son or daughter in[a] the fire, who practices divination or sorcery, interprets omens, engages in witchcraft, **11**or casts spells, or who is a medium or spiritist or who consults the dead. **12**Anyone who does these things is detestable to the LORD, and because of these detestable practices the LORD your God will drive out those nations before you. **13**You must be blameless before the LORD your God.

The Prophet

14The nations you will dispossess listen to those who practice sorcery or divination. But as for you, the LORD your God has not permitted you to do so. **15**The LORD your God will raise up for you a prophet like me from among your own brothers. You must listen to him. **16**For this is what you asked of the LORD your God at Horeb on the day of the assembly when you said, "Let us not hear the voice of the LORD our God nor see this great fire anymore, or we will die."

17The LORD said to me: "What they say is good. **18**I will raise up for them a prophet like you from among their brothers; I will put my words in his mouth, and he will tell them everything I command him. **19**If anyone does not listen to my words that the prophet speaks in my name, I myself will call him to account. **20**But a prophet who presumes to speak in my name anything I have not commanded him to say, or a prophet who speaks in the name of other gods, must be put to death."

21You may say to yourselves, "How can we know when a message has not been spoken by the LORD?" **22**If what a prophet proclaims in the name of the LORD does not take place or come true, that is a message the LORD has not spoken. That prophet has spoken presumptuously. Do not be afraid of him.

Cities of Refuge

19 When the LORD your God has destroyed the nations whose land he is giving you, and when you have driven them out and settled in their towns and houses, **2**then set aside for yourselves three cities centrally located in the land the LORD your

---

a 10 Or *who makes his son or daughter pass through*

God is giving you to possess. ³Build roads to them and divide into three parts the land the LORD your God is giving you as an inheritance, so that anyone who kills a man may flee there.

⁴This is the rule concerning the man who kills another and flees there to save his life—one who kills his neighbor unintentionally, without malice aforethought. ⁵For instance, a man may go into the forest with his neighbor to cut wood, and as he swings his ax to fell a tree, the head may fly off and hit his neighbor and kill him. That man may flee to one of these cities and save his life. ⁶Otherwise, the avenger of blood might pursue him in a rage, overtake him if the distance is too great, and kill him even though he is not deserving of death, since he did it to his neighbor without malice aforethought. ⁷This is why I command you to set aside for yourselves three cities.

⁸If the LORD your God enlarges your territory, as he promised on oath to your forefathers, and gives you the whole land he promised them, ⁹because you carefully follow all these laws I command you today—to love the LORD your God and to walk always in his ways—then you are to set aside three more cities. ¹⁰Do this so that innocent blood will not be shed in your land, which the LORD your God is giving you as your inheritance, and so that you will not be guilty of bloodshed.

¹¹But if a man hates his neighbor and lies in wait for him, assaults and kills him, and then flees to one of these cities, ¹²the elders of his town shall send for him, bring him back from the city, and hand him over to the avenger of blood to die. ¹³Show him no pity. You must purge from Israel the guilt of shedding innocent blood, so that it may go well with you.

¹⁴Do not move your neighbor's boundary stone set up by your predecessors in the inheritance you receive in the land the LORD your God is giving you to possess.

Witnesses

¹⁵One witness is not enough to convict a man accused of any crime or offense he may have committed. A matter must be established by the testimony of two or three witnesses.

¹⁶If a malicious witness takes the stand to accuse a man of a crime, ¹⁷the two men involved in the dispute must stand in the presence of the LORD before the priests and the judges who are in office at the time. ¹⁸The judges must make a thorough investigation, and if the witness proves to be a liar, giving false testimony against his brother, ¹⁹then do to him as he intended to do to his brother. You must purge the evil from among you. ²⁰The rest of the people will hear of this and be afraid, and never again will such an evil thing be done among you. ²¹Show no pity: life for life, eye for eye, tooth for tooth, hand for hand, foot for foot.

Going to War

20 When you go to war against your enemies and see horses and chariots and an army greater than yours, do not be afraid of them, because the LORD your God, who brought you up out of Egypt, will be with you. ²When you are about to go into battle, the priest shall come forward and address the army. ³He shall say: "Hear, O Israel, today you are going into battle against your enemies. Do not be fainthearted or afraid; do not be terrified or give way to panic before them. ⁴For the LORD your God is the one who goes with you to fight for you against your enemies to give you victory."

⁵The officers shall say to the army: "Has anyone built a new house and not dedicated it? Let him go home, or he may die in battle and someone else may dedicate it. ⁶Has anyone planted a vineyard and not begun to enjoy it? Let him go home, or he may die in battle and someone else enjoy it. ⁷Has anyone become pledged to a woman and not married her? Let him go home, or he may die in battle and someone else marry her." ⁸Then the officers shall add, "Is any man afraid or fainthearted? Let him go home so that his brothers will not become disheartened too." ⁹When the officers have finished speaking to the army, they shall appoint commanders over it.

¹⁰When you march up to attack a city, make its people an offer of peace. ¹¹If they accept and open their gates, all the people in it shall be subject to forced labor and shall work for you. ¹²If they refuse to make peace and they engage you in battle, lay siege to that city. ¹³When the LORD your God delivers it into your hand, put to the sword all the men in it. ¹⁴As for the women, the children, the livestock and everything else in the city, you may take these as plunder for yourselves. And you may use the plunder the LORD your God gives you from your enemies. ¹⁵This is how you are to treat all the cities that are at a distance from you and do not belong to the nations nearby.

¹⁶However, in the cities of the nations the LORD your God is giving you as an inheri-

tance, do not leave alive anything that breathes. [17]Completely destroy[a] them — the Hittites, Amorites, Canaanites, Perizzites, Hivites and Jebusites — as the LORD your God has commanded you. [18]Otherwise, they will teach you to follow all the detestable things they do in worshiping their gods, and you will sin against the LORD your God.

[19]When you lay siege to a city for a long time, fighting against it to capture it, do not destroy its trees by putting an ax to them, because you can eat their fruit. Do not cut them down. Are the trees of the field people, that you should besiege them?[b] [20]However, you may cut down trees that you know are not fruit trees and use them to build siege works until the city at war with you falls.

Atonement for an Unsolved Murder

21 If a man is found slain, lying in a field in the land the LORD your God is giving you to possess, and it is not known who killed him, [2]your elders and judges shall go out and measure the distance from the body to the neighboring towns. [3]Then the elders of the town nearest the body shall take a heifer that has never been worked and has never worn a yoke [4]and lead her down to a valley that has not been plowed or planted and where there is a flowing stream. There in the valley they are to break the heifer's neck. [5]The priests, the sons of Levi, shall step forward, for the LORD your God has chosen them to minister and to pronounce blessings in the name of the LORD and to decide all cases of dispute and assault. [6]Then all the elders of the town nearest the body shall wash their hands over the heifer whose neck was broken in the valley, [7]and they shall declare: "Our hands did not shed this blood, nor did our eyes see it done. [8]Accept this atonement for your people Israel, whom you have redeemed, O LORD, and do not hold your people guilty of the blood of an innocent man." And the bloodshed will be atoned for. [9]So you will purge from yourselves the guilt of shedding innocent blood, since you have done what is right in the eyes of the LORD.

Marrying a Captive Woman

[10]When you go to war against your enemies and the LORD your God delivers them into your hands and you take captives, [11]if you notice among the captives a beautiful woman and are attracted to her, you may take her as your wife. [12]Bring her into your home and have her shave her head, trim her nails [13]and put aside the clothes she was wearing when captured. After she has lived in your house and mourned her father and mother for a full month, then you may go to her and be her husband and she shall be your wife. [14]If you are not pleased with her, let her go wherever she wishes. You must not sell her or treat her as a slave, since you have dishonored her.

The Right of the Firstborn

[15]If a man has two wives, and he loves one but not the other, and both bear him sons but the firstborn is the son of the wife he does not love, [16]when he wills his property to his sons, he must not give the rights of the firstborn to the son of the wife he loves in preference to his actual firstborn, the son of the wife he does not love. [17]He must acknowledge the son of his unloved wife as the firstborn by giving him a double share of all he has. That son is the first sign of his father's strength. The right of the firstborn belongs to him.

A Rebellious Son

[18]If a man has a stubborn and rebellious son who does not obey his father and mother and will not listen to them when they discipline him, [19]his father and mother shall take hold of him and bring him to the elders at the gate of his town. [20]They shall say to the elders, "This son of ours is stubborn and rebellious. He will not obey us. He is a profligate and a drunkard." [21]Then all the men of his town shall stone him to death. You must purge the evil from among you. All Israel will hear of it and be afraid.

Various Laws

[22]If a man guilty of a capital offense is put to death and his body is hung on a tree, [23]you must not leave his body on the tree overnight. Be sure to bury him that same day, because anyone who is hung on a tree is under God's curse. You must not desecrate the land the LORD your God is giving you as an inheritance.

22 If you see your brother's ox or sheep straying, do not ignore it but be sure to take it back to him. [2]If the brother does not live near you or if you do not know who he is, take it home with you and keep it until

---

a 17 The Hebrew term refers to the irrevocable giving over of things or persons to the LORD, often by totally destroying them.   *b 19* Or *down to use in the siege, for the fruit trees are for the benefit of man.*

he comes looking for it. Then give it back to him. ³Do the same if you find your brother's donkey or his cloak or anything he loses. Do not ignore it.

⁴If you see your brother's donkey or his ox fallen on the road, do not ignore it. Help him get it to its feet.

⁵A woman must not wear men's clothing, nor a man wear women's clothing, for the LORD your God detests anyone who does this.

⁶If you come across a bird's nest beside the road, either in a tree or on the ground, and the mother is sitting on the young or on the eggs, do not take the mother with the young. ⁷You may take the young, but be sure to let the mother go, so that it may go well with you and you may have a long life.

⁸When you build a new house, make a parapet around your roof so that you may not bring the guilt of bloodshed on your house if someone falls from the roof.

⁹Do not plant two kinds of seed in your vineyard; if you do, not only the crops you plant but also the fruit of the vineyard will be defiled.ᵃ

¹⁰Do not plow with an ox and a donkey yoked together.

¹¹Do not wear clothes of wool and linen woven together.

¹²Make tassels on the four corners of the cloak you wear.

Marriage Violations

¹³If a man takes a wife and, after lying with her, dislikes her ¹⁴and slanders her and gives her a bad name, saying, "I married this woman, but when I approached her, I did not find proof of her virginity," ¹⁵then the girl's father and mother shall bring proof that she was a virgin to the town elders at the gate. ¹⁶The girl's father will say to the elders, "I gave my daughter in marriage to this man, but he dislikes her. ¹⁷Now he has slandered her and said, 'I did not find your daughter to be a virgin.' But here is the proof of my daughter's virginity." Then her parents shall display the cloth before the elders of the town, ¹⁸and the elders shall take the man and punish him. ¹⁹They shall fine him a hundred shekels of silverᵇ and give them to the girl's father, because this man has given an Israelite virgin a bad name. She shall continue to be his wife; he must not divorce her as long as he lives.

²⁰If, however, the charge is true and no proof of the girl's virginity can be found, ²¹she shall be brought to the door of her father's house and there the men of her town shall stone her to death. She has done a disgraceful thing in Israel by being promiscuous while still in her father's house. You must purge the evil from among you.

²²If a man is found sleeping with another man's wife, both the man who slept with her and the woman must die. You must purge the evil from Israel.

²³If a man happens to meet in a town a virgin pledged to be married and he sleeps with her, ²⁴you shall take both of them to the gate of that town and stone them to death—the girl because she was in a town and did not scream for help, and the man because he violated another man's wife. You must purge the evil from among you.

²⁵But if out in the country a man happens to meet a girl pledged to be married and rapes her, only the man who has done this shall die. ²⁶Do nothing to the girl; she has committed no sin deserving death. This case is like that of someone who attacks and murders his neighbor, ²⁷for the man found the girl out in the country, and though the betrothed girl screamed, there was no one to rescue her.

²⁸If a man happens to meet a virgin who is not pledged to be married and rapes her and they are discovered, ²⁹he shall pay the girl's father fifty shekels of silver.ᶜ He must marry the girl, for he has violated her. He can never divorce her as long as he lives.

³⁰A man is not to marry his father's wife; he must not dishonor his father's bed.

Exclusion From the Assembly

23 No one who has been emasculated by crushing or cutting may enter the assembly of the LORD.

²No one born of a forbidden marriageᵈ nor any of his descendants may enter the assembly of the LORD, even down to the tenth generation.

³No Ammonite or Moabite or any of his descendants may enter the assembly of the LORD, even down to the tenth generation. ⁴For they did not come to meet you with bread and water on your way when you came out of Egypt, and they hired Balaam son of Beor from Pethor in Aram Naharaimᵉ to pronounce a curse on you. ⁵However, the LORD your God would not listen to Balaam but turned the curse into a blessing for

---

ᵃ9 Or be forfeited to the sanctuary   ᵇ19 That is, about 2 1/2 pounds (about 1 kilogram)   ᶜ29 That is, about 1 1/4 pounds (about 0.6 kilogram)   ᵈ2 Or one of illegitimate birth   ᵉ4 That is, Northwest Mesopotamia you, because the L ORD your God loves you. ⁶Do not seek a treaty of friendship with them as long as you live.

⁷Do not abhor an Edomite, for he is your brother. Do not abhor an Egyptian, because you lived as an alien in his country. ⁸The third generation of children born to them may enter the assembly of the L ORD.

Uncleanness in the Camp

⁹When you are encamped against your enemies, keep away from everything impure. ¹⁰If one of your men is unclean because of a nocturnal emission, he is to go outside the camp and stay there. ¹¹But as evening approaches he is to wash himself, and at sunset he may return to the camp. ¹²Designate a place outside the camp where you can go to relieve yourself. ¹³As part of your equipment have something to dig with, and when you relieve yourself, dig a hole and cover up your excrement. ¹⁴For the L ORD your God moves about in your camp to protect you and to deliver your enemies to you. Your camp must be holy, so that he will not see among you anything indecent and turn away from you.

Miscellaneous Laws

¹⁵If a slave has taken refuge with you, do not hand him over to his master. ¹⁶Let him live among you wherever he likes and in whatever town he chooses. Do not oppress him.

¹⁷No Israelite man or woman is to become a shrine prostitute. ¹⁸You must not bring the earnings of a female prostitute or of a male prostitute ᵃ into the house of the L ORD your God to pay any vow, because the L ORD your God detests them both.

¹⁹Do not charge your brother interest, whether on money or food or anything else that may earn interest. ²⁰You may charge a foreigner interest, but not a brother Israelite, so that the L ORD your God may bless you in everything you put your hand to in the land you are entering to possess.

²¹If you make a vow to the L ORD your God, do not be slow to pay it, for the L ORD your God will certainly demand it of you and you will be guilty of sin. ²²But if you refrain from making a vow, you will not be guilty. ²³Whatever your lips utter you must be sure to do, because you made your vow freely to the L ORD your God with your own mouth.

²⁴If you enter your neighbor's vineyard,

you may eat all the grapes you want, but do not put any in your basket. ²⁵If you enter your neighbor's grainfield, you may pick kernels with your hands, but you must not put a sickle to his standing grain.

24 If a man marries a woman who becomes displeasing to him because he finds something indecent about her, and he writes her a certificate of divorce, gives it to her and sends her from his house, ²and if after she leaves his house she becomes the wife of another man, ³and her second husband dislikes her and writes her a certificate of divorce, gives it to her and sends her from his house, or if he dies, ⁴then her first husband, who divorced her, is not allowed to marry her again after she has been defiled. That would be detestable in the eyes of the L ORD. Do not bring sin upon the land the L ORD your God is giving you as an inheritance.

⁵If a man has recently married, he must not be sent to war or have any other duty laid on him. For one year he is to be free to stay at home and bring happiness to the wife he has married.

⁶Do not take a pair of millstones—not even the upper one—as security for a debt, because that would be taking a man's livelihood as security.

⁷If a man is caught kidnapping one of his brother Israelites and treats him as a slave or sells him, the kidnapper must die. You must purge the evil from among you.

⁸In cases of leprous ᵇ diseases be very careful to do exactly as the priests, who are Levites, instruct you. You must follow carefully what I have commanded them. ⁹Remember what the L ORD your God did to Miriam along the way after you came out of Egypt.

¹⁰When you make a loan of any kind to your neighbor, do not go into his house to get what he is offering as a pledge. ¹¹Stay outside and let the man to whom you are making the loan bring the pledge out to you. ¹²If the man is poor, do not go to sleep with his pledge in your possession. ¹³Return his cloak to him by sunset so that he may sleep in it. Then he will thank you, and it will be regarded as a righteous act in the sight of the L ORD your God.

¹⁴Do not take advantage of a hired man who is poor and needy, whether he is a brother Israelite or an alien living in one of your towns. ¹⁵Pay him his wages each day

---

ᵃ18 Hebrew *of a dog*   ᵇ8 The Hebrew word was used for various diseases affecting the skin—not necessarily leprosy.

before sunset, because he is poor and is counting on it. Otherwise he may cry to the Lord against you, and you will be guilty of sin.

¹⁶Fathers shall not be put to death for their children, nor children put to death for their fathers; each is to die for his own sin.

¹⁷Do not deprive the alien or the fatherless of justice, or take the cloak of the widow as a pledge. ¹⁸Remember that you were slaves in Egypt and the Lord your God redeemed you from there. That is why I command you to do this.

¹⁹When you are harvesting in your field and you overlook a sheaf, do not go back to get it. Leave it for the alien, the fatherless and the widow, so that the Lord your God may bless you in all the work of your hands. ²⁰When you beat the olives from your trees, do not go over the branches a second time. Leave what remains for the alien, the fatherless and the widow. ²¹When you harvest the grapes in your vineyard, do not go over the vines again. Leave what remains for the alien, the fatherless and the widow. ²²Remember that you were slaves in Egypt. That is why I command you to do this.

25 When men have a dispute, they are to take it to court and the judges will decide the case, acquitting the innocent and condemning the guilty. ²If the guilty man deserves to be beaten, the judge shall make him lie down and have him flogged in his presence with the number of lashes his crime deserves, ³but he must not give him more than forty lashes. If he is flogged more than that, your brother will be degraded in your eyes.

⁴Do not muzzle an ox while it is treading out the grain.

⁵If brothers are living together and one of them dies without a son, his widow must not marry outside the family. Her husband's brother shall take her and marry her and fulfill the duty of a brother-in-law to her. ⁶The first son she bears shall carry on the name of the dead brother so that his name will not be blotted out from Israel.

⁷However, if a man does not want to marry his brother's wife, she shall go to the elders at the town gate and say, "My husband's brother refuses to carry on his brother's name in Israel. He will not fulfill the duty of a brother-in-law to me." ⁸Then the elders of his town shall summon him and talk to him. If he persists in saying, "I do not want to marry her," ⁹his brother's widow shall go up to him in the presence of the elders, take off one of his sandals, spit in his face and say, "This is what is done to the man who will not build up his brother's family line." ¹⁰That man's line shall be known in Israel as The Family of the Unsandaled.

¹¹If two men are fighting and the wife of one of them comes to rescue her husband from his assailant, and she reaches out and seizes him by his private parts, ¹²you shall cut off her hand. Show her no pity.

¹³Do not have two differing weights in your bag—one heavy, one light. ¹⁴Do not have two differing measures in your house—one large, one small. ¹⁵You must have accurate and honest weights and measures, so that you may live long in the land the Lord your God is giving you. ¹⁶For the Lord your God detests anyone who does these things, anyone who deals dishonestly.

¹⁷Remember what the Amalekites did to you along the way when you came out of Egypt. ¹⁸When you were weary and worn out, they met you on your journey and cut off all who were lagging behind; they had no fear of God. ¹⁹When the Lord your God gives you rest from all the enemies around you in the land he is giving you to possess as an inheritance, you shall blot out the memory of Amalek from under heaven. Do not forget!

Firstfruits and Tithes

26 When you have entered the land the Lord your God is giving you as an inheritance and have taken possession of it and settled in it, ²take some of the firstfruits of all that you produce from the soil of the land the Lord your God is giving you and put them in a basket. Then go to the place the Lord your God will choose as a dwelling for his Name ³and say to the priest in office at the time, "I declare today to the Lord your God that I have come to the land the Lord swore to our forefathers to give us." ⁴The priest shall take the basket from your hands and set it down in front of the altar of the Lord your God. ⁵Then you shall declare before the Lord your God: "My father was a wandering Aramean, and he went down into Egypt with a few people and lived there and became a great nation, powerful and numerous. ⁶But the Egyptians mistreated us and made us suffer, putting us to hard labor. ⁷Then we cried out to the Lord, the God of our fathers, and the Lord heard our voice and saw our misery, toil and oppression. ⁸So the Lord brought us out of Egypt with a mighty hand and an outstretched arm, with great terror and with miraculous signs and wonders. ⁹He brought us to this place and gave us this land, a land flowing with milk and honey; [10]and now I bring the firstfruits of the soil that you, O LORD, have given me." Place the basket before the LORD your God and bow down before him. [11]And you and the Levites and the aliens among you shall rejoice in all the good things the LORD your God has given to you and your household.

[12]When you have finished setting aside a tenth of all your produce in the third year, the year of the tithe, you shall give it to the Levite, the alien, the fatherless and the widow, so that they may eat in your towns and be satisfied. [13]Then say to the LORD your God: "I have removed from my house the sacred portion and have given it to the Levite, the alien, the fatherless and the widow, according to all you commanded. I have not turned aside from your commands nor have I forgotten any of them. [14]I have not eaten any of the sacred portion while I was in mourning, nor have I removed any of it while I was unclean, nor have I offered any of it to the dead. I have obeyed the LORD my God; I have done everything you commanded me. [15]Look down from heaven, your holy dwelling place, and bless your people Israel and the land you have given us as you promised on oath to our forefathers, a land flowing with milk and honey."

Follow the LORD's Commands

[16]The LORD your God commands you this day to follow these decrees and laws; carefully observe them with all your heart and with all your soul. [17]You have declared this day that the LORD is your God and that you will walk in his ways, that you will keep his decrees, commands and laws, and that you will obey him. [18]And the LORD has declared this day that you are his people, his treasured possession as he promised, and that you are to keep all his commands. [19]He has declared that he will set you in praise, fame and honor high above all the nations he has made and that you will be a people holy to the LORD your God, as he promised.

The Altar on Mount Ebal

27 Moses and the elders of Israel commanded the people: "Keep all these commands that I give you today. [2]When you have crossed the Jordan into the land the LORD your God is giving you, set up some large stones and coat them with plaster. [3]Write on them all the words of this law when you have crossed over to enter the land the LORD your God is giving you, a land flowing with milk and honey, just as the LORD, the God of your fathers, promised you. [4]And when you have crossed the Jordan, set up these stones on Mount Ebal, as I command you today, and coat them with plaster. [5]Build there an altar to the LORD your God, an altar of stones. Do not use any iron tool upon them. [6]Build the altar of the LORD your God with fieldstones and offer burnt offerings on it to the LORD your God. [7]Sacrifice fellowship offerings[a] there, eating them and rejoicing in the presence of the LORD your God. [8]And you shall write very clearly all the words of this law on these stones you have set up."

Curses From Mount Ebal

[9]Then Moses and the priests, who are Levites, said to all Israel, "Be silent, O Israel and listen! You have now become the people of the LORD your God. [10]Obey the LORD your God and follow his commands and decrees that I give you today."

[11]On the same day Moses commanded the people:

[12]When you have crossed the Jordan, these tribes shall stand on Mount Gerizim to bless the people: Simeon, Levi, Judah, Issachar, Joseph and Benjamin. [13]And these tribes shall stand on Mount Ebal to pronounce curses: Reuben, Gad, Asher, Zebulun, Dan and Naphtali.

[14]The Levites shall recite to all the people of Israel in a loud voice:

[15]"Cursed is the man who carves an image or casts an idol — a thing detestable to the LORD, the work of the craftsman's hands — and sets it up in secret."
Then all the people shall say, "Amen!"

[16]"Cursed is the man who dishonors his father or his mother."
Then all the people shall say, "Amen!"

[17]"Cursed is the man who moves his neighbor's boundary stone."
Then all the people shall say, "Amen!"

[18]"Cursed is the man who leads the blind astray on the road."
Then all the people shall say, "Amen!"

[19]"Cursed is the man who withholds justice from the alien, the fatherless or the widow."

[a]7 Traditionally *peace offerings*

Then all the people shall say, "Amen!"

20"Cursed is the man who sleeps with his father's wife, for he dishonors his father's bed."

Then all the people shall say, "Amen!"

21"Cursed is the man who has sexual relations with any animal."

Then all the people shall say, "Amen!"

22"Cursed is the man who sleeps with his sister, the daughter of his father or the daughter of his mother."

Then all the people shall say, "Amen!"

23"Cursed is the man who sleeps with his mother-in-law."

Then all the people shall say, "Amen!"

24"Cursed is the man who kills his neighbor secretly."

Then all the people shall say, "Amen!"

25"Cursed is the man who accepts a bribe to kill an innocent person."

Then all the people shall say, "Amen!"

26"Cursed is the man who does not uphold the words of this law by carrying them out."

Then all the people shall say, "Amen!"

Blessings for Obedience

28 If you fully obey the LORD your God and carefully follow all his commands I give you today, the LORD your God will set you high above all the nations on earth. 2All these blessings will come upon you and accompany you if you obey the LORD your God:

3You will be blessed in the city and blessed in the country.

4The fruit of your womb will be blessed, and the crops of your land and the young of your livestock—the calves of your herds and the lambs of your flocks.

5Your basket and your kneading trough will be blessed.

6You will be blessed when you come in and blessed when you go out.

7The LORD will grant that the enemies who rise up against you will be defeated before

you. They will come at you from one direction but flee from you in seven.

8The LORD will send a blessing on your barns and on everything you put your hand to. The LORD your God will bless you in the land he is giving you.

9The LORD will establish you as his holy people, as he promised you on oath, if you keep the commands of the LORD your God and walk in his ways. 10Then all the peoples on earth will see that you are called by the name of the LORD, and they will fear you. 11The LORD will grant you abundant prosperity—in the fruit of your womb, the young of your livestock and the crops of your ground—in the land he swore to your forefathers to give you.

12The LORD will open the heavens, the storehouse of his bounty, to send rain on your land in season and to bless all the work of your hands. You will lend to many nations but will borrow from none. 13The LORD will make you the head, not the tail. If you pay attention to the commands of the LORD your God that I give you this day and carefully follow them, you will always be at the top, never at the bottom. 14Do not turn aside from any of the commands I give you today, to the right or to the left, following other gods and serving them.

Curses for Disobedience

15However, if you do not obey the LORD your God and do not carefully follow all his commands and decrees I am giving you today, all these curses will come upon you and overtake you:

16You will be cursed in the city and cursed in the country.

17Your basket and your kneading trough will be cursed.

18The fruit of your womb will be cursed, and the crops of your land, and the calves of your herds and the lambs of your flocks.

19You will be cursed when you come in and cursed when you go out.

20The LORD will send on you curses, confusion and rebuke in everything you put your hand to, until you are destroyed and come to sudden ruin because of the evil you have done in forsaking him.a 21The LORD will plague you with diseases until he has destroyed you from the land you are entering to possess. 22The LORD will strike you with wasting disease, with fever and inflamma-

a20 Hebrew me

tion, with scorching heat and drought, with blight and mildew, which will plague you until you perish. **23**The sky over your head will be bronze, the ground beneath you iron. **24**The LORD will turn the rain of your country into dust and powder; it will come down from the skies until you are destroyed.

25The LORD will cause you to be defeated before your enemies. You will come at them from one direction but flee from them in seven, and you will become a thing of horror to all the kingdoms on earth. **26**Your carcasses will be food for all the birds of the air and the beasts of the earth, and there will be no one to frighten them away. **27**The LORD will afflict you with the boils of Egypt and with tumors, festering sores and the itch, from which you cannot be cured. **28**The LORD will afflict you with madness, blindness and confusion of mind. **29**At midday you will grope about like a blind man in the dark. You will be unsuccessful in everything you do; day after day you will be oppressed and robbed, with no one to rescue you.

30You will be pledged to be married to a woman, but another will take her and ravish her. You will build a house, but you will not live in it. You will plant a vineyard, but you will not even begin to enjoy its fruit. **31**Your ox will be slaughtered before your eyes, but you will eat none of it. Your donkey will be forcibly taken from you and will not be returned. Your sheep will be given to your enemies, and no one will rescue them. **32**Your sons and daughters will be given to another nation, and you will wear out your eyes watching for them day after day, powerless to lift a hand. **33**A people that you do not know will eat what your land and labor produce, and you will have nothing but cruel oppression all your days. **34**The sights you see will drive you mad. **35**The LORD will afflict your knees and legs with painful boils that cannot be cured, spreading from the soles of your feet to the top of your head.

36The LORD will drive you and the king you set over you to a nation unknown to you or your fathers. There you will worship other gods, gods of wood and stone. **37**You will become a thing of horror and an object of scorn and ridicule to all the nations where the LORD will drive you.

38You will sow much seed in the field but you will harvest little, because locusts will devour it. **39**You will plant vineyards and cultivate them but you will not drink the wine or gather the grapes, because worms will eat them. **40**You will have olive trees throughout your country but you will not use the oil, because the olives will drop off. **41**You will have sons and daughters but you will not keep them, because they will go into captivity. **42**Swarms of locusts will take over all your trees and the crops of your land.

43The alien who lives among you will rise above you higher and higher, but you will sink lower and lower. **44**He will lend to you, but you will not lend to him. He will be the head, but you will be the tail.

45All these curses will come upon you. They will pursue you and overtake you until you are destroyed, because you did not obey the LORD your God and observe the commands and decrees he gave you. **46**They will be a sign and a wonder to you and your descendants forever. **47**Because you did not serve the LORD your God joyfully and gladly in the time of prosperity, **48**therefore in hunger and thirst, in nakedness and dire poverty, you will serve the enemies the LORD sends against you. He will put an iron yoke on your neck until he has destroyed you.

49The LORD will bring a nation against you from far away, from the ends of the earth, like an eagle swooping down, a nation whose language you will not understand, **50**a fierce-looking nation without respect for the old or pity for the young. **51**They will devour the young of your livestock and the crops of your land until you are destroyed. They will leave you no grain, new wine or oil, nor any calves of your herds or lambs of your flocks until you are ruined. **52**They will lay siege to all the cities throughout your land until the high fortified walls in which you trust fall down. They will besiege all the cities throughout the land the LORD your God is giving you.

53Because of the suffering that your enemy will inflict on you during the siege, you will eat the fruit of the womb, the flesh of the sons and daughters the LORD your God has given you. **54**Even the most gentle and sensitive man among you will have no compassion on his own brother or the wife he loves or his surviving children, **55**and he will not give to one of them any of the flesh of his children that he is eating. It will be all he has left because of the suffering your enemy will inflict on you during the siege of all your cities. **56**The most gentle and sensitive woman among you—so sensitive and gentle that she would not venture to touch the ground with the sole of her foot—will begrudge the husband she loves and her own son or daughter **57**the afterbirth from her womb and the children she bears. For she intends to eat them secretly during the siege and in the distress that your enemy will inflict on you in your cities.

58If you do not carefully follow all the words of this law, which are written in this book, and do not revere this glorious and awesome name — the Lord your God — **59**the Lord will send fearful plagues on you and your descendants, harsh and prolonged disasters, and severe and lingering illnesses. **60**He will bring upon you all the diseases of Egypt that you dreaded, and they will cling to you. **61**The Lord will also bring on you every kind of sickness and disaster not recorded in this Book of the Law, until you are destroyed. **62**You who were as numerous as the stars in the sky will be left but few in number, because you did not obey the Lord your God. **63**Just as it pleased the Lord to make you prosper and increase in number, so it will please him to ruin and destroy you. You will be uprooted from the land you are entering to possess.

64Then the Lord will scatter you among all nations, from one end of the earth to the other. There you will worship other gods — gods of wood and stone, which neither you nor your fathers have known. **65**Among those nations you will find no repose, no resting place for the sole of your foot. There the Lord will give you an anxious mind, eyes weary with longing, and a despairing heart. **66**You will live in constant suspense, filled with dread both night and day, never sure of your life. **67**In the morning you will say, "If only it were evening!" and in the evening, "If only it were morning!" — because of the terror that will fill your hearts and the sights that your eyes will see. **68**The Lord will send you back in ships to Egypt on a journey I said you should never make again. There you will offer yourselves for sale to your enemies as male and female slaves, but no one will buy you.

Renewal of the Covenant

29 These are the terms of the covenant the Lord commanded Moses to make with the Israelites in Moab, in addition to the covenant he had made with them at Horeb.

2Moses summoned all the Israelites and said to them:

Your eyes have seen all that the Lord did in Egypt to Pharaoh, to all his officials and to all his land. **3**With your own eyes you saw those great trials, those miraculous signs and great wonders. **4**But to this day the Lord has not given you a mind that understands or eyes that see or ears that hear. **5**During the forty years that I led you through the desert, your clothes did not wear out, nor did the sandals on your feet. **6**You ate no bread and drank no wine or other fermented drink. I did this so that you might know that I am the Lord your God.

7When you reached this place, Sihon king of Heshbon and Og king of Bashan came out to fight against us, but we defeated them. **8**We took their land and gave it as an inheritance to the Reubenites, the Gadites and the half-tribe of Manasseh.

9Carefully follow the terms of this covenant, so that you may prosper in everything you do. **10**All of you are standing today in the presence of the Lord your God — your leaders and chief men, your elders and officials, and all the other men of Israel, **11**together with your children and your wives, and the aliens living in your camps who chop your wood and carry your water. **12**You are standing here in order to enter into a covenant with the Lord your God, a covenant the Lord is making with you this day and sealing with an oath, **13**to confirm you this day as his people, that he may be your God as he promised you and as he swore to your fathers, Abraham, Isaac and Jacob. **14**I am making this covenant, with its oath, not only with you **15**who are standing here with us today in the presence of the Lord our God but also with those who are not here today.

16You yourselves know how we lived in Egypt and how we passed through the countries on the way here. **17**You saw among them their detestable images and idols of wood and stone, of silver and gold. **18**Make sure there is no man or woman, clan or tribe among you today whose heart turns away from the Lord our God to go and worship the gods of those nations; make sure there is no root among you that produces such bitter poison.

19When such a person hears the words of this oath, he invokes a blessing on himself and therefore thinks, "I will be safe, even though I persist in going my own way." This will bring disaster on the watered land as well as the dry. *a* **20**The Lord will never be willing to forgive him; his wrath and zeal will burn against that man. All the curses written in this book will fall upon him, and the Lord will blot out his name from under heaven.

a 19 Or way, in order to add drunkenness to thirst."

²¹The Lord will single him out from all the tribes of Israel for disaster, according to all the curses of the covenant written in this Book of the Law.

²²Your children who follow you in later generations and foreigners who come from distant lands will see the calamities that have fallen on the land and the diseases with which the Lord has afflicted it. ²³The whole land will be a burning waste of salt and sulfur — nothing planted, nothing sprouting, no vegetation growing on it. It will be like the destruction of Sodom and Gomorrah, Admah and Zeboiim, which the Lord overthrew in fierce anger. ²⁴All the nations will ask: "Why has the Lord done this to this land? Why this fierce, burning anger?"

²⁵And the answer will be: "It is because this people abandoned the covenant of the Lord, the God of their fathers, the covenant he made with them when he brought them out of Egypt. ²⁶They went off and worshiped other gods and bowed down to them, gods they did not know, gods he had not given them. ²⁷Therefore the Lord's anger burned against this land, so that he brought on it all the curses written in this book. ²⁸In furious anger and in great wrath the Lord uprooted them from their land and thrust them into another land, as it is now."

²⁹The secret things belong to the Lord our God, but the things revealed belong to us and to our children forever, that we may follow all the words of this law.

Prosperity After Turning to the Lord

30 When all these blessings and curses I have set before you come upon you and you take them to heart wherever the Lord your God disperses you among the nations, ²and when you and your children return to the Lord your God and obey him with all your heart and with all your soul according to everything I command you today, ³then the Lord your God will restore your fortunes[a] and have compassion on you and gather you again from all the nations where he scattered you. ⁴Even if you have been banished to the most distant land under the heavens, from there the Lord your God will gather you and bring you back. ⁵He will bring you to the land that belonged to your fathers, and you will take possession of it. He will make you more prosperous and numerous than your fathers. ⁶The Lord your

God will circumcise your hearts and the hearts of your descendants, so that you may love him with all your heart and with all your soul, and live. ⁷The Lord your God will put all these curses on your enemies who hate and persecute you. ⁸You will again obey the Lord and follow all his commands I am giving you today. ⁹Then the Lord your God will make you most prosperous in all the work of your hands and in the fruit of your womb, the young of your livestock and the crops of your land. The Lord will again delight in you and make you prosperous, just as he delighted in your fathers, ¹⁰if you obey the Lord your God and keep his commands and decrees that are written in this Book of the Law and turn to the Lord your God with all your heart and with all your soul.

The Offer of Life or Death

¹¹Now what I am commanding you today is not too difficult for you or beyond your reach. ¹²It is not up in heaven, so that you have to ask, "Who will ascend into heaven to get it and proclaim it to us so we may obey it?" ¹³Nor is it beyond the sea, so that you have to ask, "Who will cross the sea to get it and proclaim it to us so we may obey it?" ¹⁴No, the word is very near you; it is in your mouth and in your heart so you may obey it.

¹⁵See, I set before you today life and prosperity, death and destruction. ¹⁶For I command you today to love the Lord your God, to walk in his ways, and to keep his commands, decrees and laws; then you will live and increase, and the Lord your God will bless you in the land you are entering to possess.

¹⁷But if your heart turns away and you are not obedient, and if you are drawn away to bow down to other gods and worship them, ¹⁸I declare to you this day that you will certainly be destroyed. You will not live long in the land you are crossing the Jordan to enter and possess.

¹⁹This day I call heaven and earth as witnesses against you that I have set before you life and death, blessings and curses. Now choose life, so that you and your children may live ²⁰and that you may love the Lord your God, listen to his voice, and hold fast to him. For the Lord is your life, and he will give you many years in the land he swore to give to your fathers, Abraham, Isaac and Jacob.

---

a3 Or *will bring you back from captivity*

Joshua to Succeed Moses

31 Then Moses went out and spoke these words to all Israel: ²"I am now a hundred and twenty years old and I am no longer able to lead you. The LORD has said to me, 'You shall not cross the Jordan.' ³The LORD your God himself will cross over ahead of you. He will destroy these nations before you, and you will take possession of their land. Joshua also will cross over ahead of you, as the LORD said. ⁴And the LORD will do to them what he did to Sihon and Og, the kings of the Amorites, whom he destroyed along with their land. ⁵The LORD will deliver them to you, and you must do to them all that I have commanded you. ⁶Be strong and courageous. Do not be afraid or terrified because of them, for the LORD your God goes with you; he will never leave you nor forsake you."

⁷Then Moses summoned Joshua and said to him in the presence of all Israel, "Be strong and courageous, for you must go with this people into the land that the LORD swore to their forefathers to give them, and you must divide it among them as their inheritance. ⁸The LORD himself goes before you and will be with you; he will never leave you nor forsake you. Do not be afraid; do not be discouraged."

The Reading of the Law

⁹So Moses wrote down this law and gave it to the priests, the sons of Levi, who carried the ark of the covenant of the LORD, and to all the elders of Israel. ¹⁰Then Moses commanded them: "At the end of every seven years, in the year for canceling debts, during the Feast of Tabernacles, ¹¹when all Israel comes to appear before the LORD your God at the place he will choose, you shall read this law before them in their hearing. ¹²Assemble the people — men, women and children, and the aliens living in your towns — so they can listen and learn to fear the LORD your God and follow carefully all the words of this law. ¹³Their children, who do not know this law, must hear it and learn to fear the LORD your God as long as you live in the land you are crossing the Jordan to possess."

Israel's Rebellion Predicted

¹⁴The LORD said to Moses, "Now the day of your death is near. Call Joshua and present yourselves at the Tent of Meeting, where I will commission him." So Moses and Joshua came and presented themselves at the Tent of Meeting.

¹⁵Then the LORD appeared at the Tent in a pillar of cloud, and the cloud stood over the entrance to the Tent. ¹⁶And the LORD said to Moses: "You are going to rest with your fathers, and these people will soon prostitute themselves to the foreign gods of the land they are entering. They will forsake me and break the covenant I made with them. ¹⁷On that day I will become angry with them and forsake them; I will hide my face from them, and they will be destroyed. Many disasters and difficulties will come upon them, and on that day they will ask, 'Have not these disasters come upon us because our God is not with us?' ¹⁸And I will certainly hide my face on that day because of all their wickedness in turning to other gods.

¹⁹"Now write down for yourselves this song and teach it to the Israelites and have them sing it, so that it may be a witness for me against them. ²⁰When I have brought them into the land flowing with milk and honey, the land I promised on oath to their forefathers, and when they eat their fill and thrive, they will turn to other gods and worship them, rejecting me and breaking my covenant. ²¹And when many disasters and difficulties come upon them, this song will testify against them, because it will not be forgotten by their descendants. I know what they are disposed to do, even before I bring them into the land I promised them on oath." ²²So Moses wrote down this song that day and taught it to the Israelites.

²³The LORD gave this command to Joshua son of Nun: "Be strong and courageous, for you will bring the Israelites into the land I promised them on oath, and I myself will be with you."

²⁴After Moses finished writing in a book the words of this law from beginning to end, ²⁵he gave this command to the Levites who carried the ark of the covenant of the LORD: ²⁶"Take this Book of the Law and place it beside the ark of the covenant of the LORD your God. There it will remain as a witness against you. ²⁷For I know how rebellious and stiff-necked you are. If you have been rebellious against the LORD while I am still alive and with you, how much more will you rebel after I die! ²⁸Assemble before me all the elders of your tribes and all your officials, so that I can speak these words in their hearing and call heaven and earth to testify against them. ²⁹For I know that after my death you are sure to become utterly corrupt and to turn from the way I have commanded you. In days to come, disaster will fall upon you because you will do evil in the

sight of the LORD and provoke him to anger by what your hands have made."

The Song of Moses

³⁰And Moses recited the words of this song from beginning to end in the hearing of the whole assembly of Israel:

32 Listen, O heavens, and I will speak;
  hear, O earth, the words of my mouth.
²Let my teaching fall like rain
  and my words descend like dew,
 like showers on new grass,
  like abundant rain on tender plants.

³I will proclaim the name of the LORD.
  Oh, praise the greatness of our God!
⁴He is the Rock, his works are perfect,
  and all his ways are just.
 A faithful God who does no wrong,
  upright and just is he.

⁵They have acted corruptly toward him;
  to their shame they are no longer his children,
  but a warped and crooked generation.ᵃ
⁶Is this the way you repay the LORD,
  O foolish and unwise people?
 Is he not your Father, your Creator,ᵇ
  who made you and formed you?

⁷Remember the days of old;
  consider the generations long past.
 Ask your father and he will tell you,
  your elders, and they will explain to you.
⁸When the Most High gave the nations their inheritance,
  when he divided all mankind,
 he set up boundaries for the peoples
  according to the number of the sons of Israel.ᶜ
⁹For the LORD's portion is his people,
  Jacob his allotted inheritance.

¹⁰In a desert land he found him,
  in a barren and howling waste.
 He shielded him and cared for him;
  he guarded him as the apple of his eye,
¹¹like an eagle that stirs up its nest
  and hovers over its young,
 that spreads its wings to catch them
  and carries them on its pinions.
¹²The LORD alone led him;
  no foreign god was with him.

¹³He made him ride on the heights of the land
  and fed him with the fruit of the fields.
 He nourished him with honey from the rock,
  and with oil from the flinty crag,
¹⁴with curds and milk from herd and flock
  and with fattened lambs and goats,
 with choice rams of Bashan
  and the finest kernels of wheat.
 You drank the foaming blood of the grape.

¹⁵Jeshurunᵈ grew fat and kicked;
  filled with food, he became heavy and sleek.
 He abandoned the God who made him
  and rejected the Rock his Savior.
¹⁶They made him jealous with their foreign gods
  and angered him with their detestable idols.
¹⁷They sacrificed to demons, which are not God—
  gods they had not known,
 gods that recently appeared,
  gods your fathers did not fear.
¹⁸You deserted the Rock, who fathered you;
  you forgot the God who gave you birth.

¹⁹The LORD saw this and rejected them
  because he was angered by his sons and daughters.
²⁰"I will hide my face from them," he said,
  "and see what their end will be;
 for they are a perverse generation,
  children who are unfaithful.
²¹They made me jealous by what is no god
  and angered me with their worthless idols.
 I will make them envious by those who are not a people;
  I will make them angry by a nation that has no understanding.
²²For a fire has been kindled by my wrath,
  one that burns to the realm of deathᵉ below.
 It will devour the earth and its harvests

ᵃ5 Or *Corrupt are they and not his children, / a generation warped and twisted to their shame*   ᵇ6 Or *Father, who bought you*   ᶜ8 Masoretic Text; Dead Sea Scrolls (see also Septuagint) *sons of God*   ᵈ15 *Jeshurun* means *the upright one*, that is, Israel.   ᵉ22 Hebrew *to Sheol*

A GOD WHO IS WORTH KNOWING

Nicole's new word is "excellent." She uses it a lot. For example:

- "My speech class is so excellent."
- "You mean your parents aren't home? That's excellent!"
- "I can't wait to see that movie. I've heard that it's excellent!"

Anything or anyone Nicole sees that she especially likes or anything that happens that's special is immediately given the "excellent" label.

Look It Up
••••

Funny how often we forget the one who epitomizes excellence— our great God.

"Out of the north he comes in golden splendor; God comes in awesome majesty. The Almighty is beyond our reach and exalted in power" (Job 37:22–23).

"O LORD, our Lord, how majestic is your name in all the earth! You have set your glory above the heavens" (Psalm 8:1).

"The LORD Almighty, wonderful in counsel and magnificent in wisdom" (Isaiah 28:29).

Perhaps those Scripture verses don't use Nicole's favorite word in referring to God, but the same idea comes through loud and clear—God is excellent!

Think It Through
••••

Is there anything about your own life and schedule that you would rate "excellent"?

Describe an excellent date. An excellent weekend. An excellent job. An excellent vacation. What is it that makes those things excellent?

Before you could honestly rate your relationship with God "excellent," what would have to happen in your life? (Example: Any habits that need to stop? Behavior that needs to start? Values that need to change?)

Work It Out
••••

Here are thirty-one excellent things about God—one for each day of the month. He is:

Gracious, personal, loving, perfect, merciful, beyond comprehension, patient, just, wise, all-knowing, all-powerful, omnipresent, faithful, holy, righteous, unchanging, in control, good, self-existent, infinite, knowable, kind, eternal, compassionate, slow to anger, great, generous, gentle, forgiving, beautiful and unique.

Using this list, develop the daily habit of praising God. It's not difficult. Just think about how excellent he is and take a few minutes to tell him!

Nail It Down
••••

Read an excellent description of our excellent God in Deuteronomy 32:3–4.

Turn to pages 93, 1296, 1332 and 1334 for other readings on excellence.
Turn to page 229 for Thursday's reading.

Topic
••••

EXCELLENCE

and set afire the foundations of the
mountains.
23"I will heap calamities upon them
and spend my arrows against them.
24I will send wasting famine against them,
consuming pestilence and deadly
plague;
I will send against them the fangs of
wild beasts,
the venom of vipers that glide in the
dust.
25In the street the sword will make them
childless;
in their homes terror will reign.
Young men and young women will
perish,
infants and gray-haired men.
26I said I would scatter them
and blot out their memory from
mankind,
27but I dreaded the taunt of the enemy,
lest the adversary misunderstand
and say, 'Our hand has triumphed;
the LORD has not done all this.' "

28They are a nation without sense,
there is no discernment in them.
29If only they were wise and would
understand this
and discern what their end will be!
30How could one man chase a thousand,
or two put ten thousand to flight,
unless their Rock had sold them,
unless the LORD had given them up?
31For their rock is not like our Rock,
as even our enemies concede.
32Their vine comes from the vine of
Sodom
and from the fields of Gomorrah.
Their grapes are filled with poison,
and their clusters with bitterness.
33Their wine is the venom of serpents,
the deadly poison of cobras.

34"Have I not kept this in reserve
and sealed it in my vaults?
35It is mine to avenge; I will repay.
In due time their foot will slip;
their day of disaster is near
and their doom rushes upon them."

36The LORD will judge his people
and have compassion on his servants
when he sees their strength is gone
and no one is left, slave or free.
37He will say: "Now where are their gods,
the rock they took refuge in,

38the gods who ate the fat of their
sacrifices
and drank the wine of their drink
offerings?
Let them rise up to help you!
Let them give you shelter!

39"See now that I myself am He!
There is no god besides me.
I put to death and I bring to life,
I have wounded and I will heal,
and no one can deliver out of my
hand.
40I lift my hand to heaven and declare:
As surely as I live forever,
41when I sharpen my flashing sword
and my hand grasps it in judgment,
I will take vengeance on my adversaries
and repay those who hate me.
42I will make my arrows drunk with
blood,
while my sword devours flesh:
the blood of the slain and the captives,
the heads of the enemy leaders."

43Rejoice, O nations, with his people,[a,b]
for he will avenge the blood of his
servants;
he will take vengeance on his enemies
and make atonement for his land and
people.

44Moses came with Joshua[c] son of Nun
and spoke all the words of this song in the
hearing of the people. 45When Moses finished reciting all these words to all Israel,
46he said to them, "Take to heart all the
words I have solemnly declared to you this
day, so that you may command your children to obey carefully all the words of this
law. 47They are not just idle words for you—
they are your life. By them you will live long
in the land you are crossing the Jordan to
possess."

Moses to Die on Mount Nebo

48On that same day the LORD told Moses,
49"Go up into the Abarim Range to Mount
Nebo in Moab, across from Jericho, and
view Canaan, the land I am giving the Israelites as their own possession. 50There on the
mountain that you have climbed you will
die and be gathered to your people, just as
your brother Aaron died on Mount Hor and
was gathered to his people. 51This is because both of you broke faith with me in the
presence of the Israelites at the waters of

Meribah Kadesh in the Desert of Zin and because you did not uphold my holiness
among the Israelites. **52**Therefore, you will
see the land only from a distance; you will
not enter the land I am giving to the people
of Israel."

Moses Blesses the Tribes

33 This is the blessing that Moses the
man of God pronounced on the Israelites before his death. **2**He said:

"The LORD came from Sinai
  and dawned over them from Seir;
  he shone forth from Mount Paran.
He came with*a* myriads of holy ones
  from the south, from his mountain
    slopes.*b*
3Surely it is you who love the people;
  all the holy ones are in your hand.
At your feet they all bow down,
  and from you receive instruction,
4the law that Moses gave us,
  the possession of the assembly of
    Jacob.
5He was king over Jeshurun*c*
  when the leaders of the people
    assembled,
  along with the tribes of Israel.

6"Let Reuben live and not die,
  nor*d* his men be few."

7And this he said about Judah:

"Hear, O LORD, the cry of Judah;
  bring him to his people.
With his own hands he defends his
    cause.
  Oh, be his help against his foes!"

8About Levi he said:

"Your Thummim and Urim belong
  to the man you favored.
You tested him at Massah;
  you contended with him at the waters
    of Meribah.
9He said of his father and mother,
  'I have no regard for them.'
He did not recognize his brothers
  or acknowledge his own children,
but he watched over your word
  and guarded your covenant.
10He teaches your precepts to Jacob
  and your law to Israel.
He offers incense before you
  and whole burnt offerings on your
    altar.

11Bless all his skills, O LORD,
  and be pleased with the work of his
    hands.
Smite the loins of those who rise up
    against him;
  strike his foes till they rise no more."

12About Benjamin he said:

"Let the beloved of the LORD rest secure
    in him,
for he shields him all day long,
  and the one the LORD loves rests
    between his shoulders."

13About Joseph he said:

"May the LORD bless his land
  with the precious dew from heaven
    above
  and with the deep waters that lie
    below;
14with the best the sun brings forth
  and the finest the moon can yield;
15with the choicest gifts of the ancient
    mountains
  and the fruitfulness of the everlasting
    hills;
16with the best gifts of the earth and its
    fullness
  and the favor of him who dwelt in the
    burning bush.
Let all these rest on the head of Joseph,
  on the brow of the prince among*e*
    his brothers.
17In majesty he is like a firstborn bull;
  his horns are the horns of a wild ox.
With them he will gore the nations,
  even those at the ends of the earth.
Such are the ten thousands of Ephraim;
  such are the thousands of Manasseh."

18About Zebulun he said:

"Rejoice, Zebulun, in your going out,
  and you, Issachar, in your tents.
19They will summon peoples to the
    mountain
  and there offer sacrifices of
    righteousness;
they will feast on the abundance of the
    seas,
  on the treasures hidden in the sand."

20About Gad he said:

"Blessed is he who enlarges Gad's
    domain!
Gad lives there like a lion,
  tearing at arm or head.

---

*a*2 Or *from*   *b*2 The meaning of the Hebrew for this phrase is uncertain.   *c*5 *Jeshurun* means *the upright one,* that is, Israel; also in verse 26.   *d*6 Or *but let*   *e*16 Or *of the one separated from*

21He chose the best land for himself;
  the leader's portion was kept for him.
When the heads of the people
    assembled,
  he carried out the Lord's righteous
    will,
  and his judgments concerning Israel."

22About Dan he said:

"Dan is a lion's cub,
  springing out of Bashan."

23About Naphtali he said:

"Naphtali is abounding with the favor of
    the Lord
  and is full of his blessing;
  he will inherit southward to the lake."

24About Asher he said:

"Most blessed of sons is Asher;
  let him be favored by his brothers,
  and let him bathe his feet in oil.
25The bolts of your gates will be iron and
    bronze,
  and your strength will equal your
    days.

26"There is no one like the God of
    Jeshurun,
  who rides on the heavens to help you
  and on the clouds in his majesty.
27The eternal God is your refuge,
  and underneath are the everlasting
    arms.
He will drive out your enemy before
    you,
  saying, 'Destroy him!'
28So Israel will live in safety alone;
  Jacob's spring is secure
in a land of grain and new wine,
  where the heavens drop dew.
29Blessed are you, O Israel!
  Who is like you,
  a people saved by the Lord?
He is your shield and helper

and your glorious sword.
Your enemies will cower before you,
  and you will trample down their high
    places.a"

The Death of Moses

34 Then Moses climbed Mount Nebo from the plains of Moab to the top of Pisgah, across from Jericho. There the Lord showed him the whole land — from Gilead to Dan, 2all of Naphtali, the territory of Ephraim and Manasseh, all the land of Judah as far as the western sea,b 3the Negev and the whole region from the Valley of Jericho, the City of Palms, as far as Zoar. 4Then the Lord said to him, "This is the land I promised on oath to Abraham, Isaac and Jacob when I said, 'I will give it to your descendants.' I have let you see it with your eyes, but you will not cross over into it."

5And Moses the servant of the Lord died there in Moab, as the Lord had said. 6He buried himc in Moab, in the valley opposite Beth Peor, but to this day no one knows where his grave is. 7Moses was a hundred and twenty years old when he died, yet his eyes were not weak nor his strength gone. 8The Israelites grieved for Moses in the plains of Moab thirty days, until the time of weeping and mourning was over.

9Now Joshua son of Nun was filled with the spiritd of wisdom because Moses had laid his hands on him. So the Israelites listened to him and did what the Lord had commanded Moses.

10Since then, no prophet has risen in Israel like Moses, whom the Lord knew face to face, 11who did all those miraculous signs and wonders the Lord sent him to do in Egypt — to Pharaoh and to all his officials and to his whole land. 12For no one has ever shown the mighty power or performed the awesome deeds that Moses did in the sight of all Israel.

---

a29 Or will tread upon their bodies   b2 That is, the Mediterranean   c6 Or He was buried   d9 Or Spirit

JOSHUA succeeds Moses and leads the enthusiastic Israelites into the promised land. In seven years they defeat more than thirty enemy armies. By the end of this book, the land is conquered and divided among the tribes, fulfilling God's promise to Abraham. In his farewell speech Joshua challenges the people: Choose to serve yourself, and you will be defeated. Choose to serve the Lord and you will conquer. "We choose to serve the Lord," the nation promises. As you read, remember: Choose to serve the Lord, and he will conquer the enemies in your life.

Outline of Contents

The Lord Commands Joshua

1 After the death of Moses the servant of the Lord, the Lord said to Joshua son of Nun, Moses' aide: **2**"Moses my servant is dead. Now then, you and all these people, get ready to cross the Jordan River into the land I am about to give to them — to the Israelites. **3**I will give you every place where you set your foot, as I promised Moses. **4**Your territory will extend from the desert to Lebanon, and from the great river, the Euphrates — all the Hittite country — to the Great Sea*a* on the west. **5**No one will be able to stand up against you all the days of your life. As I was with Moses, so I will be with you; I will never leave you nor forsake you.

6"Be strong and courageous, because you will lead these people to inherit the land I swore to their forefathers to give them. **7**Be strong and very courageous. Be careful to obey all the law my servant Moses gave you; do not turn from it to the right or to the left, that you may be successful wherever you go. **8**Do not let this Book of the Law depart from your mouth; meditate on it day and night, so that you may be careful to do everything written in it. Then you will be prosperous and successful. **9**Have I not commanded you? Be strong and courageous. Do not be terrified; do not be discouraged, for the Lord your God will be with you wherever you go."

10So Joshua ordered the officers of the people: **11**"Go through the camp and tell the people, 'Get your supplies ready. Three days

a4 That is, the Mediterranean

from now you will cross the Jordan here to go in and take possession of the land the LORD your God is giving you for your own.' "

12But to the Reubenites, the Gadites and the half-tribe of Manasseh, Joshua said, **13**"Remember the command that Moses the servant of the LORD gave you: 'The LORD your God is giving you rest and has granted you this land.' **14**Your wives, your children and your livestock may stay in the land that Moses gave you east of the Jordan, but all your fighting men, fully armed, must cross over ahead of your brothers. You are to help your brothers **15**until the LORD gives them rest, as he has done for you, and until they too have taken possession of the land that the LORD your God is giving them. After that, you may go back and occupy your own land, which Moses the servant of the LORD gave you east of the Jordan toward the sunrise."

16Then they answered Joshua, "Whatever you have commanded us we will do, and wherever you send us we will go. **17**Just as we fully obeyed Moses, so we will obey you. Only may the LORD your God be with you as he was with Moses. **18**Whoever rebels against your word and does not obey your words, whatever you may command them, will be put to death. Only be strong and courageous!"

Rahab and the Spies

2 Then Joshua son of Nun secretly sent two spies from Shittim. "Go, look over the land," he said, "especially Jericho." So they went and entered the house of a prostitute*a* named Rahab and stayed there.

2The king of Jericho was told, "Look! Some of the Israelites have come here tonight to spy out the land." **3**So the king of Jericho sent this message to Rahab: "Bring out the men who came to you and entered your house, because they have come to spy out the whole land."

4But the woman had taken the two men and hidden them. She said, "Yes, the men came to me, but I did not know where they had come from. **5**At dusk, when it was time to close the city gate, the men left. I don't know which way they went. Go after them quickly. You may catch up with them." **6**(But she had taken them up to the roof and hidden them under the stalks of flax she had laid out on the roof.) **7**So the men set out in pursuit of the spies on the road that leads to the fords of the Jordan, and as soon as the pursuers had gone out, the gate was shut.

8Before the spies lay down for the night, she went up on the roof **9**and said to them, "I know that the LORD has given this land to you and that a great fear of you has fallen on us, so that all who live in this country are melting in fear because of you. **10**We have heard how the LORD dried up the water of the Red Sea*b* for you when you came out of Egypt, and what you did to Sihon and Og, the two kings of the Amorites east of the Jordan, whom you completely destroyed.*c* **11**When we heard of it, our hearts melted and everyone's courage failed because of you, for the LORD your God is God in heaven above and on the earth below. **12**Now then, please swear to me by the LORD that you will show kindness to my family, because I have shown kindness to you. Give me a sure sign **13**that you will spare the lives of my father and mother, my brothers and sisters, and all who belong to them, and that you will save us from death."

14"Our lives for your lives!" the men assured her. "If you don't tell what we are doing, we will treat you kindly and faithfully when the LORD gives us the land."

15So she let them down by a rope through the window, for the house she lived in was part of the city wall. **16**Now she had said to them, "Go to the hills so the pursuers will not find you. Hide yourselves there three days until they return, and then go on your way."

17The men said to her, "This oath you made us swear will not be binding on us **18**unless, when we enter the land, you have tied this scarlet cord in the window through which you let us down, and unless you have brought your father and mother, your brothers and all your family into your house. **19**If anyone goes outside your house into the street, his blood will be on his own head; we will not be responsible. As for anyone who is in the house with you, his blood will be on our head if a hand is laid on him. **20**But if you tell what we are doing, we will be released from the oath you made us swear."

21"Agreed," she replied. "Let it be as you say." So she sent them away and they departed. And she tied the scarlet cord in the window.

22When they left, they went into the hills and stayed there three days, until the pursuers had searched all along the road and returned without finding them. **23**Then the

a1 Or possibly *an innkeeper*   *b10* Hebrew *Yam Suph*; that is, Sea of Reeds   *c10* The Hebrew term refers to the irrevocable giving over of things or persons to the LORD, often by totally destroying them.

two men started back. They went down out of the hills, forded the river and came to Joshua son of Nun and told him everything that had happened to them. **24**They said to Joshua, "The Lord has surely given the whole land into our hands; all the people are melting in fear because of us."

Crossing the Jordan

3 Early in the morning Joshua and all the Israelites set out from Shittim and went to the Jordan, where they camped before crossing over. **2**After three days the officers went throughout the camp, **3**giving orders to the people: "When you see the ark of the covenant of the Lord your God, and the priests, who are Levites, carrying it, you are to move out from your positions and follow it. **4**Then you will know which way to go, since you have never been this way before. But keep a distance of about a thousand yards[a] between you and the ark; do not go near it."

5Joshua told the people, "Consecrate yourselves, for tomorrow the Lord will do amazing things among you."

6Joshua said to the priests, "Take up the ark of the covenant and pass on ahead of the people." So they took it up and went ahead of them.

7And the Lord said to Joshua, "Today I will begin to exalt you in the eyes of all Israel, so they may know that I am with you as I was with Moses. **8**Tell the priests who carry the ark of the covenant: 'When you reach the edge of the Jordan's waters, go and stand in the river.' "

9Joshua said to the Israelites, "Come here and listen to the words of the Lord your God. **10**This is how you will know that the living God is among you and that he will certainly drive out before you the Canaanites, Hittites, Hivites, Perizzites, Girgashites, Amorites and Jebusites. **11**See, the ark of the covenant of the Lord of all the earth will go into the Jordan ahead of you. **12**Now then, choose twelve men from the tribes of Israel, one from each tribe. **13**And as soon as the priests who carry the ark of the Lord — the Lord of all the earth — set foot in the Jordan, its waters flowing downstream will be cut off and stand up in a heap."

14So when the people broke camp to cross the Jordan, the priests carrying the ark of the covenant went ahead of them. **15**Now the Jordan is at flood stage all during harvest.

Yet as soon as the priests who carried the ark reached the Jordan and their feet touched the water's edge, **16**the water from upstream stopped flowing. It piled up in a heap a great distance away, at a town called Adam in the vicinity of Zarethan, while the water flowing down to the Sea of the Arabah (the Salt Sea [b]) was completely cut off. So the people crossed over opposite Jericho. **17**The priests who carried the ark of the covenant of the Lord stood firm on dry ground in the middle of the Jordan, while all Israel passed by until the whole nation had completed the crossing on dry ground.

4 When the whole nation had finished crossing the Jordan, the Lord said to Joshua, **2**"Choose twelve men from among the people, one from each tribe, **3**and tell them to take up twelve stones from the middle of the Jordan from right where the priests stood and to carry them over with you and put them down at the place where you stay tonight."

4So Joshua called together the twelve men he had appointed from the Israelites, one from each tribe, **5**and said to them, "Go over before the ark of the Lord your God into the middle of the Jordan. Each of you is to take up a stone on his shoulder, according to the number of the tribes of the Israelites, **6**to serve as a sign among you. In the future, when your children ask you, 'What do these stones mean?' **7**tell them that the flow of the Jordan was cut off before the ark of the covenant of the Lord. When it crossed the Jordan, the waters of the Jordan were cut off. These stones are to be a memorial to the people of Israel forever."

8So the Israelites did as Joshua commanded them. They took twelve stones from the middle of the Jordan, according to the number of the tribes of the Israelites, as the Lord had told Joshua; and they carried them over with them to their camp, where they put them down. **9**Joshua set up the twelve stones that had been[c] in the middle of the Jordan at the spot where the priests who carried the ark of the covenant had stood. And they are there to this day.

10Now the priests who carried the ark remained standing in the middle of the Jordan until everything the Lord had commanded Joshua was done by the people, just as Moses had directed Joshua. The people hurried over, **11**and as soon as all of them had crossed, the ark of the Lord and the priests

---

a4 Hebrew *about two thousand cubits* (about 900 meters)   *b16* That is, the Dead Sea   *c9* Or *Joshua also set up twelve stones* came to the other side while the people watched. **12**The men of Reuben, Gad and the half-tribe of Manasseh crossed over, armed, in front of the Israelites, as Moses had directed them. **13**About forty thousand armed for battle crossed over before the LORD to the plains of Jericho for war.

14That day the LORD exalted Joshua in the sight of all Israel; and they revered him all the days of his life, just as they had revered Moses.

15Then the LORD said to Joshua, **16**"Command the priests carrying the ark of the Testimony to come up out of the Jordan."

17So Joshua commanded the priests, "Come up out of the Jordan."

18And the priests came up out of the river carrying the ark of the covenant of the LORD. No sooner had they set their feet on the dry ground than the waters of the Jordan returned to their place and ran at flood stage as before.

19On the tenth day of the first month the people went up from the Jordan and camped at Gilgal on the eastern border of Jericho. **20**And Joshua set up at Gilgal the twelve stones they had taken out of the Jordan. **21**He said to the Israelites, "In the future when your descendants ask their fathers, 'What do these stones mean?' **22**tell them, 'Israel crossed the Jordan on dry ground.' **23**For the LORD your God dried up the Jordan before you until you had crossed over. The LORD your God did to the Jordan just what he had done to the Red Sea*a* when he dried it up before us until we had crossed over. **24**He did this so that all the peoples of the earth might know that the hand of the LORD is powerful and so that you might always fear the LORD your God."

Circumcision at Gilgal

5 Now when all the Amorite kings west of the Jordan and all the Canaanite kings along the coast heard how the LORD had dried up the Jordan before the Israelites until we had crossed over, their hearts melted and they no longer had the courage to face the Israelites.

2At that time the LORD said to Joshua, "Make flint knives and circumcise the Israelites again." **3**So Joshua made flint knives and circumcised the Israelites at Gibeath Haaraloth.*b*

4Now this is why he did so: All those who came out of Egypt—all the men of military age—died in the desert on the way after leaving Egypt. **5**All the people that came out had been circumcised, but all the people born in the desert during the journey from Egypt had not. **6**The Israelites had moved about in the desert forty years until all the men who were of military age when they left Egypt had died, since they had not obeyed the LORD. For the LORD had sworn to them that they would not see the land that he had solemnly promised their fathers to give us, a land flowing with milk and honey. **7**So he raised up their sons in their place, and these were the ones Joshua circumcised. They were still uncircumcised because they had not been circumcised on the way. **8**And after the whole nation had been circumcised, they remained where they were in camp until they were healed.

9Then the LORD said to Joshua, "Today I have rolled away the reproach of Egypt from you." So the place has been called Gilgal*c* to this day.

10On the evening of the fourteenth day of the month, while camped at Gilgal on the plains of Jericho, the Israelites celebrated the Passover. **11**The day after the Passover, that very day, they ate some of the produce of the land: unleavened bread and roasted grain. **12**The manna stopped the day after*d* they ate this food from the land; there was no longer any manna for the Israelites, but that year they ate of the produce of Canaan.

The Fall of Jericho

13Now when Joshua was near Jericho, he looked up and saw a man standing in front of him with a drawn sword in his hand. Joshua went up to him and asked, "Are you for us or for our enemies?"

14"Neither," he replied, "but as commander of the army of the LORD I have now come." Then Joshua fell facedown to the ground in reverence, and asked him, "What message does my Lord*e* have for his servant?"

15The commander of the LORD's army replied, "Take off your sandals, for the place where you are standing is holy." And Joshua did so.

6 Now Jericho was tightly shut up because of the Israelites. No one went out and no one came in.

2Then the LORD said to Joshua, "See, I have delivered Jericho into your hands, along with its king and its fighting men. **3**March around the city once with all the armed

---

a23 Hebrew *Yam Suph*; that is, Sea of Reeds   *b3* *Gibeath Haaraloth* means *hill of foreskins.*   *c9* *Gilgal* sounds like the Hebrew for *roll.*   *d12* Or *the day*   *e14* Or *lord* men. Do this for six days. **4**Have seven priests carry trumpets of rams' horns in front of the ark. On the seventh day, march around the city seven times, with the priests blowing the trumpets. **5**When you hear them sound a long blast on the trumpets, have all the people give a loud shout; then the wall of the city will collapse and the people will go up, every man straight in."

6So Joshua son of Nun called the priests and said to them, "Take up the ark of the covenant of the Lord and have seven priests carry trumpets in front of it." **7**And he ordered the people, "Advance! March around the city, with the armed guard going ahead of the ark of the Lord."

8When Joshua had spoken to the people, the seven priests carrying the seven trumpets before the Lord went forward, blowing their trumpets, and the ark of the Lord's covenant followed them. **9**The armed guard marched ahead of the priests who blew the trumpets, and the rear guard followed the ark. All this time the trumpets were sounding. **10**But Joshua had commanded the people, "Do not give a war cry, do not raise your voices, do not say a word until the day I tell you to shout. Then shout!" **11**So he had the ark of the Lord carried around the city, circling it once. Then the people returned to camp and spent the night there.

12Joshua got up early the next morning and the priests took up the ark of the Lord. **13**The seven priests carrying the seven trumpets went forward, marching before the ark of the Lord and blowing the trumpets. The armed men went ahead of them and the rear guard followed the ark of the Lord, while the trumpets kept sounding. **14**So on the second day they marched around the city once and returned to the camp. They did this for six days.

15On the seventh day, they got up at daybreak and marched around the city seven times in the same manner, except that on that day they circled the city seven times. **16**The seventh time around, when the priests sounded the trumpet blast, Joshua commanded the people, "Shout! For the Lord has given you the city! **17**The city and all that is in it are to be devoted*a* to the Lord. Only Rahab the prostitute*b* and all who are with her in her house shall be spared, be-

cause she hid the spies we sent. **18**But keep away from the devoted things, so that you will not bring about your own destruction by taking any of them. Otherwise you will make the camp of Israel liable to destruction and bring trouble on it. **19**All the silver and gold and the articles of bronze and iron are sacred to the Lord and must go into his treasury."

20When the trumpets sounded, the people shouted, and at the sound of the trumpet, when the people gave a loud shout, the wall collapsed; so every man charged straight in, and they took the city. **21**They devoted the city to the Lord and destroyed with the sword every living thing in it—men and women, young and old, cattle, sheep and donkeys.

22Joshua said to the two men who had spied out the land, "Go into the prostitute's house and bring her out and all who belong to her, in accordance with your oath to her." **23**So the young men who had done the spying went in and brought out Rahab, her father and mother and brothers and all who belonged to her. They brought out her entire family and put them in a place outside the camp of Israel.

24Then they burned the whole city and everything in it, but they put the silver and gold and the articles of bronze and iron into the treasury of the Lord's house. **25**But Joshua spared Rahab the prostitute, with her family and all who belonged to her, because she hid the men Joshua had sent as spies to Jericho—and she lives among the Israelites to this day.

26At that time Joshua pronounced this solemn oath: "Cursed before the Lord is the man who undertakes to rebuild this city, Jericho:

"At the cost of his firstborn son
    will he lay its foundations;
at the cost of his youngest
    will he set up its gates."

27So the Lord was with Joshua, and his fame spread throughout the land.

Achan's Sin

7 But the Israelites acted unfaithfully in regard to the devoted things*c*; Achan son of Carmi, the son of Zimri,*d* the son of

---

a17 The Hebrew term refers to the irrevocable giving over of things or persons to the Lord, often by totally destroying them; also in verses 18 and 21.   *b17* Or possibly *innkeeper*; also in verses 22 and 25   *c1* The Hebrew term refers to the irrevocable giving over of things or persons to the Lord, often by totally destroying them; also in verses 11, 12, 13 and 15.   *d1* See Septuagint and 1 Chron. 2:6; Hebrew *Zabdi*; also in verses 17 and 18.

Zerah, of the tribe of Judah, took some of them. So the LORD's anger burned against Israel.

²Now Joshua sent men from Jericho to Ai, which is near Beth Aven to the east of Bethel, and told them, "Go up and spy out the region." So the men went up and spied out Ai.

³When they returned to Joshua, they said, "Not all the people will have to go up against Ai. Send two or three thousand men to take it and do not weary all the people, for only a few men are there." ⁴So about three thousand men went up; but they were routed by the men of Ai, ⁵who killed about thirty-six of them. They chased the Israelites from the city gate as far as the stone quarries^a and struck them down on the slopes. At this the hearts of the people melted and became like water.

⁶Then Joshua tore his clothes and fell facedown to the ground before the ark of the LORD, remaining there till evening. The elders of Israel did the same, and sprinkled dust on their heads. ⁷And Joshua said, "Ah, Sovereign LORD, why did you ever bring this people across the Jordan to deliver us into the hands of the Amorites to destroy us? If only we had been content to stay on the other side of the Jordan! ⁸O Lord, what can I say, now that Israel has been routed by its enemies? ⁹The Canaanites and the other people of the country will hear about this and they will surround us and wipe out our name from the earth. What then will you do for your own great name?"

¹⁰The LORD said to Joshua, "Stand up! What are you doing down on your face? ¹¹Israel has sinned; they have violated my covenant, which I commanded them to keep. They have taken some of the devoted things; they have stolen, they have lied, they have put them with their own possessions. ¹²That is why the Israelites cannot stand against their enemies; they turn their backs and run because they have been made liable to destruction. I will not be with you anymore unless you destroy whatever among you is devoted to destruction.

¹³"Go, consecrate the people. Tell them, 'Consecrate yourselves in preparation for tomorrow; for this is what the LORD, the God of Israel, says: That which is devoted is among you, O Israel. You cannot stand against your enemies until you remove it.

¹⁴"'In the morning, present yourselves tribe by tribe. The tribe that the LORD takes shall come forward clan by clan; the clan that the LORD takes shall come forward family by family; and the family that the LORD takes shall come forward man by man. ¹⁵He who is caught with the devoted things shall be destroyed by fire, along with all that belongs to him. He has violated the covenant of the LORD and has done a disgraceful thing in Israel!'"

¹⁶Early the next morning Joshua had Israel come forward by tribes, and Judah was taken. ¹⁷The clans of Judah came forward, and he took the Zerahites. He had the clan of the Zerahites come forward by families, and Zimri was taken. ¹⁸Joshua had his family come forward man by man, and Achan son of Carmi, the son of Zimri, the son of Zerah, of the tribe of Judah, was taken.

¹⁹Then Joshua said to Achan, "My son, give glory to the LORD,^b the God of Israel, and give him the praise.^c Tell me what you have done; do not hide it from me."

²⁰Achan replied, "It is true! I have sinned against the LORD, the God of Israel. This is what I have done: ²¹When I saw in the plunder a beautiful robe from Babylonia,^d two hundred shekels^e of silver and a wedge of gold weighing fifty shekels,^f I coveted them and took them. They are hidden in the ground inside my tent, with the silver underneath."

²²So Joshua sent messengers, and they ran to the tent, and there it was, hidden in his tent, with the silver underneath. ²³They took the things from the tent, brought them to Joshua and all the Israelites and spread them out before the LORD.

²⁴Then Joshua, together with all Israel, took Achan son of Zerah, the silver, the robe, the gold wedge, his sons and daughters, his cattle, donkeys and sheep, his tent and all that he had, to the Valley of Achor. ²⁵Joshua said, "Why have you brought this trouble on us? The LORD will bring trouble on you today."

Then all Israel stoned him, and after they had stoned the rest, they burned them. ²⁶Over Achan they heaped up a large pile of rocks, which remains to this day. Then the LORD turned from his fierce anger. Therefore that place has been called the Valley of Achor^g ever since.

---

^a5 Or *as far as Shebarim*   ^b19 A solemn charge to tell the truth   ^c19 Or *and confess to him*   ^d21 Hebrew *Shinar*   ^e21 That is, about 5 pounds (about 2.3 kilograms)   ^f21 That is, about 1 1/4 pounds (about 0.6 kilogram)   ^g26 *Achor* means *trouble*.

Ai Destroyed

8 Then the LORD said to Joshua, "Do not be afraid; do not be discouraged. Take the whole army with you, and go up and attack Ai. For I have delivered into your hands the king of Ai, his people, his city and his land. **2**You shall do to Ai and its king as you did to Jericho and its king, except that you may carry off their plunder and livestock for yourselves. Set an ambush behind the city."

3So Joshua and the whole army moved out to attack Ai. He chose thirty thousand of his best fighting men and sent them out at night **4**with these orders: "Listen carefully. You are to set an ambush behind the city. Don't go very far from it. All of you be on the alert. **5**I and all those with me will advance on the city, and when the men come out against us, as they did before, we will flee from them. **6**They will pursue us until we have lured them away from the city, for they will say, 'They are running away from us as they did before.' So when we flee from them, **7**you are to rise up from ambush and take the city. The LORD your God will give it into your hand. **8**When you have taken the city, set it on fire. Do what the LORD has commanded. See to it; you have my orders."

9Then Joshua sent them off, and they went to the place of ambush and lay in wait between Bethel and Ai, to the west of Ai— but Joshua spent that night with the people.

10Early the next morning Joshua mustered his men, and he and the leaders of Israel marched before them to Ai. **11**The entire force that was with him marched up and approached the city and arrived in front of it. They set up camp north of Ai, with the valley between them and the city. **12**Joshua had taken about five thousand men and set them in ambush between Bethel and Ai, to the west of the city. **13**They had the soldiers take up their positions—all those in the camp to the north of the city and the ambush to the west of it. That night Joshua went into the valley.

14When the king of Ai saw this, he and all the men of the city hurried out early in the morning to meet Israel in battle at a certain place overlooking the Arabah. But he did not know that an ambush had been set against him behind the city. **15**Joshua and all Israel let themselves be driven back before them, and they fled toward the desert. **16**All the men of Ai were called to pursue them, and they pursued Joshua and were lured away from the city. **17**Not a man remained in Ai or Bethel who did not go after Israel. They left the city open and went in pursuit of Israel.

18Then the LORD said to Joshua, "Hold out toward Ai the javelin that is in your hand, for into your hand I will deliver the city." So Joshua held out his javelin toward Ai. **19**As soon as he did this, the men in the ambush rose quickly from their position and rushed forward. They entered the city and captured it and quickly set it on fire.

20The men of Ai looked back and saw the smoke of the city rising against the sky, but they had no chance to escape in any direction, for the Israelites who had been fleeing toward the desert had turned back against their pursuers. **21**For when Joshua and all Israel saw that the ambush had taken the city and that smoke was going up from the city, they turned around and attacked the men of Ai. **22**The men of the ambush also came out of the city against them, so that they were caught in the middle, with Israelites on both sides. Israel cut them down, leaving them neither survivors nor fugitives. **23**But they took the king of Ai alive and brought him to Joshua.

24When Israel had finished killing all the men of Ai in the fields and in the desert where they had chased them, and when every one of them had been put to the sword, all the Israelites returned to Ai and killed those who were in it. **25**Twelve thousand men and women fell that day—all the people of Ai. **26**For Joshua did not draw back the hand that held out his javelin until he had destroyed[a] all who lived in Ai. **27**But Israel did carry off for themselves the livestock and plunder of this city, as the LORD had instructed Joshua.

28So Joshua burned Ai and made it a permanent heap of ruins, a desolate place to this day. **29**He hung the king of Ai on a tree and left him there until evening. At sunset, Joshua ordered them to take his body from the tree and throw it down at the entrance of the city gate. And they raised a large pile of rocks over it, which remains to this day.

The Covenant Renewed at Mount Ebal

30Then Joshua built on Mount Ebal an altar to the LORD, the God of Israel, **31**as Moses the servant of the LORD had commanded the Israelites. He built it according to what is written in the Book of the Law of Moses—an

---

a26 The Hebrew term refers to the irrevocable giving over of things or persons to the LORD, often by totally destroying them.

altar of uncut stones, on which no iron tool had been used. On it they offered to the LORD burnt offerings and sacrificed fellowship offerings.*a* **32**There, in the presence of the Israelites, Joshua copied on stones the law of Moses, which he had written. **33**All Israel, aliens and citizens alike, with their elders, officials and judges, were standing on both sides of the ark of the covenant of the LORD, facing those who carried it — the priests, who were Levites. Half of the people stood in front of Mount Gerizim and half of them in front of Mount Ebal, as Moses the servant of the LORD had formerly commanded when he gave instructions to bless the people of Israel.

34Afterward, Joshua read all the words of the law — the blessings and the curses — just as it is written in the Book of the Law. **35**There was not a word of all that Moses had commanded that Joshua did not read to the whole assembly of Israel, including the women and children, and the aliens who lived among them.

The Gibeonite Deception

9 Now when all the kings west of the Jordan heard about these things — those in the hill country, in the western foothills, and along the entire coast of the Great Sea*b* as far as Lebanon (the kings of the Hittites, Amorites, Canaanites, Perizzites, Hivites and Jebusites) — **2**they came together to make war against Joshua and Israel.

3However, when the people of Gibeon heard what Joshua had done to Jericho and Ai, **4**they resorted to a ruse: They went as a delegation whose donkeys were loaded*c* with worn-out sacks and old wineskins, cracked and mended. **5**The men put worn and patched sandals on their feet and wore old clothes. All the bread of their food supply was dry and moldy. **6**Then they went to Joshua in the camp at Gilgal and said to him and the men of Israel, "We have come from a distant country; make a treaty with us."

7The men of Israel said to the Hivites, "But perhaps you live near us. How then can we make a treaty with you?"

8"We are your servants," they said to Joshua.

But Joshua asked, "Who are you and where do you come from?"

9They answered: "Your servants have come from a very distant country because of the fame of the LORD your God. For we have heard reports of him: all that he did in Egypt, **10**and all that he did to the two kings of the Amorites east of the Jordan — Sihon king of Heshbon, and Og king of Bashan, who reigned in Ashtaroth. **11**And our elders and all those living in our country said to us, 'Take provisions for your journey; go and meet them and say to them, "We are your servants; make a treaty with us." ' **12**This bread of ours was warm when we packed it at home on the day we left to come to you. But now see how dry and moldy it is. **13**And these wineskins that we filled were new, but see how cracked they are. And our clothes and sandals are worn out by the very long journey."

14The men of Israel sampled their provisions but did not inquire of the LORD. **15**Then Joshua made a treaty of peace with them to let them live, and the leaders of the assembly ratified it by oath.

16Three days after they made the treaty with the Gibeonites, the Israelites heard that they were neighbors, living near them. **17**So the Israelites set out and on the third day came to their cities: Gibeon, Kephirah, Beeroth and Kiriath Jearim. **18**But the Israelites did not attack them, because the leaders of the assembly had sworn an oath to them by the LORD, the God of Israel.

The whole assembly grumbled against the leaders, **19**but all the leaders answered, "We have given them our oath by the LORD, the God of Israel, and we cannot touch them now. **20**This is what we will do to them: We will let them live, so that wrath will not fall on us for breaking the oath we swore to them." **21**They continued, "Let them live, but let them be woodcutters and water carriers for the entire community." So the leaders' promise to them was kept.

22Then Joshua summoned the Gibeonites and said, "Why did you deceive us by saying, 'We live a long way from you,' while actually you live near us? **23**You are now under a curse: You will never cease to serve as woodcutters and water carriers for the house of my God."

24They answered Joshua, "Your servants were clearly told how the LORD your God had commanded his servant Moses to give you the whole land and to wipe out all its inhabitants from before you. So we feared for our lives because of you, and that is why we did this. **25**We are now in your hands. Do to us whatever seems good and right to you."

26So Joshua saved them from the Israelites, and they did not kill them. **27**That day he made the Gibeonites woodcutters and water carriers for the community and for the altar of the LORD at the place the LORD would choose. And that is what they are to this day.

The Sun Stands Still

10 Now Adoni-Zedek king of Jerusalem heard that Joshua had taken Ai and totally destroyed*a* it, doing to Ai and its king as he had done to Jericho and its king, and that the people of Gibeon had made a treaty of peace with Israel and were living near them. **2**He and his people were very much alarmed at this, because Gibeon was an important city, like one of the royal cities; it was larger than Ai, and all its men were good fighters. **3**So Adoni-Zedek king of Jerusalem appealed to Hoham king of Hebron, Piram king of Jarmuth, Japhia king of Lachish and Debir king of Eglon. **4**"Come up and help me attack Gibeon," he said, "because it has made peace with Joshua and the Israelites."

5Then the five kings of the Amorites — the kings of Jerusalem, Hebron, Jarmuth, Lachish and Eglon — joined forces. They moved up with all their troops and took up positions against Gibeon and attacked it.

6The Gibeonites then sent word to Joshua in the camp at Gilgal: "Do not abandon your servants. Come up to us quickly and save us! Help us, because all the Amorite kings from the hill country have joined forces against us."

7So Joshua marched up from Gilgal with his entire army, including all the best fighting men. **8**The LORD said to Joshua, "Do not be afraid of them; I have given them into your hand. Not one of them will be able to withstand you."

9After an all-night march from Gilgal, Joshua took them by surprise. **10**The LORD threw them into confusion before Israel, who defeated them in a great victory at Gibeon. Israel pursued them along the road going up to Beth Horon and cut them down all the way to Azekah and Makkedah. **11**As they fled before Israel on the road down from Beth Horon to Azekah, the LORD hurled large hailstones down on them from the sky, and more of them died from the hailstones than were killed by the swords of the Israelites.

12On the day the LORD gave the Amorites over to Israel, Joshua said to the LORD in the presence of Israel:

"O sun, stand still over Gibeon,
    O moon, over the Valley of Aijalon."
13So the sun stood still,
    and the moon stopped,
    till the nation avenged itself on*b* its
        enemies,

as it is written in the Book of Jashar.

The sun stopped in the middle of the sky and delayed going down about a full day. **14**There has never been a day like it before or since, a day when the LORD listened to a man. Surely the LORD was fighting for Israel!

15Then Joshua returned with all Israel to the camp at Gilgal.

Five Amorite Kings Killed

16Now the five kings had fled and hidden in the cave at Makkedah. **17**When Joshua was told that the five kings had been found hiding in the cave at Makkedah, **18**he said, "Roll large rocks up to the mouth of the cave, and post some men there to guard it. **19**But don't stop! Pursue your enemies, attack them from the rear and don't let them reach their cities, for the LORD your God has given them into your hand."

20So Joshua and the Israelites destroyed them completely — almost to a man — but the few who were left reached their fortified cities. **21**The whole army then returned safely to Joshua in the camp at Makkedah, and no one uttered a word against the Israelites.

22Joshua said, "Open the mouth of the cave and bring those five kings out to me." **23**So they brought the five kings out of the cave — the kings of Jerusalem, Hebron, Jarmuth, Lachish and Eglon. **24**When they had brought these kings to Joshua, he summoned all the men of Israel and said to the army commanders who had come with him, "Come here and put your feet on the necks of these kings." So they came forward and placed their feet on their necks.

25Joshua said to them, "Do not be afraid; do not be discouraged. Be strong and courageous. This is what the LORD will do to all the enemies you are going to fight." **26**Then Joshua struck and killed the kings and hung them on five trees, and they were left hanging on the trees until evening.

27At sunset Joshua gave the order and they took them down from the trees and threw them into the cave where they had

---

a1 The Hebrew term refers to the irrevocable giving over of things or persons to the LORD, often by totally destroying them; also in verses 28, 35, 37, 39 and 40.   *b13* Or *nation triumphed over* been hiding. At the mouth of the cave they placed large rocks, which are there to this day.

28That day Joshua took Makkedah. He put the city and its king to the sword and totally destroyed everyone in it. He left no survivors. And he did to the king of Makkedah as he had done to the king of Jericho.

Southern Cities Conquered

29Then Joshua and all Israel with him moved on from Makkedah to Libnah and attacked it. **30**The LORD also gave that city and its king into Israel's hand. The city and everyone in it Joshua put to the sword. He left no survivors there. And he did to its king as he had done to the king of Jericho.

31Then Joshua and all Israel with him moved on from Libnah to Lachish; he took up positions against it and attacked it. **32**The LORD handed Lachish over to Israel, and Joshua took it on the second day. The city and everyone in it he put to the sword, just as he had done to Libnah. **33**Meanwhile, Horam king of Gezer had come up to help Lachish, but Joshua defeated him and his army—until no survivors were left.

34Then Joshua and all Israel with him moved on from Lachish to Eglon; they took up positions against it and attacked it. **35**They captured it that same day and put it to the sword and totally destroyed everyone in it, just as they had done to Lachish.

36Then Joshua and all Israel with him went up from Eglon to Hebron and attacked it. **37**They took the city and put it to the sword, together with its king, its villages and everyone in it. They left no survivors. Just as at Eglon, they totally destroyed it and everyone in it.

38Then Joshua and all Israel with him turned around and attacked Debir. **39**They took the city, its king and its villages, and put them to the sword. Everyone in it they totally destroyed. They left no survivors. They did to Debir and its king as they had done to Libnah and its king and to Hebron.

40So Joshua subdued the whole region, including the hill country, the Negev, the western foothills and the mountain slopes, together with all their kings. He left no survivors. He totally destroyed all who breathed, just as the LORD, the God of Israel, had commanded. **41**Joshua subdued them from Kadesh Barnea to Gaza and from the whole region of Goshen to Gibeon. **42**All these kings and their lands Joshua conquered in one campaign, because the LORD, the God of Israel, fought for Israel.

43Then Joshua returned with all Israel to the camp at Gilgal.

Northern Kings Defeated

11 When Jabin king of Hazor heard of this, he sent word to Jobab king of Madon, to the kings of Shimron and Acshaph, **2**and to the northern kings who were in the mountains, in the Arabah south of Kinnereth, in the western foothills and in Naphoth Dor*a* on the west; **3**to the Canaanites in the east and west; to the Amorites, Hittites, Perizzites and Jebusites in the hill country; and to the Hivites below Hermon in the region of Mizpah. **4**They came out with all their troops and a large number of horses and chariots—a huge army, as numerous as the sand on the seashore. **5**All these kings joined forces and made camp together at the Waters of Merom, to fight against Israel.

6The LORD said to Joshua, "Do not be afraid of them, because by this time tomorrow I will hand all of them over to Israel, slain. You are to hamstring their horses and burn their chariots."

7So Joshua and his whole army came against them suddenly at the Waters of Merom and attacked them, **8**and the LORD gave them into the hand of Israel. They defeated them and pursued them all the way to Greater Sidon, to Misrephoth Maim, and to the Valley of Mizpah on the east, until no survivors were left. **9**Joshua did to them as the LORD had directed: He hamstrung their horses and burned their chariots.

10At that time Joshua turned back and captured Hazor and put its king to the sword. (Hazor had been the head of all these kingdoms.) **11**Everyone in it they put to the sword. They totally destroyed*b* them, not sparing anything that breathed, and he burned up Hazor itself.

12Joshua took all these royal cities and their kings and put them to the sword. He totally destroyed them, as Moses the servant of the LORD had commanded. **13**Yet Israel did not burn any of the cities built on their mounds—except Hazor, which Joshua burned. **14**The Israelites carried off for themselves all the plunder and livestock of these cities, but all the people they put to the sword until they completely destroyed them, not sparing anyone that breathed.

---

*a*2 Or *in the heights of Dor*   *b*11 The Hebrew term refers to the irrevocable giving over of things or persons to the LORD, often by totally destroying them; also in verses 12, 20 and 21.

¹⁵As the LORD commanded his servant Moses, so Moses commanded Joshua, and Joshua did it; he left nothing undone of all that the LORD commanded Moses.

¹⁶So Joshua took this entire land: the hill country, all the Negev, the whole region of Goshen, the western foothills, the Arabah and the mountains of Israel with their foothills, ¹⁷from Mount Halak, which rises toward Seir, to Baal Gad in the Valley of Lebanon below Mount Hermon. He captured all their kings and struck them down, putting them to death. ¹⁸Joshua waged war against all these kings for a long time. ¹⁹Except for the Hivites living in Gibeon, not one city made a treaty of peace with the Israelites, who took them all in battle. ²⁰For it was the LORD himself who hardened their hearts to wage war against Israel, so that he might destroy them totally, exterminating them without mercy, as the LORD had commanded Moses.

²¹At that time Joshua went and destroyed the Anakites from the hill country: from Hebron, Debir and Anab, from all the hill country of Judah, and from all the hill country of Israel. Joshua totally destroyed them and their towns. ²²No Anakites were left in Israelite territory; only in Gaza, Gath and Ashdod did any survive. ²³So Joshua took the entire land, just as the LORD had directed Moses, and he gave it as an inheritance to Israel according to their tribal divisions.

Then the land had rest from war.

List of Defeated Kings

12 These are the kings of the land whom the Israelites had defeated and whose territory they took over east of the Jordan, from the Arnon Gorge to Mount Hermon, including all the eastern side of the Arabah:

²Sihon king of the Amorites,
who reigned in Heshbon. He ruled from Aroer on the rim of the Arnon Gorge — from the middle of the gorge — to the Jabbok River, which is the border of the Ammonites. This included half of Gilead. ³He also ruled over the eastern Arabah from the Sea of Kinnereth*ᵃ* to the Sea of the Arabah (the Salt Sea*ᵇ*), to Beth Jeshimoth, and then southward below the slopes of Pisgah.

⁴And the territory of Og king of Bashan, one of the last of the Rephaites, who reigned in Ashtaroth and Edrei. ⁵He

ruled over Mount Hermon, Salecah, all of Bashan to the border of the people of Geshur and Maacah, and half of Gilead to the border of Sihon king of Heshbon.

⁶Moses, the servant of the LORD, and the Israelites conquered them. And Moses the servant of the LORD gave their land to the Reubenites, the Gadites and the half-tribe of Manasseh to be their possession.

⁷These are the kings of the land that Joshua and the Israelites conquered on the west side of the Jordan, from Baal Gad in the Valley of Lebanon to Mount Halak, which rises toward Seir (their lands Joshua gave as an inheritance to the tribes of Israel according to their tribal divisions — ⁸the hill country, the western foothills, the Arabah, the mountain slopes, the desert and the Negev — the lands of the Hittites, Amorites, Canaanites, Perizzites, Hivites and Jebusites):

⁹the king of Jericho	one
the king of Ai (near Bethel)	one
¹⁰the king of Jerusalem	one
the king of Hebron	one
¹¹the king of Jarmuth	one
the king of Lachish	one
¹²the king of Eglon	one
the king of Gezer	one
¹³the king of Debir	one
the king of Geder	one
¹⁴the king of Hormah	one
the king of Arad	one
¹⁵the king of Libnah	one
the king of Adullam	one
¹⁶the king of Makkedah	one
the king of Bethel	one
¹⁷the king of Tappuah	one
the king of Hepher	one
¹⁸the king of Aphek	one
the king of Lasharon	one
¹⁹the king of Madon	one
the king of Hazor	one
²⁰the king of Shimron Meron	one
the king of Acshaph	one
²¹the king of Taanach	one
the king of Megiddo	one
²²the king of Kedesh	one
the king of Jokneam in Carmel	one
²³the king of Dor (in Naphoth Dor*ᶜ*)	one
the king of Goyim in Gilgal	one
²⁴the king of Tirzah	one
thirty-one kings in all.	

ᵃ3 That is, Galilee　　*ᵇ3* That is, the Dead Sea　　*ᶜ23* Or *in the heights of Dor*

Land Still to Be Taken

13 When Joshua was old and well advanced in years, the LORD said to him, "You are very old, and there are still very large areas of land to be taken over.

2"This is the land that remains: all the regions of the Philistines and Geshurites: 3from the Shihor River on the east of Egypt to the territory of Ekron on the north, all of it counted as Canaanite (the territory of the five Philistine rulers in Gaza, Ashdod, Ashkelon, Gath and Ekron—that of the Avvites); 4from the south, all the land of the Canaanites, from Arah of the Sidonians as far as Aphek, the region of the Amorites, 5the area of the Gebalites*a*; and all Lebanon to the east, from Baal Gad below Mount Hermon to Lebo*b* Hamath.

6"As for all the inhabitants of the mountain regions from Lebanon to Misrephoth Maim, that is, all the Sidonians, I myself will drive them out before the Israelites. Be sure to allocate this land to Israel for an inheritance, as I have instructed you, 7and divide it as an inheritance among the nine tribes and half of the tribe of Manasseh."

Division of the Land East of the Jordan

8The other half of Manasseh,*c* the Reubenites and the Gadites had received the inheritance that Moses had given them east of the Jordan, as he, the servant of the LORD, had assigned it to them.

9It extended from Aroer on the rim of the Arnon Gorge, and from the town in the middle of the gorge, and included the whole plateau of Medeba as far as Dibon, 10and all the towns of Sihon king of the Amorites, who ruled in Heshbon, out to the border of the Ammonites. 11It also included Gilead, the territory of the people of Geshur and Maacah, all of Mount Hermon and all Bashan as far as Salecah— 12that is, the whole kingdom of Og in Bashan, who had reigned in Ashtaroth and Edrei and had survived as one of the last of the Rephaites. Moses had defeated them and taken over their land. 13But the Israelites did not drive out the people of Geshur and Maacah, so they continue to live among the Israelites to this day.

14But to the tribe of Levi he gave no inheritance, since the offerings made by fire to the LORD, the God of Israel, are their inheritance, as he promised them.

15This is what Moses had given to the tribe of Reuben, clan by clan:

16The territory from Aroer on the rim of the Arnon Gorge, and from the town in the middle of the gorge, and the whole plateau past Medeba 17to Heshbon and all its towns on the plateau, including Dibon, Bamoth Baal, Beth Baal Meon, 18Jahaz, Kedemoth, Mephaath, 19Kiriathaim, Sibmah, Zereth Shahar on the hill in the valley, 20Beth Peor, the slopes of Pisgah, and Beth Jeshimoth 21—all the towns on the plateau and the entire realm of Sihon king of the Amorites, who ruled at Heshbon. Moses had defeated him and the Midianite chiefs, Evi, Rekem, Zur, Hur and Reba—princes allied with Sihon—who lived in that country. 22In addition to those slain in battle, the Israelites had put to the sword Balaam son of Beor, who practiced divination. 23The boundary of the Reubenites was the bank of the Jordan. These towns and their villages were the inheritance of the Reubenites, clan by clan.

24This is what Moses had given to the tribe of Gad, clan by clan:

25The territory of Jazer, all the towns of Gilead and half the Ammonite country as far as Aroer, near Rabbah; 26and from Heshbon to Ramath Mizpah and Betonim, and from Mahanaim to the territory of Debir; 27and in the valley, Beth Haram, Beth Nimrah, Succoth and Zaphon with the rest of the realm of Sihon king of Heshbon (the east side of the Jordan, the territory up to the end of the Sea of Kinnereth*d*). 28These towns and their villages were the inheritance of the Gadites, clan by clan.

29This is what Moses had given to the half-tribe of Manasseh, that is, to half the family of the descendants of Manasseh, clan by clan:

30The territory extending from Mahanaim and including all of Bashan, the entire realm of Og king of Bashan—all the settlements of Jair in Bashan, sixty

---

a5 That is, the area of Byblos   *b5* Or *to the entrance to* Manasseh)   *d27* That is, Galilee   *c8* Hebrew *With it* (that is, with the other half of towns, [31]half of Gilead, and Ashtaroth and Edrei (the royal cities of Og in Bashan). This was for the descendants of Makir son of Manasseh—for half of the sons of Makir, clan by clan.

[32]This is the inheritance Moses had given when he was in the plains of Moab across the Jordan east of Jericho. [33]But to the tribe of Levi, Moses had given no inheritance; the LORD, the God of Israel, is their inheritance, as he promised them.

Division of the Land West of the Jordan

14 Now these are the areas the Israelites received as an inheritance in the land of Canaan, which Eleazar the priest, Joshua son of Nun and the heads of the tribal clans of Israel allotted to them. [2]Their inheritances were assigned by lot to the nine-and-a-half tribes, as the LORD had commanded through Moses. [3]Moses had granted the two-and-a-half tribes their inheritance east of the Jordan but had not granted the Levites an inheritance among the rest, [4]for the sons of Joseph had become two tribes—Manasseh and Ephraim. The Levites received no share of the land but only towns to live in, with pasturelands for their flocks and herds. [5]So the Israelites divided the land, just as the LORD had commanded Moses.

Hebron Given to Caleb

[6]Now the men of Judah approached Joshua at Gilgal, and Caleb son of Jephunneh the Kenizzite said to him, "You know what the LORD said to Moses the man of God at Kadesh Barnea about you and me. [7]I was forty years old when Moses the servant of the LORD sent me from Kadesh Barnea to explore the land. And I brought him back a report according to my convictions, [8]but my brothers who went up with me made the hearts of the people melt with fear. I, however, followed the LORD my God wholeheartedly. [9]So on that day Moses swore to me, 'The land on which your feet have walked will be your inheritance and that of your children forever, because you have followed the LORD my God wholeheartedly.'[a]

[10]"Now then, just as the LORD promised, he has kept me alive for forty-five years since the time he said this to Moses, while Israel moved about in the desert. So here I am today, eighty-five years old! [11]I am still as strong today as the day Moses sent me

out; I'm just as vigorous to go out to battle now as I was then. [12]Now give me this hill country that the LORD promised me that day. You yourself heard then that the Anakites were there and their cities were large and fortified, but, the LORD helping me, I will drive them out just as he said."

[13]Then Joshua blessed Caleb son of Jephunneh and gave him Hebron as his inheritance. [14]So Hebron has belonged to Caleb son of Jephunneh the Kenizzite ever since, because he followed the LORD, the God of Israel, wholeheartedly. [15](Hebron used to be called Kiriath Arba after Arba, who was the greatest man among the Anakites.)

Then the land had rest from war.

Allotment for Judah

15 The allotment for the tribe of Judah, clan by clan, extended down to the territory of Edom, to the Desert of Zin in the extreme south.

[2]Their southern boundary started from the bay at the southern end of the Salt Sea,[b] [3]crossed south of Scorpion[c] Pass, continued on to Zin and went over to the south of Kadesh Barnea. Then it ran past Hezron up to Addar and curved around to Karka. [4]It then passed along to Azmon and joined the Wadi of Egypt, ending at the sea. This is their[d] southern boundary.

[5]The eastern boundary is the Salt Sea as far as the mouth of the Jordan.

The northern boundary started from the bay of the sea at the mouth of the Jordan, [6]went up to Beth Hoglah and continued north of Beth Arabah to the Stone of Bohan son of Reuben. [7]The boundary then went up to Debir from the Valley of Achor and turned north to Gilgal, which faces the Pass of Adummim south of the gorge. It continued along to the waters of En Shemesh and came out at En Rogel. [8]Then it ran up the Valley of Ben Hinnom along the southern slope of the Jebusite city (that is, Jerusalem). From there it climbed to the top of the hill west of the Hinnom Valley at the northern end of the Valley of Rephaim. [9]From the hilltop the boundary headed toward the spring of the waters of Nephtoah, came out at the towns of Mount Ephron and went down toward Baalah (that is, Kiriath Jearim). [10]Then it curved westward from Baalah to Mount Seir, ran along the northern

---

[a]9 Deut. 1:36   [b]2 That is, the Dead Sea; also in verse 5   [c]3 Hebrew *Akrabbim*   [d]4 Hebrew *your*

THE CONFIDENCE OF CALEB

Individual: Jerry, fifteen.

Role Models: a really talented rock band member and a movie star with a great, muscular physique.

Description: Jerry is a Christian who's going through a rebellious period in his life. He goes to church (because his parents make him), but he'd much rather be listening to music with his fourteen-year-old girlfriend Cathy.

Result: Jerry's big thing now is to say, "Why do we always have to do everything by the Bible? How do we know all that stuff is true?"

Look It Up
••••

We've got just the role model for Jerry (or anyone else who feels like he does): Caleb. Caleb is an Old Testament character more of us should imitate. Check out Caleb's attitude—even though he was in a minority of two!

Caleb believed God completely. When the Israelites were saying they couldn't conquer Canaan because of the strength of the people who lived there, Caleb "silenced the people . . . and said, 'We should go up and take possession of the land, for we can certainly do it. . . . The LORD is with us. Do not be afraid of them' " (Numbers 13:30; 14:9).

Caleb followed God completely. Six times the Bible notes that Caleb followed God wholeheartedly (Numbers 14:24; 32:12; Deuteronomy 1:36; Joshua 14:8–9,14)!

Think It Through
••••

Caleb wasn't a "spiritual superman." He was a normal person just like you are. God promised to give Canaan to the Israelites; that settled it for Caleb. He responded, "God, I believe you, and I'll obey you."

Are you like that? Or more like Jerry who doubts God and would rather go his own way?

Work It Out
••••

Copy Caleb today.

Believe God's Word completely. That means you have to spend time in it! When God makes a promise to believers, claim it for yourself (if you are, in fact, a believer). That's what faith is—putting your confidence in what God says. Find a promise in the Bible, copy it down and claim it today.

Follow God's Word completely. If you're involved in a certain activity that is wrong—gossiping, lying, cheating, stealing, lusting, swearing—cut it out! Don't follow the Lord in some areas but not in others. Remember: Caleb was commended for following *wholeheartedly!*

Nail It Down
••••

Read Joshua 14:6–15 to find out what Caleb received for his wholeheartedness.

Turn to pages 267 and 1147 for other readings on heroes.
Turn to page 239 for Friday's reading.

Topic
••••

HEROES

slope of Mount Jearim (that is, Kesalon), continued down to Beth Shemesh and crossed to Timnah. **11**It went to the northern slope of Ekron, turned toward Shikkeron, passed along to Mount Baalah and reached Jabneel. The boundary ended at the sea.

12The western boundary is the coastline of the Great Sea.*a*

These are the boundaries around the people of Judah by their clans.

13In accordance with the Lord's command to him, Joshua gave to Caleb son of Jephunneh a portion in Judah—Kiriath Arba, that is, Hebron. (Arba was the forefather of Anak.) **14**From Hebron Caleb drove out the three Anakites—Sheshai, Ahiman and Talmai—descendants of Anak. **15**From there he marched against the people living in Debir (formerly called Kiriath Sepher). **16**And Caleb said, "I will give my daughter Acsah in marriage to the man who attacks and captures Kiriath Sepher." **17**Othniel son of Kenaz, Caleb's brother, took it; so Caleb gave his daughter Acsah to him in marriage.

18One day when she came to Othniel, she urged him*b* to ask her father for a field. When she got off her donkey, Caleb asked her, "What can I do for you?"

19She replied, "Do me a special favor. Since you have given me land in the Negev, give me also springs of water." So Caleb gave her the upper and lower springs.

20This is the inheritance of the tribe of Judah, clan by clan:

21The southernmost towns of the tribe of Judah in the Negev toward the boundary of Edom were:

Kabzeel, Eder, Jagur, **22**Kinah, Dimonah, Adadah, **23**Kedesh, Hazor, Ithnan, **24**Ziph, Telem, Bealoth, **25**Hazor Hadattah, Kerioth Hezron (that is, Hazor), **26**Amam, Shema, Moladah, **27**Hazar Gaddah, Heshmon, Beth Pelet, **28**Hazar Shual, Beersheba, Biziothiah, **29**Baalah, Iim, Ezem, **30**Eltolad, Kesil, Hormah, **31**Ziklag, Madmannah, Sansannah, **32**Lebaoth, Shilhim, Ain and Rimmon—a total of twenty-nine towns and their villages.

33In the western foothills:

Eshtaol, Zorah, Ashnah, **34**Zanoah, En Gannim, Tappuah, Enam, **35**Jar-

muth, Adullam, Socoh, Azekah, **36**Shaaraim, Adithaim and Gederah (or Gederothaim)*c*—fourteen towns and their villages.

37Zenan, Hadashah, Migdal Gad, **38**Dilean, Mizpah, Joktheel, **39**Lachish, Bozkath, Eglon, **40**Cabbon, Lahmas, Kitlish, **41**Gederoth, Beth Dagon, Naamah and Makkedah—sixteen towns and their villages.

42Libnah, Ether, Ashan, **43**Iphtah, Ashnah, Nezib, **44**Keilah, Aczib and Mareshah—nine towns and their villages.

45Ekron, with its surrounding settlements and villages; **46**west of Ekron, all that were in the vicinity of Ashdod, together with their villages; **47**Ashdod, its surrounding settlements and villages; and Gaza, its settlements and villages, as far as the Wadi of Egypt and the coastline of the Great Sea.

48In the hill country:

Shamir, Jattir, Socoh, **49**Dannah, Kiriath Sannah (that is, Debir), **50**Anab, Eshtemoh, Anim, **51**Goshen, Holon and Giloh—eleven towns and their villages.

52Arab, Dumah, Eshan, **53**Janim, Beth Tappuah, Aphekah, **54**Humtah, Kiriath Arba (that is, Hebron) and Zior—nine towns and their villages.

55Maon, Carmel, Ziph, Juttah, **56**Jezreel, Jokdeam, Zanoah, **57**Kain, Gibeah and Timnah—ten towns and their villages.

58Halhul, Beth Zur, Gedor, **59**Maarath, Beth Anoth and Eltekon—six towns and their villages.

60Kiriath Baal (that is, Kiriath Jearim) and Rabbah—two towns and their villages.

61In the desert:

Beth Arabah, Middin, Secacah, **62**Nibshan, the City of Salt and En Gedi—six towns and their villages.

63Judah could not dislodge the Jebusites, who were living in Jerusalem; to this day the Jebusites live there with the people of Judah.

Allotment for Ephraim and Manasseh

16 The allotment for Joseph began at the Jordan of Jericho,*d* east of the waters of Jericho, and went up from there through the desert into the hill country of Bethel. **2**It went on from

---

*a*12 That is, the Mediterranean; also in verse 47   *b*18 Hebrew and some Septuagint manuscripts; other Septuagint manuscripts (see also note at Judges 1:14) *Othniel, he urged her*   *c*36 Or *Gederah and Gederothaim*   *d*1 *Jordan of Jericho* was possibly an ancient name for the Jordan River.

Bethel (that is, Luz),[a] crossed over to the territory of the Arkites in Ataroth, [3]descended westward to the territory of the Japhletites as far as the region of Lower Beth Horon and on to Gezer, ending at the sea. [4]So Manasseh and Ephraim, the descendants of Joseph, received their inheritance.

[5]This was the territory of Ephraim, clan by clan:

The boundary of their inheritance went from Ataroth Addar in the east to Upper Beth Horon [6]and continued to the sea. From Micmethath on the north it curved eastward to Taanath Shiloh, passing by it to Janoah on the east. [7]Then it went down from Janoah to Ataroth and Naarah, touched Jericho and came out at the Jordan. [8]From Tappuah the border went west to the Kanah Ravine and ended at the sea. This was the inheritance of the tribe of the Ephraimites, clan by clan. [9]It also included all the towns and their villages that were set aside for the Ephraimites within the inheritance of the Manassites.

[10]They did not dislodge the Canaanites living in Gezer; to this day the Canaanites live among the people of Ephraim but are required to do forced labor.

17 This was the allotment for the tribe of Manasseh as Joseph's firstborn, that is, for Makir, Manasseh's firstborn. Makir was the ancestor of the Gileadites, who had received Gilead and Bashan because the Makirites were great soldiers. [2]So this allotment was for the rest of the people of Manasseh — the clans of Abiezer, Helek, Asriel, Shechem, Hepher and Shemida. These are the other male descendants of Manasseh son of Joseph by their clans.

[3]Now Zelophehad son of Hepher, the son of Gilead, the son of Makir, the son of Manasseh, had no sons but only daughters, whose names were Mahlah, Noah, Hoglah, Milcah and Tirzah. [4]They went to Eleazar the priest, Joshua son of Nun, and the leaders and said, "The LORD commanded Moses to give us an inheritance among our brothers." So Joshua gave them an inheritance along with the brothers of their father, according to the LORD's command. [5]Manasseh's share consisted of ten tracts of land besides Gilead and Bashan east of the Jordan, [6]because the daughters of the tribe of Ma-

nasseh received an inheritance among the sons. The land of Gilead belonged to the rest of the descendants of Manasseh.

[7]The territory of Manasseh extended from Asher to Micmethath east of Shechem. The boundary ran southward from there to include the people living at En Tappuah. [8](Manasseh had the land of Tappuah, but Tappuah itself, on the boundary of Manasseh, belonged to the Ephraimites.) [9]Then the boundary continued south to the Kanah Ravine. There were towns belonging to Ephraim lying among the towns of Manasseh, but the boundary of Manasseh was the northern side of the ravine and ended at the sea. [10]On the south the land belonged to Ephraim, on the north to Manasseh. The territory of Manasseh reached the sea and bordered Asher on the north and Issachar on the east. [11]Within Issachar and Asher, Manasseh also had Beth Shan, Ibleam and the people of Dor, Endor, Taanach and Megiddo, together with their surrounding settlements (the third in the list is Naphoth[b]).

[12]Yet the Manassites were not able to occupy these towns, for the Canaanites were determined to live in that region. [13]However, when the Israelites grew stronger, they subjected the Canaanites to forced labor but did not drive them out completely.

[14]The people of Joseph said to Joshua, "Why have you given us only one allotment and one portion for an inheritance? We are a numerous people and the LORD has blessed us abundantly."

[15]"If you are so numerous," Joshua answered, "and if the hill country of Ephraim is too small for you, go up into the forest and clear land for yourselves there in the land of the Perizzites and Rephaites."

[16]The people of Joseph replied, "The hill country is not enough for us, and all the Canaanites who live in the plain have iron chariots, both those in Beth Shan and its settlements and those in the Valley of Jezreel."

[17]But Joshua said to the house of Joseph — to Ephraim and Manasseh — "You are numerous and very powerful. You will have not only one allotment [18]but the forested hill country as well. Clear it, and its farthest limits will be yours; though the Canaanites have iron chariots and though they are strong, you can drive them out."

---

[a]2 Septuagint; Hebrew *Bethel to Luz*   [b]11 That is, Naphoth Dor

Division of the Rest of the Land

18 The whole assembly of the Israelites gathered at Shiloh and set up the Tent of Meeting there. The country was brought under their control, ²but there were still seven Israelite tribes who had not yet received their inheritance.

³So Joshua said to the Israelites: "How long will you wait before you begin to take possession of the land that the Lord, the God of your fathers, has given you? ⁴Appoint three men from each tribe. I will send them out to make a survey of the land and to write a description of it, according to the inheritance of each. Then they will return to me. ⁵You are to divide the land into seven parts. Judah is to remain in its territory on the south and the house of Joseph in its territory on the north. ⁶After you have written descriptions of the seven parts of the land, bring them here to me and I will cast lots for you in the presence of the Lord our God. ⁷The Levites, however, do not get a portion among you, because the priestly service of the Lord is their inheritance. And Gad, Reuben and the half-tribe of Manasseh have already received their inheritance on the east side of the Jordan. Moses the servant of the Lord gave it to them."

⁸As the men started on their way to map out the land, Joshua instructed them, "Go and make a survey of the land and write a description of it. Then return to me, and I will cast lots for you here at Shiloh in the presence of the Lord." ⁹So the men left and went through the land. They wrote its description on a scroll, town by town, in seven parts, and returned to Joshua in the camp at Shiloh. ¹⁰Joshua then cast lots for them in Shiloh in the presence of the Lord, and there he distributed the land to the Israelites according to their tribal divisions.

Allotment for Benjamin

¹¹The lot came up for the tribe of Benjamin, clan by clan. Their allotted territory lay between the tribes of Judah and Joseph:

¹²On the north side their boundary began at the Jordan, passed the northern slope of Jericho and headed west into the hill country, coming out at the desert of Beth Aven. ¹³From there it crossed to the south slope of Luz (that is, Bethel) and went down to Ataroth

Addar on the hill south of Lower Beth Horon.

¹⁴From the hill facing Beth Horon on the south the boundary turned south along the western side and came out at Kiriath Baal (that is, Kiriath Jearim), a town of the people of Judah. This was the western side.

¹⁵The southern side began at the outskirts of Kiriath Jearim on the west, and the boundary came out at the spring of the waters of Nephtoah. ¹⁶The boundary went down to the foot of the hill facing the Valley of Ben Hinnom, north of the Valley of Rephaim. It continued down the Hinnom Valley along the southern slope of the Jebusite city and so to En Rogel. ¹⁷It then curved north, went to En Shemesh, continued to Geliloth, which faces the Pass of Adummim, and ran down to the Stone of Bohan son of Reuben. ¹⁸It continued to the northern slope of Beth Arabah[a] and on down into the Arabah. ¹⁹It then went to the northern slope of Beth Hoglah and came out at the northern bay of the Salt Sea,[b] at the mouth of the Jordan in the south. This was the southern boundary.

²⁰The Jordan formed the boundary on the eastern side.

These were the boundaries that marked out the inheritance of the clans of Benjamin on all sides.

²¹The tribe of Benjamin, clan by clan, had the following cities:

Jericho, Beth Hoglah, Emek Keziz, ²²Beth Arabah, Zemaraim, Bethel, ²³Avvim, Parah, Ophrah, ²⁴Kephar Ammoni, Ophni and Geba — twelve towns and their villages.

²⁵Gibeon, Ramah, Beeroth, ²⁶Mizpah, Kephirah, Mozah, ²⁷Rekem, Irpeel, Taralah, ²⁸Zelah, Haeleph, the Jebusite city (that is, Jerusalem), Gibeah and Kiriath — fourteen towns and their villages.

This was the inheritance of Benjamin for its clans.

Allotment for Simeon

19 The second lot came out for the tribe of Simeon, clan by clan. Their inheritance lay within the territory of Judah. ²It included:

---

a 18 Septuagint; Hebrew *slope facing the Arabah*   *b 19* That is, the Dead Sea

Beersheba (or Sheba),[a] Moladah, [3]Hazar Shual, Balah, Ezem, [4]Eltolad, Bethul, Hormah, [5]Ziklag, Beth Marcaboth, Hazar Susah, [6]Beth Lebaoth and Sharuhen—thirteen towns and their villages;

[7]Ain, Rimmon, Ether and Ashan— four towns and their villages— [8]and all the villages around these towns as far as Baalath Beer (Ramah in the Negev).

This was the inheritance of the tribe of the Simeonites, clan by clan. [9]The inheritance of the Simeonites was taken from the share of Judah, because Judah's portion was more than they needed. So the Simeonites received their inheritance within the territory of Judah.

Allotment for Zebulun

[10]The third lot came up for Zebulun, clan by clan:

The boundary of their inheritance went as far as Sarid. [11]Going west it ran to Maralah, touched Dabbesheth, and extended to the ravine near Jokneam. [12]It turned east from Sarid toward the sunrise to the territory of Kisloth Tabor and went on to Daberath and up to Japhia. [13]Then it continued eastward to Gath Hepher and Eth Kazin; it came out at Rimmon and turned toward Neah. [14]There the boundary went around on the north to Hannathon and ended at the Valley of Iphtah El. [15]Included were Kattath, Nahalal, Shimron, Idalah and Bethlehem. There were twelve towns and their villages.

[16]These towns and their villages were the inheritance of Zebulun, clan by clan.

Allotment for Issachar

[17]The fourth lot came out for Issachar, clan by clan. [18]Their territory included:

Jezreel, Kesulloth, Shunem, [19]Hapharaim, Shion, Anaharath, [20]Rabbith, Kishion, Ebez, [21]Remeth, En Gannim, En Haddah and Beth Pazzez. [22]The boundary touched Tabor, Shahazumah and Beth Shemesh, and ended at the Jordan. There were sixteen towns and their villages.

[23]These towns and their villages were the inheritance of the tribe of Issachar, clan by clan.

Allotment for Asher

[24]The fifth lot came out for the tribe of Asher, clan by clan. [25]Their territory included:

Helkath, Hali, Beten, Acshaph, [26]Allammelech, Amad and Mishal. On the west the boundary touched Carmel and Shihor Libnath. [27]It then turned east toward Beth Dagon, touched Zebulun and the Valley of Iphtah El, and went north to Beth Emek and Neiel, passing Cabul on the left. [28]It went to Abdon,[b] Rehob, Hammon and Kanah, as far as Greater Sidon. [29]The boundary then turned back toward Ramah and went to the fortified city of Tyre, turned toward Hosah and came out at the sea in the region of Aczib, [30]Ummah, Aphek and Rehob. There were twenty-two towns and their villages.

[31]These towns and their villages were the inheritance of the tribe of Asher, clan by clan.

Allotment for Naphtali

[32]The sixth lot came out for Naphtali, clan by clan:

[33]Their boundary went from Heleph and the large tree in Zaanannim, passing Adami Nekeb and Jabneel to Lakkum and ending at the Jordan. [34]The boundary ran west through Aznoth Tabor and came out at Hukkok. It touched Zebulun on the south, Asher on the west and the Jordan[c] on the east. [35]The fortified cities were Ziddim, Zer, Hammath, Rakkath, Kinnereth, [36]Adamah, Ramah, Hazor, [37]Kedesh, Edrei, En Hazor, [38]Iron, Migdal El, Horem, Beth Anath and Beth Shemesh. There were nineteen towns and their villages.

[39]These towns and their villages were the inheritance of the tribe of Naphtali, clan by clan.

Allotment for Dan

[40]The seventh lot came out for the tribe of Dan, clan by clan. [41]The territory of their inheritance included:

Zorah, Eshtaol, Ir Shemesh, [42]Shaalabbin, Aijalon, Ithlah, [43]Elon, Timnah, Ekron, [44]Eltekeh, Gibbethon, Baalath, [45]Jehud, Bene Berak, Gath Rimmon, [46]Me Jarkon and Rakkon, with the area facing Joppa.

[47](But the Danites had difficulty taking possession of their territory, so they went up

---

[a]2 Or Beersheba, Sheba; 1 Chron. 4:28 does not have Sheba.   [b]28 Some Hebrew manuscripts (see also Joshua 21:30); most Hebrew manuscripts Ebron   [c]34 Septuagint; Hebrew west, and Judah, the Jordan,

and attacked Leshem, took it, put it to the sword and occupied it. They settled in Leshem and named it Dan after their forefather.)

⁴⁸These towns and their villages were the inheritance of the tribe of Dan, clan by clan.

Allotment for Joshua

⁴⁹When they had finished dividing the land into its allotted portions, the Israelites gave Joshua son of Nun an inheritance among them, ⁵⁰as the LORD had commanded. They gave him the town he asked for—Timnath Serahᵃ in the hill country of Ephraim. And he built up the town and settled there.

⁵¹These are the territories that Eleazar the priest, Joshua son of Nun and the heads of the tribal clans of Israel assigned by lot at Shiloh in the presence of the LORD at the entrance to the Tent of Meeting. And so they finished dividing the land.

Cities of Refuge

20 Then the LORD said to Joshua: ²"Tell the Israelites to designate the cities of refuge, as I instructed you through Moses, ³so that anyone who kills a person accidentally and unintentionally may flee there and find protection from the avenger of blood.

⁴"When he flees to one of these cities, he is to stand in the entrance of the city gate and state his case before the elders of that city. Then they are to admit him into their city and give him a place to live with them. ⁵If the avenger of blood pursues him, they must not surrender the one accused, because he killed his neighbor unintentionally and without malice aforethought. ⁶He is to stay in that city until he has stood trial before the assembly and until the death of the high priest who is serving at that time. Then he may go back to his own home in the town from which he fled."

⁷So they set apart Kedesh in Galilee in the hill country of Naphtali, Shechem in the hill country of Ephraim, and Kiriath Arba (that is, Hebron) in the hill country of Judah. ⁸On the east side of the Jordan of Jerichoᵇ they designated Bezer in the desert on the plateau in the tribe of Reuben, Ramoth in Gilead in the tribe of Gad, and Golan in Bashan in the tribe of Manasseh. ⁹Any of the Israelites or any alien living among them who killed someone accidentally could flee to these designated cities and not be killed by

the avenger of blood prior to standing trial before the assembly.

Towns for the Levites

21 Now the family heads of the Levites approached Eleazar the priest, Joshua son of Nun, and the heads of the other tribal families of Israel ²at Shiloh in Canaan and said to them, "The LORD commanded through Moses that you give us towns to live in, with pasturelands for our livestock." ³So, as the LORD had commanded, the Israelites gave the Levites the following towns and pasturelands out of their own inheritance:

⁴The first lot came out for the Kohathites, clan by clan. The Levites who were descendants of Aaron the priest were allotted thirteen towns from the tribes of Judah, Simeon and Benjamin. ⁵The rest of Kohath's descendants were allotted ten towns from the clans of the tribes of Ephraim, Dan and half of Manasseh.

⁶The descendants of Gershon were allotted thirteen towns from the clans of the tribes of Issachar, Asher, Naphtali and the half-tribe of Manasseh in Bashan.

⁷The descendants of Merari, clan by clan, received twelve towns from the tribes of Reuben, Gad and Zebulun.

⁸So the Israelites allotted to the Levites these towns and their pasturelands, as the LORD had commanded through Moses.

⁹From the tribes of Judah and Simeon they allotted the following towns by name ¹⁰(these towns were assigned to the descendants of Aaron who were from the Kohathite clans of the Levites, because the first lot fell to them):

¹¹They gave them Kiriath Arba (that is, Hebron), with its surrounding pastureland, in the hill country of Judah. (Arba was the forefather of Anak.) ¹²But the fields and villages around the city they had given to Caleb son of Jephunneh as his possession.

¹³So to the descendants of Aaron the priest they gave Hebron (a city of refuge for one accused of murder), Libnah, ¹⁴Jattir, Eshtemoa, ¹⁵Holon, Debir, ¹⁶Ain, Juttah and Beth Shemesh, together with their pasturelands—nine towns from these two tribes.

¹⁷And from the tribe of Benjamin they gave them Gibeon, Geba, ¹⁸Ana-

---

ᵃ50 Also known as *Timnath Heres* (see Judges 2:9)   ᵇ8 *Jordan of Jericho* was possibly an ancient name for the Jordan River.

thoth and Almon, together with their pasturelands—four towns. ¹⁹All the towns for the priests, the descendants of Aaron, were thirteen, together with their pasturelands.

²⁰The rest of the Kohathite clans of the Levites were allotted towns from the tribe of Ephraim:

²¹In the hill country of Ephraim they were given Shechem (a city of refuge for one accused of murder) and Gezer, ²²Kibzaim and Beth Horon, together with their pasturelands—four towns.

²³Also from the tribe of Dan they received Eltekeh, Gibbethon, ²⁴Aijalon and Gath Rimmon, together with their pasturelands—four towns.

²⁵From half the tribe of Manasseh they received Taanach and Gath Rimmon, together with their pasturelands—two towns.

²⁶All these ten towns and their pasturelands were given to the rest of the Kohathite clans.

²⁷The Levite clans of the Gershonites were given:

from the half-tribe of Manasseh,
Golan in Bashan (a city of refuge for one accused of murder) and Be Eshtarah, together with their pasturelands—two towns;

²⁸from the tribe of Issachar,
Kishion, Daberath, ²⁹Jarmuth and En Gannim, together with their pasturelands—four towns;

³⁰from the tribe of Asher,
Mishal, Abdon, ³¹Helkath and Rehob, together with their pasturelands—four towns;

³²from the tribe of Naphtali,
Kedesh in Galilee (a city of refuge for one accused of murder), Hammoth Dor and Kartan, together with their pasturelands—three towns.

³³All the towns of the Gershonite clans were thirteen, together with their pasturelands.

³⁴The Merarite clans (the rest of the Levites) were given:

from the tribe of Zebulun,
Jokneam, Kartah, ³⁵Dimnah and Nahalal, together with their pasturelands—four towns;

³⁶from the tribe of Reuben,
Bezer, Jahaz, ³⁷Kedemoth and Mephaath, together with their pasturelands—four towns;

³⁸from the tribe of Gad,
Ramoth in Gilead (a city of refuge for one accused of murder), Mahanaim, ³⁹Heshbon and Jazer, together with their pasturelands—four towns in all.

⁴⁰All the towns allotted to the Merarite clans, who were the rest of the Levites, were twelve.

⁴¹The towns of the Levites in the territory held by the Israelites were forty-eight in all, together with their pasturelands. ⁴²Each of these towns had pasturelands surrounding it; this was true for all these towns.

⁴³So the LORD gave Israel all the land he had sworn to give their forefathers, and they took possession of it and settled there. ⁴⁴The LORD gave them rest on every side, just as he had sworn to their forefathers. Not one of their enemies withstood them; the LORD handed all their enemies over to them. ⁴⁵Not one of all the LORD's good promises to the house of Israel failed; every one was fulfilled.

Eastern Tribes Return Home

22 Then Joshua summoned the Reubenites, the Gadites and the half-tribe of Manasseh ²and said to them, "You have done all that Moses the servant of the LORD commanded, and you have obeyed me in everything I commanded. ³For a long time now—to this very day—you have not deserted your brothers but have carried out the mission the LORD your God gave you. ⁴Now that the LORD your God has given your brothers rest as he promised, return to your homes in the land that Moses the servant of the LORD gave you on the other side of the Jordan. ⁵But be very careful to keep the commandment and the law that Moses the servant of the LORD gave you: to love the LORD your God, to walk in all his ways, to obey his commands, to hold fast to him and to serve him with all your heart and all your soul."

⁶Then Joshua blessed them and sent them away, and they went to their homes. ⁷(To the half-tribe of Manasseh Moses had given land in Bashan, and to the other half of the tribe Joshua gave land on the west side of the Jordan with their brothers.) When Joshua sent them home, he blessed them, ⁸saying, "Return to your homes with your great wealth—with large herds of livestock, with silver, gold, bronze and iron, and a great quantity of clothing—and divide with your brothers the plunder from your enemies."

⁹So the Reubenites, the Gadites and the half-tribe of Manasseh left the Israelites at Shiloh in Canaan to return to Gilead, their

own land, which they had acquired in accordance with the command of the Lord through Moses.

10When they came to Geliloth near the Jordan in the land of Canaan, the Reubenites, the Gadites and the half-tribe of Manasseh built an imposing altar there by the Jordan. **11**And when the Israelites heard that they had built the altar on the border of Canaan at Geliloth near the Jordan on the Israelite side, **12**the whole assembly of Israel gathered at Shiloh to go to war against them.

13So the Israelites sent Phinehas son of Eleazar, the priest, to the land of Gilead — to Reuben, Gad and the half-tribe of Manasseh. **14**With him they sent ten of the chief men, one for each of the tribes of Israel, each the head of a family division among the Israelite clans.

15When they went to Gilead — to Reuben, Gad and the half-tribe of Manasseh — they said to them: **16**"The whole assembly of the Lord says: 'How could you break faith with the God of Israel like this? How could you turn away from the Lord and build yourselves an altar in rebellion against him now? **17**Was not the sin of Peor enough for us? Up to this very day we have not cleansed ourselves from that sin, even though a plague fell on the community of the Lord! **18**And are you now turning away from the Lord?

" 'If you rebel against the Lord today, tomorrow he will be angry with the whole community of Israel. **19**If the land you possess is defiled, come over to the Lord's land, where the Lord's tabernacle stands, and share the land with us. But do not rebel against the Lord or against us by building an altar for yourselves, other than the altar of the Lord our God. **20**When Achan son of Zerah acted unfaithfully regarding the devoted things,*a* did not wrath come upon the whole community of Israel? He was not the only one who died for his sin.' "

21Then Reuben, Gad and the half-tribe of Manasseh replied to the heads of the clans of Israel: **22**"The Mighty One, God, the Lord! The Mighty One, God, the Lord! He knows! And let Israel know! If this has been in rebellion or disobedience to the Lord, do not spare us this day. **23**If we have built our own altar to turn away from the Lord and to offer burnt offerings and grain offerings, or to sacrifice fellowship offerings*b* on it, may the Lord himself call us to account.

24"No! We did it for fear that some day your descendants might say to ours, 'What do you have to do with the Lord, the God of Israel? **25**The Lord has made the Jordan a boundary between us and you — you Reubenites and Gadites! You have no share in the Lord.' So your descendants might cause ours to stop fearing the Lord.

26"That is why we said, 'Let us get ready and build an altar — but not for burnt offerings or sacrifices.' **27**On the contrary, it is to be a witness between us and you and the generations that follow, that we will worship the Lord at his sanctuary with our burnt offerings, sacrifices and fellowship offerings. Then in the future your descendants will not be able to say to ours, 'You have no share in the Lord.'

28"And we said, 'If they ever say this to us, or to our descendants, we will answer: Look at the replica of the Lord's altar, which our fathers built, not for burnt offerings and sacrifices, but as a witness between us and you.'

29"Far be it from us to rebel against the Lord and turn away from him today by building an altar for burnt offerings, grain offerings and sacrifices, other than the altar of the Lord our God that stands before his tabernacle."

30When Phinehas the priest and the leaders of the community — the heads of the clans of the Israelites — heard what Reuben, Gad and Manasseh had to say, they were pleased. **31**And Phinehas son of Eleazar, the priest, said to Reuben, Gad and Manasseh, "Today we know that the Lord is with us, because you have not acted unfaithfully toward the Lord in this matter. Now you have rescued the Israelites from the Lord's hand."

32Then Phinehas son of Eleazar, the priest, and the leaders returned to Canaan from their meeting with the Reubenites and Gadites in Gilead and reported to the Israelites. **33**They were glad to hear the report and praised God. And they talked no more about going to war against them to devastate the country where the Reubenites and the Gadites lived.

34And the Reubenites and the Gadites gave the altar this name: A Witness Between Us that the Lord is God.

Joshua's Farewell to the Leaders

23 After a long time had passed and the Lord had given Israel rest from all their enemies around them, Joshua, by then

---

a20 The Hebrew term refers to the irrevocable giving over of things or persons to the Lord, often by totally destroying them.   *b23* Traditionally *peace offerings*; also in verse 27 old and well advanced in years, **2**summoned all Israel—their elders, leaders, judges and officials—and said to them: "I am old and well advanced in years. **3**You yourselves have seen everything the Lord your God has done to all these nations for your sake; it was the Lord your God who fought for you. **4**Remember how I have allotted as an inheritance for your tribes all the land of the nations that remain—the nations I conquered—between the Jordan and the Great Sea*a* in the west. **5**The Lord your God himself will drive them out of your way. He will push them out before you, and you will take possession of their land, as the Lord your God promised you.

6"Be very strong; be careful to obey all that is written in the Book of the Law of Moses, without turning aside to the right or to the left. **7**Do not associate with these nations that remain among you; do not invoke the names of their gods or swear by them. You must not serve them or bow down to them. **8**But you are to hold fast to the Lord your God, as you have until now.

9"The Lord has driven out before you great and powerful nations; to this day no one has been able to withstand you. **10**One of you routs a thousand, because the Lord your God fights for you, just as he promised. **11**So be very careful to love the Lord your God.

12"But if you turn away and ally yourselves with the survivors of these nations that remain among you and if you intermarry with them and associate with them, **13**then you may be sure that the Lord your God will no longer drive out these nations before you. Instead, they will become snares and traps for you, whips on your backs and thorns in your eyes, until you perish from this good land, which the Lord your God has given you.

14"Now I am about to go the way of all the earth. You know with all your heart and soul that not one of all the good promises the Lord your God gave you has failed. Every promise has been fulfilled; not one has failed. **15**But just as every good promise of the Lord your God has come true, so the Lord will bring on you all the evil he has threatened, until he has destroyed you from this good land he has given you. **16**If you violate the covenant of the Lord your God, which he commanded you, and go and serve other gods and bow down to them, the Lord's an-

ger will burn against you, and you will quickly perish from the good land he has given you."

The Covenant Renewed at Shechem

24 Then Joshua assembled all the tribes of Israel at Shechem. He summoned the elders, leaders, judges and officials of Israel, and they presented themselves before God.

2Joshua said to all the people, "This is what the Lord, the God of Israel, says: 'Long ago your forefathers, including Terah the father of Abraham and Nahor, lived beyond the River*b* and worshiped other gods. **3**But I took your father Abraham from the land beyond the River and led him throughout Canaan and gave him many descendants. I gave him Isaac, **4**and to Isaac I gave Jacob and Esau. I assigned the hill country of Seir to Esau, but Jacob and his sons went down to Egypt.

5"'Then I sent Moses and Aaron, and I afflicted the Egyptians by what I did there, and I brought you out. **6**When I brought your fathers out of Egypt, you came to the sea, and the Egyptians pursued them with chariots and horsemen*c* as far as the Red Sea.*d* **7**But they cried to the Lord for help, and he put darkness between you and the Egyptians; he brought the sea over them and covered them. You saw with your own eyes what I did to the Egyptians. Then you lived in the desert for a long time.

8"'I brought you to the land of the Amorites who lived east of the Jordan. They fought against you, but I gave them into your hands. I destroyed them from before you, and you took possession of their land. **9**When Balak son of Zippor, the king of Moab, prepared to fight against Israel, he sent for Balaam son of Beor to put a curse on you. **10**But I would not listen to Balaam, so he blessed you again and again, and I delivered you out of his hand.

11"'Then you crossed the Jordan and came to Jericho. The citizens of Jericho fought against you, as did also the Amorites, Perizzites, Canaanites, Hittites, Girgashites, Hivites and Jebusites, but I gave them into your hands. **12**I sent the hornet ahead of you, which drove them out before you—also the two Amorite kings. You did not do it with your own sword and bow. **13**So I gave you a land on which you did not toil and cities you did not build; and you live in them and eat from vineyards and olive groves that you did not plant.'

[14]"Now fear the Lord and serve him with all faithfulness. Throw away the gods your forefathers worshiped beyond the River and in Egypt, and serve the Lord. [15]But if serving the Lord seems undesirable to you, then choose for yourselves this day whom you will serve, whether the gods your forefathers served beyond the River, or the gods of the Amorites, in whose land you are living. But as for me and my household, we will serve the Lord."

[16]Then the people answered, "Far be it from us to forsake the Lord to serve other gods! [17]It was the Lord our God himself who brought us and our fathers up out of Egypt, from that land of slavery, and performed those great signs before our eyes. He protected us on our entire journey and among all the nations through which we traveled. [18]And the Lord drove out before us all the nations, including the Amorites, who lived in the land. We too will serve the Lord, because he is our God."

[19]Joshua said to the people, "You are not able to serve the Lord. He is a holy God; he is a jealous God. He will not forgive your rebellion and your sins. [20]If you forsake the Lord and serve foreign gods, he will turn and bring disaster on you and make an end of you, after he has been good to you."

[21]But the people said to Joshua, "No! We will serve the Lord."

[22]Then Joshua said, "You are witnesses against yourselves that you have chosen to serve the Lord."

"Yes, we are witnesses," they replied.

[23]"Now then," said Joshua, "throw away the foreign gods that are among you and yield your hearts to the Lord, the God of Israel."

[24]And the people said to Joshua, "We will serve the Lord our God and obey him."

[25]On that day Joshua made a covenant for the people, and there at Shechem he drew up for them decrees and laws. [26]And Joshua recorded these things in the Book of the Law of God. Then he took a large stone and set it up there under the oak near the holy place of the Lord.

[27]"See!" he said to all the people. "This stone will be a witness against us. It has heard all the words the Lord has said to us. It will be a witness against you if you are untrue to your God."

Buried in the Promised Land

[28]Then Joshua sent the people away, each to his own inheritance.

[29]After these things, Joshua son of Nun, the servant of the Lord, died at the age of a hundred and ten. [30]And they buried him in the land of his inheritance, at Timnath Serah[a] in the hill country of Ephraim, north of Mount Gaash.

[31]Israel served the Lord throughout the lifetime of Joshua and of the elders who outlived him and who had experienced everything the Lord had done for Israel.

[32]And Joseph's bones, which the Israelites had brought up from Egypt, were buried at Shechem in the tract of land that Jacob bought for a hundred pieces of silver[b] from the sons of Hamor, the father of Shechem. This became the inheritance of Joseph's descendants.

[33]And Eleazar son of Aaron died and was buried at Gibeah, which had been allotted to his son Phinehas in the hill country of Ephraim.

---

[a]30 Also known as *Timnath Heres* (see Judges 2:9)   [b]32 Hebrew *hundred kesitahs*; a kesitah was a unit of money of unknown weight and value.

THE ALIBIS OF ALL THE GUYS

On the final night of a ski retreat, the students are challenged to give their lives to Jesus Christ. Thirteen do. But a few of the guys think up excuses for not making such a firm commitment.

Al reasons, "I'm too young for that right now. There's too much I want to do. I'll get serious about God when I'm older."

Keith argues, "What is this guy's problem? God loves everybody, so why all this talk about hell and this heavy pressure to 'get saved'?"

Kirby protests, "I'm not doing anything until somebody can answer all my questions. For instance, why is there so much pain and suffering in the world?"

Look It Up
••••

Those seem like pretty good excuses until you hear how God answers each one:

To those who say, "Maybe later," God replies: "I tell you, now is the time of God's favor, now is the day of salvation" (2 Corinthians 6:2).

To those who insist, "Everybody goes to heaven because God is love," the Lord responds: "Unless you repent, you too will all perish" (Luke 13:3).

To those who charge, "There are too many mysteries," the Bible warns: "The secret things belong to the LORD our God" (Deuteronomy 29:29).

Think It Through
••••

Consider these questions, which correspond to the excuses above:

1. Why is it dangerous to put off the decision to trust Christ?
2. Is it better to trust in your opinions and feelings about what you imagine God ought to be like, or to believe what he actually says he is like?
3. Does the fact that you probably can't explain how a TV works keep you from watching your favorite program?

Work It Out
••••

If you have never trusted Christ because of one of the excuses above, you're on shaky ground. Trust him now. Accept the forgiveness he offers and tell him you want to begin a real relationship with him.

If you have friends who keep using the excuses above, share with them the appropriate Bible verses on this page. Talk to them. Don't come on like a high-pressure salesperson, but gently urge them to make a decision for Christ.

Nail It Down
••••

Read Joshua 24:15 for Joshua's encouragement to make a decision for or against following the Lord.

Turn to pages 288 and 784 for other readings on excuses.
Turn to page 246 for the weekend reading.

Topic
••••
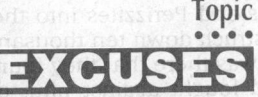

FOLLOWING the conquering of the promised land, the Israelites establish a tragic cycle of behavior. They serve idols; God sends an enemy as punishment; the oppressed people cry out in repentance; God raises up a judge (such as Deborah, Gideon or Samson) to save them; peace is restored. This cycle repeats itself seven times. As you read Judges, keep in mind that God doesn't tolerate sin—in nations or in individuals. But he always extends his unfailing love when his people confess and repent.

Outline of Contents

Israel Fights the Remaining Canaanites

1 After the death of Joshua, the Israelites asked the LORD, "Who will be the first to go up and fight for us against the Canaanites?"

²The LORD answered, "Judah is to go; I have given the land into their hands."

³Then the men of Judah said to the Simeonites their brothers, "Come up with us into the territory allotted to us, to fight against the Canaanites. We in turn will go with you into yours." So the Simeonites went with them.

⁴When Judah attacked, the LORD gave the Canaanites and Perizzites into their hands and they struck down ten thousand men at Bezek. ⁵It was there that they found Adoni-Bezek and fought against him, putting to rout the Canaanites and Perizzites. ⁶Adoni-Bezek fled, but they chased him and caught him, and cut off his thumbs and big toes.

⁷Then Adoni-Bezek said, "Seventy kings with their thumbs and big toes cut off have picked up scraps under my table. Now God has paid me back for what I did to them." They brought him to Jerusalem, and he died there.

⁸The men of Judah attacked Jerusalem also and took it. They put the city to the sword and set it on fire.

⁹After that, the men of Judah went down to fight against the Canaanites living in the hill country, the Negev and the western foothills. ¹⁰They advanced against the Canaanites living in Hebron (formerly called Kiriath

courage

How do you define courage...?

A fireman running into a burning building to rescue a child?

A person who survives a terrorist attack?

A missionary who travels to a remote village?

Jesus Christ?

What would Jesus do?

Jesus displayed courage in the face of some pretty big obstacles. Here are a few:
When Jesus returned to his hometown of Nazareth, the people in the synagogue grew so furious with what he had to say that they drove him out of town and planned to throw him off a cliff. "But he [Jesus] walked right through the crowd and went on his way" (Luke 4:30).

When Jesus was brought before the Sanhedrin, he knew these religious leaders were looking for a reason to put him to death. His life depended on how he answered their questions.

When the high priest asked him, "Are you the Christ?" Jesus answered, "I am" (Mark 14: 61-62).

While hanging on the cross, Jesus knew escape was only a word away, yet he chose to endure. He showed courage in his actions, in the things he said and in the things he didn't say.

What will you do?

You may not be facing the same trials that Jesus experienced, but there are definitely situations in your life where you can show courage. When you resist temptation, you are courageous. When you know something is wrong and you speak out, you are courageous.

You probably won't have to look very hard for ways to show courage—situations will always arise to challenge you. And Jesus will give you the courage to stand firm. Ask him to give you the courage to do what he would do.

More about courage
Acts 21:13; Philippians 1:27-30; 2 Timothy 1:7

 ?

Discrimination

Have you ever...?

been guilty of discrimination? Before you answer "no" consider this: Christians can be pretty insensitive, even downright nasty. It happens all the time in churches. People who are from different denominations are ignored. People who have disabilities are overlooked. People who just don't fit in for some reason are snubbed.

What would Jesus do?

Jesus was known for reaching out to those in his society who were considered "undesirable." He consistently befriended the tax collectors, the lepers, even the prostitutes—those individuals whom the religious establishment saw as hopeless. He spoke to Zacchaeus, a chief tax collector, and said, "Come down immediately. I must stay at your house today" (Luke 19:5). He dined at the home of Simon the Leper (Matthew 26:6). These were unthinkable acts in a world that categorized and stigmatized many social classes.

Jesus refused to discriminate. As a result, he gave hope to the hopeless. He looked beyond the sins and beyond the circumstances and saw the person. He reminded individuals by his warmth and generosity that he loved them even before they were in their mother's womb (Psalm 139:13). He demonstrated that God's love can reach everyone.

What will you do?

Following Christ and accepting the title "Christian" is more than simply knowing what words to say or going to church. Being a Christian means reaching out to those who are looked down upon. Is there someone in your school who doesn't wear the latest styles or go to your church? Christianity is not an exclusive club. Don't be guilty of shutting people out. Instead, do what Jesus would do.

More about discrimination

Job 34:18-19; Galatians 6:3-5; Philippians 2:3; James 2:1-4

W.W.J.D.?

Arba) and defeated Sheshai, Ahiman and Talmai.

[11]From there they advanced against the people living in Debir (formerly called Kiriath Sepher). [12]And Caleb said, "I will give my daughter Acsah in marriage to the man who attacks and captures Kiriath Sepher." [13]Othniel son of Kenaz, Caleb's younger brother, took it; so Caleb gave his daughter Acsah to him in marriage.

[14]One day when she came to Othniel, she urged him[a] to ask her father for a field. When she got off her donkey, Caleb asked her, "What can I do for you?"

[15]She replied, "Do me a special favor. Since you have given me land in the Negev, give me also springs of water." Then Caleb gave her the upper and lower springs.

[16]The descendants of Moses' father-in-law, the Kenite, went up from the City of Palms[b] with the men of Judah to live among the people of the Desert of Judah in the Negev near Arad.

[17]Then the men of Judah went with the Simeonites their brothers and attacked the Canaanites living in Zephath, and they totally destroyed[c] the city. Therefore it was called Hormah.[d] [18]The men of Judah also took[e] Gaza, Ashkelon and Ekron—each city with its territory.

[19]The LORD was with the men of Judah. They took possession of the hill country, but they were unable to drive the people from the plains, because they had iron chariots. [20]As Moses had promised, Hebron was given to Caleb, who drove from it the three sons of Anak. [21]The Benjamites, however, failed to dislodge the Jebusites, who were living in Jerusalem; to this day the Jebusites live there with the Benjamites.

[22]Now the house of Joseph attacked Bethel, and the LORD was with them. [23]When they sent men to spy out Bethel (formerly called Luz), [24]the spies saw a man coming out of the city and they said to him, "Show us how to get into the city and we will see that you are treated well." [25]So he showed them, and they put the city to the sword but spared the man and his whole family. [26]He then went to the land of the Hittites, where he built a city and called it Luz, which is its name to this day.

[27]But Manasseh did not drive out the people of Beth Shan or Taanach or Dor or Ible-am or Megiddo and their surrounding settlements, for the Canaanites were determined to live in that land. [28]When Israel became strong, they pressed the Canaanites into forced labor but never drove them out completely. [29]Nor did Ephraim drive out the Canaanites living in Gezer, but the Canaanites continued to live there among them. [30]Neither did Zebulun drive out the Canaanites living in Kitron or Nahalol, who remained among them; but they did subject them to forced labor. [31]Nor did Asher drive out those living in Acco or Sidon or Ahlab or Aczib or Helbah or Aphek or Rehob, [32]and because of this the people of Asher lived among the Canaanite inhabitants of the land. [33]Neither did Naphtali drive out those living in Beth Shemesh or Beth Anath; but the Naphtalites too lived among the Canaanite inhabitants of the land, and those living in Beth Shemesh and Beth Anath became forced laborers for them. [34]The Amorites confined the Danites to the hill country, not allowing them to come down into the plain. [35]And the Amorites were determined also to hold out in Mount Heres, Aijalon and Shaalbim, but when the power of the house of Joseph increased, they too were pressed into forced labor. [36]The boundary of the Amorites was from Scorpion[f] Pass to Sela and beyond.

The Angel of the LORD at Bokim

2 The angel of the LORD went up from Gilgal to Bokim and said, "I brought you up out of Egypt and led you into the land that I swore to give to your forefathers. I said, 'I will never break my covenant with you, [2]and you shall not make a covenant with the people of this land, but you shall break down their altars.' Yet you have disobeyed me. Why have you done this? [3]Now therefore I tell you that I will not drive them out before you; they will be ˌthornsˌ in your sides and their gods will be a snare to you."

[4]When the angel of the LORD had spoken these things to all the Israelites, the people wept aloud, [5]and they called that place Bokim.[g] There they offered sacrifices to the LORD.

Disobedience and Defeat

[6]After Joshua had dismissed the Israelites, they went to take possession of the land, each to his own inheritance. [7]The people

---

[a]14 Hebrew; Septuagint and Vulgate *Othniel, he urged her*   [b]16 That is, Jericho   [c]17 The Hebrew term refers to the irrevocable giving over of things or persons to the LORD, often by totally destroying them.   [d]17 *Hormah* means *destruction.*   [e]18 Hebrew; Septuagint *Judah did not take*   [f]36 Hebrew *Akrabbim*   [g]5 *Bokim* means *weepers.*

served the LORD throughout the lifetime of Joshua and of the elders who outlived him and who had seen all the great things the LORD had done for Israel.

[8]Joshua son of Nun, the servant of the LORD, died at the age of a hundred and ten. [9]And they buried him in the land of his inheritance, at Timnath Heres[a] in the hill country of Ephraim, north of Mount Gaash.

[10]After that whole generation had been gathered to their fathers, another generation grew up, who knew neither the LORD nor what he had done for Israel. [11]Then the Israelites did evil in the eyes of the LORD and served the Baals. [12]They forsook the LORD, the God of their fathers, who had brought them out of Egypt. They followed and worshiped various gods of the peoples around them. They provoked the LORD to anger [13]because they forsook him and served Baal and the Ashtoreths. [14]In his anger against Israel the LORD handed them over to raiders who plundered them. He sold them to their enemies all around, whom they were no longer able to resist. [15]Whenever Israel went out to fight, the hand of the LORD was against them to defeat them, just as he had sworn to them. They were in great distress.

[16]Then the LORD raised up judges,[b] who saved them out of the hands of these raiders. [17]Yet they would not listen to their judges but prostituted themselves to other gods and worshiped them. Unlike their fathers, they quickly turned from the way in which their fathers had walked, the way of obedience to the LORD's commands. [18]Whenever the LORD raised up a judge for them, he was with the judge and saved them out of the hands of their enemies as long as the judge lived; for the LORD had compassion on them as they groaned under those who oppressed and afflicted them. [19]But when the judge died, the people returned to ways even more corrupt than those of their fathers, following other gods and serving and worshiping them. They refused to give up their evil practices and stubborn ways.

[20]Therefore the LORD was very angry with Israel and said, "Because this nation has violated the covenant that I laid down for their forefathers and has not listened to me, [21]I will no longer drive out before them any of the nations Joshua left when he died. [22]I will use them to test Israel and see whether they will keep the way of the LORD and walk in it as their forefathers did." [23]The LORD had al-

lowed those nations to remain; he did not drive them out at once by giving them into the hands of Joshua.

3 These are the nations the LORD left to test all those Israelites who had not experienced any of the wars in Canaan [2](he did this only to teach warfare to the descendants of the Israelites who had not had previous battle experience): [3]the five rulers of the Philistines, all the Canaanites, the Sidonians, and the Hivites living in the Lebanon mountains from Mount Baal Hermon to Lebo[c] Hamath. [4]They were left to test the Israelites to see whether they would obey the LORD's commands, which he had given their forefathers through Moses.

[5]The Israelites lived among the Canaanites, Hittites, Amorites, Perizzites, Hivites and Jebusites. [6]They took their daughters in marriage and gave their own daughters to their sons, and served their gods.

Othniel

[7]The Israelites did evil in the eyes of the LORD; they forgot the LORD their God and served the Baals and the Asherahs. [8]The anger of the LORD burned against Israel so that he sold them into the hands of Cushan-Rishathaim king of Aram Naharaim,[d] to whom the Israelites were subject for eight years. [9]But when they cried out to the LORD, he raised up for them a deliverer, Othniel son of Kenaz, Caleb's younger brother, who saved them. [10]The Spirit of the LORD came upon him, so that he became Israel's judge[e] and went to war. The LORD gave Cushan-Rishathaim king of Aram into the hands of Othniel, who overpowered him. [11]So the land had peace for forty years, until Othniel son of Kenaz died.

Ehud

[12]Once again the Israelites did evil in the eyes of the LORD, and because they did this evil the LORD gave Eglon king of Moab power over Israel. [13]Getting the Ammonites and Amalekites to join him, Eglon came and attacked Israel, and they took possession of the City of Palms.[f] [14]The Israelites were subject to Eglon king of Moab for eighteen years.

[15]Again the Israelites cried out to the LORD, and he gave them a deliverer—Ehud, a left-handed man, the son of Gera the Benjamite. The Israelites sent him with tribute to Eglon king of Moab. [16]Now Ehud had made a dou-

---

[a]9 Also known as *Timnath Serah* (see Joshua 19:50 and 24:30)   [b]16 Or *leaders*; similarly in verses 17-19   [c]3 Or *to the entrance to*   [d]8 That is, Northwest Mesopotamia   [e]10 Or *leader*   [f]13 That is, Jericho

ble-edged sword about a foot and a half[a] long, which he strapped to his right thigh under his clothing. [17]He presented the tribute to Eglon king of Moab, who was a very fat man. [18]After Ehud had presented the tribute, he sent on their way the men who had carried it. [19]At the idols[b] near Gilgal he himself turned back and said, "I have a secret message for you, O king."

The king said, "Quiet!" And all his attendants left him.

[20]Ehud then approached him while he was sitting alone in the upper room of his summer palace[c] and said, "I have a message from God for you." As the king rose from his seat, [21]Ehud reached with his left hand, drew the sword from his right thigh and plunged it into the king's belly. [22]Even the handle sank in after the blade, which came out his back. Ehud did not pull the sword out, and the fat closed in over it. [23]Then Ehud went out to the porch[d]; he shut the doors of the upper room behind him and locked them.

[24]After he had gone, the servants came and found the doors of the upper room locked. They said, "He must be relieving himself in the inner room of the house." [25]They waited to the point of embarrassment, but when he did not open the doors of the room, they took a key and unlocked them. There they saw their lord fallen to the floor, dead.

[26]While they waited, Ehud got away. He passed by the idols and escaped to Seirah. [27]When he arrived there, he blew a trumpet in the hill country of Ephraim, and the Israelites went down with him from the hills, with him leading them.

[28]"Follow me," he ordered, "for the LORD has given Moab, your enemy, into your hands." So they followed him down and, taking possession of the fords of the Jordan that led to Moab, they allowed no one to cross over. [29]At that time they struck down about ten thousand Moabites, all vigorous and strong; not a man escaped. [30]That day Moab was made subject to Israel, and the land had peace for eighty years.

Shamgar

[31]After Ehud came Shamgar son of Anath, who struck down six hundred Philistines with an oxgoad. He too saved Israel.

Deborah

4 After Ehud died, the Israelites once again did evil in the eyes of the LORD. [2]So the LORD sold them into the hands of Jabin, a king of Canaan, who reigned in Hazor. The commander of his army was Sisera, who lived in Harosheth Haggoyim. [3]Because he had nine hundred iron chariots and had cruelly oppressed the Israelites for twenty years, they cried to the LORD for help.

[4]Deborah, a prophetess, the wife of Lappidoth, was leading[e] Israel at that time. [5]She held court under the Palm of Deborah between Ramah and Bethel in the hill country of Ephraim, and the Israelites came to her to have their disputes decided. [6]She sent for Barak son of Abinoam from Kedesh in Naphtali and said to him, "The LORD, the God of Israel, commands you: 'Go, take with you ten thousand men of Naphtali and Zebulun and lead the way to Mount Tabor. [7]I will lure Sisera, the commander of Jabin's army, with his chariots and his troops to the Kishon River and give him into your hands.'"

[8]Barak said to her, "If you go with me, I will go; but if you don't go with me, I won't go."

[9]"Very well," Deborah said, "I will go with you. But because of the way you are going about this,[f] the honor will not be yours, for the LORD will hand Sisera over to a woman." So Deborah went with Barak to Kedesh, [10]where he summoned Zebulun and Naphtali. Ten thousand men followed him, and Deborah also went with him.

[11]Now Heber the Kenite had left the other Kenites, the descendants of Hobab, Moses' brother-in-law,[g] and pitched his tent by the great tree in Zaanannim near Kedesh.

[12]When they told Sisera that Barak son of Abinoam had gone up to Mount Tabor, [13]Sisera gathered together his nine hundred iron chariots and all the men with him, from Harosheth Haggoyim to the Kishon River. [14]Then Deborah said to Barak, "Go! This is the day the LORD has given Sisera into your hands. Has not the LORD gone ahead of you?" So Barak went down Mount Tabor, followed by ten thousand men. [15]At Barak's advance, the LORD routed Sisera and all his chariots and army by the sword, and Sisera abandoned his chariot and fled on foot. [16]But Barak pursued the chariots and army as far as Harosheth Haggoyim. All the troops of Sisera fell by the sword; not a man was left.

---

[a]16 Hebrew *a cubit* (about 0.5 meter)   [b]19 Or *the stone quarries*; also in verse 26   [c]20 The meaning of the Hebrew for this phrase is uncertain.   [d]23 The meaning of the Hebrew for this word is uncertain.   [e]4 Traditionally *judging*   [f]9 Or *But on the expedition you are undertaking*   [g]11 Or *father-in-law*

17Sisera, however, fled on foot to the tent of Jael, the wife of Heber the Kenite, because there were friendly relations between Jabin king of Hazor and the clan of Heber the Kenite.

18Jael went out to meet Sisera and said to him, "Come, my lord, come right in. Don't be afraid." So he entered her tent, and she put a covering over him.

19"I'm thirsty," he said. "Please give me some water." She opened a skin of milk, gave him a drink, and covered him up.

20"Stand in the doorway of the tent," he told her. "If someone comes by and asks you, 'Is anyone here?' say 'No.' "

21But Jael, Heber's wife, picked up a tent peg and a hammer and went quietly to him while he lay fast asleep, exhausted. She drove the peg through his temple into the ground, and he died.

22Barak came by in pursuit of Sisera, and Jael went out to meet him. "Come," she said, "I will show you the man you're looking for." So he went in with her, and there lay Sisera with the tent peg through his temple—dead.

23On that day God subdued Jabin, the Canaanite king, before the Israelites. **24**And the hand of the Israelites grew stronger and stronger against Jabin, the Canaanite king, until they destroyed him.

The Song of Deborah

5 On that day Deborah and Barak son of Abinoam sang this song:

2"When the princes in Israel take the
　　lead,
　　when the people willingly offer
　　　　themselves—
　　praise the LORD!

3"Hear this, you kings! Listen, you rulers!
　　I will sing to*a* the LORD, I will sing;
　　I will make music to*b* the LORD, the
　　　　God of Israel.

4"O LORD, when you went out from Seir,
　　when you marched from the land of
　　　　Edom,
　the earth shook, the heavens poured,
　　the clouds poured down water.
5The mountains quaked before the LORD,
　　the One of Sinai,
　before the LORD, the God of Israel.

6"In the days of Shamgar son of Anath,
　in the days of Jael, the roads were
　　abandoned;
　travelers took to winding paths.
7Village life*c* in Israel ceased,
　　ceased until I,*d* Deborah, arose,
　　arose a mother in Israel.
8When they chose new gods,
　　war came to the city gates,
　and not a shield or spear was seen
　　among forty thousand in Israel.
9My heart is with Israel's princes,
　　with the willing volunteers among the
　　　　people.
　　Praise the LORD!

10"You who ride on white donkeys,
　　sitting on your saddle blankets,
　　and you who walk along the road,
　consider **11**the voice of the singers*e* at
　　　　the watering places.
　　They recite the righteous acts of the
　　　　LORD,
　　the righteous acts of his warriors*f* in
　　　　Israel.

　"Then the people of the LORD
　　went down to the city gates.
12'Wake up, wake up, Deborah!
　　Wake up, wake up, break out in song!
　Arise, O Barak!
　　Take captive your captives, O son of
　　　　Abinoam.'

13"Then the men who were left
　　came down to the nobles;
　the people of the LORD
　　came to me with the mighty.
14Some came from Ephraim, whose roots
　　were in Amalek;
　Benjamin was with the people who
　　followed you.
　From Makir captains came down,
　　from Zebulun those who bear a
　　　　commander's staff.
15The princes of Issachar were with
　　Deborah;
　　yes, Issachar was with Barak,
　　rushing after him into the valley.
　In the districts of Reuben
　　there was much searching of heart.
16Why did you stay among the
　　campfires*g*
　　to hear the whistling for the flocks?
　In the districts of Reuben
　　there was much searching of heart.
17Gilead stayed beyond the Jordan.

---

*a*3 Or *of*　*b*3 Or */ with song I will praise*　*c*7 Or *Warriors*　*d*7 Or *you*　*e*11 Or *archers*; the meaning of the Hebrew for this word is uncertain.　*f*11 Or *villagers*　*g*16 Or *saddlebags*

And Dan, why did he linger by the
    ships?
Asher remained on the coast
    and stayed in his coves.
¹⁸The people of Zebulun risked their very
    lives;
    so did Naphtali on the heights of the
    field.

¹⁹"Kings came, they fought;
    the kings of Canaan fought
at Taanach by the waters of Megiddo,
    but they carried off no silver, no
    plunder.
²⁰From the heavens the stars fought,
    from their courses they fought against
    Sisera.
²¹The river Kishon swept them away,
    the age-old river, the river Kishon.
March on, my soul; be strong!
²²Then thundered the horses' hoofs—
    galloping, galloping go his mighty
    steeds.
²³'Curse Meroz,' said the angel of the
    LORD.
    'Curse its people bitterly,
because they did not come to help the
    LORD,
    to help the LORD against the mighty.'

²⁴"Most blessed of women be Jael,
    the wife of Heber the Kenite,
    most blessed of tent-dwelling women.
²⁵He asked for water, and she gave him
    milk;
    in a bowl fit for nobles she brought
    him curdled milk.
²⁶Her hand reached for the tent peg,
    her right hand for the workman's
    hammer.
She struck Sisera, she crushed his head,
    she shattered and pierced his temple.
²⁷At her feet he sank,
    he fell; there he lay.
At her feet he sank, he fell;
    where he sank, there he fell—dead.

²⁸"Through the window peered Sisera's
    mother;
    behind the lattice she cried out,
'Why is his chariot so long in coming?
    Why is the clatter of his chariots
    delayed?'
²⁹The wisest of her ladies answer her;
    indeed, she keeps saying to herself,
³⁰'Are they not finding and dividing the
    spoils:
    a girl or two for each man,
    colorful garments as plunder for
    Sisera,

colorful garments embroidered,
highly embroidered garments for my
    neck—
all this as plunder?'

³¹"So may all your enemies perish,
    O LORD!
But may they who love you be like
    the sun
when it rises in its strength."

Then the land had peace forty years.

Gideon

6 Again the Israelites did evil in the eyes of the LORD, and for seven years he gave them into the hands of the Midianites. ²Because the power of Midian was so oppressive, the Israelites prepared shelters for themselves in mountain clefts, caves and strongholds. ³Whenever the Israelites planted their crops, the Midianites, Amalekites and other eastern peoples invaded the country. ⁴They camped on the land and ruined the crops all the way to Gaza and did not spare a living thing for Israel, neither sheep nor cattle nor donkeys. ⁵They came up with their livestock and their tents like swarms of locusts. It was impossible to count the men and their camels; they invaded the land to ravage it. ⁶Midian so impoverished the Israelites that they cried out to the LORD for help.

⁷When the Israelites cried to the LORD because of Midian, ⁸he sent them a prophet, who said, "This is what the LORD, the God of Israel, says: I brought you up out of Egypt, out of the land of slavery. ⁹I snatched you from the power of Egypt and from the hand of all your oppressors. I drove them from before you and gave you their land. ¹⁰I said to you, 'I am the LORD your God; do not worship the gods of the Amorites, in whose land you live.' But you have not listened to me."

¹¹The angel of the LORD came and sat down under the oak in Ophrah that belonged to Joash the Abiezrite, where his son Gideon was threshing wheat in a winepress to keep it from the Midianites. ¹²When the angel of the LORD appeared to Gideon, he said, "The LORD is with you, mighty warrior."

¹³"But sir," Gideon replied, "if the LORD is with us, why has all this happened to us? Where are all his wonders that our fathers told us about when they said, 'Did not the LORD bring us up out of Egypt?' But now the LORD has abandoned us and put us into the hand of Midian."

¹⁴The LORD turned to him and said, "Go in

ON MAKING DECISIONS

SATURDAY ☐

Work It Out

You make thousands of decisions every day, many of them without even realizing you've done it. You chose cereal instead of toast for breakfast. You decided to wear your white sweater instead of the blue one. You told your mom you'd be home at 10 P.M., which means you decided you *would* go to the girls' basketball game.

In your mind (or on paper if you wish) make a list of some of the important decisions you'll need to make in the future. The decision between cereal and toast was easy. But college, career, marriage . . . those are not simple choices. How will you decide?

God has given some pretty clear guidelines to help you in making decisions. He's the best and first place to go for help in the decision-making process.

Nail It Down

Read Judges 6:11–40 for the story of Gideon's decision-making tactics.

SUNDAY ☐

Think It Through

Most of the small decisions you make each day won't have any big impact later on. Other decisions will affect you for a lifetime. Here are some hints for helping you make the *right* decision when you must make a *big* decision:

1. Ask God. He's the one who planned your life, so make him part of the process.

2. Talk to your parents. They've had some practice making big decisions already, and they may have some good advice.

3. Examine where you want to be—not just tomorrow but next year and the next. How does this decision fit into the whole picture?

4. List the pros and cons of your decision. It will help clear up the fog a bit.

5. Don't be afraid to make a bold move into your future.

Nail It Down

Reread Gideon's story in Judges 6:11–40. For further insight ready Psalm 139.

Turn to pages 257, 1005 and 1246 for other readings on decisions.
Turn to page 257 for Monday's reading.

Topic

DECISIONS

the strength you have and save Israel out of Midian's hand. Am I not sending you?"

¹⁵"But Lord,ᵃ" Gideon asked, "how can I save Israel? My clan is the weakest in Manasseh, and I am the least in my family."

¹⁶The Lord answered, "I will be with you, and you will strike down all the Midianites together."

¹⁷Gideon replied, "If now I have found favor in your eyes, give me a sign that it is really you talking to me. ¹⁸Please do not go away until I come back and bring my offering and set it before you."

And the Lord said, "I will wait until you return."

¹⁹Gideon went in, prepared a young goat, and from an ephahᵇ of flour he made bread without yeast. Putting the meat in a basket and its broth in a pot, he brought them out and offered them to him under the oak.

²⁰The angel of God said to him, "Take the meat and the unleavened bread, place them on this rock, and pour out the broth." And Gideon did so. ²¹With the tip of the staff that was in his hand, the angel of the Lord touched the meat and the unleavened bread. Fire flared from the rock, consuming the meat and the bread. And the angel of the Lord disappeared. ²²When Gideon realized that it was the angel of the Lord, he exclaimed, "Ah, Sovereign Lord! I have seen the angel of the Lord face to face!"

²³But the Lord said to him, "Peace! Do not be afraid. You are not going to die."

²⁴So Gideon built an altar to the Lord there and called it The Lord is Peace. To this day it stands in Ophrah of the Abiezrites.

²⁵That same night the Lord said to him, "Take the second bull from your father's herd, the one seven years old.ᶜ Tear down your father's altar to Baal and cut down the Asherah poleᵈ beside it. ²⁶Then build a proper kind ofᵉ altar to the Lord your God on the top of this height. Using the wood of the Asherah pole that you cut down, offer the secondᶠ bull as a burnt offering."

²⁷So Gideon took ten of his servants and did as the Lord told him. But because he was afraid of his family and the men of the town, he did it at night rather than in the daytime.

²⁸In the morning when the men of the town got up, there was Baal's altar, demolished, with the Asherah pole beside it cut

down and the second bull sacrificed on the newly built altar!

²⁹They asked each other, "Who did this?"

When they carefully investigated, they were told, "Gideon son of Joash did it."

³⁰The men of the town demanded of Joash, "Bring out your son. He must die, because he has broken down Baal's altar and cut down the Asherah pole beside it."

³¹But Joash replied to the hostile crowd around him, "Are you going to plead Baal's cause? Are you trying to save him? Whoever fights for him shall be put to death by morning! If Baal really is a god, he can defend himself when someone breaks down his altar." ³²So that day they called Gideon "Jerub-Baal,ᵍ" saying, "Let Baal contend with him," because he broke down Baal's altar.

³³Now all the Midianites, Amalekites and other eastern peoples joined forces and crossed over the Jordan and camped in the Valley of Jezreel. ³⁴Then the Spirit of the Lord came upon Gideon, and he blew a trumpet, summoning the Abiezrites to follow him. ³⁵He sent messengers throughout Manasseh, calling them to arms, and also into Asher, Zebulun and Naphtali, so that they too went up to meet them.

³⁶Gideon said to God, "If you will save Israel by my hand as you have promised— ³⁷look, I will place a wool fleece on the threshing floor. If there is dew only on the fleece and all the ground is dry, then I will know that you will save Israel by my hand, as you said." ³⁸And that is what happened. Gideon rose early the next day; he squeezed the fleece and wrung out the dew—a bowlful of water.

³⁹Then Gideon said to God, "Do not be angry with me. Let me make just one more request. Allow me one more test with the fleece. This time make the fleece dry and the ground covered with dew." ⁴⁰That night God did so. Only the fleece was dry; all the ground was covered with dew.

Gideon Defeats the Midianites

7 Early in the morning, Jerub-Baal (that is, Gideon) and all his men camped at the spring of Harod. The camp of Midian was north of them in the valley near the hill of Moreh. ²The Lord said to Gideon, "You have too many men for me to deliver Midian into their hands. In order that Israel may not

---

ᵃ15 Or sir   ᵇ19 That is, probably about 3/5 bushel (about 22 liters)   ᶜ25 Or Take a full-grown, mature bull from your father's herd   ᵈ25 That is, a symbol of the goddess Asherah; here and elsewhere in Judges   ᵉ26 Or build with layers of stone an   ᶠ26 Or full-grown; also in verse 28   ᵍ32 Jerub-Baal means let Baal contend.

boast against me that her own strength has saved her, **3**announce now to the people, 'Anyone who trembles with fear may turn back and leave Mount Gilead.' " So twenty-two thousand men left, while ten thousand remained.

4But the LORD said to Gideon, "There are still too many men. Take them down to the water, and I will sift them for you there. If I say, 'This one shall go with you,' he shall go; but if I say, 'This one shall not go with you,' he shall not go."

5So Gideon took the men down to the water. There the LORD told him, "Separate those who lap the water with their tongues like a dog from those who kneel down to drink." **6**Three hundred men lapped with their hands to their mouths. All the rest got down on their knees to drink.

7The LORD said to Gideon, "With the three hundred men that lapped I will save you and give the Midianites into your hands. Let all the other men go, each to his own place." **8**So Gideon sent the rest of the Israelites to their tents but kept the three hundred, who took over the provisions and trumpets of the others.

Now the camp of Midian lay below him in the valley. **9**During that night the LORD said to Gideon, "Get up, go down against the camp, because I am going to give it into your hands. **10**If you are afraid to attack, go down to the camp with your servant Purah **11**and listen to what they are saying. Afterward, you will be encouraged to attack the camp." So he and Purah his servant went down to the outposts of the camp. **12**The Midianites, the Amalekites and all the other eastern peoples had settled in the valley, thick as locusts. Their camels could no more be counted than the sand on the seashore.

13Gideon arrived just as a man was telling a friend his dream. "I had a dream," he was saying. "A round loaf of barley bread came tumbling into the Midianite camp. It struck the tent with such force that the tent overturned and collapsed."

14His friend responded, "This can be nothing other than the sword of Gideon son of Joash, the Israelite. God has given the Midianites and the whole camp into his hands."

15When Gideon heard the dream and its interpretation, he worshiped God. He returned to the camp of Israel and called out, "Get up! The LORD has given the Midianite camp into your hands." **16**Dividing the three hundred men into three companies, he placed trumpets and empty jars in the hands of all of them, with torches inside.

17"Watch me," he told them. "Follow my lead. When I get to the edge of the camp, do exactly as I do. **18**When I and all who are with me blow our trumpets, then from all around the camp blow yours and shout, 'For the LORD and for Gideon.' "

19Gideon and the hundred men with him reached the edge of the camp at the beginning of the middle watch, just after they had changed the guard. They blew their trumpets and broke the jars that were in their hands. **20**The three companies blew the trumpets and smashed the jars. Grasping the torches in their left hands and holding in their right hands the trumpets they were to blow, they shouted, "A sword for the LORD and for Gideon!" **21**While each man held his position around the camp, all the Midianites ran, crying out as they fled.

22When the three hundred trumpets sounded, the LORD caused the men throughout the camp to turn on each other with their swords. The army fled to Beth Shittah toward Zererah as far as the border of Abel Meholah near Tabbath. **23**Israelites from Naphtali, Asher and all Manasseh were called out, and they pursued the Midianites. **24**Gideon sent messengers throughout the hill country of Ephraim, saying, "Come down against the Midianites and seize the waters of the Jordan ahead of them as far as Beth Barah."

So all the men of Ephraim were called out and they took the waters of the Jordan as far as Beth Barah. **25**They also captured two of the Midianite leaders, Oreb and Zeeb. They killed Oreb at the rock of Oreb, and Zeeb at the winepress of Zeeb. They pursued the Midianites and brought the heads of Oreb and Zeeb to Gideon, who was by the Jordan.

Zebah and Zalmunna

8 Now the Ephraimites asked Gideon, "Why have you treated us like this? Why didn't you call us when you went to fight Midian?" And they criticized him sharply.

2But he answered them, "What have I accomplished compared to you? Aren't the gleanings of Ephraim's grapes better than the full grape harvest of Abiezer? **3**God gave Oreb and Zeeb, the Midianite leaders, into your hands. What was I able to do compared to you?" At this, their resentment against him subsided.

4Gideon and his three hundred men, exhausted yet keeping up the pursuit, came to the Jordan and crossed it. **5**He said to the men of Succoth, "Give my troops some bread; they are worn out, and I am still pursuing Zebah and Zalmunna, the kings of Midian."

6But the officials of Succoth said, "Do you already have the hands of Zebah and Zalmunna in your possession? Why should we give bread to your troops?"

7Then Gideon replied, "Just for that, when the LORD has given Zebah and Zalmunna into my hand, I will tear your flesh with desert thorns and briers."

8From there he went up to Peniel*a* and made the same request of them, but they answered as the men of Succoth had. **9**So he said to the men of Peniel, "When I return in triumph, I will tear down this tower."

10Now Zebah and Zalmunna were in Karkor with a force of about fifteen thousand men, all that were left of the armies of the eastern peoples; a hundred and twenty thousand swordsmen had fallen. **11**Gideon went up by the route of the nomads east of Nobah and Jogbehah and fell upon the unsuspecting army. **12**Zebah and Zalmunna, the two kings of Midian, fled, but he pursued them and captured them, routing their entire army.

13Gideon son of Joash then returned from the battle by the Pass of Heres. **14**He caught a young man of Succoth and questioned him, and the young man wrote down for him the names of the seventy-seven officials of Succoth, the elders of the town. **15**Then Gideon came and said to the men of Succoth, "Here are Zebah and Zalmunna, about whom you taunted me by saying, 'Do you already have the hands of Zebah and Zalmunna in your possession? Why should we give bread to your exhausted men?' " **16**He took the elders of the town and taught the men of Succoth a lesson by punishing them with desert thorns and briers. **17**He also pulled down the tower of Peniel and killed the men of the town.

18Then he asked Zebah and Zalmunna, "What kind of men did you kill at Tabor?"

"Men like you," they answered, "each one with the bearing of a prince."

19Gideon replied, "Those were my brothers, the sons of my own mother. As surely as the LORD lives, if you had spared their lives, I would not kill you." **20**Turning to Jether, his oldest son, he said, "Kill them!" But

Jether did not draw his sword, because he was only a boy and was afraid.

21Zebah and Zalmunna said, "Come, do it yourself. 'As is the man, so is his strength.' " So Gideon stepped forward and killed them, and took the ornaments off their camels' necks.

Gideon's Ephod

22The Israelites said to Gideon, "Rule over us — you, your son and your grandson — because you have saved us out of the hand of Midian."

23But Gideon told them, "I will not rule over you, nor will my son rule over you. The LORD will rule over you." **24**And he said, "I do have one request, that each of you give me an earring from your share of the plunder." (It was the custom of the Ishmaelites to wear gold earrings.)

25They answered, "We'll be glad to give them." So they spread out a garment, and each man threw a ring from his plunder onto it. **26**The weight of the gold rings he asked for came to seventeen hundred shekels,*b* not counting the ornaments, the pendants and the purple garments worn by the kings of Midian or the chains that were on their camels' necks. **27**Gideon made the gold into an ephod, which he placed in Ophrah, his town. All Israel prostituted themselves by worshiping it there, and it became a snare to Gideon and his family.

Gideon's Death

28Thus Midian was subdued before the Israelites and did not raise its head again. During Gideon's lifetime, the land enjoyed peace forty years.

29Jerub-Baal son of Joash went back home to live. **30**He had seventy sons of his own, for he had many wives. **31**His concubine, who lived in Shechem, also bore him a son, whom he named Abimelech. **32**Gideon son of Joash died at a good old age and was buried in the tomb of his father Joash in Ophrah of the Abiezrites.

33No sooner had Gideon died than the Israelites again prostituted themselves to the Baals. They set up Baal-Berith as their god and **34**did not remember the LORD their God, who had rescued them from the hands of all their enemies on every side. **35**They also failed to show kindness to the family of Jerub-Baal (that is, Gideon) for all the good things he had done for them.

---

a8 Hebrew *Penuel*, a variant of *Peniel*; also in verses 9 and 17   *b26* That is, about 43 pounds (about 19.5 kilograms)

Abimelech

9 Abimelech son of Jerub-Baal went to his mother's brothers in Shechem and said to them and to all his mother's clan, **2**"Ask all the citizens of Shechem, 'Which is better for you: to have all seventy of Jerub-Baal's sons rule over you, or just one man?' Remember, I am your flesh and blood."

3When the brothers repeated all this to the citizens of Shechem, they were inclined to follow Abimelech, for they said, "He is our brother." **4**They gave him seventy shekels*a* of silver from the temple of Baal-Berith, and Abimelech used it to hire reckless adventurers, who became his followers. **5**He went to his father's home in Ophrah and on one stone murdered his seventy brothers, the sons of Jerub-Baal. But Jotham, the youngest son of Jerub-Baal, escaped by hiding. **6**Then all the citizens of Shechem and Beth Millo gathered beside the great tree at the pillar in Shechem to crown Abimelech king.

7When Jotham was told about this, he climbed up on the top of Mount Gerizim and shouted to them, "Listen to me, citizens of Shechem, so that God may listen to you. **8**One day the trees went out to anoint a king for themselves. They said to the olive tree, 'Be our king.'

9"But the olive tree answered, 'Should I give up my oil, by which both gods and men are honored, to hold sway over the trees?'

10"Next, the trees said to the fig tree, 'Come and be our king.'

11"But the fig tree replied, 'Should I give up my fruit, so good and sweet, to hold sway over the trees?'

12"Then the trees said to the vine, 'Come and be our king.'

13"But the vine answered, 'Should I give up my wine, which cheers both gods and men, to hold sway over the trees?'

14"Finally all the trees said to the thornbush, 'Come and be our king.'

15"The thornbush said to the trees, 'If you really want to anoint me king over you, come and take refuge in my shade; but if not, then let fire come out of the thornbush and consume the cedars of Lebanon!'

16"Now if you have acted honorably and in good faith when you made Abimelech king, and if you have been fair to Jerub-Baal and his family, and if you have treated him as he deserves— **17**and to think that my father fought for you, risked his life to rescue you from the hand of Midian **18**(but today you have revolted against my father's family, murdered his seventy sons on a single stone, and made Abimelech, the son of his slave girl, king over the citizens of Shechem because he is your brother)— **19**if then you have acted honorably and in good faith toward Jerub-Baal and his family today, may Abimelech be your joy, and may you be his, too! **20**But if you have not, let fire come out from Abimelech and consume you, citizens of Shechem and Beth Millo, and let fire come out from you, citizens of Shechem and Beth Millo, and consume Abimelech!"

21Then Jotham fled, escaping to Beer, and he lived there because he was afraid of his brother Abimelech.

22After Abimelech had governed Israel three years, **23**God sent an evil spirit between Abimelech and the citizens of Shechem, who acted treacherously against Abimelech. **24**God did this in order that the crime against Jerub-Baal's seventy sons, the shedding of their blood, might be avenged on their brother Abimelech and on the citizens of Shechem, who had helped him murder his brothers. **25**In opposition to him these citizens of Shechem set men on the hilltops to ambush and rob everyone who passed by, and this was reported to Abimelech.

26Now Gaal son of Ebed moved with his brothers into Shechem, and its citizens put their confidence in him. **27**After they had gone out into the fields and gathered the grapes and trodden them, they held a festival in the temple of their god. While they were eating and drinking, they cursed Abimelech. **28**Then Gaal son of Ebed said, "Who is Abimelech, and who is Shechem, that we should be subject to him? Isn't he Jerub-Baal's son, and isn't Zebul his deputy? Serve the men of Hamor, Shechem's father! Why should we serve Abimelech? **29**If only this people were under my command! Then I would get rid of him. I would say to Abimelech, 'Call out your whole army!'"*b*

30When Zebul the governor of the city heard what Gaal son of Ebed said, he was very angry. **31**Under cover he sent messengers to Abimelech, saying, "Gaal son of Ebed and his brothers have come to Shechem and are stirring up the city against you. **32**Now then, during the night you and your men should come and lie in wait in the fields. **33**In the morning at sunrise, advance against

---

a4 That is, about 1 3/4 pounds (about 0.8 kilogram)   *b29* Septuagint; Hebrew *him." Then he said to Abimelech, "Call out your whole army!"*

the city. When Gaal and his men come out against you, do whatever your hand finds to do."

34So Abimelech and all his troops set out by night and took up concealed positions near Shechem in four companies. **35**Now Gaal son of Ebed had gone out and was standing at the entrance to the city gate just as Abimelech and his soldiers came out from their hiding place.

36When Gaal saw them, he said to Zebul, "Look, people are coming down from the tops of the mountains!"

Zebul replied, "You mistake the shadows of the mountains for men."

37But Gaal spoke up again: "Look, people are coming down from the center of the land, and a company is coming from the direction of the soothsayers' tree."

38Then Zebul said to him, "Where is your big talk now, you who said, 'Who is Abimelech that we should be subject to him?' Aren't these the men you ridiculed? Go out and fight them!"

39So Gaal led out*a* the citizens of Shechem and fought Abimelech. **40**Abimelech chased him, and many fell wounded in the flight—all the way to the entrance to the gate. **41**Abimelech stayed in Arumah, and Zebul drove Gaal and his brothers out of Shechem.

42The next day the people of Shechem went out to the fields, and this was reported to Abimelech. **43**So he took his men, divided them into three companies and set an ambush in the fields. When he saw the people coming out of the city, he rose to attack them. **44**Abimelech and the companies with him rushed forward to a position at the entrance to the city gate. Then two companies rushed upon those in the fields and struck them down. **45**All that day Abimelech pressed his attack against the city until he had captured it and killed its people. Then he destroyed the city and scattered salt over it.

46On hearing this, the citizens in the tower of Shechem went into the stronghold of the temple of El-Berith. **47**When Abimelech heard that they had assembled there, **48**he and all his men went up Mount Zalmon. He took an ax and cut off some branches, which he lifted to his shoulders. He ordered the men with him, "Quick! Do what you have seen me do!" **49**So all the men cut branches and followed Abimelech. They piled them

against the stronghold and set it on fire over the people inside. So all the people in the tower of Shechem, about a thousand men and women, also died.

50Next Abimelech went to Thebez and besieged it and captured it. **51**Inside the city, however, was a strong tower, to which all the men and women—all the people of the city—fled. They locked themselves in and climbed up on the tower roof. **52**Abimelech went to the tower and stormed it. But as he approached the entrance to the tower to set it on fire, **53**a woman dropped an upper millstone on his head and cracked his skull.

54Hurriedly he called to his armor-bearer, "Draw your sword and kill me, so that they can't say, 'A woman killed him.' " So his servant ran him through, and he died. **55**When the Israelites saw that Abimelech was dead, they went home.

56Thus God repaid the wickedness that Abimelech had done to his father by murdering his seventy brothers. **57**God also made the men of Shechem pay for all their wickedness. The curse of Jotham son of Jerub-Baal came on them.

Tola

10 After the time of Abimelech a man of Issachar, Tola son of Puah, the son of Dodo, rose to save Israel. He lived in Shamir, in the hill country of Ephraim. **2**He led*b* Israel twenty-three years; then he died, and was buried in Shamir.

Jair

3He was followed by Jair of Gilead, who led Israel twenty-two years. **4**He had thirty sons, who rode thirty donkeys. They controlled thirty towns in Gilead, which to this day are called Havvoth Jair.*c* **5**When Jair died, he was buried in Kamon.

Jephthah

6Again the Israelites did evil in the eyes of the LORD. They served the Baals and the Ashtoreths, and the gods of Aram, the gods of Sidon, the gods of Moab, the gods of the Ammonites and the gods of the Philistines. And because the Israelites forsook the LORD and no longer served him, **7**he became angry with them. He sold them into the hands of the Philistines and the Ammonites, **8**who that year shattered and crushed them. For eighteen years they oppressed all the Israelites on the east side of the Jordan in Gilead,

---

a39 Or *Gaal went out in the sight of*   *b2* Traditionally *judged*; also in verse 3   *c4* Or *called the settlements of Jair* the land of the Amorites. **9**The Ammonites also crossed the Jordan to fight against Judah, Benjamin and the house of Ephraim; and Israel was in great distress. **10**Then the Israelites cried out to the LORD, "We have sinned against you, forsaking our God and serving the Baals."

11The LORD replied, "When the Egyptians, the Amorites, the Ammonites, the Philistines, **12**the Sidonians, the Amalekites and the Maonites*a* oppressed you and you cried to me for help, did I not save you from their hands? **13**But you have forsaken me and served other gods, so I will no longer save you. **14**Go and cry out to the gods you have chosen. Let them save you when you are in trouble!"

15But the Israelites said to the LORD, "We have sinned. Do with us whatever you think best, but please rescue us now." **16**Then they got rid of the foreign gods among them and served the LORD. And he could bear Israel's misery no longer.

17When the Ammonites were called to arms and camped in Gilead, the Israelites assembled and camped at Mizpah. **18**The leaders of the people of Gilead said to each other, "Whoever will launch the attack against the Ammonites will be the head of all those living in Gilead."

11 Jephthah the Gileadite was a mighty warrior. His father was Gilead; his mother was a prostitute. **2**Gilead's wife also bore him sons, and when they were grown up, they drove Jephthah away. "You are not going to get any inheritance in our family," they said, "because you are the son of another woman." **3**So Jephthah fled from his brothers and settled in the land of Tob, where a group of adventurers gathered around him and followed him.

4Some time later, when the Ammonites made war on Israel, **5**the elders of Gilead went to get Jephthah from the land of Tob. **6**"Come," they said, "be our commander, so we can fight the Ammonites."

7Jephthah said to them, "Didn't you hate me and drive me from my father's house? Why do you come to me now, when you're in trouble?"

8The elders of Gilead said to him, "Nevertheless, we are turning to you now; come with us to fight the Ammonites, and you will be our head over all who live in Gilead."

9Jephthah answered, "Suppose you take me back to fight the Ammonites and the LORD gives them to me — will I really be your head?"

10The elders of Gilead replied, "The LORD is our witness; we will certainly do as you say." **11**So Jephthah went with the elders of Gilead, and the people made him head and commander over them. And he repeated all his words before the LORD in Mizpah.

12Then Jephthah sent messengers to the Ammonite king with the question: "What do you have against us that you have attacked our country?"

13The king of the Ammonites answered Jephthah's messengers, "When Israel came up out of Egypt, they took away my land from the Arnon to the Jabbok, all the way to the Jordan. Now give it back peaceably."

14Jephthah sent back messengers to the Ammonite king, **15**saying:

"This is what Jephthah says: Israel did not take the land of Moab or the land of the Ammonites. **16**But when they came up out of Egypt, Israel went through the desert to the Red Sea*b* and on to Kadesh. **17**Then Israel sent messengers to the king of Edom, saying, 'Give us permission to go through your country,' but the king of Edom would not listen. They sent also to the king of Moab, and he refused. So Israel stayed at Kadesh.

18"Next they traveled through the desert, skirted the lands of Edom and Moab, passed along the eastern side of the country of Moab, and camped on the other side of the Arnon. They did not enter the territory of Moab, for the Arnon was its border.

19"Then Israel sent messengers to Sihon king of the Amorites, who ruled in Heshbon, and said to him, 'Let us pass through your country to our own place.' **20**Sihon, however, did not trust Israel*c* to pass through his territory. He mustered all his men and encamped at Jahaz and fought with Israel.

21"Then the LORD, the God of Israel, gave Sihon and all his men into Israel's hands, and they defeated them. Israel took over all the land of the Amorites who lived in that country, **22**capturing all of it from the Arnon to the Jabbok and from the desert to the Jordan.

23"Now since the LORD, the God of Israel, has driven the Amorites out before his people Israel, what right have you to

---

a 12 Hebrew; some Septuagint manuscripts *Midianites*   *b 16* Hebrew *Yam Suph*; that is, Sea of Reeds
c 20 Or *however, would not make an agreement for Israel*

take it over? **24**Will you not take what your god Chemosh gives you? Likewise, whatever the LORD our God has given us, we will possess. **25**Are you better than Balak son of Zippor, king of Moab? Did he ever quarrel with Israel or fight with them? **26**For three hundred years Israel occupied Heshbon, Aroer, the surrounding settlements and all the towns along the Arnon. Why didn't you retake them during that time? **27**I have not wronged you, but you are doing me wrong by waging war against me. Let the LORD, the Judge,*a* decide the dispute this day between the Israelites and the Ammonites."

28The king of Ammon, however, paid no attention to the message Jephthah sent him.

29Then the Spirit of the LORD came upon Jephthah. He crossed Gilead and Manasseh, passed through Mizpah of Gilead, and from there he advanced against the Ammonites. **30**And Jephthah made a vow to the LORD: "If you give the Ammonites into my hands, **31**whatever comes out of the door of my house to meet me when I return in triumph from the Ammonites will be the LORD's, and I will sacrifice it as a burnt offering."

32Then Jephthah went over to fight the Ammonites, and the LORD gave them into his hands. **33**He devastated twenty towns from Aroer to the vicinity of Minnith, as far as Abel Keramim. Thus Israel subdued Ammon.

34When Jephthah returned to his home in Mizpah, who should come out to meet him but his daughter, dancing to the sound of tambourines! She was an only child. Except for her he had neither son nor daughter. **35**When he saw her, he tore his clothes and cried, "Oh! My daughter! You have made me miserable and wretched, because I have made a vow to the LORD that I cannot break."

36"My father," she replied, "you have given your word to the LORD. Do to me just as you promised, now that the LORD has avenged you of your enemies, the Ammonites. **37**But grant me this one request," she said. "Give me two months to roam the hills and weep with my friends, because I will never marry."

38"You may go," he said. And he let her go for two months. She and the girls went into the hills and wept because she would never marry. **39**After the two months, she returned to her father and he did to her as he had vowed. And she was a virgin.

From this comes the Israelite custom **40**that each year the young women of Israel go out for four days to commemorate the daughter of Jephthah the Gileadite.

Jephthah and Ephraim

12 The men of Ephraim called out their forces, crossed over to Zaphon and said to Jephthah, "Why did you go to fight the Ammonites without calling us to go with you? We're going to burn down your house over your head."

2Jephthah answered, "I and my people were engaged in a great struggle with the Ammonites, and although I called, you didn't save me out of their hands. **3**When I saw that you wouldn't help, I took my life in my hands and crossed over to fight the Ammonites, and the LORD gave me the victory over them. Now why have you come up today to fight me?"

4Jephthah then called together the men of Gilead and fought against Ephraim. The Gileadites struck them down because the Ephraimites had said, "You Gileadites are renegades from Ephraim and Manasseh." **5**The Gileadites captured the fords of the Jordan leading to Ephraim, and whenever a survivor of Ephraim said, "Let me cross over," the men of Gilead asked him, "Are you an Ephraimite?" If he replied, "No," **6**they said, "All right, say 'Shibboleth.'" If he said, "Sibboleth," because he could not pronounce the word correctly, they seized him and killed him at the fords of the Jordan. Forty-two thousand Ephraimites were killed at that time.

7Jephthah led*b* Israel six years. Then Jephthah the Gileadite died, and was buried in a town in Gilead.

Ibzan, Elon and Abdon

8After him, Ibzan of Bethlehem led Israel. **9**He had thirty sons and thirty daughters. He gave his daughters away in marriage to those outside his clan, and for his sons he brought in thirty young women as wives from outside his clan. Ibzan led Israel seven years. **10**Then Ibzan died, and was buried in Bethlehem.

11After him, Elon the Zebulunite led Israel ten years. **12**Then Elon died, and was buried in Aijalon in the land of Zebulun.

13After him, Abdon son of Hillel, from Pirathon, led Israel. **14**He had forty sons and

a27 Or Ruler   b7 Traditionally judged; also in verses 8-14 thirty grandsons, who rode on seventy don-keys. He led Israel eight years. **15**Then Abdon son of Hillel died, and was buried at Pirathon in Ephraim, in the hill country of the Amalekites.

The Birth of Samson

13 Again the Israelites did evil in the eyes of the LORD, so the LORD delivered them into the hands of the Philistines for forty years.

2A certain man of Zorah, named Manoah, from the clan of the Danites, had a wife who was sterile and remained childless. **3**The angel of the LORD appeared to her and said, "You are sterile and childless, but you are going to conceive and have a son. **4**Now see to it that you drink no wine or other fermented drink and that you do not eat anything unclean, **5**because you will conceive and give birth to a son. No razor may be used on his head, because the boy is to be a Nazirite, set apart to God from birth, and he will begin the deliverance of Israel from the hands of the Philistines."

6Then the woman went to her husband and told him, "A man of God came to me. He looked like an angel of God, very awesome. I didn't ask him where he came from, and he didn't tell me his name. **7**But he said to me, 'You will conceive and give birth to a son. Now then, drink no wine or other fermented drink and do not eat anything unclean, because the boy will be a Nazirite of God from birth until the day of his death.'"

8Then Manoah prayed to the LORD: "O Lord, I beg you, let the man of God you sent to us come again to teach us how to bring up the boy who is to be born."

9God heard Manoah, and the angel of God came again to the woman while she was out in the field; but her husband Manoah was not with her. **10**The woman hurried to tell her husband, "He's here! The man who appeared to me the other day!"

11Manoah got up and followed his wife. When he came to the man, he said, "Are you the one who talked to my wife?"

"I am," he said.

12So Manoah asked him, "When your words are fulfilled, what is to be the rule for the boy's life and work?"

13The angel of the LORD answered, "Your wife must do all that I have told her. **14**She must not eat anything that comes from the grapevine, nor drink any wine or other fermented drink nor eat anything unclean. She must do everything I have commanded her."

15Manoah said to the angel of the LORD, "We would like you to stay until we prepare a young goat for you."

16The angel of the LORD replied, "Even though you detain me, I will not eat any of your food. But if you prepare a burnt offering, offer it to the LORD." (Manoah did not realize that it was the angel of the LORD.)

17Then Manoah inquired of the angel of the LORD, "What is your name, so that we may honor you when your word comes true?"

18He replied, "Why do you ask my name? It is beyond understanding.*a*" **19**Then Manoah took a young goat, together with the grain offering, and sacrificed it on a rock to the LORD. And the LORD did an amazing thing while Manoah and his wife watched: **20**As the flame blazed up from the altar toward heaven, the angel of the LORD ascended in the flame. Seeing this, Manoah and his wife fell with their faces to the ground. **21**When the angel of the LORD did not show himself again to Manoah and his wife, Manoah realized that it was the angel of the LORD.

22"We are doomed to die!" he said to his wife. "We have seen God!"

23But his wife answered, "If the LORD had meant to kill us, he would not have accepted a burnt offering and grain offering from our hands, nor shown us all these things or now told us this."

24The woman gave birth to a boy and named him Samson. He grew and the LORD blessed him, **25**and the Spirit of the LORD began to stir him while he was in Mahaneh Dan, between Zorah and Eshtaol.

Samson's Marriage

14 Samson went down to Timnah and saw there a young Philistine woman. **2**When he returned, he said to his father and mother, "I have seen a Philistine woman in Timnah; now get her for me as my wife."

3His father and mother replied, "Isn't there an acceptable woman among your relatives or among all our people? Must you go to the uncircumcised Philistines to get a wife?"

But Samson said to his father, "Get her for me. She's the right one for me." **4**(His parents did not know that this was from the LORD, who was seeking an occasion to confront the Philistines; for at that time they were ruling over Israel.) **5**Samson went

a18 Or is wonderful

down to Timnah together with his father and mother. As they approached the vineyards of Timnah, suddenly a young lion came roaring toward him. **6**The Spirit of the LORD came upon him in power so that he tore the lion apart with his bare hands as he might have torn a young goat. But he told neither his father nor his mother what he had done. **7**Then he went down and talked with the woman, and he liked her.

8Some time later, when he went back to marry her, he turned aside to look at the lion's carcass. In it was a swarm of bees and some honey, **9**which he scooped out with his hands and ate as he went along. When he rejoined his parents, he gave them some, and they too ate it. But he did not tell them that he had taken the honey from the lion's carcass.

10Now his father went down to see the woman. And Samson made a feast there, as was customary for bridegrooms. **11**When he appeared, he was given thirty companions.

12"Let me tell you a riddle," Samson said to them. "If you can give me the answer within the seven days of the feast, I will give you thirty linen garments and thirty sets of clothes. **13**If you can't tell me the answer, you must give me thirty linen garments and thirty sets of clothes."

"Tell us your riddle," they said. "Let's hear it."

14He replied,

"Out of the eater, something to eat;
   out of the strong, something sweet."

For three days they could not give the answer.

15On the fourth[a] day, they said to Samson's wife, "Coax your husband into explaining the riddle for us, or we will burn you and your father's household to death. Did you invite us here to rob us?"

16Then Samson's wife threw herself on him, sobbing, "You hate me! You don't really love me. You've given my people a riddle, but you haven't told me the answer."

"I haven't even explained it to my father or mother," he replied, "so why should I explain it to you?" **17**She cried the whole seven days of the feast. So on the seventh day he finally told her, because she continued to press him. She in turn explained the riddle to her people.

18Before sunset on the seventh day the men of the town said to him,

"What is sweeter than honey?
   What is stronger than a lion?"

Samson said to them,

"If you had not plowed with my heifer,
   you would not have solved my
   riddle."

19Then the Spirit of the LORD came upon him in power. He went down to Ashkelon, struck down thirty of their men, stripped them of their belongings and gave their clothes to those who had explained the riddle. Burning with anger, he went up to his father's house. **20**And Samson's wife was given to the friend who had attended him at his wedding.

Samson's Vengeance on the Philistines

15 Later on, at the time of wheat harvest, Samson took a young goat and went to visit his wife. He said, "I'm going to my wife's room." But her father would not let him go in.

2"I was so sure you thoroughly hated her," he said, "that I gave her to your friend. Isn't her younger sister more attractive? Take her instead."

3Samson said to them, "This time I have a right to get even with the Philistines; I will really harm them." **4**So he went out and caught three hundred foxes and tied them tail to tail in pairs. He then fastened a torch to every pair of tails, **5**lit the torches and let the foxes loose in the standing grain of the Philistines. He burned up the shocks and standing grain, together with the vineyards and olive groves.

6When the Philistines asked, "Who did this?" they were told, "Samson, the Timnite's son-in-law, because his wife was given to his friend."

So the Philistines went up and burned her and her father to death. **7**Samson said to them, "Since you've acted like this, I won't stop until I get my revenge on you." **8**He attacked them viciously and slaughtered many of them. Then he went down and stayed in a cave in the rock of Etam.

9The Philistines went up and camped in Judah, spreading out near Lehi. **10**The men of Judah asked, "Why have you come to fight us?"

"We have come to take Samson prisoner," they answered, "to do to him as he did to us."

11Then three thousand men from Judah

a 15 Some Septuagint manuscripts and Syriac; Hebrew seventh

went down to the cave in the rock of Etam and said to Samson, "Don't you realize that the Philistines are rulers over us? What have you done to us?"

He answered, "I merely did to them what they did to me."

¹²They said to him, "We've come to tie you up and hand you over to the Philistines."

Samson said, "Swear to me that you won't kill me yourselves."

¹³"Agreed," they answered. "We will only tie you up and hand you over to them. We will not kill you." So they bound him with two new ropes and led him up from the rock. ¹⁴As he approached Lehi, the Philistines came toward him shouting. The Spirit of the Lord came upon him in power. The ropes on his arms became like charred flax, and the bindings dropped from his hands. ¹⁵Finding a fresh jawbone of a donkey, he grabbed it and struck down a thousand men.

¹⁶Then Samson said,

"With a donkey's jawbone
  I have made donkeys of them.ᵃ
With a donkey's jawbone
  I have killed a thousand men."

¹⁷When he finished speaking, he threw away the jawbone; and the place was called Ramath Lehi.ᵇ

¹⁸Because he was very thirsty, he cried out to the Lord, "You have given your servant this great victory. Must I now die of thirst and fall into the hands of the uncircumcised?" ¹⁹Then God opened up the hollow place in Lehi, and water came out of it. When Samson drank, his strength returned and he revived. So the spring was called En Hakkore,ᶜ and it is still there in Lehi.

²⁰Samson ledᵈ Israel for twenty years in the days of the Philistines.

Samson and Delilah

16 One day Samson went to Gaza, where he saw a prostitute. He went in to spend the night with her. ²The people of Gaza were told, "Samson is here!" So they surrounded the place and lay in wait for him all night at the city gate. They made no move during the night, saying, "At dawn we'll kill him."

³But Samson lay there only until the middle of the night. Then he got up and took hold of the doors of the city gate, together with the two posts, and tore them loose, bar and all. He lifted them to his shoulders and carried them to the top of the hill that faces Hebron.

⁴Some time later, he fell in love with a woman in the Valley of Sorek whose name was Delilah. ⁵The rulers of the Philistines went to her and said, "See if you can lure him into showing you the secret of his great strength and how we can overpower him so we may tie him up and subdue him. Each one of us will give you eleven hundred shekelsᵉ of silver."

⁶So Delilah said to Samson, "Tell me the secret of your great strength and how you can be tied up and subdued."

⁷Samson answered her, "If anyone ties me with seven fresh thongsᶠ that have not been dried, I'll become as weak as any other man."

⁸Then the rulers of the Philistines brought her seven fresh thongs that had not been dried, and she tied him with them. ⁹With men hidden in the room, she called to him, "Samson, the Philistines are upon you!" But he snapped the thongs as easily as a piece of string snaps when it comes close to a flame. So the secret of his strength was not discovered.

¹⁰Then Delilah said to Samson, "You have made a fool of me; you lied to me. Come now, tell me how you can be tied."

¹¹He said, "If anyone ties me securely with new ropes that have never been used, I'll become as weak as any other man."

¹²So Delilah took new ropes and tied him with them. Then, with men hidden in the room, she called to him, "Samson, the Philistines are upon you!" But he snapped the ropes off his arms as if they were threads.

¹³Delilah then said to Samson, "Until now, you have been making a fool of me and lying to me. Tell me how you can be tied."

He replied, "If you weave the seven braids of my head into the fabric ⌊on the loom⌋ and tighten it with the pin, I'll become as weak as any other man." So while he was sleeping, Delilah took the seven braids of his head, wove them into the fabric ¹⁴andᵍ tightened it with the pin.

Again she called to him, "Samson, the Philistines are upon you!" He awoke from

---

ᵃ16 Or *made a heap or two*; the Hebrew for *donkey* sounds like the Hebrew for *heap*.   ᵇ17 *Ramath Lehi* means *jawbone hill*.   ᶜ19 *En Hakkore* means *caller's spring*.   ᵈ20 Traditionally *judged*   ᵉ5 That is, about 28 pounds (about 13 kilograms)   ᶠ7 Or *bowstrings*; also in verses 8 and 9   ᵍ13,14 Some Septuagint manuscripts; Hebrew *"I can, if you weave the seven braids of my head into the fabric ⌊on the loom⌋."* ¹⁴*So she*

DON'T JUST CHOOSE THE EASY ROAD!

Les is a smart, talented guy. He's also lazy.

Since Les wants to be an engineer, his dad recommended a challenging junior schedule of algebra, chemistry, typing, history, English, computer programming and physical education.

Les signed up for algebra, chorus, study hall, history, English, woodworking and volleyball.

"Oh, so do you like to sing and work with wood, Les?"

"No. I signed up for those classes because they're an automatic A."

Look It Up

All too often, we adopt a lazy approach to life. Rather than seeking out challenges that will stretch us and cause us to grow, we choose easy options that don't require anything at all.

Thank God that Jesus didn't make his decisions based on which option was the easiest. Had he done that, we'd still be in our sins. Instead, his decision was to do God's will—no matter what.

"Jesus took the Twelve aside and told them, 'We are going up to Jerusalem, and everything that is written by the prophets about the Son of Man will be fulfilled. He will be handed over to the Gentiles. They will mock him, insult him, spit on him, flog him and kill him' " (Luke 18:31–32).

Being crucified was not a fun plan—not something that Jesus was thrilled about. And yet his attitude was, "Father, if you are willing, take this cup from me; yet not my will, but yours be done" (Luke 22:42).

Think It Through

It doesn't seem like a big deal now, but Les made some poor academic choices last spring. He's having fun now, but when he goes off to college, he'll kick himself for not having learned to type and for not having exposed himself to more courses relevant to engineering.

Are you making decisions now (spiritual, academic, social, physical) that may come back to haunt you later?

Work It Out

Some "ABCs" for you:

Ask God to teach you how to make wise decisions.

Be sure to look up and read the verses in the "Nail It Down" section.

Commit to a lifestyle of doing what is right, not just what is easy.

Nail It Down

Read Judges 16 (especially verse 10) for how wrong choices have lasting consequences.

Turn to pages 246, 1005 and 1246 for other readings on decisions.
Turn to page 267 for Tuesday's reading.

Topic

DECISIONS

his sleep and pulled up the pin and the loom, with the fabric.

15Then she said to him, "How can you say, 'I love you,' when you won't confide in me? This is the third time you have made a fool of me and haven't told me the secret of your great strength." **16**With such nagging she prodded him day after day until he was tired to death.

17So he told her everything. "No razor has ever been used on my head," he said, "because I have been a Nazirite set apart to God since birth. If my head were shaved, my strength would leave me, and I would become as weak as any other man."

18When Delilah saw that he had told her everything, she sent word to the rulers of the Philistines, "Come back once more; he has told me everything." So the rulers of the Philistines returned with the silver in their hands. **19**Having put him to sleep on her lap, she called a man to shave off the seven braids of his hair, and so began to subdue him.*a* And his strength left him.

20Then she called, "Samson, the Philistines are upon you!"

He awoke from his sleep and thought, "I'll go out as before and shake myself free." But he did not know that the Lord had left him. **21**Then the Philistines seized him, gouged out his eyes and took him down to Gaza. Binding him with bronze shackles, they set him to grinding in the prison. **22**But the hair on his head began to grow again after it had been shaved.

The Death of Samson

23Now the rulers of the Philistines assembled to offer a great sacrifice to Dagon their god and to celebrate, saying, "Our god has delivered Samson, our enemy, into our hands."

24When the people saw him, they praised their god, saying,

"Our god has delivered our enemy
    into our hands,
the one who laid waste our land
    and multiplied our slain."

25While they were in high spirits, they shouted, "Bring out Samson to entertain us." So they called Samson out of the prison, and he performed for them.

When they stood him among the pillars, **26**Samson said to the servant who held his hand, "Put me where I can feel the pillars that support the temple, so that I may lean against them." **27**Now the temple was crowded with men and women; all the rulers of the Philistines were there, and on the roof were about three thousand men and women watching Samson perform. **28**Then Samson prayed to the Lord, "O Sovereign Lord, remember me. O God, please strengthen me just once more, and let me with one blow get revenge on the Philistines for my two eyes." **29**Then Samson reached toward the two central pillars on which the temple stood. Bracing himself against them, his right hand on the one and his left hand on the other, **30**Samson said, "Let me die with the Philistines!" Then he pushed with all his might, and down came the temple on the rulers and all the people in it. Thus he killed many more when he died than while he lived.

31Then his brothers and his father's whole family went down to get him. They brought him back and buried him between Zorah and Eshtaol in the tomb of Manoah his father. He had led*b* Israel twenty years.

Micah's Idols

17 Now a man named Micah from the hill country of Ephraim **2**said to his mother, "The eleven hundred shekels*c* of silver that were taken from you and about which I heard you utter a curse—I have that silver with me; I took it."

Then his mother said, "The Lord bless you, my son!"

3When he returned the eleven hundred shekels of silver to his mother, she said, "I solemnly consecrate my silver to the Lord for my son to make a carved image and a cast idol. I will give it back to you."

4So he returned the silver to his mother, and she took two hundred shekels*d* of silver and gave them to a silversmith, who made them into the image and the idol. And they were put in Micah's house.

5Now this man Micah had a shrine, and he made an ephod and some idols and installed one of his sons as his priest. **6**In those days Israel had no king; everyone did as he saw fit.

7A young Levite from Bethlehem in Judah, who had been living within the clan of Judah, **8**left that town in search of some other place to stay. On his way*e* he came to Mi-

---

a19 Hebrew; some Septuagint manuscripts *and he began to weaken*   *b31* Traditionally *judged*   *c2* That is, about 28 pounds (about 13 kilograms)   *d4* That is, about 5 pounds (about 2.3 kilograms)   *e8* Or *To carry on his profession* cah's house in the hill country of Ephraim. **9**Micah asked him, "Where are you from?"

"I'm a Levite from Bethlehem in Judah," he said, "and I'm looking for a place to stay."

10Then Micah said to him, "Live with me and be my father and priest, and I'll give you ten shekels*a* of silver a year, your clothes and your food." **11**So the Levite agreed to live with him, and the young man was to him like one of his sons. **12**Then Micah installed the Levite, and the young man became his priest and lived in his house. **13**And Micah said, "Now I know that the LORD will be good to me, since this Levite has become my priest."

Danites Settle in Laish

18 In those days Israel had no king.

And in those days the tribe of the Danites was seeking a place of their own where they might settle, because they had not yet come into an inheritance among the tribes of Israel. **2**So the Danites sent five warriors from Zorah and Eshtaol to spy out the land and explore it. These men represented all their clans. They told them, "Go, explore the land."

The men entered the hill country of Ephraim and came to the house of Micah, where they spent the night. **3**When they were near Micah's house, they recognized the voice of the young Levite; so they turned in there and asked him, "Who brought you here? What are you doing in this place? Why are you here?"

4He told them what Micah had done for him, and said, "He has hired me and I am his priest."

5Then they said to him, "Please inquire of God to learn whether our journey will be successful."

6The priest answered them, "Go in peace. Your journey has the LORD's approval."

7So the five men left and came to Laish, where they saw that the people were living in safety, like the Sidonians, unsuspecting and secure. And since their land lacked nothing, they were prosperous.*b* Also, they lived a long way from the Sidonians and had no relationship with anyone else.*c*

8When they returned to Zorah and Eshtaol, their brothers asked them, "How did you find things?"

9They answered, "Come on, let's attack them! We have seen that the land is very good. Aren't you going to do something?

Don't hesitate to go there and take it over. **10**When you get there, you will find an unsuspecting people and a spacious land that God has put into your hands, a land that lacks nothing whatever."

11Then six hundred men from the clan of the Danites, armed for battle, set out from Zorah and Eshtaol. **12**On their way they set up camp near Kiriath Jearim in Judah. This is why the place west of Kiriath Jearim is called Mahaneh Dan*d* to this day. **13**From there they went on to the hill country of Ephraim and came to Micah's house.

14Then the five men who had spied out the land of Laish said to their brothers, "Do you know that one of these houses has an ephod, other household gods, a carved image and a cast idol? Now you know what to do." **15**So they turned in there and went to the house of the young Levite at Micah's place and greeted him. **16**The six hundred Danites, armed for battle, stood at the entrance to the gate. **17**The five men who had spied out the land went inside and took the carved image, the ephod, the other household gods and the cast idol while the priest and the six hundred armed men stood at the entrance to the gate.

18When these men went into Micah's house and took the carved image, the ephod, the other household gods and the cast idol, the priest said to them, "What are you doing?"

19They answered him, "Be quiet! Don't say a word. Come with us, and be our father and priest. Isn't it better that you serve a tribe and clan in Israel as priest rather than just one man's household?" **20**Then the priest was glad. He took the ephod, the other household gods and the carved image and went along with the people. **21**Putting their little children, their livestock and their possessions in front of them, they turned away and left.

22When they had gone some distance from Micah's house, the men who lived near Micah were called together and overtook the Danites. **23**As they shouted after them, the Danites turned and said to Micah, "What's the matter with you that you called out your men to fight?"

24He replied, "You took the gods I made, and my priest, and went away. What else do I have? How can you ask, 'What's the matter with you?'"

25The Danites answered, "Don't argue

---

a 10 That is, about 4 ounces (about 110 grams)   *b 7* The meaning of the Hebrew for this clause is uncertain.
c 7 Hebrew; some Septuagint manuscripts *with the Arameans*   *d 12 Mahaneh Dan* means *Dan's camp.*

with us, or some hot-tempered men will attack you, and you and your family will lose your lives." **26**So the Danites went their way, and Micah, seeing that they were too strong for him, turned around and went back home.

27Then they took what Micah had made, and his priest, and went on to Laish, against a peaceful and unsuspecting people. They attacked them with the sword and burned down their city. **28**There was no one to rescue them because they lived a long way from Sidon and had no relationship with anyone else. The city was in a valley near Beth Rehob.

The Danites rebuilt the city and settled there. **29**They named it Dan after their forefather Dan, who was born to Israel — though the city used to be called Laish. **30**There the Danites set up for themselves the idols, and Jonathan son of Gershom, the son of Moses,*a* and his sons were priests for the tribe of Dan until the time of the captivity of the land. **31**They continued to use the idols Micah had made, all the time the house of God was in Shiloh.

A Levite and His Concubine

19 In those days Israel had no king.

Now a Levite who lived in a remote area in the hill country of Ephraim took a concubine from Bethlehem in Judah. **2**But she was unfaithful to him. She left him and went back to her father's house in Bethlehem, Judah. After she had been there four months, **3**her husband went to her to persuade her to return. He had with him his servant and two donkeys. She took him into her father's house, and when her father saw him, he gladly welcomed him. **4**His father-in-law, the girl's father, prevailed upon him to stay; so he remained with him three days, eating and drinking, and sleeping there.

5On the fourth day they got up early and he prepared to leave, but the girl's father said to his son-in-law, "Refresh yourself with something to eat; then you can go." **6**So the two of them sat down to eat and drink together. Afterward the girl's father said, "Please stay tonight and enjoy yourself." **7**And when the man got up to go, his father-in-law persuaded him, so he stayed there that night. **8**On the morning of the fifth day, when he rose to go, the girl's father said, "Refresh yourself. Wait till afternoon!" So the two of them ate together.

9Then when the man, with his concubine and his servant, got up to leave, his father-in-law, the girl's father, said, "Now look, it's almost evening. Spend the night here; the day is nearly over. Stay and enjoy yourself. Early tomorrow morning you can get up and be on your way home." **10**But, unwilling to stay another night, the man left and went toward Jebus (that is, Jerusalem), with his two saddled donkeys and his concubine.

11When they were near Jebus and the day was almost gone, the servant said to his master, "Come, let's stop at this city of the Jebusites and spend the night."

12His master replied, "No. We won't go into an alien city, whose people are not Israelites. We will go on to Gibeah." **13**He added, "Come, let's try to reach Gibeah or Ramah and spend the night in one of those places." **14**So they went on, and the sun set as they neared Gibeah in Benjamin. **15**There they stopped to spend the night. They went and sat in the city square, but no one took them into his home for the night.

16That evening an old man from the hill country of Ephraim, who was living in Gibeah (the men of the place were Benjamites), came in from his work in the fields. **17**When he looked and saw the traveler in the city square, the old man asked, "Where are you going? Where did you come from?"

18He answered, "We are on our way from Bethlehem in Judah to a remote area in the hill country of Ephraim where I live. I have been to Bethlehem in Judah and now I am going to the house of the LORD. No one has taken me into his house. **19**We have both straw and fodder for our donkeys and bread and wine for ourselves your servants — me, your maidservant, and the young man with us. We don't need anything."

20"You are welcome at my house," the old man said. "Let me supply whatever you need. Only don't spend the night in the square." **21**So he took him into his house and fed his donkeys. After they had washed their feet, they had something to eat and drink.

22While they were enjoying themselves, some of the wicked men of the city surrounded the house. Pounding on the door, they shouted to the old man who owned the house, "Bring out the man who came to your house so we can have sex with him."

23The owner of the house went outside and said to them, "No, my friends, don't be so vile. Since this man is my guest, don't do this disgraceful thing. **24**Look, here is my vir-

---

a30 An ancient Hebrew scribal tradition, some Septuagint manuscripts and Vulgate; Masoretic Text *Manasseh* gin daughter, and his concubine. I will bring them out to you now, and you can use them and do to them whatever you wish. But to this man, don't do such a disgraceful thing."

25But the men would not listen to him. So the man took his concubine and sent her outside to them, and they raped her and abused her throughout the night, and at dawn they let her go. **26**At daybreak the woman went back to the house where her master was staying, fell down at the door and lay there until daylight.

27When her master got up in the morning and opened the door of the house and stepped out to continue on his way, there lay his concubine, fallen in the doorway of the house, with her hands on the threshold. **28**He said to her, "Get up; let's go." But there was no answer. Then the man put her on his donkey and set out for home.

29When he reached home, he took a knife and cut up his concubine, limb by limb, into twelve parts and sent them into all the areas of Israel. **30**Everyone who saw it said, "Such a thing has never been seen or done, not since the day the Israelites came up out of Egypt. Think about it! Consider it! Tell us what to do!"

Israelites Fight the Benjamites

20 Then all the Israelites from Dan to Beersheba and from the land of Gilead came out as one man and assembled before the LORD in Mizpah. **2**The leaders of all the people of the tribes of Israel took their places in the assembly of the people of God, four hundred thousand soldiers armed with swords. **3**(The Benjamites heard that the Israelites had gone up to Mizpah.) Then the Israelites said, "Tell us how this awful thing happened."

4So the Levite, the husband of the murdered woman, said, "I and my concubine came to Gibeah in Benjamin to spend the night. **5**During the night the men of Gibeah came after me and surrounded the house, intending to kill me. They raped my concubine, and she died. **6**I took my concubine, cut her into pieces and sent one piece to each region of Israel's inheritance, because they committed this lewd and disgraceful act in Israel. **7**Now, all you Israelites, speak up and give your verdict."

8All the people rose as one man, saying, "None of us will go home. No, not one of us will return to his house. **9**But now this is what we'll do to Gibeah: We'll go up against it as the lot directs. **10**We'll take ten men out of every hundred from all the tribes of Israel, and a hundred from a thousand, and a thousand from ten thousand, to get provisions for the army. Then, when the army arrives at Gibeah*a* in Benjamin, it can give them what they deserve for all this vileness done in Israel." **11**So all the men of Israel got together and united as one man against the city.

12The tribes of Israel sent men throughout the tribe of Benjamin, saying, "What about this awful crime that was committed among you? **13**Now surrender those wicked men of Gibeah so that we may put them to death and purge the evil from Israel."

But the Benjamites would not listen to their fellow Israelites. **14**From their towns they came together at Gibeah to fight against the Israelites. **15**At once the Benjamites mobilized twenty-six thousand swordsmen from their towns, in addition to seven hundred chosen men from those living in Gibeah. **16**Among all these soldiers there were seven hundred chosen men who were left-handed, each of whom could sling a stone at a hair and not miss.

17Israel, apart from Benjamin, mustered four hundred thousand swordsmen, all of them fighting men.

18The Israelites went up to Bethel*b* and inquired of God. They said, "Who of us shall go first to fight against the Benjamites?"

The LORD replied, "Judah shall go first."

19The next morning the Israelites got up and pitched camp near Gibeah. **20**The men of Israel went out to fight the Benjamites and took up battle positions against them at Gibeah. **21**The Benjamites came out of Gibeah and cut down twenty-two thousand Israelites on the battlefield that day. **22**But the men of Israel encouraged one another and again took up their positions where they had stationed themselves the first day. **23**The Israelites went up and wept before the LORD until evening, and they inquired of the LORD. They said, "Shall we go up again to battle against the Benjamites, our brothers?"

The LORD answered, "Go up against them."

24Then the Israelites drew near to Benjamin the second day. **25**This time, when the Benjamites came out from Gibeah to oppose them, they cut down another eighteen thousand Israelites, all of them armed with swords.

---

a 10 One Hebrew manuscript; most Hebrew manuscripts *Geba*, a variant of *Gibeah*   *b* 18 Or *to the house of God*; also in verse 26

26Then the Israelites, all the people, went up to Bethel, and there they sat weeping before the Lord. They fasted that day until evening and presented burnt offerings and fellowship offerings[a] to the Lord. 27And the Israelites inquired of the Lord. (In those days the ark of the covenant of God was there, 28with Phinehas son of Eleazar, the son of Aaron, ministering before it.) They asked, "Shall we go up again to battle with Benjamin our brother, or not?"

The Lord responded, "Go, for tomorrow I will give them into your hands."

29Then Israel set an ambush around Gibeah. 30They went up against the Benjamites on the third day and took up positions against Gibeah as they had done before. 31The Benjamites came out to meet them and were drawn away from the city. They began to inflict casualties on the Israelites as before, so that about thirty men fell in the open field and on the roads—the one leading to Bethel and the other to Gibeah.

32While the Benjamites were saying, "We are defeating them as before," the Israelites were saying, "Let's retreat and draw them away from the city to the roads."

33All the men of Israel moved from their places and took up positions at Baal Tamar, and the Israelite ambush charged out of its place on the west[b] of Gibeah.[c] 34Then ten thousand of Israel's finest men made a frontal attack on Gibeah. The fighting was so heavy that the Benjamites did not realize how near disaster was. 35The Lord defeated Benjamin before Israel, and on that day the Israelites struck down 25,100 Benjamites, all armed with swords. 36Then the Benjamites saw that they were beaten.

Now the men of Israel had given way before Benjamin, because they relied on the ambush they had set near Gibeah. 37The men who had been in ambush made a sudden dash into Gibeah, spread out and put the whole city to the sword. 38The men of Israel had arranged with the ambush that they should send up a great cloud of smoke from the city, 39and then the men of Israel would turn in the battle.

The Benjamites had begun to inflict casualties on the men of Israel (about thirty), and they said, "We are defeating them as in the first battle." 40But when the column of smoke began to rise from the city, the Benjamites turned and saw the smoke of the whole city going up into the sky. 41Then the men of Israel turned on them, and the men of Benjamin were terrified, because they realized that disaster had come upon them. 42So they fled before the Israelites in the direction of the desert, but they could not escape the battle. And the men of Israel who came out of the towns cut them down there. 43They surrounded the Benjamites, chased them and easily[d] overran them in the vicinity of Gibeah on the east. 44Eighteen thousand Benjamites fell, all of them valiant fighters. 45As they turned and fled toward the desert to the rock of Rimmon, the Israelites cut down five thousand men along the roads. They kept pressing after the Benjamites as far as Gidom and struck down two thousand more.

46On that day twenty-five thousand Benjamite swordsmen fell, all of them valiant fighters. 47But six hundred men turned and fled into the desert to the rock of Rimmon, where they stayed four months. 48The men of Israel went back to Benjamin and put all the towns to the sword, including the animals and everything else they found. All the towns they came across they set on fire.

Wives for the Benjamites

21 The men of Israel had taken an oath at Mizpah: "Not one of us will give his daughter in marriage to a Benjamite."

2The people went to Bethel,[e] where they sat before God until evening, raising their voices and weeping bitterly. 3"O Lord, the God of Israel," they cried, "why has this happened to Israel? Why should one tribe be missing from Israel today?"

4Early the next day the people built an altar and presented burnt offerings and fellowship offerings.[a]

5Then the Israelites asked, "Who from all the tribes of Israel has failed to assemble before the Lord?" For they had taken a solemn oath that anyone who failed to assemble before the Lord at Mizpah should certainly be put to death.

6Now the Israelites grieved for their brothers, the Benjamites. "Today one tribe is cut off from Israel," they said. 7"How can we provide wives for those who are left, since we have taken an oath by the Lord not to give them any of our daughters in marriage?" 8Then they asked, "Which one of the tribes of Israel failed to assemble before the

---

a26,4 Traditionally *peace offerings*   b33 Some Septuagint manuscripts and Vulgate; the meaning of the Hebrew for this word is uncertain.   c33 Hebrew *Geba*, a variant of *Gibeah*   d43 The meaning of the Hebrew for this word is uncertain.   e2 Or *to the house of God*

LORD at Mizpah?" They discovered that no one from Jabesh Gilead had come to the camp for the assembly. **9**For when they counted the people, they found that none of the people of Jabesh Gilead were there.

10So the assembly sent twelve thousand fighting men with instructions to go to Jabesh Gilead and put to the sword those living there, including the women and children. **11**"This is what you are to do," they said. "Kill every male and every woman who is not a virgin." **12**They found among the people living in Jabesh Gilead four hundred young women who had never slept with a man, and they took them to the camp at Shiloh in Canaan.

13Then the whole assembly sent an offer of peace to the Benjamites at the rock of Rimmon. **14**So the Benjamites returned at that time and were given the women of Jabesh Gilead who had been spared. But there were not enough for all of them.

15The people grieved for Benjamin, because the LORD had made a gap in the tribes of Israel. **16**And the elders of the assembly said, "With the women of Benjamin destroyed, how shall we provide wives for the men who are left? **17**The Benjamite survivors must have heirs," they said, "so that a tribe of Israel will not be wiped out. **18**We can't give them our daughters as wives, since we Israelites have taken this oath: 'Cursed be anyone who gives a wife to a Benjamite.' **19**But look, there is the annual festival of the LORD in Shiloh, to the north of Bethel, and east of the road that goes from Bethel to Shechem, and to the south of Lebonah."

20So they instructed the Benjamites, saying, "Go and hide in the vineyards **21**and watch. When the girls of Shiloh come out to join in the dancing, then rush from the vineyards and each of you seize a wife from the girls of Shiloh and go to the land of Benjamin. **22**When their fathers or brothers complain to us, we will say to them, 'Do us a kindness by helping them, because we did not get wives for them during the war, and you are innocent, since you did not give your daughters to them.' "

23So that is what the Benjamites did. While the girls were dancing, each man caught one and carried her off to be his wife. Then they returned to their inheritance and rebuilt the towns and settled in them.

24At that time the Israelites left that place and went home to their tribes and clans, each to his own inheritance.

25In those days Israel had no king; everyone did as he saw fit.

RUTH

THIS is a story with a happy ending. When Naomi, widowed and childless in Moab, decides to return to her hometown of Bethlehem, her daughter-in-law Ruth chooses to accompany her. There Ruth gleans in the fields of Boaz so the two women will have food. Eventually Boaz marries Ruth. This couple has an impressive family tree; Jesus himself is one of their descendants. While reading Ruth, remember that God plans history. And even when things look bleak, he is writing his love story in the lives of individuals and nations.

Outline of Contents

Naomi and Ruth

1 In the days when the judges ruled,*a* there was a famine in the land, and a man from Bethlehem in Judah, together with his wife and two sons, went to live for a while in the country of Moab. ²The man's name was Elimelech, his wife's name Naomi, and the names of his two sons were Mahlon and Kilion. They were Ephrathites from Bethlehem, Judah. And they went to Moab and lived there.

³Now Elimelech, Naomi's husband, died, and she was left with her two sons. ⁴They married Moabite women, one named Orpah and the other Ruth. After they had lived there about ten years, ⁵both Mahlon and Kil-ion also died, and Naomi was left without her two sons and her husband.

⁶When she heard in Moab that the Lord had come to the aid of his people by providing food for them, Naomi and her daughters-in-law prepared to return home from there. ⁷With her two daughters-in-law she left the place where she had been living and set out on the road that would take them back to the land of Judah.

⁸Then Naomi said to her two daughters-in-law, "Go back, each of you, to your mother's home. May the Lord show kindness to you, as you have shown to your dead and to me. ⁹May the Lord grant that each of you will find rest in the home of another husband."

Then she kissed them and they wept

a 1 Traditionally judged

aloud [10]and said to her, "We will go back with you to your people."

[11]But Naomi said, "Return home, my daughters. Why would you come with me? Am I going to have any more sons, who could become your husbands? [12]Return home, my daughters; I am too old to have another husband. Even if I thought there was still hope for me—even if I had a husband tonight and then gave birth to sons—[13]would you wait until they grew up? Would you remain unmarried for them? No, my daughters. It is more bitter for me than for you, because the LORD's hand has gone out against me!"

[14]At this they wept again. Then Orpah kissed her mother-in-law good-by, but Ruth clung to her.

[15]"Look," said Naomi, "your sister-in-law is going back to her people and her gods. Go back with her."

[16]But Ruth replied, "Don't urge me to leave you or to turn back from you. Where you go I will go, and where you stay I will stay. Your people will be my people and your God my God. [17]Where you die I will die, and there I will be buried. May the LORD deal with me, be it ever so severely, if anything but death separates you and me." [18]When Naomi realized that Ruth was determined to go with her, she stopped urging her.

[19]So the two women went on until they came to Bethlehem. When they arrived in Bethlehem, the whole town was stirred because of them, and the women exclaimed, "Can this be Naomi?"

[20]"Don't call me Naomi,[a]" she told them. "Call me Mara,[b] because the Almighty[c] has made my life very bitter. [21]I went away full, but the LORD has brought me back empty. Why call me Naomi? The LORD has afflicted[d] me; the Almighty has brought misfortune upon me."

[22]So Naomi returned from Moab accompanied by Ruth the Moabitess, her daughter-in-law, arriving in Bethlehem as the barley harvest was beginning.

Ruth Meets Boaz

2 Now Naomi had a relative on her husband's side, from the clan of Elimelech, a man of standing, whose name was Boaz.

[2]And Ruth the Moabitess said to Naomi, "Let me go to the fields and pick up the leftover grain behind anyone in whose eyes I find favor."

Naomi said to her, "Go ahead, my daughter." [3]So she went out and began to glean in the fields behind the harvesters. As it turned out, she found herself working in a field belonging to Boaz, who was from the clan of Elimelech.

[4]Just then Boaz arrived from Bethlehem and greeted the harvesters, "The LORD be with you!"

"The LORD bless you!" they called back.

[5]Boaz asked the foreman of his harvesters, "Whose young woman is that?"

[6]The foreman replied, "She is the Moabitess who came back from Moab with Naomi. [7]She said, 'Please let me glean and gather among the sheaves behind the harvesters.' She went into the field and has worked steadily from morning till now, except for a short rest in the shelter."

[8]So Boaz said to Ruth, "My daughter, listen to me. Don't go and glean in another field and don't go away from here. Stay here with my servant girls. [9]Watch the field where the men are harvesting, and follow along after the girls. I have told the men not to touch you. And whenever you are thirsty, go and get a drink from the water jars the men have filled."

[10]At this, she bowed down with her face to the ground. She exclaimed, "Why have I found such favor in your eyes that you notice me—a foreigner?"

[11]Boaz replied, "I've been told all about what you have done for your mother-in-law since the death of your husband—how you left your father and mother and your homeland and came to live with a people you did not know before. [12]May the LORD repay you for what you have done. May you be richly rewarded by the LORD, the God of Israel, under whose wings you have come to take refuge."

[13]"May I continue to find favor in your eyes, my lord," she said. "You have given me comfort and have spoken kindly to your servant—though I do not have the standing of one of your servant girls."

[14]At mealtime Boaz said to her, "Come over here. Have some bread and dip it in the wine vinegar."

When she sat down with the harvesters, he offered her some roasted grain. She ate all she wanted and had some left over. [15]As she got up to glean, Boaz gave orders to his men, "Even if she gathers among the sheaves, don't embarrass her. [16]Rather, pull

---

[a]20 Naomi means pleasant; also in verse 21.   [b]20 Mara means bitter.   [c]20 Hebrew Shaddai; also in verse 21   [d]21 Or has testified against

out some stalks for her from the bundles and leave them for her to pick up, and don't rebuke her."

17So Ruth gleaned in the field until evening. Then she threshed the barley she had gathered, and it amounted to about an ephah. *a* **18**She carried it back to town, and her mother-in-law saw how much she had gathered. Ruth also brought out and gave her what she had left over after she had eaten enough.

19Her mother-in-law asked her, "Where did you glean today? Where did you work? Blessed be the man who took notice of you!"

Then Ruth told her mother-in-law about the one at whose place she had been working. "The name of the man I worked with today is Boaz," she said.

20"The LORD bless him!" Naomi said to her daughter-in-law. "He has not stopped showing his kindness to the living and the dead." She added, "That man is our close relative; he is one of our kinsman-redeemers."

21Then Ruth the Moabitess said, "He even said to me, 'Stay with my workers until they finish harvesting all my grain.' "

22Naomi said to Ruth her daughter-in-law, "It will be good for you, my daughter, to go with his girls, because in someone else's field you might be harmed."

23So Ruth stayed close to the servant girls of Boaz to glean until the barley and wheat harvests were finished. And she lived with her mother-in-law.

Ruth and Boaz at the Threshing Floor

3 One day Naomi her mother-in-law said to her, "My daughter, should I not try to find a home*b* for you, where you will be well provided for? **2**Is not Boaz, with whose servant girls you have been, a kinsman of ours? Tonight he will be winnowing barley on the threshing floor. **3**Wash and perfume yourself, and put on your best clothes. Then go down to the threshing floor, but don't let him know you are there until he has finished eating and drinking. **4**When he lies down, note the place where he is lying. Then go and uncover his feet and lie down. He will tell you what to do."

5"I will do whatever you say," Ruth answered. **6**So she went down to the threshing floor and did everything her mother-in-law told her to do.

7When Boaz had finished eating and drinking and was in good spirits, he went over to lie down at the far end of the grain pile. Ruth approached quietly, uncovered his feet and lay down. **8**In the middle of the night something startled the man, and he turned and discovered a woman lying at his feet.

9"Who are you?" he asked.

"I am your servant Ruth," she said. "Spread the corner of your garment over me, since you are a kinsman-redeemer."

10"The LORD bless you, my daughter," he replied. "This kindness is greater than that which you showed earlier: You have not run after the younger men, whether rich or poor. **11**And now, my daughter, don't be afraid. I will do for you all you ask. All my fellow townsmen know that you are a woman of noble character. **12**Although it is true that I am near of kin, there is a kinsman-redeemer nearer than I. **13**Stay here for the night, and in the morning if he wants to redeem, good; let him redeem. But if he is not willing, as surely as the LORD lives I will do it. Lie here until morning."

14So she lay at his feet until morning, but got up before anyone could be recognized; and he said, "Don't let it be known that a woman came to the threshing floor."

15He also said, "Bring me the shawl you are wearing and hold it out." When she did so, he poured into it six measures of barley and put it on her. Then he*c* went back to town.

16When Ruth came to her mother-in-law, Naomi asked, "How did it go, my daughter?"

Then she told her everything Boaz had done for her **17**and added, "He gave me these six measures of barley, saying, 'Don't go back to your mother-in-law empty-handed.' "

18Then Naomi said, "Wait, my daughter, until you find out what happens. For the man will not rest until the matter is settled today."

Boaz Marries Ruth

4 Meanwhile Boaz went up to the town gate and sat there. When the kinsman-redeemer he had mentioned came along, Boaz said, "Come over here, my friend, and sit down." So he went over and sat down.

2Boaz took ten of the elders of the town and said, "Sit here," and they did so. **3**Then he said to the kinsman-redeemer, "Naomi, who has come back from Moab, is selling the piece of land that belonged to our broth-

---

a17 That is, probably about 3/5 bushel (about 22 liters)   *b1* Hebrew *find rest* (see Ruth 1:9)   *c15* Most Hebrew manuscripts; many Hebrew manuscripts, Vulgate and Syriac *she*

THE FAITHFULNESS OF RUTH

Individual: Sharon, sixteen.

Role Models: Just about any female singer who is a Christian.

Description: Sharon is an aspiring singer/songwriter who wants to make it big in Christian music.

Result: Because Sharon's church is small (and the youth group is even smaller), Sharon has started going to a church with a big music program. All her friends at the old church feel rejected.

Look It Up
••••

Sharon ought to consider one name for her role model list—Ruth. The book of Ruth in the Old Testament tells the remarkable story of how this Moabite widow left her homeland to live in Palestine with her widowed Jewish mother-in-law Naomi. When Naomi begged Ruth to stay in Moab and find another husband, Ruth uttered her now famous response:

"Don't urge me to leave you or to turn back from you. Where you go I will go, and where you stay I will stay. Your people will be my people and your God my God" (Ruth 1:16).

Think It Through
••••

Ruth lived during the time of the judges (Ruth 1:1). This was a period of violence and moral decay (sort of like today!). Her unwavering devotion and faithfulness were in sharp contrast to the culture.

As a result of her faithfulness to Naomi, God guided Ruth to the field of Boaz, a relative of her dead husband. There she not only found food but also a husband!

Are you being faithful? To God? To your parents? To your responsibilities at work and at school? To your church? If so, God will reward you . . . somehow, someday.

Work It Out
••••

Pick an area of your life in which you need to be more faithful. It can be anything—doing your household chores, studying, reading your Bible, praying, getting to work on time, maintaining a friendship, spending money, calling your parents when you're out, writing letters.

Next, list some realistic goals for the next month. For instance, "I will faithfully feed Fido first thing every morning" or "I will be faithful to spend time with God every day."

Finally, write down specific ways you plan to reach your goal. "I will put a big note that says 'Feed Fido' on the bathroom mirror." Or "Every day I will get up twenty minutes earlier than usual to read the Bible and pray."

Nail It Down
••••

Read the description of Ruth's character in Ruth 3:11.

Turn to pages 229 and 1147 for other readings on heroes.
Turn to page 272 for Wednesday's reading.

Topic
••••

HEROES

er Elimelech. **4**I thought I should bring the matter to your attention and suggest that you buy it in the presence of these seated here and in the presence of the elders of my people. If you will redeem it, do so. But if you*ᵃ* will not, tell me, so I will know. For no one has the right to do it except you, and I am next in line."

"I will redeem it," he said.

5Then Boaz said, "On the day you buy the land from Naomi and from Ruth the Moabitess, you acquire*ᵇ* the dead man's widow, in order to maintain the name of the dead with his property."

6At this, the kinsman-redeemer said, "Then I cannot redeem it because I might endanger my own estate. You redeem it yourself. I cannot do it."

7(Now in earlier times in Israel, for the redemption and transfer of property to become final, one party took off his sandal and gave it to the other. This was the method of legalizing transactions in Israel.)

8So the kinsman-redeemer said to Boaz, "Buy it yourself." And he removed his sandal.

9Then Boaz announced to the elders and all the people, "Today you are witnesses that I have bought from Naomi all the property of Elimelech, Kilion and Mahlon. **10**I have also acquired Ruth the Moabitess, Mahlon's widow, as my wife, in order to maintain the name of the dead with his property, so that his name will not disappear from among his family or from the town records. Today you are witnesses!"

11Then the elders and all those at the gate said, "We are witnesses. May the Lord make the woman who is coming into your home like Rachel and Leah, who together built up the house of Israel. May you have standing in Ephrathah and be famous in Bethlehem. **12**Through the offspring the Lord gives you by this young woman, may your family be like that of Perez, whom Tamar bore to Judah."

The Genealogy of David

13So Boaz took Ruth and she became his wife. Then he went to her, and the Lord enabled her to conceive, and she gave birth to a son. **14**The women said to Naomi: "Praise be to the Lord, who this day has not left you without a kinsman-redeemer. May he become famous throughout Israel! **15**He will renew your life and sustain you in your old age. For your daughter-in-law, who loves you and who is better to you than seven sons, has given him birth."

16Then Naomi took the child, laid him in her lap and cared for him. **17**The women living there said, "Naomi has a son." And they named him Obed. He was the father of Jesse, the father of David.

18This, then, is the family line of Perez:

Perez was the father of Hezron,
19Hezron the father of Ram,
Ram the father of Amminadab,
20Amminadab the father of Nahshon,
Nahshon the father of Salmon,*ᶜ*
21Salmon the father of Boaz,
Boaz the father of Obed,
22Obed the father of Jesse,
and Jesse the father of David.

ᵃ4 Many Hebrew manuscripts, Septuagint, Vulgate and Syriac; most Hebrew manuscripts *he*   *ᵇ5* Hebrew; Vulgate and Syriac *Naomi, you acquire Ruth the Moabitess,*   *ᶜ20* A few Hebrew manuscripts, some Septuagint manuscripts and Vulgate (see also verse 21 and Septuagint of 1 Chron. 2:11); most Hebrew manuscripts *Salma*

"WE want a king!" the people cry out, and God gives them what they want. Saul becomes Israel's first monarch. But soon his disobedience causes God to reject him and choose David to take his place. Saul doesn't give up the crown easily. Jealous to keep power, he attacks David repeatedly. But David trusts God to protect him, knowing that God always fulfills his promises. As you wait for God to fulfill his plans for you, do what David did—develop a life of prayer and praise.

Outline of Contents

The Birth of Samuel

1 There was a certain man from Ramathaim, a Zuphite*a* from the hill country of Ephraim, whose name was Elkanah son of Jeroham, the son of Elihu, the son of Tohu, the son of Zuph, an Ephraimite. ²He had two wives; one was called Hannah and the other Peninnah. Peninnah had children, but Hannah had none.

³Year after year this man went up from his town to worship and sacrifice to the LORD Almighty at Shiloh, where Hophni and Phinehas, the two sons of Eli, were priests of the LORD. ⁴Whenever the day came for Elkanah to sacrifice, he would give portions of the meat to his wife Peninnah and to all her sons and daughters. ⁵But to Hannah he gave a double portion because he loved her, and the LORD had closed her womb. ⁶And because the LORD had closed her womb, her rival kept provoking her in order to irritate her. ⁷This went on year after year. Whenever Hannah went up to the house of the LORD, her rival provoked her till she wept and would not eat. ⁸Elkanah her husband would say to her, "Hannah, why are you weeping? Why don't you eat? Why are you downhearted? Don't I mean more to you than ten sons?"

⁹Once when they had finished eating and

a1 Or *from Ramathaim Zuphim*

drinking in Shiloh, Hannah stood up. Now Eli the priest was sitting on a chair by the doorpost of the LORD's temple.*a* **10**In bitterness of soul Hannah wept much and prayed to the LORD. **11**And she made a vow, saying, "O LORD Almighty, if you will only look upon your servant's misery and remember me, and not forget your servant but give her a son, then I will give him to the LORD for all the days of his life, and no razor will ever be used on his head."

12As she kept on praying to the LORD, Eli observed her mouth. **13**Hannah was praying in her heart, and her lips were moving but her voice was not heard. Eli thought she was drunk **14**and said to her, "How long will you keep on getting drunk? Get rid of your wine."

15"Not so, my lord," Hannah replied, "I am a woman who is deeply troubled. I have not been drinking wine or beer; I was pouring out my soul to the LORD. **16**Do not take your servant for a wicked woman; I have been praying here out of my great anguish and grief."

17Eli answered, "Go in peace, and may the God of Israel grant you what you have asked of him."

18She said, "May your servant find favor in your eyes." Then she went her way and ate something, and her face was no longer downcast.

19Early the next morning they arose and worshiped before the LORD and then went back to their home at Ramah. Elkanah lay with Hannah his wife, and the LORD remembered her. **20**So in the course of time Hannah conceived and gave birth to a son. She named him Samuel,*b* saying, "Because I asked the LORD for him."

Hannah Dedicates Samuel

21When the man Elkanah went up with all his family to offer the annual sacrifice to the LORD and to fulfill his vow, **22**Hannah did not go. She said to her husband, "After the boy is weaned, I will take him and present him before the LORD, and he will live there' always."

23"Do what seems best to you," Elkanah her husband told her. "Stay here until you have weaned him; only may the LORD make good his*c* word." So the woman stayed at home and nursed her son until she had weaned him.

24After he was weaned, she took the boy with her, young as he was, along with a three-year-old bull,*d* an ephah*e* of flour and a skin of wine, and brought him to the house of the LORD at Shiloh. **25**When they had slaughtered the bull, they brought the boy to Eli, **26**and she said to him, "As surely as you live, my lord, I am the woman who stood here beside you praying to the LORD. **27**I prayed for this child, and the LORD has granted me what I asked of him. **28**So now I give him to the LORD. For his whole life he will be given over to the LORD." And he worshiped the LORD there.

Hannah's Prayer

2 Then Hannah prayed and said:

"My heart rejoices in the LORD;
   in the LORD my horn*f* is lifted high.
My mouth boasts over my enemies,
   for I delight in your deliverance.

2"There is no one holy*g* like the LORD;
   there is no one besides you;
   there is no Rock like our God.

3"Do not keep talking so proudly
   or let your mouth speak such
      arrogance,
for the LORD is a God who knows,
   and by him deeds are weighed.

4"The bows of the warriors are broken,
   but those who stumbled are armed
      with strength.
5Those who were full hire themselves
      out for food,
   but those who were hungry hunger
      no more.
She who was barren has borne seven
      children,
   but she who has had many sons
      pines away.

6"The LORD brings death and makes alive;
   he brings down to the grave*h* and
      raises up.
7The LORD sends poverty and wealth;
   he humbles and he exalts.
8He raises the poor from the dust
   and lifts the needy from the ash heap;
he seats them with princes
   and has them inherit a throne of
      honor.

---

a9 That is, tabernacle   *b20 Samuel* sounds like the Hebrew for *heard of God.*   *c23* Masoretic Text; Dead Sea Scrolls, Septuagint and Syriac *your*   *d24* Dead Sea Scrolls, Septuagint and Syriac; Masoretic Text *with three bulls*   *e24* That is, probably about 3/5 bushel (about 22 liters)   *f1 Horn* here symbolizes strength; also in verse 10.   *g2* Or *no Holy One*   *h6* Hebrew *Sheol*

"For the foundations of the earth are the
   LORD's;
upon them he has set the world.
9He will guard the feet of his saints,
   but the wicked will be silenced in
     darkness.

"It is not by strength that one prevails;
10   those who oppose the LORD will be
     shattered.
He will thunder against them from
     heaven;
   the LORD will judge the ends of the
     earth.

"He will give strength to his king
   and exalt the horn of his anointed."

11Then Elkanah went home to Ramah,
but the boy ministered before the LORD under Eli the priest.

Eli's Wicked Sons

12Eli's sons were wicked men; they had no
regard for the LORD. 13Now it was the practice of the priests with the people that whenever anyone offered a sacrifice and while
the meat was being boiled, the servant of
the priest would come with a three-pronged
fork in his hand. 14He would plunge it into
the pan or kettle or caldron or pot, and the
priest would take for himself whatever the
fork brought up. This is how they treated all
the Israelites who came to Shiloh. 15But
even before the fat was burned, the servant
of the priest would come and say to the man
who was sacrificing, "Give the priest some
meat to roast; he won't accept boiled meat
from you, but only raw."

16If the man said to him, "Let the fat be
burned up first, and then take whatever you
want," the servant would then answer, "No,
hand it over now; if you don't, I'll take it by
force."

17This sin of the young men was very
great in the LORD's sight, for they[a] were
treating the LORD's offering with contempt.
18But Samuel was ministering before the
LORD—a boy wearing a linen ephod. 19Each
year his mother made him a little robe and
took it to him when she went up with her
husband to offer the annual sacrifice. 20Eli
would bless Elkanah and his wife, saying,
"May the LORD give you children by this
woman to take the place of the one she
prayed for and gave to the LORD." Then they
would go home. 21And the LORD was gracious to Hannah; she conceived and gave

birth to three sons and two daughters.
Meanwhile, the boy Samuel grew up in the
presence of the LORD.

22Now Eli, who was very old, heard about
everything his sons were doing to all Israel
and how they slept with the women who
served at the entrance to the Tent of Meeting. 23So he said to them, "Why do you do
such things? I hear from all the people about
these wicked deeds of yours. 24No, my sons;
it is not a good report that I hear spreading
among the LORD's people. 25If a man sins
against another man, God[b] may mediate
for him; but if a man sins against the LORD,
who will intercede for him?" His sons, however, did not listen to their father's rebuke,
for it was the LORD's will to put them to
death.

26And the boy Samuel continued to grow
in stature and in favor with the LORD and
with men.

Prophecy Against the House of Eli

27Now a man of God came to Eli and said
to him, "This is what the LORD says: 'Did I not
clearly reveal myself to your father's house
when they were in Egypt under Pharaoh? 28I
chose your father out of all the tribes of Israel to be my priest, to go up to my altar, to
burn incense, and to wear an ephod in my
presence. I also gave your father's house all
the offerings made with fire by the Israelites.
29Why do you[c] scorn my sacrifice and offering that I prescribed for my dwelling?
Why do you honor your sons more than me
by fattening yourselves on the choice parts
of every offering made by my people Israel?'

30"Therefore the LORD, the God of Israel,
declares: 'I promised that your house and
your father's house would minister before
me forever.' But now the LORD declares: 'Far
be it from me! Those who honor me I will
honor, but those who despise me will be disdained. 31The time is coming when I will cut
short your strength and the strength of your
father's house, so that there will not be an
old man in your family line 32and you will
see distress in my dwelling. Although good
will be done to Israel, in your family line
there will never be an old man. 33Every one
of you that I do not cut off from my altar will
be spared only to blind your eyes with tears
and to grieve your heart, and all your
descendants will die in the prime of life.

34"And what happens to your two sons,
Hophni and Phinehas, will be a sign to
you—they will both die on the same day. 35I

---

a17 Or men   b25 Or the judges   c29 The Hebrew is plural.

ACTING LIKE A SPIRITUAL GROWN-UP

L ast January, Chris was in the eighth grade. His primary interests then were riding his bike, collecting baseball cards and playing video games on his home computer.

What a difference a year makes! Now Chris wouldn't be caught dead on his bike, his baseball cards are in a box in the closet and the computer is collecting dust. What captures Chris's attention now? Girls (especially Michelle Dickinson!), clothes and trying to find a job so he can save up enough money to buy his neighbor's motorcycle.

Look It Up
••••

What is it that causes us to lose interest in the things we once loved to do? At one point in your life you probably loved to swing and dig around in the sandbox and ride on your dad's knee like it was a horse. What happened?

Obviously you grew up. You moved on to more adult activities. And that's what God expects us to do in our spiritual lives too: "When I was a child, I talked like a child, I thought like a child, I reasoned like a child. When I became a man, I put childish ways behind me" (1 Corinthians 13:11).

Think It Through
••••

No one can be a little kid forever. It's cute when a one-year-old smears chocolate cake in his or her hair and ears, but what if your best friend did that in the school cafeteria? Then it's not so cute.

We look the other way when a two-year-old throws a tantrum at the mall, but what if you did that every time you gave the wrong answer in English class?

Work It Out
••••

If you have known the Lord for several years, there is no reason that you should be: ignoring God; getting sexually involved; treating your brothers, sisters or classmates like dirt; using filthy language; cheating in school; sneaking out of the house; talking about others behind their backs; lying to your parents; participating in the party scene; or being rude to those in authority.

Those things are inexcusable. You wouldn't dare be so immature as to cry when you don't get your way during P.E. So don't do spiritually immature things either. (Which of the above things do you need to cut out today?)

Nail It Down
••••

Read about Samuel's spiritual growth in 1 Samuel 2:26.

Turn to pages 1264, 1266 and 1284 for other readings on maturity.
Turn to page 281 for Thursday's reading.

Topic
••••
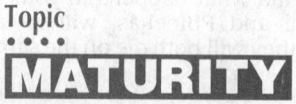

MATURITY

will raise up for myself a faithful priest, who will do according to what is in my heart and mind. I will firmly establish his house, and he will minister before my anointed one always. **36**Then everyone left in your family line will come and bow down before him for a piece of silver and a crust of bread and plead, "Appoint me to some priestly office so I can have food to eat." ' "

The Lord Calls Samuel

3 The boy Samuel ministered before the Lord under Eli. In those days the word of the Lord was rare; there were not many visions.

2One night Eli, whose eyes were becoming so weak that he could barely see, was lying down in his usual place. **3**The lamp of God had not yet gone out, and Samuel was lying down in the temple*a* of the Lord, where the ark of God was. **4**Then the Lord called Samuel.

Samuel answered, "Here I am." **5**And he ran to Eli and said, "Here I am; you called me."

But Eli said, "I did not call; go back and lie down." So he went and lay down.

6Again the Lord called, "Samuel!" And Samuel got up and went to Eli and said, "Here I am; you called me."

"My son," Eli said, "I did not call; go back and lie down."

7Now Samuel did not yet know the Lord: The word of the Lord had not yet been revealed to him.

8The Lord called Samuel a third time, and Samuel got up and went to Eli and said, "Here I am; you called me."

Then Eli realized that the Lord was calling the boy. **9**So Eli told Samuel, "Go and lie down, and if he calls you, say, 'Speak, Lord, for your servant is listening.' " So Samuel went and lay down in his place.

10The Lord came and stood there, calling as at the other times, "Samuel! Samuel!"

Then Samuel said, "Speak, for your servant is listening."

11And the Lord said to Samuel: "See, I am about to do something in Israel that will make the ears of everyone who hears of it tingle. **12**At that time I will carry out against Eli everything I spoke against his family— from beginning to end. **13**For I told him that I would judge his family forever because of the sin he knew about; his sons made themselves contemptible,*b* and he failed to re-

strain them. **14**Therefore, I swore to the house of Eli, 'The guilt of Eli's house will never be atoned for by sacrifice or offering.' "

15Samuel lay down until morning and then opened the doors of the house of the Lord. He was afraid to tell Eli the vision, **16**but Eli called him and said, "Samuel, my son."

Samuel answered, "Here I am."

17"What was it he said to you?" Eli asked. "Do not hide it from me. May God deal with you, be it ever so severely, if you hide from me anything he told you." **18**So Samuel told him everything, hiding nothing from him. Then Eli said, "He is the Lord; let him do what is good in his eyes."

19The Lord was with Samuel as he grew up, and he let none of his words fall to the ground. **20**And all Israel from Dan to Beersheba recognized that Samuel was attested as a prophet of the Lord. **21**The Lord continued to appear at Shiloh, and there he revealed himself to Samuel through his word.

4 And Samuel's word came to all Israel.

The Philistines Capture the Ark

Now the Israelites went out to fight against the Philistines. The Israelites camped at Ebenezer, and the Philistines at Aphek. **2**The Philistines deployed their forces to meet Israel, and as the battle spread, Israel was defeated by the Philistines, who killed about four thousand of them on the battlefield. **3**When the soldiers returned to camp, the elders of Israel asked, "Why did the Lord bring defeat upon us today before the Philistines? Let us bring the ark of the Lord's covenant from Shiloh, so that it*c* may go with us and save us from the hand of our enemies."

4So the people sent men to Shiloh, and they brought back the ark of the covenant of the Lord Almighty, who is enthroned between the cherubim. And Eli's two sons, Hophni and Phinehas, were there with the ark of the covenant of God.

5When the ark of the Lord's covenant came into the camp, all Israel raised such a great shout that the ground shook. **6**Hearing the uproar, the Philistines asked, "What's all this shouting in the Hebrew camp?"

When they learned that the ark of the Lord had come into the camp, **7**the Philistines were afraid. "A god has come into the

---

*a*3 That is, tabernacle   *b*13 Masoretic Text; an ancient Hebrew scribal tradition and Septuagint *sons blasphemed God*   *c*3 Or *he* camp," they said. "We're in trouble! Nothing like this has happened before. **8**Woe to us! Who will deliver us from the hand of these mighty gods? They are the gods who struck the Egyptians with all kinds of plagues in the desert. **9**Be strong, Philistines! Be men, or you will be subject to the Hebrews, as they have been to you. Be men, and fight!"

10So the Philistines fought, and the Israelites were defeated and every man fled to his tent. The slaughter was very great; Israel lost thirty thousand foot soldiers. **11**The ark of God was captured, and Eli's two sons, Hophni and Phinehas, died.

Death of Eli

12That same day a Benjamite ran from the battle line and went to Shiloh, his clothes torn and dust on his head. **13**When he arrived, there was Eli sitting on his chair by the side of the road, watching, because his heart feared for the ark of God. When the man entered the town and told what had happened, the whole town sent up a cry.

14Eli heard the outcry and asked, "What is the meaning of this uproar?"

The man hurried over to Eli, **15**who was ninety-eight years old and whose eyes were set so that he could not see. **16**He told Eli, "I have just come from the battle line; I fled from it this very day."

Eli asked, "What happened, my son?"

17The man who brought the news replied, "Israel fled before the Philistines, and the army has suffered heavy losses. Also your two sons, Hophni and Phinehas, are dead, and the ark of God has been captured."

18When he mentioned the ark of God, Eli fell backward off his chair by the side of the gate. His neck was broken and he died, for he was an old man and heavy. He had led*a* Israel forty years.

19His daughter-in-law, the wife of Phinehas, was pregnant and near the time of delivery. When she heard the news that the ark of God had been captured and that her father-in-law and her husband were dead, she went into labor and gave birth, but was overcome by her labor pains. **20**As she was dying, the women attending her said, "Don't despair; you have given birth to a son." But she did not respond or pay any attention.

21She named the boy Ichabod,*b* saying, "The glory has departed from Israel"—because of the capture of the ark of God and

the deaths of her father-in-law and her husband. **22**She said, "The glory has departed from Israel, for the ark of God has been captured."

The Ark in Ashdod and Ekron

5 After the Philistines had captured the ark of God, they took it from Ebenezer to Ashdod. **2**Then they carried the ark into Dagon's temple and set it beside Dagon. **3**When the people of Ashdod rose early the next day, there was Dagon, fallen on his face on the ground before the ark of the LORD! They took Dagon and put him back in his place. **4**But the following morning when they rose, there was Dagon, fallen on his face on the ground before the ark of the LORD! His head and hands had been broken off and were lying on the threshold; only his body remained. **5**That is why to this day neither the priests of Dagon nor any others who enter Dagon's temple at Ashdod step on the threshold.

6The LORD's hand was heavy upon the people of Ashdod and its vicinity; he brought devastation upon them and afflicted them with tumors.*c* **7**When the men of Ashdod saw what was happening, they said, "The ark of the god of Israel must not stay here with us, because his hand is heavy upon us and upon Dagon our god." **8**So they called together all the rulers of the Philistines and asked them, "What shall we do with the ark of the god of Israel?"

They answered, "Have the ark of the god of Israel moved to Gath." So they moved the ark of the God of Israel.

9But after they had moved it, the LORD's hand was against that city, throwing it into a great panic. He afflicted the people of the city, both young and old, with an outbreak of tumors.*d* **10**So they sent the ark of God to Ekron.

As the ark of God was entering Ekron, the people of Ekron cried out, "They have brought the ark of the god of Israel around to us to kill us and our people." **11**So they called together all the rulers of the Philistines and said, "Send the ark of the god of Israel away; let it go back to its own place, or it*e* will kill us and our people." For death had filled the city with panic; God's hand was very heavy upon it. **12**Those who did not die were afflicted with tumors, and the outcry of the city went up to heaven.

---

a18 Traditionally *judged*   *b21* Ichabod means *no glory.*   *c6* Hebrew; Septuagint and Vulgate *tumors. And rats appeared in their land, and death and destruction were throughout the city*   *d9* Or *with tumors in the groin* (see Septuagint)   *e11* Or *he*

The Ark Returned to Israel

6 When the ark of the Lord had been in Philistine territory seven months, **2**the Philistines called for the priests and the diviners and said, "What shall we do with the ark of the Lord? Tell us how we should send it back to its place."

3They answered, "If you return the ark of the god of Israel, do not send it away empty, but by all means send a guilt offering to him. Then you will be healed, and you will know why his hand has not been lifted from you."

4The Philistines asked, "What guilt offering should we send to him?"

They replied, "Five gold tumors and five gold rats, according to the number of the Philistine rulers, because the same plague has struck both you and your rulers. **5**Make models of the tumors and of the rats that are destroying the country, and pay honor to Israel's god. Perhaps he will lift his hand from you and your gods and your land. **6**Why do you harden your hearts as the Egyptians and Pharaoh did? When he*a* treated them harshly, did they not send the Israelites out so they could go on their way?

7"Now then, get a new cart ready, with two cows that have calved and have never been yoked. Hitch the cows to the cart, but take their calves away and pen them up. **8**Take the ark of the Lord and put it on the cart, and in a chest beside it put the gold objects you are sending back to him as a guilt offering. Send it on its way, **9**but keep watching it. If it goes up to its own territory, toward Beth Shemesh, then the Lord has brought this great disaster on us. But if it does not, then we will know that it was not his hand that struck us and that it happened to us by chance."

10So they did this. They took two such cows and hitched them to the cart and penned up their calves. **11**They placed the ark of the Lord on the cart and along with it the chest containing the gold rats and the models of the tumors. **12**Then the cows went straight up toward Beth Shemesh, keeping on the road and lowing all the way; they did not turn to the right or to the left. The rulers of the Philistines followed them as far as the border of Beth Shemesh.

13Now the people of Beth Shemesh were harvesting their wheat in the valley, and when they looked up and saw the ark, they rejoiced at the sight. **14**The cart came to the field of Joshua of Beth Shemesh, and there it stopped beside a large rock. The people chopped up the wood of the cart and sacrificed the cows as a burnt offering to the Lord. **15**The Levites took down the ark of the Lord, together with the chest containing the gold objects, and placed them on the large rock. On that day the people of Beth Shemesh offered burnt offerings and made sacrifices to the Lord. **16**The five rulers of the Philistines saw all this and then returned that same day to Ekron.

17These are the gold tumors the Philistines sent as a guilt offering to the Lord— one each for Ashdod, Gaza, Ashkelon, Gath and Ekron. **18**And the number of the gold rats was according to the number of Philistine towns belonging to the five rulers — the fortified towns with their country villages. The large rock, on which*b* they set the ark of the Lord, is a witness to this day in the field of Joshua of Beth Shemesh.

19But God struck down some of the men of Beth Shemesh, putting seventy*c* of them to death because they had looked into the ark of the Lord. The people mourned because of the heavy blow the Lord had dealt them, **20**and the men of Beth Shemesh asked, "Who can stand in the presence of the Lord, this holy God? To whom will the ark go up from here?"

21Then they sent messengers to the people of Kiriath Jearim, saying, "The Philistines have returned the ark of the Lord. Come down and take it up to your place."

7 **1**So the men of Kiriath Jearim came and took up the ark of the Lord. They took it to Abinadab's house on the hill and consecrated Eleazar his son to guard the ark of the Lord.

Samuel Subdues the Philistines at Mizpah

2It was a long time, twenty years in all, that the ark remained at Kiriath Jearim, and all the people of Israel mourned and sought after the Lord. **3**And Samuel said to the whole house of Israel, "If you are returning to the Lord with all your hearts, then rid yourselves of the foreign gods and the Ashtoreths and commit yourselves to the Lord and serve him only, and he will deliver you out of the hand of the Philistines." **4**So the Israelites put away their Baals and Ashtoreths, and served the Lord only.

5Then Samuel said, "Assemble all Israel at

---

a6 That is, God   *b18* A few Hebrew manuscripts (see also Septuagint); most Hebrew manuscripts *villages as far as Greater Abel, where*   *c19* A few Hebrew manuscripts; most Hebrew manuscripts and Septuagint *50,070*

Mizpah and I will intercede with the Lord for you." ⁶When they had assembled at Mizpah, they drew water and poured it out before the Lord. On that day they fasted and there they confessed, "We have sinned against the Lord." And Samuel was leader*a* of Israel at Mizpah.

⁷When the Philistines heard that Israel had assembled at Mizpah, the rulers of the Philistines came up to attack them. And when the Israelites heard of it, they were afraid because of the Philistines. ⁸They said to Samuel, "Do not stop crying out to the Lord our God for us, that he may rescue us from the hand of the Philistines." ⁹Then Samuel took a suckling lamb and offered it up as a whole burnt offering to the Lord. He cried out to the Lord on Israel's behalf, and the Lord answered him.

¹⁰While Samuel was sacrificing the burnt offering, the Philistines drew near to engage Israel in battle. But that day the Lord thundered with loud thunder against the Philistines and threw them into such a panic that they were routed before the Israelites. ¹¹The men of Israel rushed out of Mizpah and pursued the Philistines, slaughtering them along the way to a point below Beth Car.

¹²Then Samuel took a stone and set it up between Mizpah and Shen. He named it Ebenezer,*b* saying, "Thus far has the Lord helped us." ¹³So the Philistines were subdued and did not invade Israelite territory again.

Throughout Samuel's lifetime, the hand of the Lord was against the Philistines. ¹⁴The towns from Ekron to Gath that the Philistines had captured from Israel were restored to her, and Israel delivered the neighboring territory from the power of the Philistines. And there was peace between Israel and the Amorites.

¹⁵Samuel continued as judge over Israel all the days of his life. ¹⁶From year to year he went on a circuit from Bethel to Gilgal to Mizpah, judging Israel in all those places. ¹⁷But he always went back to Ramah, where his home was, and there he also judged Israel. And he built an altar there to the Lord.

Israel Asks for a King

8 When Samuel grew old, he appointed his sons as judges for Israel. ²The name of his firstborn was Joel and the name of his second was Abijah, and they served at Beer-sheba. ³But his sons did not walk in his ways. They turned aside after dishonest gain and accepted bribes and perverted justice.

⁴So all the elders of Israel gathered together and came to Samuel at Ramah. ⁵They said to him, "You are old, and your sons do not walk in your ways; now appoint a king to lead*c* us, such as all the other nations have."

⁶But when they said, "Give us a king to lead us," this displeased Samuel; so he prayed to the Lord. ⁷And the Lord told him: "Listen to all that the people are saying to you; it is not you they have rejected, but they have rejected me as their king. ⁸As they have done from the day I brought them up out of Egypt until this day, forsaking me and serving other gods, so they are doing to you. ⁹Now listen to them; but warn them solemnly and let them know what the king who will reign over them will do."

¹⁰Samuel told all the words of the Lord to the people who were asking him for a king. ¹¹He said, "This is what the king who will reign over you will do: He will take your sons and make them serve with his chariots and horses, and they will run in front of his chariots. ¹²Some he will assign to be commanders of thousands and commanders of fifties, and others to plow his ground and reap his harvest, and still others to make weapons of war and equipment for his chariots. ¹³He will take your daughters to be perfumers and cooks and bakers. ¹⁴He will take the best of your fields and vineyards and olive groves and give them to his attendants. ¹⁵He will take a tenth of your grain and of your vintage and give it to his officials and attendants. ¹⁶Your menservants and maidservants and the best of your cattle*d* and donkeys he will take for his own use. ¹⁷He will take a tenth of your flocks, and you yourselves will become his slaves. ¹⁸When that day comes, you will cry out for relief from the king you have chosen, and the Lord will not answer you in that day."

¹⁹But the people refused to listen to Samuel. "No!" they said. "We want a king over us. ²⁰Then we will be like all the other nations, with a king to lead us and to go out before us and fight our battles."

²¹When Samuel heard all that the people said, he repeated it before the Lord. ²²The Lord answered, "Listen to them and give them a king."

---

a6 Traditionally *judge*   *b12* Ebenezer means *stone of help.*   *c5* Traditionally *judge*; also in verses 6 and 20
d16 Septuagint; Hebrew *young men*

Then Samuel said to the men of Israel, "Everyone go back to his town."

Samuel Anoints Saul

9 There was a Benjamite, a man of standing, whose name was Kish son of Abiel, the son of Zeror, the son of Becorath, the son of Aphiah of Benjamin. ²He had a son named Saul, an impressive young man without equal among the Israelites — a head taller than any of the others.

³Now the donkeys belonging to Saul's father Kish were lost, and Kish said to his son Saul, "Take one of the servants with you and go and look for the donkeys." ⁴So he passed through the hill country of Ephraim and through the area around Shalisha, but they did not find them. They went on into the district of Shaalim, but the donkeys were not there. Then he passed through the territory of Benjamin, but they did not find them.

⁵When they reached the district of Zuph, Saul said to the servant who was with him, "Come, let's go back, or my father will stop thinking about the donkeys and start worrying about us."

⁶But the servant replied, "Look, in this town there is a man of God; he is highly respected, and everything he says comes true. Let's go there now. Perhaps he will tell us what way to take."

⁷Saul said to his servant, "If we go, what can we give the man? The food in our sacks is gone. We have no gift to take to the man of God. What do we have?"

⁸The servant answered him again. "Look," he said, "I have a quarter of a shekel*ᵃ* of silver. I will give it to the man of God so that he will tell us what way to take." ⁹(Formerly in Israel, if a man went to inquire of God, he would say, "Come, let us go to the seer," because the prophet of today used to be called a seer.)

¹⁰"Good," Saul said to his servant. "Come, let's go." So they set out for the town where the man of God was.

¹¹As they were going up the hill to the town, they met some girls coming out to draw water, and they asked them, "Is the seer here?"

¹²"He is," they answered. "He's ahead of you. Hurry now; he has just come to our town today, for the people have a sacrifice at the high place. ¹³As soon as you enter the town, you will find him before he goes up to the high place to eat. The people will not begin eating until he comes, because he must bless the sacrifice; afterward, those who are invited will eat. Go up now; you should find him about this time."

¹⁴They went up to the town, and as they were entering it, there was Samuel, coming toward them on his way up to the high place.

¹⁵Now the day before Saul came, the Lord had revealed this to Samuel: ¹⁶"About this time tomorrow I will send you a man from the land of Benjamin. Anoint him leader over my people Israel; he will deliver my people from the hand of the Philistines. I have looked upon my people, for their cry has reached me."

¹⁷When Samuel caught sight of Saul, the Lord said to him, "This is the man I spoke to you about; he will govern my people."

¹⁸Saul approached Samuel in the gateway and asked, "Would you please tell me where the seer's house is?"

¹⁹"I am the seer," Samuel replied. "Go up ahead of me to the high place, for today you are to eat with me, and in the morning I will let you go and will tell you all that is in your heart. ²⁰As for the donkeys you lost three days ago, do not worry about them; they have been found. And to whom is all the desire of Israel turned, if not to you and all your father's family?"

²¹Saul answered, "But am I not a Benjamite, from the smallest tribe of Israel, and is not my clan the least of all the clans of the tribe of Benjamin? Why do you say such a thing to me?"

²²Then Samuel brought Saul and his servant into the hall and seated them at the head of those who were invited — about thirty in number. ²³Samuel said to the cook, "Bring the piece of meat I gave you, the one I told you to lay aside."

²⁴So the cook took up the leg with what was on it and set it in front of Saul. Samuel said, "Here is what has been kept for you. Eat, because it was set aside for you for this occasion, from the time I said, 'I have invited guests.'" And Saul dined with Samuel that day.

²⁵After they came down from the high place to the town, Samuel talked with Saul on the roof of his house. ²⁶They rose about daybreak and Samuel called to Saul on the roof, "Get ready, and I will send you on your way." When Saul got ready, he and Samuel went outside together. ²⁷As they were going down to the edge of the town, Samuel said to Saul, "Tell the servant to go on ahead of

ᵃ8 That is, about 1/10 ounce (about 3 grams)

us"—and the servant did so—"but you stay here awhile, so that I may give you a message from God."

10 Then Samuel took a flask of oil and poured it on Saul's head and kissed him, saying, "Has not the LORD anointed you leader over his inheritance?*a* **2**When you leave me today, you will meet two men near Rachel's tomb, at Zelzah on the border of Benjamin. They will say to you, 'The donkeys you set out to look for have been found. And now your father has stopped thinking about them and is worried about you. He is asking, "What shall I do about my son?" '

3"Then you will go on from there until you reach the great tree of Tabor. Three men going up to God at Bethel will meet you there. One will be carrying three young goats, another three loaves of bread, and another a skin of wine. **4**They will greet you and offer you two loaves of bread, which you will accept from them.

5"After that you will go to Gibeah of God, where there is a Philistine outpost. As you approach the town, you will meet a procession of prophets coming down from the high place with lyres, tambourines, flutes and harps being played before them, and they will be prophesying. **6**The Spirit of the LORD will come upon you in power, and you will prophesy with them; and you will be changed into a different person. **7**Once these signs are fulfilled, do whatever your hand finds to do, for God is with you.

8"Go down ahead of me to Gilgal. I will surely come down to you to sacrifice burnt offerings and fellowship offerings,*b* but you must wait seven days until I come to you and tell you what you are to do."

Saul Made King

9As Saul turned to leave Samuel, God changed Saul's heart, and all these signs were fulfilled that day. **10**When they arrived at Gibeah, a procession of prophets met him; the Spirit of God came upon him in power, and he joined in their prophesying. **11**When all those who had formerly known him saw him prophesying with the prophets, they asked each other, "What is this that has happened to the son of Kish? Is Saul also among the prophets?"

12A man who lived there answered, "And

who is their father?" So it became a saying: "Is Saul also among the prophets?" **13**After Saul stopped prophesying, he went to the high place.

14Now Saul's uncle asked him and his servant, "Where have you been?"

"Looking for the donkeys," he said. "But when we saw they were not to be found, we went to Samuel."

15Saul's uncle said, "Tell me what Samuel said to you."

16Saul replied, "He assured us that the donkeys had been found." But he did not tell his uncle what Samuel had said about the kingship.

17Samuel summoned the people of Israel to the LORD at Mizpah **18**and said to them, "This is what the LORD, the God of Israel, says: 'I brought Israel up out of Egypt, and I delivered you from the power of Egypt and all the kingdoms that oppressed you.' **19**But you have now rejected your God, who saves you out of all your calamities and distresses. And you have said, 'No, set a king over us.' So now present yourselves before the LORD by your tribes and clans."

20When Samuel brought all the tribes of Israel near, the tribe of Benjamin was chosen. **21**Then he brought forward the tribe of Benjamin, clan by clan, and Matri's clan was chosen. Finally Saul son of Kish was chosen. But when they looked for him, he was not to be found. **22**So they inquired further of the LORD, "Has the man come here yet?"

And the LORD said, "Yes, he has hidden himself among the baggage."

23They ran and brought him out, and as he stood among the people he was a head taller than any of the others. **24**Samuel said to all the people, "Do you see the man the LORD has chosen? There is no one like him among all the people."

Then the people shouted, "Long live the king!"

25Samuel explained to the people the regulations of the kingship. He wrote them down on a scroll and deposited it before the LORD. Then Samuel dismissed the people, each to his own home.

26Saul also went to his home in Gibeah, accompanied by valiant men whose hearts God had touched. **27**But some troublemakers said, "How can this fellow save us?" They despised him and brought him no gifts. But Saul kept silent.

---

a1 Hebrew; Septuagint and Vulgate *over his people Israel? You will reign over the LORD's people and save them from the power of their enemies round about. And this will be a sign to you that the LORD has anointed you leader over his inheritance:* *b8* Traditionally *peace offerings*

Saul Rescues the City of Jabesh

11 Nahash the Ammonite went up and besieged Jabesh Gilead. And all the men of Jabesh said to him, "Make a treaty with us, and we will be subject to you."

2But Nahash the Ammonite replied, "I will make a treaty with you only on the condition that I gouge out the right eye of every one of you and so bring disgrace on all Israel."

3The elders of Jabesh said to him, "Give us seven days so we can send messengers throughout Israel; if no one comes to rescue us, we will surrender to you."

4When the messengers came to Gibeah of Saul and reported these terms to the people, they all wept aloud. **5**Just then Saul was returning from the fields, behind his oxen, and he asked, "What is wrong with the people? Why are they weeping?" Then they repeated to him what the men of Jabesh had said.

6When Saul heard their words, the Spirit of God came upon him in power, and he burned with anger. **7**He took a pair of oxen, cut them into pieces, and sent the pieces by messengers throughout Israel, proclaiming, "This is what will be done to the oxen of anyone who does not follow Saul and Samuel." Then the terror of the LORD fell on the people, and they turned out as one man. **8**When Saul mustered them at Bezek, the men of Israel numbered three hundred thousand and the men of Judah thirty thousand.

9They told the messengers who had come, "Say to the men of Jabesh Gilead, 'By the time the sun is hot tomorrow, you will be delivered.' " When the messengers went and reported this to the men of Jabesh, they were elated. **10**They said to the Ammonites, "Tomorrow we will surrender to you, and you can do to us whatever seems good to you."

11The next day Saul separated his men into three divisions; during the last watch of the night they broke into the camp of the Ammonites and slaughtered them until the heat of the day. Those who survived were scattered, so that no two of them were left together.

Saul Confirmed as King

12The people then said to Samuel, "Who was it that asked, 'Shall Saul reign over us?'

Bring these men to us and we will put them to death."

13But Saul said, "No one shall be put to death today, for this day the LORD has rescued Israel."

14Then Samuel said to the people, "Come, let us go to Gilgal and there reaffirm the kingship." **15**So all the people went to Gilgal and confirmed Saul as king in the presence of the LORD. There they sacrificed fellowship offerings[a] before the LORD, and Saul and all the Israelites held a great celebration.

Samuel's Farewell Speech

12 Samuel said to all Israel, "I have listened to everything you said to me and have set a king over you. **2**Now you have a king as your leader. As for me, I am old and gray, and my sons are here with you. I have been your leader from my youth until this day. **3**Here I stand. Testify against me in the presence of the LORD and his anointed. Whose ox have I taken? Whose donkey have I taken? Whom have I cheated? Whom have I oppressed? From whose hand have I accepted a bribe to make me shut my eyes? If I have done any of these, I will make it right."

4"You have not cheated or oppressed us," they replied. "You have not taken anything from anyone's hand."

5Samuel said to them, "The LORD is witness against you, and also his anointed is witness this day, that you have not found anything in my hand."

"He is witness," they said.

6Then Samuel said to the people, "It is the LORD who appointed Moses and Aaron and brought your forefathers up out of Egypt. **7**Now then, stand here, because I am going to confront you with evidence before the LORD as to all the righteous acts performed by the LORD for you and your fathers.

8"After Jacob entered Egypt, they cried to the LORD for help, and the LORD sent Moses and Aaron, who brought your forefathers out of Egypt and settled them in this place.

9"But they forgot the LORD their God; so he sold them into the hand of Sisera, the commander of the army of Hazor, and into the hands of the Philistines and the king of Moab, who fought against them. **10**They cried out to the LORD and said, 'We have sinned; we have forsaken the LORD and served the Baals and the Ashtoreths. But now deliver us from the hands of our enemies, and we will serve you.' ¹¹Then the LORD sent Jerub-Baal,*a* Barak,*b* Jephthah and Samuel,*c* and he delivered you from the hands of your enemies on every side, so that you lived securely.

¹²"But when you saw that Nahash king of the Ammonites was moving against you, you said to me, 'No, we want a king to rule over us'—even though the LORD your God was your king. ¹³Now here is the king you have chosen, the one you asked for; see, the LORD has set a king over you. ¹⁴If you fear the LORD and serve and obey him and do not rebel against his commands, and if both you and the king who reigns over you follow the LORD your God—good! ¹⁵But if you do not obey the LORD, and if you rebel against his commands, his hand will be against you, as it was against your fathers.

¹⁶"Now then, stand still and see this great thing the LORD is about to do before your eyes! ¹⁷Is it not wheat harvest now? I will call upon the LORD to send thunder and rain. And you will realize what an evil thing you did in the eyes of the LORD when you asked for a king."

¹⁸Then Samuel called upon the LORD, and that same day the LORD sent thunder and rain. So all the people stood in awe of the LORD and of Samuel.

¹⁹The people all said to Samuel, "Pray to the LORD your God for your servants so that we will not die, for we have added to all our other sins the evil of asking for a king."

²⁰"Do not be afraid," Samuel replied. "You have done all this evil; yet do not turn away from the LORD, but serve the LORD with all your heart. ²¹Do not turn away after useless idols. They can do you no good, nor can they rescue you, because they are useless. ²²For the sake of his great name the LORD will not reject his people, because the LORD was pleased to make you his own. ²³As for me, far be it from me that I should sin against the LORD by failing to pray for you. And I will teach you the way that is good and right. ²⁴But be sure to fear the LORD and serve him faithfully with all your heart; consider what great things he has done for you. ²⁵Yet if you persist in doing evil, both you and your king will be swept away."

Samuel Rebukes Saul

13 Saul was ⌐thirty⌐*d* years old when he became king, and he reigned over Israel ⌐forty-⌐*e* two years.

²Saul*f* chose three thousand men from Israel; two thousand were with him at Micmash and in the hill country of Bethel, and a thousand were with Jonathan at Gibeah in Benjamin. The rest of the men he sent back to their homes.

³Jonathan attacked the Philistine outpost at Geba, and the Philistines heard about it. Then Saul had the trumpet blown throughout the land and said, "Let the Hebrews hear!" ⁴So all Israel heard the news: "Saul has attacked the Philistine outpost, and now Israel has become a stench to the Philistines." And the people were summoned to join Saul at Gilgal.

⁵The Philistines assembled to fight Israel, with three thousand*g* chariots, six thousand charioteers, and soldiers as numerous as the sand on the seashore. They went up and camped at Micmash, east of Beth Aven. ⁶When the men of Israel saw that their situation was critical and that their army was hard pressed, they hid in caves and thickets, among the rocks, and in pits and cisterns. ⁷Some Hebrews even crossed the Jordan to the land of Gad and Gilead.

Saul remained at Gilgal, and all the troops with him were quaking with fear. ⁸He waited seven days, the time set by Samuel; but Samuel did not come to Gilgal, and Saul's men began to scatter. ⁹So he said, "Bring me the burnt offering and the fellowship offerings.*h*" And Saul offered up the burnt offering. ¹⁰Just as he finished making the offering, Samuel arrived, and Saul went out to greet him.

¹¹"What have you done?" asked Samuel.

Saul replied, "When I saw that the men were scattering, and that you did not come at the set time, and that the Philistines were assembling at Micmash, ¹²I thought, 'Now the Philistines will come down against me at Gilgal, and I have not sought the LORD's favor.' So I felt compelled to offer the burnt offering."

¹³"You acted foolishly," Samuel said. "You have not kept the command the LORD your God gave you; if you had, he would have established your kingdom over Israel for all

---

a11 Also called *Gideon*   *b11* Some Septuagint manuscripts and Syriac; Hebrew *Bedan*   *c11* Hebrew; some Septuagint manuscripts and Syriac *Samson*   *d1* A few late manuscripts of the Septuagint; Hebrew does not have *thirty.*   *e1* See the round number in Acts 13:21; Hebrew does not have *forty-.*   *f1,2* Or *and when he had reigned over Israel two years,* *2he*   *g5* Some Septuagint manuscripts and Syriac; Hebrew *thirty thousand*   *h9* Traditionally *peace offerings*

THE DANGERS OF DISOBEDIENCE

• •

D o you want to see the results of disobedience? Meet Gretchen, a tired seventeen-year-old girl at a suburban chemical dependency hospital:

"My family is very Christian. I mean, I literally grew up in the church. At thirteen I could quote all the verses and sing all the songs. I knew exactly what I was supposed to do. But I rebelled. I thought, 'I'm too cool for this. I can bend God's rules and get away with it.' Yeah, right. Look at me. I look and feel like I'm about thirty. I'm an addict who's already had two abortions. You can believe me or not, but I'm telling you the truth. You pay a high price when you reject what you know is right. And it's not even close to being worth it."

Look It Up
• • • •

From cover to cover the Bible gives sobering examples of the consequences of disobedience. Read about:
- The tragedy of Adam and Eve (Genesis 3).
- The sad story of King Saul (1 Samuel 15).
- The downfall of King Solomon (1 Kings 11).
- The judgment on Ananias and Sapphira (Acts 5:1–10).

Then spend some time reflecting on this warning:

"Do not be deceived: God cannot be mocked. A man reaps what he sows" (Galatians 6:7).

Think It Through
• • • •

Can you think of times in your life when disobedience has been devastating to you? Can you ever get away with sin? If you don't see any immediate consequences after a wrong act, does that mean that there won't be any? Why or why not?

Do you know anyone like Gretchen? Would you want to be in her place? How can you guard against ending up in her situation?

Work It Out
• • • •

List in your mind the various problems involved with each of these acts of disobedience: not reading the Word; not telling others about Christ; gossiping; lying; stealing; sexual immorality; drunkenness; ignoring the needs of the poor; refusing to pray; failing to forgive others; complaining about everything; and becoming obsessed with worldly wealth.

Now, will you make a commitment to *start* doing one thing and *stop* doing one thing in order to be more obedient to Jesus?

Nail It Down
• • • •

Read the promise and the warning in 1 Samuel 12:14–15.

Turn to pages 159, 892, 1013, 1082 and 1156 for other readings on obedience.
Turn to page 286 for Friday's reading.

Topic
• • • •

OBEDIENCE

time. **14**But now your kingdom will not endure; the LORD has sought out a man after his own heart and appointed him leader of his people, because you have not kept the LORD's command."

15Then Samuel left Gilgal[a] and went up to Gibeah in Benjamin, and Saul counted the men who were with him. They numbered about six hundred.

Israel Without Weapons

16Saul and his son Jonathan and the men with them were staying in Gibeah[b] in Benjamin, while the Philistines camped at Micmash. **17**Raiding parties went out from the Philistine camp in three detachments. One turned toward Ophrah in the vicinity of Shual, **18**another toward Beth Horon, and the third toward the borderland overlooking the Valley of Zeboim facing the desert.

19Not a blacksmith could be found in the whole land of Israel, because the Philistines had said, "Otherwise the Hebrews will make swords or spears!" **20**So all Israel went down to the Philistines to have their plowshares, mattocks, axes and sickles[c] sharpened. **21**The price was two thirds of a shekel[d] for sharpening plowshares and mattocks, and a third of a shekel[e] for sharpening forks and axes and for repointing goads.

22So on the day of the battle not a soldier with Saul and Jonathan had a sword or spear in his hand; only Saul and his son Jonathan had them.

Jonathan Attacks the Philistines

23Now a detachment of Philistines had gone out to the pass at Micmash. **14** **1**One day Jonathan son of Saul said to the young man bearing his armor, "Come, let's go over to the Philistine outpost on the other side." But he did not tell his father.

2Saul was staying on the outskirts of Gibeah under a pomegranate tree in Migron. With him were about six hundred men, **3**among whom was Ahijah, who was wearing an ephod. He was a son of Ichabod's brother Ahitub son of Phinehas, the son of Eli, the LORD's priest in Shiloh. No one was aware that Jonathan had left.

4On each side of the pass that Jonathan intended to cross to reach the Philistine outpost was a cliff; one was called Bozez, and the other Seneh. **5**One cliff stood to the north toward Micmash, the other to the south toward Geba.

6Jonathan said to his young armor-bearer, "Come, let's go over to the outpost of those uncircumcised fellows. Perhaps the LORD will act in our behalf. Nothing can hinder the LORD from saving, whether by many or by few."

7"Do all that you have in mind," his armor-bearer said. "Go ahead; I am with you heart and soul."

8Jonathan said, "Come, then; we will cross over toward the men and let them see us. **9**If they say to us, 'Wait there until we come to you,' we will stay where we are and not go up to them. **10**But if they say, 'Come up to us,' we will climb up, because that will be our sign that the LORD has given them into our hands."

11So both of them showed themselves to the Philistine outpost. "Look!" said the Philistines. "The Hebrews are crawling out of the holes they were hiding in." **12**The men of the outpost shouted to Jonathan and his armor-bearer, "Come up to us and we'll teach you a lesson."

So Jonathan said to his armor-bearer, "Climb up after me; the LORD has given them into the hand of Israel."

13Jonathan climbed up, using his hands and feet, with his armor-bearer right behind him. The Philistines fell before Jonathan, and his armor-bearer followed and killed behind him. **14**In that first attack Jonathan and his armor-bearer killed some twenty men in an area of about half an acre.[f]

Israel Routs the Philistines

15Then panic struck the whole army—those in the camp and field, and those in the outposts and raiding parties—and the ground shook. It was a panic sent by God.[g]

16Saul's lookouts at Gibeah in Benjamin saw the army melting away in all directions. **17**Then Saul said to the men who were with him, "Muster the forces and see who has left us." When they did, it was Jonathan and his armor-bearer who were not there.

18Saul said to Ahijah, "Bring the ark of God." (At that time it was with the Israel-

---

a 15 Hebrew; Septuagint *Gilgal and went his way; the rest of the people went after Saul to meet the army, and they went out of Gilgal*   *b 16* Two Hebrew manuscripts; most Hebrew manuscripts *Geba*, a variant of *Gibeah*   *c 20* Septuagint; Hebrew *plowshares*   *d 21* Hebrew *pim*; that is, about 1/4 ounce (about 8 grams)   *e 21* That is, about 1/8 ounce (about 4 grams)   *f 14* Hebrew *half a yoke*; a "yoke" was the land plowed by a yoke of oxen in one day.   *g 15* Or *a terrible panic* ites.)*a* **19**While Saul was talking to the priest, the tumult in the Philistine camp increased more and more. So Saul said to the priest, "Withdraw your hand."

20Then Saul and all his men assembled and went to the battle. They found the Philistines in total confusion, striking each other with their swords. **21**Those Hebrews who had previously been with the Philistines and had gone up with them to their camp went over to the Israelites who were with Saul and Jonathan. **22**When all the Israelites who had hidden in the hill country of Ephraim heard that the Philistines were on the run, they joined the battle in hot pursuit. **23**So the LORD rescued Israel that day, and the battle moved on beyond Beth Aven.

Jonathan Eats Honey

24Now the men of Israel were in distress that day, because Saul had bound the people under an oath, saying, "Cursed be any man who eats food before evening comes, before I have avenged myself on my enemies!" So none of the troops tasted food. **25**The entire army*b* entered the woods, and there was honey on the ground. **26**When they went into the woods, they saw the honey oozing out, yet no one put his hand to his mouth, because they feared the oath. **27**But Jonathan had not heard that his father had bound the people with the oath, so he reached out the end of the staff that was in his hand and dipped it into the honeycomb. He raised his hand to his mouth, and his eyes brightened.*c* **28**Then one of the soldiers told him, "Your father bound the army under a strict oath, saying, 'Cursed be any man who eats food today!' That is why the men are faint."

29Jonathan said, "My father has made trouble for the country. See how my eyes brightened*d* when I tasted a little of this honey. **30**How much better it would have been if the men had eaten today some of the plunder they took from their enemies. Would not the slaughter of the Philistines have been even greater?"

31That day, after the Israelites had struck down the Philistines from Micmash to Aijalon, they were exhausted. **32**They pounced on the plunder and, taking sheep, cattle and calves, they butchered them on the ground and ate them, together with the blood.

33Then someone said to Saul, "Look, the men are sinning against the LORD by eating meat that has blood in it."

"You have broken faith," he said. "Roll a large stone over here at once." **34**Then he said, "Go out among the men and tell them, 'Each of you bring me your cattle and sheep, and slaughter them here and eat them. Do not sin against the LORD by eating meat with blood still in it.'"

So everyone brought his ox that night and slaughtered it there. **35**Then Saul built an altar to the LORD; it was the first time he had done this.

36Saul said, "Let us go down after the Philistines by night and plunder them till dawn, and let us not leave one of them alive."

"Do whatever seems best to you," they replied.

But the priest said, "Let us inquire of God here."

37So Saul asked God, "Shall I go down after the Philistines? Will you give them into Israel's hand?" But God did not answer him that day.

38Saul therefore said, "Come here, all you who are leaders of the army, and let us find out what sin has been committed today. **39**As surely as the LORD who rescues Israel lives, even if it lies with my son Jonathan, he must die." But not one of the men said a word.

40Saul then said to all the Israelites, "You stand over there; I and Jonathan my son will stand over here."

"Do what seems best to you," the men replied.

41Then Saul prayed to the LORD, the God of Israel, "Give me the right answer."*e* And Jonathan and Saul were taken by lot, and the men were cleared. **42**Saul said, "Cast the lot between me and Jonathan my son." And Jonathan was taken.

43Then Saul said to Jonathan, "Tell me what you have done."

So Jonathan told him, "I merely tasted a little honey with the end of my staff. And now must I die?"

44Saul said, "May God deal with me, be it ever so severely, if you do not die, Jonathan."

45But the men said to Saul, "Should Jonathan die — he who has brought about this great deliverance in Israel? Never! As surely

---

a18 Hebrew; Septuagint *"Bring the ephod." (At that time he wore the ephod before the Israelites.)* *b25* Or *Now all the people of the land* *c27* Or *his strength was renewed* *d29* Or *my strength was renewed* *e41* Hebrew; Septuagint *"Why have you not answered your servant today? If the fault is in me or my son Jonathan, respond with Urim, but if the men of Israel are at fault, respond with Thummim."*

as the LORD lives, not a hair of his head will fall to the ground, for he did this today with God's help." So the men rescued Jonathan, and he was not put to death.

46Then Saul stopped pursuing the Philistines, and they withdrew to their own land.

47After Saul had assumed rule over Israel, he fought against their enemies on every side: Moab, the Ammonites, Edom, the kings*a* of Zobah, and the Philistines. Wherever he turned, he inflicted punishment on them.*b* **48**He fought valiantly and defeated the Amalekites, delivering Israel from the hands of those who had plundered them.

Saul's Family

49Saul's sons were Jonathan, Ishvi and Malki-Shua. The name of his older daughter was Merab, and that of the younger was Michal. **50**His wife's name was Ahinoam daughter of Ahimaaz. The name of the commander of Saul's army was Abner son of Ner, and Ner was Saul's uncle. **51**Saul's father Kish and Abner's father Ner were sons of Abiel.

52All the days of Saul there was bitter war with the Philistines, and whenever Saul saw a mighty or brave man, he took him into his service.

The LORD Rejects Saul as King

15 Samuel said to Saul, "I am the one the LORD sent to anoint you king over his people Israel; so listen now to the message from the LORD. **2**This is what the LORD Almighty says: 'I will punish the Amalekites for what they did to Israel when they waylaid them as they came up from Egypt. **3**Now go, attack the Amalekites and totally destroy*c* everything that belongs to them. Do not spare them; put to death men and women, children and infants, cattle and sheep, camels and donkeys.' "

4So Saul summoned the men and mustered them at Telaim — two hundred thousand foot soldiers and ten thousand men from Judah. **5**Saul went to the city of Amalek and set an ambush in the ravine. **6**Then he said to the Kenites, "Go away, leave the Amalekites so that I do not destroy you along with them; for you showed kindness to all the Israelites when they came up out of Egypt." So the Kenites moved away from the Amalekites.

7Then Saul attacked the Amalekites all the way from Havilah to Shur, to the east of Egypt. **8**He took Agag king of the Amalekites alive, and all his people he totally destroyed with the sword. **9**But Saul and the army spared Agag and the best of the sheep and cattle, the fat calves*d* and lambs — everything that was good. These they were unwilling to destroy completely, but everything that was despised and weak they totally destroyed.

10Then the word of the LORD came to Samuel: **11**"I am grieved that I have made Saul king, because he has turned away from me and has not carried out my instructions." Samuel was troubled, and he cried out to the LORD all that night.

12Early in the morning Samuel got up and went to meet Saul, but he was told, "Saul has gone to Carmel. There he has set up a monument in his own honor and has turned and gone on down to Gilgal."

13When Samuel reached him, Saul said, "The LORD bless you! I have carried out the LORD's instructions."

14But Samuel said, "What then is this bleating of sheep in my ears? What is this lowing of cattle that I hear?"

15Saul answered, "The soldiers brought them from the Amalekites; they spared the best of the sheep and cattle to sacrifice to the LORD your God, but we totally destroyed the rest."

16"Stop!" Samuel said to Saul. "Let me tell you what the LORD said to me last night."

"Tell me," Saul replied.

17Samuel said, "Although you were once small in your own eyes, did you not become the head of the tribes of Israel? The LORD anointed you king over Israel. **18**And he sent you on a mission, saying, 'Go and completely destroy those wicked people, the Amalekites; make war on them until you have wiped them out.' **19**Why did you not obey the LORD? Why did you pounce on the plunder and do evil in the eyes of the LORD?"

20"But I did obey the LORD," Saul said. "I went on the mission the LORD assigned me. I completely destroyed the Amalekites and brought back Agag their king. **21**The soldiers took sheep and cattle from the plunder, the best of what was devoted to God, in order to sacrifice them to the LORD your God at Gilgal."

---

a47 Masoretic Text; Dead Sea Scrolls and Septuagint *king*   *b47* Hebrew; Septuagint *he was victorious*
c3 The Hebrew term refers to the irrevocable giving over of things or persons to the LORD, often by totally destroying them; also in verses 8, 9, 15, 18, 20 and 21.   *d9* Or *the grown bulls*; the meaning of the Hebrew for this phrase is uncertain.

22But Samuel replied:

"Does the Lord delight in burnt offerings
and sacrifices
as much as in obeying the voice of
the Lord?
To obey is better than sacrifice,
and to heed is better than the fat of
rams.
23For rebellion is like the sin of
divination,
and arrogance like the evil of idolatry.
Because you have rejected the word of
the Lord,
he has rejected you as king."

24Then Saul said to Samuel, "I have
sinned. I violated the Lord's command and
your instructions. I was afraid of the people
and so I gave in to them. **25**Now I beg you,
forgive my sin and come back with me, so
that I may worship the Lord."

26But Samuel said to him, "I will not go
back with you. You have rejected the word
of the Lord, and the Lord has rejected you as
king over Israel!"

27As Samuel turned to leave, Saul caught
hold of the hem of his robe, and it tore.
28Samuel said to him, "The Lord has torn the
kingdom of Israel from you today and has
given it to one of your neighbors — to one
better than you. **29**He who is the Glory of Israel does not lie or change his mind; for he
is not a man, that he should change his
mind."

30Saul replied, "I have sinned. But please
honor me before the elders of my people
and before Israel; come back with me, so
that I may worship the Lord your God." **31**So
Samuel went back with Saul, and Saul worshiped the Lord.

32Then Samuel said, "Bring me Agag king
of the Amalekites."

Agag came to him confidently,*a* thinking,
"Surely the bitterness of death is past."

33But Samuel said,

"As your sword has made women
childless,
so will your mother be childless
among women."

And Samuel put Agag to death before the
Lord at Gilgal.

34Then Samuel left for Ramah, but Saul
went up to his home in Gibeah of Saul. **35**Until the day Samuel died, he did not go to see
Saul again, though Samuel mourned for

him. And the Lord was grieved that he had
made Saul king over Israel.

Samuel Anoints David

16 The Lord said to Samuel, "How long
will you mourn for Saul, since I have
rejected him as king over Israel? Fill your
horn with oil and be on your way; I am sending you to Jesse of Bethlehem. I have chosen
one of his sons to be king."

2But Samuel said, "How can I go? Saul will
hear about it and kill me."

The Lord said, "Take a heifer with you and
say, 'I have come to sacrifice to the Lord.'
3Invite Jesse to the sacrifice, and I will show
you what to do. You are to anoint for me the
one I indicate."

4Samuel did what the Lord said. When he
arrived at Bethlehem, the elders of the town
trembled when they met him. They asked,
"Do you come in peace?"

5Samuel replied, "Yes, in peace; I have
come to sacrifice to the Lord. Consecrate
yourselves and come to the sacrifice with
me." Then he consecrated Jesse and his
sons and invited them to the sacrifice.

6When they arrived, Samuel saw Eliab
and thought, "Surely the Lord's anointed
stands here before the Lord."

7But the Lord said to Samuel, "Do not consider his appearance or his height, for I have
rejected him. The Lord does not look at the
things man looks at. Man looks at the outward appearance, but the Lord looks at the
heart."

8Then Jesse called Abinadab and had him
pass in front of Samuel. But Samuel said,
"The Lord has not chosen this one either."
9Jesse then had Shammah pass by, but Samuel said, "Nor has the Lord chosen this one."
10Jesse had seven of his sons pass before
Samuel, but Samuel said to him, "The Lord
has not chosen these." **11**So he asked Jesse,
"Are these all the sons you have?"

"There is still the youngest," Jesse answered, "but he is tending the sheep."

Samuel said, "Send for him; we will not sit
down*b* until he arrives."

12So he sent and had him brought in. He
was ruddy, with a fine appearance and
handsome features.

Then the Lord said, "Rise and anoint him;
he is the one."

13So Samuel took the horn of oil and
anointed him in the presence of his brothers, and from that day on the Spirit of the

---

*a*32 Or *him trembling, yet*   *b*11 Some Septuagint manuscripts; Hebrew *not gather around*

YOUR TODAYS AFFECT YOUR TOMORROWS

A nne is used to getting her way. She is an only child (and the apple of her daddy's eye). Plus she's popular and pretty.

Imagine her surprise when Mr. Watson, her history teacher, refused to give her an extra day to turn in her term paper.

"But, Mr. Watson, I was sick all weekend!"

"You've had a month to work on that project. Besides, you weren't too sick to go to the football game, Anne. I saw you there."

Look It Up

Mr. Watson's response might seem harsh, but it points out that bad choices today produce bad consequences tomorrow.

The children of Israel learned this lesson when they tried to go into the promised land after initially rejecting God.

" 'We have sinned,' they said. 'We will go up to the place the LORD promised.'

"But Moses said, 'Why are you disobeying the LORD's command? This will not succeed! Do not go up, because the LORD is not with you. You will be defeated by your enemies, for the Amalekites and Canaanites will face you there. Because you have turned away from the LORD, he will not be with you and you will fall by the sword.'

"Nevertheless, in their presumption they went up toward the high hill country, though neither Moses nor the ark of the LORD's covenant moved from the camp. Then the Amalekites and Canaanites . . . came down and attacked them and beat them down all the way to Hormah" (Numbers 14:40–45).

Think It Through

Consider these two truths:

1. You can't relive your past.

2. You won't get a chance at the end of your life to reverse all your poor choices.

How should those facts affect your decisions today?

Work It Out

Grade (0–100) the choices you made last weekend (where you went, what you did, what you said, the people you chose to hang around). What's your average? Determine, with God's help, to pull up that average this weekend.

Ask a Christian friend to pray that you'll make wise choices in everything you do today.

Nail It Down

Read in 1 Samuel 15:24–26 the consequences Saul paid for his bad choice.

Turn to pages 597, 611 and 702 for other readings on time.
Turn to page 288 for the weekend reading.

Topic

LORD came upon David in power. Samuel then went to Ramah.

David in Saul's Service

14Now the Spirit of the LORD had departed from Saul, and an evil[a] spirit from the LORD tormented him.

15Saul's attendants said to him, "See, an evil spirit from God is tormenting you. **16**Let our lord command his servants here to search for someone who can play the harp. He will play when the evil spirit from God comes upon you, and you will feel better."

17So Saul said to his attendants, "Find someone who plays well and bring him to me."

18One of the servants answered, "I have seen a son of Jesse of Bethlehem who knows how to play the harp. He is a brave man and a warrior. He speaks well and is a fine-looking man. And the LORD is with him."

19Then Saul sent messengers to Jesse and said, "Send me your son David, who is with the sheep." **20**So Jesse took a donkey loaded with bread, a skin of wine and a young goat and sent them with his son David to Saul.

21David came to Saul and entered his service. Saul liked him very much, and David became one of his armor-bearers. **22**Then Saul sent word to Jesse, saying, "Allow David to remain in my service, for I am pleased with him."

23Whenever the spirit from God came upon Saul, David would take his harp and play. Then relief would come to Saul; he would feel better, and the evil spirit would leave him.

David and Goliath

17 Now the Philistines gathered their forces for war and assembled at Socoh in Judah. They pitched camp at Ephes Dammim, between Socoh and Azekah. **2**Saul and the Israelites assembled and camped in the Valley of Elah and drew up their battle line to meet the Philistines. **3**The Philistines occupied one hill and the Israelites another, with the valley between them.

4A champion named Goliath, who was from Gath, came out of the Philistine camp. He was over nine feet[b] tall. **5**He had a bronze helmet on his head and wore a coat of scale armor of bronze weighing five thousand shekels[c]; **6**on his legs he wore bronze greaves, and a bronze javelin was slung on his back. **7**His spear shaft was like a weaver's rod, and its iron point weighed six hundred shekels.[d] His shield bearer went ahead of him.

8Goliath stood and shouted to the ranks of Israel, "Why do you come out and line up for battle? Am I not a Philistine, and are you not the servants of Saul? Choose a man and have him come down to me. **9**If he is able to fight and kill me, we will become your subjects; but if I overcome him and kill him, you will become our subjects and serve us." **10**Then the Philistine said, "This day I defy the ranks of Israel! Give me a man and let us fight each other." **11**On hearing the Philistine's words, Saul and all the Israelites were dismayed and terrified.

12Now David was the son of an Ephrathite named Jesse, who was from Bethlehem in Judah. Jesse had eight sons, and in Saul's time he was old and well advanced in years. **13**Jesse's three oldest sons had followed Saul to the war: The firstborn was Eliab; the second, Abinadab; and the third, Shammah. **14**David was the youngest. The three oldest followed Saul, **15**but David went back and forth from Saul to tend his father's sheep at Bethlehem.

16For forty days the Philistine came forward every morning and evening and took his stand.

17Now Jesse said to his son David, "Take this ephah[e] of roasted grain and these ten loaves of bread for your brothers and hurry to their camp. **18**Take along these ten cheeses to the commander of their unit.[f] See how your brothers are and bring back some assurance[g] from them. **19**They are with Saul and all the men of Israel in the Valley of Elah, fighting against the Philistines."

20Early in the morning David left the flock with a shepherd, loaded up and set out, as Jesse had directed. He reached the camp as the army was going out to its battle positions, shouting the war cry. **21**Israel and the Philistines were drawing up their lines facing each other. **22**David left his things with the keeper of supplies, ran to the battle lines and greeted his brothers. **23**As he was talking with them, Goliath, the Philistine champion from Gath, stepped out from his lines and shouted his usual defiance, and David

---

a14 Or *injurious*; also in verses 15, 16 and 23   *b4* Hebrew *was six cubits and a span* (about 3 meters)
c5 That is, about 125 pounds (about 57 kilograms)   *d7* That is, about 15 pounds (about 7 kilograms)
e17 That is, probably about 3/5 bushel (about 22 liters)   *f18* Hebrew *thousand*   *g18* Or *some token*; or *some pledge of spoils*

A RECIPE FOR FAILURE

Work It Out
••••

Read the story of David and Goliath in today's Scripture reading. Don't automatically say, "I've heard that story a million times," and then not bother to read it. Turn to the passage and take a fresh look at the story, like you've never heard it before.

Young David was really quite a guy! The situation described here was desperate, but eager David jumped in with both feet. If ever there was a recipe for failure, this was it: young boy fights huge giant. But David didn't fail. He won. And he knew why. He took none of the credit for himself. He realized he was God's tool for the day (see 1 Samuel 17:45).

If little David could destroy big Goliath *in God's strength,* any ideas what you might be able to accomplish *in God's strength?*

Nail It Down
••••

Read the familiar story of David and Goliath in 1 Samuel 17.

Think It Through
•••

All throughout Scripture the people used by God in the mightiest ways were those who thought they weren't capable or talented enough for the task. Moses told God he couldn't speak fluently enough to go before Pharaoh (Exodus 4:10). Gideon thought he was too much of a nobody (Judges 6:15). Isaiah didn't think he was worthy to be used (Isaiah 6:5). Mary, the mother of Jesus, was "troubled" when an angel came and told her what was to happen to her (Luke 1:29). But God used each of these people in spectacular ways.

Most of you probably look at yourselves and think there's not much you can do for God. You're not very talented or smart or brave or strong. The thing to remember is this: God doesn't ask you to be talented or smart or brave or strong. He only asks you to be *willing.* The strongest characteristic shared by David, Moses, Gideon, Isaiah and Mary was their willingness to be used. How willing are you?

Nail It Down
••••

Enjoy the story of David and Goliath in 1 Samuel 17 again. For further insight read Psalm 51:10–19.

Turn to pages 239 and 784 for other readings on excuses.
Turn to page 291 for Monday's reading.

Topic
••••

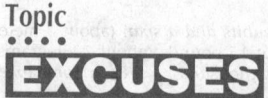

EXCUSES

heard it. **24**When the Israelites saw the man, they all ran from him in great fear.

25Now the Israelites had been saying, "Do you see how this man keeps coming out? He comes out to defy Israel. The king will give great wealth to the man who kills him. He will also give him his daughter in marriage and will exempt his father's family from taxes in Israel."

26David asked the men standing near him, "What will be done for the man who kills this Philistine and removes this disgrace from Israel? Who is this uncircumcised Philistine that he should defy the armies of the living God?"

27They repeated to him what they had been saying and told him, "This is what will be done for the man who kills him."

28When Eliab, David's oldest brother, heard him speaking with the men, he burned with anger at him and asked, "Why have you come down here? And with whom did you leave those few sheep in the desert? I know how conceited you are and how wicked your heart is; you came down only to watch the battle."

29"Now what have I done?" said David. "Can't I even speak?" **30**He then turned away to someone else and brought up the same matter, and the men answered him as before. **31**What David said was overheard and reported to Saul, and Saul sent for him.

32David said to Saul, "Let no one lose heart on account of this Philistine; your servant will go and fight him."

33Saul replied, "You are not able to go out against this Philistine and fight him; you are only a boy, and he has been a fighting man from his youth."

34But David said to Saul, "Your servant has been keeping his father's sheep. When a lion or a bear came and carried off a sheep from the flock, **35**I went after it, struck it and rescued the sheep from its mouth. When it turned on me, I seized it by its hair, struck it and killed it. **36**Your servant has killed both the lion and the bear; this uncircumcised Philistine will be like one of them, because he has defied the armies of the living God. **37**The LORD who delivered me from the paw of the lion and the paw of the bear will deliver me from the hand of this Philistine."

Saul said to David, "Go, and the LORD be with you."

38Then Saul dressed David in his own tunic. He put a coat of armor on him and a bronze helmet on his head. **39**David fastened on his sword over the tunic and tried walking around, because he was not used to them.

"I cannot go in these," he said to Saul, "because I am not used to them." So he took them off. **40**Then he took his staff in his hand, chose five smooth stones from the stream, put them in the pouch of his shepherd's bag and, with his sling in his hand, approached the Philistine.

41Meanwhile, the Philistine, with his shield bearer in front of him, kept coming closer to David. **42**He looked David over and saw that he was only a boy, ruddy and handsome, and he despised him. **43**He said to David, "Am I a dog, that you come at me with sticks?" And the Philistine cursed David by his gods. **44**"Come here," he said, "and I'll give your flesh to the birds of the air and the beasts of the field!"

45David said to the Philistine, "You come against me with sword and spear and javelin, but I come against you in the name of the LORD Almighty, the God of the armies of Israel, whom you have defied. **46**This day the LORD will hand you over to me, and I'll strike you down and cut off your head. Today I will give the carcasses of the Philistine army to the birds of the air and the beasts of the earth, and the whole world will know that there is a God in Israel. **47**All those gathered here will know that it is not by sword or spear that the LORD saves; for the battle is the LORD's, and he will give all of you into our hands."

48As the Philistine moved closer to attack him, David ran quickly toward the battle line to meet him. **49**Reaching into his bag and taking out a stone, he slung it and struck the Philistine on the forehead. The stone sank into his forehead, and he fell facedown on the ground.

50So David triumphed over the Philistine with a sling and a stone; without a sword in his hand he struck down the Philistine and killed him.

51David ran and stood over him. He took hold of the Philistine's sword and drew it from the scabbard. After he killed him, he cut off his head with the sword.

When the Philistines saw that their hero was dead, they turned and ran. **52**Then the men of Israel and Judah surged forward with a shout and pursued the Philistines to the entrance of Gath[a] and to the gates of Ekron. Their dead were strewn along the Shaaraim road to Gath and Ekron. **53**When the Israel-

---

[a]52 Some Septuagint manuscripts; Hebrew *a valley*

ites returned from chasing the Philistines, they plundered their camp. **54**David took the Philistine's head and brought it to Jerusalem, and he put the Philistine's weapons in his own tent.

55As Saul watched David going out to meet the Philistine, he said to Abner, commander of the army, "Abner, whose son is that young man?"

Abner replied, "As surely as you live, O king, I don't know."

56The king said, "Find out whose son this young man is."

57As soon as David returned from killing the Philistine, Abner took him and brought him before Saul, with David still holding the Philistine's head.

58"Whose son are you, young man?" Saul asked him.

David said, "I am the son of your servant Jesse of Bethlehem."

Saul's Jealousy of David

18 After David had finished talking with Saul, Jonathan became one in spirit with David, and he loved him as himself. **2**From that day Saul kept David with him and did not let him return to his father's house. **3**And Jonathan made a covenant with David because he loved him as himself. **4**Jonathan took off the robe he was wearing and gave it to David, along with his tunic, and even his sword, his bow and his belt.

5Whatever Saul sent him to do, David did it so successfully*a* that Saul gave him a high rank in the army. This pleased all the people, and Saul's officers as well.

6When the men were returning home after David had killed the Philistine, the women came out from all the towns of Israel to meet King Saul with singing and dancing, with joyful songs and with tambourines and lutes. **7**As they danced, they sang:

"Saul has slain his thousands,
    and David his tens of thousands."

8Saul was very angry; this refrain galled him. "They have credited David with tens of thousands," he thought, "but me with only thousands. What more can he get but the kingdom?" **9**And from that time on Saul kept a jealous eye on David.

10The next day an evil*b* spirit from God came forcefully upon Saul. He was prophesying in his house, while David was playing the harp, as he usually did. Saul had a spear in his hand **11**and he hurled it, saying to himself, "I'll pin David to the wall." But David eluded him twice.

12Saul was afraid of David, because the Lord was with David but had left Saul. **13**So he sent David away from him and gave him command over a thousand men, and David led the troops in their campaigns. **14**In everything he did he had great success,*c* because the Lord was with him. **15**When Saul saw how successful*d* he was, he was afraid of him. **16**But all Israel and Judah loved David, because he led them in their campaigns.

17Saul said to David, "Here is my older daughter Merab. I will give her to you in marriage; only serve me bravely and fight the battles of the Lord." For Saul said to himself, "I will not raise a hand against him. Let the Philistines do that!"

18But David said to Saul, "Who am I, and what is my family or my father's clan in Israel, that I should become the king's son-in-law?" **19**So*e* when the time came for Merab, Saul's daughter, to be given to David, she was given in marriage to Adriel of Meholah.

20Now Saul's daughter Michal was in love with David, and when they told Saul about it, he was pleased. **21**"I will give her to him," he thought, "so that she may be a snare to him and so that the hand of the Philistines may be against him." So Saul said to David, "Now you have a second opportunity to become my son-in-law."

22Then Saul ordered his attendants: "Speak to David privately and say, 'Look, the king is pleased with you, and his attendants all like you; now become his son-in-law.' "

23They repeated these words to David. But David said, "Do you think it is a small matter to become the king's son-in-law? I'm only a poor man and little known."

24When Saul's servants told him what David had said, **25**Saul replied, "Say to David, 'The king wants no other price for the bride than a hundred Philistine foreskins, to take revenge on his enemies.' " Saul's plan was to have David fall by the hands of the Philistines.

26When the attendants told David these things, he was pleased to become the king's son-in-law. So before the allotted time elapsed, **27**David and his men went out and killed two hundred Philistines. He brought their foreskins and presented the full number to the king so that he might become the king's son-in-law. Then Saul gave him his daughter Michal in marriage.

a5 Or *wisely*   *b10* Or *injurious*   *c14* Or *he was very wise*   *d15* Or *wise*   *e19* Or *However.*

FRIENDSHIP STARTS IN THE HEART

Craig is a new Christian who has only been going to church for a short time. Yesterday he pulled one of the youth leaders aside and said, "I don't know how to say this, but sometimes this place gives me the creeps."

"What do you mean?" the youth leader asked. "Why?"

"Well, the girls are hugging each other every fifteen minutes and saying 'I love you' to their friends. And some of the men go up and hug each other! If you ask me it looks gay."

Look It Up
• • • •

Christians—whether male or female—are expected to care deeply for their friends. One of the best examples of friendship in Scripture is the close relationship between Jonathan and David.

How unlikely! Two brave, battle-hardened warriors. Men of strength and courage . . . and yet, not ashamed to show their love for each other.

In time, a jealous King Saul determined to kill David. In an emotional farewell scene, Jonathan told his best friend to flee: "Then they kissed each other and wept together—but David wept the most. Jonathan said to David, 'Go in peace, for we have sworn friendship with each other in the name of the LORD' " (1 Samuel 20:41–42).

Think It Through
• • • •

Our culture says real males shouldn't express emotion. What a warped idea! Expressions of affection don't mean you're strange. They're completely normal. Jonathan and David were two incredibly masculine men. They lived in a culture where kissing was like shaking hands, and they never gave a second thought to expressing how they felt about each other.

Why can most girls tell each other "I love you" without batting an eyelash? Why can't guys? How come girls are not afraid to get emotional and share their feelings with each other? Why are guys usually so hesitant?

Work It Out
• • • •

If you want to see your closest friendships get even better, you need to be willing to care deeply and to express how you feel.

Perhaps right now you can't see yourself saying to your friend, "Hey, I really love and appreciate you." That's okay. At least you can start doing more to show how much you care.

Meanwhile, sit down with some friends today and discuss this idea of expressing emotion. Using Jonathan and David as an example, try to figure out why verbal declarations of love are so hard for so many people.

Nail It Down
• • • •

Read about David and Jonathan's friendship in 1 Samuel 18:1–3.

Turn to pages 195, 509, 670 and 1346 for other readings on friendship.
Turn to page 304 for Tuesday's reading.

Topic
• • • •

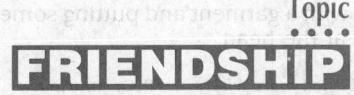

28When Saul realized that the LORD was with David and that his daughter Michal loved David, **29**Saul became still more afraid of him, and he remained his enemy the rest of his days.

30The Philistine commanders continued to go out to battle, and as often as they did, David met with more success*a* than the rest of Saul's officers, and his name became well known.

Saul Tries to Kill David

19 Saul told his son Jonathan and all the attendants to kill David. But Jonathan was very fond of David **2**and warned him, "My father Saul is looking for a chance to kill you. Be on your guard tomorrow morning; go into hiding and stay there. **3**I will go out and stand with my father in the field where you are. I'll speak to him about you and will tell you what I find out."

4Jonathan spoke well of David to Saul his father and said to him, "Let not the king do wrong to his servant David; he has not wronged you, and what he has done has benefited you greatly. **5**He took his life in his hands when he killed the Philistine. The LORD won a great victory for all Israel, and you saw it and were glad. Why then would you do wrong to an innocent man like David by killing him for no reason?"

6Saul listened to Jonathan and took this oath: "As surely as the LORD lives, David will not be put to death."

7So Jonathan called David and told him the whole conversation. He brought him to Saul, and David was with Saul as before.

8Once more war broke out, and David went out and fought the Philistines. He struck them with such force that they fled before him.

9But an evil*b* spirit from the LORD came upon Saul as he was sitting in his house with his spear in his hand. While David was playing the harp, **10**Saul tried to pin him to the wall with his spear, but David eluded him as Saul drove the spear into the wall. That night David made good his escape.

11Saul sent men to David's house to watch it and to kill him in the morning. But Michal, David's wife, warned him, "If you don't run for your life tonight, tomorrow you'll be killed." **12**So Michal let David down through a window, and he fled and escaped. **13**Then Michal took an idol*c* and laid it on the bed, covering it with a garment and putting some goats' hair at the head.

14When Saul sent the men to capture David, Michal said, "He is ill."

15Then Saul sent the men back to see David and told them, "Bring him up to me in his bed so that I may kill him." **16**But when the men entered, there was the idol in the bed, and at the head was some goats' hair.

17Saul said to Michal, "Why did you deceive me like this and send my enemy away so that he escaped?"

Michal told him, "He said to me, 'Let me get away. Why should I kill you?' "

18When David had fled and made his escape, he went to Samuel at Ramah and told him all that Saul had done to him. Then he and Samuel went to Naioth and stayed there. **19**Word came to Saul: "David is in Naioth at Ramah"; **20**so he sent men to capture him. But when they saw a group of prophets prophesying, with Samuel standing there as their leader, the Spirit of God came upon Saul's men and they also prophesied. **21**Saul was told about it, and he sent more men, and they prophesied too. Saul sent men a third time, and they also prophesied. **22**Finally, he himself left for Ramah and went to the great cistern at Secu. And he asked, "Where are Samuel and David?"

"Over in Naioth at Ramah," they said.

23So Saul went to Naioth at Ramah. But the Spirit of God came even upon him, and he walked along prophesying until he came to Naioth. **24**He stripped off his robes and also prophesied in Samuel's presence. He lay that way all that day and night. This is why people say, "Is Saul also among the prophets?"

David and Jonathan

20 Then David fled from Naioth at Ramah and went to Jonathan and asked, "What have I done? What is my crime? How have I wronged your father, that he is trying to take my life?"

2"Never!" Jonathan replied. "You are not going to die! Look, my father doesn't do anything, great or small, without confiding in me. Why would he hide this from me? It's not so!"

3But David took an oath and said, "Your father knows very well that I have found favor in your eyes, and he has said to himself, 'Jonathan must not know this or he will be grieved.' Yet as surely as the LORD lives and as you live, there is only a step between me and death."

---

a30 Or *David acted more wisely*   *b9* Or *injurious*   *c13* Hebrew *teraphim*; also in verse 16

⁴Jonathan said to David, "Whatever you want me to do, I'll do for you."

⁵So David said, "Look, tomorrow is the New Moon festival, and I am supposed to dine with the king; but let me go and hide in the field until the evening of the day after tomorrow. ⁶If your father misses me at all, tell him, 'David earnestly asked my permission to hurry to Bethlehem, his hometown, because an annual sacrifice is being made there for his whole clan.' ⁷If he says, 'Very well,' then your servant is safe. But if he loses his temper, you can be sure that he is determined to harm me. ⁸As for you, show kindness to your servant, for you have brought him into a covenant with you before the LORD. If I am guilty, then kill me yourself! Why hand me over to your father?"

⁹"Never!" Jonathan said. "If I had the least inkling that my father was determined to harm you, wouldn't I tell you?"

¹⁰David asked, "Who will tell me if your father answers you harshly?"

¹¹"Come," Jonathan said, "let's go out into the field." So they went there together.

¹²Then Jonathan said to David: "By the LORD, the God of Israel, I will surely sound out my father by this time the day after tomorrow! If he is favorably disposed toward you, will I not send you word and let you know? ¹³But if my father is inclined to harm you, may the LORD deal with me, be it ever so severely, if I do not let you know and send you away safely. May the LORD be with you as he has been with my father. ¹⁴But show me unfailing kindness like that of the LORD as long as I live, so that I may not be killed, ¹⁵and do not ever cut off your kindness from my family — not even when the LORD has cut off every one of David's enemies from the face of the earth."

¹⁶So Jonathan made a covenant with the house of David, saying, "May the LORD call David's enemies to account." ¹⁷And Jonathan had David reaffirm his oath out of love for him, because he loved him as he loved himself.

¹⁸Then Jonathan said to David: "Tomorrow is the New Moon festival. You will be missed, because your seat will be empty. ¹⁹The day after tomorrow, toward evening, go to the place where you hid when this trouble began, and wait by the stone Ezel. ²⁰I will shoot three arrows to the side of it, as though I were shooting at a target. ²¹Then I will send a boy and say, 'Go, find the arrows.' If I say to him, 'Look, the arrows are on this side of you; bring them here,' then come, because, as surely as the LORD lives, you are safe; there is no danger. ²²But if I say to the boy, 'Look, the arrows are beyond you,' then you must go, because the LORD has sent you away. ²³And about the matter you and I discussed — remember, the LORD is witness between you and me forever."

²⁴So David hid in the field, and when the New Moon festival came, the king sat down to eat. ²⁵He sat in his customary place by the wall, opposite Jonathan,ᵃ and Abner sat next to Saul, but David's place was empty. ²⁶Saul said nothing that day, for he thought, "Something must have happened to David to make him ceremonially unclean — surely he is unclean." ²⁷But the next day, the second day of the month, David's place was empty again. Then Saul said to his son Jonathan, "Why hasn't the son of Jesse come to the meal, either yesterday or today?"

²⁸Jonathan answered, "David earnestly asked me for permission to go to Bethlehem. ²⁹He said, 'Let me go, because our family is observing a sacrifice in the town and my brother has ordered me to be there. If I have found favor in your eyes, let me get away to see my brothers.' That is why he has not come to the king's table."

³⁰Saul's anger flared up at Jonathan and he said to him, "You son of a perverse and rebellious woman! Don't I know that you have sided with the son of Jesse to your own shame and to the shame of the mother who bore you? ³¹As long as the son of Jesse lives on this earth, neither you nor your kingdom will be established. Now send and bring him to me, for he must die!"

³²"Why should he be put to death? What has he done?" Jonathan asked his father. ³³But Saul hurled his spear at him to kill him. Then Jonathan knew that his father intended to kill David.

³⁴Jonathan got up from the table in fierce anger; on that second day of the month he did not eat, because he was grieved at his father's shameful treatment of David.

³⁵In the morning Jonathan went out to the field for his meeting with David. He had a small boy with him, ³⁶and he said to the boy, "Run and find the arrows I shoot." As the boy ran, he shot an arrow beyond him. ³⁷When the boy came to the place where Jonathan's arrow had fallen, Jonathan called out after him, "Isn't the arrow beyond you?" ³⁸Then he shouted, "Hurry! Go quickly! Don't stop!" The boy picked up the arrow

and returned to his master. **39**(The boy knew nothing of all this; only Jonathan and David knew.) **40**Then Jonathan gave his weapons to the boy and said, "Go, carry them back to town."

41After the boy had gone, David got up from the south side ¡of the stone¡ and bowed down before Jonathan three times, with his face to the ground. Then they kissed each other and wept together—but David wept the most.

42Jonathan said to David, "Go in peace, for we have sworn friendship with each other in the name of the LORD, saying, 'The LORD is witness between you and me, and between your descendants and my descendants forever.'" Then David left, and Jonathan went back to the town.

David at Nob

21 David went to Nob, to Ahimelech the priest. Ahimelech trembled when he met him, and asked, "Why are you alone? Why is no one with you?"

2David answered Ahimelech the priest, "The king charged me with a certain matter and said to me, 'No one is to know anything about your mission and your instructions.' As for my men, I have told them to meet me at a certain place. **3**Now then, what do you have on hand? Give me five loaves of bread, or whatever you can find."

4But the priest answered David, "I don't have any ordinary bread on hand; however, there is some consecrated bread here — provided the men have kept themselves from women."

5David replied, "Indeed women have been kept from us, as usual whenever*a* I set out. The men's things*b* are holy even on missions that are not holy. How much more so today!" **6**So the priest gave him the consecrated bread, since there was no bread there except the bread of the Presence that had been removed from before the LORD and replaced by hot bread on the day it was taken away.

7Now one of Saul's servants was there that day, detained before the LORD; he was Doeg the Edomite, Saul's head shepherd.

8David asked Ahimelech, "Don't you have a spear or a sword here? I haven't brought my sword or any other weapon, because the king's business was urgent."

9The priest replied, "The sword of Goliath the Philistine, whom you killed in the Valley of Elah, is here; it is wrapped in a cloth behind the ephod. If you want it, take it; there is no sword here but that one."

David said, "There is none like it; give it to me."

David at Gath

10That day David fled from Saul and went to Achish king of Gath. **11**But the servants of Achish said to him, "Isn't this David, the king of the land? Isn't he the one they sing about in their dances:

" 'Saul has slain his thousands,
    and David his tens of thousands'?"

12David took these words to heart and was very much afraid of Achish king of Gath. **13**So he pretended to be insane in their presence; and while he was in their hands he acted like a madman, making marks on the doors of the gate and letting saliva run down his beard.

14Achish said to his servants, "Look at the man! He is insane! Why bring him to me? **15**Am I so short of madmen that you have to bring this fellow here to carry on like this in front of me? Must this man come into my house?"

David at Adullam and Mizpah

22 David left Gath and escaped to the cave of Adullam. When his brothers and his father's household heard about it, they went down to him there. **2**All those who were in distress or in debt or discontented gathered around him, and he became their leader. About four hundred men were with him.

3From there David went to Mizpah in Moab and said to the king of Moab, "Would you let my father and mother come and stay with you until I learn what God will do for me?" **4**So he left them with the king of Moab, and they stayed with him as long as David was in the stronghold.

5But the prophet Gad said to David, "Do not stay in the stronghold. Go into the land of Judah." So David left and went to the forest of Hereth.

Saul Kills the Priests of Nob

6Now Saul heard that David and his men had been discovered. And Saul, spear in hand, was seated under the tamarisk tree on the hill at Gibeah, with all his officials standing around him. **7**Saul said to them, "Listen, men of Benjamin! Will the son of Jesse give all of you fields and vineyards? Will he make

---

a5 Or *from us in the past few days since*   *b5* Or *bodies* all of you commanders of thousands and commanders of hundreds? ⁸Is that why you have all conspired against me? No one tells me when my son makes a covenant with the son of Jesse. None of you is concerned about me or tells me that my son has incited my servant to lie in wait for me, as he does today."

⁹But Doeg the Edomite, who was standing with Saul's officials, said, "I saw the son of Jesse come to Ahimelech son of Ahitub at Nob. ¹⁰Ahimelech inquired of the LORD for him; he also gave him provisions and the sword of Goliath the Philistine."

¹¹Then the king sent for the priest Ahimelech son of Ahitub and his father's whole family, who were the priests at Nob, and they all came to the king. ¹²Saul said, "Listen now, son of Ahitub."

"Yes, my lord," he answered.

¹³Saul said to him, "Why have you conspired against me, you and the son of Jesse, giving him bread and a sword and inquiring of God for him, so that he has rebelled against me and lies in wait for me, as he does today?"

¹⁴Ahimelech answered the king, "Who of all your servants is as loyal as David, the king's son-in-law, captain of your bodyguard and highly respected in your household? ¹⁵Was that day the first time I inquired of God for him? Of course not! Let not the king accuse your servant or any of his father's family, for your servant knows nothing at all about this whole affair."

¹⁶But the king said, "You will surely die, Ahimelech, you and your father's whole family."

¹⁷Then the king ordered the guards at his side: "Turn and kill the priests of the LORD, because they too have sided with David. They knew he was fleeing, yet they did not tell me."

But the king's officials were not willing to raise a hand to strike the priests of the LORD.

¹⁸The king then ordered Doeg, "You turn and strike down the priests." So Doeg the Edomite turned and struck them down. That day he killed eighty-five men who wore the linen ephod. ¹⁹He also put to the sword Nob, the town of the priests, with its men and women, its children and infants, and its cattle, donkeys and sheep.

²⁰But Abiathar, a son of Ahimelech son of Ahitub, escaped and fled to join David. ²¹He told David that Saul had killed the priests of the LORD. ²²Then David said to Abiathar: "That day, when Doeg the Edomite was there, I knew he would be sure to tell Saul. I am responsible for the death of your father's whole family. ²³Stay with me; don't be afraid; the man who is seeking your life is seeking mine also. You will be safe with me."

David Saves Keilah

23 When David was told, "Look, the Philistines are fighting against Keilah and are looting the threshing floors," ²he inquired of the LORD, saying, "Shall I go and attack these Philistines?"

The LORD answered him, "Go, attack the Philistines and save Keilah."

³But David's men said to him, "Here in Judah we are afraid. How much more, then, if we go to Keilah against the Philistine forces!"

⁴Once again David inquired of the LORD, and the LORD answered him, "Go down to Keilah, for I am going to give the Philistines into your hand." ⁵So David and his men went to Keilah, fought the Philistines and carried off their livestock. He inflicted heavy losses on the Philistines and saved the people of Keilah. ⁶(Now Abiathar son of Ahimelech had brought the ephod down with him when he fled to David at Keilah.)

Saul Pursues David

⁷Saul was told that David had gone to Keilah, and he said, "God has handed him over to me, for David has imprisoned himself by entering a town with gates and bars." ⁸And Saul called up all his forces for battle, to go down to Keilah to besiege David and his men.

⁹When David learned that Saul was plotting against him, he said to Abiathar the priest, "Bring the ephod." ¹⁰David said, "O LORD, God of Israel, your servant has heard definitely that Saul plans to come to Keilah and destroy the town on account of me. ¹¹Will the citizens of Keilah surrender me to him? Will Saul come down, as your servant has heard? O LORD, God of Israel, tell your servant."

And the LORD said, "He will."

¹²Again David asked, "Will the citizens of Keilah surrender me and my men to Saul?"

And the LORD said, "They will."

¹³So David and his men, about six hundred in number, left Keilah and kept moving from place to place. When Saul was told that David had escaped from Keilah, he did not go there.

¹⁴David stayed in the desert strongholds and in the hills of the Desert of Ziph. Day

after day Saul searched for him, but God did not give David into his hands.

¹⁵While David was at Horesh in the Desert of Ziph, he learned that Saul had come out to take his life. ¹⁶And Saul's son Jonathan went to David at Horesh and helped him find strength in God. ¹⁷"Don't be afraid," he said. "My father Saul will not lay a hand on you. You will be king over Israel, and I will be second to you. Even my father Saul knows this." ¹⁸The two of them made a covenant before the Lord. Then Jonathan went home, but David remained at Horesh.

¹⁹The Ziphites went up to Saul at Gibeah and said, "Is not David hiding among us in the strongholds at Horesh, on the hill of Hakilah, south of Jeshimon? ²⁰Now, O king, come down whenever it pleases you to do so, and we will be responsible for handing him over to the king."

²¹Saul replied, "The Lord bless you for your concern for me. ²²Go and make further preparation. Find out where David usually goes and who has seen him there. They tell me he is very crafty. ²³Find out about all the hiding places he uses and come back to me with definite information.ᵃ Then I will go with you; if he is in the area, I will track him down among all the clans of Judah."

²⁴So they set out and went to Ziph ahead of Saul. Now David and his men were in the Desert of Maon, in the Arabah south of Jeshimon. ²⁵Saul and his men began the search, and when David was told about it, he went down to the rock and stayed in the Desert of Maon. When Saul heard this, he went into the Desert of Maon in pursuit of David.

²⁶Saul was going along one side of the mountain, and David and his men were on the other side, hurrying to get away from Saul. As Saul and his forces were closing in on David and his men to capture them, ²⁷a messenger came to Saul, saying, "Come quickly! The Philistines are raiding the land." ²⁸Then Saul broke off his pursuit of David and went to meet the Philistines. That is why they call this place Sela Hammahlekoth.ᵇ ²⁹And David went up from there and lived in the strongholds of En Gedi.

David Spares Saul's Life

24 After Saul returned from pursuing the Philistines, he was told, "David is in the Desert of En Gedi." ²So Saul took three thousand chosen men from all Israel and set out to look for David and his men near the Crags of the Wild Goats.

³He came to the sheep pens along the way; a cave was there, and Saul went in to relieve himself. David and his men were far back in the cave. ⁴The men said, "This is the day the Lord spoke of when he saidᶜ to you, 'I will give your enemy into your hands for you to deal with as you wish.'" Then David crept up unnoticed and cut off a corner of Saul's robe.

⁵Afterward, David was conscience-stricken for having cut off a corner of his robe. ⁶He said to his men, "The Lord forbid that I should do such a thing to my master, the Lord's anointed, or lift my hand against him; for he is the anointed of the Lord." ⁷With these words David rebuked his men and did not allow them to attack Saul. And Saul left the cave and went his way.

⁸Then David went out of the cave and called out to Saul, "My lord the king!" When Saul looked behind him, David bowed down and prostrated himself with his face to the ground. ⁹He said to Saul, "Why do you listen when men say, 'David is bent on harming you'? ¹⁰This day you have seen with your own eyes how the Lord delivered you into my hands in the cave. Some urged me to kill you, but I spared you; I said, 'I will not lift my hand against my master, because he is the Lord's anointed.' ¹¹See, my father, look at this piece of your robe in my hand! I cut off the corner of your robe but did not kill you. Now understand and recognize that I am not guilty of wrongdoing or rebellion. I have not wronged you, but you are hunting me down to take my life. ¹²May the Lord judge between you and me. And may the Lord avenge the wrongs you have done to me, but my hand will not touch you. ¹³As the old saying goes, 'From evildoers come evil deeds,' so my hand will not touch you.

¹⁴"Against whom has the king of Israel come out? Whom are you pursuing? A dead dog? A flea? ¹⁵May the Lord be our judge and decide between us. May he consider my cause and uphold it; may he vindicate me by delivering me from your hand."

¹⁶When David finished saying this, Saul asked, "Is that your voice, David my son?" And he wept aloud. ¹⁷"You are more righteous than I," he said. "You have treated me well, but I have treated you badly. ¹⁸You have just now told me of the good you did to me; the Lord delivered me into your hands, but you did not kill me. ¹⁹When a

---

ᵃ23 Or me at Nacon   ᵇ28 Sela Hammahlekoth means rock of parting.   ᶜ4 Or "Today the Lord is saying man finds his enemy, does he let him get away unharmed? May the LORD reward you well for the way you treated me today. [20]I know that you will surely be king and that the kingdom of Israel will be established in your hands. [21]Now swear to me by the LORD that you will not cut off my descendants or wipe out my name from my father's family."

[22]So David gave his oath to Saul. Then Saul returned home, but David and his men went up to the stronghold.

David, Nabal and Abigail

25 Now Samuel died, and all Israel assembled and mourned for him; and they buried him at his home in Ramah.

Then David moved down into the Desert of Maon.[a] [2]A certain man in Maon, who had property there at Carmel, was very wealthy. He had a thousand goats and three thousand sheep, which he was shearing in Carmel. [3]His name was Nabal and his wife's name was Abigail. She was an intelligent and beautiful woman, but her husband, a Calebite, was surly and mean in his dealings.

[4]While David was in the desert, he heard that Nabal was shearing sheep. [5]So he sent ten young men and said to them, "Go up to Nabal at Carmel and greet him in my name. [6]Say to him: 'Long life to you! Good health to you and your household! And good health to all that is yours!

[7]" 'Now I hear that it is sheep-shearing time. When your shepherds were with us, we did not mistreat them, and the whole time they were at Carmel nothing of theirs was missing. [8]Ask your own servants and they will tell you. Therefore be favorable toward my young men, since we come at a festive time. Please give your servants and your son David whatever you can find for them.' "

[9]When David's men arrived, they gave Nabal this message in David's name. Then they waited.

[10]Nabal answered David's servants, "Who is this David? Who is this son of Jesse? Many servants are breaking away from their masters these days. [11]Why should I take my bread and water, and the meat I have slaughtered for my shearers, and give it to men coming from who knows where?"

[12]David's men turned around and went back. When they arrived, they reported every word. [13]David said to his men, "Put on your swords!" So they put on their swords,

and David put on his. About four hundred men went up with David, while two hundred stayed with the supplies.

[14]One of the servants told Nabal's wife Abigail: "David sent messengers from the desert to give our master his greetings, but he hurled insults at them. [15]Yet these men were very good to us. They did not mistreat us, and the whole time we were out in the fields near them nothing was missing. [16]Night and day they were a wall around us all the time we were herding our sheep near them. [17]Now think it over and see what you can do, because disaster is hanging over our master and his whole household. He is such a wicked man that no one can talk to him."

[18]Abigail lost no time. She took two hundred loaves of bread, two skins of wine, five dressed sheep, five seahs[b] of roasted grain, a hundred cakes of raisins and two hundred cakes of pressed figs, and loaded them on donkeys. [19]Then she told her servants, "Go on ahead; I'll follow you." But she did not tell her husband Nabal.

[20]As she came riding her donkey into a mountain ravine, there were David and his men descending toward her, and she met them. [21]David had just said, "It's been useless—all my watching over this fellow's property in the desert so that nothing of his was missing. He has paid me back evil for good. [22]May God deal with David,[c] be it ever so severely, if by morning I leave alive one male of all who belong to him!"

[23]When Abigail saw David, she quickly got off her donkey and bowed down before David with her face to the ground. [24]She fell at his feet and said: "My lord, let the blame be on me alone. Please let your servant speak to you; hear what your servant has to say. [25]May my lord pay no attention to that wicked man Nabal. He is just like his name—his name is Fool, and folly goes with him. But as for me, your servant, I did not see the men my master sent.

[26]"Now since the LORD has kept you, my master, from bloodshed and from avenging yourself with your own hands, as surely as the LORD lives and as you live, may your enemies and all who intend to harm my master be like Nabal. [27]And let this gift, which your servant has brought to my master, be given to the men who follow you. [28]Please forgive your servant's offense, for the LORD will certainly make a lasting dynasty for my master, because he fights the LORD's battles. Let no

---

[a]1 Some Septuagint manuscripts; Hebrew *Paran*   [b]18 That is, probably about a bushel (about 37 liters)
[c]22 Some Septuagint manuscripts; Hebrew *with David's enemies*

wrongdoing be found in you as long as you live. **29**Even though someone is pursuing you to take your life, the life of my master will be bound securely in the bundle of the living by the LORD your God. But the lives of your enemies he will hurl away as from the pocket of a sling. **30**When the LORD has done for my master every good thing he promised concerning him and has appointed him leader over Israel, **31**my master will not have on his conscience the staggering burden of needless bloodshed or of having avenged himself. And when the LORD has brought my master success, remember your servant."

32David said to Abigail, "Praise be to the LORD, the God of Israel, who has sent you today to meet me. **33**May you be blessed for your good judgment and for keeping me from bloodshed this day and from avenging myself with my own hands. **34**Otherwise, as surely as the LORD, the God of Israel, lives, who has kept me from harming you, if you had not come quickly to meet me, not one male belonging to Nabal would have been left alive by daybreak."

35Then David accepted from her hand what she had brought him and said, "Go home in peace. I have heard your words and granted your request."

36When Abigail went to Nabal, he was in the house holding a banquet like that of a king. He was in high spirits and very drunk. So she told him nothing until daybreak. **37**Then in the morning, when Nabal was sober, his wife told him all these things, and his heart failed him and he became like a stone. **38**About ten days later, the LORD struck Nabal and he died.

39When David heard that Nabal was dead, he said, "Praise be to the LORD, who has upheld my cause against Nabal for treating me with contempt. He has kept his servant from doing wrong and has brought Nabal's wrongdoing down on his own head."

Then David sent word to Abigail, asking her to become his wife. **40**His servants went to Carmel and said to Abigail, "David has sent us to you to take you to become his wife."

41She bowed down with her face to the ground and said, "Here is your maidservant, ready to serve you and wash the feet of my master's servants." **42**Abigail quickly got on a donkey and, attended by her five maids, went with David's messengers and became his wife. **43**David had also married Ahinoam of Jezreel, and they both were his wives.

44But Saul had given his daughter Michal, David's wife, to Paltiel[a] son of Laish, who was from Gallim.

David Again Spares Saul's Life

26 The Ziphites went to Saul at Gibeah and said, "Is not David hiding on the hill of Hakilah, which faces Jeshimon?"

2So Saul went down to the Desert of Ziph, with his three thousand chosen men of Israel, to search there for David. **3**Saul made his camp beside the road on the hill of Hakilah facing Jeshimon, but David stayed in the desert. When he saw that Saul had followed him there, **4**he sent out scouts and learned that Saul had definitely arrived.[b]

5Then David set out and went to the place where Saul had camped. He saw where Saul and Abner son of Ner, the commander of the army, had lain down. Saul was lying inside the camp, with the army encamped around him.

6David then asked Ahimelech the Hittite and Abishai son of Zeruiah, Joab's brother, "Who will go down into the camp with me to Saul?"

"I'll go with you," said Abishai.

7So David and Abishai went to the army by night, and there was Saul, lying asleep inside the camp with his spear stuck in the ground near his head. Abner and the soldiers were lying around him.

8Abishai said to David, "Today God has delivered your enemy into your hands. Now let me pin him to the ground with one thrust of my spear; I won't strike him twice."

9But David said to Abishai, "Don't destroy him! Who can lay a hand on the LORD's anointed and be guiltless? **10**As surely as the LORD lives," he said, "the LORD himself will strike him; either his time will come and he will die, or he will go into battle and perish. **11**But the LORD forbid that I should lay a hand on the LORD's anointed. Now get the spear and water jug that are near his head, and let's go."

12So David took the spear and water jug near Saul's head, and they left. No one saw or knew about it, nor did anyone wake up. They were all sleeping, because the LORD had put them into a deep sleep.

13Then David crossed over to the other side and stood on top of the hill some distance away; there was a wide space between them. **14**He called out to the army and to Abner son of Ner, "Aren't you going to answer me, Abner?"

a44 Hebrew *Palti,* a variant of *Paltiel*   *b4* Or *had come to Nacon*

Abner replied, "Who are you who calls to the king?"

[15]David said, "You're a man, aren't you? And who is like you in Israel? Why didn't you guard your lord the king? Someone came to destroy your lord the king. [16]What you have done is not good. As surely as the LORD lives, you and your men deserve to die, because you did not guard your master, the LORD's anointed. Look around you. Where are the king's spear and water jug that were near his head?"

[17]Saul recognized David's voice and said, "Is that your voice, David my son?"

David replied, "Yes it is, my lord the king." [18]And he added, "Why is my lord pursuing his servant? What have I done, and what wrong am I guilty of? [19]Now let my lord the king listen to his servant's words. If the LORD has incited you against me, then may he accept an offering. If, however, men have done it, may they be cursed before the LORD! They have now driven me from my share in the LORD's inheritance and have said, 'Go, serve other gods.' [20]Now do not let my blood fall to the ground far from the presence of the LORD. The king of Israel has come out to look for a flea — as one hunts a partridge in the mountains."

[21]Then Saul said, "I have sinned. Come back, David my son. Because you considered my life precious today, I will not try to harm you again. Surely I have acted like a fool and have erred greatly."

[22]"Here is the king's spear," David answered. "Let one of your young men come over and get it. [23]The LORD rewards every man for his righteousness and faithfulness. The LORD delivered you into my hands today, but I would not lay a hand on the LORD's anointed. [24]As surely as I valued your life today, so may the LORD value my life and deliver me from all trouble."

[25]Then Saul said to David, "May you be blessed, my son David; you will do great things and surely triumph."

So David went on his way, and Saul returned home.

David Among the Philistines

27 But David thought to himself, "One of these days I will be destroyed by the hand of Saul. The best thing I can do is to escape to the land of the Philistines. Then Saul will give up searching for me anywhere in Israel, and I will slip out of his hand."

[2]So David and the six hundred men with him left and went over to Achish son of Maoch king of Gath. [3]David and his men settled in Gath with Achish. Each man had his family with him, and David had his two wives: Ahinoam of Jezreel and Abigail of Carmel, the widow of Nabal. [4]When Saul was told that David had fled to Gath, he no longer searched for him.

[5]Then David said to Achish, "If I have found favor in your eyes, let a place be assigned to me in one of the country towns, that I may live there. Why should your servant live in the royal city with you?"

[6]So on that day Achish gave him Ziklag, and it has belonged to the kings of Judah ever since. [7]David lived in Philistine territory a year and four months.

[8]Now David and his men went up and raided the Geshurites, the Girzites and the Amalekites. (From ancient times these peoples had lived in the land extending to Shur and Egypt.) [9]Whenever David attacked an area, he did not leave a man or woman alive, but took sheep and cattle, donkeys and camels, and clothes. Then he returned to Achish.

[10]When Achish asked, "Where did you go raiding today?" David would say, "Against the Negev of Judah" or "Against the Negev of Jerahmeel" or "Against the Negev of the Kenites." [11]He did not leave a man or woman alive to be brought to Gath, for he thought, "They might inform on us and say, 'This is what David did.' " And such was his practice as long as he lived in Philistine territory. [12]Achish trusted David and said to himself, "He has become so odious to his people, the Israelites, that he will be my servant forever."

Saul and the Witch of Endor

28 In those days the Philistines gathered their forces to fight against Israel. Achish said to David, "You must understand that you and your men will accompany me in the army."

[2]David said, "Then you will see for yourself what your servant can do."

Achish replied, "Very well, I will make you my bodyguard for life."

[3]Now Samuel was dead, and all Israel had mourned for him and buried him in his own town of Ramah. Saul had expelled the mediums and spiritists from the land.

[4]The Philistines assembled and came and set up camp at Shunem, while Saul gathered all the Israelites and set up camp at Gilboa. [5]When Saul saw the Philistine army, he was afraid; terror filled his heart. [6]He inquired of the LORD, but the LORD did not answer him by dreams or Urim or prophets. [7]Saul then said

to his attendants, "Find me a woman who is a medium, so I may go and inquire of her."

"There is one in Endor," they said.

8So Saul disguised himself, putting on other clothes, and at night he and two men went to the woman. "Consult a spirit for me," he said, "and bring up for me the one I name."

9But the woman said to him, "Surely you know what Saul has done. He has cut off the mediums and spiritists from the land. Why have you set a trap for my life to bring about my death?"

10Saul swore to her by the LORD, "As surely as the LORD lives, you will not be punished for this."

11Then the woman asked, "Whom shall I bring up for you?"

"Bring up Samuel," he said.

12When the woman saw Samuel, she cried out at the top of her voice and said to Saul, "Why have you deceived me? You are Saul!"

13The king said to her, "Don't be afraid. What do you see?"

The woman said, "I see a spirit*a* coming up out of the ground."

14"What does he look like?" he asked.

"An old man wearing a robe is coming up," she said.

Then Saul knew it was Samuel, and he bowed down and prostrated himself with his face to the ground.

15Samuel said to Saul, "Why have you disturbed me by bringing me up?"

"I am in great distress," Saul said. "The Philistines are fighting against me, and God has turned away from me. He no longer answers me, either by prophets or by dreams. So I have called on you to tell me what to do."

16Samuel said, "Why do you consult me, now that the LORD has turned away from you and become your enemy? **17**The LORD has done what he predicted through me. The LORD has torn the kingdom out of your hands and given it to one of your neighbors—to David. **18**Because you did not obey the LORD or carry out his fierce wrath against the Amalekites, the LORD has done this to you today. **19**The LORD will hand over both Israel and you to the Philistines, and tomorrow you and your sons will be with me. The LORD will also hand over the army of Israel to the Philistines."

20Immediately Saul fell full length on the ground, filled with fear because of Samuel's words. His strength was gone, for he had eaten nothing all that day and night.

21When the woman came to Saul and saw that he was greatly shaken, she said, "Look, your maidservant has obeyed you. I took my life in my hands and did what you told me to do. **22**Now please listen to your servant and let me give you some food so you may eat and have the strength to go on your way."

23He refused and said, "I will not eat."

But his men joined the woman in urging him, and he listened to them. He got up from the ground and sat on the couch.

24The woman had a fattened calf at the house, which she butchered at once. She took some flour, kneaded it and baked bread without yeast. **25**Then she set it before Saul and his men, and they ate. That same night they got up and left.

Achish Sends David Back to Ziklag

29 The Philistines gathered all their forces at Aphek, and Israel camped by the spring in Jezreel. **2**As the Philistine rulers marched with their units of hundreds and thousands, David and his men were marching at the rear with Achish. **3**The commanders of the Philistines asked, "What about these Hebrews?"

Achish replied, "Is this not David, who was an officer of Saul king of Israel? He has already been with me for over a year, and from the day he left Saul until now, I have found no fault in him."

4But the Philistine commanders were angry with him and said, "Send the man back, that he may return to the place you assigned him. He must not go with us into battle, or he will turn against us during the fighting. How better could he regain his master's favor than by taking the heads of our own men? **5**Isn't this the David they sang about in their dances:

" 'Saul has slain his thousands,
    and David his tens of thousands'?"

6So Achish called David and said to him, "As surely as the LORD lives, you have been reliable, and I would be pleased to have you serve with me in the army. From the day you came to me until now, I have found no fault in you, but the rulers don't approve of you. **7**Turn back and go in peace; do nothing to displease the Philistine rulers."

8"But what have I done?" asked David. "What have you found against your servant

---

a 13 Or *see spirits;* or *see gods*

from the day I came to you until now? Why can't I go and fight against the enemies of my lord the king?"

⁹Achish answered, "I know that you have been as pleasing in my eyes as an angel of God; nevertheless, the Philistine commanders have said, 'He must not go up with us into battle.' ¹⁰Now get up early, along with your master's servants who have come with you, and leave in the morning as soon as it is light."

¹¹So David and his men got up early in the morning to go back to the land of the Philistines, and the Philistines went up to Jezreel.

David Destroys the Amalekites

30 David and his men reached Ziklag on the third day. Now the Amalekites had raided the Negev and Ziklag. They had attacked Ziklag and burned it, ²and had taken captive the women and all who were in it, both young and old. They killed none of them, but carried them off as they went on their way.

³When David and his men came to Ziklag, they found it destroyed by fire and their wives and sons and daughters taken captive. ⁴So David and his men wept aloud until they had no strength left to weep. ⁵David's two wives had been captured—Ahinoam of Jezreel and Abigail, the widow of Nabal of Carmel. ⁶David was greatly distressed because the men were talking of stoning him; each one was bitter in spirit because of his sons and daughters. But David found strength in the Lord his God.

⁷Then David said to Abiathar the priest, the son of Ahimelech, "Bring me the ephod." Abiathar brought it to him, ⁸and David inquired of the Lord, "Shall I pursue this raiding party? Will I overtake them?"

"Pursue them," he answered. "You will certainly overtake them and succeed in the rescue."

⁹David and the six hundred men with him came to the Besor Ravine, where some stayed behind, ¹⁰for two hundred men were too exhausted to cross the ravine. But David and four hundred men continued the pursuit.

¹¹They found an Egyptian in a field and brought him to David. They gave him water to drink and food to eat— ¹²part of a cake of pressed figs and two cakes of raisins. He ate and was revived, for he had not eaten any food or drunk any water for three days and three nights.

¹³David asked him, "To whom do you belong, and where do you come from?"

He said, "I am an Egyptian, the slave of an Amalekite. My master abandoned me when I became ill three days ago. ¹⁴We raided the Negev of the Kerethites and the territory belonging to Judah and the Negev of Caleb. And we burned Ziklag."

¹⁵David asked him, "Can you lead me down to this raiding party?"

He answered, "Swear to me before God that you will not kill me or hand me over to my master, and I will take you down to them."

¹⁶He led David down, and there they were, scattered over the countryside, eating, drinking and reveling because of the great amount of plunder they had taken from the land of the Philistines and from Judah. ¹⁷David fought them from dusk until the evening of the next day, and none of them got away, except four hundred young men who rode off on camels and fled. ¹⁸David recovered everything the Amalekites had taken, including his two wives. ¹⁹Nothing was missing: young or old, boy or girl, plunder or anything else they had taken. David brought everything back. ²⁰He took all the flocks and herds, and his men drove them ahead of the other livestock, saying, "This is David's plunder."

²¹Then David came to the two hundred men who had been too exhausted to follow him and who were left behind at the Besor Ravine. They came out to meet David and the people with him. As David and his men approached, he greeted them. ²²But all the evil men and troublemakers among David's followers said, "Because they did not go out with us, we will not share with them the plunder we recovered. However, each man may take his wife and children and go."

²³David replied, "No, my brothers, you must not do that with what the Lord has given us. He has protected us and handed over to us the forces that came against us. ²⁴Who will listen to what you say? The share of the man who stayed with the supplies is to be the same as that of him who went down to the battle. All will share alike." ²⁵David made this a statute and ordinance for Israel from that day to this.

²⁶When David arrived in Ziklag, he sent some of the plunder to the elders of Judah, who were his friends, saying, "Here is a present for you from the plunder of the Lord's enemies."

²⁷He sent it to those who were in Bethel, Ramoth Negev and Jattir; ²⁸to those in Aroer, Siphmoth, Eshtemoa ²⁹and Racal; to those in the towns of the Jerahmeelites and the

Kenites; [30]to those in Hormah, Bor Ashan, Athach [31]and Hebron; and to those in all the other places where David and his men had roamed.

Saul Takes His Life

31 Now the Philistines fought against Israel; the Israelites fled before them, and many fell slain on Mount Gilboa. [2]The Philistines pressed hard after Saul and his sons, and they killed his sons Jonathan, Abinadab and Malki-Shua. [3]The fighting grew fierce around Saul, and when the archers overtook him, they wounded him critically.

[4]Saul said to his armor-bearer, "Draw your sword and run me through, or these uncircumcised fellows will come and run me through and abuse me."

But his armor-bearer was terrified and would not do it; so Saul took his own sword and fell on it. [5]When the armor-bearer saw that Saul was dead, he too fell on his sword and died with him. [6]So Saul and his three sons and his armor-bearer and all his men died together that same day.

[7]When the Israelites along the valley and those across the Jordan saw that the Israelite army had fled and that Saul and his sons had died, they abandoned their towns and fled. And the Philistines came and occupied them.

[8]The next day, when the Philistines came to strip the dead, they found Saul and his three sons fallen on Mount Gilboa. [9]They cut off his head and stripped off his armor, and they sent messengers throughout the land of the Philistines to proclaim the news in the temple of their idols and among their people. [10]They put his armor in the temple of the Ashtoreths and fastened his body to the wall of Beth Shan.

[11]When the people of Jabesh Gilead heard of what the Philistines had done to Saul, [12]all their valiant men journeyed through the night to Beth Shan. They took down the bodies of Saul and his sons from the wall of Beth Shan and went to Jabesh, where they burned them. [13]Then they took their bones and buried them under a tamarisk tree at Jabesh, and they fasted seven days.

2 SAMUEL

DAVID is now on the throne, leading Israel to glory. But David's success is shaken by his secret sins. Lust leads to adultery and murder, then to insurrection and incest. The results of his sin haunt David to the end of his life, but with deep sorrow he repents and experiences forgiveness. Remember as you read that sin has terrible consequences. But even in the midst of those consequences, God is faithful and ready to forgive.

Outline of Contents

David Hears of Saul's Death

1 After the death of Saul, David returned from defeating the Amalekites and stayed in Ziklag two days. ²On the third day a man arrived from Saul's camp, with his clothes torn and with dust on his head. When he came to David, he fell to the ground to pay him honor.

³"Where have you come from?" David asked him.

He answered, "I have escaped from the Israelite camp."

⁴"What happened?" David asked. "Tell me."

He said, "The men fled from the battle. Many of them fell and died. And Saul and his son Jonathan are dead."

⁵Then David said to the young man who brought him the report, "How do you know that Saul and his son Jonathan are dead?"

⁶"I happened to be on Mount Gilboa," the young man said, "and there was Saul, leaning on his spear, with the chariots and riders almost upon him. ⁷When he turned around and saw me, he called out to me, and I said, 'What can I do?'

⁸"He asked me, 'Who are you?'

" 'An Amalekite,' I answered.

⁹"Then he said to me, 'Stand over me and kill me! I am in the throes of death, but I'm still alive.'

¹⁰"So I stood over him and killed him, because I knew that after he had fallen he could not survive. And I took the crown that was on his head and the band on his arm and have brought them here to my lord."

¹¹Then David and all the men with him took hold of their clothes and tore them. ¹²They mourned and wept and fasted till evening for Saul and his son Jonathan, and for the army of the LORD and the house of Israel, because they had fallen by the sword.

PANTING FOR POPULARITY

Nora wanted so badly to be part of the "in" group. And she thought she had the perfect plan to get in—a party for all the popular crowd while her parents were away for the weekend.

Here's the result of Nora's "perfect plan": On Saturday morning, the house is trashed, the VCR is broken, some jewelry is missing. Worst of all, Nora's virginity is long gone.

Look It Up

During the time of King David, two guys named Recab and Baanah murdered a guy named Ish-Bosheth. They cut off his head and took it to David thinking he would be pleased:

"David answered Recab and his brother Baanah . . . , 'As surely as the LORD lives, who has delivered me out of all trouble, when a man told me, "Saul is dead," and thought he was bringing good news, I seized him and put him to death in Ziklag. That was the reward I gave him for his news! How much more—when wicked men have killed an innocent man in his own house and on his own bed—should I not now demand his blood from your hand and rid the earth of you!'

"So David gave an order to his men, and they killed them. They cut off their hands and feet and hung the bodies by the pool in Hebron. But they took the head of Ish-Bosheth and buried it in Abner's tomb at Hebron" (2 Samuel 4:9–12).

Recab and Baanah thought they had a plan for popularity. But their plan worked no better than Nora's.

Think It Through

Do you agree or disagree with the following statement?

"People who make you work for their friendship are not worth having as friends."

Do you make others perform for your acceptance? Have you ever tried to get on someone's good side only to have things blow up in your face?

Work It Out

Make the following personal commitments today:

1. I will not try to be someone or something I'm not.

2. I will not try to earn the acceptance of others. If certain "friends" won't accept me for who and what I am, then I'll find new friends.

3. I will not pressure others into feeling like they have to perform (especially wrong actions) in order to be on my good side.

Nail It Down

Read 2 Samuel 1:1–16 for another popularity plan that went poof!

Turn to pages 1128 and 1130 for other readings on popularity.
Turn to page 312 for Wednesday's reading.

Topic

POPULARITY

¹³David said to the young man who brought him the report, "Where are you from?"

"I am the son of an alien, an Amalekite," he answered.

¹⁴David asked him, "Why were you not afraid to lift your hand to destroy the LORD's anointed?"

¹⁵Then David called one of his men and said, "Go, strike him down!" So he struck him down, and he died. ¹⁶For David had said to him, "Your blood be on your own head. Your own mouth testified against you when you said, 'I killed the LORD's anointed.' "

David's Lament for Saul and Jonathan

¹⁷David took up this lament concerning Saul and his son Jonathan, ¹⁸and ordered that the men of Judah be taught this lament of the bow (it is written in the Book of Jashar):

¹⁹"Your glory, O Israel, lies slain on your
      heights.
    How the mighty have fallen!

²⁰"Tell it not in Gath,
      proclaim it not in the streets of
      Ashkelon,
    lest the daughters of the Philistines be
      glad,
    lest the daughters of the
      uncircumcised rejoice.

²¹"O mountains of Gilboa,
      may you have neither dew nor rain,
      nor fields that yield offerings ˻of grain˼.
    For there the shield of the mighty was
      defiled,
      the shield of Saul—no longer rubbed
      with oil.

²²From the blood of the slain,
      from the flesh of the mighty,
    the bow of Jonathan did not turn back,
      the sword of Saul did not return
      unsatisfied.

²³"Saul and Jonathan—
      in life they were loved and gracious,
      and in death they were not parted.
    They were swifter than eagles,
      they were stronger than lions.

²⁴"O daughters of Israel,
      weep for Saul,
    who clothed you in scarlet and finery,
      who adorned your garments with
      ornaments of gold.

²⁵"How the mighty have fallen in battle!
    Jonathan lies slain on your heights.
²⁶I grieve for you, Jonathan my brother;
      you were very dear to me.
    Your love for me was wonderful,
      more wonderful than that of women.

²⁷"How the mighty have fallen!
    The weapons of war have perished!"

David Anointed King Over Judah

2 In the course of time, David inquired of the LORD. "Shall I go up to one of the towns of Judah?" he asked.

The LORD said, "Go up."

David asked, "Where shall I go?"

"To Hebron," the LORD answered.

²So David went up there with his two wives, Ahinoam of Jezreel and Abigail, the widow of Nabal of Carmel. ³David also took the men who were with him, each with his family, and they settled in Hebron and its towns. ⁴Then the men of Judah came to Hebron and there they anointed David king over the house of Judah.

When David was told that it was the men of Jabesh Gilead who had buried Saul, ⁵he sent messengers to the men of Jabesh Gilead to say to them, "The LORD bless you for showing this kindness to Saul your master by burying him. ⁶May the LORD now show you kindness and faithfulness, and I too will show you the same favor because you have done this. ⁷Now then, be strong and brave, for Saul your master is dead, and the house of Judah has anointed me king over them."

War Between the Houses of David and Saul

⁸Meanwhile, Abner son of Ner, the commander of Saul's army, had taken Ish-Bosheth son of Saul and brought him over to Mahanaim. ⁹He made him king over Gilead, Ashuriᵃ and Jezreel, and also over Ephraim, Benjamin and all Israel.

¹⁰Ish-Bosheth son of Saul was forty years old when he became king over Israel, and he reigned two years. The house of Judah, however, followed David. ¹¹The length of time David was king in Hebron over the house of Judah was seven years and six months.

¹²Abner son of Ner, together with the men of Ish-Bosheth son of Saul, left Mahanaim and went to Gibeon. ¹³Joab son of Zeruiah and David's men went out and met them at the pool of Gibeon. One group sat down on

ᵃ9 Or *Asher*

one side of the pool and one group on the other side.

¹⁴Then Abner said to Joab, "Let's have some of the young men get up and fight hand to hand in front of us."

"All right, let them do it," Joab said.

¹⁵So they stood up and were counted off—twelve men for Benjamin and Ish-Bosheth son of Saul, and twelve for David. ¹⁶Then each man grabbed his opponent by the head and thrust his dagger into his opponent's side, and they fell down together. So that place in Gibeon was called Helkath Hazzurim.ᵃ

¹⁷The battle that day was very fierce, and Abner and the men of Israel were defeated by David's men.

¹⁸The three sons of Zeruiah were there: Joab, Abishai and Asahel. Now Asahel was as fleet-footed as a wild gazelle. ¹⁹He chased Abner, turning neither to the right nor to the left as he pursued him. ²⁰Abner looked behind him and asked, "Is that you, Asahel?"

"It is," he answered.

²¹Then Abner said to him, "Turn aside to the right or to the left; take on one of the young men and strip him of his weapons." But Asahel would not stop chasing him.

²²Again Abner warned Asahel, "Stop chasing me! Why should I strike you down? How could I look your brother Joab in the face?"

²³But Asahel refused to give up the pursuit; so Abner thrust the butt of his spear into Asahel's stomach, and the spear came out through his back. He fell there and died on the spot. And every man stopped when he came to the place where Asahel had fallen and died.

²⁴But Joab and Abishai pursued Abner, and as the sun was setting, they came to the hill of Ammah, near Giah on the way to the wasteland of Gibeon. ²⁵Then the men of Benjamin rallied behind Abner. They formed themselves into a group and took their stand on top of a hill.

²⁶Abner called out to Joab, "Must the sword devour forever? Don't you realize that this will end in bitterness? How long before you order your men to stop pursuing their brothers?"

²⁷Joab answered, "As surely as God lives, if you had not spoken, the men would have continued the pursuit of their brothers until morning.ᵇ"

²⁸So Joab blew the trumpet, and all the men came to a halt; they no longer pursued Israel, nor did they fight anymore.

²⁹All that night Abner and his men marched through the Arabah. They crossed the Jordan, continued through the whole Bithronᶜ and came to Mahanaim.

³⁰Then Joab returned from pursuing Abner and assembled all his men. Besides Asahel, nineteen of David's men were found missing. ³¹But David's men had killed three hundred and sixty Benjamites who were with Abner. ³²They took Asahel and buried him in his father's tomb at Bethlehem. Then Joab and his men marched all night and arrived at Hebron by daybreak.

3 The war between the house of Saul and the house of David lasted a long time. David grew stronger and stronger, while the house of Saul grew weaker and weaker.

²Sons were born to David in Hebron:

His firstborn was Amnon the son of Ahinoam of Jezreel;

³his second, Kileab the son of Abigail the widow of Nabal of Carmel;

the third, Absalom the son of Maacah daughter of Talmai king of Geshur;

⁴the fourth, Adonijah the son of Haggith;

the fifth, Shephatiah the son of Abital;

⁵and the sixth, Ithream the son of David's wife Eglah.

These were born to David in Hebron.

Abner Goes Over to David

⁶During the war between the house of Saul and the house of David, Abner had been strengthening his own position in the house of Saul. ⁷Now Saul had had a concubine named Rizpah daughter of Aiah. And Ish-Bosheth said to Abner, "Why did you sleep with my father's concubine?"

⁸Abner was very angry because of what Ish-Bosheth said and he answered, "Am I a dog's head—on Judah's side? This very day I am loyal to the house of your father Saul and to his family and friends. I haven't handed you over to David. Yet now you accuse me of an offense involving this woman! ⁹May God deal with Abner, be it ever so severely, if I do not do for David what the Lord promised him on oath ¹⁰and transfer the kingdom from the house of Saul and establish David's throne over Israel and Judah

---

ᵃ16 *Helkath Hazzurim* means *field of daggers* or *field of hostilities.*   ᵇ27 Or *spoken this morning, the men would not have taken up the pursuit of their brothers*; or *spoken, the men would have given up the pursuit of their brothers by morning*   ᶜ29 Or *morning*; or *ravine*; the meaning of the Hebrew for this word is uncertain.

from Dan to Beersheba." ¹¹Ish-Bosheth did not dare to say another word to Abner, because he was afraid of him.

¹²Then Abner sent messengers on his behalf to say to David, "Whose land is it? Make an agreement with me, and I will help you bring all Israel over to you."

¹³"Good," said David. "I will make an agreement with you. But I demand one thing of you: Do not come into my presence unless you bring Michal daughter of Saul when you come to see me." ¹⁴Then David sent messengers to Ish-Bosheth son of Saul, demanding, "Give me my wife Michal, whom I betrothed to myself for the price of a hundred Philistine foreskins."

¹⁵So Ish-Bosheth gave orders and had her taken away from her husband Paltiel son of Laish. ¹⁶Her husband, however, went with her, weeping behind her all the way to Bahurim. Then Abner said to him, "Go back home!" So he went back.

¹⁷Abner conferred with the elders of Israel and said, "For some time you have wanted to make David your king. ¹⁸Now do it! For the LORD promised David, 'By my servant David I will rescue my people Israel from the hand of the Philistines and from the hand of all their enemies.'"

¹⁹Abner also spoke to the Benjamites in person. Then he went to Hebron to tell David everything that Israel and the whole house of Benjamin wanted to do. ²⁰When Abner, who had twenty men with him, came to David at Hebron, David prepared a feast for him and his men. ²¹Then Abner said to David, "Let me go at once and assemble all Israel for my lord the king, so that they may make a compact with you, and that you may rule over all that your heart desires." So David sent Abner away, and he went in peace.

Joab Murders Abner

²²Just then David's men and Joab returned from a raid and brought with them a great deal of plunder. But Abner was no longer with David in Hebron, because David had sent him away, and he had gone in peace. ²³When Joab and all the soldiers with him arrived, he was told that Abner son of Ner had come to the king and that the king had sent him away and that he had gone in peace.

²⁴So Joab went to the king and said, "What have you done? Look, Abner came to you. Why did you let him go? Now he is gone! ²⁵You know Abner son of Ner; he came to

deceive you and observe your movements and find out everything you are doing."

²⁶Joab then left David and sent messengers after Abner, and they brought him back from the well of Sirah. But David did not know it. ²⁷Now when Abner returned to Hebron, Joab took him aside into the gateway, as though to speak with him privately. And there, to avenge the blood of his brother Asahel, Joab stabbed him in the stomach, and he died.

²⁸Later, when David heard about this, he said, "I and my kingdom are forever innocent before the LORD concerning the blood of Abner son of Ner. ²⁹May his blood fall upon the head of Joab and upon all his father's house! May Joab's house never be without someone who has a running sore or leprosy[a] or who leans on a crutch or who falls by the sword or who lacks food."

³⁰(Joab and his brother Abishai murdered Abner because he had killed their brother Asahel in the battle at Gibeon.)

³¹Then David said to Joab and all the people with him, "Tear your clothes and put on sackcloth and walk in mourning in front of Abner." King David himself walked behind the bier. ³²They buried Abner in Hebron, and the king wept aloud at Abner's tomb. All the people wept also.

³³The king sang this lament for Abner:

"Should Abner have died as the lawless die?
³⁴   Your hands were not bound,
        your feet were not fettered.
    You fell as one falls before wicked
        men."

And all the people wept over him again. ³⁵Then they all came and urged David to eat something while it was still day; but David took an oath, saying, "May God deal with me, be it ever so severely, if I taste bread or anything else before the sun sets!"

³⁶All the people took note and were pleased; indeed, everything the king did pleased them. ³⁷So on that day all the people and all Israel knew that the king had no part in the murder of Abner son of Ner.

³⁸Then the king said to his men, "Do you not realize that a prince and a great man has fallen in Israel this day? ³⁹And today, though I am the anointed king, I am weak, and these sons of Zeruiah are too strong for me. May the LORD repay the evildoer according to his evil deeds!"

---

a29 The Hebrew word was used for various diseases affecting the skin—not necessarily leprosy.

Ish-Bosheth Murdered

4 When Ish-Bosheth son of Saul heard that Abner had died in Hebron, he lost courage, and all Israel became alarmed. [2]Now Saul's son had two men who were leaders of raiding bands. One was named Baanah and the other Recab; they were sons of Rimmon the Beerothite from the tribe of Benjamin — Beeroth is considered part of Benjamin, [3]because the people of Beeroth fled to Gittaim and have lived there as aliens to this day.

[4](Jonathan son of Saul had a son who was lame in both feet. He was five years old when the news about Saul and Jonathan came from Jezreel. His nurse picked him up and fled, but as she hurried to leave, he fell and became crippled. His name was Mephibosheth.)

[5]Now Recab and Baanah, the sons of Rimmon the Beerothite, set out for the house of Ish-Bosheth, and they arrived there in the heat of the day while he was taking his noonday rest. [6]They went into the inner part of the house as if to get some wheat, and they stabbed him in the stomach. Then Recab and his brother Baanah slipped away.

[7]They had gone into the house while he was lying on the bed in his bedroom. After they stabbed and killed him, they cut off his head. Taking it with them, they traveled all night by way of the Arabah. [8]They brought the head of Ish-Bosheth to David at Hebron and said to the king, "Here is the head of Ish-Bosheth son of Saul, your enemy, who tried to take your life. This day the LORD has avenged my lord the king against Saul and his offspring."

[9]David answered Recab and his brother Baanah, the sons of Rimmon the Beerothite, "As surely as the LORD lives, who has delivered me out of all trouble, [10]when a man told me, 'Saul is dead,' and thought he was bringing good news, I seized him and put him to death in Ziklag. That was the reward I gave him for his news! [11]How much more — when wicked men have killed an innocent man in his own house and on his own bed — should I not now demand his blood from your hand and rid the earth of you!"

[12]So David gave an order to his men, and they killed them. They cut off their hands and feet and hung the bodies by the pool in Hebron. But they took the head of Ish-Bosheth and buried it in Abner's tomb at Hebron.

David Becomes King Over Israel

5 All the tribes of Israel came to David at Hebron and said, "We are your own flesh and blood. [2]In the past, while Saul was king over us, you were the one who led Israel on their military campaigns. And the LORD said to you, 'You will shepherd my people Israel, and you will become their ruler.'"

[3]When all the elders of Israel had come to King David at Hebron, the king made a compact with them at Hebron before the LORD, and they anointed David king over Israel. [4]David was thirty years old when he became king, and he reigned forty years. [5]In Hebron he reigned over Judah seven years and six months, and in Jerusalem he reigned over all Israel and Judah thirty-three years.

David Conquers Jerusalem

[6]The king and his men marched to Jerusalem to attack the Jebusites, who lived there. The Jebusites said to David, "You will not get in here; even the blind and the lame can ward you off." They thought, "David cannot get in here." [7]Nevertheless, David captured the fortress of Zion, the City of David.

[8]On that day, David said, "Anyone who conquers the Jebusites will have to use the water shaft[a] to reach those 'lame and blind' who are David's enemies.[b]" That is why they say, "The 'blind and lame' will not enter the palace."

[9]David then took up residence in the fortress and called it the City of David. He built up the area around it, from the supporting terraces[c] inward. [10]And he became more and more powerful, because the LORD God Almighty was with him.

[11]Now Hiram king of Tyre sent messengers to David, along with cedar logs and carpenters and stonemasons, and they built a palace for David. [12]And David knew that the LORD had established him as king over Israel and had exalted his kingdom for the sake of his people Israel.

[13]After he left Hebron, David took more concubines and wives in Jerusalem, and more sons and daughters were born to him. [14]These are the names of the children born to him there: Shammua, Shobab, Nathan, Solomon, [15]Ibhar, Elishua, Nepheg, Japhia, [16]Elishama, Eliada and Eliphelet.

---

a8 Or use scaling hooks   b8 Or are hated by David   c9 Or the Millo

David Defeats the Philistines

17When the Philistines heard that David had been anointed king over Israel, they went up in full force to search for him, but David heard about it and went down to the stronghold. **18**Now the Philistines had come and spread out in the Valley of Rephaim; **19**so David inquired of the Lord, "Shall I go and attack the Philistines? Will you hand them over to me?"

The Lord answered him, "Go, for I will surely hand the Philistines over to you."

20So David went to Baal Perazim, and there he defeated them. He said, "As waters break out, the Lord has broken out against my enemies before me." So that place was called Baal Perazim.*a* **21**The Philistines abandoned their idols there, and David and his men carried them off.

22Once more the Philistines came up and spread out in the Valley of Rephaim; **23**so David inquired of the Lord, and he answered, "Do not go straight up, but circle around behind them and attack them in front of the balsam trees. **24**As soon as you hear the sound of marching in the tops of the balsam trees, move quickly, because that will mean the Lord has gone out in front of you to strike the Philistine army." **25**So David did as the Lord commanded him, and he struck down the Philistines all the way from Gibeon*b* to Gezer.

The Ark Brought to Jerusalem

6 David again brought together out of Israel chosen men, thirty thousand in all. **2**He and all his men set out from Baalah of Judah*c* to bring up from there the ark of God, which is called by the Name,*d* the name of the Lord Almighty, who is enthroned between the cherubim that are on the ark. **3**They set the ark of God on a new cart and brought it from the house of Abinadab, which was on the hill. Uzzah and Ahio, sons of Abinadab, were guiding the new cart **4**with the ark of God on it,*e* and Ahio was walking in front of it. **5**David and the whole house of Israel were celebrating with all their might before the Lord, with songs*f* and with harps, lyres, tambourines, sistrums and cymbals.

6When they came to the threshing floor of Nacon, Uzzah reached out and took hold of the ark of God, because the oxen stumbled. **7**The Lord's anger burned against Uzzah because of his irreverent act; therefore God struck him down and he died there beside the ark of God.

8Then David was angry because the Lord's wrath had broken out against Uzzah, and to this day that place is called Perez Uzzah.*g*

9David was afraid of the Lord that day and said, "How can the ark of the Lord ever come to me?" **10**He was not willing to take the ark of the Lord to be with him in the City of David. Instead, he took it aside to the house of Obed-Edom the Gittite. **11**The ark of the Lord remained in the house of Obed-Edom the Gittite for three months, and the Lord blessed him and his entire household.

12Now King David was told, "The Lord has blessed the household of Obed-Edom and everything he has, because of the ark of God." So David went down and brought up the ark of God from the house of Obed-Edom to the City of David with rejoicing. **13**When those who were carrying the ark of the Lord had taken six steps, he sacrificed a bull and a fattened calf. **14**David, wearing a linen ephod, danced before the Lord with all his might, **15**while he and the entire house of Israel brought up the ark of the Lord with shouts and the sound of trumpets.

16As the ark of the Lord was entering the City of David, Michal daughter of Saul watched from a window. And when she saw King David leaping and dancing before the Lord, she despised him in her heart.

17They brought the ark of the Lord and set it in its place inside the tent that David had pitched for it, and David sacrificed burnt offerings and fellowship offerings*h* before the Lord. **18**After he had finished sacrificing the burnt offerings and fellowship offerings, he blessed the people in the name of the Lord Almighty. **19**Then he gave a loaf of bread, a cake of dates and a cake of raisins to each person in the whole crowd of Israelites, both men and women. And all the people went to their homes.

20When David returned home to bless his household, Michal daughter of Saul came

---

a20 Baal Perazim means the lord who breaks out.   *b25 Septuagint (see also 1 Chron. 14:16); Hebrew Geba*
c2 That is, Kiriath Jearim; Hebrew Baale Judah, a variant of Baalah of Judah   *d2 Hebrew; Septuagint and Vulgate do not have the Name.*   *e3,4 Dead Sea Scrolls and some Septuagint manuscripts; Masoretic Text cart*
4and they brought it with the ark of God from the house of Abinadab, which was on the hill   *f5 See Dead Sea Scrolls, Septuagint and 1 Chronicles 13:8; Masoretic Text celebrating before the Lord with all kinds of instruments made of pine.*   *g8 Perez Uzzah means outbreak against Uzzah.*   *h17 Traditionally peace offerings; also in verse 18*

out to meet him and said, "How the king of Israel has distinguished himself today, disrobing in the sight of the slave girls of his servants as any vulgar fellow would!"

²¹David said to Michal, "It was before the LORD, who chose me rather than your father or anyone from his house when he appointed me ruler over the LORD's people Israel—I will celebrate before the LORD. ²²I will become even more undignified than this, and I will be humiliated in my own eyes. But by these slave girls you spoke of, I will be held in honor."

²³And Michal daughter of Saul had no children to the day of her death.

God's Promise to David

7 After the king was settled in his palace and the LORD had given him rest from all his enemies around him, ²he said to Nathan the prophet, "Here I am, living in a palace of cedar, while the ark of God remains in a tent."

³Nathan replied to the king, "Whatever you have in mind, go ahead and do it, for the LORD is with you."

⁴That night the word of the LORD came to Nathan, saying:

⁵"Go and tell my servant David, 'This is what the LORD says: Are you the one to build me a house to dwell in? ⁶I have not dwelt in a house from the day I brought the Israelites up out of Egypt to this day. I have been moving from place to place with a tent as my dwelling. ⁷Wherever I have moved with all the Israelites, did I ever say to any of their rulers whom I commanded to shepherd my people Israel, "Why have you not built me a house of cedar?"'

⁸"Now then, tell my servant David, 'This is what the LORD Almighty says: I took you from the pasture and from following the flock to be ruler over my people Israel. ⁹I have been with you wherever you have gone, and I have cut off all your enemies from before you. Now I will make your name great, like the names of the greatest men of the earth. ¹⁰And I will provide a place for my people Israel and will plant them so that they can have a home of their own and no longer be disturbed. Wicked people will not oppress them anymore, as they did at the beginning ¹¹and have

done ever since the time I appointed leaders*ᵃ* over my people Israel. I will also give you rest from all your enemies.

"'The LORD declares to you that the LORD himself will establish a house for you: ¹²When your days are over and you rest with your fathers, I will raise up your offspring to succeed you, who will come from your own body, and I will establish his kingdom. ¹³He is the one who will build a house for my Name, and I will establish the throne of his kingdom forever. ¹⁴I will be his father, and he will be my son. When he does wrong, I will punish him with the rod of men, with floggings inflicted by men. ¹⁵But my love will never be taken away from him, as I took it away from Saul, whom I removed from before you. ¹⁶Your house and your kingdom will endure forever before me*ᵇ*; your throne will be established forever.'"

¹⁷Nathan reported to David all the words of this entire revelation.

David's Prayer

¹⁸Then King David went in and sat before the LORD, and he said:

"Who am I, O Sovereign LORD, and what is my family, that you have brought me this far? ¹⁹And as if this were not enough in your sight, O Sovereign LORD, you have also spoken about the future of the house of your servant. Is this your usual way of dealing with man, O Sovereign LORD?

²⁰"What more can David say to you? For you know your servant, O Sovereign LORD. ²¹For the sake of your word and according to your will, you have done this great thing and made it known to your servant.

²²"How great you are, O Sovereign LORD! There is no one like you, and there is no God but you, as we have heard with our own ears. ²³And who is like your people Israel—the one nation on earth that God went out to redeem as a people for himself, and to make a name for himself, and to perform great and awesome wonders by driving out nations and their gods from before your people, whom you redeemed from

Egypt?[a] [24]You have established your people Israel as your very own forever, and you, O LORD, have become their God.

[25]"And now, LORD God, keep forever the promise you have made concerning your servant and his house. Do as you promised, [26]so that your name will be great forever. Then men will say, 'The LORD Almighty is God over Israel!' And the house of your servant David will be established before you.

[27]"O LORD Almighty, God of Israel, you have revealed this to your servant, saying, 'I will build a house for you.' So your servant has found courage to offer you this prayer. [28]O Sovereign LORD, you are God! Your words are trustworthy, and you have promised these good things to your servant. [29]Now be pleased to bless the house of your servant, that it may continue forever in your sight; for you, O Sovereign LORD, have spoken, and with your blessing the house of your servant will be blessed forever."

David's Victories

8 In the course of time, David defeated the Philistines and subdued them, and he took Metheg Ammah from the control of the Philistines.

[2]David also defeated the Moabites. He made them lie down on the ground and measured them off with a length of cord. Every two lengths of them were put to death, and the third length was allowed to live. So the Moabites became subject to David and brought tribute.

[3]Moreover, David fought Hadadezer son of Rehob, king of Zobah, when he went to restore his control along the Euphrates River. [4]David captured a thousand of his chariots, seven thousand charioteers[b] and twenty thousand foot soldiers. He hamstrung all but a hundred of the chariot horses.

[5]When the Arameans of Damascus came to help Hadadezer king of Zobah, David struck down twenty-two thousand of them. [6]He put garrisons in the Aramean kingdom of Damascus, and the Arameans became

subject to him and brought tribute. The LORD gave David victory wherever he went.

[7]David took the gold shields that belonged to the officers of Hadadezer and brought them to Jerusalem. [8]From Tebah[c] and Berothai, towns that belonged to Hadadezer, King David took a great quantity of bronze.

[9]When Tou[d] king of Hamath heard that David had defeated the entire army of Hadadezer, [10]he sent his son Joram[e] to King David to greet him and congratulate him on his victory in battle over Hadadezer, who had been at war with Tou. Joram brought with him articles of silver and gold and bronze.

[11]King David dedicated these articles to the LORD, as he had done with the silver and gold from all the nations he had subdued: [12]Edom[f] and Moab, the Ammonites and the Philistines, and Amalek. He also dedicated the plunder taken from Hadadezer son of Rehob, king of Zobah.

[13]And David became famous after he returned from striking down eighteen thousand Edomites[g] in the Valley of Salt.

[14]He put garrisons throughout Edom, and all the Edomites became subject to David. The LORD gave David victory wherever he went.

David's Officials

[15]David reigned over all Israel, doing what was just and right for all his people. [16]Joab son of Zeruiah was over the army; Jehoshaphat son of Ahilud was recorder; [17]Zadok son of Ahitub and Ahimelech son of Abiathar were priests; Seraiah was secretary; [18]Benaiah son of Jehoiada was over the Kerethites and Pelethites; and David's sons were royal advisers.[h]

David and Mephibosheth

9 David asked, "Is there anyone still left of the house of Saul to whom I can show kindness for Jonathan's sake?"

[2]Now there was a servant of Saul's household named Ziba. They called him to appear before David, and the king said to him, "Are you Ziba?"

"Your servant," he replied.

[3]The king asked, "Is there no one still left

a23 See Septuagint and 1 Chron. 17:21; Hebrew *wonders for your land and before your people, whom you redeemed from Egypt, from the nations and their gods.*   b4 Septuagint (see also Dead Sea Scrolls and 1 Chron. 18:4); Masoretic Text *captured seventeen hundred of his charioteers*   c8 See some Septuagint manuscripts (see also 1 Chron. 18:8); Hebrew *Betah.*   d9 Hebrew *Toi,* a variant of *Tou*; also in verse 10   e10 A variant of *Hadoram*   f12 Some Hebrew manuscripts, Septuagint and Syriac (see also 1 Chron. 18:11); most Hebrew manuscripts *Aram*   g13 A few Hebrew manuscripts, Septuagint and Syriac (see also 1 Chron. 18:12); most Hebrew manuscripts *Aram* (that is, Arameans)   h18 Or *were priests*

WHY WOULD I WANT TO DO THAT?

"So, school just let out and you guys are already bored, huh?" Dwight and Derek, both fourteen, nod simultaneously, not even looking up from their video game.

"What if you two formed a service team and helped me out around the church this summer? I couldn't pay you anything, but I could give you plenty to do, and I'd feed you lunch every day."

Derek gives Reverend Moore a curious look. "What do you mean by 'service team'?"

"Yeah," Dwight pipes up. "Why would we want to go around serving?"

Look It Up
●●●●

Reverend Moore grabs a Bible off the shelf and spends about five minutes explaining these points to Dwight and Derek.

1. Serving is what Christ commands. "Now that I, your Lord and Teacher, have washed your feet, you also should wash one another's feet" (John 13:14).

2. Serving shows Christ that you love him (John 21:16).

3. Serving is where you find joy and contentment. "He who goes out weeping, carrying seed to sow, will return with songs of joy, carrying sheaves with him" (Psalm 126:6).

Think It Through
●●●●

Most people think they can find contentment by focusing on themselves. That explains conversations filled with self-centered pronouns like *I*, *me*, *my*, *mine* and *myself*. Yet, are most of the people you know satisfied and joyful . . . or empty and joyless?

Deep-down happiness comes when you turn your focus outward and begin serving others. The recipe for joy? *Jesus* first, *Others* second, *Yourself* last.

Work It Out
●●●●

Why serve? Because according to Jesus a lifestyle of service is the way to an obedient, more joyful walk with Christ. Look at your schedule of things you want to do today and delete one. Then pick one of the following ideas and begin serving:

• Help your mom clean up around the house.
• Run errands for your dad.
• Volunteer to baby-sit so your parents (or a neighborhood couple) can go out for the evening.
• Go wash your minister's or youth pastor's car.
• Serve food at a downtown soup kitchen.

Nail It Down
●●●●

Read how David served Mephibosheth, the son of his friend Jonathan, in 2 Samuel 9.

Turn to pages 718, 1008, 1019, 1034 and 1342 for other readings on serving.
Turn to page 315 for Thursday's reading.

Topic
●●●●

of the house of Saul to whom I can show God's kindness?"

Ziba answered the king, "There is still a son of Jonathan; he is crippled in both feet."

4"Where is he?" the king asked.

Ziba answered, "He is at the house of Makir son of Ammiel in Lo Debar."

5So King David had him brought from Lo Debar, from the house of Makir son of Ammiel.

6When Mephibosheth son of Jonathan, the son of Saul, came to David, he bowed down to pay him honor.

David said, "Mephibosheth!"

"Your servant," he replied.

7"Don't be afraid," David said to him, "for I will surely show you kindness for the sake of your father Jonathan. I will restore to you all the land that belonged to your grandfather Saul, and you will always eat at my table."

8Mephibosheth bowed down and said, "What is your servant, that you should notice a dead dog like me?"

9Then the king summoned Ziba, Saul's servant, and said to him, "I have given your master's grandson everything that belonged to Saul and his family. **10**You and your sons and your servants are to farm the land for him and bring in the crops, so that your master's grandson may be provided for. And Mephibosheth, grandson of your master, will always eat at my table." (Now Ziba had fifteen sons and twenty servants.)

11Then Ziba said to the king, "Your servant will do whatever my lord the king commands his servant to do." So Mephibosheth ate at David's*a* table like one of the king's sons.

12Mephibosheth had a young son named Mica, and all the members of Ziba's household were servants of Mephibosheth. **13**And Mephibosheth lived in Jerusalem, because he always ate at the king's table, and he was crippled in both feet.

David Defeats the Ammonites

10 In the course of time, the king of the Ammonites died, and his son Hanun succeeded him as king. **2**David thought, "I will show kindness to Hanun son of Nahash, just as his father showed kindness to me." So David sent a delegation to express his sympathy to Hanun concerning his father.

When David's men came to the land of the Ammonites, **3**the Ammonite nobles said to Hanun their lord, "Do you think David is

honoring your father by sending men to you to express sympathy? Hasn't David sent them to you to explore the city and spy it out and overthrow it?" **4**So Hanun seized David's men, shaved off half of each man's beard, cut off their garments in the middle at the buttocks, and sent them away.

5When David was told about this, he sent messengers to meet the men, for they were greatly humiliated. The king said, "Stay at Jericho till your beards have grown, and then come back."

6When the Ammonites realized that they had become a stench in David's nostrils, they hired twenty thousand Aramean foot soldiers from Beth Rehob and Zobah, as well as the king of Maacah with a thousand men, and also twelve thousand men from Tob.

7On hearing this, David sent Joab out with the entire army of fighting men. **8**The Ammonites came out and drew up in battle formation at the entrance to their city gate, while the Arameans of Zobah and Rehob and the men of Tob and Maacah were by themselves in the open country.

9Joab saw that there were battle lines in front of him and behind him; so he selected some of the best troops in Israel and deployed them against the Arameans. **10**He put the rest of the men under the command of Abishai his brother and deployed them against the Ammonites. **11**Joab said, "If the Arameans are too strong for me, then you are to come to my rescue; but if the Ammonites are too strong for you, then I will come to rescue you. **12**Be strong and let us fight bravely for our people and the cities of our God. The Lord will do what is good in his sight."

13Then Joab and the troops with him advanced to fight the Arameans, and they fled before him. **14**When the Ammonites saw that the Arameans were fleeing, they fled before Abishai and went inside the city. So Joab returned from fighting the Ammonites and came to Jerusalem.

15After the Arameans saw that they had been routed by Israel, they regrouped. **16**Hadadezer had Arameans brought from beyond the River*b*; they went to Helam, with Shobach the commander of Hadadezer's army leading them.

17When David was told of this, he gathered all Israel, crossed the Jordan and went to Helam. The Arameans formed their battle lines to meet David and fought against him.

a 11 Septuagint; Hebrew *my*   *b 16* That is, the Euphrates

[18]But they fled before Israel, and David killed seven hundred of their charioteers and forty thousand of their foot soldiers.[a] He also struck down Shobach the commander of their army, and he died there. [19]When all the kings who were vassals of Hadadezer saw that they had been defeated by Israel, they made peace with the Israelites and became subject to them.

So the Arameans were afraid to help the Ammonites anymore.

David and Bathsheba

11 In the spring, at the time when kings go off to war, David sent Joab out with the king's men and the whole Israelite army. They destroyed the Ammonites and besieged Rabbah. But David remained in Jerusalem.

[2]One evening David got up from his bed and walked around on the roof of the palace. From the roof he saw a woman bathing. The woman was very beautiful, [3]and David sent someone to find out about her. The man said, "Isn't this Bathsheba, the daughter of Eliam and the wife of Uriah the Hittite?" [4]Then David sent messengers to get her. She came to him, and he slept with her. (She had purified herself from her uncleanness.) Then[b] she went back home. [5]The woman conceived and sent word to David, saying, "I am pregnant."

[6]So David sent this word to Joab: "Send me Uriah the Hittite." And Joab sent him to David. [7]When Uriah came to him, David asked him how Joab was, how the soldiers were and how the war was going. [8]Then David said to Uriah, "Go down to your house and wash your feet." So Uriah left the palace, and a gift from the king was sent after him. [9]But Uriah slept at the entrance to the palace with all his master's servants and did not go down to his house.

[10]When David was told, "Uriah did not go home," he asked him, "Haven't you just come from a distance? Why didn't you go home?"

[11]Uriah said to David, "The ark and Israel and Judah are staying in tents, and my master Joab and my lord's men are camped in the open fields. How could I go to my house to eat and drink and lie with my wife? As surely as you live, I will not do such a thing!"

[12]Then David said to him, "Stay here one more day, and tomorrow I will send you back." So Uriah remained in Jerusalem that day and the next. [13]At David's invitation, he ate and drank with him, and David made him drunk. But in the evening Uriah went out to sleep on his mat among his master's servants; he did not go home.

[14]In the morning David wrote a letter to Joab and sent it with Uriah. [15]In it he wrote, "Put Uriah in the front line where the fighting is fiercest. Then withdraw from him so he will be struck down and die."

[16]So while Joab had the city under siege, he put Uriah at a place where he knew the strongest defenders were. [17]When the men of the city came out and fought against Joab, some of the men in David's army fell; moreover, Uriah the Hittite died.

[18]Joab sent David a full account of the battle. [19]He instructed the messenger: "When you have finished giving the king this account of the battle, [20]the king's anger may flare up, and he may ask you, 'Why did you get so close to the city to fight? Didn't you know they would shoot arrows from the wall? [21]Who killed Abimelech son of Jerub-Besheth[c]? Didn't a woman throw an upper millstone on him from the wall, so that he died in Thebez? Why did you get so close to the wall?' If he asks you this, then say to him, 'Also, your servant Uriah the Hittite is dead.'"

[22]The messenger set out, and when he arrived he told David everything Joab had sent him to say. [23]The messenger said to David, "The men overpowered us and came out against us in the open, but we drove them back to the entrance to the city gate. [24]Then the archers shot arrows at your servants from the wall, and some of the king's men died. Moreover, your servant Uriah the Hittite is dead."

[25]David told the messenger, "Say this to Joab: 'Don't let this upset you; the sword devours one as well as another. Press the attack against the city and destroy it.' Say this to encourage Joab."

[26]When Uriah's wife heard that her husband was dead, she mourned for him. [27]After the time of mourning was over, David had her brought to his house, and she became his wife and bore him a son. But the thing David had done displeased the LORD.

Nathan Rebukes David

12 The LORD sent Nathan to David. When he came to him, he said, "There were two men in a certain town, one

---

[a]18 Some Septuagint manuscripts (see also 1 Chron. 19:18); Hebrew *horsemen*   [b]4 Or *with her. When she purified herself from her uncleanness,*   [c]21 Also known as *Jerub-Baal* (that is, Gideon)

Save Yourself for the Big Day!

During a psychology lecture, Dr. Carter asked, "How many of you feel that premarital sex is wrong?"

Of thirty students, only Wendy raised her hand. Later, Shannon approached Wendy. "I can't believe you were so bold. I mean, I feel the same way you do about sex, but I guess I wimped out during class."

Look It Up

You don't have to feel embarrassed about the decision to save sex for marriage—that's God's plan.

"It is God's will that you should . . . avoid sexual immorality; that each of you should learn to control his own body in a way that is holy and honorable, not in passionate lust like the heathen, who do not know God; and that in this matter no one should wrong his brother or take advantage of him . . . . For God did not call us to be impure, but to live a holy life" (1 Thessalonians 4:3–7).

"Marriage should be honored by all, and the marriage bed kept pure, for God will judge the adulterer and all the sexually immoral" (Hebrews 13:4).

Think It Through

Look at it this way: People who are sexually involved before marriage are stealing from their own futures.

Experiences that can have only one "first time" are thoughtlessly given up in a moment of passion. And rather than being beautiful, tender and special, those acts often become bitter memories that many would rather forget.

Premarital sex may feel good at the moment, but saving sex for marriage brings long-term pleasure (and no guilt).

Work It Out

Every culture has its particular customs regarding marriage. Can you name a few customs common to your culture? Read Deuteronomy 20:5–7 for a Hebrew honeymoon custom.

Reread the verses above for God's directives on the relationship between sex and marriage.

Nail It Down

Read 2 Samuel 11—12 for the story of a king who didn't follow God's marriage plan.

Turn to pages 478, 819 and 996 for other readings on marriage.
Turn to page 336 for Friday's reading.

Topic

MARRIAGE

rich and the other poor. ²The rich man had a very large number of sheep and cattle, ³but the poor man had nothing except one little ewe lamb he had bought. He raised it, and it grew up with him and his children. It shared his food, drank from his cup and even slept in his arms. It was like a daughter to him.

⁴"Now a traveler came to the rich man, but the rich man refrained from taking one of his own sheep or cattle to prepare a meal for the traveler who had come to him. Instead, he took the ewe lamb that belonged to the poor man and prepared it for the one who had come to him."

⁵David burned with anger against the man and said to Nathan, "As surely as the Lord lives, the man who did this deserves to die! ⁶He must pay for that lamb four times over, because he did such a thing and had no pity."

⁷Then Nathan said to David, "You are the man! This is what the Lord, the God of Israel, says: 'I anointed you king over Israel, and I delivered you from the hand of Saul. ⁸I gave your master's house to you, and your master's wives into your arms. I gave you the house of Israel and Judah. And if all this had been too little, I would have given you even more. ⁹Why did you despise the word of the Lord by doing what is evil in his eyes? You struck down Uriah the Hittite with the sword and took his wife to be your own. You killed him with the sword of the Ammonites. ¹⁰Now, therefore, the sword will never depart from your house, because you despised me and took the wife of Uriah the Hittite to be your own.'

¹¹"This is what the Lord says: 'Out of your own household I am going to bring calamity upon you. Before your very eyes I will take your wives and give them to one who is close to you, and he will lie with your wives in broad daylight. ¹²You did it in secret, but I will do this thing in broad daylight before all Israel.' "

¹³Then David said to Nathan, "I have sinned against the Lord."

Nathan replied, "The Lord has taken away your sin. You are not going to die. ¹⁴But because by doing this you have made the enemies of the Lord show utter contempt,ᵃ the son born to you will die."

¹⁵After Nathan had gone home, the Lord struck the child that Uriah's wife had borne to David, and he became ill. ¹⁶David pleaded with God for the child. He fasted and went into his house and spent the nights lying on the ground. ¹⁷The elders of his household stood beside him to get him up from the ground, but he refused, and he would not eat any food with them.

¹⁸On the seventh day the child died. David's servants were afraid to tell him that the child was dead, for they thought, "While the child was still living, we spoke to David but he would not listen to us. How can we tell him the child is dead? He may do something desperate."

¹⁹David noticed that his servants were whispering among themselves and he realized the child was dead. "Is the child dead?" he asked.

"Yes," they replied, "he is dead."

²⁰Then David got up from the ground. After he had washed, put on lotions and changed his clothes, he went into the house of the Lord and worshiped. Then he went to his own house, and at his request they served him food, and he ate.

²¹His servants asked him, "Why are you acting this way? While the child was alive, you fasted and wept, but now that the child is dead, you get up and eat!"

²²He answered, "While the child was still alive, I fasted and wept. I thought, 'Who knows? The Lord may be gracious to me and let the child live.' ²³But now that he is dead, why should I fast? Can I bring him back again? I will go to him, but he will not return to me."

²⁴Then David comforted his wife Bathsheba, and he went to her and lay with her. She gave birth to a son, and they named him Solomon. The Lord loved him; ²⁵and because the Lord loved him, he sent word through Nathan the prophet to name him Jedidiah.ᵇ

²⁶Meanwhile Joab fought against Rabbah of the Ammonites and captured the royal citadel. ²⁷Joab then sent messengers to David, saying, "I have fought against Rabbah and taken its water supply. ²⁸Now muster the rest of the troops and besiege the city and capture it. Otherwise I will take the city, and it will be named after me."

²⁹So David mustered the entire army and went to Rabbah, and attacked and captured it. ³⁰He took the crown from the head of their kingᶜ—its weight was a talentᵈ of gold, and it was set with precious stones—

ᵃ14 Masoretic Text; an ancient Hebrew scribal tradition *this you have shown utter contempt for the Lord*
ᵇ25 *Jedidiah* means *loved by the Lord.*   ᶜ30 Or *of Milcom* (that is, Molech)   ᵈ30 That is, about 75 pounds (about 34 kilograms)

and it was placed on David's head. He took a great quantity of plunder from the city ³¹and brought out the people who were there, consigning them to labor with saws and with iron picks and axes, and he made them work at brickmaking.^a He did this to all the Ammonite towns. Then David and his entire army returned to Jerusalem.

Amnon and Tamar

13 In the course of time, Amnon son of David fell in love with Tamar, the beautiful sister of Absalom son of David.

²Amnon became frustrated to the point of illness on account of his sister Tamar, for she was a virgin, and it seemed impossible for him to do anything to her.

³Now Amnon had a friend named Jonadab son of Shimeah, David's brother. Jonadab was a very shrewd man. ⁴He asked Amnon, "Why do you, the king's son, look so haggard morning after morning? Won't you tell me?"

Amnon said to him, "I'm in love with Tamar, my brother Absalom's sister."

⁵"Go to bed and pretend to be ill," Jonadab said. "When your father comes to see you, say to him, 'I would like my sister Tamar to come and give me something to eat. Let her prepare the food in my sight so I may watch her and then eat it from her hand.'"

⁶So Amnon lay down and pretended to be ill. When the king came to see him, Amnon said to him, "I would like my sister Tamar to come and make some special bread in my sight, so I may eat from her hand."

⁷David sent word to Tamar at the palace: "Go to the house of your brother Amnon and prepare some food for him." ⁸So Tamar went to the house of her brother Amnon, who was lying down. She took some dough, kneaded it, made the bread in his sight and baked it. ⁹Then she took the pan and served him the bread, but he refused to eat.

"Send everyone out of here," Amnon said. So everyone left him. ¹⁰Then Amnon said to Tamar, "Bring the food here into my bedroom so I may eat from your hand." And Tamar took the bread she had prepared and brought it to her brother Amnon in his bedroom. ¹¹But when she took it to him to eat, he grabbed her and said, "Come to bed with me, my sister."

¹²"Don't, my brother!" she said to him. "Don't force me. Such a thing should not be done in Israel! Don't do this wicked thing.

¹³What about me? Where could I get rid of my disgrace? And what about you? You would be like one of the wicked fools in Israel. Please speak to the king; he will not keep me from being married to you." ¹⁴But he refused to listen to her, and since he was stronger than she, he raped her.

¹⁵Then Amnon hated her with intense hatred. In fact, he hated her more than he had loved her. Amnon said to her, "Get up and get out!"

¹⁶"No!" she said to him. "Sending me away would be a greater wrong than what you have already done to me."

But he refused to listen to her. ¹⁷He called his personal servant and said, "Get this woman out of here and bolt the door after her." ¹⁸So his servant put her out and bolted the door after her. She was wearing a richly ornamented^b robe, for this was the kind of garment the virgin daughters of the king wore. ¹⁹Tamar put ashes on her head and tore the ornamented^c robe she was wearing. She put her hand on her head and went away, weeping aloud as she went.

²⁰Her brother Absalom said to her, "Has that Amnon, your brother, been with you? Be quiet now, my sister; he is your brother. Don't take this thing to heart." And Tamar lived in her brother Absalom's house, a desolate woman.

²¹When King David heard all this, he was furious. ²²Absalom never said a word to Amnon, either good or bad; he hated Amnon because he had disgraced his sister Tamar.

Absalom Kills Amnon

²³Two years later, when Absalom's sheepshearers were at Baal Hazor near the border of Ephraim, he invited all the king's sons to come there. ²⁴Absalom went to the king and said, "Your servant has had shearers come. Will the king and his officials please join me?"

²⁵"No, my son," the king replied. "All of us should not go; we would only be a burden to you." Although Absalom urged him, he still refused to go, but gave him his blessing.

²⁶Then Absalom said, "If not, please let my brother Amnon come with us."

The king asked him, "Why should he go with you?" ²⁷But Absalom urged him, so he sent with him Amnon and the rest of the king's sons.

²⁸Absalom ordered his men, "Listen! When Amnon is in high spirits from drinking

---

^a31 The meaning of the Hebrew for this clause is uncertain.   ^b18 The meaning of the Hebrew for this phrase is uncertain.   ^c19 The meaning of the Hebrew for this word is uncertain.

wine and I say to you, 'Strike Amnon down,' then kill him. Don't be afraid. Have not I given you this order? Be strong and brave." **29**So Absalom's men did to Amnon what Absalom had ordered. Then all the king's sons got up, mounted their mules and fled.

30While they were on their way, the report came to David: "Absalom has struck down all the king's sons; not one of them is left." **31**The king stood up, tore his clothes and lay down on the ground; and all his servants stood by with their clothes torn.

32But Jonadab son of Shimeah, David's brother, said, "My lord should not think that they killed all the princes; only Amnon is dead. This has been Absalom's expressed intention ever since the day Amnon raped his sister Tamar. **33**My lord the king should not be concerned about the report that all the king's sons are dead. Only Amnon is dead."

34Meanwhile, Absalom had fled.

Now the man standing watch looked up and saw many people on the road west of him, coming down the side of the hill. The watchman went and told the king, "I see men in the direction of Horonaim, on the side of the hill."*a*

35Jonadab said to the king, "See, the king's sons are here; it has happened just as your servant said."

36As he finished speaking, the king's sons came in, wailing loudly. The king, too, and all his servants wept very bitterly.

37Absalom fled and went to Talmai son of Ammihud, the king of Geshur. But King David mourned for his son every day.

38After Absalom fled and went to Geshur, he stayed there three years. **39**And the spirit of the king*b* longed to go to Absalom, for he was consoled concerning Amnon's death.

Absalom Returns to Jerusalem

14 Joab son of Zeruiah knew that the king's heart longed for Absalom. **2**So Joab sent someone to Tekoa and had a wise woman brought from there. He said to her, "Pretend you are in mourning. Dress in mourning clothes, and don't use any cosmetic lotions. Act like a woman who has spent many days grieving for the dead. **3**Then go to the king and speak these words to him." And Joab put the words in her mouth.

4When the woman from Tekoa went*c* to the king, she fell with her face to the ground to pay him honor, and she said, "Help me, O king!"

5The king asked her, "What is troubling you?"

She said, "I am indeed a widow; my husband is dead. **6**I your servant had two sons. They got into a fight with each other in the field, and no one was there to separate them. One struck the other and killed him. **7**Now the whole clan has risen up against your servant; they say, 'Hand over the one who struck his brother down, so that we may put him to death for the life of his brother whom he killed; then we will get rid of the heir as well.' They would put out the only burning coal I have left, leaving my husband neither name nor descendant on the face of the earth."

8The king said to the woman, "Go home, and I will issue an order in your behalf."

9But the woman from Tekoa said to him, "My lord the king, let the blame rest on me and on my father's family, and let the king and his throne be without guilt."

10The king replied, "If anyone says anything to you, bring him to me, and he will not bother you again."

11She said, "Then let the king invoke the LORD his God to prevent the avenger of blood from adding to the destruction, so that my son will not be destroyed."

"As surely as the LORD lives," he said, "not one hair of your son's head will fall to the ground."

12Then the woman said, "Let your servant speak a word to my lord the king."

"Speak," he replied.

13The woman said, "Why then have you devised a thing like this against the people of God? When the king says this, does he not convict himself, for the king has not brought back his banished son? **14**Like water spilled on the ground, which cannot be recovered, so we must die. But God does not take away life; instead, he devises ways so that a banished person may not remain estranged from him.

15"And now I have come to say this to my lord the king because the people have made me afraid. Your servant thought, 'I will speak to the king; perhaps he will do what his servant asks. **16**Perhaps the king will agree to deliver his servant from the hand of the man who is trying to cut off both me and

---

a34 Septuagint; Hebrew does not have this sentence.   *b39* Dead Sea Scrolls and some Septuagint manuscripts; Masoretic Text *But the spirit of, David the king*   *c4* Many Hebrew manuscripts, Septuagint, Vulgate and Syriac; most Hebrew manuscripts *spoke* my son from the inheritance God gave us.'

17"And now your servant says, 'May the word of my lord the king bring me rest, for my lord the king is like an angel of God in discerning good and evil. May the Lord your God be with you.' "

18Then the king said to the woman, "Do not keep from me the answer to what I am going to ask you."

"Let my lord the king speak," the woman said.

19The king asked, "Isn't the hand of Joab with you in all this?"

The woman answered, "As surely as you live, my lord the king, no one can turn to the right or to the left from anything my lord the king says. Yes, it was your servant Joab who instructed me to do this and who put all these words into the mouth of your servant. **20**Your servant Joab did this to change the present situation. My lord has wisdom like that of an angel of God—he knows everything that happens in the land."

21The king said to Joab, "Very well, I will do it. Go, bring back the young man Absalom."

22Joab fell with his face to the ground to pay him honor, and he blessed the king. Joab said, "Today your servant knows that he has found favor in your eyes, my lord the king, because the king has granted his servant's request."

23Then Joab went to Geshur and brought Absalom back to Jerusalem. **24**But the king said, "He must go to his own house; he must not see my face." So Absalom went to his own house and did not see the face of the king.

25In all Israel there was not a man so highly praised for his handsome appearance as Absalom. From the top of his head to the sole of his foot there was no blemish in him. **26**Whenever he cut the hair of his head—he used to cut his hair from time to time when it became too heavy for him—he would weigh it, and its weight was two hundred shekels*a* by the royal standard.

27Three sons and a daughter were born to Absalom. The daughter's name was Tamar, and she became a beautiful woman.

28Absalom lived two years in Jerusalem without seeing the king's face. **29**Then Absalom sent for Joab in order to send him to the king, but Joab refused to come to him. So he sent a second time, but he refused to come. **30**Then he said to his servants, "Look, Joab's field is next to mine, and he has barley there. Go and set it on fire." So Absalom's servants set the field on fire.

31Then Joab did go to Absalom's house and he said to him, "Why have your servants set my field on fire?"

32Absalom said to Joab, "Look, I sent word to you and said, 'Come here so I can send you to the king to ask, "Why have I come from Geshur? It would be better for me if I were still there!" ' Now then, I want to see the king's face, and if I am guilty of anything, let him put me to death."

33So Joab went to the king and told him this. Then the king summoned Absalom, and he came in and bowed down with his face to the ground before the king. And the king kissed Absalom.

Absalom's Conspiracy

15 In the course of time, Absalom provided himself with a chariot and horses and with fifty men to run ahead of him. **2**He would get up early and stand by the side of the road leading to the city gate. Whenever anyone came with a complaint to be placed before the king for a decision, Absalom would call out to him, "What town are you from?" He would answer, "Your servant is from one of the tribes of Israel." **3**Then Absalom would say to him, "Look, your claims are valid and proper, but there is no representative of the king to hear you." **4**And Absalom would add, "If only I were appointed judge in the land! Then everyone who has a complaint or case could come to me and I would see that he gets justice."

5Also, whenever anyone approached him to bow down before him, Absalom would reach out his hand, take hold of him and kiss him. **6**Absalom behaved in this way toward all the Israelites who came to the king asking for justice, and so he stole the hearts of the men of Israel.

7At the end of four*b* years, Absalom said to the king, "Let me go to Hebron and fulfill a vow I made to the Lord. **8**While your servant was living at Geshur in Aram, I made this vow: 'If the Lord takes me back to Jerusalem, I will worship the Lord in Hebron.*c*'"

9The king said to him, "Go in peace." So he went to Hebron.

10Then Absalom sent secret messengers throughout the tribes of Israel to say, "As soon as you hear the sound of the trumpets,

---

a26 That is, about 5 pounds (about 2.3 kilograms)   *b7* Some Septuagint manuscripts, Syriac and Josephus; Hebrew *forty*   *c8* Some Septuagint manuscripts; Hebrew does not have *in Hebron*.

then say, 'Absalom is king in Hebron.' " ¹¹Two hundred men from Jerusalem had accompanied Absalom. They had been invited as guests and went quite innocently, knowing nothing about the matter. ¹²While Absalom was offering sacrifices, he also sent for Ahithophel the Gilonite, David's counselor, to come from Giloh, his hometown. And so the conspiracy gained strength, and Absalom's following kept on increasing.

David Flees

¹³A messenger came and told David, "The hearts of the men of Israel are with Absalom."

¹⁴Then David said to all his officials who were with him in Jerusalem, "Come! We must flee, or none of us will escape from Absalom. We must leave immediately, or he will move quickly to overtake us and bring ruin upon us and put the city to the sword."

¹⁵The king's officials answered him, "Your servants are ready to do whatever our lord the king chooses."

¹⁶The king set out, with his entire household following him; but he left ten concubines to take care of the palace. ¹⁷So the king set out, with all the people following him, and they halted at a place some distance away. ¹⁸All his men marched past him, along with all the Kerethites and Pelethites; and all the six hundred Gittites who had accompanied him from Gath marched before the king.

¹⁹The king said to Ittai the Gittite, "Why should you come along with us? Go back and stay with King Absalom. You are a foreigner, an exile from your homeland. ²⁰You came only yesterday. And today shall I make you wander about with us, when I do not know where I am going? Go back, and take your countrymen. May kindness and faithfulness be with you."

²¹But Ittai replied to the king, "As surely as the Lord lives, and as my lord the king lives, wherever my lord the king may be, whether it means life or death, there will your servant be."

²²David said to Ittai, "Go ahead, march on." So Ittai the Gittite marched on with all his men and the families that were with him.

²³The whole countryside wept aloud as all the people passed by. The king also crossed the Kidron Valley, and all the people moved on toward the desert.

²⁴Zadok was there, too, and all the Levites who were with him were carrying the ark of the covenant of God. They set down the ark of God, and Abiathar offered sacrifices[a] until all the people had finished leaving the city.

²⁵Then the king said to Zadok, "Take the ark of God back into the city. If I find favor in the Lord's eyes, he will bring me back and let me see it and his dwelling place again. ²⁶But if he says, 'I am not pleased with you,' then I am ready; let him do to me whatever seems good to him."

²⁷The king also said to Zadok the priest, "Aren't you a seer? Go back to the city in peace, with your son Ahimaaz and Jonathan son of Abiathar. You and Abiathar take your two sons with you. ²⁸I will wait at the fords in the desert until word comes from you to inform me." ²⁹So Zadok and Abiathar took the ark of God back to Jerusalem and stayed there.

³⁰But David continued up the Mount of Olives, weeping as he went; his head was covered and he was barefoot. All the people with him covered their heads too and were weeping as they went up. ³¹Now David had been told, "Ahithophel is among the conspirators with Absalom." So David prayed, "O Lord, turn Ahithophel's counsel into foolishness."

³²When David arrived at the summit, where people used to worship God, Hushai the Arkite was there to meet him, his robe torn and dust on his head. ³³David said to him, "If you go with me, you will be a burden to me. ³⁴But if you return to the city and say to Absalom, 'I will be your servant, O king; I was your father's servant in the past, but now I will be your servant,' then you can help me by frustrating Ahithophel's advice. ³⁵Won't the priests Zadok and Abiathar be there with you? Tell them anything you hear in the king's palace. ³⁶Their two sons, Ahimaaz son of Zadok and Jonathan son of Abiathar, are there with them. Send them to me with anything you hear."

³⁷So David's friend Hushai arrived at Jerusalem as Absalom was entering the city.

David and Ziba

16 When David had gone a short distance beyond the summit, there was Ziba, the steward of Mephibosheth, waiting to meet him. He had a string of donkeys saddled and loaded with two hundred loaves of bread, a hundred cakes of raisins, a hundred cakes of figs and a skin of wine.

---

a24 Or *Abiathar went up*

2The king asked Ziba, "Why have you brought these?"

Ziba answered, "The donkeys are for the king's household to ride on, the bread and fruit are for the men to eat, and the wine is to refresh those who become exhausted in the desert."

3The king then asked, "Where is your master's grandson?"

Ziba said to him, "He is staying in Jerusalem, because he thinks, 'Today the house of Israel will give me back my grandfather's kingdom.' "

4Then the king said to Ziba, "All that belonged to Mephibosheth is now yours."

"I humbly bow," Ziba said. "May I find favor in your eyes, my lord the king."

Shimei Curses David

5As King David approached Bahurim, a man from the same clan as Saul's family came out from there. His name was Shimei son of Gera, and he cursed as he came out. **6**He pelted David and all the king's officials with stones, though all the troops and the special guard were on David's right and left. **7**As he cursed, Shimei said, "Get out, get out, you man of blood, you scoundrel! **8**The LORD has repaid you for all the blood you shed in the household of Saul, in whose place you have reigned. The LORD has handed the kingdom over to your son Absalom. You have come to ruin because you are a man of blood!"

9Then Abishai son of Zeruiah said to the king, "Why should this dead dog curse my lord the king? Let me go over and cut off his head."

10But the king said, "What do you and I have in common, you sons of Zeruiah? If he is cursing because the LORD said to him, 'Curse David,' who can ask, 'Why do you do this?' "

11David then said to Abishai and all his officials, "My son, who is of my own flesh, is trying to take my life. How much more, then, this Benjamite! Leave him alone; let him curse, for the LORD has told him to. **12**It may be that the LORD will see my distress and repay me with good for the cursing I am receiving today."

13So David and his men continued along the road while Shimei was going along the hillside opposite him, cursing as he went and throwing stones at him and showering him with dirt. **14**The king and all the people

with him arrived at their destination exhausted. And there he refreshed himself.

The Advice of Hushai and Ahithophel

15Meanwhile, Absalom and all the men of Israel came to Jerusalem, and Ahithophel was with him. **16**Then Hushai the Arkite, David's friend, went to Absalom and said to him, "Long live the king! Long live the king!"

17Absalom asked Hushai, "Is this the love you show your friend? Why didn't you go with your friend?"

18Hushai said to Absalom, "No, the one chosen by the LORD, by these people, and by all the men of Israel — his I will be, and I will remain with him. **19**Furthermore, whom should I serve? Should I not serve the son? Just as I served your father, so I will serve you."

20Absalom said to Ahithophel, "Give us your advice. What should we do?"

21Ahithophel answered, "Lie with your father's concubines whom he left to take care of the palace. Then all Israel will hear that you have made yourself a stench in your father's nostrils, and the hands of everyone with you will be strengthened." **22**So they pitched a tent for Absalom on the roof, and he lay with his father's concubines in the sight of all Israel.

23Now in those days the advice Ahithophel gave was like that of one who inquires of God. That was how both David and Absalom regarded all of Ahithophel's advice.

17 Ahithophel said to Absalom, "I would*ᵃ* choose twelve thousand men and set out tonight in pursuit of David. **2**I would*ᵇ* attack him while he is weary and weak. I would*ᵇ* strike him with terror, and then all the people with him will flee. I would*ᵇ* strike down only the king **3**and bring all the people back to you. The death of the man you seek will mean the return of all; all the people will be unharmed." **4**This plan seemed good to Absalom and to all the elders of Israel.

5But Absalom said, "Summon also Hushai the Arkite, so we can hear what he has to say." **6**When Hushai came to him, Absalom said, "Ahithophel has given this advice. Should we do what he says? If not, give us your opinion."

7Hushai replied to Absalom, "The advice Ahithophel has given is not good this time. **8**You know your father and his men; they are fighters, and as fierce as a wild bear robbed of her cubs. Besides, your father is

ᵃ1 Or Let me   *ᵇ2 Or will*

an experienced fighter; he will not spend the night with the troops. **9**Even now, he is hidden in a cave or some other place. If he should attack your troops first,*a* whoever hears about it will say, 'There has been a slaughter among the troops who follow Absalom.' **10**Then even the bravest soldier, whose heart is like the heart of a lion, will melt with fear, for all Israel knows that your father is a fighter and that those with him are brave.

11"So I advise you: Let all Israel, from Dan to Beersheba — as numerous as the sand on the seashore — be gathered to you, with you yourself leading them into battle. **12**Then we will attack him wherever he may be found, and we will fall on him as dew settles on the ground. Neither he nor any of his men will be left alive. **13**If he withdraws into a city, then all Israel will bring ropes to that city, and we will drag it down to the valley until not even a piece of it can be found."

14Absalom and all the men of Israel said, "The advice of Hushai the Arkite is better than that of Ahithophel." For the LORD had determined to frustrate the good advice of Ahithophel in order to bring disaster on Absalom.

15Hushai told Zadok and Abiathar, the priests, "Ahithophel has advised Absalom and the elders of Israel to do such and such, but I have advised them to do so and so. **16**Now send a message immediately and tell David, 'Do not spend the night at the fords in the desert; cross over without fail, or the king and all the people with him will be swallowed up.'"

17Jonathan and Ahimaaz were staying at En Rogel. A servant girl was to go and inform them, and they were to go and tell King David, for they could not risk being seen entering the city. **18**But a young man saw them and told Absalom. So the two of them left quickly and went to the house of a man in Bahurim. He had a well in his courtyard, and they climbed down into it. **19**His wife took a covering and spread it out over the opening of the well and scattered grain over it. No one knew anything about it.

20When Absalom's men came to the woman at the house, they asked, "Where are Ahimaaz and Jonathan?"

The woman answered them, "They crossed over the brook."*b* The men searched but found no one, so they returned to Jerusalem.

21After the men had gone, the two climbed out of the well and went to inform King David. They said to him, "Set out and cross the river at once; Ahithophel has advised such and such against you." **22**So David and all the people with him set out and crossed the Jordan. By daybreak, no one was left who had not crossed the Jordan.

23When Ahithophel saw that his advice had not been followed, he saddled his donkey and set out for his house in his hometown. He put his house in order and then hanged himself. So he died and was buried in his father's tomb.

24David went to Mahanaim, and Absalom crossed the Jordan with all the men of Israel. **25**Absalom had appointed Amasa over the army in place of Joab. Amasa was the son of a man named Jether,*c* an Israelite*d* who had married Abigail,*e* the daughter of Nahash and sister of Zeruiah the mother of Joab. **26**The Israelites and Absalom camped in the land of Gilead.

27When David came to Mahanaim, Shobi son of Nahash from Rabbah of the Ammonites, and Makir son of Ammiel from Lo Debar, and Barzillai the Gileadite from Rogelim **28**brought bedding and bowls and articles of pottery. They also brought wheat and barley, flour and roasted grain, beans and lentils,*f* **29**honey and curds, sheep, and cheese from cows' milk for David and his people to eat. For they said, "The people have become hungry and tired and thirsty in the desert."

Absalom's Death

18 David mustered the men who were with him and appointed over them commanders of thousands and commanders of hundreds. **2**David sent the troops out — a third under the command of Joab, a third under Joab's brother Abishai son of Zeruiah, and a third under Ittai the Gittite. The king told the troops, "I myself will surely march out with you."

3But the men said, "You must not go out; if we are forced to flee, they won't care about us. Even if half of us die, they won't care; but you are worth ten thousand of

---

a9 Or When some of the men fall at the first attack   *b20 Or "They passed by the sheep pen toward the water."*
c25 Hebrew Ithra, a variant of Jether   *d25 Hebrew and some Septuagint manuscripts; other Septuagint manuscripts (see also 1 Chron. 2:17) Ishmaelite or Jezreelite*   *e25 Hebrew Abigal, a variant of Abigail*
f28 Most Septuagint manuscripts and Syriac; Hebrew lentils, and roasted grain

us.*a* It would be better now for you to give us support from the city."

4The king answered, "I will do whatever seems best to you."

So the king stood beside the gate while all the men marched out in units of hundreds and of thousands. **5**The king commanded Joab, Abishai and Ittai, "Be gentle with the young man Absalom for my sake." And all the troops heard the king giving orders concerning Absalom to each of the commanders.

6The army marched into the field to fight Israel, and the battle took place in the forest of Ephraim. **7**There the army of Israel was defeated by David's men, and the casualties that day were great—twenty thousand men. **8**The battle spread out over the whole countryside, and the forest claimed more lives that day than the sword.

9Now Absalom happened to meet David's men. He was riding his mule, and as the mule went under the thick branches of a large oak, Absalom's head got caught in the tree. He was left hanging in midair, while the mule he was riding kept on going.

10When one of the men saw this, he told Joab, "I just saw Absalom hanging in an oak tree."

11Joab said to the man who had told him this, "What! You saw him? Why didn't you strike him to the ground right there? Then I would have had to give you ten shekels*b* of silver and a warrior's belt."

12But the man replied, "Even if a thousand shekels*c* were weighed out into my hands, I would not lift my hand against the king's son. In our hearing the king commanded you and Abishai and Ittai, 'Protect the young man Absalom for my sake.*d*' **13**And if I had put my life in jeopardy*e*—and nothing is hidden from the king—you would have kept your distance from me."

14Joab said, "I'm not going to wait like this for you." So he took three javelins in his hand and plunged them into Absalom's heart while Absalom was still alive in the oak tree. **15**And ten of Joab's armor-bearers surrounded Absalom, struck him and killed him.

16Then Joab sounded the trumpet, and the troops stopped pursuing Israel, for Joab halted them. **17**They took Absalom, threw him into a big pit in the forest and piled up a large heap of rocks over him. Meanwhile, all the Israelites fled to their homes.

18During his lifetime Absalom had taken a pillar and erected it in the King's Valley as a monument to himself, for he thought, "I have no son to carry on the memory of my name." He named the pillar after himself, and it is called Absalom's Monument to this day.

David Mourns

19Now Ahimaaz son of Zadok said, "Let me run and take the news to the king that the LORD has delivered him from the hand of his enemies."

20"You are not the one to take the news today," Joab told him. "You may take the news another time, but you must not do so today, because the king's son is dead."

21Then Joab said to a Cushite, "Go, tell the king what you have seen." The Cushite bowed down before Joab and ran off.

22Ahimaaz son of Zadok again said to Joab, "Come what may, please let me run behind the Cushite."

But Joab replied, "My son, why do you want to go? You don't have any news that will bring you a reward."

23He said, "Come what may, I want to run."

So Joab said, "Run!" Then Ahimaaz ran by way of the plain*f* and outran the Cushite.

24While David was sitting between the inner and outer gates, the watchman went up to the roof of the gateway by the wall. As he looked out, he saw a man running alone. **25**The watchman called out to the king and reported it.

The king said, "If he is alone, he must have good news." And the man came closer and closer.

26Then the watchman saw another man running, and he called down to the gatekeeper, "Look, another man running alone!"

The king said, "He must be bringing good news, too."

27The watchman said, "It seems to me that the first one runs like Ahimaaz son of Zadok."

"He's a good man," the king said. "He comes with good news."

---

*a*3 Two Hebrew manuscripts, some Septuagint manuscripts and Vulgate; most Hebrew manuscripts *care; for now there are ten thousand like us*   *b*11 That is, about 4 ounces (about 115 grams)   *c*12 That is, about 25 pounds (about 11 kilograms)   *d*12 A few Hebrew manuscripts, Septuagint, Vulgate and Syriac; most Hebrew manuscripts may be translated *Absalom, whoever you may be.*   *e*13 Or *Otherwise, if I had acted treacherously toward him*   *f*23 That is, the plain of the Jordan

28Then Ahimaaz called out to the king, "All is well!" He bowed down before the king with his face to the ground and said, "Praise be to the LORD your God! He has delivered up the men who lifted their hands against my lord the king."

29The king asked, "Is the young man Absalom safe?"

Ahimaaz answered, "I saw great confusion just as Joab was about to send the king's servant and me, your servant, but I don't know what it was."

30The king said, "Stand aside and wait here." So he stepped aside and stood there.

31Then the Cushite arrived and said, "My lord the king, hear the good news! The LORD has delivered you today from all who rose up against you."

32The king asked the Cushite, "Is the young man Absalom safe?"

The Cushite replied, "May the enemies of my lord the king and all who rise up to harm you be like that young man."

33The king was shaken. He went up to the room over the gateway and wept. As he went, he said: "O my son Absalom! My son, my son Absalom! If only I had died instead of you — O Absalom, my son, my son!"

19 Joab was told, "The king is weeping and mourning for Absalom." **2**And for the whole army the victory that day was turned into mourning, because on that day the troops heard it said, "The king is grieving for his son." **3**The men stole into the city that day as men steal in who are ashamed when they flee from battle. **4**The king covered his face and cried aloud, "O my son Absalom! O Absalom, my son, my son!"

5Then Joab went into the house to the king and said, "Today you have humiliated all your men, who have just saved your life and the lives of your sons and daughters and the lives of your wives and concubines. **6**You love those who hate you and hate those who love you. You have made it clear today that the commanders and their men mean nothing to you. I see that you would be pleased if Absalom were alive today and all of us were dead. **7**Now go out and encourage your men. I swear by the LORD that if you don't go out, not a man will be left with you by nightfall. This will be worse for you than all the calamities that have come upon you from your youth till now."

8So the king got up and took his seat in the gateway. When the men were told, "The king is sitting in the gateway," they all came before him.

David Returns to Jerusalem

Meanwhile, the Israelites had fled to their homes. **9**Throughout the tribes of Israel, the people were all arguing with each other, saying, "The king delivered us from the hand of our enemies; he is the one who rescued us from the hand of the Philistines. But now he has fled the country because of Absalom; **10**and Absalom, whom we anointed to rule over us, has died in battle. So why do you say nothing about bringing the king back?"

11King David sent this message to Zadok and Abiathar, the priests: "Ask the elders of Judah, 'Why should you be the last to bring the king back to his palace, since what is being said throughout Israel has reached the king at his quarters? **12**You are my brothers, my own flesh and blood. So why should you be the last to bring back the king?' **13**And say to Amasa, 'Are you not my own flesh and blood? May God deal with me, be it ever so severely, if from now on you are not the commander of my army in place of Joab.' "

14He won over the hearts of all the men of Judah as though they were one man. They sent word to the king, "Return, you and all your men." **15**Then the king returned and went as far as the Jordan.

Now the men of Judah had come to Gilgal to go out and meet the king and bring him across the Jordan. **16**Shimei son of Gera, the Benjamite from Bahurim, hurried down with the men of Judah to meet King David. **17**With him were a thousand Benjamites, along with Ziba, the steward of Saul's household, and his fifteen sons and twenty servants. They rushed to the Jordan, where the king was. **18**They crossed at the ford to take the king's household over and to do whatever he wished.

When Shimei son of Gera crossed the Jordan, he fell prostrate before the king **19**and said to him, "May my lord not hold me guilty. Do not remember how your servant did wrong on the day my lord the king left Jerusalem. May the king put it out of his mind. **20**For I your servant know that I have sinned, but today I have come here as the first of the whole house of Joseph to come down and meet my lord the king."

21Then Abishai son of Zeruiah said, "Shouldn't Shimei be put to death for this? He cursed the LORD's anointed."

22David replied, "What do you and I have in common, you sons of Zeruiah? This day you have become my adversaries! Should anyone be put to death in Israel today? Do

I not know that today I am king over Israel?" ²³So the king said to Shimei, "You shall not die." And the king promised him on oath.

²⁴Mephibosheth, Saul's grandson, also went down to meet the king. He had not taken care of his feet or trimmed his mustache or washed his clothes from the day the king left until the day he returned safely. ²⁵When he came from Jerusalem to meet the king, the king asked him, "Why didn't you go with me, Mephibosheth?"

²⁶He said, "My lord the king, since I your servant am lame, I said, 'I will have my donkey saddled and will ride on it, so I can go with the king.' But Ziba my servant betrayed me. ²⁷And he has slandered your servant to my lord the king. My lord the king is like an angel of God; so do whatever pleases you. ²⁸All my grandfather's descendants deserved nothing but death from my lord the king, but you gave your servant a place among those who eat at your table. So what right do I have to make any more appeals to the king?"

²⁹The king said to him, "Why say more? I order you and Ziba to divide the fields."

³⁰Mephibosheth said to the king, "Let him take everything, now that my lord the king has arrived home safely."

³¹Barzillai the Gileadite also came down from Rogelim to cross the Jordan with the king and to send him on his way from there. ³²Now Barzillai was a very old man, eighty years of age. He had provided for the king during his stay in Mahanaim, for he was a very wealthy man. ³³The king said to Barzillai, "Cross over with me and stay with me in Jerusalem, and I will provide for you."

³⁴But Barzillai answered the king, "How many more years will I live, that I should go up to Jerusalem with the king? ³⁵I am now eighty years old. Can I tell the difference between what is good and what is not? Can your servant taste what he eats and drinks? Can I still hear the voices of men and women singers? Why should your servant be an added burden to my lord the king? ³⁶Your servant will cross over the Jordan with the king for a short distance, but why should the king reward me in this way? ³⁷Let your servant return, that I may die in my own town near the tomb of my father and mother. But here is your servant Kimham. Let him cross over with my lord the king. Do for him whatever pleases you."

³⁸The king said, "Kimham shall cross over with me, and I will do for him whatever pleases you. And anything you desire from me I will do for you."

³⁹So all the people crossed the Jordan, and then the king crossed over. The king kissed Barzillai and gave him his blessing, and Barzillai returned to his home.

⁴⁰When the king crossed over to Gilgal, Kimham crossed with him. All the troops of Judah and half the troops of Israel had taken the king over.

⁴¹Soon all the men of Israel were coming to the king and saying to him, "Why did our brothers, the men of Judah, steal the king away and bring him and his household across the Jordan, together with all his men?"

⁴²All the men of Judah answered the men of Israel, "We did this because the king is closely related to us. Why are you angry about it? Have we eaten any of the king's provisions? Have we taken anything for ourselves?"

⁴³Then the men of Israel answered the men of Judah, "We have ten shares in the king; and besides, we have a greater claim on David than you have. So why do you treat us with contempt? Were we not the first to speak of bringing back our king?"

But the men of Judah responded even more harshly than the men of Israel.

Sheba Rebels Against David

20 Now a troublemaker named Sheba son of Bicri, a Benjamite, happened to be there. He sounded the trumpet and shouted,

"We have no share in David,
  no part in Jesse's son!
Every man to his tent, O Israel!"

²So all the men of Israel deserted David to follow Sheba son of Bicri. But the men of Judah stayed by their king all the way from the Jordan to Jerusalem.

³When David returned to his palace in Jerusalem, he took the ten concubines he had left to take care of the palace and put them in a house under guard. He provided for them, but did not lie with them. They were kept in confinement till the day of their death, living as widows.

⁴Then the king said to Amasa, "Summon the men of Judah to come to me within three days, and be here yourself." ⁵But when Amasa went to summon Judah, he took longer than the time the king had set for him.

⁶David said to Abishai, "Now Sheba son of Bicri will do us more harm than Absalom did. Take your master's men and pursue him, or he will find fortified cities and escape from us." ⁷So Joab's men and the Ker-

ethites and Pelethites and all the mighty warriors went out under the command of Abishai. They marched out from Jerusalem to pursue Sheba son of Bicri.

8While they were at the great rock in Gibeon, Amasa came to meet them. Joab was wearing his military tunic, and strapped over it at his waist was a belt with a dagger in its sheath. As he stepped forward, it dropped out of its sheath.

9Joab said to Amasa, "How are you, my brother?" Then Joab took Amasa by the beard with his right hand to kiss him. **10**Amasa was not on his guard against the dagger in Joab's hand, and Joab plunged it into his belly, and his intestines spilled out on the ground. Without being stabbed again, Amasa died. Then Joab and his brother Abishai pursued Sheba son of Bicri.

11One of Joab's men stood beside Amasa and said, "Whoever favors Joab, and whoever is for David, let him follow Joab!" **12**Amasa lay wallowing in his blood in the middle of the road, and the man saw that all the troops came to a halt there. When he realized that everyone who came up to Amasa stopped, he dragged him from the road into a field and threw a garment over him. **13**After Amasa had been removed from the road, all the men went on with Joab to pursue Sheba son of Bicri.

14Sheba passed through all the tribes of Israel to Abel Beth Maacah*a* and through the entire region of the Berites, who gathered together and followed him. **15**All the troops with Joab came and besieged Sheba in Abel Beth Maacah. They built a siege ramp up to the city, and it stood against the outer fortifications. While they were battering the wall to bring it down, **16**a wise woman called from the city, "Listen! Listen! Tell Joab to come here so I can speak to him." **17**He went toward her, and she asked, "Are you Joab?"

"I am," he answered.

She said, "Listen to what your servant has to say."

"I'm listening," he said.

18She continued, "Long ago they used to say, 'Get your answer at Abel,' and that settled it. **19**We are the peaceful and faithful in Israel. You are trying to destroy a city that is a mother in Israel. Why do you want to swallow up the LORD's inheritance?"

20"Far be it from me!" Joab replied, "Far be it from me to swallow up or destroy! **21**That

is not the case. A man named Sheba son of Bicri, from the hill country of Ephraim, has lifted up his hand against the king, against David. Hand over this one man, and I'll withdraw from the city."

The woman said to Joab, "His head will be thrown to you from the wall."

22Then the woman went to all the people with her wise advice, and they cut off the head of Sheba son of Bicri and threw it to Joab. So he sounded the trumpet, and his men dispersed from the city, each returning to his home. And Joab went back to the king in Jerusalem.

23Joab was over Israel's entire army; Benaiah son of Jehoiada was over the Kerethites and Pelethites; **24**Adoniram*b* was in charge of forced labor; Jehoshaphat son of Ahilud was recorder; **25**Sheva was secretary; Zadok and Abiathar were priests; **26**and Ira the Jairite was David's priest.

The Gibeonites Avenged

21 During the reign of David, there was a famine for three successive years; so David sought the face of the LORD. The LORD said, "It is on account of Saul and his blood-stained house; it is because he put the Gibeonites to death."

2The king summoned the Gibeonites and spoke to them. (Now the Gibeonites were not a part of Israel but were survivors of the Amorites; the Israelites had sworn to ⌊spare⌋ them, but Saul in his zeal for Israel and Judah had tried to annihilate them.) **3**David asked the Gibeonites, "What shall I do for you? How shall I make amends so that you will bless the LORD's inheritance?"

4The Gibeonites answered him, "We have no right to demand silver or gold from Saul or his family, nor do we have the right to put anyone in Israel to death."

"What do you want me to do for you?" David asked.

5They answered the king, "As for the man who destroyed us and plotted against us so that we have been decimated and have no place anywhere in Israel, **6**let seven of his male descendants be given to us to be killed and exposed before the LORD at Gibeah of Saul—the LORD's chosen one."

So the king said, "I will give them to you."

7The king spared Mephibosheth son of Jonathan, the son of Saul, because of the oath before the LORD between David and Jonathan son of Saul. **8**But the king took Ar-

---

a 14 Or *Abel, even Beth Maacah*; also in verse 15   *b 24* Some Septuagint manuscripts (see also 1 Kings 4:6 and 5:14); Hebrew *Adoram* moni and Mephibosheth, the two sons of Aiah's daughter Rizpah, whom she had borne to Saul, together with the five sons of Saul's daughter Merab,*a* whom she had borne to Adriel son of Barzillai the Meholathite. **9**He handed them over to the Gibeonites, who killed and exposed them on a hill before the LORD. All seven of them fell together; they were put to death during the first days of the harvest, just as the barley harvest was beginning.

10Rizpah daughter of Aiah took sackcloth and spread it out for herself on a rock. From the beginning of the harvest till the rain poured down from the heavens on the bodies, she did not let the birds of the air touch them by day or the wild animals by night. **11**When David was told what Aiah's daughter Rizpah, Saul's concubine, had done, **12**he went and took the bones of Saul and his son Jonathan from the citizens of Jabesh Gilead. (They had taken them secretly from the public square at Beth Shan, where the Philistines had hung them after they struck Saul down on Gilboa.) **13**David brought the bones of Saul and his son Jonathan from there, and the bones of those who had been killed and exposed were gathered up.

14They buried the bones of Saul and his son Jonathan in the tomb of Saul's father Kish, at Zela in Benjamin, and did everything the king commanded. After that, God answered prayer in behalf of the land.

Wars Against the Philistines

15Once again there was a battle between the Philistines and Israel. David went down with his men to fight against the Philistines, and he became exhausted. **16**And Ishbi-Benob, one of the descendants of Rapha, whose bronze spearhead weighed three hundred shekels*b* and who was armed with a new ˌswordˌ, said he would kill David. **17**But Abishai son of Zeruiah came to David's rescue; he struck the Philistine down and killed him. Then David's men swore to him, saying, "Never again will you go out with us to battle, so that the lamp of Israel will not be extinguished."

18In the course of time, there was another battle with the Philistines, at Gob. At that time Sibbecai the Hushathite killed Saph, one of the descendants of Rapha.

19In another battle with the Philistines at Gob, Elhanan son of Jaare-Oregim*c* the Bethlehemite killed Goliath*d* the Gittite, who had a spear with a shaft like a weaver's rod.

20In still another battle, which took place at Gath, there was a huge man with six fingers on each hand and six toes on each foot—twenty-four in all. He also was descended from Rapha. **21**When he taunted Israel, Jonathan son of Shimeah, David's brother, killed him.

22These four were descendants of Rapha in Gath, and they fell at the hands of David and his men.

David's Song of Praise

22 David sang to the LORD the words of this song when the LORD delivered him from the hand of all his enemies and from the hand of Saul. **2**He said:

"The LORD is my rock, my fortress and
 my deliverer;
3 my God is my rock, in whom I take
 refuge,
 my shield and the horn*e* of my
 salvation.
He is my stronghold, my refuge and my
 savior—
 from violent men you save me.
4I call to the LORD, who is worthy of
 praise,
 and I am saved from my enemies.

5"The waves of death swirled about me;
 the torrents of destruction
 overwhelmed me.
6The cords of the grave*f* coiled around
 me;
 the snares of death confronted me.
7In my distress I called to the LORD;
 I called out to my God.
From his temple he heard my voice;
 my cry came to his ears.

8"The earth trembled and quaked,
 the foundations of the heavens*g*
 shook;
 they trembled because he was angry.
9Smoke rose from his nostrils;
 consuming fire came from his mouth,
 burning coals blazed out of it.
10He parted the heavens and came down;
 dark clouds were under his feet.

---

a8 Two Hebrew manuscripts, some Septuagint manuscripts and Syriac (see also 1 Samuel 18:19); most Hebrew and Septuagint manuscripts Michal   b16 That is, about 7 1/2 pounds (about 3.5 kilograms)   c19 Or son of Jair the weaver   d19 Hebrew and Septuagint; 1 Chron. 20:5 son of Jair killed Lahmi the brother of Goliath   e3 Horn here symbolizes strength.   f6 Hebrew Sheol   g8 Hebrew; Vulgate and Syriac (see also Psalm 18:7) mountains

11He mounted the cherubim and flew;
   he soared*a* on the wings of the wind.
12He made darkness his canopy around
      him—
   the dark*b* rain clouds of the sky.
13Out of the brightness of his presence
   bolts of lightning blazed forth.
14The LORD thundered from heaven;
   the voice of the Most High resounded.
15He shot arrows and scattered ₁the
      enemies₁,
   bolts of lightning and routed them.
16The valleys of the sea were exposed
   and the foundations of the earth laid
      bare
 at the rebuke of the LORD,
   at the blast of breath from his
      nostrils.

17"He reached down from on high and
      took hold of me;
   he drew me out of deep waters.
18He rescued me from my powerful
      enemy,
   from my foes, who were too strong
      for me.
19They confronted me in the day of my
      disaster,
   but the LORD was my support.
20He brought me out into a spacious
      place;
   he rescued me because he delighted
      in me.

21"The LORD has dealt with me according
      to my righteousness;
   according to the cleanness of my
      hands he has rewarded me.
22For I have kept the ways of the LORD;
   I have not done evil by turning from
      my God.
23All his laws are before me;
   I have not turned away from his
      decrees.
24I have been blameless before him
   and have kept myself from sin.
25The LORD has rewarded me according to
      my righteousness,
   according to my cleanness*c* in his
      sight.

26"To the faithful you show yourself
      faithful,
   to the blameless you show yourself
      blameless,
27to the pure you show yourself pure,

but to the crooked you show yourself
      shrewd.
28You save the humble,
   but your eyes are on the haughty to
      bring them low.
29You are my lamp, O LORD;
   the LORD turns my darkness into light.
30With your help I can advance against a
      troop*d*;
   with my God I can scale a wall.

31"As for God, his way is perfect;
   the word of the LORD is flawless.
 He is a shield
   for all who take refuge in him.
32For who is God besides the LORD?
   And who is the Rock except our God?
33It is God who arms me with strength*e*
   and makes my way perfect.
34He makes my feet like the feet of a
      deer;
   he enables me to stand on the
      heights.
35He trains my hands for battle;
   my arms can bend a bow of bronze.
36You give me your shield of victory;
   you stoop down to make me great.
37You broaden the path beneath me,
   so that my ankles do not turn.

38"I pursued my enemies and crushed
      them;
   I did not turn back till they were
      destroyed.
39I crushed them completely, and they
      could not rise;
   they fell beneath my feet.
40You armed me with strength for battle;
   you made my adversaries bow at my
      feet.
41You made my enemies turn their backs
      in flight,
   and I destroyed my foes.
42They cried for help, but there was no
      one to save them—
   to the LORD, but he did not answer.
43I beat them as fine as the dust of the
      earth;
   I pounded and trampled them like
      mud in the streets.

44"You have delivered me from the
      attacks of my people;
   you have preserved me as the head of
      nations.

a11 Many Hebrew manuscripts (see also Psalm 18:10); most Hebrew manuscripts *appeared*   *b12* Septuagint
and Vulgate (see also Psalm 18:11); Hebrew *massed*   *c25* Hebrew; Septuagint and Vulgate (see also Psalm
18:24) *to the cleanness of my hands*   *d30* Or *can run through a barricade*   *e33* Dead Sea Scrolls, some
Septuagint manuscripts, Vulgate and Syriac (see also Psalm 18:32); Masoretic Text *who is my strong refuge*

People I did not know are subject to
me,
45 and foreigners come cringing to me;
as soon as they hear me, they obey
me.
46They all lose heart;
they come trembling*a* from their
strongholds.

47"The LORD lives! Praise be to my Rock!
Exalted be God, the Rock, my Savior!
48He is the God who avenges me,
who puts the nations under me,
49 who sets me free from my enemies.
You exalted me above my foes;
from violent men you rescued me.
50Therefore I will praise you, O LORD,
among the nations;
I will sing praises to your name.
51He gives his king great victories;
he shows unfailing kindness to his
anointed,
to David and his descendants
forever."

The Last Words of David

23 These are the last words of David:

"The oracle of David son of Jesse,
the oracle of the man exalted by the
Most High,
the man anointed by the God of Jacob,
Israel's singer of songs*b*:

2"The Spirit of the LORD spoke through
me;
his word was on my tongue.
3The God of Israel spoke,
the Rock of Israel said to me:
'When one rules over men in
righteousness,
when he rules in the fear of God,
4he is like the light of morning at sunrise
on a cloudless morning,
like the brightness after rain
that brings the grass from the earth.'

5"Is not my house right with God?
Has he not made with me an
everlasting covenant,
arranged and secured in every part?
Will he not bring to fruition my
salvation
and grant me my every desire?

6But evil men are all to be cast aside like
thorns,
which are not gathered with the hand.
7Whoever touches thorns
uses a tool of iron or the shaft of a
spear;
they are burned up where they lie."

David's Mighty Men

8These are the names of David's mighty
men:

Josheb-Basshebeth,*c* a Tahkemonite,*d*
was chief of the Three; he raised his spear
against eight hundred men, whom he
killed*e* in one encounter.
9Next to him was Eleazar son of Dodai the
Ahohite. As one of the three mighty men, he
was with David when they taunted the Philistines gathered ₗat Pas Dammim,*f* for battle. Then the men of Israel retreated, 10but
he stood his ground and struck down the
Philistines till his hand grew tired and froze
to the sword. The LORD brought about a great
victory that day. The troops returned to Eleazar, but only to strip the dead.
11Next to him was Shammah son of Agee
the Hararite. When the Philistines banded
together at a place where there was a field
full of lentils, Israel's troops fled from them.
12But Shammah took his stand in the middle
of the field. He defended it and struck the
Philistines down, and the LORD brought
about a great victory.
13During harvest time, three of the thirty
chief men came down to David at the cave
of Adullam, while a band of Philistines was
encamped in the Valley of Rephaim. 14At
that time David was in the stronghold, and
the Philistine garrison was at Bethlehem.
15David longed for water and said, "Oh, that
someone would get me a drink of water
from the well near the gate of Bethlehem!"
16So the three mighty men broke through
the Philistine lines, drew water from the
well near the gate of Bethlehem and carried
it back to David. But he refused to drink it;
instead, he poured it out before the LORD.
17"Far be it from me, O LORD, to do this!" he
said. "Is it not the blood of men who went
at the risk of their lives?" And David would
not drink it.
Such were the exploits of the three mighty
men.

a46 Some Septuagint manuscripts and Vulgate (see also Psalm 18:45); Masoretic Text *they arm themselves.*
b1 Or *Israel's beloved singer*   *c8* Hebrew; some Septuagint manuscripts suggest *Ish-Bosheth,* that is, *Esh-Baal*
(see also 1 Chron. 11:11 *Jashobeam*).   *d8* Probably a variant of *Hacmonite* (see 1 Chron. 11:11)   *e8* Some
Septuagint manuscripts (see also 1 Chron. 11:11); Hebrew and other Septuagint manuscripts *Three; it was
Adino the Eznite who killed eight hundred men*   *f9* See 1 Chron. 11:13; Hebrew *gathered there.*

[18]Abishai the brother of Joab son of Zeruiah was chief of the Three.[a] He raised his spear against three hundred men, whom he killed, and so he became as famous as the Three. [19]Was he not held in greater honor than the Three? He became their commander, even though he was not included among them.

[20]Benaiah son of Jehoiada was a valiant fighter from Kabzeel, who performed great exploits. He struck down two of Moab's best men. He also went down into a pit on a snowy day and killed a lion. [21]And he struck down a huge Egyptian. Although the Egyptian had a spear in his hand, Benaiah went against him with a club. He snatched the spear from the Egyptian's hand and killed him with his own spear. [22]Such were the exploits of Benaiah son of Jehoiada; he too was as famous as the three mighty men. [23]He was held in greater honor than any of the Thirty, but he was not included among the Three. And David put him in charge of his bodyguard.

[24]Among the Thirty were:
Asahel the brother of Joab,
Elhanan son of Dodo from Bethlehem,
[25]Shammah the Harodite,
Elika the Harodite,
[26]Helez the Paltite,
Ira son of Ikkesh from Tekoa,
[27]Abiezer from Anathoth,
Mebunnai[b] the Hushathite,
[28]Zalmon the Ahohite,
Maharai the Netophathite,
[29]Heled[c] son of Baanah the Netophathite,
Ithai son of Ribai from Gibeah in Benjamin,
[30]Benaiah the Pirathonite,
Hiddai[d] from the ravines of Gaash,
[31]Abi-Albon the Arbathite,
Azmaveth the Barhumite,
[32]Eliahba the Shaalbonite,
the sons of Jashen,
Jonathan [33]son of[e] Shammah the Hararite,
Ahiam son of Sharar[f] the Hararite,
[34]Eliphelet son of Ahasbai the Maacathite,

Eliam son of Ahithophel the Gilonite,
[35]Hezro the Carmelite,
Paarai the Arbite,
[36]Igal son of Nathan from Zobah,
the son of Hagri,[g]
[37]Zelek the Ammonite,
Naharai the Beerothite, the armor-bearer of Joab son of Zeruiah,
[38]Ira the Ithrite,
Gareb the Ithrite
[39]and Uriah the Hittite.
There were thirty-seven in all.

David Counts the Fighting Men

24 Again the anger of the LORD burned against Israel, and he incited David against them, saying, "Go and take a census of Israel and Judah."

[2]So the king said to Joab and the army commanders[h] with him, "Go throughout the tribes of Israel from Dan to Beersheba and enroll the fighting men, so that I may know how many there are."

[3]But Joab replied to the king, "May the LORD your God multiply the troops a hundred times over, and may the eyes of my lord the king see it. But why does my lord the king want to do such a thing?"

[4]The king's word, however, overruled Joab and the army commanders; so they left the presence of the king to enroll the fighting men of Israel.

[5]After crossing the Jordan, they camped near Aroer, south of the town in the gorge, and then went through Gad and on to Jazer. [6]They went to Gilead and the region of Tahtim Hodshi, and on to Dan Jaan and around toward Sidon. [7]Then they went toward the fortress of Tyre and all the towns of the Hivites and Canaanites. Finally, they went on to Beersheba in the Negev of Judah.

[8]After they had gone through the entire land, they came back to Jerusalem at the end of nine months and twenty days.

[9]Joab reported the number of the fighting men to the king: In Israel there were eight hundred thousand able-bodied men who could handle a sword, and in Judah five hundred thousand.

[10]David was conscience-stricken after he had counted the fighting men, and he said

---

[a]18 Most Hebrew manuscripts (see also 1 Chron. 11:20); two Hebrew manuscripts and Syriac *Thirty*
[b]27 Hebrew; some Septuagint manuscripts (see also 1 Chron. 11:29) *Sibbecai*		[c]29 Some Hebrew manuscripts and Vulgate (see also 1 Chron. 11:30); most Hebrew manuscripts *Heleb*		[d]30 Hebrew; some Septuagint manuscripts (see also 1 Chron. 11:32) *Hurai*		[e]33 Some Septuagint manuscripts (see also 1 Chron. 11:34); Hebrew does not have *son of.*		[f]33 Hebrew; some Septuagint manuscripts (see also 1 Chron. 11:35) *Sacar*
[g]36 Some Septuagint manuscripts (see also 1 Chron. 11:38); Hebrew *Haggadi*		[h]2 Septuagint (see also verse 4 and 1 Chron. 21:2); Hebrew *Joab the army commander*

to the LORD, "I have sinned greatly in what I have done. Now, O LORD, I beg you, take away the guilt of your servant. I have done a very foolish thing."

¹¹Before David got up the next morning, the word of the LORD had come to Gad the prophet, David's seer: ¹²"Go and tell David, 'This is what the LORD says: I am giving you three options. Choose one of them for me to carry out against you.'"

¹³So Gad went to David and said to him, "Shall there come upon you three[a] years of famine in your land? Or three months of fleeing from your enemies while they pursue you? Or three days of plague in your land? Now then, think it over and decide how I should answer the one who sent me."

¹⁴David said to Gad, "I am in deep distress. Let us fall into the hands of the LORD, for his mercy is great; but do not let me fall into the hands of men."

¹⁵So the LORD sent a plague on Israel from that morning until the end of the time designated, and seventy thousand of the people from Dan to Beersheba died. ¹⁶When the angel stretched out his hand to destroy Jerusalem, the LORD was grieved because of the calamity and said to the angel who was afflicting the people, "Enough! Withdraw your hand." The angel of the LORD was then at the threshing floor of Araunah the Jebusite.

¹⁷When David saw the angel who was striking down the people, he said to the LORD, "I am the one who has sinned and done wrong. These are but sheep. What have they done? Let your hand fall upon me and my family."

David Builds an Altar

¹⁸On that day Gad went to David and said to him, "Go up and build an altar to the LORD on the threshing floor of Araunah the Jebusite." ¹⁹So David went up, as the LORD had commanded through Gad. ²⁰When Araunah looked and saw the king and his men coming toward him, he went out and bowed down before the king with his face to the ground.

²¹Araunah said, "Why has my lord the king come to his servant?"

"To buy your threshing floor," David answered, "so I can build an altar to the LORD, that the plague on the people may be stopped."

²²Araunah said to David, "Let my lord the king take whatever pleases him and offer it up. Here are oxen for the burnt offering, and here are threshing sledges and ox yokes for the wood. ²³O king, Araunah gives all this to the king." Araunah also said to him, "May the LORD your God accept you."

²⁴But the king replied to Araunah, "No, I insist on paying you for it. I will not sacrifice to the LORD my God burnt offerings that cost me nothing."

So David bought the threshing floor and the oxen and paid fifty shekels[b] of silver for them. ²⁵David built an altar to the LORD there and sacrificed burnt offerings and fellowship offerings.[c] Then the LORD answered prayer in behalf of the land, and the plague on Israel was stopped.

---

a13 Septuagint (see also 1 Chron. 21:12); Hebrew *seven* kilogram)   *c25* Traditionally *peace offerings*   *b24* That is, about 1 1/4 pounds (about 0.6

1 KINGS

KING David's golden reign ends, and his son Solomon inherits the throne. Wise and wealthy Solomon builds a magnificent temple for the true God, but his pagan women (seven hundred wives, three hundred concubines) draw his heart to false gods. At his death the kingdom splits into two nations. Both Israel in the north and Judah in the south begin a sad slide to destruction. God sends prophets (like Elijah) to preach God's Word and warn the rulers against idolatry. As you read, commit yourself to following God with undivided allegiance.

Outline of Contents

Adonijah Sets Himself Up as King

1 When King David was old and well advanced in years, he could not keep warm even when they put covers over him. ²So his servants said to him, "Let us look for a young virgin to attend the king and take care of him. She can lie beside him so that our lord the king may keep warm."

³Then they searched throughout Israel for a beautiful girl and found Abishag, a Shunammite, and brought her to the king. ⁴The girl was very beautiful; she took care of the king and waited on him, but the king had no intimate relations with her.

⁵Now Adonijah, whose mother was Haggith, put himself forward and said, "I will be king." So he got chariots and horses[a] ready, with fifty men to run ahead of him. ⁶(His father had never interfered with him by asking, "Why do you behave as you do?" He was also very handsome and was born next after Absalom.)

⁷Adonijah conferred with Joab son of Zeruiah and with Abiathar the priest, and they gave him their support. ⁸But Zadok the priest, Benaiah son of Jehoiada, Nathan the prophet, Shimei and Rei[b] and David's special guard did not join Adonijah.

⁹Adonijah then sacrificed sheep, cattle and fattened calves at the Stone of Zoheleth near En Rogel. He invited all his brothers, the king's sons, and all the men of Judah

a5 Or *charioteers*   *b8* Or *and his friends*

who were royal officials, **10**but he did not invite Nathan the prophet or Benaiah or the special guard or his brother Solomon.

11Then Nathan asked Bathsheba, Solomon's mother, "Have you not heard that Adonijah, the son of Haggith, has become king without our lord David's knowing it? **12**Now then, let me advise you how you can save your own life and the life of your son Solomon. **13**Go in to King David and say to him, 'My lord the king, did you not swear to me your servant: "Surely Solomon your son shall be king after me, and he will sit on my throne"? Why then has Adonijah become king?' **14**While you are still there talking to the king, I will come in and confirm what you have said."

15So Bathsheba went to see the aged king in his room, where Abishag the Shunammite was attending him. **16**Bathsheba bowed low and knelt before the king.

"What is it you want?" the king asked.

17She said to him, "My lord, you yourself swore to me your servant by the LORD your God: 'Solomon your son shall be king after me, and he will sit on my throne.' **18**But now Adonijah has become king, and you, my lord the king, do not know about it. **19**He has sacrificed great numbers of cattle, fattened calves, and sheep, and has invited all the king's sons, Abiathar the priest and Joab the commander of the army, but he has not invited Solomon your servant. **20**My lord the king, the eyes of all Israel are on you, to learn from you who will sit on the throne of my lord the king after him. **21**Otherwise, as soon as my lord the king is laid to rest with his fathers, I and my son Solomon will be treated as criminals."

22While she was still speaking with the king, Nathan the prophet arrived. **23**And they told the king, "Nathan the prophet is here." So he went before the king and bowed with his face to the ground.

24Nathan said, "Have you, my lord the king, declared that Adonijah shall be king after you, and that he will sit on your throne? **25**Today he has gone down and sacrificed great numbers of cattle, fattened calves, and sheep. He has invited all the king's sons, the commanders of the army and Abiathar the priest. Right now they are eating and drinking with him and saying, 'Long live King Adonijah!' **26**But me your servant, and Zadok the priest, and Benaiah son of Jehoiada, and your servant Solomon he did not invite. **27**Is this something my lord the king has done without letting his servants know who

should sit on the throne of my lord the king after him?"

David Makes Solomon King

28Then King David said, "Call in Bathsheba." So she came into the king's presence and stood before him.

29The king then took an oath: "As surely as the LORD lives, who has delivered me out of every trouble, **30**I will surely carry out today what I swore to you by the LORD, the God of Israel: Solomon your son shall be king after me, and he will sit on my throne in my place."

31Then Bathsheba bowed low with her face to the ground and, kneeling before the king, said, "May my lord King David live forever!"

32King David said, "Call in Zadok the priest, Nathan the prophet and Benaiah son of Jehoiada." When they came before the king, **33**he said to them: "Take your lord's servants with you and set Solomon my son on my own mule and take him down to Gihon. **34**There have Zadok the priest and Nathan the prophet anoint him king over Israel. Blow the trumpet and shout, 'Long live King Solomon!' **35**Then you are to go up with him, and he is to come and sit on my throne and reign in my place. I have appointed him ruler over Israel and Judah."

36Benaiah son of Jehoiada answered the king, "Amen! May the LORD, the God of my lord the king, so declare it. **37**As the LORD was with my lord the king, so may he be with Solomon to make his throne even greater than the throne of my lord King David!"

38So Zadok the priest, Nathan the prophet, Benaiah son of Jehoiada, the Kerethites and the Pelethites went down and put Solomon on King David's mule and escorted him to Gihon. **39**Zadok the priest took the horn of oil from the sacred tent and anointed Solomon. Then they sounded the trumpet and all the people shouted, "Long live King Solomon!" **40**And all the people went up after him, playing flutes and rejoicing greatly, so that the ground shook with the sound.

41Adonijah and all the guests who were with him heard it as they were finishing their feast. On hearing the sound of the trumpet, Joab asked, "What's the meaning of all the noise in the city?"

42Even as he was speaking, Jonathan son of Abiathar the priest arrived. Adonijah said, "Come in. A worthy man like you must be bringing good news."

43"Not at all!" Jonathan answered. "Our lord King David has made Solomon king.

44The king has sent with him Zadok the priest, Nathan the prophet, Benaiah son of Jehoiada, the Kerethites and the Pelethites, and they have put him on the king's mule, **45**and Zadok the priest and Nathan the prophet have anointed him king at Gihon. From there they have gone up cheering, and the city resounds with it. That's the noise you hear. **46**Moreover, Solomon has taken his seat on the royal throne. **47**Also, the royal officials have come to congratulate our lord King David, saying, 'May your God make Solomon's name more famous than yours and his throne greater than yours!' And the king bowed in worship on his bed **48**and said, 'Praise be to the LORD, the God of Israel, who has allowed my eyes to see a successor on my throne today.' "

49At this, all Adonijah's guests rose in alarm and dispersed. **50**But Adonijah, in fear of Solomon, went and took hold of the horns of the altar. **51**Then Solomon was told, "Adonijah is afraid of King Solomon and is clinging to the horns of the altar. He says, 'Let King Solomon swear to me today that he will not put his servant to death with the sword.' "

52Solomon replied, "If he shows himself to be a worthy man, not a hair of his head will fall to the ground; but if evil is found in him, he will die." **53**Then King Solomon sent men, and they brought him down from the altar. And Adonijah came and bowed down to King Solomon, and Solomon said, "Go to your home."

David's Charge to Solomon

2 When the time drew near for David to die, he gave a charge to Solomon his son.

2"I am about to go the way of all the earth," he said. "So be strong, show yourself a man, **3**and observe what the LORD your God requires: Walk in his ways, and keep his decrees and commands, his laws and requirements, as written in the Law of Moses, so that you may prosper in all you do and wherever you go, **4**and that the LORD may keep his promise to me: 'If your descendants watch how they live, and if they walk faithfully before me with all their heart and soul, you will never fail to have a man on the throne of Israel.'

5"Now you yourself know what Joab son of Zeruiah did to me—what he did to the two commanders of Israel's armies, Abner son of Ner and Amasa son of Jether. He

killed them, shedding their blood in peacetime as if in battle, and with that blood stained the belt around his waist and the sandals on his feet. **6**Deal with him according to your wisdom, but do not let his gray head go down to the grave*a* in peace.

7"But show kindness to the sons of Barzillai of Gilead and let them be among those who eat at your table. They stood by me when I fled from your brother Absalom.

8"And remember, you have with you Shimei son of Gera, the Benjamite from Bahurim, who called down bitter curses on me the day I went to Mahanaim. When he came down to meet me at the Jordan, I swore to him by the LORD: 'I will not put you to death by the sword.' **9**But now, do not consider him innocent. You are a man of wisdom; you will know what to do to him. Bring his gray head down to the grave in blood."

10Then David rested with his fathers and was buried in the City of David. **11**He had reigned forty years over Israel—seven years in Hebron and thirty-three in Jerusalem. **12**So Solomon sat on the throne of his father David, and his rule was firmly established.

Solomon's Throne Established

13Now Adonijah, the son of Haggith, went to Bathsheba, Solomon's mother. Bathsheba asked him, "Do you come peacefully?"

He answered, "Yes, peacefully." **14**Then he added, "I have something to say to you."

"You may say it," she replied.

15"As you know," he said, "the kingdom was mine. All Israel looked to me as their king. But things changed, and the kingdom has gone to my brother; for it has come to him from the LORD. **16**Now I have one request to make of you. Do not refuse me."

"You may make it," she said.

17So he continued, "Please ask King Solomon—he will not refuse you—to give me Abishag the Shunammite as my wife."

18"Very well," Bathsheba replied, "I will speak to the king for you."

19When Bathsheba went to King Solomon to speak to him for Adonijah, the king stood up to meet her, bowed down to her and sat down on his throne. He had a throne brought for the king's mother, and she sat down at his right hand.

20"I have one small request to make of you," she said. "Do not refuse me."

The king replied, "Make it, my mother; I will not refuse you."

21So she said, "Let Abishag the Shunam-

*a*6 Hebrew *Sheol*; also in verse 9

mite be given in marriage to your brother Adonijah."

22King Solomon answered his mother, "Why do you request Abishag the Shunammite for Adonijah? You might as well request the kingdom for him—after all, he is my older brother—yes, for him and for Abiathar the priest and Joab son of Zeruiah!"

23Then King Solomon swore by the LORD: "May God deal with me, be it ever so severely, if Adonijah does not pay with his life for this request! **24**And now, as surely as the LORD lives—he who has established me securely on the throne of my father David and has founded a dynasty for me as he promised—Adonijah shall be put to death today!" **25**So King Solomon gave orders to Benaiah son of Jehoiada, and he struck down Adonijah and he died.

26To Abiathar the priest the king said, "Go back to your fields in Anathoth. You deserve to die, but I will not put you to death now, because you carried the ark of the Sovereign LORD before my father David and shared all my father's hardships." **27**So Solomon removed Abiathar from the priesthood of the LORD, fulfilling the word the LORD had spoken at Shiloh about the house of Eli.

28When the news reached Joab, who had conspired with Adonijah though not with Absalom, he fled to the tent of the LORD and took hold of the horns of the altar. **29**King Solomon was told that Joab had fled to the tent of the LORD and was beside the altar. Then Solomon ordered Benaiah son of Jehoiada, "Go, strike him down!"

30So Benaiah entered the tent of the LORD and said to Joab, "The king says, 'Come out!'"

But he answered, "No, I will die here."

Benaiah reported to the king, "This is how Joab answered me."

31Then the king commanded Benaiah, "Do as he says. Strike him down and bury him, and so clear me and my father's house of the guilt of the innocent blood that Joab shed. **32**The LORD will repay him for the blood he shed, because without the knowledge of my father David he attacked two men and killed them with the sword. Both of them—Abner son of Ner, commander of Israel's army, and Amasa son of Jether, commander of Judah's army—were better men and more upright than he. **33**May the guilt of their blood rest on the head of Joab and his descendants forever. But on David and his

descendants, his house and his throne, may there be the LORD's peace forever."

34So Benaiah son of Jehoiada went up and struck down Joab and killed him, and he was buried on his own land[a] in the desert. **35**The king put Benaiah son of Jehoiada over the army in Joab's position and replaced Abiathar with Zadok the priest.

36Then the king sent for Shimei and said to him, "Build yourself a house in Jerusalem and live there, but do not go anywhere else. **37**The day you leave and cross the Kidron Valley, you can be sure you will die; your blood will be on your own head."

38Shimei answered the king, "What you say is good. Your servant will do as my lord the king has said." And Shimei stayed in Jerusalem for a long time.

39But three years later, two of Shimei's slaves ran off to Achish son of Maacah, king of Gath, and Shimei was told, "Your slaves are in Gath." **40**At this, he saddled his donkey and went to Achish at Gath in search of his slaves. So Shimei went away and brought the slaves back from Gath.

41When Solomon was told that Shimei had gone from Jerusalem to Gath and had returned, **42**the king summoned Shimei and said to him, "Did I not make you swear by the LORD and warn you, 'On the day you leave to go anywhere else, you can be sure you will die'? At that time you said to me, 'What you say is good. I will obey.' **43**Why then did you not keep your oath to the LORD and obey the command I gave you?"

44The king also said to Shimei, "You know in your heart all the wrong you did to my father David. Now the LORD will repay you for your wrongdoing. **45**But King Solomon will be blessed, and David's throne will remain secure before the LORD forever."

46Then the king gave the order to Benaiah son of Jehoiada, and he went out and struck Shimei down and killed him.

The kingdom was now firmly established in Solomon's hands.

Solomon Asks for Wisdom

3 Solomon made an alliance with Pharaoh king of Egypt and married his daughter. He brought her to the City of David until he finished building his palace and the temple of the LORD, and the wall around Jerusalem. **2**The people, however, were still sacrificing at the high places, because a temple had not yet been built for the Name of the LORD. **3**Solomon showed his love for

---

a34 Or buried in his tomb

WHAT TO DO IF YOU WANT WISDOM

A s Bob climbs into bed, he keeps thinking about his failing grade in chemistry and the bent fender from driving his car when he was angry. And he keeps rehearsing the things his dad told him earlier. He muses to himself:

"I guess Dad's right. I should have studied harder and been more careful. Then none of this would have ever happened. Now, I'm off the team and I owe Mom and Dad a thousand bucks . . . ."

Suddenly he sits up and clicks on the light. He reaches under his bed and pulls out a dusty Bible. "I'm stuck for now," he thinks, "but maybe I can get a little help here to keep me from getting in trouble down the line."

Look It Up
••••

Bob opens to Proverbs and reads this verse:

"The fear of the LORD is the beginning of wisdom, and knowledge of the Holy One is understanding" (Proverbs 9:10).

"I wonder what 'fear of the LORD' really means?" he reflects.

That phrase, and others similar to it, is found numerous times in the Bible. It doesn't refer to dread or shrinking away in horror. Instead it has to do with deep reverence and healthy respect. It means to worship in submission, obeying our good and loving God. To fear him means that you recognize that he is the holy, all-powerful King over your life.

The better you get to know God, the more you will develop this healthy fear.

Think It Through
••••

Think about these related truths:

1. You'll never find true wisdom until you learn to fear God.

2. You'll never develop that reverent and respectful attitude of fear for God until you get to know him.

3. You can't get to know God if you don't spend time with him—in prayer and in his Word—doing what he wants.

Work It Out
••••

Maybe, like Bob, you need some wisdom. You'll find it by learning how to fear God, which means getting to know him. It's a lifelong process. But for starters:

• Listen to what he says. Spend extra time reading and studying the Bible today. It's not just another book; it's the Word of the God of the universe!

• Do what he says. Obedience isn't optional. God didn't give Moses and the Israelites the Ten *Suggestions* but the Ten *Commandments*. He is your King. You are his servant. Your only goal should be to obey him.

Nail It Down
••••

Read the story of how Solomon got wisdom in 1 Kings 3:1–15.

Turn to pages 649 and 798 for other readings on wisdom.
Turn to page 339 for the weekend reading.

Topic
••••

WISDOM

the LORD by walking according to the statutes of his father David, except that he offered sacrifices and burned incense on the high places.

⁴The king went to Gibeon to offer sacrifices, for that was the most important high place, and Solomon offered a thousand burnt offerings on that altar. ⁵At Gibeon the LORD appeared to Solomon during the night in a dream, and God said, "Ask for whatever you want me to give you."

⁶Solomon answered, "You have shown great kindness to your servant, my father David, because he was faithful to you and righteous and upright in heart. You have continued this great kindness to him and have given him a son to sit on his throne this very day.

⁷"Now, O LORD my God, you have made your servant king in place of my father David. But I am only a little child and do not know how to carry out my duties. ⁸Your servant is here among the people you have chosen, a great people, too numerous to count or number. ⁹So give your servant a discerning heart to govern your people and to distinguish between right and wrong. For who is able to govern this great people of yours?"

¹⁰The Lord was pleased that Solomon had asked for this. ¹¹So God said to him, "Since you have asked for this and not for long life or wealth for yourself, nor have asked for the death of your enemies but for discernment in administering justice, ¹²I will do what you have asked. I will give you a wise and discerning heart, so that there will never have been anyone like you, nor will there ever be. ¹³Moreover, I will give you what you have not asked for—both riches and honor—so that in your lifetime you will have no equal among kings. ¹⁴And if you walk in my ways and obey my statutes and commands as David your father did, I will give you a long life." ¹⁵Then Solomon awoke—and he realized it had been a dream.

He returned to Jerusalem, stood before the ark of the Lord's covenant and sacrificed burnt offerings and fellowship offerings.ᵃ Then he gave a feast for all his court.

A Wise Ruling

¹⁶Now two prostitutes came to the king and stood before him. ¹⁷One of them said, "My lord, this woman and I live in the same house. I had a baby while she was there with me. ¹⁸The third day after my child was born,

this woman also had a baby. We were alone; there was no one in the house but the two of us.

¹⁹"During the night this woman's son died because she lay on him. ²⁰So she got up in the middle of the night and took my son from my side while I your servant was asleep. She put him by her breast and put her dead son by my breast. ²¹The next morning, I got up to nurse my son—and he was dead! But when I looked at him closely in the morning light, I saw that it wasn't the son I had borne."

²²The other woman said, "No! The living one is my son; the dead one is yours."

But the first one insisted, "No! The dead one is yours; the living one is mine." And so they argued before the king.

²³The king said, "This one says, 'My son is alive and your son is dead,' while that one says, 'No! Your son is dead and mine is alive.'"

²⁴Then the king said, "Bring me a sword." So they brought a sword for the king. ²⁵He then gave an order: "Cut the living child in two and give half to one and half to the other."

²⁶The woman whose son was alive was filled with compassion for her son and said to the king, "Please, my lord, give her the living baby! Don't kill him!"

But the other said, "Neither I nor you shall have him. Cut him in two!"

²⁷Then the king gave his ruling: "Give the living baby to the first woman. Do not kill him; she is his mother."

²⁸When all Israel heard the verdict the king had given, they held the king in awe, because they saw that he had wisdom from God to administer justice.

Solomon's Officials and Governors

4 So King Solomon ruled over all Israel. ²And these were his chief officials:

Azariah son of Zadok—the priest;
³Elihoreph and Ahijah, sons of Shisha—secretaries;
Jehoshaphat son of Ahilud—recorder;
⁴Benaiah son of Jehoiada—commander in chief;
Zadok and Abiathar—priests;
⁵Azariah son of Nathan—in charge of the district officers;
Zabud son of Nathan—a priest and personal adviser to the king;
⁶Ahishar—in charge of the palace;

ᵃ15 Traditionally *peace offerings*

Adoniram son of Abda—in charge of forced labor.

7Solomon also had twelve district governors over all Israel, who supplied provisions for the king and the royal household. Each one had to provide supplies for one month in the year. **8**These are their names:

Ben-Hur—in the hill country of Ephraim;

9Ben-Deker—in Makaz, Shaalbim, Beth Shemesh and Elon Bethhanan;

10Ben-Hesed—in Arubboth (Socoh and all the land of Hepher were his);

11Ben-Abinadab—in Naphoth Dor*a* (he was married to Taphath daughter of Solomon);

12Baana son of Ahilud—in Taanach and Megiddo, and in all of Beth Shan next to Zarethan below Jezreel, from Beth Shan to Abel Meholah across to Jokmeam;

13Ben-Geber—in Ramoth Gilead (the settlements of Jair son of Manasseh in Gilead were his, as well as the district of Argob in Bashan and its sixty large walled cities with bronze gate bars);

14Ahinadab son of Iddo—in Mahanaim;

15Ahimaaz—in Naphtali (he had married Basemath daughter of Solomon);

16Baana son of Hushai—in Asher and in Aloth;

17Jehoshaphat son of Paruah—in Issachar;

18Shimei son of Ela—in Benjamin;

19Geber son of Uri—in Gilead (the country of Sihon king of the Amorites and the country of Og king of Bashan). He was the only governor over the district.

Solomon's Daily Provisions

20The people of Judah and Israel were as numerous as the sand on the seashore; they ate, they drank and they were happy. **21**And Solomon ruled over all the kingdoms from the River*b* to the land of the Philistines, as far as the border of Egypt. These countries brought tribute and were Solomon's subjects all his life.

22Solomon's daily provisions were thirty cors*c* of fine flour and sixty cors*d* of meal, **23**ten head of stall-fed cattle, twenty of pasture-fed cattle and a hundred sheep and goats, as well as deer, gazelles, roebucks and choice fowl. **24**For he ruled over all the kingdoms west of the River, from Tiphsah to Gaza, and had peace on all sides. **25**During Solomon's lifetime Judah and Israel, from Dan to Beersheba, lived in safety, each man under his own vine and fig tree.

26Solomon had four*e* thousand stalls for chariot horses, and twelve thousand horses.*f*

27The district officers, each in his month, supplied provisions for King Solomon and all who came to the king's table. They saw to it that nothing was lacking. **28**They also brought to the proper place their quotas of barley and straw for the chariot horses and the other horses.

Solomon's Wisdom

29God gave Solomon wisdom and very great insight, and a breadth of understanding as measureless as the sand on the seashore. **30**Solomon's wisdom was greater than the wisdom of all the men of the East, and greater than all the wisdom of Egypt. **31**He was wiser than any other man, including Ethan the Ezrahite—wiser than Heman, Calcol and Darda, the sons of Mahol. And his fame spread to all the surrounding nations. **32**He spoke three thousand proverbs and his songs numbered a thousand and five. **33**He described plant life, from the cedar of Lebanon to the hyssop that grows out of walls. He also taught about animals and birds, reptiles and fish. **34**Men of all nations came to listen to Solomon's wisdom, sent by all the kings of the world, who had heard of his wisdom.

Preparations for Building the Temple

5 When Hiram king of Tyre heard that Solomon had been anointed king to succeed his father David, he sent his envoys to Solomon, because he had always been on friendly terms with David. **2**Solomon sent back this message to Hiram:

3"You know that because of the wars waged against my father David from all sides, he could not build a temple for the Name of the LORD his God until the LORD put his enemies under his feet. **4**But now the LORD my God has given me rest on every side, and there is no ad-

---

a11 Or *in the heights of Dor*   *b21* That is, the Euphrates; also in verse 24   *c22* That is, probably about 185 bushels (about 6.6 kiloliters)   *d22* That is, probably about 375 bushels (about 13.2 kiloliters)   *e26* Some Septuagint manuscripts (see also 2 Chron. 9:25); Hebrew *forty*   *f26* Or *charioteers*

TIME TO RELAX

Work It Out
••••

Picture the following scene in your mind: You're about to enter the 747 that will take you away for a week to just relax and get away from it all. There's only one catch. For the entire week you are limited to one, repeat *one*, leisure activity. That's all you get to do for the entire week, so choose carefully.

What will it be? Probably a lot of guys will answer, "Basketball!" But other guys would prefer swimming or biking or playing around with a computer.

Lots of girls will say, "Give me some beach and some sun, and I'll be content." But other girls would rather play tennis or hike or read.

The point is, whatever you really enjoy doing, whatever relaxes you and puts you in a fine mood, that's leisure, relaxation, rest for you.

Nail It Down
••••

Read about Solomon's leisure activities in 1 Kings 4:33.

Think It Through
••••

The primary purpose of leisure is to refresh. God has made us so that we require physical and emotional refreshment to be at our best. How you get that refreshment varies from person to person.

King Solomon got away from the pressures of ruling an entire society by taking time for his "hobby": studying the things of nature. Now maybe Solomon's hobby sounds a bit too much like work to many of you, but a few minutes with a basketball and a hoop will make you feel great after a couple of hours at the books. Others would prefer a time with headphones and great music.

A quick walk or run, baking cookies, reading a good novel, conquering a video game, wrestling with your dog—it's up to you to find out what relaxes you. You don't have to plan and prepare and plot. The best leisure can often be found in simple activities that don't require much time or preparation.

As you go through your day, look for small moments of leisure. That way, maybe it won't seem like forever between the big moments.

Nail It Down
••••

Read again about Solomon's "hobbies" in 1 Kings 4:33. For further insight read Psalm 62:1–2.

Turn to pages 81, 553, 609 and 692 for other readings on leisure.
Turn to page 348 for Monday's reading.

Topic
••••

LEISURE

versary or disaster. **5**I intend, therefore, to build a temple for the Name of the LORD my God, as the LORD told my father David, when he said, 'Your son whom I will put on the throne in your place will build the temple for my Name.'

6"So give orders that cedars of Lebanon be cut for me. My men will work with yours, and I will pay you for your men whatever wages you set. You know that we have no one so skilled in felling timber as the Sidonians."

7When Hiram heard Solomon's message, he was greatly pleased and said, "Praise be to the LORD today, for he has given David a wise son to rule over this great nation."

8So Hiram sent word to Solomon:

"I have received the message you sent me and will do all you want in providing the cedar and pine logs. **9**My men will haul them down from Lebanon to the sea, and I will float them in rafts by sea to the place you specify. There I will separate them and you can take them away. And you are to grant my wish by providing food for my royal household."

10In this way Hiram kept Solomon supplied with all the cedar and pine logs he wanted, **11**and Solomon gave Hiram twenty thousand cors*a* of wheat as food for his household, in addition to twenty thousand baths*b,c* of pressed olive oil. Solomon continued to do this for Hiram year after year. **12**The LORD gave Solomon wisdom, just as he had promised him. There were peaceful relations between Hiram and Solomon, and the two of them made a treaty.

13King Solomon conscripted laborers from all Israel—thirty thousand men. **14**He sent them off to Lebanon in shifts of ten thousand a month, so that they spent one month in Lebanon and two months at home. Adoniram was in charge of the forced labor. **15**Solomon had seventy thousand carriers and eighty thousand stonecutters in the hills, **16**as well as thirty-three hundred*d* foremen who supervised the project and directed the workmen. **17**At the king's command they removed from the quarry large blocks of quality stone to provide a foundation of dressed stone for the temple. **18**The craftsmen of Solomon and Hiram and the men of Gebal*e* cut and prepared the timber and stone for the building of the temple.

Solomon Builds the Temple

6 In the four hundred and eightieth*f* year after the Israelites had come out of Egypt, in the fourth year of Solomon's reign over Israel, in the month of Ziv, the second month, he began to build the temple of the LORD.

2The temple that King Solomon built for the LORD was sixty cubits long, twenty wide and thirty high.*g* **3**The portico at the front of the main hall of the temple extended the width of the temple, that is twenty cubits,*h* and projected ten cubits*i* from the front of the temple. **4**He made narrow clerestory windows in the temple. **5**Against the walls of the main hall and inner sanctuary he built a structure around the building, in which there were side rooms. **6**The lowest floor was five cubits*j* wide, the middle floor six cubits*k* and the third floor seven.*l* He made offset ledges around the outside of the temple so that nothing would be inserted into the temple walls.

7In building the temple, only blocks dressed at the quarry were used, and no hammer, chisel or any other iron tool was heard at the temple site while it was being built.

8The entrance to the lowest*m* floor was on the south side of the temple; a stairway led up to the middle level and from there to the third. **9**So he built the temple and completed it, roofing it with beams and cedar planks. **10**And he built the side rooms all along the temple. The height of each was five cubits, and they were attached to the temple by beams of cedar.

11The word of the LORD came to Solomon: **12**"As for this temple you are building, if you follow my decrees, carry out my regulations and keep all my commands and obey them, I will fulfill through you the promise I gave to David your father. **13**And I will live among

a11 That is, probably about 125,000 bushels (about 4,400 kiloliters)   *b11* Septuagint (see also 2 Chron. 2:10); Hebrew *twenty cors*   *c11* That is, about 115,000 gallons (about 440 kiloliters)   *d16* Hebrew; some Septuagint manuscripts (see also 2 Chron. 2:2, 18) *thirty-six hundred*   *e18* That is, Byblos   *f1* Hebrew; Septuagint *four hundred and fortieth*   *g2* That is, about 90 feet (about 27 meters) long and 30 feet (about 9 meters) wide and 45 feet (about 13.5 meters) high   *h3* That is, about 30 feet (about 9 meters)   *i3* That is, about 15 feet (about 4.5 meters)   *j6* That is, about 7 1/2 feet (about 2.3 meters); also in verses 10 and 24   *k6* That is, about 9 feet (about 2.7 meters)   *l6* That is, about 10 1/2 feet (about 3.1 meters)   *m8* Septuagint; Hebrew *middle* the Israelites and will not abandon my people Israel."

¹⁴So Solomon built the temple and completed it. ¹⁵He lined its interior walls with cedar boards, paneling them from the floor of the temple to the ceiling, and covered the floor of the temple with planks of pine. ¹⁶He partitioned off twenty cubits*ᵃ* at the rear of the temple with cedar boards from floor to ceiling to form within the temple an inner sanctuary, the Most Holy Place. ¹⁷The main hall in front of this room was forty cubits*ᵇ* long. ¹⁸The inside of the temple was cedar, carved with gourds and open flowers. Everything was cedar; no stone was to be seen.

¹⁹He prepared the inner sanctuary within the temple to set the ark of the covenant of the Lᴏʀᴅ there. ²⁰The inner sanctuary was twenty cubits long, twenty wide and twenty high.*ᶜ* He overlaid the inside with pure gold, and he also overlaid the altar of cedar. ²¹Solomon covered the inside of the temple with pure gold, and he extended gold chains across the front of the inner sanctuary, which was overlaid with gold. ²²So he overlaid the whole interior with gold. He also overlaid with gold the altar that belonged to the inner sanctuary.

²³In the inner sanctuary he made a pair of cherubim of olive wood, each ten cubits*ᵈ* high. ²⁴One wing of the first cherub was five cubits long, and the other wing five cubits — ten cubits from wing tip to wing tip. ²⁵The second cherub also measured ten cubits, for the two cherubim were identical in size and shape. ²⁶The height of each cherub was ten cubits. ²⁷He placed the cherubim inside the innermost room of the temple, with their wings spread out. The wing of one cherub touched one wall, while the wing of the other touched the other wall, and their wings touched each other in the middle of the room. ²⁸He overlaid the cherubim with gold.

²⁹On the walls all around the temple, in both the inner and outer rooms, he carved cherubim, palm trees and open flowers. ³⁰He also covered the floors of both the inner and outer rooms of the temple with gold.

³¹For the entrance of the inner sanctuary he made doors of olive wood with five-sided jambs. ³²And on the two olive wood doors he carved cherubim, palm trees and open flowers, and overlaid the cherubim and palm trees with beaten gold. ³³In the same way he made four-sided jambs of olive wood for the entrance to the main hall. ³⁴He also made two pine doors, each having two leaves that turned in sockets. ³⁵He carved cherubim, palm trees and open flowers on them and overlaid them with gold hammered evenly over the carvings.

³⁶And he built the inner courtyard of three courses of dressed stone and one course of trimmed cedar beams.

³⁷The foundation of the temple of the Lᴏʀᴅ was laid in the fourth year, in the month of Ziv. ³⁸In the eleventh year in the month of Bul, the eighth month, the temple was finished in all its details according to its specifications. He had spent seven years building it.

Solomon Builds His Palace

7 It took Solomon thirteen years, however, to complete the construction of his palace. ²He built the Palace of the Forest of Lebanon a hundred cubits long, fifty wide and thirty high,*ᵉ* with four rows of cedar columns supporting trimmed cedar beams. ³It was roofed with cedar above the beams that rested on the columns—forty-five beams, fifteen to a row. ⁴Its windows were placed high in sets of three, facing each other. ⁵All the doorways had rectangular frames; they were in the front part in sets of three, facing each other.*ᶠ*

⁶He made a colonnade fifty cubits long and thirty wide.*ᵍ* In front of it was a portico, and in front of that were pillars and an overhanging roof.

⁷He built the throne hall, the Hall of Justice, where he was to judge, and he covered it with cedar from floor to ceiling.*ʰ* ⁸And the palace in which he was to live, set farther back, was similar in design. Solomon also made a palace like this hall for Pharaoh's daughter, whom he had married.

⁹All these structures, from the outside to the great courtyard and from foundation to eaves, were made of blocks of high-grade stone cut to size and trimmed with a saw on their inner and outer faces. ¹⁰The foundations were laid with large stones of good quality, some measuring ten cubits*ᵈ* and

---

ᵃ16 That is, about 30 feet (about 9 meters)   *ᵇ17* That is, about 60 feet (about 18 meters)   *ᶜ20* That is, about 30 feet (about 9 meters) long, wide and high   *ᵈ23* That is, about 15 feet (about 4.5 meters)   *ᵉ2* That is, about 150 feet (about 46 meters) long, 75 feet (about 23 meters) wide and 45 feet (about 13.5 meters) high   *ᶠ5* The meaning of the Hebrew for this verse is uncertain.   *ᵍ6* That is, about 75 feet (about 23 meters) long and 45 feet (about 13.5 meters) wide   *ʰ7* Vulgate and Syriac; Hebrew *floor* some eight.*a* **11**Above were high-grade stones, cut to size, and cedar beams. **12**The great courtyard was surrounded by a wall of three courses of dressed stone and one course of trimmed cedar beams, as was the inner courtyard of the temple of the Lord with its portico.

The Temple's Furnishings

13King Solomon sent to Tyre and brought Huram,*b* **14**whose mother was a widow from the tribe of Naphtali and whose father was a man of Tyre and a craftsman in bronze. Huram was highly skilled and experienced in all kinds of bronze work. He came to King Solomon and did all the work assigned to him.

15He cast two bronze pillars, each eighteen cubits high and twelve cubits around,*c* by line. **16**He also made two capitals of cast bronze to set on the tops of the pillars; each capital was five cubits*d* high. **17**A network of interwoven chains festooned the capitals on top of the pillars, seven for each capital. **18**He made pomegranates in two rows*e* encircling each network to decorate the capitals on top of the pillars.*f* He did the same for each capital. **19**The capitals on top of the pillars in the portico were in the shape of lilies, four cubits*g* high. **20**On the capitals of both pillars, above the bowl-shaped part next to the network, were the two hundred pomegranates in rows all around. **21**He erected the pillars at the portico of the temple. The pillar to the south he named Jakin*h* and the one to the north Boaz.*i* **22**The capitals on top were in the shape of lilies. And so the work on the pillars was completed.

23He made the Sea of cast metal, circular in shape, measuring ten cubits*j* from rim to rim and five cubits high. It took a line of thirty cubits*k* to measure around it. **24**Below the rim, gourds encircled it — ten to a cubit. The gourds were cast in two rows in one piece with the Sea.

25The Sea stood on twelve bulls, three facing north, three facing west, three facing south and three facing east. The Sea rested on top of them, and their hindquarters were toward the center. **26**It was a handbreadth*l* in thickness, and its rim was like the rim of a cup, like a lily blossom. It held two thousand baths.*m*

27He also made ten movable stands of bronze; each was four cubits long, four wide and three high.*n* **28**This is how the stands were made: They had side panels attached to uprights. **29**On the panels between the uprights were lions, bulls and cherubim — and on the uprights as well. Above and below the lions and bulls were wreaths of hammered work. **30**Each stand had four bronze wheels with bronze axles, and each had a basin resting on four supports, cast with wreaths on each side. **31**On the inside of the stand there was an opening that had a circular frame one cubit*o* deep. This opening was round, and with its basework it measured a cubit and a half.*p* Around its opening there was engraving. The panels of the stands were square, not round. **32**The four wheels were under the panels, and the axles of the wheels were attached to the stand. The diameter of each wheel was a cubit and a half. **33**The wheels were made like chariot wheels; the axles, rims, spokes and hubs were all of cast metal.

34Each stand had four handles, one on each corner, projecting from the stand. **35**At the top of the stand there was a circular band half a cubit*q* deep. The supports and panels were attached to the top of the stand. **36**He engraved cherubim, lions and palm trees on the surfaces of the supports and on the panels, in every available space, with wreaths all around. **37**This is the way he made the ten stands. They were all cast in the same molds and were identical in size and shape.

38He then made ten bronze basins, each holding forty baths*r* and measuring four cubits across, one basin to go on each of the ten stands. **39**He placed five of the stands on the south side of the temple and five on the

---

a10 That is, about 12 feet (about 3.6 meters)　*b13* Hebrew *Hiram*, a variant of *Huram*; also in verses 40 and 45　*c15* That is, about 27 feet (about 8.1 meters) high and 18 feet (about 5.4 meters) around　*d16* That is, about 7 1/2 feet (about 2.3 meters); also in verse 23　*e18* Two Hebrew manuscripts and Septuagint; most Hebrew manuscripts *made the pillars, and there were two rows*　*f18* Many Hebrew manuscripts and Syriac; most Hebrew manuscripts *pomegranates*　*g19* That is, about 6 feet (about 1.8 meters); also in verse 38　*h21* Jakin probably means *he establishes.*　*i21* Boaz probably means *in him is strength.*　*j23* That is, about 15 feet (about 4.5 meters)　*k23* That is, about 45 feet (about 13.5 meters)　*l26* That is, about 3 inches (about 8 centimeters)　*m26* That is, probably about 11,500 gallons (about 44 kiloliters); the Septuagint does not have this sentence.　*n27* That is, about 6 feet (about 1.8 meters) long and wide and about 4 1/2 feet (about 1.3 meters) high　*o31* That is, about 1 1/2 feet (about 0.5 meter)　*p31* That is, about 2 1/4 feet (about 0.7 meter); also in verse 32　*q35* That is, about 3/4 foot (about 0.2 meter)　*r38* That is, about 230 gallons (about 880 liters) north. He placed the Sea on the south side, at the southeast corner of the temple. **40**He also made the basins and shovels and sprinkling bowls.

So Huram finished all the work he had undertaken for King Solomon in the temple of the LORD:

41the two pillars;
   the two bowl-shaped capitals on top of the pillars;
   the two sets of network decorating the two bowl-shaped capitals on top of the pillars;
42the four hundred pomegranates for the two sets of network (two rows of pomegranates for each network, decorating the bowl-shaped capitals on top of the pillars);
43the ten stands with their ten basins;
44the Sea and the twelve bulls under it;
45the pots, shovels and sprinkling bowls.

All these objects that Huram made for King Solomon for the temple of the LORD were of burnished bronze. **46**The king had them cast in clay molds in the plain of the Jordan between Succoth and Zarethan. **47**Solomon left all these things unweighed, because there were so many; the weight of the bronze was not determined.

48Solomon also made all the furnishings that were in the LORD's temple:

   the golden altar;
   the golden table on which was the bread of the Presence;
49the lampstands of pure gold (five on the right and five on the left, in front of the inner sanctuary);
   the gold floral work and lamps and tongs;
50the pure gold basins, wick trimmers, sprinkling bowls, dishes and censers;
   and the gold sockets for the doors of the innermost room, the Most Holy Place, and also for the doors of the main hall of the temple.

51When all the work King Solomon had done for the temple of the LORD was finished, he brought in the things his father David had dedicated — the silver and gold and the furnishings — and he placed them in the treasuries of the LORD's temple.

The Ark Brought to the Temple

8 Then King Solomon summoned into his presence at Jerusalem the elders of Israel, all the heads of the tribes and the chiefs of the Israelite families, to bring up the ark of the LORD's covenant from Zion, the City of David. **2**All the men of Israel came together to King Solomon at the time of the festival in the month of Ethanim, the seventh month.

3When all the elders of Israel had arrived, the priests took up the ark, **4**and they brought up the ark of the LORD and the Tent of Meeting and all the sacred furnishings in it. The priests and Levites carried them up, **5**and King Solomon and the entire assembly of Israel that had gathered about him were before the ark, sacrificing so many sheep and cattle that they could not be recorded or counted.

6The priests then brought the ark of the LORD's covenant to its place in the inner sanctuary of the temple, the Most Holy Place, and put it beneath the wings of the cherubim. **7**The cherubim spread their wings over the place of the ark and overshadowed the ark and its carrying poles. **8**These poles were so long that their ends could be seen from the Holy Place in front of the inner sanctuary, but not from outside the Holy Place; and they are still there today. **9**There was nothing in the ark except the two stone tablets that Moses had placed in it at Horeb, where the LORD made a covenant with the Israelites after they came out of Egypt.

10When the priests withdrew from the Holy Place, the cloud filled the temple of the LORD. **11**And the priests could not perform their service because of the cloud, for the glory of the LORD filled his temple.

12Then Solomon said, "The LORD has said that he would dwell in a dark cloud; **13**I have indeed built a magnificent temple for you, a place for you to dwell forever."

14While the whole assembly of Israel was standing there, the king turned around and blessed them. **15**Then he said:

"Praise be to the LORD, the God of Israel, who with his own hand has fulfilled what he promised with his own mouth to my father David. For he said, **16**'Since the day I brought my people Israel out of Egypt, I have not chosen a city in any tribe of Israel to have a temple built for my Name to be there, but I have chosen David to rule my people Israel.'

17"My father David had it in his heart to build a temple for the Name of the LORD, the God of Israel. **18**But the LORD said to my father David, 'Because it was in your heart to build a temple for my

Name, you did well to have this in your heart. **19**Nevertheless, you are not the one to build the temple, but your son, who is your own flesh and blood — he is the one who will build the temple for my Name.'

20"The Lord has kept the promise he made: I have succeeded David my father and now I sit on the throne of Israel, just as the Lord promised, and I have built the temple for the Name of the Lord, the God of Israel. **21**I have provided a place there for the ark, in which is the covenant of the Lord that he made with our fathers when he brought them out of Egypt."

Solomon's Prayer of Dedication

22Then Solomon stood before the altar of the Lord in front of the whole assembly of Israel, spread out his hands toward heaven **23**and said:

"O Lord, God of Israel, there is no God like you in heaven above or on earth below — you who keep your covenant of love with your servants who continue wholeheartedly in your way. **24**You have kept your promise to your servant David my father; with your mouth you have promised and with your hand you have fulfilled it — as it is today.

25"Now Lord, God of Israel, keep for your servant David my father the promises you made to him when you said, 'You shall never fail to have a man to sit before me on the throne of Israel, if only your sons are careful in all they do to walk before me as you have done.' **26**And now, O God of Israel, let your word that you promised your servant David my father come true.

27"But will God really dwell on earth? The heavens, even the highest heaven, cannot contain you. How much less this temple I have built! **28**Yet give attention to your servant's prayer and his plea for mercy, O Lord my God. Hear the cry and the prayer that your servant is praying in your presence this day. **29**May your eyes be open toward this temple night and day, this place of which you said, 'My Name shall be there,' so that you will hear the prayer your servant prays toward this place. **30**Hear the supplication of your servant and of your people Israel when they pray toward this place. Hear from heaven, your dwelling place, and when you hear, forgive.

31"When a man wrongs his neighbor and is required to take an oath and he comes and swears the oath before your altar in this temple, **32**then hear from heaven and act. Judge between your servants, condemning the guilty and bringing down on his own head what he has done. Declare the innocent not guilty, and so establish his innocence.

33"When your people Israel have been defeated by an enemy because they have sinned against you, and when they turn back to you and confess your name, praying and making supplication to you in this temple, **34**then hear from heaven and forgive the sin of your people Israel and bring them back to the land you gave to their fathers.

35"When the heavens are shut up and there is no rain because your people have sinned against you, and when they pray toward this place and confess your name and turn from their sin because you have afflicted them, **36**then hear from heaven and forgive the sin of your servants, your people Israel. Teach them the right way to live, and send rain on the land you gave your people for an inheritance.

37"When famine or plague comes to the land, or blight or mildew, locusts or grasshoppers, or when an enemy besieges them in any of their cities, whatever disaster or disease may come, **38**and when a prayer or plea is made by any of your people Israel — each one aware of the afflictions of his own heart, and spreading out his hands toward this temple — **39**then hear from heaven, your dwelling place. Forgive and act; deal with each man according to all he does, since you know his heart (for you alone know the hearts of all men), **40**so that they will fear you all the time they live in the land you gave our fathers.

41"As for the foreigner who does not belong to your people Israel but has come from a distant land because of your name — **42**for men will hear of your great name and your mighty hand and your outstretched arm — when he comes and prays toward this temple, **43**then hear from heaven, your dwelling place, and do whatever the foreigner asks of you, so that all the peoples of the earth may know your name and fear you, as do your own people Israel, and may know that this house I have built bears your Name.

44"When your people go to war against their enemies, wherever you send them, and when they pray to the Lord toward the city you have chosen and the temple I have built for your Name, **45**then hear from heaven their prayer and their plea, and uphold their cause.

46"When they sin against you—for there is no one who does not sin—and you become angry with them and give them over to the enemy, who takes them captive to his own land, far away or near; **47**and if they have a change of heart in the land where they are held captive, and repent and plead with you in the land of their conquerors and say, 'We have sinned, we have done wrong, we have acted wickedly'; **48**and if they turn back to you with all their heart and soul in the land of their enemies who took them captive, and pray to you toward the land you gave their fathers, toward the city you have chosen and the temple I have built for your Name; **49**then from heaven, your dwelling place, hear their prayer and their plea, and uphold their cause. **50**And forgive your people, who have sinned against you; forgive all the offenses they have committed against you, and cause their conquerors to show them mercy; **51**for they are your people and your inheritance, whom you brought out of Egypt, out of that iron-smelting furnace.

52"May your eyes be open to your servant's plea and to the plea of your people Israel, and may you listen to them whenever they cry out to you. **53**For you singled them out from all the nations of the world to be your own inheritance, just as you declared through your servant Moses when you, O Sovereign Lord, brought our fathers out of Egypt."

54When Solomon had finished all these prayers and supplications to the Lord, he rose from before the altar of the Lord, where he had been kneeling with his hands spread out toward heaven. **55**He stood and blessed the whole assembly of Israel in a loud voice, saying:

56"Praise be to the Lord, who has given rest to his people Israel just as he promised. Not one word has failed of all the good promises he gave through his servant Moses. **57**May the Lord our God be with us as he was with our fathers; may he never leave us nor forsake us. **58**May he turn our hearts to him, to walk in all his ways and to keep the commands, decrees and regulations he gave our fathers. **59**And may these words of mine, which I have prayed before the Lord, be near to the Lord our God day and night, that he may uphold the cause of his servant and the cause of his people Israel according to each day's need, **60**so that all the peoples of the earth may know that the Lord is God and that there is no other. **61**But your hearts must be fully committed to the Lord our God, to live by his decrees and obey his commands, as at this time."

The Dedication of the Temple

62Then the king and all Israel with him offered sacrifices before the Lord. **63**Solomon offered a sacrifice of fellowship offerings[a] to the Lord: twenty-two thousand cattle and a hundred and twenty thousand sheep and goats. So the king and all the Israelites dedicated the temple of the Lord.

64On that same day the king consecrated the middle part of the courtyard in front of the temple of the Lord, and there he offered burnt offerings, grain offerings and the fat of the fellowship offerings, because the bronze altar before the Lord was too small to hold the burnt offerings, the grain offerings and the fat of the fellowship offerings.

65So Solomon observed the festival at that time, and all Israel with him—a vast assembly, people from Lebo[b] Hamath to the Wadi of Egypt. They celebrated it before the Lord our God for seven days and seven days more, fourteen days in all. **66**On the following day he sent the people away. They blessed the king and then went home, joyful and glad in heart for all the good things the Lord had done for his servant David and his people Israel.

The Lord Appears to Solomon

9 When Solomon had finished building the temple of the Lord and the royal palace, and had achieved all he had desired to do, **2**the Lord appeared to him a second time, as he had appeared to him at Gibeon. **3**The Lord said to him:

"I have heard the prayer and plea you

---

a63 Traditionally *peace offerings*; also in verse 64   *b65* Or *from the entrance to* have made before me; I have consecrated this temple, which you have built, by putting my Name there forever. My eyes and my heart will always be there. 4"As for you, if you walk before me in integrity of heart and uprightness, as David your father did, and do all I command and observe my decrees and laws, 5I will establish your royal throne over Israel forever, as I promised David your father when I said, 'You shall never fail to have a man on the throne of Israel.'

6"But if you*a* or your sons turn away from me and do not observe the commands and decrees I have given you*a* and go off to serve other gods and worship them, 7then I will cut off Israel from the land I have given them and will reject this temple I have consecrated for my Name. Israel will then become a byword and an object of ridicule among all peoples. 8And though this temple is now imposing, all who pass by will be appalled and will scoff and say, 'Why has the Lord done such a thing to this land and to this temple?' 9People will answer, 'Because they have forsaken the Lord their God, who brought their fathers out of Egypt, and have embraced other gods, worshiping and serving them — that is why the Lord brought all this disaster on them.' "

Solomon's Other Activities

10At the end of twenty years, during which Solomon built these two buildings — the temple of the Lord and the royal palace — 11King Solomon gave twenty towns in Galilee to Hiram king of Tyre, because Hiram had supplied him with all the cedar and pine and gold he wanted. 12But when Hiram went from Tyre to see the towns that Solomon had given him, he was not pleased with them. 13"What kind of towns are these you have given me, my brother?" he asked. And he called them the Land of Cabul,*b* a name they have to this day. 14Now Hiram had sent to the king 120 talents*c* of gold.

15Here is the account of the forced labor King Solomon conscripted to build the Lord's temple, his own palace, the supporting terraces,*d* the wall of Jerusalem, and

Hazor, Megiddo and Gezer. 16(Pharaoh king of Egypt had attacked and captured Gezer. He had set it on fire. He killed its Canaanite inhabitants and then gave it as a wedding gift to his daughter, Solomon's wife. 17And Solomon rebuilt Gezer.) He built up Lower Beth Horon, 18Baalath, and Tadmor*e* in the desert, within his land, 19as well as all his store cities and the towns for his chariots and for his horses*f* — whatever he desired to build in Jerusalem, in Lebanon and throughout all the territory he ruled.

20All the people left from the Amorites, Hittites, Perizzites, Hivites and Jebusites (these peoples were not Israelites), 21that is, their descendants remaining in the land, whom the Israelites could not exterminate*g* — these Solomon conscripted for his slave labor force, as it is to this day. 22But Solomon did not make slaves of any of the Israelites; they were his fighting men, his government officials, his officers, his captains, and the commanders of his chariots and charioteers. 23They were also the chief officials in charge of Solomon's projects — 550 officials supervising the men who did the work.

24After Pharaoh's daughter had come up from the City of David to the palace Solomon had built for her, he constructed the supporting terraces.

25Three times a year Solomon sacrificed burnt offerings and fellowship offerings*h* on the altar he had built for the Lord, burning incense before the Lord along with them, and so fulfilled the temple obligations.

26King Solomon also built ships at Ezion Geber, which is near Elath in Edom, on the shore of the Red Sea.*i* 27And Hiram sent his men — sailors who knew the sea — to serve in the fleet with Solomon's men. 28They sailed to Ophir and brought back 420 talents*j* of gold, which they delivered to King Solomon.

The Queen of Sheba Visits Solomon

10 When the queen of Sheba heard about the fame of Solomon and his relation to the name of the Lord, she came to test him with hard questions. 2Arriving at Jerusalem with a very great caravan — with camels carrying spices, large quantities of gold, and precious stones — she came to Sol-

---

a6 The Hebrew is plural.   *b13* Cabul sounds like the Hebrew for *good-for-nothing*.   *c14* That is, about 4 1/2 tons (about 4 metric tons)   *d15* Or *the Millo*; also in verse 24   *e18* The Hebrew may also be read *Tamar*. *f19* Or *charioteers*   *g21* The Hebrew term refers to the irrevocable giving over of things or persons to the Lord, often by totally destroying them.   *h25* Traditionally *peace offerings*   *i26* Hebrew *Yam Suph*; that is, Sea of Reeds   *j28* That is, about 16 tons (about 14.5 metric tons) omon and talked with him about all that she had on her mind. ³Solomon answered all her questions; nothing was too hard for the king to explain to her. ⁴When the queen of Sheba saw all the wisdom of Solomon and the palace he had built, ⁵the food on his table, the seating of his officials, the attending servants in their robes, his cupbearers, and the burnt offerings he made at*a* the temple of the LORD, she was overwhelmed.

⁶She said to the king, "The report I heard in my own country about your achievements and your wisdom is true. ⁷But I did not believe these things until I came and saw with my own eyes. Indeed, not even half was told me; in wisdom and wealth you have far exceeded the report I heard. ⁸How happy your men must be! How happy your officials, who continually stand before you and hear your wisdom! ⁹Praise be to the LORD your God, who has delighted in you and placed you on the throne of Israel. Because of the LORD's eternal love for Israel, he has made you king, to maintain justice and righteousness."

¹⁰And she gave the king 120 talents*b* of gold, large quantities of spices, and precious stones. Never again were so many spices brought in as those the queen of Sheba gave to King Solomon.

¹¹(Hiram's ships brought gold from Ophir; and from there they brought great cargoes of almugwood*c* and precious stones. ¹²The king used the almugwood to make supports for the temple of the LORD and for the royal palace, and to make harps and lyres for the musicians. So much almugwood has never been imported or seen since that day.)

¹³King Solomon gave the queen of Sheba all she desired and asked for, besides what he had given her out of his royal bounty. Then she left and returned with her retinue to her own country.

Solomon's Splendor

¹⁴The weight of the gold that Solomon received yearly was 666 talents,*d* ¹⁵not including the revenues from merchants and traders and from all the Arabian kings and the governors of the land.

¹⁶King Solomon made two hundred large shields of hammered gold; six hundred be-kas*e* of gold went into each shield. ¹⁷He also made three hundred small shields of hammered gold, with three minas*f* of gold in each shield. The king put them in the Palace of the Forest of Lebanon.

¹⁸Then the king made a great throne inlaid with ivory and overlaid with fine gold. ¹⁹The throne had six steps, and its back had a rounded top. On both sides of the seat were armrests, with a lion standing beside each of them. ²⁰Twelve lions stood on the six steps, one at either end of each step. Nothing like it had ever been made for any other kingdom. ²¹All King Solomon's goblets were gold, and all the household articles in the Palace of the Forest of Lebanon were pure gold. Nothing was made of silver, because silver was considered of little value in Solomon's days. ²²The king had a fleet of trading ships*g* at sea along with the ships of Hiram. Once every three years it returned, carrying gold, silver and ivory, and apes and baboons.

²³King Solomon was greater in riches and wisdom than all the other kings of the earth. ²⁴The whole world sought audience with Solomon to hear the wisdom God had put in his heart. ²⁵Year after year, everyone who came brought a gift — articles of silver and gold, robes, weapons and spices, and horses and mules.

²⁶Solomon accumulated chariots and horses; he had fourteen hundred chariots and twelve thousand horses,*h* which he kept in the chariot cities and also with him in Jerusalem. ²⁷The king made silver as common in Jerusalem as stones, and cedar as plentiful as sycamore-fig trees in the foothills. ²⁸Solomon's horses were imported from Egypt*i* and from Kue*j* — the royal merchants purchased them from Kue. ²⁹They imported a chariot from Egypt for six hundred shekels*k* of silver, and a horse for a hundred and fifty.*l* They also exported them to all the kings of the Hittites and of the Arameans.

Solomon's Wives

11 King Solomon, however, loved many foreign women besides Pharaoh's daughter — Moabites, Ammonites, Edomites, Sidonians and Hittites. ²They

---

a5 Or *the ascent by which he went up to*   *b10* That is, about 4 1/2 tons (about 4 metric tons)   *c11* Probably a variant of *algumwood*; also in verse 12   *d14* That is, about 25 tons (about 23 metric tons)   *e16* That is, about 7 1/2 pounds (about 3.5 kilograms)   *f17* That is, about 3 3/4 pounds (about 1.7 kilograms)   *g22* Hebrew *of ships of Tarshish*   *h26* Or *charioteers*   *i28* Or possibly *Muzur*, a region in Cilicia; also in verse 29   *j28* Probably *Cilicia*   *k29* That is, about 15 pounds (about 7 kilograms)   *l29* That is, about 3 3/4 pounds (about 1.7 kilograms)

THE ROMANCE GOD

Twelve months ago Becky was really excited about the Lord. She spent time with him every day. She talked a lot about what he meant in her life. She was determined to please him, no matter what. In short, everyone could tell he was more important to Becky than anything or anyone else.

Now, however, Becky no longer seems quite so interested in God. What excites her these days is Eric. Now Becky spends time with Eric every day. She talks nonstop about how much Eric means to her. Her one goal seems to be to please her new boyfriend, no matter what. In short, it's obvious to everyone that Eric means more to Becky than anything or anyone—including God.

Look It Up

Becky is committed to "The Religion of Romantic Relationships." Basically she has replaced the God of the Bible with Eric "the boyfriend god." Her situation isn't new. Even wise King Solomon of Israel got caught in the same trap.

Just like Becky, Solomon started out great. He sincerely loved the Lord and eagerly sought God's wisdom. And God used him greatly. But then Solomon began to let romantic relationships rule his life. In complete disobedience to God's Word, he married hundreds of foreign women with ungodly beliefs . . . with tragic results. "As Solomon grew old, his wives turned his heart after other gods, and his heart was not fully devoted to the LORD his God, as the heart of David his father had been" (1 Kings 11:4).

Think It Through

What specific changes could Becky make in her relationship so that she's not guilty of idolatry? Is it only when a Christian dates a non-Christian that there is the danger of idolatry? Or is it possible for a Christian to become obsessed with another Christian?

Remember: Being in a dating relationship is not wrong, unless in your attitudes and actions you're more concerned with that person and more dedicated to him or her than you are to God.

Work It Out

See if you can come up with five danger signs that might indicate an idolatrous dating relationship. List some of the possible ways Becky's idolatry might come back to haunt her.

Nail It Down

Read 1 Kings 11:1–13 for consequences of Solomon's idolatrous romances.

Turn to pages 190, 483 and 713 for other readings on idols.
Turn to page 358 for Tuesday's reading.

Topic

IDOLS

were from nations about which the LORD had told the Israelites, "You must not intermarry with them, because they will surely turn your hearts after their gods." Nevertheless, Solomon held fast to them in love. ³He had seven hundred wives of royal birth and three hundred concubines, and his wives led him astray. ⁴As Solomon grew old, his wives turned his heart after other gods, and his heart was not fully devoted to the LORD his God, as the heart of David his father had been. ⁵He followed Ashtoreth the goddess of the Sidonians, and Molech*ᵃ* the detestable god of the Ammonites. ⁶So Solomon did evil in the eyes of the LORD; he did not follow the LORD completely, as David his father had done.

⁷On a hill east of Jerusalem, Solomon built a high place for Chemosh the detestable god of Moab, and for Molech the detestable god of the Ammonites. ⁸He did the same for all his foreign wives, who burned incense and offered sacrifices to their gods.

⁹The LORD became angry with Solomon because his heart had turned away from the LORD, the God of Israel, who had appeared to him twice. ¹⁰Although he had forbidden Solomon to follow other gods, Solomon did not keep the LORD's command. ¹¹So the LORD said to Solomon, "Since this is your attitude and you have not kept my covenant and my decrees, which I commanded you, I will most certainly tear the kingdom away from you and give it to one of your subordinates. ¹²Nevertheless, for the sake of David your father, I will not do it during your lifetime. I will tear it out of the hand of your son. ¹³Yet I will not tear the whole kingdom from him, but will give him one tribe for the sake of David my servant and for the sake of Jerusalem, which I have chosen."

Solomon's Adversaries

¹⁴Then the LORD raised up against Solomon an adversary, Hadad the Edomite, from the royal line of Edom. ¹⁵Earlier when David was fighting with Edom, Joab the commander of the army, who had gone up to bury the dead, had struck down all the men in Edom. ¹⁶Joab and all the Israelites stayed there for six months, until they had destroyed all the men in Edom. ¹⁷But Hadad, still only a boy, fled to Egypt with some Edomite officials who had served his father. ¹⁸They set out from Midian and went to Paran. Then taking men from Paran with them, they went to Egypt, to Pharaoh king of Egypt, who gave Hadad a house and land and provided him with food.

¹⁹Pharaoh was so pleased with Hadad that he gave him a sister of his own wife, Queen Tahpenes, in marriage. ²⁰The sister of Tahpenes bore him a son named Genubath, whom Tahpenes brought up in the royal palace. There Genubath lived with Pharaoh's own children.

²¹While he was in Egypt, Hadad heard that David rested with his fathers and that Joab the commander of the army was also dead. Then Hadad said to Pharaoh, "Let me go, that I may return to my own country."

²²"What have you lacked here that you want to go back to your own country?" Pharaoh asked.

"Nothing," Hadad replied, "but do let me go!"

²³And God raised up against Solomon another adversary, Rezon son of Eliada, who had fled from his master, Hadadezer king of Zobah. ²⁴He gathered men around him and became the leader of a band of rebels when David destroyed the forces*ᵇ* ₁of Zobah₎; the rebels went to Damascus, where they settled and took control. ²⁵Rezon was Israel's adversary as long as Solomon lived, adding to the trouble caused by Hadad. So Rezon ruled in Aram and was hostile toward Israel.

Jeroboam Rebels Against Solomon

²⁶Also, Jeroboam son of Nebat rebelled against the king. He was one of Solomon's officials, an Ephraimite from Zeredah, and his mother was a widow named Zeruah.

²⁷Here is the account of how he rebelled against the king: Solomon had built the supporting terraces*ᶜ* and had filled in the gap in the wall of the city of David his father. ²⁸Now Jeroboam was a man of standing, and when Solomon saw how well the young man did his work, he put him in charge of the whole labor force of the house of Joseph.

²⁹About that time Jeroboam was going out of Jerusalem, and Ahijah the prophet of Shiloh met him on the way, wearing a new cloak. The two of them were alone out in the country, ³⁰and Ahijah took hold of the new cloak he was wearing and tore it into twelve pieces. ³¹Then he said to Jeroboam, "Take ten pieces for yourself, for this is what the LORD, the God of Israel, says: 'See, I am going to tear the kingdom out of Solomon's hand and give you ten tribes. ³²But for the sake of my servant David and the city of Jerusalem, which I have chosen out of all the tribes of

---

*ᵃ5 Hebrew *Milcom*; also in verse 33   *ᵇ24 Hebrew *destroyed them*   *ᶜ27 Or *the Millo*

Israel, he will have one tribe. **33**I will do this because they have[a] forsaken me and worshiped Ashtoreth the goddess of the Sidonians, Chemosh the god of the Moabites, and Molech the god of the Ammonites, and have not walked in my ways, nor done what is right in my eyes, nor kept my statutes and laws as David, Solomon's father, did.

34" 'But I will not take the whole kingdom out of Solomon's hand; I have made him ruler all the days of his life for the sake of David my servant, whom I chose and who observed my commands and statutes. **35**I will take the kingdom from his son's hands and give you ten tribes. **36**I will give one tribe to his son so that David my servant may always have a lamp before me in Jerusalem, the city where I chose to put my Name. **37**However, as for you, I will take you, and you will rule over all that your heart desires; you will be king over Israel. **38**If you do whatever I command you and walk in my ways and do what is right in my eyes by keeping my statutes and commands, as David my servant did, I will be with you. I will build you a dynasty as enduring as the one I built for David and will give Israel to you. **39**I will humble David's descendants because of this, but not forever.' "

40Solomon tried to kill Jeroboam, but Jeroboam fled to Egypt, to Shishak the king, and stayed there until Solomon's death.

Solomon's Death

41As for the other events of Solomon's reign — all he did and the wisdom he displayed — are they not written in the book of the annals of Solomon? **42**Solomon reigned in Jerusalem over all Israel forty years. **43**Then he rested with his fathers and was buried in the city of David his father. And Rehoboam his son succeeded him as king.

Israel Rebels Against Rehoboam

12 Rehoboam went to Shechem, for all the Israelites had gone there to make him king. **2**When Jeroboam son of Nebat heard this (he was still in Egypt, where he had fled from King Solomon), he returned from[b] Egypt. **3**So they sent for Jeroboam, and he and the whole assembly of Israel went to Rehoboam and said to him: **4**"Your father put a heavy yoke on us, but now lighten the harsh labor and the heavy yoke he put on us, and we will serve you."

5Rehoboam answered, "Go away for three days and then come back to me." So the people went away.

6Then King Rehoboam consulted the elders who had served his father Solomon during his lifetime. "How would you advise me to answer these people?" he asked.

7They replied, "If today you will be a servant to these people and serve them and give them a favorable answer, they will always be your servants."

8But Rehoboam rejected the advice the elders gave him and consulted the young men who had grown up with him and were serving him. **9**He asked them, "What is your advice? How should we answer these people who say to me, 'Lighten the yoke your father put on us'?"

10The young men who had grown up with him replied, "Tell these people who have said to you, 'Your father put a heavy yoke on us, but make our yoke lighter' — tell them, 'My little finger is thicker than my father's waist. **11**My father laid on you a heavy yoke; I will make it even heavier. My father scourged you with whips; I will scourge you with scorpions.' "

12Three days later Jeroboam and all the people returned to Rehoboam, as the king had said, "Come back to me in three days." **13**The king answered the people harshly. Rejecting the advice given him by the elders, **14**he followed the advice of the young men and said, "My father made your yoke heavy; I will make it even heavier. My father scourged you with whips; I will scourge you with scorpions." **15**So the king did not listen to the people, for this turn of events was from the LORD, to fulfill the word the LORD had spoken to Jeroboam son of Nebat through Ahijah the Shilonite.

16When all Israel saw that the king refused to listen to them, they answered the king:

"What share do we have in David,
    what part in Jesse's son?
To your tents, O Israel!
    Look after your own house, O David!"

So the Israelites went home. **17**But as for the Israelites who were living in the towns of Judah, Rehoboam still ruled over them.

18King Rehoboam sent out Adoniram,[c] who was in charge of forced labor, but all Israel stoned him to death. King Rehoboam, however, managed to get into his chariot and escape to Jerusalem. **19**So Israel has

---

[a]33 Hebrew; Septuagint, Vulgate and Syriac *because he has*   [b]2 Or *he remained in*   [c]18 Some Septuagint manuscripts and Syriac (see also 1 Kings 4:6 and 5:14); Hebrew *Adoram*

been in rebellion against the house of David to this day.

²⁰When all the Israelites heard that Jeroboam had returned, they sent and called him to the assembly and made him king over all Israel. Only the tribe of Judah remained loyal to the house of David.

²¹When Rehoboam arrived in Jerusalem, he mustered the whole house of Judah and the tribe of Benjamin—a hundred and eighty thousand fighting men—to make war against the house of Israel and to regain the kingdom for Rehoboam son of Solomon.

²²But this word of God came to Shemaiah the man of God: ²³"Say to Rehoboam son of Solomon king of Judah, to the whole house of Judah and Benjamin, and to the rest of the people, ²⁴'This is what the LORD says: Do not go up to fight against your brothers, the Israelites. Go home, every one of you, for this is my doing.'" So they obeyed the word of the LORD and went home again, as the LORD had ordered.

Golden Calves at Bethel and Dan

²⁵Then Jeroboam fortified Shechem in the hill country of Ephraim and lived there. From there he went out and built up Peniel.ᵃ

²⁶Jeroboam thought to himself, "The kingdom will now likely revert to the house of David. ²⁷If these people go up to offer sacrifices at the temple of the LORD in Jerusalem, they will again give their allegiance to their lord, Rehoboam king of Judah. They will kill me and return to King Rehoboam."

²⁸After seeking advice, the king made two golden calves. He said to the people, "It is too much for you to go up to Jerusalem. Here are your gods, O Israel, who brought you up out of Egypt." ²⁹One he set up in Bethel, and the other in Dan. ³⁰And this thing became a sin; the people went even as far as Dan to worship the one there.

³¹Jeroboam built shrines on high places and appointed priests from all sorts of people, even though they were not Levites. ³²He instituted a festival on the fifteenth day of the eighth month, like the festival held in Judah, and offered sacrifices on the altar. This he did in Bethel, sacrificing to the calves he had made. And at Bethel he also installed priests at the high places he had made. ³³On the fifteenth day of the eighth month, a month of his own choosing, he offered sacrifices on the altar he had built at Bethel. So

he instituted the festival for the Israelites and went up to the altar to make offerings.

The Man of God From Judah

13 By the word of the LORD a man of God came from Judah to Bethel, as Jeroboam was standing by the altar to make an offering. ²He cried out against the altar by the word of the LORD: "O altar, altar! This is what the LORD says: 'A son named Josiah will be born to the house of David. On you he will sacrifice the priests of the high places who now make offerings here, and human bones will be burned on you.'" ³That same day the man of God gave a sign: "This is the sign the LORD has declared: The altar will be split apart and the ashes on it will be poured out."

⁴When King Jeroboam heard what the man of God cried out against the altar at Bethel, he stretched out his hand from the altar and said, "Seize him!" But the hand he stretched out toward the man shriveled up, so that he could not pull it back. ⁵Also, the altar was split apart and its ashes poured out according to the sign given by the man of God by the word of the LORD.

⁶Then the king said to the man of God, "Intercede with the LORD your God and pray for me that my hand may be restored." So the man of God interceded with the LORD, and the king's hand was restored and became as it was before.

⁷The king said to the man of God, "Come home with me and have something to eat, and I will give you a gift."

⁸But the man of God answered the king, "Even if you were to give me half your possessions, I would not go with you, nor would I eat bread or drink water here. ⁹For I was commanded by the word of the LORD: 'You must not eat bread or drink water or return by the way you came.'" ¹⁰So he took another road and did not return by the way he had come to Bethel.

¹¹Now there was a certain old prophet living in Bethel, whose sons came and told him all that the man of God had done there that day. They also told their father what he had said to the king. ¹²Their father asked them, "Which way did he go?" And his sons showed him which road the man of God from Judah had taken. ¹³So he said to his sons, "Saddle the donkey for me." And when they had saddled the donkey for him, he mounted it ¹⁴and rode after the man of God.

ᵃ25 Hebrew *Penuel*, a variant of *Peniel*

He found him sitting under an oak tree and asked, "Are you the man of God who came from Judah?"

"I am," he replied.

15So the prophet said to him, "Come home with me and eat."

16The man of God said, "I cannot turn back and go with you, nor can I eat bread or drink water with you in this place. **17**I have been told by the word of the LORD: 'You must not eat bread or drink water there or return by the way you came.' "

18The old prophet answered, "I too am a prophet, as you are. And an angel said to me by the word of the LORD: 'Bring him back with you to your house so that he may eat bread and drink water.' " (But he was lying to him.) **19**So the man of God returned with him and ate and drank in his house.

20While they were sitting at the table, the word of the LORD came to the old prophet who had brought him back. **21**He cried out to the man of God who had come from Judah, "This is what the LORD says: 'You have defied the word of the LORD and have not kept the command the LORD your God gave you. **22**You came back and ate bread and drank water in the place where he told you not to eat or drink. Therefore your body will not be buried in the tomb of your fathers.' "

23When the man of God had finished eating and drinking, the prophet who had brought him back saddled his donkey for him. **24**As he went on his way, a lion met him on the road and killed him, and his body was thrown down on the road, with both the donkey and the lion standing beside it. **25**Some people who passed by saw the body thrown down there, with the lion standing beside the body, and they went and reported it in the city where the old prophet lived.

26When the prophet who had brought him back from his journey heard of it, he said, "It is the man of God who defied the word of the LORD. The LORD has given him over to the lion, which has mauled him and killed him, as the word of the LORD had warned him."

27The prophet said to his sons, "Saddle the donkey for me," and they did so. **28**Then he went out and found the body thrown down on the road, with the donkey and the lion standing beside it. The lion had neither eaten the body nor mauled the donkey. **29**So the prophet picked up the body of the man of God, laid it on the donkey, and brought it back to his own city to mourn for him and bury him. **30**Then he laid the body in his

own tomb, and they mourned over him and said, "Oh, my brother!"

31After burying him, he said to his sons, "When I die, bury me in the grave where the man of God is buried; lay my bones beside his bones. **32**For the message he declared by the word of the LORD against the altar in Bethel and against all the shrines on the high places in the towns of Samaria will certainly come true."

33Even after this, Jeroboam did not change his evil ways, but once more appointed priests for the high places from all sorts of people. Anyone who wanted to become a priest he consecrated for the high places. **34**This was the sin of the house of Jeroboam that led to its downfall and to its destruction from the face of the earth.

Ahijah's Prophecy Against Jeroboam

14 At that time Abijah son of Jeroboam became ill, **2**and Jeroboam said to his wife, "Go, disguise yourself, so you won't be recognized as the wife of Jeroboam. Then go to Shiloh. Ahijah the prophet is there — the one who told me I would be king over this people. **3**Take ten loaves of bread with you, some cakes and a jar of honey, and go to him. He will tell you what will happen to the boy." **4**So Jeroboam's wife did what he said and went to Ahijah's house in Shiloh.

Now Ahijah could not see; his sight was gone because of his age. **5**But the LORD had told Ahijah, "Jeroboam's wife is coming to ask you about her son, for he is ill, and you are to give her such and such an answer. When she arrives, she will pretend to be someone else."

6So when Ahijah heard the sound of her footsteps at the door, he said, "Come in, wife of Jeroboam. Why this pretense? I have been sent to you with bad news. **7**Go, tell Jeroboam that this is what the LORD, the God of Israel, says: 'I raised you up from among the people and made you a leader over my people Israel. **8**I tore the kingdom away from the house of David and gave it to you, but you have not been like my servant David, who kept my commands and followed me with all his heart, doing only what was right in my eyes. **9**You have done more evil than all who lived before you. You have made for yourself other gods, idols made of metal; you have provoked me to anger and thrust me behind your back.

10 'Because of this, I am going to bring disaster on the house of Jeroboam. I will cut off from Jeroboam every last male in Israel — slave or free. I will burn up the house of

Jeroboam as one burns dung, until it is all gone. **11**Dogs will eat those belonging to Jeroboam who die in the city, and the birds of the air will feed on those who die in the country. The Lord has spoken!'

12"As for you, go back home. When you set foot in your city, the boy will die. **13**All Israel will mourn for him and bury him. He is the only one belonging to Jeroboam who will be buried, because he is the only one in the house of Jeroboam in whom the Lord, the God of Israel, has found anything good.

14"The Lord will raise up for himself a king over Israel who will cut off the family of Jeroboam. This is the day! What? Yes, even now.*a* **15**And the Lord will strike Israel, so that it will be like a reed swaying in the water. He will uproot Israel from this good land that he gave to their forefathers and scatter them beyond the River,*b* because they provoked the Lord to anger by making Asherah poles.*c* **16**And he will give Israel up because of the sins Jeroboam has committed and has caused Israel to commit."

17Then Jeroboam's wife got up and left and went to Tirzah. As soon as she stepped over the threshold of the house, the boy died. **18**They buried him, and all Israel mourned for him, as the Lord had said through his servant the prophet Ahijah.

19The other events of Jeroboam's reign, his wars and how he ruled, are written in the book of the annals of the kings of Israel. **20**He reigned for twenty-two years and then rested with his fathers. And Nadab his son succeeded him as king.

Rehoboam King of Judah

21Rehoboam son of Solomon was king in Judah. He was forty-one years old when he became king, and he reigned seventeen years in Jerusalem, the city the Lord had chosen out of all the tribes of Israel in which to put his Name. His mother's name was Naamah; she was an Ammonite.

22Judah did evil in the eyes of the Lord. By the sins they committed they stirred up his jealous anger more than their fathers had done. **23**They also set up for themselves high places, sacred stones and Asherah poles on every high hill and under every spreading tree. **24**There were even male shrine prostitutes in the land; the people engaged in all the detestable practices of the nations the Lord had driven out before the Israelites.

25In the fifth year of King Rehoboam, Shishak king of Egypt attacked Jerusalem. **26**He carried off the treasures of the temple of the Lord and the treasures of the royal palace. He took everything, including all the gold shields Solomon had made. **27**So King Rehoboam made bronze shields to replace them and assigned these to the commanders of the guard on duty at the entrance to the royal palace. **28**Whenever the king went to the Lord's temple, the guards bore the shields, and afterward they returned them to the guardroom.

29As for the other events of Rehoboam's reign, and all he did, are they not written in the book of the annals of the kings of Judah? **30**There was continual warfare between Rehoboam and Jeroboam. **31**And Rehoboam rested with his fathers and was buried with them in the City of David. His mother's name was Naamah; she was an Ammonite. And Abijah*d* his son succeeded him as king.

Abijah King of Judah

15 In the eighteenth year of the reign of Jeroboam son of Nebat, Abijah*e* became king of Judah, **2**and he reigned in Jerusalem three years. His mother's name was Maacah daughter of Abishalom.*f*

3He committed all the sins his father had done before him; his heart was not fully devoted to the Lord his God, as the heart of David his forefather had been. **4**Nevertheless, for David's sake the Lord his God gave him a lamp in Jerusalem by raising up a son to succeed him and by making Jerusalem strong. **5**For David had done what was right in the eyes of the Lord and had not failed to keep any of the Lord's commands all the days of his life — except in the case of Uriah the Hittite.

6There was war between Rehoboam*g* and Jeroboam throughout ⌊Abijah's⌋ lifetime. **7**As for the other events of Abijah's reign, and all he did, are they not written in the book of the annals of the kings of Judah? There was war between Abijah and Jeroboam. **8**And Abijah rested with his fathers and was buried in the City of David. And Asa his son succeeded him as king.

a14 The meaning of the Hebrew for this sentence is uncertain. *b15* That is, the Euphrates *c15* That is, symbols of the goddess Asherah; here and elsewhere in 1 Kings *d31* Some Hebrew manuscripts and Septuagint (see also 2 Chron. 12:16); most Hebrew manuscripts *Abijam* *e1* Some Hebrew manuscripts and Septuagint (see also 2 Chron. 12:16); most Hebrew manuscripts *Abijam*; also in verses 7 and 8 *f2* A variant of *Absalom*; also in verse 10 *g6* Most Hebrew manuscripts; some Hebrew manuscripts and Syriac *Abijam* (that is, Abijah)

Asa King of Judah

⁹In the twentieth year of Jeroboam king of Israel, Asa became king of Judah, ¹⁰and he reigned in Jerusalem forty-one years. His grandmother's name was Maacah daughter of Abishalom.

¹¹Asa did what was right in the eyes of the LORD, as his father David had done. ¹²He expelled the male shrine prostitutes from the land and got rid of all the idols his fathers had made. ¹³He even deposed his grandmother Maacah from her position as queen mother, because she had made a repulsive Asherah pole. Asa cut the pole down and burned it in the Kidron Valley. ¹⁴Although he did not remove the high places, Asa's heart was fully committed to the LORD all his life. ¹⁵He brought into the temple of the LORD the silver and gold and the articles that he and his father had dedicated.

¹⁶There was war between Asa and Baasha king of Israel throughout their reigns. ¹⁷Baasha king of Israel went up against Judah and fortified Ramah to prevent anyone from leaving or entering the territory of Asa king of Judah.

¹⁸Asa then took all the silver and gold that was left in the treasuries of the LORD's temple and of his own palace. He entrusted it to his officials and sent them to Ben-Hadad son of Tabrimmon, the son of Hezion, the king of Aram, who was ruling in Damascus. ¹⁹"Let there be a treaty between me and you," he said, "as there was between my father and your father. See, I am sending you a gift of silver and gold. Now break your treaty with Baasha king of Israel so he will withdraw from me."

²⁰Ben-Hadad agreed with King Asa and sent the commanders of his forces against the towns of Israel. He conquered Ijon, Dan, Abel Beth Maacah and all Kinnereth in addition to Naphtali. ²¹When Baasha heard this, he stopped building Ramah and withdrew to Tirzah. ²²Then King Asa issued an order to all Judah—no one was exempt—and they carried away from Ramah the stones and timber Baasha had been using there. With them King Asa built up Geba in Benjamin, and also Mizpah.

²³As for all the other events of Asa's reign, all his achievements, all he did and the cities he built, are they not written in the book of the annals of the kings of Judah? In his old age, however, his feet became diseased. ²⁴Then Asa rested with his fathers and was buried with them in the city of his father

David. And Jehoshaphat his son succeeded him as king.

Nadab King of Israel

²⁵Nadab son of Jeroboam became king of Israel in the second year of Asa king of Judah, and he reigned over Israel two years. ²⁶He did evil in the eyes of the LORD, walking in the ways of his father and in his sin, which he had caused Israel to commit.

²⁷Baasha son of Ahijah of the house of Issachar plotted against him, and he struck him down at Gibbethon, a Philistine town, while Nadab and all Israel were besieging it. ²⁸Baasha killed Nadab in the third year of Asa king of Judah and succeeded him as king.

²⁹As soon as he began to reign, he killed Jeroboam's whole family. He did not leave Jeroboam anyone that breathed, but destroyed them all, according to the word of the LORD given through his servant Ahijah the Shilonite— ³⁰because of the sins Jeroboam had committed and had caused Israel to commit, and because he provoked the LORD, the God of Israel, to anger.

³¹As for the other events of Nadab's reign, and all he did, are they not written in the book of the annals of the kings of Israel? ³²There was war between Asa and Baasha king of Israel throughout their reigns.

Baasha King of Israel

³³In the third year of Asa king of Judah, Baasha son of Ahijah became king of all Israel in Tirzah, and he reigned twenty-four years. ³⁴He did evil in the eyes of the LORD, walking in the ways of Jeroboam and in his sin, which he had caused Israel to commit.

16 Then the word of the LORD came to Jehu son of Hanani against Baasha: ²"I lifted you up from the dust and made you leader of my people Israel, but you walked in the ways of Jeroboam and caused my people Israel to sin and to provoke me to anger by their sins. ³So I am about to consume Baasha and his house, and I will make your house like that of Jeroboam son of Nebat. ⁴Dogs will eat those belonging to Baasha who die in the city, and the birds of the air will feed on those who die in the country."

⁵As for the other events of Baasha's reign, what he did and his achievements, are they not written in the book of the annals of the kings of Israel? ⁶Baasha rested with his fathers and was buried in Tirzah. And Elah his son succeeded him as king.

⁷Moreover, the word of the LORD came

through the prophet Jehu son of Hanani to Baasha and his house, because of all the evil he had done in the eyes of the LORD, provoking him to anger by the things he did, and becoming like the house of Jeroboam — and also because he destroyed it.

Elah King of Israel

8In the twenty-sixth year of Asa king of Judah, Elah son of Baasha became king of Israel, and he reigned in Tirzah two years.

9Zimri, one of his officials, who had command of half his chariots, plotted against him. Elah was in Tirzah at the time, getting drunk in the home of Arza, the man in charge of the palace at Tirzah. **10**Zimri came in, struck him down and killed him in the twenty-seventh year of Asa king of Judah. Then he succeeded him as king.

11As soon as he began to reign and was seated on the throne, he killed off Baasha's whole family. He did not spare a single male, whether relative or friend. **12**So Zimri destroyed the whole family of Baasha, in accordance with the word of the LORD spoken against Baasha through the prophet Jehu — **13**because of all the sins Baasha and his son Elah had committed and had caused Israel to commit, so that they provoked the LORD, the God of Israel, to anger by their worthless idols.

14As for the other events of Elah's reign, and all he did, are they not written in the book of the annals of the kings of Israel?

Zimri King of Israel

15In the twenty-seventh year of Asa king of Judah, Zimri reigned in Tirzah seven days. The army was encamped near Gibbethon, a Philistine town. **16**When the Israelites in the camp heard that Zimri had plotted against the king and murdered him, they proclaimed Omri, the commander of the army, king over Israel that very day there in the camp. **17**Then Omri and all the Israelites with him withdrew from Gibbethon and laid siege to Tirzah. **18**When Zimri saw that the city was taken, he went into the citadel of the royal palace and set the palace on fire around him. So he died, **19**because of the sins he had committed, doing evil in the eyes of the LORD and walking in the ways of Jeroboam and in the sin he had committed and had caused Israel to commit.

20As for the other events of Zimri's reign, and the rebellion he carried out, are they not written in the book of the annals of the kings of Israel?

Omri King of Israel

21Then the people of Israel were split into two factions; half supported Tibni son of Ginath for king, and the other half supported Omri. **22**But Omri's followers proved stronger than those of Tibni son of Ginath. So Tibni died and Omri became king.

23In the thirty-first year of Asa king of Judah, Omri became king of Israel, and he reigned twelve years, six of them in Tirzah. **24**He bought the hill of Samaria from Shemer for two talents*a* of silver and built a city on the hill, calling it Samaria, after Shemer, the name of the former owner of the hill.

25But Omri did evil in the eyes of the LORD and sinned more than all those before him. **26**He walked in all the ways of Jeroboam son of Nebat and in his sin, which he had caused Israel to commit, so that they provoked the LORD, the God of Israel, to anger by their worthless idols.

27As for the other events of Omri's reign, what he did and the things he achieved, are they not written in the book of the annals of the kings of Israel? **28**Omri rested with his fathers and was buried in Samaria. And Ahab his son succeeded him as king.

Ahab Becomes King of Israel

29In the thirty-eighth year of Asa king of Judah, Ahab son of Omri became king of Israel, and he reigned in Samaria over Israel twenty-two years. **30**Ahab son of Omri did more evil in the eyes of the LORD than any of those before him. **31**He not only considered it trivial to commit the sins of Jeroboam son of Nebat, but he also married Jezebel daughter of Ethbaal king of the Sidonians, and began to serve Baal and worship him. **32**He set up an altar for Baal in the temple of Baal that he built in Samaria. **33**Ahab also made an Asherah pole and did more to provoke the LORD, the God of Israel, to anger than did all the kings of Israel before him.

34In Ahab's time, Hiel of Bethel rebuilt Jericho. He laid its foundations at the cost of his firstborn son Abiram, and he set up its gates at the cost of his youngest son Segub, in accordance with the word of the LORD spoken by Joshua son of Nun.

Elijah Fed by Ravens

17 Now Elijah the Tishbite, from Tishbe*b* in Gilead, said to Ahab, "As the

---

*a*24 That is, about 150 pounds (about 70 kilograms)   *b*1 Or *Tishbite, of the settlers*

LORD, the God of Israel, lives, whom I serve, there will be neither dew nor rain in the next few years except at my word."

²Then the word of the LORD came to Elijah: ³"Leave here, turn eastward and hide in the Kerith Ravine, east of the Jordan. ⁴You will drink from the brook, and I have ordered the ravens to feed you there."

⁵So he did what the LORD had told him. He went to the Kerith Ravine, east of the Jordan, and stayed there. ⁶The ravens brought him bread and meat in the morning and bread and meat in the evening, and he drank from the brook.

The Widow at Zarephath

⁷Some time later the brook dried up because there had been no rain in the land. ⁸Then the word of the LORD came to him: ⁹"Go at once to Zarephath of Sidon and stay there. I have commanded a widow in that place to supply you with food." ¹⁰So he went to Zarephath. When he came to the town gate, a widow was there gathering sticks. He called to her and asked, "Would you bring me a little water in a jar so I may have a drink?" ¹¹As she was going to get it, he called, "And bring me, please, a piece of bread."

¹²"As surely as the LORD your God lives," she replied, "I don't have any bread—only a handful of flour in a jar and a little oil in a jug. I am gathering a few sticks to take home and make a meal for myself and my son, that we may eat it—and die."

¹³Elijah said to her, "Don't be afraid. Go home and do as you have said. But first make a small cake of bread for me from what you have and bring it to me, and then make something for yourself and your son. ¹⁴For this is what the LORD, the God of Israel, says: 'The jar of flour will not be used up and the jug of oil will not run dry until the day the LORD gives rain on the land.' "

¹⁵She went away and did as Elijah had told her. So there was food every day for Elijah and for the woman and her family. ¹⁶For the jar of flour was not used up and the jug of oil did not run dry, in keeping with the word of the LORD spoken by Elijah.

¹⁷Some time later the son of the woman who owned the house became ill. He grew worse and worse, and finally stopped breathing. ¹⁸She said to Elijah, "What do you have against me, man of God? Did you come to remind me of my sin and kill my son?"

¹⁹"Give me your son," Elijah replied. He took him from her arms, carried him to the upper room where he was staying, and laid him on his bed. ²⁰Then he cried out to the LORD, "O LORD my God, have you brought tragedy also upon this widow I am staying with, by causing her son to die?" ²¹Then he stretched himself out on the boy three times and cried to the LORD, "O LORD my God, let this boy's life return to him!"

²²The LORD heard Elijah's cry, and the boy's life returned to him, and he lived. ²³Elijah picked up the child and carried him down from the room into the house. He gave him to his mother and said, "Look, your son is alive!"

²⁴Then the woman said to Elijah, "Now I know that you are a man of God and that the word of the LORD from your mouth is the truth."

Elijah and Obadiah

18 After a long time, in the third year, the word of the LORD came to Elijah: "Go and present yourself to Ahab, and I will send rain on the land." ²So Elijah went to present himself to Ahab.

Now the famine was severe in Samaria, ³and Ahab had summoned Obadiah, who was in charge of his palace. (Obadiah was a devout believer in the LORD. ⁴While Jezebel was killing off the LORD's prophets, Obadiah had taken a hundred prophets and hidden them in two caves, fifty in each, and had supplied them with food and water.) ⁵Ahab had said to Obadiah, "Go through the land to all the springs and valleys. Maybe we can find some grass to keep the horses and mules alive so we will not have to kill any of our animals." ⁶So they divided the land they were to cover, Ahab going in one direction and Obadiah in another.

⁷As Obadiah was walking along, Elijah met him. Obadiah recognized him, bowed down to the ground, and said, "Is it really you, my lord Elijah?"

⁸"Yes," he replied. "Go tell your master, 'Elijah is here.' "

⁹"What have I done wrong," asked Obadiah, "that you are handing your servant over to Ahab to be put to death? ¹⁰As surely as the LORD your God lives, there is not a nation or kingdom where my master has not sent someone to look for you. And whenever a nation or kingdom claimed you were not there, he made them swear they could not find you. ¹¹But now you tell me to go to my master and say, 'Elijah is here.' ¹²I don't know where the Spirit of the LORD may carry you when I leave you. If I go and tell Ahab and he doesn't find you, he will kill me. Yet

I your servant have worshiped the LORD since my youth. **13**Haven't you heard, my lord, what I did while Jezebel was killing the prophets of the LORD? I hid a hundred of the LORD's prophets in two caves, fifty in each, and supplied them with food and water. **14**And now you tell me to go to my master and say, 'Elijah is here.' He will kill me!"

15Elijah said, "As the LORD Almighty lives, whom I serve, I will surely present myself to Ahab today."

Elijah on Mount Carmel

16So Obadiah went to meet Ahab and told him, and Ahab went to meet Elijah. **17**When he saw Elijah, he said to him, "Is that you, you troubler of Israel?"

18"I have not made trouble for Israel," Elijah replied. "But you and your father's family have. You have abandoned the LORD's commands and have followed the Baals. **19**Now summon the people from all over Israel to meet me on Mount Carmel. And bring the four hundred and fifty prophets of Baal and the four hundred prophets of Asherah, who eat at Jezebel's table."

20So Ahab sent word throughout all Israel and assembled the prophets on Mount Carmel. **21**Elijah went before the people and said, "How long will you waver between two opinions? If the LORD is God, follow him; but if Baal is God, follow him."

But the people said nothing.

22Then Elijah said to them, "I am the only one of the LORD's prophets left, but Baal has four hundred and fifty prophets. **23**Get two bulls for us. Let them choose one for themselves, and let them cut it into pieces and put it on the wood but not set fire to it. I will prepare the other bull and put it on the wood but not set fire to it. **24**Then you call on the name of your god, and I will call on the name of the LORD. The god who answers by fire—he is God."

Then all the people said, "What you say is good."

25Elijah said to the prophets of Baal, "Choose one of the bulls and prepare it first, since there are so many of you. Call on the name of your god, but do not light the fire." **26**So they took the bull given them and prepared it.

Then they called on the name of Baal from morning till noon. "O Baal, answer us!" they shouted. But there was no response; no one answered. And they danced around the altar they had made.

27At noon Elijah began to taunt them. "Shout louder!" he said. "Surely he is a god! Perhaps he is deep in thought, or busy, or traveling. Maybe he is sleeping and must be awakened." **28**So they shouted louder and slashed themselves with swords and spears, as was their custom, until their blood flowed. **29**Midday passed, and they continued their frantic prophesying until the time for the evening sacrifice. But there was no response, no one answered, no one paid attention.

30Then Elijah said to all the people, "Come here to me." They came to him, and he repaired the altar of the LORD, which was in ruins. **31**Elijah took twelve stones, one for each of the tribes descended from Jacob, to whom the word of the LORD had come, saying, "Your name shall be Israel." **32**With the stones he built an altar in the name of the LORD, and he dug a trench around it large enough to hold two seahs*a* of seed. **33**He arranged the wood, cut the bull into pieces and laid it on the wood. Then he said to them, "Fill four large jars with water and pour it on the offering and on the wood."

34"Do it again," he said, and they did it again.

"Do it a third time," he ordered, and they did it the third time. **35**The water ran down around the altar and even filled the trench.

36At the time of sacrifice, the prophet Elijah stepped forward and prayed: "O LORD, God of Abraham, Isaac and Israel, let it be known today that you are God in Israel and that I am your servant and have done all these things at your command. **37**Answer me, O LORD, answer me, so these people will know that you, O LORD, are God, and that you are turning their hearts back again."

38Then the fire of the LORD fell and burned up the sacrifice, the wood, the stones and the soil, and also licked up the water in the trench.

39When all the people saw this, they fell prostrate and cried, "The LORD—he is God! The LORD—he is God!"

40Then Elijah commanded them, "Seize the prophets of Baal. Don't let anyone get away!" They seized them, and Elijah had them brought down to the Kishon Valley and slaughtered there.

41And Elijah said to Ahab, "Go, eat and drink, for there is the sound of a heavy rain." **42**So Ahab went off to eat and drink, but Elijah climbed to the top of Carmel, bent down

a32 That is, probably about 13 quarts (about 15 liters)

A CLASSIC CASE OF COMMITMENT

●●●

Jon is talking to his Bible study leader.

"Richard, if I'm going to be a Christian, I mean, I want to really go for it. I don't want to play games."

"That's great, Jon. So what's the problem?"

"I guess I just feel alone. I don't know many Christians who are that serious about God. It sure would be nice to have a couple of buddies who feel the same way I do, you know?"

Look It Up
●●●●

Are you looking for someone who models true Christian commitment? You'd be hard pressed to find anyone better than the apostle Paul.

He talked about commitment. "I consider everything a loss compared to the surpassing greatness of knowing Christ Jesus my Lord, for whose sake I have lost all things" (Philippians 3:8).

He demonstrated commitment. "I have . . . been in prison . . . been flogged . . . been exposed to death again and again . . . been in danger . . . known hunger and thirst . . . gone without food . . . been cold and naked" (2 Corinthians 11:23,26–27).

Willing to give up everything. Willing to face anything. Now that's commitment.

Think It Through
●●●●

Commitment is doing the will of God even if:
• People at school make fun of your faith.
• It means losing a boyfriend or girlfriend.
• It means missing all the best parties.
• It means standing alone and saying no when everyone else is saying yes.

Could you be committed in those situations? Would you be?

Work It Out
●●●●

Commitment isn't something you can "get" once for all. It must be monitored, strengthened and guarded all the time. Here's how:

1. Take time to be alone with God and his Word today and every day.

2. Hang around mature believers. (Find a college student or married couple who really love God and see what makes them tick.)

3. Make a public commitment to Christ and then ask your friends to hold you accountable.

4. Read Paul's story in 2 Corinthians 11 each time your faith falters.

Nail It Down
●●●●

Read about the Israelites' lack of commitment in 1 Kings 18:20–21.

Turn to pages 182, 445 and 699 for other readings on commitment.
Turn to page 360 for Wednesday's reading.

Topic
●●●●

COMMITMENT

to the ground and put his face between his knees.

[43]"Go and look toward the sea," he told his servant. And he went up and looked.

"There is nothing there," he said.

Seven times Elijah said, "Go back."

[44]The seventh time the servant reported, "A cloud as small as a man's hand is rising from the sea."

So Elijah said, "Go and tell Ahab, 'Hitch up your chariot and go down before the rain stops you.'"

[45]Meanwhile, the sky grew black with clouds, the wind rose, a heavy rain came on and Ahab rode off to Jezreel. [46]The power of the LORD came upon Elijah and, tucking his cloak into his belt, he ran ahead of Ahab all the way to Jezreel.

Elijah Flees to Horeb

19 Now Ahab told Jezebel everything Elijah had done and how he had killed all the prophets with the sword. [2]So Jezebel sent a messenger to Elijah to say, "May the gods deal with me, be it ever so severely, if by this time tomorrow I do not make your life like that of one of them."

[3]Elijah was afraid[a] and ran for his life. When he came to Beersheba in Judah, he left his servant there, [4]while he himself went a day's journey into the desert. He came to a broom tree, sat down under it and prayed that he might die. "I have had enough, LORD," he said. "Take my life; I am no better than my ancestors." [5]Then he lay down under the tree and fell asleep.

All at once an angel touched him and said, "Get up and eat." [6]He looked around, and there by his head was a cake of bread baked over hot coals, and a jar of water. He ate and drank and then lay down again.

[7]The angel of the LORD came back a second time and touched him and said, "Get up and eat, for the journey is too much for you." [8]So he got up and ate and drank. Strengthened by that food, he traveled forty days and forty nights until he reached Horeb, the mountain of God. [9]There he went into a cave and spent the night.

The LORD Appears to Elijah

And the word of the LORD came to him: "What are you doing here, Elijah?"

[10]He replied, "I have been very zealous for the LORD God Almighty. The Israelites have rejected your covenant, broken down your altars, and put your prophets to death with the sword. I am the only one left, and now they are trying to kill me too."

[11]The LORD said, "Go out and stand on the mountain in the presence of the LORD, for the LORD is about to pass by."

Then a great and powerful wind tore the mountains apart and shattered the rocks before the LORD, but the LORD was not in the wind. After the wind there was an earthquake, but the LORD was not in the earthquake. [12]After the earthquake came a fire, but the LORD was not in the fire. And after the fire came a gentle whisper. [13]When Elijah heard it, he pulled his cloak over his face and went out and stood at the mouth of the cave.

Then a voice said to him, "What are you doing here, Elijah?"

[14]He replied, "I have been very zealous for the LORD God Almighty. The Israelites have rejected your covenant, broken down your altars, and put your prophets to death with the sword. I am the only one left, and now they are trying to kill me too."

[15]The LORD said to him, "Go back the way you came, and go to the Desert of Damascus. When you get there, anoint Hazael king over Aram. [16]Also, anoint Jehu son of Nimshi king over Israel, and anoint Elisha son of Shaphat from Abel Meholah to succeed you as prophet. [17]Jehu will put to death any who escape the sword of Hazael, and Elisha will put to death any who escape the sword of Jehu. [18]Yet I reserve seven thousand in Israel—all whose knees have not bowed down to Baal and all whose mouths have not kissed him."

The Call of Elisha

[19]So Elijah went from there and found Elisha son of Shaphat. He was plowing with twelve yoke of oxen, and he himself was driving the twelfth pair. Elijah went up to him and threw his cloak around him. [20]Elisha then left his oxen and ran after Elijah. "Let me kiss my father and mother goodby," he said, "and then I will come with you."

"Go back," Elijah replied. "What have I done to you?"

[21]So Elisha left him and went back. He took his yoke of oxen and slaughtered them. He burned the plowing equipment to cook the meat and gave it to the people, and they ate. Then he set out to follow Elijah and became his attendant.

a3 Or *Elijah saw*

FADED BLUE JEANS CAN'T FADE YOUR BLUES!

Mona is emotionally flat. Not excited, not suicidal . . . just blah and gloomy. The exact reason for her down cycle isn't clear. Is it because she's gained five pounds? Did it start when she failed to receive even one card on Valentine's Day? She's not sure.

After school today, at the suggestion of a friend, Mona went to the mall and purchased a new pair of faded blue jeans. She thought, "Maybe these will make me feel better."

Guess what? The jeans didn't do the trick.

Look It Up
• • • •

The Bible has a better prescription for beating the blues. Consider the case of Elijah the prophet.

After a time of great spiritual victory, he slipped into despair, " 'I have had enough, LORD. . . . Take my life.' . . . Then he lay down under the tree and fell asleep" (1 Kings 19:4–5).

That's when God went to work. He first brought him rest and refreshment (1 Kings 19:5–9). He then reassigned Elijah to service and reminded him of the other faithful servants of God (1 Kings 19:9–18).

Think It Through
• • • •

Are you experiencing feelings of hopelessness? Lack of motivation? Low energy? Difficulty communicating? A desire to sleep excessively or trouble sleeping? Low self-esteem? Behavior problems? Do you have trouble concentrating?

If so, you may be suffering from a mild case of the blues. If you have these symptoms to an extreme degree, you probably need the help of a trained professional—your family doctor, your guidance counselor or your pastor. Real recovery can begin with a simple phone call!

Work It Out
• • • •

Want to get out of the pits?

1. Ask for help. Ask God to do in your life what he did in Elijah's.

2. Tell a friend. Others cannot read your mind and are not always aware of your feelings.

3. Laugh. Spend time with a funny friend who makes you giggle.

4. Help someone else. Directing your focus outside yourself does wonders inside you.

5. Move around. You'd be amazed at how a physical fitness routine can improve your mood.

6. Be thankful. It's hard to be down when you're counting your blessings.

Nail It Down
• • • •

Read the story of Elijah's bout with the blues in 1 Kings 19:1–9.

Turn to pages 527, 601, 1197 and 1256 for other readings on depression.
Turn to page 371 for Thursday's reading.

Topic
• • • •

DEPRESSION

Ben-Hadad Attacks Samaria

20 Now Ben-Hadad king of Aram mustered his entire army. Accompanied by thirty-two kings with their horses and chariots, he went up and besieged Samaria and attacked it. **2**He sent messengers into the city to Ahab king of Israel, saying, "This is what Ben-Hadad says: **3**'Your silver and gold are mine, and the best of your wives and children are mine.' "

4The king of Israel answered, "Just as you say, my lord the king. I and all I have are yours."

5The messengers came again and said, "This is what Ben-Hadad says: 'I sent to demand your silver and gold, your wives and your children. **6**But about this time tomorrow I am going to send my officials to search your palace and the houses of your officials. They will seize everything you value and carry it away.' "

7The king of Israel summoned all the elders of the land and said to them, "See how this man is looking for trouble! When he sent for my wives and my children, my silver and my gold, I did not refuse him."

8The elders and the people all answered, "Don't listen to him or agree to his demands."

9So he replied to Ben-Hadad's messengers, "Tell my lord the king, 'Your servant will do all you demanded the first time, but this demand I cannot meet.' " They left and took the answer back to Ben-Hadad.

10Then Ben-Hadad sent another message to Ahab: "May the gods deal with me, be it ever so severely, if enough dust remains in Samaria to give each of my men a handful."

11The king of Israel answered, "Tell him: 'One who puts on his armor should not boast like one who takes it off.' "

12Ben-Hadad heard this message while he and the kings were drinking in their tents, *a* and he ordered his men: "Prepare to attack." So they prepared to attack the city.

Ahab Defeats Ben-Hadad

13Meanwhile a prophet came to Ahab king of Israel and announced, "This is what the Lord says: 'Do you see this vast army? I will give it into your hand today, and then you will know that I am the Lord.' "

14"But who will do this?" asked Ahab.

The prophet replied, "This is what the Lord says: 'The young officers of the provincial commanders will do it.' "

"And who will start the battle?" he asked.

The prophet answered, "You will."

15So Ahab summoned the young officers of the provincial commanders, 232 men. Then he assembled the rest of the Israelites, 7,000 in all. **16**They set out at noon while Ben-Hadad and the 32 kings allied with him were in their tents getting drunk. **17**The young officers of the provincial commanders went out first.

Now Ben-Hadad had dispatched scouts, who reported, "Men are advancing from Samaria."

18He said, "If they have come out for peace, take them alive; if they have come out for war, take them alive."

19The young officers of the provincial commanders marched out of the city with the army behind them **20**and each one struck down his opponent. At that, the Arameans fled, with the Israelites in pursuit. But Ben-Hadad king of Aram escaped on horseback with some of his horsemen. **21**The king of Israel advanced and overpowered the horses and chariots and inflicted heavy losses on the Arameans.

22Afterward, the prophet came to the king of Israel and said, "Strengthen your position and see what must be done, because next spring the king of Aram will attack you again."

23Meanwhile, the officials of the king of Aram advised him, "Their gods are gods of the hills. That is why they were too strong for us. But if we fight them on the plains, surely we will be stronger than they. **24**Do this: Remove all the kings from their commands and replace them with other officers. **25**You must also raise an army like the one you lost—horse for horse and chariot for chariot—so we can fight Israel on the plains. Then surely we will be stronger than they." He agreed with them and acted accordingly.

26The next spring Ben-Hadad mustered the Arameans and went up to Aphek to fight against Israel. **27**When the Israelites were also mustered and given provisions, they marched out to meet them. The Israelites camped opposite them like two small flocks of goats, while the Arameans covered the countryside.

28The man of God came up and told the king of Israel, "This is what the Lord says: 'Because the Arameans think the Lord is a god of the hills and not a god of the valleys,

a12 Or in Succoth; also in verse 16

I will deliver this vast army into your hands, and you will know that I am the LORD.' "

²⁹For seven days they camped opposite each other, and on the seventh day the battle was joined. The Israelites inflicted a hundred thousand casualties on the Aramean foot soldiers in one day. ³⁰The rest of them escaped to the city of Aphek, where the wall collapsed on twenty-seven thousand of them. And Ben-Hadad fled to the city and hid in an inner room.

³¹His officials said to him, "Look, we have heard that the kings of the house of Israel are merciful. Let us go to the king of Israel with sackcloth around our waists and ropes around our heads. Perhaps he will spare your life."

³²Wearing sackcloth around their waists and ropes around their heads, they went to the king of Israel and said, "Your servant Ben-Hadad says: 'Please let me live.' "

The king answered, "Is he still alive? He is my brother."

³³The men took this as a good sign and were quick to pick up his word. "Yes, your brother Ben-Hadad!" they said.

"Go and get him," the king said. When Ben-Hadad came out, Ahab had him come up into his chariot.

³⁴"I will return the cities my father took from your father," Ben-Hadad offered. "You may set up your own market areas in Damascus, as my father did in Samaria."

Ahab said, "On the basis of a treaty I will set you free." So he made a treaty with him, and let him go.

A Prophet Condemns Ahab

³⁵By the word of the LORD one of the sons of the prophets said to his companion, "Strike me with your weapon," but the man refused.

³⁶So the prophet said, "Because you have not obeyed the LORD, as soon as you leave me a lion will kill you." And after the man went away, a lion found him and killed him.

³⁷The prophet found another man and said, "Strike me, please." So the man struck him and wounded him. ³⁸Then the prophet went and stood by the road waiting for the king. He disguised himself with his headband down over his eyes. ³⁹As the king passed by, the prophet called out to him, "Your servant went into the thick of the battle, and someone came to me with a captive and said, 'Guard this man. If he is missing,

it will be your life for his life, or you must pay a talent[a] of silver.' ⁴⁰While your servant was busy here and there, the man disappeared."

"That is your sentence," the king of Israel said. "You have pronounced it yourself."

⁴¹Then the prophet quickly removed the headband from his eyes, and the king of Israel recognized him as one of the prophets. ⁴²He said to the king, "This is what the LORD says: 'You have set free a man I had determined should die.[b] Therefore it is your life for his life, your people for his people.' " ⁴³Sullen and angry, the king of Israel went to his palace in Samaria.

Naboth's Vineyard

21 Some time later there was an incident involving a vineyard belonging to Naboth the Jezreelite. The vineyard was in Jezreel, close to the palace of Ahab king of Samaria. ²Ahab said to Naboth, "Let me have your vineyard to use for a vegetable garden, since it is close to my palace. In exchange I will give you a better vineyard or, if you prefer, I will pay you whatever it is worth."

³But Naboth replied, "The LORD forbid that I should give you the inheritance of my fathers."

⁴So Ahab went home, sullen and angry because Naboth the Jezreelite had said, "I will not give you the inheritance of my fathers." He lay on his bed sulking and refused to eat.

⁵His wife Jezebel came in and asked him, "Why are you so sullen? Why won't you eat?"

⁶He answered her, "Because I said to Naboth the Jezreelite, 'Sell me your vineyard; or if you prefer, I will give you another vineyard in its place.' But he said, 'I will not give you my vineyard.' "

⁷Jezebel his wife said, "Is this how you act as king over Israel? Get up and eat! Cheer up. I'll get you the vineyard of Naboth the Jezreelite."

⁸So she wrote letters in Ahab's name, placed his seal on them, and sent them to the elders and nobles who lived in Naboth's city with him. ⁹In those letters she wrote:

"Proclaim a day of fasting and seat Naboth in a prominent place among the people. ¹⁰But seat two scoundrels opposite him and have them testify that

---

a39 That is, about 75 pounds (about 34 kilograms)　　b42 The Hebrew term refers to the irrevocable giving over of things or persons to the LORD, often by totally destroying them.

he has cursed both God and the king. Then take him out and stone him to death."

¹¹So the elders and nobles who lived in Naboth's city did as Jezebel directed in the letters she had written to them. ¹²They proclaimed a fast and seated Naboth in a prominent place among the people. ¹³Then two scoundrels came and sat opposite him and brought charges against Naboth before the people, saying, "Naboth has cursed both God and the king." So they took him outside the city and stoned him to death. ¹⁴Then they sent word to Jezebel: "Naboth has been stoned and is dead."

¹⁵As soon as Jezebel heard that Naboth had been stoned to death, she said to Ahab, "Get up and take possession of the vineyard of Naboth the Jezreelite that he refused to sell you. He is no longer alive, but dead." ¹⁶When Ahab heard that Naboth was dead, he got up and went down to take possession of Naboth's vineyard.

¹⁷Then the word of the LORD came to Elijah the Tishbite: ¹⁸"Go down to meet Ahab king of Israel, who rules in Samaria. He is now in Naboth's vineyard, where he has gone to take possession of it. ¹⁹Say to him, 'This is what the LORD says: Have you not murdered a man and seized his property?' Then say to him, 'This is what the LORD says: In the place where dogs licked up Naboth's blood, dogs will lick up your blood—yes, yours!' "

²⁰Ahab said to Elijah, "So you have found me, my enemy!"

"I have found you," he answered, "because you have sold yourself to do evil in the eyes of the LORD. ²¹'I am going to bring disaster on you. I will consume your descendants and cut off from Ahab every last male in Israel—slave or free. ²²I will make your house like that of Jeroboam son of Nebat and that of Baasha son of Ahijah, because you have provoked me to anger and have caused Israel to sin.'

²³"And also concerning Jezebel the LORD says: 'Dogs will devour Jezebel by the wall of[a] Jezreel.'

²⁴"Dogs will eat those belonging to Ahab who die in the city, and the birds of the air will feed on those who die in the country."

²⁵(There was never a man like Ahab, who sold himself to do evil in the eyes of the LORD, urged on by Jezebel his wife. ²⁶He behaved in the vilest manner by going after

idols, like the Amorites the LORD drove out before Israel.)

²⁷When Ahab heard these words, he tore his clothes, put on sackcloth and fasted. He lay in sackcloth and went around meekly.

²⁸Then the word of the LORD came to Elijah the Tishbite: ²⁹"Have you noticed how Ahab has humbled himself before me? Because he has humbled himself, I will not bring this disaster in his day, but I will bring it on his house in the days of his son."

Micaiah Prophesies Against Ahab

22 For three years there was no war between Aram and Israel. ²But in the third year Jehoshaphat king of Judah went down to see the king of Israel. ³The king of Israel had said to his officials, "Don't you know that Ramoth Gilead belongs to us and yet we are doing nothing to retake it from the king of Aram?"

⁴So he asked Jehoshaphat, "Will you go with me to fight against Ramoth Gilead?"

Jehoshaphat replied to the king of Israel, "I am as you are, my people as your people, my horses as your horses." ⁵But Jehoshaphat also said to the king of Israel, "First seek the counsel of the LORD."

⁶So the king of Israel brought together the prophets—about four hundred men—and asked them, "Shall I go to war against Ramoth Gilead, or shall I refrain?"

"Go," they answered, "for the Lord will give it into the king's hand."

⁷But Jehoshaphat asked, "Is there not a prophet of the LORD here whom we can inquire of?"

⁸The king of Israel answered Jehoshaphat, "There is still one man through whom we can inquire of the LORD, but I hate him because he never prophesies anything good about me, but always bad. He is Micaiah son of Imlah."

"The king should not say that," Jehoshaphat replied.

⁹So the king of Israel called one of his officials and said, "Bring Micaiah son of Imlah at once."

¹⁰Dressed in their royal robes, the king of Israel and Jehoshaphat king of Judah were sitting on their thrones at the threshing floor by the entrance of the gate of Samaria, with all the prophets prophesying before them. ¹¹Now Zedekiah son of Kenaanah had made iron horns and he declared, "This is what

---

a23 Most Hebrew manuscripts; a few Hebrew manuscripts, Vulgate and Syriac (see also 2 Kings 9:26) *the plot of ground at* the LORD says: 'With these you will gore the Arameans until they are destroyed.' "

12All the other prophets were prophesying the same thing. "Attack Ramoth Gilead and be victorious," they said, "for the LORD will give it into the king's hand."

13The messenger who had gone to summon Micaiah said to him, "Look, as one man the other prophets are predicting success for the king. Let your word agree with theirs, and speak favorably."

14But Micaiah said, "As surely as the LORD lives, I can tell him only what the LORD tells me."

15When he arrived, the king asked him, "Micaiah, shall we go to war against Ramoth Gilead, or shall I refrain?"

"Attack and be victorious," he answered, "for the LORD will give it into the king's hand."

16The king said to him, "How many times must I make you swear to tell me nothing but the truth in the name of the LORD?"

17Then Micaiah answered, "I saw all Israel scattered on the hills like sheep without a shepherd, and the LORD said, 'These people have no master. Let each one go home in peace.' "

18The king of Israel said to Jehoshaphat, "Didn't I tell you that he never prophesies anything good about me, but only bad?"

19Micaiah continued, "Therefore hear the word of the LORD: I saw the LORD sitting on his throne with all the host of heaven standing around him on his right and on his left. **20**And the LORD said, 'Who will entice Ahab into attacking Ramoth Gilead and going to his death there?'

"One suggested this, and another that. **21**Finally, a spirit came forward, stood before the LORD and said, 'I will entice him.'

22" 'By what means?' the LORD asked.

" 'I will go out and be a lying spirit in the mouths of all his prophets,' he said.

" 'You will succeed in enticing him,' said the LORD. 'Go and do it.'

23"So now the LORD has put a lying spirit in the mouths of all these prophets of yours. The LORD has decreed disaster for you."

24Then Zedekiah son of Kenaanah went up and slapped Micaiah in the face. "Which way did the spirit from*a* the LORD go when he went from me to speak to you?" he asked.

25Micaiah replied, "You will find out on the day you go to hide in an inner room."

26The king of Israel then ordered, "Take Micaiah and send him back to Amon the ruler of the city and to Joash the king's son

27and say, 'This is what the king says: Put this fellow in prison and give him nothing but bread and water until I return safely.' "

28Micaiah declared, "If you ever return safely, the LORD has not spoken through me." Then he added, "Mark my words, all you people!"

Ahab Killed at Ramoth Gilead

29So the king of Israel and Jehoshaphat king of Judah went up to Ramoth Gilead. **30**The king of Israel said to Jehoshaphat, "I will enter the battle in disguise, but you wear your royal robes." So the king of Israel disguised himself and went into battle.

31Now the king of Aram had ordered his thirty-two chariot commanders, "Do not fight with anyone, small or great, except the king of Israel." **32**When the chariot commanders saw Jehoshaphat, they thought, "Surely this is the king of Israel." So they turned to attack him, but when Jehoshaphat cried out, **33**the chariot commanders saw that he was not the king of Israel and stopped pursuing him.

34But someone drew his bow at random and hit the king of Israel between the sections of his armor. The king told his chariot driver, "Wheel around and get me out of the fighting. I've been wounded." **35**All day long the battle raged, and the king was propped up in his chariot facing the Arameans. The blood from his wound ran onto the floor of the chariot, and that evening he died. **36**As the sun was setting, a cry spread through the army: "Every man to his town; everyone to his land!"

37So the king died and was brought to Samaria, and they buried him there. **38**They washed the chariot at a pool in Samaria (where the prostitutes bathed),*b* and the dogs licked up his blood, as the word of the LORD had declared.

39As for the other events of Ahab's reign, including all he did, the palace he built and inlaid with ivory, and the cities he fortified, are they not written in the book of the annals of the kings of Israel? **40**Ahab rested with his fathers. And Ahaziah his son succeeded him as king.

Jehoshaphat King of Judah

41Jehoshaphat son of Asa became king of Judah in the fourth year of Ahab king of Israel. **42**Jehoshaphat was thirty-five years old when he became king, and he reigned in Jerusalem twenty-five years. His mother's

---

a24 Or Spirit of   b38 Or Samaria and cleaned the weapons

name was Azubah daughter of Shilhi. **43**In everything he walked in the ways of his father Asa and did not stray from them; he did what was right in the eyes of the LORD. The high places, however, were not removed, and the people continued to offer sacrifices and burn incense there. **44**Jehoshaphat was also at peace with the king of Israel.

45As for the other events of Jehoshaphat's reign, the things he achieved and his military exploits, are they not written in the book of the annals of the kings of Judah? **46**He rid the land of the rest of the male shrine prostitutes who remained there even after the reign of his father Asa. **47**There was then no king in Edom; a deputy ruled.

48Now Jehoshaphat built a fleet of trading ships*a* to go to Ophir for gold, but they never set sail — they were wrecked at Ezion Geber. **49**At that time Ahaziah son of Ahab said to Jehoshaphat, "Let my men sail with your men," but Jehoshaphat refused.

50Then Jehoshaphat rested with his fathers and was buried with them in the city of David his father. And Jehoram his son succeeded him.

Ahaziah King of Israel

51Ahaziah son of Ahab became king of Israel in Samaria in the seventeenth year of Jehoshaphat king of Judah, and he reigned over Israel two years. **52**He did evil in the eyes of the LORD, because he walked in the ways of his father and mother and in the ways of Jeroboam son of Nebat, who caused Israel to sin. **53**He served and worshiped Baal and provoked the LORD, the God of Israel, to anger, just as his father had done.

a48 Hebrew *of ships of Tarshish*

2 KINGS

"JUDGMENT is coming!" thunder the prophets, but neither Israel nor Judah is listening. Both nations continue in idolatry and sin. God finally does what he has promised, and corrupt Israel is conquered and deported by the Assyrians. A century later the people of Judah are captured by the Babylonians. These exiles are a reminder that God won't ignore sin. When you feel exiled from God's love, check your life. God's love never ceases, but whether it is tender or tough depends on your obedience.

Outline of Contents

The LORD's Judgment on Ahaziah

1 After Ahab's death, Moab rebelled against Israel. ²Now Ahaziah had fallen through the lattice of his upper room in Samaria and injured himself. So he sent messengers, saying to them, "Go and consult Baal-Zebub, the god of Ekron, to see if I will recover from this injury."

³But the angel of the LORD said to Elijah the Tishbite, "Go up and meet the messengers of the king of Samaria and ask them, 'Is it because there is no God in Israel that you are going off to consult Baal-Zebub, the god of Ekron?' ⁴Therefore this is what the LORD says: 'You will not leave the bed you are lying on. You will certainly die!' " So Elijah went.

⁵When the messengers returned to the king, he asked them, "Why have you come back?"

⁶"A man came to meet us," they replied. "And he said to us, 'Go back to the king who sent you and tell him, "This is what the LORD says: Is it because there is no God in Israel that you are sending men to consult Baal-Zebub, the god of Ekron? Therefore you will not leave the bed you are lying on. You will certainly die!" ' "

⁷The king asked them, "What kind of man was it who came to meet you and told you this?"

⁸They replied, "He was a man with a garment of hair and with a leather belt around his waist."

The king said, "That was Elijah the Tishbite."

⁹Then he sent to Elijah a captain with his company of fifty men. The captain went up to Elijah, who was sitting on the top of a hill, and said to him, "Man of God, the king says, 'Come down!'"

¹⁰Elijah answered the captain, "If I am a man of God, may fire come down from heaven and consume you and your fifty men!" Then fire fell from heaven and consumed the captain and his men.

¹¹At this the king sent to Elijah another captain with his fifty men. The captain said to him, "Man of God, this is what the king says, 'Come down at once!'"

¹²"If I am a man of God," Elijah replied, "may fire come down from heaven and consume you and your fifty men!" Then the fire of God fell from heaven and consumed him and his fifty men.

¹³So the king sent a third captain with his fifty men. This third captain went up and fell on his knees before Elijah. "Man of God," he begged, "please have respect for my life and the lives of these fifty men, your servants! ¹⁴See, fire has fallen from heaven and consumed the first two captains and all their men. But now have respect for my life!"

¹⁵The angel of the Lord said to Elijah, "Go down with him; do not be afraid of him." So Elijah got up and went down with him to the king.

¹⁶He told the king, "This is what the Lord says: Is it because there is no God in Israel for you to consult that you have sent messengers to consult Baal-Zebub, the god of Ekron? Because you have done this, you will never leave the bed you are lying on. You will certainly die!" ¹⁷So he died, according to the word of the Lord that Elijah had spoken.

Because Ahaziah had no son, Joram[a] succeeded him as king in the second year of Jehoram son of Jehoshaphat king of Judah. ¹⁸As for all the other events of Ahaziah's reign, and what he did, are they not written in the book of the annals of the kings of Israel?

Elijah Taken Up to Heaven

2 When the Lord was about to take Elijah up to heaven in a whirlwind, Elijah and Elisha were on their way from Gilgal. ²Elijah said to Elisha, "Stay here; the Lord has sent me to Bethel."

But Elisha said, "As surely as the Lord lives and as you live, I will not leave you." So they went down to Bethel.

³The company of the prophets at Bethel came out to Elisha and asked, "Do you know that the Lord is going to take your master from you today?"

"Yes, I know," Elisha replied, "but do not speak of it."

⁴Then Elijah said to him, "Stay here, Elisha; the Lord has sent me to Jericho."

And he replied, "As surely as the Lord lives and as you live, I will not leave you." So they went to Jericho.

⁵The company of the prophets at Jericho went up to Elisha and asked him, "Do you know that the Lord is going to take your master from you today?"

"Yes, I know," he replied, "but do not speak of it."

⁶Then Elijah said to him, "Stay here; the Lord has sent me to the Jordan."

And he replied, "As surely as the Lord lives and as you live, I will not leave you." So the two of them walked on.

⁷Fifty men of the company of the prophets went and stood at a distance, facing the place where Elijah and Elisha had stopped at the Jordan. ⁸Elijah took his cloak, rolled it up and struck the water with it. The water divided to the right and to the left, and the two of them crossed over on dry ground.

⁹When they had crossed, Elijah said to Elisha, "Tell me, what can I do for you before I am taken from you?"

"Let me inherit a double portion of your spirit," Elisha replied.

¹⁰"You have asked a difficult thing," Elijah said, "yet if you see me when I am taken from you, it will be yours—otherwise not."

¹¹As they were walking along and talking together, suddenly a chariot of fire and horses of fire appeared and separated the two of them, and Elijah went up to heaven in a whirlwind. ¹²Elisha saw this and cried out, "My father! My father! The chariots and horsemen of Israel!" And Elisha saw him no more. Then he took hold of his own clothes and tore them apart.

¹³He picked up the cloak that had fallen from Elijah and went back and stood on the bank of the Jordan. ¹⁴Then he took the cloak that had fallen from him and struck the water with it. "Where now is the Lord, the God of Elijah?" he asked. When he struck the water, it divided to the right and to the left, and he crossed over.

¹⁵The company of the prophets from Jericho, who were watching, said, "The spirit of Elijah is resting on Elisha." And they went to meet him and bowed to the ground before

him. [16]"Look," they said, "we your servants have fifty able men. Let them go and look for your master. Perhaps the Spirit of the LORD has picked him up and set him down on some mountain or in some valley."

"No," Elisha replied, "do not send them."

[17]But they persisted until he was too ashamed to refuse. So he said, "Send them." And they sent fifty men, who searched for three days but did not find him. [18]When they returned to Elisha, who was staying in Jericho, he said to them, "Didn't I tell you not to go?"

Healing of the Water

[19]The men of the city said to Elisha, "Look, our lord, this town is well situated, as you can see, but the water is bad and the land is unproductive."

[20]"Bring me a new bowl," he said, "and put salt in it." So they brought it to him.

[21]Then he went out to the spring and threw the salt into it, saying, "This is what the LORD says: 'I have healed this water. Never again will it cause death or make the land unproductive.'" [22]And the water has remained wholesome to this day, according to the word Elisha had spoken.

Elisha Is Jeered

[23]From there Elisha went up to Bethel. As he was walking along the road, some youths came out of the town and jeered at him. "Go on up, you baldhead!" they said. "Go on up, you baldhead!" [24]He turned around, looked at them and called down a curse on them in the name of the LORD. Then two bears came out of the woods and mauled forty-two of the youths. [25]And he went on to Mount Carmel and from there returned to Samaria.

Moab Revolts

3 Joram[a] son of Ahab became king of Israel in Samaria in the eighteenth year of Jehoshaphat king of Judah, and he reigned twelve years. [2]He did evil in the eyes of the LORD, but not as his father and mother had done. He got rid of the sacred stone of Baal that his father had made. [3]Nevertheless he clung to the sins of Jeroboam son of Nebat, which he had caused Israel to commit; he did not turn away from them.

[4]Now Mesha king of Moab raised sheep, and he had to supply the king of Israel with a hundred thousand lambs and with the wool of a hundred thousand rams. [5]But after Ahab died, the king of Moab rebelled against the king of Israel. [6]So at that time King Joram set out from Samaria and mobilized all Israel. [7]He also sent this message to Jehoshaphat king of Judah: "The king of Moab has rebelled against me. Will you go with me to fight against Moab?"

"I will go with you," he replied. "I am as you are, my people as your people, my horses as your horses."

[8]"By what route shall we attack?" he asked.

"Through the Desert of Edom," he answered.

[9]So the king of Israel set out with the king of Judah and the king of Edom. After a roundabout march of seven days, the army had no more water for themselves or for the animals with them.

[10]"What!" exclaimed the king of Israel. "Has the LORD called us three kings together only to hand us over to Moab?"

[11]But Jehoshaphat asked, "Is there no prophet of the LORD here, that we may inquire of the LORD through him?"

An officer of the king of Israel answered, "Elisha son of Shaphat is here. He used to pour water on the hands of Elijah.[b]"

[12]Jehoshaphat said, "The word of the LORD is with him." So the king of Israel and Jehoshaphat and the king of Edom went down to him.

[13]Elisha said to the king of Israel, "What do we have to do with each other? Go to the prophets of your father and the prophets of your mother."

"No," the king of Israel answered, "because it was the LORD who called us three kings together to hand us over to Moab."

[14]Elisha said, "As surely as the LORD Almighty lives, whom I serve, if I did not have respect for the presence of Jehoshaphat king of Judah, I would not look at you or even notice you. [15]But now bring me a harpist."

While the harpist was playing, the hand of the LORD came upon Elisha [16]and he said, "This is what the LORD says: Make this valley full of ditches. [17]For this is what the LORD says: You will see neither wind nor rain, yet this valley will be filled with water, and you, your cattle and your other animals will drink. [18]This is an easy thing in the eyes of the LORD; he will also hand Moab over to you. [19]You will overthrow every fortified city and every major town. You will cut down every good tree, stop up all the springs, and ruin every good field with stones."

[20]The next morning, about the time for of-

---

a 1 Hebrew *Jehoram*, a variant of *Joram*; also in verse 6　　*b 11* That is, he was Elijah's personal servant.

fering the sacrifice, there it was — water flowing from the direction of Edom! And the land was filled with water.

21Now all the Moabites had heard that the kings had come to fight against them; so every man, young and old, who could bear arms was called up and stationed on the border. 22When they got up early in the morning, the sun was shining on the water. To the Moabites across the way, the water looked red — like blood. 23"That's blood!" they said. "Those kings must have fought and slaughtered each other. Now to the plunder, Moab!"

24But when the Moabites came to the camp of Israel, the Israelites rose up and fought them until they fled. And the Israelites invaded the land and slaughtered the Moabites. 25They destroyed the towns, and each man threw a stone on every good field until it was covered. They stopped up all the springs and cut down every good tree. Only Kir Hareseth was left with its stones in place, but men armed with slings surrounded it and attacked it as well.

26When the king of Moab saw that the battle had gone against him, he took with him seven hundred swordsmen to break through to the king of Edom, but they failed. 27Then he took his firstborn son, who was to succeed him as king, and offered him as a sacrifice on the city wall. The fury against Israel was great; they withdrew and returned to their own land.

The Widow's Oil

4 The wife of a man from the company of the prophets cried out to Elisha, "Your servant my husband is dead, and you know that he revered the LORD. But now his creditor is coming to take my two boys as his slaves."

2Elisha replied to her, "How can I help you? Tell me, what do you have in your house?"

"Your servant has nothing there at all," she said, "except a little oil."

3Elisha said, "Go around and ask all your neighbors for empty jars. Don't ask for just a few. 4Then go inside and shut the door behind you and your sons. Pour oil into all the jars, and as each is filled, put it to one side."

5She left him and afterward shut the door behind her and her sons. They brought the jars to her and she kept pouring. 6When all the jars were full, she said to her son, "Bring me another one."

But he replied, "There is not a jar left." Then the oil stopped flowing.

7She went and told the man of God, and he said, "Go, sell the oil and pay your debts. You and your sons can live on what is left."

The Shunammite's Son Restored to Life

8One day Elisha went to Shunem. And a well-to-do woman was there, who urged him to stay for a meal. So whenever he came by, he stopped there to eat. 9She said to her husband, "I know that this man who often comes our way is a holy man of God. 10Let's make a small room on the roof and put in it a bed and a table, a chair and a lamp for him. Then he can stay there whenever he comes to us."

11One day when Elisha came, he went up to his room and lay down there. 12He said to his servant Gehazi, "Call the Shunammite." So he called her, and she stood before him. 13Elisha said to him, "Tell her, 'You have gone to all this trouble for us. Now what can be done for you? Can we speak on your behalf to the king or the commander of the army?' "

She replied, "I have a home among my own people."

14"What can be done for her?" Elisha asked.

Gehazi said, "Well, she has no son and her husband is old."

15Then Elisha said, "Call her." So he called her, and she stood in the doorway. 16"About this time next year," Elisha said, "you will hold a son in your arms."

"No, my lord," she objected. "Don't mislead your servant, O man of God!"

17But the woman became pregnant, and the next year about that same time she gave birth to a son, just as Elisha had told her.

18The child grew, and one day he went out to his father, who was with the reapers. 19"My head! My head!" he said to his father.

His father told a servant, "Carry him to his mother." 20After the servant had lifted him up and carried him to his mother, the boy sat on her lap until noon, and then he died. 21She went up and laid him on the bed of the man of God, then shut the door and went out.

22She called her husband and said, "Please send me one of the servants and a donkey so I can go to the man of God quickly and return."

23"Why go to him today?" he asked. "It's not the New Moon or the Sabbath."

"It's all right," she said.

24She saddled the donkey and said to her servant, "Lead on; don't slow down for me unless I tell you." **25**So she set out and came to the man of God at Mount Carmel.

When he saw her in the distance, the man of God said to his servant Gehazi, "Look! There's the Shunammite! **26**Run to meet her and ask her, 'Are you all right? Is your husband all right? Is your child all right?' "

"Everything is all right," she said.

27When she reached the man of God at the mountain, she took hold of his feet. Gehazi came over to push her away, but the man of God said, "Leave her alone! She is in bitter distress, but the Lord has hidden it from me and has not told me why."

28"Did I ask you for a son, my lord?" she said. "Didn't I tell you, 'Don't raise my hopes'?"

29Elisha said to Gehazi, "Tuck your cloak into your belt, take my staff in your hand and run. If you meet anyone, do not greet him, and if anyone greets you, do not answer. Lay my staff on the boy's face."

30But the child's mother said, "As surely as the Lord lives and as you live, I will not leave you." So he got up and followed her.

31Gehazi went on ahead and laid the staff on the boy's face, but there was no sound or response. So Gehazi went back to meet Elisha and told him, "The boy has not awakened."

32When Elisha reached the house, there was the boy lying dead on his couch. **33**He went in, shut the door on the two of them and prayed to the Lord. **34**Then he got on the bed and lay upon the boy, mouth to mouth, eyes to eyes, hands to hands. As he stretched himself out upon him, the boy's body grew warm. **35**Elisha turned away and walked back and forth in the room and then got on the bed and stretched out upon him once more. The boy sneezed seven times and opened his eyes.

36Elisha summoned Gehazi and said, "Call the Shunammite." And he did. When she came, he said, "Take your son." **37**She came in, fell at his feet and bowed to the ground. Then she took her son and went out.

Death in the Pot

38Elisha returned to Gilgal and there was a famine in that region. While the company of the prophets was meeting with him, he said to his servant, "Put on the large pot and cook some stew for these men."

39One of them went out into the fields to gather herbs and found a wild vine. He gathered some of its gourds and filled the fold of his cloak. When he returned, he cut them up into the pot of stew, though no one knew what they were. **40**The stew was poured out for the men, but as they began to eat it, they cried out, "O man of God, there is death in the pot!" And they could not eat it.

41Elisha said, "Get some flour." He put it into the pot and said, "Serve it to the people to eat." And there was nothing harmful in the pot.

Feeding of a Hundred

42A man came from Baal Shalishah, bringing the man of God twenty loaves of barley bread baked from the first ripe grain, along with some heads of new grain. "Give it to the people to eat," Elisha said.

43"How can I set this before a hundred men?" his servant asked.

But Elisha answered, "Give it to the people to eat. For this is what the Lord says: 'They will eat and have some left over.' " **44**Then he set it before them, and they ate and had some left over, according to the word of the Lord.

Naaman Healed of Leprosy

5 Now Naaman was commander of the army of the king of Aram. He was a great man in the sight of his master and highly regarded, because through him the Lord had given victory to Aram. He was a valiant soldier, but he had leprosy.*a*

2Now bands from Aram had gone out and had taken captive a young girl from Israel, and she served Naaman's wife. **3**She said to her mistress, "If only my master would see the prophet who is in Samaria! He would cure him of his leprosy."

4Naaman went to his master and told him what the girl from Israel had said. **5**"By all means, go," the king of Aram replied. "I will send a letter to the king of Israel." So Naaman left, taking with him ten talents*b* of silver, six thousand shekels*c* of gold and ten sets of clothing. **6**The letter that he took to the king of Israel read: "With this letter I am sending my servant Naaman to you so that you may cure him of his leprosy."

7As soon as the king of Israel read the letter, he tore his robes and said, "Am I God? Can I kill and bring back to life? Why does

---

a1 The Hebrew word was used for various diseases affecting the skin—not necessarily leprosy; also in verses 3, 6, 7, 11 and 27.   *b5* That is, about 750 pounds (about 340 kilograms)   *c5* That is, about 150 pounds (about 70 kilograms)

THE "BETTER THAN" SYNDROME

Mention basketball and watch Ray strut around like a peacock. That's because he knows he's the best player in the city.

Start talking about physics, chemistry or anything having to do with science and technology, and Pat will quickly try to dominate the discussion.

If there's a party, beautiful Kim is sure to be there. She knows she can get any guy's attention and can keep it for as long as she likes. Other girls aren't exactly crazy about her, but with the guys, Kim is it!

Look It Up
••••

Every individual is prideful about something. And God's Word has a good word for each one:

For the person who is proud of strength or physical ability: Hosea 10:13.

For the person who is arrogant about wealth: "But man, despite his riches, does not endure; he is like the beasts that perish" (Psalm 49:12).

For the person who is vain about looks: 1 Samuel 16:7.

For the person who is conceited about smarts: Jeremiah 9:23–24.

For the person who is spiritually cocky: Luke 18:9–14.

Perhaps Proverbs 21:4 best sums up those prideful feelings of superiority: "Haughty eyes and a proud heart, the lamp of the wicked, are sin!"

Think It Through
••••

Well-known writer C.S. Lewis wisely noted that all pride has competition or comparison at its root. People get their pleasure not out of just having something but having more of it than the next person. They get pleasure not out of being beautiful or smart or rich but out of being more beautiful or smarter or richer. It's the comparison that produces pride.

Work It Out
••••

Ask God to make you less competitive. Then make a conscious effort not to outdo others.

How? Refuse to get in arguments. Avoid comparisons. Resist the urge to make others look bad. In fact, begin saying and doing things that will make others look good.

Develop this habit, and you'll have more fun . . . not to mention more friends!

Nail It Down
••••

Read 2 Kings 5:1–15 for the story of Naaman the leper and how he was cured not only of leprosy but also of pride.

Turn to pages 65, 462 and 1113 for other readings on pride.
Turn to page 391 for Friday's reading.

Topic
••••

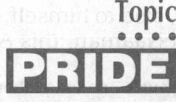

this fellow send someone to me to be cured of his leprosy? See how he is trying to pick a quarrel with me!"

⁸When Elisha the man of God heard that the king of Israel had torn his robes, he sent him this message: "Why have you torn your robes? Have the man come to me and he will know that there is a prophet in Israel." ⁹So Naaman went with his horses and chariots and stopped at the door of Elisha's house. ¹⁰Elisha sent a messenger to say to him, "Go, wash yourself seven times in the Jordan, and your flesh will be restored and you will be cleansed."

¹¹But Naaman went away angry and said, "I thought that he would surely come out to me and stand and call on the name of the LORD his God, wave his hand over the spot and cure me of my leprosy. ¹²Are not Abana and Pharpar, the rivers of Damascus, better than any of the waters of Israel? Couldn't I wash in them and be cleansed?" So he turned and went off in a rage.

¹³Naaman's servants went to him and said, "My father, if the prophet had told you to do some great thing, would you not have done it? How much more, then, when he tells you, 'Wash and be cleansed'!" ¹⁴So he went down and dipped himself in the Jordan seven times, as the man of God had told him, and his flesh was restored and became clean like that of a young boy.

¹⁵Then Naaman and all his attendants went back to the man of God. He stood before him and said, "Now I know that there is no God in all the world except in Israel. Please accept now a gift from your servant."

¹⁶The prophet answered, "As surely as the LORD lives, whom I serve, I will not accept a thing." And even though Naaman urged him, he refused.

¹⁷"If you will not," said Naaman, "please let me, your servant, be given as much earth as a pair of mules can carry, for your servant will never again make burnt offerings and sacrifices to any other god but the LORD. ¹⁸But may the LORD forgive your servant for this one thing: When my master enters the temple of Rimmon to bow down and he is leaning on my arm and I bow there also — when I bow down in the temple of Rimmon, may the LORD forgive your servant for this."

¹⁹"Go in peace," Elisha said.

After Naaman had traveled some distance, ²⁰Gehazi, the servant of Elisha the man of God, said to himself, "My master was too easy on Naaman, this Aramean, by not accepting from him what he brought. As surely as the LORD lives, I will run after him and get something from him."

²¹So Gehazi hurried after Naaman. When Naaman saw him running toward him, he got down from the chariot to meet him. "Is everything all right?" he asked.

²²"Everything is all right," Gehazi answered. "My master sent me to say, 'Two young men from the company of the prophets have just come to me from the hill country of Ephraim. Please give them a talent[a] of silver and two sets of clothing.' "

²³"By all means, take two talents," said Naaman. He urged Gehazi to accept them, and then tied up the two talents of silver in two bags, with two sets of clothing. He gave them to two of his servants, and they carried them ahead of Gehazi. ²⁴When Gehazi came to the hill, he took the things from the servants and put them away in the house. He sent the men away and they left. ²⁵Then he went in and stood before his master Elisha.

"Where have you been, Gehazi?" Elisha asked.

"Your servant didn't go anywhere," Gehazi answered.

²⁶But Elisha said to him, "Was not my spirit with you when the man got down from his chariot to meet you? Is this the time to take money, or to accept clothes, olive groves, vineyards, flocks, herds, or menservants and maidservants? ²⁷Naaman's leprosy will cling to you and to your descendants forever." Then Gehazi went from Elisha's presence and he was leprous, as white as snow.

An Axhead Floats

6 The company of the prophets said to Elisha, "Look, the place where we meet with you is too small for us. ²Let us go to the Jordan, where each of us can get a pole; and let us build a place there for us to live."

And he said, "Go."

³Then one of them said, "Won't you please come with your servants?"

"I will," Elisha replied. ⁴And he went with them.

They went to the Jordan and began to cut down trees. ⁵As one of them was cutting down a tree, the iron axhead fell into the water. "Oh, my lord," he cried out, "it was borrowed!"

⁶The man of God asked, "Where did it fall?" When he showed him the place, Elisha cut a stick and threw it there, and made the

---

a22 That is, about 75 pounds (about 34 kilograms)

iron float. ⁷"Lift it out," he said. Then the man reached out his hand and took it.

Elisha Traps Blinded Arameans

⁸Now the king of Aram was at war with Israel. After conferring with his officers, he said, "I will set up my camp in such and such a place."

⁹The man of God sent word to the king of Israel: "Beware of passing that place, because the Arameans are going down there." ¹⁰So the king of Israel checked on the place indicated by the man of God. Time and again Elisha warned the king, so that he was on his guard in such places.

¹¹This enraged the king of Aram. He summoned his officers and demanded of them, "Will you not tell me which of us is on the side of the king of Israel?"

¹²"None of us, my lord the king," said one of his officers, "but Elisha, the prophet who is in Israel, tells the king of Israel the very words you speak in your bedroom."

¹³"Go, find out where he is," the king ordered, "so I can send men and capture him." The report came back: "He is in Dothan." ¹⁴Then he sent horses and chariots and a strong force there. They went by night and surrounded the city.

¹⁵When the servant of the man of God got up and went out early the next morning, an army with horses and chariots had surrounded the city. "Oh, my lord, what shall we do?" the servant asked.

¹⁶"Don't be afraid," the prophet answered. "Those who are with us are more than those who are with them."

¹⁷And Elisha prayed, "O Lord, open his eyes so he may see." Then the Lord opened the servant's eyes, and he looked and saw the hills full of horses and chariots of fire all around Elisha.

¹⁸As the enemy came down toward him, Elisha prayed to the Lord, "Strike these people with blindness." So he struck them with blindness, as Elisha had asked.

¹⁹Elisha told them, "This is not the road and this is not the city. Follow me, and I will lead you to the man you are looking for." And he led them to Samaria.

²⁰After they entered the city, Elisha said, "Lord, open the eyes of these men so they can see." Then the Lord opened their eyes and they looked, and there they were, inside Samaria.

²¹When the king of Israel saw them, he asked Elisha, "Shall I kill them, my father? Shall I kill them?"

²²"Do not kill them," he answered. "Would you kill men you have captured with your own sword or bow? Set food and water before them so that they may eat and drink and then go back to their master." ²³So he prepared a great feast for them, and after they had finished eating and drinking, he sent them away, and they returned to their master. So the bands from Aram stopped raiding Israel's territory.

Famine in Besieged Samaria

²⁴Some time later, Ben-Hadad king of Aram mobilized his entire army and marched up and laid siege to Samaria. ²⁵There was a great famine in the city; the siege lasted so long that a donkey's head sold for eighty shekels^a of silver, and a quarter of a cab^b of seed pods^c for five shekels.^{d}

²⁶As the king of Israel was passing by on the wall, a woman cried to him, "Help me, my lord the king!"

²⁷The king replied, "If the Lord does not help you, where can I get help for you? From the threshing floor? From the winepress?" ²⁸Then he asked her, "What's the matter?"

She answered, "This woman said to me, 'Give up your son so we may eat him today, and tomorrow we'll eat my son.' ²⁹So we cooked my son and ate him. The next day I said to her, 'Give up your son so we may eat him,' but she had hidden him."

³⁰When the king heard the woman's words, he tore his robes. As he went along the wall, the people looked, and there, underneath, he had sackcloth on his body. ³¹He said, "May God deal with me, be it ever so severely, if the head of Elisha son of Shaphat remains on his shoulders today!"

³²Now Elisha was sitting in his house, and the elders were sitting with him. The king sent a messenger ahead, but before he arrived, Elisha said to the elders, "Don't you see how this murderer is sending someone to cut off my head? Look, when the messenger comes, shut the door and hold it shut against him. Is not the sound of his master's footsteps behind him?"

³³While he was still talking to them, the messenger came down to him. And ⌊the king⌋ said, "This disaster is from the Lord. Why should I wait for the Lord any longer?"

^{a}25 That is, about 2 pounds (about 1 kilogram) ^{b}25 That is, probably about 1/2 pint (about 0.3 liter) ^{c}25 Or of dove's dung ^{d}25 That is, about 2 ounces (about 55 grams)

7 Elisha said, "Hear the word of the LORD. This is what the LORD says: About this time tomorrow, a seah[a] of flour will sell for a shekel[b] and two seahs[c] of barley for a shekel at the gate of Samaria."

[2] The officer on whose arm the king was leaning said to the man of God, "Look, even if the LORD should open the floodgates of the heavens, could this happen?"

"You will see it with your own eyes," answered Elisha, "but you will not eat any of it!"

The Siege Lifted

[3] Now there were four men with leprosy[d] at the entrance of the city gate. They said to each other, "Why stay here until we die? [4] If we say, 'We'll go into the city'—the famine is there, and we will die. And if we stay here, we will die. So let's go over to the camp of the Arameans and surrender. If they spare us, we live; if they kill us, then we die."

[5] At dusk they got up and went to the camp of the Arameans. When they reached the edge of the camp, not a man was there, [6] for the Lord had caused the Arameans to hear the sound of chariots and horses and a great army, so that they said to one another, "Look, the king of Israel has hired the Hittite and Egyptian kings to attack us!" [7] So they got up and fled in the dusk and abandoned their tents and their horses and donkeys. They left the camp as it was and ran for their lives.

[8] The men who had leprosy reached the edge of the camp and entered one of the tents. They ate and drank, and carried away silver, gold and clothes, and went off and hid them. They returned and entered another tent and took some things from it and hid them also.

[9] Then they said to each other, "We're not doing right. This is a day of good news and we are keeping it to ourselves. If we wait until daylight, punishment will overtake us. Let's go at once and report this to the royal palace."

[10] So they went and called out to the city gatekeepers and told them, "We went into the Aramean camp and not a man was there—not a sound of anyone—only tethered horses and donkeys, and the tents left just as they were." [11] The gatekeepers shouted the news, and it was reported within the palace.

[12] The king got up in the night and said to his officers, "I will tell you what the Arameans have done to us. They know we are starving; so they have left the camp to hide in the countryside, thinking, 'They will surely come out, and then we will take them alive and get into the city.'"

[13] One of his officers answered, "Have some men take five of the horses that are left in the city. Their plight will be like that of all the Israelites left here—yes, they will only be like all these Israelites who are doomed. So let us send them to find out what happened."

[14] So they selected two chariots with their horses, and the king sent them after the Aramean army. He commanded the drivers, "Go and find out what has happened." [15] They followed them as far as the Jordan, and they found the whole road strewn with the clothing and equipment the Arameans had thrown away in their headlong flight. So the messengers returned and reported to the king. [16] Then the people went out and plundered the camp of the Arameans. So a seah of flour sold for a shekel, and two seahs of barley sold for a shekel, as the LORD had said.

[17] Now the king had put the officer on whose arm he leaned in charge of the gate, and the people trampled him in the gateway, and he died, just as the man of God had foretold when the king came down to his house. [18] It happened as the man of God had said to the king: "About this time tomorrow, a seah of flour will sell for a shekel and two seahs of barley for a shekel at the gate of Samaria."

[19] The officer had said to the man of God, "Look, even if the LORD should open the floodgates of the heavens, could this happen?" The man of God had replied, "You will see it with your own eyes, but you will not eat any of it!" [20] And that is exactly what happened to him, for the people trampled him in the gateway, and he died.

The Shunammite's Land Restored

8 Now Elisha had said to the woman whose son he had restored to life, "Go away with your family and stay for a while wherever you can, because the LORD has de-

a1 That is, probably about 7 quarts (about 7.3 liters); also in verses 16 and 18   b1 That is, about 2/5 ounce (about 11 grams); also in verses 16 and 18   c1 That is, probably about 13 quarts (about 15 liters); also in verses 16 and 18   d3 The Hebrew word is used for various diseases affecting the skin—not necessarily leprosy; also in verse 8.

creed a famine in the land that will last seven years." **2**The woman proceeded to do as the man of God said. She and her family went away and stayed in the land of the Philistines seven years.

3At the end of the seven years she came back from the land of the Philistines and went to the king to beg for her house and land. **4**The king was talking to Gehazi, the servant of the man of God, and had said, "Tell me about all the great things Elisha has done." **5**Just as Gehazi was telling the king how Elisha had restored the dead to life, the woman whose son Elisha had brought back to life came to beg the king for her house and land.

Gehazi said, "This is the woman, my lord the king, and this is her son whom Elisha restored to life." **6**The king asked the woman about it, and she told him.

Then he assigned an official to her case and said to him, "Give back everything that belonged to her, including all the income from her land from the day she left the country until now."

Hazael Murders Ben-Hadad

7Elisha went to Damascus, and Ben-Hadad king of Aram was ill. When the king was told, "The man of God has come all the way up here," **8**he said to Hazael, "Take a gift with you and go to meet the man of God. Consult the Lord through him; ask him, 'Will I recover from this illness?' "

9Hazael went to meet Elisha, taking with him as a gift forty camel-loads of all the finest wares of Damascus. He went in and stood before him, and said, "Your son Ben-Hadad king of Aram has sent me to ask, 'Will I recover from this illness?' "

10Elisha answered, "Go and say to him, 'You will certainly recover'; but*a* the Lord has revealed to me that he will in fact die." **11**He stared at him with a fixed gaze until Hazael felt ashamed. Then the man of God began to weep.

12"Why is my lord weeping?" asked Hazael.

"Because I know the harm you will do to the Israelites," he answered. "You will set fire to their fortified places, kill their young men with the sword, dash their little children to the ground, and rip open their pregnant women."

13Hazael said, "How could your servant, a mere dog, accomplish such a feat?"

"The Lord has shown me that you will become king of Aram," answered Elisha.

14Then Hazael left Elisha and returned to his master. When Ben-Hadad asked, "What did Elisha say to you?" Hazael replied, "He told me that you would certainly recover." **15**But the next day he took a thick cloth, soaked it in water and spread it over the king's face, so that he died. Then Hazael succeeded him as king.

Jehoram King of Judah

16In the fifth year of Joram son of Ahab king of Israel, when Jehoshaphat was king of Judah, Jehoram son of Jehoshaphat began his reign as king of Judah. **17**He was thirty-two years old when he became king, and reigned in Jerusalem eight years. **18**He walked in the ways of the kings of Israel, as the house of Ahab had done, for he married a daughter of Ahab. He did evil in the eyes of the Lord. **19**Nevertheless, for the sake of his servant David, the Lord was not willing to destroy Judah. He had promised to maintain a lamp for David and his descendants forever.

20In the time of Jehoram, Edom rebelled against Judah and set up its own king. **21**So Jehoram*b* went to Zair with all his chariots. The Edomites surrounded him and his chariot commanders, but he rose up and broke through by night; his army, however, fled back home. **22**To this day Edom has been in rebellion against Judah. Libnah revolted at the same time.

23As for the other events of Jehoram's reign, and all he did, are they not written in the book of the annals of the kings of Judah? **24**Jehoram rested with his fathers and was buried with them in the City of David. And Ahaziah his son succeeded him as king.

Ahaziah King of Judah

25In the twelfth year of Joram son of Ahab king of Israel, Ahaziah son of Jehoram king of Judah began to reign. **26**Ahaziah was twenty-two years old when he became king, and he reigned in Jerusalem one year. His mother's name was Athaliah, a granddaughter of Omri king of Israel. **27**He walked in the ways of the house of Ahab and did evil in the eyes of the Lord, as the house of Ahab had done, for he was related by marriage to Ahab's family.

28Ahaziah went with Joram son of Ahab to war against Hazael king of Aram at Ramoth

---

a 10 The Hebrew may also be read *Go and say, 'You will certainly not recover,' for.*   *b 21* Hebrew *Joram,* a variant of *Jehoram;* also in verses 23 and 24

Gilead. The Arameans wounded Joram; ²⁹so King Joram returned to Jezreel to recover from the wounds the Arameans had inflicted on him at Ramoth*ᵃ* in his battle with Hazael king of Aram.

Then Ahaziah son of Jehoram king of Judah went down to Jezreel to see Joram son of Ahab, because he had been wounded.

Jehu Anointed King of Israel

9 The prophet Elisha summoned a man from the company of the prophets and said to him, "Tuck your cloak into your belt, take this flask of oil with you and go to Ramoth Gilead. ²When you get there, look for Jehu son of Jehoshaphat, the son of Nimshi. Go to him, get him away from his companions and take him into an inner room. ³Then take the flask and pour the oil on his head and declare, 'This is what the LORD says: I anoint you king over Israel.' Then open the door and run; don't delay!"

⁴So the young man, the prophet, went to Ramoth Gilead. ⁵When he arrived, he found the army officers sitting together. "I have a message for you, commander," he said.

"For which of us?" asked Jehu.

"For you, commander," he replied.

⁶Jehu got up and went into the house. Then the prophet poured the oil on Jehu's head and declared, "This is what the LORD, the God of Israel, says: 'I anoint you king over the LORD's people Israel. ⁷You are to destroy the house of Ahab your master, and I will avenge the blood of my servants the prophets and the blood of all the LORD's servants shed by Jezebel. ⁸The whole house of Ahab will perish. I will cut off from Ahab every last male in Israel — slave or free. ⁹I will make the house of Ahab like the house of Jeroboam son of Nebat and like the house of Baasha son of Ahijah. ¹⁰As for Jezebel, dogs will devour her on the plot of ground at Jezreel, and no one will bury her.' " Then he opened the door and ran.

¹¹When Jehu went out to his fellow officers, one of them asked him, "Is everything all right? Why did this madman come to you?"

"You know the man and the sort of things he says," Jehu replied.

¹²"That's not true!" they said. "Tell us."

Jehu said, "Here is what he told me: 'This is what the LORD says: I anoint you king over Israel.' "

¹³They hurried and took their cloaks and spread them under him on the bare steps. Then they blew the trumpet and shouted, "Jehu is king!"

Jehu Kills Joram and Ahaziah

¹⁴So Jehu son of Jehoshaphat, the son of Nimshi, conspired against Joram. (Now Joram and all Israel had been defending Ramoth Gilead against Hazael king of Aram, ¹⁵but King Joram*ᵇ* had returned to Jezreel to recover from the wounds the Arameans had inflicted on him in the battle with Hazael king of Aram.) Jehu said, "If this is the way you feel, don't let anyone slip out of the city to go and tell the news in Jezreel." ¹⁶Then he got into his chariot and rode to Jezreel, because Joram was resting there and Ahaziah king of Judah had gone down to see him.

¹⁷When the lookout standing on the tower in Jezreel saw Jehu's troops approaching, he called out, "I see some troops coming."

"Get a horseman," Joram ordered. "Send him to meet them and ask, 'Do you come in peace?' "

¹⁸The horseman rode off to meet Jehu and said, "This is what the king says: 'Do you come in peace?' "

"What do you have to do with peace?" Jehu replied. "Fall in behind me."

The lookout reported, "The messenger has reached them, but he isn't coming back."

¹⁹So the king sent out a second horseman. When he came to them he said, "This is what the king says: 'Do you come in peace?' "

Jehu replied, "What do you have to do with peace? Fall in behind me."

²⁰The lookout reported, "He has reached them, but he isn't coming back either. The driving is like that of Jehu son of Nimshi — he drives like a madman."

²¹"Hitch up my chariot," Joram ordered. And when it was hitched up, Joram king of Israel and Ahaziah king of Judah rode out, each in his own chariot, to meet Jehu. They met him at the plot of ground that had belonged to Naboth the Jezreelite. ²²When Joram saw Jehu he asked, "Have you come in peace, Jehu?"

"How can there be peace," Jehu replied, "as long as all the idolatry and witchcraft of your mother Jezebel abound?"

²³Joram turned about and fled, calling out to Ahaziah, "Treachery, Ahaziah!"

²⁴Then Jehu drew his bow and shot Joram

ᵃ29 Hebrew *Ramah*, a variant of *Ramoth*   *ᵇ15* Hebrew *Jehoram*, a variant of *Joram*; also in verses 17 and 21-24 between the shoulders. The arrow pierced his heart and he slumped down in his chariot. ²⁵Jehu said to Bidkar, his chariot officer, "Pick him up and throw him on the field that belonged to Naboth the Jezreelite. Remember how you and I were riding together in chariots behind Ahab his father when the LORD made this prophecy about him: ²⁶'Yesterday I saw the blood of Naboth and the blood of his sons, declares the LORD, and I will surely make you pay for it on this plot of ground, declares the LORD.'ᵃ Now then, pick him up and throw him on that plot, in accordance with the word of the LORD."

²⁷When Ahaziah king of Judah saw what had happened, he fled up the road to Beth Haggan.ᵇ Jehu chased him, shouting, "Kill him too!" They wounded him in his chariot on the way up to Gur near Ibleam, but he escaped to Megiddo and died there. ²⁸His servants took him by chariot to Jerusalem and buried him with his fathers in his tomb in the City of David. ²⁹(In the eleventh year of Joram son of Ahab, Ahaziah had become king of Judah.)

Jezebel Killed

³⁰Then Jehu went to Jezreel. When Jezebel heard about it, she painted her eyes, arranged her hair and looked out of a window. ³¹As Jehu entered the gate, she asked, "Have you come in peace, Zimri, you murderer of your master?"ᶜ

³²He looked up at the window and called out, "Who is on my side? Who?" Two or three eunuchs looked down at him. ³³"Throw her down!" Jehu said. So they threw her down, and some of her blood spattered the wall and the horses as they trampled her underfoot.

³⁴Jehu went in and ate and drank. "Take care of that cursed woman," he said, "and bury her, for she was a king's daughter." ³⁵But when they went out to bury her, they found nothing except her skull, her feet and her hands. ³⁶They went back and told Jehu, who said, "This is the word of the LORD that he spoke through his servant Elijah the Tishbite: On the plot of ground at Jezreel dogs will devour Jezebel's flesh.ᵈ ³⁷Jezebel's body will be like refuse on the ground in the plot at Jezreel, so that no one will be able to say, 'This is Jezebel.'"

Ahab's Family Killed

10 Now there were in Samaria seventy sons of the house of Ahab. So Jehu wrote letters and sent them to Samaria: to the officials of Jezreel,ᵉ to the elders and to the guardians of Ahab's children. He said, ²"As soon as this letter reaches you, since your master's sons are with you and you have chariots and horses, a fortified city and weapons, ³choose the best and most worthy of your master's sons and set him on his father's throne. Then fight for your master's house."

⁴But they were terrified and said, "If two kings could not resist him, how can we?"

⁵So the palace administrator, the city governor, the elders and the guardians sent this message to Jehu: "We are your servants and we will do anything you say. We will not appoint anyone as king; you do whatever you think best."

⁶Then Jehu wrote them a second letter, saying, "If you are on my side and will obey me, take the heads of your master's sons and come to me in Jezreel by this time tomorrow."

Now the royal princes, seventy of them, were with the leading men of the city, who were rearing them. ⁷When the letter arrived, these men took the princes and slaughtered all seventy of them. They put their heads in baskets and sent them to Jehu in Jezreel. ⁸When the messenger arrived, he told Jehu, "They have brought the heads of the princes."

Then Jehu ordered, "Put them in two piles at the entrance of the city gate until morning."

⁹The next morning Jehu went out. He stood before all the people and said, "You are innocent. It was I who conspired against my master and killed him, but who killed all these? ¹⁰Know then, that not a word the LORD has spoken against the house of Ahab will fail. The LORD has done what he promised through his servant Elijah." ¹¹So Jehu killed everyone in Jezreel who remained of the house of Ahab, as well as all his chief men, his close friends and his priests, leaving him no survivor.

¹²Jehu then set out and went toward Samaria. At Beth Eked of the Shepherds, ¹³he met some relatives of Ahaziah king of Judah and asked, "Who are you?"

They said, "We are relatives of Ahaziah,

ᵃ26 See 1 Kings 21:19.   ᵇ27 Or fled by way of the garden house   ᶜ31 Or "Did Zimri have peace, who murdered his master?"   ᵈ36 See 1 Kings 21:23.   ᵉ1 Hebrew; some Septuagint manuscripts and Vulgate of the city and we have come down to greet the families of the king and of the queen mother."

¹⁴"Take them alive!" he ordered. So they took them alive and slaughtered them by the well of Beth Eked—forty-two men. He left no survivor.

¹⁵After he left there, he came upon Jehonadab son of Recab, who was on his way to meet him. Jehu greeted him and said, "Are you in accord with me, as I am with you?"

"I am," Jehonadab answered.

"If so," said Jehu, "give me your hand." So he did, and Jehu helped him up into the chariot. ¹⁶Jehu said, "Come with me and see my zeal for the Lord." Then he had him ride along in his chariot.

¹⁷When Jehu came to Samaria, he killed all who were left there of Ahab's family; he destroyed them, according to the word of the Lord spoken to Elijah.

Ministers of Baal Killed

¹⁸Then Jehu brought all the people together and said to them, "Ahab served Baal a little; Jehu will serve him much. ¹⁹Now summon all the prophets of Baal, all his ministers and all his priests. See that no one is missing, because I am going to hold a great sacrifice for Baal. Anyone who fails to come will no longer live." But Jehu was acting deceptively in order to destroy the ministers of Baal.

²⁰Jehu said, "Call an assembly in honor of Baal." So they proclaimed it. ²¹Then he sent word throughout Israel, and all the ministers of Baal came; not one stayed away. They crowded into the temple of Baal until it was full from one end to the other. ²²And Jehu said to the keeper of the wardrobe, "Bring robes for all the ministers of Baal." So he brought out robes for them.

²³Then Jehu and Jehonadab son of Recab went into the temple of Baal. Jehu said to the ministers of Baal, "Look around and see that no servants of the Lord are here with you—only ministers of Baal." ²⁴So they went in to make sacrifices and burnt offerings. Now Jehu had posted eighty men outside with this warning: "If one of you lets any of the men I am placing in your hands escape, it will be your life for his life."

²⁵As soon as Jehu had finished making the burnt offering, he ordered the guards and officers: "Go in and kill them; let no one escape." So they cut them down with the sword. The guards and officers threw the bodies out and then entered the inner shrine of the temple of Baal. ²⁶They brought the sacred stone out of the temple of Baal and burned it. ²⁷They demolished the sacred stone of Baal and tore down the temple of Baal, and people have used it for a latrine to this day.

²⁸So Jehu destroyed Baal worship in Israel. ²⁹However, he did not turn away from the sins of Jeroboam son of Nebat, which he had caused Israel to commit—the worship of the golden calves at Bethel and Dan.

³⁰The Lord said to Jehu, "Because you have done well in accomplishing what is right in my eyes and have done to the house of Ahab all I had in mind to do, your descendants will sit on the throne of Israel to the fourth generation." ³¹Yet Jehu was not careful to keep the law of the Lord, the God of Israel, with all his heart. He did not turn away from the sins of Jeroboam, which he had caused Israel to commit.

³²In those days the Lord began to reduce the size of Israel. Hazael overpowered the Israelites throughout their territory ³³east of the Jordan in all the land of Gilead (the region of Gad, Reuben and Manasseh), from Aroer by the Arnon Gorge through Gilead to Bashan.

³⁴As for the other events of Jehu's reign, all he did, and all his achievements, are they not written in the book of the annals of the kings of Israel?

³⁵Jehu rested with his fathers and was buried in Samaria. And Jehoahaz his son succeeded him as king. ³⁶The time that Jehu reigned over Israel in Samaria was twenty-eight years.

Athaliah and Joash

11 When Athaliah the mother of Ahaziah saw that her son was dead, she proceeded to destroy the whole royal family. ²But Jehosheba, the daughter of King Jehoram[a] and sister of Ahaziah, took Joash son of Ahaziah and stole him away from among the royal princes, who were about to be murdered. She put him and his nurse in a bedroom to hide him from Athaliah; so he was not killed. ³He remained hidden with his nurse at the temple of the Lord for six years while Athaliah ruled the land.

⁴In the seventh year Jehoiada sent for the commanders of units of a hundred, the Carites and the guards and had them brought to him at the temple of the Lord. He made a covenant with them and put them under oath at the temple of the Lord. Then he

---

a2 Hebrew *Joram*, a variant of *Jehoram*

showed them the king's son. [5]He commanded them, saying, "This is what you are to do: You who are in the three companies that are going on duty on the Sabbath—a third of you guarding the royal palace, [6]a third at the Sur Gate, and a third at the gate behind the guard, who take turns guarding the temple— [7]and you who are in the other two companies that normally go off Sabbath duty are all to guard the temple for the king. [8]Station yourselves around the king, each man with his weapon in his hand. Anyone who approaches your ranks[a] must be put to death. Stay close to the king wherever he goes."

[9]The commanders of units of a hundred did just as Jehoiada the priest ordered. Each one took his men—those who were going on duty on the Sabbath and those who were going off duty—and came to Jehoiada the priest. [10]Then he gave the commanders the spears and shields that had belonged to King David and that were in the temple of the LORD. [11]The guards, each with his weapon in his hand, stationed themselves around the king—near the altar and the temple, from the south side to the north side of the temple.

[12]Jehoiada brought out the king's son and put the crown on him; he presented him with a copy of the covenant and proclaimed him king. They anointed him, and the people clapped their hands and shouted, "Long live the king!"

[13]When Athaliah heard the noise made by the guards and the people, she went to the people at the temple of the LORD. [14]She looked and there was the king, standing by the pillar, as the custom was. The officers and the trumpeters were beside the king, and all the people of the land were rejoicing and blowing trumpets. Then Athaliah tore her robes and called out, "Treason! Treason!"

[15]Jehoiada the priest ordered the commanders of units of a hundred, who were in charge of the troops: "Bring her out between the ranks[b] and put to the sword anyone who follows her." For the priest had said, "She must not be put to death in the temple of the LORD." [16]So they seized her as she reached the place where the horses enter the palace grounds, and there she was put to death.

[17]Jehoiada then made a covenant between the LORD and the king and people that they would be the LORD's people. He also made a covenant between the king and the people. [18]All the people of the land went to the temple of Baal and tore it down. They smashed the altars and idols to pieces and killed Mattan the priest of Baal in front of the altars.

Then Jehoiada the priest posted guards at the temple of the LORD. [19]He took with him the commanders of hundreds, the Carites, the guards and all the people of the land, and together they brought the king down from the temple of the LORD and went into the palace, entering by way of the gate of the guards. The king then took his place on the royal throne, [20]and all the people of the land rejoiced. And the city was quiet, because Athaliah had been slain with the sword at the palace.

[21]Joash[c] was seven years old when he began to reign.

Joash Repairs the Temple

12 In the seventh year of Jehu, Joash[d] became king, and he reigned in Jerusalem forty years. His mother's name was Zibiah; she was from Beersheba. [2]Joash did what was right in the eyes of the LORD all the years Jehoiada the priest instructed him. [3]The high places, however, were not removed; the people continued to offer sacrifices and burn incense there.

[4]Joash said to the priests, "Collect all the money that is brought as sacred offerings to the temple of the LORD—the money collected in the census, the money received from personal vows and the money brought voluntarily to the temple. [5]Let every priest receive the money from one of the treasurers, and let it be used to repair whatever damage is found in the temple."

[6]But by the twenty-third year of King Joash the priests still had not repaired the temple. [7]Therefore King Joash summoned Jehoiada the priest and the other priests and asked them, "Why aren't you repairing the damage done to the temple? Take no more money from your treasurers, but hand it over for repairing the temple." [8]The priests agreed that they would not collect any more money from the people and that they would not repair the temple themselves.

[9]Jehoiada the priest took a chest and bored a hole in its lid. He placed it beside the altar, on the right side as one enters the temple of the LORD. The priests who guarded the

a8 Or approaches the precincts   b15 Or out from the precincts   c21 Hebrew Jehoash, a variant of Joash
d1 Hebrew Jehoash, a variant of Joash; also in verses 2, 4, 6, 7 and 18

entrance put into the chest all the money that was brought to the temple of the Lord. **10**Whenever they saw that there was a large amount of money in the chest, the royal secretary and the high priest came, counted the money that had been brought into the temple of the Lord and put it into bags. **11**When the amount had been determined, they gave the money to the men appointed to supervise the work on the temple. With it they paid those who worked on the temple of the Lord—the carpenters and builders, **12**the masons and stonecutters. They purchased timber and dressed stone for the repair of the temple of the Lord, and met all the other expenses of restoring the temple.

13The money brought into the temple was not spent for making silver basins, wick trimmers, sprinkling bowls, trumpets or any other articles of gold or silver for the temple of the Lord; **14**it was paid to the workmen, who used it to repair the temple. **15**They did not require an accounting from those to whom they gave the money to pay the workers, because they acted with complete honesty. **16**The money from the guilt offerings and sin offerings was not brought into the temple of the Lord; it belonged to the priests.

17About this time Hazael king of Aram went up and attacked Gath and captured it. Then he turned to attack Jerusalem. **18**But Joash king of Judah took all the sacred objects dedicated by his fathers—Jehoshaphat, Jehoram and Ahaziah, the kings of Judah—and the gifts he himself had dedicated and all the gold found in the treasuries of the temple of the Lord and of the royal palace, and he sent them to Hazael king of Aram, who then withdrew from Jerusalem.

19As for the other events of the reign of Joash, and all he did, are they not written in the book of the annals of the kings of Judah? **20**His officials conspired against him and assassinated him at Beth Millo, on the road down to Silla. **21**The officials who murdered him were Jozabad son of Shimeath and Jehozabad son of Shomer. He died and was buried with his fathers in the City of David. And Amaziah his son succeeded him as king.

Jehoahaz King of Israel

13 In the twenty-third year of Joash son of Ahaziah king of Judah, Jehoahaz son of Jehu became king of Israel in Samaria, and he reigned seventeen years. **2**He did

evil in the eyes of the Lord by following the sins of Jeroboam son of Nebat, which he had caused Israel to commit, and he did not turn away from them. **3**So the Lord's anger burned against Israel, and for a long time he kept them under the power of Hazael king of Aram and Ben-Hadad his son.

4Then Jehoahaz sought the Lord's favor, and the Lord listened to him, for he saw how severely the king of Aram was oppressing Israel. **5**The Lord provided a deliverer for Israel, and they escaped from the power of Aram. So the Israelites lived in their own homes as they had before. **6**But they did not turn away from the sins of the house of Jeroboam, which he had caused Israel to commit; they continued in them. Also, the Asherah pole*a* remained standing in Samaria.

7Nothing had been left of the army of Jehoahaz except fifty horsemen, ten chariots and ten thousand foot soldiers, for the king of Aram had destroyed the rest and made them like the dust at threshing time.

8As for the other events of the reign of Jehoahaz, all he did and his achievements, are they not written in the book of the annals of the kings of Israel? **9**Jehoahaz rested with his fathers and was buried in Samaria. And Jehoash*b* his son succeeded him as king.

Jehoash King of Israel

10In the thirty-seventh year of Joash king of Judah, Jehoash son of Jehoahaz became king of Israel in Samaria, and he reigned sixteen years. **11**He did evil in the eyes of the Lord and did not turn away from any of the sins of Jeroboam son of Nebat, which he had caused Israel to commit; he continued in them.

12As for the other events of the reign of Jehoash, all he did and his achievements, including his war against Amaziah king of Judah, are they not written in the book of the annals of the kings of Israel? **13**Jehoash rested with his fathers, and Jeroboam succeeded him on the throne. Jehoash was buried in Samaria with the kings of Israel.

14Now Elisha was suffering from the illness from which he died. Jehoash king of Israel went down to see him and wept over him. "My father! My father!" he cried. "The chariots and horsemen of Israel!"

15Elisha said, "Get a bow and some arrows," and he did so. **16**"Take the bow in your hands," he said to the king of Israel.

When he had taken it, Elisha put his hands on the king's hands.

[17]"Open the east window," he said, and he opened it. "Shoot!" Elisha said, and he shot. "The LORD's arrow of victory, the arrow of victory over Aram!" Elisha declared. "You will completely destroy the Arameans at Aphek."

[18]Then he said, "Take the arrows," and the king took them. Elisha told him, "Strike the ground." He struck it three times and stopped. [19]The man of God was angry with him and said, "You should have struck the ground five or six times; then you would have defeated Aram and completely destroyed it. But now you will defeat it only three times."

[20]Elisha died and was buried.

Now Moabite raiders used to enter the country every spring. [21]Once while some Israelites were burying a man, suddenly they saw a band of raiders; so they threw the man's body into Elisha's tomb. When the body touched Elisha's bones, the man came to life and stood up on his feet.

[22]Hazael king of Aram oppressed Israel throughout the reign of Jehoahaz. [23]But the LORD was gracious to them and had compassion and showed concern for them because of his covenant with Abraham, Isaac and Jacob. To this day he has been unwilling to destroy them or banish them from his presence.

[24]Hazael king of Aram died, and Ben-Hadad his son succeeded him as king. [25]Then Jehoash son of Jehoahaz recaptured from Ben-Hadad son of Hazael the towns he had taken in battle from his father Jehoahaz. Three times Jehoash defeated him, and so he recovered the Israelite towns.

Amaziah King of Judah

14 In the second year of Jehoash[a] son of Jehoahaz king of Israel, Amaziah son of Joash king of Judah began to reign. [2]He was twenty-five years old when he became king, and he reigned in Jerusalem twenty-nine years. His mother's name was Jehoaddin; she was from Jerusalem. [3]He did what was right in the eyes of the LORD, but not as his father David had done. In everything he followed the example of his father Joash. [4]The high places, however, were not removed; the people continued to offer sacrifices and burn incense there.

[5]After the kingdom was firmly in his grasp, he executed the officials who had murdered his father the king. [6]Yet he did not put the sons of the assassins to death, in accordance with what is written in the Book of the Law of Moses where the LORD commanded: "Fathers shall not be put to death for their children, nor children put to death for their fathers; each is to die for his own sins."[b]

[7]He was the one who defeated ten thousand Edomites in the Valley of Salt and captured Sela in battle, calling it Joktheel, the name it has to this day.

[8]Then Amaziah sent messengers to Jehoash son of Jehoahaz, the son of Jehu, king of Israel, with the challenge: "Come, meet me face to face."

[9]But Jehoash king of Israel replied to Amaziah king of Judah: "A thistle in Lebanon sent a message to a cedar in Lebanon, 'Give your daughter to my son in marriage.' Then a wild beast in Lebanon came along and trampled the thistle underfoot. [10]You have indeed defeated Edom and now you are arrogant. Glory in your victory, but stay at home! Why ask for trouble and cause your own downfall and that of Judah also?"

[11]Amaziah, however, would not listen, so Jehoash king of Israel attacked. He and Amaziah king of Judah faced each other at Beth Shemesh in Judah. [12]Judah was routed by Israel, and every man fled to his home. [13]Jehoash king of Israel captured Amaziah king of Judah, the son of Joash, the son of Ahaziah, at Beth Shemesh. Then Jehoash went to Jerusalem and broke down the wall of Jerusalem from the Ephraim Gate to the Corner Gate—a section about six hundred feet long.[c] [14]He took all the gold and silver and all the articles found in the temple of the LORD and in the treasuries of the royal palace. He also took hostages and returned to Samaria.

[15]As for the other events of the reign of Jehoash, what he did and his achievements, including his war against Amaziah king of Judah, are they not written in the book of the annals of the kings of Israel? [16]Jehoash rested with his fathers and was buried in Samaria with the kings of Israel. And Jeroboam his son succeeded him as king.

[17]Amaziah son of Joash king of Judah lived for fifteen years after the death of Jehoash son of Jehoahaz king of Israel. [18]As for the other events of Amaziah's reign, are they

not written in the book of the annals of the kings of Judah?

¹⁹They conspired against him in Jerusalem, and he fled to Lachish, but they sent men after him to Lachish and killed him there. ²⁰He was brought back by horse and was buried in Jerusalem with his fathers, in the City of David.

²¹Then all the people of Judah took Azariah,ᵃ who was sixteen years old, and made him king in place of his father Amaziah. ²²He was the one who rebuilt Elath and restored it to Judah after Amaziah rested with his fathers.

Jeroboam II King of Israel

²³In the fifteenth year of Amaziah son of Joash king of Judah, Jeroboam son of Jehoash king of Israel became king in Samaria, and he reigned forty-one years. ²⁴He did evil in the eyes of the Lord and did not turn away from any of the sins of Jeroboam son of Nebat, which he had caused Israel to commit. ²⁵He was the one who restored the boundaries of Israel from Leboᵇ Hamath to the Sea of the Arabah,ᶜ in accordance with the word of the Lord, the God of Israel, spoken through his servant Jonah son of Amittai, the prophet from Gath Hepher.

²⁶The Lord had seen how bitterly everyone in Israel, whether slave or free, was suffering; there was no one to help them. ²⁷And since the Lord had not said he would blot out the name of Israel from under heaven, he saved them by the hand of Jeroboam son of Jehoash.

²⁸As for the other events of Jeroboam's reign, all he did, and his military achievements, including how he recovered for Israel both Damascus and Hamath, which had belonged to Yaudi,ᵈ are they not written in the book of the annals of the kings of Israel? ²⁹Jeroboam rested with his fathers, the kings of Israel. And Zechariah his son succeeded him as king.

Azariah King of Judah

15 In the twenty-seventh year of Jeroboam king of Israel, Azariah son of Amaziah king of Judah began to reign. ²He was sixteen years old when he became king, and he reigned in Jerusalem fifty-two years. His mother's name was Jecoliah; she was from Jerusalem. ³He did what was right in the eyes of the Lord, just as his father Amaziah had done. ⁴The high places, however, were not removed; the people continued to offer sacrifices and burn incense there.

⁵The Lord afflicted the king with leprosyᵉ until the day he died, and he lived in a separate house.ᶠ Jotham the king's son had charge of the palace and governed the people of the land.

⁶As for the other events of Azariah's reign, and all he did, are they not written in the book of the annals of the kings of Judah? ⁷Azariah rested with his fathers and was buried near them in the City of David. And Jotham his son succeeded him as king.

Zechariah King of Israel

⁸In the thirty-eighth year of Azariah king of Judah, Zechariah son of Jeroboam became king of Israel in Samaria, and he reigned six months. ⁹He did evil in the eyes of the Lord, as his fathers had done. He did not turn away from the sins of Jeroboam son of Nebat, which he had caused Israel to commit.

¹⁰Shallum son of Jabesh conspired against Zechariah. He attacked him in front of the people,ᵍ assassinated him and succeeded him as king. ¹¹The other events of Zechariah's reign are written in the book of the annals of the kings of Israel. ¹²So the word of the Lord spoken to Jehu was fulfilled: "Your descendants will sit on the throne of Israel to the fourth generation."ʰ

Shallum King of Israel

¹³Shallum son of Jabesh became king in the thirty-ninth year of Uzziah king of Judah, and he reigned in Samaria one month. ¹⁴Then Menahem son of Gadi went from Tirzah up to Samaria. He attacked Shallum son of Jabesh in Samaria, assassinated him and succeeded him as king.

¹⁵The other events of Shallum's reign, and the conspiracy he led, are written in the book of the annals of the kings of Israel.

¹⁶At that time Menahem, starting out from Tirzah, attacked Tiphsah and everyone in the city and its vicinity, because they refused to open their gates. He sacked Tiphsah and ripped open all the pregnant women.

ᵃ21 Also called *Uzziah*   ᵇ25 Or *from the entrance to*   ᶜ25 That is, the Dead Sea   ᵈ28 Or *Judah*
ᵉ5 The Hebrew word was used for various diseases affecting the skin—not necessarily leprosy.   ᶠ5 Or *in a house where he was relieved of responsibility*   ᵍ10 Hebrew; some Septuagint manuscripts *in Ibleam*
ʰ12 2 Kings 10:30

Menahem King of Israel

17In the thirty-ninth year of Azariah king of Judah, Menahem son of Gadi became king of Israel, and he reigned in Samaria ten years. **18**He did evil in the eyes of the Lord. During his entire reign he did not turn away from the sins of Jeroboam son of Nebat, which he had caused Israel to commit.

19Then Pul*a* king of Assyria invaded the land, and Menahem gave him a thousand talents*b* of silver to gain his support and strengthen his own hold on the kingdom. **20**Menahem exacted this money from Israel. Every wealthy man had to contribute fifty shekels*c* of silver to be given to the king of Assyria. So the king of Assyria withdrew and stayed in the land no longer.

21As for the other events of Menahem's reign, and all he did, are they not written in the book of the annals of the kings of Israel? **22**Menahem rested with his fathers. And Pekahiah his son succeeded him as king.

Pekahiah King of Israel

23In the fiftieth year of Azariah king of Judah, Pekahiah son of Menahem became king of Israel in Samaria, and he reigned two years. **24**Pekahiah did evil in the eyes of the Lord. He did not turn away from the sins of Jeroboam son of Nebat, which he had caused Israel to commit. **25**One of his chief officers, Pekah son of Remaliah, conspired against him. Taking fifty men of Gilead with him, he assassinated Pekahiah, along with Argob and Arieh, in the citadel of the royal palace at Samaria. So Pekah killed Pekahiah and succeeded him as king.

26The other events of Pekahiah's reign, and all he did, are written in the book of the annals of the kings of Israel.

Pekah King of Israel

27In the fifty-second year of Azariah king of Judah, Pekah son of Remaliah became king of Israel in Samaria, and he reigned twenty years. **28**He did evil in the eyes of the Lord. He did not turn away from the sins of Jeroboam son of Nebat, which he had caused Israel to commit. **29**In the time of Pekah king of Israel, Tiglath-Pileser king of Assyria came and took Ijon, Abel Beth Maacah, Janoah, Kedesh and Hazor. He took Gilead and Galilee, including all the land of Naphtali, and deported the people to Assyria. **30**Then Hoshea son of Elah conspired against Pekah son of Remaliah. He attacked and assassinated him, and then succeeded him as king in the twentieth year of Jotham son of Uzziah.

31As for the other events of Pekah's reign, and all he did, are they not written in the book of the annals of the kings of Israel?

Jotham King of Judah

32In the second year of Pekah son of Remaliah king of Israel, Jotham son of Uzziah king of Judah began to reign. **33**He was twenty-five years old when he became king, and he reigned in Jerusalem sixteen years. His mother's name was Jerusha daughter of Zadok. **34**He did what was right in the eyes of the Lord, just as his father Uzziah had done. **35**The high places, however, were not removed; the people continued to offer sacrifices and burn incense there. Jotham rebuilt the Upper Gate of the temple of the Lord.

36As for the other events of Jotham's reign, and what he did, are they not written in the book of the annals of the kings of Judah? **37**(In those days the Lord began to send Rezin king of Aram and Pekah son of Remaliah against Judah.) **38**Jotham rested with his fathers and was buried with them in the City of David, the city of his father. And Ahaz his son succeeded him as king.

Ahaz King of Judah

16 In the seventeenth year of Pekah son of Remaliah, Ahaz son of Jotham king of Judah began to reign. **2**Ahaz was twenty years old when he became king, and he reigned in Jerusalem sixteen years. Unlike David his father, he did not do what was right in the eyes of the Lord his God. **3**He walked in the ways of the kings of Israel and even sacrificed his son in*d* the fire, following the detestable ways of the nations the Lord had driven out before the Israelites. **4**He offered sacrifices and burned incense at the high places, on the hilltops and under every spreading tree.

5Then Rezin king of Aram and Pekah son of Remaliah king of Israel marched up to fight against Jerusalem and besieged Ahaz, but they could not overpower him. **6**At that time, Rezin king of Aram recovered Elath for Aram by driving out the men of Judah. Edomites then moved into Elath and have lived there to this day.

7Ahaz sent messengers to say to Tiglath-Pileser king of Assyria, "I am your servant

---

a19 Also called *Tiglath-Pileser*   *b19* That is, about 37 tons (about 34 metric tons)   *c20* That is, about 1 1/4
pounds (about 0.6 kilogram)   *d3* Or *even made his son pass through*

and vassal. Come up and save me out of the hand of the king of Aram and of the king of Israel, who are attacking me." **8**And Ahaz took the silver and gold found in the temple of the Lord and in the treasuries of the royal palace and sent it as a gift to the king of Assyria. **9**The king of Assyria complied by attacking Damascus and capturing it. He deported its inhabitants to Kir and put Rezin to death.

10Then King Ahaz went to Damascus to meet Tiglath-Pileser king of Assyria. He saw an altar in Damascus and sent to Uriah the priest a sketch of the altar, with detailed plans for its construction. **11**So Uriah the priest built an altar in accordance with all the plans that King Ahaz had sent from Damascus and finished it before King Ahaz returned. **12**When the king came back from Damascus and saw the altar, he approached it and presented offerings*a* on it. **13**He offered up his burnt offering and grain offering, poured out his drink offering, and sprinkled the blood of his fellowship offerings*b* on the altar. **14**The bronze altar that stood before the Lord he brought from the front of the temple — from between the new altar and the temple of the Lord — and put it on the north side of the new altar.

15King Ahaz then gave these orders to Uriah the priest: "On the large new altar, offer the morning burnt offering and the evening grain offering, the king's burnt offering and his grain offering, and the burnt offering of all the people of the land, and their grain offering and their drink offering. Sprinkle on the altar all the blood of the burnt offerings and sacrifices. But I will use the bronze altar for seeking guidance." **16**And Uriah the priest did just as King Ahaz had ordered.

17King Ahaz took away the side panels and removed the basins from the movable stands. He removed the Sea from the bronze bulls that supported it and set it on a stone base. **18**He took away the Sabbath canopy*c* that had been built at the temple and removed the royal entryway outside the temple of the Lord, in deference to the king of Assyria.

19As for the other events of the reign of Ahaz, and what he did, are they not written in the book of the annals of the kings of Judah? **20**Ahaz rested with his fathers and was buried with them in the City of David. And Hezekiah his son succeeded him as king.

Hoshea Last King of Israel

17 In the twelfth year of Ahaz king of Judah, Hoshea son of Elah became king of Israel in Samaria, and he reigned nine years. **2**He did evil in the eyes of the Lord, but not like the kings of Israel who preceded him.

3Shalmaneser king of Assyria came up to attack Hoshea, who had been Shalmaneser's vassal and had paid him tribute. **4**But the king of Assyria discovered that Hoshea was a traitor, for he had sent envoys to So*d* king of Egypt, and he no longer paid tribute to the king of Assyria, as he had done year by year. Therefore Shalmaneser seized him and put him in prison. **5**The king of Assyria invaded the entire land, marched against Samaria and laid siege to it for three years. **6**In the ninth year of Hoshea, the king of Assyria captured Samaria and deported the Israelites to Assyria. He settled them in Halah, in Gozan on the Habor River and in the towns of the Medes.

Israel Exiled Because of Sin

7All this took place because the Israelites had sinned against the Lord their God, who had brought them up out of Egypt from under the power of Pharaoh king of Egypt. They worshiped other gods **8**and followed the practices of the nations the Lord had driven out before them, as well as the practices that the kings of Israel had introduced. **9**The Israelites secretly did things against the Lord their God that were not right. From watchtower to fortified city they built themselves high places in all their towns. **10**They set up sacred stones and Asherah poles on every high hill and under every spreading tree. **11**At every high place they burned incense, as the nations whom the Lord had driven out before them had done. They did wicked things that provoked the Lord to anger. **12**They worshiped idols, though the Lord had said, "You shall not do this."*e* **13**The Lord warned Israel and Judah through all his prophets and seers: "Turn from your evil ways. Observe my commands and decrees, in accordance with the entire Law that I commanded your fathers to obey and that I delivered to you through my servants the prophets."

14But they would not listen and were as stiff-necked as their fathers, who did not trust in the Lord their God. **15**They rejected

---

a 12 Or *and went up*   *b 13* Traditionally *peace offerings*   *c 18* Or *the dais of his throne* (see Septuagint)
d 4 Or *to Sais, to the*; *So* is possibly an abbreviation for *Osorkon.*   *e 12* Exodus 20:4, 5

his decrees and the covenant he had made with their fathers and the warnings he had given them. They followed worthless idols and themselves became worthless. They imitated the nations around them although the Lord had ordered them, "Do not do as they do," and they did the things the Lord had forbidden them to do.

¹⁶They forsook all the commands of the Lord their God and made for themselves two idols cast in the shape of calves, and an Asherah pole. They bowed down to all the starry hosts, and they worshiped Baal. ¹⁷They sacrificed their sons and daughters in ᵃ the fire. They practiced divination and sorcery and sold themselves to do evil in the eyes of the Lord, provoking him to anger.

¹⁸So the Lord was very angry with Israel and removed them from his presence. Only the tribe of Judah was left, ¹⁹and even Judah did not keep the commands of the Lord their God. They followed the practices Israel had introduced. ²⁰Therefore the Lord rejected all the people of Israel; he afflicted them and gave them into the hands of plunderers, until he thrust them from his presence.

²¹When he tore Israel away from the house of David, they made Jeroboam son of Nebat their king. Jeroboam enticed Israel away from following the Lord and caused them to commit a great sin. ²²The Israelites persisted in all the sins of Jeroboam and did not turn away from them ²³until the Lord removed them from his presence, as he had warned through all his servants the prophets. So the people of Israel were taken from their homeland into exile in Assyria, and they are still there.

Samaria Resettled

²⁴The king of Assyria brought people from Babylon, Cuthah, Avva, Hamath and Sepharvaim and settled them in the towns of Samaria to replace the Israelites. They took over Samaria and lived in its towns. ²⁵When they first lived there, they did not worship the Lord; so he sent lions among them and they killed some of the people. ²⁶It was reported to the king of Assyria: "The people you deported and resettled in the towns of Samaria do not know what the god of that country requires. He has sent lions among them, which are killing them off, because the people do not know what he requires."

²⁷Then the king of Assyria gave this order: "Have one of the priests you took captive from Samaria go back to live there and teach the people what the god of the land requires." ²⁸So one of the priests who had been exiled from Samaria came to live in Bethel and taught them how to worship the Lord.

²⁹Nevertheless, each national group made its own gods in the several towns where they settled, and set them up in the shrines the people of Samaria had made at the high places. ³⁰The men from Babylon made Succoth Benoth, the men from Cuthah made Nergal, and the men from Hamath made Ashima; ³¹the Avvites made Nibhaz and Tartak, and the Sepharvites burned their children in the fire as sacrifices to Adrammelech and Anammelech, the gods of Sepharvaim. ³²They worshiped the Lord, but they also appointed all sorts of their own people to officiate for them as priests in the shrines at the high places. ³³They worshiped the Lord, but they also served their own gods in accordance with the customs of the nations from which they had been brought.

³⁴To this day they persist in their former practices. They neither worship the Lord nor adhere to the decrees and ordinances, the laws and commands that the Lord gave the descendants of Jacob, whom he named Israel. ³⁵When the Lord made a covenant with the Israelites, he commanded them: "Do not worship any other gods or bow down to them, serve them or sacrifice to them. ³⁶But the Lord, who brought you up out of Egypt with mighty power and outstretched arm, is the one you must worship. To him you shall bow down and to him offer sacrifices. ³⁷You must always be careful to keep the decrees and ordinances, the laws and commands he wrote for you. Do not worship other gods. ³⁸Do not forget the covenant I have made with you, and do not worship other gods. ³⁹Rather, worship the Lord your God; it is he who will deliver you from the hand of all your enemies."

⁴⁰They would not listen, however, but persisted in their former practices. ⁴¹Even while these people were worshiping the Lord, they were serving their idols. To this day their children and grandchildren continue to do as their fathers did.

Hezekiah King of Judah

18 In the third year of Hoshea son of Elah king of Israel, Hezekiah son of Ahaz king of Judah began to reign. ²He was twenty-five years old when he became king,

---

ᵃ 17 Or *They made their sons and daughters pass through*

and he reigned in Jerusalem twenty-nine years. His mother's name was Abijah[a] daughter of Zechariah. [3]He did what was right in the eyes of the Lord, just as his father David had done. [4]He removed the high places, smashed the sacred stones and cut down the Asherah poles. He broke into pieces the bronze snake Moses had made, for up to that time the Israelites had been burning incense to it. (It was called[b] Nehushtan.[c])

[5]Hezekiah trusted in the Lord, the God of Israel. There was no one like him among all the kings of Judah, either before him or after him. [6]He held fast to the Lord and did not cease to follow him; he kept the commands the Lord had given Moses. [7]And the Lord was with him; he was successful in whatever he undertook. He rebelled against the king of Assyria and did not serve him. [8]From watchtower to fortified city, he defeated the Philistines, as far as Gaza and its territory.

[9]In King Hezekiah's fourth year, which was the seventh year of Hoshea son of Elah king of Israel, Shalmaneser king of Assyria marched against Samaria and laid siege to it. [10]At the end of three years the Assyrians took it. So Samaria was captured in Hezekiah's sixth year, which was the ninth year of Hoshea king of Israel. [11]The king of Assyria deported Israel to Assyria and settled them in Halah, in Gozan on the Habor River and in towns of the Medes. [12]This happened because they had not obeyed the Lord their God, but had violated his covenant—all that Moses the servant of the Lord commanded. They neither listened to the commands nor carried them out.

[13]In the fourteenth year of King Hezekiah's reign, Sennacherib king of Assyria attacked all the fortified cities of Judah and captured them. [14]So Hezekiah king of Judah sent this message to the king of Assyria at Lachish: "I have done wrong. Withdraw from me, and I will pay whatever you demand of me." The king of Assyria exacted from Hezekiah king of Judah three hundred talents[d] of silver and thirty talents[e] of gold. [15]So Hezekiah gave him all the silver that was found in the temple of the Lord and in the treasuries of the royal palace.

[16]At this time Hezekiah king of Judah stripped off the gold with which he had covered the doors and doorposts of the temple of the Lord, and gave it to the king of Assyria.

Sennacherib Threatens Jerusalem

[17]The king of Assyria sent his supreme commander, his chief officer and his field commander with a large army, from Lachish to King Hezekiah at Jerusalem. They came up to Jerusalem and stopped at the aqueduct of the Upper Pool, on the road to the Washerman's Field. [18]They called for the king; and Eliakim son of Hilkiah the palace administrator, Shebna the secretary, and Joah son of Asaph the recorder went out to them.

[19]The field commander said to them, "Tell Hezekiah:

" 'This is what the great king, the king of Assyria, says: On what are you basing this confidence of yours? [20]You say you have strategy and military strength—but you speak only empty words. On whom are you depending, that you rebel against me? [21]Look now, you are depending on Egypt, that splintered reed of a staff, which pierces a man's hand and wounds him if he leans on it! Such is Pharaoh king of Egypt to all who depend on him. [22]And if you say to me, "We are depending on the Lord our God"—isn't he the one whose high places and altars Hezekiah removed, saying to Judah and Jerusalem, "You must worship before this altar in Jerusalem"?

[23]" 'Come now, make a bargain with my master, the king of Assyria: I will give you two thousand horses—if you can put riders on them! [24]How can you repulse one officer of the least of my master's officials, even though you are depending on Egypt for chariots and horsemen[f]? [25]Furthermore, have I come to attack and destroy this place without word from the Lord? The Lord himself told me to march against this country and destroy it.' "

[26]Then Eliakim son of Hilkiah, and Shebna and Joah said to the field commander, "Please speak to your servants in Aramaic, since we understand it. Don't speak to us in Hebrew in the hearing of the people on the wall."

[27]But the commander replied, "Was it only to your master and you that my master sent me to say these things, and not to the men sitting on the wall—who, like you, will

Hebrew *Abi*, a variant of *Abijah*　　[b]4 Or *He called it*　　[c]4 *Nehushtan* sounds like the Hebrew for *bronze* ［*snake*］ and *unclean thing*.　　[d]14 That is, about 11 tons (about 10 metric tons)　　[e]14 That is, about 1 ton ［（1 metric ton）］　　[f]24 Or *charioteers* have to eat their own filth and drink their own urine?"

28Then the commander stood and called out in Hebrew: "Hear the word of the great king, the king of Assyria! **29**This is what the king says: Do not let Hezekiah deceive you. He cannot deliver you from my hand. **30**Do not let Hezekiah persuade you to trust in the Lord when he says, 'The Lord will surely deliver us; this city will not be given into the hand of the king of Assyria.'

31"Do not listen to Hezekiah. This is what the king of Assyria says: Make peace with me and come out to me. Then every one of you will eat from his own vine and fig tree and drink water from his own cistern, **32**until I come and take you to a land like your own, a land of grain and new wine, a land of bread and vineyards, a land of olive trees and honey. Choose life and not death!

"Do not listen to Hezekiah, for he is misleading you when he says, 'The Lord will deliver us.' **33**Has the god of any nation ever delivered his land from the hand of the king of Assyria? **34**Where are the gods of Hamath and Arpad? Where are the gods of Sepharvaim, Hena and Ivvah? Have they rescued Samaria from my hand? **35**Who of all the gods of these countries has been able to save his land from me? How then can the Lord deliver Jerusalem from my hand?"

36But the people remained silent and said nothing in reply, because the king had commanded, "Do not answer him."

37Then Eliakim son of Hilkiah the palace administrator, Shebna the secretary and Joah son of Asaph the recorder went to Hezekiah, with their clothes torn, and told him what the field commander had said.

Jerusalem's Deliverance Foretold

19 When King Hezekiah heard this, he tore his clothes and put on sackcloth and went into the temple of the Lord. **2**He sent Eliakim the palace administrator, Shebna the secretary and the leading priests, all wearing sackcloth, to the prophet Isaiah son of Amoz. **3**They told him, "This is what Hezekiah says: This day is a day of distress and rebuke and disgrace, as when children come to the point of birth and there is no strength to deliver them. **4**It may be that the Lord your God will hear all the words of the field commander, whom his master, the king of Assyria, has sent to ridicule the living God, and that he will rebuke him for the words the Lord your God has heard. Therefore pray for the remnant that still survives."

5When King Hezekiah's officials came to Isaiah, **6**Isaiah said to them, "Tell your master, 'This is what the Lord says: Do not be afraid of what you have heard—those words with which the underlings of the king of Assyria have blasphemed me. **7**Listen! I am going to put such a spirit in him that when he hears a certain report, he will return to his own country, and there I will have him cut down with the sword.' "

8When the field commander heard that the king of Assyria had left Lachish, he withdrew and found the king fighting against Libnah.

9Now Sennacherib received a report that Tirhakah, the Cushite*a* king ˻of Egypt˼, was marching out to fight against him. So he again sent messengers to Hezekiah with this word: **10**"Say to Hezekiah king of Judah: Do not let the god you depend on deceive you when he says, 'Jerusalem will not be handed over to the king of Assyria.' **11**Surely you have heard what the kings of Assyria have done to all the countries, destroying them completely. And will you be delivered? **12**Did the gods of the nations that were destroyed by my forefathers deliver them: the gods of Gozan, Haran, Rezeph and the people of Eden who were in Tel Assar? **13**Where is the king of Hamath, the king of Arpad, the king of the city of Sepharvaim, or of Hena or Ivvah?"

Hezekiah's Prayer

14Hezekiah received the letter from the messengers and read it. Then he went up to the temple of the Lord and spread it out before the Lord. **15**And Hezekiah prayed to the Lord: "O Lord, God of Israel, enthroned between the cherubim, you alone are God over all the kingdoms of the earth. You have made heaven and earth. **16**Give ear, O Lord, and hear; open your eyes, O Lord, and see; listen to the words Sennacherib has sent to insult the living God.

17"It is true, O Lord, that the Assyrian kings have laid waste these nations and their lands. **18**They have thrown their gods into the fire and destroyed them, for they were not gods but only wood and stone, fashioned by men's hands. **19**Now, O Lord our God, deliver us from his hand, so that all kingdoms on earth may know that you alone, O Lord, are God."

a9 That is, from the upper Nile region

Isaiah Prophesies Sennacherib's Fall

20Then Isaiah son of Amoz sent a message to Hezekiah: "This is what the LORD, the God of Israel, says: I have heard your prayer concerning Sennacherib king of Assyria. **21**This is the word that the LORD has spoken against him:

" 'The Virgin Daughter of Zion
    despises you and mocks you.
The Daughter of Jerusalem
    tosses her head as you flee.
22Who is it you have insulted and
      blasphemed?
    Against whom have you raised your
      voice
and lifted your eyes in pride?
    Against the Holy One of Israel!
23By your messengers
    you have heaped insults on the Lord.
And you have said,
    "With my many chariots
I have ascended the heights of the
      mountains,
    the utmost heights of Lebanon.
I have cut down its tallest cedars,
    the choicest of its pines.
I have reached its remotest parts,
    the finest of its forests.
24I have dug wells in foreign lands
    and drunk the water there.
With the soles of my feet
    I have dried up all the streams of
      Egypt."

25" 'Have you not heard?
    Long ago I ordained it.
In days of old I planned it;
    now I have brought it to pass,
that you have turned fortified cities
    into piles of stone.
26Their people, drained of power,
    are dismayed and put to shame.
They are like plants in the field,
    like tender green shoots,
like grass sprouting on the roof,
    scorched before it grows up.

27" 'But I know where you stay
    and when you come and go
    and how you rage against me.
Because you rage against me
    and your insolence has reached my
      ears,
'll put my hook in your nose
  d my bit in your mouth,
    will make you return
     e way you came.'

29"This will be the sign for you, O Hezekiah:

"This year you will eat what grows by
    itself,
    and the second year what springs
      from that.
But in the third year sow and reap,
    plant vineyards and eat their fruit.
30Once more a remnant of the house of
    Judah
    will take root below and bear fruit
      above.
31For out of Jerusalem will come a
    remnant,
    and out of Mount Zion a band of
      survivors.

The zeal of the LORD Almighty will accomplish this.

32"Therefore this is what the LORD says concerning the king of Assyria:

"He will not enter this city
    or shoot an arrow here.
He will not come before it with shield
    or build a siege ramp against it.
33By the way that he came he will return;
    he will not enter this city,
                declares the LORD.
34I will defend this city and save it,
    for my sake and for the sake of David
      my servant."

35That night the angel of the LORD went out and put to death a hundred and eighty-five thousand men in the Assyrian camp. When the people got up the next morning—there were all the dead bodies! **36**So Sennacherib king of Assyria broke camp and withdrew. He returned to Nineveh and stayed there.

37One day, while he was worshiping in the temple of his god Nisroch, his sons Adrammelech and Sharezer cut him down with the sword, and they escaped to the land of Ararat. And Esarhaddon his son succeeded him as king.

Hezekiah's Illness

20 In those days Hezekiah became ill and was at the point of death. The prophet Isaiah son of Amoz went to him and said, "This is what the LORD says: Put your house in order, because you are going to die; you will not recover."

2Hezekiah turned his face to the wall and prayed to the LORD, **3**"Remember, O LORD, how I have walked before you faithfully and with wholehearted devotion and have done what is good in your eyes." And Hezekiah wept bitterly.

⁴Before Isaiah had left the middle court, the word of the LORD came to him: ⁵"Go back and tell Hezekiah, the leader of my people, 'This is what the LORD, the God of your father David, says: I have heard your prayer and seen your tears; I will heal you. On the third day from now you will go up to the temple of the LORD. ⁶I will add fifteen years to your life. And I will deliver you and this city from the hand of the king of Assyria. I will defend this city for my sake and for the sake of my servant David.' "

⁷Then Isaiah said, "Prepare a poultice of figs." They did so and applied it to the boil, and he recovered.

⁸Hezekiah had asked Isaiah, "What will be the sign that the LORD will heal me and that I will go up to the temple of the LORD on the third day from now?"

⁹Isaiah answered, "This is the LORD's sign to you that the LORD will do what he has promised: Shall the shadow go forward ten steps, or shall it go back ten steps?"

¹⁰"It is a simple matter for the shadow to go forward ten steps," said Hezekiah. "Rather, have it go back ten steps."

¹¹Then the prophet Isaiah called upon the LORD, and the LORD made the shadow go back the ten steps it had gone down on the stairway of Ahaz.

Envoys From Babylon

¹²At that time Merodach-Baladan son of Baladan king of Babylon sent Hezekiah letters and a gift, because he had heard of Hezekiah's illness. ¹³Hezekiah received the messengers and showed them all that was in his storehouses — the silver, the gold, the spices and the fine oil — his armory and everything found among his treasures. There was nothing in his palace or in all his kingdom that Hezekiah did not show them.

¹⁴Then Isaiah the prophet went to King Hezekiah and asked, "What did those men say, and where did they come from?"

"From a distant land," Hezekiah replied. "They came from Babylon."

¹⁵The prophet asked, "What did they see in your palace?"

"They saw everything in my palace," Hezekiah said. "There is nothing among my treasures that I did not show them."

¹⁶Then Isaiah said to Hezekiah, "Hear the word of the LORD: ¹⁷The time will surely come when everything in your palace, and all that your fathers have stored up until this day, will be carried off to Babylon. Nothing will be left, says the LORD. ¹⁸And some of your descendants, your own flesh and blood, that will be born to you, will be taken away, and they will become eunuchs in the palace of the king of Babylon."

¹⁹"The word of the LORD you have spoken is good," Hezekiah replied. For he thought, "Will there not be peace and security in my lifetime?"

²⁰As for the other events of Hezekiah's reign, all his achievements and how he made the pool and the tunnel by which he brought water into the city, are they not written in the book of the annals of the kings of Judah? ²¹Hezekiah rested with his fathers. And Manasseh his son succeeded him as king.

Manasseh King of Judah

21 Manasseh was twelve years old when he became king, and he reigned in Jerusalem fifty-five years. His mother's name was Hephzibah. ²He did evil in the eyes of the LORD, following the detestable practices of the nations the LORD had driven out before the Israelites. ³He rebuilt the high places his father Hezekiah had destroyed; he also erected altars to Baal and made an Asherah pole, as Ahab king of Israel had done. He bowed down to all the starry hosts and worshiped them. ⁴He built altars in the temple of the LORD, of which the LORD had said, "In Jerusalem I will put my Name." ⁵In both courts of the temple of the LORD, he built altars to all the starry hosts. ⁶He sacrificed his own son in*a* the fire, practiced sorcery and divination, and consulted mediums and spiritists. He did much evil in the eyes of the LORD, provoking him to anger.

⁷He took the carved Asherah pole he had made and put it in the temple, of which the LORD had said to David and to his son Solomon, "In this temple and in Jerusalem, which I have chosen out of all the tribes of Israel, I will put my Name forever. ⁸I will not again make the feet of the Israelites wander from the land I gave their forefathers, if only they will be careful to do everything I commanded them and will keep the whole Law that my servant Moses gave them." ⁹But the people did not listen. Manasseh led them astray, so that they did more evil than the nations the LORD had destroyed before the Israelites.

a6 Or He made his own son pass through

¹⁰The LORD said through his servants the prophets: ¹¹"Manasseh king of Judah has committed these detestable sins. He has done more evil than the Amorites who preceded him and has led Judah into sin with his idols. ¹²Therefore this is what the LORD, the God of Israel, says: I am going to bring such disaster on Jerusalem and Judah that the ears of everyone who hears of it will tingle. ¹³I will stretch out over Jerusalem the measuring line used against Samaria and the plumb line used against the house of Ahab. I will wipe out Jerusalem as one wipes a dish, wiping it and turning it upside down. ¹⁴I will forsake the remnant of my inheritance and hand them over to their enemies. They will be looted and plundered by all their foes, ¹⁵because they have done evil in my eyes and have provoked me to anger from the day their forefathers came out of Egypt until this day."

¹⁶Moreover, Manasseh also shed so much innocent blood that he filled Jerusalem from end to end — besides the sin that he had caused Judah to commit, so that they did evil in the eyes of the LORD.

¹⁷As for the other events of Manasseh's reign, and all he did, including the sin he committed, are they not written in the book of the annals of the kings of Judah? ¹⁸Manasseh rested with his fathers and was buried in his palace garden, the garden of Uzza. And Amon his son succeeded him as king.

Amon King of Judah

¹⁹Amon was twenty-two years old when he became king, and he reigned in Jerusalem two years. His mother's name was Meshullemeth daughter of Haruz; she was from Jotbah. ²⁰He did evil in the eyes of the LORD, as his father Manasseh had done. ²¹He walked in all the ways of his father; he worshiped the idols his father had worshiped, and bowed down to them. ²²He forsook the LORD, the God of his fathers, and did not walk in the way of the LORD.

²³Amon's officials conspired against him and assassinated the king in his palace. ²⁴Then the people of the land killed [al]l who had plotted against King Amon, [an]d they made Josiah his son king in his [plac]e.

[²⁵A]s for the other events of Amon's reign, [and all t]hat he did, are they not written in the [book of] the annals of the kings of Judah? [²⁶He wa]s buried in his grave in the garden [...] And Josiah his son succeeded him

The Book of the Law Found

22 Josiah was eight years old when he became king, and he reigned in Jerusalem thirty-one years. His mother's name was Jedidah daughter of Adaiah; she was from Bozkath. ²He did what was right in the eyes of the LORD and walked in all the ways of his father David, not turning aside to the right or to the left.

³In the eighteenth year of his reign, King Josiah sent the secretary, Shaphan son of Azaliah, the son of Meshullam, to the temple of the LORD. He said: ⁴"Go up to Hilkiah the high priest and have him get ready the money that has been brought into the temple of the LORD, which the doorkeepers have collected from the people. ⁵Have them entrust it to the men appointed to supervise the work on the temple. And have these men pay the workers who repair the temple of the LORD — ⁶the carpenters, the builders and the masons. Also have them purchase timber and dressed stone to repair the temple. ⁷But they need not account for the money entrusted to them, because they are acting faithfully."

⁸Hilkiah the high priest said to Shaphan the secretary, "I have found the Book of the Law in the temple of the LORD." He gave it to Shaphan, who read it. ⁹Then Shaphan the secretary went to the king and reported to him: "Your officials have paid out the money that was in the temple of the LORD and have entrusted it to the workers and supervisors at the temple." ¹⁰Then Shaphan the secretary informed the king, "Hilkiah the priest has given me a book." And Shaphan read from it in the presence of the king.

¹¹When the king heard the words of the Book of the Law, he tore his robes. ¹²He gave these orders to Hilkiah the priest, Ahikam son of Shaphan, Acbor son of Micaiah, Shaphan the secretary and Asaiah the king's attendant: ¹³"Go and inquire of the LORD for me and for the people and for all Judah about what is written in this book that has been found. Great is the LORD's anger that burns against us because our fathers have not obeyed the words of this book; they have not acted in accordance with all that is written there concerning us."

¹⁴Hilkiah the priest, Ahikam, Acbor, Shaphan and Asaiah went to speak to the prophetess Huldah, who was the wife of Shallum son of Tikvah, the son of Harhas, keeper of the wardrobe. She lived in Jerusalem, in the Second District.

¹⁵She said to them, "This is what the LORD,

GODLY KIDS FROM GODLESS HOMES

Micki and Pam are sitting on Micki's bed, talking about God and about their families.

"You have such cool parents, Micki. They really love each other, and your dad is so funny. Best of all, they're both Christians. Do you know how lucky you are?"

"Yeah, I guess I am pretty lucky."

"Hey, look at my parents. They never go to church. My mom believes in reincarnation and meditation. And my atheist dad thinks we all came from baboons. I'm telling you—it's a miracle that I ever became a Christian!"

Look It Up
••••

The Bible illustrates that godly kids can come from godless homes:

King Ahaz "did not do what was right in the eyes of the LORD his God" (2 Kings 16:2). He even sacrificed one of his own sons!

But look! Despite such a horrible role model for a dad, his son Hezekiah "trusted in the LORD, the God of Israel. There was no one like him among all the kings of Judah, either before him or after him. He held fast to the LORD and did not cease to follow him; he kept the commands the LORD had given Moses. And the LORD was with him; he was successful in whatever he undertook" (2 Kings 18:5–7).

Think It Through
••••

No doubt about it, living in a non-Christian home makes it tough to walk with the Lord. However, the real issue isn't what your parents believe. No, the ultimate question is, "What do *you* believe?"

According to the example of Hezekiah, is it legitimate to blame unrighteous parents for your own unrighteousness?

Work It Out
••••

If your parents are not believers or if your home is in trouble:
• Ask God to use you to bring unsaved family members to Christ.
• Find older, more mature Christians to pattern your life after.
• Make sure you surround yourself with committed Christian friends.
• Be active in a good youth group or teen Bible study.
• Besides your daily Bible reading, spend time reading Christian books.

Nail It Down
••••

Read the story of the evil king Amon and his godly son Josiah in 2 Kings 21:19—22:2.

Turn to pages 1288 and 1304 for other readings on home.
Turn to page 397 for the weekend reading.

Topic
••••

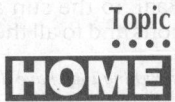

the God of Israel, says: Tell the man who sent you to me, ¹⁶'This is what the LORD says: I am going to bring disaster on this place and its people, according to everything written in the book the king of Judah has read. ¹⁷Because they have forsaken me and burned incense to other gods and provoked me to anger by all the idols their hands have made,ᵃ my anger will burn against this place and will not be quenched.' ¹⁸Tell the king of Judah, who sent you to inquire of the LORD, 'This is what the LORD, the God of Israel, says concerning the words you heard: ¹⁹Because your heart was responsive and you humbled yourself before the LORD when you heard what I have spoken against this place and its people, that they would become accursed and laid waste, and because you tore your robes and wept in my presence, I have heard you, declares the LORD. ²⁰Therefore I will gather you to your fathers, and you will be buried in peace. Your eyes will not see all the disaster I am going to bring on this place.' "

So they took her answer back to the king.

Josiah Renews the Covenant

23 Then the king called together all the elders of Judah and Jerusalem. ²He went up to the temple of the LORD with the men of Judah, the people of Jerusalem, the priests and the prophets—all the people from the least to the greatest. He read in their hearing all the words of the Book of the Covenant, which had been found in the temple of the LORD. ³The king stood by the pillar and renewed the covenant in the presence of the LORD—to follow the LORD and keep his commands, regulations and decrees with all his heart and all his soul, thus confirming the words of the covenant written in this book. Then all the people pledged themselves to the covenant.

⁴The king ordered Hilkiah the high priest, the priests next in rank and the doorkeepers to remove from the temple of the LORD all the articles made for Baal and Asherah and all the starry hosts. He burned them outside Jerusalem in the fields of the Kidron Valley and took the ashes to Bethel. ⁵He did away with the pagan priests appointed by the kings of Judah to burn incense on the high places of the towns of Judah and on those around Jerusalem—those who burned incense to Baal, to the sun and moon, to the constellations and to all the starry hosts. ⁶He

took the Asherah pole from the temple of the LORD to the Kidron Valley outside Jerusalem and burned it there. He ground it to powder and scattered the dust over the graves of the common people. ⁷He also tore down the quarters of the male shrine prostitutes, which were in the temple of the LORD and where women did weaving for Asherah.

⁸Josiah brought all the priests from the towns of Judah and desecrated the high places, from Geba to Beersheba, where the priests had burned incense. He broke down the shrinesᵇ at the gates—at the entrance to the Gate of Joshua, the city governor, which is on the left of the city gate. ⁹Although the priests of the high places did not serve at the altar of the LORD in Jerusalem, they ate unleavened bread with their fellow priests.

¹⁰He desecrated Topheth, which was in the Valley of Ben Hinnom, so no one could use it to sacrifice his son or daughter inᶜ the fire to Molech. ¹¹He removed from the entrance to the temple of the LORD the horses that the kings of Judah had dedicated to the sun. They were in the court near the room of an official named Nathan-Melech. Josiah then burned the chariots dedicated to the sun.

¹²He pulled down the altars the kings of Judah had erected on the roof near the upper room of Ahaz, and the altars Manasseh had built in the two courts of the temple of the LORD. He removed them from there, smashed them to pieces and threw the rubble into the Kidron Valley. ¹³The king also desecrated the high places that were east of Jerusalem on the south of the Hill of Corruption—the ones Solomon king of Israel had built for Ashtoreth the vile goddess of the Sidonians, for Chemosh the vile god of Moab, and for Molechᵈ the detestable god of the people of Ammon. ¹⁴Josiah smashed the sacred stones and cut down the Asherah poles and covered the sites with human bones.

¹⁵Even the altar at Bethel, the high place made by Jeroboam son of Nebat, who had caused Israel to sin—even that altar and high place he demolished. He burned the high place and ground it to powder, and burned the Asherah pole also. ¹⁶Then Josiah looked around, and when he saw the tombs that were there on the hillside, he had the bones removed from them and burned on the altar to defile it, in accordance with the

---

ᵃ17 Or by everything they have done   ᵇ8 Or high places   ᶜ10 Or to make his son or daughter pass through
ᵈ13 Hebrew Milcom

word of the LORD proclaimed by the man of God who foretold these things.

[17]The king asked, "What is that tombstone I see?"

The men of the city said, "It marks the tomb of the man of God who came from Judah and pronounced against the altar of Bethel the very things you have done to it."

[18]"Leave it alone," he said. "Don't let anyone disturb his bones." So they spared his bones and those of the prophet who had come from Samaria.

[19]Just as he had done at Bethel, Josiah removed and defiled all the shrines at the high places that the kings of Israel had built in the towns of Samaria that had provoked the LORD to anger. [20]Josiah slaughtered all the priests of those high places on the altars and burned human bones on them. Then he went back to Jerusalem.

[21]The king gave this order to all the people: "Celebrate the Passover to the LORD your God, as it is written in this Book of the Covenant." [22]Not since the days of the judges who led Israel, nor throughout the days of the kings of Israel and the kings of Judah, had any such Passover been observed. [23]But in the eighteenth year of King Josiah, this Passover was celebrated to the LORD in Jerusalem.

[24]Furthermore, Josiah got rid of the mediums and spiritists, the household gods, the idols and all the other detestable things seen in Judah and Jerusalem. This he did to fulfill the requirements of the law written in the book that Hilkiah the priest had discovered in the temple of the LORD. [25]Neither before nor after Josiah was there a king like him who turned to the LORD as he did — with all his heart and with all his soul and with all his strength, in accordance with all the Law of Moses.

[26]Nevertheless, the LORD did not turn away from the heat of his fierce anger, which burned against Judah because of all that Manasseh had done to provoke him to anger. [27]So the LORD said, "I will remove Judah also from my presence as I removed Israel, and I will reject Jerusalem, the city I chose, and this temple, about which I said, 'There shall my Name be.'[a]"

[28]As for the other events of Josiah's reign, and all he did, are they not written in the book of the annals of the kings of Judah? [29]While Josiah was king, Pharaoh Neco king of Egypt went up to the Euphrates River to help the king of Assyria. King Josiah marched out to meet him in battle, but Neco faced him and killed him at Megiddo. [30]Josiah's servants brought his body in a chariot from Megiddo to Jerusalem and buried him in his own tomb. And the people of the land took Jehoahaz son of Josiah and anointed him and made him king in place of his father.

Jehoahaz King of Judah

[31]Jehoahaz was twenty-three years old when he became king, and he reigned in Jerusalem three months. His mother's name was Hamutal daughter of Jeremiah; she was from Libnah. [32]He did evil in the eyes of the LORD, just as his fathers had done. [33]Pharaoh Neco put him in chains at Riblah in the land of Hamath[b] so that he might not reign in Jerusalem, and he imposed on Judah a levy of a hundred talents[c] of silver and a talent[d] of gold. [34]Pharaoh Neco made Eliakim son of Josiah king in place of his father Josiah and changed Eliakim's name to Jehoiakim. But he took Jehoahaz and carried him off to Egypt, and there he died. [35]Jehoiakim paid Pharaoh Neco the silver and gold he demanded. In order to do so, he taxed the land and exacted the silver and gold from the people of the land according to their assessments.

Jehoiakim King of Judah

[36]Jehoiakim was twenty-five years old when he became king, and he reigned in Jerusalem eleven years. His mother's name was Zebidah daughter of Pedaiah; she was from Rumah. [37]And he did evil in the eyes of the LORD, just as his fathers had done.

24 During Jehoiakim's reign, Nebuchadnezzar king of Babylon invaded the land, and Jehoiakim became his vassal for three years. But then he changed his mind and rebelled against Nebuchadnezzar. [2]The LORD sent Babylonian,[e] Aramean, Moabite and Ammonite raiders against him. He sent them to destroy Judah, in accordance with the word of the LORD proclaimed by his servants the prophets. [3]Surely these things happened to Judah according to the LORD's command, in order to remove them from his presence because of the sins of Manasseh and all he had done, [4]including the shedding of innocent blood. For he had filled Je-

a27 1 Kings 8:29   b33 Hebrew; Septuagint (see also 2 Chron. 36:3) *Neco at Riblah in Hamath removed him*
c33 That is, about 3 3/4 tons (about 3.4 metric tons)   d33 That is, about 75 pounds (about 34 kilograms)
e2 Or *Chaldean*

rusalem with innocent blood, and the LORD was not willing to forgive.

5As for the other events of Jehoiakim's reign, and all he did, are they not written in the book of the annals of the kings of Judah? **6**Jehoiakim rested with his fathers. And Jehoiachin his son succeeded him as king.

7The king of Egypt did not march out from his own country again, because the king of Babylon had taken all his territory, from the Wadi of Egypt to the Euphrates River.

Jehoiachin King of Judah

8Jehoiachin was eighteen years old when he became king, and he reigned in Jerusalem three months. His mother's name was Nehushta daughter of Elnathan; she was from Jerusalem. **9**He did evil in the eyes of the LORD, just as his father had done.

10At that time the officers of Nebuchadnezzar king of Babylon advanced on Jerusalem and laid siege to it, **11**and Nebuchadnezzar himself came up to the city while his officers were besieging it. **12**Jehoiachin king of Judah, his mother, his attendants, his nobles and his officials all surrendered to him.

In the eighth year of the reign of the king of Babylon, he took Jehoiachin prisoner. **13**As the LORD had declared, Nebuchadnezzar removed all the treasures from the temple of the LORD and from the royal palace, and took away all the gold articles that Solomon king of Israel had made for the temple of the LORD. **14**He carried into exile all Jerusalem: all the officers and fighting men, and all the craftsmen and artisans—a total of ten thousand. Only the poorest people of the land were left.

15Nebuchadnezzar took Jehoiachin captive to Babylon. He also took from Jerusalem to Babylon the king's mother, his wives, his officials and the leading men of the land. **16**The king of Babylon also deported to Babylon the entire force of seven thousand fighting men, strong and fit for war, and a thousand craftsmen and artisans. **17**He made Mattaniah, Jehoiachin's uncle, king in his place and changed his name to Zedekiah.

Zedekiah King of Judah

18Zedekiah was twenty-one years old when he became king, and he reigned in Jerusalem eleven years. His mother's name was Hamutal daughter of Jeremiah; she was from Libnah. **19**He did evil in the eyes of the

LORD, just as Jehoiakim had done. **20**It was because of the LORD's anger that all this happened to Jerusalem and Judah, and in the end he thrust them from his presence.

The Fall of Jerusalem

Now Zedekiah rebelled against the king of Babylon.

25 So in the ninth year of Zedekiah's reign, on the tenth day of the tenth month, Nebuchadnezzar king of Babylon marched against Jerusalem with his whole army. He encamped outside the city and built siege works all around it. **2**The city was kept under siege until the eleventh year of King Zedekiah. **3**By the ninth day of the ₍fourth₎*a* month the famine in the city had become so severe that there was no food for the people to eat. **4**Then the city wall was broken through, and the whole army fled at night through the gate between the two walls near the king's garden, though the Babylonians*b* were surrounding the city. They fled toward the Arabah,*c* **5**but the Babylonian*d* army pursued the king and overtook him in the plains of Jericho. All his soldiers were separated from him and scattered, **6**and he was captured. He was taken to the king of Babylon at Riblah, where sentence was pronounced on him. **7**They killed the sons of Zedekiah before his eyes. Then they put out his eyes, bound him with bronze shackles and took him to Babylon.

8On the seventh day of the fifth month, in the nineteenth year of Nebuchadnezzar king of Babylon, Nebuzaradan commander of the imperial guard, an official of the king of Babylon, came to Jerusalem. **9**He set fire to the temple of the LORD, the royal palace and all the houses of Jerusalem. Every important building he burned down. **10**The whole Babylonian army, under the commander of the imperial guard, broke down the walls around Jerusalem. **11**Nebuzaradan the commander of the guard carried into exile the people who remained in the city, along with the rest of the populace and those who had gone over to the king of Babylon. **12**But the commander left behind some of the poorest people of the land to work the vineyards and fields.

13The Babylonians broke up the bronze pillars, the movable stands and the bronze Sea that were at the temple of the LORD and they carried the bronze to Babylon. **14**They also took away the pots, shovels, wick trim-

*a*3 See Jer. 52:6.   *b*4 Or *Chaldeans*; also in verses 13, 25 and 26   *c*4 Or *the Jordan Valley*   *d*5 Or *Chaldean*; also in verses 10 and 24 mers, dishes and all the bronze articles used in the temple service. ¹⁵The commander of the imperial guard took away the censers and sprinkling bowls — all that were made of pure gold or silver.

¹⁶The bronze from the two pillars, the Sea and the movable stands, which Solomon had made for the temple of the LORD, was more than could be weighed. ¹⁷Each pillar was twenty-seven feet*a* high. The bronze capital on top of one pillar was four and a half feet*b* high and was decorated with a network and pomegranates of bronze all around. The other pillar, with its network, was similar.

¹⁸The commander of the guard took as prisoners Seraiah the chief priest, Zephaniah the priest next in rank and the three doorkeepers. ¹⁹Of those still in the city, he took the officer in charge of the fighting men and five royal advisers. He also took the secretary who was chief officer in charge of conscripting the people of the land and sixty of his men who were found in the city. ²⁰Nebuzaradan the commander took them all and brought them to the king of Babylon at Riblah. ²¹There at Riblah, in the land of Hamath, the king had them executed.

So Judah went into captivity, away from her land.

²²Nebuchadnezzar king of Babylon appointed Gedaliah son of Ahikam, the son of Shaphan, to be over the people he had left behind in Judah. ²³When all the army officers and their men heard that the king of Babylon had appointed Gedaliah as governor, they came to Gedaliah at Mizpah — Ishmael son of Nethaniah, Johanan son of Kareah, Seraiah son of Tanhumeth the Netophathite, Jaazaniah the son of the Maacathite, and their men. ²⁴Gedaliah took an oath to reassure them and their men. "Do not be afraid of the Babylonian officials," he said. "Settle down in the land and serve the king of Babylon, and it will go well with you."

²⁵In the seventh month, however, Ishmael son of Nethaniah, the son of Elishama, who was of royal blood, came with ten men and assassinated Gedaliah and also the men of Judah and the Babylonians who were with him at Mizpah. ²⁶At this, all the people from the least to the greatest, together with the army officers, fled to Egypt for fear of the Babylonians.

Jehoiachin Released

²⁷In the thirty-seventh year of the exile of Jehoiachin king of Judah, in the year Evil-Merodach*c* became king of Babylon, he released Jehoiachin from prison on the twenty-seventh day of the twelfth month. ²⁸He spoke kindly to him and gave him a seat of honor higher than those of the other kings who were with him in Babylon. ²⁹So Jehoiachin put aside his prison clothes and for the rest of his life ate regularly at the king's table. ³⁰Day by day the king gave Jehoiachin a regular allowance as long as he lived.

---

a17 Hebrew *eighteen cubits* (about 8.1 meters)   *b17* Hebrew *three cubits* (about 1.3 meters)   *c27* Also called *Amel-Marduk*

1 CHRONICLES

THE Chronicles give a priestly perspective on the history of God's people, sort of a divine interpretation from the time of David to the exile. First Chronicles traces David's royal line back to Adam and shows how the nation prospers under his reign. But what really shines through is the way David worshiped God—passionately and joyfully, with all kinds of prayer, a lot of music and even a dance or two. Ask yourself as you read whether worship is a priority in your life and whether it is truly from your heart.

Outline of Contents

Historical Records From Adam to Abraham

To Noah's Sons

1 Adam, Seth, Enosh, **²**Kenan, Mahalalel, Jared, **³**Enoch, Methuselah, Lamech, Noah.

⁴The sons of Noah:*ᵃ*
Shem, Ham and Japheth.

The Japhethites

⁵The sons*ᵇ* of Japheth:
Gomer, Magog, Madai, Javan, Tubal, Meshech and Tiras.
⁶The sons of Gomer:
Ashkenaz, Riphath*ᶜ* and Togarmah.
⁷The sons of Javan:
Elishah, Tarshish, the Kittim and the Rodanim.

The Hamites

⁸The sons of Ham:
Cush, Mizraim,*ᵈ* Put and Canaan.
⁹The sons of Cush:
Seba, Havilah, Sabta, Raamah and Sabteca.
The sons of Raamah:
Sheba and Dedan.
¹⁰Cush was the father*ᵉ* of
Nimrod, who grew to be a mighty warrior on earth.

ᵃ4 Septuagint; Hebrew does not have The sons of Noah: ᵇ5 Sons may mean descendants or successors or nations; also in verses 6-10, 17 and 20. ᶜ6 Many Hebrew manuscripts and Vulgate (see also Septuagint and Gen. 10:3); most Hebrew manuscripts Diphath ᵈ8 That is, Egypt; also in verse 11 ᵉ10 Father may mean ancestor or predecessor or founder; also in verses 11, 13, 18 and 20.

THANK GOD YOU'RE NOT A NOBODY

Work It Out
••••

At the back of some dictionaries is a list of names and short biographies of famous people living and dead. Out of the billions of people who have lived, the list names only several thousand. The chances are pretty slim that your name will ever be on such a list.

Does that make you feel just a bit insignificant? Don't let it! Because you're *not!* Insignificant, that is.

Your parents look at you and see the son or daughter they love. Your brothers and sisters may act like you're a pain in the neck, but deep down they probably think you're pretty special. Your friends may not always act like it, but you play an important part in their lives.

And God looks at you and sees a person he created and loves. He values you as much as a Caesar or a Lincoln or a Churchill. You're definitely not a nobody in God's eyes.

Nail It Down
••••

Read 1 Chronicles 1 for a list of names of people who seem pretty insignificant to us but never to God.

Think It Through
••••

Most of you don't have to look at a list of famous names to feel unimportant. Just a look around you—at the other kids in your classroom, at the people in your church or even at your family members at home—can bring on a serious case of "I'm-not-worth-much-itis."

What you are on the inside, what you let God make of you as a believer in him, gives you tremendous significance. He loved you enough to die for you. You've probably heard it before, but it's worth repeating: You were worth dying for. Thank God you're not a nobody!

Nail It Down
••••

Look over the list of names in 1 Chronicles 1 again. For further insight read Isaiah 43:1.

Turn to pages 1145, 1262 and 1377 for others readings on identity.
Turn to page 415 for Monday's reading.

Topic
••••

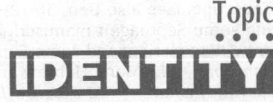

¹¹Mizraim was the father of
the Ludites, Anamites, Lehabites,
Naphtuhites, ¹²Pathrusites, Caslu-
hites (from whom the Philistines
came) and Caphtorites.
¹³Canaan was the father of
Sidon his firstborn,ᵃ and of the Hittites, ¹⁴Jebusites, Amorites, Girgashites, ¹⁵Hivites, Arkites, Sinites, ¹⁶Ar-
vadites, Zemarites and Hamathites.

The Semites

¹⁷The sons of Shem:
Elam, Asshur, Arphaxad, Lud and
Aram.
The sons of Aramᵇ:
Uz, Hul, Gether and Meshech.
¹⁸Arphaxad was the father of Shelah,
and Shelah the father of Eber.
¹⁹Two sons were born to Eber:
One was named Peleg,ᶜ because in
his time the earth was divided; his
brother was named Joktan.
²⁰Joktan was the father of
Almodad, Sheleph, Hazarmaveth,
Jerah, ²¹Hadoram, Uzal, Diklah,
²²Obal,ᵈ Abimael, Sheba, ²³Ophir,
Havilah and Jobab. All these were
sons of Joktan.

²⁴Shem, Arphaxad,ᵉ Shelah,
²⁵Eber, Peleg, Reu,
²⁶Serug, Nahor, Terah
²⁷and Abram (that is, Abraham).

The Family of Abraham

²⁸The sons of Abraham:
Isaac and Ishmael.

Descendants of Hagar

²⁹These were their descendants:
Nebaioth the firstborn of Ishmael,
Kedar, Adbeel, Mibsam, ³⁰Mishma,
Dumah, Massa, Hadad, Tema, ³¹Je-
tur, Naphish and Kedemah. These
were the sons of Ishmael.

Descendants of Keturah

³²The sons born to Keturah, Abraham's
concubine:

Zimran, Jokshan, Medan, Midian,
Ishbak and Shuah.
The sons of Jokshan:
Sheba and Dedan.
³³The sons of Midian:
Ephah, Epher, Hanoch, Abida and
Eldaah.
All these were descendants of Keturah.

Descendants of Sarah

³⁴Abraham was the father of Isaac.
The sons of Isaac:
Esau and Israel.

Esau's Sons

³⁵The sons of Esau:
Eliphaz, Reuel, Jeush, Jalam and Korah.
³⁶The sons of Eliphaz:
Teman, Omar, Zepho,ᶠ Gatam and
Kenaz;
by Timna: Amalek.ᵍ
³⁷The sons of Reuel:
Nahath, Zerah, Shammah and Mizzah.

The People of Seir in Edom

³⁸The sons of Seir:
Lotan, Shobal, Zibeon, Anah, Di-
shon, Ezer and Dishan.
³⁹The sons of Lotan:
Hori and Homam. Timna was Lo-
tan's sister.
⁴⁰The sons of Shobal:
Alvan,ʰ Manahath, Ebal, Shepho
and Onam.
The sons of Zibeon:
Aiah and Anah.
⁴¹The son of Anah:
Dishon.
The sons of Dishon:
Hemdan,ⁱ Eshban, Ithran and Ke-
ran.
⁴²The sons of Ezer:
Bilhan, Zaavan and Akan.ʲ
The sons of Dishanᵏ:
Uz and Aran.

ᵃ13 Or of the Sidonians, the foremost   ᵇ17 One Hebrew manuscript and some Septuagint manuscripts (see
also Gen. 10:23); most Hebrew manuscripts do not have this line.   ᶜ19 Peleg means division.   ᵈ22 Some
Hebrew manuscripts and Syriac (see also Gen. 10:28); most Hebrew manuscripts Ebal   ᵉ24 Hebrew; some
Septuagint manuscripts Arphaxad, Cainan (see also note at Gen. 11:10)   ᶠ36 Many Hebrew manuscripts,
some Septuagint manuscripts and Syriac (see also Gen. 36:11); most Hebrew manuscripts Zephi   ᵍ36 Some
Septuagint manuscripts (see also Gen. 36:12); Hebrew Gatam, Kenaz, Timna and Amalek   ʰ40 Many Hebrew
manuscripts and some Septuagint manuscripts (see also Gen. 36:23); most Hebrew manuscripts Alian
ⁱ41 Many Hebrew manuscripts and some Septuagint manuscripts (see also Gen. 36:26); most Hebrew
manuscripts Hamran   ʲ42 Many Hebrew and Septuagint manuscripts (see also Gen. 36:27); most Hebrew
manuscripts Zaavan, Jaakan   ᵏ42 Hebrew Dishon, a variant of Dishan

The Rulers of Edom

43These were the kings who reigned in Edom before any Israelite king reigned[a]:

Bela son of Beor, whose city was named Dinhabah. **44**When Bela died, Jobab son of Zerah from Bozrah succeeded him as king. **45**When Jobab died, Husham from the land of the Temanites succeeded him as king. **46**When Husham died, Hadad son of Bedad, who defeated Midian in the country of Moab, succeeded him as king. His city was named Avith. **47**When Hadad died, Samlah from Masrekah succeeded him as king. **48**When Samlah died, Shaul from Rehoboth on the river[b] succeeded him as king. **49**When Shaul died, Baal-Hanan son of Acbor succeeded him as king. **50**When Baal-Hanan died, Hadad succeeded him as king. His city was named Pau,[c] and his wife's name was Mehetabel daughter of Matred, the daughter of Me-Zahab. **51**Hadad also died.

The chiefs of Edom were:

Timna, Alvah, Jetheth, **52**Oholibamah, Elah, Pinon, **53**Kenaz, Teman, Mibzar, **54**Magdiel and Iram. These were the chiefs of Edom.

Israel's Sons

2 These were the sons of Israel: Reuben, Simeon, Levi, Judah, Issachar, Zebulun, **2**Dan, Joseph, Benjamin, Naphtali, Gad and Asher.

Judah

To Hezron's Sons

3The sons of Judah:

Er, Onan and Shelah. These three were born to him by a Canaanite woman, the daughter of Shua. Er, Judah's firstborn, was wicked in the LORD's sight; so the LORD put him to death. **4**Tamar, Judah's daughter-in-law, bore him Perez and Zerah. Judah had five sons in all.

5The sons of Perez:

Hezron and Hamul.

6The sons of Zerah:

Zimri, Ethan, Heman, Calcol and Darda[d]—five in all.

7The son of Carmi:

Achar,[e] who brought trouble on Israel by violating the ban on taking devoted things.[f]

8The son of Ethan:

Azariah.

9The sons born to Hezron were:

Jerahmeel, Ram and Caleb.[g]

From Ram Son of Hezron

10Ram was the father of

Amminadab, and Amminadab the father of Nahshon, the leader of the people of Judah. **11**Nahshon was the father of Salmon,[h] Salmon the father of Boaz, **12**Boaz the father of Obed and Obed the father of Jesse.

13Jesse was the father of

Eliab his firstborn; the second son was Abinadab, the third Shimea, **14**the fourth Nethanel, the fifth Raddai, **15**the sixth Ozem and the seventh David. **16**Their sisters were Zeruiah and Abigail. Zeruiah's three sons were Abishai, Joab and Asahel. **17**Abigail was the mother of Amasa, whose father was Jether the Ishmaelite.

Caleb Son of Hezron

18Caleb son of Hezron had children by his wife Azubah (and by Jerioth). These were her sons: Jesher, Shobab and Ardon. **19**When Azubah died, Caleb married Ephrath, who bore him Hur. **20**Hur was the father of Uri, and Uri the father of Bezalel.

21Later, Hezron lay with the daughter of Makir the father of Gilead (he had married her when he was sixty years old), and she bore him Segub. **22**Segub was the father of Jair, who controlled twenty-three towns in Gilead. **23**(But Geshur and Aram captured

---

a43 Or *before an Israelite king reigned over them*   *b48* Possibly the Euphrates   *c50* Many Hebrew manuscripts, some Septuagint manuscripts, Vulgate and Syriac (see also Gen. 36:39); most Hebrew manuscripts *Pai*   *d6* Many Hebrew manuscripts, some Septuagint manuscripts and Syriac (see also 1 Kings 4:31); most Hebrew manuscripts *Dara*   *e7* *Achar* means *trouble*; *Achar* is called *Achan* in Joshua.   *f7* The Hebrew term refers to the irrevocable giving over of things or persons to the LORD, often by totally destroying them.   *g9* Hebrew *Kelubai,* a variant of *Caleb*   *h11* Septuagint (see also Ruth 4:21); Hebrew *Salma*

Havvoth Jair,*a* as well as Kenath
with its surrounding settlements —
sixty towns.) All these were descendants of Makir the father of Gilead.

24After Hezron died in Caleb Ephrathah,
Abijah the wife of Hezron bore him
Ashhur the father*b* of Tekoa.

Jerahmeel Son of Hezron

25The sons of Jerahmeel the firstborn of
Hezron:
Ram his firstborn, Bunah, Oren,
Ozem and*c* Ahijah. **26**Jerahmeel
had another wife, whose name was
Atarah; she was the mother of
Onam.
27The sons of Ram the firstborn of Jerah-
meel:
Maaz, Jamin and Eker.
28The sons of Onam:
Shammai and Jada.
The sons of Shammai:
Nadab and Abishur.
29Abishur's wife was named Abihail,
who bore him Ahban and Molid.
30The sons of Nadab:
Seled and Appaim. Seled died without children.
31The son of Appaim:
Ishi, who was the father of Sheshan.
Sheshan was the father of Ahlai.
32The sons of Jada, Shammai's brother:
Jether and Jonathan. Jether died
without children.
33The sons of Jonathan:
Peleth and Zaza.
These were the descendants of Jerahmeel.
34Sheshan had no sons — only daughters.
He had an Egyptian servant named
Jarha. **35**Sheshan gave his daughter
in marriage to his servant Jarha, and
she bore him Attai.
36Attai was the father of Nathan,
Nathan the father of Zabad,
37Zabad the father of Ephlal,
Ephlal the father of Obed,
38Obed the father of Jehu,
Jehu the father of Azariah,
39Azariah the father of Helez,
Helez the father of Eleasah,
40Eleasah the father of Sismai,
Sismai the father of Shallum,
41Shallum the father of Jekamiah,
and Jekamiah the father of Elishama.

The Clans of Caleb

42The sons of Caleb the brother of Jerahmeel:
Mesha his firstborn, who was the father of Ziph, and his son Mareshah,*d* who was the father of Hebron.
43The sons of Hebron:
Korah, Tappuah, Rekem and Shema. **44**Shema was the father of Raham, and Raham the father of Jorke-
am. Rekem was the father of
Shammai. **45**The son of Shammai
was Maon, and Maon was the father
of Beth Zur.
46Caleb's concubine Ephah was the
mother of Haran, Moza and Gazez.
Haran was the father of Gazez.
47The sons of Jahdai:
Regem, Jotham, Geshan, Pelet,
Ephah and Shaaph.
48Caleb's concubine Maacah was the
mother of Sheber and Tirhanah.
49She also gave birth to Shaaph the
father of Madmannah and to Sheva
the father of Macbenah and Gibea.
Caleb's daughter was Acsah.
50These were the descendants of Caleb.

The sons of Hur the firstborn of Ephrathah:
Shobal the father of Kiriath Jearim,
51Salma the father of Bethlehem,
and Hareph the father of Beth Gader.
52The descendants of Shobal the father
of Kiriath Jearim were:
Haroeh, half the Manahathites,
53and the clans of Kiriath Jearim: the
Ithrites, Puthites, Shumathites and
Mishraites. From these descended
the Zorathites and Eshtaolites.
54The descendants of Salma:
Bethlehem, the Netophathites, Atroth Beth Joab, half the Manahathites, the Zorites, **55**and the clans of
scribes*e* who lived at Jabez: the Ti-
rathites, Shimeathites and Sucath-
ites. These are the Kenites who
came from Hammath, the father of
the house of Recab.*f*

a23 Or *captured the settlements of Jair*   *b24 Father* may mean *civic leader* or *military leader*; also in verses
42, 45, 49-52 and possibly elsewhere.   *c25* Or *Oren and Ozem, by*   *d42* The meaning of the Hebrew for
this phrase is uncertain.   *e55* Or *of the Sopherites*   *f55* Or *father of Beth Recab*

The Sons of David

3 These were the sons of David born to him in Hebron:

The firstborn was Amnon the son of Ahinoam of Jezreel;

the second, Daniel the son of Abigail of Carmel;

²the third, Absalom the son of Maacah daughter of Talmai king of Geshur;

the fourth, Adonijah the son of Haggith;

³the fifth, Shephatiah the son of Abital;

and the sixth, Ithream, by his wife Eglah.

⁴These six were born to David in Hebron, where he reigned seven years and six months.

David reigned in Jerusalem thirty-three years, ⁵and these were the children born to him there:

Shammua,ᵃ Shobab, Nathan and Solomon. These four were by Bathshebaᵇ daughter of Ammiel. ⁶There were also Ibhar, Elishua,ᶜ Eliphelet, ⁷Nogah, Nepheg, Japhia, ⁸Elishama, Eliada and Eliphelet—nine in all. ⁹All these were the sons of David, besides his sons by his concubines. And Tamar was their sister.

The Kings of Judah

¹⁰Solomon's son was Rehoboam,

Abijah his son,

Asa his son,

Jehoshaphat his son,

¹¹Jehoramᵈ his son,

Ahaziah his son,

Joash his son,

¹²Amaziah his son,

Azariah his son,

Jotham his son,

¹³Ahaz his son,

Hezekiah his son,

Manasseh his son,

¹⁴Amon his son,

Josiah his son.

¹⁵The sons of Josiah:

Johanan the firstborn,

Jehoiakim the second son,

Zedekiah the third,

Shallum the fourth.

¹⁶The successors of Jehoiakim:

Jehoiachinᵉ his son,

and Zedekiah.

The Royal Line After the Exile

¹⁷The descendants of Jehoiachin the captive:

Shealtiel his son, ¹⁸Malkiram, Pedaiah, Shenazzar, Jekamiah, Hoshama and Nedabiah.

¹⁹The sons of Pedaiah:

Zerubbabel and Shimei.

The sons of Zerubbabel:

Meshullam and Hananiah.

Shelomith was their sister.

²⁰There were also five others:

Hashubah, Ohel, Berekiah, Hasadiah and Jushab-Hesed.

²¹The descendants of Hananiah:

Pelatiah and Jeshaiah, and the sons of Rephaiah, of Arnan, of Obadiah and of Shecaniah.

²²The descendants of Shecaniah:

Shemaiah and his sons:

Hattush, Igal, Bariah, Neariah and Shaphat—six in all.

²³The sons of Neariah:

Elioenai, Hizkiah and Azrikam—three in all.

²⁴The sons of Elioenai:

Hodaviah, Eliashib, Pelaiah, Akkub, Johanan, Delaiah and Anani—seven in all.

Other Clans of Judah

4 The descendants of Judah:

Perez, Hezron, Carmi, Hur and Shobal.

²Reaiah son of Shobal was the father of Jahath, and Jahath the father of Ahumai and Lahad. These were the clans of the Zorathites.

³These were the sonsᶠ of Etam:

Jezreel, Ishma and Idbash. Their sister was named Hazzelelponi. ⁴Penuel was the father of Gedor, and Ezer the father of Hushah.

These were the descendants of Hur, the firstborn of Ephrathah and fatherᵍ of Bethlehem.

ᵃ5 Hebrew *Shimea*, a variant of *Shammua*   ᵇ5 One Hebrew manuscript and Vulgate (see also Septuagint and 2 Samuel 11:3); most Hebrew manuscripts *Bathshua*   ᶜ6 Two Hebrew manuscripts (see also 2 Samuel 5:15 and 1 Chron. 14:5); most Hebrew manuscripts *Elishama*   ᵈ11 Hebrew *Joram*, a variant of *Jehoram*   ᵉ16 Hebrew *Jeconiah*, a variant of *Jehoiachin*; also in verse 17   ᶠ3 Some Septuagint manuscripts (see also Vulgate); Hebrew *father*   ᵍ4 *Father* may mean *civic leader* or *military leader*; also in verses 12, 14, 17, 18 and possibly elsewhere.

[5]Ashhur the father of Tekoa had two wives, Helah and Naarah. [6]Naarah bore him Ahuzzam, Hepher, Temeni and Haahashtari. These were the descendants of Naarah. [7]The sons of Helah:

Zereth, Zohar, Ethnan, [8]and Koz, who was the father of Anub and Hazzobebah and of the clans of Aharhel son of Harum.

[9]Jabez was more honorable than his brothers. His mother had named him Jabez,[a] saying, "I gave birth to him in pain." [10]Jabez cried out to the God of Israel, "Oh, that you would bless me and enlarge my territory! Let your hand be with me, and keep me from harm so that I will be free from pain." And God granted his request.

[11]Kelub, Shuhah's brother, was the father of Mehir, who was the father of Eshton. [12]Eshton was the father of Beth Rapha, Paseah and Tehinnah the father of Ir Nahash.[b] These were the men of Recah. [13]The sons of Kenaz:

Othniel and Seraiah.

The sons of Othniel:

Hathath and Meonothai.[c] [14]Meonothai was the father of Ophrah.

Seraiah was the father of Joab,

the father of Ge Harashim.[d] It was called this because its people were craftsmen.

[15]The sons of Caleb son of Jephunneh:

Iru, Elah and Naam.

The son of Elah:

Kenaz.

[16]The sons of Jehallelel:

Ziph, Ziphah, Tiria and Asarel.

[17]The sons of Ezrah:

Jether, Mered, Epher and Jalon. One of Mered's wives gave birth to Miriam, Shammai and Ishbah the father of Eshtemoa. [18](His Judean wife gave birth to Jered the father of Gedor, Heber the father of Soco, and Jekuthiel the father of Zanoah.) These were the children of Pharaoh's daughter Bithiah, whom Mered had married.

[19]The sons of Hodiah's wife, the sister of Naham:

the father of Keilah the Garmite, and Eshtemoa the Maacathite.

[20]The sons of Shimon:

Amnon, Rinnah, Ben-Hanan and Tilon.

The descendants of Ishi:

Zoheth and Ben-Zoheth.

[21]The sons of Shelah son of Judah:

Er the father of Lecah, Laadah the father of Mareshah and the clans of the linen workers at Beth Ashbea, [22]Jokim, the men of Cozeba, and Joash and Saraph, who ruled in Moab and Jashubi Lehem. (These records are from ancient times.) [23]They were the potters who lived at Netaim and Gederah; they stayed there and worked for the king.

Simeon

[24]The descendants of Simeon:

Nemuel, Jamin, Jarib, Zerah and Shaul;

[25]Shallum was Shaul's son, Mibsam his son and Mishma his son.

[26]The descendants of Mishma:

Hammuel his son, Zaccur his son and Shimei his son.

[27]Shimei had sixteen sons and six daughters, but his brothers did not have many children; so their entire clan did not become as numerous as the people of Judah. [28]They lived in Beersheba, Moladah, Hazar Shual, [29]Bilhah, Ezem, Tolad, [30]Bethuel, Hormah, Ziklag, [31]Beth Marcaboth, Hazar Susim, Beth Biri and Shaaraim. These were their towns until the reign of David. [32]Their surrounding villages were Etam, Ain, Rimmon, Token and Ashan—five towns— [33]and all the villages around these towns as far as Baalath.[e] These were their settlements. And they kept a genealogical record.

[34]Meshobab, Jamlech, Joshah son of Amaziah, [35]Joel, Jehu son of Joshibiah, the son of Seraiah, the son of Asiel, [36]also Elioenai, Jaakobah, Jeshohaiah, Asaiah, Adiel, Jesimiel, Benaiah, [37]and Ziza son of Shiphi, the son of Allon, the son of Jedaiah, the son of Shimri, the son of Shemaiah.

[38]The men listed above by name were leaders of their clans. Their families increased greatly, [39]and they went to the outskirts of Gedor to the east of the valley in search of pasture for their flocks. [40]They

---

[a]9 *Jabez* sounds like the Hebrew for *pain*.   [b]12 Or *of the city of Nahash*   [c]13 Some Septuagint manuscripts and Vulgate; Hebrew does not have *and Meonothai*.   [d]14 *Ge Harashim* means *valley of craftsmen*.
[e]33 Some Septuagint manuscripts (see also Joshua 19:8); Hebrew *Baal*

found rich, good pasture, and the land was spacious, peaceful and quiet. Some Hamites had lived there formerly.

41The men whose names were listed came in the days of Hezekiah king of Judah. They attacked the Hamites in their dwellings and also the Meunites who were there and completely destroyed[a] them, as is evident to this day. Then they settled in their place, because there was pasture for their flocks. **42**And five hundred of these Simeonites, led by Pelatiah, Neariah, Rephaiah and Uzziel, the sons of Ishi, invaded the hill country of Seir. **43**They killed the remaining Amalekites who had escaped, and they have lived there to this day.

Reuben

5 The sons of Reuben the firstborn of Israel (he was the firstborn, but when he defiled his father's marriage bed, his rights as firstborn were given to the sons of Joseph son of Israel; so he could not be listed in the genealogical record in accordance with his birthright, **2**and though Judah was the strongest of his brothers and a ruler came from him, the rights of the firstborn belonged to Joseph) — **3**the sons of Reuben the firstborn of Israel:

Hanoch, Pallu, Hezron and Carmi.

4The descendants of Joel:

Shemaiah his son, Gog his son, Shimei his son, **5**Micah his son, Reaiah his son, Baal his son, **6**and Beerah his son, whom Tiglath-Pileser[b] king of Assyria took into exile. Beerah was a leader of the Reubenites.

7Their relatives by clans, listed according to their genealogical records:

Jeiel the chief, Zechariah, **8**and Bela son of Azaz, the son of Shema, the son of Joel. They settled in the area from Aroer to Nebo and Baal Meon. **9**To the east they occupied the land up to the edge of the desert that extends to the Euphrates River, because their livestock had increased in Gilead.

10During Saul's reign they waged war against the Hagrites, who were defeated at their hands; they occupied the dwellings of the Hagrites throughout the entire region east of Gilead.

Gad

11The Gadites lived next to them in Bashan, as far as Salecah:

12Joel was the chief, Shapham the second, then Janai and Shaphat, in Bashan.

13Their relatives, by families, were:

Michael, Meshullam, Sheba, Jorai, Jacan, Zia and Eber — seven in all.

14These were the sons of Abihail son of Huri, the son of Jaroah, the son of Gilead, the son of Michael, the son of Jeshishai, the son of Jahdo, the son of Buz.

15Ahi son of Abdiel, the son of Guni, was head of their family.

16The Gadites lived in Gilead, in Bashan and its outlying villages, and on all the pasturelands of Sharon as far as they extended.

17All these were entered in the genealogical records during the reigns of Jotham king of Judah and Jeroboam king of Israel.

18The Reubenites, the Gadites and the half-tribe of Manasseh had 44,760 men ready for military service — able-bodied men who could handle shield and sword, who could use a bow, and who were trained for battle. **19**They waged war against the Hagrites, Jetur, Naphish and Nodab. **20**They were helped in fighting them, and God handed the Hagrites and all their allies over to them, because they cried out to him during the battle. He answered their prayers, because they trusted in him. **21**They seized the livestock of the Hagrites — fifty thousand camels, two hundred fifty thousand sheep and two thousand donkeys. They also took one hundred thousand people captive, **22**and many others fell slain, because the battle was God's. And they occupied the land until the exile.

The Half-Tribe of Manasseh

23The people of the half-tribe of Manasseh were numerous; they settled in the land from Bashan to Baal Hermon, that is, to Senir (Mount Hermon).

24These were the heads of their families: Epher, Ishi, Eliel, Azriel, Jeremiah, Hodaviah and Jahdiel. They were brave warriors, famous men, and heads of their families. **25**But they were unfaithful to the God of their fathers and prostituted themselves to the gods of the peoples of the land, whom God

---

a41 The Hebrew term refers to the irrevocable giving over of things or persons to the LORD, often by totally destroying them.   *b6* Hebrew *Tilgath-Pilneser*, a variant of *Tiglath-Pileser*; also in verse 26 had destroyed before them. ²⁶So the God of Israel stirred up the spirit of Pul king of Assyria (that is, Tiglath-Pileser king of Assyria), who took the Reubenites, the Gadites and the half-tribe of Manasseh into exile. He took them to Halah, Habor, Hara and the river of Gozan, where they are to this day.

Levi

6 The sons of Levi:
Gershon, Kohath and Merari.
²The sons of Kohath:
Amram, Izhar, Hebron and Uzziel.
³The children of Amram:
Aaron, Moses and Miriam.
The sons of Aaron:
Nadab, Abihu, Eleazar and Ithamar.
⁴Eleazar was the father of Phinehas,
Phinehas the father of Abishua,
⁵Abishua the father of Bukki,
Bukki the father of Uzzi,
⁶Uzzi the father of Zerahiah,
Zerahiah the father of Meraioth,
⁷Meraioth the father of Amariah,
Amariah the father of Ahitub,
⁸Ahitub the father of Zadok,
Zadok the father of Ahimaaz,
⁹Ahimaaz the father of Azariah,
Azariah the father of Johanan,
¹⁰Johanan the father of Azariah (it was he who served as priest in the temple Solomon built in Jerusalem),
¹¹Azariah the father of Amariah,
Amariah the father of Ahitub,
¹²Ahitub the father of Zadok,
Zadok the father of Shallum,
¹³Shallum the father of Hilkiah,
Hilkiah the father of Azariah,
¹⁴Azariah the father of Seraiah,
and Seraiah the father of Jehozadak.
¹⁵Jehozadak was deported when the LORD sent Judah and Jerusalem into exile by the hand of Nebuchadnezzar.

¹⁶The sons of Levi:
Gershon,ᵃ Kohath and Merari.
¹⁷These are the names of the sons of Gershon:
Libni and Shimei.
¹⁸The sons of Kohath:
Amram, Izhar, Hebron and Uzziel.
¹⁹The sons of Merari:
Mahli and Mushi.

These are the clans of the Levites listed according to their fathers:
²⁰Of Gershon:
Libni his son, Jehath his son,
Zimmah his son, ²¹Joah his son,
Iddo his son, Zerah his son
and Jeatherai his son.
²²The descendants of Kohath:
Amminadab his son, Korah his son,
Assir his son, ²³Elkanah his son,
Ebiasaph his son, Assir his son,
²⁴Tahath his son, Uriel his son,
Uzziah his son and Shaul his son.
²⁵The descendants of Elkanah:
Amasai, Ahimoth,
²⁶Elkanah his son,ᵇ Zophai his son,
Nahath his son, ²⁷Eliab his son,
Jeroham his son, Elkanah his son
and Samuel his son.ᶜ
²⁸The sons of Samuel:
Joelᵈ the firstborn
and Abijah the second son.
²⁹The descendants of Merari:
Mahli, Libni his son,
Shimei his son, Uzzah his son,
³⁰Shimea his son, Haggiah his son
and Asaiah his son.

The Temple Musicians

³¹These are the men David put in charge of the music in the house of the LORD after the ark came to rest there. ³²They ministered with music before the tabernacle, the Tent of Meeting, until Solomon built the temple of the LORD in Jerusalem. They performed their duties according to the regulations laid down for them.
³³Here are the men who served, together with their sons:
From the Kohathites:
Heman, the musician,
the son of Joel, the son of Samuel,
³⁴the son of Elkanah, the son of Jeroham,
the son of Eliel, the son of Toah,
³⁵the son of Zuph, the son of Elkanah,
the son of Mahath, the son of Amasai,
³⁶the son of Elkanah, the son of Joel,
the son of Azariah, the son of Zephaniah,
³⁷the son of Tahath, the son of Assir,

ᵃ16 Hebrew *Gershom*, a variant of *Gershon*; also in verses 17, 20, 43, 62 and 71   ᵇ26 Some Hebrew manuscripts, Septuagint and Syriac; most Hebrew manuscripts *Ahimoth ²⁶and Elkanah. The sons of Elkanah:*   ᶜ27 Some Septuagint manuscripts (see also 1 Samuel 1:19,20 and 1 Chron. 6:33,34); Hebrew does not have *and Samuel his son.*   ᵈ28 Some Septuagint manuscripts and Syriac (see also 1 Samuel 8:2 and 1 Chron. 6:33); Hebrew does not have *Joel.*

the son of Ebiasaph, the son of Korah,
38the son of Izhar, the son of Kohath, the son of Levi, the son of Israel;
39and Heman's associate Asaph, who served at his right hand:
Asaph son of Berekiah, the son of Shimea,
40the son of Michael, the son of Baaseiah,*a*
the son of Malkijah, **41**the son of Ethni,
the son of Zerah, the son of Adaiah,
42the son of Ethan, the son of Zimmah, the son of Shimei, **43**the son of Jahath,
the son of Gershon, the son of Levi;
44and from their associates, the Merarites, at his left hand:
Ethan son of Kishi, the son of Abdi, the son of Malluch, **45**the son of Hashabiah,
the son of Amaziah, the son of Hilkiah,
46the son of Amzi, the son of Bani, the son of Shemer, **47**the son of Mahli,
the son of Mushi, the son of Merari, the son of Levi.

48Their fellow Levites were assigned to all the other duties of the tabernacle, the house of God. **49**But Aaron and his descendants were the ones who presented offerings on the altar of burnt offering and on the altar of incense in connection with all that was done in the Most Holy Place, making atonement for Israel, in accordance with all that Moses the servant of God had commanded.

50These were the descendants of Aaron:
Eleazar his son, Phinehas his son, Abishua his son, **51**Bukki his son, Uzzi his son, Zerahiah his son,
52Meraioth his son, Amariah his son, Ahitub his son, **53**Zadok his son and Ahimaaz his son.

54These were the locations of their settlements allotted as their territory (they were assigned to the descendants of Aaron who were from the Kohathite clan, because the first lot was for them):
55They were given Hebron in Judah with its surrounding pasturelands. **56**But the fields and villages around the city were given to Caleb son of Jephunneh.

57So the descendants of Aaron were given Hebron (a city of refuge), and Libnah,*b* Jattir, Eshtemoa, **58**Hilen, Debir, **59**Ashan, Juttah*c* and Beth Shemesh, together with their pasturelands. **60**And from the tribe of Benjamin they were given Gibeon,*d* Geba, Alemeth and Anathoth, together with their pasturelands.

These towns, which were distributed among the Kohathite clans, were thirteen in all.

61The rest of Kohath's descendants were allotted ten towns from the clans of half the tribe of Manasseh.

62The descendants of Gershon, clan by clan, were allotted thirteen towns from the tribes of Issachar, Asher and Naphtali, and from the part of the tribe of Manasseh that is in Bashan.

63The descendants of Merari, clan by clan, were allotted twelve towns from the tribes of Reuben, Gad and Zebulun.

64So the Israelites gave the Levites these towns and their pasturelands. **65**From the tribes of Judah, Simeon and Benjamin they allotted the previously named towns.

66Some of the Kohathite clans were given as their territory towns from the tribe of Ephraim.

67In the hill country of Ephraim they were given Shechem (a city of refuge), and Gezer,*e* **68**Jokmeam, Beth Horon, **69**Aijalon and Gath Rimmon, together with their pasturelands.

70And from half the tribe of Manasseh the Israelites gave Aner and Bileam, together with their pasturelands, to the rest of the Kohathite clans.

71The Gershonites received the following:
From the clan of the half-tribe of Manasseh
they received Golan in Bashan and also Ashtaroth, together with their pasturelands;
72from the tribe of Issachar
they received Kedesh, Daberath, **73**Ramoth and Anem, together with their pasturelands;
74from the tribe of Asher
they received Mashal, Abdon, **75**Hu-

---

a40 Most Hebrew manuscripts; some Hebrew manuscripts, one Septuagint manuscript and Syriac *Maaseiah*
b57 See Joshua 21:13; Hebrew *given the cities of refuge: Hebron, Libnah.*   *c59* Syriac (see also Septuagint and Joshua 21:16); Hebrew does not have *Juttah.*   *d60* See Joshua 21:17; Hebrew does not have *Gibeon.*
e67 See Joshua 21:21; Hebrew *given the cities of refuge: Shechem, Gezer.*

kok and Rehob, together with their pasturelands;

[76]and from the tribe of Naphtali
they received Kedesh in Galilee, Hammon and Kiriathaim, together with their pasturelands.

[77]The Merarites (the rest of the Levites) received the following:
From the tribe of Zebulun
they received Jokneam, Kartah,[a] Rimmono and Tabor, together with their pasturelands;
[78]from the tribe of Reuben across the Jordan east of Jericho
they received Bezer in the desert, Jahzah, [79]Kedemoth and Mephaath, together with their pasturelands;
[80]and from the tribe of Gad
they received Ramoth in Gilead, Mahanaim, [81]Heshbon and Jazer, together with their pasturelands.

Issachar

7 The sons of Issachar:
Tola, Puah, Jashub and Shimron — four in all.
[2]The sons of Tola:
Uzzi, Rephaiah, Jeriel, Jahmai, Ibsam and Samuel — heads of their families. During the reign of David, the descendants of Tola listed as fighting men in their genealogy numbered 22,600.
[3]The son of Uzzi:
Izrahiah.
The sons of Izrahiah:
Michael, Obadiah, Joel and Isshiah. All five of them were chiefs. [4]According to their family genealogy, they had 36,000 men ready for battle, for they had many wives and children.
[5]The relatives who were fighting men belonging to all the clans of Issachar, as listed in their genealogy, were 87,000 in all.

Benjamin

[6]Three sons of Benjamin:
Bela, Beker and Jediael.
[7]The sons of Bela:
Ezbon, Uzzi, Uzziel, Jerimoth and Iri, heads of families — five in all. Their genealogical record listed 22,034 fighting men.
[8]The sons of Beker:

Zemirah, Joash, Eliezer, Elioenai, Omri, Jeremoth, Abijah, Anathoth and Alemeth. All these were the sons of Beker. [9]Their genealogical record listed the heads of families and 20,200 fighting men.
[10]The son of Jediael:
Bilhan.
The sons of Bilhan:
Jeush, Benjamin, Ehud, Kenaanah, Zethan, Tarshish and Ahishahar. [11]All these sons of Jediael were heads of families. There were 17,200 fighting men ready to go out to war.
[12]The Shuppites and Huppites were the descendants of Ir, and the Hushites the descendants of Aher.

Naphtali

[13]The sons of Naphtali:
Jahziel, Guni, Jezer and Shillem[b] — the descendants of Bilhah.

Manasseh

[14]The descendants of Manasseh:
Asriel was his descendant through his Aramean concubine. She gave birth to Makir the father of Gilead. [15]Makir took a wife from among the Huppites and Shuppites. His sister's name was Maacah.
Another descendant was named Zelophehad, who had only daughters.
[16]Makir's wife Maacah gave birth to a son and named him Peresh. His brother was named Sheresh, and his sons were Ulam and Rakem.
[17]The son of Ulam:
Bedan.
These were the sons of Gilead son of Makir, the son of Manasseh. [18]His sister Hammoleketh gave birth to Ishhod, Abiezer and Mahlah.
[19]The sons of Shemida were:
Ahian, Shechem, Likhi and Aniam.

Ephraim

[20]The descendants of Ephraim:
Shuthelah, Bered his son, Tahath his son, Eleadah his son, Tahath his son, [21]Zabad his son and Shuthelah his son.
Ezer and Elead were killed by the native-born men of Gath, when they went down to seize their livestock. [22]Their

---

[a]77 See Septuagint and Joshua 21:34; Hebrew does not have *Jokneam, Kartah.*   [b]13 Some Hebrew and Septuagint manuscripts (see also Gen. 46:24 and Num. 26:49); most Hebrew manuscripts *Shallum*

father Ephraim mourned for them many days, and his relatives came to comfort him. **23**Then he lay with his wife again, and she became pregnant and gave birth to a son. He named him Beriah,[a] because there had been misfortune in his family. **24**His daughter was Sheerah, who built Lower and Upper Beth Horon as well as Uzzen Sheerah.

25Rephah was his son, Resheph his son,[b]

Telah his son, Tahan his son,

26Ladan his son, Ammihud his son, Elishama his son, **27**Nun his son and Joshua his son.

28Their lands and settlements included Bethel and its surrounding villages, Naaran to the east, Gezer and its villages to the west, and Shechem and its villages all the way to Ayyah and its villages. **29**Along the borders of Manasseh were Beth Shan, Taanach, Megiddo and Dor, together with their villages. The descendants of Joseph son of Israel lived in these towns.

Asher

30The sons of Asher:

Imnah, Ishvah, Ishvi and Beriah. Their sister was Serah.

31The sons of Beriah:

Heber and Malkiel, who was the father of Birzaith.

32Heber was the father of Japhlet, Shomer and Hotham and of their sister Shua.

33The sons of Japhlet:

Pasach, Bimhal and Ashvath. These were Japhlet's sons.

34The sons of Shomer:

Ahi, Rohgah,[c] Hubbah and Aram.

35The sons of his brother Helem:

Zophah, Imna, Shelesh and Amal.

36The sons of Zophah:

Suah, Harnepher, Shual, Beri, Imrah, **37**Bezer, Hod, Shamma, Shilshah, Ithran[d] and Beera.

38The sons of Jether:

Jephunneh, Pispah and Ara.

39The sons of Ulla:

Arah, Hanniel and Rizia.

40All these were descendants of Asher—heads of families, choice men, brave warriors and outstanding leaders. The number

of men ready for battle, as listed in their genealogy, was 26,000.

The Genealogy of Saul the Benjamite

8 Benjamin was the father of Bela his firstborn,

Ashbel the second son, Aharah the third,

2Nohah the fourth and Rapha the fifth.

3The sons of Bela were:

Addar, Gera, Abihud,[e] **4**Abishua, Naaman, Ahoah, **5**Gera, Shephuphan and Huram.

6These were the descendants of Ehud, who were heads of families of those living in Geba and were deported to Manahath:

7Naaman, Ahijah, and Gera, who deported them and who was the father of Uzza and Ahihud.

8Sons were born to Shaharaim in Moab after he had divorced his wives Hushim and Baara. **9**By his wife Hodesh he had Jobab, Zibia, Mesha, Malcam, **10**Jeuz, Sakia and Mirmah. These were his sons, heads of families. **11**By Hushim he had Abitub and Elpaal.

12The sons of Elpaal:

Eber, Misham, Shemed (who built Ono and Lod with its surrounding villages), **13**and Beriah and Shema, who were heads of families of those living in Aijalon and who drove out the inhabitants of Gath.

14Ahio, Shashak, Jeremoth, **15**Zebadiah, Arad, Eder, **16**Michael, Ishpah and Joha were the sons of Beriah.

17Zebadiah, Meshullam, Hizki, Heber, **18**Ishmerai, Izliah and Jobab were the sons of Elpaal.

19Jakim, Zicri, Zabdi, **20**Elienai, Zillethai, Eliel, **21**Adaiah, Beraiah and Shimrath were the sons of Shimei.

22Ishpan, Eber, Eliel, **23**Abdon, Zicri, Hanan, **24**Hananiah, Elam, Anthothijah, **25**Iphdeiah and Penuel were the sons of Shashak.

26Shamsherai, Shehariah, Athaliah, **27**Jaareshiah, Elijah and Zicri were the sons of Jeroham.

28All these were heads of families, chiefs as listed in their genealogy, and they lived in Jerusalem.

---

a23 *Beriah sounds like the Hebrew for* misfortune. *b25* Some Septuagint manuscripts; Hebrew does not have *his son.* *c34* Or *of his brother Shomer: Rohgah* *d37* Possibly a variant of *Jether* *e3* Or *Gera the father of Ehud*

29Jeiel[a] the father[b] of Gibeon lived in Gibeon.

His wife's name was Maacah, **30**and his firstborn son was Abdon, followed by Zur, Kish, Baal, Ner,[c] Nadab, **31**Gedor, Ahio, Zeker **32**and Mikloth, who was the father of Shimeah. They too lived near their relatives in Jerusalem.

33Ner was the father of Kish, Kish the father of Saul, and Saul the father of Jonathan, Malki-Shua, Abinadab and Esh-Baal.[d]

34The son of Jonathan:

Merib-Baal,[e] who was the father of Micah.

35The sons of Micah:

Pithon, Melech, Tarea and Ahaz.

36Ahaz was the father of Jehoaddah, Jehoaddah was the father of Alemeth, Azmaveth and Zimri, and Zimri was the father of Moza. **37**Moza was the father of Binea; Raphah was his son, Eleasah his son and Azel his son.

38Azel had six sons, and these were their names:

Azrikam, Bokeru, Ishmael, Sheariah, Obadiah and Hanan. All these were the sons of Azel.

39The sons of his brother Eshek:

Ulam his firstborn, Jeush the second son and Eliphelet the third. **40**The sons of Ulam were brave warriors who could handle the bow. They had many sons and grandsons — 150 in all.

All these were the descendants of Benjamin.

9 All Israel was listed in the genealogies recorded in the book of the kings of Israel.

The People in Jerusalem

The people of Judah were taken captive to Babylon because of their unfaithfulness. **2**Now the first to resettle on their own property in their own towns were some Israelites, priests, Levites and temple servants.

3Those from Judah, from Benjamin, and from Ephraim and Manasseh who lived in Jerusalem were:

4Uthai son of Ammihud, the son of Omri, the son of Imri, the son of Bani, a descendant of Perez son of Judah.

5Of the Shilonites:

Asaiah the firstborn and his sons.

6Of the Zerahites:

Jeuel.

The people from Judah numbered 690.

7Of the Benjamites:

Sallu son of Meshullam, the son of Hodaviah, the son of Hassenuah;

8Ibneiah son of Jeroham; Elah son of Uzzi, the son of Micri; and Meshullam son of Shephatiah, the son of Reuel, the son of Ibnijah.

9The people from Benjamin, as listed in their genealogy, numbered 956. All these men were heads of their families.

10Of the priests:

Jedaiah; Jehoiarib; Jakin;

11Azariah son of Hilkiah, the son of Meshullam, the son of Zadok, the son of Meraioth, the son of Ahitub, the official in charge of the house of God;

12Adaiah son of Jeroham, the son of Pashhur, the son of Malkijah; and Maasai son of Adiel, the son of Jahzerah, the son of Meshullam, the son of Meshillemith, the son of Immer.

13The priests, who were heads of families, numbered 1,760. They were able men, responsible for ministering in the house of God.

14Of the Levites:

Shemaiah son of Hasshub, the son of Azrikam, the son of Hashabiah, a Merarite; **15**Bakbakkar, Heresh, Galal and Mattaniah son of Mica, the son of Zicri, the son of Asaph; **16**Obadiah son of Shemaiah, the son of Galal, the son of Jeduthun; and Berekiah son of Asa, the son of Elkanah, who lived in the villages of the Netophathites.

17The gatekeepers:

Shallum, Akkub, Talmon, Ahiman and their brothers, Shallum their chief **18**being stationed at the King's Gate on the east, up to the present time. These were the gatekeepers belonging to the camp of the Levites. **19**Shallum son of Kore, the son of

---

[a]29 Some Septuagint manuscripts (see also 1 Chron. 9:35); Hebrew does not have *Jeiel*.   [b]29 *Father* may mean *civic leader* or *military leader*.   [c]30 Some Septuagint manuscripts (see also 1 Chron. 9:36); Hebrew does not have *Ner*.   [d]33 Also known as *Ish-Bosheth*   [e]34 Also known as *Mephibosheth*

Ebiasaph, the son of Korah, and his fellow gatekeepers from his family (the Korahites) were responsible for guarding the thresholds of the Tent[a] just as their fathers had been responsible for guarding the entrance to the dwelling of the LORD. [20]In earlier times Phinehas son of Eleazar was in charge of the gatekeepers, and the LORD was with him. [21]Zechariah son of Meshelemiah was the gatekeeper at the entrance to the Tent of Meeting.

[22]Altogether, those chosen to be gatekeepers at the thresholds numbered 212. They were registered by genealogy in their villages. The gatekeepers had been assigned to their positions of trust by David and Samuel the seer. [23]They and their descendants were in charge of guarding the gates of the house of the LORD — the house called the Tent. [24]The gatekeepers were on the four sides: east, west, north and south. [25]Their brothers in their villages had to come from time to time and share their duties for seven-day periods. [26]But the four principal gatekeepers, who were Levites, were entrusted with the responsibility for the rooms and treasuries in the house of God. [27]They would spend the night stationed around the house of God, because they had to guard it; and they had charge of the key for opening it each morning.

[28]Some of them were in charge of the articles used in the temple service; they counted them when they were brought in and when they were taken out. [29]Others were assigned to take care of the furnishings and all the other articles of the sanctuary, as well as the flour and wine, and the oil, incense and spices. [30]But some of the priests took care of mixing the spices. [31]A Levite named Mattithiah, the firstborn son of Shallum the Korahite, was entrusted with the responsibility for baking the offering bread. [32]Some of their Kohathite brothers were in charge of preparing for every Sabbath the bread set out on the table.

[33]Those who were musicians, heads of Levite families, stayed in the rooms of the temple and were exempt from other duties because they were responsible for the work day and night.

[34]All these were heads of Levite families, chiefs as listed in their genealogy, and they lived in Jerusalem.

The Genealogy of Saul

[35]Jeiel the father[b] of Gibeon lived in Gibeon.

His wife's name was Maacah, [36]and his firstborn son was Abdon, followed by Zur, Kish, Baal, Ner, Nadab, [37]Gedor, Ahio, Zechariah and Mikloth. [38]Mikloth was the father of Shimeam. They too lived near their relatives in Jerusalem.

[39]Ner was the father of Kish, Kish the father of Saul, and Saul the father of Jonathan, Malki-Shua, Abinadab and Esh-Baal.[c]

[40]The son of Jonathan:

Merib-Baal,[d] who was the father of Micah.

[41]The sons of Micah:

Pithon, Melech, Tahrea and Ahaz.[e]

[42]Ahaz was the father of Jadah, Jadah[f] was the father of Alemeth, Azmaveth and Zimri, and Zimri was the father of Moza. [43]Moza was the father of Binea; Rephaiah was his son, Eleasah his son and Azel his son.

[44]Azel had six sons, and these were their names:

Azrikam, Bokeru, Ishmael, Sheariah, Obadiah and Hanan. These were the sons of Azel.

Saul Takes His Life

10 Now the Philistines fought against Israel; the Israelites fled before them, and many fell slain on Mount Gilboa. [2]The Philistines pressed hard after Saul and his sons, and they killed his sons Jonathan, Abinadab and Malki-Shua. [3]The fighting grew fierce around Saul, and when the archers overtook him, they wounded him.

[4]Saul said to his armor-bearer, "Draw your sword and run me through, or these uncircumcised fellows will come and abuse me."

But his armor-bearer was terrified and would not do it; so Saul took his own sword and fell on it. [5]When the armor-bearer saw that Saul was dead, he too fell on his sword and died. [6]So Saul and his three sons died, and all his house died together.

[7]When all the Israelites in the valley saw

---

[a]19 That is, the temple; also in verses 21 and 23   [b]35 *Father* may mean *civic leader* or *military leader.*
[c]39 Also known as *Ish-Bosheth*   [d]40 Also known as *Mephibosheth*   [e]41 Vulgate and Syriac (see also
Septuagint and 1 Chron. 8:35); Hebrew does not have *and Ahaz.*   [f]42 Some Hebrew manuscripts and
Septuagint (see also 1 Chron. 8:36); most Hebrew manuscripts *Jarah, Jarah*

that the army had fled and that Saul and his sons had died, they abandoned their towns and fled. And the Philistines came and occupied them.

8The next day, when the Philistines came to strip the dead, they found Saul and his sons fallen on Mount Gilboa. **9**They stripped him and took his head and his armor, and sent messengers throughout the land of the Philistines to proclaim the news among their idols and their people. **10**They put his armor in the temple of their gods and hung up his head in the temple of Dagon.

11When all the inhabitants of Jabesh Gilead heard of everything the Philistines had done to Saul, **12**all their valiant men went and took the bodies of Saul and his sons and brought them to Jabesh. Then they buried their bones under the great tree in Jabesh, and they fasted seven days.

13Saul died because he was unfaithful to the LORD; he did not keep the word of the LORD and even consulted a medium for guidance, **14**and did not inquire of the LORD. So the LORD put him to death and turned the kingdom over to David son of Jesse.

David Becomes King Over Israel

11 All Israel came together to David at Hebron and said, "We are your own flesh and blood. **2**In the past, even while Saul was king, you were the one who led Israel on their military campaigns. And the LORD your God said to you, 'You will shepherd my people Israel, and you will become their ruler.' "

3When all the elders of Israel had come to King David at Hebron, he made a compact with them at Hebron before the LORD, and they anointed David king over Israel, as the LORD had promised through Samuel.

David Conquers Jerusalem

4David and all the Israelites marched to Jerusalem (that is, Jebus). The Jebusites who lived there **5**said to David, "You will not get in here." Nevertheless, David captured the fortress of Zion, the City of David.

6David had said, "Whoever leads the attack on the Jebusites will become commander-in-chief." Joab son of Zeruiah went up first, and so he received the command.

7David then took up residence in the fortress, and so it was called the City of David. **8**He built up the city around it, from the supporting terraces[a] to the surrounding wall, while Joab restored the rest of the city. **9**And David became more and more powerful, because the LORD Almighty was with him.

David's Mighty Men

10These were the chiefs of David's mighty men — they, together with all Israel, gave his kingship strong support to extend it over the whole land, as the LORD had promised — **11**this is the list of David's mighty men:

Jashobeam,[b] a Hacmonite, was chief of the officers[c]; he raised his spear against three hundred men, whom he killed in one encounter.

12Next to him was Eleazar son of Dodai the Ahohite, one of the three mighty men. **13**He was with David at Pas Dammim when the Philistines gathered there for battle. At a place where there was a field full of barley, the troops fled from the Philistines. **14**But they took their stand in the middle of the field. They defended it and struck the Philistines down, and the LORD brought about a great victory.

15Three of the thirty chiefs came down to David to the rock at the cave of Adullam, while a band of Philistines was encamped in the Valley of Rephaim. **16**At that time David was in the stronghold, and the Philistine garrison was at Bethlehem. **17**David longed for water and said, "Oh, that someone would get me a drink of water from the well near the gate of Bethlehem!" **18**So the Three broke through the Philistine lines, drew water from the well near the gate of Bethlehem and carried it back to David. But he refused to drink it; instead, he poured it out before the LORD. **19**"God forbid that I should do this!" he said. "Should I drink the blood of these men who went at the risk of their lives?" Because they risked their lives to bring it back, David would not drink it.

Such were the exploits of the three mighty men.

20Abishai the brother of Joab was chief of the Three. He raised his spear against three hundred men, whom he killed, and so he became as famous as the Three. **21**He was doubly honored above the Three and became their commander, even though he was not included among them.

22Benaiah son of Jehoiada was a valiant fighter from Kabzeel, who performed great exploits. He struck down two of Moab's best men. He also went down into a pit on a snowy day and killed a lion. **23**And he struck

---

a8 Or *the Millo*   *b11* Possibly a variant of *Jashob-Baal* (see also 2 Samuel 23:8)   *c11* Or *Thirty*; some Septuagint manuscripts *Three* down an Egyptian who was seven and a half feet[a] tall. Although the Egyptian had a spear like a weaver's rod in his hand, Benaiah went against him with a club. He snatched the spear from the Egyptian's hand and killed him with his own spear. ²⁴Such were the exploits of Benaiah son of Jehoiada; he too was as famous as the three mighty men. ²⁵He was held in greater honor than any of the Thirty, but he was not included among the Three. And David put him in charge of his bodyguard.

²⁶The mighty men were:
Asahel the brother of Joab,
Elhanan son of Dodo from Bethlehem,
²⁷Shammoth the Harorite,
Helez the Pelonite,
²⁸Ira son of Ikkesh from Tekoa,
Abiezer from Anathoth,
²⁹Sibbecai the Hushathite,
Ilai the Ahohite,
³⁰Maharai the Netophathite,
Heled son of Baanah the Netophathite,
³¹Ithai son of Ribai from Gibeah in Benjamin,
Benaiah the Pirathonite,
³²Hurai from the ravines of Gaash,
Abiel the Arbathite,
³³Azmaveth the Baharumite,
Eliahba the Shaalbonite,
³⁴the sons of Hashem the Gizonite,
Jonathan son of Shagee the Hararite,
³⁵Ahiam son of Sacar the Hararite,
Eliphal son of Ur,
³⁶Hepher the Mekerathite,
Ahijah the Pelonite,
³⁷Hezro the Carmelite,
Naarai son of Ezbai,
³⁸Joel the brother of Nathan,
Mibhar son of Hagri,
³⁹Zelek the Ammonite,
Naharai the Berothite, the armor-bearer of Joab son of Zeruiah,
⁴⁰Ira the Ithrite,
Gareb the Ithrite,
⁴¹Uriah the Hittite,
Zabad son of Ahlai,
⁴²Adina son of Shiza the Reubenite, who was chief of the Reubenites, and the thirty with him,
⁴³Hanan son of Maacah,
Joshaphat the Mithnite,
⁴⁴Uzzia the Ashterathite,

Shama and Jeiel the sons of Hotham the Aroerite,
⁴⁵Jediael son of Shimri,
his brother Joha the Tizite,
⁴⁶Eliel the Mahavite,
Jeribai and Joshaviah the sons of Elnaam,
Ithmah the Moabite,
⁴⁷Eliel, Obed and Jaasiel the Mezobaite.

Warriors Join David

12 These were the men who came to David at Ziklag, while he was banished from the presence of Saul son of Kish (they were among the warriors who helped him in battle; ²they were armed with bows and were able to shoot arrows or to sling stones right-handed or left-handed; they were kinsmen of Saul from the tribe of Benjamin):

³Ahiezer their chief and Joash the sons of Shemaah the Gibeathite; Jeziel and Pelet the sons of Azmaveth; Beracah, Jehu the Anathothite, ⁴and Ishmaiah the Gibeonite, a mighty man among the Thirty, who was a leader of the Thirty; Jeremiah, Jahaziel, Johanan, Jozabad the Gederathite, ⁵Eluzai, Jerimoth, Bealiah, Shemariah and Shephatiah the Haruphite; ⁶Elkanah, Isshiah, Azarel, Joezer and Jashobeam the Korahites; ⁷and Joelah and Zebadiah the sons of Jeroham from Gedor.

⁸Some Gadites defected to David at his stronghold in the desert. They were brave warriors, ready for battle and able to handle the shield and spear. Their faces were the faces of lions, and they were as swift as gazelles in the mountains.
⁹Ezer was the chief,
Obadiah the second in command, Eliab the third,
¹⁰Mishmannah the fourth, Jeremiah the fifth,
¹¹Attai the sixth, Eliel the seventh,
¹²Johanan the eighth, Elzabad the ninth,
¹³Jeremiah the tenth and Macbannai the eleventh.
¹⁴These Gadites were army commanders; the least was a match for a hundred, and the greatest for a thousand. ¹⁵It was they who crossed the Jordan in the first month when it was overflowing all its banks, and they put to flight everyone living in the valleys, to the east and to the west.

<hr>

a 23 Hebrew *five cubits* (about 2.3 meters)

¹⁶Other Benjamites and some men from Judah also came to David in his stronghold. ¹⁷David went out to meet them and said to them, "If you have come to me in peace, to help me, I am ready to have you unite with me. But if you have come to betray me to my enemies when my hands are free from violence, may the God of our fathers see it and judge you."

¹⁸Then the Spirit came upon Amasai, chief of the Thirty, and he said:

"We are yours, O David!
We are with you, O son of Jesse!
Success, success to you,
    and success to those who help you,
        for your God will help you."

So David received them and made them leaders of his raiding bands.

¹⁹Some of the men of Manasseh defected to David when he went with the Philistines to fight against Saul. (He and his men did not help the Philistines because, after consultation, their rulers sent him away. They said, "It will cost us our heads if he deserts to his master Saul.") ²⁰When David went to Ziklag, these were the men of Manasseh who defected to him: Adnah, Jozabad, Jediael, Michael, Jozabad, Elihu and Zillethai, leaders of units of a thousand in Manasseh. ²¹They helped David against raiding bands, for all of them were brave warriors, and they were commanders in his army. ²²Day after day men came to help David, until he had a great army, like the army of God.ᵃ

Others Join David at Hebron

²³These are the numbers of the men armed for battle who came to David at Hebron to turn Saul's kingdom over to him, as the Lord had said:

²⁴men of Judah, carrying shield and spear — 6,800 armed for battle;
²⁵men of Simeon, warriors ready for battle — 7,100;
²⁶men of Levi — 4,600, ²⁷including Jehoiada, leader of the family of Aaron, with 3,700 men, ²⁸and Zadok, a brave young warrior, with 22 officers from his family;
²⁹men of Benjamin, Saul's kinsmen — 3,000, most of whom had remained loyal to Saul's house until then;
³⁰men of Ephraim, brave warriors, famous in their own clans — 20,800;
³¹men of half the tribe of Manasseh, des-

ignated by name to come and make David king — 18,000;
³²men of Issachar, who understood the times and knew what Israel should do — 200 chiefs, with all their relatives under their command;
³³men of Zebulun, experienced soldiers prepared for battle with every type of weapon, to help David with undivided loyalty — 50,000;
³⁴men of Naphtali — 1,000 officers, together with 37,000 men carrying shields and spears;
³⁵men of Dan, ready for battle — 28,600;
³⁶men of Asher, experienced soldiers prepared for battle — 40,000;
³⁷and from east of the Jordan, men of Reuben, Gad and the half-tribe of Manasseh, armed with every type of weapon — 120,000.

³⁸All these were fighting men who volunteered to serve in the ranks. They came to Hebron fully determined to make David king over all Israel. All the rest of the Israelites were also of one mind to make David king. ³⁹The men spent three days there with David, eating and drinking, for their families had supplied provisions for them. ⁴⁰Also, their neighbors from as far away as Issachar, Zebulun and Naphtali came bringing food on donkeys, camels, mules and oxen. There were plentiful supplies of flour, fig cakes, raisin cakes, wine, oil, cattle and sheep, for there was joy in Israel.

Bringing Back the Ark

13 David conferred with each of his officers, the commanders of thousands and commanders of hundreds. ²He then said to the whole assembly of Israel, "If it seems good to you and if it is the will of the Lord our God, let us send word far and wide to the rest of our brothers throughout the territories of Israel, and also to the priests and Levites who are with them in their towns and pasturelands, to come and join us. ³Let us bring the ark of our God back to us, for we did not inquire ofᵇ itᶜ during the reign of Saul." ⁴The whole assembly agreed to do this, because it seemed right to all the people.

⁵So David assembled all the Israelites, from the Shihor River in Egypt to Leboᵈ Hamath, to bring the ark of God from Kiriath Jearim. ⁶David and all the Israelites with him went to Baalah of Judah (Kiriath Jearim) to bring up from there the ark of God the Lord,

---

ᵃ22 Or *a great and mighty army*   ᵇ3 Or *we neglected*   ᶜ3 Or *him*   ᵈ5 Or *to the entrance to* who is enthroned between the cherubim—the ark that is called by the Name. **7**They moved the ark of God from Abinadab's house on a new cart, with Uzzah and Ahio guiding it. **8**David and all the Israelites were celebrating with all their might before God, with songs and with harps, lyres, tambourines, cymbals and trumpets.

9When they came to the threshing floor of Kidon, Uzzah reached out his hand to steady the ark, because the oxen stumbled. **10**The LORD's anger burned against Uzzah, and he struck him down because he had put his hand on the ark. So he died there before God.

11Then David was angry because the LORD's wrath had broken out against Uzzah, and to this day that place is called Perez Uzzah.*a*

12David was afraid of God that day and asked, "How can I ever bring the ark of God to me?" **13**He did not take the ark to be with him in the City of David. Instead, he took it aside to the house of Obed-Edom the Gittite. **14**The ark of God remained with the family of Obed-Edom in his house for three months, and the LORD blessed his household and everything he had.

David's House and Family

14 Now Hiram king of Tyre sent messengers to David, along with cedar logs, stonemasons and carpenters to build a palace for him. **2**And David knew that the LORD had established him as king over Israel and that his kingdom had been highly exalted for the sake of his people Israel.

3In Jerusalem David took more wives and became the father of more sons and daughters. **4**These are the names of the children born to him there: Shammua, Shobab, Nathan, Solomon, **5**Ibhar, Elishua, Elpelet, **6**Nogah, Nepheg, Japhia, **7**Elishama, Beeliada*b* and Eliphelet.

David Defeats the Philistines

8When the Philistines heard that David had been anointed king over all Israel, they went up in full force to search for him, but David heard about it and went out to meet them. **9**Now the Philistines had come and raided the Valley of Rephaim; **10**so David inquired of God: "Shall I go and attack the Philistines? Will you hand them over to me?"

The LORD answered him, "Go, I will hand them over to you."

11So David and his men went up to Baal Perazim, and there he defeated them. He said, "As waters break out, God has broken out against my enemies by my hand." So that place was called Baal Perazim.*c* **12**The Philistines had abandoned their gods there, and David gave orders to burn them in the fire.

13Once more the Philistines raided the valley; **14**so David inquired of God again, and God answered him, "Do not go straight up, but circle around them and attack them in front of the balsam trees. **15**As soon as you hear the sound of marching in the tops of the balsam trees, move out to battle, because that will mean God has gone out in front of you to strike the Philistine army." **16**So David did as God commanded him, and they struck down the Philistine army, all the way from Gibeon to Gezer.

17So David's fame spread throughout every land, and the LORD made all the nations fear him.

The Ark Brought to Jerusalem

15 After David had constructed buildings for himself in the City of David, he prepared a place for the ark of God and pitched a tent for it. **2**Then David said, "No one but the Levites may carry the ark of God, because the LORD chose them to carry the ark of the LORD and to minister before him forever."

3David assembled all Israel in Jerusalem to bring up the ark of the LORD to the place he had prepared for it. **4**He called together the descendants of Aaron and the Levites:

5From the descendants of Kohath,
   Uriel the leader and 120 relatives;
6from the descendants of Merari,
   Asaiah the leader and 220 relatives;
7from the descendants of Gershon,*d*
   Joel the leader and 130 relatives;
8from the descendants of Elizaphan,
   Shemaiah the leader and 200 relatives;
9from the descendants of Hebron,
   Eliel the leader and 80 relatives;
10from the descendants of Uzziel,
   Amminadab the leader and 112 relatives.

11Then David summoned Zadok and Abiathar the priests, and Uriel, Asaiah, Joel, Shemaiah, Eliel and Amminadab the Levites. **12**He said to them, "You are the heads of the Levitical families; you and your fellow

---

a11 Perez Uzzah means outbreak against Uzzah.   *b7 A variant of Eliada*   *c11 Baal Perazim means the lord who breaks out.*   *d7 Hebrew Gershom, a variant of Gershon*

Levites are to consecrate yourselves and bring up the ark of the LORD, the God of Israel, to the place I have prepared for it. ¹³It was because you, the Levites, did not bring it up the first time that the LORD our God broke out in anger against us. We did not inquire of him about how to do it in the prescribed way." ¹⁴So the priests and Levites consecrated themselves in order to bring up the ark of the LORD, the God of Israel. ¹⁵And the Levites carried the ark of God with the poles on their shoulders, as Moses had commanded in accordance with the word of the LORD.

¹⁶David told the leaders of the Levites to appoint their brothers as singers to sing joyful songs, accompanied by musical instruments: lyres, harps and cymbals.

¹⁷So the Levites appointed Heman son of Joel; from his brothers, Asaph son of Berekiah; and from their brothers the Merarites, Ethan son of Kushaiah; ¹⁸and with them their brothers next in rank: Zechariah,ᵃ Jaaziel, Shemiramoth, Jehiel, Unni, Eliab, Benaiah, Maaseiah, Mattithiah, Eliphelehu, Mikneiah, Obed-Edom and Jeiel,ᵇ the gatekeepers. ¹⁹The musicians Heman, Asaph and Ethan were to sound the bronze cymbals; ²⁰Zechariah, Aziel, Shemiramoth, Jehiel, Unni, Eliab, Maaseiah and Benaiah were to play the lyres according to *alamoth,*ᶜ ²¹and Mattithiah, Eliphelehu, Mikneiah, Obed-Edom, Jeiel and Azaziah were to play the harps, directing according to *sheminith.*ᶜ ²²Kenaniah the head Levite was in charge of the singing; that was his responsibility because he was skillful at it.

²³Berekiah and Elkanah were to be doorkeepers for the ark. ²⁴Shebaniah, Joshaphat, Nethanel, Amasai, Zechariah, Benaiah and Eliezer the priests were to blow trumpets before the ark of God. Obed-Edom and Jehiah were also to be doorkeepers for the ark.

²⁵So David and the elders of Israel and the commanders of units of a thousand went to bring up the ark of the covenant of the LORD from the house of Obed-Edom, with rejoicing. ²⁶Because God had helped the Levites who were carrying the ark of the covenant of the LORD, seven bulls and seven rams were sacrificed. ²⁷Now David was clothed in a robe of fine linen, as were all the Levites who were carrying the ark, and as were the singers, and Kenaniah, who was in charge of the singing of the choirs. David also wore a linen ephod. ²⁸So all Israel brought up the ark of the covenant of the LORD with shouts, with the sounding of rams' horns and trumpets, and of cymbals, and the playing of lyres and harps.

²⁹As the ark of the covenant of the LORD was entering the City of David, Michal daughter of Saul watched from a window. And when she saw King David dancing and celebrating, she despised him in her heart.

16 They brought the ark of God and set it inside the tent that David had pitched for it, and they presented burnt offerings and fellowship offeringsᵈ before God. ²After David had finished sacrificing the burnt offerings and fellowship offerings, he blessed the people in the name of the LORD. ³Then he gave a loaf of bread, a cake of dates and a cake of raisins to each Israelite man and woman.

⁴He appointed some of the Levites to minister before the ark of the LORD, to make petition, to give thanks, and to praise the LORD, the God of Israel: ⁵Asaph was the chief, Zechariah second, then Jeiel, Shemiramoth, Jehiel, Mattithiah, Eliab, Benaiah, Obed-Edom and Jeiel. They were to play the lyres and harps, Asaph was to sound the cymbals, ⁶and Benaiah and Jahaziel the priests were to blow the trumpets regularly before the ark of the covenant of God.

David's Psalm of Thanks

⁷That day David first committed to Asaph and his associates this psalm of thanks to the LORD:

⁸Give thanks to the LORD, call on his name;
    make known among the nations what he has done.
⁹Sing to him, sing praise to him;
    tell of all his wonderful acts.
¹⁰Glory in his holy name;
    let the hearts of those who seek the LORD rejoice.
¹¹Look to the LORD and his strength;
    seek his face always.
¹²Remember the wonders he has done,
    his miracles, and the judgments he pronounced,
¹³O descendants of Israel his servant,
    O sons of Jacob, his chosen ones.

¹⁴He is the LORD our God;
    his judgments are in all the earth.

ᵃ18 Three Hebrew manuscripts and most Septuagint manuscripts (see also verse 20 and 1 Chron. 16:5); most Hebrew manuscripts *Zechariah son and* or *Zechariah, Ben and*   ᵇ18 Hebrew; Septuagint (see also verse 21) *Jeiel and Azaziah*   ᶜ20, 21 Probably a musical term   ᵈ1 Traditionally *peace offerings;* also in verse 2

GIVING GOD THE GLORY HE DESERVES
□ MONDAY

Chuck is gushing with praise for his favorite professional basketball star. "The guy is unreal. He can fly. I'm not kidding, on one fast break last night, he hung in the air for days, and then threw down a monster jam!"

Caryn is gushing with praise for Chuck. "He is soooo cute! And he's the funniest guy in the world. He cracks me up all the time. I'm serious; I think about him constantly."

"Hey, Chuck, Caryn, want to go to a praise meeting at church?"

"Praise meeting?" Chuck groans. "Why in the world would I want to do that!"

Look It Up

No one is more worthy of your praise than God. Like the heavenly creatures that John saw in his revelation, you can praise God as:

Your Creator—"You are worthy, our Lord and God, to receive glory and honor and power, for you created all things, and by your will they were created and have their being" (Revelation 4:11).

Your Redeemer—"In a loud voice they sang: 'Worthy is the Lamb, who was slain, to receive power and wealth and wisdom and strength and honor and glory and praise!' " (Revelation 5:12).

Don't you think the Almighty One, who gives both physical and spiritual life, deserves your worship?

Think It Through

Worship is not flattering God so that you can get something out of him (Malachi 3:14). It's not an escape from the problems of life (Psalm 73:16–17,26). And it's not an empty ritual (Matthew 15:8–9).

Grade yourself (A—F) in the area of worship.

Work It Out

Worship isn't an option; it's an obligation! God deserves it and you need it. If you don't spend time adoring the Lord, your Christian life will be shallow and ineffective. If you do learn to worship, you'll be plugged into the ultimate power source!

Ask God to teach you what it means to worship. And invite a friend to study the subject with you.

Nail It Down

Read 1 Chronicles 16:7–36 for David's poetic worship of God.

Turn to pages 594 and 616 for other readings on worship.
Turn to page 420 for Tuesday's reading.

Topic

WORSHIP

¹⁵He remembers^a his covenant forever,
the word he commanded, for a
thousand generations,
¹⁶the covenant he made with Abraham,
the oath he swore to Isaac.
¹⁷He confirmed it to Jacob as a decree,
to Israel as an everlasting covenant:
¹⁸"To you I will give the land of Canaan
as the portion you will inherit."

¹⁹When they were but few in number,
few indeed, and strangers in it,
²⁰they^b wandered from nation to nation,
from one kingdom to another.
²¹He allowed no man to oppress them;
for their sake he rebuked kings:
²²"Do not touch my anointed ones;
do my prophets no harm."

²³Sing to the Lord, all the earth;
proclaim his salvation day after day.
²⁴Declare his glory among the nations,
his marvelous deeds among all
peoples.
²⁵For great is the Lord and most worthy of
praise;
he is to be feared above all gods.
²⁶For all the gods of the nations are idols,
but the Lord made the heavens.
²⁷Splendor and majesty are before him;
strength and joy in his dwelling place.
²⁸Ascribe to the Lord, O families of
nations,
ascribe to the Lord glory and strength,
²⁹   ascribe to the Lord the glory due his
name.
Bring an offering and come before him;
worship the Lord in the splendor of
his^c holiness.
³⁰Tremble before him, all the earth!
The world is firmly established; it
cannot be moved.
³¹Let the heavens rejoice, let the earth be
glad;
let them say among the nations, "The
Lord reigns!"
³²Let the sea resound, and all that is in it;
let the fields be jubilant, and
everything in them!
³³Then the trees of the forest will sing,
they will sing for joy before the Lord,
for he comes to judge the earth.
³⁴Give thanks to the Lord, for he is good;
his love endures forever.
³⁵Cry out, "Save us, O God our Savior;

gather us and deliver us from the
nations,
that we may give thanks to your holy
name,
that we may glory in your praise."
³⁶Praise be to the Lord, the God of Israel,
from everlasting to everlasting.

Then all the people said "Amen" and "Praise
the Lord."

³⁷David left Asaph and his associates before the ark of the covenant of the Lord to
minister there regularly, according to each
day's requirements. ³⁸He also left Obed-
Edom and his sixty-eight associates to minister with them. Obed-Edom son of Jeduthun, and also Hosah, were gatekeepers.
³⁹David left Zadok the priest and his fellow priests before the tabernacle of the Lord
at the high place in Gibeon ⁴⁰to present
burnt offerings to the Lord on the altar of
burnt offering regularly, morning and evening, in accordance with everything written
in the Law of the Lord, which he had given
Israel. ⁴¹With them were Heman and Jeduthun and the rest of those chosen and designated by name to give thanks to the Lord,
"for his love endures forever." ⁴²Heman and
Jeduthun were responsible for the sounding
of the trumpets and cymbals and for the
playing of the other instruments for sacred
song. The sons of Jeduthun were stationed
at the gate.
⁴³Then all the people left, each for his
own home, and David returned home to
bless his family.

God's Promise to David

17 After David was settled in his palace,
he said to Nathan the prophet, "Here
I am, living in a palace of cedar, while the
ark of the covenant of the Lord is under a
tent."
²Nathan replied to David, "Whatever you
have in mind, do it, for God is with you."
³That night the word of God came to Nathan, saying:

⁴"Go and tell my servant David, 'This
is what the Lord says: You are not the
one to build me a house to dwell in. ⁵I
have not dwelt in a house from the day
I brought Israel up out of Egypt to this
day. I have moved from one tent site to
another, from one dwelling place to another. ⁶Wherever I have moved with all

---

^a15 Some Septuagint manuscripts (see also Psalm 105:8); Hebrew *Remember*   ^b18-20 One Hebrew
manuscript, Septuagint and Vulgate (see also Psalm 105:12); most Hebrew manuscripts *inherit, / ¹⁹though you
are but few in number, / few indeed, and strangers in it." / ²⁰They*   ^c29 Or *Lord with the splendor of*

the Israelites, did I ever say to any of their leaders*a* whom I commanded to shepherd my people, "Why have you not built me a house of cedar?"'

[7]"Now then, tell my servant David, 'This is what the Lord Almighty says: I took you from the pasture and from following the flock, to be ruler over my people Israel. [8]I have been with you wherever you have gone, and I have cut off all your enemies from before you. Now I will make your name like the names of the greatest men of the earth. [9]And I will provide a place for my people Israel and will plant them so that they can have a home of their own and no longer be disturbed. Wicked people will not oppress them anymore, as they did at the beginning [10]and have done ever since the time I appointed leaders over my people Israel. I will also subdue all your enemies.

" 'I declare to you that the Lord will build a house for you: [11]When your days are over and you go to be with your fathers, I will raise up your offspring to succeed you, one of your own sons, and I will establish his kingdom. [12]He is the one who will build a house for me, and I will establish his throne forever. [13]I will be his father, and he will be my son. I will never take my love away from him, as I took it away from your predecessor. [14]I will set him over my house and my kingdom forever; his throne will be established forever.' "

[15]Nathan reported to David all the words of this entire revelation.

David's Prayer

[16]Then King David went in and sat before the Lord, and he said:

"Who am I, O Lord God, and what is my family, that you have brought me this far? [17]And as if this were not enough in your sight, O God, you have spoken about the future of the house of your servant. You have looked on me as though I were the most exalted of men, O Lord God.

[18]"What more can David say to you for honoring your servant? For you know your servant, [19]O Lord. For the sake of your servant and according to your will, you have done this great

thing and made known all these great promises.

[20]"There is no one like you, O Lord, and there is no God but you, as we have heard with our own ears. [21]And who is like your people Israel—the one nation on earth whose God went out to redeem a people for himself, and to make a name for yourself, and to perform great and awesome wonders by driving out nations from before your people, whom you redeemed from Egypt? [22]You made your people Israel your very own forever, and you, O Lord, have become their God.

[23]"And now, Lord, let the promise you have made concerning your servant and his house be established forever. Do as you promised, [24]so that it will be established and that your name will be great forever. Then men will say, 'The Lord Almighty, the God over Israel, is Israel's God!' And the house of your servant David will be established before you.

[25]"You, my God, have revealed to your servant that you will build a house for him. So your servant has found courage to pray to you. [26]O Lord, you are God! You have promised these good things to your servant. [27]Now you have been pleased to bless the house of your servant, that it may continue forever in your sight; for you, O Lord, have blessed it, and it will be blessed forever."

David's Victories

18 In the course of time, David defeated the Philistines and subdued them, and he took Gath and its surrounding villages from the control of the Philistines.

[2]David also defeated the Moabites, and they became subject to him and brought tribute.

[3]Moreover, David fought Hadadezer king of Zobah, as far as Hamath, when he went to establish his control along the Euphrates River. [4]David captured a thousand of his chariots, seven thousand charioteers and twenty thousand foot soldiers. He hamstrung all but a hundred of the chariot horses.

[5]When the Arameans of Damascus came to help Hadadezer king of Zobah, David struck down twenty-two thousand of them. [6]He put garrisons in the Aramean kingdom

---

a6 Traditionally *judges*; also in verse 10

of Damascus, and the Arameans became subject to him and brought tribute. The LORD gave David victory everywhere he went.

[7]David took the gold shields carried by the officers of Hadadezer and brought them to Jerusalem. [8]From Tebah[a] and Cun, towns that belonged to Hadadezer, David took a great quantity of bronze, which Solomon used to make the bronze Sea, the pillars and various bronze articles.

[9]When Tou king of Hamath heard that David had defeated the entire army of Hadadezer king of Zobah, [10]he sent his son Hadoram to King David to greet him and congratulate him on his victory in battle over Hadadezer, who had been at war with Tou. Hadoram brought all kinds of articles of gold and silver and bronze.

[11]King David dedicated these articles to the LORD, as he had done with the silver and gold he had taken from all these nations: Edom and Moab, the Ammonites and the Philistines, and Amalek.

[12]Abishai son of Zeruiah struck down eighteen thousand Edomites in the Valley of Salt. [13]He put garrisons in Edom, and all the Edomites became subject to David. The LORD gave David victory everywhere he went.

David's Officials

[14]David reigned over all Israel, doing what was just and right for all his people. [15]Joab son of Zeruiah was over the army; Jehoshaphat son of Ahilud was recorder; [16]Zadok son of Ahitub and Ahimelech[b] son of Abiathar were priests; Shavsha was secretary; [17]Benaiah son of Jehoiada was over the Kerethites and Pelethites; and David's sons were chief officials at the king's side.

The Battle Against the Ammonites

19 In the course of time, Nahash king of the Ammonites died, and his son succeeded him as king. [2]David thought, "I will show kindness to Hanun son of Nahash, because his father showed kindness to me." So David sent a delegation to express his sympathy to Hanun concerning his father.

When David's men came to Hanun in the land of the Ammonites to express sympathy to him, [3]the Ammonite nobles said to Hanun, "Do you think David is honoring your father by sending men to you to express sympathy? Haven't his men come to you to explore and spy out the country and overthrow it?" [4]So Hanun seized David's men, shaved them, cut off their garments in the middle at the buttocks, and sent them away.

[5]When someone came and told David about the men, he sent messengers to meet them, for they were greatly humiliated. The king said, "Stay at Jericho till your beards have grown, and then come back."

[6]When the Ammonites realized that they had become a stench in David's nostrils, Hanun and the Ammonites sent a thousand talents[c] of silver to hire chariots and charioteers from Aram Naharaim,[d] Aram Maacah and Zobah. [7]They hired thirty-two thousand chariots and charioteers, as well as the king of Maacah with his troops, who came and camped near Medeba, while the Ammonites were mustered from their towns and moved out for battle.

[8]On hearing this, David sent Joab out with the entire army of fighting men. [9]The Ammonites came out and drew up in battle formation at the entrance to their city, while the kings who had come were by themselves in the open country.

[10]Joab saw that there were battle lines in front of him and behind him; so he selected some of the best troops in Israel and deployed them against the Arameans. [11]He put the rest of the men under the command of Abishai his brother, and they were deployed against the Ammonites. [12]Joab said, "If the Arameans are too strong for me, then you are to rescue me; but if the Ammonites are too strong for you, then I will rescue you. [13]Be strong and let us fight bravely for our people and the cities of our God. The LORD will do what is good in his sight."

[14]Then Joab and the troops with him advanced to fight the Arameans, and they fled before him. [15]When the Ammonites saw that the Arameans were fleeing, they too fled before his brother Abishai and went inside the city. So Joab went back to Jerusalem.

[16]After the Arameans saw that they had been routed by Israel, they sent messengers and had Arameans brought from beyond the River,[e] with Shophach the commander of Hadadezer's army leading them.

[17]When David was told of this, he gathered all Israel and crossed the Jordan; he advanced against them and formed his battle lines opposite them. David formed his lines

---

[a]8 Hebrew *Tibhath*, a variant of *Tebah*   [b]16 Some Hebrew manuscripts, Vulgate and Syriac (see also 2 Samuel 8:17); most Hebrew manuscripts *Abimelech*   [c]6 That is, about 37 tons (about 34 metric tons)
[d]6 That is, Northwest Mesopotamia   [e]16 That is, the Euphrates

to meet the Arameans in battle, and they fought against him. **18**But they fled before Israel, and David killed seven thousand of their charioteers and forty thousand of their foot soldiers. He also killed Shophach the commander of their army.

19When the vassals of Hadadezer saw that they had been defeated by Israel, they made peace with David and became subject to him.

So the Arameans were not willing to help the Ammonites anymore.

The Capture of Rabbah

20 In the spring, at the time when kings go off to war, Joab led out the armed forces. He laid waste the land of the Ammonites and went to Rabbah and besieged it, but David remained in Jerusalem. Joab attacked Rabbah and left it in ruins. **2**David took the crown from the head of their king*a*—its weight was found to be a talent*b* of gold, and it was set with precious stones—and it was placed on David's head. He took a great quantity of plunder from the city **3**and brought out the people who were there, consigning them to labor with saws and with iron picks and axes. David did this to all the Ammonite towns. Then David and his entire army returned to Jerusalem.

War With the Philistines

4In the course of time, war broke out with the Philistines, at Gezer. At that time Sibbecai the Hushathite killed Sippai, one of the descendants of the Rephaites, and the Philistines were subjugated.

5In another battle with the Philistines, Elhanan son of Jair killed Lahmi the brother of Goliath the Gittite, who had a spear with a shaft like a weaver's rod.

6In still another battle, which took place at Gath, there was a huge man with six fingers on each hand and six toes on each foot—twenty-four in all. He also was descended from Rapha. **7**When he taunted Israel, Jonathan son of Shimea, David's brother, killed him.

8These were descendants of Rapha in Gath, and they fell at the hands of David and his men.

David Numbers the Fighting Men

21 Satan rose up against Israel and incited David to take a census of Isra-el. **2**So David said to Joab and the commanders of the troops, "Go and count the Israelites from Beersheba to Dan. Then report back to me so that I may know how many there are."

3But Joab replied, "May the LORD multiply his troops a hundred times over. My lord the king, are they not all my lord's subjects? Why does my lord want to do this? Why should he bring guilt on Israel?"

4The king's word, however, overruled Joab; so Joab left and went throughout Israel and then came back to Jerusalem. **5**Joab reported the number of the fighting men to David: In all Israel there were one million one hundred thousand men who could handle a sword, including four hundred and seventy thousand in Judah.

6But Joab did not include Levi and Benjamin in the numbering, because the king's command was repulsive to him. **7**This command was also evil in the sight of God; so he punished Israel.

8Then David said to God, "I have sinned greatly by doing this. Now, I beg you, take away the guilt of your servant. I have done a very foolish thing."

9The LORD said to Gad, David's seer, **10**"Go and tell David, 'This is what the LORD says: I am giving you three options. Choose one of them for me to carry out against you.'"

11So Gad went to David and said to him, "This is what the LORD says: 'Take your choice: **12**three years of famine, three months of being swept away*c* before your enemies, with their swords overtaking you, or three days of the sword of the LORD—days of plague in the land, with the angel of the LORD ravaging every part of Israel.' Now then, decide how I should answer the one who sent me."

13David said to Gad, "I am in deep distress. Let me fall into the hands of the LORD, for his mercy is very great; but do not let me fall into the hands of men."

14So the LORD sent a plague on Israel, and seventy thousand men of Israel fell dead. **15**And God sent an angel to destroy Jerusalem. But as the angel was doing so, the LORD saw it and was grieved because of the calamity and said to the angel who was destroying the people, "Enough! Withdraw your hand." The angel of the LORD was then standing at the threshing floor of Araunah*d* the Jebusite.

---

*a*2 Or *of Milcom,* that is, Molech   *b*2 That is, about 75 pounds (about 34 kilograms)   *c*12 Hebrew; Septuagint and Vulgate (see also 2 Samuel 24:13) *of fleeing*   *d*15 Hebrew *Ornan,* a variant of *Araunah;* also in verses 18-28

WHO'S GIVING THE ORDERS?

Patti (a sophomore who struggles with bulimia) moans, "Why does God keep tempting me like this?" as she stares at all the junk food on her friend's counter.

After going too far with his girlfriend (again!), Michael tries to ease his guilty conscience: "If only Kate wasn't so beautiful," he rationalizes. "The way she looks at me, the way she dresses—it's all her fault!"

Look It Up
• • • •

Let's look at each of those excuses in light of God's Word:

First, the idea that God is the source of temptation. "When tempted, no one should say, 'God is tempting me.' For God cannot be tempted by evil, nor does he tempt anyone" (James 1:13).

Second, that others are the source of temptation. "He [Jesus] spoke plainly about this [his arrest, crucifixion and resurrection], and Peter took him aside and began to rebuke him.

"But when Jesus turned . . . he rebuked Peter. 'Get behind me, Satan!' he said" (Mark 8:32–33).

Think It Through
• • • •

Jesus' reaction to Peter is interesting. It tells us that Satan is the ultimate source of the temptations in our lives. God is involved in the sense that he allows us to undergo temptation. And people are involved in the sense that Satan uses them to tempt us to do evil. But the real tempter is the devil himself.

In what ways has Satan recently been using people to tempt you to do wrong things?

Work It Out
• • • •

Have you been blaming God or other people for the temptations in your life? Remember that people are not ultimately responsible. The engineer behind it all is the devil himself. Pray this prayer:

"Father in heaven, I am constantly tempted from every side. Thank you that you're not the one who is tempting me. Thank you for showing me who the real culprit is. Help me not to take the devil lightly. Give me wisdom to know how to fight back. And give me the desire to say no to the devil's schemes. Thank you. In Jesus' name. Amen."

Nail It Down
• • • •

Find out more about Satan, the master tempter by reading 1 Chronicles 21:1.

Turn to pages 658, 1290, 1315, 1341 and 1356 for other readings on temptation.
Turn to page 428 for Wednesday's reading.

Topic
• • • •

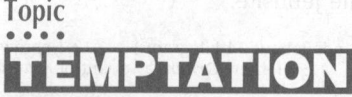

16David looked up and saw the angel of the LORD standing between heaven and earth, with a drawn sword in his hand extended over Jerusalem. Then David and the elders, clothed in sackcloth, fell facedown. 17David said to God, "Was it not I who ordered the fighting men to be counted? I am the one who has sinned and done wrong. These are but sheep. What have they done? O LORD my God, let your hand fall upon me and my family, but do not let this plague remain on your people."

18Then the angel of the LORD ordered Gad to tell David to go up and build an altar to the LORD on the threshing floor of Araunah the Jebusite. 19So David went up in obedience to the word that Gad had spoken in the name of the LORD.

20While Araunah was threshing wheat, he turned and saw the angel; his four sons who were with him hid themselves. 21Then David approached, and when Araunah looked and saw him, he left the threshing floor and bowed down before David with his face to the ground.

22David said to him, "Let me have the site of your threshing floor so I can build an altar to the LORD, that the plague on the people may be stopped. Sell it to me at the full price."

23Araunah said to David, "Take it! Let my lord the king do whatever pleases him. Look, I will give the oxen for the burnt offerings, the threshing sledges for the wood, and the wheat for the grain offering. I will give all this."

24But King David replied to Araunah, "No, I insist on paying the full price. I will not take for the LORD what is yours, or sacrifice a burnt offering that costs me nothing."

25So David paid Araunah six hundred shekels*a* of gold for the site. 26David built an altar to the LORD there and sacrificed burnt offerings and fellowship offerings.*b* He called on the LORD, and the LORD answered him with fire from heaven on the altar of burnt offering.

27Then the LORD spoke to the angel, and he put his sword back into its sheath. 28At that time, when David saw that the LORD had answered him on the threshing floor of Araunah the Jebusite, he offered sacrifices there. 29The tabernacle of the LORD, which Moses had made in the desert, and the altar of burnt offering were at that time on the high place at Gibeon. 30But David could not

go before it to inquire of God, because he was afraid of the sword of the angel of the LORD.

22 Then David said, "The house of the LORD God is to be here, and also the altar of burnt offering for Israel."

Preparations for the Temple

2So David gave orders to assemble the aliens living in Israel, and from among them he appointed stonecutters to prepare dressed stone for building the house of God. 3He provided a large amount of iron to make nails for the doors of the gateways and for the fittings, and more bronze than could be weighed. 4He also provided more cedar logs than could be counted, for the Sidonians and Tyrians had brought large numbers of them to David.

5David said, "My son Solomon is young and inexperienced, and the house to be built for the LORD should be of great magnificence and fame and splendor in the sight of all the nations. Therefore I will make preparations for it." So David made extensive preparations before his death.

6Then he called for his son Solomon and charged him to build a house for the LORD, the God of Israel. 7David said to Solomon: "My son, I had it in my heart to build a house for the Name of the LORD my God. 8But this word of the LORD came to me: 'You have shed much blood and have fought many wars. You are not to build a house for my Name, because you have shed much blood on the earth in my sight. 9But you will have a son who will be a man of peace and rest, and I will give him rest from all his enemies on every side. His name will be Solomon,*c* and I will grant Israel peace and quiet during his reign. 10He is the one who will build a house for my Name. He will be my son, and I will be his father. And I will establish the throne of his kingdom over Israel forever.'

11"Now, my son, the LORD be with you, and may you have success and build the house of the LORD your God, as he said you would. 12May the LORD give you discretion and understanding when he puts you in command over Israel, so that you may keep the law of the LORD your God. 13Then you will have success if you are careful to observe the decrees and laws that the LORD gave Moses for Israel. Be strong and courageous. Do not be afraid or discouraged.

14"I have taken great pains to provide for

---

*a*25 That is, about 15 pounds (about 7 kilograms)   *b*26 Traditionally *peace offerings*   *c*9 *Solomon* sounds like and may be derived from the Hebrew for *peace*.

the temple of the Lord a hundred thousand talents[a] of gold, a million talents[b] of silver, quantities of bronze and iron too great to be weighed, and wood and stone. And you may add to them. **15**You have many workmen: stonecutters, masons and carpenters, as well as men skilled in every kind of work **16**in gold and silver, bronze and iron— craftsmen beyond number. Now begin the work, and the Lord be with you."

17Then David ordered all the leaders of Israel to help his son Solomon. **18**He said to them, "Is not the Lord your God with you? And has he not granted you rest on every side? For he has handed the inhabitants of the land over to me, and the land is subject to the Lord and to his people. **19**Now devote your heart and soul to seeking the Lord your God. Begin to build the sanctuary of the Lord God, so that you may bring the ark of the covenant of the Lord and the sacred articles belonging to God into the temple that will be built for the Name of the Lord."

The Levites

23 When David was old and full of years, he made his son Solomon king over Israel.

2He also gathered together all the leaders of Israel, as well as the priests and Levites. **3**The Levites thirty years old or more were counted, and the total number of men was thirty-eight thousand. **4**David said, "Of these, twenty-four thousand are to supervise the work of the temple of the Lord and six thousand are to be officials and judges. **5**Four thousand are to be gatekeepers and four thousand are to praise the Lord with the musical instruments I have provided for that purpose."

6David divided the Levites into groups corresponding to the sons of Levi: Gershon, Kohath and Merari.

Gershonites

7Belonging to the Gershonites:
Ladan and Shimei.

8The sons of Ladan:
Jehiel the first, Zetham and Joel— three in all.

9The sons of Shimei:
Shelomoth, Haziel and Haran— three in all.
These were the heads of the families of Ladan.

10And the sons of Shimei:
Jahath, Ziza,[c] Jeush and Beriah.
These were the sons of Shimei— four in all.

11Jahath was the first and Ziza the second, but Jeush and Beriah did not have many sons; so they were counted as one family with one assignment.

Kohathites

12The sons of Kohath:
Amram, Izhar, Hebron and Uzziel— four in all.

13The sons of Amram:
Aaron and Moses.
Aaron was set apart, he and his descendants forever, to consecrate the most holy things, to offer sacrifices before the Lord, to minister before him and to pronounce blessings in his name forever. **14**The sons of Moses the man of God were counted as part of the tribe of Levi.

15The sons of Moses:
Gershom and Eliezer.

16The descendants of Gershom:
Shubael was the first.

17The descendants of Eliezer:
Rehabiah was the first.
Eliezer had no other sons, but the sons of Rehabiah were very numerous.

18The sons of Izhar:
Shelomith was the first.

19The sons of Hebron:
Jeriah the first, Amariah the second, Jahaziel the third and Jekameam the fourth.

20The sons of Uzziel:
Micah the first and Isshiah the second.

Merarites

21The sons of Merari:
Mahli and Mushi.
The sons of Mahli:
Eleazar and Kish.

22Eleazar died without having sons: he had only daughters. Their cousins, the sons of Kish, married them.

23The sons of Mushi:
Mahli, Eder and Jerimoth—three in all.

---

a 14 That is, about 3,750 tons (about 3,450 metric tons)   *b 14* That is, about 37,500 tons (about 34,500 metric tons)   *c 10* One Hebrew manuscript, Septuagint and Vulgate (see also verse 11); most Hebrew manuscripts Zina

24These were the descendants of Levi by their families — the heads of families as they were registered under their names and counted individually, that is, the workers twenty years old or more who served in the temple of the LORD. **25**For David had said, "Since the LORD, the God of Israel, has granted rest to his people and has come to dwell in Jerusalem forever, **26**the Levites no longer need to carry the tabernacle or any of the articles used in its service." **27**According to the last instructions of David, the Levites were counted from those twenty years old or more.

28The duty of the Levites was to help Aaron's descendants in the service of the temple of the LORD: to be in charge of the courtyards, the side rooms, the purification of all sacred things and the performance of other duties at the house of God. **29**They were in charge of the bread set out on the table, the flour for the grain offerings, the unleavened wafers, the baking and the mixing, and all measurements of quantity and size. **30**They were also to stand every morning to thank and praise the LORD. They were to do the same in the evening **31**and whenever burnt offerings were presented to the LORD on Sabbaths and at New Moon festivals and at appointed feasts. They were to serve before the LORD regularly in the proper number and in the way prescribed for them.

32And so the Levites carried out their responsibilities for the Tent of Meeting, for the Holy Place and, under their brothers the descendants of Aaron, for the service of the temple of the LORD.

The Divisions of Priests

24 These were the divisions of the sons of Aaron:

The sons of Aaron were Nadab, Abihu, Eleazar and Ithamar. **2**But Nadab and Abihu died before their father did, and they had no sons; so Eleazar and Ithamar served as the priests. **3**With the help of Zadok a descendant of Eleazar and Ahimelech a descendant of Ithamar, David separated them into divisions for their appointed order of ministering. **4**A larger number of leaders were found among Eleazar's descendants than among Ithamar's, and they were divided accordingly: sixteen heads of families from Eleazar's descendants and eight heads of families from Ithamar's descendants. **5**They divided them impartially by drawing lots, for

there were officials of the sanctuary and officials of God among the descendants of both Eleazar and Ithamar.

6The scribe Shemaiah son of Nethanel, a Levite, recorded their names in the presence of the king and of the officials: Zadok the priest, Ahimelech son of Abiathar and the heads of families of the priests and of the Levites — one family being taken from Eleazar and then one from Ithamar.

7The first lot fell to Jehoiarib,
   the second to Jedaiah,
8the third to Harim,
   the fourth to Seorim,
9the fifth to Malkijah,
   the sixth to Mijamin,
10the seventh to Hakkoz,
   the eighth to Abijah,
11the ninth to Jeshua,
   the tenth to Shecaniah,
12the eleventh to Eliashib,
   the twelfth to Jakim,
13the thirteenth to Huppah,
   the fourteenth to Jeshebeab,
14the fifteenth to Bilgah,
   the sixteenth to Immer,
15the seventeenth to Hezir,
   the eighteenth to Happizzez,
16the nineteenth to Pethahiah,
   the twentieth to Jehezkel,
17the twenty-first to Jakin,
   the twenty-second to Gamul,
18the twenty-third to Delaiah
   and the twenty-fourth to Maaziah.

19This was their appointed order of ministering when they entered the temple of the LORD, according to the regulations prescribed for them by their forefather Aaron, as the LORD, the God of Israel, had commanded him.

The Rest of the Levites

20As for the rest of the descendants of Levi:
   from the sons of Amram: Shubael;
      from the sons of Shubael: Jehdeiah.
   21As for Rehabiah, from his sons:
      Isshiah was the first.
22From the Izharites: Shelomoth;
   from the sons of Shelomoth: Jahath.
23The sons of Hebron: Jeriah the first,[a]
   Amariah the second, Jahaziel the third and Jekameam the fourth.
24The son of Uzziel: Micah;
   from the sons of Micah: Shamir.
25The brother of Micah: Isshiah;

---

[a]23 Two Hebrew manuscripts and some Septuagint manuscripts (see also 1 Chron. 23:19); most Hebrew manuscripts *The sons of Jeriah:*

from the sons of Isshiah: Zechariah.
²⁶The sons of Merari: Mahli and Mushi.
The son of Jaaziah: Beno.
²⁷The sons of Merari:
from Jaaziah: Beno, Shoham, Zaccur
and Ibri.
²⁸From Mahli: Eleazar, who had no sons.
²⁹From Kish: the son of Kish:
Jerahmeel.
³⁰And the sons of Mushi: Mahli, Eder and
Jerimoth.

These were the Levites, according to their families. ³¹They also cast lots, just as their brothers the descendants of Aaron did, in the presence of King David and of Zadok, Ahimelech, and the heads of families of the priests and of the Levites. The families of the oldest brother were treated the same as those of the youngest.

The Singers

25 David, together with the commanders of the army, set apart some of the sons of Asaph, Heman and Jeduthun for the ministry of prophesying, accompanied by harps, lyres and cymbals. Here is the list of the men who performed this service:

²From the sons of Asaph:
Zaccur, Joseph, Nethaniah and Asarelah. The sons of Asaph were under the supervision of Asaph, who prophesied under the king's supervision.
³As for Jeduthun, from his sons:
Gedaliah, Zeri, Jeshaiah, Shimei,ᵃ Hashabiah and Mattithiah, six in all, under the supervision of their father Jeduthun, who prophesied, using the harp in thanking and praising the LORD.
⁴As for Heman, from his sons:
Bukkiah, Mattaniah, Uzziel, Shubael and Jerimoth; Hananiah, Hanani, Eliathah, Giddalti and Romamti-Ezer; Joshbekashah, Mallothi, Hothir and Mahazioth. ⁵All these were sons of Heman the king's seer. They were given him through the promises of God to exalt him.ᵇ God gave Heman fourteen sons and three daughters.

⁶All these men were under the supervision of their fathers for the music of the temple of the LORD, with cymbals, lyres and harps, for the ministry at the house of God. Asaph, Jeduthun and Heman were under

the supervision of the king. ⁷Along with their relatives — all of them trained and skilled in music for the LORD — they numbered 288. ⁸Young and old alike, teacher as well as student, cast lots for their duties.

⁹The first lot, which was for Asaph,
fell to Joseph,
his sons and relatives,ᶜ   12ᵈ
the second to Gedaliah,
he and his relatives and sons,   12
¹⁰the third to Zaccur,
his sons and relatives,   12
¹¹the fourth to Izri,ᵉ
his sons and relatives,   12
¹²the fifth to Nethaniah,
his sons and relatives,   12
¹³the sixth to Bukkiah,
his sons and relatives,   12
¹⁴the seventh to Jesarelah,ᶠ
his sons and relatives,   12
¹⁵the eighth to Jeshaiah,
his sons and relatives,   12
¹⁶the ninth to Mattaniah,
his sons and relatives,   12
¹⁷the tenth to Shimei,
his sons and relatives,   12
¹⁸the eleventh to Azarel,ᵍ
his sons and relatives,   12
¹⁹the twelfth to Hashabiah,
his sons and relatives,   12
²⁰the thirteenth to Shubael,
his sons and relatives,   12
²¹the fourteenth to Mattithiah,
his sons and relatives,   12
²²the fifteenth to Jerimoth,
his sons and relatives,   12
²³the sixteenth to Hananiah,
his sons and relatives,   12
²⁴the seventeenth to
Joshbekashah,
his sons and relatives,   12
²⁵the eighteenth to Hanani,
his sons and relatives,   12
²⁶the nineteenth to Mallothi,
his sons and relatives,   12
²⁷the twentieth to Eliathah,
his sons and relatives,   12
²⁸the twenty-first to Hothir,
his sons and relatives,   12
²⁹the twenty-second to Giddalti,
his sons and relatives,   12
³⁰the twenty-third to
Mahazioth,
his sons and relatives,   12

31the twenty-fourth to Romamti-Ezer,
his sons and relatives,   12

The Gatekeepers

26 The divisions of the gatekeepers:

From the Korahites: Meshelemiah
son of Kore, one of the sons of
Asaph.
2Meshelemiah had sons:
Zechariah the firstborn,
Jediael the second,
Zebadiah the third,
Jathniel the fourth,
3Elam the fifth,
Jehohanan the sixth
and Eliehoenai the seventh.
4Obed-Edom also had sons:
Shemaiah the firstborn,
Jehozabad the second,
Joah the third,
Sacar the fourth,
Nethanel the fifth,
5Ammiel the sixth,
Issachar the seventh
and Peullethai the eighth.
(For God had blessed Obed-Edom.)

6His son Shemaiah also had sons, who
were leaders in their father's family
because they were very capable
men. **7**The sons of Shemaiah: Othni,
Rephael, Obed and Elzabad; his relatives Elihu and Semakiah were also
able men. **8**All these were descendants of Obed-Edom; they and their
sons and their relatives were capable men with the strength to do the
work—descendants of Obed-Edom,
62 in all.
9Meshelemiah had sons and relatives,
who were able men—18 in all.

10Hosah the Merarite had sons: Shimri
the first (although he was not the
firstborn, his father had appointed
him the first), **11**Hilkiah the second,
Tabaliah the third and Zechariah the
fourth. The sons and relatives of Hosah were 13 in all.
12These divisions of the gatekeepers,
through their chief men, had duties for ministering in the temple of the LORD, just as
their relatives had. **13**Lots were cast for each
gate, according to their families, young and
old alike.
14The lot for the East Gate fell to Shelemi-
ah.ª Then lots were cast for his son Zecha-

riah, a wise counselor, and the lot for the
North Gate fell to him. **15**The lot for the
South Gate fell to Obed-Edom, and the lot
for the storehouse fell to his sons. **16**The lots
for the West Gate and the Shalleketh Gate on
the upper road fell to Shuppim and Hosah.
Guard was alongside of guard: **17**There
were six Levites a day on the east, four a day
on the north, four a day on the south and
two at a time at the storehouse. **18**As for the
court to the west, there were four at the road
and two at the court itself.
19These were the divisions of the gatekeepers who were descendants of Korah
and Merari.

The Treasurers and Other Officials

20Their fellow Levites wereᵇ in charge of
the treasuries of the house of God and the
treasuries for the dedicated things.
21The descendants of Ladan, who were
Gershonites through Ladan and who were
heads of families belonging to Ladan the
Gershonite, were Jehieli, **22**the sons of Jehieli, Zetham and his brother Joel. They were in
charge of the treasuries of the temple of the
LORD.
23From the Amramites, the Izharites, the
Hebronites and the Uzzielites:

24Shubael, a descendant of Gershom son
of Moses, was the officer in charge of
the treasuries. **25**His relatives
through Eliezer: Rehabiah his son,
Jeshaiah his son, Joram his son, Zicri
his son and Shelomith his son.
26Shelomith and his relatives were
in charge of all the treasuries for the
things dedicated by King David, by
the heads of families who were the
commanders of thousands and
commanders of hundreds, and by
the other army commanders.
27Some of the plunder taken in battle they dedicated for the repair of
the temple of the LORD. **28**And everything dedicated by Samuel the seer
and by Saul son of Kish, Abner son
of Ner and Joab son of Zeruiah, and
all the other dedicated things were
in the care of Shelomith and his relatives.
29From the Izharites: Kenaniah and his
sons were assigned duties away
from the temple, as officials and
judges over Israel.
30From the Hebronites: Hashabiah and

his relatives — seventeen hundred able men — were responsible in Israel west of the Jordan for all the work of the LORD and for the king's service. **31**As for the Hebronites, Jeriah was their chief according to the genealogical records of their families. In the fortieth year of David's reign a search was made in the records, and capable men among the Hebronites were found at Jazer in Gilead. **32**Jeriah had twenty-seven hundred relatives, who were able men and heads of families, and King David put them in charge of the Reubenites, the Gadites and the half-tribe of Manasseh for every matter pertaining to God and for the affairs of the king.

Army Divisions

27 This is the list of the Israelites — heads of families, commanders of thousands and commanders of hundreds, and their officers, who served the king in all that concerned the army divisions that were on duty month by month throughout the year. Each division consisted of 24,000 men.

2In charge of the first division, for the first month, was Jashobeam son of Zabdiel. There were 24,000 men in his division. **3**He was a descendant of Perez and chief of all the army officers for the first month. **4**In charge of the division for the second month was Dodai the Ahohite; Mikloth was the leader of his division. There were 24,000 men in his division. **5**The third army commander, for the third month, was Benaiah son of Jehoiada the priest. He was chief and there were 24,000 men in his division. **6**This was the Benaiah who was a mighty man among the Thirty and was over the Thirty. His son Ammizabad was in charge of his division. **7**The fourth, for the fourth month, was Asahel the brother of Joab; his son Zebadiah was his successor. There were 24,000 men in his division. **8**The fifth, for the fifth month, was the commander Shamhuth the Izrahite. There were 24,000 men in his division. **9**The sixth, for the sixth month, was Ira the son of Ikkesh the Tekoite. There were 24,000 men in his division.

10The seventh, for the seventh month, was Helez the Pelonite, an Ephraimite. There were 24,000 men in his division. **11**The eighth, for the eighth month, was Sibbecai the Hushathite, a Zerahite. There were 24,000 men in his division. **12**The ninth, for the ninth month, was Abiezer the Anathothite, a Benjamite. There were 24,000 men in his division. **13**The tenth, for the tenth month, was Maharai the Netophathite, a Zerahite. There were 24,000 men in his division. **14**The eleventh, for the eleventh month, was Benaiah the Pirathonite, an Ephraimite. There were 24,000 men in his division. **15**The twelfth, for the twelfth month, was Heldai the Netophathite, from the family of Othniel. There were 24,000 men in his division.

Officers of the Tribes

16The officers over the tribes of Israel:

over the Reubenites: Eliezer son of Zicri;
over the Simeonites: Shephatiah son of Maacah;
17over Levi: Hashabiah son of Kemuel;
over Aaron: Zadok;
18over Judah: Elihu, a brother of David;
over Issachar: Omri son of Michael;
19over Zebulun: Ishmaiah son of Obadiah;
over Naphtali: Jerimoth son of Azriel;
20over the Ephraimites: Hoshea son of Azaziah;
over half the tribe of Manasseh: Joel son of Pedaiah;
21over the half-tribe of Manasseh in Gilead: Iddo son of Zechariah;
over Benjamin: Jaasiel son of Abner;
22over Dan: Azarel son of Jeroham.

These were the officers over the tribes of Israel.

23David did not take the number of the men twenty years old or less, because the LORD had promised to make Israel as numerous as the stars in the sky. **24**Joab son of Zeruiah began to count the men but did not finish. Wrath came on Israel on account of this numbering, and the number was not entered in the book[a] of the annals of King David.

The King's Overseers

25Azmaveth son of Adiel was in charge of the royal storehouses.

a24 Septuagint; Hebrew *number*

Jonathan son of Uzziah was in charge of the storehouses in the outlying districts, in the towns, the villages and the watchtowers. **26**Ezri son of Kelub was in charge of the field workers who farmed the land. **27**Shimei the Ramathite was in charge of the vineyards.

Zabdi the Shiphmite was in charge of the produce of the vineyards for the wine vats. **28**Baal-Hanan the Gederite was in charge of the olive and sycamore-fig trees in the western foothills.

Joash was in charge of the supplies of olive oil. **29**Shitrai the Sharonite was in charge of the herds grazing in Sharon.

Shaphat son of Adlai was in charge of herds in the valleys. **30**Obil the Ishmaelite was in charge of the camels.

Jehdeiah the Meronothite was in charge of the donkeys. **31**Jaziz the Hagrite was in charge of the flocks.

All these were the officials in charge of King David's property.

32Jonathan, David's uncle, was a counselor, a man of insight and a scribe. Jehiel son of Hacmoni took care of the king's sons. **33**Ahithophel was the king's counselor.

Hushai the Arkite was the king's friend. **34**Ahithophel was succeeded by Jehoiada son of Benaiah and by Abiathar.

Joab was the commander of the royal army.

David's Plans for the Temple

28 David summoned all the officials of Israel to assemble at Jerusalem: the officers over the tribes, the commanders of the divisions in the service of the king, the commanders of thousands and commanders of hundreds, and the officials in charge of all the property and livestock belonging to the king and his sons, together with the palace officials, the mighty men and all the brave warriors.

2King David rose to his feet and said: "Listen to me, my brothers and my people. I had it in my heart to build a house as a place of rest for the ark of the covenant of the LORD, for the footstool of our God, and I made plans to build it. **3**But God said to me, 'You are not to build a house for my Name, because you are a warrior and have shed blood.'

4"Yet the LORD, the God of Israel, chose me from my whole family to be king over Israel forever. He chose Judah as leader, and from the house of Judah he chose my family, and from my father's sons he was pleased to make me king over all Israel. **5**Of all my sons—and the LORD has given me many—he has chosen my son Solomon to sit on the throne of the kingdom of the LORD over Israel. **6**He said to me: 'Solomon your son is the one who will build my house and my courts, for I have chosen him to be my son, and I will be his father. **7**I will establish his kingdom forever if he is unswerving in carrying out my commands and laws, as is being done at this time.'

8"So now I charge you in the sight of all Israel and of the assembly of the LORD, and in the hearing of our God: Be careful to follow all the commands of the LORD your God, that you may possess this good land and pass it on as an inheritance to your descendants forever.

9"And you, my son Solomon, acknowledge the God of your father, and serve him with wholehearted devotion and with a willing mind, for the LORD searches every heart and understands every motive behind the thoughts. If you seek him, he will be found by you; but if you forsake him, he will reject you forever. **10**Consider now, for the LORD has chosen you to build a temple as a sanctuary. Be strong and do the work."

11Then David gave his son Solomon the plans for the portico of the temple, its buildings, its storerooms, its upper parts, its inner rooms and the place of atonement. **12**He gave him the plans of all that the Spirit had put in his mind for the courts of the temple of the LORD and all the surrounding rooms, for the treasuries of the temple of God and for the treasuries for the dedicated things. **13**He gave him instructions for the divisions of the priests and Levites, and for all the work of serving in the temple of the LORD, as well as for all the articles to be used in its service. **14**He designated the weight of gold for all the gold articles to be used in various kinds of service, and the weight of silver for all the silver articles to be used in various kinds of service: **15**the weight of gold for the gold lampstands and their lamps, with the weight for each lampstand and its lamps; and the weight of silver for each silver lampstand and its lamps, according to the use of each lampstand; **16**the weight of gold for each table for consecrated bread; the weight of silver for the silver tables; **17**the weight of pure gold for the forks, sprinkling bowls and pitchers; the weight of gold for each gold dish; the weight of silver for each silver dish;

GETTING TO THE HEART OF THE MATTER

I can't believe this," Jennifer thought to herself. "Holly, the weirdest girl at school, is sitting at my lunch table. Will you look at her outfit? Does she wash? She's rambling on to me like we're best friends or something. I'm so embarrassed."

Holly's voice trailed off to a whisper. "I know you need to study. But I sat down because I don't know where else to turn. I know you're a Christian, and I've been wondering a lot lately about God and stuff. Can you help me?"

Look It Up
• • • •

Jennifer swallowed hard as she remembered what she had read that morning in her Bible. "The LORD does not look at the things man looks at. Man looks at the outward appearance, but the LORD looks at the heart" (1 Samuel 16:7).

She had always ignored Holly because of her outward appearance. She would never have guessed that Holly was hungry to know more about God. "How could I be so mean and insensitive?" Jennifer thought.

A few weeks later, Jennifer said to another friend, "I had Holly figured all wrong. She's different for sure, but really sweet and a lot of fun when you get to know her. I'm glad to have a friend like her. And I'm really glad I can be a witness to her."

When God looks at people, he doesn't see the clothes they wear, their makeup, hairstyles or reputation. God sees the desire of each person's heart. He gets past the superficial stuff to discover what an individual is really about.

Think It Through
• • • •

Which matters more to you, outer credentials or inner potential?

Looking at others from God's perspective demands that you not reject them for the way they seem on the outside. It's best to try to get to know them on the inside.

You are responsible to discover the potential in others and encourage them to achieve their best in God's kingdom. Think about it: What a privilege it is to be able to share God's unconditional love with those who have felt the sting of rejection.

Work It Out
• • • •

Right now think of someone you know who gets rejected because he or she is different. Ask God to grant you the insight to see as he sees, not just external characteristics, but internal character. Then determine to go out of your way to encourage that person.

Nail It Down
• • • •

Meditate on 1 Chronicles 28:9.

Turn to pages 544, 569 and 755 for other readings on rejection.
Turn to page 432 for Thursday's reading.

Topic
• • • •

REJECTION

18and the weight of the refined gold for the altar of incense. He also gave him the plan for the chariot, that is, the cherubim of gold that spread their wings and shelter the ark of the covenant of the LORD.

19"All this," David said, "I have in writing from the hand of the LORD upon me, and he gave me understanding in all the details of the plan."

20David also said to Solomon his son, "Be strong and courageous, and do the work. Do not be afraid or discouraged, for the LORD God, my God, is with you. He will not fail you or forsake you until all the work for the service of the temple of the LORD is finished. **21**The divisions of the priests and Levites are ready for all the work on the temple of God, and every willing man skilled in any craft will help you in all the work. The officials and all the people will obey your every command."

Gifts for Building the Temple

29 Then King David said to the whole assembly: "My son Solomon, the one whom God has chosen, is young and inexperienced. The task is great, because this palatial structure is not for man but for the LORD God. **2**With all my resources I have provided for the temple of my God—gold for the gold work, silver for the silver, bronze for the bronze, iron for the iron and wood for the wood, as well as onyx for the settings, turquoise,*a* stones of various colors, and all kinds of fine stone and marble—all of these in large quantities. **3**Besides, in my devotion to the temple of my God I now give my personal treasures of gold and silver for the temple of my God, over and above everything I have provided for this holy temple: **4**three thousand talents*b* of gold (gold of Ophir) and seven thousand talents*c* of refined silver, for the overlaying of the walls of the buildings, **5**for the gold work and the silver work, and for all the work to be done by the craftsmen. Now, who is willing to consecrate himself today to the LORD?"

6Then the leaders of families, the officers of the tribes of Israel, the commanders of thousands and commanders of hundreds, and the officials in charge of the king's work gave willingly. **7**They gave toward the work on the temple of God five thousand talents*d*

and ten thousand darics*e* of gold, ten thousand talents*f* of silver, eighteen thousand talents*g* of bronze and a hundred thousand talents*h* of iron. **8**Any who had precious stones gave them to the treasury of the temple of the LORD in the custody of Jehiel the Gershonite. **9**The people rejoiced at the willing response of their leaders, for they had given freely and wholeheartedly to the LORD. David the king also rejoiced greatly.

David's Prayer

10David praised the LORD in the presence of the whole assembly, saying,

"Praise be to you, O LORD,
  God of our father Israel,
  from everlasting to everlasting.
11Yours, O LORD, is the greatness and the
    power
  and the glory and the majesty and the
    splendor,
  for everything in heaven and earth is
    yours.
Yours, O LORD, is the kingdom;
  you are exalted as head over all.
12Wealth and honor come from you;
  you are the ruler of all things.
In your hands are strength and power
  to exalt and give strength to all.
13Now, our God, we give you thanks,
  and praise your glorious name.

14"But who am I, and who are my people, that we should be able to give as generously as this? Everything comes from you, and we have given you only what comes from your hand. **15**We are aliens and strangers in your sight, as were all our forefathers. Our days on earth are like a shadow, without hope. **16**O LORD our God, as for all this abundance that we have provided for building you a temple for your Holy Name, it comes from your hand, and all of it belongs to you. **17**I know, my God, that you test the heart and are pleased with integrity. All these things have I given willingly and with honest intent. And now I have seen with joy how willingly your people who are here have given to you. **18**O LORD, God of our fathers Abraham, Isaac and Israel, keep this desire in the hearts of your people forever, and keep their hearts loyal to you. **19**And give my son

---

a2 The meaning of the Hebrew for this word is uncertain.   *b4* That is, about 110 tons (about 100 metric tons)   *c4* That is, about 260 tons (about 240 metric tons)   *d7* That is, about 190 tons (about 170 metric tons)   *e7* That is, about 185 pounds (about 84 kilograms)   *f7* That is, about 375 tons (about 345 metric tons)   *g7* That is, about 675 tons (about 610 metric tons)   *h7* That is, about 3,750 tons (about 3,450 metric tons)

Solomon the wholehearted devotion to keep your commands, requirements and decrees and to do everything to build the palatial structure for which I have provided."

²⁰Then David said to the whole assembly, "Praise the Lord your God." So they all praised the Lord, the God of their fathers; they bowed low and fell prostrate before the Lord and the king.

Solomon Acknowledged as King

²¹The next day they made sacrifices to the Lord and presented burnt offerings to him: a thousand bulls, a thousand rams and a thousand male lambs, together with their drink offerings, and other sacrifices in abundance for all Israel. ²²They ate and drank with great joy in the presence of the Lord that day.

Then they acknowledged Solomon son of David as king a second time, anointing him before the Lord to be ruler and Zadok to be priest. ²³So Solomon sat on the throne of the Lord as king in place of his father David. He prospered and all Israel obeyed him. ²⁴All the officers and mighty men, as well as all of King David's sons, pledged their submission to King Solomon.

²⁵The Lord highly exalted Solomon in the sight of all Israel and bestowed on him royal splendor such as no king over Israel ever had before.

The Death of David

²⁶David son of Jesse was king over all Israel. ²⁷He ruled over Israel forty years — seven in Hebron and thirty-three in Jerusalem. ²⁸He died at a good old age, having enjoyed long life, wealth and honor. His son Solomon succeeded him as king.

²⁹As for the events of King David's reign, from beginning to end, they are written in the records of Samuel the seer, the records of Nathan the prophet and the records of Gad the seer, ³⁰together with the details of his reign and power, and the circumstances that surrounded him and Israel and the kingdoms of all the other lands.

INTERPRETING the four centuries between the reign of Solomon (the high point) and the Babylonian captivity (the low point), 2 Chronicles gives the priestly perspective on the nation of Judah. A few good kings among the many wicked ones can't stop the nation's downward plunge. The effect? Economic, military, moral and spiritual decay—and ultimately, defeat and captivity. But after seventy years, the Persian King Cyrus allows people to return to their homeland. Remember this: At their place of greatest failure God gives his people another chance.

Outline of Contents

Solomon Asks for Wisdom

1 Solomon son of David established himself firmly over his kingdom, for the LORD his God was with him and made him exceedingly great.

²Then Solomon spoke to all Israel — to the commanders of thousands and commanders of hundreds, to the judges and to all the leaders in Israel, the heads of families — ³and Solomon and the whole assembly went to the high place at Gibeon, for God's Tent of Meeting was there, which Moses the LORD's servant had made in the desert. ⁴Now David had brought up the ark of God from Kiriath Jearim to the place he had prepared for it, because he had pitched a tent for it in Jerusalem. ⁵But the bronze altar that Bezalel son of Uri, the son of Hur, had made was in Gibeon in front of the tabernacle of the LORD; so Solomon and the assembly inquired of him there. ⁶Solomon went up to the bronze altar before the LORD in the Tent of Meeting and offered a thousand burnt offerings on it.

⁷That night God appeared to Solomon and said to him, "Ask for whatever you want me to give you."

⁸Solomon answered God, "You have shown great kindness to David my father and have made me king in his place. ⁹Now, LORD God, let your promise to my father David be confirmed, for you have made me king over a people who are as numerous as the dust of the earth. ¹⁰Give me wisdom and knowledge, that I may lead this people, for who is able to govern this great people of yours?"

¹¹God said to Solomon, "Since this is your heart's desire and you have not asked for wealth, riches or honor, nor for the death of your enemies, and since you have not asked for a long life but for wisdom and knowledge

A "NEW AND IMPROVED" SET OF PRIORITIES

The coach has just asked Kurt and Christopher to play summer league baseball. That'll take a lot of time. Doing it right will mean making it a high priority. Should they play? Consider:

Kurt loves baseball, but he's so competitive that he throws a bat or gets into a heated argument at almost every game. Christopher loves baseball too, but it doesn't have such a negative effect on him. He sees the summer team as a good opportunity to increase his skills and to interact with some of his non-Christian friends.

Look It Up
••••

If, like Kurt and Christopher, you're trying to set priorities and you're wondering about a certain activity, use these guidelines:

1. Is it Biblical? "I have chosen the way of truth; I have set my heart on your laws" (Psalm 119:30).

2. Does it help you or hurt you? " 'Everything is permissible for me'—but not everything is beneficial. 'Everything is permissible for me'—but I will not be mastered by anything" (1 Corinthians 6:12).

3. Is it the best use of your limited time (Psalm 90:12; Ephesians 5:16)?

4. Will it result in right or wrong thoughts (Philippians 4:8)?

Think It Through
••••

Remember: If you do not actively set your own schedule and priorities, other people and situations will do it for you!

Suppose Kurt and Christopher came to you for advice. What course would you recommend to each?

Work It Out
••••

Using the guidelines listed above, evaluate your own schedule— things you do at home, at school, at church, with friends and at work.

If necessary set some "new and improved" priorities for yourself. Pray for the wisdom and strength to go after the things that are truly important and will last.

Nail It Down
••••

Read about Solomon's priorities in 2 Chronicles 1:11–12.

Turn to pages 796, 1015, 1142 and 1292 for other readings on priorities.
Turn to page 439 for Friday's reading.

Topic
••••

PRIORITIES

to govern my people over whom I have made you king, **12**therefore wisdom and knowledge will be given you. And I will also give you wealth, riches and honor, such as no king who was before you ever had and none after you will have."

13Then Solomon went to Jerusalem from the high place at Gibeon, from before the Tent of Meeting. And he reigned over Israel.

14Solomon accumulated chariots and horses; he had fourteen hundred chariots and twelve thousand horses,*a* which he kept in the chariot cities and also with him in Jerusalem. **15**The king made silver and gold as common in Jerusalem as stones, and cedar as plentiful as sycamore-fig trees in the foothills. **16**Solomon's horses were imported from Egypt*b* and from Kue*c* — the royal merchants purchased them from Kue. **17**They imported a chariot from Egypt for six hundred shekels*d* of silver, and a horse for a hundred and fifty.*e* They also exported them to all the kings of the Hittites and of the Arameans.

Preparations for Building the Temple

2 Solomon gave orders to build a temple for the Name of the LORD and a royal palace for himself. **2**He conscripted seventy thousand men as carriers and eighty thousand as stonecutters in the hills and thirty-six hundred as foremen over them.

3Solomon sent this message to Hiram*f* king of Tyre:

"Send me cedar logs as you did for my father David when you sent him cedar to build a palace to live in. **4**Now I am about to build a temple for the Name of the LORD my God and to dedicate it to him for burning fragrant incense before him, for setting out the consecrated bread regularly, and for making burnt offerings every morning and evening and on Sabbaths and New Moons and at the appointed feasts of the LORD our God. This is a lasting ordinance for Israel.

5"The temple I am going to build will be great, because our God is greater than all other gods. **6**But who is able to build a temple for him, since the heavens, even the highest heavens, cannot contain him? Who then am I to build a temple for him, except as a place to burn sacrifices before him?

7"Send me, therefore, a man skilled to work in gold and silver, bronze and iron, and in purple, crimson and blue yarn, and experienced in the art of engraving, to work in Judah and Jerusalem with my skilled craftsmen, whom my father David provided.

8"Send me also cedar, pine and algum*g* logs from Lebanon, for I know that your men are skilled in cutting timber there. My men will work with yours **9**to provide me with plenty of lumber, because the temple I build must be large and magnificent. **10**I will give your servants, the woodsmen who cut the timber, twenty thousand cors*h* of ground wheat, twenty thousand cors of barley, twenty thousand baths*i* of wine and twenty thousand baths of olive oil."

11Hiram king of Tyre replied by letter to Solomon:

"Because the LORD loves his people, he has made you their king."

12And Hiram added:

"Praise be to the LORD, the God of Israel, who made heaven and earth! He has given King David a wise son, endowed with intelligence and discernment, who will build a temple for the LORD and a palace for himself.

13"I am sending you Huram-Abi, a man of great skill, **14**whose mother was from Dan and whose father was from Tyre. He is trained to work in gold and silver, bronze and iron, stone and wood, and with purple and blue and crimson yarn and fine linen. He is experienced in all kinds of engraving and can execute any design given to him. He will work with your craftsmen and with those of my lord, David your father.

15"Now let my lord send his servants the wheat and barley and the olive oil and wine he promised, **16**and we will cut all the logs from Lebanon that you need and will float them in rafts by sea

---

a14 Or *charioteers*   *b16* Or possibly *Muzur,* a region in Cilicia; also in verse 17   *c16* Probably Cilicia   *d17* That is, about 15 pounds (about 7 kilograms)   *e17* That is, about 3 3/4 pounds (about 1.7 kilograms)   *f3* Hebrew *Huram,* a variant of *Hiram*; also in verses 11 and 12   *g8* Probably a variant of *almug*; possibly juniper   *h10* That is, probably about 125,000 bushels (about 4,400 kiloliters)   *i10* That is, probably about 115,000 gallons (about 440 kiloliters) down to Joppa. You can then take them up to Jerusalem."

[17]Solomon took a census of all the aliens who were in Israel, after the census his father David had taken; and they were found to be 153,600. [18]He assigned 70,000 of them to be carriers and 80,000 to be stonecutters in the hills, with 3,600 foremen over them to keep the people working.

Solomon Builds the Temple

3 Then Solomon began to build the temple of the LORD in Jerusalem on Mount Moriah, where the LORD had appeared to his father David. It was on the threshing floor of Araunah[a] the Jebusite, the place provided by David. [2]He began building on the second day of the second month in the fourth year of his reign.

[3]The foundation Solomon laid for building the temple of God was sixty cubits long and twenty cubits wide[b] (using the cubit of the old standard). [4]The portico at the front of the temple was twenty cubits[c] long across the width of the building and twenty cubits[d] high.

He overlaid the inside with pure gold. [5]He paneled the main hall with pine and covered it with fine gold and decorated it with palm tree and chain designs. [6]He adorned the temple with precious stones. And the gold he used was gold of Parvaim. [7]He overlaid the ceiling beams, doorframes, walls and doors of the temple with gold, and he carved cherubim on the walls.

[8]He built the Most Holy Place, its length corresponding to the width of the temple — twenty cubits long and twenty cubits wide. He overlaid the inside with six hundred talents[e] of fine gold. [9]The gold nails weighed fifty shekels.[f] He also overlaid the upper parts with gold.

[10]In the Most Holy Place he made a pair of sculptured cherubim and overlaid them with gold. [11]The total wingspan of the cherubim was twenty cubits. One wing of the first cherub was five cubits[g] long and touched the temple wall, while its other wing, also five cubits long, touched the wing of the other cherub. [12]Similarly one wing of the second cherub was five cubits long and touched the other temple wall, and its other wing, also five cubits long, touched the wing of the first cherub. [13]The wings of these cherubim extended twenty cubits. They stood on their feet, facing the main hall.[h]

[14]He made the curtain of blue, purple and crimson yarn and fine linen, with cherubim worked into it.

[15]In the front of the temple he made two pillars, which ⌊together⌋ were thirty-five cubits[i] long, each with a capital on top measuring five cubits. [16]He made interwoven chains[j] and put them on top of the pillars. He also made a hundred pomegranates and attached them to the chains. [17]He erected the pillars in the front of the temple, one to the south and one to the north. The one to the south he named Jakin[k] and the one to the north Boaz.[l]

The Temple's Furnishings

4 He made a bronze altar twenty cubits long, twenty cubits wide and ten cubits high.[m] [2]He made the Sea of cast metal, circular in shape, measuring ten cubits from rim to rim and five cubits[n] high. It took a line of thirty cubits[o] to measure around it. [3]Below the rim, figures of bulls encircled it — ten to a cubit.[p] The bulls were cast in two rows in one piece with the Sea.

[4]The Sea stood on twelve bulls, three facing north, three facing west, three facing south and three facing east. The Sea rested on top of them, and their hindquarters were toward the center. [5]It was a handbreadth[q] in thickness, and its rim was like the rim of a cup, like a lily blossom. It held three thousand baths.[r]

[6]He then made ten basins for washing and placed five on the south side and five on the north. In them the things to be used for the burnt offerings were rinsed, but the Sea was to be used by the priests for washing.

[7]He made ten gold lampstands according to the specifications for them and placed

---

[a]1 Hebrew *Ornan*, a variant of *Araunah*   [b]3 That is, about 90 feet (about 27 meters) long and 30 feet (about 9 meters) wide   [c]4 That is, about 30 feet (about 9 meters); also in verses 8, 11 and 13   [d]4 Some Septuagint and Syriac manuscripts; Hebrew *and a hundred and twenty*   [e]8 That is, about 23 tons (about 21 metric tons)   [f]9 That is, about 1 1/4 pounds (about 0.6 kilogram)   [g]11 That is, about 7 1/2 feet (about 2.3 meters); also in verse 15   [h]13 Or *facing inward*   [i]15 That is, about 52 feet (about 16 meters)   [j]16 Or possibly *made chains in the inner sanctuary*; the meaning of the Hebrew for this phrase is uncertain.   [k]17 *Jakin* probably means *he establishes*.   [l]17 *Boaz* probably means *in him is strength*.   [m]1 That is, about 30 feet (about 9 meters) long and wide, and about 15 feet (about 4.5 meters) high   [n]2 That is, about 7 1/2 feet (about 2.3 meters)   [o]2 That is, about 45 feet (about 13.5 meters)   [p]3 That is, about 1 1/2 feet (about 0.5 meter)   [q]5 That is, about 3 inches (about 8 centimeters)   [r]5 That is, about 17,500 gallons (about 66 kiloliters)

them in the temple, five on the south side and five on the north.

⁸He made ten tables and placed them in the temple, five on the south side and five on the north. He also made a hundred gold sprinkling bowls.

⁹He made the courtyard of the priests, and the large court and the doors for the court, and overlaid the doors with bronze. ¹⁰He placed the Sea on the south side, at the southeast corner.

¹¹He also made the pots and shovels and sprinkling bowls.

So Huram finished the work he had undertaken for King Solomon in the temple of God:

¹²the two pillars;

the two bowl-shaped capitals on top of the pillars;

the two sets of network decorating the two bowl-shaped capitals on top of the pillars;

¹³the four hundred pomegranates for the two sets of network (two rows of pomegranates for each network, decorating the bowl-shaped capitals on top of the pillars);

¹⁴the stands with their basins;

¹⁵the Sea and the twelve bulls under it;

¹⁶the pots, shovels, meat forks and all related articles.

All the objects that Huram-Abi made for King Solomon for the temple of the LORD were of polished bronze. ¹⁷The king had them cast in clay molds in the plain of the Jordan between Succoth and Zarethan.ᵃ ¹⁸All these things that Solomon made amounted to so much that the weight of the bronze was not determined.

¹⁹Solomon also made all the furnishings that were in God's temple:

the golden altar;

the tables on which was the bread of the Presence;

²⁰the lampstands of pure gold with their lamps, to burn in front of the inner sanctuary as prescribed;

²¹the gold floral work and lamps and tongs (they were solid gold);

²²the pure gold wick trimmers, sprinkling bowls, dishes and censers; and the gold doors of the temple: the inner doors to the Most Holy Place and the doors of the main hall.

5 When all the work Solomon had done for the temple of the LORD was finished, he brought in the things his father David had dedicated — the silver and gold and all the furnishings — and he placed them in the treasuries of God's temple.

The Ark Brought to the Temple

²Then Solomon summoned to Jerusalem the elders of Israel, all the heads of the tribes and the chiefs of the Israelite families, to bring up the ark of the LORD's covenant from Zion, the City of David. ³And all the men of Israel came together to the king at the time of the festival in the seventh month.

⁴When all the elders of Israel had arrived, the Levites took up the ark, ⁵and they brought up the ark and the Tent of Meeting and all the sacred furnishings in it. The priests, who were Levites, carried them up; ⁶and King Solomon and the entire assembly of Israel that had gathered about him were before the ark, sacrificing so many sheep and cattle that they could not be recorded or counted.

⁷The priests then brought the ark of the LORD's covenant to its place in the inner sanctuary of the temple, the Most Holy Place, and put it beneath the wings of the cherubim. ⁸The cherubim spread their wings over the place of the ark and covered the ark and its carrying poles. ⁹These poles were so long that their ends, extending from the ark, could be seen from in front of the inner sanctuary, but not from outside the Holy Place; and they are still there today. ¹⁰There was nothing in the ark except the two tablets that Moses had placed in it at Horeb, where the LORD made a covenant with the Israelites after they came out of Egypt.

¹¹The priests then withdrew from the Holy Place. All the priests who were there had consecrated themselves, regardless of their divisions. ¹²All the Levites who were musicians — Asaph, Heman, Jeduthun and their sons and relatives — stood on the east side of the altar, dressed in fine linen and playing cymbals, harps and lyres. They were accompanied by 120 priests sounding trumpets. ¹³The trumpeters and singers joined in unison, as with one voice, to give praise and thanks to the LORD. Accompanied by trumpets, cymbals and other instruments, they raised their voices in praise to the LORD and sang:

ᵃ17 Hebrew Zeredatha, a variant of Zarethan

"He is good;
    his love endures forever."

Then the temple of the LORD was filled with a cloud, **14**and the priests could not perform their service because of the cloud, for the glory of the LORD filled the temple of God.

6 Then Solomon said, "The LORD has said that he would dwell in a dark cloud; **2**I have built a magnificent temple for you, a place for you to dwell forever."

3While the whole assembly of Israel was standing there, the king turned around and blessed them. **4**Then he said:

"Praise be to the LORD, the God of Israel, who with his hands has fulfilled what he promised with his mouth to my father David. For he said, **5**'Since the day I brought my people out of Egypt, I have not chosen a city in any tribe of Israel to have a temple built for my Name to be there, nor have I chosen anyone to be the leader over my people Israel. **6**But now I have chosen Jerusalem for my Name to be there, and I have chosen David to rule my people Israel.'

7"My father David had it in his heart to build a temple for the Name of the LORD, the God of Israel. **8**But the LORD said to my father David, 'Because it was in your heart to build a temple for my Name, you did well to have this in your heart. **9**Nevertheless, you are not the one to build the temple, but your son, who is your own flesh and blood—he is the one who will build the temple for my Name.'

10"The LORD has kept the promise he made. I have succeeded David my father and now I sit on the throne of Israel, just as the LORD promised, and I have built the temple for the Name of the LORD, the God of Israel. **11**There I have placed the ark, in which is the covenant of the LORD that he made with the people of Israel."

Solomon's Prayer of Dedication

12Then Solomon stood before the altar of the LORD in front of the whole assembly of Israel and spread out his hands. **13**Now he had made a bronze platform, five cubits*a* long, five cubits wide and three cubits*b* high, and had placed it in the center of the outer court. He stood on the platform and then knelt down before the whole assembly

of Israel and spread out his hands toward heaven. **14**He said:

"O LORD, God of Israel, there is no God like you in heaven or on earth—you who keep your covenant of love with your servants who continue wholeheartedly in your way. **15**You have kept your promise to your servant David my father; with your mouth you have promised and with your hand you have fulfilled it—as it is today.

16"Now LORD, God of Israel, keep for your servant David my father the promises you made to him when you said, 'You shall never fail to have a man to sit before me on the throne of Israel, if only your sons are careful in all they do to walk before me according to my law, as you have done.' **17**And now, O LORD, God of Israel, let your word that you promised your servant David come true.

18"But will God really dwell on earth with men? The heavens, even the highest heavens, cannot contain you. How much less this temple I have built! **19**Yet give attention to your servant's prayer and his plea for mercy, O LORD my God. Hear the cry and the prayer that your servant is praying in your presence. **20**May your eyes be open toward this temple day and night, this place of which you said you would put your Name there. May you hear the prayer your servant prays toward this place. **21**Hear the supplications of your servant and of your people Israel when they pray toward this place. Hear from heaven, your dwelling place; and when you hear, forgive.

22"When a man wrongs his neighbor and is required to take an oath and he comes and swears the oath before your altar in this temple, **23**then hear from heaven and act. Judge between your servants, repaying the guilty by bringing down on his own head what he has done. Declare the innocent not guilty and so establish his innocence.

24"When your people Israel have been defeated by an enemy because they have sinned against you and when they turn back and confess your name, praying and making supplication before you in this temple, **25**then hear from heaven and forgive the sin of your

---

a 13 That is, about 7 1/2 feet (about 2.3 meters)   *b 13* That is, about 4 1/2 feet (about 1.3 meters) people Israel and bring them back to the land you gave to them and their fathers. **26**"When the heavens are shut up and there is no rain because your people have sinned against you, and when they pray toward this place and confess your name and turn from their sin because you have afflicted them, **27**then hear from heaven and forgive the sin of your servants, your people Israel. Teach them the right way to live, and send rain on the land you gave your people for an inheritance.

28"When famine or plague comes to the land, or blight or mildew, locusts or grasshoppers, or when enemies besiege them in any of their cities, whatever disaster or disease may come, **29**and when a prayer or plea is made by any of your people Israel — each one aware of his afflictions and pains, and spreading out his hands toward this temple — **30**then hear from heaven, your dwelling place. Forgive, and deal with each man according to all he does, since you know his heart (for you alone know the hearts of men), **31**so that they will fear you and walk in your ways all the time they live in the land you gave our fathers.

32"As for the foreigner who does not belong to your people Israel but has come from a distant land because of your great name and your mighty hand and your outstretched arm — when he comes and prays toward this temple, **33**then hear from heaven, your dwelling place, and do whatever the foreigner asks of you, so that all the peoples of the earth may know your name and fear you, as do your own people Israel, and may know that this house I have built bears your Name.

34"When your people go to war against their enemies, wherever you send them, and when they pray to you toward this city you have chosen and the temple I have built for your Name, **35**then hear from heaven their prayer and their plea, and uphold their cause.

36"When they sin against you — for there is no one who does not sin — and you become angry with them and give them over to the enemy, who takes them captive to a land far away or near; **37**and if they have a change of heart in the land where they are held captive, and repent and plead with you in the land of their captivity and say, 'We have sinned, we have done wrong and acted wickedly'; **38**and if they turn back to you with all their heart and soul in the land of their captivity where they were taken, and pray toward the land you gave their fathers, toward the city you have chosen and toward the temple I have built for your Name; **39**then from heaven, your dwelling place, hear their prayer and their pleas, and uphold their cause. And forgive your people, who have sinned against you.

40"Now, my God, may your eyes be open and your ears attentive to the prayers offered in this place.

41"Now arise, O Lord God, and come
    to your resting place,
    you and the ark of your might.
May your priests, O Lord God, be
    clothed with salvation,
    may your saints rejoice in your
    goodness.
42O Lord God, do not reject your
    anointed one.
    Remember the great love
    promised to David your
    servant."

The Dedication of the Temple

7 When Solomon finished praying, fire came down from heaven and consumed the burnt offering and the sacrifices, and the glory of the Lord filled the temple. **2**The priests could not enter the temple of the Lord because the glory of the Lord filled it. **3**When all the Israelites saw the fire coming down and the glory of the Lord above the temple, they knelt on the pavement with their faces to the ground, and they worshiped and gave thanks to the Lord, saying,

"He is good;
    his love endures forever."

4Then the king and all the people offered sacrifices before the Lord. **5**And King Solomon offered a sacrifice of twenty-two thousand head of cattle and a hundred and twenty thousand sheep and goats. So the king and all the people dedicated the temple of God. **6**The priests took their positions, as did the Levites with the Lord's musical instruments, which King David had made for praising the Lord and which were used when he gave thanks, saying, "His love endures forever." Opposite the Levites, the priests blew their trumpets, and all the Israelites were standing.

[7]Solomon consecrated the middle part of the courtyard in front of the temple of the Lord, and there he offered burnt offerings and the fat of the fellowship offerings,[a] because the bronze altar he had made could not hold the burnt offerings, the grain offerings and the fat portions.

[8]So Solomon observed the festival at that time for seven days, and all Israel with him—a vast assembly, people from Lebo[b] Hamath to the Wadi of Egypt. [9]On the eighth day they held an assembly, for they had celebrated the dedication of the altar for seven days and the festival for seven days more. [10]On the twenty-third day of the seventh month he sent the people to their homes, joyful and glad in heart for the good things the Lord had done for David and Solomon and for his people Israel.

The Lord Appears to Solomon

[11]When Solomon had finished the temple of the Lord and the royal palace, and had succeeded in carrying out all he had in mind to do in the temple of the Lord and in his own palace, [12]the Lord appeared to him at night and said:

"I have heard your prayer and have chosen this place for myself as a temple for sacrifices.

[13]"When I shut up the heavens so that there is no rain, or command locusts to devour the land or send a plague among my people, [14]if my people, who are called by my name, will humble themselves and pray and seek my face and turn from their wicked ways, then will I hear from heaven and will forgive their sin and will heal their land. [15]Now my eyes will be open and my ears attentive to the prayers offered in this place. [16]I have chosen and consecrated this temple so that my Name may be there forever. My eyes and my heart will always be there.

[17]"As for you, if you walk before me as David your father did, and do all I command, and observe my decrees and laws, [18]I will establish your royal throne, as I covenanted with David your father when I said, 'You shall never fail to have a man to rule over Israel.'

[19]"But if you[c] turn away and forsake the decrees and commands I have given you[c] and go off to serve other gods

and worship them, [20]then I will uproot Israel from my land, which I have given them, and will reject this temple I have consecrated for my Name. I will make it a byword and an object of ridicule among all peoples. [21]And though this temple is now so imposing, all who pass by will be appalled and say, 'Why has the Lord done such a thing to this land and to this temple?' [22]People will answer, 'Because they have forsaken the Lord, the God of their fathers, who brought them out of Egypt, and have embraced other gods, worshiping and serving them—that is why he brought all this disaster on them.'"

Solomon's Other Activities

8 At the end of twenty years, during which Solomon built the temple of the Lord and his own palace, [2]Solomon rebuilt the villages that Hiram[d] had given him, and settled Israelites in them. [3]Solomon then went to Hamath Zobah and captured it. [4]He also built up Tadmor in the desert and all the store cities he had built in Hamath. [5]He rebuilt Upper Beth Horon and Lower Beth Horon as fortified cities, with walls and with gates and bars, [6]as well as Baalath and all his store cities, and all the cities for his chariots and for his horses[e]—whatever he desired to build in Jerusalem, in Lebanon and throughout all the territory he ruled.

[7]All the people left from the Hittites, Amorites, Perizzites, Hivites and Jebusites (these peoples were not Israelites), [8]that is, their descendants remaining in the land, whom the Israelites had not destroyed—these Solomon conscripted for his slave labor force, as it is to this day. [9]But Solomon did not make slaves of the Israelites for his work; they were his fighting men, commanders of his captains, and commanders of his chariots and charioteers. [10]They were also King Solomon's chief officials—two hundred and fifty officials supervising the men.

[11]Solomon brought Pharaoh's daughter up from the City of David to the palace he had built for her, for he said, "My wife must not live in the palace of David king of Israel, because the places the ark of the Lord has entered are holy."

[12]On the altar of the Lord that he had built in front of the portico, Solomon sacrificed burnt offerings to the Lord, [13]according to the daily requirement for offerings com-

---

[a]7 Traditionally *peace offerings*   [b]8 Or *from the entrance to Hamath*, a variant of *Hiram*; also in verse 18   [c]19 The Hebrew is plural.   [d]2 Hebrew   [e]6 Or *charioteers*

MYTH: HUMANS CAN SAVE THEMSELVES

Kim clicks the TV on and begins watching a program about the future.

The show's point is that the human race is capable of solving its own problems. At the conclusion, the narrator intones:

"We do not need ancient myths, superstition or the baggage of religion weighing us down. Through scientific research, technology, human reason and progressive secular education, we cannot only save humanity from all of its problems, but we can also build a humane and prosperous global community."

Look It Up
••••

Can humanity save itself? Are we really self-sufficient? No and no. People desperately need the Lord.

God alone can save. "For the LORD is our judge, the LORD is our lawgiver, the LORD is our king; it is he who will save us" (Isaiah 33:22).

Depending on anything or anyone other than God is idolatry. "Ignorant are those who carry about idols of wood, who pray to gods that cannot save" (Isaiah 45:20).

God's salvation depends on man's humility. "You save the humble but bring low those whose eyes are haughty" (Psalm 18:27).

Think It Through
••••

The U.S. is facing some serious problems: drug abuse, pollution, crime, educational failure, the breakdown of the family, economic hardships, the threat of terrorism.

All U.S. coins bear the phrase, "In God We Trust." Do you think that's true? Do you think that the U.S. is looking to God for deliverance? What are some idols in this country?

Work It Out
••••

You've got two assignments today.

Ask God to bring about revival in your life. If you don't know Christ, trust him right now to forgive your sins and to lead you in his ways, giving your life meaning. If you are a Christian, ask God to help you to obey him better.

Ask God to bring about a national revival. The U.S. is rapidly turning its back on God. Only a return to Biblical truth can deliver it from the problems brought about by abandoning that truth. Pray that the church will strengthen its witness to all areas of life—including law, government and the media.

Nail It Down
••••

Read the promise in 2 Chronicles 7:14.

Turn to pages 768, 1282 and 1311 for other readings on human nature.
Turn to page 441 for the weekend reading.

Topic
••••

HUMAN NATURE

manded by Moses for Sabbaths, New Moons and the three annual feasts—the Feast of Unleavened Bread, the Feast of Weeks and the Feast of Tabernacles. ¹⁴In keeping with the ordinance of his father David, he appointed the divisions of the priests for their duties, and the Levites to lead the praise and to assist the priests according to each day's requirement. He also appointed the gatekeepers by divisions for the various gates, because this was what David the man of God had ordered. ¹⁵They did not deviate from the king's commands to the priests or to the Levites in any matter, including that of the treasuries.

¹⁶All Solomon's work was carried out, from the day the foundation of the temple of the LORD was laid until its completion. So the temple of the LORD was finished.

¹⁷Then Solomon went to Ezion Geber and Elath on the coast of Edom. ¹⁸And Hiram sent him ships commanded by his own officers, men who knew the sea. These, with Solomon's men, sailed to Ophir and brought back four hundred and fifty talents[a] of gold, which they delivered to King Solomon.

The Queen of Sheba Visits Solomon

9 When the queen of Sheba heard of Solomon's fame, she came to Jerusalem to test him with hard questions. Arriving with a very great caravan—with camels carrying spices, large quantities of gold, and precious stones—she came to Solomon and talked with him about all she had on her mind. ²Solomon answered all her questions; nothing was too hard for him to explain to her. ³When the queen of Sheba saw the wisdom of Solomon, as well as the palace he had built, ⁴the food on his table, the seating of his officials, the attending servants in their robes, the cupbearers in their robes and the burnt offerings he made at[b] the temple of the LORD, she was overwhelmed.

⁵She said to the king, "The report I heard in my own country about your achievements and your wisdom is true. ⁶But I did not believe what they said until I came and saw with my own eyes. Indeed, not even half the greatness of your wisdom was told me; you have far exceeded the report I heard. ⁷How happy your men must be! How happy your officials, who continually stand before you and hear your wisdom! ⁸Praise

be to the LORD your God, who has delighted in you and placed you on his throne as king to rule for the LORD your God. Because of the love of your God for Israel and his desire to uphold them forever, he has made you king over them, to maintain justice and righteousness."

⁹Then she gave the king 120 talents[c] of gold, large quantities of spices, and precious stones. There had never been such spices as those the queen of Sheba gave to King Solomon.

¹⁰(The men of Hiram and the men of Solomon brought gold from Ophir; they also brought algumwood[d] and precious stones. ¹¹The king used the algumwood to make steps for the temple of the LORD and for the royal palace, and to make harps and lyres for the musicians. Nothing like them had ever been seen in Judah.)

¹²King Solomon gave the queen of Sheba all she desired and asked for; he gave her more than she had brought to him. Then she left and returned with her retinue to her own country.

Solomon's Splendor

¹³The weight of the gold that Solomon received yearly was 666 talents,[e] ¹⁴not including the revenues brought in by merchants and traders. Also all the kings of Arabia and the governors of the land brought gold and silver to Solomon.

¹⁵King Solomon made two hundred large shields of hammered gold; six hundred bekas[f] of hammered gold went into each shield. ¹⁶He also made three hundred small shields of hammered gold, with three hundred bekas[g] of gold in each shield. The king put them in the Palace of the Forest of Lebanon.

¹⁷Then the king made a great throne inlaid with ivory and overlaid with pure gold. ¹⁸The throne had six steps, and a footstool of gold was attached to it. On both sides of the seat were armrests, with a lion standing beside each of them. ¹⁹Twelve lions stood on the six steps, one at either end of each step. Nothing like it had ever been made for any other kingdom. ²⁰All King Solomon's goblets were gold, and all the household articles in the Palace of the Forest of Lebanon were pure gold. Nothing was made of silver, because silver was considered of little value

---

[a]18 That is, about 17 tons (about 16 metric tons)   [b]4 Or the ascent by which he went up to   [c]9 That is, about 4 1/2 tons (about 4 metric tons)   [d]10 Probably a variant of almugwood   [e]13 That is, about 25 tons (about 23 metric tons)   [f]15 That is, about 7 1/2 pounds (about 3.5 kilograms)   [g]16 That is, about 3 3/4 pounds (about 1.7 kilograms)

HOW WEALTHY ARE YOU?

Work It Out • • • •

You may not be as wealthy as Solomon was, but you probably have more than you really need of just about everything. You have jeans you no longer wear, shoes you've outgrown, books you don't read, cassettes you don't like and don't listen to. Items you don't use and have forgotten you even own gather dust on the closet shelf.

You live in an affluent society, a society where even those who are poor are wealthy by much of the world's standards. You may think you're poor when you compare yourself with Amy, who has a mall-sized wardrobe, or Jerry, who has a brand new sports car. But you're wealthy when you compare yourself with the majority of the people in the world.

Go into your room, open your closet and take inventory of the clothes and shoes you no longer wear and the other items you no longer use. Why not pack those things up and take them to the local thrift store or ministry that works with the poor? You have so much, why not share some of it with those who have so little?

Nail It Down • • • •

Read about the great wealth of Solomon in 2 Chronicles 9:13–28 (note especially verse 27).

Think It Through • • • •

God tells us many times and many places in his Word that money and wealth don't satisfy and that they can easily rule us instead of us ruling them. Most people who are wealthy still are not content; they just want more.

Sometimes those who are wealthy are the poorest of all (read Proverbs 15:17). Someone who is hungry can be fed. Someone who needs clothing can be given something to wear. But those who, in their wealth, are lonely, unwanted, unloved, unhappy . . . they are truly the poorest of the poor.

Nail It Down • • • •

Reread the story of Solomon's wealth in 2 Chronicles 9:13–28. For further insight read Ecclesiastes 5:10.

Turn to pages 1110, 1374 and 1396 for other readings on wealth.
Turn to page 445 for Monday's reading.

Topic
• • • •
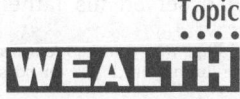

in Solomon's day. **21**The king had a fleet of trading ships*a* manned by Hiram's*b* men. Once every three years it returned, carrying gold, silver and ivory, and apes and baboons.

22King Solomon was greater in riches and wisdom than all the other kings of the earth. **23**All the kings of the earth sought audience with Solomon to hear the wisdom God had put in his heart. **24**Year after year, everyone who came brought a gift—articles of silver and gold, and robes, weapons and spices, and horses and mules.

25Solomon had four thousand stalls for horses and chariots, and twelve thousand horses,*c* which he kept in the chariot cities and also with him in Jerusalem. **26**He ruled over all the kings from the River*d* to the land of the Philistines, as far as the border of Egypt. **27**The king made silver as common in Jerusalem as stones, and cedar as plentiful as sycamore-fig trees in the foothills. **28**Solomon's horses were imported from Egypt*e* and from all other countries.

Solomon's Death

29As for the other events of Solomon's reign, from beginning to end, are they not written in the records of Nathan the prophet, in the prophecy of Ahijah the Shilonite and in the visions of Iddo the seer concerning Jeroboam son of Nebat? **30**Solomon reigned in Jerusalem over all Israel forty years. **31**Then he rested with his fathers and was buried in the city of David his father. And Rehoboam his son succeeded him as king.

Israel Rebels Against Rehoboam

10 Rehoboam went to Shechem, for all the Israelites had gone there to make him king. **2**When Jeroboam son of Nebat heard this (he was in Egypt, where he had fled from King Solomon), he returned from Egypt. **3**So they sent for Jeroboam, and he and all Israel went to Rehoboam and said to him: **4**"Your father put a heavy yoke on us, but now lighten the harsh labor and the heavy yoke he put on us, and we will serve you."

5Rehoboam answered, "Come back to me in three days." So the people went away.

6Then King Rehoboam consulted the elders who had served his father Solomon during his lifetime. "How would you advise me to answer these people?" he asked.

7They replied, "If you will be kind to these people and please them and give them a favorable answer, they will always be your servants."

8But Rehoboam rejected the advice the elders gave him and consulted the young men who had grown up with him and were serving him. **9**He asked them, "What is your advice? How should we answer these people who say to me, 'Lighten the yoke your father put on us'?"

10The young men who had grown up with him replied, "Tell the people who have said to you, 'Your father put a heavy yoke on us, but make our yoke lighter'—tell them, 'My little finger is thicker than my father's waist. **11**My father laid on you a heavy yoke; I will make it even heavier. My father scourged you with whips; I will scourge you with scorpions.'"

12Three days later Jeroboam and all the people returned to Rehoboam, as the king had said, "Come back to me in three days." **13**The king answered them harshly. Rejecting the advice of the elders, **14**he followed the advice of the young men and said, "My father made your yoke heavy; I will make it even heavier. My father scourged you with whips; I will scourge you with scorpions." **15**So the king did not listen to the people, for this turn of events was from God, to fulfill the word the LORD had spoken to Jeroboam son of Nebat through Ahijah the Shilonite.

16When all Israel saw that the king refused to listen to them, they answered the king:

"What share do we have in David,
  what part in Jesse's son?
To your tents, O Israel!
  Look after your own house, O David!"

So all the Israelites went home. **17**But as for the Israelites who were living in the towns of Judah, Rehoboam still ruled over them.

18King Rehoboam sent out Adoniram,*f* who was in charge of forced labor, but the Israelites stoned him to death. King Rehoboam, however, managed to get into his chariot and escape to Jerusalem. **19**So Israel has been in rebellion against the house of David to this day.

11 When Rehoboam arrived in Jerusalem, he mustered the house of Ju-

---

a21 Hebrew *of ships that could go to Tarshish*   *b21* Hebrew *Huram,* a variant of *Hiram*   *c25* Or *charioteers*
d26 That is, the Euphrates   *e28* Or possibly *Muzur,* a region in Cilicia   *f18* Hebrew *Hadoram,* a variant of *Adoniram*

dah and Benjamin—a hundred and eighty thousand fighting men—to make war against Israel and to regain the kingdom for Rehoboam.

²But this word of the LORD came to Shemaiah the man of God: ³"Say to Rehoboam son of Solomon king of Judah and to all the Israelites in Judah and Benjamin, ⁴'This is what the LORD says: Do not go up to fight against your brothers. Go home, every one of you, for this is my doing.'" So they obeyed the words of the LORD and turned back from marching against Jeroboam.

Rehoboam Fortifies Judah

⁵Rehoboam lived in Jerusalem and built up towns for defense in Judah: ⁶Bethlehem, Etam, Tekoa, ⁷Beth Zur, Soco, Adullam, ⁸Gath, Mareshah, Ziph, ⁹Adoraim, Lachish, Azekah, ¹⁰Zorah, Aijalon and Hebron. These were fortified cities in Judah and Benjamin. ¹¹He strengthened their defenses and put commanders in them, with supplies of food, olive oil and wine. ¹²He put shields and spears in all the cities, and made them very strong. So Judah and Benjamin were his.

¹³The priests and Levites from all their districts throughout Israel sided with him. ¹⁴The Levites even abandoned their pasturelands and property, and came to Judah and Jerusalem because Jeroboam and his sons had rejected them as priests of the LORD. ¹⁵And he appointed his own priests for the high places and for the goat and calf idols he had made. ¹⁶Those from every tribe of Israel who set their hearts on seeking the LORD, the God of Israel, followed the Levites to Jerusalem to offer sacrifices to the LORD, the God of their fathers. ¹⁷They strengthened the kingdom of Judah and supported Rehoboam son of Solomon three years, walking in the ways of David and Solomon during this time.

Rehoboam's Family

¹⁸Rehoboam married Mahalath, who was the daughter of David's son Jerimoth and of Abihail, the daughter of Jesse's son Eliab. ¹⁹She bore him sons: Jeush, Shemariah and Zaham. ²⁰Then he married Maacah daughter of Absalom, who bore him Abijah, Attai, Ziza and Shelomith. ²¹Rehoboam loved Maacah daughter of Absalom more than any of his other wives and concubines. In all, he had eighteen wives and sixty concubines, twenty-eight sons and sixty daughters.

²²Rehoboam appointed Abijah son of Ma-

acah to be the chief prince among his brothers, in order to make him king. ²³He acted wisely, dispersing some of his sons throughout the districts of Judah and Benjamin, and to all the fortified cities. He gave them abundant provisions and took many wives for them.

Shishak Attacks Jerusalem

12 After Rehoboam's position as king was established and he had become strong, he and all Israel[a] with him abandoned the law of the LORD. ²Because they had been unfaithful to the LORD, Shishak king of Egypt attacked Jerusalem in the fifth year of King Rehoboam. ³With twelve hundred chariots and sixty thousand horsemen and the innumerable troops of Libyans, Sukkites and Cushites[b] that came with him from Egypt, ⁴he captured the fortified cities of Judah and came as far as Jerusalem.

⁵Then the prophet Shemaiah came to Rehoboam and to the leaders of Judah who had assembled in Jerusalem for fear of Shishak, and he said to them, "This is what the LORD says, 'You have abandoned me; therefore, I now abandon you to Shishak.'"

⁶The leaders of Israel and the king humbled themselves and said, "The LORD is just."

⁷When the LORD saw that they humbled themselves, this word of the LORD came to Shemaiah: "Since they have humbled themselves, I will not destroy them but will soon give them deliverance. My wrath will not be poured out on Jerusalem through Shishak. ⁸They will, however, become subject to him, so that they may learn the difference between serving me and serving the kings of other lands."

⁹When Shishak king of Egypt attacked Jerusalem, he carried off the treasures of the temple of the LORD and the treasures of the royal palace. He took everything, including the gold shields Solomon had made. ¹⁰So King Rehoboam made bronze shields to replace them and assigned these to the commanders of the guard on duty at the entrance to the royal palace. ¹¹Whenever the king went to the LORD's temple, the guards went with him, bearing the shields, and afterward they returned them to the guardroom.

¹²Because Rehoboam humbled himself, the LORD's anger turned from him, and he was not totally destroyed. Indeed, there was some good in Judah.

¹³King Rehoboam established himself

---

a1 That is, Judah, as frequently in 2 Chronicles   b3 That is, people from the upper Nile region firmly in Jerusalem and continued as king. He was forty-one years old when he became king, and he reigned seventeen years in Jerusalem, the city the LORD had chosen out of all the tribes of Israel in which to put his Name. His mother's name was Naamah; she was an Ammonite. **14**He did evil because he had not set his heart on seeking the LORD.

15As for the events of Rehoboam's reign, from beginning to end, are they not written in the records of Shemaiah the prophet and of Iddo the seer that deal with genealogies? There was continual warfare between Rehoboam and Jeroboam. **16**Rehoboam rested with his fathers and was buried in the City of David. And Abijah his son succeeded him as king.

Abijah King of Judah

13 In the eighteenth year of the reign of Jeroboam, Abijah became king of Judah, **2**and he reigned in Jerusalem three years. His mother's name was Maacah,*a* a daughter*b* of Uriel of Gibeah.

There was war between Abijah and Jeroboam. **3**Abijah went into battle with a force of four hundred thousand able fighting men, and Jeroboam drew up a battle line against him with eight hundred thousand able troops.

4Abijah stood on Mount Zemaraim, in the hill country of Ephraim, and said, "Jeroboam and all Israel, listen to me! **5**Don't you know that the LORD, the God of Israel, has given the kingship of Israel to David and his descendants forever by a covenant of salt? **6**Yet Jeroboam son of Nebat, an official of Solomon son of David, rebelled against his master. **7**Some worthless scoundrels gathered around him and opposed Rehoboam son of Solomon when he was young and indecisive and not strong enough to resist them.

8"And now you plan to resist the kingdom of the LORD, which is in the hands of David's descendants. You are indeed a vast army and have with you the golden calves that Jeroboam made to be your gods. **9**But didn't you drive out the priests of the LORD, the sons of Aaron, and the Levites, and make priests of your own as the peoples of other lands do? Whoever comes to consecrate himself with a young bull and seven rams may become a priest of what are not gods.

10"As for us, the LORD is our God, and we have not forsaken him. The priests who serve the LORD are sons of Aaron, and the Levites assist them. **11**Every morning and evening they present burnt offerings and fragrant incense to the LORD. They set out the bread on the ceremonially clean table and light the lamps on the gold lampstand every evening. We are observing the requirements of the LORD our God. But you have forsaken him. **12**God is with us; he is our leader. His priests with their trumpets will sound the battle cry against you. Men of Israel, do not fight against the LORD, the God of your fathers, for you will not succeed."

13Now Jeroboam had sent troops around to the rear, so that while he was in front of Judah the ambush was behind them. **14**Judah turned and saw that they were being attacked at both front and rear. Then they cried out to the LORD. The priests blew their trumpets **15**and the men of Judah raised the battle cry. At the sound of their battle cry, God routed Jeroboam and all Israel before Abijah and Judah. **16**The Israelites fled before Judah, and God delivered them into their hands. **17**Abijah and his men inflicted heavy losses on them, so that there were five hundred thousand casualties among Israel's able men. **18**The men of Israel were subdued on that occasion, and the men of Judah were victorious because they relied on the LORD, the God of their fathers.

19Abijah pursued Jeroboam and took from him the towns of Bethel, Jeshanah and Ephron, with their surrounding villages. **20**Jeroboam did not regain power during the time of Abijah. And the LORD struck him down and he died.

21But Abijah grew in strength. He married fourteen wives and had twenty-two sons and sixteen daughters.

22The other events of Abijah's reign, what he did and what he said, are written in the annotations of the prophet Iddo.

14 And Abijah rested with his fathers and was buried in the City of David. Asa his son succeeded him as king, and in his days the country was at peace for ten years.

Asa King of Judah

2Asa did what was good and right in the eyes of the LORD his God. **3**He removed the foreign altars and the high places, smashed the sacred stones and cut down the Asherah poles.*c* **4**He commanded Judah to seek the LORD, the God of their fathers, and to obey

---

a2 Most Septuagint manuscripts and Syriac (see also 2 Chron. 11:20 and 1 Kings 15:2); Hebrew *Micaiah*
b2 Or *granddaughter*   *c3* That is, symbols of the goddess Asherah; here and elsewhere in 2 Chronicles

ARE YOU SUFFERING FROM "HEART" DISEASE?

• •

Imagine these two romantic situations:
• As he proposes marriage in the moonlight, Stewart grabs Estelle, looks deeply into her eyes and gushes, "I just want you to know that I love you . . . with 60 percent of my heart!"
• Emily turns to Reed and says, "I love you and I'm totally committed to our relationship . . . maybe. No, wait a minute. Let me think about that. Well, I sort of like you. Last Friday, I really was sure, but now I . . . ."
Great relationships, huh?

Look It Up
• • • •

The Bible often uses the word heart when describing the center of an individual's life, emotions, will and character. A careful reading of God's Word shows that true commitment takes:
1. A whole heart—"Love the LORD your God with all your heart" (Deuteronomy 6:5). Committed individuals hold nothing back. They seek God (Deuteronomy 4:29), obey God (1 Kings 8:61), serve God (Joshua 22:5), rejoice in God (Zephaniah 3:14), and give thanks to God (Psalm 9:1) with all their hearts.
2. A steadfast heart—"My heart is steadfast, O God, my heart is steadfast" (Psalm 57:7). Committed people are steady, solid and unwavering.
3. A pure heart—"Create in me a pure heart, O God" (Psalm 51:10). Committed people confess their sins quickly and move on.

Think It Through
• • • •

Is your heart completely committed to the Lord? That is, are you giving him 100 percent? If not, what areas of your life are not under his control? Why are you reluctant to give him those things?
Does your commitment waver from day to day? What sort of situations cause you to become shaky in your walk with Christ?

Work It Out
• • • •

The Great Physician specializes in healing diseased hearts.
First, ask him to search your heart (pray the prayer of Psalm 139:23–24).
Second, get on his treatment program.
Remove from your diet the dangerous "fats" (questionable TV shows, sexually explicit videos, violent movies and raunchy magazines) that contribute to spiritual heart disease.
Exercise your heart regularly—through prayer and by talking about your faith.

Nail It Down
• • • •

Read about King Asa's commitment to God in 2 Chronicles 14—15.

Turn to pages 182, 358 and 699 for other readings on commitment.
Turn to page 462 for Tuesday's reading.

Topic
• • • •

his laws and commands. **⁵**He removed the high places and incense altars in every town in Judah, and the kingdom was at peace under him. **⁶**He built up the fortified cities of Judah, since the land was at peace. No one was at war with him during those years, for the Lᴏʀᴅ gave him rest.

⁷"Let us build up these towns," he said to Judah, "and put walls around them, with towers, gates and bars. The land is still ours, because we have sought the Lᴏʀᴅ our God; we sought him and he has given us rest on every side." So they built and prospered.

⁸Asa had an army of three hundred thousand men from Judah, equipped with large shields and with spears, and two hundred and eighty thousand from Benjamin, armed with small shields and with bows. All these were brave fighting men.

⁹Zerah the Cushite marched out against them with a vast army*ᵃ* and three hundred chariots, and came as far as Mareshah. **¹⁰**Asa went out to meet him, and they took up battle positions in the Valley of Zephathah near Mareshah.

¹¹Then Asa called to the Lᴏʀᴅ his God and said, "Lᴏʀᴅ, there is no one like you to help the powerless against the mighty. Help us, O Lᴏʀᴅ our God, for we rely on you, and in your name we have come against this vast army. O Lᴏʀᴅ, you are our God; do not let man prevail against you."

¹²The Lᴏʀᴅ struck down the Cushites before Asa and Judah. The Cushites fled, **¹³**and Asa and his army pursued them as far as Gerar. Such a great number of Cushites fell that they could not recover; they were crushed before the Lᴏʀᴅ and his forces. The men of Judah carried off a large amount of plunder. **¹⁴**They destroyed all the villages around Gerar, for the terror of the Lᴏʀᴅ had fallen upon them. They plundered all these villages, since there was much booty there. **¹⁵**They also attacked the camps of the herdsmen and carried off droves of sheep and goats and camels. Then they returned to Jerusalem.

Asa's Reform

15 The Spirit of God came upon Azariah son of Oded. **²**He went out to meet Asa and said to him, "Listen to me, Asa and all Judah and Benjamin. The Lᴏʀᴅ is with you when you are with him. If you seek him, he will be found by you, but if you forsake him, he will forsake you. **³**For a long time

Israel was without the true God, without a priest to teach and without the law. **⁴**But in their distress they turned to the Lᴏʀᴅ, the God of Israel, and sought him, and he was found by them. **⁵**In those days it was not safe to travel about, for all the inhabitants of the lands were in great turmoil. **⁶**One nation was being crushed by another and one city by another, because God was troubling them with every kind of distress. **⁷**But as for you, be strong and do not give up, for your work will be rewarded."

⁸When Asa heard these words and the prophecy of Azariah son of*ᵇ* Oded the prophet, he took courage. He removed the detestable idols from the whole land of Judah and Benjamin and from the towns he had captured in the hills of Ephraim. He repaired the altar of the Lᴏʀᴅ that was in front of the portico of the Lᴏʀᴅ's temple.

⁹Then he assembled all Judah and Benjamin and the people from Ephraim, Manasseh and Simeon who had settled among them, for large numbers had come over to him from Israel when they saw that the Lᴏʀᴅ his God was with him.

¹⁰They assembled at Jerusalem in the third month of the fifteenth year of Asa's reign. **¹¹**At that time they sacrificed to the Lᴏʀᴅ seven hundred head of cattle and seven thousand sheep and goats from the plunder they had brought back. **¹²**They entered into a covenant to seek the Lᴏʀᴅ, the God of their fathers, with all their heart and soul. **¹³**All who would not seek the Lᴏʀᴅ, the God of Israel, were to be put to death, whether small or great, man or woman. **¹⁴**They took an oath to the Lᴏʀᴅ with loud acclamation, with shouting and with trumpets and horns. **¹⁵**All Judah rejoiced about the oath because they had sworn it wholeheartedly. They sought God eagerly, and he was found by them. So the Lᴏʀᴅ gave them rest on every side.

¹⁶King Asa also deposed his grandmother Maacah from her position as queen mother, because she had made a repulsive Asherah pole. Asa cut the pole down, broke it up and burned it in the Kidron Valley. **¹⁷**Although he did not remove the high places from Israel, Asa's heart was fully committed ₍to the Lᴏʀᴅ₎ all his life. **¹⁸**He brought into the temple of God the silver and gold and the articles that he and his father had dedicated.

¹⁹There was no more war until the thirty-fifth year of Asa's reign.

ᵃ9 Hebrew *with an army of a thousand thousands* or *with an army of thousands upon thousands*　　*ᵇ8* Vulgate and Syriac (see also Septuagint and verse 1); Hebrew does not have *Azariah son of.*

Asa's Last Years

16 In the thirty-sixth year of Asa's reign Baasha king of Israel went up against Judah and fortified Ramah to prevent anyone from leaving or entering the territory of Asa king of Judah.

²Asa then took the silver and gold out of the treasuries of the LORD's temple and of his own palace and sent it to Ben-Hadad king of Aram, who was ruling in Damascus. ³"Let there be a treaty between me and you," he said, "as there was between my father and your father. See, I am sending you silver and gold. Now break your treaty with Baasha king of Israel so he will withdraw from me."

⁴Ben-Hadad agreed with King Asa and sent the commanders of his forces against the towns of Israel. They conquered Ijon, Dan, Abel Maim*a* and all the store cities of Naphtali. ⁵When Baasha heard this, he stopped building Ramah and abandoned his work. ⁶Then King Asa brought all the men of Judah, and they carried away from Ramah the stones and timber Baasha had been using. With them he built up Geba and Mizpah.

⁷At that time Hanani the seer came to Asa king of Judah and said to him: "Because you relied on the king of Aram and not on the LORD your God, the army of the king of Aram has escaped from your hand. ⁸Were not the Cushites*b* and Libyans a mighty army with great numbers of chariots and horsemen*c*? Yet when you relied on the LORD, he delivered them into your hand. ⁹For the eyes of the LORD range throughout the earth to strengthen those whose hearts are fully committed to him. You have done a foolish thing, and from now on you will be at war."

¹⁰Asa was angry with the seer because of this; he was so enraged that he put him in prison. At the same time Asa brutally oppressed some of the people.

¹¹The events of Asa's reign, from beginning to end, are written in the book of the kings of Judah and Israel. ¹²In the thirty-ninth year of his reign Asa was afflicted with a disease in his feet. Though his disease was severe, even in his illness he did not seek help from the LORD, but only from the physicians. ¹³Then in the forty-first year of his reign Asa died and rested with his fathers. ¹⁴They buried him in the tomb that he had cut out for himself in the City of David. They laid him on a bier covered with spices and various blended perfumes, and they made a huge fire in his honor.

Jehoshaphat King of Judah

17 Jehoshaphat his son succeeded him as king and strengthened himself against Israel. ²He stationed troops in all the fortified cities of Judah and put garrisons in Judah and in the towns of Ephraim that his father Asa had captured.

³The LORD was with Jehoshaphat because in his early years he walked in the ways his father David had followed. He did not consult the Baals ⁴but sought the God of his father and followed his commands rather than the practices of Israel. ⁵The LORD established the kingdom under his control; and all Judah brought gifts to Jehoshaphat, so that he had great wealth and honor. ⁶His heart was devoted to the ways of the LORD; furthermore, he removed the high places and the Asherah poles from Judah.

⁷In the third year of his reign he sent his officials Ben-Hail, Obadiah, Zechariah, Nethanel and Micaiah to teach in the towns of Judah. ⁸With them were certain Levites—Shemaiah, Nethaniah, Zebadiah, Asahel, Shemiramoth, Jehonathan, Adonijah, Tobijah and Tob-Adonijah—and the priests Elishama and Jehoram. ⁹They taught throughout Judah, taking with them the Book of the Law of the LORD; they went around to all the towns of Judah and taught the people.

¹⁰The fear of the LORD fell on all the kingdoms of the lands surrounding Judah, so that they did not make war with Jehoshaphat. ¹¹Some Philistines brought Jehoshaphat gifts and silver as tribute, and the Arabs brought him flocks: seven thousand seven hundred rams and seven thousand seven hundred goats.

¹²Jehoshaphat became more and more powerful; he built forts and store cities in Judah ¹³and had large supplies in the towns of Judah. He also kept experienced fighting men in Jerusalem. ¹⁴Their enrollment by families was as follows:

From Judah, commanders of units of 1,000:
Adnah the commander, with 300,000 fighting men;
¹⁵next, Jehohanan the commander, with 280,000;
¹⁶next, Amasiah son of Zicri, who vol-

---

a4 Also known as *Abel Beth Maacah*   *b8* That is, people from the upper Nile region   *c8* Or *charioteers* unteered himself for the service of the LORD, with 200,000.

17From Benjamin:

Eliada, a valiant soldier, with 200,000 men armed with bows and shields; **18**next, Jehozabad, with 180,000 men armed for battle.

19These were the men who served the king, besides those he stationed in the fortified cities throughout Judah.

Micaiah Prophesies Against Ahab

18 Now Jehoshaphat had great wealth and honor, and he allied himself with Ahab by marriage. **2**Some years later he went down to visit Ahab in Samaria. Ahab slaughtered many sheep and cattle for him and the people with him and urged him to attack Ramoth Gilead. **3**Ahab king of Israel asked Jehoshaphat king of Judah, "Will you go with me against Ramoth Gilead?"

Jehoshaphat replied, "I am as you are, and my people as your people; we will join you in the war." **4**But Jehoshaphat also said to the king of Israel, "First seek the counsel of the LORD."

5So the king of Israel brought together the prophets—four hundred men—and asked them, "Shall we go to war against Ramoth Gilead, or shall I refrain?"

"Go," they answered, "for God will give it into the king's hand."

6But Jehoshaphat asked, "Is there not a prophet of the LORD here whom we can inquire of?"

7The king of Israel answered Jehoshaphat, "There is still one man through whom we can inquire of the LORD, but I hate him because he never prophesies anything good about me, but always bad. He is Micaiah son of Imlah."

"The king should not say that," Jehoshaphat replied.

8So the king of Israel called one of his officials and said, "Bring Micaiah son of Imlah at once."

9Dressed in their royal robes, the king of Israel and Jehoshaphat king of Judah were sitting on their thrones at the threshing floor by the entrance to the gate of Samaria, with all the prophets prophesying before them. **10**Now Zedekiah son of Kenaanah had made iron horns, and he declared, "This is what the LORD says: 'With these you will gore the Arameans until they are destroyed.' "

11All the other prophets were prophesying the same thing. "Attack Ramoth Gilead and be victorious," they said, "for the LORD will give it into the king's hand."

12The messenger who had gone to summon Micaiah said to him, "Look, as one man the other prophets are predicting success for the king. Let your word agree with theirs, and speak favorably."

13But Micaiah said, "As surely as the LORD lives, I can tell him only what my God says."

14When he arrived, the king asked him, "Micaiah, shall we go to war against Ramoth Gilead, or shall I refrain?"

"Attack and be victorious," he answered, "for they will be given into your hand."

15The king said to him, "How many times must I make you swear to tell me nothing but the truth in the name of the LORD?"

16Then Micaiah answered, "I saw all Israel scattered on the hills like sheep without a shepherd, and the LORD said, 'These people have no master. Let each one go home in peace.' "

17The king of Israel said to Jehoshaphat, "Didn't I tell you that he never prophesies anything good about me, but only bad?"

18Micaiah continued, "Therefore hear the word of the LORD: I saw the LORD sitting on his throne with all the host of heaven standing on his right and on his left. **19**And the LORD said, 'Who will entice Ahab king of Israel into attacking Ramoth Gilead and going to his death there?'

"One suggested this, and another that. **20**Finally, a spirit came forward, stood before the LORD and said, 'I will entice him.'

" 'By what means?' the LORD asked.

21" 'I will go and be a lying spirit in the mouths of all his prophets,' he said.

" 'You will succeed in enticing him,' said the LORD. 'Go and do it.'

22"So now the LORD has put a lying spirit in the mouths of these prophets of yours. The LORD has decreed disaster for you."

23Then Zedekiah son of Kenaanah went up and slapped Micaiah in the face. "Which way did the spirit from*a* the LORD go when he went from me to speak to you?" he asked.

24Micaiah replied, "You will find out on the day you go to hide in an inner room."

25The king of Israel then ordered, "Take Micaiah and send him back to Amon the ruler of the city and to Joash the king's son, **26**and say, 'This is what the king says: Put this fellow in prison and give him nothing but bread and water until I return safely.' "

27Micaiah declared, "If you ever return

a23 Or Spirit of

safely, the LORD has not spoken through me." Then he added, "Mark my words, all you people!"

Ahab Killed at Ramoth Gilead

28So the king of Israel and Jehoshaphat king of Judah went up to Ramoth Gilead. **29**The king of Israel said to Jehoshaphat, "I will enter the battle in disguise, but you wear your royal robes." So the king of Israel disguised himself and went into battle.

30Now the king of Aram had ordered his chariot commanders, "Do not fight with anyone, small or great, except the king of Israel." **31**When the chariot commanders saw Jehoshaphat, they thought, "This is the king of Israel." So they turned to attack him, but Jehoshaphat cried out, and the LORD helped him. God drew them away from him, **32**for when the chariot commanders saw that he was not the king of Israel, they stopped pursuing him.

33But someone drew his bow at random and hit the king of Israel between the sections of his armor. The king told the chariot driver, "Wheel around and get me out of the fighting. I've been wounded." **34**All day long the battle raged, and the king of Israel propped himself up in his chariot facing the Arameans until evening. Then at sunset he died.

19 When Jehoshaphat king of Judah returned safely to his palace in Jerusalem, **2**Jehu the seer, the son of Hanani, went out to meet him and said to the king, "Should you help the wicked and love*a* those who hate the LORD? Because of this, the wrath of the LORD is upon you. **3**There is, however, some good in you, for you have rid the land of the Asherah poles and have set your heart on seeking God."

Jehoshaphat Appoints Judges

4Jehoshaphat lived in Jerusalem, and he went out again among the people from Beersheba to the hill country of Ephraim and turned them back to the LORD, the God of their fathers. **5**He appointed judges in the land, in each of the fortified cities of Judah. **6**He told them, "Consider carefully what you do, because you are not judging for man but for the LORD, who is with you whenever you give a verdict. **7**Now let the fear of the LORD be upon you. Judge carefully, for with the LORD our God there is no injustice or partiality or bribery."

8In Jerusalem also, Jehoshaphat appointed some of the Levites, priests and heads of Israelite families to administer the law of the LORD and to settle disputes. And they lived in Jerusalem. **9**He gave them these orders: "You must serve faithfully and wholeheartedly in the fear of the LORD. **10**In every case that comes before you from your fellow countrymen who live in the cities—whether bloodshed or other concerns of the law, commands, decrees or ordinances—you are to warn them not to sin against the LORD; otherwise his wrath will come on you and your brothers. Do this, and you will not sin.

11"Amariah the chief priest will be over you in any matter concerning the LORD, and Zebadiah son of Ishmael, the leader of the tribe of Judah, will be over you in any matter concerning the king, and the Levites will serve as officials before you. Act with courage, and may the LORD be with those who do well."

Jehoshaphat Defeats Moab and Ammon

20 After this, the Moabites and Ammonites with some of the Meunites*b* came to make war on Jehoshaphat.

2Some men came and told Jehoshaphat, "A vast army is coming against you from Edom,*c* from the other side of the Sea.*d* It is already in Hazazon Tamar" (that is, En Gedi). **3**Alarmed, Jehoshaphat resolved to inquire of the LORD, and he proclaimed a fast for all Judah. **4**The people of Judah came together to seek help from the LORD; indeed, they came from every town in Judah to seek him.

5Then Jehoshaphat stood up in the assembly of Judah and Jerusalem at the temple of the LORD in the front of the new courtyard **6**and said:

"O LORD, God of our fathers, are you not the God who is in heaven? You rule over all the kingdoms of the nations. Power and might are in your hand, and no one can withstand you. **7**O our God, did you not drive out the inhabitants of this land before your people Israel and give it forever to the descendants of Abraham your friend? **8**They have lived in it and have built in it a sanctuary for your Name, saying, **9**'If calamity comes upon us, whether the sword of judgment, or plague or famine, we will stand in your presence before this tem-

---

a2 Or *and make alliances with*   *b1* Some Septuagint manuscripts; Hebrew *Ammonites*   *c2* One Hebrew manuscript; most Hebrew manuscripts, Septuagint and Vulgate *Aram*   *d2* That is, the Dead Sea ple that bears your Name and will cry out to you in our distress, and you will hear us and save us.'

¹⁰"But now here are men from Ammon, Moab and Mount Seir, whose territory you would not allow Israel to invade when they came from Egypt; so they turned away from them and did not destroy them. ¹¹See how they are repaying us by coming to drive us out of the possession you gave us as an inheritance. ¹²O our God, will you not judge them? For we have no power to face this vast army that is attacking us. We do not know what to do, but our eyes are upon you."

¹³All the men of Judah, with their wives and children and little ones, stood there before the LORD.

¹⁴Then the Spirit of the LORD came upon Jahaziel son of Zechariah, the son of Benaiah, the son of Jeiel, the son of Mattaniah, a Levite and descendant of Asaph, as he stood in the assembly.

¹⁵He said: "Listen, King Jehoshaphat and all who live in Judah and Jerusalem! This is what the LORD says to you: 'Do not be afraid or discouraged because of this vast army. For the battle is not yours, but God's. ¹⁶Tomorrow march down against them. They will be climbing up by the Pass of Ziz, and you will find them at the end of the gorge in the Desert of Jeruel. ¹⁷You will not have to fight this battle. Take up your positions; stand firm and see the deliverance the LORD will give you, O Judah and Jerusalem. Do not be afraid; do not be discouraged. Go out to face them tomorrow, and the LORD will be with you.' "

¹⁸Jehoshaphat bowed with his face to the ground, and all the people of Judah and Jerusalem fell down in worship before the LORD. ¹⁹Then some Levites from the Kohathites and Korahites stood up and praised the LORD, the God of Israel, with very loud voice.

²⁰Early in the morning they left for the Desert of Tekoa. As they set out, Jehoshaphat stood and said, "Listen to me, Judah and people of Jerusalem! Have faith in the LORD your God and you will be upheld; have faith in his prophets and you will be successful." ²¹After consulting the people, Jehoshaphat appointed men to sing to the LORD and to praise him for the splendor of his[a] holiness as they went out at the head of the army, saying:

"Give thanks to the LORD,
    for his love endures forever."

²²As they began to sing and praise, the LORD set ambushes against the men of Ammon and Moab and Mount Seir who were invading Judah, and they were defeated. ²³The men of Ammon and Moab rose up against the men from Mount Seir to destroy and annihilate them. After they finished slaughtering the men from Seir, they helped to destroy one another.

²⁴When the men of Judah came to the place that overlooks the desert and looked toward the vast army, they saw only dead bodies lying on the ground; no one had escaped. ²⁵So Jehoshaphat and his men went to carry off their plunder, and they found among them a great amount of equipment and clothing[b] and also articles of value—more than they could take away. There was so much plunder that it took three days to collect it. ²⁶On the fourth day they assembled in the Valley of Beracah, where they praised the LORD. This is why it is called the Valley of Beracah[c] to this day.

²⁷Then, led by Jehoshaphat, all the men of Judah and Jerusalem returned joyfully to Jerusalem, for the LORD had given them cause to rejoice over their enemies. ²⁸They entered Jerusalem and went to the temple of the LORD with harps and lutes and trumpets.

²⁹The fear of God came upon all the kingdoms of the countries when they heard how the LORD had fought against the enemies of Israel. ³⁰And the kingdom of Jehoshaphat was at peace, for his God had given him rest on every side.

The End of Jehoshaphat's Reign

³¹So Jehoshaphat reigned over Judah. He was thirty-five years old when he became king of Judah, and he reigned in Jerusalem twenty-five years. His mother's name was Azubah daughter of Shilhi. ³²He walked in the ways of his father Asa and did not stray from them; he did what was right in the eyes of the LORD. ³³The high places, however, were not removed, and the people still had not set their hearts on the God of their fathers.

³⁴The other events of Jehoshaphat's reign, from beginning to end, are written in the an-

---

[a]21 Or him with the splendor of   [b]25 Some Hebrew manuscripts and Vulgate; most Hebrew manuscripts corpses   [c]26 Beracah means praise.

nals of Jehu son of Hanani, which are recorded in the book of the kings of Israel.

35Later, Jehoshaphat king of Judah made an alliance with Ahaziah king of Israel, who was guilty of wickedness. **36**He agreed with him to construct a fleet of trading ships.*a* After these were built at Ezion Geber, **37**Eliezer son of Dodavahu of Mareshah prophesied against Jehoshaphat, saying, "Because you have made an alliance with Ahaziah, the LORD will destroy what you have made." The ships were wrecked and were not able to set sail to trade.*b*

21 Then Jehoshaphat rested with his fathers and was buried with them in the City of David. And Jehoram his son succeeded him as king. **2**Jehoram's brothers, the sons of Jehoshaphat, were Azariah, Jehiel, Zechariah, Azariahu, Michael and Shephatiah. All these were sons of Jehoshaphat king of Israel.*c* **3**Their father had given them many gifts of silver and gold and articles of value, as well as fortified cities in Judah, but he had given the kingdom to Jehoram because he was his firstborn son.

Jehoram King of Judah

4When Jehoram established himself firmly over his father's kingdom, he put all his brothers to the sword along with some of the princes of Israel. **5**Jehoram was thirty-two years old when he became king, and he reigned in Jerusalem eight years. **6**He walked in the ways of the kings of Israel, as the house of Ahab had done, for he married a daughter of Ahab. He did evil in the eyes of the LORD. **7**Nevertheless, because of the covenant the LORD had made with David, the LORD was not willing to destroy the house of David. He had promised to maintain a lamp for him and his descendants forever.

8In the time of Jehoram, Edom rebelled against Judah and set up its own king. **9**So Jehoram went there with his officers and all his chariots. The Edomites surrounded him and his chariot commanders, but he rose up and broke through by night. **10**To this day Edom has been in rebellion against Judah.

Libnah revolted at the same time, because Jehoram had forsaken the LORD, the God of his fathers. **11**He had also built high places on the hills of Judah and had caused the people of Jerusalem to prostitute themselves and had led Judah astray.

12Jehoram received a letter from Elijah the prophet, which said:

"This is what the LORD, the God of your father David, says: 'You have not walked in the ways of your father Jehoshaphat or of Asa king of Judah. **13**But you have walked in the ways of the kings of Israel, and you have led Judah and the people of Jerusalem to prostitute themselves, just as the house of Ahab did. You have also murdered your own brothers, members of your father's house, men who were better than you. **14**So now the LORD is about to strike your people, your sons, your wives and everything that is yours, with a heavy blow. **15**You yourself will be very ill with a lingering disease of the bowels, until the disease causes your bowels to come out.'"

16The LORD aroused against Jehoram the hostility of the Philistines and of the Arabs who lived near the Cushites. **17**They attacked Judah, invaded it and carried off all the goods found in the king's palace, together with his sons and wives. Not a son was left to him except Ahaziah,*d* the youngest.

18After all this, the LORD afflicted Jehoram with an incurable disease of the bowels. **19**In the course of time, at the end of the second year, his bowels came out because of the disease, and he died in great pain. His people made no fire in his honor, as they had for his fathers.

20Jehoram was thirty-two years old when he became king, and he reigned in Jerusalem eight years. He passed away, to no one's regret, and was buried in the City of David, but not in the tombs of the kings.

Ahaziah King of Judah

22 The people of Jerusalem made Ahaziah, Jehoram's youngest son, king in his place, since the raiders, who came with the Arabs into the camp, had killed all the older sons. So Ahaziah son of Jehoram king of Judah began to reign.

2Ahaziah was twenty-two*e* years old when he became king, and he reigned in Jerusalem one year. His mother's name was Athaliah, a granddaughter of Omri.

3He too walked in the ways of the house of Ahab, for his mother encouraged him in doing wrong. **4**He did evil in the eyes of the

---

a36 Hebrew *of ships that could go to Tarshish*   *b37* Hebrew *sail for Tarshish*   *c2* That is, Judah, as frequently in 2 Chronicles   *d17* Hebrew *Jehoahaz*, a variant of *Ahaziah*   *e2* Some Septuagint manuscripts and Syriac (see also 2 Kings 8:26); Hebrew *forty-two*

LORD, as the house of Ahab had done, for after his father's death they became his advisers, to his undoing. **5**He also followed their counsel when he went with Joram*a* son of Ahab king of Israel to war against Hazael king of Aram at Ramoth Gilead. The Arameans wounded Joram; **6**so he returned to Jezreel to recover from the wounds they had inflicted on him at Ramoth*b* in his battle with Hazael king of Aram.

Then Ahaziah*c* son of Jehoram king of Judah went down to Jezreel to see Joram son of Ahab because he had been wounded.

7Through Ahaziah's visit to Joram, God brought about Ahaziah's downfall. When Ahaziah arrived, he went out with Joram to meet Jehu son of Nimshi, whom the LORD had anointed to destroy the house of Ahab. **8**While Jehu was executing judgment on the house of Ahab, he found the princes of Judah and the sons of Ahaziah's relatives, who had been attending Ahaziah, and he killed them. **9**He then went in search of Ahaziah, and his men captured him while he was hiding in Samaria. He was brought to Jehu and put to death. They buried him, for they said, "He was a son of Jehoshaphat, who sought the LORD with all his heart." So there was no one in the house of Ahaziah powerful enough to retain the kingdom.

Athaliah and Joash

10When Athaliah the mother of Ahaziah saw that her son was dead, she proceeded to destroy the whole royal family of the house of Judah. **11**But Jehosheba,*d* the daughter of King Jehoram, took Joash son of Ahaziah and stole him away from among the royal princes who were about to be murdered and put him and his nurse in a bedroom. Because Jehosheba,*d* the daughter of King Jehoram and wife of the priest Jehoiada, was Ahaziah's sister, she hid the child from Athaliah so she could not kill him. **12**He remained hidden with them at the temple of God for six years while Athaliah ruled the land.

23 In the seventh year Jehoiada showed his strength. He made a covenant with the commanders of units of a hundred: Azariah son of Jeroham, Ishmael son of Jehohanan, Azariah son of Obed, Maaseiah son of Adaiah, and Elishaphat son of Zicri. **2**They went throughout Judah and gathered the Levites and the heads of Israelite families from all the towns. When they came to Jerusalem, **3**the whole assembly made a covenant with the king at the temple of God.

Jehoiada said to them, "The king's son shall reign, as the LORD promised concerning the descendants of David. **4**Now this is what you are to do: A third of you priests and Levites who are going on duty on the Sabbath are to keep watch at the doors, **5**a third of you at the royal palace and a third at the Foundation Gate, and all the other men are to be in the courtyards of the temple of the LORD. **6**No one is to enter the temple of the LORD except the priests and Levites on duty; they may enter because they are consecrated, but all the other men are to guard what the LORD has assigned to them.*e* **7**The Levites are to station themselves around the king, each man with his weapons in his hand. Anyone who enters the temple must be put to death. Stay close to the king wherever he goes."

8The Levites and all the men of Judah did just as Jehoiada the priest ordered. Each one took his men—those who were going on duty on the Sabbath and those who were going off duty—for Jehoiada the priest had not released any of the divisions. **9**Then he gave the commanders of units of a hundred the spears and the large and small shields that had belonged to King David and that were in the temple of God. **10**He stationed all the men, each with his weapon in his hand, around the king—near the altar and the temple, from the south side to the north side of the temple.

11Jehoiada and his sons brought out the king's son and put the crown on him; they presented him with a copy of the covenant and proclaimed him king. They anointed him and shouted, "Long live the king!"

12When Athaliah heard the noise of the people running and cheering the king, she went to them at the temple of the LORD. **13**She looked, and there was the king, standing by his pillar at the entrance. The officers and the trumpeters were beside the king, and all the people of the land were rejoicing and blowing trumpets, and singers with musical instruments were leading the praises. Then Athaliah tore her robes and shouted, "Treason! Treason!"

*a*5 Hebrew *Jehoram*, a variant of *Joram*; also in verses 6 and 7   *b*6 Hebrew *Ramah*, a variant of *Ramoth*
*c*6 Some Hebrew manuscripts, Septuagint, Vulgate and Syriac (see also 2 Kings 8:29); most Hebrew manuscripts *Azariah*   *d*11 Hebrew *Jehoshabeath*, a variant of *Jehosheba*   *e*6 Or *to observe the LORD's command ⌊not to enter⌋*

[14]Jehoiada the priest sent out the commanders of units of a hundred, who were in charge of the troops, and said to them: "Bring her out between the ranks[a] and put to the sword anyone who follows her." For the priest had said, "Do not put her to death at the temple of the LORD." [15]So they seized her as she reached the entrance of the Horse Gate on the palace grounds, and there they put her to death.

[16]Jehoiada then made a covenant that he and the people and the king[b] would be the LORD's people. [17]All the people went to the temple of Baal and tore it down. They smashed the altars and idols and killed Mattan the priest of Baal in front of the altars.

[18]Then Jehoiada placed the oversight of the temple of the LORD in the hands of the priests, who were Levites, to whom David had made assignments in the temple, to present the burnt offerings of the LORD as written in the Law of Moses, with rejoicing and singing, as David had ordered. [19]He also stationed doorkeepers at the gates of the LORD's temple so that no one who was in any way unclean might enter.

[20]He took with him the commanders of hundreds, the nobles, the rulers of the people and all the people of the land and brought the king down from the temple of the LORD. They went into the palace through the Upper Gate and seated the king on the royal throne, [21]and all the people of the land rejoiced. And the city was quiet, because Athaliah had been slain with the sword.

Joash Repairs the Temple

24 Joash was seven years old when he became king, and he reigned in Jerusalem forty years. His mother's name was Zibiah; she was from Beersheba. [2]Joash did what was right in the eyes of the LORD all the years of Jehoiada the priest. [3]Jehoiada chose two wives for him, and he had sons and daughters.

[4]Some time later Joash decided to restore the temple of the LORD. [5]He called together the priests and Levites and said to them, "Go to the towns of Judah and collect the money due annually from all Israel, to repair the temple of your God. Do it now." But the Levites did not act at once.

[6]Therefore the king summoned Jehoiada the chief priest and said to him, "Why haven't you required the Levites to bring in from Judah and Jerusalem the tax imposed by Moses the servant of the LORD and by the assembly of Israel for the Tent of the Testimony?"

[7]Now the sons of that wicked woman Athaliah had broken into the temple of God and had used even its sacred objects for the Baals.

[8]At the king's command, a chest was made and placed outside, at the gate of the temple of the LORD. [9]A proclamation was then issued in Judah and Jerusalem that they should bring to the LORD the tax that Moses the servant of God had required of Israel in the desert. [10]All the officials and all the people brought their contributions gladly, dropping them into the chest until it was full. [11]Whenever the chest was brought in by the Levites to the king's officials and they saw that there was a large amount of money, the royal secretary and the officer of the chief priest would come and empty the chest and carry it back to its place. They did this regularly and collected a great amount of money. [12]The king and Jehoiada gave it to the men who carried out the work required for the temple of the LORD. They hired masons and carpenters to restore the LORD's temple, and also workers in iron and bronze to repair the temple.

[13]The men in charge of the work were diligent, and the repairs progressed under them. They rebuilt the temple of God according to its original design and reinforced it. [14]When they had finished, they brought the rest of the money to the king and Jehoiada, and with it were made articles for the LORD's temple: articles for the service and for the burnt offerings, and also dishes and other objects of gold and silver. As long as Jehoiada lived, burnt offerings were presented continually in the temple of the LORD.

[15]Now Jehoiada was old and full of years, and he died at the age of a hundred and thirty. [16]He was buried with the kings in the City of David, because of the good he had done in Israel for God and his temple.

The Wickedness of Joash

[17]After the death of Jehoiada, the officials of Judah came and paid homage to the king, and he listened to them. [18]They abandoned the temple of the LORD, the God of their fathers, and worshiped Asherah poles and idols. Because of their guilt, God's anger came upon Judah and Jerusalem. [19]Although the LORD sent prophets to the people

---

a 14 Or *out from the precincts*   *b 16* Or *covenant between* ⸤*the LORD*⸥ *and the people and the king that they* (see 2 Kings 11:17) to bring them back to him, and though they testified against them, they would not listen.

20Then the Spirit of God came upon Zechariah son of Jehoiada the priest. He stood before the people and said, "This is what God says: 'Why do you disobey the Lord's commands? You will not prosper. Because you have forsaken the Lord, he has forsaken you.' "

21But they plotted against him, and by order of the king they stoned him to death in the courtyard of the Lord's temple. **22**King Joash did not remember the kindness Zechariah's father Jehoiada had shown him but killed his son, who said as he lay dying, "May the Lord see this and call you to account."

23At the turn of the year,*a* the army of Aram marched against Joash; it invaded Judah and Jerusalem and killed all the leaders of the people. They sent all the plunder to their king in Damascus. **24**Although the Aramean army had come with only a few men, the Lord delivered into their hands a much larger army. Because Judah had forsaken the Lord, the God of their fathers, judgment was executed on Joash. **25**When the Arameans withdrew, they left Joash severely wounded. His officials conspired against him for murdering the son of Jehoiada the priest, and they killed him in his bed. So he died and was buried in the City of David, but not in the tombs of the kings.

26Those who conspired against him were Zabad,*b* son of Shimeath an Ammonite woman, and Jehozabad, son of Shimrith*c* a Moabite woman. **27**The account of his sons, the many prophecies about him, and the record of the restoration of the temple of God are written in the annotations on the book of the kings. And Amaziah his son succeeded him as king.

Amaziah King of Judah

25 Amaziah was twenty-five years old when he became king, and he reigned in Jerusalem twenty-nine years. His mother's name was Jehoaddin*d*; she was from Jerusalem. **2**He did what was right in the eyes of the Lord, but not wholeheartedly. **3**After the kingdom was firmly in his control, he executed the officials who had murdered his father the king. **4**Yet he did not put their sons to death, but acted in accordance

with what is written in the Law, in the Book of Moses, where the Lord commanded: "Fathers shall not be put to death for their children, nor children put to death for their fathers; each is to die for his own sins."*e*

5Amaziah called the people of Judah together and assigned them according to their families to commanders of thousands and commanders of hundreds for all Judah and Benjamin. He then mustered those twenty years old or more and found that there were three hundred thousand men ready for military service, able to handle the spear and shield. **6**He also hired a hundred thousand fighting men from Israel for a hundred talents*f* of silver.

7But a man of God came to him and said, "O king, these troops from Israel must not march with you, for the Lord is not with Israel—not with any of the people of Ephraim. **8**Even if you go and fight courageously in battle, God will overthrow you before the enemy, for God has the power to help or to overthrow."

9Amaziah asked the man of God, "But what about the hundred talents I paid for these Israelite troops?"

The man of God replied, "The Lord can give you much more than that."

10So Amaziah dismissed the troops who had come to him from Ephraim and sent them home. They were furious with Judah and left for home in a great rage.

11Amaziah then marshaled his strength and led his army to the Valley of Salt, where he killed ten thousand men of Seir. **12**The army of Judah also captured ten thousand men alive, took them to the top of a cliff and threw them down so that all were dashed to pieces.

13Meanwhile the troops that Amaziah had sent back and had not allowed to take part in the war raided Judean towns from Samaria to Beth Horon. They killed three thousand people and carried off great quantities of plunder.

14When Amaziah returned from slaughtering the Edomites, he brought back the gods of the people of Seir. He set them up as his own gods, bowed down to them and burned sacrifices to them. **15**The anger of the Lord burned against Amaziah, and he sent a prophet to him, who said, "Why do you consult this people's gods, which could not save their own people from your hand?"

a23 Probably in the spring   *b26* A variant of *Jozabad*   *c26* A variant of *Shomer*   *d1* Hebrew *Jehoaddan,* a variant of *Jehoaddin*   *e4* Deut. 24:16   *f6* That is, about 3 3/4 tons (about 3.4 metric tons); also in verse 9

[16]While he was still speaking, the king said to him, "Have we appointed you an adviser to the king? Stop! Why be struck down?"

So the prophet stopped but said, "I know that God has determined to destroy you, because you have done this and have not listened to my counsel."

[17]After Amaziah king of Judah consulted his advisers, he sent this challenge to Jehoash[a] son of Jehoahaz, the son of Jehu, king of Israel: "Come, meet me face to face."

[18]But Jehoash king of Israel replied to Amaziah king of Judah: "A thistle in Lebanon sent a message to a cedar in Lebanon, 'Give your daughter to my son in marriage.' Then a wild beast in Lebanon came along and trampled the thistle underfoot. [19]You say to yourself that you have defeated Edom, and now you are arrogant and proud. But stay at home! Why ask for trouble and cause your own downfall and that of Judah also?"

[20]Amaziah, however, would not listen, for God so worked that he might hand them over to ⌊Jehoash⌋, because they sought the gods of Edom. [21]So Jehoash king of Israel attacked. He and Amaziah king of Judah faced each other at Beth Shemesh in Judah. [22]Judah was routed by Israel, and every man fled to his home. [23]Jehoash king of Israel captured Amaziah king of Judah, the son of Joash, the son of Ahaziah,[b] at Beth Shemesh. Then Jehoash brought him to Jerusalem and broke down the wall of Jerusalem from the Ephraim Gate to the Corner Gate—a section about six hundred feet[c] long. [24]He took all the gold and silver and all the articles found in the temple of God that had been in the care of Obed-Edom, together with the palace treasures and the hostages, and returned to Samaria.

[25]Amaziah son of Joash king of Judah lived for fifteen years after the death of Jehoash son of Jehoahaz king of Israel. [26]As for the other events of Amaziah's reign, from beginning to end, are they not written in the book of the kings of Judah and Israel? [27]From the time that Amaziah turned away from following the LORD, they conspired against him in Jerusalem and he fled to Lachish, but they sent men after him to Lachish and killed him there. [28]He was brought back by horse and was buried with his fathers in the City of Judah.

Uzziah King of Judah

26 Then all the people of Judah took Uzziah,[d] who was sixteen years old, and made him king in place of his father Amaziah. [2]He was the one who rebuilt Elath and restored it to Judah after Amaziah rested with his fathers.

[3]Uzziah was sixteen years old when he became king, and he reigned in Jerusalem fifty-two years. His mother's name was Jecoliah; she was from Jerusalem. [4]He did what was right in the eyes of the LORD, just as his father Amaziah had done. [5]He sought God during the days of Zechariah, who instructed him in the fear[e] of God. As long as he sought the LORD, God gave him success.

[6]He went to war against the Philistines and broke down the walls of Gath, Jabneh and Ashdod. He then rebuilt towns near Ashdod and elsewhere among the Philistines. [7]God helped him against the Philistines and against the Arabs who lived in Gur Baal and against the Meunites. [8]The Ammonites brought tribute to Uzziah, and his fame spread as far as the border of Egypt, because he had become very powerful.

[9]Uzziah built towers in Jerusalem at the Corner Gate, at the Valley Gate and at the angle of the wall, and he fortified them. [10]He also built towers in the desert and dug many cisterns, because he had much livestock in the foothills and in the plain. He had people working his fields and vineyards in the hills and in the fertile lands, for he loved the soil. [11]Uzziah had a well-trained army, ready to go out by divisions according to their numbers as mustered by Jeiel the secretary and Maaseiah the officer under the direction of Hananiah, one of the royal officials. [12]The total number of family leaders over the fighting men was 2,600. [13]Under their command was an army of 307,500 men trained for war, a powerful force to support the king against his enemies. [14]Uzziah provided shields, spears, helmets, coats of armor, bows and slingstones for the entire army. [15]In Jerusalem he made machines designed by skillful men for use on the towers and on the corner defenses to shoot arrows and hurl large stones. His fame spread far and wide, for he was greatly helped until he became powerful.

[16]But after Uzziah became powerful, his pride led to his downfall. He was unfaithful to the LORD his God, and entered the temple

---

[a]17 Hebrew *Joash*, a variant of *Jehoash*; also in verses 18, 21, 23 and 25   [b]23 Hebrew *Jehoahaz*, a variant of *Ahaziah*   [c]23 Hebrew *four hundred cubits* (about 180 meters)   [d]1 Also called *Azariah*   [e]5 Many Hebrew manuscripts, Septuagint and Syriac; other Hebrew manuscripts *vision*

of the LORD to burn incense on the altar of incense. ¹⁷Azariah the priest with eighty other courageous priests of the LORD followed him in. ¹⁸They confronted him and said, "It is not right for you, Uzziah, to burn incense to the LORD. That is for the priests, the descendants of Aaron, who have been consecrated to burn incense. Leave the sanctuary, for you have been unfaithful; and you will not be honored by the LORD God."

¹⁹Uzziah, who had a censer in his hand ready to burn incense, became angry. While he was raging at the priests in their presence before the incense altar in the LORD's temple, leprosy*a* broke out on his forehead. ²⁰When Azariah the chief priest and all the other priests looked at him, they saw that he had leprosy on his forehead, so they hurried him out. Indeed, he himself was eager to leave, because the LORD had afflicted him. ²¹King Uzziah had leprosy until the day he died. He lived in a separate house*b* — leprous, and excluded from the temple of the LORD. Jotham his son had charge of the palace and governed the people of the land.

²²The other events of Uzziah's reign, from beginning to end, are recorded by the prophet Isaiah son of Amoz. ²³Uzziah rested with his fathers and was buried near them in a field for burial that belonged to the kings, for people said, "He had leprosy." And Jotham his son succeeded him as king.

Jotham King of Judah

27 Jotham was twenty-five years old when he became king, and he reigned in Jerusalem sixteen years. His mother's name was Jerusha daughter of Zadok. ²He did what was right in the eyes of the LORD, just as his father Uzziah had done, but unlike him he did not enter the temple of the LORD. The people, however, continued their corrupt practices. ³Jotham rebuilt the Upper Gate of the temple of the LORD and did extensive work on the wall at the hill of Ophel. ⁴He built towns in the Judean hills and forts and towers in the wooded areas.

⁵Jotham made war on the king of the Ammonites and conquered them. That year the Ammonites paid him a hundred talents*c* of silver, ten thousand cors*d* of wheat and ten thousand cors of barley. The Ammonites brought him the same amount also in the second and third years.

⁶Jotham grew powerful because he walked steadfastly before the LORD his God.

⁷The other events in Jotham's reign, including all his wars and the other things he did, are written in the book of the kings of Israel and Judah. ⁸He was twenty-five years old when he became king, and he reigned in Jerusalem sixteen years. ⁹Jotham rested with his fathers and was buried in the City of David. And Ahaz his son succeeded him as king.

Ahaz King of Judah

28 Ahaz was twenty years old when he became king, and he reigned in Jerusalem sixteen years. Unlike David his father, he did not do what was right in the eyes of the LORD. ²He walked in the ways of the kings of Israel and also made cast idols for worshiping the Baals. ³He burned sacrifices in the Valley of Ben Hinnom and sacrificed his sons in the fire, following the detestable ways of the nations the LORD had driven out before the Israelites. ⁴He offered sacrifices and burned incense at the high places, on the hilltops and under every spreading tree.

⁵Therefore the LORD his God handed him over to the king of Aram. The Arameans defeated him and took many of his people as prisoners and brought them to Damascus.

He was also given into the hands of the king of Israel, who inflicted heavy casualties on him. ⁶In one day Pekah son of Remaliah killed a hundred and twenty thousand soldiers in Judah — because Judah had forsaken the LORD, the God of their fathers. ⁷Zicri, an Ephraimite warrior, killed Maaseiah the king's son, Azrikam the officer in charge of the palace, and Elkanah, second to the king. ⁸The Israelites took captive from their kinsmen two hundred thousand wives, sons and daughters. They also took a great deal of plunder, which they carried back to Samaria.

⁹But a prophet of the LORD named Oded was there, and he went out to meet the army when it returned to Samaria. He said to them, "Because the LORD, the God of your fathers, was angry with Judah, he gave them into your hand. But you have slaughtered them in a rage that reaches to heaven. ¹⁰And now you intend to make the men and women of Judah and Jerusalem your slaves. But aren't you also guilty of sins against the LORD your God? ¹¹Now listen to me! Send back your fellow countrymen you have taken as

---

a19 The Hebrew word was used for various diseases affecting the skin—not necessarily leprosy; also in verses 20, 21 and 23.   *b21* Or *in a house where he was relieved of responsibilities*   *c5* That is, about 3 3/4 tons (about 3.4 metric tons)   *d5* That is, probably about 62,000 bushels (about 2,200 kiloliters) prisoners, for the LORD's fierce anger rests on you."

¹²Then some of the leaders in Ephraim — Azariah son of Jehohanan, Berekiah son of Meshillemoth, Jehizkiah son of Shallum, and Amasa son of Hadlai — confronted those who were arriving from the war. ¹³"You must not bring those prisoners here," they said, "or we will be guilty before the LORD. Do you intend to add to our sin and guilt? For our guilt is already great, and his fierce anger rests on Israel."

¹⁴So the soldiers gave up the prisoners and plunder in the presence of the officials and all the assembly. ¹⁵The men designated by name took the prisoners, and from the plunder they clothed all who were naked. They provided them with clothes and sandals, food and drink, and healing balm. All those who were weak they put on donkeys. So they took them back to their fellow countrymen at Jericho, the City of Palms, and returned to Samaria.

¹⁶At that time King Ahaz sent to the king[a] of Assyria for help. ¹⁷The Edomites had again come and attacked Judah and carried away prisoners, ¹⁸while the Philistines had raided towns in the foothills and in the Negev of Judah. They captured and occupied Beth Shemesh, Aijalon and Gederoth, as well as Soco, Timnah and Gimzo, with their surrounding villages. ¹⁹The LORD had humbled Judah because of Ahaz king of Israel,[b] for he had promoted wickedness in Judah and had been most unfaithful to the LORD. ²⁰Tiglath-Pileser[c] king of Assyria came to him, but he gave him trouble instead of help. ²¹Ahaz took some of the things from the temple of the LORD and from the royal palace and from the princes and presented them to the king of Assyria, but that did not help him.

²²In his time of trouble King Ahaz became even more unfaithful to the LORD. ²³He offered sacrifices to the gods of Damascus, who had defeated him; for he thought, "Since the gods of the kings of Aram have helped them, I will sacrifice to them so they will help me." But they were his downfall and the downfall of all Israel.

²⁴Ahaz gathered together the furnishings from the temple of God and took them away.[d] He shut the doors of the LORD's temple and set up altars at every street corner in Jerusalem. ²⁵In every town in Judah he built high places to burn sacrifices to other gods and provoked the LORD, the God of his fathers, to anger.

²⁶The other events of his reign and all his ways, from beginning to end, are written in the book of the kings of Judah and Israel. ²⁷Ahaz rested with his fathers and was buried in the city of Jerusalem, but he was not placed in the tombs of the kings of Israel. And Hezekiah his son succeeded him as king.

Hezekiah Purifies the Temple

29 Hezekiah was twenty-five years old when he became king, and he reigned in Jerusalem twenty-nine years. His mother's name was Abijah daughter of Zechariah. ²He did what was right in the eyes of the LORD, just as his father David had done.

³In the first month of the first year of his reign, he opened the doors of the temple of the LORD and repaired them. ⁴He brought in the priests and the Levites, assembled them in the square on the east side ⁵and said: "Listen to me, Levites! Consecrate yourselves now and consecrate the temple of the LORD, the God of your fathers. Remove all defilement from the sanctuary. ⁶Our fathers were unfaithful; they did evil in the eyes of the LORD our God and forsook him. They turned their faces away from the LORD's dwelling place and turned their backs on him. ⁷They also shut the doors of the portico and put out the lamps. They did not burn incense or present any burnt offerings at the sanctuary to the God of Israel. ⁸Therefore, the anger of the LORD has fallen on Judah and Jerusalem; he has made them an object of dread and horror and scorn, as you can see with your own eyes. ⁹This is why our fathers have fallen by the sword and why our sons and daughters and our wives are in captivity. ¹⁰Now I intend to make a covenant with the LORD, the God of Israel, so that his fierce anger will turn away from us. ¹¹My sons, do not be negligent now, for the LORD has chosen you to stand before him and serve him, to minister before him and to burn incense."

¹²Then these Levites set to work:

from the Kohathites,

Mahath son of Amasai and Joel son of Azariah;

from the Merarites,

---

[a]16 One Hebrew manuscript, Septuagint and Vulgate (see also 2 Kings 16:7); most Hebrew manuscripts *kings*   [b]19 That is, Judah, as frequently in 2 Chronicles   [c]20 Hebrew *Tilgath-Pilneser*, a variant of *Tiglath-Pileser*   [d]24 Or *and cut them up*

Kish son of Abdi and Azariah son of
　　Jehallelel;
from the Gershonites,
　　Joah son of Zimmah and Eden son of
　　　　Joah;
13from the descendants of Elizaphan,
　　Shimri and Jeiel;
from the descendants of Asaph,
　　Zechariah and Mattaniah;
14from the descendants of Heman,
　　Jehiel and Shimei;
from the descendants of Jeduthun,
　　Shemaiah and Uzziel.

15When they had assembled their brothers and consecrated themselves, they went
in to purify the temple of the LORD, as the
king had ordered, following the word of the
LORD. **16**The priests went into the sanctuary
of the LORD to purify it. They brought out to
the courtyard of the LORD's temple everything unclean that they found in the temple
of the LORD. The Levites took it and carried
it out to the Kidron Valley. **17**They began the
consecration on the first day of the first
month, and by the eighth day of the month
they reached the portico of the LORD. For
eight more days they consecrated the temple of the LORD itself, finishing on the sixteenth day of the first month.

18Then they went in to King Hezekiah and
reported: "We have purified the entire temple of the LORD, the altar of burnt offering
with all its utensils, and the table for setting
out the consecrated bread, with all its articles. **19**We have prepared and consecrated
all the articles that King Ahaz removed in his
unfaithfulness while he was king. They are
now in front of the LORD's altar."

20Early the next morning King Hezekiah
gathered the city officials together and went
up to the temple of the LORD. **21**They brought
seven bulls, seven rams, seven male lambs
and seven male goats as a sin offering for
the kingdom, for the sanctuary and for Judah. The king commanded the priests, the
descendants of Aaron, to offer these on
the altar of the LORD. **22**So they slaughtered
the bulls, and the priests took the blood and
sprinkled it on the altar; next they slaughtered the rams and sprinkled their blood on
the altar; then they slaughtered the lambs
and sprinkled their blood on the altar. **23**The
goats for the sin offering were brought before the king and the assembly, and they
laid their hands on them. **24**The priests then
slaughtered the goats and presented their
blood on the altar for a sin offering to atone

for all Israel, because the king had ordered
the burnt offering and the sin offering for all
Israel.

25He stationed the Levites in the temple of
the LORD with cymbals, harps and lyres in
the way prescribed by David and Gad the
king's seer and Nathan the prophet; this was
commanded by the LORD through his prophets. **26**So the Levites stood ready with David's instruments, and the priests with their
trumpets.

27Hezekiah gave the order to sacrifice the
burnt offering on the altar. As the offering
began, singing to the LORD began also, accompanied by trumpets and the instruments of David king of Israel. **28**The whole
assembly bowed in worship, while the singers sang and the trumpeters played. All this
continued until the sacrifice of the burnt offering was completed.

29When the offerings were finished, the
king and everyone present with him knelt
down and worshiped. **30**King Hezekiah and
his officials ordered the Levites to praise the
LORD with the words of David and of Asaph
the seer. So they sang praises with gladness
and bowed their heads and worshiped.

31Then Hezekiah said, "You have now
dedicated yourselves to the LORD. Come and
bring sacrifices and thank offerings to the
temple of the LORD." So the assembly
brought sacrifices and thank offerings, and
all whose hearts were willing brought burnt
offerings.

32The number of burnt offerings the assembly brought was seventy bulls, a hundred rams and two hundred male lambs—
all of them for burnt offerings to the LORD.
33The animals consecrated as sacrifices
amounted to six hundred bulls and three
thousand sheep and goats. **34**The priests,
however, were too few to skin all the burnt
offerings; so their kinsmen the Levites
helped them until the task was finished and
until other priests had been consecrated, for
the Levites had been more conscientious in
consecrating themselves than the priests
had been. **35**There were burnt offerings in
abundance, together with the fat of the fellowship offerings*a* and the drink offerings
that accompanied the burnt offerings.

So the service of the temple of the LORD
was reestablished. **36**Hezekiah and all the
people rejoiced at what God had brought
about for his people, because it was done so
quickly.

a35 Traditionally *peace offerings*

Hezekiah Celebrates the Passover

30 Hezekiah sent word to all Israel and Judah and also wrote letters to Ephraim and Manasseh, inviting them to come to the temple of the LORD in Jerusalem and celebrate the Passover to the LORD, the God of Israel. ²The king and his officials and the whole assembly in Jerusalem decided to celebrate the Passover in the second month. ³They had not been able to celebrate it at the regular time because not enough priests had consecrated themselves and the people had not assembled in Jerusalem. ⁴The plan seemed right both to the king and to the whole assembly. ⁵They decided to send a proclamation throughout Israel, from Beersheba to Dan, calling the people to come to Jerusalem and celebrate the Passover to the LORD, the God of Israel. It had not been celebrated in large numbers according to what was written.

⁶At the king's command, couriers went throughout Israel and Judah with letters from the king and from his officials, which read:

"People of Israel, return to the LORD, the God of Abraham, Isaac and Israel, that he may return to you who are left, who have escaped from the hand of the kings of Assyria. ⁷Do not be like your fathers and brothers, who were unfaithful to the LORD, the God of their fathers, so that he made them an object of horror, as you see. ⁸Do not be stiff-necked, as your fathers were; submit to the LORD. Come to the sanctuary, which he has consecrated forever. Serve the LORD your God, so that his fierce anger will turn away from you. ⁹If you return to the LORD, then your brothers and your children will be shown compassion by their captors and will come back to this land, for the LORD your God is gracious and compassionate. He will not turn his face from you if you return to him."

¹⁰The couriers went from town to town in Ephraim and Manasseh, as far as Zebulun, but the people scorned and ridiculed them. ¹¹Nevertheless, some men of Asher, Manasseh and Zebulun humbled themselves and went to Jerusalem. ¹²Also in Judah the hand of God was on the people to give them unity of mind to carry out what the king and his officials had ordered, following the word of the LORD.

¹³A very large crowd of people assembled in Jerusalem to celebrate the Feast of Unleavened Bread in the second month. ¹⁴They removed the altars in Jerusalem and cleared away the incense altars and threw them into the Kidron Valley.

¹⁵They slaughtered the Passover lamb on the fourteenth day of the second month. The priests and the Levites were ashamed and consecrated themselves and brought burnt offerings to the temple of the LORD. ¹⁶Then they took up their regular positions as prescribed in the Law of Moses the man of God. The priests sprinkled the blood handed to them by the Levites. ¹⁷Since many in the crowd had not consecrated themselves, the Levites had to kill the Passover lambs for all those who were not ceremonially clean and could not consecrate ⌊their lambs⌋ to the LORD. ¹⁸Although most of the many people who came from Ephraim, Manasseh, Issachar and Zebulun had not purified themselves, yet they ate the Passover, contrary to what was written. But Hezekiah prayed for them, saying, "May the LORD, who is good, pardon everyone ¹⁹who sets his heart on seeking God—the LORD, the God of his fathers—even if he is not clean according to the rules of the sanctuary." ²⁰And the LORD heard Hezekiah and healed the people.

²¹The Israelites who were present in Jerusalem celebrated the Feast of Unleavened Bread for seven days with great rejoicing, while the Levites and priests sang to the LORD every day, accompanied by the LORD's instruments of praise.*ᵃ*

²²Hezekiah spoke encouragingly to all the Levites, who showed good understanding of the service of the LORD. For the seven days they ate their assigned portion and offered fellowship offerings*ᵇ* and praised the LORD, the God of their fathers.

²³The whole assembly then agreed to celebrate the festival seven more days; so for another seven days they celebrated joyfully. ²⁴Hezekiah king of Judah provided a thousand bulls and seven thousand sheep and goats for the assembly, and the officials provided them with a thousand bulls and ten thousand sheep and goats. A great number of priests consecrated themselves. ²⁵The entire assembly of Judah rejoiced, along with the priests and Levites and all who had

---

ᵃ21 Or *priests praised the LORD every day with resounding instruments belonging to the LORD*
ᵇ22 Traditionally *peace offerings*

assembled from Israel, including the aliens who had come from Israel and those who lived in Judah. **26**There was great joy in Jerusalem, for since the days of Solomon son of David king of Israel there had been nothing like this in Jerusalem. **27**The priests and the Levites stood to bless the people, and God heard them, for their prayer reached heaven, his holy dwelling place.

31 When all this had ended, the Israelites who were there went out to the towns of Judah, smashed the sacred stones and cut down the Asherah poles. They destroyed the high places and the altars throughout Judah and Benjamin and in Ephraim and Manasseh. After they had destroyed all of them, the Israelites returned to their own towns and to their own property.

Contributions for Worship

2Hezekiah assigned the priests and Levites to divisions — each of them according to their duties as priests or Levites — to offer burnt offerings and fellowship offerings,*a* to minister, to give thanks and to sing praises at the gates of the LORD's dwelling. **3**The king contributed from his own possessions for the morning and evening burnt offerings and for the burnt offerings on the Sabbaths, New Moons and appointed feasts as written in the Law of the LORD. **4**He ordered the people living in Jerusalem to give the portion due the priests and Levites so they could devote themselves to the Law of the LORD. **5**As soon as the order went out, the Israelites generously gave the firstfruits of their grain, new wine, oil and honey and all that the fields produced. They brought a great amount, a tithe of everything. **6**The men of Israel and Judah who lived in the towns of Judah also brought a tithe of their herds and flocks and a tithe of the holy things dedicated to the LORD their God, and they piled them in heaps. **7**They began doing this in the third month and finished in the seventh month. **8**When Hezekiah and his officials came and saw the heaps, they praised the LORD and blessed his people Israel.

9Hezekiah asked the priests and Levites about the heaps; **10**and Azariah the chief priest, from the family of Zadok, answered, "Since the people began to bring their contributions to the temple of the LORD, we have had enough to eat and plenty to spare, because the LORD has blessed his people, and this great amount is left over."

11Hezekiah gave orders to prepare storerooms in the temple of the LORD, and this was done. **12**Then they faithfully brought in the contributions, tithes and dedicated gifts. Conaniah, a Levite, was in charge of these things, and his brother Shimei was next in rank. **13**Jehiel, Azaziah, Nahath, Asahel, Jerimoth, Jozabad, Eliel, Ismakiah, Mahath and Benaiah were supervisors under Conaniah and Shimei his brother, by appointment of King Hezekiah and Azariah the official in charge of the temple of God.

14Kore son of Imnah the Levite, keeper of the East Gate, was in charge of the freewill offerings given to God, distributing the contributions made to the LORD and also the consecrated gifts. **15**Eden, Miniamin, Jeshua, Shemaiah, Amariah and Shecaniah assisted him faithfully in the towns of the priests, distributing to their fellow priests according to their divisions, old and young alike.

16In addition, they distributed to the males three years old or more whose names were in the genealogical records — all who would enter the temple of the LORD to perform the daily duties of their various tasks, according to their responsibilities and their divisions. **17**And they distributed to the priests enrolled by their families in the genealogical records and likewise to the Levites twenty years old or more, according to their responsibilities and their divisions. **18**They included all the little ones, the wives, and the sons and daughters of the whole community listed in these genealogical records. For they were faithful in consecrating themselves.

19As for the priests, the descendants of Aaron, who lived on the farm lands around their towns or in any other towns, men were designated by name to distribute portions to every male among them and to all who were recorded in the genealogies of the Levites.

20This is what Hezekiah did throughout Judah, doing what was good and right and faithful before the LORD his God. **21**In everything that he undertook in the service of God's temple and in obedience to the law and the commands, he sought his God and worked wholeheartedly. And so he prospered.

Sennacherib Threatens Jerusalem

32 After all that Hezekiah had so faithfully done, Sennacherib king of Assyria came and invaded Judah. He laid siege

a2 Traditionally peace offerings

to the fortified cities, thinking to conquer them for himself. ²When Hezekiah saw that Sennacherib had come and that he intended to make war on Jerusalem, ³he consulted with his officials and military staff about blocking off the water from the springs outside the city, and they helped him. ⁴A large force of men assembled, and they blocked all the springs and the stream that flowed through the land. "Why should the kings*a* of Assyria come and find plenty of water?" they said. ⁵Then he worked hard repairing all the broken sections of the wall and building towers on it. He built another wall outside that one and reinforced the supporting terraces*b* of the City of David. He also made large numbers of weapons and shields.

⁶He appointed military officers over the people and assembled them before him in the square at the city gate and encouraged them with these words: ⁷"Be strong and courageous. Do not be afraid or discouraged because of the king of Assyria and the vast army with him, for there is a greater power with us than with him. ⁸With him is only the arm of flesh, but with us is the LORD our God to help us and to fight our battles." And the people gained confidence from what Hezekiah the king of Judah said.

⁹Later, when Sennacherib king of Assyria and all his forces were laying siege to Lachish, he sent his officers to Jerusalem with this message for Hezekiah king of Judah and for all the people of Judah who were there:

¹⁰"This is what Sennacherib king of Assyria says: On what are you basing your confidence, that you remain in Jerusalem under siege? ¹¹When Hezekiah says, 'The LORD our God will save us from the hand of the king of Assyria,' he is misleading you, to let you die of hunger and thirst. ¹²Did not Hezekiah himself remove this god's high places and altars, saying to Judah and Jerusalem, 'You must worship before one altar and burn sacrifices on it'?

¹³"Do you not know what I and my fathers have done to all the peoples of the other lands? Were the gods of those nations ever able to deliver their land from my hand? ¹⁴Who of all the gods of these nations that my fathers destroyed has been able to save his people from me? How then can your god deliver you from my hand? ¹⁵Now do not let Heze-

kiah deceive you and mislead you like this. Do not believe him, for no god of any nation or kingdom has been able to deliver his people from my hand or the hand of my fathers. How much less will your god deliver you from my hand!"

¹⁶Sennacherib's officers spoke further against the LORD God and against his servant Hezekiah. ¹⁷The king also wrote letters insulting the LORD, the God of Israel, and saying this against him: "Just as the gods of the peoples of the other lands did not rescue their people from my hand, so the god of Hezekiah will not rescue his people from my hand." ¹⁸Then they called out in Hebrew to the people of Jerusalem who were on the wall, to terrify them and make them afraid in order to capture the city. ¹⁹They spoke about the God of Jerusalem as they did about the gods of the other peoples of the world — the work of men's hands.

²⁰King Hezekiah and the prophet Isaiah son of Amoz cried out in prayer to heaven about this. ²¹And the LORD sent an angel, who annihilated all the fighting men and the leaders and officers in the camp of the Assyrian king. So he withdrew to his own land in disgrace. And when he went into the temple of his god, some of his sons cut him down with the sword.

²²So the LORD saved Hezekiah and the people of Jerusalem from the hand of Sennacherib king of Assyria and from the hand of all others. He took care of them*c* on every side. ²³Many brought offerings to Jerusalem for the LORD and valuable gifts for Hezekiah king of Judah. From then on he was highly regarded by all the nations.

Hezekiah's Pride, Success and Death

²⁴In those days Hezekiah became ill and was at the point of death. He prayed to the LORD, who answered him and gave him a miraculous sign. ²⁵But Hezekiah's heart was proud and he did not respond to the kindness shown him; therefore the LORD's wrath was on him and on Judah and Jerusalem. ²⁶Then Hezekiah repented of the pride of his heart, as did the people of Jerusalem; therefore the LORD's wrath did not come upon them during the days of Hezekiah.

²⁷Hezekiah had very great riches and honor, and he made treasuries for his silver and gold and for his precious stones, spices, shields and all kinds of valuables. ²⁸He also

---

a4 Hebrew; Septuagint and Syriac *king*   *b5* Or *the Millo*   *c22* Hebrew; Septuagint and Vulgate *He gave them rest*

PRIDE'S OPPOSITE ATTRACTS

Belinda isn't very popular. Maybe it's because she constantly brags about all the things she's accomplished. Or perhaps it has to do with the fact that she can never admit to her friends when she is wrong. Then again, it might just be the result of her always trying to be the center of attention.

Ben, on the other hand, is well liked. Not in the sense that he gets voted class favorite but in the sense that people respect him and consider him a good friend. His popularity probably results from the fact that Ben puts the interests of others ahead of his own.

Look It Up •••• Have you heard the old expression, "Opposites attract"? Well, consider this new expression: "Pride's opposite—humility—is very attractive!"

Here in a nutshell is the scoop on humility: "All of you, clothe yourselves with humility toward one another, because, 'God opposes the proud but gives grace to the humble.' Humble yourselves, therefore, under God's mighty hand, that he may lift you up in due time" (1 Peter 5:5–6).

Think It Through •••• Reflect on this statement: "Usually if we are humble, we don't realize it. The moment we consider ourselves humble, we are surely wrong." Do you agree or disagree?

Would you rather be friends with someone like Belinda or someone like Ben? Which one are you most like?

Work It Out •••• How can you cultivate humility?

1. Spend time getting to know God. (It's hard to be impressed with yourself once you see how great God is!)
2. Take the spotlight off yourself by focusing on others (Philippians 2:3–8).
3. Admit your faults and own up to your mistakes.
4. Submit to those who are in authority over you (Ephesians 5:21).
5. Resist the urge to praise yourself (Proverbs 27:2).
6. Do good deeds secretly (Matthew 6:1–4).
7. Show kindness even to people who are undeserving and unappreciative (Matthew 5:43–47).

Nail It Down •••• Read today about Hezekiah's brief bout with pride in 2 Chronicles 32:24–26.

Turn to pages 65, 371 and 1113 for other readings on pride.
Turn to page 472 for Wednesday's reading.

Topic ••••

made buildings to store the harvest of grain, new wine and oil; and he made stalls for various kinds of cattle, and pens for the flocks. **29**He built villages and acquired great numbers of flocks and herds, for God had given him very great riches.

30It was Hezekiah who blocked the upper outlet of the Gihon spring and channeled the water down to the west side of the City of David. He succeeded in everything he undertook. **31**But when envoys were sent by the rulers of Babylon to ask him about the miraculous sign that had occurred in the land, God left him to test him and to know everything that was in his heart.

32The other events of Hezekiah's reign and his acts of devotion are written in the vision of the prophet Isaiah son of Amoz in the book of the kings of Judah and Israel. **33**Hezekiah rested with his fathers and was buried on the hill where the tombs of David's descendants are. All Judah and the people of Jerusalem honored him when he died. And Manasseh his son succeeded him as king.

Manasseh King of Judah

33 Manasseh was twelve years old when he became king, and he reigned in Jerusalem fifty-five years. **2**He did evil in the eyes of the LORD, following the detestable practices of the nations the LORD had driven out before the Israelites. **3**He rebuilt the high places his father Hezekiah had demolished; he also erected altars to the Baals and made Asherah poles. He bowed down to all the starry hosts and worshiped them. **4**He built altars in the temple of the LORD, of which the LORD had said, "My Name will remain in Jerusalem forever." **5**In both courts of the temple of the LORD, he built altars to all the starry hosts. **6**He sacrificed his sons in*a* the fire in the Valley of Ben Hinnom, practiced sorcery, divination and witchcraft, and consulted mediums and spiritists. He did much evil in the eyes of the LORD, provoking him to anger.

7He took the carved image he had made and put it in God's temple, of which God had said to David and to his son Solomon, "In this temple and in Jerusalem, which I have chosen out of all the tribes of Israel, I will put my Name forever. **8**I will not again make the feet of the Israelites leave the land I assigned to your forefathers, if only they will be careful to do everything I commanded

them concerning all the laws, decrees and ordinances given through Moses." **9**But Manasseh led Judah and the people of Jerusalem astray, so that they did more evil than the nations the LORD had destroyed before the Israelites.

10The LORD spoke to Manasseh and his people, but they paid no attention. **11**So the LORD brought against them the army commanders of the king of Assyria, who took Manasseh prisoner, put a hook in his nose, bound him with bronze shackles and took him to Babylon. **12**In his distress he sought the favor of the LORD his God and humbled himself greatly before the God of his fathers. **13**And when he prayed to him, the LORD was moved by his entreaty and listened to his plea; so he brought him back to Jerusalem and to his kingdom. Then Manasseh knew that the LORD is God.

14Afterward he rebuilt the outer wall of the City of David, west of the Gihon spring in the valley, as far as the entrance of the Fish Gate and encircling the hill of Ophel; he also made it much higher. He stationed military commanders in all the fortified cities in Judah.

15He got rid of the foreign gods and removed the image from the temple of the LORD, as well as all the altars he had built on the temple hill and in Jerusalem; and he threw them out of the city. **16**Then he restored the altar of the LORD and sacrificed fellowship offerings*b* and thank offerings on it, and told Judah to serve the LORD, the God of Israel. **17**The people, however, continued to sacrifice at the high places, but only to the LORD their God.

18The other events of Manasseh's reign, including his prayer to his God and the words the seers spoke to him in the name of the LORD, the God of Israel, are written in the annals of the kings of Israel.*c* **19**His prayer and how God was moved by his entreaty, as well as all his sins and unfaithfulness, and the sites where he built high places and set up Asherah poles and idols before he humbled himself—all are written in the records of the seers.*d* **20**Manasseh rested with his fathers and was buried in his palace. And Amon his son succeeded him as king.

Amon King of Judah

21Amon was twenty-two years old when he became king, and he reigned in Jerusalem two years. **22**He did evil in the eyes of

---

a6 Or *He made his sons pass through*   *b16* Traditionally *peace offerings*   *c18* That is, Judah, as frequently in 2 Chronicles   *d19* One Hebrew manuscript and Septuagint; most Hebrew manuscripts *of Hozai* the LORD, as his father Manasseh had done. Amon worshiped and offered sacrifices to all the idols Manasseh had made. ²³But unlike his father Manasseh, he did not humble himself before the LORD; Amon increased his guilt.

²⁴Amon's officials conspired against him and assassinated him in his palace. ²⁵Then the people of the land killed all who had plotted against King Amon, and they made Josiah his son king in his place.

Josiah's Reforms

34 Josiah was eight years old when he became king, and he reigned in Jerusalem thirty-one years. ²He did what was right in the eyes of the LORD and walked in the ways of his father David, not turning aside to the right or to the left.

³In the eighth year of his reign, while he was still young, he began to seek the God of his father David. In his twelfth year he began to purge Judah and Jerusalem of high places, Asherah poles, carved idols and cast images. ⁴Under his direction the altars of the Baals were torn down; he cut to pieces the incense altars that were above them, and smashed the Asherah poles, the idols and the images. These he broke to pieces and scattered over the graves of those who had sacrificed to them. ⁵He burned the bones of the priests on their altars, and so he purged Judah and Jerusalem. ⁶In the towns of Manasseh, Ephraim and Simeon, as far as Naphtali, and in the ruins around them, ⁷he tore down the altars and the Asherah poles and crushed the idols to powder and cut to pieces all the incense altars throughout Israel. Then he went back to Jerusalem.

⁸In the eighteenth year of Josiah's reign, to purify the land and the temple, he sent Shaphan son of Azaliah and Maaseiah the ruler of the city, with Joah son of Joahaz, the recorder, to repair the temple of the LORD his God.

⁹They went to Hilkiah the high priest and gave him the money that had been brought into the temple of God, which the Levites who were the doorkeepers had collected from the people of Manasseh, Ephraim and the entire remnant of Israel and from all the people of Judah and Benjamin and the inhabitants of Jerusalem. ¹⁰Then they entrusted it to the men appointed to supervise the work on the LORD's temple. These men paid the workers who repaired and restored the temple. ¹¹They also gave money to the carpenters and builders to purchase dressed stone, and timber for joists and beams for the buildings that the kings of Judah had allowed to fall into ruin.

¹²The men did the work faithfully. Over them to direct them were Jahath and Obadiah, Levites descended from Merari, and Zechariah and Meshullam, descended from Kohath. The Levites—all who were skilled in playing musical instruments— ¹³had charge of the laborers and supervised all the workers from job to job. Some of the Levites were secretaries, scribes and doorkeepers.

The Book of the Law Found

¹⁴While they were bringing out the money that had been taken into the temple of the LORD, Hilkiah the priest found the Book of the Law of the LORD that had been given through Moses. ¹⁵Hilkiah said to Shaphan the secretary, "I have found the Book of the Law in the temple of the LORD." He gave it to Shaphan.

¹⁶Then Shaphan took the book to the king and reported to him: "Your officials are doing everything that has been committed to them. ¹⁷They have paid out the money that was in the temple of the LORD and have entrusted it to the supervisors and workers." ¹⁸Then Shaphan the secretary informed the king, "Hilkiah the priest has given me a book." And Shaphan read from it in the presence of the king.

¹⁹When the king heard the words of the Law, he tore his robes. ²⁰He gave these orders to Hilkiah, Ahikam son of Shaphan, Abdon son of Micah,ᵃ Shaphan the secretary and Asaiah the king's attendant: ²¹"Go and inquire of the LORD for me and for the remnant in Israel and Judah about what is written in this book that has been found. Great is the LORD's anger that is poured out on us because our fathers have not kept the word of the LORD; they have not acted in accordance with all that is written in this book."

²²Hilkiah and those the king had sent with himᵇ went to speak to the prophetess Huldah, who was the wife of Shallum son of Tokhath,ᶜ the son of Hasrah,ᵈ keeper of the wardrobe. She lived in Jerusalem, in the Second District.

²³She said to them, "This is what the LORD, the God of Israel, says: Tell the man who sent you to me, ²⁴'This is what the LORD says: I am going to bring disaster on this place and

---

ᵃ20 Also called *Acbor son of Micaiah*   ᵇ22 One Hebrew manuscript, Vulgate and Syriac; most Hebrew manuscripts do not have *had sent with him.*   ᶜ22 Also called *Tikvah*   ᵈ22 Also called *Harhas* its people—all the curses written in the book that has been read in the presence of the king of Judah. **25**Because they have forsaken me and burned incense to other gods and provoked me to anger by all that their hands have made,*a* my anger will be poured out on this place and will not be quenched.' **26**Tell the king of Judah, who sent you to inquire of the LORD, 'This is what the LORD, the God of Israel, says concerning the words you heard: **27**Because your heart was responsive and you humbled yourself before God when you heard what he spoke against this place and its people, and because you humbled yourself before me and tore your robes and wept in my presence, I have heard you, declares the LORD. **28**Now I will gather you to your fathers, and you will be buried in peace. Your eyes will not see all the disaster I am going to bring on this place and on those who live here.' "

So they took her answer back to the king.

29Then the king called together all the elders of Judah and Jerusalem. **30**He went up to the temple of the LORD with the men of Judah, the people of Jerusalem, the priests and the Levites—all the people from the least to the greatest. He read in their hearing all the words of the Book of the Covenant, which had been found in the temple of the LORD. **31**The king stood by his pillar and renewed the covenant in the presence of the LORD—to follow the LORD and keep his commands, regulations and decrees with all his heart and all his soul, and to obey the words of the covenant written in this book.

32Then he had everyone in Jerusalem and Benjamin pledge themselves to it; the people of Jerusalem did this in accordance with the covenant of God, the God of their fathers.

33Josiah removed all the detestable idols from all the territory belonging to the Israelites, and he had all who were present in Israel serve the LORD their God. As long as he lived, they did not fail to follow the LORD, the God of their fathers.

Josiah Celebrates the Passover

35 Josiah celebrated the Passover to the LORD in Jerusalem, and the Passover lamb was slaughtered on the fourteenth day of the first month. **2**He appointed the priests to their duties and encouraged them in the service of the LORD's temple. **3**He said to the Levites, who instructed all Israel and who had been consecrated to the LORD: "Put the sacred ark in the temple that Solomon son of David king of Israel built. It is not to be carried about on your shoulders. Now serve the LORD your God and his people Israel. **4**Prepare yourselves by families in your divisions, according to the directions written by David king of Israel and by his son Solomon.

5"Stand in the holy place with a group of Levites for each subdivision of the families of your fellow countrymen, the lay people. **6**Slaughter the Passover lambs, consecrate yourselves and prepare ˌthe lambsˌ for your fellow countrymen, doing what the LORD commanded through Moses."

7Josiah provided for all the lay people who were there a total of thirty thousand sheep and goats for the Passover offerings, and also three thousand cattle—all from the king's own possessions.

8His officials also contributed voluntarily to the people and the priests and Levites. Hilkiah, Zechariah and Jehiel, the administrators of God's temple, gave the priests twenty-six hundred Passover offerings and three hundred cattle. **9**Also Conaniah along with Shemaiah and Nethanel, his brothers, and Hashabiah, Jeiel and Jozabad, the leaders of the Levites, provided five thousand Passover offerings and five hundred head of cattle for the Levites.

10The service was arranged and the priests stood in their places with the Levites in their divisions as the king had ordered. **11**The Passover lambs were slaughtered, and the priests sprinkled the blood handed to them, while the Levites skinned the animals. **12**They set aside the burnt offerings to give them to the subdivisions of the families of the people to offer to the LORD, as is written in the Book of Moses. They did the same with the cattle. **13**They roasted the Passover animals over the fire as prescribed, and boiled the holy offerings in pots, caldrons and pans and served them quickly to all the people. **14**After this, they made preparations for themselves and for the priests, because the priests, the descendants of Aaron, were sacrificing the burnt offerings and the fat portions until nightfall. So the Levites made preparations for themselves and for the Aaronic priests.

15The musicians, the descendants of Asaph, were in the places prescribed by David, Asaph, Heman and Jeduthun the king's seer. The gatekeepers at each gate did not need to leave their posts, because their fellow Levites made the preparations for them.

a25 Or by everything they have done

[16]So at that time the entire service of the Lord was carried out for the celebration of the Passover and the offering of burnt offerings on the altar of the Lord, as King Josiah had ordered. [17]The Israelites who were present celebrated the Passover at that time and observed the Feast of Unleavened Bread for seven days. [18]The Passover had not been observed like this in Israel since the days of the prophet Samuel; and none of the kings of Israel had ever celebrated such a Passover as did Josiah, with the priests, the Levites and all Judah and Israel who were there with the people of Jerusalem. [19]This Passover was celebrated in the eighteenth year of Josiah's reign.

The Death of Josiah

[20]After all this, when Josiah had set the temple in order, Neco king of Egypt went up to fight at Carchemish on the Euphrates, and Josiah marched out to meet him in battle. [21]But Neco sent messengers to him, saying, "What quarrel is there between you and me, O king of Judah? It is not you I am attacking at this time, but the house with which I am at war. God has told me to hurry; so stop opposing God, who is with me, or he will destroy you."

[22]Josiah, however, would not turn away from him, but disguised himself to engage him in battle. He would not listen to what Neco had said at God's command but went to fight him on the plain of Megiddo.

[23]Archers shot King Josiah, and he told his officers, "Take me away; I am badly wounded." [24]So they took him out of his chariot, put him in the other chariot he had and brought him to Jerusalem, where he died. He was buried in the tombs of his fathers, and all Judah and Jerusalem mourned for him.

[25]Jeremiah composed laments for Josiah, and to this day all the men and women singers commemorate Josiah in the laments. These became a tradition in Israel and are written in the Laments.

[26]The other events of Josiah's reign and his acts of devotion, according to what is written in the Law of the Lord— [27]all the events, from beginning to end, are written in the book of the kings of Israel and Judah.

36

[1]And the people of the land took Jehoahaz son of Josiah and made him king in Jerusalem in place of his father.

Jehoahaz King of Judah

[2]Jehoahaz[a] was twenty-three years old when he became king, and he reigned in Jerusalem three months. [3]The king of Egypt dethroned him in Jerusalem and imposed on Judah a levy of a hundred talents[b] of silver and a talent[c] of gold. [4]The king of Egypt made Eliakim, a brother of Jehoahaz, king over Judah and Jerusalem and changed Eliakim's name to Jehoiakim. But Neco took Eliakim's brother Jehoahaz and carried him off to Egypt.

Jehoiakim King of Judah

[5]Jehoiakim was twenty-five years old when he became king, and he reigned in Jerusalem eleven years. He did evil in the eyes of the Lord his God. [6]Nebuchadnezzar king of Babylon attacked him and bound him with bronze shackles to take him to Babylon. [7]Nebuchadnezzar also took to Babylon articles from the temple of the Lord and put them in his temple[d] there.

[8]The other events of Jehoiakim's reign, the detestable things he did and all that was found against him, are written in the book of the kings of Israel and Judah. And Jehoiachin his son succeeded him as king.

Jehoiachin King of Judah

[9]Jehoiachin was eighteen[e] years old when he became king, and he reigned in Jerusalem three months and ten days. He did evil in the eyes of the Lord. [10]In the spring, King Nebuchadnezzar sent for him and brought him to Babylon, together with articles of value from the temple of the Lord, and he made Jehoiachin's uncle,[f] Zedekiah, king over Judah and Jerusalem.

Zedekiah King of Judah

[11]Zedekiah was twenty-one years old when he became king, and he reigned in Jerusalem eleven years. [12]He did evil in the eyes of the Lord his God and did not humble himself before Jeremiah the prophet, who spoke the word of the Lord. [13]He also rebelled against King Nebuchadnezzar, who had made him take an oath in God's name. He became stiff-necked and hardened his

---

[a]2 Hebrew Joahaz, a variant of Jehoahaz; also in verse 4　[b]3 That is, about 3 3/4 tons (about 3.4 metric tons)　[c]3 That is, about 75 pounds (about 34 kilograms)　[d]7 Or palace　[e]9 One Hebrew manuscript, some Septuagint manuscripts and Syriac (see also 2 Kings 24:8); most Hebrew manuscripts eight　[f]10 Hebrew brother, that is, relative (see 2 Kings 24:17)

heart and would not turn to the Lord, the God of Israel. ¹⁴Furthermore, all the leaders of the priests and the people became more and more unfaithful, following all the detestable practices of the nations and defiling the temple of the Lord, which he had consecrated in Jerusalem.

The Fall of Jerusalem

¹⁵The Lord, the God of their fathers, sent word to them through his messengers again and again, because he had pity on his people and on his dwelling place. ¹⁶But they mocked God's messengers, despised his words and scoffed at his prophets until the wrath of the Lord was aroused against his people and there was no remedy. ¹⁷He brought up against them the king of the Babylonians,ᵃ who killed their young men with the sword in the sanctuary, and spared neither young man nor young woman, old man or aged. God handed all of them over to Nebuchadnezzar. ¹⁸He carried to Babylon all the articles from the temple of God, both large and small, and the treasures of the Lord's temple and the treasures of the king and his officials. ¹⁹They set fire to God's temple and broke down the wall of Jerusalem; they burned all the palaces and destroyed everything of value there.

²⁰He carried into exile to Babylon the remnant, who escaped from the sword, and they became servants to him and his sons until the kingdom of Persia came to power. ²¹The land enjoyed its sabbath rests; all the time of its desolation it rested, until the seventy years were completed in fulfillment of the word of the Lord spoken by Jeremiah.

²²In the first year of Cyrus king of Persia, in order to fulfill the word of the Lord spoken by Jeremiah, the Lord moved the heart of Cyrus king of Persia to make a proclamation throughout his realm and to put it in writing:

²³"This is what Cyrus king of Persia says:

"'The Lord, the God of heaven, has given me all the kingdoms of the earth and he has appointed me to build a temple for him at Jerusalem in Judah. Anyone of his people among you — may the Lord his God be with him, and let him go up.'"

ᵃ17 Or *Chaldeans*

EZRA

AFTER seventy years in Babylon, it's time for the Jews to come home. The first group comes with Zerubbabel to rebuild the temple (Ezra 1—6); the second wave comes with Ezra to rebuild the hearts of the people (Ezra 7—10). Ezra sees the sinful intermarriages with women from neighboring nations and calls for total commitment to the Lord. The people respond with serious repentance. As you read Ezra, acknowledge that the process of righting wrongs is painful, difficult and time-consuming. But a life of purity before the Lord is worth whatever it takes.

Outline of Contents

Cyrus Helps the Exiles to Return

1 In the first year of Cyrus king of Persia, in order to fulfill the word of the LORD spoken by Jeremiah, the LORD moved the heart of Cyrus king of Persia to make a proclamation throughout his realm and to put it in writing:

²"This is what Cyrus king of Persia says:

" 'The LORD, the God of heaven, has given me all the kingdoms of the earth and he has appointed me to build a temple for him at Jerusalem in Judah. ³Anyone of his people among you— may his God be with him, and let him go up to Jerusalem in Judah and build the temple of the LORD, the God of Israel, the God who is in Jerusalem. ⁴And

the people of any place where survivors may now be living are to provide him with silver and gold, with goods and livestock, and with freewill offerings for the temple of God in Jerusalem.' "

⁵Then the family heads of Judah and Benjamin, and the priests and Levites—everyone whose heart God had moved—prepared to go up and build the house of the LORD in Jerusalem. ⁶All their neighbors assisted them with articles of silver and gold, with goods and livestock, and with valuable gifts, in addition to all the freewill offerings. ⁷Moreover, King Cyrus brought out the articles belonging to the temple of the LORD, which Nebuchadnezzar had carried away from Jerusalem and had placed in the tem-

ple of his god.[a] **8**Cyrus king of Persia had them brought by Mithredath the treasurer, who counted them out to Sheshbazzar the prince of Judah. **9**This was the inventory:

gold dishes	30
silver dishes	1,000
silver pans[b]	29
10gold bowls	30
matching silver bowls	410
other articles	1,000

11In all, there were 5,400 articles of gold and of silver. Sheshbazzar brought all these along when the exiles came up from Babylon to Jerusalem.

The List of the Exiles Who Returned

2 Now these are the people of the province who came up from the captivity of the exiles, whom Nebuchadnezzar king of Babylon had taken captive to Babylon (they returned to Jerusalem and Judah, each to his own town, **2**in company with Zerubbabel, Jeshua, Nehemiah, Seraiah, Reelaiah, Mordecai, Bilshan, Mispar, Bigvai, Rehum and Baanah):

The list of the men of the people of Israel:

3the descendants of Parosh	2,172
4of Shephatiah	372
5of Arah	775
6of Pahath-Moab (through the line of Jeshua and Joab)	2,812
7of Elam	1,254
8of Zattu	945
9of Zaccai	760
10of Bani	642
11of Bebai	623
12of Azgad	1,222
13of Adonikam	666
14of Bigvai	2,056
15of Adin	454
16of Ater (through Hezekiah)	98
17of Bezai	323
18of Jorah	112
19of Hashum	223
20of Gibbar	95
21the men of Bethlehem	123
22of Netophah	56
23of Anathoth	128
24of Azmaveth	42
25of Kiriath Jearim,[c] Kephirah and Beeroth	743
26of Ramah and Geba	621
27of Micmash	122
28of Bethel and Ai	223
29of Nebo	52
30of Magbish	156
31of the other Elam	1,254
32of Harim	320
33of Lod, Hadid and Ono	725
34of Jericho	345
35of Senaah	3,630

36The priests:

the descendants of Jedaiah (through the family of Jeshua)	973
37of Immer	1,052
38of Pashhur	1,247
39of Harim	1,017

40The Levites:

the descendants of Jeshua and Kadmiel (through the line of Hodaviah)	74

41The singers:

the descendants of Asaph	128

42The gatekeepers of the temple:

the descendants of Shallum, Ater, Talmon, Akkub, Hatita and Shobai	139

43The temple servants:

the descendants of
Ziha, Hasupha, Tabbaoth,
44Keros, Siaha, Padon,
45Lebanah, Hagabah, Akkub,
46Hagab, Shalmai, Hanan,
47Giddel, Gahar, Reaiah,
48Rezin, Nekoda, Gazzam,
49Uzza, Paseah, Besai,
50Asnah, Meunim, Nephussim,
51Bakbuk, Hakupha, Harhur,
52Bazluth, Mehida, Harsha,
53Barkos, Sisera, Temah,
54Neziah and Hatipha

55The descendants of the servants of Solomon:

the descendants of
Sotai, Hassophereth, Peruda,
56Jaala, Darkon, Giddel,
57Shephatiah, Hattil,
Pokereth-Hazzebaim and Ami

---

[a]7 Or *gods*   [b]9 The meaning of the Hebrew for this word is uncertain.   [c]25 See Septuagint (see also Neh. 7:29); Hebrew *Kiriath Arim*.

58The temple servants and the
descendants of the servants of
Solomon   392

59The following came up from the
towns of Tel Melah, Tel Harsha, Kerub,
Addon and Immer, but they could not
show that their families were descended from Israel:

60The descendants of
Delaiah, Tobiah and Nekoda   652

61And from among the priests:

The descendants of
Hobaiah, Hakkoz and Barzillai (a
man who had married a daughter
of Barzillai the Gileadite and was
called by that name).

62These searched for their family
records, but they could not find them
and so were excluded from the priesthood as unclean. 63The governor ordered them not to eat any of the most
sacred food until there was a priest
ministering with the Urim and Thummim.

64The whole company numbered
42,360, 65besides their 7,337 menservants and maidservants; and they also
had 200 men and women singers.
66They had 736 horses, 245 mules,
67435 camels and 6,720 donkeys.

68When they arrived at the house of the
Lord in Jerusalem, some of the heads of
the families gave freewill offerings toward
the rebuilding of the house of God on its site.
69According to their ability they gave to the
treasury for this work 61,000 drachmas*a* of
gold, 5,000 minas*b* of silver and 100 priestly garments.

70The priests, the Levites, the singers, the
gatekeepers and the temple servants settled
in their own towns, along with some of the
other people, and the rest of the Israelites
settled in their towns.

Rebuilding the Altar

3 When the seventh month came and the
Israelites had settled in their towns, the
people assembled as one man in Jerusalem.
2Then Jeshua son of Jozadak and his fellow
priests and Zerubbabel son of Shealtiel and
his associates began to build the altar of the
God of Israel to sacrifice burnt offerings on
it, in accordance with what is written in the
Law of Moses the man of God. 3Despite their
fear of the peoples around them, they built
the altar on its foundation and sacrificed
burnt offerings on it to the Lord, both the
morning and evening sacrifices. 4Then in
accordance with what is written, they celebrated the Feast of Tabernacles with the required number of burnt offerings prescribed
for each day. 5After that, they presented the
regular burnt offerings, the New Moon sacrifices and the sacrifices for all the appointed
sacred feasts of the Lord, as well as those
brought as freewill offerings to the Lord. 6On
the first day of the seventh month they began to offer burnt offerings to the Lord,
though the foundation of the Lord's temple
had not yet been laid.

Rebuilding the Temple

7Then they gave money to the masons
and carpenters, and gave food and drink
and oil to the people of Sidon and Tyre, so
that they would bring cedar logs by sea from
Lebanon to Joppa, as authorized by Cyrus
king of Persia.

8In the second month of the second year
after their arrival at the house of God in Jerusalem, Zerubbabel son of Shealtiel, Jeshua
son of Jozadak and the rest of their brothers
(the priests and the Levites and all who had
returned from the captivity to Jerusalem)
began the work, appointing Levites twenty
years of age and older to supervise the
building of the house of the Lord. 9Jeshua
and his sons and brothers and Kadmiel
and his sons (descendants of Hodaviah*c*) and
the sons of Henadad and their sons and
brothers — all Levites — joined together in
supervising those working on the house of
God.

10When the builders laid the foundation
of the temple of the Lord, the priests in their
vestments and with trumpets, and the Levites (the sons of Asaph) with cymbals, took
their places to praise the Lord, as prescribed
by David king of Israel. 11With praise and
thanksgiving they sang to the Lord:

"He is good;
his love to Israel endures forever."

And all the people gave a great shout of
praise to the Lord, because the foundation
of the house of the Lord was laid. 12But
many of the older priests and Levites and
family heads, who had seen the former temple, wept aloud when they saw the founda-

*a69 That is, about 1,100 pounds (about 500 kilograms)
c9 Hebrew Yehudah, probably a variant of Hodaviah

b69 That is, about 3 tons (about 2.9 metric tons)

tion of this temple being laid, while many others shouted for joy. **13**No one could distinguish the sound of the shouts of joy from the sound of weeping, because the people made so much noise. And the sound was heard far away.

Opposition to the Rebuilding

4 When the enemies of Judah and Benjamin heard that the exiles were building a temple for the LORD, the God of Israel, **2**they came to Zerubbabel and to the heads of the families and said, "Let us help you build because, like you, we seek your God and have been sacrificing to him since the time of Esarhaddon king of Assyria, who brought us here."

3But Zerubbabel, Jeshua and the rest of the heads of the families of Israel answered, "You have no part with us in building a temple to our God. We alone will build it for the LORD, the God of Israel, as King Cyrus, the king of Persia, commanded us."

4Then the peoples around them set out to discourage the people of Judah and make them afraid to go on building.*a* **5**They hired counselors to work against them and frustrate their plans during the entire reign of Cyrus king of Persia and down to the reign of Darius king of Persia.

Later Opposition Under Xerxes and Artaxerxes

6At the beginning of the reign of Xerxes,*b* they lodged an accusation against the people of Judah and Jerusalem.

7And in the days of Artaxerxes king of Persia, Bishlam, Mithredath, Tabeel and the rest of his associates wrote a letter to Artaxerxes. The letter was written in Aramaic script and in the Aramaic language.*c, d*

8Rehum the commanding officer and Shimshai the secretary wrote a letter against Jerusalem to Artaxerxes the king as follows:

9Rehum the commanding officer and Shimshai the secretary, together with the rest of their associates — the judges and officials over the men from Tripolis, Persia,*e* Erech and Babylon, the Elamites of Susa, **10**and the other people whom the great and honorable Ashurbanipal*f* deported and settled in the city of Samaria and elsewhere in Trans-Euphrates.

11(This is a copy of the letter they sent him.)

To King Artaxerxes,

From your servants, the men of Trans-Euphrates:

12The king should know that the Jews who came up to us from you have gone to Jerusalem and are rebuilding that rebellious and wicked city. They are restoring the walls and repairing the foundations.

13Furthermore, the king should know that if this city is built and its walls are restored, no more taxes, tribute or duty will be paid, and the royal revenues will suffer. **14**Now since we are under obligation to the palace and it is not proper for us to see the king dishonored, we are sending this message to inform the king, **15**so that a search may be made in the archives of your predecessors. In these records you will find that this city is a rebellious city, troublesome to kings and provinces, a place of rebellion from ancient times. That is why this city was destroyed. **16**We inform the king that if this city is built and its walls are restored, you will be left with nothing in Trans-Euphrates.

17The king sent this reply:

To Rehum the commanding officer, Shimshai the secretary and the rest of their associates living in Samaria and elsewhere in Trans-Euphrates:

Greetings.

18The letter you sent us has been read and translated in my presence. **19**I issued an order and a search was made, and it was found that this city has a long history of revolt against kings and has been a place of rebellion and sedition. **20**Jerusalem has had powerful kings ruling over the whole of Trans-Euphrates, and taxes, tribute and duty were paid to them. **21**Now issue an order to these men to stop work, so that this city will not be rebuilt until I so order. **22**Be careful not to neglect this matter. Why let this threat grow, to the detriment of the royal interests?

23As soon as the copy of the letter of King

---

a4 Or *and troubled them as they built*   *b6* Hebrew *Ahasuerus*, a variant of Xerxes' Persian name
c7 Or *written in Aramaic and translated*   *d7* The text of Ezra 4:8–6:18 is in Aramaic.   *e9* Or *officials*,
magistrates and governors over the men from   *f10* Aramaic *Osnappar*, a variant of *Ashurbanipal*

DON'T THROW IN THE TOWEL!

Catherine is opening her locker when her best friend Melody suddenly grabs her.

"Let's go! Coach K. just posted the results of the tennis team tryouts!"

As the two girls race across campus, Catherine's heart is pounding. Thinking of how disappointed she felt last year when she didn't make the team, she prays silently, "Oh, God, please let my name be on that list. That's all I ask!"

Scanning the list, Catherine's pounding heart skips a beat. Her name isn't there. Melody's is.

As Melody squeals and begins jumping up and down, Catherine's big blue eyes fill with tears.

Look It Up
●●●●

When reality doesn't meet your expectations, the result is disappointment. And if the disappointment runs deep enough (and long enough), the result can often be discouragement. Have you ever felt it—that futile feeling of, "It's no use . . . I quit"?

If you know that feeling (and no doubt you do), don't feel like you're the Lone Ranger. Even a Bible hero like General Joshua felt tempted to throw in the towel. In fact, God had to remind him on at least four different occasions:

"Do not be afraid; do not be discouraged" (Deuteronomy 31:8; see also Joshua 1:9; 8:1; 10:25).

Think It Through
●●●●

In the Hebrew language, the word for discouraged can also be translated "shattered or broken, dismayed or terrified." In English it literally means "to lose courage"—you lose confidence that your situation will ever change for the better. Your dreams are broken. Your hope is dimmed. You're discouraged.

Without a renewed sense of hope, discouragement can lead to depression, disillusionment—even despair!

Work It Out
●●●●

Can you relate to Catherine's feelings—those feelings of brokenness inside? Then pray this:

"Lord, I was hoping (maybe even expecting) that the situation involving _____ would turn out differently. But it didn't, and now I feel downright discouraged. God, please teach me how to take courage in you. Use this set of circumstances to draw me closer to you. Amen."

Nail It Down
●●●●

Read about the discouraging enemies of Judah in Ezra 4.

Turn to pages 663 and 1205 for other readings on encouragement.
Turn to page 478 for Thursday's reading.

Topic
●●●●

ENCOURAGEMENT

Artaxerxes was read to Rehum and Shimshai the secretary and their associates, they went immediately to the Jews in Jerusalem and compelled them by force to stop.

²⁴Thus the work on the house of God in Jerusalem came to a standstill until the second year of the reign of Darius king of Persia.

Tattenai's Letter to Darius

5 Now Haggai the prophet and Zechariah the prophet, a descendant of Iddo, prophesied to the Jews in Judah and Jerusalem in the name of the God of Israel, who was over them. ²Then Zerubbabel son of Shealtiel and Jeshua son of Jozadak set to work to rebuild the house of God in Jerusalem. And the prophets of God were with them, helping them.

³At that time Tattenai, governor of Trans-Euphrates, and Shethar-Bozenai and their associates went to them and asked, "Who authorized you to rebuild this temple and restore this structure?" ⁴They also asked, "What are the names of the men constructing this building?"ᵃ ⁵But the eye of their God was watching over the elders of the Jews, and they were not stopped until a report could go to Darius and his written reply be received.

⁶This is a copy of the letter that Tattenai, governor of Trans-Euphrates, and Shethar-Bozenai and their associates, the officials of Trans-Euphrates, sent to King Darius. ⁷The report they sent him read as follows:

To King Darius:

Cordial greetings.

⁸The king should know that we went to the district of Judah, to the temple of the great God. The people are building it with large stones and placing the timbers in the walls. The work is being carried on with diligence and is making rapid progress under their direction.

⁹We questioned the elders and asked them, "Who authorized you to rebuild this temple and restore this structure?" ¹⁰We also asked them their names, so that we could write down the names of their leaders for your information.

¹¹This is the answer they gave us:

"We are the servants of the God of heaven and earth, and we are rebuilding the temple that was built many years ago, one that a great king of Israel built and finished. ¹²But because our fathers angered the God of heaven, he handed them over to Nebuchadnezzar the Chaldean, king of Babylon, who destroyed this temple and deported the people to Babylon.

¹³"However, in the first year of Cyrus king of Babylon, King Cyrus issued a decree to rebuild this house of God. ¹⁴He even removed from the templeᵇ of Babylon the gold and silver articles of the house of God, which Nebuchadnezzar had taken from the temple in Jerusalem and brought to the templeᵇ in Babylon.

"Then King Cyrus gave them to a man named Sheshbazzar, whom he had appointed governor, ¹⁵and he told him, 'Take these articles and go and deposit them in the temple in Jerusalem. And rebuild the house of God on its site.' ¹⁶So this Sheshbazzar came and laid the foundations of the house of God in Jerusalem. From that day to the present it has been under construction but is not yet finished."

¹⁷Now if it pleases the king, let a search be made in the royal archives of Babylon to see if King Cyrus did in fact issue a decree to rebuild this house of God in Jerusalem. Then let the king send us his decision in this matter.

The Decree of Darius

6 King Darius then issued an order, and they searched in the archives stored in the treasury at Babylon. ²A scroll was found in the citadel of Ecbatana in the province of Media, and this was written on it:

Memorandum:

³In the first year of King Cyrus, the king issued a decree concerning the temple of God in Jerusalem:

Let the temple be rebuilt as a place to present sacrifices, and let its foundations be laid. It is to be ninety feetᶜ high and ninety feet wide, ⁴with three courses of large stones and one of timbers. The costs are to be paid by the royal treasury. ⁵Also, the gold and silver articles of the house of God, which Neb-

---

ᵃ4 See Septuagint; Aramaic ⁴We told them the names of the men constructing this building.   ᵇ14 Or palace
ᶜ3 Aramaic sixty cubits (about 27 meters)

uchadnezzar took from the temple in Jerusalem and brought to Babylon, are to be returned to their places in the temple in Jerusalem; they are to be deposited in the house of God.

⁶Now then, Tattenai, governor of Trans-Euphrates, and Shethar-Bozenai and you, their fellow officials of that province, stay away from there. ⁷Do not interfere with the work on this temple of God. Let the governor of the Jews and the Jewish elders rebuild this house of God on its site.

⁸Moreover, I hereby decree what you are to do for these elders of the Jews in the construction of this house of God:

The expenses of these men are to be fully paid out of the royal treasury, from the revenues of Trans-Euphrates, so that the work will not stop. ⁹Whatever is needed—young bulls, rams, male lambs for burnt offerings to the God of heaven, and wheat, salt, wine and oil, as requested by the priests in Jerusalem—must be given them daily without fail, ¹⁰so that they may offer sacrifices pleasing to the God of heaven and pray for the well-being of the king and his sons.

¹¹Furthermore, I decree that if anyone changes this edict, a beam is to be pulled from his house and he is to be lifted up and impaled on it. And for this crime his house is to be made a pile of rubble. ¹²May God, who has caused his Name to dwell there, overthrow any king or people who lifts a hand to change this decree or to destroy this temple in Jerusalem.

I Darius have decreed it. Let it be carried out with diligence.

Completion and Dedication of the Temple

¹³Then, because of the decree King Darius had sent, Tattenai, governor of Trans-Euphrates, and Shethar-Bozenai and their associates carried it out with diligence. ¹⁴So the elders of the Jews continued to build and prosper under the preaching of Haggai the prophet and Zechariah, a descendant of Iddo. They finished building the temple according to the command of the God of Israel and the decrees of Cyrus, Darius and Artaxerxes, kings of Persia. ¹⁵The temple was completed on the third day of the month Adar, in the sixth year of the reign of King Darius.

¹⁶Then the people of Israel—the priests, the Levites and the rest of the exiles—celebrated the dedication of the house of God with joy. ¹⁷For the dedication of this house of God they offered a hundred bulls, two hundred rams, four hundred male lambs and, as a sin offering for all Israel, twelve male goats, one for each of the tribes of Israel. ¹⁸And they installed the priests in their divisions and the Levites in their groups for the service of God at Jerusalem, according to what is written in the Book of Moses.

The Passover

¹⁹On the fourteenth day of the first month, the exiles celebrated the Passover. ²⁰The priests and Levites had purified themselves and were all ceremonially clean. The Levites slaughtered the Passover lamb for all the exiles, for their brothers the priests and for themselves. ²¹So the Israelites who had returned from the exile ate it, together with all who had separated themselves from the unclean practices of their Gentile neighbors in order to seek the LORD, the God of Israel. ²²For seven days they celebrated with joy the Feast of Unleavened Bread, because the LORD had filled them with joy by changing the attitude of the king of Assyria, so that he assisted them in the work on the house of God, the God of Israel.

Ezra Comes to Jerusalem

7 After these things, during the reign of Artaxerxes king of Persia, Ezra son of Seraiah, the son of Azariah, the son of Hilkiah, ²the son of Shallum, the son of Zadok, the son of Ahitub, ³the son of Amariah, the son of Azariah, the son of Meraioth, ⁴the son of Zerahiah, the son of Uzzi, the son of Bukki, ⁵the son of Abishua, the son of Phinehas, the son of Eleazar, the son of Aaron the chief priest— ⁶this Ezra came up from Babylon. He was a teacher well versed in the Law of Moses, which the LORD, the God of Israel, had given. The king had granted him everything he asked, for the hand of the LORD his God was on him. ⁷Some of the Israelites, including priests, Levites, singers, gatekeepers and temple servants, also came up to Jerusalem in the seventh year of King Artaxerxes.

⁸Ezra arrived in Jerusalem in the fifth month of the seventh year of the king. ⁹He had begun his journey from Babylon on the first day of the first month, and he arrived in Jerusalem on the first day of the fifth month, for the gracious hand of his God was on him. ¹⁰For Ezra had devoted himself to the study

and observance of the Law of the Lord, and to teaching its decrees and laws in Israel.

King Artaxerxes' Letter to Ezra

11This is a copy of the letter King Artaxerxes had given to Ezra the priest and teacher, a man learned in matters concerning the commands and decrees of the Lord for Israel:

12*a*Artaxerxes, king of kings,

To Ezra the priest, a teacher of the Law of the God of heaven:

Greetings.

13Now I decree that any of the Israelites in my kingdom, including priests and Levites, who wish to go to Jerusalem with you, may go. **14**You are sent by the king and his seven advisers to inquire about Judah and Jerusalem with regard to the Law of your God, which is in your hand. **15**Moreover, you are to take with you the silver and gold that the king and his advisers have freely given to the God of Israel, whose dwelling is in Jerusalem, **16**together with all the silver and gold you may obtain from the province of Babylon, as well as the freewill offerings of the people and priests for the temple of their God in Jerusalem. **17**With this money be sure to buy bulls, rams and male lambs, together with their grain offerings and drink offerings, and sacrifice them on the altar of the temple of your God in Jerusalem.

18You and your brother Jews may then do whatever seems best with the rest of the silver and gold, in accordance with the will of your God. **19**Deliver to the God of Jerusalem all the articles entrusted to you for worship in the temple of your God. **20**And anything else needed for the temple of your God that you may have occasion to supply, you may provide from the royal treasury.

21Now I, King Artaxerxes, order all the treasurers of Trans-Euphrates to provide with diligence whatever Ezra the priest, a teacher of the Law of the God of heaven, may ask of you— **22**up to a hundred talents*b* of silver, a hundred cors*c* of wheat, a hundred baths*d*

of wine, a hundred baths*d* of olive oil, and salt without limit. **23**Whatever the God of heaven has prescribed, let it be done with diligence for the temple of the God of heaven. Why should there be wrath against the realm of the king and of his sons? **24**You are also to know that you have no authority to impose taxes, tribute or duty on any of the priests, Levites, singers, gatekeepers, temple servants or other workers at this house of God.

25And you, Ezra, in accordance with the wisdom of your God, which you possess, appoint magistrates and judges to administer justice to all the people of Trans-Euphrates—all who know the laws of your God. And you are to teach any who do not know them. **26**Whoever does not obey the law of your God and the law of the king must surely be punished by death, banishment, confiscation of property, or imprisonment.

27Praise be to the Lord, the God of our fathers, who has put it into the king's heart to bring honor to the house of the Lord in Jerusalem in this way **28**and who has extended his good favor to me before the king and his advisers and all the king's powerful officials. Because the hand of the Lord my God was on me, I took courage and gathered leading men from Israel to go up with me.

List of the Family Heads Returning With Ezra

8 These are the family heads and those registered with them who came up with me from Babylon during the reign of King Artaxerxes:

2of the descendants of Phinehas, Gershom;

of the descendants of Ithamar, Daniel;

of the descendants of David, Hattush **3**of the descendants of Shecaniah;

of the descendants of Parosh, Zechariah, and with him were registered 150 men;

4of the descendants of Pahath-Moab, Eliehoenai son of Zerahiah, and with him 200 men;

5of the descendants of Zattu,*e* Shecaniah son of Jahaziel, and with him 300 men;

⁶of the descendants of Adin, Ebed son of Jonathan, and with him 50 men; ⁷of the descendants of Elam, Jeshaiah son of Athaliah, and with him 70 men; ⁸of the descendants of Shephatiah, Zebadiah son of Michael, and with him 80 men; ⁹of the descendants of Joab, Obadiah son of Jehiel, and with him 218 men; ¹⁰of the descendants of Bani,ᵃ Shelomith son of Josiphiah, and with him 160 men; ¹¹of the descendants of Bebai, Zechariah son of Bebai, and with him 28 men; ¹²of the descendants of Azgad, Johanan son of Hakkatan, and with him 110 men; ¹³of the descendants of Adonikam, the last ones, whose names were Eliphelet, Jeuel and Shemaiah, and with them 60 men; ¹⁴of the descendants of Bigvai, Uthai and Zaccur, and with them 70 men.

The Return to Jerusalem

¹⁵I assembled them at the canal that flows toward Ahava, and we camped there three days. When I checked among the people and the priests, I found no Levites there. ¹⁶So I summoned Eliezer, Ariel, Shemaiah, Elnathan, Jarib, Elnathan, Nathan, Zechariah and Meshullam, who were leaders, and Joiarib and Elnathan, who were men of learning, ¹⁷and I sent them to Iddo, the leader in Casiphia. I told them what to say to Iddo and his kinsmen, the temple servants in Casiphia, so that they might bring attendants to us for the house of our God. ¹⁸Because the gracious hand of our God was on us, they brought us Sherebiah, a capable man, from the descendants of Mahli son of Levi, the son of Israel, and Sherebiah's sons and brothers, 18 men; ¹⁹and Hashabiah, together with Jeshaiah from the descendants of Merari, and his brothers and nephews, 20 men. ²⁰They also brought 220 of the temple servants—a body that David and the officials had established to assist the Levites. All were registered by name.

²¹There, by the Ahava Canal, I proclaimed a fast, so that we might humble ourselves before our God and ask him for a safe journey for us and our children, with all our possessions. ²²I was ashamed to ask the king for soldiers and horsemen to protect us from enemies on the road, because we had told the king, "The gracious hand of our God is on everyone who looks to him, but his great anger is against all who forsake him." ²³So we fasted and petitioned our God about this, and he answered our prayer.

²⁴Then I set apart twelve of the leading priests, together with Sherebiah, Hashabiah and ten of their brothers, ²⁵and I weighed out to them the offering of silver and gold and the articles that the king, his advisers, his officials and all Israel present there had donated for the house of our God. ²⁶I weighed out to them 650 talentsᵇ of silver, silver articles weighing 100 talents,ᶜ 100 talentsᶜ of gold, ²⁷20 bowls of gold valued at 1,000 darics,ᵈ and two fine articles of polished bronze, as precious as gold.

²⁸I said to them, "You as well as these articles are consecrated to the Lᴏʀᴅ. The silver and gold are a freewill offering to the Lᴏʀᴅ, the God of your fathers. ²⁹Guard them carefully until you weigh them out in the chambers of the house of the Lᴏʀᴅ in Jerusalem before the leading priests and the Levites and the family heads of Israel." ³⁰Then the priests and Levites received the silver and gold and sacred articles that had been weighed out to be taken to the house of our God in Jerusalem.

³¹On the twelfth day of the first month we set out from the Ahava Canal to go to Jerusalem. The hand of our God was on us, and he protected us from enemies and bandits along the way. ³²So we arrived in Jerusalem, where we rested three days.

³³On the fourth day, in the house of our God, we weighed out the silver and gold and the sacred articles into the hands of Meremoth son of Uriah, the priest. Eleazar son of Phinehas was with him, and so were the Levites Jozabad son of Jeshua and Noadiah son of Binnui. ³⁴Everything was accounted for by number and weight, and the entire weight was recorded at that time.

³⁵Then the exiles who had returned from captivity sacrificed burnt offerings to the God of Israel: twelve bulls for all Israel, ninety-six rams, seventy-seven male lambs and, as a sin offering, twelve male goats. All this was a burnt offering to the Lᴏʀᴅ. ³⁶They also delivered the king's orders to the royal sa-

---

ᵃ10 Some Septuagint manuscripts (also 1 Esdras 8:36); Hebrew does not have *Bani.*   ᵇ26 That is, about 25 tons (about 22 metric tons)   ᶜ26 That is, about 3 3/4 tons (about 3.4 metric tons)   ᵈ27 That is, about 19 pounds (about 8.5 kilograms) traps and to the governors of Trans-Euphrates, who then gave assistance to the people and to the house of God.

Ezra's Prayer About Intermarriage

9 After these things had been done, the leaders came to me and said, "The people of Israel, including the priests and the Levites, have not kept themselves separate from the neighboring peoples with their detestable practices, like those of the Canaanites, Hittites, Perizzites, Jebusites, Ammonites, Moabites, Egyptians and Amorites. ²They have taken some of their daughters as wives for themselves and their sons, and have mingled the holy race with the peoples around them. And the leaders and officials have led the way in this unfaithfulness."

³When I heard this, I tore my tunic and cloak, pulled hair from my head and beard and sat down appalled. ⁴Then everyone who trembled at the words of the God of Israel gathered around me because of this unfaithfulness of the exiles. And I sat there appalled until the evening sacrifice.

⁵Then, at the evening sacrifice, I rose from my self-abasement, with my tunic and cloak torn, and fell on my knees with my hands spread out to the Lord my God ⁶and prayed:

"O my God, I am too ashamed and disgraced to lift up my face to you, my God, because our sins are higher than our heads and our guilt has reached to the heavens. ⁷From the days of our forefathers until now, our guilt has been great. Because of our sins, we and our kings and our priests have been subjected to the sword and captivity, to pillage and humiliation at the hand of foreign kings, as it is today.

⁸"But now, for a brief moment, the Lord our God has been gracious in leaving us a remnant and giving us a firm place in his sanctuary, and so our God gives light to our eyes and a little relief in our bondage. ⁹Though we are slaves, our God has not deserted us in our bondage. He has shown us kindness in the sight of the kings of Persia: He has granted us new life to rebuild the house of our God and repair its ruins, and he has given us a wall of protection in Judah and Jerusalem.

¹⁰"But now, O our God, what can we say after this? For we have disregarded the commands ¹¹you gave through your servants the prophets when you said: 'The land you are entering to pos-

sess is a land polluted by the corruption of its peoples. By their detestable practices they have filled it with their impurity from one end to the other. ¹²Therefore, do not give your daughters in marriage to their sons or take their daughters for your sons. Do not seek a treaty of friendship with them at any time, that you may be strong and eat the good things of the land and leave it to your children as an everlasting inheritance.'

¹³"What has happened to us is a result of our evil deeds and our great guilt, and yet, our God, you have punished us less than our sins have deserved and have given us a remnant like this. ¹⁴Shall we again break your commands and intermarry with the peoples who commit such detestable practices? Would you not be angry enough with us to destroy us, leaving us no remnant or survivor? ¹⁵O Lord, God of Israel, you are righteous! We are left this day as a remnant. Here we are before you in our guilt, though because of it not one of us can stand in your presence."

The People's Confession of Sin

10 While Ezra was praying and confessing, weeping and throwing himself down before the house of God, a large crowd of Israelites — men, women and children — gathered around him. They too wept bitterly. ²Then Shecaniah son of Jehiel, one of the descendants of Elam, said to Ezra, "We have been unfaithful to our God by marrying foreign women from the peoples around us. But in spite of this, there is still hope for Israel. ³Now let us make a covenant before our God to send away all these women and their children, in accordance with the counsel of my lord and of those who fear the commands of our God. Let it be done according to the Law. ⁴Rise up; this matter is in your hands. We will support you, so take courage and do it."

⁵So Ezra rose up and put the leading priests and Levites and all Israel under oath to do what had been suggested. And they took the oath. ⁶Then Ezra withdrew from before the house of God and went to the room of Jehohanan son of Eliashib. While he was there, he ate no food and drank no water, because he continued to mourn over the unfaithfulness of the exiles.

⁷A proclamation was then issued throughout Judah and Jerusalem for all the exiles to assemble in Jerusalem. ⁸Anyone who failed

PICKY, PICKY, PICKY!

People accuse Mark of being too picky about girls.

"Why are you so particular, Mark?"

"I don't want to get involved with the wrong person. I know that if I'm not careful, I could very well fall in love with someone who's not even a Christian. Then where would I be?"

"Mark, chill out! We're not talking about marriage here—just a simple date for the weekend!"

"Hey, I want to develop good habits now. I'm only seventeen, but one of these days, I hope to marry one of the girls I date."

Look It Up
••••

Mark's a perceptive guy! It pays to be picky when it comes to the opposite sex because marriage is a serious proposition. And being married to the wrong person can be a nightmare.

"A quarrelsome wife is like a constant dripping" (Proverbs 19:13).

"Better to live on a corner of the roof than share a house with a quarrelsome wife" (Proverbs 21:9).

"Better to live in a desert than with a quarrelsome and ill-tempered wife" (Proverbs 21:19).

And don't forget—it isn't just women who cause problems in marriage. Guys can be real jerks too. So don't be in a rush to get hitched, girls.

Think It Through
••••

Many Christians believe that God has one perfect person for you to marry and that everyone else is less than the best. Others feel strongly that there are a wide variety of possible mates for each believer.

Which view do you hold? Why?

Is it possible that both sides are actually in harmony? Maybe they're like two sides of the same coin—one viewed from God's perspective and the other from ours.

Work It Out
••••

If you have never done so, sit down and write out some dating standards for yourself. Think about these questions, do some serious Bible study, then talk them over with your parents and/or youth leader.

1. Should I go out with non-Christians?
2. How far should I go physically on a date?
3. Is it okay to date just one person?
4. What is the best age for marriage?
5. What is my purpose for dating?
6. What dangers should I avoid in dating?

Nail It Down
••••

Read about the exiles with messed-up marriages and what they did to solve the problem in Ezra 9—10.

Turn to pages 315, 819 and 996 for other readings on marriage.
Turn to page 483 for Friday's reading.

Topic
••••

MARRIAGE

to appear within three days would forfeit all his property, in accordance with the decision of the officials and elders, and would himself be expelled from the assembly of the exiles.

⁹Within the three days, all the men of Judah and Benjamin had gathered in Jerusalem. And on the twentieth day of the ninth month, all the people were sitting in the square before the house of God, greatly distressed by the occasion and because of the rain. ¹⁰Then Ezra the priest stood up and said to them, "You have been unfaithful; you have married foreign women, adding to Israel's guilt. ¹¹Now make confession to the LORD, the God of your fathers, and do his will. Separate yourselves from the peoples around you and from your foreign wives."

¹²The whole assembly responded with a loud voice: "You are right! We must do as you say. ¹³But there are many people here and it is the rainy season; so we cannot stand outside. Besides, this matter cannot be taken care of in a day or two, because we have sinned greatly in this thing. ¹⁴Let our officials act for the whole assembly. Then let everyone in our towns who has married a foreign woman come at a set time, along with the elders and judges of each town, until the fierce anger of our God in this matter is turned away from us." ¹⁵Only Jonathan son of Asahel and Jahzeiah son of Tikvah, supported by Meshullam and Shabbethai the Levite, opposed this.

¹⁶So the exiles did as was proposed. Ezra the priest selected men who were family heads, one from each family division, and all of them designated by name. On the first day of the tenth month they sat down to investigate the cases, ¹⁷and by the first day of the first month they finished dealing with all the men who had married foreign women.

Those Guilty of Intermarriage

¹⁸Among the descendants of the priests, the following had married foreign women:

From the descendants of Jeshua son of Jozadak, and his brothers: Maaseiah, Eliezer, Jarib and Gedaliah. ¹⁹(They all gave their hands in pledge to put away their wives, and for their guilt they each presented a ram from the flock as a guilt offering.)

²⁰From the descendants of Immer:
Hanani and Zebadiah.
²¹From the descendants of Harim:
Maaseiah, Elijah, Shemaiah, Jehiel and Uzziah.
²²From the descendants of Pashhur:
Elioenai, Maaseiah, Ishmael, Nethanel, Jozabad and Elasah.

²³Among the Levites:

Jozabad, Shimei, Kelaiah (that is, Kelita), Pethahiah, Judah and Eliezer.
²⁴From the singers:
Eliashib.
From the gatekeepers:
Shallum, Telem and Uri.

²⁵And among the other Israelites:

From the descendants of Parosh:
Ramiah, Izziah, Malkijah, Mijamin, Eleazar, Malkijah and Benaiah.
²⁶From the descendants of Elam:
Mattaniah, Zechariah, Jehiel, Abdi, Jeremoth and Elijah.
²⁷From the descendants of Zattu:
Elioenai, Eliashib, Mattaniah, Jeremoth, Zabad and Aziza.
²⁸From the descendants of Bebai:
Jehohanan, Hananiah, Zabbai and Athlai.
²⁹From the descendants of Bani:
Meshullam, Malluch, Adaiah, Jashub, Sheal and Jeremoth.
³⁰From the descendants of Pahath-Moab:
Adna, Kelal, Benaiah, Maaseiah, Mattaniah, Bezalel, Binnui and Manasseh.
³¹From the descendants of Harim:
Eliezer, Ishijah, Malkijah, Shemaiah, Shimeon, ³²Benjamin, Malluch and Shemariah.
³³From the descendants of Hashum:
Mattenai, Mattattah, Zabad, Eliphelet, Jeremai, Manasseh and Shimei.
³⁴From the descendants of Bani:
Maadai, Amram, Uel, ³⁵Benaiah, Bedeiah, Keluhi, ³⁶Vaniah, Meremoth, Eliashib, ³⁷Mattaniah, Mattenai and Jaasu.

³⁸From the descendants of Binnui:ᵃ Shimei, ³⁹Shelemiah, Nathan, Adaiah, ⁴⁰Macnadebai, Shashai, Sharai, ⁴¹Azarel, Shelemiah, Shemariah, ⁴²Shallum, Amariah and Joseph.

⁴³From the descendants of Nebo:

Jeiel, Mattithiah, Zabad, Zebina, Jaddai, Joel and Benaiah.

⁴⁴All these had married foreign women, and some of them had children by these wives.ᵇ

ᵃ37,38 See Septuagint (also 1 Esdras 9:34); Hebrew *Jaasu* ³⁸*and Bani and Binnui,*   ᵇ44 Or *and they sent them away with their children*

NEHEMIAH

CUPBEARER to the Persian king, Nehemiah receives permission to lead an expedition to rebuild Jerusalem's walls. Because of stiff opposition, the people must work with weapons in one hand and tools in the other. But because of Nehemiah's inspired leadership, they get the job done—in record time. As you read this book, notice the relationship between how Nehemiah leads and how he prays. Learn to pray now so you'll be ready to lead when God gives you the opportunity.

Outline of Contents

Nehemiah's Prayer

1 The words of Nehemiah son of Hacaliah:

In the month of Kislev in the twentieth year, while I was in the citadel of Susa, ²Hanani, one of my brothers, came from Judah with some other men, and I questioned them about the Jewish remnant that survived the exile, and also about Jerusalem.

³They said to me, "Those who survived the exile and are back in the province are in great trouble and disgrace. The wall of Jerusalem is broken down, and its gates have been burned with fire."

⁴When I heard these things, I sat down and wept. For some days I mourned and fasted and prayed before the God of heaven. ⁵Then I said:

"O Lord, God of heaven, the great and awesome God, who keeps his covenant of love with those who love him and obey his commands, ⁶let your ear be attentive and your eyes open to hear the prayer your servant is praying before you day and night for your servants, the people of Israel. I confess the sins we Israelites, including myself and my father's house, have committed against you. ⁷We have acted very wickedly toward you. We have not obeyed the commands, decrees and laws you gave your servant Moses.

⁸"Remember the instruction you gave your servant Moses, saying, 'If you are unfaithful, I will scatter you among the nations, ⁹but if you return to me and obey my commands, then even if your exiled people are at the farthest horizon, I will gather them from there

and bring them to the place I have chosen as a dwelling for my Name.'

¹⁰"They are your servants and your people, whom you redeemed by your great strength and your mighty hand. ¹¹O Lord, let your ear be attentive to the prayer of this your servant and to the prayer of your servants who delight in revering your name. Give your servant success today by granting him favor in the presence of this man."

I was cupbearer to the king.

Artaxerxes Sends Nehemiah to Jerusalem

2 In the month of Nisan in the twentieth year of King Artaxerxes, when wine was brought for him, I took the wine and gave it to the king. I had not been sad in his presence before; ²so the king asked me, "Why does your face look so sad when you are not ill? This can be nothing but sadness of heart."

I was very much afraid, ³but I said to the king, "May the king live forever! Why should my face not look sad when the city where my fathers are buried lies in ruins, and its gates have been destroyed by fire?"

⁴The king said to me, "What is it you want?"

Then I prayed to the God of heaven, ⁵and I answered the king, "If it pleases the king and if your servant has found favor in his sight, let him send me to the city in Judah where my fathers are buried so that I can rebuild it."

⁶Then the king, with the queen sitting beside him, asked me, "How long will your journey take, and when will you get back?" It pleased the king to send me; so I set a time.

⁷I also said to him, "If it pleases the king, may I have letters to the governors of Trans-Euphrates, so that they will provide me safe-conduct until I arrive in Judah? ⁸And may I have a letter to Asaph, keeper of the king's forest, so he will give me timber to make beams for the gates of the citadel by the temple and for the city wall and for the residence I will occupy?" And because the gracious hand of my God was upon me, the king granted my requests. ⁹So I went to the governors of Trans-Euphrates and gave them the king's letters. The king had also sent army officers and cavalry with me.

¹⁰When Sanballat the Horonite and Tobi-ah the Ammonite official heard about this, they were very much disturbed that someone had come to promote the welfare of the Israelites.

Nehemiah Inspects Jerusalem's Walls

¹¹I went to Jerusalem, and after staying there three days ¹²I set out during the night with a few men. I had not told anyone what my God had put in my heart to do for Jerusalem. There were no mounts with me except the one I was riding on. ¹³By night I went out through the Valley Gate toward the Jackal[a] Well and the Dung Gate, examining the walls of Jerusalem, which had been broken down, and its gates, which had been destroyed by fire. ¹⁴Then I moved on toward the Fountain Gate and the King's Pool, but there was not enough room for my mount to get through; ¹⁵so I went up the valley by night, examining the wall. Finally, I turned back and reentered through the Valley Gate. ¹⁶The officials did not know where I had gone or what I was doing, because as yet I had said nothing to the Jews or the priests or nobles or officials or any others who would be doing the work.

¹⁷Then I said to them, "You see the trouble we are in: Jerusalem lies in ruins, and its gates have been burned with fire. Come, let us rebuild the wall of Jerusalem, and we will no longer be in disgrace." ¹⁸I also told them about the gracious hand of my God upon me and what the king had said to me.

They replied, "Let us start rebuilding." So they began this good work.

¹⁹But when Sanballat the Horonite, Tobiah the Ammonite official and Geshem the Arab heard about it, they mocked and ridiculed us. "What is this you are doing?" they asked. "Are you rebelling against the king?"

²⁰I answered them by saying, "The God of heaven will give us success. We his servants will start rebuilding, but as for you, you have no share in Jerusalem or any claim or historic right to it."

Builders of the Wall

3 Eliashib the high priest and his fellow priests went to work and rebuilt the Sheep Gate. They dedicated it and set its doors in place, building as far as the Tower of the Hundred, which they dedicated, and as far as the Tower of Hananel. ²The men of Jericho built the adjoining section, and Zaccur son of Imri built next to them.

a 13 Or Serpent or Fig

THE SECRET OF YOUR SUCCESS

□ FRIDAY

Bruce and Peter are two very different guys with one thing in common. Both are obsessed with the prospect of success—Bruce on the athletic field, Peter in the classroom. They want to succeed so badly they can taste it. If Bruce can up his batting average and if Peter can maintain his 4.0 GPA, they'll probably both get scholarships. Each has this attitude, "Hey, this is everything to me. It's something I've worked my whole life for, and I'm not going to blow it now. Being successful means paying whatever price it takes to get to the top. If some things have to slide for a while, well then, that's just the way it's got to be."

Look It Up ••••

The Bruces and Peters of the world need to know what God's Word says about success.

"Do not let this Book of the Law depart from your mouth; meditate on it day and night, so that you may be careful to do everything written in it. Then you will be prosperous and successful" (Joshua 1:8).

God is telling Joshua, the young leader of the Israelites, the secret to true success. Here it is: Real success comes when God's children obey his Word!

Christians are not to forget God's commandments in order to achieve worldly success. That's idolatry! Rather, Christians are to focus on him, obey the principles in his Word and then work as hard as they can.

Think It Through ••••

Peter and Bruce have an element of the truth in their thinking: Success is usually the result of hard work toward a goal. (The Biblical term for that concept is faithfulness.) And yes, it's a good thing, even admirable, to work hard to be a good athlete or good student. But here's where Peter's and Bruce's thinking goes terribly wrong: Their success means more than God to them . Their idol can't be seen, smelled, tasted, touched or heard. But to God, it's as sinful as the golden calf Moses destroyed.

Work It Out ••••

In what areas are you tempted to pursue success more than God? If God has given you ability and granted you success in athletics, academics, business, making friends, the arts or any other area, stop right now and give him thanks.

And make sure you demonstrate that you are grateful to him by keeping your gifts and goals in proper perspective.

Nail It Down ••••

Read Nehemiah 2:20 for one man's perspective on success.

Turn to pages 190, 348 and 713 for other readings on idols.
Turn to page 486 for the weekend reading.

Topic
••••
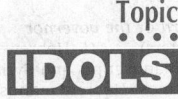

[3]The Fish Gate was rebuilt by the sons of Hassenaah. They laid its beams and put its doors and bolts and bars in place. [4]Meremoth son of Uriah, the son of Hakkoz, repaired the next section. Next to him Meshullam son of Berekiah, the son of Meshezabel, made repairs, and next to him Zadok son of Baana also made repairs. [5]The next section was repaired by the men of Tekoa, but their nobles would not put their shoulders to the work under their supervisors.[a]

[6]The Jeshanah[b] Gate was repaired by Joiada son of Paseah and Meshullam son of Besodeiah. They laid its beams and put its doors and bolts and bars in place. [7]Next to them, repairs were made by men from Gibeon and Mizpah — Melatiah of Gibeon and Jadon of Meronoth — places under the authority of the governor of Trans-Euphrates. [8]Uzziel son of Harhaiah, one of the goldsmiths, repaired the next section; and Hananiah, one of the perfume-makers, made repairs next to that. They restored[c] Jerusalem as far as the Broad Wall. [9]Rephaiah son of Hur, ruler of a half-district of Jerusalem, repaired the next section. [10]Adjoining this, Jedaiah son of Harumaph made repairs opposite his house, and Hattush son of Hashabneiah made repairs next to him. [11]Malkijah son of Harim and Hasshub son of Pahath-Moab repaired another section and the Tower of the Ovens. [12]Shallum son of Hallohesh, ruler of a half-district of Jerusalem, repaired the next section with the help of his daughters.

[13]The Valley Gate was repaired by Hanun and the residents of Zanoah. They rebuilt it and put its doors and bolts and bars in place. They also repaired five hundred yards[d] of the wall as far as the Dung Gate.

[14]The Dung Gate was repaired by Malkijah son of Recab, ruler of the district of Beth Hakkerem. He rebuilt it and put its doors and bolts and bars in place.

[15]The Fountain Gate was repaired by Shallun son of Col-Hozeh, ruler of the district of Mizpah. He rebuilt it, roofing it over and putting its doors and bolts and bars in place. He also repaired the wall of the Pool of Siloam,[e] by the King's Garden, as far as the steps going down from the City of David. [16]Beyond him, Nehemiah son of Azbuk, ruler of a half-district of Beth Zur, made repairs up to a point opposite the tombs[f] of David, as far as the artificial pool and the House of the Heroes.

[17]Next to him, the repairs were made by the Levites under Rehum son of Bani. Beside him, Hashabiah, ruler of half the district of Keilah, carried out repairs for his district. [18]Next to him, the repairs were made by their countrymen under Binnui[g] son of Henadad, ruler of the other half-district of Keilah. [19]Next to him, Ezer son of Jeshua, ruler of Mizpah, repaired another section, from a point facing the ascent to the armory as far as the angle. [20]Next to him, Baruch son of Zabbai zealously repaired another section, from the angle to the entrance of the house of Eliashib the high priest. [21]Next to him, Meremoth son of Uriah, the son of Hakkoz, repaired another section, from the entrance of Eliashib's house to the end of it.

[22]The repairs next to him were made by the priests from the surrounding region. [23]Beyond them, Benjamin and Hasshub made repairs in front of their house; and next to them, Azariah son of Maaseiah, the son of Ananiah, made repairs beside his house. [24]Next to him, Binnui son of Henadad repaired another section, from Azariah's house to the angle and the corner, [25]and Palal son of Uzai worked opposite the angle and the tower projecting from the upper palace near the court of the guard. Next to him, Pedaiah son of Parosh [26]and the temple servants living on the hill of Ophel made repairs up to a point opposite the Water Gate toward the east and the projecting tower. [27]Next to them, the men of Tekoa repaired another section, from the great projecting tower to the wall of Ophel.

[28]Above the Horse Gate, the priests made repairs, each in front of his own house. [29]Next to them, Zadok son of Immer made repairs opposite his house. Next to him, Shemaiah son of Shecaniah, the guard at the East Gate, made repairs. [30]Next to him, Hananiah son of Shelemiah, and Hanun, the sixth son of Zalaph, repaired another section. Next to them, Meshullam son of Berekiah made repairs opposite his living quarters. [31]Next to him, Malkijah, one of the goldsmiths, made repairs as far as the house of the temple servants and the merchants, opposite the Inspection Gate, and as far as

---

[a]5 Or their Lord or the governor　　[b]6 Or Old　　[c]8 Or They left out part of　　[d]13 Hebrew a thousand cubits (about 450 meters)　　[e]15 Hebrew Shelah, a variant of Shiloah, that is, Siloam　　[f]16 Hebrew; Septuagint, some Vulgate manuscripts and Syriac tomb　　[g]18 Two Hebrew manuscripts and Syriac (see also Septuagint and verse 24); most Hebrew manuscripts Bavvai

the room above the corner; ³²and between the room above the corner and the Sheep Gate the goldsmiths and merchants made repairs.

Opposition to the Rebuilding

4 When Sanballat heard that we were rebuilding the wall, he became angry and was greatly incensed. He ridiculed the Jews, ²and in the presence of his associates and the army of Samaria, he said, "What are those feeble Jews doing? Will they restore their wall? Will they offer sacrifices? Will they finish in a day? Can they bring the stones back to life from those heaps of rubble — burned as they are?"

³Tobiah the Ammonite, who was at his side, said, "What they are building — if even a fox climbed up on it, he would break down their wall of stones!"

⁴Hear us, O our God, for we are despised. Turn their insults back on their own heads. Give them over as plunder in a land of captivity. ⁵Do not cover up their guilt or blot out their sins from your sight, for they have thrown insults in the face of[a] the builders.

⁶So we rebuilt the wall till all of it reached half its height, for the people worked with all their heart.

⁷But when Sanballat, Tobiah, the Arabs, the Ammonites and the men of Ashdod heard that the repairs to Jerusalem's walls had gone ahead and that the gaps were being closed, they were very angry. ⁸They all plotted together to come and fight against Jerusalem and stir up trouble against it. ⁹But we prayed to our God and posted a guard day and night to meet this threat.

¹⁰Meanwhile, the people in Judah said, "The strength of the laborers is giving out, and there is so much rubble that we cannot rebuild the wall."

¹¹Also our enemies said, "Before they know it or see us, we will be right there among them and will kill them and put an end to the work."

¹²Then the Jews who lived near them came and told us ten times over, "Wherever you turn, they will attack us."

¹³Therefore I stationed some of the people behind the lowest points of the wall at the exposed places, posting them by families, with their swords, spears and bows. ¹⁴After I looked things over, I stood up and said to the nobles, the officials and the rest of the people, "Don't be afraid of them. Remember the Lord, who is great and awesome, and fight for your brothers, your sons and your daughters, your wives and your homes."

¹⁵When our enemies heard that we were aware of their plot and that God had frustrated it, we all returned to the wall, each to his own work.

¹⁶From that day on, half of my men did the work, while the other half were equipped with spears, shields, bows and armor. The officers posted themselves behind all the people of Judah ¹⁷who were building the wall. Those who carried materials did their work with one hand and held a weapon in the other, ¹⁸and each of the builders wore his sword at his side as he worked. But the man who sounded the trumpet stayed with me.

¹⁹Then I said to the nobles, the officials and the rest of the people, "The work is extensive and spread out, and we are widely separated from each other along the wall. ²⁰Wherever you hear the sound of the trumpet, join us there. Our God will fight for us!"

²¹So we continued the work with half the men holding spears, from the first light of dawn till the stars came out. ²²At that time I also said to the people, "Have every man and his helper stay inside Jerusalem at night, so they can serve us as guards by night and workmen by day." ²³Neither I nor my brothers nor my men nor the guards with me took off our clothes; each had his weapon, even when he went for water.[b]

Nehemiah Helps the Poor

5 Now the men and their wives raised a great outcry against their Jewish brothers. ²Some were saying, "We and our sons and daughters are numerous; in order for us to eat and stay alive, we must get grain."

³Others were saying, "We are mortgaging our fields, our vineyards and our homes to get grain during the famine."

⁴Still others were saying, "We have had to borrow money to pay the king's tax on our fields and vineyards. ⁵Although we are of the same flesh and blood as our countrymen and though our sons are as good as theirs, yet we have to subject our sons and daughters to slavery. Some of our daughters have already been enslaved, but we are powerless, because our fields and our vineyards belong to others."

⁶When I heard their outcry and these charges, I was very angry. ⁷I pondered them

DON'T LET OTHERS MAKE YOU GIVE UP

Work It Out
••••

"You can't. . . ." "You'll never. . . ." "You're better off not even trying. . . ." Those are the words of discouragers.

In the past year, have you had anyone say these words, or words like them, to you? Maybe you were going to try out for the tennis team. Or go out for debate. Or maybe you were going to audition for the choir. Usually, when you're trying something new, there will be someone around with words of *discouragement* rather than *encouragement*.

Well, don't let the discouragers cause you to give up. Try out for the team. Join the debate club. Audition for the choir. If you don't make the team or if you're not the world's greatest debater or vocalist, hey, at least you tried. And in your trying you made a worthwhile contribution.

Nail It Down
••••

Read about a prime discourager, Sanballat, in Nehemiah 4.

Think It Through
••••

God has given each of you a gift, an ability, that no one else has exactly like you do. And he wants—no, he *expects*—you to use it. Don't let others force you into their ideas of what you should or shouldn't be interested in doing. While there's nothing wrong with wanting to be with your friends, you shouldn't try out for the choir just because your best friend is trying out. Especially if you can't sing a note, but you can talk circles around everyone else. You need to check out the debate team.

The whole point is to follow your own course in life. Don't let the words of discouragement stop you. You'll be most content in life if you're where God wants you. And you'll enjoy life best if you're using the gifts God has given you.

Nail It Down
••••

Reread the story of Sanballat in Nehemiah 4. For further insight read Psalm 142.

Turn to pages 1056, 1087, 1248 and 1367 for other readings on obstacles.
Turn to page 488 for Monday's reading.

Topic
••••

OBSTACLES

in my mind and then accused the nobles and officials. I told them, "You are exacting usury from your own countrymen!" So I called together a large meeting to deal with them [8]and said: "As far as possible, we have bought back our Jewish brothers who were sold to the Gentiles. Now you are selling your brothers, only for them to be sold back to us!" They kept quiet, because they could find nothing to say.

[9]So I continued, "What you are doing is not right. Shouldn't you walk in the fear of our God to avoid the reproach of our Gentile enemies? [10]I and my brothers and my men are also lending the people money and grain. But let the exacting of usury stop! [11]Give back to them immediately their fields, vineyards, olive groves and houses, and also the usury you are charging them — the hundredth part of the money, grain, new wine and oil."

[12]"We will give it back," they said. "And we will not demand anything more from them. We will do as you say."

Then I summoned the priests and made the nobles and officials take an oath to do what they had promised. [13]I also shook out the folds of my robe and said, "In this way may God shake out of his house and possessions every man who does not keep this promise. So may such a man be shaken out and emptied!"

At this the whole assembly said, "Amen," and praised the LORD. And the people did as they had promised.

[14]Moreover, from the twentieth year of King Artaxerxes, when I was appointed to be their governor in the land of Judah, until his thirty-second year — twelve years — neither I nor my brothers ate the food allotted to the governor. [15]But the earlier governors — those preceding me — placed a heavy burden on the people and took forty shekels[a] of silver from them in addition to food and wine. Their assistants also lorded it over the people. But out of reverence for God I did not act like that. [16]Instead, I devoted myself to the work on this wall. All my men were assembled there for the work; we[b] did not acquire any land.

[17]Furthermore, a hundred and fifty Jews and officials ate at my table, as well as those who came to us from the surrounding nations. [18]Each day one ox, six choice sheep and some poultry were prepared for me, and every ten days an abundant supply of wine of all kinds. In spite of all this, I never demanded the food allotted to the governor, because the demands were heavy on these people.

[19]Remember me with favor, O my God, for all I have done for these people.

Further Opposition to the Rebuilding

6 When word came to Sanballat, Tobiah, Geshem the Arab and the rest of our enemies that I had rebuilt the wall and not a gap was left in it — though up to that time I had not set the doors in the gates — [2]Sanballat and Geshem sent me this message: "Come, let us meet together in one of the villages[c] on the plain of Ono."

But they were scheming to harm me; [3]so I sent messengers to them with this reply: "I am carrying on a great project and cannot go down. Why should the work stop while I leave it and go down to you?" [4]Four times they sent me the same message, and each time I gave them the same answer.

[5]Then, the fifth time, Sanballat sent his aide to me with the same message, and in his hand was an unsealed letter [6]in which was written:

"It is reported among the nations — and Geshem[d] says it is true — that you and the Jews are plotting to revolt, and therefore you are building the wall. Moreover, according to these reports you are about to become their king [7]and have even appointed prophets to make this proclamation about you in Jerusalem: 'There is a king in Judah!' Now this report will get back to the king; so come, let us confer together."

[8]I sent him this reply: "Nothing like what you are saying is happening; you are just making it up out of your head."

[9]They were all trying to frighten us, thinking, "Their hands will get too weak for the work, and it will not be completed."

⌊But I prayed,⌋ "Now strengthen my hands."

[10]One day I went to the house of Shemaiah son of Delaiah, the son of Mehetabel, who was shut in at his home. He said, "Let us meet in the house of God, inside the temple, and let us close the temple doors, because men are coming to kill you — by night they are coming to kill you."

[11]But I said, "Should a man like me run away? Or should one like me go into the

---

[a]15 That is, about 1 pound (about 0.5 kilogram)   [b]16 Most Hebrew manuscripts; some Hebrew manuscripts, Septuagint, Vulgate and Syriac *I*   [c]2 Or *in Kephirim*   [d]6 Hebrew *Gashmu*, a variant of *Geshem*

APPEARING TO BE BAD?

The following are three very questionable situations:

1. Sixteen-year-old Randy is seen hanging out in front of a local liquor store.

2. Carol and her boyfriend Taylor, both sophomores at college, are taking a weekend trip with another couple to a nearby resort. The two guys and two girls are staying in the same motel room.

3. Kyle is seen giving money to Billy on the same day that everyone knows Billy has been selling copies of Mrs. Schenk's English test.

Look It Up
• • • •

One of the recurring themes of the New Testament is that a Christian must be extremely careful to avoid the appearance of wrongdoing and to strive for a good reputation.

"But among you there must not be even a hint of sexual immorality, or of any kind of impurity, or of greed, because these are improper for God's holy people" (Ephesians 5:3).

"Avoid every kind of evil" (1 Thessalonians 5:22).

"He must also have a good reputation with outsiders, so that he will not fall into disgrace and into the devil's trap" (1 Timothy 3:7).

Think It Through
• • • •

Going back to the examples cited, what behaviors do those situations suggest? Do we know that Randy is buying booze? Or that Carol and Taylor are having sex? Or that Kyle is purchasing a hot test? Maybe not. But at the same time their behavior does raise serious questions.

Work It Out
• • • •

Sit down with a close Christian friend and discuss the stories of Randy, Carol and Taylor, and Kyle. Assume that in each of the situations nothing sinful is taking place. Now, can you come up with a better plan in each case?

Take a few moments to examine your own lives. Are you making ambiguous remarks or doing questionable things or going to suspicious places? Determine to be careful about every activity that might be misunderstood.

Hold each other accountable in the days ahead. A little carelessness can cause a lot of heartache!

Nail It Down
• • • •

In Nehemiah 5:1–11 check out Nehemiah's concern with appearances.

Turn to pages 560, 1300 and 1358 for other readings on appearance.
Turn to page 502 for Tuesday's reading.

Topic
• • • •

temple to save his life? I will not go!" [12]I realized that God had not sent him, but that he had prophesied against me because Tobiah and Sanballat had hired him. [13]He had been hired to intimidate me so that I would commit a sin by doing this, and then they would give me a bad name to discredit me.

[14]Remember Tobiah and Sanballat, O my God, because of what they have done; remember also the prophetess Noadiah and the rest of the prophets who have been trying to intimidate me.

The Completion of the Wall

[15]So the wall was completed on the twenty-fifth of Elul, in fifty-two days. [16]When all our enemies heard about this, all the surrounding nations were afraid and lost their self-confidence, because they realized that this work had been done with the help of our God.

[17]Also, in those days the nobles of Judah were sending many letters to Tobiah, and replies from Tobiah kept coming to them. [18]For many in Judah were under oath to him, since he was son-in-law to Shecaniah son of Arah, and his son Jehohanan had married the daughter of Meshullam son of Berekiah. [19]Moreover, they kept reporting to me his good deeds and then telling him what I said. And Tobiah sent letters to intimidate me.

7 After the wall had been rebuilt and I had set the doors in place, the gatekeepers and the singers and the Levites were appointed. [2]I put in charge of Jerusalem my brother Hanani, along with[a] Hananiah the commander of the citadel, because he was a man of integrity and feared God more than most men do. [3]I said to them, "The gates of Jerusalem are not to be opened until the sun is hot. While the gatekeepers are still on duty, have them shut the doors and bar them. Also appoint residents of Jerusalem as guards, some at their posts and some near their own houses."

The List of the Exiles Who Returned

[4]Now the city was large and spacious, but there were few people in it, and the houses had not yet been rebuilt. [5]So my God put it into my heart to assemble the nobles, the officials and the common people for registration by families. I found the genealogical record of those who had been the first to return. This is what I found written there:

[6]These are the people of the province who came up from the captivity of the exiles whom Nebuchadnezzar king of Babylon had taken captive (they returned to Jerusalem and Judah, each to his own town, [7]in company with Zerubbabel, Jeshua, Nehemiah, Azariah, Raamiah, Nahamani, Mordecai, Bilshan, Mispereth, Bigvai, Nehum and Baanah):

The list of the men of Israel:

[8]the descendants of Parosh	2,172
[9]of Shephatiah	372
[10]of Arah	652
[11]of Pahath-Moab (through the line of Jeshua and Joab)	2,818
[12]of Elam	1,254
[13]of Zattu	845
[14]of Zaccai	760
[15]of Binnui	648
[16]of Bebai	628
[17]of Azgad	2,322
[18]of Adonikam	667
[19]of Bigvai	2,067
[20]of Adin	655
[21]of Ater (through Hezekiah)	98
[22]of Hashum	328
[23]of Bezai	324
[24]of Hariph	112
[25]of Gibeon	95
[26]the men of Bethlehem and Netophah	188
[27]of Anathoth	128
[28]of Beth Azmaveth	42
[29]of Kiriath Jearim, Kephirah and Beeroth	743
[30]of Ramah and Geba	621
[31]of Micmash	122
[32]of Bethel and Ai	123
[33]of the other Nebo	52
[34]of the other Elam	1,254
[35]of Harim	320
[36]of Jericho	345
[37]of Lod, Hadid and Ono	721
[38]of Senaah	3,930

[39]The priests:

the descendants of Jedaiah (through the family of Jeshua)	973
[40]of Immer	1,052
[41]of Pashhur	1,247
[42]of Harim	1,017

[43]The Levites:

the descendants of Jeshua (through Kadmiel through the line of Hodaviah) 74

44The singers:

the descendants of Asaph 148

45The gatekeepers:

the descendants of Shallum, Ater, Talmon, Akkub, Hatita and Shobai 138

46The temple servants:

the descendants of Ziha, Hasupha, Tabbaoth, **47**Keros, Sia, Padon, **48**Lebana, Hagaba, Shalmai, **49**Hanan, Giddel, Gahar, **50**Reaiah, Rezin, Nekoda, **51**Gazzam, Uzza, Paseah, **52**Besai, Meunim, Nephussim, **53**Bakbuk, Hakupha, Harhur, **54**Bazluth, Mehida, Harsha, **55**Barkos, Sisera, Temah, **56**Neziah and Hatipha

57The descendants of the servants of Solomon:

the descendants of Sotai, Sophereth, Perida, **58**Jaala, Darkon, Giddel, **59**Shephatiah, Hattil, Pokereth-Hazzebaim and Amon

60The temple servants and the descendants of the servants of Solomon 392

61The following came up from the towns of Tel Melah, Tel Harsha, Kerub, Addon and Immer, but they could not show that their families were descended from Israel:

62the descendants of Delaiah, Tobiah and Nekoda 642

63And from among the priests:

the descendants of Hobaiah, Hakkoz and Barzillai (a man who had married a daughter of Barzillai the Gileadite and was called by that name).

64These searched for their family records, but they could not find them and so were excluded from the priesthood as unclean. **65**The governor, therefore, ordered them not to eat any of the most sacred food until there should be a priest ministering with the Urim and Thummim.

66The whole company numbered 42,360, **67**besides their 7,337 menservants and maidservants; and they also had 245 men and women singers. **68**There were 736 horses, 245 mules,[a] **69**435 camels and 6,720 donkeys.

70Some of the heads of the families contributed to the work. The governor gave to the treasury 1,000 drachmas[b] of gold, 50 bowls and 530 garments for priests. **71**Some of the heads of the families gave to the treasury for the work 20,000 drachmas[c] of gold and 2,200 minas[d] of silver. **72**The total given by the rest of the people was 20,000 drachmas of gold, 2,000 minas[e] of silver and 67 garments for priests.

73The priests, the Levites, the gatekeepers, the singers and the temple servants, along with certain of the people and the rest of the Israelites, settled in their own towns.

Ezra Reads the Law

When the seventh month came and the Israelites had settled in their towns, **1**all the people assembled as one man in the square before the Water Gate. They told Ezra the scribe to bring out the Book of the Law of Moses, which the Lord had commanded for Israel.

2So on the first day of the seventh month Ezra the priest brought the Law before the assembly, which was made up of men and women and all who were able to understand. **3**He read it aloud from daybreak till noon as he faced the square before the Water Gate in the presence of the men, women and others who could understand. And all the people listened attentively to the Book of the Law.

4Ezra the scribe stood on a high wooden platform built for the occasion. Beside him on his right stood Mattithiah, Shema, Anaiah, Uriah, Hilkiah and Maaseiah; and on his left were Pedaiah, Mishael, Malkijah, Hashum, Hashbaddanah, Zechariah and Meshullam.

---

a68 Some Hebrew manuscripts (see also Ezra 2:66); most Hebrew manuscripts do not have this verse.
b70 That is, about 19 pounds (about 8.5 kilograms) *c71* That is, about 375 pounds (about 170 kilograms); also in verse 72 *d71* That is, about 1 1/3 tons (about 1.2 metric tons) *e72* That is, about 1 1/4 tons (about 1.1 metric tons)

[5]Ezra opened the book. All the people could see him because he was standing above them; and as he opened it, the people all stood up. [6]Ezra praised the LORD, the great God; and all the people lifted their hands and responded, "Amen! Amen!" Then they bowed down and worshiped the LORD with their faces to the ground.

[7]The Levites—Jeshua, Bani, Sherebiah, Jamin, Akkub, Shabbethai, Hodiah, Maaseiah, Kelita, Azariah, Jozabad, Hanan and Pelaiah—instructed the people in the Law while the people were standing there. [8]They read from the Book of the Law of God, making it clear[a] and giving the meaning so that the people could understand what was being read.

[9]Then Nehemiah the governor, Ezra the priest and scribe, and the Levites who were instructing the people said to them all, "This day is sacred to the LORD your God. Do not mourn or weep." For all the people had been weeping as they listened to the words of the Law.

[10]Nehemiah said, "Go and enjoy choice food and sweet drinks, and send some to those who have nothing prepared. This day is sacred to our Lord. Do not grieve, for the joy of the LORD is your strength."

[11]The Levites calmed all the people, saying, "Be still, for this is a sacred day. Do not grieve."

[12]Then all the people went away to eat and drink, to send portions of food and to celebrate with great joy, because they now understood the words that had been made known to them.

[13]On the second day of the month, the heads of all the families, along with the priests and the Levites, gathered around Ezra the scribe to give attention to the words of the Law. [14]They found written in the Law, which the LORD had commanded through Moses, that the Israelites were to live in booths during the feast of the seventh month [15]and that they should proclaim this word and spread it throughout their towns and in Jerusalem: "Go out into the hill country and bring back branches from olive and wild olive trees, and from myrtles, palms and shade trees, to make booths"—as it is written.[b]

[16]So the people went out and brought back branches and built themselves booths on their own roofs, in their courtyards, in the courts of the house of God and in the square by the Water Gate and the one by the Gate of Ephraim. [17]The whole company that had returned from exile built booths and lived in them. From the days of Joshua son of Nun until that day, the Israelites had not celebrated it like this. And their joy was very great.

[18]Day after day, from the first day to the last, Ezra read from the Book of the Law of God. They celebrated the feast for seven days, and on the eighth day, in accordance with the regulation, there was an assembly.

The Israelites Confess Their Sins

9 On the twenty-fourth day of the same month, the Israelites gathered together, fasting and wearing sackcloth and having dust on their heads. [2]Those of Israelite descent had separated themselves from all foreigners. They stood in their places and confessed their sins and the wickedness of their fathers. [3]They stood where they were and read from the Book of the Law of the LORD their God for a quarter of the day, and spent another quarter in confession and in worshiping the LORD their God. [4]Standing on the stairs were the Levites—Jeshua, Bani, Kadmiel, Shebaniah, Bunni, Sherebiah, Bani and Kenani—who called with loud voices to the LORD their God. [5]And the Levites—Jeshua, Kadmiel, Bani, Hashabneiah, Sherebiah, Hodiah, Shebaniah and Pethahiah—said: "Stand up and praise the LORD your God, who is from everlasting to everlasting.[c]"

"Blessed be your glorious name, and may it be exalted above all blessing and praise. [6]You alone are the LORD. You made the heavens, even the highest heavens, and all their starry host, the earth and all that is on it, the seas and all that is in them. You give life to everything, and the multitudes of heaven worship you.

[7]"You are the LORD God, who chose Abram and brought him out of Ur of the Chaldeans and named him Abraham. [8]You found his heart faithful to you, and you made a covenant with him to give to his descendants the land of the Canaanites, Hittites, Amorites, Perizzites, Jebusites and Girgashites. You have kept your promise because you are righteous.

[9]"You saw the suffering of our forefa-

---

[a]8 Or God, translating it   [b]15 See Lev. 23:37-40.   [c]5 Or God for ever and ever

thers in Egypt; you heard their cry at the Red Sea.[a] **10**You sent miraculous signs and wonders against Pharaoh, against all his officials and all the people of his land, for you knew how arrogantly the Egyptians treated them. You made a name for yourself, which remains to this day. **11**You divided the sea before them, so that they passed through it on dry ground, but you hurled their pursuers into the depths, like a stone into mighty waters. **12**By day you led them with a pillar of cloud, and by night with a pillar of fire to give them light on the way they were to take.

13"You came down on Mount Sinai; you spoke to them from heaven. You gave them regulations and laws that are just and right, and decrees and commands that are good. **14**You made known to them your holy Sabbath and gave them commands, decrees and laws through your servant Moses. **15**In their hunger you gave them bread from heaven and in their thirst you brought them water from the rock; you told them to go in and take possession of the land you had sworn with uplifted hand to give them.

16"But they, our forefathers, became arrogant and stiff-necked, and did not obey your commands. **17**They refused to listen and failed to remember the miracles you performed among them. They became stiff-necked and in their rebellion appointed a leader in order to return to their slavery. But you are a forgiving God, gracious and compassionate, slow to anger and abounding in love. Therefore you did not desert them, **18**even when they cast for themselves an image of a calf and said, 'This is your god, who brought you up out of Egypt,' or when they committed awful blasphemies.

19"Because of your great compassion you did not abandon them in the desert. By day the pillar of cloud did not cease to guide them on their path, nor the pillar of fire by night to shine on the way they were to take. **20**You gave your good Spirit to instruct them. You did not withhold your manna from their mouths, and you gave them water for their thirst. **21**For forty years you sustained them in the desert; they lacked nothing, their clothes did not wear out nor did their feet become swollen.

22"You gave them kingdoms and nations, allotting to them even the remotest frontiers. They took over the country of Sihon[b] king of Heshbon and the country of Og king of Bashan. **23**You made their sons as numerous as the stars in the sky, and you brought them into the land that you told their fathers to enter and possess. **24**Their sons went in and took possession of the land. You subdued before them the Canaanites, who lived in the land; you handed the Canaanites over to them, along with their kings and the peoples of the land, to deal with them as they pleased. **25**They captured fortified cities and fertile land; they took possession of houses filled with all kinds of good things, wells already dug, vineyards, olive groves and fruit trees in abundance. They ate to the full and were well-nourished; they reveled in your great goodness.

26"But they were disobedient and rebelled against you; they put your law behind their backs. They killed your prophets, who had admonished them in order to turn them back to you; they committed awful blasphemies. **27**So you handed them over to their enemies, who oppressed them. But when they were oppressed they cried out to you. From heaven you heard them, and in your great compassion you gave them deliverers, who rescued them from the hand of their enemies.

28"But as soon as they were at rest, they again did what was evil in your sight. Then you abandoned them to the hand of their enemies so that they ruled over them. And when they cried out to you again, you heard from heaven, and in your compassion you delivered them time after time.

29"You warned them to return to your law, but they became arrogant and disobeyed your commands. They sinned against your ordinances, by which a man will live if he obeys them. Stubbornly they turned their backs on you, became stiff-necked and refused to listen. **30**For many years you were patient with them. By your Spirit you admonished them through your prophets. Yet

---

[a]9 Hebrew *Yam Suph*; that is, Sea of Reeds   [b]22 One Hebrew manuscript and Septuagint; most Hebrew manuscripts *Sihon, that is, the country of the*

they paid no attention, so you handed them over to the neighboring peoples. **31**But in your great mercy you did not put an end to them or abandon them, for you are a gracious and merciful God.

32"Now therefore, O our God, the great, mighty and awesome God, who keeps his covenant of love, do not let all this hardship seem trifling in your eyes—the hardship that has come upon us, upon our kings and leaders, upon our priests and prophets, upon our fathers and all your people, from the days of the kings of Assyria until today. **33**In all that has happened to us, you have been just; you have acted faithfully, while we did wrong. **34**Our kings, our leaders, our priests and our fathers did not follow your law; they did not pay attention to your commands or the warnings you gave them. **35**Even while they were in their kingdom, enjoying your great goodness to them in the spacious and fertile land you gave them, they did not serve you or turn from their evil ways.

36"But see, we are slaves today, slaves in the land you gave our forefathers so they could eat its fruit and the other good things it produces. **37**Because of our sins, its abundant harvest goes to the kings you have placed over us. They rule over our bodies and our cattle as they please. We are in great distress.

The Agreement of the People

38"In view of all this, we are making a binding agreement, putting it in writing, and our leaders, our Levites and our priests are affixing their seals to it."

10 Those who sealed it were:

Nehemiah the governor, the son of Hacaliah.

Zedekiah, **2**Seraiah, Azariah, Jeremiah, **3**Pashhur, Amariah, Malkijah, **4**Hattush, Shebaniah, Malluch, **5**Harim, Meremoth, Obadiah, **6**Daniel, Ginnethon, Baruch, **7**Meshullam, Abijah, Mijamin, **8**Maaziah, Bilgai and Shemaiah.

These were the priests.

9The Levites:

Jeshua son of Azaniah, Binnui of the sons of Henadad, Kadmiel,

10and their associates: Shebaniah, Hodiah, Kelita, Pelaiah, Hanan, **11**Mica, Rehob, Hashabiah, **12**Zaccur, Sherebiah, Shebaniah, **13**Hodiah, Bani and Beninu.

14The leaders of the people:

Parosh, Pahath-Moab, Elam, Zattu, Bani, **15**Bunni, Azgad, Bebai, **16**Adonijah, Bigvai, Adin, **17**Ater, Hezekiah, Azzur, **18**Hodiah, Hashum, Bezai, **19**Hariph, Anathoth, Nebai, **20**Magpiash, Meshullam, Hezir, **21**Meshezabel, Zadok, Jaddua, **22**Pelatiah, Hanan, Anaiah, **23**Hoshea, Hananiah, Hasshub, **24**Hallohesh, Pilha, Shobek, **25**Rehum, Hashabnah, Maaseiah, **26**Ahiah, Hanan, Anan, **27**Malluch, Harim and Baanah.

28"The rest of the people—priests, Levites, gatekeepers, singers, temple servants and all who separated themselves from the neighboring peoples for the sake of the Law of God, together with their wives and all their sons and daughters who are able to understand— **29**all these now join their brothers the nobles, and bind themselves with a curse and an oath to follow the Law of God given through Moses the servant of God and to obey carefully all the commands, regulations and decrees of the LORD our Lord.

30"We promise not to give our daughters in marriage to the peoples around us or take their daughters for our sons.

31"When the neighboring peoples bring merchandise or grain to sell on the Sabbath, we will not buy from them on the Sabbath or on any holy day. Every seventh year we will forgo working the land and will cancel all debts.

32"We assume the responsibility for carrying out the commands to give a third of a shekel[a] each year for the service of the house of our God: **33**for the bread set out on the table; for the regular grain offerings and burnt offerings; for the offerings on the Sabbaths, New Moon festivals and appointed feasts; for the holy offerings; for sin offerings to

a32 That is, about 1/8 ounce (about 4 grams)

make atonement for Israel; and for all the duties of the house of our God.

34"We — the priests, the Levites and the people — have cast lots to determine when each of our families is to bring to the house of our God at set times each year a contribution of wood to burn on the altar of the LORD our God, as it is written in the Law.

35"We also assume responsibility for bringing to the house of the LORD each year the firstfruits of our crops and of every fruit tree.

36"As it is also written in the Law, we will bring the firstborn of our sons and of our cattle, of our herds and of our flocks to the house of our God, to the priests ministering there.

37"Moreover, we will bring to the storerooms of the house of our God, to the priests, the first of our ground meal, of our grain, offerings, of the fruit of all our trees and of our new wine and oil. And we will bring a tithe of our crops to the Levites, for it is the Levites who collect the tithes in all the towns where we work. **38**A priest descended from Aaron is to accompany the Levites when they receive the tithes, and the Levites are to bring a tenth of the tithes up to the house of our God, to the storerooms of the treasury. **39**The people of Israel, including the Levites, are to bring their contributions of grain, new wine and oil to the storerooms where the articles for the sanctuary are kept and where the ministering priests, the gatekeepers and the singers stay.

"We will not neglect the house of our God."

The New Residents of Jerusalem

11 Now the leaders of the people settled in Jerusalem, and the rest of the people cast lots to bring one out of every ten to live in Jerusalem, the holy city, while the remaining nine were to stay in their own towns. **2**The people commended all the men who volunteered to live in Jerusalem.

3These are the provincial leaders who settled in Jerusalem (now some Israelites, priests, Levites, temple servants and descendants of Solomon's servants lived in the towns of Judah, each on his own property in the various towns, **4**while other people from both Judah and Benjamin lived in Jerusalem):

From the descendants of Judah:

Athaiah son of Uzziah, the son of Zechariah, the son of Amariah, the son of Shephatiah, the son of Mahalalel, a descendant of Perez; **5**and Maaseiah son of Baruch, the son of Col-Hozeh, the son of Hazaiah, the son of Adaiah, the son of Joiarib, the son of Zechariah, a descendant of Shelah. **6**The descendants of Perez who lived in Jerusalem totaled 468 able men.

7From the descendants of Benjamin:

Sallu son of Meshullam, the son of Joed, the son of Pedaiah, the son of Kolaiah, the son of Maaseiah, the son of Ithiel, the son of Jeshaiah, **8**and his followers, Gabbai and Sallai — 928 men. **9**Joel son of Zicri was their chief officer, and Judah son of Hassenuah was over the Second District of the city.

10From the priests:

Jedaiah; the son of Joiarib; Jakin; **11**Seraiah son of Hilkiah, the son of Meshullam, the son of Zadok, the son of Meraioth, the son of Ahitub, supervisor in the house of God, **12**and their associates, who carried on work for the temple — 822 men; Adaiah son of Jeroham, the son of Pelaliah, the son of Amzi, the son of Zechariah, the son of Pashhur, the son of Malkijah, **13**and his associates, who were heads of families — 242 men; Amashsai son of Azarel, the son of Ahzai, the son of Meshillemoth, the son of Immer, **14**and his[a] associates, who were able men — 128. Their chief officer was Zabdiel son of Haggedolim.

15From the Levites:

Shemaiah son of Hasshub, the son of Azrikam, the son of Hashabiah, the son of Bunni; **16**Shabbethai and Jozabad, two of the heads of the Levites, who had charge of the outside work of the house of God; **17**Mattaniah son of Mica, the son of Zabdi, the son of Asaph, the director who led in thanksgiving and prayer; Bakbukiah, second among his associates; and Abda son of Shammua, the son of Galal, the son of Jeduthun. **18**The Levites in the holy city totaled 284.

19The gatekeepers:

---

a 14 Most Septuagint manuscripts; Hebrew *their*

Akkub, Talmon and their associates, who kept watch at the gates — 172 men.

20The rest of the Israelites, with the priests and Levites, were in all the towns of Judah, each on his ancestral property.

21The temple servants lived on the hill of Ophel, and Ziha and Gishpa were in charge of them.

22The chief officer of the Levites in Jerusalem was Uzzi son of Bani, the son of Hashabiah, the son of Mattaniah, the son of Mica. Uzzi was one of Asaph's descendants, who were the singers responsible for the service of the house of God. **23**The singers were under the king's orders, which regulated their daily activity.

24Pethahiah son of Meshezabel, one of the descendants of Zerah son of Judah, was the king's agent in all affairs relating to the people.

25As for the villages with their fields, some of the people of Judah lived in Kiriath Arba and its surrounding settlements, in Dibon and its settlements, in Jekabzeel and its villages, **26**in Jeshua, in Moladah, in Beth Pelet, **27**in Hazar Shual, in Beersheba and its settlements, **28**in Ziklag, in Meconah and its settlements, **29**in En Rimmon, in Zorah, in Jarmuth, **30**Zanoah, Adullam and their villages, in Lachish and its fields, and in Azekah and its settlements. So they were living all the way from Beersheba to the Valley of Hinnom.

31The descendants of the Benjamites from Geba lived in Micmash, Aija, Bethel and its settlements, **32**in Anathoth, Nob and Ananiah, **33**in Hazor, Ramah and Gittaim, **34**in Hadid, Zeboim and Neballat, **35**in Lod and Ono, and in the Valley of the Craftsmen.

36Some of the divisions of the Levites of Judah settled in Benjamin.

Priests and Levites

12 These were the priests and Levites who returned with Zerubbabel son of Shealtiel and with Jeshua:

Seraiah, Jeremiah, Ezra,

2Amariah, Malluch, Hattush,

3Shecaniah, Rehum, Meremoth,

4Iddo, Ginnethon,^{a} Abijah,

5Mijamin,^{b} Moadiah, Bilgah,

6Shemaiah, Joiarib, Jedaiah,

7Sallu, Amok, Hilkiah and Jedaiah.

These were the leaders of the priests and their associates in the days of Jeshua.

8The Levites were Jeshua, Binnui, Kadmiel, Sherebiah, Judah, and also Mattaniah, who, together with his associates, was in charge of the songs of thanksgiving. **9**Bakbukiah and Unni, their associates, stood opposite them in the services.

10Jeshua was the father of Joiakim, Joiakim the father of Eliashib, Eliashib the father of Joiada, **11**Joiada the father of Jonathan, and Jonathan the father of Jaddua.

12In the days of Joiakim, these were the heads of the priestly families:

of Seraiah's family, Meraiah;

of Jeremiah's, Hananiah;

13of Ezra's, Meshullam;

of Amariah's, Jehohanan;

14of Malluch's, Jonathan;

of Shecaniah's,^{c} Joseph;

15of Harim's, Adna;

of Meremoth's,^{d} Helkai;

16of Iddo's, Zechariah;

of Ginnethon's, Meshullam;

17of Abijah's, Zicri;

of Miniamin's and of Moadiah's, Piltai;

18of Bilgah's, Shammua;

of Shemaiah's, Jehonathan;

19of Joiarib's, Mattenai;

of Jedaiah's, Uzzi;

20of Sallu's, Kallai;

of Amok's, Eber;

21of Hilkiah's, Hashabiah;

of Jedaiah's, Nethanel.

22The family heads of the Levites in the days of Eliashib, Joiada, Johanan and Jaddua, as well as those of the priests, were recorded in the reign of Darius the Persian. **23**The family heads among the descendants of Levi up to the time of Johanan son of Eliashib were recorded in the book of the annals. **24**And the leaders of the Levites were Hashabiah, Sherebiah, Jeshua son of Kadmiel, and their associates, who stood opposite them to give praise and thanksgiving, one section responding to the other, as prescribed by David the man of God.

25Mattaniah, Bakbukiah, Obadiah, Meshullam, Talmon and Akkub were gatekeepers who guarded the storerooms at the gates. **26**They served in the days of Joiakim son of Jeshua, the son of Jozadak, and in the days of Nehemiah the governor and of Ezra the priest and scribe.

---

^{a}4 Many Hebrew manuscripts and Vulgate (see also Neh. 12:16); most Hebrew manuscripts *Ginnethoi* ^{b}5 A variant of *Miniamin* ^{c}14 Very many Hebrew manuscripts, some Septuagint manuscripts and Syriac (see also Neh. 12:3); most Hebrew manuscripts *Shebaniah's* ^{d}15 Some Septuagint manuscripts (see also Neh. 12:3); Hebrew *Meraioth's*

Dedication of the Wall of Jerusalem

27At the dedication of the wall of Jerusalem, the Levites were sought out from where they lived and were brought to Jerusalem to celebrate joyfully the dedication with songs of thanksgiving and with the music of cymbals, harps and lyres. **28**The singers also were brought together from the region around Jerusalem — from the villages of the Netophathites, **29**from Beth Gilgal, and from the area of Geba and Azmaveth, for the singers had built villages for themselves around Jerusalem. **30**When the priests and Levites had purified themselves ceremonially, they purified the people, the gates and the wall.

31I had the leaders of Judah go up on top*a* of the wall. I also assigned two large choirs to give thanks. One was to proceed on top*b* of the wall to the right, toward the Dung Gate. **32**Hoshaiah and half the leaders of Judah followed them, **33**along with Azariah, Ezra, Meshullam, **34**Judah, Benjamin, Shemaiah, Jeremiah, **35**as well as some priests with trumpets, and also Zechariah son of Jonathan, the son of Shemaiah, the son of Mattaniah, the son of Micaiah, the son of Zaccur, the son of Asaph, **36**and his associates — Shemaiah, Azarel, Milalai, Gilalai, Maai, Nethanel, Judah and Hanani — with musical instruments ⌊prescribed by⌋ David the man of God. Ezra the scribe led the procession. **37**At the Fountain Gate they continued directly up the steps of the City of David on the ascent to the wall and passed above the house of David to the Water Gate on the east.

38The second choir proceeded in the opposite direction. I followed them on top*c* of the wall, together with half the people — past the Tower of the Ovens to the Broad Wall, **39**over the Gate of Ephraim, the Jeshanah*d* Gate, the Fish Gate, the Tower of Hananel and the Tower of the Hundred, as far as the Sheep Gate. At the Gate of the Guard they stopped.

40The two choirs that gave thanks then took their places in the house of God; so did I, together with half the officials, **41**as well as the priests — Eliakim, Maaseiah, Miniamin, Micaiah, Elioenai, Zechariah and Hananiah with their trumpets — **42**and also Maaseiah, Shemaiah, Eleazar, Uzzi, Jehohanan, Malkijah, Elam and Ezer. The choirs sang under the direction of Jezrahiah. **43**And on that day they offered great sacrifices, rejoicing because God had given them great joy. The women and children also rejoiced. The sound of rejoicing in Jerusalem could be heard far away.

44At that time men were appointed to be in charge of the storerooms for the contributions, firstfruits and tithes. From the fields around the towns they were to bring into the storerooms the portions required by the Law for the priests and the Levites, for Judah was pleased with the ministering priests and Levites. **45**They performed the service of their God and the service of purification, as did also the singers and gatekeepers, according to the commands of David and his son Solomon. **46**For long ago, in the days of David and Asaph, there had been directors for the singers and for the songs of praise and thanksgiving to God. **47**So in the days of Zerubbabel and of Nehemiah, all Israel contributed the daily portions for the singers and gatekeepers. They also set aside the portion for the other Levites, and the Levites set aside the portion for the descendants of Aaron.

Nehemiah's Final Reforms

13 On that day the Book of Moses was read aloud in the hearing of the people and there it was found written that no Ammonite or Moabite should ever be admitted into the assembly of God, **2**because they had not met the Israelites with food and water but had hired Balaam to call a curse down on them. (Our God, however, turned the curse into a blessing.) **3**When the people heard this law, they excluded from Israel all who were of foreign descent.

4Before this, Eliashib the priest had been put in charge of the storerooms of the house of our God. He was closely associated with Tobiah, **5**and he had provided him with a large room formerly used to store the grain offerings and incense and temple articles, and also the tithes of grain, new wine and oil prescribed for the Levites, singers and gatekeepers, as well as the contributions for the priests.

6But while all this was going on, I was not in Jerusalem, for in the thirty-second year of Artaxerxes king of Babylon I had returned to the king. Some time later I asked his permission **7**and came back to Jerusalem. Here I learned about the evil thing Eliashib had done in providing Tobiah a room in the courts of the house of God. **8**I was greatly displeased and threw all Tobiah's household goods out of the room. **9**I gave orders

a31 Or *go alongside*   *b31* Or *proceed alongside*   *c38* Or *them alongside*   *d39* Or *Old* to purify the rooms, and then I put back into them the equipment of the house of God, with the grain offerings and the incense.

¹⁰I also learned that the portions assigned to the Levites had not been given to them, and that all the Levites and singers responsible for the service had gone back to their own fields. ¹¹So I rebuked the officials and asked them, "Why is the house of God neglected?" Then I called them together and stationed them at their posts.

¹²All Judah brought the tithes of grain, new wine and oil into the storerooms. ¹³I put Shelemiah the priest, Zadok the scribe, and a Levite named Pedaiah in charge of the storerooms and made Hanan son of Zaccur, the son of Mattaniah, their assistant, because these men were considered trustworthy. They were made responsible for distributing the supplies to their brothers.

¹⁴Remember me for this, O my God, and do not blot out what I have so faithfully done for the house of my God and its services.

¹⁵In those days I saw men in Judah treading winepresses on the Sabbath and bringing in grain and loading it on donkeys, together with wine, grapes, figs and all other kinds of loads. And they were bringing all this into Jerusalem on the Sabbath. Therefore I warned them against selling food on that day. ¹⁶Men from Tyre who lived in Jerusalem were bringing in fish and all kinds of merchandise and selling them in Jerusalem on the Sabbath to the people of Judah. ¹⁷I rebuked the nobles of Judah and said to them, "What is this wicked thing you are doing—desecrating the Sabbath day? ¹⁸Didn't your forefathers do the same things, so that our God brought all this calamity upon us and upon this city? Now you are stirring up more wrath against Israel by desecrating the Sabbath."

¹⁹When evening shadows fell on the gates of Jerusalem before the Sabbath, I ordered the doors to be shut and not opened until the Sabbath was over. I stationed some of my own men at the gates so that no load could be brought in on the Sabbath day. ²⁰Once or twice the merchants and sellers of all kinds of goods spent the night outside Jerusalem. ²¹But I warned them and said, "Why do you spend the night by the wall? If you do this again, I will lay hands on you." From that time on they no longer came on the Sabbath. ²²Then I commanded the Levites to purify themselves and go and guard the gates in order to keep the Sabbath day holy.

Remember me for this also, O my God, and show mercy to me according to your great love.

²³Moreover, in those days I saw men of Judah who had married women from Ashdod, Ammon and Moab. ²⁴Half of their children spoke the language of Ashdod or the language of one of the other peoples, and did not know how to speak the language of Judah. ²⁵I rebuked them and called curses down on them. I beat some of the men and pulled out their hair. I made them take an oath in God's name and said: "You are not to give your daughters in marriage to their sons, nor are you to take their daughters in marriage for your sons or for yourselves. ²⁶Was it not because of marriages like these that Solomon king of Israel sinned? Among the many nations there was no king like him. He was loved by his God, and God made him king over all Israel, but even he was led into sin by foreign women. ²⁷Must we hear now that you too are doing all this terrible wickedness and are being unfaithful to our God by marrying foreign women?"

²⁸One of the sons of Joiada son of Eliashib the high priest was son-in-law to Sanballat the Horonite. And I drove him away from me.

²⁹Remember them, O my God, because they defiled the priestly office and the covenant of the priesthood and of the Levites.

³⁰So I purified the priests and the Levites of everything foreign, and assigned them duties, each to his own task. ³¹I also made provision for contributions of wood at designated times, and for the firstfruits.

Remember me with favor, O my God.

ESTHER

SOME Jews return to their homeland after the seventy-year captivity; many more remain in Persia. In fact, Esther, a beautiful Jewish woman, actually becomes the queen of Persia. While Zerubbabel and Ezra labor to reestablish the Jews in Jerusalem, in Persia the villain Haman plots to destroy those who remain there. But the story has a surprise twist. Esther is a heroine, and God works through her to save his people. As you read, be encouraged. If you are willing, God will use you wherever you are.

Queen Vashti Deposed

1 This is what happened during the time of Xerxes,[a] the Xerxes who ruled over 127 provinces stretching from India to Cush[b]: ²At that time King Xerxes reigned from his royal throne in the citadel of Susa, ³and in the third year of his reign he gave a banquet for all his nobles and officials. The military leaders of Persia and Media, the princes, and the nobles of the provinces were present.

⁴For a full 180 days he displayed the vast wealth of his kingdom and the splendor and glory of his majesty. ⁵When these days were over, the king gave a banquet, lasting seven days, in the enclosed garden of the king's palace, for all the people from the least to the greatest, who were in the citadel of Susa.

⁶The garden had hangings of white and blue linen, fastened with cords of white linen and purple material to silver rings on marble pillars. There were couches of gold and silver on a mosaic pavement of porphyry, marble, mother-of-pearl and other costly stones. ⁷Wine was served in goblets of gold, each one different from the other, and the royal wine was abundant, in keeping with the king's liberality. ⁸By the king's command each guest was allowed to drink in his own way, for the king instructed all the wine stewards to serve each man what he wished.

⁹Queen Vashti also gave a banquet for the women in the royal palace of King Xerxes.

¹⁰On the seventh day, when King Xerxes was in high spirits from wine, he command-

---

a1 Hebrew *Ahasuerus*, a variant of Xerxes' Persian name; here and throughout Esther   *b1* That is, the upper Nile region ed the seven eunuchs who served him— Mehuman, Biztha, Harbona, Bigtha, Abagtha, Zethar and Carcas— [11]to bring before him Queen Vashti, wearing her royal crown, in order to display her beauty to the people and nobles, for she was lovely to look at. [12]But when the attendants delivered the king's command, Queen Vashti refused to come. Then the king became furious and burned with anger.

[13]Since it was customary for the king to consult experts in matters of law and justice, he spoke with the wise men who understood the times [14]and were closest to the king—Carshena, Shethar, Admatha, Tarshish, Meres, Marsena and Memucan, the seven nobles of Persia and Media who had special access to the king and were highest in the kingdom.

[15]"According to law, what must be done to Queen Vashti?" he asked. "She has not obeyed the command of King Xerxes that the eunuchs have taken to her."

[16]Then Memucan replied in the presence of the king and the nobles, "Queen Vashti has done wrong, not only against the king but also against all the nobles and the peoples of all the provinces of King Xerxes. [17]For the queen's conduct will become known to all the women, and so they will despise their husbands and say, 'King Xerxes commanded Queen Vashti to be brought before him, but she would not come.' [18]This very day the Persian and Median women of the nobility who have heard about the queen's conduct will respond to all the king's nobles in the same way. There will be no end of disrespect and discord.

[19]"Therefore, if it pleases the king, let him issue a royal decree and let it be written in the laws of Persia and Media, which cannot be repealed, that Vashti is never again to enter the presence of King Xerxes. Also let the king give her royal position to someone else who is better than she. [20]Then when the king's edict is proclaimed throughout all his vast realm, all the women will respect their husbands, from the least to the greatest."

[21]The king and his nobles were pleased with this advice, so the king did as Memucan proposed. [22]He sent dispatches to all parts of the kingdom, to each province in its own script and to each people in its own language, proclaiming in each people's tongue that every man should be ruler over his own household.

Esther Made Queen

2 Later when the anger of King Xerxes had subsided, he remembered Vashti and what she had done and what he had decreed about her. [2]Then the king's personal attendants proposed, "Let a search be made for beautiful young virgins for the king. [3]Let the king appoint commissioners in every province of his realm to bring all these beautiful girls into the harem at the citadel of Susa. Let them be placed under the care of Hegai, the king's eunuch, who is in charge of the women; and let beauty treatments be given to them. [4]Then let the girl who pleases the king be queen instead of Vashti." This advice appealed to the king, and he followed it.

[5]Now there was in the citadel of Susa a Jew of the tribe of Benjamin, named Mordecai son of Jair, the son of Shimei, the son of Kish, [6]who had been carried into exile from Jerusalem by Nebuchadnezzar king of Babylon, among those taken captive with Jehoiachin[a] king of Judah. [7]Mordecai had a cousin named Hadassah, whom he had brought up because she had neither father nor mother. This girl, who was also known as Esther, was lovely in form and features, and Mordecai had taken her as his own daughter when her father and mother died.

[8]When the king's order and edict had been proclaimed, many girls were brought to the citadel of Susa and put under the care of Hegai. Esther also was taken to the king's palace and entrusted to Hegai, who had charge of the harem. [9]The girl pleased him and won his favor. Immediately he provided her with her beauty treatments and special food. He assigned to her seven maids selected from the king's palace and moved her and her maids into the best place in the harem.

[10]Esther had not revealed her nationality and family background, because Mordecai had forbidden her to do so. [11]Every day he walked back and forth near the courtyard of the harem to find out how Esther was and what was happening to her.

[12]Before a girl's turn came to go in to King Xerxes, she had to complete twelve months of beauty treatments prescribed for the women, six months with oil of myrrh and six with perfumes and cosmetics. [13]And this is how she would go to the king: Anything she wanted was given her to take with her from the harem to the king's palace. [14]In the eve-

---

[a]6 Hebrew *Jeconiah,* a variant of *Jehoiachin*

ning she would go there and in the morning return to another part of the harem to the care of Shaashgaz, the king's eunuch who was in charge of the concubines. She would not return to the king unless he was pleased with her and summoned her by name.

15When the turn came for Esther (the girl Mordecai had adopted, the daughter of his uncle Abihail) to go to the king, she asked for nothing other than what Hegai, the king's eunuch who was in charge of the harem, suggested. And Esther won the favor of everyone who saw her. **16**She was taken to King Xerxes in the royal residence in the tenth month, the month of Tebeth, in the seventh year of his reign.

17Now the king was attracted to Esther more than to any of the other women, and she won his favor and approval more than any of the other virgins. So he set a royal crown on her head and made her queen instead of Vashti. **18**And the king gave a great banquet, Esther's banquet, for all his nobles and officials. He proclaimed a holiday throughout the provinces and distributed gifts with royal liberality.

Mordecai Uncovers a Conspiracy

19When the virgins were assembled a second time, Mordecai was sitting at the king's gate. **20**But Esther had kept secret her family background and nationality just as Mordecai had told her to do, for she continued to follow Mordecai's instructions as she had done when he was bringing her up.

21During the time Mordecai was sitting at the king's gate, Bigthana[a] and Teresh, two of the king's officers who guarded the doorway, became angry and conspired to assassinate King Xerxes. **22**But Mordecai found out about the plot and told Queen Esther, who in turn reported it to the king, giving credit to Mordecai. **23**And when the report was investigated and found to be true, the two officials were hanged on a gallows.[b] All this was recorded in the book of the annals in the presence of the king.

Haman's Plot to Destroy the Jews

3 After these events, King Xerxes honored Haman son of Hammedatha, the Agagite, elevating him and giving him a seat of honor higher than that of all the other nobles. **2**All the royal officials at the king's gate knelt down and paid honor to Haman, for

the king had commanded this concerning him. But Mordecai would not kneel down or pay him honor.

3Then the royal officials at the king's gate asked Mordecai, "Why do you disobey the king's command?" **4**Day after day they spoke to him but he refused to comply. Therefore they told Haman about it to see whether Mordecai's behavior would be tolerated, for he had told them he was a Jew.

5When Haman saw that Mordecai would not kneel down or pay him honor, he was enraged. **6**Yet having learned who Mordecai's people were, he scorned the idea of killing only Mordecai. Instead Haman looked for a way to destroy all Mordecai's people, the Jews, throughout the whole kingdom of Xerxes.

7In the twelfth year of King Xerxes, in the first month, the month of Nisan, they cast the *pur* (that is, the lot) in the presence of Haman to select a day and month. And the lot fell on[c] the twelfth month, the month of Adar.

8Then Haman said to King Xerxes, "There is a certain people dispersed and scattered among the peoples in all the provinces of your kingdom whose customs are different from those of all other people and who do not obey the king's laws; it is not in the king's best interest to tolerate them. **9**If it pleases the king, let a decree be issued to destroy them, and I will put ten thousand talents[d] of silver into the royal treasury for the men who carry out this business."

10So the king took his signet ring from his finger and gave it to Haman son of Hammedatha, the Agagite, the enemy of the Jews. **11**"Keep the money," the king said to Haman, "and do with the people as you please."

12Then on the thirteenth day of the first month the royal secretaries were summoned. They wrote out in the script of each province and in the language of each people all Haman's orders to the king's satraps, the governors of the various provinces and the nobles of the various peoples. These were written in the name of King Xerxes himself and sealed with his own ring. **13**Dispatches were sent by couriers to all the king's provinces with the order to destroy, kill and annihilate all the Jews—young and old, women and little children—on a single day, the thirteenth day of the twelfth month, the

---

a21 Hebrew *Bigthan*, a variant of *Bigthana*   *b23* Or *were hung* (or *impaled*) *on poles*; similarly elsewhere in Esther   *c7* Septuagint; Hebrew does not have *And the lot fell on.*   *d9* That is, about 375 tons (about 345 metric tons) month of Adar, and to plunder their goods. [14]A copy of the text of the edict was to be issued as law in every province and made known to the people of every nationality so they would be ready for that day.

[15]Spurred on by the king's command, the couriers went out, and the edict was issued in the citadel of Susa. The king and Haman sat down to drink, but the city of Susa was bewildered.

Mordecai Persuades Esther to Help

4 When Mordecai learned of all that had been done, he tore his clothes, put on sackcloth and ashes, and went out into the city, wailing loudly and bitterly. [2]But he went only as far as the king's gate, because no one clothed in sackcloth was allowed to enter it. [3]In every province to which the edict and order of the king came, there was great mourning among the Jews, with fasting, weeping and wailing. Many lay in sackcloth and ashes.

[4]When Esther's maids and eunuchs came and told her about Mordecai, she was in great distress. She sent clothes for him to put on instead of his sackcloth, but he would not accept them. [5]Then Esther summoned Hathach, one of the king's eunuchs assigned to attend her, and ordered him to find out what was troubling Mordecai and why.

[6]So Hathach went out to Mordecai in the open square of the city in front of the king's gate. [7]Mordecai told him everything that had happened to him, including the exact amount of money Haman had promised to pay into the royal treasury for the destruction of the Jews. [8]He also gave him a copy of the text of the edict for their annihilation, which had been published in Susa, to show to Esther and explain it to her, and he told him to urge her to go into the king's presence to beg for mercy and plead with him for her people.

[9]Hathach went back and reported to Esther what Mordecai had said. [10]Then she instructed him to say to Mordecai, [11]"All the king's officials and the people of the royal provinces know that for any man or woman who approaches the king in the inner court without being summoned the king has but one law: that he be put to death. The only exception to this is for the king to extend the gold scepter to him and spare his life. But thirty days have passed since I was called to go to the king."

[12]When Esther's words were reported to Mordecai, [13]he sent back this answer: "Do not think that because you are in the king's house you alone of all the Jews will escape. [14]For if you remain silent at this time, relief and deliverance for the Jews will arise from another place, but you and your father's family will perish. And who knows but that you have come to royal position for such a time as this?"

[15]Then Esther sent this reply to Mordecai: [16]"Go, gather together all the Jews who are in Susa, and fast for me. Do not eat or drink for three days, night or day. I and my maids will fast as you do. When this is done, I will go to the king, even though it is against the law. And if I perish, I perish."

[17]So Mordecai went away and carried out all of Esther's instructions.

Esther's Request to the King

5 On the third day Esther put on her royal robes and stood in the inner court of the palace, in front of the king's hall. The king was sitting on his royal throne in the hall, facing the entrance. [2]When he saw Queen Esther standing in the court, he was pleased with her and held out to her the gold scepter that was in his hand. So Esther approached and touched the tip of the scepter.

[3]Then the king asked, "What is it, Queen Esther? What is your request? Even up to half the kingdom, it will be given you."

[4]"If it pleases the king," replied Esther, "let the king, together with Haman, come today to a banquet I have prepared for him."

[5]"Bring Haman at once," the king said, "so that we may do what Esther asks."

So the king and Haman went to the banquet Esther had prepared. [6]As they were drinking wine, the king again asked Esther, "Now what is your petition? It will be given you. And what is your request? Even up to half the kingdom, it will be granted."

[7]Esther replied, "My petition and my request is this: [8]If the king regards me with favor and if it pleases the king to grant my petition and fulfill my request, let the king and Haman come tomorrow to the banquet I will prepare for them. Then I will answer the king's question."

Haman's Rage Against Mordecai

[9]Haman went out that day happy and in high spirits. But when he saw Mordecai at the king's gate and observed that he neither rose nor showed fear in his presence, he was filled with rage against Mordecai. [10]Nevertheless, Haman restrained himself and went home.

Calling together his friends and Zeresh,

ARE YOU DOING THE WILL OF GOD?

Darla, a junior at Peabody Academy, is all hung up on God's will.

"I don't know what to do with my life. I'm not sure if I should go into nursing or business. It's all so confusing. How am I supposed to know what's right? I wish God would write it all out in the clouds."

Sixteen-year-old Jessica nods, "I know what you mean. I'm dying to know if Mike and I will ever get married."

Look It Up
•••

Too many Christians picture God's will as a giant scroll: "If only he would let me peek at my future—let me see it laid out."

But it doesn't work that way. God's purpose for us is that we prepare for the future by doing his will today. " 'My food,' said Jesus, 'is to do the will of him who sent me and to finish his work' " (John 4:34).

And that purpose involves our good works! "For we are God's workmanship, created in Christ Jesus to do good works, which God prepared in advance for us to do" (Ephesians 2:10).

Think It Through
•••

Do you ever get confused about God's will? Do you ever wonder what his purpose is for you?

Instead of fretting over your future, persevere in the present! Take a few simple steps of obedience today. Over the course of time, you'll be able to look back and see how God directed your future through your present actions.

Work It Out
•••

Repeat: Your purpose in life is to do God's will. And what is the will of God? It's to prepare for—not fret about—the future by living for him today.

Questions like, "What should I do with the rest of my life?" and, "Where will I be in ten years?" are important. But the first step toward answering those questions is to ask yourself, "God, what do you want me to do here and now?"

The Word of God gives the principles that answer that question. To apply those principles, just look around at the needs in your part of the world. Then meet one of those needs . . . today. (Now that's doing God's will!)

Nail It Down
•••

Read Esther 4:12–16 and notice how Queen Esther saw her circumstances as being part of God's purpose.

Turn to pages 1102, 1158 and 1220 for other readings on purpose.
Turn to page 509 for Wednesday's reading.

Topic
••••
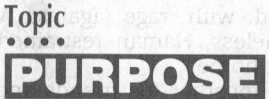

his wife, [11]Haman boasted to them about his vast wealth, his many sons, and all the ways the king had honored him and how he had elevated him above the other nobles and officials. [12]"And that's not all," Haman added. "I'm the only person Queen Esther invited to accompany the king to the banquet she gave. And she has invited me along with the king tomorrow. [13]But all this gives me no satisfaction as long as I see that Jew Mordecai sitting at the king's gate."

[14]His wife Zeresh and all his friends said to him, "Have a gallows built, seventy-five feet[a] high, and ask the king in the morning to have Mordecai hanged on it. Then go with the king to the dinner and be happy." This suggestion delighted Haman, and he had the gallows built.

Mordecai Honored

6 That night the king could not sleep; so he ordered the book of the chronicles, the record of his reign, to be brought in and read to him. [2]It was found recorded there that Mordecai had exposed Bigthana and Teresh, two of the king's officers who guarded the doorway, who had conspired to assassinate King Xerxes.

[3]"What honor and recognition has Mordecai received for this?" the king asked.

"Nothing has been done for him," his attendants answered.

[4]The king said, "Who is in the court?" Now Haman had just entered the outer court of the palace to speak to the king about hanging Mordecai on the gallows he had erected for him.

[5]His attendants answered, "Haman is standing in the court."

"Bring him in," the king ordered.

[6]When Haman entered, the king asked him, "What should be done for the man the king delights to honor?"

Now Haman thought to himself, "Who is there that the king would rather honor than me?" [7]So he answered the king, "For the man the king delights to honor, [8]have them bring a royal robe the king has worn and a horse the king has ridden, one with a royal crest placed on its head. [9]Then let the robe and horse be entrusted to one of the king's most noble princes. Let them robe the man the king delights to honor, and lead him on the horse through the city streets, proclaiming before him, 'This is what is done for the man the king delights to honor!' "

[10]"Go at once," the king commanded Haman. "Get the robe and the horse and do just as you have suggested for Mordecai the Jew, who sits at the king's gate. Do not neglect anything you have recommended."

[11]So Haman got the robe and the horse. He robed Mordecai, and led him on horseback through the city streets, proclaiming before him, "This is what is done for the man the king delights to honor!"

[12]Afterward Mordecai returned to the king's gate. But Haman rushed home, with his head covered in grief, [13]and told Zeresh his wife and all his friends everything that had happened to him.

His advisers and his wife Zeresh said to him, "Since Mordecai, before whom your downfall has started, is of Jewish origin, you cannot stand against him — you will surely come to ruin!" [14]While they were still talking with him, the king's eunuchs arrived and hurried Haman away to the banquet Esther had prepared.

Haman Hanged

7 So the king and Haman went to dine with Queen Esther, [2]and as they were drinking wine on that second day, the king again asked, "Queen Esther, what is your petition? It will be given you. What is your request? Even up to half the kingdom, it will be granted."

[3]Then Queen Esther answered, "If I have found favor with you, O king, and if it pleases your majesty, grant me my life — this is my petition. And spare my people — this is my request. [4]For I and my people have been sold for destruction and slaughter and annihilation. If we had merely been sold as male and female slaves, I would have kept quiet, because no such distress would justify disturbing the king.[b]

[5]King Xerxes asked Queen Esther, "Who is he? Where is the man who has dared to do such a thing?"

[6]Esther said, "The adversary and enemy is this vile Haman."

Then Haman was terrified before the king and queen. [7]The king got up in a rage, left his wine and went out into the palace garden. But Haman, realizing that the king had already decided his fate, stayed behind to beg Queen Esther for his life.

[8]Just as the king returned from the palace garden to the banquet hall, Haman was fall-

---

a14 Hebrew *fifty cubits* (about 23 meters)   b4 Or *quiet, but the compensation our adversary offers cannot be compared with the loss the king would suffer* ing on the couch where Esther was reclining.

The king exclaimed, "Will he even molest the queen while she is with me in the house?"

As soon as the word left the king's mouth, they covered Haman's face. **9**Then Harbona, one of the eunuchs attending the king, said, "A gallows seventy-five feet*a* high stands by Haman's house. He had it made for Mordecai, who spoke up to help the king."

The king said, "Hang him on it!" **10**So they hanged Haman on the gallows he had prepared for Mordecai. Then the king's fury subsided.

The King's Edict in Behalf of the Jews

8 That same day King Xerxes gave Queen Esther the estate of Haman, the enemy of the Jews. And Mordecai came into the presence of the king, for Esther had told how he was related to her. **2**The king took off his signet ring, which he had reclaimed from Haman, and presented it to Mordecai. And Esther appointed him over Haman's estate.

3Esther again pleaded with the king, falling at his feet and weeping. She begged him to put an end to the evil plan of Haman the Agagite, which he had devised against the Jews. **4**Then the king extended the gold scepter to Esther and she arose and stood before him.

5"If it pleases the king," she said, "and if he regards me with favor and thinks it the right thing to do, and if he is pleased with me, let an order be written overruling the dispatches that Haman son of Hammedatha, the Agagite, devised and wrote to destroy the Jews in all the king's provinces. **6**For how can I bear to see disaster fall on my people? How can I bear to see the destruction of my family?"

7King Xerxes replied to Queen Esther and to Mordecai the Jew, "Because Haman attacked the Jews, I have given his estate to Esther, and they have hanged him on the gallows. **8**Now write another decree in the king's name in behalf of the Jews as seems best to you, and seal it with the king's signet ring—for no document written in the king's name and sealed with his ring can be revoked."

9At once the royal secretaries were summoned—on the twenty-third day of the third month, the month of Sivan. They wrote out all Mordecai's orders to the Jews, and to the satraps, governors and nobles of the 127 provinces stretching from India to Cush.*b* These orders were written in the script of each province and the language of each people and also to the Jews in their own script and language. **10**Mordecai wrote in the name of King Xerxes, sealed the dispatches with the king's signet ring, and sent them by mounted couriers, who rode fast horses especially bred for the king.

11The king's edict granted the Jews in every city the right to assemble and protect themselves; to destroy, kill and annihilate any armed force of any nationality or province that might attack them and their women and children; and to plunder the property of their enemies. **12**The day appointed for the Jews to do this in all the provinces of King Xerxes was the thirteenth day of the twelfth month, the month of Adar. **13**A copy of the text of the edict was to be issued as law in every province and made known to the people of every nationality so that the Jews would be ready on that day to avenge themselves on their enemies.

14The couriers, riding the royal horses, raced out, spurred on by the king's command. And the edict was also issued in the citadel of Susa.

15Mordecai left the king's presence wearing royal garments of blue and white, a large crown of gold and a purple robe of fine linen. And the city of Susa held a joyous celebration. **16**For the Jews it was a time of happiness and joy, gladness and honor. **17**In every province and in every city, wherever the edict of the king went, there was joy and gladness among the Jews, with feasting and celebrating. And many people of other nationalities became Jews because fear of the Jews had seized them.

Triumph of the Jews

9 On the thirteenth day of the twelfth month, the month of Adar, the edict commanded by the king was to be carried out. On this day the enemies of the Jews had hoped to overpower them, but now the tables were turned and the Jews got the upper hand over those who hated them. **2**The Jews assembled in their cities in all the provinces of King Xerxes to attack those seeking their destruction. No one could stand against them, because the people of all the other nationalities were afraid of them. **3**And all the nobles of the provinces, the satraps, the governors and the king's administrators helped the Jews, because fear of Mordecai had

---

*a*9 Hebrew *fifty cubits* (about 23 meters)   *b*9 That is, the upper Nile region seized them. **4**Mordecai was prominent in the palace; his reputation spread throughout the provinces, and he became more and more powerful.

5The Jews struck down all their enemies with the sword, killing and destroying them, and they did what they pleased to those who hated them. **6**In the citadel of Susa, the Jews killed and destroyed five hundred men. **7**They also killed Parshandatha, Dalphon, Aspatha, **8**Poratha, Adalia, Aridatha, **9**Parmashta, Arisai, Aridai and Vaizatha, **10**the ten sons of Haman son of Hammedatha, the enemy of the Jews. But they did not lay their hands on the plunder.

11The number of those slain in the citadel of Susa was reported to the king that same day. **12**The king said to Queen Esther, "The Jews have killed and destroyed five hundred men and the ten sons of Haman in the citadel of Susa. What have they done in the rest of the king's provinces? Now what is your petition? It will be given you. What is your request? It will also be granted."

13"If it pleases the king," Esther answered, "give the Jews in Susa permission to carry out this day's edict tomorrow also, and let Haman's ten sons be hanged on gallows."

14So the king commanded that this be done. An edict was issued in Susa, and they hanged the ten sons of Haman. **15**The Jews in Susa came together on the fourteenth day of the month of Adar, and they put to death in Susa three hundred men, but they did not lay their hands on the plunder.

16Meanwhile, the remainder of the Jews who were in the king's provinces also assembled to protect themselves and get relief from their enemies. They killed seventy-five thousand of them but did not lay their hands on the plunder. **17**This happened on the thirteenth day of the month of Adar, and on the fourteenth they rested and made it a day of feasting and joy.

Purim Celebrated

18The Jews in Susa, however, had assembled on the thirteenth and fourteenth, and then on the fifteenth they rested and made it a day of feasting and joy.

19That is why rural Jews—those living in villages—observe the fourteenth of the month of Adar as a day of joy and feasting, a day for giving presents to each other.

20Mordecai recorded these events, and he sent letters to all the Jews throughout the provinces of King Xerxes, near and far, **21**to have them celebrate annually the fourteenth and fifteenth days of the month of Adar **22**as the time when the Jews got relief from their enemies, and as the month when their sorrow was turned into joy and their mourning into a day of celebration. He wrote them to observe the days as days of feasting and joy and giving presents of food to one another and gifts to the poor.

23So the Jews agreed to continue the celebration they had begun, doing what Mordecai had written to them. **24**For Haman son of Hammedatha, the Agagite, the enemy of all the Jews, had plotted against the Jews to destroy them and had cast the *pur* (that is, the lot) for their ruin and destruction. **25**But when the plot came to the king's attention,ᵃ he issued written orders that the evil scheme Haman had devised against the Jews should come back onto his own head, and that he and his sons should be hanged on the gallows. **26**(Therefore these days were called Purim, from the word *pur.*) Because of everything written in this letter and because of what they had seen and what had happened to them, **27**the Jews took it upon themselves to establish the custom that they and their descendants and all who join them should without fail observe these two days every year, in the way prescribed and at the time appointed. **28**These days should be remembered and observed in every generation by every family, and in every province and in every city. And these days of Purim should never cease to be celebrated by the Jews, nor should the memory of them die out among their descendants.

29So Queen Esther, daughter of Abihail, along with Mordecai the Jew, wrote with full authority to confirm this second letter concerning Purim. **30**And Mordecai sent letters to all the Jews in the 127 provinces of the kingdom of Xerxes—words of goodwill and assurance— **31**to establish these days of Purim at their designated times, as Mordecai the Jew and Queen Esther had decreed for them, and as they had established for themselves and their descendants in regard to their times of fasting and lamentation. **32**Esther's decree confirmed these regulations about Purim, and it was written down in the records.

The Greatness of Mordecai

10 King Xerxes imposed tribute throughout the empire, to its distant shores. **2**And all his acts of power and might,

---

ᵃ25 Or *when Esther came before the king*

together with a full account of the greatness of Mordecai to which the king had raised him, are they not written in the book of the annals of the kings of Media and Persia? ³Mordecai the Jew was second in rank to King Xerxes, preeminent among the Jews, and held in high esteem by his many fellow Jews, because he worked for the good of his people and spoke up for the welfare of all the Jews.

JOB

FOR no apparent reason, a string of disasters bombard Job. Family, fame, fortune and fitness vanish. Job responds by asking why. But no answer comes. Only when God himself challenges Job, does Job realize that he has been in God's hands all along. God's sovereignty is a fundamental fact of the universe. As you read Job's story, remember that God may not always answer your why questions, but he's always there, and he's in control.

Outline of Contents

Prologue

1 In the land of Uz there lived a man whose name was Job. This man was blameless and upright; he feared God and shunned evil. ²He had seven sons and three daughters, ³and he owned seven thousand sheep, three thousand camels, five hundred yoke of oxen and five hundred donkeys, and had a large number of servants. He was the greatest man among all the people of the East.

⁴His sons used to take turns holding feasts in their homes, and they would invite their three sisters to eat and drink with them.

⁵When a period of feasting had run its course, Job would send and have them purified. Early in the morning he would sacrifice a burnt offering for each of them, thinking, "Perhaps my children have sinned and cursed God in their hearts." This was Job's regular custom.

Job's First Test

⁶One day the angels*a* came to present themselves before the LORD, and Satan*b* also came with them. ⁷The LORD said to Satan, "Where have you come from?"

Satan answered the LORD, "From roaming

---

a6 Hebrew the sons of God   *b6 Satan means accuser.*

through the earth and going back and forth in it."

8Then the Lord said to Satan, "Have you considered my servant Job? There is no one on earth like him; he is blameless and upright, a man who fears God and shuns evil."

9"Does Job fear God for nothing?" Satan replied. **10**"Have you not put a hedge around him and his household and everything he has? You have blessed the work of his hands, so that his flocks and herds are spread throughout the land. **11**But stretch out your hand and strike everything he has, and he will surely curse you to your face."

12The Lord said to Satan, "Very well, then, everything he has is in your hands, but on the man himself do not lay a finger."

Then Satan went out from the presence of the Lord.

13One day when Job's sons and daughters were feasting and drinking wine at the oldest brother's house, **14**a messenger came to Job and said, "The oxen were plowing and the donkeys were grazing nearby, **15**and the Sabeans attacked and carried them off. They put the servants to the sword, and I am the only one who has escaped to tell you!"

16While he was still speaking, another messenger came and said, "The fire of God fell from the sky and burned up the sheep and the servants, and I am the only one who has escaped to tell you!"

17While he was still speaking, another messenger came and said, "The Chaldeans formed three raiding parties and swept down on your camels and carried them off. They put the servants to the sword, and I am the only one who has escaped to tell you!"

18While he was still speaking, yet another messenger came and said, "Your sons and daughters were feasting and drinking wine at the oldest brother's house, **19**when suddenly a mighty wind swept in from the desert and struck the four corners of the house. It collapsed on them and they are dead, and I am the only one who has escaped to tell you!"

20At this, Job got up and tore his robe and shaved his head. Then he fell to the ground in worship **21**and said:

"Naked I came from my mother's womb,
    and naked I will depart.*a*
The Lord gave and the Lord has taken
    away;

may the name of the Lord be
    praised."

22In all this, Job did not sin by charging God with wrongdoing.

Job's Second Test

2 On another day the angels*b* came to present themselves before the Lord, and Satan also came with them to present himself before him. **2**And the Lord said to Satan, "Where have you come from?"

Satan answered the Lord, "From roaming through the earth and going back and forth in it."

3Then the Lord said to Satan, "Have you considered my servant Job? There is no one on earth like him; he is blameless and upright, a man who fears God and shuns evil. And he still maintains his integrity, though you incited me against him to ruin him without any reason."

4"Skin for skin!" Satan replied. "A man will give all he has for his own life. **5**But stretch out your hand and strike his flesh and bones, and he will surely curse you to your face."

6The Lord said to Satan, "Very well, then, he is in your hands; but you must spare his life."

7So Satan went out from the presence of the Lord and afflicted Job with painful sores from the soles of his feet to the top of his head. **8**Then Job took a piece of broken pottery and scraped himself with it as he sat among the ashes.

9His wife said to him, "Are you still holding on to your integrity? Curse God and die!"

10He replied, "You are talking like a foolish*c* woman. Shall we accept good from God, and not trouble?"

In all this, Job did not sin in what he said.

Job's Three Friends

11When Job's three friends, Eliphaz the Temanite, Bildad the Shuhite and Zophar the Naamathite, heard about all the troubles that had come upon him, they set out from their homes and met together by agreement to go and sympathize with him and comfort him. **12**When they saw him from a distance, they could hardly recognize him; they began to weep aloud, and they tore their robes and sprinkled dust on their heads. **13**Then they sat on the ground with him for seven days and seven nights. No one said a word

a21 Or *will return there*   *b1* Hebrew *the sons of God*   *c10* The Hebrew word rendered *foolish* denotes moral deficiency.

THE HANDS AND FEET OF FRIENDSHIP

Early on a rainy Monday morning the dreaded phone call finally came. Walt's dad had died after a long struggle with lung cancer.

While the family huddled together at the hospital, their friends swung into action. People from church brought food, cleaned the house and volunteered to house out-of-town funeral guests. Walt's two best friends left school to come by and sit with their dazed friend. They didn't say much, but just being there was a huge support.

Look It Up
• • • •

Walt's family was blessed by people who understood the Biblical principle that true friendship involves sacrifice.

"Two are better than one, because they have a good return for their work: If one falls down, his friend can help him up. But pity the man who falls and has no one to help him up! Also, if two lie down together, they will keep warm. But how can one keep warm alone? Though one may be overpowered, two can defend themselves. A cord of three strands is not quickly broken" (Ecclesiastes 4:9–12).

"Julius, in kindness to Paul, allowed him to go to his friends so they might provide for his needs" (Acts 27:3).

Think It Through
• • • •

Sometimes friendship requires that you go out of your way to provide help and caring. Sometimes friendship requires moving outside of your own comfort zone to give support to a friend who is in the middle of a hard time.

Can your chosen friends count on you for communication, caring, commitment and sacrifice?

Work It Out
• • • •

Use your hands and feet today to develop deeper friendships. This means more than just empty talk or warm, fuzzy feelings. It means action. It means being willing to sacrifice your time, emotion, energy and even material wealth if necessary for your friends.

Today, use your hands to support friends with a pat on the back, a hug or help in doing something difficult. Pick them up when they're down.

Also today, use your feet to walk with friends in times of hurt and to go to whatever lengths are necessary to meet their needs. Take presents, flowers or surprise "pick-me-ups" to them. Go out of your way to help.

Nail It Down
• • • •

Read what Job's friends did for him in Job 2:13.

Turn to pages 195, 291, 670 and 1346 for other readings on friendship.
Turn to page 518 for Thursday's reading.

Topic
• • • •

FRIENDSHIP

to him, because they saw how great his suffering was.

Job Speaks

3 After this, Job opened his mouth and cursed the day of his birth. ²He said:

³"May the day of my birth perish,
  and the night it was said, 'A boy is born!'
⁴That day—may it turn to darkness;
  may God above not care about it;
  may no light shine upon it.
⁵May darkness and deep shadow*ᵃ* claim
    it once more;
  may a cloud settle over it;
  may blackness overwhelm its light.
⁶That night—may thick darkness seize it;
  may it not be included among the
    days of the year
  nor be entered in any of the months.
⁷May that night be barren;
  may no shout of joy be heard in it.
⁸May those who curse days*ᵇ* curse that
    day,
  those who are ready to rouse
    Leviathan.
⁹May its morning stars become dark;
  may it wait for daylight in vain
  and not see the first rays of dawn,
¹⁰for it did not shut the doors of the
    womb on me
  to hide trouble from my eyes.

¹¹"Why did I not perish at birth,
  and die as I came from the womb?
¹²Why were there knees to receive me
  and breasts that I might be nursed?
¹³For now I would be lying down in
    peace;
  I would be asleep and at rest
¹⁴with kings and counselors of the earth,
  who built for themselves places now
    lying in ruins,
¹⁵with rulers who had gold,
  who filled their houses with silver.
¹⁶Or why was I not hidden in the ground
    like a stillborn child,
  like an infant who never saw the light
    of day?
¹⁷There the wicked cease from turmoil,
  and there the weary are at rest.
¹⁸Captives also enjoy their ease;
  they no longer hear the slave driver's
    shout.
¹⁹The small and the great are there,
  and the slave is freed from his
    master.

²⁰"Why is light given to those in misery,
  and life to the bitter of soul,
²¹to those who long for death that does
    not come,
  who search for it more than for
    hidden treasure,
²²who are filled with gladness
  and rejoice when they reach the
    grave?
²³Why is life given to a man
  whose way is hidden,
  whom God has hedged in?
²⁴For sighing comes to me instead of
    food;
  my groans pour out like water.
²⁵What I feared has come upon me;
  what I dreaded has happened to me.
²⁶I have no peace, no quietness;
  I have no rest, but only turmoil."

Eliphaz

4 Then Eliphaz the Temanite replied:

²"If someone ventures a word with
    you, will you be impatient?
  But who can keep from speaking?
³Think how you have instructed many,
  how you have strengthened feeble
    hands.
⁴Your words have supported those who
    stumbled;
  you have strengthened faltering
    knees.
⁵But now trouble comes to you, and you
    are discouraged;
  it strikes you, and you are dismayed.
⁶Should not your piety be your
    confidence
  and your blameless ways your hope?

⁷"Consider now: Who, being innocent,
    has ever perished?
  Where were the upright ever
    destroyed?
⁸As I have observed, those who plow evil
  and those who sow trouble reap it.
⁹At the breath of God they are destroyed;
  at the blast of his anger they perish.
¹⁰The lions may roar and growl,
  yet the teeth of the great lions are
    broken.
¹¹The lion perishes for lack of prey,
  and the cubs of the lioness are
    scattered.

¹²"A word was secretly brought to me,
  my ears caught a whisper of it.
¹³Amid disquieting dreams in the night,

ᵃ5 Or *and the shadow of death*   ᵇ8 Or *the sea*

when deep sleep falls on men,
¹⁴fear and trembling seized me
and made all my bones shake.
¹⁵A spirit glided past my face,
and the hair on my body stood on
end.
¹⁶It stopped,
but I could not tell what it was.
A form stood before my eyes,
and I heard a hushed voice:
¹⁷'Can a mortal be more righteous than
God?
Can a man be more pure than his
Maker?
¹⁸If God places no trust in his servants,
if he charges his angels with error,
¹⁹how much more those who live in
houses of clay,
whose foundations are in the dust,
who are crushed more readily than a
moth!
²⁰Between dawn and dusk they are
broken to pieces;
unnoticed, they perish forever.
²¹Are not the cords of their tent pulled
up,
so that they die without wisdom?'^a

5 "Call if you will, but who will answer
you?
To which of the holy ones will you
turn?
²Resentment kills a fool,
and envy slays the simple.
³I myself have seen a fool taking root,
but suddenly his house was cursed.
⁴His children are far from safety,
crushed in court without a defender.
⁵The hungry consume his harvest,
taking it even from among thorns,
and the thirsty pant after his wealth.
⁶For hardship does not spring from the
soil,
nor does trouble sprout from the
ground.
⁷Yet man is born to trouble
as surely as sparks fly upward.

⁸"But if it were I, I would appeal to God;
I would lay my cause before him.
⁹He performs wonders that cannot be
fathomed,
miracles that cannot be counted.
¹⁰He bestows rain on the earth;
he sends water upon the countryside.
¹¹The lowly he sets on high,
and those who mourn are lifted to
safety.
¹²He thwarts the plans of the crafty,
so that their hands achieve no
success.
¹³He catches the wise in their craftiness,
and the schemes of the wily are
swept away.
¹⁴Darkness comes upon them in the
daytime;
at noon they grope as in the night.
¹⁵He saves the needy from the sword in
their mouth;
he saves them from the clutches of
the powerful.
¹⁶So the poor have hope,
and injustice shuts its mouth.

¹⁷"Blessed is the man whom God corrects;
so do not despise the discipline of the
Almighty.^b
¹⁸For he wounds, but he also binds up;
he injures, but his hands also heal.
¹⁹From six calamities he will rescue you;
in seven no harm will befall you.
²⁰In famine he will ransom you from
death,
and in battle from the stroke of the
sword.
²¹You will be protected from the lash of
the tongue,
and need not fear when destruction
comes.
²²You will laugh at destruction and
famine,
and need not fear the beasts of the
earth.
²³For you will have a covenant with the
stones of the field,
and the wild animals will be at peace
with you.
²⁴You will know that your tent is secure;
you will take stock of your property
and find nothing missing.
²⁵You will know that your children will be
many,
and your descendants like the grass
of the earth.
²⁶You will come to the grave in full vigor,
like sheaves gathered in season.

²⁷"We have examined this, and it is true.
So hear it and apply it to yourself."

Job

6 Then Job replied:

²"If only my anguish could be
weighed

---

^a21 Some interpreters end the quotation after verse 17.   ^b17 Hebrew *Shaddai*; here and throughout Job

and all my misery be placed on the
scales!
³It would surely outweigh the sand of the
seas —
no wonder my words have been
impetuous.
⁴The arrows of the Almighty are in me,
my spirit drinks in their poison;
God's terrors are marshaled against
me.
⁵Does a wild donkey bray when it has
grass,
or an ox bellow when it has fodder?
⁶Is tasteless food eaten without salt,
or is there flavor in the white of an
egg*ᵃ*?
⁷I refuse to touch it;
such food makes me ill.

⁸"Oh, that I might have my request,
that God would grant what I hope for,
⁹that God would be willing to crush me,
to let loose his hand and cut me off!
¹⁰Then I would still have this
consolation —
my joy in unrelenting pain —
that I had not denied the words of the
Holy One.

¹¹"What strength do I have, that I should
still hope?
What prospects, that I should be
patient?
¹²Do I have the strength of stone?
Is my flesh bronze?
¹³Do I have any power to help myself,
now that success has been driven
from me?

¹⁴"A despairing man should have the
devotion of his friends,
even though he forsakes the fear of
the Almighty.
¹⁵But my brothers are as undependable
as intermittent streams,
as the streams that overflow
¹⁶when darkened by thawing ice
and swollen with melting snow,
¹⁷but that cease to flow in the dry season,
and in the heat vanish from their
channels.
¹⁸Caravans turn aside from their routes;
they go up into the wasteland and
perish.
¹⁹The caravans of Tema look for water,
the traveling merchants of Sheba look
in hope.

²⁰They are distressed, because they had
been confident;
they arrive there, only to be
disappointed.
²¹Now you too have proved to be of no
help;
you see something dreadful and are
afraid.
²²Have I ever said, 'Give something on my
behalf,
pay a ransom for me from your
wealth,
²³deliver me from the hand of the enemy,
ransom me from the clutches of the
ruthless'?

²⁴"Teach me, and I will be quiet;
show me where I have been wrong.
²⁵How painful are honest words!
But what do your arguments prove?
²⁶Do you mean to correct what I say,
and treat the words of a despairing
man as wind?
²⁷You would even cast lots for the
fatherless
and barter away your friend.

²⁸"But now be so kind as to look at me.
Would I lie to your face?
²⁹Relent, do not be unjust;
reconsider, for my integrity is at
stake.*ᵇ*
³⁰Is there any wickedness on my lips?
Can my mouth not discern malice?

7 "Does not man have hard service on
earth?
Are not his days like those of a hired
man?
²Like a slave longing for the evening
shadows,
or a hired man waiting eagerly for his
wages,
³so I have been allotted months of
futility,
and nights of misery have been
assigned to me.
⁴When I lie down I think, 'How long
before I get up?'
The night drags on, and I toss till
dawn.
⁵My body is clothed with worms and
scabs,
my skin is broken and festering.

⁶"My days are swifter than a weaver's
shuttle,
and they come to an end without
hope.

ᵃ6 The meaning of the Hebrew for this phrase is uncertain.   ᵇ29 Or *my righteousness still stands*

7Remember, O God, that my life is but a
   breath;
   my eyes will never see happiness
   again.
8The eye that now sees me will see me
   no longer;
   you will look for me, but I will be no
   more.
9As a cloud vanishes and is gone,
   so he who goes down to the grave*a*
   does not return.
10He will never come to his house again;
   his place will know him no more.

11"Therefore I will not keep silent;
   I will speak out in the anguish of my
   spirit,
   I will complain in the bitterness of my
   soul.
12Am I the sea, or the monster of the
   deep,
   that you put me under guard?
13When I think my bed will comfort me
   and my couch will ease my
   complaint,
14even then you frighten me with dreams
   and terrify me with visions,
15so that I prefer strangling and death,
   rather than this body of mine.
16I despise my life; I would not live
   forever.
   Let me alone; my days have no
   meaning.

17"What is man that you make so much
   of him,
   that you give him so much attention,
18that you examine him every morning
   and test him every moment?
19Will you never look away from me,
   or let me alone even for an instant?
20If I have sinned, what have I done to
   you,
   O watcher of men?
   Why have you made me your target?
   Have I become a burden to you?*b*
21Why do you not pardon my offenses
   and forgive my sins?
   For I will soon lie down in the dust;
   you will search for me, but I will be
   no more."

Bildad

8 Then Bildad the Shuhite replied:

   2"How long will you say such things?
   Your words are a blustering wind.

3Does God pervert justice?
   Does the Almighty pervert what is
   right?
4When your children sinned against him,
   he gave them over to the penalty of
   their sin.
5But if you will look to God
   and plead with the Almighty,
6if you are pure and upright,
   even now he will rouse himself on
   your behalf
   and restore you to your rightful place.
7Your beginnings will seem humble,
   so prosperous will your future be.

8"Ask the former generations
   and find out what their fathers
   learned,
9for we were born only yesterday and
   know nothing,
   and our days on earth are but a
   shadow.
10Will they not instruct you and tell you?
   Will they not bring forth words from
   their understanding?
11Can papyrus grow tall where there is no
   marsh?
   Can reeds thrive without water?
12While still growing and uncut,
   they wither more quickly than grass.
13Such is the destiny of all who forget
   God;
   so perishes the hope of the godless.
14What he trusts in is fragile*c*;
   what he relies on is a spider's web.
15He leans on his web, but it gives way;
   he clings to it, but it does not hold.
16He is like a well-watered plant in the
   sunshine,
   spreading its shoots over the garden;
17it entwines its roots around a pile of
   rocks
   and looks for a place among the
   stones.
18But when it is torn from its spot,
   that place disowns it and says, 'I
   never saw you.'
19Surely its life withers away,
   and*d* from the soil other plants grow.

20"Surely God does not reject a blameless
   man
   or strengthen the hands of evildoers.
21He will yet fill your mouth with laughter
   and your lips with shouts of joy.
22Your enemies will be clothed in shame,

---

a9 Hebrew *Sheol*   *b20* A few manuscripts of the Masoretic Text, an ancient Hebrew scribal tradition and
Septuagint; most manuscripts of the Masoretic Text *I have become a burden to myself.*   *c14* The meaning of
the Hebrew for this word is uncertain.   *d19* Or *Surely all the joy it has / is that*

and the tents of the wicked will be no more."

Job

9 Then Job replied:

2"Indeed, I know that this is true.
But how can a mortal be righteous before God?
3Though one wished to dispute with him,
he could not answer him one time out of a thousand.
4His wisdom is profound, his power is vast.
Who has resisted him and come out unscathed?
5He moves mountains without their knowing it
and overturns them in his anger.
6He shakes the earth from its place
and makes its pillars tremble.
7He speaks to the sun and it does not shine;
he seals off the light of the stars.
8He alone stretches out the heavens
and treads on the waves of the sea.
9He is the Maker of the Bear and Orion,
the Pleiades and the constellations of the south.
10He performs wonders that cannot be fathomed,
miracles that cannot be counted.
11When he passes me, I cannot see him;
when he goes by, I cannot perceive him.
12If he snatches away, who can stop him?
Who can say to him, 'What are you doing?'
13God does not restrain his anger;
even the cohorts of Rahab cowered at his feet.

14"How then can I dispute with him?
How can I find words to argue with him?
15Though I were innocent, I could not answer him;
I could only plead with my Judge for mercy.
16Even if I summoned him and he responded,
I do not believe he would give me a hearing.
17He would crush me with a storm
and multiply my wounds for no reason.
18He would not let me regain my breath
but would overwhelm me with misery.
19If it is a matter of strength, he is mighty!
And if it is a matter of justice, who will summon him[a]?
20Even if I were innocent, my mouth would condemn me;
if I were blameless, it would pronounce me guilty.

21"Although I am blameless,
I have no concern for myself;
I despise my own life.
22It is all the same; that is why I say,
'He destroys both the blameless and the wicked.'
23When a scourge brings sudden death,
he mocks the despair of the innocent.
24When a land falls into the hands of the wicked,
he blindfolds its judges.
If it is not he, then who is it?

25"My days are swifter than a runner;
they fly away without a glimpse of joy.
26They skim past like boats of papyrus,
like eagles swooping down on their prey.
27If I say, 'I will forget my complaint,
I will change my expression, and smile,'
28I still dread all my sufferings,
for I know you will not hold me innocent.
29Since I am already found guilty,
why should I struggle in vain?
30Even if I washed myself with soap[b]
and my hands with washing soda,
31you would plunge me into a slime pit
so that even my clothes would detest me.

32"He is not a man like me that I might answer him,
that we might confront each other in court.
33If only there were someone to arbitrate between us,
to lay his hand upon us both,
34someone to remove God's rod from me,
so that his terror would frighten me no more.
35Then I would speak up without fear of him,
but as it now stands with me, I cannot.

a 19 See Septuagint; Hebrew me.   b 30 Or snow

10

"I loathe my very life;
therefore I will give free rein to
my complaint
and speak out in the bitterness of my
soul.
²I will say to God: Do not condemn me,
but tell me what charges you have
against me.
³Does it please you to oppress me,
to spurn the work of your hands,
while you smile on the schemes of
the wicked?
⁴Do you have eyes of flesh?
Do you see as a mortal sees?
⁵Are your days like those of a mortal
or your years like those of a man,
⁶that you must search out my faults
and probe after my sin—
⁷though you know that I am not guilty
and that no one can rescue me from
your hand?

⁸"Your hands shaped me and made me.
Will you now turn and destroy me?
⁹Remember that you molded me like
clay.
Will you now turn me to dust again?
¹⁰Did you not pour me out like milk
and curdle me like cheese,
¹¹clothe me with skin and flesh
and knit me together with bones and
sinews?
¹²You gave me life and showed me
kindness,
and in your providence watched over
my spirit.

¹³"But this is what you concealed in your
heart,
and I know that this was in your
mind:
¹⁴If I sinned, you would be watching me
and would not let my offense go
unpunished.
¹⁵If I am guilty—woe to me!
Even if I am innocent, I cannot lift my
head,
for I am full of shame
and drowned in[a] my affliction.
¹⁶If I hold my head high, you stalk me
like a lion
and again display your awesome
power against me.
¹⁷You bring new witnesses against me
and increase your anger toward me;
your forces come against me wave
upon wave.

¹⁸"Why then did you bring me out of the
womb?
I wish I had died before any eye saw
me.
¹⁹If only I had never come into being,
or had been carried straight from the
womb to the grave!
²⁰Are not my few days almost over?
Turn away from me so I can have a
moment's joy
²¹before I go to the place of no return,
to the land of gloom and deep
shadow,[b]
²²to the land of deepest night,
of deep shadow and disorder,
where even the light is like darkness."

Zophar

11

Then Zophar the Naamathite replied:

²"Are all these words to go unanswered?
Is this talker to be vindicated?
³Will your idle talk reduce men to
silence?
Will no one rebuke you when you
mock?
⁴You say to God, 'My beliefs are flawless
and I am pure in your sight.'
⁵Oh, how I wish that God would speak,
that he would open his lips against
you
⁶and disclose to you the secrets of
wisdom,
for true wisdom has two sides.
Know this: God has even forgotten
some of your sin.

⁷"Can you fathom the mysteries of God?
Can you probe the limits of the
Almighty?
⁸They are higher than the
heavens—what can you do?
They are deeper than the depths of
the grave[c]—what can you know?
⁹Their measure is longer than the earth
and wider than the sea.

¹⁰"If he comes along and confines you in
prison
and convenes a court, who can
oppose him?
¹¹Surely he recognizes deceitful men;
and when he sees evil, does he not
take note?
¹²But a witless man can no more become
wise

---

[a]15 Or *and aware of*   [b]21 Or *and the shadow of death*; also in verse 22   [c]8 Hebrew *than Sheol*

than a wild donkey's colt can be born
a man.^a

¹³"Yet if you devote your heart to him
and stretch out your hands to him,
¹⁴if you put away the sin that is in your
hand
and allow no evil to dwell in your
tent,
¹⁵then you will lift up your face without
shame;
you will stand firm and without fear.
¹⁶You will surely forget your trouble,
recalling it only as waters gone by.
¹⁷Life will be brighter than noonday,
and darkness will become like
morning.
¹⁸You will be secure, because there is
hope;
you will look about you and take your
rest in safety.
¹⁹You will lie down, with no one to make
you afraid,
and many will court your favor.
²⁰But the eyes of the wicked will fail,
and escape will elude them;
their hope will become a dying gasp."

Job

12

Then Job replied:

²"Doubtless you are the people,
and wisdom will die with you!
³But I have a mind as well as you;
I am not inferior to you.
Who does not know all these things?

⁴"I have become a laughingstock to my
friends,
though I called upon God and he
answered—
a mere laughingstock, though
righteous and blameless!
⁵Men at ease have contempt for
misfortune
as the fate of those whose feet are
slipping.
⁶The tents of marauders are undisturbed,
and those who provoke God are
secure—
those who carry their god in their
hands.^b

⁷"But ask the animals, and they will
teach you,
or the birds of the air, and they will
tell you;

⁸or speak to the earth, and it will teach
you,
or let the fish of the sea inform you.
⁹Which of all these does not know
that the hand of the LORD has done
this?
¹⁰In his hand is the life of every creature
and the breath of all mankind.
¹¹Does not the ear test words
as the tongue tastes food?
¹²Is not wisdom found among the aged?
Does not long life bring
understanding?

¹³"To God belong wisdom and power;
counsel and understanding are his.
¹⁴What he tears down cannot be rebuilt;
the man he imprisons cannot be
released.
¹⁵If he holds back the waters, there is
drought;
if he lets them loose, they devastate
the land.
¹⁶To him belong strength and victory;
both deceived and deceiver are his.
¹⁷He leads counselors away stripped
and makes fools of judges.
¹⁸He takes off the shackles put on by
kings
and ties a loincloth^c around their
waist.
¹⁹He leads priests away stripped
and overthrows men long established.
²⁰He silences the lips of trusted advisers
and takes away the discernment of
elders.
²¹He pours contempt on nobles
and disarms the mighty.
²²He reveals the deep things of darkness
and brings deep shadows into the
light.
²³He makes nations great, and destroys
them;
he enlarges nations, and disperses
them.
²⁴He deprives the leaders of the earth of
their reason;
he sends them wandering through a
trackless waste.
²⁵They grope in darkness with no light;
he makes them stagger like
drunkards.

13

"My eyes have seen all this,
my ears have heard and
understood it.
²What you know, I also know;

---

^a12 Or *wild donkey can be born tame*   ^b6 Or *secure / in what God's hand brings them*   ^c18 Or *shackles of kings / and ties a belt*

I am not inferior to you.
³But I desire to speak to the Almighty
and to argue my case with God.
⁴You, however, smear me with lies;
you are worthless physicians, all of
you!
⁵If only you would be altogether silent!
For you, that would be wisdom.
⁶Hear now my argument;
listen to the plea of my lips.
⁷Will you speak wickedly on God's
behalf?
Will you speak deceitfully for him?
⁸Will you show him partiality?
Will you argue the case for God?
⁹Would it turn out well if he examined
you?
Could you deceive him as you might
deceive men?
¹⁰He would surely rebuke you
if you secretly showed partiality.
¹¹Would not his splendor terrify you?
Would not the dread of him fall on
you?
¹²Your maxims are proverbs of ashes;
your defenses are defenses of clay.

¹³"Keep silent and let me speak;
then let come to me what may.
¹⁴Why do I put myself in jeopardy
and take my life in my hands?
¹⁵Though he slay me, yet will I hope in
him;
I will surely*a* defend my ways to his
face.
¹⁶Indeed, this will turn out for my
deliverance,
for no godless man would dare come
before him!
¹⁷Listen carefully to my words;
let your ears take in what I say.
¹⁸Now that I have prepared my case,
I know I will be vindicated.
¹⁹Can anyone bring charges against me?
If so, I will be silent and die.

²⁰"Only grant me these two things, O God,
and then I will not hide from you:
²¹Withdraw your hand far from me,
and stop frightening me with your
terrors.
²²Then summon me and I will answer,
or let me speak, and you reply.
²³How many wrongs and sins have I
committed?
Show me my offense and my sin.
²⁴Why do you hide your face

and consider me your enemy?
²⁵Will you torment a windblown leaf?
Will you chase after dry chaff?
²⁶For you write down bitter things against
me
and make me inherit the sins of my
youth.
²⁷You fasten my feet in shackles;
you keep close watch on all my paths
by putting marks on the soles of my
feet.

²⁸"So man wastes away like something
rotten,
like a garment eaten by moths.

14 "Man born of woman
is of few days and full of trouble.
²He springs up like a flower and withers
away;
like a fleeting shadow, he does not
endure.
³Do you fix your eye on such a one?
Will you bring him*b* before you for
judgment?
⁴Who can bring what is pure from the
impure?
No one!
⁵Man's days are determined;
you have decreed the number of his
months
and have set limits he cannot exceed.
⁶So look away from him and let him
alone,
till he has put in his time like a hired
man.

⁷"At least there is hope for a tree:
If it is cut down, it will sprout again,
and its new shoots will not fail.
⁸Its roots may grow old in the ground
and its stump die in the soil,
⁹yet at the scent of water it will bud
and put forth shoots like a plant.
¹⁰But man dies and is laid low;
he breathes his last and is no more.
¹¹As water disappears from the sea
or a riverbed becomes parched and
dry,
¹²so man lies down and does not rise;
till the heavens are no more, men will
not awake
or be roused from their sleep.

¹³"If only you would hide me in the
grave*c*
and conceal me till your anger has
passed!

---

a15 Or *He will surely slay me; I have no hope — / yet I will*   *b3* Septuagint, Vulgate and Syriac; Hebrew *me*
c13 Hebrew *Sheol*

THE ANSWER TO WHY IS WHO

Maria is sobbing. Angrily she yells at Albert, "It's not fair! How can a loving God just sit there while my father gets gunned down? If God is so good, how come my father's dead and those drug dealers are still alive? My father was trying to make this a better place. He only cared about helping people. And now he's gone, and they're still out there pushing drugs. Why, Al?"

"I don't know," Al replies quietly. "I just don't have an answer."

Look It Up
● ● ● ●

In the book of Job, Job undergoes an unbelievable series of personal tragedies (Job 1—2). Friends offer all sorts of possible reasons for his suffering (Job 3—37), but there is no comfort for Job until God finally speaks (Job 38—41). Interestingly, God never addresses the "why" question. He simply reveals himself.

Reminded of God's sovereignty, Job responds, "Surely I spoke of things I did not understand, things too wonderful for me to know . . . . My ears had heard of you but now my eyes have seen you" (Job 42:3,5).

It may not take away the pain, but somehow it helps to remember that God is good and that he's in control.

Think It Through
● ● ● ●

An artisan unveils his latest tapestry—a motley mass of jumbled and knotted threads. "What's that?" you mumble. The craftsman laughs and flips the ugly textile over, revealing a magnificent design. You had been looking at it from the back side!

God's use of suffering in our lives is like that. From where we sit, pain is ugly and useless. But one day we'll see things from a different perspective. We'll finally understand how he weaves all our sorrow into a wonderful work of art.

Work It Out
● ● ● ●

Go to your church library or to your local Christian bookstore and get a copy of a book that covers the issue of suffering from the Christian's perspective. Do you agree with what is said? You may need to read several books in order to get a grasp on why there is pain in the world and how God uses suffering.

Nail It Down
● ● ● ●

Read Job's words in the face of tremendous suffering in Job 13:15.

Turn to pages 525, 1261, 1309 and 1369 for other readings on suffering.
Turn to page 525 for Friday's reading.

Topic
● ● ● ●

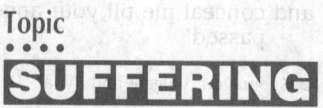

SUFFERING

If only you would set me a time
and then remember me!
¹⁴If a man dies, will he live again?
All the days of my hard service
I will wait for my renewal^a to come.
¹⁵You will call and I will answer you;
you will long for the creature your
hands have made.
¹⁶Surely then you will count my steps
but not keep track of my sin.
¹⁷My offenses will be sealed up in a bag;
you will cover over my sin.

¹⁸"But as a mountain erodes and
crumbles
and as a rock is moved from its place,
¹⁹as water wears away stones
and torrents wash away the soil,
so you destroy man's hope.
²⁰You overpower him once for all, and he
is gone;
you change his countenance and send
him away.
²¹If his sons are honored, he does not
know it;
if they are brought low, he does not
see it.
²²He feels but the pain of his own body
and mourns only for himself."

Eliphaz

15

Then Eliphaz the Temanite replied:

²"Would a wise man answer with
empty notions
or fill his belly with the hot east
wind?
³Would he argue with useless words,
with speeches that have no value?
⁴But you even undermine piety
and hinder devotion to God.
⁵Your sin prompts your mouth;
you adopt the tongue of the crafty.
⁶Your own mouth condemns you, not
mine;
your own lips testify against you.

⁷"Are you the first man ever born?
Were you brought forth before the
hills?
⁸Do you listen in on God's council?
Do you limit wisdom to yourself?
⁹What do you know that we do not
know?
What insights do you have that we do
not have?
¹⁰The gray-haired and the aged are on
our side,

men even older than your father.
¹¹Are God's consolations not enough for
you,
words spoken gently to you?
¹²Why has your heart carried you away,
and why do your eyes flash,
¹³so that you vent your rage against God
and pour out such words from your
mouth?

¹⁴"What is man, that he could be pure,
or one born of woman, that he could
be righteous?
¹⁵If God places no trust in his holy ones,
if even the heavens are not pure in
his eyes,
¹⁶how much less man, who is vile and
corrupt,
who drinks up evil like water!

¹⁷"Listen to me and I will explain to you;
let me tell you what I have seen,
¹⁸what wise men have declared,
hiding nothing received from their
fathers
¹⁹(to whom alone the land was given
when no alien passed among them):
²⁰All his days the wicked man suffers
torment,
the ruthless through all the years
stored up for him.
²¹Terrifying sounds fill his ears;
when all seems well, marauders
attack him.
²²He despairs of escaping the darkness;
he is marked for the sword.
²³He wanders about—food for vultures^b;
he knows the day of darkness is at
hand.
²⁴Distress and anguish fill him with terror;
they overwhelm him, like a king
poised to attack,
²⁵because he shakes his fist at God
and vaunts himself against the
Almighty,
²⁶defiantly charging against him
with a thick, strong shield.

²⁷"Though his face is covered with fat
and his waist bulges with flesh,
²⁸he will inhabit ruined towns
and houses where no one lives,
houses crumbling to rubble.
²⁹He will no longer be rich and his wealth
will not endure,
nor will his possessions spread over
the land.
³⁰He will not escape the darkness;

^a14 Or *release*   ^b23 Or *about, looking for food*

a flame will wither his shoots,
and the breath of God's mouth will
carry him away.
³¹Let him not deceive himself by trusting
what is worthless,
for he will get nothing in return.
³²Before his time he will be paid in full,
and his branches will not flourish.
³³He will be like a vine stripped of its
unripe grapes,
like an olive tree shedding its
blossoms.
³⁴For the company of the godless will be
barren,
and fire will consume the tents of
those who love bribes.
³⁵They conceive trouble and give birth to
evil;
their womb fashions deceit."

Job

16

Then Job replied:

²"I have heard many things like
these;
miserable comforters are you all!
³Will your long-winded speeches never
end?
What ails you that you keep on
arguing?
⁴I also could speak like you,
if you were in my place;
I could make fine speeches against you
and shake my head at you.
⁵But my mouth would encourage you;
comfort from my lips would bring you
relief.

⁶"Yet if I speak, my pain is not relieved;
and if I refrain, it does not go away.
⁷Surely, O God, you have worn me out;
you have devastated my entire
household.
⁸You have bound me—and it has
become a witness;
my gauntness rises up and testifies
against me.
⁹God assails me and tears me in his
anger
and gnashes his teeth at me;
my opponent fastens on me his
piercing eyes.
¹⁰Men open their mouths to jeer at me;
they strike my cheek in scorn
and unite together against me.
¹¹God has turned me over to evil men
and thrown me into the clutches of
the wicked.

¹²All was well with me, but he shattered
me;
he seized me by the neck and
crushed me.
He has made me his target;
¹³   his archers surround me.
Without pity, he pierces my kidneys
and spills my gall on the ground.
¹⁴Again and again he bursts upon me;
he rushes at me like a warrior.

¹⁵"I have sewed sackcloth over my skin
and buried my brow in the dust.
¹⁶My face is red with weeping,
deep shadows ring my eyes;
¹⁷yet my hands have been free of
violence
and my prayer is pure.

¹⁸"O earth, do not cover my blood;
may my cry never be laid to rest!
¹⁹Even now my witness is in heaven;
my advocate is on high.
²⁰My intercessor is my friend^a
as my eyes pour out tears to God;
²¹on behalf of a man he pleads with God
as a man pleads for his friend.

²²"Only a few years will pass
before I go on the journey of no
return.

17

¹My spirit is broken,
my days are cut short,
the grave awaits me.
²Surely mockers surround me;
my eyes must dwell on their hostility.

³"Give me, O God, the pledge you
demand.
Who else will put up security for me?
⁴You have closed their minds to
understanding;
therefore you will not let them
triumph.
⁵If a man denounces his friends for
reward,
the eyes of his children will fail.

⁶"God has made me a byword to
everyone,
a man in whose face people spit.
⁷My eyes have grown dim with grief;
my whole frame is but a shadow.
⁸Upright men are appalled at this;
the innocent are aroused against the
ungodly.
⁹Nevertheless, the righteous will hold to
their ways,

^a20 Or *My friends treat me with scorn*

and those with clean hands will grow
    stronger.
10"But come on, all of you, try again!
    I will not find a wise man among you.
11My days have passed, my plans are
    shattered,
    and so are the desires of my heart.
12These men turn night into day;
    in the face of darkness they say,
    'Light is near.'
13If the only home I hope for is the
    grave,ᵃ
    if I spread out my bed in darkness,
14if I say to corruption, 'You are my
    father,'
    and to the worm, 'My mother' or 'My
    sister,'
15where then is my hope?
    Who can see any hope for me?
16Will it go down to the gates of deathᵃ?
    Will we descend together into the
    dust?"

Bildad

18 Then Bildad the Shuhite replied:

2"When will you end these
    speeches?
    Be sensible, and then we can talk.
3Why are we regarded as cattle
    and considered stupid in your sight?
4You who tear yourself to pieces in your
    anger,
    is the earth to be abandoned for your
    sake?
    Or must the rocks be moved from
    their place?

5"The lamp of the wicked is snuffed out;
    the flame of his fire stops burning.
6The light in his tent becomes dark;
    the lamp beside him goes out.
7The vigor of his step is weakened;
    his own schemes throw him down.
8His feet thrust him into a net
    and he wanders into its mesh.
9A trap seizes him by the heel;
    a snare holds him fast.
10A noose is hidden for him on the
    ground;
    a trap lies in his path.
11Terrors startle him on every side
    and dog his every step.
12Calamity is hungry for him;
    disaster is ready for him when he
    falls.
13It eats away parts of his skin;

death's firstborn devours his limbs.
14He is torn from the security of his tent
    and marched off to the king of
    terrors.
15Fire residesᵇ in his tent;
    burning sulfur is scattered over his
    dwelling.
16His roots dry up below
    and his branches wither above.
17The memory of him perishes from the
    earth;
    he has no name in the land.
18He is driven from light into darkness
    and is banished from the world.
19He has no offspring or descendants
    among his people,
    no survivor where once he lived.
20Men of the west are appalled at his fate;
    men of the east are seized with
    horror.
21Surely such is the dwelling of an evil
    man;
    such is the place of one who knows
    not God."

Job

19 Then Job replied:

2"How long will you torment me
    and crush me with words?
3Ten times now you have reproached
    me;
    shamelessly you attack me.
4If it is true that I have gone astray,
    my error remains my concern alone.
5If indeed you would exalt yourselves
    above me
    and use my humiliation against me,
6then know that God has wronged me
    and drawn his net around me.

7"Though I cry, 'I've been wronged!' I get
    no response;
    though I call for help, there is no
    justice.
8He has blocked my way so I cannot
    pass;
    he has shrouded my paths in
    darkness.
9He has stripped me of my honor
    and removed the crown from my
    head.
10He tears me down on every side till I
    am gone;
    he uproots my hope like a tree.
11His anger burns against me;
    he counts me among his enemies.

ᵃ13,16 Hebrew Sheol   ᵇ15 Or Nothing he had remains

¹²His troops advance in force;
    they build a siege ramp against me
        and encamp around my tent.

¹³"He has alienated my brothers from me;
    my acquaintances are completely
        estranged from me.
¹⁴My kinsmen have gone away;
    my friends have forgotten me.
¹⁵My guests and my maidservants count
        me a stranger;
    they look upon me as an alien.
¹⁶I summon my servant, but he does not
        answer,
    though I beg him with my own
        mouth.
¹⁷My breath is offensive to my wife;
    I am loathsome to my own brothers.
¹⁸Even the little boys scorn me;
    when I appear, they ridicule me.
¹⁹All my intimate friends detest me;
    those I love have turned against me.
²⁰I am nothing but skin and bones;
    I have escaped with only the skin of
        my teeth.ᵃ

²¹"Have pity on me, my friends, have pity,
    for the hand of God has struck me.
²²Why do you pursue me as God does?
    Will you never get enough of my
        flesh?

²³"Oh, that my words were recorded,
    that they were written on a scroll,
²⁴that they were inscribed with an iron
        tool onᵇ lead,
    or engraved in rock forever!
²⁵I know that my Redeemerᶜ lives,
    and that in the end he will stand
        upon the earth.ᵈ
²⁶And after my skin has been destroyed,
    yetᵉ inᶠ my flesh I will see God;
²⁷I myself will see him
    with my own eyes—I, and not
        another.
    How my heart yearns within me!

²⁸"If you say, 'How we will hound him,
    since the root of the trouble lies in
        him,ᵍ'
²⁹you should fear the sword yourselves;
    for wrath will bring punishment by
        the sword,
    and then you will know that there is
        judgment.ʰ"

Zophar

20 Then Zophar the Naamathite replied:

²"My troubled thoughts prompt me to
        answer
    because I am greatly disturbed.
³I hear a rebuke that dishonors me,
    and my understanding inspires me to
        reply.

⁴"Surely you know how it has been from
        of old,
    ever since manⁱ was placed on the
        earth,
⁵that the mirth of the wicked is brief,
    the joy of the godless lasts but a
        moment.
⁶Though his pride reaches to the
        heavens
    and his head touches the clouds,
⁷he will perish forever, like his own
        dung;
    those who have seen him will say,
        'Where is he?'
⁸Like a dream he flies away, no more to
        be found,
    banished like a vision of the night.
⁹The eye that saw him will not see him
        again;
    his place will look on him no more.
¹⁰His children must make amends to the
        poor;
    his own hands must give back his
        wealth.
¹¹The youthful vigor that fills his bones
    will lie with him in the dust.

¹²"Though evil is sweet in his mouth
    and he hides it under his tongue,
¹³though he cannot bear to let it go
    and keeps it in his mouth,
¹⁴yet his food will turn sour in his
        stomach;
    it will become the venom of serpents
        within him.
¹⁵He will spit out the riches he
        swallowed;
    God will make his stomach vomit
        them up.
¹⁶He will suck the poison of serpents;
    the fangs of an adder will kill him.
¹⁷He will not enjoy the streams,
    the rivers flowing with honey and
        cream.

ᵃ20 Or only my gums   ᵇ24 Or and   ᶜ25 Or defender
awake, / though this body, has been destroyed, / then   ᵈ25 Or upon my grave   ᵉ26 Or And after I
Septuagint and Vulgate; most Hebrew manuscripts me   ᶠ26 Or / apart from   ᵍ28 Many Hebrew manuscripts.
ⁱ4 Or Adam   ʰ29 Or / that you may come to know the Almighty

18What he toiled for he must give back
   uneaten;
   he will not enjoy the profit from his
   trading.
19For he has oppressed the poor and left
   them destitute;
   he has seized houses he did not
   build.

20"Surely he will have no respite from his
   craving;
   he cannot save himself by his
   treasure.
21Nothing is left for him to devour;
   his prosperity will not endure.
22In the midst of his plenty, distress will
   overtake him;
   the full force of misery will come
   upon him.
23When he has filled his belly,
   God will vent his burning anger
   against him
   and rain down his blows upon him.
24Though he flees from an iron weapon,
   a bronze-tipped arrow pierces him.
25He pulls it out of his back,
   the gleaming point out of his liver.
   Terrors will come over him;
26   total darkness lies in wait for his
   treasures.
   A fire unfanned will consume him
   and devour what is left in his tent.
27The heavens will expose his guilt;
   the earth will rise up against him.
28A flood will carry off his house,
   rushing watersa on the day of God's
   wrath.
29Such is the fate God allots the wicked,
   the heritage appointed for them by
   God."

Job
21
Then Job replied:

2"Listen carefully to my words;
   let this be the consolation you give
   me.
3Bear with me while I speak,
   and after I have spoken, mock on.

4"Is my complaint directed to man?
   Why should I not be impatient?
5Look at me and be astonished;
   clap your hand over your mouth.
6When I think about this, I am terrified;
   trembling seizes my body.
7Why do the wicked live on,

   growing old and increasing in power?
8They see their children established
   around them,
   their offspring before their eyes.
9Their homes are safe and free from fear;
   the rod of God is not upon them.
10Their bulls never fail to breed;
   their cows calve and do not miscarry.
11They send forth their children as a
   flock;
   their little ones dance about.
12They sing to the music of tambourine
   and harp;
   they make merry to the sound of the
   flute.
13They spend their years in prosperity
   and go down to the graveb in
   peace.c
14Yet they say to God, 'Leave us alone!
   We have no desire to know your
   ways.
15Who is the Almighty, that we should
   serve him?
   What would we gain by praying to
   him?'
16But their prosperity is not in their own
   hands,
   so I stand aloof from the counsel of
   the wicked.

17"Yet how often is the lamp of the
   wicked snuffed out?
   How often does calamity come upon
   them,
   the fate God allots in his anger?
18How often are they like straw before the
   wind,
   like chaff swept away by a gale?
19It is said, 'God stores up a man's
   punishment for his sons.'
   Let him repay the man himself, so
   that he will know it!
20Let his own eyes see his destruction;
   let him drink of the wrath of the
   Almighty.d
21For what does he care about the family
   he leaves behind
   when his allotted months come to an
   end?

22"Can anyone teach knowledge to God,
   since he judges even the highest?
23One man dies in full vigor,
   completely secure and at ease,
24his bodye well nourished,
   his bones rich with marrow.

---

a28 Or *The possessions in his house will be carried off, / washed away*   b13 Hebrew *Sheol*   c13 Or *in an instant*   d17-20 Verses 17 and 18 may be taken as exclamations and 19 and 20 as declarations.   e24 The meaning of the Hebrew for this word is uncertain.

²⁵Another man dies in bitterness of soul,
  never having enjoyed anything good.
²⁶Side by side they lie in the dust,
  and worms cover them both.

²⁷"I know full well what you are thinking,
  the schemes by which you would
    wrong me.
²⁸You say, 'Where now is the great man's
    house,
  the tents where wicked men lived?'
²⁹Have you never questioned those who
    travel?
  Have you paid no regard to their
    accounts—
³⁰that the evil man is spared from the day
    of calamity,
  that he is delivered from ᵃ the day of
    wrath?
³¹Who denounces his conduct to his face?
  Who repays him for what he has
    done?
³²He is carried to the grave,
  and watch is kept over his tomb.
³³The soil in the valley is sweet to him;
  all men follow after him,
  and a countless throng goes ᵇ before
    him.

³⁴"So how can you console me with your
    nonsense?
  Nothing is left of your answers but
    falsehood!"

Eliphaz

22 Then Eliphaz the Temanite replied:

²"Can a man be of benefit to God?
  Can even a wise man benefit him?
³What pleasure would it give the
    Almighty if you were righteous?
  What would he gain if your ways
    were blameless?

⁴"Is it for your piety that he rebukes you
  and brings charges against you?
⁵Is not your wickedness great?
  Are not your sins endless?
⁶You demanded security from your
    brothers for no reason;
  you stripped men of their clothing,
    leaving them naked.
⁷You gave no water to the weary
  and you withheld food from the
    hungry,
⁸though you were a powerful man,
    owning land—
  an honored man, living on it.

⁹And you sent widows away
    empty-handed
  and broke the strength of the
    fatherless.
¹⁰That is why snares are all around you,
  why sudden peril terrifies you,
¹¹why it is so dark you cannot see,
  and why a flood of water covers you.

¹²"Is not God in the heights of heaven?
  And see how lofty are the highest
    stars!
¹³Yet you say, 'What does God know?
  Does he judge through such
    darkness?
¹⁴Thick clouds veil him, so he does not
    see us
  as he goes about in the vaulted
    heavens.'
¹⁵Will you keep to the old path
  that evil men have trod?
¹⁶They were carried off before their time,
  their foundations washed away by a
    flood.
¹⁷They said to God, 'Leave us alone!
  What can the Almighty do to us?'
¹⁸Yet it was he who filled their houses
    with good things,
  so I stand aloof from the counsel of
    the wicked.

¹⁹"The righteous see their ruin and
    rejoice;
  the innocent mock them, saying,
²⁰'Surely our foes are destroyed,
  and fire devours their wealth.'

²¹"Submit to God and be at peace with
    him;
  in this way prosperity will come to
    you.
²²Accept instruction from his mouth
  and lay up his words in your heart.
²³If you return to the Almighty, you will
    be restored:
  If you remove wickedness far from
    your tent
²⁴and assign your nuggets to the dust,
  your gold of Ophir to the rocks in the
    ravines,
²⁵then the Almighty will be your gold,
  the choicest silver for you.
²⁶Surely then you will find delight in the
    Almighty
  and will lift up your face to God.
²⁷You will pray to him, and he will hear
    you,

ᵃ30 Or *man is reserved for the day of calamity, / that he is brought forth to*   ᵇ33 Or / *as a countless throng*
went

A NEW LOOK AT AN OLD PROBLEM

• •

Two tragedies, two responses:
When she was fifteen, Ellen broke her neck in an automobile accident. Paralyzed from the neck down, she has spent the last nine years in a wheelchair. Yet most of the time she is happy and joyful. She has an unusually deep walk with God. People like to be around her.

At age 10, Carl lost his parents in a plane crash. In the years that followed, the initial shock and grief turned into bitterness. Carl is an alcoholic with no real friends.

Look It Up
• • • •

We often see pain and suffering as horrible enemies to be avoided at all costs. Yet the Bible charges that suffering can have tremendous value:

"We also rejoice in our sufferings, because we know that suffering produces perseverance; perseverance, character; and character, hope" (Romans 5:3–4).

"I consider that our present sufferings are not worth comparing with the glory that will be revealed in us" (Romans 8:18).

Present character. Future glory. How can something that results in so much good be so bad?

Think It Through
• • • •

Consider this poem by an unknown author:

> I walked a mile with pleasure;
> She chattered all the way,
> But left me none the wiser
> For all she had to say.
> I walked a mile with sorrow;
> And ne'er a word said she;
> But, oh, the things I learned from her
> When sorrow walked with me.

Work It Out
• • • •

Does your view of or reaction to suffering need an overhaul? Here are four positive reactions to pain:

Put yourself in God's hands (Psalm 31:5), remembering that he is good (Psalm 34:8).

Acknowledge that you may never fully understand the reasons for your suffering (Deuteronomy 29:29).

Include sincere thanksgiving (1 Thessalonians 5:18) and rejoicing (James 1:2) in your times of prayer.

Nourish your faith by memorizing appropriate Bible verses on suffering (e.g., 2 Corinthians 4:16–18).

Nail It Down
• • • •

Memorize Job 23:10.

Turn to pages 518, 1261, 1309 and 1369 for other readings on suffering.
Turn to page 527 the weekend reading.

Topic
• • • •

SUFFERING

and you will fulfill your vows.
²⁸What you decide on will be done,
    and light will shine on your ways.
²⁹When men are brought low and you
        say, 'Lift them up!'
    then he will save the downcast.
³⁰He will deliver even one who is not
        innocent,
    who will be delivered through the
        cleanness of your hands."

Job

23

Then Job replied:

²"Even today my complaint is
        bitter;
    his hand*ᵃ* is heavy in spite of*ᵇ* my
        groaning.
³If only I knew where to find him;
    if only I could go to his dwelling!
⁴I would state my case before him
    and fill my mouth with arguments.
⁵I would find out what he would answer
        me,
    and consider what he would say.
⁶Would he oppose me with great power?
    No, he would not press charges
        against me.
⁷There an upright man could present his
        case before him,
    and I would be delivered forever from
        my judge.

⁸"But if I go to the east, he is not there;
    if I go to the west, I do not find him.
⁹When he is at work in the north, I do
        not see him;
    when he turns to the south, I catch
        no glimpse of him.
¹⁰But he knows the way that I take;
    when he has tested me, I will come
        forth as gold.
¹¹My feet have closely followed his steps;
    I have kept to his way without turning
        aside.
¹²I have not departed from the commands
        of his lips;
    I have treasured the words of his
        mouth more than my daily bread.

¹³"But he stands alone, and who can
        oppose him?
    He does whatever he pleases.
¹⁴He carries out his decree against me,
    and many such plans he still has in
        store.
¹⁵That is why I am terrified before him;

when I think of all this, I fear him.
¹⁶God has made my heart faint;
    the Almighty has terrified me.
¹⁷Yet I am not silenced by the darkness,
    by the thick darkness that covers my
        face.

24

"Why does the Almighty not set
        times for judgment?
    Why must those who know him look
        in vain for such days?
²Men move boundary stones;
    they pasture flocks they have stolen.
³They drive away the orphan's donkey
    and take the widow's ox in pledge.
⁴They thrust the needy from the path
    and force all the poor of the land into
        hiding.
⁵Like wild donkeys in the desert,
    the poor go about their labor of
        foraging food;
    the wasteland provides food for their
        children.
⁶They gather fodder in the fields
    and glean in the vineyards of the
        wicked.
⁷Lacking clothes, they spend the night
        naked;
    they have nothing to cover themselves
        in the cold.
⁸They are drenched by mountain rains
    and hug the rocks for lack of shelter.
⁹The fatherless child is snatched from
        the breast;
    the infant of the poor is seized for a
        debt.
¹⁰Lacking clothes, they go about naked;
    they carry the sheaves, but still go
        hungry.
¹¹They crush olives among the terracesᶜ;
    they tread the winepresses, yet suffer
        thirst.
¹²The groans of the dying rise from the
        city,
    and the souls of the wounded cry out
        for help.
    But God charges no one with
        wrongdoing.

¹³"There are those who rebel against the
        light,
    who do not know its ways
    or stay in its paths.
¹⁴When daylight is gone, the murderer
        rises up
    and kills the poor and needy;

ᵃ2 Septuagint and Syriac; Hebrew / the hand on me   ᵇ2 Or heavy on me in   ᶜ11 Or olives between the millstones; the meaning of the Hebrew for this word is uncertain.

THE LOW-DOWN ON FEELING LOW

Work It Out
• • • •

Do a quick study of depression. Look up a definition in the dictionary. Check out a book on the subject. What causes depression? What are some obvious symptoms?

Do you know someone who has been depressed? Have you ever been depressed? Not just in a bad mood but truly down and depressed? And not just for a few hours but for several days? What was it like? What did you do to get over it?

Depression itself is not a sin. The Bible says that Job was "blameless and upright." Yet after all the terrible things that happened to him, the loss of all his belongings and the death of his children, he felt pretty low. So low, in fact, that he said he wished he had never been born (Job 3:1–2).

There was one thing Job didn't do, though. He didn't ignore how he felt. He didn't pretend everything was okay when it wasn't. He faced his feelings, talked with his friends and went to God for help.

The same resources are there for you if you're depressed. Face your feelings and get some help. Your friends, a youth pastor, a parent, a teacher—find someone to help you work through your feelings. And talk to God, too. He offers help no one else can offer.

Nail It Down
• • • •

Read Job 23:17 for a description of Job's depression.

Think It Through
• • • •

Depression is an outer evidence of inner problems. Anger, bitterness, sorrow or sickness can all cause depression. Usually in order for depression to go away, the problems behind it must be dealt with, gotten into the open.

Job didn't hesitate to let God know exactly how he, Job, felt about all that had happened to him. So can you. Tell God exactly what you think and how you feel. He's a big God—big enough to listen to all you have to say and to help you when you need him most.

Nail It Down
• • • •

Reread Job's description of depression in Job 23:17. For further insight read Psalm 130.

Turn to page 360, 601, 1197 and 1256 for other readings on depression.
Turn to page 529 for Monday's reading.

Topic
• • • •

DEPRESSION

in the night he steals forth like a
　　thief.
¹⁵The eye of the adulterer watches for
　　dusk;
　he thinks, 'No eye will see me,'
　and he keeps his face concealed.
¹⁶In the dark, men break into houses,
　but by day they shut themselves in;
　they want nothing to do with the
　　light.
¹⁷For all of them, deep darkness is their
　　morning[a];
　they make friends with the terrors of
　　darkness.[b]

¹⁸"Yet they are foam on the surface of the
　　water;
　their portion of the land is cursed,
　so that no one goes to the vineyards.
¹⁹As heat and drought snatch away the
　　melted snow,
　so the grave[c] snatches away those
　　who have sinned.
²⁰The womb forgets them,
　the worm feasts on them;
　evil men are no longer remembered
　but are broken like a tree.
²¹They prey on the barren and childless
　　woman,
　and to the widow show no kindness.
²²But God drags away the mighty by his
　　power;
　though they become established, they
　　have no assurance of life.
²³He may let them rest in a feeling of
　　security,
　but his eyes are on their ways.
²⁴For a little while they are exalted, and
　　then they are gone;
　they are brought low and gathered up
　　like all others;
　they are cut off like heads of grain.

²⁵"If this is not so, who can prove me
　　false
　and reduce my words to nothing?"

Bildad

25 Then Bildad the Shuhite replied:

²"Dominion and awe belong to
　　God;
　he establishes order in the heights of
　　heaven.
³Can his forces be numbered?
　Upon whom does his light not rise?

⁴How then can a man be righteous
　　before God?
　How can one born of woman be
　　pure?
⁵If even the moon is not bright
　and the stars are not pure in his
　　eyes,
⁶how much less man, who is but a
　　maggot—
　a son of man, who is only a worm!"

Job

26 Then Job replied:

²"How you have helped the
　　powerless!
　How you have saved the arm that is
　　feeble!
³What advice you have offered to one
　　without wisdom!
　And what great insight you have
　　displayed!
⁴Who has helped you utter these words?
　And whose spirit spoke from your
　　mouth?

⁵"The dead are in deep anguish,
　those beneath the waters and all that
　　live in them.
⁶Death[c] is naked before God;
　Destruction[d] lies uncovered.
⁷He spreads out the northern ⌊skies⌋ over
　　empty space;
　he suspends the earth over nothing.
⁸He wraps up the waters in his clouds,
　yet the clouds do not burst under
　　their weight.
⁹He covers the face of the full moon,
　spreading his clouds over it.
¹⁰He marks out the horizon on the face of
　　the waters
　for a boundary between light and
　　darkness.
¹¹The pillars of the heavens quake,
　aghast at his rebuke.
¹²By his power he churned up the sea;
　by his wisdom he cut Rahab to
　　pieces.
¹³By his breath the skies became fair;
　his hand pierced the gliding serpent.
¹⁴And these are but the outer fringe of his
　　works;
　how faint the whisper we hear of him!
　Who then can understand the thunder
　　of his power?"

---

a 17 Or *them, their morning is like the shadow of death*
Sheol　　d 6 Hebrew *Abaddon*　　　　b 17 Or *of the shadow of death*　　c 19,6 Hebrew

ARE THERE LIMITS TO OUR KNOWLEDGE?

Confused and concerned, Alene pays a visit to her science teacher after school. Mrs. Turner's friendliness and willingness to listen make her a favorite with the students. (She's also very intelligent.)

After Alene explains the inner struggle she feels because of the conflict between the theory of evolution and her belief in creation, Mrs. Turner points to recent issues of several scientific magazines.

"Alene, I know what you're feeling, believe me. I was brought up in a religious home too. But I had to come to a point where I had to decide, 'Am I going to believe a Bible story or the findings of modern science?' "

Look It Up

Many advocates of the theory of evolution belittle other viewpoints—especially the belief in special creation. They glorify, instead, science and human reason. Yet, note these verses about human "wisdom":

"I am the LORD, who has made all things, who alone stretched out the heavens, who spread out the earth by myself, . . . who overthrows the learning of the wise and turns it into nonsense" (Isaiah 44:24–25).

"The man who thinks he knows something does not yet know as he ought to know" (1 Corinthians 8:2).

Think It Through

Some critics label creationism a "religious doctrine" and discount it because it is cited in the Bible. "You can't really believe that! It's in the Bible." As if being in the Bible automatically makes a thing untrue and not worth consideration.

Be sure you don't accept all you're taught without doing some of your own research into the issues.

Work It Out

Find out if there are any Christians in your community who are knowledgeable on the creation/evolution issue. Ask your youth director or Bible study leader to invite them in for a special series on origins.

Think through and talk over with a Christian friend what you would say if someone called evolution a "fact" and creation a "crock."

Nail It Down

Read what Job had to say about God as creator in Job 26:7.

Turn to pages 2, 621, 1188 and 1348 for other readings on origins.
Turn to page 544 for Tuesday's reading.

Topic
. . . .
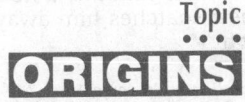

27

And Job continued his discourse:

²"As surely as God lives, who has
    denied me justice,
the Almighty, who has made me taste
    bitterness of soul,
³as long as I have life within me,
    the breath of God in my nostrils,
⁴my lips will not speak wickedness,
    and my tongue will utter no deceit.
⁵I will never admit you are in the right;
    till I die, I will not deny my integrity.
⁶I will maintain my righteousness and
    never let go of it;
my conscience will not reproach me
    as long as I live.

⁷"May my enemies be like the wicked,
    my adversaries like the unjust!
⁸For what hope has the godless when he
    is cut off,
when God takes away his life?
⁹Does God listen to his cry
    when distress comes upon him?
¹⁰Will he find delight in the Almighty?
    Will he call upon God at all times?

¹¹"I will teach you about the power of
    God;
the ways of the Almighty I will not
    conceal.
¹²You have all seen this yourselves.
    Why then this meaningless talk?

¹³"Here is the fate God allots to the
    wicked,
the heritage a ruthless man receives
    from the Almighty:
¹⁴However many his children, their fate is
    the sword;
his offspring will never have enough
    to eat.
¹⁵The plague will bury those who survive
    him,
and their widows will not weep for
    them.
¹⁶Though he heaps up silver like dust
    and clothes like piles of clay,
¹⁷what he lays up the righteous will wear,
    and the innocent will divide his silver.
¹⁸The house he builds is like a moth's
    cocoon,
like a hut made by a watchman.
¹⁹He lies down wealthy, but will do so no
    more;
when he opens his eyes, all is gone.
²⁰Terrors overtake him like a flood;
    a tempest snatches him away in the
    night.

²¹The east wind carries him off, and he is
    gone;
it sweeps him out of his place.
²²It hurls itself against him without mercy
    as he flees headlong from its power.
²³It claps its hands in derision
    and hisses him out of his place.

28

"There is a mine for silver
    and a place where gold is refined.
²Iron is taken from the earth,
    and copper is smelted from ore.
³Man puts an end to the darkness;
    he searches the farthest recesses
    for ore in the blackest darkness.
⁴Far from where people dwell he cuts a
    shaft,
in places forgotten by the foot of
    man;
far from men he dangles and sways.
⁵The earth, from which food comes,
    is transformed below as by fire;
⁶sapphires*ᵃ* come from its rocks,
    and its dust contains nuggets of gold.
⁷No bird of prey knows that hidden path,
    no falcon's eye has seen it.
⁸Proud beasts do not set foot on it,
    and no lion prowls there.
⁹Man's hand assaults the flinty rock
    and lays bare the roots of the
    mountains.
¹⁰He tunnels through the rock;
    his eyes see all its treasures.
¹¹He searches*ᵇ* the sources of the rivers
    and brings hidden things to light.

¹²"But where can wisdom be found?
    Where does understanding dwell?
¹³Man does not comprehend its worth;
    it cannot be found in the land of the
    living.
¹⁴The deep says, 'It is not in me';
    the sea says, 'It is not with me.'
¹⁵It cannot be bought with the finest gold,
    nor can its price be weighed in silver.
¹⁶It cannot be bought with the gold of
    Ophir,
with precious onyx or sapphires.
¹⁷Neither gold nor crystal can compare
    with it,
nor can it be had for jewels of gold.
¹⁸Coral and jasper are not worthy of
    mention;
the price of wisdom is beyond rubies.
¹⁹The topaz of Cush cannot compare with
    it;
it cannot be bought with pure gold.

ᵃ6 Or *lapis lazuli*; also in verse 16   *ᵇ11* Septuagint, Aquila and Vulgate; Hebrew *He dams up*

²⁰"Where then does wisdom come from?
   Where does understanding dwell?
²¹It is hidden from the eyes of every
       living thing,
   concealed even from the birds of the
       air.
²²Destruction*ᵃ* and Death say,
   'Only a rumor of it has reached our
       ears.'
²³God understands the way to it
   and he alone knows where it dwells,
²⁴for he views the ends of the earth
   and sees everything under the
       heavens.
²⁵When he established the force of the
       wind
   and measured out the waters,
²⁶when he made a decree for the rain
   and a path for the thunderstorm,
²⁷then he looked at wisdom and
       appraised it;
   he confirmed it and tested it.
²⁸And he said to man,
   'The fear of the Lord—that is wisdom,
   and to shun evil is understanding.'"

29
Job continued his discourse:

²"How I long for the months gone
       by,
   for the days when God watched over
       me,
³when his lamp shone upon my head
   and by his light I walked through
       darkness!
⁴Oh, for the days when I was in my
       prime,
   when God's intimate friendship
       blessed my house,
⁵when the Almighty was still with me
   and my children were around me,
⁶when my path was drenched with
       cream
   and the rock poured out for me
       streams of olive oil.

⁷"When I went to the gate of the city
   and took my seat in the public
       square,
⁸the young men saw me and stepped
       aside
   and the old men rose to their feet;
⁹the chief men refrained from speaking
   and covered their mouths with their
       hands;
¹⁰the voices of the nobles were hushed,
   and their tongues stuck to the roof of
       their mouths.

¹¹Whoever heard me spoke well of me,
   and those who saw me commended
       me,
¹²because I rescued the poor who cried
       for help,
   and the fatherless who had none to
       assist him.
¹³The man who was dying blessed me;
   I made the widow's heart sing.
¹⁴I put on righteousness as my clothing;
   justice was my robe and my turban.
¹⁵I was eyes to the blind
   and feet to the lame.
¹⁶I was a father to the needy;
   I took up the case of the stranger.
¹⁷I broke the fangs of the wicked
   and snatched the victims from their
       teeth.

¹⁸"I thought, 'I will die in my own house,
   my days as numerous as the grains of
       sand.
¹⁹My roots will reach to the water,
   and the dew will lie all night on my
       branches.
²⁰My glory will remain fresh in me,
   the bow ever new in my hand.'

²¹"Men listened to me expectantly,
   waiting in silence for my counsel.
²²After I had spoken, they spoke no more;
   my words fell gently on their ears.
²³They waited for me as for showers
   and drank in my words as the spring
       rain.
²⁴When I smiled at them, they scarcely
       believed it;
   the light of my face was precious to
       them.*ᵇ*
²⁵I chose the way for them and sat as
       their chief;
   I dwelt as a king among his troops;
   I was like one who comforts
       mourners.

30
"But now they mock me,
   men younger than I,
whose fathers I would have disdained
   to put with my sheep dogs.
²Of what use was the strength of their
       hands to me,
   since their vigor had gone from them?
³Haggard from want and hunger,
   they roamed*ᶜ* the parched land
   in desolate wastelands at night.
⁴In the brush they gathered salt herbs,

---

*ᵃ*22 Hebrew *Abaddon*   *ᵇ*24 The meaning of the Hebrew for this clause is uncertain.   *ᶜ*3 Or *gnawed*

and their food*a* was the root of the
broom tree.
⁵They were banished from their fellow
men,
shouted at as if they were thieves.
⁶They were forced to live in the dry
stream beds,
among the rocks and in holes in the
ground.
⁷They brayed among the bushes
and huddled in the undergrowth.
⁸A base and nameless brood,
they were driven out of the land.

⁹"And now their sons mock me in song;
I have become a byword among
them.
¹⁰They detest me and keep their distance;
they do not hesitate to spit in my
face.
¹¹Now that God has unstrung my bow
and afflicted me,
they throw off restraint in my
presence.
¹²On my right the tribe*b* attacks;
they lay snares for my feet,
they build their siege ramps against
me.
¹³They break up my road;
they succeed in destroying me—
without anyone's helping them.*c*
¹⁴They advance as through a gaping
breach;
amid the ruins they come rolling in.
¹⁵Terrors overwhelm me;
my dignity is driven away as by the
wind,
my safety vanishes like a cloud.

¹⁶"And now my life ebbs away;
days of suffering grip me.
¹⁷Night pierces my bones;
my gnawing pains never rest.
¹⁸In his great power ⌐God⌐ becomes like
clothing to me*d*;
he binds me like the neck of my
garment.
¹⁹He throws me into the mud,
and I am reduced to dust and ashes.

²⁰"I cry out to you, O God, but you do not
answer;
I stand up, but you merely look at
me.
²¹You turn on me ruthlessly;
with the might of your hand you
attack me.

²²You snatch me up and drive me before
the wind;
you toss me about in the storm.
²³I know you will bring me down to
death,
to the place appointed for all the
living.

²⁴"Surely no one lays a hand on a broken
man
when he cries for help in his distress.
²⁵Have I not wept for those in trouble?
Has not my soul grieved for the poor?
²⁶Yet when I hoped for good, evil came;
when I looked for light, then came
darkness.
²⁷The churning inside me never stops;
days of suffering confront me.
²⁸I go about blackened, but not by the
sun;
I stand up in the assembly and cry for
help.
²⁹I have become a brother of jackals,
a companion of owls.
³⁰My skin grows black and peels;
my body burns with fever.
³¹My harp is tuned to mourning,
and my flute to the sound of wailing.

31

"I made a covenant with my eyes
not to look lustfully at a girl.
²For what is man's lot from God above,
his heritage from the Almighty on
high?
³Is it not ruin for the wicked,
disaster for those who do wrong?
⁴Does he not see my ways
and count my every step?

⁵"If I have walked in falsehood
or my foot has hurried after deceit—
⁶let God weigh me in honest scales
and he will know that I am
blameless—
⁷if my steps have turned from the path,
if my heart has been led by my eyes,
or if my hands have been defiled,
⁸then may others eat what I have sown,
and may my crops be uprooted.

⁹"If my heart has been enticed by a
woman,
or if I have lurked at my neighbor's
door,
¹⁰then may my wife grind another man's
grain,
and may other men sleep with her.
¹¹For that would have been shameful,

---

a4 Or *fuel*   *b12* The meaning of the Hebrew for this word is uncertain.   *c13* Or *me. / 'No one can help him,'*
they say.   *d18* Hebrew; Septuagint ⌐God⌐ *grasps my clothing*

a sin to be judged.
12It is a fire that burns to Destruction[a];
    it would have uprooted my harvest.

13"If I have denied justice to my
        menservants and maidservants
    when they had a grievance against
        me,
14what will I do when God confronts me?
    What will I answer when called to
        account?
15Did not he who made me in the womb
        make them?
    Did not the same one form us both
        within our mothers?

16"If I have denied the desires of the poor
    or let the eyes of the widow grow
        weary,
17if I have kept my bread to myself,
    not sharing it with the fatherless—
18but from my youth I reared him as
        would a father,
    and from my birth I guided the
        widow—
19if I have seen anyone perishing for lack
        of clothing,
    or a needy man without a garment,
20and his heart did not bless me
    for warming him with the fleece from
        my sheep,
21if I have raised my hand against the
        fatherless,
    knowing that I had influence in court,
22then let my arm fall from the shoulder,
    let it be broken off at the joint.
23For I dreaded destruction from God,
    and for fear of his splendor I could
        not do such things.

24"If I have put my trust in gold
    or said to pure gold, 'You are my
        security,'
25if I have rejoiced over my great wealth,
    the fortune my hands had gained,
26if I have regarded the sun in its
        radiance
    or the moon moving in splendor,
27so that my heart was secretly enticed
    and my hand offered them a kiss of
        homage,
28then these also would be sins to be
        judged,
    for I would have been unfaithful to
        God on high.

29"If I have rejoiced at my enemy's
        misfortune

or gloated over the trouble that came
        to him—
30I have not allowed my mouth to sin
    by invoking a curse against his life—
31if the men of my household have never
        said,
    'Who has not had his fill of Job's
        meat?'—
32but no stranger had to spend the night
        in the street,
    for my door was always open to the
        traveler—
33if I have concealed my sin as men do,[b]
    by hiding my guilt in my heart
34because I so feared the crowd
    and so dreaded the contempt of the
        clans
    that I kept silent and would not go
        outside

35("Oh, that I had someone to hear me!
    I sign now my defense—let the
        Almighty answer me;
    let my accuser put his indictment in
        writing.
36Surely I would wear it on my shoulder,
    I would put it on like a crown.
37I would give him an account of my
        every step;
    like a prince I would approach
        him.)—

38"if my land cries out against me
    and all its furrows are wet with tears,
39if I have devoured its yield without
        payment
    or broken the spirit of its tenants,
40then let briers come up instead of
        wheat
    and weeds instead of barley."

The words of Job are ended.

Elihu

32 So these three men stopped answering Job, because he was righteous in his own eyes. 2But Elihu son of Barakel the Buzite, of the family of Ram, became very angry with Job for justifying himself rather than God. 3He was also angry with the three friends, because they had found no way to refute Job, and yet had condemned him.[c] 4Now Elihu had waited before speaking to Job because they were older than he. 5But when he saw that the three men had nothing more to say, his anger was aroused.

6So Elihu son of Barakel the Buzite said:

---

[a]12 Hebrew *Abaddon*   [b]33 Or *as Adam did*   [c]3 Masoretic Text; an ancient Hebrew scribal tradition *Job,*
and so had condemned God

"I am young in years,
   and you are old;
that is why I was fearful,
   not daring to tell you what I know.
⁷I thought, 'Age should speak;
   advanced years should teach wisdom.'
⁸But it is the spirit ᵃ in a man,
   the breath of the Almighty, that gives
     him understanding.
⁹It is not only the old ᵇ who are wise,
   not only the aged who understand
     what is right.

¹⁰"Therefore I say: Listen to me;
   I too will tell you what I know.
¹¹I waited while you spoke,
   I listened to your reasoning;
while you were searching for words,
¹²   I gave you my full attention.
But not one of you has proved Job
     wrong;
   none of you has answered his
     arguments.
¹³Do not say, 'We have found wisdom;
   let God refute him, not man.'
¹⁴But Job has not marshaled his words
     against me,
   and I will not answer him with your
     arguments.

¹⁵"They are dismayed and have no more
     to say;
   words have failed them.
¹⁶Must I wait, now that they are silent,
   now that they stand there with no
     reply?
¹⁷I too will have my say;
   I too will tell what I know.
¹⁸For I am full of words,
   and the spirit within me compels me;
¹⁹inside I am like bottled-up wine,
   like new wineskins ready to burst.
²⁰I must speak and find relief;
   I must open my lips and reply.
²¹I will show partiality to no one,
   nor will I flatter any man;
²²for if I were skilled in flattery,
   my Maker would soon take me away.

33 "But now, Job, listen to my words;
   pay attention to everything I say.
²I am about to open my mouth;
   my words are on the tip of my
     tongue.
³My words come from an upright heart;
   my lips sincerely speak what I know.
⁴The Spirit of God has made me;

   the breath of the Almighty gives me
     life.
⁵Answer me then, if you can;
   prepare yourself and confront me.
⁶I am just like you before God;
   I too have been taken from clay.
⁷No fear of me should alarm you,
   nor should my hand be heavy upon
     you.

⁸"But you have said in my hearing—
   I heard the very words—
⁹'I am pure and without sin;
   I am clean and free from guilt.
¹⁰Yet God has found fault with me;
   he considers me his enemy.
¹¹He fastens my feet in shackles;
   he keeps close watch on all my
     paths.'

¹²"But I tell you, in this you are not right,
   for God is greater than man.
¹³Why do you complain to him
   that he answers none of man's
     words ᶜ?
¹⁴For God does speak—now one way,
     now another—
   though man may not perceive it.
¹⁵In a dream, in a vision of the night,
   when deep sleep falls on men
     as they slumber in their beds,
¹⁶he may speak in their ears
   and terrify them with warnings,
¹⁷to turn man from wrongdoing
   and keep him from pride,
¹⁸to preserve his soul from the pit, ᵈ
   his life from perishing by the sword. ᵉ
¹⁹Or a man may be chastened on a bed
     of pain
   with constant distress in his bones,
²⁰so that his very being finds food
     repulsive
   and his soul loathes the choicest
     meal.
²¹His flesh wastes away to nothing,
   and his bones, once hidden, now
     stick out.
²²His soul draws near to the pit, ᶠ
   and his life to the messengers of
     death. ᵍ

²³"Yet if there is an angel on his side
   as a mediator, one out of a thousand,
   to tell a man what is right for him,
²⁴to be gracious to him and say,
   'Spare him from going down to the
     pit ʰ;

ᵃ8 Or *Spirit*; also in verse 18   ᵇ9 Or *many*; or *great*   ᶜ13 Or *that he does not answer for any of his actions*
ᵈ18 Or *preserve him from the grave*   ᵉ18 Or *from crossing the River*   ᶠ22 Or *He draws near to the grave*
ᵍ22 Or *to the dead*   ʰ24 Or *grave*

I have found a ransom for him'—
25then his flesh is renewed like a child's;
  it is restored as in the days of his
    youth.
26He prays to God and finds favor with
    him,
  he sees God's face and shouts for joy;
  he is restored by God to his righteous
    state.
27Then he comes to men and says,
  'I sinned, and perverted what was
    right,
  but I did not get what I deserved.
28He redeemed my soul from going down
    to the pit,ᵃ
  and I will live to enjoy the light.'

29"God does all these things to a man—
  twice, even three times—
30to turn back his soul from the pit,ᵇ
  that the light of life may shine on
    him.

31"Pay attention, Job, and listen to me;
  be silent, and I will speak.
32If you have anything to say, answer me;
  speak up, for I want you to be
    cleared.
33But if not, then listen to me;
  be silent, and I will teach you
    wisdom."

34 Then Elihu said:

2"Hear my words, you wise men;
  listen to me, you men of learning.
3For the ear tests words
  as the tongue tastes food.
4Let us discern for ourselves what is
    right;
  let us learn together what is good.

5"Job says, 'I am innocent,
  but God denies me justice.
6Although I am right,
  I am considered a liar;
  although I am guiltless,
  his arrow inflicts an incurable wound.'
7What man is like Job,
  who drinks scorn like water?
8He keeps company with evildoers;
  he associates with wicked men.
9For he says, 'It profits a man nothing
  when he tries to please God.'

10"So listen to me, you men of
    understanding.
  Far be it from God to do evil,
  from the Almighty to do wrong.

11He repays a man for what he has done;
  he brings upon him what his conduct
    deserves.
12It is unthinkable that God would do
    wrong,
  that the Almighty would pervert
    justice.
13Who appointed him over the earth?
  Who put him in charge of the whole
    world?
14If it were his intention
  and he withdrew his spiritᶜ and
    breath,
15all mankind would perish together
  and man would return to the dust.

16"If you have understanding, hear this;
  listen to what I say.
17Can he who hates justice govern?
  Will you condemn the just and
    mighty One?
18Is he not the One who says to kings,
  'You are worthless,'
  and to nobles, 'You are wicked,'
19who shows no partiality to princes
  and does not favor the rich over the
    poor,
  for they are all the work of his hands?
20They die in an instant, in the middle of
    the night;
  the people are shaken and they pass
    away;
  the mighty are removed without
    human hand.

21"His eyes are on the ways of men;
  he sees their every step.
22There is no dark place, no deep
    shadow,
  where evildoers can hide.
23God has no need to examine men
    further,
  that they should come before him for
    judgment.
24Without inquiry he shatters the mighty
  and sets up others in their place.
25Because he takes note of their deeds,
  he overthrows them in the night and
    they are crushed.
26He punishes them for their wickedness
  where everyone can see them,
27because they turned from following him
  and had no regard for any of his
    ways.
28They caused the cry of the poor to
    come before him,
  so that he heard the cry of the needy.

ᵃ28 Or redeemed me from going down to the grave   ᵇ30 Or turn him back from the grave   ᶜ14 Or Spirit

²⁹But if he remains silent, who can
condemn him?
If he hides his face, who can see him?
Yet he is over man and nation alike,
³⁰ to keep a godless man from ruling,
from laying snares for the people.

³¹"Suppose a man says to God,
'I am guilty but will offend no more.
³²Teach me what I cannot see;
if I have done wrong, I will not do so
again.'
³³Should God then reward you on your
terms,
when you refuse to repent?
You must decide, not I;
so tell me what you know.

³⁴"Men of understanding declare,
wise men who hear me say to me,
³⁵'Job speaks without knowledge;
his words lack insight.'
³⁶Oh, that Job might be tested to the
utmost
for answering like a wicked man!
³⁷To his sin he adds rebellion;
scornfully he claps his hands among
us
and multiplies his words against God."

35

Then Elihu said:

²"Do you think this is just?
You say, 'I will be cleared by God.ᵃ'
³Yet you ask him, 'What profit is it to
me,ᵇ
and what do I gain by not sinning?'

⁴"I would like to reply to you
and to your friends with you.
⁵Look up at the heavens and see;
gaze at the clouds so high above you.
⁶If you sin, how does that affect him?
If your sins are many, what does that
do to him?
⁷If you are righteous, what do you give
to him,
or what does he receive from your
hand?
⁸Your wickedness affects only a man like
yourself,
and your righteousness only the sons
of men.

⁹"Men cry out under a load of
oppression;
they plead for relief from the arm of
the powerful.

¹⁰But no one says, 'Where is God my
Maker,
who gives songs in the night,
¹¹who teaches more to us than toᶜ the
beasts of the earth
and makes us wiser thanᵈ the birds
of the air?'
¹²He does not answer when men cry out
because of the arrogance of the
wicked.
¹³Indeed, God does not listen to their
empty plea;
the Almighty pays no attention to it.
¹⁴How much less, then, will he listen
when you say that you do not see
him,
that your case is before him
and you must wait for him,
¹⁵and further, that his anger never
punishes
and he does not take the least notice
of wickedness.ᵉ
¹⁶So Job opens his mouth with empty
talk;
without knowledge he multiplies
words."

36

Elihu continued:

²"Bear with me a little longer and I
will show you
that there is more to be said in God's
behalf.
³I get my knowledge from afar;
I will ascribe justice to my Maker.
⁴Be assured that my words are not false;
one perfect in knowledge is with you.

⁵"God is mighty, but does not despise
men;
he is mighty, and firm in his purpose.
⁶He does not keep the wicked alive
but gives the afflicted their rights.
⁷He does not take his eyes off the
righteous;
he enthrones them with kings
and exalts them forever.
⁸But if men are bound in chains,
held fast by cords of affliction,
⁹he tells them what they have done—
that they have sinned arrogantly.
¹⁰He makes them listen to correction
and commands them to repent of
their evil.
¹¹If they obey and serve him,
they will spend the rest of their days
in prosperity

ᵃ2 Or *My righteousness is more than God's*   ᵇ3 Or *you*   ᶜ11 Or *teaches us by*   ᵈ11 Or *us wise by*
ᵉ15 Symmachus, Theodotion and Vulgate; the meaning of the Hebrew for this word is uncertain.

and their years in contentment.
¹²But if they do not listen,
  they will perish by the sword[a]
  and die without knowledge.

¹³"The godless in heart harbor
      resentment;
  even when he fetters them, they do
      not cry for help.
¹⁴They die in their youth,
  among male prostitutes of the shrines.
¹⁵But those who suffer he delivers in their
      suffering;
  he speaks to them in their affliction.

¹⁶"He is wooing you from the jaws of
      distress
  to a spacious place free from
      restriction,
  to the comfort of your table laden
      with choice food.
¹⁷But now you are laden with the
      judgment due the wicked;
  judgment and justice have taken hold
      of you.
¹⁸Be careful that no one entices you by
      riches;
  do not let a large bribe turn you
      aside.
¹⁹Would your wealth
  or even all your mighty efforts
  sustain you so you would not be in
      distress?
²⁰Do not long for the night,
  to drag people away from their
      homes.[b]
²¹Beware of turning to evil,
  which you seem to prefer to affliction.

²²"God is exalted in his power.
  Who is a teacher like him?
²³Who has prescribed his ways for him,
  or said to him, 'You have done
      wrong'?
²⁴Remember to extol his work,
  which men have praised in song.
²⁵All mankind has seen it;
  men gaze on it from afar.
²⁶How great is God—beyond our
      understanding!
  The number of his years is past
      finding out.

²⁷"He draws up the drops of water,
  which distill as rain to the streams[c];
²⁸the clouds pour down their moisture

and abundant showers fall on
      mankind.
²⁹Who can understand how he spreads
      out the clouds,
  how he thunders from his pavilion?
³⁰See how he scatters his lightning about
      him,
  bathing the depths of the sea.
³¹This is the way he governs[d] the nations
  and provides food in abundance.
³²He fills his hands with lightning
  and commands it to strike its mark.
³³His thunder announces the coming
      storm;
  even the cattle make known its
      approach.[e]

37 "At this my heart pounds
      and leaps from its place.
²Listen! Listen to the roar of his voice,
  to the rumbling that comes from his
      mouth.
³He unleashes his lightning beneath the
      whole heaven
  and sends it to the ends of the earth.
⁴After that comes the sound of his roar;
  he thunders with his majestic voice.
  When his voice resounds,
  he holds nothing back.
⁵God's voice thunders in marvelous ways;
  he does great things beyond our
      understanding.
⁶He says to the snow, 'Fall on the earth,'
  and to the rain shower, 'Be a mighty
      downpour.'
⁷So that all men he has made may know
      his work,
  he stops every man from his labor.[f]
⁸The animals take cover;
  they remain in their dens.
⁹The tempest comes out from its
      chamber,
  the cold from the driving winds.
¹⁰The breath of God produces ice,
  and the broad waters become frozen.
¹¹He loads the clouds with moisture;
  he scatters his lightning through
      them.
¹²At his direction they swirl around
  over the face of the whole earth
  to do whatever he commands them.
¹³He brings the clouds to punish men,
  or to water his earth[g] and show his
      love.

¹⁴"Listen to this, Job;

---

[a]12 Or *will cross the River*   [b]20 The meaning of the Hebrew for verses 18-20 is uncertain.   [c]27 Or *distill from the mist as rain*   [d]31 Or *nourishes*   [e]33 Or *announces his coming— / the One zealous against evil*   [f]7 Or / *he fills all men with fear by his power*   [g]13 Or *to favor them*

stop and consider God's wonders.
15Do you know how God controls the
clouds
and makes his lightning flash?
16Do you know how the clouds hang
poised,
those wonders of him who is perfect
in knowledge?
17You who swelter in your clothes
when the land lies hushed under the
south wind,
18can you join him in spreading out the
skies,
hard as a mirror of cast bronze?

19"Tell us what we should say to him;
we cannot draw up our case because
of our darkness.
20Should he be told that I want to speak?
Would any man ask to be swallowed
up?
21Now no one can look at the sun,
bright as it is in the skies
after the wind has swept them clean.
22Out of the north he comes in golden
splendor;
God comes in awesome majesty.
23The Almighty is beyond our reach and
exalted in power;
in his justice and great righteousness,
he does not oppress.
24Therefore, men revere him,
for does he not have regard for all the
wise in heart?a"

The Lord Speaks

38 Then the Lord answered Job out of
the storm. He said:

2"Who is this that darkens my counsel
with words without knowledge?
3Brace yourself like a man;
I will question you,
and you shall answer me.

4"Where were you when I laid the earth's
foundation?
Tell me, if you understand.
5Who marked off its dimensions? Surely
you know!
Who stretched a measuring line
across it?
6On what were its footings set,
or who laid its cornerstone—
7while the morning stars sang together
and all the angelsb shouted for joy?

8"Who shut up the sea behind doors

when it burst forth from the womb,
9when I made the clouds its garment
and wrapped it in thick darkness,
10when I fixed limits for it
and set its doors and bars in place,
11when I said, 'This far you may come
and no farther;
here is where your proud waves halt'?

12"Have you ever given orders to the
morning,
or shown the dawn its place,
13that it might take the earth by the edges
and shake the wicked out of it?
14The earth takes shape like clay under a
seal;
its features stand out like those of a
garment.
15The wicked are denied their light,
and their upraised arm is broken.

16"Have you journeyed to the springs of
the sea
or walked in the recesses of the deep?
17Have the gates of death been shown to
you?
Have you seen the gates of the
shadow of deathc?
18Have you comprehended the vast
expanses of the earth?
Tell me, if you know all this.

19"What is the way to the abode of light?
And where does darkness reside?
20Can you take them to their places?
Do you know the paths to their
dwellings?
21Surely you know, for you were already
born!
You have lived so many years!

22"Have you entered the storehouses of
the snow
or seen the storehouses of the hail,
23which I reserve for times of trouble,
for days of war and battle?
24What is the way to the place where the
lightning is dispersed,
or the place where the east winds are
scattered over the earth?
25Who cuts a channel for the torrents of
rain,
and a path for the thunderstorm,
26to water a land where no man lives,
a desert with no one in it,
27to satisfy a desolate wasteland
and make it sprout with grass?
28Does the rain have a father?

---

a24 Or for he does not have regard for any who think they are wise.   b7 Hebrew the sons of God   c17 Or
gates of deep shadows

Who fathers the drops of dew?
29From whose womb comes the ice?
  Who gives birth to the frost from the
    heavens
30when the waters become hard as stone,
  when the surface of the deep is
    frozen?

31"Can you bind the beautiful[a] Pleiades?
  Can you loose the cords of Orion?
32Can you bring forth the constellations in
    their seasons[b]
  or lead out the Bear[c] with its cubs?
33Do you know the laws of the heavens?
  Can you set up ⸤God's[d]⸥ dominion
    over the earth?

34"Can you raise your voice to the clouds
  and cover yourself with a flood of
    water?
35Do you send the lightning bolts on their
    way?
  Do they report to you, 'Here we are'?
36Who endowed the heart[e] with wisdom
  or gave understanding to the mind[e]?
37Who has the wisdom to count the
    clouds?
  Who can tip over the water jars of the
    heavens
38when the dust becomes hard
  and the clods of earth stick together?

39"Do you hunt the prey for the lioness
  and satisfy the hunger of the lions
40when they crouch in their dens
  or lie in wait in a thicket?
41Who provides food for the raven
  when its young cry out to God
  and wander about for lack of food?

39 "Do you know when the mountain
    goats give birth?
  Do you watch when the doe bears her
    fawn?
2Do you count the months till they bear?
  Do you know the time they give birth?
3They crouch down and bring forth their
    young;
  their labor pains are ended.
4Their young thrive and grow strong in
    the wilds;
  they leave and do not return.

5"Who let the wild donkey go free?
  Who untied his ropes?
6I gave him the wasteland as his home,
  the salt flats as his habitat.

7He laughs at the commotion in the
    town;
  he does not hear a driver's shout.
8He ranges the hills for his pasture
  and searches for any green thing.

9"Will the wild ox consent to serve you?
  Will he stay by your manger at night?
10Can you hold him to the furrow with a
    harness?
  Will he till the valleys behind you?
11Will you rely on him for his great
    strength?
  Will you leave your heavy work to
    him?
12Can you trust him to bring in your grain
  and gather it to your threshing floor?

13"The wings of the ostrich flap joyfully,
  but they cannot compare with the
    pinions and feathers of the stork.
14She lays her eggs on the ground
  and lets them warm in the sand,
15unmindful that a foot may crush them,
  that some wild animal may trample
    them.
16She treats her young harshly, as if they
    were not hers;
  she cares not that her labor was in
    vain,
17for God did not endow her with wisdom
  or give her a share of good sense.
18Yet when she spreads her feathers to
    run,
  she laughs at horse and rider.

19"Do you give the horse his strength
  or clothe his neck with a flowing
    mane?
20Do you make him leap like a locust,
  striking terror with his proud
    snorting?
21He paws fiercely, rejoicing in his
    strength,
  and charges into the fray.
22He laughs at fear, afraid of nothing;
  he does not shy away from the sword.
23The quiver rattles against his side,
  along with the flashing spear and
    lance.
24In frenzied excitement he eats up the
    ground;
  he cannot stand still when the
    trumpet sounds.
25At the blast of the trumpet he snorts,
  'Aha!'

a31 Or the twinkling; or the chains of the   b32 Or the morning star in its season   c32 Or out Leo
d33 Or his; or their   e36 The meaning of the Hebrew for this word is uncertain.

He catches the scent of battle from afar,
the shout of commanders and the battle cry.

26"Does the hawk take flight by your wisdom
and spread his wings toward the south?
27Does the eagle soar at your command
and build his nest on high?
28He dwells on a cliff and stays there at night;
a rocky crag is his stronghold.
29From there he seeks out his food;
his eyes detect it from afar.
30His young ones feast on blood,
and where the slain are, there is he."

40 The LORD said to Job:

2"Will the one who contends with the Almighty correct him?
Let him who accuses God answer him!"

3Then Job answered the LORD:

4"I am unworthy—how can I reply to you?
I put my hand over my mouth.
5I spoke once, but I have no answer—
twice, but I will say no more."

6Then the LORD spoke to Job out of the storm:

7"Brace yourself like a man;
I will question you,
and you shall answer me.

8"Would you discredit my justice?
Would you condemn me to justify yourself?
9Do you have an arm like God's,
and can your voice thunder like his?
10Then adorn yourself with glory and splendor,
and clothe yourself in honor and majesty.
11Unleash the fury of your wrath,
look at every proud man and bring him low,
12look at every proud man and humble him,
crush the wicked where they stand.
13Bury them all in the dust together;
shroud their faces in the grave.
14Then I myself will admit to you

that your own right hand can save you.

15"Look at the behemoth,a
which I made along with you
and which feeds on grass like an ox.
16What strength he has in his loins,
what power in the muscles of his belly!
17His tailb sways like a cedar;
the sinews of his thighs are close-knit.
18His bones are tubes of bronze,
his limbs like rods of iron.
19He ranks first among the works of God,
yet his Maker can approach him with his sword.
20The hills bring him their produce,
and all the wild animals play nearby.
21Under the lotus plants he lies,
hidden among the reeds in the marsh.
22The lotuses conceal him in their shadow;
the poplars by the stream surround him.
23When the river rages, he is not alarmed;
he is secure, though the Jordan should surge against his mouth.
24Can anyone capture him by the eyes,c
or trap him and pierce his nose?

41 "Can you pull in the leviathand
with a fishhook
or tie down his tongue with a rope?
2Can you put a cord through his nose
or pierce his jaw with a hook?
3Will he keep begging you for mercy?
Will he speak to you with gentle words?
4Will he make an agreement with you
for you to take him as your slave for life?
5Can you make a pet of him like a bird
or put him on a leash for your girls?
6Will traders barter for him?
Will they divide him up among the merchants?
7Can you fill his hide with harpoons
or his head with fishing spears?
8If you lay a hand on him,
you will remember the struggle and never do it again!
9Any hope of subduing him is false;
the mere sight of him is overpowering.
10No one is fierce enough to rouse him.
Who then is able to stand against me?

---

a15 Possibly the hippopotamus or the elephant   b17 Possibly trunk   c24 Or by a water hole   d1 Possibly the crocodile

11Who has a claim against me that I must pay?

Everything under heaven belongs to me.

12"I will not fail to speak of his limbs,
his strength and his graceful form.
13Who can strip off his outer coat?
Who would approach him with a bridle?
14Who dares open the doors of his mouth,
ringed about with his fearsome teeth?
15His back has*a* rows of shields
tightly sealed together;
16each is so close to the next
that no air can pass between.
17They are joined fast to one another;
they cling together and cannot be parted.
18His snorting throws out flashes of light;
his eyes are like the rays of dawn.
19Firebrands stream from his mouth;
sparks of fire shoot out.
20Smoke pours from his nostrils
as from a boiling pot over a fire of reeds.
21His breath sets coals ablaze,
and flames dart from his mouth.
22Strength resides in his neck;
dismay goes before him.
23The folds of his flesh are tightly joined;
they are firm and immovable.
24His chest is hard as rock,
hard as a lower millstone.
25When he rises up, the mighty are terrified;
they retreat before his thrashing.
26The sword that reaches him has no effect,
nor does the spear or the dart or the javelin.
27Iron he treats like straw
and bronze like rotten wood.
28Arrows do not make him flee;
slingstones are like chaff to him.
29A club seems to him but a piece of straw;
he laughs at the rattling of the lance.
30His undersides are jagged potsherds,
leaving a trail in the mud like a threshing sledge.
31He makes the depths churn like a boiling caldron
and stirs up the sea like a pot of ointment.
32Behind him he leaves a glistening wake;
one would think the deep had white hair.
33Nothing on earth is his equal—
a creature without fear.
34He looks down on all that are haughty;
he is king over all that are proud."

Job

42 Then Job replied to the LORD:

2"I know that you can do all things;
no plan of yours can be thwarted.
3⌊You asked,⌋ 'Who is this that obscures my counsel without knowledge?'
Surely I spoke of things I did not understand,
things too wonderful for me to know.

4⌊"You said,⌋ 'Listen now, and I will speak;
I will question you,
and you shall answer me.'
5My ears had heard of you
but now my eyes have seen you.
6Therefore I despise myself
and repent in dust and ashes."

Epilogue

7After the LORD had said these things to Job, he said to Eliphaz the Temanite, "I am angry with you and your two friends, because you have not spoken of me what is right, as my servant Job has. 8So now take seven bulls and seven rams and go to my servant Job and sacrifice a burnt offering for yourselves. My servant Job will pray for you, and I will accept his prayer and not deal with you according to your folly. You have not spoken of me what is right, as my servant Job has." 9So Eliphaz the Temanite, Bildad the Shuhite and Zophar the Naamathite did what the LORD told them; and the LORD accepted Job's prayer.

10After Job had prayed for his friends, the LORD made him prosperous again and gave him twice as much as he had before. 11All his brothers and sisters and everyone who had known him before came and ate with him in his house. They comforted and consoled him over all the trouble the LORD had brought upon him, and each one gave him a piece of silver*b* and a gold ring.

12The LORD blessed the latter part of Job's life more than the first. He had fourteen

a15 Or *His pride is his value.*   *b11* Hebrew *him a kesitah*; a kesitah was a unit of money of unknown weight and thousand sheep, six thousand camels, a thousand yoke of oxen and a thousand donkeys. ¹³And he also had seven sons and three daughters. ¹⁴The first daughter he named Jemimah, the second Keziah and the third Keren-Happuch. ¹⁵Nowhere in all the land were there found women as beautiful as Job's daughters, and their father granted them an inheritance along with their brothers.

¹⁶After this, Job lived a hundred and forty years; he saw his children and their children to the fourth generation. ¹⁷And so he died, old and full of years.

PSALMS

IN the psalms (or songs), primarily written by David, no feelings are taboo. With joy, excitement, sorrow, compassion, love, fear, anger, grief and depression, the psalm writers cry out passionately to God, utterly confident that he listens and cares. As you read these Hebrew songs, remember: You too can tell God how you really feel with complete confidence that he cares for you.

BOOK I
Psalms 1–41

Psalm 1

¹Blessed is the man
  who does not walk in the counsel of
    the wicked
 or stand in the way of sinners
  or sit in the seat of mockers.
²But his delight is in the law of the
    LORD,
  and on his law he meditates day and
    night.

³He is like a tree planted by streams of
    water,
  which yields its fruit in season
 and whose leaf does not wither.
  Whatever he does prospers.
⁴Not so the wicked!
  They are like chaff
   that the wind blows away.
⁵Therefore the wicked will not stand in
    the judgment,
  nor sinners in the assembly of the
    righteous.

⁶For the LORD watches over the way of
    the righteous,
  but the way of the wicked will
    perish.

FEELING GOOD ABOUT FEELING BAD

• •

Jim sat at home in his room alone. Two hours ago, he was having a great time at a friend's house. But when the NC-17 movie went into the VCR, Jim went out of the house.

Jim said to his mom: "Man, Mom, it sure hurts. The guys looked at me like I was some kind of freak when I told them I wouldn't feel right seeing that movie."

"It may not feel great," his mom replied, "but you did the right thing. It's probably not the last time your non-Christian friends will ridicule you when you follow Christ. Why don't you see if a couple of your friends from church would like to come over. I'll order a pizza and you can watch the game on television."

"Good idea. Thanks, Mom."

Look It Up
• • • •

"If you suffer as a Christian, do not be ashamed, but praise God that you bear that name" (1 Peter 4:16).

As Christians, we are sometimes limited in our relationships with non-Christians. They don't see the world the same way we do.

Like Jim, then, we'll sometimes have to make decisions that are unpopular with our friends. As a result, we may feel rejected by those who either can't understand why or don't like the fact that our commitment to Christ comes first.

Many times, though, these feelings of rejection are only in our own minds. Our non-Christian friends often actually respect rather than reject us for having the courage to stand up for what we believe.

But even when the rejection is real, we can find comfort in God's nearness (Psalm 34:18) and in his promise to reward our faithfulness to him (Matthew 5:10–12).

Think It Through
• • • •

Do you ever fear you will be rejected if you refuse to go along with some of your non-Christian friends' behavior? Do you think if you had been in Jim's shoes you would have done what he did?

It's important to have relationships with unbelievers so that you can be a witness for Christ. But it's also crucial that you not compromise your convictions just to avoid catching grief from your friends. In trying to please everybody, you end up pleasing nobody.

Work It Out
• • • •

Try to envision a typical day at school and the different opportunities for either courage or compromise that come your way.

Pray for the courage to stand up for what you believe. Then commit your fear of rejection to God.

Nail It Down
• • • •

Memorize Psalm 1:1–3.

Turn to pages 428, 569 and 755 for other readings on rejection.
Turn to page 546 for Wednesday's reading.

Topic
• • • •

REJECTION

Psalm 2

[1]Why do the nations conspire[a]
and the peoples plot in vain?
[2]The kings of the earth take their stand
and the rulers gather together
against the LORD
and against his Anointed One.[b]
[3]"Let us break their chains," they say,
"and throw off their fetters."

[4]The One enthroned in heaven laughs;
the Lord scoffs at them.
[5]Then he rebukes them in his anger
and terrifies them in his wrath,
saying,
[6]"I have installed my King[c]
on Zion, my holy hill."

[7]I will proclaim the decree of the LORD:

He said to me, "You are my Son[d];
today I have become your Father.[e]
[8]Ask of me,
and I will make the nations your
inheritance,
the ends of the earth your possession.
[9]You will rule them with an iron
scepter[f];
you will dash them to pieces like
pottery."

[10]Therefore, you kings, be wise;
be warned, you rulers of the earth.
[11]Serve the LORD with fear
and rejoice with trembling.
[12]Kiss the Son, lest he be angry
and you be destroyed in your way,
for his wrath can flare up in a moment.
Blessed are all who take refuge in
him.

Psalm 3

A psalm of David. When he fled from his
son Absalom.

[1]O LORD, how many are my foes!
How many rise up against me!
[2]Many are saying of me,
"God will not deliver him."   Selah[g]

[3]But you are a shield around me, O LORD;
you bestow glory on me and lift[h] up
my head.

[4]To the LORD I cry aloud,
and he answers me from his holy hill.
Selah

[5]I lie down and sleep;
I wake again, because the LORD
sustains me.
[6]I will not fear the tens of thousands
drawn up against me on every side.

[7]Arise, O LORD!
Deliver me, O my God!
Strike all my enemies on the jaw;
break the teeth of the wicked.

[8]From the LORD comes deliverance.
May your blessing be on your people.
Selah

Psalm 4

For the director of music. With stringed
instruments. A psalm of David.

[1]Answer me when I call to you,
O my righteous God.
Give me relief from my distress;
be merciful to me and hear my
prayer.

[2]How long, O men, will you turn my
glory into shame[i]?
How long will you love delusions and
seek false gods[j]?   Selah
[3]Know that the LORD has set apart the
godly for himself;
the LORD will hear when I call to him.

[4]In your anger do not sin;
when you are on your beds,
search your hearts and be silent.
Selah

[5]Offer right sacrifices
and trust in the LORD.

[6]Many are asking, "Who can show us
any good?"
Let the light of your face shine upon
us, O LORD.
[7]You have filled my heart with greater
joy
than when their grain and new wine
abound.

---

[a]1 Hebrew; Septuagint *rage*   [b]2 Or *anointed one*   [c]6 Or *king*   [d]7 Or *son*; also in verse 12   [e]7 Or *have begotten you*   [f]9 Or *will break them with a rod of iron*   [g]2 A word of uncertain meaning, occurring frequently in the Psalms; possibly a musical term   [h]3 Or LORD, / *my Glorious One, who lifts*   [i]2 Or *you dishonor my Glorious One*   [j]2 Or *seek lies*

TALK TO GOD DURING STRESS'S MESSES

What would you do in the following situations?

Biff, the largest senior on the football team, has vowed to beat up Tommy for giving Biff's girlfriend a ride home.

Carla has been wrongly accused of cheating during a history exam.

Melinda just learned that her father is being transferred. She'll be moving away from the town she's lived in all her life.

David, who has a mortal fear of speaking to large groups, has to give an oral report in class tomorrow.

Look It Up
••••

No matter what you're facing, remember the stressful experience of David in Psalm 18:

First, David prayed. "In my distress I called to the LORD; I cried to my God for help" (Psalm 18:6).

Second, God answered. "From his temple he heard my voice; my cry came before him into his ears" (Psalm 18:6).

Turning to God was David's immediate response. On the heels of another tense occasion, David proclaimed: "Surely God is my help; the Lord is the one who sustains me . . . . For he has delivered me from all my troubles" (Psalm 54:4,7).

Think It Through
••••

The words to an old hymn underscore the truth that prayer is the best response to stress:

I must tell Jesus all of my trials;
I cannot bear these burdens alone.
In my distress he kindly will help me;
He ever loves and cares for his own.

That one little stanza contains a lot of truth, doesn't it?

Work It Out
••••

Some people, when facing a stressful situation, do everything but pray. They toss and turn, agonize, plan, scheme, fret, connive, plot, consult friends, worry, calculate and finally trust in their own abilities to overcome the pressure. Why not just turn all the headaches over to God—right away?

Here's what we're talking about: "Lord, I feel really stressed out because of _____. I don't know what to do. I'm tired and scared. The problem is too big for me to handle. Please take control of the situation. Give me your peace. Keep reminding me that you will take care of things. Amen."

Nail It Down
••••

Read David's prayer for help in Psalm 4:1.

Turn to pages 778, 1058, 1219 and 1280 for other readings on stress.
Turn to page 550 for Thursday's reading.

Topic
••••
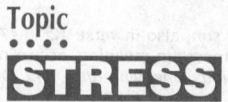

8I will lie down and sleep in peace,
  for you alone, O LORD,
  make me dwell in safety.

Psalm 5

*For the director of music. For flutes.
A psalm of David.*

1Give ear to my words, O LORD,
  consider my sighing.
2Listen to my cry for help,
  my King and my God,
  for to you I pray.
3In the morning, O LORD, you hear my
    voice;
  in the morning I lay my requests
    before you
  and wait in expectation.

4You are not a God who takes pleasure
    in evil;
  with you the wicked cannot dwell.
5The arrogant cannot stand in your
    presence;
  you hate all who do wrong.
6You destroy those who tell lies;
  bloodthirsty and deceitful men
  the LORD abhors.

7But I, by your great mercy,
  will come into your house;
  in reverence will I bow down
    toward your holy temple.
8Lead me, O LORD, in your righteousness
  because of my enemies—
  make straight your way before me.

9Not a word from their mouth can be
    trusted;
  their heart is filled with destruction.
  Their throat is an open grave;
  with their tongue they speak deceit.
10Declare them guilty, O God!
  Let their intrigues be their downfall.
  Banish them for their many sins,
  for they have rebelled against you.

11But let all who take refuge in you be
    glad;
  let them ever sing for joy.
  Spread your protection over them,
  that those who love your name may
    rejoice in you.
12For surely, O LORD, you bless the
    righteous;
  you surround them with your favor as
    with a shield.

Psalm 6

*For the director of music. With stringed
instruments. According to sheminith.*[a]
A psalm of David.

1O LORD, do not rebuke me in your anger
  or discipline me in your wrath.
2Be merciful to me, LORD, for I am faint;
  O LORD, heal me, for my bones are in
    agony.
3My soul is in anguish.
  How long, O LORD, how long?

4Turn, O LORD, and deliver me;
  save me because of your unfailing
    love.
5No one remembers you when he is
    dead.
  Who praises you from the grave[b]?

6I am worn out from groaning;
  all night long I flood my bed with
    weeping
  and drench my couch with tears.
7My eyes grow weak with sorrow;
  they fail because of all my foes.

8Away from me, all you who do evil,
  for the LORD has heard my weeping.
9The LORD has heard my cry for mercy;
  the LORD accepts my prayer.
10All my enemies will be ashamed and
    dismayed;
  they will turn back in sudden
    disgrace.

Psalm 7

A shiggaion[c] *of David, which he sang to
the LORD concerning Cush, a Benjamite.*

1O LORD my God, I take refuge in you;
  save and deliver me from all who
    pursue me,
2or they will tear me like a lion
  and rip me to pieces with no one to
    rescue me.

3O LORD my God, if I have done this
  and there is guilt on my hands—
4if I have done evil to him who is at
    peace with me
  or without cause have robbed my
    foe—
5then let my enemy pursue and overtake
    me;
  let him trample my life to the ground
  and make me sleep in the dust. *Selah*

---

*a*Title: Probably a musical term   *b5* Hebrew *Sheol*   *c*Title: Probably a literary or musical term

[6]Arise, O Lord, in your anger;
   rise up against the rage of my
      enemies.
   Awake, my God; decree justice.
[7]Let the assembled peoples gather
      around you.
   Rule over them from on high;
[8] let the Lord judge the peoples.
 Judge me, O Lord, according to my
      righteousness,
   according to my integrity, O Most
      High.
[9]O righteous God,
   who searches minds and hearts,
 bring to an end the violence of the
      wicked
 and make the righteous secure.

[10]My shield[a] is God Most High,
   who saves the upright in heart.
[11]God is a righteous judge,
   a God who expresses his wrath every
      day.
[12]If he does not relent,
   he[b] will sharpen his sword;
   he will bend and string his bow.
[13]He has prepared his deadly weapons;
   he makes ready his flaming arrows.

[14]He who is pregnant with evil
   and conceives trouble gives birth to
      disillusionment.
[15]He who digs a hole and scoops it out
   falls into the pit he has made.
[16]The trouble he causes recoils on
      himself;
   his violence comes down on his own
      head.

[17]I will give thanks to the Lord because of
      his righteousness
   and will sing praise to the name of
      the Lord Most High.

Psalm 8

For the director of music. According to
gittith.[c] A psalm of David.

[1]O Lord, our Lord,
   how majestic is your name in all the
      earth!

You have set your glory
   above the heavens.
[2]From the lips of children and infants
   you have ordained praise[d]
because of your enemies,

to silence the foe and the avenger.

[3]When I consider your heavens,
   the work of your fingers,
 the moon and the stars,
   which you have set in place,
[4]what is man that you are mindful of
      him,
   the son of man that you care for him?
[5]You made him a little lower than the
      heavenly beings[e]
   and crowned him with glory and
      honor.

[6]You made him ruler over the works of
      your hands;
   you put everything under his feet:
[7]all flocks and herds,
   and the beasts of the field,
[8]the birds of the air,
   and the fish of the sea,
   all that swim the paths of the seas.

[9]O Lord, our Lord,
   how majestic is your name in all the
      earth!

Psalm 9[f]

For the director of music. To ˌthe tune ofˌ
"The Death of the Son." A psalm of David.

[1]I will praise you, O Lord, with all my
      heart;
   I will tell of all your wonders.
[2]I will be glad and rejoice in you;
   I will sing praise to your name,
      O Most High.

[3]My enemies turn back;
   they stumble and perish before you.
[4]For you have upheld my right and my
      cause;
   you have sat on your throne, judging
      righteously.
[5]You have rebuked the nations and
      destroyed the wicked;
   you have blotted out their name for
      ever and ever.
[6]Endless ruin has overtaken the enemy,
   you have uprooted their cities;
   even the memory of them has
      perished.

[7]The Lord reigns forever;
   he has established his throne for
      judgment.

---

[a]10 Or *sovereign*   [b]12 Or *If a man does not repent, / God*   [c]Title: Probably a musical term   [d]2 Or
strength   [e]5 Or *than God*   [f]Psalms 9 and 10 may have been originally a single acrostic poem, the stanzas
of which begin with the successive letters of the Hebrew alphabet. In the Septuagint they constitute one psalm.

⁸He will judge the world in
   righteousness;
  he will govern the peoples with
   justice.
⁹The Lord is a refuge for the oppressed,
  a stronghold in times of trouble.
¹⁰Those who know your name will trust
   in you,
  for you, Lord, have never forsaken
   those who seek you.

¹¹Sing praises to the Lord, enthroned in
   Zion;
  proclaim among the nations what he
   has done.
¹²For he who avenges blood remembers;
  he does not ignore the cry of the
   afflicted.

¹³O Lord, see how my enemies persecute
   me!
  Have mercy and lift me up from the
   gates of death,
¹⁴that I may declare your praises
  in the gates of the Daughter of Zion
  and there rejoice in your salvation.
¹⁵The nations have fallen into the pit they
   have dug;
  their feet are caught in the net they
   have hidden.
¹⁶The Lord is known by his justice;
  the wicked are ensnared by the work
   of their hands.   *Higgaion.* ᵃ *Selah*
¹⁷The wicked return to the grave,ᵇ
  all the nations that forget God.
¹⁸But the needy will not always be
   forgotten,
  nor the hope of the afflicted ever
   perish.

¹⁹Arise, O Lord, let not man triumph;
  let the nations be judged in your
   presence.
²⁰Strike them with terror, O Lord;
  let the nations know they are but
   men.   *Selah*

Psalm 10ᶜ

¹Why, O Lord, do you stand far off?
  Why do you hide yourself in times of
   trouble?

²In his arrogance the wicked man hunts
   down the weak,
  who are caught in the schemes he
   devises.

³He boasts of the cravings of his heart;
  he blesses the greedy and reviles the
   Lord.
⁴In his pride the wicked does not seek
   him;
  in all his thoughts there is no room
   for God.
⁵His ways are always prosperous;
  he is haughty and your laws are far
   from him;
  he sneers at all his enemies.
⁶He says to himself, "Nothing will shake
   me;
  I'll always be happy and never have
   trouble."
⁷His mouth is full of curses and lies and
   threats;
  trouble and evil are under his tongue.
⁸He lies in wait near the villages;
  from ambush he murders the
   innocent,
  watching in secret for his victims.
⁹He lies in wait like a lion in cover;
  he lies in wait to catch the helpless;
  he catches the helpless and drags
   them off in his net.
¹⁰His victims are crushed, they collapse;
  they fall under his strength.
¹¹He says to himself, "God has forgotten;
  he covers his face and never sees."

¹²Arise, Lord! Lift up your hand, O God.
  Do not forget the helpless.
¹³Why does the wicked man revile God?
  Why does he say to himself,
  "He won't call me to account"?
¹⁴But you, O God, do see trouble and
   grief;
  you consider it to take it in hand.
  The victim commits himself to you;
  you are the helper of the fatherless.
¹⁵Break the arm of the wicked and evil
   man;
  call him to account for his wickedness
   that would not be found out.

¹⁶The Lord is King for ever and ever;
  the nations will perish from his land.
¹⁷You hear, O Lord, the desire of the
   afflicted;
  you encourage them, and you listen
   to their cry,
¹⁸defending the fatherless and the
   oppressed,
  in order that man, who is of the
   earth, may terrify no more.

ᵃ16 Or *Meditation*; possibly a musical notation   ᵇ17 Hebrew *Sheol*   ᶜPsalms 9 and 10 may have been
originally a single acrostic poem, the stanzas of which begin with the successive letters of the Hebrew alphabet.
In the Septuagint they constitute one psalm.

AN UNBRIDLED THOUGHT LIFE

The gym at 2:30, Friday afternoon:
Enter Doug and Gene who suddenly notice about a dozen members of the school dance team going through a routine.

Gene (excitedly whispering): "Would you look at Pam Powers! She's unbelievable! I sure wish . . . ."

Doug looks at Pam. Then again. Then a third time. In fact, he can't get his eyes or his mind off her. And, as you might imagine, it's not because he's marveling at the talent God has given her in the art of dance.

Look It Up
One of the toughest assignments Christians have is self-control of the mind. How can you make sure your thought life is pleasing to God?

"Set your minds on things above, not on earthly things" (Colossians 3:2).

"Finally, brothers, whatever is true, whatever is noble, whatever is right, whatever is pure, whatever is lovely, whatever is admirable—if anything is excellent or praiseworthy—think about such things" (Philippians 4:8).

In short, self-control of the mind doesn't come about by magic or mystery. It happens when you deliberately choose moment by moment to fill your mind with pure, godly thoughts and not with impure, godless ones.

Think It Through
The human mind is an incredible creation. It's there that you reason, think, predict, use stored information, decide, analyze, believe and develop attitudes. And, of course, how you think determines how you live—your behavior.

No wonder God's Word is so insistent that you "renew [your] minds" (Romans 12:2; Ephesians 4:23). Your ability to live for God depends directly on the way you use your mind.

Work It Out
Guys, when you encounter a scene that tempts you to sin, look away! Given our pagan, sex-crazed culture, that's a tall order. But God's law is a tall standard.

Girls, the temptations in your thought life are different. You're less likely to lust, more likely to fantasize. Be careful! Too much fantasy can be just as dangerous.

Here's a guarantee: Spend time every day reading, memorizing and studying God's Word, and you'll have more control over your thought life.

Nail It Down
Spend some time thinking about Psalm 10:4.

Turn to pages 665 and 1276 for other readings on self-control.
Turn to page 553 for Friday's reading.

Topic

SELF-CONTROL

Psalm 11

For the director of music. Of David.

[1] In the LORD I take refuge.
  How then can you say to me:
  "Flee like a bird to your mountain.
[2] For look, the wicked bend their bows;
  they set their arrows against the
    strings
to shoot from the shadows
  at the upright in heart.
[3] When the foundations are being
    destroyed,
  what can the righteous do[a]?"

[4] The LORD is in his holy temple;
  the LORD is on his heavenly throne.
He observes the sons of men;
  his eyes examine them.
[5] The LORD examines the righteous,
  but the wicked[b] and those who love
    violence
  his soul hates.
[6] On the wicked he will rain
  fiery coals and burning sulfur;
  a scorching wind will be their lot.

[7] For the LORD is righteous,
  he loves justice;
  upright men will see his face.

Psalm 12

For the director of music. According to
sheminith.[c] A psalm of David.

[1] Help, LORD, for the godly are no more;
  the faithful have vanished from
    among men.
[2] Everyone lies to his neighbor;
  their flattering lips speak with
    deception.

[3] May the LORD cut off all flattering lips
  and every boastful tongue
[4] that says, "We will triumph with our
    tongues;
  we own our lips[d] — who is our
    master?"

[5] "Because of the oppression of the weak
  and the groaning of the needy,
  I will now arise," says the LORD.
  "I will protect them from those who
    malign them."
[6] And the words of the LORD are flawless,
  like silver refined in a furnace of clay,

purified seven times.
[7] O LORD, you will keep us safe
  and protect us from such people
    forever.
[8] The wicked freely strut about
  when what is vile is honored among
    men.

Psalm 13

For the director of music. A psalm
of David.

[1] How long, O LORD? Will you forget me
    forever?
  How long will you hide your face
    from me?
[2] How long must I wrestle with my
    thoughts
  and every day have sorrow in my
    heart?
  How long will my enemy triumph
    over me?

[3] Look on me and answer, O LORD my
    God.
  Give light to my eyes, or I will sleep
    in death;
[4] my enemy will say, "I have overcome
    him,"
  and my foes will rejoice when I fall.

[5] But I trust in your unfailing love;
  my heart rejoices in your salvation.
[6] I will sing to the LORD,
  for he has been good to me.

Psalm 14

For the director of music. Of David.

[1] The fool[e] says in his heart,
  "There is no God."
They are corrupt, their deeds are vile;
  there is no one who does good.

[2] The LORD looks down from heaven
  on the sons of men
to see if there are any who understand,
  any who seek God.
[3] All have turned aside,
  they have together become corrupt;
there is no one who does good,
  not even one.

[4] Will evildoers never learn —

---

[a]3 Or *what is the Righteous One doing*   [b]5 Or *The LORD, the Righteous One, examines the wicked, /*   [c]Title:
Probably a musical term   [d]4 Or */ our lips are our plowshares*   [e]1 The Hebrew words rendered *fool* in
Psalms denote one who is morally deficient.

those who devour my people as men
eat bread
and who do not call on the LORD?
⁵There they are, overwhelmed with
dread,
for God is present in the company of
the righteous.
⁶You evildoers frustrate the plans of the
poor,
but the LORD is their refuge.

⁷Oh, that salvation for Israel would come
out of Zion!
When the LORD restores the fortunes
of his people,
let Jacob rejoice and Israel be glad!

Psalm 15

A psalm of David.

¹LORD, who may dwell in your sanctuary?
Who may live on your holy hill?

²He whose walk is blameless
and who does what is righteous,
who speaks the truth from his heart
³ and has no slander on his tongue,
who does his neighbor no wrong
and casts no slur on his fellowman,
⁴who despises a vile man
but honors those who fear the LORD,
who keeps his oath
even when it hurts,
⁵who lends his money without usury
and does not accept a bribe against
the innocent.

He who does these things
will never be shaken.

Psalm 16

A miktamᵃ of David.

¹Keep me safe, O God,
for in you I take refuge.

²I said to the LORD, "You are my Lord;
apart from you I have no good thing."
³As for the saints who are in the land,
they are the glorious ones in whom is
all my delight.ᵇ
⁴The sorrows of those will increase
who run after other gods.
I will not pour out their libations of
blood
or take up their names on my lips.

⁵LORD, you have assigned me my portion
and my cup;
you have made my lot secure.
⁶The boundary lines have fallen for me
in pleasant places;
surely I have a delightful inheritance.

⁷I will praise the LORD, who counsels me;
even at night my heart instructs me.
⁸I have set the LORD always before me.
Because he is at my right hand,
I will not be shaken.

⁹Therefore my heart is glad and my
tongue rejoices;
my body also will rest secure,
¹⁰because you will not abandon me to the
grave,ᶜ
nor will you let your Holy Oneᵈ see
decay.
¹¹You have madeᵉ known to me the path
of life;
you will fill me with joy in your
presence,
with eternal pleasures at your right
hand.

Psalm 17

A prayer of David.

¹Hear, O LORD, my righteous plea;
listen to my cry.
Give ear to my prayer—
it does not rise from deceitful lips.
²May my vindication come from you;
may your eyes see what is right.

³Though you probe my heart and
examine me at night,
though you test me, you will find
nothing;
I have resolved that my mouth will
not sin.
⁴As for the deeds of men—
by the word of your lips
I have kept myself
from the ways of the violent.
⁵My steps have held to your paths;
my feet have not slipped.

⁶I call on you, O God, for you will
answer me;
give ear to me and hear my prayer.
⁷Show the wonder of your great love,
you who save by your right hand
those who take refuge in you from
their foes.

ᵃTitle: Probably a literary or musical term   ᵇ3 Or *As for the pagan priests who are in the land / and the nobles in whom all delight, I said:*   ᶜ10 Hebrew *Sheol*   ᵈ10 Or *your faithful one*   ᵉ11 Or *You will make*

MAKING EVERY DAY A HOLIDAY

Almost everybody at Clifford High likes to hang out at the Hunter's house—not just because the Hunters have three teenagers but because there's always something fun going on there.

They play goofy games. They organize cookouts and lead bike hikes and make crazy home videos. And they laugh—they laugh a lot!

Candy, the oldest daughter, sometimes gets embarrassed by her parents' antics. But she admits, "It's fun because you never know what's gonna happen next. They make every day seem like a holiday."

Look It Up
• • • •

Isn't that great? Don't you wish you could seize life like that and squeeze all the goodness out of it? Hey, guess what? You can! It's called living under the control of the Holy Spirit of God:

"But the fruit of the Spirit is love, joy, peace, patience, kindness, goodness, faithfulness, gentleness and self-control. . . . Since we live by the Spirit, let us keep in step with the Spirit" (Galatians 5:22,25).

Think It Through
• • • •

Where is it written that leisure has to cost a lot of money? Can you think of five creative leisure activities that don't require a lot of money?

Who says that leisure has to involve huge chunks of time? See if you can come up with five unique activities that can bring the refreshment of leisure in just a few minutes.

Work It Out
• • • •

Don't be boring! Christians should be the most fun, the most alive, the most creative people on earth. Attack each day with exuberance. Find joy and refreshment in life's simple pleasures (and invite a non-Christian friend along for the ride):
- Make an exotic dessert and eat it slowly, savoring each bite.
- Teach your dog a new trick.
- Learn how to juggle or to ride a unicycle.
- Borrow a telescope and locate the various constellations.
- Memorize 1 Corinthians 13.
- Build something with your hands.
- Feed the ducks at a city park.
- Plan an around-the-world vacation.

Nail It Down
• • • •

Read Psalm 16:11 for David's view on life and leisure.

Turn to pages 81, 339, 609 and 692 for other readings on leisure.
Turn to page 557 for the weekend reading.

Topic
• • • •

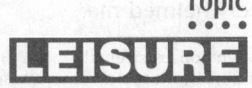

8Keep me as the apple of your eye;
  hide me in the shadow of your wings
9from the wicked who assail me,
  from my mortal enemies who
    surround me.

10They close up their callous hearts,
  and their mouths speak with
    arrogance.
11They have tracked me down, they now
    surround me,
  with eyes alert, to throw me to the
    ground.
12They are like a lion hungry for prey,
  like a great lion crouching in cover.

13Rise up, O LORD, confront them, bring
    them down;
  rescue me from the wicked by your
    sword.
14O LORD, by your hand save me from
    such men,
  from men of this world whose reward
    is in this life.

You still the hunger of those you
    cherish;
  their sons have plenty,
  and they store up wealth for their
    children.
15And I—in righteousness I will see your
    face;
  when I awake, I will be satisfied with
    seeing your likeness.

Psalm 18

For the director of music. Of David the
servant of the LORD. He sang to the LORD
the words of this song when the LORD
delivered him from the hand of all his
enemies and from the hand of Saul.
He said:

1I love you, O LORD, my strength.

2The LORD is my rock, my fortress and
    my deliverer;
  my God is my rock, in whom I take
    refuge.
  He is my shield and the horn[a] of my
    salvation, my stronghold.
3I call to the LORD, who is worthy of
    praise,
  and I am saved from my enemies.

4The cords of death entangled me;
  the torrents of destruction
    overwhelmed me.

5The cords of the grave[b] coiled around
    me;
  the snares of death confronted me.
6In my distress I called to the LORD;
  I cried to my God for help.
From his temple he heard my voice;
  my cry came before him, into his
    ears.

7The earth trembled and quaked,
  and the foundations of the mountains
    shook;
  they trembled because he was angry.
8Smoke rose from his nostrils;
  consuming fire came from his mouth,
  burning coals blazed out of it.
9He parted the heavens and came down;
  dark clouds were under his feet.
10He mounted the cherubim and flew;
  he soared on the wings of the wind.
11He made darkness his covering, his
    canopy around him—
  the dark rain clouds of the sky.
12Out of the brightness of his presence
    clouds advanced,
  with hailstones and bolts of lightning.
13The LORD thundered from heaven;
  the voice of the Most High
    resounded.[c]
14He shot his arrows and scattered ₍the
    enemies₎,
  great bolts of lightning and routed
    them.
15The valleys of the sea were exposed
  and the foundations of the earth laid
    bare
  at your rebuke, O LORD,
  at the blast of breath from your
    nostrils.

16He reached down from on high and
    took hold of me;
  he drew me out of deep waters.
17He rescued me from my powerful
    enemy,
  from my foes, who were too strong
    for me.
18They confronted me in the day of my
    disaster,
  but the LORD was my support.
19He brought me out into a spacious
    place;
  he rescued me because he delighted
    in me.

20The LORD has dealt with me according to
    my righteousness;

---

a2 Horn here symbolizes strength.   *b5* Hebrew *Sheol*   *c13* Some Hebrew manuscripts and Septuagint (see
also 2 Samuel 22:14); most Hebrew manuscripts *resounded, / amid hailstones and bolts of lightning*

according to the cleanness of my
hands he has rewarded me.
²¹For I have kept the ways of the LORD;
I have not done evil by turning from
my God.
²²All his laws are before me;
I have not turned away from his
decrees.
²³I have been blameless before him
and have kept myself from sin.
²⁴The LORD has rewarded me according to
my righteousness,
according to the cleanness of my
hands in his sight.

²⁵To the faithful you show yourself
faithful,
to the blameless you show yourself
blameless,
²⁶to the pure you show yourself pure,
but to the crooked you show yourself
shrewd.
²⁷You save the humble
but bring low those whose eyes are
haughty.
²⁸You, O LORD, keep my lamp burning;
my God turns my darkness into light.
²⁹With your help I can advance against a
troop^a;
with my God I can scale a wall.

³⁰As for God, his way is perfect;
the word of the LORD is flawless.
He is a shield
for all who take refuge in him.
³¹For who is God besides the LORD?
And who is the Rock except our God?
³²It is God who arms me with strength
and makes my way perfect.
³³He makes my feet like the feet of a
deer;
he enables me to stand on the
heights.
³⁴He trains my hands for battle;
my arms can bend a bow of bronze.
³⁵You give me your shield of victory,
and your right hand sustains me;
you stoop down to make me great.
³⁶You broaden the path beneath me,
so that my ankles do not turn.

³⁷I pursued my enemies and overtook
them;
I did not turn back till they were
destroyed.
³⁸I crushed them so that they could not
rise;

they fell beneath my feet.
³⁹You armed me with strength for battle;
you made my adversaries bow at my
feet.
⁴⁰You made my enemies turn their backs
in flight,
and I destroyed my foes.
⁴¹They cried for help, but there was no
one to save them—
to the LORD, but he did not answer.
⁴²I beat them as fine as dust borne on the
wind;
I poured them out like mud in the
streets.

⁴³You have delivered me from the attacks
of the people;
you have made me the head of
nations;
people I did not know are subject to
me.
⁴⁴As soon as they hear me, they obey me;
foreigners cringe before me.
⁴⁵They all lose heart;
they come trembling from their
strongholds.

⁴⁶The LORD lives! Praise be to my Rock!
Exalted be God my Savior!
⁴⁷He is the God who avenges me,
who subdues nations under me,
⁴⁸ who saves me from my enemies.
You exalted me above my foes;
from violent men you rescued me.
⁴⁹Therefore I will praise you among the
nations, O LORD;
I will sing praises to your name.
⁵⁰He gives his king great victories;
he shows unfailing kindness to his
anointed,
to David and his descendants forever.

Psalm 19

For the director of music. A psalm
of David.

¹The heavens declare the glory of God;
the skies proclaim the work of his
hands.
²Day after day they pour forth speech;
night after night they display
knowledge.
³There is no speech or language
where their voice is not heard.^b
⁴Their voice^c goes out into all the earth,
their words to the ends of the world.

---

^a29 Or can run through a barricade ^b3 Or They have no speech, there are no words; / no sound is heard
from them ^c4 Septuagint, Jerome and Syriac; Hebrew line

In the heavens he has pitched a tent for
the sun,

5 which is like a bridegroom coming
forth from his pavilion,
like a champion rejoicing to run his
course.

[6]It rises at one end of the heavens
and makes its circuit to the other;
nothing is hidden from its heat.

[7]The law of the Lord is perfect,
reviving the soul.
The statutes of the Lord are trustworthy,
making wise the simple.

[8]The precepts of the Lord are right,
giving joy to the heart.
The commands of the Lord are radiant,
giving light to the eyes.

[9]The fear of the Lord is pure,
enduring forever.
The ordinances of the Lord are sure
and altogether righteous.

[10]They are more precious than gold,
than much pure gold;
they are sweeter than honey,
than honey from the comb.

[11]By them is your servant warned;
in keeping them there is great reward.

[12]Who can discern his errors?
Forgive my hidden faults.

[13]Keep your servant also from willful sins;
may they not rule over me.
Then will I be blameless,
innocent of great transgression.

[14]May the words of my mouth and the
meditation of my heart
be pleasing in your sight,
O Lord, my Rock and my Redeemer.

Psalm 20

For the director of music. A psalm
of David.

[1]May the Lord answer you when you are
in distress;
may the name of the God of Jacob
protect you.

[2]May he send you help from the
sanctuary
and grant you support from Zion.

[3]May he remember all your sacrifices
and accept your burnt offerings. *Selah*

[4]May he give you the desire of your
heart
and make all your plans succeed.

[5]We will shout for joy when you are
victorious
and will lift up our banners in the
name of our God.
May the Lord grant all your requests.

[6]Now I know that the Lord saves his
anointed;
he answers him from his holy heaven
with the saving power of his right
hand.

[7]Some trust in chariots and some in
horses,
but we trust in the name of the Lord
our God.

[8]They are brought to their knees and fall,
but we rise up and stand firm.

[9]O Lord, save the king!
Answer[a] us when we call!

Psalm 21

For the director of music. A psalm
of David.

[1]O Lord, the king rejoices in your
strength.
How great is his joy in the victories
you give!

[2]You have granted him the desire of his
heart
and have not withheld the request of
his lips. *Selah*

[3]You welcomed him with rich blessings
and placed a crown of pure gold on
his head.

[4]He asked you for life, and you gave it to
him—
length of days, for ever and ever.

[5]Through the victories you gave, his glory
is great;
you have bestowed on him splendor
and majesty.

[6]Surely you have granted him eternal
blessings
and made him glad with the joy of
your presence.

[7]For the king trusts in the Lord;
through the unfailing love of the Most
High
he will not be shaken.

[8]Your hand will lay hold on all your
enemies;
your right hand will seize your foes.

[9]At the time of your appearing
you will make them like a fiery
furnace.

---

[a]9 Or *save! / O King, answer*

A DEVOTION TO DEVOTIONS

●●●

Work It Out
●●●●

Having devotions on a regular basis is something just about everyone struggles with at one time or another. Some people get up at 6:09 A.M. every morning without fail in order to spend time alone with God. Others struggle to make time even once or twice a week. Others will manage to have devotions every day for about two weeks and then quit for a year or more. How about you? Where does your devotional life fit in this picture?

If you find it hard to maintain a regular time alone with God, here's a hint:

Buy yourself a little notebook. Each time you have devotions, jot down what you read, what you learned, how you felt. At the end of a few months or a year, look back at this little book. You'll probably be surprised at what you've read and how much God has taught you.

Nail It Down
●●●●

Read Psalm 19:7–11 for a beautiful description of what God's Word meant to David.

●●●

Think It Through
●●●●

You can't, of course, call God on the phone or invite him over for pizza in order to spend time with him. But that doesn't mean you can't communicate with him. God's primary way of communicating with you is through prayer and the Bible. As you read and study and pray, the Holy Spirit communicates God's love and plan for you.

Time spent with God and his Word on a regular basis will give your life meaning and direction. He promises! It will revive your soul, make you wise and give you joy (Psalm 19:7–8). Why not take advantage of those good things for your life? You'll never regret it!

Nail It Down
●●●●

Read again David's description of God's Word in Psalm 19:7–11. For further insight read Psalm 119:57–64.

Turn to pages 587, 974, 1050 and 1053 for other readings on devotions.
Turn to page 560 for Monday's reading.

Topic
●●●●

In his wrath the Lord will swallow them
up,
and his fire will consume them.
[10]You will destroy their descendants from
the earth,
their posterity from mankind.
[11]Though they plot evil against you
and devise wicked schemes, they
cannot succeed;
[12]for you will make them turn their backs
when you aim at them with drawn
bow.

[13]Be exalted, O Lord, in your strength;
we will sing and praise your might.

Psalm 22

For the director of music. To the tune of
"The Doe of the Morning." A psalm
of David.

[1]My God, my God, why have you
forsaken me?
Why are you so far from saving me,
so far from the words of my groaning?
[2]O my God, I cry out by day, but you do
not answer,
by night, and am not silent.

[3]Yet you are enthroned as the Holy One;
you are the praise of Israel.[a]
[4]In you our fathers put their trust;
they trusted and you delivered them.
[5]They cried to you and were saved;
in you they trusted and were not
disappointed.

[6]But I am a worm and not a man,
scorned by men and despised by the
people.
[7]All who see me mock me;
they hurl insults, shaking their heads:
[8]"He trusts in the Lord;
let the Lord rescue him.
Let him deliver him,
since he delights in him."

[9]Yet you brought me out of the womb;
you made me trust in you
even at my mother's breast.
[10]From birth I was cast upon you;
from my mother's womb you have
been my God.
[11]Do not be far from me,
for trouble is near
and there is no one to help.

[12]Many bulls surround me;
strong bulls of Bashan encircle me.
[13]Roaring lions tearing their prey
open their mouths wide against me.
[14]I am poured out like water,
and all my bones are out of joint.
My heart has turned to wax;
it has melted away within me.
[15]My strength is dried up like a potsherd,
and my tongue sticks to the roof of
my mouth;
you lay me[b] in the dust of death.
[16]Dogs have surrounded me;
a band of evil men has encircled me,
they have pierced[c] my hands and my
feet.
[17]I can count all my bones;
people stare and gloat over me.
[18]They divide my garments among them
and cast lots for my clothing.

[19]But you, O Lord, be not far off;
O my Strength, come quickly to help
me.
[20]Deliver my life from the sword,
my precious life from the power of
the dogs.
[21]Rescue me from the mouth of the lions;
save[d] me from the horns of the wild
oxen.

[22]I will declare your name to my brothers;
in the congregation I will praise you.
[23]You who fear the Lord, praise him!
All you descendants of Jacob, honor
him!
Revere him, all you descendants of
Israel!
[24]For he has not despised or disdained
the suffering of the afflicted one;
he has not hidden his face from him
but has listened to his cry for help.

[25]From you comes the theme of my
praise in the great assembly;
before those who fear you[e] will I
fulfill my vows.
[26]The poor will eat and be satisfied;
they who seek the Lord will praise
him—
may your hearts live forever!
[27]All the ends of the earth
will remember and turn to the Lord,
and all the families of the nations
will bow down before him,
[28]for dominion belongs to the Lord
and he rules over the nations.

---

[a]3 Or *Yet you are holy, / enthroned on the praises of Israel*   [b]15 Or *I am laid*   [c]16 Some Hebrew
manuscripts, Septuagint and Syriac; most Hebrew manuscripts / *like the lion,*   [d]21 Or / *you have heard*
[e]25 Hebrew *him*

²⁹All the rich of the earth will feast and
    worship;
  all who go down to the dust will
    kneel before him—
  those who cannot keep themselves
    alive.
³⁰Posterity will serve him;
  future generations will be told about
    the Lord.
³¹They will proclaim his righteousness
  to a people yet unborn—
  for he has done it.

Psalm 23

A psalm of David.

¹The Lord is my shepherd, I shall not be
    in want.
² He makes me lie down in green
    pastures,
  he leads me beside quiet waters,
³ he restores my soul.
  He guides me in paths of righteousness
    for his name's sake.
⁴Even though I walk
    through the valley of the shadow of
    death,ᵃ
  I will fear no evil,
    for you are with me;
  your rod and your staff,
    they comfort me.

⁵You prepare a table before me
  in the presence of my enemies.
  You anoint my head with oil;
    my cup overflows.
⁶Surely goodness and love will follow me
  all the days of my life,
  and I will dwell in the house of the Lord
    forever.

Psalm 24

Of David. A psalm.

¹The earth is the Lord's, and everything
    in it,
  the world, and all who live in it;
²for he founded it upon the seas
  and established it upon the waters.

³Who may ascend the hill of the Lord?
  Who may stand in his holy place?
⁴He who has clean hands and a pure
    heart,

who does not lift up his soul to an
    idol
  or swear by what is false.ᵇ
⁵He will receive blessing from the Lord
  and vindication from God his Savior.
⁶Such is the generation of those who
    seek him,
  who seek your face, O God of Jacob.ᶜ
                                    Selah

⁷Lift up your heads, O you gates;
  be lifted up, you ancient doors,
  that the King of glory may come in.
⁸Who is this King of glory?
  The Lord strong and mighty,
  the Lord mighty in battle.
⁹Lift up your heads, O you gates;
  lift them up, you ancient doors,
  that the King of glory may come in.
¹⁰Who is he, this King of glory?
  The Lord Almighty—
  he is the King of glory.   Selah

Psalm 25ᵈ

Of David.

¹To you, O Lord, I lift up my soul;
² in you I trust, O my God.
  Do not let me be put to shame,
    nor let my enemies triumph over me.
³No one whose hope is in you
  will ever be put to shame,
  but they will be put to shame
    who are treacherous without excuse.

⁴Show me your ways, O Lord,
    teach me your paths;
⁵guide me in your truth and teach me,
  for you are God my Savior,
    and my hope is in you all day long.
⁶Remember, O Lord, your great mercy
    and love,
  for they are from of old.
⁷Remember not the sins of my youth
    and my rebellious ways;
  according to your love remember me,
    for you are good, O Lord.

⁸Good and upright is the Lord;
  therefore he instructs sinners in his
    ways.
⁹He guides the humble in what is right
  and teaches them his way.
¹⁰All the ways of the Lord are loving and
    faithful

ᵃ4 Or *through the darkest valley*   ᵇ4 Or *swear falsely*   ᶜ6 Two Hebrew manuscripts and Syriac (see also
Septuagint); most Hebrew manuscripts *face, Jacob*   ᵈThis psalm is an acrostic poem, the verses of which
begin with the successive letters of the Hebrew alphabet.

THE ULTIMATE DISAPPEARING ACT

Randy, who just became a Christian a few weeks ago, was seen last night hanging out in front of a local liquor store.

Faith in Christ is totally new to Randy. On the one hand, he has made some big changes. But on the other hand, he still has some glaring faults—like his fighting, his swearing and his thought life.

Look It Up
••••

When we consider appearances, we automatically stress that we need to be careful about how things appear. But we also want to emphasize the things that need to *disappear*!

"Put to death, therefore, whatever belongs to your earthly nature: sexual immorality, impurity, lust, evil desires and greed, which is idolatry. Because of these, the wrath of God is coming. You used to walk in these ways, in the life you once lived. But now you must rid yourselves of all such things as these: anger, rage, malice, slander, and filthy language from your lips. Do not lie to each other, since you have taken off your old self with its practices and have put on the new self, which is being renewed in knowledge in the image of its Creator" (Colossians 3:5–10).

Think It Through
••••

If Randy were your friend, how would you try to help him?

Is growth something you must wait for God to do? Or do you also have a responsibility in the maturing process? What does Colossians 3:5–10 say?

Work It Out
••••

Check whether the behaviors and/or attitudes described in the above passage are present in your life today. You can answer each with a simple yes or no.
1. Sexual immorality.
2. Impurity.
3. Lust.
4. Evil desires.
5. Greed.
6. Anger/Rage.
7. Malice.
8. Slander.
9. Filthy language.
10. Lying.
For the next week, keep in mind each of the items to which you answered yes. And whenever a situation comes up involving one of the items, do what's right. It's pretty easy to read a devotion like this, realize that there are areas where you need to change, and then forget all about it within a few hours. Make this time different! Make a conscious effort to remember and to correct what needs to change.

Nail It Down
••••

Read Psalm 24:3–4 for more about the need to make evil disappear from your life.

Turn to pages 488, 1300 and 1358 for other readings on appearance.
Turn to page 565 for Tuesday's reading.

Topic
••••

APPEARANCE

kindness

Commit random acts of kindness!

You've probably either heard that phrase or seen it on a bumper sticker. So what does it mean? How can you show kindness to people you come in contact with every day?

What would Jesus do?

To say that Jesus was kind is probably like saying flowers bloom. It's obvious. But Jesus expressed kindness in many different ways, radical ways. He said to love and pray for those who don't show the same love in return (Matthew 5:43-48). He said to give to the needy without looking for praise in return (Matthew 6:1-4).

According to Jesus' example, kindness also meant helping people see their sinfulness and repent. When a rich young man came to Jesus and asked what he could do to get eternal life, Jesus replied frankly that he would have to sell all his possessions and give the proceeds to the poor.

Matthew 19:22 says, "When the young man heard this, he went away sad, because he had great wealth." Jesus' kindness consisted in helping the young man see what he really valued and giving him an opportunity to change.

What will you do?

As a Christian, acts of kindness should be a constant part of your life because they reflect the character of Christ. There should be nothing "random" about them. In real life, kindness is giving to someone in need or being kind to someone who has been rude or inconsiderate. Kindness is helping someone see sin for what it is and turn away from it. Be known for committing consistent acts of kindness. That's what Jesus did.

More about kindness

Romans 2:4; Ephesians 2:6-9; Titus 3:4-7

W.W.J.D. ?

Racism

There's a lot of talk...

about racism these days, and "racial reconciliation" is a phrase that many people toss around. But what does it mean? How do you reach past stereotypes and get to know and understand people whose skin color is different from yours?

What would Jesus do?

During Jesus' time, the Jews despised the Samaritans, a mixed race of people who lived among them. The feeling was mutual. With a long history of religious and political disagreement between them, the Samaritans despised the Jews as well.

In reading the Gospels, it is very clear that Jesus' primary target of ministry was the Jews. But sprinkled throughout his ministry are encounters with Gentiles, like the Samaritans, that changed people's lives and spread the gospel throughout their communities. From the Samaritan woman at the well (John 4) to the Canaanite woman who begged Jesus to deliver her demon-possessed daughter (Matthew 15:22-28), Jesus looked past the racism that filled his society and reached out to individuals. As a result, the apostles were instructed in to preach to all Jerusalem, Judea, and Samaria (Acts 1:8).

What will you do?

The best way to fight racism is to avoid judging others by their outward appearance or race. If you tend to stereotype people based on how they dress or look, it helps to remember that God does not look on the outside. He looks at the heart. Jesus changed lives when he reached out to those whom others avoided and despised. Can you reach out to those who are different from you? Those who are outside your circle of friends? Can you show them what Jesus would do?

More about racism

Acts 10:24-35; Acts 15:5-11; Galatians 3:28; 1 John 2:9-11

for those who keep the demands of
his covenant.
¹¹For the sake of your name, O Lord,
forgive my iniquity, though it is great.
¹²Who, then, is the man that fears the
Lord?
He will instruct him in the way
chosen for him.
¹³He will spend his days in prosperity,
and his descendants will inherit the
land.
¹⁴The Lord confides in those who fear
him;
he makes his covenant known to
them.
¹⁵My eyes are ever on the Lord,
for only he will release my feet from
the snare.

¹⁶Turn to me and be gracious to me,
for I am lonely and afflicted.
¹⁷The troubles of my heart have
multiplied;
free me from my anguish.
¹⁸Look upon my affliction and my distress
and take away all my sins.
¹⁹See how my enemies have increased
and how fiercely they hate me!
²⁰Guard my life and rescue me;
let me not be put to shame,
for I take refuge in you.
²¹May integrity and uprightness protect
me,
because my hope is in you.

²²Redeem Israel, O God,
from all their troubles!

Psalm 26

Of David.

¹Vindicate me, O Lord,
for I have led a blameless life;
I have trusted in the Lord
without wavering.
²Test me, O Lord, and try me,
examine my heart and my mind;
³for your love is ever before me,
and I walk continually in your truth.
⁴I do not sit with deceitful men,
nor do I consort with hypocrites;
⁵I abhor the assembly of evildoers
and refuse to sit with the wicked.
⁶I wash my hands in innocence,
and go about your altar, O Lord,
⁷proclaiming aloud your praise

and telling of all your wonderful
deeds.
⁸I love the house where you live, O Lord,
the place where your glory dwells.

⁹Do not take away my soul along with
sinners,
my life with bloodthirsty men,
¹⁰in whose hands are wicked schemes,
whose right hands are full of bribes.
¹¹But I lead a blameless life;
redeem me and be merciful to me.

¹²My feet stand on level ground;
in the great assembly I will praise the
Lord.

Psalm 27

Of David.

¹The Lord is my light and my salvation—
whom shall I fear?
The Lord is the stronghold of my life—
of whom shall I be afraid?
²When evil men advance against me
to devour my flesh,ᵃ
when my enemies and my foes attack
me,
they will stumble and fall.
³Though an army besiege me,
my heart will not fear;
though war break out against me,
even then will I be confident.

⁴One thing I ask of the Lord,
this is what I seek:
that I may dwell in the house of the
Lord
all the days of my life,
to gaze upon the beauty of the Lord
and to seek him in his temple.
⁵For in the day of trouble
he will keep me safe in his dwelling;
he will hide me in the shelter of his
tabernacle
and set me high upon a rock.
⁶Then my head will be exalted
above the enemies who surround me;
at his tabernacle will I sacrifice with
shouts of joy;
I will sing and make music to the
Lord.

⁷Hear my voice when I call, O Lord;
be merciful to me and answer me.
⁸My heart says of you, "Seek hisᵇ face!"
Your face, Lord, I will seek.
⁹Do not hide your face from me,

ᵃ2 Or to slander me   ᵇ8 Or To you, O my heart, he has said, "Seek my

do not turn your servant away in
anger;
you have been my helper.
Do not reject me or forsake me,
O God my Savior.
[10]Though my father and mother forsake
me,
the LORD will receive me.
[11]Teach me your way, O LORD;
lead me in a straight path
because of my oppressors.
[12]Do not turn me over to the desire of my
foes,
for false witnesses rise up against me,
breathing out violence.

[13]I am still confident of this:
I will see the goodness of the LORD
in the land of the living.
[14]Wait for the LORD;
be strong and take heart
and wait for the LORD.

Psalm 28

Of David.

[1]To you I call, O LORD my Rock;
do not turn a deaf ear to me.
For if you remain silent,
I will be like those who have gone
down to the pit.
[2]Hear my cry for mercy
as I call to you for help,
as I lift up my hands
toward your Most Holy Place.

[3]Do not drag me away with the wicked,
with those who do evil,
who speak cordially with their neighbors
but harbor malice in their hearts.
[4]Repay them for their deeds
and for their evil work;
repay them for what their hands have
done
and bring back upon them what they
deserve.
[5]Since they show no regard for the works
of the LORD
and what his hands have done,
he will tear them down
and never build them up again.

[6]Praise be to the LORD,
for he has heard my cry for mercy.
[7]The LORD is my strength and my shield;
my heart trusts in him, and I am
helped.

My heart leaps for joy
and I will give thanks to him in song.
[8]The LORD is the strength of his people,
a fortress of salvation for his anointed
one.
[9]Save your people and bless your
inheritance;
be their shepherd and carry them
forever.

Psalm 29

A psalm of David.

[1]Ascribe to the LORD, O mighty ones,
ascribe to the LORD glory and strength.
[2]Ascribe to the LORD the glory due his
name;
worship the LORD in the splendor of
his[a] holiness.

[3]The voice of the LORD is over the waters;
the God of glory thunders,
the LORD thunders over the mighty
waters.
[4]The voice of the LORD is powerful;
the voice of the LORD is majestic.
[5]The voice of the LORD breaks the cedars;
the LORD breaks in pieces the cedars
of Lebanon.
[6]He makes Lebanon skip like a calf,
Sirion[b] like a young wild ox.
[7]The voice of the LORD strikes
with flashes of lightning.
[8]The voice of the LORD shakes the desert;
the LORD shakes the Desert of Kadesh.
[9]The voice of the LORD twists the oaks[c]
and strips the forests bare.
And in his temple all cry, "Glory!"

[10]The LORD sits[d] enthroned over the
flood;
the LORD is enthroned as King forever.
[11]The LORD gives strength to his people;
the LORD blesses his people with
peace.

Psalm 30

A psalm. A song. For the dedication of the
temple.[e] Of David.

[1]I will exalt you, O LORD,
for you lifted me out of the depths
and did not let my enemies gloat over
me.
[2]O LORD my God, I called to you for help

---

[a]2 Or LORD with the splendor of   [b]6 That is, Mount Hermon   [c]9 Or LORD makes the deer give birth
[d]10 Or sat   [e]Title: Or palace

and you healed me.
3O Lord, you brought me up from the
      grave[a];
   you spared me from going down into
      the pit.

4Sing to the Lord, you saints of his;
   praise his holy name.
5For his anger lasts only a moment,
   but his favor lasts a lifetime;
weeping may remain for a night,
   but rejoicing comes in the morning.

6When I felt secure, I said,
   "I will never be shaken."
7O Lord, when you favored me,
   you made my mountain[b] stand firm;
but when you hid your face,
   I was dismayed.

8To you, O Lord, I called;
   to the Lord I cried for mercy:
9"What gain is there in my destruction,[c]
   in my going down into the pit?
Will the dust praise you?
   Will it proclaim your faithfulness?
10Hear, O Lord, and be merciful to me;
   O Lord, be my help."

11You turned my wailing into dancing;
   you removed my sackcloth and
      clothed me with joy,
12that my heart may sing to you and not
      be silent.
   O Lord my God, I will give you thanks
      forever.

Psalm 31

For the director of music. A psalm
of David.

1In you, O Lord, I have taken refuge;
   let me never be put to shame;
   deliver me in your righteousness.
2Turn your ear to me,
   come quickly to my rescue;
be my rock of refuge,
   a strong fortress to save me.
3Since you are my rock and my fortress,
   for the sake of your name lead and
      guide me.
4Free me from the trap that is set for me,
   for you are my refuge.
5Into your hands I commit my spirit;
   redeem me, O Lord, the God of truth.

6I hate those who cling to worthless
      idols;
   I trust in the Lord.

7I will be glad and rejoice in your love,
   for you saw my affliction
   and knew the anguish of my soul.
8You have not handed me over to the
      enemy
   but have set my feet in a spacious
      place.

9Be merciful to me, O Lord, for I am in
      distress;
   my eyes grow weak with sorrow,
   my soul and my body with grief.
10My life is consumed by anguish
   and my years by groaning;
my strength fails because of my
      affliction,[d]
   and my bones grow weak.
11Because of all my enemies,
   I am the utter contempt of my
      neighbors;
I am a dread to my friends—
   those who see me on the street flee
      from me.
12I am forgotten by them as though I
      were dead;
   I have become like broken pottery.
13For I hear the slander of many;
   there is terror on every side;
they conspire against me
   and plot to take my life.

14But I trust in you, O Lord;
   I say, "You are my God."
15My times are in your hands;
   deliver me from my enemies
   and from those who pursue me.
16Let your face shine on your servant;
   save me in your unfailing love.
17Let me not be put to shame, O Lord,
   for I have cried out to you;
but let the wicked be put to shame
   and lie silent in the grave.[a]
18Let their lying lips be silenced,
   for with pride and contempt
   they speak arrogantly against the
      righteous.

19How great is your goodness,
   which you have stored up for those
      who fear you,
which you bestow in the sight of men
   on those who take refuge in you.
20In the shelter of your presence you hide
      them
   from the intrigues of men;
in your dwelling you keep them safe
   from accusing tongues.

21Praise be to the Lord,

a3,17 Hebrew Sheol   *b7 Or* hill country   *c9 Or* there if I am silenced   *d10 Or* guilt

for he showed his wonderful love to
    me
when I was in a besieged city.
²²In my alarm I said,
    "I am cut off from your sight!"
Yet you heard my cry for mercy
    when I called to you for help.

²³Love the LORD, all his saints!
    The LORD preserves the faithful,
    but the proud he pays back in full.
²⁴Be strong and take heart,
    all you who hope in the LORD.

Psalm 32

Of David. A *maskil.* [a]

¹Blessed is he
    whose transgressions are forgiven,
    whose sins are covered.
²Blessed is the man
    whose sin the LORD does not count
        against him
    and in whose spirit is no deceit.

³When I kept silent,
    my bones wasted away
    through my groaning all day long.
⁴For day and night
    your hand was heavy upon me;
my strength was sapped
    as in the heat of summer.   *Selah*
⁵Then I acknowledged my sin to you
    and did not cover up my iniquity.
I said, "I will confess
    my transgressions to the LORD" —
and you forgave
    the guilt of my sin.   *Selah*

⁶Therefore let everyone who is godly
        pray to you
    while you may be found;
surely when the mighty waters rise,
    they will not reach him.
⁷You are my hiding place;
    you will protect me from trouble
    and surround me with songs of
        deliverance.   *Selah*

⁸I will instruct you and teach you in the
        way you should go;
    I will counsel you and watch over
        you.
⁹Do not be like the horse or the mule,
    which have no understanding
but must be controlled by bit and bridle
    or they will not come to you.
¹⁰Many are the woes of the wicked,

but the LORD's unfailing love
    surrounds the man who trusts in him.
¹¹Rejoice in the LORD and be glad, you
        righteous;
    sing, all you who are upright in heart!

Psalm 33

¹Sing joyfully to the LORD, you righteous;
    it is fitting for the upright to praise
        him.
²Praise the LORD with the harp;
    make music to him on the
        ten-stringed lyre.
³Sing to him a new song;
    play skillfully, and shout for joy.

⁴For the word of the LORD is right and
        true;
    he is faithful in all he does.
⁵The LORD loves righteousness and
        justice;
    the earth is full of his unfailing love.

⁶By the word of the LORD were the
        heavens made,
    their starry host by the breath of his
        mouth.
⁷He gathers the waters of the sea into
        jars [b];
    he puts the deep into storehouses.
⁸Let all the earth fear the LORD;
    let all the people of the world revere
        him.
⁹For he spoke, and it came to be;
    he commanded, and it stood firm.
¹⁰The LORD foils the plans of the nations;
    he thwarts the purposes of the
        peoples.
¹¹But the plans of the LORD stand firm
        forever,
    the purposes of his heart through all
        generations.

¹²Blessed is the nation whose God is the
        LORD,
    the people he chose for his
        inheritance.
¹³From heaven the LORD looks down
    and sees all mankind;
¹⁴from his dwelling place he watches
    all who live on earth —
¹⁵he who forms the hearts of all,
    who considers everything they do.
¹⁶No king is saved by the size of his
        army;
    no warrior escapes by his great
        strength.

---

[a]Title: Probably a literary or musical term   [b]7 Or *sea as into a heap*

IS GUILT EVER GOOD?

••

Try as she might, Jenny cannot stop thinking about her overly passionate date on Saturday night. The guilt is like a giant weight. She feels a deep sadness in her heart and a sick feeling in her stomach. Unable to concentrate on anything, Jenny is unsettled and extremely restless.

In desperation, she finally pulls out her Bible and turns to Psalm 51. As she reads the words, she begins to cry.

Look It Up ••••

Guilt can actually end up being a good thing. Often it is not until we are broken and helpless that we sense our need for God. Only individuals who recognize their sin can understand their need for God's forgiveness and restoration.

Do you remember the story of the lost son—the guy who left home, wasted his inheritance in a spree of wild living and hit rock bottom? What happened next?

"When he came to his senses, he said, . . . 'I will set out and go back to my father and say to him: Father, I have sinned against heaven and against you.' . . . So he got up and went to his father" (Luke 15:17–18,20).

Let your guilt serve as a help—not a hindrance—to point you back to God.

Think It Through ••••

Kudzu is an Asian vine that grows like crazy and is practically impossible to exterminate. People chop it, burn it and poison it; but killing it for good takes extreme measures.

Guilt is kind of like kudzu. You can, by your own efforts, get rid of it; but it will take a long time and a lot of effort. And in the process, you'll probably damage your conscience (1 Timothy 4:2)!

Work It Out ••••

Don't try to eliminate guilty feelings without facing up to the cause of those feelings. That's like treating the symptoms but ignoring the real disease. Instead, let your guilt propel you toward God.

Ask God to show you why you feel guilty. Because he is kind, he will do that. Then let that kindness lead you to repentance (Romans 2:4).

Hey, why wallow around in a pigpen of guilt (Luke 15:15–16) when you can enjoy the forgiveness and the blessing of God (Luke 15:20–24)?

Nail It Down ••••

Read Psalm 32:5 for how King David responded to guilt.

Turn to pages 6, 957 and 1213 for other readings on guilt.
Turn to page 569 for Wednesday's reading.

Topic ••••

GUILT

¹⁷A horse is a vain hope for deliverance;
    despite all its great strength it cannot
        save.
¹⁸But the eyes of the Lord are on those
        who fear him,
    on those whose hope is in his
        unfailing love,
¹⁹to deliver them from death
    and keep them alive in famine.

²⁰We wait in hope for the Lord;
    he is our help and our shield.
²¹In him our hearts rejoice,
    for we trust in his holy name.
²²May your unfailing love rest upon us,
    O Lord,
    even as we put our hope in you.

Psalm 34^a

Of David. When he pretended to be insane
before Abimelech, who drove him away,
and he left.

¹I will extol the Lord at all times;
    his praise will always be on my lips.
²My soul will boast in the Lord;
    let the afflicted hear and rejoice.
³Glorify the Lord with me;
    let us exalt his name together.

⁴I sought the Lord, and he answered me;
    he delivered me from all my fears.
⁵Those who look to him are radiant;
    their faces are never covered with
        shame.
⁶This poor man called, and the Lord
        heard him;
    he saved him out of all his troubles.
⁷The angel of the Lord encamps around
        those who fear him,
    and he delivers them.

⁸Taste and see that the Lord is good;
    blessed is the man who takes refuge
        in him.
⁹Fear the Lord, you his saints,
    for those who fear him lack nothing.
¹⁰The lions may grow weak and hungry,
    but those who seek the Lord lack no
        good thing.
¹¹Come, my children, listen to me;
    I will teach you the fear of the Lord.
¹²Whoever of you loves life
    and desires to see many good days,
¹³keep your tongue from evil
    and your lips from speaking lies.

¹⁴Turn from evil and do good;
    seek peace and pursue it.

¹⁵The eyes of the Lord are on the
        righteous
    and his ears are attentive to their cry;
¹⁶the face of the Lord is against those
        who do evil,
    to cut off the memory of them from
        the earth.

¹⁷The righteous cry out, and the Lord
        hears them;
    he delivers them from all their
        troubles.
¹⁸The Lord is close to the brokenhearted
    and saves those who are crushed in
        spirit.

¹⁹A righteous man may have many
        troubles,
    but the Lord delivers him from them
        all;
²⁰he protects all his bones,
    not one of them will be broken.

²¹Evil will slay the wicked;
    the foes of the righteous will be
        condemned.
²²The Lord redeems his servants;
    no one will be condemned who takes
        refuge in him.

Psalm 35

Of David.

¹Contend, O Lord, with those who
        contend with me;
    fight against those who fight against
        me.
²Take up shield and buckler;
    arise and come to my aid.
³Brandish spear and javelin^b
    against those who pursue me.
Say to my soul,
    "I am your salvation."

⁴May those who seek my life
    be disgraced and put to shame;
may those who plot my ruin
    be turned back in dismay.
⁵May they be like chaff before the wind,
    with the angel of the Lord driving
        them away;
⁶may their path be dark and slippery,
    with the angel of the Lord pursuing
        them.

^aThis psalm is an acrostic poem, the verses of which begin with the successive letters of the Hebrew alphabet.
^b3 Or *and block the way*

⁷Since they hid their net for me without
    cause
  and without cause dug a pit for me,
⁸may ruin overtake them by surprise—
  may the net they hid entangle them,
  may they fall into the pit, to their
    ruin.
⁹Then my soul will rejoice in the Lord
  and delight in his salvation.
¹⁰My whole being will exclaim,
  "Who is like you, O Lord?
  You rescue the poor from those too
    strong for them,
  the poor and needy from those who
    rob them."

¹¹Ruthless witnesses come forward;
  they question me on things I know
    nothing about.
¹²They repay me evil for good
  and leave my soul forlorn.
¹³Yet when they were ill, I put on
    sackcloth
  and humbled myself with fasting.
  When my prayers returned to me
    unanswered,
¹⁴ I went about mourning
  as though for my friend or brother.
  I bowed my head in grief
  as though weeping for my mother.
¹⁵But when I stumbled, they gathered in
    glee;
  attackers gathered against me when I
    was unaware.
  They slandered me without ceasing.
¹⁶Like the ungodly they maliciously
    mocked[a];
  they gnashed their teeth at me.
¹⁷O Lord, how long will you look on?
  Rescue my life from their ravages,
  my precious life from these lions.
¹⁸I will give you thanks in the great
    assembly;
  among throngs of people I will praise
    you.

¹⁹Let not those gloat over me
  who are my enemies without cause;
  let not those who hate me without
    reason
  maliciously wink the eye.
²⁰They do not speak peaceably,
  but devise false accusations
  against those who live quietly in the
    land.
²¹They gape at me and say, "Aha! Aha!
  With our own eyes we have seen it."

²²O Lord, you have seen this; be not
    silent.
  Do not be far from me, O Lord.
²³Awake, and rise to my defense!
  Contend for me, my God and Lord.
²⁴Vindicate me in your righteousness,
    O Lord my God;
  do not let them gloat over me.
²⁵Do not let them think, "Aha, just what
    we wanted!"
  or say, "We have swallowed him up."

²⁶May all who gloat over my distress
  be put to shame and confusion;
  may all who exalt themselves over me
  be clothed with shame and disgrace.
²⁷May those who delight in my
    vindication
  shout for joy and gladness;
  may they always say, "The Lord be
    exalted,
  who delights in the well-being of his
    servant."
²⁸My tongue will speak of your
    righteousness
  and of your praises all day long.

Psalm 36

For the director of music. Of David the
    servant of the Lord.

¹An oracle is within my heart
  concerning the sinfulness of the
    wicked:[b]
  There is no fear of God
  before his eyes.
²For in his own eyes he flatters himself
  too much to detect or hate his sin.
³The words of his mouth are wicked and
    deceitful;
  he has ceased to be wise and to do
    good.
⁴Even on his bed he plots evil;
  he commits himself to a sinful course
  and does not reject what is wrong.

⁵Your love, O Lord, reaches to the
    heavens,
  your faithfulness to the skies.
⁶Your righteousness is like the mighty
    mountains,
  your justice like the great deep.
  O Lord, you preserve both man and
    beast.
⁷ How priceless is your unfailing love!
  Both high and low among men

---

a16 Septuagint; Hebrew may mean *ungodly circle of mockers.*   *b1* Or *heart: / Sin proceeds from the wicked.*

find^a refuge in the shadow of your
   wings.
8They feast on the abundance of your
   house;
   you give them drink from your river
      of delights.
9For with you is the fountain of life;
   in your light we see light.

10Continue your love to those who know
      you,
   your righteousness to the upright in
      heart.
11May the foot of the proud not come
      against me,
   nor the hand of the wicked drive me
      away.
12See how the evildoers lie fallen—
   thrown down, not able to rise!

Psalm 37^b

Of David.

1Do not fret because of evil men
   or be envious of those who do wrong;
2for like the grass they will soon wither,
   like green plants they will soon die
      away.

3Trust in the LORD and do good;
   dwell in the land and enjoy safe
      pasture.
4Delight yourself in the LORD
   and he will give you the desires of
      your heart.

5Commit your way to the LORD;
   trust in him and he will do this:
6He will make your righteousness shine
      like the dawn,
   the justice of your cause like the
      noonday sun.

7Be still before the LORD and wait
      patiently for him;
   do not fret when men succeed in
      their ways,
   when they carry out their wicked
      schemes.

8Refrain from anger and turn from wrath;
   do not fret—it leads only to evil.
9For evil men will be cut off,
   but those who hope in the LORD will
      inherit the land.

10A little while, and the wicked will be no
   more;

though you look for them, they will
   not be found.
11But the meek will inherit the land
   and enjoy great peace.

12The wicked plot against the righteous
   and gnash their teeth at them;
13but the Lord laughs at the wicked,
   for he knows their day is coming.

14The wicked draw the sword
   and bend the bow
to bring down the poor and needy,
   to slay those whose ways are upright.
15But their swords will pierce their own
      hearts,
   and their bows will be broken.

16Better the little that the righteous have
   than the wealth of many wicked;
17for the power of the wicked will be
      broken,
   but the LORD upholds the righteous.

18The days of the blameless are known to
      the LORD,
   and their inheritance will endure
      forever.
19In times of disaster they will not wither;
   in days of famine they will enjoy
      plenty.

20But the wicked will perish:
   The LORD's enemies will be like the
      beauty of the fields,
   they will vanish—vanish like smoke.

21The wicked borrow and do not repay,
   but the righteous give generously;
22those the LORD blesses will inherit the
      land,
   but those he curses will be cut off.

23If the LORD delights in a man's way,
   he makes his steps firm;
24though he stumble, he will not fall,
   for the LORD upholds him with his
      hand.

25I was young and now I am old,
   yet I have never seen the righteous
      forsaken
   or their children begging bread.
26They are always generous and lend
      freely;
   their children will be blessed.

27Turn from evil and do good;
   then you will dwell in the land
      forever.

---

^{a}7 Or *love, O God! / Men* find; or *love! / Both heavenly beings and men / find* ^{b}This psalm is an acrostic
poem, the stanzas of which begin with the successive letters of the Hebrew alphabet.

WHEN REJECTION COMES HOME

Greg is having a hard time getting to sleep. He just can't stop thinking about all the family problems Bill is having. Last week Bill told him that his parents were thinking about getting a divorce.

Today he listened in shock as Bill, who was crying, described his parents' most recent argument:

"I'm sick of all of you! That's why I'm leaving!"

"Fine! Go ahead! But you're not going to stick me with these kids. I can't control them and you know it!"

"Oh, yeah? Well, if you don't get the kids, you don't get the house or the savings account!"

Greg didn't say anything. He didn't know what to say. Now he keeps tossing and turning in bed. What in the world can he say or do to help his hurting friend?

Look It Up
•••

The next morning as Greg is reading his Bible, he comes across a verse that intrigues him: "All that the Father gives me will come to me, and whoever comes to me I will never drive away" (John 6:37). In other words, those who turn to Christ will find complete acceptance in him. Greg knows he's found something he can share with Bill.

Think It Through
•••

Greg realizes he can't make Bill's parents act differently. Nor can he really understand what it must be like to live in a home full of conflict, to feel like nobody cares.

But Greg decides to do what he can. He can be a great friend to Bill, providing support and comfort through the rough times. He can share with Bill the love and acceptance that God has for him. And he can pray regularly and fervently for God to work a miracle in Bill's family. In short, Greg can show acceptance to Bill.

Work It Out
•••

Can you relate to what Greg or Bill is facing? Chances are you or one of your friends is going through a tough time at home, perhaps feeling rejected and unloved. Ask God to give you the sensitivity to know when your friends are hurting and the wisdom to know what to say.

If you find yourself in Bill's situation, find comfort in the love and acceptance Christ offers. And find a good friend like Greg who'll be there for you.

Nail It Down
•••

Read Psalm 37:5–7 for your commitment to God and the response he promises.

Turn to pages 428, 544 and 755 for other readings on rejection.
Turn to page 572 for Thursday's reading.

Topic
••••

28For the Lord loves the just
  and will not forsake his faithful ones.

They will be protected forever,
  but the offspring of the wicked will be
  cut off;
29the righteous will inherit the land
  and dwell in it forever.

30The mouth of the righteous man utters
  wisdom,
  and his tongue speaks what is just.
31The law of his God is in his heart;
  his feet do not slip.

32The wicked lie in wait for the righteous,
  seeking their very lives;
33but the Lord will not leave them in their
  power
  or let them be condemned when
  brought to trial.

34Wait for the Lord
  and keep his way.
He will exalt you to inherit the land;
  when the wicked are cut off, you will
  see it.

35I have seen a wicked and ruthless man
  flourishing like a green tree in its
  native soil,
36but he soon passed away and was no
  more;
  though I looked for him, he could not
  be found.

37Consider the blameless, observe the
  upright;
  there is a future*a* for the man of
  peace.
38But all sinners will be destroyed;
  the future*b* of the wicked will be cut
  off.

39The salvation of the righteous comes
  from the Lord;
  he is their stronghold in time of
  trouble.
40The Lord helps them and delivers them;
  he delivers them from the wicked and
  saves them,
  because they take refuge in him.

Psalm 38

A psalm of David. A petition.

1O Lord, do not rebuke me in your anger
  or discipline me in your wrath.
2For your arrows have pierced me,
  and your hand has come down upon me.
3Because of your wrath there is no
  health in my body;
  my bones have no soundness because
  of my sin.
4My guilt has overwhelmed me
  like a burden too heavy to bear.

5My wounds fester and are loathsome
  because of my sinful folly.
6I am bowed down and brought very
  low;
  all day long I go about mourning.
7My back is filled with searing pain;
  there is no health in my body.
8I am feeble and utterly crushed;
  I groan in anguish of heart.

9All my longings lie open before you,
  O Lord;
  my sighing is not hidden from you.
10My heart pounds, my strength fails me;
  even the light has gone from my eyes.
11My friends and companions avoid me
  because of my wounds;
  my neighbors stay far away.
12Those who seek my life set their traps,
  those who would harm me talk of my
  ruin;
  all day long they plot deception.

13I am like a deaf man, who cannot hear,
  like a mute, who cannot open his
  mouth;
14I have become like a man who does not
  hear,
  whose mouth can offer no reply.
15I wait for you, O Lord;
  you will answer, O Lord my God.
16For I said, "Do not let them gloat
  or exalt themselves over me when my
  foot slips."

17For I am about to fall,
  and my pain is ever with me.
18I confess my iniquity;
  I am troubled by my sin.
19Many are those who are my vigorous
  enemies;
  those who hate me without reason
  are numerous.
20Those who repay my good with evil
  slander me when I pursue what is
  good.

21O Lord, do not forsake me;
  be not far from me, O my God.
22Come quickly to help me,
  O Lord my Savior.

a37 Or *there will be posterity*   *b38* Or *posterity*

Psalm 39

For the director of music. For Jeduthun.
A psalm of David.

[1] I said, "I will watch my ways
and keep my tongue from sin;
I will put a muzzle on my mouth
as long as the wicked are in my
presence."
[2] But when I was silent and still,
not even saying anything good,
my anguish increased.
[3] My heart grew hot within me,
and as I meditated, the fire burned;
then I spoke with my tongue:

[4] "Show me, O LORD, my life's end
and the number of my days;
let me know how fleeting is my life.
[5] You have made my days a mere
handbreadth;
the span of my years is as nothing
before you.
Each man's life is but a breath.   *Selah*
[6] Man is a mere phantom as he goes to
and fro:
He bustles about, but only in vain;
he heaps up wealth, not knowing who
will get it.

[7] "But now, Lord, what do I look for?
My hope is in you.
[8] Save me from all my transgressions;
do not make me the scorn of fools.
[9] I was silent; I would not open my
mouth,
for you are the one who has done
this.
[10] Remove your scourge from me;
I am overcome by the blow of your
hand.
[11] You rebuke and discipline men for their
sin;
you consume their wealth like a
moth—
each man is but a breath.   *Selah*

[12] "Hear my prayer, O LORD,
listen to my cry for help;
be not deaf to my weeping.
For I dwell with you as an alien,
a stranger, as all my fathers were.
[13] Look away from me, that I may rejoice
again
before I depart and am no more."

Psalm 40

For the director of music. Of David.
A psalm.

[1] I waited patiently for the LORD;
he turned to me and heard my cry.
[2] He lifted me out of the slimy pit,
out of the mud and mire;
he set my feet on a rock
and gave me a firm place to stand.
[3] He put a new song in my mouth,
a hymn of praise to our God.
Many will see and fear
and put their trust in the LORD.

[4] Blessed is the man
who makes the LORD his trust,
who does not look to the proud,
to those who turn aside to false
gods.[a]
[5] Many, O LORD my God,
are the wonders you have done.
The things you planned for us
no one can recount to you;
were I to speak and tell of them,
they would be too many to declare.

[6] Sacrifice and offering you did not
desire,
but my ears you have pierced[b,c];
burnt offerings and sin offerings
you did not require.
[7] Then I said, "Here I am, I have come—
it is written about me in the scroll.[d]
[8] I desire to do your will, O my God;
your law is within my heart."

[9] I proclaim righteousness in the great
assembly;
I do not seal my lips,
as you know, O LORD.
[10] I do not hide your righteousness in my
heart;
I speak of your faithfulness and
salvation.
I do not conceal your love and your
truth
from the great assembly.

[11] Do not withhold your mercy from me,
O LORD;
may your love and your truth always
protect me.
[12] For troubles without number surround
me;
my sins have overtaken me, and I
cannot see.

*a*4 Or *to falsehood*   *b*6 Hebrew; Septuagint *but a body you have prepared for me* (see also Symmachus and
Theodotion)   *c*6 Or *opened*   *d*7 Or *come / with the scroll written for me*

DON'T LET DEPRESSION DESTROY YOU!

She slumps in the last desk of the last row with her face buried in a book so Mrs. Whitten can't see that she's not really there. On the outside Diane looks like a typical high school student. But on the inside . . . well, that's another story.

"I feel like I'm in a black hole," she wrote in her diary just that morning. "And it's scary because I don't see any way out. What's the use anyway? I don't like my family. No one likes me. I don't even like myself. If I had any guts, I'd end it all. I'm not sure if I could work up the courage, but how hard can it be to swallow a bunch of pills?"

Look It Up
••••
If you get depressed sometimes, you're not alone. In the space of one day, Elijah called down fire from heaven, executed the prophets of Baal and outran a horse to Jezreel (1 Kings 18:16–46)! That night he rejoiced at the victory God gave him, right? Wrong.

Elijah was afraid and ran for his life. He came to a broom tree, sat down under it and prayed that he would die. "I have had enough LORD. Take my life; I am no better than my ancestors" (1 Kings 19:3–4).

Pretty extreme mood swing, wouldn't you say?

Think It Through
••••
If Elijah could get that depressed, is there any reason to think that a strong Christian couldn't? Can you think of any other Bible characters who showed signs of depression?

Do you have a close friend or two who would stick with you and encourage you through low times?

Do any of your friends seem down? How could you encourage them?

Work It Out
••••
Most teens sometimes suffer from mild depression. Here are some suggestions for defeating it:

Obey Christ's Word. Sometimes you get depressed because of sin.

Develop close friendships. "A friend loves at all times, and a brother is born for adversity" (Proverbs 17:17).

Reach out! Do you know anyone—a struggling student, an elderly neighbor, a less fortunate family—with needs to be met? Sometimes inward problems are greatly helped by outward service.

And if you or someone you know is severely depressed or even suicidal (like Diane), seek professional help. Contact your pastor or a doctor you trust.

Nail It Down
••••
Read about David's deliverance from depression in Psalm 40:1–3.

Turn to pages 686, 694, 939, 1026, 1148 and 1178 for other readings on feelings.
Turn to page 576 for Friday's reading.

Topic
••••
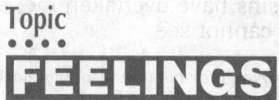

They are more than the hairs of my
    head,
    and my heart fails within me.

¹³Be pleased, O LORD, to save me;
    O LORD, come quickly to help me.
¹⁴May all who seek to take my life
    be put to shame and confusion;
    may all who desire my ruin
    be turned back in disgrace.
¹⁵May those who say to me, "Aha! Aha!"
    be appalled at their own shame.
¹⁶But may all who seek you
    rejoice and be glad in you;
    may those who love your salvation
        always say,
    "The LORD be exalted!"

¹⁷Yet I am poor and needy;
    may the Lord think of me.
    You are my help and my deliverer;
    O my God, do not delay.

Psalm 41

For the director of music. A psalm
of David.

¹Blessed is he who has regard for the
    weak;
    the LORD delivers him in times of
    trouble.
²The LORD will protect him and preserve
    his life;
    he will bless him in the land
    and not surrender him to the desire
        of his foes.
³The LORD will sustain him on his sickbed
    and restore him from his bed of
    illness.

⁴I said, "O LORD, have mercy on me;
    heal me, for I have sinned against
    you."
⁵My enemies say of me in malice,
    "When will he die and his name
        perish?"
⁶Whenever one comes to see me,
    he speaks falsely, while his heart
        gathers slander;
    then he goes out and spreads it
    abroad.

⁷All my enemies whisper together against
    me;
    they imagine the worst for me, saying,
⁸"A vile disease has beset him;

he will never get up from the place
    where he lies."
⁹Even my close friend, whom I trusted,
    he who shared my bread,
    has lifted up his heel against me.

¹⁰But you, O LORD, have mercy on me;
    raise me up, that I may repay them.
¹¹I know that you are pleased with me,
    for my enemy does not triumph over
    me.
¹²In my integrity you uphold me
    and set me in your presence forever.

¹³Praise be to the LORD, the God of Israel,
    from everlasting to everlasting.
        Amen and Amen.

BOOK II

Psalms 42–72

Psalm 42 ᵃ

For the director of music. A *maskil* ᵇ of
the Sons of Korah.

¹As the deer pants for streams of water,
    so my soul pants for you, O God.
²My soul thirsts for God, for the living
    God.
    When can I go and meet with God?
³My tears have been my food
    day and night,
    while men say to me all day long,
    "Where is your God?"
⁴These things I remember
    as I pour out my soul:
    how I used to go with the multitude,
    leading the procession to the house of
        God,
    with shouts of joy and thanksgiving
    among the festive throng.

⁵Why are you downcast, O my soul?
    Why so disturbed within me?
    Put your hope in God,
    for I will yet praise him,
    my Savior and ⁶my God.

My ᶜ soul is downcast within me;
    therefore I will remember you
    from the land of the Jordan,
    the heights of Hermon — from Mount
        Mizar.
⁷Deep calls to deep
    in the roar of your waterfalls;
    all your waves and breakers

ᵃIn many Hebrew manuscripts Psalms 42 and 43 constitute one psalm.   ᵇTitle: Probably a literary or musical
term   ᶜ5,6 A few Hebrew manuscripts, Septuagint and Syriac; most Hebrew manuscripts *praise him for his
saving help. / ⁶O my God, my*

have swept over me.

8By day the LORD directs his love,
    at night his song is with me—
    a prayer to the God of my life.

9I say to God my Rock,
    "Why have you forgotten me?
Why must I go about mourning,
    oppressed by the enemy?"
10My bones suffer mortal agony
    as my foes taunt me,
saying to me all day long,
    "Where is your God?"

11Why are you downcast, O my soul?
    Why so disturbed within me?
Put your hope in God,
    for I will yet praise him,
    my Savior and my God.

Psalm 43 *a*

1Vindicate me, O God,
    and plead my cause against an
        ungodly nation;
    rescue me from deceitful and wicked
        men.
2You are God my stronghold.
    Why have you rejected me?
Why must I go about mourning,
    oppressed by the enemy?
3Send forth your light and your truth,
    let them guide me;
let them bring me to your holy
        mountain,
    to the place where you dwell.
4Then will I go to the altar of God,
    to God, my joy and my delight.
I will praise you with the harp,
    O God, my God.

5Why are you downcast, O my soul?
    Why so disturbed within me?
Put your hope in God,
    for I will yet praise him,
    my Savior and my God.

Psalm 44

For the director of music. Of the Sons
of Korah. A *maskil.* *b*

1We have heard with our ears, O God;
    our fathers have told us
what you did in their days,
    in days long ago.

2With your hand you drove out the
        nations
    and planted our fathers;
you crushed the peoples
    and made our fathers flourish.
3It was not by their sword that they won
        the land,
    nor did their arm bring them victory;
it was your right hand, your arm,
    and the light of your face, for you
        loved them.

4You are my King and my God,
    who decrees *c* victories for Jacob.
5Through you we push back our
        enemies;
    through your name we trample our
        foes.
6I do not trust in my bow,
    my sword does not bring me victory;
7but you give us victory over our
        enemies,
    you put our adversaries to shame.
8In God we make our boast all day long,
    and we will praise your name forever.
                        Selah

9But now you have rejected and
        humbled us;
    you no longer go out with our armies.
10You made us retreat before the enemy,
    and our adversaries have plundered
        us.
11You gave us up to be devoured like
        sheep
    and have scattered us among the
        nations.
12You sold your people for a pittance,
    gaining nothing from their sale.

13You have made us a reproach to our
        neighbors,
    the scorn and derision of those
        around us.
14You have made us a byword among the
        nations;
    the peoples shake their heads at us.
15My disgrace is before me all day long,
    and my face is covered with shame
16at the taunts of those who reproach and
        revile me,
    because of the enemy, who is bent on
        revenge.

17All this happened to us,
    though we had not forgotten you
    or been false to your covenant.
18Our hearts had not turned back;

---

*a*In many Hebrew manuscripts Psalms 42 and 43 constitute one psalm.   *b*Title: Probably a literary or musical
term   *c*4 Septuagint, Aquila and Syriac; Hebrew *King, O God;* / *command*

our feet had not strayed from your
path.
¹⁹But you crushed us and made us a
haunt for jackals
and covered us over with deep
darkness.
²⁰If we had forgotten the name of our
God
or spread out our hands to a foreign
god,
²¹would not God have discovered it,
since he knows the secrets of the
heart?
²²Yet for your sake we face death all day
long;
we are considered as sheep to be
slaughtered.

²³Awake, O Lord! Why do you sleep?
Rouse yourself! Do not reject us
forever.
²⁴Why do you hide your face
and forget our misery and
oppression?

²⁵We are brought down to the dust;
our bodies cling to the ground.
²⁶Rise up and help us;
redeem us because of your unfailing
love.

Psalm 45

For the director of music. To the tune of
"Lilies." Of the Sons of Korah. A *maskil.*ᵃ
A wedding song.

¹My heart is stirred by a noble theme
as I recite my verses for the king;
my tongue is the pen of a skillful
writer.

²You are the most excellent of men
and your lips have been anointed
with grace,
since God has blessed you forever.
³Gird your sword upon your side,
O mighty one;
clothe yourself with splendor and
majesty.
⁴In your majesty ride forth victoriously
in behalf of truth, humility and
righteousness;
let your right hand display awesome
deeds.
⁵Let your sharp arrows pierce the hearts
of the king's enemies;

let the nations fall beneath your feet.
⁶Your throne, O God, will last for ever
and ever;
a scepter of justice will be the scepter
of your kingdom.
⁷You love righteousness and hate
wickedness;
therefore God, your God, has set you
above your companions
by anointing you with the oil of joy.
⁸All your robes are fragrant with myrrh
and aloes and cassia;
from palaces adorned with ivory
the music of the strings makes you
glad.
⁹Daughters of kings are among your
honored women;
at your right hand is the royal bride
in gold of Ophir.

¹⁰Listen, O daughter, consider and give
ear:
Forget your people and your father's
house.
¹¹The king is enthralled by your beauty;
honor him, for he is your lord.
¹²The Daughter of Tyre will come with a
gift,ᵇ
men of wealth will seek your favor.
¹³All glorious is the princess within her
chamber;
her gown is interwoven with gold.
¹⁴In embroidered garments she is led to
the king;
her virgin companions follow her
and are brought to you.
¹⁵They are led in with joy and gladness;
they enter the palace of the king.

¹⁶Your sons will take the place of your
fathers;
you will make them princes
throughout the land.
¹⁷I will perpetuate your memory through
all generations;
therefore the nations will praise you
for ever and ever.

Psalm 46

For the director of music. Of the Sons of
Korah. According to *alamoth.*ᶜ A song.

¹God is our refuge and strength,
an ever-present help in trouble.
²Therefore we will not fear, though the
earth give way

WHEN CHANGE CHURNS UP YOUR FAMILY

Everybody at church feels bad for fifteen-year-old John and his sister Allie. Why? Because their father deserted the family a few months ago, and this week their mother was put into a psychiatric hospital.

Over at the Matlack's, everyone is trying to get used to a new baby and the arrival of Grandpa Matlack, who can no longer live by himself. Nancy, the oldest girl and a sophomore at Webster High, not only has to sleep in a makeshift room in the basement, she also feels forgotten in all the uproar.

Look It Up
• • • •

When Job's sons and daughters were killed in a mighty windstorm, "Job got up and tore his robe and shaved his head. Then he fell to the ground in worship and said: 'Naked I came from my mother's womb, and naked I will depart. The LORD gave and the LORD has taken away; may the name of the LORD be praised' " (Job 1:20–21).

Job learned the hard lesson that only by trusting in God's wisdom, his justice and his control over the universe could Job face life's harsh trials. God is the constant protector who makes family changes, whether big or small, bearable.

Think It Through
• • • •

How do you think you'd react if your family was changed by the death of a parent or sister or brother? By severe marital problems? By the sudden addition of a new family member? By the severe illness of a family member? By the criminal conduct of a family member? By the sudden fame of a family member?

Work It Out
• • • •

Changes at home are some of the most difficult changes to deal with. But you may want to start by praying this: "Dear God, things at home are so confusing right now. I don't know what to do or where to go. Help me. Make yourself real to me. Show me that you are always the same even though the situation at home is always changing. I need you. Give me the strength to hang on during these rough times, through Christ. Amen."

If you have a friend who's facing a family crisis, go spend some time with him or her. Take your friend out for a burger. You don't have to have all the answers. Just be willing to listen and be there for your friend to lean on. The love of Christ within you can begin the healing process within him or her.

Nail It Down
• • • •

Memorize Psalm 46:1.

Turn to pages 591 and 984 for other readings on change.
Turn to page 580 for the weekend reading.

Topic
• • • •

and the mountains fall into the heart
  of the sea,
³though its waters roar and foam
  and the mountains quake with their
    surging.   *Selah*

⁴There is a river whose streams make
  glad the city of God,
  the holy place where the Most High
    dwells.
⁵God is within her, she will not fall;
  God will help her at break of day.
⁶Nations are in uproar, kingdoms fall;
  he lifts his voice, the earth melts.

⁷The LORD Almighty is with us;
  the God of Jacob is our fortress. *Selah*

⁸Come and see the works of the LORD,
  the desolations he has brought on the
    earth.
⁹He makes wars cease to the ends of the
    earth;
  he breaks the bow and shatters the
    spear,
  he burns the shields*ᵃ* with fire.
¹⁰"Be still, and know that I am God;
  I will be exalted among the nations,
  I will be exalted in the earth."

¹¹The LORD Almighty is with us;
  the God of Jacob is our fortress. *Selah*

Psalm 47

*For the director of music. Of the Sons
of Korah. A psalm.*

¹Clap your hands, all you nations;
  shout to God with cries of joy.
²How awesome is the LORD Most High,
  the great King over all the earth!
³He subdued nations under us,
  peoples under our feet.
⁴He chose our inheritance for us,
  the pride of Jacob, whom he loved.
            Selah

⁵God has ascended amid shouts of joy,
  the LORD amid the sounding of
    trumpets.
⁶Sing praises to God, sing praises;
  sing praises to our King, sing praises.

⁷For God is the King of all the earth;
  sing to him a psalm*ᵇ* of praise.
⁸God reigns over the nations;
  God is seated on his holy throne.
⁹The nobles of the nations assemble

as the people of the God of Abraham,
for the kings*ᶜ* of the earth belong to
    God;
  he is greatly exalted.

Psalm 48

A song. A psalm of the Sons of Korah.

¹Great is the LORD, and most worthy of
    praise,
  in the city of our God, his holy
    mountain.
²It is beautiful in its loftiness,
  the joy of the whole earth.
Like the utmost heights of Zaphon*ᵈ* is
    Mount Zion,
  the*ᵉ* city of the Great King.
³God is in her citadels;
  he has shown himself to be her
    fortress.

⁴When the kings joined forces,
  when they advanced together,
⁵they saw ˻her˼ and were astounded;
  they fled in terror.
⁶Trembling seized them there,
  pain like that of a woman in labor.
⁷You destroyed them like ships of
    Tarshish
  shattered by an east wind.

⁸As we have heard,
  so have we seen
in the city of the LORD Almighty,
  in the city of our God:
  God makes her secure forever.   *Selah*

⁹Within your temple, O God,
  we meditate on your unfailing love.
¹⁰Like your name, O God,
  your praise reaches to the ends of the
    earth;
  your right hand is filled with
    righteousness.
¹¹Mount Zion rejoices,
  the villages of Judah are glad
  because of your judgments.

¹²Walk about Zion, go around her,
  count her towers,
¹³consider well her ramparts,
  view her citadels,
  that you may tell of them to the next
    generation.
¹⁴For this God is our God for ever and
    ever;
  he will be our guide even to the end.

---

*ᵃ9 Or chariots   ᵇ7 Or a maskil (probably a literary or musical term)   ᶜ9 Or shields   ᵈ2 Zaphon can refer
to a sacred mountain or the direction north.   ᵉ2 Or earth, / Mount Zion, on the northern side / of the*

Psalm 49

For the director of music. Of the Sons
of Korah. A psalm.

¹Hear this, all you peoples;
   listen, all who live in this world,
²both low and high,
   rich and poor alike:
³My mouth will speak words of wisdom;
   the utterance from my heart will give
      understanding.
⁴I will turn my ear to a proverb;
   with the harp I will expound my
      riddle:

⁵Why should I fear when evil days come,
   when wicked deceivers surround
      me—
⁶those who trust in their wealth
   and boast of their great riches?
⁷No man can redeem the life of another
   or give to God a ransom for him—
⁸the ransom for a life is costly,
   no payment is ever enough—
⁹that he should live on forever
   and not see decay.

¹⁰For all can see that wise men die;
   the foolish and the senseless alike
      perish
   and leave their wealth to others.
¹¹Their tombs will remain their houses*ᵃ*
      forever,
   their dwellings for endless
      generations,
   though they had*ᵇ* named lands after
      themselves.

¹²But man, despite his riches, does not
      endure;
   he is*ᶜ* like the beasts that perish.

¹³This is the fate of those who trust in
      themselves,
   and of their followers, who approve
      their sayings.   *Selah*
¹⁴Like sheep they are destined for the
      grave,*ᵈ*
   and death will feed on them.
   The upright will rule over them in the
      morning;
   their forms will decay in the grave,*ᵈ*
   far from their princely mansions.
¹⁵But God will redeem my life*ᵉ* from the
      grave;
   he will surely take me to himself.
                             Selah

¹⁶Do not be overawed when a man grows
      rich,
   when the splendor of his house
      increases;
¹⁷for he will take nothing with him when
      he dies,
   his splendor will not descend with
      him.
¹⁸Though while he lived he counted
      himself blessed—
   and men praise you when you
      prosper—
¹⁹he will join the generation of his
      fathers,
   who will never see the light ⌞of life⌟.

²⁰A man who has riches without
      understanding
   is like the beasts that perish.

Psalm 50

A psalm of Asaph.

¹The Mighty One, God, the LORD,
   speaks and summons the earth
   from the rising of the sun to the place
      where it sets.
²From Zion, perfect in beauty,
   God shines forth.
³Our God comes and will not be silent;
   a fire devours before him,
   and around him a tempest rages.
⁴He summons the heavens above,
   and the earth, that he may judge his
      people:
⁵"Gather to me my consecrated ones,
   who made a covenant with me by
      sacrifice."
⁶And the heavens proclaim his
      righteousness,
   for God himself is judge.   *Selah*

⁷"Hear, O my people, and I will speak,
   O Israel, and I will testify against you:
   I am God, your God.
⁸I do not rebuke you for your sacrifices
   or your burnt offerings, which are
      ever before me.
⁹I have no need of a bull from your stall
   or of goats from your pens,
¹⁰for every animal of the forest is mine,
   and the cattle on a thousand hills.
¹¹I know every bird in the mountains,
   and the creatures of the field are
      mine.

ᵃ11 Septuagint and Syriac; Hebrew *In their thoughts their houses will remain*   *ᵇ11* Or *I for they have*
ᶜ12 Hebrew; Septuagint and Syriac read verse 12 the same as verse 20.   *ᵈ14* Hebrew *Sheol*; also in verse 15
ᵉ15 Or *soul*

¹²If I were hungry I would not tell you,
   for the world is mine, and all that is
      in it.
¹³Do I eat the flesh of bulls
   or drink the blood of goats?
¹⁴Sacrifice thank offerings to God,
   fulfill your vows to the Most High,
¹⁵and call upon me in the day of trouble;
   I will deliver you, and you will honor
      me."

¹⁶But to the wicked, God says:

"What right have you to recite my laws
   or take my covenant on your lips?
¹⁷You hate my instruction
   and cast my words behind you.
¹⁸When you see a thief, you join with
      him;
   you throw in your lot with adulterers.
¹⁹You use your mouth for evil
   and harness your tongue to deceit.
²⁰You speak continually against your
      brother
   and slander your own mother's son.
²¹These things you have done and I kept
      silent;
   you thought I was altogether^a like
      you.
But I will rebuke you
   and accuse you to your face.

²²"Consider this, you who forget God,
   or I will tear you to pieces, with none
      to rescue:
²³He who sacrifices thank offerings
      honors me,
   and he prepares the way
   so that I may show him^b the
      salvation of God."

Psalm 51

For the director of music. A psalm of
David. When the prophet Nathan came to
him after David had committed adultery
with Bathsheba.

¹Have mercy on me, O God,
   according to your unfailing love;
according to your great compassion
   blot out my transgressions.
²Wash away all my iniquity
   and cleanse me from my sin.

³For I know my transgressions,
   and my sin is always before me.

⁴Against you, you only, have I sinned
   and done what is evil in your sight,
so that you are proved right when you
      speak
   and justified when you judge.
⁵Surely I was sinful at birth,
   sinful from the time my mother
      conceived me.
⁶Surely you desire truth in the inner
      parts^c;
   you teach^d me wisdom in the inmost
      place.
⁷Cleanse me with hyssop, and I will be
      clean;
   wash me, and I will be whiter than
      snow.
⁸Let me hear joy and gladness;
   let the bones you have crushed
      rejoice.
⁹Hide your face from my sins
   and blot out all my iniquity.

¹⁰Create in me a pure heart, O God,
   and renew a steadfast spirit within
      me.
¹¹Do not cast me from your presence
   or take your Holy Spirit from me.
¹²Restore to me the joy of your salvation
   and grant me a willing spirit, to
      sustain me.

¹³Then I will teach transgressors your
      ways,
   and sinners will turn back to you.
¹⁴Save me from bloodguilt, O God,
   the God who saves me,
   and my tongue will sing of your
      righteousness.
¹⁵O Lord, open my lips,
   and my mouth will declare your
      praise.
¹⁶You do not delight in sacrifice, or I
      would bring it;
   you do not take pleasure in burnt
      offerings.
¹⁷The sacrifices of God are^e a broken
      spirit;
   a broken and contrite heart,
   O God, you will not despise.

¹⁸In your good pleasure make Zion
      prosper;
   build up the walls of Jerusalem.

---

^{a}21 Or *thought the 'I AM' was* ^{b}23 Or *and to him who considers his way / I will show* ^{c}6 The meaning of the Hebrew for this phrase is uncertain. ^{d}6 Or *you desired . . . ; / you taught* ^{e}17 Or *My sacrifice, O God, is*

FORGIVENESS MEANS THEY'RE GONE

Work It Out
• • • •

Take a sheet of paper. On it write all the things for which you need to be forgiven. Write down things you've never asked God to forgive. Write down things you've asked God to forgive but which keep bugging your conscience anyway.

Now take that sheet of paper and tear it up. Into tiny, itsy-bitsy pieces. On a windy day, take the pieces, throw them into the wind and watch them scatter and fly away.

Admittedly, littering isn't the most environmentally conscious thing to do. However, the picture is there. The sins you wrote down are gone. You couldn't pick up the scattered pieces and put them back together again even if you wanted to.

That's the way God views your sins when you ask his forgiveness. Scattered. Gone. *Forgiven.*

Nail It Down

Read David's confession of sin in Psalm 51.

Think It Through
• • • •

The writers of the Bible didn't hesitate to show their historical characters as they really were. The sin David was confessing when he wrote Psalm 51 was the sin described in 2 Samuel 11. It wasn't a pretty picture.

David had really blown it. He was guilty of adultery and murder. He saw Bathsheba, he wanted her, and as king he took what he wanted. When husband Uriah got in the way, he was simply removed from the picture. By murder. Still, David was called "a man after his [God's] own heart" (1 Samuel 13:14).

David wasn't a man after God's own heart because he was perfect but because he was willing to seek God's forgiveness when he sinned. If God could forgive David for murder and adultery, he can forgive you, whatever your sin. He not only *can,* he *wants* to forgive. You just have to ask.

Nail It Down

Reread Psalm 51. For further insight read Psalm 130:1–4.

Turn to pages 771, 809, 966, 1068, 1302 and 1352 for other readings on forgiveness.
Turn to page 584 for Monday's reading.

Topic
• • • •

FORGIVENESS

¹⁹Then there will be righteous sacrifices,
    whole burnt offerings to delight you;
    then bulls will be offered on your
        altar.

Psalm 52

For the director of music. A *maskil*[a]
of David. When Doeg the Edomite had
gone to Saul and told him: "David has
gone to the house of Ahimelech."

¹Why do you boast of evil, you mighty
    man?
    Why do you boast all day long,
    you who are a disgrace in the eyes of
        God?
²Your tongue plots destruction;
    it is like a sharpened razor,
    you who practice deceit.
³You love evil rather than good,
    falsehood rather than speaking the
        truth.   *Selah*
⁴You love every harmful word,
    O you deceitful tongue!

⁵Surely God will bring you down to
    everlasting ruin:
    He will snatch you up and tear you
        from your tent;
    he will uproot you from the land of
        the living.   *Selah*
⁶The righteous will see and fear;
    they will laugh at him, saying,
⁷"Here now is the man
    who did not make God his stronghold
  but trusted in his great wealth
    and grew strong by destroying
        others!"

⁸But I am like an olive tree
    flourishing in the house of God;
  I trust in God's unfailing love
    for ever and ever.
⁹I will praise you forever for what you
    have done;
    in your name I will hope, for your
        name is good.
    I will praise you in the presence of
        your saints.

Psalm 53

For the director of music. According to
mahalath.[b] A *maskil*[a] of David.

¹The fool says in his heart,
    "There is no God."

They are corrupt, and their ways are
    vile;
    there is no one who does good.

²God looks down from heaven
    on the sons of men
  to see if there are any who understand,
    any who seek God.
³Everyone has turned away,
    they have together become corrupt;
  there is no one who does good,
    not even one.

⁴Will the evildoers never learn—
    those who devour my people as men
        eat bread
    and who do not call on God?
⁵There they were, overwhelmed with
    dread,
    where there was nothing to dread.
  God scattered the bones of those who
        attacked you;
    you put them to shame, for God
        despised them.

⁶Oh, that salvation for Israel would come
    out of Zion!
    When God restores the fortunes of his
        people,
    let Jacob rejoice and Israel be glad!

Psalm 54

For the director of music. With stringed
instruments. A *maskil*[a] of David. When
the Ziphites had gone to Saul and said, "Is
not David hiding among us?"

¹Save me, O God, by your name;
    vindicate me by your might.
²Hear my prayer, O God;
    listen to the words of my mouth.

³Strangers are attacking me;
    ruthless men seek my life—
    men without regard for God.   *Selah*

⁴Surely God is my help;
    the Lord is the one who sustains me.

⁵Let evil recoil on those who slander me;
    in your faithfulness destroy them.

⁶I will sacrifice a freewill offering to you;
    I will praise your name, O LORD,
    for it is good.
⁷For he has delivered me from all my
    troubles,
    and my eyes have looked in triumph
    on my foes.

---

[a]Title: Probably a literary or musical term   [b]Title: Probably a musical term

Psalm 55

For the director of music. With stringed
instruments. A *maskil*[a] of David.

[1]Listen to my prayer, O God,
do not ignore my plea;
[2] hear me and answer me.
My thoughts trouble me and I am
distraught
[3] at the voice of the enemy,
at the stares of the wicked;
for they bring down suffering upon me
and revile me in their anger.

[4]My heart is in anguish within me;
the terrors of death assail me.
[5]Fear and trembling have beset me;
horror has overwhelmed me.
[6]I said, "Oh, that I had the wings of a
dove!
I would fly away and be at rest—
[7]I would flee far away
and stay in the desert;   *Selah*
[8]I would hurry to my place of shelter,
far from the tempest and storm."

[9]Confuse the wicked, O Lord, confound
their speech,
for I see violence and strife in the
city.
[10]Day and night they prowl about on its
walls;
malice and abuse are within it.
[11]Destructive forces are at work in the
city;
threats and lies never leave its streets.

[12]If an enemy were insulting me,
I could endure it;
if a foe were raising himself against me,
I could hide from him.
[13]But it is you, a man like myself,
my companion, my close friend,
[14]with whom I once enjoyed sweet
fellowship
as we walked with the throng at the
house of God.

[15]Let death take my enemies by surprise;
let them go down alive to the grave,[b]
for evil finds lodging among them.

[16]But I call to God,
and the LORD saves me.
[17]Evening, morning and noon
I cry out in distress,
and he hears my voice.
[18]He ransoms me unharmed
from the battle waged against me,

even though many oppose me.
[19]God, who is enthroned forever,
will hear them and afflict them—
Selah
men who never change their ways
and have no fear of God.

[20]My companion attacks his friends;
he violates his covenant.
[21]His speech is smooth as butter,
yet war is in his heart;
his words are more soothing than oil,
yet they are drawn swords.

[22]Cast your cares on the LORD
and he will sustain you;
he will never let the righteous fall.
[23]But you, O God, will bring down the
wicked
into the pit of corruption;
bloodthirsty and deceitful men
will not live out half their days.

But as for me, I trust in you.

Psalm 56

For the director of music. To ˌthe tune ofˌ
"A Dove on Distant Oaks." Of David. A
miktam.[a] When the Philistines had seized
him in Gath.

[1]Be merciful to me, O God, for men hotly
pursue me;
all day long they press their attack.
[2]My slanderers pursue me all day long;
many are attacking me in their pride.

[3]When I am afraid,
I will trust in you.
[4]In God, whose word I praise,
in God I trust; I will not be afraid.
What can mortal man do to me?

[5]All day long they twist my words;
they are always plotting to harm me.
[6]They conspire, they lurk,
they watch my steps,
eager to take my life.

[7]On no account let them escape;
in your anger, O God, bring down the
nations.
[8]Record my lament;
list my tears on your scroll[c]—
are they not in your record?

[9]Then my enemies will turn back
when I call for help.
By this I will know that God is for me.

---

[a]Title: Probably a literary or musical term   [b]15 Hebrew *Sheol*   [c]8 Or / *put my tears in your wineskin*

[10]In God, whose word I praise,
   in the LORD, whose word I praise—
[11]in God I trust; I will not be afraid.
   What can man do to me?

[12]I am under vows to you, O God;
   I will present my thank offerings to
      you.
[13]For you have delivered me[a] from death
   and my feet from stumbling,
that I may walk before God
   in the light of life.[b]

Psalm 57

For the director of music. ⸤To the tune of⸥
"Do Not Destroy." Of David. A *miktam*.[c]
When he had fled from Saul into the cave.

[1]Have mercy on me, O God, have mercy
      on me,
   for in you my soul takes refuge.
I will take refuge in the shadow of your
      wings
   until the disaster has passed.

[2]I cry out to God Most High,
   to God, who fulfills ⸤his purpose⸥ for
      me.
[3]He sends from heaven and saves me,
   rebuking those who hotly pursue me;
                                    Selah
God sends his love and his
   faithfulness.

[4]I am in the midst of lions;
   I lie among ravenous beasts—
men whose teeth are spears and arrows,
   whose tongues are sharp swords.

[5]Be exalted, O God, above the heavens;
   let your glory be over all the earth.

[6]They spread a net for my feet—
   I was bowed down in distress.
They dug a pit in my path—
   but they have fallen into it
      themselves.   *Selah*

[7]My heart is steadfast, O God,
   my heart is steadfast;
   I will sing and make music.
[8]Awake, my soul!
   Awake, harp and lyre!
   I will awaken the dawn.

[9]I will praise you, O Lord, among the
      nations;

I will sing of you among the peoples.
[10]For great is your love, reaching to the
      heavens;
   your faithfulness reaches to the skies.

[11]Be exalted, O God, above the heavens;
   let your glory be over all the earth.

Psalm 58

For the director of music. ⸤To the tune of⸥
"Do Not Destroy." Of David. A *miktam*.[c]

[1]Do you rulers indeed speak justly?
   Do you judge uprightly among men?
[2]No, in your heart you devise injustice,
   and your hands mete out violence on
      the earth.
[3]Even from birth the wicked go astray;
   from the womb they are wayward and
      speak lies.
[4]Their venom is like the venom of a
      snake,
   like that of a cobra that has stopped
      its ears,
[5]that will not heed the tune of the
      charmer,
   however skillful the enchanter may
      be.

[6]Break the teeth in their mouths, O God;
   tear out, O LORD, the fangs of the
      lions!
[7]Let them vanish like water that flows
      away;
   when they draw the bow, let their
      arrows be blunted.
[8]Like a slug melting away as it moves
      along,
   like a stillborn child, may they not
      see the sun.

[9]Before your pots can feel ⸤the heat of⸥
      the thorns—
   whether they be green or dry—the
      wicked will be swept away.[d]
[10]The righteous will be glad when they
      are avenged,
   when they bathe their feet in the
      blood of the wicked.
[11]Then men will say,
   "Surely the righteous still are
      rewarded;
   surely there is a God who judges the
      earth."

a13 Or *my soul*   b13 Or *the land of the living*   cTitle: Probably a literary or musical term   d9 The
meaning of the Hebrew for this verse is uncertain.

THE DEADLINESS OF DESPAIR

Emergency room personnel worked feverishly to save the thin patient—a seventeen-year-old high school junior named Davey. About forty-five minutes earlier Davey had taken a .38 pistol, put it in his mouth and pulled the trigger.

Police found this haphazard note at the scene: "I can't stand it anymore. We're all alone in a cold, dark universe. Life makes no sense. Since no one can give me a reason to live, I'm checking out. Please play 'The Wall' by Pink Floyd at my funeral. Davey."

Look It Up
••••

Davey's cry? "Life is pointless!" Our response? "No! Life has real purpose!" Why do we believe that?

The Bible tells of a Deity who created us. "Then God said, 'Let us make man in our image, in our likeness' " (Genesis 1:26). We didn't evolve by chance. We were specially created by God!

The Bible further explains that God is personally and purposely involved in our lives: "And we know that in all things God works for the good of those who love him, who have been called according to his purpose" (Romans 8:28).

Think It Through
••••

If you take God out of the equation, Davey's right. Nothing adds up. There are no absolutes to anchor us. We spin in space, a pointless people on a puny planet. And to what do we owe our existence? Blind chance.

On the other hand, if you recognize the reality and true nature of God, and if you anchor your life to him, everything makes sense. You have purpose, and your existence has real meaning.

Work It Out
••••

You don't have to live with a bunch of negative feelings about yourself. Take some steps to improve your self-esteem in a major way. Begin today by praying: "God, I'm so glad that you are real; that I'm not all alone in the cosmos. Help me to base my feelings about myself on the fact that you created me in your image. Thank you for being at work in the world and in my life. Help me to see, more and more, your purpose for my life. Amen."

Nail It Down
••••

Read David's cry to God for help in Psalm 57.

Turn to pages 641, 1029, 1100 and 1379 for other readings on self-esteem.
Turn to page 587 for Tuesday's reading.

Topic
••••

SELF-ESTEEM

Psalm 59

For the director of music. ⌊To the tune of⌋
"Do Not Destroy." Of David. A *miktam.* [a]
When Saul had sent men to watch David's
house in order to kill him.

[1] Deliver me from my enemies, O God;
    protect me from those who rise up
    against me.
[2] Deliver me from evildoers
    and save me from bloodthirsty men.

[3] See how they lie in wait for me!
    Fierce men conspire against me
    for no offense or sin of mine, O LORD.
[4] I have done no wrong, yet they are
    ready to attack me.
    Arise to help me; look on my plight!
[5] O LORD God Almighty, the God of Israel,
    rouse yourself to punish all the
    nations;
    show no mercy to wicked traitors.
                                    Selah

[6] They return at evening,
    snarling like dogs,
    and prowl about the city.
[7] See what they spew from their
    mouths —
    they spew out swords from their lips,
    and they say, "Who can hear us?"
[8] But you, O LORD, laugh at them;
    you scoff at all those nations.

[9] O my Strength, I watch for you;
    you, O God, are my fortress, [10] my
    loving God.

God will go before me
    and will let me gloat over those who
    slander me.
[11] But do not kill them, O Lord our
    shield, [b]
    or my people will forget.
In your might make them wander
    about,
    and bring them down.
[12] For the sins of their mouths,
    for the words of their lips,
    let them be caught in their pride.
For the curses and lies they utter,
[13] consume them in wrath,
    consume them till they are no more.
Then it will be known to the ends of the
    earth
    that God rules over Jacob.   *Selah*

[14] They return at evening,
    snarling like dogs,
    and prowl about the city.
[15] They wander about for food
    and howl if not satisfied.
[16] But I will sing of your strength,
    in the morning I will sing of your
    love;
    for you are my fortress,
    my refuge in times of trouble.

[17] O my Strength, I sing praise to you;
    you, O God, are my fortress, my
    loving God.

Psalm 60

For the director of music. To ⌊the tune of⌋
"The Lily of the Covenant." A *miktam* [a] of
David. For teaching. When he fought Aram
Naharaim [c] and Aram Zobah, [d] and when
Joab returned and struck down twelve
thousand Edomites in the Valley of Salt.

[1] You have rejected us, O God, and burst
    forth upon us;
    you have been angry — now restore
    us!
[2] You have shaken the land and torn it
    open;
    mend its fractures, for it is quaking.
[3] You have shown your people desperate
    times;
    you have given us wine that makes us
    stagger.

[4] But for those who fear you, you have
    raised a banner
    to be unfurled against the bow. *Selah*

[5] Save us and help us with your right
    hand,
    that those you love may be delivered.
[6] God has spoken from his sanctuary:
    "In triumph I will parcel out Shechem
    and measure off the Valley of
    Succoth.
[7] Gilead is mine, and Manasseh is mine;
    Ephraim is my helmet,
    Judah my scepter.
[8] Moab is my washbasin,
    upon Edom I toss my sandal;
    over Philistia I shout in triumph."

[9] Who will bring me to the fortified city?
    Who will lead me to Edom?
[10] Is it not you, O God, you who have
    rejected us
    and no longer go out with our armies?

---

[a]Title: Probably a literary or musical term   [b]11 Or *sovereign*   [c]Title: That is, Arameans of Northwest
Mesopotamia   [d]Title: That is, Arameans of central Syria

11Give us aid against the enemy,
for the help of man is worthless.
12With God we will gain the victory,
and he will trample down our
enemies.

Psalm 61

For the director of music. With stringed
instruments. Of David.

1Hear my cry, O God;
listen to my prayer.

2From the ends of the earth I call to you,
I call as my heart grows faint;
lead me to the rock that is higher
than I.
3For you have been my refuge,
a strong tower against the foe.

4I long to dwell in your tent forever
and take refuge in the shelter of your
wings.   *Selah*
5For you have heard my vows, O God;
you have given me the heritage of
those who fear your name.

6Increase the days of the king's life,
his years for many generations.
7May he be enthroned in God's presence
forever;
appoint your love and faithfulness to
protect him.

8Then will I ever sing praise to your
name
and fulfill my vows day after day.

Psalm 62

For the director of music. For Jeduthun.
A psalm of David.

1My soul finds rest in God alone;
my salvation comes from him.
2He alone is my rock and my salvation;
he is my fortress, I will never be
shaken.

3How long will you assault a man?
Would all of you throw him down—
this leaning wall, this tottering fence?
4They fully intend to topple him
from his lofty place;
they take delight in lies.
With their mouths they bless,
but in their hearts they curse.   *Selah*

5Find rest, O my soul, in God alone;
my hope comes from him.
6He alone is my rock and my salvation;
he is my fortress, I will not be
shaken.
7My salvation and my honor depend on
God[a];
he is my mighty rock, my refuge.
8Trust in him at all times, O people;
pour out your hearts to him,
for God is our refuge.   *Selah*

9Lowborn men are but a breath,
the highborn are but a lie;
if weighed on a balance, they are
nothing;
together they are only a breath.
10Do not trust in extortion
or take pride in stolen goods;
though your riches increase,
do not set your heart on them.

11One thing God has spoken,
two things have I heard:
that you, O God, are strong,
12 and that you, O Lord, are loving.
Surely you will reward each person
according to what he has done.

Psalm 63

A psalm of David. When he was in the
Desert of Judah.

1O God, you are my God,
earnestly I seek you;
my soul thirsts for you,
my body longs for you,
in a dry and weary land
where there is no water.

2I have seen you in the sanctuary
and beheld your power and your
glory.
3Because your love is better than life,
my lips will glorify you.
4I will praise you as long as I live,
and in your name I will lift up my
hands.
5My soul will be satisfied as with the
richest of foods;
with singing lips my mouth will praise
you.

6On my bed I remember you;
I think of you through the watches of
the night.

---

[a]7 Or / *God Most High is my salvation and my honor*

WHY DIDN'T I DO THIS SOONER?

When Jack set aside 6:15—6:45 each morning as his "appointment with God," he noticed a big spurt in his spiritual growth.

Carol's evening devotions became more meaningful when she began to spend a few minutes softly singing her favorite praise songs to God.

A month ago Brady found a quiet corner of the school library where he could spend twenty minutes every day at lunch, praying, memorizing Scripture and getting his thoughts back on God. This practice revolutionized his Christian life! He now laments, "Why didn't I do this sooner?"

Look It Up
••••

Remember that effective devotions depend on:
- Determination. "But if from there you seek the LORD your God, you will find him if you look for him with all your heart and with all your soul" (Deuteronomy 4:29).
- Discipline. "Train yourself to be godly" (1 Timothy 4:7).
- Doing what God says. "Do not merely listen to the word . . . . Do what it says" (James 1:22).

Think It Through
••••

Is there a right time for devotions? No! Some prefer the morning (Psalm 5:3). Others find that evening works better (Psalm 119:55,62,148). Still others take short times with God all through the day (Psalm 55:17; Daniel 6:10). The point is to have your devotional time whenever you can concentrate best.

Work It Out
••••

See if these tips can help improve your devotional life:
1. Begin by asking God to speak to you (1 Samuel 3:10).
2. Use the devotions in this Bible as a starting—not a finishing—point. Let them propel you toward further thinking and reading.
3. Meditate on the verses you read each day. Biblical meditation (Psalm 119:97–99) involves concentrating on the meaning of a passage. It's like marinating or soaking your mind in a portion of God's Word until that truth becomes a part of your life.
4. As you read, ask yourself questions like these: Is there a sin to avoid? Is there a promise to claim? Is there a new insight about God? Is there a command or an example to follow?

Nail It Down
••••

Meditate on Psalm 63.

Turn to pages 557, 974, 1050 and 1053 for other readings on devotions.
Turn to page 591 for Wednesday's reading.

Topic
••••

DEVOTIONS

⁷Because you are my help,
    I sing in the shadow of your wings.
⁸My soul clings to you;
    your right hand upholds me.

⁹They who seek my life will be
    destroyed;
    they will go down to the depths of the
    earth.
¹⁰They will be given over to the sword
    and become food for jackals.

¹¹But the king will rejoice in God;
    all who swear by God's name will
    praise him,
    while the mouths of liars will be
    silenced.

Psalm 64

For the director of music. A psalm
of David.

¹Hear me, O God, as I voice my
    complaint;
    protect my life from the threat of the
    enemy.
²Hide me from the conspiracy of the
    wicked,
    from that noisy crowd of evildoers.

³They sharpen their tongues like swords
    and aim their words like deadly
    arrows.
⁴They shoot from ambush at the
    innocent man;
    they shoot at him suddenly, without
    fear.

⁵They encourage each other in evil plans,
    they talk about hiding their snares;
    they say, "Who will see them^a?"
⁶They plot injustice and say,
    "We have devised a perfect plan!"
    Surely the mind and heart of man are
    cunning.

⁷But God will shoot them with arrows;
    suddenly they will be struck down.
⁸He will turn their own tongues against
    them
    and bring them to ruin;
    all who see them will shake their
    heads in scorn.

⁹All mankind will fear;
    they will proclaim the works of God
    and ponder what he has done.

¹⁰Let the righteous rejoice in the LORD
    and take refuge in him;
    let all the upright in heart praise him!

Psalm 65

For the director of music. A psalm
of David. A song.

¹Praise awaits^b you, O God, in Zion;
    to you our vows will be fulfilled.
²O you who hear prayer,
    to you all men will come.
³When we were overwhelmed by sins,
    you forgave^c our transgressions.
⁴Blessed are those you choose
    and bring near to live in your courts!
We are filled with the good things of
    your house,
    of your holy temple.

⁵You answer us with awesome deeds of
    righteousness,
    O God our Savior,
    the hope of all the ends of the earth
    and of the farthest seas,
⁶who formed the mountains by your
    power,
    having armed yourself with strength,
⁷who stilled the roaring of the seas,
    the roaring of their waves,
    and the turmoil of the nations.
⁸Those living far away fear your
    wonders;
    where morning dawns and evening
    fades
    you call forth songs of joy.

⁹You care for the land and water it;
    you enrich it abundantly.
The streams of God are filled with water
    to provide the people with grain,
    for so you have ordained it.^d
¹⁰You drench its furrows
    and level its ridges;
    you soften it with showers
    and bless its crops.
¹¹You crown the year with your bounty,
    and your carts overflow with
    abundance.
¹²The grasslands of the desert overflow;
    the hills are clothed with gladness.
¹³The meadows are covered with flocks
    and the valleys are mantled with
    grain;
    they shout for joy and sing.

^a5 Or *us*   ^b1 Or *befits*; the meaning of the Hebrew for this word is uncertain.   ^c3 Or *made atonement for*
^d9 Or *for that is how you prepare the land*

Psalm 66

For the director of music. A song. A psalm.

¹Shout with joy to God, all the earth!
² Sing the glory of his name;
  make his praise glorious!
³Say to God, "How awesome are your
    deeds!
  So great is your power
  that your enemies cringe before you.
⁴All the earth bows down to you;
  they sing praise to you,
  they sing praise to your name." *Selah*

⁵Come and see what God has done,
  how awesome his works in man's
    behalf!
⁶He turned the sea into dry land,
  they passed through the waters on
    foot —
  come, let us rejoice in him.
⁷He rules forever by his power,
  his eyes watch the nations —
  let not the rebellious rise up against
    him.   *Selah*

⁸Praise our God, O peoples,
  let the sound of his praise be heard;
⁹he has preserved our lives
  and kept our feet from slipping.
¹⁰For you, O God, tested us;
  you refined us like silver.
¹¹You brought us into prison
  and laid burdens on our backs.
¹²You let men ride over our heads;
  we went through fire and water,
  but you brought us to a place of
    abundance.

¹³I will come to your temple with burnt
    offerings
  and fulfill my vows to you —
¹⁴vows my lips promised and my mouth
    spoke
  when I was in trouble.
¹⁵I will sacrifice fat animals to you
  and an offering of rams;
  I will offer bulls and goats.   *Selah*

¹⁶Come and listen, all you who fear God;
  let me tell you what he has done for
    me.
¹⁷I cried out to him with my mouth;
  his praise was on my tongue.
¹⁸If I had cherished sin in my heart,
  the Lord would not have listened;
¹⁹but God has surely listened
  and heard my voice in prayer.

²⁰Praise be to God,
  who has not rejected my prayer
  or withheld his love from me!

Psalm 67

For the director of music. With stringed
  instruments. A psalm. A song.

¹May God be gracious to us and bless us
  and make his face shine upon us,
          Selah
²that your ways may be known on earth,
  your salvation among all nations.

³May the peoples praise you, O God;
  may all the peoples praise you.
⁴May the nations be glad and sing for
    joy,
  for you rule the peoples justly
  and guide the nations of the earth.
          Selah
⁵May the peoples praise you, O God;
  may all the peoples praise you.

⁶Then the land will yield its harvest,
  and God, our God, will bless us.
⁷God will bless us,
  and all the ends of the earth will fear
    him.

Psalm 68

For the director of music. Of David.
          A psalm. A song.

¹May God arise, may his enemies be
    scattered;
  may his foes flee before him.
²As smoke is blown away by the wind,
  may you blow them away;
  as wax melts before the fire,
  may the wicked perish before God.
³But may the righteous be glad
  and rejoice before God;
  may they be happy and joyful.

⁴Sing to God, sing praise to his name,
  extol him who rides on the
    clouds ᵃ—
  his name is the Lord —
  and rejoice before him.
⁵A father to the fatherless, a defender of
    widows,
  is God in his holy dwelling.
⁶God sets the lonely in families,ᵇ
  he leads forth the prisoners with
    singing;

ᵃ4 Or *I prepare the way for him who rides through the deserts*   ᵇ6 Or *the desolate in a homeland*

but the rebellious live in a
   sun-scorched land.

7When you went out before your people,
   O God,
   when you marched through the
      wasteland,   *Selah*
8the earth shook,
   the heavens poured down rain,
 before God, the One of Sinai,
   before God, the God of Israel.
9You gave abundant showers, O God;
   you refreshed your weary inheritance.
10Your people settled in it,
   and from your bounty, O God, you
      provided for the poor.

11The Lord announced the word,
   and great was the company of those
      who proclaimed it:
12"Kings and armies flee in haste;
   in the camps men divide the plunder.
13Even while you sleep among the
      campfires,*a*
   the wings of ˻my˼ dove are sheathed
      with silver,
   its feathers with shining gold."
14When the Almighty*b* scattered the kings
      in the land,
   it was like snow fallen on Zalmon.

15The mountains of Bashan are majestic
      mountains;
   rugged are the mountains of Bashan.
16Why gaze in envy, O rugged mountains,
   at the mountain where God chooses
      to reign,
   where the LORD himself will dwell
      forever?
17The chariots of God are tens of
      thousands
   and thousands of thousands;
   the Lord ˻has come˼ from Sinai into
      his sanctuary.
18When you ascended on high,
   you led captives in your train;
   you received gifts from men,
 even from*c* the rebellious—
   that you,*d* O LORD God, might dwell
      there.

19Praise be to the Lord, to God our Savior,
   who daily bears our burdens.   *Selah*
20Our God is a God who saves;
   from the Sovereign LORD comes
      escape from death.

21Surely God will crush the heads of his
      enemies,
   the hairy crowns of those who go on
      in their sins.
22The Lord says, "I will bring them from
      Bashan;
   I will bring them from the depths of
      the sea,
23that you may plunge your feet in the
      blood of your foes,
   while the tongues of your dogs have
      their share."

24Your procession has come into view,
      O God,
   the procession of my God and King
      into the sanctuary.
25In front are the singers, after them the
      musicians;
   with them are the maidens playing
      tambourines.
26Praise God in the great congregation;
   praise the LORD in the assembly of
      Israel.
27There is the little tribe of Benjamin,
      leading them,
   there the great throng of Judah's
      princes,
   and there the princes of Zebulun and
      of Naphtali.

28Summon your power, O God*e*;
   show us your strength, O God, as you
      have done before.
29Because of your temple at Jerusalem
   kings will bring you gifts.
30Rebuke the beast among the reeds,
   the herd of bulls among the calves of
      the nations.
   Humbled, may it bring bars of silver.
   Scatter the nations who delight in war.
31Envoys will come from Egypt;
   Cush*f* will submit herself to God.

32Sing to God, O kingdoms of the earth,
   sing praise to the Lord,   *Selah*
33to him who rides the ancient skies above,
   who thunders with mighty voice.
34Proclaim the power of God,
   whose majesty is over Israel,
   whose power is in the skies.
35You are awesome, O God, in your
      sanctuary;
   the God of Israel gives power and
      strength to his people.

   Praise be to God!

---

a13 Or *saddlebags*   *b14* Hebrew *Shaddai*   *c18* Or *gifts for men, / even*   *d18* Or *they*   *e28* Many Hebrew
manuscripts, Septuagint and Syriac; most Hebrew manuscripts *Your God has summoned power for you*
f31 That is, the upper Nile region

WHEN YOU LOSE FINANCES OR FRIENDS

How would you like to trade places with sixteen-year-old Dean?

His father has been out of work for about four months and finally started doing lawn work a few days ago. To make ends meet, the family is having a big emergency garage sale.

In the fall Dean will have to leave the small Christian school he's been attending, where all his friends are (the family can no longer afford it), and begin attending a huge public school.

Dean feels like a social outcast.

Everyone knows all about his family's financial problems. And at the new school he won't have any friends.

Look It Up

What can you do when big social or financial changes smack you in the face? You can start by leaning on these comforting Biblical truths:

1. God will never change, even if your whole world collapses. His love for you is always the same (Malachi 3:6; James 1:17).

2. God is the source of comfort. "Praise be to the God and Father of our Lord Jesus Christ, the Father of compassion and the God of all comfort, who comforts us in all our troubles" (2 Corinthians 1:3–4).

3. God can make you content in any situation (Philippians 4:11–13).

4. Friends in a good church will stand beside you. "Carry each other's burdens, and in this way you will fulfill the law of Christ" (Galatians 6:2).

Think It Through

When the bottom falls out, it's natural to want to grab hold of something steady and secure. But nothing in this changing world can provide the ultimate support for which you're looking. Only God can give you the security you need in the face of big social or financial changes.

In a world as fickle as this one, only the Rock-solid God can give true security.

Work It Out

Is your family having financial difficulties? Stop right now and thank God for being in control of your life. Ask him to help you learn whatever lessons you can from your adverse circumstances.

Or are you thinking, "I guess this stuff doesn't apply to me. I'm off the hook"? Sorry. You've got an assignment too: Find someone who is dealing with disturbing social or economic changes. Help to ease the burden. Be a friend. Listen, and then help in any way you can.

Nail It Down

Read in Psalm 68:19 about a God who's there for you every day.

Turn to pages 576 and 984 for other readings on change.
Turn to page 594 for Thursday's reading.

Topic

CHANGE

Psalm 69

For the director of music. To ₍the tune of₎ "Lilies." Of David.

¹Save me, O God,
  for the waters have come up to my
    neck.
²I sink in the miry depths,
  where there is no foothold.
I have come into the deep waters;
  the floods engulf me.
³I am worn out calling for help;
  my throat is parched.
My eyes fail,
  looking for my God.
⁴Those who hate me without reason
  outnumber the hairs of my head;
many are my enemies without cause,
  those who seek to destroy me.
I am forced to restore
  what I did not steal.

⁵You know my folly, O God;
  my guilt is not hidden from you.

⁶May those who hope in you
  not be disgraced because of me,
  O Lord, the LORD Almighty;
may those who seek you
  not be put to shame because of me,
  O God of Israel.
⁷For I endure scorn for your sake,
  and shame covers my face.
⁸I am a stranger to my brothers,
  an alien to my own mother's sons;
⁹for zeal for your house consumes me,
  and the insults of those who insult
    you fall on me.
¹⁰When I weep and fast,
  I must endure scorn;
¹¹when I put on sackcloth,
  people make sport of me.
¹²Those who sit at the gate mock me,
  and I am the song of the drunkards.

¹³But I pray to you, O LORD,
  in the time of your favor;
in your great love, O God,
  answer me with your sure salvation.
¹⁴Rescue me from the mire,
  do not let me sink;
deliver me from those who hate me,
  from the deep waters.
¹⁵Do not let the floodwaters engulf me
  or the depths swallow me up
  or the pit close its mouth over me.
¹⁶Answer me, O LORD, out of the goodness
  of your love;

in your great mercy turn to me.
¹⁷Do not hide your face from your
    servant;
  answer me quickly, for I am in
    trouble.
¹⁸Come near and rescue me;
  redeem me because of my foes.

¹⁹You know how I am scorned, disgraced
    and shamed;
  all my enemies are before you.
²⁰Scorn has broken my heart
  and has left me helpless;
I looked for sympathy, but there was
    none,
  for comforters, but I found none.
²¹They put gall in my food
  and gave me vinegar for my thirst.

²²May the table set before them become a
    snare;
  may it become retribution andᵃ a
    trap.
²³May their eyes be darkened so they
    cannot see,
  and their backs be bent forever.
²⁴Pour out your wrath on them;
  let your fierce anger overtake them.
²⁵May their place be deserted;
  let there be no one to dwell in their
    tents.
²⁶For they persecute those you wound
  and talk about the pain of those you
    hurt.
²⁷Charge them with crime upon crime;
  do not let them share in your
    salvation.
²⁸May they be blotted out of the book of
    life
  and not be listed with the righteous.

²⁹I am in pain and distress;
  may your salvation, O God, protect
    me.

³⁰I will praise God's name in song
  and glorify him with thanksgiving.
³¹This will please the LORD more than an
    ox,
  more than a bull with its horns and
    hoofs.
³²The poor will see and be glad—
  you who seek God, may your hearts
    live!
³³The LORD hears the needy
  and does not despise his captive
    people.

ᵃ22 Or snare / and their fellowship become

34Let heaven and earth praise him,
  the seas and all that move in them,
35for God will save Zion
  and rebuild the cities of Judah.
Then people will settle there and
  possess it;
36 the children of his servants will
    inherit it,
  and those who love his name will
    dwell there.

Psalm 70

For the director of music. Of David.
A petition.

1Hasten, O God, to save me;
  O LORD, come quickly to help me.
2May those who seek my life
  be put to shame and confusion;
may all who desire my ruin
  be turned back in disgrace.
3May those who say to me, "Aha! Aha!"
  turn back because of their shame.
4But may all who seek you
  rejoice and be glad in you;
may those who love your salvation
    always say,
  "Let God be exalted!"

5Yet I am poor and needy;
  come quickly to me, O God.
You are my help and my deliverer;
  O LORD, do not delay.

Psalm 71

1In you, O LORD, I have taken refuge;
  let me never be put to shame.
2Rescue me and deliver me in your
    righteousness;
  turn your ear to me and save me.
3Be my rock of refuge,
  to which I can always go;
give the command to save me,
  for you are my rock and my fortress.
4Deliver me, O my God, from the hand
    of the wicked,
  from the grasp of evil and cruel men.

5For you have been my hope,
  O Sovereign LORD,
  my confidence since my youth.
6From birth I have relied on you;
  you brought me forth from my
    mother's womb.
  I will ever praise you.
7I have become like a portent to many,
  but you are my strong refuge.
8My mouth is filled with your praise,
  declaring your splendor all day long.

9Do not cast me away when I am old;
  do not forsake me when my strength
    is gone.
10For my enemies speak against me;
  those who wait to kill me conspire
    together.
11They say, "God has forsaken him;
  pursue him and seize him,
  for no one will rescue him."
12Be not far from me, O God;
  come quickly, O my God, to help me.
13May my accusers perish in shame;
  may those who want to harm me
  be covered with scorn and disgrace.

14But as for me, I will always have hope;
  I will praise you more and more.
15My mouth will tell of your
    righteousness,
  of your salvation all day long,
  though I know not its measure.
16I will come and proclaim your mighty
    acts, O Sovereign LORD;
  I will proclaim your righteousness,
    yours alone.
17Since my youth, O God, you have
    taught me,
  and to this day I declare your
    marvelous deeds.
18Even when I am old and gray,
  do not forsake me, O God,
  till I declare your power to the next
    generation,
  your might to all who are to come.

19Your righteousness reaches to the skies,
    O God,
  you who have done great things.
  Who, O God, is like you?
20Though you have made me see
    troubles, many and bitter,
  you will restore my life again;
from the depths of the earth
  you will again bring me up.
21You will increase my honor
  and comfort me once again.

22I will praise you with the harp
  for your faithfulness, O my God;
  I will sing praise to you with the lyre,
    O Holy One of Israel.
23My lips will shout for joy
  when I sing praise to you—
  I, whom you have redeemed.
24My tongue will tell of your righteous
    acts
  all day long,

NATURE IS WORSHIPING; ARE YOU?

Walt's high school group takes a "One-day Getaway" at the beginning of each summer. It works like this:

The students and leaders leave early in the morning for a nearby state park. They spend the morning in individual worship. Some sit by the lake reading their Bibles and praying. Others walk on the mountain trails and marvel at God's magnificent creation.

In the afternoon they gather for a time of group sharing and praise. Each time, someone notices the chirping birds and the blooming flowers and says, "Hey, look! We're not the only ones worshiping God today!"

**Look
It Up
••••**

Have you ever stopped to think that nature is busy praising God? It's true.

> Praise him, sun and moon,
>   praise him, all you shining stars.
> Praise him, you highest heavens
>   and you waters above the skies.
>
> Praise the LORD from the earth,
>   you great sea creatures and all ocean depths,
> lightning and hail, snow and clouds,
>   stormy winds that do his bidding,
> you mountains and all hills,
>   fruit trees and all cedars,
> wild animals and all cattle,
>   small creatures and flying birds
>   (Psalm 148:3–4, 7–10).

**Think It
Through
••••**

Match the following two lists. Which part of nature matches which aspect of God (more than one answer may apply)?

mountains	a. God's creativity
clouds and rain	b. God's sense of humor
thunder and lightning	c. God's wisdom
rivers and streams	d. God's power
giraffes and monkeys	e. God's majesty

**Work It
Out
••••**

Steal Walt's idea: Go alone or with some Christian friends to a quiet park and spend some time with God.

1. Look up the verses listed under "worship" in a concordance or in the index at the back of this Bible.

2. Reflect on all the ways nature praises God.

3. Renew your commitment to be a worshiping Christian. (Begin right where you are by praising God for who he is.)

**Nail It
Down
••••**

Read another verse on nature's praise of God in Psalm 69:34.

**Turn to pages 415 and 616 for other readings on worship.
Turn to page 597 for Friday's reading.**

**Topic
••••**

WORSHIP

for those who wanted to harm me
have been put to shame and
confusion.

Psalm 72

Of Solomon.

[1]Endow the king with your justice,
O God,
the royal son with your righteousness.
[2]He will[a] judge your people in
righteousness,
your afflicted ones with justice.
[3]The mountains will bring prosperity to
the people,
the hills the fruit of righteousness.
[4]He will defend the afflicted among the
people
and save the children of the needy;
he will crush the oppressor.

[5]He will endure[b] as long as the sun,
as long as the moon, through all
generations.
[6]He will be like rain falling on a mown
field,
like showers watering the earth.
[7]In his days the righteous will flourish;
prosperity will abound till the moon is
no more.

[8]He will rule from sea to sea
and from the River[c] to the ends of
the earth.[d]
[9]The desert tribes will bow before him
and his enemies will lick the dust.
[10]The kings of Tarshish and of distant
shores
will bring tribute to him;
the kings of Sheba and Seba
will present him gifts.
[11]All kings will bow down to him
and all nations will serve him.

[12]For he will deliver the needy who cry
out,
the afflicted who have no one to help.
[13]He will take pity on the weak and the
needy
and save the needy from death.
[14]He will rescue them from oppression
and violence,
for precious is their blood in his sight.

[15]Long may he live!
May gold from Sheba be given him.

May people ever pray for him
and bless him all day long.
[16]Let grain abound throughout the land;
on the tops of the hills may it sway.
Let its fruit flourish like Lebanon;
let it thrive like the grass of the field.
[17]May his name endure forever;
may it continue as long as the sun.

All nations will be blessed through him,
and they will call him blessed.

[18]Praise be to the Lord God, the God of
Israel,
who alone does marvelous deeds.
[19]Praise be to his glorious name forever;
may the whole earth be filled with his
glory.
Amen and Amen.

[20]This concludes the prayers of David son
of Jesse.

BOOK III

Psalms 73–89

Psalm 73

A psalm of Asaph.

[1]Surely God is good to Israel,
to those who are pure in heart.

[2]But as for me, my feet had almost
slipped;
I had nearly lost my foothold.
[3]For I envied the arrogant
when I saw the prosperity of the
wicked.

[4]They have no struggles;
their bodies are healthy and strong.[e]
[5]They are free from the burdens
common to man;
they are not plagued by human ills.
[6]Therefore pride is their necklace;
they clothe themselves with violence.
[7]From their callous hearts comes
iniquity[f];
the evil conceits of their minds know
no limits.
[8]They scoff, and speak with malice;
in their arrogance they threaten
oppression.

---

a2 Or May he; similarly in verses 3-11 and 17   *b5 Septuagint; Hebrew You will be feared*   *c8 That is, the
Euphrates*   *d8 Or the end of the land*   *e4 With a different word division of the Hebrew; Masoretic Text
struggles at their death; / their bodies are healthy*   *f7 Syriac (see also Septuagint); Hebrew Their eyes bulge
with fat*

[9]Their mouths lay claim to heaven,
  and their tongues take possession of
  the earth.
[10]Therefore their people turn to them
  and drink up waters in abundance.[a]
[11]They say, "How can God know?
  Does the Most High have knowledge?"

[12]This is what the wicked are like—
  always carefree, they increase in
  wealth.

[13]Surely in vain have I kept my heart
  pure;
  in vain have I washed my hands in
  innocence.
[14]All day long I have been plagued;
  I have been punished every morning.

[15]If I had said, "I will speak thus,"
  I would have betrayed your children.
[16]When I tried to understand all this,
  it was oppressive to me
[17]till I entered the sanctuary of God;
  then I understood their final destiny.

[18]Surely you place them on slippery
  ground;
  you cast them down to ruin.
[19]How suddenly are they destroyed,
  completely swept away by terrors!
[20]As a dream when one awakes,
  so when you arise, O Lord,
  you will despise them as fantasies.

[21]When my heart was grieved
  and my spirit embittered,
[22]I was senseless and ignorant;
  I was a brute beast before you.

[23]Yet I am always with you;
  you hold me by my right hand.
[24]You guide me with your counsel,
  and afterward you will take me into
  glory.
[25]Whom have I in heaven but you?
  And earth has nothing I desire
  besides you.
[26]My flesh and my heart may fail,
  but God is the strength of my heart
  and my portion forever.

[27]Those who are far from you will perish;
  you destroy all who are unfaithful to
  you.
[28]But as for me, it is good to be near God.
  I have made the Sovereign Lord my
  refuge;
  I will tell of all your deeds.

Psalm 74

A maskil[b] of Asaph.

[1]Why have you rejected us forever,
  O God?
  Why does your anger smolder against
  the sheep of your pasture?
[2]Remember the people you purchased of
  old,
  the tribe of your inheritance, whom
  you redeemed—
  Mount Zion, where you dwelt.
[3]Turn your steps toward these everlasting
  ruins,
  all this destruction the enemy has
  brought on the sanctuary.

[4]Your foes roared in the place where you
  met with us;
  they set up their standards as signs.
[5]They behaved like men wielding axes
  to cut through a thicket of trees.
[6]They smashed all the carved paneling
  with their axes and hatchets.
[7]They burned your sanctuary to the
  ground;
  they defiled the dwelling place of
  your Name.
[8]They said in their hearts, "We will crush
  them completely!"
  They burned every place where God
  was worshiped in the land.
[9]We are given no miraculous signs;
  no prophets are left,
  and none of us knows how long this
  will be.

[10]How long will the enemy mock you,
  O God?
  Will the foe revile your name forever?
[11]Why do you hold back your hand, your
  right hand?
  Take it from the folds of your garment
  and destroy them!

[12]But you, O God, are my king from of
  old;
  you bring salvation upon the earth.
[13]It was you who split open the sea by
  your power;
  you broke the heads of the monster
  in the waters.
[14]It was you who crushed the heads of
  Leviathan
  and gave him as food to the creatures
  of the desert.
[15]It was you who opened up springs and
  streams;

---

[a]10 The meaning of the Hebrew for this verse is uncertain.   [b]Title: Probably a literary or musical term

GOD'S ABSOLUTELY PERFECT TIMING

Unlike most of the people in his class, Doug is extremely organized. He carries a massive notebook with everything in it—class schedules, monthly planning guides, a master calendar and various "to do" lists.

His friends kid him that he has the next ten years of his life all planned out and that if he lost his notebook he'd go crazy.

Those statements are exaggerations, but it's not an exaggeration to say that Doug gets pretty upset when life doesn't go according to his notebook.

Look It Up
••••

In a world where things don't always work out the way you'd like, isn't it great to know that God has flawless timing?

1. He brought salvation at the perfect time. "You see, at just the right time, when we were still powerless, Christ died for the ungodly" (Romans 5:6).

2. He guides your life and governs the world according to his timetable (1 Chronicles 17:1–14).

3. He brings judgment in his time. "We give thanks to you, O God, we give thanks, for your Name is near; men tell of your wonderful deeds. You say, 'I choose the appointed time; it is I who judge uprightly' " (Psalm 75:1–2).

Think It Through
••••

Why is it that God sometimes seems to be so slow in acting? Perhaps it's because of the truth of 2 Peter 3:8. (Look up that verse and contemplate its profound meaning.)

And remember that Jesus, the Savior of the world, didn't begin his ministry until he was thirty years old. He spent the bulk of his life working in a carpenter's shop! A waste of time? No . . . God's perfect timing.

Work It Out
••••

List the situations in your life where you find yourself saying, "C'mon, God, when are you going to do something?" (Examples might be an unsaved family member, the apparent success of evil people, a lack of friends, a problem at church, difficulties at school.)

Ask God to show you if anything in your own life is preventing him from working in those situations. If so, do what you can to eliminate that wrong attitude or action. If not, tell him you are trusting him to work things out . . . in his time.

Nail It Down
••••

Read what the psalmist thought about God's timing in Psalm 74.

Turn to pages 286, 611 and 702 for other readings on time.
Turn to page 599 for the weekend reading.

Topic
••••

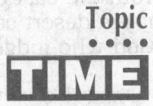

you dried up the ever flowing rivers.
¹⁶The day is yours, and yours also the
    night;
    you established the sun and moon.
¹⁷It was you who set all the boundaries of
    the earth;
    you made both summer and winter.

¹⁸Remember how the enemy has mocked
    you, O Lᴏʀᴅ,
    how foolish people have reviled your
    name.
¹⁹Do not hand over the life of your dove
    to wild beasts;
    do not forget the lives of your afflicted
    people forever.
²⁰Have regard for your covenant,
    because haunts of violence fill the
    dark places of the land.
²¹Do not let the oppressed retreat in
    disgrace;
    may the poor and needy praise your
    name.

²²Rise up, O God, and defend your cause;
    remember how fools mock you all
    day long.
²³Do not ignore the clamor of your
    adversaries,
    the uproar of your enemies, which
    rises continually.

Psalm 75

For the director of music. ⸢To the tune of⸣
"Do Not Destroy." A psalm of Asaph.
A song.

¹We give thanks to you, O God,
    we give thanks, for your Name is
    near;
    men tell of your wonderful deeds.

²You say, "I choose the appointed time;
    it is I who judge uprightly.
³When the earth and all its people
    quake,
    it is I who hold its pillars firm.   *Selah*
⁴To the arrogant I say, 'Boast no more,'
    and to the wicked, 'Do not lift up your
    horns.
⁵Do not lift your horns against heaven;
    do not speak with outstretched
    neck.' "

⁶No one from the east or the west
    or from the desert can exalt a man.
⁷But it is God who judges:

He brings one down, he exalts
    another.
⁸In the hand of the Lᴏʀᴅ is a cup
    full of foaming wine mixed with
    spices;
    he pours it out, and all the wicked of
    the earth
    drink it down to its very dregs.

⁹As for me, I will declare this forever;
    I will sing praise to the God of Jacob.
¹⁰I will cut off the horns of all the wicked,
    but the horns of the righteous will be
    lifted up.

Psalm 76

For the director of music. With stringed
instruments. A psalm of Asaph. A song.

¹In Judah God is known;
    his name is great in Israel.
²His tent is in Salem,
    his dwelling place in Zion.
³There he broke the flashing arrows,
    the shields and the swords, the
    weapons of war.   *Selah*

⁴You are resplendent with light,
    more majestic than mountains rich
    with game.
⁵Valiant men lie plundered,
    they sleep their last sleep;
not one of the warriors
    can lift his hands.
⁶At your rebuke, O God of Jacob,
    both horse and chariot lie still.

⁷You alone are to be feared.
    Who can stand before you when you
    are angry?
⁸From heaven you pronounced
    judgment,
    and the land feared and was quiet—
⁹when you, O God, rose up to judge,
    to save all the afflicted of the land.
                               Selah
¹⁰Surely your wrath against men brings
    you praise,
    and the survivors of your wrath are
    restrained.ᵃ

¹¹Make vows to the Lᴏʀᴅ your God and
    fulfill them;
    let all the neighboring lands
    bring gifts to the One to be feared.
¹²He breaks the spirit of rulers;
    he is feared by the kings of the earth.

ᵃ10 Or *Surely the wrath of men brings you praise, / and with the remainder of wrath you arm yourself*

RECOGNIZING WHO GOD IS

Work It Out
••••

Make a list of all the characteristics of God you can think of. List the things that make him a kind God (he protects, he heals). List the things that make him a God to be feared (he judges sin). Also list the things that make him a loving God (he forgives, he comforts).

God's kindness makes him good to believer and unbeliever alike. He makes sure the sun goes down in the evening and that winter is followed by spring.

As a human being you fear God because he sees you as you really are. The perfect God sees the sinful human being.

But this God is also a loving God. He sees you as you really are, but he loves you enough to give you an opportunity to be saved from what he sees.

Don't let your list of God's characteristics drive you away from him. Look that list over. Let it draw you to him as you realize how great your God is and how much he loves you.

Nail It Down
••••

Read the psalmist's description of God in Psalm 75.

Think It Through
••••

Part of knowing God is recognizing who he really is. He is not just a nameless supreme being. He's not just some benevolent force. He's not just some kindly gentleman. He is the God of the universe.

This great God of the universe knows you intimately. And he is not afraid to pass judgment on what he sees. Nor is he afraid or unwilling to provide a way for you to be free from the sin he sees and, therefore, from that judgment. When God looks at you through the blood of your Savior (a Savior he provided), he doesn't see your sin, he sees the Savior's perfection.

Pretty great plan of salvation, don't you agree? All brought to you by a tremendously great God.

Nail It Down
••••

Reread Psalm 75. For further insight read Psalm 99.

Turn to pages 980, 998, 1126, 1235 and 1330 for other readings on knowing God.
Turn to page 601 for Monday's reading.

Topic
••••

KNOWING GOD

Psalm 77

For the director of music. For Jeduthun.
Of Asaph. A psalm.

1I cried out to God for help;
   I cried out to God to hear me.
2When I was in distress, I sought the
      Lord;
   at night I stretched out untiring hands
   and my soul refused to be comforted.

3I remembered you, O God, and I
      groaned;
   I mused, and my spirit grew faint.
                                    Selah

4You kept my eyes from closing;
   I was too troubled to speak.
5I thought about the former days,
   the years of long ago;
6I remembered my songs in the night.
   My heart mused and my spirit
      inquired:

7"Will the Lord reject forever?
   Will he never show his favor again?
8Has his unfailing love vanished forever?
   Has his promise failed for all time?
9Has God forgotten to be merciful?
   Has he in anger withheld his
      compassion?"   *Selah*

10Then I thought, "To this I will appeal:
   the years of the right hand of the
      Most High."
11I will remember the deeds of the LORD;
   yes, I will remember your miracles of
      long ago.
12I will meditate on all your works
   and consider all your mighty deeds.

13Your ways, O God, are holy.
   What god is so great as our God?
14You are the God who performs miracles;
   you display your power among the
      peoples.
15With your mighty arm you redeemed
      your people,
   the descendants of Jacob and Joseph.
                                    Selah

16The waters saw you, O God,
   the waters saw you and writhed;
   the very depths were convulsed.
17The clouds poured down water,
   the skies resounded with thunder;
   your arrows flashed back and forth.
18Your thunder was heard in the
      whirlwind,
   your lightning lit up the world;

the earth trembled and quaked.
19Your path led through the sea,
   your way through the mighty waters,
   though your footprints were not seen.

20You led your people like a flock
   by the hand of Moses and Aaron.

Psalm 78

A *maskil*[a] of Asaph.

1O my people, hear my teaching;
   listen to the words of my mouth.
2I will open my mouth in parables,
   I will utter hidden things, things from
      of old—
3what we have heard and known,
   what our fathers have told us.
4We will not hide them from their
      children;
   we will tell the next generation
the praiseworthy deeds of the LORD,
   his power, and the wonders he has
      done.
5He decreed statutes for Jacob
   and established the law in Israel,
which he commanded our forefathers
   to teach their children,
6so the next generation would know
      them,
   even the children yet to be born,
   and they in turn would tell their
      children.
7Then they would put their trust in God
   and would not forget his deeds
   but would keep his commands.
8They would not be like their
      forefathers—
   a stubborn and rebellious generation,
whose hearts were not loyal to God,
   whose spirits were not faithful to him.

9The men of Ephraim, though armed
      with bows,
   turned back on the day of battle;
10they did not keep God's covenant
   and refused to live by his law.
11They forgot what he had done,
   the wonders he had shown them.
12He did miracles in the sight of their
      fathers
   in the land of Egypt, in the region of
      Zoan.
13He divided the sea and led them
      through;
   he made the water stand firm like a
      wall.

Depression is so... Depressing!

It's a cold, wet miserable day, and the cafeteria is like a morgue. People aren't talking much; they aren't smiling at all. A fellow student committed suicide over the weekend.

Rebecca and Tina are at a table by themselves whispering in low tones.

"I feel so depressed."

"You mean about Reggie?"

"Well, yeah. But I've been feeling blah for months now—long before this weekend. I try and try, but I can't seem to snap out of it, Tina. And that makes me feel even worse—Christians should never get down like this."

Look It Up
••••

The idea that a committed Christian can't get depressed is downright wrong! The Bible is full of examples of godly, depressed individuals:

Moses (Numbers 11:10–15).

Job (Job 6).

King David—"How long, O LORD? Will you forget me forever? How long will you hide your face from me? How long must I wrestle with my thoughts and every day have sorrow in my heart?" (Psalm 13:1–2).

The prophet Jeremiah—"Why did I ever come out of the womb to see trouble and sorrow and to end my days in shame?" (Jeremiah 20:18).

Think It Through
••••

Other famous individuals have also battled depression—painter Vincent van Gogh, U. S. president Abraham Lincoln and British statesman Winston Churchill. Even Charles Haddon Spurgeon, one of the greatest preachers who ever lived, struggled with depression. In fact, he was sometimes confined to his bed for weeks at a time.

The point? If you suffer from occasional blues or even from a more serious form of depression, you are not alone. Others have felt as you feel . . . and have found their way back to joy.

Work It Out
••••

Each person who reads this fits into one of these two categories right now:

1. You feel depressed.

2. You know someone who feels depressed.

Either way, here's what to do. Declare war on the blues. Determine to learn all you can about the crippling emotional disorder called depression. And remember: There are no quick fixes, but in Christ there is real hope and healing!

Nail It Down
••••

Can you relate to the feelings expressed in Psalm 77:1–15?

Turn to pages 360, 527, 1197 and 1256 for other readings on depression.
Turn to page 609 for Tuesday's reading.

Topic
••••

DEPRESSION

¹⁴He guided them with the cloud by day
  and with light from the fire all night.
¹⁵He split the rocks in the desert
  and gave them water as abundant as
    the seas;
¹⁶he brought streams out of a rocky crag
  and made water flow down like rivers.

¹⁷But they continued to sin against him,
  rebelling in the desert against the
    Most High.
¹⁸They willfully put God to the test
  by demanding the food they craved.
¹⁹They spoke against God, saying,
  "Can God spread a table in the desert?
²⁰When he struck the rock, water gushed
    out,
  and streams flowed abundantly.
  But can he also give us food?
  Can he supply meat for his people?"
²¹When the LORD heard them, he was very
    angry;
  his fire broke out against Jacob,
  and his wrath rose against Israel,
²²for they did not believe in God
  or trust in his deliverance.
²³Yet he gave a command to the skies
    above
  and opened the doors of the heavens;
²⁴he rained down manna for the people
    to eat,
  he gave them the grain of heaven.
²⁵Men ate the bread of angels;
  he sent them all the food they could
    eat.
²⁶He let loose the east wind from the
    heavens
  and led forth the south wind by his
    power.
²⁷He rained meat down on them like
    dust,
  flying birds like sand on the seashore.
²⁸He made them come down inside their
    camp,
  all around their tents.
²⁹They ate till they had more than
    enough,
  for he had given them what they
    craved.
³⁰But before they turned from the food
    they craved,
  even while it was still in their mouths,
³¹God's anger rose against them;
  he put to death the sturdiest among
    them,
  cutting down the young men of Israel.

³²In spite of all this, they kept on sinning;
  in spite of his wonders, they did not
    believe.

³³So he ended their days in futility
  and their years in terror.
³⁴Whenever God slew them, they would
    seek him;
  they eagerly turned to him again.
³⁵They remembered that God was their
    Rock,
  that God Most High was their
    Redeemer.
³⁶But then they would flatter him with
    their mouths,
  lying to him with their tongues;
³⁷their hearts were not loyal to him,
  they were not faithful to his covenant.
³⁸Yet he was merciful;
  he forgave their iniquities
  and did not destroy them.
  Time after time he restrained his anger
  and did not stir up his full wrath.
³⁹He remembered that they were but
    flesh,
  a passing breeze that does not return.

⁴⁰How often they rebelled against him in
    the desert
  and grieved him in the wasteland!
⁴¹Again and again they put God to the
    test;
  they vexed the Holy One of Israel.
⁴²They did not remember his power—
  the day he redeemed them from the
    oppressor,
⁴³the day he displayed his miraculous
    signs in Egypt,
  his wonders in the region of Zoan.
⁴⁴He turned their rivers to blood;
  they could not drink from their
    streams.
⁴⁵He sent swarms of flies that devoured
    them,
  and frogs that devastated them.
⁴⁶He gave their crops to the grasshopper,
  their produce to the locust.
⁴⁷He destroyed their vines with hail
  and their sycamore-figs with sleet.
⁴⁸He gave over their cattle to the hail,
  their livestock to bolts of lightning.
⁴⁹He unleashed against them his hot
    anger,
  his wrath, indignation and hostility—
  a band of destroying angels.
⁵⁰He prepared a path for his anger;
  he did not spare them from death
  but gave them over to the plague.
⁵¹He struck down all the firstborn of
    Egypt,
  the firstfruits of manhood in the tents
    of Ham.

⁵²But he brought his people out like a
flock;
he led them like sheep through the
desert.
⁵³He guided them safely, so they were
unafraid;
but the sea engulfed their enemies.
⁵⁴Thus he brought them to the border of
his holy land,
to the hill country his right hand had
taken.
⁵⁵He drove out nations before them
and allotted their lands to them as an
inheritance;
he settled the tribes of Israel in their
homes.
⁵⁶But they put God to the test
and rebelled against the Most High;
they did not keep his statutes.
⁵⁷Like their fathers they were disloyal and
faithless,
as unreliable as a faulty bow.
⁵⁸They angered him with their high
places;
they aroused his jealousy with their
idols.
⁵⁹When God heard them, he was very
angry;
he rejected Israel completely.
⁶⁰He abandoned the tabernacle of Shiloh,
the tent he had set up among men.
⁶¹He sent ⌊the ark of⌋ his might into
captivity,
his splendor into the hands of the
enemy.
⁶²He gave his people over to the sword;
he was very angry with his
inheritance.
⁶³Fire consumed their young men,
and their maidens had no wedding
songs;
⁶⁴their priests were put to the sword,
and their widows could not weep.

⁶⁵Then the Lord awoke as from sleep,
as a man wakes from the stupor of
wine.
⁶⁶He beat back his enemies;
he put them to everlasting shame.
⁶⁷Then he rejected the tents of Joseph,
he did not choose the tribe of
Ephraim;
⁶⁸but he chose the tribe of Judah,
Mount Zion, which he loved.
⁶⁹He built his sanctuary like the heights,
like the earth that he established
forever.
⁷⁰He chose David his servant
and took him from the sheep pens;

⁷¹from tending the sheep he brought him
to be the shepherd of his people
Jacob,
of Israel his inheritance.
⁷²And David shepherded them with
integrity of heart;
with skillful hands he led them.

Psalm 79

A psalm of Asaph.

¹O God, the nations have invaded your
inheritance;
they have defiled your holy temple,
they have reduced Jerusalem to
rubble.
²They have given the dead bodies of
your servants
as food to the birds of the air,
the flesh of your saints to the beasts
of the earth.
³They have poured out blood like water
all around Jerusalem,
and there is no one to bury the dead.
⁴We are objects of reproach to our
neighbors,
of scorn and derision to those around
us.

⁵How long, O Lord? Will you be angry
forever?
How long will your jealousy burn like
fire?
⁶Pour out your wrath on the nations
that do not acknowledge you,
on the kingdoms
that do not call on your name;
⁷for they have devoured Jacob
and destroyed his homeland.
⁸Do not hold against us the sins of the
fathers;
may your mercy come quickly to
meet us,
for we are in desperate need.

⁹Help us, O God our Savior,
for the glory of your name;
deliver us and forgive our sins
for your name's sake.
¹⁰Why should the nations say,
"Where is their God?"
Before our eyes, make known among
the nations
that you avenge the outpoured blood
of your servants.
¹¹May the groans of the prisoners come
before you;
by the strength of your arm
preserve those condemned to die.

¹²Pay back into the laps of our neighbors
　　seven times
　　the reproach they have hurled at you,
　　O Lord.
¹³Then we your people, the sheep of your
　　pasture,
　　will praise you forever;
from generation to generation
　　we will recount your praise.

Psalm 80

For the director of music. To ˻the tune of˼
"The Lilies of the Covenant." Of Asaph.
A psalm.

¹Hear us, O Shepherd of Israel,
　　you who lead Joseph like a flock;
you who sit enthroned between the
　　cherubim, shine forth
2　before Ephraim, Benjamin and
　　Manasseh.
Awaken your might;
　　come and save us.

³Restore us, O God;
　　make your face shine upon us,
　　that we may be saved.

⁴O Lᴏʀᴅ God Almighty,
　　how long will your anger smolder
　　against the prayers of your people?
⁵You have fed them with the bread of
　　tears;
　　you have made them drink tears by
　　the bowlful.
⁶You have made us a source of
　　contention to our neighbors,
　　and our enemies mock us.

⁷Restore us, O God Almighty;
　　make your face shine upon us,
　　that we may be saved.

⁸You brought a vine out of Egypt;
　　you drove out the nations and planted
　　it.
⁹You cleared the ground for it,
　　and it took root and filled the land.
¹⁰The mountains were covered with its
　　shade,
　　the mighty cedars with its branches.
¹¹It sent out its boughs to the Sea,ᵃ
　　its shoots as far as the River.ᵇ

¹²Why have you broken down its walls
　　so that all who pass by pick its
　　grapes?
¹³Boars from the forest ravage it

　　and the creatures of the field feed on
　　it.
¹⁴Return to us, O God Almighty!
　　Look down from heaven and see!
　Watch over this vine,
15　the root your right hand has planted,
　　the sonᶜ you have raised up for
　　yourself.

¹⁶Your vine is cut down, it is burned with
　　fire;
　　at your rebuke your people perish.
¹⁷Let your hand rest on the man at your
　　right hand,
　　the son of man you have raised up
　　for yourself.
¹⁸Then we will not turn away from you;
　　revive us, and we will call on your
　　name.

¹⁹Restore us, O Lᴏʀᴅ God Almighty;
　　make your face shine upon us,
　　that we may be saved.

Psalm 81

For the director of music. According
to gittith.ᵈ Of Asaph.

¹Sing for joy to God our strength;
　　shout aloud to the God of Jacob!
²Begin the music, strike the tambourine,
　　play the melodious harp and lyre.

³Sound the ram's horn at the New Moon,
　　and when the moon is full, on the
　　day of our Feast;
⁴this is a decree for Israel,
　　an ordinance of the God of Jacob.
⁵He established it as a statute for Joseph
　　when he went out against Egypt,
　　where we heard a language we did
　　not understand.ᵉ

⁶He says, "I removed the burden from
　　their shoulders;
　　their hands were set free from the
　　basket.
⁷In your distress you called and I
　　rescued you,
　　I answered you out of a thundercloud;
　　I tested you at the waters of Meribah.
　　　　　　　　　　　　　　　Selah

⁸"Hear, O my people, and I will warn
　　you—
　　if you would but listen to me,
　　O Israel!

ᵃ11 Probably the Mediterranean　　ᵇ11 That is, the Euphrates　　ᶜ15 Or branch　　ᵈTitle: Probably a musical
term　　ᵉ5 Or / and we heard a voice we had not known

[9]You shall have no foreign god among
  you;
    you shall not bow down to an alien
    god.
[10]I am the LORD your God,
    who brought you up out of Egypt.
    Open wide your mouth and I will fill
    it.

[11]"But my people would not listen to me;
    Israel would not submit to me.
[12]So I gave them over to their stubborn
    hearts
    to follow their own devices.

[13]"If my people would but listen to me,
    if Israel would follow my ways,
[14]how quickly would I subdue their
    enemies
    and turn my hand against their foes!
[15]Those who hate the LORD would cringe
    before him,
    and their punishment would last
    forever.
[16]But you would be fed with the finest of
    wheat;
    with honey from the rock I would
    satisfy you."

Psalm 82

A psalm of Asaph.

[1]God presides in the great assembly;
    he gives judgment among the "gods":

[2]"How long will you[a] defend the unjust
    and show partiality to the wicked?
                                    Selah

[3]Defend the cause of the weak and
    fatherless;
    maintain the rights of the poor and
    oppressed.
[4]Rescue the weak and needy;
    deliver them from the hand of the
    wicked.

[5]"They know nothing, they understand
    nothing.
    They walk about in darkness;
    all the foundations of the earth are
    shaken.

[6]"I said, 'You are "gods";
    you are all sons of the Most High.'
[7]But you will die like mere men;
    you will fall like every other ruler."

[8]Rise up, O God, judge the earth,

for all the nations are your
  inheritance.

Psalm 83

A song. A psalm of Asaph.

[1]O God, do not keep silent;
    be not quiet, O God, be not still.
[2]See how your enemies are astir,
    how your foes rear their heads.
[3]With cunning they conspire against your
    people;
    they plot against those you cherish.
[4]"Come," they say, "let us destroy them
    as a nation,
    that the name of Israel be
    remembered no more."

[5]With one mind they plot together;
    they form an alliance against you—
[6]the tents of Edom and the Ishmaelites,
    of Moab and the Hagrites,
[7]Gebal,[b] Ammon and Amalek,
    Philistia, with the people of Tyre.
[8]Even Assyria has joined them
    to lend strength to the descendants of
    Lot.   *Selah*

[9]Do to them as you did to Midian,
    as you did to Sisera and Jabin at the
    river Kishon,
[10]who perished at Endor
    and became like refuse on the
    ground.
[11]Make their nobles like Oreb and Zeeb,
    all their princes like Zebah and
    Zalmunna,
[12]who said, "Let us take possession
    of the pasturelands of God."

[13]Make them like tumbleweed, O my God,
    like chaff before the wind.
[14]As fire consumes the forest
    or a flame sets the mountains ablaze,
[15]so pursue them with your tempest
    and terrify them with your storm.
[16]Cover their faces with shame
    so that men will seek your name,
    O LORD.

[17]May they ever be ashamed and
    dismayed;
    may they perish in disgrace.
[18]Let them know that you, whose name is
    the LORD—
    that you alone are the Most High over
    all the earth.

---

a2 The Hebrew is plural.   *b7* That is, Byblos

Psalm 84

For the director of music. According to *gittith*.[a] Of the Sons of Korah. A psalm.

[1]How lovely is your dwelling place,
　O LORD Almighty!
[2]My soul yearns, even faints,
　for the courts of the LORD;
my heart and my flesh cry out
　for the living God.

[3]Even the sparrow has found a home,
　and the swallow a nest for herself,
　where she may have her young —
a place near your altar,
　O LORD Almighty, my King and my
　God.
[4]Blessed are those who dwell in your
　house;
　they are ever praising you.　　*Selah*

[5]Blessed are those whose strength is in
　you,
　who have set their hearts on
　pilgrimage.
[6]As they pass through the Valley of Baca,
　they make it a place of springs;
　the autumn rains also cover it with
　pools.[b]
[7]They go from strength to strength,
　till each appears before God in Zion.

[8]Hear my prayer, O LORD God Almighty;
　listen to me, O God of Jacob.　　*Selah*
[9]Look upon our shield,[c] O God;
　look with favor on your anointed one.

[10]Better is one day in your courts
　than a thousand elsewhere;
I would rather be a doorkeeper in the
　house of my God
　than dwell in the tents of the wicked.
[11]For the LORD God is a sun and shield;
　the LORD bestows favor and honor;
no good thing does he withhold
　from those whose walk is blameless.

[12]O LORD Almighty,
　blessed is the man who trusts in you.

Psalm 85

For the director of music. Of the Sons
of Korah. A psalm.

[1]You showed favor to your land, O LORD;
　you restored the fortunes of Jacob.
[2]You forgave the iniquity of your people
　and covered all their sins.　　*Selah*

[3]You set aside all your wrath
　and turned from your fierce anger.

[4]Restore us again, O God our Savior,
　and put away your displeasure toward
　us.
[5]Will you be angry with us forever?
　Will you prolong your anger through
　all generations?
[6]Will you not revive us again,
　that your people may rejoice in you?
[7]Show us your unfailing love, O LORD,
　and grant us your salvation.

[8]I will listen to what God the LORD will
　say;
　he promises peace to his people, his
　saints —
　but let them not return to folly.
[9]Surely his salvation is near those who
　fear him,
　that his glory may dwell in our land.

[10]Love and faithfulness meet together;
　righteousness and peace kiss each
　other.
[11]Faithfulness springs forth from the
　earth,
　and righteousness looks down from
　heaven.
[12]The LORD will indeed give what is good,
　and our land will yield its harvest.
[13]Righteousness goes before him
　and prepares the way for his steps.

Psalm 86

A prayer of David.

[1]Hear, O LORD, and answer me,
　for I am poor and needy.
[2]Guard my life, for I am devoted to you.
　You are my God; save your servant
　who trusts in you.
[3]Have mercy on me, O Lord,
　for I call to you all day long.
[4]Bring joy to your servant,
　for to you, O Lord,
　I lift up my soul.

[5]You are forgiving and good, O Lord,
　abounding in love to all who call to
　you.
[6]Hear my prayer, O LORD;
　listen to my cry for mercy.
[7]In the day of my trouble I will call to
　you,
　for you will answer me.

---

aTitle: Probably a musical term　　b6 Or *blessings*　　c9 Or *sovereign*

8Among the gods there is none like you,
O Lord;
no deeds can compare with yours.
9All the nations you have made
will come and worship before you,
O Lord;
they will bring glory to your name.
10For you are great and do marvelous
deeds;
you alone are God.

11Teach me your way, O Lord,
and I will walk in your truth;
give me an undivided heart,
that I may fear your name.
12I will praise you, O Lord my God, with
all my heart;
I will glorify your name forever.
13For great is your love toward me;
you have delivered me from the
depths of the grave.*a*

14The arrogant are attacking me, O God;
a band of ruthless men seeks my
life—
men without regard for you.
15But you, O Lord, are a compassionate
and gracious God,
slow to anger, abounding in love and
faithfulness.
16Turn to me and have mercy on me;
grant your strength to your servant
and save the son of your
maidservant.*b*
17Give me a sign of your goodness,
that my enemies may see it and be
put to shame,
for you, O Lord, have helped me and
comforted me.

Psalm 87

Of the Sons of Korah. A psalm. A song.

1He has set his foundation on the holy
mountain;
2   the Lord loves the gates of Zion
more than all the dwellings of Jacob.
3Glorious things are said of you,
O city of God: *Selah*
4"I will record Rahab*c* and Babylon
among those who acknowledge me—
Philistia too, and Tyre, along with
Cush*d*—
and will say, 'This*e* one was born in
Zion.'"

5Indeed, of Zion it will be said,
"This one and that one were born in
her,
and the Most High himself will
establish her."
6The Lord will write in the register of the
peoples:
"This one was born in Zion."   *Selah*
7As they make music they will sing,
"All my fountains are in you."

Psalm 88

A song. A psalm of the Sons of Korah. For
the director of music. According to
mahalath leannoth.f A *maskilg* of
Heman the Ezrahite.

1O Lord, the God who saves me,
day and night I cry out before you.
2May my prayer come before you;
turn your ear to my cry.

3For my soul is full of trouble
and my life draws near the grave.*a*
4I am counted among those who go
down to the pit;
I am like a man without strength.
5I am set apart with the dead,
like the slain who lie in the grave,
whom you remember no more,
who are cut off from your care.

6You have put me in the lowest pit,
in the darkest depths.
7Your wrath lies heavily upon me;
you have overwhelmed me with all
your waves.   *Selah*
8You have taken from me my closest
friends
and have made me repulsive to them.
I am confined and cannot escape;
9   my eyes are dim with grief.

I call to you, O Lord, every day;
I spread out my hands to you.
10Do you show your wonders to the dead?
Do those who are dead rise up and
praise you?   *Selah*
11Is your love declared in the grave,
your faithfulness in Destruction*h*?
12Are your wonders known in the place of
darkness,
or your righteous deeds in the land of
oblivion?

13But I cry to you for help, O Lord;

---

a13,3 Hebrew *Sheol*   *b16* Or *save your faithful son*   *c4* A poetic name for Egypt   *d4* That is, the upper
Nile region   *e4* Or *"O Rahab and Babylon, / Philistia, Tyre and Cush, / I will record concerning those who
acknowledge me: / 'This   f*Title: Possibly a tune, "The Suffering of Affliction"   *g*Title: Probably a literary or
musical term   *h11* Hebrew *Abaddon*

in the morning my prayer comes
before you.
¹⁴Why, O Lᴏʀᴅ, do you reject me
and hide your face from me?

¹⁵From my youth I have been afflicted
and close to death;
I have suffered your terrors and am in
despair.
¹⁶Your wrath has swept over me;
your terrors have destroyed me.
¹⁷All day long they surround me like a
flood;
they have completely engulfed me.
¹⁸You have taken my companions and
loved ones from me;
the darkness is my closest friend.

Psalm 89

A *maskil*ᵃ of Ethan the Ezrahite.

¹I will sing of the Lᴏʀᴅ's great love
forever;
with my mouth I will make your
faithfulness known through all
generations.
²I will declare that your love stands firm
forever,
that you established your faithfulness
in heaven itself.

³You said, "I have made a covenant with
my chosen one,
I have sworn to David my servant,
⁴'I will establish your line forever
and make your throne firm through
all generations.' "   *Selah*

⁵The heavens praise your wonders,
O Lᴏʀᴅ,
your faithfulness too, in the assembly
of the holy ones.
⁶For who in the skies above can compare
with the Lᴏʀᴅ?
Who is like the Lᴏʀᴅ among the
heavenly beings?
⁷In the council of the holy ones God is
greatly feared;
he is more awesome than all who
surround him.
⁸O Lᴏʀᴅ God Almighty, who is like you?
You are mighty, O Lᴏʀᴅ, and your
faithfulness surrounds you.

⁹You rule over the surging sea;
when its waves mount up, you still
them.

¹⁰You crushed Rahab like one of the
slain;
with your strong arm you scattered
your enemies.
¹¹The heavens are yours, and yours also
the earth;
you founded the world and all that is
in it.
¹²You created the north and the south;
Tabor and Hermon sing for joy at
your name.
¹³Your arm is endued with power;
your hand is strong, your right hand
exalted.

¹⁴Righteousness and justice are the
foundation of your throne;
love and faithfulness go before you.
¹⁵Blessed are those who have learned to
acclaim you,
who walk in the light of your
presence, O Lᴏʀᴅ.
¹⁶They rejoice in your name all day long;
they exult in your righteousness.
¹⁷For you are their glory and strength,
and by your favor you exalt our
horn.ᵇ
¹⁸Indeed, our shieldᶜ belongs to the Lᴏʀᴅ,
our king to the Holy One of Israel.

¹⁹Once you spoke in a vision,
to your faithful people you said:
"I have bestowed strength on a warrior;
I have exalted a young man from
among the people.
²⁰I have found David my servant;
with my sacred oil I have anointed
him.
²¹My hand will sustain him;
surely my arm will strengthen him.
²²No enemy will subject him to tribute;
no wicked man will oppress him.
²³I will crush his foes before him
and strike down his adversaries.
²⁴My faithful love will be with him,
and through my name his hornᵈ will
be exalted.
²⁵I will set his hand over the sea,
his right hand over the rivers.
²⁶He will call out to me, 'You are my
Father,
my God, the Rock my Savior.'
²⁷I will also appoint him my firstborn,
the most exalted of the kings of the
earth.
²⁸I will maintain my love to him forever,

ᵃTitle: Probably a literary or musical term   ᵇ17 *Horn* here symbolizes strong one.   ᶜ18 Or *sovereign*
ᵈ24 *Horn* here symbolizes strength.

WHO HAS TIME TO RELAX?

• •

Marcy: "Hey, guys, I need a break. What do you say we get up early on Saturday and hike up to Buck Creek Falls?"

Shelby: "Marcy, that would take all day! I can't afford to waste a whole day. I've got to study. Plus, I've got to work Saturday night and do some things around the house. Maybe when summer gets here."

Carl: "Yeah, I'm busy too. Besides, have you forgotten what that youth speaker talked about at camp? God didn't put us here to have fun! We goof off too much as it is. We need to get serious about serving God."

Look It Up
• • • •

Shelby and Carl need to rethink what they're saying.

The Bible is clear that we need regular breaks from the routine of life. When Jesus noticed that his busy, hardworking disciples had not even had "a chance to eat, he said to them, 'Come with me by yourselves to a quiet place and get some rest.' So they went away by themselves in a boat to a solitary place" (Mark 6:31–32).

The Bible also says that it's okay to enjoy life. "God . . . richly provides us with everything for our enjoyment" (1 Timothy 6:17; also see John 10:10).

Think It Through
• • • •

Why do many Christians get so intense—"No time for play . . . I have important things to do"? Where did we ever get the idea that it's a sin to find pleasure in life?

Granted, the pursuit of enjoyment can be taken to the extreme, but God doesn't mind if we laugh or if we pause to appreciate his creation. Really.

In the story above, which character do you relate to the most?

Work It Out
• • • •

Working too hard? Take a brief break:

1. Walk around the block. Breathe deeply and drink in the sights.

2. Go to the mall to watch people. Write down all the funny things they do and say.

3. Get a joke book from the library and make yourself laugh out loud ten times.

4. Play for thirty minutes with someone under five years of age. Forget about being cool and become a kid again. You'll have a blast!

5. Find a friend and go eat ice cream sundaes!

Nail It Down
• • • •

Reflect on Psalm 89:15.

Turn to pages 81, 339, 553 and 692 for other readings on leisure.
Turn to page 611 for Wednesday's reading.

Topic
• • • •

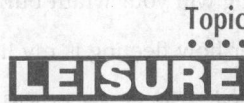
LEISURE

and my covenant with him will never
  fail.
²⁹I will establish his line forever,
  his throne as long as the heavens
    endure.

³⁰"If his sons forsake my law
  and do not follow my statutes,
³¹if they violate my decrees
  and fail to keep my commands,
³²I will punish their sin with the rod,
  their iniquity with flogging;
³³but I will not take my love from him,
  nor will I ever betray my faithfulness.
³⁴I will not violate my covenant
  or alter what my lips have uttered.
³⁵Once for all, I have sworn by my
    holiness—
  and I will not lie to David—
³⁶that his line will continue forever
  and his throne endure before me like
    the sun;
³⁷it will be established forever like the
    moon,
  the faithful witness in the sky." *Selah*

³⁸But you have rejected, you have
    spurned,
  you have been very angry with your
    anointed one.
³⁹You have renounced the covenant with
    your servant
  and have defiled his crown in the
    dust.
⁴⁰You have broken through all his walls
  and reduced his strongholds to ruins.
⁴¹All who pass by have plundered him;
  he has become the scorn of his
    neighbors.
⁴²You have exalted the right hand of his
    foes;
  you have made all his enemies
    rejoice.
⁴³You have turned back the edge of his
    sword
  and have not supported him in battle.
⁴⁴You have put an end to his splendor
  and cast his throne to the ground.
⁴⁵You have cut short the days of his
    youth;
  you have covered him with a mantle
    of shame.   *Selah*

⁴⁶How long, O LORD? Will you hide
    yourself forever?
  How long will your wrath burn like
    fire?
⁴⁷Remember how fleeting is my life.

For what futility you have created all
    men!
⁴⁸What man can live and not see death,
  or save himself from the power of the
    grave*ᵃ*?   *Selah*
⁴⁹O Lord, where is your former great love,
  which in your faithfulness you swore
    to David?
⁵⁰Remember, Lord, how your servant
    has*ᵇ* been mocked,
  how I bear in my heart the taunts of
    all the nations,
⁵¹the taunts with which your enemies
    have mocked, O LORD,
  with which they have mocked every
    step of your anointed one.

⁵²Praise be to the LORD forever!
  Amen and Amen.

BOOK IV

Psalms 90–106

Psalm 90

A prayer of Moses the man of God.

¹Lord, you have been our dwelling place
  throughout all generations.
²Before the mountains were born
  or you brought forth the earth and the
    world,
  from everlasting to everlasting you are
    God.

³You turn men back to dust,
  saying, "Return to dust, O sons of
    men."
⁴For a thousand years in your sight
  are like a day that has just gone by,
  or like a watch in the night.
⁵You sweep men away in the sleep of
    death;
  they are like the new grass of the
    morning—
⁶though in the morning it springs up
    new,
  by evening it is dry and withered.

⁷We are consumed by your anger
  and terrified by your indignation.
⁸You have set our iniquities before you,
  our secret sins in the light of your
    presence.
⁹All our days pass away under your
    wrath;
  we finish our years with a moan.

ᵃ48 Hebrew *Sheol*   *ᵇ50 Or your servants have*

NUMBERING OUR NUMBERED DAYS

On Friday, Angie's Aunt Madge had a massive heart attack and died. She was only forty-five.

Last night Tommy, a popular sophomore at Angie's school, was killed when a truck blew a tire on the expressway and jackknifed into his path. Tommy was sixteen.

Today, Angie is thinking a lot about death and about how short and unsure this life really is. "All this makes me realize I need to quit playing games with God."

Look It Up
••••

God's Word speaks clearly and repeatedly about our need to understand how brief this life is.

> You sweep men away in the sleep of death;
> they are like the new grass of the morning—
> though in the morning it springs up new,
> by evening it is dry and withered.
> The length of our days is seventy years—
> or eighty, if we have the strength;
> yet their span is but trouble and sorrow,
> for they quickly pass, and we fly away.
> Teach us to number our days aright,
> that we may gain a heart of wisdom
>   (Psalm 90:5–6,10,12).

Think It Through
••••

Scripture uses some interesting imagery to help us grasp just how temporary our time on this earth is. Life is compared to a shadow (Job 8:9; 14:2), a breath (Psalm 39:5) and a mist (James 4:14). And if you want a shock, read Genesis 47:9. There 130-year-old Jacob is quoted as saying that his years have been few!

Can you think of other ways to express the passing nature of this earthly life? When are you most aware of how short life is?

Work It Out
••••

Take a moment to number your days. Based on Psalm 90:10, assume a life span of 70 years. Subtract your present age from 70. Multiply the remaining number by 365. That's approximately how many days you have to live . . . if you don't die prematurely!

If you think that 20,000 days is a long time, remember the old saying: "Time flies." And reread Psalm 90:5—we're like grass!

Before you end your time with God, spend a few minutes praying about the things you would like to accomplish in the time you have left on this earth.

Nail It Down
••••

Read about the timelessness of God in Psalm 90:1–4.

Turn to pages 286, 597 and 702 for other readings on time.
Turn to page 616 for Thursday's reading.

Topic
••••

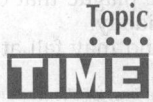

TIME

¹⁰The length of our days is seventy
　　　years—
　　or eighty, if we have the strength;
　yet their span*ᵃ* is but trouble and
　　　sorrow,
　　for they quickly pass, and we fly
　　　away.
¹¹Who knows the power of your anger?
　　For your wrath is as great as the fear
　　　that is due you.
¹²Teach us to number our days aright,
　　that we may gain a heart of wisdom.

¹³Relent, O Lᴏʀᴅ! How long will it be?
　　Have compassion on your servants.
¹⁴Satisfy us in the morning with your
　　　unfailing love,
　　that we may sing for joy and be glad
　　　all our days.
¹⁵Make us glad for as many days as you
　　　have afflicted us,
　　for as many years as we have seen
　　　trouble.
¹⁶May your deeds be shown to your
　　　servants,
　　your splendor to their children.

¹⁷May the favor*ᵇ* of the Lord our God rest
　　　upon us;
　　establish the work of our hands for
　　　us—
　　yes, establish the work of our hands.

Psalm 91

¹He who dwells in the shelter of the
　　　Most High
　　will rest in the shadow of the
　　　Almighty.*ᶜ*
²I will say*ᵈ* of the Lᴏʀᴅ, "He is my refuge
　　　and my fortress,
　　my God, in whom I trust."

³Surely he will save you from the
　　　fowler's snare
　　and from the deadly pestilence.
⁴He will cover you with his feathers,
　　and under his wings you will find
　　　refuge;
　　his faithfulness will be your shield
　　　and rampart.
⁵You will not fear the terror of night,
　　nor the arrow that flies by day,
⁶nor the pestilence that stalks in the
　　　darkness,
　　nor the plague that destroys at
　　　midday.
⁷A thousand may fall at your side,

　　ten thousand at your right hand,
　　but it will not come near you.
⁸You will only observe with your eyes
　　and see the punishment of the
　　　wicked.

⁹If you make the Most High your
　　　dwelling—
　　even the Lᴏʀᴅ, who is my refuge—
¹⁰then no harm will befall you,
　　no disaster will come near your tent.
¹¹For he will command his angels
　　　concerning you
　　to guard you in all your ways;
¹²they will lift you up in their hands,
　　so that you will not strike your foot
　　　against a stone.
¹³You will tread upon the lion and the
　　　cobra;
　　you will trample the great lion and
　　　the serpent.

¹⁴"Because he loves me," says the Lᴏʀᴅ, "I
　　　will rescue him;
　　I will protect him, for he
　　　acknowledges my name.
¹⁵He will call upon me, and I will answer
　　　him;
　　I will be with him in trouble,
　　I will deliver him and honor him.
¹⁶With long life will I satisfy him
　　and show him my salvation."

Psalm 92

A psalm. A song. For the Sabbath day.

¹It is good to praise the Lᴏʀᴅ
　　and make music to your name,
　　　O Most High,
²to proclaim your love in the morning
　　and your faithfulness at night,
³to the music of the ten-stringed lyre
　　and the melody of the harp.

⁴For you make me glad by your deeds,
　　　O Lᴏʀᴅ;
　　I sing for joy at the works of your
　　　hands.
⁵How great are your works, O Lᴏʀᴅ,
　　how profound your thoughts!
⁶The senseless man does not know,
　　fools do not understand,
⁷that though the wicked spring up like
　　　grass
　　and all evildoers flourish,
　　they will be forever destroyed.

⁸But you, O Lᴏʀᴅ, are exalted forever.

ᵃ10 Or *yet the best of them*　　*ᵇ17* Or *beauty*　　*ᶜ1* Hebrew *Shaddai*　　*ᵈ2* Or *He says*

9For surely your enemies, O Lord,
　surely your enemies will perish;
　all evildoers will be scattered.
10You have exalted my horn^a like that of
　a wild ox;
　fine oils have been poured upon me.
11My eyes have seen the defeat of my
　adversaries;
　my ears have heard the rout of my
　wicked foes.

12The righteous will flourish like a palm
　tree,
　they will grow like a cedar of
　Lebanon;
13planted in the house of the Lord,
　they will flourish in the courts of our
　God.
14They will still bear fruit in old age,
　they will stay fresh and green,
15proclaiming, "The Lord is upright;
　he is my Rock, and there is no
　wickedness in him."

Psalm 93

1The Lord reigns, he is robed in majesty;
　the Lord is robed in majesty
　and is armed with strength.
The world is firmly established;
　it cannot be moved.
2Your throne was established long ago;
　you are from all eternity.

3The seas have lifted up, O Lord,
　the seas have lifted up their voice;
　the seas have lifted up their pounding
　waves.
4Mightier than the thunder of the great
　waters,
　mightier than the breakers of the
　sea—
　the Lord on high is mighty.

5Your statutes stand firm;
　holiness adorns your house
　for endless days, O Lord.

Psalm 94

1O Lord, the God who avenges,
　O God who avenges, shine forth.
2Rise up, O Judge of the earth;
　pay back to the proud what they
　deserve.
3How long will the wicked, O Lord,
　how long will the wicked be jubilant?

4They pour out arrogant words;

all the evildoers are full of boasting.
5They crush your people, O Lord;
　they oppress your inheritance.
6They slay the widow and the alien;
　they murder the fatherless.
7They say, "The Lord does not see;
　the God of Jacob pays no heed."

8Take heed, you senseless ones among
　the people;
　you fools, when will you become
　wise?
9Does he who implanted the ear not
　hear?
　Does he who formed the eye not see?
10Does he who disciplines nations not
　punish?
　Does he who teaches man lack
　knowledge?
11The Lord knows the thoughts of man;
　he knows that they are futile.

12Blessed is the man you discipline,
　O Lord,
　the man you teach from your law;
13you grant him relief from days of
　trouble,
　till a pit is dug for the wicked.
14For the Lord will not reject his people;
　he will never forsake his inheritance.
15Judgment will again be founded on
　righteousness,
　and all the upright in heart will follow
　it.

16Who will rise up for me against the
　wicked?
　Who will take a stand for me against
　evildoers?
17Unless the Lord had given me help,
　I would soon have dwelt in the
　silence of death.
18When I said, "My foot is slipping,"
　your love, O Lord, supported me.
19When anxiety was great within me,
　your consolation brought joy to my
　soul.

20Can a corrupt throne be allied with
　you—
　one that brings on misery by its
　decrees?
21They band together against the
　righteous
　and condemn the innocent to death.
22But the Lord has become my fortress,
　and my God the rock in whom I take
　refuge.
23He will repay them for their sins

---

a10 Horn here symbolizes strength.

and destroy them for their
wickedness;
the LORD our God will destroy them.

Psalm 95

[1]Come, let us sing for joy to the LORD;
let us shout aloud to the Rock of our
salvation.
[2]Let us come before him with
thanksgiving
and extol him with music and song.

[3]For the LORD is the great God,
the great King above all gods.
[4]In his hand are the depths of the earth,
and the mountain peaks belong to
him.
[5]The sea is his, for he made it,
and his hands formed the dry land.

[6]Come, let us bow down in worship,
let us kneel before the LORD our
Maker;
[7]for he is our God
and we are the people of his pasture,
the flock under his care.

Today, if you hear his voice,
[8]   do not harden your hearts as you did
at Meribah,[a]
as you did that day at Massah[b] in
the desert,
[9]where your fathers tested and tried me,
though they had seen what I did.
[10]For forty years I was angry with that
generation;
I said, "They are a people whose
hearts go astray,
and they have not known my ways."
[11]So I declared on oath in my anger,
"They shall never enter my rest."

Psalm 96

[1]Sing to the LORD a new song;
sing to the LORD, all the earth.
[2]Sing to the LORD, praise his name;
proclaim his salvation day after day.
[3]Declare his glory among the nations,
his marvelous deeds among all
peoples.

[4]For great is the LORD and most worthy of
praise;
he is to be feared above all gods.
[5]For all the gods of the nations are idols,
but the LORD made the heavens.
[6]Splendor and majesty are before him;

strength and glory are in his
sanctuary.

[7]Ascribe to the LORD, O families of
nations,
ascribe to the LORD glory and strength.
[8]Ascribe to the LORD the glory due his
name;
bring an offering and come into his
courts.
[9]Worship the LORD in the splendor of
his[c] holiness;
tremble before him, all the earth.

[10]Say among the nations, "The LORD
reigns."
The world is firmly established, it
cannot be moved;
he will judge the peoples with equity.
[11]Let the heavens rejoice, let the earth be
glad;
let the sea resound, and all that is in
it;
[12]   let the fields be jubilant, and
everything in them.
Then all the trees of the forest will sing
for joy;
[13]   they will sing before the LORD, for he
comes,
he comes to judge the earth.
He will judge the world in righteousness
and the peoples in his truth.

Psalm 97

[1]The LORD reigns, let the earth be glad;
let the distant shores rejoice.
[2]Clouds and thick darkness surround
him;
righteousness and justice are the
foundation of his throne.
[3]Fire goes before him
and consumes his foes on every side.
[4]His lightning lights up the world;
the earth sees and trembles.
[5]The mountains melt like wax before the
LORD,
before the Lord of all the earth.
[6]The heavens proclaim his righteousness,
and all the peoples see his glory.

[7]All who worship images are put to
shame,
those who boast in idols—
worship him, all you gods!

[8]Zion hears and rejoices
and the villages of Judah are glad

---

[a]8 Meribah means quarreling.   [b]8 Massah means testing.   [c]9 Or LORD with the splendor of

because of your judgments, O LORD.
⁹For you, O LORD, are the Most High over
  all the earth;
  you are exalted far above all gods.

¹⁰Let those who love the LORD hate evil,
  for he guards the lives of his faithful
    ones
  and delivers them from the hand of
    the wicked.
¹¹Light is shed upon the righteous
  and joy on the upright in heart.
¹²Rejoice in the LORD, you who are
    righteous,
  and praise his holy name.

Psalm 98

A psalm.

¹Sing to the LORD a new song,
  for he has done marvelous things;
  his right hand and his holy arm
  have worked salvation for him.
²The LORD has made his salvation known
  and revealed his righteousness to the
    nations.
³He has remembered his love
  and his faithfulness to the house of
    Israel;
  all the ends of the earth have seen
  the salvation of our God.

⁴Shout for joy to the LORD, all the earth,
  burst into jubilant song with music;
⁵make music to the LORD with the harp,
  with the harp and the sound of
    singing,
⁶with trumpets and the blast of the ram's
    horn—
  shout for joy before the LORD, the
    King.

⁷Let the sea resound, and everything in
    it,
  the world, and all who live in it.
⁸Let the rivers clap their hands,
  let the mountains sing together for
    joy;
⁹let them sing before the LORD,
  for he comes to judge the earth.
He will judge the world in righteousness
  and the peoples with equity.

Psalm 99

¹The LORD reigns,
  let the nations tremble;

he sits enthroned between the
    cherubim,
  let the earth shake.
²Great is the LORD in Zion;
  he is exalted over all the nations.
³Let them praise your great and
    awesome name—
  he is holy.

⁴The King is mighty, he loves justice—
  you have established equity;
  in Jacob you have done
  what is just and right.
⁵Exalt the LORD our God
  and worship at his footstool;
  he is holy.

⁶Moses and Aaron were among his
    priests,
  Samuel was among those who called
    on his name;
  they called on the LORD
  and he answered them.
⁷He spoke to them from the pillar of
    cloud;
  they kept his statutes and the decrees
  he gave them.

⁸O LORD our God,
  you answered them;
  you were to Israel[a] a forgiving God,
    though you punished their
    misdeeds.[b]
⁹Exalt the LORD our God
  and worship at his holy mountain,
  for the LORD our God is holy.

Psalm 100

A psalm. For giving thanks.

¹Shout for joy to the LORD, all the earth.
² Worship the LORD with gladness;
  come before him with joyful songs.
³Know that the LORD is God.
  It is he who made us, and we are
    his[c];
  we are his people, the sheep of his
    pasture.
⁴Enter his gates with thanksgiving
  and his courts with praise;
  give thanks to him and praise his
    name.
⁵For the LORD is good and his love
    endures forever;
  his faithfulness continues through all
    generations.

a8 Hebrew them   b8 Or / an avenger of the wrongs done to them   c3 Or and not we ourselves

WORSHIP IS A WAY OF LIFE

Consider these comments from a youth group discussion on worship:

Ann: "I'm more into private worship. I don't like big church meetings."

DeWayne: "I worship God. He knows I love him. Isn't that enough? Why do I have to *do* anything?"

Ramona: "It gives me the creeps the way some churches get all emotional in their worship services!"

Look It Up
••••

Now consider what the Bible says:

1. Worship is both private (Psalm 63) and public. "I remember . . . how I used to go with the multitude, leading the procession to the house of God, with shouts of joy and thanksgiving among the festive throng" (Psalm 42:4).

2. Worship involves attitudes (Psalm 92:4) and actions (Hebrews 13:16).

3. Worship involves the head and the heart. "God is spirit, and his worshipers must worship in spirit and in truth" (John 4:24).

Think It Through
••••

You can use this devotion in one of two ways: (a) as a quick fast-food snack or (b) as an appetizer for a gourmet meal.

People with the first view read hurriedly and don't bother to look up or reflect on the verses. They get only a tiny bit of spiritual nourishment and rarely sit still long enough to have a genuine encounter with God. People with the second view take time to linger in God's presence. They come away filled and satisfied because they have truly worshiped.

Which view describes you?

Work It Out
••••

Find a hymnbook, grab your Bible and go to a quiet place. Spend at least thirty minutes (you can do it!) worshiping God. Use these incomplete sentences to help guide your thoughts:

"My two favorite psalms are _____ and _____ because _____."

"My two favorite hymns are _____ and _____ because _____."

"I want to praise you, God, because you are _____."

"I want to thank you, God, for these five blessings:

1. _____
2. _____
3. _____
4. _____
5. _____

Sing softly, kneel if you like, raise your hands if you desire (1 Timothy 2:8). The important thing is to worship out of love.

Nail It Down
••••

Use the words of Psalm 100 to praise and worship God.

Turn to pages 415 and 594 for other readings on worship.
Turn to page 619 for Friday's reading.

Topic
••••

WORSHIP

Psalm 101

Of David. A psalm.

1I will sing of your love and justice;
  to you, O Lord, I will sing praise.
2I will be careful to lead a blameless
      life—
  when will you come to me?

I will walk in my house
  with blameless heart.
3I will set before my eyes
  no vile thing.

The deeds of faithless men I hate;
  they will not cling to me.
4Men of perverse heart shall be far from
      me;
  I will have nothing to do with evil.

5Whoever slanders his neighbor in
      secret,
  him will I put to silence;
whoever has haughty eyes and a proud
      heart,
  him will I not endure.

6My eyes will be on the faithful in the
      land,
  that they may dwell with me;
he whose walk is blameless
  will minister to me.

7No one who practices deceit
  will dwell in my house;
no one who speaks falsely
  will stand in my presence.

8Every morning I will put to silence
  all the wicked in the land;
I will cut off every evildoer
  from the city of the Lord.

Psalm 102

*A prayer of an afflicted man. When he is
faint and pours out his lament before the
Lord.*

1Hear my prayer, O Lord;
  let my cry for help come to you.
2Do not hide your face from me
  when I am in distress.
Turn your ear to me;
  when I call, answer me quickly.

3For my days vanish like smoke;
  my bones burn like glowing embers.
4My heart is blighted and withered like
      grass;

  I forget to eat my food.
5Because of my loud groaning
  I am reduced to skin and bones.
6I am like a desert owl,
  like an owl among the ruins.
7I lie awake; I have become
  like a bird alone on a roof.
8All day long my enemies taunt me;
  those who rail against me use my
      name as a curse.
9For I eat ashes as my food
  and mingle my drink with tears
10because of your great wrath,
  for you have taken me up and thrown
      me aside.
11My days are like the evening shadow;
  I wither away like grass.

12But you, O Lord, sit enthroned forever;
  your renown endures through all
      generations.
13You will arise and have compassion on
      Zion,
  for it is time to show favor to her;
  the appointed time has come.
14For her stones are dear to your
      servants;
  her very dust moves them to pity.
15The nations will fear the name of the
      Lord,
  all the kings of the earth will revere
      your glory.
16For the Lord will rebuild Zion
  and appear in his glory.
17He will respond to the prayer of the
      destitute;
  he will not despise their plea.

18Let this be written for a future
      generation,
  that a people not yet created may
      praise the Lord:
19"The Lord looked down from his
      sanctuary on high,
  from heaven he viewed the earth,
20to hear the groans of the prisoners
  and release those condemned to
      death."
21So the name of the Lord will be
      declared in Zion
  and his praise in Jerusalem
22when the peoples and the kingdoms
  assemble to worship the Lord.

23In the course of my life[a] he broke my
      strength;
  he cut short my days.
24So I said:

a23 Or By his power

"Do not take me away, O my God, in
   the midst of my days;
your years go on through all
   generations.
25In the beginning you laid the
   foundations of the earth,
and the heavens are the work of your
   hands.
26They will perish, but you remain;
   they will all wear out like a garment.
Like clothing you will change them
   and they will be discarded.
27But you remain the same,
   and your years will never end.
28The children of your servants will live in
   your presence;
   their descendants will be established
      before you."

Psalm 103

Of David.

1Praise the LORD, O my soul;
   all my inmost being, praise his holy
      name.
2Praise the LORD, O my soul,
   and forget not all his benefits—
3who forgives all your sins
   and heals all your diseases,
4who redeems your life from the pit
   and crowns you with love and
      compassion,
5who satisfies your desires with good
   things
so that your youth is renewed like the
   eagle's.

6The LORD works righteousness
   and justice for all the oppressed.

7He made known his ways to Moses,
   his deeds to the people of Israel:
8The LORD is compassionate and gracious,
   slow to anger, abounding in love.
9He will not always accuse,
   nor will he harbor his anger forever;
10he does not treat us as our sins deserve
   or repay us according to our
      iniquities.
11For as high as the heavens are above
   the earth,
so great is his love for those who fear
   him;
12as far as the east is from the west,
   so far has he removed our
      transgressions from us.

13As a father has compassion on his
   children,
so the LORD has compassion on those
   who fear him;
14for he knows how we are formed,
   he remembers that we are dust.
15As for man, his days are like grass,
   he flourishes like a flower of the field;
16the wind blows over it and it is gone,
   and its place remembers it no more.
17But from everlasting to everlasting
   the LORD's love is with those who fear
      him,
   and his righteousness with their
      children's children—
18with those who keep his covenant
   and remember to obey his precepts.

19The LORD has established his throne in
   heaven,
   and his kingdom rules over all.

20Praise the LORD, you his angels,
   you mighty ones who do his bidding,
   who obey his word.
21Praise the LORD, all his heavenly hosts,
   you his servants who do his will.
22Praise the LORD, all his works
   everywhere in his dominion.

   Praise the LORD, O my soul.

Psalm 104

1Praise the LORD, O my soul.

O LORD my God, you are very great;
   you are clothed with splendor and
      majesty.
2He wraps himself in light as with a
   garment;
   he stretches out the heavens like a
      tent
3   and lays the beams of his upper
      chambers on their waters.
He makes the clouds his chariot
   and rides on the wings of the wind.
4He makes winds his messengers,a
   flames of fire his servants.

5He set the earth on its foundations;
   it can never be moved.
6You covered it with the deep as with a
   garment;
   the waters stood above the
      mountains.
7But at your rebuke the waters fled,
   at the sound of your thunder they
      took to flight;

a4 Or angels

OUR FAITHFUL FRIEND

Bill: "So, let's say you have a major problem. Who are you gonna talk to first?"

Beth: "Either Christi or Julie, I guess. They're probably my best friends. But it bugs me because sometimes Christi can't keep a secret. And Julie, well, she's so busy all the time, I hardly ever see her anymore."

Bill: "What about God?"

Beth: "Well, sure, I'd pray and everything. But God is . . . well, he's God, not really a friend. I mean, I don't think of him like I do Christi and Julie."

Look It Up
• • • •

We can sometimes emphasize so much God's roles as Creator, Father, King and Judge, that we often forget he can also be a Friend.

1. Abraham enjoyed a friendship with God: "And the scripture was fulfilled that says, 'Abraham believed God, and it was credited to him as righteousness,' and he was called God's friend" (James 2:23).

2. Moses enjoyed a friendship with God: "The LORD would speak to Moses face to face, as a man speaks with his friend" (Exodus 33:11).

3. Jesus Christ emphasized divine-human friendship: "I no longer call you servants . . . . Instead, I have called you friends" (John 15:15).

Think It Through
• • • •

What an amazing truth. You can actually be friends with the God of the universe!

What are the things that make for close friendships? Are those ingredients a part of your relationship with God? If not, why not?

Work It Out
• • • •

Friends spend time together and talk to each other, right? Right! So spend time with God today and every day.

Get your Bible and go to a quiet place—just you and the Lord. Tell him everything you're thinking. Then pick a portion of Scripture and let him tell you what's on his mind.

But don't stop there. Converse with him all day—as you drive, when you're walking to classes, while opening your locker—just as you do with your other friends. Because that's what he is, your closest, most faithful Friend.

Nail It Down
• • • •

Read the beautiful praise in Psalm 103.

Turn to pages 761, 1208, 1210 and 1243 for other readings on God.
Turn to page 621 for the weekend reading.

Topic
• • • •

8they flowed over the mountains,
they went down into the valleys,
to the place you assigned for them.
9You set a boundary they cannot cross;
never again will they cover the earth.

10He makes springs pour water into the
ravines;
it flows between the mountains.
11They give water to all the beasts of the
field;
the wild donkeys quench their thirst.
12The birds of the air nest by the waters;
they sing among the branches.
13He waters the mountains from his
upper chambers;
the earth is satisfied by the fruit of his
work.
14He makes grass grow for the cattle,
and plants for man to cultivate—
bringing forth food from the earth:
15wine that gladdens the heart of man,
oil to make his face shine,
and bread that sustains his heart.
16The trees of the LORD are well watered,
the cedars of Lebanon that he
planted.
17There the birds make their nests;
the stork has its home in the pine
trees.
18The high mountains belong to the wild
goats;
the crags are a refuge for the
coneys.a

19The moon marks off the seasons,
and the sun knows when to go down.
20You bring darkness, it becomes night,
and all the beasts of the forest prowl.
21The lions roar for their prey
and seek their food from God.
22The sun rises, and they steal away;
they return and lie down in their
dens.
23Then man goes out to his work,
to his labor until evening.

24How many are your works, O LORD!
In wisdom you made them all;
the earth is full of your creatures.
25There is the sea, vast and spacious,
teeming with creatures beyond
number—
living things both large and small.
26There the ships go to and fro,
and the leviathan, which you formed
to frolic there.

27These all look to you
to give them their food at the proper
time.
28When you give it to them,
they gather it up;
when you open your hand,
they are satisfied with good things.
29When you hide your face,
they are terrified;
when you take away their breath,
they die and return to the dust.
30When you send your Spirit,
they are created,
and you renew the face of the earth.

31May the glory of the LORD endure
forever;
may the LORD rejoice in his works—
32he who looks at the earth, and it
trembles,
who touches the mountains, and they
smoke.

33I will sing to the LORD all my life;
I will sing praise to my God as long as
I live.
34May my meditation be pleasing to him,
as I rejoice in the LORD.
35But may sinners vanish from the earth
and the wicked be no more.

Praise the LORD, O my soul.

Praise the LORD.b

Psalm 105

1Give thanks to the LORD, call on his
name;
make known among the nations what
he has done.
2Sing to him, sing praise to him;
tell of all his wonderful acts.
3Glory in his holy name;
let the hearts of those who seek the
LORD rejoice.
4Look to the LORD and his strength;
seek his face always.

5Remember the wonders he has done,
his miracles, and the judgments he
pronounced,
6O descendants of Abraham his servant,
O sons of Jacob, his chosen ones.
7He is the LORD our God;
his judgments are in all the earth.

8He remembers his covenant forever,

a18 That is, the hyrax or rock badger   b35 Hebrew Hallelu Yah; in the Septuagint this line stands at the
beginning of Psalm 105.

GOD'S CREATIVE GENIUS

Work It Out ••••

After it gets dark tonight, go outside and take a serious look at the moon and the stars. Bring a blanket with you, lie down and gaze. There's a big difference between looking and gazing. Tonight, try gazing.

Pretty astounding sight, isn't it? God made the moon and stars and gave them a pattern for existence. The stars shine just brightly enough to be seen at night. They shine just as brightly during the day, but you can't see them. The moon shows up mostly at night. Sometimes, however, you'll see it in the daytime. Imagine the sun shining at night. Everyone would be astonished and afraid. God's correct pattern would be broken.

And now for the punch line: the very same God who made sun, moon and stars made you. If God cared enough about the universe to devise a pattern for the continued function and existence of the sun, moon and stars, he certainly loves you enough to create an order, a plan for your life.

Nail It Down ••••

Read about God's creative genius in Psalm 104:19–35.

Think It Through ••••

The sun, moon and stars have no choice in the matter. They're capable only of following God's created order for them. That's why the sun doesn't shine at night and frighten everyone; it only knows how to rise in the morning.

But you're different. You can choose to live inside or outside of God's plan for your life.

Living outside of God's pattern for your life produces disappointment and, ultimately, judgment. Living inside the pattern produces the joy and contentment of abundant life that Jesus promised (John 10:10) and a future you can't begin to imagine (1 Corinthians 2:9).

You choose!

Nail It Down ••••

Reread God's order for creation in Psalm 104:19–35. For further insight memorize and think about Psalm 104:24.

Turn to pages 2, 529, 1188 and 1348 for other readings on origins.
Turn to page 633 for Monday's reading.

Topic
••••

the word he commanded, for a
thousand generations,
[9]the covenant he made with Abraham,
the oath he swore to Isaac.
[10]He confirmed it to Jacob as a decree,
to Israel as an everlasting covenant:
[11]"To you I will give the land of Canaan
as the portion you will inherit."

[12]When they were but few in number,
few indeed, and strangers in it,
[13]they wandered from nation to nation,
from one kingdom to another.
[14]He allowed no one to oppress them;
for their sake he rebuked kings:
[15]"Do not touch my anointed ones;
do my prophets no harm."

[16]He called down famine on the land
and destroyed all their supplies of
food;
[17]and he sent a man before them—
Joseph, sold as a slave.
[18]They bruised his feet with shackles,
his neck was put in irons,
[19]till what he foretold came to pass,
till the word of the Lord proved him
true.
[20]The king sent and released him,
the ruler of peoples set him free.
[21]He made him master of his household,
ruler over all he possessed,
[22]to instruct his princes as he pleased
and teach his elders wisdom.

[23]Then Israel entered Egypt;
Jacob lived as an alien in the land of
Ham.
[24]The Lord made his people very fruitful;
he made them too numerous for their
foes,
[25]whose hearts he turned to hate his
people,
to conspire against his servants.
[26]He sent Moses his servant,
and Aaron, whom he had chosen.
[27]They performed his miraculous signs
among them,
his wonders in the land of Ham.
[28]He sent darkness and made the land
dark—
for had they not rebelled against his
words?
[29]He turned their waters into blood,
causing their fish to die.
[30]Their land teemed with frogs,
which went up into the bedrooms of
their rulers.

[31]He spoke, and there came swarms of
flies,
and gnats throughout their country.
[32]He turned their rain into hail,
with lightning throughout their land;
[33]he struck down their vines and fig trees
and shattered the trees of their
country.
[34]He spoke, and the locusts came,
grasshoppers without number;
[35]they ate up every green thing in their
land,
ate up the produce of their soil.
[36]Then he struck down all the firstborn in
their land,
the firstfruits of all their manhood.

[37]He brought out Israel, laden with silver
and gold,
and from among their tribes no one
faltered.
[38]Egypt was glad when they left,
because dread of Israel had fallen on
them.
[39]He spread out a cloud as a covering,
and a fire to give light at night.
[40]They asked, and he brought them quail
and satisfied them with the bread of
heaven.
[41]He opened the rock, and water gushed
out;
like a river it flowed in the desert.

[42]For he remembered his holy promise
given to his servant Abraham.
[43]He brought out his people with
rejoicing,
his chosen ones with shouts of joy;
[44]he gave them the lands of the nations,
and they fell heir to what others had
toiled for—
[45]that they might keep his precepts
and observe his laws.

Praise the Lord.[a]

Psalm 106

[1]Praise the Lord.[b]

Give thanks to the Lord, for he is good;
his love endures forever.
[2]Who can proclaim the mighty acts of
the Lord
or fully declare his praise?
[3]Blessed are they who maintain justice,
who constantly do what is right.
[4]Remember me, O Lord, when you show
favor to your people,

come to my aid when you save them,
5that I may enjoy the prosperity of your
chosen ones,
that I may share in the joy of your
nation
and join your inheritance in giving
praise.

6We have sinned, even as our fathers
did;
we have done wrong and acted
wickedly.
7When our fathers were in Egypt,
they gave no thought to your
miracles;
they did not remember your many
kindnesses,
and they rebelled by the sea, the Red
Sea.*a*
8Yet he saved them for his name's sake,
to make his mighty power known.
9He rebuked the Red Sea, and it dried
up;
he led them through the depths as
through a desert.
10He saved them from the hand of the
foe;
from the hand of the enemy he
redeemed them.
11The waters covered their adversaries;
not one of them survived.
12Then they believed his promises
and sang his praise.

13But they soon forgot what he had done
and did not wait for his counsel.
14In the desert they gave in to their
craving;
in the wasteland they put God to the
test.
15So he gave them what they asked for,
but sent a wasting disease upon
them.

16In the camp they grew envious of Moses
and of Aaron, who was consecrated to
the LORD.
17The earth opened up and swallowed
Dathan;
it buried the company of Abiram.
18Fire blazed among their followers;
a flame consumed the wicked.

19At Horeb they made a calf
and worshiped an idol cast from
metal.
20They exchanged their Glory

for an image of a bull, which eats
grass.
21They forgot the God who saved them,
who had done great things in Egypt,
22miracles in the land of Ham
and awesome deeds by the Red Sea.
23So he said he would destroy them—
had not Moses, his chosen one,
stood in the breach before him
to keep his wrath from destroying
them.

24Then they despised the pleasant land;
they did not believe his promise.
25They grumbled in their tents
and did not obey the LORD.
26So he swore to them with uplifted hand
that he would make them fall in the
desert,
27make their descendants fall among the
nations
and scatter them throughout the
lands.

28They yoked themselves to the Baal of
Peor
and ate sacrifices offered to lifeless
gods;
29they provoked the LORD to anger by their
wicked deeds,
and a plague broke out among them.
30But Phinehas stood up and intervened,
and the plague was checked.
31This was credited to him as
righteousness
for endless generations to come.

32By the waters of Meribah they angered
the LORD,
and trouble came to Moses because
of them;
33for they rebelled against the Spirit of
God,
and rash words came from Moses'
lips.*b*

34They did not destroy the peoples
as the LORD had commanded them,
35but they mingled with the nations
and adopted their customs.
36They worshiped their idols,
which became a snare to them.
37They sacrificed their sons
and their daughters to demons.
38They shed innocent blood,
the blood of their sons and daughters,
whom they sacrificed to the idols of
Canaan,

*a7 Hebrew Yam Suph; that is, Sea of Reeds; also in verses 9 and 22   b33 Or against his spirit, / and rash
words came from his lips*

and the land was desecrated by their
blood.
39They defiled themselves by what they
did;
by their deeds they prostituted
themselves.

40Therefore the LORD was angry with his
people
and abhorred his inheritance.
41He handed them over to the nations,
and their foes ruled over them.
42Their enemies oppressed them
and subjected them to their power.
43Many times he delivered them,
but they were bent on rebellion
and they wasted away in their sin.

44But he took note of their distress
when he heard their cry;
45for their sake he remembered his
covenant
and out of his great love he relented.
46He caused them to be pitied
by all who held them captive.

47Save us, O LORD our God,
and gather us from the nations,
that we may give thanks to your holy
name
and glory in your praise.

48Praise be to the LORD, the God of Israel,
from everlasting to everlasting.
Let all the people say, "Amen!"

Praise the LORD.

BOOK V

Psalms 107–150

Psalm 107

1Give thanks to the LORD, for he is good;
his love endures forever.
2Let the redeemed of the LORD say this—
those he redeemed from the hand of
the foe,
3those he gathered from the lands,
from east and west, from north and
south.*a*

4Some wandered in desert wastelands,
finding no way to a city where they
could settle.
5They were hungry and thirsty,
and their lives ebbed away.
6Then they cried out to the LORD in their
trouble,

and he delivered them from their
distress.
7He led them by a straight way
to a city where they could settle.
8Let them give thanks to the LORD for his
unfailing love
and his wonderful deeds for men,
9for he satisfies the thirsty
and fills the hungry with good things.

10Some sat in darkness and the deepest
gloom,
prisoners suffering in iron chains,
11for they had rebelled against the words
of God
and despised the counsel of the Most
High.
12So he subjected them to bitter labor;
they stumbled, and there was no one
to help.
13Then they cried to the LORD in their
trouble,
and he saved them from their
distress.
14He brought them out of darkness and
the deepest gloom
and broke away their chains.
15Let them give thanks to the LORD for his
unfailing love
and his wonderful deeds for men,
16for he breaks down gates of bronze
and cuts through bars of iron.

17Some became fools through their
rebellious ways
and suffered affliction because of
their iniquities.
18They loathed all food
and drew near the gates of death.
19Then they cried to the LORD in their
trouble,
and he saved them from their
distress.
20He sent forth his word and healed
them;
he rescued them from the grave.
21Let them give thanks to the LORD for his
unfailing love
and his wonderful deeds for men.
22Let them sacrifice thank offerings
and tell of his works with songs of
joy.

23Others went out on the sea in ships;
they were merchants on the mighty
waters.
24They saw the works of the LORD,
his wonderful deeds in the deep.

*a*3 Hebrew *north and the sea*

25For he spoke and stirred up a tempest
  that lifted high the waves.
26They mounted up to the heavens and
    went down to the depths;
  in their peril their courage melted
    away.
27They reeled and staggered like drunken
    men;
  they were at their wits' end.
28Then they cried out to the LORD in their
    trouble,
  and he brought them out of their
    distress.
29He stilled the storm to a whisper;
  the waves of the sea were hushed.
30They were glad when it grew calm,
  and he guided them to their desired
    haven.
31Let them give thanks to the LORD for his
    unfailing love
  and his wonderful deeds for men.
32Let them exalt him in the assembly of
    the people
  and praise him in the council of the
    elders.

33He turned rivers into a desert,
  flowing springs into thirsty ground,
34and fruitful land into a salt waste,
  because of the wickedness of those
    who lived there.
35He turned the desert into pools of water
  and the parched ground into flowing
    springs;
36there he brought the hungry to live,
  and they founded a city where they
    could settle.
37They sowed fields and planted
    vineyards
  that yielded a fruitful harvest;
38he blessed them, and their numbers
    greatly increased,
  and he did not let their herds
    diminish.

39Then their numbers decreased, and
    they were humbled
  by oppression, calamity and sorrow;
40he who pours contempt on nobles
  made them wander in a trackless
    waste.
41But he lifted the needy out of their
    affliction
  and increased their families like
    flocks.
42The upright see and rejoice,
  but all the wicked shut their mouths.

43Whoever is wise, let him heed these
    things
and consider the great love of the
  LORD.

Psalm 108

A song. A psalm of David.

1My heart is steadfast, O God;
  I will sing and make music with all
    my soul.
2Awake, harp and lyre!
  I will awaken the dawn.
3I will praise you, O LORD, among the
    nations;
  I will sing of you among the peoples.
4For great is your love, higher than the
    heavens;
  your faithfulness reaches to the skies.
5Be exalted, O God, above the heavens,
  and let your glory be over all the
    earth.

6Save us and help us with your right
    hand,
  that those you love may be delivered.
7God has spoken from his sanctuary:
  "In triumph I will parcel out Shechem
  and measure off the Valley of
    Succoth.
8Gilead is mine, Manasseh is mine;
  Ephraim is my helmet,
  Judah my scepter.
9Moab is my washbasin,
  upon Edom I toss my sandal;
  over Philistia I shout in triumph."

10Who will bring me to the fortified city?
  Who will lead me to Edom?
11Is it not you, O God, you who have
    rejected us
  and no longer go out with our armies?
12Give us aid against the enemy,
  for the help of man is worthless.
13With God we will gain the victory,
  and he will trample down our
    enemies.

Psalm 109

*For the director of music. Of David.
A psalm.*

1O God, whom I praise,
  do not remain silent,
2for wicked and deceitful men
  have opened their mouths against me;
  they have spoken against me with
    lying tongues.
3With words of hatred they surround me;
  they attack me without cause.

⁴In return for my friendship they accuse
    me,
  but I am a man of prayer.
⁵They repay me evil for good,
  and hatred for my friendship.

⁶Appoint*a* an evil man*b* to oppose him;
  let an accuser*c* stand at his right
    hand.
⁷When he is tried, let him be found
    guilty,
  and may his prayers condemn him.
⁸May his days be few;
  may another take his place of
    leadership.
⁹May his children be fatherless
  and his wife a widow.
¹⁰May his children be wandering beggars;
  may they be driven*d* from their
    ruined homes.
¹¹May a creditor seize all he has;
  may strangers plunder the fruits of his
    labor.
¹²May no one extend kindness to him
  or take pity on his fatherless children.
¹³May his descendants be cut off,
  their names blotted out from the next
    generation.
¹⁴May the iniquity of his fathers be
    remembered before the LORD;
  may the sin of his mother never be
    blotted out.
¹⁵May their sins always remain before the
    LORD,
  that he may cut off the memory of
    them from the earth.

¹⁶For he never thought of doing a
    kindness,
  but hounded to death the poor
  and the needy and the brokenhearted.
¹⁷He loved to pronounce a curse—
  may it*e* come on him;
  he found no pleasure in blessing—
  may it be*f* far from him.
¹⁸He wore cursing as his garment;
  it entered into his body like water,
  into his bones like oil.
¹⁹May it be like a cloak wrapped about
    him,
  like a belt tied forever around him.
²⁰May this be the LORD's payment to my
    accusers,
  to those who speak evil of me.

²¹But you, O Sovereign LORD,
  deal well with me for your name's
    sake;
  out of the goodness of your love,
    deliver me.
²²For I am poor and needy,
  and my heart is wounded within me.
²³I fade away like an evening shadow;
  I am shaken off like a locust.
²⁴My knees give way from fasting;
  my body is thin and gaunt.
²⁵I am an object of scorn to my accusers;
  when they see me, they shake their
    heads.

²⁶Help me, O LORD my God;
  save me in accordance with your love.
²⁷Let them know that it is your hand,
  that you, O LORD, have done it.
²⁸They may curse, but you will bless;
  when they attack they will be put to
    shame,
  but your servant will rejoice.
²⁹My accusers will be clothed with
    disgrace
  and wrapped in shame as in a cloak.

³⁰With my mouth I will greatly extol the
    LORD;
  in the great throng I will praise him.
³¹For he stands at the right hand of the
    needy one,
  to save his life from those who
    condemn him.

Psalm 110

Of David. A psalm.

¹The LORD says to my Lord:
  "Sit at my right hand
until I make your enemies
  a footstool for your feet."

²The LORD will extend your mighty
    scepter from Zion;
  you will rule in the midst of your
    enemies.
³Your troops will be willing
  on your day of battle.
Arrayed in holy majesty,
  from the womb of the dawn
you will receive the dew of your
    youth.*g*

*a6 Or ⌊They say:⌋ "Appoint (with quotation marks at the end of verse 19)   b6 Or the Evil One   c6 Or let
Satan   d10 Septuagint; Hebrew sought   e17 Or curse, / and it has   f17 Or blessing, / and it is   g3 Or /
your young men will come to you like the dew*

4The Lord has sworn
  and will not change his mind:
"You are a priest forever,
  in the order of Melchizedek."

5The Lord is at your right hand;
  he will crush kings on the day of his
    wrath.
6He will judge the nations, heaping up
    the dead
  and crushing the rulers of the whole
    earth.
7He will drink from a brook beside the
    way^a;
  therefore he will lift up his head.

Psalm 111^b

1Praise the Lord.^c

  I will extol the Lord with all my heart
    in the council of the upright and in
    the assembly.

2Great are the works of the Lord;
  they are pondered by all who delight
    in them.
3Glorious and majestic are his deeds,
  and his righteousness endures
    forever.
4He has caused his wonders to be
    remembered;
  the Lord is gracious and
    compassionate.
5He provides food for those who fear
    him;
  he remembers his covenant forever.
6He has shown his people the power of
    his works,
  giving them the lands of other
    nations.
7The works of his hands are faithful and
    just;
  all his precepts are trustworthy.
8They are steadfast for ever and ever,
  done in faithfulness and uprightness.
9He provided redemption for his people;
  he ordained his covenant forever—
  holy and awesome is his name.

10The fear of the Lord is the beginning of
    wisdom;
  all who follow his precepts have good
    understanding.
  To him belongs eternal praise.

Psalm 112^b

1Praise the Lord.^c

  Blessed is the man who fears the Lord,
  who finds great delight in his
    commands.

2His children will be mighty in the land;
  the generation of the upright will be
    blessed.
3Wealth and riches are in his house,
  and his righteousness endures
    forever.
4Even in darkness light dawns for the
    upright,
  for the gracious and compassionate
    and righteous man.^d
5Good will come to him who is generous
    and lends freely,
  who conducts his affairs with justice.
6Surely he will never be shaken;
  a righteous man will be remembered
    forever.
7He will have no fear of bad news;
  his heart is steadfast, trusting in the
    Lord.
8His heart is secure, he will have no fear;
  in the end he will look in triumph on
    his foes.
9He has scattered abroad his gifts to the
    poor,
  his righteousness endures forever;
  his horn^e will be lifted high in honor.

10The wicked man will see and be vexed,
  he will gnash his teeth and waste
    away;
  the longings of the wicked will come
    to nothing.

Psalm 113

1Praise the Lord.^f

  Praise, O servants of the Lord,
  praise the name of the Lord.
2Let the name of the Lord be praised,
  both now and forevermore.
3From the rising of the sun to the place
    where it sets,
  the name of the Lord is to be praised.

4The Lord is exalted over all the nations,
  his glory above the heavens.
5Who is like the Lord our God,
  the One who sits enthroned on high,

*a*7 Or / *The One who grants succession will set him in authority* of which begin with the successive letters of the Hebrew alphabet. *b*This psalm is an acrostic poem, the lines *c*1 Hebrew *Hallelu Yah* *d*4 Or / *for the Lord, is gracious and compassionate and righteous* *e*9 *Horn* here symbolizes dignity. *f*1 Hebrew *Hallelu Yah*; also in verse 9

6who stoops down to look
　　on the heavens and the earth?

7He raises the poor from the dust
　　and lifts the needy from the ash heap;
8he seats them with princes,
　　with the princes of their people.
9He settles the barren woman in her
　　　home
　　as a happy mother of children.

Praise the LORD.

Psalm 114

1When Israel came out of Egypt,
　　the house of Jacob from a people of
　　　foreign tongue,
2Judah became God's sanctuary,
　　Israel his dominion.

3The sea looked and fled,
　　the Jordan turned back;
4the mountains skipped like rams,
　　the hills like lambs.

5Why was it, O sea, that you fled,
　　O Jordan, that you turned back,
6you mountains, that you skipped like
　　　rams,
　　you hills, like lambs?

7Tremble, O earth, at the presence of the
　　　Lord,
　　at the presence of the God of Jacob,
8who turned the rock into a pool,
　　the hard rock into springs of water.

Psalm 115

1Not to us, O LORD, not to us
　　but to your name be the glory,
　　because of your love and faithfulness.

2Why do the nations say,
　　"Where is their God?"
3Our God is in heaven;
　　he does whatever pleases him.
4But their idols are silver and gold,
　　made by the hands of men.
5They have mouths, but cannot speak,
　　eyes, but they cannot see;
6they have ears, but cannot hear,
　　noses, but they cannot smell;
7they have hands, but cannot feel,
　　feet, but they cannot walk;
　　nor can they utter a sound with their
　　　throats.
8Those who make them will be like
　　them,

and so will all who trust in them.

9O house of Israel, trust in the LORD—
　　he is their help and shield.
10O house of Aaron, trust in the LORD—
　　he is their help and shield.
11You who fear him, trust in the LORD—
　　he is their help and shield.

12The LORD remembers us and will bless
　　　us:
　　He will bless the house of Israel,
　　he will bless the house of Aaron,
13he will bless those who fear the LORD—
　　small and great alike.

14May the LORD make you increase,
　　both you and your children.
15May you be blessed by the LORD,
　　the Maker of heaven and earth.

16The highest heavens belong to the LORD,
　　but the earth he has given to man.
17It is not the dead who praise the LORD,
　　those who go down to silence;
18it is we who extol the LORD,
　　both now and forevermore.

Praise the LORD.a

Psalm 116

1I love the LORD, for he heard my voice;
　　he heard my cry for mercy.
2Because he turned his ear to me,
　　I will call on him as long as I live.

3The cords of death entangled me,
　　the anguish of the graveb came upon
　　　me;
　　I was overcome by trouble and
　　　sorrow.
4Then I called on the name of the LORD:
　　"O LORD, save me!"

5The LORD is gracious and righteous;
　　our God is full of compassion.
6The LORD protects the simplehearted;
　　when I was in great need, he saved
　　　me.

7Be at rest once more, O my soul,
　　for the LORD has been good to you.

8For you, O LORD, have delivered my soul
　　　from death,
　　my eyes from tears,
　　my feet from stumbling,
9that I may walk before the LORD
　　in the land of the living.
10I believed; thereforec I said,

---

a18 Hebrew *Hallelu Yah*　　b3 Hebrew *Sheol*　　c10 Or *believed even when*

"I am greatly afflicted."
[11]And in my dismay I said,
"All men are liars."

[12]How can I repay the LORD
for all his goodness to me?
[13]I will lift up the cup of salvation
and call on the name of the LORD.
[14]I will fulfill my vows to the LORD
in the presence of all his people.

[15]Precious in the sight of the LORD
is the death of his saints.
[16]O LORD, truly I am your servant;
I am your servant, the son of your
maidservant[a];
you have freed me from my chains.

[17]I will sacrifice a thank offering to you
and call on the name of the LORD.
[18]I will fulfill my vows to the LORD
in the presence of all his people,
[19]in the courts of the house of the LORD—
in your midst, O Jerusalem.

Praise the LORD.[b]

Psalm 117

[1]Praise the LORD, all you nations;
extol him, all you peoples.
[2]For great is his love toward us,
and the faithfulness of the LORD
endures forever.

Praise the LORD.[b]

Psalm 118

[1]Give thanks to the LORD, for he is good;
his love endures forever.

[2]Let Israel say:
"His love endures forever."
[3]Let the house of Aaron say:
"His love endures forever."
[4]Let those who fear the LORD say:
"His love endures forever."

[5]In my anguish I cried to the LORD,
and he answered by setting me free.
[6]The LORD is with me; I will not be afraid.
What can man do to me?
[7]The LORD is with me; he is my helper.
I will look in triumph on my enemies.

[8]It is better to take refuge in the LORD
than to trust in man.
[9]It is better to take refuge in the LORD
than to trust in princes.

[10]All the nations surrounded me,
but in the name of the LORD I cut
them off.
[11]They surrounded me on every side,
but in the name of the LORD I cut
them off.
[12]They swarmed around me like bees,
but they died out as quickly as
burning thorns;
in the name of the LORD I cut them
off.
[13]I was pushed back and about to fall,
but the LORD helped me.
[14]The LORD is my strength and my song;
he has become my salvation.

[15]Shouts of joy and victory
resound in the tents of the righteous:
"The LORD's right hand has done mighty
things!
[16]   The LORD's right hand is lifted high;
the LORD's right hand has done mighty
things!"
[17]I will not die but live,
and will proclaim what the LORD has
done.
[18]The LORD has chastened me severely,
but he has not given me over to
death.

[19]Open for me the gates of righteousness;
I will enter and give thanks to the
LORD.
[20]This is the gate of the LORD
through which the righteous may
enter.
[21]I will give you thanks, for you answered
me;
you have become my salvation.

[22]The stone the builders rejected
has become the capstone;
[23]the LORD has done this,
and it is marvelous in our eyes.
[24]This is the day the LORD has made;
let us rejoice and be glad in it.

[25]O LORD, save us;
O LORD, grant us success.
[26]Blessed is he who comes in the name of
the LORD.
From the house of the LORD we bless
you.[c]
[27]The LORD is God,
and he has made his light shine upon
us.
With boughs in hand, join in the festal
procession

---

[a]16 Or servant, your faithful son   [b]19,2 Hebrew Hallelu Yah   [c]26 The Hebrew is plural.

up[a] to the horns of the altar.
[28]You are my God, and I will give you
thanks;
you are my God, and I will exalt you.

[29]Give thanks to the LORD, for he is good;
his love endures forever.

Psalm 119[b]

א Aleph

[1]Blessed are they whose ways are
blameless,
who walk according to the law of the
LORD.
[2]Blessed are they who keep his statutes
and seek him with all their heart.
[3]They do nothing wrong;
they walk in his ways.
[4]You have laid down precepts
that are to be fully obeyed.
[5]Oh, that my ways were steadfast
in obeying your decrees!
[6]Then I would not be put to shame
when I consider all your commands.
[7]I will praise you with an upright heart
as I learn your righteous laws.
[8]I will obey your decrees;
do not utterly forsake me.

ב Beth

[9]How can a young man keep his way
pure?
By living according to your word.
[10]I seek you with all my heart;
do not let me stray from your
commands.
[11]I have hidden your word in my heart
that I might not sin against you.
[12]Praise be to you, O LORD;
teach me your decrees.
[13]With my lips I recount
all the laws that come from your
mouth.
[14]I rejoice in following your statutes
as one rejoices in great riches.
[15]I meditate on your precepts
and consider your ways.
[16]I delight in your decrees;
I will not neglect your word.

ג Gimel

[17]Do good to your servant, and I will live;
I will obey your word.
[18]Open my eyes that I may see

wonderful things in your law.
[19]I am a stranger on earth;
do not hide your commands from me.
[20]My soul is consumed with longing
for your laws at all times.
[21]You rebuke the arrogant, who are
cursed
and who stray from your commands.
[22]Remove from me scorn and contempt,
for I keep your statutes.
[23]Though rulers sit together and slander
me,
your servant will meditate on your
decrees.
[24]Your statutes are my delight;
they are my counselors.

ד Daleth

[25]I am laid low in the dust;
preserve my life according to your
word.
[26]I recounted my ways and you answered
me;
teach me your decrees.
[27]Let me understand the teaching of your
precepts;
then I will meditate on your wonders.
[28]My soul is weary with sorrow;
strengthen me according to your
word.
[29]Keep me from deceitful ways;
be gracious to me through your law.
[30]I have chosen the way of truth;
I have set my heart on your laws.
[31]I hold fast to your statutes, O LORD;
do not let me be put to shame.
[32]I run in the path of your commands,
for you have set my heart free.

ה He

[33]Teach me, O LORD, to follow your
decrees;
then I will keep them to the end.
[34]Give me understanding, and I will keep
your law
and obey it with all my heart.
[35]Direct me in the path of your
commands,
for there I find delight.
[36]Turn my heart toward your statutes
and not toward selfish gain.
[37]Turn my eyes away from worthless
things;
preserve my life according to your
word.[c]

---

[a]27 Or *Bind the festal sacrifice with ropes / and take it*   [b]This psalm is an acrostic poem; the verses of each
stanza begin with the same letter of the Hebrew alphabet.   [c]37 Two manuscripts of the Masoretic Text and
Dead Sea Scrolls; most manuscripts of the Masoretic Text *life in your way*

38Fulfill your promise to your servant,
   so that you may be feared.
39Take away the disgrace I dread,
   for your laws are good.
40How I long for your precepts!
   Preserve my life in your
      righteousness.

    ו   Waw

41May your unfailing love come to me,
   O LORD,
   your salvation according to your
      promise;
42then I will answer the one who taunts
      me,
   for I trust in your word.
43Do not snatch the word of truth from
      my mouth,
   for I have put my hope in your laws.
44I will always obey your law,
   for ever and ever.
45I will walk about in freedom,
   for I have sought out your precepts.
46I will speak of your statutes before
      kings
   and will not be put to shame,
47for I delight in your commands
   because I love them.
48I lift up my hands to[a] your commands,
      which I love,
   and I meditate on your decrees.

    ז   Zayin

49Remember your word to your servant,
   for you have given me hope.
50My comfort in my suffering is this:
   Your promise preserves my life.
51The arrogant mock me without restraint,
   but I do not turn from your law.
52I remember your ancient laws, O LORD,
   and I find comfort in them.
53Indignation grips me because of the
      wicked,
   who have forsaken your law.
54Your decrees are the theme of my song
   wherever I lodge.
55In the night I remember your name,
   O LORD,
   and I will keep your law.
56This has been my practice:
   I obey your precepts.

    ח   Heth

57You are my portion, O LORD;
   I have promised to obey your words.
58I have sought your face with all my
      heart;

   be gracious to me according to your
      promise.
59I have considered my ways
   and have turned my steps to your
      statutes.
60I will hasten and not delay
   to obey your commands.
61Though the wicked bind me with ropes,
   I will not forget your law.
62At midnight I rise to give you thanks
   for your righteous laws.
63I am a friend to all who fear you,
   to all who follow your precepts.
64The earth is filled with your love,
   O LORD;
   teach me your decrees.

    ט   Teth

65Do good to your servant
   according to your word, O LORD.
66Teach me knowledge and good
      judgment,
   for I believe in your commands.
67Before I was afflicted I went astray,
   but now I obey your word.
68You are good, and what you do is good;
   teach me your decrees.
69Though the arrogant have smeared me
      with lies,
   I keep your precepts with all my
      heart.
70Their hearts are callous and unfeeling,
   but I delight in your law.
71It was good for me to be afflicted
   so that I might learn your decrees.
72The law from your mouth is more
      precious to me
   than thousands of pieces of silver and
      gold.

    י   Yodh

73Your hands made me and formed me;
   give me understanding to learn your
      commands.
74May those who fear you rejoice when
      they see me,
   for I have put my hope in your word.
75I know, O LORD, that your laws are
      righteous,
   and in faithfulness you have afflicted
      me.
76May your unfailing love be my comfort,
   according to your promise to your
      servant.
77Let your compassion come to me that I
      may live,
   for your law is my delight.

a48 Or for

78May the arrogant be put to shame for
   wronging me without cause;
   but I will meditate on your precepts.
79May those who fear you turn to me,
   those who understand your statutes.
80May my heart be blameless toward your
   decrees,
   that I may not be put to shame.

ﬠ   Kaph

81My soul faints with longing for your
   salvation,
   but I have put my hope in your word.
82My eyes fail, looking for your promise;
   I say, "When will you comfort me?"
83Though I am like a wineskin in the
   smoke,
   I do not forget your decrees.
84How long must your servant wait?
   When will you punish my
   persecutors?
85The arrogant dig pitfalls for me,
   contrary to your law.
86All your commands are trustworthy;
   help me, for men persecute me
   without cause.
87They almost wiped me from the earth,
   but I have not forsaken your precepts.
88Preserve my life according to your love,
   and I will obey the statutes of your
   mouth.

ל   Lamedh

89Your word, O LORD, is eternal;
   it stands firm in the heavens.
90Your faithfulness continues through all
   generations;
   you established the earth, and it
   endures.
91Your laws endure to this day,
   for all things serve you.
92If your law had not been my delight,
   I would have perished in my
   affliction.
93I will never forget your precepts,
   for by them you have preserved my
   life.
94Save me, for I am yours;
   I have sought out your precepts.
95The wicked are waiting to destroy me,
   but I will ponder your statutes.
96To all perfection I see a limit;
   but your commands are boundless.

מ   Mem

97Oh, how I love your law!
   I meditate on it all day long.
98Your commands make me wiser than
   my enemies,
   for they are ever with me.
99I have more insight than all my
   teachers,
   for I meditate on your statutes.
100I have more understanding than the
   elders,
   for I obey your precepts.
101I have kept my feet from every evil
   path
   so that I might obey your word.
102I have not departed from your laws,
   for you yourself have taught me.
103 How sweet are your words to my taste,
   sweeter than honey to my mouth!
104I gain understanding from your
   precepts;
   therefore I hate every wrong path.

נ   Nun

105 Your word is a lamp to my feet
   and a light for my path.
106I have taken an oath and confirmed it,
   that I will follow your righteous laws.
107I have suffered much;
   preserve my life, O LORD, according to
   your word.
108 Accept, O LORD, the willing praise of my
   mouth,
   and teach me your laws.
109 Though I constantly take my life in my
   hands,
   I will not forget your law.
110 The wicked have set a snare for me,
   but I have not strayed from your
   precepts.
111 Your statutes are my heritage forever;
   they are the joy of my heart.
112 My heart is set on keeping your
   decrees
   to the very end.

ס   Samekh

113I hate double-minded men,
   but I love your law.
114 You are my refuge and my shield;
   I have put my hope in your word.
115 Away from me, you evildoers,
   that I may keep the commands of my
   God!
116 Sustain me according to your promise,
   and I will live;
   do not let my hopes be dashed.
117 Uphold me, and I will be delivered;
   I will always have regard for your
   decrees.
118 You reject all who stray from your
   decrees,
   for their deceitfulness is in vain.

THE BOOK IS NOT JUST ANY BOOK

Colleen and Paula are talking with Tom, their youth pastor. He's holding a bunch of strange-looking books.

"What's all that?" Colleen asks.

"Well, this Sunday we're going to study about how we know the Bible is really from God. These are all books considered holy by other religions."

Paula is stunned. "You mean some religious people don't believe the Bible?"

Tom smiles. "Well, most religions depend on other writings. The Mormons have the Book of Mormon; Muslims follow the Koran; Hare Krishnas use a book I can't even pronounce; Christian Scientists read stuff written by Mary Baker Eddy . . . ."

Look It Up

With so many groups claiming to have "God's Word," it's nice to know the Bible is trustworthy.

The Old Testament is constantly punctuated by the phrases "this is the word of the LORD" and "then the LORD said." The New Testament says "all Scripture is God-breathed" (2 Timothy 3:16) and "prophecy never had its origin in the will of man, but men spoke from God as they were carried along by the Holy Spirit" (2 Peter 1:21).

Perhaps the authors of all those more recent books listed above should consider this warning:

"Every word of God is flawless. . . . Do not add to his words, or he will rebuke you and prove you a liar" (Proverbs 30:5–6).

Think It Through

Despite being written by more than forty authors over a period of about 1,600 years, the Bible displays amazing unity and continuity.

Despite persecution, misinterpretation, criticism, abuse and time, the Bible has survived virtually intact. What's more, the Bible is completely accurate with respect to history, archaeology and prophecy.

Finally, the Bible has had a greater impact on culture, thought and the lives of individuals than any other book.

What other book can truthfully make such claims?

Work It Out

Since the Bible is really the Word of the living God, then it only makes sense to learn as much about it as you can. A daily habit of reading, thinking about and memorizing God's Word will strengthen you in your Christian walk.

Nail It Down

Read Psalm 119:105 for a poetic description of God's Word.

Turn to pages 1136, 1172 and 1370 for other readings on tough questions.
Turn to page 641 for Tuesday's reading.

Topic

TOUGH QUESTIONS

¹¹⁹All the wicked of the earth you discard
    like dross;
  therefore I love your statutes.
¹²⁰My flesh trembles in fear of you;
  I stand in awe of your laws.

ע   Ayin

¹²¹I have done what is righteous and just;
  do not leave me to my oppressors.
¹²²Ensure your servant's well-being;
  let not the arrogant oppress me.
¹²³My eyes fail, looking for your salvation,
  looking for your righteous promise.
¹²⁴Deal with your servant according to
    your love
  and teach me your decrees.
¹²⁵I am your servant; give me
    discernment
  that I may understand your statutes.
¹²⁶It is time for you to act, O Lord;
  your law is being broken.
¹²⁷Because I love your commands
  more than gold, more than pure gold,
¹²⁸and because I consider all your
    precepts right,
  I hate every wrong path.

פ   Pe

¹²⁹Your statutes are wonderful;
  therefore I obey them.
¹³⁰The unfolding of your words gives
    light;
  it gives understanding to the simple.
¹³¹I open my mouth and pant,
  longing for your commands.
¹³²Turn to me and have mercy on me,
  as you always do to those who love
    your name.
¹³³Direct my footsteps according to your
    word;
  let no sin rule over me.
¹³⁴Redeem me from the oppression of
    men,
  that I may obey your precepts.
¹³⁵Make your face shine upon your
    servant
  and teach me your decrees.
¹³⁶Streams of tears flow from my eyes,
  for your law is not obeyed.

צ   Tsadhe

¹³⁷Righteous are you, O Lord,
  and your laws are right.
¹³⁸The statutes you have laid down are
    righteous;
  they are fully trustworthy.
¹³⁹My zeal wears me out,
  for my enemies ignore your words.

¹⁴⁰Your promises have been thoroughly
    tested,
  and your servant loves them.
¹⁴¹Though I am lowly and despised,
  I do not forget your precepts.
¹⁴²Your righteousness is everlasting
  and your law is true.
¹⁴³Trouble and distress have come
    upon me,
  but your commands are my delight.
¹⁴⁴Your statutes are forever right;
  give me understanding that I may
    live.

ק   Qoph

¹⁴⁵I call with all my heart; answer me,
    O Lord,
  and I will obey your decrees.
¹⁴⁶I call out to you; save me
  and I will keep your statutes.
¹⁴⁷I rise before dawn and cry for help;
  I have put my hope in your word.
¹⁴⁸My eyes stay open through the watches
    of the night,
  that I may meditate on your promises.
¹⁴⁹Hear my voice in accordance with your
    love;
  preserve my life, O Lord, according to
    your laws.
¹⁵⁰Those who devise wicked schemes are
    near,
  but they are far from your law.
¹⁵¹Yet you are near, O Lord,
  and all your commands are true.
¹⁵²Long ago I learned from your statutes
  that you established them to last
    forever.

ר   Resh

¹⁵³Look upon my suffering and
    deliver me,
  for I have not forgotten your law.
¹⁵⁴Defend my cause and redeem me;
  preserve my life according to your
    promise.
¹⁵⁵Salvation is far from the wicked,
  for they do not seek out your decrees.
¹⁵⁶Your compassion is great, O Lord;
  preserve my life according to your
    laws.
¹⁵⁷Many are the foes who persecute me,
  but I have not turned from your
    statutes.
¹⁵⁸I look on the faithless with loathing,
  for they do not obey your word.
¹⁵⁹See how I love your precepts;
  preserve my life, O Lord, according to
    your love.

160All your words are true;
  all your righteous laws are eternal.

ש   Sin and Shin

161Rulers persecute me without cause,
  but my heart trembles at your word.
162I rejoice in your promise
  like one who finds great spoil.
163I hate and abhor falsehood
  but I love your law.
164Seven times a day I praise you
  for your righteous laws.
165Great peace have they who love your
    law,
  and nothing can make them stumble.
166I wait for your salvation, O LORD,
  and I follow your commands.
167I obey your statutes,
  for I love them greatly.
168I obey your precepts and your statutes,
  for all my ways are known to you.

ת   Taw

169May my cry come before you, O LORD;
  give me understanding according to
    your word.
170May my supplication come before you;
  deliver me according to your promise.
171May my lips overflow with praise,
  for you teach me your decrees.
172May my tongue sing of your word,
  for all your commands are righteous.
173May your hand be ready to help me,
  for I have chosen your precepts.
174I long for your salvation, O LORD,
  and your law is my delight.
175Let me live that I may praise you,
  and may your laws sustain me.
176I have strayed like a lost sheep.
  Seek your servant,
  for I have not forgotten your
    commands.

Psalm 120

A song of ascents.

1I call on the LORD in my distress,
  and he answers me.
2Save me, O LORD, from lying lips
  and from deceitful tongues.

3What will he do to you,
  and what more besides, O deceitful
    tongue?
4He will punish you with a warrior's
    sharp arrows,
  with burning coals of the broom tree.

5Woe to me that I dwell in Meshech,
  that I live among the tents of Kedar!

6Too long have I lived
  among those who hate peace.
7I am a man of peace;
  but when I speak, they are for war.

Psalm 121

A song of ascents.

1I lift up my eyes to the hills—
  where does my help come from?
2My help comes from the LORD,
  the Maker of heaven and earth.

3He will not let your foot slip—
  he who watches over you will not
    slumber;
4indeed, he who watches over Israel
  will neither slumber nor sleep.

5The LORD watches over you—
  the LORD is your shade at your right
    hand;
6the sun will not harm you by day,
  nor the moon by night.

7The LORD will keep you from all harm—
  he will watch over your life;
8the LORD will watch over your coming
    and going
  both now and forevermore.

Psalm 122

A song of ascents. Of David.

1I rejoiced with those who said to me,
  "Let us go to the house of the LORD."
2Our feet are standing
  in your gates, O Jerusalem.

3Jerusalem is built like a city
  that is closely compacted together.
4That is where the tribes go up,
  the tribes of the LORD,
  to praise the name of the LORD
  according to the statute given to
    Israel.
5There the thrones for judgment stand,
  the thrones of the house of David.

6Pray for the peace of Jerusalem:
  "May those who love you be secure.
7May there be peace within your walls
  and security within your citadels."
8For the sake of my brothers and friends,
  I will say, "Peace be within you."
9For the sake of the house of the LORD
    our God,
  I will seek your prosperity.

Psalm 123

A song of ascents.

[1] I lift up my eyes to you,
    to you whose throne is in heaven.
[2] As the eyes of slaves look to the hand
        of their master,
    as the eyes of a maid look to the
        hand of her mistress,
    so our eyes look to the LORD our God,
        till he shows us his mercy.

[3] Have mercy on us, O LORD, have mercy
        on us,
    for we have endured much contempt.
[4] We have endured much ridicule from
        the proud,
    much contempt from the arrogant.

Psalm 124

A song of ascents. Of David.

[1] If the LORD had not been on our side—
    let Israel say—
[2] if the LORD had not been on our side
    when men attacked us,
[3] when their anger flared against us,
    they would have swallowed us alive;
[4] the flood would have engulfed us,
    the torrent would have swept over us,
[5] the raging waters
    would have swept us away.

[6] Praise be to the LORD,
    who has not let us be torn by their
        teeth.
[7] We have escaped like a bird
    out of the fowler's snare;
    the snare has been broken,
    and we have escaped.
[8] Our help is in the name of the LORD,
    the Maker of heaven and earth.

Psalm 125

A song of ascents.

[1] Those who trust in the LORD are like
        Mount Zion,
    which cannot be shaken but endures
        forever.
[2] As the mountains surround Jerusalem,
    so the LORD surrounds his people
    both now and forevermore.

[3] The scepter of the wicked will not
        remain
    over the land allotted to the righteous,
    for then the righteous might use
    their hands to do evil.

[4] Do good, O LORD, to those who are
        good,
    to those who are upright in heart.
[5] But those who turn to crooked ways
    the LORD will banish with the
        evildoers.

Peace be upon Israel.

Psalm 126

A song of ascents.

[1] When the LORD brought back the
        captives to[a] Zion,
    we were like men who dreamed.[b]
[2] Our mouths were filled with laughter,
    our tongues with songs of joy.
    Then it was said among the nations,
    "The LORD has done great things for
        them."
[3] The LORD has done great things for us,
    and we are filled with joy.

[4] Restore our fortunes,[c] O LORD,
    like streams in the Negev.
[5] Those who sow in tears
    will reap with songs of joy.
[6] He who goes out weeping,
    carrying seed to sow,
    will return with songs of joy,
    carrying sheaves with him.

Psalm 127

A song of ascents. Of Solomon.

[1] Unless the LORD builds the house,
    its builders labor in vain.
    Unless the LORD watches over the city,
    the watchmen stand guard in vain.
[2] In vain you rise early
    and stay up late,
    toiling for food to eat—
    for he grants sleep to[d] those he
        loves.

[3] Sons are a heritage from the LORD,
    children a reward from him.

---

[a]1 Or LORD restored the fortunes of   [b]1 Or men restored to health   [c]4 Or Bring back our captives
[d]2 Or eat— / for while they sleep he provides for

⁴Like arrows in the hands of a warrior
   are sons born in one's youth.
⁵Blessed is the man
   whose quiver is full of them.
They will not be put to shame
   when they contend with their
      enemies in the gate.

Psalm 128

A song of ascents.

¹Blessed are all who fear the LORD,
   who walk in his ways.
²You will eat the fruit of your labor;
   blessings and prosperity will be yours.
³Your wife will be like a fruitful vine
   within your house;
your sons will be like olive shoots
   around your table.
⁴Thus is the man blessed
   who fears the LORD.

⁵May the LORD bless you from Zion
   all the days of your life;
may you see the prosperity of
      Jerusalem,
⁶ and may you live to see your
      children's children.

Peace be upon Israel.

Psalm 129

A song of ascents.

¹They have greatly oppressed me from
      my youth—
   let Israel say—
²they have greatly oppressed me from
      my youth,
   but they have not gained the victory
      over me.
³Plowmen have plowed my back
   and made their furrows long.
⁴But the LORD is righteous;
   he has cut me free from the cords of
      the wicked.

⁵May all who hate Zion
   be turned back in shame.
⁶May they be like grass on the roof,
   which withers before it can grow;
⁷with it the reaper cannot fill his hands,
   nor the one who gathers fill his arms.
⁸May those who pass by not say,
   "The blessing of the LORD be upon
      you;
   we bless you in the name of the
      LORD."

Psalm 130

A song of ascents.

¹Out of the depths I cry to you, O LORD;
² O Lord, hear my voice.
Let your ears be attentive
   to my cry for mercy.

³If you, O LORD, kept a record of sins,
   O Lord, who could stand?
⁴But with you there is forgiveness;
   therefore you are feared.

⁵I wait for the LORD, my soul waits,
   and in his word I put my hope.
⁶My soul waits for the Lord
   more than watchmen wait for the
      morning,
   more than watchmen wait for the
      morning.

⁷O Israel, put your hope in the LORD,
   for with the LORD is unfailing love
   and with him is full redemption.
⁸He himself will redeem Israel
   from all their sins.

Psalm 131

A song of ascents. Of David.

¹My heart is not proud, O LORD,
   my eyes are not haughty;
I do not concern myself with great
      matters
   or things too wonderful for me.
²But I have stilled and quieted my soul;
   like a weaned child with its mother,
   like a weaned child is my soul within
      me.

³O Israel, put your hope in the LORD
   both now and forevermore.

Psalm 132

A song of ascents.

¹O LORD, remember David
   and all the hardships he endured.

²He swore an oath to the LORD
   and made a vow to the Mighty One of
      Jacob:
³"I will not enter my house
   or go to my bed—
⁴I will allow no sleep to my eyes,
   no slumber to my eyelids,
⁵till I find a place for the LORD,
   a dwelling for the Mighty One of
      Jacob."

⁶We heard it in Ephrathah,
  we came upon it in the fields of
    Jaar^{a;b}
⁷"Let us go to his dwelling place;
  let us worship at his footstool —
⁸arise, O LORD, and come to your resting
    place,
  you and the ark of your might.
⁹May your priests be clothed with
    righteousness;
  may your saints sing for joy."

¹⁰For the sake of David your servant,
  do not reject your anointed one.

¹¹The LORD swore an oath to David,
  a sure oath that he will not revoke:
"One of your own descendants
  I will place on your throne —
¹²if your sons keep my covenant
  and the statutes I teach them,
then their sons will sit
  on your throne for ever and ever."

¹³For the LORD has chosen Zion,
  he has desired it for his dwelling:
¹⁴"This is my resting place for ever and
    ever;
  here I will sit enthroned, for I have
    desired it —
¹⁵I will bless her with abundant
    provisions;
  her poor will I satisfy with food.
¹⁶I will clothe her priests with salvation,
  and her saints will ever sing for joy.

¹⁷"Here I will make a horn^c grow for
    David
  and set up a lamp for my anointed
    one.
¹⁸I will clothe his enemies with shame,
  but the crown on his head will be
    resplendent."

Psalm 133

A song of ascents. Of David.

¹How good and pleasant it is
  when brothers live together in unity!
²It is like precious oil poured on the
    head,
  running down on the beard,
running down on Aaron's beard,
  down upon the collar of his robes.
³It is as if the dew of Hermon
  were falling on Mount Zion.

For there the LORD bestows his blessing,
  even life forevermore.

Psalm 134

A song of ascents.

¹Praise the LORD, all you servants of the
    LORD
  who minister by night in the house of
    the LORD.
²Lift up your hands in the sanctuary
  and praise the LORD.

³May the LORD, the Maker of heaven and
    earth,
  bless you from Zion.

Psalm 135

¹Praise the LORD.^d

Praise the name of the LORD;
  praise him, you servants of the LORD,
²you who minister in the house of the
    LORD,
  in the courts of the house of our God.

³Praise the LORD, for the LORD is good;
  sing praise to his name, for that is
    pleasant.
⁴For the LORD has chosen Jacob to be his
    own,
  Israel to be his treasured possession.

⁵I know that the LORD is great,
  that our Lord is greater than all gods.
⁶The LORD does whatever pleases him,
  in the heavens and on the earth,
  in the seas and all their depths.
⁷He makes clouds rise from the ends of
    the earth;
  he sends lightning with the rain
  and brings out the wind from his
    storehouses.

⁸He struck down the firstborn of Egypt,
  the firstborn of men and animals.
⁹He sent his signs and wonders into your
    midst, O Egypt,
  against Pharaoh and all his servants.
¹⁰He struck down many nations
  and killed mighty kings —
¹¹Sihon king of the Amorites,
  Og king of Bashan
  and all the kings of Canaan —
¹²and he gave their land as an
    inheritance,

---

^a6 That is, Kiriath Jearim   ^b6 Or *heard of it in Ephrathah, / we found it in the fields of Jaar*. (And no quotes around verses 7-9)   ^c17 *Horn* here symbolizes strong one, that is, king.   ^d1 Hebrew *Hallelu Yah*; also in verses 3 and 21

an inheritance to his people Israel.

¹³Your name, O LORD, endures forever,
  your renown, O LORD, through all
    generations.
¹⁴For the LORD will vindicate his people
  and have compassion on his servants.

¹⁵The idols of the nations are silver and
    gold,
  made by the hands of men.
¹⁶They have mouths, but cannot speak,
  eyes, but they cannot see;
¹⁷they have ears, but cannot hear,
  nor is there breath in their mouths.
¹⁸Those who make them will be like
    them,
  and so will all who trust in them.

¹⁹O house of Israel, praise the LORD;
  O house of Aaron, praise the LORD;
²⁰O house of Levi, praise the LORD;
  you who fear him, praise the LORD.
²¹Praise be to the LORD from Zion,
  to him who dwells in Jerusalem.

    Praise the LORD.

Psalm 136

¹Give thanks to the LORD, for he is good.
  His love endures forever.
²Give thanks to the God of gods.
  His love endures forever.
³Give thanks to the Lord of lords:
  His love endures forever.

⁴to him who alone does great wonders,
  His love endures forever.
⁵who by his understanding made the
    heavens,
  His love endures forever.
⁶who spread out the earth upon the
    waters,
  His love endures forever.
⁷who made the great lights—
  His love endures forever.
⁸the sun to govern the day,
  His love endures forever.
⁹the moon and stars to govern the night;
  His love endures forever.

¹⁰to him who struck down the firstborn of
    Egypt
  His love endures forever.
¹¹and brought Israel out from among
    them
  His love endures forever.

¹²with a mighty hand and outstretched
    arm;
  His love endures forever.

¹³to him who divided the Red Sea*ᵃ*
    asunder
  His love endures forever.
¹⁴and brought Israel through the midst of
    it,
  His love endures forever.
¹⁵but swept Pharaoh and his army into
    the Red Sea;
  His love endures forever.

¹⁶to him who led his people through the
    desert,
  His love endures forever.
¹⁷who struck down great kings,
  His love endures forever.
¹⁸and killed mighty kings—
  His love endures forever.
¹⁹Sihon king of the Amorites
  His love endures forever.
²⁰and Og king of Bashan—
  His love endures forever.
²¹and gave their land as an inheritance,
  His love endures forever.
²²an inheritance to his servant Israel;
  His love endures forever.

²³to the One who remembered us in our
    low estate
  His love endures forever.
²⁴and freed us from our enemies,
  His love endures forever.
²⁵and who gives food to every creature.
  His love endures forever.

²⁶Give thanks to the God of heaven.
  His love endures forever.

Psalm 137

¹By the rivers of Babylon we sat and
    wept
  when we remembered Zion.
²There on the poplars
  we hung our harps,
³for there our captors asked us for songs,
  our tormentors demanded songs of
    joy;
  they said, "Sing us one of the songs
    of Zion!"

⁴How can we sing the songs of the LORD
  while in a foreign land?

ᵃ13 Hebrew *Yam Suph*; that is, Sea of Reeds; also in verse 15

⁵If I forget you, O Jerusalem,
  may my right hand forget ⌊its skill⌋.
⁶May my tongue cling to the roof of my
  mouth
    if I do not remember you,
  if I do not consider Jerusalem
    my highest joy.

⁷Remember, O LORD, what the Edomites
  did
    on the day Jerusalem fell.
  "Tear it down," they cried,
    "tear it down to its foundations!"

⁸O Daughter of Babylon, doomed to
  destruction,
    happy is he who repays you
  for what you have done to us—
⁹he who seizes your infants
  and dashes them against the rocks.

Psalm 138

Of David.

¹I will praise you, O LORD, with all my
  heart;
    before the "gods" I will sing your
    praise.
²I will bow down toward your holy
  temple
    and will praise your name
  for your love and your faithfulness,
  for you have exalted above all things
    your name and your word.
³When I called, you answered me;
  you made me bold and stouthearted.

⁴May all the kings of the earth praise
  you, O LORD,
    when they hear the words of your
    mouth.
⁵May they sing of the ways of the LORD,
  for the glory of the LORD is great.

⁶Though the LORD is on high, he looks
  upon the lowly,
    but the proud he knows from afar.
⁷Though I walk in the midst of trouble,
  you preserve my life;
  you stretch out your hand against the
    anger of my foes,
  with your right hand you save me.
⁸The LORD will fulfill ⌊his purpose⌋
  for me;
    your love, O LORD, endures forever—
  do not abandon the works of your
    hands.

Psalm 139

For the director of music. Of David.
A psalm.

¹O LORD, you have searched me
  and you know me.
²You know when I sit and when I rise;
  you perceive my thoughts from afar.
³You discern my going out and my lying
  down;
    you are familiar with all my ways.
⁴Before a word is on my tongue
  you know it completely, O LORD.

⁵You hem me in—behind and before;
  you have laid your hand upon me.
⁶Such knowledge is too wonderful for
  me,
    too lofty for me to attain.

⁷Where can I go from your Spirit?
  Where can I flee from your presence?
⁸If I go up to the heavens, you are there;
  if I make my bed in the depths,ᵃ you
    are there.
⁹If I rise on the wings of the dawn,
  if I settle on the far side of the sea,
¹⁰even there your hand will guide me,
  your right hand will hold me fast.
¹¹If I say, "Surely the darkness will hide
  me
    and the light become night around
    me,"
¹²even the darkness will not be dark to
  you;
    the night will shine like the day,
  for darkness is as light to you.

¹³For you created my inmost being;
  you knit me together in my mother's
    womb.
¹⁴I praise you because I am fearfully and
  wonderfully made;
    your works are wonderful,
  I know that full well.
¹⁵My frame was not hidden from you
  when I was made in the secret place.
  When I was woven together in the
    depths of the earth,
¹⁶ your eyes saw my unformed body.
  All the days ordained for me
    were written in your book
  before one of them came to be.

¹⁷How precious toᵇ me are your
    thoughts, O God!
  How vast is the sum of them!
¹⁸Were I to count them,

ᵃ8 Hebrew *Sheol*   ᵇ17 Or *concerning*

WHAT THE MIRROR DOESN'T SHOW YOU

Liz was supposed to pick up her friend Robyn fifteen minutes ago. Crying, she buries her face in a pillow. Her mother enters the room.

"Honey, you look fine, really you do."

"No, I don't, Mother! My hair looks stupid and my face is all broken out!" She gets up and looks into the mirror, "Besides, look at my eyes now. They're all red and swollen."

"I bet if you washed your face with a cold cloth—"

"Mother, don't you see? It'll just be the same old story! I'll walk in with Robyn, and everyone will rave about how cute she is. And I'll just be ignored!"

Look It Up
••••

One of the hardest things to believe is the Bible's declaration that each one of us is specially designed by God:

"For we are God's workmanship" (Ephesians 2:10).

"I praise you because I am fearfully and wonderfully made; your works are wonderful, I know that full well" (Psalm 139:14).

According to the Bible, you are a one-of-a-kind, original masterpiece! You have been beautifully designed by God.

Think It Through
••••

Do you really believe that? Or are you constantly comparing yourself with others—top fashion models or movie stars—and feeling like a loser?

Comparisons are both stifling and a waste of time. The Rocky Mountains aren't better than the Smoky Mountains. Each is beautiful in its own unique way.

Work It Out
••••

Here are some practical tips for overcoming the "I'm-so-ugly" syndrome:

1. Improve your physical appearance. Ask a parent or a Christian friend to help you think of ways, within reason, to enhance your looks. Take the best advice and go for it. Then relax, knowing you've done all you can do.

2. Most important, work on improving your spiritual appearance (1 Samuel 16:7). Remember that God values inner beauty. Many people who are merely average in physical appearance are incredibly attractive to others. Why? Because these individuals have radiant walks with Christ. They're full of his life, and nothing is more beautiful than that!

Nail It Down
••••

Meditate on Psalm 139:13–14.

**Turn to pages 584, 1029, 1100 and 1379 for other readings on self-esteem.
Turn to page 644 for Wednesday's reading.**

Topic
•••

they would outnumber the grains of
sand.
When I awake,
I am still with you.

19If only you would slay the wicked,
O God!
Away from me, you bloodthirsty men!
20They speak of you with evil intent;
your adversaries misuse your name.
21Do I not hate those who hate you,
O LORD,
and abhor those who rise up against
you?
22I have nothing but hatred for them;
I count them my enemies.

23Search me, O God, and know my heart;
test me and know my anxious
thoughts.
24See if there is any offensive way in me,
and lead me in the way everlasting.

Psalm 140

For the director of music. A psalm
of David.

1Rescue me, O LORD, from evil men;
protect me from men of violence,
2who devise evil plans in their hearts
and stir up war every day.
3They make their tongues as sharp as a
serpent's;
the poison of vipers is on their lips.
Selah

4Keep me, O LORD, from the hands of the
wicked;
protect me from men of violence
who plan to trip my feet.
5Proud men have hidden a snare for me;
they have spread out the cords of
their net
and have set traps for me along my
path.   *Selah*

6O LORD, I say to you, "You are my God."
Hear, O LORD, my cry for mercy.
7O Sovereign LORD, my strong deliverer,
who shields my head in the day of
battle—
8do not grant the wicked their desires,
O LORD;
do not let their plans succeed,
or they will become proud.   *Selah*

9Let the heads of those who surround
me

be covered with the trouble their lips
have caused.
10Let burning coals fall upon them;
may they be thrown into the fire,
into miry pits, never to rise.
11Let slanderers not be established in the
land;
may disaster hunt down men of
violence.

12I know that the LORD secures justice for
the poor
and upholds the cause of the needy.
13Surely the righteous will praise your
name
and the upright will live before you.

Psalm 141

A psalm of David.

1O LORD, I call to you; come quickly to
me.
Hear my voice when I call to you.
2May my prayer be set before you like
incense;
may the lifting up of my hands be
like the evening sacrifice.

3Set a guard over my mouth, O LORD;
keep watch over the door of my lips.
4Let not my heart be drawn to what is
evil,
to take part in wicked deeds
with men who are evildoers;
let me not eat of their delicacies.

5Let a righteous man*a* strike me—it is a
kindness;
let him rebuke me—it is oil on my
head.
My head will not refuse it.

Yet my prayer is ever against the deeds
of evildoers;
6   their rulers will be thrown down from
the cliffs,
and the wicked will learn that my
words were well spoken.
7⌊They will say,⌋ "As one plows and
breaks up the earth,
so our bones have been scattered at
the mouth of the grave.*b*"

8But my eyes are fixed on you,
O Sovereign LORD;
in you I take refuge—do not give me
over to death.
9Keep me from the snares they have laid
for me,

a5 Or *Let the Righteous One*   *b7* Hebrew *Sheol*

from the traps set by evildoers.
¹⁰Let the wicked fall into their own nets,
while I pass by in safety.

Psalm 142

*A maskil[a] of David. When he was in the
cave. A prayer.*

¹I cry aloud to the LORD;
I lift up my voice to the LORD for
mercy.
²I pour out my complaint before him;
before him I tell my trouble.

³When my spirit grows faint within me,
it is you who know my way.
In the path where I walk
men have hidden a snare for me.
⁴Look to my right and see;
no one is concerned for me.
I have no refuge;
no one cares for my life.

⁵I cry to you, O LORD;
I say, "You are my refuge,
my portion in the land of the living."
⁶Listen to my cry,
for I am in desperate need;
rescue me from those who pursue me,
for they are too strong for me.
⁷Set me free from my prison,
that I may praise your name.

Then the righteous will gather about me
because of your goodness to me.

Psalm 143

A psalm of David.

¹O LORD, hear my prayer,
listen to my cry for mercy;
in your faithfulness and righteousness
come to my relief.
²Do not bring your servant into
judgment,
for no one living is righteous before
you.

³The enemy pursues me,
he crushes me to the ground;
he makes me dwell in darkness
like those long dead.
⁴So my spirit grows faint within me;
my heart within me is dismayed.
⁵I remember the days of long ago;
I meditate on all your works

and consider what your hands have
done.
⁶I spread out my hands to you;
my soul thirsts for you like a parched
land.   *Selah*

⁷Answer me quickly, O LORD;
my spirit fails.
Do not hide your face from me
or I will be like those who go down to
the pit.
⁸Let the morning bring me word of your
unfailing love,
for I have put my trust in you.
Show me the way I should go,
for to you I lift up my soul.
⁹Rescue me from my enemies, O LORD,
for I hide myself in you.
¹⁰Teach me to do your will,
for you are my God;
may your good Spirit
lead me on level ground.

¹¹For your name's sake, O LORD, preserve
my life;
in your righteousness, bring me out of
trouble.
¹²In your unfailing love, silence my
enemies;
destroy all my foes,
for I am your servant.

Psalm 144

Of David.

¹Praise be to the LORD my Rock,
who trains my hands for war,
my fingers for battle.
²He is my loving God and my fortress,
my stronghold and my deliverer,
my shield, in whom I take refuge,
who subdues peoples[b] under me.

³O LORD, what is man that you care for
him,
the son of man that you think of him?
⁴Man is like a breath;
his days are like a fleeting shadow.

⁵Part your heavens, O LORD, and come
down;
touch the mountains, so that they
smoke.
⁶Send forth lightning and scatter ⌞the
enemies⌟;
shoot your arrows and rout them.
⁷Reach down your hand from on high;

---

aTitle: Probably a literary or musical term   b2 Many manuscripts of the Masoretic Text, Dead Sea Scrolls,
Aquila, Jerome and Syriac; most manuscripts of the Masoretic Text *subdues my people*

THE MYSTERY IS HISTORY!

Can you relate to this?
Grant is facing some big decisions—where to go to college, what to major in, if he and Susan have any sort of future—and he hasn't got the foggiest idea of what to do. He complains:

"I want to do the right thing, but I'm so confused. I mean, I know God must have some sort of plan for my life, but for some reason, I can't figure out what it is. What if I make the wrong choices? What if I go in the wrong direction? It's kind of scary, because I don't want to end up regretting the decisions I make."

Look It Up
● ● ● ●

Discovering God's will for your life is not like searching for buried treasure in the ocean. His will *can* be known.

Paul urged the Christians in Rome to "be transformed by the renewing of your mind. Then you will be able to test and approve what God's will is—his good, pleasing and perfect will" (Romans 12:2).

Paul also prayed for the believers in Colosse, "asking God to fill [them] with the knowledge of his will through all spiritual wisdom and understanding" (Colossians 1:9).

Obviously, Paul thought it was possible—and essential—to know God's will.

Think It Through
● ● ● ●

Most parents are always giving their kids advice, telling them, "You need to do this" or "If I were in your shoes, I'd do that." Why? Usually because they love their kids and don't want them to make wrong choices.

In a much greater way God loves you and wants the best for you. He isn't just sitting up in heaven, tight-lipped and unwilling to give you guidance when you need it.

Work It Out
● ● ● ●

Why not start off your study of God's will this week with a prayer: "Father in heaven, thank you so much for loving me. Thank you so much for making your will for my life something that I can discover and not some impossible mystery. Teach me about the different ways you lead and guide your children as I look at your Word the next few days. You know I want my life to count for you. You know I want to do your will. Help me through Christ. Amen."

Nail It Down
● ● ● ●

Use the words of Psalm 143:10 to pray for God's leading in your life.

Turn to pages 78, 1286 and 1298 for other readings on God's will.
Turn to page 649 for Thursday's reading.

Topic
● ● ● ●

deliver me and rescue me
from the mighty waters,
from the hands of foreigners
8whose mouths are full of lies,
whose right hands are deceitful.

9I will sing a new song to you, O God;
on the ten-stringed lyre I will make
music to you,
10to the One who gives victory to kings,
who delivers his servant David from
the deadly sword.

11Deliver me and rescue me
from the hands of foreigners
whose mouths are full of lies,
whose right hands are deceitful.

12Then our sons in their youth
will be like well-nurtured plants,
and our daughters will be like pillars
carved to adorn a palace.
13Our barns will be filled
with every kind of provision.
Our sheep will increase by thousands,
by tens of thousands in our fields;
14   our oxen will draw heavy loads.*a*
There will be no breaching of walls,
no going into captivity,
no cry of distress in our streets.

15Blessed are the people of whom this is
true;
blessed are the people whose God is
the LORD.

Psalm 145*b*

A psalm of praise. Of David.

1I will exalt you, my God the King;
I will praise your name for ever and
ever.
2Every day I will praise you
and extol your name for ever and
ever.

3Great is the LORD and most worthy of
praise;
his greatness no one can fathom.
4One generation will commend your
works to another;
they will tell of your mighty acts.
5They will speak of the glorious splendor
of your majesty,

and I will meditate on your wonderful
works.*c*
6They will tell of the power of your
awesome works,
and I will proclaim your great deeds.
7They will celebrate your abundant
goodness
and joyfully sing of your
righteousness.

8The LORD is gracious and compassionate,
slow to anger and rich in love.
9The LORD is good to all;
he has compassion on all he has
made.
10All you have made will praise you,
O LORD;
your saints will extol you.
11They will tell of the glory of your
kingdom
and speak of your might,
12so that all men may know of your
mighty acts
and the glorious splendor of your
kingdom.
13Your kingdom is an everlasting
kingdom,
and your dominion endures through
all generations.

The LORD is faithful to all his promises
and loving toward all he has made.*d*
14The LORD upholds all those who fall
and lifts up all who are bowed down.
15The eyes of all look to you,
and you give them their food at the
proper time.
16You open your hand
and satisfy the desires of every living
thing.

17The LORD is righteous in all his ways
and loving toward all he has made.
18The LORD is near to all who call on him,
to all who call on him in truth.
19He fulfills the desires of those who fear
him;
he hears their cry and saves them.
20The LORD watches over all who love
him,
but all the wicked he will destroy.

21My mouth will speak in praise of the
LORD.

---

a14 Or *our chieftains will be firmly established*   *b*This psalm is an acrostic poem, the verses of which
(including verse 13b) begin with the successive letters of the Hebrew alphabet.   *c5* Dead Sea Scrolls and
Syriac (see also Septuagint); Masoretic Text *On the glorious splendor of your majesty / and on your wonderful
works I will meditate*   *d13* One manuscript of the Masoretic Text, Dead Sea Scrolls and Syriac (see also
Septuagint); most manuscripts of the Masoretic Text do not have the last two lines of verse 13.

Let every creature praise his holy
  name
for ever and ever.

Psalm 146

[1]Praise the LORD.[a]

Praise the LORD, O my soul.
2 I will praise the LORD all my life;
   I will sing praise to my God as long as
     I live.

[3]Do not put your trust in princes,
   in mortal men, who cannot save.
[4]When their spirit departs, they return to
     the ground;
   on that very day their plans come to
     nothing.

[5]Blessed is he whose help is the God of
     Jacob,
   whose hope is in the LORD his God,
[6]the Maker of heaven and earth,
   the sea, and everything in them—
   the LORD, who remains faithful forever.
[7]He upholds the cause of the oppressed
   and gives food to the hungry.
   The LORD sets prisoners free,
8   the LORD gives sight to the blind,
   the LORD lifts up those who are bowed
     down,
   the LORD loves the righteous.
[9]The LORD watches over the alien
   and sustains the fatherless and the
     widow,
   but he frustrates the ways of the
     wicked.

[10]The LORD reigns forever,
   your God, O Zion, for all generations.

Praise the LORD.

Psalm 147

[1]Praise the LORD.[b]

How good it is to sing praises to our
     God,
   how pleasant and fitting to praise
     him!

[2]The LORD builds up Jerusalem;
   he gathers the exiles of Israel.
[3]He heals the brokenhearted
   and binds up their wounds.

[4]He determines the number of the stars
   and calls them each by name.

[5]Great is our Lord and mighty in power;
   his understanding has no limit.
[6]The LORD sustains the humble
   but casts the wicked to the ground.

[7]Sing to the LORD with thanksgiving;
   make music to our God on the harp.
[8]He covers the sky with clouds;
   he supplies the earth with rain
   and makes grass grow on the hills.
[9]He provides food for the cattle
   and for the young ravens when they
     call.

[10]His pleasure is not in the strength of the
     horse,
   nor his delight in the legs of a man;
[11]the LORD delights in those who fear him,
   who put their hope in his unfailing
     love.

[12]Extol the LORD, O Jerusalem;
   praise your God, O Zion,
[13]for he strengthens the bars of your
     gates
   and blesses your people within you.
[14]He grants peace to your borders
   and satisfies you with the finest of
     wheat.

[15]He sends his command to the earth;
   his word runs swiftly.
[16]He spreads the snow like wool
   and scatters the frost like ashes.
[17]He hurls down his hail like pebbles.
   Who can withstand his icy blast?
[18]He sends his word and melts them;
   he stirs up his breezes, and the
     waters flow.

[19]He has revealed his word to Jacob,
   his laws and decrees to Israel.
[20]He has done this for no other nation;
   they do not know his laws.

Praise the LORD.

Psalm 148

[1]Praise the LORD.[c]

Praise the LORD from the heavens,
   praise him in the heights above.
[2]Praise him, all his angels,
   praise him, all his heavenly hosts.
[3]Praise him, sun and moon,
   praise him, all you shining stars.
[4]Praise him, you highest heavens
   and you waters above the skies.
[5]Let them praise the name of the LORD,

---

[a]1 Hebrew *Hallelu Yah*; also in verse 10   [b]1 Hebrew *Hallelu Yah*; also in verse 20   [c]1 Hebrew *Hallelu Yah*;
also in verse 14

for he commanded and they were
created.
6He set them in place for ever and ever;
he gave a decree that will never pass
away.

7Praise the LORD from the earth,
you great sea creatures and all ocean
depths,
8lightning and hail, snow and clouds,
stormy winds that do his bidding,
9you mountains and all hills,
fruit trees and all cedars,
10wild animals and all cattle,
small creatures and flying birds,
11kings of the earth and all nations,
you princes and all rulers on earth,
12young men and maidens,
old men and children.

13Let them praise the name of the LORD,
for his name alone is exalted;
his splendor is above the earth and
the heavens.
14He has raised up for his people a
horn,*a*
the praise of all his saints,
of Israel, the people close to his heart.

Praise the LORD.

Psalm 149

1Praise the LORD.*b*

Sing to the LORD a new song,
his praise in the assembly of the
saints.
2Let Israel rejoice in their Maker;
let the people of Zion be glad in their
King.
3Let them praise his name with dancing

and make music to him with
tambourine and harp.
4For the LORD takes delight in his people;
he crowns the humble with salvation.
5Let the saints rejoice in this honor
and sing for joy on their beds.

6May the praise of God be in their
mouths
and a double-edged sword in their
hands,
7to inflict vengeance on the nations
and punishment on the peoples,
8to bind their kings with fetters,
their nobles with shackles of iron,
9to carry out the sentence written against
them.
This is the glory of all his saints.

Praise the LORD.

Psalm 150

1Praise the LORD.*c*

Praise God in his sanctuary;
praise him in his mighty heavens.
2Praise him for his acts of power;
praise him for his surpassing
greatness.
3Praise him with the sounding of the
trumpet,
praise him with the harp and lyre,
4praise him with tambourine and
dancing,
praise him with the strings and flute,
5praise him with the clash of cymbals,
praise him with resounding cymbals.

6Let everything that has breath praise the
LORD.

Praise the LORD.

---

a14 Horn here symbolizes strong one, that is, king.   *b1* Hebrew *Hallelu Yah*; also in verse 9   *c1* Hebrew
Hallelu Yah; also in verse 6

PROVERBS

WRITTEN primarily by Solomon, Proverbs is an inspired collection of practical, wise sayings that touch on every age group and all relationships. Their fundamental instruction is: Fear and trust the Lord, seeking his wisdom in every decision, and he will steer you in the right direction. If you want to find God's solutions for the problems you face, Proverbs is a good place to begin.

Prologue: Purpose and Theme

1 The proverbs of Solomon son of David, king of Israel:

²for attaining wisdom and discipline;
for understanding words of insight;
³for acquiring a disciplined and prudent life,
doing what is right and just and fair;
⁴for giving prudence to the simple,
knowledge and discretion to the young —
⁵let the wise listen and add to their learning,
and let the discerning get guidance —
⁶for understanding proverbs and parables,
the sayings and riddles of the wise.

⁷The fear of the LORD is the beginning of knowledge,
but fools^a despise wisdom and discipline.

---

^{a}7 The Hebrew words rendered *fool* in Proverbs, and often elsewhere in the Old Testament, denote one who is morally deficient.

WONDERING ABOUT WISDOM

Bob goofed off in school so much during the past six weeks that he ended up flunking chemistry. After school he tried talking to his teacher, Mrs. Mellish, but she said there was nothing to discuss. Really ticked off, Bob jumped in his car and spun out of the parking lot—right into a ditch!

Look at what he's facing now: a failing grade, being dropped from the baseball team, an angry father, snickering classmates, a huge car repair bill and higher car insurance rates.

Bob needs wisdom, wouldn't you say?

Look It Up
••••

Some answers to your basic questions about wisdom:

Q: Where can we get ultimate wisdom?

A: From God. "For the LORD gives wisdom, and from his mouth come knowledge and understanding" (Proverbs 2:6).

Q: Who can have wisdom?

A: Anyone. "Does not wisdom call out? . . . To you, O men, I call out; I raise my voice to all mankind" (Proverbs 8:1,4).

Q: Is wisdom easy to get?

A: No. Becoming wise involves diligent searching (Proverbs 2:1–5).

Q: Why should we pursue wisdom?

A: Because it is extremely valuable (Proverbs 3:13–18) and can save you from making huge mistakes (Proverbs 4:5–6).

Think It Through
••••

Did you notice all these verses are found in the same Biblical book? Proverbs is probably the most practical book in the Old Testament. It contains hundreds of short sayings that are crammed with wise advice. What's the overall topic? Living for God in an ungodly world.

Hey, if you need wisdom, Proverbs is the place to go!

Work It Out
••••

Here's a prayer for the week:

"Lord, I need wisdom. I'm not facing exactly what Bob faces, but I do need understanding in order to deal with _____. Work in my life this week. Change me. Show me how to live skillfully for you. Amen."

(If you want an extra challenge, make the commitment to read through the 31 chapters of Proverbs this month. A chapter a day may just keep foolishness away!)

Nail It Down
••••

Read about the purpose of Proverbs in Proverbs 1:1–6.

Turn to pages 336 and 798 for other readings on wisdom.
Turn to page 654 for Friday's reading.

Topic
••••

Exhortations to Embrace Wisdom

Warning Against Enticement

8Listen, my son, to your father's
  instruction
  and do not forsake your mother's
  teaching.
9They will be a garland to grace your
  head
  and a chain to adorn your neck.

10My son, if sinners entice you,
  do not give in to them.
11If they say, "Come along with us;
  let's lie in wait for someone's blood,
  let's waylay some harmless soul;
12let's swallow them alive, like the
  grave,*a*
  and whole, like those who go down to
  the pit;
13we will get all sorts of valuable things
  and fill our houses with plunder;
14throw in your lot with us,
  and we will share a common
  purse"—
15my son, do not go along with them,
  do not set foot on their paths;
16for their feet rush into sin,
  they are swift to shed blood.
17How useless to spread a net
  in full view of all the birds!
18These men lie in wait for their own
  blood;
  they waylay only themselves!
19Such is the end of all who go after
  ill-gotten gain;
  it takes away the lives of those who
  get it.

Warning Against Rejecting Wisdom

20Wisdom calls aloud in the street,
  she raises her voice in the public
  squares;
21at the head of the noisy streets*b* she
  cries out,
  in the gateways of the city she makes
  her speech:

22"How long will you simple ones*c* love
  your simple ways?
  How long will mockers delight in
  mockery
  and fools hate knowledge?
23If you had responded to my rebuke,
  I would have poured out my heart to
  you
  and made my thoughts known to you.

24But since you rejected me when I called
  and no one gave heed when I
  stretched out my hand,
25since you ignored all my advice
  and would not accept my rebuke,
26I in turn will laugh at your disaster;
  I will mock when calamity overtakes
  you—
27when calamity overtakes you like a
  storm,
  when disaster sweeps over you like a
  whirlwind,
  when distress and trouble overwhelm
  you.

28"Then they will call to me but I will not
  answer;
  they will look for me but will not find
  me.
29Since they hated knowledge
  and did not choose to fear the Lord,
30since they would not accept my advice
  and spurned my rebuke,
31they will eat the fruit of their ways
  and be filled with the fruit of their
  schemes.
32For the waywardness of the simple will
  kill them,
  and the complacency of fools will
  destroy them;
33but whoever listens to me will live in
  safety
  and be at ease, without fear of harm."

Moral Benefits of Wisdom

2 My son, if you accept my words
  and store up my commands within
  you,
2turning your ear to wisdom
  and applying your heart to
  understanding,
3and if you call out for insight
  and cry aloud for understanding,
4and if you look for it as for silver
  and search for it as for hidden
  treasure,
5then you will understand the fear of the
  Lord
  and find the knowledge of God.
6For the Lord gives wisdom,
  and from his mouth come knowledge
  and understanding.
7He holds victory in store for the upright,
  he is a shield to those whose walk is
  blameless,
8for he guards the course of the just

---

a12 Hebrew *Sheol*   *b21* Hebrew; Septuagint / *on the tops of the walls*   *c22* The Hebrew word rendered
simple in Proverbs generally denotes one without moral direction and inclined to evil.

and protects the way of his faithful ones.

⁹Then you will understand what is right and just
and fair—every good path.
¹⁰For wisdom will enter your heart,
and knowledge will be pleasant to your soul.
¹¹Discretion will protect you,
and understanding will guard you.

¹²Wisdom will save you from the ways of wicked men,
from men whose words are perverse,
¹³who leave the straight paths
to walk in dark ways,
¹⁴who delight in doing wrong
and rejoice in the perverseness of evil,
¹⁵whose paths are crooked
and who are devious in their ways.

¹⁶It will save you also from the adulteress,
from the wayward wife with her seductive words,
¹⁷who has left the partner of her youth
and ignored the covenant she made before God. ᵃ
¹⁸For her house leads down to death
and her paths to the spirits of the dead.
¹⁹None who go to her return
or attain the paths of life.

²⁰Thus you will walk in the ways of good men
and keep to the paths of the righteous.
²¹For the upright will live in the land,
and the blameless will remain in it;
²²but the wicked will be cut off from the land,
and the unfaithful will be torn from it.

Further Benefits of Wisdom

3 My son, do not forget my teaching,
but keep my commands in your heart,
²for they will prolong your life many years
and bring you prosperity.

³Let love and faithfulness never leave you;
bind them around your neck,
write them on the tablet of your heart.

⁴Then you will win favor and a good name
in the sight of God and man.
⁵Trust in the LORD with all your heart
and lean not on your own understanding;
⁶in all your ways acknowledge him,
and he will make your paths straight. ᵇ
⁷Do not be wise in your own eyes;
fear the LORD and shun evil.
⁸This will bring health to your body
and nourishment to your bones.

⁹Honor the LORD with your wealth,
with the firstfruits of all your crops;
¹⁰then your barns will be filled to overflowing,
and your vats will brim over with new wine.

¹¹My son, do not despise the LORD's discipline
and do not resent his rebuke,
¹²because the LORD disciplines those he loves,
as a fatherᶜ the son he delights in.

¹³Blessed is the man who finds wisdom,
the man who gains understanding,
¹⁴for she is more profitable than silver
and yields better returns than gold.
¹⁵She is more precious than rubies;
nothing you desire can compare with her.
¹⁶Long life is in her right hand;
in her left hand are riches and honor.
¹⁷Her ways are pleasant ways,
and all her paths are peace.
¹⁸She is a tree of life to those who embrace her;
those who lay hold of her will be blessed.

¹⁹By wisdom the LORD laid the earth's foundations,
by understanding he set the heavens in place;
²⁰by his knowledge the deeps were divided,
and the clouds let drop the dew.

²¹My son, preserve sound judgment and discernment,
do not let them out of your sight;
²²they will be life for you,
an ornament to grace your neck.
²³Then you will go on your way in safety,

ᵃ17 Or covenant of her God   ᵇ6 Or will direct your paths   ᶜ12 Hebrew; Septuagint / and he punishes

and your foot will not stumble;
²⁴when you lie down, you will not be
afraid;
when you lie down, your sleep will be
sweet.
²⁵Have no fear of sudden disaster
or of the ruin that overtakes the
wicked,
²⁶for the LORD will be your confidence
and will keep your foot from being
snared.

²⁷Do not withhold good from those who
deserve it,
when it is in your power to act.
²⁸Do not say to your neighbor,
"Come back later; I'll give it
tomorrow"—
when you now have it with you.

²⁹Do not plot harm against your neighbor,
who lives trustfully near you.
³⁰Do not accuse a man for no reason—
when he has done you no harm.

³¹Do not envy a violent man
or choose any of his ways,
³²for the LORD detests a perverse man
but takes the upright into his
confidence.

³³The LORD's curse is on the house of the
wicked,
but he blesses the home of the
righteous.
³⁴He mocks proud mockers
but gives grace to the humble.
³⁵The wise inherit honor,
but fools he holds up to shame.

Wisdom Is Supreme

4 Listen, my sons, to a father's
instruction;
pay attention and gain understanding.
²I give you sound learning,
so do not forsake my teaching.
³When I was a boy in my father's house,
still tender, and an only child of my
mother,
⁴he taught me and said,
"Lay hold of my words with all your
heart;
keep my commands and you will live.
⁵Get wisdom, get understanding;
do not forget my words or swerve
from them.
⁶Do not forsake wisdom, and she will
protect you;
love her, and she will watch over you.

⁷Wisdom is supreme; therefore get
wisdom.
Though it cost all you have,^a get
understanding.
⁸Esteem her, and she will exalt you;
embrace her, and she will honor you.
⁹She will set a garland of grace on your
head
and present you with a crown of
splendor."

¹⁰Listen, my son, accept what I say,
and the years of your life will be
many.
¹¹I guide you in the way of wisdom
and lead you along straight paths.
¹²When you walk, your steps will not be
hampered;
when you run, you will not stumble.
¹³Hold on to instruction, do not let it go;
guard it well, for it is your life.
¹⁴Do not set foot on the path of the
wicked
or walk in the way of evil men.
¹⁵Avoid it, do not travel on it;
turn from it and go on your way.
¹⁶For they cannot sleep till they do evil;
they are robbed of slumber till they
make someone fall.
¹⁷They eat the bread of wickedness
and drink the wine of violence.
¹⁸The path of the righteous is like the first
gleam of dawn,
shining ever brighter till the full light
of day.
¹⁹But the way of the wicked is like deep
darkness;
they do not know what makes them
stumble.

²⁰My son, pay attention to what I say;
listen closely to my words.
²¹Do not let them out of your sight,
keep them within your heart;
²²for they are life to those who find them
and health to a man's whole body.
²³Above all else, guard your heart,
for it is the wellspring of life.
²⁴Put away perversity from your mouth;
keep corrupt talk far from your lips.
²⁵Let your eyes look straight ahead,
fix your gaze directly before you.
²⁶Make level^b paths for your feet
and take only ways that are firm.
²⁷Do not swerve to the right or the left;
keep your foot from evil.

^a7 Or *Whatever else you get*   ^b26 Or *Consider the*

Warning Against Adultery

5 My son, pay attention to my wisdom,
   listen well to my words of insight,
[2]that you may maintain discretion
   and your lips may preserve
      knowledge.
[3]For the lips of an adulteress drip honey,
   and her speech is smoother than oil;
[4]but in the end she is bitter as gall,
   sharp as a double-edged sword.
[5]Her feet go down to death;
   her steps lead straight to the grave.[a]
[6]She gives no thought to the way of life;
   her paths are crooked, but she knows
      it not.

[7]Now then, my sons, listen to me;
   do not turn aside from what I say.
[8]Keep to a path far from her,
   do not go near the door of her house,
[9]lest you give your best strength to
      others
   and your years to one who is cruel,
[10]lest strangers feast on your wealth
   and your toil enrich another man's
      house.
[11]At the end of your life you will groan,
   when your flesh and body are spent.
[12]You will say, "How I hated discipline!
   How my heart spurned correction!
[13]I would not obey my teachers
   or listen to my instructors.
[14]I have come to the brink of utter ruin
   in the midst of the whole assembly."

[15]Drink water from your own cistern,
   running water from your own well.
[16]Should your springs overflow in the
      streets,
   your streams of water in the public
      squares?
[17]Let them be yours alone,
   never to be shared with strangers.
[18]May your fountain be blessed,
   and may you rejoice in the wife of
      your youth.
[19]A loving doe, a graceful deer—
   may her breasts satisfy you always,
   may you ever be captivated by her
      love.
[20]Why be captivated, my son, by an
      adulteress?
   Why embrace the bosom of another
      man's wife?

[21]For a man's ways are in full view of the
      Lord,
   and he examines all his paths.

[22]The evil deeds of a wicked man ensnare
      him;
   the cords of his sin hold him fast.
[23]He will die for lack of discipline,
   led astray by his own great folly.

Warnings Against Folly

6 My son, if you have put up security
   for your neighbor,
   if you have struck hands in pledge for
      another,
[2]if you have been trapped by what you
      said,
   ensnared by the words of your
      mouth,
[3]then do this, my son, to free yourself,
   since you have fallen into your
      neighbor's hands:
   Go and humble yourself;
   press your plea with your neighbor!
[4]Allow no sleep to your eyes,
   no slumber to your eyelids.
[5]Free yourself, like a gazelle from the
      hand of the hunter,
   like a bird from the snare of the
      fowler.

[6]Go to the ant, you sluggard;
   consider its ways and be wise!
[7]It has no commander,
   no overseer or ruler,
[8]yet it stores its provisions in summer
   and gathers its food at harvest.

[9]How long will you lie there, you
      sluggard?
   When will you get up from your
      sleep?
[10]A little sleep, a little slumber,
   a little folding of the hands to rest—
[11]and poverty will come on you like a
      bandit
   and scarcity like an armed man.[b]

[12]A scoundrel and villain,
   who goes about with a corrupt mouth,
[13] who winks with his eye,
   signals with his feet
   and motions with his fingers,
[14] who plots evil with deceit in his
      heart—
   he always stirs up dissension.
[15]Therefore disaster will overtake him in
      an instant;
   he will suddenly be
      destroyed—without remedy.

[16]There are six things the Lord hates,
   seven that are detestable to him:

---

[a]5 Hebrew *Sheol*   [b]11 Or *like a vagrant / and scarcity like a beggar*

WHY IT'S WISEST TO WAIT

• •

After her honeymoon with Steve, twenty-three-year-old Paula is talking with some of the girls in her high school Bible study group.

"Was it hard to wait? You better believe it! The temptations were incredible, and it would have been so easy to rationalize, 'We'll be married in a few days.' But because we held out, we had no reason to feel guilty or weird on our wedding night. Hey, the world may mock virginity, but I know a lot of people who wish they had waited. I don't know any who wish they hadn't."

Look It Up
• • • •

After citing the dangers of sex outside of marriage, the writer of Proverbs expounds on the blessings of sex within marriage:

> Drink water from your own cistern,
>   running water from your own well.
> May your fountain be blessed,
>   and may you rejoice in the wife of your youth.
> A loving doe, a graceful deer . . .
>   may you ever be captivated by her love.
> Why be captivated, my son, by an adulteress?
> Why embrace the bosom of another man's
>   wife?
> For a man's ways are in full view of the LORD,
>   and he examines all his paths (Proverbs
>   5:15,18–21).

In short, waiting until marriage for sex will bring long-term physical and emotional satisfaction, plus the spiritual benefit of a life that is pleasing to God.

Think It Through
• • • •

First, consider the following poem that a brokenhearted woman once sent to newspaper columnist Ann Landers:

> I met him; I liked him.
> I liked him; I loved him.
> I loved him; I let him.
> I let him; I lost him.

Second, reflect on this statement: "There is only one first time. Once you give away your virginity, you can never, ever get it back."

Work It Out
• • • •

Buy (and begin reading) any of the excellent Christian books that have been written recently on the subject of sex. Maybe you could even get some friends together and do a group study.

Nail It Down
• • • •

Read the warning against adultery in Proverbs 5:1–14.

Turn to pages 124, 705 and 1237 for other readings on sex.
Turn to page 656 for the weekend reading.

Topic
• • • •

17   haughty eyes,
      a lying tongue,
      hands that shed innocent blood,
18   a heart that devises wicked
      schemes,
      feet that are quick to rush into evil,
19   a false witness who pours out lies
      and a man who stirs up dissension
      among brothers.

Warning Against Adultery

20My son, keep your father's commands
    and do not forsake your mother's
    teaching.
21Bind them upon your heart forever;
    fasten them around your neck.
22When you walk, they will guide you;
    when you sleep, they will watch over
    you;
    when you awake, they will speak to
    you.
23For these commands are a lamp,
    this teaching is a light,
  and the corrections of discipline
    are the way to life,
24keeping you from the immoral woman,
    from the smooth tongue of the
    wayward wife.
25Do not lust in your heart after her
    beauty
  or let her captivate you with her eyes,
26for the prostitute reduces you to a loaf
    of bread,
    and the adulteress preys upon your
    very life.
27Can a man scoop fire into his lap
    without his clothes being burned?
28Can a man walk on hot coals
    without his feet being scorched?
29So is he who sleeps with another man's
    wife;
    no one who touches her will go
    unpunished.

30Men do not despise a thief if he steals
    to satisfy his hunger when he is
    starving.
31Yet if he is caught, he must pay
    sevenfold,
    though it costs him all the wealth of
    his house.
32But a man who commits adultery lacks
    judgment;
    whoever does so destroys himself.
33Blows and disgrace are his lot,
    and his shame will never be wiped
    away;

34for jealousy arouses a husband's fury,
    and he will show no mercy when he
    takes revenge.
35He will not accept any compensation;
    he will refuse the bribe, however
    great it is.

Warning Against the Adulteress

7 My son, keep my words
    and store up my commands within
    you.
2Keep my commands and you will live;
    guard my teachings as the apple of
    your eye.
3Bind them on your fingers;
    write them on the tablet of your
    heart.
4Say to wisdom, "You are my sister,"
    and call understanding your kinsman;
5they will keep you from the adulteress,
    from the wayward wife with her
    seductive words.

6At the window of my house
    I looked out through the lattice.
7I saw among the simple,
    I noticed among the young men,
    a youth who lacked judgment.
8He was going down the street near her
    corner,
    walking along in the direction of her
    house
9at twilight, as the day was fading,
    as the dark of night set in.
10Then out came a woman to meet him,
    dressed like a prostitute and with
    crafty intent.
11(She is loud and defiant,
    her feet never stay at home;
12now in the street, now in the squares,
    at every corner she lurks.)
13She took hold of him and kissed him
    and with a brazen face she said:

14"I have fellowship offerings*a* at home;
    today I fulfilled my vows.
15So I came out to meet you;
    I looked for you and have found you!
16I have covered my bed
    with colored linens from Egypt.
17I have perfumed my bed
    with myrrh, aloes and cinnamon.
18Come, let's drink deep of love till
    morning;
    let's enjoy ourselves with love!
19My husband is not at home;
    he has gone on a long journey.

a14 Traditionally peace offerings

WHAT YOU LEARN (OR DON'T LEARN) AT HOME

Work It Out
····

Think about this for a moment: What is the one thing your mom or dad tells you to do most frequently? Is it, "Make your bed"? Or "Be careful with the car"? Or "Leave your brother/sister alone"?

Who you are has a lot to do with where you come from. What you learn (or don't learn) at home affects how you act when you're away from home and will have an enormous impact on your actions as an adult.

There's just no getting away from it. The teachings of the home affect every part of life. Home is where you learn that burping in public is not acceptable behavior (some of you probably do it anyway, right?). Home is where you learn that beating on your sister doesn't solve any problems (besides, God says murder is out!). Home is where you learn that accomplishing anything worthwhile takes work (that's why you stay up late to get ready for your exam in physics).

All your parents' suggestions, rules and commands were designed to prepare you to handle life on your own. How are you doing?

Nail It Down
····

Read Proverbs 6:20–23 for what that writer thought you should do with what you learned at home.

Think It Through
····

How often have you gotten angry with your parents when you were told, "Do this," or "Don't do that"? Most of you get irritated at least some of the time when adults try to control your life. Those feelings are pretty natural. You're almost an adult yourself.

However, next time you feel out of sorts and ornery when told what to do and when to do it and how to do it . . . take a deep breath and try to remember just what your parents are trying to accomplish: acceptable behavior and a satisfactory lifestyle when you get to adulthood. Don't be quick to turn your back on what you were taught when you were young and what you're being taught even now.

Nail It Down
····

Reread Proverbs 6:20–23. For further insight read Ecclesiastes 12:1.

Turn to pages 947 and 1032 for other readings on behavior.
Turn to page 658 for Monday's reading.

Topic
····

BEHAVIOR

20He took his purse filled with money
　and will not be home till full moon."

21With persuasive words she led him
　　astray;
　she seduced him with her smooth
　　talk.
22All at once he followed her
　like an ox going to the slaughter,
　like a deer[a] stepping into a noose[b]
23　till an arrow pierces his liver,
　like a bird darting into a snare,
　　little knowing it will cost him his life.

24Now then, my sons, listen to me;
　pay attention to what I say.
25Do not let your heart turn to her ways
　or stray into her paths.
26Many are the victims she has brought
　　down;
　her slain are a mighty throng.
27Her house is a highway to the grave,[c]
　leading down to the chambers of
　　death.

Wisdom's Call

8 Does not wisdom call out?
　Does not understanding raise her
　　voice?
2On the heights along the way,
　where the paths meet, she takes her
　　stand;
3beside the gates leading into the city,
　at the entrances, she cries aloud:
4"To you, O men, I call out;
　I raise my voice to all mankind.
5You who are simple, gain prudence;
　you who are foolish, gain
　　understanding.
6Listen, for I have worthy things to say;
　I open my lips to speak what is right.
7My mouth speaks what is true,
　for my lips detest wickedness.
8All the words of my mouth are just;
　none of them is crooked or perverse.
9To the discerning all of them are right;
　they are faultless to those who have
　　knowledge.
10Choose my instruction instead of silver,
　knowledge rather than choice gold,
11for wisdom is more precious than
　　rubies,
　and nothing you desire can compare
　　with her.

12"I, wisdom, dwell together with
　　prudence;
　I possess knowledge and discretion.
13To fear the LORD is to hate evil;
　I hate pride and arrogance,
　　evil behavior and perverse speech.
14Counsel and sound judgment are mine;
　I have understanding and power.
15By me kings reign
　and rulers make laws that are just;
16by me princes govern,
　and all nobles who rule on earth.[d]
17I love those who love me,
　and those who seek me find me.
18With me are riches and honor,
　enduring wealth and prosperity.
19My fruit is better than fine gold;
　what I yield surpasses choice silver.
20I walk in the way of righteousness,
　along the paths of justice,
21bestowing wealth on those who love me
　and making their treasuries full.

22"The LORD brought me forth as the first
　　of his works,[e][f]
　before his deeds of old;
23I was appointed[g] from eternity,
　from the beginning, before the world
　　began.
24When there were no oceans, I was
　　given birth,
　when there were no springs
　　abounding with water;
25before the mountains were settled in
　　place,
　before the hills, I was given birth,
26before he made the earth or its fields
　or any of the dust of the world.
27I was there when he set the heavens in
　　place,
　when he marked out the horizon on
　　the face of the deep,
28when he established the clouds above
　and fixed securely the fountains of
　　the deep,
29when he gave the sea its boundary
　　so the waters would not overstep his
　　command,
　and when he marked out the
　　foundations of the earth.
30　Then I was the craftsman at his side.
　I was filled with delight day after day,
　rejoicing always in his presence,
31rejoicing in his whole world
　and delighting in mankind.

---

a22 Syriac (see also Septuagint); Hebrew *fool*　　b22 The meaning of the Hebrew for this line is uncertain.
c27 Hebrew *Sheol*　　d16 Many Hebrew manuscripts and Septuagint; most Hebrew manuscripts *and
nobles—all righteous rulers*　　e22 Or *way*; or *dominion*　　f22 Or *The LORD possessed me at the beginning of
his work*; or *The LORD brought me forth at the beginning of his work*　　g23 Or *fashioned*

THE GOOD NEWS ABOUT TEMPTATION

Keith, fifteen, has a problem with lust. As a Christian, he feels really guilty when he yields to this temptation. He's prayed about his problem, has read everything he can find on the topic and has seriously vowed to stop; but nothing seems to work.

"What can I do to make this temptation go away?"

Look It Up

The bad news is that, in this life, we will always face temptation. The good news is that we can avoid some temptations and we can flee all the rest.

Remember Joseph? When his master's wife begged him to sleep with her, notice his reaction:

"And though she spoke to Joseph day after day, he refused to go to bed with her or even be with her.

"One day he went into the house to attend to his duties, and none of the household servants was inside. She caught him by his cloak and said, 'Come to bed with me!' But he left his cloak in her hand and ran out of the house" (Genesis 39:10–12).

As much as possible, Joseph avoided his master's wife. And when she cornered him, he literally ran away!

Think It Through

Why is it important to stop temptations in their tracks? Because temptations are like stray cats—feed one, and it will soon return with all its friends!

Do *you* avoid tempting situations? When you find yourself in a potentially dangerous situation, do you immediately run the other way (2 Timothy 2:22)?

Work It Out

If you are tempted to:

Lust—avoid certain movies, magazines and TV shows. (Note: Keith doesn't do this! He sees almost every movie that comes out; no wonder his hormones give him so much trouble!)

Be sexually involved—go on group dates and avoid dark, secluded places.

Cheat at school—study hard and then sit by yourself.

Drink—stay away from parties and other places where alcohol is served.

Be materialistic—don't go to the mall.

Part of the solution to temptation is just using common sense!

Nail It Down

Read Proverbs 7:6–27 for the wrong way to respond to temptation.

Turn to pages 420, 1290, 1315, 1341 and 1356 for other readings on temptation.
Turn to page 663 for Tuesday's reading.

Topic

TEMPTATION

32"Now then, my sons, listen to me;
  blessed are those who keep my ways.
33Listen to my instruction and be wise;
  do not ignore it.
34Blessed is the man who listens to me,
  watching daily at my doors,
  waiting at my doorway.
35For whoever finds me finds life
  and receives favor from the LORD.
36But whoever fails to find me harms
  himself;
  all who hate me love death."

Invitations of Wisdom and of Folly

9 Wisdom has built her house;
  she has hewn out its seven pillars.
2She has prepared her meat and mixed
  her wine;
  she has also set her table.
3She has sent out her maids, and she
  calls
  from the highest point of the city.
4"Let all who are simple come in here!"
  she says to those who lack judgment.
5"Come, eat my food
  and drink the wine I have mixed.
6Leave your simple ways and you will
  live;
  walk in the way of understanding.

7"Whoever corrects a mocker invites
  insult;
  whoever rebukes a wicked man incurs
  abuse.
8Do not rebuke a mocker or he will hate
  you;
  rebuke a wise man and he will love
  you.
9Instruct a wise man and he will be
  wiser still;
  teach a righteous man and he will
  add to his learning.

10"The fear of the LORD is the beginning of
  wisdom,
  and knowledge of the Holy One is
  understanding.
11For through me your days will be many,
  and years will be added to your life.
12If you are wise, your wisdom will
  reward you;
  if you are a mocker, you alone will
  suffer."

13The woman Folly is loud;
  she is undisciplined and without
  knowledge.
14She sits at the door of her house,
on a seat at the highest point of the
  city,
15calling out to those who pass by,
  who go straight on their way.
16"Let all who are simple come in here!"
  she says to those who lack judgment.
17"Stolen water is sweet;
  food eaten in secret is delicious!"
18But little do they know that the dead
  are there,
  that her guests are in the depths of
  the grave.*a*

Proverbs of Solomon

10 The proverbs of Solomon:

  A wise son brings joy to his father,
  but a foolish son grief to his mother.

2Ill-gotten treasures are of no value,
  but righteousness delivers from death.

3The LORD does not let the righteous go
  hungry
  but he thwarts the craving of the
  wicked.

4Lazy hands make a man poor,
  but diligent hands bring wealth.

5He who gathers crops in summer is a
  wise son,
  but he who sleeps during harvest is a
  disgraceful son.

6Blessings crown the head of the
  righteous,
  but violence overwhelms the mouth
  of the wicked.*b*

7The memory of the righteous will be a
  blessing,
  but the name of the wicked will rot.

8The wise in heart accept commands,
  but a chattering fool comes to ruin.

9The man of integrity walks securely,
  but he who takes crooked paths will
  be found out.

10He who winks maliciously causes grief,
  and a chattering fool comes to ruin.

11The mouth of the righteous is a
  fountain of life,
  but violence overwhelms the mouth
  of the wicked.

12Hatred stirs up dissension,
  but love covers over all wrongs.

---

a18 Hebrew *Sheol*   *b6* Or *but the mouth of the wicked conceals violence*; also in verse 11

¹³Wisdom is found on the lips of the
  discerning,
    but a rod is for the back of him who
    lacks judgment.

¹⁴Wise men store up knowledge,
    but the mouth of a fool invites ruin.

¹⁵The wealth of the rich is their fortified
  city,
    but poverty is the ruin of the poor.

¹⁶The wages of the righteous bring them
  life,
    but the income of the wicked brings
    them punishment.

¹⁷He who heeds discipline shows the way
  to life,
    but whoever ignores correction leads
    others astray.

¹⁸He who conceals his hatred has lying
  lips,
    and whoever spreads slander is a fool.

¹⁹When words are many, sin is not
  absent,
    but he who holds his tongue is wise.

²⁰The tongue of the righteous is choice
  silver,
    but the heart of the wicked is of little
    value.

²¹The lips of the righteous nourish many,
    but fools die for lack of judgment.

²²The blessing of the Lord brings wealth,
    and he adds no trouble to it.

²³A fool finds pleasure in evil conduct,
    but a man of understanding delights
    in wisdom.

²⁴What the wicked dreads will overtake
  him;
    what the righteous desire will be
    granted.

²⁵When the storm has swept by, the
  wicked are gone,
    but the righteous stand firm forever.

²⁶As vinegar to the teeth and smoke to
  the eyes,
    so is a sluggard to those who send
    him.

²⁷The fear of the Lord adds length to life,
    but the years of the wicked are cut
    short.

²⁸The prospect of the righteous is joy,
    but the hopes of the wicked come to
    nothing.

²⁹The way of the Lord is a refuge for the
  righteous,
    but it is the ruin of those who do evil.

³⁰The righteous will never be uprooted,
    but the wicked will not remain in the
    land.

³¹The mouth of the righteous brings forth
  wisdom,
    but a perverse tongue will be cut out.

³²The lips of the righteous know what is
  fitting,
    but the mouth of the wicked only
    what is perverse.

11 The Lord abhors dishonest scales,
    but accurate weights are his
    delight.

²When pride comes, then comes
  disgrace,
    but with humility comes wisdom.

³The integrity of the upright guides them,
    but the unfaithful are destroyed by
    their duplicity.

⁴Wealth is worthless in the day of wrath,
    but righteousness delivers from death.

⁵The righteousness of the blameless
    makes a straight way for them,
    but the wicked are brought down by
    their own wickedness.

⁶The righteousness of the upright
  delivers them,
    but the unfaithful are trapped by evil
    desires.

⁷When a wicked man dies, his hope
  perishes;
    all he expected from his power comes
    to nothing.

⁸The righteous man is rescued from
  trouble,
    and it comes on the wicked instead.

⁹With his mouth the godless destroys his
  neighbor,
    but through knowledge the righteous
    escape.

¹⁰When the righteous prosper, the city
  rejoices;
    when the wicked perish, there are
    shouts of joy.

¹¹Through the blessing of the upright a
  city is exalted,
    but by the mouth of the wicked it is
    destroyed.

¹²A man who lacks judgment derides his
    neighbor,
  but a man of understanding holds his
    tongue.

¹³A gossip betrays a confidence,
  but a trustworthy man keeps a secret.

¹⁴For lack of guidance a nation falls,
  but many advisers make victory sure.

¹⁵He who puts up security for another will
    surely suffer,
  but whoever refuses to strike hands in
    pledge is safe.

¹⁶A kindhearted woman gains respect,
  but ruthless men gain only wealth.

¹⁷A kind man benefits himself,
  but a cruel man brings trouble on
    himself.

¹⁸The wicked man earns deceptive wages,
  but he who sows righteousness reaps
    a sure reward.

¹⁹The truly righteous man attains life,
  but he who pursues evil goes to his
    death.

²⁰The LORD detests men of perverse heart
  but he delights in those whose ways
    are blameless.

²¹Be sure of this: The wicked will not go
    unpunished,
  but those who are righteous will go
    free.

²²Like a gold ring in a pig's snout
  is a beautiful woman who shows no
    discretion.

²³The desire of the righteous ends only in
    good,
  but the hope of the wicked only in
    wrath.

²⁴One man gives freely, yet gains even
    more;
  another withholds unduly, but comes
    to poverty.

²⁵A generous man will prosper;
  he who refreshes others will himself
    be refreshed.

²⁶People curse the man who hoards grain,
  but blessing crowns him who is
    willing to sell.

²⁷He who seeks good finds goodwill,
  but evil comes to him who searches
    for it.

²⁸Whoever trusts in his riches will fall,
  but the righteous will thrive like a
    green leaf.

²⁹He who brings trouble on his family will
    inherit only wind,
  and the fool will be servant to the
    wise.

³⁰The fruit of the righteous is a tree of
    life,
  and he who wins souls is wise.

³¹If the righteous receive their due on
    earth,
  how much more the ungodly and the
    sinner!

12 Whoever loves discipline loves
      knowledge,
  but he who hates correction is stupid.

²A good man obtains favor from the
    LORD,
  but the LORD condemns a crafty man.

³A man cannot be established through
    wickedness,
  but the righteous cannot be uprooted.

⁴A wife of noble character is her
    husband's crown,
  but a disgraceful wife is like decay in
    his bones.

⁵The plans of the righteous are just,
  but the advice of the wicked is
    deceitful.

⁶The words of the wicked lie in wait for
    blood,
  but the speech of the upright rescues
    them.

⁷Wicked men are overthrown and are no
    more,
  but the house of the righteous stands
    firm.

⁸A man is praised according to his
    wisdom,
  but men with warped minds are
    despised.

⁹Better to be a nobody and yet have a
    servant
  than pretend to be somebody and
    have no food.

¹⁰A righteous man cares for the needs of
    his animal,
  but the kindest acts of the wicked are
    cruel.

¹¹He who works his land will have
    abundant food,

but he who chases fantasies lacks
judgment.

¹²The wicked desire the plunder of evil
men,
but the root of the righteous
flourishes.

¹³An evil man is trapped by his sinful
talk,
but a righteous man escapes trouble.

¹⁴From the fruit of his lips a man is filled
with good things
as surely as the work of his hands
rewards him.

¹⁵The way of a fool seems right to him,
but a wise man listens to advice.

¹⁶A fool shows his annoyance at once,
but a prudent man overlooks an
insult.

¹⁷A truthful witness gives honest
testimony,
but a false witness tells lies.

¹⁸Reckless words pierce like a sword,
but the tongue of the wise brings
healing.

¹⁹Truthful lips endure forever,
but a lying tongue lasts only a
moment.

²⁰There is deceit in the hearts of those
who plot evil,
but joy for those who promote peace.

²¹No harm befalls the righteous,
but the wicked have their fill of
trouble.

²²The LORD detests lying lips,
but he delights in men who are
truthful.

²³A prudent man keeps his knowledge to
himself,
but the heart of fools blurts out folly.

²⁴Diligent hands will rule,
but laziness ends in slave labor.

²⁵An anxious heart weighs a man down,
but a kind word cheers him up.

²⁶A righteous man is cautious in
friendship,ᵃ
but the way of the wicked leads them
astray.

²⁷The lazy man does not roastᵇ his
game,

but the diligent man prizes his
possessions.

²⁸In the way of righteousness there is life;
along that path is immortality.

13 A wise son heeds his father's
instruction,
but a mocker does not listen to
rebuke.

²From the fruit of his lips a man enjoys
good things,
but the unfaithful have a craving for
violence.

³He who guards his lips guards his life,
but he who speaks rashly will come
to ruin.

⁴The sluggard craves and gets nothing,
but the desires of the diligent are fully
satisfied.

⁵The righteous hate what is false,
but the wicked bring shame and
disgrace.

⁶Righteousness guards the man of
integrity,
but wickedness overthrows the sinner.

⁷One man pretends to be rich, yet has
nothing;
another pretends to be poor, yet has
great wealth.

⁸A man's riches may ransom his life,
but a poor man hears no threat.

⁹The light of the righteous shines
brightly,
but the lamp of the wicked is snuffed
out.

¹⁰Pride only breeds quarrels,
but wisdom is found in those who
take advice.

¹¹Dishonest money dwindles away,
but he who gathers money little by
little makes it grow.

¹²Hope deferred makes the heart sick,
but a longing fulfilled is a tree of life.

¹³He who scorns instruction will pay for
it,
but he who respects a command is
rewarded.

¹⁴The teaching of the wise is a fountain of
life,

ᵃ26 Or *man is a guide to his neighbor*   ᵇ27 The meaning of the Hebrew for this word is uncertain.

YOUR TONGUE CAN WORK WONDERS!

Melody has been doing her best to encourage her friend Catherine. Catherine didn't make the school tennis team, and she's feeling pretty discouraged. Melody wrote Catherine a note and took her out to lunch in order to help her through.

Catherine is surprised (and a little embarrassed) by Melody's thoughtfulness. As the girls sit in the restaurant, the following conversation takes place:

Catherine: "I really appreciate all this. But you really didn't need to go to all this—"

Melody (interrupting): "I know I didn't need to, but I wanted to. Cath, you're my best friend! I'd give anything if you could be on the team. Really I would. And I don't care what Coach K. thinks, I still say you're a great player."

A broad grin slowly spreads across Catherine's face.

Look It Up
••••

Scripture is clear. Your words have the power to heal . . . or to hurt:

"The tongue that brings healing is a tree of life, but a deceitful tongue crushes the spirit" (Proverbs 15:4).

"Pleasant words are a honeycomb, sweet to the soul and healing to the bones" (Proverbs 16:24).

"The tongue has the power of life and death" (Proverbs 18:21).

"Life and death." Pretty obvious, isn't it? You can opt for life, and you can choose to heal others by the things you say.

Think It Through
••••

The old song, "Home, Home on the Range," praises the range as a place "where seldom is heard a discouraging word." If you were to adapt those lyrics to fit your world, they would probably read, "where seldom is heard an encouraging word"!

Mark Twain once said, "I can live two months on one good compliment." Do you agree?

Work It Out
••••

Discouraged people are everywhere. So here's the mission: Just by using the power of your tongue, see how many people you can encourage today. Look for:

- The store clerk who is having a horrible day.
- The quiet classmate who usually sits alone at lunch.
- The friend who has just flunked the biggest test of the year.
- The girl at school or church who never has a date.
- The teacher who is constantly run over by her "bus" of a class.

Nail It Down
••••

Reflect on Proverbs 12:25.

Turn to pages 472 and 1205 for other readings on encouragement.
Turn to page 665 for Wednesday's reading.

Topic
••••

ENCOURAGEMENT

turning a man from the snares of
death.

[15]Good understanding wins favor,
but the way of the unfaithful is
hard.[a]

[16]Every prudent man acts out of
knowledge,
but a fool exposes his folly.

[17]A wicked messenger falls into trouble,
but a trustworthy envoy brings
healing.

[18]He who ignores discipline comes to
poverty and shame,
but whoever heeds correction is
honored.

[19]A longing fulfilled is sweet to the soul,
but fools detest turning from evil.

[20]He who walks with the wise grows wise,
but a companion of fools suffers
harm.

[21]Misfortune pursues the sinner,
but prosperity is the reward of the
righteous.

[22]A good man leaves an inheritance for
his children's children,
but a sinner's wealth is stored up for
the righteous.

[23]A poor man's field may produce
abundant food,
but injustice sweeps it away.

[24]He who spares the rod hates his son,
but he who loves him is careful to
discipline him.

[25]The righteous eat to their hearts'
content,
but the stomach of the wicked goes
hungry.

14 The wise woman builds her
house,
but with her own hands the foolish
one tears hers down.

[2]He whose walk is upright fears the Lord,
but he whose ways are devious
despises him.

[3]A fool's talk brings a rod to his back,
but the lips of the wise protect them.

[4]Where there are no oxen, the manger is
empty,

but from the strength of an ox comes
an abundant harvest.

[5]A truthful witness does not deceive,
but a false witness pours out lies.

[6]The mocker seeks wisdom and finds
none,
but knowledge comes easily to the
discerning.

[7]Stay away from a foolish man,
for you will not find knowledge on his
lips.

[8]The wisdom of the prudent is to give
thought to their ways,
but the folly of fools is deception.

[9]Fools mock at making amends for sin,
but goodwill is found among the
upright.

[10]Each heart knows its own bitterness,
and no one else can share its joy.

[11]The house of the wicked will be
destroyed,
but the tent of the upright will
flourish.

[12]There is a way that seems right to a
man,
but in the end it leads to death.

[13]Even in laughter the heart may ache,
and joy may end in grief.

[14]The faithless will be fully repaid for
their ways,
and the good man rewarded for his.

[15]A simple man believes anything,
but a prudent man gives thought to
his steps.

[16]A wise man fears the Lord and shuns
evil,
but a fool is hotheaded and reckless.

[17]A quick-tempered man does foolish
things,
and a crafty man is hated.

[18]The simple inherit folly,
but the prudent are crowned with
knowledge.

[19]Evil men will bow down in the presence
of the good,
and the wicked at the gates of the
righteous.

[20]The poor are shunned even by their
neighbors,

[a]15 Or *unfaithful does not endure*

AN UNRULY TEMPER

It's Friday, 5:45 P.M., at the Macklin residence. Tempers are flaring.

Kirk (his voice rising): "I'm not telling you again—get off the phone!"

Donna: "Shut up, Kirk! This is important. I'll be off in a minute."

Kirk (yelling): "No! Get off now! You just talked to her at school. I swear, you can't even go to the bathroom without your stupid friends."

Donna (into the phone): "Hold on, Cathy." (To Kirk): "At least I have friends."

Kirk: "Only because they feel sorry for you because Corey dumped you for Melissa!"

Donna (throwing a shoe at Kirk): "You pig! Get out!"

Kirk (dodging the shoe and lunging at Donna): "You're history!"

Look It Up

In a world full of bully brothers and sarcastic sisters, it's easy for a minor squabble to turn into a major conflict. In Proverbs Solomon gives some advice for controlling tempers:

"Better a patient man than a warrior, a man who controls his temper than one who takes a city" (Proverbs 16:32).

"Do not make friends with a hot-tempered man, do not associate with one easily angered, or you may learn his ways and get yourself ensnared" (Proverbs 22:24–25).

"An angry man stirs up dissension, and a hot-tempered one commits many sins" (Proverbs 29:22).

Think It Through

Have you ever been a bystander and watched a couple of people completely lose their tempers? Didn't they look silly? By allowing their tempers to get the best of them, they ended up making fools of themselves and embarrassing everyone around them.

Do you know someone who is quick-tempered? Are you? What situations tend to make you the angriest in the shortest amount of time?

Work It Out

The next time you get in a high-voltage situation (like the one above), call a literal timeout. Go somewhere else for as long as it takes to get a clear head.

When you can be more objective, ask yourself, "Who's in control of my life right now? Is God? Or am I?"

Stop. Make sure his Spirit is calling the shots.

Then go back and resolve the problem without ranting and raving, without saying and doing things you'll regret later.

Nail It Down

Read Proverbs 14:17 for what can happen to someone with a quick temper.

Turn to pages 550 and 1276 for other readings on self-control.
Turn to page 670 for Thursday's reading.

Topic
....

SELF-CONTROL

but the rich have many friends.

21He who despises his neighbor sins,
  but blessed is he who is kind to the
    needy.

22Do not those who plot evil go astray?
  But those who plan what is good
    find*a* love and faithfulness.

23All hard work brings a profit,
  but mere talk leads only to poverty.

24The wealth of the wise is their crown,
  but the folly of fools yields folly.

25A truthful witness saves lives,
  but a false witness is deceitful.

26He who fears the Lord has a secure
    fortress,
  and for his children it will be a
    refuge.

27The fear of the Lord is a fountain of life,
  turning a man from the snares of
    death.

28A large population is a king's glory,
  but without subjects a prince is
    ruined.

29A patient man has great understanding,
  but a quick-tempered man displays
    folly.

30A heart at peace gives life to the body,
  but envy rots the bones.

31He who oppresses the poor shows
    contempt for their Maker,
  but whoever is kind to the needy
    honors God.

32When calamity comes, the wicked are
    brought down,
  but even in death the righteous have
    a refuge.

33Wisdom reposes in the heart of the
    discerning
  and even among fools she lets herself
    be known.*b*

34Righteousness exalts a nation,
  but sin is a disgrace to any people.

35A king delights in a wise servant,
  but a shameful servant incurs his
    wrath.

15 A gentle answer turns away wrath,
   but a harsh word stirs up anger.

2The tongue of the wise commends
    knowledge,
  but the mouth of the fool gushes
    folly.

3The eyes of the Lord are everywhere,
  keeping watch on the wicked and the
    good.

4The tongue that brings healing is a tree
    of life,
  but a deceitful tongue crushes the
    spirit.

5A fool spurns his father's discipline,
  but whoever heeds correction shows
    prudence.

6The house of the righteous contains
    great treasure,
  but the income of the wicked brings
    them trouble.

7The lips of the wise spread knowledge;
  not so the hearts of fools.

8The Lord detests the sacrifice of the
    wicked,
  but the prayer of the upright pleases
    him.

9The Lord detests the way of the wicked
  but he loves those who pursue
    righteousness.

10Stern discipline awaits him who leaves
    the path;
  he who hates correction will die.

11Death and Destruction*c* lie open before
    the Lord —
  how much more the hearts of men!

12A mocker resents correction;
  he will not consult the wise.

13A happy heart makes the face cheerful,
  but heartache crushes the spirit.

14The discerning heart seeks knowledge,
  but the mouth of a fool feeds on folly.

15All the days of the oppressed are
    wretched,
  but the cheerful heart has a continual
    feast.

16Better a little with the fear of the Lord
  than great wealth with turmoil.

17Better a meal of vegetables where there
    is love
  than a fattened calf with hatred.

a22 Or show   *b33 Hebrew; Septuagint and Syriac / but in the heart of fools she is not known*   *c11 Hebrew
Sheol and Abaddon*

[18]A hot-tempered man stirs up dissension,
  but a patient man calms a quarrel.

[19]The way of the sluggard is blocked with
    thorns,
  but the path of the upright is a
    highway.

[20]A wise son brings joy to his father,
  but a foolish man despises his
    mother.

[21]Folly delights a man who lacks
    judgment,
  but a man of understanding keeps a
    straight course.

[22]Plans fail for lack of counsel,
  but with many advisers they succeed.

[23]A man finds joy in giving an apt reply—
  and how good is a timely word!

[24]The path of life leads upward for the
    wise
  to keep him from going down to the
    grave.[a]

[25]The LORD tears down the proud man's
    house
  but he keeps the widow's boundaries
    intact.

[26]The LORD detests the thoughts of the
    wicked,
  but those of the pure are pleasing to
    him.

[27]A greedy man brings trouble to his
    family,
  but he who hates bribes will live.

[28]The heart of the righteous weighs its
    answers,
  but the mouth of the wicked gushes
    evil.

[29]The LORD is far from the wicked
  but he hears the prayer of the
    righteous.

[30]A cheerful look brings joy to the heart,
  and good news gives health to the
    bones.

[31]He who listens to a life-giving rebuke
  will be at home among the wise.

[32]He who ignores discipline despises
    himself,
  but whoever heeds correction gains
    understanding.

[33]The fear of the LORD teaches a man
    wisdom,[b]
  and humility comes before honor.

16 To man belong the plans of the
    heart,
  but from the LORD comes the reply of
    the tongue.

[2]All a man's ways seem innocent to him,
  but motives are weighed by the LORD.

[3]Commit to the LORD whatever you do,
  and your plans will succeed.

[4]The LORD works out everything for his
    own ends—
  even the wicked for a day of disaster.

[5]The LORD detests all the proud of heart.
  Be sure of this: They will not go
    unpunished.

[6]Through love and faithfulness sin is
    atoned for;
  through the fear of the LORD a man
    avoids evil.

[7]When a man's ways are pleasing to the
    LORD,
  he makes even his enemies live at
    peace with him.

[8]Better a little with righteousness
  than much gain with injustice.

[9]In his heart a man plans his course,
  but the LORD determines his steps.

[10]The lips of a king speak as an oracle,
  and his mouth should not betray
    justice.

[11]Honest scales and balances are from the
    LORD;
  all the weights in the bag are of his
    making.

[12]Kings detest wrongdoing,
  for a throne is established through
    righteousness.

[13]Kings take pleasure in honest lips;
  they value a man who speaks the
    truth.

[14]A king's wrath is a messenger of death,
  but a wise man will appease it.

[15]When a king's face brightens, it means
    life;
  his favor is like a rain cloud in spring.

[16]How much better to get wisdom than
    gold,

---

[a]24 Hebrew *Sheol*   [b]33 Or *Wisdom teaches the fear of the* LORD

to choose understanding rather than silver!

17The highway of the upright avoids evil;
he who guards his way guards his life.

18Pride goes before destruction,
a haughty spirit before a fall.

19Better to be lowly in spirit and among the oppressed
than to share plunder with the proud.

20Whoever gives heed to instruction prospers,
and blessed is he who trusts in the LORD.

21The wise in heart are called discerning,
and pleasant words promote instruction.*a*

22Understanding is a fountain of life to those who have it,
but folly brings punishment to fools.

23A wise man's heart guides his mouth,
and his lips promote instruction.*b*

24Pleasant words are a honeycomb,
sweet to the soul and healing to the bones.

25There is a way that seems right to a man,
but in the end it leads to death.

26The laborer's appetite works for him;
his hunger drives him on.

27A scoundrel plots evil,
and his speech is like a scorching fire.

28A perverse man stirs up dissension,
and a gossip separates close friends.

29A violent man entices his neighbor
and leads him down a path that is not good.

30He who winks with his eye is plotting perversity;
he who purses his lips is bent on evil.

31Gray hair is a crown of splendor;
it is attained by a righteous life.

32Better a patient man than a warrior,
a man who controls his temper than one who takes a city.

33The lot is cast into the lap,
but its every decision is from the LORD.

17 Better a dry crust with peace and quiet
than a house full of feasting,*c* with strife.

2A wise servant will rule over a disgraceful son,
and will share the inheritance as one of the brothers.

3The crucible for silver and the furnace for gold,
but the LORD tests the heart.

4A wicked man listens to evil lips;
a liar pays attention to a malicious tongue.

5He who mocks the poor shows contempt for their Maker;
whoever gloats over disaster will not go unpunished.

6Children's children are a crown to the aged,
and parents are the pride of their children.

7Arrogant*d* lips are unsuited to a fool—
how much worse lying lips to a ruler!

8A bribe is a charm to the one who gives it;
wherever he turns, he succeeds.

9He who covers over an offense promotes love,
but whoever repeats the matter separates close friends.

10A rebuke impresses a man of discernment
more than a hundred lashes a fool.

11An evil man is bent only on rebellion;
a merciless official will be sent against him.

12Better to meet a bear robbed of her cubs
than a fool in his folly.

13If a man pays back evil for good,
evil will never leave his house.

14Starting a quarrel is like breaching a dam;
so drop the matter before a dispute breaks out.

a21 Or words make a man persuasive   *b23 Or mouth / and makes his lips persuasive*   *c1 Hebrew sacrifices*
d7 Or Eloquent

¹⁵Acquitting the guilty and condemning
　　the innocent—
　the Lord detests them both.

¹⁶Of what use is money in the hand of a
　　fool,
　since he has no desire to get wisdom?

¹⁷A friend loves at all times,
　and a brother is born for adversity.

¹⁸A man lacking in judgment strikes
　　hands in pledge
　and puts up security for his neighbor.

¹⁹He who loves a quarrel loves sin;
　he who builds a high gate invites
　　destruction.

²⁰A man of perverse heart does not
　　prosper;
　he whose tongue is deceitful falls into
　　trouble.

²¹To have a fool for a son brings grief;
　there is no joy for the father of a fool.

²²A cheerful heart is good medicine,
　but a crushed spirit dries up the
　　bones.

²³A wicked man accepts a bribe in secret
　to pervert the course of justice.

²⁴A discerning man keeps wisdom in
　　view,
　but a fool's eyes wander to the ends
　　of the earth.

²⁵A foolish son brings grief to his father
　and bitterness to the one who bore
　　him.

²⁶It is not good to punish an innocent
　　man,
　or to flog officials for their integrity.

²⁷A man of knowledge uses words with
　　restraint,
　and a man of understanding is
　　even-tempered.

²⁸Even a fool is thought wise if he keeps
　　silent,
　and discerning if he holds his tongue.

18 An unfriendly man pursues selfish
　　ends;
　he defies all sound judgment.

²A fool finds no pleasure in
　　understanding
　but delights in airing his own
　　opinions.

³When wickedness comes, so does
　contempt,

and with shame comes disgrace.

⁴The words of a man's mouth are deep
　　waters,
　but the fountain of wisdom is a
　　bubbling brook.

⁵It is not good to be partial to the wicked
　or to deprive the innocent of justice.

⁶A fool's lips bring him strife,
　and his mouth invites a beating.

⁷A fool's mouth is his undoing,
　and his lips are a snare to his soul.

⁸The words of a gossip are like choice
　　morsels;
　they go down to a man's inmost parts.

⁹One who is slack in his work
　is brother to one who destroys.

¹⁰The name of the Lord is a strong tower;
　the righteous run to it and are safe.

¹¹The wealth of the rich is their fortified
　　city;
　they imagine it an unscalable wall.

¹²Before his downfall a man's heart is
　　proud,
　but humility comes before honor.

¹³He who answers before listening—
　that is his folly and his shame.

¹⁴A man's spirit sustains him in sickness,
　but a crushed spirit who can bear?

¹⁵The heart of the discerning acquires
　　knowledge;
　the ears of the wise seek it out.

¹⁶A gift opens the way for the giver
　and ushers him into the presence of
　　the great.

¹⁷The first to present his case seems right,
　till another comes forward and
　　questions him.

¹⁸Casting the lot settles disputes
　and keeps strong opponents apart.

¹⁹An offended brother is more unyielding
　　than a fortified city,
　and disputes are like the barred gates
　　of a citadel.

²⁰From the fruit of his mouth a man's
　　stomach is filled;
　with the harvest from his lips he is
　　satisfied.

²¹The tongue has the power of life and
　　death,
　and those who love it will eat its fruit.

IT TAKES GUTS AND AN IRON WILL

Everybody knows Jason. He's one of the biggest (and best) players on the football team. He's hilarious. All the members of the "in" crowd at school love to be around him.

Drew is a different story. He's not very athletic or funny or cool. It's not that people dislike him. They just ignore him. Everyone, that is, except Jason. You can believe it or not, but Jason and Drew are best friends. They go hunting and fishing together, and they always have a great time.

Look It Up

Drew and Jason first became friends when they were little kids. Since then they've stayed close even while pursuing different interests. How? Because they understand that true friendship requires that our commitment to our friends be unconditional. Consider these wise sayings:

"Do not forsake your friend and the friend of your father, and do not go to your brother's house when disaster strikes you—better a neighbor nearby than a brother far away" (Proverbs 27:10).

"A man of many companions may come to ruin, but there is a friend who sticks closer than a brother" (Proverbs 18:24).

Both of these verses stress the importance of commitment in friendship . . . no matter what happens, no matter what the situation.

Think It Through

Commitment means you stick up for a friend when everyone else is turning their backs. It means you keep in touch. It means you can be counted on when trouble is brewing. It means you don't let minor differences or petty arguments diminish your relationship. It means being consistent, regardless of how you feel.

Work It Out

Here are a few steps you can take to become a more committed friend:

• Pray for your friends today and every day.

• Approach a friend with whom you've had a strained relationship lately. Talk about and resolve whatever problem is hampering your friendship.

• Find a friend who is in trouble and who needs someone to believe in him or her. This doesn't mean that you condone the wrong actions, only that you stand with your friend and continue loving no matter what.

• Comfort a friend who is going through a traumatic or difficult experience. It might not be convenient to go out of your way to help, but that's what commitment requires.

• Ask God to make you a more committed friend.

Nail It Down

Read Proverbs 17:17.

Turn to pages 195, 291, 509 and 1346 for other readings on friendship.
Turn to page 674 for Friday's reading.

Topic

FRIENDSHIP

22He who finds a wife finds what is good
and receives favor from the LORD.

23A poor man pleads for mercy,
but a rich man answers harshly.

24A man of many companions may come
to ruin,
but there is a friend who sticks closer
than a brother.

19 Better a poor man whose walk is
blameless
than a fool whose lips are perverse.

2It is not good to have zeal without
knowledge,
nor to be hasty and miss the way.

3A man's own folly ruins his life,
yet his heart rages against the LORD.

4Wealth brings many friends,
but a poor man's friend deserts him.

5A false witness will not go unpunished,
and he who pours out lies will not go
free.

6Many curry favor with a ruler,
and everyone is the friend of a man
who gives gifts.

7A poor man is shunned by all his
relatives—
how much more do his friends avoid
him!
Though he pursues them with pleading,
they are nowhere to be found.ᵃ

8He who gets wisdom loves his own soul;
he who cherishes understanding
prospers.

9A false witness will not go unpunished,
and he who pours out lies will perish.

10It is not fitting for a fool to live in
luxury—
how much worse for a slave to rule
over princes!

11A man's wisdom gives him patience;
it is to his glory to overlook an
offense.

12A king's rage is like the roar of a lion,
but his favor is like dew on the grass.

13A foolish son is his father's ruin,
and a quarrelsome wife is like a
constant dripping.

14Houses and wealth are inherited from
parents,

but a prudent wife is from the LORD.

15Laziness brings on deep sleep,
and the shiftless man goes hungry.

16He who obeys instructions guards his
life,
but he who is contemptuous of his
ways will die.

17He who is kind to the poor lends to the
LORD,
and he will reward him for what he
has done.

18Discipline your son, for in that there is
hope;
do not be a willing party to his death.

19A hot-tempered man must pay the
penalty;
if you rescue him, you will have to do
it again.

20Listen to advice and accept instruction,
and in the end you will be wise.

21Many are the plans in a man's heart,
but it is the LORD's purpose that
prevails.

22What a man desires is unfailing loveᵇ;
better to be poor than a liar.

23The fear of the LORD leads to life:
Then one rests content, untouched by
trouble.

24The sluggard buries his hand in the
dish;
he will not even bring it back to his
mouth!

25Flog a mocker, and the simple will learn
prudence;
rebuke a discerning man, and he will
gain knowledge.

26He who robs his father and drives out
his mother
is a son who brings shame and
disgrace.

27Stop listening to instruction, my son,
and you will stray from the words of
knowledge.

28A corrupt witness mocks at justice,
and the mouth of the wicked gulps
down evil.

29Penalties are prepared for mockers,
and beatings for the backs of fools.

ᵃ7 The meaning of the Hebrew for this sentence is uncertain.   ᵇ22 Or *A man's greed is his shame*

20 Wine is a mocker and beer a
brawler;
   whoever is led astray by them is not
   wise.

²A king's wrath is like the roar of a lion;
   he who angers him forfeits his life.

³It is to a man's honor to avoid strife,
   but every fool is quick to quarrel.

⁴A sluggard does not plow in season;
   so at harvest time he looks but finds
   nothing.

⁵The purposes of a man's heart are deep
   waters,
   but a man of understanding draws
   them out.

⁶Many a man claims to have unfailing
   love,
   but a faithful man who can find?

⁷The righteous man leads a blameless
   life;
   blessed are his children after him.

⁸When a king sits on his throne to judge,
   he winnows out all evil with his eyes.

⁹Who can say, "I have kept my heart
   pure;
   I am clean and without sin"?

¹⁰Differing weights and differing
   measures—
   the LORD detests them both.

¹¹Even a child is known by his actions,
   by whether his conduct is pure and
   right.

¹²Ears that hear and eyes that see—
   the LORD has made them both.

¹³Do not love sleep or you will grow poor;
   stay awake and you will have food to
   spare.

¹⁴"It's no good, it's no good!" says the
   buyer;
   then off he goes and boasts about his
   purchase.

¹⁵Gold there is, and rubies in abundance,
   but lips that speak knowledge are a
   rare jewel.

¹⁶Take the garment of one who puts up
   security for a stranger;
   hold it in pledge if he does it for a
   wayward woman.

¹⁷Food gained by fraud tastes sweet to a
   man,
   but he ends up with a mouth full of
   gravel.

¹⁸Make plans by seeking advice;
   if you wage war, obtain guidance.

¹⁹A gossip betrays a confidence;
   so avoid a man who talks too much.

²⁰If a man curses his father or mother,
   his lamp will be snuffed out in pitch
   darkness.

²¹An inheritance quickly gained at the
   beginning
   will not be blessed at the end.

²²Do not say, "I'll pay you back for this
   wrong!"
   Wait for the LORD, and he will deliver
   you.

²³The LORD detests differing weights,
   and dishonest scales do not please
   him.

²⁴A man's steps are directed by the LORD.
   How then can anyone understand his
   own way?

²⁵It is a trap for a man to dedicate
   something rashly
   and only later to consider his vows.

²⁶A wise king winnows out the wicked;
   he drives the threshing wheel over
   them.

²⁷The lamp of the LORD searches the spirit
   of a man*ᵃ*;
   it searches out his inmost being.

²⁸Love and faithfulness keep a king safe;
   through love his throne is made
   secure.

²⁹The glory of young men is their
   strength,
   gray hair the splendor of the old.

³⁰Blows and wounds cleanse away evil,
   and beatings purge the inmost being.

21 The king's heart is in the hand of
the LORD;
   he directs it like a watercourse
   wherever he pleases.

²All a man's ways seem right to him,
   but the LORD weighs the heart.

³To do what is right and just

ᵃ27 Or The spirit of man is the LORD's lamp

is more acceptable to the LORD than
sacrifice.

4Haughty eyes and a proud heart,
the lamp of the wicked, are sin!

5The plans of the diligent lead to profit
as surely as haste leads to poverty.

6A fortune made by a lying tongue
is a fleeting vapor and a deadly
snare.*a*

7The violence of the wicked will drag
them away,
for they refuse to do what is right.

8The way of the guilty is devious,
but the conduct of the innocent is
upright.

9Better to live on a corner of the roof
than share a house with a
quarrelsome wife.

10The wicked man craves evil;
his neighbor gets no mercy from him.

11When a mocker is punished, the simple
gain wisdom;
when a wise man is instructed, he
gets knowledge.

12The Righteous One*b* takes note of the
house of the wicked
and brings the wicked to ruin.

13If a man shuts his ears to the cry of the
poor,
he too will cry out and not be
answered.

14A gift given in secret soothes anger,
and a bribe concealed in the cloak
pacifies great wrath.

15When justice is done, it brings joy to
the righteous
but terror to evildoers.

16A man who strays from the path of
understanding
comes to rest in the company of the
dead.

17He who loves pleasure will become
poor;
whoever loves wine and oil will never
be rich.

18The wicked become a ransom for the
righteous,
and the unfaithful for the upright.

19Better to live in a desert
than with a quarrelsome and
ill-tempered wife.

20In the house of the wise are stores of
choice food and oil,
but a foolish man devours all he has.

21He who pursues righteousness and love
finds life, prosperity*c* and honor.

22A wise man attacks the city of the
mighty
and pulls down the stronghold in
which they trust.

23He who guards his mouth and his
tongue
keeps himself from calamity.

24The proud and arrogant man—"Mocker"
is his name;
he behaves with overweening pride.

25The sluggard's craving will be the death
of him,
because his hands refuse to work.
26All day long he craves for more,
but the righteous give without
sparing.

27The sacrifice of the wicked is
detestable—
how much more so when brought
with evil intent!

28A false witness will perish,
and whoever listens to him will be
destroyed forever.*d*

29A wicked man puts up a bold front,
but an upright man gives thought to
his ways.

30There is no wisdom, no insight, no plan
that can succeed against the LORD.

31The horse is made ready for the day of
battle,
but victory rests with the LORD.

22 A good name is more desirable
than great riches;
to be esteemed is better than silver or
gold.

2Rich and poor have this in common:
The LORD is the Maker of them all.

3A prudent man sees danger and takes
refuge,

---

*a6 Some Hebrew manuscripts, Septuagint and Vulgate; most Hebrew manuscripts vapor for those who seek
death   b12 Or The righteous man   c21 Or righteousness   d28 Or / but the words of an obedient man will
live on*

WORTH MORE THAN SILVER OR GOLD

Sarah is walking down a hall at school. As she threads her way through the clusters of students, a strange phenomenon is taking place. The people who look her way automatically review her reputation. They do it without thinking.

Here are some of the thoughts that pop into their heads when they consider the name and face of Sarah: "Sweet." "Nice—but a little too serious about God." "Christian." "Friendly." "Smart."

From the other direction comes Bart. People take one glance at him and instantly think to themselves: "Jerk." "Wild." "Handsome." "Arrogant." "Unpredictable." "Headed for trouble."

Look It Up
••••

Have you ever watched a wildlife show on TV and seen those sucker fishes (properly called remoras) that attach themselves to sharks and whales? Your reputation is like a remora. It's stuck to you and everything related to you—especially your name. It goes with you everywhere. No wonder the Bible warns you to seek a good reputation by having a good name.

"Let love and faithfulness never leave you; . . . Then you will win favor and a good name in the sight of God and man" (Proverbs 3:3–4).

"A good name is better than fine perfume" (Ecclesiastes 7:1).

Think It Through
••••

What do people think of you? When they hear your name, what one word or phrase do you think comes to their minds? Why?

If you died today and your family and friends were going to put your name and a description of you on your tombstone, how would it read? Are you pleased with that reputation?

Work It Out
••••

Rate your own reputation in the following areas using a scale of one to five (one represents "what a joke!"—five represents "an accurate description"):
• Hardworking
• Honest
• Dependable
• Godly
• Joyful
• Compassionate
• Fun
• Unselfish
• Wise
• Faithful
• Teachable

Based on what you see in this chart, in which area(s) could you use a reputation overhaul?

Nail It Down
••••

Read Proverbs 22:1 to find out what a good reputation is worth.

Turn to pages 150, 1074, 1078 and 1306 for other readings on reputation.
Turn to page 678 for the weekend reading.

Topic
••••

REPUTATION

but the simple keep going and suffer
for it.

4Humility and the fear of the Lord
bring wealth and honor and life.

5In the paths of the wicked lie thorns
and snares,
but he who guards his soul stays far
from them.

6Train*a* a child in the way he should go,
and when he is old he will not turn
from it.

7The rich rule over the poor,
and the borrower is servant to the
lender.

8He who sows wickedness reaps trouble,
and the rod of his fury will be
destroyed.

9A generous man will himself be blessed,
for he shares his food with the poor.

10Drive out the mocker, and out goes
strife;
quarrels and insults are ended.

11He who loves a pure heart and whose
speech is gracious
will have the king for his friend.

12The eyes of the Lord keep watch over
knowledge,
but he frustrates the words of the
unfaithful.

13The sluggard says, "There is a lion
outside!"
or, "I will be murdered in the streets!"

14The mouth of an adulteress is a deep
pit;
he who is under the Lord's wrath will
fall into it.

15Folly is bound up in the heart of a
child,
but the rod of discipline will drive it
far from him.

16He who oppresses the poor to increase
his wealth
and he who gives gifts to the
rich—both come to poverty.

Sayings of the Wise

17Pay attention and listen to the sayings
of the wise;
apply your heart to what I teach,

18for it is pleasing when you keep them
in your heart
and have all of them ready on your
lips.

19So that your trust may be in the Lord,
I teach you today, even you.

20Have I not written thirty*b* sayings for
you,
sayings of counsel and knowledge,

21teaching you true and reliable words,
so that you can give sound answers
to him who sent you?

22Do not exploit the poor because they
are poor
and do not crush the needy in court,

23for the Lord will take up their case
and will plunder those who plunder
them.

24Do not make friends with a
hot-tempered man,
do not associate with one easily
angered,

25or you may learn his ways
and get yourself ensnared.

26Do not be a man who strikes hands in
pledge
or puts up security for debts;

27if you lack the means to pay,
your very bed will be snatched from
under you.

28Do not move an ancient boundary stone
set up by your forefathers.

29Do you see a man skilled in his work?
He will serve before kings;
he will not serve before obscure men.

23 When you sit to dine with a ruler,
note well what*c* is before you,
2and put a knife to your throat
if you are given to gluttony.
3Do not crave his delicacies,
for that food is deceptive.

4Do not wear yourself out to get rich;
have the wisdom to show restraint.
5Cast but a glance at riches, and they are
gone,
for they will surely sprout wings
and fly off to the sky like an eagle.

6Do not eat the food of a stingy man,
do not crave his delicacies;
7for he is the kind of man
who is always thinking about the
cost.*d*

---

a6 Or *Start*   *b20* Or *not formerly written; or not written excellent*   *c1* Or *who*   *d7* Or *for as he thinks*
within himself. / so he is; or for as he puts on a feast, / so he is

"Eat and drink," he says to you,
    but his heart is not with you.
⁸You will vomit up the little you have
    eaten
    and will have wasted your
    compliments.

⁹Do not speak to a fool,
    for he will scorn the wisdom of your
    words.

¹⁰Do not move an ancient boundary stone
    or encroach on the fields of the
    fatherless,
¹¹for their Defender is strong;
    he will take up their case against you.

¹²Apply your heart to instruction
    and your ears to words of knowledge.

¹³Do not withhold discipline from a child;
    if you punish him with the rod, he
    will not die.
¹⁴Punish him with the rod
    and save his soul from death. ᵃ

¹⁵My son, if your heart is wise,
    then my heart will be glad;
¹⁶my inmost being will rejoice
    when your lips speak what is right.

¹⁷Do not let your heart envy sinners,
    but always be zealous for the fear of
    the LORD.
¹⁸There is surely a future hope for you,
    and your hope will not be cut off.

¹⁹Listen, my son, and be wise,
    and keep your heart on the right path.
²⁰Do not join those who drink too much
    wine
    or gorge themselves on meat,
²¹for drunkards and gluttons become
    poor,
    and drowsiness clothes them in rags.

²²Listen to your father, who gave you life,
    and do not despise your mother when
    she is old.
²³Buy the truth and do not sell it;
    get wisdom, discipline and
    understanding.
²⁴The father of a righteous man has great
    joy;
    he who has a wise son delights in
    him.
²⁵May your father and mother be glad;
    may she who gave you birth rejoice!

²⁶My son, give me your heart
    and let your eyes keep to my ways,

²⁷for a prostitute is a deep pit
    and a wayward wife is a narrow well.
²⁸Like a bandit she lies in wait,
    and multiplies the unfaithful among
    men.

²⁹Who has woe? Who has sorrow?
    Who has strife? Who has complaints?
    Who has needless bruises? Who has
    bloodshot eyes?
³⁰Those who linger over wine,
    who go to sample bowls of mixed
    wine.
³¹Do not gaze at wine when it is red,
    when it sparkles in the cup,
    when it goes down smoothly!
³²In the end it bites like a snake
    and poisons like a viper.
³³Your eyes will see strange sights
    and your mind imagine confusing
    things.
³⁴You will be like one sleeping on the
    high seas,
    lying on top of the rigging.
³⁵"They hit me," you will say, "but I'm not
    hurt!
    They beat me, but I don't feel it!
When will I wake up
    so I can find another drink?"

24 Do not envy wicked men,
    do not desire their company;
²for their hearts plot violence,
    and their lips talk about making
    trouble.

³By wisdom a house is built,
    and through understanding it is
    established;
⁴through knowledge its rooms are filled
    with rare and beautiful treasures.

⁵A wise man has great power,
    and a man of knowledge increases
    strength;
⁶for waging war you need guidance,
    and for victory many advisers.

⁷Wisdom is too high for a fool;
    in the assembly at the gate he has
    nothing to say.

⁸He who plots evil
    will be known as a schemer.
⁹The schemes of folly are sin,
    and men detest a mocker.

¹⁰If you falter in times of trouble,
    how small is your strength!

¹¹Rescue those being led away to death;

hold back those staggering toward
    slaughter.
¹²If you say, "But we knew nothing about
    this,"
    does not he who weighs the heart
        perceive it?
Does not he who guards your life know
    it?
Will he not repay each person
    according to what he has done?

¹³Eat honey, my son, for it is good;
    honey from the comb is sweet to your
        taste.
¹⁴Know also that wisdom is sweet to your
    soul;
    if you find it, there is a future hope
        for you,
    and your hope will not be cut off.

¹⁵Do not lie in wait like an outlaw against
    a righteous man's house,
    do not raid his dwelling place;
¹⁶for though a righteous man falls seven
    times, he rises again,
    but the wicked are brought down by
        calamity.

¹⁷Do not gloat when your enemy falls;
    when he stumbles, do not let your
        heart rejoice,
¹⁸or the LORD will see and disapprove
    and turn his wrath away from him.

¹⁹Do not fret because of evil men
    or be envious of the wicked,
²⁰for the evil man has no future hope,
    and the lamp of the wicked will be
        snuffed out.

²¹Fear the LORD and the king, my son,
    and do not join with the rebellious,
²²for those two will send sudden
    destruction upon them,
    and who knows what calamities they
        can bring?

Further Sayings of the Wise

²³These also are sayings of the wise:

To show partiality in judging is not
    good:
²⁴Whoever says to the guilty, "You are
    innocent"—
    peoples will curse him and nations
        denounce him.
²⁵But it will go well with those who
    convict the guilty,

and rich blessing will come upon
    them.

²⁶An honest answer
    is like a kiss on the lips.

²⁷Finish your outdoor work
    and get your fields ready;
    after that, build your house.

²⁸Do not testify against your neighbor
    without cause,
    or use your lips to deceive.
²⁹Do not say, "I'll do to him as he has
    done to me;
    I'll pay that man back for what he
        did."

³⁰I went past the field of the sluggard,
    past the vineyard of the man who
        lacks judgment;
³¹thorns had come up everywhere,
    the ground was covered with weeds,
    and the stone wall was in ruins.
³²I applied my heart to what I observed
    and learned a lesson from what I saw:
³³A little sleep, a little slumber,
    a little folding of the hands to rest—
³⁴and poverty will come on you like a
    bandit
    and scarcity like an armed man.ᵃ

More Proverbs of Solomon

25 These are more proverbs of Solomon, copied by the men of Hezekiah
king of Judah:

²It is the glory of God to conceal a
    matter;
    to search out a matter is the glory of
        kings.

³As the heavens are high and the earth is
    deep,
    so the hearts of kings are
        unsearchable.

⁴Remove the dross from the silver,
    and out comes material forᵇ the
        silversmith;
⁵remove the wicked from the king's
    presence,
    and his throne will be established
        through righteousness.

⁶Do not exalt yourself in the king's
    presence,
    and do not claim a place among great
        men;

ᵃ34 Or like a vagrant / and scarcity like a beggar   ᵇ4 Or comes a vessel from

A KISS ON THE LIPS

Work It Out

Take an index card and, with plenty of lipstick on your lips (guys, you may want to ask a female friend to do this for you), give that index card a big kiss. Now take that card and hang it up where you'll see it every day, near your bed or on the bathroom mirror.

What exactly is that kiss supposed to remind you of each time you look at it? It will remind you that "an honest answer is like a kiss on the lips."

That's right! That's exactly what Proverbs 24:26 says. An honest answer is that special, that precious.

So, the next time your mom asks you something and you answer her honestly, you can say to her, "There. I just gave you a kiss on the lips!"

Nail It Down

Memorize Proverbs 24:26.

Think It Through

Honesty and its opposite, dishonesty, are not always as clear as black and white. Dishonesty can be a subtle thing. Instead of a clear and honest "Yes," you answer, "Maybe" or "Sort of." You leave out just a few details of a story. Or you add a few. You exaggerate "just a little." Or you "forget" to return something you borrowed. Even if it seems only "sort of" dishonest, it is still dishonest.

However subtle dishonesty can seem, however easy to slip into, God still condemns it. Proverbs 11:1 states that "the LORD abhors dishonest scales." The verse is speaking of merchant's scales, but this is God's attitude toward any sort of dishonesty. *Abhors* is a pretty strong word. The dictionary gives its meaning as "hates, loathes, detests utterly." Those strong words accurately describe what God thinks of dishonesty.

Dishonesty sounds like something you'd want to stay miles away from, doesn't it? Use your little "kisser card" to remind you to be honest. Always.

Nail It Down

Reread Proverbs 24:26. For further insight read Proverbs 12:17,19,22.

Turn to pages 751, 853, 1278 and 1325 for other readings on character.
Turn to page 680 for Monday's reading.

Topic

CHARACTER

⁷it is better for him to say to you, "Come
  up here,"
than for him to humiliate you before
  a nobleman.

What you have seen with your eyes
8 do not bring[a] hastily to court,
for what will you do in the end
  if your neighbor puts you to shame?

⁹If you argue your case with a neighbor,
  do not betray another man's
    confidence,
¹⁰or he who hears it may shame you
  and you will never lose your bad
    reputation.

¹¹A word aptly spoken
  is like apples of gold in settings of
    silver.

¹²Like an earring of gold or an ornament
    of fine gold
  is a wise man's rebuke to a listening
    ear.

¹³Like the coolness of snow at harvest
    time
  is a trustworthy messenger to those
    who send him;
  he refreshes the spirit of his masters.

¹⁴Like clouds and wind without rain
  is a man who boasts of gifts he does
    not give.

¹⁵Through patience a ruler can be
    persuaded,
  and a gentle tongue can break a
    bone.

¹⁶If you find honey, eat just enough—
  too much of it, and you will vomit.
¹⁷Seldom set foot in your neighbor's
    house—
  too much of you, and he will hate
    you.

¹⁸Like a club or a sword or a sharp arrow
  is the man who gives false testimony
    against his neighbor.

¹⁹Like a bad tooth or a lame foot
  is reliance on the unfaithful in times
    of trouble.

²⁰Like one who takes away a garment on
    a cold day,
  or like vinegar poured on soda,
  is one who sings songs to a heavy
    heart.

²¹If your enemy is hungry, give him food
    to eat;
  if he is thirsty, give him water to
    drink.
²²In doing this, you will heap burning
    coals on his head,
  and the LORD will reward you.

²³As a north wind brings rain,
  so a sly tongue brings angry looks.

²⁴Better to live on a corner of the roof
  than share a house with a
    quarrelsome wife.

²⁵Like cold water to a weary soul
  is good news from a distant land.

²⁶Like a muddied spring or a polluted
    well
  is a righteous man who gives way to
    the wicked.

²⁷It is not good to eat too much honey,
  nor is it honorable to seek one's own
    honor.

²⁸Like a city whose walls are broken
    down
  is a man who lacks self-control.

26 Like snow in summer or rain in
    harvest,
  honor is not fitting for a fool.

²Like a fluttering sparrow or a darting
    swallow,
  an undeserved curse does not come
    to rest.

³A whip for the horse, a halter for the
    donkey,
  and a rod for the backs of fools!

⁴Do not answer a fool according to his
    folly,
  or you will be like him yourself.

⁵Answer a fool according to his folly,
  or he will be wise in his own eyes.

⁶Like cutting off one's feet or drinking
    violence
  is the sending of a message by the
    hand of a fool.

⁷Like a lame man's legs that hang limp
  is a proverb in the mouth of a fool.

⁸Like tying a stone in a sling
  is the giving of honor to a fool.

⁹Like a thornbush in a drunkard's hand
  is a proverb in the mouth of a fool.

a7,8 Or nobleman / on whom you had set your eyes. / 8Do not go

WHEN PARENTS MISTRUST YOU

❚am so furious! Can you believe my mom's been snooping around in my room?"

"Oh, yeah, I can believe it. My dad thinks he's Sherlock Holmes. He plugged the clock into the light switch the other night. When I came home after my date with Steve and cut off the lights, I didn't know it, but I also cut off the clock!"

"So?"

"So, when I said I made it home by my 11:00 P.M. curfew, my dad knew I was lying. The clock said 11:25!"

"And now you're grounded?"

"You got it."

Look It Up
••••

How can you get your parents to trust you?

• Be honest. "Truthful lips endure forever, but a lying tongue lasts only a moment" (Proverbs 12:19). Hey, you're not eager to trust someone who has lied to you in the past. Why should your parents be any different?

• Show maturity. "When I was a child, I talked like a child, I thought like a child, I reasoned like a child. When I became a man, I put childish ways behind me" (1 Corinthians 13:11). Question: Would you put your confidence in an irresponsible little kid?

• Show respect (Deuteronomy 27:16).

In short, you gain trust by being trustworthy!

Think It Through
••••

Do your parents trust you? Why or why not? Should they trust you?

Put it this way: If you knew your friends acted behind your back the way you act behind your parents' back, would you trust them?

Work It Out
••••

What can you do if your mom or dad mistrust you?

1. Humbly admit where you've been wrong. "Mom, Dad, I acted [dishonestly, immaturely, disrespectfully] when I _____."

2. Ask for forgiveness. "I'm sorry. I have no excuses. I was wrong. Will you please forgive me?"

3. Express your desire to change. "I don't want to be like that. I want to put all that behind us, and I want to regain your respect. Will you tell me how I can do that?"

4. Work hard to show your sincerity. Keep your word. Don't do irresponsible things. You'll have to win back that lost trust bit by bit.

Nail It Down
••••

A trustworthy person is refreshing—see Proverbs 25:13.

Turn to pages 62, 122 and 1384 for other readings on parents.
Turn to page 683 for Tuesday's reading.

Topic
••••

¹⁰Like an archer who wounds at random
  is he who hires a fool or any
    passer-by.

¹¹As a dog returns to its vomit,
  so a fool repeats his folly.

¹²Do you see a man wise in his own
    eyes?
  There is more hope for a fool than for
    him.

¹³The sluggard says, "There is a lion in
    the road,
  a fierce lion roaming the streets!"

¹⁴As a door turns on its hinges,
  so a sluggard turns on his bed.

¹⁵The sluggard buries his hand in the
    dish;
  he is too lazy to bring it back to his
    mouth.

¹⁶The sluggard is wiser in his own eyes
  than seven men who answer
    discreetly.

¹⁷Like one who seizes a dog by the ears
  is a passer-by who meddles in a
    quarrel not his own.

¹⁸Like a madman shooting
    firebrands or deadly arrows
¹⁹is a man who deceives his neighbor
  and says, "I was only joking!"

²⁰Without wood a fire goes out;
  without gossip a quarrel dies down.

²¹As charcoal to embers and as wood to
    fire,
  so is a quarrelsome man for kindling
    strife.

²²The words of a gossip are like choice
    morsels;
  they go down to a man's inmost parts.

²³Like a coating of glaze*a* over
    earthenware
  are fervent lips with an evil heart.

²⁴A malicious man disguises himself with
    his lips,
  but in his heart he harbors deceit.
²⁵Though his speech is charming, do not
    believe him,
  for seven abominations fill his heart.
²⁶His malice may be concealed by
    deception,
  but his wickedness will be exposed in
    the assembly.

²⁷If a man digs a pit, he will fall into it;
  if a man rolls a stone, it will roll back
    on him.

²⁸A lying tongue hates those it hurts,
  and a flattering mouth works ruin.

27 Do not boast about tomorrow,
  for you do not know what a day
    may bring forth.

²Let another praise you, and not your
    own mouth;
  someone else, and not your own lips.

³Stone is heavy and sand a burden,
  but provocation by a fool is heavier
    than both.

⁴Anger is cruel and fury overwhelming,
  but who can stand before jealousy?

⁵Better is open rebuke
  than hidden love.

⁶Wounds from a friend can be trusted,
  but an enemy multiplies kisses.

⁷He who is full loathes honey,
  but to the hungry even what is bitter
    tastes sweet.

⁸Like a bird that strays from its nest
  is a man who strays from his home.

⁹Perfume and incense bring joy to the
    heart,
  and the pleasantness of one's friend
    springs from his earnest counsel.

¹⁰Do not forsake your friend and the
    friend of your father,
  and do not go to your brother's house
    when disaster strikes you—
  better a neighbor nearby than a
    brother far away.

¹¹Be wise, my son, and bring joy to my
    heart;
  then I can answer anyone who treats
    me with contempt.

¹²The prudent see danger and take
    refuge,
  but the simple keep going and suffer
    for it.

¹³Take the garment of one who puts up
    security for a stranger;
  hold it in pledge if he does it for a
    wayward woman.

¹⁴If a man loudly blesses his neighbor
    early in the morning,

---

a23 With a different word division of the Hebrew; Masoretic Text *of silver dross* it will be taken as a curse.

15A quarrelsome wife is like
a constant dripping on a rainy day;
16restraining her is like restraining the
wind
or grasping oil with the hand.

17As iron sharpens iron,
so one man sharpens another.

18He who tends a fig tree will eat its fruit,
and he who looks after his master will
be honored.

19As water reflects a face,
so a man's heart reflects the man.

20Death and Destruction[a] are never
satisfied,
and neither are the eyes of man.

21The crucible for silver and the furnace
for gold,
but man is tested by the praise he
receives.

22Though you grind a fool in a mortar,
grinding him like grain with a pestle,
you will not remove his folly from
him.

23Be sure you know the condition of your
flocks,
give careful attention to your herds;
24for riches do not endure forever,
and a crown is not secure for all
generations.
25When the hay is removed and new
growth appears
and the grass from the hills is
gathered in,
26the lambs will provide you with
clothing,
and the goats with the price of a field.
27You will have plenty of goats' milk
to feed you and your family
and to nourish your servant girls.

28 The wicked man flees though no
one pursues,
but the righteous are as bold as a
lion.

2When a country is rebellious, it has
many rulers,
but a man of understanding and
knowledge maintains order.

3A ruler[b] who oppresses the poor
is like a driving rain that leaves no
crops.

4Those who forsake the law praise the
wicked,
but those who keep the law resist
them.

5Evil men do not understand justice,
but those who seek the LORD
understand it fully.

6Better a poor man whose walk is
blameless
than a rich man whose ways are
perverse.

7He who keeps the law is a discerning
son,
but a companion of gluttons disgraces
his father.

8He who increases his wealth by
exorbitant interest
amasses it for another, who will be
kind to the poor.

9If anyone turns a deaf ear to the law,
even his prayers are detestable.

10He who leads the upright along an evil
path
will fall into his own trap,
but the blameless will receive a good
inheritance.

11A rich man may be wise in his own
eyes,
but a poor man who has discernment
sees through him.

12When the righteous triumph, there is
great elation;
but when the wicked rise to power,
men go into hiding.

13He who conceals his sins does not
prosper,
but whoever confesses and renounces
them finds mercy.

14Blessed is the man who always fears
the LORD,
but he who hardens his heart falls
into trouble.

15Like a roaring lion or a charging bear
is a wicked man ruling over a helpless
people.

16A tyrannical ruler lacks judgment,
but he who hates ill-gotten gain will
enjoy a long life.

17A man tormented by the guilt of murder
will be a fugitive till death;

---

a20 Hebrew *Sheol and Abaddon*   *b3* Or *A poor man*

I JUST WANT TO FIT IN!

Matt attended a small Christian school from kindergarten through eighth grade. This year he made the transition to a very large public high school. It's been a whole new world for Matt. It's also been a time of great inner turmoil.

Friday night Matt went out with some sophomore guys at his new school. About nine o'clock, as they drove around town, someone said, "Hey, let's cruise into the city."

Matt thought to himself, "That's seventy miles away! I'm supposed to be home by 11:00." But he didn't say a word. And he didn't get home until after 1:00 A.M.!

Look It Up

Peer pressure is the emotional force friends apply to try to get you to do (or not do) certain things. It's an old phenomenon; in fact, Solomon warned his son about it long ago.

> My son, if sinners entice you,
> do not give in to them.
> If they say, 'Come along with us; . . .
> throw in your lot with us,
> and we will share a common purse'—
> my son, do not go along with them,
> do not set foot on their paths;
> for their feet rush into sin,
> they are swift to shed blood.
> These men lie in wait for their own blood;
> they waylay only themselves!
> (Proverbs 1:10–11,14–16,18).

Think It Through

Why do you think peer pressure is so intense? Where does peer pressure hit you the hardest? If you found yourself in a situation like the one Matt faced, how do you think you would respond?

Work It Out

We all need to pray this prayer:
"Father, I need wisdom to both understand and learn to deal with peer pressure. Give me an open heart to hear what you want to say to me. And give me a willing spirit, so that I will put into practice the things I learn. In Jesus' name I pray. Amen."

Then do this experiment: Today at school, watch for examples of peer pressure in action. Observe how your classmates are affected. See if you can isolate and identify some of the techniques people use to pressure each other.

Nail It Down

Read the warning in Proverbs 28:10—especially if you're applying negative peer pressure to others.

Turn to pages 163, 1174 and 1386 for other readings on peer pressure.
Turn to page 686 for Wednesday's reading.

Topic

PEER PRESSURE

let no one support him.

¹⁸He whose walk is blameless is kept
    safe,
  but he whose ways are perverse will
    suddenly fall.

¹⁹He who works his land will have
    abundant food,
  but the one who chases fantasies will
    have his fill of poverty.

²⁰A faithful man will be richly blessed,
  but one eager to get rich will not go
    unpunished.

²¹To show partiality is not good—
  yet a man will do wrong for a piece of
    bread.

²²A stingy man is eager to get rich
  and is unaware that poverty awaits
    him.

²³He who rebukes a man will in the end
    gain more favor
  than he who has a flattering tongue.

²⁴He who robs his father or mother
  and says, "It's not wrong"—
  he is partner to him who destroys.

²⁵A greedy man stirs up dissension,
  but he who trusts in the Lord will
    prosper.

²⁶He who trusts in himself is a fool,
  but he who walks in wisdom is kept
    safe.

²⁷He who gives to the poor will lack
    nothing,
  but he who closes his eyes to them
    receives many curses.

²⁸When the wicked rise to power, people
    go into hiding;
  but when the wicked perish, the
    righteous thrive.

29 A man who remains stiff-necked
    after many rebukes
  will suddenly be destroyed—without
    remedy.

²When the righteous thrive, the people
    rejoice;
  when the wicked rule, the people
    groan.

³A man who loves wisdom brings joy to
    his father,
  but a companion of prostitutes
    squanders his wealth.

⁴By justice a king gives a country
    stability,
  but one who is greedy for bribes tears
    it down.

⁵Whoever flatters his neighbor
  is spreading a net for his feet.

⁶An evil man is snared by his own sin,
  but a righteous one can sing and be
    glad.

⁷The righteous care about justice for the
    poor,
  but the wicked have no such concern.

⁸Mockers stir up a city,
  but wise men turn away anger.

⁹If a wise man goes to court with a fool,
  the fool rages and scoffs, and there is
    no peace.

¹⁰Bloodthirsty men hate a man of
    integrity
  and seek to kill the upright.

¹¹A fool gives full vent to his anger,
  but a wise man keeps himself under
    control.

¹²If a ruler listens to lies,
  all his officials become wicked.

¹³The poor man and the oppressor have
    this in common:
  The Lord gives sight to the eyes of
    both.

¹⁴If a king judges the poor with fairness,
  his throne will always be secure.

¹⁵The rod of correction imparts wisdom,
  but a child left to himself disgraces
    his mother.

¹⁶When the wicked thrive, so does sin,
  but the righteous will see their
    downfall.

¹⁷Discipline your son, and he will give
    you peace;
  he will bring delight to your soul.

¹⁸Where there is no revelation, the people
    cast off restraint;
  but blessed is he who keeps the law.

¹⁹A servant cannot be corrected by mere
    words;
  though he understands, he will not
    respond.

²⁰Do you see a man who speaks in haste?
  There is more hope for a fool than for
    him.

²¹If a man pampers his servant from
     youth,
   he will bring grief*a* in the end.

²²An angry man stirs up dissension,
   and a hot-tempered one commits
     many sins.

²³A man's pride brings him low,
   but a man of lowly spirit gains honor.

²⁴The accomplice of a thief is his own
     enemy;
   he is put under oath and dare not
     testify.

²⁵Fear of man will prove to be a snare,
   but whoever trusts in the LORD is kept
     safe.

²⁶Many seek an audience with a ruler,
   but it is from the LORD that man gets
     justice.

²⁷The righteous detest the dishonest;
   the wicked detest the upright.

Sayings of Agur

30 The sayings of Agur son of Jakeh—
     an oracle*b*:

This man declared to Ithiel,
   to Ithiel and to Ucal:*c*

²"I am the most ignorant of men;
   I do not have a man's understanding.
³I have not learned wisdom,
   nor have I knowledge of the Holy
     One.
⁴Who has gone up to heaven and come
     down?
   Who has gathered up the wind in the
     hollow of his hands?
   Who has wrapped up the waters in his
     cloak?
   Who has established all the ends of
     the earth?
   What is his name, and the name of his
     son?
   Tell me if you know!

⁵"Every word of God is flawless;
   he is a shield to those who take
     refuge in him.
⁶Do not add to his words,
   or he will rebuke you and prove you
     a liar.

⁷"Two things I ask of you, O LORD;

do not refuse me before I die:
⁸Keep falsehood and lies far from me;
   give me neither poverty nor riches,
   but give me only my daily bread.
⁹Otherwise, I may have too much and
     disown you
   and say, 'Who is the LORD?'
   Or I may become poor and steal,
   and so dishonor the name of my God.

¹⁰"Do not slander a servant to his master,
   or he will curse you, and you will pay
     for it.

¹¹"There are those who curse their fathers
   and do not bless their mothers;
¹²those who are pure in their own eyes
   and yet are not cleansed of their filth;
¹³those whose eyes are ever so haughty,
   whose glances are so disdainful;
¹⁴those whose teeth are swords
   and whose jaws are set with knives
   to devour the poor from the earth,
   the needy from among mankind.

¹⁵"The leech has two daughters.
   'Give! Give!' they cry.

"There are three things that are never
     satisfied,
   four that never say, 'Enough!':
¹⁶the grave,*d* the barren womb,
   land, which is never satisfied with
     water,
   and fire, which never says, 'Enough!'

¹⁷"The eye that mocks a father,
   that scorns obedience to a mother,
   will be pecked out by the ravens of the
     valley,
   will be eaten by the vultures.

¹⁸"There are three things that are too
     amazing for me,
   four that I do not understand:
¹⁹the way of an eagle in the sky,
   the way of a snake on a rock,
   the way of a ship on the high seas,
   and the way of a man with a maiden.

²⁰"This is the way of an adulteress:
   She eats and wipes her mouth
   and says, 'I've done nothing wrong.'

²¹"Under three things the earth trembles,
   under four it cannot bear up:
²²a servant who becomes king,
   a fool who is full of food,
²³an unloved woman who is married,

a21 The meaning of the Hebrew for this word is uncertain.   *b1* Or *Jakeh of Massa*   *c1* Masoretic Text; with
a different word division of the Hebrew *declared, "I am weary, O God; / I am weary, O God, and faint.*
d16 Hebrew *Sheol*

AMBUSHED BY ANGER

R ight in the middle of English class, Anne suddenly shrieks, "No!" Everyone, except Mrs. Whitten, who's hard of hearing, turns just in time to see Sherri put a note on Brad's desk.

Anne buries her face in her arms, dying of embarrassment. She had just passed a note to Sherri about how cute Brad is and how she really wishes he'd call her sometime. All of a sudden, Sherri, with a devilish grin, had leaned forward and given the note to Brad!

In a few minutes Anne is more than embarrassed; she's mad! "How can a good friend do something so rotten?" she wonders.

Look It Up
••••

Anger is powerful, isn't it? One minute, you're smiling; the next, smoke is coming out of your ears!

Consider these verses:

" 'In your anger do not sin': Do not let the sun go down while you are still angry" (Ephesians 4:26).

"Everyone should be . . . slow to become angry, for man's anger does not bring about the righteous life that God desires" (James 1:19–20).

Hey, what gives? The first passage seems to condone anger. But the second seems to be saying that anger is to be avoided. Is this one of those famous contradictions that people say the Bible is full of?

Think It Through
••••

Paul and James are talking about different kinds of anger. The anger of Ephesians 4:26 might be called righteous indignation. It's the justifiable anger you feel when you or others have clearly been wronged. Jesus felt this kind of anger when he cleared the money changers from the temple.

But James warns against a selfish tendency to rationalize anger too quickly and for trivial reasons.

Work It Out
••••

When you feel your temperature rising, don't explode! Count to ten and pray immediately (Proverbs 29:11).

With the Bible as your guide, try to honestly assess the situation. Is your anger justifiable, or is it selfish?

If it's selfish, ask God to help you drop it.

If it's justifiable, don't bury your feelings and burn! Talk gently with the offending party (Luke 17:3). If they repent, forgive them immediately. If they refuse, give the situation to God (Romans 12:17–21). He will handle it with perfect justice.

Nail It Down
••••

Read the warning in Proverbs 29:22

Turn to pages 572, 694, 939, 1026, 1148 and 1178 for other readings on feelings.
Turn to page 692 for Thursday's reading.

Topic
••••

FEELINGS

and a maidservant who displaces her
   mistress.

24"Four things on earth are small,
   yet they are extremely wise:
25Ants are creatures of little strength,
   yet they store up their food in the
     summer;
26coneys*a* are creatures of little power,
   yet they make their home in the
     crags;
27locusts have no king,
   yet they advance together in ranks;
28a lizard can be caught with the hand,
   yet it is found in kings' palaces.

29"There are three things that are stately
   in their stride,
   four that move with stately bearing:
30a lion, mighty among beasts,
   who retreats before nothing;
31a strutting rooster, a he-goat,
   and a king with his army around
     him.*b*

32"If you have played the fool and exalted
   yourself,
   or if you have planned evil,
   clap your hand over your mouth!
33For as churning the milk produces
   butter,
   and as twisting the nose produces
     blood,
   so stirring up anger produces strife."

Sayings of King Lemuel

31 The sayings of King Lemuel—an oracle*c* his mother taught him:

2"O my son, O son of my womb,
   O son of my vows,*d*
3do not spend your strength on women,
   your vigor on those who ruin kings.

4"It is not for kings, O Lemuel—
   not for kings to drink wine,
   not for rulers to crave beer,
5lest they drink and forget what the law
   decrees,
   and deprive all the oppressed of their
     rights.
6Give beer to those who are perishing,
   wine to those who are in anguish;
7let them drink and forget their poverty
   and remember their misery no more.

8"Speak up for those who cannot speak
   for themselves,
   for the rights of all who are destitute.
9Speak up and judge fairly;
   defend the rights of the poor and
     needy."

Epilogue: The Wife of Noble Character

10*e*A wife of noble character who can
   find?
   She is worth far more than rubies.
11Her husband has full confidence in her
   and lacks nothing of value.
12She brings him good, not harm,
   all the days of her life.
13She selects wool and flax
   and works with eager hands.
14She is like the merchant ships,
   bringing her food from afar.
15She gets up while it is still dark;
   she provides food for her family
   and portions for her servant girls.
16She considers a field and buys it;
   out of her earnings she plants a
     vineyard.
17She sets about her work vigorously;
   her arms are strong for her tasks.
18She sees that her trading is profitable,
   and her lamp does not go out at
     night.
19In her hand she holds the distaff
   and grasps the spindle with her
     fingers.
20She opens her arms to the poor
   and extends her hands to the needy.
21When it snows, she has no fear for her
   household;
   for all of them are clothed in scarlet.
22She makes coverings for her bed;
   she is clothed in fine linen and
     purple.
23Her husband is respected at the city
   gate,
   where he takes his seat among the
     elders of the land.
24She makes linen garments and sells
   them,
   and supplies the merchants with
     sashes.
25She is clothed with strength and dignity;
   she can laugh at the days to come.

---

a26 That is, the hyrax or rock badger   *b31* Or *king secure against revolt*   *c1* Or *of Lemuel king of Massa,*
which   *d2* Or / *the answer to my prayers*   *e10* Verses 10-31 are an acrostic, each verse beginning with a
successive letter of the Hebrew alphabet.

²⁶She speaks with wisdom,
　　and faithful instruction is on her
　　　tongue.
²⁷She watches over the affairs of her
　　household
　　and does not eat the bread of
　　　idleness.
²⁸Her children arise and call her blessed;
　　her husband also, and he praises her:

²⁹"Many women do noble things,
　　but you surpass them all."
³⁰Charm is deceptive, and beauty is
　　fleeting;
　　but a woman who fears the LORD is to
　　　be praised.
³¹Give her the reward she has earned,
　　and let her works bring her praise at
　　the city gate.

ECCLESIASTES

WHERE can you find meaning and purpose for life? That is the age-old question raised by the writer of Ecclesiastes, who searches long and hard to find satisfaction "under the sun"—apart from God. His conclusion? Without God, life is a useless passion. If what you see is all there is, nothing really matters. As you read, keep in mind that satisfaction comes only when you fear, honor and obey God. And the very best time to start loving him is when you are young (Ecclesiastes 12:1).

Outline of Contents

Everything Is Meaningless

1 The words of the Teacher,[a] son of David, king in Jerusalem:

[2] "Meaningless! Meaningless!"
    says the Teacher.
"Utterly meaningless!
    Everything is meaningless."

[3] What does man gain from all his labor
    at which he toils under the sun?
[4] Generations come and generations go,
    but the earth remains forever.
[5] The sun rises and the sun sets,
    and hurries back to where it rises.
[6] The wind blows to the south
    and turns to the north;
round and round it goes,
    ever returning on its course.
[7] All streams flow into the sea,
    yet the sea is never full.
To the place the streams come
    from,
    there they return again.
[8] All things are wearisome,
    more than one can say.
The eye never has enough of seeing,
    nor the ear its fill of hearing.

[a]1 Or leader of the assembly; also in verses 2 and 12

[9]What has been will be again,
    what has been done will be done
        again;
    there is nothing new under the sun.
[10]Is there anything of which one can say,
    "Look! This is something new"?
  It was here already, long ago;
    it was here before our time.
[11]There is no remembrance of men of
       old,
    and even those who are yet to come
will not be remembered
    by those who follow.

Wisdom Is Meaningless

[12]I, the Teacher, was king over Israel in Jerusalem. [13]I devoted myself to study and to explore by wisdom all that is done under heaven. What a heavy burden God has laid on men! [14]I have seen all the things that are done under the sun; all of them are meaningless, a chasing after the wind.

[15]What is twisted cannot be straightened;
    what is lacking cannot be counted.

[16]I thought to myself, "Look, I have grown and increased in wisdom more than anyone who has ruled over Jerusalem before me; I have experienced much of wisdom and knowledge." [17]Then I applied myself to the understanding of wisdom, and also of madness and folly, but I learned that this, too, is a chasing after the wind.

[18]For with much wisdom comes much
      sorrow;
    the more knowledge, the more grief.

Pleasures Are Meaningless

2 I thought in my heart, "Come now, I will test you with pleasure to find out what is good." But that also proved to be meaningless. [2]"Laughter," I said, "is foolish. And what does pleasure accomplish?" [3]I tried cheering myself with wine, and embracing folly—my mind still guiding me with wisdom. I wanted to see what was worthwhile for men to do under heaven during the few days of their lives.

[4]I undertook great projects: I built houses for myself and planted vineyards. [5]I made gardens and parks and planted all kinds of fruit trees in them. [6]I made reservoirs to water groves of flourishing trees. [7]I bought male and female slaves and had other slaves who were born in my house. I also owned more herds and flocks than anyone in Jeru-

salem before me. [8]I amassed silver and gold for myself, and the treasure of kings and provinces. I acquired men and women singers, and a harem[a] as well—the delights of the heart of man. [9]I became greater by far than anyone in Jerusalem before me. In all this my wisdom stayed with me.

[10]I denied myself nothing my eyes
      desired;
  I refused my heart no pleasure.
My heart took delight in all my work,
    and this was the reward for all my
      labor.
[11]Yet when I surveyed all that my hands
      had done
  and what I had toiled to achieve,
everything was meaningless, a chasing
      after the wind;
  nothing was gained under the sun.

Wisdom and Folly Are Meaningless

[12]Then I turned my thoughts to consider
      wisdom,
    and also madness and folly.
What more can the king's successor do
    than what has already been done?
[13]I saw that wisdom is better than folly,
    just as light is better than darkness.
[14]The wise man has eyes in his head,
    while the fool walks in the darkness;
but I came to realize
    that the same fate overtakes them
      both.

[15]Then I thought in my heart,

"The fate of the fool will overtake me
      also.
    What then do I gain by being wise?"
I said in my heart,
    "This too is meaningless."
[16]For the wise man, like the fool, will not
      be long remembered;
    in days to come both will be
      forgotten.
Like the fool, the wise man too must
      die!

Toil Is Meaningless

[17]So I hated life, because the work that is done under the sun was grievous to me. All of it is meaningless, a chasing after the wind. [18]I hated all the things I had toiled for under the sun, because I must leave them to the one who comes after me. [19]And who knows whether he will be a wise man or a fool? Yet he will have control over all the

---

[a]8 The meaning of the Hebrew for this phrase is uncertain.

work into which I have poured my effort and skill under the sun. This too is meaningless. ²⁰So my heart began to despair over all my toilsome labor under the sun. ²¹For a man may do his work with wisdom, knowledge and skill, and then he must leave all he owns to someone who has not worked for it. This too is meaningless and a great misfortune. ²²What does a man get for all the toil and anxious striving with which he labors under the sun? ²³All his days his work is pain and grief; even at night his mind does not rest. This too is meaningless.

²⁴A man can do nothing better than to eat and drink and find satisfaction in his work. This too, I see, is from the hand of God, ²⁵for without him, who can eat or find enjoyment? ²⁶To the man who pleases him, God gives wisdom, knowledge and happiness, but to the sinner he gives the task of gathering and storing up wealth to hand it over to the one who pleases God. This too is meaningless, a chasing after the wind.

A Time for Everything

3 There is a time for everything,
　　and a season for every activity under
　　　heaven:

²　a time to be born and a time to die,
　　a time to plant and a time to uproot,
³　a time to kill and a time to heal,
　　a time to tear down and a time to
　　　build,
⁴　a time to weep and a time to laugh,
　　a time to mourn and a time to dance,
⁵　a time to scatter stones and a time to
　　　gather them,
　　a time to embrace and a time to
　　　refrain,
⁶　a time to search and a time to give
　　　up,
　　a time to keep and a time to throw
　　　away,
⁷　a time to tear and a time to mend,
　　a time to be silent and a time to
　　　speak,
⁸　a time to love and a time to hate,
　　a time for war and a time for peace.

⁹What does the worker gain from his toil? ¹⁰I have seen the burden God has laid on men. ¹¹He has made everything beautiful in its time. He has also set eternity in the hearts of men; yet they cannot fathom what God has done from beginning to end. ¹²I know that there is nothing better for men than to

be happy and do good while they live. ¹³That everyone may eat and drink, and find satisfaction in all his toil—this is the gift of God. ¹⁴I know that everything God does will endure forever; nothing can be added to it and nothing taken from it. God does it so that men will revere him.

¹⁵Whatever is has already been,
　　and what will be has been before;
　　and God will call the past to
　　　account.^a

¹⁶And I saw something else under the sun:

In the place of judgment—wickedness
　　　was there,
　　in the place of justice—wickedness
　　　was there.

¹⁷I thought in my heart,

"God will bring to judgment
　　both the righteous and the wicked,
for there will be a time for every
　　　activity,
　　a time for every deed."

¹⁸I also thought, "As for men, God tests them so that they may see that they are like the animals. ¹⁹Man's fate is like that of the animals; the same fate awaits them both: As one dies, so dies the other. All have the same breath^b; man has no advantage over the animal. Everything is meaningless. ²⁰All go to the same place; all come from dust, and to dust all return. ²¹Who knows if the spirit of man rises upward and if the spirit of the animal^c goes down into the earth?"

²²So I saw that there is nothing better for a man than to enjoy his work, because that is his lot. For who can bring him to see what will happen after him?

Oppression, Toil, Friendlessness

4 Again I looked and saw all the oppression that was taking place under the sun:

I saw the tears of the oppressed—
　　and they have no comforter;
power was on the side of their
　　　oppressors—
　　and they have no comforter.
²And I declared that the dead,
　　who had already died,
are happier than the living,
　　who are still alive.

---

^a15 Or *God calls back the past*　^b19 Or *spirit*　^c21 Or *Who knows the spirit of man, which rises upward, or the spirit of the animal, which*

LEISURE DOES NOT EQUAL LAZINESS!

Nobody needs to urge sixteen-year-old Darrin to include leisure in his lifestyle. The guy lives (so it seems) solely to relax and have fun. Consider:

He sleeps about ten hours a day (in the summer—about twelve). He never lifts a finger around the house. He seldom brings home a book. He spends almost all his waking hours hanging out with friends, listening to music, watching videos, talking on the phone, and cruising around on his motorcycle.

Look It Up
••••

Does God want us to have some leisure and find enjoyment in life? No doubt about it. Is it possible to go overboard in seeking the good life? The apostle Paul seemed to think so:

"In the name of the Lord Jesus Christ, we command you, brothers, to keep away from every brother who is idle. . . . We were not idle when we were with you. . . . On the contrary, we worked night and day. . . . We hear that some among you are idle. They are not busy; they are busybodies. Such people we command and urge in the Lord Jesus Christ to settle down and earn the bread they eat" (2 Thessalonians 3:6–8,11–12).

From this passage we can conclude that true leisure does not equal laziness!

Think It Through
••••

As in every area of life, we must find a balance. None of the things Darrin does are inherently wrong. It's just that he does them to the exclusion of almost everything else!

Do you agree or disagree with the following statements?
• Our culture places too much emphasis on entertainment.
• My friends aren't concerned about having fun.
• Too much pursuit of pleasure is a form of selfishness.

Work It Out
••••

Have you been acting like Darrin? Have you let recreation and amusements become too important in your life?

Pray this prayer: "Lord, forgive me for getting my priorities mixed up. I've made leisure more important than serving you. That's wrong and I want to change. Help me get back on track today. Amen."

Now, take a look at your schedule and make the tough decision to cut out some of the fluff.

Nail It Down
••••

Read Ecclesiastes 3:1–8 where we're told that there is a time for everything, even work and play.

Turn to pages 81, 339, 553 and 609 for other readings on leisure.
Turn to page 694 for Friday's reading.

Topic
••••

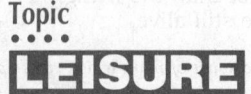

3But better than both
  is he who has not yet been,
who has not seen the evil
  that is done under the sun.

4And I saw that all labor and all achievement spring from man's envy of his neighbor. This too is meaningless, a chasing after the wind.

5The fool folds his hands
  and ruins himself.
6Better one handful with tranquillity
  than two handfuls with toil
  and chasing after the wind.

7Again I saw something meaningless under the sun:

8There was a man all alone;
  he had neither son nor brother.
There was no end to his toil,
  yet his eyes were not content with his
    wealth.
"For whom am I toiling," he asked,
"and why am I depriving myself of
    enjoyment?"
This too is meaningless—
  a miserable business!

9Two are better than one,
  because they have a good return for
    their work:
10If one falls down,
  his friend can help him up.
But pity the man who falls
  and has no one to help him up!
11Also, if two lie down together, they will
    keep warm.
But how can one keep warm alone?
12Though one may be overpowered,
  two can defend themselves.
A cord of three strands is not quickly
    broken.

Advancement Is Meaningless

13Better a poor but wise youth than an old but foolish king who no longer knows how to take warning. **14**The youth may have come from prison to the kingship, or he may have been born in poverty within his kingdom. **15**I saw that all who lived and walked under the sun followed the youth, the king's successor. **16**There was no end to all the people who were before them. But those who came later were not pleased with the successor. This too is meaningless, a chasing after the wind.

Stand in Awe of God

5 Guard your steps when you go to the house of God. Go near to listen rather than to offer the sacrifice of fools, who do not know that they do wrong.

2Do not be quick with your mouth,
  do not be hasty in your heart
  to utter anything before God.
God is in heaven
  and you are on earth,
  so let your words be few.
3As a dream comes when there are many
    cares,
  so the speech of a fool when there
    are many words.

4When you make a vow to God, do not delay in fulfilling it. He has no pleasure in fools; fulfill your vow. **5**It is better not to vow than to make a vow and not fulfill it. **6**Do not let your mouth lead you into sin. And do not protest to the ⌞temple⌟ messenger, "My vow was a mistake." Why should God be angry at what you say and destroy the work of your hands? **7**Much dreaming and many words are meaningless. Therefore stand in awe of God.

Riches Are Meaningless

8If you see the poor oppressed in a district, and justice and rights denied, do not be surprised at such things; for one official is eyed by a higher one, and over them both are others higher still. **9**The increase from the land is taken by all; the king himself profits from the fields.

10Whoever loves money never has money
    enough;
  whoever loves wealth is never
    satisfied with his income.
This too is meaningless.

11As goods increase,
  so do those who consume them.
And what benefit are they to the owner
  except to feast his eyes on them?

12The sleep of a laborer is sweet,
  whether he eats little or much,
but the abundance of a rich man
  permits him no sleep.

13I have seen a grievous evil under the sun:

wealth hoarded to the harm of its
    owner,
14 or wealth lost through some
    misfortune,
so that when he has a son

REACH OUT AND TOUCH SOMEONE

As the bell rings to end Mrs. Whitten's English class on Friday, everyone jumps up and rushes to the gym. A big pep rally has been scheduled to get the basketball team pumped up for the state championship game tonight. After the game is a "Victory Dance." (Plus there's no school on Monday because of a teacher's work day.)

Everyone's celebrating. Everyone but Leanne.

You see, Leanne lives out in the "boonies." She's an only child. Her one good friend is going to visit relatives. With no driver's license, no date, no other friends and no plans, Leanne isn't exactly excited about the weekend.

Isn't it strange that a person can feel incredibly lonely even in the middle of a pep rally, even when surrounded by 1,500 people?

Look It Up
••••

Loneliness is feeling like you're cut off from the human race; like there's no one to call; like no one cares about you or even knows if you're alive. Does God's Word offer the lonely Leannes of the world any hope? Yes! Here are three great principles:

Tell God how you feel. That's what David did. "Turn to me and be gracious to me, for I am lonely and afflicted . . . . my hope is in you" (Psalm 25:16,21).

Thank God for his companionship. He's always with you (Hebrews 13:5).

Ask God to provide opportunities for new friendships. That's a prayer he'll answer. He doesn't want you to be lonely (Ecclesiastes 4:9–10).

Think It Through
••••

Suppose Leanne lived in a big neighborhood, had sixteen brothers and sisters, had every guy in the school calling her for dates and had lots of girls wanting to be her friend. Could she still feel lonely? She might (and lots of "popular" people do!). It takes close relationships to overcome the "lonelies." And you only make friends when you are a friend—one who reaches out to others.

Work It Out
••••

Seek out someone you suspect may be feeling lonely today. Include that person in your plans this weekend.

If *you* feel lonely, follow the steps above. Don't sit around having your own "pity party"! Overcoming loneliness often begins with a prayer and a phone call or two.

Nail It Down
••••

Read Ecclesiastes 4:8 for a description of true loneliness.

Turn to pages 572, 686, 939, 1026, 1148 and 1178 for other readings on feelings.
Turn to page 696 for the weekend reading.

Topic
••••

there is nothing left for him.
¹⁵Naked a man comes from his mother's
womb,
and as he comes, so he departs.
He takes nothing from his labor
that he can carry in his hand.

¹⁶This too is a grievous evil:

As a man comes, so he departs,
and what does he gain,
since he toils for the wind?
¹⁷All his days he eats in darkness,
with great frustration, affliction and
anger.

¹⁸Then I realized that it is good and proper
for a man to eat and drink, and to find satisfaction in his toilsome labor under the sun
during the few days of life God has given
him—for this is his lot. ¹⁹Moreover, when
God gives any man wealth and possessions,
and enables him to enjoy them, to accept
his lot and be happy in his work—this is a
gift of God. ²⁰He seldom reflects on the days
of his life, because God keeps him occupied
with gladness of heart.

6 I have seen another evil under the sun,
and it weighs heavily on men: ²God
gives a man wealth, possessions and honor,
so that he lacks nothing his heart desires,
but God does not enable him to enjoy them,
and a stranger enjoys them instead. This is
meaningless, a grievous evil.

³A man may have a hundred children and
live many years; yet no matter how long he
lives, if he cannot enjoy his prosperity and
does not receive proper burial, I say that a
stillborn child is better off than he. ⁴It comes
without meaning, it departs in darkness,
and in darkness its name is shrouded.
⁵Though it never saw the sun or knew anything, it has more rest than does that man—
⁶even if he lives a thousand years twice over
but fails to enjoy his prosperity. Do not all
go to the same place?

⁷All man's efforts are for his mouth,
yet his appetite is never satisfied.
⁸What advantage has a wise man
over a fool?
What does a poor man gain
by knowing how to conduct himself
before others?
⁹Better what the eye sees
than the roving of the appetite.
This too is meaningless,
a chasing after the wind.

¹⁰Whatever exists has already been
named,

and what man is has been known;
no man can contend
with one who is stronger than he.
¹¹The more the words,
the less the meaning,
and how does that profit anyone?

¹²For who knows what is good for a man
in life, during the few and meaningless days
he passes through like a shadow? Who can
tell him what will happen under the sun after he is gone?

Wisdom

7 A good name is better than fine
perfume,
and the day of death better than the
day of birth.
²It is better to go to a house of mourning
than to go to a house of feasting,
for death is the destiny of every man;
the living should take this to heart.
³Sorrow is better than laughter,
because a sad face is good for the
heart.
⁴The heart of the wise is in the house of
mourning,
but the heart of fools is in the house
of pleasure.
⁵It is better to heed a wise man's rebuke
than to listen to the song of fools.
⁶Like the crackling of thorns under the
pot,
so is the laughter of fools.
This too is meaningless.

⁷Extortion turns a wise man into a fool,
and a bribe corrupts the heart.

⁸The end of a matter is better than its
beginning,
and patience is better than pride.
⁹Do not be quickly provoked in your
spirit,
for anger resides in the lap of fools.

¹⁰Do not say, "Why were the old days
better than these?"
For it is not wise to ask such
questions.

¹¹Wisdom, like an inheritance, is a good
thing
and benefits those who see the sun.
¹²Wisdom is a shelter
as money is a shelter,
but the advantage of knowledge is this:
that wisdom preserves the life of its
possessor.

¹³Consider what God has done:

CONTENTMENT DESCRIBED

....

**Work It
Out**
....

The next time you watch TV, write down all the things the advertisers think you need: hairspray, deodorant, cars, fast food, appliances. The list is almost endless.

Now take a close look at just how the advertisements try to get you to purchase their products. Mostly, they try to make you discontent with what you already have. The subtle (and sometimes not so subtle) claim of the commercials is that if you purchase the product your life will be in great shape. You won't need another thing to be happy . . . you'll be content.

It doesn't take much brain power to figure out that a new facial cleansing cream isn't going to make your life radically different. Nail polish can't change attitudes. And attitude is where contentment begins, not with new cars, cleaner teeth or brighter whites. Contentment is an inner quality, not something to be achieved by outward possessions.

Don't let the advertisers pull you into their trap. They have nothing to offer that will bring satisfaction or contentment. Only God can offer that. If the commercials continue to bother your feelings of contentment, turn off the TV.

**Nail It
Down**
....

Read the Teacher's description of contentment in Ecclesiastes 5:18–20.

....

**Think It
Through**
....

It's a pretty sad fact, but it's still a true one: the more you have the less content you become. Possessions are a bit like an itch that needs to be scratched. The more it itches, the more you scratch; the more you scratch, the more it itches.

If you are having a hard time being content, go to the source of all contentment: God. You won't need any money; he gives it away freely. You'll never run short; he's got plenty. And almost without realizing it, you'll find yourself enjoying your life a whole lot more.

**Nail It
Down**
....

Reread the passage on contentment in Ecclesiastes 5:18–20. For further insight read Ecclesiastes 5:10.

Turn to pages 1294, 1321 and 1354 for other readings on contentment.
Turn to page 699 for Monday's reading.

Topic
....

CONTENTMENT

Who can straighten
    what he has made crooked?
14When times are good, be happy;
    but when times are bad, consider:
God has made the one
    as well as the other.
Therefore, a man cannot discover
    anything about his future.

15In this meaningless life of mine I have
seen both of these:

a righteous man perishing in his
    righteousness,
and a wicked man living long in his
    wickedness.
16Do not be overrighteous,
    neither be overwise—
    why destroy yourself?
17Do not be overwicked,
    and do not be a fool—
    why die before your time?
18It is good to grasp the one
    and not let go of the other.
The man who fears God will avoid all
    extremes. *a*

19Wisdom makes one wise man more
    powerful
    than ten rulers in a city.

20There is not a righteous man on earth
    who does what is right and never
    sins.

21Do not pay attention to every word
    people say,
    or you may hear your servant cursing
    you—
22for you know in your heart
    that many times you yourself have
    cursed others.

23All this I tested by wisdom and I said,

"I am determined to be wise"—
    but this was beyond me.
24Whatever wisdom may be,
    it is far off and most profound—
    who can discover it?
25So I turned my mind to understand,
    to investigate and to search out
      wisdom and the scheme of things
and to understand the stupidity of
    wickedness
and the madness of folly.
26I find more bitter than death
    the woman who is a snare,
    whose heart is a trap

and whose hands are chains.
The man who pleases God will escape
    her,
    but the sinner she will ensnare.

27"Look," says the Teacher, *b* "this is what
I have discovered:

"Adding one thing to another to discover
    the scheme of things—
28 while I was still searching
    but not finding—
I found one upright man among a
    thousand,
    but not one upright woman among
    them all.
29This only have I found:
    God made mankind upright,
    but men have gone in search of many
    schemes."

8 Who is like the wise man?
    Who knows the explanation of
      things?
Wisdom brightens a man's face
    and changes its hard appearance.

Obey the King

2Obey the king's command, I say, because you took an oath before God. **3**Do not
be in a hurry to leave the king's presence. Do
not stand up for a bad cause, for he will do
whatever he pleases. **4**Since a king's word is
supreme, who can say to him, "What are
you doing?"

5Whoever obeys his command will come
    to no harm,
    and the wise heart will know the
      proper time and procedure.
6For there is a proper time and
    procedure for every matter,
    though a man's misery weighs heavily
      upon him.

7Since no man knows the future,
    who can tell him what is to come?
8No man has power over the wind to
    contain it*c*;
    so no one has power over the day of
      his death.
As no one is discharged in time of war,
    so wickedness will not release those
      who practice it.

9All this I saw, as I applied my mind to
everything done under the sun. There is a
time when a man lords it over others to his
own*d* hurt. **10**Then too, I saw the wicked

---

a18 Or *will follow them both*   *b27* Or *leader of the assembly*   *c8* Or *over his spirit to retain it*   *d9* Or *to*
their

buried—those who used to come and go from the holy place and receive praise[a] in the city where they did this. This too is meaningless.

[11]When the sentence for a crime is not quickly carried out, the hearts of the people are filled with schemes to do wrong. [12]Although a wicked man commits a hundred crimes and still lives a long time, I know that it will go better with God-fearing men, who are reverent before God. [13]Yet because the wicked do not fear God, it will not go well with them, and their days will not lengthen like a shadow.

[14]There is something else meaningless that occurs on earth: righteous men who get what the wicked deserve, and wicked men who get what the righteous deserve. This too, I say, is meaningless. [15]So I commend the enjoyment of life, because nothing is better for a man under the sun than to eat and drink and be glad. Then joy will accompany him in his work all the days of the life God has given him under the sun.

[16]When I applied my mind to know wisdom and to observe man's labor on earth—his eyes not seeing sleep day or night—[17]then I saw all that God has done. No one can comprehend what goes on under the sun. Despite all his efforts to search it out, man cannot discover its meaning. Even if a wise man claims he knows, he cannot really comprehend it.

A Common Destiny for All

9 So I reflected on all this and concluded that the righteous and the wise and what they do are in God's hands, but no man knows whether love or hate awaits him. [2]All share a common destiny—the righteous and the wicked, the good and the bad,[b] the clean and the unclean, those who offer sacrifices and those who do not.

As it is with the good man,
   so with the sinner;
as it is with those who take oaths,
   so with those who are afraid to take
     them.

[3]This is the evil in everything that happens under the sun: The same destiny overtakes all. The hearts of men, moreover, are full of evil and there is madness in their hearts while they live, and afterward they join the dead. [4]Anyone who is among the

living has hope[c]—even a live dog is better off than a dead lion!

[5]For the living know that they will die,
   but the dead know nothing;
they have no further reward,
   and even the memory of them is
     forgotten.
[6]Their love, their hate
   and their jealousy have long since
     vanished;
never again will they have a part
   in anything that happens under the
     sun.

[7]Go, eat your food with gladness, and drink your wine with a joyful heart, for it is now that God favors what you do. [8]Always be clothed in white, and always anoint your head with oil. [9]Enjoy life with your wife, whom you love, all the days of this meaningless life that God has given you under the sun—all your meaningless days. For this is your lot in life and in your toilsome labor under the sun. [10]Whatever your hand finds to do, do it with all your might, for in the grave,[d] where you are going, there is neither working nor planning nor knowledge nor wisdom.

[11]I have seen something else under the sun:

The race is not to the swift
   or the battle to the strong,
nor does food come to the wise
   or wealth to the brilliant
   or favor to the learned;
but time and chance happen to them
     all.

[12]Moreover, no man knows when his hour will come:

As fish are caught in a cruel net,
   or birds are taken in a snare,
so men are trapped by evil times
   that fall unexpectedly upon them.

Wisdom Better Than Folly

[13]I also saw under the sun this example of wisdom that greatly impressed me: [14]There was once a small city with only a few people in it. And a powerful king came against it, surrounded it and built huge siegeworks against it. [15]Now there lived in that city a man poor but wise, and he saved the city by his wisdom. But nobody remembered that

---

[a]10 Some Hebrew manuscripts and Septuagint (Aquila); most Hebrew manuscripts *and are forgotten*
[b]2 Septuagint (Aquila), Vulgate and Syriac; Hebrew does not have *and the bad*.   [c]4 Or *What then is to be chosen? With all who live, there is hope*   [d]10 Hebrew *Sheol*

THE CULT OF THE UNCOMMITTED

Scene 1: "You can't quit now! The youth musical is only two weeks away!"

"Look, I just decided I don't want to do it."

"But you promised . . . everybody's counting on you."

"Well, that's too bad, because I changed my mind."

Scene 2: "Hey, see you at the beach outreach, okay?"

"Uh, Vic, something . . . er, came up. I can't make it."

"Can't make it? You told me yesterday you'd be there. I'm counting on you to drive."

"I'm sorry, but something urgent came up at the last minute."

Look It Up

When the famous explorer Cortez set foot on the shores of Mexico, he did an amazing thing. He ordered his soldiers to set fire to the ships that had carried them from Spain to Central America!

No backing out at a later date. No boats in the bushes just in case. Only ashes on the beach. Cortez was committed.

Are you that committed to Christ? Or are you like the Jewish leaders in John 12?

"At the same time many even among the leaders believed in him [Jesus]. But because of the Pharisees they would not confess their faith for fear they would be put out of the synagogue; for they loved praise from men more than praise from God" (John 12:42–43).

Think It Through

Job-hoppers, church-shoppers, spouse-swappers—most people aren't very dedicated to anything! Check where you are in your Christian commitment:

• I usually live for Christ only as long as it's convenient, comfortable and cool. (I don't want to get too radical or be too weird!)

• I honestly try to do what's right regardless of feelings, the opinions of others or how demanding things become.

Work It Out

Without God's direct intervention, all the vows and promises and pledges in the world won't mean a thing. To be truly committed, you need the touch of the Holy Spirit in your life. Pray:

"Father, deepen my commitment this week. Give me a deeper love for you, a more fervent desire to know you, and a greater willingness to obey you. Amen."

Nail It Down

Read Solomon's reply to the uncommitted in Ecclesiates 9:10.

Turn to pages 182, 358 and 445 for other readings on commitment.
Turn to page 702 for Tuesday's reading.

Topic

poor man. [16]So I said, "Wisdom is better than strength." But the poor man's wisdom is despised, and his words are no longer heeded.

[17]The quiet words of the wise are more to be heeded
than the shouts of a ruler of fools.
[18]Wisdom is better than weapons of war,
but one sinner destroys much good.

10 As dead flies give perfume a bad smell,
so a little folly outweighs wisdom and honor.
[2]The heart of the wise inclines to the right,
but the heart of the fool to the left.
[3]Even as he walks along the road,
the fool lacks sense
and shows everyone how stupid he is.
[4]If a ruler's anger rises against you,
do not leave your post;
calmness can lay great errors to rest.

[5]There is an evil I have seen under the sun,
the sort of error that arises from a ruler:
[6]Fools are put in many high positions,
while the rich occupy the low ones.
[7]I have seen slaves on horseback,
while princes go on foot like slaves.

[8]Whoever digs a pit may fall into it;
whoever breaks through a wall may be bitten by a snake.
[9]Whoever quarries stones may be injured by them;
whoever splits logs may be endangered by them.

[10]If the ax is dull
and its edge unsharpened,
more strength is needed
but skill will bring success.

[11]If a snake bites before it is charmed,
there is no profit for the charmer.

[12]Words from a wise man's mouth are gracious,
but a fool is consumed by his own lips.
[13]At the beginning his words are folly;
at the end they are wicked madness—
[14] and the fool multiplies words.

No one knows what is coming—

who can tell him what will happen after him?

[15]A fool's work wearies him;
he does not know the way to town.

[16]Woe to you, O land whose king was a servant[a]
and whose princes feast in the morning.
[17]Blessed are you, O land whose king is of noble birth
and whose princes eat at a proper time—
for strength and not for drunkenness.

[18]If a man is lazy, the rafters sag;
if his hands are idle, the house leaks.

[19]A feast is made for laughter,
and wine makes life merry,
but money is the answer for everything.

[20]Do not revile the king even in your thoughts,
or curse the rich in your bedroom,
because a bird of the air may carry your words,
and a bird on the wing may report what you say.

Bread Upon the Waters

11 Cast your bread upon the waters,
for after many days you will find it again.
[2]Give portions to seven, yes to eight,
for you do not know what disaster may come upon the land.

[3]If clouds are full of water,
they pour rain upon the earth.
Whether a tree falls to the south or to the north,
in the place where it falls, there will it lie.
[4]Whoever watches the wind will not plant;
whoever looks at the clouds will not reap.

[5]As you do not know the path of the wind,
or how the body is formed[b] in a mother's womb,
so you cannot understand the work of God,
the Maker of all things.

[6]Sow your seed in the morning,

---

[a]16 Or *king is a child*   [b]5 Or *know how life* (or *the spirit*) / *enters the body being formed*

and at evening let not your hands be
idle,
for you do not know which will
succeed,
whether this or that,
or whether both will do equally well.

Remember Your Creator While Young

7Light is sweet,
and it pleases the eyes to see the sun.
8However many years a man may live,
let him enjoy them all.
But let him remember the days of
darkness,
for they will be many.
Everything to come is meaningless.

9Be happy, young man, while you are
young,
and let your heart give you joy in the
days of your youth.
Follow the ways of your heart
and whatever your eyes see,
but know that for all these things
God will bring you to judgment.
10So then, banish anxiety from your heart
and cast off the troubles of your
body,
for youth and vigor are meaningless.

12 Remember your Creator
in the days of your youth,
before the days of trouble come
and the years approach when you will
say,
"I find no pleasure in them" —
2before the sun and the light
and the moon and the stars grow
dark,
and the clouds return after the rain;
3when the keepers of the house tremble,
and the strong men stoop,
when the grinders cease because they
are few,
and those looking through the
windows grow dim;
4when the doors to the street are closed
and the sound of grinding fades;
when men rise up at the sound of birds,

but all their songs grow faint;
5when men are afraid of heights
and of dangers in the streets;
when the almond tree blossoms
and the grasshopper drags himself
along
and desire no longer is stirred.
Then man goes to his eternal home
and mourners go about the streets.

6Remember him — before the silver cord
is severed,
or the golden bowl is broken;
before the pitcher is shattered at the
spring,
or the wheel broken at the well,
7and the dust returns to the ground it
came from,
and the spirit returns to God who
gave it.

8"Meaningless! Meaningless!" says the
Teacher.*ᵃ*
"Everything is meaningless!"

The Conclusion of the Matter

9Not only was the Teacher wise, but also
he imparted knowledge to the people. He
pondered and searched out and set in order
many proverbs. **10**The Teacher searched to
find just the right words, and what he wrote
was upright and true.

11The words of the wise are like goads,
their collected sayings like firmly embedded
nails — given by one Shepherd. **12**Be
warned, my son, of anything in addition to
them.

Of making many books there is no end,
and much study wearies the body.

13Now all has been heard;
here is the conclusion of the matter:
Fear God and keep his commandments,
for this is the whole ⌊duty⌋ of man.
14For God will bring every deed into
judgment,
including every hidden thing,
whether it is good or evil.

ᵃ8 Or the leader of the assembly; also in verses 9 and 10

WHAT TIME IS IT? TIME TO SEEK GOD!

Because of several recent encounters with death (her aunt and a close friend from school both died unexpectedly), Angie is understandably sad . . . and scared.

See, she's been going to church all her life, but she's never really thought about why. Angie has always considered the sermons just irrelevant words and youth group just another social activity.

Now things are different. Angie admits, "I don't know what would happen if I died. Where would I go? Do I really know who God is? It's getting to where I can't even sleep at night!"

Grabbing the phone book, she calls her youth leader and makes an appointment to meet with him tomorrow after school.

Look It Up
••••

Without knowing it, Angie is doing exactly what the Bible commands. She is using the present to prepare for her future.

Non-Christians need to get right with God today: "For he says, 'In the time of my favor I heard you, and in the day of salvation I helped you.' I tell you, now is the time of God's favor, now is the day of salvation" (2 Corinthians 6:2).

Christians should also seek God today: "Therefore let everyone who is godly pray to you while you may be found; surely when the mighty waters rise, they will not reach him" (Psalm 32:6).

"But I pray to you, O LORD, in the time of your favor; in your great love, O God, answer me with your sure salvation" (Psalm 69:13).

Think It Through
••••

Why the big fuss about getting right with God today? Why not wait until you're older to get serious about spiritual matters? Consider the things that could happen if you put off such a decision.

Work It Out
••••

If you're not sure about your relationship with God or if you have questions about what it means to trust Christ as your Savior, do what Angie did. Make an appointment with your pastor or youth minister. Don't put it off. That's an issue you need to settle right now. ("NOW is the day of salvation.")

If you already know Christ, use today to deepen your walk with him. Seek him now, while you have the opportunity. You don't know what the future holds.

Nail It Down
••••

Meditate on the message of Ecclesiastes 12:1–7.

Turn to pages 286, 597 and 611 for other readings on time.
Turn to page 705 for Wednesday's reading.

Topic
••••

SONG OF SONGS

TALK about explicit lyrics! Called the Song of Songs by its author King Solomon, this robust love poem exalts the beauty of love and sex within marriage. Some interpreters also see the book as an allegory of the love Christ has for his bride, the church. As you read remember this: Sex is a beautiful part of God's design for men and women, but only within marriage. Commit yourself to a life of purity until your wedding night, and you'll never regret it.

Outline of Contents

1 Solomon's Song of Songs.

Beloved[a]

²Let him kiss me with the kisses of his mouth —
 for your love is more delightful than wine.
³Pleasing is the fragrance of your perfumes;
 your name is like perfume poured out.
 No wonder the maidens love you!
⁴Take me away with you — let us hurry!

Let the king bring me into his chambers.

Friends

We rejoice and delight in you[b];
 we will praise your love more than wine.

Beloved

How right they are to adore you!

⁵Dark am I, yet lovely,
 O daughters of Jerusalem,
 dark like the tents of Kedar,

---

[a]Primarily on the basis of the gender of the Hebrew pronouns used, male and female speakers are indicated in the margins by the captions *Lover* and *Beloved* respectively. The words of others are marked *Friends*. In some instances the divisions and their captions are debatable.   [b]4 The Hebrew is masculine singular.

like the tent curtains of Solomon.[a]
⁶Do not stare at me because I am dark,
    because I am darkened by the sun.
My mother's sons were angry with me
    and made me take care of the
        vineyards;
    my own vineyard I have neglected.
⁷Tell me, you whom I love, where you
        graze your flock
    and where you rest your sheep at
        midday.
Why should I be like a veiled woman
    beside the flocks of your friends?

Friends

⁸If you do not know, most beautiful of
        women,
    follow the tracks of the sheep
and graze your young goats
    by the tents of the shepherds.

Lover

⁹I liken you, my darling, to a mare
    harnessed to one of the chariots of
        Pharaoh.
¹⁰Your cheeks are beautiful with earrings,
    your neck with strings of jewels.
¹¹We will make you earrings of gold,
    studded with silver.

Beloved

¹²While the king was at his table,
    my perfume spread its fragrance.
¹³My lover is to me a sachet of myrrh
    resting between my breasts.
¹⁴My lover is to me a cluster of henna
        blossoms
    from the vineyards of En Gedi.

Lover

¹⁵How beautiful you are, my darling!
    Oh, how beautiful!
    Your eyes are doves.

Beloved

¹⁶How handsome you are, my lover!
    Oh, how charming!
    And our bed is verdant.

Lover

¹⁷The beams of our house are cedars;
    our rafters are firs.

Beloved[b]

2   I am a rose[c] of Sharon,
    a lily of the valleys.

Lover

²Like a lily among thorns
    is my darling among the maidens.

Beloved

³Like an apple tree among the trees of
        the forest
    is my lover among the young men.
I delight to sit in his shade,
    and his fruit is sweet to my taste.
⁴He has taken me to the banquet hall,
    and his banner over me is love.
⁵Strengthen me with raisins,
    refresh me with apples,
    for I am faint with love.
⁶His left arm is under my head,
    and his right arm embraces me.
⁷Daughters of Jerusalem, I charge you
    by the gazelles and by the does of the
        field:
Do not arouse or awaken love
    until it so desires.

⁸Listen! My lover!
    Look! Here he comes,
leaping across the mountains,
    bounding over the hills.
⁹My lover is like a gazelle or a young
        stag.
    Look! There he stands behind our
        wall,
gazing through the windows,
    peering through the lattice.
¹⁰My lover spoke and said to me,
    "Arise, my darling,
    my beautiful one, and come with me.
¹¹See! The winter is past;
    the rains are over and gone.
¹²Flowers appear on the earth;
    the season of singing has come,
    the cooing of doves
    is heard in our land.
¹³The fig tree forms its early fruit;
    the blossoming vines spread their
        fragrance.
Arise, come, my darling;
    my beautiful one, come with me."

Lover

¹⁴My dove in the clefts of the rock,
    in the hiding places on the
        mountainside,
show me your face,
    let me hear your voice;
for your voice is sweet,
    and your face is lovely.
¹⁵Catch for us the foxes,

---

[a]5 Or *Salma*   [b]1 Or *Lover*   [c]1 Possibly a member of the crocus family

Revelations for the (Sexual) Revolution

Katie is reading an article in *Worldly Woman* magazine entitled, "How an Affair Can Save Your Marriage." Suddenly she realizes it's time for her favorite TV talk show. Tuning in, she discovers today's topic: bisexual parents.

At first she thinks, "Yuck!" Afterward she reasons, "Maybe my views on sex are too closed-minded. After all, this is the twentieth century."

Look It Up
••••

The so-called sexual revolution is not really new at all. "Alternative lifestyles" have been around for a long time. Notice what God once told the nation of Israel:

"You must not do as they do in Egypt, where you used to live, and you must not do as they do in the land of Canaan, where I am bringing you. Do not follow their practices. . . . No one is to approach any close relative to have sexual relations. I am the LORD. . . . Do not have sexual relations with your neighbor's wife and defile yourself with her. . . . Do not lie with a man as one lies with a woman; that is detestable. Do not have sexual relations with an animal and defile yourself with it. . . . That is a perversion. Do not defile yourselves in any of these ways, because this is how the nations that I am going to drive out before you became defiled" (Leviticus 18:3,6,20,22–24).

Think It Through
••••

In a few paragraphs, God condemns incest, adultery, homosexuality and bestiality (sex with animals). All such practices are disgusting to God.

In what ways does today's "liberated" society try to make any or all of those behaviors acceptable?

Does the fact that a command is old automatically mean it is no longer appropriate?

Work It Out
••••

Start your day off with this prayer:

"Father, my society is obsessed with sex. Give me wisdom. Remind me of what is right and wrong. And grant me the grace to live a pure life in a very impure world. I want my friends (and the world) to see that sex is best when it is reserved for marriage. In Jesus' name. Amen."

Nail It Down
••••

Read Song of Songs 2 for a beautiful description of sexual love in marriage.

Turn to pages 124, 654 and 1237 for other readings on sex.
Turn to page 713 for Thursday's reading.

Topic
••••

the little foxes
that ruin the vineyards,
   our vineyards that are in bloom.

Beloved

16My lover is mine and I am his;
   he browses among the lilies.
17Until the day breaks
   and the shadows flee,
turn, my lover,
   and be like a gazelle
or like a young stag
   on the rugged hills.*a*

3 All night long on my bed
   I looked for the one my heart loves;
   I looked for him but did not find him.
2I will get up now and go about the city,
   through its streets and squares;
I will search for the one my heart loves.
   So I looked for him but did not find
      him.
3The watchmen found me
   as they made their rounds in the city.
   "Have you seen the one my heart
      loves?"
4Scarcely had I passed them
   when I found the one my heart loves.
I held him and would not let him go
   till I had brought him to my mother's
      house,
   to the room of the one who conceived
      me.
5Daughters of Jerusalem, I charge you
   by the gazelles and by the does of the
      field:
Do not arouse or awaken love
   until it so desires.

6Who is this coming up from the desert
   like a column of smoke,
perfumed with myrrh and incense
   made from all the spices of the
      merchant?
7Look! It is Solomon's carriage,
   escorted by sixty warriors,
   the noblest of Israel,
8all of them wearing the sword,
   all experienced in battle,
each with his sword at his side,
   prepared for the terrors of the night.
9King Solomon made for himself the
      carriage;
   he made it of wood from Lebanon.
10Its posts he made of silver,
   its base of gold.
Its seat was upholstered with purple,

its interior lovingly inlaid
   by*b* the daughters of Jerusalem.
11Come out, you daughters of Zion,
   and look at King Solomon wearing the
      crown,
the crown with which his mother
      crowned him
on the day of his wedding,
   the day his heart rejoiced.

Lover

4 How beautiful you are, my darling!
   Oh, how beautiful!
   Your eyes behind your veil are doves.
Your hair is like a flock of goats
   descending from Mount Gilead.
2Your teeth are like a flock of sheep just
      shorn,
   coming up from the washing.
Each has its twin;
   not one of them is alone.
3Your lips are like a scarlet ribbon;
   your mouth is lovely.
Your temples behind your veil
   are like the halves of a pomegranate.
4Your neck is like the tower of David,
   built with elegance*c*;
on it hang a thousand shields,
   all of them shields of warriors.
5Your two breasts are like two fawns,
   like twin fawns of a gazelle
   that browse among the lilies.
6Until the day breaks
   and the shadows flee,
I will go to the mountain of myrrh
   and to the hill of incense.
7All beautiful you are, my darling;
   there is no flaw in you.

8Come with me from Lebanon, my bride,
   come with me from Lebanon.
Descend from the crest of Amana,
   from the top of Senir, the summit of
      Hermon,
from the lions' dens
   and the mountain haunts of the
      leopards.
9You have stolen my heart, my sister, my
      bride;
   you have stolen my heart
with one glance of your eyes,
   with one jewel of your necklace.
10How delightful is your love, my sister,
      my bride!
How much more pleasing is your love
      than wine,

a 17 Or *the hills of Bether*   *b 10* Or *its inlaid interior a gift of love / from*   *c 4* The meaning of the Hebrew
for this word is uncertain.

and the fragrance of your perfume
    than any spice!
11Your lips drop sweetness as the
    honeycomb, my bride;
  milk and honey are under your
    tongue.
  The fragrance of your garments is like
    that of Lebanon.
12You are a garden locked up, my sister,
    my bride;
  you are a spring enclosed, a sealed
    fountain.
13Your plants are an orchard of
    pomegranates
  with choice fruits,
  with henna and nard,
14 nard and saffron,
  calamus and cinnamon,
  with every kind of incense tree,
  with myrrh and aloes
  and all the finest spices.
15You are^a a garden fountain,
  a well of flowing water
  streaming down from Lebanon.

Beloved

16Awake, north wind,
  and come, south wind!
Blow on my garden,
  that its fragrance may spread abroad.
Let my lover come into his garden
  and taste its choice fruits.

Lover

5   I have come into my garden, my
    sister, my bride;
  I have gathered my myrrh with my
    spice.
I have eaten my honeycomb and my
    honey;
I have drunk my wine and my milk.

Friends

Eat, O friends, and drink;
  drink your fill, O lovers.

Beloved

2I slept but my heart was awake.
  Listen! My lover is knocking:
"Open to me, my sister, my darling,
  my dove, my flawless one.
My head is drenched with dew,
  my hair with the dampness of the
    night."
3I have taken off my robe —
  must I put it on again?
I have washed my feet —

must I soil them again?
4My lover thrust his hand through the
    latch-opening;
  my heart began to pound for him.
5I arose to open for my lover,
  and my hands dripped with myrrh,
  my fingers with flowing myrrh,
    on the handles of the lock.
6I opened for my lover,
  but my lover had left; he was gone.
  My heart sank at his departure.^b
I looked for him but did not find him.
  I called him but he did not answer.
7The watchmen found me
  as they made their rounds in the city.
They beat me, they bruised me;
  they took away my cloak,
  those watchmen of the walls!
8O daughters of Jerusalem, I charge
    you —
  if you find my lover,
what will you tell him?
  Tell him I am faint with love.

Friends

9How is your beloved better than others,
  most beautiful of women?
How is your beloved better than others,
  that you charge us so?

Beloved

10My lover is radiant and ruddy,
  outstanding among ten thousand.
11His head is purest gold;
  his hair is wavy
  and black as a raven.
12His eyes are like doves
  by the water streams,
washed in milk,
  mounted like jewels.
13His cheeks are like beds of spice
  yielding perfume.
His lips are like lilies
  dripping with myrrh.
14His arms are rods of gold
  set with chrysolite.
His body is like polished ivory
  decorated with sapphires.^c
15His legs are pillars of marble
  set on bases of pure gold.
His appearance is like Lebanon,
  choice as its cedars.
16His mouth is sweetness itself;
  he is altogether lovely.
This is my lover, this my friend,
  O daughters of Jerusalem.

---

^a15 Or *I am* (spoken by the *Beloved*)   ^b6 Or *heart had gone out to him when he spoke*   ^c14 Or *lapis lazuli*

Friends

6 Where has your lover gone,
  most beautiful of women?
Which way did your lover turn,
  that we may look for him with you?

Beloved

²My lover has gone down to his garden,
  to the beds of spices,
to browse in the gardens
  and to gather lilies.
³I am my lover's and my lover is mine;
  he browses among the lilies.

Lover

⁴You are beautiful, my darling, as Tirzah,
  lovely as Jerusalem,
  majestic as troops with banners.
⁵Turn your eyes from me;
  they overwhelm me.
Your hair is like a flock of goats
  descending from Gilead.
⁶Your teeth are like a flock of sheep
  coming up from the washing.
Each has its twin,
  not one of them is alone.
⁷Your temples behind your veil
  are like the halves of a pomegranate.
⁸Sixty queens there may be,
  and eighty concubines,
  and virgins beyond number;
⁹but my dove, my perfect one, is unique,
  the only daughter of her mother,
  the favorite of the one who bore her.
The maidens saw her and called her
    blessed;
  the queens and concubines praised
    her.

Friends

¹⁰Who is this that appears like the dawn,
  fair as the moon, bright as the sun,
  majestic as the stars in procession?

Lover

¹¹I went down to the grove of nut trees
  to look at the new growth in the
    valley,
  to see if the vines had budded
  or the pomegranates were in bloom.
¹²Before I realized it,
  my desire set me among the royal
    chariots of my people.ᵃ

Friends

¹³Come back, come back, O Shulammite;
  come back, come back, that we may
    gaze on you!

Lover

Why would you gaze on the
    Shulammite
  as on the dance of Mahanaim?

7 How beautiful your sandaled feet,
  O prince's daughter!
Your graceful legs are like jewels,
  the work of a craftsman's hands.
²Your navel is a rounded goblet
  that never lacks blended wine.
Your waist is a mound of wheat
  encircled by lilies.
³Your breasts are like two fawns,
  twins of a gazelle.
⁴Your neck is like an ivory tower.
Your eyes are the pools of Heshbon
  by the gate of Bath Rabbim.
Your nose is like the tower of Lebanon
  looking toward Damascus.
⁵Your head crowns you like Mount
    Carmel.
  Your hair is like royal tapestry;
  the king is held captive by its tresses.
⁶How beautiful you are and how
    pleasing,
  O love, with your delights!
⁷Your stature is like that of the palm,
  and your breasts like clusters of fruit.
⁸I said, "I will climb the palm tree;
  I will take hold of its fruit."
May your breasts be like the clusters of
    the vine,
  the fragrance of your breath like
    apples,
⁹ and your mouth like the best wine.

Beloved

May the wine go straight to my lover,
  flowing gently over lips and teeth.ᵇ
¹⁰I belong to my lover,
  and his desire is for me.
¹¹Come, my lover, let us go to the
    countryside,
  let us spend the night in the
    villages.ᶜ
¹²Let us go early to the vineyards
  to see if the vines have budded,
  if their blossoms have opened,
  and if the pomegranates are in
    bloom—

ᵃ12 Or among the chariots of Amminadab; or among the chariots of the people of the prince   ᵇ9 Septuagint,
Aquila, Vulgate and Syriac; Hebrew lips of sleepers   ᶜ11 Or henna bushes

there I will give you my love.
13The mandrakes send out their
    fragrance,
and at our door is every delicacy,
both new and old,
    that I have stored up for you, my
    lover.

8 If only you were to me like a brother,
    who was nursed at my mother's
    breasts!
Then, if I found you outside,
    I would kiss you,
    and no one would despise me.
2I would lead you
    and bring you to my mother's
    house—
    she who has taught me.
I would give you spiced wine to drink,
    the nectar of my pomegranates.
3His left arm is under my head
    and his right arm embraces me.
4Daughters of Jerusalem, I charge you:
    Do not arouse or awaken love
    until it so desires.

Friends

5Who is this coming up from the desert
    leaning on her lover?

Beloved

Under the apple tree I roused you;
    there your mother conceived you,
    there she who was in labor gave you
    birth.
6Place me like a seal over your heart,
    like a seal on your arm;
for love is as strong as death,
    its jealousy[a] unyielding as the
    grave.[b]
It burns like blazing fire,
    like a mighty flame.[c]
7Many waters cannot quench love;

rivers cannot wash it away.
If one were to give
    all the wealth of his house for love,
    it[d] would be utterly scorned.

Friends

8We have a young sister,
    and her breasts are not yet grown.
What shall we do for our sister
    for the day she is spoken for?
9If she is a wall,
    we will build towers of silver on her.
If she is a door,
    we will enclose her with panels of
    cedar.

Beloved

10I am a wall,
    and my breasts are like towers.
Thus I have become in his eyes
    like one bringing contentment.
11Solomon had a vineyard in Baal Hamon;
    he let out his vineyard to tenants.
Each was to bring for its fruit
    a thousand shekels[e] of silver.
12But my own vineyard is mine to give;
    the thousand shekels are for you,
    O Solomon,
    and two hundred[f] are for those who
    tend its fruit.

Lover

13You who dwell in the gardens
    with friends in attendance,
    let me hear your voice!

Beloved

14Come away, my lover,
    and be like a gazelle
or like a young stag
    on the spice-laden mountains.

---

[a]6 Or *ardor*   [b]6 Hebrew *Sheol*   [c]6 Or / *like the very flame of the* LORD   [d]7 Or *he*   [e]11 That is, about 25
pounds (about 11.5 kilograms); also in verse 12   [f]12 That is, about 5 pounds (about 2.3 kilograms)

PROPHETS are not always popular. They have a habit of telling the truth, and the truth often hurts. Isaiah is no exception. His message to the wicked kings and corrupt people of Judah is simple: repent or experience God's wrath. He doesn't hesitate to boldly proclaim their sins — idolatry, hypocrisy, materialism and oppression of the poor. While Isaiah sees the people groan under God's judgment, he also sees the glory of the coming Messiah. As you read, ask yourself this question: Have I repented of my sin and bowed to the Messiah, Jesus Christ?

Outline of Contents

1 The vision concerning Judah and Jerusalem that Isaiah son of Amoz saw during the reigns of Uzziah, Jotham, Ahaz and Hezekiah, kings of Judah.

A Rebellious Nation

²Hear, O heavens! Listen, O earth!
    For the LORD has spoken:
"I reared children and brought them
        up,
    but they have rebelled against me.
³The ox knows his master,
    the donkey his owner's manger,
but Israel does not know,

    my people do not understand."

⁴Ah, sinful nation,
    a people loaded with guilt,
a brood of evildoers,
    children given to corruption!
They have forsaken the LORD;
    they have spurned the Holy One of
        Israel
    and turned their backs on him.

⁵Why should you be beaten anymore?
    Why do you persist in rebellion?
Your whole head is injured,
    your whole heart afflicted.

⁶From the sole of your foot to the top of
      your head
    there is no soundness—
only wounds and welts
    and open sores,
not cleansed or bandaged
    or soothed with oil.

⁷Your country is desolate,
    your cities burned with fire;
your fields are being stripped by
      foreigners
    right before you,
    laid waste as when overthrown by
      strangers.
⁸The Daughter of Zion is left
    like a shelter in a vineyard,
like a hut in a field of melons,
    like a city under siege.
⁹Unless the LORD Almighty
    had left us some survivors,
we would have become like Sodom,
    we would have been like Gomorrah.

¹⁰Hear the word of the LORD,
    you rulers of Sodom;
listen to the law of our God,
    you people of Gomorrah!
¹¹"The multitude of your sacrifices—
    what are they to me?" says the LORD.
"I have more than enough of burnt
      offerings,
    of rams and the fat of fattened
      animals;
I have no pleasure
    in the blood of bulls and lambs and
      goats.
¹²When you come to appear before me,
    who has asked this of you,
    this trampling of my courts?
¹³Stop bringing meaningless offerings!
    Your incense is detestable to me.
New Moons, Sabbaths and
      convocations—
    I cannot bear your evil assemblies.
¹⁴Your New Moon festivals and your
      appointed feasts
    my soul hates.
They have become a burden to me;
    I am weary of bearing them.
¹⁵When you spread out your hands in
      prayer,
    I will hide my eyes from you;
even if you offer many prayers,
    I will not listen.
Your hands are full of blood;
¹⁶   wash and make yourselves clean.
    Take your evil deeds

out of my sight!
Stop doing wrong,
¹⁷   learn to do right!
Seek justice,
    encourage the oppressed.ᵃ
Defend the cause of the fatherless,
    plead the case of the widow.

¹⁸"Come now, let us reason together,"
    says the LORD.
"Though your sins are like scarlet,
    they shall be as white as snow;
though they are red as crimson,
    they shall be like wool.
¹⁹If you are willing and obedient,
    you will eat the best from the land;
²⁰but if you resist and rebel,
    you will be devoured by the sword."
            For the mouth of the LORD
                        has spoken.

²¹See how the faithful city
    has become a harlot!
She once was full of justice;
    righteousness used to dwell in her—
    but now murderers!
²²Your silver has become dross,
    your choice wine is diluted with
      water.
²³Your rulers are rebels,
    companions of thieves;
they all love bribes
    and chase after gifts.
They do not defend the cause of the
      fatherless;
    the widow's case does not come
      before them.
²⁴Therefore the Lord, the LORD Almighty,
    the Mighty One of Israel, declares:
"Ah, I will get relief from my foes
    and avenge myself on my enemies.
²⁵I will turn my hand against you;
    I will thoroughly purge away your
      dross
    and remove all your impurities.
²⁶I will restore your judges as in days of
      old,
    your counselors as at the beginning.
Afterward you will be called
    the City of Righteousness,
    the Faithful City."

²⁷Zion will be redeemed with justice,
    her penitent ones with righteousness.
²⁸But rebels and sinners will both be
      broken,
    and those who forsake the LORD will
      perish.

ᵃ17 Or / rebuke the oppressor

²⁹"You will be ashamed because of the
        sacred oaks
    in which you have delighted;
    you will be disgraced because of the
        gardens
        that you have chosen.
³⁰You will be like an oak with fading
        leaves,
    like a garden without water.
³¹The mighty man will become tinder
    and his work a spark;
    both will burn together,
    with no one to quench the fire."

The Mountain of the LORD

2 This is what Isaiah son of Amoz saw
  concerning Judah and Jerusalem:

²In the last days

    the mountain of the LORD's temple will
        be established
    as chief among the mountains;
    it will be raised above the hills,
    and all nations will stream to it.

³Many peoples will come and say,

"Come, let us go up to the mountain of
    the LORD,
    to the house of the God of Jacob.
He will teach us his ways,
    so that we may walk in his paths."
The law will go out from Zion,
    the word of the LORD from Jerusalem.
⁴He will judge between the nations
    and will settle disputes for many
        peoples.
They will beat their swords into
        plowshares
    and their spears into pruning hooks.
Nation will not take up sword against
        nation,
    nor will they train for war anymore.

⁵Come, O house of Jacob,
    let us walk in the light of the LORD.

The Day of the LORD

⁶You have abandoned your people,
    the house of Jacob.
They are full of superstitions from the
    East;
    they practice divination like the
        Philistines
    and clasp hands with pagans.
⁷Their land is full of silver and gold;
    there is no end to their treasures.
Their land is full of horses;

there is no end to their chariots.
⁸Their land is full of idols;
    they bow down to the work of their
        hands,
    to what their fingers have made.
⁹So man will be brought low
    and mankind humbled—
    do not forgive them.ᵃ

¹⁰Go into the rocks,
    hide in the ground
from dread of the LORD
    and the splendor of his majesty!
¹¹The eyes of the arrogant man will be
        humbled
    and the pride of men brought low;
    the LORD alone will be exalted in that
        day.

¹²The LORD Almighty has a day in store
    for all the proud and lofty,
    for all that is exalted
    (and they will be humbled),
¹³for all the cedars of Lebanon, tall and
        lofty,
    and all the oaks of Bashan,
¹⁴for all the towering mountains
    and all the high hills,
¹⁵for every lofty tower
    and every fortified wall,
¹⁶for every trading shipᵇ
    and every stately vessel.
¹⁷The arrogance of man will be brought
        low
    and the pride of men humbled;
    the LORD alone will be exalted in that
        day,
¹⁸   and the idols will totally disappear.

¹⁹Men will flee to caves in the rocks
    and to holes in the ground
from dread of the LORD
    and the splendor of his majesty,
    when he rises to shake the earth.
²⁰In that day men will throw away
    to the rodents and bats
their idols of silver and idols of gold,
    which they made to worship.
²¹They will flee to caverns in the rocks
    and to the overhanging crags
from dread of the LORD
    and the splendor of his majesty,
    when he rises to shake the earth.

²²Stop trusting in man,
    who has but a breath in his nostrils.
Of what account is he?

ᵃ9 Or *not raise them up*   ᵇ16 Hebrew *every ship of Tarshish*

LIVING IN A MATERIAL WORLD

Mingle with the crowd at Dale's Friday night party. Out front is Steve in his great new little sports car, impressing a crowd of admirers with his car's CD player. In the living room, as several girls rave about Stephanie's new $400 outfit, one whispers, "She's got enough clothes to open her own mall!" In the kitchen, John, the popular but overweight class clown, is finishing off the contents of Dale's refrigerator. And Kris, the cutest and best school cheerleader, is in the bathroom for the fourth time, checking her hair and make-up.

Look It Up • • • •

Dale's party is a good place to see some of the things that can become idols in our lives.

About cars and clothes, remember: "Every good and perfect gift is from above, coming down from the Father of the heavenly lights" (James 1:17). Don't fall into the trap of valuing created things more than the Creator!

About food, remember that God's Word condemns gluttony and being controlled by our appetite (Philippians 3:19). Concentrate on spiritual as well as physical food.

About appearance, remember that God doesn't see us the way we see each other (1 Samuel 16:7). We need to focus on how we look on the inside as well as on the outside.

Think It Through • • • •

An idol is anything that becomes more important to us than God. (It doesn't have to be a stone statue—and usually it isn't in the twentieth century!)

Friendships, dating relationships, music, success, cars, clothes, food and appearance—they're not always idols. They only become idols or false gods when we place more emphasis on them than we do on our relationship with God. We can enjoy all those things without guilt as long as God remains our ultimate priority.

Work It Out • • • •

We can check for idols in our lives by answering these three questions: What do I think about most? How do I spend my free time? If someone closely examined my life, what would he or she say was most important to me?

We can tear down any idols we find by confessing our sin and changing our actions. We can make the Lord number one in our life by spending more time with him. He'll give us the strength to overcome the temptations to idolatry all around us.

Nail It Down • • • •

Read Isaiah 2:12–18 for information on what will eventually happen to all idols.

Turn to pages 190, 348 and 483 for other readings on idols.
Turn to page 716 for Friday's reading.

Topic
• • • •
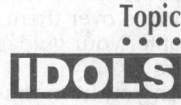

Judgment on Jerusalem and Judah

3 See now, the Lord,
    the Lord Almighty,
  is about to take from Jerusalem and
        Judah
  both supply and support:
all supplies of food and all supplies of
        water,
² the hero and warrior,
  the judge and prophet,
  the soothsayer and elder,
³the captain of fifty and man of rank,
  the counselor, skilled craftsman and
        clever enchanter.

⁴I will make boys their officials;
  mere children will govern them.
⁵People will oppress each other—
  man against man, neighbor against
        neighbor.
The young will rise up against the old,
  the base against the honorable.

⁶A man will seize one of his brothers
  at his father's home, and say,
"You have a cloak, you be our leader;
  take charge of this heap of ruins!"
⁷But in that day he will cry out,
  "I have no remedy.
I have no food or clothing in my house;
  do not make me the leader of the
        people."

⁸Jerusalem staggers,
  Judah is falling;
their words and deeds are against the
        Lord,
  defying his glorious presence.
⁹The look on their faces testifies against
        them;
  they parade their sin like Sodom;
  they do not hide it.
Woe to them!
  They have brought disaster upon
        themselves.

¹⁰Tell the righteous it will be well with
        them,
  for they will enjoy the fruit of their
        deeds.
¹¹Woe to the wicked! Disaster is upon
        them!
  They will be paid back for what their
        hands have done.

¹²Youths oppress my people,
  women rule over them.
O my people, your guides lead you
        astray;
  they turn you from the path.

¹³The Lord takes his place in court;
  he rises to judge the people.
¹⁴The Lord enters into judgment
  against the elders and leaders of his
        people:
"It is you who have ruined my vineyard;
  the plunder from the poor is in your
        houses.
¹⁵What do you mean by crushing my
        people
  and grinding the faces of the poor?"
  declares the Lord, the Lord Almighty.

¹⁶The Lord says,
  "The women of Zion are haughty,
walking along with outstretched necks,
  flirting with their eyes,
tripping along with mincing steps,
  with ornaments jingling on their
        ankles.
¹⁷Therefore the Lord will bring sores on
        the heads of the women of Zion;
  the Lord will make their scalps bald."

¹⁸In that day the Lord will snatch away
their finery: the bangles and headbands
and crescent necklaces, ¹⁹the earrings and
bracelets and veils, ²⁰the headdresses and
ankle chains and sashes, the perfume bot-
tles and charms, ²¹the signet rings and nose
rings, ²²the fine robes and the capes and
cloaks, the purses ²³and mirrors, and the
linen garments and tiaras and shawls.

²⁴Instead of fragrance there will be a
        stench;
  instead of a sash, a rope;
instead of well-dressed hair, baldness;
  instead of fine clothing, sackcloth;
  instead of beauty, branding.
²⁵Your men will fall by the sword,
  your warriors in battle.
²⁶The gates of Zion will lament and
        mourn;
  destitute, she will sit on the ground.

4 In that day seven women
    will take hold of one man
  and say, "We will eat our own food
  and provide our own clothes;
only let us be called by your name.
  Take away our disgrace!"

The Branch of the Lord

²In that day the Branch of the Lord will be
beautiful and glorious, and the fruit of the
land will be the pride and glory of the survivors in Israel. ³Those who are left in Zion,
who remain in Jerusalem, will be called
holy, all who are recorded among the living
in Jerusalem. ⁴The Lord will wash away the

filth of the women of Zion; he will cleanse the bloodstains from Jerusalem by a spirit[a] of judgment and a spirit[a] of fire. [5]Then the LORD will create over all of Mount Zion and over those who assemble there a cloud of smoke by day and a glow of flaming fire by night; over all the glory will be a canopy. [6]It will be a shelter and shade from the heat of the day, and a refuge and hiding place from the storm and rain.

The Song of the Vineyard

5 I will sing for the one I love
   a song about his vineyard:
My loved one had a vineyard
   on a fertile hillside.
[2]He dug it up and cleared it of stones
   and planted it with the choicest vines.
He built a watchtower in it
   and cut out a winepress as well.
Then he looked for a crop of good
      grapes,
   but it yielded only bad fruit.

[3]"Now you dwellers in Jerusalem and
      men of Judah,
   judge between me and my vineyard.
[4]What more could have been done for
      my vineyard
   than I have done for it?
When I looked for good grapes,
   why did it yield only bad?
[5]Now I will tell you
   what I am going to do to my vineyard:
I will take away its hedge,
   and it will be destroyed;
I will break down its wall,
   and it will be trampled.
[6]I will make it a wasteland,
   neither pruned nor cultivated,
   and briers and thorns will grow there.
I will command the clouds
   not to rain on it."

[7]The vineyard of the LORD Almighty
   is the house of Israel,
and the men of Judah
   are the garden of his delight.
And he looked for justice, but saw
      bloodshed;
   for righteousness, but heard cries of
      distress.

Woes and Judgments

[8]Woe to you who add house to house
and join field to field
till no space is left
   and you live alone in the land.

[9]The LORD Almighty has declared in my hearing:

"Surely the great houses will become
      desolate,
   the fine mansions left without
      occupants.
[10]A ten-acre[b] vineyard will produce only
      a bath[c] of wine,
   a homer[d] of seed only an ephah[e] of
      grain."

[11]Woe to those who rise early in the
      morning
   to run after their drinks,
who stay up late at night
   till they are inflamed with wine.
[12]They have harps and lyres at their
      banquets,
   tambourines and flutes and wine,
but they have no regard for the deeds of
      the LORD,
   no respect for the work of his hands.
[13]Therefore my people will go into exile
   for lack of understanding;
their men of rank will die of hunger
   and their masses will be parched with
      thirst.
[14]Therefore the grave[f] enlarges its
      appetite
   and opens its mouth without limit;
into it will descend their nobles and
      masses
   with all their brawlers and revelers.
[15]So man will be brought low
   and mankind humbled,
   the eyes of the arrogant humbled.
[16]But the LORD Almighty will be exalted by
      his justice,
   and the holy God will show himself
      holy by his righteousness.
[17]Then sheep will graze as in their own
      pasture;
   lambs will feed[g] among the ruins of
      the rich.

[18]Woe to those who draw sin along with
      cords of deceit,
   and wickedness as with cart ropes,
[19]to those who say, "Let God hurry,
   let him hasten his work
   so we may see it.

---

[a]4 Or *the Spirit*   [b]10 Hebrew *ten-yoke,* that is, the land plowed by 10 yoke of oxen in one day   [c]10 That is, probably about 6 gallons (about 22 liters)   [d]10 That is, probably about 6 bushels (about 220 liters)   [e]10 That is, probably about 3/5 bushel (about 22 liters)   [f]14 Hebrew *Sheol*   [g]17 Septuagint; Hebrew / *strangers will eat*

VALUES TO LAST A LIFETIME

"Look," Pam says, "I have to have my own values. I'll never be a strong person if I'm always borrowing someone else's beliefs. I have to really feel something in my heart or it won't last.

"Besides, it makes me so mad when my parents tell me how to live, and then they don't even live like that themselves. My dad goes crazy if I tell a lie, but sometimes when people call, I hear him say to my mom, 'Tell whoever it is that I'm not home'!"

Look It Up
••••

Wise words, Pam! You're right on target about having your own personal values. Personal doesn't mean different from everyone else. It simply means you've struggled with your values until you understand not only what you believe, but also why.

Only then will you be able "to give an answer to everyone who asks you to give the reason for the hope that you have" (1 Peter 3:15).

Only then will you be able to resist the devil, "standing . . . firm in the faith" (1 Peter 5:9).

Think It Through
••••

If an authority figure preaches certain Biblical values but then doesn't practice them, does that mean those values are worthless? No!

Mistakes by a doctor don't nullify the principles of medicine. Incompetence by a pilot doesn't undo the laws of aerodynamics. In the same way, don't toss out good values just because a person who advocates them is a hypocrite.

Work It Out
••••

Over the centuries, Biblical values have proven to be best. Such standards may seem old-fashioned, but you'll find (and many of us have to learn these things the hard way) that they're true and they bring ultimate satisfaction.

1. DON'T stop asking why. "Why do we believe that? Why don't we do that?" Questioning your faith isn't bad. Christianity can stand the scrutiny. But you'll never feel secure until you know why you believe what you believe.

2. DO develop a close relationship with a more mature Christian (a youth leader, a counselor) who can help you sort through your values.

Nail It Down
••••

Read Isaiah 5:20 about those who spread confusing values.

Turn to pages 1000, 1192 and 1259 for other readings on values.
Turn to page 718 for the weekend reading.

Topic
••••

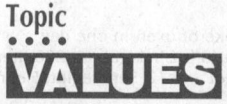

Let it approach,
    let the plan of the Holy One of Israel
      come,
    so we may know it."

20Woe to those who call evil good
    and good evil,
  who put darkness for light
    and light for darkness,
  who put bitter for sweet
    and sweet for bitter.

21Woe to those who are wise in their own
      eyes
    and clever in their own sight.

22Woe to those who are heroes at
      drinking wine
    and champions at mixing drinks,
23who acquit the guilty for a bribe,
    but deny justice to the innocent.
24Therefore, as tongues of fire lick up
      straw
    and as dry grass sinks down in the
      flames,
  so their roots will decay
    and their flowers blow away like dust;
  for they have rejected the law of the
      Lord Almighty
    and spurned the word of the Holy
      One of Israel.
25Therefore the Lord's anger burns against
      his people;
    his hand is raised and he strikes them
      down.
  The mountains shake,
    and the dead bodies are like refuse in
      the streets.

Yet for all this, his anger is not turned
      away,
    his hand is still upraised.

26He lifts up a banner for the distant
      nations,
    he whistles for those at the ends of
      the earth.
  Here they come,
    swiftly and speedily!
27Not one of them grows tired or
      stumbles,
    not one slumbers or sleeps;
  not a belt is loosened at the waist,
    not a sandal thong is broken.
28Their arrows are sharp,
    all their bows are strung;
  their horses' hoofs seem like flint,
    their chariot wheels like a whirlwind.

29Their roar is like that of the lion,
    they roar like young lions;
  they growl as they seize their prey
    and carry it off with no one to rescue.
30In that day they will roar over it
    like the roaring of the sea.
  And if one looks at the land,
    he will see darkness and distress;
  even the light will be darkened by the
      clouds.

Isaiah's Commission

6 In the year that King Uzziah died, I saw the Lord seated on a throne, high and exalted, and the train of his robe filled the temple. 2Above him were seraphs, each with six wings: With two wings they covered their faces, with two they covered their feet, and with two they were flying. 3And they were calling to one another:

"Holy, holy, holy is the Lord Almighty;
    the whole earth is full of his glory."

4At the sound of their voices the doorposts and thresholds shook and the temple was filled with smoke.

5"Woe to me!" I cried. "I am ruined! For I am a man of unclean lips, and I live among a people of unclean lips, and my eyes have seen the King, the Lord Almighty."

6Then one of the seraphs flew to me with a live coal in his hand, which he had taken with tongs from the altar. 7With it he touched my mouth and said, "See, this has touched your lips; your guilt is taken away and your sin atoned for."

8Then I heard the voice of the Lord saying, "Whom shall I send? And who will go for us?"

And I said, "Here am I. Send me!"

9He said, "Go and tell this people:

" 'Be ever hearing, but never
      understanding;
    be ever seeing, but never perceiving.'
10Make the heart of this people calloused;
    make their ears dull
    and close their eyes.a
  Otherwise they might see with their
      eyes,
    hear with their ears,
    understand with their hearts,
  and turn and be healed."

11Then I said, "For how long, O Lord?"
And he answered:

---

a9,10 Hebrew; Septuagint 'You will be ever hearing, but never understanding; / you will be ever seeing, but never perceiving.' / 10This people's heart has become calloused; / they hardly hear with their ears, / and they have closed their eyes

RESPONDING TO GOD'S CALL TO SERVE

Work It Out
• • • •

You may be as willing to serve as Isaiah was when he said, "Here I am! You can send me!" You'd be willing to do just about anything to serve God. But you may not be able to go away somewhere for an entire summer on a service project. Maybe it isn't financially feasible; or maybe you're needed at home while your mom works (that's a service project in itself!).

You don't need to leave your home to be of service to God. Here are a few ideas for at-home service projects:

• Offer to do the dishes after supper tonight.
• Go and rake your grandma's leaves.
• Baby-sit (no fee) so a young mom in your neighborhood can do some shopping.
• Take your little brother or sister with you when you run to the store or go to the mall.
• Offer to do typing or filing for your youth pastor.
• Be available to help out in the church nursery.

These are pretty simple, everyday tasks that you can do to be of service to God. You don't need to travel any farther than your own home to be on a service project.

Nail It Down
• • • •

Read Isaiah's response to God's call to service in Isaiah 6:8.

Think It Through
• • • •

Serving God doesn't mean you have to fly away to a foreign country or give weeks and weeks of your summer. It begins a lot closer to home. In fact, it begins right where you are, right now.

Serving God doesn't have to be dangerous or expensive or flashy. It doesn't have to be serious or pious or boring. But it does have to be sincere. And it does have to help someone in some way. And it will make you feel great. That's guaranteed.

Try it and see!

Nail It Down
• • • •

Reread Isaiah 6:8. For further insight read Proverbs 12:14.

Turn to pages 312, 1008, 1019, 1034 and 1342 for other readings on serving.
Turn to page 724 for Monday's reading.

Topic
• • • •

SERVING

"Until the cities lie ruined
  and without inhabitant,
until the houses are left deserted
  and the fields ruined and ravaged,
[12]until the LORD has sent everyone far
    away
  and the land is utterly forsaken.
[13]And though a tenth remains in the land,
  it will again be laid waste.
But as the terebinth and oak
  leave stumps when they are cut
    down,
  so the holy seed will be the stump in
    the land."

The Sign of Immanuel

7 When Ahaz son of Jotham, the son of
  Uzziah, was king of Judah, King Rezin
of Aram and Pekah son of Remaliah king of
Israel marched up to fight against Jerusalem, but they could not overpower it.

[2]Now the house of David was told, "Aram
has allied itself with[a] Ephraim"; so the
hearts of Ahaz and his people were shaken,
as the trees of the forest are shaken by the
wind.

[3]Then the LORD said to Isaiah, "Go out, you
and your son Shear-Jashub,[b] to meet Ahaz
at the end of the aqueduct of the Upper
Pool, on the road to the Washerman's Field.
[4]Say to him, 'Be careful, keep calm and don't
be afraid. Do not lose heart because of these
two smoldering stubs of firewood — because
of the fierce anger of Rezin and Aram and of
the son of Remaliah. [5]Aram, Ephraim and
Remaliah's son have plotted your ruin, saying, [6]"Let us invade Judah; let us tear it apart
and divide it among ourselves, and make
the son of Tabeel king over it." [7]Yet this is
what the Sovereign LORD says:

" 'It will not take place,
  it will not happen,
[8]for the head of Aram is Damascus,
  and the head of Damascus is only
    Rezin.
Within sixty-five years
  Ephraim will be too shattered to be a
    people.
[9]The head of Ephraim is Samaria,
  and the head of Samaria is only
    Remaliah's son.
If you do not stand firm in your faith,
  you will not stand at all.' "

[10]Again the LORD spoke to Ahaz, [11]"Ask the
LORD your God for a sign, whether in the
deepest depths or in the highest heights."
[12]But Ahaz said, "I will not ask; I will not
put the LORD to the test."

[13]Then Isaiah said, "Hear now, you house
of David! Is it not enough to try the patience
of men? Will you try the patience of my God
also? [14]Therefore the Lord himself will give
you[c] a sign: The virgin will be with child
and will give birth to a son, and[d] will call
him Immanuel.[e] [15]He will eat curds and
honey when he knows enough to reject the
wrong and choose the right. [16]But before the
boy knows enough to reject the wrong and
choose the right, the land of the two kings
you dread will be laid waste. [17]The LORD will
bring on you and on your people and on the
house of your father a time unlike any since
Ephraim broke away from Judah — he will
bring the king of Assyria."

[18]In that day the LORD will whistle for flies
from the distant streams of Egypt and for
bees from the land of Assyria. [19]They will all
come and settle in the steep ravines and in
the crevices in the rocks, on all the thornbushes and at all the water holes. [20]In that
day the Lord will use a razor hired from beyond the River[f] — the king of Assyria — to
shave your head and the hair of your legs,
and to take off your beards also. [21]In that
day, a man will keep alive a young cow and
two goats. [22]And because of the abundance
of the milk they give, he will have curds to
eat. All who remain in the land will eat curds
and honey. [23]In that day, in every place
where there were a thousand vines worth a
thousand silver shekels,[g] there will be only
briers and thorns. [24]Men will go there with
bow and arrow, for the land will be covered
with briers and thorns. [25]As for all the hills
once cultivated by the hoe, you will no longer go there for fear of the briers and thorns;
they will become places where cattle are
turned loose and where sheep run.

Assyria, the LORD's Instrument

8 The LORD said to me, "Take a large scroll
  and write on it with an ordinary pen:
Maher-Shalal-Hash-Baz.[h] [2]And I will call in
Uriah the priest and Zechariah son of Jeberekiah as reliable witnesses for me."

[3]Then I went to the prophetess, and she
conceived and gave birth to a son. And the

---

[a]2 Or has set up camp in   [b]3 Shear-Jashub means a remnant will return.   [c]14 The Hebrew is plural.
[d]14 Masoretic Text; Dead Sea Scrolls and he or and they   [e]14 Immanuel means God with us.   [f]20 That is,
the Euphrates   [g]23 That is, about 25 pounds (about 11.5 kilograms)   [h]1 Maher-Shalal-Hash-Baz means
quick to the plunder, swift to the spoil; also in verse 3.

LORD said to me, "Name him Maher-Shalal-Hash-Baz. **4**Before the boy knows how to say 'My father' or 'My mother,' the wealth of Damascus and the plunder of Samaria will be carried off by the king of Assyria."

5The LORD spoke to me again:

6"Because this people has rejected
  the gently flowing waters of Shiloah
and rejoices over Rezin
  and the son of Remaliah,
7therefore the Lord is about to bring
    against them
  the mighty floodwaters of the
    River*a*—
  the king of Assyria with all his pomp.
It will overflow all its channels,
  run over all its banks
8and sweep on into Judah, swirling over
    it,
  passing through it and reaching up to
    the neck.
Its outspread wings will cover the
    breadth of your land,
  O Immanuel*b*!"

9Raise the war cry,*c* you nations, and be
    shattered!
  Listen, all you distant lands.
Prepare for battle, and be shattered!
Prepare for battle, and be shattered!
10Devise your strategy, but it will be
    thwarted;
  propose your plan, but it will not
    stand,
for God is with us.*d*

Fear God

11The LORD spoke to me with his strong hand upon me, warning me not to follow the way of this people. He said:

12"Do not call conspiracy
  everything that these people call
    conspiracy*e*;
do not fear what they fear,
  and do not dread it.
13The LORD Almighty is the one you are to
    regard as holy,
  he is the one you are to fear,
  he is the one you are to dread,
14and he will be a sanctuary;
  but for both houses of Israel he will
    be
a stone that causes men to stumble
  and a rock that makes them fall.

And for the people of Jerusalem he will
    be
  a trap and a snare.
15Many of them will stumble;
  they will fall and be broken,
  they will be snared and captured."

16Bind up the testimony
  and seal up the law among my
    disciples.
17I will wait for the LORD,
  who is hiding his face from the house
    of Jacob.
I will put my trust in him.

18Here am I, and the children the LORD has given me. We are signs and symbols in Israel from the LORD Almighty, who dwells on Mount Zion.

19When men tell you to consult mediums and spiritists, who whisper and mutter, should not a people inquire of their God? Why consult the dead on behalf of the living? **20**To the law and to the testimony! If they do not speak according to this word, they have no light of dawn. **21**Distressed and hungry, they will roam through the land; when they are famished, they will become enraged and, looking upward, will curse their king and their God. **22**Then they will look toward the earth and see only distress and darkness and fearful gloom, and they will be thrust into utter darkness.

To Us a Child Is Born

9 Nevertheless, there will be no more gloom for those who were in distress. In the past he humbled the land of Zebulun and the land of Naphtali, but in the future he will honor Galilee of the Gentiles, by the way of the sea, along the Jordan—

2The people walking in darkness
  have seen a great light;
on those living in the land of the
    shadow of death*f*
  a light has dawned.
3You have enlarged the nation
  and increased their joy;
they rejoice before you
  as people rejoice at the harvest,
as men rejoice
  when dividing the plunder.
4For as in the day of Midian's defeat,
  you have shattered
the yoke that burdens them,
  the bar across their shoulders,

---

a7 That is, the Euphrates   *b8 Immanuel* means *God with us.*   *c9* Or *Do your worst*   *d10* Hebrew
Immanuel   *e12* Or *Do not call for a treaty / every time these people call for a treaty*   *f2* Or *land of darkness*

the rod of their oppressor.
[5]Every warrior's boot used in battle
    and every garment rolled in blood
will be destined for burning,
    will be fuel for the fire.
[6]For to us a child is born,
    to us a son is given,
    and the government will be on his
        shoulders.
And he will be called
    Wonderful Counselor,[a] Mighty God,
    Everlasting Father, Prince of Peace.
[7]Of the increase of his government and
        peace
    there will be no end.
He will reign on David's throne
    and over his kingdom,
establishing and upholding it
    with justice and righteousness
    from that time on and forever.
The zeal of the LORD Almighty
    will accomplish this.

The LORD's Anger Against Israel

[8]The Lord has sent a message against
        Jacob;
    it will fall on Israel.
[9]All the people will know it—
    Ephraim and the inhabitants of
        Samaria—
who say with pride
    and arrogance of heart,
[10]"The bricks have fallen down,
    but we will rebuild with dressed
        stone;
the fig trees have been felled,
    but we will replace them with cedars."
[11]But the LORD has strengthened Rezin's
        foes against them
    and has spurred their enemies on.
[12]Arameans from the east and Philistines
        from the west
    have devoured Israel with open
        mouth.

Yet for all this, his anger is not turned
        away,
    his hand is still upraised.

[13]But the people have not returned to him
        who struck them,
    nor have they sought the LORD
        Almighty.
[14]So the LORD will cut off from Israel both
        head and tail,
    both palm branch and reed in a single
        day;

[15]the elders and prominent men are the
        head,
    the prophets who teach lies are the
        tail.
[16]Those who guide this people mislead
        them,
    and those who are guided are led
        astray.
[17]Therefore the Lord will take no pleasure
        in the young men,
    nor will he pity the fatherless and
        widows,
for everyone is ungodly and wicked,
    every mouth speaks vileness.

Yet for all this, his anger is not turned
        away,
    his hand is still upraised.

[18]Surely wickedness burns like a fire;
    it consumes briers and thorns,
it sets the forest thickets ablaze,
    so that it rolls upward in a column of
        smoke.
[19]By the wrath of the LORD Almighty
    the land will be scorched
and the people will be fuel for the fire;
    no one will spare his brother.
[20]On the right they will devour,
    but still be hungry;
on the left they will eat,
    but not be satisfied.
Each will feed on the flesh of his own
        offspring[b]:
[21]   Manasseh will feed on Ephraim, and
            Ephraim on Manasseh;
    together they will turn against Judah.

Yet for all this, his anger is not turned
        away,
    his hand is still upraised.

10 Woe to those who make unjust
        laws,
    to those who issue oppressive
        decrees,
[2]to deprive the poor of their rights
    and withhold justice from the
        oppressed of my people,
making widows their prey
    and robbing the fatherless.
[3]What will you do on the day of
        reckoning,
    when disaster comes from afar?
To whom will you run for help?
    Where will you leave your riches?
[4]Nothing will remain but to cringe among
        the captives

---

[a]6 Or Wonderful, Counselor   [b]20 Or arm

or fall among the slain.

Yet for all this, his anger is not turned
away,
his hand is still upraised.

God's Judgment on Assyria

⁵"Woe to the Assyrian, the rod of my
anger,
in whose hand is the club of my
wrath!
⁶I send him against a godless nation,
I dispatch him against a people who
anger me,
to seize loot and snatch plunder,
and to trample them down like mud
in the streets.
⁷But this is not what he intends,
this is not what he has in mind;
his purpose is to destroy,
to put an end to many nations.
⁸'Are not my commanders all kings?' he
says.
⁹ 'Has not Calno fared like Carchemish?
Is not Hamath like Arpad,
and Samaria like Damascus?
¹⁰As my hand seized the kingdoms of the
idols,
kingdoms whose images excelled
those of Jerusalem and
Samaria—
¹¹shall I not deal with Jerusalem and her
images
as I dealt with Samaria and her
idols?' "

¹²When the Lord has finished all his work
against Mount Zion and Jerusalem, he will
say, "I will punish the king of Assyria for the
willful pride of his heart and the haughty
look in his eyes. ¹³For he says:

" 'By the strength of my hand I have
done this,
and by my wisdom, because I have
understanding.
I removed the boundaries of nations,
I plundered their treasures;
like a mighty one I subdued*a their
kings.
¹⁴As one reaches into a nest,
so my hand reached for the wealth of
the nations;
as men gather abandoned eggs,
so I gathered all the countries;
not one flapped a wing,
or opened its mouth to chirp.' "

¹⁵Does the ax raise itself above him who
swings it,
or the saw boast against him who
uses it?
As if a rod were to wield him who lifts it
up,
or a club brandish him who is not
wood!
¹⁶Therefore, the Lord, the LORD Almighty,
will send a wasting disease upon his
sturdy warriors;
under his pomp a fire will be kindled
like a blazing flame.
¹⁷The Light of Israel will become a fire,
their Holy One a flame;
in a single day it will burn and consume
his thorns and his briers.
¹⁸The splendor of his forests and fertile
fields
it will completely destroy,
as when a sick man wastes away.
¹⁹And the remaining trees of his forests
will be so few
that a child could write them down.

The Remnant of Israel

²⁰In that day the remnant of Israel,
the survivors of the house of Jacob,
will no longer rely on him
who struck them down
but will truly rely on the LORD,
the Holy One of Israel.
²¹A remnant will return,ᵇ a remnant of
Jacob
will return to the Mighty God.
²²Though your people, O Israel, be like
the sand by the sea,
only a remnant will return.
Destruction has been decreed,
overwhelming and righteous.
²³The Lord, the LORD Almighty, will carry
out
the destruction decreed upon the
whole land.

²⁴Therefore, this is what the Lord, the
LORD Almighty, says:

"O my people who live in Zion,
do not be afraid of the Assyrians,
who beat you with a rod
and lift up a club against you, as
Egypt did.
²⁵Very soon my anger against you will
end
and my wrath will be directed to their
destruction."

a13 Or / I subdued the mighty,   b21 Hebrew shear-jashub; also in verse 22

²⁶The Lᴏʀᴅ Almighty will lash them with a
    whip,
  as when he struck down Midian at
      the rock of Oreb;
  and he will raise his staff over the
      waters,
  as he did in Egypt.
²⁷In that day their burden will be lifted
    from your shoulders,
  their yoke from your neck;
  the yoke will be broken
  because you have grown so fat.ᵃ

²⁸They enter Aiath;
  they pass through Migron;
  they store supplies at Micmash.
²⁹They go over the pass, and say,
  "We will camp overnight at Geba."
Ramah trembles;
  Gibeah of Saul flees.
³⁰Cry out, O Daughter of Gallim!
  Listen, O Laishah!
  Poor Anathoth!
³¹Madmenah is in flight;
  the people of Gebim take cover.
³²This day they will halt at Nob;
  they will shake their fist
at the mount of the Daughter of Zion,
  at the hill of Jerusalem.

³³See, the Lord, the Lᴏʀᴅ Almighty,
  will lop off the boughs with great
      power.
The lofty trees will be felled,
  the tall ones will be brought low.
³⁴He will cut down the forest thickets
    with an ax;
  Lebanon will fall before the Mighty
    One.

The Branch From Jesse

11 A shoot will come up from the
    stump of Jesse;
  from his roots a Branch will bear fruit.
²The Spirit of the Lᴏʀᴅ will rest on him —
  the Spirit of wisdom and of
      understanding,
  the Spirit of counsel and of power,
  the Spirit of knowledge and of the
      fear of the Lᴏʀᴅ —
³and he will delight in the fear of the
    Lᴏʀᴅ.

He will not judge by what he sees with
    his eyes,
  or decide by what he hears with his
    ears;

⁴but with righteousness he will judge the
    needy,
  with justice he will give decisions for
      the poor of the earth.
He will strike the earth with the rod of
    his mouth;
  with the breath of his lips he will slay
      the wicked.
⁵Righteousness will be his belt
  and faithfulness the sash around his
      waist.

⁶The wolf will live with the lamb,
  the leopard will lie down with the
      goat,
the calf and the lion and the yearlingᵇ
    together;
  and a little child will lead them.
⁷The cow will feed with the bear,
  their young will lie down together,
  and the lion will eat straw like the ox.
⁸The infant will play near the hole of the
    cobra,
  and the young child put his hand into
      the viper's nest.
⁹They will neither harm nor destroy
  on all my holy mountain,
for the earth will be full of the
    knowledge of the Lᴏʀᴅ
  as the waters cover the sea.

¹⁰In that day the Root of Jesse will stand
as a banner for the peoples; the nations will
rally to him, and his place of rest will be glorious. ¹¹In that day the Lord will reach out
his hand a second time to reclaim the remnant that is left of his people from Assyria, from Lower Egypt, from Upper Egypt,ᶜ
from Cush,ᵈ from Elam, from Babylonia,ᵉ
from Hamath and from the islands of the
sea.

¹²He will raise a banner for the nations
  and gather the exiles of Israel;
he will assemble the scattered people of
    Judah
  from the four quarters of the earth.
¹³Ephraim's jealousy will vanish,
  and Judah's enemiesᶠ will be cut off;
Ephraim will not be jealous of Judah,
  nor Judah hostile toward Ephraim.
¹⁴They will swoop down on the slopes of
    Philistia to the west;
  together they will plunder the people
      to the east.
They will lay hands on Edom and Moab,

ᵃ27 Hebrew; Septuagint *broken / from your shoulders*   ᵇ6 Hebrew; Septuagint *lion will feed*   ᶜ11 Hebrew
from Pathros   ᵈ11 That is, the upper Nile region   ᵉ11 Hebrew *Shinar*   ᶠ13 Or *hostility*

WHEN ALL THE "PEACES" FALL INTO PLACE

Hillary's older sister comes home from college with a bumper sticker on her car that says, "Visualize World Peace."

"What does that mean, Kate?" Hillary asks.

"It's to get everyone to meditate together on love and harmony so that we can usher in the beginning of genuine world peace."

Look It Up
• • • •

Nice thought, Kate. Unfortunately, it just won't work. The book of Revelation reveals that ultimate peace won't be possible until Christ returns and brings about a whole new world order:

"Then I saw a new heaven and a new earth, for the first heaven and the first earth had passed away, and there was no longer any sea. . . . 'Now the dwelling of God is with men, and he will live with them. They will be his people, and God himself will be with them and be their God. He will wipe every tear from their eyes. There will be no more death or mourning or crying or pain, for the old order of things has passed away' " (Revelation 21:1,3–4).

Think It Through
• • • •

Here's an amazing fact: Since 3600 B.C., humans have fought approximately 15,000 wars. That's an average of more than 2.5 wars every year for the almost 5,600 years of recorded human history!

Do you think that the human race will ever be able to engineer a lasting peace on earth without God's help? Without a fundamental change in human nature?

Work It Out
• • • •

Though ultimate peace will not be possible until Christ comes and makes everything right, Christians are still expected to be peacemakers. You can:

1. Pray for peace. Ask God to raise up world leaders with the courage and character to pursue diplomacy rather than war (1 Timothy 2:1–2).

2. Be an example of peace in your own life (1 Thessalonians 5:13). Reach out in love to an "enemy."

3. Urge your elected officials to use their power and position to promote peace.

4. Tell one person this weekend how he or she can know the Lord of peace.

Nail It Down
• • • •

Read Isaiah's description of peace in Isaiah 11:6–9.

Turn to pages 736, 991 and 1270 for other readings on peace.
Turn to page 736 for Tuesday's reading.

Topic
• • • •

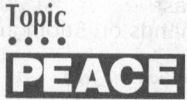

and the Ammonites will be subject to
them.
¹⁵The Lord will dry up
the gulf of the Egyptian sea;
with a scorching wind he will sweep his
hand
over the Euphrates River.ᵃ
He will break it up into seven streams
so that men can cross over in sandals.
¹⁶There will be a highway for the remnant
of his people
that is left from Assyria,
as there was for Israel
when they came up from Egypt.

Songs of Praise

12 In that day you will say:

"I will praise you, O Lord.
Although you were angry with me,
your anger has turned away
and you have comforted me.
²Surely God is my salvation;
I will trust and not be afraid.
The Lord, the Lord, is my strength and
my song;
he has become my salvation."
³With joy you will draw water
from the wells of salvation.

⁴In that day you will say:

"Give thanks to the Lord, call on his
name;
make known among the nations what
he has done,
and proclaim that his name is exalted.
⁵Sing to the Lord, for he has done
glorious things;
let this be known to all the world.
⁶Shout aloud and sing for joy, people of
Zion,
for great is the Holy One of Israel
among you."

A Prophecy Against Babylon

13 An oracle concerning Babylon that
Isaiah son of Amoz saw:

²Raise a banner on a bare hilltop,
shout to them;
beckon to them
to enter the gates of the nobles.
³I have commanded my holy ones;
I have summoned my warriors to
carry out my wrath—
those who rejoice in my triumph.

⁴Listen, a noise on the mountains,

like that of a great multitude!
Listen, an uproar among the kingdoms,
like nations massing together!
The Lord Almighty is mustering
an army for war.
⁵They come from faraway lands,
from the ends of the heavens—
the Lord and the weapons of his
wrath—
to destroy the whole country.

⁶Wail, for the day of the Lord is near;
it will come like destruction from the
Almighty.ᵇ
⁷Because of this, all hands will go limp,
every man's heart will melt.
⁸Terror will seize them,
pain and anguish will grip them;
they will writhe like a woman in
labor.
They will look aghast at each other,
their faces aflame.

⁹See, the day of the Lord is coming
—a cruel day, with wrath and fierce
anger—
to make the land desolate
and destroy the sinners within it.
¹⁰The stars of heaven and their
constellations
will not show their light.
The rising sun will be darkened
and the moon will not give its light.
¹¹I will punish the world for its evil,
the wicked for their sins.
I will put an end to the arrogance of the
haughty
and will humble the pride of the
ruthless.
¹²I will make man scarcer than pure gold,
more rare than the gold of Ophir.
¹³Therefore I will make the heavens
tremble;
and the earth will shake from its
place
at the wrath of the Lord Almighty,
in the day of his burning anger.

¹⁴Like a hunted gazelle,
like sheep without a shepherd,
each will return to his own people,
each will flee to his native land.
¹⁵Whoever is captured will be thrust
through;
all who are caught will fall by the
sword.
¹⁶Their infants will be dashed to pieces
before their eyes;

ᵃ15 Hebrew *the River*   ᵇ6 Hebrew *Shaddai*

their houses will be looted and their
wives ravished.
[17]See, I will stir up against them the
Medes,
who do not care for silver
and have no delight in gold.
[18]Their bows will strike down the young
men;
they will have no mercy on infants
nor will they look with compassion on
children.
[19]Babylon, the jewel of kingdoms,
the glory of the Babylonians'[a] pride,
will be overthrown by God
like Sodom and Gomorrah.
[20]She will never be inhabited
or lived in through all generations;
no Arab will pitch his tent there,
no shepherd will rest his flocks there.
[21]But desert creatures will lie there,
jackals will fill her houses;
there the owls will dwell,
and there the wild goats will leap
about.
[22]Hyenas will howl in her strongholds,
jackals in her luxurious palaces.
Her time is at hand,
and her days will not be prolonged.

14 The LORD will have compassion on
Jacob;
once again he will choose Israel
and will settle them in their own land.
Aliens will join them
and unite with the house of Jacob.
[2]Nations will take them
and bring them to their own place.
And the house of Israel will possess the
nations
as menservants and maidservants in
the LORD's land.
They will make captives of their captors
and rule over their oppressors.

[3]On the day the LORD gives you relief from
suffering and turmoil and cruel bondage,
[4]you will take up this taunt against the king
of Babylon:

How the oppressor has come to an end!
How his fury[b] has ended!
[5]The LORD has broken the rod of the
wicked,
the scepter of the rulers,
[6]which in anger struck down peoples
with unceasing blows,

and in fury subdued nations
with relentless aggression.
[7]All the lands are at rest and at peace;
they break into singing.
[8]Even the pine trees and the cedars of
Lebanon
exult over you and say,
"Now that you have been laid low,
no woodsman comes to cut us down."
[9]The grave[c] below is all astir
to meet you at your coming;
it rouses the spirits of the departed to
greet you—
all those who were leaders in the
world;
it makes them rise from their thrones—
all those who were kings over the
nations.
[10]They will all respond,
they will say to you,
"You also have become weak, as we
are;
you have become like us."
[11]All your pomp has been brought down
to the grave,
along with the noise of your harps;
maggots are spread out beneath you
and worms cover you.
[12]How you have fallen from heaven,
O morning star, son of the dawn!
You have been cast down to the earth,
you who once laid low the nations!
[13]You said in your heart,
"I will ascend to heaven;
I will raise my throne
above the stars of God;
I will sit enthroned on the mount of
assembly,
on the utmost heights of the sacred
mountain.[d]
[14]I will ascend above the tops of the
clouds;
I will make myself like the Most
High."
[15]But you are brought down to the grave,
to the depths of the pit.
[16]Those who see you stare at you,
they ponder your fate:
"Is this the man who shook the earth
and made kingdoms tremble,
[17]the man who made the world a desert,
who overthrew its cities
and would not let his captives go
home?"

a19 Or Chaldeans'   b4 Dead Sea Scrolls, Septuagint and Syriac; the meaning of the word in the Masoretic
Text is uncertain.   c9 Hebrew Sheol; also in verses 11 and 15   d13 Or the north; Hebrew Zaphon

18All the kings of the nations lie in state,
  each in his own tomb.
19But you are cast out of your tomb
  like a rejected branch;
you are covered with the slain,
  with those pierced by the sword,
  those who descend to the stones of
    the pit.
Like a corpse trampled underfoot,
20 you will not join them in burial,
for you have destroyed your land
  and killed your people.

The offspring of the wicked
  will never be mentioned again.
21Prepare a place to slaughter his sons
  for the sins of their forefathers;
they are not to rise to inherit the land
  and cover the earth with their cities.

22"I will rise up against them,"
  declares the Lord Almighty.
"I will cut off from Babylon her name
    and survivors,
  her offspring and descendants,"
                declares the Lord.
23"I will turn her into a place for owls
  and into swampland;
I will sweep her with the broom of
    destruction,"
  declares the Lord Almighty.

A Prophecy Against Assyria

24The Lord Almighty has sworn,

"Surely, as I have planned, so it will be,
  and as I have purposed, so it will
    stand.
25I will crush the Assyrian in my land;
  on my mountains I will trample him
    down.
His yoke will be taken from my people,
  and his burden removed from their
    shoulders."
26This is the plan determined for the
    whole world;
  this is the hand stretched out over all
    nations.
27For the Lord Almighty has purposed,
  and who can thwart him?
His hand is stretched out, and who
  can turn it back?

A Prophecy Against the Philistines

28This oracle came in the year King Ahaz
died:

29Do not rejoice, all you Philistines,
  that the rod that struck you is broken;

from the root of that snake will spring
    up a viper,
  its fruit will be a darting, venomous
    serpent.
30The poorest of the poor will find
    pasture,
  and the needy will lie down in safety.
But your root I will destroy by famine;
  it will slay your survivors.

31Wail, O gate! Howl, O city!
  Melt away, all you Philistines!
A cloud of smoke comes from the north,
  and there is not a straggler in its
    ranks.
32What answer shall be given
  to the envoys of that nation?
"The Lord has established Zion,
  and in her his afflicted people will
    find refuge."

A Prophecy Against Moab

15 An oracle concerning Moab:

Ar in Moab is ruined,
  destroyed in a night!
Kir in Moab is ruined,
  destroyed in a night!
2Dibon goes up to its temple,
  to its high places to weep;
  Moab wails over Nebo and Medeba.
Every head is shaved
  and every beard cut off.
3In the streets they wear sackcloth;
  on the roofs and in the public squares
they all wail,
  prostrate with weeping.
4Heshbon and Elealeh cry out,
  their voices are heard all the way to
    Jahaz.
Therefore the armed men of Moab cry
    out,
  and their hearts are faint.

5My heart cries out over Moab;
  her fugitives flee as far as Zoar,
  as far as Eglath Shelishiyah.
They go up the way to Luhith,
  weeping as they go;
on the road to Horonaim
  they lament their destruction.
6The waters of Nimrim are dried up
  and the grass is withered;
the vegetation is gone
  and nothing green is left.
7So the wealth they have acquired and
    stored up
  they carry away over the Ravine of
    the Poplars.

[8]Their outcry echoes along the border of
      Moab;
   their wailing reaches as far as Eglaim,
   their lamentation as far as Beer Elim.
[9]Dimon's[a] waters are full of blood,
   but I will bring still more upon
      Dimon[a] —
a lion upon the fugitives of Moab
   and upon those who remain in the
      land.

16
Send lambs as tribute
to the ruler of the land,
from Sela, across the desert,
   to the mount of the Daughter of Zion.
[2]Like fluttering birds
   pushed from the nest,
so are the women of Moab
   at the fords of the Arnon.

[3]"Give us counsel,
   render a decision.
Make your shadow like night—
   at high noon.
Hide the fugitives,
   do not betray the refugees.
[4]Let the Moabite fugitives stay with you;
   be their shelter from the destroyer."

The oppressor will come to an end,
   and destruction will cease;
the aggressor will vanish from the
      land.
[5]In love a throne will be established;
   in faithfulness a man will sit on it—
   one from the house[b] of David—
one who in judging seeks justice
   and speeds the cause of
      righteousness.

[6]We have heard of Moab's pride—
   her overweening pride and conceit,
   her pride and her insolence—
   but her boasts are empty.
[7]Therefore the Moabites wail,
   they wail together for Moab.
Lament and grieve
   for the men[c] of Kir Hareseth.
[8]The fields of Heshbon wither,
   the vines of Sibmah also.
The rulers of the nations
   have trampled down the choicest
      vines,
which once reached Jazer
   and spread toward the desert.
Their shoots spread out
   and went as far as the sea.

[9]So I weep, as Jazer weeps,
   for the vines of Sibmah.
O Heshbon, O Elealeh,
   I drench you with tears!
The shouts of joy over your ripened
      fruit
   and over your harvests have been
      stilled.
[10]Joy and gladness are taken away from
      the orchards;
   no one sings or shouts in the vineyards;
no one treads out wine at the presses,
   for I have put an end to the shouting.
[11]My heart laments for Moab like a harp,
   my inmost being for Kir Hareseth.
[12]When Moab appears at her high place,
   she only wears herself out;
when she goes to her shrine to pray,
   it is to no avail.

[13]This is the word the LORD has already
spoken concerning Moab. [14]But now the
LORD says: "Within three years, as a servant
bound by contract would count them,
Moab's splendor and all her many people
will be despised, and her survivors will be
very few and feeble."

An Oracle Against Damascus

17
An oracle concerning Damascus:

   "See, Damascus will no longer be
      a city
   but will become a heap of ruins.
[2]The cities of Aroer will be deserted
   and left to flocks, which will lie down,
   with no one to make them afraid.
[3]The fortified city will disappear from
      Ephraim,
   and royal power from Damascus;
the remnant of Aram will be
   like the glory of the Israelites,"
      declares the LORD Almighty.

[4]"In that day the glory of Jacob will fade;
   the fat of his body will waste away.
[5]It will be as when a reaper gathers the
      standing grain
   and harvests the grain with his arm—
as when a man gleans heads of grain
   in the Valley of Rephaim.
[6]Yet some gleanings will remain,
   as when an olive tree is beaten,
leaving two or three olives on the
      topmost branches,
   four or five on the fruitful boughs,"
      declares the LORD, the God of Israel.

---

[a]9 Masoretic Text; Dead Sea Scrolls, some Septuagint manuscripts and Vulgate *Dibon*   [b]5 Hebrew *tent*
[c]7 Or "*raisin cakes*," a wordplay

7In that day men will look to their Maker
  and turn their eyes to the Holy One of
    Israel.
8They will not look to the altars,
  the work of their hands,
and they will have no regard for the
    Asherah poles*a*
and the incense altars their fingers
  have made.

9In that day their strong cities, which they left because of the Israelites, will be like places abandoned to thickets and undergrowth. And all will be desolation.

10You have forgotten God your Savior;
  you have not remembered the Rock,
    your fortress.
Therefore, though you set out the finest
    plants
  and plant imported vines,
11though on the day you set them out,
  you make them grow,
and on the morning when you plant
    them, you bring them to bud,
yet the harvest will be as nothing
  in the day of disease and incurable
    pain.

12Oh, the raging of many nations—
  they rage like the raging sea!
Oh, the uproar of the peoples—
  they roar like the roaring of great
    waters!
13Although the peoples roar like the roar
    of surging waters,
  when he rebukes them they flee far
    away,
driven before the wind like chaff on the
    hills,
  like tumbleweed before a gale.
14In the evening, sudden terror!
  Before the morning, they are gone!
This is the portion of those who loot us,
  the lot of those who plunder us.

A Prophecy Against Cush

18 Woe to the land of whirring
      wings*b*
  along the rivers of Cush,*c*
2which sends envoys by sea
  in papyrus boats over the water.

Go, swift messengers,
  to a people tall and smooth-skinned,
    to a people feared far and wide,
an aggressive nation of strange speech,
  whose land is divided by rivers.

3All you people of the world,
  you who live on the earth,
when a banner is raised on the
    mountains,
  you will see it,
and when a trumpet sounds,
  you will hear it.
4This is what the LORD says to me:
  "I will remain quiet and will look on
    from my dwelling place,
like shimmering heat in the sunshine,
  like a cloud of dew in the heat of
    harvest."
5For, before the harvest, when the
    blossom is gone
  and the flower becomes a ripening
    grape,
he will cut off the shoots with pruning
    knives,
  and cut down and take away the
    spreading branches.
6They will all be left to the mountain
    birds of prey
  and to the wild animals;
the birds will feed on them all summer,
  the wild animals all winter.

7At that time gifts will be brought to the
LORD Almighty

from a people tall and smooth-skinned,
  from a people feared far and wide,
an aggressive nation of strange speech,
  whose land is divided by rivers—

the gifts will be brought to Mount Zion, the
place of the Name of the LORD Almighty.

A Prophecy About Egypt

19 An oracle concerning Egypt:

  See, the LORD rides on a swift
      cloud
  and is coming to Egypt.
The idols of Egypt tremble before him,
  and the hearts of the Egyptians melt
    within them.

2"I will stir up Egyptian against
    Egyptian—
  brother will fight against brother,
  neighbor against neighbor,
  city against city,
  kingdom against kingdom.
3The Egyptians will lose heart,
  and I will bring their plans to nothing;
they will consult the idols and the
    spirits of the dead,

---

a8 That is, symbols of the goddess Asherah   *b1* Or *of locusts*   *c1* That is, the upper Nile region

the mediums and the spiritists.
⁴I will hand the Egyptians over
  to the power of a cruel master,
and a fierce king will rule over them,"
  declares the Lord, the Lord Almighty.

⁵The waters of the river will dry up,
  and the riverbed will be parched and
    dry.
⁶The canals will stink;
  the streams of Egypt will dwindle and
    dry up.
The reeds and rushes will wither,
⁷ also the plants along the Nile,
  at the mouth of the river.
Every sown field along the Nile
  will become parched, will blow away
    and be no more.
⁸The fishermen will groan and lament,
  all who cast hooks into the Nile;
those who throw nets on the water
  will pine away.
⁹Those who work with combed flax will
    despair,
  the weavers of fine linen will lose
    hope.
¹⁰The workers in cloth will be dejected,
  and all the wage earners will be sick
    at heart.

¹¹The officials of Zoan are nothing but
    fools;
  the wise counselors of Pharaoh give
    senseless advice.
How can you say to Pharaoh,
  "I am one of the wise men,
  a disciple of the ancient kings"?

¹²Where are your wise men now?
  Let them show you and make known
what the Lord Almighty
  has planned against Egypt.
¹³The officials of Zoan have become fools,
  the leaders of Memphisᵃ are
    deceived;
  the cornerstones of her peoples
  have led Egypt astray.
¹⁴The Lord has poured into them
  a spirit of dizziness;
they make Egypt stagger in all that she
    does,
  as a drunkard staggers around in his
    vomit.
¹⁵There is nothing Egypt can do—
  head or tail, palm branch or reed.

¹⁶In that day the Egyptians will be like

women. They will shudder with fear at the uplifted hand that the Lord Almighty raises against them. ¹⁷And the land of Judah will bring terror to the Egyptians; everyone to whom Judah is mentioned will be terrified, because of what the Lord Almighty is planning against them.

¹⁸In that day five cities in Egypt will speak the language of Canaan and swear allegiance to the Lord Almighty. One of them will be called the City of Destruction.ᵇ

¹⁹In that day there will be an altar to the Lord in the heart of Egypt, and a monument to the Lord at its border. ²⁰It will be a sign and witness to the Lord Almighty in the land of Egypt. When they cry out to the Lord because of their oppressors, he will send them a savior and defender, and he will rescue them. ²¹So the Lord will make himself known to the Egyptians, and in that day they will acknowledge the Lord. They will worship with sacrifices and grain offerings; they will make vows to the Lord and keep them. ²²The Lord will strike Egypt with a plague; he will strike them and heal them. They will turn to the Lord, and he will respond to their pleas and heal them.

²³In that day there will be a highway from Egypt to Assyria. The Assyrians will go to Egypt and the Egyptians to Assyria. The Egyptians and Assyrians will worship together. ²⁴In that day Israel will be the third, along with Egypt and Assyria, a blessing on the earth. ²⁵The Lord Almighty will bless them, saying, "Blessed be Egypt my people, Assyria my handiwork, and Israel my inheritance."

A Prophecy Against Egypt and Cush

20 In the year that the supreme commander, sent by Sargon king of Assyria, came to Ashdod and attacked and captured it— ²at that time the Lord spoke through Isaiah son of Amoz. He said to him, "Take off the sackcloth from your body and the sandals from your feet." And he did so, going around stripped and barefoot.

³Then the Lord said, "Just as my servant Isaiah has gone stripped and barefoot for three years, as a sign and portent against Egypt and Cush,ᶜ ⁴so the king of Assyria will lead away stripped and barefoot the Egyptian captives and Cushite exiles, young and old, with buttocks bared—to Egypt's shame. ⁵Those who trusted in Cush and

ᵃ13 Hebrew *Noph*   ᵇ18 Most manuscripts of the Masoretic Text; some manuscripts of the Masoretic Text, Dead Sea Scrolls and Vulgate *City of the Sun* (that is, Heliopolis)   ᶜ3 That is, the upper Nile region; also in verse 5 boasted in Egypt will be afraid and put to shame. **6**In that day the people who live on this coast will say, 'See what has happened to those we relied on, those we fled to for help and deliverance from the king of Assyria! How then can we escape?' "

A Prophecy Against Babylon

21 An oracle concerning the Desert by the Sea:

Like whirlwinds sweeping through the
 southland,
 an invader comes from the desert,
 from a land of terror.
2A dire vision has been shown to me:
 The traitor betrays, the looter takes
  loot.
Elam, attack! Media, lay siege!
 I will bring to an end all the groaning
  she caused.

3At this my body is racked with pain,
 pangs seize me, like those of a
  woman in labor;
I am staggered by what I hear,
 I am bewildered by what I see.
4My heart falters,
 fear makes me tremble;
the twilight I longed for
 has become a horror to me.

5They set the tables,
 they spread the rugs,
 they eat, they drink!
Get up, you officers,
 oil the shields!

6This is what the Lord says to me:

"Go, post a lookout
 and have him report what he sees.
7When he sees chariots
 with teams of horses,
riders on donkeys
 or riders on camels,
let him be alert,
 fully alert."

8And the lookout[a] shouted,

"Day after day, my lord, I stand on the
 watchtower;
 every night I stay at my post.
9Look, here comes a man in a chariot
 with a team of horses.
And he gives back the answer:
 'Babylon has fallen, has fallen!

All the images of its gods
 lie shattered on the ground!' "

10O my people, crushed on the threshing
  floor,
 I tell you what I have heard
from the Lord Almighty,
 from the God of Israel.

A Prophecy Against Edom

11An oracle concerning Dumah[b]:

Someone calls to me from Seir,
 "Watchman, what is left of the night?
 Watchman, what is left of the night?"
12The watchman replies,
 "Morning is coming, but also the
  night.
If you would ask, then ask;
 and come back yet again."

A Prophecy Against Arabia

13An oracle concerning Arabia:

You caravans of Dedanites,
 who camp in the thickets of Arabia,
14 bring water for the thirsty;
you who live in Tema,
 bring food for the fugitives.
15They flee from the sword,
 from the drawn sword,
from the bent bow
 and from the heat of battle.

16This is what the Lord says to me: "Within one year, as a servant bound by contract would count it, all the pomp of Kedar will come to an end. **17**The survivors of the bowmen, the warriors of Kedar, will be few." The Lord, the God of Israel, has spoken.

A Prophecy About Jerusalem

22 An oracle concerning the Valley of Vision:

What troubles you now,
 that you have all gone up on the
  roofs,
2O town full of commotion,
 O city of tumult and revelry?
Your slain were not killed by the sword,
 nor did they die in battle.
3All your leaders have fled together;
 they have been captured without
  using the bow.
All you who were caught were taken
 prisoner together,

---

[a] 8 Dead Sea Scrolls and Syriac; Masoretic Text *A lion* a wordplay on *Edom*.

[b] 11 *Dumah* means *silence* or *stillness,*

having fled while the enemy was still
    far away.
4Therefore I said, "Turn away from me;
    let me weep bitterly.
Do not try to console me
    over the destruction of my people."

5The Lord, the LORD Almighty, has a day
    of tumult and trampling and terror
    in the Valley of Vision,
a day of battering down walls
    and of crying out to the mountains.
6Elam takes up the quiver,
    with her charioteers and horses;
Kir uncovers the shield.
7Your choicest valleys are full of chariots,
    and horsemen are posted at the city
        gates;
8 the defenses of Judah are stripped
        away.

And you looked in that day
    to the weapons in the Palace of the
        Forest;
9you saw that the City of David
    had many breaches in its defenses;
you stored up water
    in the Lower Pool.
10You counted the buildings in Jerusalem
    and tore down houses to strengthen
        the wall.
11You built a reservoir between the two
        walls
    for the water of the Old Pool,
but you did not look to the One who
        made it,
    or have regard for the One who
        planned it long ago.

12The Lord, the LORD Almighty,
    called you on that day
to weep and to wail,
    to tear out your hair and put on
        sackcloth.
13But see, there is joy and revelry,
    slaughtering of cattle and killing of
        sheep,
    eating of meat and drinking of wine!
"Let us eat and drink," you say,
    "for tomorrow we die!"

14The LORD Almighty has revealed this in
my hearing: "Till your dying day this sin will
not be atoned for," says the Lord, the LORD
Almighty.

15This is what the Lord, the LORD Almighty,
says:

"Go, say to this steward,
    to Shebna, who is in charge of the
        palace:
16What are you doing here and who gave
        you permission
    to cut out a grave for yourself here,
hewing your grave on the height
    and chiseling your resting place in the
        rock?

17"Beware, the LORD is about to take firm
        hold of you
    and hurl you away, O you mighty
        man.
18He will roll you up tightly like a ball
    and throw you into a large country.
There you will die
    and there your splendid chariots will
        remain—
    you disgrace to your master's house!
19I will depose you from your office,
    and you will be ousted from your
        position.

20"In that day I will summon my servant,
Eliakim son of Hilkiah. **21**I will clothe him
with your robe and fasten your sash around
him and hand your authority over to him.
He will be a father to those who live in Jerusalem and to the house of Judah. **22**I will
place on his shoulder the key to the house
of David; what he opens no one can shut,
and what he shuts no one can open. **23**I will
drive him like a peg into a firm place; he will
be a seat*a* of honor for the house of his father. **24**All the glory of his family will hang on
him: its offspring and offshoots—all its lesser vessels, from the bowls to all the jars.

25"In that day," declares the LORD Almighty, "the peg driven into the firm place
will give way; it will be sheared off and will
fall, and the load hanging on it will be cut
down." The LORD has spoken.

A Prophecy About Tyre

23 An oracle concerning Tyre:

    Wail, O ships of Tarshish!
For Tyre is destroyed
    and left without house or harbor.
From the land of Cyprus*b*
    word has come to them.

2Be silent, you people of the island
    and you merchants of Sidon,
    whom the seafarers have enriched.
3On the great waters
    came the grain of the Shihor;

a23 Or throne   b1 Hebrew Kittim

the harvest of the Nile[a] was the
  revenue of Tyre,
and she became the marketplace of
  the nations.

[4]Be ashamed, O Sidon, and you,
  O fortress of the sea,
for the sea has spoken:
"I have neither been in labor nor given
  birth;
I have neither reared sons nor
  brought up daughters."
[5]When word comes to Egypt,
  they will be in anguish at the report
  from Tyre.

[6]Cross over to Tarshish;
  wail, you people of the island.
[7]Is this your city of revelry,
  the old, old city,
whose feet have taken her
  to settle in far-off lands?
[8]Who planned this against Tyre,
  the bestower of crowns,
whose merchants are princes,
  whose traders are renowned in the
  earth?
[9]The LORD Almighty planned it,
  to bring low the pride of all glory
and to humble all who are renowned
  on the earth.

[10]Till[b] your land as along the Nile,
  O Daughter of Tarshish,
  for you no longer have a harbor.
[11]The LORD has stretched out his hand
  over the sea
  and made its kingdoms tremble.
He has given an order concerning
  Phoenicia[c]
  that her fortresses be destroyed.
[12]He said, "No more of your reveling,
  O Virgin Daughter of Sidon, now
  crushed!

"Up, cross over to Cyprus[d];
  even there you will find no rest."
[13]Look at the land of the Babylonians,[e]
  this people that is now of no account!
The Assyrians have made it
  a place for desert creatures;
they raised up their siege towers,
  they stripped its fortresses bare
  and turned it into a ruin.

[14]Wail, you ships of Tarshish;
  your fortress is destroyed!

[15]At that time Tyre will be forgotten for
seventy years, the span of a king's life. But
at the end of these seventy years, it will happen to Tyre as in the song of the prostitute:

[16]"Take up a harp, walk through the city,
  O prostitute forgotten;
play the harp well, sing many a song,
  so that you will be remembered."

[17]At the end of seventy years, the LORD will
deal with Tyre. She will return to her hire as
a prostitute and will ply her trade with all the
kingdoms on the face of the earth. [18]Yet her
profit and her earnings will be set apart for
the LORD; they will not be stored up or hoarded. Her profits will go to those who live before the LORD, for abundant food and fine
clothes.

The LORD's Devastation of the Earth

24   See, the LORD is going to lay waste
    the earth
  and devastate it;
he will ruin its face
  and scatter its inhabitants—
[2]it will be the same
  for priest as for people,
  for master as for servant,
  for mistress as for maid,
  for seller as for buyer,
  for borrower as for lender,
  for debtor as for creditor.
[3]The earth will be completely laid waste
  and totally plundered.
      The LORD has spoken this word.

[4]The earth dries up and withers,
  the world languishes and withers,
  the exalted of the earth languish.
[5]The earth is defiled by its people;
  they have disobeyed the laws,
violated the statutes
  and broken the everlasting covenant.
[6]Therefore a curse consumes the earth;
  its people must bear their guilt.
Therefore earth's inhabitants are burned
  up,
  and very few are left.
[7]The new wine dries up and the vine
  withers;
  all the merrymakers groan.
[8]The gaiety of the tambourines is stilled,
  the noise of the revelers has stopped,
  the joyful harp is silent.
[9]No longer do they drink wine with a
  song;

---

[a]2,3 Masoretic Text; one Dead Sea Scroll *Sidon, / who cross over the sea; / your envoys* [3]*are on the great
waters. / The grain of the Shihor, / the harvest of the Nile,*   [b]10 Dead Sea Scrolls and some Septuagint
manuscripts; Masoretic Text *Go through*   [c]11 Hebrew *Canaan*   [d]12 Hebrew *Kittim*   [e]13 Or *Chaldeans*

the beer is bitter to its drinkers.
¹⁰The ruined city lies desolate;
  the entrance to every house is barred.
¹¹In the streets they cry out for wine;
  all joy turns to gloom,
  all gaiety is banished from the earth.
¹²The city is left in ruins,
  its gate is battered to pieces.
¹³So will it be on the earth
  and among the nations,
as when an olive tree is beaten,
  or as when gleanings are left after the
    grape harvest.

¹⁴They raise their voices, they shout for
    joy;
  from the west they acclaim the LORD's
    majesty.
¹⁵Therefore in the east give glory to the
    LORD;
  exalt the name of the LORD, the God of
    Israel,
  in the islands of the sea.
¹⁶From the ends of the earth we hear
    singing:
  "Glory to the Righteous One."

But I said, "I waste away, I waste away!
    Woe to me!
The treacherous betray!
  With treachery the treacherous
    betray!"
¹⁷Terror and pit and snare await you,
  O people of the earth.
¹⁸Whoever flees at the sound of terror
  will fall into a pit;
whoever climbs out of the pit
  will be caught in a snare.

The floodgates of the heavens are
    opened,
  the foundations of the earth shake.
¹⁹The earth is broken up,
  the earth is split asunder,
  the earth is thoroughly shaken.
²⁰The earth reels like a drunkard,
  it sways like a hut in the wind;
so heavy upon it is the guilt of its
    rebellion
  that it falls—never to rise again.

²¹In that day the LORD will punish
  the powers in the heavens above
  and the kings on the earth below.
²²They will be herded together
  like prisoners bound in a dungeon;
they will be shut up in prison
  and be punished[a] after many days.

²³The moon will be abashed, the sun
    ashamed;
  for the LORD Almighty will reign
on Mount Zion and in Jerusalem,
  and before its elders, gloriously.

Praise to the LORD

25 O LORD, you are my God;
  I will exalt you and praise your
    name,
for in perfect faithfulness
  you have done marvelous things,
  things planned long ago.
²You have made the city a heap of
    rubble,
  the fortified town a ruin,
the foreigners' stronghold a city no
    more;
  it will never be rebuilt.
³Therefore strong peoples will honor you;
  cities of ruthless nations will revere
    you.
⁴You have been a refuge for the poor,
  a refuge for the needy in his distress,
a shelter from the storm
  and a shade from the heat.
For the breath of the ruthless
  is like a storm driving against a wall
⁵ and like the heat of the desert.
You silence the uproar of foreigners;
  as heat is reduced by the shadow of a
    cloud,
so the song of the ruthless is stilled.

⁶On this mountain the LORD Almighty will
    prepare
  a feast of rich food for all peoples,
a banquet of aged wine—
  the best of meats and the finest of
    wines.
⁷On this mountain he will destroy
  the shroud that enfolds all peoples,
the sheet that covers all nations;
⁸ he will swallow up death forever.
The Sovereign LORD will wipe away the
    tears
  from all faces;
he will remove the disgrace of his
    people
  from all the earth.
        The LORD has spoken.

⁹In that day they will say,

"Surely this is our God;
  we trusted in him, and he saved us.
This is the LORD, we trusted in him;

ᵃ22 Or *released*

let us rejoice and be glad in his
  salvation."

¹⁰The hand of the L<small>ORD</small> will rest on this
    mountain;
  but Moab will be trampled under him
    as straw is trampled down in the
    manure.
¹¹They will spread out their hands in it,
    as a swimmer spreads out his hands
    to swim.
  God will bring down their pride
    despite the cleverness*ᵃ* of their
    hands.
¹²He will bring down your high fortified
    walls
    and lay them low;
  he will bring them down to the ground,
    to the very dust.

A Song of Praise

26 In that day this song will be sung in
      the land of Judah:

  We have a strong city;
    God makes salvation
    its walls and ramparts.
²Open the gates
    that the righteous nation may enter,
    the nation that keeps faith.
³You will keep in perfect peace
    him whose mind is steadfast,
    because he trusts in you.
⁴Trust in the L<small>ORD</small> forever,
    for the L<small>ORD</small>, the L<small>ORD</small>, is the Rock
    eternal.
⁵He humbles those who dwell on high,
    he lays the lofty city low;
  he levels it to the ground
    and casts it down to the dust.
⁶Feet trample it down—
    the feet of the oppressed,
    the footsteps of the poor.

⁷The path of the righteous is level;
    O upright One, you make the way of
    the righteous smooth.
⁸Yes, L<small>ORD</small>, walking in the way of your
    laws,*ᵇ*
  we wait for you;
  your name and renown
    are the desire of our hearts.
⁹My soul yearns for you in the night;
    in the morning my spirit longs for
    you.
  When your judgments come upon the
    earth,

the people of the world learn
  righteousness.
¹⁰Though grace is shown to the wicked,
    they do not learn righteousness;
  even in a land of uprightness they go on
    doing evil
  and regard not the majesty of the
    L<small>ORD</small>.
¹¹O L<small>ORD</small>, your hand is lifted high,
    but they do not see it.
  Let them see your zeal for your people
    and be put to shame;
  let the fire reserved for your enemies
    consume them.

¹²L<small>ORD</small>, you establish peace for us;
    all that we have accomplished you
    have done for us.
¹³O L<small>ORD</small>, our God, other lords besides
    you have ruled over us,
  but your name alone do we honor.
¹⁴They are now dead, they live no more;
    those departed spirits do not rise.
  You punished them and brought them
    to ruin;
  you wiped out all memory of them.
¹⁵You have enlarged the nation, O L<small>ORD</small>;
    you have enlarged the nation.
  You have gained glory for yourself;
    you have extended all the borders of
    the land.

¹⁶L<small>ORD</small>, they came to you in their distress;
    when you disciplined them,
    they could barely whisper a prayer.*ᶜ*
¹⁷As a woman with child and about to
      give birth
    writhes and cries out in her pain,
    so were we in your presence, O L<small>ORD</small>.
¹⁸We were with child, we writhed in pain,
    but we gave birth to wind.
  We have not brought salvation to the
    earth;
  we have not given birth to people of
    the world.

¹⁹But your dead will live;
    their bodies will rise.
  You who dwell in the dust,
    wake up and shout for joy.
  Your dew is like the dew of the
    morning;
    the earth will give birth to her dead.

²⁰Go, my people, enter your rooms
    and shut the doors behind you;
  hide yourselves for a little while
    until his wrath has passed by.

ᵃ11 The meaning of the Hebrew for this word is uncertain.   *ᵇ8* Or *judgments*   *ᶜ16* The meaning of the
Hebrew for this clause is uncertain.

THE PATH TO PERSONAL PEACE

After youth group, Amelia, Blaine and Tyler stop for some frozen yogurt.

Blaine: "This scholarship thing is making me insane. I've got a horrible feeling that if it doesn't work out, my parents are going to be really disappointed. I haven't been able to sleep all week!"

Amelia: "Me either. I *still* haven't talked to Mike."

Tyler: "I thought you were going to break up with him last weekend!"

Amelia: "I was. But I chickened out. And it's like this heavy cloud hanging over my head. I know I need to do it. I just can't find the nerve. I'm going crazy inside!"

Look It Up
••••

The Bible mentions several stepping stones on the path to personal peace:

1. A focus on God's Word. "Great peace have they who love your law, and nothing can make them stumble" (Psalm 119:165).

2. An emphasis on prayer. "Do not be anxious about anything, but in everything, by prayer and petition, with thanksgiving, present your requests to God. And the peace of God, which transcends all understanding, will guard your hearts and your minds in Christ Jesus" (Philippians 4:6–7).

3. A dependence on the Holy Spirit. "But the fruit of the Spirit is . . . peace" (Galatians 5:22).

Think It Through
••••

Rate your level of peacefulness in each of the following areas: school, home, social, your future. Would you rate your level of peacefulness as: "Volcanic Alert!" or "Frequent Anxiety" or "Occasional Restlessness" or "Couldn't Be Calmer"? Which rating sounds best to you?

Work It Out
••••

Visit someone who has small children. When the kids fall asleep, observe them. Do they look uptight? Anxious? Deeply worried? No! When little kids fall asleep, they crash! They really rest! And they have such peaceful looks on their faces.

Who says little kids can't teach us anything?

We need to relearn how to be that calm and trusting (see Matthew 18:3–4).

Spend extra time in God's Word today meditating on his goodness, power and control. Pray about every single thing that is robbing you of peace. Ask God to fill you with his Spirit of peace.

Nail It Down
••••

Read Isaiah's prescription for peace in Isaiah 26:3.

Turn to pages 724, 991 and 1270 for other readings on peace.
Turn to page 742 for Wednesday's reading.

Topic
••••

²¹See, the LORD is coming out of his
    dwelling
  to punish the people of the earth for
    their sins.
  The earth will disclose the blood shed
    upon her;
  she will conceal her slain no longer.

Deliverance of Israel

27 In that day,
    the LORD will punish with his
      sword,
  his fierce, great and powerful sword,
  Leviathan the gliding serpent,
    Leviathan the coiling serpent;
  he will slay the monster of the sea.

  ²In that day—

  "Sing about a fruitful vineyard:
  ³ I, the LORD, watch over it;
    I water it continually.
  I guard it day and night
    so that no one may harm it.
  ⁴ I am not angry.
  If only there were briers and thorns
      confronting me!
    I would march against them in battle;
    I would set them all on fire.
  ⁵Or else let them come to me for refuge;
    let them make peace with me,
    yes, let them make peace with me."

  ⁶In days to come Jacob will take root,
    Israel will bud and blossom
    and fill all the world with fruit.

  ⁷Has ˌthe LORDˌ struck her
    as he struck down those who struck
      her?
  Has she been killed
    as those were killed who killed her?
  ⁸By warfareᵃ and exile you contend with
      her—
    with his fierce blast he drives her out,
    as on a day the east wind blows.
  ⁹By this, then, will Jacob's guilt be
      atoned for,
    and this will be the full fruitage of the
      removal of his sin:
  When he makes all the altar stones
    to be like chalk stones crushed to
      pieces,
  no Asherah polesᵇ or incense altars
    will be left standing.
  ¹⁰The fortified city stands desolate,

an abandoned settlement, forsaken
    like the desert;
  there the calves graze,
    there they lie down;
    they strip its branches bare.
  ¹¹When its twigs are dry, they are broken
      off
    and women come and make fires
      with them.
  For this is a people without
      understanding;
    so their Maker has no compassion on
      them,
    and their Creator shows them no
      favor.

  ¹²In that day the LORD will thresh from the
flowing Euphratesᶜ to the Wadi of Egypt,
and you, O Israelites, will be gathered up
one by one. ¹³And in that day a great trumpet will sound. Those who were perishing in
Assyria and those who were exiled in Egypt
will come and worship the LORD on the holy
mountain in Jerusalem.

Woe to Ephraim

28 Woe to that wreath, the pride of
    Ephraim's drunkards,
  to the fading flower, his glorious
    beauty,
  set on the head of a fertile valley—
    to that city, the pride of those laid
      low by wine!
  ²See, the Lord has one who is powerful
      and strong.
  Like a hailstorm and a destructive
      wind,
  like a driving rain and a flooding
      downpour,
    he will throw it forcefully to the
      ground.
  ³That wreath, the pride of Ephraim's
      drunkards,
    will be trampled underfoot.
  ⁴That fading flower, his glorious beauty,
    set on the head of a fertile valley,
  will be like a fig ripe before harvest—
    as soon as someone sees it and takes
      it in his hand,
    he swallows it.

  ⁵In that day the LORD Almighty
    will be a glorious crown,
  a beautiful wreath
    for the remnant of his people.
  ⁶He will be a spirit of justice
    to him who sits in judgment,

ᵃ8 See Septuagint; the meaning of the Hebrew for this word is uncertain.   ᵇ9 That is, symbols of the goddess
Asherah   ᶜ12 Hebrew *River*

a source of strength
  to those who turn back the battle at
    the gate.
7And these also stagger from wine
  and reel from beer:
Priests and prophets stagger from beer
  and are befuddled with wine;
they reel from beer,
  they stagger when seeing visions,
  they stumble when rendering
    decisions.
8All the tables are covered with vomit
  and there is not a spot without filth.

9"Who is it he is trying to teach?
  To whom is he explaining his
    message?
To children weaned from their milk,
  to those just taken from the breast?
10For it is:
  Do and do, do and do,
  rule on rule, rule on rule*a*;
  a little here, a little there."

11Very well then, with foreign lips and
    strange tongues
  God will speak to this people,
12to whom he said,
  "This is the resting place, let the
    weary rest";
and, "This is the place of repose"—
  but they would not listen.
13So then, the word of the LORD to them
    will become:
  Do and do, do and do,
  rule on rule, rule on rule;
  a little here, a little there—
so that they will go and fall backward,
  be injured and snared and captured.

14Therefore hear the word of the LORD,
    you scoffers
  who rule this people in Jerusalem.
15You boast, "We have entered into a
    covenant with death,
  with the grave*b* we have made an
    agreement.
When an overwhelming scourge sweeps
    by,
  it cannot touch us,
for we have made a lie our refuge
  and falsehood*c* our hiding place."

16So this is what the Sovereign LORD says:

"See, I lay a stone in Zion,
  a tested stone,

a precious cornerstone for a sure
    foundation;
  the one who trusts will never be
    dismayed.
17I will make justice the measuring line
  and righteousness the plumb line;
hail will sweep away your refuge, the
    lie,
  and water will overflow your hiding
    place.
18Your covenant with death will be
    annulled;
  your agreement with the grave will
    not stand.
When the overwhelming scourge sweeps
    by,
  you will be beaten down by it.
19As often as it comes it will carry you
    away;
  morning after morning, by day and by
    night,
  it will sweep through."

The understanding of this message
  will bring sheer terror.
20The bed is too short to stretch out on,
  the blanket too narrow to wrap
    around you.
21The LORD will rise up as he did at Mount
    Perazim,
  he will rouse himself as in the Valley
    of Gibeon—
to do his work, his strange work,
  and perform his task, his alien task.
22Now stop your mocking,
  or your chains will become heavier;
the Lord, the LORD Almighty, has told me
  of the destruction decreed against the
    whole land.

23Listen and hear my voice;
  pay attention and hear what I say.
24When a farmer plows for planting, does
    he plow continually?
  Does he keep on breaking up and
    harrowing the soil?
25When he has leveled the surface,
  does he not sow caraway and scatter
    cummin?
Does he not plant wheat in its place,*d*
  barley in its plot,*d*
  and spelt in its field?
26His God instructs him
  and teaches him the right way.

27Caraway is not threshed with a sledge,

---

a 10 Hebrew / *sav lasav sav lasav / kav lakav kav lakav* (possibly meaningless sounds; perhaps a mimicking of
the prophet's words); also in verse 13   *b 15* Hebrew *Sheol*; also in verse 18   *c 15* 'Or *false gods*   *d 25* The
meaning of the Hebrew for this word is uncertain.

nor is a cartwheel rolled over
     cummin;
caraway is beaten out with a rod,
     and cummin with a stick.
²⁸Grain must be ground to make bread;
     so one does not go on threshing it
          forever.
Though he drives the wheels of his
          threshing cart over it,
     his horses do not grind it.
²⁹All this also comes from the Lord
          Almighty,
     wonderful in counsel and magnificent
          in wisdom.

Woe to David's City

29 Woe to you, Ariel, Ariel,
          the city where David settled!
Add year to year
     and let your cycle of festivals go on.
²Yet I will besiege Ariel;
     she will mourn and lament,
     she will be to me like an altar
          hearth.ᵃ
³I will encamp against you all around;
     I will encircle you with towers
     and set up my siege works against
          you.
⁴Brought low, you will speak from the
          ground;
     your speech will mumble out of the
          dust.
Your voice will come ghostlike from the
          earth;
     out of the dust your speech will
          whisper.

⁵But your many enemies will become
          like fine dust,
     the ruthless hordes like blown chaff.
Suddenly, in an instant,
⁶   the Lord Almighty will come
with thunder and earthquake and great
          noise,
     with windstorm and tempest and
          flames of a devouring fire.
⁷Then the hordes of all the nations that
          fight against Ariel,
     that attack her and her fortress and
          besiege her,
will be as it is with a dream,
     with a vision in the night—
⁸as when a hungry man dreams that he
          is eating,
     but he awakens, and his hunger
          remains;

as when a thirsty man dreams that he is
          drinking,
     but he awakens faint, with his thirst
          unquenched.
So will it be with the hordes of all the
          nations
     that fight against Mount Zion.

⁹Be stunned and amazed,
     blind yourselves and be sightless;
be drunk, but not from wine,
     stagger, but not from beer.
¹⁰The Lord has brought over you a deep
          sleep:
     He has sealed your eyes (the
          prophets);
     he has covered your heads (the
          seers).

¹¹For you this whole vision is nothing but
words sealed in a scroll. And if you give the
scroll to someone who can read, and say to
him, "Read this, please," he will answer, "I
can't; it is sealed." ¹²Or if you give the scroll
to someone who cannot read, and say,
"Read this, please," he will answer, "I don't
know how to read."

¹³The Lord says:

"These people come near to me with
          their mouth
     and honor me with their lips,
     but their hearts are far from me.
Their worship of me
     is made up only of rules taught by
          men.ᵇ
¹⁴Therefore once more I will astound
          these people
     with wonder upon wonder;
the wisdom of the wise will perish,
     the intelligence of the intelligent will
          vanish."
¹⁵Woe to those who go to great depths
     to hide their plans from the Lord,
who do their work in darkness and
          think,
     "Who sees us? Who will know?"
¹⁶You turn things upside down,
     as if the potter were thought to be
          like the clay!
Shall what is formed say to him who
          formed it,
     "He did not make me"?
Can the pot say of the potter,
     "He knows nothing"?

ᵃ2 The Hebrew for *altar hearth* sounds like the Hebrew for *Ariel*.   ᵇ13 Hebrew; Septuagint *They worship me in vain; / their teachings are but rules taught by men*

¹⁷In a very short time, will not Lebanon
    be turned into a fertile field
and the fertile field seem like a
    forest?
¹⁸In that day the deaf will hear the words
    of the scroll,
and out of gloom and darkness
    the eyes of the blind will see.
¹⁹Once more the humble will rejoice in
    the LORD;
    the needy will rejoice in the Holy One
    of Israel.
²⁰The ruthless will vanish,
    the mockers will disappear,
and all who have an eye for evil will
    be cut down—
²¹those who with a word make a man out
    to be guilty,
who ensnare the defender in court
and with false testimony deprive the
    innocent of justice.

²²Therefore this is what the LORD, who redeemed Abraham, says to the house of Jacob:

"No longer will Jacob be ashamed;
    no longer will their faces grow pale.
²³When they see among them their
    children,
    the work of my hands,
they will keep my name holy;
    they will acknowledge the holiness of
    the Holy One of Jacob,
    and will stand in awe of the God of
    Israel.
²⁴Those who are wayward in spirit will
    gain understanding;
    those who complain will accept
    instruction."

Woe to the Obstinate Nation

30 "Woe to the obstinate children,"
    declares the LORD,
"to those who carry out plans that are
    not mine,
    forming an alliance, but not by my
    Spirit,
    heaping sin upon sin;
²who go down to Egypt
    without consulting me;
who look for help to Pharaoh's
    protection,
    to Egypt's shade for refuge.
³But Pharaoh's protection will be to your
    shame,
    Egypt's shade will bring you disgrace.
⁴Though they have officials in Zoan
    and their envoys have arrived in
    Hanes,

⁵everyone will be put to shame
    because of a people useless to them,
who bring neither help nor advantage,
    but only shame and disgrace."

⁶An oracle concerning the animals of the
Negev:

Through a land of hardship and distress,
    of lions and lionesses,
    of adders and darting snakes,
the envoys carry their riches on
    donkeys' backs,
    their treasures on the humps of
    camels,
to that unprofitable nation,
⁷   to Egypt, whose help is utterly
    useless.
Therefore I call her
    Rahab the Do-Nothing.

⁸Go now, write it on a tablet for them,
    inscribe it on a scroll,
that for the days to come
    it may be an everlasting witness.
⁹These are rebellious people, deceitful
    children,
    children unwilling to listen to the
    LORD's instruction.
¹⁰They say to the seers,
    "See no more visions!"
and to the prophets,
    "Give us no more visions of what is
    right!
Tell us pleasant things,
    prophesy illusions.
¹¹Leave this way,
    get off this path,
and stop confronting us
    with the Holy One of Israel!"

¹²Therefore, this is what the Holy One of
Israel says:

"Because you have rejected this
    message,
    relied on oppression
    and depended on deceit,
¹³this sin will become for you
    like a high wall, cracked and bulging,
    that collapses suddenly, in an instant.
¹⁴It will break in pieces like pottery,
    shattered so mercilessly
that among its pieces not a fragment
    will be found
    for taking coals from a hearth
    or scooping water out of a cistern."

¹⁵This is what the Sovereign LORD, the
Holy One of Israel, says:

"In repentance and rest is your
    salvation,
  in quietness and trust is your
    strength,
  but you would have none of it.
¹⁶You said, 'No, we will flee on horses.'
  Therefore you will flee!
  You said, 'We will ride off on swift
    horses.'
  Therefore your pursuers will be swift!
¹⁷A thousand will flee
    at the threat of one;
  at the threat of five
    you will all flee away,
  till you are left
    like a flagstaff on a mountaintop,
    like a banner on a hill."

¹⁸Yet the LORD longs to be gracious to you;
  he rises to show you compassion.
  For the LORD is a God of justice.
    Blessed are all who wait for him!

¹⁹O people of Zion, who live in Jerusalem,
you will weep no more. How gracious he
will be when you cry for help! As soon as he
hears, he will answer you. ²⁰Although the
Lord gives you the bread of adversity and
the water of affliction, your teachers will be
hidden no more; with your own eyes you
will see them. ²¹Whether you turn to the
right or to the left, your ears will hear a voice
behind you, saying, "This is the way; walk in
it." ²²Then you will defile your idols overlaid
with silver and your images covered with
gold; you will throw them away like a men-
strual cloth and say to them, "Away with
you!"

²³He will also send you rain for the seed
you sow in the ground, and the food that
comes from the land will be rich and plentiful. In that day your cattle will graze in broad
meadows. ²⁴The oxen and donkeys that
work the soil will eat fodder and mash,
spread out with fork and shovel. ²⁵In the day
of great slaughter, when the towers fall,
streams of water will flow on every high
mountain and every lofty hill. ²⁶The moon
will shine like the sun, and the sunlight will
be seven times brighter, like the light of sev-
en full days, when the LORD binds up the
bruises of his people and heals the wounds
he inflicted.

²⁷See, the Name of the LORD comes from
    afar,
  with burning anger and dense clouds
    of smoke;
  his lips are full of wrath,
    and his tongue is a consuming fire.

²⁸His breath is like a rushing torrent,
    rising up to the neck.
  He shakes the nations in the sieve of
    destruction;
  he places in the jaws of the peoples
    a bit that leads them astray.
²⁹And you will sing
    as on the night you celebrate a holy
    festival;
  your hearts will rejoice
    as when people go up with flutes
  to the mountain of the LORD,
    to the Rock of Israel.
³⁰The LORD will cause men to hear his
    majestic voice
  and will make them see his arm
    coming down
  with raging anger and consuming fire,
    with cloudburst, thunderstorm and
    hail.
³¹The voice of the LORD will shatter
    Assyria;
  with his scepter he will strike them
    down.
³²Every stroke the LORD lays on them
    with his punishing rod
  will be to the music of tambourines and
    harps,
  as he fights them in battle with the
    blows of his arm.
³³Topheth has long been prepared;
    it has been made ready for the king.
  Its fire pit has been made deep and
    wide,
  with an abundance of fire and wood;
  the breath of the LORD,
    like a stream of burning sulfur,
    sets it ablaze.

Woe to Those Who Rely on Egypt

31 Woe to those who go down to
        Egypt for help,
  who rely on horses,
  who trust in the multitude of their
    chariots
    and in the great strength of their
    horsemen,
  but do not look to the Holy One of
    Israel,
    or seek help from the LORD.
²Yet he too is wise and can bring
    disaster;
  he does not take back his words.
  He will rise up against the house of the
    wicked,
    against those who help evildoers.
³But the Egyptians are men and not God;
    their horses are flesh and not spirit.
  When the LORD stretches out his hand,

DON'T PUT YOUR TRUST IN PEOPLE!

In August Kay started going with Jerry. Handsome, funny and athletic, Jerry was everything Kay ever dreamed of in a guy.

The problem is that without realizing it, Kay has built her whole world around Jerry. For two months, her whole self-worth was based on how he treated her. Compliments made her feel terrific. Criticism made her feel like scum.

This yo-yo lifestyle of security/insecurity hit rock bottom last night. Jerry suddenly cut the string. Kay is pretty much devastated . . . and feeling totally insecure.

Look It Up ••••

The Bible sternly warns us not to depend on other people to provide the security we crave.

"It is better to take refuge in the LORD than to trust in princes" (Psalm 118:9).

"Stop trusting in man, who has but a breath in his nostrils. Of what account is he?" (Isaiah 2:22).

"This is what the LORD says: 'Cursed is the one who trusts in man, who depends on flesh for his strength and whose heart turns away from the LORD' " (Jeremiah 17:5).

Think It Through ••••

Do you base your security on how others treat you? What's the danger in that kind of approach to life?

In a world of sinful people, is it realistic to expect to find anyone who will never let you down?

Work It Out ••••

Take this quiz. Answer each statement with either true or false.
1. It would destroy me if my friends suddenly ignored me.
2. I just can't stand it when I'm not going with someone.
3. What the kids at school think of me matters more than anything else.
4. I hate to be alone.
5. I am not happy unless I am together with my family and/or friends.
6. If someone close to me died or if my parents divorced, I don't think I'd want to live.

If you answered "true" to any or all of the questions above, you may be depending too much on people to give you a sense of security. Discuss the verses, the quiz and the other ideas on this page with some mature Christian friends—and then pray for each other.

Nail It Down ••••

Read Isaiah 31:1 to find out what the Israelites were depending on rather than on God.

Turn to pages 805, 954 and 976 for other readings on security.
Turn to page 751 for Thursday's reading.

Topic ••••
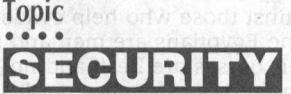

he who helps will stumble,
he who is helped will fall;
both will perish together.

⁴This is what the LORD says to me:

"As a lion growls,
a great lion over his prey—
and though a whole band of shepherds
is called together against him,
he is not frightened by their shouts
or disturbed by their clamor—
so the LORD Almighty will come down
to do battle on Mount Zion and on its
heights.
⁵Like birds hovering overhead,
the LORD Almighty will shield
Jerusalem;
he will shield it and deliver it,
he will 'pass over' it and will rescue
it."

⁶Return to him you have so greatly revolted against, O Israelites. ⁷For in that day every one of you will reject the idols of silver and gold your sinful hands have made.

⁸"Assyria will fall by a sword that is not
of man;
a sword, not of mortals, will devour
them.
They will flee before the sword
and their young men will be put to
forced labor.
⁹Their stronghold will fall because of
terror;
at sight of the battle standard their
commanders will panic,"
declares the LORD,
whose fire is in Zion,
whose furnace is in Jerusalem.

The Kingdom of Righteousness

32 See, a king will reign in
righteousness
and rulers will rule with justice.
²Each man will be like a shelter from the
wind
and a refuge from the storm,
like streams of water in the desert
and the shadow of a great rock in a
thirsty land.

³Then the eyes of those who see will no
longer be closed,
and the ears of those who hear will
listen.
⁴The mind of the rash will know and
understand,
and the stammering tongue will be
fluent and clear.

⁵No longer will the fool be called noble
nor the scoundrel be highly respected.
⁶For the fool speaks folly,
his mind is busy with evil:
He practices ungodliness
and spreads error concerning the
LORD;
the hungry he leaves empty
and from the thirsty he withholds
water.
⁷The scoundrel's methods are wicked,
he makes up evil schemes
to destroy the poor with lies,
even when the plea of the needy is
just.
⁸But the noble man makes noble plans,
and by noble deeds he stands.

The Women of Jerusalem

⁹You women who are so complacent,
rise up and listen to me;
you daughters who feel secure,
hear what I have to say!
¹⁰In little more than a year
you who feel secure will tremble;
the grape harvest will fail,
and the harvest of fruit will not come.
¹¹Tremble, you complacent women;
shudder, you daughters who feel
secure!
Strip off your clothes,
put sackcloth around your waists.
¹²Beat your breasts for the pleasant fields,
for the fruitful vines
¹³and for the land of my people,
a land overgrown with thorns and
briers—
yes, mourn for all houses of merriment
and for this city of revelry.
¹⁴The fortress will be abandoned,
the noisy city deserted;
citadel and watchtower will become a
wasteland forever,
the delight of donkeys, a pasture for
flocks,
¹⁵till the Spirit is poured upon us from on
high,
and the desert becomes a fertile field,
and the fertile field seems like a
forest.
¹⁶Justice will dwell in the desert
and righteousness live in the fertile
field.
¹⁷The fruit of righteousness will be peace;
the effect of righteousness will be
quietness and confidence forever.
¹⁸My people will live in peaceful dwelling
places,
in secure homes,

in undisturbed places of rest.
19Though hail flattens the forest
  and the city is leveled completely,
20how blessed you will be,
  sowing your seed by every stream,
  and letting your cattle and donkeys
    range free.

Distress and Help

33 Woe to you, O destroyer,
  you who have not been destroyed!
Woe to you, O traitor,
  you who have not been betrayed!
When you stop destroying,
  you will be destroyed;
when you stop betraying,
  you will be betrayed.

2O LORD, be gracious to us;
  we long for you.
Be our strength every morning,
  our salvation in time of distress.
3At the thunder of your voice, the
    peoples flee;
  when you rise up, the nations scatter.
4Your plunder, O nations, is harvested as
    by young locusts;
  like a swarm of locusts men pounce
    on it.

5The LORD is exalted, for he dwells on
    high;
  he will fill Zion with justice and
    righteousness.
6He will be the sure foundation for your
    times,
  a rich store of salvation and wisdom
    and knowledge;
  the fear of the LORD is the key to this
    treasure. *a*

7Look, their brave men cry aloud in the
    streets;
  the envoys of peace weep bitterly.
8The highways are deserted,
  no travelers are on the roads.
The treaty is broken,
  its witnesses *b* are despised,
  no one is respected.
9The land mourns *c* and wastes away,
  Lebanon is ashamed and withers;
Sharon is like the Arabah,
  and Bashan and Carmel drop their
    leaves.

10"Now will I arise," says the LORD.
  "Now will I be exalted;
  now will I be lifted up.
11You conceive chaff,

you give birth to straw;
  your breath is a fire that consumes
    you.
12The peoples will be burned as if to
    lime;
  like cut thornbushes they will be set
    ablaze."

13You who are far away, hear what I have
    done;
  you who are near, acknowledge my
    power!
14The sinners in Zion are terrified;
  trembling grips the godless:
"Who of us can dwell with the
    consuming fire?
  Who of us can dwell with everlasting
    burning?"
15He who walks righteously
  and speaks what is right,
who rejects gain from extortion
  and keeps his hand from accepting
    bribes,
who stops his ears against plots of
    murder
  and shuts his eyes against
    contemplating evil —
16this is the man who will dwell on the
    heights,
  whose refuge will be the mountain
    fortress.
His bread will be supplied,
  and water will not fail him.

17Your eyes will see the king in his
    beauty
  and view a land that stretches afar.
18In your thoughts you will ponder the
    former terror:
  "Where is that chief officer?
  Where is the one who took the
    revenue?
  Where is the officer in charge of the
    towers?"
19You will see those arrogant people no
    more,
  those people of an obscure speech,
  with their strange, incomprehensible
    tongue.

20Look upon Zion, the city of our festivals;
  your eyes will see Jerusalem,
  a peaceful abode, a tent that will not
    be moved;
  its stakes will never be pulled up,
    nor any of its ropes broken.
21There the LORD will be our Mighty One.

---

a6 Or *is a treasure from him*   *b8* Dead Sea Scrolls; Masoretic Text / *the cities*   *c9* Or *dries up*

It will be like a place of broad rivers
    and streams.
No galley with oars will ride them,
    no mighty ship will sail them.
22For the Lord is our judge,
    the Lord is our lawgiver,
    the Lord is our king;
    it is he who will save us.

23Your rigging hangs loose:
    The mast is not held secure,
    the sail is not spread.
Then an abundance of spoils will be
    divided
    and even the lame will carry off
    plunder.
24No one living in Zion will say, "I am ill";
    and the sins of those who dwell there
    will be forgiven.

Judgment Against the Nations

34 Come near, you nations, and
    listen;
    pay attention, you peoples!
Let the earth hear, and all that is in it,
    the world, and all that comes out of
    it!
2The Lord is angry with all nations;
    his wrath is upon all their armies.
He will totally destroy*a* them,
    he will give them over to slaughter.
3Their slain will be thrown out,
    their dead bodies will send up a
    stench;
    the mountains will be soaked with
    their blood.
4All the stars of the heavens will be
    dissolved
    and the sky rolled up like a scroll;
all the starry host will fall
    like withered leaves from the vine,
    like shriveled figs from the fig tree.

5My sword has drunk its fill in the
    heavens;
    see, it descends in judgment on
    Edom,
    the people I have totally destroyed.
6The sword of the Lord is bathed in
    blood,
    it is covered with fat—
the blood of lambs and goats,
    fat from the kidneys of rams.
For the Lord has a sacrifice in Bozrah
    and a great slaughter in Edom.
7And the wild oxen will fall with them,
    the bull calves and the great bulls.

Their land will be drenched with blood,
    and the dust will be soaked with fat.

8For the Lord has a day of vengeance,
    a year of retribution, to uphold Zion's
    cause.
9Edom's streams will be turned into
    pitch,
    her dust into burning sulfur;
    her land will become blazing pitch!
10It will not be quenched night and day;
    its smoke will rise forever.
From generation to generation it will lie
    desolate;
    no one will ever pass through it again.
11The desert owl*b* and screech owl*b* will
    possess it;
    the great owl*b* and the raven will
    nest there.
God will stretch out over Edom
    the measuring line of chaos
    and the plumb line of desolation.
12Her nobles will have nothing there to be
    called a kingdom,
    all her princes will vanish away.
13Thorns will overrun her citadels,
    nettles and brambles her strongholds.
She will become a haunt for jackals,
    a home for owls.
14Desert creatures will meet with hyenas,
    and wild goats will bleat to each
    other;
    there the night creatures will also
    repose
    and find for themselves places of rest.
15The owl will nest there and lay eggs,
    she will hatch them, and care for her
    young under the shadow of her
    wings;
    there also the falcons will gather,
    each with its mate.

16Look in the scroll of the Lord and read:

None of these will be missing,
    not one will lack her mate.
For it is his mouth that has given the
    order,
    and his Spirit will gather them
    together.
17He allots their portions;
    his hand distributes them by
    measure.
They will possess it forever
    and dwell there from generation to
    generation.

---

a2 The Hebrew term refers to the irrevocable giving over of things or persons to the Lord, often by totally
destroying them; also in verse 5.   *b11* The precise identification of these birds is uncertain.

Joy of the Redeemed

35 The desert and the parched land
will be glad;
the wilderness will rejoice and
blossom.
Like the crocus, ²it will burst into
bloom;
it will rejoice greatly and shout for
joy.
The glory of Lebanon will be given to it,
the splendor of Carmel and Sharon;
they will see the glory of the LORD,
the splendor of our God.

³Strengthen the feeble hands,
steady the knees that give way;
⁴say to those with fearful hearts,
"Be strong, do not fear;
your God will come,
he will come with vengeance;
with divine retribution
he will come to save you."

⁵Then will the eyes of the blind be
opened
and the ears of the deaf unstopped.
⁶Then will the lame leap like a deer,
and the mute tongue shout for joy.
Water will gush forth in the wilderness
and streams in the desert.
⁷The burning sand will become a pool,
the thirsty ground bubbling springs.
In the haunts where jackals once lay,
grass and reeds and papyrus will
grow.

⁸And a highway will be there;
it will be called the Way of Holiness.
The unclean will not journey on it;
it will be for those who walk in that
Way;
wicked fools will not go about on it.ᵃ
⁹No lion will be there,
nor will any ferocious beast get up on
it;
they will not be found there.
But only the redeemed will walk there,
¹⁰ and the ransomed of the LORD will
return.
They will enter Zion with singing;
everlasting joy will crown their heads.
Gladness and joy will overtake them,
and sorrow and sighing will flee away.

Sennacherib Threatens Jerusalem

36 In the fourteenth year of King Hezekiah's reign, Sennacherib king of Assyria attacked all the fortified cities of Judah

and captured them. ²Then the king of Assyria sent his field commander with a large
army from Lachish to King Hezekiah at Jerusalem. When the commander stopped at the
aqueduct of the Upper Pool, on the road to
the Washerman's Field, ³Eliakim son of Hilkiah the palace administrator, Shebna the
secretary, and Joah son of Asaph the recorder went out to him.

⁴The field commander said to them, "Tell
Hezekiah,

"'This is what the great king, the
king of Assyria, says: On what are you
basing this confidence of yours? ⁵You
say you have strategy and military
strength—but you speak only empty
words. On whom are you depending,
that you rebel against me? ⁶Look now,
you are depending on Egypt, that
splintered reed of a staff, which pierces
a man's hand and wounds him if he
leans on it! Such is Pharaoh king of
Egypt to all who depend on him. ⁷And
if you say to me, "We are depending on
the LORD our God"—isn't he the one
whose high places and altars Hezekiah
removed, saying to Judah and Jerusalem, "You must worship before this altar"?

⁸"'Come now, make a bargain with
my master, the king of Assyria: I will
give you two thousand horses—if you
can put riders on them! ⁹How then can
you repulse one officer of the least of
my master's officials, even though you
are depending on Egypt for chariots
and horsemen? ¹⁰Furthermore, have I
come to attack and destroy this land
without the LORD? The LORD himself told
me to march against this country and
destroy it.'"

¹¹Then Eliakim, Shebna and Joah said to
the field commander, "Please speak to your
servants in Aramaic, since we understand it.
Don't speak to us in Hebrew in the hearing
of the people on the wall."

¹²But the commander replied, "Was it
only to your master and you that my master
sent me to say these things, and not to the
men sitting on the wall—who, like you, will
have to eat their own filth and drink their
own urine?"

¹³Then the commander stood and called
out in Hebrew, "Hear the words of the great
king, the king of Assyria! ¹⁴This is what the
king says: Do not let Hezekiah deceive you.

ᵃ8 Or / the simple will not stray from it

He cannot deliver you! **15**Do not let Hezekiah persuade you to trust in the LORD when he says, 'The LORD will surely deliver us; this city will not be given into the hand of the king of Assyria.'

16"Do not listen to Hezekiah. This is what the king of Assyria says: Make peace with me and come out to me. Then every one of you will eat from his own vine and fig tree and drink water from his own cistern, **17**until I come and take you to a land like your own — a land of grain and new wine, a land of bread and vineyards.

18"Do not let Hezekiah mislead you when he says, 'The LORD will deliver us.' Has the god of any nation ever delivered his land from the hand of the king of Assyria? **19**Where are the gods of Hamath and Arpad? Where are the gods of Sepharvaim? Have they rescued Samaria from my hand? **20**Who of all the gods of these countries has been able to save his land from me? How then can the LORD deliver Jerusalem from my hand?"

21But the people remained silent and said nothing in reply, because the king had commanded, "Do not answer him."

22Then Eliakim son of Hilkiah the palace administrator, Shebna the secretary, and Joah son of Asaph the recorder went to Hezekiah, with their clothes torn, and told him what the field commander had said.

Jerusalem's Deliverance Foretold

37 When King Hezekiah heard this, he tore his clothes and put on sackcloth and went into the temple of the LORD. **2**He sent Eliakim the palace administrator, Shebna the secretary, and the leading priests, all wearing sackcloth, to the prophet Isaiah son of Amoz. **3**They told him, "This is what Hezekiah says: This day is a day of distress and rebuke and disgrace, as when children come to the point of birth and there is no strength to deliver them. **4**It may be that the LORD your God will hear the words of the field commander, whom his master, the king of Assyria, has sent to ridicule the living God, and that he will rebuke him for the words the LORD your God has heard. Therefore pray for the remnant that still survives."

5When King Hezekiah's officials came to Isaiah, **6**Isaiah said to them, "Tell your master, 'This is what the LORD says: Do not be afraid of what you have heard — those words with which the underlings of the king of As-

syria have blasphemed me. **7**Listen! I am going to put a spirit in him so that when he hears a certain report, he will return to his own country, and there I will have him cut down with the sword.' "

8When the field commander heard that the king of Assyria had left Lachish, he withdrew and found the king fighting against Libnah.

9Now Sennacherib received a report that Tirhakah, the Cushite*a* king ˻of Egypt˼, was marching out to fight against him. When he heard it, he sent messengers to Hezekiah with this word: **10**"Say to Hezekiah king of Judah: Do not let the god you depend on deceive you when he says, 'Jerusalem will not be handed over to the king of Assyria.' **11**Surely you have heard what the kings of Assyria have done to all the countries, destroying them completely. And will you be delivered? **12**Did the gods of the nations that were destroyed by my forefathers deliver them — the gods of Gozan, Haran, Rezeph and the people of Eden who were in Tel Assar? **13**Where is the king of Hamath, the king of Arpad, the king of the city of Sepharvaim, or of Hena or Ivvah?"

Hezekiah's Prayer

14Hezekiah received the letter from the messengers and read it. Then he went up to the temple of the LORD and spread it out before the LORD. **15**And Hezekiah prayed to the LORD: **16**"O LORD Almighty, God of Israel, enthroned between the cherubim, you alone are God over all the kingdoms of the earth. You have made heaven and earth. **17**Give ear, O LORD, and hear; open your eyes, O LORD, and see; listen to all the words Sennacherib has sent to insult the living God.

18"It is true, O LORD, that the Assyrian kings have laid waste all these peoples and their lands. **19**They have thrown their gods into the fire and destroyed them, for they were not gods but only wood and stone, fashioned by human hands. **20**Now, O LORD our God, deliver us from his hand, so that all kingdoms on earth may know that you alone, O LORD, are God.*b*"

Sennacherib's Fall

21Then Isaiah son of Amoz sent a message to Hezekiah: "This is what the LORD, the God of Israel, says: Because you have prayed to me concerning Sennacherib king of Assyria,

a9 That is, from the upper Nile region   b20 Dead Sea Scrolls (see also 2 Kings 19:19); Masoretic Text alone are the LORD

22this is the word the Lord has spoken against him:

"The Virgin Daughter of Zion
  despises and mocks you.
The Daughter of Jerusalem
  tosses her head as you flee.
23Who is it you have insulted and
    blasphemed?
  Against whom have you raised your
    voice
and lifted your eyes in pride?
  Against the Holy One of Israel!
24By your messengers
  you have heaped insults on the Lord.
And you have said,
  'With my many chariots
I have ascended the heights of the
    mountains,
  the utmost heights of Lebanon.
I have cut down its tallest cedars,
  the choicest of its pines.
I have reached its remotest heights,
  the finest of its forests.
25I have dug wells in foreign lands*a*
  and drunk the water there.
With the soles of my feet
  I have dried up all the streams of
    Egypt.'

26"Have you not heard?
  Long ago I ordained it.
In days of old I planned it;
  now I have brought it to pass,
that you have turned fortified cities
  into piles of stone.
27Their people, drained of power,
  are dismayed and put to shame.
They are like plants in the field,
  like tender green shoots,
like grass sprouting on the roof,
  scorched*b* before it grows up.

28"But I know where you stay
  and when you come and go
  and how you rage against me.
29Because you rage against me
  and because your insolence has
    reached my ears,
I will put my hook in your nose
  and my bit in your mouth,
and I will make you return
  by the way you came.

30"This will be the sign for you,
O Hezekiah:

"This year you will eat what grows by
    itself,
  and the second year what springs
    from that.
But in the third year sow and reap,
  plant vineyards and eat their fruit.
31Once more a remnant of the house of
    Judah
  will take root below and bear fruit
    above.
32For out of Jerusalem will come a
    remnant,
  and out of Mount Zion a band of
    survivors.
The zeal of the Lord Almighty
  will accomplish this.

33"Therefore this is what the Lord says concerning the king of Assyria:

"He will not enter this city
  or shoot an arrow here.
He will not come before it with shield
  or build a siege ramp against it.
34By the way that he came he will return;
  he will not enter this city,"
                          declares the Lord.
35"I will defend this city and save it,
  for my sake and for the sake of David
    my servant!"

36Then the angel of the Lord went out and put to death a hundred and eighty-five thousand men in the Assyrian camp. When the people got up the next morning—there were all the dead bodies! **37**So Sennacherib king of Assyria broke camp and withdrew. He returned to Nineveh and stayed there.

38One day, while he was worshiping in the temple of his god Nisroch, his sons Adrammelech and Sharezer cut him down with the sword, and they escaped to the land of Ararat. And Esarhaddon his son succeeded him as king.

Hezekiah's Illness

38 In those days Hezekiah became ill and was at the point of death. The prophet Isaiah son of Amoz went to him and said, "This is what the Lord says: Put your house in order, because you are going to die; you will not recover."

2Hezekiah turned his face to the wall and prayed to the Lord, **3**"Remember, O Lord, how I have walked before you faithfully and with wholehearted devotion and have done

---

*a*25 Dead Sea Scrolls (see also 2 Kings 19:24); Masoretic Text does not have *in foreign lands.*   *b*27 Some manuscripts of the Masoretic Text, Dead Sea Scrolls and some Septuagint manuscripts (see also 2 Kings 19:26); most manuscripts of the Masoretic Text *roof / and terraced fields* what is good in your eyes." And Hezekiah wept bitterly.

⁴Then the word of the Lord came to Isaiah: ⁵"Go and tell Hezekiah, 'This is what the Lord, the God of your father David, says: I have heard your prayer and seen your tears; I will add fifteen years to your life. ⁶And I will deliver you and this city from the hand of the king of Assyria. I will defend this city.

⁷" 'This is the Lord's sign to you that the Lord will do what he has promised: ⁸I will make the shadow cast by the sun go back the ten steps it has gone down on the stairway of Ahaz.' " So the sunlight went back the ten steps it had gone down.

⁹A writing of Hezekiah king of Judah after his illness and recovery:

¹⁰I said, "In the prime of my life
    must I go through the gates of death*a*
    and be robbed of the rest of my
        years?"
¹¹I said, "I will not again see the Lord,
    the Lord, in the land of the living;
no longer will I look on mankind,
    or be with those who now dwell in
        this world.*b*
¹²Like a shepherd's tent my house
    has been pulled down and taken from
        me.
Like a weaver I have rolled up my life,
    and he has cut me off from the loom;
    day and night you made an end of
        me.
¹³I waited patiently till dawn,
    but like a lion he broke all my bones;
    day and night you made an end of
        me.
¹⁴I cried like a swift or thrush,
    I moaned like a mourning dove.
My eyes grew weak as I looked to the
    heavens.
    I am troubled; O Lord, come to my
        aid!"

¹⁵But what can I say?
    He has spoken to me, and he himself
        has done this.
I will walk humbly all my years
    because of this anguish of my soul.
¹⁶Lord, by such things men live;
    and my spirit finds life in them too.
You restored me to health
    and let me live.
¹⁷Surely it was for my benefit
    that I suffered such anguish.
In your love you kept me

from the pit of destruction;
    you have put all my sins
        behind your back.
¹⁸For the grave*a* cannot praise you,
    death cannot sing your praise;
those who go down to the pit
    cannot hope for your faithfulness.
¹⁹The living, the living—they praise you,
    as I am doing today;
fathers tell their children
    about your faithfulness.

²⁰The Lord will save me,
    and we will sing with stringed
        instruments
all the days of our lives
    in the temple of the Lord.

²¹Isaiah had said, "Prepare a poultice of figs and apply it to the boil, and he will recover."

²²Hezekiah had asked, "What will be the sign that I will go up to the temple of the Lord?"

Envoys From Babylon

39 At that time Merodach-Baladan son of Baladan king of Babylon sent Hezekiah letters and a gift, because he had heard of his illness and recovery. ²Hezekiah received the envoys gladly and showed them what was in his storehouses—the silver, the gold, the spices, the fine oil, his entire armory and everything found among his treasures. There was nothing in his palace or in all his kingdom that Hezekiah did not show them.

³Then Isaiah the prophet went to King Hezekiah and asked, "What did those men say, and where did they come from?"

"From a distant land," Hezekiah replied. "They came to me from Babylon."

⁴The prophet asked, "What did they see in your palace?"

"They saw everything in my palace," Hezekiah said. "There is nothing among my treasures that I did not show them."

⁵Then Isaiah said to Hezekiah, "Hear the word of the Lord Almighty: ⁶The time will surely come when everything in your palace, and all that your fathers have stored up until this day, will be carried off to Babylon. Nothing will be left, says the Lord. ⁷And some of your descendants, your own flesh and blood who will be born to you, will be taken away, and they will become eunuchs in the palace of the king of Babylon."

⁸"The word of the Lord you have spoken

---

a 10,18 Hebrew *Sheol*   *b 11* A few Hebrew manuscripts; most Hebrew manuscripts *in the place of cessation* is good," Hezekiah replied. For he thought, "There will be peace and security in my lifetime."

Comfort for God's People

40 Comfort, comfort my people, says your God.
²Speak tenderly to Jerusalem,
  and proclaim to her
that her hard service has been
    completed,
  that her sin has been paid for,
that she has received from the Lord's
    hand
  double for all her sins.

³A voice of one calling:
"In the desert prepare
  the way for the Lord*a*;
make straight in the wilderness
  a highway for our God.*b*
⁴Every valley shall be raised up,
  every mountain and hill made low;
the rough ground shall become level,
  the rugged places a plain.
⁵And the glory of the Lord will be
    revealed,
  and all mankind together will see it.
      For the mouth of the Lord
        has spoken."

⁶A voice says, "Cry out."
  And I said, "What shall I cry?"

"All men are like grass,
  and all their glory is like the flowers
    of the field.
⁷The grass withers and the flowers fall,
  because the breath of the Lord blows
    on them.
  Surely the people are grass.
⁸The grass withers and the flowers fall,
  but the word of our God stands
    forever."

⁹You who bring good tidings to Zion,
  go up on a high mountain.
You who bring good tidings to
    Jerusalem,*c*
  lift up your voice with a shout,
  lift it up, do not be afraid;
  say to the towns of Judah,
  "Here is your God!"
¹⁰See, the Sovereign Lord comes with
    power,
  and his arm rules for him.
  See, his reward is with him,

and his recompense accompanies
    him.
¹¹He tends his flock like a shepherd:
  He gathers the lambs in his arms
and carries them close to his heart;
  he gently leads those that have
    young.

¹²Who has measured the waters in the
    hollow of his hand,
  or with the breadth of his hand
    marked off the heavens?
Who has held the dust of the earth in a
    basket,
  or weighed the mountains on the
    scales
  and the hills in a balance?
¹³Who has understood the mind*d* of the
    Lord,
  or instructed him as his counselor?
¹⁴Whom did the Lord consult to enlighten
    him,
  and who taught him the right way?
Who was it that taught him knowledge
  or showed him the path of
    understanding?

¹⁵Surely the nations are like a drop in a
    bucket;
  they are regarded as dust on the
    scales;
  he weighs the islands as though they
    were fine dust.
¹⁶Lebanon is not sufficient for altar fires,
  nor its animals enough for burnt
    offerings.
¹⁷Before him all the nations are as
    nothing;
  they are regarded by him as worthless
    and less than nothing.

¹⁸To whom, then, will you compare God?
  What image will you compare him to?
¹⁹As for an idol, a craftsman casts it,
  and a goldsmith overlays it with gold
    and fashions silver chains for it.
²⁰A man too poor to present such an
    offering
  selects wood that will not rot.
He looks for a skilled craftsman
  to set up an idol that will not topple.

²¹Do you not know?
  Have you not heard?
Has it not been told you from the
    beginning?

---

a3 Or *A voice of one calling in the desert:* / *"Prepare the way for the Lord*   *b3* Hebrew; Septuagint *make straight the paths of our God*   *c9* Or *O Zion, bringer of good tidings,* / *go up on a high mountain.* / *O Jerusalem, bringer of good tidings*   *d13* Or *Spirit*; or *spirit*

GENTLENESS = GREATNESS IN GOD'S EYES
□ THURSDAY

Elaine still can't believe what she saw last night. The news briefly mentioned a crisis in Russia, peace talks in the Middle East and the million-dollar contract a superstar basketball player had just signed. Then the network devoted the rest of the newscast to seventeen-year-old Betsy of Overland Park, Kansas.

Five different correspondents went on and on about how gentle Betsy is. They told about how she always treats others with tenderness and consideration. The newscast then closed with the newscaster encouraging everyone to be gentle like Betsy.

Look It Up
••••

A far-fetched idea, right? Obviously! But can you imagine how much better the world might be if gentleness were such a valued attribute?

Guess what? It *is* that important to God.

He wants you to be gentle in your speech: "A gentle answer turns away wrath, but a harsh word stirs up anger" (Proverbs 15:1).

He also wants you to be gentle in your actions:

"Let your gentleness be evident to all. The Lord is near" (Philippians 4:5).

"But you, man of God, flee from all this [i.e. envy, strife, friction, love of money], and pursue . . . gentleness" (1 Timothy 6:11).

Think It Through
••••

Consider the way Christ treated people during his earthly ministry. Would you say that he was gentle?

How many times did he ridicule or pick on or make fun of those who were less fortunate? Was he ever harsh or insensitive to the feelings of others? What about you?

Work It Out
••••

Ask the Lord to reproduce his gentleness in you. Pray for a considerate, soothing, sensitive attitude toward the people in your life. Make a plan for how you could (and would!) deal gently with others in the following situations: 1. Your little brother or sister hits you and calls you a dirty name. 2. A group of people at school are having some laughs at the expense of an embarrassed classmate. 3. The class klutz spills his cafeteria tray all over you. 4. A good friend is messing up spiritually (hint: see Galatians 6:1).

Nail It Down
••••

Read about God's gentleness toward you in Isaiah 40:11.

Turn to pages 678, 853, 1278 and 1325 for other readings on character.
Turn to page 755 for Friday's reading.

Topic
••••

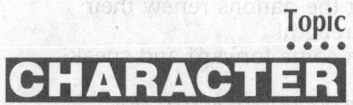
CHARACTER

Have you not understood since the
      earth was founded?
²²He sits enthroned above the circle of
      the earth,
   and its people are like grasshoppers.
He stretches out the heavens like a
      canopy,
   and spreads them out like a tent to
      live in.
²³He brings princes to naught
   and reduces the rulers of this world to
      nothing.
²⁴No sooner are they planted,
   no sooner are they sown,
   no sooner do they take root in the
      ground,
than he blows on them and they wither,
   and a whirlwind sweeps them away
      like chaff.

²⁵"To whom will you compare me?
   Or who is my equal?" says the Holy
      One.
²⁶Lift your eyes and look to the heavens:
   Who created all these?
He who brings out the starry host one
      by one,
   and calls them each by name.
Because of his great power and mighty
      strength,
   not one of them is missing.

²⁷Why do you say, O Jacob,
   and complain, O Israel,
"My way is hidden from the Lord;
   my cause is disregarded by my God"?
²⁸Do you not know?
   Have you not heard?
The Lord is the everlasting God,
   the Creator of the ends of the earth.
He will not grow tired or weary,
   and his understanding no one can
      fathom.
²⁹He gives strength to the weary
   and increases the power of the weak.
³⁰Even youths grow tired and weary,
   and young men stumble and fall;
³¹but those who hope in the Lord
   will renew their strength.
They will soar on wings like eagles;
   they will run and not grow weary,
   they will walk and not be faint.

The Helper of Israel

41 "Be silent before me, you islands!
      Let the nations renew their
      strength!
Let them come forward and speak;

   let us meet together at the place of
      judgment.
²"Who has stirred up one from the east,
   calling him in righteousness to his
      service[a]?
He hands nations over to him
   and subdues kings before him.
He turns them to dust with his sword,
   to windblown chaff with his bow.
³He pursues them and moves on
      unscathed,
   by a path his feet have not traveled
      before.
⁴Who has done this and carried it
      through,
   calling forth the generations from the
      beginning?
I, the Lord—with the first of them
   and with the last—I am he."

⁵The islands have seen it and fear;
   the ends of the earth tremble.
They approach and come forward;
⁶   each helps the other
   and says to his brother, "Be strong!"
⁷The craftsman encourages the
      goldsmith,
   and he who smooths with the
      hammer
spurs on him who strikes the anvil.
He says of the welding, "It is good."
   He nails down the idol so it will not
      topple.

⁸"But you, O Israel, my servant,
   Jacob, whom I have chosen,
   you descendants of Abraham my
      friend,
⁹I took you from the ends of the earth,
   from its farthest corners I called you.
I said, 'You are my servant';
   I have chosen you and have not
      rejected you.
¹⁰So do not fear, for I am with you;
   do not be dismayed, for I am your
      God.
I will strengthen you and help you;
   I will uphold you with my righteous
      right hand.

¹¹"All who rage against you
   will surely be ashamed and disgraced;
those who oppose you
   will be as nothing and perish.
¹²Though you search for your enemies,
   you will not find them.
Those who wage war against you
   will be as nothing at all.

a2 Or / whom victory meets at every step

¹³For I am the LORD, your God,
  who takes hold of your right hand
  and says to you, Do not fear;
    I will help you.
¹⁴Do not be afraid, O worm Jacob,
  O little Israel,
  for I myself will help you," declares the
    LORD,
    your Redeemer, the Holy One of
      Israel.
¹⁵"See, I will make you into a threshing
    sledge,
    new and sharp, with many teeth.
  You will thresh the mountains and
    crush them,
    and reduce the hills to chaff.
¹⁶You will winnow them, the wind will
    pick them up,
    and a gale will blow them away.
  But you will rejoice in the LORD
    and glory in the Holy One of Israel.

¹⁷"The poor and needy search for water,
    but there is none;
    their tongues are parched with thirst.
  But I the LORD will answer them;
    I, the God of Israel, will not forsake
      them.
¹⁸I will make rivers flow on barren
    heights,
    and springs within the valleys.
  I will turn the desert into pools of water,
    and the parched ground into springs.
¹⁹I will put in the desert
    the cedar and the acacia, the myrtle
      and the olive.
  I will set pines in the wasteland,
    the fir and the cypress together,
²⁰so that people may see and know,
    may consider and understand,
    that the hand of the LORD has done this,
    that the Holy One of Israel has
      created it.

²¹"Present your case," says the LORD.
    "Set forth your arguments," says
      Jacob's King.
²²"Bring in ⌊your idols⌋ to tell us
    what is going to happen.
  Tell us what the former things were,
    so that we may consider them
    and know their final outcome.
  Or declare to us the things to come,
²³ tell us what the future holds,
    so we may know that you are gods.
  Do something, whether good or bad,
    so that we will be dismayed and filled
      with fear.
²⁴But you are less than nothing
    and your works are utterly worthless;

he who chooses you is detestable.
²⁵"I have stirred up one from the north,
    and he comes—
    one from the rising sun who calls on
      my name.
  He treads on rulers as if they were
    mortar,
    as if he were a potter treading the
      clay.
²⁶Who told of this from the beginning, so
    we could know,
    or beforehand, so we could say, 'He
      was right'?
  No one told of this,
    no one foretold it,
    no one heard any words from you.
²⁷I was the first to tell Zion, 'Look, here
    they are!'
  I gave to Jerusalem a messenger of
    good tidings.
²⁸I look but there is no one—
    no one among them to give counsel,
    no one to give answer when I ask
      them.
²⁹See, they are all false!
    Their deeds amount to nothing;
    their images are but wind and
      confusion.

The Servant of the LORD

42 "Here is my servant, whom I
    uphold,
    my chosen one in whom I delight;
  I will put my Spirit on him
    and he will bring justice to the
      nations.
²He will not shout or cry out,
    or raise his voice in the streets.
³A bruised reed he will not break,
    and a smoldering wick he will not
      snuff out.
  In faithfulness he will bring forth justice;
⁴ he will not falter or be discouraged
    till he establishes justice on earth.
    In his law the islands will put their
      hope."

⁵This is what God the LORD says—
  he who created the heavens and
    stretched them out,
    who spread out the earth and all that
      comes out of it,
  who gives breath to its people,
    and life to those who walk on it:
⁶"I, the LORD, have called you in
    righteousness;
    I will take hold of your hand.
  I will keep you and will make you
    to be a covenant for the people

and a light for the Gentiles,
[7]to open eyes that are blind,
  to free captives from prison
  and to release from the dungeon
    those who sit in darkness.

[8]"I am the LORD; that is my name!
  I will not give my glory to another
  or my praise to idols.
[9]See, the former things have taken place,
  and new things I declare;
  before they spring into being
  I announce them to you."

Song of Praise to the LORD

[10]Sing to the LORD a new song,
  his praise from the ends of the earth,
  you who go down to the sea, and all
    that is in it,
  you islands, and all who live in them.
[11]Let the desert and its towns raise their
    voices;
  let the settlements where Kedar lives
    rejoice.
  Let the people of Sela sing for joy;
  let them shout from the
    mountaintops.
[12]Let them give glory to the LORD
  and proclaim his praise in the islands.
[13]The LORD will march out like a mighty
    man,
  like a warrior he will stir up his zeal;
  with a shout he will raise the battle cry
  and will triumph over his enemies.

[14]"For a long time I have kept silent,
  I have been quiet and held myself
    back.
  But now, like a woman in childbirth,
  I cry out, I gasp and pant.
[15]I will lay waste the mountains and hills
  and dry up all their vegetation;
  I will turn rivers into islands
  and dry up the pools.
[16]I will lead the blind by ways they have
    not known,
  along unfamiliar paths I will guide
    them;
  I will turn the darkness into light before
    them
  and make the rough places smooth.
  These are the things I will do;
  I will not forsake them.
[17]But those who trust in idols,
  who say to images, 'You are our
    gods,'
  will be turned back in utter shame.

Israel Blind and Deaf

[18]"Hear, you deaf;

  look, you blind, and see!
[19]Who is blind but my servant,
  and deaf like the messenger I send?
  Who is blind like the one committed to
    me,
  blind like the servant of the LORD?
[20]You have seen many things, but have
    paid no attention;
  your ears are open, but you hear
    nothing."
[21]It pleased the LORD
  for the sake of his righteousness
  to make his law great and glorious.
[22]But this is a people plundered and
    looted,
  all of them trapped in pits
  or hidden away in prisons.
  They have become plunder,
  with no one to rescue them;
  they have been made loot,
  with no one to say, "Send them
    back."

[23]Which of you will listen to this
  or pay close attention in time to
    come?
[24]Who handed Jacob over to become loot,
  and Israel to the plunderers?
  Was it not the LORD,
  against whom we have sinned?
  For they would not follow his ways;
  they did not obey his law.
[25]So he poured out on them his burning
    anger,
  the violence of war.
  It enveloped them in flames, yet they
    did not understand;
  it consumed them, but they did not
    take it to heart.

Israel's Only Savior

43 But now, this is what the LORD
    says —
  he who created you, O Jacob,
  he who formed you, O Israel:
"Fear not, for I have redeemed you;
  I have summoned you by name; you
    are mine.
[2]When you pass through the waters,
  I will be with you;
  and when you pass through the rivers,
  they will not sweep over you.
  When you walk through the fire,
  you will not be burned;
  the flames will not set you ablaze.
[3]For I am the LORD, your God,
  the Holy One of Israel, your Savior;
  I give Egypt for your ransom,

A LARGE ORDER OF ACCEPTANCE TO GO

Brian is not having a good day. He's new at Adams High School. No one sits by him at lunch. During P.E. class, nobody chooses him to participate. In fact, three bigger guys pick on him in front of some girls. Brian feels humiliated.

Patti is in tears. She just found out that her two best friends are having a pool party. They've invited everybody, except her. When she walks to her locker after school, her two "friends" giggle as she passes by.

Look It Up
••••

Brian and Patti are going through tough situations. But they're not alone. Every person who has ever lived has experienced similar circumstances.

Feeling rejected and unloved is lousy. And while it's true that you can't control how others treat you, you can control one thing . . . how you react.

When you're feeling hurt, these truths can make a big difference:

Because God created you in his image, he considers you precious and valuable (Genesis 1:26; Psalm 139:13–16).

God loves you more than you can comprehend (Romans 5:8).

God is there to care for you even when it seems nobody else is (Matthew 10:29–31).

God is "the Father of compassion and the God of all comfort, who comforts us in all our troubles, so that we can comfort those in any trouble with the comfort we ourselves have received from God" (2 Corinthians 1:3–4).

Think It Through
••••

Since God created you, loves you, is there when you need him, and comforts you, you have several great reasons to rejoice!

Regardless of how rejected you may feel, regardless of how unkind others have been, you can know without a doubt that God feels differently about you than those who have rejected you. He'll never be cruel to you or toss you aside. He's a friend you can depend on.

Work It Out
••••

If you're feeling like Brian or Patti for some reason, take a few minutes right now to open yourself up to God. Tell him just how you feel.

But don't stop there: Let him tell you about how much you matter to him. Look up the verses above and think about them. Be willing to share what you think with others who feel the bitter pain of rejection.

Nail It Down
••••

Read God's promise to you in Isaiah 43:1–7.

Turn to pages 428, 544 and 569 for other readings on rejection.
Turn to page 761 for the weekend reading.

Topic
••••

Cush[a] and Seba in your stead.
4Since you are precious and honored in
my sight,
and because I love you,
I will give men in exchange for you,
and people in exchange for your life.
5Do not be afraid, for I am with you;
I will bring your children from the
east
and gather you from the west.
6I will say to the north, 'Give them up!'
and to the south, 'Do not hold them
back.'
Bring my sons from afar
and my daughters from the ends of
the earth —
7everyone who is called by my name,
whom I created for my glory,
whom I formed and made."

8Lead out those who have eyes but are
blind,
who have ears but are deaf.
9All the nations gather together
and the peoples assemble.
Which of them foretold this
and proclaimed to us the former
things?
Let them bring in their witnesses to
prove they were right,
so that others may hear and say, "It is
true."
10"You are my witnesses," declares the
LORD,
"and my servant whom I have chosen,
so that you may know and believe me
and understand that I am he.
Before me no god was formed,
nor will there be one after me.
11I, even I, am the LORD,
and apart from me there is no savior.
12I have revealed and saved and
proclaimed —
I, and not some foreign god among
you.
You are my witnesses," declares the
LORD, "that I am God.
13 Yes, and from ancient days I am he.
No one can deliver out of my hand.
When I act, who can reverse it?"

God's Mercy and Israel's Unfaithfulness

14This is what the LORD says —
your Redeemer, the Holy One of
Israel:
"For your sake I will send to Babylon

and bring down as fugitives all the
Babylonians,[b]
in the ships in which they took pride.
15I am the LORD, your Holy One,
Israel's Creator, your King."

16This is what the LORD says —
he who made a way through the sea,
a path through the mighty waters,
17who drew out the chariots and horses,
the army and reinforcements together,
and they lay there, never to rise again,
extinguished, snuffed out like a wick:
18"Forget the former things;
do not dwell on the past.
19See, I am doing a new thing!
Now it springs up; do you not
perceive it?
I am making a way in the desert
and streams in the wasteland.
20The wild animals honor me,
the jackals and the owls,
because I provide water in the desert
and streams in the wasteland,
to give drink to my people, my chosen,
21 the people I formed for myself
that they may proclaim my praise.

22"Yet you have not called upon me,
O Jacob,
you have not wearied yourselves for
me, O Israel.
23You have not brought me sheep for
burnt offerings,
nor honored me with your sacrifices.
I have not burdened you with grain
offerings
nor wearied you with demands for
incense.
24You have not bought any fragrant
calamus for me,
or lavished on me the fat of your
sacrifices.
But you have burdened me with your
sins
and wearied me with your offenses.

25"I, even I, am he who blots out
your transgressions, for my own sake,
and remembers your sins no more.
26Review the past for me,
let us argue the matter together;
state the case for your innocence.
27Your first father sinned;
your spokesmen rebelled against me.
28So I will disgrace the dignitaries of your
temple,

a3 That is, the upper Nile region   b14 Or Chaldeans

and I will consign Jacob to
destruction[a]
and Israel to scorn.

Israel the Chosen

44 "But now listen, O Jacob, my
servant,
Israel, whom I have chosen.
²This is what the LORD says —
he who made you, who formed you
in the womb,
and who will help you:
Do not be afraid, O Jacob, my servant,
Jeshurun, whom I have chosen.
³For I will pour water on the thirsty land,
and streams on the dry ground;
I will pour out my Spirit on your
offspring,
and my blessing on your descendants.
⁴They will spring up like grass in a
meadow,
like poplar trees by flowing streams.
⁵One will say, 'I belong to the LORD';
another will call himself by the name
of Jacob;
still another will write on his hand, 'The
LORD's,'
and will take the name Israel.

The LORD, Not Idols

⁶"This is what the LORD says —
Israel's King and Redeemer, the LORD
Almighty:
I am the first and I am the last;
apart from me there is no God.
⁷Who then is like me? Let him proclaim
it.
Let him declare and lay out before
me
what has happened since I established
my ancient people,
and what is yet to come —
yes, let him foretell what will come.
⁸Do not tremble, do not be afraid.
Did I not proclaim this and foretell it
long ago?
You are my witnesses. Is there any God
besides me?
No, there is no other Rock; I know
not one."

⁹All who make idols are nothing,
and the things they treasure are
worthless.
Those who would speak up for them are
blind;

they are ignorant, to their own shame.
¹⁰Who shapes a god and casts an idol,
which can profit him nothing?
¹¹He and his kind will be put to shame;
craftsmen are nothing but men.
Let them all come together and take
their stand;
they will be brought down to terror
and infamy.

¹²The blacksmith takes a tool
and works with it in the coals;
he shapes an idol with hammers,
he forges it with the might of his arm.
He gets hungry and loses his strength;
he drinks no water and grows faint.
¹³The carpenter measures with a line
and makes an outline with a marker;
he roughs it out with chisels
and marks it with compasses.
He shapes it in the form of man,
of man in all his glory,
that it may dwell in a shrine.
¹⁴He cut down cedars,
or perhaps took a cypress or oak.
He let it grow among the trees of the
forest,
or planted a pine, and the rain made
it grow.
¹⁵It is man's fuel for burning;
some of it he takes and warms
himself,
he kindles a fire and bakes bread.
But he also fashions a god and worships
it;
he makes an idol and bows down to
it.
¹⁶Half of the wood he burns in the fire;
over it he prepares his meal,
he roasts his meat and eats his fill.
He also warms himself and says,
"Ah! I am warm; I see the fire."
¹⁷From the rest he makes a god, his idol;
he bows down to it and worships.
He prays to it and says,
"Save me; you are my god."
¹⁸They know nothing, they understand
nothing;
their eyes are plastered over so they
cannot see,
and their minds closed so they cannot
understand.
¹⁹No one stops to think,
no one has the knowledge or
understanding to say,
"Half of it I used for fuel;

---

[a]28 The Hebrew term refers to the irrevocable giving over of things or persons to the LORD, often by totally
destroying them.

I even baked bread over its coals,
I roasted meat and I ate.
Shall I make a detestable thing from
      what is left?
Shall I bow down to a block of
      wood?"
20He feeds on ashes, a deluded heart
      misleads him;
he cannot save himself, or say,
"Is not this thing in my right hand a
      lie?"

21"Remember these things, O Jacob,
for you are my servant, O Israel.
I have made you, you are my servant;
O Israel, I will not forget you.
22I have swept away your offenses like a
      cloud,
your sins like the morning mist.
Return to me,
for I have redeemed you."

23Sing for joy, O heavens, for the LORD has
      done this;
shout aloud, O earth beneath.
Burst into song, you mountains,
you forests and all your trees,
for the LORD has redeemed Jacob,
he displays his glory in Israel.

Jerusalem to Be Inhabited

24"This is what the LORD says—
your Redeemer, who formed you in
      the womb:

I am the LORD,
who has made all things,
who alone stretched out the heavens,
who spread out the earth by myself,

25who foils the signs of false prophets
and makes fools of diviners,
who overthrows the learning of the wise
and turns it into nonsense,
26who carries out the words of his
      servants
and fulfills the predictions of his
      messengers,

who says of Jerusalem, 'It shall be
      inhabited,'
of the towns of Judah, 'They shall be
      built,'
and of their ruins, 'I will restore
      them,'
27who says to the watery deep, 'Be dry,
and I will dry up your streams,'
28who says of Cyrus, 'He is my shepherd
and will accomplish all that I please;

he will say of Jerusalem, "Let it be
      rebuilt,"
and of the temple, "Let its
      foundations be laid." '

45 "This is what the LORD says to his
      anointed,
to Cyrus, whose right hand I take
      hold of
to subdue nations before him
and to strip kings of their armor,
to open doors before him
so that gates will not be shut:
2I will go before you
and will level the mountains[a];
I will break down gates of bronze
and cut through bars of iron.
3I will give you the treasures of darkness,
riches stored in secret places,
so that you may know that I am the
      LORD,
the God of Israel, who summons you
      by name.
4For the sake of Jacob my servant,
of Israel my chosen,
I summon you by name
and bestow on you a title of honor,
though you do not acknowledge me.
5I am the LORD, and there is no other;
apart from me there is no God.
I will strengthen you,
though you have not acknowledged
      me,
6so that from the rising of the sun
to the place of its setting
men may know there is none besides
      me.
I am the LORD, and there is no other.
7I form the light and create darkness,
I bring prosperity and create disaster;
I, the LORD, do all these things.

8"You heavens above, rain down
      righteousness;
let the clouds shower it down.
Let the earth open wide,
let salvation spring up,
let righteousness grow with it;
I, the LORD, have created it.

9"Woe to him who quarrels with his
      Maker,
to him who is but a potsherd among
      the potsherds on the ground.
Does the clay say to the potter,
'What are you making?'
Does your work say,
'He has no hands'?

---

*a*2 Dead Sea Scrolls and Septuagint; the meaning of the word in the Masoretic Text is uncertain.

10Woe to him who says to his father,
  'What have you begotten?'
or to his mother,
  'What have you brought to birth?'

11"This is what the LORD says—
  the Holy One of Israel, and its Maker:
Concerning things to come,
  do you question me about my
    children,
  or give me orders about the work of
    my hands?
12It is I who made the earth
  and created mankind upon it.
My own hands stretched out the
    heavens;
  I marshaled their starry hosts.
13I will raise up Cyrus[a] in my
    righteousness:
  I will make all his ways straight.
He will rebuild my city
  and set my exiles free,
but not for a price or reward,
  says the LORD Almighty."

14This is what the LORD says:

"The products of Egypt and the
    merchandise of Cush,[b]
  and those tall Sabeans—
they will come over to you
  and will be yours;
they will trudge behind you,
  coming over to you in chains.
They will bow down before you
  and plead with you, saying,
'Surely God is with you, and there is no
    other;
  there is no other god.'"

15Truly you are a God who hides himself,
  O God and Savior of Israel.
16All the makers of idols will be put to
    shame and disgraced;
  they will go off into disgrace together.
17But Israel will be saved by the LORD
  with an everlasting salvation;
you will never be put to shame or
    disgraced,
  to ages everlasting.

18For this is what the LORD says—
he who created the heavens,
  he is God;
he who fashioned and made the earth,
  he founded it;
he did not create it to be empty,
  but formed it to be inhabited—
he says:

"I am the LORD,
  and there is no other.
19I have not spoken in secret,
  from somewhere in a land of
    darkness;
I have not said to Jacob's descendants,
  'Seek me in vain.'
I, the LORD, speak the truth;
  I declare what is right.

20"Gather together and come;
  assemble, you fugitives from the
    nations.
Ignorant are those who carry about idols
    of wood,
  who pray to gods that cannot save.
21Declare what is to be, present it—
  let them take counsel together.
Who foretold this long ago,
  who declared it from the distant past?
Was it not I, the LORD?
  And there is no God apart from me,
a righteous God and a Savior;
  there is none but me.

22"Turn to me and be saved,
  all you ends of the earth;
  for I am God, and there is no other.
23By myself I have sworn,
  my mouth has uttered in all integrity
    a word that will not be revoked:
Before me every knee will bow;
  by me every tongue will swear.
24They will say of me, 'In the LORD alone
  are righteousness and strength.'"
All who have raged against him
  will come to him and be put to
    shame.
25But in the LORD all the descendants of
    Israel
  will be found righteous and will exult.

Gods of Babylon

46 Bel bows down, Nebo stoops low;
  their idols are borne by beasts of
    burden.[c]
The images that are carried about are
    burdensome,
  a burden for the weary.
2They stoop and bow down together;
  unable to rescue the burden,
  they themselves go off into captivity.

3"Listen to me, O house of Jacob,
  all you who remain of the house of
    Israel,
you whom I have upheld since you
    were conceived,

---

a13 Hebrew him   b14 That is, the upper Nile region   c1 Or are but beasts and cattle

and have carried since your birth.
⁴Even to your old age and gray hairs
    I am he, I am he who will sustain
        you.
I have made you and I will carry you;
    I will sustain you and I will rescue
        you.

⁵"To whom will you compare me or
        count me equal?
    To whom will you liken me that we
        may be compared?
⁶Some pour out gold from their bags
    and weigh out silver on the scales;
they hire a goldsmith to make it into a
        god,
    and they bow down and worship it.
⁷They lift it to their shoulders and carry
        it;
    they set it up in its place, and there it
        stands.
    From that spot it cannot move.
Though one cries out to it, it does not
        answer;
    it cannot save him from his troubles.

⁸"Remember this, fix it in mind,
    take it to heart, you rebels.
⁹Remember the former things, those of
        long ago;
    I am God, and there is no other;
    I am God, and there is none like me.
¹⁰I make known the end from the
        beginning,
    from ancient times, what is still to
        come.
I say: My purpose will stand,
    and I will do all that I please.
¹¹From the east I summon a bird of prey;
    from a far-off land, a man to fulfill my
        purpose.
What I have said, that will I bring about;
    what I have planned, that will I do.
¹²Listen to me, you stubborn-hearted,
    you who are far from righteousness.
¹³I am bringing my righteousness near,
    it is not far away;
    and my salvation will not be delayed.
I will grant salvation to Zion,
    my splendor to Israel.

The Fall of Babylon

47 "Go down, sit in the dust,
      Virgin Daughter of Babylon;
sit on the ground without a throne,
    Daughter of the Babylonians.ᵃ
No more will you be called
    tender or delicate.

²Take millstones and grind flour;
    take off your veil.
Lift up your skirts, bare your legs,
    and wade through the streams.
³Your nakedness will be exposed
    and your shame uncovered.
I will take vengeance;
    I will spare no one."

⁴Our Redeemer—the Lord Almighty is
        his name—
    is the Holy One of Israel.

⁵"Sit in silence, go into darkness,
    Daughter of the Babylonians;
no more will you be called
    queen of kingdoms.
⁶I was angry with my people
    and desecrated my inheritance;
I gave them into your hand,
    and you showed them no mercy.
Even on the aged
    you laid a very heavy yoke.
⁷You said, 'I will continue forever—
    the eternal queen!'
But you did not consider these things
    or reflect on what might happen.

⁸"Now then, listen, you wanton creature,
    lounging in your security
and saying to yourself,
    'I am, and there is none besides me.
I will never be a widow
    or suffer the loss of children.'
⁹Both of these will overtake you
    in a moment, on a single day:
    loss of children and widowhood.
They will come upon you in full
        measure,
    in spite of your many sorceries
    and all your potent spells.
¹⁰You have trusted in your wickedness
    and have said, 'No one sees me.'
Your wisdom and knowledge mislead
        you
    when you say to yourself,
    'I am, and there is none besides me.'
¹¹Disaster will come upon you,
    and you will not know how to conjure
        it away.
A calamity will fall upon you
    that you cannot ward off with a
        ransom;
a catastrophe you cannot foresee
    will suddenly come upon you.

¹²"Keep on, then, with your magic spells
    and with your many sorceries,

ᵃ1 Or *Chaldeans*; also in verse 5

THE ONE AND ONLY

Work It Out
•••

Think for a minute of things that there are only one of. Things like:
- the Great Wall of China
- the Grand Canyon
- Westminster Abby
- Mount Everest
- the Mona Lisa
- God

The Eiffel Tower wouldn't be all that amazing if there were ten of them. Neither would Pike's Peak or the Sistine Chapel. But because they are the only one and they are extraordinary in some way—the highest, the most beautiful, the most unusual—they are looked on with awe and respect.

You know, of course, that God is the one and only God of the universe. You look on him with awe and respect because he is the superlative of every adjective you could apply to him and because he is the only God.

It only makes sense to follow him, don't you think?

Nail It Down
•••

Read Isaiah's confession of God as the one and only in Isaiah 46:8–13.

Think It Through
•••

Now here's an even more amazing fact: this one and only God of the universe loves you.

He could have chosen to ignore you. He could have chosen to destroy you. He could have chosen not to create you at all.

Instead, he chose to love you and to provide salvation for you through his Son. Who needs any other god? This God, the one and only, is all you'll ever need. Praise him!

Nail It Down
•••

Reread Isaiah's confession in Isaiah 46:8–13. For further insight read Psalm 145.

Turn to pages 619, 1208, 1210 and 1243 for other readings on God.
Turn to page 768 for Monday's reading.

Topic

GOD

which you have labored at since
   childhood.
Perhaps you will succeed,
   perhaps you will cause terror.
¹³All the counsel you have received has
   only worn you out!
Let your astrologers come forward,
   those stargazers who make predictions
     month by month,
   let them save you from what is
     coming upon you.
¹⁴Surely they are like stubble;
   the fire will burn them up.
They cannot even save themselves
   from the power of the flame.
Here are no coals to warm anyone;
   here is no fire to sit by.
¹⁵That is all they can do for you—
   these you have labored with
   and trafficked with since childhood.
Each of them goes on in his error;
   there is not one that can save you.

Stubborn Israel

48 "Listen to this, O house of Jacob,
   you who are called by the name
     of Israel
and come from the line of Judah,
you who take oaths in the name of the
   LORD
and invoke the God of Israel—
but not in truth or righteousness—
²you who call yourselves citizens of the
     holy city
and rely on the God of Israel—
   the LORD Almighty is his name:
³I foretold the former things long ago,
   my mouth announced them and I
     made them known;
   then suddenly I acted, and they came
     to pass.
⁴For I knew how stubborn you were;
   the sinews of your neck were iron,
   your forehead was bronze.
⁵Therefore I told you these things long
     ago;
   before they happened I announced
     them to you
so that you could not say,
   'My idols did them;
   my wooden image and metal god
     ordained them.'
⁶You have heard these things; look at
     them all.
   Will you not admit them?

"From now on I will tell you of new
     things,
   of hidden things unknown to you.
⁷They are created now, and not long ago;
   you have not heard of them before
     today.
So you cannot say,
   'Yes, I knew of them.'
⁸You have neither heard nor understood;
   from of old your ear has not been
     open.
Well do I know how treacherous you
     are;
   you were called a rebel from birth.
⁹For my own name's sake I delay my
     wrath;
   for the sake of my praise I hold it
     back from you,
   so as not to cut you off.
¹⁰See, I have refined you, though not as
     silver;
   I have tested you in the furnace of
     affliction.
¹¹For my own sake, for my own sake, I
     do this.
   How can I let myself be defamed?
   I will not yield my glory to another.

Israel Freed

¹²"Listen to me, O Jacob,
   Israel, whom I have called:
I am he;
   I am the first and I am the last.
¹³My own hand laid the foundations of
     the earth,
   and my right hand spread out the
     heavens;
when I summon them,
   they all stand up together.

¹⁴"Come together, all of you, and listen:
   Which of ⌊the idols⌋ has foretold these
     things?
The LORD's chosen ally
   will carry out his purpose against
     Babylon;
   his arm will be against the
     Babylonians.[a]
¹⁵I, even I, have spoken;
   yes, I have called him.
I will bring him,
   and he will succeed in his mission.

¹⁶"Come near me and listen to this:

"From the first announcement I have
     not spoken in secret;
   at the time it happens, I am there."

---

[a]14 Or *Chaldeans*; also in verse 20

And now the Sovereign Lord has sent
    me,
    with his Spirit.

¹⁷This is what the Lord says—
    your Redeemer, the Holy One of
        Israel:
"I am the Lord your God,
    who teaches you what is best for you,
    who directs you in the way you
        should go.
¹⁸If only you had paid attention to my
        commands,
    your peace would have been like a
        river,
    your righteousness like the waves of
        the sea.
¹⁹Your descendants would have been like
        the sand,
    your children like its numberless
        grains;
    their name would never be cut off
    nor destroyed from before me."

²⁰Leave Babylon,
    flee from the Babylonians!
Announce this with shouts of joy
    and proclaim it.
Send it out to the ends of the earth;
    say, "The Lord has redeemed his
        servant Jacob."
²¹They did not thirst when he led them
        through the deserts;
    he made water flow for them from
        the rock;
    he split the rock
    and water gushed out.

²²"There is no peace," says the Lord, "for
    the wicked."

The Servant of the Lord

49 Listen to me, you islands;
        hear this, you distant nations:
Before I was born the Lord called me;
    from my birth he has made mention
        of my name.
²He made my mouth like a sharpened
        sword,
    in the shadow of his hand he hid me;
    he made me into a polished arrow
    and concealed me in his quiver.
³He said to me, "You are my servant,
    Israel, in whom I will display my
        splendor."
⁴But I said, "I have labored to no
        purpose;
    I have spent my strength in vain and
        for nothing.

Yet what is due me is in the Lord's
        hand,
    and my reward is with my God."

⁵And now the Lord says—
    he who formed me in the womb to be
        his servant
to bring Jacob back to him
    and gather Israel to himself,
for I am honored in the eyes of the Lord
    and my God has been my strength—
⁶he says:
"It is too small a thing for you to be my
        servant
    to restore the tribes of Jacob
    and bring back those of Israel I have
        kept.
I will also make you a light for the
        Gentiles,
    that you may bring my salvation to
        the ends of the earth."

⁷This is what the Lord says—
    the Redeemer and Holy One of
        Israel—
to him who was despised and abhorred
        by the nation,
    to the servant of rulers:
"Kings will see you and rise up,
    princes will see and bow down,
because of the Lord, who is faithful,
    the Holy One of Israel, who has
        chosen you."

Restoration of Israel

⁸This is what the Lord says:

"In the time of my favor I will answer
        you,
    and in the day of salvation I will help
        you;
I will keep you and will make you
    to be a covenant for the people,
to restore the land
    and to reassign its desolate
        inheritances,
⁹to say to the captives, 'Come out,'
    and to those in darkness, 'Be free!'

"They will feed beside the roads
    and find pasture on every barren hill.
¹⁰They will neither hunger nor thirst,
    nor will the desert heat or the sun
        beat upon them.
He who has compassion on them will
        guide them
    and lead them beside springs of
        water.
¹¹I will turn all my mountains into roads,
    and my highways will be raised up.
¹²See, they will come from afar—

some from the north, some from the
        west,
some from the region of Aswan. *a*"

¹³Shout for joy, O heavens;
    rejoice, O earth;
    burst into song, O mountains!
For the LORD comforts his people
    and will have compassion on his
        afflicted ones.

¹⁴But Zion said, "The LORD has forsaken
        me,
    the Lord has forgotten me."

¹⁵"Can a mother forget the baby at her
        breast
    and have no compassion on the child
        she has borne?
Though she may forget,
    I will not forget you!
¹⁶See, I have engraved you on the palms
        of my hands;
    your walls are ever before me.
¹⁷Your sons hasten back,
    and those who laid you waste depart
        from you.
¹⁸Lift up your eyes and look around;
    all your sons gather and come to you.
As surely as I live," declares the LORD,
    "you will wear them all as ornaments;
    you will put them on, like a bride.

¹⁹"Though you were ruined and made
        desolate
    and your land laid waste,
now you will be too small for your
        people,
    and those who devoured you will be
        far away.
²⁰The children born during your
        bereavement
    will yet say in your hearing,
'This place is too small for us;
    give us more space to live in.'
²¹Then you will say in your heart,
    'Who bore me these?
I was bereaved and barren;
    I was exiled and rejected.
Who brought these up?
I was left all alone,
    but these—where have they come
        from?' "

²²This is what the Sovereign LORD says:

"See, I will beckon to the Gentiles,

I will lift up my banner to the
        peoples;
they will bring your sons in their arms
    and carry your daughters on their
        shoulders.
²³Kings will be your foster fathers,
    and their queens your nursing
        mothers.
They will bow down before you with
        their faces to the ground;
    they will lick the dust at your feet.
Then you will know that I am the LORD;
    those who hope in me will not be
        disappointed."

²⁴Can plunder be taken from warriors,
    or captives rescued from the fierce *b*?

²⁵But this is what the LORD says:

"Yes, captives will be taken from
        warriors,
    and plunder retrieved from the fierce;
I will contend with those who contend
        with you,
    and your children I will save.
²⁶I will make your oppressors eat their
        own flesh;
    they will be drunk on their own
        blood, as with wine.
Then all mankind will know
    that I, the LORD, am your Savior,
    your Redeemer, the Mighty One of
        Jacob."

Israel's Sin and the Servant's Obedience

50 This is what the LORD says:

"Where is your mother's certificate
        of divorce
    with which I sent her away?
Or to which of my creditors
    did I sell you?
Because of your sins you were sold;
    because of your transgressions your
        mother was sent away.
²When I came, why was there no one?
    When I called, why was there no one
        to answer?
Was my arm too short to ransom you?
    Do I lack the strength to rescue you?
By a mere rebuke I dry up the sea,
    I turn rivers into a desert;
their fish rot for lack of water
    and die of thirst.
³I clothe the sky with darkness
    and make sackcloth its covering."

4The Sovereign Lord has given me an
  instructed tongue,
    to know the word that sustains the
      weary.
He wakens me morning by morning,
  wakens my ear to listen like one
    being taught.
5The Sovereign Lord has opened my
  ears,
    and I have not been rebellious;
    I have not drawn back.
6I offered my back to those who beat
  me,
    my cheeks to those who pulled out
      my beard;
I did not hide my face
  from mocking and spitting.
7Because the Sovereign Lord helps me,
  I will not be disgraced.
Therefore have I set my face like flint,
  and I know I will not be put to
    shame.
8He who vindicates me is near.
  Who then will bring charges against
    me?
  Let us face each other!
Who is my accuser?
  Let him confront me!
9It is the Sovereign Lord who helps me.
  Who is he that will condemn me?
They will all wear out like a garment;
  the moths will eat them up.

10Who among you fears the Lord
  and obeys the word of his servant?
Let him who walks in the dark,
  who has no light,
trust in the name of the Lord
  and rely on his God.
11But now, all you who light fires
  and provide yourselves with flaming
    torches,
go, walk in the light of your fires
  and of the torches you have set
    ablaze.
This is what you shall receive from my
  hand:
  You will lie down in torment.

Everlasting Salvation for Zion

51 "Listen to me, you who pursue
  righteousness
  and who seek the Lord:
Look to the rock from which you were
  cut
  and to the quarry from which you
    were hewn;
2look to Abraham, your father,
  and to Sarah, who gave you birth.

When I called him he was but one,
  and I blessed him and made him
    many.
3The Lord will surely comfort Zion
  and will look with compassion on all
    her ruins;
he will make her deserts like Eden,
  her wastelands like the garden of the
    Lord.
Joy and gladness will be found in her,
  thanksgiving and the sound of
    singing.

4"Listen to me, my people;
  hear me, my nation:
The law will go out from me;
  my justice will become a light to the
    nations.
5My righteousness draws near speedily,
  my salvation is on the way,
and my arm will bring justice to the
  nations.
The islands will look to me
  and wait in hope for my arm.
6Lift up your eyes to the heavens,
  look at the earth beneath;
the heavens will vanish like smoke,
  the earth will wear out like a garment
  and its inhabitants die like flies.
But my salvation will last forever,
  my righteousness will never fail.

7"Hear me, you who know what is right,
  you people who have my law in your
    hearts:
Do not fear the reproach of men
  or be terrified by their insults.
8For the moth will eat them up like a
    garment;
  the worm will devour them like wool.
But my righteousness will last forever,
  my salvation through all generations."

9Awake, awake! Clothe yourself with
    strength,
  O arm of the Lord;
awake, as in days gone by,
  as in generations of old.
Was it not you who cut Rahab to
    pieces,
  who pierced that monster through?
10Was it not you who dried up the sea,
  the waters of the great deep,
who made a road in the depths of the
    sea
  so that the redeemed might cross
    over?
11The ransomed of the Lord will return.
  They will enter Zion with singing;
  everlasting joy will crown their heads.

Gladness and joy will overtake them,
and sorrow and sighing will flee away.

12"I, even I, am he who comforts you.
Who are you that you fear mortal
men,
the sons of men, who are but grass,
13that you forget the LORD your Maker,
who stretched out the heavens
and laid the foundations of the earth,
that you live in constant terror every
day
because of the wrath of the
oppressor,
who is bent on destruction?
For where is the wrath of the oppressor?
14   The cowering prisoners will soon be
set free;
they will not die in their dungeon,
nor will they lack bread.
15For I am the LORD your God,
who churns up the sea so that its
waves roar—
the LORD Almighty is his name.
16I have put my words in your mouth
and covered you with the shadow of
my hand—
I who set the heavens in place,
who laid the foundations of the earth,
and who say to Zion, 'You are my
people.' "

The Cup of the LORD's Wrath

17Awake, awake!
Rise up, O Jerusalem,
you who have drunk from the hand of
the LORD
the cup of his wrath,
you who have drained to its dregs
the goblet that makes men stagger.
18Of all the sons she bore
there was none to guide her;
of all the sons she reared
there was none to take her by the
hand.
19These double calamities have come
upon you—
who can comfort you?
ruin and destruction, famine and
sword—
who can*a* console you?
20Your sons have fainted;
they lie at the head of every street,
like antelope caught in a net.
They are filled with the wrath of the
LORD

and the rebuke of your God.

21Therefore hear this, you afflicted one,
made drunk, but not with wine.
22This is what your Sovereign LORD says,
your God, who defends his people:
"See, I have taken out of your hand
the cup that made you stagger;
from that cup, the goblet of my wrath,
you will never drink again.
23I will put it into the hands of your
tormentors,
who said to you,
'Fall prostrate that we may walk over
you.'
And you made your back like the
ground,
like a street to be walked over."

52 Awake, awake, O Zion,
clothe yourself with strength.
Put on your garments of splendor,
O Jerusalem, the holy city.
The uncircumcised and defiled
will not enter you again.
2Shake off your dust;
rise up, sit enthroned, O Jerusalem.
Free yourself from the chains on your
neck,
O captive Daughter of Zion.

3For this is what the LORD says:

"You were sold for nothing,
and without money you will be
redeemed."

4For this is what the Sovereign LORD says:

"At first my people went down to Egypt
to live;
lately, Assyria has oppressed them.

5"And now what do I have here?" declares
the LORD.

"For my people have been taken away
for nothing,
and those who rule them mock,*b*"
declares the LORD.
"And all day long
my name is constantly blasphemed.
6Therefore my people will know my
name;
therefore in that day they will know
that it is I who foretold it.
Yes, it is I."

7How beautiful on the mountains

a19 Dead Sea Scrolls, Septuagint, Vulgate and Syriac; Masoretic Text / *how can I*   *b5* Dead Sea Scrolls and Vulgate; Masoretic Text *wail*

are the feet of those who bring good
news,
who proclaim peace,
who bring good tidings,
who proclaim salvation,
who say to Zion,
"Your God reigns!"
8Listen! Your watchmen lift up their
voices;
together they shout for joy.
When the LORD returns to Zion,
they will see it with their own eyes.
9Burst into songs of joy together,
you ruins of Jerusalem,
for the LORD has comforted his people,
he has redeemed Jerusalem.
10The LORD will lay bare his holy arm
in the sight of all the nations,
and all the ends of the earth will see
the salvation of our God.

11Depart, depart, go out from there!
Touch no unclean thing!
Come out from it and be pure,
you who carry the vessels of the LORD.
12But you will not leave in haste
or go in flight;
for the LORD will go before you,
the God of Israel will be your rear
guard.

The Suffering and Glory of the Servant

13See, my servant will act wisely[a];
he will be raised and lifted up and
highly exalted.
14Just as there were many who were
appalled at him[b]—
his appearance was so disfigured
beyond that of any man
and his form marred beyond human
likeness—
15so will he sprinkle many nations,[c]
and kings will shut their mouths
because of him.
For what they were not told, they will
see,
and what they have not heard, they
will understand.

53 Who has believed our message
and to whom has the arm of the
LORD been revealed?
2He grew up before him like a tender
shoot,
and like a root out of dry ground.

He had no beauty or majesty to attract
us to him,
nothing in his appearance that we
should desire him.
3He was despised and rejected by men,
a man of sorrows, and familiar with
suffering.
Like one from whom men hide their
faces
he was despised, and we esteemed
him not.

4Surely he took up our infirmities
and carried our sorrows,
yet we considered him stricken by God,
smitten by him, and afflicted.
5But he was pierced for our
transgressions,
he was crushed for our iniquities;
the punishment that brought us peace
was upon him,
and by his wounds we are healed.
6We all, like sheep, have gone astray,
each of us has turned to his own way;
and the LORD has laid on him
the iniquity of us all.

7He was oppressed and afflicted,
yet he did not open his mouth;
he was led like a lamb to the slaughter,
and as a sheep before her shearers is
silent,
so he did not open his mouth.
8By oppression[d] and judgment he was
taken away.
And who can speak of his
descendants?
For he was cut off from the land of the
living;
for the transgression of my people he
was stricken.[e]
9He was assigned a grave with the
wicked,
and with the rich in his death,
though he had done no violence,
nor was any deceit in his mouth.

10Yet it was the LORD's will to crush him
and cause him to suffer,
and though the LORD makes[f] his life
a guilt offering,
he will see his offspring and prolong his
days,
and the will of the LORD will prosper
in his hand.
11After the suffering of his soul,

---

a13 Or *will prosper*   b14 Hebrew *you*   c15 Hebrew; Septuagint *so will many nations marvel at him*
d8 Or *From arrest*   e8 Or *away. / Yet who of his generation considered / that he was cut off from the land of
the living / for the transgression of my people, / to whom the blow was due?*   f10 Hebrew *though you make*

MYTH: HUMANS ARE BASICALLY GOOD

• •

Kim's first hour class is sociology with Mrs. Kaufman. Always optimistic and cheerful, Mrs. Kaufman is popular with all the students. Let's listen in.

"So you see, class, no one is born 'evil' or 'sinful.' We're simply products of our environment. Why does a ghetto kid turn to crime? Is it because he's evil? No! He doesn't have the benefits of a positive home and good education. Take that kid, educate him and change his surroundings, and you'll lessen and possibly eliminate his negative behavior."

Look It Up
• • • •

Mrs. Kaufman's lecture seems to make sense. But, according to the Word of God, it simply isn't true.

In fact, the very nature of the human race is sinful: "As for you, you were dead in your transgressions and sins, in which you used to live when you followed the ways of this world . . . gratifying the cravings of our sinful nature and following its desires and thoughts. Like the rest, we were by nature objects of wrath" (Ephesians 2:1–3).

Think It Through
• • • •

In making her claim, Mrs. Kaufman ignored some relevant evidence: For example, many criminals grew up in a very positive environment. If environment were the only influencing factor, wouldn't the bad guys all live in only one kind of neighborhood?

Sure, environment is a factor in people's personalities. But it's one factor—not the only factor. Unfortunately, sinful human beings who need to be changed from the inside often exhibit "negative behavior" regardless of the environment they live in.

Work It Out
• • • •

The bad news is that people are sinful and separated from God. The good news is that Jesus died on the cross to solve the problem. When you trust him to forgive you, he comes into your life and begins to change you from the inside out. He exchanges your evil and lifelessness for his goodness and life.

Ask your friends if they think humans are basically good or evil. If they respond, "good," ask why. Think about their answer. Does it take into account the terrible things people have done? Share with them the Scripture's view of human nature. Point out how it rings true considering the facts of history.

If your friends say, "evil," ask them where they can find a solution for that evil. It's a great way to share your faith in Christ.

Nail It Down
• • • •

Read Isaiah's assessment of human nature in Isaiah 53:6.

Turn to pages 439, 1282 and 1311 for other readings on human nature.
Turn to page 771 for Tuesday's reading.

Topic
• • • •

HUMAN NATURE

he will see the light ˻of life˼ᵃ and be
    satisfiedᵇ;
by his knowledgeᶜ my righteous
    servant will justify many,
and he will bear their iniquities.
¹²Therefore I will give him a portion
    among the great,ᵈ
and he will divide the spoils with the
    strong,ᵉ
because he poured out his life unto
    death,
and was numbered with the
    transgressors.
For he bore the sin of many,
and made intercession for the
    transgressors.

The Future Glory of Zion

54 "Sing, O barren woman,
    you who never bore a child;
burst into song, shout for joy,
    you who were never in labor;
because more are the children of the
    desolate woman
than of her who has a husband,"
                        says the LORD.
²"Enlarge the place of your tent,
    stretch your tent curtains wide,
    do not hold back;
lengthen your cords,
    strengthen your stakes.
³For you will spread out to the right and
    to the left;
your descendants will dispossess
    nations
and settle in their desolate cities.

⁴"Do not be afraid; you will not suffer
    shame.
Do not fear disgrace; you will not be
    humiliated.
You will forget the shame of your youth
and remember no more the reproach
    of your widowhood.
⁵For your Maker is your husband—
    the LORD Almighty is his name—
the Holy One of Israel is your
    Redeemer;
he is called the God of all the earth.
⁶The LORD will call you back
as if you were a wife deserted and
    distressed in spirit—
a wife who married young,
    only to be rejected," says your God.
⁷"For a brief moment I abandoned you,

but with deep compassion I will bring
    you back.
⁸In a surge of anger
I hid my face from you for a moment,
but with everlasting kindness
I will have compassion on you,"
    says the LORD your Redeemer.

⁹"To me this is like the days of Noah,
when I swore that the waters of Noah
    would never again cover the
    earth.
So now I have sworn not to be angry
    with you,
never to rebuke you again.
¹⁰Though the mountains be shaken
    and the hills be removed,
yet my unfailing love for you will not be
    shaken
nor my covenant of peace be
    removed,"
says the LORD, who has compassion
    on you.

¹¹"O afflicted city, lashed by storms and
    not comforted,
I will build you with stones of
    turquoise,ᶠ
your foundations with sapphires.ᵍ
¹²I will make your battlements of rubies,
    your gates of sparkling jewels,
and all your walls of precious stones.
¹³All your sons will be taught by the LORD,
and great will be your children's
    peace.
¹⁴In righteousness you will be established:
Tyranny will be far from you;
    you will have nothing to fear.
Terror will be far removed;
    it will not come near you.
¹⁵If anyone does attack you, it will not be
    my doing;
whoever attacks you will surrender to
    you.

¹⁶"See, it is I who created the blacksmith
who fans the coals into flame
and forges a weapon fit for its work.
And it is I who have created the
    destroyer to work havoc;
¹⁷ no weapon forged against you will
    prevail,
and you will refute every tongue that
    accuses you.
This is the heritage of the servants of
    the LORD,

ᵃ11 Dead Sea Scrolls (see also Septuagint); Masoretic Text does not have *the light ˻of life˼*.   ᵇ11 Or (with Masoretic Text) *¹¹He will see the result of the suffering of his soul / and be satisfied*   ᶜ11 Or *by knowledge of him*   ᵈ12 Or *many*   ᵉ12 Or *numerous*   ᶠ11 The meaning of the Hebrew for this word is uncertain.   ᵍ11 Or *lapis lazuli*

and this is their vindication from me,"
                              declares the Lord.

Invitation to the Thirsty

55 "Come, all you who are thirsty,
          come to the waters;
and you who have no money,
   come, buy and eat!
Come, buy wine and milk
   without money and without cost.
²Why spend money on what is not
      bread,
   and your labor on what does not
      satisfy?
Listen, listen to me, and eat what is
      good,
   and your soul will delight in the
      richest of fare.
³Give ear and come to me;
   hear me, that your soul may live.
I will make an everlasting covenant with
      you,
   my faithful love promised to David.
⁴See, I have made him a witness to the
      peoples,
   a leader and commander of the
      peoples.
⁵Surely you will summon nations you
      know not,
   and nations that do not know you will
      hasten to you,
because of the Lord your God,
   the Holy One of Israel,
   for he has endowed you with
      splendor."

⁶Seek the Lord while he may be found;
   call on him while he is near.
⁷Let the wicked forsake his way
   and the evil man his thoughts.
Let him turn to the Lord, and he will
      have mercy on him,
   and to our God, for he will freely
      pardon.

⁸"For my thoughts are not your thoughts,
   neither are your ways my ways,"
                              declares the Lord.
⁹"As the heavens are higher than the
      earth,
   so are my ways higher than your
      ways
   and my thoughts than your thoughts.
¹⁰As the rain and the snow
   come down from heaven,
   and do not return to it
   without watering the earth
and making it bud and flourish,
   so that it yields seed for the sower
      and bread for the eater,

¹¹so is my word that goes out from my
      mouth:
   It will not return to me empty,
but will accomplish what I desire
   and achieve the purpose for which I
      sent it.
¹²You will go out in joy
   and be led forth in peace;
the mountains and hills
   will burst into song before you,
and all the trees of the field
   will clap their hands.
¹³Instead of the thornbush will grow the
      pine tree,
   and instead of briers the myrtle will
      grow.
This will be for the Lord's renown,
   for an everlasting sign,
   which will not be destroyed."

Salvation for Others

56 This is what the Lord says:

"Maintain justice
   and do what is right,
for my salvation is close at hand
   and my righteousness will soon be
      revealed.
²Blessed is the man who does this,
   the man who holds it fast,
who keeps the Sabbath without
      desecrating it,
   and keeps his hand from doing any
      evil."

³Let no foreigner who has bound himself
      to the Lord say,
   "The Lord will surely exclude me from
      his people."
And let not any eunuch complain,
   "I am only a dry tree."

⁴For this is what the Lord says:

"To the eunuchs who keep my
      Sabbaths,
   who choose what pleases me
   and hold fast to my covenant—
⁵to them I will give within my temple
      and its walls
   a memorial and a name
   better than sons and daughters;
I will give them an everlasting name
   that will not be cut off.
⁶And foreigners who bind themselves to
      the Lord
   to serve him,
to love the name of the Lord,
   and to worship him,
all who keep the Sabbath without
      desecrating it

YOUR BIGGEST DEBT HAS BEEN PAID IN FULL
☐ TUESDAY

At a freshman Bible study three years ago, Judy and Kirby heard this: "Because of sin, the entire human race was under a death sentence. But Jesus came and paid the penalty for all of us by dying in our place. If you trust in him, you can experience total forgiveness!"

"But don't I also have to live a good life?" Kirby inquired.

"Forgiveness isn't based on anything you do to earn it. It's based on what Jesus has already done. He paid for your sins. Now the question is: Will you accept the payment he made?"

Judy said yes. Kirby said no, reasoning, "That can't be right! Surely God must expect me to do something to make up for my sins."

Look It Up
•••

The book of Acts tells how the followers of Christ went all over the known world with the message of forgiveness:

"All the prophets testify about him that everyone who believes in him receives forgiveness of sins through his name" (Acts 10:43).

"Therefore, my brothers, I want you to know that through Jesus the forgiveness of sins is proclaimed to you" (Acts 13:38).

No wonder they were excited: Jesus completely paid the debt we could never pay!

Think It Through
•••

You break the law and are caught. Because of your crime, the judge fines you $1,000. What are you going to do? You deserve to be punished. Yet you don't have the money to pay the penalty.

Suddenly, the judge pulls out his checkbook and pays the fine you owe. Your debt to society has been cancelled. Your offense is completely forgiven.

God has done that for us on a grander scale. The very payment he demanded for sin—death—he has also supplied!

Work It Out
•••

If you've already experienced forgiveness through Christ, tell God how thankful you are. Then tell someone else.

If you're not sure, you can be sure by sincerely praying: "God, I know I've sinned. I need and want to be forgiven. Right now, I am trusting Jesus to be my Savior. I believe the message of the Bible, that his death on the cross paid the penalty for all my sins. Amen."

Nail It Down
•••

Read the message of forgiveness in Isaiah 55:6–7.

Turn to pages 580, 809, 966, 1068, 1302 and 1352 for other readings on forgiveness.
Turn to page 778 for Wednesday's reading.

Topic
••••

FORGIVENESS

and who hold fast to my covenant—
7these I will bring to my holy mountain
  and give them joy in my house of
    prayer.
Their burnt offerings and sacrifices
  will be accepted on my altar;
for my house will be called
  a house of prayer for all nations."
8The Sovereign Lord declares—
  he who gathers the exiles of Israel:
"I will gather still others to them
  besides those already gathered."

God's Accusation Against the Wicked

9Come, all you beasts of the field,
  come and devour, all you beasts of
    the forest!
10Israel's watchmen are blind,
  they all lack knowledge;
they are all mute dogs,
  they cannot bark;
they lie around and dream,
  they love to sleep.
11They are dogs with mighty appetites;
  they never have enough.
They are shepherds who lack
    understanding;
  they all turn to their own way,
  each seeks his own gain.
12"Come," each one cries, "let me get
    wine!
  Let us drink our fill of beer!
And tomorrow will be like today,
  or even far better."

57 The righteous perish,
     and no one ponders it in his
       heart;
devout men are taken away,
  and no one understands
that the righteous are taken away
  to be spared from evil.
2Those who walk uprightly
  enter into peace;
  they find rest as they lie in death.

3"But you—come here, you sons of a
    sorceress,
  you offspring of adulterers and
    prostitutes!
4Whom are you mocking?
  At whom do you sneer
  and stick out your tongue?
Are you not a brood of rebels,
  the offspring of liars?
5You burn with lust among the oaks
  and under every spreading tree;

you sacrifice your children in the
    ravines
  and under the overhanging crags.
6⌊The idols⌋ among the smooth stones of
    the ravines are your portion;
  they, they are your lot.
Yes, to them you have poured out drink
    offerings
  and offered grain offerings.
In the light of these things, should I
    relent?
7You have made your bed on a high and
    lofty hill;
  there you went up to offer your
    sacrifices.
8Behind your doors and your doorposts
  you have put your pagan symbols.
Forsaking me, you uncovered your bed,
  you climbed into it and opened it
    wide;
you made a pact with those whose beds
    you love,
  and you looked on their nakedness.
9You went to Molecha with olive oil
  and increased your perfumes.
You sent your ambassadorsb far away;
  you descended to the gravec itself!
10You were wearied by all your ways,
  but you would not say, 'It is hopeless.'
You found renewal of your strength,
  and so you did not faint.

11"Whom have you so dreaded and feared
    that you have been false to me,
and have neither remembered me
  nor pondered this in your hearts?
Is it not because I have long been silent
  that you do not fear me?
12I will expose your righteousness and
    your works,
  and they will not benefit you.
13When you cry out for help,
  let your collection ⌊of idols⌋ save you!
The wind will carry all of them off,
  a mere breath will blow them away.
But the man who makes me his refuge
  will inherit the land
  and possess my holy mountain."

Comfort for the Contrite

14And it will be said:

"Build up, build up, prepare the road!
  Remove the obstacles out of the way
    of my people."
15For this is what the high and lofty One
    says—

a9 Or to the king   b9 Or idols   c9 Hebrew Sheol

he who lives forever, whose name is
　holy:
"I live in a high and holy place,
　but also with him who is contrite and
　　lowly in spirit,
to revive the spirit of the lowly
　and to revive the heart of the contrite.
¹⁶I will not accuse forever,
　nor will I always be angry,
for then the spirit of man would grow
　　faint before me —
　the breath of man that I have created.
¹⁷I was enraged by his sinful greed;
　I punished him, and hid my face in
　　anger,
yet he kept on in his willful ways.
¹⁸I have seen his ways, but I will heal
　　him;
　I will guide him and restore comfort
　　to him,
¹⁹　creating praise on the lips of the
　　mourners in Israel.
Peace, peace, to those far and near,"
says the LORD. "And I will heal them."
²⁰But the wicked are like the tossing sea,
　which cannot rest,
　whose waves cast up mire and mud.
²¹"There is no peace," says my God, "for
　the wicked."

True Fasting

58 "Shout it aloud, do not hold back.
　Raise your voice like a trumpet.
Declare to my people their rebellion
　and to the house of Jacob their sins.
²For day after day they seek me out;
　they seem eager to know my ways,
as if they were a nation that does what
　　is right
　and has not forsaken the commands
　　of its God.
They ask me for just decisions
　and seem eager for God to come near
　　them.
³'Why have we fasted,' they say,
　'and you have not seen it?
Why have we humbled ourselves,
　and you have not noticed?'

"Yet on the day of your fasting, you do
　　as you please
　and exploit all your workers.
⁴Your fasting ends in quarreling and
　　strife,
　and in striking each other with wicked
　　fists.
You cannot fast as you do today

and expect your voice to be heard on
　high.
⁵Is this the kind of fast I have chosen,
　only a day for a man to humble
　　himself?
Is it only for bowing one's head like a
　　reed
　and for lying on sackcloth and ashes?
Is that what you call a fast,
　a day acceptable to the LORD?

⁶"Is not this the kind of fasting I have
　　chosen:
to loose the chains of injustice
　and untie the cords of the yoke,
to set the oppressed free
　and break every yoke?
⁷Is it not to share your food with the
　　hungry
　and to provide the poor wanderer
　　with shelter —
when you see the naked, to clothe him,
　and not to turn away from your own
　　flesh and blood?
⁸Then your light will break forth like the
　　dawn,
　and your healing will quickly appear;
then your righteousness*a* will go before
　you,
　and the glory of the LORD will be your
　　rear guard.
⁹Then you will call, and the LORD will
　　answer;
　you will cry for help, and he will say:
　　Here am I.

"If you do away with the yoke of
　　oppression,
　with the pointing finger and malicious
　　talk,
¹⁰and if you spend yourselves in behalf of
　　the hungry
　and satisfy the needs of the
　　oppressed,
then your light will rise in the darkness,
　and your night will become like the
　　noonday.
¹¹The LORD will guide you always;
　he will satisfy your needs in a
　　sun-scorched land
　and will strengthen your frame.
You will be like a well-watered garden,
　like a spring whose waters never fail.
¹²Your people will rebuild the ancient
　　ruins
　and will raise up the age-old
　　foundations;

a8 Or your righteous One

you will be called Repairer of Broken
    Walls,
    Restorer of Streets with Dwellings.

[13]"If you keep your feet from breaking the
    Sabbath
    and from doing as you please on my
        holy day,
if you call the Sabbath a delight
    and the Lord's holy day honorable,
and if you honor it by not going your
        own way
    and not doing as you please or
        speaking idle words,
[14]then you will find your joy in the Lord,
    and I will cause you to ride on the
        heights of the land
    and to feast on the inheritance of
        your father Jacob."
    The mouth of the Lord has spoken.

Sin, Confession and Redemption

59 Surely the arm of the Lord is not
      too short to save,
    nor his ear too dull to hear.
[2]But your iniquities have separated
    you from your God;
your sins have hidden his face from
    you,
    so that he will not hear.
[3]For your hands are stained with blood,
    your fingers with guilt.
Your lips have spoken lies,
    and your tongue mutters wicked
        things.
[4]No one calls for justice;
    no one pleads his case with integrity.
They rely on empty arguments and
        speak lies;
    they conceive trouble and give birth
        to evil.
[5]They hatch the eggs of vipers
    and spin a spider's web.
Whoever eats their eggs will die,
    and when one is broken, an adder is
        hatched.
[6]Their cobwebs are useless for clothing;
    they cannot cover themselves with
        what they make.
Their deeds are evil deeds,
    and acts of violence are in their
        hands.
[7]Their feet rush into sin;
    they are swift to shed innocent blood.
Their thoughts are evil thoughts;
    ruin and destruction mark their ways.
[8]The way of peace they do not know;
    there is no justice in their paths.

They have turned them into crooked
    roads;
no one who walks in them will know
    peace.

[9]So justice is far from us,
    and righteousness does not reach us.
We look for light, but all is darkness;
    for brightness, but we walk in deep
        shadows.
[10]Like the blind we grope along the wall,
    feeling our way like men without
        eyes.
At midday we stumble as if it were
        twilight;
    among the strong, we are like the
        dead.
[11]We all growl like bears;
    we moan mournfully like doves.
We look for justice, but find none;
    for deliverance, but it is far away.

[12]For our offenses are many in your sight,
    and our sins testify against us.
Our offenses are ever with us,
    and we acknowledge our iniquities:
[13]rebellion and treachery against the Lord,
    turning our backs on our God,
fomenting oppression and revolt,
    uttering lies our hearts have
        conceived.
[14]So justice is driven back,
    and righteousness stands at a
        distance;
truth has stumbled in the streets,
    honesty cannot enter.
[15]Truth is nowhere to be found,
    and whoever shuns evil becomes a
        prey.

The Lord looked and was displeased
    that there was no justice.
[16]He saw that there was no one,
    he was appalled that there was no
        one to intervene;
so his own arm worked salvation for
        him,
    and his own righteousness sustained
        him.
[17]He put on righteousness as his
        breastplate,
    and the helmet of salvation on his
        head;
he put on the garments of vengeance
    and wrapped himself in zeal as in a
        cloak.
[18]According to what they have done,
    so will he repay
wrath to his enemies
    and retribution to his foes;

he will repay the islands their due.
¹⁹From the west, men will fear the name
of the Lord,
and from the rising of the sun, they
will revere his glory.
For he will come like a pent-up flood
that the breath of the Lord drives
along.^a

²⁰"The Redeemer will come to Zion,
to those in Jacob who repent of their
sins,"
declares the Lord.

²¹"As for me, this is my covenant with
them," says the Lord. "My Spirit, who is on
you, and my words that I have put in your
mouth will not depart from your mouth, or
from the mouths of your children, or from
the mouths of their descendants from this
time on and forever," says the Lord.

The Glory of Zion

60 "Arise, shine, for your light has
come,
and the glory of the Lord rises upon
you.
²See, darkness covers the earth
and thick darkness is over the
peoples,
but the Lord rises upon you
and his glory appears over you.
³Nations will come to your light,
and kings to the brightness of your
dawn.

⁴"Lift up your eyes and look about you:
All assemble and come to you;
your sons come from afar,
and your daughters are carried on the
arm.
⁵Then you will look and be radiant,
your heart will throb and swell with
joy;
the wealth on the seas will be brought
to you,
to you the riches of the nations will
come.
⁶Herds of camels will cover your land,
young camels of Midian and Ephah.
And all from Sheba will come,
bearing gold and incense
and proclaiming the praise of the
Lord.
⁷All Kedar's flocks will be gathered to
you,
the rams of Nebaioth will serve you;

they will be accepted as offerings on my
altar,
and I will adorn my glorious temple.

⁸"Who are these that fly along like
clouds,
like doves to their nests?
⁹Surely the islands look to me;
in the lead are the ships of
Tarshish,^b
bringing your sons from afar,
with their silver and gold,
to the honor of the Lord your God,
the Holy One of Israel,
for he has endowed you with
splendor.

¹⁰"Foreigners will rebuild your walls,
and their kings will serve you.
Though in anger I struck you,
in favor I will show you compassion.
¹¹Your gates will always stand open,
they will never be shut, day or night,
so that men may bring you the wealth
of the nations—
their kings led in triumphal
procession.
¹²For the nation or kingdom that will not
serve you will perish;
it will be utterly ruined.

¹³"The glory of Lebanon will come to you,
the pine, the fir and the cypress
together,
to adorn the place of my sanctuary;
and I will glorify the place of my feet.
¹⁴The sons of your oppressors will come
bowing before you;
all who despise you will bow down at
your feet
and will call you the City of the Lord,
Zion of the Holy One of Israel.

¹⁵"Although you have been forsaken and
hated,
with no one traveling through,
I will make you the everlasting pride
and the joy of all generations.
¹⁶You will drink the milk of nations
and be nursed at royal breasts.
Then you will know that I, the Lord, am
your Savior,
your Redeemer, the Mighty One of
Jacob.
¹⁷Instead of bronze I will bring you gold,
and silver in place of iron.
Instead of wood I will bring you bronze,

^a19 Or When the enemy comes in like a flood, / the Spirit of the Lord will put him to flight   ^b9 Or the trading
ships

and iron in place of stones.
I will make peace your governor
    and righteousness your ruler.
¹⁸No longer will violence be heard in your
        land,
    nor ruin or destruction within your
        borders,
but you will call your walls Salvation
    and your gates Praise.
¹⁹The sun will no more be your light by
        day,
    nor will the brightness of the moon
        shine on you,
for the LORD will be your everlasting
        light,
    and your God will be your glory.
²⁰Your sun will never set again,
    and your moon will wane no more;
the LORD will be your everlasting light,
    and your days of sorrow will end.
²¹Then will all your people be righteous
    and they will possess the land forever.
They are the shoot I have planted,
    the work of my hands,
    for the display of my splendor.
²²The least of you will become a
        thousand,
    the smallest a mighty nation.
I am the LORD;
    in its time I will do this swiftly."

The Year of the LORD's Favor

61 The Spirit of the Sovereign LORD is
        on me,
    because the LORD has anointed me
    to preach good news to the poor.
He has sent me to bind up the
        brokenhearted,
    to proclaim freedom for the captives
    and release from darkness for the
        prisoners,[a]
²to proclaim the year of the LORD's favor
    and the day of vengeance of our God,
to comfort all who mourn,
³   and provide for those who grieve in
        Zion —
    to bestow on them a crown of beauty
        instead of ashes,
    the oil of gladness
        instead of mourning,
    and a garment of praise
        instead of a spirit of despair.
They will be called oaks of
        righteousness,
    a planting of the LORD
    for the display of his splendor.

⁴They will rebuild the ancient ruins
    and restore the places long
        devastated;
they will renew the ruined cities
    that have been devastated for
        generations.
⁵Aliens will shepherd your flocks;
    foreigners will work your fields and
        vineyards.
⁶And you will be called priests of the
        LORD,
    you will be named ministers of our
        God.
You will feed on the wealth of nations,
    and in their riches you will boast.

⁷Instead of their shame
    my people will receive a double
        portion,
and instead of disgrace
    they will rejoice in their inheritance;
and so they will inherit a double portion
        in their land,
    and everlasting joy will be theirs.

⁸"For I, the LORD, love justice;
    I hate robbery and iniquity.
In my faithfulness I will reward them
    and make an everlasting covenant
        with them.
⁹Their descendants will be known among
        the nations
    and their offspring among the
        peoples.
All who see them will acknowledge
    that they are a people the LORD has
        blessed."

¹⁰I delight greatly in the LORD;
    my soul rejoices in my God.
For he has clothed me with garments of
        salvation
    and arrayed me in a robe of
        righteousness,
as a bridegroom adorns his head like a
        priest,
    and as a bride adorns herself with her
        jewels.
¹¹For as the soil makes the sprout come
        up
    and a garden causes seeds to grow,
so the Sovereign LORD will make
        righteousness and praise
    spring up before all nations.

Zion's New Name

62 For Zion's sake I will not keep
        silent,

---

a 1 Hebrew; Septuagint *the blind*

for Jerusalem's sake I will not remain
    quiet,
till her righteousness shines out like the
    dawn,
    her salvation like a blazing torch.
²The nations will see your righteousness,
    and all kings your glory;
you will be called by a new name
    that the mouth of the LORD will
        bestow.
³You will be a crown of splendor in the
    LORD's hand,
    a royal diadem in the hand of your
        God.
⁴No longer will they call you Deserted,
    or name your land Desolate.
But you will be called Hephzibah,ᵃ
    and your land Beulahᵇ;
for the LORD will take delight in you,
    and your land will be married.
⁵As a young man marries a maiden,
    so will your sonsᶜ marry you;
as a bridegroom rejoices over his bride,
    so will your God rejoice over you.

⁶I have posted watchmen on your walls,
    O Jerusalem;
    they will never be silent day or night.
You who call on the LORD,
    give yourselves no rest,
⁷and give him no rest till he establishes
    Jerusalem
    and makes her the praise of the earth.

⁸The LORD has sworn by his right hand
    and by his mighty arm:
"Never again will I give your grain
    as food for your enemies,
and never again will foreigners drink the
    new wine
    for which you have toiled;
⁹but those who harvest it will eat it
    and praise the LORD,
and those who gather the grapes will
    drink it
    in the courts of my sanctuary."

¹⁰Pass through, pass through the gates!
    Prepare the way for the people.
Build up, build up the highway!
    Remove the stones.
Raise a banner for the nations.

¹¹The LORD has made proclamation
    to the ends of the earth:
"Say to the Daughter of Zion,
    'See, your Savior comes!
See, his reward is with him,

and his recompense accompanies
    him.'"
¹²They will be called the Holy People,
    the Redeemed of the LORD;
and you will be called Sought After,
    the City No Longer Deserted.

God's Day of Vengeance and Redemption

63 Who is this coming from Edom,
    from Bozrah, with his garments
        stained crimson?
Who is this, robed in splendor,
    striding forward in the greatness of
        his strength?

"It is I, speaking in righteousness,
    mighty to save."

²Why are your garments red,
    like those of one treading the
        winepress?

³"I have trodden the winepress alone;
    from the nations no one was with me.
I trampled them in my anger
    and trod them down in my wrath;
their blood spattered my garments,
    and I stained all my clothing.
⁴For the day of vengeance was in my
    heart,
    and the year of my redemption has
        come.
⁵I looked, but there was no one to help,
    I was appalled that no one gave
        support;
so my own arm worked salvation for
    me,
    and my own wrath sustained me.
⁶I trampled the nations in my anger;
    in my wrath I made them drunk
    and poured their blood on the
        ground."

Praise and Prayer

⁷I will tell of the kindnesses of the LORD,
    the deeds for which he is to be
        praised,
    according to all the LORD has done for
        us —
yes, the many good things he has done
    for the house of Israel,
    according to his compassion and
        many kindnesses.
⁸He said, "Surely they are my people,
    sons who will not be false to me";
and so he became their Savior.

ᵃ4 *Hephzibah* means *my delight is in her.*   ᵇ4 *Beulah* means *married.*   ᶜ5 Or *Builder*

WHO'S FIGHTING YOUR BATTLES?

Louis is as nervous as a long-tailed cat in a room full of rocking chairs. On Saturday he takes the SAT test for the third time. His parents want him to improve his scores radically (and his chances for getting into a top-notch college).

Every night they're after him to study. "You need at least a 1350 or 1400, Lou!" Mr. Watkins insists (for about the 200th time!). "Make us proud, Son. No goofing off till after this weekend, okay?"

Lou nods weakly, his stomach in knots.

Look It Up

Have you ever battled extreme pressure like Lou is facing? Have you ever felt so tense you wondered if you could even function? If so, you're not alone. Consider this charge given to Israel:

"When you go to war against your enemies . . . do not be afraid . . . Do not be fainthearted or afraid; do not be terrified or give way to panic before them. For the LORD your God is the one who goes with you to fight for you against your enemies to give you victory" (Deuteronomy 20:1,3–4).

What a promise! The pressure for success isn't on you . . . it's on God! Your obligation is simply to "go to war." It's up to God to "give you the victory."

Think It Through

What would you do if you had parents like Lou? How would you handle such stress? Is it right for parents to put that much pressure on their children? Is it right for you to put that much pressure on yourself?

Work It Out

Don't lose the Biblical perspective. When your back is to the wall, all you have to do is your part. What is your part in the stresses you face?

• In academics, your part is to study.
• In a relational conflict, your part is to apologize and be kind.
• In athletics, your part is to be well-prepared and in shape.
• In a tempting situation, your part is to turn away from sin.
• In a pressure-filled job, your part is to work hard and be cheerful.

Once you know your part, simply do your part. Then give the pressure to God. He can handle it. (He can also bring victory when we trust him!)

Nail It Down

Read about what God will do in a difficult situation in Isaiah 63:7–9.

Turn to pages 546, 1058, 1219 and 1280 for other readings on stress.
Turn to page 784 for Thursday's reading.

Topic

⁹In all their distress he too was
    distressed,
  and the angel of his presence saved
    them.
In his love and mercy he redeemed
    them;
  he lifted them up and carried them
    all the days of old.
¹⁰Yet they rebelled
  and grieved his Holy Spirit.
So he turned and became their enemy
  and he himself fought against them.

¹¹Then his people recalled*a* the days of
    old,
  the days of Moses and his people—
where is he who brought them through
    the sea,
  with the shepherd of his flock?
Where is he who set
  his Holy Spirit among them,
¹²who sent his glorious arm of power
  to be at Moses' right hand,
who divided the waters before them,
  to gain for himself everlasting renown,
¹³who led them through the depths?
Like a horse in open country,
  they did not stumble;
¹⁴like cattle that go down to the plain,
  they were given rest by the Spirit of
    the LORD.
This is how you guided your people
  to make for yourself a glorious name.

¹⁵Look down from heaven and see
  from your lofty throne, holy and
    glorious.
Where are your zeal and your might?
  Your tenderness and compassion are
    withheld from us.
¹⁶But you are our Father,
  though Abraham does not know us
  or Israel acknowledge us;
you, O LORD, are our Father,
  our Redeemer from of old is your
    name.
¹⁷Why, O LORD, do you make us wander
    from your ways
  and harden our hearts so we do not
    revere you?
Return for the sake of your servants,
  the tribes that are your inheritance.
¹⁸For a little while your people possessed
    your holy place,
  but now our enemies have trampled
    down your sanctuary.

¹⁹We are yours from of old;
  but you have not ruled over them,
  they have not been called by your
    name.*b*

64 Oh, that you would rend the
    heavens and come down,
  that the mountains would tremble
    before you!
²As when fire sets twigs ablaze
  and causes water to boil,
come down to make your name known
    to your enemies
  and cause the nations to quake before
    you!
³For when you did awesome things that
    we did not expect,
  you came down, and the mountains
    trembled before you.
⁴Since ancient times no one has heard,
  no ear has perceived,
no eye has seen any God besides you,
  who acts on behalf of those who wait
    for him.
⁵You come to the help of those who
    gladly do right,
  who remember your ways.
But when we continued to sin against
    them,
  you were angry.
How then can we be saved?
⁶All of us have become like one who is
    unclean,
  and all our righteous acts are like
    filthy rags;
we all shrivel up like a leaf,
  and like the wind our sins sweep us
    away.
⁷No one calls on your name
  or strives to lay hold of you;
for you have hidden your face from us
  and made us waste away because of
    our sins.

⁸Yet, O LORD, you are our Father.
  We are the clay, you are the potter;
  we are all the work of your hand.
⁹Do not be angry beyond measure,
    O LORD;
  do not remember our sins forever.
Oh, look upon us, we pray,
  for we are all your people.
¹⁰Your sacred cities have become a
    desert;
  even Zion is a desert, Jerusalem a
    desolation.

a11 Or *But may he recall*   *b19* Or *We are like those you have never ruled, / like those never called by your
name*

¹¹Our holy and glorious temple, where
        our fathers praised you,
    has been burned with fire,
    and all that we treasured lies in ruins.
¹²After all this, O Lord, will you hold
        yourself back?
    Will you keep silent and punish us
        beyond measure?

Judgment and Salvation

65 "I revealed myself to those who
        did not ask for me;
    I was found by those who did not
        seek me.
    To a nation that did not call on my
        name,
    I said, 'Here am I, here am I.'
²All day long I have held out my hands
    to an obstinate people,
    who walk in ways not good,
        pursuing their own imaginations—
³a people who continually provoke me
    to my very face,
    offering sacrifices in gardens
        and burning incense on altars of
        brick;
⁴who sit among the graves
    and spend their nights keeping secret
        vigil;
    who eat the flesh of pigs,
        and whose pots hold broth of unclean
        meat;
⁵who say, 'Keep away; don't come near
        me,
    for I am too sacred for you!'
    Such people are smoke in my nostrils,
    a fire that keeps burning all day.

⁶"See, it stands written before me:
    I will not keep silent but will pay back
        in full;
    I will pay it back into their laps—
⁷both your sins and the sins of your
        fathers,"
    says the Lord.
    "Because they burned sacrifices on the
        mountains
    and defied me on the hills,
    I will measure into their laps
    the full payment for their former
        deeds."

⁸This is what the Lord says:

"As when juice is still found in a cluster
        of grapes
    and men say, 'Don't destroy it,
    there is yet some good in it,'
    so will I do in behalf of my servants;
    I will not destroy them all.

⁹I will bring forth descendants from
        Jacob,
    and from Judah those who will
        possess my mountains;
    my chosen people will inherit them,
    and there will my servants live.
¹⁰Sharon will become a pasture for flocks,
    and the Valley of Achor a resting
        place for herds,
    for my people who seek me.

¹¹"But as for you who forsake the Lord
    and forget my holy mountain,
    who spread a table for Fortune
    and fill bowls of mixed wine for
        Destiny,
¹²I will destine you for the sword,
    and you will all bend down for the
        slaughter;
    for I called but you did not answer,
    I spoke but you did not listen.
    You did evil in my sight
    and chose what displeases me."

¹³Therefore this is what the Sovereign
Lord says:

"My servants will eat,
    but you will go hungry;
    my servants will drink,
    but you will go thirsty;
    my servants will rejoice,
    but you will be put to shame.
¹⁴My servants will sing
    out of the joy of their hearts,
    but you will cry out
    from anguish of heart
    and wail in brokenness of spirit.
¹⁵You will leave your name
    to my chosen ones as a curse;
    the Sovereign Lord will put you to
        death,
    but to his servants he will give
        another name.
¹⁶Whoever invokes a blessing in the land
    will do so by the God of truth;
    he who takes an oath in the land
    will swear by the God of truth.
    For the past troubles will be forgotten
    and hidden from my eyes.

New Heavens and a New Earth

¹⁷"Behold, I will create
    new heavens and a new earth.
    The former things will not be
        remembered,
    nor will they come to mind.
¹⁸But be glad and rejoice forever
    in what I will create,

for I will create Jerusalem to be a
delight
and its people a joy.
¹⁹I will rejoice over Jerusalem
and take delight in my people;
the sound of weeping and of crying
will be heard in it no more.

²⁰"Never again will there be in it
an infant who lives but a few days,
or an old man who does not live out
his years;
he who dies at a hundred
will be thought a mere youth;
he who fails to reach^a a hundred
will be considered accursed.
²¹They will build houses and dwell in
them;
they will plant vineyards and eat their
fruit.
²²No longer will they build houses and
others live in them,
or plant and others eat.
For as the days of a tree,
so will be the days of my people;
my chosen ones will long enjoy
the works of their hands.
²³They will not toil in vain
or bear children doomed to
misfortune;
for they will be a people blessed by the
Lord,
they and their descendants with
them.
²⁴Before they call I will answer;
while they are still speaking I will
hear.
²⁵The wolf and the lamb will feed
together,
and the lion will eat straw like the ox,
but dust will be the serpent's food.
They will neither harm nor destroy
on all my holy mountain,"
says the Lord.

Judgment and Hope

66 This is what the Lord says:

"Heaven is my throne,
and the earth is my footstool.
Where is the house you will build for
me?
Where will my resting place be?
²Has not my hand made all these things,
and so they came into being?"
declares the Lord.

"This is the one I esteem:

he who is humble and contrite in
spirit,
and trembles at my word.
³But whoever sacrifices a bull
is like one who kills a man,
and whoever offers a lamb,
like one who breaks a dog's neck;
whoever makes a grain offering
is like one who presents pig's blood,
and whoever burns memorial incense,
like one who worships an idol.
They have chosen their own ways,
and their souls delight in their
abominations;
⁴so I also will choose harsh treatment for
them
and will bring upon them what they
dread.
For when I called, no one answered,
when I spoke, no one listened.
They did evil in my sight
and chose what displeases me."

⁵Hear the word of the Lord,
you who tremble at his word:
"Your brothers who hate you,
and exclude you because of my
name, have said,
'Let the Lord be glorified,
that we may see your joy!'
Yet they will be put to shame.
⁶Hear that uproar from the city,
hear that noise from the temple!
It is the sound of the Lord
repaying his enemies all they deserve.

⁷"Before she goes into labor,
she gives birth;
before the pains come upon her,
she delivers a son.
⁸Who has ever heard of such a thing?
Who has ever seen such things?
Can a country be born in a day
or a nation be brought forth in a
moment?
Yet no sooner is Zion in labor
than she gives birth to her children.
⁹Do I bring to the moment of birth
and not give delivery?" says the Lord.
"Do I close up the womb
when I bring to delivery?" says your
God.
¹⁰"Rejoice with Jerusalem and be glad for
her,
all you who love her;
rejoice greatly with her,
all you who mourn over her.
¹¹For you will nurse and be satisfied

---

^a20 Or / the sinner who reaches

at her comforting breasts;
you will drink deeply
　and delight in her overflowing
　　abundance."

12For this is what the LORD says:

"I will extend peace to her like a river,
　and the wealth of nations like a
　　flooding stream;
you will nurse and be carried on her
　arm
and dandled on her knees.
13As a mother comforts her child,
　so will I comfort you;
and you will be comforted over
　Jerusalem."

14When you see this, your heart will
　rejoice
and you will flourish like grass;
the hand of the LORD will be made
　known to his servants,
but his fury will be shown to his foes.
15See, the LORD is coming with fire,
　and his chariots are like a whirlwind;
he will bring down his anger with fury,
　and his rebuke with flames of fire.
16For with fire and with his sword
　the LORD will execute judgment upon
　　all men,
and many will be those slain by the
　LORD.

17"Those who consecrate and purify
themselves to go into the gardens, following
the one in the midst of[a] those who eat the
flesh of pigs and rats and other abominable
things — they will meet their end together,"
declares the LORD.

18"And I, because of their actions and
their imaginations, am about to come[b] and
gather all nations and tongues, and they will
come and see my glory.

19"I will set a sign among them, and I will
send some of those who survive to the nations — to Tarshish, to the Libyans[c] and
Lydians (famous as archers), to Tubal and
Greece, and to the distant islands that have
not heard of my fame or seen my glory.
They will proclaim my glory among the nations. **20**And they will bring all your brothers, from all the nations, to my holy mountain in Jerusalem as an offering to the
LORD — on horses, in chariots and wagons,
and on mules and camels," says the LORD.
"They will bring them, as the Israelites bring
their grain offerings, to the temple of the
LORD in ceremonially clean vessels. **21**And I
will select some of them also to be priests
and Levites," says the LORD.

22"As the new heavens and the new earth
that I make will endure before me," declares
the LORD, "so will your name and descendants endure. **23**From one New Moon to another and from one Sabbath to another, all
mankind will come and bow down before
me," says the LORD. **24**"And they will go out
and look upon the dead bodies of those who
rebelled against me; their worm will not die,
nor will their fire be quenched, and they will
be loathsome to all mankind."

---

a17 Or *gardens behind one of your temples, and*　　*b18* The meaning of the Hebrew for this clause is
uncertain.　　*c19* Some Septuagint manuscripts *Put* (Libyans); Hebrew *Pul*

JEREMIAH sees it coming. Babylon will conquer Judah unless the people repent. So Jeremiah preaches, weeps, and preaches some more. But Judah's moral decay is deep and deadly. The self-satisfied people respond by imprisoning Jeremiah and ignoring his pleas. But turning a deaf ear to God's Word doesn't keep it from taking effect. The Babylonian army arrives, and the ax of vengeance falls. As you read Jeremiah consider any sins in your own life that are revealed by God's Word. Don't close the book; you have much to gain by reading the words of this prophet.

Outline of Contents

1 The words of Jeremiah son of Hilkiah, one of the priests at Anathoth in the territory of Benjamin. ²The word of the LORD came to him in the thirteenth year of the reign of Josiah son of Amon king of Judah, ³and through the reign of Jehoiakim son of Josiah king of Judah, down to the fifth month of the eleventh year of Zedekiah son of Josiah king of Judah, when the people of Jerusalem went into exile.

The Call of Jeremiah

⁴The word of the LORD came to me, saying,

⁵"Before I formed you in the womb I
    knew[a] you,
  before you were born I set you apart;
  I appointed you as a prophet to the
    nations."

⁶"Ah, Sovereign LORD," I said, "I do not know how to speak; I am only a child."

⁷But the LORD said to me, "Do not say, 'I am only a child.' You must go to everyone I send you to and say whatever I command you. ⁸Do not be afraid of them, for I am with you and will rescue you," declares the LORD. ⁹Then the LORD reached out his hand and

---

THE LOUSY REASONS OF HELEN STEPHENS

Every time her Bible study leader asks her to do something—it doesn't matter what—Helen comes up with some excuse for not helping out.

"I'd like to, Mrs. Miley. I'm not kidding. It's just that I've never spoken to a group that size before. I just don't feel capable."

"Who's gonna listen to me? Those girls dress really nice and live near the country club. My dad is a cop, and we live in a run-down apartment!"

"Do you think an inner-city outreach like that would be safe?"

The reasons are always different, but the answer is always the same: No.

Look It Up
••••

One by one, the Bible shoots down the excuses you and others give for neglecting your responsibilities as Christians:

"I'm not qualified"—See Exodus 4:10–16.

"I'm nobody"—" 'But Lord,' Gideon asked, 'how can I save Israel? My clan is the weakest in Manasseh, and I am the least in my family.' The LORD answered, 'I will be with you' " (Judges 6:15–16).

"It's too risky"—"The sluggard says, 'There is a lion outside!' or, 'I will be murdered in the streets!' " (Proverbs 22:13).

Think It Through
••••

If you don't feel qualified to perform some type of Christian service, remember this: The God of the universe promises not only to be with you but also to give you the power to succeed. You may be weak, but he is strong!

Work It Out
••••

If you're overinvolved in Christian activity (Bible study, ministry to others, etc.) because you can never say no, your assignment today is to relax. Seriously, take a break! Spend a few minutes with God looking over your schedule and evaluating your priorities. Maybe you need to cut back.

If, on the other hand, you're underinvolved because you always make excuses and say no, you need to take on a responsibility today. Sign up to be on a ministry team in your youth group. Volunteer to help with outreach. Commit to working with the elderly or with younger kids. Remember: There's no excuse for a Christian to sit around and do nothing.

Nail It Down
••••

Read God's response to Jeremiah in Jeremiah 1:6–7.

Turn to pages 239 and 288 for other readings on excuses.
Turn to page 796 for Friday's reading.

Topic
••••

EXCUSES

touched my mouth and said to me, "Now, I have put my words in your mouth. [10]See, today I appoint you over nations and kingdoms to uproot and tear down, to destroy and overthrow, to build and to plant."

[11]The word of the LORD came to me: "What do you see, Jeremiah?"

"I see the branch of an almond tree," I replied.

[12]The LORD said to me, "You have seen correctly, for I am watching[a] to see that my word is fulfilled."

[13]The word of the LORD came to me again: "What do you see?"

"I see a boiling pot, tilting away from the north," I answered.

[14]The LORD said to me, "From the north disaster will be poured out on all who live in the land. [15]I am about to summon all the peoples of the northern kingdoms," declares the LORD.

"Their kings will come and set up their
    thrones
  in the entrance of the gates of
    Jerusalem;
they will come against all her
    surrounding walls
  and against all the towns of Judah.
[16]I will pronounce my judgments on my
    people
because of their wickedness in
    forsaking me,
in burning incense to other gods
  and in worshiping what their hands
    have made.

[17]"Get yourself ready! Stand up and say to them whatever I command you. Do not be terrified by them, or I will terrify you before them. [18]Today I have made you a fortified city, an iron pillar and a bronze wall to stand against the whole land — against the kings of Judah, its officials, its priests and the people of the land. [19]They will fight against you but will not overcome you, for I am with you and will rescue you," declares the LORD.

Israel Forsakes God

2 The word of the LORD came to me: [2]"Go and proclaim in the hearing of Jerusalem:

" 'I remember the devotion of your
    youth,
  how as a bride you loved me
and followed me through the desert,

through a land not sown.
[3]Israel was holy to the LORD,
  the firstfruits of his harvest;
all who devoured her were held guilty,
  and disaster overtook them,' "
                declares the LORD.

[4]Hear the word of the LORD, O house of
    Jacob,
  all you clans of the house of Israel.

[5]This is what the LORD says:

"What fault did your fathers find in me,
  that they strayed so far from me?
They followed worthless idols
  and became worthless themselves.
[6]They did not ask, 'Where is the LORD,
  who brought us up out of Egypt
and led us through the barren
    wilderness,
  through a land of deserts and rifts,
a land of drought and darkness,[b]
  a land where no one travels and no
    one lives?'
[7]I brought you into a fertile land
  to eat its fruit and rich produce.
But you came and defiled my land
  and made my inheritance detestable.
[8]The priests did not ask,
  'Where is the LORD?'
Those who deal with the law did not
    know me;
  the leaders rebelled against me.
The prophets prophesied by Baal,
  following worthless idols.

[9]"Therefore I bring charges against you
    again,"
                declares the LORD.
"And I will bring charges against your
    children's children.
[10]Cross over to the coasts of Kittim[c] and
    look,
  send to Kedar[d] and observe closely;
  see if there has ever been anything
    like this:
[11]Has a nation ever changed its gods?
  (Yet they are not gods at all.)
But my people have exchanged their[e]
    Glory
  for worthless idols.
[12]Be appalled at this, O heavens,
  and shudder with great horror,"
                declares the LORD.
[13]"My people have committed two sins:
  They have forsaken me,

---

[a]12 The Hebrew for *watching* sounds like the Hebrew for *almond tree*.   [b]6 Or *and the shadow of death*
[c]10 That is, Cyprus and western coastlands   [d]10 The home of Bedouin tribes in the Syro-Arabian desert
[e]11 Masoretic Text; an ancient Hebrew scribal tradition *my*

the spring of living water,
and have dug their own cisterns,
    broken cisterns that cannot hold
        water.
¹⁴Is Israel a servant, a slave by birth?
    Why then has he become plunder?
¹⁵Lions have roared;
    they have growled at him.
They have laid waste his land;
    his towns are burned and deserted.
¹⁶Also, the men of Memphis*ᵃ* and
        Tahpanhes
    have shaved the crown of your
        head.ᵇ
¹⁷Have you not brought this on yourselves
    by forsaking the Lᴏʀᴅ your God
    when he led you in the way?
¹⁸Now why go to Egypt
    to drink water from the Shihorᶜ?
And why go to Assyria
    to drink water from the Riverᵈ?
¹⁹Your wickedness will punish you;
    your backsliding will rebuke you.
Consider then and realize
    how evil and bitter it is for you
when you forsake the Lᴏʀᴅ your God
    and have no awe of me,"

                        declares the Lord,
                        the Lᴏʀᴅ Almighty.

²⁰"Long ago you broke off your yoke
    and tore off your bonds;
    you said, 'I will not serve you!'
Indeed, on every high hill
    and under every spreading tree
    you lay down as a prostitute.
²¹I had planted you like a choice vine
    of sound and reliable stock.
How then did you turn against me
    into a corrupt, wild vine?
²²Although you wash yourself with soda
    and use an abundance of soap,
    the stain of your guilt is still before
        me,"
                        declares the Sovereign Lᴏʀᴅ.
²³"How can you say, 'I am not defiled;
    I have not run after the Baals'?
See how you behaved in the valley;
    consider what you have done.
You are a swift she-camel
    running here and there,
²⁴a wild donkey accustomed to the desert,
    sniffing the wind in her craving—
    in her heat who can restrain her?
Any males that pursue her need not tire
        themselves;

at mating time they will find her.
²⁵Do not run until your feet are bare
    and your throat is dry.
But you said, 'It's no use!
    I love foreign gods,
    and I must go after them.'

²⁶"As a thief is disgraced when he is
        caught,
    so the house of Israel is disgraced—
they, their kings and their officials,
    their priests and their prophets.
²⁷They say to wood, 'You are my father,'
    and to stone, 'You gave me birth.'
They have turned their backs to me
    and not their faces;
yet when they are in trouble, they say,
    'Come and save us!'
²⁸Where then are the gods you made for
        yourselves?
    Let them come if they can save you
    when you are in trouble!
For you have as many gods
    as you have towns, O Judah.

²⁹"Why do you bring charges against me?
    You have all rebelled against me,"
                        declares the Lᴏʀᴅ.
³⁰"In vain I punished your people;
    they did not respond to correction.
Your sword has devoured your prophets
    like a ravening lion.

³¹"You of this generation, consider the
word of the Lᴏʀᴅ:

"Have I been a desert to Israel
    or a land of great darkness?
Why do my people say, 'We are free to
        roam;
    we will come to you no more'?
³²Does a maiden forget her jewelry,
    a bride her wedding ornaments?
Yet my people have forgotten me,
    days without number.
³³How skilled you are at pursuing love!
    Even the worst of women can learn
        from your ways.
³⁴On your clothes men find
    the lifeblood of the innocent poor,
    though you did not catch them
        breaking in.
Yet in spite of all this
³⁵   you say, 'I am innocent;
    he is not angry with me.'
But I will pass judgment on you
    because you say, 'I have not sinned.'
³⁶Why do you go about so much,

ᵃ16 Hebrew *Noph*   *ᵇ16* Or *have cracked your skull*   *ᶜ18* That is, a branch of the Nile   *ᵈ18* That is, the
Euphrates

changing your ways?
You will be disappointed by Egypt
    as you were by Assyria.
37You will also leave that place
    with your hands on your head,
for the LORD has rejected those you
        trust;
    you will not be helped by them.

3 "If a man divorces his wife
    and she leaves him and marries
        another man,
should he return to her again?
    Would not the land be completely
        defiled?
But you have lived as a prostitute with
        many lovers —
    would you now return to me?"
                        declares the LORD.
2"Look up to the barren heights and see.
    Is there any place where you have not
        been ravished?
By the roadside you sat waiting for
        lovers,
    sat like a nomad*a* in the desert.
You have defiled the land
    with your prostitution and
        wickedness.
3Therefore the showers have been
        withheld,
    and no spring rains have fallen.
Yet you have the brazen look of a
        prostitute;
    you refuse to blush with shame.
4Have you not just called to me:
    'My Father, my friend from my youth,
5will you always be angry?
    Will your wrath continue forever?'
This is how you talk,
    but you do all the evil you can."

Unfaithful Israel

6During the reign of King Josiah, the LORD
said to me, "Have you seen what faithless
Israel has done? She has gone up on every
high hill and under every spreading tree and
has committed adultery there. **7**I thought
that after she had done all this she would
return to me but she did not, and her unfaithful sister Judah saw it. **8**I gave faithless
Israel her certificate of divorce and sent her
away because of all her adulteries. Yet I saw
that her unfaithful sister Judah had no fear;
she also went out and committed adultery.
9Because Israel's immorality mattered so little to her, she defiled the land and committed adultery with stone and wood. **10**In spite

of all this, her unfaithful sister Judah did not
return to me with all her heart, but only in
pretense," declares the LORD.

11The LORD said to me, "Faithless Israel is
more righteous than unfaithful Judah. **12**Go,
proclaim this message toward the north:

" 'Return, faithless Israel,' declares the
        LORD,
    'I will frown on you no longer,
for I am merciful,' declares the LORD,
    'I will not be angry forever.
13Only acknowledge your guilt —
    you have rebelled against the LORD
        your God,
you have scattered your favors to
        foreign gods
    under every spreading tree,
    and have not obeyed me,' "
                        declares the LORD.

14"Return, faithless people," declares the
LORD, "for I am your husband. I will choose
you — one from a town and two from a
clan — and bring you to Zion. **15**Then I will
give you shepherds after my own heart, who
will lead you with knowledge and understanding. **16**In those days, when your numbers have increased greatly in the land," declares the LORD, "men will no longer say,
'The ark of the covenant of the LORD.' It will
never enter their minds or be remembered;
it will not be missed, nor will another one be
made. **17**At that time they will call Jerusalem
The Throne of the LORD, and all nations will
gather in Jerusalem to honor the name of
the LORD. No longer will they follow the stubbornness of their evil hearts. **18**In those days
the house of Judah will join the house of Israel, and together they will come from a
northern land to the land I gave your forefathers as an inheritance.

19"I myself said,

" 'How gladly would I treat you like sons
    and give you a desirable land,
    the most beautiful inheritance of any
        nation.'
I thought you would call me 'Father'
    and not turn away from following me.
20But like a woman unfaithful to her
        husband,
    so you have been unfaithful to me,
    O house of Israel,"
                        declares the LORD.

21A cry is heard on the barren heights,
    the weeping and pleading of the
        people of Israel,

a2 Or an Arab

because they have perverted their ways
    and have forgotten the LORD their God.

22"Return, faithless people;
    I will cure you of backsliding."

"Yes, we will come to you,
    for you are the LORD our God.
23Surely the ¡idolatrous¡ commotion on the hills
    and mountains is a deception;
surely in the LORD our God
    is the salvation of Israel.
24From our youth shameful gods have consumed
    the fruits of our fathers' labor—
their flocks and herds,
    their sons and daughters.
25Let us lie down in our shame,
    and let our disgrace cover us.
We have sinned against the LORD our God,
    both we and our fathers;
from our youth till this day
    we have not obeyed the LORD our God."

4 "If you will return, O Israel,
    return to me,"
                        declares the LORD.
"If you put your detestable idols out of my sight
    and no longer go astray,
2and if in a truthful, just and righteous way
    you swear, 'As surely as the LORD lives,'
then the nations will be blessed by him
    and in him they will glory."

3This is what the LORD says to the men of Judah and to Jerusalem:

"Break up your unplowed ground
    and do not sow among thorns.
4Circumcise yourselves to the LORD,
    circumcise your hearts,
    you men of Judah and people of Jerusalem,
or my wrath will break out and burn like fire
    because of the evil you have done—
    burn with no one to quench it.

Disaster From the North

5"Announce in Judah and proclaim in Jerusalem and say:
    'Sound the trumpet throughout the land!'

Cry aloud and say:
    'Gather together!
Let us flee to the fortified cities!'
6Raise the signal to go to Zion!
    Flee for safety without delay!
For I am bringing disaster from the north,
    even terrible destruction."

7A lion has come out of his lair;
    a destroyer of nations has set out.
He has left his place
    to lay waste your land.
Your towns will lie in ruins
    without inhabitant.
8So put on sackcloth,
    lament and wail,
for the fierce anger of the LORD
    has not turned away from us.

9"In that day," declares the LORD,
    "the king and the officials will lose heart,
the priests will be horrified,
    and the prophets will be appalled."

10Then I said, "Ah, Sovereign LORD, how completely you have deceived this people and Jerusalem by saying, 'You will have peace,' when the sword is at our throats."

11At that time this people and Jerusalem will be told, "A scorching wind from the barren heights in the desert blows toward my people, but not to winnow or cleanse; 12a wind too strong for that comes from me.[a] Now I pronounce my judgments against them."

13Look! He advances like the clouds,
    his chariots come like a whirlwind,
    his horses are swifter than eagles.
    Woe to us! We are ruined!
14O Jerusalem, wash the evil from your heart and be saved.
    How long will you harbor wicked thoughts?
15A voice is announcing from Dan,
    proclaiming disaster from the hills of Ephraim.
16"Tell this to the nations,
    proclaim it to Jerusalem:
'A besieging army is coming from a distant land,
    raising a war cry against the cities of Judah.
17They surround her like men guarding a field,
    because she has rebelled against me,' "
                        declares the LORD.

a12 Or comes at my command

18"Your own conduct and actions
    have brought this upon you.
This is your punishment.
    How bitter it is!
    How it pierces to the heart!"

19Oh, my anguish, my anguish!
    I writhe in pain.
Oh, the agony of my heart!
    My heart pounds within me,
    I cannot keep silent.
For I have heard the sound of the
    trumpet;
    I have heard the battle cry.
20Disaster follows disaster;
    the whole land lies in ruins.
In an instant my tents are destroyed,
    my shelter in a moment.
21How long must I see the battle standard
    and hear the sound of the trumpet?

22"My people are fools;
    they do not know me.
They are senseless children;
    they have no understanding.
They are skilled in doing evil;
    they know not how to do good."

23I looked at the earth,
    and it was formless and empty;
and at the heavens,
    and their light was gone.
24I looked at the mountains,
    and they were quaking;
    all the hills were swaying.
25I looked, and there were no people;
    every bird in the sky had flown away.
26I looked, and the fruitful land was a
    desert;
    all its towns lay in ruins
before the LORD, before his fierce
    anger.

27This is what the LORD says:

"The whole land will be ruined,
    though I will not destroy it
    completely.
28Therefore the earth will mourn
    and the heavens above grow dark,
because I have spoken and will not
    relent,
    I have decided and will not turn
    back."

29At the sound of horsemen and archers
    every town takes to flight.
Some go into the thickets;
    some climb up among the rocks.
All the towns are deserted;
    no one lives in them.

30What are you doing, O devastated one?
    Why dress yourself in scarlet
    and put on jewels of gold?
Why shade your eyes with paint?
    You adorn yourself in vain.
Your lovers despise you;
    they seek your life.

31I hear a cry as of a woman in labor,
    a groan as of one bearing her first
    child—
the cry of the Daughter of Zion gasping
    for breath,
    stretching out her hands and saying,
"Alas! I am fainting;
    my life is given over to murderers."

Not One Is Upright

5 "Go up and down the streets of
    Jerusalem,
look around and consider,
    search through her squares.
If you can find but one person
    who deals honestly and seeks the
    truth,
    I will forgive this city.
2Although they say, 'As surely as the
    LORD lives,'
    still they are swearing falsely."

3O LORD, do not your eyes look for truth?
    You struck them, but they felt no
    pain;
    you crushed them, but they refused
    correction.
They made their faces harder than
    stone
    and refused to repent.
4I thought, "These are only the poor;
    they are foolish,
for they do not know the way of the
    LORD,
    the requirements of their God.
5So I will go to the leaders
    and speak to them;
surely they know the way of the LORD,
    the requirements of their God."
But with one accord they too had
    broken off the yoke
    and torn off the bonds.
6Therefore a lion from the forest will
    attack them,
    a wolf from the desert will ravage
    them,
a leopard will lie in wait near their
    towns
    to tear to pieces any who venture out,
for their rebellion is great
    and their backslidings many.

7"Why should I forgive you?
  Your children have forsaken me
  and sworn by gods that are not gods.
I supplied all their needs,
  yet they committed adultery
  and thronged to the houses of
    prostitutes.
8They are well-fed, lusty stallions,
  each neighing for another man's wife.
9Should I not punish them for this?"
  declares the LORD.
"Should I not avenge myself
  on such a nation as this?

10"Go through her vineyards and ravage
    them,
  but do not destroy them completely.
Strip off her branches,
  for these people do not belong to the
    LORD.
11The house of Israel and the house of
    Judah
  have been utterly unfaithful to me,"
                    declares the LORD.

12They have lied about the LORD;
  they said, "He will do nothing!
No harm will come to us;
  we will never see sword or famine.
13The prophets are but wind
  and the word is not in them;
  so let what they say be done to
    them."

14Therefore this is what the LORD God Almighty says:

"Because the people have spoken these
    words,
  I will make my words in your mouth
    a fire
  and these people the wood it
    consumes.
15O house of Israel," declares the LORD,
"I am bringing a distant nation against
    you—
an ancient and enduring nation,
  a people whose language you do not
    know,
  whose speech you do not understand.
16Their quivers are like an open grave;
  all of them are mighty warriors.
17They will devour your harvests and
    food,
  devour your sons and daughters;
they will devour your flocks and herds,
  devour your vines and fig trees.
With the sword they will destroy
  the fortified cities in which you trust.

18"Yet even in those days," declares the
LORD, "I will not destroy you completely.
19And when the people ask, 'Why has the
LORD our God done all this to us?' you will tell
them, 'As you have forsaken me and served
foreign gods in your own land, so now you
will serve foreigners in a land not your own.'

20"Announce this to the house of Jacob
  and proclaim it in Judah:
21Hear this, you foolish and senseless
    people,
  who have eyes but do not see,
  who have ears but do not hear:
22Should you not fear me?" declares the
    LORD.
  "Should you not tremble in my
    presence?
I made the sand a boundary for the sea,
  an everlasting barrier it cannot cross.
The waves may roll, but they cannot
    prevail;
  they may roar, but they cannot cross
    it.
23But these people have stubborn and
    rebellious hearts;
  they have turned aside and gone
    away.
24They do not say to themselves,
  'Let us fear the LORD our God,
who gives autumn and spring rains in
    season,
  who assures us of the regular weeks
    of harvest.'
25Your wrongdoings have kept these
    away;
  your sins have deprived you of good.

26"Among my people are wicked men
  who lie in wait like men who snare
    birds
  and like those who set traps to catch
    men.
27Like cages full of birds,
  their houses are full of deceit;
they have become rich and powerful
28 and have grown fat and sleek.
  Their evil deeds have no limit;
  they do not plead the case of the
    fatherless to win it,
  they do not defend the rights of the
    poor.
29Should I not punish them for this?"
  declares the LORD.
"Should I not avenge myself
  on such a nation as this?

30"A horrible and shocking thing
  has happened in the land:
31The prophets prophesy lies,

the priests rule by their own
authority,
and my people love it this way.
But what will you do in the end?

Jerusalem Under Siege

6 "Flee for safety, people of Benjamin!
Flee from Jerusalem!
Sound the trumpet in Tekoa!
Raise the signal over Beth Hakkerem!
For disaster looms out of the north,
even terrible destruction.
²I will destroy the Daughter of Zion,
so beautiful and delicate.
³Shepherds with their flocks will come
against her;
they will pitch their tents around her,
each tending his own portion."

⁴"Prepare for battle against her!
Arise, let us attack at noon!
But, alas, the daylight is fading,
and the shadows of evening grow
long.
⁵So arise, let us attack at night
and destroy her fortresses!"

⁶This is what the LORD Almighty says:

"Cut down the trees
and build siege ramps against
Jerusalem.
This city must be punished;
it is filled with oppression.
⁷As a well pours out its water,
so she pours out her wickedness.
Violence and destruction resound in
her;
her sickness and wounds are ever
before me.
⁸Take warning, O Jerusalem,
or I will turn away from you
and make your land desolate
so no one can live in it."

⁹This is what the LORD Almighty says:

"Let them glean the remnant of Israel
as thoroughly as a vine;
pass your hand over the branches again,
like one gathering grapes."

¹⁰To whom can I speak and give warning?
Who will listen to me?
Their ears are closed[a]
so they cannot hear.
The word of the LORD is offensive to
them;
they find no pleasure in it.
¹¹But I am full of the wrath of the LORD,
and I cannot hold it in.

"Pour it out on the children in the street
and on the young men gathered
together;
both husband and wife will be caught in
it,
and the old, those weighed down with
years.
¹²Their houses will be turned over to
others,
together with their fields and their
wives,
when I stretch out my hand
against those who live in the land,"
declares the LORD.
¹³"From the least to the greatest,
all are greedy for gain;
prophets and priests alike,
all practice deceit.
¹⁴They dress the wound of my people
as though it were not serious.
'Peace, peace,' they say,
when there is no peace.
¹⁵Are they ashamed of their loathsome
conduct?
No, they have no shame at all;
they do not even know how to blush.
So they will fall among the fallen;
they will be brought down when I
punish them,"
says the LORD.

¹⁶This is what the LORD says:

"Stand at the crossroads and look;
ask for the ancient paths,
ask where the good way is, and walk in
it,
and you will find rest for your souls.
But you said, 'We will not walk in it.'
¹⁷I appointed watchmen over you and
said,
'Listen to the sound of the trumpet!'
But you said, 'We will not listen.'
¹⁸Therefore hear, O nations;
observe, O witnesses,
what will happen to them.
¹⁹Hear, O earth:
I am bringing disaster on this people,
the fruit of their schemes,
because they have not listened to my
words
and have rejected my law.
²⁰What do I care about incense from
Sheba
or sweet calamus from a distant land?
Your burnt offerings are not acceptable;

---

a 10 Hebrew *uncircumcised*

your sacrifices do not please me."

²¹Therefore this is what the LORD says:

"I will put obstacles before this people.
Fathers and sons alike will stumble
over them;
neighbors and friends will perish."

²²This is what the LORD says:

"Look, an army is coming
from the land of the north;
a great nation is being stirred up
from the ends of the earth.
²³They are armed with bow and spear;
they are cruel and show no mercy.
They sound like the roaring sea
as they ride on their horses;
they come like men in battle formation
to attack you, O Daughter of Zion."

²⁴We have heard reports about them,
and our hands hang limp.
Anguish has gripped us,
pain like that of a woman in labor.
²⁵Do not go out to the fields
or walk on the roads,
for the enemy has a sword,
and there is terror on every side.
²⁶O my people, put on sackcloth
and roll in ashes;
mourn with bitter wailing
as for an only son,
for suddenly the destroyer
will come upon us.

²⁷"I have made you a tester of metals
and my people the ore,
that you may observe
and test their ways.
²⁸They are all hardened rebels,
going about to slander.
They are bronze and iron;
they all act corruptly.
²⁹The bellows blow fiercely
to burn away the lead with fire,
but the refining goes on in vain;
the wicked are not purged out.
³⁰They are called rejected silver,
because the LORD has rejected them."

False Religion Worthless

7 This is the word that came to Jeremiah from the LORD: ²"Stand at the gate of the LORD's house and there proclaim this message:

" 'Hear the word of the LORD, all you people of Judah who come through these gates to worship the LORD. ³This is what the LORD Almighty, the God of Israel, says: Reform your ways and your actions, and I will let you live in this place. ⁴Do not trust in deceptive words and say, "This is the temple of the LORD, the temple of the LORD, the temple of the LORD!" ⁵If you really change your ways and your actions and deal with each other justly, ⁶if you do not oppress the alien, the fatherless or the widow and do not shed innocent blood in this place, and if you do not follow other gods to your own harm, ⁷then I will let you live in this place, in the land I gave your forefathers for ever and ever. ⁸But look, you are trusting in deceptive words that are worthless.

⁹" 'Will you steal and murder, commit adultery and perjury,ᵃ burn incense to Baal and follow other gods you have not known, ¹⁰and then come and stand before me in this house, which bears my Name, and say, "We are safe"—safe to do all these detestable things? ¹¹Has this house, which bears my Name, become a den of robbers to you? But I have been watching! declares the LORD.

¹²" 'Go now to the place in Shiloh where I first made a dwelling for my Name, and see what I did to it because of the wickedness of my people Israel. ¹³While you were doing all these things, declares the LORD, I spoke to you again and again, but you did not listen; I called you, but you did not answer. ¹⁴Therefore, what I did to Shiloh I will now do to the house that bears my Name, the temple you trust in, the place I gave to you and your fathers. ¹⁵I will thrust you from my presence, just as I did all your brothers, the people of Ephraim.'

¹⁶"So do not pray for this people nor offer any plea or petition for them; do not plead with me, for I will not listen to you. ¹⁷Do you not see what they are doing in the towns of Judah and in the streets of Jerusalem? ¹⁸The children gather wood, the fathers light the fire, and the women knead the dough and make cakes of bread for the Queen of Heaven. They pour out drink offerings to other gods to provoke me to anger. ¹⁹But am I the one they are provoking? declares the LORD. Are they not rather harming themselves, to their own shame?

²⁰" 'Therefore this is what the Sovereign LORD says: My anger and my wrath will be poured out on this place, on man and beast, on the trees of the field and on the fruit of the ground, and it will burn and not be quenched.

²¹" 'This is what the LORD Almighty, the

ᵃ9 Or and swear by false gods

God of Israel, says: Go ahead, add your burnt offerings to your other sacrifices and eat the meat yourselves! **22**For when I brought your forefathers out of Egypt and spoke to them, I did not just give them commands about burnt offerings and sacrifices, **23**but I gave them this command: Obey me, and I will be your God and you will be my people. Walk in all the ways I command you, that it may go well with you. **24**But they did not listen or pay attention; instead, they followed the stubborn inclinations of their evil hearts. They went backward and not forward. **25**From the time your forefathers left Egypt until now, day after day, again and again I sent you my servants the prophets. **26**But they did not listen to me or pay attention. They were stiff-necked and did more evil than their forefathers.'

27"When you tell them all this, they will not listen to you; when you call to them, they will not answer. **28**Therefore say to them, 'This is the nation that has not obeyed the LORD its God or responded to correction. Truth has perished; it has vanished from their lips. **29**Cut off your hair and throw it away; take up a lament on the barren heights, for the LORD has rejected and abandoned this generation that is under his wrath.

The Valley of Slaughter

30" 'The people of Judah have done evil in my eyes, declares the LORD. They have set up their detestable idols in the house that bears my Name and have defiled it. **31**They have built the high places of Topheth in the Valley of Ben Hinnom to burn their sons and daughters in the fire — something I did not command, nor did it enter my mind. **32**So beware, the days are coming, declares the LORD, when people will no longer call it Topheth or the Valley of Ben Hinnom, but the Valley of Slaughter, for they will bury the dead in Topheth until there is no more room. **33**Then the carcasses of this people will become food for the birds of the air and the beasts of the earth, and there will be no one to frighten them away. **34**I will bring an end to the sounds of joy and gladness and to the voices of bride and bridegroom in the towns of Judah and the streets of Jerusalem, for the land will become desolate.

8 " 'At that time, declares the LORD, the bones of the kings and officials of Judah, the bones of the priests and prophets, and the bones of the people of Jerusalem will be removed from their graves. **2**They will be exposed to the sun and the moon and all the stars of the heavens, which they have loved and served and which they have followed and consulted and worshiped. They will not be gathered up or buried, but will be like refuse lying on the ground. **3**Wherever I banish them, all the survivors of this evil nation will prefer death to life, declares the LORD Almighty.'

Sin and Punishment

4"Say to them, 'This is what the LORD says:

" 'When men fall down, do they not get up?
When a man turns away, does he not return?
5Why then have these people turned away?
Why does Jerusalem always turn away?
They cling to deceit;
they refuse to return.
6I have listened attentively,
but they do not say what is right.
No one repents of his wickedness,
saying, "What have I done?"
Each pursues his own course
like a horse charging into battle.
7Even the stork in the sky
knows her appointed seasons,
and the dove, the swift and the thrush
observe the time of their migration.
But my people do not know
the requirements of the LORD.

8" 'How can you say, "We are wise,
for we have the law of the LORD,"
when actually the lying pen of the
scribes
has handled it falsely?
9The wise will be put to shame;
they will be dismayed and trapped.
Since they have rejected the word of the
LORD,
what kind of wisdom do they have?
10Therefore I will give their wives to other
men
and their fields to new owners.
From the least to the greatest,
all are greedy for gain;
prophets and priests alike,
all practice deceit.
11They dress the wound of my people
as though it were not serious.
"Peace, peace," they say,
when there is no peace.
12Are they ashamed of their loathsome
conduct?
No, they have no shame at all;
they do not even know how to blush.

So they will fall among the fallen;
  they will be brought down when they
    are punished,
                says the Lord.

13" 'I will take away their harvest,
          declares the Lord.
There will be no grapes on the vine.
There will be no figs on the tree,
  and their leaves will wither.
What I have given them
  will be taken from them.*a*' "

14"Why are we sitting here?
  Gather together!
Let us flee to the fortified cities
  and perish there!
For the Lord our God has doomed us to
  perish
and given us poisoned water to drink,
  because we have sinned against him.
15We hoped for peace
  but no good has come,
for a time of healing
  but there was only terror.
16The snorting of the enemy's horses
  is heard from Dan;
at the neighing of their stallions
  the whole land trembles.
They have come to devour
  the land and everything in it,
  the city and all who live there."

17"See, I will send venomous snakes
    among you,
  vipers that cannot be charmed,
  and they will bite you,"
         declares the Lord.

18O my Comforter*b* in sorrow,
  my heart is faint within me.
19Listen to the cry of my people
  from a land far away:
"Is the Lord not in Zion?
  Is her King no longer there?"

"Why have they provoked me to anger
    with their images,
  with their worthless foreign idols?"

20"The harvest is past,
  the summer has ended,
  and we are not saved."

21Since my people are crushed, I am
    crushed;
I mourn, and horror grips me.
22Is there no balm in Gilead?
  Is there no physician there?

Why then is there no healing
  for the wound of my people?

9 1Oh, that my head were a spring of
    water
and my eyes a fountain of tears!
I would weep day and night
  for the slain of my people.
2Oh, that I had in the desert
  a lodging place for travelers,
so that I might leave my people
  and go away from them;
for they are all adulterers,
  a crowd of unfaithful people.

3"They make ready their tongue
  like a bow, to shoot lies;
it is not by truth
  that they triumph*c* in the land.
They go from one sin to another;
  they do not acknowledge me,"
         declares the Lord.
4"Beware of your friends;
  do not trust your brothers.
For every brother is a deceiver,*d*
  and every friend a slanderer.
5Friend deceives friend,
  and no one speaks the truth.
They have taught their tongues to lie;
  they weary themselves with sinning.
6You*e* live in the midst of deception;
  in their deceit they refuse to
    acknowledge me,"
         declares the Lord.

7Therefore this is what the Lord Almighty
says:

"See, I will refine and test them,
  for what else can I do
  because of the sin of my people?
8Their tongue is a deadly arrow;
  it speaks with deceit.
With his mouth each speaks cordially to
    his neighbor,
  but in his heart he sets a trap for him.
9Should I not punish them for this?"
  declares the Lord.
"Should I not avenge myself
  on such a nation as this?"

10I will weep and wail for the mountains
  and take up a lament concerning the
    desert pastures.
They are desolate and untraveled,
  and the lowing of cattle is not heard.
The birds of the air have fled
  and the animals are gone.

---

a13 The meaning of the Hebrew for this sentence is uncertain.   *b18* The meaning of the Hebrew for this
word is uncertain.   *c3* Or *lies; / they are not valiant for truth*   *d4* Or *a deceiving Jacob*   *e6* That is,
Jeremiah (the Hebrew is singular)

11"I will make Jerusalem a heap of ruins,
  a haunt of jackals;
and I will lay waste the towns of Judah
  so no one can live there."

12What man is wise enough to understand this? Who has been instructed by the LORD and can explain it? Why has the land been ruined and laid waste like a desert that no one can cross?

13The LORD said, "It is because they have forsaken my law, which I set before them; they have not obeyed me or followed my law. **14**Instead, they have followed the stubbornness of their hearts; they have followed the Baals, as their fathers taught them." **15**Therefore, this is what the LORD Almighty, the God of Israel, says: "See, I will make this people eat bitter food and drink poisoned water. **16**I will scatter them among nations that neither they nor their fathers have known, and I will pursue them with the sword until I have destroyed them."

17This is what the LORD Almighty says:

"Consider now! Call for the wailing
    women to come;
  send for the most skillful of them.
18Let them come quickly
    and wail over us
till our eyes overflow with tears
    and water streams from our eyelids.
19The sound of wailing is heard from
    Zion:
  'How ruined we are!
  How great is our shame!
  We must leave our land
    because our houses are in ruins.' "

20Now, O women, hear the word of the
    LORD;
  open your ears to the words of his
    mouth.
Teach your daughters how to wail;
  teach one another a lament.
21Death has climbed in through our
    windows
  and has entered our fortresses;
it has cut off the children from the
    streets
  and the young men from the public
    squares.

22Say, "This is what the LORD declares:

" 'The dead bodies of men will lie
    like refuse on the open field,
like cut grain behind the reaper,
    with no one to gather them.' "

23This is what the LORD says:

"Let not the wise man boast of his
    wisdom
  or the strong man boast of his
    strength
  or the rich man boast of his riches,
24but let him who boasts boast about this:
  that he understands and knows me,
that I am the LORD, who exercises
    kindness,
  justice and righteousness on earth,
  for in these I delight,"
                    declares the LORD.

25"The days are coming," declares the LORD, "when I will punish all who are circumcised only in the flesh — **26**Egypt, Judah, Edom, Ammon, Moab and all who live in the desert in distant places.*a* For all these nations are really uncircumcised, and even the whole house of Israel is uncircumcised in heart."

God and Idols

10 Hear what the LORD says to you, O house of Israel. **2**This is what the LORD says:

"Do not learn the ways of the nations
  or be terrified by signs in the sky,
  though the nations are terrified by
    them.
3For the customs of the peoples are
    worthless;
  they cut a tree out of the forest,
  and a craftsman shapes it with his
    chisel.
4They adorn it with silver and gold;
  they fasten it with hammer and nails
  so it will not totter.
5Like a scarecrow in a melon patch,
  their idols cannot speak;
they must be carried
  because they cannot walk.
Do not fear them;
  they can do no harm
  nor can they do any good."

6No one is like you, O LORD;
  you are great,
  and your name is mighty in power.
7Who should not revere you,
  O King of the nations?
  This is your due.
Among all the wise men of the nations
  and in all their kingdoms,
  there is no one like you.
8They are all senseless and foolish;

a26 Or desert and who clip the hair by their foreheads

IS CHRIST RANKED #1 IN YOUR LIFE?

Kevin, fourteen, runs around like the proverbial chicken with its head chopped off. He is always rushing about frantically, desperately trying to do everything—band, Boy Scouts, youth group, homework, freestyle biking, chores around the house, athletic events at school, time with God. All the activities wear him out (not to mention his poor mom who has to drive him everywhere!).

One day in his youth group, during a lesson on priorities, Kevin is hit with this question: "Is your relationship with God the most important thing in your life? If not, what is?"

Look It Up
• • • •

The Old Testament says that the Lord should be more important than anything else: "Love the LORD your God with all your heart and with all your soul and with all your strength" (Deuteronomy 6:5).

The New Testament echoes the idea that the Lord wants to have the top spot: "And he is the head of the body, the church; he is the beginning and the firstborn from among the dead, so that in everything he might have the supremacy" (Colossians 1:18).

Think It Through
• • • •

It's a good idea now and then to examine your priorities—the things you are doing, the things you are not doing, and why. When was the last time you did that?

Are Kevin's activities wrong? How would you respond to the question Kevin's youth leader put to the class?

Is it possible to have the right priorities but to have them in the wrong order?

Work It Out
• • • •

As you study priorities, take a few moments to think about your own. What things are most important to you?

Here's how you can tell: When you're not actively doing anything, what sort of thoughts run through your mind? Do you think a lot about money? Being popular? Your friends? Having a boyfriend/girlfriend? Athletics? Good grades? Your body? Telling others about Christ?

Make a list of the things that matter most to you.

Nail It Down
• • • •

Read Jeremiah 9:23–24 to see the one thing that is really worth pursuing in this life.

Turn to pages 432, 1015, 1142 and 1292 for other readings on priorities.
Turn to page 798 for the weekend reading.

Topic
• • • •
PRIORITIES

they are taught by worthless wooden
    idols.
9Hammered silver is brought from
    Tarshish
  and gold from Uphaz.
What the craftsman and goldsmith have
    made
  is then dressed in blue and purple—
  all made by skilled workers.
10But the LORD is the true God;
  he is the living God, the eternal King.
When he is angry, the earth trembles;
  the nations cannot endure his wrath.

11"Tell them this: 'These gods, who did
not make the heavens and the earth, will
perish from the earth and from under the
heavens.' "[a]

12But God made the earth by his power;
  he founded the world by his wisdom
  and stretched out the heavens by his
    understanding.
13When he thunders, the waters in the
    heavens roar;
  he makes clouds rise from the ends
    of the earth.
He sends lightning with the rain
  and brings out the wind from his
    storehouses.

14Everyone is senseless and without
    knowledge;
  every goldsmith is shamed by his
    idols.
His images are a fraud;
  they have no breath in them.
15They are worthless, the objects of
    mockery;
  when their judgment comes, they will
    perish.
16He who is the Portion of Jacob is not
    like these,
  for he is the Maker of all things,
including Israel, the tribe of his
    inheritance—
  the LORD Almighty is his name.

Coming Destruction

17Gather up your belongings to leave the
    land,
  you who live under siege.
18For this is what the LORD says:
  "At this time I will hurl out
    those who live in this land;
  I will bring distress on them
    so that they may be captured."

19Woe to me because of my injury!

My wound is incurable!
Yet I said to myself,
  "This is my sickness, and I must
    endure it."
20My tent is destroyed;
  all its ropes are snapped.
My sons are gone from me and are no
    more;
  no one is left now to pitch my tent
  or to set up my shelter.
21The shepherds are senseless
  and do not inquire of the LORD;
so they do not prosper
  and all their flock is scattered.
22Listen! The report is coming—
  a great commotion from the land of
    the north!
It will make the towns of Judah
    desolate,
  a haunt of jackals.

Jeremiah's Prayer

23I know, O LORD, that a man's life is not
    his own;
  it is not for man to direct his steps.
24Correct me, LORD, but only with
    justice—
  not in your anger,
  lest you reduce me to nothing.
25Pour out your wrath on the nations
  that do not acknowledge you,
  on the peoples who do not call on
    your name.
For they have devoured Jacob;
  they have devoured him completely
  and destroyed his homeland.

The Covenant Is Broken

11 This is the word that came to Jeremiah from the LORD: 2"Listen to the
terms of this covenant and tell them to the
people of Judah and to those who live in Jerusalem. 3Tell them that this is what the
LORD, the God of Israel, says: 'Cursed is the
man who does not obey the terms of this
covenant— 4the terms I commanded your
forefathers when I brought them out of
Egypt, out of the iron-smelting furnace.' I
said, 'Obey me and do everything I command you, and you will be my people, and
I will be your God. 5Then I will fulfill the oath
I swore to your forefathers, to give them a
land flowing with milk and honey'—the
land you possess today."

I answered, "Amen, LORD."

6The LORD said to me, "Proclaim all these
words in the towns of Judah and in the

---

[a] *11* The text of this verse is in Aramaic.

THE WISDOM IN FOLLOWING GOD

Work It Out

Probably at some time in your life you've felt pretty dumb. You can remember the incident without difficulty. You answered, "Ten" in a math class when everyone else in the class knew the answer was eight. You made a major mistake in some competitive sport, like shooting the ball in the opponent's basket or running the wrong way on the football field. Or maybe you stumbled down some steps in front of about a million people.

Of course, you probably can also remember a time in your life when you felt pretty smart. You won a game of trivia by answering a question no one else could. You helped your parents solve a major problem with your brother. Or you decided to follow Jesus.

You bet! The last one is probably the smartest move you or anyone else has ever made. God has promised to make it a wise move and one you'll never regret.

Nail It Down

God's promise to the Israelites in Jeremiah 11:1–5 is true for you too.

Think It Through

What are some benefits that make following Jesus a wise move, you ask? Here are just a few:
- Contentment.
- Satisfaction with life.
- Purpose
- Direction.
- Hope.
- Joy.

As a follower of Jesus you have his promise of a full life here and an exciting eternity with him. What more could you ask?

If you haven't already done so, make the wise decision to follow Jesus today. He'll make it worth your while.

Nail It Down

Reread Jeremiah 11:1–5. For further insight read Proverbs 1:1–7.

Turn to pages 336 and 649 for other readings on wisdom.
Turn to page 805 for Monday's reading.

Topic

WISDOM

streets of Jerusalem: 'Listen to the terms of this covenant and follow them. **7**From the time I brought your forefathers up from Egypt until today, I warned them again and again, saying, "Obey me." **8**But they did not listen or pay attention; instead, they followed the stubbornness of their evil hearts. So I brought on them all the curses of the covenant I had commanded them to follow but that they did not keep.' "

9Then the LORD said to me, "There is a conspiracy among the people of Judah and those who live in Jerusalem. **10**They have returned to the sins of their forefathers, who refused to listen to my words. They have followed other gods to serve them. Both the house of Israel and the house of Judah have broken the covenant I made with their forefathers. **11**Therefore this is what the LORD says: 'I will bring on them a disaster they cannot escape. Although they cry out to me, I will not listen to them. **12**The towns of Judah and the people of Jerusalem will go and cry out to the gods to whom they burn incense, but they will not help them at all when disaster strikes. **13**You have as many gods as you have towns, O Judah; and the altars you have set up to burn incense to that shameful god Baal are as many as the streets of Jerusalem.'

14"Do not pray for this people nor offer any plea or petition for them, because I will not listen when they call to me in the time of their distress.

15"What is my beloved doing in my temple
  as she works out her evil schemes with many?
Can consecrated meat avert ∟your punishment⌟?
When you engage in your wickedness,
  then you rejoice.*a*"

16The LORD called you a thriving olive tree
  with fruit beautiful in form.
But with the roar of a mighty storm
  he will set it on fire,
  and its branches will be broken.

17The LORD Almighty, who planted you, has decreed disaster for you, because the house of Israel and the house of Judah have done evil and provoked me to anger by burning incense to Baal.

Plot Against Jeremiah

18Because the LORD revealed their plot to me, I knew it, for at that time he showed me what they were doing. **19**I had been like a gentle lamb led to the slaughter; I did not realize that they had plotted against me, saying,

"Let us destroy the tree and its fruit;
  let us cut him off from the land of the living,
  that his name be remembered no more."

20But, O LORD Almighty, you who judge righteously
  and test the heart and mind,
let me see your vengeance upon them,
  for to you I have committed my cause.

21"Therefore this is what the LORD says about the men of Anathoth who are seeking your life and saying, 'Do not prophesy in the name of the LORD or you will die by our hands'— **22**therefore this is what the LORD Almighty says: 'I will punish them. Their young men will die by the sword, their sons and daughters by famine. **23**Not even a remnant will be left to them, because I will bring disaster on the men of Anathoth in the year of their punishment.' "

Jeremiah's Complaint

12 You are always righteous, O LORD, when I bring a case before you.
Yet I would speak with you about your justice:
  Why does the way of the wicked prosper?
  Why do all the faithless live at ease?
2You have planted them, and they have taken root;
  they grow and bear fruit.
You are always on their lips
  but far from their hearts.
3Yet you know me, O LORD;
  you see me and test my thoughts about you.
Drag them off like sheep to be butchered!
  Set them apart for the day of slaughter!
4How long will the land lie parched*b*
  and the grass in every field be withered?
Because those who live in it are wicked,
  the animals and birds have perished.
Moreover, the people are saying,
  "He will not see what happens to us."

---

a15 Or Could consecrated meat avert your punishment? / Then you would rejoice   *b4 Or land mourn*

God's Answer

5"If you have raced with men on foot
   and they have worn you out,
   how can you compete with horses?
If you stumble in safe country,*a*
   how will you manage in the thickets
      by*b* the Jordan?
6Your brothers, your own family—
   even they have betrayed you;
   they have raised a loud cry against
      you.
Do not trust them,
   though they speak well of you.

7"I will forsake my house,
   abandon my inheritance;
I will give the one I love
   into the hands of her enemies.
8My inheritance has become to me
   like a lion in the forest.
She roars at me;
   therefore I hate her.
9Has not my inheritance become to me
   like a speckled bird of prey
   that other birds of prey surround and
      attack?
Go and gather all the wild beasts;
   bring them to devour.
10Many shepherds will ruin my vineyard
   and trample down my field;
they will turn my pleasant field
   into a desolate wasteland.
11It will be made a wasteland,
   parched and desolate before me;
the whole land will be laid waste
   because there is no one who cares.
12Over all the barren heights in the desert
   destroyers will swarm,
for the sword of the LORD will devour
   from one end of the land to the other;
   no one will be safe.
13They will sow wheat but reap thorns;
   they will wear themselves out but
      gain nothing.
So bear the shame of your harvest
   because of the LORD's fierce anger."

14This is what the LORD says: "As for all my
wicked neighbors who seize the inheritance
I gave my people Israel, I will uproot them
from their lands and I will uproot the house
of Judah from among them. 15But after I uproot them, I will again have compassion and
will bring each of them back to his own inheritance and his own country. 16And if they
learn well the ways of my people and swear

by my name, saying, 'As surely as the LORD
lives'—even as they once taught my people
to swear by Baal—then they will be established among my people. 17But if any nation
does not listen, I will completely uproot and
destroy it," declares the LORD.

A Linen Belt

13 This is what the LORD said to me: "Go
and buy a linen belt and put it
around your waist, but do not let it touch
water." 2So I bought a belt, as the LORD directed, and put it around my waist.

3Then the word of the LORD came to me a
second time: 4"Take the belt you bought and
are wearing around your waist, and go now
to Perath*c* and hide it there in a crevice in
the rocks." 5So I went and hid it at Perath,
as the LORD told me.

6Many days later the LORD said to me, "Go
now to Perath and get the belt I told you to
hide there." 7So I went to Perath and dug up
the belt and took it from the place where I
had hidden it, but now it was ruined and
completely useless.

8Then the word of the LORD came to me:
9"This is what the LORD says: 'In the same
way I will ruin the pride of Judah and the
great pride of Jerusalem. 10These wicked
people, who refuse to listen to my words,
who follow the stubbornness of their hearts
and go after other gods to serve and worship
them, will be like this belt—completely useless! 11For as a belt is bound around a man's
waist, so I bound the whole house of Israel
and the whole house of Judah to me,' declares the LORD, 'to be my people for my renown and praise and honor. But they have
not listened.'

Wineskins

12"Say to them: 'This is what the LORD, the
God of Israel, says: Every wineskin should
be filled with wine.' And if they say to you,
'Don't we know that every wineskin should
be filled with wine?' 13then tell them, 'This
is what the LORD says: I am going to fill with
drunkenness all who live in this land, including the kings who sit on David's throne,
the priests, the prophets and all those living
in Jerusalem. 14I will smash them one
against the other, fathers and sons alike, declares the LORD. I will allow no pity or mercy
or compassion to keep me from destroying
them.' "

---

*a*5 Or *If you put your trust in a land of safety*   *b*5 Or *the flooding of*   *c*4 Or possibly *the Euphrates*; also in
verses 5-7

Threat of Captivity

15Hear and pay attention,
    do not be arrogant,
    for the LORD has spoken.
16Give glory to the LORD your God
    before he brings the darkness,
    before your feet stumble
    on the darkening hills.
You hope for light,
    but he will turn it to thick darkness
    and change it to deep gloom.
17But if you do not listen,
    I will weep in secret
    because of your pride;
my eyes will weep bitterly,
    overflowing with tears,
    because the LORD's flock will be taken
        captive.

18Say to the king and to the queen
        mother,
    "Come down from your thrones,
for your glorious crowns
    will fall from your heads."
19The cities in the Negev will be shut up,
    and there will be no one to open
        them.
All Judah will be carried into exile,
    carried completely away.

20Lift up your eyes and see
    those who are coming from the north.
Where is the flock that was entrusted to
        you,
    the sheep of which you boasted?
21What will you say when ⌊the LORD⌋ sets
        over you
    those you cultivated as your special
        allies?
Will not pain grip you
    like that of a woman in labor?
22And if you ask yourself,
    "Why has this happened to me?"—
it is because of your many sins
    that your skirts have been torn off
    and your body mistreated.
23Can the Ethiopian[a] change his skin
    or the leopard its spots?
Neither can you do good
    who are accustomed to doing evil.

24"I will scatter you like chaff
    driven by the desert wind.
25This is your lot,
    the portion I have decreed for you,"
                declares the LORD,
    "because you have forgotten me
    and trusted in false gods.

26I will pull up your skirts over your face
    that your shame may be seen—
27your adulteries and lustful neighings,
    your shameless prostitution!
I have seen your detestable acts
    on the hills and in the fields.
Woe to you, O Jerusalem!
    How long will you be unclean?"

Drought, Famine, Sword

14 This is the word of the LORD to Jeremiah concerning the drought:

2"Judah mourns,
    her cities languish;
they wail for the land,
    and a cry goes up from Jerusalem.
3The nobles send their servants for
        water;
    they go to the cisterns
    but find no water.
They return with their jars unfilled;
    dismayed and despairing,
    they cover their heads.
4The ground is cracked
    because there is no rain in the land;
the farmers are dismayed
    and cover their heads.
5Even the doe in the field
    deserts her newborn fawn
    because there is no grass.
6Wild donkeys stand on the barren
        heights
    and pant like jackals;
their eyesight fails
    for lack of pasture."

7Although our sins testify against us,
    O LORD, do something for the sake of
        your name.
For our backsliding is great;
    we have sinned against you.
8O Hope of Israel,
    its Savior in times of distress,
why are you like a stranger in the land,
    like a traveler who stays only a night?
9Why are you like a man taken by
        surprise,
    like a warrior powerless to save?
You are among us, O LORD,
    and we bear your name;
    do not forsake us!

10This is what the LORD says about this
people:

"They greatly love to wander;
    they do not restrain their feet.
So the LORD does not accept them;

a23 Hebrew *Cushite* (probably a person from the upper Nile region)

he will now remember their
    wickedness
and punish them for their sins."

11Then the Lord said to me, "Do not pray
for the well-being of this people. **12**Although
they fast, I will not listen to their cry; though
they offer burnt offerings and grain offerings, I will not accept them. Instead, I will
destroy them with the sword, famine and
plague."

13But I said, "Ah, Sovereign Lord, the
prophets keep telling them, 'You will not see
the sword or suffer famine. Indeed, I will
give you lasting peace in this place.'"

14Then the Lord said to me, "The prophets
are prophesying lies in my name. I have not
sent them or appointed them or spoken to
them. They are prophesying to you false visions, divinations, idolatries*a* and the delusions of their own minds. **15**Therefore, this
is what the Lord says about the prophets
who are prophesying in my name: I did not
send them, yet they are saying, 'No sword or
famine will touch this land.' Those same
prophets will perish by sword and famine.
16And the people they are prophesying to
will be thrown out into the streets of Jerusalem because of the famine and sword. There
will be no one to bury them or their wives,
their sons or their daughters. I will pour out
on them the calamity they deserve.

17"Speak this word to them:

" 'Let my eyes overflow with tears
    night and day without ceasing;
for my virgin daughter—my people—
    has suffered a grievous wound,
    a crushing blow.
18If I go into the country,
    I see those slain by the sword;
if I go into the city,
    I see the ravages of famine.
Both prophet and priest
    have gone to a land they know not.'"

19Have you rejected Judah completely?
    Do you despise Zion?
Why have you afflicted us
    so that we cannot be healed?
We hoped for peace
    but no good has come,
for a time of healing
    but there is only terror.
20O Lord, we acknowledge our wickedness
    and the guilt of our fathers;
    we have indeed sinned against you.

21For the sake of your name do not
        despise us;
    do not dishonor your glorious throne.
Remember your covenant with us
    and do not break it.
22Do any of the worthless idols of the
        nations bring rain?
    Do the skies themselves send down
        showers?
No, it is you, O Lord our God.
    Therefore our hope is in you,
    for you are the one who does all this.

15   Then the Lord said to me: "Even if
    Moses and Samuel were to stand be-
fore me, my heart would not go out to this
people. Send them away from my presence!
Let them go! **2**And if they ask you, 'Where
shall we go?' tell them, 'This is what the Lord
says:

" 'Those destined for death, to death;
those for the sword, to the sword;
those for starvation, to starvation;
those for captivity, to captivity.'

3"I will send four kinds of destroyers
against them," declares the Lord, "the sword
to kill and the dogs to drag away and the
birds of the air and the beasts of the earth
to devour and destroy. **4**I will make them abhorrent to all the kingdoms of the earth because of what Manasseh son of Hezekiah
king of Judah did in Jerusalem.

5"Who will have pity on you,
        O Jerusalem?
    Who will mourn for you?
    Who will stop to ask how you are?
6You have rejected me," declares the
        Lord.
    "You keep on backsliding.
So I will lay hands on you and destroy
        you;
    I can no longer show compassion.
7I will winnow them with a winnowing
        fork
    at the city gates of the land.
I will bring bereavement and destruction
        on my people,
    for they have not changed their ways.
8I will make their widows more
        numerous
    than the sand of the sea.
At midday I will bring a destroyer
    against the mothers of their young
        men;
suddenly I will bring down on them
    anguish and terror.

a14 Or *visions, worthless divinations*

⁹The mother of seven will grow faint
    and breathe her last.
Her sun will set while it is still day;
    she will be disgraced and humiliated.
I will put the survivors to the sword
    before their enemies,"
                    declares the LORD.

¹⁰Alas, my mother, that you gave me
        birth,
    a man with whom the whole land
        strives and contends!
I have neither lent nor borrowed,
    yet everyone curses me.

¹¹The LORD said,

"Surely I will deliver you for a good
        purpose;
    surely I will make your enemies plead
        with you
    in times of disaster and times of
        distress.

¹²"Can a man break iron—
    iron from the north—or bronze?
¹³Your wealth and your treasures
    I will give as plunder, without charge,
because of all your sins
    throughout your country.
¹⁴I will enslave you to your enemies
    in[a] a land you do not know,
for my anger will kindle a fire
    that will burn against you."

¹⁵You understand, O LORD;
    remember me and care for me.
    Avenge me on my persecutors.
You are long-suffering—do not take me
        away;
    think of how I suffer reproach for
        your sake.
¹⁶When your words came, I ate them;
    they were my joy and my heart's
        delight,
for I bear your name,
    O LORD God Almighty.
¹⁷I never sat in the company of revelers,
    never made merry with them;
I sat alone because your hand was on
        me
    and you had filled me with
        indignation.
¹⁸Why is my pain unending
    and my wound grievous and
        incurable?
Will you be to me like a deceptive
        brook,

like a spring that fails?

¹⁹Therefore this is what the LORD says:

"If you repent, I will restore you
    that you may serve me;
if you utter worthy, not worthless,
        words,
    you will be my spokesman.
Let this people turn to you,
    but you must not turn to them.
²⁰I will make you a wall to this people,
    a fortified wall of bronze;
they will fight against you
    but will not overcome you,
for I am with you
    to rescue and save you,"
                    declares the LORD.
²¹"I will save you from the hands of the
        wicked
    and redeem you from the grasp of the
        cruel."

Day of Disaster

16 Then the word of the LORD came to
me: ²"You must not marry and have
sons or daughters in this place." ³For this is
what the LORD says about the sons and
daughters born in this land and about the
women who are their mothers and the men
who are their fathers: ⁴"They will die of
deadly diseases. They will not be mourned
or buried but will be like refuse lying on the
ground. They will perish by sword and famine, and their dead bodies will become food
for the birds of the air and the beasts of the
earth."

⁵For this is what the LORD says: "Do not
enter a house where there is a funeral meal;
do not go to mourn or show sympathy, because I have withdrawn my blessing, my
love and my pity from this people," declares
the LORD. ⁶"Both high and low will die in this
land. They will not be buried or mourned,
and no one will cut himself or shave his
head for them. ⁷No one will offer food to
comfort those who mourn for the dead—
not even for a father or a mother—nor will
anyone give them a drink to console them.

⁸"And do not enter a house where there is
feasting and sit down to eat and drink. ⁹For
this is what the LORD Almighty, the God of
Israel, says: Before your eyes and in your
days I will bring an end to the sounds of joy
and gladness and to the voices of bride and
bridegroom in this place.

¹⁰"When you tell these people all this and

---

*a14 Some Hebrew manuscripts, Septuagint and Syriac (see also Jer. 17:4); most Hebrew manuscripts I will
cause your enemies to bring you / into*

they ask you, 'Why has the LORD decreed such a great disaster against us? What wrong have we done? What sin have we committed against the LORD our God?' ¹¹then say to them, 'It is because your fathers forsook me,' declares the LORD, 'and followed other gods and served and worshiped them. They forsook me and did not keep my law. ¹²But you have behaved more wickedly than your fathers. See how each of you is following the stubbornness of his evil heart instead of obeying me. ¹³So I will throw you out of this land into a land neither you nor your fathers have known, and there you will serve other gods day and night, for I will show you no favor.'

¹⁴"However, the days are coming," declares the LORD, "when men will no longer say, 'As surely as the LORD lives, who brought the Israelites up out of Egypt,' ¹⁵but they will say, 'As surely as the LORD lives, who brought the Israelites up out of the land of the north and out of all the countries where he had banished them.' For I will restore them to the land I gave their forefathers.

¹⁶"But now I will send for many fishermen," declares the LORD, "and they will catch them. After that I will send for many hunters, and they will hunt them down on every mountain and hill and from the crevices of the rocks. ¹⁷My eyes are on all their ways; they are not hidden from me, nor is their sin concealed from my eyes. ¹⁸I will repay them double for their wickedness and their sin, because they have defiled my land with the lifeless forms of their vile images and have filled my inheritance with their detestable idols."

¹⁹O LORD, my strength and my fortress,
my refuge in time of distress,
to you the nations will come
from the ends of the earth and say,
"Our fathers possessed nothing but false gods,
worthless idols that did them no good.
²⁰Do men make their own gods?
Yes, but they are not gods!"

²¹"Therefore I will teach them—
this time I will teach them
my power and might.
Then they will know
that my name is the LORD.

17 "Judah's sin is engraved with an iron tool,

inscribed with a flint point,
on the tablets of their hearts
and on the horns of their altars.
²Even their children remember
their altars and Asherah poles^a
beside the spreading trees
and on the high hills.
³My mountain in the land
and your^b wealth and all your treasures
I will give away as plunder,
together with your high places,
because of sin throughout your country.
⁴Through your own fault you will lose
the inheritance I gave you.
I will enslave you to your enemies
in a land you do not know,
for you have kindled my anger,
and it will burn forever."

⁵This is what the LORD says:

"Cursed is the one who trusts in man,
who depends on flesh for his strength
and whose heart turns away from the LORD.
⁶He will be like a bush in the wastelands;
he will not see prosperity when it comes.
He will dwell in the parched places of the desert,
in a salt land where no one lives.

⁷"But blessed is the man who trusts in the LORD,
whose confidence is in him.
⁸He will be like a tree planted by the water
that sends out its roots by the stream.
It does not fear when heat comes;
its leaves are always green.
It has no worries in a year of drought
and never fails to bear fruit."

⁹The heart is deceitful above all things
and beyond cure.
Who can understand it?

¹⁰"I the LORD search the heart
and examine the mind,
to reward a man according to his conduct,
according to what his deeds deserve."

¹¹Like a partridge that hatches eggs it did not lay
is the man who gains riches by unjust means.

---

^a2 That is, symbols of the goddess Asherah　^b2,3 Or hills / ³and the mountains of the land. / Your

Seeking Out the Source of Security
☐ **Monday**

• •

Tammy comes home from school in tears. During sixth hour she found out her "friends" have been spreading a very vicious rumor about her. Talk about embarrassed!

"I'll never be able to show my face there ever again," she sobs. Tammy's dad puts his arms around her, pulls her close and gives her a long hug.

"Sweetie, I'm so sorry. I know it doesn't change your situation, but . . . I love you."

"Thanks, Dad," Tammy sniffles.

Look It Up
• • • •

Isn't it great to have an earthly dad who cares? Isn't it even greater to have a heavenly Father who cares perfectly and all the time?

"I have set the LORD always before me. Because he is at my right hand, I will not be shaken" (Psalm 16:8).

"For the king trusts in the LORD; through the unfailing love of the Most High he will not be shaken" (Psalm 21:7).

"So we say with confidence, 'The Lord is my helper; I will not be afraid. What can man do to me?' " (Hebrews 13:6).

Do you see the common thread that runs through these passages? It's this: The source of ultimate security is the Lord!

Think It Through
• • • •

It's okay to go to friends and/or family members with your problems. But remember this: People will eventually let you down. They have bad days and problems of their own. If your trust is in them alone, you'll definitely be disappointed.

Look first to the Lord. With him as your security, you won't fall apart when your world does.

Work It Out
• • • •

People look for security in all kinds of places—romantic relationships, a high grade point average, a close family, a good job, a promising future, a special talent or natural ability, a group of friends, a certain routine, good looks and material possessions.

List the potential problems that face people who make one of the above the basis for their security and well-being.

If you sense that you are trusting in one of those things more than you are the Lord, ask God to show you how to change.

Nail It Down
• • • •

Read Jeremiah 17:5–8 for what Jeremiah has to say about trusting in people or in God.

Turn to pages 742, 954 and 976 for other readings on security.
Turn to page 809 for Tuesday's reading.

Topic
• • • •

SECURITY

When his life is half gone, they will
    desert him,
  and in the end he will prove to be a
    fool.

[12]A glorious throne, exalted from the
    beginning,
  is the place of our sanctuary.
[13]O Lord, the hope of Israel,
  all who forsake you will be put to
    shame.
Those who turn away from you will be
    written in the dust
because they have forsaken the Lord,
  the spring of living water.

[14]Heal me, O Lord, and I will be healed;
  save me and I will be saved,
  for you are the one I praise.
[15]They keep saying to me,
  "Where is the word of the Lord?
  Let it now be fulfilled!"
[16]I have not run away from being your
    shepherd;
  you know I have not desired the day
    of despair.
  What passes my lips is open before
    you.
[17]Do not be a terror to me;
  you are my refuge in the day of
    disaster.
[18]Let my persecutors be put to shame,
  but keep me from shame;
  let them be terrified,
  but keep me from terror.
Bring on them the day of disaster;
  destroy them with double destruction.

Keeping the Sabbath Holy

[19]This is what the Lord said to me: "Go and stand at the gate of the people, through which the kings of Judah go in and out; stand also at all the other gates of Jerusalem. [20]Say to them, 'Hear the word of the Lord, O kings of Judah and all people of Judah and everyone living in Jerusalem who come through these gates. [21]This is what the Lord says: Be careful not to carry a load on the Sabbath day or bring it through the gates of Jerusalem. [22]Do not bring a load out of your houses or do any work on the Sabbath, but keep the Sabbath day holy, as I commanded your forefathers. [23]Yet they did not listen or pay attention; they were stiff-necked and would not listen or respond to discipline. [24]But if you are careful to obey me, declares the Lord, and bring no load through the gates of this city on the Sabbath, but keep the Sabbath day holy by not doing any work on it, [25]then kings who sit on David's throne will come through the gates of this city with their officials. They and their officials will come riding in chariots and on horses, accompanied by the men of Judah and those living in Jerusalem, and this city will be inhabited forever. [26]People will come from the towns of Judah and the villages around Jerusalem, from the territory of Benjamin and the western foothills, from the hill country and the Negev, bringing burnt offerings and sacrifices, grain offerings, incense and thank offerings to the house of the Lord. [27]But if you do not obey me to keep the Sabbath day holy by not carrying any load as you come through the gates of Jerusalem on the Sabbath day, then I will kindle an unquenchable fire in the gates of Jerusalem that will consume her fortresses.' "

At the Potter's House

18 This is the word that came to Jeremiah from the Lord: [2]"Go down to the potter's house, and there I will give you my message." [3]So I went down to the potter's house, and I saw him working at the wheel. [4]But the pot he was shaping from the clay was marred in his hands; so the potter formed it into another pot, shaping it as seemed best to him.

[5]Then the word of the Lord came to me: [6]"O house of Israel, can I not do with you as this potter does?" declares the Lord. "Like clay in the hand of the potter, so are you in my hand, O house of Israel. [7]If at any time I announce that a nation or kingdom is to be uprooted, torn down and destroyed, [8]and if that nation I warned repents of its evil, then I will relent and not inflict on it the disaster I had planned. [9]And if at another time I announce that a nation or kingdom is to be built up and planted, [10]and if it does evil in my sight and does not obey me, then I will reconsider the good I had intended to do for it.

[11]"Now therefore say to the people of Judah and those living in Jerusalem, 'This is what the Lord says: Look! I am preparing a disaster for you and devising a plan against you. So turn from your evil ways, each one of you, and reform your ways and your actions.' [12]But they will reply, 'It's no use. We will continue with our own plans; each of us will follow the stubbornness of his evil heart.' "

[13]Therefore this is what the Lord says:

"Inquire among the nations:
  Who has ever heard anything like
    this?

A most horrible thing has been done
  by Virgin Israel.
14Does the snow of Lebanon
  ever vanish from its rocky slopes?
Do its cool waters from distant sources
  ever cease to flow?[a]
15Yet my people have forgotten me;
  they burn incense to worthless idols,
which made them stumble in their ways
  and in the ancient paths.
They made them walk in bypaths
  and on roads not built up.
16Their land will be laid waste,
  an object of lasting scorn;
all who pass by will be appalled
  and will shake their heads.
17Like a wind from the east,
  I will scatter them before their
    enemies;
I will show them my back and not my
    face
  in the day of their disaster."

18They said, "Come, let's make plans
against Jeremiah; for the teaching of the law
by the priest will not be lost, nor will counsel
from the wise, nor the word from the prophets. So come, let's attack him with our
tongues and pay no attention to anything he
says."

19Listen to me, O Lord;
  hear what my accusers are saying!
20Should good be repaid with evil?
  Yet they have dug a pit for me.
Remember that I stood before you
  and spoke in their behalf
  to turn your wrath away from them.
21So give their children over to famine;
  hand them over to the power of the
    sword.
Let their wives be made childless and
    widows;
  let their men be put to death,
  their young men slain by the sword in
    battle.
22Let a cry be heard from their houses
  when you suddenly bring invaders
    against them,
for they have dug a pit to capture me
  and have hidden snares for my feet.
23But you know, O Lord,
  all their plots to kill me.
Do not forgive their crimes
  or blot out their sins from your sight.
Let them be overthrown before you;

deal with them in the time of your
  anger.

19 This is what the Lord says: "Go and
  buy a clay jar from a potter. Take
along some of the elders of the people and
of the priests **2**and go out to the Valley of Ben
Hinnom, near the entrance of the Potsherd
Gate. There proclaim the words I tell you,
3and say, 'Hear the word of the Lord, O kings
of Judah and people of Jerusalem. This is
what the Lord Almighty, the God of Israel,
says: Listen! I am going to bring a disaster on
this place that will make the ears of everyone who hears of it tingle. **4**For they have
forsaken me and made this a place of foreign gods; they have burned sacrifices in it
to gods that neither they nor their fathers
nor the kings of Judah ever knew, and they
have filled this place with the blood of the
innocent. **5**They have built the high places
of Baal to burn their sons in the fire as offerings to Baal—something I did not command
or mention, nor did it enter my mind. **6**So
beware, the days are coming, declares the
Lord, when people will no longer call this
place Topheth or the Valley of Ben Hinnom,
but the Valley of Slaughter.

7"'In this place I will ruin[b] the plans of
Judah and Jerusalem. I will make them fall
by the sword before their enemies, at the
hands of those who seek their lives, and I
will give their carcasses as food to the birds
of the air and the beasts of the earth. **8**I will
devastate this city and make it an object of
scorn; all who pass by will be appalled and
will scoff because of all its wounds. **9**I will
make them eat the flesh of their sons and
daughters, and they will eat one another's
flesh during the stress of the siege imposed
on them by the enemies who seek their
lives.'

10"Then break the jar while those who go
with you are watching, **11**and say to them,
'This is what the Lord Almighty says: I will
smash this nation and this city just as this
potter's jar is smashed and cannot be repaired. They will bury the dead in Topheth
until there is no more room. **12**This is what
I will do to this place and to those who live
here, declares the Lord. I will make this city
like Topheth. **13**The houses in Jerusalem
and those of the kings of Judah will be defiled like this place, Topheth—all the
houses where they burned incense on the

---

a 14 The meaning of the Hebrew for this sentence is uncertain.   *b 7* The Hebrew for *ruin* sounds like the
Hebrew for *jar* (see verses 1 and 10).

roofs to all the starry hosts and poured out drink offerings to other gods.'"

¹⁴Jeremiah then returned from Topheth, where the Lord had sent him to prophesy, and stood in the court of the Lord's temple and said to all the people, ¹⁵"This is what the Lord Almighty, the God of Israel, says: 'Listen! I am going to bring on this city and the villages around it every disaster I pronounced against them, because they were stiff-necked and would not listen to my words.'"

Jeremiah and Pashhur

20 When the priest Pashhur son of Immer, the chief officer in the temple of the Lord, heard Jeremiah prophesying these things, ²he had Jeremiah the prophet beaten and put in the stocks at the Upper Gate of Benjamin at the Lord's temple. ³The next day, when Pashhur released him from the stocks, Jeremiah said to him, "The Lord's name for you is not Pashhur, but Magor-Missabib.ᵃ ⁴For this is what the Lord says: 'I will make you a terror to yourself and to all your friends; with your own eyes you will see them fall by the sword of their enemies. I will hand all Judah over to the king of Babylon, who will carry them away to Babylon or put them to the sword. ⁵I will hand over to their enemies all the wealth of this city — all its products, all its valuables and all the treasures of the kings of Judah. They will take it away as plunder and carry it off to Babylon. ⁶And you, Pashhur, and all who live in your house will go into exile to Babylon. There you will die and be buried, you and all your friends to whom you have prophesied lies.'"

Jeremiah's Complaint

⁷O Lord, you deceivedᵇ me, and I was deceivedᵇ;
  you overpowered me and prevailed.
I am ridiculed all day long;
  everyone mocks me.
⁸Whenever I speak, I cry out
  proclaiming violence and destruction.
So the word of the Lord has brought me
  insult and reproach all day long.
⁹But if I say, "I will not mention him
  or speak any more in his name,"
his word is in my heart like a fire,
  a fire shut up in my bones.
I am weary of holding it in;
  indeed, I cannot.

¹⁰I hear many whispering,
  "Terror on every side!
  Report him! Let's report him!"
All my friends
  are waiting for me to slip, saying,
"Perhaps he will be deceived;
  then we will prevail over him
  and take our revenge on him."

¹¹But the Lord is with me like a mighty
    warrior;
  so my persecutors will stumble and
    not prevail.
They will fail and be thoroughly
    disgraced;
  their dishonor will never be forgotten.
¹²O Lord Almighty, you who examine the
    righteous
  and probe the heart and mind,
let me see your vengeance upon them,
  for to you I have committed my
    cause.

¹³Sing to the Lord!
  Give praise to the Lord!
He rescues the life of the needy
  from the hands of the wicked.

¹⁴Cursed be the day I was born!
  May the day my mother bore me not
    be blessed!
¹⁵Cursed be the man who brought my
    father the news,
  who made him very glad, saying,
  "A child is born to you — a son!"
¹⁶May that man be like the towns
  the Lord overthrew without pity.
May he hear wailing in the morning,
  a battle cry at noon.
¹⁷For he did not kill me in the womb,
  with my mother as my grave,
  her womb enlarged forever.
¹⁸Why did I ever come out of the womb
  to see trouble and sorrow
  and to end my days in shame?

God Rejects Zedekiah's Request

21 The word came to Jeremiah from the Lord when King Zedekiah sent to him Pashhur son of Malkijah and the priest Zephaniah son of Maaseiah. They said: ²"Inquire now of the Lord for us because Nebuchadnezzarᶜ king of Babylon is attacking us. Perhaps the Lord will perform wonders for us as in times past so that he will withdraw from us."

³But Jeremiah answered them, "Tell Zede-

ᵃ3 Magor-Missabib means terror on every side.   ᵇ7 Or persuaded   ᶜ2 Hebrew Nebuchadrezzar, of which Nebuchadnezzar is a variant; here and often in Jeremiah and Ezekiel

DOES GOD NEED OUR FORGIVENESS?

Judy and Kirby went together for about four months during their sophomore year. The relationship was getting pretty physical when Kirby suddenly quit calling. When Judy began to understand and accept God's forgiveness, her spiritual journey got back on track. Learning to forgive herself was her first big obstacle. Later, she took another giant step by realizing the need to forgive others—especially Kirby.

The other day Judy was telling a friend some of the things she's been learning. When the subject of forgiveness came up, the friend exploded:

"God forgive *me!*? If anything I need to be forgiving *him*. How could he allow my dad to die when I was only two? Why did he let that happen?"

Look It Up
••••

Most people blame God when life turns sour. They feel abandoned and often angry. King David was no exception:

> My God, my God, why have you forsaken me?
> Why are you so far from saving me . . . ?
> O my God, I cry out by day, but you do not
> answer,
> by night, and am not silent (Psalm 22:1–2).

For David, relief finally came when he remembered God's perfection and his faithfulness (Psalm 22:4–5).

Think It Through
••••

Some people would suggest that you need to forgive God for being unable to prevent bad experiences from entering your life. Such an idea is outrageous! God is perfect and needs no forgiveness. He has never wronged anyone. In spite of that, you may *feel* wronged. And that causes you to feel angry toward God. Those emotions must be dealt with if you want to enjoy a close relationship with the Lord.

Work It Out
••••

Are you mad at God? You might want to pray something like this: "Lord, I feel angry at you because of _____. I admit that I've been prideful and stubborn, believing that I know better than you what's best for me. Right now I give up my angry demands for an explanation. I willingly accept the circumstances that you have allowed in my life. I choose to trust you in this situation. Keep reminding me that you are totally wise and completely good. Amen."

Nail It Down
••••

Read about Jeremiah's anger at God in Jeremiah 20:7–18.

Turn to pages 580, 771, 966, 1068, 1302 and 1352 for other readings on forgiveness.
Turn to page 816 for Wednesday's reading.

Topic
••••

FORGIVENESS

kiah, **4**'This is what the Lord, the God of Israel, says: I am about to turn against you the weapons of war that are in your hands, which you are using to fight the king of Babylon and the Babylonians*a* who are outside the wall besieging you. And I will gather them inside this city. **5**I myself will fight against you with an outstretched hand and a mighty arm in anger and fury and great wrath. **6**I will strike down those who live in this city — both men and animals — and they will die of a terrible plague. **7**After that, declares the Lord, I will hand over Zedekiah king of Judah, his officials and the people in this city who survive the plague, sword and famine, to Nebuchadnezzar king of Babylon and to their enemies who seek their lives. He will put them to the sword; he will show them no mercy or pity or compassion.'

8"Furthermore, tell the people, 'This is what the Lord says: See, I am setting before you the way of life and the way of death. **9**Whoever stays in this city will die by the sword, famine or plague. But whoever goes out and surrenders to the Babylonians who are besieging you will live; he will escape with his life. **10**I have determined to do this city harm and not good, declares the Lord. It will be given into the hands of the king of Babylon, and he will destroy it with fire.'

11"Moreover, say to the royal house of Judah, 'Hear the word of the Lord; **12**O house of David, this is what the Lord says:

" 'Administer justice every morning;
rescue from the hand of his oppressor
the one who has been robbed,
or my wrath will break out and burn
like fire
because of the evil you have done —
burn with no one to quench it.
13I am against you, ˎJerusalemˌ
you who live above this valley
on the rocky plateau,
              declares the Lord —
you who say, "Who can come against
us?
Who can enter our refuge?"
14I will punish you as your deeds deserve,
              declares the Lord.
I will kindle a fire in your forests
that will consume everything around
you.' "

Judgment Against Evil Kings

22 This is what the Lord says: "Go down to the palace of the king of Judah and proclaim this message there: **2**'Hear the word of the Lord, O king of Judah, you who sit on David's throne — you, your officials and your people who come through these gates. **3**This is what the Lord says: Do what is just and right. Rescue from the hand of his oppressor the one who has been robbed. Do no wrong or violence to the alien, the fatherless or the widow, and do not shed innocent blood in this place. **4**For if you are careful to carry out these commands, then kings who sit on David's throne will come through the gates of this palace, riding in chariots and on horses, accompanied by their officials and their people. **5**But if you do not obey these commands, declares the Lord, I swear by myself that this palace will become a ruin.' "

6For this is what the Lord says about the palace of the king of Judah:

"Though you are like Gilead to me,
like the summit of Lebanon,
I will surely make you like a desert,
like towns not inhabited.
7I will send destroyers against you,
each man with his weapons,
and they will cut up your fine cedar
beams
and throw them into the fire.

8"People from many nations will pass by this city and will ask one another, 'Why has the Lord done such a thing to this great city?' **9**And the answer will be: 'Because they have forsaken the covenant of the Lord their God and have worshiped and served other gods.' "

10Do not weep for the dead ˎkingˌ or
mourn his loss;
rather, weep bitterly for him who is
exiled,
because he will never return
nor see his native land again.

11For this is what the Lord says about Shallum*b* son of Josiah, who succeeded his father as king of Judah but has gone from this place: "He will never return. **12**He will die in the place where they have led him captive; he will not see this land again."

13"Woe to him who builds his palace by
unrighteousness,
his upper rooms by injustice,
making his countrymen work for
nothing,
not paying them for their labor.

---

a4 Or *Chaldeans*; also in verse 9   *b11* Also called *Jehoahaz*

14He says, 'I will build myself a great
palace
with spacious upper rooms.'
So he makes large windows in it,
panels it with cedar
and decorates it in red.

15"Does it make you a king
to have more and more cedar?
Did not your father have food and
drink?
He did what was right and just,
so all went well with him.
16He defended the cause of the poor and
needy,
and so all went well.
Is that not what it means to know me?"
declares the LORD.
17"But your eyes and your heart
are set only on dishonest gain,
on shedding innocent blood
and on oppression and extortion."

18Therefore this is what the LORD says about
Jehoiakim son of Josiah king of Judah:

"They will not mourn for him:
'Alas, my brother! Alas, my sister!'
They will not mourn for him:
'Alas, my master! Alas, his splendor!'
19He will have the burial of a donkey—
dragged away and thrown
outside the gates of Jerusalem."

20"Go up to Lebanon and cry out,
let your voice be heard in Bashan,
cry out from Abarim,
for all your allies are crushed.
21I warned you when you felt secure,
but you said, 'I will not listen!'
This has been your way from your
youth;
you have not obeyed me.
22The wind will drive all your shepherds
away,
and your allies will go into exile.
Then you will be ashamed and
disgraced
because of all your wickedness.
23You who live in 'Lebanon,'ª
who are nestled in cedar buildings,
how you will groan when pangs come
upon you,
pain like that of a woman in labor!

24"As surely as I live," declares the LORD,
"even if you, Jehoiachinᵇ son of Jehoiakim
king of Judah, were a signet ring on my right

hand, I would still pull you off. **25**I will hand
you over to those who seek your life, those
you fear—to Nebuchadnezzar king of Babylon and to the Babylonians.ᶜ **26**I will hurl
you and the mother who gave you birth into
another country, where neither of you was
born, and there you both will die. **27**You will
never come back to the land you long to return to."

28Is this man Jehoiachin a despised,
broken pot,
an object no one wants?
Why will he and his children be hurled
out,
cast into a land they do not know?
29O land, land, land,
hear the word of the LORD!
30This is what the LORD says:
"Record this man as if childless,
a man who will not prosper in his
lifetime,
for none of his offspring will prosper,
none will sit on the throne of David
or rule anymore in Judah."

The Righteous Branch

23 "Woe to the shepherds who are destroying and scattering the sheep of
my pasture!" declares the LORD. **2**Therefore
this is what the LORD, the God of Israel, says
to the shepherds who tend my people: "Because you have scattered my flock and driv-
en them away and have not bestowed care
on them, I will bestow punishment on you
for the evil you have done," declares the
LORD. **3**"I myself will gather the remnant of
my flock out of all the countries where I
have driven them and will bring them back
to their pasture, where they will be fruitful
and increase in number. **4**I will place shepherds over them who will tend them, and
they will no longer be afraid or terrified, nor
will any be missing," declares the LORD.

5"The days are coming," declares the
LORD,
"when I will raise up to Davidᵈ a
righteous Branch,
a King who will reign wisely
and do what is just and right in the
land.
6In his days Judah will be saved
and Israel will live in safety.
This is the name by which he will be
called:
The LORD Our Righteousness.

ª23 That is, the palace in Jerusalem (see 1 Kings 7:2)   ᵇ24 Hebrew *Coniah*, a variant of *Jehoiachin*; also in
verse 28   ᶜ25 Or *Chaldeans*   ᵈ5 Or *up from David's line*

⁷"So then, the days are coming," declares the LORD, "when people will no longer say, 'As surely as the LORD lives, who brought the Israelites up out of Egypt,' ⁸but they will say, 'As surely as the LORD lives, who brought the descendants of Israel up out of the land of the north and out of all the countries where he had banished them.' Then they will live in their own land."

Lying Prophets

⁹Concerning the prophets:

My heart is broken within me;
  all my bones tremble.
I am like a drunken man,
  like a man overcome by wine,
because of the LORD
  and his holy words.
¹⁰The land is full of adulterers;
  because of the curse*ᵃ* the land lies parched*ᵇ*
and the pastures in the desert are withered.
The ₗprophetsₗ follow an evil course
  and use their power unjustly.

¹¹"Both prophet and priest are godless;
  even in my temple I find their wickedness,"
            declares the LORD.
¹²"Therefore their path will become slippery;
  they will be banished to darkness
  and there they will fall.
I will bring disaster on them
  in the year they are punished,"
            declares the LORD.

¹³"Among the prophets of Samaria
  I saw this repulsive thing:
They prophesied by Baal
  and led my people Israel astray.
¹⁴And among the prophets of Jerusalem
  I have seen something horrible:
They commit adultery and live a lie.
They strengthen the hands of evildoers,
  so that no one turns from his wickedness.
They are all like Sodom to me;
  the people of Jerusalem are like Gomorrah."

¹⁵Therefore, this is what the LORD Almighty says concerning the prophets:

"I will make them eat bitter food
  and drink poisoned water,
because from the prophets of Jerusalem

ungodliness has spread throughout the land."

¹⁶This is what the LORD Almighty says:

"Do not listen to what the prophets are prophesying to you;
  they fill you with false hopes.
They speak visions from their own minds,
  not from the mouth of the LORD.
¹⁷They keep saying to those who despise me,
  'The LORD says: You will have peace.'
And to all who follow the stubbornness of their hearts
  they say, 'No harm will come to you.'
¹⁸But which of them has stood in the council of the LORD
  to see or to hear his word?
Who has listened and heard his word?
¹⁹See, the storm of the LORD
  will burst out in wrath,
a whirlwind swirling down
  on the heads of the wicked.
²⁰The anger of the LORD will not turn back
  until he fully accomplishes
  the purposes of his heart.
In days to come
  you will understand it clearly.
²¹I did not send these prophets,
  yet they have run with their message;
I did not speak to them,
  yet they have prophesied.
²²But if they had stood in my council,
  they would have proclaimed my words to my people
and would have turned them from their evil ways
  and from their evil deeds.

²³"Am I only a God nearby,"
  "and not a God far away?
²⁴Can anyone hide in secret places
  so that I cannot see him?"
            declares the LORD.
"Do not I fill heaven and earth?"
            declares the LORD.

²⁵"I have heard what the prophets say who prophesy lies in my name. They say, 'I had a dream! I had a dream!' ²⁶How long will this continue in the hearts of these lying prophets, who prophesy the delusions of their own minds? ²⁷They think the dreams they tell one another will make my people forget my name, just as their fathers forgot my name through Baal worship. ²⁸Let the prophet who has a dream tell his dream, but

ᵃ10 Or *because of these things*   *ᵇ10* Or *land mourns* let the one who has my word speak it faithfully. For what has straw to do with grain?" declares the LORD. **29**"Is not my word like fire," declares the LORD, "and like a hammer that breaks a rock in pieces?

30"Therefore," declares the LORD, "I am against the prophets who steal from one another words supposedly from me. **31**Yes," declares the LORD, "I am against the prophets who wag their own tongues and yet declare, 'The LORD declares.' **32**Indeed, I am against those who prophesy false dreams," declares the LORD. "They tell them and lead my people astray with their reckless lies, yet I did not send or appoint them. They do not benefit these people in the least," declares the LORD.

False Oracles and False Prophets

33"When these people, or a prophet or a priest, ask you, 'What is the oracle*a* of the LORD?' say to them, 'What oracle?*b* I will forsake you, declares the LORD.' **34**If a prophet or a priest or anyone else claims, 'This is the oracle of the LORD,' I will punish that man and his household. **35**This is what each of you keeps on saying to his friend or relative: 'What is the LORD's answer?' or 'What has the LORD spoken?' **36**But you must not mention 'the oracle of the LORD' again, because every man's own word becomes his oracle and so you distort the words of the living God, the LORD Almighty, our God. **37**This is what you keep saying to a prophet: 'What is the LORD's answer to you?' or 'What has the LORD spoken?' **38**Although you claim, 'This is the oracle of the LORD,' this is what the LORD says: You used the words, 'This is the oracle of the LORD,' even though I told you that you must not claim, 'This is the oracle of the LORD.' **39**Therefore, I will surely forget you and cast you out of my presence along with the city I gave to you and your fathers. **40**I will bring upon you everlasting disgrace — everlasting shame that will not be forgotten."

Two Baskets of Figs

24 After Jehoiachin*c* son of Jehoiakim king of Judah and the officials, the craftsmen and the artisans of Judah were carried into exile from Jerusalem to Babylon by Nebuchadnezzar king of Babylon, the LORD showed me two baskets of figs placed in front of the temple of the LORD. **2**One basket had very good figs, like those that ripen early; the other basket had very poor figs, so bad they could not be eaten.

3Then the LORD asked me, "What do you see, Jeremiah?"

"Figs," I answered. "The good ones are very good, but the poor ones are so bad they cannot be eaten."

4Then the word of the LORD came to me: **5**"This is what the LORD, the God of Israel, says: 'Like these good figs, I regard as good the exiles from Judah, whom I sent away from this place to the land of the Babylonians.*d* **6**My eyes will watch over them for their good, and I will bring them back to this land. I will build them up and not tear them down; I will plant them and not uproot them. **7**I will give them a heart to know me, that I am the LORD. They will be my people, and I will be their God, for they will return to me with all their heart.

8" 'But like the poor figs, which are so bad they cannot be eaten,' says the LORD, 'so will I deal with Zedekiah king of Judah, his officials and the survivors from Jerusalem, whether they remain in this land or live in Egypt. **9**I will make them abhorrent and an offense to all the kingdoms of the earth, a reproach and a byword, an object of ridicule and cursing, wherever I banish them. **10**I will send the sword, famine and plague against them until they are destroyed from the land I gave to them and their fathers.' "

Seventy Years of Captivity

25 The word came to Jeremiah concerning all the people of Judah in the fourth year of Jehoiakim son of Josiah king of Judah, which was the first year of Nebuchadnezzar king of Babylon. **2**So Jeremiah the prophet said to all the people of Judah and to all those living in Jerusalem: **3**For twenty-three years — from the thirteenth year of Josiah son of Amon king of Judah until this very day — the word of the LORD has come to me and I have spoken to you again and again, but you have not listened.

4And though the LORD has sent all his servants the prophets to you again and again, you have not listened or paid any attention. **5**They said, "Turn now, each of you, from your evil ways and your evil practices, and you can stay in the land the LORD gave to you and your fathers for ever and ever. **6**Do not follow other gods to serve and worship them; do not provoke me to anger with what

---

a33 Or *burden* (see Septuagint and Vulgate)   *b33* Hebrew; Septuagint and Vulgate *You are the burden.* (The Hebrew for *oracle* and *burden* is the same.)   *c1* Hebrew *Jeconiah,* a variant of *Jehoiachin*   *d5* Or *Chaldeans* your hands have made. Then I will not harm you."

⁷"But you did not listen to me," declares the LORD, "and you have provoked me with what your hands have made, and you have brought harm to yourselves."

⁸Therefore the LORD Almighty says this: "Because you have not listened to my words, ⁹I will summon all the peoples of the north and my servant Nebuchadnezzar king of Babylon," declares the LORD, "and I will bring them against this land and its inhabitants and against all the surrounding nations. I will completely destroy*ᵃ* them and make them an object of horror and scorn, and an everlasting ruin. ¹⁰I will banish from them the sounds of joy and gladness, the voices of bride and bridegroom, the sound of millstones and the light of the lamp. ¹¹This whole country will become a desolate wasteland, and these nations will serve the king of Babylon seventy years.

¹²"But when the seventy years are fulfilled, I will punish the king of Babylon and his nation, the land of the Babylonians,*ᵇ* for their guilt," declares the LORD, "and will make it desolate forever. ¹³I will bring upon that land all the things I have spoken against it, all that are written in this book and prophesied by Jeremiah against all the nations. ¹⁴They themselves will be enslaved by many nations and great kings; I will repay them according to their deeds and the work of their hands."

The Cup of God's Wrath

¹⁵This is what the LORD, the God of Israel, said to me: "Take from my hand this cup filled with the wine of my wrath and make all the nations to whom I send you drink it. ¹⁶When they drink it, they will stagger and go mad because of the sword I will send among them."

¹⁷So I took the cup from the LORD's hand and made all the nations to whom he sent me drink it: ¹⁸Jerusalem and the towns of Judah, its kings and officials, to make them a ruin and an object of horror and scorn and cursing, as they are today; ¹⁹Pharaoh king of Egypt, his attendants, his officials and all his people, ²⁰and all the foreign people there; all the kings of Uz; all the kings of the Philistines (those of Ashkelon, Gaza, Ekron, and the people left at Ashdod); ²¹Edom, Moab and Ammon; ²²all the kings of Tyre and Si-

don; the kings of the coastlands across the sea; ²³Dedan, Tema, Buz and all who are in distant places*ᶜ*; ²⁴all the kings of Arabia and all the kings of the foreign people who live in the desert; ²⁵all the kings of Zimri, Elam and Media; ²⁶and all the kings of the north, near and far, one after the other — all the kingdoms on the face of the earth. And after all of them, the king of Sheshach*ᵈ* will drink it too.

²⁷"Then tell them, 'This is what the LORD Almighty, the God of Israel, says: Drink, get drunk and vomit, and fall to rise no more because of the sword I will send among you.' ²⁸But if they refuse to take the cup from your hand and drink, tell them, 'This is what the LORD Almighty says: You must drink it! ²⁹See, I am beginning to bring disaster on the city that bears my Name, and will you indeed go unpunished? You will not go unpunished, for I am calling down a sword upon all who live on the earth, declares the LORD Almighty.'

³⁰"Now prophesy all these words against them and say to them:

" 'The LORD will roar from on high;
    he will thunder from his holy dwelling
    and roar mightily against his land.
He will shout like those who tread the
        grapes,
    shout against all who live on the
        earth.
³¹The tumult will resound to the ends of
        the earth,
    for the LORD will bring charges against
        the nations;
    he will bring judgment on all mankind
    and put the wicked to the sword,' "
                        declares the LORD.

³²This is what the LORD Almighty says:

"Look! Disaster is spreading
    from nation to nation;
a mighty storm is rising
    from the ends of the earth."

³³At that time those slain by the LORD will be everywhere — from one end of the earth to the other. They will not be mourned or gathered up or buried, but will be like refuse lying on the ground.

³⁴Weep and wail, you shepherds;
    roll in the dust, you leaders of the
        flock.

ᵃ9 The Hebrew term refers to the irrevocable giving over of things or persons to the LORD, often by totally destroying them.   *ᵇ12* Or *Chaldeans*   *ᶜ23* Or *who clip the hair by their foreheads*   *ᵈ26* *Sheshach* is a cryptogram for Babylon.

For your time to be slaughtered has
    come;
  you will fall and be shattered like fine
    pottery.
35The shepherds will have nowhere to
    flee,
  the leaders of the flock no place to
    escape.
36Hear the cry of the shepherds,
  the wailing of the leaders of the flock,
  for the LORD is destroying their
    pasture.
37The peaceful meadows will be laid
    waste
  because of the fierce anger of the
    LORD.
38Like a lion he will leave his lair,
  and their land will become desolate
  because of the sword*a* of the oppressor
  and because of the LORD's fierce
    anger.

Jeremiah Threatened With Death

26 Early in the reign of Jehoiakim son of Josiah king of Judah, this word came from the LORD: **2**"This is what the LORD says: Stand in the courtyard of the LORD's house and speak to all the people of the towns of Judah who come to worship in the house of the LORD. Tell them everything I command you; do not omit a word. **3**Perhaps they will listen and each will turn from his evil way. Then I will relent and not bring on them the disaster I was planning because of the evil they have done. **4**Say to them, 'This is what the LORD says: If you do not listen to me and follow my law, which I have set before you, **5**and if you do not listen to the words of my servants the prophets, whom I have sent to you again and again (though you have not listened), **6**then I will make this house like Shiloh and this city an object of cursing among all the nations of the earth.' "

7The priests, the prophets and all the people heard Jeremiah speak these words in the house of the LORD. **8**But as soon as Jeremiah finished telling all the people everything the LORD had commanded him to say, the priests, the prophets and all the people seized him and said, "You must die! **9**Why do you prophesy in the LORD's name that this house will be like Shiloh and this city will be desolate and deserted?" And all the people crowded around Jeremiah in the house of the LORD.

10When the officials of Judah heard about these things, they went up from the royal palace to the house of the LORD and took their places at the entrance of the New Gate of the LORD's house. **11**Then the priests and the prophets said to the officials and all the people, "This man should be sentenced to death because he has prophesied against this city. You have heard it with your own ears!"

12Then Jeremiah said to all the officials and all the people: "The LORD sent me to prophesy against this house and this city all the things you have heard. **13**Now reform your ways and your actions and obey the LORD your God. Then the LORD will relent and not bring the disaster he has pronounced against you. **14**As for me, I am in your hands; do with me whatever you think is good and right. **15**Be assured, however, that if you put me to death, you will bring the guilt of innocent blood on yourselves and on this city and on those who live in it, for in truth the LORD has sent me to you to speak all these words in your hearing."

16Then the officials and all the people said to the priests and the prophets, "This man should not be sentenced to death! He has spoken to us in the name of the LORD our God."

17Some of the elders of the land stepped forward and said to the entire assembly of people, **18**"Micah of Moresheth prophesied in the days of Hezekiah king of Judah. He told all the people of Judah, 'This is what the LORD Almighty says:

" 'Zion will be plowed like a field,
  Jerusalem will become a heap of
    rubble,
  the temple hill a mound overgrown
    with thickets.'*b*

19"Did Hezekiah king of Judah or anyone else in Judah put him to death? Did not Hezekiah fear the LORD and seek his favor? And did not the LORD relent, so that he did not bring the disaster he pronounced against them? We are about to bring a terrible disaster on ourselves!"

20(Now Uriah son of Shemaiah from Kiriath Jearim was another man who prophesied in the name of the LORD; he prophesied the same things against this city and this land as Jeremiah did. **21**When King Jehoiakim and all his officers and officials heard his words, the king sought to put him to death. But Uriah heard of it and fled in fear

---

a38 Some Hebrew manuscripts and Septuagint (see also Jer. 46:16 and 50:16); most Hebrew manuscripts *anger*
b18 Micah 3:12

THE LONELINESS OF OBEDIENCE

Last week Frank was in a busy restaurant with a group of friends. Suddenly someone said, "Let's split!" One by one the guys—under the pretense of going to the rest room—slipped outside without paying their bills.

Soon only Gordon and Frank were left. "C'mon," Gordon urged. "Let's go before we get caught."

"No way. I'm paying for my dinner. You guys are wrong."

Well, Gordon split, the manager was really upset, the police arrived, and now Frank is catching serious heat from his so-called friends.

Look It Up
••••

Living for God and being obedient to his will often result in loneliness. Consider:

• The career of Jeremiah the prophet: "But as soon as Jeremiah finished telling all the people everything the LORD had commanded him to say, the priests, the prophets and all the people seized him and said, 'You must die!' " (Jeremiah 26:8).

• The words of Christ: "All men will hate you because of me, but he who stands firm to the end will be saved" (Matthew 10:22).

• The experience of Paul: "In fact, everyone who wants to live a godly life in Christ Jesus will be persecuted" (2 Timothy 3:12).

Think It Through
••••

Has obedience to Christ ever cost you anything? Have you ever felt the pain of loneliness because you refused to join others in doing something wrong?

What would you have done in Frank's situation?

Work It Out
••••

Determine your response in each of these instances:

1. Friends invite you to a wild celebration (complete with alcohol and without adults).

2. At the movie theater, everyone in the group votes to see a popular R-rated horror flick.

3. You are grounded, but your parents are out for the evening. Some classmates drop by and urge you to come with them "for just a few minutes."

4. In a classroom discussion about sex, the instructor says, "If you think that it is wrong to have sex before marriage, will you raise your hand?"

5. Everyone is standing around making fun of Chester, a clumsy kid in your class.

Nail It Down
••••

In Jeremiah 26:20–23 read how obedience to God can result in death.

Turn to pages 5, 1047 and 1222 for other readings on loneliness.
Turn to page 819 for Thursday's reading.

Topic
••••

LONELINESS

to Egypt. [22]King Jehoiakim, however, sent Elnathan son of Acbor to Egypt, along with some other men. [23]They brought Uriah out of Egypt and took him to King Jehoiakim, who had him struck down with a sword and his body thrown into the burial place of the common people.)

[24]Furthermore, Ahikam son of Shaphan supported Jeremiah, and so he was not handed over to the people to be put to death.

Judah to Serve Nebuchadnezzar

27 Early in the reign of Zedekiah[a] son of Josiah king of Judah, this word came to Jeremiah from the LORD: [2]This is what the LORD said to me: "Make a yoke out of straps and crossbars and put it on your neck. [3]Then send word to the kings of Edom, Moab, Ammon, Tyre and Sidon through the envoys who have come to Jerusalem to Zedekiah king of Judah. [4]Give them a message for their masters and say, 'This is what the LORD Almighty, the God of Israel, says: "Tell this to your masters: [5]With my great power and outstretched arm I made the earth and its people and the animals that are on it, and I give it to anyone I please. [6]Now I will hand all your countries over to my servant Nebuchadnezzar king of Babylon; I will make even the wild animals subject to him. [7]All nations will serve him and his son and his grandson until the time for his land comes; then many nations and great kings will subjugate him.

[8]" ' "If, however, any nation or kingdom will not serve Nebuchadnezzar king of Babylon or bow its neck under his yoke, I will punish that nation with the sword, famine and plague, declares the LORD, until I destroy it by his hand. [9]So do not listen to your prophets, your diviners, your interpreters of dreams, your mediums or your sorcerers who tell you, 'You will not serve the king of Babylon.' [10]They prophesy lies to you that will only serve to remove you far from your lands; I will banish you and you will perish. [11]But if any nation will bow its neck under the yoke of the king of Babylon and serve him, I will let that nation remain in its own land to till it and to live there, declares the LORD." ' "

[12]I gave the same message to Zedekiah king of Judah. I said, "Bow your neck under the yoke of the king of Babylon; serve him and his people, and you will live. [13]Why will

you and your people die by the sword, famine and plague with which the LORD has threatened any nation that will not serve the king of Babylon? [14]Do not listen to the words of the prophets who say to you, 'You will not serve the king of Babylon,' for they are prophesying lies to you. [15]I have not sent them,' declares the LORD. 'They are prophesying lies in my name. Therefore, I will banish you and you will perish, both you and the prophets who prophesy to you.' "

[16]Then I said to the priests and all these people, "This is what the LORD says: Do not listen to the prophets who say, 'Very soon now the articles from the LORD's house will be brought back from Babylon.' They are prophesying lies to you. [17]Do not listen to them. Serve the king of Babylon, and you will live. Why should this city become a ruin? [18]If they are prophets and have the word of the LORD, let them plead with the LORD Almighty that the furnishings remaining in the house of the LORD and in the palace of the king of Judah and in Jerusalem not be taken to Babylon. [19]For this is what the LORD Almighty says about the pillars, the Sea, the movable stands and the other furnishings that are left in this city, [20]which Nebuchadnezzar king of Babylon did not take away when he carried Jehoiachin[b] son of Jehoiakim king of Judah into exile from Jerusalem to Babylon, along with all the nobles of Judah and Jerusalem— [21]yes, this is what the LORD Almighty, the God of Israel, says about the things that are left in the house of the LORD and in the palace of the king of Judah and in Jerusalem: [22]'They will be taken to Babylon and there they will remain until the day I come for them,' declares the LORD. 'Then I will bring them back and restore them to this place.' "

The False Prophet Hananiah

28 In the fifth month of that same year, the fourth year, early in the reign of Zedekiah king of Judah, the prophet Hananiah son of Azzur, who was from Gibeon, said to me in the house of the LORD in the presence of the priests and all the people: [2]"This is what the LORD Almighty, the God of Israel, says: 'I will break the yoke of the king of Babylon. [3]Within two years I will bring back to this place all the articles of the LORD's house that Nebuchadnezzar king of Babylon removed from here and took to Babylon. [4]I will also bring back to this place Jehoia-

---

[a]1 A few Hebrew manuscripts and Syriac (see also Jer. 27:3, 12 and 28:1); most Hebrew manuscripts *Jehoiakim* (Most Septuagint manuscripts do not have this verse.)　　[b]20 Hebrew *Jeconiah*, a variant of *Jehoiachin*

chin[a] son of Jehoiakim king of Judah and all the other exiles from Judah who went to Babylon,' declares the LORD, 'for I will break the yoke of the king of Babylon.' "

[5]Then the prophet Jeremiah replied to the prophet Hananiah before the priests and all the people who were standing in the house of the LORD. [6]He said, "Amen! May the LORD do so! May the LORD fulfill the words you have prophesied by bringing the articles of the LORD's house and all the exiles back to this place from Babylon. [7]Nevertheless, listen to what I have to say in your hearing and in the hearing of all the people: [8]From early times the prophets who preceded you and me have prophesied war, disaster and plague against many countries and great kingdoms. [9]But the prophet who prophesies peace will be recognized as one truly sent by the LORD only if his prediction comes true."

[10]Then the prophet Hananiah took the yoke off the neck of the prophet Jeremiah and broke it, [11]and he said before all the people, "This is what the LORD says: 'In the same way will I break the yoke of Nebuchadnezzar king of Babylon off the neck of all the nations within two years.' " At this, the prophet Jeremiah went on his way.

[12]Shortly after the prophet Hananiah had broken the yoke off the neck of the prophet Jeremiah, the word of the LORD came to Jeremiah: [13]"Go and tell Hananiah, 'This is what the LORD says: You have broken a wooden yoke, but in its place you will get a yoke of iron. [14]This is what the LORD Almighty, the God of Israel, says: I will put an iron yoke on the necks of all these nations to make them serve Nebuchadnezzar king of Babylon, and they will serve him. I will even give him control over the wild animals.' "

[15]Then the prophet Jeremiah said to Hananiah the prophet, "Listen, Hananiah! The LORD has not sent you, yet you have persuaded this nation to trust in lies. [16]Therefore, this is what the LORD says: 'I am about to remove you from the face of the earth. This very year you are going to die, because you have preached rebellion against the LORD.' "

[17]In the seventh month of that same year, Hananiah the prophet died.

A Letter to the Exiles

29 This is the text of the letter that the prophet Jeremiah sent from Jerusalem to the surviving elders among the exiles and to the priests, the prophets and all the other people Nebuchadnezzar had carried into exile from Jerusalem to Babylon. [2](This was after King Jehoiachin[a] and the queen mother, the court officials and the leaders of Judah and Jerusalem, the craftsmen and the artisans had gone into exile from Jerusalem.) [3]He entrusted the letter to Elasah son of Shaphan and to Gemariah son of Hilkiah, whom Zedekiah king of Judah sent to King Nebuchadnezzar in Babylon. It said:

[4]This is what the LORD Almighty, the God of Israel, says to all those I carried into exile from Jerusalem to Babylon: [5]"Build houses and settle down; plant gardens and eat what they produce. [6]Marry and have sons and daughters; find wives for your sons and give your daughters in marriage, so that they too may have sons and daughters. Increase in number there; do not decrease. [7]Also, seek the peace and prosperity of the city to which I have carried you into exile. Pray to the LORD for it, because if it prospers, you too will prosper." [8]Yes, this is what the LORD Almighty, the God of Israel, says: "Do not let the prophets and diviners among you deceive you. Do not listen to the dreams you encourage them to have. [9]They are prophesying lies to you in my name. I have not sent them," declares the LORD.

[10]This is what the LORD says: "When seventy years are completed for Babylon, I will come to you and fulfill my gracious promise to bring you back to this place. [11]For I know the plans I have for you," declares the LORD, "plans to prosper you and not to harm you, plans to give you hope and a future. [12]Then you will call upon me and come and pray to me, and I will listen to you. [13]You will seek me and find me when you seek me with all your heart. [14]I will be found by you," declares the LORD, "and will bring you back from captivity.[b] I will gather you from all the nations and places where I have banished you," declares the LORD, "and will bring you back to the place from which I carried you into exile."

[15]You may say, "The LORD has raised up prophets for us in Babylon," [16]but this is what the LORD says about the king who sits on David's throne and all the people who remain in this city, your countrymen who did not go with you into exile — [17]yes, this is what the LORD

---

[a]4,2 Hebrew *Jeconiah*, a variant of *Jehoiachin*　　[b]14 Or *will restore your fortunes*

WHO GAVE MARRIAGE SUCH A BAD RAP?

☐ THURSDAY

A ngie is adamant. "No way! I'm never getting married. Not after watching how my parents treat each other."

"But, Angie, just because your parents had a bad experience and divorced doesn't mean that you have to follow in their footsteps. You can still have a really good marriage one day."

"Nope. It isn't worth the risk. Too many of my friends tell the same horror stories. I'm not going to put myself through all that mess."

Look It Up
•••

The way people talk and act, you'd think that marriage is the worst idea anyone ever came up with. But listen to King Solomon—a man who had more than seven hundred wives: "He who finds a wife finds what is good and receives favor from the LORD" (Proverbs 18:22).

And listen to this encouragement from the apostle Paul, a bachelor who helped lead the early church: "A deacon must be the husband of but one wife and must manage his children and his household well" (1 Timothy 3:12).

"So I counsel younger widows to marry, to have children, to manage their homes and to give the enemy no opportunity for slander" (1 Timothy 5:14).

Think It Through
•••

When we hear about a quack doctor, we don't decide that medical principles are suddenly invalid. And when an airplane crashes, we don't conclude that the laws of aerodynamics no longer work.

So why, when a lot of people bail out of their marriages, do we write marriage off as a bad deal?

Is the institution of marriage defective, or are the people involved defective?

Work It Out
•••

Don't let a warped and twisted culture brainwash you into believing that marriage doesn't work. Marriage does work— amazingly well—when those involved follow the principles God has given in his Word.

Ask God to open your spiritual eyes and spiritual ears to the truth about Christian marriage. (And begin now praying that, if it is his will for you to marry, God will prepare you and your potential mate for each other and his service.)

Nail It Down
•••

Read God's command to the Hebrews who were in exile in Babylon—Jeremiah 29:6—then read Jeremiah 29:11.

Turn to pages 315, 478 and 996 for other readings on marriage.
Turn to page 853 for Friday's reading.

Topic
••••

MARRIAGE

Almighty says: "I will send the sword, famine and plague against them and I will make them like poor figs that are so bad they cannot be eaten. **18**I will pursue them with the sword, famine and plague and will make them abhorrent to all the kingdoms of the earth and an object of cursing and horror, of scorn and reproach, among all the nations where I drive them. **19**For they have not listened to my words," declares the LORD, "words that I sent to them again and again by my servants the prophets. And you exiles have not listened either," declares the LORD.

20Therefore, hear the word of the LORD, all you exiles whom I have sent away from Jerusalem to Babylon. **21**This is what the LORD Almighty, the God of Israel, says about Ahab son of Kolaiah and Zedekiah son of Maaseiah, who are prophesying lies to you in my name: "I will hand them over to Nebuchadnezzar king of Babylon, and he will put them to death before your very eyes. **22**Because of them, all the exiles from Judah who are in Babylon will use this curse: 'The LORD treat you like Zedekiah and Ahab, whom the king of Babylon burned in the fire.' **23**For they have done outrageous things in Israel; they have committed adultery with their neighbors' wives and in my name have spoken lies, which I did not tell them to do. I know it and am a witness to it," declares the LORD.

Message to Shemaiah

24Tell Shemaiah the Nehelamite, **25**"This is what the LORD Almighty, the God of Israel, says: You sent letters in your own name to all the people in Jerusalem, to Zephaniah son of Maaseiah the priest, and to all the other priests. You said to Zephaniah, **26**'The LORD has appointed you priest in place of Jehoiada to be in charge of the house of the LORD; you should put any madman who acts like a prophet into the stocks and neckirons. **27**So why have you not reprimanded Jeremiah from Anathoth, who poses as a prophet among you? **28**He has sent this message to us in Babylon: It will be a long time. Therefore build houses and settle down; plant gardens and eat what they produce.' "

29Zephaniah the priest, however, read the letter to Jeremiah the prophet. **30**Then the word of the LORD came to Jeremiah: **31**"Send

this message to all the exiles: 'This is what the LORD says about Shemaiah the Nehelamite: Because Shemaiah has prophesied to you, even though I did not send him, and has led you to believe a lie, **32**this is what the LORD says: I will surely punish Shemaiah the Nehelamite and his descendants. He will have no one left among this people, nor will he see the good things I will do for my people, declares the LORD, because he has preached rebellion against me.' "

Restoration of Israel

30 This is the word that came to Jeremiah from the LORD: **2**"This is what the LORD, the God of Israel, says: 'Write in a book all the words I have spoken to you. **3**The days are coming,' declares the LORD, 'when I will bring my people Israel and Judah back from captivity*a* and restore them to the land I gave their forefathers to possess,' says the LORD."

4These are the words the LORD spoke concerning Israel and Judah: **5**"This is what the LORD says:

" 'Cries of fear are heard—
    terror, not peace.
6Ask and see:
    Can a man bear children?
Then why do I see every strong man
    with his hands on his stomach like a
        woman in labor,
    every face turned deathly pale?
7How awful that day will be!
    None will be like it.
It will be a time of trouble for Jacob,
    but he will be saved out of it.

8" ' In that day,' declares the LORD
        Almighty,
    'I will break the yoke off their necks
and will tear off their bonds;
    no longer will foreigners enslave
        them.
9Instead, they will serve the LORD their
        God
    and David their king,
    whom I will raise up for them.

10" 'So do not fear, O Jacob my servant;
    do not be dismayed, O Israel,'
                declares the LORD.
'I will surely save you out of a distant
        place,
    your descendants from the land of
        their exile.

---

a3 Or *will restore the fortunes of my people Israel and Judah*

Jacob will again have peace and
  security,
  and no one will make him afraid.
[11]I am with you and will save you,'
  declares the Lord.
'Though I completely destroy all the
  nations
  among which I scatter you,
  I will not completely destroy you.
I will discipline you but only with
  justice;
  I will not let you go entirely
  unpunished.'

[12]"This is what the Lord says:

" 'Your wound is incurable,
  your injury beyond healing.
[13]There is no one to plead your cause,
  no remedy for your sore,
  no healing for you.
[14]All your allies have forgotten you;
  they care nothing for you.
I have struck you as an enemy would
  and punished you as would the cruel,
because your guilt is so great
  and your sins so many.
[15]Why do you cry out over your wound,
  your pain that has no cure?
Because of your great guilt and many
  sins
  I have done these things to you.

[16]" 'But all who devour you will be
  devoured;
  all your enemies will go into exile.
Those who plunder you will be
  plundered;
  all who make spoil of you I will
  despoil.
[17]But I will restore you to health
  and heal your wounds,'
                  declares the Lord,
'because you are called an outcast,
  Zion for whom no one cares.'

[18]"This is what the Lord says:

" 'I will restore the fortunes of Jacob's
  tents
  and have compassion on his
  dwellings;
the city will be rebuilt on her ruins,
  and the palace will stand in its proper
  place.
[19]From them will come songs of
  thanksgiving
  and the sound of rejoicing.
I will add to their numbers,

and they will not be decreased;
I will bring them honor,
  and they will not be disdained.
[20]Their children will be as in days of old,
  and their community will be
  established before me;
I will punish all who oppress them.
[21]Their leader will be one of their own;
  their ruler will arise from among
  them.
I will bring him near and he will come
  close to me,
  for who is he who will devote himself
  to be close to me?'
                  declares the Lord.
[22]" 'So you will be my people,
  and I will be your God.' "

[23]See, the storm of the Lord
  will burst out in wrath,
  a driving wind swirling down
  on the heads of the wicked.
[24]The fierce anger of the Lord will not
  turn back
  until he fully accomplishes
  the purposes of his heart.
In days to come
  you will understand this.

31 "At that time," declares the Lord, "I
  will be the God of all the clans of Israel, and they will be my people."
[2]This is what the Lord says:

"The people who survive the sword
  will find favor in the desert;
  I will come to give rest to Israel."

[3]The Lord appeared to us in the past,[a]
saying:

"I have loved you with an everlasting
  love;
  I have drawn you with
  loving-kindness.
[4]I will build you up again
  and you will be rebuilt, O Virgin
  Israel.
Again you will take up your
  tambourines
  and go out to dance with the joyful.
[5]Again you will plant vineyards
  on the hills of Samaria;
the farmers will plant them
  and enjoy their fruit.
[6]There will be a day when watchmen cry
  out
  on the hills of Ephraim,
'Come, let us go up to Zion,

[a]3 Or Lord has appeared to us from afar

to the L‌ord our God.' "

⁷This is what the L‌ord says:

"Sing with joy for Jacob;
    shout for the foremost of the nations.
Make your praises heard, and say,
    'O L‌ord, save your people,
    the remnant of Israel.'
⁸See, I will bring them from the land of
      the north
    and gather them from the ends of the
      earth.
Among them will be the blind and the
      lame,
    expectant mothers and women in
      labor;
    a great throng will return.
⁹They will come with weeping;
    they will pray as I bring them back.
I will lead them beside streams of water
    on a level path where they will not
      stumble,
because I am Israel's father,
    and Ephraim is my firstborn son.

¹⁰"Hear the word of the L‌ord, O nations;
    proclaim it in distant coastlands:
'He who scattered Israel will gather
      them
    and will watch over his flock like a
      shepherd.'
¹¹For the L‌ord will ransom Jacob
    and redeem them from the hand of
      those stronger than they.
¹²They will come and shout for joy on the
      heights of Zion;
    they will rejoice in the bounty of the
      L‌ord—
the grain, the new wine and the oil,
    the young of the flocks and herds.
They will be like a well-watered garden,
    and they will sorrow no more.
¹³Then maidens will dance and be glad,
    young men and old as well.
I will turn their mourning into gladness;
    I will give them comfort and joy
      instead of sorrow.
¹⁴I will satisfy the priests with abundance,
    and my people will be filled with my
      bounty,"
                declares the L‌ord.

¹⁵This is what the L‌ord says:

"A voice is heard in Ramah,
    mourning and great weeping,
Rachel weeping for her children
    and refusing to be comforted,

because her children are no more."

¹⁶This is what the L‌ord says:

"Restrain your voice from weeping
    and your eyes from tears,
for your work will be rewarded,"
                declares the L‌ord.
"They will return from the land of the
      enemy.
¹⁷So there is hope for your future,"
                declares the L‌ord.
"Your children will return to their own
      land.

¹⁸"I have surely heard Ephraim's
      moaning:
'You disciplined me like an unruly
      calf,
    and I have been disciplined.
Restore me, and I will return,
    because you are the L‌ord my God.
¹⁹After I strayed,
    I repented;
after I came to understand,
    I beat my breast.
I was ashamed and humiliated
    because I bore the disgrace of my
      youth.'
²⁰Is not Ephraim my dear son,
    the child in whom I delight?
Though I often speak against him,
    I still remember him.
Therefore my heart yearns for him;
    I have great compassion for him,"
                declares the L‌ord.

²¹"Set up road signs;
    put up guideposts.
Take note of the highway,
    the road that you take.
Return, O Virgin Israel,
    return to your towns.
²²How long will you wander,
    O unfaithful daughter?
The L‌ord will create a new thing on
      earth—
    a woman will surround^a a man."

²³This is what the L‌ord Almighty, the God
of Israel, says: "When I bring them back
from captivity,^b the people in the land of
Judah and in its towns will once again use
these words: 'The L‌ord bless you, O righteous dwelling, O sacred mountain.' ²⁴Peo-
ple will live together in Judah and all its
towns—farmers and those who move about
with their flocks. ²⁵I will refresh the weary
and satisfy the faint."

---

^a22 Or *will go about* ⌊*seeking*⌋; or *will protect*   ^b23 Or *I restore their fortunes*

26At this I awoke and looked around. My sleep had been pleasant to me.

27"The days are coming," declares the LORD, "when I will plant the house of Israel and the house of Judah with the offspring of men and of animals. **28**Just as I watched over them to uproot and tear down, and to overthrow, destroy and bring disaster, so I will watch over them to build and to plant," declares the LORD. **29**"In those days people will no longer say,

'The fathers have eaten sour grapes,
    and the children's teeth are set on
        edge.'

30Instead, everyone will die for his own sin; whoever eats sour grapes — his own teeth will be set on edge.

31"The time is coming," declares the LORD,
    "when I will make a new covenant
    with the house of Israel
        and with the house of Judah.
32It will not be like the covenant
        I made with their forefathers
    when I took them by the hand
        to lead them out of Egypt,
because they broke my covenant,
    though I was a husband to*ᵃ* them,*ᵇ*"
            declares the LORD.
33"This is the covenant I will make with
        the house of Israel
    after that time," declares the LORD.
    "I will put my law in their minds
        and write it on their hearts.
    I will be their God,
        and they will be my people.
34No longer will a man teach his
            neighbor,
    or a man his brother, saying, 'Know
        the LORD,'
because they will all know me,
    from the least of them to the
            greatest,"
            declares the LORD.
"For I will forgive their wickedness
    and will remember their sins no
        more."

35This is what the LORD says,

he who appoints the sun
    to shine by day,
who decrees the moon and stars
    to shine by night,
who stirs up the sea
    so that its waves roar —

the LORD Almighty is his name:
36"Only if these decrees vanish from my
        sight,"
        declares the LORD,
"will the descendants of Israel ever
        cease
    to be a nation before me."

37This is what the LORD says:

"Only if the heavens above can be
        measured
    and the foundations of the earth
        below be searched out
will I reject all the descendants of Israel
    because of all they have done,"
            declares the LORD.

38"The days are coming," declares the LORD, "when this city will be rebuilt for me from the Tower of Hananel to the Corner Gate. **39**The measuring line will stretch from there straight to the hill of Gareb and then turn to Goah. **40**The whole valley where dead bodies and ashes are thrown, and all the terraces out to the Kidron Valley on the east as far as the corner of the Horse Gate, will be holy to the LORD. The city will never again be uprooted or demolished."

Jeremiah Buys a Field

32 This is the word that came to Jeremiah from the LORD in the tenth year of Zedekiah king of Judah, which was the eighteenth year of Nebuchadnezzar. **2**The army of the king of Babylon was then besieging Jerusalem, and Jeremiah the prophet was confined in the courtyard of the guard in the royal palace of Judah.

3Now Zedekiah king of Judah had imprisoned him there, saying, "Why do you prophesy as you do? You say, 'This is what the LORD says: I am about to hand this city over to the king of Babylon, and he will capture it. **4**Zedekiah king of Judah will not escape out of the hands of the Babylonians*ᶜ* but will certainly be handed over to the king of Babylon, and will speak with him face to face and see him with his own eyes. **5**He will take Zedekiah to Babylon, where he will remain until I deal with him, declares the LORD. If you fight against the Babylonians, you will not succeed.' "

6Jeremiah said, "The word of the LORD came to me: **7**Hanamel son of Shallum your uncle is going to come to you and say, 'Buy

---

ᵃ32 Hebrew; Septuagint and Syriac / *and I turned away from*   *ᵇ32* Or *was their master*   *ᶜ4* Or *Chaldeans;* also in verses 5, 24, 25, 28, 29 and 43 my field at Anathoth, because as nearest relative it is your right and duty to buy it.'

8"Then, just as the Lord had said, my cousin Hanamel came to me in the courtyard of the guard and said, 'Buy my field at Anathoth in the territory of Benjamin. Since it is your right to redeem it and possess it, buy it for yourself.'

"I knew that this was the word of the Lord; **9**so I bought the field at Anathoth from my cousin Hanamel and weighed out for him seventeen shekels*a* of silver. **10**I signed and sealed the deed, had it witnessed, and weighed out the silver on the scales. **11**I took the deed of purchase — the sealed copy containing the terms and conditions, as well as the unsealed copy — **12**and I gave this deed to Baruch son of Neriah, the son of Mahseiah, in the presence of my cousin Hanamel and of the witnesses who had signed the deed and of all the Jews sitting in the courtyard of the guard.

13"In their presence I gave Baruch these instructions: **14**'This is what the Lord Almighty, the God of Israel, says: Take these documents, both the sealed and unsealed copies of the deed of purchase, and put them in a clay jar so they will last a long time. **15**For this is what the Lord Almighty, the God of Israel, says: Houses, fields and vineyards will again be bought in this land.'

16"After I had given the deed of purchase to Baruch son of Neriah, I prayed to the Lord:

17"Ah, Sovereign Lord, you have made the heavens and the earth by your great power and outstretched arm. Nothing is too hard for you. **18**You show love to thousands but bring the punishment for the fathers' sins into the laps of their children after them. O great and powerful God, whose name is the Lord Almighty, **19**great are your purposes and mighty are your deeds. Your eyes are open to all the ways of men; you reward everyone according to his conduct and as his deeds deserve. **20**You performed miraculous signs and wonders in Egypt and have continued them to this day, both in Israel and among all mankind, and have gained the renown that is still yours. **21**You brought your people Israel out of Egypt with signs and wonders, by a mighty hand and an outstretched arm and with great terror. **22**You gave them this land you had sworn to give their forefathers, a land flowing with milk and honey. **23**They came in and took possession of it, but they did not obey you or follow your law; they did not do what you commanded them to do. So you brought all this disaster upon them.

24"See how the siege ramps are built up to take the city. Because of the sword, famine and plague, the city will be handed over to the Babylonians who are attacking it. What you said has happened, as you now see. **25**And though the city will be handed over to the Babylonians, you, O Sovereign Lord, say to me, 'Buy the field with silver and have the transaction witnessed.'"

26Then the word of the Lord came to Jeremiah: **27**"I am the Lord, the God of all mankind. Is anything too hard for me? **28**Therefore, this is what the Lord says: I am about to hand this city over to the Babylonians and to Nebuchadnezzar king of Babylon, who will capture it. **29**The Babylonians who are attacking this city will come in and set it on fire; they will burn it down, along with the houses where the people provoked me to anger by burning incense on the roofs to Baal and by pouring out drink offerings to other gods.

30"The people of Israel and Judah have done nothing but evil in my sight from their youth; indeed, the people of Israel have done nothing but provoke me with what their hands have made, declares the Lord. **31**From the day it was built until now, this city has so aroused my anger and wrath that I must remove it from my sight. **32**The people of Israel and Judah have provoked me by all the evil they have done — they, their kings and officials, their priests and prophets, the men of Judah and the people of Jerusalem. **33**They turned their backs to me and not their faces; though I taught them again and again, they would not listen or respond to discipline. **34**They set up their abominable idols in the house that bears my Name and defiled it. **35**They built high places for Baal in the Valley of Ben Hinnom to sacrifice their sons and daughters*b* to Molech, though I never commanded, nor did it enter my mind, that they should do such a detestable thing and so make Judah sin.

36"You are saying about this city, 'By the sword, famine and plague it will be handed over to the king of Babylon'; but this is what

a9 That is, about 7 ounces (about 200 grams)   *b35* Or *to make their sons and daughters pass through ⸤the fire⸥*

the Lord, the God of Israel, says: **37**I will surely gather them from all the lands where I banish them in my furious anger and great wrath; I will bring them back to this place and let them live in safety. **38**They will be my people, and I will be their God. **39**I will give them singleness of heart and action, so that they will always fear me for their own good and the good of their children after them. **40**I will make an everlasting covenant with them: I will never stop doing good to them, and I will inspire them to fear me, so that they will never turn away from me. **41**I will rejoice in doing them good and will assuredly plant them in this land with all my heart and soul.

42"This is what the Lord says: As I have brought all this great calamity on this people, so I will give them all the prosperity I have promised them. **43**Once more fields will be bought in this land of which you say, 'It is a desolate waste, without men or animals, for it has been handed over to the Babylonians.' **44**Fields will be bought for silver, and deeds will be signed, sealed and witnessed in the territory of Benjamin, in the villages around Jerusalem, in the towns of Judah and in the towns of the hill country, of the western foothills and of the Negev, because I will restore their fortunes,*a* declares the Lord."

Promise of Restoration

33 While Jeremiah was still confined in the courtyard of the guard, the word of the Lord came to him a second time: **2**"This is what the Lord says, he who made the earth, the Lord who formed it and established it — the Lord is his name: **3**'Call to me and I will answer you and tell you great and unsearchable things you do not know.' **4**For this is what the Lord, the God of Israel, says about the houses in this city and the royal palaces of Judah that have been torn down to be used against the siege ramps and the sword **5**in the fight with the Babylonians*b*: 'They will be filled with the dead bodies of the men I will slay in my anger and wrath. I will hide my face from this city because of all its wickedness.

6" 'Nevertheless, I will bring health and healing to it; I will heal my people and will let them enjoy abundant peace and security. **7**I will bring Judah and Israel back from captivity*c* and will rebuild them as they were before. **8**I will cleanse them from all

the sin they have committed against me and will forgive all their sins of rebellion against me. **9**Then this city will bring me renown, joy, praise and honor before all nations on earth that hear of all the good things I do for it; and they will be in awe and will tremble at the abundant prosperity and peace I provide for it.'

10"This is what the Lord says: 'You say about this place, "It is a desolate waste, without men or animals." Yet in the towns of Judah and the streets of Jerusalem that are deserted, inhabited by neither men nor animals, there will be heard once more **11**the sounds of joy and gladness, the voices of bride and bridegroom, and the voices of those who bring thank offerings to the house of the Lord, saying,

"Give thanks to the Lord Almighty,
    for the Lord is good;
    his love endures forever."

For I will restore the fortunes of the land as they were before,' says the Lord.

12"This is what the Lord Almighty says: 'In this place, desolate and without men or animals — in all its towns there will again be pastures for shepherds to rest their flocks. **13**In the towns of the hill country, of the western foothills and of the Negev, in the territory of Benjamin, in the villages around Jerusalem and in the towns of Judah, flocks will again pass under the hand of the one who counts them,' says the Lord.

14" 'The days are coming,' declares the Lord, 'when I will fulfill the gracious promise I made to the house of Israel and to the house of Judah.

15" 'In those days and at that time
    I will make a righteous Branch sprout
        from David's line;
    he will do what is just and right in the
        land.
16In those days Judah will be saved
    and Jerusalem will live in safety.
This is the name by which it*d* will be
        called:
    The Lord Our Righteousness.'

17For this is what the Lord says: 'David will never fail to have a man to sit on the throne of the house of Israel, **18**nor will the priests, who are Levites, ever fail to have a man to stand before me continually to offer burnt offerings, to burn grain offerings and to present sacrifices.' "

---

a44 Or *will bring them back from captivity*   *b5* Or *Chaldeans*   *c7* Or *will restore the fortunes of Judah and Israel*   *d16* Or *he*

[19]The word of the Lord came to Jeremiah: [20]"This is what the Lord says: 'If you can break my covenant with the day and my covenant with the night, so that day and night no longer come at their appointed time, [21]then my covenant with David my servant—and my covenant with the Levites who are priests ministering before me—can be broken and David will no longer have a descendant to reign on his throne. [22]I will make the descendants of David my servant and the Levites who minister before me as countless as the stars of the sky and as measureless as the sand on the seashore.'"

[23]The word of the Lord came to Jeremiah: [24]"Have you not noticed that these people are saying, 'The Lord has rejected the two kingdoms[a] he chose'? So they despise my people and no longer regard them as a nation. [25]This is what the Lord says: 'If I have not established my covenant with day and night and the fixed laws of heaven and earth, [26]then I will reject the descendants of Jacob and David my servant and will not choose one of his sons to rule over the descendants of Abraham, Isaac and Jacob. For I will restore their fortunes[b] and have compassion on them.'"

Warning to Zedekiah

34 While Nebuchadnezzar king of Babylon and all his army and all the kingdoms and peoples in the empire he ruled were fighting against Jerusalem and all its surrounding towns, this word came to Jeremiah from the Lord: [2]"This is what the Lord, the God of Israel, says: Go to Zedekiah king of Judah and tell him, 'This is what the Lord says: I am about to hand this city over to the king of Babylon, and he will burn it down. [3]You will not escape from his grasp but will surely be captured and handed over to him. You will see the king of Babylon with your own eyes, and he will speak with you face to face. And you will go to Babylon.

[4]" 'Yet hear the promise of the Lord, O Zedekiah king of Judah. This is what the Lord says concerning you: You will not die by the sword; [5]you will die peacefully. As people made a funeral fire in honor of your fathers, the former kings who preceded you, so they will make a fire in your honor and lament, "Alas, O master!" I myself make this promise, declares the Lord.'"

[6]Then Jeremiah the prophet told all this to Zedekiah king of Judah, in Jerusalem, [7]while the army of the king of Babylon was fighting against Jerusalem and the other cities of Judah that were still holding out—Lachish and Azekah. These were the only fortified cities left in Judah.

Freedom for Slaves

[8]The word came to Jeremiah from the Lord after King Zedekiah had made a covenant with all the people in Jerusalem to proclaim freedom for the slaves. [9]Everyone was to free his Hebrew slaves, both male and female; no one was to hold a fellow Jew in bondage. [10]So all the officials and people who entered into this covenant agreed that they would free their male and female slaves and no longer hold them in bondage. They agreed, and set them free. [11]But afterward they changed their minds and took back the slaves they had freed and enslaved them again.

[12]Then the word of the Lord came to Jeremiah: [13]"This is what the Lord, the God of Israel, says: I made a covenant with your forefathers when I brought them out of Egypt, out of the land of slavery. I said, [14]'Every seventh year each of you must free any fellow Hebrew who has sold himself to you. After he has served you six years, you must let him go free.'[c] Your fathers, however, did not listen to me or pay attention to me. [15]Recently you repented and did what is right in my sight: Each of you proclaimed freedom to his countrymen. You even made a covenant before me in the house that bears my Name. [16]But now you have turned around and profaned my name; each of you has taken back the male and female slaves you had set free to go where they wished. You have forced them to become your slaves again.

[17]"Therefore, this is what the Lord says: You have not obeyed me; you have not proclaimed freedom for your fellow countrymen. So I now proclaim 'freedom' for you, declares the Lord—'freedom' to fall by the sword, plague and famine. I will make you abhorrent to all the kingdoms of the earth. [18]The men who have violated my covenant and have not fulfilled the terms of the covenant they made before me, I will treat like the calf they cut in two and then walked between its pieces. [19]The leaders of Judah and Jerusalem, the court officials, the priests and all the people of the land who walked between the pieces of the calf, [20]I will hand over to their enemies who seek their lives. Their dead bodies will become food for the birds of the air and the beasts of the earth.

---

[a]24 Or families   [b]26 Or will bring them back from captivity   [c]14 Deut. 15:12

²¹"I will hand Zedekiah king of Judah and his officials over to their enemies who seek their lives, to the army of the king of Babylon, which has withdrawn from you. ²²I am going to give the order, declares the LORD, and I will bring them back to this city. They will fight against it, take it and burn it down. And I will lay waste the towns of Judah so no one can live there."

The Recabites

35 This is the word that came to Jeremiah from the LORD during the reign of Jehoiakim son of Josiah king of Judah: ²"Go to the Recabite family and invite them to come to one of the side rooms of the house of the LORD and give them wine to drink."

³So I went to get Jaazaniah son of Jeremiah, the son of Habazziniah, and his brothers and all his sons—the whole family of the Recabites. ⁴I brought them into the house of the LORD, into the room of the sons of Hanan son of Igdaliah the man of God. It was next to the room of the officials, which was over that of Maaseiah son of Shallum the doorkeeper. ⁵Then I set bowls full of wine and some cups before the men of the Recabite family and said to them, "Drink some wine."

⁶But they replied, "We do not drink wine, because our forefather Jonadab son of Recab gave us this command: 'Neither you nor your descendants must ever drink wine. ⁷Also you must never build houses, sow seed or plant vineyards; you must never have any of these things, but must always live in tents. Then you will live a long time in the land where you are nomads.' ⁸We have obeyed everything our forefather Jonadab son of Recab commanded us. Neither we nor our wives nor our sons and daughters have ever drunk wine ⁹or built houses to live in or had vineyards, fields or crops. ¹⁰We have lived in tents and have fully obeyed everything our forefather Jonadab commanded us. ¹¹But when Nebuchadnezzar king of Babylon invaded this land, we said, 'Come, we must go to Jerusalem to escape the Babylonian*a* and Aramean armies.' So we have remained in Jerusalem."

¹²Then the word of the LORD came to Jeremiah, saying: ¹³"This is what the LORD Almighty, the God of Israel, says: Go and tell the men of Judah and the people of Jerusalem, 'Will you not learn a lesson and obey my words?' declares the LORD. ¹⁴'Jonadab son of Recab ordered his sons not to drink wine and this command has been kept. To

this day they do not drink wine, because they obey their forefather's command. But I have spoken to you again and again, yet you have not obeyed me. ¹⁵Again and again I sent all my servants the prophets to you. They said, "Each of you must turn from your wicked ways and reform your actions; do not follow other gods to serve them. Then you will live in the land I have given to you and your fathers." But you have not paid attention or listened to me. ¹⁶The descendants of Jonadab son of Recab have carried out the command their forefather gave them, but these people have not obeyed me.'

¹⁷"Therefore, this is what the LORD God Almighty, the God of Israel, says: 'Listen! I am going to bring on Judah and on everyone living in Jerusalem every disaster I pronounced against them. I spoke to them, but they did not listen; I called to them, but they did not answer.'"

¹⁸Then Jeremiah said to the family of the Recabites, "This is what the LORD Almighty, the God of Israel, says: 'You have obeyed the command of your forefather Jonadab and have followed all his instructions and have done everything he ordered.' ¹⁹Therefore, this is what the LORD Almighty, the God of Israel, says: 'Jonadab son of Recab will never fail to have a man to serve me.'"

Jehoiakim Burns Jeremiah's Scroll

36 In the fourth year of Jehoiakim son of Josiah king of Judah, this word came to Jeremiah from the LORD: ²"Take a scroll and write on it all the words I have spoken to you concerning Israel, Judah and all the other nations from the time I began speaking to you in the reign of Josiah till now. ³Perhaps when the people of Judah hear about every disaster I plan to inflict on them, each of them will turn from his wicked way; then I will forgive their wickedness and their sin."

⁴So Jeremiah called Baruch son of Neriah, and while Jeremiah dictated all the words the LORD had spoken to him, Baruch wrote them on the scroll. ⁵Then Jeremiah told Baruch, "I am restricted; I cannot go to the LORD's temple. ⁶So you go to the house of the LORD on a day of fasting and read to the people from the scroll the words of the LORD that you wrote as I dictated. Read them to all the people of Judah who come in from their towns. ⁷Perhaps they will bring their petition before the LORD, and each will turn from

a 11 Or Chaldean

his wicked ways, for the anger and wrath pronounced against this people by the LORD are great."

⁸Baruch son of Neriah did everything Jeremiah the prophet told him to do; at the LORD's temple he read the words of the LORD from the scroll. ⁹In the ninth month of the fifth year of Jehoiakim son of Josiah king of Judah, a time of fasting before the LORD was proclaimed for all the people in Jerusalem and those who had come from the towns of Judah. ¹⁰From the room of Gemariah son of Shaphan the secretary, which was in the upper courtyard at the entrance of the New Gate of the temple, Baruch read to all the people at the LORD's temple the words of Jeremiah from the scroll.

¹¹When Micaiah son of Gemariah, the son of Shaphan, heard all the words of the LORD from the scroll, ¹²he went down to the secretary's room in the royal palace, where all the officials were sitting: Elishama the secretary, Delaiah son of Shemaiah, Elnathan son of Acbor, Gemariah son of Shaphan, Zedekiah son of Hananiah, and all the other officials. ¹³After Micaiah told them everything he had heard Baruch read to the people from the scroll, ¹⁴all the officials sent Jehudi son of Nethaniah, the son of Shelemiah, the son of Cushi, to say to Baruch, "Bring the scroll from which you have read to the people and come." So Baruch son of Neriah went to them with the scroll in his hand. ¹⁵They said to him, "Sit down, please, and read it to us."

So Baruch read it to them. ¹⁶When they heard all these words, they looked at each other in fear and said to Baruch, "We must report all these words to the king." ¹⁷Then they asked Baruch, "Tell us, how did you come to write all this? Did Jeremiah dictate it?"

¹⁸"Yes," Baruch replied, "he dictated all these words to me, and I wrote them in ink on the scroll."

¹⁹Then the officials said to Baruch, "You and Jeremiah, go and hide. Don't let anyone know where you are."

²⁰After they put the scroll in the room of Elishama the secretary, they went to the king in the courtyard and reported everything to him. ²¹The king sent Jehudi to get the scroll, and Jehudi brought it from the room of Elishama the secretary and read it to the king and all the officials standing beside him. ²²It was the ninth month and the king was sitting in the winter apartment,

with a fire burning in the firepot in front of him. ²³Whenever Jehudi had read three or four columns of the scroll, the king cut them off with a scribe's knife and threw them into the firepot, until the entire scroll was burned in the fire. ²⁴The king and all his attendants who heard all these words showed no fear, nor did they tear their clothes. ²⁵Even though Elnathan, Delaiah and Gemariah urged the king not to burn the scroll, he would not listen to them. ²⁶Instead, the king commanded Jerahmeel, a son of the king, Seraiah son of Azriel and Shelemiah son of Abdeel to arrest Baruch the scribe and Jeremiah the prophet. But the LORD had hidden them.

²⁷After the king burned the scroll containing the words that Baruch had written at Jeremiah's dictation, the word of the LORD came to Jeremiah: ²⁸"Take another scroll and write on it all the words that were on the first scroll, which Jehoiakim king of Judah burned up. ²⁹Also tell Jehoiakim king of Judah, 'This is what the LORD says: You burned that scroll and said, "Why did you write on it that the king of Babylon would certainly come and destroy this land and cut off both men and animals from it?" ³⁰Therefore, this is what the LORD says about Jehoiakim king of Judah: He will have no one to sit on the throne of David; his body will be thrown out and exposed to the heat by day and the frost by night. ³¹I will punish him and his children and his attendants for their wickedness; I will bring on them and those living in Jerusalem and the people of Judah every disaster I pronounced against them, because they have not listened.' "

³²So Jeremiah took another scroll and gave it to the scribe Baruch son of Neriah, and as Jeremiah dictated, Baruch wrote on it all the words of the scroll that Jehoiakim king of Judah had burned in the fire. And many similar words were added to them.

Jeremiah in Prison

37 Zedekiah son of Josiah was made king of Judah by Nebuchadnezzar king of Babylon; he reigned in place of Jehoiachin[a] son of Jehoiakim. ²Neither he nor his attendants nor the people of the land paid any attention to the words the LORD had spoken through Jeremiah the prophet.

³King Zedekiah, however, sent Jehucal son of Shelemiah with the priest Zephaniah son of Maaseiah to Jeremiah the prophet

---

ª1 Hebrew *Coniah*, a variant of *Jehoiachin*

with this message: "Please pray to the Lord our God for us."

⁴Now Jeremiah was free to come and go among the people, for he had not yet been put in prison. ⁵Pharaoh's army had marched out of Egypt, and when the Babylonians[a] who were besieging Jerusalem heard the report about them, they withdrew from Jerusalem.

⁶Then the word of the Lord came to Jeremiah the prophet: ⁷"This is what the Lord, the God of Israel, says: Tell the king of Judah, who sent you to inquire of me, 'Pharaoh's army, which has marched out to support you, will go back to its own land, to Egypt. ⁸Then the Babylonians will return and attack this city; they will capture it and burn it down.'

⁹"This is what the Lord says: Do not deceive yourselves, thinking, 'The Babylonians will surely leave us.' They will not! ¹⁰Even if you were to defeat the entire Babylonian[b] army that is attacking you and only wounded men were left in their tents, they would come out and burn this city down."

¹¹After the Babylonian army had withdrawn from Jerusalem because of Pharaoh's army, ¹²Jeremiah started to leave the city to go to the territory of Benjamin to get his share of the property among the people there. ¹³But when he reached the Benjamin Gate, the captain of the guard, whose name was Irijah son of Shelemiah, the son of Hananiah, arrested him and said, "You are deserting to the Babylonians!"

¹⁴"That's not true!" Jeremiah said. "I am not deserting to the Babylonians." But Irijah would not listen to him; instead, he arrested Jeremiah and brought him to the officials. ¹⁵They were angry with Jeremiah and had him beaten and imprisoned in the house of Jonathan the secretary, which they had made into a prison.

¹⁶Jeremiah was put into a vaulted cell in a dungeon, where he remained a long time. ¹⁷Then King Zedekiah sent for him and had him brought to the palace, where he asked him privately, "Is there any word from the Lord?"

"Yes," Jeremiah replied, "you will be handed over to the king of Babylon."

¹⁸Then Jeremiah said to King Zedekiah, "What crime have I committed against you or your officials or this people, that you have

put me in prison? ¹⁹Where are your prophets who prophesied to you, 'The king of Babylon will not attack you or this land'? ²⁰But now, my lord the king, please listen. Let me bring my petition before you: Do not send me back to the house of Jonathan the secretary, or I will die there."

²¹King Zedekiah then gave orders for Jeremiah to be placed in the courtyard of the guard and given bread from the street of the bakers each day until all the bread in the city was gone. So Jeremiah remained in the courtyard of the guard.

Jeremiah Thrown Into a Cistern

38 Shephatiah son of Mattan, Gedaliah son of Pashhur, Jehucal[c] son of Shelemiah, and Pashhur son of Malkijah heard what Jeremiah was telling all the people when he said, ²"This is what the Lord says: 'Whoever stays in this city will die by the sword, famine or plague, but whoever goes over to the Babylonians[d] will live. He will escape with his life; he will live.' ³And this is what the Lord says: 'This city will certainly be handed over to the army of the king of Babylon, who will capture it.'"

⁴Then the officials said to the king, "This man should be put to death. He is discouraging the soldiers who are left in this city, as well as all the people, by the things he is saying to them. This man is not seeking the good of these people but their ruin."

⁵"He is in your hands," King Zedekiah answered. "The king can do nothing to oppose you."

⁶So they took Jeremiah and put him into the cistern of Malkijah, the king's son, which was in the courtyard of the guard. They lowered Jeremiah by ropes into the cistern; it had no water in it, only mud, and Jeremiah sank down into the mud.

⁷But Ebed-Melech, a Cushite,[e] an official[f] in the royal palace, heard that they had put Jeremiah into the cistern. While the king was sitting in the Benjamin Gate, ⁸Ebed-Melech went out of the palace and said to him, ⁹"My lord the king, these men have acted wickedly in all they have done to Jeremiah the prophet. They have thrown him into a cistern, where he will starve to death when there is no longer any bread in the city."

¹⁰Then the king commanded Ebed-Melech the Cushite, "Take thirty men from here

a5 Or Chaldeans; also in verses 8, 9, 13 and 14   b10 Or Chaldean; also in verse 11   c1 Hebrew Jucal, a variant of Jehucal   d2 Or Chaldeans; also in verses 18, 19 and 23   e7 Probably from the upper Nile region   f7 Or a eunuch with you and lift Jeremiah the prophet out of the cistern before he dies."

[11]So Ebed-Melech took the men with him and went to a room under the treasury in the palace. He took some old rags and worn-out clothes from there and let them down with ropes to Jeremiah in the cistern. [12]Ebed-Melech the Cushite said to Jeremiah, "Put these old rags and worn-out clothes under your arms to pad the ropes." Jeremiah did so, [13]and they pulled him up with the ropes and lifted him out of the cistern. And Jeremiah remained in the courtyard of the guard.

Zedekiah Questions Jeremiah Again

[14]Then King Zedekiah sent for Jeremiah the prophet and had him brought to the third entrance to the temple of the Lord. "I am going to ask you something," the king said to Jeremiah. "Do not hide anything from me."

[15]Jeremiah said to Zedekiah, "If I give you an answer, will you not kill me? Even if I did give you counsel, you would not listen to me."

[16]But King Zedekiah swore this oath secretly to Jeremiah: "As surely as the Lord lives, who has given us breath, I will neither kill you nor hand you over to those who are seeking your life."

[17]Then Jeremiah said to Zedekiah, "This is what the Lord God Almighty, the God of Israel, says: 'If you surrender to the officers of the king of Babylon, your life will be spared and this city will not be burned down; you and your family will live. [18]But if you will not surrender to the officers of the king of Babylon, this city will be handed over to the Babylonians and they will burn it down; you yourself will not escape from their hands.' "

[19]King Zedekiah said to Jeremiah, "I am afraid of the Jews who have gone over to the Babylonians, for the Babylonians may hand me over to them and they will mistreat me."

[20]"They will not hand you over," Jeremiah replied. "Obey the Lord by doing what I tell you. Then it will go well with you, and your life will be spared. [21]But if you refuse to surrender, this is what the Lord has revealed to me: [22]All the women left in the palace of the king of Judah will be brought out to the officials of the king of Babylon. Those women will say to you:

" 'They misled you and overcame you—
    those trusted friends of yours.

Your feet are sunk in the mud;
    your friends have deserted you.'

[23]"All your wives and children will be brought out to the Babylonians. You yourself will not escape from their hands but will be captured by the king of Babylon; and this city will[a] be burned down."

[24]Then Zedekiah said to Jeremiah, "Do not let anyone know about this conversation, or you may die. [25]If the officials hear that I talked with you, and they come to you and say, 'Tell us what you said to the king and what the king said to you; do not hide it from us or we will kill you,' [26]then tell them, 'I was pleading with the king not to send me back to Jonathan's house to die there.' "

[27]All the officials did come to Jeremiah and question him, and he told them everything the king had ordered him to say. So they said no more to him, for no one had heard his conversation with the king.

[28]And Jeremiah remained in the courtyard of the guard until the day Jerusalem was captured.

The Fall of Jerusalem

39 This is how Jerusalem was taken: [1]In the ninth year of Zedekiah king of Judah, in the tenth month, Nebuchadnezzar king of Babylon marched against Jerusalem with his whole army and laid siege to it. [2]And on the ninth day of the fourth month of Zedekiah's eleventh year, the city wall was broken through. [3]Then all the officials of the king of Babylon came and took seats in the Middle Gate: Nergal-Sharezer of Samgar, Nebo-Sarsekim[b] a chief officer, Nergal-Sharezer a high official and all the other officials of the king of Babylon. [4]When Zedekiah king of Judah and all the soldiers saw them, they fled; they left the city at night by way of the king's garden, through the gate between the two walls, and headed toward the Arabah.[c]

[5]But the Babylonian[d] army pursued them and overtook Zedekiah in the plains of Jericho. They captured him and took him to Nebuchadnezzar king of Babylon at Riblah in the land of Hamath, where he pronounced sentence on him. [6]There at Riblah the king of Babylon slaughtered the sons of Zedekiah before his eyes and also killed all the nobles of Judah. [7]Then he put out Zede-

---

[a]23 Or and you will cause this city to   [b]3 Or Nergal-Sharezer, Samgar-Nebo, Sarsekim   [c]4 Or the Jordan
Valley   [d]5 Or Chaldean

kiah's eyes and bound him with bronze shackles to take him to Babylon.

8The Babylonians*ª* set fire to the royal palace and the houses of the people and broke down the walls of Jerusalem. **9**Nebuzaradan commander of the imperial guard carried into exile to Babylon the people who remained in the city, along with those who had gone over to him, and the rest of the people. **10**But Nebuzaradan the commander of the guard left behind in the land of Judah some of the poor people, who owned nothing; and at that time he gave them vineyards and fields.

11Now Nebuchadnezzar king of Babylon had given these orders about Jeremiah through Nebuzaradan commander of the imperial guard: **12**"Take him and look after him; don't harm him but do for him whatever he asks." **13**So Nebuzaradan the commander of the guard, Nebushazban a chief officer, Nergal-Sharezer a high official and all the other officers of the king of Babylon **14**sent and had Jeremiah taken out of the courtyard of the guard. They turned him over to Gedaliah son of Ahikam, the son of Shaphan, to take him back to his home. So he remained among his own people.

15While Jeremiah had been confined in the courtyard of the guard, the word of the Lord came to him: **16**"Go and tell Ebed-Melech the Cushite, 'This is what the Lord Almighty, the God of Israel, says: I am about to fulfill my words against this city through disaster, not prosperity. At that time they will be fulfilled before your eyes. **17**But I will rescue you on that day, declares the Lord; you will not be handed over to those you fear. **18**I will save you; you will not fall by the sword but will escape with your life, because you trust in me, declares the Lord.' "

Jeremiah Freed

40 The word came to Jeremiah from the Lord after Nebuzaradan commander of the imperial guard had released him at Ramah. He had found Jeremiah bound in chains among all the captives from Jerusalem and Judah who were being carried into exile to Babylon. **2**When the commander of the guard found Jeremiah, he said to him, "The Lord your God decreed this disaster for this place. **3**And now the Lord has brought it about; he has done just as he said he would. All this happened because you people sinned against the Lord and did not obey

him. **4**But today I am freeing you from the chains on your wrists. Come with me to Babylon, if you like, and I will look after you; but if you do not want to, then don't come. Look, the whole country lies before you; go wherever you please." **5**However, before Jeremiah turned to go,*ᵇ* Nebuzaradan added, "Go back to Gedaliah son of Ahikam, the son of Shaphan, whom the king of Babylon has appointed over the towns of Judah, and live with him among the people, or go anywhere else you please."

Then the commander gave him provisions and a present and let him go. **6**So Jeremiah went to Gedaliah son of Ahikam at Mizpah and stayed with him among the people who were left behind in the land.

Gedaliah Assassinated

7When all the army officers and their men who were still in the open country heard that the king of Babylon had appointed Gedaliah son of Ahikam as governor over the land and had put him in charge of the men, women and children who were the poorest in the land and who had not been carried into exile to Babylon, **8**they came to Gedaliah at Mizpah — Ishmael son of Nethaniah, Johanan and Jonathan the sons of Kareah, Seraiah son of Tanhumeth, the sons of Ephai the Netophathite, and Jaazaniah*ᶜ* the son of the Maacathite, and their men. **9**Gedaliah son of Ahikam, the son of Shaphan, took an oath to reassure them and their men. "Do not be afraid to serve the Babylonians,*ᵈ*" he said. "Settle down in the land and serve the king of Babylon, and it will go well with you. **10**I myself will stay at Mizpah to represent you before the Babylonians who come to us, but you are to harvest the wine, summer fruit and oil, and put them in your storage jars, and live in the towns you have taken over."

11When all the Jews in Moab, Ammon, Edom and all the other countries heard that the king of Babylon had left a remnant in Judah and had appointed Gedaliah son of Ahikam, the son of Shaphan, as governor over them, **12**they all came back to the land of Judah, to Gedaliah at Mizpah, from all the countries where they had been scattered. And they harvested an abundance of wine and summer fruit.

13Johanan son of Kareah and all the army officers still in the open country came to Gedaliah at Mizpah **14**and said to him, "Don't

---

ª8 Or *Chaldeans*   *ᵇ5* Or *Jeremiah answered*   *ᶜ8* Hebrew *Jezaniah,* a variant of *Jaazaniah*   *ᵈ9* Or *Chaldeans*; also in verse 10 you know that Baalis king of the Ammonites has sent Ishmael son of Nethaniah to take your life?" But Gedaliah son of Ahikam did not believe them.

15Then Johanan son of Kareah said privately to Gedaliah in Mizpah, "Let me go and kill Ishmael son of Nethaniah, and no one will know it. Why should he take your life and cause all the Jews who are gathered around you to be scattered and the remnant of Judah to perish?"

16But Gedaliah son of Ahikam said to Johanan son of Kareah, "Don't do such a thing! What you are saying about Ishmael is not true."

41 In the seventh month Ishmael son of Nethaniah, the son of Elishama, who was of royal blood and had been one of the king's officers, came with ten men to Gedaliah son of Ahikam at Mizpah. While they were eating together there, **2**Ishmael son of Nethaniah and the ten men who were with him got up and struck down Gedaliah son of Ahikam, the son of Shaphan, with the sword, killing the one whom the king of Babylon had appointed as governor over the land. **3**Ishmael also killed all the Jews who were with Gedaliah at Mizpah, as well as the Babylonian*a* soldiers who were there.

4The day after Gedaliah's assassination, before anyone knew about it, **5**eighty men who had shaved off their beards, torn their clothes and cut themselves came from Shechem, Shiloh and Samaria, bringing grain offerings and incense with them to the house of the LORD. **6**Ishmael son of Nethaniah went out from Mizpah to meet them, weeping as he went. When he met them, he said, "Come to Gedaliah son of Ahikam." **7**When they went into the city, Ishmael son of Nethaniah and the men who were with him slaughtered them and threw them into a cistern. **8**But ten of them said to Ishmael, "Don't kill us! We have wheat and barley, oil and honey, hidden in a field." So he let them alone and did not kill them with the others. **9**Now the cistern where he threw all the bodies of the men he had killed along with Gedaliah was the one King Asa had made as part of his defense against Baasha king of Israel. Ishmael son of Nethaniah filled it with the dead.

10Ishmael made captives of all the rest of the people who were in Mizpah — the king's daughters along with all the others who were left there, over whom Nebuzaradan commander of the imperial guard had ap-

pointed Gedaliah son of Ahikam. Ishmael son of Nethaniah took them captive and set out to cross over to the Ammonites.

11When Johanan son of Kareah and all the army officers who were with him heard about all the crimes Ishmael son of Nethaniah had committed, **12**they took all their men and went to fight Ishmael son of Nethaniah. They caught up with him near the great pool in Gibeon. **13**When all the people Ishmael had with him saw Johanan son of Kareah and the army officers who were with him, they were glad. **14**All the people Ishmael had taken captive at Mizpah turned and went over to Johanan son of Kareah. **15**But Ishmael son of Nethaniah and eight of his men escaped from Johanan and fled to the Ammonites.

Flight to Egypt

16Then Johanan son of Kareah and all the army officers who were with him led away all the survivors from Mizpah whom he had recovered from Ishmael son of Nethaniah after he had assassinated Gedaliah son of Ahikam: the soldiers, women, children and court officials he had brought from Gibeon. **17**And they went on, stopping at Geruth Kimham near Bethlehem on their way to Egypt **18**to escape the Babylonians.*b* They were afraid of them because Ishmael son of Nethaniah had killed Gedaliah son of Ahikam, whom the king of Babylon had appointed as governor over the land.

42 Then all the army officers, including Johanan son of Kareah and Jezaniah*c* son of Hoshaiah, and all the people from the least to the greatest approached **2**Jeremiah the prophet and said to him, "Please hear our petition and pray to the LORD your God for this entire remnant. For as you now see, though we were once many, now only a few are left. **3**Pray that the LORD your God will tell us where we should go and what we should do."

4"I have heard you," replied Jeremiah the prophet. "I will certainly pray to the LORD your God as you have requested; I will tell you everything the LORD says and will keep nothing back from you."

5Then they said to Jeremiah, "May the LORD be a true and faithful witness against us if we do not act in accordance with everything the LORD your God sends you to tell us. **6**Whether it is favorable or unfavorable, we will obey the LORD our God, to whom we are

---

*a*3 Or *Chaldean*   *b*18 Or *Chaldeans*   *c*1 Hebrew; Septuagint (see also 43:2) *Azariah* sending you, so that it will go well with us, for we will obey the LORD our God."

[7]Ten days later the word of the LORD came to Jeremiah. [8]So he called together Johanan son of Kareah and all the army officers who were with him and all the people from the least to the greatest. [9]He said to them, "This is what the LORD, the God of Israel, to whom you sent me to present your petition, says: [10]'If you stay in this land, I will build you up and not tear you down; I will plant you and not uproot you, for I am grieved over the disaster I have inflicted on you. [11]Do not be afraid of the king of Babylon, whom you now fear. Do not be afraid of him, declares the LORD, for I am with you and will save you and deliver you from his hands. [12]I will show you compassion so that he will have compassion on you and restore you to your land.'

[13]"However, if you say, 'We will not stay in this land,' and so disobey the LORD your God, [14]and if you say, 'No, we will go and live in Egypt, where we will not see war or hear the trumpet or be hungry for bread,' [15]then hear the word of the LORD, O remnant of Judah. This is what the LORD Almighty, the God of Israel, says: 'If you are determined to go to Egypt and you do go to settle there, [16]then the sword you fear will overtake you there, and the famine you dread will follow you into Egypt, and there you will die. [17]Indeed, all who are determined to go to Egypt to settle there will die by the sword, famine and plague; not one of them will survive or escape the disaster I will bring on them.' [18]This is what the LORD Almighty, the God of Israel, says: 'As my anger and wrath have been poured out on those who lived in Jerusalem, so will my wrath be poured out on you when you go to Egypt. You will be an object of cursing and horror, of condemnation and reproach; you will never see this place again.'

[19]"O remnant of Judah, the LORD has told you, 'Do not go to Egypt.' Be sure of this: I warn you today [20]that you made a fatal mistake[a] when you sent me to the LORD your God and said, 'Pray to the LORD our God for us; tell us everything he says and we will do it.' [21]I have told you today, but you still have not obeyed the LORD your God in all he sent me to tell you. [22]So now, be sure of this: You will die by the sword, famine and plague in the place where you want to go to settle."

43 When Jeremiah finished telling the people all the words of the LORD their God—everything the LORD had sent him to tell them— [2]Azariah son of Hoshaiah and Johanan son of Kareah and all the arrogant men said to Jeremiah, "You are lying! The LORD our God has not sent you to say, 'You must not go to Egypt to settle there.' [3]But Baruch son of Neriah is inciting you against us to hand us over to the Babylonians,[b] so they may kill us or carry us into exile to Babylon."

[4]So Johanan son of Kareah and all the army officers and all the people disobeyed the LORD's command to stay in the land of Judah. [5]Instead, Johanan son of Kareah and all the army officers led away all the remnant of Judah who had come back to live in the land of Judah from all the nations where they had been scattered. [6]They also led away all the men, women and children and the king's daughters whom Nebuzaradan commander of the imperial guard had left with Gedaliah son of Ahikam, the son of Shaphan, and Jeremiah the prophet and Baruch son of Neriah. [7]So they entered Egypt in disobedience to the LORD and went as far as Tahpanhes.

[8]In Tahpanhes the word of the LORD came to Jeremiah: [9]"While the Jews are watching, take some large stones with you and bury them in clay in the brick pavement at the entrance to Pharaoh's palace in Tahpanhes. [10]Then say to them, 'This is what the LORD Almighty, the God of Israel, says: I will send for my servant Nebuchadnezzar king of Babylon, and I will set his throne over these stones I have buried here; he will spread his royal canopy above them. [11]He will come and attack Egypt, bringing death to those destined for death, captivity to those destined for captivity, and the sword to those destined for the sword. [12]He[c] will set fire to the temples of the gods of Egypt; he will burn their temples and take their gods captive. As a shepherd wraps his garment around him, so will he wrap Egypt around himself and depart from there unscathed. [13]There in the temple of the sun[d] in Egypt he will demolish the sacred pillars and will burn down the temples of the gods of Egypt.'"

Disaster Because of Idolatry

44 This word came to Jeremiah concerning all the Jews living in Lower Egypt—in Migdol, Tahpanhes and Mem-

---

[a]20 Or *you erred in your hearts*   [b]3 Or *Chaldeans*   [c]12 Or *I*   [d]13 Or *in Heliopolis*

phis^a — and in Upper Egypt^b: **2**"This is what the LORD Almighty, the God of Israel, says: You saw the great disaster I brought on Jerusalem and on all the towns of Judah. Today they lie deserted and in ruins **3**because of the evil they have done. They provoked me to anger by burning incense and by worshiping other gods that neither they nor you nor your fathers ever knew. **4**Again and again I sent my servants the prophets, who said, 'Do not do this detestable thing that I hate!' **5**But they did not listen or pay attention; they did not turn from their wickedness or stop burning incense to other gods. **6**Therefore, my fierce anger was poured out; it raged against the towns of Judah and the streets of Jerusalem and made them the desolate ruins they are today.

7"Now this is what the LORD God Almighty, the God of Israel, says: Why bring such great disaster on yourselves by cutting off from Judah the men and women, the children and infants, and so leave yourselves without a remnant? **8**Why provoke me to anger with what your hands have made, burning incense to other gods in Egypt, where you have come to live? You will destroy yourselves and make yourselves an object of cursing and reproach among all the nations on earth. **9**Have you forgotten the wickedness committed by your fathers and by the kings and queens of Judah and the wickedness committed by you and your wives in the land of Judah and the streets of Jerusalem? **10**To this day they have not humbled themselves or shown reverence, nor have they followed my law and the decrees I set before you and your fathers.

11"Therefore, this is what the LORD Almighty, the God of Israel, says: I am determined to bring disaster on you and to destroy all Judah. **12**I will take away the remnant of Judah who were determined to go to Egypt to settle there. They will all perish in Egypt; they will fall by the sword or die from famine. From the least to the greatest, they will die by sword or famine. They will become an object of cursing and horror, of condemnation and reproach. **13**I will punish those who live in Egypt with the sword, famine and plague, as I punished Jerusalem. **14**None of the remnant of Judah who have gone to live in Egypt will escape or survive to return to the land of Judah, to which they long to return and live; none will return except a few fugitives."

15Then all the men who knew that their wives were burning incense to other gods, along with all the women who were present — a large assembly — and all the people living in Lower and Upper Egypt,^{c} said to Jeremiah, **16**"We will not listen to the message you have spoken to us in the name of the LORD! **17**We will certainly do everything we said we would: We will burn incense to the Queen of Heaven and will pour out drink offerings to her just as we and our fathers, our kings and our officials did in the towns of Judah and in the streets of Jerusalem. At that time we had plenty of food and were well off and suffered no harm. **18**But ever since we stopped burning incense to the Queen of Heaven and pouring out drink offerings to her, we have had nothing and have been perishing by sword and famine."

19The women added, "When we burned incense to the Queen of Heaven and poured out drink offerings to her, did not our husbands know that we were making cakes like her image and pouring out drink offerings to her?"

20Then Jeremiah said to all the people, both men and women, who were answering him, **21**"Did not the LORD remember and think about the incense burned in the towns of Judah and the streets of Jerusalem by you and your fathers, your kings and your officials and the people of the land? **22**When the LORD could no longer endure your wicked actions and the detestable things you did, your land became an object of cursing and a desolate waste without inhabitants, as it is today. **23**Because you have burned incense and have sinned against the LORD and have not obeyed him or followed his law or his decrees or his stipulations, this disaster has come upon you, as you now see."

24Then Jeremiah said to all the people, including the women, "Hear the word of the LORD, all you people of Judah in Egypt. **25**This is what the LORD Almighty, the God of Israel, says: You and your wives have shown by your actions what you promised when you said, 'We will certainly carry out the vows we made to burn incense and pour out drink offerings to the Queen of Heaven.'

"Go ahead then, do what you promised! Keep your vows! **26**But hear the word of the LORD, all Jews living in Egypt: 'I swear by my great name,' says the LORD, 'that no one from Judah living anywhere in Egypt will ever again invoke my name or swear, "As surely as the Sovereign LORD lives." **27**For I am watching over them for harm, not for good;

---

^{a}1 Hebrew *Noph* ^{b}1 Hebrew *in Pathros* ^{c}15 Hebrew *in Egypt and Pathros* the Jews in Egypt will perish by sword and famine until they are all destroyed. **28**Those who escape the sword and return to the land of Judah from Egypt will be very few. Then the whole remnant of Judah who came to live in Egypt will know whose word will stand—mine or theirs.

29"This will be the sign to you that I will punish you in this place,' declares the Lord, 'so that you will know that my threats of harm against you will surely stand.' **30**This is what the Lord says: 'I am going to hand Pharaoh Hophra king of Egypt over to his enemies who seek his life, just as I handed Zedekiah king of Judah over to Nebuchadnezzar king of Babylon, the enemy who was seeking his life.' "

A Message to Baruch

45 This is what Jeremiah the prophet told Baruch son of Neriah in the fourth year of Jehoiakim son of Josiah king of Judah, after Baruch had written on a scroll the words Jeremiah was then dictating: **2**"This is what the Lord, the God of Israel, says to you, Baruch: **3**You said, 'Woe to me! The Lord has added sorrow to my pain; I am worn out with groaning and find no rest.' "

4The Lord said, "Say this to him: 'This is what the Lord says: I will overthrow what I have built and uproot what I have planted, throughout the land. **5**Should you then seek great things for yourself? Seek them not. For I will bring disaster on all people, declares the Lord, but wherever you go I will let you escape with your life.' "

A Message About Egypt

46 This is the word of the Lord that came to Jeremiah the prophet concerning the nations:

2Concerning Egypt:

This is the message against the army of Pharaoh Neco king of Egypt, which was defeated at Carchemish on the Euphrates River by Nebuchadnezzar king of Babylon in the fourth year of Jehoiakim son of Josiah king of Judah:

3"Prepare your shields, both large and small,
  and march out for battle!
4Harness the horses,
  mount the steeds!
Take your positions
  with helmets on!

Polish your spears,
  put on your armor!
5What do I see?
  They are terrified,
they are retreating,
  their warriors are defeated.
They flee in haste
  without looking back,
  and there is terror on every side,"
            declares the Lord.
6"The swift cannot flee
  nor the strong escape.
In the north by the River Euphrates
  they stumble and fall.

7"Who is this that rises like the Nile,
  like rivers of surging waters?
8Egypt rises like the Nile,
  like rivers of surging waters.
She says, 'I will rise and cover the earth;
  I will destroy cities and their people.'
9Charge, O horses!
  Drive furiously, O charioteers!
March on, O warriors—
  men of Cush*a* and Put who carry
    shields,
  men of Lydia who draw the bow.
10But that day belongs to the Lord, the
    Lord Almighty—
  a day of vengeance, for vengeance on
    his foes.
The sword will devour till it is satisfied,
  till it has quenched its thirst with
    blood.
For the Lord, the Lord Almighty, will
    offer sacrifice
  in the land of the north by the River
    Euphrates.

11"Go up to Gilead and get balm,
  O Virgin Daughter of Egypt.
But you multiply remedies in vain;
  there is no healing for you.
12The nations will hear of your shame;
  your cries will fill the earth.
One warrior will stumble over another;
  both will fall down together."

13This is the message the Lord spoke to Jeremiah the prophet about the coming of Nebuchadnezzar king of Babylon to attack Egypt:

14"Announce this in Egypt, and proclaim it in Migdol;
  proclaim it also in Memphis*b* and
    Tahpanhes:
'Take your positions and get ready,

---

a9 That is, the upper Nile region   *b14* Hebrew *Noph*; also in verse 19

for the sword devours those around
    you.'
15Why will your warriors be laid low?
    They cannot stand, for the LORD will
        push them down.
16They will stumble repeatedly;
    they will fall over each other.
They will say, 'Get up, let us go back
    to our own people and our native
        lands,
    away from the sword of the
        oppressor.'
17There they will exclaim,
    'Pharaoh king of Egypt is only a loud
        noise;
    he has missed his opportunity.'

18"As surely as I live," declares the King,
    whose name is the LORD Almighty,
"one will come who is like Tabor among
        the mountains,
    like Carmel by the sea.
19Pack your belongings for exile,
    you who live in Egypt,
for Memphis will be laid waste
    and lie in ruins without inhabitant.

20"Egypt is a beautiful heifer,
    but a gadfly is coming
    against her from the north.
21The mercenaries in her ranks
    are like fattened calves.
They too will turn and flee together,
    they will not stand their ground,
for the day of disaster is coming upon
        them,
    the time for them to be punished.
22Egypt will hiss like a fleeing serpent
    as the enemy advances in force;
they will come against her with axes,
    like men who cut down trees.
23They will chop down her forest,"
                    declares the LORD,
    "dense though it be.
They are more numerous than locusts,
    they cannot be counted.
24The Daughter of Egypt will be put to
        shame,
    handed over to the people of the
        north."

25The LORD Almighty, the God of Israel,
says: "I am about to bring punishment on
Amon god of Thebes,a on Pharaoh, on
Egypt and her gods and her kings, and
on those who rely on Pharaoh. 26I will hand
them over to those who seek their lives, to
Nebuchadnezzar king of Babylon and his of-

ficers. Later, however, Egypt will be inhabited as in times past," declares the LORD.

27"Do not fear, O Jacob my servant;
    do not be dismayed, O Israel.
I will surely save you out of a distant
        place,
    your descendants from the land of
        their exile.
Jacob will again have peace and
        security,
    and no one will make him afraid.
28Do not fear, O Jacob my servant,
    for I am with you," declares the LORD.
"Though I completely destroy all the
        nations
    among which I scatter you,
    I will not completely destroy you.
I will discipline you but only with
        justice;
    I will not let you go entirely
        unpunished."

A Message About the Philistines

47 This is the word of the LORD that
came to Jeremiah the prophet concerning the Philistines before Pharaoh attacked Gaza:

2This is what the LORD says:

"See how the waters are rising in the
        north;
    they will become an overflowing
        torrent.
They will overflow the land and
        everything in it,
    the towns and those who live in
        them.
The people will cry out;
    all who dwell in the land will wail
3at the sound of the hoofs of galloping
        steeds,
    at the noise of enemy chariots
    and the rumble of their wheels.
Fathers will not turn to help their
        children;
    their hands will hang limp.
4For the day has come
    to destroy all the Philistines
and to cut off all survivors
    who could help Tyre and Sidon.
The LORD is about to destroy the
        Philistines,
    the remnant from the coasts of
        Caphtor.b
5Gaza will shave her head in mourning;
    Ashkelon will be silenced.

a25 Hebrew No   b4 That is, Crete

O remnant on the plain,
how long will you cut yourselves?

6 " 'Ah, sword of the LORD,' ⌐you cry⌐
'how long till you rest?
Return to your scabbard;
cease and be still.'
7 But how can it rest
when the LORD has commanded it,
when he has ordered it
to attack Ashkelon and the coast?"

A Message About Moab

48 Concerning Moab:

This is what the LORD Almighty, the
God of Israel, says:

"Woe to Nebo, for it will be ruined.
Kiriathaim will be disgraced and
captured;
the stronghold[a] will be disgraced and
shattered.
2 Moab will be praised no more;
in Heshbon[b] men will plot her
downfall:
'Come, let us put an end to that
nation.'
You too, O Madmen,[c] will be silenced;
the sword will pursue you.
3 Listen to the cries from Horonaim,
cries of great havoc and destruction.
4 Moab will be broken;
her little ones will cry out.[d]
5 They go up the way to Luhith,
weeping bitterly as they go;
on the road down to Horonaim
anguished cries over the destruction
are heard.
6 Flee! Run for your lives;
become like a bush[e] in the desert.
7 Since you trust in your deeds and
riches,
you too will be taken captive,
and Chemosh will go into exile,
together with his priests and officials.
8 The destroyer will come against every
town,
and not a town will escape.
The valley will be ruined
and the plateau destroyed,
because the LORD has spoken.
9 Put salt on Moab,
for she will be laid waste;[f]
her towns will become desolate,
with no one to live in them.

10 "A curse on him who is lax in doing the
LORD's work!
A curse on him who keeps his sword
from bloodshed!

11 "Moab has been at rest from youth,
like wine left on its dregs,
not poured from one jar to another—
she has not gone into exile.
So she tastes as she did,
and her aroma is unchanged.
12 But days are coming,"
declares the LORD,
"when I will send men who pour from
jars,
and they will pour her out;
they will empty her jars
and smash her jugs.
13 Then Moab will be ashamed of
Chemosh,
as the house of Israel was ashamed
when they trusted in Bethel.

14 "How can you say, 'We are warriors,
men valiant in battle'?
15 Moab will be destroyed and her towns
invaded;
her finest young men will go down in
the slaughter,"
declares the King, whose name is the
LORD Almighty.
16 "The fall of Moab is at hand;
her calamity will come quickly.
17 Mourn for her, all who live around her,
all who know her fame;
say, 'How broken is the mighty scepter,
how broken the glorious staff!'

18 "Come down from your glory
and sit on the parched ground,
O inhabitants of the Daughter of
Dibon,
for he who destroys Moab
will come up against you
and ruin your fortified cities.
19 Stand by the road and watch,
you who live in Aroer.
Ask the man fleeing and the woman
escaping,
ask them, 'What has happened?'
20 Moab is disgraced, for she is shattered.
Wail and cry out!
Announce by the Arnon
that Moab is destroyed.
21 Judgment has come to the plateau—
to Holon, Jahzah and Mephaath,
22   to Dibon, Nebo and Beth Diblathaim,

---

a 1 Or / *Misgab*   *b 2* The Hebrew for *Heshbon* sounds like the Hebrew for *plot*.   *c 2* The name of the Moabite
town Madmen sounds like the Hebrew for *be silenced.*   *d 4* Hebrew; Septuagint / *proclaim it to Zoar*   *e 6* Or
like Aroer   *f 9* Or *Give wings to Moab, / for she will fly away*

23 to Kiriathaim, Beth Gamul and Beth
   Meon,
24 to Kerioth and Bozrah —
   to all the towns of Moab, far and
      near.
25Moab's horn[a] is cut off;
   her arm is broken,"
                                    declares the LORD.

26"Make her drunk,
   for she has defied the LORD.
Let Moab wallow in her vomit;
   let her be an object of ridicule.
27Was not Israel the object of your
      ridicule?
   Was she caught among thieves,
that you shake your head in scorn
   whenever you speak of her?
28Abandon your towns and dwell among
      the rocks,
   you who live in Moab.
Be like a dove that makes its nest
   at the mouth of a cave.

29"We have heard of Moab's pride —
   her overweening pride and conceit,
her pride and arrogance
   and the haughtiness of her heart.
30I know her insolence but it is futile,"
                                    declares the LORD,
   "and her boasts accomplish nothing.
31Therefore I wail over Moab,
   for all Moab I cry out,
I moan for the men of Kir Hareseth.
32I weep for you, as Jazer weeps,
   O vines of Sibmah.
Your branches spread as far as the sea;
   they reached as far as the sea of
      Jazer.
The destroyer has fallen
   on your ripened fruit and grapes.
33Joy and gladness are gone
   from the orchards and fields of Moab.
I have stopped the flow of wine from
      the presses;
   no one treads them with shouts of
      joy.
Although there are shouts,
   they are not shouts of joy.

34"The sound of their cry rises
   from Heshbon to Elealeh and Jahaz,
from Zoar as far as Horonaim and
      Eglath Shelishiyah,
   for even the waters of Nimrim are
      dried up.
35In Moab I will put an end

to those who make offerings on the
      high places
and burn incense to their gods,"
                                    declares the LORD.
36"So my heart laments for Moab like a
      flute;
   it laments like a flute for the men of
      Kir Hareseth.
The wealth they acquired is gone.
37Every head is shaved
   and every beard cut off;
every hand is slashed
   and every waist is covered with
      sackcloth.
38On all the roofs in Moab
   and in the public squares
there is nothing but mourning,
   for I have broken Moab
like a jar that no one wants,"
                                    declares the LORD.
39"How shattered she is! How they wail!
   How Moab turns her back in shame!
Moab has become an object of ridicule,
   an object of horror to all those around
      her."

40This is what the LORD says:

"Look! An eagle is swooping down,
   spreading its wings over Moab.
41Kerioth[b] will be captured
   and the strongholds taken.
In that day the hearts of Moab's
      warriors
   will be like the heart of a woman in
      labor.
42Moab will be destroyed as a nation
   because she defied the LORD.
43Terror and pit and snare await you,
   O people of Moab,"
                                    declares the LORD.
44"Whoever flees from the terror
   will fall into a pit,
whoever climbs out of the pit
   will be caught in a snare;
for I will bring upon Moab
   the year of her punishment,"
                                    declares the LORD.
45"In the shadow of Heshbon
   the fugitives stand helpless,
for a fire has gone out from Heshbon,
   a blaze from the midst of Sihon;
it burns the foreheads of Moab,
   the skulls of the noisy boasters.
46Woe to you, O Moab!
   The people of Chemosh are
      destroyed;

---

[a]25 *Horn* here symbolizes strength.   [b]41 Or *The cities*

your sons are taken into exile
and your daughters into captivity.

47"Yet I will restore the fortunes of Moab
in days to come,"
> declares the LORD.

Here ends the judgment on Moab.

A Message About Ammon

49 Concerning the Ammonites:

This is what the LORD says:

"Has Israel no sons?
Has she no heirs?
Why then has Molech[a] taken
possession of Gad?
Why do his people live in its towns?
2But the days are coming,"
declares the LORD,
"when I will sound the battle cry
against Rabbah of the Ammonites;
it will become a mound of ruins,
and its surrounding villages will be set
on fire.
Then Israel will drive out
those who drove her out,"
> says the LORD.
3"Wail, O Heshbon, for Ai is destroyed!
Cry out, O inhabitants of Rabbah!
Put on sackcloth and mourn;
rush here and there inside the walls,
for Molech will go into exile,
together with his priests and officials.
4Why do you boast of your valleys,
boast of your valleys so fruitful?
O unfaithful daughter,
you trust in your riches and say,
'Who will attack me?'
5I will bring terror on you
from all those around you,"
> declares the Lord,
> the LORD Almighty.
"Every one of you will be driven away,
and no one will gather the fugitives.

6"Yet afterward, I will restore the
fortunes of the Ammonites,"
> declares the LORD.

A Message About Edom

7Concerning Edom:

This is what the LORD Almighty says:

"Is there no longer wisdom in Teman?
Has counsel perished from the
prudent?
Has their wisdom decayed?

8Turn and flee, hide in deep caves,
you who live in Dedan,
for I will bring disaster on Esau
at the time I punish him.
9If grape pickers came to you,
would they not leave a few grapes?
If thieves came during the night,
would they not steal only as much as
they wanted?
10But I will strip Esau bare;
I will uncover his hiding places,
so that he cannot conceal himself.
His children, relatives and neighbors
will perish,
and he will be no more.
11Leave your orphans; I will protect their
lives.
Your widows too can trust in me."

12This is what the LORD says: "If those who
do not deserve to drink the cup must drink
it, why should you go unpunished? You will
not go unpunished, but must drink it. **13**I
swear by myself," declares the LORD, "that
Bozrah will become a ruin and an object of
horror, of reproach and of cursing; and all its
towns will be in ruins forever."

14I have heard a message from the LORD:
An envoy was sent to the nations to
say,
"Assemble yourselves to attack it!
Rise up for battle!"

15"Now I will make you small among the
nations,
despised among men.
16The terror you inspire
and the pride of your heart have
deceived you,
you who live in the clefts of the rocks,
who occupy the heights of the hill.
Though you build your nest as high as
the eagle's,
from there I will bring you down,"
> declares the LORD.
17"Edom will become an object of horror;
all who pass by will be appalled and
will scoff
because of all its wounds.
18As Sodom and Gomorrah were
overthrown,
along with their neighboring towns,"
> says the LORD,
"so no one will live there;
no man will dwell in it.
19"Like a lion coming up from Jordan's
thickets

---

a 1 Or their king; Hebrew *malcam*; also in verse 3

to a rich pastureland,
I will chase Edom from its land in an
    instant.
    Who is the chosen one I will appoint
        for this?
    Who is like me and who can challenge
        me?
    And what shepherd can stand against
        me?"
²⁰Therefore, hear what the LORD has
    planned against Edom,
    what he has purposed against those
        who live in Teman:
    The young of the flock will be dragged
        away;
    he will completely destroy their
        pasture because of them.
²¹At the sound of their fall the earth will
    tremble;
    their cry will resound to the Red
        Sea.ᵃ
²²Look! An eagle will soar and swoop
    down,
    spreading its wings over Bozrah.
    In that day the hearts of Edom's
        warriors
    will be like the heart of a woman in
        labor.

A Message About Damascus

²³Concerning Damascus:

"Hamath and Arpad are dismayed,
    for they have heard bad news.
They are disheartened,
    troubled likeᵇ the restless sea.
²⁴Damascus has become feeble,
    she has turned to flee
    and panic has gripped her;
anguish and pain have seized her,
    pain like that of a woman in labor.
²⁵Why has the city of renown not been
    abandoned,
    the town in which I delight?
²⁶Surely, her young men will fall in the
    streets;
    all her soldiers will be silenced in that
        day,"
                declares the LORD Almighty.
²⁷"I will set fire to the walls of Damascus;
    it will consume the fortresses of
        Ben-Hadad."

A Message About Kedar and Hazor

²⁸Concerning Kedar and the kingdoms of

Hazor, which Nebuchadnezzar king of Babylon attacked:

    This is what the LORD says:

"Arise, and attack Kedar
    and destroy the people of the East.
²⁹Their tents and their flocks will be
    taken;
    their shelters will be carried off
    with all their goods and camels.
Men will shout to them,
    'Terror on every side!'

³⁰"Flee quickly away!
    Stay in deep caves, you who live in
        Hazor,"
                declares the LORD.
"Nebuchadnezzar king of Babylon has
    plotted against you;
    he has devised a plan against you.

³¹"Arise and attack a nation at ease,
    which lives in confidence,"
                declares the LORD,
"a nation that has neither gates nor
    bars;
    its people live alone.
³²Their camels will become plunder,
    and their large herds will be booty.
I will scatter to the winds those who are
    in distant placesᶜ
    and will bring disaster on them from
        every side,"
                declares the LORD.
³³"Hazor will become a haunt of jackals,
    a desolate place forever.
No one will live there;
    no man will dwell in it."

A Message About Elam

³⁴This is the word of the LORD that came
to Jeremiah the prophet concerning Elam,
early in the reign of Zedekiah king of Judah:

³⁵This is what the LORD Almighty says:

"See, I will break the bow of Elam,
    the mainstay of their might.
³⁶I will bring against Elam the four winds
    from the four quarters of the heavens;
I will scatter them to the four winds,
    and there will not be a nation
    where Elam's exiles do not go.
³⁷I will shatter Elam before their foes,
    before those who seek their lives;
I will bring disaster upon them,
    even my fierce anger,"
                declares the LORD.

ᵃ21 Hebrew Yam Suph; that is, Sea of Reeds   ᵇ23 Hebrew on or by   ᶜ32 Or who clip the hair by their
foreheads

"I will pursue them with the sword
  until I have made an end of them.
38I will set my throne in Elam
  and destroy her king and officials,"
                              declares the LORD.

39"Yet I will restore the fortunes of Elam
  in days to come,"
                              declares the LORD.

A Message About Babylon

50 This is the word the LORD spoke
      through Jeremiah the prophet con-
cerning Babylon and the land of the Babylonians*a*:

2"Announce and proclaim among the
      nations,
  lift up a banner and proclaim it;
  keep nothing back, but say,
'Babylon will be captured;
  Bel will be put to shame,
  Marduk filled with terror.
Her images will be put to shame
  and her idols filled with terror.'
3A nation from the north will attack her
  and lay waste her land.
No one will live in it;
  both men and animals will flee away.

4"In those days, at that time,"
      declares the LORD,
"the people of Israel and the people of
      Judah together
  will go in tears to seek the LORD their
      God.
5They will ask the way to Zion
  and turn their faces toward it.
They will come and bind themselves to
      the LORD
  in an everlasting covenant
  that will not be forgotten.

6"My people have been lost sheep;
  their shepherds have led them astray
  and caused them to roam on the
      mountains.
They wandered over mountain and hill
  and forgot their own resting place.
7Whoever found them devoured them;
  their enemies said, 'We are not guilty,
for they sinned against the LORD, their
      true pasture,
  the LORD, the hope of their fathers.'

8"Flee out of Babylon;
  leave the land of the Babylonians,
  and be like the goats that lead the
      flock.

9For I will stir up and bring against
      Babylon
  an alliance of great nations from the
      land of the north.
They will take up their positions against
      her,
  and from the north she will be
      captured.
Their arrows will be like skilled warriors
  who do not return empty-handed.
10So Babylonia*b* will be plundered;
  all who plunder her will have their
      fill,"
                              declares the LORD.

11"Because you rejoice and are glad,
  you who pillage my inheritance,
because you frolic like a heifer
      threshing grain
  and neigh like stallions,
12your mother will be greatly ashamed;
  she who gave you birth will be
      disgraced.
She will be the least of the nations—
  a wilderness, a dry land, a desert.
13Because of the LORD's anger she will not
      be inhabited
  but will be completely desolate.
All who pass Babylon will be horrified
      and scoff
  because of all her wounds.

14"Take up your positions around
      Babylon,
  all you who draw the bow.
Shoot at her! Spare no arrows,
  for she has sinned against the LORD.
15Shout against her on every side!
  She surrenders, her towers fall,
  her walls are torn down.
Since this is the vengeance of the LORD,
      take vengeance on her;
  do to her as she has done to others.
16Cut off from Babylon the sower,
  and the reaper with his sickle at
      harvest.
Because of the sword of the oppressor
  let everyone return to his own people,
  let everyone flee to his own land.

17"Israel is a scattered flock
  that lions have chased away.
The first to devour him
  was the king of Assyria;
the last to crush his bones
  was Nebuchadnezzar king of
      Babylon."

*a*1 Or *Chaldeans*; also in verses 8, 25, 35 and 45   *b*10 Or *Chaldea*

¹⁸Therefore this is what the L<small>ORD</small> Almighty, the God of Israel, says:

"I will punish the king of Babylon and
his land
    as I punished the king of Assyria.
¹⁹But I will bring Israel back to his own
pasture
    and he will graze on Carmel and
Bashan;
his appetite will be satisfied
    on the hills of Ephraim and Gilead.
²⁰In those days, at that time,"
    declares the L<small>ORD</small>,
"search will be made for Israel's guilt,
    but there will be none,
and for the sins of Judah,
    but none will be found,
for I will forgive the remnant I spare.

²¹"Attack the land of Merathaim
    and those who live in Pekod.
Pursue, kill and completely destroy^a
them,"
                declares the L<small>ORD</small>.
"Do everything I have commanded
you.
²²The noise of battle is in the land,
    the noise of great destruction!
²³How broken and shattered
    is the hammer of the whole earth!
How desolate is Babylon
    among the nations!
²⁴I set a trap for you, O Babylon,
    and you were caught before you knew
it;
you were found and captured
    because you opposed the L<small>ORD</small>.
²⁵The L<small>ORD</small> has opened his arsenal
    and brought out the weapons of his
wrath,
for the Sovereign L<small>ORD</small> Almighty has
work to do
    in the land of the Babylonians.
²⁶Come against her from afar.
    Break open her granaries;
    pile her up like heaps of grain.
Completely destroy her
    and leave her no remnant.
²⁷Kill all her young bulls;
    let them go down to the slaughter!
Woe to them! For their day has come,
    the time for them to be punished.
²⁸Listen to the fugitives and refugees from
Babylon
    declaring in Zion

how the L<small>ORD</small> our God has taken
vengeance,
    vengeance for his temple.
²⁹"Summon archers against Babylon,
    all those who draw the bow.
Encamp all around her;
    let no one escape.
Repay her for her deeds;
    do to her as she has done.
For she has defied the L<small>ORD</small>,
    the Holy One of Israel.
³⁰Therefore, her young men will fall in
the streets;
    all her soldiers will be silenced in that
day,"
                declares the L<small>ORD</small>.
³¹"See, I am against you, O arrogant one,"
    declares the Lord, the L<small>ORD</small> Almighty,
"for your day has come,
    the time for you to be punished.
³²The arrogant one will stumble and fall
    and no one will help her up;
I will kindle a fire in her towns
    that will consume all who are around
her."

³³This is what the L<small>ORD</small> Almighty says:

"The people of Israel are oppressed,
    and the people of Judah as well.
All their captors hold them fast,
    refusing to let them go.
³⁴Yet their Redeemer is strong;
    the L<small>ORD</small> Almighty is his name.
He will vigorously defend their cause
    so that he may bring rest to their
land,
    but unrest to those who live in
Babylon.

³⁵"A sword against the Babylonians!"
    declares the L<small>ORD</small> —
"against those who live in Babylon
    and against her officials and wise
men!
³⁶A sword against her false prophets!
    They will become fools.
A sword against her warriors!
    They will be filled with terror.
³⁷A sword against her horses and chariots
    and all the foreigners in her ranks!
    They will become women.
A sword against her treasures!
    They will be plundered.
³⁸A drought on^b her waters!

---

^a21 The Hebrew term refers to the irrevocable giving over of things or persons to the L<small>ORD</small>, often by totally destroying them; also in verse 26.   ^b38 Or *A sword against*

They will dry up.
For it is a land of idols,
    idols that will go mad with terror.

39"So desert creatures and hyenas will live
        there,
    and there the owl will dwell.
It will never again be inhabited
    or lived in from generation to
        generation.
40As God overthrew Sodom and Gomorrah
    along with their neighboring towns,"
                              declares the LORD,
    "so no one will live there;
    no man will dwell in it.

41"Look! An army is coming from the
        north;
    a great nation and many kings
    are being stirred up from the ends of
        the earth.
42They are armed with bows and spears;
    they are cruel and without mercy.
They sound like the roaring sea
    as they ride on their horses;
they come like men in battle formation
    to attack you, O Daughter of Babylon.
43The king of Babylon has heard reports
        about them,
    and his hands hang limp.
Anguish has gripped him,
    pain like that of a woman in labor.
44Like a lion coming up from Jordan's
        thickets
    to a rich pastureland,
I will chase Babylon from its land in an
        instant.
    Who is the chosen one I will appoint
        for this?
Who is like me and who can challenge
        me?
    And what shepherd can stand against
        me?"
45Therefore, hear what the LORD has
        planned against Babylon,
    what he has purposed against the
        land of the Babylonians:
The young of the flock will be dragged
        away;
    he will completely destroy their
        pasture because of them.
46At the sound of Babylon's capture the
        earth will tremble;
    its cry will resound among the
        nations.

51 This is what the LORD says:

"See, I will stir up the spirit of a
        destroyer
    against Babylon and the people of Leb
        Kamai.[a]
2I will send foreigners to Babylon
    to winnow her and to devastate her
        land;
they will oppose her on every side
    in the day of her disaster.
3Let not the archer string his bow,
    nor let him put on his armor.
Do not spare her young men;
    completely destroy[b] her army.
4They will fall down slain in Babylon,[c]
    fatally wounded in her streets.
5For Israel and Judah have not been
        forsaken
    by their God, the LORD Almighty,
though their land[d] is full of guilt
    before the Holy One of Israel.

6"Flee from Babylon!
    Run for your lives!
Do not be destroyed because of her
        sins.
It is time for the LORD's vengeance;
    he will pay her what she deserves.
7Babylon was a gold cup in the LORD's
        hand;
    she made the whole earth drunk.
The nations drank her wine;
    therefore they have now gone mad.
8Babylon will suddenly fall and be
        broken.
    Wail over her!
Get balm for her pain;
    perhaps she can be healed.

9" 'We would have healed Babylon,
    but she cannot be healed;
let us leave her and each go to his own
        land,
    for her judgment reaches to the skies,
    it rises as high as the clouds.'

10" 'The LORD has vindicated us;
    come, let us tell in Zion
    what the LORD our God has done.'

11"Sharpen the arrows,
    take up the shields!
The LORD has stirred up the kings of the
        Medes,
    because his purpose is to destroy
        Babylon.
The LORD will take vengeance,

---

a1 Leb Kamai is a cryptogram for Chaldea, that is, Babylonia.   *b3* The Hebrew term refers to the irrevocable
giving over of things or persons to the LORD, often by totally destroying them.   *c4* Or Chaldea   *d5* Or / and
the land of the Babylonians

vengeance for his temple.
¹²Lift up a banner against the walls of
    Babylon!
Reinforce the guard,
   station the watchmen,
   prepare an ambush!
The Lord will carry out his purpose,
   his decree against the people of
    Babylon.
¹³You who live by many waters
   and are rich in treasures,
your end has come,
   the time for you to be cut off.
¹⁴The Lord Almighty has sworn by
    himself:
I will surely fill you with men, as with
   a swarm of locusts,
   and they will shout in triumph over
    you.

¹⁵"He made the earth by his power;
   he founded the world by his wisdom
   and stretched out the heavens by his
    understanding.
¹⁶When he thunders, the waters in the
    heavens roar;
   he makes clouds rise from the ends
    of the earth.
He sends lightning with the rain
   and brings out the wind from his
    storehouses.

¹⁷"Every man is senseless and without
    knowledge;
   every goldsmith is shamed by his
    idols.
His images are a fraud;
   they have no breath in them.
¹⁸They are worthless, the objects of
    mockery;
   when their judgment comes, they will
    perish.
¹⁹He who is the Portion of Jacob is not
   like these,
   for he is the Maker of all things,
including the tribe of his inheritance—
   the Lord Almighty is his name.

²⁰"You are my war club,
   my weapon for battle—
with you I shatter nations,
   with you I destroy kingdoms,
²¹with you I shatter horse and rider,
   with you I shatter chariot and driver,
²²with you I shatter man and woman,
   with you I shatter old man and youth,
   with you I shatter young man and
    maiden,

²³with you I shatter shepherd and flock,
   with you I shatter farmer and oxen,
   with you I shatter governors and
    officials.

²⁴"Before your eyes I will repay Babylon
and all who live in Babylonia^a for all the
wrong they have done in Zion," declares the
Lord.

²⁵"I am against you, O destroying
    mountain,
   you who destroy the whole earth,"
             declares the Lord.
"I will stretch out my hand against you,
   roll you off the cliffs,
   and make you a burned-out
    mountain.
²⁶No rock will be taken from you for a
    cornerstone,
   nor any stone for a foundation,
   for you will be desolate forever,"
             declares the Lord.

²⁷"Lift up a banner in the land!
   Blow the trumpet among the nations!
Prepare the nations for battle against
    her;
   summon against her these kingdoms:
   Ararat, Minni and Ashkenaz.
Appoint a commander against her;
   send up horses like a swarm of
    locusts.
²⁸Prepare the nations for battle against
    her—
the kings of the Medes,
   their governors and all their officials,
   and all the countries they rule.
²⁹The land trembles and writhes,
   for the Lord's purposes against
    Babylon stand—
to lay waste the land of Babylon
   so that no one will live there.
³⁰Babylon's warriors have stopped
    fighting;
   they remain in their strongholds.
Their strength is exhausted;
   they have become like women.
Her dwellings are set on fire;
   the bars of her gates are broken.
³¹One courier follows another
   and messenger follows messenger
to announce to the king of Babylon
   that his entire city is captured,
³²the river crossings seized,
   the marshes set on fire,
   and the soldiers terrified."

^a24 Or *Chaldea*; also in verse 35

³³This is what the LORD Almighty, the God of Israel, says:

"The Daughter of Babylon is like a
        threshing floor
    at the time it is trampled;
    the time to harvest her will soon
        come."

³⁴"Nebuchadnezzar king of Babylon has
        devoured us,
    he has thrown us into confusion,
    he has made us an empty jar.
Like a serpent he has swallowed us
    and filled his stomach with our
        delicacies,
    and then has spewed us out.
³⁵May the violence done to our flesh*ᵃ* be
        upon Babylon,"
    say the inhabitants of Zion.
"May our blood be on those who live in
        Babylonia,"
    says Jerusalem.

³⁶Therefore, this is what the LORD says:

"See, I will defend your cause
    and avenge you;
I will dry up her sea
    and make her springs dry.
³⁷Babylon will be a heap of ruins,
    a haunt of jackals,
an object of horror and scorn,
    a place where no one lives.
³⁸Her people all roar like young lions,
    they growl like lion cubs.
³⁹But while they are aroused,
    I will set out a feast for them
    and make them drunk,
so that they shout with laughter—
    then sleep forever and not awake,"
                        declares the LORD.
⁴⁰"I will bring them down
    like lambs to the slaughter,
    like rams and goats.

⁴¹"How Sheshach*ᵇ* will be captured,
    the boast of the whole earth seized!
What a horror Babylon will be
    among the nations!
⁴²The sea will rise over Babylon;
    its roaring waves will cover her.
⁴³Her towns will be desolate,
    a dry and desert land,
a land where no one lives,
    through which no man travels.
⁴⁴I will punish Bel in Babylon
    and make him spew out what he has
        swallowed.

The nations will no longer stream to
        him.
    And the wall of Babylon will fall.
⁴⁵"Come out of her, my people!
    Run for your lives!
    Run from the fierce anger of the LORD.
⁴⁶Do not lose heart or be afraid
    when rumors are heard in the land;
one rumor comes this year, another the
        next,
    rumors of violence in the land
    and of ruler against ruler.
⁴⁷For the time will surely come
    when I will punish the idols of
        Babylon;
her whole land will be disgraced
    and her slain will all lie fallen within
        her.
⁴⁸Then heaven and earth and all that is in
        them
    will shout for joy over Babylon,
for out of the north
    destroyers will attack her,"
                        declares the LORD.

⁴⁹"Babylon must fall because of Israel's
        slain,
    just as the slain in all the earth
    have fallen because of Babylon.
⁵⁰You who have escaped the sword,
    leave and do not linger!
Remember the LORD in a distant land,
    and think on Jerusalem."

⁵¹"We are disgraced,
    for we have been insulted
    and shame covers our faces,
because foreigners have entered
    the holy places of the LORD's house."

⁵²"But days are coming," declares the
        LORD,
    "when I will punish her idols,
and throughout her land
    the wounded will groan.
⁵³Even if Babylon reaches the sky
    and fortifies her lofty stronghold,
    I will send destroyers against her,"
                        declares the LORD.

⁵⁴"The sound of a cry comes from
        Babylon,
    the sound of great destruction
    from the land of the Babylonians.*ᶜ*
⁵⁵The LORD will destroy Babylon;
    he will silence her noisy din.
Waves ⌊of enemies⌋ will rage like great
        waters;

ᵃ35 Or *done to us and to our children*   *ᵇ41 Sheshach* is a cryptogram for Babylon.   *ᶜ54* Or *Chaldeans*

the roar of their voices will resound.
56A destroyer will come against Babylon;
　　her warriors will be captured,
　　and their bows will be broken.
　For the Lord is a God of retribution;
　　he will repay in full.
57I will make her officials and wise men
　　drunk,
　　her governors, officers and warriors as
　　　well;
　they will sleep forever and not awake,"
　　declares the King, whose name is the
　　　Lord Almighty.

58This is what the Lord Almighty says:

"Babylon's thick wall will be leveled
　　and her high gates set on fire;
　the peoples exhaust themselves for
　　nothing,
　　the nations' labor is only fuel for the
　　　flames."

59This is the message Jeremiah gave to the
staff officer Seraiah son of Neriah, the son of
Mahseiah, when he went to Babylon with
Zedekiah king of Judah in the fourth year of
his reign. **60**Jeremiah had written on a scroll
about all the disasters that would come
upon Babylon—all that had been recorded
concerning Babylon. **61**He said to Seraiah,
"When you get to Babylon, see that you read
all these words aloud. **62**Then say, 'O Lord,
you have said you will destroy this place, so
that neither man nor animal will live in it; it
will be desolate forever.' **63**When you finish
reading this scroll, tie a stone to it and throw
it into the Euphrates. **64**Then say, 'So will
Babylon sink to rise no more because of the
disaster I will bring upon her. And her people will fall.' "

The words of Jeremiah end here.

The Fall of Jerusalem

52 Zedekiah was twenty-one years old
when he became king, and he
reigned in Jerusalem eleven years. His
mother's name was Hamutal daughter of
Jeremiah; she was from Libnah. **2**He did evil
in the eyes of the Lord, just as Jehoiakim had
done. **3**It was because of the Lord's anger
that all this happened to Jerusalem and Judah, and in the end he thrust them from his
presence.

Now Zedekiah rebelled against the king of
Babylon.

4So in the ninth year of Zedekiah's reign,
on the tenth day of the tenth month, Nebuchadnezzar king of Babylon marched
against Jerusalem with his whole army.
They camped outside the city and built
siege works all around it. **5**The city was kept
under siege until the eleventh year of King
Zedekiah.

6By the ninth day of the fourth month the
famine in the city had become so severe that
there was no food for the people to eat.
7Then the city wall was broken through, and
the whole army fled. They left the city at
night through the gate between the two
walls near the king's garden, though the
Babylonians*a* were surrounding the city.
They fled toward the Arabah,*b* **8**but the
Babylonian*c* army pursued King Zedekiah
and overtook him in the plains of Jericho. All
his soldiers were separated from him and
scattered, **9**and he was captured.

He was taken to the king of Babylon at
Riblah in the land of Hamath, where he pronounced sentence on him. **10**There at Riblah
the king of Babylon slaughtered the sons of
Zedekiah before his eyes; he also killed all
the officials of Judah. **11**Then he put out Zedekiah's eyes, bound him with bronze shackles and took him to Babylon, where he put
him in prison till the day of his death.

12On the tenth day of the fifth month, in
the nineteenth year of Nebuchadnezzar
king of Babylon, Nebuzaradan commander
of the imperial guard, who served the king
of Babylon, came to Jerusalem. **13**He set fire
to the temple of the Lord, the royal palace
and all the houses of Jerusalem. Every important building he burned down. **14**The
whole Babylonian army under the commander of the imperial guard broke down
all the walls around Jerusalem. **15**Nebuzaradan the commander of the guard carried
into exile some of the poorest people and
those who remained in the city, along with
the rest of the craftsmen*d* and those who
had gone over to the king of Babylon. **16**But
Nebuzaradan left behind the rest of the
poorest people of the land to work the vineyards and fields.

17The Babylonians broke up the bronze
pillars, the movable stands and the bronze
Sea that were at the temple of the Lord and
they carried all the bronze to Babylon.
18They also took away the pots, shovels,
wick trimmers, sprinkling bowls, dishes and
all the bronze articles used in the temple

---

*a*7 Or *Chaldeans*; also in verse 17　　*b*7 Or *the Jordan Valley*　　*c*8 Or *Chaldean*; also in verse 14　　*d*15 Or
populace

service. [19]The commander of the imperial guard took away the basins, censers, sprinkling bowls, pots, lampstands, dishes and bowls used for drink offerings — all that were made of pure gold or silver.

[20]The bronze from the two pillars, the Sea and the twelve bronze bulls under it, and the movable stands, which King Solomon had made for the temple of the LORD, was more than could be weighed. [21]Each of the pillars was eighteen cubits high and twelve cubits in circumference[a]; each was four fingers thick, and hollow. [22]The bronze capital on top of the one pillar was five cubits[b] high and was decorated with a network and pomegranates of bronze all around. The other pillar, with its pomegranates, was similar. [23]There were ninety-six pomegranates on the sides; the total number of pomegranates above the surrounding network was a hundred.

[24]The commander of the guard took as prisoners Seraiah the chief priest, Zephaniah the priest next in rank and the three doorkeepers. [25]Of those still in the city, he took the officer in charge of the fighting men, and seven royal advisers. He also took the secretary who was chief officer in charge of conscripting the people of the land and sixty of his men who were found in the city. [26]Nebuzaradan the commander took them all and brought them to the king of Babylon at Riblah. [27]There at Riblah, in the land of Hamath, the king had them executed.

So Judah went into captivity, away from her land. [28]This is the number of the people Nebuchadnezzar carried into exile:

in the seventh year, 3,023 Jews;
[29]in Nebuchadnezzar's eighteenth year,
    832 people from Jerusalem;
[30]in his twenty-third year,
    745 Jews taken into exile by Nebuzaradan the commander of the imperial guard.
There were 4,600 people in all.

Jehoiachin Released

[31]In the thirty-seventh year of the exile of Jehoiachin king of Judah, in the year Evil-Merodach[c] became king of Babylon, he released Jehoiachin king of Judah and freed him from prison on the twenty-fifth day of the twelfth month. [32]He spoke kindly to him and gave him a seat of honor higher than those of the other kings who were with him in Babylon. [33]So Jehoiachin put aside his prison clothes and for the rest of his life ate regularly at the king's table. [34]Day by day the king of Babylon gave Jehoiachin a regular allowance as long as he lived, till the day of his death.

---

[a]21 That is, about 27 feet (about 8.1 meters) high and 18 feet (about 5.4 meters) in circumference   [b]22 That is, about 7 1/2 feet (about 2.3 meters)   [c]31 Also called *Amel-Marduk*

LAMENTATIONS

IT happens just the way God says it will. Judah refuses to listen; judgment comes. As Jeremiah watches Jerusalem fall, he weeps, and his sorrow spills over into a poem of lament. Yet even now he finds a spark of hope. The period of judgment is limited. God promises forgiveness. He is faithful and will restore his people. As you read this book, keep in mind that unless you are willing to repent when sin is revealed, you will weep tears of sorrow when judgment falls.

1 *a* How deserted lies the city,
   once so full of people!
How like a widow is she,
   who once was great among the
      nations!
She who was queen among the
      provinces
has now become a slave.

²Bitterly she weeps at night,
   tears are upon her cheeks.
Among all her lovers
   there is none to comfort her.
All her friends have betrayed her;
   they have become her enemies.

³After affliction and harsh labor,
   Judah has gone into exile.
She dwells among the nations;
   she finds no resting place.
All who pursue her have overtaken her
   in the midst of her distress.

⁴The roads to Zion mourn,
   for no one comes to her appointed
      feasts.
All her gateways are desolate,
   her priests groan,
her maidens grieve,
   and she is in bitter anguish.

*a*This chapter is an acrostic poem, the verses of which begin with the successive letters of the Hebrew alphabet.

⁵Her foes have become her masters;
    her enemies are at ease.
The Lord has brought her grief
    because of her many sins.
Her children have gone into exile,
    captive before the foe.

⁶All the splendor has departed
    from the Daughter of Zion.
Her princes are like deer
    that find no pasture;
in weakness they have fled
    before the pursuer.

⁷In the days of her affliction and
        wandering
    Jerusalem remembers all the treasures
    that were hers in days of old.
When her people fell into enemy hands,
    there was no one to help her.
Her enemies looked at her
    and laughed at her destruction.

⁸Jerusalem has sinned greatly
    and so has become unclean.
All who honored her despise her,
    for they have seen her nakedness;
she herself groans
    and turns away.

⁹Her filthiness clung to her skirts;
    she did not consider her future.
Her fall was astounding;
    there was none to comfort her.
"Look, O Lord, on my affliction,
    for the enemy has triumphed."

¹⁰The enemy laid hands
    on all her treasures;
she saw pagan nations
    enter her sanctuary—
those you had forbidden
    to enter your assembly.

¹¹All her people groan
    as they search for bread;
they barter their treasures for food
    to keep themselves alive.
"Look, O Lord, and consider,
    for I am despised."

¹²"Is it nothing to you, all you who pass
        by?
    Look around and see.
Is any suffering like my suffering
    that was inflicted on me,
that the Lord brought on me
    in the day of his fierce anger?

¹³"From on high he sent fire,
    sent it down into my bones.
He spread a net for my feet
    and turned me back.
He made me desolate,
    faint all the day long.

¹⁴"My sins have been bound into a
        yoke[a];
    by his hands they were woven
        together.
They have come upon my neck
    and the Lord has sapped my strength.
He has handed me over
    to those I cannot withstand.

¹⁵"The Lord has rejected
    all the warriors in my midst;
he has summoned an army against me
    to[b] crush my young men.
In his winepress the Lord has trampled
    the Virgin Daughter of Judah.

¹⁶"This is why I weep
    and my eyes overflow with tears.
No one is near to comfort me,
    no one to restore my spirit.
My children are destitute
    because the enemy has prevailed."

¹⁷Zion stretches out her hands,
    but there is no one to comfort her.
The Lord has decreed for Jacob
    that his neighbors become his foes;
Jerusalem has become
    an unclean thing among them.

¹⁸"The Lord is righteous,
    yet I rebelled against his command.
Listen, all you peoples;
    look upon my suffering.
My young men and maidens
    have gone into exile.

¹⁹"I called to my allies
    but they betrayed me.
My priests and my elders
    perished in the city
while they searched for food
    to keep themselves alive.

²⁰"See, O Lord, how distressed I am!
    I am in torment within,
and in my heart I am disturbed,
    for I have been most rebellious.
Outside, the sword bereaves;
    inside, there is only death.

²¹"People have heard my groaning,
    but there is no one to comfort me.

a 14 Most Hebrew manuscripts; Septuagint *He kept watch over my sins*   b 15 Or *has set a time for me / when he will*

All my enemies have heard of my
　　distress;
　they rejoice at what you have done.
May you bring the day you have
　　announced
　so they may become like me.

22"Let all their wickedness come before
　　you;
　deal with them
as you have dealt with me
　because of all my sins.
My groans are many
　and my heart is faint."

2 *a* How the Lord has covered the
　　Daughter of Zion
　with the cloud of his anger*b*!
He has hurled down the splendor of
　　Israel
　from heaven to earth;
he has not remembered his footstool
　in the day of his anger.

2Without pity the Lord has swallowed up
　all the dwellings of Jacob;
in his wrath he has torn down
　the strongholds of the Daughter of
　　Judah.
He has brought her kingdom and its
　　princes
　down to the ground in dishonor.

3In fierce anger he has cut off
　every horn*c* of Israel.
He has withdrawn his right hand
　at the approach of the enemy.
He has burned in Jacob like a flaming
　　fire
　that consumes everything around it.

4Like an enemy he has strung his bow;
　his right hand is ready.
Like a foe he has slain
　all who were pleasing to the eye;
he has poured out his wrath like fire
　on the tent of the Daughter of Zion.

5The Lord is like an enemy;
　he has swallowed up Israel.
He has swallowed up all her palaces
　and destroyed her strongholds.
He has multiplied mourning and
　　lamentation
　for the Daughter of Judah.

6He has laid waste his dwelling like a
　　garden;

he has destroyed his place of
　　meeting.
The Lord has made Zion forget
　her appointed feasts and her
　　Sabbaths;
in his fierce anger he has spurned
　both king and priest.

7The Lord has rejected his altar
　and abandoned his sanctuary.
He has handed over to the enemy
　the walls of her palaces;
they have raised a shout in the house of
　　the Lord
　as on the day of an appointed feast.

8The Lord determined to tear down
　the wall around the Daughter of Zion.
He stretched out a measuring line
　and did not withhold his hand from
　　destroying.
He made ramparts and walls lament;
　together they wasted away.

9Her gates have sunk into the ground;
　their bars he has broken and
　　destroyed.
Her king and her princes are exiled
　among the nations,
　the law is no more,
and her prophets no longer find
　visions from the Lord.

10The elders of the Daughter of Zion
　sit on the ground in silence;
they have sprinkled dust on their heads
　and put on sackcloth.
The young women of Jerusalem
　have bowed their heads to the
　　ground.

11My eyes fail from weeping,
　I am in torment within,
my heart is poured out on the ground
　because my people are destroyed,
because children and infants faint
　in the streets of the city.

12They say to their mothers,
　"Where is bread and wine?"
as they faint like wounded men
　in the streets of the city,
as their lives ebb away
　in their mothers' arms.

13What can I say for you?
　With what can I compare you,
　O Daughter of Jerusalem?
To what can I liken you,

---

*a*This chapter is an acrostic poem, the verses of which begin with the successive letters of the Hebrew
alphabet.　　*b*1 Or *How the Lord in his anger / has treated the Daughter of Zion with contempt*　　*c*3 Or / *all
the strength*; or *every king*; *horn* here symbolizes strength.

that I may comfort you,
O Virgin Daughter of Zion?
Your wound is as deep as the sea.
Who can heal you?

¹⁴The visions of your prophets
were false and worthless;
they did not expose your sin
to ward off your captivity.
The oracles they gave you
were false and misleading.

¹⁵All who pass your way
clap their hands at you;
they scoff and shake their heads
at the Daughter of Jerusalem:
"Is this the city that was called
the perfection of beauty,
the joy of the whole earth?"

¹⁶All your enemies open their mouths
wide against you;
they scoff and gnash their teeth
and say, "We have swallowed her up.
This is the day we have waited for;
we have lived to see it."

¹⁷The Lord has done what he planned;
he has fulfilled his word,
which he decreed long ago.
He has overthrown you without pity,
he has let the enemy gloat over you,
he has exalted the horn[a] of your
foes.

¹⁸The hearts of the people
cry out to the Lord.
O wall of the Daughter of Zion,
let your tears flow like a river
day and night;
give yourself no relief,
your eyes no rest.

¹⁹Arise, cry out in the night,
as the watches of the night begin;
pour out your heart like water
in the presence of the Lord.
Lift up your hands to him
for the lives of your children,
who faint from hunger
at the head of every street.

²⁰"Look, O Lord, and consider:
Whom have you ever treated like this?
Should women eat their offspring,
the children they have cared for?
Should priest and prophet be killed
in the sanctuary of the Lord?

²¹"Young and old lie together

in the dust of the streets;
my young men and maidens
have fallen by the sword.
You have slain them in the day of your
anger;
you have slaughtered them without
pity.

²²"As you summon to a feast day,
so you summoned against me terrors
on every side.
In the day of the Lord's anger
no one escaped or survived;
those I cared for and reared,
my enemy has destroyed."

3[b]I am the man who has seen affliction
by the rod of his wrath.
²He has driven me away and made me
walk
in darkness rather than light;
³indeed, he has turned his hand against
me
again and again, all day long.

⁴He has made my skin and my flesh
grow old
and has broken my bones.
⁵He has besieged me and surrounded me
with bitterness and hardship.
⁶He has made me dwell in darkness
like those long dead.

⁷He has walled me in so I cannot escape;
he has weighed me down with chains.
⁸Even when I call out or cry for help,
he shuts out my prayer.
⁹He has barred my way with blocks of
stone;
he has made my paths crooked.

¹⁰Like a bear lying in wait,
like a lion in hiding,
¹¹he dragged me from the path and
mangled me
and left me without help.
¹²He drew his bow
and made me the target for his
arrows.

¹³He pierced my heart
with arrows from his quiver.
¹⁴I became the laughingstock of all my
people;
they mock me in song all day long.
¹⁵He has filled me with bitter herbs
and sated me with gall.

¹⁶He has broken my teeth with gravel;

---

a 17 Horn here symbolizes strength.   *b* This chapter is an acrostic poem; the verses of each stanza begin with
the successive letters of the Hebrew alphabet, and the verses within each stanza begin with the same letter.

he has trampled me in the dust.
¹⁷I have been deprived of peace;
I have forgotten what prosperity is.
¹⁸So I say, "My splendor is gone
and all that I had hoped from the
LORD."

¹⁹I remember my affliction and my
wandering,
the bitterness and the gall.
²⁰I well remember them,
and my soul is downcast within me.
²¹Yet this I call to mind
and therefore I have hope:

²²Because of the LORD's great love we are
not consumed,
for his compassions never fail.
²³They are new every morning;
great is your faithfulness.
²⁴I say to myself, "The LORD is my portion;
therefore I will wait for him."

²⁵The LORD is good to those whose hope is
in him,
to the one who seeks him;
²⁶it is good to wait quietly
for the salvation of the LORD.
²⁷It is good for a man to bear the yoke
while he is young.

²⁸Let him sit alone in silence,
for the LORD has laid it on him.
²⁹Let him bury his face in the dust—
there may yet be hope.
³⁰Let him offer his cheek to one who
would strike him,
and let him be filled with disgrace.

³¹For men are not cast off
by the Lord forever.
³²Though he brings grief, he will show
compassion,
so great is his unfailing love.
³³For he does not willingly bring affliction
or grief to the children of men.

³⁴To crush underfoot
all prisoners in the land,
³⁵to deny a man his rights
before the Most High,
³⁶to deprive a man of justice—
would not the Lord see such things?

³⁷Who can speak and have it happen
if the Lord has not decreed it?
³⁸Is it not from the mouth of the Most
High
that both calamities and good things
come?
³⁹Why should any living man complain
when punished for his sins?

⁴⁰Let us examine our ways and test them,
and let us return to the LORD.
⁴¹Let us lift up our hearts and our hands
to God in heaven, and say:
⁴²"We have sinned and rebelled
and you have not forgiven.

⁴³"You have covered yourself with anger
and pursued us;
you have slain without pity.
⁴⁴You have covered yourself with a cloud
so that no prayer can get through.
⁴⁵You have made us scum and refuse
among the nations.

⁴⁶"All our enemies have opened their
mouths
wide against us.
⁴⁷We have suffered terror and pitfalls,
ruin and destruction."
⁴⁸Streams of tears flow from my eyes
because my people are destroyed.

⁴⁹My eyes will flow unceasingly,
without relief,
⁵⁰until the LORD looks down
from heaven and sees.
⁵¹What I see brings grief to my soul
because of all the women of my city.

⁵²Those who were my enemies without
cause
hunted me like a bird.
⁵³They tried to end my life in a pit
and threw stones at me;
⁵⁴the waters closed over my head,
and I thought I was about to be cut
off.

⁵⁵I called on your name, O LORD,
from the depths of the pit.
⁵⁶You heard my plea: "Do not close your
ears
to my cry for relief."
⁵⁷You came near when I called you,
and you said, "Do not fear."

⁵⁸O Lord, you took up my case;
you redeemed my life.
⁵⁹You have seen, O LORD, the wrong done
to me.
Uphold my cause!
⁶⁰You have seen the depth of their
vengeance,
all their plots against me.

⁶¹O LORD, you have heard their insults,
all their plots against me—
⁶²what my enemies whisper and mutter
against me all day long.
⁶³Look at them! Sitting or standing,
they mock me in their songs.

WINNING THE GOLD MEDAL IN PATIENCE

☐ FRIDAY

I t's all over!" the announcer screamed. "John has won the Patience Pentathlon. He's going to take home the gold!"

"An unbelievable performance!" the commentator added. "First, John had to wear braces for two years! Then his parents made him wait three extra months before letting him get his driver's license. As soon as that happened, he had to baby-sit his little brothers for five Saturday nights in a row! Meanwhile his coach kept promising him some playing time and never delivered. Last, Susan turned him down for dates on six consecutive weekends. And never once during all that did John give up or get anxious! I don't know when we've seen such patience!"

Look It Up

Okay, there's no such Olympic competition. Apparently running and jumping are considered more valuable than having the important character quality of patience. But not to God!

"But the fruit of the Spirit is . . . patience" (Galatians 5:22).

"Be patient with everyone" (1 Thessalonians 5:14).

"Be patient, then, brothers, until the Lord's coming. See how the farmer waits for the land to yield its valuable crop and how patient he is for the autumn and spring rains. You too, be patient and stand firm, because the Lord's coming is near" (James 5:7–8).

Think It Through

Since nobody enjoys waiting, our culture is geared toward immediate gratification. That explains fast food, one-hour film developing, convenience stores, instant coffee and microwave ovens. With each new time-saving breakthrough, patience becomes less valued and more obsolete.

How would you survive the situations John went through?

Work It Out

Think of the things during a typical day that cause you to become impatient. Ask God to teach you how to deal with those trying situations and/or people. (Caution: This is one of the most dangerous prayers you can ever pray! The only way to acquire patience is to face the things that help you develop it. But if you'll let the Holy Spirit produce this quality in you, life will become much more enjoyable!)

Nail It Down

Read Lamentations 3:22–24 for a beautiful statement on waiting or being patient.

Turn to pages 678, 751, 1278 and 1325 for other readings on character.
Turn to page 864 for the weekend reading.

Topic
····

64Pay them back what they deserve,
     O Lord,
  for what their hands have done.
65Put a veil over their hearts,
  and may your curse be on them!
66Pursue them in anger and destroy them
  from under the heavens of the Lord.

4ᵃ How the gold has lost its luster,
     the fine gold become dull!
  The sacred gems are scattered
  at the head of every street.

2How the precious sons of Zion,
  once worth their weight in gold,
are now considered as pots of clay,
  the work of a potter's hands!

3Even jackals offer their breasts
  to nurse their young,
but my people have become heartless
  like ostriches in the desert.

4Because of thirst the infant's tongue
  sticks to the roof of its mouth;
the children beg for bread,
  but no one gives it to them.

5Those who once ate delicacies
  are destitute in the streets.
Those nurtured in purple
  now lie on ash heaps.

6The punishment of my people
  is greater than that of Sodom,
which was overthrown in a moment
  without a hand turned to help her.

7Their princes were brighter than snow
  and whiter than milk,
their bodies more ruddy than rubies,
  their appearance like sapphires.ᵇ

8But now they are blacker than soot;
  they are not recognized in the streets.
Their skin has shriveled on their bones;
  it has become as dry as a stick.

9Those killed by the sword are better off
  than those who die of famine;
racked with hunger, they waste away
  for lack of food from the field.

10With their own hands compassionate
     women
  have cooked their own children,
who became their food
  when my people were destroyed.

11The Lord has given full vent to his
     wrath;

he has poured out his fierce anger.
He kindled a fire in Zion
  that consumed her foundations.

12The kings of the earth did not believe,
  nor did any of the world's people,
that enemies and foes could enter
  the gates of Jerusalem.

13But it happened because of the sins of
     her prophets
  and the iniquities of her priests,
who shed within her
  the blood of the righteous.

14Now they grope through the streets
  like men who are blind.
They are so defiled with blood
  that no one dares to touch their
     garments.

15"Go away! You are unclean!" men cry to
     them.
  "Away! Away! Don't touch us!"
When they flee and wander about,
  people among the nations say,
  "They can stay here no longer."

16The Lord himself has scattered them;
  he no longer watches over them.
The priests are shown no honor,
  the elders no favor.

17Moreover, our eyes failed,
  looking in vain for help;
from our towers we watched
  for a nation that could not save us.

18Men stalked us at every step,
  so we could not walk in our streets.
Our end was near, our days were
     numbered,
  for our end had come.

19Our pursuers were swifter
  than eagles in the sky;
they chased us over the mountains
  and lay in wait for us in the desert.

20The Lord's anointed, our very life
     breath,
  was caught in their traps.
We thought that under his shadow
  we would live among the nations.

21Rejoice and be glad, O Daughter of
     Edom,
  you who live in the land of Uz.
But to you also the cup will be passed;
  you will be drunk and stripped naked.

ᵃThis chapter is an acrostic poem, the verses of which begin with the successive letters of the Hebrew alphabet.   ᵇ7 Or *lapis lazuli*

²²O Daughter of Zion, your punishment
  will end;
  he will not prolong your exile.
But, O Daughter of Edom, he will
  punish your sin
  and expose your wickedness.

5 Remember, O LORD, what has
  happened to us;
  look, and see our disgrace.
²Our inheritance has been turned over to
  aliens,
  our homes to foreigners.
³We have become orphans and
  fatherless,
  our mothers like widows.
⁴We must buy the water we drink;
  our wood can be had only at a price.
⁵Those who pursue us are at our heels;
  we are weary and find no rest.
⁶We submitted to Egypt and Assyria
  to get enough bread.
⁷Our fathers sinned and are no more,
  and we bear their punishment.
⁸Slaves rule over us,
  and there is none to free us from
  their hands.
⁹We get our bread at the risk of our lives
  because of the sword in the desert.
¹⁰Our skin is hot as an oven,
  feverish from hunger.

¹¹Women have been ravished in Zion,
  and virgins in the towns of Judah.
¹²Princes have been hung up by their
  hands;
  elders are shown no respect.
¹³Young men toil at the millstones;
  boys stagger under loads of wood.
¹⁴The elders are gone from the city
  gate;
  the young men have stopped their
  music.
¹⁵Joy is gone from our hearts;
  our dancing has turned to mourning.
¹⁶The crown has fallen from our head.
  Woe to us, for we have sinned!
¹⁷Because of this our hearts are faint,
  because of these things our eyes grow
  dim
¹⁸for Mount Zion, which lies desolate,
  with jackals prowling over it.

¹⁹You, O LORD, reign forever;
  your throne endures from generation
  to generation.
²⁰Why do you always forget us?
  Why do you forsake us so long?
²¹Restore us to yourself, O LORD, that we
  may return;
  renew our days as of old
²²unless you have utterly rejected us
  and are angry with us beyond
  measure.

EZEKIEL

LIVING among the exiles in Babylon, Ezekiel's own body is more than once the stage on which God's message is wordlessly acted out. And more than once it's a frightening experience. But Ezekiel's message is ultimately one of hope and comfort. He knows God will restore his nation. Then all nations will know that God is the Lord. As you read, think about the way you live. Is your life such a dramatic demonstration of God's love that people around you stop and take notice?

Outline of Contents

The Living Creatures and the Glory of the LORD

1 In the*a* thirtieth year, in the fourth month on the fifth day, while I was among the exiles by the Kebar River, the heavens were opened and I saw visions of God.

²On the fifth of the month—it was the fifth year of the exile of King Jehoiachin—³the word of the LORD came to Ezekiel the priest, the son of Buzi,*b* by the Kebar River in the land of the Babylonians.*c* There the hand of the LORD was upon him.

⁴I looked, and I saw a windstorm coming out of the north—an immense cloud with flashing lightning and surrounded by brilliant light. The center of the fire looked like glowing metal, ⁵and in the fire was what looked like four living creatures. In appearance their form was that of a man, ⁶but each of them had four faces and four wings. ⁷Their legs were straight; their feet were like those of a calf and gleamed like burnished bronze. ⁸Under their wings on their four sides they had the hands of a man. All four of them had faces and wings, ⁹and their wings touched one another. Each one went straight ahead; they did not turn as they moved.

¹⁰Their faces looked like this: Each of the

a1 Or my   *b3 Or Ezekiel son of Buzi the priest*   *c3 Or Chaldeans* four had the face of a man, and on the right side each had the face of a lion, and on the left the face of an ox; each also had the face of an eagle. ¹¹Such were their faces. Their wings were spread out upward; each had two wings, one touching the wing of another creature on either side, and two wings covering its body. ¹²Each one went straight ahead. Wherever the spirit would go, they would go, without turning as they went. ¹³The appearance of the living creatures was like burning coals of fire or like torches. Fire moved back and forth among the creatures; it was bright, and lightning flashed out of it. ¹⁴The creatures sped back and forth like flashes of lightning.

¹⁵As I looked at the living creatures, I saw a wheel on the ground beside each creature with its four faces. ¹⁶This was the appearance and structure of the wheels: They sparkled like chrysolite, and all four looked alike. Each appeared to be made like a wheel intersecting a wheel. ¹⁷As they moved, they would go in any one of the four directions the creatures faced; the wheels did not turn about*a* as the creatures went. ¹⁸Their rims were high and awesome, and all four rims were full of eyes all around.

¹⁹When the living creatures moved, the wheels beside them moved; and when the living creatures rose from the ground, the wheels also rose. ²⁰Wherever the spirit would go, they would go, and the wheels would rise along with them, because the spirit of the living creatures was in the wheels. ²¹When the creatures moved, they also moved; when the creatures stood still, they also stood still; and when the creatures rose from the ground, the wheels rose along with them, because the spirit of the living creatures was in the wheels.

²²Spread out above the heads of the living creatures was what looked like an expanse, sparkling like ice, and awesome. ²³Under the expanse their wings were stretched out one toward the other, and each had two wings covering its body. ²⁴When the creatures moved, I heard the sound of their wings, like the roar of rushing waters, like the voice of the Almighty,*b* like the tumult of an army. When they stood still, they lowered their wings.

²⁵Then there came a voice from above the expanse over their heads as they stood with lowered wings. ²⁶Above the expanse over their heads was what looked like a throne of sapphire,*c* and high above on the throne

was a figure like that of a man. ²⁷I saw that from what appeared to be his waist up he looked like glowing metal, as if full of fire, and that from there down he looked like fire; and brilliant light surrounded him. ²⁸Like the appearance of a rainbow in the clouds on a rainy day, so was the radiance around him.

This was the appearance of the likeness of the glory of the LORD. When I saw it, I fell facedown, and I heard the voice of one speaking.

Ezekiel's Call

2 He said to me, "Son of man, stand up on your feet and I will speak to you." ²As he spoke, the Spirit came into me and raised me to my feet, and I heard him speaking to me.

³He said: "Son of man, I am sending you to the Israelites, to a rebellious nation that has rebelled against me; they and their fathers have been in revolt against me to this very day. ⁴The people to whom I am sending you are obstinate and stubborn. Say to them, 'This is what the Sovereign LORD says.' ⁵And whether they listen or fail to listen—for they are a rebellious house—they will know that a prophet has been among them. ⁶And you, son of man, do not be afraid of them or their words. Do not be afraid, though briers and thorns are all around you and you live among scorpions. Do not be afraid of what they say or terrified by them, though they are a rebellious house. ⁷You must speak my words to them, whether they listen or fail to listen, for they are rebellious. ⁸But you, son of man, listen to what I say to you. Do not rebel like that rebellious house; open your mouth and eat what I give you."

⁹Then I looked, and I saw a hand stretched out to me. In it was a scroll, ¹⁰which he unrolled before me. On both sides of it were written words of lament and mourning and woe.

3 And he said to me, "Son of man, eat what is before you, eat this scroll; then go and speak to the house of Israel." ²So I opened my mouth, and he gave me the scroll to eat.

³Then he said to me, "Son of man, eat this scroll I am giving you and fill your stomach with it." So I ate it, and it tasted as sweet as honey in my mouth.

⁴He then said to me: "Son of man, go now to the house of Israel and speak my words

---

a17 Or *aside*   *b24* Hebrew *Shaddai*   *c26* Or *lapis lazuli* to them. **5**You are not being sent to a people of obscure speech and difficult language, but to the house of Israel— **6**not to many peoples of obscure speech and difficult language, whose words you cannot understand. Surely if I had sent you to them, they would have listened to you. **7**But the house of Israel is not willing to listen to you because they are not willing to listen to me, for the whole house of Israel is hardened and obstinate. **8**But I will make you as unyielding and hardened as they are. **9**I will make your forehead like the hardest stone, harder than flint. Do not be afraid of them or terrified by them, though they are a rebellious house."

10And he said to me, "Son of man, listen carefully and take to heart all the words I speak to you. **11**Go now to your countrymen in exile and speak to them. Say to them, 'This is what the Sovereign LORD says,' whether they listen or fail to listen."

12Then the Spirit lifted me up, and I heard behind me a loud rumbling sound— May the glory of the LORD be praised in his dwelling place!— **13**the sound of the wings of the living creatures brushing against each other and the sound of the wheels beside them, a loud rumbling sound. **14**The Spirit then lifted me up and took me away, and I went in bitterness and in the anger of my spirit, with the strong hand of the LORD upon me. **15**I came to the exiles who lived at Tel Abib near the Kebar River. And there, where they were living, I sat among them for seven days— overwhelmed.

Warning to Israel

16At the end of seven days the word of the LORD came to me: **17**"Son of man, I have made you a watchman for the house of Israel; so hear the word I speak and give them warning from me. **18**When I say to a wicked man, 'You will surely die,' and you do not warn him or speak out to dissuade him from his evil ways in order to save his life, that wicked man will die for*ᵃ* his sin, and I will hold you accountable for his blood. **19**But if you do warn the wicked man and he does not turn from his wickedness or from his evil ways, he will die for his sin; but you will have saved yourself.

20"Again, when a righteous man turns from his righteousness and does evil, and I put a stumbling block before him, he will die. Since you did not warn him, he will die for his sin. The righteous things he did will not be remembered, and I will hold you ac-

countable for his blood. **21**But if you do warn the righteous man not to sin and he does not sin, he will surely live because he took warning, and you will have saved yourself."

22The hand of the LORD was upon me there, and he said to me, "Get up and go out to the plain, and there I will speak to you." **23**So I got up and went out to the plain. And the glory of the LORD was standing there, like the glory I had seen by the Kebar River, and I fell facedown.

24Then the Spirit came into me and raised me to my feet. He spoke to me and said: "Go, shut yourself inside your house. **25**And you, son of man, they will tie with ropes; you will be bound so that you cannot go out among the people. **26**I will make your tongue stick to the roof of your mouth so that you will be silent and unable to rebuke them, though they are a rebellious house. **27**But when I speak to you, I will open your mouth and you shall say to them, 'This is what the Sovereign LORD says.' Whoever will listen let him listen, and whoever will refuse let him refuse; for they are a rebellious house.

Siege of Jerusalem Symbolized

4 "Now, son of man, take a clay tablet, put it in front of you and draw the city of Jerusalem on it. **2**Then lay siege to it: Erect siege works against it, build a ramp up to it, set up camps against it and put battering rams around it. **3**Then take an iron pan, place it as an iron wall between you and the city and turn your face toward it. It will be under siege, and you shall besiege it. This will be a sign to the house of Israel.

4"Then lie on your left side and put the sin of the house of Israel upon yourself.*ᵇ* You are to bear their sin for the number of days you lie on your side. **5**I have assigned you the same number of days as the years of their sin. So for 390 days you will bear the sin of the house of Israel.

6"After you have finished this, lie down again, this time on your right side, and bear the sin of the house of Judah. I have assigned you 40 days, a day for each year. **7**Turn your face toward the siege of Jerusalem and with bared arm prophesy against her. **8**I will tie you up with ropes so that you cannot turn from one side to the other until you have finished the days of your siege.

9"Take wheat and barley, beans and lentils, millet and spelt; put them in a storage jar and use them to make bread for yourself. You are to eat it during the 390 days you lie

---

ᵃ18 Or *in*; also in verses 19 and 20   *ᵇ4* Or *your side* on your side. **10**Weigh out twenty shekels*a* of food to eat each day and eat it at set times. **11**Also measure out a sixth of a hin*b* of water and drink it at set times. **12**Eat the food as you would a barley cake; bake it in the sight of the people, using human excrement for fuel." **13**The LORD said, "In this way the people of Israel will eat defiled food among the nations where I will drive them."

14Then I said, "Not so, Sovereign LORD! I have never defiled myself. From my youth until now I have never eaten anything found dead or torn by wild animals. No unclean meat has ever entered my mouth."

15"Very well," he said, "I will let you bake your bread over cow manure instead of human excrement."

16He then said to me: "Son of man, I will cut off the supply of food in Jerusalem. The people will eat rationed food in anxiety and drink rationed water in despair, **17**for food and water will be scarce. They will be appalled at the sight of each other and will waste away because of*c* their sin.

5 "Now, son of man, take a sharp sword and use it as a barber's razor to shave your head and your beard. Then take a set of scales and divide up the hair. **2**When the days of your siege come to an end, burn a third of the hair with fire inside the city. Take a third and strike it with the sword all around the city. And scatter a third to the wind. For I will pursue them with drawn sword. **3**But take a few strands of hair and tuck them away in the folds of your garment. **4**Again, take a few of these and throw them into the fire and burn them up. A fire will spread from there to the whole house of Israel.

5"This is what the Sovereign LORD says: This is Jerusalem, which I have set in the center of the nations, with countries all around her. **6**Yet in her wickedness she has rebelled against my laws and decrees more than the nations and countries around her. She has rejected my laws and has not followed my decrees.

7"Therefore this is what the Sovereign LORD says: You have been more unruly than the nations around you and have not followed my decrees or kept my laws. You have not even*d* conformed to the standards of the nations around you.

8"Therefore this is what the Sovereign LORD says: I myself am against you, Jerusalem, and I will inflict punishment on you in the sight of the nations. **9**Because of all your detestable idols, I will do to you what I have never done before and will never do again. **10**Therefore in your midst fathers will eat their children, and children will eat their fathers. I will inflict punishment on you and will scatter all your survivors to the winds. **11**Therefore as surely as I live, declares the Sovereign LORD, because you have defiled my sanctuary with all your vile images and detestable practices, I myself will withdraw my favor; I will not look on you with pity or spare you. **12**A third of your people will die of the plague or perish by famine inside you; a third will fall by the sword outside your walls; and a third I will scatter to the winds and pursue with drawn sword.

13"Then my anger will cease and my wrath against them will subside, and I will be avenged. And when I have spent my wrath upon them, they will know that I the LORD have spoken in my zeal.

14"I will make you a ruin and a reproach among the nations around you, in the sight of all who pass by. **15**You will be a reproach and a taunt, a warning and an object of horror to the nations around you when I inflict punishment on you in anger and in wrath and with stinging rebuke. I the LORD have spoken. **16**When I shoot at you with my deadly and destructive arrows of famine, I will shoot to destroy you. I will bring more and more famine upon you and cut off your supply of food. **17**I will send famine and wild beasts against you, and they will leave you childless. Plague and bloodshed will sweep through you, and I will bring the sword against you. I the LORD have spoken."

A Prophecy Against the Mountains of Israel

6 The word of the LORD came to me: **2**"Son of man, set your face against the mountains of Israel; prophesy against them **3**and say: 'O mountains of Israel, hear the word of the Sovereign LORD. This is what the Sovereign LORD says to the mountains and hills, to the ravines and valleys: I am about to bring a sword against you, and I will destroy your high places. **4**Your altars will be demolished and your incense altars will be smashed; and I will slay your people in front of your idols. **5**I will lay the dead bodies of the Israelites in front of their idols, and I will scatter your bones around your altars. **6**Wherever you live, the towns will be laid waste and the

---

a 10 That is, about 8 ounces (about 0.2 kilogram)   *b 11* That is, about 2/3 quart (about 0.6 liter)   *c 17* Or *away in*   *d 7* Most Hebrew manuscripts; some Hebrew manuscripts and Syriac *You have* high places demolished, so that your altars will be laid waste and devastated, your idols smashed and ruined, your incense altars broken down, and what you have made wiped out. **7**Your people will fall slain among you, and you will know that I am the LORD.

8" 'But I will spare some, for some of you will escape the sword when you are scattered among the lands and nations. **9**Then in the nations where they have been carried captive, those who escape will remember me—how I have been grieved by their adulterous hearts, which have turned away from me, and by their eyes, which have lusted after their idols. They will loathe themselves for the evil they have done and for all their detestable practices. **10**And they will know that I am the LORD; I did not threaten in vain to bring this calamity on them.

11" 'This is what the Sovereign LORD says: Strike your hands together and stamp your feet and cry out "Alas!" because of all the wicked and detestable practices of the house of Israel, for they will fall by the sword, famine and plague. **12**He that is far away will die of the plague, and he that is near will fall by the sword, and he that survives and is spared will die of famine. So will I spend my wrath upon them. **13**And they will know that I am the LORD, when their people lie slain among their idols around their altars, on every high hill and on all the mountaintops, under every spreading tree and every leafy oak—places where they offered fragrant incense to all their idols. **14**And I will stretch out my hand against them and make the land a desolate waste from the desert to Diblah*a*—wherever they live. Then they will know that I am the LORD.' "

The End Has Come

7 The word of the LORD came to me: **2**"Son of man, this is what the Sovereign LORD says to the land of Israel: The end! The end has come upon the four corners of the land. **3**The end is now upon you and I will unleash my anger against you. I will judge you according to your conduct and repay you for all your detestable practices. **4**I will not look on you with pity or spare you; I will surely repay you for your conduct and the detestable practices among you. Then you will know that I am the LORD.

5"This is what the Sovereign LORD says: Di-

saster! An unheard-of*b* disaster is coming. **6**The end has come! The end has come! It has roused itself against you. It has come! **7**Doom has come upon you—you who dwell in the land. The time has come, the day is near; there is panic, not joy, upon the mountains. **8**I am about to pour out my wrath on you and spend my anger against you; I will judge you according to your conduct and repay you for all your detestable practices. **9**I will not look on you with pity or spare you; I will repay you in accordance with your conduct and the detestable practices among you. Then you will know that it is I the LORD who strikes the blow.

10"The day is here! It has come! Doom has burst forth, the rod has budded, arrogance has blossomed! **11**Violence has grown into*c* a rod to punish wickedness; none of the people will be left, none of that crowd—no wealth, nothing of value. **12**The time has come, the day has arrived. Let not the buyer rejoice nor the seller grieve, for wrath is upon the whole crowd. **13**The seller will not recover the land he has sold as long as both of them live, for the vision concerning the whole crowd will not be reversed. Because of their sins, not one of them will preserve his life. **14**Though they blow the trumpet and get everything ready, no one will go into battle, for my wrath is upon the whole crowd.

15"Outside is the sword, inside are plague and famine; those in the country will die by the sword, and those in the city will be devoured by famine and plague. **16**All who survive and escape will be in the mountains, moaning like doves of the valleys, each because of his sins. **17**Every hand will go limp, and every knee will become as weak as water. **18**They will put on sackcloth and be clothed with terror. Their faces will be covered with shame and their heads will be shaved. **19**They will throw their silver into the streets, and their gold will be an unclean thing. Their silver and gold will not be able to save them in the day of the LORD's wrath. They will not satisfy their hunger or fill their stomachs with it, for it has made them stumble into sin. **20**They were proud of their beautiful jewelry and used it to make their detestable idols and vile images. Therefore I will turn these into an unclean thing for them. **21**I will hand it all over as plunder to foreigners and as loot to the wicked of the earth, and they will defile it. **22**I will turn my face away from them, and they will dese-

---

a14 Most Hebrew manuscripts; a few Hebrew manuscripts *Riblah*   *b5* Most Hebrew manuscripts; some Hebrew manuscripts and Syriac *Disaster after*   *c11* Or *The violent one has become* crate my treasured place; robbers will enter it and desecrate it.

²³"Prepare chains, because the land is full of bloodshed and the city is full of violence. ²⁴I will bring the most wicked of the nations to take possession of their houses; I will put an end to the pride of the mighty, and their sanctuaries will be desecrated. ²⁵When terror comes, they will seek peace, but there will be none. ²⁶Calamity upon calamity will come, and rumor upon rumor. They will try to get a vision from the prophet; the teaching of the law by the priest will be lost, as will the counsel of the elders. ²⁷The king will mourn, the prince will be clothed with despair, and the hands of the people of the land will tremble. I will deal with them according to their conduct, and by their own standards I will judge them. Then they will know that I am the Lord."

Idolatry in the Temple

8 In the sixth year, in the sixth month on the fifth day, while I was sitting in my house and the elders of Judah were sitting before me, the hand of the Sovereign Lord came upon me there. ²I looked, and I saw a figure like that of a man.ᵃ From what appeared to be his waist down he was like fire, and from there up his appearance was as bright as glowing metal. ³He stretched out what looked like a hand and took me by the hair of my head. The Spirit lifted me up between earth and heaven and in visions of God he took me to Jerusalem, to the entrance to the north gate of the inner court, where the idol that provokes to jealousy stood. ⁴And there before me was the glory of the God of Israel, as in the vision I had seen in the plain.

⁵Then he said to me, "Son of man, look toward the north." So I looked, and in the entrance north of the gate of the altar I saw this idol of jealousy.

⁶And he said to me, "Son of man, do you see what they are doing—the utterly detestable things the house of Israel is doing here, things that will drive me far from my sanctuary? But you will see things that are even more detestable."

⁷Then he brought me to the entrance to the court. I looked, and I saw a hole in the wall. ⁸He said to me, "Son of man, now dig into the wall." So I dug into the wall and saw a doorway there.

⁹And he said to me, "Go in and see the wicked and detestable things they are doing

here." ¹⁰So I went in and looked, and I saw portrayed all over the walls all kinds of crawling things and detestable animals and all the idols of the house of Israel. ¹¹In front of them stood seventy elders of the house of Israel, and Jaazaniah son of Shaphan was standing among them. Each had a censer in his hand, and a fragrant cloud of incense was rising.

¹²He said to me, "Son of man, have you seen what the elders of the house of Israel are doing in the darkness, each at the shrine of his own idol? They say, 'The Lord does not see us; the Lord has forsaken the land.' " ¹³Again, he said, "You will see them doing things that are even more detestable."

¹⁴Then he brought me to the entrance to the north gate of the house of the Lord, and I saw women sitting there, mourning for Tammuz. ¹⁵He said to me, "Do you see this, son of man? You will see things that are even more detestable than this."

¹⁶He then brought me into the inner court of the house of the Lord, and there at the entrance to the temple, between the portico and the altar, were about twenty-five men. With their backs toward the temple of the Lord and their faces toward the east, they were bowing down to the sun in the east.

¹⁷He said to me, "Have you seen this, son of man? Is it a trivial matter for the house of Judah to do the detestable things they are doing here? Must they also fill the land with violence and continually provoke me to anger? Look at them putting the branch to their nose! ¹⁸Therefore I will deal with them in anger; I will not look on them with pity or spare them. Although they shout in my ears, I will not listen to them."

Idolaters Killed

9 Then I heard him call out in a loud voice, "Bring the guards of the city here, each with a weapon in his hand." ²And I saw six men coming from the direction of the upper gate, which faces north, each with a deadly weapon in his hand. With them was a man clothed in linen who had a writing kit at his side. They came in and stood beside the bronze altar.

³Now the glory of the God of Israel went up from above the cherubim, where it had been, and moved to the threshold of the temple. Then the Lord called to the man clothed in linen who had the writing kit at his side ⁴and said to him, "Go throughout the city of Jerusalem and put a mark on the

ᵃ2 Or saw a fiery figure

foreheads of those who grieve and lament over all the detestable things that are done in it."

⁵As I listened, he said to the others, "Follow him through the city and kill, without showing pity or compassion. ⁶Slaughter old men, young men and maidens, women and children, but do not touch anyone who has the mark. Begin at my sanctuary." So they began with the elders who were in front of the temple.

⁷Then he said to them, "Defile the temple and fill the courts with the slain. Go!" So they went out and began killing throughout the city. ⁸While they were killing and I was left alone, I fell facedown, crying out, "Ah, Sovereign Lord! Are you going to destroy the entire remnant of Israel in this outpouring of your wrath on Jerusalem?"

⁹He answered me, "The sin of the house of Israel and Judah is exceedingly great; the land is full of bloodshed and the city is full of injustice. They say, 'The Lord has forsaken the land; the Lord does not see.' ¹⁰So I will not look on them with pity or spare them, but I will bring down on their own heads what they have done."

¹¹Then the man in linen with the writing kit at his side brought back word, saying, "I have done as you commanded."

The Glory Departs From the Temple

10 I looked, and I saw the likeness of a throne of sapphire[a] above the expanse that was over the heads of the cherubim. ²The Lord said to the man clothed in linen, "Go in among the wheels beneath the cherubim. Fill your hands with burning coals from among the cherubim and scatter them over the city." And as I watched, he went in.

³Now the cherubim were standing on the south side of the temple when the man went in, and a cloud filled the inner court. ⁴Then the glory of the Lord rose from above the cherubim and moved to the threshold of the temple. The cloud filled the temple, and the court was full of the radiance of the glory of the Lord. ⁵The sound of the wings of the cherubim could be heard as far away as the outer court, like the voice of God Almighty[b] when he speaks.

⁶When the Lord commanded the man in linen, "Take fire from among the wheels, from among the cherubim," the man went in and stood beside a wheel. ⁷Then one of the cherubim reached out his hand to the

fire that was among them. He took up some of it and put it into the hands of the man in linen, who took it and went out. ⁸(Under the wings of the cherubim could be seen what looked like the hands of a man.)

⁹I looked, and I saw beside the cherubim four wheels, one beside each of the cherubim; the wheels sparkled like chrysolite. ¹⁰As for their appearance, the four of them looked alike; each was like a wheel intersecting a wheel. ¹¹As they moved, they would go in any one of the four directions the cherubim faced; the wheels did not turn about[c] as the cherubim went. The cherubim went in whatever direction the head faced, without turning as they went. ¹²Their entire bodies, including their backs, their hands and their wings, were completely full of eyes, as were their four wheels. ¹³I heard the wheels being called "the whirling wheels." ¹⁴Each of the cherubim had four faces: One face was that of a cherub, the second the face of a man, the third the face of a lion, and the fourth the face of an eagle.

¹⁵Then the cherubim rose upward. These were the living creatures I had seen by the Kebar River. ¹⁶When the cherubim moved, the wheels beside them moved; and when the cherubim spread their wings to rise from the ground, the wheels did not leave their side. ¹⁷When the cherubim stood still, they also stood still; and when the cherubim rose, they rose with them, because the spirit of the living creatures was in them.

¹⁸Then the glory of the Lord departed from over the threshold of the temple and stopped above the cherubim. ¹⁹While I watched, the cherubim spread their wings and rose from the ground, and as they went, the wheels went with them. They stopped at the entrance to the east gate of the Lord's house, and the glory of the God of Israel was above them.

²⁰These were the living creatures I had seen beneath the God of Israel by the Kebar River, and I realized that they were cherubim. ²¹Each had four faces and four wings, and under their wings was what looked like the hands of a man. ²²Their faces had the same appearance as those I had seen by the Kebar River. Each one went straight ahead.

Judgment on Israel's Leaders

11 Then the Spirit lifted me up and brought me to the gate of the house of the Lord that faces east. There at the entrance to the gate were twenty-five men, and

---

a1 Or *lapis lazuli*   *b5* Hebrew *El-Shaddai*   *c11* Or *aside*

I saw among them Jaazaniah son of Azzur and Pelatiah son of Benaiah, leaders of the people. **2**The LORD said to me, "Son of man, these are the men who are plotting evil and giving wicked advice in this city. **3**They say, 'Will it not soon be time to build houses?*a* This city is a cooking pot, and we are the meat.' **4**Therefore prophesy against them; prophesy, son of man."

5Then the Spirit of the LORD came upon me, and he told me to say: "This is what the LORD says: That is what you are saying, O house of Israel, but I know what is going through your mind. **6**You have killed many people in this city and filled its streets with the dead.

7"Therefore this is what the Sovereign LORD says: The bodies you have thrown there are the meat and this city is the pot, but I will drive you out of it. **8**You fear the sword, and the sword is what I will bring against you, declares the Sovereign LORD. **9**I will drive you out of the city and hand you over to foreigners and inflict punishment on you. **10**You will fall by the sword, and I will execute judgment on you at the borders of Israel. Then you will know that I am the LORD. **11**This city will not be a pot for you, nor will you be the meat in it; I will execute judgment on you at the borders of Israel. **12**And you will know that I am the LORD, for you have not followed my decrees or kept my laws but have conformed to the standards of the nations around you."

13Now as I was prophesying, Pelatiah son of Benaiah died. Then I fell facedown and cried out in a loud voice, "Ah, Sovereign LORD! Will you completely destroy the remnant of Israel?"

14The word of the LORD came to me: **15**"Son of man, your brothers—your brothers who are your blood relatives*b* and the whole house of Israel—are those of whom the people of Jerusalem have said, 'They are*c* far away from the LORD; this land was given to us as our possession.'

Promised Return of Israel

16"Therefore say: 'This is what the Sovereign LORD says: Although I sent them far away among the nations and scattered them among the countries, yet for a little while I have been a sanctuary for them in the countries where they have gone.'

17"Therefore say: 'This is what the Sovereign LORD says: I will gather you from the na-

tions and bring you back from the countries where you have been scattered, and I will give you back the land of Israel again.'

18"They will return to it and remove all its vile images and detestable idols. **19**I will give them an undivided heart and put a new spirit in them; I will remove from them their heart of stone and give them a heart of flesh. **20**Then they will follow my decrees and be careful to keep my laws. They will be my people, and I will be their God. **21**But as for those whose hearts are devoted to their vile images and detestable idols, I will bring down on their own heads what they have done, declares the Sovereign LORD."

22Then the cherubim, with the wheels beside them, spread their wings, and the glory of the God of Israel was above them. **23**The glory of the LORD went up from within the city and stopped above the mountain east of it. **24**The Spirit lifted me up and brought me to the exiles in Babylonia*d* in the vision given by the Spirit of God.

Then the vision I had seen went up from me, **25**and I told the exiles everything the LORD had shown me.

The Exile Symbolized

12 The word of the LORD came to me: **2**"Son of man, you are living among a rebellious people. They have eyes to see but do not see and ears to hear but do not hear, for they are a rebellious people.

3"Therefore, son of man, pack your belongings for exile and in the daytime, as they watch, set out and go from where you are to another place. Perhaps they will understand, though they are a rebellious house. **4**During the daytime, while they watch, bring out your belongings packed for exile. Then in the evening, while they are watching, go out like those who go into exile. **5**While they watch, dig through the wall and take your belongings out through it. **6**Put them on your shoulder as they are watching and carry them out at dusk. Cover your face so that you cannot see the land, for I have made you a sign to the house of Israel."

7So I did as I was commanded. During the day I brought out my things packed for exile. Then in the evening I dug through the wall with my hands. I took my belongings out at dusk, carrying them on my shoulders while they watched.

8In the morning the word of the LORD

---

a3 Or *This is not the time to build houses.*   *b15* Or *are in exile with you* (see Septuagint and Syriac)
c15 Or *those to whom the people of Jerusalem have said, 'Stay*   *d24* Or *Chaldea*

SATURDAY ☐

**Work It
Out**
••••

Think about the last twelve months of your life. In that time did you ever feel sort of cold toward God? Did you feel like you didn't really care? Did you feel like following him, being "godly," was just too hard, too much work? Everyone feels that way at one time or another. The important thing is what you do about it.

In order to get rid of that cold, weary feeling, tell God about it. That's right. Tell him exactly how you feel. He can take it. Say:

"God, if I'm honest, I just don't feel very godly. I don't feel like trying. So, God, I'm asking you to do whatever you have to do in order to make me *want* to put you first. Please deepen my love for you. Thanks, God. Amen.

**Nail It
Down**
••••

Read Ezekiel 11:19–20 for how God responds to this sort of prayer.

SUNDAY ☐

**Think It
Through**
••••

True godliness is something that can be a bit hard to define. It's not just doing things but how they're done and with what sort of attitude. Anyone can teach Bible school, but the students of a godly person will know they are loved. Raking leaves or shoveling snow for an elderly neighbor can be done by almost anyone, but the godly person does it willingly and with a smile. Anyone can sing a solo in church (well, almost anyone), but the godly person knows who gets the credit.

Godliness *is* and *does* all from a heart so full of love for God and others that there's no room for grumbling or irritation or pride.

Godliness sounds like a pretty tall order, doesn't it? That's why God's promise in Ezekiel is so important. The promise wasn't just for Ezekiel and his contemporaries. It's for you too. Have you taken advantage of such a wonderful promise from God?

**Nail It
Down**
••••

Reread Ezekiel 11:19–20. For further insight read Psalm 86:11–13.

Turn to pages 9 and 1372 for other readings on godliness.
Turn to page 867 for Monday's reading.

Topic
••••

GODLINESS

came to me: **9**"Son of man, did not that rebellious house of Israel ask you, 'What are you doing?'

10"Say to them, 'This is what the Sovereign LORD says: This oracle concerns the prince in Jerusalem and the whole house of Israel who are there.' **11**Say to them, 'I am a sign to you.'

"As I have done, so it will be done to them. They will go into exile as captives.

12"The prince among them will put his things on his shoulder at dusk and leave, and a hole will be dug in the wall for him to go through. He will cover his face so that he cannot see the land. **13**I will spread my net for him, and he will be caught in my snare; I will bring him to Babylonia, the land of the Chaldeans, but he will not see it, and there he will die. **14**I will scatter to the winds all those around him—his staff and all his troops—and I will pursue them with drawn sword.

15"They will know that I am the LORD, when I disperse them among the nations and scatter them through the countries. **16**But I will spare a few of them from the sword, famine and plague, so that in the nations where they go they may acknowledge all their detestable practices. Then they will know that I am the LORD."

17The word of the LORD came to me: **18**"Son of man, tremble as you eat your food, and shudder in fear as you drink your water. **19**Say to the people of the land: 'This is what the Sovereign LORD says about those living in Jerusalem and in the land of Israel: They will eat their food in anxiety and drink their water in despair, for their land will be stripped of everything in it because of the violence of all who live there. **20**The inhabited towns will be laid waste and the land will be desolate. Then you will know that I am the LORD.' "

21The word of the LORD came to me: **22**"Son of man, what is this proverb you have in the land of Israel: 'The days go by and every vision comes to nothing'? **23**Say to them, 'This is what the Sovereign LORD says: I am going to put an end to this proverb, and they will no longer quote it in Israel.' Say to them, 'The days are near when every vision will be fulfilled. **24**For there will be no more false visions or flattering divinations among the people of Israel. **25**But I the LORD will speak what I will, and it shall be fulfilled without delay. For in your days, you rebellious

house, I will fulfill whatever I say, declares the Sovereign LORD.' "

26The word of the LORD came to me: **27**"Son of man, the house of Israel is saying, 'The vision he sees is for many years from now, and he prophesies about the distant future.'

28"Therefore say to them, 'This is what the Sovereign LORD says: None of my words will be delayed any longer; whatever I say will be fulfilled, declares the Sovereign LORD.' "

False Prophets Condemned

13 The word of the LORD came to me: **2**"Son of man, prophesy against the prophets of Israel who are now prophesying. Say to those who prophesy out of their own imagination: 'Hear the word of the LORD! **3**This is what the Sovereign LORD says: Woe to the foolish[a] prophets who follow their own spirit and have seen nothing! **4**Your prophets, O Israel, are like jackals among ruins. **5**You have not gone up to the breaks in the wall to repair it for the house of Israel so that it will stand firm in the battle on the day of the LORD. **6**Their visions are false and their divinations a lie. They say, "The LORD declares," when the LORD has not sent them; yet they expect their words to be fulfilled. **7**Have you not seen false visions and uttered lying divinations when you say, "The LORD declares," though I have not spoken?

8" 'Therefore this is what the Sovereign LORD says: Because of your false words and lying visions, I am against you, declares the Sovereign LORD. **9**My hand will be against the prophets who see false visions and utter lying divinations. They will not belong to the council of my people or be listed in the records of the house of Israel, nor will they enter the land of Israel. Then you will know that I am the Sovereign LORD.

10" 'Because they lead my people astray, saying, "Peace," when there is no peace, and because, when a flimsy wall is built, they cover it with whitewash, **11**therefore tell those who cover it with whitewash that it is going to fall. Rain will come in torrents, and I will send hailstones hurtling down, and violent winds will burst forth. **12**When the wall collapses, will people not ask you, "Where is the whitewash you covered it with?"

13" 'Therefore this is what the Sovereign LORD says: In my wrath I will unleash a violent wind, and in my anger hailstones and torrents of rain will fall with destructive fury.

---

a3 Or *wicked*

14I will tear down the wall you have covered with whitewash and will level it to the ground so that its foundation will be laid bare. When it*a* falls, you will be destroyed in it; and you will know that I am the LORD. **15**So I will spend my wrath against the wall and against those who covered it with whitewash. I will say to you, "The wall is gone and so are those who whitewashed it, **16**those prophets of Israel who prophesied to Jerusalem and saw visions of peace for her when there was no peace, declares the Sovereign LORD." '

17"Now, son of man, set your face against the daughters of your people who prophesy out of their own imagination. Prophesy against them **18**and say, 'This is what the Sovereign LORD says: Woe to the women who sew magic charms on all their wrists and make veils of various lengths for their heads in order to ensnare people. Will you ensnare the lives of my people but preserve your own? **19**You have profaned me among my people for a few handfuls of barley and scraps of bread. By lying to my people, who listen to lies, you have killed those who should not have died and have spared those who should not live.

20" 'Therefore this is what the Sovereign LORD says: I am against your magic charms with which you ensnare people like birds and I will tear them from your arms; I will set free the people that you ensnare like birds. **21**I will tear off your veils and save my people from your hands, and they will no longer fall prey to your power. Then you will know that I am the LORD. **22**Because you disheartened the righteous with your lies, when I had brought them no grief, and because you encouraged the wicked not to turn from their evil ways and so save their lives, **23**therefore you will no longer see false visions or practice divination. I will save my people from your hands. And then you will know that I am the LORD.' "

Idolaters Condemned

14 Some of the elders of Israel came to me and sat down in front of me. **2**Then the word of the LORD came to me: **3**"Son of man, these men have set up idols in their hearts and put wicked stumbling blocks before their faces. Should I let them inquire of me at all? **4**Therefore speak to them and tell them, 'This is what the Sover-

eign LORD says: When any Israelite sets up idols in his heart and puts a wicked stumbling block before his face and then goes to a prophet, I the LORD will answer him myself in keeping with his great idolatry. **5**I will do this to recapture the hearts of the people of Israel, who have all deserted me for their idols.'

6"Therefore say to the house of Israel, 'This is what the Sovereign LORD says: Repent! Turn from your idols and renounce all your detestable practices!

7" 'When any Israelite or any alien living in Israel separates himself from me and sets up idols in his heart and puts a wicked stumbling block before his face and then goes to a prophet to inquire of me, I the LORD will answer him myself. **8**I will set my face against that man and make him an example and a byword. I will cut him off from my people. Then you will know that I am the LORD.

9" 'And if the prophet is enticed to utter a prophecy, I the LORD have enticed that prophet, and I will stretch out my hand against him and destroy him from among my people Israel. **10**They will bear their guilt—the prophet will be as guilty as the one who consults him. **11**Then the people of Israel will no longer stray from me, nor will they defile themselves anymore with all their sins. They will be my people, and I will be their God, declares the Sovereign LORD.' "

Judgment Inescapable

12The word of the LORD came to me: **13**"Son of man, if a country sins against me by being unfaithful and I stretch out my hand against it to cut off its food supply and send famine upon it and kill its men and their animals, **14**even if these three men—Noah, Daniel*b* and Job—were in it, they could save only themselves by their righteousness, declares the Sovereign LORD.

15"Or if I send wild beasts through that country and they leave it childless and it becomes desolate so that no one can pass through it because of the beasts, **16**as surely as I live, declares the Sovereign LORD, even if these three men were in it, they could not save their own sons or daughters. They alone would be saved, but the land would be desolate.

17"Or if I bring a sword against that country and say, 'Let the sword pass throughout

---

a 14 Or *the city*   *b 14* Or *Danel*; the Hebrew spelling may suggest a person other than the prophet Daniel; also in verse 20.

YOU CAN'T TELL ME WHAT TO DO

☐ MONDAY

Eric's parents have tried everything to curb their son's rebellious behavior. They took away his privileges, grounded him and cut off his money. Nothing worked. Eric's basic attitude was, "I can do what I want when I want." When his mom and dad announced that they were enrolling Eric in a military school, his response was to run away to New York City.

After a week of living on the streets that included seeing a gang fight, being mugged, getting propositioned and eating out of a dumpster, Eric returned home with a different attitude.

Look It Up

Rebelling against authority by running away doesn't work for several reasons.

1. You might be able to get out from under your parents' hands, but you can't escape from God, the ultimate authority. "Where can I go from your Spirit? Where can I flee from your presence?" (Psalm 139:7).

2. God will not allow his children, because of a rebellious attitude, to "escape" from their responsibilities. (Remember Jonah?)

3. Pride (do you see the pride reflected in the title of this article?) carries severe consequences: "Pride goes before destruction, a haughty spirit before a fall" (Proverbs 16:18).

In short, it's better to humble yourself, than to have God bring you back down to earth.

Think It Through

It seems like it would be fun and exciting to be out on your own, doing what you want. The truth is that most teenage runaways lead nightmarish lives of addiction, prostitution and despair. They are perhaps the most preyed upon members of society. Running away to find freedom is one of Satan's wildest lies.

Work It Out

Go to the library or search the Internet for articles about the life of runaways. If you read just one or two stories, you quickly see running away as the dead end it really is.

Then pray: "God, keep me from ever thinking that running away is a solution. Help me to see that my situation at home, though not perfect, is still paradise compared to life on the streets. And God, work through your church so that thousands of runaways will return home even today. Amen."

Nail It Down

Read Ezekiel 14:12–14 for a warning that we cannot escape the results of our behavior.

Turn to pages 1021, 1365 and 1390 for other readings on escape.
Turn to page 892 for Tuesday's reading.

Topic

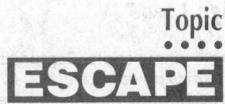

ESCAPE

the land,' and I kill its men and their animals, **18**as surely as I live, declares the Sovereign LORD, even if these three men were in it, they could not save their own sons or daughters. They alone would be saved.

19"Or if I send a plague into that land and pour out my wrath upon it through bloodshed, killing its men and their animals, **20**as surely as I live, declares the Sovereign LORD, even if Noah, Daniel and Job were in it, they could save neither son nor daughter. They would save only themselves by their righteousness.

21"For this is what the Sovereign LORD says: How much worse will it be when I send against Jerusalem my four dreadful judgments—sword and famine and wild beasts and plague—to kill its men and their animals! **22**Yet there will be some survivors—sons and daughters who will be brought out of it. They will come to you, and when you see their conduct and their actions, you will be consoled regarding the disaster I have brought upon Jerusalem—every disaster I have brought upon it. **23**You will be consoled when you see their conduct and their actions, for you will know that I have done nothing in it without cause, declares the Sovereign LORD."

Jerusalem, A Useless Vine

15 The word of the LORD came to me: **2**"Son of man, how is the wood of a vine better than that of a branch on any of the trees in the forest? **3**Is wood ever taken from it to make anything useful? Do they make pegs from it to hang things on? **4**And after it is thrown on the fire as fuel and the fire burns both ends and chars the middle, is it then useful for anything? **5**If it was not useful for anything when it was whole, how much less can it be made into something useful when the fire has burned it and it is charred?

6"Therefore this is what the Sovereign LORD says: As I have given the wood of the vine among the trees of the forest as fuel for the fire, so will I treat the people living in Jerusalem. **7**I will set my face against them. Although they have come out of the fire, the fire will yet consume them. And when I set my face against them, you will know that I am the LORD. **8**I will make the land desolate because they have been unfaithful, declares the Sovereign LORD."

An Allegory of Unfaithful Jerusalem

16 The word of the LORD came to me: **2**"Son of man, confront Jerusalem with her detestable practices **3**and say, 'This is what the Sovereign LORD says to Jerusalem: Your ancestry and birth were in the land of the Canaanites; your father was an Amorite and your mother a Hittite. **4**On the day you were born your cord was not cut, nor were you washed with water to make you clean, nor were you rubbed with salt or wrapped in cloths. **5**No one looked on you with pity or had compassion enough to do any of these things for you. Rather, you were thrown out into the open field, for on the day you were born you were despised.

6"'Then I passed by and saw you kicking about in your blood, and as you lay there in your blood I said to you, "Live!"*a* **7**I made you grow like a plant of the field. You grew up and developed and became the most beautiful of jewels.*b* Your breasts were formed and your hair grew, you who were naked and bare.

8"'Later I passed by, and when I looked at you and saw that you were old enough for love, I spread the corner of my garment over you and covered your nakedness. I gave you my solemn oath and entered into a covenant with you, declares the Sovereign LORD, and you became mine.

9"'I bathed*c* you with water and washed the blood from you and put ointments on you. **10**I clothed you with an embroidered dress and put leather sandals on you. I dressed you in fine linen and covered you with costly garments. **11**I adorned you with jewelry: I put bracelets on your arms and a necklace around your neck, **12**and I put a ring on your nose, earrings on your ears and a beautiful crown on your head. **13**So you were adorned with gold and silver; your clothes were of fine linen and costly fabric and embroidered cloth. Your food was fine flour, honey and olive oil. You became very beautiful and rose to be a queen. **14**And your fame spread among the nations on account of your beauty, because the splendor I had given you made your beauty perfect, declares the Sovereign LORD.

15"'But you trusted in your beauty and used your fame to become a prostitute. You lavished your favors on anyone who passed by and your beauty became his.*d* **16**You took some of your garments to make gaudy

---

a6 A few Hebrew manuscripts, Septuagint and Syriac; most Hebrew manuscripts *"Live!" And as you lay there in your blood I said to you, "Live!"*   *b7* Or *became mature*   *c9* Or *I had bathed*   *d15* Most Hebrew manuscripts; one Hebrew manuscript (see some Septuagint manuscripts) *by. Such a thing should not happen* high places, where you carried on your prostitution. Such things should not happen, nor should they ever occur. **17**You also took the fine jewelry I gave you, the jewelry made of my gold and silver, and you made for yourself male idols and engaged in prostitution with them. **18**And you took your embroidered clothes to put on them, and you offered my oil and incense before them. **19**Also the food I provided for you — the fine flour, olive oil and honey I gave you to eat — you offered as fragrant incense before them. That is what happened, declares the Sovereign Lord.

20" 'And you took your sons and daughters whom you bore to me and sacrificed them as food to the idols. Was your prostitution not enough? **21**You slaughtered my children and sacrificed them*a* to the idols. **22**In all your detestable practices and your prostitution you did not remember the days of your youth, when you were naked and bare, kicking about in your blood.

23" 'Woe! Woe to you, declares the Sovereign Lord. In addition to all your other wickedness, **24**you built a mound for yourself and made a lofty shrine in every public square. **25**At the head of every street you built your lofty shrines and degraded your beauty, offering your body with increasing promiscuity to anyone who passed by. **26**You engaged in prostitution with the Egyptians, your lustful neighbors, and provoked me to anger with your increasing promiscuity. **27**So I stretched out my hand against you and reduced your territory; I gave you over to the greed of your enemies, the daughters of the Philistines, who were shocked by your lewd conduct. **28**You engaged in prostitution with the Assyrians too, because you were insatiable; and even after that, you still were not satisfied. **29**Then you increased your promiscuity to include Babylonia,*b* a land of merchants, but even with this you were not satisfied.

30" 'How weak-willed you are, declares the Sovereign Lord, when you do all these things, acting like a brazen prostitute! **31**When you built your mounds at the head of every street and made your lofty shrines in every public square, you were unlike a prostitute, because you scorned payment.

32" 'You adulterous wife! You prefer strangers to your own husband! **33**Every prostitute receives a fee, but you give gifts to all your lovers, bribing them to come to you from everywhere for your illicit favors. **34**So in your prostitution you are the opposite of others; no one runs after you for your favors. You are the very opposite, for you give payment and none is given to you.

35" 'Therefore, you prostitute, hear the word of the Lord! **36**This is what the Sovereign Lord says: Because you poured out your wealth*c* and exposed your nakedness in your promiscuity with your lovers, and because of all your detestable idols, and because you gave them your children's blood, **37**therefore I am going to gather all your lovers, with whom you found pleasure, those you loved as well as those you hated. I will gather them against you from all around and will strip you in front of them, and they will see all your nakedness. **38**I will sentence you to the punishment of women who commit adultery and who shed blood; I will bring upon you the blood vengeance of my wrath and jealous anger. **39**Then I will hand you over to your lovers, and they will tear down your mounds and destroy your lofty shrines. They will strip you of your clothes and take your fine jewelry and leave you naked and bare. **40**They will bring a mob against you, who will stone you and hack you to pieces with their swords. **41**They will burn down your houses and inflict punishment on you in the sight of many women. I will put a stop to your prostitution, and you will no longer pay your lovers. **42**Then my wrath against you will subside and my jealous anger will turn away from you; I will be calm and no longer angry.

43" 'Because you did not remember the days of your youth but enraged me with all these things, I will surely bring down on your head what you have done, declares the Sovereign Lord. Did you not add lewdness to all your other detestable practices?

44" 'Everyone who quotes proverbs will quote this proverb about you: "Like mother, like daughter." **45**You are a true daughter of your mother, who despised her husband and her children; and you are a true sister of your sisters, who despised their husbands and their children. Your mother was a Hittite and your father an Amorite. **46**Your older sister was Samaria, who lived to the north of you with her daughters; and your younger sister, who lived to the south of you with her daughters, was Sodom. **47**You not only walked in their ways and copied their detestable practices, but in all your ways you soon became more depraved than they. **48**As surely as I live, declares the Sovereign

---

a21 Or *and made them pass through* *the fire*   *b29* Or *Chaldea*   *c36* Or *lust*

LORD, your sister Sodom and her daughters never did what you and your daughters have done.

⁴⁹" 'Now this was the sin of your sister Sodom: She and her daughters were arrogant, overfed and unconcerned; they did not help the poor and needy. ⁵⁰They were haughty and did detestable things before me. Therefore I did away with them as you have seen. ⁵¹Samaria did not commit half the sins you did. You have done more detestable things than they, and have made your sisters seem righteous by all these things you have done. ⁵²Bear your disgrace, for you have furnished some justification for your sisters. Because your sins were more vile than theirs, they appear more righteous than you. So then, be ashamed and bear your disgrace, for you have made your sisters appear righteous.

⁵³" 'However, I will restore the fortunes of Sodom and her daughters and of Samaria and her daughters, and your fortunes along with them, ⁵⁴so that you may bear your disgrace and be ashamed of all you have done in giving them comfort. ⁵⁵And your sisters, Sodom with her daughters and Samaria with her daughters, will return to what they were before; and you and your daughters will return to what you were before. ⁵⁶You would not even mention your sister Sodom in the day of your pride, ⁵⁷before your wickedness was uncovered. Even so, you are now scorned by the daughters of Edom*a* and all her neighbors and the daughters of the Philistines—all those around you who despise you. ⁵⁸You will bear the consequences of your lewdness and your detestable practices, declares the LORD.

⁵⁹" 'This is what the Sovereign LORD says: I will deal with you as you deserve, because you have despised my oath by breaking the covenant. ⁶⁰Yet I will remember the covenant I made with you in the days of your youth, and I will establish an everlasting covenant with you. ⁶¹Then you will remember your ways and be ashamed when you receive your sisters, both those who are older than you and those who are younger. I will give them to you as daughters, but not on the basis of my covenant with you. ⁶²So I will establish my covenant with you, and you will know that I am the LORD. ⁶³Then, when I make atonement for you for all you have done, you will remember and be ashamed and never again open your mouth because of your humiliation, declares the Sovereign LORD.' "

Two Eagles and a Vine

17 The word of the LORD came to me: ²"Son of man, set forth an allegory and tell the house of Israel a parable. ³Say to them, 'This is what the Sovereign LORD says: A great eagle with powerful wings, long feathers and full plumage of varied colors came to Lebanon. Taking hold of the top of a cedar, ⁴he broke off its topmost shoot and carried it away to a land of merchants, where he planted it in a city of traders.

⁵" 'He took some of the seed of your land and put it in fertile soil. He planted it like a willow by abundant water, ⁶and it sprouted and became a low, spreading vine. Its branches turned toward him, but its roots remained under it. So it became a vine and produced branches and put out leafy boughs.

⁷" 'But there was another great eagle with powerful wings and full plumage. The vine now sent out its roots toward him from the plot where it was planted and stretched out its branches to him for water. ⁸It had been planted in good soil by abundant water so that it would produce branches, bear fruit and become a splendid vine.'

⁹"Say to them, 'This is what the Sovereign LORD says: Will it thrive? Will it not be uprooted and stripped of its fruit so that it withers? All its new growth will wither. It will not take a strong arm or many people to pull it up by the roots. ¹⁰Even if it is transplanted, will it thrive? Will it not wither completely when the east wind strikes it—wither away in the plot where it grew?' "

¹¹Then the word of the LORD came to me: ¹²"Say to this rebellious house, 'Do you not know what these things mean?' Say to them: 'The king of Babylon went to Jerusalem and carried off her king and her nobles, bringing them back with him to Babylon. ¹³Then he took a member of the royal family and made a treaty with him, putting him under oath. He also carried away the leading men of the land, ¹⁴so that the kingdom would be brought low, unable to rise again, surviving only by keeping his treaty. ¹⁵But the king rebelled against him by sending his envoys to Egypt to get horses and a large army. Will he succeed? Will he who does such things escape? Will he break the treaty and yet escape?

¹⁶" 'As surely as I live, declares the Sover-

---

a57 Many Hebrew manuscripts and Syriac; most Hebrew manuscripts, Septuagint and Vulgate *Aram* eign LORD, he shall die in Babylon, in the land of the king who put him on the throne, whose oath he despised and whose treaty he broke. [17]Pharaoh with his mighty army and great horde will be of no help to him in war, when ramps are built and siege works erected to destroy many lives. [18]He despised the oath by breaking the covenant. Because he had given his hand in pledge and yet did all these things, he shall not escape.

[19]" 'Therefore this is what the Sovereign LORD says: As surely as I live, I will bring down on his head my oath that he despised and my covenant that he broke. [20]I will spread my net for him, and he will be caught in my snare. I will bring him to Babylon and execute judgment upon him there because he was unfaithful to me. [21]All his fleeing troops will fall by the sword, and the survivors will be scattered to the winds. Then you will know that I the LORD have spoken.

[22]" 'This is what the Sovereign LORD says: I myself will take a shoot from the very top of a cedar and plant it; I will break off a tender sprig from its topmost shoots and plant it on a high and lofty mountain. [23]On the mountain heights of Israel I will plant it; it will produce branches and bear fruit and become a splendid cedar. Birds of every kind will nest in it; they will find shelter in the shade of its branches. [24]All the trees of the field will know that I the LORD bring down the tall tree and make the low tree grow tall. I dry up the green tree and make the dry tree flourish.

" 'I the LORD have spoken, and I will do it.' "

The Soul Who Sins Will Die

18 The word of the LORD came to me: [2]"What do you people mean by quoting this proverb about the land of Israel:

" 'The fathers eat sour grapes,
    and the children's teeth are set on
        edge'?

[3]"As surely as I live, declares the Sovereign LORD, you will no longer quote this proverb in Israel. [4]For every living soul belongs to me, the father as well as the son—both alike belong to me. The soul who sins is the one who will die.

[5]"Suppose there is a righteous man
    who does what is just and right.
[6]He does not eat at the mountain shrines

or look to the idols of the house of
    Israel.
He does not defile his neighbor's wife
    or lie with a woman during her
        period.
[7]He does not oppress anyone,
    but returns what he took in pledge for
        a loan.
He does not commit robbery
    but gives his food to the hungry
    and provides clothing for the naked.
[8]He does not lend at usury
    or take excessive interest.[a]
He withholds his hand from doing
        wrong
    and judges fairly between man and
        man.
[9]He follows my decrees
    and faithfully keeps my laws.
That man is righteous;
    he will surely live,
            declares the Sovereign LORD.

[10]"Suppose he has a violent son, who sheds blood or does any of these other things[b] [11](though the father has done none of them):

"He eats at the mountain shrines.
He defiles his neighbor's wife.
[12]He oppresses the poor and needy.
He commits robbery.
He does not return what he took in
        pledge.
He looks to the idols.
He does detestable things.
[13]He lends at usury and takes excessive
        interest.

Will such a man live? He will not! Because he has done all these detestable things, he will surely be put to death and his blood will be on his own head.

[14]"But suppose this son has a son who sees all the sins his father commits, and though he sees them, he does not do such things:

[15]"He does not eat at the mountain
        shrines
    or look to the idols of the house of
        Israel.
He does not defile his neighbor's wife.
[16]He does not oppress anyone
    or require a pledge for a loan.
He does not commit robbery
    but gives his food to the hungry
    and provides clothing for the naked.

---

[a]8 Or *take interest*; similarly in verses 13 and 17   [b]10 Or *things to a brother*

[17]He withholds his hand from sin[a]
and takes no usury or excessive
interest.
He keeps my laws and follows my
decrees.

He will not die for his father's sin; he will
surely live. [18]But his father will die for his
own sin, because he practiced extortion,
robbed his brother and did what was wrong
among his people.

[19]"Yet you ask, 'Why does the son not
share the guilt of his father?' Since the son
has done what is just and right and has been
careful to keep all my decrees, he will surely
live. [20]The soul who sins is the one who will
die. The son will not share the guilt of the
father, nor will the father share the guilt of
the son. The righteousness of the righteous
man will be credited to him, and the wickedness of the wicked will be charged against
him.

[21]"But if a wicked man turns away from all
the sins he has committed and keeps all my
decrees and does what is just and right, he
will surely live; he will not die. [22]None of the
offenses he has committed will be remembered against him. Because of the righteous
things he has done, he will live. [23]Do I take
any pleasure in the death of the wicked? declares the Sovereign LORD. Rather, am I not
pleased when they turn from their ways and
live?

[24]"But if a righteous man turns from his
righteousness and commits sin and does the
same detestable things the wicked man
does, will he live? None of the righteous
things he has done will be remembered. Because of the unfaithfulness he is guilty of
and because of the sins he has committed,
he will die.

[25]"Yet you say, 'The way of the Lord is not
just.' Hear, O house of Israel: Is my way unjust? Is it not your ways that are unjust? [26]If
a righteous man turns from his righteousness and commits sin, he will die for it; because of the sin he has committed he will
die. [27]But if a wicked man turns away from
the wickedness he has committed and does
what is just and right, he will save his life.
[28]Because he considers all the offenses he
has committed and turns away from them,
he will surely live; he will not die. [29]Yet the
house of Israel says, 'The way of the Lord is
not just.' Are my ways unjust, O house of
Israel? Is it not your ways that are unjust?

[30]"Therefore, O house of Israel, I will
judge you, each one according to his ways,
declares the Sovereign LORD. Repent! Turn
away from all your offenses; then sin will
not be your downfall. [31]Rid yourselves of all
the offenses you have committed, and get a
new heart and a new spirit. Why will you
die, O house of Israel? [32]For I take no pleasure in the death of anyone, declares the
Sovereign LORD. Repent and live!

A Lament for Israel's Princes

19 "Take up a lament concerning the
princes of Israel [2]and say:

" 'What a lioness was your mother
among the lions!
She lay down among the young lions
and reared her cubs.
[3]She brought up one of her cubs,
and he became a strong lion.
He learned to tear the prey
and he devoured men.
[4]The nations heard about him,
and he was trapped in their pit.
They led him with hooks
to the land of Egypt.

[5]" 'When she saw her hope unfulfilled,
her expectation gone,
she took another of her cubs
and made him a strong lion.
[6]He prowled among the lions,
for he was now a strong lion.
He learned to tear the prey
and he devoured men.
[7]He broke down[b] their strongholds
and devastated their towns.
The land and all who were in it
were terrified by his roaring.
[8]Then the nations came against him,
those from regions round about.
They spread their net for him,
and he was trapped in their pit.
[9]With hooks they pulled him into a cage
and brought him to the king of
Babylon.
They put him in prison,
so his roar was heard no longer
on the mountains of Israel.

[10]" 'Your mother was like a vine in your
vineyard[c]
planted by the water;
it was fruitful and full of branches
because of abundant water.
[11]Its branches were strong,

fit for a ruler's scepter.
It towered high
   above the thick foliage,
conspicuous for its height
   and for its many branches.
¹²But it was uprooted in fury
   and thrown to the ground.
The east wind made it shrivel,
   it was stripped of its fruit;
its strong branches withered
   and fire consumed them.
¹³Now it is planted in the desert,
   in a dry and thirsty land.
¹⁴Fire spread from one of its main*ᵃ*
      branches
   and consumed its fruit.
No strong branch is left on it
   fit for a ruler's scepter.'

This is a lament and is to be used as a lament."

Rebellious Israel

20 In the seventh year, in the fifth month on the tenth day, some of the elders of Israel came to inquire of the LORD, and they sat down in front of me.

²Then the word of the LORD came to me: ³"Son of man, speak to the elders of Israel and say to them, 'This is what the Sovereign LORD says: Have you come to inquire of me? As surely as I live, I will not let you inquire of me, declares the Sovereign LORD.'

⁴"Will you judge them? Will you judge them, son of man? Then confront them with the detestable practices of their fathers ⁵and say to them: 'This is what the Sovereign LORD says: On the day I chose Israel, I swore with uplifted hand to the descendants of the house of Jacob and revealed myself to them in Egypt. With uplifted hand I said to them, "I am the LORD your God." ⁶On that day I swore to them that I would bring them out of Egypt into a land I had searched out for them, a land flowing with milk and honey, the most beautiful of all lands. ⁷And I said to them, "Each of you, get rid of the vile images you have set your eyes on, and do not defile yourselves with the idols of Egypt. I am the LORD your God."

⁸" 'But they rebelled against me and would not listen to me; they did not get rid of the vile images they had set their eyes on, nor did they forsake the idols of Egypt. So I said I would pour out my wrath on them and spend my anger against them in Egypt. ⁹But for the sake of my name I did what would keep it from being profaned in the eyes of the nations they lived among and in whose sight I had revealed myself to the Israelites by bringing them out of Egypt. ¹⁰Therefore I led them out of Egypt and brought them into the desert. ¹¹I gave them my decrees and made known to them my laws, for the man who obeys them will live by them. ¹²Also I gave them my Sabbaths as a sign between us, so they would know that I the LORD made them holy.

¹³" 'Yet the people of Israel rebelled against me in the desert. They did not follow my decrees but rejected my laws—although the man who obeys them will live by them—and they utterly desecrated my Sabbaths. So I said I would pour out my wrath on them and destroy them in the desert. ¹⁴But for the sake of my name I did what would keep it from being profaned in the eyes of the nations in whose sight I had brought them out. ¹⁵Also with uplifted hand I swore to them in the desert that I would not bring them into the land I had given them—a land flowing with milk and honey, most beautiful of all lands— ¹⁶because they rejected my laws and did not follow my decrees and desecrated my Sabbaths. For their hearts were devoted to their idols. ¹⁷Yet I looked on them with pity and did not destroy them or put an end to them in the desert. ¹⁸I said to their children in the desert, "Do not follow the statutes of your fathers or keep their laws or defile yourselves with their idols. ¹⁹I am the LORD your God; follow my decrees and be careful to keep my laws. ²⁰Keep my Sabbaths holy, that they may be a sign between us. Then you will know that I am the LORD your God."

²¹" 'But the children rebelled against me: They did not follow my decrees, they were not careful to keep my laws—although the man who obeys them will live by them—and they desecrated my Sabbaths. So I said I would pour out my wrath on them and spend my anger against them in the desert. ²²But I withheld my hand, and for the sake of my name I did what would keep it from being profaned in the eyes of the nations in whose sight I had brought them out. ²³Also with uplifted hand I swore to them in the desert that I would disperse them among the nations and scatter them through the countries, ²⁴because they had not obeyed my laws but had rejected my decrees and desecrated my Sabbaths, and their eyes lusted after their fathers' idols. ²⁵I also gave

---

ᵃ*14 Or from under its*

them over to statutes that were not good and laws they could not live by; **26**I let them become defiled through their gifts — the sacrifice of every firstborn*a* — that I might fill them with horror so they would know that I am the LORD.'

27"Therefore, son of man, speak to the people of Israel and say to them, 'This is what the Sovereign LORD says: In this also your fathers blasphemed me by forsaking me: **28**When I brought them into the land I had sworn to give them and they saw any high hill or any leafy tree, there they offered their sacrifices, made offerings that provoked me to anger, presented their fragrant incense and poured out their drink offerings. **29**Then I said to them: What is this high place you go to?' " (It is called Bamah*b* to this day.)

Judgment and Restoration

30"Therefore say to the house of Israel: 'This is what the Sovereign LORD says: Will you defile yourselves the way your fathers did and lust after their vile images? **31**When you offer your gifts — the sacrifice of your sons in*c* the fire — you continue to defile yourselves with all your idols to this day. Am I to let you inquire of me, O house of Israel? As surely as I live, declares the Sovereign LORD, I will not let you inquire of me.

32" 'You say, "We want to be like the nations, like the peoples of the world, who serve wood and stone." But what you have in mind will never happen. **33**As surely as I live, declares the Sovereign LORD, I will rule over you with a mighty hand and an outstretched arm and with outpoured wrath. **34**I will bring you from the nations and gather you from the countries where you have been scattered — with a mighty hand and an outstretched arm and with outpoured wrath. **35**I will bring you into the desert of the nations and there, face to face, I will execute judgment upon you. **36**As I judged your fathers in the desert of the land of Egypt, so I will judge you, declares the Sovereign LORD. **37**I will take note of you as you pass under my rod, and I will bring you into the bond of the covenant. **38**I will purge you of those who revolt and rebel against me. Although I will bring them out of the land where they are living, yet they will not enter the land of Israel. Then you will know that I am the LORD.

39" 'As for you, O house of Israel, this is

what the Sovereign LORD says: Go and serve your idols, every one of you! But afterward you will surely listen to me and no longer profane my holy name with your gifts and idols. **40**For on my holy mountain, the high mountain of Israel, declares the Sovereign LORD, there in the land the entire house of Israel will serve me, and there I will accept them. There I will require your offerings and your choice gifts,*d* along with all your holy sacrifices. **41**I will accept you as fragrant incense when I bring you out from the nations and gather you from the countries where you have been scattered, and I will show myself holy among you in the sight of the nations. **42**Then you will know that I am the LORD, when I bring you into the land of Israel, the land I had sworn with uplifted hand to give to your fathers. **43**There you will remember your conduct and all the actions by which you have defiled yourselves, and you will loathe yourselves for all the evil you have done. **44**You will know that I am the LORD, when I deal with you for my name's sake and not according to your evil ways and your corrupt practices, O house of Israel, declares the Sovereign LORD.' "

Prophecy Against the South

45The word of the LORD came to me: **46**"Son of man, set your face toward the south; preach against the south and prophesy against the forest of the southland. **47**Say to the southern forest: 'Hear the word of the LORD. This is what the Sovereign LORD says: I am about to set fire to you, and it will consume all your trees, both green and dry. The blazing flame will not be quenched, and every face from south to north will be scorched by it. **48**Everyone will see that I the LORD have kindled it; it will not be quenched.' "

49Then I said, "Ah, Sovereign LORD! They are saying of me, 'Isn't he just telling parables?' "

Babylon, God's Sword of Judgment

21 The word of the LORD came to me: **2**"Son of man, set your face against Jerusalem and preach against the sanctuary. Prophesy against the land of Israel **3**and say to her: 'This is what the LORD says: I am against you. I will draw my sword from its scabbard and cut off from you both the righteous and the wicked. **4**Because I am going to cut off the righteous and the wicked, my

---

a26 Or —making every firstborn pass through ⸢the fire⸣ *b29 Bamah means high place.* *c31 Or —making your sons pass through* *d40 Or and the gifts of your firstfruits* sword will be unsheathed against everyone from south to north. **5**Then all people will know that I the LORD have drawn my sword from its scabbard; it will not return again.'

6"Therefore groan, son of man! Groan before them with broken heart and bitter grief. **7**And when they ask you, 'Why are you groaning?' you shall say, 'Because of the news that is coming. Every heart will melt and every hand go limp; every spirit will become faint and every knee become as weak as water.' It is coming! It will surely take place, declares the Sovereign LORD."

8The word of the LORD came to me: **9**"Son of man, prophesy and say, 'This is what the Lord says:

" 'A sword, a sword,
    sharpened and polished —
10sharpened for the slaughter,
    polished to flash like lightning!

" 'Shall we rejoice in the scepter of my son ⌊Judah⌋? The sword despises every such stick.

11" 'The sword is appointed to be
        polished,
    to be grasped with the hand;
it is sharpened and polished,
    made ready for the hand of the
        slayer.
12Cry out and wail, son of man,
    for it is against my people;
it is against all the princes of Israel.
They are thrown to the sword
    along with my people.
Therefore beat your breast.

13" 'Testing will surely come. And what if the scepter ⌊of Judah⌋, which the sword despises, does not continue? declares the Sovereign LORD.'

14"So then, son of man, prophesy
    and strike your hands together.
Let the sword strike twice,
    even three times.
It is a sword for slaughter —
    a sword for great slaughter,
    closing in on them from every side.
15So that hearts may melt
    and the fallen be many,
I have stationed the sword for
        slaughter[a]
    at all their gates.
Oh! It is made to flash like lightning,
    it is grasped for slaughter.
16O sword, slash to the right,

then to the left,
    wherever your blade is turned.
17I too will strike my hands together,
    and my wrath will subside.
I the LORD have spoken."

18The word of the LORD came to me: **19**"Son of man, mark out two roads for the sword of the king of Babylon to take, both starting from the same country. Make a signpost where the road branches off to the city. **20**Mark out one road for the sword to come against Rabbah of the Ammonites and another against Judah and fortified Jerusalem. **21**For the king of Babylon will stop at the fork in the road, at the junction of the two roads, to seek an omen: He will cast lots with arrows, he will consult his idols, he will examine the liver. **22**Into his right hand will come the lot for Jerusalem, where he is to set up battering rams, to give the command to slaughter, to sound the battle cry, to set battering rams against the gates, to build a ramp and to erect siege works. **23**It will seem like a false omen to those who have sworn allegiance to him, but he will remind them of their guilt and take them captive.

24"Therefore this is what the Sovereign LORD says: 'Because you people have brought to mind your guilt by your open rebellion, revealing your sins in all that you do — because you have done this, you will be taken captive.

25" 'O profane and wicked prince of Israel, whose day has come, whose time of punishment has reached its climax, **26**this is what the Sovereign LORD says: Take off the turban, remove the crown. It will not be as it was: The lowly will be exalted and the exalted will be brought low. **27**A ruin! A ruin! I will make it a ruin! It will not be restored until he comes to whom it rightfully belongs; to him I will give it.'

28"And you, son of man, prophesy and say, 'This is what the Sovereign LORD says about the Ammonites and their insults:

" 'A sword, a sword,
    drawn for the slaughter,
polished to consume
    and to flash like lightning!
29Despite false visions concerning you
    and lying divinations about you,
it will be laid on the necks
    of the wicked who are to be slain,
whose day has come,
    whose time of punishment has
        reached its climax.

---

a15 Septuagint; the meaning of the Hebrew for this word is uncertain.

30Return the sword to its scabbard.
In the place where you were created,
　in the land of your ancestry,
　　I will judge you.
31I will pour out my wrath upon you
　and breathe out my fiery anger
　　against you;
I will hand you over to brutal men,
　men skilled in destruction.
32You will be fuel for the fire,
　your blood will be shed in your land,
you will be remembered no more;
　for I the LORD have spoken.' "

Jerusalem's Sins

22 The word of the LORD came to me: **2**"Son of man, will you judge her? Will you judge this city of bloodshed? Then confront her with all her detestable practices **3**and say: 'This is what the Sovereign LORD says: O city that brings on herself doom by shedding blood in her midst and defiles herself by making idols, **4**you have become guilty because of the blood you have shed and have become defiled by the idols you have made. You have brought your days to a close, and the end of your years has come. Therefore I will make you an object of scorn to the nations and a laughingstock to all the countries. **5**Those who are near and those who are far away will mock you, O infamous city, full of turmoil.

6" 'See how each of the princes of Israel who are in you uses his power to shed blood. **7**In you they have treated father and mother with contempt; in you they have oppressed the alien and mistreated the fatherless and the widow. **8**You have despised my holy things and desecrated my Sabbaths. **9**In you are slanderous men bent on shedding blood; in you are those who eat at the mountain shrines and commit lewd acts. **10**In you are those who dishonor their fathers' bed; in you are those who violate women during their period, when they are ceremonially unclean. **11**In you one man commits a detestable offense with his neighbor's wife, another shamefully defiles his daughter-in-law, and another violates his sister, his own father's daughter. **12**In you men accept bribes to shed blood; you take usury and excessive interest*a* and make unjust gain from your neighbors by extortion. And you have forgotten me, declares the Sovereign LORD.

13" 'I will surely strike my hands together

at the unjust gain you have made and at the blood you have shed in your midst. **14**Will your courage endure or your hands be strong in the day I deal with you? I the LORD have spoken, and I will do it. **15**I will disperse you among the nations and scatter you through the countries; and I will put an end to your uncleanness. **16**When you have been defiled*b* in the eyes of the nations, you will know that I am the LORD.' "

17Then the word of the LORD came to me: **18**"Son of man, the house of Israel has become dross to me; all of them are the copper, tin, iron and lead left inside a furnace. They are but the dross of silver. **19**Therefore this is what the Sovereign LORD says: 'Because you have all become dross, I will gather you into Jerusalem. **20**As men gather silver, copper, iron, lead and tin into a furnace to melt it with a fiery blast, so will I gather you in my anger and my wrath and put you inside the city and melt you. **21**I will gather you and I will blow on you with my fiery wrath, and you will be melted inside her. **22**As silver is melted in a furnace, so you will be melted inside her, and you will know that I the LORD have poured out my wrath upon you.' "

23Again the word of the LORD came to me: **24**"Son of man, say to the land, 'You are a land that has had no rain or showers*c* in the day of wrath.' **25**There is a conspiracy of her princes*d* within her like a roaring lion tearing its prey; they devour people, take treasures and precious things and make many widows within her. **26**Her priests do violence to my law and profane my holy things; they do not distinguish between the holy and the common; they teach that there is no difference between the unclean and the clean; and they shut their eyes to the keeping of my Sabbaths, so that I am profaned among them. **27**Her officials within her are like wolves tearing their prey; they shed blood and kill people to make unjust gain. **28**Her prophets whitewash these deeds for them by false visions and lying divinations. They say, 'This is what the Sovereign LORD says'—when the LORD has not spoken. **29**The people of the land practice extortion and commit robbery; they oppress the poor and needy and mistreat the alien, denying them justice.

30"I looked for a man among them who would build up the wall and stand before me in the gap on behalf of the land so I

---

*a*12 Or *usury and interest*　　*b*16 Or *When I have allotted you your inheritance*　　*c*24 Septuagint; Hebrew *has not been cleansed or rained on*　　*d*25 Septuagint; Hebrew *prophets* would not have to destroy it, but I found none. ³¹So I will pour out my wrath on them and consume them with my fiery anger, bringing down on their own heads all they have done, declares the Sovereign LORD."

Two Adulterous Sisters

23 The word of the LORD came to me: ²"Son of man, there were two women, daughters of the same mother. ³They became prostitutes in Egypt, engaging in prostitution from their youth. In that land their breasts were fondled and their virgin bosoms caressed. ⁴The older was named Oholah, and her sister was Oholibah. They were mine and gave birth to sons and daughters. Oholah is Samaria, and Oholibah is Jerusalem.

⁵"Oholah engaged in prostitution while she was still mine; and she lusted after her lovers, the Assyrians—warriors ⁶clothed in blue, governors and commanders, all of them handsome young men, and mounted horsemen. ⁷She gave herself as a prostitute to all the elite of the Assyrians and defiled herself with all the idols of everyone she lusted after. ⁸She did not give up the prostitution she began in Egypt, when during her youth men slept with her, caressed her virgin bosom and poured out their lust upon her.

⁹"Therefore I handed her over to her lovers, the Assyrians, for whom she lusted. ¹⁰They stripped her naked, took away her sons and daughters and killed her with the sword. She became a byword among women, and punishment was inflicted on her.

¹¹"Her sister Oholibah saw this, yet in her lust and prostitution she was more depraved than her sister. ¹²She too lusted after the Assyrians—governors and commanders, warriors in full dress, mounted horsemen, all handsome young men. ¹³I saw that she too defiled herself; both of them went the same way.

¹⁴"But she carried her prostitution still further. She saw men portrayed on a wall, figures of Chaldeans[a] portrayed in red, ¹⁵with belts around their waists and flowing turbans on their heads; all of them looked like Babylonian chariot officers, natives of Chaldea.[b] ¹⁶As soon as she saw them, she lusted after them and sent messengers to them in Chaldea. ¹⁷Then the Babylonians came to her, to the bed of love, and in their lust they defiled her. After she had been de-

filed by them, she turned away from them in disgust. ¹⁸When she carried on her prostitution openly and exposed her nakedness, I turned away from her in disgust, just as I had turned away from her sister. ¹⁹Yet she became more and more promiscuous as she recalled the days of her youth, when she was a prostitute in Egypt. ²⁰There she lusted after her lovers, whose genitals were like those of donkeys and whose emission was like that of horses. ²¹So you longed for the lewdness of your youth, when in Egypt your bosom was caressed and your young breasts fondled.[c]

²²"Therefore, Oholibah, this is what the Sovereign LORD says: I will stir up your lovers against you, those you turned away from in disgust, and I will bring them against you from every side— ²³the Babylonians and all the Chaldeans, the men of Pekod and Shoa and Koa, and all the Assyrians with them, handsome young men, all of them governors and commanders, chariot officers and men of high rank, all mounted on horses. ²⁴They will come against you with weapons,[d] chariots and wagons and with a throng of people; they will take up positions against you on every side with large and small shields and with helmets. I will turn you over to them for punishment, and they will punish you according to their standards. ²⁵I will direct my jealous anger against you, and they will deal with you in fury. They will cut off your noses and your ears, and those of you who are left will fall by the sword. They will take away your sons and daughters, and those of you who are left will be consumed by fire. ²⁶They will also strip you of your clothes and take your fine jewelry. ²⁷So I will put a stop to the lewdness and prostitution you began in Egypt. You will not look on these things with longing or remember Egypt anymore.

²⁸"For this is what the Sovereign LORD says: I am about to hand you over to those you hate, to those you turned away from in disgust. ²⁹They will deal with you in hatred and take away everything you have worked for. They will leave you naked and bare, and the shame of your prostitution will be exposed. Your lewdness and promiscuity ³⁰have brought this upon you, because you lusted after the nations and defiled yourself with their idols. ³¹You have gone the way of your sister; so I will put her cup into your hand.

---

a14 Or *Babylonians*   b15 Or *Babylonia*; also in verse 16   c21 Syriac (see also verse 3); Hebrew *caressed because of your young breasts*   d24 The meaning of the Hebrew for this word is uncertain.

³²"This is what the Sovereign Lord says:

"You will drink your sister's cup,
  a cup large and deep;
it will bring scorn and derision,
  for it holds so much.
³³You will be filled with drunkenness and
    sorrow,
  the cup of ruin and desolation,
  the cup of your sister Samaria.
³⁴You will drink it and drain it dry;
  you will dash it to pieces
  and tear your breasts.

I have spoken, declares the Sovereign Lord.

³⁵"Therefore this is what the Sovereign Lord says: Since you have forgotten me and thrust me behind your back, you must bear the consequences of your lewdness and prostitution."

³⁶The Lord said to me: "Son of man, will you judge Oholah and Oholibah? Then confront them with their detestable practices, ³⁷for they have committed adultery and blood is on their hands. They committed adultery with their idols; they even sacrificed their children, whom they bore to me,^a as food for them. ³⁸They have also done this to me: At that same time they defiled my sanctuary and desecrated my Sabbaths. ³⁹On the very day they sacrificed their children to their idols, they entered my sanctuary and desecrated it. That is what they did in my house.

⁴⁰"They even sent messengers for men who came from far away, and when they arrived you bathed yourself for them, painted your eyes and put on your jewelry. ⁴¹You sat on an elegant couch, with a table spread before it on which you had placed the incense and oil that belonged to me.

⁴²"The noise of a carefree crowd was around her; Sabeans^b were brought from the desert along with men from the rabble, and they put bracelets on the arms of the woman and her sister and beautiful crowns on their heads. ⁴³Then I said about the one worn out by adultery, 'Now let them use her as a prostitute, for that is all she is.' ⁴⁴And they slept with her. As men sleep with a prostitute, so they slept with those lewd women, Oholah and Oholibah. ⁴⁵But righteous men will sentence them to the punishment of women who commit adultery and shed blood, because they are adulterous and blood is on their hands.

⁴⁶"This is what the Sovereign Lord says:

Bring a mob against them and give them over to terror and plunder. ⁴⁷The mob will stone them and cut them down with their swords; they will kill their sons and daughters and burn down their houses.

⁴⁸"So I will put an end to lewdness in the land, that all women may take warning and not imitate you. ⁴⁹You will suffer the penalty for your lewdness and bear the consequences of your sins of idolatry. Then you will know that I am the Sovereign Lord."

The Cooking Pot

24 In the ninth year, in the tenth month on the tenth day, the word of the Lord came to me: ²"Son of man, record this date, this very date, because the king of Babylon has laid siege to Jerusalem this very day. ³Tell this rebellious house a parable and say to them: 'This is what the Sovereign Lord says:

" 'Put on the cooking pot; put it on
  and pour water into it.
⁴Put into it the pieces of meat,
  all the choice pieces—the leg and the
    shoulder.
Fill it with the best of these bones;
⁵ take the pick of the flock.
Pile wood beneath it for the bones;
  bring it to a boil
  and cook the bones in it.

⁶" 'For this is what the Sovereign Lord says:

" 'Woe to the city of bloodshed,
  to the pot now encrusted,
  whose deposit will not go away!
Empty it piece by piece
  without casting lots for them.

⁷" 'For the blood she shed is in her
    midst:
  She poured it on the bare rock;
she did not pour it on the ground,
  where the dust would cover it.
⁸To stir up wrath and take revenge
  I put her blood on the bare rock,
  so that it would not be covered.

⁹" 'Therefore this is what the Sovereign Lord says:

" 'Woe to the city of bloodshed!
  I, too, will pile the wood high.
¹⁰So heap on the wood
  and kindle the fire.
Cook the meat well,
  mixing in the spices;
  and let the bones be charred.

---

^a37 Or even made the children they bore to me pass through ⌊the fire⌋   ^b42 Or drunkards

11Then set the empty pot on the coals
    till it becomes hot and its copper
      glows
  so its impurities may be melted
    and its deposit burned away.
12It has frustrated all efforts;
    its heavy deposit has not been
      removed,
  not even by fire.

13" 'Now your impurity is lewdness. Because I tried to cleanse you but you would not be cleansed from your impurity, you will not be clean again until my wrath against you has subsided.

14" 'I the Lord have spoken. The time has come for me to act. I will not hold back; I will not have pity, nor will I relent. You will be judged according to your conduct and your actions, declares the Sovereign Lord.' "

Ezekiel's Wife Dies

15The word of the Lord came to me: **16**"Son of man, with one blow I am about to take away from you the delight of your eyes. Yet do not lament or weep or shed any tears. **17**Groan quietly; do not mourn for the dead. Keep your turban fastened and your sandals on your feet; do not cover the lower part of your face or eat the customary food ₒof mournersₒ."

18So I spoke to the people in the morning, and in the evening my wife died. The next morning I did as I had been commanded.

19Then the people asked me, "Won't you tell us what these things have to do with us?"

20So I said to them, "The word of the Lord came to me: **21**Say to the house of Israel, 'This is what the Sovereign Lord says: I am about to desecrate my sanctuary — the stronghold in which you take pride, the delight of your eyes, the object of your affection. The sons and daughters you left behind will fall by the sword. **22**And you will do as I have done. You will not cover the lower part of your face or eat the customary food ₒof mournersₒ. **23**You will keep your turbans on your heads and your sandals on your feet. You will not mourn or weep but will waste away because of*a* your sins and groan among yourselves. **24**Ezekiel will be a sign to you; you will do just as he has done. When this happens, you will know that I am the Sovereign Lord.'

25"And you, son of man, on the day I take away their stronghold, their joy and glory, the delight of their eyes, their heart's desire, and their sons and daughters as well — **26**on that day a fugitive will come to tell you the news. **27**At that time your mouth will be opened; you will speak with him and will no longer be silent. So you will be a sign to them, and they will know that I am the Lord."

A Prophecy Against Ammon

25 The word of the Lord came to me: **2**"Son of man, set your face against the Ammonites and prophesy against them. **3**Say to them, 'Hear the word of the Sovereign Lord. This is what the Sovereign Lord says: Because you said "Aha!" over my sanctuary when it was desecrated and over the land of Israel when it was laid waste and over the people of Judah when they went into exile, **4**therefore I am going to give you to the people of the East as a possession. They will set up their camps and pitch their tents among you; they will eat your fruit and drink your milk. **5**I will turn Rabbah into a pasture for camels and Ammon into a resting place for sheep. Then you will know that I am the Lord. **6**For this is what the Sovereign Lord says: Because you have clapped your hands and stamped your feet, rejoicing with all the malice of your heart against the land of Israel, **7**therefore I will stretch out my hand against you and give you as plunder to the nations. I will cut you off from the nations and exterminate you from the countries. I will destroy you, and you will know that I am the Lord.' "

A Prophecy Against Moab

8"This is what the Sovereign Lord says: 'Because Moab and Seir said, "Look, the house of Judah has become like all the other nations," **9**therefore I will expose the flank of Moab, beginning at its frontier towns — Beth Jeshimoth, Baal Meon and Kiriathaim — the glory of that land. **10**I will give Moab along with the Ammonites to the people of the East as a possession, so that the Ammonites will not be remembered among the nations; **11**and I will inflict punishment on Moab. Then they will know that I am the Lord.' "

A Prophecy Against Edom

12"This is what the Sovereign Lord says: 'Because Edom took revenge on the house of Judah and became very guilty by doing so, **13**therefore this is what the Sovereign Lord says: I will stretch out my hand against

a23 Or away in

Edom and kill its men and their animals. I will lay it waste, and from Teman to Dedan they will fall by the sword. **14**I will take vengeance on Edom by the hand of my people Israel, and they will deal with Edom in accordance with my anger and my wrath; they will know my vengeance, declares the Sovereign LORD.' "

A Prophecy Against Philistia

15"This is what the Sovereign LORD says: 'Because the Philistines acted in vengeance and took revenge with malice in their hearts, and with ancient hostility sought to destroy Judah, **16**therefore this is what the Sovereign LORD says: I am about to stretch out my hand against the Philistines, and I will cut off the Kerethites and destroy those remaining along the coast. **17**I will carry out great vengeance on them and punish them in my wrath. Then they will know that I am the LORD, when I take vengeance on them.' "

A Prophecy Against Tyre

26 In the eleventh year, on the first day of the month, the word of the LORD came to me: **2**"Son of man, because Tyre has said of Jerusalem, 'Aha! The gate to the nations is broken, and its doors have swung open to me; now that she lies in ruins I will prosper,' **3**therefore this is what the Sovereign LORD says: I am against you, O Tyre, and I will bring many nations against you, like the sea casting up its waves. **4**They will destroy the walls of Tyre and pull down her towers; I will scrape away her rubble and make her a bare rock. **5**Out in the sea she will become a place to spread fishnets, for I have spoken, declares the Sovereign LORD. She will become plunder for the nations, **6**and her settlements on the mainland will be ravaged by the sword. Then they will know that I am the LORD.

7"For this is what the Sovereign LORD says: From the north I am going to bring against Tyre Nebuchadnezzar[a] king of Babylon, king of kings, with horses and chariots, with horsemen and a great army. **8**He will ravage your settlements on the mainland with the sword; he will set up siege works against you, build a ramp up to your walls and raise his shields against you. **9**He will direct the blows of his battering rams against your walls and demolish your towers with his weapons. **10**His horses will be so many that

they will cover you with dust. Your walls will tremble at the noise of the war horses, wagons and chariots when he enters your gates as men enter a city whose walls have been broken through. **11**The hoofs of his horses will trample all your streets; he will kill your people with the sword, and your strong pillars will fall to the ground. **12**They will plunder your wealth and loot your merchandise; they will break down your walls and demolish your fine houses and throw your stones, timber and rubble into the sea. **13**I will put an end to your noisy songs, and the music of your harps will be heard no more. **14**I will make you a bare rock, and you will become a place to spread fishnets. You will never be rebuilt, for I the LORD have spoken, declares the Sovereign LORD.

15"This is what the Sovereign LORD says to Tyre: Will not the coastlands tremble at the sound of your fall, when the wounded groan and the slaughter takes place in you? **16**Then all the princes of the coast will step down from their thrones and lay aside their robes and take off their embroidered garments. Clothed with terror, they will sit on the ground, trembling every moment, appalled at you. **17**Then they will take up a lament concerning you and say to you:

" 'How you are destroyed, O city of renown,
  peopled by men of the sea!
You were a power on the seas,
  you and your citizens;
you put your terror
  on all who lived there.
18Now the coastlands tremble
  on the day of your fall;
the islands in the sea
  are terrified at your collapse.'

19"This is what the Sovereign LORD says: When I make you a desolate city, like cities no longer inhabited, and when I bring the ocean depths over you and its vast waters cover you, **20**then I will bring you down with those who go down to the pit, to the people of long ago. I will make you dwell in the earth below, as in ancient ruins, with those who go down to the pit, and you will not return or take your place[b] in the land of the living. **21**I will bring you to a horrible end and you will be no more. You will be sought, but you will never again be found, declares the Sovereign LORD."

---

[a]7 Hebrew Nebuchadrezzar, of which Nebuchadnezzar is a variant; here and often in Ezekiel and Jeremiah
[b]20 Septuagint; Hebrew return, and I will give glory

Rejection

Have you felt the sting of rejection?

A good friend gives you the cold shoulder.

A family member turns away when you need help and support.

A boyfriend or girlfriend rejects you.

A person to whom you are witnessing laughs at your beliefs.

What would Jesus do?

"Nazareth! Can anything good come from there?" (John 1:46). Many people asked that question when news spread that the long-awaited Messiah was a carpenter's son from Nazareth. Jesus was well-acquainted with rejection. Throughout his ministry and in the events leading up to his death, he confronted disbelief and scorn. But the ultimate rejection occurred when Jesus was on the cross. When God the Father turned away from his Son, Jesus cried, "My God, my God, why have you forsaken me?" (Matthew 27:46). Rejected. Ignored. Cast off. The spotless lamb carried the weight of our sin alone.

What will you do?

From Jesus' example, you can see clearly how to handle rejection—you go on. Jesus knew God's plan, and he simply followed it. Even in his darkest moment, he chose to pay the price so that you would never have to know God's rejection.

Jesus knew that his message would be received by some, mocked by others. He knew that the truth of his message would eventually cause the ultimate form of rejection: his crucifixion. But he stayed the course, forgiving those who caused his death (Luke 23:24).

If you are sharing your faith with your friends or family and they reject the truth, don't become discouraged or bitter. If a friend turns away, don't hold a grudge. Do what Jesus did. Forgive, and then go on.

More about rejection

Psalm 69:4-7; John 7:25-31; 2 Timothy 4:16

W.W.J.D.?

Stress

You just want to scream!

Do you battle stress? With homework, after-school activities, maybe a part-time job, youth group—how do you get it all done? And then add to it the stress of relationships and planning for the future! Wow!

What would Jesus do?

Do you think Jesus can't understand the pressures you face today? Consider this: Everywhere Jesus went a crowd followed him. Anytime he tried to enjoy a few moments of solitude, he was interrupted. Everyone wanted something from him. The crowds were constantly pushing in. The Pharisees were constantly trying to trap him with verbal attacks. The disciples fluctuated between believing one moment and being clueless the next. And this was a typical day!

But despite the crowds clamoring for him (Mark 6:54-56), Jesus had compassion on the people. He taught them. He healed them. He fed them. And despite the frustration with his disciples, Jesus never gave up. He loved them and encouraged them, and through it all he demonstrated a peace that was pretty amazing (Philippians 4:7).

What will you do?

By all visible accounts, Jesus should have been the most stressed out individual to ever walk the earth. He dealt with overwhelming daily pressures and the knowledge that his life would soon end. So what does that have to do with your stress? The same peace that Jesus had—that defies comprehension—is available to you. Your life is in the Father's hands. Isn't it comforting to know that the Jesus who dealt with stress while here on earth is the same Jesus who lives within you and knows what you're going through? As you study his life and obey his Word, you can know what he would do when you feel overwhelmed.

More about stress

Matthew 11:28-30; Hebrews 6:19-20; Revelation 21:1-5

W.W.J.D.?

A Lament for Tyre

27 The word of the LORD came to me: [2]"Son of man, take up a lament concerning Tyre. [3]Say to Tyre, situated at the gateway to the sea, merchant of peoples on many coasts, 'This is what the Sovereign LORD says:

" 'You say, O Tyre,
"I am perfect in beauty."
[4]Your domain was on the high seas;
   your builders brought your beauty to
      perfection.
[5]They made all your timbers
   of pine trees from Senir[a];
they took a cedar from Lebanon
   to make a mast for you.
[6]Of oaks from Bashan
   they made your oars;
of cypress wood[b] from the coasts of
      Cyprus[c]
they made your deck, inlaid with
   ivory.
[7]Fine embroidered linen from Egypt was
      your sail
   and served as your banner;
your awnings were of blue and purple
   from the coasts of Elishah.
[8]Men of Sidon and Arvad were your
      oarsmen;
   your skilled men, O Tyre, were
      aboard as your seamen.
[9]Veteran craftsmen of Gebal[d] were on
      board
   as shipwrights to caulk your seams.
All the ships of the sea and their sailors
   came alongside to trade for your
      wares.

[10]" 'Men of Persia, Lydia and Put
   served as soldiers in your army.
They hung their shields and helmets on
      your walls,
   bringing you splendor.
[11]Men of Arvad and Helech
   manned your walls on every side;
men of Gammad
   were in your towers.
They hung their shields around your
      walls;
   they brought your beauty to
      perfection.

[12]" 'Tarshish did business with you because of your great wealth of goods; they ex-changed silver, iron, tin and lead for your merchandise.

[13]" 'Greece, Tubal and Meshech traded with you; they exchanged slaves and articles of bronze for your wares.

[14]" 'Men of Beth Togarmah exchanged work horses, war horses and mules for your merchandise.

[15]" 'The men of Rhodes[e] traded with you, and many coastlands were your customers; they paid you with ivory tusks and ebony.

[16]" 'Aram[f] did business with you because of your many products; they exchanged turquoise, purple fabric, embroidered work, fine linen, coral and rubies for your merchandise.

[17]" 'Judah and Israel traded with you; they exchanged wheat from Minnith and confections,[g] honey, oil and balm for your wares.

[18]" 'Damascus, because of your many products and great wealth of goods, did business with you in wine from Helbon and wool from Zahar.

[19]" 'Danites and Greeks from Uzal bought your merchandise; they exchanged wrought iron, cassia and calamus for your wares.

[20]" 'Dedan traded in saddle blankets with you.

[21]" 'Arabia and all the princes of Kedar were your customers; they did business with you in lambs, rams and goats.

[22]" 'The merchants of Sheba and Raamah traded with you; for your merchandise they exchanged the finest of all kinds of spices and precious stones, and gold.

[23]" 'Haran, Canneh and Eden and merchants of Sheba, Asshur and Kilmad traded with you. [24]In your marketplace they traded with you beautiful garments, blue fabric, embroidered work and multicolored rugs with cords twisted and tightly knotted.

[25]" 'The ships of Tarshish serve
   as carriers for your wares.
You are filled with heavy cargo
   in the heart of the sea.
[26]Your oarsmen take you
   out to the high seas.
But the east wind will break you to
      pieces
   in the heart of the sea.
[27]Your wealth, merchandise and wares,
   your mariners, seamen and
      shipwrights,
your merchants and all your soldiers,

---

[a]5 That is, Hermon   [b]6 Targum; the Masoretic Text has a different division of the consonants.   [c]6 Hebrew *Kittim*   [d]9 That is, Byblos   [e]15 Septuagint; Hebrew *Dedan*   [f]16 Most Hebrew manuscripts; some Hebrew manuscripts and Syriac *Edom*   [g]17 The meaning of the Hebrew for this word is uncertain.

and everyone else on board
will sink into the heart of the sea
    on the day of your shipwreck.
28The shorelands will quake
    when your seamen cry out.
29All who handle the oars
    will abandon their ships;
the mariners and all the seamen
    will stand on the shore.
30They will raise their voice
    and cry bitterly over you;
they will sprinkle dust on their heads
    and roll in ashes.
31They will shave their heads because of
        you
    and will put on sackcloth.
They will weep over you with anguish
        of soul
    and with bitter mourning.
32As they wail and mourn over you,
    they will take up a lament concerning
        you:
"Who was ever silenced like Tyre,
    surrounded by the sea?"
33When your merchandise went out on
        the seas,
    you satisfied many nations;
with your great wealth and your wares
    you enriched the kings of the earth.
34Now you are shattered by the sea
    in the depths of the waters;
your wares and all your company
    have gone down with you.
35All who live in the coastlands
    are appalled at you;
their kings shudder with horror
    and their faces are distorted with fear.
36The merchants among the nations hiss
        at you;
    you have come to a horrible end
    and will be no more.' "

A Prophecy Against the King of Tyre

28 The word of the LORD came to me:
2"Son of man, say to the ruler of
Tyre, 'This is what the Sovereign LORD says:

" 'In the pride of your heart
    you say, "I am a god;
I sit on the throne of a god
    in the heart of the seas."
But you are a man and not a god,
    though you think you are as wise as a
        god.
3Are you wiser than Daniela?

Is no secret hidden from you?
4By your wisdom and understanding
    you have gained wealth for yourself
and amassed gold and silver
    in your treasuries.
5By your great skill in trading
    you have increased your wealth,
and because of your wealth
    your heart has grown proud.

6" 'Therefore this is what the Sovereign
LORD says:

" 'Because you think you are wise,
    as wise as a god,
7I am going to bring foreigners against
        you,
    the most ruthless of nations;
they will draw their swords against your
        beauty and wisdom
    and pierce your shining splendor.
8They will bring you down to the pit,
    and you will die a violent death
    in the heart of the seas.
9Will you then say, "I am a god,"
    in the presence of those who kill you?
You will be but a man, not a god,
    in the hands of those who slay you.
10You will die the death of the
        uncircumcised
    at the hands of foreigners.

I have spoken, declares the Sovereign
LORD.' "

11The word of the LORD came to me:
12"Son of man, take up a lament concerning
the king of Tyre and say to him: 'This is what
the Sovereign LORD says:

" 'You were the model of perfection,
    full of wisdom and perfect in beauty.
13You were in Eden,
    the garden of God;
every precious stone adorned you:
    ruby, topaz and emerald,
    chrysolite, onyx and jasper,
    sapphire,b turquoise and beryl.c
Your settings and mountingsd were
        made of gold;
    on the day you were created they
        were prepared.
14You were anointed as a guardian
        cherub,
    for so I ordained you.
You were on the holy mount of God;
    you walked among the fiery stones.
15You were blameless in your ways

---

a3 Or Danel; the Hebrew spelling may suggest a person other than the prophet Daniel.   b13 Or lapis lazuli
c13 The precise identification of some of these precious stones is uncertain.   d13 The meaning of the
Hebrew for this phrase is uncertain.

from the day you were created
till wickedness was found in you.
[16]Through your widespread trade
you were filled with violence,
and you sinned.
So I drove you in disgrace from the
mount of God,
and I expelled you, O guardian
cherub,
from among the fiery stones.
[17]Your heart became proud
on account of your beauty,
and you corrupted your wisdom
because of your splendor.
So I threw you to the earth;
I made a spectacle of you before
kings.
[18]By your many sins and dishonest trade
you have desecrated your sanctuaries.
So I made a fire come out from you,
and it consumed you,
and I reduced you to ashes on the
ground
in the sight of all who were watching.
[19]All the nations who knew you
are appalled at you;
you have come to a horrible end
and will be no more.' "

A Prophecy Against Sidon

[20]The word of the LORD came to me:
[21]"Son of man, set your face against Sidon;
prophesy against her [22]and say: 'This is
what the Sovereign LORD says:

" 'I am against you, O Sidon,
and I will gain glory within you.
They will know that I am the LORD,
when I inflict punishment on her
and show myself holy within her.
[23]I will send a plague upon her
and make blood flow in her streets.
The slain will fall within her,
with the sword against her on every
side.
Then they will know that I am the LORD.

[24]" 'No longer will the people of Israel
have malicious neighbors who are painful
briers and sharp thorns. Then they will
know that I am the Sovereign LORD.

[25]" 'This is what the Sovereign LORD says:
When I gather the people of Israel from the
nations where they have been scattered, I
will show myself holy among them in the
sight of the nations. Then they will live in
their own land, which I gave to my servant
Jacob. [26]They will live there in safety and
will build houses and plant vineyards; they
will live in safety when I inflict punishment
on all their neighbors who maligned them.
Then they will know that I am the LORD their
God.' "

A Prophecy Against Egypt

29 In the tenth year, in the tenth month
on the twelfth day, the word of the
LORD came to me: [2]"Son of man, set your
face against Pharaoh king of Egypt and
prophesy against him and against all Egypt.
[3]Speak to him and say: 'This is what the Sovereign LORD says:

" 'I am against you, Pharaoh king of
Egypt,
you great monster lying among your
streams.
You say, "The Nile is mine;
I made it for myself."
[4]But I will put hooks in your jaws
and make the fish of your streams
stick to your scales.
I will pull you out from among your
streams,
with all the fish sticking to your
scales.
[5]I will leave you in the desert,
you and all the fish of your streams.
You will fall on the open field
and not be gathered or picked up.
I will give you as food
to the beasts of the earth and the
birds of the air.

[6]Then all who live in Egypt will know that I
am the LORD.

" 'You have been a staff of reed for the
house of Israel. [7]When they grasped you
with their hands, you splintered and you
tore open their shoulders; when they leaned
on you, you broke and their backs were
wrenched.[a]

[8]" 'Therefore this is what the Sovereign
LORD says: I will bring a sword against you
and kill your men and their animals. [9]Egypt
will become a desolate wasteland. Then
they will know that I am the LORD.

" 'Because you said, "The Nile is mine; I
made it," [10]therefore I am against you and
against your streams, and I will make the
land of Egypt a ruin and a desolate waste
from Migdol to Aswan, as far as the border
of Cush.[b] [11]No foot of man or animal will

---

[a]7 Syriac (see also Septuagint and Vulgate); Hebrew *and you caused their backs to stand*   [b]10 That is, the
upper Nile region

pass through it; no one will live there for forty years. **12**I will make the land of Egypt desolate among devastated lands, and her cities will lie desolate forty years among ruined cities. And I will disperse the Egyptians among the nations and scatter them through the countries.

13" 'Yet this is what the Sovereign LORD says: At the end of forty years I will gather the Egyptians from the nations where they were scattered. **14**I will bring them back from captivity and return them to Upper Egypt,*a* the land of their ancestry. There they will be a lowly kingdom. **15**It will be the lowliest of kingdoms and will never again exalt itself above the other nations. I will make it so weak that it will never again rule over the nations. **16**Egypt will no longer be a source of confidence for the people of Israel but will be a reminder of their sin in turning to her for help. Then they will know that I am the Sovereign LORD.' "

17In the twenty-seventh year, in the first month on the first day, the word of the LORD came to me: **18**"Son of man, Nebuchadnezzar king of Babylon drove his army in a hard campaign against Tyre; every head was rubbed bare and every shoulder made raw. Yet he and his army got no reward from the campaign he led against Tyre. **19**Therefore this is what the Sovereign LORD says: I am going to give Egypt to Nebuchadnezzar king of Babylon, and he will carry off its wealth. He will loot and plunder the land as pay for his army. **20**I have given him Egypt as a reward for his efforts because he and his army did it for me, declares the Sovereign LORD. **21**"On that day I will make a horn*b* grow for the house of Israel, and I will open your mouth among them. Then they will know that I am the LORD."

A Lament for Egypt

30 The word of the LORD came to me: **2**"Son of man, prophesy and say: 'This is what the Sovereign LORD says:

" 'Wail and say,
  "Alas for that day!"
3For the day is near,
  the day of the LORD is near—
a day of clouds,
  a time of doom for the nations.
4A sword will come against Egypt,
  and anguish will come upon Cush.*c*
When the slain fall in Egypt,

her wealth will be carried away
  and her foundations torn down.

5Cush and Put, Lydia and all Arabia, Libya*d* and the people of the covenant land will fall by the sword along with Egypt.

6" 'This is what the LORD says:

" 'The allies of Egypt will fall
  and her proud strength will fail.
From Migdol to Aswan
  they will fall by the sword within her,
    declares the Sovereign LORD.
7" 'They will be desolate
  among desolate lands,
and their cities will lie
  among ruined cities.
8Then they will know that I am the LORD,
  when I set fire to Egypt
  and all her helpers are crushed.

9" 'On that day messengers will go out from me in ships to frighten Cush out of her complacency. Anguish will take hold of them on the day of Egypt's doom, for it is sure to come.

10" 'This is what the Sovereign LORD says:

" 'I will put an end to the hordes of
    Egypt
  by the hand of Nebuchadnezzar king
    of Babylon.
11He and his army—the most ruthless of
    nations—
  will be brought in to destroy the land.
They will draw their swords against
    Egypt
  and fill the land with the slain.
12I will dry up the streams of the Nile
  and sell the land to evil men;
by the hand of foreigners
  I will lay waste the land and
    everything in it.

I the LORD have spoken.

13" 'This is what the Sovereign LORD says:

" 'I will destroy the idols
  and put an end to the images in
    Memphis.*e*
No longer will there be a prince in
    Egypt,
  and I will spread fear throughout the
    land.
14I will lay waste Upper Egypt,*f*
  set fire to Zoan

---

a14 Hebrew *to Pathros*   *b21 Horn* here symbolizes strength.   *c4* That is, the upper Nile region; also in verses 5 and 9   *d5* Hebrew *Cub*   *e13* Hebrew *Noph*; also in verse 16   *f14* Hebrew *waste Pathros* and inflict punishment on Thebes.*a*

15I will pour out my wrath on Pelusium,*b*
    the stronghold of Egypt,
    and cut off the hordes of Thebes.
16I will set fire to Egypt;
    Pelusium will writhe in agony.
Thebes will be taken by storm;
    Memphis will be in constant distress.
17The young men of Heliopolis*c* and
        Bubastis*d*
    will fall by the sword,
    and the cities themselves will go into
        captivity.
18Dark will be the day at Tahpanhes
    when I break the yoke of Egypt;
    there her proud strength will come to
        an end.
She will be covered with clouds,
    and her villages will go into captivity.
19So I will inflict punishment on Egypt,
    and they will know that I am the
        Lord.' "

20In the eleventh year, in the first month on the seventh day, the word of the Lord came to me: **21**"Son of man, I have broken the arm of Pharaoh king of Egypt. It has not been bound up for healing or put in a splint so as to become strong enough to hold a sword. **22**Therefore this is what the Sovereign Lord says: I am against Pharaoh king of Egypt. I will break both his arms, the good arm as well as the broken one, and make the sword fall from his hand. **23**I will disperse the Egyptians among the nations and scatter them through the countries. **24**I will strengthen the arms of the king of Babylon and put my sword in his hand, but I will break the arms of Pharaoh, and he will groan before him like a mortally wounded man. **25**I will strengthen the arms of the king of Babylon, but the arms of Pharaoh will fall limp. Then they will know that I am the Lord, when I put my sword into the hand of the king of Babylon and he brandishes it against Egypt. **26**I will disperse the Egyptians among the nations and scatter them through the countries. Then they will know that I am the Lord."

A Cedar in Lebanon

31 In the eleventh year, in the third month on the first day, the word of the Lord came to me: **2**"Son of man, say to Pharaoh king of Egypt and to his hordes:

" 'Who can be compared with you in
    majesty?
3Consider Assyria, once a cedar in
        Lebanon,
    with beautiful branches
        overshadowing the forest;
it towered on high,
    its top above the thick foliage.
4The waters nourished it,
    deep springs made it grow tall;
their streams flowed
    all around its base
and sent their channels
    to all the trees of the field.
5So it towered higher
    than all the trees of the field;
its boughs increased
    and its branches grew long,
    spreading because of abundant
        waters.
6All the birds of the air
    nested in its boughs,
all the beasts of the field
    gave birth under its branches;
all the great nations
    lived in its shade.
7It was majestic in beauty,
    with its spreading boughs,
for its roots went down
    to abundant waters.
8The cedars in the garden of God
    could not rival it,
nor could the pine trees
    equal its boughs,
nor could the plane trees
    compare with its branches—
no tree in the garden of God
    could match its beauty.
9I made it beautiful
    with abundant branches,
the envy of all the trees of Eden
    in the garden of God.

10" 'Therefore this is what the Sovereign Lord says: Because it towered on high, lifting its top above the thick foliage, and because it was proud of its height, **11**I handed it over to the ruler of the nations, for him to deal with according to its wickedness. I cast it aside, **12**and the most ruthless of foreign nations cut it down and left it. Its boughs fell on the mountains and in all the valleys; its branches lay broken in all the ravines of the land. All the nations of the earth came out from under its shade and left it. **13**All the birds of the air settled on the fallen tree, and all the beasts of the field were among its branches. [14]Therefore no other trees by the waters are ever to tower proudly on high, lifting their tops above the thick foliage. No other trees so well-watered are ever to reach such a height; they are all destined for death, for the earth below, among mortal men, with those who go down to the pit.

[15]" 'This is what the Sovereign LORD says: On the day it was brought down to the grave[a] I covered the deep springs with mourning for it; I held back its streams, and its abundant waters were restrained. Because of it I clothed Lebanon with gloom, and all the trees of the field withered away. [16]I made the nations tremble at the sound of its fall when I brought it down to the grave with those who go down to the pit. Then all the trees of Eden, the choicest and best of Lebanon, all the trees that were well-watered, were consoled in the earth below. [17]Those who lived in its shade, its allies among the nations, had also gone down to the grave with it, joining those killed by the sword.

[18]" 'Which of the trees of Eden can be compared with you in splendor and majesty? Yet you, too, will be brought down with the trees of Eden to the earth below; you will lie among the uncircumcised, with those killed by the sword.

" 'This is Pharaoh and all his hordes, declares the Sovereign LORD.' "

A Lament for Pharaoh

32 In the twelfth year, in the twelfth month on the first day, the word of the LORD came to me: [2]"Son of man, take up a lament concerning Pharaoh king of Egypt and say to him:

" 'You are like a lion among the nations;
   you are like a monster in the seas
thrashing about in your streams,
   churning the water with your feet
   and muddying the streams.

[3]" 'This is what the Sovereign LORD says:

" 'With a great throng of people
   I will cast my net over you,
   and they will haul you up in my net.
[4]I will throw you on the land
   and hurl you on the open field.
I will let all the birds of the air settle on
   you

and all the beasts of the earth gorge
   themselves on you.
[5]I will spread your flesh on the
   mountains
   and fill the valleys with your remains.
[6]I will drench the land with your flowing
   blood
   all the way to the mountains,
   and the ravines will be filled with
     your flesh.
[7]When I snuff you out, I will cover the
   heavens
   and darken their stars;
 I will cover the sun with a cloud,
   and the moon will not give its light.
[8]All the shining lights in the heavens
   I will darken over you;
   I will bring darkness over your land,
       declares the Sovereign LORD.
[9]I will trouble the hearts of many
   peoples
   when I bring about your destruction
   among the nations,
   among[b] lands you have not known.
[10]I will cause many peoples to be
   appalled at you,
   and their kings will shudder with
   horror because of you
   when I brandish my sword before
   them.
On the day of your downfall
   each of them will tremble
   every moment for his life.

[11]" 'For this is what the Sovereign LORD says:

" 'The sword of the king of Babylon
   will come against you.
[12]I will cause your hordes to fall
   by the swords of mighty men—
   the most ruthless of all nations.
They will shatter the pride of Egypt,
   and all her hordes will be overthrown.
[13]I will destroy all her cattle
   from beside abundant waters
no longer to be stirred by the foot of
   man
   or muddied by the hoofs of cattle.
[14]Then I will let her waters settle
   and make her streams flow like oil,
       declares the Sovereign LORD.
[15]When I make Egypt desolate
   and strip the land of everything in it,
when I strike down all who live there,
   then they will know that I am the
   LORD.'

---

[a]15 Hebrew *Sheol*; also in verses 16 and 17   [b]9 Hebrew; Septuagint *bring you into captivity among the nations, / to*

¹⁶"This is the lament they will chant for her. The daughters of the nations will chant it; for Egypt and all her hordes they will chant it, declares the Sovereign LORD."

¹⁷In the twelfth year, on the fifteenth day of the month, the word of the LORD came to me: ¹⁸"Son of man, wail for the hordes of Egypt and consign to the earth below both her and the daughters of mighty nations, with those who go down to the pit. ¹⁹Say to them, 'Are you more favored than others? Go down and be laid among the uncircumcised.' ²⁰They will fall among those killed by the sword. The sword is drawn; let her be dragged off with all her hordes. ²¹From within the grave*a* the mighty leaders will say of Egypt and her allies, 'They have come down and they lie with the uncircumcised, with those killed by the sword.'

²²"Assyria is there with her whole army; she is surrounded by the graves of all her slain, all who have fallen by the sword. ²³Their graves are in the depths of the pit and her army lies around her grave. All who had spread terror in the land of the living are slain, fallen by the sword.

²⁴"Elam is there, with all her hordes around her grave. All of them are slain, fallen by the sword. All who had spread terror in the land of the living went down uncircumcised to the earth below. They bear their shame with those who go down to the pit. ²⁵A bed is made for her among the slain, with all her hordes around her grave. All of them are uncircumcised, killed by the sword. Because their terror had spread in the land of the living, they bear their shame with those who go down to the pit; they are laid among the slain.

²⁶"Meshech and Tubal are there, with all their hordes around their graves. All of them are uncircumcised, killed by the sword because they spread their terror in the land of the living. ²⁷Do they not lie with the other uncircumcised warriors who have fallen, who went down to the grave with their weapons of war, whose swords were placed under their heads? The punishment for their sins rested on their bones, though the terror of these warriors had stalked through the land of the living.

²⁸"You too, O Pharaoh, will be broken and will lie among the uncircumcised, with those killed by the sword.

²⁹"Edom is there, her kings and all her princes; despite their power, they are laid with those killed by the sword. They lie with the uncircumcised, with those who go down to the pit.

³⁰"All the princes of the north and all the Sidonians are there; they went down with the slain in disgrace despite the terror caused by their power. They lie uncircumcised with those killed by the sword and bear their shame with those who go down to the pit.

³¹"Pharaoh—he and all his army—will see them and he will be consoled for all his hordes that were killed by the sword, declares the Sovereign LORD. ³²Although I had him spread terror in the land of the living, Pharaoh and all his hordes will be laid among the uncircumcised, with those killed by the sword, declares the Sovereign LORD."

Ezekiel a Watchman

33 The word of the LORD came to me: ²"Son of man, speak to your countrymen and say to them: 'When I bring the sword against a land, and the people of the land choose one of their men and make him their watchman, ³and he sees the sword coming against the land and blows the trumpet to warn the people, ⁴then if anyone hears the trumpet but does not take warning and the sword comes and takes his life, his blood will be on his own head. ⁵Since he heard the sound of the trumpet but did not take warning, his blood will be on his own head. If he had taken warning, he would have saved himself. ⁶But if the watchman sees the sword coming and does not blow the trumpet to warn the people and the sword comes and takes the life of one of them, that man will be taken away because of his sin, but I will hold the watchman accountable for his blood.'

⁷"Son of man, I have made you a watchman for the house of Israel; so hear the word I speak and give them warning from me. ⁸When I say to the wicked, 'O wicked man, you will surely die,' and you do not speak out to dissuade him from his ways, that wicked man will die for*b* his sin, and I will hold you accountable for his blood. ⁹But if you do warn the wicked man to turn from his ways and he does not do so, he will die for his sin, but you will have saved yourself.

¹⁰"Son of man, say to the house of Israel, 'This is what you are saying: "Our offenses and sins weigh us down, and we are wasting away because of*c* them. How then can we live?" ' ¹¹Say to them, 'As surely as I live, de-

a21 Hebrew *Sheol*; also in verse 27   *b8* Or *in*; also in verse 9   *c10* Or *away in* clares the Sovereign LORD, I take no pleasure in the death of the wicked, but rather that they turn from their ways and live. Turn! Turn from your evil ways! Why will you die, O house of Israel?'

12"Therefore, son of man, say to your countrymen, 'The righteousness of the righteous man will not save him when he disobeys, and the wickedness of the wicked man will not cause him to fall when he turns from it. The righteous man, if he sins, will not be allowed to live because of his former righteousness.' 13If I tell the righteous man that he will surely live, but then he trusts in his righteousness and does evil, none of the righteous things he has done will be remembered; he will die for the evil he has done. 14And if I say to the wicked man, 'You will surely die,' but he then turns away from his sin and does what is just and right — 15if he gives back what he took in pledge for a loan, returns what he has stolen, follows the decrees that give life, and does no evil, he will surely live; he will not die. 16None of the sins he has committed will be remembered against him. He has done what is just and right; he will surely live.

17"Yet your countrymen say, 'The way of the Lord is not just.' But it is their way that is not just. 18If a righteous man turns from his righteousness and does evil, he will die for it. 19And if a wicked man turns away from his wickedness and does what is just and right, he will live by doing so. 20Yet, O house of Israel, you say, 'The way of the Lord is not just.' But I will judge each of you according to his own ways."

Jerusalem's Fall Explained

21In the twelfth year of our exile, in the tenth month on the fifth day, a man who had escaped from Jerusalem came to me and said, "The city has fallen!" 22Now the evening before the man arrived, the hand of the LORD was upon me, and he opened my mouth before the man came to me in the morning. So my mouth was opened and I was no longer silent.

23Then the word of the LORD came to me: 24"Son of man, the people living in those ruins in the land of Israel are saying, 'Abraham was only one man, yet he possessed the land. But we are many; surely the land has been given to us as our possession.' 25Therefore say to them, 'This is what the Sovereign LORD says: Since you eat meat with the blood still in it and look to your idols and shed blood, should you then possess the land? 26You rely on your sword, you do detestable things, and each of you defiles his neighbor's wife. Should you then possess the land?'

27"Say this to them: 'This is what the Sovereign LORD says: As surely as I live, those who are left in the ruins will fall by the sword, those out in the country I will give to the wild animals to be devoured, and those in strongholds and caves will die of a plague. 28I will make the land a desolate waste, and her proud strength will come to an end, and the mountains of Israel will become desolate so that no one will cross them. 29Then they will know that I am the LORD, when I have made the land a desolate waste because of all the detestable things they have done.'

30"As for you, son of man, your countrymen are talking together about you by the walls and at the doors of the houses, saying to each other, 'Come and hear the message that has come from the LORD.' 31My people come to you, as they usually do, and sit before you to listen to your words, but they do not put them into practice. With their mouths they express devotion, but their hearts are greedy for unjust gain. 32Indeed, to them you are nothing more than one who sings love songs with a beautiful voice and plays an instrument well, for they hear your words but do not put them into practice.

33"When all this comes true — and it surely will — then they will know that a prophet has been among them."

Shepherds and Sheep

34 The word of the LORD came to me: 2"Son of man, prophesy against the shepherds of Israel; prophesy and say to them: 'This is what the Sovereign LORD says: Woe to the shepherds of Israel who only take care of themselves! Should not shepherds take care of the flock? 3You eat the curds, clothe yourselves with the wool and slaughter the choice animals, but you do not take care of the flock. 4You have not strengthened the weak or healed the sick or bound up the injured. You have not brought back the strays or searched for the lost. You have ruled them harshly and brutally. 5So they were scattered because there was no shepherd, and when they were scattered they became food for all the wild animals. 6My sheep wandered over all the mountains and on every high hill. They were scattered over the whole earth, and no one searched or looked for them.

7" 'Therefore, you shepherds, hear the word of the LORD: 8As surely as I live, declares the Sovereign LORD, because my flock lacks a shepherd and so has been plundered and has become food for all the wild animals, and because my shepherds did not search for my flock but cared for themselves rather than for my flock, **9**therefore, O shepherds, hear the word of the LORD: **10**This is what the Sovereign LORD says: I am against the shepherds and will hold them accountable for my flock. I will remove them from tending the flock so that the shepherds can no longer feed themselves. I will rescue my flock from their mouths, and it will no longer be food for them.

11" 'For this is what the Sovereign LORD says: I myself will search for my sheep and look after them. **12**As a shepherd looks after his scattered flock when he is with them, so will I look after my sheep. I will rescue them from all the places where they were scattered on a day of clouds and darkness. **13**I will bring them out from the nations and gather them from the countries, and I will bring them into their own land. I will pasture them on the mountains of Israel, in the ravines and in all the settlements in the land. **14**I will tend them in a good pasture, and the mountain heights of Israel will be their grazing land. There they will lie down in good grazing land, and there they will feed in a rich pasture on the mountains of Israel. **15**I myself will tend my sheep and have them lie down, declares the Sovereign LORD. **16**I will search for the lost and bring back the strays. I will bind up the injured and strengthen the weak, but the sleek and the strong I will destroy. I will shepherd the flock with justice.

17" 'As for you, my flock, this is what the Sovereign LORD says: I will judge between one sheep and another, and between rams and goats. **18**Is it not enough for you to feed on the good pasture? Must you also trample the rest of your pasture with your feet? Is it not enough for you to drink clear water? Must you also muddy the rest with your feet? **19**Must my flock feed on what you have trampled and drink what you have muddied with your feet?

20" 'Therefore this is what the Sovereign LORD says to them: See, I myself will judge between the fat sheep and the lean sheep. **21**Because you shove with flank and shoulder, butting all the weak sheep with your horns until you have driven them away, **22**I will save my flock, and they will no longer be plundered. I will judge between one sheep and another. **23**I will place over them

one shepherd, my servant David, and he will tend them; he will tend them and be their shepherd. **24**I the LORD will be their God, and my servant David will be prince among them. I the LORD have spoken.

25" 'I will make a covenant of peace with them and rid the land of wild beasts so that they may live in the desert and sleep in the forests in safety. **26**I will bless them and the places surrounding my hill.*a* I will send down showers in season; there will be showers of blessing. **27**The trees of the field will yield their fruit and the ground will yield its crops; the people will be secure in their land. They will know that I am the LORD, when I break the bars of their yoke and rescue them from the hands of those who enslaved them. **28**They will no longer be plundered by the nations, nor will wild animals devour them. They will live in safety, and no one will make them afraid. **29**I will provide for them a land renowned for its crops, and they will no longer be victims of famine in the land or bear the scorn of the nations. **30**Then they will know that I, the LORD their God, am with them and that they, the house of Israel, are my people, declares the Sovereign LORD. **31**You my sheep, the sheep of my pasture, are people, and I am your God, declares the Sovereign LORD.' "

A Prophecy Against Edom

35 The word of the LORD came to me: **2**"Son of man, set your face against Mount Seir; prophesy against it **3**and say: 'This is what the Sovereign LORD says: I am against you, Mount Seir, and I will stretch out my hand against you and make you a desolate waste. **4**I will turn your towns into ruins and you will be desolate. Then you will know that I am the LORD.

5" 'Because you harbored an ancient hostility and delivered the Israelites over to the sword at the time of their calamity, the time their punishment reached its climax, **6**therefore as surely as I live, declares the Sovereign LORD, I will give you over to bloodshed and it will pursue you. Since you did not hate bloodshed, bloodshed will pursue you. **7**I will make Mount Seir a desolate waste and cut off from it all who come and go. **8**I will fill your mountains with the slain; those killed by the sword will fall on your hills and in your valleys and in all your ravines. **9**I will make you desolate forever; your towns will not be inhabited. Then you will know that I am the LORD.

a26 Or I will make them and the places surrounding my hill a blessing

¹⁰" 'Because you have said, "These two nations and countries will be ours and we will take possession of them," even though I the Lᴏʀᴅ was there, ¹¹therefore as surely as I live, declares the Sovereign Lᴏʀᴅ, I will treat you in accordance with the anger and jealousy you showed in your hatred of them and I will make myself known among them when I judge you. ¹²Then you will know that I the Lᴏʀᴅ have heard all the contemptible things you have said against the mountains of Israel. You said, "They have been laid waste and have been given over to us to devour." ¹³You boasted against me and spoke against me without restraint, and I heard it. ¹⁴This is what the Sovereign Lᴏʀᴅ says: While the whole earth rejoices, I will make you desolate. ¹⁵Because you rejoiced when the inheritance of the house of Israel became desolate, that is how I will treat you. You will be desolate, O Mount Seir, you and all of Edom. Then they will know that I am the Lᴏʀᴅ.' "

A Prophecy to the Mountains of Israel

36 "Son of man, prophesy to the mountains of Israel and say, 'O mountains of Israel, hear the word of the Lᴏʀᴅ. ²This is what the Sovereign Lᴏʀᴅ says: The enemy said of you, "Aha! The ancient heights have become our possession." ' ³Therefore prophesy and say, 'This is what the Sovereign Lᴏʀᴅ says: Because they ravaged and hounded you from every side so that you became the possession of the rest of the nations and the object of people's malicious talk and slander, ⁴therefore, O mountains of Israel, hear the word of the Sovereign Lᴏʀᴅ: This is what the Sovereign Lᴏʀᴅ says to the mountains and hills, to the ravines and valleys, to the desolate ruins and the deserted towns that have been plundered and ridiculed by the rest of the nations around you— ⁵this is what the Sovereign Lᴏʀᴅ says: In my burning zeal I have spoken against the rest of the nations, and against all Edom, for with glee and with malice in their hearts they made my land their own possession so that they might plunder its pastureland.' ⁶Therefore prophesy concerning the land of Israel and say to the mountains and hills, to the ravines and valleys: 'This is what the Sovereign Lᴏʀᴅ says: I speak in my jealous wrath because you have suffered the scorn of the nations. ⁷Therefore this is what the Sovereign Lᴏʀᴅ says: I swear with uplifted hand that the nations around you will also suffer scorn.

⁸" 'But you, O mountains of Israel, will produce branches and fruit for my people Israel, for they will soon come home. ⁹I am concerned for you and will look on you with favor; you will be plowed and sown, ¹⁰and I will multiply the number of people upon you, even the whole house of Israel. The towns will be inhabited and the ruins rebuilt. ¹¹I will increase the number of men and animals upon you, and they will be fruitful and become numerous. I will settle people on you as in the past and will make you prosper more than before. Then you will know that I am the Lᴏʀᴅ. ¹²I will cause people, my people Israel, to walk upon you. They will possess you, and you will be their inheritance; you will never again deprive them of their children.

¹³" 'This is what the Sovereign Lᴏʀᴅ says: Because people say to you, "You devour men and deprive your nation of its children," ¹⁴therefore you will no longer devour men or make your nation childless, declares the Sovereign Lᴏʀᴅ. ¹⁵No longer will I make you hear the taunts of the nations, and no longer will you suffer the scorn of the peoples or cause your nation to fall, declares the Sovereign Lᴏʀᴅ.' "

¹⁶Again the word of the Lᴏʀᴅ came to me: ¹⁷"Son of man, when the people of Israel were living in their own land, they defiled it by their conduct and their actions. Their conduct was like a woman's monthly uncleanness in my sight. ¹⁸So I poured out my wrath on them because they had shed blood in the land and because they had defiled it with their idols. ¹⁹I dispersed them among the nations, and they were scattered through the countries; I judged them according to their conduct and their actions. ²⁰And wherever they went among the nations they profaned my holy name, for it was said of them, 'These are the Lᴏʀᴅ's people, and yet they had to leave his land.' ²¹I had concern for my holy name, which the house of Israel profaned among the nations where they had gone.

²²"Therefore say to the house of Israel, 'This is what the Sovereign Lᴏʀᴅ says: It is not for your sake, O house of Israel, that I am going to do these things, but for the sake of my holy name, which you have profaned among the nations where you have gone. ²³I will show the holiness of my great name, which has been profaned among the nations, the name you have profaned among them. Then the nations will know that I am the Lᴏʀᴅ, declares the Sovereign Lᴏʀᴅ, when I show myself holy through you before their eyes.

24" 'For I will take you out of the nations; I will gather you from all the countries and bring you back into your own land. **25**I will sprinkle clean water on you, and you will be clean; I will cleanse you from all your impurities and from all your idols. **26**I will give you a new heart and put a new spirit in you; I will remove from you your heart of stone and give you a heart of flesh. **27**And I will put my Spirit in you and move you to follow my decrees and be careful to keep my laws. **28**You will live in the land I gave your forefathers; you will be my people, and I will be your God. **29**I will save you from all your uncleanness. I will call for the grain and make it plentiful and will not bring famine upon you. **30**I will increase the fruit of the trees and the crops of the field, so that you will no longer suffer disgrace among the nations because of famine. **31**Then you will remember your evil ways and wicked deeds, and you will loathe yourselves for your sins and detestable practices. **32**I want you to know that I am not doing this for your sake, declares the Sovereign Lord. Be ashamed and disgraced for your conduct, O house of Israel!

33" 'This is what the Sovereign Lord says: On the day I cleanse you from all your sins, I will resettle your towns, and the ruins will be rebuilt. **34**The desolate land will be cultivated instead of lying desolate in the sight of all who pass through it. **35**They will say, "This land that was laid waste has become like the garden of Eden; the cities that were lying in ruins, desolate and destroyed, are now fortified and inhabited." **36**Then the nations around you that remain will know that I the Lord have rebuilt what was destroyed and have replanted what was desolate. I the Lord have spoken, and I will do it.'

37"This is what the Sovereign Lord says: Once again I will yield to the plea of the house of Israel and do this for them: I will make their people as numerous as sheep, **38**as numerous as the flocks for offerings at Jerusalem during her appointed feasts. So will the ruined cities be filled with flocks of people. Then they will know that I am the Lord."

The Valley of Dry Bones

37 The hand of the Lord was upon me, and he brought me out by the Spirit of the Lord and set me in the middle of a valley; it was full of bones. **2**He led me back and forth among them, and I saw a great many bones on the floor of the valley, bones that were very dry. **3**He asked me, "Son of man, can these bones live?"

I said, "O Sovereign Lord, you alone know."

4Then he said to me, "Prophesy to these bones and say to them, 'Dry bones, hear the word of the Lord! **5**This is what the Sovereign Lord says to these bones: I will make breath*a* enter you, and you will come to life. **6**I will attach tendons to you and make flesh come upon you and cover you with skin; I will put breath in you, and you will come to life. Then you will know that I am the Lord.' "

7So I prophesied as I was commanded. And as I was prophesying, there was a noise, a rattling sound, and the bones came together, bone to bone. **8**I looked, and tendons and flesh appeared on them and skin covered them, but there was no breath in them.

9Then he said to me, "Prophesy to the breath; prophesy, son of man, and say to it, 'This is what the Sovereign Lord says: Come from the four winds, O breath, and breathe into these slain, that they may live.' " **10**So I prophesied as he commanded me, and breath entered them; they came to life and stood up on their feet—a vast army.

11Then he said to me: "Son of man, these bones are the whole house of Israel. They say, 'Our bones are dried up and our hope is gone; we are cut off.' **12**Therefore prophesy and say to them: 'This is what the Sovereign Lord says: O my people, I am going to open your graves and bring you up from them; I will bring you back to the land of Israel. **13**Then you, my people, will know that I am the Lord, when I open your graves and bring you up from them. **14**I will put my Spirit in you and you will live, and I will settle you in your own land. Then you will know that I the Lord have spoken, and I have done it, declares the Lord.' "

One Nation Under One King

15The word of the Lord came to me: **16**"Son of man, take a stick of wood and write on it, 'Belonging to Judah and the Israelites associated with him.' Then take another stick of wood, and write on it, 'Ephraim's stick, belonging to Joseph and all the house of Israel associated with him.' **17**Join them together into one stick so that they will become one in your hand.

18"When your countrymen ask you, 'Won't you tell us what you mean by this?'

---

a5 The Hebrew for this word can also mean *wind* or *spirit* (see verses 6-14).

SERVICE – OBEDIENCE = WORTHLESSNESS

After a night of severe partying, Bill slips a $10 bill in the offering plate at church and thinks, "Hopefully, God will overlook some of the things I did last night!"

Nancy feels guilty because she and her boyfriend have been getting too physical. So she turns down a chance to go with friends to the beach for the weekend and volunteers instead to work with an inner-city outreach. "Maybe this will help make up for all my mistakes," she says to herself.

Look It Up • • • •

Is that the way the Christian life works? Can we disobey God and then make up for it by "bribing" him with our money or time?

King Saul tried such an approach, disobeying God in his dealings with the Amalekites. He then tried to cover up his sin with all sorts of sacrifices. Note the prophet Samuel's response:

> Does the LORD delight in burnt offerings and
> sacrifices
>   as much as in obeying the voice of the LORD?
> To obey is better than sacrifice,
>   and to heed is better than the fat of rams.
> For rebellion is like the sin of divination,
>   and arrogance like the evil of idolatry
>   (1 Samuel 15:22–23).

Think It Through • • • •

Imagine owing the government $1,000 in taxes and not paying by the April 15 deadline. How would Internal Revenue Service agents respond if, when they questioned you, you said, "Hey, I say the pledge of allegiance every day. Plus I spend all my time trying to make this a better country!"?

Would such an answer satisfy the IRS? Do they want to hear all about your sacrifices for the country, or do they want you to obey the law?

Work It Out • • • •

Perhaps you have some areas of disobedience in your life where you might even be thinking, "Well, I'll make up for those little things by doing something extra great for the Lord." Forget it! God wants you to obey him, not to try to buy him off.

Pick out the one or two areas that really stand out and commit yourself to obedience. Ask God for the strength to do what is right . . . no matter what.

Nail It Down • • • •

Read how God will make you *want* to obey him in Ezekiel 36:26–27.

Turn to pages 159, 281, 1013, 1082 and 1156 for other readings on obedience.
Turn to page 906 for Wednesday's reading.

Topic • • • •

OBEDIENCE

[19]say to them, 'This is what the Sovereign Lord says: I am going to take the stick of Joseph—which is in Ephraim's hand—and of the Israelite tribes associated with him, and join it to Judah's stick, making them a single stick of wood, and they will become one in my hand.' [20]Hold before their eyes the sticks you have written on [21]and say to them, 'This is what the Sovereign Lord says: I will take the Israelites out of the nations where they have gone. I will gather them from all around and bring them back into their own land. [22]I will make them one nation in the land, on the mountains of Israel. There will be one king over all of them and they will never again be two nations or be divided into two kingdoms. [23]They will no longer defile themselves with their idols and vile images or with any of their offenses, for I will save them from all their sinful backsliding,[a] and I will cleanse them. They will be my people, and I will be their God.

[24]"'My servant David will be king over them, and they will all have one shepherd. They will follow my laws and be careful to keep my decrees. [25]They will live in the land I gave to my servant Jacob, the land where your fathers lived. They and their children and their children's children will live there forever, and David my servant will be their prince forever. [26]I will make a covenant of peace with them; it will be an everlasting covenant. I will establish them and increase their numbers, and I will put my sanctuary among them forever. [27]My dwelling place will be with them; I will be their God, and they will be my people. [28]Then the nations will know that I the Lord make Israel holy, when my sanctuary is among them forever.'"

A Prophecy Against Gog

38 The word of the Lord came to me: [2]"Son of man, set your face against Gog, of the land of Magog, the chief prince of[b] Meshech and Tubal; prophesy against him [3]and say: 'This is what the Sovereign Lord says: I am against you, O Gog, chief prince of[c] Meshech and Tubal. [4]I will turn you around, put hooks in your jaws and bring you out with your whole army—your horses, your horsemen fully armed, and a great horde with large and small shields, all of them brandishing their swords. [5]Persia, Cush[d] and Put will be with them, all with shields and helmets, [6]also Gomer with all its troops, and Beth Togarmah from the far north with all its troops—the many nations with you.

[7]"'Get ready; be prepared, you and all the hordes gathered around you, and take command of them. [8]After many days you will be called to arms. In future years you will invade a land that has recovered from war, whose people were gathered from many nations to the mountains of Israel, which had long been desolate. They had been brought out from the nations, and now all of them live in safety. [9]You and all your troops and the many nations with you will go up, advancing like a storm; you will be like a cloud covering the land.

[10]"'This is what the Sovereign Lord says: On that day thoughts will come into your mind and you will devise an evil scheme. [11]You will say, "I will invade a land of unwalled villages; I will attack a peaceful and unsuspecting people—all of them living without walls and without gates and bars. [12]I will plunder and loot and turn my hand against the resettled ruins and the people gathered from the nations, rich in livestock and goods, living at the center of the land." [13]Sheba and Dedan and the merchants of Tarshish and all her villages[e] will say to you, "Have you come to plunder? Have you gathered your hordes to loot, to carry off silver and gold, to take away livestock and goods and to seize much plunder?"'

[14]"Therefore, son of man, prophesy and say to Gog: 'This is what the Sovereign Lord says: In that day, when my people Israel are living in safety, will you not take notice of it? [15]You will come from your place in the far north, you and many nations with you, all of them riding on horses, a great horde, a mighty army. [16]You will advance against my people Israel like a cloud that covers the land. In days to come, O Gog, I will bring you against my land, so that the nations may know me when I show myself holy through you before their eyes.

[17]"'This is what the Sovereign Lord says: Are you not the one I spoke of in former days by my servants the prophets of Israel? At that time they prophesied for years that I would bring you against them. [18]This is what will happen in that day: When Gog attacks the land of Israel, my hot anger will be aroused, declares the Sovereign Lord. [19]In

---

a23 Many Hebrew manuscripts (see also Septuagint); most Hebrew manuscripts *all their dwelling places where they sinned*   *b2* Or *the prince of Rosh,*   *c3* Or *Gog, prince of Rosh,*   *d5* That is, the upper Nile region   *e13* Or *her strong lions* my zeal and fiery wrath I declare that at that time there shall be a great earthquake in the land of Israel. **20**The fish of the sea, the birds of the air, the beasts of the field, every creature that moves along the ground, and all the people on the face of the earth will tremble at my presence. The mountains will be overturned, the cliffs will crumble and every wall will fall to the ground. **21**I will summon a sword against Gog on all my mountains, declares the Sovereign Lord. Every man's sword will be against his brother. **22**I will execute judgment upon him with plague and bloodshed; I will pour down torrents of rain, hailstones and burning sulfur on him and on his troops and on the many nations with him. **23**And so I will show my greatness and my holiness, and I will make myself known in the sight of many nations. Then they will know that I am the Lord.'

39 "Son of man, prophesy against Gog and say: 'This is what the Sovereign Lord says: I am against you, O Gog, chief prince of*a* Meshech and Tubal. **2**I will turn you around and drag you along. I will bring you from the far north and send you against the mountains of Israel. **3**Then I will strike your bow from your left hand and make your arrows drop from your right hand. **4**On the mountains of Israel you will fall, you and all your troops and the nations with you. I will give you as food to all kinds of carrion birds and to the wild animals. **5**You will fall in the open field, for I have spoken, declares the Sovereign Lord. **6**I will send fire on Magog and on those who live in safety in the coastlands, and they will know that I am the Lord.

7" 'I will make known my holy name among my people Israel. I will no longer let my holy name be profaned, and the nations will know that I the Lord am the Holy One in Israel. **8**It is coming! It will surely take place, declares the Sovereign Lord. This is the day I have spoken of.

9" 'Then those who live in the towns of Israel will go out and use the weapons for fuel and burn them up—the small and large shields, the bows and arrows, the war clubs and spears. For seven years they will use them for fuel. **10**They will not need to gather wood from the fields or cut it from the forests, because they will use the weapons for fuel. And they will plunder those who plundered them and loot those who looted them, declares the Sovereign Lord.

11" 'On that day I will give Gog a burial place in Israel, in the valley of those who travel east toward*b* the Sea.*c* It will block the way of travelers, because Gog and all his hordes will be buried there. So it will be called the Valley of Hamon Gog.*d*

12" 'For seven months the house of Israel will be burying them in order to cleanse the land. **13**All the people of the land will bury them, and the day I am glorified will be a memorable day for them, declares the Sovereign Lord.

14" 'Men will be regularly employed to cleanse the land. Some will go throughout the land and, in addition to them, others will bury those that remain on the ground. At the end of the seven months they will begin their search. **15**As they go through the land and one of them sees a human bone, he will set up a marker beside it until the gravediggers have buried it in the Valley of Hamon Gog. **16**(Also a town called Hamonah*e* will be there.) And so they will cleanse the land.'

17"Son of man, this is what the Sovereign Lord says: Call out to every kind of bird and all the wild animals: 'Assemble and come together from all around to the sacrifice I am preparing for you, the great sacrifice on the mountains of Israel. There you will eat flesh and drink blood. **18**You will eat the flesh of mighty men and drink the blood of the princes of the earth as if they were rams and lambs, goats and bulls—all of them fattened animals from Bashan. **19**At the sacrifice I am preparing for you, you will eat fat till you are glutted and drink blood till you are drunk. **20**At my table you will eat your fill of horses and riders, mighty men and soldiers of every kind,' declares the Sovereign Lord.

21"I will display my glory among the nations, and all the nations will see the punishment I inflict and the hand I lay upon them. **22**From that day forward the house of Israel will know that I am the Lord their God. **23**And the nations will know that the people of Israel went into exile for their sin, because they were unfaithful to me. So I hid my face from them and handed them over to their enemies, and they all fell by the sword. **24**I dealt with them according to their uncleanness and their offenses, and I hid my face from them.

25"Therefore this is what the Sovereign Lord says: I will now bring Jacob back from captivity*f* and will have compassion on all the people of Israel, and I will be zealous for

---

a1 Or *Gog, prince of Rosh,*   *b11* Or *of*   *c11* That is, the Dead Sea   *d11* *Hamon Gog* means *hordes of Gog.*
e16 *Hamonah* means *horde.*   *f25* Or *now restore the fortunes of Jacob*

my holy name. 26They will forget their shame and all the unfaithfulness they showed toward me when they lived in safety in their land with no one to make them afraid. 27When I have brought them back from the nations and have gathered them from the countries of their enemies, I will show myself holy through them in the sight of many nations. 28Then they will know that I am the Lord their God, for though I sent them into exile among the nations, I will gather them to their own land, not leaving any behind. 29I will no longer hide my face from them, for I will pour out my Spirit on the house of Israel, declares the Sovereign Lord."

The New Temple Area

40 In the twenty-fifth year of our exile, at the beginning of the year, on the tenth of the month, in the fourteenth year after the fall of the city — on that very day the hand of the Lord was upon me and he took me there. 2In visions of God he took me to the land of Israel and set me on a very high mountain, on whose south side were some buildings that looked like a city. 3He took me there, and I saw a man whose appearance was like bronze; he was standing in the gateway with a linen cord and a measuring rod in his hand. 4The man said to me, "Son of man, look with your eyes and hear with your ears and pay attention to everything I am going to show you, for that is why you have been brought here. Tell the house of Israel everything you see."

The East Gate to the Outer Court

5I saw a wall completely surrounding the temple area. The length of the measuring rod in the man's hand was six long cubits, each of which was a cubit[a] and a handbreadth.[b] He measured the wall; it was one measuring rod thick and one rod high.

6Then he went to the gate facing east. He climbed its steps and measured the threshold of the gate; it was one rod deep.[c] 7The alcoves for the guards were one rod long and one rod wide, and the projecting walls between the alcoves were five cubits thick. And the threshold of the gate next to the portico facing the temple was one rod deep. 8Then he measured the portico of the gateway; 9it[d] was eight cubits deep and its jambs were two cubits thick. The portico of the gateway faced the temple.

10Inside the east gate were three alcoves on each side; the three had the same measurements, and the faces of the projecting walls on each side had the same measurements. 11Then he measured the width of the entrance to the gateway; it was ten cubits and its length was thirteen cubits. 12In front of each alcove was a wall one cubit high, and the alcoves were six cubits square. 13Then he measured the gateway from the top of the rear wall of one alcove to the top of the opposite one; the distance was twenty-five cubits from one parapet opening to the opposite one. 14He measured along the faces of the projecting walls all around the inside of the gateway — sixty cubits. The measurement was up to the portico[e] facing the courtyard.[f] 15The distance from the entrance of the gateway to the far end of its portico was fifty cubits. 16The alcoves and the projecting walls inside the gateway were surmounted by narrow parapet openings all around, as was the portico; the openings all around faced inward. The faces of the projecting walls were decorated with palm trees.

The Outer Court

17Then he brought me into the outer court. There I saw some rooms and a pavement that had been constructed all around the court; there were thirty rooms along the pavement. 18It abutted the sides of the gateways and was as wide as they were long; this was the lower pavement. 19Then he measured the distance from the inside of the lower gateway to the outside of the inner court; it was a hundred cubits on the east side as well as on the north.

The North Gate

20Then he measured the length and width of the gate facing north, leading into the outer court. 21Its alcoves — three on each side — its projecting walls and its portico had the same measurements as those of the first gateway. It was fifty cubits long and twenty-five cubits wide. 22Its openings, its portico and its palm tree decorations had the same measurements as those of the gate facing

---

a5 The common cubit was about 1 1/2 feet (about 0.5 meter).   b5 That is, about 3 inches (about 8 centimeters)   c6 Septuagint; Hebrew deep, the first threshold, one rod deep   d8,9 Many Hebrew manuscripts, Septuagint, Vulgate and Syriac; most Hebrew manuscripts gateway facing the temple; it was one rod deep. 9Then he measured the portico of the gateway; it   e14 Septuagint; Hebrew projecting wall   f14 The meaning of the Hebrew for this verse is uncertain.

east. Seven steps led up to it, with its portico opposite them. **23**There was a gate to the inner court facing the north gate, just as there was on the east. He measured from one gate to the opposite one; it was a hundred cubits.

The South Gate

24Then he led me to the south side and I saw a gate facing south. He measured its jambs and its portico, and they had the same measurements as the others. **25**The gateway and its portico had narrow openings all around, like the openings of the others. It was fifty cubits long and twenty-five cubits wide. **26**Seven steps led up to it, with its portico opposite them; it had palm tree decorations on the faces of the projecting walls on each side. **27**The inner court also had a gate facing south, and he measured from this gate to the outer gate on the south side; it was a hundred cubits.

Gates to the Inner Court

28Then he brought me into the inner court through the south gate, and he measured the south gate; it had the same measurements as the others. **29**Its alcoves, its projecting walls and its portico had the same measurements as the others. The gateway and its portico had openings all around. It was fifty cubits long and twenty-five cubits wide. **30**(The porticoes of the gateways around the inner court were twenty-five cubits wide and five cubits deep.) **31**Its portico faced the outer court; palm trees decorated its jambs, and eight steps led up to it.

32Then he brought me to the inner court on the east side, and he measured the gateway; it had the same measurements as the others. **33**Its alcoves, its projecting walls and its portico had the same measurements as the others. The gateway and its portico had openings all around. It was fifty cubits long and twenty-five cubits wide. **34**Its portico faced the outer court; palm trees decorated the jambs on either side, and eight steps led up to it.

35Then he brought me to the north gate and measured it. It had the same measurements as the others, **36**as did its alcoves, its projecting walls and its portico, and it had openings all around. It was fifty cubits long and twenty-five cubits wide. **37**Its portico*a* faced the outer court; palm trees decorated

the jambs on either side, and eight steps led up to it.

The Rooms for Preparing Sacrifices

38A room with a doorway was by the portico in each of the inner gateways, where the burnt offerings were washed. **39**In the portico of the gateway were two tables on each side, on which the burnt offerings, sin offerings and guilt offerings were slaughtered. **40**By the outside wall of the portico of the gateway, near the steps at the entrance to the north gateway were two tables, and on the other side of the steps were two tables. **41**So there were four tables on one side of the gateway and four on the other — eight tables in all — on which the sacrifices were slaughtered. **42**There were also four tables of dressed stone for the burnt offerings, each a cubit and a half long, a cubit and a half wide and a cubit high. On them were placed the utensils for slaughtering the burnt offerings and the other sacrifices. **43**And double-pronged hooks, each a handbreadth long, were attached to the wall all around. The tables were for the flesh of the offerings.

Rooms for the Priests

44Outside the inner gate, within the inner court, were two rooms, one*b* at the side of the north gate and facing south, and another at the side of the south*c* gate and facing north. **45**He said to me, "The room facing south is for the priests who have charge of the temple, **46**and the room facing north is for the priests who have charge of the altar. These are the sons of Zadok, who are the only Levites who may draw near to the Lord to minister before him."

47Then he measured the court: It was square — a hundred cubits long and a hundred cubits wide. And the altar was in front of the temple.

The Temple

48He brought me to the portico of the temple and measured the jambs of the portico; they were five cubits wide on either side. The width of the entrance was fourteen cubits and its projecting walls were*d* three cubits wide on either side. **49**The portico was twenty cubits wide, and twelve*e* cubits from front to back. It was reached by a flight of stairs,*f* and there were pillars on each side of the jambs.

---

a37 Septuagint (see also verses 31 and 34); Hebrew *jambs*   *b44* Septuagint; Hebrew *were rooms for singers,*
which were   *c44* Septuagint; Hebrew *east*   *d48* Septuagint; Hebrew *entrance was*   *e49* Septuagint;
Hebrew *eleven*   *f49* Hebrew; Septuagint *Ten steps led up to it*

41 Then the man brought me to the outer sanctuary and measured the jambs; the width of the jambs was six cubits[a] on each side.[b] **2**The entrance was ten cubits wide, and the projecting walls on each side of it were five cubits wide. He also measured the outer sanctuary; it was forty cubits long and twenty cubits wide.

3Then he went into the inner sanctuary and measured the jambs of the entrance; each was two cubits wide. The entrance was six cubits wide, and the projecting walls on each side of it were seven cubits wide. **4**And he measured the length of the inner sanctuary; it was twenty cubits, and its width was twenty cubits across the end of the outer sanctuary. He said to me, "This is the Most Holy Place."

5Then he measured the wall of the temple; it was six cubits thick, and each side room around the temple was four cubits wide. **6**The side rooms were on three levels, one above another, thirty on each level. There were ledges all around the wall of the temple to serve as supports for the side rooms, so that the supports were not inserted into the wall of the temple. **7**The side rooms all around the temple were wider at each successive level. The structure surrounding the temple was built in ascending stages, so that the rooms widened as one went upward. A stairway went up from the lowest floor to the top floor through the middle floor.

8I saw that the temple had a raised base all around it, forming the foundation of the side rooms. It was the length of the rod, six long cubits. **9**The outer wall of the side rooms was five cubits thick. The open area between the side rooms of the temple **10**and the ⌊priests'⌋ rooms was twenty cubits wide all around the temple. **11**There were entrances to the side rooms from the open area, one on the north and another on the south; and the base adjoining the open area was five cubits wide all around.

12The building facing the temple courtyard on the west side was seventy cubits wide. The wall of the building was five cubits thick all around, and its length was ninety cubits.

13Then he measured the temple; it was a hundred cubits long, and the temple courtyard and the building with its walls were also a hundred cubits long. **14**The width of the temple courtyard on the east, including the front of the temple, was a hundred cubits.

15Then he measured the length of the building facing the courtyard at the rear of the temple, including its galleries on each side; it was a hundred cubits.

The outer sanctuary, the inner sanctuary and the portico facing the court, **16**as well as the thresholds and the narrow windows and galleries around the three of them—everything beyond and including the threshold was covered with wood. The floor, the wall up to the windows, and the windows were covered. **17**In the space above the outside of the entrance to the inner sanctuary and on the walls at regular intervals all around the inner and outer sanctuary **18**were carved cherubim and palm trees. Palm trees alternated with cherubim. Each cherub had two faces: **19**the face of a man toward the palm tree on one side and the face of a lion toward the palm tree on the other. They were carved all around the whole temple. **20**From the floor to the area above the entrance, cherubim and palm trees were carved on the wall of the outer sanctuary.

21The outer sanctuary had a rectangular doorframe, and the one at the front of the Most Holy Place was similar. **22**There was a wooden altar three cubits high and two cubits square[c]; its corners, its base[d] and its sides were of wood. The man said to me, "This is the table that is before the Lord." **23**Both the outer sanctuary and the Most Holy Place had double doors. **24**Each door had two leaves—two hinged leaves for each door. **25**And on the doors of the outer sanctuary were carved cherubim and palm trees like those carved on the walls, and there was a wooden overhang on the front of the portico. **26**On the sidewalls of the portico were narrow windows with palm trees carved on each side. The side rooms of the temple also had overhangs.

Rooms for the Priests

42 Then the man led me northward into the outer court and brought me to the rooms opposite the temple courtyard and opposite the outer wall on the north side. **2**The building whose door faced north was a hundred cubits[e] long and fifty cubits wide. **3**Both in the section twenty cubits from the inner court and in the section op-

a1 The common cubit was about 1 1/2 feet (about 0.5 meter).   b1 One Hebrew manuscript and Septuagint; most Hebrew manuscripts *side, the width of the tent*   c22 Septuagint; Hebrew *long*   d22 Septuagint; Hebrew *length*   e2 The common cubit was about 1 1/2 feet (about 0.5 meter).

posite the pavement of the outer court, gallery faced gallery at the three levels. [4]In front of the rooms was an inner passageway ten cubits wide and a hundred cubits[a] long. Their doors were on the north. [5]Now the upper rooms were narrower, for the galleries took more space from them than from the rooms on the lower and middle floors of the building. [6]The rooms on the third floor had no pillars, as the courts had; so they were smaller in floor space than those on the lower and middle floors. [7]There was an outer wall parallel to the rooms and the outer court; it extended in front of the rooms for fifty cubits. [8]While the row of rooms on the side next to the outer court was fifty cubits long, the row on the side nearest the sanctuary was a hundred cubits long. [9]The lower rooms had an entrance on the east side as one enters them from the outer court.

[10]On the south side[b] along the length of the wall of the outer court, adjoining the temple courtyard and opposite the outer wall, were rooms [11]with a passageway in front of them. These were like the rooms on the north; they had the same length and width, with similar exits and dimensions. Similar to the doorways on the north [12]were the doorways of the rooms on the south. There was a doorway at the beginning of the passageway that was parallel to the corresponding wall extending eastward, by which one enters the rooms.

[13]Then he said to me, "The north and south rooms facing the temple courtyard are the priests' rooms, where the priests who approach the LORD will eat the most holy offerings. There they will put the most holy offerings — the grain offerings, the sin offerings and the guilt offerings — for the place is holy. [14]Once the priests enter the holy precincts, they are not to go into the outer court until they leave behind the garments in which they minister, for these are holy. They are to put on other clothes before they go near the places that are for the people."

[15]When he had finished measuring what was inside the temple area, he led me out by the east gate and measured the area all around: [16]He measured the east side with the measuring rod; it was five hundred cubits.[c] [17]He measured the north side; it was five hundred cubits[d] by the measuring rod.

[18]He measured the south side; it was five hundred cubits by the measuring rod. [19]Then he turned to the west side and measured; it was five hundred cubits by the measuring rod. [20]So he measured the area on all four sides. It had a wall around it, five hundred cubits long and five hundred cubits wide, to separate the holy from the common.

The Glory Returns to the Temple

43 Then the man brought me to the gate facing east, [2]and I saw the glory of the God of Israel coming from the east. His voice was like the roar of rushing waters, and the land was radiant with his glory. [3]The vision I saw was like the vision I had seen when he[e] came to destroy the city and like the visions I had seen by the Kebar River, and I fell facedown. [4]The glory of the LORD entered the temple through the gate facing east. [5]Then the Spirit lifted me up and brought me into the inner court, and the glory of the LORD filled the temple.

[6]While the man was standing beside me, I heard someone speaking to me from inside the temple. [7]He said: "Son of man, this is the place of my throne and the place for the soles of my feet. This is where I will live among the Israelites forever. The house of Israel will never again defile my holy name — neither they nor their kings — by their prostitution[f] and the lifeless idols[g] of their kings at their high places. [8]When they placed their threshold next to my threshold and their doorposts beside my doorposts, with only a wall between me and them, they defiled my holy name by their detestable practices. So I destroyed them in my anger. [9]Now let them put away from me their prostitution and the lifeless idols of their kings, and I will live among them forever.

[10]"Son of man, describe the temple to the people of Israel, that they may be ashamed of their sins. Let them consider the plan, [11]and if they are ashamed of all they have done, make known to them the design of the temple — its arrangement, its exits and entrances — its whole design and all its regulations[h] and laws. Write these down before them so that they may be faithful to its design and follow all its regulations.

[12]"This is the law of the temple: All the

a4 Septuagint and Syriac; Hebrew and one cubit   b10 Septuagint; Hebrew Eastward   c16 See Septuagint of verse 17; Hebrew rods; also in verses 18 and 19.   d17 Septuagint; Hebrew rods   e3 Some Hebrew manuscripts and Vulgate; most Hebrew manuscripts I   f7 Or their spiritual adultery; also in verse 9   g7 Or the corpses; also in verse 9   h11 Some Hebrew manuscripts and Septuagint; most Hebrew manuscripts regulations and its whole design surrounding area on top of the mountain will be most holy. Such is the law of the temple.

The Altar

13"These are the measurements of the altar in long cubits, that cubit being a cubit[a] and a handbreadth[b]: Its gutter is a cubit deep and a cubit wide, with a rim of one span[c] around the edge. And this is the height of the altar: **14**From the gutter on the ground up to the lower ledge it is two cubits high and a cubit wide, and from the smaller ledge up to the larger ledge it is four cubits high and a cubit wide. **15**The altar hearth is four cubits high, and four horns project upward from the hearth. **16**The altar hearth is square, twelve cubits long and twelve cubits wide. **17**The upper ledge also is square, fourteen cubits long and fourteen cubits wide, with a rim of half a cubit and a gutter of a cubit all around. The steps of the altar face east."

18Then he said to me, "Son of man, this is what the Sovereign Lord says: These will be the regulations for sacrificing burnt offerings and sprinkling blood upon the altar when it is built: **19**You are to give a young bull as a sin offering to the priests, who are Levites, of the family of Zadok, who come near to minister before me, declares the Sovereign Lord. **20**You are to take some of its blood and put it on the four horns of the altar and on the four corners of the upper ledge and all around the rim, and so purify the altar and make atonement for it. **21**You are to take the bull for the sin offering and burn it in the designated part of the temple area outside the sanctuary.

22"On the second day you are to offer a male goat without defect for a sin offering, and the altar is to be purified as it was purified with the bull. **23**When you have finished purifying it, you are to offer a young bull and a ram from the flock, both without defect. **24**You are to offer them before the Lord, and the priests are to sprinkle salt on them and sacrifice them as a burnt offering to the Lord.

25"For seven days you are to provide a male goat daily for a sin offering; you are also to provide a young bull and a ram from the flock, both without defect. **26**For seven days they are to make atonement for the altar and cleanse it; thus they will dedicate it. **27**At the end of these days, from the eighth

day on, the priests are to present your burnt offerings and fellowship offerings[d] on the altar. Then I will accept you, declares the Sovereign Lord."

The Prince, the Levites, the Priests

44 Then the man brought me back to the outer gate of the sanctuary, the one facing east, and it was shut. **2**The Lord said to me, "This gate is to remain shut. It must not be opened; no one may enter through it. It is to remain shut because the Lord, the God of Israel, has entered through it. **3**The prince himself is the only one who may sit inside the gateway to eat in the presence of the Lord. He is to enter by way of the portico of the gateway and go out the same way."

4Then the man brought me by way of the north gate to the front of the temple. I looked and saw the glory of the Lord filling the temple of the Lord, and I fell facedown.

5The Lord said to me, "Son of man, look carefully, listen closely and give attention to everything I tell you concerning all the regulations regarding the temple of the Lord. Give attention to the entrance of the temple and all the exits of the sanctuary. **6**Say to the rebellious house of Israel, 'This is what the Sovereign Lord says: Enough of your detestable practices, O house of Israel! **7**In addition to all your other detestable practices, you brought foreigners uncircumcised in heart and flesh into my sanctuary, desecrating my temple while you offered me food, fat and blood, and you broke my covenant. **8**Instead of carrying out your duty in regard to my holy things, you put others in charge of my sanctuary. **9**This is what the Sovereign Lord says: No foreigner uncircumcised in heart and flesh is to enter my sanctuary, not even the foreigners who live among the Israelites.

10" 'The Levites who went far from me when Israel went astray and who wandered from me after their idols must bear the consequences of their sin. **11**They may serve in my sanctuary, having charge of the gates of the temple and serving in it; they may slaughter the burnt offerings and sacrifices for the people and stand before the people and serve them. **12**But because they served them in the presence of their idols and made the house of Israel fall into sin, therefore I have sworn with uplifted hand that they must bear the consequences of their

---

a13 The common cubit was about 1 1/2 feet (about 0.5 meter).   *b13* That is, about 3 inches (about 8 centimeters)   *c13* That is, about 9 inches (about 22 centimeters)   *d27* Traditionally *peace offerings* sin, declares the Sovereign Lord. [13]They are not to come near to serve me as priests or come near any of my holy things or my most holy offerings; they must bear the shame of their detestable practices. [14]Yet I will put them in charge of the duties of the temple and all the work that is to be done in it.

[15]" 'But the priests, who are Levites and descendants of Zadok and who faithfully carried out the duties of my sanctuary when the Israelites went astray from me, are to come near to minister before me; they are to stand before me to offer sacrifices of fat and blood, declares the Sovereign Lord. [16]They alone are to enter my sanctuary; they alone are to come near my table to minister before me and perform my service.

[17]" 'When they enter the gates of the inner court, they are to wear linen clothes; they must not wear any woolen garment while ministering at the gates of the inner court or inside the temple. [18]They are to wear linen turbans on their heads and linen undergarments around their waists. They must not wear anything that makes them perspire. [19]When they go out into the outer court where the people are, they are to take off the clothes they have been ministering in and are to leave them in the sacred rooms, and put on other clothes, so that they do not consecrate the people by means of their garments.

[20]" 'They must not shave their heads or let their hair grow long, but they are to keep the hair of their heads trimmed. [21]No priest is to drink wine when he enters the inner court. [22]They must not marry widows or divorced women; they may marry only virgins of Israelite descent or widows of priests. [23]They are to teach my people the difference between the holy and the common and show them how to distinguish between the unclean and the clean.

[24]" 'In any dispute, the priests are to serve as judges and decide it according to my ordinances. They are to keep my laws and my decrees for all my appointed feasts, and they are to keep my Sabbaths holy.

[25]" 'A priest must not defile himself by going near a dead person; however, if the dead person was his father or mother, son or daughter, brother or unmarried sister, then he may defile himself. [26]After he is cleansed, he must wait seven days. [27]On the day he goes into the inner court of the sanctuary to minister in the sanctuary, he is to offer a sin offering for himself, declares the Sovereign Lord.

[28]" 'I am to be the only inheritance the priests have. You are to give them no possession in Israel; I will be their possession. [29]They will eat the grain offerings, the sin offerings and the guilt offerings; and everything in Israel devoted[a] to the Lord will belong to them. [30]The best of all the firstfruits and of all your special gifts will belong to the priests. You are to give them the first portion of your ground meal so that a blessing may rest on your household. [31]The priests must not eat anything, bird or animal, found dead or torn by wild animals.

Division of the Land

45 " 'When you allot the land as an inheritance, you are to present to the Lord a portion of the land as a sacred district, 25,000 cubits long and 20,000[b] cubits wide; the entire area will be holy. [2]Of this, a section 500 cubits square is to be for the sanctuary, with 50 cubits around it for open land. [3]In the sacred district, measure off a section 25,000 cubits[c] long and 10,000 cubits[d] wide. In it will be the sanctuary, the Most Holy Place. [4]It will be the sacred portion of the land for the priests, who minister in the sanctuary and who draw near to minister before the Lord. It will be a place for their houses as well as a holy place for the sanctuary. [5]An area 25,000 cubits long and 10,000 cubits wide will belong to the Levites, who serve in the temple, as their possession for towns to live in.[e]

[6]" 'You are to give the city as its property an area 5,000 cubits wide and 25,000 cubits long, adjoining the sacred portion; it will belong to the whole house of Israel.

[7]" 'The prince will have the land bordering each side of the area formed by the sacred district and the property of the city. It will extend westward from the west side and eastward from the east side, running lengthwise from the western to the eastern border parallel to one of the tribal portions. [8]This land will be his possession in Israel. And my princes will no longer oppress my people but will allow the house of Israel to possess the land according to their tribes.

[9]" 'This is what the Sovereign Lord says:

---

[a]29 The Hebrew term refers to the irrevocable giving over of things or persons to the Lord.   [b]1 Septuagint (see also verses 3 and 5 and 48:9); Hebrew *10,000*   [c]3 That is, about 7 miles (about 12 kilometers)
[d]3 That is, about 3 miles (about 5 kilometers)   [e]5 Septuagint; Hebrew *temple; they will have as their possession 20 rooms*

You have gone far enough, O princes of Israel! Give up your violence and oppression and do what is just and right. Stop dispossessing my people, declares the Sovereign LORD. [10]You are to use accurate scales, an accurate ephah[a] and an accurate bath.[b] [11]The ephah and the bath are to be the same size, the bath containing a tenth of a homer[c] and the ephah a tenth of a homer; the homer is to be the standard measure for both. [12]The shekel[d] is to consist of twenty gerahs. Twenty shekels plus twenty-five shekels plus fifteen shekels equal one mina.[e]

Offerings and Holy Days

[13]" 'This is the special gift you are to offer: a sixth of an ephah from each homer of wheat and a sixth of an ephah from each homer of barley. [14]The prescribed portion of oil, measured by the bath, is a tenth of a bath from each cor (which consists of ten baths or one homer, for ten baths are equivalent to a homer). [15]Also one sheep is to be taken from every flock of two hundred from the well-watered pastures of Israel. These will be used for the grain offerings, burnt offerings and fellowship offerings[f] to make atonement for the people, declares the Sovereign LORD. [16]All the people of the land will participate in this special gift for the use of the prince in Israel. [17]It will be the duty of the prince to provide the burnt offerings, grain offerings and drink offerings at the festivals, the New Moons and the Sabbaths — at all the appointed feasts of the house of Israel. He will provide the sin offerings, grain offerings, burnt offerings and fellowship offerings to make atonement for the house of Israel.

[18]" 'This is what the Sovereign LORD says: In the first month on the first day you are to take a young bull without defect and purify the sanctuary. [19]The priest is to take some of the blood of the sin offering and put it on the doorposts of the temple, on the four corners of the upper ledge of the altar and on the gateposts of the inner court. [20]You are to do the same on the seventh day of the month for anyone who sins unintentionally or through ignorance; so you are to make atonement for the temple.

[21]" 'In the first month on the fourteenth day you are to observe the Passover, a feast lasting seven days, during which you shall eat bread made without yeast. [22]On that day the prince is to provide a bull as a sin offering for himself and for all the people of the land. [23]Every day during the seven days of the Feast he is to provide seven bulls and seven rams without defect as a burnt offering to the LORD, and a male goat for a sin offering. [24]He is to provide as a grain offering an ephah for each bull and an ephah for each ram, along with a hin[g] of oil for each ephah.

[25]" 'During the seven days of the Feast, which begins in the seventh month on the fifteenth day, he is to make the same provision for sin offerings, burnt offerings, grain offerings and oil.

46 " 'This is what the Sovereign LORD says: The gate of the inner court facing east is to be shut on the six working days, but on the Sabbath day and on the day of the New Moon it is to be opened. [2]The prince is to enter from the outside through the portico of the gateway and stand by the gatepost. The priests are to sacrifice his burnt offering and his fellowship offerings.[h] He is to worship at the threshold of the gateway and then go out, but the gate will not be shut until evening. [3]On the Sabbaths and New Moons the people of the land are to worship in the presence of the LORD at the entrance to that gateway. [4]The burnt offering the prince brings to the LORD on the Sabbath day is to be six male lambs and a ram, all without defect. [5]The grain offering given with the ram is to be an ephah,[i] and the grain offering with the lambs is to be as much as he pleases, along with a hin[g] of oil for each ephah. [6]On the day of the New Moon he is to offer a young bull, six lambs and a ram, all without defect. [7]He is to provide as a grain offering one ephah with the bull, one ephah with the ram, and with the lambs as much as he wants to give, along with a hin of oil with each ephah. [8]When the prince enters, he is to go in through the portico of the gateway, and he is to come out the same way.

[9]" 'When the people of the land come before the LORD at the appointed feasts, whoever enters by the north gate to worship is to go out the south gate; and whoever enters

[a]10 An ephah was a dry measure.   [b]10 A bath was a liquid measure.   [c]11 A homer was a dry measure.
[d]12 A shekel weighed about 2/5 ounce (about 11.5 grams).   [e]12 That is, 60 shekels; the common mina was 50 shekels.   [f]15 Traditionally peace offerings; also in verse 17   [g]24,5 That is, probably about 4 quarts (about 4 liters)   [h]2 Traditionally peace offerings; also in verse 12   [i]5 That is, probably about 3/5 bushel (about 22 liters)

by the south gate is to go out the north gate. No one is to return through the gate by which he entered, but each is to go out the opposite gate. **10**The prince is to be among them, going in when they go in and going out when they go out.

11" 'At the festivals and the appointed feasts, the grain offering is to be an ephah with a bull, an ephah with a ram, and with the lambs as much as one pleases, along with a hin of oil for each ephah. **12**When the prince provides a freewill offering to the Lord—whether a burnt offering or fellowship offerings—the gate facing east is to be opened for him. He shall offer his burnt offering or his fellowship offerings as he does on the Sabbath day. Then he shall go out, and after he has gone out, the gate will be shut.

13" 'Every day you are to provide a year-old lamb without defect for a burnt offering to the Lord; morning by morning you shall provide it. **14**You are also to provide with it morning by morning a grain offering, consisting of a sixth of an ephah with a third of a hin of oil to moisten the flour. The presenting of this grain offering to the Lord is a lasting ordinance. **15**So the lamb and the grain offering and the oil shall be provided morning by morning for a regular burnt offering.

16" 'This is what the Sovereign Lord says: If the prince makes a gift from his inheritance to one of his sons, it will also belong to his descendants; it is to be their property by inheritance. **17**If, however, he makes a gift from his inheritance to one of his servants, the servant may keep it until the year of freedom; then it will revert to the prince. His inheritance belongs to his sons only; it is theirs. **18**The prince must not take any of the inheritance of the people, driving them off their property. He is to give his sons their inheritance out of his own property, so that none of my people will be separated from his property.' "

19Then the man brought me through the entrance at the side of the gate to the sacred rooms facing north, which belonged to the priests, and showed me a place at the western end. **20**He said to me, "This is the place where the priests will cook the guilt offering and the sin offering and bake the grain offering, to avoid bringing them into the outer court and consecrating the people."

21He then brought me to the outer court and led me around to its four corners, and I saw in each corner another court. **22**In the four corners of the outer court were enclosed*a* courts, forty cubits long and thirty cubits wide; each of the courts in the four corners was the same size. **23**Around the inside of each of the four courts was a ledge of stone, with places for fire built all around under the ledge. **24**He said to me, "These are the kitchens where those who minister at the temple will cook the sacrifices of the people."

The River From the Temple

47 The man brought me back to the entrance of the temple, and I saw water coming out from under the threshold of the temple toward the east (for the temple faced east). The water was coming down from under the south side of the temple, south of the altar. **2**He then brought me out through the north gate and led me around the outside to the outer gate facing east, and the water was flowing from the south side.

3As the man went eastward with a measuring line in his hand, he measured off a thousand cubits*b* and then led me through water that was ankle-deep. **4**He measured off another thousand cubits and led me through water that was knee-deep. He measured off another thousand and led me through water that was up to the waist. **5**He measured off another thousand, but now it was a river that I could not cross, because the water had risen and was deep enough to swim in—a river that no one could cross. **6**He asked me, "Son of man, do you see this?"

Then he led me back to the bank of the river. **7**When I arrived there, I saw a great number of trees on each side of the river. **8**He said to me, "This water flows toward the eastern region and goes down into the Arabah,*c* where it enters the Sea.*d* When it empties into the Sea,*d* the water there becomes fresh. **9**Swarms of living creatures will live wherever the river flows. There will be large numbers of fish, because this water flows there and makes the salt water fresh; so where the river flows everything will live. **10**Fishermen will stand along the shore; from En Gedi to En Eglaim there will be places for spreading nets. The fish will be of many kinds—like the fish of the Great Sea.*e* **11**But the swamps and marshes will not become fresh; they will be left for salt. [12]Fruit trees of all kinds will grow on both banks of the river. Their leaves will not wither, nor will their fruit fail. Every month they will bear, because the water from the sanctuary flows to them. Their fruit will serve for food and their leaves for healing."

The Boundaries of the Land

[13]This is what the Sovereign LORD says: "These are the boundaries by which you are to divide the land for an inheritance among the twelve tribes of Israel, with two portions for Joseph. [14]You are to divide it equally among them. Because I swore with uplifted hand to give it to your forefathers, this land will become your inheritance.

[15]"This is to be the boundary of the land:

"On the north side it will run from the Great Sea by the Hethlon road past Lebo[a] Hamath to Zedad, [16]Berothah[b] and Sibraim (which lies on the border between Damascus and Hamath), as far as Hazer Hatticon, which is on the border of Hauran. [17]The boundary will extend from the sea to Hazer Enan,[c] along the northern border of Damascus, with the border of Hamath to the north. This will be the north boundary. [18]"On the east side the boundary will run between Hauran and Damascus, along the Jordan between Gilead and the land of Israel, to the eastern sea and as far as Tamar.[d] This will be the east boundary. [19]"On the south side it will run from Tamar as far as the waters of Meribah Kadesh, then along the Wadi ⌊of Egypt⌋ to the Great Sea. This will be the south boundary. [20]"On the west side, the Great Sea will be the boundary to a point opposite Lebo[e] Hamath. This will be the west boundary.

[21]"You are to distribute this land among yourselves according to the tribes of Israel. [22]You are to allot it as an inheritance for yourselves and for the aliens who have settled among you and who have children. You are to consider them as native-born Israelites; along with you they are to be allotted an inheritance among the tribes of Israel. [23]In whatever tribe the alien settles, there

you are to give him his inheritance," declares the Sovereign LORD.

The Division of the Land

48 "These are the tribes, listed by name: At the northern frontier, Dan will have one portion; it will follow the Hethlon road to Lebo[f] Hamath; Hazar Enan and the northern border of Damascus next to Hamath will be part of its border from the east side to the west side.

[2]"Asher will have one portion; it will border the territory of Dan from east to west.

[3]"Naphtali will have one portion; it will border the territory of Asher from east to west.

[4]"Manasseh will have one portion; it will border the territory of Naphtali from east to west.

[5]"Ephraim will have one portion; it will border the territory of Manasseh from east to west.

[6]"Reuben will have one portion; it will border the territory of Ephraim from east to west.

[7]"Judah will have one portion; it will border the territory of Reuben from east to west.

[8]"Bordering the territory of Judah from east to west will be the portion you are to present as a special gift. It will be 25,000 cubits[g] wide, and its length from east to west will equal one of the tribal portions; the sanctuary will be in the center of it.

[9]"The special portion you are to offer to the LORD will be 25,000 cubits long and 10,000 cubits[h] wide. [10]This will be the sacred portion for the priests. It will be 25,000 cubits long on the north side, 10,000 cubits wide on the west side, 10,000 cubits wide on the east side and 25,000 cubits long on the south side. In the center of it will be the sanctuary of the LORD. [11]This will be for the consecrated priests, the Zadokites, who were faithful in serving me and did not go astray as the Levites did when the Israelites went astray. [12]It will be a special gift to them from the sacred portion of the land, a most holy portion, bordering the territory of the Levites.

[13]"Alongside the territory of the priests, the Levites will have an allotment 25,000 cubits long and 10,000 cubits wide. Its total length will be 25,000 cubits and its width

---

a15 Or past the entrance to   b15,16 See Septuagint and Ezekiel 48:1; Hebrew road to go into Zedad, 16Hamath, Berothah   c17 Hebrew Enon, a variant of Enan   d18 Septuagint and Syriac; Hebrew Israel. You will measure to the eastern sea   e20 Or opposite the entrance to   f1 Or to the entrance to   g8 That is, about 7 miles (about 12 kilometers)   h9 That is, about 3 miles (about 5 kilometers)

10,000 cubits. **14**They must not sell or exchange any of it. This is the best of the land and must not pass into other hands, because it is holy to the Lᴏʀᴅ.

15"The remaining area, 5,000 cubits wide and 25,000 cubits long, will be for the common use of the city, for houses and for pastureland. The city will be in the center of it **16**and will have these measurements: the north side 4,500 cubits, the south side 4,500 cubits, the east side 4,500 cubits, and the west side 4,500 cubits. **17**The pastureland for the city will be 250 cubits on the north, 250 cubits on the south, 250 cubits on the east, and 250 cubits on the west. **18**What remains of the area, bordering on the sacred portion and running the length of it, will be 10,000 cubits on the east side and 10,000 cubits on the west side. Its produce will supply food for the workers of the city. **19**The workers from the city who farm it will come from all the tribes of Israel. **20**The entire portion will be a square, 25,000 cubits on each side. As a special gift you will set aside the sacred portion, along with the property of the city.

21"What remains on both sides of the area formed by the sacred portion and the city property will belong to the prince. It will extend eastward from the 25,000 cubits of the sacred portion to the eastern border, and westward from the 25,000 cubits to the western border. Both these areas running the length of the tribal portions will belong to the prince, and the sacred portion with the temple sanctuary will be in the center of them. **22**So the property of the Levites and the property of the city will lie in the center of the area that belongs to the prince. The area belonging to the prince will lie between the border of Judah and the border of Benjamin.

23"As for the rest of the tribes: Benjamin will have one portion; it will extend from the east side to the west side.

24"Simeon will have one portion; it will border the territory of Benjamin from east to west.

25"Issachar will have one portion; it will border the territory of Simeon from east to west.

26"Zebulun will have one portion; it will border the territory of Issachar from east to west.

27"Gad will have one portion; it will border the territory of Zebulun from east to west.

28"The southern boundary of Gad will run south from Tamar to the waters of Meribah Kadesh, then along the Wadi ⌊of Egypt⌋ to the Great Sea.*ª*

29"This is the land you are to allot as an inheritance to the tribes of Israel, and these will be their portions," declares the Sovereign Lᴏʀᴅ.

The Gates of the City

30"These will be the exits of the city: Beginning on the north side, which is 4,500 cubits long, **31**the gates of the city will be named after the tribes of Israel. The three gates on the north side will be the gate of Reuben, the gate of Judah and the gate of Levi.

32"On the east side, which is 4,500 cubits long, will be three gates: the gate of Joseph, the gate of Benjamin and the gate of Dan.

33"On the south side, which measures 4,500 cubits, will be three gates: the gate of Simeon, the gate of Issachar and the gate of Zebulun.

34"On the west side, which is 4,500 cubits long, will be three gates: the gate of Gad, the gate of Asher and the gate of Naphtali.

35"The distance all around will be 18,000 cubits.

"And the name of the city from that time on will be:

ᴛʜᴇ Lᴏʀᴅ ɪs ᴛʜᴇʀᴇ."

ª28 That is, the Mediterranean

DANIEL

THOUGH Daniel is a captive in Babylon, he remains obedient to the Lord. Through his adventures he learns that God never forgets his people—even in the most trying circumstances. Through his God-given dreams Daniel learns that God is in control—not only of the present, but also of the future. As you read, ask God to build your commitment to obedience so that you, like Daniel, can rest in the presence of lions.

Outline of Contents

Daniel's Training in Babylon

1 In the third year of the reign of Jehoiakim king of Judah, Nebuchadnezzar king of Babylon came to Jerusalem and besieged it. ²And the Lord delivered Jehoiakim king of Judah into his hand, along with some of the articles from the temple of God. These he carried off to the temple of his god in Babylonia*a* and put in the treasure house of his god.

³Then the king ordered Ashpenaz, chief of his court officials, to bring in some of the Israelites from the royal family and the nobility— ⁴young men without any physical defect, handsome, showing aptitude for every kind of learning, well informed, quick to understand, and qualified to serve in the king's palace. He was to teach them the language and literature of the Babylonians.*b* ⁵The king assigned them a daily amount of food and wine from the king's table. They were to be trained for three years, and after that they were to enter the king's service. ⁶Among these were some from Judah:

a2 Hebrew *Shinar*   *b4* Or *Chaldeans*

THE NECESSITY OF CONVICTION

B randon is new at school. On Friday a classmate says, "Hey, we've got a case of beer in the trunk, and we're heading out to the Point [a popular hangout] tonight. Wanna go?"

In his desire to fit in, Brandon can shrug off his Christian beliefs and go out drinking with the guys. Or Brandon can say: "Hey, I appreciate the offer, but no thanks. Don't get me wrong, I like to have fun, and I'd like to spend some time with you and the guys. But the Point sounds a little too wild for me."

Look It Up
••••

As teenagers Daniel and some other young Israelites were taken from their families and homeland and carried off to Babylon.

No doubt Daniel felt fearful. He must have wondered, "How can I make the best of this situation?" Surely the temptation to compromise was present: "If I just go along with what the Babylonians say, everything will be cool."

The first test came right off the bat. Daniel was offered the king's rich food. Would he violate the strict dietary laws of the Israelite faith?

"But Daniel resolved not to defile himself with the royal food and wine, and he asked the chief official for permission not to defile himself this way" (Daniel 1:8).

Think It Through
••••

Beliefs alone aren't enough to make you stand strong for Christ. You also need convictions. Beliefs are in your head. With enough pressure they can be swayed, challenged—even changed! But convictions are cemented in your heart and no trial is able to dislodge them.

Is your code of conduct a series of loosely held beliefs, or is it a list of rock-solid convictions? Only convictions will keep you from compromise and give you a positive influence on the people in your life.

Work It Out
••••

Sit down and write out your true convictions—those things you feel the strongest about, those principles you are committed to no matter what the cost or risk.

If you have no convictions, or if you have very few, ask God to turn your beliefs into convictions. Ask him to give you the resolve and commitment of Daniel. Tell him you want to have an influence in your school and in your neighborhood.

Nail It Down
••••

Read Daniel 1 for the story of Daniel and his convictions.

Turn to pages 910, 913, 919 and 921 for other readings on influence.
Turn to page 910 for Thursday's reading.

Topic
••••
INFLUENCE

Daniel, Hananiah, Mishael and Azariah. [7]The chief official gave them new names: to Daniel, the name Belteshazzar; to Hananiah, Shadrach; to Mishael, Meshach; and to Azariah, Abednego.

[8]But Daniel resolved not to defile himself with the royal food and wine, and he asked the chief official for permission not to defile himself this way. [9]Now God had caused the official to show favor and sympathy to Daniel, [10]but the official told Daniel, "I am afraid of my lord the king, who has assigned your[a] food and drink. Why should he see you looking worse than the other young men your age? The king would then have my head because of you."

[11]Daniel then said to the guard whom the chief official had appointed over Daniel, Hananiah, Mishael and Azariah, [12]"Please test your servants for ten days: Give us nothing but vegetables to eat and water to drink. [13]Then compare our appearance with that of the young men who ate the royal food, and treat your servants in accordance with what you see." [14]So he agreed to this and tested them for ten days.

[15]At the end of the ten days they looked healthier and better nourished than any of the young men who ate the royal food. [16]So the guard took away their choice food and the wine they were to drink and gave them vegetables instead.

[17]To these four young men God gave knowledge and understanding of all kinds of literature and learning. And Daniel could understand visions and dreams of all kinds.

[18]At the end of the time set by the king to bring them in, the chief official presented them to Nebuchadnezzar. [19]The king talked with them, and he found none equal to Daniel, Hananiah, Mishael and Azariah; so they entered the king's service. [20]In every matter of wisdom and understanding about which the king questioned them, he found them ten times better than all the magicians and enchanters in his whole kingdom.

[21]And Daniel remained there until the first year of King Cyrus.

Nebuchadnezzar's Dream

2 In the second year of his reign, Nebuchadnezzar had dreams; his mind was troubled and he could not sleep. [2]So the king summoned the magicians, enchanters, sorcerers and astrologers[b] to tell him what he had dreamed. When they came in and stood before the king, [3]he said to them, "I have had a dream that troubles me and I want to know what it means.[c]"

[4]Then the astrologers answered the king in Aramaic,[d] "O king, live forever! Tell your servants the dream, and we will interpret it."

[5]The king replied to the astrologers, "This is what I have firmly decided: If you do not tell me what my dream was and interpret it, I will have you cut into pieces and your houses turned into piles of rubble. [6]But if you tell me the dream and explain it, you will receive from me gifts and rewards and great honor. So tell me the dream and interpret it for me."

[7]Once more they replied, "Let the king tell his servants the dream, and we will interpret it."

[8]Then the king answered, "I am certain that you are trying to gain time, because you realize that this is what I have firmly decided: [9]If you do not tell me the dream, there is just one penalty for you. You have conspired to tell me misleading and wicked things, hoping the situation will change. So then, tell me the dream, and I will know that you can interpret it for me."

[10]The astrologers answered the king, "There is not a man on earth who can do what the king asks! No king, however great and mighty, has ever asked such a thing of any magician or enchanter or astrologer. [11]What the king asks is too difficult. No one can reveal it to the king except the gods, and they do not live among men."

[12]This made the king so angry and furious that he ordered the execution of all the wise men of Babylon. [13]So the decree was issued to put the wise men to death, and men were sent to look for Daniel and his friends to put them to death.

[14]When Arioch, the commander of the king's guard, had gone out to put to death the wise men of Babylon, Daniel spoke to him with wisdom and tact. [15]He asked the king's officer, "Why did the king issue such a harsh decree?" Arioch then explained the matter to Daniel. [16]At this, Daniel went in to the king and asked for time, so that he might interpret the dream for him.

[17]Then Daniel returned to his house and explained the matter to his friends Hananiah, Mishael and Azariah. [18]He urged them to plead for mercy from the God of heaven concerning this mystery, so that he and his

---

[a]10 The Hebrew for *your* and *you* in this verse is plural.   [b]2 Or *Chaldeans*; also in verses 4, 5 and 10
[c]3 Or *was*   [d]4 The text from here through chapter 7 is in Aramaic.

friends might not be executed with the rest of the wise men of Babylon. ¹⁹During the night the mystery was revealed to Daniel in a vision. Then Daniel praised the God of heaven ²⁰and said:

"Praise be to the name of God for ever
and ever;
wisdom and power are his.
²¹He changes times and seasons;
he sets up kings and deposes them.
He gives wisdom to the wise
and knowledge to the discerning.
²²He reveals deep and hidden things;
he knows what lies in darkness,
and light dwells with him.
²³I thank and praise you, O God of my
fathers:
You have given me wisdom and
power,
you have made known to me what we
asked of you,
you have made known to us the
dream of the king."

Daniel Interprets the Dream

²⁴Then Daniel went to Arioch, whom the king had appointed to execute the wise men of Babylon, and said to him, "Do not execute the wise men of Babylon. Take me to the king, and I will interpret his dream for him." ²⁵Arioch took Daniel to the king at once and said, "I have found a man among the exiles from Judah who can tell the king what his dream means."

²⁶The king asked Daniel (also called Belteshazzar), "Are you able to tell me what I saw in my dream and interpret it?"

²⁷Daniel replied, "No wise man, enchanter, magician or diviner can explain to the king the mystery he has asked about, ²⁸but there is a God in heaven who reveals mysteries. He has shown King Nebuchadnezzar what will happen in days to come. Your dream and the visions that passed through your mind as you lay on your bed are these: ²⁹"As you were lying there, O king, your mind turned to things to come, and the revealer of mysteries showed you what is going to happen. ³⁰As for me, this mystery has been revealed to me, not because I have greater wisdom than other living men, but so that you, O king, may know the interpretation and that you may understand what went through your mind.

³¹"You looked, O king, and there before you stood a large statue—an enormous, dazzling statue, awesome in appearance. ³²The head of the statue was made of pure gold, its chest and arms of silver, its belly and thighs of bronze, ³³its legs of iron, its feet partly of iron and partly of baked clay. ³⁴While you were watching, a rock was cut out, but not by human hands. It struck the statue on its feet of iron and clay and smashed them. ³⁵Then the iron, the clay, the bronze, the silver and the gold were broken to pieces at the same time and became like chaff on a threshing floor in the summer. The wind swept them away without leaving a trace. But the rock that struck the statue became a huge mountain and filled the whole earth.

³⁶"This was the dream, and now we will interpret it to the king. ³⁷You, O king, are the king of kings. The God of heaven has given you dominion and power and might and glory; ³⁸in your hands he has placed mankind and the beasts of the field and the birds of the air. Wherever they live, he has made you ruler over them all. You are that head of gold.

³⁹"After you, another kingdom will rise, inferior to yours. Next, a third kingdom, one of bronze, will rule over the whole earth. ⁴⁰Finally, there will be a fourth kingdom, strong as iron—for iron breaks and smashes everything—and as iron breaks things to pieces, so it will crush and break all the others. ⁴¹Just as you saw that the feet and toes were partly of baked clay and partly of iron, so this will be a divided kingdom; yet it will have some of the strength of iron in it, even as you saw iron mixed with clay. ⁴²As the toes were partly iron and partly clay, so this kingdom will be partly strong and partly brittle. ⁴³And just as you saw the iron mixed with baked clay, so the people will be a mixture and will not remain united, any more than iron mixes with clay.

⁴⁴"In the time of those kings, the God of heaven will set up a kingdom that will never be destroyed, nor will it be left to another people. It will crush all those kingdoms and bring them to an end, but it will itself endure forever. ⁴⁵This is the meaning of the vision of the rock cut out of a mountain, but not by human hands—a rock that broke the iron, the bronze, the clay, the silver and the gold to pieces.

"The great God has shown the king what will take place in the future. The dream is true and the interpretation is trustworthy."

⁴⁶Then King Nebuchadnezzar fell prostrate before Daniel and paid him honor and ordered that an offering and incense be presented to him. ⁴⁷The king said to Daniel, "Surely your God is the God of gods and the

Lord of kings and a revealer of mysteries, for you were able to reveal this mystery."

48Then the king placed Daniel in a high position and lavished many gifts on him. He made him ruler over the entire province of Babylon and placed him in charge of all its wise men. 49Moreover, at Daniel's request the king appointed Shadrach, Meshach and Abednego administrators over the province of Babylon, while Daniel himself remained at the royal court.

The Image of Gold and the Fiery Furnace

3 King Nebuchadnezzar made an image of gold, ninety feet high and nine feet[a] wide, and set it up on the plain of Dura in the province of Babylon. 2He then summoned the satraps, prefects, governors, advisers, treasurers, judges, magistrates and all the other provincial officials to come to the dedication of the image he had set up. 3So the satraps, prefects, governors, advisers, treasurers, judges, magistrates and all the other provincial officials assembled for the dedication of the image that King Nebuchadnezzar had set up, and they stood before it.

4Then the herald loudly proclaimed, "This is what you are commanded to do, O peoples, nations and men of every language: 5As soon as you hear the sound of the horn, flute, zither, lyre, harp, pipes and all kinds of music, you must fall down and worship the image of gold that King Nebuchadnezzar has set up. 6Whoever does not fall down and worship will immediately be thrown into a blazing furnace."

7Therefore, as soon as they heard the sound of the horn, flute, zither, lyre, harp and all kinds of music, all the peoples, nations and men of every language fell down and worshiped the image of gold that King Nebuchadnezzar had set up.

8At this time some astrologers[b] came forward and denounced the Jews. 9They said to King Nebuchadnezzar, "O king, live forever! 10You have issued a decree, O king, that everyone who hears the sound of the horn, flute, zither, lyre, harp, pipes and all kinds of music must fall down and worship the image of gold, 11and that whoever does not fall down and worship will be thrown into a blazing furnace. 12But there are some Jews whom you have set over the affairs of the

province of Babylon—Shadrach, Meshach and Abednego—who pay no attention to you, O king. They neither serve your gods nor worship the image of gold you have set up."

13Furious with rage, Nebuchadnezzar summoned Shadrach, Meshach and Abednego. So these men were brought before the king, 14and Nebuchadnezzar said to them, "Is it true, Shadrach, Meshach and Abednego, that you do not serve my gods or worship the image of gold I have set up? 15Now when you hear the sound of the horn, flute, zither, lyre, harp, pipes and all kinds of music, if you are ready to fall down and worship the image I made, very good. But if you do not worship it, you will be thrown immediately into a blazing furnace. Then what god will be able to rescue you from my hand?"

16Shadrach, Meshach and Abednego replied to the king, "O Nebuchadnezzar, we do not need to defend ourselves before you in this matter. 17If we are thrown into the blazing furnace, the God we serve is able to save us from it, and he will rescue us from your hand, O king. 18But even if he does not, we want you to know, O king, that we will not serve your gods or worship the image of gold you have set up."

19Then Nebuchadnezzar was furious with Shadrach, Meshach and Abednego, and his attitude toward them changed. He ordered the furnace heated seven times hotter than usual 20and commanded some of the strongest soldiers in his army to tie up Shadrach, Meshach and Abednego and throw them into the blazing furnace. 21So these men, wearing their robes, trousers, turbans and other clothes, were bound and thrown into the blazing furnace. 22The king's command was so urgent and the furnace so hot that the flames of the fire killed the soldiers who took up Shadrach, Meshach and Abednego, 23and these three men, firmly tied, fell into the blazing furnace.

24Then King Nebuchadnezzar leaped to his feet in amazement and asked his advisers, "Weren't there three men that we tied up and threw into the fire?"

They replied, "Certainly, O king."

25He said, "Look! I see four men walking around in the fire, unbound and unharmed, and the fourth looks like a son of the gods."

26Nebuchadnezzar then approached the opening of the blazing furnace and shouted,

---

a1 Aramaic *sixty cubits high and six cubits wide* (about 27 meters high and 2.7 meters wide)   b8 Or *Chaldeans*

THE POWER OF BOLDNESS

Some of Carla's Christian friends have started a once-a-week noontime Bible study at school. These students, in an effort to have more of a witness on campus, bring their Bibles to school and urge other believers to do the same.

Yesterday, Carla was in the hall talking with Paige and Sandi, two of her non-Christian friends. One of the Carla's Christian friends walked by and reminded her, "Hey, don't forget Bible study today at lunch!"

Paige's jaw dropped. "Carla, don't tell me you hang out with the 'Born Agains'?"

Look It Up

Having trouble standing up for Christ? Take a boldness lesson from Daniel and his friends:

At the risk of being burned alive, Shadrach, Meshach and Abednego refused to bow down to an idol. "If we are thrown into the blazing furnace, the God we serve is able to save us from it, and he will rescue us from your hand, O king. But even if he does not, we want you to know, O king, that we will not serve your gods or worship the image of gold you have set up" (Daniel 3:17–18).

And Daniel twice was courageous enough to tell rulers that they would be punished by God because of pride (Daniel 4:24–27; 5:18–31).

Think It Through

Have you ever heard this little song?

> Dare to be a Daniel,
> Dare to stand alone!
> Dare to have a purpose firm!
> Dare to make it known!

Imagine being bold enough to stand up to the leader of a nation, courageous enough to say no to evil—even though it could cost you your life!

What would you have done in the above situations?

Work It Out

Being bold for Christ is risky. Some people will laugh and make fun. But do you know what? They'll also be checking you out to see if your walk matches your talk. And if it does—if they see God at work in your life—those same individuals will be forced to deal with the claims of Christ.

Stand up for Christ today by: saying no to the temptation to cheat; refusing to join the crowd in a wrong activity; sharing your faith in Christ with a friend; taking your Bible to school; inviting others to church or to a youth group function.

Nail It Down

Read more about Daniel and his friends in Daniel 3–4.

Turn to pages 906, 913, 919 and 921 for other readings on influence.
Turn to page 913 for Friday's reading.

Topic

INFLUENCE

"Shadrach, Meshach and Abednego, servants of the Most High God, come out! Come here!"

So Shadrach, Meshach and Abednego came out of the fire, **27**and the satraps, prefects, governors and royal advisers crowded around them. They saw that the fire had not harmed their bodies, nor was a hair of their heads singed; their robes were not scorched, and there was no smell of fire on them.

28Then Nebuchadnezzar said, "Praise be to the God of Shadrach, Meshach and Abednego, who has sent his angel and rescued his servants! They trusted in him and defied the king's command and were willing to give up their lives rather than serve or worship any god except their own God. **29**Therefore I decree that the people of any nation or language who say anything against the God of Shadrach, Meshach and Abednego be cut into pieces and their houses be turned into piles of rubble, for no other god can save in this way."

30Then the king promoted Shadrach, Meshach and Abednego in the province of Babylon.

Nebuchadnezzar's Dream of a Tree

4 King Nebuchadnezzar,

To the peoples, nations and men of every language, who live in all the world:

May you prosper greatly!

2It is my pleasure to tell you about the miraculous signs and wonders that the Most High God has performed for me.

3How great are his signs,
    how mighty his wonders!
His kingdom is an eternal kingdom;
    his dominion endures from
        generation to generation.

4I, Nebuchadnezzar, was at home in my palace, contented and prosperous. **5**I had a dream that made me afraid. As I was lying in my bed, the images and visions that passed through my mind terrified me. **6**So I commanded that all the wise men of Babylon be brought before me to interpret the dream for me. **7**When the magicians, enchanters, as-

trologers*a* and diviners came, I told them the dream, but they could not interpret it for me. **8**Finally, Daniel came into my presence and I told him the dream. (He is called Belteshazzar, after the name of my god, and the spirit of the holy gods is in him.)

9I said, "Belteshazzar, chief of the magicians, I know that the spirit of the holy gods is in you, and no mystery is too difficult for you. Here is my dream; interpret it for me. **10**These are the visions I saw while lying in my bed: I looked, and there before me stood a tree in the middle of the land. Its height was enormous. **11**The tree grew large and strong and its top touched the sky; it was visible to the ends of the earth. **12**Its leaves were beautiful, its fruit abundant, and on it was food for all. Under it the beasts of the field found shelter, and the birds of the air lived in its branches; from it every creature was fed.

13"In the visions I saw while lying in my bed, I looked, and there before me was a messenger,*b* a holy one, coming down from heaven. **14**He called in a loud voice: 'Cut down the tree and trim off its branches; strip off its leaves and scatter its fruit. Let the animals flee from under it and the birds from its branches. **15**But let the stump and its roots, bound with iron and bronze, remain in the ground, in the grass of the field.

" 'Let him be drenched with the dew of heaven, and let him live with the animals among the plants of the earth. **16**Let his mind be changed from that of a man and let him be given the mind of an animal, till seven times*c* pass by for him.

17" 'The decision is announced by messengers, the holy ones declare the verdict, so that the living may know that the Most High is sovereign over the kingdoms of men and gives them to anyone he wishes and sets over them the lowliest of men.'

18"This is the dream that I, King Nebuchadnezzar, had. Now, Belteshazzar, tell me what it means, for none of the wise men in my kingdom can interpret it for me. But you can, because the spirit of the holy gods is in you."

---

a7 Or *Chaldeans*   *b13* Or *watchman*; also in verses 17 and 23   *c16* Or *years*; also in verses 23, 25 and 32

Daniel Interprets the Dream

19Then Daniel (also called Belteshazzar) was greatly perplexed for a time, and his thoughts terrified him. So the king said, "Belteshazzar, do not let the dream or its meaning alarm you."

Belteshazzar answered, "My lord, if only the dream applied to your enemies and its meaning to your adversaries! **20**The tree you saw, which grew large and strong, with its top touching the sky, visible to the whole earth, **21**with beautiful leaves and abundant fruit, providing food for all, giving shelter to the beasts of the field, and having nesting places in its branches for the birds of the air— **22**you, O king, are that tree! You have become great and strong; your greatness has grown until it reaches the sky, and your dominion extends to distant parts of the earth.

23"You, O king, saw a messenger, a holy one, coming down from heaven and saying, 'Cut down the tree and destroy it, but leave the stump, bound with iron and bronze, in the grass of the field, while its roots remain in the ground. Let him be drenched with the dew of heaven; let him live like the wild animals, until seven times pass by for him.'

24"This is the interpretation, O king, and this is the decree the Most High has issued against my lord the king: **25**You will be driven away from people and will live with the wild animals; you will eat grass like cattle and be drenched with the dew of heaven. Seven times will pass by for you until you acknowledge that the Most High is sovereign over the kingdoms of men and gives them to anyone he wishes. **26**The command to leave the stump of the tree with its roots means that your kingdom will be restored to you when you acknowledge that Heaven rules. **27**Therefore, O king, be pleased to accept my advice: Renounce your sins by doing what is right, and your wickedness by being kind to the oppressed. It may be that then your prosperity will continue."

The Dream Is Fulfilled

28All this happened to King Nebuchadnezzar. **29**Twelve months later, as the king was walking on the roof of the royal palace of Babylon, **30**he said, "Is not this the great Babylon I have built as the royal residence, by my mighty power and for the glory of my majesty?"

31The words were still on his lips when a voice came from heaven, "This is what is decreed for you, King Nebuchadnezzar: Your royal authority has been taken from you. **32**You will be driven away from people and will live with the wild animals; you will eat grass like cattle. Seven times will pass by for you until you acknowledge that the Most High is sovereign over the kingdoms of men and gives them to anyone he wishes."

33Immediately what had been said about Nebuchadnezzar was fulfilled. He was driven away from people and ate grass like cattle. His body was drenched with the dew of heaven until his hair grew like the feathers of an eagle and his nails like the claws of a bird.

34At the end of that time, I, Nebuchadnezzar, raised my eyes toward heaven, and my sanity was restored. Then I praised the Most High; I honored and glorified him who lives forever.

His dominion is an eternal dominion;
　his kingdom endures from generation
　　to generation.
35All the peoples of the earth
　are regarded as nothing.
He does as he pleases
　with the powers of heaven
　and the peoples of the earth.
No one can hold back his hand
　or say to him: "What have you done?"

36At the same time that my sanity was restored, my honor and splendor were returned to me for the glory of my kingdom. My advisers and nobles sought me out, and I was restored to my throne and became even greater than before. **37**Now I, Nebuchadnezzar, praise and exalt and glorify the King of heaven, because everything he does is right and all his ways are just. And those who walk in pride he is able to humble.

The Writing on the Wall

5 King Belshazzar gave a great banquet for a thousand of his nobles and drank wine with them. **2**While Belshazzar was drinking his wine, he gave orders to bring in the gold and silver goblets that Nebuchad-

THE IMPORTANCE OF REPUTATION ☐ FRIDAY

D on is a member of a Christian band called LifeRock. The group performs frequently for churches all over his area. *Performs*. That's the perfect word to describe Don. He sings songs about faith and commitment and he goes to church regularly, but talk to the people with whom he hangs out every day. Ask them to tell you how much credibility Don has as a Christian.

In short, Don's reputation stinks.

Look It Up

The Bible says that Christian leaders must be "above reproach" (1 Timothy 3:2). In other words: respectable, of good reputation. That was Daniel. He was respected; his reputation was spotless:

He was "highly esteemed" (Daniel 9:23; 10:11,19).

He was considered extremely wise (Ezekiel 28:3).

He was tactful: "When Arioch, the commander of the king's guard, had gone out to put to death the wise men of Babylon, Daniel spoke to him with wisdom and tact" (Daniel 2:14).

He was known for his spirituality (Daniel 4:8,18; 5:11–12,14).

Think It Through

What do other people honestly think about you? When you're not around, and somehow you become the subject of the conversation of your friends and classmates, what kind of things do you think they say?

Suppose that you *do* have a bad reputation for certain reasons, how could you go about changing the way other people think of you?

Work It Out

The topic today is reputation—making sure yours is respectable. Write down an action that would help correct each of the following bad reputations:

(a) "You're such a liar!"
(b) "Take her out. She'll let you do anything!"
(c) "Don't tell her . . . unless you want it all over the school."
(d) "He'll use anybody to get what he wants!"
(e) "Why are you always such a downer?"
(f) "Oh, great! Here comes Mr. Holy."
(g) "She thinks she's so great!"
(h) "Don't go out with him unless you want to be attacked."
(If any of these apply to you, start working today to change your image!)

Nail It Down

Read about Daniel's wisdom and bravery in Daniel 5—6.

Turn to pages 906, 910, 919 and 921 for other readings on influence.
Turn to page 919 for the weekend reading.

Topic

INFLUENCE

nezzar his father[a] had taken from the temple in Jerusalem, so that the king and his nobles, his wives and his concubines might drink from them. [3]So they brought in the gold goblets that had been taken from the temple of God in Jerusalem, and the king and his nobles, his wives and his concubines drank from them. [4]As they drank the wine, they praised the gods of gold and silver, of bronze, iron, wood and stone.

[5]Suddenly the fingers of a human hand appeared and wrote on the plaster of the wall, near the lampstand in the royal palace. The king watched the hand as it wrote. [6]His face turned pale and he was so frightened that his knees knocked together and his legs gave way.

[7]The king called out for the enchanters, astrologers[b] and diviners to be brought and said to these wise men of Babylon, "Whoever reads this writing and tells me what it means will be clothed in purple and have a gold chain placed around his neck, and he will be made the third highest ruler in the kingdom."

[8]Then all the king's wise men came in, but they could not read the writing or tell the king what it meant. [9]So King Belshazzar became even more terrified and his face grew more pale. His nobles were baffled.

[10]The queen,[c] hearing the voices of the king and his nobles, came into the banquet hall. "O king, live forever!" she said. "Don't be alarmed! Don't look so pale! [11]There is a man in your kingdom who has the spirit of the holy gods in him. In the time of your father he was found to have insight and intelligence and wisdom like that of the gods. King Nebuchadnezzar your father—your father the king, I say—appointed him chief of the magicians, enchanters, astrologers and diviners. [12]This man Daniel, whom the king called Belteshazzar, was found to have a keen mind and knowledge and understanding, and also the ability to interpret dreams, explain riddles and solve difficult problems. Call for Daniel, and he will tell you what the writing means."

[13]So Daniel was brought before the king, and the king said to him, "Are you Daniel, one of the exiles my father the king brought from Judah? [14]I have heard that the spirit of the gods is in you and that you have insight, intelligence and outstanding wisdom. [15]The wise men and enchanters were brought before me to read this writing and tell me what it means, but they could not explain it. [16]Now I have heard that you are able to give interpretations and to solve difficult problems. If you can read this writing and tell me what it means, you will be clothed in purple and have a gold chain placed around your neck, and you will be made the third highest ruler in the kingdom."

[17]Then Daniel answered the king, "You may keep your gifts for yourself and give your rewards to someone else. Nevertheless, I will read the writing for the king and tell him what it means.

[18]"O king, the Most High God gave your father Nebuchadnezzar sovereignty and greatness and glory and splendor. [19]Because of the high position he gave him, all the peoples and nations and men of every language dreaded and feared him. Those the king wanted to put to death, he put to death; those he wanted to spare, he spared; those he wanted to promote, he promoted; and those he wanted to humble, he humbled. [20]But when his heart became arrogant and hardened with pride, he was deposed from his royal throne and stripped of his glory. [21]He was driven away from people and given the mind of an animal; he lived with the wild donkeys and ate grass like cattle; and his body was drenched with the dew of heaven, until he acknowledged that the Most High God is sovereign over the kingdoms of men and sets over them anyone he wishes.

[22]"But you his son,[d] O Belshazzar, have not humbled yourself, though you knew all this. [23]Instead, you have set yourself up against the Lord of heaven. You had the goblets from his temple brought to you, and you and your nobles, your wives and your concubines drank wine from them. You praised the gods of silver and gold, of bronze, iron, wood and stone, which cannot see or hear or understand. But you did not honor the God who holds in his hand your life and all your ways. [24]Therefore he sent the hand that wrote the inscription.

[25]"This is the inscription that was written:

MENE, MENE, TEKEL, PARSIN[e]

[26]"This is what these words mean:

Mene[f]: God has numbered the days of your reign and brought it to an end.

[a]2 Or ancestor; or predecessor; also in verses 11, 13 and 18   [b]7 Or Chaldeans; also in verse 11   [c]10 Or queen mother   [d]22 Or descendant; or successor   [e]25 Aramaic UPARSIN (that is, AND PARSIN)   [f]26 Mene can mean numbered or mina (a unit of money).

²⁷*Tekel*ᵃ: You have been weighed on the scales and found wanting.

²⁸*Peres*ᵇ: Your kingdom is divided and given to the Medes and Persians."

²⁹Then at Belshazzar's command, Daniel was clothed in purple, a gold chain was placed around his neck, and he was proclaimed the third highest ruler in the kingdom.

³⁰That very night Belshazzar, king of the Babylonians,ᶜ was slain, ³¹and Darius the Mede took over the kingdom, at the age of sixty-two.

Daniel in the Den of Lions

6 It pleased Darius to appoint 120 satraps to rule throughout the kingdom, ²with three administrators over them, one of whom was Daniel. The satraps were made accountable to them so that the king might not suffer loss. ³Now Daniel so distinguished himself among the administrators and the satraps by his exceptional qualities that the king planned to set him over the whole kingdom. ⁴At this, the administrators and the satraps tried to find grounds for charges against Daniel in his conduct of government affairs, but they were unable to do so. They could find no corruption in him, because he was trustworthy and neither corrupt nor negligent. ⁵Finally these men said, "We will never find any basis for charges against this man Daniel unless it has something to do with the law of his God."

⁶So the administrators and the satraps went as a group to the king and said: "O King Darius, live forever! ⁷The royal administrators, prefects, satraps, advisers and governors have all agreed that the king should issue an edict and enforce the decree that anyone who prays to any god or man during the next thirty days, except to you, O king, shall be thrown into the lions' den. ⁸Now, O king, issue the decree and put it in writing so that it cannot be altered—in accordance with the laws of the Medes and Persians, which cannot be repealed." ⁹So King Darius put the decree in writing.

¹⁰Now when Daniel learned that the decree had been published, he went home to his upstairs room where the windows opened toward Jerusalem. Three times a day he got down on his knees and prayed, giving thanks to his God, just as he had done before. ¹¹Then these men went as a group and found Daniel praying and asking God for help. ¹²So they went to the king and spoke to him about his royal decree: "Did you not publish a decree that during the next thirty days anyone who prays to any god or man except to you, O king, would be thrown into the lions' den?"

The king answered, "The decree stands—in accordance with the laws of the Medes and Persians, which cannot be repealed."

¹³Then they said to the king, "Daniel, who is one of the exiles from Judah, pays no attention to you, O king, or to the decree you put in writing. He still prays three times a day." ¹⁴When the king heard this, he was greatly distressed; he was determined to rescue Daniel and made every effort until sundown to save him.

¹⁵Then the men went as a group to the king and said to him, "Remember, O king, that according to the law of the Medes and Persians no decree or edict that the king issues can be changed."

¹⁶So the king gave the order, and they brought Daniel and threw him into the lions' den. The king said to Daniel, "May your God, whom you serve continually, rescue you!"

¹⁷A stone was brought and placed over the mouth of the den, and the king sealed it with his own signet ring and with the rings of his nobles, so that Daniel's situation might not be changed. ¹⁸Then the king returned to his palace and spent the night without eating and without any entertainment being brought to him. And he could not sleep.

¹⁹At the first light of dawn, the king got up and hurried to the lions' den. ²⁰When he came near the den, he called to Daniel in an anguished voice, "Daniel, servant of the living God, has your God, whom you serve continually, been able to rescue you from lions?"

²¹Daniel answered, "O king, live forever! ²²My God sent his angel, and he shut the mouths of the lions. They have not hurt me, because I was found innocent in his sight. Nor have I ever done any wrong before you, O king."

²³The king was overjoyed and gave orders to lift Daniel out of the den. And when Daniel was lifted from the den, no wound was found on him, because he had trusted in his God.

ᵃ27 *Tekel* can mean *weighed* or *shekel*.   ᵇ28 *Peres* (the singular of *Parsin*) can mean *divided* or *Persia* or *a half mina* or *a half shekel*.   ᶜ30 Or *Chaldeans*

²⁴At the king's command, the men who had falsely accused Daniel were brought in and thrown into the lions' den, along with their wives and children. And before they reached the floor of the den, the lions overpowered them and crushed all their bones.

²⁵Then King Darius wrote to all the peoples, nations and men of every language throughout the land:

"May you prosper greatly!

²⁶"I issue a decree that in every part of my kingdom people must fear and reverence the God of Daniel.

"For he is the living God
and he endures forever;
his kingdom will not be destroyed,
his dominion will never end.
²⁷He rescues and he saves;
he performs signs and wonders
in the heavens and on the earth.
He has rescued Daniel
from the power of the lions."

²⁸So Daniel prospered during the reign of Darius and the reign of Cyrus*a* the Persian.

Daniel's Dream of Four Beasts

7 In the first year of Belshazzar king of Babylon, Daniel had a dream, and visions passed through his mind as he was lying on his bed. He wrote down the substance of his dream.

²Daniel said: "In my vision at night I looked, and there before me were the four winds of heaven churning up the great sea. ³Four great beasts, each different from the others, came up out of the sea.

⁴"The first was like a lion, and it had the wings of an eagle. I watched until its wings were torn off and it was lifted from the ground so that it stood on two feet like a man, and the heart of a man was given to it.

⁵"And there before me was a second beast, which looked like a bear. It was raised up on one of its sides, and it had three ribs in its mouth between its teeth. It was told, 'Get up and eat your fill of flesh!'

⁶"After that, I looked, and there before me was another beast, one that looked like a leopard. And on its back it had four wings like those of a bird. This beast had four heads, and it was given authority to rule.

⁷"After that, in my vision at night I looked, and there before me was a fourth beast—terrifying and frightening and very powerful. It had large iron teeth; it crushed and de-voured its victims and trampled underfoot whatever was left. It was different from all the former beasts, and it had ten horns.

⁸"While I was thinking about the horns, there before me was another horn, a little one, which came up among them; and three of the first horns were uprooted before it. This horn had eyes like the eyes of a man and a mouth that spoke boastfully.

⁹"As I looked,

"thrones were set in place,
and the Ancient of Days took his seat.
His clothing was as white as snow;
the hair of his head was white like
wool. .
His throne was flaming with fire,
and its wheels were all ablaze.
¹⁰A river of fire was flowing,
coming out from before him.
Thousands upon thousands attended
him;
ten thousand times ten thousand
stood before him.
The court was seated,
and the books were opened.

¹¹"Then I continued to watch because of the boastful words the horn was speaking. I kept looking until the beast was slain and its body destroyed and thrown into the blazing fire. ¹²(The other beasts had been stripped of their authority, but were allowed to live for a period of time.)

¹³"In my vision at night I looked, and there before me was one like a son of man, coming with the clouds of heaven. He approached the Ancient of Days and was led into his presence. ¹⁴He was given authority, glory and sovereign power; all peoples, nations and men of every language worshiped him. His dominion is an everlasting dominion that will not pass away, and his kingdom is one that will never be destroyed.

The Interpretation of the Dream

¹⁵"I, Daniel, was troubled in spirit, and the visions that passed through my mind disturbed me. ¹⁶I approached one of those standing there and asked him the true meaning of all this.

"So he told me and gave me the interpretation of these things: ¹⁷'The four great beasts are four kingdoms that will rise from the earth. ¹⁸But the saints of the Most High will receive the kingdom and will possess it forever—yes, for ever and ever.'

¹⁹"Then I wanted to know the true mean-

---

a28 Or Darius, that is, the reign of Cyrus

ing of the fourth beast, which was different from all the others and most terrifying, with its iron teeth and bronze claws—the beast that crushed and devoured its victims and trampled underfoot whatever was left. **20**I also wanted to know about the ten horns on its head and about the other horn that came up, before which three of them fell—the horn that looked more imposing than the others and that had eyes and a mouth that spoke boastfully. **21**As I watched, this horn was waging war against the saints and defeating them, **22**until the Ancient of Days came and pronounced judgment in favor of the saints of the Most High, and the time came when they possessed the kingdom.

23"He gave me this explanation: 'The fourth beast is a fourth kingdom that will appear on earth. It will be different from all the other kingdoms and will devour the whole earth, trampling it down and crushing it. **24**The ten horns are ten kings who will come from this kingdom. After them another king will arise, different from the earlier ones; he will subdue three kings. **25**He will speak against the Most High and oppress his saints and try to change the set times and the laws. The saints will be handed over to him for a time, times and half a time.*a*

26" 'But the court will sit, and his power will be taken away and completely destroyed forever. **27**Then the sovereignty, power and greatness of the kingdoms under the whole heaven will be handed over to the saints, the people of the Most High. His kingdom will be an everlasting kingdom, and all rulers will worship and obey him.'

28"This is the end of the matter. I, Daniel, was deeply troubled by my thoughts, and my face turned pale, but I kept the matter to myself."

Daniel's Vision of a Ram and a Goat

8 In the third year of King Belshazzar's reign, I, Daniel, had a vision, after the one that had already appeared to me. **2**In my vision I saw myself in the citadel of Susa in the province of Elam; in the vision I was beside the Ulai Canal. **3**I looked up, and there before me was a ram with two horns, standing beside the canal, and the horns were long. One of the horns was longer than the other but grew up later. **4**I watched the ram as he charged toward the west and the north and the south. No animal could stand against him, and none could rescue from his

power. He did as he pleased and became great.

5As I was thinking about this, suddenly a goat with a prominent horn between his eyes came from the west, crossing the whole earth without touching the ground. **6**He came toward the two-horned ram I had seen standing beside the canal and charged at him in great rage. **7**I saw him attack the ram furiously, striking the ram and shattering his two horns. The ram was powerless to stand against him; the goat knocked him to the ground and trampled on him, and none could rescue the ram from his power. **8**The goat became very great, but at the height of his power his large horn was broken off, and in its place four prominent horns grew up toward the four winds of heaven.

9Out of one of them came another horn, which started small but grew in power to the south and to the east and toward the Beautiful Land. **10**It grew until it reached the host of the heavens, and it threw some of the starry host down to the earth and trampled on them. **11**It set itself up to be as great as the Prince of the host; it took away the daily sacrifice from him, and the place of his sanctuary was brought low. **12**Because of rebellion, the host ₍of the saints₎*b* and the daily sacrifice were given over to it. It prospered in everything it did, and truth was thrown to the ground.

13Then I heard a holy one speaking, and another holy one said to him, "How long will it take for the vision to be fulfilled—the vision concerning the daily sacrifice, the rebellion that causes desolation, and the surrender of the sanctuary and of the host that will be trampled underfoot?"

14He said to me, "It will take 2,300 evenings and mornings; then the sanctuary will be reconsecrated."

The Interpretation of the Vision

15While I, Daniel, was watching the vision and trying to understand it, there before me stood one who looked like a man. **16**And I heard a man's voice from the Ulai calling, "Gabriel, tell this man the meaning of the vision."

17As he came near the place where I was standing, I was terrified and fell prostrate. "Son of man," he said to me, "understand that the vision concerns the time of the end."

18While he was speaking to me, I was in a deep sleep, with my face to the ground.

a25 Or for a year, two years and half a year   *b12 Or rebellion, the armies*

Then he touched me and raised me to my feet.

[19]He said: "I am going to tell you what will happen later in the time of wrath, because the vision concerns the appointed time of the end.[a] [20]The two-horned ram that you saw represents the kings of Media and Persia. [21]The shaggy goat is the king of Greece, and the large horn between his eyes is the first king. [22]The four horns that replaced the one that was broken off represent four kingdoms that will emerge from his nation but will not have the same power.

[23]"In the latter part of their reign, when rebels have become completely wicked, a stern-faced king, a master of intrigue, will arise. [24]He will become very strong, but not by his own power. He will cause astounding devastation and will succeed in whatever he does. He will destroy the mighty men and the holy people. [25]He will cause deceit to prosper, and he will consider himself superior. When they feel secure, he will destroy many and take his stand against the Prince of princes. Yet he will be destroyed, but not by human power.

[26]"The vision of the evenings and mornings that has been given you is true, but seal up the vision, for it concerns the distant future."

[27]I, Daniel, was exhausted and lay ill for several days. Then I got up and went about the king's business. I was appalled by the vision; it was beyond understanding.

Daniel's Prayer

9 In the first year of Darius son of Xerxes[b] (a Mede by descent), who was made ruler over the Babylonian[c] kingdom— [2]in the first year of his reign, I, Daniel, understood from the Scriptures, according to the word of the Lord given to Jeremiah the prophet, that the desolation of Jerusalem would last seventy years. [3]So I turned to the Lord God and pleaded with him in prayer and petition, in fasting, and in sackcloth and ashes.

[4]I prayed to the Lord my God and confessed:

"O Lord, the great and awesome God, who keeps his covenant of love with all who love him and obey his commands, [5]we have sinned and done wrong. We have been wicked and have rebelled; we have turned away from your commands and laws. [6]We have not listened to your servants the prophets, who spoke in your name to our kings, our princes and our fathers, and to all the people of the land.

[7]"Lord, you are righteous, but this day we are covered with shame—the men of Judah and people of Jerusalem and all Israel, both near and far, in all the countries where you have scattered us because of our unfaithfulness to you. [8]O Lord, we and our kings, our princes and our fathers are covered with shame because we have sinned against you. [9]The Lord our God is merciful and forgiving, even though we have rebelled against him; [10]we have not obeyed the Lord our God or kept the laws he gave us through his servants the prophets. [11]All Israel has transgressed your law and turned away, refusing to obey you.

"Therefore the curses and sworn judgments written in the Law of Moses, the servant of God, have been poured out on us, because we have sinned against you. [12]You have fulfilled the words spoken against us and against our rulers by bringing upon us great disaster. Under the whole heaven nothing has ever been done like what has been done to Jerusalem. [13]Just as it is written in the Law of Moses, all this disaster has come upon us, yet we have not sought the favor of the Lord our God by turning from our sins and giving attention to your truth. [14]The Lord did not hesitate to bring the disaster upon us, for the Lord our God is righteous in everything he does; yet we have not obeyed him.

[15]"Now, O Lord our God, who brought your people out of Egypt with a mighty hand and who made for yourself a name that endures to this day, we have sinned, we have done wrong. [16]O Lord, in keeping with all your righteous acts, turn away your anger and your wrath from Jerusalem, your city, your holy hill. Our sins and the iniquities of our fathers have made Jerusalem and your people an object of scorn to all those around us.

[17]"Now, our God, hear the prayers and petitions of your servant. For your

---

[a]19 Or because the end will be at the appointed time   [b]1 Hebrew Ahasuerus   [c]1 Or Chaldean

THE IMPACT OF PRAYER

Work It Out •••

On a sheet of paper list the names of five people. Beside each name write what you would like God to accomplish in that person's life. You could write, "salvation" or "healing" or "protection" or whatever the need is. If you want to list two or three needs, go ahead and do that.

Now comes the hard part: commit yourself to praying daily for each person on your list. Don't take the commitment lightly. Be sure you pray every day.

Now get yourself prepared. Prepared for what? For God's answers. Because he will hear your prayers, and he will answer. The answers may not always be exactly what you expected or wanted. But God won't just ignore your request. He will answer your prayer. He has promised.

Nail It Down •••

Read Daniel's prayer in Daniel 9.

Think It Through •••

The most effective way to influence people and situations for good is to pray for them. Many times there doesn't seem to be anything you can do to change a situation or influence a person. But there is always something you can do. You can pray.

Someone once said, "More things are wrought by prayer than this world dreams of." James said the same thing in a little different way: "The prayer of a righteous man is powerful and effective" (James 5:16). God hears your sincere prayers and answers them. That's what makes them "powerful and effective."

Of course, the benefit doesn't all go to the person or situation for whom you're praying. You get some benefits yourself: a closer walk with God and the satisfaction of seeing the lives of others changed. With two such great benefits, what are you waiting for? Why not get started today?

Nail It Down •••

Read Daniel's prayer again in Daniel 9. For further insight read Psalm 86:5–7.

Turn to pages 906, 910, 913 and 921 for other readings on influence.
Turn to page 921 for Monday's reading.

Topic ••••

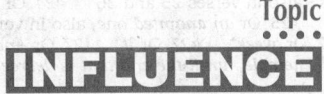

INFLUENCE

sake, O Lord, look with favor on your desolate sanctuary. [18]Give ear, O God, and hear; open your eyes and see the desolation of the city that bears your Name. We do not make requests of you because we are righteous, but because of your great mercy. [19]O Lord, listen! O Lord, forgive! O Lord, hear and act! For your sake, O my God, do not delay, because your city and your people bear your Name."

The Seventy "Sevens"

[20]While I was speaking and praying, confessing my sin and the sin of my people Israel and making my request to the Lord my God for his holy hill— [21]while I was still in prayer, Gabriel, the man I had seen in the earlier vision, came to me in swift flight about the time of the evening sacrifice. [22]He instructed me and said to me, "Daniel, I have now come to give you insight and understanding. [23]As soon as you began to pray, an answer was given, which I have come to tell you, for you are highly esteemed. Therefore, consider the message and understand the vision:

[24]"Seventy 'sevens'[a] are decreed for your people and your holy city to finish[b] transgression, to put an end to sin, to atone for wickedness, to bring in everlasting righteousness, to seal up vision and prophecy and to anoint the most holy.[c]

[25]"Know and understand this: From the issuing of the decree[d] to restore and rebuild Jerusalem until the Anointed One,[e] the ruler, comes, there will be seven 'sevens,' and sixty-two 'sevens.' It will be rebuilt with streets and a trench, but in times of trouble. [26]After the sixty-two 'sevens,' the Anointed One will be cut off and will have nothing.[f] The people of the ruler who will come will destroy the city and the sanctuary. The end will come like a flood: War will continue until the end, and desolations have been decreed. [27]He will confirm a covenant with many for one 'seven.'[g] In the middle of the 'seven'[g] he will put an end to sacrifice and offering. And on a wing of the temple, he will set up an abomination that causes desolation, until the end that is decreed is poured out on him.[h]"[i]

Daniel's Vision of a Man

10 In the third year of Cyrus king of Persia, a revelation was given to Daniel (who was called Belteshazzar). Its message was true and it concerned a great war.[j] The understanding of the message came to him in a vision.

[2]At that time I, Daniel, mourned for three weeks. [3]I ate no choice food; no meat or wine touched my lips; and I used no lotions at all until the three weeks were over.

[4]On the twenty-fourth day of the first month, as I was standing on the bank of the great river, the Tigris, [5]I looked up and there before me was a man dressed in linen, with a belt of the finest gold around his waist. [6]His body was like chrysolite, his face like lightning, his eyes like flaming torches, his arms and legs like the gleam of burnished bronze, and his voice like the sound of a multitude.

[7]I, Daniel, was the only one who saw the vision; the men with me did not see it, but such terror overwhelmed them that they fled and hid themselves. [8]So I was left alone, gazing at this great vision; I had no strength left, my face turned deathly pale and I was helpless. [9]Then I heard him speaking, and as I listened to him, I fell into a deep sleep, my face to the ground.

[10]A hand touched me and set me trembling on my hands and knees. [11]He said, "Daniel, you who are highly esteemed, consider carefully the words I am about to speak to you, and stand up, for I have now been sent to you." And when he said this to me, I stood up trembling.

[12]Then he continued, "Do not be afraid, Daniel. Since the first day that you set your mind to gain understanding and to humble yourself before your God, your words were heard, and I have come in response to them. [13]But the prince of the Persian kingdom resisted me twenty-one days. Then Michael, one of the chief princes, came to help me, because I was detained there with the king of Persia. [14]Now I have come to explain to you what will happen to your people in the future, for the vision concerns a time yet to come."

[15]While he was saying this to me, I bowed with my face toward the ground and was speechless. [16]Then one who looked like a

---

[a]24 Or 'weeks'; also in verses 25 and 26   [b]24 Or restrain   [c]24 Or Most Holy Place; or most holy One
[d]25 Or word   [e]25 Or an anointed one; also in verse 26   [f]26 Or off and will have no one; or off, but not for himself   [g]27 Or 'week'   [h]27 Or it   [i]27 Or And one who causes desolation will come upon the pinnacle of the abominable temple, until the end that is decreed is poured out on the desolated city,   [j]1 Or true and burdensome

THE CRUCIALITY OF CHARACTER

● ●

Paul, a junior at Coolidge High, recently won the Coolidge Leadership Award. This honor is given each year by the student body to the student who best demonstrates high character and leadership ability.

A sophomore girl later explained the vote, "There's nothing fake about Paul. Everybody respects him—even those people who think he's a little too religious. That's because he treats everybody the same, and he's not afraid to stand up for what he believes."

Look It Up
● ● ● ●

Paul's not the only one. In every way and in every situation, Daniel demonstrated godly character.

He possessed such absolute integrity that the worst charge his enemies could pin on him was that he was godly!

They could find no corruption in him, because he was trustworthy and neither corrupt nor negligent. Finally these men said, "We will never find any basis for charges against this man Daniel unless it has something to do with the law of his God" (Daniel 6:5).

He was a standard of human righteousness (Ezekiel 14:14,20).

Think It Through
● ● ● ●

Daniel made an impact even though he was a young man and even though he wasn't a full-time minister (he worked for the Babylonian government). That means excuses like, "I can't do anything—I'm just a kid" and "It's the pastor's job to try to influence others for Christ" just won't wash! Every Christian can be influential if he or she has conviction, a consistent prayer life, boldness, a good reputation and godly character.

Work It Out
● ● ● ●

Reputation and character—they're related but not the same. Reputation is what others think you are. Character is what you really are. Both are important, but character is definitely the more crucial of the two.

Take the big risk of asking a close friend to point out your biggest character flaws. The words might sting, but at least you'll know where to begin work. Once you identify your weaknesses, pick one, pray about it and begin to change.

Nail It Down
● ● ● ●

Continue your study of Daniel by reading Daniel 10—12.

**Turn to pages 906, 910, 913 and 919 for other readings on influence.
Turn to page 932 for Tuesday's reading.**

Topic
● ● ● ●

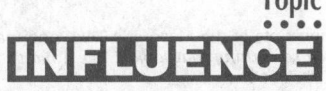

man[a] touched my lips, and I opened my mouth and began to speak. I said to the one standing before me, "I am overcome with anguish because of the vision, my lord, and I am helpless. [17]How can I, your servant, talk with you, my lord? My strength is gone and I can hardly breathe."

[18]Again the one who looked like a man touched me and gave me strength. [19]"Do not be afraid, O man highly esteemed," he said. "Peace! Be strong now; be strong."

When he spoke to me, I was strengthened and said, "Speak, my lord, since you have given me strength."

[20]So he said, "Do you know why I have come to you? Soon I will return to fight against the prince of Persia, and when I go, the prince of Greece will come; [21]but first I will tell you what is written in the Book of Truth. (No one supports me against them except Michael, your prince. [1]And in the first year of Darius the Mede, I took my stand to support and protect him.)

11

The Kings of the South and the North

[2]"Now then, I tell you the truth: Three more kings will appear in Persia, and then a fourth, who will be far richer than all the others. When he has gained power by his wealth, he will stir up everyone against the kingdom of Greece. [3]Then a mighty king will appear, who will rule with great power and do as he pleases. [4]After he has appeared, his empire will be broken up and parceled out toward the four winds of heaven. It will not go to his descendants, nor will it have the power he exercised, because his empire will be uprooted and given to others.

[5]"The king of the South will become strong, but one of his commanders will become even stronger than he and will rule his own kingdom with great power. [6]After some years, they will become allies. The daughter of the king of the South will go to the king of the North to make an alliance, but she will not retain her power, and he and his power[b] will not last. In those days she will be handed over, together with her royal escort and her father[c] and the one who supported her.

[7]"One from her family line will arise to take her place. He will attack the forces of the king of the North and enter his fortress; he will fight against them and be victorious. [8]He will also seize their gods, their metal im-

ages and their valuable articles of silver and gold and carry them off to Egypt. For some years he will leave the king of the North alone. [9]Then the king of the North will invade the realm of the king of the South but will retreat to his own country. [10]His sons will prepare for war and assemble a great army, which will sweep on like an irresistible flood and carry the battle as far as his fortress.

[11]"Then the king of the South will march out in a rage and fight against the king of the North, who will raise a large army, but it will be defeated. [12]When the army is carried off, the king of the South will be filled with pride and will slaughter many thousands, yet he will not remain triumphant. [13]For the king of the North will muster another army, larger than the first; and after several years, he will advance with a huge army fully equipped.

[14]"In those times many will rise against the king of the South. The violent men among your own people will rebel in fulfillment of the vision, but without success. [15]Then the king of the North will come and build up siege ramps and will capture a fortified city. The forces of the South will be powerless to resist; even their best troops will not have the strength to stand. [16]The invader will do as he pleases; no one will be able to stand against him. He will establish himself in the Beautiful Land and will have the power to destroy it. [17]He will determine to come with the might of his entire kingdom and will make an alliance with the king of the South. And he will give him a daughter in marriage in order to overthrow the kingdom, but his plans[d] will not succeed or help him. [18]Then he will turn his attention to the coastlands and will take many of them, but a commander will put an end to his insolence and will turn his insolence back upon him. [19]After this, he will turn back toward the fortresses of his own country but will stumble and fall, to be seen no more.

[20]"His successor will send out a tax collector to maintain the royal splendor. In a few years, however, he will be destroyed, yet not in anger or in battle.

[21]"He will be succeeded by a contemptible person who has not been given the honor of royalty. He will invade the kingdom when its people feel secure, and he will seize it through intrigue. [22]Then an over-

---

[a]16 Most manuscripts of the Masoretic Text; one manuscript of the Masoretic Text, Dead Sea Scrolls and Septuagint *Then something that looked like a man's hand*   [b]6 Or *offspring*   [c]6 Or *child* (see Vulgate and Syriac)   [d]17 Or *but she*

whelming army will be swept away before him; both it and a prince of the covenant will be destroyed. ²³After coming to an agreement with him, he will act deceitfully, and with only a few people he will rise to power. ²⁴When the richest provinces feel secure, he will invade them and will achieve what neither his fathers nor his forefathers did. He will distribute plunder, loot and wealth among his followers. He will plot the overthrow of fortresses — but only for a time.

²⁵"With a large army he will stir up his strength and courage against the king of the South. The king of the South will wage war with a large and very powerful army, but he will not be able to stand because of the plots devised against him. ²⁶Those who eat from the king's provisions will try to destroy him; his army will be swept away, and many will fall in battle. ²⁷The two kings, with their hearts bent on evil, will sit at the same table and lie to each other, but to no avail, because an end will still come at the appointed time. ²⁸The king of the North will return to his own country with great wealth, but his heart will be set against the holy covenant. He will take action against it and then return to his own country.

²⁹"At the appointed time he will invade the South again, but this time the outcome will be different from what it was before. ³⁰Ships of the western coastlands[a] will oppose him, and he will lose heart. Then he will turn back and vent his fury against the holy covenant. He will return and show favor to those who forsake the holy covenant.

³¹"His armed forces will rise up to desecrate the temple fortress and will abolish the daily sacrifice. Then they will set up the abomination that causes desolation. ³²With flattery he will corrupt those who have violated the covenant, but the people who know their God will firmly resist him.

³³"Those who are wise will instruct many, though for a time they will fall by the sword or be burned or captured or plundered. ³⁴When they fall, they will receive a little help, and many who are not sincere will join them. ³⁵Some of the wise will stumble, so that they may be refined, purified and made spotless until the time of the end, for it will still come at the appointed time.

The King Who Exalts Himself

³⁶"The king will do as he pleases. He will exalt and magnify himself above every god and will say unheard-of things against the

God of gods. He will be successful until the time of wrath is completed, for what has been determined must take place. ³⁷He will show no regard for the gods of his fathers or for the one desired by women, nor will he regard any god, but will exalt himself above them all. ³⁸Instead of them, he will honor a god of fortresses; a god unknown to his fathers he will honor with gold and silver, with precious stones and costly gifts. ³⁹He will attack the mightiest fortresses with the help of a foreign god and will greatly honor those who acknowledge him. He will make them rulers over many people and will distribute the land at a price.[b]

⁴⁰"At the time of the end the king of the South will engage him in battle, and the king of the North will storm out against him with chariots and cavalry and a great fleet of ships. He will invade many countries and sweep through them like a flood. ⁴¹He will also invade the Beautiful Land. Many countries will fall, but Edom, Moab and the leaders of Ammon will be delivered from his hand. ⁴²He will extend his power over many countries; Egypt will not escape. ⁴³He will gain control of the treasures of gold and silver and all the riches of Egypt, with the Libyans and Nubians in submission. ⁴⁴But reports from the east and the north will alarm him, and he will set out in a great rage to destroy and annihilate many. ⁴⁵He will pitch his royal tents between the seas at[c] the beautiful holy mountain. Yet he will come to his end, and no one will help him.

The End Times

12 "At that time Michael, the great prince who protects your people, will arise. There will be a time of distress such as has not happened from the beginning of nations until then. But at that time your people — everyone whose name is found written in the book — will be delivered. ²Multitudes who sleep in the dust of the earth will awake: some to everlasting life, others to shame and everlasting contempt. ³Those who are wise[d] will shine like the brightness of the heavens, and those who lead many to righteousness, like the stars for ever and ever. ⁴But you, Daniel, close up and seal the words of the scroll until the time of the end. Many will go here and there to increase knowledge."

⁵Then I, Daniel, looked, and there before me stood two others, one on this bank of the

---

a30 Hebrew *of Kittim*   b39 Or *land for a reward*   c45 Or *the sea and*   d3 Or *who impart wisdom* river and one on the opposite bank. **6**One of them said to the man clothed in linen, who was above the waters of the river, "How long will it be before these astonishing things are fulfilled?"

7The man clothed in linen, who was above the waters of the river, lifted his right hand and his left hand toward heaven, and I heard him swear by him who lives forever, saying, "It will be for a time, times and half a time.*a* When the power of the holy people has been finally broken, all these things will be completed."

8I heard, but I did not understand. So I asked, "My lord, what will the outcome of all this be?"

9He replied, "Go your way, Daniel, because the words are closed up and sealed until the time of the end. **10**Many will be purified, made spotless and refined, but the wicked will continue to be wicked. None of the wicked will understand, but those who are wise will understand.

11"From the time that the daily sacrifice is abolished and the abomination that causes desolation is set up, there will be 1,290 days. **12**Blessed is the one who waits for and reaches the end of the 1,335 days.

13"As for you, go your way till the end. You will rest, and then at the end of the days you will rise to receive your allotted inheritance."

a7 Or a year, two years and half a year

HOSEA

"MARRY whom?" Imagine Hosea's surprise when God tells him to marry Gomer, an adulteress. Because the Israelites are worshiping idols, Hosea's faithless wife is a picture of God's idolatrous people. When Gomer deserts her husband and ends up as a slave, Hosea is commanded to buy her back, for she is still his wife. In the same way God pledges continuing love for his people, even though their spiritual adultery will bring captivity at the hands of Assyria. The message is clear: God is faithful to his people, and his love never fails.

1 The word of the LORD that came to Hosea son of Beeri during the reigns of Uzziah, Jotham, Ahaz and Hezekiah, kings of Judah, and during the reign of Jeroboam son of Jehoash*ᵃ* king of Israel:

Hosea's Wife and Children

2 When the LORD began to speak through Hosea, the LORD said to him, "Go, take to yourself an adulterous wife and children of unfaithfulness, because the land is guilty of the vilest adultery in departing from the LORD." **3** So he married Gomer daughter of Diblaim, and she conceived and bore him a son.

4 Then the LORD said to Hosea, "Call him Jezreel, because I will soon punish the house of Jehu for the massacre at Jezreel, and I will put an end to the kingdom of Israel. **5** In that day I will break Israel's bow in the Valley of Jezreel."

6 Gomer conceived again and gave birth to a daughter. Then the LORD said to Hosea, "Call her Lo-Ruhamah,*ᵇ* for I will no longer show love to the house of Israel, that I should at all forgive them. **7** Yet I will show love to the house of Judah; and I will save them—not by bow, sword or battle, or by horses and horsemen, but by the LORD their God."

8 After she had weaned Lo-Ruhamah, Gomer had another son. **9** Then the LORD said, "Call him Lo-Ammi,*ᶜ* for you are not my people, and I am not your God.

ᵃ1 Hebrew *Joash*, a variant of *Jehoash*   *ᵇ6 Lo-Ruhamah* means *not loved.*   *ᶜ9 Lo-Ammi* means *not my people.*

[10]"Yet the Israelites will be like the sand on the seashore, which cannot be measured or counted. In the place where it was said to them, 'You are not my people,' they will be called 'sons of the living God.' [11]The people of Judah and the people of Israel will be reunited, and they will appoint one leader and will come up out of the land, for great will be the day of Jezreel.

[2] "Say of your brothers, 'My people,' and of your sisters, 'My loved one.'

Israel Punished and Restored

[2]"Rebuke your mother, rebuke her,
    for she is not my wife,
    and I am not her husband.
Let her remove the adulterous look from
    her face
    and the unfaithfulness from between
    her breasts.
[3]Otherwise I will strip her naked
    and make her as bare as on the day
    she was born;
I will make her like a desert,
    turn her into a parched land,
    and slay her with thirst.
[4]I will not show my love to her children,
    because they are the children of
    adultery.
[5]Their mother has been unfaithful
    and has conceived them in disgrace.
She said, 'I will go after my lovers,
    who give me my food and my
    water,
    my wool and my linen, my oil
    and my drink.'
[6]Therefore I will block her path with
    thornbushes;
    I will wall her in so that she cannot
    find her way.
[7]She will chase after her lovers but not
    catch them;
    she will look for them but not find
    them.
Then she will say,
    'I will go back to my husband as at
    first,
    for then I was better off than now.'
[8]She has not acknowledged that I was
    the one
    who gave her the grain, the new wine
    and oil,
    who lavished on her the silver and
    gold—
    which they used for Baal.

[9]"Therefore I will take away my grain
    when it ripens,
    and my new wine when it is ready.
I will take back my wool and my linen,
    intended to cover her nakedness.
[10]So now I will expose her lewdness
    before the eyes of her lovers;
    no one will take her out of my hands.
[11]I will stop all her celebrations:
    her yearly festivals, her New Moons,
    her Sabbath days—all her appointed
    feasts.
[12]I will ruin her vines and her fig trees,
    which she said were her pay from her
    lovers;
I will make them a thicket,
    and wild animals will devour them.
[13]I will punish her for the days
    she burned incense to the Baals;
    she decked herself with rings and
    jewelry,
    and went after her lovers,
    but me she forgot,"
                        declares the LORD.

[14]"Therefore I am now going to allure her;
    I will lead her into the desert
    and speak tenderly to her.
[15]There I will give her back her vineyards,
    and will make the Valley of Achor[a] a
    door of hope.
There she will sing[b] as in the days of
    her youth,
    as in the day she came up out of
    Egypt.

[16]"In that day," declares the LORD,
    "you will call me 'my husband';
    you will no longer call me 'my
    master.[c]'
[17]I will remove the names of the Baals
    from her lips;
    no longer will their names be
    invoked.
[18]In that day I will make a covenant for
    them
    with the beasts of the field and the
    birds of the air
    and the creatures that move along the
    ground.
Bow and sword and battle
    I will abolish from the land,
    so that all may lie down in safety.
[19]I will betroth you to me forever;
    I will betroth you in[d] righteousness
    and justice,
    in[e] love and compassion.

---

[a]15 Achor means trouble.   [b]15 Or respond   [c]16 Hebrew baal   [d]19 Or with; also in verse 20
[e]19 Or with

20I will betroth you in faithfulness,
  and you will acknowledge the LORD.

21"In that day I will respond,"
  declares the LORD—
"I will respond to the skies,
  and they will respond to the earth;
22and the earth will respond to the grain,
  the new wine and oil,
  and they will respond to Jezreel.*a*
23I will plant her for myself in the land;
  I will show my love to the one I
    called 'Not my loved one.'*b*
I will say to those called 'Not my
    people,'*c* 'You are my people';
  and they will say, 'You are my God.' "

Hosea's Reconciliation With His Wife

3 The LORD said to me, "Go, show your love to your wife again, though she is loved by another and is an adulteress. Love her as the LORD loves the Israelites, though they turn to other gods and love the sacred raisin cakes."

2So I bought her for fifteen shekels*d* of silver and about a homer and a lethek*e* of barley. 3Then I told her, "You are to live with*f* me many days; you must not be a prostitute or be intimate with any man, and I will live with*f* you."

4For the Israelites will live many days without king or prince, without sacrifice or sacred stones, without ephod or idol. 5Afterward the Israelites will return and seek the LORD their God and David their king. They will come trembling to the LORD and to his blessings in the last days.

The Charge Against Israel

4 Hear the word of the LORD, you Israelites,
  because the LORD has a charge to
    bring
  against you who live in the land:
"There is no faithfulness, no love,
  no acknowledgment of God in the
    land.
2There is only cursing,*g* lying and
    murder,
  stealing and adultery;
they break all bounds,
  and bloodshed follows bloodshed.
3Because of this the land mourns,*h*
  and all who live in it waste away;

the beasts of the field and the birds of
    the air
  and the fish of the sea are dying.

4"But let no man bring a charge,
  let no man accuse another,
for your people are like those
  who bring charges against a priest.
5You stumble day and night,
  and the prophets stumble with you.
So I will destroy your mother—
6 my people are destroyed from lack of
    knowledge.

"Because you have rejected knowledge,
  I also reject you as my priests;
because you have ignored the law of
    your God,
  I also will ignore your children.
7The more the priests increased,
  the more they sinned against me;
  they exchanged*i* their*j* Glory for
    something disgraceful.
8They feed on the sins of my people
  and relish their wickedness.
9And it will be: Like people, like priests.
  I will punish both of them for their
    ways
  and repay them for their deeds.

10"They will eat but not have enough;
  they will engage in prostitution but
    not increase,
because they have deserted the LORD
  to give themselves 11to prostitution,
to old wine and new,
  which take away the understanding
    12of my people.
They consult a wooden idol
  and are answered by a stick of wood.
A spirit of prostitution leads them
    astray;
  they are unfaithful to their God.
13They sacrifice on the mountaintops
  and burn offerings on the hills,
under oak, poplar and terebinth,
  where the shade is pleasant.
Therefore your daughters turn to
    prostitution
  and your daughters-in-law to adultery.

14"I will not punish your daughters
  when they turn to prostitution,
nor your daughters-in-law
  when they commit adultery,

---

a22 Jezreel means *God plants.*   *b23* Hebrew *Lo-Ruhamah*   *c23* Hebrew *Lo-Ammi*   *d2* That is, about 6 ounces (about 170 grams)   *e2* That is, probably about 10 bushels (about 330 liters)   *f3* Or *wait for* *g2* That is, to pronounce a curse upon   *h3* Or *dries up*   *i7* Syriac and an ancient Hebrew scribal tradition; Masoretic Text *I will exchange*   *j7* Masoretic Text; an ancient Hebrew scribal tradition *my*

because the men themselves consort
with harlots
and sacrifice with shrine prostitutes—
a people without understanding will
come to ruin!

¹⁵"Though you commit adultery, O Israel,
let not Judah become guilty.

"Do not go to Gilgal;
do not go up to Beth Aven.ᵃ
And do not swear, 'As surely as the
LORD lives!'
¹⁶The Israelites are stubborn,
like a stubborn heifer.
How then can the LORD pasture them
like lambs in a meadow?
¹⁷Ephraim is joined to idols;
leave him alone!
¹⁸Even when their drinks are gone,
they continue their prostitution;
their rulers dearly love shameful
ways.
¹⁹A whirlwind will sweep them away,
and their sacrifices will bring them
shame.

Judgment Against Israel

5 "Hear this, you priests!
Pay attention, you Israelites!
Listen, O royal house!
This judgment is against you:
You have been a snare at Mizpah,
a net spread out on Tabor.
²The rebels are deep in slaughter.
I will discipline all of them.
³I know all about Ephraim;
Israel is not hidden from me.
Ephraim, you have now turned to
prostitution;
Israel is corrupt.

⁴"Their deeds do not permit them
to return to their God.
A spirit of prostitution is in their heart;
they do not acknowledge the LORD.
⁵Israel's arrogance testifies against them;
the Israelites, even Ephraim, stumble
in their sin;
Judah also stumbles with them.
⁶When they go with their flocks and
herds
to seek the LORD,
they will not find him;
he has withdrawn himself from them.
⁷They are unfaithful to the LORD;
they give birth to illegitimate children.

Now their New Moon festivals
will devour them and their fields.

⁸"Sound the trumpet in Gibeah,
the horn in Ramah.
Raise the battle cry in Beth Avenᵃ;
lead on, O Benjamin.
⁹Ephraim will be laid waste
on the day of reckoning.
Among the tribes of Israel
I proclaim what is certain.
¹⁰Judah's leaders are like those
who move boundary stones.
I will pour out my wrath on them
like a flood of water.
¹¹Ephraim is oppressed,
trampled in judgment,
intent on pursuing idols.ᵇ
¹²I am like a moth to Ephraim,
like rot to the people of Judah.

¹³"When Ephraim saw his sickness,
and Judah his sores,
then Ephraim turned to Assyria,
and sent to the great king for help.
But he is not able to cure you,
not able to heal your sores.
¹⁴For I will be like a lion to Ephraim,
like a great lion to Judah.
I will tear them to pieces and go away;
I will carry them off, with no one to
rescue them.
¹⁵Then I will go back to my place
until they admit their guilt.
And they will seek my face;
in their misery they will earnestly
seek me."

Israel Unrepentant

6 "Come, let us return to the LORD.
He has torn us to pieces
but he will heal us;
he has injured us
but he will bind up our wounds.
²After two days he will revive us;
on the third day he will restore us,
that we may live in his presence.
³Let us acknowledge the LORD;
let us press on to acknowledge him.
As surely as the sun rises,
he will appear;
he will come to us like the winter rains,
like the spring rains that water the
earth."

⁴"What can I do with you, Ephraim?
What can I do with you, Judah?

ᵃ 15,8 Beth Aven means house of wickedness (a name for Bethel, which means house of God).   ᵇ 11 The
meaning of the Hebrew for this word is uncertain.

Your love is like the morning mist,
  like the early dew that disappears.
5Therefore I cut you in pieces with my
    prophets,
  I killed you with the words of my
    mouth;
  my judgments flashed like lightning
    upon you.
6For I desire mercy, not sacrifice,
  and acknowledgment of God rather
    than burnt offerings.
7Like Adam,*a* they have broken the
    covenant—
  they were unfaithful to me there.
8Gilead is a city of wicked men,
  stained with footprints of blood.
9As marauders lie in ambush for a man,
  so do bands of priests;
  they murder on the road to Shechem,
    committing shameful crimes.
10I have seen a horrible thing
  in the house of Israel.
  There Ephraim is given to prostitution
    and Israel is defiled.

11"Also for you, Judah,
  a harvest is appointed.

"Whenever I would restore the fortunes
    of my people,
7 **1**whenever I would heal Israel,
  the sins of Ephraim are exposed
    and the crimes of Samaria revealed.
  They practice deceit,
    thieves break into houses,
    bandits rob in the streets;
2but they do not realize
  that I remember all their evil deeds.
  Their sins engulf them;
    they are always before me.

3"They delight the king with their
    wickedness,
  the princes with their lies.
4They are all adulterers,
  burning like an oven
  whose fire the baker need not stir
    from the kneading of the dough till it
      rises.
5On the day of the festival of our king
  the princes become inflamed with
    wine,
  and he joins hands with the mockers.
6Their hearts are like an oven;
  they approach him with intrigue.
  Their passion smolders all night;

in the morning it blazes like a flaming
    fire.
7All of them are hot as an oven;
  they devour their rulers.
  All their kings fall,
    and none of them calls on me.

8"Ephraim mixes with the nations;
  Ephraim is a flat cake not turned
    over.
9Foreigners sap his strength,
  but he does not realize it.
  His hair is sprinkled with gray,
    but he does not notice.
10Israel's arrogance testifies against him,
  but despite all this
  he does not return to the LORD his God
    or search for him.

11"Ephraim is like a dove,
  easily deceived and senseless—
  now calling to Egypt,
    now turning to Assyria.
12When they go, I will throw my net over
    them;
  I will pull them down like birds of the
    air.
  When I hear them flocking together,
    I will catch them.
13Woe to them,
  because they have strayed from me!
  Destruction to them,
    because they have rebelled against
      me!
  I long to redeem them
    but they speak lies against me.
14They do not cry out to me from their
    hearts
  but wail upon their beds.
  They gather together*b* for grain and
    new wine
  but turn away from me.
15I trained them and strengthened them,
  but they plot evil against me.
16They do not turn to the Most High;
  they are like a faulty bow.
  Their leaders will fall by the sword
    because of their insolent words.
  For this they will be ridiculed
    in the land of Egypt.

Israel to Reap the Whirlwind

8 "Put the trumpet to your lips!
  An eagle is over the house of the
    LORD
  because the people have broken my
    covenant

---

*a*7 Or *As at Adam*; or *Like men*   *b*14 Most Hebrew manuscripts; some Hebrew manuscripts and Septuagint
They slash themselves

and rebelled against my law.
²Israel cries out to me,
   'O our God, we acknowledge you!'
³But Israel has rejected what is good;
   an enemy will pursue him.
⁴They set up kings without my consent;
   they choose princes without my
      approval.
With their silver and gold
   they make idols for themselves
   to their own destruction.
⁵Throw out your calf-idol, O Samaria!
   My anger burns against them.
How long will they be incapable of
      purity?
⁶   They are from Israel!
This calf—a craftsman has made it;
   it is not God.
It will be broken in pieces,
   that calf of Samaria.

⁷"They sow the wind
   and reap the whirlwind.
The stalk has no head;
   it will produce no flour.
Were it to yield grain,
   foreigners would swallow it up.
⁸Israel is swallowed up;
   now she is among the nations
   like a worthless thing.
⁹For they have gone up to Assyria
   like a wild donkey wandering alone.
   Ephraim has sold herself to lovers.
¹⁰Although they have sold themselves
   among the nations,
   I will now gather them together.
They will begin to waste away
   under the oppression of the mighty
      king.

¹¹"Though Ephraim built many altars for
      sin offerings,
   these have become altars for sinning.
¹²I wrote for them the many things of my
      law,
   but they regarded them as something
      alien.
¹³They offer sacrifices given to me
   and they eat the meat,
   but the Lᴏʀᴅ is not pleased with them.
Now he will remember their wickedness
   and punish their sins:
   They will return to Egypt.
¹⁴Israel has forgotten his Maker
   and built palaces;
   Judah has fortified many towns.
But I will send fire upon their cities
   that will consume their fortresses."

Punishment for Israel

9 Do not rejoice, O Israel;
   do not be jubilant like the other
      nations.
For you have been unfaithful to your
      God;
   you love the wages of a prostitute
   at every threshing floor.
²Threshing floors and winepresses will
      not feed the people;
   the new wine will fail them.
³They will not remain in the Lᴏʀᴅ's land;
   Ephraim will return to Egypt
   and eat unclean^a food in Assyria.
⁴They will not pour out wine offerings to
      the Lᴏʀᴅ,
   nor will their sacrifices please him.
Such sacrifices will be to them like the
      bread of mourners;
   all who eat them will be unclean.
This food will be for themselves;
   it will not come into the temple of the
      Lᴏʀᴅ.

⁵What will you do on the day of your
      appointed feasts,
   on the festival days of the Lᴏʀᴅ?
⁶Even if they escape from destruction,
   Egypt will gather them,
   and Memphis will bury them.
Their treasures of silver will be taken
      over by briers,
   and thorns will overrun their tents.
⁷The days of punishment are coming,
   the days of reckoning are at hand.
   Let Israel know this.
Because your sins are so many
   and your hostility so great,
the prophet is considered a fool,
   the inspired man a maniac.
⁸The prophet, along with my God,
   is the watchman over Ephraim,^{b}
yet snares await him on all his paths,
   and hostility in the house of his
      God.
⁹They have sunk deep into corruption,
   as in the days of Gibeah.
God will remember their wickedness
   and punish them for their sins.

¹⁰"When I found Israel,
   it was like finding grapes in the
      desert;
when I saw your fathers,
   it was like seeing the early fruit on
      the fig tree.
But when they came to Baal Peor,

---

^{a}3 That is, ceremonially unclean ^{b}8 Or *The prophet is the watchman over Ephraim, / the people of my God*

they consecrated themselves to that
   shameful idol
and became as vile as the thing they
   loved.
[11]Ephraim's glory will fly away like a
   bird—
no birth, no pregnancy, no
   conception.
[12]Even if they rear children,
   I will bereave them of every one.
Woe to them
   when I turn away from them!
[13]I have seen Ephraim, like Tyre,
   planted in a pleasant place.
But Ephraim will bring out
   their children to the slayer."

[14]Give them, O LORD—
   what will you give them?
Give them wombs that miscarry
   and breasts that are dry.

[15]"Because of all their wickedness in
   Gilgal,
   I hated them there.
Because of their sinful deeds,
   I will drive them out of my house.
I will no longer love them;
   all their leaders are rebellious.
[16]Ephraim is blighted,
   their root is withered,
   they yield no fruit.
Even if they bear children,
   I will slay their cherished offspring."

[17]My God will reject them
   because they have not obeyed him;
they will be wanderers among the
   nations.

10

Israel was a spreading vine;
   he brought forth fruit for himself.
As his fruit increased,
   he built more altars;
as his land prospered,
   he adorned his sacred stones.
[2]Their heart is deceitful,
   and now they must bear their guilt.
The LORD will demolish their altars
   and destroy their sacred stones.

[3]Then they will say, "We have no king
   because we did not revere the LORD.
But even if we had a king,
   what could he do for us?"
[4]They make many promises,
   take false oaths
   and make agreements;

therefore lawsuits spring up
   like poisonous weeds in a plowed
   field.
[5]The people who live in Samaria fear
   for the calf-idol of Beth Aven.[a]
Its people will mourn over it,
   and so will its idolatrous priests,
those who had rejoiced over its
   splendor,
   because it is taken from them into
   exile.
[6]It will be carried to Assyria
   as tribute for the great king.
Ephraim will be disgraced;
   Israel will be ashamed of its wooden
   idols.[b]
[7]Samaria and its king will float away
   like a twig on the surface of the
   waters.
[8]The high places of wickedness[c] will be
   destroyed—
   it is the sin of Israel.
Thorns and thistles will grow up
   and cover their altars.
Then they will say to the mountains,
   "Cover us!"
   and to the hills, "Fall on us!"

[9]"Since the days of Gibeah, you have
   sinned, O Israel,
   and there you have remained.[d]
Did not war overtake
   the evildoers in Gibeah?
[10]When I please, I will punish them;
   nations will be gathered against them
to put them in bonds for their double
   sin.
[11]Ephraim is a trained heifer
   that loves to thresh;
so I will put a yoke
   on her fair neck.
I will drive Ephraim,
   Judah must plow,
   and Jacob must break up the ground.
[12]Sow for yourselves righteousness,
   reap the fruit of unfailing love,
and break up your unplowed ground;
   for it is time to seek the LORD,
until he comes
   and showers righteousness on you.
[13]But you have planted wickedness,
   you have reaped evil,
   you have eaten the fruit of deception.
Because you have depended on your
   own strength
   and on your many warriors,

---

a5 Beth Aven means house of wickedness (a name for Bethel, which means house of God).   *b6 Or its counsel*
c8 Hebrew aven, a reference to Beth Aven (a derogatory name for Bethel)   *d9 Or there a stand was taken*

UNCOVERING THE REAL DIRT IN YOUR LIFE

Last summer at a Christian youth conference, Jeff told Steve that he had asked Christ into his life and that he really wanted to live for God. Steve was excited.

But when school started, Jeff got more and more involved in the party scene. He went to church less and less. Now he avoids Steve.

"What happened?" Steve asks. "Last summer, Jeff was so fired up about God. Now if I even mention church to him, he looks at me like, 'What are you talking about?' "

Look It Up
• • • •

People respond to God's Word in different ways. Jesus demonstrated this fact in a story about a farmer who threw seed on a path, on rocky ground, among thorns and on good soil.

"This is the meaning of the parable: The seed is the word of God. Those along the path are the ones who hear, and then the devil comes and takes away the word from their hearts, so that they may not believe and be saved. Those on the rock are the ones who receive the word with joy when they hear it, but they have no root. They believe for a while, but in the time of testing they fall away. The seed that fell among thorns stands for those who hear, but as they go on their way they are choked by life's worries, riches and pleasures, and they do not mature. But the seed on good soil stands for those with a noble and good heart, who hear the word, retain it, and by persevering produce a crop" (Luke 8:11–15).

Think It Through
• • • •

Should Steve feel responsible for the way Jeff is responding to God's Word? Is it Steve's fault that Jeff isn't "good soil" at this time?

What kind of soil are you? Are there thorns and weeds in your life that need to be rooted out? Is your heart hard, rocky or good soil?

Work It Out
• • • •

Do you want to sow some seed? Invite your non-Christian friends to youth group. Bring them to hear special speakers or Christian music groups. Remember—your responsibility is to faithfully sow the seed, not to get them to respond in a certain way. It's up to God to work on their hearts.

If you don't think you're good soil, ask God to cause his Word to take root in your life and to produce the good crop he desires.

Nail It Down
• • • •

Read what Hosea has to say about sowing seed in Hosea 10:12.

Turn to pages 1098, 1108 and 1228 for other readings on parables.
Turn to page 939 for Wednesday's reading.

Topic
• • • •

PARABLES

14the roar of battle will rise against your
people,
so that all your fortresses will be
devastated —
as Shalman devastated Beth Arbel on
the day of battle,
when mothers were dashed to the
ground with their children.
15Thus will it happen to you, O Bethel,
because your wickedness is great.
When that day dawns,
the king of Israel will be completely
destroyed.

God's Love for Israel

11 "When Israel was a child, I loved
him,
and out of Egypt I called my son.
2But the more I*a* called Israel,
the further they went from me.*b*
They sacrificed to the Baals
and they burned incense to images.
3It was I who taught Ephraim to walk,
taking them by the arms;
but they did not realize
it was I who healed them.
4I led them with cords of human
kindness,
with ties of love;
I lifted the yoke from their neck
and bent down to feed them.

5"Will they not return to Egypt
and will not Assyria rule over them
because they refuse to repent?
6Swords will flash in their cities,
will destroy the bars of their gates
and put an end to their plans.
7My people are determined to turn from
me.
Even if they call to the Most High,
he will by no means exalt them.

8"How can I give you up, Ephraim?
How can I hand you over, Israel?
How can I treat you like Admah?
How can I make you like Zeboiim?
My heart is changed within me;
all my compassion is aroused.
9I will not carry out my fierce anger,
nor will I turn and devastate Ephraim.
For I am God, and not man —
the Holy One among you.
I will not come in wrath.*c*
10They will follow the Lord;
he will roar like a lion.
When he roars,

his children will come trembling from
the west.
11They will come trembling
like birds from Egypt,
like doves from Assyria.
I will settle them in their homes,"
declares the Lord.

Israel's Sin

12Ephraim has surrounded me with lies,
the house of Israel with deceit.
And Judah is unruly against God,
even against the faithful Holy One.

12 1Ephraim feeds on the wind;
he pursues the east wind all day
and multiplies lies and violence.
He makes a treaty with Assyria
and sends olive oil to Egypt.
2The Lord has a charge to bring against
Judah;
he will punish Jacob*d* according to
his ways
and repay him according to his deeds.
3In the womb he grasped his brother's
heel;
as a man he struggled with God.
4He struggled with the angel and
overcame him;
he wept and begged for his favor.
He found him at Bethel
and talked with him there —
5the Lord God Almighty,
the Lord is his name of renown!
6But you must return to your God;
maintain love and justice,
and wait for your God always.

7The merchant uses dishonest scales;
he loves to defraud.
8Ephraim boasts,
"I am very rich; I have become
wealthy.
With all my wealth they will not find in
me
any iniquity or sin."

9"I am the Lord your God,
⌊who brought you⌋ out of*e* Egypt;
I will make you live in tents again,
as in the days of your appointed
feasts.
10I spoke to the prophets,
gave them many visions
and told parables through them."

11Is Gilead wicked?
Its people are worthless!

---

a2 Some Septuagint manuscripts; Hebrew *they*   *b2* Septuagint; Hebrew *them*   *c9* Or *come against any city*
d2 Jacob means *he grasps the heel* (figuratively, *he deceives*).   *e9* Or *God / ever since you were in*

Do they sacrifice bulls in Gilgal?
Their altars will be like piles of stones
on a plowed field.
[12]Jacob fled to the country of Aram[a];
Israel served to get a wife,
and to pay for her he tended sheep.
[13]The LORD used a prophet to bring Israel
up from Egypt,
by a prophet he cared for him.
[14]But Ephraim has bitterly provoked him
to anger;
his Lord will leave upon him the guilt
of his bloodshed
and will repay him for his contempt.

The LORD's Anger Against Israel

13 When Ephraim spoke, men
trembled;
he was exalted in Israel.
But he became guilty of Baal worship
and died.
[2]Now they sin more and more;
they make idols for themselves from
their silver,
cleverly fashioned images,
all of them the work of craftsmen.
It is said of these people,
"They offer human sacrifice
and kiss[b] the calf-idols."
[3]Therefore they will be like the morning
mist,
like the early dew that disappears,
like chaff swirling from a threshing
floor,
like smoke escaping through a
window.

[4]"But I am the LORD your God,
⌊who brought you⌋ out of[c] Egypt.
You shall acknowledge no God but me,
no Savior except me.
[5]I cared for you in the desert,
in the land of burning heat.
[6]When I fed them, they were satisfied;
when they were satisfied, they
became proud;
then they forgot me.
[7]So I will come upon them like a lion,
like a leopard I will lurk by the path.
[8]Like a bear robbed of her cubs,
I will attack them and rip them open.
Like a lion I will devour them;
a wild animal will tear them apart.
[9]"You are destroyed, O Israel,
because you are against me, against
your helper.

[10]Where is your king, that he may save
you?
Where are your rulers in all your
towns,
of whom you said,
'Give me a king and princes'?
[11]So in my anger I gave you a king,
and in my wrath I took him away.
[12]The guilt of Ephraim is stored up,
his sins are kept on record.
[13]Pains as of a woman in childbirth come
to him,
but he is a child without wisdom;
when the time arrives,
he does not come to the opening of
the womb.

[14]"I will ransom them from the power of
the grave[d];
I will redeem them from death.
Where, O death, are your plagues?
Where, O grave,[d] is your destruction?

"I will have no compassion,
[15]   even though he thrives among his
brothers.
An east wind from the LORD will come,
blowing in from the desert;
his spring will fail
and his well dry up.
His storehouse will be plundered
of all its treasures.
[16]The people of Samaria must bear their
guilt,
because they have rebelled against
their God.
They will fall by the sword;
their little ones will be dashed to the
ground,
their pregnant women ripped open."

Repentance to Bring Blessing

14 Return, O Israel, to the LORD your
God.
Your sins have been your downfall!
[2]Take words with you
and return to the LORD.
Say to him:
"Forgive all our sins
and receive us graciously,
that we may offer the fruit of our
lips.[e]
[3]Assyria cannot save us;
we will not mount war-horses.
We will never again say 'Our gods'
to what our own hands have made,

---

[a]12 That is, Northwest Mesopotamia   [b]2 Or "Men who sacrifice / kiss   [c]4 Or God / ever since you were in
[d]14 Hebrew Sheol   [e]2 Or offer our lips as sacrifices of bulls

for in you the fatherless find
   compassion."

[4]"I will heal their waywardness
   and love them freely,
   for my anger has turned away from
     them.
[5]I will be like the dew to Israel;
   he will blossom like a lily.
Like a cedar of Lebanon
   he will send down his roots;
[6] his young shoots will grow.
His splendor will be like an olive tree,
   his fragrance like a cedar of Lebanon.
[7]Men will dwell again in his shade.
   He will flourish like the grain.

He will blossom like a vine,
   and his fame will be like the wine
     from Lebanon.
[8]O Ephraim, what more have I[a] to do
   with idols?
I will answer him and care for him.
I am like a green pine tree;
   your fruitfulness comes from me."

[9]Who is wise? He will realize these
   things.
Who is discerning? He will understand
   them.
The ways of the LORD are right;
   the righteous walk in them,
   but the rebellious stumble in them.

[a]8 Or *What more has Ephraim*

JOEL

THE locusts come. Suddenly everything green is gone, and famine extends throughout the land. The prophet Joel uses a recent national disaster to warn of an even greater catastrophe: Unless the people repent, an army from the north will devour their land. You may not see a connection between your life and the locusts of Joel's day, but don't be complacent. Repentance can spare you from a personal plague—spiritual "locusts" that might strip you of God's blessing.

Outline of Contents

1 The word of the LORD that came to Joel son of Pethuel.

An Invasion of Locusts

²Hear this, you elders;
  listen, all who live in the land.
Has anything like this ever happened in your days
  or in the days of your forefathers?
³Tell it to your children,
  and let your children tell it to their children,
  and their children to the next generation.
⁴What the locust swarm has left
  the great locusts have eaten;
what the great locusts have left
  the young locusts have eaten;
what the young locusts have left
  other locusts*a* have eaten.

⁵Wake up, you drunkards, and weep!
  Wail, all you drinkers of wine;
wail because of the new wine,
  for it has been snatched from your lips.
⁶A nation has invaded my land,
  powerful and without number;
it has the teeth of a lion,
  the fangs of a lioness.
⁷It has laid waste my vines
  and ruined my fig trees.
It has stripped off their bark
  and thrown it away,
  leaving their branches white.

---

a4 The precise meaning of the four Hebrew words used here for locusts is uncertain.

8Mourn like a virgin[a] in sackcloth
    grieving for the husband[b] of her
        youth.
9Grain offerings and drink offerings
    are cut off from the house of the
        Lord.
The priests are in mourning,
    those who minister before the Lord.
10The fields are ruined,
    the ground is dried up[c];
the grain is destroyed,
    the new wine is dried up,
    the oil fails.
11Despair, you farmers,
    wail, you vine growers;
grieve for the wheat and the barley,
    because the harvest of the field is
        destroyed.
12The vine is dried up
    and the fig tree is withered;
the pomegranate, the palm and the
        apple tree—
    all the trees of the field—are dried
        up.
Surely the joy of mankind
    is withered away.

A Call to Repentance

13Put on sackcloth, O priests, and mourn;
    wail, you who minister before the
        altar.
Come, spend the night in sackcloth,
    you who minister before my God;
for the grain offerings and drink
        offerings
    are withheld from the house of your
        God.
14Declare a holy fast;
    call a sacred assembly.
Summon the elders
    and all who live in the land
to the house of the Lord your God,
    and cry out to the Lord.

15Alas for that day!
    For the day of the Lord is near;
    it will come like destruction from the
        Almighty.[d]

16Has not the food been cut off
    before our very eyes—
joy and gladness
    from the house of our God?
17The seeds are shriveled
    beneath the clods.[e]
The storehouses are in ruins,
    the granaries have been broken down,

for the grain has dried up.
18How the cattle moan!
    The herds mill about
because they have no pasture;
    even the flocks of sheep are suffering.

19To you, O Lord, I call,
    for fire has devoured the open
        pastures
    and flames have burned up all the
        trees of the field.
20Even the wild animals pant for you;
    the streams of water have dried up
    and fire has devoured the open
        pastures.

An Army of Locusts

2 Blow the trumpet in Zion;
    sound the alarm on my holy hill.
Let all who live in the land tremble,
    for the day of the Lord is coming.
It is close at hand—
2   a day of darkness and gloom,
    a day of clouds and blackness.
Like dawn spreading across the
        mountains
    a large and mighty army comes,
such as never was of old
    nor ever will be in ages to come.

3Before them fire devours,
    behind them a flame blazes.
Before them the land is like the garden
        of Eden,
    behind them, a desert waste—
        nothing escapes them.
4They have the appearance of horses;
    they gallop along like cavalry.
5With a noise like that of chariots
    they leap over the mountaintops,
like a crackling fire consuming stubble,
    like a mighty army drawn up for
        battle.
6At the sight of them, nations are in
        anguish;
    every face turns pale.
7They charge like warriors;
    they scale walls like soldiers.
They all march in line,
    not swerving from their course.
8They do not jostle each other;
    each marches straight ahead.
They plunge through defenses
    without breaking ranks.
9They rush upon the city;
    they run along the wall.

---

[a]8 Or *young woman*   [b]8 Or *betrothed*   [c]10 Or *ground mourns*   [d]15 Hebrew *Shaddai*   [e]17 The
meaning of the Hebrew for this word is uncertain.

They climb into the houses;
  like thieves they enter through the
    windows.

¹⁰Before them the earth shakes,
  the sky trembles,
the sun and moon are darkened,
  and the stars no longer shine.
¹¹The LORD thunders
  at the head of his army;
his forces are beyond number,
  and mighty are those who obey his
    command.
The day of the LORD is great;
  it is dreadful.
Who can endure it?

Rend Your Heart

¹²"Even now," declares the LORD,
  "return to me with all your heart,
  with fasting and weeping and
    mourning."

¹³Rend your heart
  and not your garments.
Return to the LORD your God,
  for he is gracious and compassionate,
slow to anger and abounding in love,
  and he relents from sending calamity.
¹⁴Who knows? He may turn and have pity
  and leave behind a blessing—
grain offerings and drink offerings
  for the LORD your God.

¹⁵Blow the trumpet in Zion,
  declare a holy fast,
  call a sacred assembly.
¹⁶Gather the people,
  consecrate the assembly;
bring together the elders,
  gather the children,
  those nursing at the breast.
Let the bridegroom leave his room
  and the bride her chamber.
¹⁷Let the priests, who minister before the
    LORD,
  weep between the temple porch and
    the altar.
Let them say, "Spare your people,
  O LORD.
Do not make your inheritance an
  object of scorn,
a byword among the nations.
Why should they say among the
  peoples,
'Where is their God?'"

The LORD's Answer

¹⁸Then the LORD will be jealous for his
    land
  and take pity on his people.

¹⁹The LORD will reply[a] to them:

"I am sending you grain, new wine and
    oil,
  enough to satisfy you fully;
never again will I make you
  an object of scorn to the nations.

²⁰"I will drive the northern army far from
    you,
  pushing it into a parched and barren
    land,
with its front columns going into the
    eastern sea[b]
  and those in the rear into the western
    sea.[c]
And its stench will go up;
  its smell will rise."

Surely he has done great things.[d]
21   Be not afraid, O land;
    be glad and rejoice.
Surely the LORD has done great things.
22   Be not afraid, O wild animals,
    for the open pastures are becoming
      green.
The trees are bearing their fruit;
  the fig tree and the vine yield their
    riches.
²³Be glad, O people of Zion,
  rejoice in the LORD your God,
for he has given you
  the autumn rains in righteousness.[e]
He sends you abundant showers,
  both autumn and spring rains, as
    before.
²⁴The threshing floors will be filled with
    grain;
  the vats will overflow with new wine
    and oil.

²⁵"I will repay you for the years the
    locusts have eaten—
  the great locust and the young locust,
  the other locusts and the locust
    swarm[f]—
my great army that I sent among you.
²⁶You will have plenty to eat, until you
    are full,
  and you will praise the name of the
    LORD your God,
  who has worked wonders for you;

ᵃ18,19 Or LORD was jealous . . . / and took pity . . . / ¹⁹The LORD replied   ᵇ20 That is, the Dead Sea
ᶜ20 That is, the Mediterranean   ᵈ20 Or rise. / Surely it has done great things."   ᵉ23 Or / the teacher for
righteousness: ᶠ25 The precise meaning of the four Hebrew words used here for locusts is uncertain.

WHY ARE YOU SO GOOD TO ME, LORD?

Fifteen-year-old Rachel is lying in a girls' bunkhouse at a missionary compound in Haiti. In the last five days she has witnessed abject poverty (both material and spiritual). She has seen people wracked by sickness (of both body and soul). This afternoon she visited an orphanage where dozens of kids have bloated bellies and bleak futures.

As she listens to the chorus of crickets outside, she prays, "God, why are you so good to me? Why was I born into a Christian family, a loving home with so many material blessings?"

Look It Up
••••

Certain circumstances create strong feelings of gratitude within us. Sometimes we may even feel like falling on our faces and thanking God for how good he has been to us.

Many of the psalms were written during times when God's people were overcome by strong feelings of thanksgiving, but consider just one—Psalm 65.

> Praise awaits you, O God, in Zion;
>   to you our vows will be fulfilled.
> When we were overwhelmed by sins,
>   you forgave our transgressions.
> Blessed are those you choose
>   and bring near to live in your courts!
> We are filled with the good things of your house,
>   of your holy temple.
> The streams of God are filled with water
>   to provide the people with grain,
>   for so you have ordained it (Psalm 65:1,3–4,9).

Think It Through
••••

When was the last time you found yourself overwhelmed by feelings like the ones Rachel felt on her mission trip?

Why do you think God has so abundantly blessed this nation and the Christians in this nation?

What blessings are you most grateful for?

Work It Out
••••

Don't wait until Thanksgiving rolls around to express your thanks to God. Make a list of the things for which you are grateful. Then spend some time telling God you appreciate what he has done.

Guess what? Even if you don't feel thankful right now, chances are you *will* by the time you finish this exercise!

Nail It Down
••••

Read Joel 2:12–14 to discover that God will respond with blessings when we are true to him.

Turn to pages 572, 686, 694, 1026, 1148 and 1178 for other readings on feelings.
Turn to page 947 for Thursday's reading.

Topic
••••

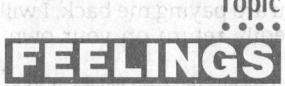

never again will my people be shamed.
²⁷Then you will know that I am in Israel,
  that I am the Lord your God,
  and that there is no other;
never again will my people be shamed.

The Day of the Lord

²⁸"And afterward,
  I will pour out my Spirit on all
    people.
Your sons and daughters will prophesy,
  your old men will dream dreams,
  your young men will see visions.
²⁹Even on my servants, both men and
    women,
  I will pour out my Spirit in those
    days.
³⁰I will show wonders in the heavens
    and on the earth,
  blood and fire and billows of smoke.
³¹The sun will be turned to darkness
    and the moon to blood
  before the coming of the great and
    dreadful day of the Lord.
³²And everyone who calls
  on the name of the Lord will be
    saved;
for on Mount Zion and in Jerusalem
  there will be deliverance,
  as the Lord has said,
among the survivors
  whom the Lord calls.

The Nations Judged

3 "In those days and at that time,
  when I restore the fortunes of Judah
    and Jerusalem,
²I will gather all nations
  and bring them down to the Valley of
    Jehoshaphat.ᵃ
There I will enter into judgment against
    them
  concerning my inheritance, my people
    Israel,
for they scattered my people among the
    nations
  and divided up my land.
³They cast lots for my people
  and traded boys for prostitutes;
they sold girls for wine
  that they might drink.

⁴"Now what have you against me, O Tyre
and Sidon and all you regions of Philistia?
Are you repaying me for something I have
done? If you are paying me back, I will swiftly and speedily return on your own heads

what you have done. ⁵For you took my silver
and my gold and carried off my finest treasures to your temples. ⁶You sold the people
of Judah and Jerusalem to the Greeks, that
you might send them far from their homeland.

⁷"See, I am going to rouse them out of the
places to which you sold them, and I will
return on your own heads what you have
done. ⁸I will sell your sons and daughters to
the people of Judah, and they will sell them
to the Sabeans, a nation far away." The Lord
has spoken.

⁹Proclaim this among the nations:
  Prepare for war!
Rouse the warriors!
  Let all the fighting men draw near
    and attack.
¹⁰Beat your plowshares into swords
  and your pruning hooks into spears.
Let the weakling say,
  "I am strong!"
¹¹Come quickly, all you nations from
    every side,
  and assemble there.

Bring down your warriors, O Lord!

¹²"Let the nations be roused;
  let them advance into the Valley of
    Jehoshaphat,
for there I will sit
  to judge all the nations on every side.
¹³Swing the sickle,
  for the harvest is ripe.
Come, trample the grapes,
  for the winepress is full
  and the vats overflow—
so great is their wickedness!"

¹⁴Multitudes, multitudes
  in the valley of decision!
For the day of the Lord is near
  in the valley of decision.
¹⁵The sun and moon will be darkened,
  and the stars no longer shine.
¹⁶The Lord will roar from Zion
  and thunder from Jerusalem;
  the earth and the sky will tremble.
But the Lord will be a refuge for his
    people,
  a stronghold for the people of Israel.

Blessings for God's People

¹⁷"Then you will know that I, the Lord
    your God,
  dwell in Zion, my holy hill.
Jerusalem will be holy;

ᵃ2 Jehoshaphat means the Lord judges; also in verse 12.

never again will foreigners invade her.

18"In that day the mountains will drip
        new wine,
    and the hills will flow with milk;
    all the ravines of Judah will run with
        water.
    A fountain will flow out of the Lord's
        house
    and will water the valley of acacias.ª
19But Egypt will be desolate,
    Edom a desert waste,

because of violence done to the people
        of Judah,
    in whose land they shed innocent
        blood.
20Judah will be inhabited forever
    and Jerusalem through all
        generations.
21Their bloodguilt, which I have not
        pardoned,
    I will pardon."

The Lord dwells in Zion!

AMOS

ISRAEL looks peaceful, prosperous and secure. But that's on the outside. Underneath the surface of respectability bubbles a rotten sewer of immorality, oppression, injustice and apostasy. So when the prophet Amos symbolically holds up the plumbline of God's perfect standard, the crookedness of the nation is exposed. As you think of Amos and his plumbline, don't forget that confessing your sin and repenting will bring you in line with God's will.

Outline of Contents

1 The words of Amos, one of the shepherds of Tekoa—what he saw concerning Israel two years before the earthquake, when Uzziah was king of Judah and Jeroboam son of Jehoash*a* was king of Israel. ²He said:

"The Lord roars from Zion
  and thunders from Jerusalem;
the pastures of the shepherds dry up,*b*
  and the top of Carmel withers."

Judgment on Israel's Neighbors

³This is what the Lord says:

"For three sins of Damascus,
  even for four, I will not turn back ⌊my wrath⌋.
Because she threshed Gilead
  with sledges having iron teeth,
⁴I will send fire upon the house of Hazael
  that will consume the fortresses of Ben-Hadad.
⁵I will break down the gate of Damascus;
  I will destroy the king who is in*c* the Valley of Aven*d*
and the one who holds the scepter in Beth Eden.

---

*a*1 Hebrew *Joash*, a variant of *Jehoash*   *b*2 Or *shepherds mourn*   *c*5 Or *the inhabitants of*   *d*5 *Aven* means *wickedness*.

The people of Aram will go into exile
  to Kir,"
                          says the LORD.

6This is what the LORD says:

"For three sins of Gaza,
  even for four, I will not turn back ⌐my
    wrath⌐.
Because she took captive whole
    communities
  and sold them to Edom,
7I will send fire upon the walls of Gaza
  that will consume her fortresses.
8I will destroy the king*a* of Ashdod
  and the one who holds the scepter in
    Ashkelon.
I will turn my hand against Ekron,
  till the last of the Philistines is dead,"
                    says the Sovereign LORD.

9This is what the LORD says:

"For three sins of Tyre,
  even for four, I will not turn back ⌐my
    wrath⌐.
Because she sold whole communities of
    captives to Edom,
  disregarding a treaty of brotherhood,
10I will send fire upon the walls of Tyre
  that will consume her fortresses."

11This is what the LORD says:

"For three sins of Edom,
  even for four, I will not turn back ⌐my
    wrath⌐.
Because he pursued his brother with a
    sword,
  stifling all compassion,*b*
because his anger raged continually
  and his fury flamed unchecked,
12I will send fire upon Teman
  that will consume the fortresses of
    Bozrah."

13This is what the LORD says:

"For three sins of Ammon,
  even for four, I will not turn back ⌐my
    wrath⌐.
Because he ripped open the pregnant
    women of Gilead
  in order to extend his borders,
14I will set fire to the walls of Rabbah
  that will consume her fortresses
amid war cries on the day of battle,
  amid violent winds on a stormy day.
15Her king*c* will go into exile,

he and his officials together,"
                          says the LORD.

2 This is what the LORD says:

"For three sins of Moab,
  even for four, I will not turn back ⌐my
    wrath⌐.
Because he burned, as if to lime,
  the bones of Edom's king,
2I will send fire upon Moab
  that will consume the fortresses of
    Kerioth.*d*
Moab will go down in great tumult
  amid war cries and the blast of the
    trumpet.
3I will destroy her ruler
  and kill all her officials with him,"
                          says the LORD.

4This is what the LORD says:

"For three sins of Judah,
  even for four, I will not turn back ⌐my
    wrath⌐.
Because they have rejected the law of
    the LORD
  and have not kept his decrees,
because they have been led astray by
    false gods,*e*
  the gods*f* their ancestors followed,
5I will send fire upon Judah
  that will consume the fortresses of
    Jerusalem."

Judgment on Israel

6This is what the LORD says:

"For three sins of Israel,
  even for four, I will not turn back ⌐my
    wrath⌐.
They sell the righteous for silver,
  and the needy for a pair of sandals.
7They trample on the heads of the poor
  as upon the dust of the ground
  and deny justice to the oppressed.
Father and son use the same girl
  and so profane my holy name.
8They lie down beside every altar
  on garments taken in pledge.
In the house of their god
  they drink wine taken as fines.
9"I destroyed the Amorite before them,
  though he was tall as the cedars
  and strong as the oaks.
I destroyed his fruit above
  and his roots below.

---

a8 Or inhabitants   *b11 Or sword / and destroyed his allies*   *c15 Or / Molech;* Hebrew *malcam*   *d2 Or of*
her cities   *e4 Or by lies*   *f4 Or lies*

¹⁰"I brought you up out of Egypt,
  and I led you forty years in the desert
  to give you the land of the Amorites.
¹¹I also raised up prophets from among
      your sons
  and Nazirites from among your young
      men.
  Is this not true, people of Israel?"
                    declares the LORD.
¹²"But you made the Nazirites drink wine
  and commanded the prophets not to
      prophesy.

¹³"Now then, I will crush you
  as a cart crushes when loaded with
      grain.
¹⁴The swift will not escape,
  the strong will not muster their
      strength,
  and the warrior will not save his life.
¹⁵The archer will not stand his ground,
  the fleet-footed soldier will not get
      away,
  and the horseman will not save his
      life.
¹⁶Even the bravest warriors
  will flee naked on that day,"
                    declares the LORD.

Witnesses Summoned Against Israel

3 Hear this word the LORD has spoken
  against you, O people of Israel—
against the whole family I brought up out of
Egypt:

²"You only have I chosen
  of all the families of the earth;
therefore I will punish you
  for all your sins."

³Do two walk together
  unless they have agreed to do so?
⁴Does a lion roar in the thicket
  when he has no prey?
Does he growl in his den
  when he has caught nothing?
⁵Does a bird fall into a trap on the
      ground
  where no snare has been set?
Does a trap spring up from the earth
  when there is nothing to catch?
⁶When a trumpet sounds in a city,
  do not the people tremble?
When disaster comes to a city,
  has not the LORD caused it?

⁷Surely the Sovereign LORD does nothing
  without revealing his plan
  to his servants the prophets.

⁸The lion has roared—
  who will not fear?
The Sovereign LORD has spoken—
  who can but prophesy?

⁹Proclaim to the fortresses of Ashdod
  and to the fortresses of Egypt:
"Assemble yourselves on the mountains
    of Samaria;
  see the great unrest within her
  and the oppression among her
      people."

¹⁰"They do not know how to do right,"
    declares the LORD,
  "who hoard plunder and loot in their
      fortresses."

¹¹Therefore this is what the Sovereign
LORD says:

"An enemy will overrun the land;
  he will pull down your strongholds
  and plunder your fortresses."

¹²This is what the LORD says:

"As a shepherd saves from the lion's
      mouth
  only two leg bones or a piece of an
      ear,
  so will the Israelites be saved,
those who sit in Samaria
  on the edge of their beds
  and in Damascus on their couches.ᵃ"

¹³"Hear this and testify against the house
of Jacob," declares the Lord, the LORD God
Almighty.

¹⁴"On the day I punish Israel for her sins,
  I will destroy the altars of Bethel;
the horns of the altar will be cut off
  and fall to the ground.
¹⁵I will tear down the winter house
  along with the summer house;
the houses adorned with ivory will be
      destroyed
  and the mansions will be
      demolished,"
                    declares the LORD.

Israel Has Not Returned to God

4 Hear this word, you cows of Bashan
    on Mount Samaria,
  you women who oppress the poor
    and crush the needy
  and say to your husbands, "Bring us
      some drinks!"
²The Sovereign LORD has sworn by his
      holiness:

ᵃ12 The meaning of the Hebrew for this line is uncertain.

"The time will surely come
when you will be taken away with
  hooks,
  the last of you with fishhooks.
³You will each go straight out
  through breaks in the wall,
  and you will be cast out toward
  Harmon,ᵃ"
                              declares the Lᴏʀᴅ.
⁴"Go to Bethel and sin;
  go to Gilgal and sin yet more.
Bring your sacrifices every morning,
  your tithes every three years.ᵇ
⁵Burn leavened bread as a thank offering
  and brag about your freewill
    offerings—
boast about them, you Israelites,
  for this is what you love to do,"
                      declares the Sovereign Lᴏʀᴅ.

⁶"I gave you empty stomachsᶜ in every
    city
  and lack of bread in every town,
  yet you have not returned to me,"
                              declares the Lᴏʀᴅ.

⁷"I also withheld rain from you
  when the harvest was still three
    months away.
I sent rain on one town,
  but withheld it from another.
One field had rain;
  another had none and dried up.
⁸People staggered from town to town for
    water
  but did not get enough to drink,
  yet you have not returned to me,"
                              declares the Lᴏʀᴅ.

⁹"Many times I struck your gardens and
    vineyards,
  I struck them with blight and mildew.
Locusts devoured your fig and olive
    trees,
  yet you have not returned to me,"
                              declares the Lᴏʀᴅ.

¹⁰"I sent plagues among you
  as I did to Egypt.
I killed your young men with the sword,
  along with your captured horses.
I filled your nostrils with the stench of
    your camps,
  yet you have not returned to me,"
                              declares the Lᴏʀᴅ.

¹¹"I overthrew some of you

as Iᵈ overthrew Sodom and
    Gomorrah.
You were like a burning stick snatched
    from the fire,
  yet you have not returned to me,"
                              declares the Lᴏʀᴅ.

¹²"Therefore this is what I will do to you,
    Israel,
  and because I will do this to you,
  prepare to meet your God, O Israel."

¹³He who forms the mountains,
  creates the wind,
  and reveals his thoughts to man,
he who turns dawn to darkness,
  and treads the high places of the
    earth—
  the Lᴏʀᴅ God Almighty is his name.

A Lament and Call to Repentance

5 Hear this word, O house of Israel, this
  lament I take up concerning you:

²"Fallen is Virgin Israel,
  never to rise again,
deserted in her own land,
  with no one to lift her up."

³This is what the Sovereign Lᴏʀᴅ says:

"The city that marches out a thousand
    strong for Israel
  will have only a hundred left;
the town that marches out a hundred
    strong
  will have only ten left."

⁴This is what the Lᴏʀᴅ says to the house
of Israel:

"Seek me and live;
⁵ do not seek Bethel,
do not go to Gilgal,
  do not journey to Beersheba.
For Gilgal will surely go into exile,
  and Bethel will be reduced to
    nothing.ᵉ"
⁶Seek the Lᴏʀᴅ and live,
  or he will sweep through the house of
    Joseph like a fire;
it will devour,
  and Bethel will have no one to
    quench it.

⁷You who turn justice into bitterness
  and cast righteousness to the ground
⁸(he who made the Pleiades and Orion,
  who turns blackness into dawn

ᵃ3 Masoretic Text; with a different word division of the Hebrew (see Septuagint) *out, O mountain of oppression*
ᵇ4 Or *tithes on the third day*   ᶜ6 Hebrew *you cleanness of teeth*   ᵈ11 Hebrew *God*   ᵉ5 Or *grief*; or
wickedness; Hebrew *aven*, a reference to Beth Aven (a derogatory name for Bethel)

and darkens day into night,
who calls for the waters of the sea
  and pours them out over the face of
    the land—
  the Lord is his name—
⁹he flashes destruction on the stronghold
  and brings the fortified city to ruin),
¹⁰you hate the one who reproves in court
  and despise him who tells the truth.

¹¹You trample on the poor
  and force him to give you grain.
  Therefore, though you have built stone
    mansions,
  you will not live in them;
  though you have planted lush vineyards,
  you will not drink their wine.
¹²For I know how many are your offenses
  and how great your sins.

You oppress the righteous and take
  bribes
  and you deprive the poor of justice in
    the courts.
¹³Therefore the prudent man keeps quiet
  in such times,
  for the times are evil.

¹⁴Seek good, not evil,
  that you may live.
  Then the Lord God Almighty will be with
    you,
  just as you say he is.
¹⁵Hate evil, love good;
  maintain justice in the courts.
  Perhaps the Lord God Almighty will
    have mercy
  on the remnant of Joseph.

¹⁶Therefore this is what the Lord, the Lord
God Almighty, says:

"There will be wailing in all the streets
  and cries of anguish in every public
    square.
The farmers will be summoned to weep
  and the mourners to wail.
¹⁷There will be wailing in all the
    vineyards,
  for I will pass through your midst,"
                        says the Lord.

The Day of the Lord

¹⁸Woe to you who long
  for the day of the Lord!
  Why do you long for the day of the
    Lord?
  That day will be darkness, not light.

¹⁹It will be as though a man fled from a
    lion
  only to meet a bear,
  as though he entered his house
  and rested his hand on the wall
  only to have a snake bite him.
²⁰Will not the day of the Lord be
    darkness, not light—
  pitch-dark, without a ray of
    brightness?

²¹"I hate, I despise your religious feasts;
  I cannot stand your assemblies.
²²Even though you bring me burnt
    offerings and grain offerings,
  I will not accept them.
  Though you bring choice fellowship
    offerings,ᵃ
  I will have no regard for them.
²³Away with the noise of your songs!
  I will not listen to the music of your
    harps.
²⁴But let justice roll on like a river,
  righteousness like a never-failing
    stream!

²⁵"Did you bring me sacrifices and
    offerings
  forty years in the desert, O house of
    Israel?
²⁶You have lifted up the shrine of your
    king,
  the pedestal of your idols,
  the star of your godᵇ—
  which you made for yourselves.
²⁷Therefore I will send you into exile
    beyond Damascus,"
  says the Lord, whose name is God
    Almighty.

Woe to the Complacent

6 Woe to you who are complacent in
  Zion,
  and to you who feel secure on Mount
    Samaria,
you notable men of the foremost nation,
  to whom the people of Israel come!
²Go to Calneh and look at it;
  go from there to great Hamath,
  and then go down to Gath in Philistia.
  Are they better off than your two
    kingdoms?
  Is their land larger than yours?
³You put off the evil day
  and bring near a reign of terror.
⁴You lie on beds inlaid with ivory
  and lounge on your couches.

ᵃ22 Traditionally *peace offerings*   ᵇ26 Or *lifted up Sakkuth your king / and Kaiwan your idols, / your
star-gods*; Septuagint *lifted up the shrine of Molech / and the star of your god Rephan, / their idols*

SWEEPING AWAY HOLLOW HYPOCRISY

• •

M eet Stuart, a modern-day Dr. Jekyll and Mr. Hyde.
He goes to a Christian school and puts on a good front for his teachers—especially Mrs. Sibley in Bible class. He says all the right things in church and prays at all the youth functions. The youth leaders think Stuart is terrific. He even reads his devotional guide every day.

But here's the real Stuart behind the mask. Though he knows what's right—sexual purity, honesty, spending time with God, watching his tongue—he rarely does it. See, for Stuart, the Christian life is a show.

Look It Up
• • • •

Even though everyone else may be impressed, God says the performance of a hypocrite stinks. Listen to this scathing denunciation:

> Stop bringing meaningless offerings!
>   Your incense is detestable to me . . . .
> Your New Moon festivals and your appointed feasts
>   my soul hates.
> They have become a burden to me;
>   I am weary of bearing them.
> When you spread out your hands in prayer,
>   I will hide my eyes from you;
> even if you offer many prayers,
>   I will not listen. . . .
> Take your evil deeds out of my sight!
> Stop doing wrong,
>   learn to do right! (Isaiah 1:13–17).

How much clearer can God be?

Think It Through
• • • •

If your life is full of sin, it doesn't matter how many good deeds you do. No amount of religious activity will make up for sinful behavior and wrong attitudes. Look again at what God says: "Even if you offer many prayers, I will not listen."

Is that the case in your life? Are you living like Stuart? Is unconfessed sin creating a wall between you and God?

Work It Out
• • • •

Turn in your Bible to Isaiah 1:18–20. There you'll see the solution to hypocritical behavior. Humble repentance and obedience lead to blessing. But continued resistance and rebellion result in further discipline from God.

Take a short walk today—just you and God. Ask him to forgive you and help you get back on track. Tell him you want to get rid of the hypocrisy in your life. Then tell a friend about your commitment.

Nail It Down
• • • •

Read the warning in Amos 5:21–24.

Turn to pages 656 and 1032 for other readings on behavior.
Turn to page 949 for Friday's reading.

Topic
• • • •

BEHAVIOR

You dine on choice lambs
and fattened calves.
⁵You strum away on your harps like
David
and improvise on musical
instruments.
⁶You drink wine by the bowlful
and use the finest lotions,
but you do not grieve over the ruin of
Joseph.
⁷Therefore you will be among the first to
go into exile;
your feasting and lounging will end.

The Lord Abhors the Pride of Israel

⁸The Sovereign Lord has sworn by himself—the Lord God Almighty declares:

"I abhor the pride of Jacob
and detest his fortresses;
I will deliver up the city
and everything in it."

⁹If ten men are left in one house, they too will die. ¹⁰And if a relative who is to burn the bodies comes to carry them out of the house and asks anyone still hiding there, "Is anyone with you?" and he says, "No," then he will say, "Hush! We must not mention the name of the Lord."

¹¹For the Lord has given the command,
and he will smash the great house
into pieces
and the small house into bits.

¹²Do horses run on the rocky crags?
Does one plow there with oxen?
But you have turned justice into poison
and the fruit of righteousness into
bitterness—
¹³you who rejoice in the conquest of Lo
Debarᵃ
and say, "Did we not take Karnaimᵇ
by our own strength?"

¹⁴For the Lord God Almighty declares,
"I will stir up a nation against you,
O house of Israel,
that will oppress you all the way
from Leboᶜ Hamath to the valley of
the Arabah."

Locusts, Fire and a Plumb Line

7 This is what the Sovereign Lord showed me: He was preparing swarms of locusts after the king's share had been harvested and just as the second crop was coming up. ²When they had stripped the land clean, I cried out, "Sovereign Lord, forgive! How can Jacob survive? He is so small!"

³So the Lord relented.

"This will not happen," the Lord said.

⁴This is what the Sovereign Lord showed me: The Sovereign Lord was calling for judgment by fire; it dried up the great deep and devoured the land. ⁵Then I cried out, "Sovereign Lord, I beg you, stop! How can Jacob survive? He is so small!"

⁶So the Lord relented.

"This will not happen either," the Sovereign Lord said.

⁷This is what he showed me: The Lord was standing by a wall that had been built true to plumb, with a plumb line in his hand. ⁸And the Lord asked me, "What do you see, Amos?"

"A plumb line," I replied.

Then the Lord said, "Look, I am setting a plumb line among my people Israel; I will spare them no longer.

⁹"The high places of Isaac will be
destroyed
and the sanctuaries of Israel will be
ruined;
with my sword I will rise against the
house of Jeroboam."

Amos and Amaziah

¹⁰Then Amaziah the priest of Bethel sent a message to Jeroboam king of Israel: "Amos is raising a conspiracy against you in the very heart of Israel. The land cannot bear all his words. ¹¹For this is what Amos is saying:

" 'Jeroboam will die by the sword,
and Israel will surely go into exile,
away from their native land.' "

¹²Then Amaziah said to Amos, "Get out, you seer! Go back to the land of Judah. Earn your bread there and do your prophesying there. ¹³Don't prophesy anymore at Bethel, because this is the king's sanctuary and the temple of the kingdom."

¹⁴Amos answered Amaziah, "I was neither a prophet nor a prophet's son, but I was a shepherd, and I also took care of sycamore-fig trees. ¹⁵But the Lord took me from tending the flock and said to me, 'Go, prophesy to my people Israel.' ¹⁶Now then, hear the word of the Lord. You say,

" 'Do not prophesy against Israel,

ᵃ13 Lo Debar means nothing.   ᵇ13 Karnaim means horns; horn here symbolizes strength.   ᶜ14 Or from the entrance to

PRAYING FOR THE PROPHETS OF GOD

● ●

During a debate in speech class on the topic of teenage sexuality, outspoken Anita finally can't take it anymore. She explodes: "Why can't you just admit that God's standards are best? The issue isn't birth control; it's self-control! We need a return to morality! Face it—until guys and girls learn to handle their hormones, teenagers are going to keep getting pregnant, and they're going to keep catching sexual diseases!"

You can imagine how well those remarks were received.

Look It Up
● ● ● ●

God always raises up prophetic voices to speak hard words to hard hearts. And almost always the response is negative.

Noah faced scorn when he preached righteousness to his neighbors (2 Peter 2:5).

Jeremiah's sermons produced a response of rage. He was beaten (Jeremiah 20:2) and thrown into a muddy cistern (Jeremiah 38:6). Typical of his career is this verse: "As soon as Jeremiah finished telling all the people everything the LORD had commanded him to say, the priests, the prophets and all the people seized him and said, 'You must die!' " (Jeremiah 26:8).

As you can see, proclaiming God's truth to people wallowing in sin is never easy!

Think It Through
● ● ● ●

What moral issue do you feel most strongly about? What would happen if, like Anita, you took a stand in front of your classmates and friends? Which is worse: to speak up and face possible ridicule and persecution or to be quiet and let evil continue unchecked?

Work It Out
● ● ● ●

Pray daily for the leaders of churches and ministries that are working to preserve traditional family values, those that are struggling to restore decency to the media, and those fighting against abortion and injustice. Ask for protection from Satan's attacks, for strength to carry on the battle, for boldness in proclaiming the truth, and for success in their efforts.

Then pick one issue and let your voice be heard. (Imagine what would happen if every Christian teenager actively stood against one wrong thing in this society!)

Nail It Down
● ● ● ●

Read about the rejection Amos faced and his response in Amos 7:10–17.

Turn to pages 23 and 1017 for other readings on society.
Turn to page 951 for the weekend reading.

Topic
● ● ● ●

and stop preaching against the house of Isaac.'

17"Therefore this is what the Lord says:

" 'Your wife will become a prostitute in
the city,
and your sons and daughters will fall
by the sword.
Your land will be measured and divided
up,
and you yourself will die in a pagan*a*
country.
And Israel will certainly go into exile,
away from their native land.' "

A Basket of Ripe Fruit

8 This is what the Sovereign Lord showed me: a basket of ripe fruit. **2**"What do you see, Amos?" he asked.

"A basket of ripe fruit," I answered.

Then the Lord said to me, "The time is ripe for my people Israel; I will spare them no longer.

3"In that day," declares the Sovereign Lord, "the songs in the temple will turn to wailing.*b* Many, many bodies—flung everywhere! Silence!"

4Hear this, you who trample the needy
and do away with the poor of the
land,

5saying,

"When will the New Moon be over
that we may sell grain,
and the Sabbath be ended
that we may market wheat?"—
skimping the measure,
boosting the price
and cheating with dishonest scales,
6buying the poor with silver
and the needy for a pair of sandals,
selling even the sweepings with the
wheat.

7The Lord has sworn by the Pride of Jacob: "I will never forget anything they have done.

8"Will not the land tremble for this,
and all who live in it mourn?
The whole land will rise like the Nile;
it will be stirred up and then sink
like the river of Egypt.

9"In that day," declares the Sovereign Lord,

"I will make the sun go down at noon

and darken the earth in broad
daylight.
10I will turn your religious feasts into
mourning
and all your singing into weeping.
I will make all of you wear sackcloth
and shave your heads.
I will make that time like mourning for
an only son
and the end of it like a bitter day.

11"The days are coming," declares the
Sovereign Lord,
"when I will send a famine through
the land—
not a famine of food or a thirst for
water,
but a famine of hearing the words of
the Lord.
12Men will stagger from sea to sea
and wander from north to east,
searching for the word of the Lord,
but they will not find it.

13"In that day

"the lovely young women and strong
young men
will faint because of thirst.
14They who swear by the shame*c* of
Samaria,
or say, 'As surely as your god lives,
O Dan,'
or, 'As surely as the god*d* of
Beersheba lives'—
they will fall,
never to rise again."

Israel to Be Destroyed

9 I saw the Lord standing by the altar, and he said:

"Strike the tops of the pillars
so that the thresholds shake.
Bring them down on the heads of all the
people;
those who are left I will kill with the
sword.
Not one will get away,
none will escape.
2Though they dig down to the depths of
the grave,*e*
from there my hand will take them.
Though they climb up to the heavens,
from there I will bring them down.
3Though they hide themselves on the top
of Carmel,

---

a17 Hebrew *an unclean*　　*b3* Or *"the temple singers will wail*　　*c14* Or *by Ashima;* or *by the idol*　　*d14* Or *power*　　*e2* Hebrew *to Sheol*

A FAMINE OF HEARING GOD'S WORD

Work It Out

I magine for a minute that there was a famine in your community. You won't be physically hungry, because it isn't a famine of food. You won't be physically thirsty, because it isn't a famine of water. But it is a famine of hearing God's Word.

Imagine what your world would be like if there suddenly were no Bibles, no hymnbooks, no churches, no worship services. What would your life be like if starting today you never again heard God's Word?

Would your life lack direction? Would your life's purpose be removed? Would joy leave?

Or would your life go on pretty much the same as it always has? Think about it.

Nail It Down

Read about the spiritual famine in Amos 8:11.

Think It Through

R eal life in Christ can be exciting and fulfilling. But you need communication with the designer of real life to experience it. His manual, the Bible, communicates to you all you need for real life. His love for you and your commitment to him are communicated through the words and music of many hymns and praise songs. The fellowship and teaching that you receive when you attend your local church can't be found anywhere else.

If in your life there is "a famine of hearing the words of the LORD," you can do something about it.

Put your left hand on the front cover of a Bible. Put your right hand on the back cover. Open and read.

Nail It Down

Reread Amos 8:11. For further insight read Psalm 119:11–16.

Turn to pages 1160, 1164, 1167, 1217 and 1319 for other readings on real life.
Turn to page 954 for Monday's reading.

Topic

REAL LIFE

there I will hunt them down and seize
    them.
Though they hide from me at the
    bottom of the sea,
    there I will command the serpent to
        bite them.
⁴Though they are driven into exile by
    their enemies,
    there I will command the sword to
        slay them.
I will fix my eyes upon them
    for evil and not for good."

⁵The Lord, the LORD Almighty,
    he who touches the earth and it
        melts,
    and all who live in it mourn—
the whole land rises like the Nile,
    then sinks like the river of Egypt—
⁶he who builds his lofty palaceᵃ in the
    heavens
    and sets its foundationᵇ on the earth,
who calls for the waters of the sea
    and pours them out over the face of
        the land—
    the LORD is his name.

⁷"Are not you Israelites
    the same to me as the Cushitesᶜ?"
                    declares the LORD.
"Did I not bring Israel up from Egypt,
    the Philistines from Caphtorᵈ
    and the Arameans from Kir?

⁸"Surely the eyes of the Sovereign LORD
    are on the sinful kingdom.
I will destroy it
    from the face of the earth—
    yet I will not totally destroy
    the house of Jacob,"
                    declares the LORD.
⁹"For I will give the command,
    and I will shake the house of Israel
    among all the nations

as grain is shaken in a sieve,
    and not a pebble will reach the
        ground.
¹⁰All the sinners among my people
    will die by the sword,
all those who say,
    'Disaster will not overtake or meet us.'

Israel's Restoration

¹¹"In that day I will restore
    David's fallen tent.
I will repair its broken places,
    restore its ruins,
    and build it as it used to be,
¹²so that they may possess the remnant
    of Edom
    and all the nations that bear my
        name,ᵉ"
                declares the LORD, who
                    will do these things.

¹³"The days are coming," declares the
LORD,

"when the reaper will be overtaken by
    the plowman
    and the planter by the one treading
        grapes.
New wine will drip from the mountains
    and flow from all the hills.
¹⁴I will bring back my exiledᶠ people
    Israel;
    they will rebuild the ruined cities and
    live in them.
They will plant vineyards and drink
    their wine;
    they will make gardens and eat their
    fruit.
¹⁵I will plant Israel in their own land,
    never again to be uprooted
    from the land I have given them,"
                says the LORD your God.

ᵃ6 The meaning of the Hebrew for this phrase is uncertain.   ᵇ6 The meaning of the Hebrew for this word is uncertain.   ᶜ7 That is, people from the upper Nile region   ᵈ7 That is, Crete   ᵉ12 Hebrew; Septuagint *so that the remnant of men / and all the nations that bear my name may seek ⸤the Lord⸥*   ᶠ14 Or *will restore the fortunes of my*

OBADIAH

IT should have been a family affair. After all, Israel and Edom were descended from the brothers Jacob and Esau. But when Israel's enemies came pounding on the gates of Jerusalem, Edom rushed in to help . . . the enemy! As a result God's prophet Obadiah prophesies extinction for the haughty Edomites. As you read, remember: No one can fight against God's people and win. The final victory belongs to the Lord.

Outline of Contents

The doom of Edom (1–14)
Edom in the day of the Lord (15–21)

---

¹The vision of Obadiah.

This is what the Sovereign Lord says about Edom—

We have heard a message from the
    Lord:
    An envoy was sent to the nations to
        say,
    "Rise, and let us go against her for
        battle"—

²"See, I will make you small among the
    nations;
    you will be utterly despised.
³The pride of your heart has deceived
    you,
    you who live in the clefts of the
        rocksª

and make your home on the heights,
    you who say to yourself,
    'Who can bring me down to the
        ground?'
⁴Though you soar like the eagle
    and make your nest among the stars,
    from there I will bring you down,"
                        declares the Lord.
⁵"If thieves came to you,
    if robbers in the night—
Oh, what a disaster awaits you—
    would they not steal only as much as
        they wanted?
If grape pickers came to you,
    would they not leave a few grapes?
⁶But how Esau will be ransacked,
    his hidden treasures pillaged!
⁷All your allies will force you to the
        border;

ª3 Or of Sela

INSTALLING YOUR OWN SECURITY SYSTEM

Mark just knew he was going to make first string on the football team. He made sure his parents, girlfriend and other classmates knew it too. Imagine Mark's surprise (and embarrassment) when he didn't start. (He only played about ten plays in the first two games!)

Martha has felt panicky and uptight for three weeks now. She and her boyfriend went all the way. She's terribly afraid she might be pregnant.

Look It Up
••••

Your actions will often determine whether you experience security or insecurity in your life. You will find security when you:

• Obey Christ—"Therefore everyone who hears these words of mine and puts them into practice is like a wise man who built his house on the rock. The rain came down, the streams rose, and the winds blew and beat against that house; yet it did not fall, because it had its foundation on the rock" (Matthew 7:24–25);

• Live wisely—"He who trusts in himself is a fool, but he who walks in wisdom is kept safe" (Proverbs 28:26);

• Humbly depend on God (2 Chronicles 20:20).

But you will probably experience insecurity when you:

• Are proud—"So, if you think you are standing firm, be careful that you don't fall!" (1 Corinthians 10:12);

• Are disobedient to God—(Matthew 7:26–27).

Think It Through
••••

What could Mark and Martha have done to prevent the insecurity they now feel?

Work It Out
••••

Install your own security system.

1. Obey God's Word. (The commands that seem so negative—no sex, no partying, no filthy talk, no cheating—are actually positive. Following them builds security!)

2. Hang around people who want to live for God. (Rebellious, insecure people want to drag you down. Misery loves company, right?)

3. Seek to know Jesus Christ. (He loves and accepts you totally and completely. He'll never reject you. You can count on him!)

Nail It Down
••••

Read in Obadiah 3–4 how pride brought destruction (and ultimate insecurity) to Edom.

Turn to pages 742, 805 and 976 for other readings on security.
Turn to page 957 for Tuesday's reading.

Topic
••••

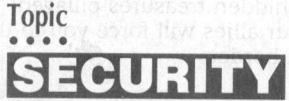
SECURITY

your friends will deceive and
    overpower you;
those who eat your bread will set a trap
    for you,[a]
but you will not detect it.

⁸"In that day," declares the LORD,
    "will I not destroy the wise men of
        Edom,
    men of understanding in the
        mountains of Esau?
⁹Your warriors, O Teman, will be
    terrified,
and everyone in Esau's mountains
    will be cut down in the slaughter.
¹⁰Because of the violence against your
    brother Jacob,
you will be covered with shame;
    you will be destroyed forever.
¹¹On the day you stood aloof
    while strangers carried off his wealth
and foreigners entered his gates
    and cast lots for Jerusalem,
you were like one of them.
¹²You should not look down on your
    brother
    in the day of his misfortune,
nor rejoice over the people of Judah
    in the day of their destruction,
nor boast so much
    in the day of their trouble.
¹³You should not march through the gates
    of my people
    in the day of their disaster,
nor look down on them in their
    calamity
    in the day of their disaster,
nor seize their wealth
    in the day of their disaster.
¹⁴You should not wait at the crossroads
    to cut down their fugitives,
nor hand over their survivors
    in the day of their trouble.

¹⁵"The day of the LORD is near
    for all nations.
As you have done, it will be done to
    you;
    your deeds will return upon your own
        head.
¹⁶Just as you drank on my holy hill,
    so all the nations will drink
        continually;
they will drink and drink
    and be as if they had never been.
¹⁷But on Mount Zion will be deliverance;
    it will be holy,
and the house of Jacob
    will possess its inheritance.
¹⁸The house of Jacob will be a fire
    and the house of Joseph a flame;
the house of Esau will be stubble,
    and they will set it on fire and
        consume it.
There will be no survivors
    from the house of Esau."
                The LORD has spoken.

¹⁹People from the Negev will occupy
    the mountains of Esau,
and people from the foothills will
        possess
    the land of the Philistines.
They will occupy the fields of Ephraim
    and Samaria,
and Benjamin will possess Gilead.
²⁰This company of Israelite exiles who are
    in Canaan
    will possess ˌthe landˌ as far as
        Zarephath;
the exiles from Jerusalem who are in
        Sepharad
    will possess the towns of the Negev.
²¹Deliverers will go up on[b] Mount Zion
    to govern the mountains of Esau.
And the kingdom will be the
        LORD's.

---

[a]7 The meaning of the Hebrew for this clause is uncertain.   [b]21 Or *from*

JONAH

THERE'S a lot more to the story of Jonah than what's on the surface. When told to preach at Nineveh, the capital city of the brutal Assyrians, Jonah sets sail—in the opposite direction. Using a storm at sea and a large fish, God brings his reluctant prophet to Nineveh. Jonah finally preaches in the city, but when the Ninevites repent Jonah sulks. God then uses a plant, a worm and scorching heat to teach the prophet a lesson in compassion. As you read Jonah, remember: God loves all people, not just those you love.

Outline of Contents

Jonah Flees From the Lord

1 The word of the Lord came to Jonah son of Amittai: 2"Go to the great city of Nineveh and preach against it, because its wickedness has come up before me."

3But Jonah ran away from the Lord and headed for Tarshish. He went down to Joppa, where he found a ship bound for that port. After paying the fare, he went aboard and sailed for Tarshish to flee from the Lord.

4Then the Lord sent a great wind on the sea, and such a violent storm arose that the ship threatened to break up. 5All the sailors were afraid and each cried out to his own god. And they threw the cargo into the sea to lighten the ship.

But Jonah had gone below deck, where he lay down and fell into a deep sleep. 6The captain went to him and said, "How can you sleep? Get up and call on your god! Maybe he will take notice of us, and we will not perish."

7Then the sailors said to each other, "Come, let us cast lots to find out who is responsible for this calamity." They cast lots and the lot fell on Jonah.

8So they asked him, "Tell us, who is responsible for making all this trouble for us? What do you do? Where do you come from? What is your country? From what people are you?"

9He answered, "I am a Hebrew and I worship the Lord, the God of heaven, who made the sea and the land."

10This terrified them and they asked, "What have you done?" (They knew he was running away from the Lord, because he had already told them so.)

THE MARKS OF A GUILTY PERSON

It's Tuesday and Jenny is still feeling bad over getting too physical with her boyfriend on Saturday night. The more she replays the scene in her head, the sadder she gets. "Why did I let that happen? I knew better. I'm such an idiot!"

Feeling too unworthy to pray, Jenny tries to escape her guilt by doing her homework. When that doesn't work, she picks up a novel she has been reading. She can't concentrate at all.

Finally, in desperation, she clicks on the TV.

Look It Up
••••

How do people respond to guilt?

Some don't even know they're guilty!—"They are darkened in their understanding and separated from the life of God because of the ignorance that is in them due to the hardening of their hearts" (Ephesians 4:18).

Some feel bad (Matthew 26:74–75).

Some get depressed (Psalm 40:12).

Some get physically sick:

> When I kept silent,
> my bones wasted away
> through my groaning all day long.
> For day and night
> your hand was heavy upon me;
> my strength was sapped
> as in the heat of summer (Psalm 32:3–4).

In extreme cases, some commit suicide (Matthew 27:3–5).

A few repent (Psalm 51:1–12).

Think It Through
••••

According to at least one survey of mental health professionals, many of the patients in mental health institutions today could be restored to health if they could just know that they are forgiven!

How successful do you think Jenny will be in dealing with her guilt using the approach she has chosen?

Is guilt a regular part of your life right now? How are you dealing with it?

Work It Out
••••

Try to list some additional methods that people use to try to avoid a sense of guilt.

If you're struggling with guilt, pray this prayer: "Lord, please search my heart and show me where I am guilty of wrong actions, thoughts or words. Then, Lord, reassure me that I am forgiven and help me to forgive myself. More than anything else, I want to be right with you. In Jesus' name, Amen."

Nail It Down
••••

Read how Jonah tried to escape the guilt he felt for not following what God asked him to do in Jonah 1:1–6.

Turn to pages 6, 565 and 1213 for other readings on guilt.
Turn to page 966 for Wednesday's reading.

Topic
••••
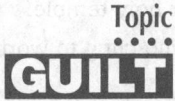
GUILT

[11]The sea was getting rougher and rougher. So they asked him, "What should we do to you to make the sea calm down for us?" [12]"Pick me up and throw me into the sea," he replied, "and it will become calm. I know that it is my fault that this great storm has come upon you."

[13]Instead, the men did their best to row back to land. But they could not, for the sea grew even wilder than before. [14]Then they cried to the LORD, "O LORD, please do not let us die for taking this man's life. Do not hold us accountable for killing an innocent man, for you, O LORD, have done as you pleased." [15]Then they took Jonah and threw him overboard, and the raging sea grew calm. [16]At this the men greatly feared the LORD, and they offered a sacrifice to the LORD and made vows to him.

[17]But the LORD provided a great fish to swallow Jonah, and Jonah was inside the fish three days and three nights.

Jonah's Prayer

2 From inside the fish Jonah prayed to the LORD his God. [2]He said:

"In my distress I called to the LORD,
    and he answered me.
From the depths of the grave[a] I called
        for help,
    and you listened to my cry.
[3]You hurled me into the deep,
    into the very heart of the seas,
    and the currents swirled about me;
all your waves and breakers
    swept over me.
[4]I said, 'I have been banished
    from your sight;
yet I will look again
    toward your holy temple.'
[5]The engulfing waters threatened me,[b]
    the deep surrounded me;
    seaweed was wrapped around my
        head.
[6]To the roots of the mountains I sank
        down;
    the earth beneath barred me in
        forever.
But you brought my life up from the pit,
    O LORD my God.

[7]"When my life was ebbing away,
    I remembered you, LORD,
and my prayer rose to you,
    to your holy temple.

[8]"Those who cling to worthless idols
forfeit the grace that could be theirs.
[9]But I, with a song of thanksgiving,
    will sacrifice to you.
What I have vowed I will make good.
    Salvation comes from the LORD."

[10]And the LORD commanded the fish, and it vomited Jonah onto dry land.

Jonah Goes to Nineveh

3 Then the word of the LORD came to Jonah a second time: [2]"Go to the great city of Nineveh and proclaim to it the message I give you."

[3]Jonah obeyed the word of the LORD and went to Nineveh. Now Nineveh was a very important city—a visit required three days. [4]On the first day, Jonah started into the city. He proclaimed: "Forty more days and Nineveh will be overturned." [5]The Ninevites believed God. They declared a fast, and all of them, from the greatest to the least, put on sackcloth.

[6]When the news reached the king of Nineveh, he rose from his throne, took off his royal robes, covered himself with sackcloth and sat down in the dust. [7]Then he issued a proclamation in Nineveh:

"By the decree of the king and his nobles:

Do not let any man or beast, herd or flock, taste anything; do not let them eat or drink. [8]But let man and beast be covered with sackcloth. Let everyone call urgently on God. Let them give up their evil ways and their violence. [9]Who knows? God may yet relent and with compassion turn from his fierce anger so that we will not perish."

[10]When God saw what they did and how they turned from their evil ways, he had compassion and did not bring upon them the destruction he had threatened.

Jonah's Anger at the LORD's Compassion

4 But Jonah was greatly displeased and became angry. [2]He prayed to the LORD, "O LORD, is this not what I said when I was still at home? That is why I was so quick to flee to Tarshish. I knew that you are a gracious and compassionate God, slow to anger and abounding in love, a God who relents from sending calamity. [3]Now, O LORD, take away my life, for it is better for me to die than to live."

[4]But the LORD replied, "Have you any right to be angry?"

---

[a]2 Hebrew *Sheol*   [b]5 Or *waters were at my throat*

⁵Jonah went out and sat down at a place east of the city. There he made himself a shelter, sat in its shade and waited to see what would happen to the city. ⁶Then the LORD God provided a vine and made it grow up over Jonah to give shade for his head to ease his discomfort, and Jonah was very happy about the vine. ⁷But at dawn the next day God provided a worm, which chewed the vine so that it withered. ⁸When the sun rose, God provided a scorching east wind, and the sun blazed on Jonah's head so that he grew faint. He wanted to die, and said, "It would be better for me to die than to live."

⁹But God said to Jonah, "Do you have a right to be angry about the vine?"

"I do," he said. "I am angry enough to die."

¹⁰But the LORD said, "You have been concerned about this vine, though you did not tend it or make it grow. It sprang up overnight and died overnight. ¹¹But Nineveh has more than a hundred and twenty thousand people who cannot tell their right hand from their left, and many cattle as well. Should I not be concerned about that great city?"

MICAH

IN this short prophecy, God aims his charges at those in Judah who cheat the poor, abuse the powerless and corrupt justice. Such sin will not go unpunished. God wants justice in society. Judgment will be swift. But once the punishment is complete, justice will be tempered with mercy. As you read, remember that God is the judge of all the earth. And through the Messiah, he will bring peace and justice.

1 The word of the LORD that came to Micah of Moresheth during the reigns of Jotham, Ahaz and Hezekiah, kings of Judah—the vision he saw concerning Samaria and Jerusalem.

²Hear, O peoples, all of you,
   listen, O earth and all who are in it,
that the Sovereign LORD may witness
      against you,
   the Lord from his holy temple.

Judgment Against Samaria and Jerusalem

³Look! The LORD is coming from his
      dwelling place;
   he comes down and treads the high
      places of the earth.

⁴The mountains melt beneath him
   and the valleys split apart,
like wax before the fire,
   like water rushing down a slope.
⁵All this is because of Jacob's
      transgression,
   because of the sins of the house of
      Israel.
What is Jacob's transgression?
   Is it not Samaria?
What is Judah's high place?
   Is it not Jerusalem?
⁶"Therefore I will make Samaria a heap
      of rubble,
   a place for planting vineyards.
I will pour her stones into the valley
   and lay bare her foundations.
⁷All her idols will be broken to pieces;

all her temple gifts will be burned
with fire;
I will destroy all her images.
Since she gathered her gifts from the
wages of prostitutes,
as the wages of prostitutes they will
again be used."

Weeping and Mourning

8Because of this I will weep and wail;
I will go about barefoot and naked.
I will howl like a jackal
and moan like an owl.
9For her wound is incurable;
it has come to Judah.
It*a* has reached the very gate of my
people,
even to Jerusalem itself.
10Tell it not in Gath*b*;
weep not at all.*c*
In Beth Ophrah*d*
roll in the dust.
11Pass on in nakedness and shame,
you who live in Shaphir.*e*
Those who live in Zaanan*f*
will not come out.
Beth Ezel is in mourning;
its protection is taken from you.
12Those who live in Maroth*g* writhe in
pain,
waiting for relief,
because disaster has come from the
LORD,
even to the gate of Jerusalem.
13You who live in Lachish,*h*
harness the team to the chariot.
You were the beginning of sin
to the Daughter of Zion,
for the transgressions of Israel
were found in you.
14Therefore you will give parting gifts
to Moresheth Gath.
The town of Aczib*i* will prove deceptive
to the kings of Israel.
15I will bring a conqueror against you
who live in Mareshah.*j*
He who is the glory of Israel
will come to Adullam.
16Shave your heads in mourning
for the children in whom you delight;
make yourselves as bald as the vulture,
for they will go from you into exile.

Man's Plans and God's

2 Woe to those who plan iniquity,
to those who plot evil on their beds!
At morning's light they carry it out
because it is in their power to do it.
2They covet fields and seize them,
and houses, and take them.
They defraud a man of his home,
a fellowman of his inheritance.

3Therefore, the LORD says:

"I am planning disaster against this
people,
from which you cannot save
yourselves.
You will no longer walk proudly,
for it will be a time of calamity.
4In that day men will ridicule you;
they will taunt you with this mournful
song:
'We are utterly ruined;
my people's possession is divided up.
He takes it from me!
He assigns our fields to traitors.' "

5Therefore you will have no one in the
assembly of the LORD
to divide the land by lot.

False Prophets

6"Do not prophesy," their prophets say.
"Do not prophesy about these things;
disgrace will not overtake us."
7Should it be said, O house of Jacob:
"Is the Spirit of the LORD angry?
Does he do such things?"

"Do not my words do good
to him whose ways are upright?
8Lately my people have risen up
like an enemy.
You strip off the rich robe
from those who pass by without a
care,
like men returning from battle.
9You drive the women of my people
from their pleasant homes.
You take away my blessing
from their children forever.
10Get up, go away!
For this is not your resting place,
because it is defiled,
it is ruined, beyond all remedy.
11If a liar and deceiver comes and says,

---

*a*9 Or *He*   *b*10 *Gath sounds like the Hebrew for tell.*
Hebrew for *in Acco sounds like the Hebrew for weep.*   *c*10 Hebrew; Septuagint may suggest *not in Acco.* The
*d*10 *Beth Ophrah means house of dust.*   *e*11 *Shaphir*
means *pleasant.*   *f*11 *Zaanan sounds like the Hebrew for come out.*   *g*12 *Maroth sounds like the Hebrew*
for *bitter.*   *h*13 *Lachish sounds like the Hebrew for team.*   *i*14 *Aczib means deception.*   *j*15 *Mareshah*
sounds like the Hebrew for *conqueror.*

'I will prophesy for you plenty of wine
and beer,'
he would be just the prophet for this
people!

Deliverance Promised

¹²"I will surely gather all of you, O Jacob;
I will surely bring together the
remnant of Israel.
I will bring them together like sheep in
a pen,
like a flock in its pasture;
the place will throng with people.
¹³One who breaks open the way will go
up before them;
they will break through the gate and
go out.
Their king will pass through before
them,
the LORD at their head."

Leaders and Prophets Rebuked

3 Then I said,

"Listen, you leaders of Jacob,
you rulers of the house of Israel.
Should you not know justice,
² you who hate good and love evil;
who tear the skin from my people
and the flesh from their bones;
³who eat my people's flesh,
strip off their skin
and break their bones in pieces;
who chop them up like meat for the
pan,
like flesh for the pot?"

⁴Then they will cry out to the LORD,
but he will not answer them.
At that time he will hide his face from
them
because of the evil they have done.

⁵This is what the LORD says:

"As for the prophets
who lead my people astray,
if one feeds them,
they proclaim 'peace';
if he does not,
they prepare to wage war against him.
⁶Therefore night will come over you,
without visions,
and darkness, without divination.
The sun will set for the prophets,
and the day will go dark for them.
⁷The seers will be ashamed
and the diviners disgraced.
They will all cover their faces
because there is no answer from
God."

⁸But as for me, I am filled with power,
with the Spirit of the LORD,
and with justice and might,
to declare to Jacob his transgression,
to Israel his sin.
⁹Hear this, you leaders of the house of
Jacob,
you rulers of the house of Israel,
who despise justice
and distort all that is right;
¹⁰who build Zion with bloodshed,
and Jerusalem with wickedness.
¹¹Her leaders judge for a bribe,
her priests teach for a price,
and her prophets tell fortunes for
money.
Yet they lean upon the LORD and say,
"Is not the LORD among us?
No disaster will come upon us."
¹²Therefore because of you,
Zion will be plowed like a field,
Jerusalem will become a heap of rubble,
the temple hill a mound overgrown
with thickets.

The Mountain of the LORD

4 In the last days

the mountain of the LORD's temple
will be established
as chief among the mountains;
it will be raised above the hills,
and peoples will stream to it.

²Many nations will come and say,

"Come, let us go up to the mountain of
the LORD,
to the house of the God of Jacob.
He will teach us his ways,
so that we may walk in his paths."
The law will go out from Zion,
the word of the LORD from Jerusalem.
³He will judge between many peoples
and will settle disputes for strong
nations far and wide.
They will beat their swords into
plowshares
and their spears into pruning hooks.
Nation will not take up sword against
nation,
nor will they train for war anymore.
⁴Every man will sit under his own vine
and under his own fig tree,
and no one will make them afraid,
for the LORD Almighty has spoken.
⁵All the nations may walk
in the name of their gods;
we will walk in the name of the LORD
our God for ever and ever.

The LORD's Plan

6"In that day," declares the LORD,

"I will gather the lame;
I will assemble the exiles
and those I have brought to grief.
7I will make the lame a remnant,
those driven away a strong nation.
The LORD will rule over them in Mount
Zion
from that day and forever.
8As for you, O watchtower of the flock,
O stronghold*a* of the Daughter of
Zion,
the former dominion will be restored to
you;
kingship will come to the Daughter of
Jerusalem."

9Why do you now cry aloud—
have you no king?
Has your counselor perished,
that pain seizes you like that of a
woman in labor?
10Writhe in agony, O Daughter of Zion,
like a woman in labor,
for now you must leave the city
to camp in the open field.
You will go to Babylon;
there you will be rescued.
There the LORD will redeem you
out of the hand of your enemies.

11But now many nations
are gathered against you.
They say, "Let her be defiled,
let our eyes gloat over Zion!"
12But they do not know
the thoughts of the LORD;
they do not understand his plan,
he who gathers them like sheaves to
the threshing floor.
13"Rise and thresh, O Daughter of Zion,
for I will give you horns of iron;
I will give you hoofs of bronze
and you will break to pieces many
nations."

You will devote their ill-gotten gains to
the LORD,
their wealth to the Lord of all the
earth.

A Promised Ruler From Bethlehem

5 Marshal your troops, O city of
troops,*b*
for a siege is laid against us.

They will strike Israel's ruler
on the cheek with a rod.

2"But you, Bethlehem Ephrathah,
though you are small among the
clans*c* of Judah,
out of you will come for me
one who will be ruler over Israel,
whose origins*d* are from of old,
from ancient times.*e*"

3Therefore Israel will be abandoned
until the time when she who is in
labor gives birth
and the rest of his brothers return
to join the Israelites.

4He will stand and shepherd his flock
in the strength of the LORD,
in the majesty of the name of the
LORD his God.
And they will live securely, for then his
greatness
will reach to the ends of the earth.
5   And he will be their peace.

Deliverance and Destruction

When the Assyrian invades our land
and marches through our fortresses,
we will raise against him seven
shepherds,
even eight leaders of men.
6They will rule*f* the land of Assyria with
the sword,
the land of Nimrod with drawn
sword.*g*
He will deliver us from the Assyrian
when he invades our land
and marches into our borders.

7The remnant of Jacob will be
in the midst of many peoples
like dew from the LORD,
like showers on the grass,
which do not wait for man
or linger for mankind.
8The remnant of Jacob will be among the
nations,
in the midst of many peoples,
like a lion among the beasts of the
forest,
like a young lion among flocks of
sheep,
which mauls and mangles as it goes,
and no one can rescue.
9Your hand will be lifted up in triumph
over your enemies,
and all your foes will be destroyed.

*a8 Or hill   b1 Or Strengthen your walls, O walled city   c2 Or rulers   d2 Hebrew goings out   e2 Or
from days of eternity   f6 Or crush   g6 Or Nimrod in its gates*

¹⁰"In that day," declares the LORD,

"I will destroy your horses from among
    you
    and demolish your chariots.
¹¹I will destroy the cities of your land
    and tear down all your strongholds.
¹²I will destroy your witchcraft
    and you will no longer cast spells.
¹³I will destroy your carved images
    and your sacred stones from among
        you;
    you will no longer bow down
    to the work of your hands.
¹⁴I will uproot from among you your
        Asherah poles*a*
    and demolish your cities.
¹⁵I will take vengeance in anger and
        wrath
    upon the nations that have not
        obeyed me."

The LORD's Case Against Israel

6 Listen to what the LORD says:

"Stand up, plead your case before the
    mountains;
    let the hills hear what you have to
        say.
²Hear, O mountains, the LORD's
        accusation;
    listen, you everlasting foundations of
        the earth.
For the LORD has a case against his
        people;
    he is lodging a charge against Israel.

³"My people, what have I done to you?
    How have I burdened you? Answer
        me.
⁴I brought you up out of Egypt
    and redeemed you from the land of
        slavery.
I sent Moses to lead you,
    also Aaron and Miriam.
⁵My people, remember
    what Balak king of Moab counseled
    and what Balaam son of Beor
        answered.
Remember ⌐your journey⌐ from Shittim
        to Gilgal,
    that you may know the righteous acts
        of the LORD."

⁶With what shall I come before the LORD
    and bow down before the exalted
        God?

Shall I come before him with burnt
        offerings,
    with calves a year old?
⁷Will the LORD be pleased with thousands
        of rams,
    with ten thousand rivers of oil?
Shall I offer my firstborn for my
        transgression,
    the fruit of my body for the sin of my
        soul?
⁸He has showed you, O man, what is
        good.
    And what does the LORD require of
        you?
To act justly and to love mercy
    and to walk humbly with your God.

Israel's Guilt and Punishment

⁹Listen! The LORD is calling to the
        city—
    and to fear your name is wisdom—
"Heed the rod and the One who
        appointed it.*b*
¹⁰Am I still to forget, O wicked house,
        your ill-gotten treasures
    and the short ephah,*c* which is
        accursed?
¹¹Shall I acquit a man with dishonest
        scales,
    with a bag of false weights?
¹²Her rich men are violent;
    her people are liars
    and their tongues speak deceitfully.
¹³Therefore, I have begun to destroy
        you,
    to ruin you because of your sins.
¹⁴You will eat but not be satisfied;
    your stomach will still be empty.*d*
You will store up but save nothing,
    because what you save I will give to
        the sword.
¹⁵You will plant but not harvest;
    you will press olives but not use the
        oil on yourselves,
    you will crush grapes but not drink
        the wine.
¹⁶You have observed the statutes of Omri
    and all the practices of Ahab's house,
    and you have followed their
        traditions.
Therefore I will give you over to ruin
    and your people to derision;
    you will bear the scorn of the
        nations.*e*"

a14 That is, symbols of the goddess Asherah   *b9* The meaning of the Hebrew for this line is uncertain.
c10 An ephah was a dry measure.   *d14* The meaning of the Hebrew for this word is uncertain.
e16 Septuagint; Hebrew *scorn due my people*

Israel's Misery

7 What misery is mine!
I am like one who gathers summer
fruit
at the gleaning of the vineyard;
there is no cluster of grapes to eat,
none of the early figs that I crave.
2The godly have been swept from the
land;
not one upright man remains.
All men lie in wait to shed blood;
each hunts his brother with a net.
3Both hands are skilled in doing evil;
the ruler demands gifts,
the judge accepts bribes,
the powerful dictate what they
desire—
they all conspire together.
4The best of them is like a brier,
the most upright worse than a thorn
hedge.
The day of your watchmen has come,
the day God visits you.
Now is the time of their confusion.
5Do not trust a neighbor;
put no confidence in a friend.
Even with her who lies in your embrace
be careful of your words.
6For a son dishonors his father,
a daughter rises up against her
mother,
a daughter-in-law against her
mother-in-law—
a man's enemies are the members of
his own household.

7But as for me, I watch in hope for the
Lord,
I wait for God my Savior;
my God will hear me.

Israel Will Rise

8Do not gloat over me, my enemy!
Though I have fallen, I will rise.
Though I sit in darkness,
the Lord will be my light.
9Because I have sinned against him,
I will bear the Lord's wrath,
until he pleads my case
and establishes my right.
He will bring me out into the light;
I will see his righteousness.
10Then my enemy will see it
and will be covered with shame,
she who said to me,
"Where is the Lord your God?"

My eyes will see her downfall;
even now she will be trampled
underfoot
like mire in the streets.

11The day for building your walls will
come,
the day for extending your
boundaries.
12In that day people will come to you
from Assyria and the cities of Egypt,
even from Egypt to the Euphrates
and from sea to sea
and from mountain to mountain.
13The earth will become desolate because
of its inhabitants,
as the result of their deeds.

Prayer and Praise

14Shepherd your people with your staff,
the flock of your inheritance,
which lives by itself in a forest,
in fertile pasturelands. *a*
Let them feed in Bashan and Gilead
as in days long ago.

15"As in the days when you came out of
Egypt,
I will show them my wonders."

16Nations will see and be ashamed,
deprived of all their power.
They will lay their hands on their
mouths
and their ears will become deaf.
17They will lick dust like a snake,
like creatures that crawl on the
ground.
They will come trembling out of their
dens;
they will turn in fear to the Lord our
God
and will be afraid of you.
18Who is a God like you,
who pardons sin and forgives the
transgression
of the remnant of his inheritance?
You do not stay angry forever
but delight to show mercy.
19You will again have compassion on us;
you will tread our sins underfoot
and hurl all our iniquities into the
depths of the sea.
20You will be true to Jacob,
and show mercy to Abraham,
as you pledged on oath to our fathers
in days long ago.

a 14 Or in the middle of Carmel

966

TURN OFF THE TAPE PLAYER!

WEDNESDAY ☐

Two years ago, during their sophomore year, Kirby and Judy went out for about four months. The relationship had gotten extremely physical when suddenly Kirby quit calling.

Hurt and confused, Judy couldn't understand the unreturned phone calls. As she tried to work through the pain and guilt, she said, "I know that God has forgiven me for what I did. I'm just not sure that I can forgive myself."

Look It Up
Refusing to forgive ourselves when God says he's forgiven us makes no sense! It's like saying that we know more about dealing with sin than God does. Notice that he not only forgives, he also forgets:
• "I have swept away your offenses like a cloud, your sins like the morning mist" (Isaiah 44:22).
• "As far as the east is from the west, so far has he removed our transgressions from us" (Psalm 103:12).
• "I, even I, am he who blots out your transgressions, for my own sake, and remembers your sins no more" (Isaiah 43:25).

Think It Through
Satan doesn't miss a trick. Every time you really determine to walk with God and serve him, the devil plays taped reruns of all your sins (especially the "big" ones) and whispers, "You're no good. God could never use a sinner like you." Maybe this explains why Judy was like a spiritual yo-yo for almost a year.

Work It Out
If you can't seem to forgive yourself for certain actions, pray: "God, though you say I am totally forgiven, I realize I have never forgiven myself for _____. Right now I choose not only to believe what you say, but also to forgive myself. Once and for all, I release myself from that burden."

Then, as Satan brings up sins from your past, fight back. Tell him, "You're right. I did do those things. But 2,000 years ago Jesus died on the cross and paid for every sin I have ever or will ever commit. God has forgiven me. I have forgiven myself. Thanks for the reminder."

Nail It Down
Read the assurance of forgiveness in Micah 7:19.

Turn to pages 580, 771, 809, 1068, 1302 and 1352 for other readings on forgiveness.
Turn to page 968 for Thursday's reading.

Topic
FORGIVENESS

Nahum

ABOUT a hundred years after Jonah's visit, Nineveh is again a terror to the whole world. She is filled with pride. No enemy can touch her, she boasts. But gloating days are over, Nahum says, because a "flood" will destroy the city. God's Word comes true to the letter when the overflowing Tigris River crumbles Nineveh's walls, allowing the Babylonian army to flood violently into the city. Nahum (whose name means comfort) can bring you comfort with this thought: God is the judge of the nations; he is the Lord of history.

Outline of Contents

1 An oracle concerning Nineveh. The book of the vision of Nahum the Elkoshite.

The Lord's Anger Against Nineveh

²The LORD is a jealous and avenging God;
    the LORD takes vengeance and is filled with wrath.
The LORD takes vengeance on his foes
    and maintains his wrath against his enemies.
³The LORD is slow to anger and great in power;
    the LORD will not leave the guilty unpunished.
His way is in the whirlwind and the storm,
    and clouds are the dust of his feet.
⁴He rebukes the sea and dries it up;
    he makes all the rivers run dry.
Bashan and Carmel wither
    and the blossoms of Lebanon fade.
⁵The mountains quake before him
    and the hills melt away.
The earth trembles at his presence,
    the world and all who live in it.
⁶Who can withstand his indignation?
    Who can endure his fierce anger?
His wrath is poured out like fire;
    the rocks are shattered before him.

⁷The LORD is good,
    a refuge in times of trouble.
He cares for those who trust in him,
⁸ but with an overwhelming flood
he will make an end of ₎Nineveh₎;
    he will pursue his foes into darkness.

⁹Whatever they plot against the LORD

THE ONE WHO WANTS OUR WORRIES

Last year Stephanie was a nervous wreck—always biting her nails and panicking about one thing or another. This year she's like a new person. How did she manage to become so calm?

"I finally got sick of being anxious all the time. My worrying never changed anything—except I felt torn up on the inside.

"Then one day it hit me: I'm trusting Christ to get me to heaven, but I don't even trust him for everyday problems. How ridiculous!

"Since then, whenever I start to freak out over a situation, I remember that he's promised to take care of all the things I can't handle."

Look It Up •••• Is it really possible to become less of a worrier? Yes! How?

1. Rest in the fact that God cares for you. "Cast all your anxiety on him because he cares for you" (1 Peter 5:7).

2. Rest in the fact that God is in control. "Be still, and know that I am God; I will be exalted among the nations, I will be exalted in the earth" (Psalm 46:10).

In short, peace comes when you focus on the God of peace!

Think It Through •••• Have you ever watched a little kid sleep? We're talking hibernation! No tossing and turning. No fretting about paying the rent or rising grocery prices or whether the car is going to last another year. About all a kid knows is that mom and/or dad will take care of things.

Do you trust in your heavenly Father that much? As much as Stephanie? If not, why not?

Work It Out •••• Get into the habit of looking to God whenever you face a tough problem. (Obstacles that are impossible for you are a breeze for him!)

How do you develop that habit of turning your problems over to him? In the same way you develop any habit—by practice. You may forget to turn to him at first, but if you make the effort for a long enough time, you can eventually train yourself to "cast all your anxiety on him."

Nail It Down •••• Meditate on the promise given in Nahum 1:7.

Turn to pages 1011 and 1119 for other readings on worry.
Turn to page 974 for Friday's reading.

Topic ••••

he[a] will bring to an end;
trouble will not come a second time.
¹⁰They will be entangled among thorns
and drunk from their wine;
they will be consumed like dry
stubble.[b]
¹¹From you, ⌊O Nineveh⌋ has one come
forth
who plots evil against the Lord
and counsels wickedness.

¹²This is what the Lord says:

"Although they have allies and are
numerous,
they will be cut off and pass away.
Although I have afflicted you, ⌊O Judah⌋
I will afflict you no more.
¹³Now I will break their yoke from your
neck
and tear your shackles away."

¹⁴The Lord has given a command
concerning you, ⌊Nineveh⌋:
"You will have no descendants to bear
your name.
I will destroy the carved images and
cast idols
that are in the temple of your gods.
I will prepare your grave,
for you are vile."

¹⁵Look, there on the mountains,
the feet of one who brings good news,
who proclaims peace!
Celebrate your festivals, O Judah,
and fulfill your vows.
No more will the wicked invade you;
they will be completely destroyed.

Nineveh to Fall

2 An attacker advances against you,
⌊Nineveh⌋.
Guard the fortress,
watch the road,
brace yourselves,
marshal all your strength!

²The Lord will restore the splendor of
Jacob
like the splendor of Israel,
though destroyers have laid them waste
and have ruined their vines.

³The shields of his soldiers are red;
the warriors are clad in scarlet.
The metal on the chariots flashes
on the day they are made ready;

the spears of pine are brandished.[c]
⁴The chariots storm through the streets,
rushing back and forth through the
squares.
They look like flaming torches;
they dart about like lightning.

⁵He summons his picked troops,
yet they stumble on their way.
They dash to the city wall;
the protective shield is put in place.
⁶The river gates are thrown open
and the palace collapses.
⁷It is decreed[d] that ⌊the city⌋
be exiled and carried away.
Its slave girls moan like doves
and beat upon their breasts.
⁸Nineveh is like a pool,
and its water is draining away.
"Stop! Stop!" they cry,
but no one turns back.
⁹Plunder the silver!
Plunder the gold!
The supply is endless,
the wealth from all its treasures!
¹⁰She is pillaged, plundered, stripped!
Hearts melt, knees give way,
bodies tremble, every face grows pale.

¹¹Where now is the lions' den,
the place where they fed their young,
where the lion and lioness went,
and the cubs, with nothing to fear?
¹²The lion killed enough for his cubs
and strangled the prey for his mate,
filling his lairs with the kill
and his dens with the prey.
¹³"I am against you,"
declares the Lord Almighty.
"I will burn up your chariots in smoke,
and the sword will devour your young
lions.
I will leave you no prey on the earth.
The voices of your messengers
will no longer be heard."

Woe to Nineveh

3 Woe to the city of blood,
full of lies,
full of plunder,
never without victims!
²The crack of whips,
the clatter of wheels,
galloping horses
and jolting chariots!
³Charging cavalry,

---

[a]9 Or *What do you foes plot against the Lord? / He*   [b]10 The meaning of the Hebrew for this verse is
uncertain.   [c]3 Hebrew; Septuagint and Syriac / *the horsemen rush to and fro*   [d]7 The meaning of the
Hebrew for this word is uncertain.

flashing swords
and glittering spears!
Many casualties,
piles of dead,
bodies without number,
people stumbling over the corpses —
4all because of the wanton lust of a
harlot,
alluring, the mistress of sorceries,
who enslaved nations by her
prostitution
and peoples by her witchcraft.

5"I am against you," declares the Lord
Almighty.
"I will lift your skirts over your face.
I will show the nations your nakedness
and the kingdoms your shame.
6I will pelt you with filth,
I will treat you with contempt
and make you a spectacle.
7All who see you will flee from you and
say,
'Nineveh is in ruins — who will mourn
for her?'
Where can I find anyone to comfort
you?"

8Are you better than Thebes,[a]
situated on the Nile,
with water around her?
The river was her defense,
the waters her wall.
9Cush[b] and Egypt were her boundless
strength;
Put and Libya were among her allies.
10Yet she was taken captive
and went into exile.
Her infants were dashed to pieces
at the head of every street.
Lots were cast for her nobles,
and all her great men were put in
chains.
11You too will become drunk;
you will go into hiding
and seek refuge from the enemy.

12All your fortresses are like fig trees

with their first ripe fruit;
when they are shaken,
the figs fall into the mouth of the
eater.
13Look at your troops —
they are all women!
The gates of your land
are wide open to your enemies;
fire has consumed their bars.

14Draw water for the siege,
strengthen your defenses!
Work the clay,
tread the mortar,
repair the brickwork!
15There the fire will devour you;
the sword will cut you down
and, like grasshoppers, consume you.
Multiply like grasshoppers,
multiply like locusts!
16You have increased the number of your
merchants
till they are more than the stars of the
sky,
but like locusts they strip the land
and then fly away.
17Your guards are like locusts,
your officials like swarms of locusts
that settle in the walls on a cold
day —
but when the sun appears they fly
away,
and no one knows where.

18O king of Assyria, your shepherds[c]
slumber;
your nobles lie down to rest.
Your people are scattered on the
mountains
with no one to gather them.
19Nothing can heal your wound;
your injury is fatal.
Everyone who hears the news about
you
claps his hands at your fall,
for who has not felt
your endless cruelty?

---

a8 Hebrew *No Amon*   *b9* That is, the upper Nile region   *c18* Or *rulers*

HABAKKUK

HABAKKUK prophesies in Judah when the power of Babylon is growing. He questions God's justice in allowing evil to go unchecked and demands an answer. And God does answer—not with explanation, but with revelation. The Babylonians will be his instruments of judgment against Judah. God leads Habakkuk to understand that God will deal with the wicked in his way and in his time. When you have questions for God, try to see the world through the eyes of faith. No matter what happens to you, God is in control of your life.

Outline of Contents

1 The oracle that Habakkuk the prophet received.

Habakkuk's Complaint

²How long, O Lord, must I call for help,
  but you do not listen?
Or cry out to you, "Violence!"
  but you do not save?
³Why do you make me look at injustice?
  Why do you tolerate wrong?
Destruction and violence are before me;
  there is strife, and conflict abounds.
⁴Therefore the law is paralyzed,
  and justice never prevails.
The wicked hem in the righteous,
  so that justice is perverted.

The Lord's Answer

⁵"Look at the nations and watch—
  and be utterly amazed.
For I am going to do something in your
    days
  that you would not believe,
  even if you were told.
⁶I am raising up the Babylonians,ᵃ
  that ruthless and impetuous people,
who sweep across the whole earth
  to seize dwelling places not their own.
⁷They are a feared and dreaded people;
  they are a law to themselves
  and promote their own honor.
⁸Their horses are swifter than leopards,
  fiercer than wolves at dusk.
Their cavalry gallops headlong;

ᵃ6 Or Chaldeans

their horsemen come from afar.
They fly like a vulture swooping to
    devour;
9   they all come bent on violence.
Their hordes^a advance like a desert
    wind
and gather prisoners like sand.
¹⁰They deride kings
    and scoff at rulers.
They laugh at all fortified cities;
    they build earthen ramps and capture
    them.
¹¹Then they sweep past like the wind and
    go on—
guilty men, whose own strength is
    their god."

Habakkuk's Second Complaint

¹²O Lord, are you not from everlasting?
    My God, my Holy One, we will not
    die.
O Lord, you have appointed them to
    execute judgment;
    O Rock, you have ordained them to
    punish.
¹³Your eyes are too pure to look on evil;
    you cannot tolerate wrong.
Why then do you tolerate the
    treacherous?
    Why are you silent while the wicked
    swallow up those more righteous than
    themselves?
¹⁴You have made men like fish in the sea,
    like sea creatures that have no ruler.
¹⁵The wicked foe pulls all of them up
    with hooks,
he catches them in his net,
    he gathers them up in his dragnet;
and so he rejoices and is glad.
¹⁶Therefore he sacrifices to his net
    and burns incense to his dragnet,
for by his net he lives in luxury
    and enjoys the choicest food.
¹⁷Is he to keep on emptying his net,
    destroying nations without mercy?

2   I will stand at my watch
    and station myself on the ramparts;
I will look to see what he will say to
    me,
    and what answer I am to give to this
    complaint.^b

The Lord's Answer

²Then the Lord replied:

"Write down the revelation
    and make it plain on tablets
    so that a herald^c may run with it.
³For the revelation awaits an appointed
    time;
    it speaks of the end
    and will not prove false.
Though it linger, wait for it;
    it^d will certainly come and will not
    delay.

⁴"See, he is puffed up;
    his desires are not upright—
but the righteous will live by his
    faith^e—
⁵indeed, wine betrays him;
    he is arrogant and never at rest.
Because he is as greedy as the grave^f
    and like death is never satisfied,
he gathers to himself all the nations
    and takes captive all the peoples.

⁶"Will not all of them taunt him with ridi-
cule and scorn, saying,

" 'Woe to him who piles up stolen goods
    and makes himself wealthy by
    extortion!
    How long must this go on?'
⁷Will not your debtors^g suddenly arise?
    Will they not wake up and make you
    tremble?
    Then you will become their victim.
⁸Because you have plundered many
    nations,
    the peoples who are left will plunder
    you.
For you have shed man's blood;
    you have destroyed lands and cities
    and everyone in them.

⁹"Woe to him who builds his realm by
    unjust gain
    to set his nest on high,
    to escape the clutches of ruin!
¹⁰You have plotted the ruin of many
    peoples,
    shaming your own house and
    forfeiting your life.
¹¹The stones of the wall will cry out,
    and the beams of the woodwork will
    echo it.

¹²"Woe to him who builds a city with
    bloodshed
    and establishes a town by crime!
¹³Has not the Lord Almighty determined

---

^a9 The meaning of the Hebrew for this word is uncertain.   ^b1 Or and what to answer when I am rebuked
^c2 Or so that whoever reads it   ^d3 Or Though he linger, wait for him; / he   ^e4 Or faithfulness   ^f5 Hebrew
Sheol   ^g7 Or creditors

that the people's labor is only fuel for
  the fire,
that the nations exhaust themselves
  for nothing?
14For the earth will be filled with the
  knowledge of the glory of the
  LORD,
  as the waters cover the sea.

15"Woe to him who gives drink to his
  neighbors,
  pouring it from the wineskin till they
  are drunk,
  so that he can gaze on their naked
  bodies.
16You will be filled with shame instead of
  glory.
  Now it is your turn! Drink and be
  exposed[a]!
The cup from the LORD's right hand is
  coming around to you,
  and disgrace will cover your glory.
17The violence you have done to Lebanon
  will overwhelm you,
  and your destruction of animals will
  terrify you.
For you have shed man's blood;
  you have destroyed lands and cities
  and everyone in them.

18"Of what value is an idol, since a man
  has carved it?
  Or an image that teaches lies?
For he who makes it trusts in his own
  creation;
  he makes idols that cannot speak.
19Woe to him who says to wood, 'Come
  to life!'
  Or to lifeless stone, 'Wake up!'
Can it give guidance?
  It is covered with gold and silver;
  there is no breath in it.
20But the LORD is in his holy temple;
  let all the earth be silent before him."

Habakkuk's Prayer

3 A prayer of Habakkuk the prophet. On
  shigionoth.[b]

2LORD, I have heard of your fame;
  I stand in awe of your deeds, O LORD.
Renew them in our day,
  in our time make them known;
  in wrath remember mercy.

3God came from Teman,

the Holy One from Mount Paran.
                        Selah[c]
His glory covered the heavens
  and his praise filled the earth.
4His splendor was like the sunrise;
  rays flashed from his hand,
  where his power was hidden.
5Plague went before him;
  pestilence followed his steps.
6He stood, and shook the earth;
  he looked, and made the nations
  tremble.
The ancient mountains crumbled
  and the age-old hills collapsed.
His ways are eternal.
7I saw the tents of Cushan in distress,
  the dwellings of Midian in anguish.

8Were you angry with the rivers, O LORD?
  Was your wrath against the streams?
Did you rage against the sea
  when you rode with your horses
  and your victorious chariots?
9You uncovered your bow,
  you called for many arrows.   Selah
You split the earth with rivers;
10 the mountains saw you and writhed.
Torrents of water swept by;
  the deep roared
  and lifted its waves on high.

11Sun and moon stood still in the heavens
  at the glint of your flying arrows,
  at the lightning of your flashing spear.
12In wrath you strode through the earth
  and in anger you threshed the
  nations.
13You came out to deliver your people,
  to save your anointed one.
You crushed the leader of the land of
  wickedness,
  you stripped him from head to foot.
                          Selah
14With his own spear you pierced his
  head
  when his warriors stormed out to
  scatter us,
  gloating as though about to devour
  the wretched who were in hiding.
15You trampled the sea with your horses,
  churning the great waters.

16I heard and my heart pounded,
  my lips quivered at the sound;
  decay crept into my bones,
  and my legs trembled.

a16 Masoretic Text; Dead Sea Scrolls, Aquila, Vulgate and Syriac (see also Septuagint) and stagger
b1 Probably a literary or musical term   c3 A word of uncertain meaning; possibly a musical term; also in
verses 9 and 13

WHY ISN'T GOD MORE REAL TO ME?

Reed is a committed Christian. He wants to please God. He's involved in a lot of youth group activities. He has a devotional time every day.

Despite all his spiritual activity, Reed wonders, "Why isn't God more real to me?"

Look It Up
• • • •

Like everyone else around you, your life is filled with noise. From the time you get up until the time you go to sleep, your ears (and minds) are bombarded with sounds—blaring alarm clocks, honking horns, screeching brakes, wailing sirens, constant music, obnoxious TV sounds, lecturing teachers and talkative friends.

Granted, many of these noises are both necessary and good. However, you need to remember the message of God's Word that silence is also good (Ecclesiastes 3:7) and that you often need quiet moments to hear his voice:

"Be still and know that I am God" (Psalm 46:10).

"I have stilled and quieted my soul; like a weaned child with its mother, like a weaned child is my soul within me" (Psalm 131:2).

Think It Through
• • • •

Does silence make you uncomfortable? Do you always have to play the radio when you are in your room or alone in your car? Why?

One writer says that we seek out noise for three reasons: (1) It lets us focus our attention on what's outside us rather than what's inside. (2) It gives us a false sense of control. (3) It shuts out God. Do you agree?

Work It Out
• • • •

Seek some silence in your life:
1. Get up before everyone else.
2. Take a walk in the snow, or ride down a seldom-traveled street.
3. Visit an empty church.
4. Plan a personal retreat (a half day or even a full day of quiet contemplation).

Once you find a quiet place, stay there until you've heard from God. Be still. Read the Psalms. Look around. Listen. Sing softly. Pray conversationally.

Nail It Down

Read the command to be silent in Habakkuk 2:20.

Turn to pages 557, 587, 1050 and 1053 for other readings on devotions.
Turn to page 976 for the weekend reading.

Topic
• • • •

DEVOTIONS

Yet I will wait patiently for the day of
    calamity
to come on the nation invading us.
[17]Though the fig tree does not bud
    and there are no grapes on the vines,
though the olive crop fails
    and the fields produce no food,
though there are no sheep in the pen
    and no cattle in the stalls,

[18]yet I will rejoice in the LORD,
    I will be joyful in God my Savior.

[19]The Sovereign LORD is my strength;
    he makes my feet like the feet of a
    deer,
    he enables me to go on the heights.

For the director of music. On my
    stringed instruments.

A SENSE OF SECURITY

Work It Out
••••

Think about your life over the last year: all the things that have happened to you, all the things you've done, all the changes you've experienced. Was it all good? Did it make you happy and excited? Or were some of the things you experienced not so great? Even bad?

Habakkuk could relate. Habakkuk had a hard time dealing with the terrible things that were going on in his life and all around him in Judah. But even when life got truly hard—when there was a famine and no food to eat—Habakkuk knew where to turn and to whom to go for security. Do you?

Nail It Down
••••

Read Habakkuk's confession of security in Habakkuk 3:17–18.

Think It Through
••••

Hardly anyone gets through an entire year without some bad experiences. Your girlfriend or boyfriend broke up with you. Your parents split. Or your grandmother died. Maybe you moved to a new city, and the change was terribly hard.

No matter how life has hurt you, God has been there in the middle of it. Perhaps you forgot he was there, or perhaps you were so angry you ignored him. That doesn't change the fact that *God was there.*

Even when life is one vicious struggle after another, God is with you, willing to give you a sense of security, even joy, when the going gets tough. Habakkuk found that he could praise God even when his stomach was growling. Pretty radical, don't you think?

If God was with Habakkuk in his difficult circumstances, you can be sure he's with you in yours. And he's not just there watching you suffer. He's there willing to give you hope and security and even joy.

Nail It Down
••••

Reread Habakkuk's hymn of praise in Habakkuk 3:17–18. For further insight read Psalm 16.

Turn to pages 742, 805 and 954 for other readings on security.
Turn to page 980 for Monday's reading.

Topic
••••

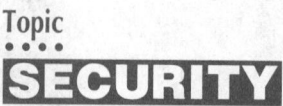
SECURITY

WRITING early in Josiah's reign, Zephaniah prophesies about the day of the Lord. That's his focus and his hope. The day of the Lord will come with ferocity, fury and finality. But there is a wonderful future for those who humble themselves, seek the Lord and live righteously. As you read this book, be encouraged. The Lord will destroy his enemies and bless his people. A day of judgment is coming, but you can escape by turning to the Lord Jesus Christ.

Outline of Contents

1 The word of the LORD that came to Zephaniah son of Cushi, the son of Gedaliah, the son of Amariah, the son of Hezekiah, during the reign of Josiah son of Amon king of Judah:

Warning of Coming Destruction

2"I will sweep away everything
  from the face of the earth,"
                declares the LORD.
3"I will sweep away both men and
      animals;
  I will sweep away the birds of the air
  and the fish of the sea.
The wicked will have only heaps of
      rubble[a]
  when I cut off man from the face of
      the earth,"
                declares the LORD.

Against Judah

4"I will stretch out my hand against
      Judah
  and against all who live in Jerusalem.
I will cut off from this place every
      remnant of Baal,
  the names of the pagan and the
      idolatrous priests—
5those who bow down on the roofs
  to worship the starry host,
those who bow down and swear by the
      LORD
  and who also swear by Molech,[b]
6those who turn back from following the
      LORD
  and neither seek the LORD nor inquire
      of him.
7Be silent before the Sovereign LORD,
  for the day of the LORD is near.

---

a3 The meaning of the Hebrew for this line is uncertain.   b5 Hebrew *Malcam*, that is, Milcom

The LORD has prepared a sacrifice;
he has consecrated those he has
invited.
⁸On the day of the LORD's sacrifice
I will punish the princes
and the king's sons
and all those clad
in foreign clothes.
⁹On that day I will punish
all who avoid stepping on the
threshold,ᵃ
who fill the temple of their gods
with violence and deceit.

¹⁰"On that day," declares the LORD,
"a cry will go up from the Fish Gate,
wailing from the New Quarter,
and a loud crash from the hills.
¹¹Wail, you who live in the market
districtᵇ;
all your merchants will be wiped out,
all who trade withᶜ silver will be
ruined.
¹²At that time I will search Jerusalem with
lamps
and punish those who are
complacent,
who are like wine left on its dregs,
who think, 'The LORD will do nothing,
either good or bad.'
¹³Their wealth will be plundered,
their houses demolished.
They will build houses
but not live in them;
they will plant vineyards
but not drink the wine.

The Great Day of the LORD

¹⁴"The great day of the LORD is near—
near and coming quickly.
Listen! The cry on the day of the LORD
will be bitter,
the shouting of the warrior there.
¹⁵That day will be a day of wrath,
a day of distress and anguish,
a day of trouble and ruin,
a day of darkness and gloom,
a day of clouds and blackness,
¹⁶a day of trumpet and battle cry
against the fortified cities
and against the corner towers.
¹⁷I will bring distress on the people
and they will walk like blind men,
because they have sinned against the
LORD.
Their blood will be poured out like dust

and their entrails like filth.
¹⁸Neither their silver nor their gold
will be able to save them
on the day of the LORD's wrath.
In the fire of his jealousy
the whole world will be consumed,
for he will make a sudden end
of all who live in the earth."

2 Gather together, gather together,
O shameful nation,
²before the appointed time arrives
and that day sweeps on like chaff,
before the fierce anger of the LORD
comes upon you,
before the day of the LORD's wrath
comes upon you.
³Seek the LORD, all you humble of the
land,
you who do what he commands.
Seek righteousness, seek humility;
perhaps you will be sheltered
on the day of the LORD's anger.

Against Philistia

⁴Gaza will be abandoned
and Ashkelon left in ruins.
At midday Ashdod will be emptied
and Ekron uprooted.
⁵Woe to you who live by the sea,
O Kerethite people;
the word of the LORD is against you,
O Canaan, land of the Philistines.

"I will destroy you,
and none will be left."

⁶The land by the sea, where the
Kerethitesᵈ dwell,
will be a place for shepherds and
sheep pens.
⁷It will belong to the remnant of the
house of Judah;
there they will find pasture.
In the evening they will lie down
in the houses of Ashkelon.
The LORD their God will care for them;
he will restore their fortunes.ᵉ

Against Moab and Ammon

⁸"I have heard the insults of Moab
and the taunts of the Ammonites,
who insulted my people
and made threats against their land.
⁹Therefore, as surely as I live,"
declares the LORD Almighty, the God of
Israel,

ᵃ9 See 1 Samuel 5:5.   ᵇ11 Or the Mortar   ᶜ11 Or in
uncertain.   ᵉ7 Or will bring back their captives   ᵈ6 The meaning of the Hebrew for this word is

"surely Moab will become like Sodom,
  the Ammonites like Gomorrah—
a place of weeds and salt pits,
  a wasteland forever.
The remnant of my people will plunder
    them;
  the survivors of my nation will inherit
    their land."

¹⁰This is what they will get in return for
      their pride,
  for insulting and mocking the people
    of the Lord Almighty.
¹¹The Lord will be awesome to them
  when he destroys all the gods of the
    land.
  The nations on every shore will worship
    him,
  every one in its own land.

Against Cush

¹²"You too, O Cushites,ᵃ
  will be slain by my sword."

Against Assyria

¹³He will stretch out his hand against the
      north
  and destroy Assyria,
  leaving Nineveh utterly desolate
  and dry as the desert.
¹⁴Flocks and herds will lie down there,
    creatures of every kind.
  The desert owl and the screech owl
  will roost on her columns.
  Their calls will echo through the
      windows,
  rubble will be in the doorways,
  the beams of cedar will be exposed.
¹⁵This is the carefree city
  that lived in safety.
  She said to herself,
  "I am, and there is none besides me."
What a ruin she has become,
  a lair for wild beasts!
All who pass by her scoff
  and shake their fists.

The Future of Jerusalem

3 Woe to the city of oppressors,
  rebellious and defiled!
²She obeys no one,
  she accepts no correction.
She does not trust in the Lord,
  she does not draw near to her God.
³Her officials are roaring lions,
  her rulers are evening wolves,

who leave nothing for the morning.
⁴Her prophets are arrogant;
  they are treacherous men.
Her priests profane the sanctuary
  and do violence to the law.
⁵The Lord within her is righteous;
  he does no wrong.
Morning by morning he dispenses his
      justice,
  and every new day he does not fail,
  yet the unrighteous know no shame.

⁶"I have cut off nations;
  their strongholds are demolished.
I have left their streets deserted,
  with no one passing through.
Their cities are destroyed;
  no one will be left—no one at all.
⁷I said to the city,
  'Surely you will fear me
  and accept correction!'
Then her dwelling would not be cut off,
  nor all my punishments come upon
    her.
But they were still eager
  to act corruptly in all they did.
⁸Therefore wait for me," declares the
    Lord,
  "for the day I will stand up to
    testify.ᵇ
I have decided to assemble the nations,
  to gather the kingdoms
and to pour out my wrath on them—
  all my fierce anger.
The whole world will be consumed
  by the fire of my jealous anger.

⁹"Then will I purify the lips of the
      peoples,
  that all of them may call on the name
    of the Lord
  and serve him shoulder to shoulder.
¹⁰From beyond the rivers of Cushᶜ
  my worshipers, my scattered people,
  will bring me offerings.
¹¹On that day you will not be put to
      shame
  for all the wrongs you have done to
    me,
because I will remove from this city
  those who rejoice in their pride.
Never again will you be haughty
  on my holy hill.
¹²But I will leave within you
  the meek and humble,
  who trust in the name of the Lord.
¹³The remnant of Israel will do no wrong;

ᵃ12 That is, people from the upper Nile region   ᵇ8 Septuagint and Syriac; Hebrew *will rise up to plunder*
ᶜ10 That is, the upper Nile region

A BIG GOD = SMALL PROBLEMS

Brent is the kind of guy who's always "up." Today, however, Brent is depressed. In science class he saw a movie about what might happen if there were a nuclear war. At church he heard a visiting missionary talk about the billions of people in hundreds of countries around the world who are lost without Christ. Suddenly, Brent feels overwhelmed—very small, very insignificant and very powerless.

What can he possibly do to make a difference in such a desperate and dying world?

Look It Up
••••
Isaiah can help Brent remember the greatness and power of God: "Who has measured the waters in the hollow of his hand, or with the breadth of his hand marked off the heavens?" (Isaiah 40:12). In other words, God is so big he could (if he wanted to) "palm" the universe like a professional basketball player palms a basketball!

That's not all: "Surely the nations are like a drop in a bucket; they are regarded as dust on the scales" (Isaiah 40:15). Imagine all of Canada and the United States, thousands of miles of plains, deserts, forests, lakes, rivers, mountains and valleys. Yet God is so big that, to him, both of these nations are like tiny specks of dust or little drops of water.

Wait, there's more: "He brings princes to naught and reduces the rulers of this world to nothing" (Isaiah 40:23). God, not world leaders, is ultimately in charge of his world.

Think It Through
••••
If God really is as awesome and powerful as these verses say he is, why do you think we often get so worried about so many things? Do most Christians treat their majestic and great God as they should? Do you?

Work It Out
••••
List all the things that you feel incapable of doing or facing today. Write across the top of the list, "Glory and power belong to our God" (Revelation 19:1). Across the bottom write, "He gives strength to the weary and increases the power of the weak" (Isaiah 40:29).

You can make a difference in God's world because he gives his power to you.

Nail It Down
••••
Read God's promise to handle your troubles in Zephaniah 3:17–20.

Turn to pages 599, 998, 1126, 1235 and 1330 for other readings on knowing God.
Turn to page 984 for Tuesday's reading.

Topic
••••

KNOWING GOD

they will speak no lies,
   nor will deceit be found in their
     mouths.
They will eat and lie down
   and no one will make them afraid."

14Sing, O Daughter of Zion;
   shout aloud, O Israel!
Be glad and rejoice with all your heart,
   O Daughter of Jerusalem!
15The Lord has taken away your
     punishment,
   he has turned back your enemy.
The Lord, the King of Israel, is with you;
   never again will you fear any harm.
16On that day they will say to Jerusalem,
   "Do not fear, O Zion;
   do not let your hands hang limp.
17The Lord your God is with you,
   he is mighty to save.
He will take great delight in you,

he will quiet you with his love,
   he will rejoice over you with singing."
18"The sorrows for the appointed feasts
   I will remove from you;
   they are a burden and a reproach to
     you.*a*
19At that time I will deal
   with all who oppressed you;
I will rescue the lame
   and gather those who have been
     scattered.
I will give them praise and honor
   in every land where they were put to
     shame.
20At that time I will gather you;
   at that time I will bring you home.
I will give you honor and praise
   among all the peoples of the earth
when I restore your fortunes*b*
   before your very eyes,"
                  says the Lord.

---

a 18 Or "I will gather you who mourn for the appointed feasts; / your reproach is a burden to you   *b20* Or I
bring back your captives

HAGGAI

THE exiles are back after a long stay in Babylon. Jerusalem is in shambles, so they set about rebuilding. They start construction on a new temple but soon turn away to rebuild their own houses. For sixteen years they ignore the unfinished temple until Haggai urges them to get their priorities straight. With renewed courage and commitment, the people clear the rubble and complete the temple. As you read Haggai, get your priorities straight. Clear away any worldly rubble that might be in your life and seek God's kingdom first.

Outline of Contents

A Call to Build the House of the LORD

1 In the second year of King Darius, on the first day of the sixth month, the word of the LORD came through the prophet Haggai to Zerubbabel son of Shealtiel, governor of Judah, and to Joshua*a* son of Jehozadak, the high priest:

²This is what the LORD Almighty says: "These people say, 'The time has not yet come for the LORD's house to be built.'"

³Then the word of the LORD came through the prophet Haggai: ⁴"Is it a time for you yourselves to be living in your paneled houses, while this house remains a ruin?"

⁵Now this is what the LORD Almighty says: "Give careful thought to your ways. ⁶You have planted much, but have harvested lit-

tle. You eat, but never have enough. You drink, but never have your fill. You put on clothes, but are not warm. You earn wages, only to put them in a purse with holes in it."

⁷This is what the LORD Almighty says: "Give careful thought to your ways. ⁸Go up into the mountains and bring down timber and build the house, so that I may take pleasure in it and be honored," says the LORD. ⁹"You expected much, but see, it turned out to be little. What you brought home, I blew away. Why?" declares the LORD Almighty. "Because of my house, which remains a ruin, while each of you is busy with his own house. ¹⁰Therefore, because of you the heavens have withheld their dew and the

a1 A variant of *Jeshua*; here and elsewhere in Haggai

earth its crops. ¹¹I called for a drought on the fields and the mountains, on the grain, the new wine, the oil and whatever the ground produces, on men and cattle, and on the labor of your hands."

¹²Then Zerubbabel son of Shealtiel, Joshua son of Jehozadak, the high priest, and the whole remnant of the people obeyed the voice of the Lord their God and the message of the prophet Haggai, because the Lord their God had sent him. And the people feared the Lord.

¹³Then Haggai, the Lord's messenger, gave this message of the Lord to the people: "I am with you," declares the Lord. ¹⁴So the Lord stirred up the spirit of Zerubbabel son of Shealtiel, governor of Judah, and the spirit of Joshua son of Jehozadak, the high priest, and the spirit of the whole remnant of the people. They came and began to work on the house of the Lord Almighty, their God, ¹⁵on the twenty-fourth day of the sixth month in the second year of King Darius.

The Promised Glory of the New House

2 On the twenty-first day of the seventh month, the word of the Lord came through the prophet Haggai: ²"Speak to Zerubbabel son of Shealtiel, governor of Judah, to Joshua son of Jehozadak, the high priest, and to the remnant of the people. Ask them, ³'Who of you is left who saw this house in its former glory? How does it look to you now? Does it not seem to you like nothing? ⁴But now be strong, O Zerubbabel,' declares the Lord. 'Be strong, O Joshua son of Jehozadak, the high priest. Be strong, all you people of the land,' declares the Lord, 'and work. For I am with you,' declares the Lord Almighty. ⁵'This is what I covenanted with you when you came out of Egypt. And my Spirit remains among you. Do not fear.'

⁶"This is what the Lord Almighty says: 'In a little while I will once more shake the heavens and the earth, the sea and the dry land. ⁷I will shake all nations, and the desired of all nations will come, and I will fill this house with glory,' says the Lord Almighty. ⁸'The silver is mine and the gold is mine,' declares the Lord Almighty. ⁹'The glory of this present house will be greater than the glory of the former house,' says the Lord Almighty. 'And in this place I will grant peace,' declares the Lord Almighty."

Blessings for a Defiled People

¹⁰On the twenty-fourth day of the ninth month, in the second year of Darius, the word of the Lord came to the prophet Haggai: ¹¹"This is what the Lord Almighty says: 'Ask the priests what the law says: ¹²If a person carries consecrated meat in the fold of his garment, and that fold touches some bread or stew, some wine, oil or other food, does it become consecrated?' "

The priests answered, "No."

¹³Then Haggai said, "If a person defiled by contact with a dead body touches one of these things, does it become defiled?"

"Yes," the priests replied, "it becomes defiled."

¹⁴Then Haggai said, " 'So it is with this people and this nation in my sight,' declares the Lord. 'Whatever they do and whatever they offer there is defiled.

¹⁵" 'Now give careful thought to this from this day onᵃ—consider how things were before one stone was laid on another in the Lord's temple. ¹⁶When anyone came to a heap of twenty measures, there were only ten. When anyone went to a wine vat to draw fifty measures, there were only twenty. ¹⁷I struck all the work of your hands with blight, mildew and hail, yet you did not turn to me,' declares the Lord. ¹⁸'From this day on, from this twenty-fourth day of the ninth month, give careful thought to the day when the foundation of the Lord's temple was laid. Give careful thought: ¹⁹Is there yet any seed left in the barn? Until now, the vine and the fig tree, the pomegranate and the olive tree have not borne fruit.

" 'From this day on I will bless you.' "

Zerubbabel the Lord's Signet Ring

²⁰The word of the Lord came to Haggai a second time on the twenty-fourth day of the month: ²¹"Tell Zerubbabel governor of Judah that I will shake the heavens and the earth. ²²I will overturn royal thrones and shatter the power of the foreign kingdoms. I will overthrow chariots and their drivers; horses and their riders will fall, each by the sword of his brother.

²³" 'On that day,' declares the Lord Almighty, 'I will take you, my servant Zerubbabel son of Shealtiel,' declares the Lord, 'and I will make you like my signet ring, for I have chosen you,' declares the Lord Almighty."

ᵃ15 Or to the days past

WHEN YOU'RE YANKED UP BY YOUR ROOTS

Two months ago, life for Susan was going perfectly. She had a great circle of friends, a leadership position in the drama club, and she was part of a good youth group. Plus she had lined up the one summer job everyone wanted—being a lifeguard at the neighborhood swimming pool.

A month ago her dad came home with the news. "The company wants to promote me—move me to the home office in Chicago! Isn't that great?" Today Susan sits in the Hewitt's new home in the Chicago suburbs—alone and really depressed.

Look It Up
••••

Few things are as difficult as geographical change. Does God offer any comfort when your family pulls up its stakes and makes a move, dragging you along? Yes! When God's people go to a new place, he goes with them. God told:

• Jacob: "I am with you and will watch over you wherever you go" (Genesis 28:15);

• The children of Israel: "Be strong and courageous. Do not be afraid or terrified because of them, for the LORD your God goes with you; he will never leave you nor forsake you" (Deuteronomy 31:6);

• Paul: "Do not be afraid . . . . For I am with you" (Acts 18:9–10).

Think It Through
••••

Imagine that your family suddenly moved a thousand miles away. But suppose your best friend's family moved to the same place. The transition would be a whole lot easier, wouldn't it?

As a Christian, when you move, you get to bring your best friend with you. Because God goes wherever you go! In fact, he's already at your new destination—ready to listen, comfort, and give you the courage to start over.

Work It Out
••••

Here's how to avoid the depression of a major move.

Be honest with God about your feelings. You can't hide them from him. Why try?

Don't fool yourself into thinking the situation is worse than it is with thoughts like, "I'll never fit in." Look at it this way: You're not the first (and you won't be the last) person who has had to move. In time, you'll do just fine.

At the earliest opportunity, get involved at school and church. Try a new activity or join the same activities you enjoyed in your old community.

Nail It Down
••••

Read God's promise to be with you in Haggai 1:13.

Turn to pages 576 and 591 for other readings on change.
Turn to page 991 for Wednesday's reading.

Topic
••••

CHANGE

ZECHARIAH joins Haggai to encourage the people to finish the temple. And his motivational messages are riveting. He tells of horses, horns, craftsmen, a lampstand and two olive trees, a flying scroll, a woman in a basket, and four chariots—technicolor visions and a divine commentary that show God's control over everything and the coming new kingdom of the Messiah. In a final, glorious vision Zechariah sees Messiah himself inhabiting the temple. As you read, be sure you have turned to the Lord and let these visions of hope inspire you to serve him.

Outline of Contents

A Call to Return to the LORD

1 In the eighth month of the second year of Darius, the word of the LORD came to the prophet Zechariah son of Berekiah, the son of Iddo:

2"The LORD was very angry with your forefathers. 3Therefore tell the people: This is what the LORD Almighty says: 'Return to me,' declares the LORD Almighty, 'and I will return to you,' says the LORD Almighty. 4Do not be like your forefathers, to whom the earlier prophets proclaimed: This is what the LORD Almighty says: 'Turn from your evil ways and your evil practices.' But they would not listen or pay attention to me, declares the LORD. 5Where are your forefathers now? And the prophets, do they live forever? 6But did not my words and my decrees, which I com- manded my servants the prophets, overtake your forefathers?

"Then they repented and said, 'The LORD Almighty has done to us what our ways and practices deserve, just as he determined to do.'"

The Man Among the Myrtle Trees

7On the twenty-fourth day of the eleventh month, the month of Shebat, in the second year of Darius, the word of the LORD came to the prophet Zechariah son of Berekiah, the son of Iddo.

8During the night I had a vision—and there before me was a man riding a red horse! He was standing among the myrtle trees in a ravine. Behind him were red, brown and white horses.

[9]I asked, "What are these, my lord?"

The angel who was talking with me answered, "I will show you what they are."

[10]Then the man standing among the myrtle trees explained, "They are the ones the LORD has sent to go throughout the earth."

[11]And they reported to the angel of the LORD, who was standing among the myrtle trees, "We have gone throughout the earth and found the whole world at rest and in peace."

[12]Then the angel of the LORD said, "LORD Almighty, how long will you withhold mercy from Jerusalem and from the towns of Judah, which you have been angry with these seventy years?" [13]So the LORD spoke kind and comforting words to the angel who talked with me.

[14]Then the angel who was speaking to me said, "Proclaim this word: This is what the LORD Almighty says: 'I am very jealous for Jerusalem and Zion, [15]but I am very angry with the nations that feel secure. I was only a little angry, but they added to the calamity.'

[16]"Therefore, this is what the LORD says: 'I will return to Jerusalem with mercy, and there my house will be rebuilt. And the measuring line will be stretched out over Jerusalem,' declares the LORD Almighty.

[17]"Proclaim further: This is what the LORD Almighty says: 'My towns will again overflow with prosperity, and the LORD will again comfort Zion and choose Jerusalem.'"

Four Horns and Four Craftsmen

[18]Then I looked up—and there before me were four horns! [19]I asked the angel who was speaking to me, "What are these?"

He answered me, "These are the horns that scattered Judah, Israel and Jerusalem."

[20]Then the LORD showed me four craftsmen. [21]I asked, "What are these coming to do?"

He answered, "These are the horns that scattered Judah so that no one could raise his head, but the craftsmen have come to terrify them and throw down these horns of the nations who lifted up their horns against the land of Judah to scatter its people."

A Man With a Measuring Line

2 Then I looked up—and there before me was a man with a measuring line in his hand! [2]I asked, "Where are you going?"

He answered me, "To measure Jerusalem, to find out how wide and how long it is."

[3]Then the angel who was speaking to me left, and another angel came to meet him [4]and said to him: "Run, tell that young man, 'Jerusalem will be a city without walls because of the great number of men and livestock in it. [5]And I myself will be a wall of fire around it,' declares the LORD, 'and I will be its glory within.'

[6]"Come! Come! Flee from the land of the north," declares the LORD, "for I have scattered you to the four winds of heaven," declares the LORD.

[7]"Come, O Zion! Escape, you who live in the Daughter of Babylon!" [8]For this is what the LORD Almighty says: "After he has honored me and has sent me against the nations that have plundered you—for whoever touches you touches the apple of his eye— [9]I will surely raise my hand against them so that their slaves will plunder them.[a] Then you will know that the LORD Almighty has sent me.

[10]"Shout and be glad, O Daughter of Zion. For I am coming, and I will live among you," declares the LORD. [11]"Many nations will be joined with the LORD in that day and will become my people. I will live among you and you will know that the LORD Almighty has sent me to you. [12]The LORD will inherit Judah as his portion in the holy land and will again choose Jerusalem. [13]Be still before the LORD, all mankind, because he has roused himself from his holy dwelling."

Clean Garments for the High Priest

3 Then he showed me Joshua[b] the high priest standing before the angel of the LORD, and Satan[c] standing at his right side to accuse him. [2]The LORD said to Satan, "The LORD rebuke you, Satan! The LORD, who has chosen Jerusalem, rebuke you! Is not this man a burning stick snatched from the fire?"

[3]Now Joshua was dressed in filthy clothes as he stood before the angel. [4]The angel said to those who were standing before him, "Take off his filthy clothes."

Then he said to Joshua, "See, I have taken away your sin, and I will put rich garments on you."

[5]Then I said, "Put a clean turban on his head." So they put a clean turban on his head and clothed him, while the angel of the LORD stood by.

---

a8,9 Or says after . . . eye: [9]*"I . . . plunder them."*   *b1 A variant of Jeshua; here and elsewhere in Zechariah*
c1 Satan means accuser.

⁶The angel of the Lord gave this charge to Joshua: ⁷"This is what the Lord Almighty says: 'If you will walk in my ways and keep my requirements, then you will govern my house and have charge of my courts, and I will give you a place among these standing here.

⁸" 'Listen, O high priest Joshua and your associates seated before you, who are men symbolic of things to come: I am going to bring my servant, the Branch. ⁹See, the stone I have set in front of Joshua! There are seven eyes[a] on that one stone, and I will engrave an inscription on it,' says the Lord Almighty, 'and I will remove the sin of this land in a single day.

¹⁰ 'In that day each of you will invite his neighbor to sit under his vine and fig tree,' declares the Lord Almighty."

The Gold Lampstand and the Two Olive Trees

4 Then the angel who talked with me returned and wakened me, as a man is wakened from his sleep. ²He asked me, "What do you see?"

I answered, "I see a solid gold lampstand with a bowl at the top and seven lights on it, with seven channels to the lights. ³Also there are two olive trees by it, one on the right of the bowl and the other on its left."

⁴I asked the angel who talked with me, "What are these, my lord?"

⁵He answered, "Do you not know what these are?"

"No, my lord," I replied.

⁶So he said to me, "This is the word of the Lord to Zerubbabel: 'Not by might nor by power, but by my Spirit,' says the Lord Almighty.

⁷"What[b] are you, O mighty mountain? Before Zerubbabel you will become level ground. Then he will bring out the capstone to shouts of 'God bless it! God bless it!' "

⁸Then the word of the Lord came to me: ⁹"The hands of Zerubbabel have laid the foundation of this temple; his hands will also complete it. Then you will know that the Lord Almighty has sent me to you.

¹⁰"Who despises the day of small things? Men will rejoice when they see the plumb line in the hand of Zerubbabel.

"(These seven are the eyes of the Lord, which range throughout the earth.)"

¹¹Then I asked the angel, "What are these two olive trees on the right and the left of the lampstand?"

¹²Again I asked him, "What are these two olive branches beside the two gold pipes that pour out golden oil?"

¹³He replied, "Do you not know what these are?"

"No, my lord," I said.

¹⁴So he said, "These are the two who are anointed to[c] serve the Lord of all the earth."

The Flying Scroll

5 I looked again—and there before me was a flying scroll!

²He asked me, "What do you see?"

I answered, "I see a flying scroll, thirty feet long and fifteen feet wide.[d]"

³And he said to me, "This is the curse that is going out over the whole land; for according to what it says on one side, every thief will be banished, and according to what it says on the other, everyone who swears falsely will be banished. ⁴The Lord Almighty declares, 'I will send it out, and it will enter the house of the thief and the house of him who swears falsely by my name. It will remain in his house and destroy it, both its timbers and its stones.' "

The Woman in a Basket

⁵Then the angel who was speaking to me came forward and said to me, "Look up and see what this is that is appearing."

⁶I asked, "What is it?"

He replied, "It is a measuring basket.[e]" And he added, "This is the iniquity[f] of the people throughout the land."

⁷Then the cover of lead was raised, and there in the basket sat a woman! ⁸He said, "This is wickedness," and he pushed her back into the basket and pushed the lead cover down over its mouth.

⁹Then I looked up—and there before me were two women, with the wind in their wings! They had wings like those of a stork, and they lifted up the basket between heaven and earth.

¹⁰"Where are they taking the basket?" I asked the angel who was speaking to me.

¹¹He replied, "To the country of Babylonia[g] to build a house for it. When it is ready, the basket will be set there in its place."

---

a9 Or *facets*   *b7* Or *Who*   *c14* Or *two who bring oil and wide* (about 9 meters long and 4.5 meters wide)   *d2* Hebrew *twenty cubits long and ten cubits*   *e6* Hebrew *an ephah*; also in verses 7-11   *f6* Or *appearance*   *g11* Hebrew *Shinar*

Four Chariots

6 I looked up again—and there before me were four chariots coming out from between two mountains—mountains of bronze! **2**The first chariot had red horses, the second black, **3**the third white, and the fourth dappled—all of them powerful. **4**I asked the angel who was speaking to me, "What are these, my lord?"

5The angel answered me, "These are the four spirits*a* of heaven, going out from standing in the presence of the Lord of the whole world. **6**The one with the black horses is going toward the north country, the one with the white horses toward the west,*b* and the one with the dappled horses toward the south."

7When the powerful horses went out, they were straining to go throughout the earth. And he said, "Go throughout the earth!" So they went throughout the earth.

8Then he called to me, "Look, those going toward the north country have given my Spirit*c* rest in the land of the north."

A Crown for Joshua

9The word of the Lord came to me: **10**"Take ₁silver and gold₎ from the exiles Heldai, Tobijah and Jedaiah, who have arrived from Babylon. Go the same day to the house of Josiah son of Zephaniah. **11**Take the silver and gold and make a crown, and set it on the head of the high priest, Joshua son of Jehozadak. **12**Tell him this is what the Lord Almighty says: 'Here is the man whose name is the Branch, and he will branch out from his place and build the temple of the Lord. **13**It is he who will build the temple of the Lord, and he will be clothed with majesty and will sit and rule on his throne. And he will be a priest on his throne. And there will be harmony between the two.' **14**The crown will be given to Heldai,*d* Tobijah, Jedaiah and Hen*e* son of Zephaniah as a memorial in the temple of the Lord. **15**Those who are far away will come and help to build the temple of the Lord, and you will know that the Lord Almighty has sent me to you. This will happen if you diligently obey the Lord your God."

Justice and Mercy, Not Fasting

7 In the fourth year of King Darius, the word of the Lord came to Zechariah on the fourth day of the ninth month, the month of Kislev. **2**The people of Bethel had sent Sharezer and Regem-Melech, together with their men, to entreat the Lord **3**by asking the priests of the house of the Lord Almighty and the prophets, "Should I mourn and fast in the fifth month, as I have done for so many years?"

4Then the word of the Lord Almighty came to me: **5**"Ask all the people of the land and the priests, 'When you fasted and mourned in the fifth and seventh months for the past seventy years, was it really for me that you fasted? **6**And when you were eating and drinking, were you not just feasting for yourselves? **7**Are these not the words the Lord proclaimed through the earlier prophets when Jerusalem and its surrounding towns were at rest and prosperous, and the Negev and the western foothills were settled?' "

8And the word of the Lord came again to Zechariah: **9**"This is what the Lord Almighty says: 'Administer true justice; show mercy and compassion to one another. **10**Do not oppress the widow or the fatherless, the alien or the poor. In your hearts do not think evil of each other.'

11"But they refused to pay attention; stubbornly they turned their backs and stopped up their ears. **12**They made their hearts as hard as flint and would not listen to the law or to the words that the Lord Almighty had sent by his Spirit through the earlier prophets. So the Lord Almighty was very angry.

13" 'When I called, they did not listen; so when they called, I would not listen,' says the Lord Almighty. **14**'I scattered them with a whirlwind among all the nations, where they were strangers. The land was left so desolate behind them that no one could come or go. This is how they made the pleasant land desolate.' "

The Lord Promises to Bless Jerusalem

8 Again the word of the Lord Almighty came to me. **2**This is what the Lord Almighty says: "I am very jealous for Zion; I am burning with jealousy for her."

3This is what the Lord says: "I will return to Zion and dwell in Jerusalem. Then Jerusalem will be called the City of Truth, and the mountain of the Lord Almighty will be called the Holy Mountain."

4This is what the Lord Almighty says: "Once again men and women of ripe old age will sit in the streets of Jerusalem, each with

---

*a*5 Or *winds*   *b*6 Or *horses after them*   *c*8 Or *spirit*
*d*14 Syriac; Hebrew *Helem*   *e*14 Or *and the*
gracious one, the

cane in hand because of his age. [5]The city streets will be filled with boys and girls playing there."

[6]This is what the LORD Almighty says: "It may seem marvelous to the remnant of this people at that time, but will it seem marvelous to me?" declares the LORD Almighty.

[7]This is what the LORD Almighty says: "I will save my people from the countries of the east and the west. [8]I will bring them back to live in Jerusalem; they will be my people, and I will be faithful and righteous to them as their God."

[9]This is what the LORD Almighty says: "You who now hear these words spoken by the prophets who were there when the foundation was laid for the house of the LORD Almighty, let your hands be strong so that the temple may be built. [10]Before that time there were no wages for man or beast. No one could go about his business safely because of his enemy, for I had turned every man against his neighbor. [11]But now I will not deal with the remnant of this people as I did in the past," declares the LORD Almighty.

[12]"The seed will grow well, the vine will yield its fruit, the ground will produce its crops, and the heavens will drop their dew. I will give all these things as an inheritance to the remnant of this people. [13]As you have been an object of cursing among the nations, O Judah and Israel, so will I save you, and you will be a blessing. Do not be afraid, but let your hands be strong."

[14]This is what the LORD Almighty says: "Just as I had determined to bring disaster upon you and showed no pity when your fathers angered me," says the LORD Almighty, [15]"so now I have determined to do good again to Jerusalem and Judah. Do not be afraid. [16]These are the things you are to do: Speak the truth to each other, and render true and sound judgment in your courts; [17]do not plot evil against your neighbor, and do not love to swear falsely. I hate all this," declares the LORD.

[18]Again the word of the LORD Almighty came to me. [19]This is what the LORD Almighty says: "The fasts of the fourth, fifth, seventh and tenth months will become joyful and glad occasions and happy festivals for Judah. Therefore love truth and peace."

[20]This is what the LORD Almighty says: "Many peoples and the inhabitants of many cities will yet come, [21]and the inhabitants of one city will go to another and say, 'Let us go at once to entreat the LORD and seek the LORD Almighty. I myself am going.' [22]And many peoples and powerful nations will come to Jerusalem to seek the LORD Almighty and to entreat him."

[23]This is what the LORD Almighty says: "In those days ten men from all languages and nations will take firm hold of one Jew by the hem of his robe and say, 'Let us go with you, because we have heard that God is with you.' "

Judgment on Israel's Enemies

An Oracle

9 The word of the LORD is against the land of Hadrach
and will rest upon Damascus—
for the eyes of men and all the tribes of Israel
are on the LORD — [a]
[2]and upon Hamath too, which borders on it,
and upon Tyre and Sidon, though they are very skillful.
[3]Tyre has built herself a stronghold;
she has heaped up silver like dust,
and gold like the dirt of the streets.
[4]But the Lord will take away her possessions
and destroy her power on the sea,
and she will be consumed by fire.
[5]Ashkelon will see it and fear;
Gaza will writhe in agony,
and Ekron too, for her hope will wither.
Gaza will lose her king
and Ashkelon will be deserted.
[6]Foreigners will occupy Ashdod,
and I will cut off the pride of the Philistines.
[7]I will take the blood from their mouths,
the forbidden food from between their teeth.
Those who are left will belong to our God
and become leaders in Judah,
and Ekron will be like the Jebusites.
[8]But I will defend my house
against marauding forces.
Never again will an oppressor overrun my people,
for now I am keeping watch.

The Coming of Zion's King

[9]Rejoice greatly, O Daughter of Zion!
Shout, Daughter of Jerusalem!

---

[a]1 Or *Damascus. / For the eye of the* LORD *is on all mankind, / as well as on the tribes of Israel,*

See, your king[a] comes to you,
  righteous and having salvation,
  gentle and riding on a donkey,
  on a colt, the foal of a donkey.
[10]I will take away the chariots from
        Ephraim
  and the war-horses from Jerusalem,
  and the battle bow will be broken.
  He will proclaim peace to the nations.
  His rule will extend from sea to sea
  and from the River[b] to the ends of
        the earth.[c]
[11]As for you, because of the blood of my
        covenant with you,
  I will free your prisoners from the
        waterless pit.
[12]Return to your fortress, O prisoners of
        hope;
  even now I announce that I will
        restore twice as much to you.
[13]I will bend Judah as I bend my bow
  and fill it with Ephraim.
  I will rouse your sons, O Zion,
  against your sons, O Greece,
  and make you like a warrior's sword.

The LORD Will Appear

[14]Then the LORD will appear over them;
  his arrow will flash like lightning.
  The Sovereign LORD will sound the
        trumpet;
  he will march in the storms of the
        south,
[15] and the LORD Almighty will shield
        them.
  They will destroy
  and overcome with slingstones.
  They will drink and roar as with wine;
  they will be full like a bowl
  used for sprinkling[d] the corners of
        the altar.
[16]The LORD their God will save them on
        that day
  as the flock of his people.
  They will sparkle in his land
  like jewels in a crown.
[17]How attractive and beautiful they will
        be!
  Grain will make the young men
        thrive,
  and new wine the young women.

The LORD Will Care for Judah

10 Ask the LORD for rain in the
        springtime;

it is the LORD who makes the storm
        clouds.
  He gives showers of rain to men,
  and plants of the field to everyone.
[2]The idols speak deceit,
  diviners see visions that lie;
  they tell dreams that are false,
  they give comfort in vain.
  Therefore the people wander like sheep
  oppressed for lack of a shepherd.

[3]"My anger burns against the shepherds,
  and I will punish the leaders;
  for the LORD Almighty will care
  for his flock, the house of Judah,
  and make them like a proud horse in
        battle.
[4]From Judah will come the cornerstone,
  from him the tent peg,
  from him the battle bow,
  from him every ruler.
[5]Together they[e] will be like mighty men
  trampling the muddy streets in battle.
  Because the LORD is with them,
  they will fight and overthrow the
        horsemen.

[6]"I will strengthen the house of Judah
  and save the house of Joseph.
  I will restore them
  because I have compassion on them.
  They will be as though
  I had not rejected them,
  for I am the LORD their God
  and I will answer them.
[7]The Ephraimites will become like
        mighty men,
  and their hearts will be glad as with
        wine.
  Their children will see it and be joyful;
  their hearts will rejoice in the LORD.
[8]I will signal for them
  and gather them in.
  Surely I will redeem them;
  they will be as numerous as before.
[9]Though I scatter them among the
        peoples,
  yet in distant lands they will
        remember me.
  They and their children will survive,
  and they will return.
[10]I will bring them back from Egypt
  and gather them from Assyria.
  I will bring them to Gilead and Lebanon,
  and there will not be room enough
        for them.

[a]9 Or King   [b]10 That is, the Euphrates   [c]10 Or the end of the land   [d]15 Or bowl, / like   [e]4,5 Or ruler,
all of them together. / [5]They

PEACE FOR A WORLD IN PIECES

Consider four teens whose lives are in an uproar:

Camille's father is gay and has AIDS. Camille's afraid people will find out and then shun her.

Maria recently had an abortion. She feels extremely depressed and guilty.

Alvin is being pressured to join a neighborhood gang . . . or else.

Clark's parents have wild fights and yelling matches almost every night.

All four say the pressure is unreal. And all four say they'd give almost anything for just a little peace.

Look It Up

The Bible discusses humanity's desperate search for peace:

"What does a man get for all the toil and anxious striving with which he labors under the sun? All his days his work is pain and grief; even at night his mind does not rest" (Ecclesiastes 2:22–23).

Yet the Bible also offers hope for the seemingly hopeless:

"Peace I leave with you; my peace I give you. I do not give to you as the world gives. Do not let your hearts be troubled and do not be afraid" (John 14:27).

Think It Through

What's worse?

1. To have a horrible secret that is eating you alive, that you can't share with anyone?

2. To be so consumed with guilt that you can't sleep night after night?

3. To live in a high crime area or a war zone with the constant fear that your life might end at any point?

4. To live in a home filled with fighting and strife?

Are any of those scenarios too close for comfort? Is there a solution in each case?

Work It Out

Take an opinion poll on the subject of peace. Ask your friends and family members these questions:

• What percentage of the time do you feel truly peaceful?

• What would you say are the biggest barriers to peace—both personal and world peace?

• How does a troubled person or a troubled world find peace?

Don't just ignore this assignment—really do it. You'll be surprised at what people will tell you . . . and it might just provide a chance for you to share your faith in Christ!

Nail It Down

Read Zechariah 9:10 to find out who brings true peace to nations as well as to individuals.

Turn to pages 724, 736 and 1270 for other readings on peace.
Turn to page 996 for Thursday's reading.

Topic

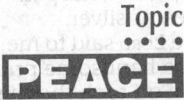

PEACE

[11]They will pass through the sea of
      trouble;
   the surging sea will be subdued
      and all the depths of the Nile will dry
         up.
   Assyria's pride will be brought down
      and Egypt's scepter will pass away.
[12]I will strengthen them in the LORD
      and in his name they will walk,"
                     declares the LORD.

11 Open your doors, O Lebanon,
      so that fire may devour your
      cedars!
[2]Wail, O pine tree, for the cedar has
      fallen;
   the stately trees are ruined!
   Wail, oaks of Bashan;
      the dense forest has been cut down!
[3]Listen to the wail of the shepherds;
      their rich pastures are destroyed!
   Listen to the roar of the lions;
      the lush thicket of the Jordan is
         ruined!

Two Shepherds

[4]This is what the LORD my God says: "Pasture the flock marked for slaughter. [5]Their
buyers slaughter them and go unpunished.
Those who sell them say, 'Praise the LORD, I
am rich!' Their own shepherds do not spare
them. [6]For I will no longer have pity on the
people of the land," declares the LORD. "I will
hand everyone over to his neighbor and his
king. They will oppress the land, and I will
not rescue them from their hands."

[7]So I pastured the flock marked for
slaughter, particularly the oppressed of the
flock. Then I took two staffs and called one
Favor and the other Union, and I pastured
the flock. [8]In one month I got rid of the three
shepherds.

The flock detested me, and I grew weary
of them [9]and said, "I will not be your shepherd. Let the dying die, and the perishing
perish. Let those who are left eat one another's flesh."

[10]Then I took my staff called Favor and
broke it, revoking the covenant I had made
with all the nations. [11]It was revoked on that
day, and so the afflicted of the flock who
were watching me knew it was the word of
the LORD.

[12]I told them, "If you think it best, give me
my pay; but if not, keep it." So they paid me
thirty pieces of silver.

[13]And the LORD said to me, "Throw it to the
potter"—the handsome price at which they
priced me! So I took the thirty pieces of sil-

ver and threw them into the house of the
LORD to the potter.

[14]Then I broke my second staff called
Union, breaking the brotherhood between
Judah and Israel.

[15]Then the LORD said to me, "Take again
the equipment of a foolish shepherd. [16]For
I am going to raise up a shepherd over the
land who will not care for the lost, or seek
the young, or heal the injured, or feed the
healthy, but will eat the meat of the choice
sheep, tearing off their hoofs.

[17]"Woe to the worthless shepherd,
   who deserts the flock!
   May the sword strike his arm and his
      right eye!
   May his arm be completely withered,
      his right eye totally blinded!"

Jerusalem's Enemies to Be Destroyed

An Oracle

12 This is the word of the LORD concern-
      ing Israel. The LORD, who stretches
out the heavens, who lays the foundation of
the earth, and who forms the spirit of man
within him, declares: [2]"I am going to make
Jerusalem a cup that sends all the surrounding peoples reeling. Judah will be besieged
as well as Jerusalem. [3]On that day, when all
the nations of the earth are gathered against
her, I will make Jerusalem an immovable
rock for all the nations. All who try to move
it will injure themselves. [4]On that day I will
strike every horse with panic and its rider
with madness," declares the LORD. "I will
keep a watchful eye over the house of Judah, but I will blind all the horses of the nations. [5]Then the leaders of Judah will say in
their hearts, 'The people of Jerusalem are
strong, because the LORD Almighty is their
God.'

[6]"On that day I will make the leaders of
Judah like a firepot in a woodpile, like a
flaming torch among sheaves. They will
consume right and left all the surrounding
peoples, but Jerusalem will remain intact in
her place.

[7]"The LORD will save the dwellings of Judah first, so that the honor of the house of
David and of Jerusalem's inhabitants may
not be greater than that of Judah. [8]On that
day the LORD will shield those who live in Jerusalem, so that the feeblest among them will
be like David, and the house of David will
be like God, like the Angel of the LORD going
before them. [9]On that day I will set out to
destroy all the nations that attack Jerusalem.

Mourning for the One They Pierced

10"And I will pour out on the house of David and the inhabitants of Jerusalem a spirit[a] of grace and supplication. They will look on[b] me, the one they have pierced, and they will mourn for him as one mourns for an only child, and grieve bitterly for him as one grieves for a firstborn son. **11**On that day the weeping in Jerusalem will be great, like the weeping of Hadad Rimmon in the plain of Megiddo. **12**The land will mourn, each clan by itself, with their wives by themselves: the clan of the house of David and their wives, the clan of the house of Nathan and their wives, **13**the clan of the house of Levi and their wives, the clan of Shimei and their wives, **14**and all the rest of the clans and their wives.

Cleansing From Sin

13 "On that day a fountain will be opened to the house of David and the inhabitants of Jerusalem, to cleanse them from sin and impurity.

2"On that day, I will banish the names of the idols from the land, and they will be remembered no more," declares the LORD Almighty. "I will remove both the prophets and the spirit of impurity from the land. **3**And if anyone still prophesies, his father and mother, to whom he was born, will say to him, 'You must die, because you have told lies in the LORD's name.' When he prophesies, his own parents will stab him.

4"On that day every prophet will be ashamed of his prophetic vision. He will not put on a prophet's garment of hair in order to deceive. **5**He will say, 'I am not a prophet. I am a farmer; the land has been my livelihood since my youth.[c]' **6**If someone asks him, 'What are these wounds on your body[d]?' he will answer, 'The wounds I was given at the house of my friends.'

The Shepherd Struck, the Sheep Scattered

7"Awake, O sword, against my shepherd,
    against the man who is close to me!"
    declares the LORD Almighty.
"Strike the shepherd,
    and the sheep will be scattered,
    and I will turn my hand against the
      little ones.
8In the whole land," declares the LORD,

"two-thirds will be struck down and
    perish;
  yet one-third will be left in it.
9This third I will bring into the fire;
  I will refine them like silver
    and test them like gold.
They will call on my name
    and I will answer them;
I will say, 'They are my people,'
    and they will say, 'The LORD is our
      God.'"

The LORD Comes and Reigns

14 A day of the LORD is coming when your plunder will be divided among you.

2I will gather all the nations to Jerusalem to fight against it; the city will be captured, the houses ransacked, and the women raped. Half of the city will go into exile, but the rest of the people will not be taken from the city. **3**Then the LORD will go out and fight against those nations, as he fights in the day of battle. **4**On that day his feet will stand on the Mount of Olives, east of Jerusalem, and the Mount of Olives will be split in two from east to west, forming a great valley, with half of the mountain moving north and half moving south. **5**You will flee by my mountain valley, for it will extend to Azel. You will flee as you fled from the earthquake[e] in the days of Uzziah king of Judah. Then the LORD my God will come, and all the holy ones with him.

6On that day there will be no light, no cold or frost. **7**It will be a unique day, without daytime or nighttime—a day known to the LORD. When evening comes, there will be light.

8On that day living water will flow out from Jerusalem, half to the eastern sea[f] and half to the western sea,[g] in summer and in winter.

9The LORD will be king over the whole earth. On that day there will be one LORD, and his name the only name.

10The whole land, from Geba to Rimmon, south of Jerusalem, will become like the Arabah. But Jerusalem will be raised up and remain in its place, from the Benjamin Gate to the site of the First Gate, to the Corner Gate, and from the Tower of Hananel to the royal winepresses. **11**It will be inhabited;

---

*a*10 Or *the Spirit*   *b*10 Or *to*   *c*5 Or *farmer; a man sold me in my youth*   *d*6 Or *wounds between your hands*   *e*5 Or *5My mountain valley will be blocked and will extend to Azel. It will be blocked as it was blocked because of the earthquake*   *f*8 That is, the Dead Sea   *g*8 That is, the Mediterranean never again will it be destroyed. Jerusalem will be secure.

¹²This is the plague with which the LORD will strike all the nations that fought against Jerusalem: Their flesh will rot while they are still standing on their feet, their eyes will rot in their sockets, and their tongues will rot in their mouths. ¹³On that day men will be stricken by the LORD with great panic. Each man will seize the hand of another, and they will attack each other. ¹⁴Judah too will fight at Jerusalem. The wealth of all the surrounding nations will be collected — great quantities of gold and silver and clothing. ¹⁵A similar plague will strike the horses and mules, the camels and donkeys, and all the animals in those camps.

¹⁶Then the survivors from all the nations that have attacked Jerusalem will go up year after year to worship the King, the LORD Almighty, and to celebrate the Feast of Taber-nacles. ¹⁷If any of the peoples of the earth do not go up to Jerusalem to worship the King, the LORD Almighty, they will have no rain. ¹⁸If the Egyptian people do not go up and take part, they will have no rain. The LORD*a* will bring on them the plague he inflicts on the nations that do not go up to celebrate the Feast of Tabernacles. ¹⁹This will be the punishment of Egypt and the punishment of all the nations that do not go up to celebrate the Feast of Tabernacles.

²⁰On that day HOLY TO THE LORD will be inscribed on the bells of the horses, and the cooking pots in the LORD's house will be like the sacred bowls in front of the altar. ²¹Every pot in Jerusalem and Judah will be holy to the LORD Almighty, and all who come to sacrifice will take some of the pots and cook in them. And on that day there will no longer be a Canaanite*b* in the house of the LORD Almighty.

a18 Or part, then the LORD   b21 Or merchant

THERE they go again. Malachi prophesies during the deplorable conditions described in Nehemiah 13, years after the Israelites return from exile. The people don't tithe, they marry foreigners, they ignore the Sabbath. But Malachi's words of judgment have little effect. After a final warning about the purifying day of the Lord, the Old Testament closes. Four hundred silent years will pass before God sends another prophet, John the Baptist, to announce the coming of the Messiah, Jesus. As you read this book, commit yourself to loving the Lord wholeheartedly and putting his concerns before your own.

Outline of Contents

God's love for Israel (1:1–5)
Israel insults God (1:6–2:16)
God's judgment and promise (2:17–4:6)

1 An oracle: The word of the LORD to Israel through Malachi.[a]

Jacob Loved, Esau Hated

2"I have loved you," says the LORD.

"But you ask, 'How have you loved us?'

"Was not Esau Jacob's brother?" the LORD says. "Yet I have loved Jacob, 3but Esau I have hated, and I have turned his mountains into a wasteland and left his inheritance to the desert jackals."

4Edom may say, "Though we have been crushed, we will rebuild the ruins."

But this is what the LORD Almighty says: "They may build, but I will demolish. They will be called the Wicked Land, a people always under the wrath of the LORD. 5You will see it with your own eyes and say, 'Great is the LORD — even beyond the borders of Israel!'

Blemished Sacrifices

6"A son honors his father, and a servant his master. If I am a father, where is the honor due me? If I am a master, where is the respect due me?" says the LORD Almighty. "It is you, O priests, who show contempt for my name.

"But you ask, 'How have we shown contempt for your name?'

7"You place defiled food on my altar.

"But you ask, 'How have we defiled you?'

"By saying that the LORD's table is contemptible. 8When you bring blind animals for sacrifice, is that not wrong? When you sacrifice crippled or diseased animals, is

a1 Malachi means my messenger.

MARRIAGE IS FOR *LIFE!*

When the phone rang just after dinner last night, Blair expected it to be her friend Jenny. (So did everyone else in the house, since Jenny has called Blair after dinner every night for two months!)

What Blair did not expect was what Jenny had to say:

"No!" she screamed in utter shock. "I can't believe this. Mr. and Mrs. Brooks are getting a divorce? They've been married for almost twenty years!"

The next day, as Blair was driving to the mall, she thought about the phone call. "Well, I guess twenty years is a long time. Who knows? Maybe it's the best thing for the kids."

Look It Up
••••

From the very beginning, God meant for marriage to last.

"For this reason a man will leave his father and mother and be united to his wife, and they will become one flesh" (Genesis 2:24).

Jesus Christ, commenting on this verse, added, "So they are no longer two, but one. Therefore what God has joined together, let man not separate" (Mark 10:8–9).

And the apostle Paul charged, "To the married I give this command (not I, but the Lord): A wife must not separate from her husband. But if she does, she must remain unmarried or else be reconciled to her husband. And a husband must not divorce his wife" (1 Corinthians 7:10–11).

Think It Through
••••

Some Christians interpret the Bible as teaching, "No divorce for any reason." Others insist that God permits divorce in cases of marital unfaithfulness. Still others allow divorce for other reasons such as abandonment or abuse. ,

Views on remarriage are just as diverse.

Use a concordance to look up the words *marry*, *marriage* and *divorce*. What do you think Scripture teaches regarding marriage and divorce?

Work It Out
••••

If your parents are separated, pray fervently that their problems might be resolved and that your family might be restored.

If your parents are divorced, determine that by God's grace you won't make the same mistakes.

If you have a friend whose family is in a messy divorce battle right now, take him or her out for pizza. Be a listening ear and a shoulder to cry on.

Nail It Down
••••

Read the strong statement about divorce found in Malachi 2:13–16.

Turn to pages 315, 478 and 819 for other readings on marriage.
Turn to page 998 for Friday's reading.

Topic
••••

MARRIAGE

that not wrong? Try offering them to your governor! Would he be pleased with you? Would he accept you?" says the Lord Almighty.

⁹"Now implore God to be gracious to us. With such offerings from your hands, will he accept you?" — says the Lord Almighty.

¹⁰"Oh, that one of you would shut the temple doors, so that you would not light useless fires on my altar! I am not pleased with you," says the Lord Almighty, "and I will accept no offering from your hands. ¹¹My name will be great among the nations, from the rising to the setting of the sun. In every place incense and pure offerings will be brought to my name, because my name will be great among the nations," says the Lord Almighty.

¹²"But you profane it by saying of the Lord's table, 'It is defiled,' and of its food, 'It is contemptible.' ¹³And you say, 'What a burden!' and you sniff at it contemptuously," says the Lord Almighty.

"When you bring injured, crippled or diseased animals and offer them as sacrifices, should I accept them from your hands?" says the Lord. ¹⁴"Cursed is the cheat who has an acceptable male in his flock and vows to give it, but then sacrifices a blemished animal to the Lord. For I am a great king," says the Lord Almighty, "and my name is to be feared among the nations.

Admonition for the Priests

2 "And now this admonition is for you, O priests. ²If you do not listen, and if you do not set your heart to honor my name," says the Lord Almighty, "I will send a curse upon you, and I will curse your blessings. Yes, I have already cursed them, because you have not set your heart to honor me.

³"Because of you I will rebukeᵃ your descendantsᵇ; I will spread on your faces the offal from your festival sacrifices, and you will be carried off with it. ⁴And you will know that I have sent you this admonition so that my covenant with Levi may continue," says the Lord Almighty. ⁵"My covenant was with him, a covenant of life and peace, and I gave them to him; this called for reverence and he revered me and stood in awe of my name. ⁶True instruction was in his mouth and nothing false was found on his lips. He walked with me in peace and uprightness, and turned many from sin.

⁷"For the lips of a priest ought to preserve knowledge, and from his mouth men should seek instruction — because he is the messenger of the Lord Almighty. ⁸But you have turned from the way and by your teaching have caused many to stumble; you have violated the covenant with Levi," says the Lord Almighty. ⁹"So I have caused you to be despised and humiliated before all the people, because you have not followed my ways but have shown partiality in matters of the law."

Judah Unfaithful

¹⁰Have we not all one Fatherᶜ? Did not one God create us? Why do we profane the covenant of our fathers by breaking faith with one another?

¹¹Judah has broken faith. A detestable thing has been committed in Israel and in Jerusalem: Judah has desecrated the sanctuary the Lord loves, by marrying the daughter of a foreign god. ¹²As for the man who does this, whoever he may be, may the Lord cut him off from the tents of Jacobᵈ — even though he brings offerings to the Lord Almighty.

¹³Another thing you do: You flood the Lord's altar with tears. You weep and wail because he no longer pays attention to your offerings or accepts them with pleasure from your hands. ¹⁴You ask, "Why?" It is because the Lord is acting as the witness between you and the wife of your youth, because you have broken faith with her, though she is your partner, the wife of your marriage covenant.

¹⁵Has not ₗthe Lordⱼ made them one? In flesh and spirit they are his. And why one? Because he was seeking godly offspring.ᵉ So guard yourself in your spirit, and do not break faith with the wife of your youth.

¹⁶"I hate divorce," says the Lord God of Israel, "and I hate a man's covering himselfᶠ with violence as well as with his garment," says the Lord Almighty.

So guard yourself in your spirit, and do not break faith.

The Day of Judgment

¹⁷You have wearied the Lord with your words.

ᵃ3 Or cut off (see Septuagint)   ᵇ3 Or will blight your grain   ᶜ10 Or father   ᵈ12 Or ¹²May the Lord cut off from the tents of Jacob anyone who gives testimony in behalf of the man who does this   ᵉ15 Or ¹⁵But the one who is our father, did not do this, not as long as life remained in him. And what was he seeking? An offspring from God   ᶠ16 Or his wife

ALWAYS THE SAME IN AN EVER-CHANGING WORLD

Changes. Everybody goes through some changes, but Karen feels like she's in a whirlwind. When her family recently moved from Idaho to Alabama, she had to break up with her boyfriend, leave all her friends, and kiss her favorite pastime—snow-skiing—good-bye.

Besides being in a new school, she's having a hard time getting used to her dad's new sales job, which has him home only on weekends.

Maybe you can identify with her anger: "Everything is always so new and different. Everything's always changing! I hate it! Why do we keep moving every other year? Why can't we just settle down somewhere and be normal?"

Look It Up Sometimes change is for the better, but sometimes it isn't. In a changing world, where can we find security? Consider these verses describing God:

"The Father of the heavenly lights . . . does not change" (James 1:17).

"Jesus Christ is the same yesterday and today and forever" (Hebrews 13:8).

God is the solid rock you can cling to and count on. Since he's perfect, he can't get better. Since he's perfect, he can't become anything less. His character is constant day after day. The truth of his Word never goes out of style. He does not waver in his plans or purposes. He can't love you any more than he already does, and he'll never love you any less.

What security! What comfort! What a changeless truth for a changing world!

Think It Through Since everyone feels like Karen sooner or later, spend a couple of minutes thinking about the consistency of God. If God doesn't change, what does that say about: (1) his love for you and (2) his attitude toward sin?

Work It Out Think of the most faithful, dependable person you know. Ask that person to share with you some tips on dependability. Then do at least one thing he or she suggests today.

God will never, ever change in his nature, his Word, or his dealings with you! He is dependable and sure. Now that's good news!

Nail It Down Read Malachi 3:6 for God's promise that he won't change.

Turn to pages 599, 980, 1126, 1235 and 1330 for other readings on knowing God.
Turn to page 1000 for the weekend reading.

Topic
KNOWING GOD

"How have we wearied him?" you ask.

By saying, "All who do evil are good in the eyes of the LORD, and he is pleased with them" or "Where is the God of justice?"

3 "See, I will send my messenger, who will prepare the way before me. Then suddenly the Lord you are seeking will come to his temple; the messenger of the covenant, whom you desire, will come," says the LORD Almighty.

²But who can endure the day of his coming? Who can stand when he appears? For he will be like a refiner's fire or a launderer's soap. ³He will sit as a refiner and purifier of silver; he will purify the Levites and refine them like gold and silver. Then the LORD will have men who will bring offerings in righteousness, ⁴and the offerings of Judah and Jerusalem will be acceptable to the LORD, as in days gone by, as in former years.

⁵"So I will come near to you for judgment. I will be quick to testify against sorcerers, adulterers and perjurers, against those who defraud laborers of their wages, who oppress the widows and the fatherless, and deprive aliens of justice, but do not fear me," says the LORD Almighty.

Robbing God

⁶"I the LORD do not change. So you, O descendants of Jacob, are not destroyed. ⁷Ever since the time of your forefathers you have turned away from my decrees and have not kept them. Return to me, and I will return to you," says the LORD Almighty.

"But you ask, 'How are we to return?'

⁸"Will a man rob God? Yet you rob me.

"But you ask, 'How do we rob you?'

"In tithes and offerings. ⁹You are under a curse — the whole nation of you — because you are robbing me. ¹⁰Bring the whole tithe into the storehouse, that there may be food in my house. Test me in this," says the LORD Almighty, "and see if I will not throw open the floodgates of heaven and pour out so much blessing that you will not have room enough for it. ¹¹I will prevent pests from devouring your crops, and the vines in your fields will not cast their fruit," says the LORD Almighty. ¹²"Then all the nations will call

you blessed, for yours will be a delightful land," says the LORD Almighty.

¹³"You have said harsh things against me," says the LORD.

"Yet you ask, 'What have we said against you?'

¹⁴"You have said, 'It is futile to serve God. What did we gain by carrying out his requirements and going about like mourners before the LORD Almighty? ¹⁵But now we call the arrogant blessed. Certainly the evildoers prosper, and even those who challenge God escape.' "

¹⁶Then those who feared the LORD talked with each other, and the LORD listened and heard. A scroll of remembrance was written in his presence concerning those who feared the LORD and honored his name.

¹⁷"They will be mine," says the LORD Almighty, "in the day when I make up my treasured possession.ᵃ I will spare them, just as in compassion a man spares his son who serves him. ¹⁸And you will again see the distinction between the righteous and the wicked, between those who serve God and those who do not.

The Day of the LORD

4 "Surely the day is coming; it will burn like a furnace. All the arrogant and every evildoer will be stubble, and that day that is coming will set them on fire," says the LORD Almighty. "Not a root or a branch will be left to them. ²But for you who revere my name, the sun of righteousness will rise with healing in its wings. And you will go out and leap like calves released from the stall. ³Then you will trample down the wicked; they will be ashes under the soles of your feet on the day when I do these things," says the LORD Almighty.

⁴"Remember the law of my servant Moses, the decrees and laws I gave him at Horeb for all Israel.

⁵"See, I will send you the prophet Elijah before that great and dreadful day of the LORD comes. ⁶He will turn the hearts of the fathers to their children, and the hearts of the children to their fathers; or else I will come and strike the land with a curse."

ᵃ17 Or Almighty, "my treasured possession, in the day when I act

WHAT DO YOU VALUE MORE?

Work It Out
••••

Go over your finances for the last month. You're probably already laughing and saying, "What finances?" or "That should take about two minutes!"

Seriously, though, look at how much money you took in last month. Maybe you baby-sit regularly; maybe you have a part-time job; maybe you get a regular allowance. No matter how you get your money, add up how much you earned over the last month.

Now for the fun part. List how you spent that money. Can you even remember? Gas in the car, new shoes, lunch and a movie on Saturday, new jeans, tithe.

Say what!? Yes, tithe. God expects even you to give him part of the money you earn. Whether you put it in the offering plate in church or give to a local ministry, part of your money should go back to God to help others in some way.

Nail It Down
••••

Read Malachi 3:10–12 for God's response to our obedience in the area of giving.

Think It Through
••••

Does the thought of giving away some of your hard-earned income make you a little uptight, nervous? Even squeamish? Maybe it will help to put things into perspective a bit.

The first thing to remember is that the money isn't really yours anyway. Sure, you earned it, but ultimately, everything you have belongs to God. So you're only returning to him part of what is already his. And he lets you keep all the rest! When you look at it that way, it doesn't seem quite so hard, does it?

The second thing to remember is that there is something much larger at stake here than your few dollars in a collection plate. It has to do with what you value most: your few dollars or your obedience to God.

The third thing to remember is the promise that God attaches to giving to him: he'll bless you in return. The promise in Malachi is that he will "pour out so much blessing that you will not have room enough for it." That's a pretty extravagant promise. And God always keeps his promises!

Nail It Down
••••

Reread Malachi 3:10–12 for the great things God will do when you give. For further insight read Proverbs 10:16–22.

Turn to pages 716, 1192 and 1259 for other readings on values.
Turn to page 1005 for Monday's reading.

Topic
••••

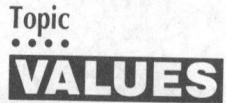

NEW TESTAMENT

MATTHEW

A Jewish audience needs a Jewish message. Matthew the tax collector writes to convince a Jewish audience that their Messiah, their king, has come. Matthew shows how Jesus' life fulfills more than three hundred specific Old Testament prophecies about the coming king. Jesus possesses the credentials of the Messiah, preaches the messages only the Messiah could deliver, and finally dies the death only the Messiah could die. As you read, make sure that Jesus is King of your own heart and kneel before him.

Outline of Contents

The Genealogy of Jesus

1 A record of the genealogy of Jesus Christ the son of David, the son of Abraham:

²Abraham was the father of Isaac,
Isaac the father of Jacob,
Jacob the father of Judah and his brothers,
³Judah the father of Perez and Zerah, whose mother was Tamar,
Perez the father of Hezron,
Hezron the father of Ram,
⁴Ram the father of Amminadab,
Amminadab the father of Nahshon,
Nahshon the father of Salmon,
⁵Salmon the father of Boaz, whose mother was Rahab,
Boaz the father of Obed, whose mother was Ruth,
Obed the father of Jesse,
⁶and Jesse the father of King David.

David was the father of Solomon, whose mother had been Uriah's wife,
⁷Solomon the father of Rehoboam,
Rehoboam the father of Abijah,
Abijah the father of Asa,
⁸Asa the father of Jehoshaphat,

Jehoshaphat the father of Jehoram,
Jehoram the father of Uzziah,
9Uzziah the father of Jotham,
Jotham the father of Ahaz,
Ahaz the father of Hezekiah,
10Hezekiah the father of Manasseh,
Manasseh the father of Amon,
Amon the father of Josiah,
11and Josiah the father of Jeconiah*a*
and his brothers at the time of the
exile to Babylon.

12After the exile to Babylon:
Jeconiah was the father of Shealtiel,
Shealtiel the father of Zerubbabel,
13Zerubbabel the father of Abiud,
Abiud the father of Eliakim,
Eliakim the father of Azor,
14Azor the father of Zadok,
Zadok the father of Akim,
Akim the father of Eliud,
15Eliud the father of Eleazar,
Eleazar the father of Matthan,
Matthan the father of Jacob,
16and Jacob the father of Joseph, the
husband of Mary, of whom was
born Jesus, who is called Christ.

17Thus there were fourteen generations in
all from Abraham to David, fourteen from
David to the exile to Babylon, and fourteen
from the exile to the Christ.*b*

The Birth of Jesus Christ

18This is how the birth of Jesus Christ
came about: His mother Mary was pledged
to be married to Joseph, but before they
came together, she was found to be with
child through the Holy Spirit. **19**Because Joseph her husband was a righteous man and
did not want to expose her to public disgrace, he had in mind to divorce her quietly.
20But after he had considered this, an angel of the Lord appeared to him in a dream
and said, "Joseph son of David, do not be
afraid to take Mary home as your wife, because what is conceived in her is from the
Holy Spirit. **21**She will give birth to a son, and
you are to give him the name Jesus,*c* because he will save his people from their
sins."
22All this took place to fulfill what the Lord
had said through the prophet: **23**"The virgin
will be with child and will give birth to a son,

and they will call him Immanuel"*d*—which
means, "God with us."
24When Joseph woke up, he did what the
angel of the Lord had commanded him and
took Mary home as his wife. **25**But he had no
union with her until she gave birth to a son.
And he gave him the name Jesus.

The Visit of the Magi

2 After Jesus was born in Bethlehem in
Judea, during the time of King Herod,
Magi*e* from the east came to Jerusalem
2and asked, "Where is the one who has been
born king of the Jews? We saw his star in the
east*f* and have come to worship him."
3When King Herod heard this he was disturbed, and all Jerusalem with him. **4**When
he had called together all the people's chief
priests and teachers of the law, he asked
them where the Christ*g* was to be born. **5**"In
Bethlehem in Judea," they replied, "for this
is what the prophet has written:

6" 'But you, Bethlehem, in the land of
Judah,
are by no means least among the
rulers of Judah;
for out of you will come a ruler
who will be the shepherd of my
people Israel.'*h* "

7Then Herod called the Magi secretly and
found out from them the exact time the star
had appeared. **8**He sent them to Bethlehem
and said, "Go and make a careful search for
the child. As soon as you find him, report to
me, so that I too may go and worship him."
9After they had heard the king, they went
on their way, and the star they had seen in
the east*i* went ahead of them until it
stopped over the place where the child was.
10When they saw the star, they were overjoyed. **11**On coming to the house, they saw
the child with his mother Mary, and they
bowed down and worshiped him. Then they
opened their treasures and presented him
with gifts of gold and of incense and of
myrrh. **12**And having been warned in a
dream not to go back to Herod, they returned to their country by another route.

The Escape to Egypt

13When they had gone, an angel of the
Lord appeared to Joseph in a dream. "Get
up," he said, "take the child and his mother

---

a11 That is, Jehoiachin; also in verse 12   *b17* Or *Messiah.* "The Christ" (Greek) and "the Messiah" (Hebrew)
both mean "the Anointed One."   *c21* *Jesus* is the Greek form of *Joshua,* which means *the LORD saves.*
d23 Isaiah 7:14   *e1* Traditionally *Wise Men*   *f2* Or *star when it rose*   *g4* Or *Messiah*   *h6* Micah 5:2
i9 Or *seen when it rose*

WHEN QUICK "FIXES" DON'T FIX THINGS!

Debbie is stunned. "Matt wants to ask me to his prom?"
"That's what he said."
"How excellent! I've been wanting to go out with Matt since early last summer."
"But what about your date with Donnie?"
"Kim, why would I go to a movie with Donnie when I could go to the prom with Matt?"
Three weeks later, Matt is finished with Debbie. And because of what she did to Donnie, so is everyone else.

Look It Up

When the Israelites demanded a king, the prophet Samuel spelled out the consequences of such a choice:
"He said, 'This is what the king who will reign over you will do: He will take your sons and make them serve. . . . He will take your daughters to be perfumers and cooks and bakers. He will take the best of your fields and vineyards and olive groves . . . . Your menservants and maidservants and the best of your cattle and donkeys he will take for his own use. He will take a tenth of your flocks, and you yourselves will become his slaves. When that day comes, you will cry out for relief from the king you have chosen, and the LORD will not answer you in that day.'
"But the people refused to listen to Samuel. 'No!' they said. 'We want a king over us. Then we will be like all the other nations, with a king to lead us and to go out before us and fight our battles' " (1 Samuel 8:11,13–14,16–20).
Things happened just as Samuel said!

Think It Through

What did Debbie fail to consider when she broke her movie date with Donnie for a prom date with Matt?
Do you tend to think through the consequences of your choices before you make decisions? If not, why not?

Work It Out

Try the "Options & Consequences" method next time you face a big decision.
1. Identify the decision you are facing.
2. Ask God to help you list all the options you could choose.
3. Ask God to help you see the possible consequences of each choice.
4. Select the option that results in the best, most Biblical consequences.

Nail It Down

Read about how an angel of the Lord showed Joseph an option he had failed to consider in Matthew 1:18–25.

Turn to pages 246, 257 and 1246 for other readings on decisions.
Turn to page 1008 for Tuesday's reading.

Topic

DECISIONS

and escape to Egypt. Stay there until I tell you, for Herod is going to search for the child to kill him."

14So he got up, took the child and his mother during the night and left for Egypt, **15**where he stayed until the death of Herod. And so was fulfilled what the Lord had said through the prophet: "Out of Egypt I called my son."*a*

16When Herod realized that he had been outwitted by the Magi, he was furious, and he gave orders to kill all the boys in Bethlehem and its vicinity who were two years old and under, in accordance with the time he had learned from the Magi. **17**Then what was said through the prophet Jeremiah was fulfilled:

18"A voice is heard in Ramah,
    weeping and great mourning,
Rachel weeping for her children
    and refusing to be comforted,
because they are no more."*b*

The Return to Nazareth

19After Herod died, an angel of the Lord appeared in a dream to Joseph in Egypt **20**and said, "Get up, take the child and his mother and go to the land of Israel, for those who were trying to take the child's life are dead."

21So he got up, took the child and his mother and went to the land of Israel. **22**But when he heard that Archelaus was reigning in Judea in place of his father Herod, he was afraid to go there. Having been warned in a dream, he withdrew to the district of Galilee, **23**and he went and lived in a town called Nazareth. So was fulfilled what was said through the prophets: "He will be called a Nazarene."

John the Baptist Prepares the Way

3 In those days John the Baptist came, preaching in the Desert of Judea **2**and saying, "Repent, for the kingdom of heaven is near." **3**This is he who was spoken of through the prophet Isaiah:

"A voice of one calling in the desert,
'Prepare the way for the Lord,
    make straight paths for him.' "*c*

4John's clothes were made of camel's hair, and he had a leather belt around his waist. His food was locusts and wild honey. **5**People went out to him from Jerusalem and all Judea and the whole region of the Jordan.

6Confessing their sins, they were baptized by him in the Jordan River.

7But when he saw many of the Pharisees and Sadducees coming to where he was baptizing, he said to them: "You brood of vipers! Who warned you to flee from the coming wrath? **8**Produce fruit in keeping with repentance. **9**And do not think you can say to yourselves, 'We have Abraham as our father.' I tell you that out of these stones God can raise up children for Abraham. **10**The ax is already at the root of the trees, and every tree that does not produce good fruit will be cut down and thrown into the fire.

11"I baptize you with*d* water for repentance. But after me will come one who is more powerful than I, whose sandals I am not fit to carry. He will baptize you with the Holy Spirit and with fire. **12**His winnowing fork is in his hand, and he will clear his threshing floor, gathering his wheat into the barn and burning up the chaff with unquenchable fire."

The Baptism of Jesus

13Then Jesus came from Galilee to the Jordan to be baptized by John. **14**But John tried to deter him, saying, "I need to be baptized by you, and do you come to me?"

15Jesus replied, "Let it be so now; it is proper for us to do this to fulfill all righteousness." Then John consented.

16As soon as Jesus was baptized, he went up out of the water. At that moment heaven was opened, and he saw the Spirit of God descending like a dove and lighting on him. **17**And a voice from heaven said, "This is my Son, whom I love; with him I am well pleased."

The Temptation of Jesus

4 Then Jesus was led by the Spirit into the desert to be tempted by the devil. **2**After fasting forty days and forty nights, he was hungry. **3**The tempter came to him and said, "If you are the Son of God, tell these stones to become bread."

4Jesus answered, "It is written: 'Man does not live on bread alone, but on every word that comes from the mouth of God.'*e*"

5Then the devil took him to the holy city and had him stand on the highest point of the temple. **6**"If you are the Son of God," he said, "throw yourself down. For it is written:

" 'He will command his angels
        concerning you,

a15 Hosea 11:1   *b18* Jer. 31:15   *c3* Isaiah 40:3   *d11* Or *in*   *e4* Deut. 8:3

and they will lift you up in their
hands,
so that you will not strike your foot
against a stone.'*a*"

7Jesus answered him, "It is also written:
'Do not put the Lord your God to the test.'*b*"
8Again, the devil took him to a very high
mountain and showed him all the kingdoms
of the world and their splendor. **9**"All this I
will give you," he said, "if you will bow down
and worship me."
10Jesus said to him, "Away from me, Satan! For it is written: 'Worship the Lord your
God, and serve him only.'*c*"
11Then the devil left him, and angels
came and attended him.

Jesus Begins to Preach

12When Jesus heard that John had been
put in prison, he returned to Galilee. **13**Leaving Nazareth, he went and lived in Capernaum, which was by the lake in the area of
Zebulun and Naphtali— **14**to fulfill what was
said through the prophet Isaiah:

15"Land of Zebulun and land of Naphtali,
the way to the sea, along the Jordan,
Galilee of the Gentiles—
16the people living in darkness
have seen a great light;
on those living in the land of the
shadow of death
a light has dawned."*d*

17From that time on Jesus began to
preach, "Repent, for the kingdom of heaven
is near."

The Calling of the First Disciples

18As Jesus was walking beside the Sea of
Galilee, he saw two brothers, Simon called
Peter and his brother Andrew. They were
casting a net into the lake, for they were
fishermen. **19**"Come, follow me," Jesus said,
"and I will make you fishers of men." **20**At
once they left their nets and followed him.
21Going on from there, he saw two other
brothers, James son of Zebedee and his
brother John. They were in a boat with their
father Zebedee, preparing their nets. Jesus
called them, **22**and immediately they left the
boat and their father and followed him.

Jesus Heals the Sick

23Jesus went throughout Galilee, teaching
in their synagogues, preaching the good
news of the kingdom, and healing every

disease and sickness among the people.
24News about him spread all over Syria, and
people brought to him all who were ill with
various diseases, those suffering severe
pain, the demon-possessed, those having
seizures, and the paralyzed, and he healed
them. **25**Large crowds from Galilee, the Decapolis,*e* Jerusalem, Judea and the region
across the Jordan followed him.

The Beatitudes

5 Now when he saw the crowds, he went
up on a mountainside and sat down.
His disciples came to him, **2**and he began to
teach them, saying:

3"Blessed are the poor in spirit,
for theirs is the kingdom of heaven.
4Blessed are those who mourn,
for they will be comforted.
5Blessed are the meek,
for they will inherit the earth.
6Blessed are those who hunger and thirst
for righteousness,
for they will be filled.
7Blessed are the merciful,
for they will be shown mercy.
8Blessed are the pure in heart,
for they will see God.
9Blessed are the peacemakers,
for they will be called sons of God.
10Blessed are those who are persecuted
because of righteousness,
for theirs is the kingdom of heaven.

11"Blessed are you when people insult
you, persecute you and falsely say all kinds
of evil against you because of me. **12**Rejoice
and be glad, because great is your reward in
heaven, for in the same way they persecuted the prophets who were before you.

Salt and Light

13"You are the salt of the earth. But if the
salt loses its saltiness, how can it be made
salty again? It is no longer good for anything,
except to be thrown out and trampled by
men.
14"You are the light of the world. A city on
a hill cannot be hidden. **15**Neither do people
light a lamp and put it under a bowl. Instead
they put it on its stand, and it gives light to
everyone in the house. **16**In the same way,
let your light shine before men, that they
may see your good deeds and praise your
Father in heaven.

a6 Psalm 91:11,12   *b7* Deut. 6:16   *c10* Deut. 6:13   *d16* Isaiah 9:1,2   *e25* That is, the Ten Cities

THE CHARACTER OF A SERVANT

Dwight and Derek are spending their summer as part of a service team in their church. This week they're helping out with vacation Bible school. It's been raining. The kids are restless from being cooped up inside.

Suddenly, one first grader, an obnoxious little kid who's been whining all week, barfs all over himself and all over the floor. Mrs. Perez asks Derek to clean up the kid; she asks Dwight to get a mop and clean up the floor.

The two friends look at each other. Dwight is just about to say, "Who do you think I am, Mother Teresa?" when Reverend Moore peeks in the door.

Look It Up

What qualities make up the character of a servant?

A humble spirit: "Jesus called them together and said, 'You know that the rulers of the Gentiles lord it over them, and their high officials exercise authority over them. Not so with you. Instead, whoever wants to become great among you must be your servant, and whoever wants to be first must be your slave' " (Matthew 20:25–27).

A forgiving spirit (Matthew 18:21–34).

A generous spirit (2 Corinthians 8:1–5).

An obedient spirit (John 13:13–17).

We could probably list others, but these are enough to keep you busy for quite a while!

Think It Through

It has been said that true character is determined by what a person does when nobody else is watching. Some Christians see what they can get away with; others keep serving God faithfully.

Consider these questions: How eager are you to do acts of service that no one else will ever see? Do you serve only when you know you're going to get credit? If so, why?

Work It Out

Ask God to create a servant spirit in your heart. Tell him you want to learn humility, forgiveness, generosity and obedience. Then pick a course and start working on your servanthood degree:

1. Do some yard work without your mom or dad even asking.
2. Wash the dishes after supper.
3. Ask your mom what job she hates doing the most; then volunteer to do it for her.
4. Entertain your kid brother(s) and/or sister(s) tonight.
5. Bake cookies for an older person in the neighborhood.

Nail It Down

Read what Jesus had to say about servanthood in Matthew 5:3–12.

Turn to pages 312, 718, 1019, 1034 and 1342 for other readings on serving.
Turn to page 1011 for Wednesday's reading.

Topic

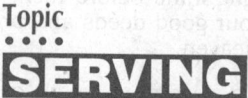
SERVING

The Fulfillment of the Law

17"Do not think that I have come to abolish the Law or the Prophets; I have not come to abolish them but to fulfill them. **18**I tell you the truth, until heaven and earth disappear, not the smallest letter, not the least stroke of a pen, will by any means disappear from the Law until everything is accomplished. **19**Anyone who breaks one of the least of these commandments and teaches others to do the same will be called least in the kingdom of heaven, but whoever practices and teaches these commands will be called great in the kingdom of heaven. **20**For I tell you that unless your righteousness surpasses that of the Pharisees and the teachers of the law, you will certainly not enter the kingdom of heaven.

Murder

21"You have heard that it was said to the people long ago, 'Do not murder,ᵃ and anyone who murders will be subject to judgment.' **22**But I tell you that anyone who is angry with his brotherᵇ will be subject to judgment. Again, anyone who says to his brother, 'Raca,ᶜ' is answerable to the Sanhedrin. But anyone who says, 'You fool!' will be in danger of the fire of hell.

23"Therefore, if you are offering your gift at the altar and there remember that your brother has something against you, **24**leave your gift there in front of the altar. First go and be reconciled to your brother; then come and offer your gift.

25"Settle matters quickly with your adversary who is taking you to court. Do it while you are still with him on the way, or he may hand you over to the judge, and the judge may hand you over to the officer, and you may be thrown into prison. **26**I tell you the truth, you will not get out until you have paid the last penny.ᵈ

Adultery

27"You have heard that it was said, 'Do not commit adultery.'ᵉ **28**But I tell you that anyone who looks at a woman lustfully has already committed adultery with her in his heart. **29**If your right eye causes you to sin, gouge it out and throw it away. It is better for you to lose one part of your body than for your whole body to be thrown into hell. **30**And if your right hand causes you to sin,

cut it off and throw it away. It is better for you to lose one part of your body than for your whole body to go into hell.

Divorce

31"It has been said, 'Anyone who divorces his wife must give her a certificate of divorce.'ᶠ **32**But I tell you that anyone who divorces his wife, except for marital unfaithfulness, causes her to become an adulteress, and anyone who marries the divorced woman commits adultery.

Oaths

33"Again, you have heard that it was said to the people long ago, 'Do not break your oath, but keep the oaths you have made to the Lord.' **34**But I tell you, Do not swear at all: either by heaven, for it is God's throne; **35**or by the earth, for it is his footstool; or by Jerusalem, for it is the city of the Great King. **36**And do not swear by your head, for you cannot make even one hair white or black. **37**Simply let your 'Yes' be 'Yes,' and your 'No,' 'No'; anything beyond this comes from the evil one.

An Eye for an Eye

38"You have heard that it was said, 'Eye for eye, and tooth for tooth.'ᵍ **39**But I tell you, Do not resist an evil person. If someone strikes you on the right cheek, turn to him the other also. **40**And if someone wants to sue you and take your tunic, let him have your cloak as well. **41**If someone forces you to go one mile, go with him two miles. **42**Give to the one who asks you, and do not turn away from the one who wants to borrow from you.

Love for Enemies

43"You have heard that it was said, 'Love your neighborʰ and hate your enemy.' **44**But I tell you: Love your enemiesⁱ and pray for those who persecute you, **45**that you may be sons of your Father in heaven. He causes his sun to rise on the evil and the good, and sends rain on the righteous and the unrighteous. **46**If you love those who love you, what reward will you get? Are not even the tax collectors doing that? **47**And if you greet only your brothers, what are you doing more than others? Do not even pa-

---

ᵃ21 Exodus 20:13   ᵇ22 Some manuscripts *brother without cause*   ᶜ22 An Aramaic term of contempt
ᵈ26 Greek *kodrantes*   ᵉ27 Exodus 20:14   ᶠ31 Deut. 24:1   ᵍ38 Exodus 21:24; Lev. 24:20; Deut. 19:21
ʰ43 Lev. 19:18   ⁱ44 Some late manuscripts *enemies, bless those who curse you, do good to those who hate you*

gans do that? **48**Be perfect, therefore, as your heavenly Father is perfect.

Giving to the Needy

6 "Be careful not to do your 'acts of righteousness' before men, to be seen by them. If you do, you will have no reward from your Father in heaven.

2"So when you give to the needy, do not announce it with trumpets, as the hypocrites do in the synagogues and on the streets, to be honored by men. I tell you the truth, they have received their reward in full. **3**But when you give to the needy, do not let your left hand know what your right hand is doing, **4**so that your giving may be in secret. Then your Father, who sees what is done in secret, will reward you.

Prayer

5"And when you pray, do not be like the hypocrites, for they love to pray standing in the synagogues and on the street corners to be seen by men. I tell you the truth, they have received their reward in full. **6**But when you pray, go into your room, close the door and pray to your Father, who is unseen. Then your Father, who sees what is done in secret, will reward you. **7**And when you pray, do not keep on babbling like pagans, for they think they will be heard because of their many words. **8**Do not be like them, for your Father knows what you need before you ask him.

9"This, then, is how you should pray:

" 'Our Father in heaven,
hallowed be your name,
10your kingdom come,
your will be done
on earth as it is in heaven.
11Give us today our daily bread.
12Forgive us our debts,
as we also have forgiven our debtors.
13And lead us not into temptation,
but deliver us from the evil one.ᵃ'

14For if you forgive men when they sin against you, your heavenly Father will also forgive you. **15**But if you do not forgive men their sins, your Father will not forgive your sins.

Fasting

16"When you fast, do not look somber as the hypocrites do, for they disfigure their faces to show men they are fasting. I tell you

the truth, they have received their reward in full. **17**But when you fast, put oil on your head and wash your face, **18**so that it will not be obvious to men that you are fasting, but only to your Father, who is unseen; and your Father, who sees what is done in secret, will reward you.

Treasures in Heaven

19"Do not store up for yourselves treasures on earth, where moth and rust destroy, and where thieves break in and steal. **20**But store up for yourselves treasures in heaven, where moth and rust do not destroy, and where thieves do not break in and steal. **21**For where your treasure is, there your heart will be also.

22"The eye is the lamp of the body. If your eyes are good, your whole body will be full of light. **23**But if your eyes are bad, your whole body will be full of darkness. If then the light within you is darkness, how great is that darkness!

24"No one can serve two masters. Either he will hate the one and love the other, or he will be devoted to the one and despise the other. You cannot serve both God and Money.

Do Not Worry

25"Therefore I tell you, do not worry about your life, what you will eat or drink; or about your body, what you will wear. Is not life more important than food, and the body more important than clothes? **26**Look at the birds of the air; they do not sow or reap or store away in barns, and yet your heavenly Father feeds them. Are you not much more valuable than they? **27**Who of you by worrying can add a single hour to his lifeᵇ?

28"And why do you worry about clothes? See how the lilies of the field grow. They do not labor or spin. **29**Yet I tell you that not even Solomon in all his splendor was dressed like one of these. **30**If that is how God clothes the grass of the field, which is here today and tomorrow is thrown into the fire, will he not much more clothe you, O you of little faith? **31**So do not worry, saying, 'What shall we eat?' or 'What shall we drink?' or 'What shall we wear?' **32**For the pagans run after all these things, and your heavenly Father knows that you need them. **33**But seek first his kingdom and his righteousness, and all these things will be given to you as well. **34**Therefore do not worry about

---

ᵃ13 Or *from evil*; some late manuscripts *one, / for yours is the kingdom and the power and the glory forever. Amen.*   ᵇ27 Or *single cubit to his height*

THE FUTILITY OF ANXIETY

Van is stressed out about the game this weekend. "What if I miss another open field tackle like I did last week? I guarantee the coach will bench me! Worse than that, what if I blow my coverages? What if I get burned and give up three or even four touchdown passes? Oh man, this could be a real disaster! Then there's the whole question of my hamstring. What if . . . ?"

Look It Up
• • • •

Someone has suggested that about 90 percent of the things we worry about never happen anyway. In fact, worrying is just an exercise in futility!

"Then Jesus said to his disciples: 'Therefore I tell you, do not worry about your life, what you will eat; or about your body, what you will wear. Life is more than food, and the body more than clothes. Consider the ravens: They do not sow or reap, they have no storeroom or barn; yet God feeds them. And how much more valuable you are than birds! Who of you by worrying can add a single hour to his life? Since you cannot do this very little thing, why do you worry about the rest?' " (Luke 12:22–26).

Think It Through
• • • •

Consider these observations about anxiety:

1. Playing the "what if" game doesn't change anything.
2. Stewing over a situation eats up time that could be better spent praying about or working to change the situation.
3. Getting upset and uptight consumes emotional energy and keeps you from being productive in other areas of life.
4. Fretting may even result in physical damage to your body— zits, ulcers, headaches, weight gain, sleeplessness. (And in severe amounts, worry may lead to depression, heart attacks or even strokes!)

The one big benefit of worry? Easy. It's the same as what you see when you close your eyes!

Work It Out
• • • •

Learn to take life less seriously. The next time you face an unpleasant situation or tough decision in your life, try finding the humor in the situation instead of focusing on the worst possible scenario.

It will help to search out some Christians who have a more relaxed, less stressed-out attitude about life.

Nail It Down
• • • •

Read Jesus' lesson on worry in Matthew 6:25–34.

Turn to pages 968 and 1119 for other readings on worry.
Turn to page 1013 for Thursday's reading.

Topic
• • • •
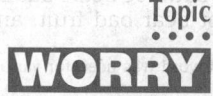
WORRY

tomorrow, for tomorrow will worry about it-self. Each day has enough trouble of its own.

Judging Others

7 "Do not judge, or you too will be judged. ²For in the same way you judge others, you will be judged, and with the measure you use, it will be measured to you.

³"Why do you look at the speck of saw-dust in your brother's eye and pay no atten-tion to the plank in your own eye? ⁴How can you say to your brother, 'Let me take the speck out of your eye,' when all the time there is a plank in your own eye? ⁵You hypo-crite, first take the plank out of your own eye, and then you will see clearly to remove the speck from your brother's eye.

⁶"Do not give dogs what is sacred; do not throw your pearls to pigs. If you do, they may trample them under their feet, and then turn and tear you to pieces.

Ask, Seek, Knock

⁷"Ask and it will be given to you; seek and you will find; knock and the door will be opened to you. ⁸For everyone who asks re-ceives; he who seeks finds; and to him who knocks, the door will be opened.

⁹"Which of you, if his son asks for bread, will give him a stone? ¹⁰Or if he asks for a fish, will give him a snake? ¹¹If you, then, though you are evil, know how to give good gifts to your children, how much more will your Father in heaven give good gifts to those who ask him! ¹²So in everything, do to others what you would have them do to you, for this sums up the Law and the Prophets.

The Narrow and Wide Gates

¹³"Enter through the narrow gate. For wide is the gate and broad is the road that leads to destruction, and many enter through it. ¹⁴But small is the gate and nar-row the road that leads to life, and only a few find it.

A Tree and Its Fruit

¹⁵"Watch out for false prophets. They come to you in sheep's clothing, but inward-ly they are ferocious wolves. ¹⁶By their fruit you will recognize them. Do people pick grapes from thornbushes, or figs from this-tles? ¹⁷Likewise every good tree bears good fruit, but a bad tree bears bad fruit. ¹⁸A good tree cannot bear bad fruit, and a bad tree

cannot bear good fruit. ¹⁹Every tree that does not bear good fruit is cut down and thrown into the fire. ²⁰Thus, by their fruit you will recognize them.

²¹"Not everyone who says to me, 'Lord, Lord,' will enter the kingdom of heaven, but only he who does the will of my Father who is in heaven. ²²Many will say to me on that day, 'Lord, Lord, did we not prophesy in your name, and in your name drive out de-mons and perform many miracles?' ²³Then I will tell them plainly, 'I never knew you. Away from me, you evildoers!'

The Wise and Foolish Builders

²⁴"Therefore everyone who hears these words of mine and puts them into practice is like a wise man who built his house on the rock. ²⁵The rain came down, the streams rose, and the winds blew and beat against that house; yet it did not fall, because it had its foundation on the rock. ²⁶But everyone who hears these words of mine and does not put them into practice is like a foolish man who built his house on sand. ²⁷The rain came down, the streams rose, and the winds blew and beat against that house, and it fell with a great crash."

²⁸When Jesus had finished saying these things, the crowds were amazed at his teaching, ²⁹because he taught as one who had authority, and not as their teachers of the law.

The Man With Leprosy

8 When he came down from the moun-tainside, large crowds followed him. ²A man with leprosyᵃ came and knelt before him and said, "Lord, if you are willing, you can make me clean."

³Jesus reached out his hand and touched the man. "I am willing," he said. "Be clean!" Immediately he was curedᵇ of his leprosy. ⁴Then Jesus said to him, "See that you don't tell anyone. But go, show yourself to the priest and offer the gift Moses commanded, as a testimony to them."

The Faith of the Centurion

⁵When Jesus had entered Capernaum, a centurion came to him, asking for help. ⁶"Lord," he said, "my servant lies at home paralyzed and in terrible suffering."

⁷Jesus said to him, "I will go and heal him."

ᵃ2 The Greek word was used for various diseases affecting the skin—not necessarily leprosy.   ᵇ3 Greek *made clean*

STANDARD EQUIPMENT FOR THE CHRISTIAN LIFE ☐ THURSDAY

● ●

Joel's attitude pretty much sums up the way a lot of believers feel about obedience: "I can get into most of what the Bible teaches. But when our pastor starts talking about some things, I think, 'No way! Nobody does that!' For instance, last week he started talking about 'turning the other cheek.' You tell me. If some dude punches you in the face, are you gonna just stand there and let him do it again? Not me, man! I'd knock his teeth down his throat!"

Look It Up
● ● ● ●

Uh, thanks for that loving thought, Joel. Now, here's the question for you: Is obedience an option? Can believers pick and choose the commands of Christ they plan to obey . . . and just ignore the rest? Note the penetrating question Jesus asks:

"Why do you call me, 'Lord, Lord,' and do not do what I say?" (Luke 6:46).

Do you see his point? The synonyms *lord* and *master* were used during New Testament times to describe an owner (Matthew 20:8), a king or ruler (Acts 25:26), or one to whom service was due (Matthew 24:45–51). In other words, to call someone "lord" automatically meant that you had an obligation to obey that person. Obedience is not an option; it's a requirement!

Think It Through
● ● ● ●

How would you respond to these commands:
• Your teacher says, "See me after school."
• A policeman motions you to pull over.
• A parent says, "Go to your room."
• A coach orders you to participate in a certain drill.

Hopefully, you would comply with the wishes of each one of these authority figures. How much more should you do what Jesus, the ultimate authority, tells you to do?

Work It Out
● ● ● ●

Here's a prayer to get you off to a good (and obedient) start: "Jesus, you are Lord whether I act like it or not. So help me begin to act like it. I need to treat you as my Owner, King and Master, because that is what you are. I want to learn to obey you. Teach me the lessons I need to know. Amen."

Now think of one thing that you know Jesus wants you to do today . . . and do it.

Nail It Down
● ● ● ●

Read the warning in Matthew 7:21.

Turn to pages 159, 281, 892, 1082 and 1156 for other readings on obedience.
Turn to page 1015 for Friday's reading.

Topic
● ● ● ●

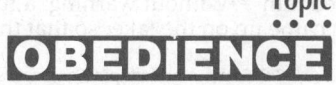

8The centurion replied, "Lord, I do not deserve to have you come under my roof. But just say the word, and my servant will be healed. **9**For I myself am a man under authority, with soldiers under me. I tell this one, 'Go,' and he goes; and that one, 'Come,' and he comes. I say to my servant, 'Do this,' and he does it."

10When Jesus heard this, he was astonished and said to those following him, "I tell you the truth, I have not found anyone in Israel with such great faith. **11**I say to you that many will come from the east and the west, and will take their places at the feast with Abraham, Isaac and Jacob in the kingdom of heaven. **12**But the subjects of the kingdom will be thrown outside, into the darkness, where there will be weeping and gnashing of teeth."

13Then Jesus said to the centurion, "Go! It will be done just as you believed it would." And his servant was healed at that very hour.

Jesus Heals Many

14When Jesus came into Peter's house, he saw Peter's mother-in-law lying in bed with a fever. **15**He touched her hand and the fever left her, and she got up and began to wait on him.

16When evening came, many who were demon-possessed were brought to him, and he drove out the spirits with a word and healed all the sick. **17**This was to fulfill what was spoken through the prophet Isaiah:

"He took up our infirmities
  and carried our diseases."[a]

The Cost of Following Jesus

18When Jesus saw the crowd around him, he gave orders to cross to the other side of the lake. **19**Then a teacher of the law came to him and said, "Teacher, I will follow you wherever you go."

20Jesus replied, "Foxes have holes and birds of the air have nests, but the Son of Man has no place to lay his head."

21Another disciple said to him, "Lord, first let me go and bury my father."

22But Jesus told him, "Follow me, and let the dead bury their own dead."

Jesus Calms the Storm

23Then he got into the boat and his disciples followed him. **24**Without warning, a furious storm came up on the lake, so that the waves swept over the boat. But Jesus was sleeping. **25**The disciples went and woke him, saying, "Lord, save us! We're going to drown!"

26He replied, "You of little faith, why are you so afraid?" Then he got up and rebuked the winds and the waves, and it was completely calm.

27The men were amazed and asked, "What kind of man is this? Even the winds and the waves obey him!"

The Healing of Two Demon-possessed Men

28When he arrived at the other side in the region of the Gadarenes,[b] two demon-possessed men coming from the tombs met him. They were so violent that no one could pass that way. **29**"What do you want with us, Son of God?" they shouted. "Have you come here to torture us before the appointed time?"

30Some distance from them a large herd of pigs was feeding. **31**The demons begged Jesus, "If you drive us out, send us into the herd of pigs."

32He said to them, "Go!" So they came out and went into the pigs, and the whole herd rushed down the steep bank into the lake and died in the water. **33**Those tending the pigs ran off, went into the town and reported all this, including what had happened to the demon-possessed men. **34**Then the whole town went out to meet Jesus. And when they saw him, they pleaded with him to leave their region.

Jesus Heals a Paralytic

9 Jesus stepped into a boat, crossed over and came to his own town. **2**Some men brought to him a paralytic, lying on a mat. When Jesus saw their faith, he said to the paralytic, "Take heart, son; your sins are forgiven."

3At this, some of the teachers of the law said to themselves, "This fellow is blaspheming!"

4Knowing their thoughts, Jesus said, "Why do you entertain evil thoughts in your hearts? **5**Which is easier: to say, 'Your sins are forgiven,' or to say, 'Get up and walk'? **6**But so that you may know that the Son of Man has authority on earth to forgive sins...." Then he said to the paralytic, "Get up, take your mat and go home." **7**And the man got up and went home. **8**When the crowd saw this, they were filled with awe;

FORGET *STUFF*–FOCUS ON PEOPLE!

Mark is into "stuff." He thinks almost exclusively about cars and stereos and clothes. He'd rather have a new shirt or a new CD than a conversation with Mom any day. Give him a choice between being with people and getting a new possession . . . and, hey, there really is no choice.

"Hey, Mark! We're doing a service project down in the inner city this Saturday. Want to come help out? It'll be fun."

"Uh . . . can't. Gotta put some new speakers in my Mustang."

Look It Up
Consider the implications of this passage: "The end of all things is near. Therefore be clear minded and self-controlled so that you can pray. Above all, love each other deeply, because love covers over a multitude of sins. Offer hospitality to one another without grumbling" (1 Peter 4:7–9).

In view of the fact that Christ is returning, should you be spending your time loving things? Should you be focusing on acquiring more stuff?

No! Possessions aren't eternal. God's people are called instead to invest their time and resources in what will last—people!

Think It Through
So often in life the urgent things, the things that must be taken care of *now* (deadlines, projects, possessions), crowd out the really important things (spending time with friends and family, getting to know God).

Are you so involved in life's urgent situations that you are neglecting life's important priorities?

Work It Out
Try an experiment. For the rest of this week, forget watching TV, listening to your stereo, buying new clothes, working on your car, playing video games or messing with your other possessions. Concentrate instead on building relationships with others. Talk to your parents, your grandparents, your brothers and sisters, your friends. Ask questions and then listen.

Personal relationships are far more rewarding than material possessions!

Nail It Down
Read in Matthew 8:28–34 about the people who valued their pigs more than they valued knowing Christ.

Turn to pages 432, 796, 1142 and 1292 for other readings on priorities.
Turn to page 1017 for the weekend reading.

Topic

PRIORITIES

and they praised God, who had given such authority to men.

The Calling of Matthew

9As Jesus went on from there, he saw a man named Matthew sitting at the tax collector's booth. "Follow me," he told him, and Matthew got up and followed him.

10While Jesus was having dinner at Matthew's house, many tax collectors and "sinners" came and ate with him and his disciples. **11**When the Pharisees saw this, they asked his disciples, "Why does your teacher eat with tax collectors and 'sinners'?"

12On hearing this, Jesus said, "It is not the healthy who need a doctor, but the sick. **13**But go and learn what this means: 'I desire mercy, not sacrifice.'*a* For I have not come to call the righteous, but sinners."

Jesus Questioned About Fasting

14Then John's disciples came and asked him, "How is it that we and the Pharisees fast, but your disciples do not fast?"

15Jesus answered, "How can the guests of the bridegroom mourn while he is with them? The time will come when the bridegroom will be taken from them; then they will fast.

16"No one sews a patch of unshrunk cloth on an old garment, for the patch will pull away from the garment, making the tear worse. **17**Neither do men pour new wine into old wineskins. If they do, the skins will burst, the wine will run out and the wineskins will be ruined. No, they pour new wine into new wineskins, and both are preserved."

A Dead Girl and a Sick Woman

18While he was saying this, a ruler came and knelt before him and said, "My daughter has just died. But come and put your hand on her, and she will live." **19**Jesus got up and went with him, and so did his disciples.

20Just then a woman who had been subject to bleeding for twelve years came up behind him and touched the edge of his cloak. **21**She said to herself, "If I only touch his cloak, I will be healed."

22Jesus turned and saw her. "Take heart, daughter," he said, "your faith has healed you." And the woman was healed from that moment.

23When Jesus entered the ruler's house and saw the flute players and the noisy crowd, **24**he said, "Go away. The girl is not dead but asleep." But they laughed at him. **25**After the crowd had been put outside, he went in and took the girl by the hand, and she got up. **26**News of this spread through all that region.

Jesus Heals the Blind and Mute

27As Jesus went on from there, two blind men followed him, calling out, "Have mercy on us, Son of David!"

28When he had gone indoors, the blind men came to him, and he asked them, "Do you believe that I am able to do this?"

"Yes, Lord," they replied.

29Then he touched their eyes and said, "According to your faith will it be done to you"; **30**and their sight was restored. Jesus warned them sternly, "See that no one knows about this." **31**But they went out and spread the news about him all over that region.

32While they were going out, a man who was demon-possessed and could not talk was brought to Jesus. **33**And when the demon was driven out, the man who had been mute spoke. The crowd was amazed and said, "Nothing like this has ever been seen in Israel."

34But the Pharisees said, "It is by the prince of demons that he drives out demons."

The Workers Are Few

35Jesus went through all the towns and villages, teaching in their synagogues, preaching the good news of the kingdom and healing every disease and sickness. **36**When he saw the crowds, he had compassion on them, because they were harassed and helpless, like sheep without a shepherd. **37**Then he said to his disciples, "The harvest is plentiful but the workers are few. **38**Ask the Lord of the harvest, therefore, to send out workers into his harvest field."

Jesus Sends Out the Twelve

10 He called his twelve disciples to him and gave them authority to drive out evil*b* spirits and to heal every disease and sickness.

2These are the names of the twelve apostles: first, Simon (who is called Peter) and his brother Andrew; James son of Zebedee, and his brother John; **3**Philip and Bartholomew; Thomas and Matthew the tax collector; James son of Alphaeus, and Thaddaeus;

---

a13 Hosea 6:6   *b1* Greek *unclean*

SERVING SOCIETY IN SMALL WAYS

Work It Out
••••

Next time you go to the mall or some other busy place, don't hurry through. Take a few minutes to watch the people. How many of them seem rushed? Do some look worried? Do many seem irritated or out of sorts? Do they look tired or hassled?

When Jesus was in a crowded place, he looked at the people around him, and "he had compassion on them." Jesus didn't just rush through the crowd or ignore those around him, he really *looked* at the people.

Life is so hectic that it's pretty easy to look right past those around you. But if you look, and if you truly *see*, you'll view a lot of people who are in need. Today's society is full of people who have more than enough to eat, plenty of clothes to wear, beautiful houses to live in—but who are needy. They don't need a meal or a place to stay, they need a smile or a word of encouragement.

Are you willing to be a servant in small ways to your needy society?

Nail It Down
••••

Read Matthew 9:35–38 for how Jesus viewed the crowds around him.

Think It Through
••••

Jesus didn't just look at the crowds around him, feel sorry for them, and then move on to the next town. He "healed every disease and sickness" (Matthew 9:35). And he told his disciples that he needed workers to help (Matthew 9:37–38). In fact, he even stated that there weren't enough workers to assist these people who were "harassed and helpless."

The need is the same today. Multitudes of people in your society are in need. And most Christians are too busy to even see the need, much less minister to it.

Are you too busy—with school, dating, job, sports, all the things that fill your life—to serve the people around you? Or are you willing to be one of the workers that Jesus was calling to help those in need?

Nail It Down
••••

Reread Matthew 9:35–38. For further insight read Proverbs 14:21,31.

Turn to pages 23 and 949 for other readings on society.
Turn to page 1019 for Monday's reading.

Topic
••••

⁴Simon the Zealot and Judas Iscariot, who betrayed him.

⁵These twelve Jesus sent out with the following instructions: "Do not go among the Gentiles or enter any town of the Samaritans. ⁶Go rather to the lost sheep of Israel. ⁷As you go, preach this message: 'The kingdom of heaven is near.' ⁸Heal the sick, raise the dead, cleanse those who have leprosy,ᵃ drive out demons. Freely you have received, freely give. ⁹Do not take along any gold or silver or copper in your belts; ¹⁰take no bag for the journey, or extra tunic, or sandals or a staff; for the worker is worth his keep.

¹¹"Whatever town or village you enter, search for some worthy person there and stay at his house until you leave. ¹²As you enter the home, give it your greeting. ¹³If the home is deserving, let your peace rest on it; if it is not, let your peace return to you. ¹⁴If anyone will not welcome you or listen to your words, shake the dust off your feet when you leave that home or town. ¹⁵I tell you the truth, it will be more bearable for Sodom and Gomorrah on the day of judgment than for that town. ¹⁶I am sending you out like sheep among wolves. Therefore be as shrewd as snakes and as innocent as doves.

¹⁷"Be on your guard against men; they will hand you over to the local councils and flog you in their synagogues. ¹⁸On my account you will be brought before governors and kings as witnesses to them and to the Gentiles. ¹⁹But when they arrest you, do not worry about what to say or how to say it. At that time you will be given what to say, ²⁰for it will not be you speaking, but the Spirit of your Father speaking through you.

²¹"Brother will betray brother to death, and a father his child; children will rebel against their parents and have them put to death. ²²All men will hate you because of me, but he who stands firm to the end will be saved. ²³When you are persecuted in one place, flee to another. I tell you the truth, you will not finish going through the cities of Israel before the Son of Man comes.

²⁴"A student is not above his teacher, nor a servant above his master. ²⁵It is enough for the student to be like his teacher, and the servant like his master. If the head of the house has been called Beelzebub,ᵇ how much more the members of his household!

²⁶"So do not be afraid of them. There is nothing concealed that will not be dis-closed, or hidden that will not be made known. ²⁷What I tell you in the dark, speak in the daylight; what is whispered in your ear, proclaim from the roofs. ²⁸Do not be afraid of those who kill the body but cannot kill the soul. Rather, be afraid of the One who can destroy both soul and body in hell. ²⁹Are not two sparrows sold for a pennyᶜ? Yet not one of them will fall to the ground apart from the will of your Father. ³⁰And even the very hairs of your head are all numbered. ³¹So don't be afraid; you are worth more than many sparrows.

³²"Whoever acknowledges me before men, I will also acknowledge him before my Father in heaven. ³³But whoever disowns me before men, I will disown him before my Father in heaven.

³⁴"Do not suppose that I have come to bring peace to the earth. I did not come to bring peace, but a sword. ³⁵For I have come to turn

> " 'a man against his father,
>   a daughter against her mother,
>   a daughter-in-law against her
>   mother-in-law—
> ³⁶   a man's enemies will be the members
>   of his own household.'ᵈ

³⁷"Anyone who loves his father or mother more than me is not worthy of me; anyone who loves his son or daughter more than me is not worthy of me; ³⁸and anyone who does not take his cross and follow me is not worthy of me. ³⁹Whoever finds his life will lose it, and whoever loses his life for my sake will find it.

⁴⁰"He who receives you receives me, and he who receives me receives the one who sent me. ⁴¹Anyone who receives a prophet because he is a prophet will receive a prophet's reward, and anyone who receives a righteous man because he is a righteous man will receive a righteous man's reward. ⁴²And if anyone gives even a cup of cold water to one of these little ones because he is my disciple, I tell you the truth, he will certainly not lose his reward."

Jesus and John the Baptist

11 After Jesus had finished instructing his twelve disciples, he went on from there to teach and preach in the towns of Galilee.ᵉ

²When John heard in prison what Christ was doing, he sent his disciples ³to ask him,

---

ᵃ8 The Greek word was used for various diseases affecting the skin—not necessarily leprosy.   ᵇ25 Greek *Beezeboul* or *Beelzeboul*   ᶜ29 Greek *an assarion*   ᵈ36 Micah 7:6   ᵉ1 Greek *in their towns*

THE REWARDS ARE WORTH IT ALL!

☐ MONDAY

At the end of the summer, Derek and Dwight are recognized by Reverend Moore during an evening church service. They spent their entire summer as part of a service team working for their church.

"These guys have been working hard all summer. They've done everything from paint classrooms to serve food at the once-a-month church potluck dinners. I don't know what I would have done without them."

The two friends stare sheepishly at the ground, uncomfortable with all the attention but feeling good about their summertime accomplishments.

Look It Up •••

The Bible is clear—a lifestyle of service is rewarding!

"If any man builds . . . using gold, silver, costly stones, wood, hay or straw, his work will be shown for what it is, because the Day will bring it to light. It will be revealed with fire, and the fire will test the quality of each man's work. If what he has built survives, he will receive his reward" (1 Corinthians 3:12–14).

In building God's kingdom, what kind of materials (that is, actions and motives) are you using?

Think It Through •••

You may be thinking, "Serving is a drag. There are too many problems, too much opposition and not enough recognition. Forget it!" Before ruling out a lifestyle of service because of the risks involved, remember the benefits—short-term satisfaction here and long-term joy in heaven.

How many heavenly rewards do you think you're accumulating by your present lifestyle of service?

Work It Out •••

Servanthood isn't just for right now; it's for the rest of your life. It brings satisfaction now and eternal rewards later. Close with this prayer:

"Father, I want to continue learning what it means to be your servant. Keep changing my attitude so that I come to the place where my only desire is to give myself away. Thanks for sending Jesus Christ, the ultimate Servant, to die for me, so that I might know you. In his name I pray, Amen."

Nail It Down •••

Read Jesus' promise to servants in Matthew 10:42.

Turn to pages 312, 718, 1008, 1034 and 1342 for other readings on serving.
Turn to page 1021 for Tuesday's reading.

Topic •••

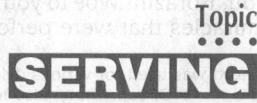

"Are you the one who was to come, or should we expect someone else?"

[4]Jesus replied, "Go back and report to John what you hear and see: [5]The blind receive sight, the lame walk, those who have leprosy[a] are cured, the deaf hear, the dead are raised, and the good news is preached to the poor. [6]Blessed is the man who does not fall away on account of me."

[7]As John's disciples were leaving, Jesus began to speak to the crowd about John: "What did you go out into the desert to see? A reed swayed by the wind? [8]If not, what did you go out to see? A man dressed in fine clothes? No, those who wear fine clothes are in kings' palaces. [9]Then what did you go out to see? A prophet? Yes, I tell you, and more than a prophet. [10]This is the one about whom it is written:

> " 'I will send my messenger ahead of
>   you,
>   who will prepare your way before
>   you.'[b]

[11]I tell you the truth: Among those born of women there has not risen anyone greater than John the Baptist; yet he who is least in the kingdom of heaven is greater than he. [12]From the days of John the Baptist until now, the kingdom of heaven has been forcefully advancing, and forceful men lay hold of it. [13]For all the Prophets and the Law prophesied until John. [14]And if you are willing to accept it, he is the Elijah who was to come. [15]He who has ears, let him hear.

[16]"To what can I compare this generation? They are like children sitting in the marketplaces and calling out to others:

[17]" 'We played the flute for you,
>   and you did not dance;
>   we sang a dirge,
>   and you did not mourn.'

[18]For John came neither eating nor drinking, and they say, 'He has a demon.' [19]The Son of Man came eating and drinking, and they say, 'Here is a glutton and a drunkard, a friend of tax collectors and "sinners." ' But wisdom is proved right by her actions."

Woe on Unrepentant Cities

[20]Then Jesus began to denounce the cities in which most of his miracles had been performed, because they did not repent. [21]"Woe to you, Korazin! Woe to you, Bethsaida! If the miracles that were performed in you had been performed in Tyre and Sidon, they would have repented long ago in sackcloth and ashes. [22]But I tell you, it will be more bearable for Tyre and Sidon on the day of judgment than for you. [23]And you, Capernaum, will you be lifted up to the skies? No, you will go down to the depths.[c] If the miracles that were performed in you had been performed in Sodom, it would have remained to this day. [24]But I tell you that it will be more bearable for Sodom on the day of judgment than for you."

Rest for the Weary

[25]At that time Jesus said, "I praise you, Father, Lord of heaven and earth, because you have hidden these things from the wise and learned, and revealed them to little children. [26]Yes, Father, for this was your good pleasure.

[27]"All things have been committed to me by my Father. No one knows the Son except the Father, and no one knows the Father except the Son and those to whom the Son chooses to reveal him.

[28]"Come to me, all you who are weary and burdened, and I will give you rest. [29]Take my yoke upon you and learn from me, for I am gentle and humble in heart, and you will find rest for your souls. [30]For my yoke is easy and my burden is light."

Lord of the Sabbath

12 At that time Jesus went through the grainfields on the Sabbath. His disciples were hungry and began to pick some heads of grain and eat them. [2]When the Pharisees saw this, they said to him, "Look! Your disciples are doing what is unlawful on the Sabbath."

[3]He answered, "Haven't you read what David did when he and his companions were hungry? [4]He entered the house of God, and he and his companions ate the consecrated bread—which was not lawful for them to do, but only for the priests. [5]Or haven't you read in the Law that on the Sabbath the priests in the temple desecrate the day and yet are innocent? [6]I tell you that one[d] greater than the temple is here. [7]If you had known what these words mean, 'I desire mercy, not sacrifice,'[e] you would not have condemned the innocent. [8]For the Son of Man is Lord of the Sabbath."

[9]Going on from that place, he went into their synagogue, [10]and a man with a shriv-

---

a5 The Greek word was used for various diseases affecting the skin—not necessarily leprosy.   b10 Mal. 3:1
c23 Greek Hades   d6 Or something; also in verses 41 and 42   e7 Hosea 6:6

I CAN'T STAND THE PAIN

In June Stan was found literally "at the end of his rope" down in the basement . . . just in the nick of time. He has since come to grips with the pain that drove him to try the ultimate escape. His poem describes what he's learned:

> Grab a pizza from the freezer,
> MTV or VCR?
> Try to blank out all your troubles,
> In the back seat of a car.
>
> Drown your sorrows with Jack Daniels,
> Oversleep or run away,
> But you can't escape the problems
> That you're facing every day.
>
> There's a permanent solution
> For the pressure that you face,
> Not to leave your loved ones . . . hanging,
> But to call upon his grace.
>
> Not to leave your classmates . . . dangling,
> But to call upon his grace.

Look It Up
••••

Are you spending your life trying to find ways to escape your emotional hurts? Here's good news: Turn to Jesus, and your running can be over. Don't wait, he's calling you, and he's ready to give you all you need to face the pain:
"My grace is sufficient for you, for my power is made perfect in weakness" (2 Corinthians 12:9).

Think It Through
••••

Think about it . . . and be very honest with yourself. Has anything you've ever tried to escape the hurt in your life worked? If your answer is no, read on.

Work It Out
••••

If serious thoughts of suicide are filling your mind, ask for help. Please! There's a better way to be free. You can talk to Jesus now, just like you talk to the person next to you. Let him help you.

Talk to an adult you trust: a parent, a teacher, a guidance counselor, a youth leader, a favorite aunt or uncle.

If this kind of pain isn't a problem in your life, pray that God will make you more sensitive to your classmates today. Someone you know may be about to believe the lie of the final good-by!

Nail It Down
••••

Read Jesus' assurance that he's willing to help in Matthew 11:28–29.

Turn to pages 867, 1365 and 1390 for other readings on escape.
Turn to page 1026 for Wednesday's reading.

Topic
••••

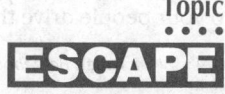

eled hand was there. Looking for a reason to accuse Jesus, they asked him, "Is it lawful to heal on the Sabbath?"

[11]He said to them, "If any of you has a sheep and it falls into a pit on the Sabbath, will you not take hold of it and lift it out? [12]How much more valuable is a man than a sheep! Therefore it is lawful to do good on the Sabbath."

[13]Then he said to the man, "Stretch out your hand." So he stretched it out and it was completely restored, just as sound as the other. [14]But the Pharisees went out and plotted how they might kill Jesus.

God's Chosen Servant

[15]Aware of this, Jesus withdrew from that place. Many followed him, and he healed all their sick, [16]warning them not to tell who he was. [17]This was to fulfill what was spoken through the prophet Isaiah:

[18]"Here is my servant whom I have
    chosen,
  the one I love, in whom I delight;
I will put my Spirit on him,
  and he will proclaim justice to the
    nations.
[19]He will not quarrel or cry out;
  no one will hear his voice in the
    streets.
[20]A bruised reed he will not break,
  and a smoldering wick he will not
    snuff out,
till he leads justice to victory.
[21] In his name the nations will put their
    hope."[a]

Jesus and Beelzebub

[22]Then they brought him a demon-possessed man who was blind and mute, and Jesus healed him, so that he could both talk and see. [23]All the people were astonished and said, "Could this be the Son of David?"

[24]But when the Pharisees heard this, they said, "It is only by Beelzebub,[b] the prince of demons, that this fellow drives out demons."

[25]Jesus knew their thoughts and said to them, "Every kingdom divided against itself will be ruined, and every city or household divided against itself will not stand. [26]If Satan drives out Satan, he is divided against himself. How then can his kingdom stand? [27]And if I drive out demons by Beelzebub, by whom do your people drive them out? So

then, they will be your judges. [28]But if I drive out demons by the Spirit of God, then the kingdom of God has come upon you.

[29]"Or again, how can anyone enter a strong man's house and carry off his possessions unless he first ties up the strong man? Then he can rob his house.

[30]"He who is not with me is against me, and he who does not gather with me scatters. [31]And so I tell you, every sin and blasphemy will be forgiven men, but the blasphemy against the Spirit will not be forgiven. [32]Anyone who speaks a word against the Son of Man will be forgiven, but anyone who speaks against the Holy Spirit will not be forgiven, either in this age or in the age to come.

[33]"Make a tree good and its fruit will be good, or make a tree bad and its fruit will be bad, for a tree is recognized by its fruit. [34]You brood of vipers, how can you who are evil say anything good? For out of the overflow of the heart the mouth speaks. [35]The good man brings good things out of the good stored up in him, and the evil man brings evil things out of the evil stored up in him. [36]But I tell you that men will have to give account on the day of judgment for every careless word they have spoken. [37]For by your words you will be acquitted, and by your words you will be condemned."

The Sign of Jonah

[38]Then some of the Pharisees and teachers of the law said to him, "Teacher, we want to see a miraculous sign from you."

[39]He answered, "A wicked and adulterous generation asks for a miraculous sign! But none will be given it except the sign of the prophet Jonah. [40]For as Jonah was three days and three nights in the belly of a huge fish, so the Son of Man will be three days and three nights in the heart of the earth. [41]The men of Nineveh will stand up at the judgment with this generation and condemn it; for they repented at the preaching of Jonah, and now one[c] greater than Jonah is here. [42]The Queen of the South will rise at the judgment with this generation and condemn it; for she came from the ends of the earth to listen to Solomon's wisdom, and now one greater than Solomon is here.

[43]"When an evil[d] spirit comes out of a man, it goes through arid places seeking rest and does not find it. [44]Then it says, 'I will return to the house I left.' When it arrives, it

---

[a]21 Isaiah 42:1-4   [b]24 Greek *Beezeboul* or *Beelzeboul*; also in verse 27   [c]41 Or *something*; also in verse 42
[d]43 Greek *unclean*

finds the house unoccupied, swept clean and put in order. **45**Then it goes and takes with it seven other spirits more wicked than itself, and they go and live there. And the final condition of that man is worse than the first. That is how it will be with this wicked generation."

Jesus' Mother and Brothers

46While Jesus was still talking to the crowd, his mother and brothers stood outside, wanting to speak to him. **47**Someone told him, "Your mother and brothers are standing outside, wanting to speak to you."[a]

48He replied to him, "Who is my mother, and who are my brothers?" **49**Pointing to his disciples, he said, "Here are my mother and my brothers. **50**For whoever does the will of my Father in heaven is my brother and sister and mother."

The Parable of the Sower

13 That same day Jesus went out of the house and sat by the lake. **2**Such large crowds gathered around him that he got into a boat and sat in it, while all the people stood on the shore. **3**Then he told them many things in parables, saying: "A farmer went out to sow his seed. **4**As he was scattering the seed, some fell along the path, and the birds came and ate it up. **5**Some fell on rocky places, where it did not have much soil. It sprang up quickly, because the soil was shallow. **6**But when the sun came up, the plants were scorched, and they withered because they had no root. **7**Other seed fell among thorns, which grew up and choked the plants. **8**Still other seed fell on good soil, where it produced a crop — a hundred, sixty or thirty times what was sown. **9**He who has ears, let him hear."

10The disciples came to him and asked, "Why do you speak to the people in parables?"

11He replied, "The knowledge of the secrets of the kingdom of heaven has been given to you, but not to them. **12**Whoever has will be given more, and he will have an abundance. Whoever does not have, even what he has will be taken from him. **13**This is why I speak to them in parables:

"Though seeing, they do not see;
  though hearing, they do not hear or
    understand.

14In them is fulfilled the prophecy of Isaiah:

" 'You will be ever hearing but never
    understanding;
  you will be ever seeing but never
    perceiving.
15For this people's heart has become
    calloused;
  they hardly hear with their ears,
  and they have closed their eyes.
Otherwise they might see with their
    eyes,
  hear with their ears,
  understand with their hearts
and turn, and I would heal them.'[b]

16But blessed are your eyes because they see, and your ears because they hear. **17**For I tell you the truth, many prophets and righteous men longed to see what you see but did not see it, and to hear what you hear but did not hear it.

18"Listen then to what the parable of the sower means: **19**When anyone hears the message about the kingdom and does not understand it, the evil one comes and snatches away what was sown in his heart. This is the seed sown along the path. **20**The one who received the seed that fell on rocky places is the man who hears the word and at once receives it with joy. **21**But since he has no root, he lasts only a short time. When trouble or persecution comes because of the word, he quickly falls away. **22**The one who received the seed that fell among the thorns is the man who hears the word, but the worries of this life and the deceitfulness of wealth choke it, making it unfruitful. **23**But the one who received the seed that fell on good soil is the man who hears the word and understands it. He produces a crop, yielding a hundred, sixty or thirty times what was sown."

The Parable of the Weeds

24Jesus told them another parable: "The kingdom of heaven is like a man who sowed good seed in his field. **25**But while everyone was sleeping, his enemy came and sowed weeds among the wheat, and went away. **26**When the wheat sprouted and formed heads, then the weeds also appeared.

27"The owner's servants came to him and said, 'Sir, didn't you sow good seed in your field? Where then did the weeds come from?'

28" 'An enemy did this,' he replied.

"The servants asked him, 'Do you want us to go and pull them up?'

---

[a]47 Some manuscripts do not have verse 47.   [b]15 Isaiah 6:9,10

²⁹" 'No,' he answered, 'because while you are pulling the weeds, you may root up the wheat with them. ³⁰Let both grow together until the harvest. At that time I will tell the harvesters: First collect the weeds and tie them in bundles to be burned; then gather the wheat and bring it into my barn.' "

The Parables of the Mustard Seed and the Yeast

³¹He told them another parable: "The kingdom of heaven is like a mustard seed, which a man took and planted in his field. ³²Though it is the smallest of all your seeds, yet when it grows, it is the largest of garden plants and becomes a tree, so that the birds of the air come and perch in its branches."

³³He told them still another parable: "The kingdom of heaven is like yeast that a woman took and mixed into a large amount*ᵃ* of flour until it worked all through the dough."

³⁴Jesus spoke all these things to the crowd in parables; he did not say anything to them without using a parable. ³⁵So was fulfilled what was spoken through the prophet:

"I will open my mouth in parables,
I will utter things hidden since the creation of the world."*ᵇ*

The Parable of the Weeds Explained

³⁶Then he left the crowd and went into the house. His disciples came to him and said, "Explain to us the parable of the weeds in the field."

³⁷He answered, "The one who sowed the good seed is the Son of Man. ³⁸The field is the world, and the good seed stands for the sons of the kingdom. The weeds are the sons of the evil one, ³⁹and the enemy who sows them is the devil. The harvest is the end of the age, and the harvesters are angels.

⁴⁰"As the weeds are pulled up and burned in the fire, so it will be at the end of the age. ⁴¹The Son of Man will send out his angels, and they will weed out of his kingdom everything that causes sin and all who do evil. ⁴²They will throw them into the fiery furnace, where there will be weeping and gnashing of teeth. ⁴³Then the righteous will shine like the sun in the kingdom of their Father. He who has ears, let him hear.

The Parables of the Hidden Treasure and the Pearl

⁴⁴"The kingdom of heaven is like treasure hidden in a field. When a man found it, he hid it again, and then in his joy went and sold all he had and bought that field.

⁴⁵"Again, the kingdom of heaven is like a merchant looking for fine pearls. ⁴⁶When he found one of great value, he went away and sold everything he had and bought it.

The Parable of the Net

⁴⁷"Once again, the kingdom of heaven is like a net that was let down into the lake and caught all kinds of fish. ⁴⁸When it was full, the fishermen pulled it up on the shore. Then they sat down and collected the good fish in baskets, but threw the bad away. ⁴⁹This is how it will be at the end of the age. The angels will come and separate the wicked from the righteous ⁵⁰and throw them into the fiery furnace, where there will be weeping and gnashing of teeth.

⁵¹"Have you understood all these things?" Jesus asked.

"Yes," they replied.

⁵²He said to them, "Therefore every teacher of the law who has been instructed about the kingdom of heaven is like the owner of a house who brings out of his storeroom new treasures as well as old."

A Prophet Without Honor

⁵³When Jesus had finished these parables, he moved on from there. ⁵⁴Coming to his hometown, he began teaching the people in their synagogue, and they were amazed. "Where did this man get this wisdom and these miraculous powers?" they asked. ⁵⁵"Isn't this the carpenter's son? Isn't his mother's name Mary, and aren't his brothers James, Joseph, Simon and Judas? ⁵⁶Aren't all his sisters with us? Where then did this man get all these things?" ⁵⁷And they took offense at him.

But Jesus said to them, "Only in his hometown and in his own house is a prophet without honor."

⁵⁸And he did not do many miracles there because of their lack of faith.

John the Baptist Beheaded

14 At that time Herod the tetrarch heard the reports about Jesus, ²and he said to his attendants, "This is John the Baptist; he has risen from the dead! That is why miraculous powers are at work in him."

³Now Herod had arrested John and bound him and put him in prison because of Herodias, his brother Philip's wife, ⁴for John had

---

ᵃ33 Greek *three satas* (probably about 1/2 bushel or 22 liters)   *ᵇ35* Psalm 78:2

been saying to him: "It is not lawful for you to have her." ⁵Herod wanted to kill John, but he was afraid of the people, because they considered him a prophet.

⁶On Herod's birthday the daughter of Herodias danced for them and pleased Herod so much ⁷that he promised with an oath to give her whatever she asked. ⁸Prompted by her mother, she said, "Give me here on a platter the head of John the Baptist." ⁹The king was distressed, but because of his oaths and his dinner guests, he ordered that her request be granted ¹⁰and had John beheaded in the prison. ¹¹His head was brought in on a platter and given to the girl, who carried it to her mother. ¹²John's disciples came and took his body and buried it. Then they went and told Jesus.

Jesus Feeds the Five Thousand

¹³When Jesus heard what had happened, he withdrew by boat privately to a solitary place. Hearing of this, the crowds followed him on foot from the towns. ¹⁴When Jesus landed and saw a large crowd, he had compassion on them and healed their sick.

¹⁵As evening approached, the disciples came to him and said, "This is a remote place, and it's already getting late. Send the crowds away, so they can go to the villages and buy themselves some food."

¹⁶Jesus replied, "They do not need to go away. You give them something to eat."

¹⁷"We have here only five loaves of bread and two fish," they answered.

¹⁸"Bring them here to me," he said. ¹⁹And he directed the people to sit down on the grass. Taking the five loaves and the two fish and looking up to heaven, he gave thanks and broke the loaves. Then he gave them to the disciples, and the disciples gave them to the people. ²⁰They all ate and were satisfied, and the disciples picked up twelve basketfuls of broken pieces that were left over. ²¹The number of those who ate was about five thousand men, besides women and children.

Jesus Walks on the Water

²²Immediately Jesus made the disciples get into the boat and go on ahead of him to the other side, while he dismissed the crowd. ²³After he had dismissed them, he went up on a mountainside by himself to pray. When evening came, he was there alone, ²⁴but the boat was already a considerable distance[a] from land, buffeted by the waves because the wind was against it.

²⁵During the fourth watch of the night Jesus went out to them, walking on the lake. ²⁶When the disciples saw him walking on the lake, they were terrified. "It's a ghost," they said, and cried out in fear.

²⁷But Jesus immediately said to them: "Take courage! It is I. Don't be afraid."

²⁸"Lord, if it's you," Peter replied, "tell me to come to you on the water."

²⁹"Come," he said.

Then Peter got down out of the boat, walked on the water and came toward Jesus. ³⁰But when he saw the wind, he was afraid and, beginning to sink, cried out, "Lord, save me!"

³¹Immediately Jesus reached out his hand and caught him. "You of little faith," he said, "why did you doubt?"

³²And when they climbed into the boat, the wind died down. ³³Then those who were in the boat worshiped him, saying, "Truly you are the Son of God."

³⁴When they had crossed over, they landed at Gennesaret. ³⁵And when the men of that place recognized Jesus, they sent word to all the surrounding country. People brought all their sick to him ³⁶and begged him to let the sick just touch the edge of his cloak, and all who touched him were healed.

Clean and Unclean

15 Then some Pharisees and teachers of the law came to Jesus from Jerusalem and asked, ²"Why do your disciples break the tradition of the elders? They don't wash their hands before they eat!"

³Jesus replied, "And why do you break the command of God for the sake of your tradition? ⁴For God said, 'Honor your father and mother'[b] and 'Anyone who curses his father or mother must be put to death.'[c] ⁵But you say that if a man says to his father or mother, 'Whatever help you might otherwise have received from me is a gift devoted to God,' ⁶he is not to 'honor his father[d]' with it. Thus you nullify the word of God for the sake of your tradition. ⁷You hypocrites! Isaiah was right when he prophesied about you:

⁸" 'These people honor me with their lips,
but their hearts are far from me.

LORD, I FEEL SO WEARY!

W hen Donna heard about a youth group weekend retreat at a conference center up in the mountains she thought, "Perfect! That's exactly what I need. A chance to get away and get my act together. Since my relationship with God has been practically nonexistent the last few weeks, this'll be a great opportunity to rest and reflect."

She signed up immediately.

On Sunday night, after the retreat was over, Donna felt even more pooped than she did before she left town on Friday afternoon!

Look It Up • • • •

We are frenzied, wild-and-crazy, never-sit-still, always-in-motion people who live in a hectic, action-packed, chaotic culture. No wonder we feel so worn out all the time! Listen to the psalmist.

> I remember the days of long ago;
> I meditate on all your works
> and consider what your hands have done.
> I spread out my hands to you;
> my soul thirsts for you like a parched land.
> Answer me quickly, O LORD;
> my spirit fails.
> Do not hide your face from me
> or I will be like those who go down to the pit
> (Psalm 143:5–7).

When was the last time you took time for such reflection?

Think It Through • • • •

If retreats are supposed to be times of solitude and rest, why do most people who go on them come home exhausted?

What would happen if your church or youth group had a retreat with no games or scheduled activities—just time for reading God's Word, quiet meditation and sleeping? What if there was a rule that no one could talk during the entire weekend—except to God? Would anyone sign up? Would you?

Work It Out • • • •

Feeling spiritually dry and blah?

Take your own personal retreat. Grab your Bible, a notebook and a pen. Find a peaceful place, and spend a whole morning (nine to noon) talking to God, praising him, reading his Word and singing your favorite praise choruses.

Personal retreats aren't just refreshing . . . they're also a lot of fun! You may find that three hours are too short!

Nail It Down • • • •

Read about Jesus' own spiritual personal retreat in Matthew 14:22–23.

Turn to pages 572, 686, 694, 939, 1148 and 1178 for other readings on feelings.
Turn to page 1029 for Thursday's reading.

Topic • • • •

FEELINGS

[9]They worship me in vain;
their teachings are but rules taught by
men.'[a]"

[10]Jesus called the crowd to him and said,
"Listen and understand. [11]What goes into a
man's mouth does not make him 'unclean,'
but what comes out of his mouth, that is
what makes him 'unclean.'"

[12]Then the disciples came to him and
asked, "Do you know that the Pharisees
were offended when they heard this?"

[13]He replied, "Every plant that my heavenly Father has not planted will be pulled up
by the roots. [14]Leave them; they are blind
guides.[b] If a blind man leads a blind man,
both will fall into a pit."

[15]Peter said, "Explain the parable to us."

[16]"Are you still so dull?" Jesus asked them.
[17]"Don't you see that whatever enters the
mouth goes into the stomach and then out
of the body? [18]But the things that come out
of the mouth come from the heart, and
these make a man 'unclean.' [19]For out of the
heart come evil thoughts, murder, adultery,
sexual immorality, theft, false testimony,
slander. [20]These are what make a man 'unclean'; but eating with unwashed hands
does not make him 'unclean.'"

The Faith of the Canaanite Woman

[21]Leaving that place, Jesus withdrew to
the region of Tyre and Sidon. [22]A Canaanite
woman from that vicinity came to him, crying out, "Lord, Son of David, have mercy on
me! My daughter is suffering terribly from
demon-possession."

[23]Jesus did not answer a word. So his disciples came to him and urged him, "Send
her away, for she keeps crying out after us."

[24]He answered, "I was sent only to the lost
sheep of Israel."

[25]The woman came and knelt before him.
"Lord, help me!" she said.

[26]He replied, "It is not right to take the
children's bread and toss it to their dogs."

[27]"Yes, Lord," she said, "but even the dogs
eat the crumbs that fall from their masters'
table."

[28]Then Jesus answered, "Woman, you
have great faith! Your request is granted."
And her daughter was healed from that very
hour.

Jesus Feeds the Four Thousand

[29]Jesus left there and went along the Sea
of Galilee. Then he went up on a mountainside and sat down. [30]Great crowds came to
him, bringing the lame, the blind, the crippled, the mute and many others, and laid
them at his feet; and he healed them. [31]The
people were amazed when they saw the
mute speaking, the crippled made well,
the lame walking and the blind seeing. And
they praised the God of Israel.

[32]Jesus called his disciples to him and
said, "I have compassion for these people;
they have already been with me three days
and have nothing to eat. I do not want to
send them away hungry, or they may collapse on the way."

[33]His disciples answered, "Where could
we get enough bread in this remote place to
feed such a crowd?"

[34]"How many loaves do you have?" Jesus
asked.

"Seven," they replied, "and a few small
fish."

[35]He told the crowd to sit down on the
ground. [36]Then he took the seven loaves
and the fish, and when he had given thanks,
he broke them and gave them to the disciples, and they in turn to the people. [37]They
all ate and were satisfied. Afterward the disciples picked up seven basketfuls of broken
pieces that were left over. [38]The number of
those who ate was four thousand, besides
women and children. [39]After Jesus had sent
the crowd away, he got into the boat and
went into the vicinity of Magadan.

The Demand for a Sign

16 The Pharisees and Sadducees came
to Jesus and tested him by asking
him to show them a sign from heaven.

[2]He replied,[c] "When evening comes, you
say, 'It will be fair weather, for the sky is red,'
[3]and in the morning, 'Today it will be
stormy, for the sky is red and overcast.' You
know how to interpret the appearance of the
sky, but you cannot interpret the signs of the
times. [4]A wicked and adulterous generation
looks for a miraculous sign, but none will be
given it except the sign of Jonah." Jesus then
left them and went away.

The Yeast of the Pharisees and Sadducees

[5]When they went across the lake, the disciples forgot to take bread. [6]"Be careful,"

---

[a]9 Isaiah 29:13   [b]14 Some manuscripts *guides of the blind*   [c]2 Some early manuscripts do not have the rest of verse 2 and all of verse 3.

Jesus said to them. "Be on your guard against the yeast of the Pharisees and Sadducees."

7They discussed this among themselves and said, "It is because we didn't bring any bread."

8Aware of their discussion, Jesus asked, "You of little faith, why are you talking among yourselves about having no bread? **9**Do you still not understand? Don't you remember the five loaves for the five thousand, and how many basketfuls you gathered? **10**Or the seven loaves for the four thousand, and how many basketfuls you gathered? **11**How is it you don't understand that I was not talking to you about bread? But be on your guard against the yeast of the Pharisees and Sadducees." **12**Then they understood that he was not telling them to guard against the yeast used in bread, but against the teaching of the Pharisees and Sadducees.

Peter's Confession of Christ

13When Jesus came to the region of Caesarea Philippi, he asked his disciples, "Who do people say the Son of Man is?"

14They replied, "Some say John the Baptist; others say Elijah; and still others, Jeremiah or one of the prophets."

15"But what about you?" he asked. "Who do you say I am?"

16Simon Peter answered, "You are the Christ,*a* the Son of the living God."

17Jesus replied, "Blessed are you, Simon son of Jonah, for this was not revealed to you by man, but by my Father in heaven. **18**And I tell you that you are Peter,*b* and on this rock I will build my church, and the gates of Hades*c* will not overcome it.*d* **19**I will give you the keys of the kingdom of heaven; whatever you bind on earth will be*e* bound in heaven, and whatever you loose on earth will be*e* loosed in heaven." **20**Then he warned his disciples not to tell anyone that he was the Christ.

Jesus Predicts His Death

21From that time on Jesus began to explain to his disciples that he must go to Jerusalem and suffer many things at the hands of the elders, chief priests and teachers of the law, and that he must be killed and on the third day be raised to life.

22Peter took him aside and began to rebuke him. "Never, Lord!" he said. "This shall never happen to you!"

23Jesus turned and said to Peter, "Get behind me, Satan! You are a stumbling block to me; you do not have in mind the things of God, but the things of men."

24Then Jesus said to his disciples, "If anyone would come after me, he must deny himself and take up his cross and follow me. **25**For whoever wants to save his life*f* will lose it, but whoever loses his life for me will find it. **26**What good will it be for a man if he gains the whole world, yet forfeits his soul? Or what can a man give in exchange for his soul? **27**For the Son of Man is going to come in his Father's glory with his angels, and then he will reward each person according to what he has done. **28**I tell you the truth, some who are standing here will not taste death before they see the Son of Man coming in his kingdom."

The Transfiguration

17 After six days Jesus took with him Peter, James and John the brother of James, and led them up a high mountain by themselves. **2**There he was transfigured before them. His face shone like the sun, and his clothes became as white as the light. **3**Just then there appeared before them Moses and Elijah, talking with Jesus.

4Peter said to Jesus, "Lord, it is good for us to be here. If you wish, I will put up three shelters — one for you, one for Moses and one for Elijah."

5While he was still speaking, a bright cloud enveloped them, and a voice from the cloud said, "This is my Son, whom I love; with him I am well pleased. Listen to him!"

6When the disciples heard this, they fell facedown to the ground, terrified. **7**But Jesus came and touched them. "Get up," he said. "Don't be afraid." **8**When they looked up, they saw no one except Jesus.

9As they were coming down the mountain, Jesus instructed them, "Don't tell anyone what you have seen, until the Son of Man has been raised from the dead."

10The disciples asked him, "Why then do the teachers of the law say that Elijah must come first?"

11Jesus replied, "To be sure, Elijah comes and will restore all things. **12**But I tell you, Elijah has already come, and they did not

*a*16 Or *Messiah*; also in verse 20   *b*18 *Peter* means *rock*.   *c*18 Or *hell*   *d*18 Or *not prove stronger than it*   *e*19 Or *have been*   *f*25 The Greek word means either *life* or *soul*; also in verse 26.

GOD'S MVP'S (MUCH VALUED PEOPLE)

Mark's older brother, right out of college, makes $40,000 a year as a computer programmer.

Mark's older sister just received an academic scholarship to Yale.

Mark's younger brother was recently named to the All-State baseball team.

And Mark? Well, he flips hamburgers for less than $4.00 an hour, gets average grades and has never made any kind of sports team. His interest is poetry. Thinking that's weird, his parents are always on him to "make something of yourself . . . do something worthwhile . . . be like one of your brothers."

Is it any wonder that Mark feels worthless?

Look It Up

Listen up! No matter what parents or coaches or teachers or others say, you are extremely valuable to God. He really cares about you. Are you ready for all the evidence?

• You are constantly in God's thoughts (Psalm 139:17–18).
• God keeps track of all your hurts (Psalm 56:8).
• Because you are so precious to him, God is aware of every detail of your life: "Are not five sparrows sold for two pennies? Yet not one of them is forgotten by God. Indeed, the very hairs of your head are all numbered. Don't be afraid; you are worth more than many sparrows" (Luke 12:6–7).

Think It Through

Society says you have worth if, and only if, you are beautiful or smart or talented. This explains why illiterate, disabled, poor and elderly people are considered to be of little value.

God says you matter just because you are created in his image. That's all. You don't have to do anything. You just have to be.

Work It Out

First, praise God that your worth is not dependent on what you do. He values you just because you are.

Second, thank God for caring about every aspect of your life. (A big boost to your self-esteem will come when you realize that God is deeply concerned about you and about how you feel.)

Third, go out of your way to let others today know how valuable they are. Tell someone how much God cares for him or her.

Nail It Down

Read Matthew 16:26 for more insight about your value to God.

Turn to pages 584, 641, 1100 and 1379 for other readings on self-esteem.
Turn to page 1032 for Friday's reading.

Topic

SELF-ESTEEM

recognize him, but have done to him everything they wished. In the same way the Son of Man is going to suffer at their hands." ¹³Then the disciples understood that he was talking to them about John the Baptist.

The Healing of a Boy With a Demon

¹⁴When they came to the crowd, a man approached Jesus and knelt before him. ¹⁵"Lord, have mercy on my son," he said. "He has seizures and is suffering greatly. He often falls into the fire or into the water. ¹⁶I brought him to your disciples, but they could not heal him."

¹⁷"O unbelieving and perverse generation," Jesus replied, "how long shall I stay with you? How long shall I put up with you? Bring the boy here to me." ¹⁸Jesus rebuked the demon, and it came out of the boy, and he was healed from that moment.

¹⁹Then the disciples came to Jesus in private and asked, "Why couldn't we drive it out?"

²⁰He replied, "Because you have so little faith. I tell you the truth, if you have faith as small as a mustard seed, you can say to this mountain, 'Move from here to there' and it will move. Nothing will be impossible for you.ᵃ"

²²When they came together in Galilee, he said to them, "The Son of Man is going to be betrayed into the hands of men. ²³They will kill him, and on the third day he will be raised to life." And the disciples were filled with grief.

The Temple Tax

²⁴After Jesus and his disciples arrived in Capernaum, the collectors of the two-drachma tax came to Peter and asked, "Doesn't your teacher pay the temple taxᵇ?"

²⁵"Yes, he does," he replied.

When Peter came into the house, Jesus was the first to speak. "What do you think, Simon?" he asked. "From whom do the kings of the earth collect duty and taxes — from their own sons or from others?"

²⁶"From others," Peter answered.

"Then the sons are exempt," Jesus said to him. ²⁷"But so that we may not offend them, go to the lake and throw out your line. Take the first fish you catch; open its mouth and you will find a four-drachma coin. Take it and give it to them for my tax and yours."

The Greatest in the Kingdom of Heaven

18 At that time the disciples came to Jesus and asked, "Who is the greatest in the kingdom of heaven?"

²He called a little child and had him stand among them. ³And he said: "I tell you the truth, unless you change and become like little children, you will never enter the kingdom of heaven. ⁴Therefore, whoever humbles himself like this child is the greatest in the kingdom of heaven.

⁵"And whoever welcomes a little child like this in my name welcomes me. ⁶But if anyone causes one of these little ones who believe in me to sin, it would be better for him to have a large millstone hung around his neck and to be drowned in the depths of the sea.

⁷"Woe to the world because of the things that cause people to sin! Such things must come, but woe to the man through whom they come! ⁸If your hand or your foot causes you to sin, cut it off and throw it away. It is better for you to enter life maimed or crippled than to have two hands or two feet and be thrown into eternal fire. ⁹And if your eye causes you to sin, gouge it out and throw it away. It is better for you to enter life with one eye than to have two eyes and be thrown into the fire of hell.

The Parable of the Lost Sheep

¹⁰"See that you do not look down on one of these little ones. For I tell you that their angels in heaven always see the face of my Father in heaven.ᶜ

¹²"What do you think? If a man owns a hundred sheep, and one of them wanders away, will he not leave the ninety-nine on the hills and go to look for the one that wandered off? ¹³And if he finds it, I tell you the truth, he is happier about that one sheep than about the ninety-nine that did not wander off. ¹⁴In the same way your Father in heaven is not willing that any of these little ones should be lost.

A Brother Who Sins Against You

¹⁵"If your brother sins against you,ᵈ go and show him his fault, just between the two of you. If he listens to you, you have won your brother over. ¹⁶But if he will not listen, take one or two others along, so that 'every matter may be established by the testimony of two or three witnesses.'ᵉ ¹⁷If he

---

ᵃ20 Some manuscripts you. ²¹But this kind does not go out except by prayer and fasting.   ᵇ24 Greek the two drachmas   ᶜ10 Some manuscripts heaven. ¹¹The Son of Man came to save what was lost.   ᵈ15 Some manuscripts do not have against you.   ᵉ16 Deut. 19:15

refuses to listen to them, tell it to the church; and if he refuses to listen even to the church, treat him as you would a pagan or a tax collector.

18"I tell you the truth, whatever you bind on earth will be[a] bound in heaven, and whatever you loose on earth will be[a] loosed in heaven.

19"Again, I tell you that if two of you on earth agree about anything you ask for, it will be done for you by my Father in heaven. **20**For where two or three come together in my name, there am I with them."

The Parable of the Unmerciful Servant

21Then Peter came to Jesus and asked, "Lord, how many times shall I forgive my brother when he sins against me? Up to seven times?"

22Jesus answered, "I tell you, not seven times, but seventy-seven times.[b]

23"Therefore, the kingdom of heaven is like a king who wanted to settle accounts with his servants. **24**As he began the settlement, a man who owed him ten thousand talents[c] was brought to him. **25**Since he was not able to pay, the master ordered that he and his wife and his children and all that he had be sold to repay the debt.

26"The servant fell on his knees before him. 'Be patient with me,' he begged, 'and I will pay back everything.' **27**The servant's master took pity on him, canceled the debt and let him go.

28"But when that servant went out, he found one of his fellow servants who owed him a hundred denarii.[d] He grabbed him and began to choke him. 'Pay back what you owe me!' he demanded.

29"His fellow servant fell to his knees and begged him, 'Be patient with me, and I will pay you back.'

30"But he refused. Instead, he went off and had the man thrown into prison until he could pay the debt. **31**When the other servants saw what had happened, they were greatly distressed and went and told their master everything that had happened.

32"Then the master called the servant in. 'You wicked servant,' he said, 'I canceled all that debt of yours because you begged me to. **33**Shouldn't you have had mercy on your fellow servant just as I had on you?' **34**In anger his master turned him over to the jailers to be tortured, until he should pay back all he owed.

35"This is how my heavenly Father will treat each of you unless you forgive your brother from your heart."

Divorce

19 When Jesus had finished saying these things, he left Galilee and went into the region of Judea to the other side of the Jordan. **2**Large crowds followed him, and he healed them there.

3Some Pharisees came to him to test him. They asked, "Is it lawful for a man to divorce his wife for any and every reason?"

4"Haven't you read," he replied, "that at the beginning the Creator 'made them male and female,'[e] **5**and said, 'For this reason a man will leave his father and mother and be united to his wife, and the two will become one flesh'[f]? **6**So they are no longer two, but one. Therefore what God has joined together, let man not separate."

7"Why then," they asked, "did Moses command that a man give his wife a certificate of divorce and send her away?"

8Jesus replied, "Moses permitted you to divorce your wives because your hearts were hard. But it was not this way from the beginning. **9**I tell you that anyone who divorces his wife, except for marital unfaithfulness, and marries another woman commits adultery."

10The disciples said to him, "If this is the situation between a husband and wife, it is better not to marry."

11Jesus replied, "Not everyone can accept this word, but only those to whom it has been given. **12**For some are eunuchs because they were born that way; others were made that way by men; and others have renounced marriage[g] because of the kingdom of heaven. The one who can accept this should accept it."

The Little Children and Jesus

13Then little children were brought to Jesus for him to place his hands on them and pray for them. But the disciples rebuked those who brought them.

14Jesus said, "Let the little children come to me, and do not hinder them, for the kingdom of heaven belongs to such as these." **15**When he had placed his hands on them, he went on from there.

The Rich Young Man

16Now a man came up to Jesus and asked,

---

a18 Or *have been*   *b22* Or *seventy times seven*   *c24* That is, millions of dollars   *d28* That is, a few dollars
e4 Gen. 1:27   *f5* Gen. 2:24   *g12* Or *have made themselves eunuchs*

THE FIASCO OF A FRACTURED FAMILY

Word just leaked out that Mike and Christine, married for twenty years, parents of two teens, long-time church members, are filing for divorce.

"Hasn't anybody talked with them?" another member asks.

"I don't think so. I mean, it was such a total surprise. Besides, I think their minds are made up."

"What a shame."

"I know. I feel so bad for their kids. How old are they? Thirteen and sixteen?"

"I think so."

Look It Up

With frightening regularity, judges utter the sobering words, "Divorce granted." Even Christians are flocking to the courts! What does God think about all this?

The testimony of the Old Testament is clear: " 'I hate divorce,' says the LORD God of Israel" (Malachi 2:16).

The testimony of the New Testament is equally clear: "What God has joined together, let man not separate" (Matthew 19:6).

Think It Through

Our society sees divorce as an acceptable alternative when marital problems arise. The message is, "If it gets too tough, just bail out."

You need to begin rejecting that false philosophy now, while you're a teenager. Otherwise, it will infect and then affect you when you do marry later on.

(Remember, you have no control over what your parents do or may have already done. But you can decide for yourself what marriage will mean to you and the kind of commitment you will make to it.)

Work It Out

God not only hates it when parents decide to divorce, but he is also saddened when kids cause friction in the family. Are you creating strife in your home? Fighting with a brother or sister? Arguing with your parents? Not helping out around the house?

Pick out a behavior in your life that needs to change in order to make things more peaceful at home. Before the clock strikes midnight, correct that situation (and then ask God to protect your family in the future).

Nail It Down

See what Jesus has to say about marriage and divorce in Matthew 19:4–7.

Turn to pages 656 and 947 for other readings on behavior.
Turn to page 1034 for the weekend reading.

Topic

"Teacher, what good thing must I do to get eternal life?"

[17]"Why do you ask me about what is good?" Jesus replied. "There is only One who is good. If you want to enter life, obey the commandments."

[18]"Which ones?" the man inquired.

Jesus replied, " 'Do not murder, do not commit adultery, do not steal, do not give false testimony, [19]honor your father and mother,'[a] and 'love your neighbor as yourself.'[b]"

[20]"All these I have kept," the young man said. "What do I still lack?"

[21]Jesus answered, "If you want to be perfect, go, sell your possessions and give to the poor, and you will have treasure in heaven. Then come, follow me."

[22]When the young man heard this, he went away sad, because he had great wealth.

[23]Then Jesus said to his disciples, "I tell you the truth, it is hard for a rich man to enter the kingdom of heaven. [24]Again I tell you, it is easier for a camel to go through the eye of a needle than for a rich man to enter the kingdom of God."

[25]When the disciples heard this, they were greatly astonished and asked, "Who then can be saved?"

[26]Jesus looked at them and said, "With man this is impossible, but with God all things are possible."

[27]Peter answered him, "We have left everything to follow you! What then will there be for us?"

[28]Jesus said to them, "I tell you the truth, at the renewal of all things, when the Son of Man sits on his glorious throne, you who have followed me will also sit on twelve thrones, judging the twelve tribes of Israel. [29]And everyone who has left houses or brothers or sisters or father or mother[c] or children or fields for my sake will receive a hundred times as much and will inherit eternal life. [30]But many who are first will be last, and many who are last will be first.

The Parable of the Workers in the Vineyard

20 "For the kingdom of heaven is like a landowner who went out early in the morning to hire men to work in his vineyard. [2]He agreed to pay them a denarius for the day and sent them into his vineyard.

[3]"About the third hour he went out and saw others standing in the marketplace doing nothing. [4]He told them, 'You also go and work in my vineyard, and I will pay you whatever is right.' [5]So they went.

"He went out again about the sixth hour and the ninth hour and did the same thing. [6]About the eleventh hour he went out and found still others standing around. He asked them, 'Why have you been standing here all day long doing nothing?'

[7]" 'Because no one has hired us,' they answered.

"He said to them, 'You also go and work in my vineyard.'

[8]"When evening came, the owner of the vineyard said to his foreman, 'Call the workers and pay them their wages, beginning with the last ones hired and going on to the first.'

[9]"The workers who were hired about the eleventh hour came and each received a denarius. [10]So when those came who were hired first, they expected to receive more. But each one of them also received a denarius. [11]When they received it, they began to grumble against the landowner. [12]'These men who were hired last worked only one hour,' they said, 'and you have made them equal to us who have borne the burden of the work and the heat of the day.'

[13]"But he answered one of them, 'Friend, I am not being unfair to you. Didn't you agree to work for a denarius? [14]Take your pay and go. I want to give the man who was hired last the same as I gave you. [15]Don't I have the right to do what I want with my own money? Or are you envious because I am generous?'

[16]"So the last will be first, and the first will be last."

Jesus Again Predicts His Death

[17]Now as Jesus was going up to Jerusalem, he took the twelve disciples aside and said to them, [18]"We are going up to Jerusalem, and the Son of Man will be betrayed to the chief priests and the teachers of the law. They will condemn him to death [19]and will turn him over to the Gentiles to be mocked and flogged and crucified. On the third day he will be raised to life!"

A Mother's Request

[20]Then the mother of Zebedee's sons came to Jesus with her sons and, kneeling down, asked a favor of him.

[21]"What is it you want?" he asked.

She said, "Grant that one of these two

---

[a]19 Exodus 20:12-16; Deut. 5:16-20   [b]19 Lev. 19:18   [c]29 Some manuscripts *mother or wife*

THE GOAL OF SERVICE

Work It Out
••••

Take a few minutes to write down your goals for the next year. You could write:
- Graduate from high school.
- Win ten tennis matches.
- Find a good part-time job.
- Convince my parents I don't need a curfew.
- Find ways to serve others.

Does that last one seem out of place? It shouldn't. As a Christian, serving others should be a primary goal in your life. As you work toward graduating from high school, Christ asks you to serve. As you look for a part-time job, Christ asks you to be a servant.

What are you looking for in life? Popularity? Honor? Praise? Or are you looking for ways to serve?

Nail It Down
••••

Read Matthew 20:20–28 to find out how Jesus responded when his disciples had their goals out of order.

Think It Through
••••

Jesus was quick to set the mother of James and John straight. She wanted them to have a place of honor next to Jesus. Jesus made sure that she and the rest of the disciples knew that the place wouldn't be given as a favor but would be given to the one willing to serve in spite of hardship or difficulty.

Today's world isn't in the business of honoring servants. For the most part, the honor, the prestige, the big salaries, go to those who are aggressive or flashy, to those who are "looking out for number one."

What is one of the main ways you can identify true Christianity in action? The true Christian's primary goal is not to gain power or wealth or status; the primary goal is to serve. Are your goals in their proper order?

Nail It Down
••••

Reread Jesus' call to servant leadership in Matthew 20:20–28. For further insight read Psalm 34.

Turn to pages 312, 718, 1008, 1019 and 1342 for other readings on serving.
Turn to page 1042 for Monday's reading.

Topic
••••
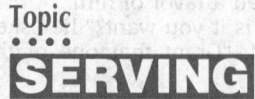

sons of mine may sit at your right and the other at your left in your kingdom."

22"You don't know what you are asking," Jesus said to them. "Can you drink the cup I am going to drink?"

"We can," they answered.

23Jesus said to them, "You will indeed drink from my cup, but to sit at my right or left is not for me to grant. These places belong to those for whom they have been prepared by my Father."

24When the ten heard about this, they were indignant with the two brothers. **25**Jesus called them together and said, "You know that the rulers of the Gentiles lord it over them, and their high officials exercise authority over them. **26**Not so with you. Instead, whoever wants to become great among you must be your servant, **27**and whoever wants to be first must be your slave— **28**just as the Son of Man did not come to be served, but to serve, and to give his life as a ransom for many."

Two Blind Men Receive Sight

29As Jesus and his disciples were leaving Jericho, a large crowd followed him. **30**Two blind men were sitting by the roadside, and when they heard that Jesus was going by, they shouted, "Lord, Son of David, have mercy on us!"

31The crowd rebuked them and told them to be quiet, but they shouted all the louder, "Lord, Son of David, have mercy on us!"

32Jesus stopped and called them. "What do you want me to do for you?" he asked.

33"Lord," they answered, "we want our sight."

34Jesus had compassion on them and touched their eyes. Immediately they received their sight and followed him.

The Triumphal Entry

21 As they approached Jerusalem and came to Bethphage on the Mount of Olives, Jesus sent two disciples, **2**saying to them, "Go to the village ahead of you, and at once you will find a donkey tied there, with her colt by her. Untie them and bring them to me. **3**If anyone says anything to you, tell him that the Lord needs them, and he will send them right away."

4This took place to fulfill what was spoken through the prophet:

5"Say to the Daughter of Zion,

'See, your king comes to you,
gentle and riding on a donkey,
on a colt, the foal of a donkey.' "[a]

6The disciples went and did as Jesus had instructed them. **7**They brought the donkey and the colt, placed their cloaks on them, and Jesus sat on them. **8**A very large crowd spread their cloaks on the road, while others cut branches from the trees and spread them on the road. **9**The crowds that went ahead of him and those that followed shouted,

"Hosanna[b] to the Son of David!"

"Blessed is he who comes in the name
of the Lord!"[c]

"Hosanna[b] in the highest!"

10When Jesus entered Jerusalem, the whole city was stirred and asked, "Who is this?"

11The crowds answered, "This is Jesus, the prophet from Nazareth in Galilee."

Jesus at the Temple

12Jesus entered the temple area and drove out all who were buying and selling there. He overturned the tables of the money changers and the benches of those selling doves. **13**"It is written," he said to them, " 'My house will be called a house of prayer,'[d] but you are making it a 'den of robbers.'[e]"

14The blind and the lame came to him at the temple, and he healed them. **15**But when the chief priests and the teachers of the law saw the wonderful things he did and the children shouting in the temple area, "Hosanna to the Son of David," they were indignant.

16"Do you hear what these children are saying?" they asked him.

"Yes," replied Jesus, "have you never read,

" 'From the lips of children and infants
you have ordained praise'[f]?"

17And he left them and went out of the city to Bethany, where he spent the night.

The Fig Tree Withers

18Early in the morning, as he was on his way back to the city, he was hungry. **19**Seeing a fig tree by the road, he went up to it but found nothing on it except leaves. Then he

---

a5 Zech. 9:9 *b9* A Hebrew expression meaning "Save!" which became an exclamation of praise; also in verse 15 *c9* Psalm 118:26 *d13* Isaiah 56:7 *e13* Jer. 7:11 *f16* Psalm 8:2

said to it, "May you never bear fruit again!" Immediately the tree withered.

²⁰When the disciples saw this, they were amazed. "How did the fig tree wither so quickly?" they asked.

²¹Jesus replied, "I tell you the truth, if you have faith and do not doubt, not only can you do what was done to the fig tree, but also you can say to this mountain, 'Go, throw yourself into the sea,' and it will be done. ²²If you believe, you will receive whatever you ask for in prayer."

The Authority of Jesus Questioned

²³Jesus entered the temple courts, and, while he was teaching, the chief priests and the elders of the people came to him. "By what authority are you doing these things?" they asked. "And who gave you this authority?"

²⁴Jesus replied, "I will also ask you one question. If you answer me, I will tell you by what authority I am doing these things. ²⁵John's baptism—where did it come from? Was it from heaven, or from men?"

They discussed it among themselves and said, "If we say, 'From heaven,' he will ask, 'Then why didn't you believe him?' ²⁶But if we say, 'From men'—we are afraid of the people, for they all hold that John was a prophet."

²⁷So they answered Jesus, "We don't know."

Then he said, "Neither will I tell you by what authority I am doing these things.

The Parable of the Two Sons

²⁸"What do you think? There was a man who had two sons. He went to the first and said, 'Son, go and work today in the vineyard.'

²⁹"'I will not,' he answered, but later he changed his mind and went.

³⁰"Then the father went to the other son and said the same thing. He answered, 'I will, sir,' but he did not go.

³¹"Which of the two did what his father wanted?"

"The first," they answered.

Jesus said to them, "I tell you the truth, the tax collectors and the prostitutes are entering the kingdom of God ahead of you. ³²For John came to you to show you the way of righteousness, and you did not believe him, but the tax collectors and the prostitutes did. And even after you saw this, you did not repent and believe him.

The Parable of the Tenants

³³"Listen to another parable: There was a landowner who planted a vineyard. He put a wall around it, dug a winepress in it and built a watchtower. Then he rented the vineyard to some farmers and went away on a journey. ³⁴When the harvest time approached, he sent his servants to the tenants to collect his fruit.

³⁵"The tenants seized his servants; they beat one, killed another, and stoned a third. ³⁶Then he sent other servants to them, more than the first time, and the tenants treated them the same way. ³⁷Last of all, he sent his son to them. 'They will respect my son,' he said.

³⁸"But when the tenants saw the son, they said to each other, 'This is the heir. Come, let's kill him and take his inheritance.' ³⁹So they took him and threw him out of the vineyard and killed him.

⁴⁰"Therefore, when the owner of the vineyard comes, what will he do to those tenants?"

⁴¹"He will bring those wretches to a wretched end," they replied, "and he will rent the vineyard to other tenants, who will give him his share of the crop at harvest time."

⁴²Jesus said to them, "Have you never read in the Scriptures:

" 'The stone the builders rejected
    has become the capstone^a;
the Lord has done this,
    and it is marvelous in our eyes'^b?

⁴³"Therefore I tell you that the kingdom of God will be taken away from you and given to a people who will produce its fruit. ⁴⁴He who falls on this stone will be broken to pieces, but he on whom it falls will be crushed."^c

⁴⁵When the chief priests and the Pharisees heard Jesus' parables, they knew he was talking about them. ⁴⁶They looked for a way to arrest him, but they were afraid of the crowd because the people held that he was a prophet.

The Parable of the Wedding Banquet

22 Jesus spoke to them again in parables, saying: ²"The kingdom of heaven is like a king who prepared a wedding banquet for his son. ³He sent his servants to those who had been invited to the banquet

^a42 Or *cornerstone*   ^b42 Psalm 118:22,23   ^c44 Some manuscripts do not have verse 44.

to tell them to come, but they refused to come.

⁴"Then he sent some more servants and said, 'Tell those who have been invited that I have prepared my dinner: My oxen and fattened cattle have been butchered, and everything is ready. Come to the wedding banquet.'

⁵"But they paid no attention and went off—one to his field, another to his business. ⁶The rest seized his servants, mistreated them and killed them. ⁷The king was enraged. He sent his army and destroyed those murderers and burned their city.

⁸"Then he said to his servants, 'The wedding banquet is ready, but those I invited did not deserve to come. ⁹Go to the street corners and invite to the banquet anyone you find.' ¹⁰So the servants went out into the streets and gathered all the people they could find, both good and bad, and the wedding hall was filled with guests.

¹¹"But when the king came in to see the guests, he noticed a man there who was not wearing wedding clothes. ¹²'Friend,' he asked, 'how did you get in here without wedding clothes?' The man was speechless.

¹³"Then the king told the attendants, 'Tie him hand and foot, and throw him outside, into the darkness, where there will be weeping and gnashing of teeth.'

¹⁴"For many are invited, but few are chosen."

Paying Taxes to Caesar

¹⁵Then the Pharisees went out and laid plans to trap him in his words. ¹⁶They sent their disciples to him along with the Herodians. "Teacher," they said, "we know you are a man of integrity and that you teach the way of God in accordance with the truth. You aren't swayed by men, because you pay no attention to who they are. ¹⁷Tell us then, what is your opinion? Is it right to pay taxes to Caesar or not?"

¹⁸But Jesus, knowing their evil intent, said, "You hypocrites, why are you trying to trap me? ¹⁹Show me the coin used for paying the tax." They brought him a denarius, ²⁰and he asked them, "Whose portrait is this? And whose inscription?"

²¹"Caesar's," they replied.

Then he said to them, "Give to Caesar what is Caesar's, and to God what is God's."

²²When they heard this, they were amazed. So they left him and went away.

Marriage at the Resurrection

²³That same day the Sadducees, who say there is no resurrection, came to him with a question. ²⁴"Teacher," they said, "Moses told us that if a man dies without having children, his brother must marry the widow and have children for him. ²⁵Now there were seven brothers among us. The first one married and died, and since he had no children, he left his wife to his brother. ²⁶The same thing happened to the second and third brother, right on down to the seventh. ²⁷Finally, the woman died. ²⁸Now then, at the resurrection, whose wife will she be of the seven, since all of them were married to her?"

²⁹Jesus replied, "You are in error because you do not know the Scriptures or the power of God. ³⁰At the resurrection people will neither marry nor be given in marriage; they will be like the angels in heaven. ³¹But about the resurrection of the dead—have you not read what God said to you, ³²'I am the God of Abraham, the God of Isaac, and the God of Jacob'ᵃ? He is not the God of the dead but of the living."

³³When the crowds heard this, they were astonished at his teaching.

The Greatest Commandment

³⁴Hearing that Jesus had silenced the Sadducees, the Pharisees got together. ³⁵One of them, an expert in the law, tested him with this question: ³⁶"Teacher, which is the greatest commandment in the Law?"

³⁷Jesus replied: " 'Love the Lord your God with all your heart and with all your soul and with all your mind.'ᵇ ³⁸This is the first and greatest commandment. ³⁹And the second is like it: 'Love your neighbor as yourself.'ᶜ ⁴⁰All the Law and the Prophets hang on these two commandments."

Whose Son Is the Christ?

⁴¹While the Pharisees were gathered together, Jesus asked them, ⁴²"What do you think about the Christᵈ? Whose son is he?"

"The son of David," they replied.

⁴³He said to them, "How is it then that David, speaking by the Spirit, calls him 'Lord'? For he says,

⁴⁴" 'The Lord said to my Lord:
  "Sit at my right hand
until I put your enemies
  under your feet." 'ᵉ

ᵃ32 Exodus 3:6   ᵇ37 Deut. 6:5   ᶜ39 Lev. 19:18   ᵈ42 Or Messiah   ᵉ44 Psalm 110:1

45If then David calls him 'Lord,' how can he be his son?" 46No one could say a word in reply, and from that day on no one dared to ask him any more questions.

Seven Woes

23 Then Jesus said to the crowds and to his disciples: 2"The teachers of the law and the Pharisees sit in Moses' seat. 3So you must obey them and do everything they tell you. But do not do what they do, for they do not practice what they preach. 4They tie up heavy loads and put them on men's shoulders, but they themselves are not willing to lift a finger to move them.

5"Everything they do is done for men to see: They make their phylacteries[a] wide and the tassels on their garments long; 6they love the place of honor at banquets and the most important seats in the synagogues; 7they love to be greeted in the marketplaces and to have men call them 'Rabbi.'

8"But you are not to be called 'Rabbi,' for you have only one Master and you are all brothers. 9And do not call anyone on earth 'father,' for you have one Father, and he is in heaven. 10Nor are you to be called 'teacher,' for you have one Teacher, the Christ.[b] 11The greatest among you will be your servant. 12For whoever exalts himself will be humbled, and whoever humbles himself will be exalted.

13"Woe to you, teachers of the law and Pharisees, you hypocrites! You shut the kingdom of heaven in men's faces. You yourselves do not enter, nor will you let those enter who are trying to.[c]

15"Woe to you, teachers of the law and Pharisees, you hypocrites! You travel over land and sea to win a single convert, and when he becomes one, you make him twice as much a son of hell as you are.

16"Woe to you, blind guides! You say, 'If anyone swears by the temple, it means nothing; but if anyone swears by the gold of the temple, he is bound by his oath.' 17You blind fools! Which is greater: the gold, or the temple that makes the gold sacred? 18You also say, 'If anyone swears by the altar, it means nothing; but if anyone swears by the gift on it, he is bound by his oath.' 19You blind men! Which is greater: the gift, or the altar that makes the gift sacred? 20Therefore, he who swears by the altar swears by it and by everything on it. 21And he who swears by the temple swears by it and by the one who dwells in it. 22And he who swears by heaven swears by God's throne and by the one who sits on it.

23"Woe to you, teachers of the law and Pharisees, you hypocrites! You give a tenth of your spices—mint, dill and cummin. But you have neglected the more important matters of the law—justice, mercy and faithfulness. You should have practiced the latter, without neglecting the former. 24You blind guides! You strain out a gnat but swallow a camel.

25"Woe to you, teachers of the law and Pharisees, you hypocrites! You clean the outside of the cup and dish, but inside they are full of greed and self-indulgence. 26Blind Pharisee! First clean the inside of the cup and dish, and then the outside also will be clean.

27"Woe to you, teachers of the law and Pharisees, you hypocrites! You are like whitewashed tombs, which look beautiful on the outside but on the inside are full of dead men's bones and everything unclean. 28In the same way, on the outside you appear to people as righteous but on the inside you are full of hypocrisy and wickedness.

29"Woe to you, teachers of the law and Pharisees, you hypocrites! You build tombs for the prophets and decorate the graves of the righteous. 30And you say, 'If we had lived in the days of our forefathers, we would not have taken part with them in shedding the blood of the prophets.' 31So you testify against yourselves that you are the descendants of those who murdered the prophets. 32Fill up, then, the measure of the sin of your forefathers!

33"You snakes! You brood of vipers! How will you escape being condemned to hell? 34Therefore I am sending you prophets and wise men and teachers. Some of them you will kill and crucify; others you will flog in your synagogues and pursue from town to town. 35And so upon you will come all the righteous blood that has been shed on earth, from the blood of righteous Abel to the blood of Zechariah son of Berekiah, whom you murdered between the temple and the altar. 36I tell you the truth, all this will come upon this generation.

37"O Jerusalem, Jerusalem, you who kill the prophets and stone those sent to you, how often I have longed to gather your chil-

---

a5 That is, boxes containing Scripture verses, worn on forehead and arm   b10 Or Messiah   c13 Some manuscripts to. 14Woe to you, teachers of the law and Pharisees, you hypocrites! You devour widows' houses and for a show make lengthy prayers. Therefore you will be punished more severely.

dren together, as a hen gathers her chicks under her wings, but you were not willing. [38]Look, your house is left to you desolate. [39]For I tell you, you will not see me again until you say, 'Blessed is he who comes in the name of the Lord.'[a]"

Signs of the End of the Age

24 Jesus left the temple and was walking away when his disciples came up to him to call his attention to its buildings. [2]"Do you see all these things?" he asked. "I tell you the truth, not one stone here will be left on another; every one will be thrown down."

[3]As Jesus was sitting on the Mount of Olives, the disciples came to him privately. "Tell us," they said, "when will this happen, and what will be the sign of your coming and of the end of the age?"

[4]Jesus answered: "Watch out that no one deceives you. [5]For many will come in my name, claiming, 'I am the Christ,[b]' and will deceive many. [6]You will hear of wars and rumors of wars, but see to it that you are not alarmed. Such things must happen, but the end is still to come. [7]Nation will rise against nation, and kingdom against kingdom. There will be famines and earthquakes in various places. [8]All these are the beginning of birth pains.

[9]"Then you will be handed over to be persecuted and put to death, and you will be hated by all nations because of me. [10]At that time many will turn away from the faith and will betray and hate each other, [11]and many false prophets will appear and deceive many people. [12]Because of the increase of wickedness, the love of most will grow cold, [13]but he who stands firm to the end will be saved. [14]And this gospel of the kingdom will be preached in the whole world as a testimony to all nations, and then the end will come.

[15]"So when you see standing in the holy place 'the abomination that causes desolation,'[c] spoken of through the prophet Daniel—let the reader understand— [16]then let those who are in Judea flee to the mountains. [17]Let no one on the roof of his house go down to take anything out of the house. [18]Let no one in the field go back to get his cloak. [19]How dreadful it will be in those days for pregnant women and nursing mothers! [20]Pray that your flight will not take place in winter or on the Sabbath. [21]For then

there will be great distress, unequaled from the beginning of the world until now—and never to be equaled again. [22]If those days had not been cut short, no one would survive, but for the sake of the elect those days will be shortened. [23]At that time if anyone says to you, 'Look, here is the Christ!' or, 'There he is!' do not believe it. [24]For false Christs and false prophets will appear and perform great signs and miracles to deceive even the elect—if that were possible. [25]See, I have told you ahead of time.

[26]"So if anyone tells you, 'There he is, out in the desert,' do not go out; or, 'Here he is, in the inner rooms,' do not believe it. [27]For as lightning that comes from the east is visible even in the west, so will be the coming of the Son of Man. [28]Wherever there is a carcass, there the vultures will gather.

[29]"Immediately after the distress of those days

" 'the sun will be darkened,
   and the moon will not give its light;
the stars will fall from the sky,
   and the heavenly bodies will be
      shaken.'[d]

[30]"At that time the sign of the Son of Man will appear in the sky, and all the nations of the earth will mourn. They will see the Son of Man coming on the clouds of the sky, with power and great glory. [31]And he will send his angels with a loud trumpet call, and they will gather his elect from the four winds, from one end of the heavens to the other.

[32]"Now learn this lesson from the fig tree: As soon as its twigs get tender and its leaves come out, you know that summer is near. [33]Even so, when you see all these things, you know that it[e] is near, right at the door. [34]I tell you the truth, this generation[f] will certainly not pass away until all these things have happened. [35]Heaven and earth will pass away, but my words will never pass away.

The Day and Hour Unknown

[36]"No one knows about that day or hour, not even the angels in heaven, nor the Son,[g] but only the Father. [37]As it was in the days of Noah, so it will be at the coming of the Son of Man. [38]For in the days before the flood, people were eating and drinking, marrying and giving in marriage, up to the day Noah entered the ark; [39]and they knew nothing about what would happen until the

---

[a]39 Psalm 118:26   [b]5 Or *Messiah*; also in verse 23   [c]15 Daniel 9:27; 11:31; 12:11   [d]29 Isaiah 13:10; 34:4   [e]33 Or *he*   [f]34 Or *race*   [g]36 Some manuscripts do not have *nor the Son*.

flood came and took them all away. That is how it will be at the coming of the Son of Man. **40**Two men will be in the field; one will be taken and the other left. **41**Two women will be grinding with a hand mill; one will be taken and the other left.

42"Therefore keep watch, because you do not know on what day your Lord will come. **43**But understand this: If the owner of the house had known at what time of night the thief was coming, he would have kept watch and would not have let his house be broken into. **44**So you also must be ready, because the Son of Man will come at an hour when you do not expect him.

45"Who then is the faithful and wise servant, whom the master has put in charge of the servants in his household to give them their food at the proper time? **46**It will be good for that servant whose master finds him doing so when he returns. **47**I tell you the truth, he will put him in charge of all his possessions. **48**But suppose that servant is wicked and says to himself, 'My master is staying away a long time,' **49**and he then begins to beat his fellow servants and to eat and drink with drunkards. **50**The master of that servant will come on a day when he does not expect him and at an hour he is not aware of. **51**He will cut him to pieces and assign him a place with the hypocrites, where there will be weeping and gnashing of teeth.

The Parable of the Ten Virgins

25 "At that time the kingdom of heaven will be like ten virgins who took their lamps and went out to meet the bridegroom. **2**Five of them were foolish and five were wise. **3**The foolish ones took their lamps but did not take any oil with them. **4**The wise, however, took oil in jars along with their lamps. **5**The bridegroom was a long time in coming, and they all became drowsy and fell asleep.

6"At midnight the cry rang out: 'Here's the bridegroom! Come out to meet him!'

7"Then all the virgins woke up and trimmed their lamps. **8**The foolish ones said to the wise, 'Give us some of your oil; our lamps are going out.'

9" 'No,' they replied, 'there may not be enough for both us and you. Instead, go to those who sell oil and buy some for yourselves.'

10"But while they were on their way to buy the oil, the bridegroom arrived. The virgins who were ready went in with him

to the wedding banquet. And the door was shut.

11"Later the others also came. 'Sir! Sir!' they said. 'Open the door for us!'

12"But he replied, 'I tell you the truth, I don't know you.'

13"Therefore keep watch, because you do not know the day or the hour.

The Parable of the Talents

14"Again, it will be like a man going on a journey, who called his servants and entrusted his property to them. **15**To one he gave five talents*a* of money, to another two talents, and to another one talent, each according to his ability. Then he went on his journey. **16**The man who had received the five talents went at once and put his money to work and gained five more. **17**So also, the one with the two talents gained two more. **18**But the man who had received the one talent went off, dug a hole in the ground and hid his master's money.

19"After a long time the master of those servants returned and settled accounts with them. **20**The man who had received the five talents brought the other five. 'Master,' he said, 'you entrusted me with five talents. See, I have gained five more.'

21"His master replied, 'Well done, good and faithful servant! You have been faithful with a few things; I will put you in charge of many things. Come and share your master's happiness!'

22"The man with the two talents also came. 'Master,' he said, 'you entrusted me with two talents; see, I have gained two more.'

23"His master replied, 'Well done, good and faithful servant! You have been faithful with a few things; I will put you in charge of many things. Come and share your master's happiness!'

24"Then the man who had received the one talent came. 'Master,' he said, 'I knew that you are a hard man, harvesting where you have not sown and gathering where you have not scattered seed. **25**So I was afraid and went out and hid your talent in the ground. See, here is what belongs to you.'

26"His master replied, 'You wicked, lazy servant! So you knew that I harvest where I have not sown and gather where I have not scattered seed? **27**Well then, you should have put my money on deposit with the bankers, so that when I returned I would have received it back with interest.

a 15 A talent was worth more than a thousand dollars.

28" 'Take the talent from him and give it to the one who has the ten talents. 29For everyone who has will be given more, and he will have an abundance. Whoever does not have, even what he has will be taken from him. 30And throw that worthless servant outside, into the darkness, where there will be weeping and gnashing of teeth.'

The Sheep and the Goats

31"When the Son of Man comes in his glory, and all the angels with him, he will sit on his throne in heavenly glory. 32All the nations will be gathered before him, and he will separate the people one from another as a shepherd separates the sheep from the goats. 33He will put the sheep on his right and the goats on his left.

34"Then the King will say to those on his right, 'Come, you who are blessed by my Father; take your inheritance, the kingdom prepared for you since the creation of the world. 35For I was hungry and you gave me something to eat, I was thirsty and you gave me something to drink, I was a stranger and you invited me in, 36I needed clothes and you clothed me, I was sick and you looked after me, I was in prison and you came to visit me.'

37"Then the righteous will answer him, 'Lord, when did we see you hungry and feed you, or thirsty and give you something to drink? 38When did we see you a stranger and invite you in, or needing clothes and clothe you? 39When did we see you sick or in prison and go to visit you?'

40"The King will reply, 'I tell you the truth, whatever you did for one of the least of these brothers of mine, you did for me.'

41"Then he will say to those on his left, 'Depart from me, you who are cursed, into the eternal fire prepared for the devil and his angels. 42For I was hungry and you gave me nothing to eat, I was thirsty and you gave me nothing to drink, 43I was a stranger and you did not invite me in, I needed clothes and you did not clothe me, I was sick and in prison and you did not look after me.'

44"They also will answer, 'Lord, when did we see you hungry or thirsty or a stranger or needing clothes or sick or in prison, and did not help you?'

45"He will reply, 'I tell you the truth, whatever you did not do for one of the least of these, you did not do for me.'

46"Then they will go away to eternal punishment, but the righteous to eternal life."

The Plot Against Jesus

26 When Jesus had finished saying all these things, he said to his disciples, 2"As you know, the Passover is two days away—and the Son of Man will be handed over to be crucified."

3Then the chief priests and the elders of the people assembled in the palace of the high priest, whose name was Caiaphas, 4and they plotted to arrest Jesus in some sly way and kill him. 5"But not during the Feast," they said, "or there may be a riot among the people."

Jesus Anointed at Bethany

6While Jesus was in Bethany in the home of a man known as Simon the Leper, 7a woman came to him with an alabaster jar of very expensive perfume, which she poured on his head as he was reclining at the table.

8When the disciples saw this, they were indignant. "Why this waste?" they asked. 9"This perfume could have been sold at a high price and the money given to the poor."

10Aware of this, Jesus said to them, "Why are you bothering this woman? She has done a beautiful thing to me. 11The poor you will always have with you, but you will not always have me. 12When she poured this perfume on my body, she did it to prepare me for burial. 13I tell you the truth, wherever this gospel is preached throughout the world, what she has done will also be told, in memory of her."

Judas Agrees to Betray Jesus

14Then one of the Twelve—the one called Judas Iscariot—went to the chief priests 15and asked, "What are you willing to give me if I hand him over to you?" So they counted out for him thirty silver coins. 16From then on Judas watched for an opportunity to hand him over.

The Lord's Supper

17On the first day of the Feast of Unleavened Bread, the disciples came to Jesus and asked, "Where do you want us to make preparations for you to eat the Passover?"

18He replied, "Go into the city to a certain man and tell him, 'The Teacher says: My appointed time is near. I am going to celebrate the Passover with my disciples at your house.' " 19So the disciples did as Jesus had directed them and prepared the Passover.

20When evening came, Jesus was reclining at the table with the Twelve. 21And while

THE REALITY WE'D LIKE TO FORGET

Seven juniors—three guys and four girls—are sitting at a picnic table during lunch. They talk about snow-skiing, why anybody would want to eat Vienna sausages, and hell. (Don't ask how they got from Vienna sausages to hell; you wouldn't believe it!)

Doug: "C'mon, Gretchen, you don't really believe that, do you? A place where people burn forever?"

Sue: "Really. If there even is a God, I doubt if he's cruel enough to send people somewhere like that."

Look It Up
••••

Hell is not a pleasant topic. People would rather pretend it doesn't exist. Yet according to the Bible:

Hell is real (Matthew 5:29–30).

Hell is horrible. It is likened to a place of burning and fire (Matthew 5:22; Mark 9:42–48), darkness and weeping (Matthew 8:11–12), torment (Revelation 14:9–11) and wrath (John 3:36). It is also described as a dungeon (2 Peter 2:4), a furnace (Matthew 13:40–42) and a lake of burning sulfur (Revelation 19:20).

Hell is eternal. "He will punish those who do not know God and do not obey the gospel of our Lord Jesus. They will be punished with everlasting destruction and shut out from the presence of the Lord and from the majesty of his power" (2 Thessalonians 1:8–9).

Think It Through
••••

According to Matthew 25:41, God created hell as a place of judgment for Satan and the other angels who rebelled against God (see also Isaiah 14:12–20 and Ezekiel 28:14–19). But since humans have sinned against God too, hell also includes those who don't repent. God is holy and just and must punish sin.

Jesus talked a lot about hell—much more than he talked about heaven. To say there is no hell is to say that Jesus was either lying or badly mistaken.

Work It Out
••••

Here's a prayer for today: "God, the Bible is filled with references to a real, horrible, eternal place called hell. Cause that truth to sink into my head and heart so that I will have more concern for people who don't know you. Make me more compassionate for those who are headed to hell."

At lunch today or tomorrow, bring up the topic of hell and see what happens. Many people are more willing to hear about Christ when they finally understand the reality of hell.

Nail It Down
••••

Read the description of eternal judgment found in Matthew 25:31–46.

Turn to pages 1080, 1382, 1403 and 1407 for other readings on destiny.
Turn to page 1047 for Tuesday's reading.

Topic
••••

they were eating, he said, "I tell you the truth, one of you will betray me."

22They were very sad and began to say to him one after the other, "Surely not I, Lord?"

23Jesus replied, "The one who has dipped his hand into the bowl with me will betray me. **24**The Son of Man will go just as it is written about him. But woe to that man who betrays the Son of Man! It would be better for him if he had not been born."

25Then Judas, the one who would betray him, said, "Surely not I, Rabbi?"

Jesus answered, "Yes, it is you."*a*

26While they were eating, Jesus took bread, gave thanks and broke it, and gave it to his disciples, saying, "Take and eat; this is my body."

27Then he took the cup, gave thanks and offered it to them, saying, "Drink from it, all of you. **28**This is my blood of the*b* covenant, which is poured out for many for the forgiveness of sins. **29**I tell you, I will not drink of this fruit of the vine from now on until that day when I drink it anew with you in my Father's kingdom."

30When they had sung a hymn, they went out to the Mount of Olives.

Jesus Predicts Peter's Denial

31Then Jesus told them, "This very night you will all fall away on account of me, for it is written:

" 'I will strike the shepherd,
    and the sheep of the flock will be
        scattered.'*c*

32But after I have risen, I will go ahead of you into Galilee."

33Peter replied, "Even if all fall away on account of you, I never will."

34"I tell you the truth," Jesus answered, "this very night, before the rooster crows, you will disown me three times."

35But Peter declared, "Even if I have to die with you, I will never disown you." And all the other disciples said the same.

Gethsemane

36Then Jesus went with his disciples to a place called Gethsemane, and he said to them, "Sit here while I go over there and pray." **37**He took Peter and the two sons of Zebedee along with him, and he began to be sorrowful and troubled. **38**Then he said to them, "My soul is overwhelmed with sorrow

to the point of death. Stay here and keep watch with me."

39Going a little farther, he fell with his face to the ground and prayed, "My Father, if it is possible, may this cup be taken from me. Yet not as I will, but as you will."

40Then he returned to his disciples and found them sleeping. "Could you men not keep watch with me for one hour?" he asked Peter. **41**"Watch and pray so that you will not fall into temptation. The spirit is willing, but the body is weak."

42He went away a second time and prayed, "My Father, if it is not possible for this cup to be taken away unless I drink it, may your will be done."

43When he came back, he again found them sleeping, because their eyes were heavy. **44**So he left them and went away once more and prayed the third time, saying the same thing.

45Then he returned to the disciples and said to them, "Are you still sleeping and resting? Look, the hour is near, and the Son of Man is betrayed into the hands of sinners. **46**Rise, let us go! Here comes my betrayer!"

Jesus Arrested

47While he was still speaking, Judas, one of the Twelve, arrived. With him was a large crowd armed with swords and clubs, sent from the chief priests and the elders of the people. **48**Now the betrayer had arranged a signal with them: "The one I kiss is the man; arrest him." **49**Going at once to Jesus, Judas said, "Greetings, Rabbi!" and kissed him.

50Jesus replied, "Friend, do what you came for."*d*

Then the men stepped forward, seized Jesus and arrested him. **51**With that, one of Jesus' companions reached for his sword, drew it out and struck the servant of the high priest, cutting off his ear.

52"Put your sword back in its place," Jesus said to him, "for all who draw the sword will die by the sword. **53**Do you think I cannot call on my Father, and he will at once put at my disposal more than twelve legions of angels? **54**But how then would the Scriptures be fulfilled that say it must happen in this way?"

55At that time Jesus said to the crowd, "Am I leading a rebellion, that you have come out with swords and clubs to capture me? Every day I sat in the temple courts teaching, and you did not arrest me. **56**But

---

a25 Or "You yourself have said it" have come?"   *b28 Some manuscripts the new*   *c31 Zech. 13:7*   *d50 Or "Friend, why* this has all taken place that the writings of the prophets might be fulfilled." Then all the disciples deserted him and fled.

Before the Sanhedrin

⁵⁷Those who had arrested Jesus took him to Caiaphas, the high priest, where the teachers of the law and the elders had assembled. ⁵⁸But Peter followed him at a distance, right up to the courtyard of the high priest. He entered and sat down with the guards to see the outcome.

⁵⁹The chief priests and the whole Sanhedrin were looking for false evidence against Jesus so that they could put him to death. ⁶⁰But they did not find any, though many false witnesses came forward.

Finally two came forward ⁶¹and declared, "This fellow said, 'I am able to destroy the temple of God and rebuild it in three days.'"

⁶²Then the high priest stood up and said to Jesus, "Are you not going to answer? What is this testimony that these men are bringing against you?" ⁶³But Jesus remained silent.

The high priest said to him, "I charge you under oath by the living God: Tell us if you are the Christ,ᵃ the Son of God."

⁶⁴"Yes, it is as you say," Jesus replied. "But I say to all of you: In the future you will see the Son of Man sitting at the right hand of the Mighty One and coming on the clouds of heaven."

⁶⁵Then the high priest tore his clothes and said, "He has spoken blasphemy! Why do we need any more witnesses? Look, now you have heard the blasphemy. ⁶⁶What do you think?"

"He is worthy of death," they answered.

⁶⁷Then they spit in his face and struck him with their fists. Others slapped him ⁶⁸and said, "Prophesy to us, Christ. Who hit you?"

Peter Disowns Jesus

⁶⁹Now Peter was sitting out in the courtyard, and a servant girl came to him. "You also were with Jesus of Galilee," she said.

⁷⁰But he denied it before them all. "I don't know what you're talking about," he said.

⁷¹Then he went out to the gateway, where another girl saw him and said to the people there, "This fellow was with Jesus of Nazareth."

⁷²He denied it again, with an oath: "I don't know the man!"

⁷³After a little while, those standing there went up to Peter and said, "Surely you are one of them, for your accent gives you away."

⁷⁴Then he began to call down curses on himself and he swore to them, "I don't know the man!"

Immediately a rooster crowed. ⁷⁵Then Peter remembered the word Jesus had spoken: "Before the rooster crows, you will disown me three times." And he went outside and wept bitterly.

Judas Hangs Himself

27 Early in the morning, all the chief priests and the elders of the people came to the decision to put Jesus to death. ²They bound him, led him away and handed him over to Pilate, the governor.

³When Judas, who had betrayed him, saw that Jesus was condemned, he was seized with remorse and returned the thirty silver coins to the chief priests and the elders. ⁴"I have sinned," he said, "for I have betrayed innocent blood."

"What is that to us?" they replied. "That's your responsibility."

⁵So Judas threw the money into the temple and left. Then he went away and hanged himself.

⁶The chief priests picked up the coins and said, "It is against the law to put this into the treasury, since it is blood money." ⁷So they decided to use the money to buy the potter's field as a burial place for foreigners. ⁸That is why it has been called the Field of Blood to this day. ⁹Then what was spoken by Jeremiah the prophet was fulfilled: "They took the thirty silver coins, the price set on him by the people of Israel, ¹⁰and they used them to buy the potter's field, as the Lord commanded me."ᵇ

Jesus Before Pilate

¹¹Meanwhile Jesus stood before the governor, and the governor asked him, "Are you the king of the Jews?"

"Yes, it is as you say," Jesus replied.

¹²When he was accused by the chief priests and the elders, he gave no answer. ¹³Then Pilate asked him, "Don't you hear the testimony they are bringing against you?" ¹⁴But Jesus made no reply, not even to a single charge—to the great amazement of the governor.

¹⁵Now it was the governor's custom at the Feast to release a prisoner chosen by the crowd. ¹⁶At that time they had a notorious prisoner, called Barabbas. ¹⁷So when the

---

ᵃ63 Or Messiah; also in verse 68   ᵇ10 See Zech. 11:12,13; Jer. 19:1-13; 32:6-9.

crowd had gathered, Pilate asked them, "Which one do you want me to release to you: Barabbas, or Jesus who is called Christ?" [18]For he knew it was out of envy that they had handed Jesus over to him.

[19]While Pilate was sitting on the judge's seat, his wife sent him this message: "Don't have anything to do with that innocent man, for I have suffered a great deal today in a dream because of him."

[20]But the chief priests and the elders persuaded the crowd to ask for Barabbas and to have Jesus executed.

[21]"Which of the two do you want me to release to you?" asked the governor.

"Barabbas," they answered.

[22]"What shall I do, then, with Jesus who is called Christ?" Pilate asked.

They all answered, "Crucify him!"

[23]"Why? What crime has he committed?" asked Pilate.

But they shouted all the louder, "Crucify him!"

[24]When Pilate saw that he was getting nowhere, but that instead an uproar was starting, he took water and washed his hands in front of the crowd. "I am innocent of this man's blood," he said. "It is your responsibility!"

[25]All the people answered, "Let his blood be on us and on our children!"

[26]Then he released Barabbas to them. But he had Jesus flogged, and handed him over to be crucified.

The Soldiers Mock Jesus

[27]Then the governor's soldiers took Jesus into the Praetorium and gathered the whole company of soldiers around him. [28]They stripped him and put a scarlet robe on him, [29]and then twisted together a crown of thorns and set it on his head. They put a staff in his right hand and knelt in front of him and mocked him. "Hail, king of the Jews!" they said. [30]They spit on him, and took the staff and struck him on the head again and again. [31]After they had mocked him, they took off the robe and put his own clothes on him. Then they led him away to crucify him.

The Crucifixion

[32]As they were going out, they met a man from Cyrene, named Simon, and they forced him to carry the cross. [33]They came to a place called Golgotha (which means The Place of the Skull). [34]There they offered Jesus wine to drink, mixed with gall; but after tasting it, he refused to drink it. [35]When they had crucified him, they divided up his clothes by casting lots.[a] [36]And sitting down, they kept watch over him there. [37]Above his head they placed the written charge against him: THIS IS JESUS, THE KING OF THE JEWS. [38]Two robbers were crucified with him, one on his right and one on his left. [39]Those who passed by hurled insults at him, shaking their heads [40]and saying, "You who are going to destroy the temple and build it in three days, save yourself! Come down from the cross, if you are the Son of God!"

[41]In the same way the chief priests, the teachers of the law and the elders mocked him. [42]"He saved others," they said, "but he can't save himself! He's the King of Israel! Let him come down now from the cross, and we will believe in him. [43]He trusts in God. Let God rescue him now if he wants him, for he said, 'I am the Son of God.'" [44]In the same way the robbers who were crucified with him also heaped insults on him.

The Death of Jesus

[45]From the sixth hour until the ninth hour darkness came over all the land. [46]About the ninth hour Jesus cried out in a loud voice, "Eloi, Eloi,[b] lama sabachthani?"—which means, "My God, my God, why have you forsaken me?"[c]

[47]When some of those standing there heard this, they said, "He's calling Elijah."

[48]Immediately one of them ran and got a sponge. He filled it with wine vinegar, put it on a stick, and offered it to Jesus to drink. [49]The rest said, "Now leave him alone. Let's see if Elijah comes to save him."

[50]And when Jesus had cried out again in a loud voice, he gave up his spirit.

[51]At that moment the curtain of the temple was torn in two from top to bottom. The earth shook and the rocks split. [52]The tombs broke open and the bodies of many holy people who had died were raised to life. [53]They came out of the tombs, and after Jesus' resurrection they went into the holy city and appeared to many people.

[54]When the centurion and those with him who were guarding Jesus saw the earthquake and all that had happened, they were

---

[a]35 A few late manuscripts *lots that the word spoken by the prophet might be fulfilled: "They divided my garments among themselves and cast lots for my clothing"* (Psalm 22:18)   [b]46 Some manuscripts *Eli, Eli*   [c]46 Psalm 22:1

terrified, and exclaimed, "Surely he was the Son*a* of God!"

55Many women were there, watching from a distance. They had followed Jesus from Galilee to care for his needs. 56Among them were Mary Magdalene, Mary the mother of James and Joses, and the mother of Zebedee's sons.

The Burial of Jesus

57As evening approached, there came a rich man from Arimathea, named Joseph, who had himself become a disciple of Jesus. 58Going to Pilate, he asked for Jesus' body, and Pilate ordered that it be given to him. 59Joseph took the body, wrapped it in a clean linen cloth, 60and placed it in his own new tomb that he had cut out of the rock. He rolled a big stone in front of the entrance to the tomb and went away. 61Mary Magdalene and the other Mary were sitting there opposite the tomb.

The Guard at the Tomb

62The next day, the one after Preparation Day, the chief priests and the Pharisees went to Pilate. 63"Sir," they said, "we remember that while he was still alive that deceiver said, 'After three days I will rise again.' 64So give the order for the tomb to be made secure until the third day. Otherwise, his disciples may come and steal the body and tell the people that he has been raised from the dead. This last deception will be worse than the first."

65"Take a guard," Pilate answered. "Go, make the tomb as secure as you know how." 66So they went and made the tomb secure by putting a seal on the stone and posting the guard.

The Resurrection

28 After the Sabbath, at dawn on the first day of the week, Mary Magdalene and the other Mary went to look at the tomb.

2There was a violent earthquake, for an angel of the Lord came down from heaven and, going to the tomb, rolled back the stone and sat on it. 3His appearance was like light-ning, and his clothes were white as snow. 4The guards were so afraid of him that they shook and became like dead men.

5The angel said to the women, "Do not be afraid, for I know that you are looking for Jesus, who was crucified. 6He is not here; he has risen, just as he said. Come and see the place where he lay. 7Then go quickly and tell his disciples: 'He has risen from the dead and is going ahead of you into Galilee. There you will see him.' Now I have told you."

8So the women hurried away from the tomb, afraid yet filled with joy, and ran to tell his disciples. 9Suddenly Jesus met them. "Greetings," he said. They came to him, clasped his feet and worshiped him. 10Then Jesus said to them, "Do not be afraid. Go and tell my brothers to go to Galilee; there they will see me."

The Guards' Report

11While the women were on their way, some of the guards went into the city and reported to the chief priests everything that had happened. 12When the chief priests had met with the elders and devised a plan, they gave the soldiers a large sum of money, 13telling them, "You are to say, 'His disciples came during the night and stole him away while we were asleep.' 14If this report gets to the governor, we will satisfy him and keep you out of trouble." 15So the soldiers took the money and did as they were instructed. And this story has been widely circulated among the Jews to this very day.

The Great Commission

16Then the eleven disciples went to Galilee, to the mountain where Jesus had told them to go. 17When they saw him, they worshiped him; but some doubted. 18Then Jesus came to them and said, "All authority in heaven and on earth has been given to me. 19Therefore go and make disciples of all nations, baptizing them in*b* the name of the Father and of the Son and of the Holy Spirit, 20and teaching them to obey everything I have commanded you. And surely I am with you always, to the very end of the age."

---

*a*54 Or *a son*   *b*19 Or *into*; see Acts 8:16; 19:5; Romans 6:3; 1 Cor. 1:13; 10:2 and Gal. 3:27.

LONELY... BUT NEVER ALONE

Sara has just moved with her family to a new community. She did not want to leave her hometown a month before her long-awaited freshman year at Clark High School, but did anyone bother to consult her? No way!

So on her first day at the new school, Sara doesn't know a soul. She feels ignored, stared at, forgotten, insignificant, isolated, left out, ugly, unloved, misunderstood and abandoned.

In a word, Sara is experiencing loneliness.

Look It Up Sara feels alone. But is she? Not according to the Bible. God's Word tells you that you are never alone. You may have feelings of loneliness, but the fact is that you always have a near and dear friend in the Lord.

> Can a mother forget the baby at her breast
> and have no compassion on the child she has
> borne?
> Though she may forget,
> I will not forget you!
> See, I have engraved you on the palms of my
> hands (Isaiah 49:15–16).

"I will not leave you as orphans; I will come to you" (John 14:18).

"God has said, 'Never will I leave you; never will I forsake you' " (Hebrews 13:5).

Hey, even when everyone else leaves you or no one else knows you, God is right there, always ready to comfort you. Now that's good news!

Think It Through Have you ever been in a situation similar to the one Sara is facing? How did you feel at the time? How did you handle it? Did your plan work?

Have any new families moved into your neighborhood this year? Anyone your age? What could you do to make that new person feel more welcome?

Work It Out Are you lonely right now? Don't sit there and have a pity party! Do something! Take a walk (or even a jog)—just you and Jesus. Tell him everything that's on your heart and mind. Yes, he already knows, but telling him somehow makes things better.

Then softly sing your favorite old hymn or praise chorus and think about the words. (Warning: If you jog and sing at the same time, you need to be in good shape. Otherwise you'll sound like a bagpipe!)

Nail It Down Consider the last sentence of Matthew 28:20.

Turn to pages 5, 816 and 1222 for other readings on loneliness.
Turn to page 1050 for Wednesday's reading.

Topic

LONELINESS

MARK

JESUS is King as Matthew shows, but he's not aloof from his subjects. Mark reveals Jesus as the perfect servant, intimately involved with people and working among them. He heals the sick, casts out demons and preaches messages that change lives. He finishes his work as a servant when he is crucified, dying for sinners. As you read Mark, take the initiative to be a servant and give a gift of love to other people in gratitude for the gift of love God has given to you.

Outline of Contents

John the Baptist Prepares the Way

1 The beginning of the gospel about Jesus Christ, the Son of God.[a]

²It is written in Isaiah the prophet:

"I will send my messenger ahead of you,
who will prepare your way"[b] —
³"a voice of one calling in the desert,
'Prepare the way for the Lord,
make straight paths for him.' "[c]

⁴And so John came, baptizing in the desert region and preaching a baptism of repentance for the forgiveness of sins. ⁵The whole Judean countryside and all the people of Jerusalem went out to him. Confessing their sins, they were baptized by him in the Jordan River. ⁶John wore clothing made of camel's hair, with a leather belt around his waist, and he ate locusts and wild honey. ⁷And this was his message: "After me will come one more powerful than I, the thongs of whose sandals I am not worthy to stoop down and untie. ⁸I baptize you with[d] water, but he will baptize you with the Holy Spirit."

[a]1 Some manuscripts do not have the Son of God.   [b]2 Mal. 3:1   [c]3 Isaiah 40:3   [d]8 Or in

The Baptism and Temptation of Jesus

9At that time Jesus came from Nazareth in Galilee and was baptized by John in the Jordan. **10**As Jesus was coming up out of the water, he saw heaven being torn open and the Spirit descending on him like a dove. **11**And a voice came from heaven: "You are my Son, whom I love; with you I am well pleased."

12At once the Spirit sent him out into the desert, **13**and he was in the desert forty days, being tempted by Satan. He was with the wild animals, and angels attended him.

The Calling of the First Disciples

14After John was put in prison, Jesus went into Galilee, proclaiming the good news of God. **15**"The time has come," he said. "The kingdom of God is near. Repent and believe the good news!"

16As Jesus walked beside the Sea of Galilee, he saw Simon and his brother Andrew casting a net into the lake, for they were fishermen. **17**"Come, follow me," Jesus said, "and I will make you fishers of men." **18**At once they left their nets and followed him.

19When he had gone a little farther, he saw James son of Zebedee and his brother John in a boat, preparing their nets. **20**Without delay he called them, and they left their father Zebedee in the boat with the hired men and followed him.

Jesus Drives Out an Evil Spirit

21They went to Capernaum, and when the Sabbath came, Jesus went into the synagogue and began to teach. **22**The people were amazed at his teaching, because he taught them as one who had authority, not as the teachers of the law. **23**Just then a man in their synagogue who was possessed by an evil*a* spirit cried out, **24**"What do you want with us, Jesus of Nazareth? Have you come to destroy us? I know who you are—the Holy One of God!"

25"Be quiet!" said Jesus sternly. "Come out of him!" **26**The evil spirit shook the man violently and came out of him with a shriek.

27The people were all so amazed that they asked each other, "What is this? A new teaching—and with authority! He even gives orders to evil spirits and they obey him." **28**News about him spread quickly over the whole region of Galilee.

Jesus Heals Many

29As soon as they left the synagogue, they went with James and John to the home of Simon and Andrew. **30**Simon's mother-in-law was in bed with a fever, and they told Jesus about her. **31**So he went to her, took her hand and helped her up. The fever left her and she began to wait on them.

32That evening after sunset the people brought to Jesus all the sick and demon-possessed. **33**The whole town gathered at the door, **34**and Jesus healed many who had various diseases. He also drove out many demons, but he would not let the demons speak because they knew who he was.

Jesus Prays in a Solitary Place

35Very early in the morning, while it was still dark, Jesus got up, left the house and went off to a solitary place, where he prayed. **36**Simon and his companions went to look for him, **37**and when they found him, they exclaimed: "Everyone is looking for you!"

38Jesus replied, "Let us go somewhere else—to the nearby villages—so I can preach there also. That is why I have come." **39**So he traveled throughout Galilee, preaching in their synagogues and driving out demons.

A Man With Leprosy

40A man with leprosy*b* came to him and begged him on his knees, "If you are willing, you can make me clean."

41Filled with compassion, Jesus reached out his hand and touched the man. "I am willing," he said. "Be clean!" **42**Immediately the leprosy left him and he was cured.

43Jesus sent him away at once with a strong warning: **44**"See that you don't tell this to anyone. But go, show yourself to the priest and offer the sacrifices that Moses commanded for your cleansing, as a testimony to them." **45**Instead he went out and began to talk freely, spreading the news. As a result, Jesus could no longer enter a town openly but stayed outside in lonely places. Yet the people still came to him from everywhere.

Jesus Heals a Paralytic

2 A few days later, when Jesus again entered Capernaum, the people heard that he had come home. **2**So many gathered

---

a23 Greek *unclean*; also in verses 26 and 27   *b40* The Greek word was used for various diseases affecting the skin—not necessarily leprosy.

WHY IS MY QUIET TIME IN SUCH A RUT?

Reed feels so desperate that he drops by his older brother's college dorm room.

"Hey, Spencer, can I talk to you for a minute?"

"Sure, Reed, what's up?"

"Man, I don't know. It's like my quiet times have gradually gotten so stale. I used to be all excited. I used to feel like I was really meeting with God. I always looked forward to them. Now I feel like I'm in a rut. What's wrong with me?"

Look It Up
••••

When your time with God is in a rut, it may be a case of "devotionless devotions." That's when individuals just go through the motions. They treat devotions as though they were a mindless assignment.

Contrast this with the thirst of the psalmist: "As the deer pants for streams of water, so my soul pants for you, O God" (Psalm 42:1).

Spiritual staleness may also be caused by a case of "distracted devotions." That's when individuals are so busy thinking about other things, they never really give God's Word their full attention.

Jesus likened these people to seed sown among thorns. "But the worries of this life, the deceitfulness of wealth and the desires for other things come in and choke the word, making it unfruitful" (Mark 4:19).

Think It Through
••••

Pick the best answer:

1. My times with God lately have been: (a) nonexistent; (b) something I look forward to and get a lot out of; (c) kind of blah; (d) just something I know I'm supposed to do.

2. When I spend time alone with God, I: (a) go blank; (b) think about him and about my own spiritual state; (c) daydream.

Work It Out
••••

If you are suffering from "devotionless devotions"—that is, your heart just isn't in it—ask the Lord to create within you a deeper desire, a greater thirst to know him better. No prayer could please him more than that one!

You might also want to try something as simple as changing the material you use, the time or place you have devotions or what you do during your devotional time. Small changes can sometimes make a big difference.

Nail It Down
••••

Read Mark 1:35 to see how Jesus met with the Father.

Turn to pages 557, 587, 974 and 1053 for other readings on devotions.
Turn to page 1053 for Thursday's reading.

Topic
••••

DEVOTIONS

that there was no room left, not even outside the door, and he preached the word to them. ³Some men came, bringing to him a paralytic, carried by four of them. ⁴Since they could not get him to Jesus because of the crowd, they made an opening in the roof above Jesus and, after digging through it, lowered the mat the paralyzed man was lying on. ⁵When Jesus saw their faith, he said to the paralytic, "Son, your sins are forgiven."

⁶Now some teachers of the law were sitting there, thinking to themselves, ⁷"Why does this fellow talk like that? He's blaspheming! Who can forgive sins but God alone?"

⁸Immediately Jesus knew in his spirit that this was what they were thinking in their hearts, and he said to them, "Why are you thinking these things? ⁹Which is easier: to say to the paralytic, 'Your sins are forgiven,' or to say, 'Get up, take your mat and walk'? ¹⁰But that you may know that the Son of Man has authority on earth to forgive sins . . . ." He said to the paralytic, ¹¹"I tell you, get up, take your mat and go home." ¹²He got up, took his mat and walked out in full view of them all. This amazed everyone and they praised God, saying, "We have never seen anything like this!"

The Calling of Levi

¹³Once again Jesus went out beside the lake. A large crowd came to him, and he began to teach them. ¹⁴As he walked along, he saw Levi son of Alphaeus sitting at the tax collector's booth. "Follow me," Jesus told him, and Levi got up and followed him.

¹⁵While Jesus was having dinner at Levi's house, many tax collectors and "sinners" were eating with him and his disciples, for there were many who followed him. ¹⁶When the teachers of the law who were Pharisees saw him eating with the "sinners" and tax collectors, they asked his disciples: "Why does he eat with tax collectors and 'sinners'?"

¹⁷On hearing this, Jesus said to them, "It is not the healthy who need a doctor, but the sick. I have not come to call the righteous, but sinners."

Jesus Questioned About Fasting

¹⁸Now John's disciples and the Pharisees were fasting. Some people came and asked Jesus, "How is it that John's disciples and the disciples of the Pharisees are fasting, but yours are not?"

¹⁹Jesus answered, "How can the guests of the bridegroom fast while he is with them? They cannot, so long as they have him with them. ²⁰But the time will come when the bridegroom will be taken from them, and on that day they will fast.

²¹"No one sews a patch of unshrunk cloth on an old garment. If he does, the new piece will pull away from the old, making the tear worse. ²²And no one pours new wine into old wineskins. If he does, the wine will burst the skins, and both the wine and the wineskins will be ruined. No, he pours new wine into new wineskins."

Lord of the Sabbath

²³One Sabbath Jesus was going through the grainfields, and as his disciples walked along, they began to pick some heads of grain. ²⁴The Pharisees said to him, "Look, why are they doing what is unlawful on the Sabbath?"

²⁵He answered, "Have you never read what David did when he and his companions were hungry and in need? ²⁶In the days of Abiathar the high priest, he entered the house of God and ate the consecrated bread, which is lawful only for priests to eat. And he also gave some to his companions."

²⁷Then he said to them, "The Sabbath was made for man, not man for the Sabbath. ²⁸So the Son of Man is Lord even of the Sabbath."

3 Another time he went into the synagogue, and a man with a shriveled hand was there. ²Some of them were looking for a reason to accuse Jesus, so they watched him closely to see if he would heal him on the Sabbath. ³Jesus said to the man with the shriveled hand, "Stand up in front of everyone."

⁴Then Jesus asked them, "Which is lawful on the Sabbath: to do good or to do evil, to save life or to kill?" But they remained silent.

⁵He looked around at them in anger and, deeply distressed at their stubborn hearts, said to the man, "Stretch out your hand." He stretched it out, and his hand was completely restored. ⁶Then the Pharisees went out and began to plot with the Herodians how they might kill Jesus.

Crowds Follow Jesus

⁷Jesus withdrew with his disciples to the lake, and a large crowd from Galilee followed. ⁸When they heard all he was doing, many people came to him from Judea, Jerusalem, Idumea, and the regions across the Jordan and around Tyre and Sidon. ⁹Because of the crowd he told his disciples to have a small boat ready for him, to keep the

people from crowding him. [10]For he had healed many, so that those with diseases were pushing forward to touch him. [11]Whenever the evil[a] spirits saw him, they fell down before him and cried out, "You are the Son of God." [12]But he gave them strict orders not to tell who he was.

The Appointing of the Twelve Apostles

[13]Jesus went up on a mountainside and called to him those he wanted, and they came to him. [14]He appointed twelve — designating them apostles[b] — that they might be with him and that he might send them out to preach [15]and to have authority to drive out demons. [16]These are the twelve he appointed: Simon (to whom he gave the name Peter); [17]James son of Zebedee and his brother John (to them he gave the name Boanerges, which means Sons of Thunder); [18]Andrew, Philip, Bartholomew, Matthew, Thomas, James son of Alphaeus, Thaddaeus, Simon the Zealot [19]and Judas Iscariot, who betrayed him.

Jesus and Beelzebub

[20]Then Jesus entered a house, and again a crowd gathered, so that he and his disciples were not even able to eat. [21]When his family heard about this, they went to take charge of him, for they said, "He is out of his mind."

[22]And the teachers of the law who came down from Jerusalem said, "He is possessed by Beelzebub[c]! By the prince of demons he is driving out demons."

[23]So Jesus called them and spoke to them in parables: "How can Satan drive out Satan? [24]If a kingdom is divided against itself, that kingdom cannot stand. [25]If a house is divided against itself, that house cannot stand. [26]And if Satan opposes himself and is divided, he cannot stand; his end has come. [27]In fact, no one can enter a strong man's house and carry off his possessions unless he first ties up the strong man. Then he can rob his house. [28]I tell you the truth, all the sins and blasphemies of men will be forgiven them. [29]But whoever blasphemes against the Holy Spirit will never be forgiven; he is guilty of an eternal sin."

[30]He said this because they were saying, "He has an evil spirit."

Jesus' Mother and Brothers

[31]Then Jesus' mother and brothers arrived. Standing outside, they sent someone in to call him. [32]A crowd was sitting around him, and they told him, "Your mother and brothers are outside looking for you."

[33]"Who are my mother and my brothers?" he asked.

[34]Then he looked at those seated in a circle around him and said, "Here are my mother and my brothers! [35]Whoever does God's will is my brother and sister and mother."

The Parable of the Sower

4 Again Jesus began to teach by the lake. The crowd that gathered around him was so large that he got into a boat and sat in it out on the lake, while all the people were along the shore at the water's edge. [2]He taught them many things by parables, and in his teaching said: [3]"Listen! A farmer went out to sow his seed. [4]As he was scattering the seed, some fell along the path, and the birds came and ate it up. [5]Some fell on rocky places, where it did not have much soil. It sprang up quickly, because the soil was shallow. [6]But when the sun came up, the plants were scorched, and they withered because they had no root. [7]Other seed fell among thorns, which grew up and choked the plants, so that they did not bear grain. [8]Still other seed fell on good soil. It came up, grew and produced a crop, multiplying thirty, sixty, or even a hundred times."

[9]Then Jesus said, "He who has ears to hear, let him hear."

[10]When he was alone, the Twelve and the others around him asked him about the parables. [11]He told them, "The secret of the kingdom of God has been given to you. But to those on the outside everything is said in parables [12]so that,

> " 'they may be ever seeing but never
>   perceiving,
>   and ever hearing but never
>   understanding;
>   otherwise they might turn and be
>   forgiven!'[d] "

[13]Then Jesus said to them, "Don't you understand this parable? How then will you understand any parable? [14]The farmer sows the word. [15]Some people are like seed along the path, where the word is sown. As soon as they hear it, Satan comes and takes away the word that was sown in them. [16]Others, like seed sown on rocky places, hear the

WHAT DOES GOD WANT MOST FROM ME?

Erica is totally exhausted.

When you look at her schedule, it's not hard to figure out why. As a student leader in her youth group, a typical week for her includes a full day at church on Sunday; a Monday morning, before school prayer group; discipleship group on Tuesday afternoon; Bible study on Wednesday night; youth visitation on Thursday; and an aftergame get-together on Friday nights.

Yet, even with all that spiritual activity, Erica feels far from God.

Look It Up
••••

Do you remember what happened the time Jesus visited the home of the sisters Mary and Martha?

While Martha worked frantically to prepare an elaborate meal for Jesus, Mary "sat at the Lord's feet listening to what he said" (Luke 10:39). Finally Martha got really ticked. She stormed into the room where Jesus was and interrupted the conversation, " 'Lord, don't you care that my sister has left me to do the work by myself? Tell her to help me!' "

" 'Martha, Martha,' the Lord answered, 'you are worried and upset about many things, but only one thing is needed. Mary has chosen what is better, and it will not be taken away from her' " (Luke 10:40–42).

Think It Through
••••

What Jesus was saying is this: Serving God is good. You ought to be involved in service. But the thing that God wants most is your worship, not your works! First, you need to be with God . . . then you can go out and do things for him.

Are you frazzled like Erica or Martha? Are you ready for a change?

Work It Out
••••

Imitate Mary. In other words, take time out today (and every day) just to be with Jesus. Listen to him speak to you through his Word. Then tell him what's on your heart and mind.

Serving God is important, but your first need, as one old preacher put it, is to "sit near the spout where the glory runs out." According to Jesus those devotional times are more important than anything else. And those precious moments can never be taken away from you!

Nail It Down
••••

Notice how being *with* God comes before being *busy* for God in Mark 3:14.

Turn to pages 557, 587, 974 and 1050 for other readings on devotions.
Turn to page 1056 for Friday's reading.

Topic
••••

DEVOTIONS

word and at once receive it with joy. [17]But since they have no root, they last only a short time. When trouble or persecution comes because of the word, they quickly fall away. [18]Still others, like seed sown among thorns, hear the word; [19]but the worries of this life, the deceitfulness of wealth and the desires for other things come in and choke the word, making it unfruitful. [20]Others, like seed sown on good soil, hear the word, accept it, and produce a crop — thirty, sixty or even a hundred times what was sown."

A Lamp on a Stand

[21]He said to them, "Do you bring in a lamp to put it under a bowl or a bed? Instead, don't you put it on its stand? [22]For whatever is hidden is meant to be disclosed, and whatever is concealed is meant to be brought out into the open. [23]If anyone has ears to hear, let him hear."

[24]"Consider carefully what you hear," he continued. "With the measure you use, it will be measured to you — and even more. [25]Whoever has will be given more; whoever does not have, even what he has will be taken from him."

The Parable of the Growing Seed

[26]He also said, "This is what the kingdom of God is like. A man scatters seed on the ground. [27]Night and day, whether he sleeps or gets up, the seed sprouts and grows, though he does not know how. [28]All by itself the soil produces grain — first the stalk, then the head, then the full kernel in the head. [29]As soon as the grain is ripe, he puts the sickle to it, because the harvest has come."

The Parable of the Mustard Seed

[30]Again he said, "What shall we say the kingdom of God is like, or what parable shall we use to describe it? [31]It is like a mustard seed, which is the smallest seed you plant in the ground. [32]Yet when planted, it grows and becomes the largest of all garden plants, with such big branches that the birds of the air can perch in its shade."

[33]With many similar parables Jesus spoke the word to them, as much as they could understand. [34]He did not say anything to them without using a parable. But when he was alone with his own disciples, he explained everything.

Jesus Calms the Storm

[35]That day when evening came, he said to his disciples, "Let us go over to the other side." [36]Leaving the crowd behind, they took him along, just as he was, in the boat. There were also other boats with him. [37]A furious squall came up, and the waves broke over the boat, so that it was nearly swamped. [38]Jesus was in the stern, sleeping on a cushion. The disciples woke him and said to him, "Teacher, don't you care if we drown?"

[39]He got up, rebuked the wind and said to the waves, "Quiet! Be still!" Then the wind died down and it was completely calm.

[40]He said to his disciples, "Why are you so afraid? Do you still have no faith?"

[41]They were terrified and asked each other, "Who is this? Even the wind and the waves obey him!"

The Healing of a Demon-possessed Man

5 They went across the lake to the region of the Gerasenes.[a] [2]When Jesus got out of the boat, a man with an evil[b] spirit came from the tombs to meet him. [3]This man lived in the tombs, and no one could bind him any more, not even with a chain. [4]For he had often been chained hand and foot, but he tore the chains apart and broke the irons on his feet. No one was strong enough to subdue him. [5]Night and day among the tombs and in the hills he would cry out and cut himself with stones.

[6]When he saw Jesus from a distance, he ran and fell on his knees in front of him. [7]He shouted at the top of his voice, "What do you want with me, Jesus, Son of the Most High God? Swear to God that you won't torture me!" [8]For Jesus had said to him, "Come out of this man, you evil spirit!"

[9]Then Jesus asked him, "What is your name?"

"My name is Legion," he replied, "for we are many." [10]And he begged Jesus again and again not to send them out of the area.

[11]A large herd of pigs was feeding on the nearby hillside. [12]The demons begged Jesus, "Send us among the pigs; allow us to go into them." [13]He gave them permission, and the evil spirits came out and went into the pigs. The herd, about two thousand in number, rushed down the steep bank into the lake and were drowned.

[14]Those tending the pigs ran off and reported this in the town and countryside, and the people went out to see what had happened. [15]When they came to Jesus, they saw the man who had been possessed by the legion of demons, sitting there, dressed and in

---

[a]1 Some manuscripts Gadarenes; other manuscripts Gergesenes   [b]2 Greek unclean; also in verses 8 and 13

his right mind; and they were afraid.
16Those who had seen it told the people
what had happened to the demon-pos-
sessed man — and told about the pigs as
well. **17**Then the people began to plead with
Jesus to leave their region.

18As Jesus was getting into the boat, the
man who had been demon-possessed
begged to go with him. **19**Jesus did not let
him, but said, "Go home to your family and
tell them how much the Lord has done for
you, and how he has had mercy on you."
20So the man went away and began to tell in
the Decapolis*a* how much Jesus had done
for him. And all the people were amazed.

A Dead Girl and a Sick Woman

21When Jesus had again crossed over by
boat to the other side of the lake, a large
crowd gathered around him while he was by
the lake. **22**Then one of the synagogue rulers, named Jairus, came there. Seeing Jesus,
he fell at his feet **23**and pleaded earnestly
with him, "My little daughter is dying. Please
come and put your hands on her so that she
will be healed and live." **24**So Jesus went
with him.

A large crowd followed and pressed
around him. **25**And a woman was there who
had been subject to bleeding for twelve
years. **26**She had suffered a great deal under
the care of many doctors and had spent all
she had, yet instead of getting better she
grew worse. **27**When she heard about Jesus,
she came up behind him in the crowd and
touched his cloak, **28**because she thought,
"If I just touch his clothes, I will be healed."
29Immediately her bleeding stopped and
she felt in her body that she was freed from
her suffering.

30At once Jesus realized that power had
gone out from him. He turned around in the
crowd and asked, "Who touched my
clothes?"

31"You see the people crowding against
you," his disciples answered, "and yet you
can ask, 'Who touched me?'"

32But Jesus kept looking around to see
who had done it. **33**Then the woman, knowing what had happened to her, came and fell
at his feet and, trembling with fear, told him
the whole truth. **34**He said to her, "Daughter,
your faith has healed you. Go in peace and
be freed from your suffering."

35While Jesus was still speaking, some
men came from the house of Jairus, the synagogue ruler. "Your daughter is dead," they

said. "Why bother the teacher any more?"
36Ignoring what they said, Jesus told the
synagogue ruler, "Don't be afraid; just believe."

37He did not let anyone follow him except
Peter, James and John the brother of James.
38When they came to the home of the synagogue ruler, Jesus saw a commotion, with
people crying and wailing loudly. **39**He went
in and said to them, "Why all this commotion and wailing? The child is not dead but
asleep." **40**But they laughed at him.

After he put them all out, he took the
child's father and mother and the disciples
who were with him, and went in where the
child was. **41**He took her by the hand and
said to her, *"Talitha koum!"* (which means,
"Little girl, I say to you, get up!"). **42**Immediately the girl stood up and walked around
(she was twelve years old). At this they were
completely astonished. **43**He gave strict orders not to let anyone know about this, and
told them to give her something to eat.

A Prophet Without Honor

6 Jesus left there and went to his hometown, accompanied by his disciples.
2When the Sabbath came, he began to teach
in the synagogue, and many who heard him
were amazed.

"Where did this man get these things?"
they asked. "What's this wisdom that has
been given him, that he even does miracles!
3Isn't this the carpenter? Isn't this Mary's son
and the brother of James, Joseph,*b* Judas
and Simon? Aren't his sisters here with us?"
And they took offense at him.

4Jesus said to them, "Only in his hometown, among his relatives and in his own
house is a prophet without honor." **5**He
could not do any miracles there, except lay
his hands on a few sick people and heal
them. **6**And he was amazed at their lack of
faith.

Jesus Sends Out the Twelve

Then Jesus went around teaching from
village to village. **7**Calling the Twelve to him,
he sent them out two by two and gave them
authority over evil*c* spirits.

8These were his instructions: "Take nothing for the journey except a staff — no bread,
no bag, no money in your belts. **9**Wear sandals but not an extra tunic. **10**Whenever you
enter a house, stay there until you leave that
town. **11**And if any place will not welcome

---

a20 That is, the Ten Cities   *b3* Greek *Joses*, a variant of *Joseph*   *c7* Greek *unclean*

THE BOOBY TRAP OF BAD ADVICE

Shay has been cruising down the narrow road, doing his best to live for Jesus. Now, just when he was getting over the big faith hurdles in his path, he encountered another obstacle: the booby trap of bad advice.

Suddenly, it seems that all his friends are trying to drag him down:

Arnie: "What's the big deal? Nobody's going to make you drink. It's just a chance to party while Sue's parents are gone for the weekend."

Stephen: "Forget the church retreat! You hang out with those people all the time. Come with us this weekend."

Beth: "I'm telling you, it's not that bad. There are only three sex scenes in the whole movie."

Look It Up
• • • •

Sound familiar? Probably so. And that just may be the reason the Bible contains frequent warnings to weigh very carefully the advice your friends give you.

"Do not follow the crowd in doing wrong" (Exodus 23:2).

"Blessed is the man who does not walk in the counsel of the wicked or stand in the way of sinners or sit in the seat of mockers" (Psalm 1:1).

"Do not set foot on the path of the wicked or walk in the way of evil men" (Proverbs 4:14).

The point? Wrong friends who give bad advice can bring your Christian life to a screeching halt!

Think It Through
• • • •

What's the worst advice a friend ever gave you that you followed? How long did it take you to get back on track? What's the best advice a friend ever gave you that you followed? What was the result?

In your life right now, are you mainly getting (and following) good advice or bad?

Work It Out
• • • •

Rate each of your closest friendships in these three ways:
1. How much good advice do you get in the relationship?
2. How much does the relationship help you grow in Christ?
3. How much trouble does the relationship cause you?

Does this survey show you anything you didn't realize before? What action will you take as a result?

Nail It Down
• • • •

Read an example of bad advice in Mark 5:35–36.

Turn to pages 486, 1087, 1248 and 1367 for other readings on obstacles.
Turn to page 1058 for the weekend reading.

Topic
• • • •

OBSTACLES

you or listen to you, shake the dust off your feet when you leave, as a testimony against them."

[12]They went out and preached that people should repent. [13]They drove out many demons and anointed many sick people with oil and healed them.

John the Baptist Beheaded

[14]King Herod heard about this, for Jesus' name had become well known. Some were saying,[a] "John the Baptist has been raised from the dead, and that is why miraculous powers are at work in him."

[15]Others said, "He is Elijah."

And still others claimed, "He is a prophet, like one of the prophets of long ago."

[16]But when Herod heard this, he said, "John, the man I beheaded, has been raised from the dead!"

[17]For Herod himself had given orders to have John arrested, and he had him bound and put in prison. He did this because of Herodias, his brother Philip's wife, whom he had married. [18]For John had been saying to Herod, "It is not lawful for you to have your brother's wife." [19]So Herodias nursed a grudge against John and wanted to kill him. But she was not able to, [20]because Herod feared John and protected him, knowing him to be a righteous and holy man. When Herod heard John, he was greatly puzzled[b]; yet he liked to listen to him.

[21]Finally the opportune time came. On his birthday Herod gave a banquet for his high officials and military commanders and the leading men of Galilee. [22]When the daughter of Herodias came in and danced, she pleased Herod and his dinner guests.

The king said to the girl, "Ask me for anything you want, and I'll give it to you." [23]And he promised her with an oath, "Whatever you ask I will give you, up to half my kingdom."

[24]She went out and said to her mother, "What shall I ask for?"

"The head of John the Baptist," she answered.

[25]At once the girl hurried in to the king with the request: "I want you to give me right now the head of John the Baptist on a platter."

[26]The king was greatly distressed, but because of his oaths and his dinner guests, he did not want to refuse her. [27]So he immediately sent an executioner with orders to bring John's head. The man went, beheaded John in the prison, [28]and brought back his head on a platter. He presented it to the girl, and she gave it to her mother. [29]On hearing of this, John's disciples came and took his body and laid it in a tomb.

Jesus Feeds the Five Thousand

[30]The apostles gathered around Jesus and reported to him all they had done and taught. [31]Then, because so many people were coming and going that they did not even have a chance to eat, he said to them, "Come with me by yourselves to a quiet place and get some rest."

[32]So they went away by themselves in a boat to a solitary place. [33]But many who saw them leaving recognized them and ran on foot from all the towns and got there ahead of them. [34]When Jesus landed and saw a large crowd, he had compassion on them, because they were like sheep without a shepherd. So he began teaching them many things.

[35]By this time it was late in the day, so his disciples came to him. "This is a remote place," they said, "and it's already very late. [36]Send the people away so they can go to the surrounding countryside and villages and buy themselves something to eat."

[37]But he answered, "You give them something to eat."

They said to him, "That would take eight months of a man's wages[c]! Are we to go and spend that much on bread and give it to them to eat?"

[38]"How many loaves do you have?" he asked. "Go and see."

When they found out, they said, "Five — and two fish."

[39]Then Jesus directed them to have all the people sit down in groups on the green grass. [40]So they sat down in groups of hundreds and fifties. [41]Taking the five loaves and the two fish and looking up to heaven, he gave thanks and broke the loaves. Then he gave them to his disciples to set before the people. He also divided the two fish among them all. [42]They all ate and were satisfied, [43]and the disciples picked up twelve basketfuls of broken pieces of bread and fish. [44]The number of the men who had eaten was five thousand.

Jesus Walks on the Water

[45]Immediately Jesus made his disciples

---

[a]14 Some early manuscripts *He was saying*   [b]20 Some early manuscripts *he did many things*   [c]37 Greek *take two hundred denarii*

JESUS' PRESCRIPTION FOR STRESS

• •

Work It Out
• • • •

How many of you would answer "Yes!" to the following question:

Are you too busy?

When you look at your schedule for the next few days, do you feel overwhelmed? Do you sometimes wish you could just drop out of the rat race for a while? Do you often think you'll never get it all done?

Then you're experiencing stress. Of course, that's probably not a revelation to you. You knew it already. But maybe you didn't think there was anything you could do about it.

Think again! Jesus includes a prescription for stress in the book of Mark. Jesus and his disciples were so busy caring for the needs of the people around them that they "didn't even have a chance to eat." That's when Jesus gave his prescription for stress: "Come with me by yourselves to a quiet place and get some rest." The needy people were still there, the demands of the job were still there, but they left it all to get away and rest.

When the demands of your life get too hectic to handle, take a lesson from the disciples and get some rest.

Nail It Down
• • • •

Read Mark 6:31 for Jesus' prescription for stress.

• •

Think It Through
• • • •

Don't ever feel guilty when you just have to slow down—even stop—for a while. Rest is often the best cure for stress. You may have to omit doing something that ordinarily would be important. You may have to cut something worthwhile out of your schedule. Because *more* important and *more* worthwhile are the rest and relief you need in order to keep going. There is nothing holy or godly about being so busy doing so many good things that you don't enjoy any of them and you're only barely effective.

When your car runs low on gas, you go to the station and put some gas in the tank. The same should be true for you emotionally and spiritually. You need a fill-up after a busy schedule has worn you out. Take a rest. Relax. And then go back to your schedule with renewed energy and enthusiasm.

Nail It Down
• • • •

Reread the prescription for stress in Mark 6:31. For further insight read Psalm 91:1.

Turn to pages 546, 778, 1219 and 1280 for other readings on stress.
Turn to page 1060 for Monday's reading.

Topic
• • • •

get into the boat and go on ahead of him to Bethsaida, while he dismissed the crowd. **46**After leaving them, he went up on a mountainside to pray.

47When evening came, the boat was in the middle of the lake, and he was alone on land. **48**He saw the disciples straining at the oars, because the wind was against them. About the fourth watch of the night he went out to them, walking on the lake. He was about to pass by them, **49**but when they saw him walking on the lake, they thought he was a ghost. They cried out, **50**because they all saw him and were terrified.

Immediately he spoke to them and said, "Take courage! It is I. Don't be afraid." **51**Then he climbed into the boat with them, and the wind died down. They were completely amazed, **52**for they had not understood about the loaves; their hearts were hardened.

53When they had crossed over, they landed at Gennesaret and anchored there. **54**As soon as they got out of the boat, people recognized Jesus. **55**They ran throughout that whole region and carried the sick on mats to wherever they heard he was. **56**And wherever he went—into villages, towns or countryside—they placed the sick in the marketplaces. They begged him to let them touch even the edge of his cloak, and all who touched him were healed.

Clean and Unclean

7 The Pharisees and some of the teachers of the law who had come from Jerusalem gathered around Jesus and **2**saw some of his disciples eating food with hands that were "unclean," that is, unwashed. **3**(The Pharisees and all the Jews do not eat unless they give their hands a ceremonial washing, holding to the tradition of the elders. **4**When they come from the marketplace they do not eat unless they wash. And they observe many other traditions, such as the washing of cups, pitchers and kettles.*a*)

5So the Pharisees and teachers of the law asked Jesus, "Why don't your disciples live according to the tradition of the elders instead of eating their food with 'unclean' hands?"

6He replied, "Isaiah was right when he prophesied about you hypocrites; as it is written:

" 'These people honor me with their lips,
    but their hearts are far from me.
7They worship me in vain;
    their teachings are but rules taught by men.'*b*

8You have let go of the commands of God and are holding on to the traditions of men."

9And he said to them: "You have a fine way of setting aside the commands of God in order to observe*c* your own traditions! **10**For Moses said, 'Honor your father and your mother,'*d* and, 'Anyone who curses his father or mother must be put to death.'*e* **11**But you say that if a man says to his father or mother: 'Whatever help you might otherwise have received from me is Corban' (that is, a gift devoted to God), **12**then you no longer let him do anything for his father or mother. **13**Thus you nullify the word of God by your tradition that you have handed down. And you do many things like that."

14Again Jesus called the crowd to him and said, "Listen to me, everyone, and understand this. **15**Nothing outside a man can make him 'unclean' by going into him. Rather, it is what comes out of a man that makes him 'unclean.'*f*"

17After he had left the crowd and entered the house, his disciples asked him about this parable. **18**"Are you so dull?" he asked. "Don't you see that nothing that enters a man from the outside can make him 'unclean'? **19**For it doesn't go into his heart but into his stomach, and then out of his body." (In saying this, Jesus declared all foods "clean.")

20He went on: "What comes out of a man is what makes him 'unclean.' **21**For from within, out of men's hearts, come evil thoughts, sexual immorality, theft, murder, adultery, **22**greed, malice, deceit, lewdness, envy, slander, arrogance and folly. **23**All these evils come from inside and make a man 'unclean.' "

The Faith of a Syrophoenician Woman

24Jesus left that place and went to the vicinity of Tyre.*g* He entered a house and did not want anyone to know it; yet he could not keep his presence secret. **25**In fact, as soon as she heard about him, a woman whose little daughter was possessed by an evil*h* spirit came and fell at his feet. **26**The woman

---

a4 Some early manuscripts *pitchers, kettles and dining couches*   *b6,7* Isaiah 29:13   *c9* Some manuscripts *set up*   *d10* Exodus 20:12; Deut. 5:16   *e10* Exodus 21:17; Lev. 20:9   *f15* Some early manuscripts *'unclean.' 16If anyone has ears to hear, let him hear.*   *g24* Many early manuscripts *Tyre and Sidon*   *h25* Greek *unclean*

DIFFERENT... BUT IN WHAT WAYS?

Wednesday was Mark's turn to lead the discussion at youth group, and he let them have it!

"Our biggest problem is worldliness. We're just like all the non-Christians at school. We go to the same parties and dances and movies. We wear the same clothes. We treat people just like they do.

"Why should any of them want to be Christians? They don't see anything different about our lives!"

Look It Up
• • • •

Mark is on the right track. Christians should be careful about where they go, what they wear and how they act. And yet, according to Jesus, being different means much more than just being different on the outside. It also means being different on the inside. Consider what he told the religious leaders of Israel (who carefully avoided all questionable activities):

"Woe to you . . . you hypocrites! You give a tenth of your spices—mint, dill and cummin. But you have neglected the more important matters of the law—justice, mercy and faithfulness . . . . You blind guides! You strain out a gnat but swallow a camel . . . . on the outside you appear to people as righteous but on the inside you are full of hypocrisy and wickedness" (Matthew 23:23–24,28).

Think It Through
• • • •

Don't fall into the trap of thinking that you can avoid worldliness merely by giving up activities like drinking, smoking, card playing, dancing or going to movies. Anyone—an atheist, a devout Muslim, even a Christian—can stay away from those things and still be filled with worldly attitudes like selfishness, pride and materialism.

Work It Out
• • • •

Evaluate your outward behavior. Does being a Christian make any difference in the kinds of things you choose to do? It should. Are you involved in questionable activities? If so, you need to follow the commands given in 1 Thessalonians 5:21–22.

Examine your inner character. Do you find worldly values and attitudes? If so, pray for a deeper love for the things of God and a lesser desire for the things of this world.

Nail It Down
• • • •

Read more about the need to be different on the inside in Mark 7:20–23.

Turn to pages 1241 and 1393 for other readings on worldliness.
Turn to page 1063 for Tuesday's reading.

Topic
• • • •

WORLDLINESS

was a Greek, born in Syrian Phoenicia. She begged Jesus to drive the demon out of her daughter.

27"First let the children eat all they want," he told her, "for it is not right to take the children's bread and toss it to their dogs."

28"Yes, Lord," she replied, "but even the dogs under the table eat the children's crumbs."

29Then he told her, "For such a reply, you may go; the demon has left your daughter."

30She went home and found her child lying on the bed, and the demon gone.

The Healing of a Deaf and Mute Man

31Then Jesus left the vicinity of Tyre and went through Sidon, down to the Sea of Galilee and into the region of the Decapolis.*a* 32There some people brought to him a man who was deaf and could hardly talk, and they begged him to place his hand on the man.

33After he took him aside, away from the crowd, Jesus put his fingers into the man's ears. Then he spit and touched the man's tongue. 34He looked up to heaven and with a deep sigh said to him, *"Ephphatha!"* (which means, "Be opened!"). 35At this, the man's ears were opened, his tongue was loosened and he began to speak plainly.

36Jesus commanded them not to tell anyone. But the more he did so, the more they kept talking about it. 37People were overwhelmed with amazement. "He has done everything well," they said. "He even makes the deaf hear and the mute speak."

Jesus Feeds the Four Thousand

8 During those days another large crowd gathered. Since they had nothing to eat, Jesus called his disciples to him and said, 2"I have compassion for these people; they have already been with me three days and have nothing to eat. 3If I send them home hungry, they will collapse on the way, because some of them have come a long distance."

4His disciples answered, "But where in this remote place can anyone get enough bread to feed them?"

5"How many loaves do you have?" Jesus asked.

"Seven," they replied.

6He told the crowd to sit down on the ground. When he had taken the seven loaves and given thanks, he broke them and gave them to his disciples to set before the people, and they did so. 7They had a few small fish as well; he gave thanks for them also and told the disciples to distribute them. 8The people ate and were satisfied. Afterward the disciples picked up seven basketfuls of broken pieces that were left over. 9About four thousand men were present. And having sent them away, 10he got into the boat with his disciples and went to the region of Dalmanutha.

11The Pharisees came and began to question Jesus. To test him, they asked him for a sign from heaven. 12He sighed deeply and said, "Why does this generation ask for a miraculous sign? I tell you the truth, no sign will be given to it." 13Then he left them, got back into the boat and crossed to the other side.

The Yeast of the Pharisees and Herod

14The disciples had forgotten to bring bread, except for one loaf they had with them in the boat. 15"Be careful," Jesus warned them. "Watch out for the yeast of the Pharisees and that of Herod."

16They discussed this with one another and said, "It is because we have no bread."

17Aware of their discussion, Jesus asked them: "Why are you talking about having no bread? Do you still not see or understand? Are your hearts hardened? 18Do you have eyes but fail to see, and ears but fail to hear? And don't you remember? 19When I broke the five loaves for the five thousand, how many basketfuls of pieces did you pick up?"

"Twelve," they replied.

20"And when I broke the seven loaves for the four thousand, how many basketfuls of pieces did you pick up?"

They answered, "Seven."

21He said to them, "Do you still not understand?"

The Healing of a Blind Man at Bethsaida

22They came to Bethsaida, and some people brought a blind man and begged Jesus to touch him. 23He took the blind man by the hand and led him outside the village. When he had spit on the man's eyes and put his hands on him, Jesus asked, "Do you see anything?"

24He looked up and said, "I see people; they look like trees walking around."

25Once more Jesus put his hands on the man's eyes. Then his eyes were opened, his sight was restored, and he saw everything

a31 That is, the Ten Cities

clearly. **26**Jesus sent him home, saying, "Don't go into the village. *a* "

Peter's Confession of Christ

27Jesus and his disciples went on to the villages around Caesarea Philippi. On the way he asked them, "Who do people say I am?"

28They replied, "Some say John the Baptist; others say Elijah; and still others, one of the prophets."

29"But what about you?" he asked. "Who do you say I am?"

Peter answered, "You are the Christ. *b* "

30Jesus warned them not to tell anyone about him.

Jesus Predicts His Death

31He then began to teach them that the Son of Man must suffer many things and be rejected by the elders, chief priests and teachers of the law, and that he must be killed and after three days rise again. **32**He spoke plainly about this, and Peter took him aside and began to rebuke him.

33But when Jesus turned and looked at his disciples, he rebuked Peter. "Get behind me, Satan!" he said. "You do not have in mind the things of God, but the things of men."

34Then he called the crowd to him along with his disciples and said: "If anyone would come after me, he must deny himself and take up his cross and follow me. **35**For whoever wants to save his life *c* will lose it, but whoever loses his life for me and for the gospel will save it. **36**What good is it for a man to gain the whole world, yet forfeit his soul? **37**Or what can a man give in exchange for his soul? **38**If anyone is ashamed of me and my words in this adulterous and sinful generation, the Son of Man will be ashamed of him when he comes in his Father's glory with the holy angels."

9 And he said to them, "I tell you the truth, some who are standing here will not taste death before they see the kingdom of God come with power."

The Transfiguration

2After six days Jesus took Peter, James and John with him and led them up a high mountain, where they were all alone. There he was transfigured before them. **3**His clothes became dazzling white, whiter than anyone in the world could bleach them.

4And there appeared before them Elijah and Moses, who were talking with Jesus.

5Peter said to Jesus, "Rabbi, it is good for us to be here. Let us put up three shelters — one for you, one for Moses and one for Elijah." **6**(He did not know what to say, they were so frightened.)

7Then a cloud appeared and enveloped them, and a voice came from the cloud: "This is my Son, whom I love. Listen to him!"

8Suddenly, when they looked around, they no longer saw anyone with them except Jesus.

9As they were coming down the mountain, Jesus gave them orders not to tell anyone what they had seen until the Son of Man had risen from the dead. **10**They kept the matter to themselves, discussing what "rising from the dead" meant.

11And they asked him, "Why do the teachers of the law say that Elijah must come first?"

12Jesus replied, "To be sure, Elijah does come first, and restores all things. Why then is it written that the Son of Man must suffer much and be rejected? **13**But I tell you, Elijah has come, and they have done to him everything they wished, just as it is written about him."

The Healing of a Boy With an Evil Spirit

14When they came to the other disciples, they saw a large crowd around them and the teachers of the law arguing with them. **15**As soon as all the people saw Jesus, they were overwhelmed with wonder and ran to greet him.

16"What are you arguing with them about?" he asked.

17A man in the crowd answered, "Teacher, I brought you my son, who is possessed by a spirit that has robbed him of speech. **18**Whenever it seizes him, it throws him to the ground. He foams at the mouth, gnashes his teeth and becomes rigid. I asked your disciples to drive out the spirit, but they could not."

19"O unbelieving generation," Jesus replied, "how long shall I stay with you? How long shall I put up with you? Bring the boy to me."

20So they brought him. When the spirit saw Jesus, it immediately threw the boy into a convulsion. He fell to the ground and rolled around, foaming at the mouth.

---

a26 Some manuscripts *Don't go and tell anyone in the village*   *b29* Or *Messiah*. "The Christ" (Greek) and "the Messiah" (Hebrew) both mean "the Anointed One."   *c35* The Greek word means either *life* or *soul*; also in verse 36.

ARE YOU ASHAMED OF THE LORD?

Betty is feeling guilty. Why? Because after reading Mark 8:38 last night, she started realizing that:

• She is reluctant to tell her friends at school where she goes on Wednesday nights—to her youth group Bible study.

• She's too embarrassed to bow her head and thank God for her food before eating in the school cafeteria.

• She and her friends constantly make fun of one particular classmate who is very outspoken about his faith.

• She hides her Bible whenever friends come over.

Look It Up
••••

Betty's not the first believer to act ashamed of the Lord. Do you remember what happened the night Jesus was arrested? A servant girl recognized Peter as one of Jesus' disciples. Peter played dumb.

"After a little while, those standing near said to Peter, 'Surely you are one of them, for you are a Galilean.'

"He began to call down curses on himself, and he swore to them, 'I don't know this man you're talking about' " (Mark 14:70–71).

Strong words, huh? Now get your Bible and read Acts 5:27–42. It's the same guy (and a similar situation), but the results are vastly different.

Think It Through
••••

In one instance, Peter acts totally ashamed of Christ; in the next, he's like a spiritual superman. How do you explain the amazing change?

Do people (friends, classmates, neighbors) know about your belief in Christ? Or do you keep your commitment a secret like Peter did the night Jesus was arrested or like the individuals mentioned in John 12:42–43?

Work It Out
••••

Maybe you've been acting like Betty. And maybe you feel pretty rotten. Don't despair—God waits to forgive you, and he still wants to use you!

How about praying:

"Lord, I'm sorry for the way I've acted ashamed of you. I don't want to be like that. Make me strong. Help me to stand up for you today, no matter what the situation. Thanks for forgiving me. Amen."

Nail It Down
••••

Read the stern warning in Mark 8:38.

Turn to pages 52 and 1272 for other readings on embarrassment.
Turn to page 1068 for Wednesday's reading.

Topic
••••

EMBARRASSMENT

²¹Jesus asked the boy's father, "How long has he been like this?"

"From childhood," he answered. ²²"It has often thrown him into fire or water to kill him. But if you can do anything, take pity on us and help us."

²³"'If you can'?" said Jesus. "Everything is possible for him who believes."

²⁴Immediately the boy's father exclaimed, "I do believe; help me overcome my unbelief!"

²⁵When Jesus saw that a crowd was running to the scene, he rebuked the evilª spirit. "You deaf and mute spirit," he said, "I command you, come out of him and never enter him again."

²⁶The spirit shrieked, convulsed him violently and came out. The boy looked so much like a corpse that many said, "He's dead." ²⁷But Jesus took him by the hand and lifted him to his feet, and he stood up.

²⁸After Jesus had gone indoors, his disciples asked him privately, "Why couldn't we drive it out?"

²⁹He replied, "This kind can come out only by prayer.ᵇ"

³⁰They left that place and passed through Galilee. Jesus did not want anyone to know where they were, ³¹because he was teaching his disciples. He said to them, "The Son of Man is going to be betrayed into the hands of men. They will kill him, and after three days he will rise." ³²But they did not understand what he meant and were afraid to ask him about it.

Who Is the Greatest?

³³They came to Capernaum. When he was in the house, he asked them, "What were you arguing about on the road?" ³⁴But they kept quiet because on the way they had argued about who was the greatest.

³⁵Sitting down, Jesus called the Twelve and said, "If anyone wants to be first, he must be the very last, and the servant of all."

³⁶He took a little child and had him stand among them. Taking him in his arms, he said to them, ³⁷"Whoever welcomes one of these little children in my name welcomes me; and whoever welcomes me does not welcome me but the one who sent me."

Whoever Is Not Against Us Is for Us

³⁸"Teacher," said John, "we saw a man driving out demons in your name and we told him to stop, because he was not one of us."

³⁹"Do not stop him," Jesus said. "No one who does a miracle in my name can in the next moment say anything bad about me, ⁴⁰for whoever is not against us is for us. ⁴¹I tell you the truth, anyone who gives you a cup of water in my name because you belong to Christ will certainly not lose his reward.

Causing to Sin

⁴²"And if anyone causes one of these little ones who believe in me to sin, it would be better for him to be thrown into the sea with a large millstone tied around his neck. ⁴³If your hand causes you to sin, cut it off. It is better for you to enter life maimed than with two hands to go into hell, where the fire never goes out.ᶜ ⁴⁵And if your foot causes you to sin, cut it off. It is better for you to enter life crippled than to have two feet and be thrown into hell.ᵈ ⁴⁷And if your eye causes you to sin, pluck it out. It is better for you to enter the kingdom of God with one eye than to have two eyes and be thrown into hell, ⁴⁸where

" 'their worm does not die,
    and the fire is not quenched.'ᵉ

⁴⁹Everyone will be salted with fire.

⁵⁰"Salt is good, but if it loses its saltiness, how can you make it salty again? Have salt in yourselves, and be at peace with each other."

Divorce

10 Jesus then left that place and went into the region of Judea and across the Jordan. Again crowds of people came to him, and as was his custom, he taught them.

²Some Pharisees came and tested him by asking, "Is it lawful for a man to divorce his wife?"

³"What did Moses command you?" he replied.

⁴They said, "Moses permitted a man to write a certificate of divorce and send her away."

⁵"It was because your hearts were hard that Moses wrote you this law," Jesus replied. ⁶"But at the beginning of creation God 'made them male and female.'ᶠ ⁷For this reason a man will leave his father and moth-

ª25 Greek *unclean*   ᵇ29 Some manuscripts *prayer and fasting*   ᶜ43 Some manuscripts *out, ⁴⁴where /*
" 'their worm does not die, / and the fire is not quenched.'   ᵈ45 Some manuscripts *hell, ⁴⁶where / " 'their*
worm does not die, / and the fire is not quenched.'   ᵉ48 Isaiah 66:24   ᶠ6 Gen. 1:27

er and be united to his wife,^a **8**and the two will become one flesh.'^b So they are no longer two, but one. **9**Therefore what God has joined together, let man not separate."

10When they were in the house again, the disciples asked Jesus about this. **11**He answered, "Anyone who divorces his wife and marries another woman commits adultery against her. **12**And if she divorces her husband and marries another man, she commits adultery."

The Little Children and Jesus

13People were bringing little children to Jesus to have him touch them, but the disciples rebuked them. **14**When Jesus saw this, he was indignant. He said to them, "Let the little children come to me, and do not hinder them, for the kingdom of God belongs to such as these. **15**I tell you the truth, anyone who will not receive the kingdom of God like a little child will never enter it." **16**And he took the children in his arms, put his hands on them and blessed them.

The Rich Young Man

17As Jesus started on his way, a man ran up to him and fell on his knees before him. "Good teacher," he asked, "what must I do to inherit eternal life?"

18"Why do you call me good?" Jesus answered. "No one is good—except God alone. **19**You know the commandments: 'Do not murder, do not commit adultery, do not steal, do not give false testimony, do not defraud, honor your father and mother.'^c "

20"Teacher," he declared, "all these I have kept since I was a boy."

21Jesus looked at him and loved him. "One thing you lack," he said. "Go, sell everything you have and give to the poor, and you will have treasure in heaven. Then come, follow me."

22At this the man's face fell. He went away sad, because he had great wealth.

23Jesus looked around and said to his disciples, "How hard it is for the rich to enter the kingdom of God!"

24The disciples were amazed at his words. But Jesus said again, "Children, how hard it is^d to enter the kingdom of God! **25**It is easier for a camel to go through the eye of a needle than for a rich man to enter the kingdom of God."

26The disciples were even more amazed, and said to each other, "Who then can be saved?"

27Jesus looked at them and said, "With man this is impossible, but not with God; all things are possible with God."

28Peter said to him, "We have left everything to follow you!"

29"I tell you the truth," Jesus replied, "no one who has left home or brothers or sisters or mother or father or children or fields for me and the gospel **30**will fail to receive a hundred times as much in this present age (homes, brothers, sisters, mothers, children and fields—and with them, persecutions) and in the age to come, eternal life. **31**But many who are first will be last, and the last first."

Jesus Again Predicts His Death

32They were on their way up to Jerusalem, with Jesus leading the way, and the disciples were astonished, while those who followed were afraid. Again he took the Twelve aside and told them what was going to happen to him. **33**"We are going up to Jerusalem," he said, "and the Son of Man will be betrayed to the chief priests and teachers of the law. They will condemn him to death and will hand him over to the Gentiles, **34**who will mock him and spit on him, flog him and kill him. Three days later he will rise."

The Request of James and John

35Then James and John, the sons of Zebedee, came to him. "Teacher," they said, "we want you to do for us whatever we ask."

36"What do you want me to do for you?" he asked.

37They replied, "Let one of us sit at your right and the other at your left in your glory."

38"You don't know what you are asking," Jesus said. "Can you drink the cup I drink or be baptized with the baptism I am baptized with?"

39"We can," they answered.

Jesus said to them, "You will drink the cup I drink and be baptized with the baptism I am baptized with, **40**but to sit at my right or left is not for me to grant. These places belong to those for whom they have been prepared."

41When the ten heard about this, they became indignant with James and John. **42**Jesus called them together and said, "You know that those who are regarded as rulers of the Gentiles lord it over them, and their

---

^a7 Some early manuscripts do not have *and be united to his wife.*   ^b8 Gen. 2:24   ^c19 Exodus 20:12-16; Deut. 5:16-20   ^d24 Some manuscripts *is for those who trust in riches*

high officials exercise authority over them. [43]Not so with you. Instead, whoever wants to become great among you must be your servant, [44]and whoever wants to be first must be slave of all. [45]For even the Son of Man did not come to be served, but to serve, and to give his life as a ransom for many."

Blind Bartimaeus Receives His Sight

[46]Then they came to Jericho. As Jesus and his disciples, together with a large crowd, were leaving the city, a blind man, Bartimaeus (that is, the Son of Timaeus), was sitting by the roadside begging. [47]When he heard that it was Jesus of Nazareth, he began to shout, "Jesus, Son of David, have mercy on me!"

[48]Many rebuked him and told him to be quiet, but he shouted all the more, "Son of David, have mercy on me!"

[49]Jesus stopped and said, "Call him."

So they called to the blind man, "Cheer up! On your feet! He's calling you." [50]Throwing his cloak aside, he jumped to his feet and came to Jesus.

[51]"What do you want me to do for you?" Jesus asked him.

The blind man said, "Rabbi, I want to see."

[52]"Go," said Jesus, "your faith has healed you." Immediately he received his sight and followed Jesus along the road.

The Triumphal Entry

11 As they approached Jerusalem and came to Bethphage and Bethany at the Mount of Olives, Jesus sent two of his disciples, [2]saying to them, "Go to the village ahead of you, and just as you enter it, you will find a colt tied there, which no one has ever ridden. Untie it and bring it here. [3]If anyone asks you, 'Why are you doing this?' tell him, 'The Lord needs it and will send it back here shortly.' "

[4]They went and found a colt outside in the street, tied at a doorway. As they untied it, [5]some people standing there asked, "What are you doing, untying that colt?" [6]They answered as Jesus had told them to, and the people let them go. [7]When they brought the colt to Jesus and threw their cloaks over it, he sat on it. [8]Many people spread their cloaks on the road, while others spread branches they had cut in the fields. [9]Those

who went ahead and those who followed shouted,

"Hosanna![a]"

"Blessed is he who comes in the name
    of the Lord!"[b]

[10]"Blessed is the coming kingdom of our
    father David!"

"Hosanna in the highest!"

[11]Jesus entered Jerusalem and went to the temple. He looked around at everything, but since it was already late, he went out to Bethany with the Twelve.

Jesus Clears the Temple

[12]The next day as they were leaving Bethany, Jesus was hungry. [13]Seeing in the distance a fig tree in leaf, he went to find out if it had any fruit. When he reached it, he found nothing but leaves, because it was not the season for figs. [14]Then he said to the tree, "May no one ever eat fruit from you again." And his disciples heard him say it.

[15]On reaching Jerusalem, Jesus entered the temple area and began driving out those who were buying and selling there. He overturned the tables of the money changers and the benches of those selling doves, [16]and would not allow anyone to carry merchandise through the temple courts. [17]And as he taught them, he said, "Is it not written:

" 'My house will be called
    a house of prayer for all nations'[c]?

But you have made it 'a den of robbers.'[d] "

[18]The chief priests and the teachers of the law heard this and began looking for a way to kill him, for they feared him, because the whole crowd was amazed at his teaching.

[19]When evening came, they[e] went out of the city.

The Withered Fig Tree

[20]In the morning, as they went along, they saw the fig tree withered from the roots. [21]Peter remembered and said to Jesus, "Rabbi, look! The fig tree you cursed has withered!"

[22]"Have[f] faith in God," Jesus answered. [23]"I tell you the truth, if anyone says to this mountain, 'Go, throw yourself into the sea,' and does not doubt in his heart but believes that what he says will happen, it will be done for him. [24]Therefore I tell you, whatev-

---

[a]9 A Hebrew expression meaning "Save!" which became an exclamation of praise; also in verse 10   [b]9 Psalm 118:25,26   [c]17 Isaiah 56:7   [d]17 Jer. 7:11   [e]19 Some early manuscripts he   [f]22 Some early manuscripts If you have

er you ask for in prayer, believe that you have received it, and it will be yours. **25**And when you stand praying, if you hold anything against anyone, forgive him, so that your Father in heaven may forgive you your sins. *a* "

The Authority of Jesus Questioned

27They arrived again in Jerusalem, and while Jesus was walking in the temple courts, the chief priests, the teachers of the law and the elders came to him. **28**"By what authority are you doing these things?" they asked. "And who gave you authority to do this?"

29Jesus replied, "I will ask you one question. Answer me, and I will tell you by what authority I am doing these things. **30**John's baptism—was it from heaven, or from men? Tell me!"

31They discussed it among themselves and said, "If we say, 'From heaven,' he will ask, 'Then why didn't you believe him?' **32**But if we say, 'From men' . . . ." (They feared the people, for everyone held that John really was a prophet.)

33So they answered Jesus, "We don't know."

Jesus said, "Neither will I tell you by what authority I am doing these things."

The Parable of the Tenants

12 He then began to speak to them in parables: "A man planted a vineyard. He put a wall around it, dug a pit for the winepress and built a watchtower. Then he rented the vineyard to some farmers and went away on a journey. **2**At harvest time he sent a servant to the tenants to collect from them some of the fruit of the vineyard. **3**But they seized him, beat him and sent him away empty-handed. **4**Then he sent another servant to them; they struck this man on the head and treated him shamefully. **5**He sent still another, and that one they killed. He sent many others; some of them they beat, others they killed.

6"He had one left to send, a son, whom he loved. He sent him last of all, saying, 'They will respect my son.'

7"But the tenants said to one another, 'This is the heir. Come, let's kill him, and the inheritance will be ours.' **8**So they took him and killed him, and threw him out of the vineyard.

9"What then will the owner of the vineyard do? He will come and kill those tenants and give the vineyard to others. **10**Haven't you read this scripture:

" 'The stone the builders rejected
  has become the capstone *b*;
11the Lord has done this,
  and it is marvelous in our eyes' *c*?"

12Then they looked for a way to arrest him because they knew he had spoken the parable against them. But they were afraid of the crowd; so they left him and went away.

Paying Taxes to Caesar

13Later they sent some of the Pharisees and Herodians to Jesus to catch him in his words. **14**They came to him and said, "Teacher, we know you are a man of integrity. You aren't swayed by men, because you pay no attention to who they are; but you teach the way of God in accordance with the truth. Is it right to pay taxes to Caesar or not? **15**Should we pay or shouldn't we?"

But Jesus knew their hypocrisy. "Why are you trying to trap me?" he asked. "Bring me a denarius and let me look at it." **16**They brought the coin, and he asked them, "Whose portrait is this? And whose inscription?"

"Caesar's," they replied.

17Then Jesus said to them, "Give to Caesar what is Caesar's and to God what is God's." And they were amazed at him.

Marriage at the Resurrection

18Then the Sadducees, who say there is no resurrection, came to him with a question. **19**"Teacher," they said, "Moses wrote for us that if a man's brother dies and leaves a wife but no children, the man must marry the widow and have children for his brother. **20**Now there were seven brothers. The first one married and died without leaving any children. **21**The second one married the widow, but he also died, leaving no child. It was the same with the third. **22**In fact, none of the seven left any children. Last of all, the woman died too. **23**At the resurrection *d* whose wife will she be, since the seven were married to her?"

24Jesus replied, "Are you not in error because you do not know the Scriptures or the power of God? **25**When the dead rise, they will neither marry nor be given in marriage;

---

a25 Some manuscripts sins. 26But if you do not forgive, neither will your Father who is in heaven forgive your sins. b10 Or cornerstone c11 Psalm 118:22,23 d23 Some manuscripts resurrection, when men rise from the dead,

FORGIVENESS IS FOR GIVING

Up until a month ago, Judy couldn't stand even the thought of Kirby. Though they had broken up over two years ago, she still felt angry about their whole experience. She felt used and terribly mistreated.

To get back, she avoided Kirby at school. And any time he came to youth group activities, she ignored him. "Until he apologizes for what he did to me, I'll never even speak to him."

Four weeks ago something happened. Judy's pastor talked about forgiveness, and Judy hasn't been the same since.

Look It Up •••• The following facts prompted the change in Judy's attitude:

God has forgiven you for all the wrong things you have done (Psalm 103:3).

Because God has forgiven you, you must forgive others. "Bear with each other and forgive whatever grievances you may have against one another. Forgive as the Lord forgave you" (Colossians 3:13).

Your fellowship with God is interrupted when you refuse to forgive others. "For if you forgive men when they sin against you, your heavenly Father will also forgive you. But if you do not forgive men their sins, your Father will not forgive your sins" (Matthew 6:14–15).

Think It Through •••• Forgiveness is not (a) denying that you've been hurt, (b) explaining away the wrong behavior of someone, or (c) trying to understand why a person has acted a certain way. Forgiveness is: (d) consciously choosing to release others from debts you feel they owe you because of hurts they have caused in your life.

Work It Out •••• Do you have someone in your life that you need to forgive? You can experience the freedom Judy found by praying:

"God, I am angry and hurt because of what _____ has done to me. I don't feel like forgiving, and in my own strength I know I can't. But because you have completely forgiven me, right now I choose to forgive. Today, by your grace I will begin accepting _____, and I will seek to rebuild our broken relationship."

Nail It Down •••• Read the instructions on forgiveness in Mark 11:25.

Turn to pages 580, 771, 809, 966, 1302 and 1352 for other readings on forgiveness.
Turn to page 1074 for Thursday's reading.

Topic ••••

FORGIVENESS

they will be like the angels in heaven. **26**Now about the dead rising — have you not read in the book of Moses, in the account of the bush, how God said to him, 'I am the God of Abraham, the God of Isaac, and the God of Jacob'*a*? **27**He is not the God of the dead, but of the living. You are badly mistaken!"

The Greatest Commandment

28One of the teachers of the law came and heard them debating. Noticing that Jesus had given them a good answer, he asked him, "Of all the commandments, which is the most important?"

29"The most important one," answered Jesus, "is this: 'Hear, O Israel, the Lord our God, the Lord is one.*b* **30**Love the Lord your God with all your heart and with all your soul and with all your mind and with all your strength.'*c* **31**The second is this: 'Love your neighbor as yourself.'*d* There is no commandment greater than these."

32"Well said, teacher," the man replied. "You are right in saying that God is one and there is no other but him. **33**To love him with all your heart, with all your understanding and with all your strength, and to love your neighbor as yourself is more important than all burnt offerings and sacrifices."

34When Jesus saw that he had answered wisely, he said to him, "You are not far from the kingdom of God." And from then on no one dared ask him any more questions.

Whose Son Is the Christ?

35While Jesus was teaching in the temple courts, he asked, "How is it that the teachers of the law say that the Christ*e* is the son of David? **36**David himself, speaking by the Holy Spirit, declared:

" 'The Lord said to my Lord:
    "Sit at my right hand
until I put your enemies
    under your feet." '*f*

37David himself calls him 'Lord.' How then can he be his son?"

The large crowd listened to him with delight.

38As he taught, Jesus said, "Watch out for the teachers of the law. They like to walk around in flowing robes and be greeted in the marketplaces, **39**and have the most important seats in the synagogues and the places of honor at banquets. **40**They devour widows' houses and for a show make lengthy prayers. Such men will be punished most severely."

The Widow's Offering

41Jesus sat down opposite the place where the offerings were put and watched the crowd putting their money into the temple treasury. Many rich people threw in large amounts. **42**But a poor widow came and put in two very small copper coins,*g* worth only a fraction of a penny.*h*

43Calling his disciples to him, Jesus said, "I tell you the truth, this poor widow has put more into the treasury than all the others. **44**They all gave out of their wealth; but she, out of her poverty, put in everything — all she had to live on."

Signs of the End of the Age

13 As he was leaving the temple, one of his disciples said to him, "Look, Teacher! What massive stones! What magnificent buildings!"

2"Do you see all these great buildings?" replied Jesus. "Not one stone here will be left on another; every one will be thrown down."

3As Jesus was sitting on the Mount of Olives opposite the temple, Peter, James, John and Andrew asked him privately, **4**"Tell us, when will these things happen? And what will be the sign that they are all about to be fulfilled?"

5Jesus said to them: "Watch out that no one deceives you. **6**Many will come in my name, claiming, 'I am he,' and will deceive many. **7**When you hear of wars and rumors of wars, do not be alarmed. Such things must happen, but the end is still to come. **8**Nation will rise against nation, and kingdom against kingdom. There will be earthquakes in various places, and famines. These are the beginning of birth pains.

9"You must be on your guard. You will be handed over to the local councils and flogged in the synagogues. On account of me you will stand before governors and kings as witnesses to them. **10**And the gospel must first be preached to all nations. **11**Whenever you are arrested and brought to trial, do not worry beforehand about what to say. Just say whatever is given you at the time, for it is not you speaking, but the Holy Spirit.

12"Brother will betray brother to death, and a father his child. Children will rebel

---

a26 Exodus 3:6   *b29* Or *the Lord our God is one Lord*   *c30* Deut. 6:4,5   *d31* Lev. 19:18   *e35* Or *Messiah*   *f36* Psalm 110:1   *g42* Greek *two lepta*   *h42* Greek *kodrantes* against their parents and have them put to death. [13]All men will hate you because of me, but he who stands firm to the end will be saved.

[14]"When you see 'the abomination that causes desolation'[a] standing where it[b] does not belong—let the reader understand—then let those who are in Judea flee to the mountains. [15]Let no one on the roof of his house go down or enter the house to take anything out. [16]Let no one in the field go back to get his cloak. [17]How dreadful it will be in those days for pregnant women and nursing mothers! [18]Pray that this will not take place in winter, [19]because those will be days of distress unequaled from the beginning, when God created the world, until now—and never to be equaled again. [20]If the Lord had not cut short those days, no one would survive. But for the sake of the elect, whom he has chosen, he has shortened them. [21]At that time if anyone says to you, 'Look, here is the Christ[c]!' or, 'Look, there he is!' do not believe it. [22]For false Christs and false prophets will appear and perform signs and miracles to deceive the elect—if that were possible. [23]So be on your guard; I have told you everything ahead of time.

[24]"But in those days, following that distress,

" 'the sun will be darkened,
     and the moon will not give its light;
[25]the stars will fall from the sky,
     and the heavenly bodies will be
         shaken.'[d]

[26]"At that time men will see the Son of Man coming in clouds with great power and glory. [27]And he will send his angels and gather his elect from the four winds, from the ends of the earth to the ends of the heavens.

[28]"Now learn this lesson from the fig tree: As soon as its twigs get tender and its leaves come out, you know that summer is near. [29]Even so, when you see these things happening, you know that it is near, right at the door. [30]I tell you the truth, this generation[e] will certainly not pass away until all these things have happened. [31]Heaven and earth will pass away, but my words will never pass away.

The Day and Hour Unknown

[32]"No one knows about that day or hour, not even the angels in heaven, nor the Son, but only the Father. [33]Be on guard! Be alert[f]! You do not know when that time will come. [34]It's like a man going away: He leaves his house and puts his servants in charge, each with his assigned task, and tells the one at the door to keep watch.

[35]"Therefore keep watch because you do not know when the owner of the house will come back—whether in the evening, or at midnight, or when the rooster crows, or at dawn. [36]If he comes suddenly, do not let him find you sleeping. [37]What I say to you, I say to everyone: 'Watch!' "

Jesus Anointed at Bethany

14 Now the Passover and the Feast of Unleavened Bread were only two days away, and the chief priests and the teachers of the law were looking for some sly way to arrest Jesus and kill him. [2]"But not during the Feast," they said, "or the people may riot."

[3]While he was in Bethany, reclining at the table in the home of a man known as Simon the Leper, a woman came with an alabaster jar of very expensive perfume, made of pure nard. She broke the jar and poured the perfume on his head.

[4]Some of those present were saying indignantly to one another, "Why this waste of perfume? [5]It could have been sold for more than a year's wages[g] and the money given to the poor." And they rebuked her harshly.

[6]"Leave her alone," said Jesus. "Why are you bothering her? She has done a beautiful thing to me. [7]The poor you will always have with you, and you can help them any time you want. But you will not always have me. [8]She did what she could. She poured perfume on my body beforehand to prepare for my burial. [9]I tell you the truth, wherever the gospel is preached throughout the world, what she has done will also be told, in memory of her."

[10]Then Judas Iscariot, one of the Twelve, went to the chief priests to betray Jesus to them. [11]They were delighted to hear this and promised to give him money. So he watched for an opportunity to hand him over.

The Lord's Supper

[12]On the first day of the Feast of Unleavened Bread, when it was customary to sacrifice the Passover lamb, Jesus' disciples

---

[a]14 Daniel 9:27; 11:31; 12:11   [b]14 Or he; also in verse 29   [c]21 Or Messiah   [d]25 Isaiah 13:10; 34:4   [e]30 Or race   [f]33 Some manuscripts alert and pray   [g]5 Greek than three hundred denarii

asked him, "Where do you want us to go and make preparations for you to eat the Passover?"

13So he sent two of his disciples, telling them, "Go into the city, and a man carrying a jar of water will meet you. Follow him. **14**Say to the owner of the house he enters, 'The Teacher asks: Where is my guest room, where I may eat the Passover with my disciples?' **15**He will show you a large upper room, furnished and ready. Make preparations for us there."

16The disciples left, went into the city and found things just as Jesus had told them. So they prepared the Passover.

17When evening came, Jesus arrived with the Twelve. **18**While they were reclining at the table eating, he said, "I tell you the truth, one of you will betray me—one who is eating with me."

19They were saddened, and one by one they said to him, "Surely not I?"

20"It is one of the Twelve," he replied, "one who dips bread into the bowl with me. **21**The Son of Man will go just as it is written about him. But woe to that man who betrays the Son of Man! It would be better for him if he had not been born."

22While they were eating, Jesus took bread, gave thanks and broke it, and gave it to his disciples, saying, "Take it; this is my body."

23Then he took the cup, gave thanks and offered it to them, and they all drank from it.

24"This is my blood of the[a] covenant, which is poured out for many," he said to them. **25**"I tell you the truth, I will not drink again of the fruit of the vine until that day when I drink it anew in the kingdom of God."

26When they had sung a hymn, they went out to the Mount of Olives.

Jesus Predicts Peter's Denial

27"You will all fall away," Jesus told them, "for it is written:

" 'I will strike the shepherd,
   and the sheep will be scattered.'[b]

28But after I have risen, I will go ahead of you into Galilee."

29Peter declared, "Even if all fall away, I will not."

30"I tell you the truth," Jesus answered, "today—yes, tonight—before the rooster crows twice[c] you yourself will disown me three times."

31But Peter insisted emphatically, "Even if I have to die with you, I will never disown you." And all the others said the same.

Gethsemane

32They went to a place called Gethsemane, and Jesus said to his disciples, "Sit here while I pray." **33**He took Peter, James and John along with him, and he began to be deeply distressed and troubled. **34**"My soul is overwhelmed with sorrow to the point of death," he said to them. "Stay here and keep watch."

35Going a little farther, he fell to the ground and prayed that if possible the hour might pass from him. **36**"*Abba*,[d] Father," he said, "everything is possible for you. Take this cup from me. Yet not what I will, but what you will."

37Then he returned to his disciples and found them sleeping. "Simon," he said to Peter, "are you asleep? Could you not keep watch for one hour? **38**Watch and pray so that you will not fall into temptation. The spirit is willing, but the body is weak."

39Once more he went away and prayed the same thing. **40**When he came back, he again found them sleeping, because their eyes were heavy. They did not know what to say to him.

41Returning the third time, he said to them, "Are you still sleeping and resting? Enough! The hour has come. Look, the Son of Man is betrayed into the hands of sinners. **42**Rise! Let us go! Here comes my betrayer!"

Jesus Arrested

43Just as he was speaking, Judas, one of the Twelve, appeared. With him was a crowd armed with swords and clubs, sent from the chief priests, the teachers of the law, and the elders.

44Now the betrayer had arranged a signal with them: "The one I kiss is the man; arrest him and lead him away under guard." **45**Going at once to Jesus, Judas said, "Rabbi!" and kissed him. **46**The men seized Jesus and arrested him. **47**Then one of those standing near drew his sword and struck the servant of the high priest, cutting off his ear.

48"Am I leading a rebellion," said Jesus, "that you have come out with swords and clubs to capture me? **49**Every day I was with you, teaching in the temple courts, and you

---

a24 Some manuscripts *the new*   *b27* Zech. 13:7   *c30* Some early manuscripts do not have *twice*.
d36 Aramaic for *Father*

did not arrest me. But the Scriptures must be fulfilled." **50**Then everyone deserted him and fled.

51A young man, wearing nothing but a linen garment, was following Jesus. When they seized him, **52**he fled naked, leaving his garment behind.

Before the Sanhedrin

53They took Jesus to the high priest, and all the chief priests, elders and teachers of the law came together. **54**Peter followed him at a distance, right into the courtyard of the high priest. There he sat with the guards and warmed himself at the fire.

55The chief priests and the whole Sanhedrin were looking for evidence against Jesus so that they could put him to death, but they did not find any. **56**Many testified falsely against him, but their statements did not agree.

57Then some stood up and gave this false testimony against him: **58**"We heard him say, 'I will destroy this man-made temple and in three days will build another, not made by man.' " **59**Yet even then their testimony did not agree.

60Then the high priest stood up before them and asked Jesus, "Are you not going to answer? What is this testimony that these men are bringing against you?" **61**But Jesus remained silent and gave no answer.

Again the high priest asked him, "Are you the Christ,*a* the Son of the Blessed One?"

62"I am," said Jesus. "And you will see the Son of Man sitting at the right hand of the Mighty One and coming on the clouds of heaven."

63The high priest tore his clothes. "Why do we need any more witnesses?" he asked. **64**"You have heard the blasphemy. What do you think?"

They all condemned him as worthy of death. **65**Then some began to spit at him; they blindfolded him, struck him with their fists, and said, "Prophesy!" And the guards took him and beat him.

Peter Disowns Jesus

66While Peter was below in the courtyard, one of the servant girls of the high priest came by. **67**When she saw Peter warming himself, she looked closely at him.

"You also were with that Nazarene, Jesus," she said.

68But he denied it. "I don't know or understand what you're talking about," he said, and went out into the entryway.*b*

69When the servant girl saw him there, she said again to those standing around, "This fellow is one of them." **70**Again he denied it.

After a little while, those standing near said to Peter, "Surely you are one of them, for you are a Galilean."

71He began to call down curses on himself, and he swore to them, "I don't know this man you're talking about."

72Immediately the rooster crowed the second time.*c* Then Peter remembered the word Jesus had spoken to him: "Before the rooster crows twice*d* you will disown me three times." And he broke down and wept.

Jesus Before Pilate

15 Very early in the morning, the chief priests, with the elders, the teachers of the law and the whole Sanhedrin, reached a decision. They bound Jesus, led him away and handed him over to Pilate.

2"Are you the king of the Jews?" asked Pilate.

"Yes, it is as you say," Jesus replied.

3The chief priests accused him of many things. **4**So again Pilate asked him, "Aren't you going to answer? See how many things they are accusing you of."

5But Jesus still made no reply, and Pilate was amazed.

6Now it was the custom at the Feast to release a prisoner whom the people requested. **7**A man called Barabbas was in prison with the insurrectionists who had committed murder in the uprising. **8**The crowd came up and asked Pilate to do for them what he usually did.

9"Do you want me to release to you the king of the Jews?" asked Pilate, **10**knowing it was out of envy that the chief priests had handed Jesus over to him. **11**But the chief priests stirred up the crowd to have Pilate release Barabbas instead.

12"What shall I do, then, with the one you call the king of the Jews?" Pilate asked them.

13"Crucify him!" they shouted.

14"Why? What crime has he committed?" asked Pilate.

But they shouted all the louder, "Crucify him!"

15Wanting to satisfy the crowd, Pilate released Barabbas to them. He had Jesus

---

a61 Or *Messiah*   *b68* Some early manuscripts *entryway and the rooster crowed*   *c72* Some early manuscripts do not have *the second time.*   *d72* Some early manuscripts do not have *twice.*

flogged, and handed him over to be crucified.

The Soldiers Mock Jesus

16The soldiers led Jesus away into the palace (that is, the Praetorium) and called together the whole company of soldiers. **17**They put a purple robe on him, then twisted together a crown of thorns and set it on him. **18**And they began to call out to him, "Hail, king of the Jews!" **19**Again and again they struck him on the head with a staff and spit on him. Falling on their knees, they paid homage to him. **20**And when they had mocked him, they took off the purple robe and put his own clothes on him. Then they led him out to crucify him.

The Crucifixion

21A certain man from Cyrene, Simon, the father of Alexander and Rufus, was passing by on his way in from the country, and they forced him to carry the cross. **22**They brought Jesus to the place called Golgotha (which means The Place of the Skull). **23**Then they offered him wine mixed with myrrh, but he did not take it. **24**And they crucified him. Dividing up his clothes, they cast lots to see what each would get.

25It was the third hour when they crucified him. **26**The written notice of the charge against him read: THE KING OF THE JEWS. **27**They crucified two robbers with him, one on his right and one on his left.*a* **29**Those who passed by hurled insults at him, shaking their heads and saying, "So! You who are going to destroy the temple and build it in three days, **30**come down from the cross and save yourself!"

31In the same way the chief priests and the teachers of the law mocked him among themselves. "He saved others," they said, "but he can't save himself! **32**Let this Christ,*b* this King of Israel, come down now from the cross, that we may see and believe." Those crucified with him also heaped insults on him.

The Death of Jesus

33At the sixth hour darkness came over the whole land until the ninth hour. **34**And at the ninth hour Jesus cried out in a loud voice, *"Eloi, Eloi, lama sabachthani?"* — which means, "My God, my God, why have you forsaken me?"*c*

35When some of those standing near heard this, they said, "Listen, he's calling Elijah."

36One man ran, filled a sponge with wine vinegar, put it on a stick, and offered it to Jesus to drink. "Now leave him alone. Let's see if Elijah comes to take him down," he said.

37With a loud cry, Jesus breathed his last.

38The curtain of the temple was torn in two from top to bottom. **39**And when the centurion, who stood there in front of Jesus, heard his cry and*d* saw how he died, he said, "Surely this man was the Son*e* of God!"

40Some women were watching from a distance. Among them were Mary Magdalene, Mary the mother of James the younger and of Joses, and Salome. **41**In Galilee these women had followed him and cared for his needs. Many other women who had come up with him to Jerusalem were also there.

The Burial of Jesus

42It was Preparation Day (that is, the day before the Sabbath). So as evening approached, **43**Joseph of Arimathea, a prominent member of the Council, who was himself waiting for the kingdom of God, went boldly to Pilate and asked for Jesus' body. **44**Pilate was surprised to hear that he was already dead. Summoning the centurion, he asked him if Jesus had already died. **45**When he learned from the centurion that it was so, he gave the body to Joseph. **46**So Joseph bought some linen cloth, took down the body, wrapped it in the linen, and placed it in a tomb cut out of rock. Then he rolled a stone against the entrance of the tomb. **47**Mary Magdalene and Mary the mother of Joses saw where he was laid.

The Resurrection

16 When the Sabbath was over, Mary Magdalene, Mary the mother of James, and Salome bought spices so that they might go to anoint Jesus' body. **2**Very early on the first day of the week, just after sunrise, they were on their way to the tomb **3**and they asked each other, "Who will roll the stone away from the entrance of the tomb?"

4But when they looked up, they saw that the stone, which was very large, had been rolled away. **5**As they entered the tomb, they

---

a27 Some manuscripts left, 28and the scripture was fulfilled which says, "He was counted with the lawless ones" (Isaiah 53:12)   *b32 Or Messiah   c34 Psalm 22:1   d39 Some manuscripts do not have heard his cry and* *e39 Or a son*

REPAIRING A ROTTEN REPUTATION

During junior high school, Betty had sex with four different guys. Not surprisingly, she quickly developed a reputation for being "loose." Classmates began pronouncing her name "Beddy."

When she got to high school, Betty gave her life to Jesus Christ. No kidding, she is really a new person. But now the "loose" reputation won't die. Even though Betty is no longer sexually active, the rumors and whispering persist.

"How can I show people that I've changed?" Betty groans.

Look It Up
• • • •

After a history of "breathing out murderous threats against the Lord's disciples" (Acts 9:1), Saul did not exactly have a great reputation among Christians. Even after his conversion on the road to Damascus, he had a hard time convincing the members of the first century church that he had truly changed. In fact, "When he came to Jerusalem, he tried to join the disciples, but they were all afraid of him, not believing that he really was a disciple" (Acts 9:26).

However, because Barnabas, an older, more mature Christian, stood up for him (Acts 9:27), and because Saul continued to exhibit a changed lifestyle (Acts 9:28–30), he was able to repair his rotten reputation. Over time Saul, the Christian hater, became know as Paul, an apostle of Jesus Christ.

Think It Through
• • • •

A warning about the subject of reputation:

A religious reputation will not get you into heaven. The apostle Paul had a lot of religious credentials, but it was not until he trusted Christ that he found eternal life (Philippians 3:4–11).

Work It Out
• • • •

Are you trying to revamp your reputation? Remember the lessons from Saul's life:

• Trust Christ—Changing your outer image is a waste unless you also have a changed inner identity (2 Corinthians 5:17).

• Find a "Barnabas" who will believe in you and disciple you.

• Be consistent. It takes many months (maybe even years) to undo a bad reputation. Don't give up (Galatians 6:9).

Nail It Down
• • • •

Read Mark 15:40–41 as well as Luke 8:2 and consider how Mary Magdalene's reputation changed.

Turn to pages 150, 674, 1078 and 1306 for other readings on reputation.
Turn to page 1078 for Friday's reading.

Topic
• • • •
REPUTATION

saw a young man dressed in a white robe sitting on the right side, and they were alarmed.

⁶"Don't be alarmed," he said. "You are looking for Jesus the Nazarene, who was crucified. He has risen! He is not here. See the place where they laid him. ⁷But go, tell his disciples and Peter, 'He is going ahead of you into Galilee. There you will see him, just as he told you.'"

⁸Trembling and bewildered, the women went out and fled from the tomb. They said nothing to anyone, because they were afraid.

[The earliest manuscripts and some other ancient witnesses do not have Mark 16:9–20.]

⁹When Jesus rose early on the first day of the week, he appeared first to Mary Magdalene, out of whom he had driven seven demons. ¹⁰She went and told those who had been with him and who were mourning and weeping. ¹¹When they heard that Jesus was alive and that she had seen him, they did not believe it.

¹²Afterward Jesus appeared in a different form to two of them while they were walking in the country. ¹³These returned and reported it to the rest; but they did not believe them either.

¹⁴Later Jesus appeared to the Eleven as they were eating; he rebuked them for their lack of faith and their stubborn refusal to believe those who had seen him after he had risen.

¹⁵He said to them, "Go into all the world and preach the good news to all creation. ¹⁶Whoever believes and is baptized will be saved, but whoever does not believe will be condemned. ¹⁷And these signs will accompany those who believe: In my name they will drive out demons; they will speak in new tongues; ¹⁸they will pick up snakes with their hands; and when they drink deadly poison, it will not hurt them at all; they will place their hands on sick people, and they will get well."

¹⁹After the Lord Jesus had spoken to them, he was taken up into heaven and he sat at the right hand of God. ²⁰Then the disciples went out and preached everywhere, and the Lord worked with them and confirmed his word by the signs that accompanied it.

LUKE

ADAM, the first man, brings sin into the whole human race through his disobedience. The book of Luke shows that Jesus, the perfect man, brings salvation for all people through his obedience to God. Luke shows that as a human being, Jesus faces everything that we will ever face, and wins. As the perfect man Jesus meets all the real needs of young and old, rich and poor, men, women and children. As you read this book, be sure that you have asked Jesus to meet your greatest need: to have your sins forgiven.

Outline of Contents

Introduction

1 Many have undertaken to draw up an account of the things that have been fulfilled[a] among us, ²just as they were handed down to us by those who from the first were eyewitnesses and servants of the word. ³Therefore, since I myself have carefully investigated everything from the beginning, it seemed good also to me to write an orderly account for you, most excellent Theophilus, ⁴so that you may know the certainty of the things you have been taught.

The Birth of John the Baptist Foretold

⁵In the time of Herod king of Judea there was a priest named Zechariah, who belonged to the priestly division of Abijah; his wife Elizabeth was also a descendant of Aaron. ⁶Both of them were upright in the sight of God, observing all the Lord's commandments and regulations blamelessly. ⁷But they had no children, because Elizabeth

---

a1 Or *been surely believed*

was barren; and they were both well along in years.

8Once when Zechariah's division was on duty and he was serving as priest before God, **9**he was chosen by lot, according to the custom of the priesthood, to go into the temple of the Lord and burn incense. **10**And when the time for the burning of incense came, all the assembled worshipers were praying outside.

11Then an angel of the Lord appeared to him, standing at the right side of the altar of incense. **12**When Zechariah saw him, he was startled and was gripped with fear. **13**But the angel said to him: "Do not be afraid, Zechariah; your prayer has been heard. Your wife Elizabeth will bear you a son, and you are to give him the name John. **14**He will be a joy and delight to you, and many will rejoice because of his birth, **15**for he will be great in the sight of the Lord. He is never to take wine or other fermented drink, and he will be filled with the Holy Spirit even from birth.*a* **16**Many of the people of Israel will he bring back to the Lord their God. **17**And he will go on before the Lord, in the spirit and power of Elijah, to turn the hearts of the fathers to their children and the disobedient to the wisdom of the righteous — to make ready a people prepared for the Lord."

18Zechariah asked the angel, "How can I be sure of this? I am an old man and my wife is well along in years."

19The angel answered, "I am Gabriel. I stand in the presence of God, and I have been sent to speak to you and to tell you this good news. **20**And now you will be silent and not able to speak until the day this happens, because you did not believe my words, which will come true at their proper time."

21Meanwhile, the people were waiting for Zechariah and wondering why he stayed so long in the temple. **22**When he came out, he could not speak to them. They realized he had seen a vision in the temple, for he kept making signs to them but remained unable to speak.

23When his time of service was completed, he returned home. **24**After this his wife Elizabeth became pregnant and for five months remained in seclusion. **25**"The Lord has done this for me," she said. "In these days he has shown his favor and taken away my disgrace among the people."

The Birth of Jesus Foretold

26In the sixth month, God sent the angel Gabriel to Nazareth, a town in Galilee, **27**to a virgin pledged to be married to a man named Joseph, a descendant of David. The virgin's name was Mary. **28**The angel went to her and said, "Greetings, you who are highly favored! The Lord is with you."

29Mary was greatly troubled at his words and wondered what kind of greeting this might be. **30**But the angel said to her, "Do not be afraid, Mary, you have found favor with God. **31**You will be with child and give birth to a son, and you are to give him the name Jesus. **32**He will be great and will be called the Son of the Most High. The Lord God will give him the throne of his father David, **33**and he will reign over the house of Jacob forever; his kingdom will never end."

34"How will this be," Mary asked the angel, "since I am a virgin?"

35The angel answered, "The Holy Spirit will come upon you, and the power of the Most High will overshadow you. So the holy one to be born will be called*b* the Son of God. **36**Even Elizabeth your relative is going to have a child in her old age, and she who was said to be barren is in her sixth month. **37**For nothing is impossible with God."

38"I am the Lord's servant," Mary answered. "May it be to me as you have said." Then the angel left her.

Mary Visits Elizabeth

39At that time Mary got ready and hurried to a town in the hill country of Judea, **40**where she entered Zechariah's home and greeted Elizabeth. **41**When Elizabeth heard Mary's greeting, the baby leaped in her womb, and Elizabeth was filled with the Holy Spirit. **42**In a loud voice she exclaimed: "Blessed are you among women, and blessed is the child you will bear! **43**But why am I so favored, that the mother of my Lord should come to me? **44**As soon as the sound of your greeting reached my ears, the baby in my womb leaped for joy. **45**Blessed is she who has believed that what the Lord has said to her will be accomplished!"

Mary's Song

46And Mary said:

"My soul glorifies the Lord
47 and my spirit rejoices in God my
        Savior,
48for he has been mindful
      of the humble state of his servant.

---

*a*15 Or *from his mother's womb*   *b*35 Or *So the child to be born will be called holy,*

RIGHTING A WRONG REPUTATION

A week ago, a scared friend confided to Anita, "I think I'm pregnant. Will you go with me to have a test done?" Wanting to show compassion, Anita agreed.

The next day the girls drove to a crisis pregnancy center. While they were waiting for the results of the test, Anita ran out to the car to get her purse.

As Anita was hurrying back toward the building, some classmates drove by and saw her going inside. Now the whole school is passing the rumor that Anita is pregnant! Poor Anita can't really tell the whole truth—she'd be ratting on her friend.

"My reputation is ruined! What can I do?"

Look It Up
••••

Consider a similar situation from the New Testament:

"This is how the birth of Jesus Christ came about: His mother Mary was pledged to be married to Joseph, but before they came together, she was found to be with child through the Holy Spirit. Because Joseph her husband was a righteous man and did not want to expose her to public disgrace, he had in mind to divorce her quietly" (Matthew 1:18–19).

They weren't married yet . . . but Mary was pregnant! Imagine the whispers, the stares, the juicy gossip.

But Mary didn't groan and complain. Knowing that she was innocent of any wrong, she willingly accepted her situation as being a part of God's plan.

Think It Through
••••

Be careful not to value your reputation more than you value God and his will.

In certain situations, do you worry more about looking good in front of others, or is your primary concern doing whatever pleases God?

Work It Out
••••

Should you be concerned about your reputation? Yes! Is reputation the most important thing in the world? No!

Write this saying on a card and carry it with you today:

"I will be more concerned with my character than with my reputation. My character is what I really am. My reputation is just what others think I am."

Nail It Down
••••

Read Luke 1:26–38 and consider again how Mary dealt with the possibility of a bad reputation.

Turn to pages 150, 674, 1074 and 1306 for other readings on reputation.
Turn to page 1080 for the weekend reading.

Topic
••••

REPUTATION

From now on all generations will call
  me blessed,
49 for the Mighty One has done great
  things for me —
  holy is his name.
50His mercy extends to those who fear
  him,
  from generation to generation.
51He has performed mighty deeds with
  his arm;
  he has scattered those who are proud
  in their inmost thoughts.
52He has brought down rulers from their
  thrones
  but has lifted up the humble.
53He has filled the hungry with good
  things
  but has sent the rich away empty.
54He has helped his servant Israel,
  remembering to be merciful
55to Abraham and his descendants
  forever,
  even as he said to our fathers."

56Mary stayed with Elizabeth for about three months and then returned home.

The Birth of John the Baptist

57When it was time for Elizabeth to have her baby, she gave birth to a son. **58**Her neighbors and relatives heard that the Lord had shown her great mercy, and they shared her joy.

59On the eighth day they came to circumcise the child, and they were going to name him after his father Zechariah, **60**but his mother spoke up and said, "No! He is to be called John."

61They said to her, "There is no one among your relatives who has that name."

62Then they made signs to his father, to find out what he would like to name the child. **63**He asked for a writing tablet, and to everyone's astonishment he wrote, "His name is John." **64**Immediately his mouth was opened and his tongue was loosed, and he began to speak, praising God. **65**The neighbors were all filled with awe, and throughout the hill country of Judea people were talking about all these things. **66**Everyone who heard this wondered about it, asking, "What then is this child going to be?" For the Lord's hand was with him.

Zechariah's Song

67His father Zechariah was filled with the Holy Spirit and prophesied:

68"Praise be to the Lord, the God of Israel,
  because he has come and has
  redeemed his people.
69He has raised up a horn^a of salvation
  for us
  in the house of his servant David
70(as he said through his holy prophets of
  long ago),
71salvation from our enemies
  and from the hand of all who hate
  us —
72to show mercy to our fathers
  and to remember his holy covenant,
73 the oath he swore to our father
  Abraham:
74to rescue us from the hand of our
  enemies,
  and to enable us to serve him without
  fear
75 in holiness and righteousness before
  him all our days.

76And you, my child, will be called a
  prophet of the Most High;
  for you will go on before the Lord to
  prepare the way for him,
77to give his people the knowledge of
  salvation
  through the forgiveness of their sins,
78because of the tender mercy of our God,
  by which the rising sun will come to
  us from heaven
79to shine on those living in darkness
  and in the shadow of death,
  to guide our feet into the path of
  peace."

80And the child grew and became strong in spirit; and he lived in the desert until he appeared publicly to Israel.

The Birth of Jesus

2 In those days Caesar Augustus issued a decree that a census should be taken of the entire Roman world. **2**(This was the first census that took place while Quirinius was governor of Syria.) **3**And everyone went to his own town to register.

4So Joseph also went up from the town of Nazareth in Galilee to Judea, to Bethlehem the town of David, because he belonged to the house and line of David. **5**He went there to register with Mary, who was pledged to be married to him and was expecting a child. **6**While they were there, the time came for the baby to be born, **7**and she gave birth to her firstborn, a son. She wrapped him in

---

^a69 *Horn* here symbolizes strength.

WHAT WILL YOU BE?

Work It Out
• • • •

"What do you want to be when you grow up?" Were you asked that question over and over again when you were young?

Think back over the years. How did you answer when you were three? When you were six? Ten? Thirteen? Now that you're older, you're probably asked the same question in a little different way: "What do you plan to do after you graduate?"

The question that was easy to answer when you were only eight is much more difficult today. In fact, it's one of the most difficult decisions you'll have to make.

You may change your mind ten times before you settle into a particular job or occupation. There's nothing wrong with that. Just don't make the decision alone. God has been in the business of directing people's lives for thousands of years. He cares about your satisfaction and contentment. Go to him for guidance.

Nail It Down
• • • •

In Luke 1:46–55 Mary reveals that she knew her purpose in life, her destiny.

Think It Through
• • • •

When making career decisions, keep one thing in mind: the most important thing is not *what* you do but *why* you do it. Is your primary concern to make money or gain honor or become famous? Or is your primary concern to serve Christ and others?

No matter what you decide to do in life—drive a bulldozer, sell insurance, fix cars, nurse the sick, sing in the opera, teach children—if serving others and serving Christ is your motivation, you'll succeed. And your life will ultimately be one of purpose and satisfaction.

Nail It Down
• • • •

Read Mary's testimony again in Luke 1:46–55. For further insight read Psalm 27.

Turn to pages 1042, 1382, 1403 and 1407 for other readings on destiny.
Turn to page 1082 for Monday's reading.

Topic
• • • •

DESTINY

cloths and placed him in a manger, because there was no room for them in the inn.

The Shepherds and the Angels

8And there were shepherds living out in the fields nearby, keeping watch over their flocks at night. **9**An angel of the Lord appeared to them, and the glory of the Lord shone around them, and they were terrified. **10**But the angel said to them, "Do not be afraid. I bring you good news of great joy that will be for all the people. **11**Today in the town of David a Savior has been born to you; he is Christ*a* the Lord. **12**This will be a sign to you: You will find a baby wrapped in cloths and lying in a manger."

13Suddenly a great company of the heavenly host appeared with the angel, praising God and saying,

14"Glory to God in the highest,
    and on earth peace to men on whom
        his favor rests."

15When the angels had left them and gone into heaven, the shepherds said to one another, "Let's go to Bethlehem and see this thing that has happened, which the Lord has told us about."

16So they hurried off and found Mary and Joseph, and the baby, who was lying in the manger. **17**When they had seen him, they spread the word concerning what had been told them about this child, **18**and all who heard it were amazed at what the shepherds said to them. **19**But Mary treasured up all these things and pondered them in her heart. **20**The shepherds returned, glorifying and praising God for all the things they had heard and seen, which were just as they had been told.

Jesus Presented in the Temple

21On the eighth day, when it was time to circumcise him, he was named Jesus, the name the angel had given him before he had been conceived.

22When the time of their purification according to the Law of Moses had been completed, Joseph and Mary took him to Jerusalem to present him to the Lord **23**(as it is written in the Law of the Lord, "Every firstborn male is to be consecrated to the Lord"*b*), **24**and to offer a sacrifice in keeping with what is said in the Law of the Lord: "a pair of doves or two young pigeons."*c*

25Now there was a man in Jerusalem called Simeon, who was righteous and devout. He was waiting for the consolation of Israel, and the Holy Spirit was upon him. **26**It had been revealed to him by the Holy Spirit that he would not die before he had seen the Lord's Christ. **27**Moved by the Spirit, he went into the temple courts. When the parents brought in the child Jesus to do for him what the custom of the Law required, **28**Simeon took him in his arms and praised God, saying:

29"Sovereign Lord, as you have promised,
    you now dismiss*d* your servant in
        peace.
30For my eyes have seen your salvation,
31   which you have prepared in the sight
        of all people,
32a light for revelation to the Gentiles
    and for glory to your people Israel."

33The child's father and mother marveled at what was said about him. **34**Then Simeon blessed them and said to Mary, his mother: "This child is destined to cause the falling and rising of many in Israel, and to be a sign that will be spoken against, **35**so that the thoughts of many hearts will be revealed. And a sword will pierce your own soul too."

36There was also a prophetess, Anna, the daughter of Phanuel, of the tribe of Asher. She was very old; she had lived with her husband seven years after her marriage, **37**and then was a widow until she was eighty-four.*e* She never left the temple but worshiped night and day, fasting and praying. **38**Coming up to them at that very moment, she gave thanks to God and spoke about the child to all who were looking forward to the redemption of Jerusalem.

39When Joseph and Mary had done everything required by the Law of the Lord, they returned to Galilee to their own town of Nazareth. **40**And the child grew and became strong; he was filled with wisdom, and the grace of God was upon him.

The Boy Jesus at the Temple

41Every year his parents went to Jerusalem for the Feast of the Passover. **42**When he was twelve years old, they went up to the Feast, according to the custom. **43**After the Feast was over, while his parents were returning home, the boy Jesus stayed behind in Jerusalem, but they were unaware of it.

a11 Or *Messiah.* "The Christ" (Greek) and "the Messiah" (Hebrew) both mean "the Anointed One"; also in verse 26.   *b23* Exodus 13:2,12   *c24* Lev. 12:8   *d29* Or *promised, / now dismiss*   *e37* Or *widow for eighty-four years*

FEELINGS ARE IRRELEVANT!

Predict the response in each situation:

Scene One: "Susan! I told you this morning to clean up your room. Why haven't you done it?"

"Sorry, Mom. I just haven't felt like it."

Scene Two: "Tucker, get in there for Raymond."

"Coach, I'd rather not. I'm feeling kind of scared."

Look It Up

Now check out these servants who were submissive to God, in spite of all the negative emotions they must have felt:

• Noah, after being told to build an ark and fill it with animals— "Noah did everything just as God commanded him" (Genesis 6:22).

• Joshua, when told to conquer the intimidating enemies in the land of Canaan—"As the LORD commanded his servant Moses, so Moses commanded Joshua, and Joshua did it; he left nothing undone of all that the LORD commanded Moses" (Joshua 11:15).

• Peter and the apostles, when told to quit preaching about Jesus . . . or else—"We must obey God rather than men!" (Acts 5:29).

Think It Through

Put yourself in the shoes of one of these characters. Do you think you would have been confused by God's commands? How about scared? Reluctant to obey?

It took Noah about a hundred years to finish the ark. Do you think he felt like getting up every day and working on the project? Remember, he was probably building miles from any water. Do you think he was ever tempted to say, "God, this makes no sense! Forget it!"? Think about the implications if he had disobeyed.

Work It Out

What command of God are you having the hardest time obeying? The decree to remain sexually pure (1 Thessalonians 4:3)? The charge to guard your mouth (Proverbs 13:3)? The mandate to be honest (Psalm 15:2–3)?

Make a list of five positive results of obedience in each one of those areas. Get together with a Christian friend sometime today and pray that you might become more obedient in every way. Then go out and obey, imitating Christ (John 14:31), as well as the role models we discussed today—no matter how you feel!

Nail It Down

Read about the obedience of Mary and Joseph in Luke 2:39–40.

Turn to pages 159, 281, 892, 1013 and 1156 for other readings on obedience.
Turn to page 1087 for Tuesday's reading.

Topic

44Thinking he was in their company, they traveled on for a day. Then they began looking for him among their relatives and friends. 45When they did not find him, they went back to Jerusalem to look for him. 46After three days they found him in the temple courts, sitting among the teachers, listening to them and asking them questions. 47Everyone who heard him was amazed at his understanding and his answers. 48When his parents saw him, they were astonished. His mother said to him, "Son, why have you treated us like this? Your father and I have been anxiously searching for you."

49"Why were you searching for me?" he asked. "Didn't you know I had to be in my Father's house?" 50But they did not understand what he was saying to them.

51Then he went down to Nazareth with them and was obedient to them. But his mother treasured all these things in her heart. 52And Jesus grew in wisdom and stature, and in favor with God and men.

John the Baptist Prepares the Way

3 In the fifteenth year of the reign of Tiberius Caesar—when Pontius Pilate was governor of Judea, Herod tetrarch of Galilee, his brother Philip tetrarch of Iturea and Traconitis, and Lysanias tetrarch of Abilene— 2during the high priesthood of Annas and Caiaphas, the word of God came to John son of Zechariah in the desert. 3He went into all the country around the Jordan, preaching a baptism of repentance for the forgiveness of sins. 4As is written in the book of the words of Isaiah the prophet:

"A voice of one calling in the desert,
'Prepare the way for the Lord,
    make straight paths for him.
5Every valley shall be filled in,
    every mountain and hill made low.
The crooked roads shall become
        straight,
    the rough ways smooth.
6And all mankind will see God's
        salvation.' "a

7John said to the crowds coming out to be baptized by him, "You brood of vipers! Who warned you to flee from the coming wrath? 8Produce fruit in keeping with repentance. And do not begin to say to yourselves, 'We have Abraham as our father.' For I tell you that out of these stones God can raise up children for Abraham. 9The ax is already at the root of the trees, and every tree that does not produce good fruit will be cut down and thrown into the fire."

10"What should we do then?" the crowd asked.

11John answered, "The man with two tunics should share with him who has none, and the one who has food should do the same."

12Tax collectors also came to be baptized. "Teacher," they asked, "what should we do?"

13"Don't collect any more than you are required to," he told them.

14Then some soldiers asked him, "And what should we do?"

He replied, "Don't extort money and don't accuse people falsely—be content with your pay."

15The people were waiting expectantly and were all wondering in their hearts if John might possibly be the Christ.b 16John answered them all, "I baptize you withc water. But one more powerful than I will come, the thongs of whose sandals I am not worthy to untie. He will baptize you with the Holy Spirit and with fire. 17His winnowing fork is in his hand to clear his threshing floor and to gather the wheat into his barn, but he will burn up the chaff with unquenchable fire." 18And with many other words John exhorted the people and preached the good news to them.

19But when John rebuked Herod the tetrarch because of Herodias, his brother's wife, and all the other evil things he had done, 20Herod added this to them all: He locked John up in prison.

The Baptism and Genealogy of Jesus

21When all the people were being baptized, Jesus was baptized too. And as he was praying, heaven was opened 22and the Holy Spirit descended on him in bodily form like a dove. And a voice came from heaven: "You are my Son, whom I love; with you I am well pleased."

23Now Jesus himself was about thirty years old when he began his ministry. He was the son, so it was thought, of Joseph,

the son of Heli, 24the son of Matthat,
    the son of Levi, the son of Melki,
    the son of Jannai, the son of Joseph,
25the son of Mattathias, the son of Amos,
    the son of Nahum, the son of Esli,
    the son of Naggai, 26the son of Maath,

a6 Isaiah 40:3-5   b15 Or Messiah   c16 Or in

the son of Mattathias, the son of Sem-
ein,
the son of Josech, the son of Joda,
[27]the son of Joanan, the son of Rhesa,
the son of Zerubbabel, the son of Shealtiel,
the son of Neri, [28]the son of Melki,
the son of Addi, the son of Cosam,
the son of Elmadam, the son of Er,
[29]the son of Joshua, the son of Eliezer,
the son of Jorim, the son of Matthat,
the son of Levi, [30]the son of Simeon,
the son of Judah, the son of Joseph,
the son of Jonam, the son of Eliakim,
[31]the son of Melea, the son of Menna,
the son of Mattatha, the son of Nathan,
the son of David, [32]the son of Jesse,
the son of Obed, the son of Boaz,
the son of Salmon,[a] the son of Nahshon,
[33]the son of Amminadab, the son of
Ram,[b]
the son of Hezron, the son of Perez,
the son of Judah, [34]the son of Jacob,
the son of Isaac, the son of Abraham,
the son of Terah, the son of Nahor,
[35]the son of Serug, the son of Reu,
the son of Peleg, the son of Eber,
the son of Shelah, [36]the son of Cainan,
the son of Arphaxad, the son of Shem,
the son of Noah, the son of Lamech,
[37]the son of Methuselah, the son of
Enoch,
the son of Jared, the son of Mahalalel,
the son of Kenan, [38]the son of Enosh,
the son of Seth, the son of Adam,
the son of God.

The Temptation of Jesus

4 Jesus, full of the Holy Spirit, returned
from the Jordan and was led by the
Spirit in the desert, [2]where for forty days he
was tempted by the devil. He ate nothing
during those days, and at the end of them he
was hungry.

[3]The devil said to him, "If you are the Son
of God, tell this stone to become bread."

[4]Jesus answered, "It is written: 'Man does
not live on bread alone.'[c]"

[5]The devil led him up to a high place and
showed him in an instant all the kingdoms
of the world. [6]And he said to him, "I will give
you all their authority and splendor, for it
has been given to me, and I can give it to

anyone I want to. [7]So if you worship me, it
will all be yours."

[8]Jesus answered, "It is written: 'Worship
the Lord your God and serve him only.'[d]"

[9]The devil led him to Jerusalem and had
him stand on the highest point of the temple. "If you are the Son of God," he said,
"throw yourself down from here. [10]For it is
written:

" 'He will command his angels
      concerning you
   to guard you carefully;
[11]they will lift you up in their hands,
   so that you will not strike your foot
      against a stone.'[e]"

[12]Jesus answered, "It says: 'Do not put the
Lord your God to the test.'[f]"

[13]When the devil had finished all this
tempting, he left him until an opportune
time.

Jesus Rejected at Nazareth

[14]Jesus returned to Galilee in the power of
the Spirit, and news about him spread
through the whole countryside. [15]He taught
in their synagogues, and everyone praised
him.

[16]He went to Nazareth, where he had
been brought up, and on the Sabbath day he
went into the synagogue, as was his custom.
And he stood up to read. [17]The scroll of the
prophet Isaiah was handed to him. Unroll-
ing it, he found the place where it is written:

[18]"The Spirit of the Lord is on me,
   because he has anointed me
   to preach good news to the poor.
He has sent me to proclaim freedom for
      the prisoners
   and recovery of sight for the blind,
to release the oppressed,
[19]   to proclaim the year of the Lord's
      favor."[g]

[20]Then he rolled up the scroll, gave it back
to the attendant and sat down. The eyes of
everyone in the synagogue were fastened on
him, [21]and he began by saying to them, "Today this scripture is fulfilled in your hearing."

[22]All spoke well of him and were amazed
at the gracious words that came from his
lips. "Isn't this Joseph's son?" they asked.

[23]Jesus said to them, "Surely you will
quote this proverb to me: 'Physician, heal

---

[a]32 Some early manuscripts *Sala*   [b]33 Some manuscripts *Amminadab, the son of Admin, the son of Arni*;
other manuscripts vary widely.   [c]4 Deut. 8:3   [d]8 Deut. 6:13   [e]11 Psalm 91:11,12   [f]12 Deut. 6:16
[g]19 Isaiah 61:1,2

yourself! Do here in your hometown what we have heard that you did in Capernaum.' "

24"I tell you the truth," he continued, "no prophet is accepted in his hometown. **25**I assure you that there were many widows in Israel in Elijah's time, when the sky was shut for three and a half years and there was a severe famine throughout the land. **26**Yet Elijah was not sent to any of them, but to a widow in Zarephath in the region of Sidon. **27**And there were many in Israel with leprosy*ª* in the time of Elisha the prophet, yet not one of them was cleansed—only Naaman the Syrian."

28All the people in the synagogue were furious when they heard this. **29**They got up, drove him out of the town, and took him to the brow of the hill on which the town was built, in order to throw him down the cliff. **30**But he walked right through the crowd and went on his way.

Jesus Drives Out an Evil Spirit

31Then he went down to Capernaum, a town in Galilee, and on the Sabbath began to teach the people. **32**They were amazed at his teaching, because his message had authority.

33In the synagogue there was a man possessed by a demon, an evil*ᵇ* spirit. He cried out at the top of his voice, **34**"Ha! What do you want with us, Jesus of Nazareth? Have you come to destroy us? I know who you are—the Holy One of God!"

35"Be quiet!" Jesus said sternly. "Come out of him!" Then the demon threw the man down before them all and came out without injuring him.

36All the people were amazed and said to each other, "What is this teaching? With authority and power he gives orders to evil spirits and they come out!" **37**And the news about him spread throughout the surrounding area.

Jesus Heals Many

38Jesus left the synagogue and went to the home of Simon. Now Simon's mother-in-law was suffering from a high fever, and they asked Jesus to help her. **39**So he bent over her and rebuked the fever, and it left her. She got up at once and began to wait on them.

40When the sun was setting, the people brought to Jesus all who had various kinds of sickness, and laying his hands on each one, he healed them. **41**Moreover, demons came out of many people, shouting, "You are the Son of God!" But he rebuked them and would not allow them to speak, because they knew he was the Christ.*ᶜ*

42At daybreak Jesus went out to a solitary place. The people were looking for him and when they came to where he was, they tried to keep him from leaving them. **43**But he said, "I must preach the good news of the kingdom of God to the other towns also, because that is why I was sent." **44**And he kept on preaching in the synagogues of Judea.*ᵈ*

The Calling of the First Disciples

5 One day as Jesus was standing by the Lake of Gennesaret,*ᵉ* with the people crowding around him and listening to the word of God, **2**he saw at the water's edge two boats, left there by the fishermen, who were washing their nets. **3**He got into one of the boats, the one belonging to Simon, and asked him to put out a little from shore. Then he sat down and taught the people from the boat.

4When he had finished speaking, he said to Simon, "Put out into deep water, and let down*ᶠ* the nets for a catch."

5Simon answered, "Master, we've worked hard all night and haven't caught anything. But because you say so, I will let down the nets."

6When they had done so, they caught such a large number of fish that their nets began to break. **7**So they signaled their partners in the other boat to come and help them, and they came and filled both boats so full that they began to sink.

8When Simon Peter saw this, he fell at Jesus' knees and said, "Go away from me, Lord; I am a sinful man!" **9**For he and all his companions were astonished at the catch of fish they had taken, **10**and so were James and John, the sons of Zebedee, Simon's partners.

Then Jesus said to Simon, "Don't be afraid; from now on you will catch men." **11**So they pulled their boats up on shore, left everything and followed him.

The Man With Leprosy

12While Jesus was in one of the towns, a man came along who was covered with leprosy.*ª* When he saw Jesus, he fell with his

---

ª27,12 The Greek word was used for various diseases affecting the skin—not necessarily leprosy.   *ᵇ33* Greek *unclean*; also in verse 36   *ᶜ41* Or *Messiah*   *ᵈ44* Or *the land of the Jews*; some manuscripts *Galilee*
ᵉ1 That is, Sea of Galilee   *ᶠ4* The Greek verb is plural.

face to the ground and begged him, "Lord, if you are willing, you can make me clean."
[13]Jesus reached out his hand and touched the man. "I am willing," he said. "Be clean!" And immediately the leprosy left him. [14]Then Jesus ordered him, "Don't tell anyone, but go, show yourself to the priest and offer the sacrifices that Moses commanded for your cleansing, as a testimony to them." [15]Yet the news about him spread all the more, so that crowds of people came to hear him and to be healed of their sicknesses. [16]But Jesus often withdrew to lonely places and prayed.

Jesus Heals a Paralytic

[17]One day as he was teaching, Pharisees and teachers of the law, who had come from every village of Galilee and from Judea and Jerusalem, were sitting there. And the power of the Lord was present for him to heal the sick. [18]Some men came carrying a paralytic on a mat and tried to take him into the house to lay him before Jesus. [19]When they could not find a way to do this because of the crowd, they went up on the roof and lowered him on his mat through the tiles into the middle of the crowd, right in front of Jesus.
[20]When Jesus saw their faith, he said, "Friend, your sins are forgiven."
[21]The Pharisees and the teachers of the law began thinking to themselves, "Who is this fellow who speaks blasphemy? Who can forgive sins but God alone?"
[22]Jesus knew what they were thinking and asked, "Why are you thinking these things in your hearts? [23]Which is easier: to say, 'Your sins are forgiven,' or to say, 'Get up and walk'? [24]But that you may know that the Son of Man has authority on earth to forgive sins. . . ." He said to the paralyzed man, "I tell you, get up, take your mat and go home." [25]Immediately he stood up in front of them, took what he had been lying on and went home praising God. [26]Everyone was amazed and gave praise to God. They were filled with awe and said, "We have seen remarkable things today."

The Calling of Levi

[27]After this, Jesus went out and saw a tax collector by the name of Levi sitting at his tax booth. "Follow me," Jesus said to him, [28]and Levi got up, left everything and followed him.
[29]Then Levi held a great banquet for Jesus at his house, and a large crowd of tax collectors and others were eating with them. [30]But the Pharisees and the teachers of the law who belonged to their sect complained to his disciples, "Why do you eat and drink with tax collectors and 'sinners'?"
[31]Jesus answered them, "It is not the healthy who need a doctor, but the sick. [32]I have not come to call the righteous, but sinners to repentance."

Jesus Questioned About Fasting

[33]They said to him, "John's disciples often fast and pray, and so do the disciples of the Pharisees, but yours go on eating and drinking."
[34]Jesus answered, "Can you make the guests of the bridegroom fast while he is with them? [35]But the time will come when the bridegroom will be taken from them; in those days they will fast."
[36]He told them this parable: "No one tears a patch from a new garment and sews it on an old one. If he does, he will have torn the new garment, and the patch from the new will not match the old. [37]And no one pours new wine into old wineskins. If he does, the new wine will burst the skins, the wine will run out and the wineskins will be ruined. [38]No, new wine must be poured into new wineskins. [39]And no one after drinking old wine wants the new, for he says, 'The old is better.' "

Lord of the Sabbath

6 One Sabbath Jesus was going through the grainfields, and his disciples began to pick some heads of grain, rub them in their hands and eat the kernels. [2]Some of the Pharisees asked, "Why are you doing what is unlawful on the Sabbath?"
[3]Jesus answered them, "Have you never read what David did when he and his companions were hungry? [4]He entered the house of God, and taking the consecrated bread, he ate what is lawful only for priests to eat. And he also gave some to his companions." [5]Then Jesus said to them, "The Son of Man is Lord of the Sabbath."
[6]On another Sabbath he went into the synagogue and was teaching, and a man was there whose right hand was shriveled. [7]The Pharisees and the teachers of the law were looking for a reason to accuse Jesus, so they watched him closely to see if he would heal on the Sabbath. [8]But Jesus knew what they were thinking and said to the man with the shriveled hand, "Get up and stand in front of everyone." So he got up and stood there.
[9]Then Jesus said to them, "I ask you,

THE DEAD END OF DISCOURAGEMENT

Humming down the narrow road, Shay is determined not to get off track in his Christian life this school year.

Sometimes, however, the obstacles along the way are tough. Like earlier this week when he flunked his first big algebra test—despite studying till 1:00 A.M. the night before! And like yesterday when he missed his wrestling weight limit—despite starving himself and exercising like a maniac for three weeks!

Look It Up

For a great lesson in how to avoid the dead end of discouragement, consider the Old Testament book of Nehemiah. (Nehemiah was the man commissioned to oversee the rebuilding of the walls of Jerusalem in 444 B.C.)

What Nehemiah and his workers faced was enough to discourage anyone: ridicule (Nehemiah 4:1–3), violent plots (Nehemiah 4:7–8) and physical exhaustion (Nehemiah 4:10). But by focusing on the power and ability of God (Nehemiah 4:9,14) rather than on the size of their problems, and through careful, steady work (Nehemiah 4:15–21), the Jews experienced victory.

"So the wall was completed . . . in fifty-two days. When all our enemies heard about this . . . they realized that this work had been done with the help of our God" (Nehemiah 6:15–16).

Think It Through

Usually it's not too difficult to spot a discouraged individual. He or she looks just like an old, worn-out, broken-down car on the side of the road, hood raised weakly in surrender.

Does that description fit you today? Do you find yourself out of commission on the dead end of discouragement?

Work It Out

Without looking too hard, you could find numerous reasons to get discouraged any day of the week. But before you go that route, remember the example of Nehemiah:

1. Pray about your situation.
2. Concentrate on God, not the obstacles you face.
3. Do what you can do (drawing upon God's strength).

There's no guarantee, but those are excellent directions for avoiding the dead end of discouragement.

Nail It Down

Read about some other people who overcame a potentially discouraging situation in Luke 5:18–19.

Turn to pages 486, 1056, 1248 and 1367 for other readings on obstacles.
Turn to page 1089 for Wednesday's reading.

Topic

OBSTACLES

which is lawful on the Sabbath: to do good or to do evil, to save life or to destroy it?" [10]He looked around at them all, and then said to the man, "Stretch out your hand." He did so, and his hand was completely restored. [11]But they were furious and began to discuss with one another what they might do to Jesus.

The Twelve Apostles

[12]One of those days Jesus went out to a mountainside to pray, and spent the night praying to God. [13]When morning came, he called his disciples to him and chose twelve of them, whom he also designated apostles: [14]Simon (whom he named Peter), his brother Andrew, James, John, Philip, Bartholomew, [15]Matthew, Thomas, James son of Alphaeus, Simon who was called the Zealot, [16]Judas son of James, and Judas Iscariot, who became a traitor.

Blessings and Woes

[17]He went down with them and stood on a level place. A large crowd of his disciples was there and a great number of people from all over Judea, from Jerusalem, and from the coast of Tyre and Sidon, [18]who had come to hear him and to be healed of their diseases. Those troubled by evil[a] spirits were cured, [19]and the people all tried to touch him, because power was coming from him and healing them all.

[20]Looking at his disciples, he said:

"Blessed are you who are poor,
　for yours is the kingdom of God.
[21]Blessed are you who hunger now,
　for you will be satisfied.
Blessed are you who weep now,
　for you will laugh.
[22]Blessed are you when men hate you,
　when they exclude you and insult you
　and reject your name as evil,
　　because of the Son of Man.

[23]"Rejoice in that day and leap for joy, because great is your reward in heaven. For that is how their fathers treated the prophets.

[24]"But woe to you who are rich,
　for you have already received your
　　comfort.
[25]Woe to you who are well fed now,
　for you will go hungry.
Woe to you who laugh now,
　for you will mourn and weep.

[26]Woe to you when all men speak well of
　you,
　for that is how their fathers treated
　　the false prophets.

Love for Enemies

[27]"But I tell you who hear me: Love your enemies, do good to those who hate you, [28]bless those who curse you, pray for those who mistreat you. [29]If someone strikes you on one cheek, turn to him the other also. If someone takes your cloak, do not stop him from taking your tunic. [30]Give to everyone who asks you, and if anyone takes what belongs to you, do not demand it back. [31]Do to others as you would have them do to you.

[32]"If you love those who love you, what credit is that to you? Even 'sinners' love those who love them. [33]And if you do good to those who are good to you, what credit is that to you? Even 'sinners' do that. [34]And if you lend to those from whom you expect repayment, what credit is that to you? Even 'sinners' lend to 'sinners,' expecting to be repaid in full. [35]But love your enemies, do good to them, and lend to them without expecting to get anything back. Then your reward will be great, and you will be sons of the Most High, because he is kind to the ungrateful and wicked. [36]Be merciful, just as your Father is merciful.

Judging Others

[37]"Do not judge, and you will not be judged. Do not condemn, and you will not be condemned. Forgive, and you will be forgiven. [38]Give, and it will be given to you. A good measure, pressed down, shaken together and running over, will be poured into your lap. For with the measure you use, it will be measured to you."

[39]He also told them this parable: "Can a blind man lead a blind man? Will they not both fall into a pit? [40]A student is not above his teacher, but everyone who is fully trained will be like his teacher.

[41]"Why do you look at the speck of sawdust in your brother's eye and pay no attention to the plank in your own eye? [42]How can you say to your brother, 'Brother, let me take the speck out of your eye,' when you yourself fail to see the plank in your own eye? You hypocrite, first take the plank out of your eye, and then you will see clearly to remove the speck from your brother's eye.

[a]18 Greek unclean

BE MERCIFUL–NOT MERCILESS!

•••

Nearly three months after the Davises, a black family, moved into an all-white neighborhood, the police arrested three men and charged them with spray painting racial slurs on the Davises' garage. The youngest of the suspects eventually signed a confession admitting that they had also poisoned the Davises' dog.

But then an amazing thing happened. Mr. Davis refused to press charges.

"That's not necessary. Those men had my forgiveness long ago. I just want to live in peace here with my family. Please, that's all I want."

Look It Up
••••

Mr. Davis is unusual. Most people in his situation would be screaming for justice. But the Bible gently reminds us of a more tolerant way.

1. Our heavenly Father is merciful (Micah 7:18).

2. We are to be like our heavenly Father. "Be imitators of God, therefore, as dearly loved children" (Ephesians 5:1).

3. Therefore, we must be merciful to others. "Be merciful, just as your Father is merciful" (Luke 6:36).

Think It Through
••••

Mercy means loving and accepting others even when they don't deserve it. It means choosing to overlook their shortcomings and differences.

You can't be prejudiced or bigoted and also be merciful. Like oil and water, intolerance and mercy simply do not mix.

Are you a merciful person? Could you have done what Mr. Davis did? Would you have done that?

If God suddenly refused to deal with you mercifully, where would you be?

Work It Out
••••

Intolerance is intolerable for believers. Instead, practice mercy today.

• Forgive that family member who recently hurt your feelings.

• Resist the urge to strike back at that classmate who has it in for you.

• Cancel a debt (financial or emotional) that someone owes you.

• Refuse to answer back when someone gossips about you.

• Show compassion to someone who is trapped in sin. Don't turn away from such people! On the contrary, let them see the love of Christ through you.

Nail It Down
••••

Think about the implications of Luke 6:27–35.

Turn to pages 1132, 1182 and 1274 for other readings on intolerance.
Turn to page 1095 for Thursday's reading.

Topic
••••

INTOLERANCE

A Tree and Its Fruit

43"No good tree bears bad fruit, nor does a bad tree bear good fruit. **44**Each tree is recognized by its own fruit. People do not pick figs from thornbushes, or grapes from briers. **45**The good man brings good things out of the good stored up in his heart, and the evil man brings evil things out of the evil stored up in his heart. For out of the overflow of his heart his mouth speaks.

The Wise and Foolish Builders

46"Why do you call me, 'Lord, Lord,' and do not do what I say? **47**I will show you what he is like who comes to me and hears my words and puts them into practice. **48**He is like a man building a house, who dug down deep and laid the foundation on rock. When a flood came, the torrent struck that house but could not shake it, because it was well built. **49**But the one who hears my words and does not put them into practice is like a man who built a house on the ground without a foundation. The moment the torrent struck that house, it collapsed and its destruction was complete."

The Faith of the Centurion

7 When Jesus had finished saying all this in the hearing of the people, he entered Capernaum. **2**There a centurion's servant, whom his master valued highly, was sick and about to die. **3**The centurion heard of Jesus and sent some elders of the Jews to him, asking him to come and heal his servant. **4**When they came to Jesus, they pleaded earnestly with him, "This man deserves to have you do this, **5**because he loves our nation and has built our synagogue." **6**So Jesus went with them.

He was not far from the house when the centurion sent friends to say to him: "Lord, don't trouble yourself, for I do not deserve to have you come under my roof. **7**That is why I did not even consider myself worthy to come to you. But say the word, and my servant will be healed. **8**For I myself am a man under authority, with soldiers under me. I tell this one, 'Go,' and he goes; and that one, 'Come,' and he comes. I say to my servant, 'Do this,' and he does it."

9When Jesus heard this, he was amazed at him, and turning to the crowd following him, he said, "I tell you, I have not found such great faith even in Israel." **10**Then the

men who had been sent returned to the house and found the servant well.

Jesus Raises a Widow's Son

11Soon afterward, Jesus went to a town called Nain, and his disciples and a large crowd went along with him. **12**As he approached the town gate, a dead person was being carried out—the only son of his mother, and she was a widow. And a large crowd from the town was with her. **13**When the Lord saw her, his heart went out to her and he said, "Don't cry."

14Then he went up and touched the coffin, and those carrying it stood still. He said, "Young man, I say to you, get up!" **15**The dead man sat up and began to talk, and Jesus gave him back to his mother.

16They were all filled with awe and praised God. "A great prophet has appeared among us," they said. "God has come to help his people." **17**This news about Jesus spread throughout Judea*a* and the surrounding country.

Jesus and John the Baptist

18John's disciples told him about all these things. Calling two of them, **19**he sent them to the Lord to ask, "Are you the one who was to come, or should we expect someone else?"

20When the men came to Jesus, they said, "John the Baptist sent us to you to ask, 'Are you the one who was to come, or should we expect someone else?'"

21At that very time Jesus cured many who had diseases, sicknesses and evil spirits, and gave sight to many who were blind. **22**So he replied to the messengers, "Go back and report to John what you have seen and heard: The blind receive sight, the lame walk, those who have leprosy*b* are cured, the deaf hear, the dead are raised, and the good news is preached to the poor. **23**Blessed is the man who does not fall away on account of me."

24After John's messengers left, Jesus began to speak to the crowd about John: "What did you go out into the desert to see? A reed swayed by the wind? **25**If not, what did you go out to see? A man dressed in fine clothes? No, those who wear expensive clothes and indulge in luxury are in palaces. **26**But what did you go out to see? A prophet? Yes, I tell you, and more than a prophet. **27**This is the one about whom it is written:

*a*17 Or *the land of the Jews*   *b*22 The Greek word was used for various diseases affecting the skin—not necessarily leprosy.

" 'I will send my messenger ahead of
        you,
    who will prepare your way before
        you.' *a*

28I tell you, among those born of women
there is no one greater than John; yet the
one who is least in the kingdom of God is
greater than he."

29(All the people, even the tax collectors,
when they heard Jesus' words, acknowledged that God's way was right, because
they had been baptized by John. **30**But the
Pharisees and experts in the law rejected
God's purpose for themselves, because they
had not been baptized by John.)

31"To what, then, can I compare the people of this generation? What are they like?
32They are like children sitting in the marketplace and calling out to each other:

    " 'We played the flute for you,
        and you did not dance;
    we sang a dirge,
        and you did not cry.'

33For John the Baptist came neither eating
bread nor drinking wine, and you say, 'He
has a demon.' **34**The Son of Man came eating and drinking, and you say, 'Here is a
glutton and a drunkard, a friend of tax collectors and "sinners." ' **35**But wisdom is
proved right by all her children."

Jesus Anointed by a Sinful Woman

36Now one of the Pharisees invited Jesus
to have dinner with him, so he went to the
Pharisee's house and reclined at the table.
37When a woman who had lived a sinful life
in that town learned that Jesus was eating at
the Pharisee's house, she brought an alabaster jar of perfume, **38**and as she stood behind him at his feet weeping, she began to
wet his feet with her tears. Then she wiped
them with her hair, kissed them and poured
perfume on them.

39When the Pharisee who had invited him
saw this, he said to himself, "If this man
were a prophet, he would know who is
touching him and what kind of woman she
is — that she is a sinner."

40Jesus answered him, "Simon, I have
something to tell you."

"Tell me, teacher," he said.

41"Two men owed money to a certain
moneylender. One owed him five hundred
denarii, *b* and the other fifty. **42**Neither of
them had the money to pay him back, so he

canceled the debts of both. Now which of
them will love him more?"

43Simon replied, "I suppose the one who
had the bigger debt canceled."

"You have judged correctly," Jesus said.

44Then he turned toward the woman and
said to Simon, "Do you see this woman? I
came into your house. You did not give me
any water for my feet, but she wet my feet
with her tears and wiped them with her hair.
45You did not give me a kiss, but this woman, from the time I entered, has not stopped
kissing my feet. **46**You did not put oil on my
head, but she has poured perfume on my
feet. **47**Therefore, I tell you, her many sins
have been forgiven — for she loved much.
But he who has been forgiven little loves little."

48Then Jesus said to her, "Your sins are
forgiven."

49The other guests began to say among
themselves, "Who is this who even forgives
sins?"

50Jesus said to the woman, "Your faith has
saved you; go in peace."

The Parable of the Sower

8 After this, Jesus traveled about from
one town and village to another, proclaiming the good news of the kingdom of
God. The Twelve were with him, **2**and also
some women who had been cured of evil
spirits and diseases: Mary (called Magdalene) from whom seven demons had come
out; **3**Joanna the wife of Cuza, the manager
of Herod's household; Susanna; and many
others. These women were helping to support them out of their own means.

4While a large crowd was gathering and
people were coming to Jesus from town after town, he told this parable: **5**"A farmer
went out to sow his seed. As he was scattering the seed, some fell along the path; it was
trampled on, and the birds of the air ate it
up. **6**Some fell on rock, and when it came
up, the plants withered because they had no
moisture. **7**Other seed fell among thorns,
which grew up with it and choked the
plants. **8**Still other seed fell on good soil. It
came up and yielded a crop, a hundred
times more than was sown."

When he said this, he called out, "He who
has ears to hear, let him hear."

9His disciples asked him what this parable meant. **10**He said, "The knowledge of the
secrets of the kingdom of God has been giv-

---

a27 Mal. 3:1   *b41* A denarius was a coin worth about a day's wages.

en to you, but to others I speak in parables, so that,

" 'though seeing, they may not see;
    though hearing, they may not
        understand.'*a*

11"This is the meaning of the parable: The seed is the word of God. **12**Those along the path are the ones who hear, and then the devil comes and takes away the word from their hearts, so that they may not believe and be saved. **13**Those on the rock are the ones who receive the word with joy when they hear it, but they have no root. They believe for a while, but in the time of testing they fall away. **14**The seed that fell among thorns stands for those who hear, but as they go on their way they are choked by life's worries, riches and pleasures, and they do not mature. **15**But the seed on good soil stands for those with a noble and good heart, who hear the word, retain it, and by persevering produce a crop.

A Lamp on a Stand

16"No one lights a lamp and hides it in a jar or puts it under a bed. Instead, he puts it on a stand, so that those who come in can see the light. **17**For there is nothing hidden that will not be disclosed, and nothing concealed that will not be known or brought out into the open. **18**Therefore consider carefully how you listen. Whoever has will be given more; whoever does not have, even what he thinks he has will be taken from him."

Jesus' Mother and Brothers

19Now Jesus' mother and brothers came to see him, but they were not able to get near him because of the crowd. **20**Someone told him, "Your mother and brothers are standing outside, wanting to see you."

21He replied, "My mother and brothers are those who hear God's word and put it into practice."

Jesus Calms the Storm

22One day Jesus said to his disciples, "Let's go over to the other side of the lake." So they got into a boat and set out. **23**As they sailed, he fell asleep. A squall came down on the lake, so that the boat was being swamped, and they were in great danger.

24The disciples went and woke him, saying, "Master, Master, we're going to drown!"

He got up and rebuked the wind and the raging waters; the storm subsided, and all was calm. **25**"Where is your faith?" he asked his disciples.

In fear and amazement they asked one another, "Who is this? He commands even the winds and the water, and they obey him."

The Healing of a Demon-possessed Man

26They sailed to the region of the Gerasenes,*b* which is across the lake from Galilee. **27**When Jesus stepped ashore, he was met by a demon-possessed man from the town. For a long time this man had not worn clothes or lived in a house, but had lived in the tombs. **28**When he saw Jesus, he cried out and fell at his feet, shouting at the top of his voice, "What do you want with me, Jesus, Son of the Most High God? I beg you, don't torture me!" **29**For Jesus had commanded the evil*c* spirit to come out of the man. Many times it had seized him, and though he was chained hand and foot and kept under guard, he had broken his chains and had been driven by the demon into solitary places.

30Jesus asked him, "What is your name?"

"Legion," he replied, because many demons had gone into him. **31**And they begged him repeatedly not to order them to go into the Abyss.

32A large herd of pigs was feeding there on the hillside. The demons begged Jesus to let them go into them, and he gave them permission. **33**When the demons came out of the man, they went into the pigs, and the herd rushed down the steep bank into the lake and was drowned.

34When those tending the pigs saw what had happened, they ran off and reported this in the town and countryside, **35**and the people went out to see what had happened. When they came to Jesus, they found the man from whom the demons had gone out, sitting at Jesus' feet, dressed and in his right mind; and they were afraid. **36**Those who had seen it told the people how the demon-possessed man had been cured. **37**Then all the people of the region of the Gerasenes asked Jesus to leave them, because they were overcome with fear. So he got into the boat and left.

38The man from whom the demons had gone out begged to go with him, but Jesus sent him away, saying, **39**"Return home and tell how much God has done for you." So the

---

*a*10 Isaiah 6:9   *b*26 Some manuscripts *Gadarenes*; other manuscripts *Gergesenes*; also in verse 37
*c*29 Greek *unclean*

man went away and told all over town how much Jesus had done for him.

A Dead Girl and a Sick Woman

40Now when Jesus returned, a crowd welcomed him, for they were all expecting him. **41**Then a man named Jairus, a ruler of the synagogue, came and fell at Jesus' feet, pleading with him to come to his house **42**because his only daughter, a girl of about twelve, was dying.

As Jesus was on his way, the crowds almost crushed him. **43**And a woman was there who had been subject to bleeding for twelve years,*ª* but no one could heal her. **44**She came up behind him and touched the edge of his cloak, and immediately her bleeding stopped.

45"Who touched me?" Jesus asked.

When they all denied it, Peter said, "Master, the people are crowding and pressing against you."

46But Jesus said, "Someone touched me; I know that power has gone out from me."

47Then the woman, seeing that she could not go unnoticed, came trembling and fell at his feet. In the presence of all the people, she told why she had touched him and how she had been instantly healed. **48**Then he said to her, "Daughter, your faith has healed you. Go in peace."

49While Jesus was still speaking, someone came from the house of Jairus, the synagogue ruler. "Your daughter is dead," he said. "Don't bother the teacher any more."

50Hearing this, Jesus said to Jairus, "Don't be afraid; just believe, and she will be healed."

51When he arrived at the house of Jairus, he did not let anyone go in with him except Peter, John and James, and the child's father and mother. **52**Meanwhile, all the people were wailing and mourning for her. "Stop wailing," Jesus said. "She is not dead but asleep."

53They laughed at him, knowing that she was dead. **54**But he took her by the hand and said, "My child, get up!" **55**Her spirit returned, and at once she stood up. Then Jesus told them to give her something to eat. **56**Her parents were astonished, but he ordered them not to tell anyone what had happened.

Jesus Sends Out the Twelve

9 When Jesus had called the Twelve together, he gave them power and authority to drive out all demons and to cure diseases, **2**and he sent them out to preach the kingdom of God and to heal the sick. **3**He told them: "Take nothing for the journey — no staff, no bag, no bread, no money, no extra tunic. **4**Whatever house you enter, stay there until you leave that town. **5**If people do not welcome you, shake the dust off your feet when you leave their town, as a testimony against them." **6**So they set out and went from village to village, preaching the gospel and healing people everywhere.

7Now Herod the tetrarch heard about all that was going on. And he was perplexed, because some were saying that John had been raised from the dead, **8**others that Elijah had appeared, and still others that one of the prophets of long ago had come back to life. **9**But Herod said, "I beheaded John. Who, then, is this I hear such things about?" And he tried to see him.

Jesus Feeds the Five Thousand

10When the apostles returned, they reported to Jesus what they had done. Then he took them with him and they withdrew by themselves to a town called Bethsaida, **11**but the crowds learned about it and followed him. He welcomed them and spoke to them about the kingdom of God, and healed those who needed healing.

12Late in the afternoon the Twelve came to him and said, "Send the crowd away so they can go to the surrounding villages and countryside and find food and lodging, because we are in a remote place here."

13He replied, "You give them something to eat."

They answered, "We have only five loaves of bread and two fish — unless we go and buy food for all this crowd." **14**(About five thousand men were there.)

But he said to his disciples, "Have them sit down in groups of about fifty each." **15**The disciples did so, and everybody sat down. **16**Taking the five loaves and the two fish and looking up to heaven, he gave thanks and broke them. Then he gave them to the disciples to set before the people. **17**They all ate and were satisfied, and the disciples picked up twelve basketfuls of broken pieces that were left over.

Peter's Confession of Christ

18Once when Jesus was praying in private and his disciples were with him, he asked them, "Who do the crowds say I am?"

ª43 Many manuscripts *years, and she had spent all she had on doctors*

¹⁹They replied, "Some say John the Baptist; others say Elijah; and still others, that one of the prophets of long ago has come back to life."

²⁰"But what about you?" he asked. "Who do you say I am?"

Peter answered, "The Christ*a* of God."

²¹Jesus strictly warned them not to tell this to anyone. ²²And he said, "The Son of Man must suffer many things and be rejected by the elders, chief priests and teachers of the law, and he must be killed and on the third day be raised to life."

²³Then he said to them all: "If anyone would come after me, he must deny himself and take up his cross daily and follow me. ²⁴For whoever wants to save his life will lose it, but whoever loses his life for me will save it. ²⁵What good is it for a man to gain the whole world, and yet lose or forfeit his very self? ²⁶If anyone is ashamed of me and my words, the Son of Man will be ashamed of him when he comes in his glory and in the glory of the Father and of the holy angels. ²⁷I tell you the truth, some who are standing here will not taste death before they see the kingdom of God."

The Transfiguration

²⁸About eight days after Jesus said this, he took Peter, John and James with him and went up onto a mountain to pray. ²⁹As he was praying, the appearance of his face changed, and his clothes became as bright as a flash of lightning. ³⁰Two men, Moses and Elijah, ³¹appeared in glorious splendor, talking with Jesus. They spoke about his departure, which he was about to bring to fulfillment at Jerusalem. ³²Peter and his companions were very sleepy, but when they became fully awake, they saw his glory and the two men standing with him. ³³As the men were leaving Jesus, Peter said to him, "Master, it is good for us to be here. Let us put up three shelters — one for you, one for Moses and one for Elijah." (He did not know what he was saying.)

³⁴While he was speaking, a cloud appeared and enveloped them, and they were afraid as they entered the cloud. ³⁵A voice came from the cloud, saying, "This is my Son, whom I have chosen; listen to him." ³⁶When the voice had spoken, they found that Jesus was alone. The disciples kept this to themselves, and told no one at that time what they had seen.

The Healing of a Boy With an Evil Spirit

³⁷The next day, when they came down from the mountain, a large crowd met him. ³⁸A man in the crowd called out, "Teacher, I beg you to look at my son, for he is my only child. ³⁹A spirit seizes him and he suddenly screams; it throws him into convulsions so that he foams at the mouth. It scarcely ever leaves him and is destroying him. ⁴⁰I begged your disciples to drive it out, but they could not."

⁴¹"O unbelieving and perverse generation," Jesus replied, "how long shall I stay with you and put up with you? Bring your son here."

⁴²Even while the boy was coming, the demon threw him to the ground in a convulsion. But Jesus rebuked the evil*b* spirit, healed the boy and gave him back to his father. ⁴³And they were all amazed at the greatness of God.

While everyone was marveling at all that Jesus did, he said to his disciples, ⁴⁴"Listen carefully to what I am about to tell you: The Son of Man is going to be betrayed into the hands of men." ⁴⁵But they did not understand what this meant. It was hidden from them, so that they did not grasp it, and they were afraid to ask him about it.

Who Will Be the Greatest?

⁴⁶An argument started among the disciples as to which of them would be the greatest. ⁴⁷Jesus, knowing their thoughts, took a little child and had him stand beside him. ⁴⁸Then he said to them, "Whoever welcomes this little child in my name welcomes me; and whoever welcomes me welcomes the one who sent me. For he who is least among you all — he is the greatest."

⁴⁹"Master," said John, "we saw a man driving out demons in your name and we tried to stop him, because he is not one of us."

⁵⁰"Do not stop him," Jesus said, "for whoever is not against you is for you."

Samaritan Opposition

⁵¹As the time approached for him to be taken up to heaven, Jesus resolutely set out for Jerusalem. ⁵²And he sent messengers on ahead, who went into a Samaritan village to get things ready for him; ⁵³but the people there did not welcome him, because he was heading for Jerusalem. ⁵⁴When the disciples James and John saw this, they asked, "Lord, do you want us to call fire down from heav-

*a*20 Or *Messiah*   *b*42 Greek *unclean*

Serving: the cure for selfishness!

It's really hard to believe that the Monica of last fall and the Monica of this summer are the same person. Talk about a transformation!

Then: Monica was totally into herself—dating, clothes and keeping up her grade point average.

Now: Monica spends more time helping others. On Mondays she does peer counseling at a teen drop-in center. On Saturdays she and a friend regularly visit a shelter for abused children.

Why the change? Monica has discovered that true joy is found in obeying Christ and serving others.

Look It Up
••••

Perhaps the most famous passage about selfishness in all of Scripture is found in Philippians 2:3–7:

"Do nothing out of selfish ambition or vain conceit, but in humility consider others better than yourselves. Each of you should look not only to your own interests, but also to the interests of others.

"Your attitude should be the same as that of Christ Jesus: Who . . . made himself nothing, taking the very nature of a servant."

The message? Consider others. Think about their interests and needs. Be a servant.

Think It Through
••••

Try to imagine what would happen if each of your Christian friends adopted a Christlike attitude of service. What would happen to your friendships? To your witness at school? At your church?

What keeps you from doing that . . . starting right now?

Work It Out
••••

Plan and participate in a service project for next weekend. Here are a few ideas for serving others:
• Have a garage sale for world hunger.
• Do free yard work for the elderly.
• Baby-sit for a neighbor who needs a break.
• Sponsor a car wash and donate the proceeds to a mission.
• Collect canned goods for your church's food bank.
• Plan a romantic evening for your parents.
• Clean the garage.
• Organize a games day for the kids in your neighborhood (and give some weary parents a few hours of rest).
• Wash and wax the family car.
Now pick one and go for it!

Nail It Down
••••

Read Luke 9:23 for a word on being unselfish.

Turn to pages 1106 and 1362 for other readings on selfishness.
Turn to page 1098 for Friday's reading.

Topic
••••

SELFISHNESS

en to destroy them[a]?" [55]But Jesus turned and rebuked them, [56]and[b] they went to another village.

The Cost of Following Jesus

[57]As they were walking along the road, a man said to him, "I will follow you wherever you go."

[58]Jesus replied, "Foxes have holes and birds of the air have nests, but the Son of Man has no place to lay his head."

[59]He said to another man, "Follow me." But the man replied, "Lord, first let me go and bury my father."

[60]Jesus said to him, "Let the dead bury their own dead, but you go and proclaim the kingdom of God."

[61]Still another said, "I will follow you, Lord; but first let me go back and say goodby to my family."

[62]Jesus replied, "No one who puts his hand to the plow and looks back is fit for service in the kingdom of God."

Jesus Sends Out the Seventy-two

10 After this the Lord appointed seventy-two[c] others and sent them two by two ahead of him to every town and place where he was about to go. [2]He told them, "The harvest is plentiful, but the workers are few. Ask the Lord of the harvest, therefore, to send out workers into his harvest field. [3]Go! I am sending you out like lambs among wolves. [4]Do not take a purse or bag or sandals; and do not greet anyone on the road.

[5]"When you enter a house, first say, 'Peace to this house.' [6]If a man of peace is there, your peace will rest on him; if not, it will return to you. [7]Stay in that house, eating and drinking whatever they give you, for the worker deserves his wages. Do not move around from house to house.

[8]"When you enter a town and are welcomed, eat what is set before you. [9]Heal the sick who are there and tell them, 'The kingdom of God is near you.' [10]But when you enter a town and are not welcomed, go into its streets and say, [11]'Even the dust of your town that sticks to our feet we wipe off against you. Yet be sure of this: The kingdom of God is near.' [12]I tell you, it will be more bearable on that day for Sodom than for that town.

[13]"Woe to you, Korazin! Woe to you, Bethsaida! For if the miracles that were performed in you had been performed in Tyre and Sidon, they would have repented long ago, sitting in sackcloth and ashes. [14]But it will be more bearable for Tyre and Sidon at the judgment than for you. [15]And you, Capernaum, will you be lifted up to the skies? No, you will go down to the depths.[d]

[16]"He who listens to you listens to me; he who rejects you rejects me; but he who rejects me rejects him who sent me."

[17]The seventy-two returned with joy and said, "Lord, even the demons submit to us in your name."

[18]He replied, "I saw Satan fall like lightning from heaven. [19]I have given you authority to trample on snakes and scorpions and to overcome all the power of the enemy; nothing will harm you. [20]However, do not rejoice that the spirits submit to you, but rejoice that your names are written in heaven."

[21]At that time Jesus, full of joy through the Holy Spirit, said, "I praise you, Father, Lord of heaven and earth, because you have hidden these things from the wise and learned, and revealed them to little children. Yes, Father, for this was your good pleasure.

[22]"All things have been committed to me by my Father. No one knows who the Son is except the Father, and no one knows who the Father is except the Son and those to whom the Son chooses to reveal him."

[23]Then he turned to his disciples and said privately, "Blessed are the eyes that see what you see. [24]For I tell you that many prophets and kings wanted to see what you see but did not see it, and to hear what you hear but did not hear it."

The Parable of the Good Samaritan

[25]On one occasion an expert in the law stood up to test Jesus. "Teacher," he asked, "what must I do to inherit eternal life?"

[26]"What is written in the Law?" he replied. "How do you read it?"

[27]He answered: " 'Love the Lord your God with all your heart and with all your soul and with all your strength and with all your mind'[e]; and, 'Love your neighbor as yourself.'[f]"

[28]"You have answered correctly," Jesus replied. "Do this and you will live."

[29]But he wanted to justify himself, so he asked Jesus, "And who is my neighbor?"

[30]In reply Jesus said: "A man was going

---

[a]54 Some manuscripts them, even as Elijah did   [b]55,56 Some manuscripts them. And he said, "You do not know what kind of spirit you are of, for the Son of Man did not come to destroy men's lives, but to save them." [56]And   [c]1 Some manuscripts seventy; also in verse 17   [d]15 Greek Hades   [e]27 Deut. 6:5   [f]27 Lev. 19:18

down from Jerusalem to Jericho, when he fell into the hands of robbers. They stripped him of his clothes, beat him and went away, leaving him half dead. **31**A priest happened to be going down the same road, and when he saw the man, he passed by on the other side. **32**So too, a Levite, when he came to the place and saw him, passed by on the other side. **33**But a Samaritan, as he traveled, came where the man was; and when he saw him, he took pity on him. **34**He went to him and bandaged his wounds, pouring on oil and wine. Then he put the man on his own donkey, took him to an inn and took care of him. **35**The next day he took out two silver coins*a* and gave them to the innkeeper. 'Look after him,' he said, 'and when I return, I will reimburse you for any extra expense you may have.'

36"Which of these three do you think was a neighbor to the man who fell into the hands of robbers?"

37The expert in the law replied, "The one who had mercy on him."

Jesus told him, "Go and do likewise."

At the Home of Martha and Mary

38As Jesus and his disciples were on their way, he came to a village where a woman named Martha opened her home to him. **39**She had a sister called Mary, who sat at the Lord's feet listening to what he said. **40**But Martha was distracted by all the preparations that had to be made. She came to him and asked, "Lord, don't you care that my sister has left me to do the work by myself? Tell her to help me!"

41"Martha, Martha," the Lord answered, "you are worried and upset about many things, **42**but only one thing is needed.*b* Mary has chosen what is better, and it will not be taken away from her."

Jesus' Teaching on Prayer

11 One day Jesus was praying in a certain place. When he finished, one of his disciples said to him, "Lord, teach us to pray, just as John taught his disciples."

2He said to them, "When you pray, say:

" 'Father,*c*
hallowed be your name,
your kingdom come.*d*
3Give us each day our daily bread.

4Forgive us our sins,
for we also forgive everyone who sins
against us.*e*
And lead us not into temptation.*f* ' "

5Then he said to them, "Suppose one of you has a friend, and he goes to him at midnight and says, 'Friend, lend me three loaves of bread, **6**because a friend of mine on a journey has come to me, and I have nothing to set before him.'

7"Then the one inside answers, 'Don't bother me. The door is already locked, and my children are with me in bed. I can't get up and give you anything.' **8**I tell you, though he will not get up and give him the bread because he is his friend, yet because of the man's boldness*g* he will get up and give him as much as he needs.

9"So I say to you: Ask and it will be given to you; seek and you will find; knock and the door will be opened to you. **10**For everyone who asks receives; he who seeks finds; and to him who knocks, the door will be opened.

11"Which of you fathers, if your son asks for*h* a fish, will give him a snake instead? **12**Or if he asks for an egg, will give him a scorpion? **13**If you then, though you are evil, know how to give good gifts to your children, how much more will your Father in heaven give the Holy Spirit to those who ask him!"

Jesus and Beelzebub

14Jesus was driving out a demon that was mute. When the demon left, the man who had been mute spoke, and the crowd was amazed. **15**But some of them said, "By Beelzebub,*i* the prince of demons, he is driving out demons." **16**Others tested him by asking for a sign from heaven.

17Jesus knew their thoughts and said to them: "Any kingdom divided against itself will be ruined, and a house divided against itself will fall. **18**If Satan is divided against himself, how can his kingdom stand? I say this because you claim that I drive out demons by Beelzebub. **19**Now if I drive out demons by Beelzebub, by whom do your followers drive them out? So then, they will be your judges. **20**But if I drive out demons by the finger of God, then the kingdom of God has come to you.

---

a35 Greek *two denarii*   *b42* Some manuscripts *but few things are needed—or only one*   *c2* Some manuscripts *Our Father in heaven*   *d2* Some manuscripts *come. May your will be done on earth as it is in heaven.*   *e4* Greek *everyone who is indebted to us*   *f4* Some manuscripts *temptation but deliver us from the evil one*   *g8* Or *persistence*   *h11* Some manuscripts *for bread, will give him a stone; or if he asks for* *i15* Greek *Beezeboul* or *Beelzeboul*; also in verses 18 and 19

PERSISTENT PRAYING PAYS OFF

Sometimes Robin forgets to feed the cat, and sometimes she forgets the birthdays in her family (she's got five brothers and two sisters!). But one thing Robin never forgets is to pray before she goes to bed.

Robin has prayed every day for the last four years for her grandfather's soul. She quips, "I tell him, 'Grandpa, you might as well give your life to the Lord now 'cause you will sooner or later. I'm going to keep praying for you if it takes twenty years—you don't have a chance!' "

Look It Up ....

Jesus "told his disciples a parable to show them that they should always pray and not give up" (Luke 18:1–8).

In short, the parable goes like this: An old widow kept coming to an unjust judge, saying, "Grant me justice against my adversary" (Luke 18:3). For a long time the judge refused to help the woman. Finally he realized that she was going to wear him out until he gave in.

"And the Lord said, 'Listen to what the unjust judge says. And will not God bring about justice for his chosen ones, who cry out to him day and night? Will he keep putting them off? I tell you, he will see that they get justice, and quickly' " (Luke 18:6–8).

Think It Through ....

If constant nagging can force even an unjust judge to act, how do you think our loving heavenly Father will respond to our continual prayers?

Imagine you're married and have an adorable little three-year-old girl. One Monday morning she comes bounding into your room, jumps in your lap, looks at you with her big brown eyes and pleads, "Can we go to the zoo on Saturday? Oh, pleeeeeeeze!" Suppose she does this every morning for a whole week.

It's pretty easy to figure out where you'll be on Saturday.

Work It Out ....

Have you been praying for something for a long time without any results? Don't give up! God will honor your persistence. As long as you're walking with Christ (John 15:7–8) and praying according to God's will revealed in his Word (1 John 5:14–15), he will answer.

If prayer has never been your strong point, grab an old notebook and make out a prayer list. List your family, friends, personal needs, dreams and goals. Mark the date you begin to pray for each item. Then when God answers, jot down the date. You'll see him do some incredible things. And you'll have a written record of his faithfulness.

Nail It Down ....

Read another story about a persistent person in Luke 11:5–13.

Turn to pages 932, 1108 and 1228 for other readings on parables.
Turn to page 1100 for the weekend reading.

Topic ....

PARABLES

²¹"When a strong man, fully armed, guards his own house, his possessions are safe. ²²But when someone stronger attacks and overpowers him, he takes away the armor in which the man trusted and divides up the spoils.

²³"He who is not with me is against me, and he who does not gather with me, scatters.

²⁴"When an evil*a* spirit comes out of a man, it goes through arid places seeking rest and does not find it. Then it says, 'I will return to the house I left.' ²⁵When it arrives, it finds the house swept clean and put in order. ²⁶Then it goes and takes seven other spirits more wicked than itself, and they go in and live there. And the final condition of that man is worse than the first."

²⁷As Jesus was saying these things, a woman in the crowd called out, "Blessed is the mother who gave you birth and nursed you."

²⁸He replied, "Blessed rather are those who hear the word of God and obey it."

The Sign of Jonah

²⁹As the crowds increased, Jesus said, "This is a wicked generation. It asks for a miraculous sign, but none will be given it except the sign of Jonah. ³⁰For as Jonah was a sign to the Ninevites, so also will the Son of Man be to this generation. ³¹The Queen of the South will rise at the judgment with the men of this generation and condemn them; for she came from the ends of the earth to listen to Solomon's wisdom, and now one*b* greater than Solomon is here. ³²The men of Nineveh will stand up at the judgment with this generation and condemn it; for they repented at the preaching of Jonah, and now one greater than Jonah is here.

The Lamp of the Body

³³"No one lights a lamp and puts it in a place where it will be hidden, or under a bowl. Instead he puts it on its stand, so that those who come in may see the light. ³⁴Your eye is the lamp of your body. When your eyes are good, your whole body also is full of light. But when they are bad, your body also is full of darkness. ³⁵See to it, then, that the light within you is not darkness. ³⁶Therefore, if your whole body is full of light, and no part of it is dark, it will be completely lighted, as when the light of a lamp shines on you."

Six Woes

³⁷When Jesus had finished speaking, a Pharisee invited him to eat with him; so he went in and reclined at the table. ³⁸But the Pharisee, noticing that Jesus did not first wash before the meal, was surprised.

³⁹Then the Lord said to him, "Now then, you Pharisees clean the outside of the cup and dish, but inside you are full of greed and wickedness. ⁴⁰You foolish people! Did not the one who made the outside make the inside also? ⁴¹But give what is inside ⌊the dish⌋*c* to the poor, and everything will be clean for you.

⁴²"Woe to you Pharisees, because you give God a tenth of your mint, rue and all other kinds of garden herbs, but you neglect justice and the love of God. You should have practiced the latter without leaving the former undone.

⁴³"Woe to you Pharisees, because you love the most important seats in the synagogues and greetings in the marketplaces.

⁴⁴"Woe to you, because you are like unmarked graves, which men walk over without knowing it."

⁴⁵One of the experts in the law answered him, "Teacher, when you say these things, you insult us also."

⁴⁶Jesus replied, "And you experts in the law, woe to you, because you load people down with burdens they can hardly carry, and you yourselves will not lift one finger to help them.

⁴⁷"Woe to you, because you build tombs for the prophets, and it was your forefathers who killed them. ⁴⁸So you testify that you approve of what your forefathers did; they killed the prophets, and you build their tombs. ⁴⁹Because of this, God in his wisdom said, 'I will send them prophets and apostles, some of whom they will kill and others they will persecute.' ⁵⁰Therefore this generation will be held responsible for the blood of all the prophets that has been shed since the beginning of the world, ⁵¹from the blood of Abel to the blood of Zechariah, who was killed between the altar and the sanctuary. Yes, I tell you, this generation will be held responsible for it all.

⁵²"Woe to you experts in the law, because you have taken away the key to knowledge. You yourselves have not entered, and you have hindered those who were entering."

⁵³When Jesus left there, the Pharisees and the teachers of the law began to oppose him

---

a24 Greek *unclean*   *b31* Or *something*; also in verse 32   *c41* Or *what you have*

WHOSE OPINION COUNTS?

●●

Work It Out
●●●●

Think of four people whose opinion of you matters. Perhaps your parents, your best friend, your youth pastor, a teacher or a neighbor will be on your list. Whoever the people are, what they think of you is important to you.

Those people will often judge you by outward things: what you look like, how you act, what others say about you, how you treat them. And if you fail, if you don't measure up in some way, they may reject you. That sort of rejection does little for your self-esteem.

There's someone you can put on your list, however, who will never reject you. Through Jesus, God cares about you simply because you belong to him. He doesn't ask you to measure up or achieve or perform before he accepts you. And he won't reject you if you fail. Now what does that do for your self-esteem?

Nail It Down
●●●●

Read about God's care for the sparrow and for you in Luke 12:6–7.

●●

Think It Through
●●●●

If you're having trouble with self-esteem, if you sometimes think you're not worth much, maybe you've been looking in the wrong place for help.

What you are in the eyes of your friends and neighbors and teachers and parents is important. But not nearly as important as who you are in God's eyes.

God values you because he created you, he provided salvation through Jesus for you and he loves you. If your self-esteem is shattered, if you think you're worth very little, stop looking at yourself through your own eyes or through the eyes of others. Start to look at yourself through God's eyes. You'll like what you see!

Nail It Down
●●●●

Reread Luke 12:6–7. For further insight read Psalm 8.

Turn to pages 584, 641, 1029 and 1379 for other readings on self-esteem.
Turn to page 1102 for Monday's reading.

Topic
●●●●

SELF-ESTEEM

fiercely and to besiege him with questions, **54**waiting to catch him in something he might say.

Warnings and Encouragements

12 Meanwhile, when a crowd of many thousands had gathered, so that they were trampling on one another, Jesus began to speak first to his disciples, saying: "Be on your guard against the yeast of the Pharisees, which is hypocrisy. **2**There is nothing concealed that will not be disclosed, or hidden that will not be made known. **3**What you have said in the dark will be heard in the daylight, and what you have whispered in the ear in the inner rooms will be proclaimed from the roofs.

4"I tell you, my friends, do not be afraid of those who kill the body and after that can do no more. **5**But I will show you whom you should fear: Fear him who, after the killing of the body, has power to throw you into hell. Yes, I tell you, fear him. **6**Are not five sparrows sold for two pennies*a*? Yet not one of them is forgotten by God. **7**Indeed, the very hairs of your head are all numbered. Don't be afraid; you are worth more than many sparrows.

8"I tell you, whoever acknowledges me before men, the Son of Man will also acknowledge him before the angels of God. **9**But he who disowns me before men will be disowned before the angels of God. **10**And everyone who speaks a word against the Son of Man will be forgiven, but anyone who blasphemes against the Holy Spirit will not be forgiven.

11"When you are brought before synagogues, rulers and authorities, do not worry about how you will defend yourselves or what you will say, **12**for the Holy Spirit will teach you at that time what you should say."

The Parable of the Rich Fool

13Someone in the crowd said to him, "Teacher, tell my brother to divide the inheritance with me."

14Jesus replied, "Man, who appointed me a judge or an arbiter between you?" **15**Then he said to them, "Watch out! Be on your guard against all kinds of greed; a man's life does not consist in the abundance of his possessions."

16And he told them this parable: "The ground of a certain rich man produced a good crop. **17**He thought to himself, 'What shall I do? I have no place to store my crops.'

18"Then he said, 'This is what I'll do. I will tear down my barns and build bigger ones, and there I will store all my grain and my goods. **19**And I'll say to myself, "You have plenty of good things laid up for many years. Take life easy; eat, drink and be merry." '

20"But God said to him, 'You fool! This very night your life will be demanded from you. Then who will get what you have prepared for yourself?'

21"This is how it will be with anyone who stores up things for himself but is not rich toward God."

Do Not Worry

22Then Jesus said to his disciples: "Therefore I tell you, do not worry about your life, what you will eat; or about your body, what you will wear. **23**Life is more than food, and the body more than clothes. **24**Consider the ravens: They do not sow or reap, they have no storeroom or barn; yet God feeds them. And how much more valuable you are than birds! **25**Who of you by worrying can add a single hour to his life*b*? **26**Since you cannot do this very little thing, why do you worry about the rest?

27"Consider how the lilies grow. They do not labor or spin. Yet I tell you, not even Solomon in all his splendor was dressed like one of these. **28**If that is how God clothes the grass of the field, which is here today, and tomorrow is thrown into the fire, how much more will he clothe you, O you of little faith! **29**And do not set your heart on what you will eat or drink; do not worry about it. **30**For the pagan world runs after all such things, and your Father knows that you need them. **31**But seek his kingdom, and these things will be given to you as well.

32"Do not be afraid, little flock, for your Father has been pleased to give you the kingdom. **33**Sell your possessions and give to the poor. Provide purses for yourselves that will not wear out, a treasure in heaven that will not be exhausted, where no thief comes near and no moth destroys. **34**For where your treasure is, there your heart will be also.

Watchfulness

35"Be dressed ready for service and keep your lamps burning, **36**like men waiting for their master to return from a wedding banquet, so that when he comes and knocks they can immediately open the door for him. **37**It will be good for those servants

---

*a*6 Greek *two assaria*   *b*25 Or *single cubit to his height*

ARE YOU SEEKING GOD'S KINGDOM?

Terrance works out for hours at a neighborhood health club (spending most of that time looking in the mirrors and admiring his own physique). He is obsessed with his clothing and the way his hair looks. He talks a lot about starting his own business and becoming a tycoon.

Because he's so stuck on himself, Terrance can't understand Kenitra's deep commitment to Christ. "Hey, I believe in God too. I just think she takes it too far. She's a fanatic!"

Look It Up

Do you remember what Jesus told his disciples when they were getting anxious about the trivial things of this world?

"So do not worry, saying, 'What shall we eat?' or 'What shall we drink?' or 'What shall we wear?' For the pagans run after all these things, and your heavenly Father knows that you need them. But seek first his kingdom and his righteousness, and all these things will be given to you as well" (Matthew 6:31-33).

God not only knows your needs, but he meets them when you seek him first.

Think It Through

Are you acting like a "pagan" (that is, a non-Christian) and running after the things of this world? Is your main concern you—how you look, how you dress, building your own career, taking care of yourself?

Which goal sounds more noble and more enduring?
1. I'm here to build the kingdom of God.
2. I'm here to take care of me.

Work It Out

Some people worry that if they don't look out for themselves, no one will. Not true. God promises to care for his children when they put him and his kingdom first.

Begin your week with this prayer:

"Father, I don't want to be like the people who foolishly chase after the things of this world. I don't want to spend my life selfishly running after things for me. I want to be involved in building your kingdom. Change me as I read and study your Word. In Jesus' name I pray. Amen."

Nail It Down

Read the sad story of the guy who was more concerned about building his own kingdom than about building the kingdom of God—Luke 12:16-21.

Turn to pages 502, 1158 and 1220 for other readings on purpose.
Turn to page 1104 for Tuesday's reading.

Topic

PURPOSE

whose master finds them watching when he comes. I tell you the truth, he will dress himself to serve, will have them recline at the table and will come and wait on them. ³⁸It will be good for those servants whose master finds them ready, even if he comes in the second or third watch of the night. ³⁹But understand this: If the owner of the house had known at what hour the thief was coming, he would not have let his house be broken into. ⁴⁰You also must be ready, because the Son of Man will come at an hour when you do not expect him."

⁴¹Peter asked, "Lord, are you telling this parable to us, or to everyone?"

⁴²The Lord answered, "Who then is the faithful and wise manager, whom the master puts in charge of his servants to give them their food allowance at the proper time? ⁴³It will be good for that servant whom the master finds doing so when he returns. ⁴⁴I tell you the truth, he will put him in charge of all his possessions. ⁴⁵But suppose the servant says to himself, 'My master is taking a long time in coming,' and he then begins to beat the menservants and maidservants and to eat and drink and get drunk. ⁴⁶The master of that servant will come on a day when he does not expect him and at an hour he is not aware of. He will cut him to pieces and assign him a place with the unbelievers.

⁴⁷"That servant who knows his master's will and does not get ready or does not do what his master wants will be beaten with many blows. ⁴⁸But the one who does not know and does things deserving punishment will be beaten with few blows. From everyone who has been given much, much will be demanded; and from the one who has been entrusted with much, much more will be asked.

Not Peace but Division

⁴⁹"I have come to bring fire on the earth, and how I wish it were already kindled! ⁵⁰But I have a baptism to undergo, and how distressed I am until it is completed! ⁵¹Do you think I came to bring peace on earth? No, I tell you, but division. ⁵²From now on there will be five in one family divided against each other, three against two and two against three. ⁵³They will be divided, father against son and son against father, mother against daughter and daughter against mother, mother-in-law

against daughter-in-law and daughter-in-law against mother-in-law."

Interpreting the Times

⁵⁴He said to the crowd: "When you see a cloud rising in the west, immediately you say, 'It's going to rain,' and it does. ⁵⁵And when the south wind blows, you say, 'It's going to be hot,' and it is. ⁵⁶Hypocrites! You know how to interpret the appearance of the earth and the sky. How is it that you don't know how to interpret this present time?

⁵⁷"Why don't you judge for yourselves what is right? ⁵⁸As you are going with your adversary to the magistrate, try hard to be reconciled to him on the way, or he may drag you off to the judge, and the judge turn you over to the officer, and the officer throw you into prison. ⁵⁹I tell you, you will not get out until you have paid the last penny.ᵃ"

Repent or Perish

13 Now there were some present at that time who told Jesus about the Galileans whose blood Pilate had mixed with their sacrifices. ²Jesus answered, "Do you think that these Galileans were worse sinners than all the other Galileans because they suffered this way? ³I tell you, no! But unless you repent, you too will all perish. ⁴Or those eighteen who died when the tower in Siloam fell on them — do you think they were more guilty than all the others living in Jerusalem? ⁵I tell you, no! But unless you repent, you too will all perish."

⁶Then he told this parable: "A man had a fig tree, planted in his vineyard, and he went to look for fruit on it, but did not find any. ⁷So he said to the man who took care of the vineyard, 'For three years now I've been coming to look for fruit on this fig tree and haven't found any. Cut it down! Why should it use up the soil?'

⁸" 'Sir,' the man replied, 'leave it alone for one more year, and I'll dig around it and fertilize it. ⁹If it bears fruit next year, fine! If not, then cut it down.' "

A Crippled Woman Healed
on the Sabbath

¹⁰On a Sabbath Jesus was teaching in one of the synagogues, ¹¹and a woman was there who had been crippled by a spirit for eighteen years. She was bent over and could not straighten up at all. ¹²When Jesus saw her, he called her forward and said to her, "Woman, you are set free from your infirmi-

ᵃ59 Greek *lepton*

FRUITLESSNESS = HYPOCRISY

Scott had just spent a weekend with his cousin Eddie. They had gone on a service project with Eddie's youth group. Scott had been amazed. Everyone was so enthusiastic and committed. On the way home, Scott didn't say much to his parents. He was too busy thinking about the weekend and about his own life and youth group. "Our youth group is nothing like Eddie's," he thought. "His group is different . . . and maybe that's why they're really making an impact."

The comparisons rushed and tumbled through his head. "We just go through the motions. They really practice what they preach. We're just a bunch of talk. They're really committed. We just sit around selfishly waiting for the next swim party or ski trip. They're concerned for others—they look forward to serving and sharing."

Look It Up
● ● ● ●

There is an incident in one of the Gospels that shows that Jesus was not pleased with fruitlessness.

"Seeing in the distance a fig tree in leaf, [Jesus] went to find out if it had any fruit. When he reached it, he found nothing but leaves, because it was not the season for figs. Then he said to the tree, 'May no one ever eat fruit from you again' " (Mark 11:13–14).

In the Bible, the fig tree is often used as a symbol for God's people. With a powerful illustration, Jesus was teaching that God curses hypocrites—people who claim to be his but don't bear any fruit for him.

Think It Through
● ● ● ●

Think about how blessed the Israelites were. Chosen by God, he protected them, cared for them, gave them his law and finally sent them his Son. But, rather than live for him in a productive way, they rebelled, resisted and finally rejected the Savior, Jesus Christ. What a tragedy!

Think about how blessed you are. Are you responding to God's goodness and bearing fruit for him, or are you a hypocrite?

Work It Out
● ● ● ●

Some Christians look great from a distance. They go to church, read the Bible and do all those easy-to-spot activities. But when you get up close and examine their lives, you just don't find any fruit. They aren't really any different from unbelievers.

Don't be like that. Sit down today with one or two Christian friends. Ask yourselves, "Are we serious about the Lord and about being productive for him? Or are we just being a bunch of hypocrites?" Read these passages together. Pray for and with each other. Encourage each other to go for it—to be like the people in Eddie's youth group.

Nail It Down
● ● ● ●

Read the story of the fig tree in Luke 13:6–9.

Turn to pages 1134 and 1184 for other readings on fruitfulness.
Turn to page 1106 for Wednesday's reading.

Topic
● ● ● ●

FRUITFULNESS

ty." **13**Then he put his hands on her, and immediately she straightened up and praised God.

14Indignant because Jesus had healed on the Sabbath, the synagogue ruler said to the people, "There are six days for work. So come and be healed on those days, not on the Sabbath."

15The Lord answered him, "You hypocrites! Doesn't each of you on the Sabbath untie his ox or donkey from the stall and lead it out to give it water? **16**Then should not this woman, a daughter of Abraham, whom Satan has kept bound for eighteen long years, be set free on the Sabbath day from what bound her?"

17When he said this, all his opponents were humiliated, but the people were delighted with all the wonderful things he was doing.

The Parables of the Mustard Seed and the Yeast

18Then Jesus asked, "What is the kingdom of God like? What shall I compare it to? **19**It is like a mustard seed, which a man took and planted in his garden. It grew and became a tree, and the birds of the air perched in its branches."

20Again he asked, "What shall I compare the kingdom of God to? **21**It is like yeast that a woman took and mixed into a large amount*a* of flour until it worked all through the dough."

The Narrow Door

22Then Jesus went through the towns and villages, teaching as he made his way to Jerusalem. **23**Someone asked him, "Lord, are only a few people going to be saved?"

He said to them, **24**"Make every effort to enter through the narrow door, because many, I tell you, will try to enter and will not be able to. **25**Once the owner of the house gets up and closes the door, you will stand outside knocking and pleading, 'Sir, open the door for us.'

"But he will answer, 'I don't know you or where you come from.'

26"Then you will say, 'We ate and drank with you, and you taught in our streets.'

27"But he will reply, 'I don't know you or where you come from. Away from me, all you evildoers!'

28"There will be weeping there, and gnashing of teeth, when you see Abraham, Isaac and Jacob and all the prophets in the kingdom of God, but you yourselves thrown out. **29**People will come from east and west and north and south, and will take their places at the feast in the kingdom of God. **30**Indeed there are those who are last who will be first, and first who will be last."

Jesus' Sorrow for Jerusalem

31At that time some Pharisees came to Jesus and said to him, "Leave this place and go somewhere else. Herod wants to kill you."

32He replied, "Go tell that fox, 'I will drive out demons and heal people today and tomorrow, and on the third day I will reach my goal.' **33**In any case, I must keep going today and tomorrow and the next day—for surely no prophet can die outside Jerusalem!

34"O Jerusalem, Jerusalem, you who kill the prophets and stone those sent to you, how often I have longed to gather your children together, as a hen gathers her chicks under her wings, but you were not willing! **35**Look, your house is left to you desolate. I tell you, you will not see me again until you say, 'Blessed is he who comes in the name of the Lord.'*b*"

Jesus at a Pharisee's House

14 One Sabbath, when Jesus went to eat in the house of a prominent Pharisee, he was being carefully watched. **2**There in front of him was a man suffering from dropsy. **3**Jesus asked the Pharisees and experts in the law, "Is it lawful to heal on the Sabbath or not?" **4**But they remained silent. So taking hold of the man, he healed him and sent him away.

5Then he asked them, "If one of you has a son*c* or an ox that falls into a well on the Sabbath day, will you not immediately pull him out?" **6**And they had nothing to say.

7When he noticed how the guests picked the places of honor at the table, he told them this parable: **8**"When someone invites you to a wedding feast, do not take the place of honor, for a person more distinguished than you may have been invited. **9**If so, the host who invited both of you will come and say to you, 'Give this man your seat.' Then, humiliated, you will have to take the least important place. **10**But when you are invited, take the lowest place, so that when your host comes, he will say to you, 'Friend, move up to a better place.' Then you will be

---

a21 Greek *three satas* (probably about 1/2 bushel or 22 liters)   *b35* Psalm 118:26   *c5* Some manuscripts donkey

DO YOU CARE? THEN DARE TO SHARE!

The Richmonds are wealthy—there's no doubt about it. But they're also one of the most generous families around! They give a lot of money to their church, various ministries and other social causes.

What's more, Mrs. Richmond works with a literacy program, and Mr. Richmond takes a month each year to help build churches overseas. In addition, the Richmond's home includes a guest apartment that is always filled with visitors. (The Richmond kids jokingly call it "the hotel"!) This month it is housing a missionary couple from Africa. Last year it was home for an unwed mother.

Look It Up
••••

The Bible talks a lot about giving.

1. You are to share your material goods. "Give to the one who asks you, and do not turn away from the one who wants to borrow from you" (Matthew 5:42).

2. You are to give without a thought about being repaid (Luke 14:12–14).

3. You are to be generous when sharing your material blessings. "Remember this: Whoever sows sparingly will also reap sparingly, and whoever sows generously will also reap generously" (2 Corinthians 9:6).

Think It Through
••••

Which matters more to God? How much money he allows a person to have, or what that person does with the money?

Do you share with others what God has given you? Why or why not?

If you were homeless (or in a similar tight spot) and everyone treated you the way you respond to those in need, would you be eating tonight? Would your future be bright or bleak?

Work It Out
••••

Be daring and caring—start sharing!
• Give your allowance to someone in need.
• Give a whole day's pay to a missionary.
• Buy a Bible for someone who can't afford one.
• Share some of your duplicate possessions with others. (Who needs fourteen pairs of jeans or seven Bibles?)
• Take a possession you really value and give it to someone who needs it more than you.

Nail It Down
••••

Read Luke 14:7–11 for the danger in thinking more of yourself and your possessions than you should.

Turn to pages 1095 and 1362 for other readings on selfishness.
Turn to page 1108 for Thursday's reading.

Topic
••••

SELFISHNESS

honored in the presence of all your fellow guests. **11**For everyone who exalts himself will be humbled, and he who humbles himself will be exalted."

12Then Jesus said to his host, "When you give a luncheon or dinner, do not invite your friends, your brothers or relatives, or your rich neighbors; if you do, they may invite you back and so you will be repaid. **13**But when you give a banquet, invite the poor, the crippled, the lame, the blind, **14**and you will be blessed. Although they cannot repay you, you will be repaid at the resurrection of the righteous."

The Parable of the Great Banquet

15When one of those at the table with him heard this, he said to Jesus, "Blessed is the man who will eat at the feast in the kingdom of God."

16Jesus replied: "A certain man was preparing a great banquet and invited many guests. **17**At the time of the banquet he sent his servant to tell those who had been invited, 'Come, for everything is now ready.'

18"But they all alike began to make excuses. The first said, 'I have just bought a field, and I must go and see it. Please excuse me.'

19"Another said, 'I have just bought five yoke of oxen, and I'm on my way to try them out. Please excuse me.'

20"Still another said, 'I just got married, so I can't come.'

21"The servant came back and reported this to his master. Then the owner of the house became angry and ordered his servant, 'Go out quickly into the streets and alleys of the town and bring in the poor, the crippled, the blind and the lame.'

22" 'Sir,' the servant said, 'what you ordered has been done, but there is still room.'

23"Then the master told his servant, 'Go out to the roads and country lanes and make them come in, so that my house will be full. **24**I tell you, not one of those men who were invited will get a taste of my banquet.' "

The Cost of Being a Disciple

25Large crowds were traveling with Jesus, and turning to them he said: **26**"If anyone comes to me and does not hate his father and mother, his wife and children, his brothers and sisters — yes, even his own life — he cannot be my disciple. **27**And anyone who does not carry his cross and follow me cannot be my disciple.

28"Suppose one of you wants to build a tower. Will he not first sit down and estimate the cost to see if he has enough money to complete it? **29**For if he lays the foundation and is not able to finish it, everyone who sees it will ridicule him, **30**saying, 'This fellow began to build and was not able to finish.'

31"Or suppose a king is about to go to war against another king. Will he not first sit down and consider whether he is able with ten thousand men to oppose the one coming against him with twenty thousand? **32**If he is not able, he will send a delegation while the other is still a long way off and will ask for terms of peace. **33**In the same way, any of you who does not give up everything he has cannot be my disciple.

34"Salt is good, but if it loses its saltiness, how can it be made salty again? **35**It is fit neither for the soil nor for the manure pile; it is thrown out.

"He who has ears to hear, let him hear."

The Parable of the Lost Sheep

15 Now the tax collectors and "sinners" were all gathering around to hear him. **2**But the Pharisees and the teachers of the law muttered, "This man welcomes sinners and eats with them."

3Then Jesus told them this parable: **4**"Suppose one of you has a hundred sheep and loses one of them. Does he not leave the ninety-nine in the open country and go after the lost sheep until he finds it? **5**And when he finds it, he joyfully puts it on his shoulders **6**and goes home. Then he calls his friends and neighbors together and says, 'Rejoice with me; I have found my lost sheep.' **7**I tell you that in the same way there will be more rejoicing in heaven over one sinner who repents than over ninety-nine righteous persons who do not need to repent.

The Parable of the Lost Coin

8"Or suppose a woman has ten silver coins*a* and loses one. Does she not light a lamp, sweep the house and search carefully until she finds it? **9**And when she finds it, she calls her friends and neighbors together and says, 'Rejoice with me; I have found my lost coin.' **10**In the same way, I tell you, there is rejoicing in the presence of the angels of God over one sinner who repents."

a8 Greek ten drachmas, each worth about a day's wages

PLAYING HEAVENLY HIDE-AND-GO-SEEK

Patti is a committed Christian. So why are some of her church friends giving her such a hard time? Because she also spends time with a bunch of people who don't know Jesus Christ from the latest rock star.

These friends of Patti dress weird and have a pretty crazy lifestyle. But they all know Patti is different, that she's committed to the Lord, and that she cares about them. They give her a lot of grief, calling her Sister Patti, but they also come to her for counsel and comfort. Patti is praying hard that God's love will break through and save her wild friends.

Look It Up When the Pharisees criticized Jesus for being a friend to sinners, he responded by telling them the parable of the lost son (Luke 15:11–32).

A young man took his inheritance and spent it on a wild partying spree. When the money ran out and he hit rock bottom, the son returned to his father to beg forgiveness. He planned to say, "I am no longer worthy to be called your son; make me like one of your hired men" (Luke 15:19).

But the father surprised him by running out to greet him and then hugging and kissing him. Rather than a lecture, the father gave his son a gigantic party, saying, "Let's have a feast and celebrate. For this son of mine was dead and is alive again; he was lost and is found" (Luke 15:23–24).

Think It Through Jesus told the parable of the lost son to illustrate that God doesn't hate sinners. He loves and searches for them. And when one of them turns to him, all heaven rejoices (Luke 15:10).

Do you tend to be more like Patti or more like the Pharisees in your attitudes toward non-Christians? If you don't really have any relationships with non-Christians, how can you ever influence them for Christ?

Work It Out Maybe like the lost son, you've done some wild things in your search for satisfaction, but now you're realizing that's all a dead-end street. Hey, guess what? If you return to the God who made you, he will welcome you with open arms into his family.

Or maybe you're like a Pharisee and don't want to have any contact with non-Christians. If that's the case, you need to look at Jesus' example and begin reaching out. This doesn't mean that you join in all their behavior. It does mean that you show them that God is real by your life and your words.

Nail It Down Read Luke 15:1–10 for parables about other lost items that were found.

Turn to pages 932, 1098 and 1228 for other readings on parables.
Turn to page 1110 for Friday's reading.

Topic

PARABLES

The Parable of the Lost Son

[11]Jesus continued: "There was a man who had two sons. [12]The younger one said to his father, 'Father, give me my share of the estate.' So he divided his property between them.

[13]"Not long after that, the younger son got together all he had, set off for a distant country and there squandered his wealth in wild living. [14]After he had spent everything, there was a severe famine in that whole country, and he began to be in need. [15]So he went and hired himself out to a citizen of that country, who sent him to his fields to feed pigs. [16]He longed to fill his stomach with the pods that the pigs were eating, but no one gave him anything.

[17]"When he came to his senses, he said, 'How many of my father's hired men have food to spare, and here I am starving to death! [18]I will set out and go back to my father and say to him: Father, I have sinned against heaven and against you. [19]I am no longer worthy to be called your son; make me like one of your hired men.' [20]So he got up and went to his father.

"But while he was still a long way off, his father saw him and was filled with compassion for him; he ran to his son, threw his arms around him and kissed him.

[21]"The son said to him, 'Father, I have sinned against heaven and against you. I am no longer worthy to be called your son.[a]'

[22]"But the father said to his servants, 'Quick! Bring the best robe and put it on him. Put a ring on his finger and sandals on his feet. [23]Bring the fattened calf and kill it. Let's have a feast and celebrate. [24]For this son of mine was dead and is alive again; he was lost and is found.' So they began to celebrate.

[25]"Meanwhile, the older son was in the field. When he came near the house, he heard music and dancing. [26]So he called one of the servants and asked him what was going on. [27]'Your brother has come,' he replied, 'and your father has killed the fattened calf because he has him back safe and sound.'

[28]"The older brother became angry and refused to go in. So his father went out and pleaded with him. [29]But he answered his father, 'Look! All these years I've been slaving for you and never disobeyed your orders. Yet you never gave me even a young goat so I could celebrate with my friends. [30]But when this son of yours who has squandered your property with prostitutes comes home, you kill the fattened calf for him!'

[31]"'My son,' the father said, 'you are always with me, and everything I have is yours. [32]But we had to celebrate and be glad, because this brother of yours was dead and is alive again; he was lost and is found.'"

The Parable of the Shrewd Manager

16 Jesus told his disciples: "There was a rich man whose manager was accused of wasting his possessions. [2]So he called him in and asked him, 'What is this I hear about you? Give an account of your management, because you cannot be manager any longer.'

[3]"The manager said to himself, 'What shall I do now? My master is taking away my job. I'm not strong enough to dig, and I'm ashamed to beg— [4]I know what I'll do so that, when I lose my job here, people will welcome me into their houses.'

[5]"So he called in each one of his master's debtors. He asked the first, 'How much do you owe my master?'

[6]"'Eight hundred gallons[b] of olive oil,' he replied.

"The manager told him, 'Take your bill, sit down quickly, and make it four hundred.'

[7]"Then he asked the second, 'And how much do you owe?'

"'A thousand bushels[c] of wheat,' he replied.

"He told him, 'Take your bill and make it eight hundred.'

[8]"The master commended the dishonest manager because he had acted shrewdly. For the people of this world are more shrewd in dealing with their own kind than are the people of the light. [9]I tell you, use worldly wealth to gain friends for yourselves, so that when it is gone, you will be welcomed into eternal dwellings.

[10]"Whoever can be trusted with very little can also be trusted with much, and whoever is dishonest with very little will also be dishonest with much. [11]So if you have not been trustworthy in handling worldly wealth, who will trust you with true riches? [12]And if you have not been trustworthy with someone else's property, who will give you property of your own?

[13]"No servant can serve two masters. Ei-

---

[a]21 Some early manuscripts son. Make me like one of your hired men.   [b]6 Greek one hundred batous (probably about 3 kiloliters)   [c]7 Greek one hundred korous (probably about 35 kiloliters)

WE'RE TO USE WEALTH, NOT ABUSE IT

H i kids, and welcome to today's version of 'Get Rich Quick!' It's the show where teens have the opportunity to earn some serious cash! I'm your host, Buck Burke. Players, tell us your name, a little bit about yourselves, and why you want the money!"

"Okay, like, my name is Mark. I'm sixteen, and I enjoy skiing and hanging out in the parking lot after school. If I win the money, I'm going to buy a new Porsche, and I guess just spend the rest on myself."

"Buck, I'm Elizabeth. I'm seventeen, and I'll set aside a portion to give to charity (you know, my church and a pro-life organization), then I'll buy a car, and then I'll save the rest for my college education. Stuff like that."

Look It Up
••••

How should you handle worldly wealth?

"Command those who are rich in this present world not to be arrogant nor to put their hope in wealth, which is so uncertain, but to put their hope in God, who richly provides us with everything for our enjoyment. Command them to do good, to be rich in good deeds, and to be generous and willing to share. In this way they will lay up treasure for themselves as a firm foundation for the coming age, so that they may take hold of the life that is truly life" (1 Timothy 6:17–19).

You're to use worldly wealth reasonably, investing it, like Elizabeth, in things that are truly important.

Think It Through
••••

What if Mexico decided to change its currency from pesos to dollars? And what if the government wouldn't say when the change was to take place, only that when it did, all pesos would be worthless? The sensible thing for Mexicans to do would be to change almost all their pesos into dollars, keeping only enough pesos to live day by day.

Likewise, you need to invest most of your wealth in things that matter, spending only what you need to live.

Work It Out
••••

Figure out how much money you spend in an average month on: clothes, records/tapes/CD's, magazines, movies, eating out. Now figure how much per month you give to your church, needy people, pro-life and pro-family organizations, groups that fight world hunger.

Is there an imbalance? Try giving at least $1 for every $10 you spend on entertainment or luxury items.

Nail It Down
••••

Read Luke 16:10–15 for Jesus' views on wealth.

Turn to pages 441, 1374 and 1396 for other readings on wealth.
Turn to page 1113 for the weekend reading.

Topic
••••
WEALTH

ther he will hate the one and love the other, or he will be devoted to the one and despise the other. You cannot serve both God and Money."

¹⁴The Pharisees, who loved money, heard all this and were sneering at Jesus. ¹⁵He said to them, "You are the ones who justify yourselves in the eyes of men, but God knows your hearts. What is highly valued among men is detestable in God's sight.

Additional Teachings

¹⁶"The Law and the Prophets were proclaimed until John. Since that time, the good news of the kingdom of God is being preached, and everyone is forcing his way into it. ¹⁷It is easier for heaven and earth to disappear than for the least stroke of a pen to drop out of the Law.

¹⁸"Anyone who divorces his wife and marries another woman commits adultery, and the man who marries a divorced woman commits adultery.

The Rich Man and Lazarus

¹⁹"There was a rich man who was dressed in purple and fine linen and lived in luxury every day. ²⁰At his gate was laid a beggar named Lazarus, covered with sores ²¹and longing to eat what fell from the rich man's table. Even the dogs came and licked his sores.

²²"The time came when the beggar died and the angels carried him to Abraham's side. The rich man also died and was buried. ²³In hell,ᵃ where he was in torment, he looked up and saw Abraham far away, with Lazarus by his side. ²⁴So he called to him, 'Father Abraham, have pity on me and send Lazarus to dip the tip of his finger in water and cool my tongue, because I am in agony in this fire.'

²⁵"But Abraham replied, 'Son, remember that in your lifetime you received your good things, while Lazarus received bad things, but now he is comforted here and you are in agony. ²⁶And besides all this, between us and you a great chasm has been fixed, so that those who want to go from here to you cannot, nor can anyone cross over from there to us.'

²⁷"He answered, 'Then I beg you, father, send Lazarus to my father's house, ²⁸for I have five brothers. Let him warn them, so that they will not also come to this place of torment.'

²⁹"Abraham replied, 'They have Moses and the Prophets; let them listen to them.'

³⁰" 'No, father Abraham,' he said, 'but if someone from the dead goes to them, they will repent.'

³¹"He said to him, 'If they do not listen to Moses and the Prophets, they will not be convinced even if someone rises from the dead.'"

Sin, Faith, Duty

17 Jesus said to his disciples: "Things that cause people to sin are bound to come, but woe to that person through whom they come. ²It would be better for him to be thrown into the sea with a millstone tied around his neck than for him to cause one of these little ones to sin. ³So watch yourselves.

"If your brother sins, rebuke him, and if he repents, forgive him. ⁴If he sins against you seven times in a day, and seven times comes back to you and says, 'I repent,' forgive him."

⁵The apostles said to the Lord, "Increase our faith!"

⁶He replied, "If you have faith as small as a mustard seed, you can say to this mulberry tree, 'Be uprooted and planted in the sea,' and it will obey you.

⁷"Suppose one of you had a servant plowing or looking after the sheep. Would he say to the servant when he comes in from the field, 'Come along now and sit down to eat'? ⁸Would he not rather say, 'Prepare my supper, get yourself ready and wait on me while I eat and drink; after that you may eat and drink'? ⁹Would he thank the servant because he did what he was told to do? ¹⁰So you also, when you have done everything you were told to do, should say, 'We are unworthy servants; we have only done our duty.'"

Ten Healed of Leprosy

¹¹Now on his way to Jerusalem, Jesus traveled along the border between Samaria and Galilee. ¹²As he was going into a village, ten men who had leprosyᵇ met him. They stood at a distance ¹³and called out in a loud voice, "Jesus, Master, have pity on us!"

¹⁴When he saw them, he said, "Go, show yourselves to the priests." And as they went, they were cleansed.

¹⁵One of them, when he saw he was healed, came back, praising God in a loud

ᵃ23 Greek Hades   ᵇ12 The Greek word was used for various diseases affecting the skin—not necessarily leprosy.

voice. [16]He threw himself at Jesus' feet and thanked him — and he was a Samaritan.

[17]Jesus asked, "Were not all ten cleansed? Where are the other nine? [18]Was no one found to return and give praise to God except this foreigner?" [19]Then he said to him, "Rise and go; your faith has made you well."

The Coming of the Kingdom of God

[20]Once, having been asked by the Pharisees when the kingdom of God would come, Jesus replied, "The kingdom of God does not come with your careful observation, [21]nor will people say, 'Here it is,' or 'There it is,' because the kingdom of God is within[a] you."

[22]Then he said to his disciples, "The time is coming when you will long to see one of the days of the Son of Man, but you will not see it. [23]Men will tell you, 'There he is!' or 'Here he is!' Do not go running off after them. [24]For the Son of Man in his day[b] will be like the lightning, which flashes and lights up the sky from one end to the other. [25]But first he must suffer many things and be rejected by this generation.

[26]"Just as it was in the days of Noah, so also will it be in the days of the Son of Man. [27]People were eating, drinking, marrying and being given in marriage up to the day Noah entered the ark. Then the flood came and destroyed them all.

[28]"It was the same in the days of Lot. People were eating and drinking, buying and selling, planting and building. [29]But the day Lot left Sodom, fire and sulfur rained down from heaven and destroyed them all.

[30]"It will be just like this on the day the Son of Man is revealed. [31]On that day no one who is on the roof of his house, with his goods inside, should go down to get them. Likewise, no one in the field should go back for anything. [32]Remember Lot's wife! [33]Whoever tries to keep his life will lose it, and whoever loses his life will preserve it. [34]I tell you, on that night two people will be in one bed; one will be taken and the other left. [35]Two women will be grinding grain together; one will be taken and the other left.[c]"

[37]"Where, Lord?" they asked.

He replied, "Where there is a dead body, there the vultures will gather."

The Parable of the Persistent Widow

18 Then Jesus told his disciples a parable to show them that they should always pray and not give up. [2]He said: "In a certain town there was a judge who neither feared God nor cared about men. [3]And there was a widow in that town who kept coming to him with the plea, 'Grant me justice against my adversary.'

[4]"For some time he refused. But finally he said to himself, 'Even though I don't fear God or care about men, [5]yet because this widow keeps bothering me, I will see that she gets justice, so that she won't eventually wear me out with her coming!' "

[6]And the Lord said, "Listen to what the unjust judge says. [7]And will not God bring about justice for his chosen ones, who cry out to him day and night? Will he keep putting them off? [8]I tell you, he will see that they get justice, and quickly. However, when the Son of Man comes, will he find faith on the earth?"

The Parable of the Pharisee and the Tax Collector

[9]To some who were confident of their own righteousness and looked down on everybody else, Jesus told this parable: [10]"Two men went up to the temple to pray, one a Pharisee and the other a tax collector. [11]The Pharisee stood up and prayed about[d] himself: 'God, I thank you that I am not like other men — robbers, evildoers, adulterers — or even like this tax collector. [12]I fast twice a week and give a tenth of all I get.'

[13]"But the tax collector stood at a distance. He would not even look up to heaven, but beat his breast and said, 'God, have mercy on me, a sinner.'

[14]"I tell you that this man, rather than the other, went home justified before God. For everyone who exalts himself will be humbled, and he who humbles himself will be exalted."

The Little Children and Jesus

[15]People were also bringing babies to Jesus to have him touch them. When the disciples saw this, they rebuked them. [16]But Jesus called the children to him and said, "Let the little children come to me, and do not hinder them, for the kingdom of God belongs to such as these. [17]I tell you the truth, anyone who will not receive the kingdom of God like a little child will never enter it."

The Rich Ruler

[18]A certain ruler asked him, "Good teach-

---

[a]21 Or among   [b]24 Some manuscripts do not have in his day.   [c]35 Some manuscripts left. [36]Two men will be in the field; one will be taken and the other left.   [d]11 Or to

PROUD VERSUS HUMBLE

Work It Out
••••

The next time you watch a famous guest on a talk show, listen closely to what that person has to say. Before very long you'll be able to tell whether that person is proud or humble.

Proud speaks mainly of itself; humble speaks of others. Proud runs to the front of the line; humble lets others go first. Proud shouts to let opinions be known; humble listens to others' opinions first. Proud rejects others as unimportant; humble accepts others as worthwhile. Proud knows it all; humble is teachable. Proud cheers when others fall; humble picks up those who have fallen.

Nail It Down
••••

Read the parable Jesus used to teach about pride and humility in Luke 18:9–14.

Think It Through
••••

Luke 18:9 says that Jesus told this story "to some who were confident of their own righteousness and looked down on everyone else." Those who are self-righteous, who are proud, put themselves not only above others but above God.

Eventually, those who are proud are alone. Pride alienates others because it puts others down instead of building others up.

Worse, pride separates the person from God. The proud person can't accept the fact that he or she needs God and can learn from God. Soon pride separates the person from others, from God and eventually from self. Pride alone is pretty poor company.

Self-examination isn't always easy nor is it always enjoyable. But it's important. Are you proud? Or are you humble? How you treat others and how you view God are good indicators.

Nail It Down
••••

Reread Jesus' parable in Luke 18:9–14. For further insight read Psalm 25:8–9.

Turn to pages 65, 371 and 462 for other readings on pride.
Turn to page 1115 for Monday's reading.

Topic
••••

er, what must I do to inherit eternal life?"

[19]"Why do you call me good?" Jesus answered. "No one is good—except God alone. [20]You know the commandments: 'Do not commit adultery, do not murder, do not steal, do not give false testimony, honor your father and mother.'ᵃ"

[21]"All these I have kept since I was a boy," he said.

[22]When Jesus heard this, he said to him, "You still lack one thing. Sell everything you have and give to the poor, and you will have treasure in heaven. Then come, follow me."

[23]When he heard this, he became very sad, because he was a man of great wealth. [24]Jesus looked at him and said, "How hard it is for the rich to enter the kingdom of God! [25]Indeed, it is easier for a camel to go through the eye of a needle than for a rich man to enter the kingdom of God."

[26]Those who heard this asked, "Who then can be saved?"

[27]Jesus replied, "What is impossible with men is possible with God."

[28]Peter said to him, "We have left all we had to follow you!"

[29]"I tell you the truth," Jesus said to them, "no one who has left home or wife or brothers or parents or children for the sake of the kingdom of God [30]will fail to receive many times as much in this age and, in the age to come, eternal life."

Jesus Again Predicts His Death

[31]Jesus took the Twelve aside and told them, "We are going up to Jerusalem, and everything that is written by the prophets about the Son of Man will be fulfilled. [32]He will be handed over to the Gentiles. They will mock him, insult him, spit on him, flog him and kill him. [33]On the third day he will rise again."

[34]The disciples did not understand any of this. Its meaning was hidden from them, and they did not know what he was talking about.

A Blind Beggar Receives His Sight

[35]As Jesus approached Jericho, a blind man was sitting by the roadside begging. [36]When he heard the crowd going by, he asked what was happening. [37]They told him, "Jesus of Nazareth is passing by."

[38]He called out, "Jesus, Son of David, have mercy on me!"

[39]Those who led the way rebuked him and told him to be quiet, but he shouted all the more, "Son of David, have mercy on me!"

[40]Jesus stopped and ordered the man to be brought to him. When he came near, Jesus asked him, [41]"What do you want me to do for you?"

"Lord, I want to see," he replied.

[42]Jesus said to him, "Receive your sight; your faith has healed you." [43]Immediately he received his sight and followed Jesus, praising God. When all the people saw it, they also praised God.

Zacchaeus the Tax Collector

19 Jesus entered Jericho and was passing through. [2]A man was there by the name of Zacchaeus; he was a chief tax collector and was wealthy. [3]He wanted to see who Jesus was, but being a short man he could not, because of the crowd. [4]So he ran ahead and climbed a sycamore-fig tree to see him, since Jesus was coming that way.

[5]When Jesus reached the spot, he looked up and said to him, "Zacchaeus, come down immediately. I must stay at your house today." [6]So he came down at once and welcomed him gladly.

[7]All the people saw this and began to mutter, "He has gone to be the guest of a 'sinner.'"

[8]But Zacchaeus stood up and said to the Lord, "Look, Lord! Here and now I give half of my possessions to the poor, and if I have cheated anybody out of anything, I will pay back four times the amount."

[9]Jesus said to him, "Today salvation has come to this house, because this man, too, is a son of Abraham. [10]For the Son of Man came to seek and to save what was lost."

The Parable of the Ten Minas

[11]While they were listening to this, he went on to tell them a parable, because he was near Jerusalem and the people thought that the kingdom of God was going to appear at once. [12]He said: "A man of noble birth went to a distant country to have himself appointed king and then to return. [13]So he called ten of his servants and gave them ten minas.ᵇ 'Put this money to work,' he said, 'until I come back.'

[14]"But his subjects hated him and sent a delegation after him to say, 'We don't want this man to be our king.'

[15]"He was made king, however, and returned home. Then he sent for the servants

---

ᵃ20 Exodus 20:12-16; Deut. 5:16-20　　ᵇ13 A mina was about three months' wages.

JESUS LOVES DRUGGIES!

As he passes through a parking lot on the way to youth group, Richard, sixteen, looks with disgust at a group of "druggies" standing by a pickup truck. "What a bunch of losers!" he thinks.

One of the girls, seventeen-year-old Julia, is hooked on crack. Her addiction is such that she'll do anything—beg on the street, steal, even sell herself as a prostitute—just to get enough cash for one more hit. To be truthful, Julia is about as low as a person can go.

Look It Up
• • • •

From a human standpoint, it seems that certain sins are especially bad, and that God, if he forgives them at all, does so only reluctantly.

No. The good news of Christ is that anyone can be forgiven. In fact, Jesus is the best friend a sinner could ever have.

"While Jesus was having dinner at Matthew's house, many tax collectors and 'sinners' came and ate with him and his disciples. When the Pharisees saw this, they asked his disciples, 'Why does your teacher eat with tax collectors and "sinners"?'

"On hearing this, Jesus said, 'It is not the healthy who need a doctor, but the sick' " (Matthew 9:10–12).

Think It Through
• • • •

How can you tell if someone you love is using drugs? By looking for the following symptoms:
- A decline in school or work performance.
- Mood changes that can't be explained.
- Less concern with physical appearance.
- Secretiveness or vagueness when asked about social activities.
- Disinterest in school activities or hobbies.

Work It Out
• • • •

If you think you might have a drug problem, remember first that you have a forgiving friend in Jesus. Second, talk to your youth leader or school counselor about getting some help.

If you have friends who are experimenting with drugs, pray for wisdom. Then gently communicate your concern, love, acceptance, and desire to see them get help.

If someone you know is addicted to drugs, share that information with a mature Christian leader. This is one situation where snitching on a friend is the best, most loving thing you can do. It may even make the difference between life and death!

Nail It Down
• • • •

Read the message of Luke 19:1–10.

Turn to pages 1151, 1239 and 1350 for other readings on drugs.
Turn to page 1119 for Tuesday's reading.

Topic
• • • •

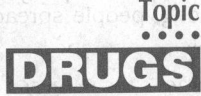

DRUGS

to whom he had given the money, in order to find out what they had gained with it.

¹⁶"The first one came and said, 'Sir, your mina has earned ten more.'

¹⁷" 'Well done, my good servant!' his master replied. 'Because you have been trustworthy in a very small matter, take charge of ten cities.'

¹⁸"The second came and said, 'Sir, your mina has earned five more.'

¹⁹"His master answered, 'You take charge of five cities.'

²⁰"Then another servant came and said, 'Sir, here is your mina; I have kept it laid away in a piece of cloth. ²¹I was afraid of you, because you are a hard man. You take out what you did not put in and reap what you did not sow.'

²²"His master replied, 'I will judge you by your own words, you wicked servant! You knew, did you, that I am a hard man, taking out what I did not put in, and reaping what I did not sow? ²³Why then didn't you put my money on deposit, so that when I came back, I could have collected it with interest?'

²⁴"Then he said to those standing by, 'Take his mina away from him and give it to the one who has ten minas.'

²⁵" 'Sir,' they said, 'he already has ten!'

²⁶"He replied, 'I tell you that to everyone who has, more will be given, but as for the one who has nothing, even what he has will be taken away. ²⁷But those enemies of mine who did not want me to be king over them — bring them here and kill them in front of me.' "

The Triumphal Entry

²⁸After Jesus had said this, he went on ahead, going up to Jerusalem. ²⁹As he approached Bethphage and Bethany at the hill called the Mount of Olives, he sent two of his disciples, saying to them, ³⁰"Go to the village ahead of you, and as you enter it, you will find a colt tied there, which no one has ever ridden. Untie it and bring it here. ³¹If anyone asks you, 'Why are you untying it?' tell him, 'The Lord needs it.' "

³²Those who were sent ahead went and found it just as he had told them. ³³As they were untying the colt, its owners asked them, "Why are you untying the colt?"

³⁴They replied, "The Lord needs it."

³⁵They brought it to Jesus, threw their cloaks on the colt and put Jesus on it. ³⁶As he went along, people spread their cloaks on the road.

³⁷When he came near the place where the road goes down the Mount of Olives, the whole crowd of disciples began joyfully to praise God in loud voices for all the miracles they had seen:

³⁸"Blessed is the king who comes in the name of the Lord!"ᵃ

"Peace in heaven and glory in the highest!"

³⁹Some of the Pharisees in the crowd said to Jesus, "Teacher, rebuke your disciples!"

⁴⁰"I tell you," he replied, "if they keep quiet, the stones will cry out."

⁴¹As he approached Jerusalem and saw the city, he wept over it ⁴²and said, "If you, even you, had only known on this day what would bring you peace — but now it is hidden from your eyes. ⁴³The days will come upon you when your enemies will build an embankment against you and encircle you and hem you in on every side. ⁴⁴They will dash you to the ground, you and the children within your walls. They will not leave one stone on another, because you did not recognize the time of God's coming to you."

Jesus at the Temple

⁴⁵Then he entered the temple area and began driving out those who were selling. ⁴⁶"It is written," he said to them, " 'My house will be a house of prayer'ᵇ; but you have made it 'a den of robbers.'ᶜ"

⁴⁷Every day he was teaching at the temple. But the chief priests, the teachers of the law and the leaders among the people were trying to kill him. ⁴⁸Yet they could not find any way to do it, because all the people hung on his words.

The Authority of Jesus Questioned

20 One day as he was teaching the people in the temple courts and preaching the gospel, the chief priests and the teachers of the law, together with the elders, came up to him. ²"Tell us by what authority you are doing these things," they said. "Who gave you this authority?"

³He replied, "I will also ask you a question. Tell me, ⁴John's baptism — was it from heaven, or from men?"

⁵They discussed it among themselves and said, "If we say, 'From heaven,' he will ask, 'Why didn't you believe him?' ⁶But if we say, 'From men,' all the people will stone us, be-

ᵃ38 Psalm 118:26   ᵇ46 Isaiah 56:7   ᶜ46 Jer. 7:11

cause they are persuaded that John was a prophet."

7So they answered, "We don't know where it was from."

8Jesus said, "Neither will I tell you by what authority I am doing these things."

The Parable of the Tenants

9He went on to tell the people this parable: "A man planted a vineyard, rented it to some farmers and went away for a long time. **10**At harvest time he sent a servant to the tenants so they would give him some of the fruit of the vineyard. But the tenants beat him and sent him away empty-handed. **11**He sent another servant, but that one also they beat and treated shamefully and sent away empty-handed. **12**He sent still a third, and they wounded him and threw him out.

13"Then the owner of the vineyard said, 'What shall I do? I will send my son, whom I love; perhaps they will respect him.'

14"But when the tenants saw him, they talked the matter over. 'This is the heir,' they said. 'Let's kill him, and the inheritance will be ours.' **15**So they threw him out of the vineyard and killed him.

"What then will the owner of the vineyard do to them? **16**He will come and kill those tenants and give the vineyard to others."

When the people heard this, they said, "May this never be!"

17Jesus looked directly at them and asked, "Then what is the meaning of that which is written:

" 'The stone the builders rejected
has become the capstone*a* '*b*?

18Everyone who falls on that stone will be broken to pieces, but he on whom it falls will be crushed."

19The teachers of the law and the chief priests looked for a way to arrest him immediately, because they knew he had spoken this parable against them. But they were afraid of the people.

Paying Taxes to Caesar

20Keeping a close watch on him, they sent spies, who pretended to be honest. They hoped to catch Jesus in something he said so that they might hand him over to the power and authority of the governor. **21**So the spies questioned him: "Teacher, we know that you speak and teach what is right, and that you do not show partiality but teach the way of God in accordance with the truth. **22**Is it right for us to pay taxes to Caesar or not?"

23He saw through their duplicity and said to them, **24**"Show me a denarius. Whose portrait and inscription are on it?"

25"Caesar's," they replied.

He said to them, "Then give to Caesar what is Caesar's, and to God what is God's."

26They were unable to trap him in what he had said there in public. And astonished by his answer, they became silent.

The Resurrection and Marriage

27Some of the Sadducees, who say there is no resurrection, came to Jesus with a question. **28**"Teacher," they said, "Moses wrote for us that if a man's brother dies and leaves a wife but no children, the man must marry the widow and have children for his brother. **29**Now there were seven brothers. The first one married a woman and died childless. **30**The second **31**and then the third married her, and in the same way the seven died, leaving no children. **32**Finally, the woman died too. **33**Now then, at the resurrection whose wife will she be, since the seven were married to her?"

34Jesus replied, "The people of this age marry and are given in marriage. **35**But those who are considered worthy of taking part in that age and in the resurrection from the dead will neither marry nor be given in marriage, **36**and they can no longer die; for they are like the angels. They are God's children, since they are children of the resurrection. **37**But in the account of the bush, even Moses showed that the dead rise, for he calls the Lord 'the God of Abraham, and the God of Isaac, and the God of Jacob.'*c* **38**He is not the God of the dead, but of the living, for to him all are alive."

39Some of the teachers of the law responded, "Well said, teacher!" **40**And no one dared to ask him any more questions.

Whose Son Is the Christ?

41Then Jesus said to them, "How is it that they say the Christ*d* is the Son of David? **42**David himself declares in the Book of Psalms:

" 'The Lord said to my Lord:
"Sit at my right hand
43until I make your enemies
a footstool for your feet." '*e*

44David calls him 'Lord.' How then can he be his son?"

---

a17 Or *cornerstone*   *b17* Psalm 118:22   *c37* Exodus 3:6   *d41* Or *Messiah*   *e43* Psalm 110:1

45While all the people were listening, Jesus said to his disciples, **46**"Beware of the teachers of the law. They like to walk around in flowing robes and love to be greeted in the marketplaces and have the most important seats in the synagogues and the places of honor at banquets. **47**They devour widows' houses and for a show make lengthy prayers. Such men will be punished most severely."

The Widow's Offering

21 As he looked up, Jesus saw the rich putting their gifts into the temple treasury. **2**He also saw a poor widow put in two very small copper coins. *a* **3**"I tell you the truth," he said, "this poor widow has put in more than all the others. **4**All these people gave their gifts out of their wealth; but she out of her poverty put in all she had to live on."

Signs of the End of the Age

5Some of his disciples were remarking about how the temple was adorned with beautiful stones and with gifts dedicated to God. But Jesus said, **6**"As for what you see here, the time will come when not one stone will be left on another; every one of them will be thrown down."

7"Teacher," they asked, "when will these things happen? And what will be the sign that they are about to take place?"

8He replied: "Watch out that you are not deceived. For many will come in my name, claiming, 'I am he,' and, 'The time is near.' Do not follow them. **9**When you hear of wars and revolutions, do not be frightened. These things must happen first, but the end will not come right away."

10Then he said to them: "Nation will rise against nation, and kingdom against kingdom. **11**There will be great earthquakes, famines and pestilences in various places, and fearful events and great signs from heaven.

12"But before all this, they will lay hands on you and persecute you. They will deliver you to synagogues and prisons, and you will be brought before kings and governors, and all on account of my name. **13**This will result in your being witnesses to them. **14**But make up your mind not to worry beforehand how you will defend yourselves. **15**For I will give you words and wisdom that none of your adversaries will be able to resist or contradict. **16**You will be betrayed even by parents,

brothers, relatives and friends, and they will put some of you to death. **17**All men will hate you because of me. **18**But not a hair of your head will perish. **19**By standing firm you will gain life.

20"When you see Jerusalem being surrounded by armies, you will know that its desolation is near. **21**Then let those who are in Judea flee to the mountains, let those in the city get out, and let those in the country not enter the city. **22**For this is the time of punishment in fulfillment of all that has been written. **23**How dreadful it will be in those days for pregnant women and nursing mothers! There will be great distress in the land and wrath against this people. **24**They will fall by the sword and will be taken as prisoners to all the nations. Jerusalem will be trampled on by the Gentiles until the times of the Gentiles are fulfilled.

25"There will be signs in the sun, moon and stars. On the earth, nations will be in anguish and perplexity at the roaring and tossing of the sea. **26**Men will faint from terror, apprehensive of what is coming on the world, for the heavenly bodies will be shaken. **27**At that time they will see the Son of Man coming in a cloud with power and great glory. **28**When these things begin to take place, stand up and lift up your heads, because your redemption is drawing near."

29He told them this parable: "Look at the fig tree and all the trees. **30**When they sprout leaves, you can see for yourselves and know that summer is near. **31**Even so, when you see these things happening, you know that the kingdom of God is near.

32"I tell you the truth, this generation *b* will certainly not pass away until all these things have happened. **33**Heaven and earth will pass away, but my words will never pass away.

34"Be careful, or your hearts will be weighed down with dissipation, drunkenness and the anxieties of life, and that day will close on you unexpectedly like a trap. **35**For it will come upon all those who live on the face of the whole earth. **36**Be always on the watch, and pray that you may be able to escape all that is about to happen, and that you may be able to stand before the Son of Man."

37Each day Jesus was teaching at the temple, and each evening he went out to spend the night on the hill called the Mount of Olives, **38**and all the people came early in the morning to hear him at the temple.

---

a2 Greek *two lepta*   *b32* Or *race*

A WORLD WALLOPED BY WORRY

During an unusually boring lecture on the Pythagorean theorem in Mrs. Baxter's fourth hour geometry class, at least three students have, within their own minds, left the room.

Mark is frantically trying to figure out which girl to ask to the Friday night banquet. (Last night this problem kept him up till 3:30 A.M.!)

Sandy is fretting over something Elaine said to her about Ryan. "I wonder if she meant that he . . . "

Jared is worried about his mom, who is back in the hospital for the third time this month. The doctors still can't figure out what's wrong with her.

Look It Up ••••

Feelings of worry have nipped at the hearts and minds of everyone who has ever lived. Take, for example, Martha, a friend of Jesus:

"But Martha was distracted by all the preparations that had to be made. She came to him [Jesus] and asked, 'Lord, don't you care that my sister has left me to do the work by myself? Tell her to help me!'

" 'Martha, Martha,' the Lord answered, 'you are worried and upset about many things, but only one thing is needed. Mary has chosen what is better, and it will not be taken away from her' " (Luke 10:40–42).

We're all a bit like Martha. We get all upset over life's problems—both big and small. It's no wonder Jesus said, "So do not worry, . . . For the pagans run after all these things, and your heavenly Father knows that you need them" (Matthew 6:31–32).

Think It Through ••••

What are your biggest worries today? Why do those things bother you so much?

Who is the most relaxed and peaceful person you know? What is that person's secret?

Work It Out ••••

You don't have to be paralyzed by anxiety. Ask God to show you how to overcome your worries.

"Lord, I really need to learn how to deal with worry. Too many times I drive myself crazy thinking about my problems, and I totally stress out. Teach me what your Word says about worry. More than that, show me what I can do to have victory over those nagging fears. Amen."

Nail It Down ••••

Read Jesus' warning against worrying in Luke 21:34.

Turn to pages 968 and 1011 for other readings on worry.
Turn to page 1126 for Wednesday's reading.

Topic
••••

WORRY

Judas Agrees to Betray Jesus

22 Now the Feast of Unleavened Bread, called the Passover, was approaching, ²and the chief priests and the teachers of the law were looking for some way to get rid of Jesus, for they were afraid of the people. ³Then Satan entered Judas, called Iscariot, one of the Twelve. ⁴And Judas went to the chief priests and the officers of the temple guard and discussed with them how he might betray Jesus. ⁵They were delighted and agreed to give him money. ⁶He consented, and watched for an opportunity to hand Jesus over to them when no crowd was present.

The Last Supper

⁷Then came the day of Unleavened Bread on which the Passover lamb had to be sacrificed. ⁸Jesus sent Peter and John, saying, "Go and make preparations for us to eat the Passover."

⁹"Where do you want us to prepare for it?" they asked.

¹⁰He replied, "As you enter the city, a man carrying a jar of water will meet you. Follow him to the house that he enters, ¹¹and say to the owner of the house, 'The Teacher asks: Where is the guest room, where I may eat the Passover with my disciples?' ¹²He will show you a large upper room, all furnished. Make preparations there."

¹³They left and found things just as Jesus had told them. So they prepared the Passover.

¹⁴When the hour came, Jesus and his apostles reclined at the table. ¹⁵And he said to them, "I have eagerly desired to eat this Passover with you before I suffer. ¹⁶For I tell you, I will not eat it again until it finds fulfillment in the kingdom of God."

¹⁷After taking the cup, he gave thanks and said, "Take this and divide it among you. ¹⁸For I tell you I will not drink again of the fruit of the vine until the kingdom of God comes."

¹⁹And he took bread, gave thanks and broke it, and gave it to them, saying, "This is my body given for you; do this in remembrance of me."

²⁰In the same way, after the supper he took the cup, saying, "This cup is the new covenant in my blood, which is poured out for you. ²¹But the hand of him who is going to betray me is with mine on the table. ²²The Son of Man will go as it has been decreed, but woe to that man who betrays him." ²³They began to question among themselves which of them it might be who would do this.

²⁴Also a dispute arose among them as to which of them was considered to be greatest. ²⁵Jesus said to them, "The kings of the Gentiles lord it over them; and those who exercise authority over them call themselves Benefactors. ²⁶But you are not to be like that. Instead, the greatest among you should be like the youngest, and the one who rules like the one who serves. ²⁷For who is greater, the one who is at the table or the one who serves? Is it not the one who is at the table? But I am among you as one who serves. ²⁸You are those who have stood by me in my trials. ²⁹And I confer on you a kingdom, just as my Father conferred one on me, ³⁰so that you may eat and drink at my table in my kingdom and sit on thrones, judging the twelve tribes of Israel.

³¹"Simon, Simon, Satan has asked to sift you*ᵃ* as wheat. ³²But I have prayed for you, Simon, that your faith may not fail. And when you have turned back, strengthen your brothers."

³³But he replied, "Lord, I am ready to go with you to prison and to death."

³⁴Jesus answered, "I tell you, Peter, before the rooster crows today, you will deny three times that you know me."

³⁵Then Jesus asked them, "When I sent you without purse, bag or sandals, did you lack anything?"

"Nothing," they answered.

³⁶He said to them, "But now if you have a purse, take it, and also a bag; and if you don't have a sword, sell your cloak and buy one. ³⁷It is written: 'And he was numbered with the transgressors'ᵇ; and I tell you that this must be fulfilled in me. Yes, what is written about me is reaching its fulfillment."

³⁸The disciples said, "See, Lord, here are two swords."

"That is enough," he replied.

Jesus Prays on the Mount of Olives

³⁹Jesus went out as usual to the Mount of Olives, and his disciples followed him. ⁴⁰On reaching the place, he said to them, "Pray that you will not fall into temptation." ⁴¹He withdrew about a stone's throw beyond them, knelt down and prayed, ⁴²"Father, if you are willing, take this cup from me; yet not my will, but yours be done." ⁴³An angel from heaven appeared to him and strength-

ᵃ31 The Greek is plural.   ᵇ37 Isaiah 53:12

ened him. **44**And being in anguish, he prayed more earnestly, and his sweat was like drops of blood falling to the ground.*a*

45When he rose from prayer and went back to the disciples, he found them asleep, exhausted from sorrow. **46**"Why are you sleeping?" he asked them. "Get up and pray so that you will not fall into temptation."

Jesus Arrested

47While he was still speaking a crowd came up, and the man who was called Judas, one of the Twelve, was leading them. He approached Jesus to kiss him, **48**but Jesus asked him, "Judas, are you betraying the Son of Man with a kiss?"

49When Jesus' followers saw what was going to happen, they said, "Lord, should we strike with our swords?" **50**And one of them struck the servant of the high priest, cutting off his right ear.

51But Jesus answered, "No more of this!" And he touched the man's ear and healed him.

52Then Jesus said to the chief priests, the officers of the temple guard, and the elders, who had come for him, "Am I leading a rebellion, that you have come with swords and clubs? **53**Every day I was with you in the temple courts, and you did not lay a hand on me. But this is your hour—when darkness reigns."

Peter Disowns Jesus

54Then seizing him, they led him away and took him into the house of the high priest. Peter followed at a distance. **55**But when they had kindled a fire in the middle of the courtyard and had sat down together, Peter sat down with them. **56**A servant girl saw him seated there in the firelight. She looked closely at him and said, "This man was with him."

57But he denied it. "Woman, I don't know him," he said.

58A little later someone else saw him and said, "You also are one of them."

"Man, I am not!" Peter replied.

59About an hour later another asserted, "Certainly this fellow was with him, for he is a Galilean."

60Peter replied, "Man, I don't know what you're talking about!" Just as he was speaking, the rooster crowed. **61**The Lord turned and looked straight at Peter. Then Peter remembered the word the Lord had spoken to

him: "Before the rooster crows today, you will disown me three times." **62**And he went outside and wept bitterly.

The Guards Mock Jesus

63The men who were guarding Jesus began mocking and beating him. **64**They blindfolded him and demanded, "Prophesy! Who hit you?" **65**And they said many other insulting things to him.

Jesus Before Pilate and Herod

66At daybreak the council of the elders of the people, both the chief priests and teachers of the law, met together, and Jesus was led before them. **67**"If you are the Christ,*b*" they said, "tell us."

Jesus answered, "If I tell you, you will not believe me, **68**and if I asked you, you would not answer. **69**But from now on, the Son of Man will be seated at the right hand of the mighty God."

70They all asked, "Are you then the Son of God?"

He replied, "You are right in saying I am."

71Then they said, "Why do we need any more testimony? We have heard it from his own lips."

23 Then the whole assembly rose and led him off to Pilate. **2**And they began to accuse him, saying, "We have found this man subverting our nation. He opposes payment of taxes to Caesar and claims to be Christ,*c* a king."

3So Pilate asked Jesus, "Are you the king of the Jews?"

"Yes, it is as you say," Jesus replied.

4Then Pilate announced to the chief priests and the crowd, "I find no basis for a charge against this man."

5But they insisted, "He stirs up the people all over Judea*d* by his teaching. He started in Galilee and has come all the way here."

6On hearing this, Pilate asked if the man was a Galilean. **7**When he learned that Jesus was under Herod's jurisdiction, he sent him to Herod, who was also in Jerusalem at that time.

8When Herod saw Jesus, he was greatly pleased, because for a long time he had been wanting to see him. From what he had heard about him, he hoped to see him perform some miracle. **9**He plied him with many questions, but Jesus gave him no answer. **10**The chief priests and the teachers of the law were standing there, vehemently ac-

---

a44 Some early manuscripts do not have verses 43 and 44.   *b67* Or *Messiah*   *c2* Or *Messiah*; also in verses 35 and 39   *d5* Or *over the land of the Jews* cusing him. **11**Then Herod and his soldiers ridiculed and mocked him. Dressing him in an elegant robe, they sent him back to Pilate. **12**That day Herod and Pilate became friends — before this they had been enemies.

13Pilate called together the chief priests, the rulers and the people, **14**and said to them, "You brought me this man as one who was inciting the people to rebellion. I have examined him in your presence and have found no basis for your charges against him. **15**Neither has Herod, for he sent him back to us; as you can see, he has done nothing to deserve death. **16**Therefore, I will punish him and then release him.*a*"

18With one voice they cried out, "Away with this man! Release Barabbas to us!" **19**(Barabbas had been thrown into prison for an insurrection in the city, and for murder.)

20Wanting to release Jesus, Pilate appealed to them again. **21**But they kept shouting, "Crucify him! Crucify him!"

22For the third time he spoke to them: "Why? What crime has this man committed? I have found in him no grounds for the death penalty. Therefore I will have him punished and then release him."

23But with loud shouts they insistently demanded that he be crucified, and their shouts prevailed. **24**So Pilate decided to grant their demand. **25**He released the man who had been thrown into prison for insurrection and murder, the one they asked for, and surrendered Jesus to their will.

The Crucifixion

26As they led him away, they seized Simon from Cyrene, who was on his way in from the country, and put the cross on him and made him carry it behind Jesus. **27**A large number of people followed him, including women who mourned and wailed for him. **28**Jesus turned and said to them, "Daughters of Jerusalem, do not weep for me; weep for yourselves and for your children. **29**For the time will come when you will say, 'Blessed are the barren women, the wombs that never bore and the breasts that never nursed!' **30**Then

" 'they will say to the mountains, "Fall on us!"
and to the hills, "Cover us!" '*b*

31For if men do these things when the tree is green, what will happen when it is dry?"

32Two other men, both criminals, were also led out with him to be executed. **33**When they came to the place called the Skull, there they crucified him, along with the criminals — one on his right, the other on his left. **34**Jesus said, "Father, forgive them, for they do not know what they are doing."*c* And they divided up his clothes by casting lots.

35The people stood watching, and the rulers even sneered at him. They said, "He saved others; let him save himself if he is the Christ of God, the Chosen One."

36The soldiers also came up and mocked him. They offered him wine vinegar **37**and said, "If you are the king of the Jews, save yourself."

38There was a written notice above him, which read: THIS IS THE KING OF THE JEWS.

39One of the criminals who hung there hurled insults at him: "Aren't you the Christ? Save yourself and us!"

40But the other criminal rebuked him. "Don't you fear God," he said, "since you are under the same sentence? **41**We are punished justly, for we are getting what our deeds deserve. But this man has done nothing wrong."

42Then he said, "Jesus, remember me when you come into your kingdom.*d*"

43Jesus answered him, "I tell you the truth, today you will be with me in paradise."

Jesus' Death

44It was now about the sixth hour, and darkness came over the whole land until the ninth hour, **45**for the sun stopped shining. And the curtain of the temple was torn in two. **46**Jesus called out with a loud voice, "Father, into your hands I commit my spirit." When he had said this, he breathed his last.

47The centurion, seeing what had happened, praised God and said, "Surely this was a righteous man." **48**When all the people who had gathered to witness this sight saw what took place, they beat their breasts and went away. **49**But all those who knew him, including the women who had followed him from Galilee, stood at a distance, watching these things.

Jesus' Burial

50Now there was a man named Joseph, a member of the Council, a good and upright

---

a16 Some manuscripts *him."* *17Now he was obliged to release one man to them at the Feast.*   *b30* Hosea 10:8
c34 Some early manuscripts do not have this sentence.   *d42* Some manuscripts *come with your kingly power*

man, **51**who had not consented to their decision and action. He came from the Judean town of Arimathea and he was waiting for the kingdom of God. **52**Going to Pilate, he asked for Jesus' body. **53**Then he took it down, wrapped it in linen cloth and placed it in a tomb cut in the rock, one in which no one had yet been laid. **54**It was Preparation Day, and the Sabbath was about to begin.

55The women who had come with Jesus from Galilee followed Joseph and saw the tomb and how his body was laid in it. **56**Then they went home and prepared spices and perfumes. But they rested on the Sabbath in obedience to the commandment.

The Resurrection

24 On the first day of the week, very early in the morning, the women took the spices they had prepared and went to the tomb. **2**They found the stone rolled away from the tomb, **3**but when they entered, they did not find the body of the Lord Jesus. **4**While they were wondering about this, suddenly two men in clothes that gleamed like lightning stood beside them. **5**In their fright the women bowed down with their faces to the ground, but the men said to them, "Why do you look for the living among the dead? **6**He is not here; he has risen! Remember how he told you, while he was still with you in Galilee: **7**'The Son of Man must be delivered into the hands of sinful men, be crucified and on the third day be raised again.' " **8**Then they remembered his words.

9When they came back from the tomb, they told all these things to the Eleven and to all the others. **10**It was Mary Magdalene, Joanna, Mary the mother of James, and the others with them who told this to the apostles. **11**But they did not believe the women, because their words seemed to them like nonsense. **12**Peter, however, got up and ran to the tomb. Bending over, he saw the strips of linen lying by themselves, and he went away, wondering to himself what had happened.

On the Road to Emmaus

13Now that same day two of them were going to a village called Emmaus, about seven miles*a* from Jerusalem. **14**They were talking with each other about everything that had happened. **15**As they talked and discussed these things with each other, Jesus himself came up and walked along with them; **16**but they were kept from recognizing him.

17He asked them, "What are you discussing together as you walk along?"

They stood still, their faces downcast. **18**One of them, named Cleopas, asked him, "Are you only a visitor to Jerusalem and do not know the things that have happened there in these days?"

19"What things?" he asked.

"About Jesus of Nazareth," they replied. "He was a prophet, powerful in word and deed before God and all the people. **20**The chief priests and our rulers handed him over to be sentenced to death, and they crucified him; **21**but we had hoped that he was the one who was going to redeem Israel. And what is more, it is the third day since all this took place. **22**In addition, some of our women amazed us. They went to the tomb early this morning **23**but didn't find his body. They came and told us that they had seen a vision of angels, who said he was alive. **24**Then some of our companions went to the tomb and found it just as the women had said, but him they did not see."

25He said to them, "How foolish you are, and how slow of heart to believe all that the prophets have spoken! **26**Did not the Christ*b* have to suffer these things and then enter his glory?" **27**And beginning with Moses and all the Prophets, he explained to them what was said in all the Scriptures concerning himself.

28As they approached the village to which they were going, Jesus acted as if he were going farther. **29**But they urged him strongly, "Stay with us, for it is nearly evening; the day is almost over." So he went in to stay with them.

30When he was at the table with them, he took bread, gave thanks, broke it and began to give it to them. **31**Then their eyes were opened and they recognized him, and he disappeared from their sight. **32**They asked each other, "Were not our hearts burning within us while he talked with us on the road and opened the Scriptures to us?"

33They got up and returned at once to Jerusalem. There they found the Eleven and those with them, assembled together **34**and saying, "It is true! The Lord has risen and has appeared to Simon." **35**Then the two told what had happened on the way, and how

a13 Greek *sixty stadia* (about 11 kilometers)   *b26* Or *Messiah*; also in verse 46

Jesus was recognized by them when he broke the bread.

Jesus Appears to the Disciples

36While they were still talking about this, Jesus himself stood among them and said to them, "Peace be with you."

37They were startled and frightened, thinking they saw a ghost. **38**He said to them, "Why are you troubled, and why do doubts rise in your minds? **39**Look at my hands and my feet. It is I myself! Touch me and see; a ghost does not have flesh and bones, as you see I have."

40When he had said this, he showed them his hands and feet. **41**And while they still did not believe it because of joy and amazement, he asked them, "Do you have anything here to eat?" **42**They gave him a piece of broiled fish, **43**and he took it and ate it in their presence.

44He said to them, "This is what I told you while I was still with you: Everything must be fulfilled that is written about me in the Law of Moses, the Prophets and the Psalms."

45Then he opened their minds so they could understand the Scriptures. **46**He told them, "This is what is written: The Christ will suffer and rise from the dead on the third day, **47**and repentance and forgiveness of sins will be preached in his name to all nations, beginning at Jerusalem. **48**You are witnesses of these things. **49**I am going to send you what my Father has promised; but stay in the city until you have been clothed with power from on high."

The Ascension

50When he had led them out to the vicinity of Bethany, he lifted up his hands and blessed them. **51**While he was blessing them, he left them and was taken up into heaven. **52**Then they worshiped him and returned to Jerusalem with great joy. **53**And they stayed continually at the temple, praising God.

JOHN

"IN the beginning," begins John's gospel. Starting before the beginning of time, John shows how the Son of God becomes a man in order to bring eternal life to the human race and die as the sacrifice for human sin. John gives an account of seven miracles and seven "I am" declarations that prove Jesus is God. John also records prayers and teachings that reveal how very much God loves us, and his book contains one of the most famous verses in the Bible—John 3:16. If you've never memorized this verse, make that a goal as you read this book.

Outline of Contents

The Word Became Flesh

1 In the beginning was the Word, and the Word was with God, and the Word was God. **2**He was with God in the beginning. **3**Through him all things were made; without him nothing was made that has been made. **4**In him was life, and that life was the light of men. **5**The light shines in the darkness, but the darkness has not understood[a] it.

6There came a man who was sent from God; his name was John. **7**He came as a witness to testify concerning that light, so that through him all men might believe. **8**He himself was not the light; he came only as a witness to the light. **9**The true light that gives light to every man was coming into the world.[b]

10He was in the world, and though the world was made through him, the world did not recognize him. **11**He came to that which was his own, but his own did not receive him. **12**Yet to all who received him, to those who believed in his name, he gave the right

---

[a]5 Or *darkness, and the darkness has not overcome*
man who comes into the world

[b]9 Or *This was the true light that gives light to every*

UNDERSTANDING GOD'S INVISIBLE TOUCH

Ellen feels frustrated.

All her life she's heard about God. In her Bible she's read about God. She and her Christian friends talk about God. Ellen believes in God, and seven years ago she became a child of God by trusting Christ as her Savior. So why the frustration, Ellen?

"I don't know. It's just that sometimes I wish I could actually see God. Or when I feel really down, have him reach out and give me a big hug. Wouldn't it be great to have him right here with us all the time? Wow! Then we'd never doubt again!"

Look It Up

Do you ever feel like Ellen? Most people do at one time or another. Our skeptical society usually dismisses whatever we can't see, feel or touch. This attitude even affects Christians, making us doubt. The frustration comes because God can't be known on those terms.

Why? Because "God is spirit" (John 4:24).

What does that mean? It means he is, by nature, invisible. He doesn't have a material body like we do. And since he's not confined to a body in a specific location, he can be everywhere at once! He is right there with Ellen wherever she is, and at the same time he is right here with us!

Think It Through

If God doesn't have a physical body, why do some Bible verses mention his "ears" (1 Peter 3:12) or his "hands" (Psalm 19:1)? Such passages don't mean that God literally has hands and ears. They are figures of speech intended to show that God can hear our prayers and help us in our time of need.

Yes, sometimes the Bible records instances in which men "saw" God (Genesis 18:1; Exodus 24:10; Isaiah 6:1). But these individuals saw some manifestation of God, not his invisible essence (John 1:18).

Work It Out

Thank God that, because he is spirit, not limited to a material body, he can be everywhere at once. Thank him for being right here this very minute. And remember, we are always in his presence.

The next step? Live like it!

Nail It Down

Read John 1:1–18 for instructions on how we can get to know God.

Turn to pages 599, 980, 998, 1235 and 1330 for other readings on knowing God.
Turn to page 1128 for Thursday's reading.

Topic

KNOWING GOD

to become children of God— [13]children born not of natural descent,[a] nor of human decision or a husband's will, but born of God.

[14]The Word became flesh and made his dwelling among us. We have seen his glory, the glory of the One and Only,[b] who came from the Father, full of grace and truth.

[15]John testifies concerning him. He cries out, saying, "This was he of whom I said, 'He who comes after me has surpassed me because he was before me.'" [16]From the fullness of his grace we have all received one blessing after another. [17]For the law was given through Moses; grace and truth came through Jesus Christ. [18]No one has ever seen God, but God the One and Only,[b,c] who is at the Father's side, has made him known.

John the Baptist Denies Being the Christ

[19]Now this was John's testimony when the Jews of Jerusalem sent priests and Levites to ask him who he was. [20]He did not fail to confess, but confessed freely, "I am not the Christ.[d]"

[21]They asked him, "Then who are you? Are you Elijah?"

He said, "I am not."

"Are you the Prophet?"

He answered, "No."

[22]Finally they said, "Who are you? Give us an answer to take back to those who sent us. What do you say about yourself?"

[23]John replied in the words of Isaiah the prophet, "I am the voice of one calling in the desert, 'Make straight the way for the Lord.'"[e]

[24]Now some Pharisees who had been sent [25]questioned him, "Why then do you baptize if you are not the Christ, nor Elijah, nor the Prophet?"

[26]"I baptize with[f] water," John replied, "but among you stands one you do not know. [27]He is the one who comes after me, the thongs of whose sandals I am not worthy to untie."

[28]This all happened at Bethany on the other side of the Jordan, where John was baptizing.

Jesus the Lamb of God

[29]The next day John saw Jesus coming toward him and said, "Look, the Lamb of God, who takes away the sin of the world! [30]This is the one I meant when I said, 'A man who comes after me has surpassed me because he was before me.' [31]I myself did not know him, but the reason I came baptizing with water was that he might be revealed to Israel."

[32]Then John gave this testimony: "I saw the Spirit come down from heaven as a dove and remain on him. [33]I would not have known him, except that the one who sent me to baptize with water told me, 'The man on whom you see the Spirit come down and remain is he who will baptize with the Holy Spirit.' [34]I have seen and I testify that this is the Son of God."

Jesus' First Disciples

[35]The next day John was there again with two of his disciples. [36]When he saw Jesus passing by, he said, "Look, the Lamb of God!"

[37]When the two disciples heard him say this, they followed Jesus. [38]Turning around, Jesus saw them following and asked, "What do you want?"

They said, "Rabbi" (which means Teacher), "where are you staying?"

[39]"Come," he replied, "and you will see."

So they went and saw where he was staying, and spent that day with him. It was about the tenth hour.

[40]Andrew, Simon Peter's brother, was one of the two who heard what John had said and who had followed Jesus. [41]The first thing Andrew did was to find his brother Simon and tell him, "We have found the Messiah" (that is, the Christ). [42]And he brought him to Jesus.

Jesus looked at him and said, "You are Simon son of John. You will be called Cephas" (which, when translated, is Peter[g]).

Jesus Calls Philip and Nathanael

[43]The next day Jesus decided to leave for Galilee. Finding Philip, he said to him, "Follow me."

[44]Philip, like Andrew and Peter, was from the town of Bethsaida. [45]Philip found Nathanael and told him, "We have found the one Moses wrote about in the Law, and about whom the prophets also wrote— Jesus of Nazareth, the son of Joseph."

[46]"Nazareth! Can anything good come from there?" Nathanael asked.

---

a13 Greek of bloods   b14,18 Or the Only Begotten   c18 Some manuscripts but the only (or only begotten) Son
d20 Or Messiah. "The Christ" (Greek) and "the Messiah" (Hebrew) both mean "the Anointed One"; also in verse
25.   e23 Isaiah 40:3   f26 Or in; also in verses 31 and 33   g42 Both Cephas (Aramaic) and Peter (Greek)
mean rock.

WHY THE GOSPEL ISN'T MORE POPULAR

The big fall outreach that Marci and her youth group have been planning for two months turned out to be, so it seems, a huge bust.

Twenty-seven kids showed up, and all of them were already believers in Jesus.

"I don't get it," Marci moans. "We prayed, we advertised, we worked so hard. Why can't we get non-Christians interested in the gospel?"

Look It Up
••••

You'd think that people would be lining up to trust Christ . . . scrambling like mad to know that their sins were forgiven and that their eternal destiny was secure, but it doesn't work that way.

The gospel message isn't very popular because:
• It demands that you acknowledge your need for the spiritual healing only Christ can bring (Matthew 9:11–13);
• Until God opens a person's heart, it is impossible to fully comprehend (1 Corinthians 2:14);
• Embracing it completely will lead to hardship and persecution: "This is my gospel, for which I am suffering even to the point of being chained like a criminal. . . . You, however, know all about my . . . persecutions, sufferings—what kinds of things happened to me in Antioch, Iconium and Lystra, the persecutions I endured. Yet the Lord rescued me from all of them. In fact, everyone who wants to live a godly life in Christ Jesus will be persecuted (2 Timothy 2:8–9; 3:10–12).

Think It Through
••••

In what specific ways is the message of Christ's death on the cross "foolish"? (See 1 Corinthians 1:18–29.)

Work It Out
••••

God has called you to share the story of Christ's love regardless of how people respond.

Ask him for an opportunity to do that today. Then be sensitive to the Spirit's leading. Who knows? You may see a miracle!

(Remember—just because many people are uninterested, doesn't mean that *all* of them are. In fact, some of your friends may be ready to respond right now!)

Nail It Down
••••

Reflect on the manner in which Jesus regarded his popularity in John 2:23–25.

Turn to pages 304 and 1130 for other readings on popularity.
Turn to page 1130 for Friday's reading.

Topic
••••
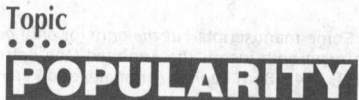
POPULARITY

"Come and see," said Philip.

47When Jesus saw Nathanael approaching, he said of him, "Here is a true Israelite, in whom there is nothing false."

48"How do you know me?" Nathanael asked.

Jesus answered, "I saw you while you were still under the fig tree before Philip called you."

49Then Nathanael declared, "Rabbi, you are the Son of God; you are the King of Israel."

50Jesus said, "You believe[a] because I told you I saw you under the fig tree. You shall see greater things than that." **51**He then added, "I tell you[b] the truth, you[b] shall see heaven open, and the angels of God ascending and descending on the Son of Man."

Jesus Changes Water to Wine

2 On the third day a wedding took place at Cana in Galilee. Jesus' mother was there, **2**and Jesus and his disciples had also been invited to the wedding. **3**When the wine was gone, Jesus' mother said to him, "They have no more wine."

4"Dear woman, why do you involve me?" Jesus replied. "My time has not yet come."

5His mother said to the servants, "Do whatever he tells you."

6Nearby stood six stone water jars, the kind used by the Jews for ceremonial washing, each holding from twenty to thirty gallons.[c]

7Jesus said to the servants, "Fill the jars with water"; so they filled them to the brim.

8Then he told them, "Now draw some out and take it to the master of the banquet."

They did so, **9**and the master of the banquet tasted the water that had been turned into wine. He did not realize where it had come from, though the servants who had drawn the water knew. Then he called the bridegroom aside **10**and said, "Everyone brings out the choice wine first and then the cheaper wine after the guests have had too much to drink; but you have saved the best till now."

11This, the first of his miraculous signs, Jesus performed at Cana in Galilee. He thus revealed his glory, and his disciples put their faith in him.

Jesus Clears the Temple

12After this he went down to Capernaum with his mother and brothers and his disciples. There they stayed for a few days.

13When it was almost time for the Jewish Passover, Jesus went up to Jerusalem. **14**In the temple courts he found men selling cattle, sheep and doves, and others sitting at tables exchanging money. **15**So he made a whip out of cords, and drove all from the temple area, both sheep and cattle; he scattered the coins of the money changers and overturned their tables. **16**To those who sold doves he said, "Get these out of here! How dare you turn my Father's house into a market!"

17His disciples remembered that it is written: "Zeal for your house will consume me."[d]

18Then the Jews demanded of him, "What miraculous sign can you show us to prove your authority to do all this?"

19Jesus answered them, "Destroy this temple, and I will raise it again in three days."

20The Jews replied, "It has taken forty-six years to build this temple, and you are going to raise it in three days?" **21**But the temple he had spoken of was his body. **22**After he was raised from the dead, his disciples recalled what he had said. Then they believed the Scripture and the words that Jesus had spoken.

23Now while he was in Jerusalem at the Passover Feast, many people saw the miraculous signs he was doing and believed in his name.[e] **24**But Jesus would not entrust himself to them, for he knew all men. **25**He did not need man's testimony about man, for he knew what was in a man.

Jesus Teaches Nicodemus

3 Now there was a man of the Pharisees named Nicodemus, a member of the Jewish ruling council. **2**He came to Jesus at night and said, "Rabbi, we know you are a teacher who has come from God. For no one could perform the miraculous signs you are doing if God were not with him."

3In reply Jesus declared, "I tell you the truth, no one can see the kingdom of God unless he is born again.[f]"

4"How can a man be born when he is old?" Nicodemus asked. "Surely he cannot enter a second time into his mother's womb to be born!"

5Jesus answered, "I tell you the truth, no one can enter the kingdom of God unless he

---

a50 Or *Do you believe . . . ?*   *b51* The Greek is plural.   *c6* Greek *two to three metretes* (probably about 75 to 115 liters)   *d17* Psalm 69:9   *e23* Or *and believed in him*   *f3* Or *born from above*; also in verse 7

THE POWER AND PULL OF POPULARITY

Melissa can't stand Kaycee, a classmate who lives up the street. Kaycee is very popular. Not only is she a senior class officer, but she also was recently named homecoming queen.

"What has she got that I haven't got? I'm a nice person too. I'm not bad looking. Why don't I ever get any honors like that?"

Meanwhile Kaycee is beginning her campaign to try to get a date with Kurt (the school heartthrob).

Look It Up

Popularity is dangerous for at least two reasons.

1. It can become a major source of jealousy.

"When Saul saw how successful he [David] was, he was afraid of him. But all Israel and Judah loved David, because he led them in their campaigns" (1 Samuel 18:15–16).

2. It can become an obsession.

"So he [Haman] answered the king, 'For the man the king delights to honor, have them bring a royal robe the king has worn and a horse the king has ridden, one with a royal crest placed on its head. Then let the robe and horse be entrusted to one of the king's most noble princes. Let them robe the man the king delights to honor, and lead him on the horse through the city streets, proclaiming before him, "This is what is done for the man the king delights to honor!" ' " (Esther 6:7–9).

Think It Through

Like Melissa, are you jealous of someone at school who is especially popular? Do you ever catch yourself doing certain things just to try to gain a little more popularity?

After such feelings and/or actions, do you generally like yourself more or less?

Work It Out

Ask God to help you deal with popularity. If you aren't especially popular with your peers, ask him to give you needed insights and proper attitudes.

If you are part of the popular crowd, ask the Lord to keep you from getting a big head. Honestly analyze your behavior and lifestyle for any actions that might not be pleasing in the sight of God.

Nail It Down

Observe in John 3:25–30 how John the Baptist dealt with his decreasing popularity—and the increasing popularity of Christ.

Turn to pages 304 and 1128 for other readings on popularity.
Turn to page 1132 for the weekend reading.

Topic

POPULARITY

is born of water and the Spirit. **6**Flesh gives birth to flesh, but the Spirit*a* gives birth to spirit. **7**You should not be surprised at my saying, 'You*b* must be born again.' **8**The wind blows wherever it pleases. You hear its sound, but you cannot tell where it comes from or where it is going. So it is with everyone born of the Spirit."

9"How can this be?" Nicodemus asked.

10"You are Israel's teacher," said Jesus, "and do you not understand these things? **11**I tell you the truth, we speak of what we know, and we testify to what we have seen, but still you people do not accept our testimony. **12**I have spoken to you of earthly things and you do not believe; how then will you believe if I speak of heavenly things? **13**No one has ever gone into heaven except the one who came from heaven—the Son of Man.*c* **14**Just as Moses lifted up the snake in the desert, so the Son of Man must be lifted up, **15**that everyone who believes in him may have eternal life.*d*

16"For God so loved the world that he gave his one and only Son,*e* that whoever believes in him shall not perish but have eternal life. **17**For God did not send his Son into the world to condemn the world, but to save the world through him. **18**Whoever believes in him is not condemned, but whoever does not believe stands condemned already because he has not believed in the name of God's one and only Son.*f* **19**This is the verdict: Light has come into the world, but men loved darkness instead of light because their deeds were evil. **20**Everyone who does evil hates the light, and will not come into the light for fear that his deeds will be exposed. **21**But whoever lives by the truth comes into the light, so that it may be seen plainly that what he has done has been done through God."*g*

John the Baptist's Testimony About Jesus

22After this, Jesus and his disciples went out into the Judean countryside, where he spent some time with them, and baptized. **23**Now John also was baptizing at Aenon near Salim, because there was plenty of water, and people were constantly coming to be baptized. **24**(This was before John was put in prison.) **25**An argument developed between some of John's disciples and a certain Jew*h* over the matter of ceremonial washing. **26**They came to John and said to him, "Rabbi, that man who was with you on the other side of the Jordan—the one you testified about—well, he is baptizing, and everyone is going to him."

27To this John replied, "A man can receive only what is given him from heaven. **28**You yourselves can testify that I said, 'I am not the Christ*i* but am sent ahead of him.' **29**The bride belongs to the bridegroom. The friend who attends the bridegroom waits and listens for him, and is full of joy when he hears the bridegroom's voice. That joy is mine, and it is now complete. **30**He must become greater; I must become less.

31"The one who comes from above is above all; the one who is from the earth belongs to the earth, and speaks as one from the earth. The one who comes from heaven is above all. **32**He testifies to what he has seen and heard, but no one accepts his testimony. **33**The man who has accepted it has certified that God is truthful. **34**For the one whom God has sent speaks the words of God, for God*j* gives the Spirit without limit. **35**The Father loves the Son and has placed everything in his hands. **36**Whoever believes in the Son has eternal life, but whoever rejects the Son will not see life, for God's wrath remains on him."*k*

Jesus Talks With a Samaritan Woman

4 The Pharisees heard that Jesus was gaining and baptizing more disciples than John, **2**although in fact it was not Jesus who baptized, but his disciples. **3**When the Lord learned of this, he left Judea and went back once more to Galilee.

4Now he had to go through Samaria. **5**So he came to a town in Samaria called Sychar, near the plot of ground Jacob had given to his son Joseph. **6**Jacob's well was there, and Jesus, tired as he was from the journey, sat down by the well. It was about the sixth hour.

7When a Samaritan woman came to draw water, Jesus said to her, "Will you give me a drink?" **8**(His disciples had gone into the town to buy food.)

9The Samaritan woman said to him, "You are a Jew and I am a Samaritan woman. How

*a*6 Or *but spirit*   *b*7 The Greek is plural.   *c*13 Some manuscripts *Man, who is in heaven*   *d*15 Or *believes may have eternal life in him*   *e*16 Or *his only begotten Son*   *f*18 Or *God's only begotten Son*   *g*21 Some interpreters end the quotation after verse 15.   *h*25 Some manuscripts *and certain Jews*   *i*28 Or *Messiah*   *j*34 Greek *he*   *k*36 Some interpreters end the quotation after verse 30.

DO YOU FIND INTOLERANCE INTOLERABLE?

● ●

Work It Out
● ● ● ●

The worship service is just about to begin. The organ is playing, the congregation is quiet and worshipful. There is a stir at the back of the church, and you turn around just in time to see a young man enter the sanctuary. His hair is messy, he's wearing an old tee shirt and jeans, and he's barefoot.

There are no seats in sight as this young man makes his way down the aisle. When he reaches the front, he still hasn't found a seat, so he calmly bends his knees and sits in the aisle.

Now an older gentleman, someone who's been involved in church all his life, makes his way to the front. You hold your breath, wondering what he's going to do to or with the young man sitting on the floor in the aisle.

Instead of moving or scolding the young man, which is what everyone expects, the older man moves down the aisle, and when he gets to the front, he calmly, and with some difficulty, sits on the floor, right next to the young man.*

There's a person who obviously found intolerance intolerable. And he did something about it.

Nail It Down
● ● ● ●

Read John 4:1–26 to learn about a time when Jesus accepted someone society had rejected.

*Adapted from *Out of the Saltshaker & Into the World* by Rebecca Manley Pippert. ©1979 by InterVarsity Christian Fellowship of the USA. Used by permission of InterVarsity Press.

● ●

Think It Through
● ● ● ●

The story you read yesterday isn't just a nice story. It really happened. If you had been in that congregation, would you have reacted like the older gentleman? Or would you have stayed in your seat and whispered horrified words of judgment? Or would you have done nothing?

Christians must reject society's intolerance of those who are "different." Do you turn your back on those whom society doesn't find acceptable? That's intolerance. Do you do nothing when others are rejected or treated with discourtesy? That's intolerance. Do you ignore the "different" person in your class? That's intolerance. Or do you move to sit alongside of those whom society has cast aside? That's finding intolerance intolerable.

Nail It Down
● ● ● ●

Reread John 4:1–26. For further insight read Proverbs 14:20–21,31.

Turn to pages 1089, 1182 and 1274 for other readings on intolerance.
Turn to page 1134 for Monday's reading.

Topic
● ● ● ●

INTOLERANCE

can you ask me for a drink?" (For Jews do not associate with Samaritans.*a*)

10Jesus answered her, "If you knew the gift of God and who it is that asks you for a drink, you would have asked him and he would have given you living water."

11"Sir," the woman said, "you have nothing to draw with and the well is deep. Where can you get this living water? **12**Are you greater than our father Jacob, who gave us the well and drank from it himself, as did also his sons and his flocks and herds?"

13Jesus answered, "Everyone who drinks this water will be thirsty again, **14**but whoever drinks the water I give him will never thirst. Indeed, the water I give him will become in him a spring of water welling up to eternal life."

15The woman said to him, "Sir, give me this water so that I won't get thirsty and have to keep coming here to draw water."

16He told her, "Go, call your husband and come back."

17"I have no husband," she replied.

Jesus said to her, "You are right when you say you have no husband. **18**The fact is, you have had five husbands, and the man you now have is not your husband. What you have just said is quite true."

19"Sir," the woman said, "I can see that you are a prophet. **20**Our fathers worshiped on this mountain, but you Jews claim that the place where we must worship is in Jerusalem."

21Jesus declared, "Believe me, woman, a time is coming when you will worship the Father neither on this mountain nor in Jerusalem. **22**You Samaritans worship what you do not know; we worship what we do know, for salvation is from the Jews. **23**Yet a time is coming and has now come when the true worshipers will worship the Father in spirit and truth, for they are the kind of worshipers the Father seeks. **24**God is spirit, and his worshipers must worship in spirit and in truth."

25The woman said, "I know that Messiah" (called Christ) "is coming. When he comes, he will explain everything to us."

26Then Jesus declared, "I who speak to you am he."

The Disciples Rejoin Jesus

27Just then his disciples returned and were surprised to find him talking with a woman. But no one asked, "What do you want?" or "Why are you talking with her?"

28Then, leaving her water jar, the woman went back to the town and said to the people, **29**"Come, see a man who told me everything I ever did. Could this be the Christ*b*?" **30**They came out of the town and made their way toward him.

31Meanwhile his disciples urged him, "Rabbi, eat something."

32But he said to them, "I have food to eat that you know nothing about."

33Then his disciples said to each other, "Could someone have brought him food?"

34"My food," said Jesus, "is to do the will of him who sent me and to finish his work. **35**Do you not say, 'Four months more and then the harvest'? I tell you, open your eyes and look at the fields! They are ripe for harvest. **36**Even now the reaper draws his wages, even now he harvests the crop for eternal life, so that the sower and the reaper may be glad together. **37**Thus the saying 'One sows and another reaps' is true. **38**I sent you to reap what you have not worked for. Others have done the hard work, and you have reaped the benefits of their labor."

Many Samaritans Believe

39Many of the Samaritans from that town believed in him because of the woman's testimony, "He told me everything I ever did." **40**So when the Samaritans came to him, they urged him to stay with them, and he stayed two days. **41**And because of his words many more became believers.

42They said to the woman, "We no longer believe just because of what you said; now we have heard for ourselves, and we know that this man really is the Savior of the world."

Jesus Heals the Official's Son

43After the two days he left for Galilee. **44**(Now Jesus himself had pointed out that a prophet has no honor in his own country.) **45**When he arrived in Galilee, the Galileans welcomed him. They had seen all that he had done in Jerusalem at the Passover Feast, for they also had been there.

46Once more he visited Cana in Galilee, where he had turned the water into wine. And there was a certain royal official whose son lay sick at Capernaum. **47**When this man heard that Jesus had arrived in Galilee from Judea, he went to him and begged him to come and heal his son, who was close to death.

48"Unless you people see miraculous

---

a9 Or do not use dishes Samaritans have used   *b29 Or Messiah*

WHAT IS A FRUITFUL CHRISTIAN?

Scott visited his cousin Eddie in Detroit last weekend. On Saturday, the two of them helped out with an inner-city project that Eddie's youth group had been planning for several months. Scott couldn't believe what he was seeing. Everyone was so enthusiastic, so committed to the Lord, so excited about reaching out. At lunch he pulled Eddie aside and said, "Hey, man, what's going on here?"

"What do you mean?" Eddie inquired.

"I mean the way you guys care about each other and about these poor people. It's like nothing I've ever seen. Everybody's all happy and friendly."

Scott became even more amazed. By the end of the day, the group had distributed food and clothes to thirty-two families and had seen thirteen kids profess faith in Jesus Christ!

Look It Up
••••

The secret of Eddie's group (it's not really a secret when you read the New Testament) is called "fruitfulness." All Christians are expected to bear fruit in their lives. This fruit grows in at least two forms:
- Character: "The fruit of the Spirit is love, joy, peace, patience, kindness, goodness, faithfulness, gentleness and self-control" (Galatians 5:22–23);
- Concern: "The harvest is plentiful, but the workers are few. Ask the Lord of the harvest, therefore, to send out workers into his harvest field" (Luke 10:2).

Think It Through
••••

That first kind of fruitbearing comes when you live according to the Holy Spirit. As you obey his Word, your character becomes like his character. The result? Greater godliness and therefore greater effectiveness in God's world.

The second kind of fruitbearing refers to being involved in the process of planting the seed of God's Word in other people's lives, nurturing it, watching it grow and then finally reaping the harvest of seeing them turn to Jesus Christ.

How about you? Are you a fruitful Christian?

Work It Out
••••

Perhaps this whole idea of being fruitful is new to you. If it is, sincerely pray this prayer to God:

"Father, I want to be an effective Christian in your world. Help me learn more about fruitfulness. Change me as I study the Word of Christ. Amen."

Nail It Down
••••

Read what Jesus had to say about fruitfulness in John 4:35–38.

Turn to pages 1104 and 1184 for other readings on fruitfulness.
Turn to page 1136 for Tuesday's reading.

Topic
••••

FRUITFULNESS

signs and wonders," Jesus told him, "you will never believe."

⁴⁹The royal official said, "Sir, come down before my child dies."

⁵⁰Jesus replied, "You may go. Your son will live."

The man took Jesus at his word and departed. ⁵¹While he was still on the way, his servants met him with the news that his boy was living. ⁵²When he inquired as to the time when his son got better, they said to him, "The fever left him yesterday at the seventh hour."

⁵³Then the father realized that this was the exact time at which Jesus had said to him, "Your son will live." So he and all his household believed.

⁵⁴This was the second miraculous sign that Jesus performed, having come from Judea to Galilee.

The Healing at the Pool

5 Some time later, Jesus went up to Jerusalem for a feast of the Jews. ²Now there is in Jerusalem near the Sheep Gate a pool, which in Aramaic is called Bethesda*a* and which is surrounded by five covered colonnades. ³Here a great number of disabled people used to lie—the blind, the lame, the paralyzed.*b* ⁵One who was there had been an invalid for thirty-eight years. ⁶When Jesus saw him lying there and learned that he had been in this condition for a long time, he asked him, "Do you want to get well?"

⁷"Sir," the invalid replied, "I have no one to help me into the pool when the water is stirred. While I am trying to get in, someone else goes down ahead of me."

⁸Then Jesus said to him, "Get up! Pick up your mat and walk." ⁹At once the man was cured; he picked up his mat and walked.

The day on which this took place was a Sabbath, ¹⁰and so the Jews said to the man who had been healed, "It is the Sabbath; the law forbids you to carry your mat."

¹¹But he replied, "The man who made me well said to me, 'Pick up your mat and walk.' "

¹²So they asked him, "Who is this fellow who told you to pick it up and walk?"

¹³The man who was healed had no idea who it was, for Jesus had slipped away into the crowd that was there.

¹⁴Later Jesus found him at the temple and said to him, "See, you are well again. Stop sinning or something worse may happen to you." ¹⁵The man went away and told the Jews that it was Jesus who had made him well.

Life Through the Son

¹⁶So, because Jesus was doing these things on the Sabbath, the Jews persecuted him. ¹⁷Jesus said to them, "My Father is always at his work to this very day, and I, too, am working." ¹⁸For this reason the Jews tried all the harder to kill him; not only was he breaking the Sabbath, but he was even calling God his own Father, making himself equal with God.

¹⁹Jesus gave them this answer: "I tell you the truth, the Son can do nothing by himself; he can do only what he sees his Father doing, because whatever the Father does the Son also does. ²⁰For the Father loves the Son and shows him all he does. Yes, to your amazement he will show him even greater things than these. ²¹For just as the Father raises the dead and gives them life, even so the Son gives life to whom he is pleased to give it. ²²Moreover, the Father judges no one, but has entrusted all judgment to the Son, ²³that all may honor the Son just as they honor the Father. He who does not honor the Son does not honor the Father, who sent him.

²⁴"I tell you the truth, whoever hears my word and believes him who sent me has eternal life and will not be condemned; he has crossed over from death to life. ²⁵I tell you the truth, a time is coming and has now come when the dead will hear the voice of the Son of God and those who hear will live. ²⁶For as the Father has life in himself, so he has granted the Son to have life in himself. ²⁷And he has given him authority to judge because he is the Son of Man.

²⁸"Do not be amazed at this, for a time is coming when all who are in their graves will hear his voice ²⁹and come out—those who have done good will rise to live, and those who have done evil will rise to be condemned. ³⁰By myself I can do nothing; I judge only as I hear, and my judgment is just, for I seek not to please myself but him who sent me.

---

a2 Some manuscripts Bethzatha; other manuscripts Bethsaida   b3 Some less important manuscripts paralyzed—and they waited for the moving of the waters. ⁴From time to time an angel of the Lord would come down and stir up the waters. The first one into the pool after each such disturbance would be cured of whatever disease he had.

HOW TO KNOW WHERE YOU'RE GONNA GO

Debbie sits in front of Gil in English class. One day, while staying after school to work on their term papers, they somehow got into a conversation about church. That led to a serious discussion about Christianity (not a typical conversation in the library!).

"Look, I don't understand everything about it . . . I just know when I die, I'm going to heaven," Debbie finally said.

Gil couldn't believe it. "How can you say that? How can you be so sure? You really can't know about all that until after you die. I mean, I try to live a pretty decent life. I think I'm an okay person. But I'm sure not going to act like heaven's a definite thing!"

Look It Up
••••

You may be surprised at how many people think like Gil. They believe that when you die, God takes all your good works and bad works and dumps them on a huge, cosmic scale. If the good outweighs the bad, you're in. If the opposite is true . . . well, you know what that means.

No way.

When it comes to something so important, God spells it right out so there's no guesswork.

"God has given us eternal life, and this life is in his Son. He who has the Son has life; he who does not have the Son of God does not have life. I write these things to you who believe in the name of the Son of God so that you may know that you have eternal life" (1 John 5:11–13).

Think It Through
••••

It boils down to this: If you "have the Son," you have eternal life and are headed for heaven.

To say you "have the Son" is just another way of saying you believe in Jesus. You trust him (and him alone) to forgive your sins and make you right with God.

Work It Out
••••

Maybe for a class in sociology, psychology or even history, your teacher would let you do a project on "Religious Beliefs of Students at _____ High School." If so, you could conduct a survey with your classmates. One of the questions might be: "Assuming you believe in God and in a real place called heaven, how does one get to heaven?"

Not only would this help you find out what your friends believe, but it also might give you the opportunity to share with some of them what the Bible says on the subject. Plus you'd end up with a really interesting paper!

Nail It Down
••••

Read John 5:24 for clear-cut directions to eternal life.

Turn to pages 633, 1172 and 1370 for other readings on tough questions.
Turn to page 1142 for Wednesday's reading.

Topic
••••

TOUGH QUESTIONS

Testimonies About Jesus

31"If I testify about myself, my testimony is not valid. **32**There is another who testifies in my favor, and I know that his testimony about me is valid.

33"You have sent to John and he has testified to the truth. **34**Not that I accept human testimony; but I mention it that you may be saved. **35**John was a lamp that burned and gave light, and you chose for a time to enjoy his light.

36"I have testimony weightier than that of John. For the very work that the Father has given me to finish, and which I am doing, testifies that the Father has sent me. **37**And the Father who sent me has himself testified concerning me. You have never heard his voice nor seen his form, **38**nor does his word dwell in you, for you do not believe the one he sent. **39**You diligently study*a* the Scriptures because you think that by them you possess eternal life. These are the Scriptures that testify about me, **40**yet you refuse to come to me to have life.

41"I do not accept praise from men, **42**but I know you. I know that you do not have the love of God in your hearts. **43**I have come in my Father's name, and you do not accept me; but if someone else comes in his own name, you will accept him. **44**How can you believe if you accept praise from one another, yet make no effort to obtain the praise that comes from the only God*b*?

45"But do not think I will accuse you before the Father. Your accuser is Moses, on whom your hopes are set. **46**If you believed Moses, you would believe me, for he wrote about me. **47**But since you do not believe what he wrote, how are you going to believe what I say?"

Jesus Feeds the Five Thousand

6 Some time after this, Jesus crossed to the far shore of the Sea of Galilee (that is, the Sea of Tiberias), **2**and a great crowd of people followed him because they saw the miraculous signs he had performed on the sick. **3**Then Jesus went up on a mountainside and sat down with his disciples. **4**The Jewish Passover Feast was near.

5When Jesus looked up and saw a great crowd coming toward him, he said to Philip, "Where shall we buy bread for these people to eat?" **6**He asked this only to test him, for he already had in mind what he was going to do.

7Philip answered him, "Eight months' wages*c* would not buy enough bread for each one to have a bite!"

8Another of his disciples, Andrew, Simon Peter's brother, spoke up, **9**"Here is a boy with five small barley loaves and two small fish, but how far will they go among so many?"

10Jesus said, "Have the people sit down." There was plenty of grass in that place, and the men sat down, about five thousand of them. **11**Jesus then took the loaves, gave thanks, and distributed to those who were seated as much as they wanted. He did the same with the fish.

12When they had all had enough to eat, he said to his disciples, "Gather the pieces that are left over. Let nothing be wasted." **13**So they gathered them and filled twelve baskets with the pieces of the five barley loaves left over by those who had eaten.

14After the people saw the miraculous sign that Jesus did, they began to say, "Surely this is the Prophet who is to come into the world." **15**Jesus, knowing that they intended to come and make him king by force, withdrew again to a mountain by himself.

Jesus Walks on the Water

16When evening came, his disciples went down to the lake, **17**where they got into a boat and set off across the lake for Capernaum. By now it was dark, and Jesus had not yet joined them. **18**A strong wind was blowing and the waters grew rough. **19**When they had rowed three or three and a half miles,*d* they saw Jesus approaching the boat, walking on the water; and they were terrified. **20**But he said to them, "It is I; don't be afraid." **21**Then they were willing to take him into the boat, and immediately the boat reached the shore where they were heading.

22The next day the crowd that had stayed on the opposite shore of the lake realized that only one boat had been there, and that Jesus had not entered it with his disciples, but that they had gone away alone. **23**Then some boats from Tiberias landed near the place where the people had eaten the bread after the Lord had given thanks. **24**Once the crowd realized that neither Jesus nor his disciples were there, they got into the boats and went to Capernaum in search of Jesus.

a39 Or *Study diligently* (the imperative)   *b44* Some early manuscripts *the Only One*   *c7* Greek *two hundred denarii*   *d19* Greek *rowed twenty-five or thirty stadia* (about 5 or 6 kilometers)

Jesus the Bread of Life

25When they found him on the other side of the lake, they asked him, "Rabbi, when did you get here?"

26Jesus answered, "I tell you the truth, you are looking for me, not because you saw miraculous signs but because you ate the loaves and had your fill. **27**Do not work for food that spoils, but for food that endures to eternal life, which the Son of Man will give you. On him God the Father has placed his seal of approval."

28Then they asked him, "What must we do to do the works God requires?"

29Jesus answered, "The work of God is this: to believe in the one he has sent."

30So they asked him, "What miraculous sign then will you give that we may see it and believe you? What will you do? **31**Our forefathers ate the manna in the desert; as it is written: 'He gave them bread from heaven to eat.'*a*"

32Jesus said to them, "I tell you the truth, it is not Moses who has given you the bread from heaven, but it is my Father who gives you the true bread from heaven. **33**For the bread of God is he who comes down from heaven and gives life to the world."

34"Sir," they said, "from now on give us this bread."

35Then Jesus declared, "I am the bread of life. He who comes to me will never go hungry, and he who believes in me will never be thirsty. **36**But as I told you, you have seen me and still you do not believe. **37**All that the Father gives me will come to me, and whoever comes to me I will never drive away. **38**For I have come down from heaven not to do my will but to do the will of him who sent me. **39**And this is the will of him who sent me, that I shall lose none of all that he has given me, but raise them up at the last day. **40**For my Father's will is that everyone who looks to the Son and believes in him shall have eternal life, and I will raise him up at the last day."

41At this the Jews began to grumble about him because he said, "I am the bread that came down from heaven." **42**They said, "Is this not Jesus, the son of Joseph, whose father and mother we know? How can he now say, 'I came down from heaven'?"

43"Stop grumbling among yourselves," Jesus answered. **44**"No one can come to me unless the Father who sent him draws him, and I will raise him up at the last day. **45**It is written in the Prophets: 'They will all be taught by God.'*b* Everyone who listens to the Father and learns from him comes to me. **46**No one has seen the Father except the one who is from God; only he has seen the Father. **47**I tell you the truth, he who believes has everlasting life. **48**I am the bread of life. **49**Your forefathers ate the manna in the desert, yet they died. **50**But here is the bread that comes down from heaven, which a man may eat and not die. **51**I am the living bread that came down from heaven. If anyone eats of this bread, he will live forever. This bread is my flesh, which I will give for the life of the world."

52Then the Jews began to argue sharply among themselves, "How can this man give us his flesh to eat?"

53Jesus said to them, "I tell you the truth, unless you eat the flesh of the Son of Man and drink his blood, you have no life in you. **54**Whoever eats my flesh and drinks my blood has eternal life, and I will raise him up at the last day. **55**For my flesh is real food and my blood is real drink. **56**Whoever eats my flesh and drinks my blood remains in me, and I in him. **57**Just as the living Father sent me and I live because of the Father, so the one who feeds on me will live because of me. **58**This is the bread that came down from heaven. Your forefathers ate manna and died, but he who feeds on this bread will live forever." **59**He said this while teaching in the synagogue in Capernaum.

Many Disciples Desert Jesus

60On hearing it, many of his disciples said, "This is a hard teaching. Who can accept it?"

61Aware that his disciples were grumbling about this, Jesus said to them, "Does this offend you? **62**What if you see the Son of Man ascend to where he was before! **63**The Spirit gives life; the flesh counts for nothing. The words I have spoken to you are spirit*c* and they are life. **64**Yet there are some of you who do not believe." For Jesus had known from the beginning which of them did not believe and who would betray him. **65**He went on to say, "This is why I told you that no one can come to me unless the Father has enabled him."

66From this time many of his disciples turned back and no longer followed him.

67"You do not want to leave too, do you?" Jesus asked the Twelve.

68Simon Peter answered him, "Lord, to

a31 Exodus 16:4; Neh. 9:15; Psalm 78:24,25   *b45* Isaiah 54:13   *c63* Or *Spirit* whom shall we go? You have the words of eternal life. **69**We believe and know that you are the Holy One of God."

70Then Jesus replied, "Have I not chosen you, the Twelve? Yet one of you is a devil!" **71**(He meant Judas, the son of Simon Iscariot, who, though one of the Twelve, was later to betray him.)

Jesus Goes to the Feast of Tabernacles

7 After this, Jesus went around in Galilee, purposely staying away from Judea because the Jews there were waiting to take his life. **2**But when the Jewish Feast of Tabernacles was near, **3**Jesus' brothers said to him, "You ought to leave here and go to Judea, so that your disciples may see the miracles you do. **4**No one who wants to become a public figure acts in secret. Since you are doing these things, show yourself to the world." **5**For even his own brothers did not believe in him.

6Therefore Jesus told them, "The right time for me has not yet come; for you any time is right. **7**The world cannot hate you, but it hates me because I testify that what it does is evil. **8**You go to the Feast. I am not yet[a] going up to this Feast, because for me the right time has not yet come." **9**Having said this, he stayed in Galilee.

10However, after his brothers had left for the Feast, he went also, not publicly, but in secret. **11**Now at the Feast the Jews were watching for him and asking, "Where is that man?"

12Among the crowds there was widespread whispering about him. Some said, "He is a good man."

Others replied, "No, he deceives the people." **13**But no one would say anything publicly about him for fear of the Jews.

Jesus Teaches at the Feast

14Not until halfway through the Feast did Jesus go up to the temple courts and begin to teach. **15**The Jews were amazed and asked, "How did this man get such learning without having studied?"

16Jesus answered, "My teaching is not my own. It comes from him who sent me. **17**If anyone chooses to do God's will, he will find out whether my teaching comes from God or whether I speak on my own. **18**He who speaks on his own does so to gain honor for himself, but he who works for the honor of the one who sent him is a man of truth; there is nothing false about him. **19**Has not

Moses given you the law? Yet not one of you keeps the law. Why are you trying to kill me?"

20"You are demon-possessed," the crowd answered. "Who is trying to kill you?"

21Jesus said to them, "I did one miracle, and you are all astonished. **22**Yet, because Moses gave you circumcision (though actually it did not come from Moses, but from the patriarchs), you circumcise a child on the Sabbath. **23**Now if a child can be circumcised on the Sabbath so that the law of Moses may not be broken, why are you angry with me for healing the whole man on the Sabbath? **24**Stop judging by mere appearances, and make a right judgment."

Is Jesus the Christ?

25At that point some of the people of Jerusalem began to ask, "Isn't this the man they are trying to kill? **26**Here he is, speaking publicly, and they are not saying a word to him. Have the authorities really concluded that he is the Christ[b]? **27**But we know where this man is from; when the Christ comes, no one will know where he is from."

28Then Jesus, still teaching in the temple courts, cried out, "Yes, you know me, and you know where I am from. I am not here on my own, but he who sent me is true. You do not know him, **29**but I know him because I am from him and he sent me."

30At this they tried to seize him, but no one laid a hand on him, because his time had not yet come. **31**Still, many in the crowd put their faith in him. They said, "When the Christ comes, will he do more miraculous signs than this man?"

32The Pharisees heard the crowd whispering such things about him. Then the chief priests and the Pharisees sent temple guards to arrest him.

33Jesus said, "I am with you for only a short time, and then I go to the one who sent me. **34**You will look for me, but you will not find me; and where I am, you cannot come."

35The Jews said to one another, "Where does this man intend to go that we cannot find him? Will he go where our people live scattered among the Greeks, and teach the Greeks? **36**What did he mean when he said, 'You will look for me, but you will not find me,' and 'Where I am, you cannot come'?"

37On the last and greatest day of the Feast, Jesus stood and said in a loud voice, "If anyone is thirsty, let him come to me and drink.

---

a8 Some early manuscripts do not have *yet.*   *b26* Or *Messiah*; also in verses 27, 31, 41 and 42

38Whoever believes in me, as[a] the Scripture has said, streams of living water will flow from within him." **39**By this he meant the Spirit, whom those who believed in him were later to receive. Up to that time the Spirit had not been given, since Jesus had not yet been glorified.

40On hearing his words, some of the people said, "Surely this man is the Prophet." **41**Others said, "He is the Christ."

Still others asked, "How can the Christ come from Galilee? **42**Does not the Scripture say that the Christ will come from David's family[b] and from Bethlehem, the town where David lived?" **43**Thus the people were divided because of Jesus. **44**Some wanted to seize him, but no one laid a hand on him.

Unbelief of the Jewish Leaders

45Finally the temple guards went back to the chief priests and Pharisees, who asked them, "Why didn't you bring him in?"

46"No one ever spoke the way this man does," the guards declared.

47"You mean he has deceived you also?" the Pharisees retorted. **48**"Has any of the rulers or of the Pharisees believed in him? **49**No! But this mob that knows nothing of the law — there is a curse on them."

50Nicodemus, who had gone to Jesus earlier and who was one of their own number, asked, **51**"Does our law condemn anyone without first hearing him to find out what he is doing?"

52They replied, "Are you from Galilee, too? Look into it, and you will find that a prophet[c] does not come out of Galilee."

[The earliest manuscripts
and many other ancient witnesses
do not have John 7:53–8:11.]

53Then each went to his own home.

8 But Jesus went to the Mount of Olives. **2**At dawn he appeared again in the temple courts, where all the people gathered around him, and he sat down to teach them. **3**The teachers of the law and the Pharisees brought in a woman caught in adultery. They made her stand before the group **4**and said to Jesus, "Teacher, this woman was caught in the act of adultery. **5**In the Law Moses commanded us to stone such wom-

en. Now what do you say?" **6**They were using this question as a trap, in order to have a basis for accusing him.

But Jesus bent down and started to write on the ground with his finger. **7**When they kept on questioning him, he straightened up and said to them, "If any one of you is without sin, let him be the first to throw a stone at her." **8**Again he stooped down and wrote on the ground.

9At this, those who heard began to go away one at a time, the older ones first, until only Jesus was left, with the woman still standing there. **10**Jesus straightened up and asked her, "Woman, where are they? Has no one condemned you?"

11"No one, sir," she said.

"Then neither do I condemn you," Jesus declared. "Go now and leave your life of sin."

The Validity of Jesus' Testimony

12When Jesus spoke again to the people, he said, "I am the light of the world. Whoever follows me will never walk in darkness, but will have the light of life."

13The Pharisees challenged him, "Here you are, appearing as your own witness; your testimony is not valid."

14Jesus answered, "Even if I testify on my own behalf, my testimony is valid, for I know where I came from and where I am going. But you have no idea where I come from or where I am going. **15**You judge by human standards; I pass judgment on no one. **16**But if I do judge, my decisions are right, because I am not alone. I stand with the Father, who sent me. **17**In your own Law it is written that the testimony of two men is valid. **18**I am one who testifies for myself; my other witness is the Father, who sent me."

19Then they asked him, "Where is your father?"

"You do not know me or my Father," Jesus replied. "If you knew me, you would know my Father also." **20**He spoke these words while teaching in the temple area near the place where the offerings were put. Yet no one seized him, because his time had not yet come.

21Once more Jesus said to them, "I am going away, and you will look for me, and you

---

[a] *37,38* Or / *If anyone is thirsty, let him come to me. / And let him drink,* **38***who believes in me. / As*　[b] *42* Greek *seed*　[c] *52* Two early manuscripts *the Prophet*

will die in your sin. Where I go, you cannot come."

²²This made the Jews ask, "Will he kill himself? Is that why he says, 'Where I go, you cannot come'?"

²³But he continued, "You are from below; I am from above. You are of this world; I am not of this world. ²⁴I told you that you would die in your sins; if you do not believe that I am ˌthe one I claim to beˌ,ᵃ you will indeed die in your sins."

²⁵"Who are you?" they asked.

"Just what I have been claiming all along," Jesus replied. ²⁶"I have much to say in judgment of you. But he who sent me is reliable, and what I have heard from him I tell the world."

²⁷They did not understand that he was telling them about his Father. ²⁸So Jesus said, "When you have lifted up the Son of Man, then you will know that I am ˌthe one I claim to beˌ and that I do nothing on my own but speak just what the Father has taught me. ²⁹The one who sent me is with me; he has not left me alone, for I always do what pleases him." ³⁰Even as he spoke, many put their faith in him.

The Children of Abraham

³¹To the Jews who had believed him, Jesus said, "If you hold to my teaching, you are really my disciples. ³²Then you will know the truth, and the truth will set you free."

³³They answered him, "We are Abraham's descendants ᵇ and have never been slaves of anyone. How can you say that we shall be set free?"

³⁴Jesus replied, "I tell you the truth, everyone who sins is a slave to sin. ³⁵Now a slave has no permanent place in the family, but a son belongs to it forever. ³⁶So if the Son sets you free, you will be free indeed. ³⁷I know you are Abraham's descendants. Yet you are ready to kill me, because you have no room for my word. ³⁸I am telling you what I have seen in the Father's presence, and you do what you have heard from your father.ᶜ

³⁹"Abraham is our father," they answered.

"If you were Abraham's children," said Jesus, "then you wouldᵈ do the things Abraham did. ⁴⁰As it is, you are determined to kill me, a man who has told you the truth that I heard from God. Abraham did not do such things. ⁴¹You are doing the things your own father does."

"We are not illegitimate children," they protested. "The only Father we have is God himself."

The Children of the Devil

⁴²Jesus said to them, "If God were your Father, you would love me, for I came from God and now am here. I have not come on my own; but he sent me. ⁴³Why is my language not clear to you? Because you are unable to hear what I say. ⁴⁴You belong to your father, the devil, and you want to carry out your father's desire. He was a murderer from the beginning, not holding to the truth, for there is no truth in him. When he lies, he speaks his native language, for he is a liar and the father of lies. ⁴⁵Yet because I tell the truth, you do not believe me! ⁴⁶Can any of you prove me guilty of sin? If I am telling the truth, why don't you believe me? ⁴⁷He who belongs to God hears what God says. The reason you do not hear is that you do not belong to God."

The Claims of Jesus About Himself

⁴⁸The Jews answered him, "Aren't we right in saying that you are a Samaritan and demon-possessed?"

⁴⁹"I am not possessed by a demon," said Jesus, "but I honor my Father and you dishonor me. ⁵⁰I am not seeking glory for myself; but there is one who seeks it, and he is the judge. ⁵¹I tell you the truth, if anyone keeps my word, he will never see death."

⁵²At this the Jews exclaimed, "Now we know that you are demon-possessed! Abraham died and so did the prophets, yet you say that if anyone keeps your word, he will never taste death. ⁵³Are you greater than our father Abraham? He died, and so did the prophets. Who do you think you are?"

⁵⁴Jesus replied, "If I glorify myself, my glory means nothing. My Father, whom you claim as your God, is the one who glorifies me. ⁵⁵Though you do not know him, I know him. If I said I did not, I would be a liar like you, but I do know him and keep his word. ⁵⁶Your father Abraham rejoiced at the thought of seeing my day; he saw it and was glad."

⁵⁷"You are not yet fifty years old," the Jews said to him, "and you have seen Abraham!"

⁵⁸"I tell you the truth," Jesus answered, "before Abraham was born, I am!" ⁵⁹At this, they picked up stones to stone him, but

---

ᵃ24 Or *I am he*; also in verse 28   ᵇ33 Greek *seed*; also in verse 37   ᶜ38 Or *presence. Therefore do what you have heard from the Father.*   ᵈ39 Some early manuscripts *"If you are Abraham's children," said Jesus, "then*

PLEASING PEOPLE OR PLEASING GOD?

The most popular students at Ridgely High are the top jocks and their girlfriends. Attractive and well-to-do, these individuals form a close-knit group. They're the elite, and they know it.

Kathy hangs around these individuals, but she's not really included by them. This rejection eats at her because she wants—more than anything else—for them to like her. Everything she does—the way she acts, the way she talks, the way she dresses—is a calculated attempt to work her way into this inner circle.

Look It Up • • • •

It is so tempting for us to try to please our peers, to do whatever it takes to get others to like us. But the Bible suggests a different set of priorities.

"So we make it our goal to please him [the Lord]" (2 Corinthians 5:9).

"We are not trying to please men but God, who tests our hearts" (1 Thessalonians 2:4).

"Brothers, we instructed you how to live in order to please God. . . . Now we ask you and urge you in the Lord Jesus to do this more and more" (1 Thessalonians 4:1).

"And we pray . . . that you may live a life worthy of the Lord and may please him in every way" (Colossians 1:10).

Think It Through • • • •

Which is more important to you—pleasing people or pleasing God?

Note: Some Bible verses do tell you to please other people (Romans 15:1–2; 1 Corinthians 10:33). Does this mean you can or should do whatever you want in order to get others to like you? No. Pleasing others in this sense means looking out for their spiritual good, seeking to do things that will help them grow as Christians.

Work It Out • • • •

Make a list of all the things you do in a typical week. Then think about the motives behind those activities.

Does your life contain habits or behaviors that you do just to try to get others to like you (drinking, cheating, smoking, cursing, sexual involvement, lying, skipping school, being cruel to certain people)? If so, eliminate those wrong activities. In their place, substitute actions that you know will please the Lord.

Nail It Down • • • •

Notice what Christ's top priority was in John 8:29.

Turn to pages 432, 796, 1015 and 1292 for other readings on priorities.
Turn to page 1145 for Thursday's reading.

Topic • • • •

PRIORITIES

Jesus hid himself, slipping away from the temple grounds.

Jesus Heals a Man Born Blind

9 As he went along, he saw a man blind from birth. **2**His disciples asked him, "Rabbi, who sinned, this man or his parents, that he was born blind?"

3"Neither this man nor his parents sinned," said Jesus, "but this happened so that the work of God might be displayed in his life. **4**As long as it is day, we must do the work of him who sent me. Night is coming, when no one can work. **5**While I am in the world, I am the light of the world."

6Having said this, he spit on the ground, made some mud with the saliva, and put it on the man's eyes. **7**"Go," he told him, "wash in the Pool of Siloam" (this word means Sent). So the man went and washed, and came home seeing.

8His neighbors and those who had formerly seen him begging asked, "Isn't this the same man who used to sit and beg?" **9**Some claimed that he was.

Others said, "No, he only looks like him."

But he himself insisted, "I am the man."

10"How then were your eyes opened?" they demanded.

11He replied, "The man they call Jesus made some mud and put it on my eyes. He told me to go to Siloam and wash. So I went and washed, and then I could see."

12"Where is this man?" they asked him.

"I don't know," he said.

The Pharisees Investigate the Healing

13They brought to the Pharisees the man who had been blind. **14**Now the day on which Jesus had made the mud and opened the man's eyes was a Sabbath. **15**Therefore the Pharisees also asked him how he had received his sight. "He put mud on my eyes," the man replied, "and I washed, and now I see."

16Some of the Pharisees said, "This man is not from God, for he does not keep the Sabbath."

But others asked, "How can a sinner do such miraculous signs?" So they were divided.

17Finally they turned again to the blind man, "What have you to say about him? It was your eyes he opened."

The man replied, "He is a prophet."

18The Jews still did not believe that he had been blind and had received his sight until they sent for the man's parents. **19**"Is this your son?" they asked. "Is this the one you say was born blind? How is it that now he can see?"

20"We know he is our son," the parents answered, "and we know he was born blind. **21**But how he can see now, or who opened his eyes, we don't know. Ask him. He is of age; he will speak for himself." **22**His parents said this because they were afraid of the Jews, for already the Jews had decided that anyone who acknowledged that Jesus was the Christ*a* would be put out of the synagogue. **23**That was why his parents said, "He is of age; ask him."

24A second time they summoned the man who had been blind. "Give glory to God,*b*" they said. "We know this man is a sinner."

25He replied, "Whether he is a sinner or not, I don't know. One thing I do know. I was blind but now I see!"

26Then they asked him, "What did he do to you? How did he open your eyes?"

27He answered, "I have told you already and you did not listen. Why do you want to hear it again? Do you want to become his disciples, too?"

28Then they hurled insults at him and said, "You are this fellow's disciple! We are disciples of Moses! **29**We know that God spoke to Moses, but as for this fellow, we don't even know where he comes from."

30The man answered, "Now that is remarkable! You don't know where he comes from, yet he opened my eyes. **31**We know that God does not listen to sinners. He listens to the godly man who does his will. **32**Nobody has ever heard of opening the eyes of a man born blind. **33**If this man were not from God, he could do nothing."

34To this they replied, "You were steeped in sin at birth; how dare you lecture us!" And they threw him out.

Spiritual Blindness

35Jesus heard that they had thrown him out, and when he found him, he said, "Do you believe in the Son of Man?"

36"Who is he, sir?" the man asked. "Tell me so that I may believe in him."

37Jesus said, "You have now seen him; in fact, he is the one speaking with you."

38Then the man said, "Lord, I believe," and he worshiped him.

39Jesus said, "For judgment I have come into this world, so that the blind will see and those who see will become blind."

a22 Or *Messiah*   *b24* A solemn charge to tell the truth (see Joshua 7:19)

[40]Some Pharisees who were with him heard him say this and asked, "What? Are we blind too?"

[41]Jesus said, "If you were blind, you would not be guilty of sin; but now that you claim you can see, your guilt remains.

The Shepherd and His Flock

10 "I tell you the truth, the man who does not enter the sheep pen by the gate, but climbs in by some other way, is a thief and a robber. [2]The man who enters by the gate is the shepherd of his sheep. [3]The watchman opens the gate for him, and the sheep listen to his voice. He calls his own sheep by name and leads them out. [4]When he has brought out all his own, he goes on ahead of them, and his sheep follow him because they know his voice. [5]But they will never follow a stranger; in fact, they will run away from him because they do not recognize a stranger's voice." [6]Jesus used this figure of speech, but they did not understand what he was telling them.

[7]Therefore Jesus said again, "I tell you the truth, I am the gate for the sheep. [8]All who ever came before me were thieves and robbers, but the sheep did not listen to them. [9]I am the gate; whoever enters through me will be saved.[a] He will come in and go out, and find pasture. [10]The thief comes only to steal and kill and destroy; I have come that they may have life, and have it to the full.

[11]"I am the good shepherd. The good shepherd lays down his life for the sheep. [12]The hired hand is not the shepherd who owns the sheep. So when he sees the wolf coming, he abandons the sheep and runs away. Then the wolf attacks the flock and scatters it. [13]The man runs away because he is a hired hand and cares nothing for the sheep.

[14]"I am the good shepherd; I know my sheep and my sheep know me— [15]just as the Father knows me and I know the Father—and I lay down my life for the sheep. [16]I have other sheep that are not of this sheep pen. I must bring them also. They too will listen to my voice, and there shall be one flock and one shepherd. [17]The reason my Father loves me is that I lay down my life—only to take it up again. [18]No one takes it from me, but I lay it down of my own accord. I have authority to lay it down and authority to take it up again. This command I received from my Father."

[19]At these words the Jews were again divided. [20]Many of them said, "He is demon-possessed and raving mad. Why listen to him?"

[21]But others said, "These are not the sayings of a man possessed by a demon. Can a demon open the eyes of the blind?"

The Unbelief of the Jews

[22]Then came the Feast of Dedication[b] at Jerusalem. It was winter, [23]and Jesus was in the temple area walking in Solomon's Colonnade. [24]The Jews gathered around him, saying, "How long will you keep us in suspense? If you are the Christ,[c] tell us plainly."

[25]Jesus answered, "I did tell you, but you do not believe. The miracles I do in my Father's name speak for me, [26]but you do not believe because you are not my sheep. [27]My sheep listen to my voice; I know them, and they follow me. [28]I give them eternal life, and they shall never perish; no one can snatch them out of my hand. [29]My Father, who has given them to me, is greater than all[d]; no one can snatch them out of my Father's hand. [30]I and the Father are one."

[31]Again the Jews picked up stones to stone him, [32]but Jesus said to them, "I have shown you many great miracles from the Father. For which of these do you stone me?"

[33]"We are not stoning you for any of these," replied the Jews, "but for blasphemy, because you, a mere man, claim to be God."

[34]Jesus answered them, "Is it not written in your Law, 'I have said you are gods'[e]? [35]If he called them 'gods,' to whom the word of God came—and the Scripture cannot be broken— [36]what about the one whom the Father set apart as his very own and sent into the world? Why then do you accuse me of blasphemy because I said, 'I am God's Son'? [37]Do not believe me unless I do what my Father does. [38]But if I do it, even though you do not believe me, believe the miracles, that you may know and understand that the Father is in me, and I in the Father." [39]Again they tried to seize him, but he escaped their grasp.

[40]Then Jesus went back across the Jordan to the place where John had been baptizing in the early days. Here he stayed [41]and many people came to him. They said, "Though John never performed a miraculous sign, all that John said about this man

---

[a]9 Or kept safe   [b]22 That is, Hanukkah   [c]24 Or Messiah   [d]29 Many early manuscripts What my Father has given me is greater than all   [e]34 Psalm 82:6

YOU ARE GOD'S SHEEP

W hat's the deal with this Kent Clark guy? What's his secret? While most Christians in Metropolis play games with God and see nothing exciting happening in their spiritual lives, it seems that Kent is always in the middle of something wild. Let's eavesdrop on his prayer time and see if we can find out his secret:

". . . and your Word is so true. You are the Good Shepherd! O, Lord, keep me from wandering away from you today. Help me to realize that you'll keep me safe and provide everything I need if I'll just stay close to you. Thank you for loving me in Christ my Lord. Amen."

Look It Up
● ● ● ●

Kent had these verses in mind when he was talking to God:

The LORD is my shepherd, I shall not be in want.
    He makes me lie down in green pastures,
he leads me beside quiet waters,
    he restores my soul.
He guides me in paths of righteousness
    for his name's sake (Psalm 23:1–3).

Come, let us bow down in worship,
    let us kneel before the LORD our Maker;
for he is our God
    and we are the people of his pasture,
    the flock under his care (Psalm 95:6–7).

What a great analogy! Like a shepherd, God lovingly cares for us, his flock. In him, we "sheep" find nourishment, guidance and rest.

Think It Through
● ● ● ●

According to Phillip Keller, a former shepherd, sheep are dependent animals. As long as they remain close to their owner, they enjoy prosperity, protection and peace. However, as soon as they wander away from their keeper, they open themselves up to danger and possible death.

As a sheep, are you listening to and staying close to the Good Shepherd? If not, why not?

Work It Out
● ● ● ●

A big part of Kent's spiritual success is the fact that he begins each day by expressing both his dependence on God and his desire to walk closely with God.

Is that how you start your day? Why not try it? Start out tomorrow and each day after that with a prayer similar to Kent's prayer. And be ready for God to involve himself in your life in wonderful ways you can't even imagine.

Nail It Down
● ● ● ●

Read Jesus' description of shepherd and sheep in John 10:1–18.

Turn to pages 397, 1262 and 1377 for other readings on identity.
Turn to page 1147 for Friday's reading.

Topic
● ● ● ●

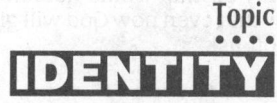
IDENTITY

was true." ⁴²And in that place many believed in Jesus.

The Death of Lazarus

11 Now a man named Lazarus was sick. He was from Bethany, the village of Mary and her sister Martha. ²This Mary, whose brother Lazarus now lay sick, was the same one who poured perfume on the Lord and wiped his feet with her hair. ³So the sisters sent word to Jesus, "Lord, the one you love is sick."

⁴When he heard this, Jesus said, "This sickness will not end in death. No, it is for God's glory so that God's Son may be glorified through it." ⁵Jesus loved Martha and her sister and Lazarus. ⁶Yet when he heard that Lazarus was sick, he stayed where he was two more days.

⁷Then he said to his disciples, "Let us go back to Judea."

⁸"But Rabbi," they said, "a short while ago the Jews tried to stone you, and yet you are going back there?"

⁹Jesus answered, "Are there not twelve hours of daylight? A man who walks by day will not stumble, for he sees by this world's light. ¹⁰It is when he walks by night that he stumbles, for he has no light."

¹¹After he had said this, he went on to tell them, "Our friend Lazarus has fallen asleep; but I am going there to wake him up."

¹²His disciples replied, "Lord, if he sleeps, he will get better." ¹³Jesus had been speaking of his death, but his disciples thought he meant natural sleep.

¹⁴So then he told them plainly, "Lazarus is dead, ¹⁵and for your sake I am glad I was not there, so that you may believe. But let us go to him."

¹⁶Then Thomas (called Didymus) said to the rest of the disciples, "Let us also go, that we may die with him."

Jesus Comforts the Sisters

¹⁷On his arrival, Jesus found that Lazarus had already been in the tomb for four days. ¹⁸Bethany was less than two miles^a from Jerusalem, ¹⁹and many Jews had come to Martha and Mary to comfort them in the loss of their brother. ²⁰When Martha heard that Jesus was coming, she went out to meet him, but Mary stayed at home.

²¹"Lord," Martha said to Jesus, "if you had been here, my brother would not have died. ²²But I know that even now God will give you whatever you ask."

²³Jesus said to her, "Your brother will rise again."

²⁴Martha answered, "I know he will rise again in the resurrection at the last day."

²⁵Jesus said to her, "I am the resurrection and the life. He who believes in me will live, even though he dies; ²⁶and whoever lives and believes in me will never die. Do you believe this?"

²⁷"Yes, Lord," she told him, "I believe that you are the Christ,^b the Son of God, who was to come into the world."

²⁸And after she had said this, she went back and called her sister Mary aside. "The Teacher is here," she said, "and is asking for you." ²⁹When Mary heard this, she got up quickly and went to him. ³⁰Now Jesus had not yet entered the village, but was still at the place where Martha had met him. ³¹When the Jews who had been with Mary in the house, comforting her, noticed how quickly she got up and went out, they followed her, supposing she was going to the tomb to mourn there.

³²When Mary reached the place where Jesus was and saw him, she fell at his feet and said, "Lord, if you had been here, my brother would not have died."

³³When Jesus saw her weeping, and the Jews who had come along with her also weeping, he was deeply moved in spirit and troubled. ³⁴"Where have you laid him?" he asked.

"Come and see, Lord," they replied.

³⁵Jesus wept.

³⁶Then the Jews said, "See how he loved him!"

³⁷But some of them said, "Could not he who opened the eyes of the blind man have kept this man from dying?"

Jesus Raises Lazarus From the Dead

³⁸Jesus, once more deeply moved, came to the tomb. It was a cave with a stone laid across the entrance. ³⁹"Take away the stone," he said.

"But, Lord," said Martha, the sister of the dead man, "by this time there is a bad odor, for he has been there four days."

⁴⁰Then Jesus said, "Did I not tell you that if you believed, you would see the glory of God?"

⁴¹So they took away the stone. Then Jesus looked up and said, "Father, I thank you that you have heard me. ⁴²I knew that you al-

---

^a18 Greek fifteen stadia (about 3 kilometers)   ^b27 Or Messiah

THE DEVOTION OF MARY

Individual: Kelly, fourteen.

Role Models: A well-known model with sleek hair and body to match; a popular singer with a great voice and charismatic personality; her mother who places a lot of emphasis on nice things, looking good and keeping up with all the other members of the club.

Description: Kelly is a Christian, but within recent weeks she's only thought of one thing—David Tanner. In her own words, "I'm so in love I can't stand it!"

Result: Kelly doesn't feel very close to God anymore. She's considering not going to youth camp so she can see more of David.

Look It Up
••••

Kelly could use a new role model. She'd be much better off if she'd imitate the life of Mary, the sister of Lazarus and Martha.

Mary had her priorities in the correct order. While her sister Martha hurried about putting together an elaborate meal, Mary "sat at the Lord's feet listening to what he said" (Luke 10:39).

Jesus praised this willingness to hear and obey his Word. "Mary has chosen what is better, and it will not be taken away from her" (Luke 10:42).

As a result, Mary developed a deep love for Jesus Christ. She demonstrated this when she poured perfume worth thousands of dollars on his feet to prepare him for his burial (John 12:1–8).

Think It Through
••••

When people spend time listening to Jesus Christ through his Word, they realize how much he loves them. That love frees them to love him in return. His importance in their lives grows as they spend time in his Word and experience his love for them. Eventually, there is nothing they won't do for him.

That's what happened in Mary's life. That's what needs to happen in Kelly's life.

Work It Out
••••

Do a priority check today. Do you have time for friends, romantic relationships, exercise, TV, studying, phone calls, meetings, but no time to spend with the Lord?

The solution is to fall in love with Jesus Christ. When he is your first love, you'll find the strength and motivation to live in a way that is pleasing to him.

With that in mind, make the following commitment: "Lord, by your grace, I want to begin spending at least ten minutes every day getting to know you better. Deepen my love for you so that, like Mary, I would be willing to make any sacrifice for you. Signed, _____."

Nail It Down
••••

Read Mary's response to Jesus' call in John 11:28–29.

Turn to pages 229 and 267 for other readings on heroes.
Turn to page 1148 for the weekend reading.

Topic
••••

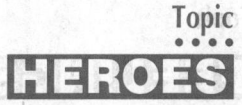

HEROES

FEELINGS: DON'T BE AFRAID TO EXPRESS THEM

Work It Out
••••

Have you been in a tough situation recently when you found it hard to express your feelings? Maybe someone in your family was very sick, or your parents were going through a divorce. Perhaps your boyfriend or girlfriend broke up with you. Whatever the situation, you were hurting. Were you able to get all of your feelings out into the open? Or did you have a hard time expressing how you felt?

Everyone has been in a tough situation at one time or another. Jesus was in one when his friend Lazarus died. Jesus loved Lazarus and his sisters. They were his close friends. Now Lazarus was dead, and Mary and Martha were hurting. Jesus stood in front of the tomb, and he cried.

The next time you're in a situation and it hurts, take a lesson from the Teacher of all teachers: Cry about it.

Nail It Down
••••

Read John 11:35 where Jesus expressed his feelings.

Think It Through
••••

Why are people uncomfortable when someone cries? Even when a loved one dies, people will often pat on the back the one who is crying and say, "Oh, don't cry." Crying gives outward evidence of inward pain. It's like drawing a picture of the pain for everyone to look at, and people are often uncomfortable with such pictures.

Crying is as beautiful a way to express hurt as laughter is to express happiness. Don't be afraid of it. Crying releases the tension that grief causes. Crying can blunt the sharp edges of hurt. Crying eases the pain of tough situations.

The next time you're in a hard situation, if someone tells you, "Oh, don't cry about it," politely ignore them and go on expressing your feelings—just as Jesus did.

Nail It Down
••••

Reread the little verse in John 11:35. For further insight read Psalm 126:5–6.

Turn to pages 572, 686, 694, 939, 1026 and 1178 for other readings on feelings.
Turn to page 1151 for Monday's reading.

Topic
••••

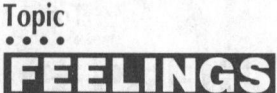

ways hear me, but I said this for the benefit of the people standing here, that they may believe that you sent me."

43When he had said this, Jesus called in a loud voice, "Lazarus, come out!" **44**The dead man came out, his hands and feet wrapped with strips of linen, and a cloth around his face.

Jesus said to them, "Take off the grave clothes and let him go."

The Plot to Kill Jesus

45Therefore many of the Jews who had come to visit Mary, and had seen what Jesus did, put their faith in him. **46**But some of them went to the Pharisees and told them what Jesus had done. **47**Then the chief priests and the Pharisees called a meeting of the Sanhedrin.

"What are we accomplishing?" they asked. "Here is this man performing many miraculous signs. **48**If we let him go on like this, everyone will believe in him, and then the Romans will come and take away both our place*a* and our nation."

49Then one of them, named Caiaphas, who was high priest that year, spoke up, "You know nothing at all! **50**You do not realize that it is better for you that one man die for the people than that the whole nation perish."

51He did not say this on his own, but as high priest that year he prophesied that Jesus would die for the Jewish nation, **52**and not only for that nation but also for the scattered children of God, to bring them together and make them one. **53**So from that day on they plotted to take his life.

54Therefore Jesus no longer moved about publicly among the Jews. Instead he withdrew to a region near the desert, to a village called Ephraim, where he stayed with his disciples.

55When it was almost time for the Jewish Passover, many went up from the country to Jerusalem for their ceremonial cleansing before the Passover. **56**They kept looking for Jesus, and as they stood in the temple area they asked one another, "What do you think? Isn't he coming to the Feast at all?" **57**But the chief priests and Pharisees had given orders that if anyone found out where Jesus was, he should report it so that they might arrest him.

Jesus Anointed at Bethany

12 Six days before the Passover, Jesus arrived at Bethany, where Lazarus lived, whom Jesus had raised from the dead. **2**Here a dinner was given in Jesus' honor. Martha served, while Lazarus was among those reclining at the table with him. **3**Then Mary took about a pint*b* of pure nard, an expensive perfume; she poured it on Jesus' feet and wiped his feet with her hair. And the house was filled with the fragrance of the perfume.

4But one of his disciples, Judas Iscariot, who was later to betray him, objected, **5**"Why wasn't this perfume sold and the money given to the poor? It was worth a year's wages.*c*" **6**He did not say this because he cared about the poor but because he was a thief; as keeper of the money bag, he used to help himself to what was put into it.

7"Leave her alone," Jesus replied. "It was intended, that she should save this perfume for the day of my burial. **8**You will always have the poor among you, but you will not always have me."

9Meanwhile a large crowd of Jews found out that Jesus was there and came, not only because of him but also to see Lazarus, whom he had raised from the dead. **10**So the chief priests made plans to kill Lazarus as well, **11**for on account of him many of the Jews were going over to Jesus and putting their faith in him.

The Triumphal Entry

12The next day the great crowd that had come for the Feast heard that Jesus was on his way to Jerusalem. **13**They took palm branches and went out to meet him, shouting,

"Hosanna!*d*"

"Blessed is he who comes in the name
  of the Lord!"*e*

"Blessed is the King of Israel!"

14Jesus found a young donkey and sat upon it, as it is written,

15"Do not be afraid, O Daughter of Zion;
  see, your king is coming,
  seated on a donkey's colt."*f*

16At first his disciples did not understand all this. Only after Jesus was glorified did

---

*a*48 Or *temple*   *b*3 Greek *a litra* (probably about 0.5 liter)   *c*5 Greek *three hundred denarii*   *d*13 A Hebrew expression meaning "Save!" which became an exclamation of praise   *e*13 Psalm 118:25, 26   *f*15 Zech. 9:9

they realize that these things had been written about him and that they had done these things to him.

[17]Now the crowd that was with him when he called Lazarus from the tomb and raised him from the dead continued to spread the word. [18]Many people, because they had heard that he had given this miraculous sign, went out to meet him. [19]So the Pharisees said to one another, "See, this is getting us nowhere. Look how the whole world has gone after him!"

Jesus Predicts His Death

[20]Now there were some Greeks among those who went up to worship at the Feast. [21]They came to Philip, who was from Bethsaida in Galilee, with a request. "Sir," they said, "we would like to see Jesus." [22]Philip went to tell Andrew; Andrew and Philip in turn told Jesus.

[23]Jesus replied, "The hour has come for the Son of Man to be glorified. [24]I tell you the truth, unless a kernel of wheat falls to the ground and dies, it remains only a single seed. But if it dies, it produces many seeds. [25]The man who loves his life will lose it, while the man who hates his life in this world will keep it for eternal life. [26]Whoever serves me must follow me; and where I am, my servant also will be. My Father will honor the one who serves me.

[27]"Now my heart is troubled, and what shall I say? 'Father, save me from this hour'? No, it was for this very reason I came to this hour. [28]Father, glorify your name!"

Then a voice came from heaven, "I have glorified it, and will glorify it again." [29]The crowd that was there and heard it said it had thundered; others said an angel had spoken to him.

[30]Jesus said, "This voice was for your benefit, not mine. [31]Now is the time for judgment on this world; now the prince of this world will be driven out. [32]But I, when I am lifted up from the earth, will draw all men to myself." [33]He said this to show the kind of death he was going to die.

[34]The crowd spoke up, "We have heard from the Law that the Christ[a] will remain forever, so how can you say, 'The Son of Man must be lifted up'? Who is this 'Son of Man'?"

[35]Then Jesus told them, "You are going to have the light just a little while longer. Walk while you have the light, before darkness overtakes you. The man who walks in the dark does not know where he is going. [36]Put your trust in the light while you have it, so that you may become sons of light." When he had finished speaking, Jesus left and hid himself from them.

The Jews Continue in Their Unbelief

[37]Even after Jesus had done all these miraculous signs in their presence, they still would not believe in him. [38]This was to fulfill the word of Isaiah the prophet:

"Lord, who has believed our message
　　and to whom has the arm of the Lord
　　　been revealed?"[b]

[39]For this reason they could not believe, because, as Isaiah says elsewhere:

[40]"He has blinded their eyes
　　and deadened their hearts,
so they can neither see with their eyes,
　　nor understand with their hearts,
　　nor turn—and I would heal them."[c]

[41]Isaiah said this because he saw Jesus' glory and spoke about him.

[42]Yet at the same time many even among the leaders believed in him. But because of the Pharisees they would not confess their faith for fear they would be put out of the synagogue; [43]for they loved praise from men more than praise from God.

[44]Then Jesus cried out, "When a man believes in me, he does not believe in me only, but in the one who sent me. [45]When he looks at me, he sees the one who sent me. [46]I have come into the world as a light, so that no one who believes in me should stay in darkness.

[47]"As for the person who hears my words but does not keep them, I do not judge him. For I did not come to judge the world, but to save it. [48]There is a judge for the one who rejects me and does not accept my words; that very word which I spoke will condemn him at the last day. [49]For I did not speak of my own accord, but the Father who sent me commanded me what to say and how to say it. [50]I know that his command leads to eternal life. So whatever I say is just what the Father has told me to say."

Jesus Washes His Disciples' Feet

13 It was just before the Passover Feast. Jesus knew that the time had come for him to leave this world and go to the Father. Having loved his own who were in the

THE BIG LIE OF THE CHEMICAL HIGH

☐ MONDAY

For two nightmarish years at Devlin High, Sheila was heavily involved with drugs. She's now drug-free. It wasn't easy—three months of almost total isolation in a drug rehabilitation hospital followed by lots of counseling—but Sheila has come face to face with one of life's greatest mysteries.

"It might sound corny or something, but with not much else to do in the hospital, I started reading the Bible my mom sent me. And it hit me—like never before—that drugs are a big lie. They can't bring you happiness or take away your pain. Only Jesus can do that."

Look It Up
••••

Did you catch what Sheila just said? If not, here's the same truth again from the lips of Jesus Christ:

"If anyone would come after me, he must deny himself and take up his cross and follow me. For whoever wants to save his life will lose it, but whoever loses his life for me and for the gospel will save it. What good is it for a man to gain the whole world, yet forfeit his soul? Or what can a man give in exchange for his soul?" (Mark 8:34–37).

What a profound truth! You can never find real satisfaction or long-term happiness in drugs (or any other selfish pursuit). True fulfillment is found only in Christ.

Think It Through
••••

Anti-drug campaigns are only a partial answer to the drug problem. People who say no to drugs—if they don't know Christ—still have emotional needs. Granted, they may not turn to drugs, but they will continue to look for something to fill the holes in their souls.

A more complete answer to the drug problem? Say no to drugs and yes to Christ.

Work It Out
••••

In a concordance look under the word *life* and check how often that word is used in the gospel of John. Carefully read each reference Jesus makes to life. How does his definition compare to what the world says life is all about?

Conclude your study with prayer. Ask God to help you grasp the fact that ultimate satisfaction is found only in Christ.

Nail It Down
••••

Contemplate the words of Christ found in John 12:23–25.

Turn to pages 1115, 1239 and 1350 for other readings on drugs.
Turn to page 1153 for Tuesday's reading.

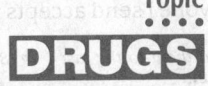

Topic
••••
DRUGS

world, he now showed them the full extent of his love. *a*

2The evening meal was being served, and the devil had already prompted Judas Iscariot, son of Simon, to betray Jesus. **3**Jesus knew that the Father had put all things under his power, and that he had come from God and was returning to God; **4**so he got up from the meal, took off his outer clothing, and wrapped a towel around his waist. **5**After that, he poured water into a basin and began to wash his disciples' feet, drying them with the towel that was wrapped around him.

6He came to Simon Peter, who said to him, "Lord, are you going to wash my feet?" **7**Jesus replied, "You do not realize now what I am doing, but later you will understand."

8"No," said Peter, "you shall never wash my feet."

Jesus answered, "Unless I wash you, you have no part with me."

9"Then, Lord," Simon Peter replied, "not just my feet but my hands and my head as well!"

10Jesus answered, "A person who has had a bath needs only to wash his feet; his whole body is clean. And you are clean, though not every one of you." **11**For he knew who was going to betray him, and that was why he said not every one was clean.

12When he had finished washing their feet, he put on his clothes and returned to his place. "Do you understand what I have done for you?" he asked them. **13**"You call me 'Teacher' and 'Lord,' and rightly so, for that is what I am. **14**Now that I, your Lord and Teacher, have washed your feet, you also should wash one another's feet. **15**I have set you an example that you should do as I have done for you. **16**I tell you the truth, no servant is greater than his master, nor is a messenger greater than the one who sent him. **17**Now that you know these things, you will be blessed if you do them.

Jesus Predicts His Betrayal

18"I am not referring to all of you; I know those I have chosen. But this is to fulfill the scripture: 'He who shares my bread has lifted up his heel against me.'*b*

19"I am telling you now before it happens, so that when it does happen you will believe that I am He. **20**I tell you the truth, whoever accepts anyone I send accepts me; and whoever accepts me accepts the one who sent me."

21After he had said this, Jesus was troubled in spirit and testified, "I tell you the truth, one of you is going to betray me."

22His disciples stared at one another, at a loss to know which of them he meant. **23**One of them, the disciple whom Jesus loved, was reclining next to him. **24**Simon Peter motioned to this disciple and said, "Ask him which one he means."

25Leaning back against Jesus, he asked him, "Lord, who is it?"

26Jesus answered, "It is the one to whom I will give this piece of bread when I have dipped it in the dish." Then, dipping the piece of bread, he gave it to Judas Iscariot, son of Simon. **27**As soon as Judas took the bread, Satan entered into him.

"What you are about to do, do quickly," Jesus told him, **28**but no one at the meal understood why Jesus said this to him. **29**Since Judas had charge of the money, some thought Jesus was telling him to buy what was needed for the Feast, or to give something to the poor. **30**As soon as Judas had taken the bread, he went out. And it was night.

Jesus Predicts Peter's Denial

31When he was gone, Jesus said, "Now is the Son of Man glorified and God is glorified in him. **32**If God is glorified in him,*c* God will glorify the Son in himself, and will glorify him at once.

33"My children, I will be with you only a little longer. You will look for me, and just as I told the Jews, so I tell you now: Where I am going, you cannot come.

34"A new command I give you: Love one another. As I have loved you, so you must love one another. **35**By this all men will know that you are my disciples, if you love one another."

36Simon Peter asked him, "Lord, where are you going?"

Jesus replied, "Where I am going, you cannot follow now, but you will follow later."

37Peter asked, "Lord, why can't I follow you now? I will lay down my life for you."

38Then Jesus answered, "Will you really lay down your life for me? I tell you the truth, before the rooster crows, you will disown me three times!

---

a1 Or *he loved them to the last*   *b18* Psalm 41:9   *c32* Many early manuscripts do not have *If God is glorified in him.*

THE DEMANDS OF LOVE

Imagine the following situations:
1. You're in the middle of a major crisis. You ask your parents for support, and they respond: "Look, we're busy right now. Our favorite TV show is on. And after its over we have to go to the store and pick up a few things. But, honey, we do love you. Really we do."

2. On the weekend your boyfriend or girlfriend is affectionate and sweet, gushing about how much he or she loves you. But during the week he or she says, "Hey, what can I say? I just don't feel anything for you right now. Maybe my love for you is dying out. I don't know. Gimme some space, okay?"

Look It Up • • • •

What a nightmare! And yet a lot of people actually think like that. Some imagine that love is shown merely by words. Others believe that love is just a feeling. When the feeling fades, the relationship is over. These people desperately need to take Love U. course 103: The Demands of Love.

In that class students find out that love is action. "Dear children, let us not love with words or tongue but with actions and in truth" (1 John 3:18).

Students there also discover that love is primarily a commitment, not a feeling—an action, not a goose bump. God's love for the people of Israel was shown by his constant faithfulness to them, even when he was angered by their actions (see Judges 10:6–16).

Think It Through • • • •

What if God sat up in heaven and just kept saying over and over to the human race, "I love you," but he never did anything to show his love? What if his goodness to you depended on his feelings? What if he loved you only as long as you performed perfectly for him?

The point? Love and actions cannot be separated. You need to be committed to doing loving actions for others even when you don't feel like it.

Work It Out • • • •

In each one of your close relationships (parents, siblings, special friends) show your love today by doing something. It doesn't have to cost money or take a lot of time. Try one of these: a note, a hug, a helping hand, a surprise. Perhaps the best way to show your love is by *not* doing something that annoys, disturbs, hurts or offends.

Remember: Love is more than just talk, and feelings are the result, not the goal. You do your part—performing acts of love—and the feelings will probably follow.

Nail It Down • • • •

Read John 13:34 for whose loving example you are to follow.

Turn to pages 1215, 1250 and 1313 for other readings on love.
Turn to page 1156 for Wednesday's reading.

Topic
• • • •

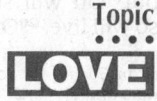
LOVE

Jesus Comforts His Disciples

14 "Do not let your hearts be troubled. Trust in God[a]; trust also in me. [2]In my Father's house are many rooms; if it were not so, I would have told you. I am going there to prepare a place for you. [3]And if I go and prepare a place for you, I will come back and take you to be with me that you also may be where I am. [4]You know the way to the place where I am going."

Jesus the Way to the Father

[5]Thomas said to him, "Lord, we don't know where you are going, so how can we know the way?"

[6]Jesus answered, "I am the way and the truth and the life. No one comes to the Father except through me. [7]If you really knew me, you would know[b] my Father as well. From now on, you do know him and have seen him."

[8]Philip said, "Lord, show us the Father and that will be enough for us."

[9]Jesus answered: "Don't you know me, Philip, even after I have been among you such a long time? Anyone who has seen me has seen the Father. How can you say, 'Show us the Father'? [10]Don't you believe that I am in the Father, and that the Father is in me? The words I say to you are not just my own. Rather, it is the Father, living in me, who is doing his work. [11]Believe me when I say that I am in the Father and the Father is in me; or at least believe on the evidence of the miracles themselves. [12]I tell you the truth, anyone who has faith in me will do what I have been doing. He will do even greater things than these, because I am going to the Father. [13]And I will do whatever you ask in my name, so that the Son may bring glory to the Father. [14]You may ask me for anything in my name, and I will do it.

Jesus Promises the Holy Spirit

[15]"If you love me, you will obey what I command. [16]And I will ask the Father, and he will give you another Counselor to be with you forever— [17]the Spirit of truth. The world cannot accept him, because it neither sees him nor knows him. But you know him, for he lives with you and will be[c] in you. [18]I will not leave you as orphans; I will come to you. [19]Before long, the world will not see me anymore, but you will see me. Because I live, you also will live. [20]On that day you will

realize that I am in my Father, and you are in me, and I am in you. [21]Whoever has my commands and obeys them, he is the one who loves me. He who loves me will be loved by my Father, and I too will love him and show myself to him."

[22]Then Judas (not Judas Iscariot) said, "But, Lord, why do you intend to show yourself to us and not to the world?"

[23]Jesus replied, "If anyone loves me, he will obey my teaching. My Father will love him, and we will come to him and make our home with him. [24]He who does not love me will not obey my teaching. These words you hear are not my own; they belong to the Father who sent me.

[25]"All this I have spoken while still with you. [26]But the Counselor, the Holy Spirit, whom the Father will send in my name, will teach you all things and will remind you of everything I have said to you. [27]Peace I leave with you; my peace I give you. I do not give to you as the world gives. Do not let your hearts be troubled and do not be afraid.

[28]"You heard me say, 'I am going away and I am coming back to you.' If you loved me, you would be glad that I am going to the Father, for the Father is greater than I. [29]I have told you now before it happens, so that when it does happen you will believe. [30]I will not speak with you much longer, for the prince of this world is coming. He has no hold on me, [31]but the world must learn that I love the Father and that I do exactly what my Father has commanded me.

"Come now; let us leave.

The Vine and the Branches

15 "I am the true vine, and my Father is the gardener. [2]He cuts off every branch in me that bears no fruit, while every branch that does bear fruit he prunes[d] so that it will be even more fruitful. [3]You are already clean because of the word I have spoken to you. [4]Remain in me, and I will remain in you. No branch can bear fruit by itself; it must remain in the vine. Neither can you bear fruit unless you remain in me.

[5]"I am the vine; you are the branches. If a man remains in me and I in him, he will bear much fruit; apart from me you can do nothing. [6]If anyone does not remain in me, he is like a branch that is thrown away and withers; such branches are picked up, thrown into the fire and burned. [7]If you remain in me and my words remain in you,

a1 Or *You trust in God*　b7 Some early manuscripts *If you really have known me, you will know*　c17 Some early manuscripts *and is*　d2 The Greek for *prunes* also means *cleans*.

ask whatever you wish, and it will be given you. **8**This is to my Father's glory, that you bear much fruit, showing yourselves to be my disciples.

9"As the Father has loved me, so have I loved you. Now remain in my love. **10**If you obey my commands, you will remain in my love, just as I have obeyed my Father's commands and remain in his love. **11**I have told you this so that my joy may be in you and that your joy may be complete. **12**My command is this: Love each other as I have loved you. **13**Greater love has no one than this, that he lay down his life for his friends. **14**You are my friends if you do what I command. **15**I no longer call you servants, because a servant does not know his master's business. Instead, I have called you friends, for everything that I learned from my Father I have made known to you. **16**You did not choose me, but I chose you and appointed you to go and bear fruit—fruit that will last. Then the Father will give you whatever you ask in my name. **17**This is my command: Love each other.

The World Hates the Disciples

18"If the world hates you, keep in mind that it hated me first. **19**If you belonged to the world, it would love you as its own. As it is, you do not belong to the world, but I have chosen you out of the world. That is why the world hates you. **20**Remember the words I spoke to you: 'No servant is greater than his master.'*a* If they persecuted me, they will persecute you also. If they obeyed my teaching, they will obey yours also. **21**They will treat you this way because of my name, for they do not know the One who sent me. **22**If I had not come and spoken to them, they would not be guilty of sin. Now, however, they have no excuse for their sin. **23**He who hates me hates my Father as well. **24**If I had not done among them what no one else did, they would not be guilty of sin. But now they have seen these miracles, and yet they have hated both me and my Father. **25**But this is to fulfill what is written in their Law: 'They hated me without reason.'*b*

26"When the Counselor comes, whom I will send to you from the Father, the Spirit of truth who goes out from the Father, he will testify about me. **27**And you also must testify, for you have been with me from the beginning.

16 "All this I have told you so that you will not go astray. **2**They will put you out of the synagogue; in fact, a time is coming when anyone who kills you will think he is offering a service to God. **3**They will do such things because they have not known the Father or me. **4**I have told you this, so that when the time comes you will remember that I warned you. I did not tell you this at first because I was with you.

The Work of the Holy Spirit

5"Now I am going to him who sent me, yet none of you asks me, 'Where are you going?' **6**Because I have said these things, you are filled with grief. **7**But I tell you the truth: It is for your good that I am going away. Unless I go away, the Counselor will not come to you; but if I go, I will send him to you. **8**When he comes, he will convict the world of guilt*c* in regard to sin and righteousness and judgment: **9**in regard to sin, because men do not believe in me; **10**in regard to righteousness, because I am going to the Father, where you can see me no longer; **11**and in regard to judgment, because the prince of this world now stands condemned.

12"I have much more to say to you, more than you can now bear. **13**But when he, the Spirit of truth, comes, he will guide you into all truth. He will not speak on his own; he will speak only what he hears, and he will tell you what is yet to come. **14**He will bring glory to me by taking from what is mine and making it known to you. **15**All that belongs to the Father is mine. That is why I said the Spirit will take from what is mine and make it known to you.

16"In a little while you will see me no more, and then after a little while you will see me."

The Disciples' Grief Will Turn to Joy

17Some of his disciples said to one another, "What does he mean by saying, 'In a little while you will see me no more, and then after a little while you will see me,' and 'Because I am going to the Father'?" **18**They kept asking, "What does he mean by 'a little while'? We don't understand what he is saying."

19Jesus saw that they wanted to ask him about this, so he said to them, "Are you asking one another what I meant when I said, 'In a little while you will see me no more, and then after a little while you will see me'? **20**I tell you the truth, you will weep and mourn while the world rejoices. You will grieve, but your grief will turn to joy. **21**A

a20 John 13:16   *b25* Psalms 35:19; 69:4   *c8* Or *will expose the guilt of the world*

PUTTING YOUR MONEY WHERE YOUR MOUTH IS

What's wrong with the following scene? Jill goes to church on Sunday night and sings the hymn, "Oh, How I Love Jesus." Later that night she goes home, calls a friend and proceeds to rip to shreds someone named Leslie.

"She makes me so mad! I mean, what a total fake! Did you see the way she was acting around the guys? She's about as much of a Christian as my dog. I know I should just probably ignore her — and I would if it wasn't for what she did to me last summer! But that was the worst! I'll never forgive her for that lie she told Steve about me."

Look It Up
• • • •

Hey, you can't really say (or sing) about how much you love Jesus unless you're also doing what he says:

"If anyone loves me, he will obey my teaching. My Father will love him, and we will come to him and make our home with him" (John 14:23).

And Jesus didn't just tell you to obey, he also gave you an example to follow:

"The world must learn that I love the Father and that I do exactly what my Father has commanded me" (John 14:31).

Think It Through
• • • •

Philippians 2:8 says that Christ was "obedient to death — even death on a cross!" How great is your willingness to be obedient? Are you willing to do whatever God commands — even if it means you have to suffer? If it came down to it, would you be willing to give up friends, family, a good job, a relationship or a valued possession in order to be obedient to Christ?

Has your obedience to Christ ever cost you something?

Work It Out
• • • •

Scan through the Sermon on the Mount (Matthew 5 — 7). Pick out two or three commands of Christ that relate to weak areas in your walk with the Lord.

First, pray, asking God to help you to be obedient in these areas. Second, call a good Christian friend and share your commitment with him or her. Ask your friend to check up on you and to keep encouraging you to do the things that Jesus commands.

Nail It Down
• • • •

Read Jesus' promise in John 15:10.

Turn to pages 159, 281, 892, 1013 and 1082 for other readings on obedience.
Turn to page 1158 for Thursday's reading.

Topic
• • • •

OBEDIENCE

woman giving birth to a child has pain because her time has come; but when her baby is born she forgets the anguish because of her joy that a child is born into the world. ²²So with you: Now is your time of grief, but I will see you again and you will rejoice, and no one will take away your joy. ²³In that day you will no longer ask me anything. I tell you the truth, my Father will give you whatever you ask in my name. ²⁴Until now you have not asked for anything in my name. Ask and you will receive, and your joy will be complete.

²⁵"Though I have been speaking figuratively, a time is coming when I will no longer use this kind of language but will tell you plainly about my Father. ²⁶In that day you will ask in my name. I am not saying that I will ask the Father on your behalf. ²⁷No, the Father himself loves you because you have loved me and have believed that I came from God. ²⁸I came from the Father and entered the world; now I am leaving the world and going back to the Father."

²⁹Then Jesus' disciples said, "Now you are speaking clearly and without figures of speech. ³⁰Now we can see that you know all things and that you do not even need to have anyone ask you questions. This makes us believe that you came from God."

³¹"You believe at last!"ᵃ Jesus answered. ³²"But a time is coming, and has come, when you will be scattered, each to his own home. You will leave me all alone. Yet I am not alone, for my Father is with me.

³³"I have told you these things, so that in me you may have peace. In this world you will have trouble. But take heart! I have overcome the world."

Jesus Prays for Himself

17 After Jesus said this, he looked toward heaven and prayed:

"Father, the time has come. Glorify your Son, that your Son may glorify you. ²For you granted him authority over all people that he might give eternal life to all those you have given him. ³Now this is eternal life: that they may know you, the only true God, and Jesus Christ, whom you have sent. ⁴I have brought you glory on earth by completing the work you gave me to do. ⁵And now, Father, glorify me in your presence with the glory I had with you before the world began.

Jesus Prays for His Disciples

⁶"I have revealed youᵇ to those whom you gave me out of the world. They were yours; you gave them to me and they have obeyed your word. ⁷Now they know that everything you have given me comes from you. ⁸For I gave them the words you gave me and they accepted them. They knew with certainty that I came from you, and they believed that you sent me. ⁹I pray for them. I am not praying for the world, but for those you have given me, for they are yours. ¹⁰All I have is yours, and all you have is mine. And glory has come to me through them. ¹¹I will remain in the world no longer, but they are still in the world, and I am coming to you. Holy Father, protect them by the power of your name—the name you gave me—so that they may be one as we are one. ¹²While I was with them, I protected them and kept them safe by that name you gave me. None has been lost except the one doomed to destruction so that Scripture would be fulfilled.

¹³"I am coming to you now, but I say these things while I am still in the world, so that they may have the full measure of my joy within them. ¹⁴I have given them your word and the world has hated them, for they are not of the world any more than I am of the world. ¹⁵My prayer is not that you take them out of the world but that you protect them from the evil one. ¹⁶They are not of the world, even as I am not of it. ¹⁷Sanctifyᶜ them by the truth; your word is truth. ¹⁸As you sent me into the world, I have sent them into the world. ¹⁹For them I sanctify myself, that they too may be truly sanctified.

Jesus Prays for All Believers

²⁰"My prayer is not for them alone. I pray also for those who will believe in me through their message, ²¹that all of them may be one, Father, just as you are in me and I am in you. May they also be in us so that the world may believe that you have sent me. ²²I have given them the glory that you gave me, that they may be one as we are one: ²³I

ᵃ31 Or *"Do you now believe?"*   ᵇ6 Greek *your name*; also in verse 26   ᶜ17 Greek *hagiazo (set apart for sacred use or make holy)*; also in verse 19

ARE YOU FINISHING YOUR ASSIGNMENTS?

On Wednesday in her advanced literature class, Blair agreed to read (for extra credit) *War and Peace,* a huge Russian novel. By Friday she was kicking herself.

"Why did I say I would do this?" she moaned. "This is the longest book in the history of the world! I couldn't finish it in three months much less one!"

But Blair stayed at it, faithfully reading a little bit every night. And guess what? She finished Tolstoy's classic!

Look It Up

The principle Blair learned at school is one we want to apply to our spiritual lives: By daily obedience we can accomplish God's purposes for our lives.

Ruth did it by refusing to be turned aside or distracted from the purpose of one event in her life: going with Naomi back to Judah. That one incident lead to a lifetime of doing God's will day by day and eventually made Ruth an ancestress of Jesus Christ (Ruth 1–4).

The apostle Paul also made that his goal—"If only I may finish the race and complete the task the Lord Jesus has given me—the task of testifying to the gospel of God's grace" (Acts 20:24). And he was successful—"I have fought the good fight, I have finished the race, I have kept the faith" (2 Timothy 4:7).

Think It Through

History is littered with quitters and the unfinished business they leave behind. Many people begin great projects. Few people stick with the projects until they are complete.

What qualities does it take to hang in there until the very end?

Work It Out

How can you make sure that you accomplish God's purpose for your life?

1. Be single-minded, concentrating on one task at a time (1 Chronicles 12:38).

2. Get in the habit of pausing to evaluate your life. Many times the children of Israel took time out to regroup. They reminded themselves of what God had done for them and remembered their priorities (see Deuteronomy and Joshua).

3. When troubles and discouragement come, remember that God has you in his hands. He will watch over you to see that his purposes are always carried out in your life (1 Samuel 16:14; 18:10–12; 19:9–10).

Nail It Down

Read John 17:4 for how Christ followed God's will for him.

Turn to pages 502, 1102 and 1220 for other readings on purpose.
Turn to page 1160 for Friday's reading.

Topic

PURPOSE

in them and you in me. May they be brought to complete unity to let the world know that you sent me and have loved them even as you have loved me.

24"Father, I want those you have given me to be with me where I am, and to see my glory, the glory you have given me because you loved me before the creation of the world.

25"Righteous Father, though the world does not know you, I know you, and they know that you have sent me. **26**I have made you known to them, and will continue to make you known in order that the love you have for me may be in them and that I myself may be in them."

Jesus Arrested

18 When he had finished praying, Jesus left with his disciples and crossed the Kidron Valley. On the other side there was an olive grove, and he and his disciples went into it.

2Now Judas, who betrayed him, knew the place, because Jesus had often met there with his disciples. **3**So Judas came to the grove, guiding a detachment of soldiers and some officials from the chief priests and Pharisees. They were carrying torches, lanterns and weapons.

4Jesus, knowing all that was going to happen to him, went out and asked them, "Who is it you want?"

5"Jesus of Nazareth," they replied.

"I am he," Jesus said. (And Judas the traitor was standing there with them.) **6**When Jesus said, "I am he," they drew back and fell to the ground.

7Again he asked them, "Who is it you want?"

And they said, "Jesus of Nazareth."

8"I told you that I am he," Jesus answered. "If you are looking for me, then let these men go." **9**This happened so that the words he had spoken would be fulfilled: "I have not lost one of those you gave me."*a*

10Then Simon Peter, who had a sword, drew it and struck the high priest's servant, cutting off his right ear. (The servant's name was Malchus.)

11Jesus commanded Peter, "Put your sword away! Shall I not drink the cup the Father has given me?"

Jesus Taken to Annas

12Then the detachment of soldiers with its commander and the Jewish officials arrested Jesus. They bound him **13**and brought him first to Annas, who was the father-in-law of Caiaphas, the high priest that year. **14**Caiaphas was the one who had advised the Jews that it would be good if one man died for the people.

Peter's First Denial

15Simon Peter and another disciple were following Jesus. Because this disciple was known to the high priest, he went with Jesus into the high priest's courtyard, **16**but Peter had to wait outside at the door. The other disciple, who was known to the high priest, came back, spoke to the girl on duty there and brought Peter in.

17"You are not one of his disciples, are you?" the girl at the door asked Peter.

He replied, "I am not."

18It was cold, and the servants and officials stood around a fire they had made to keep warm. Peter also was standing with them, warming himself.

The High Priest Questions Jesus

19Meanwhile, the high priest questioned Jesus about his disciples and his teaching.

20"I have spoken openly to the world," Jesus replied. "I always taught in synagogues or at the temple, where all the Jews come together. I said nothing in secret. **21**Why question me? Ask those who heard me. Surely they know what I said."

22When Jesus said this, one of the officials nearby struck him in the face. "Is this the way you answer the high priest?" he demanded.

23"If I said something wrong," Jesus replied, "testify as to what is wrong. But if I spoke the truth, why did you strike me?" **24**Then Annas sent him, still bound, to Caiaphas the high priest.*b*

Peter's Second and Third Denials

25As Simon Peter stood warming himself, he was asked, "You are not one of his disciples, are you?"

He denied it, saying, "I am not."

26One of the high priest's servants, a relative of the man whose ear Peter had cut off, challenged him, "Didn't I see you with him in the olive grove?" **27**Again Peter denied it, and at that moment a rooster began to crow.

Jesus Before Pilate

28Then the Jews led Jesus from Caiaphas

a9 John 6:39   *b24* Or *(Now Annas had sent him, still bound, to Caiaphas the high priest.)*

LATCHING ON TO THE LIFE SOURCE

Kurt drives a sporty little car with a "Party Naked" bumper sticker on it. He's a great athlete and a good student. His family has some serious cash. He dates the cutest girl at school.

Kurt's got it made, right? He's enjoying the good life, right? He's completely happy, right?

Wrong.

If you could ever get Kurt to be totally honest, he'd tell you he's not really so together on the inside. Oh, sure, he has a lot of fun. But when he crawls into bed at night and turns out the light, he lies there in the dark silence and wonders, "If my life is so great, like everybody keeps telling me, how come I feel so awful?"

Look It Up
••••

A lamp has to be plugged into a power source before it will work. Likewise, people have to be plugged into the life source before they can experience real life.

Who is that life source? "Jesus answered, 'I am the way and the truth and the life. No one comes to the Father except through me' " (John 14:6).

As Jesus told the religious leaders of his day, "You diligently study the Scriptures because you think that by them you possess eternal life. These are the Scriptures that testify about me, yet you refuse to come to me to have life" (John 5:39–40).

In short, what these passages are saying is that life—real life, eternal life—has one source: Jesus Christ.

Think It Through
••••

Why can't you or anyone else find real satisfaction from boyfriends, girlfriends, money or social status? Because you were created in God's image and therefore you need your Creator. But you come into this world cut off from God (Ephesians 2:1–3). Your most urgent need is not a new designer dress or a dream vacation. It is the life that only God can give.

Work It Out
••••

Do some experiments. Watch the people at your school today to see if you can figure out what they are counting on to bring them fulfillment in life.

Examine your own behavior and attitudes. Do others see you as full of the life, joy and peace that only God can give? If not, why not?

Here's a prayer for the week: "Dear God, I give you thanks for giving me life—real life—through your Son, Jesus Christ. Help me to see that real satisfaction and fulfillment are found only in you, through Christ. Amen."

Nail It Down
••••

Read John 17:25-26 to find out where the real source of life can be found.

Turn to pages 951, 1164, 1167, 1217 and 1319 for other readings on real life.
Turn to page 1164 for the weekend reading.

Topic
••••

REAL LIFE

to the palace of the Roman governor. By now it was early morning, and to avoid ceremonial uncleanness the Jews did not enter the palace; they wanted to be able to eat the Passover. ²⁹So Pilate came out to them and asked, "What charges are you bringing against this man?"

³⁰"If he were not a criminal," they replied, "we would not have handed him over to you."

³¹Pilate said, "Take him yourselves and judge him by your own law."

"But we have no right to execute anyone," the Jews objected. ³²This happened so that the words Jesus had spoken indicating the kind of death he was going to die would be fulfilled.

³³Pilate then went back inside the palace, summoned Jesus and asked him, "Are you the king of the Jews?"

³⁴"Is that your own idea," Jesus asked, "or did others talk to you about me?"

³⁵"Am I a Jew?" Pilate replied. "It was your people and your chief priests who handed you over to me. What is it you have done?"

³⁶Jesus said, "My kingdom is not of this world. If it were, my servants would fight to prevent my arrest by the Jews. But now my kingdom is from another place."

³⁷"You are a king, then!" said Pilate.

Jesus answered, "You are right in saying I am a king. In fact, for this reason I was born, and for this I came into the world, to testify to the truth. Everyone on the side of truth listens to me."

³⁸"What is truth?" Pilate asked. With this he went out again to the Jews and said, "I find no basis for a charge against him. ³⁹But it is your custom for me to release to you one prisoner at the time of the Passover. Do you want me to release 'the king of the Jews'?"

⁴⁰They shouted back, "No, not him! Give us Barabbas!" Now Barabbas had taken part in a rebellion.

Jesus Sentenced to be Crucified

19 Then Pilate took Jesus and had him flogged. ²The soldiers twisted together a crown of thorns and put it on his head. They clothed him in a purple robe ³and went up to him again and again, saying, "Hail, king of the Jews!" And they struck him in the face.

⁴Once more Pilate came out and said to the Jews, "Look, I am bringing him out to you to let you know that I find no basis for a charge against him." ⁵When Jesus came out wearing the crown of thorns and the purple robe, Pilate said to them, "Here is the man!"

⁶As soon as the chief priests and their officials saw him, they shouted, "Crucify! Crucify!"

But Pilate answered, "You take him and crucify him. As for me, I find no basis for a charge against him."

⁷The Jews insisted, "We have a law, and according to that law he must die, because he claimed to be the Son of God."

⁸When Pilate heard this, he was even more afraid, ⁹and he went back inside the palace. "Where do you come from?" he asked Jesus, but Jesus gave him no answer. ¹⁰"Do you refuse to speak to me?" Pilate said. "Don't you realize I have power either to free you or to crucify you?"

¹¹Jesus answered, "You would have no power over me if it were not given to you from above. Therefore the one who handed me over to you is guilty of a greater sin."

¹²From then on, Pilate tried to set Jesus free, but the Jews kept shouting, "If you let this man go, you are no friend of Caesar. Anyone who claims to be a king opposes Caesar."

¹³When Pilate heard this, he brought Jesus out and sat down on the judge's seat at a place known as the Stone Pavement (which in Aramaic is Gabbatha). ¹⁴It was the day of Preparation of Passover Week, about the sixth hour.

"Here is your king," Pilate said to the Jews.

¹⁵But they shouted, "Take him away! Take him away! Crucify him!"

"Shall I crucify your king?" Pilate asked.

"We have no king but Caesar," the chief priests answered.

¹⁶Finally Pilate handed him over to them to be crucified.

The Crucifixion

So the soldiers took charge of Jesus. ¹⁷Carrying his own cross, he went out to the place of the Skull (which in Aramaic is called Golgotha). ¹⁸Here they crucified him, and with him two others—one on each side and Jesus in the middle.

¹⁹Pilate had a notice prepared and fastened to the cross. It read: JESUS OF NAZARETH, THE KING OF THE JEWS. ²⁰Many of the Jews read this sign, for the place where Jesus was crucified was near the city, and the sign was written in Aramaic, Latin and Greek. ²¹The chief priests of the Jews protested to Pilate, "Do not write 'The King of the Jews,' but that this man claimed to be king of the Jews."

22Pilate answered, "What I have written, I have written."

23When the soldiers crucified Jesus, they took his clothes, dividing them into four shares, one for each of them, with the undergarment remaining. This garment was seamless, woven in one piece from top to bottom.

24"Let's not tear it," they said to one another. "Let's decide by lot who will get it."

This happened that the scripture might be fulfilled which said,

"They divided my garments among
    them
  and cast lots for my clothing."[a]

So this is what the soldiers did.

25Near the cross of Jesus stood his mother, his mother's sister, Mary the wife of Clopas, and Mary Magdalene. **26**When Jesus saw his mother there, and the disciple whom he loved standing nearby, he said to his mother, "Dear woman, here is your son," **27**and to the disciple, "Here is your mother." From that time on, this disciple took her into his home.

The Death of Jesus

28Later, knowing that all was now completed, and so that the Scripture would be fulfilled, Jesus said, "I am thirsty." **29**A jar of wine vinegar was there, so they soaked a sponge in it, put the sponge on a stalk of the hyssop plant, and lifted it to Jesus' lips. **30**When he had received the drink, Jesus said, "It is finished." With that, he bowed his head and gave up his spirit.

31Now it was the day of Preparation, and the next day was to be a special Sabbath. Because the Jews did not want the bodies left on the crosses during the Sabbath, they asked Pilate to have the legs broken and the bodies taken down. **32**The soldiers therefore came and broke the legs of the first man who had been crucified with Jesus, and then those of the other. **33**But when they came to Jesus and found that he was already dead, they did not break his legs. **34**Instead, one of the soldiers pierced Jesus' side with a spear, bringing a sudden flow of blood and water. **35**The man who saw it has given testimony, and his testimony is true. He knows that he tells the truth, and he testifies so that you also may believe. **36**These things happened so that the scripture would be fulfilled: "Not one of his bones will be broken,"[b] **37**and, as

another scripture says, "They will look on the one they have pierced."[c]

The Burial of Jesus

38Later, Joseph of Arimathea asked Pilate for the body of Jesus. Now Joseph was a disciple of Jesus, but secretly because he feared the Jews. With Pilate's permission, he came and took the body away. **39**He was accompanied by Nicodemus, the man who earlier had visited Jesus at night. Nicodemus brought a mixture of myrrh and aloes, about seventy-five pounds.[d] **40**Taking Jesus' body, the two of them wrapped it, with the spices, in strips of linen. This was in accordance with Jewish burial customs. **41**At the place where Jesus was crucified, there was a garden, and in the garden a new tomb, in which no one had ever been laid. **42**Because it was the Jewish day of Preparation and since the tomb was nearby, they laid Jesus there.

The Empty Tomb

20 Early on the first day of the week, while it was still dark, Mary Magdalene went to the tomb and saw that the stone had been removed from the entrance. **2**So she came running to Simon Peter and the other disciple, the one Jesus loved, and said, "They have taken the Lord out of the tomb, and we don't know where they have put him!"

3So Peter and the other disciple started for the tomb. **4**Both were running, but the other disciple outran Peter and reached the tomb first. **5**He bent over and looked in at the strips of linen lying there but did not go in. **6**Then Simon Peter, who was behind him, arrived and went into the tomb. He saw the strips of linen lying there, **7**as well as the burial cloth that had been around Jesus' head. The cloth was folded up by itself, separate from the linen. **8**Finally the other disciple, who had reached the tomb first, also went inside. He saw and believed. **9**(They still did not understand from Scripture that Jesus had to rise from the dead.)

Jesus Appears to Mary Magdalene

10Then the disciples went back to their homes, **11**but Mary stood outside the tomb crying. As she wept, she bent over to look into the tomb **12**and saw two angels in white, seated where Jesus' body had been, one at the head and the other at the foot.

---

a24 Psalm 22:18   *b36* Exodus 12:46; Num. 9:12; Psalm 34:20   *c37* Zech. 12:10   *d39* Greek *a hundred litrai* (about 34 kilograms)

¹³They asked her, "Woman, why are you crying?"

"They have taken my Lord away," she said, "and I don't know where they have put him." ¹⁴At this, she turned around and saw Jesus standing there, but she did not realize that it was Jesus.

¹⁵"Woman," he said, "why are you crying? Who is it you are looking for?"

Thinking he was the gardener, she said, "Sir, if you have carried him away, tell me where you have put him, and I will get him."

¹⁶Jesus said to her, "Mary."

She turned toward him and cried out in Aramaic, "Rabboni!" (which means Teacher).

¹⁷Jesus said, "Do not hold on to me, for I have not yet returned to the Father. Go instead to my brothers and tell them, 'I am returning to my Father and your Father, to my God and your God.'"

¹⁸Mary Magdalene went to the disciples with the news: "I have seen the Lord!" And she told them that he had said these things to her.

Jesus Appears to His Disciples

¹⁹On the evening of that first day of the week, when the disciples were together, with the doors locked for fear of the Jews, Jesus came and stood among them and said, "Peace be with you!" ²⁰After he said this, he showed them his hands and side. The disciples were overjoyed when they saw the Lord.

²¹Again Jesus said, "Peace be with you! As the Father has sent me, I am sending you." ²²And with that he breathed on them and said, "Receive the Holy Spirit. ²³If you forgive anyone his sins, they are forgiven; if you do not forgive them, they are not forgiven."

Jesus Appears to Thomas

²⁴Now Thomas (called Didymus), one of the Twelve, was not with the disciples when Jesus came. ²⁵So the other disciples told him, "We have seen the Lord!"

But he said to them, "Unless I see the nail marks in his hands and put my finger where the nails were, and put my hand into his side, I will not believe it."

²⁶A week later his disciples were in the house again, and Thomas was with them. Though the doors were locked, Jesus came and stood among them and said, "Peace be with you!" ²⁷Then he said to Thomas, "Put your finger here; see my hands. Reach out your hand and put it into my side. Stop doubting and believe."

²⁸Thomas said to him, "My Lord and my God!"

²⁹Then Jesus told him, "Because you have seen me, you have believed; blessed are those who have not seen and yet have believed."

³⁰Jesus did many other miraculous signs in the presence of his disciples, which are not recorded in this book. ³¹But these are written that you may*ᵃ* believe that Jesus is the Christ, the Son of God, and that by believing you may have life in his name.

Jesus and the Miraculous Catch of Fish

21 Afterward Jesus appeared again to his disciples, by the Sea of Tiberias.*ᵇ* It happened this way: ²Simon Peter, Thomas (called Didymus), Nathanael from Cana in Galilee, the sons of Zebedee, and two other disciples were together. ³"I'm going out to fish," Simon Peter told them, and they said, "We'll go with you." So they went out and got into the boat, but that night they caught nothing.

⁴Early in the morning, Jesus stood on the shore, but the disciples did not realize that it was Jesus.

⁵He called out to them, "Friends, haven't you any fish?"

"No," they answered.

⁶He said, "Throw your net on the right side of the boat and you will find some." When they did, they were unable to haul the net in because of the large number of fish.

⁷Then the disciple whom Jesus loved said to Peter, "It is the Lord!" As soon as Simon Peter heard him say, "It is the Lord," he wrapped his outer garment around him (for he had taken it off) and jumped into the water. ⁸The other disciples followed in the boat, towing the net full of fish, for they were not far from shore, about a hundred yards.*ᶜ* ⁹When they landed, they saw a fire of burning coals there with fish on it, and some bread.

¹⁰Jesus said to them, "Bring some of the fish you have just caught."

¹¹Simon Peter climbed aboard and dragged the net ashore. It was full of large fish, 153, but even with so many the net was not torn. ¹²Jesus said to them, "Come and have breakfast." None of the disciples dared

---

ᵃ31 Some manuscripts *may continue to*   ᵇ1 That is, Sea of Galilee   ᶜ8 Greek *about two hundred cubits*
(about 90 meters)

REAL LIFE'S UPS AND DOWNS

Work It Out
• • • •

How often have you failed to live up to the expectations others have for you? Or to the expectations you have for yourself?

You expected to get an A on your Algebra test, but you only managed a B. You expected to make the winning shot in Friday night's basketball game, but you sat out the entire fourth quarter. You expected to win a prize in the school art contest, but your work was ignored.

Probably Thomas didn't expect to be remembered as the one who doubted Jesus' resurrection. He loved Jesus just as much as the other disciples and had followed him just as faithfully. But when he came face to face with real life, he didn't live up to expectation. What we should really remember Thomas for, however, is not that he doubted but that he so quickly turned from doubting to confession.

When you feel like you haven't lived up to your own or someone else's expectations, when real life slaps you around a bit, remember Thomas. Don't just sit in a corner and moan about failure. Turn immediately to do right, to try again, to move forward.

Nail It Down

Read the story of Thomas in John 20:24–29.

Think It Through
• • • •

Failure isn't fun. When you don't succeed, it hurts you and often those around you. But, unfortunately, failure is as much a part of life as success.

There can be success in failure, however. Thomas showed it beautifully. Instead of wallowing around in self-pity because he had doubted, instead of sitting in a corner because he hadn't lived up to expectation, he did what he should have done right away. He confessed Jesus as his Lord.

If you've failed at something, don't moan and feel sorry for yourself; move ahead. If you feel like you've let yourself and others down, don't sit in a corner; get up and try again. It's the only way to bring success out of failure.

Nail It Down

Reread the story of Thomas in John 20:24–29. For further insight and reassurance read Psalm 119:73–80.

Turn to pages 951, 1160, 1167, 1217 and 1319 for other readings on real life.
Turn to page 1167 for Monday's reading.

Topic
• • • •

REAL LIFE

ask him, "Who are you?" They knew it was the Lord. [13]Jesus came, took the bread and gave it to them, and did the same with the fish. [14]This was now the third time Jesus appeared to his disciples after he was raised from the dead.

Jesus Reinstates Peter

[15]When they had finished eating, Jesus said to Simon Peter, "Simon son of John, do you truly love me more than these?"

"Yes, Lord," he said, "you know that I love you."

Jesus said, "Feed my lambs."

[16]Again Jesus said, "Simon son of John, do you truly love me?"

He answered, "Yes, Lord, you know that I love you."

Jesus said, "Take care of my sheep."

[17]The third time he said to him, "Simon son of John, do you love me?"

Peter was hurt because Jesus asked him the third time, "Do you love me?" He said, "Lord, you know all things; you know that I love you."

Jesus said, "Feed my sheep. [18]I tell you the truth, when you were younger you dressed yourself and went where you want-

ed; but when you are old you will stretch out your hands, and someone else will dress you and lead you where you do not want to go." [19]Jesus said this to indicate the kind of death by which Peter would glorify God. Then he said to him, "Follow me!"

[20]Peter turned and saw that the disciple whom Jesus loved was following them. (This was the one who had leaned back against Jesus at the supper and had said, "Lord, who is going to betray you?") [21]When Peter saw him, he asked, "Lord, what about him?"

[22]Jesus answered, "If I want him to remain alive until I return, what is that to you? You must follow me." [23]Because of this, the rumor spread among the brothers that this disciple would not die. But Jesus did not say that he would not die; he only said, "If I want him to remain alive until I return, what is that to you?"

[24]This is the disciple who testifies to these things and who wrote them down. We know that his testimony is true.

[25]Jesus did many other things as well. If every one of them were written down, I suppose that even the whole world would not have room for the books that would be written.

ACTS

TRANSFORMED from frightened cowards to fearless champions of the gospel by the divine outpouring of the Holy Spirit, Jesus' followers begin to fulfill the Great Commission. Acts, the second part of Luke's history of Christianity, documents the growth of the early church as the disciples preach the message of salvation everywhere they go. Luke introduces the apostle Paul, who spearheads the outreach to the Gentiles and establishes churches in many cities. As you read, keep in mind that the gospel is the power of God for salvation. And share that gospel with boldness.

Outline of Contents

Jesus Taken Up Into Heaven

1 In my former book, Theophilus, I wrote about all that Jesus began to do and to teach ²until the day he was taken up to heaven, after giving instructions through the Holy Spirit to the apostles he had chosen. ³After his suffering, he showed himself to these men and gave many convincing proofs that he was alive. He appeared to them over a period of forty days and spoke about the kingdom of God. ⁴On one occa-sion, while he was eating with them, he gave them this command: "Do not leave Jerusa-lem, but wait for the gift my Father prom-ised, which you have heard me speak about. ⁵For John baptized with*a* water, but in a few days you will be baptized with the Holy Spirit."

⁶So when they met together, they asked him, "Lord, are you at this time going to re-store the kingdom to Israel?"

⁷He said to them: "It is not for you to know the times or dates the Father has set by his

---

*a*5 Or *in*

ETERNAL LIFE IS CONTAGIOUS!

Jesse is not perfect. Far from it. Sometimes he pounds his little brother. And he struggles with other temptations—to lie or cheat or lust, to give in to peer pressure.

But for the most part, Jesse is happy, because deep down he's at peace. He has a growing relationship with God. Plus he's learning how to depend on Christ for direction and strength.

And guess what? Because people know he's a person of character, and because he's fun to be around, Jesse is becoming a real witness for Christ at his school.

Look It Up
Jesus told his followers that he is the source of real life. And he told them he is the only way to life (John 14:6). He explained to them what eternal life meant and how they could experience it. He also revealed that people who receive eternal life will want to share it, not hoard it.

In 1 John 5:20 God's Word explains the source of our eternal life:

"We know also that the Son of God has come and has given us understanding, so that we may know him who is true. And we are in him who is true—even in his Son Jesus Christ. He is the true God and eternal life."

Think It Through
Your Aunt Winifred (who's so old she may have come over on the *Mayflower*) gives you a chemistry set for your birthday. Your mom won't let you exchange it for that new pair of jeans you've been wanting. So you go down in the basement to play mad scientist.

Three hours and two small explosions later, you discover a new formula that can eliminate every known disease. Would you (a) forget it, or (b) call a press conference, announce your amazing find, collect the Nobel Prize and tons of money—in short, make the world a better place?

Work It Out
Christians have the answer that gives true meaning to existence: eternal life in this world and the next, through Jesus Christ. What a contrast to the cheap, empty substitutes of this age!

Be a witness for Christ today by your life and by your words. The more you talk about him in everyday situations, the more normal it will seem to you and to those listening.

Nail It Down
Read the last thing Jesus had to say to his followers in Acts 1:8.

Turn to pages 951, 1160, 1164, 1217 and 1319 for other readings on real life.
Turn to page 1172 for Tuesday's reading.

Topic

REAL LIFE

own authority. **8**But you will receive power when the Holy Spirit comes on you; and you will be my witnesses in Jerusalem, and in all Judea and Samaria, and to the ends of the earth."

9After he said this, he was taken up before their very eyes, and a cloud hid him from their sight.

10They were looking intently up into the sky as he was going, when suddenly two men dressed in white stood beside them. **11**"Men of Galilee," they said, "why do you stand here looking into the sky? This same Jesus, who has been taken from you into heaven, will come back in the same way you have seen him go into heaven."

Matthias Chosen to Replace Judas

12Then they returned to Jerusalem from the hill called the Mount of Olives, a Sabbath day's walk*a* from the city. **13**When they arrived, they went upstairs to the room where they were staying. Those present were Peter, John, James and Andrew; Philip and Thomas, Bartholomew and Matthew; James son of Alphaeus and Simon the Zealot, and Judas son of James. **14**They all joined together constantly in prayer, along with the women and Mary the mother of Jesus, and with his brothers.

15In those days Peter stood up among the believers*b* (a group numbering about a hundred and twenty) **16**and said, "Brothers, the Scripture had to be fulfilled which the Holy Spirit spoke long ago through the mouth of David concerning Judas, who served as guide for those who arrested Jesus— **17**he was one of our number and shared in this ministry."

18(With the reward he got for his wickedness, Judas bought a field; there he fell headlong, his body burst open and all his intestines spilled out. **19**Everyone in Jerusalem heard about this, so they called that field in their language Akeldama, that is, Field of Blood.)

20"For," said Peter, "it is written in the book of Psalms,

" 'May his place be deserted;
    let there be no one to dwell in it,'*c*

and,

" 'May another take his place of
    leadership.'*d*

21Therefore it is necessary to choose one of the men who have been with us the whole time the Lord Jesus went in and out among us, **22**beginning from John's baptism to the time when Jesus was taken up from us. For one of these must become a witness with us of his resurrection."

23So they proposed two men: Joseph called Barsabbas (also known as Justus) and Matthias. **24**Then they prayed, "Lord, you know everyone's heart. Show us which of these two you have chosen **25**to take over this apostolic ministry, which Judas left to go where he belongs." **26**Then they cast lots, and the lot fell to Matthias; so he was added to the eleven apostles.

The Holy Spirit Comes at Pentecost

2 When the day of Pentecost came, they were all together in one place. **2**Suddenly a sound like the blowing of a violent wind came from heaven and filled the whole house where they were sitting. **3**They saw what seemed to be tongues of fire that separated and came to rest on each of them. **4**All of them were filled with the Holy Spirit and began to speak in other tongues*e* as the Spirit enabled them.

5Now there were staying in Jerusalem God-fearing Jews from every nation under heaven. **6**When they heard this sound, a crowd came together in bewilderment, because each one heard them speaking in his own language. **7**Utterly amazed, they asked: "Are not all these men who are speaking Galileans? **8**Then how is it that each of us hears them in his own native language? **9**Parthians, Medes and Elamites; residents of Mesopotamia, Judea and Cappadocia, Pontus and Asia, **10**Phrygia and Pamphylia, Egypt and the parts of Libya near Cyrene; visitors from Rome **11**(both Jews and converts to Judaism); Cretans and Arabs—we hear them declaring the wonders of God in our own tongues!" **12**Amazed and perplexed, they asked one another, "What does this mean?"

13Some, however, made fun of them and said, "They have had too much wine.*f*"

Peter Addresses the Crowd

14Then Peter stood up with the Eleven, raised his voice and addressed the crowd: "Fellow Jews and all of you who live in Jerusalem, let me explain this to you; listen carefully to what I say. **15**These men are not drunk, as you suppose. It's only nine in the

---

a12 That is, about 3/4 mile (about 1,100 meters)   *b15* Greek *brothers*   *c20* Psalm 69:25   *d20* Psalm 109:8   *e4* Or *languages*; also in verse 11   *f13* Or *sweet wine* morning! **16**No, this is what was spoken by the prophet Joel:

17"'In the last days, God says,
　I will pour out my Spirit on all
　　people.
Your sons and daughters will prophesy,
　your young men will see visions,
　your old men will dream dreams.
18Even on my servants, both men and
　　women,
　I will pour out my Spirit in those
　　days,
　and they will prophesy.
19I will show wonders in the heaven
　　above
　and signs on the earth below,
　blood and fire and billows of smoke.
20The sun will be turned to darkness
　and the moon to blood
　before the coming of the great and
　　glorious day of the Lord.
21And everyone who calls
　on the name of the Lord will be
　　saved.'*a*

22"Men of Israel, listen to this: Jesus of Nazareth was a man accredited by God to you by miracles, wonders and signs, which God did among you through him, as you yourselves know. **23**This man was handed over to you by God's set purpose and foreknowledge; and you, with the help of wicked men,*b* put him to death by nailing him to the cross. **24**But God raised him from the dead, freeing him from the agony of death, because it was impossible for death to keep its hold on him. **25**David said about him:

" 'I saw the Lord always before me.
　Because he is at my right hand,
　I will not be shaken.
26Therefore my heart is glad and my
　　tongue rejoices;
　my body also will live in hope,
27because you will not abandon me to the
　　grave,
　nor will you let your Holy One see
　　decay.
28You have made known to me the paths
　　of life;
　you will fill me with joy in your
　　presence.'*c*

29"Brothers, I can tell you confidently that the patriarch David died and was buried, and his tomb is here to this day. **30**But he was a prophet and knew that God had promised him on oath that he would place one of his descendants on his throne. **31**Seeing what was ahead, he spoke of the resurrection of the Christ,*d* that he was not abandoned to the grave, nor did his body see decay. **32**God has raised this Jesus to life, and we are all witnesses of the fact. **33**Exalted to the right hand of God, he has received from the Father the promised Holy Spirit and has poured out what you now see and hear. **34**For David did not ascend to heaven, and yet he said,

" 'The Lord said to my Lord:
　"Sit at my right hand
35until I make your enemies
　a footstool for your feet." '*e*

36"Therefore let all Israel be assured of this: God has made this Jesus, whom you crucified, both Lord and Christ."

37When the people heard this, they were cut to the heart and said to Peter and the other apostles, "Brothers, what shall we do?"

38Peter replied, "Repent and be baptized, every one of you, in the name of Jesus Christ for the forgiveness of your sins. And you will receive the gift of the Holy Spirit. **39**The promise is for you and your children and for all who are far off—for all whom the Lord our God will call."

40With many other words he warned them; and he pleaded with them, "Save yourselves from this corrupt generation." **41**Those who accepted his message were baptized, and about three thousand were added to their number that day.

The Fellowship of the Believers

42They devoted themselves to the apostles' teaching and to the fellowship, to the breaking of bread and to prayer. **43**Everyone was filled with awe, and many wonders and miraculous signs were done by the apostles. **44**All the believers were together and had everything in common. **45**Selling their possessions and goods, they gave to anyone as he had need. **46**Every day they continued to meet together in the temple courts. They broke bread in their homes and ate together with glad and sincere hearts, **47**praising God and enjoying the favor of all the people. And the Lord added to their number daily those who were being saved.

---

a21 Joel 2:28-32　　*b23* Or *of those not having the law* (that is, Gentiles)　　*c28* Psalm 16:8-11　　*d31* Or *Messiah*. "The Christ" (Greek) and "the Messiah" (Hebrew) both mean "the Anointed One"; also in verse 36. *e35* Psalm 110:1

Peter Heals the Crippled Beggar

3 One day Peter and John were going up to the temple at the time of prayer — at three in the afternoon. ²Now a man crippled from birth was being carried to the temple gate called Beautiful, where he was put every day to beg from those going into the temple courts. ³When he saw Peter and John about to enter, he asked them for money. ⁴Peter looked straight at him, as did John. Then Peter said, "Look at us!" ⁵So the man gave them his attention, expecting to get something from them.

⁶Then Peter said, "Silver or gold I do not have, but what I have I give you. In the name of Jesus Christ of Nazareth, walk." ⁷Taking him by the right hand, he helped him up, and instantly the man's feet and ankles became strong. ⁸He jumped to his feet and began to walk. Then he went with them into the temple courts, walking and jumping, and praising God. ⁹When all the people saw him walking and praising God, ¹⁰they recognized him as the same man who used to sit begging at the temple gate called Beautiful, and they were filled with wonder and amazement at what had happened to him.

Peter Speaks to the Onlookers

¹¹While the beggar held on to Peter and John, all the people were astonished and came running to them in the place called Solomon's Colonnade. ¹²When Peter saw this, he said to them: "Men of Israel, why does this surprise you? Why do you stare at us as if by our own power or godliness we had made this man walk? ¹³The God of Abraham, Isaac and Jacob, the God of our fathers, has glorified his servant Jesus. You handed him over to be killed, and you disowned him before Pilate, though he had decided to let him go. ¹⁴You disowned the Holy and Righteous One and asked that a murderer be released to you. ¹⁵You killed the author of life, but God raised him from the dead. We are witnesses of this. ¹⁶By faith in the name of Jesus, this man whom you see and know was made strong. It is Jesus' name and the faith that comes through him that has given this complete healing to him, as you can all see.

¹⁷"Now, brothers, I know that you acted in ignorance, as did your leaders. ¹⁸But this is how God fulfilled what he had foretold through all the prophets, saying that his Christ[a] would suffer. ¹⁹Repent, then, and turn to God, so that your sins may be wiped out, that times of refreshing may come from the Lord, ²⁰and that he may send the Christ, who has been appointed for you — even Jesus. ²¹He must remain in heaven until the time comes for God to restore everything, as he promised long ago through his holy prophets. ²²For Moses said, 'The Lord your God will raise up for you a prophet like me from among your own people; you must listen to everything he tells you. ²³Anyone who does not listen to him will be completely cut off from among his people.'[b]

²⁴"Indeed, all the prophets from Samuel on, as many as have spoken, have foretold these days. ²⁵And you are heirs of the prophets and of the covenant God made with your fathers. He said to Abraham, 'Through your offspring all peoples on earth will be blessed.'[c] ²⁶When God raised up his servant, he sent him first to you to bless you by turning each of you from your wicked ways."

Peter and John Before the Sanhedrin

4 The priests and the captain of the temple guard and the Sadducees came up to Peter and John while they were speaking to the people. ²They were greatly disturbed because the apostles were teaching the people and proclaiming in Jesus the resurrection of the dead. ³They seized Peter and John, and because it was evening, they put them in jail until the next day. ⁴But many who heard the message believed, and the number of men grew to about five thousand.

⁵The next day the rulers, elders and teachers of the law met in Jerusalem. ⁶Annas the high priest was there, and so were Caiaphas, John, Alexander and the other men of the high priest's family. ⁷They had Peter and John brought before them and began to question them: "By what power or what name did you do this?"

⁸Then Peter, filled with the Holy Spirit, said to them: "Rulers and elders of the people! ⁹If we are being called to account today for an act of kindness shown to a cripple and are asked how he was healed, ¹⁰then know this, you and all the people of Israel: It is by the name of Jesus Christ of Nazareth, whom you crucified but whom God raised from the dead, that this man stands before you healed. ¹¹He is

" 'the stone you builders rejected,

---

a18 Or *Messiah*; also in verse 20   *b23* Deut. 18:15,18,19   *c25* Gen. 22:18; 26:4

which has become the capstone.$^{a'b}$

¹²Salvation is found in no one else, for there is no other name under heaven given to men by which we must be saved."

¹³When they saw the courage of Peter and John and realized that they were unschooled, ordinary men, they were astonished and they took note that these men had been with Jesus. ¹⁴But since they could see the man who had been healed standing there with them, there was nothing they could say. ¹⁵So they ordered them to withdraw from the Sanhedrin and then conferred together. ¹⁶"What are we going to do with these men?" they asked. "Everybody living in Jerusalem knows they have done an outstanding miracle, and we cannot deny it. ¹⁷But to stop this thing from spreading any further among the people, we must warn these men to speak no longer to anyone in this name."

¹⁸Then they called them in again and commanded them not to speak or teach at all in the name of Jesus. ¹⁹But Peter and John replied, "Judge for yourselves whether it is right in God's sight to obey you rather than God. ²⁰For we cannot help speaking about what we have seen and heard."

²¹After further threats they let them go. They could not decide how to punish them, because all the people were praising God for what had happened. ²²For the man who was miraculously healed was over forty years old.

The Believers' Prayer

²³On their release, Peter and John went back to their own people and reported all that the chief priests and elders had said to them. ²⁴When they heard this, they raised their voices together in prayer to God. "Sovereign Lord," they said, "you made the heaven and the earth and the sea, and everything in them. ²⁵You spoke by the Holy Spirit through the mouth of your servant, our father David:

" 'Why do the nations rage
    and the peoples plot in vain?
²⁶The kings of the earth take their stand
    and the rulers gather together
against the Lord
    and against his Anointed One.$^{c'd}$

²⁷Indeed Herod and Pontius Pilate met together with the Gentiles and the people^{e} of Israel in this city to conspire against your holy servant Jesus, whom you anointed. ²⁸They did what your power and will had decided beforehand should happen. ²⁹Now, Lord, consider their threats and enable your servants to speak your word with great boldness. ³⁰Stretch out your hand to heal and perform miraculous signs and wonders through the name of your holy servant Jesus."

³¹After they prayed, the place where they were meeting was shaken. And they were all filled with the Holy Spirit and spoke the word of God boldly.

The Believers Share Their Possessions

³²All the believers were one in heart and mind. No one claimed that any of his possessions was his own, but they shared everything they had. ³³With great power the apostles continued to testify to the resurrection of the Lord Jesus, and much grace was upon them all. ³⁴There were no needy persons among them. For from time to time those who owned lands or houses sold them, brought the money from the sales ³⁵and put it at the apostles' feet, and it was distributed to anyone as he had need.

³⁶Joseph, a Levite from Cyprus, whom the apostles called Barnabas (which means Son of Encouragement), ³⁷sold a field he owned and brought the money and put it at the apostles' feet.

Ananias and Sapphira

5 Now a man named Ananias, together with his wife Sapphira, also sold a piece of property. ²With his wife's full knowledge he kept back part of the money for himself, but brought the rest and put it at the apostles' feet.

³Then Peter said, "Ananias, how is it that Satan has so filled your heart that you have lied to the Holy Spirit and have kept for yourself some of the money you received for the land? ⁴Didn't it belong to you before it was sold? And after it was sold, wasn't the money at your disposal? What made you think of doing such a thing? You have not lied to men but to God."

⁵When Ananias heard this, he fell down and died. And great fear seized all who heard what had happened. ⁶Then the young men came forward, wrapped up his body, and carried him out and buried him.

⁷About three hours later his wife came in,

---

^{a}11 Or *cornerstone* ^{b}11 Psalm 118:22 ^{c}26 That is, Christ or Messiah ^{d}26 Psalm 2:1,2 ^{e}27 The Greek is plural.

A NARROW WAY IS BETTER THAN NO WAY

Claire is thumbing through the newspaper when she sees a popular advice column. Its headline says: "Heaven Big Enough for Everyone." A woman has written in to complain that her grown children, who are committed Christians, are trying to persuade her to believe in Jesus Christ. She resents their "preaching," but at the same time she wonders if what they say is true.

The columnist replies that all religions worship the same God and, because he is a God of love, he allows everyone into heaven—Christians, Jews, Muslims, Hindus and Buddhists. She concludes, "There are many ways to God."

Look It Up
••••

A lot of people share that viewpoint. But the problem is that if you believe that, what do you do with these statements of Jesus?

"I am the way and the truth and the life. No one comes to the Father except through me" (John 14:6).

"I am the gate; whoever enters through me will be saved" (John 10:9).

Jesus didn't say, "I am *a* way" or "I am *a* gate." He said, "No one comes to the Father except through me." That's exclusive.

Now, either Jesus was telling the truth or else he was lying or mistaken. Those are the only options.

Think It Through
••••

Imagine that everyone in your city is starving. But let's say that a gigantic grocery store is giving out free food to anyone who will come inside and receive it.

Would it make sense to stand outside and complain that the store only had one entrance? Can you imagine someone saying, "I want to get inside by going through the roof and they're saying I can't. How unfair can you get?" Of course not! People would be thrilled just to be getting food. It's unlikely you'd hear any grumbling about the number of entrances.

So why do people complain about Christ being the only way to God? At least there *is* a way!

Work It Out
••••

Are you counting on reaching God by being a good person or by being religious? Forget it. Jesus is the only way to God.

If you've never trusted him for salvation, you can do so right now! Simply pray, "Lord Jesus, thank you for dying for my sins. I want to trust you as Savior and follow you as Lord."

If you've already trusted in Jesus, ask God for a chance to discuss your beliefs today. Lots of your friends are standing outside the "grocery store" of heaven, starving spiritually. Show them the entrance: Jesus Christ!

Nail It Down
••••

Memorize Acts 4:12.

Turn to pages 633, 1136 and 1370 for other readings on tough questions.
Turn to page 1174 for Wednesday's reading.

Topic
••••

TOUGH QUESTIONS

not knowing what had happened. **8**Peter asked her, "Tell me, is this the price you and Ananias got for the land?"

"Yes," she said, "that is the price."

9Peter said to her, "How could you agree to test the Spirit of the Lord? Look! The feet of the men who buried your husband are at the door, and they will carry you out also."

10At that moment she fell down at his feet and died. Then the young men came in and, finding her dead, carried her out and buried her beside her husband. **11**Great fear seized the whole church and all who heard about these events.

The Apostles Heal Many

12The apostles performed many miraculous signs and wonders among the people. And all the believers used to meet together in Solomon's Colonnade. **13**No one else dared join them, even though they were highly regarded by the people. **14**Nevertheless, more and more men and women believed in the Lord and were added to their number. **15**As a result, people brought the sick into the streets and laid them on beds and mats so that at least Peter's shadow might fall on some of them as he passed by. **16**Crowds gathered also from the towns around Jerusalem, bringing their sick and those tormented by evil*a* spirits, and all of them were healed.

The Apostles Persecuted

17Then the high priest and all his associates, who were members of the party of the Sadducees, were filled with jealousy. **18**They arrested the apostles and put them in the public jail. **19**But during the night an angel of the Lord opened the doors of the jail and brought them out. **20**"Go, stand in the temple courts," he said, "and tell the people the full message of this new life."

21At daybreak they entered the temple courts, as they had been told, and began to teach the people.

When the high priest and his associates arrived, they called together the Sanhedrin—the full assembly of the elders of Israel—and sent to the jail for the apostles. **22**But on arriving at the jail, the officers did not find them there. So they went back and reported, **23**"We found the jail securely locked, with the guards standing at the doors; but when we opened them, we found no one inside." **24**On hearing this report, the captain of the temple guard and the chief priests were puzzled, wondering what would come of this.

25Then someone came and said, "Look! The men you put in jail are standing in the temple courts teaching the people." **26**At that, the captain went with his officers and brought the apostles. They did not use force, because they feared that the people would stone them.

27Having brought the apostles, they made them appear before the Sanhedrin to be questioned by the high priest. **28**"We gave you strict orders not to teach in this name," he said. "Yet you have filled Jerusalem with your teaching and are determined to make us guilty of this man's blood."

29Peter and the other apostles replied: "We must obey God rather than men! **30**The God of our fathers raised Jesus from the dead—whom you had killed by hanging him on a tree. **31**God exalted him to his own right hand as Prince and Savior that he might give repentance and forgiveness of sins to Israel. **32**We are witnesses of these things, and so is the Holy Spirit, whom God has given to those who obey him."

33When they heard this, they were furious and wanted to put them to death. **34**But a Pharisee named Gamaliel, a teacher of the law, who was honored by all the people, stood up in the Sanhedrin and ordered that the men be put outside for a little while. **35**Then he addressed them: "Men of Israel, consider carefully what you intend to do to these men. **36**Some time ago Theudas appeared, claiming to be somebody, and about four hundred men rallied to him. He was killed, all his followers were dispersed, and it all came to nothing. **37**After him, Judas the Galilean appeared in the days of the census and led a band of people in revolt. He too was killed, and all his followers were scattered. **38**Therefore, in the present case I advise you: Leave these men alone! Let them go! For if their purpose or activity is of human origin, it will fail. **39**But if it is from God, you will not be able to stop these men; you will only find yourselves fighting against God."

40His speech persuaded them. They called the apostles in and had them flogged. Then they ordered them not to speak in the name of Jesus, and let them go.

41The apostles left the Sanhedrin, rejoicing because they had been counted worthy of suffering disgrace for the Name. **42**Day after day, in the temple courts and from house

a 16 Greek *unclean*

YOU CAN STEER YOUR PEERS!

After two Thompson Senior High School students died in separate alcohol-related accidents, Martha decided it was time to exert a positive influence.

She first wrote a stirring editorial for the school paper. Then, with the help of her youth pastor and guidance counselor, she organized "Weekend Workout."

What is Weekend Workout? It's a Friday night function at Martha's church gymnasium. From nine until midnight each week, teens play volleyball and basketball and participate in aerobic classes.

And guess what? Everyone just loves it!

Look It Up
• • • •

Can one person really affect a whole group? Is it possible to steer your peers in the right direction when they're going the wrong way? Yes!

"You are the light of the world. A city on a hill cannot be hidden. Neither do people light a lamp and put it under a bowl. Instead they put it on its stand, and it gives light to everyone in the house. In the same way, let your light shine before men, that they may see your good deeds and praise your Father in heaven" (Matthew 5:14–16).

Think It Through

Martha is one of those people who make things happen. Rather than let peer pressure always influence *her,* she influences *it.* That's not always easy, but it makes a worthwhile goal for anyone.

Work It Out
• • • •

List the problems and predicaments that your friends most often fall into. Now list some ways you could steer your peers away from those troublesome situations. When the time comes, will you make the tough choice to stand up and encourage your friends to do the right thing?

If you won't, who will?

Nail It Down
• • • •

Check out how Gamaliel's cool-headed response altered his peer group's actions in Acts 5:29–40.

Turn to pages 163, 683 and 1386 for other readings on peer pressure.
Turn to page 1178 for Thursday's reading.

Topic
• • • •

PEER PRESSURE

to house, they never stopped teaching and proclaiming the good news that Jesus is the Christ.[a]

The Choosing of the Seven

6 In those days when the number of disciples was increasing, the Grecian Jews among them complained against the Hebraic Jews because their widows were being overlooked in the daily distribution of food. [2]So the Twelve gathered all the disciples together and said, "It would not be right for us to neglect the ministry of the word of God in order to wait on tables. [3]Brothers, choose seven men from among you who are known to be full of the Spirit and wisdom. We will turn this responsibility over to them [4]and will give our attention to prayer and the ministry of the word."

[5]This proposal pleased the whole group. They chose Stephen, a man full of faith and of the Holy Spirit; also Philip, Procorus, Nicanor, Timon, Parmenas, and Nicolas from Antioch, a convert to Judaism. [6]They presented these men to the apostles, who prayed and laid their hands on them.

[7]So the word of God spread. The number of disciples in Jerusalem increased rapidly, and a large number of priests became obedient to the faith.

Stephen Seized

[8]Now Stephen, a man full of God's grace and power, did great wonders and miraculous signs among the people. [9]Opposition arose, however, from members of the Synagogue of the Freedmen (as it was called) — Jews of Cyrene and Alexandria as well as the provinces of Cilicia and Asia. These men began to argue with Stephen, [10]but they could not stand up against his wisdom or the Spirit by whom he spoke.

[11]Then they secretly persuaded some men to say, "We have heard Stephen speak words of blasphemy against Moses and against God."

[12]So they stirred up the people and the elders and the teachers of the law. They seized Stephen and brought him before the Sanhedrin. [13]They produced false witnesses, who testified, "This fellow never stops speaking against this holy place and against the law. [14]For we have heard him say that this Jesus of Nazareth will destroy this place and change the customs Moses handed down to us."

[15]All who were sitting in the Sanhedrin looked intently at Stephen, and they saw that his face was like the face of an angel.

Stephen's Speech to the Sanhedrin

7 Then the high priest asked him, "Are these charges true?"

[2]To this he replied: "Brothers and fathers, listen to me! The God of glory appeared to our father Abraham while he was still in Mesopotamia, before he lived in Haran. [3]'Leave your country and your people,' God said, 'and go to the land I will show you.'[b]

[4]"So he left the land of the Chaldeans and settled in Haran. After the death of his father, God sent him to this land where you are now living. [5]He gave him no inheritance here, not even a foot of ground. But God promised him that he and his descendants after him would possess the land, even though at that time Abraham had no child. [6]God spoke to him in this way: 'Your descendants will be strangers in a country not their own, and they will be enslaved and mistreated four hundred years. [7]But I will punish the nation they serve as slaves,' God said, 'and afterward they will come out of that country and worship me in this place.'[c] [8]Then he gave Abraham the covenant of circumcision. And Abraham became the father of Isaac and circumcised him eight days after his birth. Later Isaac became the father of Jacob, and Jacob became the father of the twelve patriarchs.

[9]"Because the patriarchs were jealous of Joseph, they sold him as a slave into Egypt. But God was with him [10]and rescued him from all his troubles. He gave Joseph wisdom and enabled him to gain the goodwill of Pharaoh king of Egypt; so he made him ruler over Egypt and all his palace.

[11]"Then a famine struck all Egypt and Canaan, bringing great suffering, and our fathers could not find food. [12]When Jacob heard that there was grain in Egypt, he sent our fathers on their first visit. [13]On their second visit, Joseph told his brothers who he was, and Pharaoh learned about Joseph's family. [14]After this, Joseph sent for his father Jacob and his whole family, seventy-five in all. [15]Then Jacob went down to Egypt, where he and our fathers died. [16]Their bodies were brought back to Shechem and placed in the tomb that Abraham had bought from the sons of Hamor at Shechem for a certain sum of money.

[17]"As the time drew near for God to fulfill his promise to Abraham, the number of our

a42 Or *Messiah*   b3 Gen. 12:1   c7 Gen. 15:13,14

people in Egypt greatly increased. ¹⁸Then another king, who knew nothing about Joseph, became ruler of Egypt. ¹⁹He dealt treacherously with our people and oppressed our forefathers by forcing them to throw out their newborn babies so that they would die.

²⁰"At that time Moses was born, and he was no ordinary child.ᵃ For three months he was cared for in his father's house. ²¹When he was placed outside, Pharaoh's daughter took him and brought him up as her own son. ²²Moses was educated in all the wisdom of the Egyptians and was powerful in speech and action.

²³"When Moses was forty years old, he decided to visit his fellow Israelites. ²⁴He saw one of them being mistreated by an Egyptian, so he went to his defense and avenged him by killing the Egyptian. ²⁵Moses thought that his own people would realize that God was using him to rescue them, but they did not. ²⁶The next day Moses came upon two Israelites who were fighting. He tried to reconcile them by saying, 'Men, you are brothers; why do you want to hurt each other?'

²⁷"But the man who was mistreating the other pushed Moses aside and said, 'Who made you ruler and judge over us? ²⁸Do you want to kill me as you killed the Egyptian yesterday?'ᵇ ²⁹When Moses heard this, he fled to Midian, where he settled as a foreigner and had two sons.

³⁰"After forty years had passed, an angel appeared to Moses in the flames of a burning bush in the desert near Mount Sinai. ³¹When he saw this, he was amazed at the sight. As he went over to look more closely, he heard the Lord's voice: ³²'I am the God of your fathers, the God of Abraham, Isaac and Jacob.'ᶜ Moses trembled with fear and did not dare to look.

³³"Then the Lord said to him, 'Take off your sandals; the place where you are standing is holy ground. ³⁴I have indeed seen the oppression of my people in Egypt. I have heard their groaning and have come down to set them free. Now come, I will send you back to Egypt.'ᵈ

³⁵"This is the same Moses whom they had rejected with the words, 'Who made you ruler and judge?' He was sent to be their ruler and deliverer by God himself, through the angel who appeared to him in the bush.

³⁶He led them out of Egypt and did wonders and miraculous signs in Egypt, at the Red Seaᵉ and for forty years in the desert.

³⁷"This is that Moses who told the Israelites, 'God will send you a prophet like me from your own people.'ᶠ ³⁸He was in the assembly in the desert, with the angel who spoke to him on Mount Sinai, and with our fathers; and he received living words to pass on to us.

³⁹"But our fathers refused to obey him. Instead, they rejected him and in their hearts turned back to Egypt. ⁴⁰They told Aaron, 'Make us gods who will go before us. As for this fellow Moses who led us out of Egypt— we don't know what has happened to him!'ᵍ ⁴¹That was the time they made an idol in the form of a calf. They brought sacrifices to it and held a celebration in honor of what their hands had made. ⁴²But God turned away and gave them over to the worship of the heavenly bodies. This agrees with what is written in the book of the prophets:

" 'Did you bring me sacrifices and
      offerings
   forty years in the desert, O house of
      Israel?
⁴³You have lifted up the shrine of Molech
   and the star of your god Rephan,
   the idols you made to worship.
Therefore I will send you into exile'ʰ
   beyond Babylon.

⁴⁴"Our forefathers had the tabernacle of the Testimony with them in the desert. It had been made as God directed Moses, according to the pattern he had seen. ⁴⁵Having received the tabernacle, our fathers under Joshua brought it with them when they took the land from the nations God drove out before them. It remained in the land until the time of David, ⁴⁶who enjoyed God's favor and asked that he might provide a dwelling place for the God of Jacob.ⁱ ⁴⁷But it was Solomon who built the house for him.

⁴⁸"However, the Most High does not live in houses made by men. As the prophet says:

⁴⁹" 'Heaven is my throne,
   and the earth is my footstool.
What kind of house will you build for
      me?
                     says the Lord.
   Or where will my resting place be?

ᵃ20 Or *was fair in the sight of God*   ᵇ28 Exodus 2:14   ᶜ32 Exodus 3:6   ᵈ34 Exodus 3:5,7,8,10
ᵉ36 That is, Sea of Reeds   ᶠ37 Deut. 18:15   ᵍ40 Exodus 32:1   ʰ43 Amos 5:25-27   ⁱ46 Some early
manuscripts *the house of Jacob*

50Has not my hand made all these things?'[a]

51"You stiff-necked people, with uncircumcised hearts and ears! You are just like your fathers: You always resist the Holy Spirit! **52**Was there ever a prophet your fathers did not persecute? They even killed those who predicted the coming of the Righteous One. And now you have betrayed and murdered him— **53**you who have received the law that was put into effect through angels but have not obeyed it."

The Stoning of Stephen

54When they heard this, they were furious and gnashed their teeth at him. **55**But Stephen, full of the Holy Spirit, looked up to heaven and saw the glory of God, and Jesus standing at the right hand of God. **56**"Look," he said, "I see heaven open and the Son of Man standing at the right hand of God."

57At this they covered their ears and, yelling at the top of their voices, they all rushed at him, **58**dragged him out of the city and began to stone him. Meanwhile, the witnesses laid their clothes at the feet of a young man named Saul.

59While they were stoning him, Stephen prayed, "Lord Jesus, receive my spirit." **60**Then he fell on his knees and cried out, "Lord, do not hold this sin against them." When he had said this, he fell asleep.

8 And Saul was there, giving approval to his death.

The Church Persecuted and Scattered

On that day a great persecution broke out against the church at Jerusalem, and all except the apostles were scattered throughout Judea and Samaria. **2**Godly men buried Stephen and mourned deeply for him. **3**But Saul began to destroy the church. Going from house to house, he dragged off men and women and put them in prison.

Philip in Samaria

4Those who had been scattered preached the word wherever they went. **5**Philip went down to a city in Samaria and proclaimed the Christ[b] there. **6**When the crowds heard Philip and saw the miraculous signs he did, they all paid close attention to what he said. **7**With shrieks, evil[c] spirits came out of many, and many paralytics and cripples were healed. **8**So there was great joy in that city.

Simon the Sorcerer

9Now for some time a man named Simon had practiced sorcery in the city and amazed all the people of Samaria. He boasted that he was someone great, **10**and all the people, both high and low, gave him their attention and exclaimed, "This man is the divine power known as the Great Power." **11**They followed him because he had amazed them for a long time with his magic. **12**But when they believed Philip as he preached the good news of the kingdom of God and the name of Jesus Christ, they were baptized, both men and women. **13**Simon himself believed and was baptized. And he followed Philip everywhere, astonished by the great signs and miracles he saw.

14When the apostles in Jerusalem heard that Samaria had accepted the word of God, they sent Peter and John to them. **15**When they arrived, they prayed for them that they might receive the Holy Spirit, **16**because the Holy Spirit had not yet come upon any of them; they had simply been baptized into[d] the name of the Lord Jesus. **17**Then Peter and John placed their hands on them, and they received the Holy Spirit.

18When Simon saw that the Spirit was given at the laying on of the apostles' hands, he offered them money **19**and said, "Give me also this ability so that everyone on whom I lay my hands may receive the Holy Spirit."

20Peter answered: "May your money perish with you, because you thought you could buy the gift of God with money! **21**You have no part or share in this ministry, because your heart is not right before God. **22**Repent of this wickedness and pray to the Lord. Perhaps he will forgive you for having such a thought in your heart. **23**For I see that you are full of bitterness and captive to sin."

24Then Simon answered, "Pray to the Lord for me so that nothing you have said may happen to me."

25When they had testified and proclaimed the word of the Lord, Peter and John returned to Jerusalem, preaching the gospel in many Samaritan villages.

Philip and the Ethiopian

26Now an angel of the Lord said to Philip, "Go south to the road—the desert road—that goes down from Jerusalem to Gaza." **27**So he started out, and on his way he met

---

[a]50 Isaiah 66:1,2   [b]5 Or Messiah   [c]7 Greek unclean   [d]16 Or in

BITTER IS "BADDER" NOT BETTER!

Barry's not the greatest student in the world, normally making C's and D's. However, his parents told him that if he could pull a B in English for the year, they'd see about helping him get a car. He's been studying his brains out all year!

But get this—in December during the English mid-term exam, Mrs. Whitten accused Barry of cheating and flunked him. He went to talk to her twice, but it was no use. She wouldn't listen, and she wouldn't believe him. Now the B and the car look pretty doubtful.

Maybe now you can see why Barry can't stand Mrs. Whitten.

Look It Up
••••

Barry doesn't realize that bitterness, like a cancerous tumor, is eating him up on the inside. But tomorrow morning, during his daily Bible reading, he's going to come across this verse: "Get rid of all bitterness, rage and anger, brawling and slander, along with every form of malice" (Ephesians 4:31). And all of a sudden, it's going to hit him.

Bitterness usually comes when you think you've been treated unfairly. Whether the offense is real or imagined doesn't really matter. The point is that if you're not careful to deal with those initial angry feelings by taking them to God and forgiving the wrongdoer, they can turn into bitterness. It's sort of like a small cut on your hand. Left untreated, infection can set in . . . and then you've got serious problems!

Think It Through
••••

Put yourself in Barry's situation. You could: (1) Take revenge. But that only dishonors God (Romans 12:19). (2) Turn bitter. But that's also a bad choice. Not only is it disobedient (Ephesians 4:31), but it also ruins your own life by tearing you up on the inside. (3) Forgive in God's strength. That pleases God and saves you a lot of grief in the long run (Colossians 3:13).

Work It Out
••••

If someone pushes you around, chances are good you'll be tempted to become bitter. Don't! You'll only hurt yourself. One of the devil's biggest lies is that you can "get back" at someone by hating them. And revenge is not an option for a Christian. The proper, Biblical response is to ask God to give you the grace to forgive. "Do not be overcome by evil, but overcome evil with good" (Romans 12:21).

Nail It Down
••••

Read how Peter and John handled their anger against Simon in Acts 8:9–24.

Turn to pages 572, 686, 694, 939, 1026 and 1148 for other readings on feelings.
Turn to page 1182 for Friday's reading.

Topic
••••

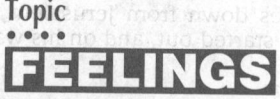
FEELINGS

an Ethiopian[a] eunuch, an important official in charge of all the treasury of Candace, queen of the Ethiopians. This man had gone to Jerusalem to worship, **28**and on his way home was sitting in his chariot reading the book of Isaiah the prophet. **29**The Spirit told Philip, "Go to that chariot and stay near it." **30**Then Philip ran up to the chariot and heard the man reading Isaiah the prophet. "Do you understand what you are reading?" Philip asked.

31"How can I," he said, "unless someone explains it to me?" So he invited Philip to come up and sit with him.

32The eunuch was reading this passage of Scripture:

"He was led like a sheep to the
     slaughter,
and as a lamb before the shearer is
     silent,
so he did not open his mouth.
33In his humiliation he was deprived of
     justice.
Who can speak of his descendants?
For his life was taken from the
     earth."[b]

34The eunuch asked Philip, "Tell me, please, who is the prophet talking about, himself or someone else?" **35**Then Philip began with that very passage of Scripture and told him the good news about Jesus.

36As they traveled along the road, they came to some water and the eunuch said, "Look, here is water. Why shouldn't I be baptized?"[c] **38**And he gave orders to stop the chariot. Then both Philip and the eunuch went down into the water and Philip baptized him. **39**When they came up out of the water, the Spirit of the Lord suddenly took Philip away, and the eunuch did not see him again, but went on his way rejoicing. **40**Philip, however, appeared at Azotus and traveled about, preaching the gospel in all the towns until he reached Caesarea.

Saul's Conversion

9 Meanwhile, Saul was still breathing out murderous threats against the Lord's disciples. He went to the high priest **2**and asked him for letters to the synagogues in Damascus, so that if he found any there who belonged to the Way, whether men or women, he might take them as prisoners to Jerusalem. **3**As he neared Damascus on his jour-

ney, suddenly a light from heaven flashed around him. **4**He fell to the ground and heard a voice say to him, "Saul, Saul, why do you persecute me?"

5"Who are you, Lord?" Saul asked.

"I am Jesus, whom you are persecuting," he replied. **6**"Now get up and go into the city, and you will be told what you must do."

7The men traveling with Saul stood there speechless; they heard the sound but did not see anyone. **8**Saul got up from the ground, but when he opened his eyes he could see nothing. So they led him by the hand into Damascus. **9**For three days he was blind, and did not eat or drink anything.

10In Damascus there was a disciple named Ananias. The Lord called to him in a vision, "Ananias!"

"Yes, Lord," he answered.

11The Lord told him, "Go to the house of Judas on Straight Street and ask for a man from Tarsus named Saul, for he is praying. **12**In a vision he has seen a man named Ananias come and place his hands on him to restore his sight."

13"Lord," Ananias answered, "I have heard many reports about this man and all the harm he has done to your saints in Jerusalem. **14**And he has come here with authority from the chief priests to arrest all who call on your name."

15But the Lord said to Ananias, "Go! This man is my chosen instrument to carry my name before the Gentiles and their kings and before the people of Israel. **16**I will show him how much he must suffer for my name."

17Then Ananias went to the house and entered it. Placing his hands on Saul, he said, "Brother Saul, the Lord—Jesus, who appeared to you on the road as you were coming here—has sent me so that you may see again and be filled with the Holy Spirit." **18**Immediately, something like scales fell from Saul's eyes, and he could see again. He got up and was baptized, **19**and after taking some food, he regained his strength.

Saul in Damascus and Jerusalem

Saul spent several days with the disciples in Damascus. **20**At once he began to preach in the synagogues that Jesus is the Son of God. **21**All those who heard him were astonished and asked, "Isn't he the man who raised havoc in Jerusalem among those who

a27 That is, from the upper Nile region   b33 Isaiah 53:7,8   c36 Some late manuscripts baptized?" 37Philip said, "If you believe with all your heart, you may." The eunuch answered, "I believe that Jesus Christ is the Son of God."

call on this name? And hasn't he come here to take them as prisoners to the chief priests?" **22**Yet Saul grew more and more powerful and baffled the Jews living in Damascus by proving that Jesus is the Christ.*ᵃ*

23After many days had gone by, the Jews conspired to kill him, **24**but Saul learned of their plan. Day and night they kept close watch on the city gates in order to kill him. **25**But his followers took him by night and lowered him in a basket through an opening in the wall.

26When he came to Jerusalem, he tried to join the disciples, but they were all afraid of him, not believing that he really was a disciple. **27**But Barnabas took him and brought him to the apostles. He told them how Saul on his journey had seen the Lord and that the Lord had spoken to him, and how in Damascus he had preached fearlessly in the name of Jesus. **28**So Saul stayed with them and moved about freely in Jerusalem, speaking boldly in the name of the Lord. **29**He talked and debated with the Grecian Jews, but they tried to kill him. **30**When the brothers learned of this, they took him down to Caesarea and sent him off to Tarsus.

31Then the church throughout Judea, Galilee and Samaria enjoyed a time of peace. It was strengthened; and encouraged by the Holy Spirit, it grew in numbers, living in the fear of the Lord.

Aeneas and Dorcas

32As Peter traveled about the country, he went to visit the saints in Lydda. **33**There he found a man named Aeneas, a paralytic who had been bedridden for eight years. **34**"Aeneas," Peter said to him, "Jesus Christ heals you. Get up and take care of your mat." Immediately Aeneas got up. **35**All those who lived in Lydda and Sharon saw him and turned to the Lord.

36In Joppa there was a disciple named Tabitha (which, when translated, is Dorcas*ᵇ*), who was always doing good and helping the poor. **37**About that time she became sick and died, and her body was washed and placed in an upstairs room. **38**Lydda was near Joppa; so when the disciples heard that Peter was in Lydda, they sent two men to him and urged him, "Please come at once!"

39Peter went with them, and when he arrived he was taken upstairs to the room. All the widows stood around him, crying and showing him the robes and other clothing

that Dorcas had made while she was still with them.

40Peter sent them all out of the room; then he got down on his knees and prayed. Turning toward the dead woman, he said, "Tabitha, get up." She opened her eyes, and seeing Peter she sat up. **41**He took her by the hand and helped her to her feet. Then he called the believers and the widows and presented her to them alive. **42**This became known all over Joppa, and many people believed in the Lord. **43**Peter stayed in Joppa for some time with a tanner named Simon.

Cornelius Calls for Peter

10 At Caesarea there was a man named Cornelius, a centurion in what was known as the Italian Regiment. **2**He and all his family were devout and God-fearing; he gave generously to those in need and prayed to God regularly. **3**One day at about three in the afternoon he had a vision. He distinctly saw an angel of God, who came to him and said, "Cornelius!"

4Cornelius stared at him in fear. "What is it, Lord?" he asked.

The angel answered, "Your prayers and gifts to the poor have come up as a memorial offering before God. **5**Now send men to Joppa to bring back a man named Simon who is called Peter. **6**He is staying with Simon the tanner, whose house is by the sea."

7When the angel who spoke to him had gone, Cornelius called two of his servants and a devout soldier who was one of his attendants. **8**He told them everything that had happened and sent them to Joppa.

Peter's Vision

9About noon the following day as they were on their journey and approaching the city, Peter went up on the roof to pray. **10**He became hungry and wanted something to eat, and while the meal was being prepared, he fell into a trance. **11**He saw heaven opened and something like a large sheet being let down to earth by its four corners. **12**It contained all kinds of four-footed animals, as well as reptiles of the earth and birds of the air. **13**Then a voice told him, "Get up, Peter. Kill and eat."

14"Surely not, Lord!" Peter replied. "I have never eaten anything impure or unclean."

15The voice spoke to him a second time, "Do not call anything impure that God has made clean."

16This happened three times, and imme-

---

*ᵃ*22 Or *Messiah*   *ᵇ*36 Both *Tabitha* (Aramaic) and *Dorcas* (Greek) mean *gazelle.*

diately the sheet was taken back to heaven.
[17]While Peter was wondering about the meaning of the vision, the men sent by Cornelius found out where Simon's house was and stopped at the gate. [18]They called out, asking if Simon who was known as Peter was staying there.

[19]While Peter was still thinking about the vision, the Spirit said to him, "Simon, three[a] men are looking for you. [20]So get up and go downstairs. Do not hesitate to go with them, for I have sent them."

[21]Peter went down and said to the men, "I'm the one you're looking for. Why have you come?"

[22]The men replied, "We have come from Cornelius the centurion. He is a righteous and God-fearing man, who is respected by all the Jewish people. A holy angel told him to have you come to his house so that he could hear what you have to say." [23]Then Peter invited the men into the house to be his guests.

Peter at Cornelius' House

The next day Peter started out with them, and some of the brothers from Joppa went along. [24]The following day he arrived in Caesarea. Cornelius was expecting them and had called together his relatives and close friends. [25]As Peter entered the house, Cornelius met him and fell at his feet in reverence. [26]But Peter made him get up. "Stand up," he said, "I am only a man myself."

[27]Talking with him, Peter went inside and found a large gathering of people. [28]He said to them: "You are well aware that it is against our law for a Jew to associate with a Gentile or visit him. But God has shown me that I should not call any man impure or unclean. [29]So when I was sent for, I came without raising any objection. May I ask why you sent for me?"

[30]Cornelius answered: "Four days ago I was in my house praying at this hour, at three in the afternoon. Suddenly a man in shining clothes stood before me [31]and said, 'Cornelius, God has heard your prayer and remembered your gifts to the poor. [32]Send to Joppa for Simon who is called Peter. He is a guest in the home of Simon the tanner, who lives by the sea.' [33]So I sent for you immediately, and it was good of you to come. Now we are all here in the presence of God to listen to everything the Lord has commanded you to tell us."

[34]Then Peter began to speak: "I now realize how true it is that God does not show favoritism [35]but accepts men from every nation who fear him and do what is right. [36]You know the message God sent to the people of Israel, telling the good news of peace through Jesus Christ, who is Lord of all. [37]You know what has happened throughout Judea, beginning in Galilee after the baptism that John preached— [38]how God anointed Jesus of Nazareth with the Holy Spirit and power, and how he went around doing good and healing all who were under the power of the devil, because God was with him.

[39]"We are witnesses of everything he did in the country of the Jews and in Jerusalem. They killed him by hanging him on a tree, [40]but God raised him from the dead on the third day and caused him to be seen. [41]He was not seen by all the people, but by witnesses whom God had already chosen—by us who ate and drank with him after he rose from the dead. [42]He commanded us to preach to the people and to testify that he is the one whom God appointed as judge of the living and the dead. [43]All the prophets testify about him that everyone who believes in him receives forgiveness of sins through his name."

[44]While Peter was still speaking these words, the Holy Spirit came on all who heard the message. [45]The circumcised believers who had come with Peter were astonished that the gift of the Holy Spirit had been poured out even on the Gentiles. [46]For they heard them speaking in tongues[b] and praising God.

Then Peter said, [47]"Can anyone keep these people from being baptized with water? They have received the Holy Spirit just as we have." [48]So he ordered that they be baptized in the name of Jesus Christ. Then they asked Peter to stay with them for a few days.

Peter Explains His Actions

11 The apostles and the brothers throughout Judea heard that the Gentiles also had received the word of God. [2]So when Peter went up to Jerusalem, the circumcised believers criticized him [3]and said, "You went into the house of uncircumcised men and ate with them."

[4]Peter began and explained everything to them precisely as it had happened: [5]"I was in the city of Joppa praying, and in a trance I saw a vision. I saw something like a large

BYE-BYE TO BIGOTRY

Raymond is the new guy in the neighborhood. An all-white neighborhood. That is, it was all white until Raymond and his family moved in. They're black. And some people in the neighborhood have been making life very unpleasant for the new family.

As Larry and his sister drive past Raymond's house, Larry starts fuming.

"Okay, I know I probably have some prejudice, but I would never do anything like that! These are supposed to be civilized people in this neighborhood. This is supposed to be the twentieth century! Who cares if the Davises are black?"

Pam just shakes her head, "Obviously some people care a lot."

"Well, I'm embarrassed to say that I'm even partly prejudiced."

Pam shrugs, "Me too. So how do we change?"

Look It Up
••••

Never fear, Pam and Larry. God's Word has lots of ideas about how to respond to prejudice.

1. We must look to Christ. Only he can tear down the barriers that separate individuals and races (Ephesians 2:11–12).

2. We must be willing to befriend those who are different. In Acts 9:43 we read about Peter, a Jew, staying with a man who tanned skins for a living. Most Jews would not have gone near a person who worked with animal carcasses and hides, much less stayed in his house!

3. We must be able to say as Peter did, "I now realize how true it is that God does not show favoritism but accepts men from every nation who fear him and do what is right" (Acts 10:34–35).

4. We must stand up against those who are intolerant (Galatians 2:11–14).

Think It Through
••••

If you had a good friend from a different race who was being persecuted, how would you respond?

What do you think Jesus Christ thinks about those individuals who are trying to run the Davises out of their neighborhood?

What is the most prejudicial thing you've ever done? Why do you think you did it?

Work It Out
••••

Here are some practical ways to begin to overcome your own bigotry:

• Pray that God will help you change your attitudes.
• Eat lunch with someone from a different race or background.
• Visit an ethnic church.
• Read a magazine that expresses a different racial or cultural viewpoint.
• Write an article on racism for your school newspaper.

Nail It Down
••••

Read about how God shattered religious prejudice in Acts 11:1–18.

Turn to pages 1089, 1132 and 1274 for other readings on intolerance.
Turn to page 1184 for the weekend reading.

Topic
••••

INTOLERANCE

sheet being let down from heaven by its four corners, and it came down to where I was. [6]I looked into it and saw four-footed animals of the earth, wild beasts, reptiles, and birds of the air. [7]Then I heard a voice telling me, 'Get up, Peter. Kill and eat.'

[8]"I replied, 'Surely not, Lord! Nothing impure or unclean has ever entered my mouth.'

[9]"The voice spoke from heaven a second time, 'Do not call anything impure that God has made clean.' [10]This happened three times, and then it was all pulled up to heaven again.

[11]"Right then three men who had been sent to me from Caesarea stopped at the house where I was staying. [12]The Spirit told me to have no hesitation about going with them. These six brothers also went with me, and we entered the man's house. [13]He told us how he had seen an angel appear in his house and say, 'Send to Joppa for Simon who is called Peter. [14]He will bring you a message through which you and all your household will be saved.'

[15]"As I began to speak, the Holy Spirit came on them as he had come on us at the beginning. [16]Then I remembered what the Lord had said: 'John baptized with[a] water, but you will be baptized with the Holy Spirit.' [17]So if God gave them the same gift as he gave us, who believed in the Lord Jesus Christ, who was I to think that I could oppose God?"

[18]When they heard this, they had no further objections and praised God, saying, "So then, God has granted even the Gentiles repentance unto life."

The Church in Antioch

[19]Now those who had been scattered by the persecution in connection with Stephen traveled as far as Phoenicia, Cyprus and Antioch, telling the message only to Jews. [20]Some of them, however, men from Cyprus and Cyrene, went to Antioch and began to speak to Greeks also, telling them the good news about the Lord Jesus. [21]The Lord's hand was with them, and a great number of people believed and turned to the Lord.

[22]News of this reached the ears of the church at Jerusalem, and they sent Barnabas to Antioch. [23]When he arrived and saw the evidence of the grace of God, he was glad and encouraged them all to remain true to the Lord with all their hearts. [24]He was a good man, full of the Holy Spirit and faith,

and a great number of people were brought to the Lord.

[25]Then Barnabas went to Tarsus to look for Saul, [26]and when he found him, he brought him to Antioch. So for a whole year Barnabas and Saul met with the church and taught great numbers of people. The disciples were called Christians first at Antioch.

[27]During this time some prophets came down from Jerusalem to Antioch. [28]One of them, named Agabus, stood up and through the Spirit predicted that a severe famine would spread over the entire Roman world. (This happened during the reign of Claudius.) [29]The disciples, each according to his ability, decided to provide help for the brothers living in Judea. [30]This they did, sending their gift to the elders by Barnabas and Saul.

Peter's Miraculous Escape From Prison

12 It was about this time that King Herod arrested some who belonged to the church, intending to persecute them. [2]He had James, the brother of John, put to death with the sword. [3]When he saw that this pleased the Jews, he proceeded to seize Peter also. This happened during the Feast of Unleavened Bread. [4]After arresting him, he put him in prison, handing him over to be guarded by four squads of four soldiers each. Herod intended to bring him out for public trial after the Passover.

[5]So Peter was kept in prison, but the church was earnestly praying to God for him.

[6]The night before Herod was to bring him to trial, Peter was sleeping between two soldiers, bound with two chains, and sentries stood guard at the entrance. [7]Suddenly an angel of the Lord appeared and a light shone in the cell. He struck Peter on the side and woke him up. "Quick, get up!" he said, and the chains fell off Peter's wrists.

[8]Then the angel said to him, "Put on your clothes and sandals." And Peter did so. "Wrap your cloak around you and follow me," the angel told him. [9]Peter followed him out of the prison, but he had no idea that what the angel was doing was really happening; he thought he was seeing a vision. [10]They passed the first and second guards and came to the iron gate leading to the city. It opened for them by itself, and they went through it. When they had walked the length of one street, suddenly the angel left him.

[a]16 Or *in*

A FORMULA FOR FRUITFULNESS

Work It Out

How many of you have watched an apple tree produce apples? If you watch closely, will you see the tree straining, working, toiling to produce apples? Does the tree look worn out with the effort?

You're probably thinking, "Now that's a silly question!" Of course an apple tree doesn't strain and have a heart attack over producing apples. It just does what it was meant to do—be an apple tree—naturally.

Perhaps you've been straining and toiling and working overtime to be a fruitful Christian. And you still feel like you're not doing enough. You need to remind yourself of the apple tree. To be a fruitful Christian, you need only be what God created you to be—his child. The fruit will then come—naturally.

Nail It Down

Read about a fruitful Christian named Barnabas in Acts 11:22–24.

Think It Through

Some Christians think it takes hours and hours of straining, toiling, pounding the streets and banging on doors to be a fruitful Christian. Those things aren't wrong or out of place, but they're not the way to be fruitful either.

Barnabas, an early church worker, had the right formula. Acts 11:24 says that Barnabas "was a good man, full of the Holy Spirit and faith, and a great number of people were brought to the Lord." Notice, it doesn't say Barnabas used just the right tract or knocked on so many doors per day or spent so many hours witnessing on the beaches. This passage tells you who Barnabas *was*, not what he *did*.

An apple tree doesn't have to work and strain to produce apples. It just has to be what it's supposed to be—an apple tree. You, as a Christian, will produce fruit *naturally* if you're being what you're supposed to be—"a good [person], full of the Holy Spirit and faith." Be a Barnabas and be fruitful.

Nail It Down

Read about Barnabas again in Acts 11:22–24. For further insight read Psalm 37:1–11.

Turn to pages 1104 and 1134 for other readings on fruitfulness.
Turn to page 1188 for Monday's reading.

Topic

FRUITFULNESS

11Then Peter came to himself and said, "Now I know without a doubt that the Lord sent his angel and rescued me from Herod's clutches and from everything the Jewish people were anticipating."

12When this had dawned on him, he went to the house of Mary the mother of John, also called Mark, where many people had gathered and were praying. **13**Peter knocked at the outer entrance, and a servant girl named Rhoda came to answer the door. **14**When she recognized Peter's voice, she was so overjoyed she ran back without opening it and exclaimed, "Peter is at the door!"

15"You're out of your mind," they told her. When she kept insisting that it was so, they said, "It must be his angel."

16But Peter kept on knocking, and when they opened the door and saw him, they were astonished. **17**Peter motioned with his hand for them to be quiet and described how the Lord had brought him out of prison. "Tell James and the brothers about this," he said, and then he left for another place.

18In the morning, there was no small commotion among the soldiers as to what had become of Peter. **19**After Herod had a thorough search made for him and did not find him, he cross-examined the guards and ordered that they be executed.

Herod's Death

Then Herod went from Judea to Caesarea and stayed there a while. **20**He had been quarreling with the people of Tyre and Sidon; they now joined together and sought an audience with him. Having secured the support of Blastus, a trusted personal servant of the king, they asked for peace, because they depended on the king's country for their food supply.

21On the appointed day Herod, wearing his royal robes, sat on his throne and delivered a public address to the people. **22**They shouted, "This is the voice of a god, not of a man." **23**Immediately, because Herod did not give praise to God, an angel of the Lord struck him down, and he was eaten by worms and died.

24But the word of God continued to increase and spread.

25When Barnabas and Saul had finished their mission, they returned from*a* Jerusalem, taking with them John, also called Mark.

Barnabas and Saul Sent Off

13 In the church at Antioch there were prophets and teachers: Barnabas, Simeon called Niger, Lucius of Cyrene, Manaen (who had been brought up with Herod the tetrarch) and Saul. **2**While they were worshiping the Lord and fasting, the Holy Spirit said, "Set apart for me Barnabas and Saul for the work to which I have called them." **3**So after they had fasted and prayed, they placed their hands on them and sent them off.

On Cyprus

4The two of them, sent on their way by the Holy Spirit, went down to Seleucia and sailed from there to Cyprus. **5**When they arrived at Salamis, they proclaimed the word of God in the Jewish synagogues. John was with them as their helper.

6They traveled through the whole island until they came to Paphos. There they met a Jewish sorcerer and false prophet named Bar-Jesus, **7**who was an attendant of the proconsul, Sergius Paulus. The proconsul, an intelligent man, sent for Barnabas and Saul because he wanted to hear the word of God. **8**But Elymas the sorcerer (for that is what his name means) opposed them and tried to turn the proconsul from the faith. **9**Then Saul, who was also called Paul, filled with the Holy Spirit, looked straight at Elymas and said, **10**"You are a child of the devil and an enemy of everything that is right! You are full of all kinds of deceit and trickery. Will you never stop perverting the right ways of the Lord? **11**Now the hand of the Lord is against you. You are going to be blind, and for a time you will be unable to see the light of the sun."

Immediately mist and darkness came over him, and he groped about, seeking someone to lead him by the hand. **12**When the proconsul saw what had happened, he believed, for he was amazed at the teaching about the Lord.

In Pisidian Antioch

13From Paphos, Paul and his companions sailed to Perga in Pamphylia, where John left them to return to Jerusalem. **14**From Perga they went on to Pisidian Antioch. On the Sabbath they entered the synagogue and sat down. **15**After the reading from the Law and the Prophets, the synagogue rulers sent word to them, saying, "Brothers, if you have

a25 Some manuscripts to

a message of encouragement for the people, please speak."

¹⁶Standing up, Paul motioned with his hand and said: "Men of Israel and you Gentiles who worship God, listen to me! ¹⁷The God of the people of Israel chose our fathers; he made the people prosper during their stay in Egypt, with mighty power he led them out of that country, ¹⁸he endured their conduct*a* for about forty years in the desert, ¹⁹he overthrew seven nations in Canaan and gave their land to his people as their inheritance. ²⁰All this took about 450 years.

"After this, God gave them judges until the time of Samuel the prophet. ²¹Then the people asked for a king, and he gave them Saul son of Kish, of the tribe of Benjamin, who ruled forty years. ²²After removing Saul, he made David their king. He testified concerning him: 'I have found David son of Jesse a man after my own heart; he will do everything I want him to do.'

²³"From this man's descendants God has brought to Israel the Savior Jesus, as he promised. ²⁴Before the coming of Jesus, John preached repentance and baptism to all the people of Israel. ²⁵As John was completing his work, he said: 'Who do you think I am? I am not that one. No, but he is coming after me, whose sandals I am not worthy to untie.'

²⁶"Brothers, children of Abraham, and you God-fearing Gentiles, it is to us that this message of salvation has been sent. ²⁷The people of Jerusalem and their rulers did not recognize Jesus, yet in condemning him they fulfilled the words of the prophets that are read every Sabbath. ²⁸Though they found no proper ground for a death sentence, they asked Pilate to have him executed. ²⁹When they had carried out all that was written about him, they took him down from the tree and laid him in a tomb. ³⁰But God raised him from the dead, ³¹and for many days he was seen by those who had traveled with him from Galilee to Jerusalem. They are now his witnesses to our people.

³²"We tell you the good news: What God promised our fathers ³³he has fulfilled for us, their children, by raising up Jesus. As it is written in the second Psalm:

" 'You are my Son;
today I have become your Father.'*b'c*

³⁴The fact that God raised him from the

dead, never to decay, is stated in these words:

" 'I will give you the holy and sure
blessings promised to David.'*d*

³⁵So it is stated elsewhere:

" 'You will not let your Holy One see
decay.'*e*

³⁶"For when David had served God's purpose in his own generation, he fell asleep; he was buried with his fathers and his body decayed. ³⁷But the one whom God raised from the dead did not see decay.

³⁸"Therefore, my brothers, I want you to know that through Jesus the forgiveness of sins is proclaimed to you. ³⁹Through him everyone who believes is justified from everything you could not be justified from by the law of Moses. ⁴⁰Take care that what the prophets have said does not happen to you:

⁴¹" 'Look, you scoffers,
wonder and perish,
for I am going to do something in your
days
that you would never believe,
even if someone told you.'*f*"

⁴²As Paul and Barnabas were leaving the synagogue, the people invited them to speak further about these things on the next Sabbath. ⁴³When the congregation was dismissed, many of the Jews and devout converts to Judaism followed Paul and Barnabas, who talked with them and urged them to continue in the grace of God.

⁴⁴On the next Sabbath almost the whole city gathered to hear the word of the Lord. ⁴⁵When the Jews saw the crowds, they were filled with jealousy and talked abusively against what Paul was saying.

⁴⁶Then Paul and Barnabas answered them boldly: "We had to speak the word of God to you first. Since you reject it and do not consider yourselves worthy of eternal life, we now turn to the Gentiles. ⁴⁷For this is what the Lord has commanded us:

" 'I have made you*g* a light for the
Gentiles,
that you*g* may bring salvation to the
ends of the earth.'*h*"

⁴⁸When the Gentiles heard this, they were glad and honored the word of the Lord; and all who were appointed for eternal life believed.

---

a18 Some manuscripts *and cared for them*   *b33* Or *have begotten you*   *c33* Psalm 2:7   *d34* Isaiah 55:3
e35 Psalm 16:10   *f41* Hab. 1:5   *g47* The Greek is singular.   *h47* Isaiah 49:6

49The word of the Lord spread through the whole region. **50**But the Jews incited the God-fearing women of high standing and the leading men of the city. They stirred up persecution against Paul and Barnabas, and expelled them from their region. **51**So they shook the dust from their feet in protest against them and went to Iconium. **52**And the disciples were filled with joy and with the Holy Spirit.

In Iconium

14 At Iconium Paul and Barnabas went as usual into the Jewish synagogue. There they spoke so effectively that a great number of Jews and Gentiles believed. **2**But the Jews who refused to believe stirred up the Gentiles and poisoned their minds against the brothers. **3**So Paul and Barnabas spent considerable time there, speaking boldly for the Lord, who confirmed the message of his grace by enabling them to do miraculous signs and wonders. **4**The people of the city were divided; some sided with the Jews, others with the apostles. **5**There was a plot afoot among the Gentiles and Jews, together with their leaders, to mistreat them and stone them. **6**But they found out about it and fled to the Lycaonian cities of Lystra and Derbe and to the surrounding country, **7**where they continued to preach the good news.

In Lystra and Derbe

8In Lystra there sat a man crippled in his feet, who was lame from birth and had never walked. **9**He listened to Paul as he was speaking. Paul looked directly at him, saw that he had faith to be healed **10**and called out, "Stand up on your feet!" At that, the man jumped up and began to walk.

11When the crowd saw what Paul had done, they shouted in the Lycaonian language, "The gods have come down to us in human form!" **12**Barnabas they called Zeus, and Paul they called Hermes because he was the chief speaker. **13**The priest of Zeus, whose temple was just outside the city, brought bulls and wreaths to the city gates because he and the crowd wanted to offer sacrifices to them.

14But when the apostles Barnabas and Paul heard of this, they tore their clothes and rushed out into the crowd, shouting: **15**"Men, why are you doing this? We too are only men, human like you. We are bringing you good news, telling you to turn from these worthless things to the living God, who made heaven and earth and sea and everything in them. **16**In the past, he let all nations go their own way. **17**Yet he has not left himself without testimony: He has shown kindness by giving you rain from heaven and crops in their seasons; he provides you with plenty of food and fills your hearts with joy." **18**Even with these words, they had difficulty keeping the crowd from sacrificing to them.

19Then some Jews came from Antioch and Iconium and won the crowd over. They stoned Paul and dragged him outside the city, thinking he was dead. **20**But after the disciples had gathered around him, he got up and went back into the city. The next day he and Barnabas left for Derbe.

The Return to Antioch in Syria

21They preached the good news in that city and won a large number of disciples. Then they returned to Lystra, Iconium and Antioch, **22**strengthening the disciples and encouraging them to remain true to the faith. "We must go through many hardships to enter the kingdom of God," they said. **23**Paul and Barnabas appointed elders*a* for them in each church and, with prayer and fasting, committed them to the Lord, in whom they had put their trust. **24**After going through Pisidia, they came into Pamphylia, **25**and when they had preached the word in Perga, they went down to Attalia.

26From Attalia they sailed back to Antioch, where they had been committed to the grace of God for the work they had now completed. **27**On arriving there, they gathered the church together and reported all that God had done through them and how he had opened the door of faith to the Gentiles. **28**And they stayed there a long time with the disciples.

The Council at Jerusalem

15 Some men came down from Judea to Antioch and were teaching the brothers: "Unless you are circumcised, according to the custom taught by Moses, you cannot be saved." **2**This brought Paul and Barnabas into sharp dispute and debate with them. So Paul and Barnabas were appointed, along with some other believers, to go up to Jerusalem to see the apostles and elders about this question. **3**The church sent them on their way, and as they traveled through Phoenicia and Samaria, they told

a23 Or Barnabas ordained elders; or Barnabas had elders elected

WHAT ARE THE REAL FACTS OF LIFE?

For her science term paper, Alene wrote on "Problems with Evolution, Proofs for Creation." She read tons of material, learned a lot of good things and came away feeling more confident in her faith.

Alene's science teacher Mrs. Turner wasn't wild about the project, but she did say later that some of Alene's research made her think.

Good for you, Alene! That was definitely a gutsy move.

Look It Up
● ● ● ●

It's always nice to know what Jesus said about certain matters. And fortunately for us, he spoke out clearly on:

• The origin of the universe:
"God created the world" (Mark 13:19).
• The origin of humanity:
"But at the beginning of creation God made them 'male and female' " (Mark 10:6).

These statements leave us with only three options: (1) Jesus didn't know what he was talking about; (2) he was lying; or (3) he was telling the truth.

Think It Through
● ● ● ●

Are you the product of chance? Or were you created by God? If chance is the reason you exist today, your existence is a joke and is pretty much pointless. However, if you were formed by a God who has the power to create the beauty of a hummingbird, the orderly succession of seasons and the grandeur of the Rocky Mountains, your existence immediately gains value and worth. If you think of yourself as the product of chance, how does that make you feel about yourself? If you think of yourself as the creation of a loving and powerful God, does that change how you view yourself? How you view others?

Work It Out
● ● ● ●

Could the marvelous world all around you have happened simply by chance? Try this experiment:

On a sheet of paper print this sentence: "Our complex universe came into existence by chance, over a long period of time." Cut the sentence into individual letters and characters (you should have sixty-six slips of paper). Put these in a jar and shake them up. Dump the letters onto the table. Do they spell anything? Do this several times. Is the result intelligible?

Maybe the characters need to fall for a longer time before they will finally end up in the right combination. Stand on a chair and drop them to the floor. Go up on your roof and drop them to the ground. Any luck?

Nail It Down
● ● ● ●

Read what Paul and Barnabas had to say about the creator God in Acts 14:15.

Turn to pages 2, 529, 621 and 1348 for other readings on origins.
Turn to page 1192 for Tuesday's reading.

Topic
● ● ● ●

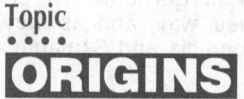

how the Gentiles had been converted. This news made all the brothers very glad. ⁴When they came to Jerusalem, they were welcomed by the church and the apostles and elders, to whom they reported everything God had done through them.

⁵Then some of the believers who belonged to the party of the Pharisees stood up and said, "The Gentiles must be circumcised and required to obey the law of Moses."

⁶The apostles and elders met to consider this question. ⁷After much discussion, Peter got up and addressed them: "Brothers, you know that some time ago God made a choice among you that the Gentiles might hear from my lips the message of the gospel and believe. ⁸God, who knows the heart, showed that he accepted them by giving the Holy Spirit to them, just as he did to us. ⁹He made no distinction between us and them, for he purified their hearts by faith. ¹⁰Now then, why do you try to test God by putting on the necks of the disciples a yoke that neither we nor our fathers have been able to bear? ¹¹No! We believe it is through the grace of our Lord Jesus that we are saved, just as they are."

¹²The whole assembly became silent as they listened to Barnabas and Paul telling about the miraculous signs and wonders God had done among the Gentiles through them. ¹³When they finished, James spoke up: "Brothers, listen to me. ¹⁴Simonᵃ has described to us how God at first showed his concern by taking from the Gentiles a people for himself. ¹⁵The words of the prophets are in agreement with this, as it is written:

¹⁶" 'After this I will return
    and rebuild David's fallen tent.
  Its ruins I will rebuild,
    and I will restore it,
¹⁷that the remnant of men may seek the
    Lord,
  and all the Gentiles who bear my
    name,
  says the Lord, who does these things'ᵇ
¹⁸   that have been known for ages.ᶜ

¹⁹"It is my judgment, therefore, that we should not make it difficult for the Gentiles who are turning to God. ²⁰Instead we should write to them, telling them to abstain from food polluted by idols, from sexual immorality, from the meat of strangled animals and from blood. ²¹For Moses has been preached in every city from the earliest times and is read in the synagogues on every Sabbath."

The Council's Letter to Gentile Believers

²²Then the apostles and elders, with the whole church, decided to choose some of their own men and send them to Antioch with Paul and Barnabas. They chose Judas (called Barsabbas) and Silas, two men who were leaders among the brothers. ²³With them they sent the following letter:

The apostles and elders, your brothers,

To the Gentile believers in Antioch, Syria and Cilicia:

Greetings.

²⁴We have heard that some went out from us without our authorization and disturbed you, troubling your minds by what they said. ²⁵So we all agreed to choose some men and send them to you with our dear friends Barnabas and Paul— ²⁶men who have risked their lives for the name of our Lord Jesus Christ. ²⁷Therefore we are sending Judas and Silas to confirm by word of mouth what we are writing. ²⁸It seemed good to the Holy Spirit and to us not to burden you with anything beyond the following requirements: ²⁹You are to abstain from food sacrificed to idols, from blood, from the meat of strangled animals and from sexual immorality. You will do well to avoid these things.

Farewell.

³⁰The men were sent off and went down to Antioch, where they gathered the church together and delivered the letter. ³¹The people read it and were glad for its encouraging message. ³²Judas and Silas, who themselves were prophets, said much to encourage and strengthen the brothers. ³³After spending some time there, they were sent off by the brothers with the blessing of peace to return to those who had sent them.ᵈ ³⁵But Paul and Barnabas remained in Antioch, where they and many others taught and preached the word of the Lord.

ᵃ14 Greek Simeon, a variant of Simon; that is, Peter   ᵇ17 Amos 9:11,12   ᶜ17,18 Some manuscripts things'— / ¹⁸known to the Lord for ages is his work   ᵈ33 Some manuscripts them, ³⁴but Silas decided to remain there

Disagreement Between Paul and Barnabas

36Some time later Paul said to Barnabas, "Let us go back and visit the brothers in all the towns where we preached the word of the Lord and see how they are doing." **37**Barnabas wanted to take John, also called Mark, with them, **38**but Paul did not think it wise to take him, because he had deserted them in Pamphylia and had not continued with them in the work. **39**They had such a sharp disagreement that they parted company. Barnabas took Mark and sailed for Cyprus, **40**but Paul chose Silas and left, commended by the brothers to the grace of the Lord. **41**He went through Syria and Cilicia, strengthening the churches.

Timothy Joins Paul and Silas

16 He came to Derbe and then to Lystra, where a disciple named Timothy lived, whose mother was a Jewess and a believer, but whose father was a Greek. **2**The brothers at Lystra and Iconium spoke well of him. **3**Paul wanted to take him along on the journey, so he circumcised him because of the Jews who lived in that area, for they all knew that his father was a Greek. **4**As they traveled from town to town, they delivered the decisions reached by the apostles and elders in Jerusalem for the people to obey. **5**So the churches were strengthened in the faith and grew daily in numbers.

Paul's Vision of the Man of Macedonia

6Paul and his companions traveled throughout the region of Phrygia and Galatia, having been kept by the Holy Spirit from preaching the word in the province of Asia. **7**When they came to the border of Mysia, they tried to enter Bithynia, but the Spirit of Jesus would not allow them to. **8**So they passed by Mysia and went down to Troas. **9**During the night Paul had a vision of a man of Macedonia standing and begging him, "Come over to Macedonia and help us." **10**After Paul had seen the vision, we got ready at once to leave for Macedonia, concluding that God had called us to preach the gospel to them.

Lydia's Conversion in Philippi

11From Troas we put out to sea and sailed straight for Samothrace, and the next day on to Neapolis. **12**From there we traveled to Philippi, a Roman colony and the leading city of that district of Macedonia. And we stayed there several days.

13On the Sabbath we went outside the city gate to the river, where we expected to find a place of prayer. We sat down and began to speak to the women who had gathered there. **14**One of those listening was a woman named Lydia, a dealer in purple cloth from the city of Thyatira, who was a worshiper of God. The Lord opened her heart to respond to Paul's message. **15**When she and the members of her household were baptized, she invited us to her home. "If you consider me a believer in the Lord," she said, "come and stay at my house." And she persuaded us.

Paul and Silas in Prison

16Once when we were going to the place of prayer, we were met by a slave girl who had a spirit by which she predicted the future. She earned a great deal of money for her owners by fortune-telling. **17**This girl followed Paul and the rest of us, shouting, "These men are servants of the Most High God, who are telling you the way to be saved." **18**She kept this up for many days. Finally Paul became so troubled that he turned around and said to the spirit, "In the name of Jesus Christ I command you to come out of her!" At that moment the spirit left her.

19When the owners of the slave girl realized that their hope of making money was gone, they seized Paul and Silas and dragged them into the marketplace to face the authorities. **20**They brought them before the magistrates and said, "These men are Jews, and are throwing our city into an uproar **21**by advocating customs unlawful for us Romans to accept or practice."

22The crowd joined in the attack against Paul and Silas, and the magistrates ordered them to be stripped and beaten. **23**After they had been severely flogged, they were thrown into prison, and the jailer was commanded to guard them carefully. **24**Upon receiving such orders, he put them in the inner cell and fastened their feet in the stocks.

25About midnight Paul and Silas were praying and singing hymns to God, and the other prisoners were listening to them. **26**Suddenly there was such a violent earthquake that the foundations of the prison were shaken. At once all the prison doors flew open, and everybody's chains came loose. **27**The jailer woke up, and when he saw the prison doors open, he drew his sword and was about to kill himself because he thought the prisoners had escaped. **28**But

Paul shouted, "Don't harm yourself! We are all here!"

29The jailer called for lights, rushed in and fell trembling before Paul and Silas. **30**He then brought them out and asked, "Sirs, what must I do to be saved?"

31They replied, "Believe in the Lord Jesus, and you will be saved—you and your household." **32**Then they spoke the word of the Lord to him and to all the others in his house. **33**At that hour of the night the jailer took them and washed their wounds; then immediately he and all his family were baptized. **34**The jailer brought them into his house and set a meal before them; he was filled with joy because he had come to believe in God—he and his whole family.

35When it was daylight, the magistrates sent their officers to the jailer with the order: "Release those men." **36**The jailer told Paul, "The magistrates have ordered that you and Silas be released. Now you can leave. Go in peace."

37But Paul said to the officers: "They beat us publicly without a trial, even though we are Roman citizens, and threw us into prison. And now do they want to get rid of us quietly? No! Let them come themselves and escort us out."

38The officers reported this to the magistrates, and when they heard that Paul and Silas were Roman citizens, they were alarmed. **39**They came to appease them and escorted them from the prison, requesting them to leave the city. **40**After Paul and Silas came out of the prison, they went to Lydia's house, where they met with the brothers and encouraged them. Then they left.

In Thessalonica

17 When they had passed through Amphipolis and Apollonia, they came to Thessalonica, where there was a Jewish synagogue. **2**As his custom was, Paul went into the synagogue, and on three Sabbath days he reasoned with them from the Scriptures, **3**explaining and proving that the Christ*a* had to suffer and rise from the dead. "This Jesus I am proclaiming to you is the Christ,*a*" he said. **4**Some of the Jews were persuaded and joined Paul and Silas, as did a large number of God-fearing Greeks and not a few prominent women.

5But the Jews were jealous; so they rounded up some bad characters from the marketplace, formed a mob and started a riot in the city. They rushed to Jason's house in search of Paul and Silas in order to bring them out to the crowd.*b* **6**But when they did not find them, they dragged Jason and some other brothers before the city officials, shouting: "These men who have caused trouble all over the world have now come here, **7**and Jason has welcomed them into his house. They are all defying Caesar's decrees, saying that there is another king, one called Jesus." **8**When they heard this, the crowd and the city officials were thrown into turmoil. **9**Then they made Jason and the others post bond and let them go.

In Berea

10As soon as it was night, the brothers sent Paul and Silas away to Berea. On arriving there, they went to the Jewish synagogue. **11**Now the Bereans were of more noble character than the Thessalonians, for they received the message with great eagerness and examined the Scriptures every day to see if what Paul said was true. **12**Many of the Jews believed, as did also a number of prominent Greek women and many Greek men.

13When the Jews in Thessalonica learned that Paul was preaching the word of God at Berea, they went there too, agitating the crowds and stirring them up. **14**The brothers immediately sent Paul to the coast, but Silas and Timothy stayed at Berea. **15**The men who escorted Paul brought him to Athens and then left with instructions for Silas and Timothy to join him as soon as possible.

In Athens

16While Paul was waiting for them in Athens, he was greatly distressed to see that the city was full of idols. **17**So he reasoned in the synagogue with the Jews and the God-fearing Greeks, as well as in the marketplace day by day with those who happened to be there. **18**A group of Epicurean and Stoic philosophers began to dispute with him. Some of them asked, "What is this babbler trying to say?" Others remarked, "He seems to be advocating foreign gods." They said this because Paul was preaching the good news about Jesus and the resurrection. **19**Then they took him and brought him to a meeting of the Areopagus, where they said to him, "May we know what this new teaching is that you are presenting? **20**You are bringing some strange ideas to our ears, and we want to know what they mean." **21**(All the Athenians and the foreigners who lived there spent

---

*a*3 Or *Messiah*   *b*5 Or *the assembly of the people*

BECOMING A VALUE EVALUATOR

Stacey and her friends were bombarded by values at the mall today without even realizing it.

In a record store they drooled over a poster of a popular singer. In the theater, they screamed at a new horror flick. In a clothing store they developed a serious case of the "I wants!" In a department store Stacey felt humiliated when a beautiful cosmetician bluntly told her that her makeup was all wrong. In the food court the girls made fun of an overweight woman who was eating an order of french fries.

Look It Up
••••

All day every day you are hit with a barrage of different values. Statements and claims are made. Ideas and philosophies are introduced. In the face of this vast array of values, the Bible counsels you to become critical thinkers:

"We demolish arguments and every pretension that sets itself up against the knowledge of God, and we take captive every thought to make it obedient to Christ" (2 Corinthians 10:5).

The goal? To analyze all the ideas that come your way, keeping those that are true and good and discarding those that are shallow or worthless.

Think It Through
••••

Do you actively guard your mind from bogus values by capturing wrong thoughts as 1 Corinthians 10:5 suggests? Or is your mind a place where any and all values are welcomed and entertained?

Satan is battling for your mind. Can you guess how he makes the most headway? By attacking the fortress of your mind with hundreds of false values!

Work It Out
••••

Don't leave your mind unattended! Even a few minutes in neutral means you're a sitting duck for wrong thoughts.

Develop the habit of thinking critically. Begin questioning the things you see and hear. During and after movies, songs, classroom lectures, sermons, speeches, commercials, TV programs, videos, magazine articles, textbook chapters or conversations with friends, ask yourself:

1. What about this is true?
2. What conflicts with my values?
3. How might this undermine my values?
4. How can I use this to strengthen my values?

Nail It Down
••••

Read Acts 17:11 for how the Bereans were value evaluators.

Turn to pages 716, 1000 and 1259 for other readings on values.
Turn to page 1197 for Wednesday's reading.

Topic
••••

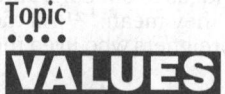
VALUES

their time doing nothing but talking about and listening to the latest ideas.)

22Paul then stood up in the meeting of the Areopagus and said: "Men of Athens! I see that in every way you are very religious. 23For as I walked around and looked carefully at your objects of worship, I even found an altar with this inscription: TO AN UNKNOWN GOD. Now what you worship as something unknown I am going to proclaim to you.

24"The God who made the world and everything in it is the Lord of heaven and earth and does not live in temples built by hands. 25And he is not served by human hands, as if he needed anything, because he himself gives all men life and breath and everything else. 26From one man he made every nation of men, that they should inhabit the whole earth; and he determined the times set for them and the exact places where they should live. 27God did this so that men would seek him and perhaps reach out for him and find him, though he is not far from each one of us. 28'For in him we live and move and have our being.' As some of your own poets have said, 'We are his offspring.'

29"Therefore since we are God's offspring, we should not think that the divine being is like gold or silver or stone—an image made by man's design and skill. 30In the past God overlooked such ignorance, but now he commands all people everywhere to repent. 31For he has set a day when he will judge the world with justice by the man he has appointed. He has given proof of this to all men by raising him from the dead."

32When they heard about the resurrection of the dead, some of them sneered, but others said, "We want to hear you again on this subject." 33At that, Paul left the Council. 34A few men became followers of Paul and believed. Among them was Dionysius, a member of the Areopagus, also a woman named Damaris, and a number of others.

In Corinth

18 After this, Paul left Athens and went to Corinth. 2There he met a Jew named Aquila, a native of Pontus, who had recently come from Italy with his wife Priscilla, because Claudius had ordered all the Jews to leave Rome. Paul went to see them, 3and because he was a tentmaker as they were, he stayed and worked with them. 4Every Sabbath he reasoned in the synagogue, trying to persuade Jews and Greeks.

5When Silas and Timothy came from Macedonia, Paul devoted himself exclusively to preaching, testifying to the Jews that Jesus was the Christ.*a* 6But when the Jews opposed Paul and became abusive, he shook out his clothes in protest and said to them, "Your blood be on your own heads! I am clear of my responsibility. From now on I will go to the Gentiles."

7Then Paul left the synagogue and went next door to the house of Titius Justus, a worshiper of God. 8Crispus, the synagogue ruler, and his entire household believed in the Lord; and many of the Corinthians who heard him believed and were baptized.

9One night the Lord spoke to Paul in a vision: "Do not be afraid; keep on speaking, do not be silent. 10For I am with you, and no one is going to attack and harm you, because I have many people in this city." 11So Paul stayed for a year and a half, teaching them the word of God.

12While Gallio was proconsul of Achaia, the Jews made a united attack on Paul and brought him into court. 13"This man," they charged, "is persuading the people to worship God in ways contrary to the law."

14Just as Paul was about to speak, Gallio said to the Jews, "If you Jews were making a complaint about some misdemeanor or serious crime, it would be reasonable for me to listen to you. 15But since it involves questions about words and names and your own law—settle the matter yourselves. I will not be a judge of such things." 16So he had them ejected from the court. 17Then they all turned on Sosthenes the synagogue ruler and beat him in front of the court. But Gallio showed no concern whatever.

Priscilla, Aquila and Apollos

18Paul stayed on in Corinth for some time. Then he left the brothers and sailed for Syria, accompanied by Priscilla and Aquila. Before he sailed, he had his hair cut off at Cenchrea because of a vow he had taken. 19They arrived at Ephesus, where Paul left Priscilla and Aquila. He himself went into the synagogue and reasoned with the Jews. 20When they asked him to spend more time with them, he declined. 21But as he left, he promised, "I will come back if it is God's will." Then he set sail from Ephesus. 22When he landed at Caesarea, he went up and greeted the church and then went down to Antioch.

23After spending some time in Antioch, Paul set out from there and traveled from

a5 Or Messiah; also in verse 28

place to place throughout the region of Galatia and Phrygia, strengthening all the disciples.

24Meanwhile a Jew named Apollos, a native of Alexandria, came to Ephesus. He was a learned man, with a thorough knowledge of the Scriptures. **25**He had been instructed in the way of the Lord, and he spoke with great fervor*a* and taught about Jesus accurately, though he knew only the baptism of John. **26**He began to speak boldly in the synagogue. When Priscilla and Aquila heard him, they invited him to their home and explained to him the way of God more adequately.

27When Apollos wanted to go to Achaia, the brothers encouraged him and wrote to the disciples there to welcome him. On arriving, he was a great help to those who by grace had believed. **28**For he vigorously refuted the Jews in public debate, proving from the Scriptures that Jesus was the Christ.

Paul in Ephesus

19 While Apollos was at Corinth, Paul took the road through the interior and arrived at Ephesus. There he found some disciples **2**and asked them, "Did you receive the Holy Spirit when*b* you believed?"

They answered, "No, we have not even heard that there is a Holy Spirit."

3So Paul asked, "Then what baptism did you receive?"

"John's baptism," they replied.

4Paul said, "John's baptism was a baptism of repentance. He told the people to believe in the one coming after him, that is, in Jesus." **5**On hearing this, they were baptized into*c* the name of the Lord Jesus. **6**When Paul placed his hands on them, the Holy Spirit came on them, and they spoke in tongues*d* and prophesied. **7**There were about twelve men in all.

8Paul entered the synagogue and spoke boldly there for three months, arguing persuasively about the kingdom of God. **9**But some of them became obstinate; they refused to believe and publicly maligned the Way. So Paul left them. He took the disciples with him and had discussions daily in the lecture hall of Tyrannus. **10**This went on for two years, so that all the Jews and Greeks who lived in the province of Asia heard the word of the Lord.

11God did extraordinary miracles through Paul, **12**so that even handkerchiefs and aprons that had touched him were taken to the sick, and their illnesses were cured and the evil spirits left them.

13Some Jews who went around driving out evil spirits tried to invoke the name of the Lord Jesus over those who were demon-possessed. They would say, "In the name of Jesus, whom Paul preaches, I command you to come out." **14**Seven sons of Sceva, a Jewish chief priest, were doing this. **15**One day, the evil spirit answered them, "Jesus I know, and I know about Paul, but who are you?" **16**Then the man who had the evil spirit jumped on them and overpowered them all. He gave them such a beating that they ran out of the house naked and bleeding.

17When this became known to the Jews and Greeks living in Ephesus, they were all seized with fear, and the name of the Lord Jesus was held in high honor. **18**Many of those who believed now came and openly confessed their evil deeds. **19**A number who had practiced sorcery brought their scrolls together and burned them publicly. When they calculated the value of the scrolls, the total came to fifty thousand drachmas.*e* **20**In this way the word of the Lord spread widely and grew in power.

21After all this had happened, Paul decided to go to Jerusalem, passing through Macedonia and Achaia. "After I have been there," he said, "I must visit Rome also." **22**He sent two of his helpers, Timothy and Erastus, to Macedonia, while he stayed in the province of Asia a little longer.

The Riot in Ephesus

23About that time there arose a great disturbance about the Way. **24**A silversmith named Demetrius, who made silver shrines of Artemis, brought in no little business for the craftsmen. **25**He called them together, along with the workmen in related trades, and said: "Men, you know we receive a good income from this business. **26**And you see and hear how this fellow Paul has convinced and led astray large numbers of people here in Ephesus and in practically the whole province of Asia. He says that man-made gods are no gods at all. **27**There is danger not only that our trade will lose its good name, but also that the temple of the great goddess Artemis will be discredited, and the goddess herself, who is worshiped throughout the

---

*a*25 Or *with fervor in the Spirit*   *b*2 Or *after*   *c*5 Or *in*   *d*6 Or *other languages*   *e*19 A drachma was a silver coin worth about a day's wages.

province of Asia and the world, will be robbed of her divine majesty."

28When they heard this, they were furious and began shouting: "Great is Artemis of the Ephesians!" **29**Soon the whole city was in an uproar. The people seized Gaius and Aristarchus, Paul's traveling companions from Macedonia, and rushed as one man into the theater. **30**Paul wanted to appear before the crowd, but the disciples would not let him. **31**Even some of the officials of the province, friends of Paul, sent him a message begging him not to venture into the theater.

32The assembly was in confusion: Some were shouting one thing, some another. Most of the people did not even know why they were there. **33**The Jews pushed Alexander to the front, and some of the crowd shouted instructions to him. He motioned for silence in order to make a defense before the people. **34**But when they realized he was a Jew, they all shouted in unison for about two hours: "Great is Artemis of the Ephesians!"

35The city clerk quieted the crowd and said: "Men of Ephesus, doesn't all the world know that the city of Ephesus is the guardian of the temple of the great Artemis and of her image, which fell from heaven? **36**Therefore, since these facts are undeniable, you ought to be quiet and not do anything rash. **37**You have brought these men here, though they have neither robbed temples nor blasphemed our goddess. **38**If, then, Demetrius and his fellow craftsmen have a grievance against anybody, the courts are open and there are proconsuls. They can press charges. **39**If there is anything further you want to bring up, it must be settled in a legal assembly. **40**As it is, we are in danger of being charged with rioting because of today's events. In that case we would not be able to account for this commotion, since there is no reason for it." **41**After he had said this, he dismissed the assembly.

Through Macedonia and Greece

20 When the uproar had ended, Paul sent for the disciples and, after encouraging them, said good-by and set out for Macedonia. **2**He traveled through that area, speaking many words of encouragement to the people, and finally arrived in Greece, **3**where he stayed three months. Because the Jews made a plot against him just as he was about to sail for Syria, he decided to go back through Macedonia. **4**He was accompanied by Sopater son of Pyrrhus from Berea, Aristarchus and Secundus from Thessalonica, Gaius from Derbe, Timothy also, and Tychicus and Trophimus from the province of Asia. **5**These men went on ahead and waited for us at Troas. **6**But we sailed from Philippi after the Feast of Unleavened Bread, and five days later joined the others at Troas, where we stayed seven days.

Eutychus Raised From the Dead at Troas

7On the first day of the week we came together to break bread. Paul spoke to the people and, because he intended to leave the next day, kept on talking until midnight. **8**There were many lamps in the upstairs room where we were meeting. **9**Seated in a window was a young man named Eutychus, who was sinking into a deep sleep as Paul talked on and on. When he was sound asleep, he fell to the ground from the third story and was picked up dead. **10**Paul went down, threw himself on the young man and put his arms around him. "Don't be alarmed," he said. "He's alive!" **11**Then he went upstairs again and broke bread and ate. After talking until daylight, he left. **12**The people took the young man home alive and were greatly comforted.

Paul's Farewell to the Ephesian Elders

13We went on ahead to the ship and sailed for Assos, where we were going to take Paul aboard. He had made this arrangement because he was going there on foot. **14**When he met us at Assos, we took him aboard and went on to Mitylene. **15**The next day we set sail from there and arrived off Kios. The day after that we crossed over to Samos, and on the following day arrived at Miletus. **16**Paul had decided to sail past Ephesus to avoid spending time in the province of Asia, for he was in a hurry to reach Jerusalem, if possible, by the day of Pentecost.

17From Miletus, Paul sent to Ephesus for the elders of the church. **18**When they arrived, he said to them: "You know how I lived the whole time I was with you, from the first day I came into the province of Asia. **19**I served the Lord with great humility and with tears, although I was severely tested by the plots of the Jews. **20**You know that I have not hesitated to preach anything that would be helpful to you but have taught you publicly and from house to house. **21**I have declared to both Jews and Greeks that they must turn to God in repentance and have faith in our Lord Jesus.

22"And now, compelled by the Spirit, I am

going to Jerusalem, not knowing what will happen to me there. **23**I only know that in every city the Holy Spirit warns me that prison and hardships are facing me. **24**However, I consider my life worth nothing to me, if only I may finish the race and complete the task the Lord Jesus has given me — the task of testifying to the gospel of God's grace.

25"Now I know that none of you among whom I have gone about preaching the kingdom will ever see me again. **26**Therefore, I declare to you today that I am innocent of the blood of all men. **27**For I have not hesitated to proclaim to you the whole will of God. **28**Keep watch over yourselves and all the flock of which the Holy Spirit has made you overseers.*a* Be shepherds of the church of God,*b* which he bought with his own blood. **29**I know that after I leave, savage wolves will come in among you and will not spare the flock. **30**Even from your own number men will arise and distort the truth in order to draw away disciples after them. **31**So be on your guard! Remember that for three years I never stopped warning each of you night and day with tears.

32"Now I commit you to God and to the word of his grace, which can build you up and give you an inheritance among all those who are sanctified. **33**I have not coveted anyone's silver or gold or clothing. **34**You yourselves know that these hands of mine have supplied my own needs and the needs of my companions. **35**In everything I did, I showed you that by this kind of hard work we must help the weak, remembering the words the Lord Jesus himself said: 'It is more blessed to give than to receive.' "

36When he had said this, he knelt down with all of them and prayed. **37**They all wept as they embraced him and kissed him. **38**What grieved them most was his statement that they would never see his face again. Then they accompanied him to the ship.

On to Jerusalem

21 After we had torn ourselves away from them, we put out to sea and sailed straight to Cos. The next day we went to Rhodes and from there to Patara. **2**We found a ship crossing over to Phoenicia, went on board and set sail. **3**After sighting Cyprus and passing to the south of it, we sailed on to Syria. We landed at Tyre, where our ship was to unload its cargo. **4**Finding the disciples there, we stayed with them

seven days. Through the Spirit they urged Paul not to go on to Jerusalem. **5**But when our time was up, we left and continued on our way. All the disciples and their wives and children accompanied us out of the city, and there on the beach we knelt to pray. **6**After saying good-by to each other, we went aboard the ship, and they returned home.

7We continued our voyage from Tyre and landed at Ptolemais, where we greeted the brothers and stayed with them for a day. **8**Leaving the next day, we reached Caesarea and stayed at the house of Philip the evangelist, one of the Seven. **9**He had four unmarried daughters who prophesied.

10After we had been there a number of days, a prophet named Agabus came down from Judea. **11**Coming over to us, he took Paul's belt, tied his own hands and feet with it and said, "The Holy Spirit says, 'In this way the Jews of Jerusalem will bind the owner of this belt and will hand him over to the Gentiles.' "

12When we heard this, we and the people there pleaded with Paul not to go up to Jerusalem. **13**Then Paul answered, "Why are you weeping and breaking my heart? I am ready not only to be bound, but also to die in Jerusalem for the name of the Lord Jesus." **14**When he would not be dissuaded, we gave up and said, "The Lord's will be done."

15After this, we got ready and went up to Jerusalem. **16**Some of the disciples from Caesarea accompanied us and brought us to the home of Mnason, where we were to stay. He was a man from Cyprus and one of the early disciples.

Paul's Arrival at Jerusalem

17When we arrived at Jerusalem, the brothers received us warmly. **18**The next day Paul and the rest of us went to see James, and all the elders were present. **19**Paul greeted them and reported in detail what God had done among the Gentiles through his ministry.

20When they heard this, they praised God. Then they said to Paul: "You see, brother, how many thousands of Jews have believed, and all of them are zealous for the law. **21**They have been informed that you teach all the Jews who live among the Gentiles to turn away from Moses, telling them not to circumcise their children or live according to our customs. **22**What shall we do? They will certainly hear that you have come, **23**so do what we tell you. There are four men

---

a28 Traditionally *bishops*   *b28* Many manuscripts *of the Lord*

INFLATING THE DEPRESSED

A fter struggling with depression for nearly three months, Rebecca finally is recapturing a sense of joy in life. She has a bounce in her step. Her room-brightening smile is back too.

How did she recover?

Well, there were no quick fixes, no easy answers. The healing came from a variety of factors. But surely one of the biggest reasons was Tina. Rebecca's friend Tina showed patient love for her friend through the entire ordeal.

Look It Up
• • • •

Over and over again the Bible requires that Christians sympathize with those who hurt:

"Rejoice with those who rejoice; mourn with those who mourn" (Romans 12:15).

"Carry each other's burdens, and in this way you will fulfill the law of Christ" (Galatians 6:2).

"Therefore, as God's chosen people, holy and dearly loved, clothe yourselves with compassion, kindness, humility, gentleness and patience" (Colossians 3:12).

Tina put those verses into practice in her relationship with Rebecca. Perhaps you need to do the same with the Rebeccas in your life.

Think It Through
• • • •

Depressed individuals need your support, love, patience and encouragement. They do not need for you to blame them, lecture them or argue with them about their condition.

Is there someone in your life who is down in the dumps? What can you do to help pull that individual out of the pits?

Work It Out
• • • •

Pick one of these practical things, and reach out in love to someone who's dealing with depression:
1. Send a card.
2. Call and express your love and concern.
3. Visit the person and listen to him or her.
4. Give a hug.
5. Share a favorite joke.
6. Pray for your friend.
7. Invite that person to participate with you in a service project.
8. Go jogging together.
9. Bring that person to youth group and church.
10. Make a special surprise package.

Nail It Down
• • • •

Read Acts 20:35 to find out your responsibility to those dealing with depression.

Turn to pages 360, 527, 601 and 1256 for other readings on depression.
Turn to page 1205 for Thursday's reading.

Topic
• • • •

DEPRESSION

with us who have made a vow. **24**Take these men, join in their purification rites and pay their expenses, so that they can have their heads shaved. Then everybody will know there is no truth in these reports about you, but that you yourself are living in obedience to the law. **25**As for the Gentile believers, we have written to them our decision that they should abstain from food sacrificed to idols, from blood, from the meat of strangled animals and from sexual immorality."

26The next day Paul took the men and purified himself along with them. Then he went to the temple to give notice of the date when the days of purification would end and the offering would be made for each of them.

Paul Arrested

27When the seven days were nearly over, some Jews from the province of Asia saw Paul at the temple. They stirred up the whole crowd and seized him, **28**shouting, "Men of Israel, help us! This is the man who teaches all men everywhere against our people and our law and this place. And besides, he has brought Greeks into the temple area and defiled this holy place." **29**(They had previously seen Trophimus the Ephesian in the city with Paul and assumed that Paul had brought him into the temple area.)

30The whole city was aroused, and the people came running from all directions. Seizing Paul, they dragged him from the temple, and immediately the gates were shut. **31**While they were trying to kill him, news reached the commander of the Roman troops that the whole city of Jerusalem was in an uproar. **32**He at once took some officers and soldiers and ran down to the crowd. When the rioters saw the commander and his soldiers, they stopped beating Paul.

33The commander came up and arrested him and ordered him to be bound with two chains. Then he asked who he was and what he had done. **34**Some in the crowd shouted one thing and some another, and since the commander could not get at the truth because of the uproar, he ordered that Paul be taken into the barracks. **35**When Paul reached the steps, the violence of the mob was so great he had to be carried by the soldiers. **36**The crowd that followed kept shouting, "Away with him!"

Paul Speaks to the Crowd

37As the soldiers were about to take Paul into the barracks, he asked the commander, "May I say something to you?"

"Do you speak Greek?" he replied. **38**"Aren't you the Egyptian who started a revolt and led four thousand terrorists out into the desert some time ago?"

39Paul answered, "I am a Jew, from Tarsus in Cilicia, a citizen of no ordinary city. Please let me speak to the people."

40Having received the commander's permission, Paul stood on the steps and motioned to the crowd. When they were all silent, he said to them in Aramaic*a*:

22

1"Brothers and fathers, listen now to my defense."

2When they heard him speak to them in Aramaic, they became very quiet.

Then Paul said: **3**"I am a Jew, born in Tarsus of Cilicia, but brought up in this city. Under Gamaliel I was thoroughly trained in the law of our fathers and was just as zealous for God as any of you are today. **4**I persecuted the followers of this Way to their death, arresting both men and women and throwing them into prison, **5**as also the high priest and all the Council can testify. I even obtained letters from them to their brothers in Damascus, and went there to bring these people as prisoners to Jerusalem to be punished.

6"About noon as I came near Damascus, suddenly a bright light from heaven flashed around me. **7**I fell to the ground and heard a voice say to me, 'Saul! Saul! Why do you persecute me?'

8" 'Who are you, Lord?' I asked.

" 'I am Jesus of Nazareth, whom you are persecuting,' he replied. **9**My companions saw the light, but they did not understand the voice of him who was speaking to me.

10" 'What shall I do, Lord?' I asked.

" 'Get up,' the Lord said, 'and go into Damascus. There you will be told all that you have been assigned to do.' **11**My companions led me by the hand into Damascus, because the brilliance of the light had blinded me.

12"A man named Ananias came to see me. He was a devout observer of the law and highly respected by all the Jews living there. **13**He stood beside me and said, 'Brother Saul, receive your sight!' And at that very moment I was able to see him.

14"Then he said: 'The God of our fathers

a40 Or possibly *Hebrew*; also in 22:2

has chosen you to know his will and to see the Righteous One and to hear words from his mouth. **15**You will be his witness to all men of what you have seen and heard. **16**And now what are you waiting for? Get up, be baptized and wash your sins away, calling on his name.'

17"When I returned to Jerusalem and was praying at the temple, I fell into a trance **18**and saw the Lord speaking. 'Quick!' he said to me. 'Leave Jerusalem immediately, because they will not accept your testimony about me.'

19" 'Lord,' I replied, 'these men know that I went from one synagogue to another to imprison and beat those who believe in you. **20**And when the blood of your martyr*a* Stephen was shed, I stood there giving my approval and guarding the clothes of those who were killing him.'

21"Then the Lord said to me, 'Go; I will send you far away to the Gentiles.' "

Paul the Roman Citizen

22The crowd listened to Paul until he said this. Then they raised their voices and shouted, "Rid the earth of him! He's not fit to live!"

23As they were shouting and throwing off their cloaks and flinging dust into the air, **24**the commander ordered Paul to be taken into the barracks. He directed that he be flogged and questioned in order to find out why the people were shouting at him like this. **25**As they stretched him out to flog him, Paul said to the centurion standing there, "Is it legal for you to flog a Roman citizen who hasn't even been found guilty?"

26When the centurion heard this, he went to the commander and reported it. "What are you going to do?" he asked. "This man is a Roman citizen."

27The commander went to Paul and asked, "Tell me, are you a Roman citizen?"

"Yes, I am," he answered.

28Then the commander said, "I had to pay a big price for my citizenship."

"But I was born a citizen," Paul replied.

29Those who were about to question him withdrew immediately. The commander himself was alarmed when he realized that he had put Paul, a Roman citizen, in chains.

Before the Sanhedrin

30The next day, since the commander wanted to find out exactly why Paul was being accused by the Jews, he released him and ordered the chief priests and all the Sanhedrin to assemble. Then he brought Paul and had him stand before them.

23 Paul looked straight at the Sanhedrin and said, "My brothers, I have fulfilled my duty to God in all good conscience to this day." **2**At this the high priest Ananias ordered those standing near Paul to strike him on the mouth. **3**Then Paul said to him, "God will strike you, you whitewashed wall! You sit there to judge me according to the law, yet you yourself violate the law by commanding that I be struck!"

4Those who were standing near Paul said, "You dare to insult God's high priest?"

5Paul replied, "Brothers, I did not realize that he was the high priest; for it is written: 'Do not speak evil about the ruler of your people.'*b* "

6Then Paul, knowing that some of them were Sadducees and the others Pharisees, called out in the Sanhedrin, "My brothers, I am a Pharisee, the son of a Pharisee. I stand on trial because of my hope in the resurrection of the dead." **7**When he said this, a dispute broke out between the Pharisees and the Sadducees, and the assembly was divided. **8**(The Sadducees say that there is no resurrection, and that there are neither angels nor spirits, but the Pharisees acknowledge them all.)

9There was a great uproar, and some of the teachers of the law who were Pharisees stood up and argued vigorously. "We find nothing wrong with this man," they said. "What if a spirit or an angel has spoken to him?" **10**The dispute became so violent that the commander was afraid Paul would be torn to pieces by them. He ordered the troops to go down and take him away from them by force and bring him into the barracks.

11The following night the Lord stood near Paul and said, "Take courage! As you have testified about me in Jerusalem, so you must also testify in Rome."

The Plot to Kill Paul

12The next morning the Jews formed a conspiracy and bound themselves with an oath not to eat or drink until they had killed Paul. **13**More than forty men were involved in this plot. **14**They went to the chief priests and elders and said, "We have taken a solemn oath not to eat anything until we have killed Paul. **15**Now then, you and the Sanhedrin petition the commander to bring him

---

*a*20 Or *witness*   *b*5 Exodus 22:28

before you on the pretext of wanting more accurate information about his case. We are ready to kill him before he gets here."

[16]But when the son of Paul's sister heard of this plot, he went into the barracks and told Paul.

[17]Then Paul called one of the centurions and said, "Take this young man to the commander; he has something to tell him." [18]So he took him to the commander.

The centurion said, "Paul, the prisoner, sent for me and asked me to bring this young man to you because he has something to tell you."

[19]The commander took the young man by the hand, drew him aside and asked, "What is it you want to tell me?"

[20]He said: "The Jews have agreed to ask you to bring Paul before the Sanhedrin tomorrow on the pretext of wanting more accurate information about him. [21]Don't give in to them, because more than forty of them are waiting in ambush for him. They have taken an oath not to eat or drink until they have killed him. They are ready now, waiting for your consent to their request."

[22]The commander dismissed the young man and cautioned him, "Don't tell anyone that you have reported this to me."

Paul Transferred to Caesarea

[23]Then he called two of his centurions and ordered them, "Get ready a detachment of two hundred soldiers, seventy horsemen and two hundred spearmen[a] to go to Caesarea at nine tonight. [24]Provide mounts for Paul so that he may be taken safely to Governor Felix."

[25]He wrote a letter as follows:

[26]Claudius Lysias,

To His Excellency, Governor Felix:

Greetings.

[27]This man was seized by the Jews and they were about to kill him, but I came with my troops and rescued him, for I had learned that he is a Roman citizen. [28]I wanted to know why they were accusing him, so I brought him to their Sanhedrin. [29]I found that the accusation had to do with questions about their law, but there was no charge against him that deserved death or im-

prisonment. [30]When I was informed of a plot to be carried out against the man, I sent him to you at once. I also ordered his accusers to present to you their case against him.

[31]So the soldiers, carrying out their orders, took Paul with them during the night and brought him as far as Antipatris. [32]The next day they let the cavalry go on with him, while they returned to the barracks. [33]When the cavalry arrived in Caesarea, they delivered the letter to the governor and handed Paul over to him. [34]The governor read the letter and asked what province he was from. Learning that he was from Cilicia, [35]he said, "I will hear your case when your accusers get here." Then he ordered that Paul be kept under guard in Herod's palace.

The Trial Before Felix

24 Five days later the high priest Ananias went down to Caesarea with some of the elders and a lawyer named Tertullus, and they brought their charges against Paul before the governor. [2]When Paul was called in, Tertullus presented his case before Felix: "We have enjoyed a long period of peace under you, and your foresight has brought about reforms in this nation. [3]Everywhere and in every way, most excellent Felix, we acknowledge this with profound gratitude. [4]But in order not to weary you further, I would request that you be kind enough to hear us briefly.

[5]"We have found this man to be a troublemaker, stirring up riots among the Jews all over the world. He is a ringleader of the Nazarene sect [6]and even tried to desecrate the temple; so we seized him. [8]By[b] examining him yourself you will be able to learn the truth about all these charges we are bringing against him."

[9]The Jews joined in the accusation, asserting that these things were true.

[10]When the governor motioned for him to speak, Paul replied: "I know that for a number of years you have been a judge over this nation; so I gladly make my defense. [11]You can easily verify that no more than twelve days ago I went up to Jerusalem to worship. [12]My accusers did not find me arguing with anyone at the temple, or stirring up a crowd in the synagogues or anywhere else in the city. [13]And they cannot prove to you the

---

a23 The meaning of the Greek for this word is uncertain.   *b6-8* Some manuscripts *him and wanted to judge him according to our law.* [7]*But the commander, Lysias, came and with the use of much force snatched him from our hands* [8]*and ordered his accusers to come before you. By*

Temptation

Have you ever been tempted to...

Lie to your parents to avoid getting in trouble?

Rent a movie you know you shouldn't watch?

Go "all the way" with your boyfriend or girlfriend?

What would Jesus do?

You may already know the story of Jesus being tempted by Satan (Matthew 4:1-11). Satan tempted Jesus three times, and each time Jesus responded by quoting Scripture. Let's take a closer look.

Many people know the Bible very well. But quoting Scripture and actually basing your actions on it can be two very different things. You probably know that pre-marital sex is wrong. You can find Bible verses to tell you so. But when the time comes and you are tempted, you must choose your way or God's way.

That's what Jesus did. Not only did he quote the words that "had been written," he acted on them. The words were firmly planted in his heart. He already knew what to do. By acting on Scripture, Jesus chose his Father's way.

What will you do?

You too have a choice. You can choose to do the "right thing"— the thing that pleases God. Even though your particular tempting situation may seem overwhelming, there is always a way out (1 Corinthians 10:13).

You will constantly encounter temptation. Luke 4:13 says that when Satan had finished tempting Jesus, he left him until an "opportune time." But as you read the Bible and learn to resist temptation, you will become stronger in those weak areas and better prepared to stand against temptation. You will be better prepared to ask, "What would Jesus do?" And then do it!

More about temptation

Matthew 26:41; 1 Timothy 6:9; James 1:13-15

Witnessing

Do you have to be great...
to fulfill the great commission? Or should you leave witnessing to the professionals like pastors, youth leaders or missionaries?

What would Jesus do?
A Samaritan woman brought an empty bucket to the well. She left filled with the living water of eternal life (John 4:1-26). A tax collector climbed a tree to catch a glimpse of the Messiah. When he climbed down, not only had Zacchaeus made room in his home for Jesus, but he had also made room in his heart (Luke 19:2-10). Throughout his life, Jesus told the Good News to everyone he came in contact with. And people walked away changed forever.

Jesus' greatest call is found in the great commission. In Matthew 28:19, Jesus tells his followers to "go and make disciples of all nations."

What will you do?
There are two ways you can let your light shine. The first is to verbally share your belief in Jesus Christ. Look for opportunities. Tell people what God has done in your life. Tell them what your relationship with him means to you. When someone you know is going through a tough time, encourage him or her with Scripture.

The second way to let your light shine is in your actions—how you act every day. It means following Christ's example and living according to his teaching—not just reading the Bible but doing what it says. In every situation learn to ask yourself, "What would Jesus do?" Then go about doing it!

More about witnessing
John 1:7; John 20:21; Acts 5:42

W.W.J.D. ?

charges they are now making against me. [14]However, I admit that I worship the God of our fathers as a follower of the Way, which they call a sect. I believe everything that agrees with the Law and that is written in the Prophets, [15]and I have the same hope in God as these men, that there will be a resurrection of both the righteous and the wicked. [16]So I strive always to keep my conscience clear before God and man.

[17]"After an absence of several years, I came to Jerusalem to bring my people gifts for the poor and to present offerings. [18]I was ceremonially clean when they found me in the temple courts doing this. There was no crowd with me, nor was I involved in any disturbance. [19]But there are some Jews from the province of Asia, who ought to be here before you and bring charges if they have anything against me. [20]Or these who are here should state what crime they found in me when I stood before the Sanhedrin — [21]unless it was this one thing I shouted as I stood in their presence: 'It is concerning the resurrection of the dead that I am on trial before you today.'"

[22]Then Felix, who was well acquainted with the Way, adjourned the proceedings. "When Lysias the commander comes," he said, "I will decide your case." [23]He ordered the centurion to keep Paul under guard but to give him some freedom and permit his friends to take care of his needs.

[24]Several days later Felix came with his wife Drusilla, who was a Jewess. He sent for Paul and listened to him as he spoke about faith in Christ Jesus. [25]As Paul discoursed on righteousness, self-control and the judgment to come, Felix was afraid and said, "That's enough for now! You may leave. When I find it convenient, I will send for you." [26]At the same time he was hoping that Paul would offer him a bribe, so he sent for him frequently and talked with him.

[27]When two years had passed, Felix was succeeded by Porcius Festus, but because Felix wanted to grant a favor to the Jews, he left Paul in prison.

The Trial Before Festus

25 Three days after arriving in the province, Festus went up from Caesarea to Jerusalem, [2]where the chief priests and Jewish leaders appeared before him and presented the charges against Paul. [3]They urgently requested Festus, as a favor to them, to have Paul transferred to Jerusalem, for they were preparing an ambush to kill him along the way. [4]Festus answered, "Paul is being held at Caesarea, and I myself am going there soon. [5]Let some of your leaders come with me and press charges against the man there, if he has done anything wrong."

[6]After spending eight or ten days with them, he went down to Caesarea, and the next day he convened the court and ordered that Paul be brought before him. [7]When Paul appeared, the Jews who had come down from Jerusalem stood around him, bringing many serious charges against him, which they could not prove.

[8]Then Paul made his defense: "I have done nothing wrong against the law of the Jews or against the temple or against Caesar."

[9]Festus, wishing to do the Jews a favor, said to Paul, "Are you willing to go up to Jerusalem and stand trial before me there on these charges?"

[10]Paul answered: "I am now standing before Caesar's court, where I ought to be tried. I have not done any wrong to the Jews, as you yourself know very well. [11]If, however, I am guilty of doing anything deserving death, I do not refuse to die. But if the charges brought against me by these Jews are not true, no one has the right to hand me over to them. I appeal to Caesar!"

[12]After Festus had conferred with his council, he declared: "You have appealed to Caesar. To Caesar you will go!"

Festus Consults King Agrippa

[13]A few days later King Agrippa and Bernice arrived at Caesarea to pay their respects to Festus. [14]Since they were spending many days there, Festus discussed Paul's case with the king. He said: "There is a man here whom Felix left as a prisoner. [15]When I went to Jerusalem, the chief priests and elders of the Jews brought charges against him and asked that he be condemned.

[16]"I told them that it is not the Roman custom to hand over any man before he has faced his accusers and has had an opportunity to defend himself against their charges. [17]When they came here with me, I did not delay the case, but convened the court the next day and ordered the man to be brought in. [18]When his accusers got up to speak, they did not charge him with any of the crimes I had expected. [19]Instead, they had some points of dispute with him about their own religion and about a dead man named Jesus who Paul claimed was alive. [20]I was at a loss how to investigate such matters; so I asked if he would be willing to go to Jerusalem and stand trial there on these charges.

²¹When Paul made his appeal to be held over for the Emperor's decision, I ordered him held until I could send him to Caesar."

²²Then Agrippa said to Festus, "I would like to hear this man myself."

He replied, "Tomorrow you will hear him."

Paul Before Agrippa

²³The next day Agrippa and Bernice came with great pomp and entered the audience room with the high ranking officers and the leading men of the city. At the command of Festus, Paul was brought in. ²⁴Festus said: "King Agrippa, and all who are present with us, you see this man! The whole Jewish community has petitioned me about him in Jerusalem and here in Caesarea, shouting that he ought not to live any longer. ²⁵I found he had done nothing deserving of death, but because he made his appeal to the Emperor I decided to send him to Rome. ²⁶But I have nothing definite to write to His Majesty about him. Therefore I have brought him before all of you, and especially before you, King Agrippa, so that as a result of this investigation I may have something to write. ²⁷For I think it is unreasonable to send on a prisoner without specifying the charges against him."

26 Then Agrippa said to Paul, "You have permission to speak for yourself."

So Paul motioned with his hand and began his defense: ²"King Agrippa, I consider myself fortunate to stand before you today as I make my defense against all the accusations of the Jews, ³and especially so because you are well acquainted with all the Jewish customs and controversies. Therefore, I beg you to listen to me patiently.

⁴"The Jews all know the way I have lived ever since I was a child, from the beginning of my life in my own country, and also in Jerusalem. ⁵They have known me for a long time and can testify, if they are willing, that according to the strictest sect of our religion, I lived as a Pharisee. ⁶And now it is because of my hope in what God has promised our fathers that I am on trial today. ⁷This is the promise our twelve tribes are hoping to see fulfilled as they earnestly serve God day and night. O king, it is because of this hope that the Jews are accusing me. ⁸Why should any of you consider it incredible that God raises the dead?

⁹"I too was convinced that I ought to do all

that was possible to oppose the name of Jesus of Nazareth. ¹⁰And that is just what I did in Jerusalem. On the authority of the chief priests I put many of the saints in prison, and when they were put to death, I cast my vote against them. ¹¹Many a time I went from one synagogue to another to have them punished, and I tried to force them to blaspheme. In my obsession against them, I even went to foreign cities to persecute them.

¹²"On one of these journeys I was going to Damascus with the authority and commission of the chief priests. ¹³About noon, O king, as I was on the road, I saw a light from heaven, brighter than the sun, blazing around me and my companions. ¹⁴We all fell to the ground, and I heard a voice saying to me in Aramaic,ᵃ 'Saul, Saul, why do you persecute me? It is hard for you to kick against the goads.'

¹⁵"Then I asked, 'Who are you, Lord?'

" 'I am Jesus, whom you are persecuting,' the Lord replied. ¹⁶'Now get up and stand on your feet. I have appeared to you to appoint you as a servant and as a witness of what you have seen of me and what I will show you. ¹⁷I will rescue you from your own people and from the Gentiles. I am sending you to them ¹⁸to open their eyes and turn them from darkness to light, and from the power of Satan to God, so that they may receive forgiveness of sins and a place among those who are sanctified by faith in me.'

¹⁹"So then, King Agrippa, I was not disobedient to the vision from heaven. ²⁰First to those in Damascus, then to those in Jerusalem and in all Judea, and to the Gentiles also, I preached that they should repent and turn to God and prove their repentance by their deeds. ²¹That is why the Jews seized me in the temple courts and tried to kill me. ²²But I have had God's help to this very day, and so I stand here and testify to small and great alike. I am saying nothing beyond what the prophets and Moses said would happen— ²³that the Christᵇ would suffer and, as the first to rise from the dead, would proclaim light to his own people and to the Gentiles."

²⁴At this point Festus interrupted Paul's defense. "You are out of your mind, Paul!" he shouted. "Your great learning is driving you insane."

²⁵"I am not insane, most excellent Festus," Paul replied. "What I am saying is true and reasonable. ²⁶The king is familiar with

ᵃ14 Or Hebrew   ᵇ23 Or Messiah

these things, and I can speak freely to him. I am convinced that none of this has escaped his notice, because it was not done in a corner. ²⁷King Agrippa, do you believe the prophets? I know you do."

²⁸Then Agrippa said to Paul, "Do you think that in such a short time you can persuade me to be a Christian?"

²⁹Paul replied, "Short time or long—I pray God that not only you but all who are listening to me today may become what I am, except for these chains."

³⁰The king rose, and with him the governor and Bernice and those sitting with them. ³¹They left the room, and while talking with one another, they said, "This man is not doing anything that deserves death or imprisonment."

³²Agrippa said to Festus, "This man could have been set free if he had not appealed to Caesar."

Paul Sails for Rome

27 When it was decided that we would sail for Italy, Paul and some other prisoners were handed over to a centurion named Julius, who belonged to the Imperial Regiment. ²We boarded a ship from Adramyttium about to sail for ports along the coast of the province of Asia, and we put out to sea. Aristarchus, a Macedonian from Thessalonica, was with us.

³The next day we landed at Sidon; and Julius, in kindness to Paul, allowed him to go to his friends so they might provide for his needs. ⁴From there we put out to sea again and passed to the lee of Cyprus because the winds were against us. ⁵When we had sailed across the open sea off the coast of Cilicia and Pamphylia, we landed at Myra in Lycia. ⁶There the centurion found an Alexandrian ship sailing for Italy and put us on board. ⁷We made slow headway for many days and had difficulty arriving off Cnidus. When the wind did not allow us to hold our course, we sailed to the lee of Crete, opposite Salmone. ⁸We moved along the coast with difficulty and came to a place called Fair Havens, near the town of Lasea.

⁹Much time had been lost, and sailing had already become dangerous because by now it was after the Fast.^a So Paul warned them, ¹⁰"Men, I can see that our voyage is going to be disastrous and bring great loss to ship and cargo, and to our own lives also." ¹¹But the centurion, instead of listening to what

Paul said, followed the advice of the pilot and of the owner of the ship. ¹²Since the harbor was unsuitable to winter in, the majority decided that we should sail on, hoping to reach Phoenix and winter there. This was a harbor in Crete, facing both southwest and northwest.

The Storm

¹³When a gentle south wind began to blow, they thought they had obtained what they wanted; so they weighed anchor and sailed along the shore of Crete. ¹⁴Before very long, a wind of hurricane force, called the "northeaster," swept down from the island. ¹⁵The ship was caught by the storm and could not head into the wind; so we gave way to it and were driven along. ¹⁶As we passed to the lee of a small island called Cauda, we were hardly able to make the lifeboat secure. ¹⁷When the men had hoisted it aboard, they passed ropes under the ship itself to hold it together. Fearing that they would run aground on the sandbars of Syrtis, they lowered the sea anchor and let the ship be driven along. ¹⁸We took such a violent battering from the storm that the next day they began to throw the cargo overboard. ¹⁹On the third day, they threw the ship's tackle overboard with their own hands. ²⁰When neither sun nor stars appeared for many days and the storm continued raging, we finally gave up all hope of being saved.

²¹After the men had gone a long time without food, Paul stood up before them and said: "Men, you should have taken my advice not to sail from Crete; then you would have spared yourselves this damage and loss. ²²But now I urge you to keep up your courage, because not one of you will be lost; only the ship will be destroyed. ²³Last night an angel of the God whose I am and whom I serve stood beside me ²⁴and said, 'Do not be afraid, Paul. You must stand trial before Caesar; and God has graciously given you the lives of all who sail with you.' ²⁵So keep up your courage, men, for I have faith in God that it will happen just as he told me. ²⁶Nevertheless, we must run aground on some island."

The Shipwreck

²⁷On the fourteenth night we were still being driven across the Adriatic^b Sea, when about midnight the sailors sensed they were

---

^a9 That is, the Day of Atonement (Yom Kippur)   ^b27 In ancient times the name referred to an area extending well south of Italy.

approaching land. **28**They took soundings and found that the water was a hundred and twenty feet*a* deep. A short time later they took soundings again and found it was ninety feet*b* deep. **29**Fearing that we would be dashed against the rocks, they dropped four anchors from the stern and prayed for daylight. **30**In an attempt to escape from the ship, the sailors let the lifeboat down into the sea, pretending they were going to lower some anchors from the bow. **31**Then Paul said to the centurion and the soldiers, "Unless these men stay with the ship, you cannot be saved." **32**So the soldiers cut the ropes that held the lifeboat and let it fall away.

33Just before dawn Paul urged them all to eat. "For the last fourteen days," he said, "you have been in constant suspense and have gone without food — you haven't eaten anything. **34**Now I urge you to take some food. You need it to survive. Not one of you will lose a single hair from his head." **35**After he said this, he took some bread and gave thanks to God in front of them all. Then he broke it and began to eat. **36**They were all encouraged and ate some food themselves. **37**Altogether there were 276 of us on board. **38**When they had eaten as much as they wanted, they lightened the ship by throwing the grain into the sea.

39When daylight came, they did not recognize the land, but they saw a bay with a sandy beach, where they decided to run the ship aground if they could. **40**Cutting loose the anchors, they left them in the sea and at the same time untied the ropes that held the rudders. Then they hoisted the foresail to the wind and made for the beach. **41**But the ship struck a sandbar and ran aground. The bow stuck fast and would not move, and the stern was broken to pieces by the pounding of the surf.

42The soldiers planned to kill the prisoners to prevent any of them from swimming away and escaping. **43**But the centurion wanted to spare Paul's life and kept them from carrying out their plan. He ordered those who could swim to jump overboard first and get to land. **44**The rest were to get there on planks or on pieces of the ship. In this way everyone reached land in safety.

Ashore on Malta

28 Once safely on shore, we found out that the island was called Malta. **2**The islanders showed us unusual kindness. They built a fire and welcomed us all because it was raining and cold. **3**Paul gathered a pile of brushwood and, as he put it on the fire, a viper, driven out by the heat, fastened itself on his hand. **4**When the islanders saw the snake hanging from his hand, they said to each other, "This man must be a murderer; for though he escaped from the sea, Justice has not allowed him to live." **5**But Paul shook the snake off into the fire and suffered no ill effects. **6**The people expected him to swell up or suddenly fall dead, but after waiting a long time and seeing nothing unusual happen to him, they changed their minds and said he was a god.

7There was an estate nearby that belonged to Publius, the chief official of the island. He welcomed us to his home and for three days entertained us hospitably. **8**His father was sick in bed, suffering from fever and dysentery. Paul went in to see him and, after prayer, placed his hands on him and healed him. **9**When this had happened, the rest of the sick on the island came and were cured. **10**They honored us in many ways and when we were ready to sail, they furnished us with the supplies we needed.

Arrival at Rome

11After three months we put out to sea in a ship that had wintered in the island. It was an Alexandrian ship with the figurehead of the twin gods Castor and Pollux. **12**We put in at Syracuse and stayed there three days. **13**From there we set sail and arrived at Rhegium. The next day the south wind came up, and on the following day we reached Puteoli. **14**There we found some brothers who invited us to spend a week with them. And so we came to Rome. **15**The brothers there had heard that we were coming, and they traveled as far as the Forum of Appius and the Three Taverns to meet us. At the sight of these men Paul thanked God and was encouraged. **16**When we got to Rome, Paul was allowed to live by himself, with a soldier to guard him.

Paul Preaches at Rome Under Guard

17Three days later he called together the leaders of the Jews. When they had assembled, Paul said to them: "My brothers, although I have done nothing against our people or against the customs of our ancestors, I was arrested in Jerusalem and handed over to the Romans. **18**They examined me and wanted to release me, because I was not guilty of any crime deserving death. **19**But

---

a28 Greek *twenty orguias* (about 37 meters)   *b28* Greek *fifteen orguias* (about 27 meters)

Want to Get Into the Act?

Melody is feeling pretty bad. She made the school tennis team, but her friend Catherine was cut. Catherine is so discouraged, and Melody isn't sure that there's anything she can do. But, after talking with her father, Melody is excited.

"Why wasn't I thinking?" she wonders aloud. "I don't have to sit here twiddling my thumbs. I can be the one God uses to encourage Catherine!"

Melody pulls out her stationery and writes a sweet note to her discouraged friend. Part of it reads, "I'm so glad you're my best friend. You may not believe this, but I really look up to you, and . . . I love you!"

Melody then picks up the phone to invite Catherine out for lunch at their favorite fast-food hangout.

Look It Up

The Greek word *encourage* literally means "to come alongside and help." Encouragement can come through a variety of means:

A word of challenge—"And we urge you, brothers . . . encourage the timid" (1 Thessalonians 5:14; also see Acts 11:23; 14:22).

A word of comfort or cheer (Colossians 4:7–9).

A word of strength—"Then the church . . . enjoyed a time of peace. It was strengthened; and encouraged by the Holy Spirit, it grew in numbers" (Acts 9:31; also see 1 Samuel 30:6 and 1 Thessalonians 5:11).

A word of affirmation (Acts 18:27).

A word of instruction—"Encourage others by sound doctrine" (Titus 1:9).

Think It Through

The beauty of encouragement is that anyone can do it. It doesn't take lots of money, and there are no age restrictions.

What's the most encouraging thing anyone has ever done for you or said to you?

Can you think of five really creative ways to encourage someone who's down?

Work It Out

Practice the power of encouragement. Pick one of the following messages, expand on it and modify it for a discouraged person you know. Then go out and deliver it in Christian love today!

1. "Don't be afraid to go for it!"
2. "Think on the bright side."
3. "Because God is behind you, you're going to make it!"
4. "Keep it up! You're on the right track!"
5. "Can I share something with you that really helped me?"

Nail It Down

Read how just your presence can encourage someone in need in Acts 28:15.

Turn to pages 472 and 663 for other readings on encouragement.
Turn to page 1208 for Friday's reading.

Topic

ENCOURAGEMENT

when the Jews objected, I was compelled to appeal to Caesar — not that I had any charge to bring against my own people. **20**For this reason I have asked to see you and talk with you. It is because of the hope of Israel that I am bound with this chain."

21They replied, "We have not received any letters from Judea concerning you, and none of the brothers who have come from there has reported or said anything bad about you. **22**But we want to hear what your views are, for we know that people everywhere are talking against this sect."

23They arranged to meet Paul on a certain day, and came in even larger numbers to the place where he was staying. From morning till evening he explained and declared to them the kingdom of God and tried to convince them about Jesus from the Law of Moses and from the Prophets. **24**Some were convinced by what he said, but others would not believe. **25**They disagreed among themselves and began to leave after Paul had made this final statement: "The Holy Spirit spoke the truth to your forefathers when he said through Isaiah the prophet:

26" 'Go to this people and say,
"You will be ever hearing but never understanding;
you will be ever seeing but never perceiving."
27For this people's heart has become calloused;
they hardly hear with their ears,
and they have closed their eyes.
Otherwise they might see with their eyes,
hear with their ears,
understand with their hearts
and turn, and I would heal them.'*a*

28"Therefore I want you to know that God's salvation has been sent to the Gentiles, and they will listen!"*b*

30For two whole years Paul stayed there in his own rented house and welcomed all who came to see him. **31**Boldly and without hindrance he preached the kingdom of God and taught about the Lord Jesus Christ.

a27 Isaiah 6:9,10   *b28* Some manuscripts *listen!"* *29After he said this, the Jews left, arguing vigorously among themselves.*

ROMANS

PAUL writes this letter to introduce himself to the church at Rome, which he has not yet visited. In a systematic way he teaches about sin, salvation by faith, life in the Spirit, God's plan for Jews and Gentiles, and how to live day by day with other believers. Everything you need to know about God's great plan for redemption lies in these sixteen chapters. As you read, remember that God is holy, people are sinful, and Jesus Christ paid in full the price required to save sinners.

Outline of Contents

1 Paul, a servant of Christ Jesus, called to be an apostle and set apart for the gospel of God— ²the gospel he promised beforehand through his prophets in the Holy Scriptures ³regarding his Son, who as to his human nature was a descendant of David, ⁴and who through the Spirit*a* of holiness was declared with power to be the Son of God*b* by his resurrection from the dead: Jesus Christ our Lord. ⁵Through him and for his name's sake, we received grace and apostleship to call people from among all the Gentiles to the obedience that comes from faith. ⁶And you also are among those who are called to belong to Jesus Christ.

⁷To all in Rome who are loved by God and called to be saints:

Grace and peace to you from God our Father and from the Lord Jesus Christ.

Paul's Longing to Visit Rome

⁸First, I thank my God through Jesus Christ for all of you, because your faith is being reported all over the world. ⁹God, whom I serve with my whole heart in preaching the gospel of his Son, is my witness how constantly I remember you ¹⁰in my prayers at all times; and I pray that now at last by God's will the way may be opened for me to come to you.

a4 Or *who as to his spirit*   *b4* Or *was appointed to be the Son of God with power*

OUR AWESOME CREATOR

On a camping trip to the mountains, Kyle gets up early one morning and hikes up to Eagle's Peak. From there he has a panoramic view of the hills and valleys to the east.

As a cool morning breeze blows gently through his hair, Kyle sits back against a boulder to watch the sun rise. This spectacular display is made all the more dramatic by an unreal silence that blankets the ridge.

Just before seven, a large trout begins splashing about in the mountain pool nearby. As he stares at the beauty on every side, Kyle begins to wonder about God.

Look It Up
••••

Wouldn't it be great to be at Eagle's Peak right now? It's not surprising that such a place prompts Kyle to consider God. The beauties of nature are supposed to have that effect:

"The heavens declare the glory of God; the skies proclaim the work of his hands" (Psalm 19:1).

"You alone are the LORD. You made the heavens, even the highest heavens, and all their starry host, the earth and all that is on it, the seas and all that is in them. You give life to everything, and the multitudes of heaven worship you" (Nehemiah 9:6).

Think It Through
••••

The Bible indicates that the wonders of creation are designed to make you reflect on your Creator! Isn't it strange that while nature is shouting about the glory and power of God, many scientists are ignoring him, and New Age devotees are praising the physical universe instead of its creator?

When was the last time you consciously acknowledged God for who he is—the mighty Creator of the universe?

Work It Out
••••

Today, try to forget asphalt, high-rise buildings and man-made gadgets. Instead notice God's magnificent creation: the sky, the clouds, the birds and flowers. Then pray this prayer:

"God, I praise you as the awesome Creator of the universe. Your power is limitless, and your creativity is staggering. Thank you for revealing yourself through nature. Help me to know you better. Amen."

Nail It Down
••••

Read Paul's statement about creation and its Creator in Romans 1:20.

Turn to pages 619, 761, 1210 and 1243 for other readings on God.
Turn to page 1210 for the weekend reading.

Topic
••••

[11]I long to see you so that I may impart to you some spiritual gift to make you strong— [12]that is, that you and I may be mutually encouraged by each other's faith. [13]I do not want you to be unaware, brothers, that I planned many times to come to you (but have been prevented from doing so until now) in order that I might have a harvest among you, just as I have had among the other Gentiles.

[14]I am obligated both to Greeks and non-Greeks, both to the wise and the foolish. [15]That is why I am so eager to preach the gospel also to you who are at Rome.

[16]I am not ashamed of the gospel, because it is the power of God for the salvation of everyone who believes: first for the Jew, then for the Gentile. [17]For in the gospel a righteousness from God is revealed, a righteousness that is by faith from first to last,[a] just as it is written: "The righteous will live by faith."[b]

God's Wrath Against Mankind

[18]The wrath of God is being revealed from heaven against all the godlessness and wickedness of men who suppress the truth by their wickedness, [19]since what may be known about God is plain to them, because God has made it plain to them. [20]For since the creation of the world God's invisible qualities—his eternal power and divine nature—have been clearly seen, being understood from what has been made, so that men are without excuse.

[21]For although they knew God, they neither glorified him as God nor gave thanks to him, but their thinking became futile and their foolish hearts were darkened. [22]Although they claimed to be wise, they became fools [23]and exchanged the glory of the immortal God for images made to look like mortal man and birds and animals and reptiles.

[24]Therefore God gave them over in the sinful desires of their hearts to sexual impurity for the degrading of their bodies with one another. [25]They exchanged the truth of God for a lie, and worshiped and served created things rather than the Creator—who is forever praised. Amen.

[26]Because of this, God gave them over to shameful lusts. Even their women exchanged natural relations for unnatural ones. [27]In the same way the men also abandoned natural relations with women and were inflamed with lust for one another. Men committed indecent acts with other men, and received in themselves the due penalty for their perversion.

[28]Furthermore, since they did not think it worthwhile to retain the knowledge of God, he gave them over to a depraved mind, to do what ought not to be done. [29]They have become filled with every kind of wickedness, evil, greed and depravity. They are full of envy, murder, strife, deceit and malice. They are gossips, [30]slanderers, God-haters, insolent, arrogant and boastful; they invent ways of doing evil; they disobey their parents; [31]they are senseless, faithless, heartless, ruthless. [32]Although they know God's righteous decree that those who do such things deserve death, they not only continue to do these very things but also approve of those who practice them.

God's Righteous Judgment

2 You, therefore, have no excuse, you who pass judgment on someone else, for at whatever point you judge the other, you are condemning yourself, because you who pass judgment do the same things. [2]Now we know that God's judgment against those who do such things is based on truth. [3]So when you, a mere man, pass judgment on them and yet do the same things, do you think you will escape God's judgment? [4]Or do you show contempt for the riches of his kindness, tolerance and patience, not realizing that God's kindness leads you toward repentance?

[5]But because of your stubbornness and your unrepentant heart, you are storing up wrath against yourself for the day of God's wrath, when his righteous judgment will be revealed. [6]God "will give to each person according to what he has done."[c] [7]To those who by persistence in doing good seek glory, honor and immortality, he will give eternal life. [8]But for those who are self-seeking and who reject the truth and follow evil, there will be wrath and anger. [9]There will be trouble and distress for every human being who does evil: first for the Jew, then for the Gentile; [10]but glory, honor and peace for everyone who does good: first for the Jew, then for the Gentile. [11]For God does not show favoritism.

[12]All who sin apart from the law will also perish apart from the law, and all who sin under the law will be judged by the law.

---

[a]17 Or is from faith to faith   [b]17 Hab. 2:4   [c]6 Psalm 62:12; Prov. 24:12

GOD'S KINDNESS TO YOU

● ●

**Work It
Out**
● ● ● ●

Do you ever have trouble being kind? If you're totally honest, you will have to answer yes. Being kind isn't too difficult in most circumstances. But what if you've been baby-sitting five pre-schoolers all day on Saturday? Or what if you're trying to satisfy an especially cranky customer at work? Or how about if your brother keeps coming into your room when you've told him ten times to *please* stay out? Is it easy then? Or does it take self-control?

Thank goodness God doesn't have to work at being kind to you. Kindness is something that comes natural to God. It's just part of his nature. He loves you, and he keeps on being kind to you in order to lead you to him.

**Nail It
Down**
● ● ● ●

Read about God's kindness in Romans 2:4.

● ●

**Think It
Through**
● ● ● ●

How has God been kind to you? You can probably name ten or twenty ways within just a few minutes. But if God's kindness only gave you one thing—salvation—he would be kind enough. You could still talk about the "riches" of God's kindness.

So then, how much richer is God's kindness because he doesn't stop there! He not only leads you to repentance, he is willing and ready to forgive you when you come. And he then continues to be kind by giving you peace, joy, contentment and an abundant life.

"The riches of his kindness." What more could you ask for?

**Nail It
Down**
● ● ● ●

Read about God's kindness again in Romans 2:4. For further insight read Isaiah 63:7–8.

Turn to pages 619, 761, 1208 and 1243 for other readings on God.
Turn to page 1213 for Monday's reading.

Topic
● ● ● ●

¹³For it is not those who hear the law who are righteous in God's sight, but it is those who obey the law who will be declared righteous. ¹⁴(Indeed, when Gentiles, who do not have the law, do by nature things required by the law, they are a law for themselves, even though they do not have the law, ¹⁵since they show that the requirements of the law are written on their hearts, their consciences also bearing witness, and their thoughts now accusing, now even defending them.) ¹⁶This will take place on the day when God will judge men's secrets through Jesus Christ, as my gospel declares.

The Jews and the Law

¹⁷Now you, if you call yourself a Jew; if you rely on the law and brag about your relationship to God; ¹⁸if you know his will and approve of what is superior because you are instructed by the law; ¹⁹if you are convinced that you are a guide for the blind, a light for those who are in the dark, ²⁰an instructor of the foolish, a teacher of infants, because you have in the law the embodiment of knowledge and truth— ²¹you, then, who teach others, do you not teach yourself? You who preach against stealing, do you steal? ²²You who say that people should not commit adultery, do you commit adultery? You who abhor idols, do you rob temples? ²³You who brag about the law, do you dishonor God by breaking the law? ²⁴As it is written: "God's name is blasphemed among the Gentiles because of you."^a

²⁵Circumcision has value if you observe the law, but if you break the law, you have become as though you had not been circumcised. ²⁶If those who are not circumcised keep the law's requirements, will they not be regarded as though they were circumcised? ²⁷The one who is not circumcised physically and yet obeys the law will condemn you who, even though you have the^b written code and circumcision, are a lawbreaker.

²⁸A man is not a Jew if he is only one outwardly, nor is circumcision merely outward and physical. ²⁹No, a man is a Jew if he is one inwardly; and circumcision is circumcision of the heart, by the Spirit, not by the written code. Such a man's praise is not from men, but from God.

God's Faithfulness

3 What advantage, then, is there in being a Jew, or what value is there in circumcision? ²Much in every way! First of all, they have been entrusted with the very words of God.

³What if some did not have faith? Will their lack of faith nullify God's faithfulness? ⁴Not at all! Let God be true, and every man a liar. As it is written:

"So that you may be proved right when you speak
    and prevail when you judge."^c

⁵But if our unrighteousness brings out God's righteousness more clearly, what shall we say? That God is unjust in bringing his wrath on us? (I am using a human argument.) ⁶Certainly not! If that were so, how could God judge the world? ⁷Someone might argue, "If my falsehood enhances God's truthfulness and so increases his glory, why am I still condemned as a sinner?" ⁸Why not say—as we are being slanderously reported as saying and as some claim that we say—"Let us do evil that good may result"? Their condemnation is deserved.

No One Is Righteous

⁹What shall we conclude then? Are we any better^d? Not at all! We have already made the charge that Jews and Gentiles alike are all under sin. ¹⁰As it is written:

"There is no one righteous, not even one;
¹¹   there is no one who understands,
        no one who seeks God.
¹²All have turned away,
        they have together become worthless;
    there is no one who does good,
        not even one."^e
¹³"Their throats are open graves;
        their tongues practice deceit."^f
    "The poison of vipers is on their lips."^g
¹⁴   "Their mouths are full of cursing and bitterness."^h
¹⁵"Their feet are swift to shed blood;
¹⁶   ruin and misery mark their ways,
¹⁷and the way of peace they do not know."ⁱ
¹⁸   "There is no fear of God before their eyes."^j

¹⁹Now we know that whatever the law says, it says to those who are under the law,

so that every mouth may be silenced and the whole world held accountable to God. [20]Therefore no one will be declared righteous in his sight by observing the law; rather, through the law we become conscious of sin.

Righteousness Through Faith

[21]But now a righteousness from God, apart from law, has been made known, to which the Law and the Prophets testify. [22]This righteousness from God comes through faith in Jesus Christ to all who believe. There is no difference, [23]for all have sinned and fall short of the glory of God, [24]and are justified freely by his grace through the redemption that came by Christ Jesus. [25]God presented him as a sacrifice of atonement,[a] through faith in his blood. He did this to demonstrate his justice, because in his forbearance he had left the sins committed beforehand unpunished— [26]he did it to demonstrate his justice at the present time, so as to be just and the one who justifies those who have faith in Jesus.

[27]Where, then, is boasting? It is excluded. On what principle? On that of observing the law? No, but on that of faith. [28]For we maintain that a man is justified by faith apart from observing the law. [29]Is God the God of Jews only? Is he not the God of Gentiles too? Yes, of Gentiles too, [30]since there is only one God, who will justify the circumcised by faith and the uncircumcised through that same faith. [31]Do we, then, nullify the law by this faith? Not at all! Rather, we uphold the law.

Abraham Justified by Faith

4 What then shall we say that Abraham, our forefather, discovered in this matter? [2]If, in fact, Abraham was justified by works, he had something to boast about— but not before God. [3]What does the Scripture say? "Abraham believed God, and it was credited to him as righteousness."[b]

[4]Now when a man works, his wages are not credited to him as a gift, but as an obligation. [5]However, to the man who does not work but trusts God who justifies the wicked, his faith is credited as righteousness. [6]David says the same thing when he speaks of the blessedness of the man to whom God credits righteousness apart from works:

[7]"Blessed are they

whose transgressions are forgiven,
  whose sins are covered.
[8]Blessed is the man
  whose sin the Lord will never count
    against him."[c]

[9]Is this blessedness only for the circumcised, or also for the uncircumcised? We have been saying that Abraham's faith was credited to him as righteousness. [10]Under what circumstances was it credited? Was it after he was circumcised, or before? It was not after, but before! [11]And he received the sign of circumcision, a seal of the righteousness that he had by faith while he was still uncircumcised. So then, he is the father of all who believe but have not been circumcised, in order that righteousness might be credited to them. [12]And he is also the father of the circumcised who not only are circumcised but who also walk in the footsteps of the faith that our father Abraham had before he was circumcised.

[13]It was not through law that Abraham and his offspring received the promise that he would be heir of the world, but through the righteousness that comes by faith. [14]For if those who live by law are heirs, faith has no value and the promise is worthless, [15]because law brings wrath. And where there is no law there is no transgression.

[16]Therefore, the promise comes by faith, so that it may be by grace and may be guaranteed to all Abraham's offspring— not only to those who are of the law but also to those who are of the faith of Abraham. He is the father of us all. [17]As it is written: "I have made you a father of many nations."[d] He is our father in the sight of God, in whom he believed— the God who gives life to the dead and calls things that are not as though they were.

[18]Against all hope, Abraham in hope believed and so became the father of many nations, just as it had been said to him, "So shall your offspring be."[e] [19]Without weakening in his faith, he faced the fact that his body was as good as dead— since he was about a hundred years old— and that Sarah's womb was also dead. [20]Yet he did not waver through unbelief regarding the promise of God, but was strengthened in his faith and gave glory to God, [21]being fully persuaded that God had power to do what he had promised. [22]This is why "it was credited to him as righteousness." [23]The words "it was

---

a25 Or *as the one who would turn aside his wrath, taking away sin*   *b3* Gen. 15:6; also in verse 22
c8 Psalm 32:1,2   *d17* Gen. 17:5   *e18* Gen. 15:5

THE RIGHT WAY TO GET RID OF GUILT   □ MONDAY

J enny has been struggling all week with guilty feelings over getting much too physical with her boyfriend last Saturday night. But notice what she's doing now. She's talking with God about her guilt; she's looking to him for forgiveness.

Notice also all the things Jenny is *not* doing to end her guilt— she isn't trying to pay for her own sins; she isn't seeking to earn forgiveness; she isn't attempting to explain away her failure; and she isn't blaming anyone else.

Afterward, Jenny doesn't feel forgiven, but she believes that she is, based on the promises of God's Word.

Look It Up
••••

If you're about to wilt because of guilt, Jenny's actions are worth another look:

1. Admit your sin (Hosea 5:15). You must be willing to face up to your guilt and take full responsibility for your actions and attitudes.

2. Believe that God is willing to forgive you. "If we confess our sins, he is faithful and just and will forgive us our sins and purify us from all unrighteousness" (1 John 1:9).

3. Renew your commitment to obey God. "Now make confession to the LORD, the God of your fathers, and do his will" (Ezra 10:11).

Think It Through
••••

Let's repeat an important point: You cannot remove your own guilt. Lady Macbeth (of Shakespearean fame) couldn't. Pontius Pilate also tried (and failed) to wash his hands of the blood of Christ and clear his guilty conscience (Matthew 27:24–26).

Is it really possible that Jenny has found forgiveness, even though she doesn't feel forgiven?

Work It Out
••••

If you have never trusted Jesus Christ to forgive your sins, you stand "guilty" before a holy God. But there is a way you can be declared "not guilty." Carefully (and prayerfully) go to God with your guilt. Admit that you need him, through the blood of Jesus Christ, to cover your guilt. Tell him you want to live for him and in obedience to him from now on.

Or perhaps you already have trusted Christ as your Savior (that is, you already are a Christian), but you haven't been living like a child of God. If that is the case, acknowledge your disobedience to God, claim the forgiveness you enjoy in Christ, and trust him for the power to "live a new life" (Romans 6:4).

Nail It Down
••••

Read the story of sin, guilt and forgiveness in Romans 3:21–31.

Turn to pages 6, 565 and 957 for other readings on guilt.
Turn to page 1215 for Tuesday's reading.

Topic
••••

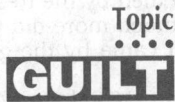

GUILT

credited to him" were written not for him alone, **24**but also for us, to whom God will credit righteousness — for us who believe in him who raised Jesus our Lord from the dead. **25**He was delivered over to death for our sins and was raised to life for our justification.

Peace and Joy

5 Therefore, since we have been justified through faith, we*a* have peace with God through our Lord Jesus Christ, **2**through whom we have gained access by faith into this grace in which we now stand. And we*a* rejoice in the hope of the glory of God. **3**Not only so, but we*a* also rejoice in our sufferings, because we know that suffering produces perseverance; **4**perseverance, character; and character, hope. **5**And hope does not disappoint us, because God has poured out his love into our hearts by the Holy Spirit, whom he has given us.

6You see, at just the right time, when we were still powerless, Christ died for the ungodly. **7**Very rarely will anyone die for a righteous man, though for a good man someone might possibly dare to die. **8**But God demonstrates his own love for us in this: While we were still sinners, Christ died for us.

9Since we have now been justified by his blood, how much more shall we be saved from God's wrath through him! **10**For if, when we were God's enemies, we were reconciled to him through the death of his Son, how much more, having been reconciled, shall we be saved through his life! **11**Not only is this so, but we also rejoice in God through our Lord Jesus Christ, through whom we have now received reconciliation.

Death Through Adam, Life Through Christ

12Therefore, just as sin entered the world through one man, and death through sin, and in this way death came to all men, because all sinned — **13**for before the law was given, sin was in the world. But sin is not taken into account when there is no law. **14**Nevertheless, death reigned from the time of Adam to the time of Moses, even over those who did not sin by breaking a command, as did Adam, who was a pattern of the one to come.

15But the gift is not like the trespass. For if the many died by the trespass of the one man, how much more did God's grace and the gift that came by the grace of the one

man, Jesus Christ, overflow to the many! **16**Again, the gift of God is not like the result of the one man's sin: The judgment followed one sin and brought condemnation, but the gift followed many trespasses and brought justification. **17**For if, by the trespass of the one man, death reigned through that one man, how much more will those who receive God's abundant provision of grace and of the gift of righteousness reign in life through the one man, Jesus Christ.

18Consequently, just as the result of one trespass was condemnation for all men, so also the result of one act of righteousness was justification that brings life for all men. **19**For just as through the disobedience of the one man the many were made sinners, so also through the obedience of the one man the many will be made righteous.

20The law was added so that the trespass might increase. But where sin increased, grace increased all the more, **21**so that, just as sin reigned in death, so also grace might reign through righteousness to bring eternal life through Jesus Christ our Lord.

Dead to Sin, Alive in Christ

6 What shall we say, then? Shall we go on sinning so that grace may increase? **2**By no means! We died to sin; how can we live in it any longer? **3**Or don't you know that all of us who were baptized into Christ Jesus were baptized into his death? **4**We were therefore buried with him through baptism into death in order that, just as Christ was raised from the dead through the glory of the Father, we too may live a new life.

5If we have been united with him like this in his death, we will certainly also be united with him in his resurrection. **6**For we know that our old self was crucified with him so that the body of sin might be done away with,*b* that we should no longer be slaves to sin — **7**because anyone who has died has been freed from sin.

8Now if we died with Christ, we believe that we will also live with him. **9**For we know that since Christ was raised from the dead, he cannot die again; death no longer has mastery over him. **10**The death he died, he died to sin once for all; but the life he lives, he lives to God.

11In the same way, count yourselves dead to sin but alive to God in Christ Jesus. **12**Therefore do not let sin reign in your mortal body so that you obey its evil desires. **13**Do not offer the parts of your body to sin,

---

a 1,2,3 Or *let us*   *b 6* Or *be rendered powerless*

THE SOURCE OF LOVE

Meet Randy, seventeen, who has one year of high school left. Randy plans to go to the state university next fall and major in accounting. He says it's because accountants make a lot of money. But the truth (and maybe he doesn't even realize it) is that he's trying to earn approval from his workaholic father (who's an accountant for a big firm).

Randy's pretty normal. He just wants to be loved and accepted. The best way for him to find what he's looking for would be for him to go to Love U. and sit in on course 101: The Source of Love.

Look It Up
• • • •

It's not wrong to want to be loved and accepted. The problem comes when you go looking for love in the wrong places. You need to go right to the source—the God of the universe. Why? Because:

• His very nature is love: "God is love" (1 John 4:16).
• His love never stops. (Note that the phrase "his love endures forever" occurs twenty-six times in Psalm 136!)
• He alone is able to give you the ability to love: "But the fruit of the Spirit is love" (Galatians 5:22).

Think It Through
• • • •

Imagine this scenario: You're lost in a hot, dry desert. You encounter some other wanderers sitting around a dusty riverbed trying to quench their thirst with a tiny trickle of water. A man comes over a dune and shouts, "Hey, if you'll follow that trickle a few miles east, you'll find a giant spring of refreshing cool water!"

Which would make more sense: to settle for a few drops or to go to the source and have all the water you could ever want?

Work It Out
• • • •

Everyone craves love and acceptance. But no human love—from parents, family or friends—can ever completely satisfy your deepest needs. Only God's love is perfect and able to truly meet your needs. That's the first lesson to learn at Love U.

Assignment Time: If you're feeling unloved just now, take a quick dip in the refreshing waters of God's Word. Splash around in these verses for a few minutes: Romans 8:35–39; Ephesians 3:17–19; 1 John 4:7–21.

When it comes to love, there's no one like the God who is love. He created you. He redeemed you. He left you his written instructions in the Bible. He will one day resurrect you to live in a perfect world.

No doubt about it: Jesus is the world's greatest example of true love.

Nail It Down
• • • •

Read about Jesus' ultimate act of love for you in Romans 5:8.

Turn to pages 1153, 1250 and 1313 for other readings on love.
Turn to page 1217 for Wednesday's reading.

Topic
• • • •
LOVE

as instruments of wickedness, but rather offer yourselves to God, as those who have been brought from death to life; and offer the parts of your body to him as instruments of righteousness. **14**For sin shall not be your master, because you are not under law, but under grace.

Slaves to Righteousness

15What then? Shall we sin because we are not under law but under grace? By no means! **16**Don't you know that when you offer yourselves to someone to obey him as slaves, you are slaves to the one whom you obey—whether you are slaves to sin, which leads to death, or to obedience, which leads to righteousness? **17**But thanks be to God that, though you used to be slaves to sin, you wholeheartedly obeyed the form of teaching to which you were entrusted. **18**You have been set free from sin and have become slaves to righteousness.

19I put this in human terms because you are weak in your natural selves. Just as you used to offer the parts of your body in slavery to impurity and to ever-increasing wickedness, so now offer them in slavery to righteousness leading to holiness. **20**When you were slaves to sin, you were free from the control of righteousness. **21**What benefit did you reap at that time from the things you are now ashamed of? Those things result in death! **22**But now that you have been set free from sin and have become slaves to God, the benefit you reap leads to holiness, and the result is eternal life. **23**For the wages of sin is death, but the gift of God is eternal life in*a* Christ Jesus our Lord.

An Illustration From Marriage

7 Do you not know, brothers—for I am speaking to men who know the law—that the law has authority over a man only as long as he lives? **2**For example, by law a married woman is bound to her husband as long as he is alive, but if her husband dies, she is released from the law of marriage. **3**So then, if she marries another man while her husband is still alive, she is called an adulteress. But if her husband dies, she is released from that law and is not an adulteress, even though she marries another man.

4So, my brothers, you also died to the law through the body of Christ, that you might belong to another, to him who was raised from the dead, in order that we might bear fruit to God. **5**For when we were controlled by the sinful nature,*b* the sinful passions aroused by the law were at work in our bodies, so that we bore fruit for death. **6**But now, by dying to what once bound us, we have been released from the law so that we serve in the new way of the Spirit, and not in the old way of the written code.

Struggling With Sin

7What shall we say, then? Is the law sin? Certainly not! Indeed I would not have known what sin was except through the law. For I would not have known what coveting really was if the law had not said, "Do not covet."*c* **8**But sin, seizing the opportunity afforded by the commandment, produced in me every kind of covetous desire. For apart from law, sin is dead. **9**Once I was alive apart from law; but when the commandment came, sin sprang to life and I died. **10**I found that the very commandment that was intended to bring life actually brought death. **11**For sin, seizing the opportunity afforded by the commandment, deceived me, and through the commandment put me to death. **12**So then, the law is holy, and the commandment is holy, righteous and good.

13Did that which is good, then, become death to me? By no means! But in order that sin might be recognized as sin, it produced death in me through what was good, so that through the commandment sin might become utterly sinful.

14We know that the law is spiritual; but I am unspiritual, sold as a slave to sin. **15**I do not understand what I do. For what I want to do I do not do, but what I hate I do. **16**And if I do what I do not want to do, I agree that the law is good. **17**As it is, it is no longer I myself who do it, but it is sin living in me. **18**I know that nothing good lives in me, that is, in my sinful nature.*d* For I have the desire to do what is good, but I cannot carry it out. **19**For what I do is not the good I want to do; no, the evil I do not want to do—this I keep on doing. **20**Now if I do what I do not want to do, it is no longer I who do it, but it is sin living in me that does it.

21So I find this law at work: When I want to do good, evil is right there with me. **22**For in my inner being I delight in God's law; **23**but I see another law at work in the members of my body, waging war against the law of my mind and making me a prisoner of the law of sin at work within my members. **24**What a wretched man I am! Who will rescue me from this body of death? **25**Thanks

PIE IN THE SKY WHEN YOU DIE?

☐ WEDNESDAY

• •

Does this sound familiar?
Erin, a sixteen-year-old sophomore, says: "Okay, I became a Christian about a year ago. And the speaker there said if you have Jesus in your heart that means you get eternal life. I always thought it meant that when you die you go to heaven. But I heard some preacher on TV the other day say that God gives you eternal life right now. How can you have eternal life right now without dying and going to heaven?"

Look It Up
• • • •

Actually, Erin, you and the TV preacher are both right. Eternal life means that when you die you go to be with the Lord in heaven (2 Corinthians 5:8). And it also refers to a new quality of life that you enjoy here and now.

"Father . . . you granted [your son] authority over all people that he might give eternal life to all those you have given him. Now this is eternal life: that they may know you, the only true God, and Jesus Christ, whom you have sent" (John 17:1–3).

Do you understand what Jesus was saying? Eternal life isn't so much about quantity as it is about quality. It means knowing God. It means having a relationship with the Creator of the universe, now and forever.

Think It Through
• • • •

Eternal life begins the moment you put your faith in Christ. It means a rich, satisfying relationship right now (John 10:10). It also means a future home in heaven (John 14:2–3).

Are you experiencing eternal life right now?

Work It Out
• • • •

Don't sit around thinking, "When I die, I'll get to have eternal life. Won't that be great?" Know God and enjoy eternal life right now. How?

Be clean. Are there sins you need to confess to God? This is the crucial first step to a deeper relationship with the Lord.

Be communicative. Relationships can only be good when there is close communication. That means talking and listening. Let God speak to you by jotting down a couple of Bible verses on an index card. Take the card to school and look at it throughout the day.

Be consistent. Knowing God is a lifelong process. Plan to meet with him every morning or every night. Make knowing him your top priority.

Nail It Down
• • • •

Memorize Romans 6:23.

Turn to pages 951, 1160, 1164, 1167 and 1319 for other readings on real life.
Turn to page 1219 for Thursday's reading.

Topic
• • • •

REAL LIFE

be to God—through Jesus Christ our Lord!

So then, I myself in my mind am a slave to God's law, but in the sinful nature a slave to the law of sin.

Life Through the Spirit

8 Therefore, there is now no condemnation for those who are in Christ Jesus,[a] ²because through Christ Jesus the law of the Spirit of life set me free from the law of sin and death. ³For what the law was powerless to do in that it was weakened by the sinful nature,[b] God did by sending his own Son in the likeness of sinful man to be a sin offering.[c] And so he condemned sin in sinful man,[d] ⁴in order that the righteous requirements of the law might be fully met in us, who do not live according to the sinful nature but according to the Spirit.

⁵Those who live according to the sinful nature have their minds set on what that nature desires; but those who live in accordance with the Spirit have their minds set on what the Spirit desires. ⁶The mind of sinful man[e] is death, but the mind controlled by the Spirit is life and peace; ⁷the sinful mind[f] is hostile to God. It does not submit to God's law, nor can it do so. ⁸Those controlled by the sinful nature cannot please God.

⁹You, however, are controlled not by the sinful nature but by the Spirit, if the Spirit of God lives in you. And if anyone does not have the Spirit of Christ, he does not belong to Christ. ¹⁰But if Christ is in you, your body is dead because of sin, yet your spirit is alive because of righteousness. ¹¹And if the Spirit of him who raised Jesus from the dead is living in you, he who raised Christ from the dead will also give life to your mortal bodies through his Spirit, who lives in you.

¹²Therefore, brothers, we have an obligation—but it is not to the sinful nature, to live according to it. ¹³For if you live according to the sinful nature, you will die; but if by the Spirit you put to death the misdeeds of the body, you will live, ¹⁴because those who are led by the Spirit of God are sons of God. ¹⁵For you did not receive a spirit that makes you a slave again to fear, but you received the Spirit of sonship.[g] And by him we cry, "Abba,[h] Father." ¹⁶The Spirit himself testifies with our spirit that we are God's children. ¹⁷Now if we are children, then we are heirs—heirs of God and co-heirs with Christ, if indeed we share in his sufferings in order that we may also share in his glory.

Future Glory

¹⁸I consider that our present sufferings are not worth comparing with the glory that will be revealed in us. ¹⁹The creation waits in eager expectation for the sons of God to be revealed. ²⁰For the creation was subjected to frustration, not by its own choice, but by the will of the one who subjected it, in hope ²¹that[i] the creation itself will be liberated from its bondage to decay and brought into the glorious freedom of the children of God.

²²We know that the whole creation has been groaning as in the pains of childbirth right up to the present time. ²³Not only so, but we ourselves, who have the firstfruits of the Spirit, groan inwardly as we wait eagerly for our adoption as sons, the redemption of our bodies. ²⁴For in this hope we were saved. But hope that is seen is no hope at all. Who hopes for what he already has? ²⁵But if we hope for what we do not yet have, we wait for it patiently.

²⁶In the same way, the Spirit helps us in our weakness. We do not know what we ought to pray for, but the Spirit himself intercedes for us with groans that words cannot express. ²⁷And he who searches our hearts knows the mind of the Spirit, because the Spirit intercedes for the saints in accordance with God's will.

More Than Conquerors

²⁸And we know that in all things God works for the good of those who love him,[j] who[k] have been called according to his purpose. ²⁹For those God foreknew he also predestined to be conformed to the likeness of his Son, that he might be the firstborn among many brothers. ³⁰And those he predestined, he also called; those he called, he also justified; those he justified, he also glorified.

³¹What, then, shall we say in response to this? If God is for us, who can be against us? ³²He who did not spare his own Son, but

---

a1 Some later manuscripts *Jesus, who do not live according to the sinful nature but according to the Spirit,* *b3* Or *the flesh;* also in verses 4, 5, 8, 9, 12 and 13   *c3* Or *man, for sin*   *d3* Or *in the flesh*   *e6* Or *mind set on the flesh*   *f7* Or *the mind set on the flesh*   *g15* Or *adoption*   *h15* Aramaic for *Father*   *i20,21* Or *subjected it in hope. ²¹For*   *j28* Some manuscripts *And we know that all things work together for good to those who love God*   *k28* Or *works together with those who love him to bring about what is good—with those who*

STRESS CAN RESULT IN THE BEST

Melinda was horrified when she learned that her dad had been transferred and the family was moving away from the town where she had lived all her life. Now, nine months later, she's finally beginning to see that the situation may not be so horrible after all. She comments:

"The move was so hard. We were all totally bummed out at first. But what could we do? We had to lean on each other—and especially on God.

"I still miss my friends. But, I'm meeting some great people here too, and I'm actually starting to like this place. My family is closer, and God is a bigger part of our lives now."

Look It Up
••••

It's important to remember that since God is in control, stressful circumstances can have positive results. For example, stress can:

1. Bring about real character in your life. "When he has tested me, I will come forth as gold" (Job 23:10).

2. Cause you to have a closer walk with Christ (2 Corinthians 12:7–10).

3. Provide opportunities for you to be a good example to others. "In spite of severe suffering, you welcomed the message with the joy given by the Holy Spirit. And so you became a model to all the believers in Macedonia and Achaia" (1 Thessalonians 1:6–7).

4. Result in future reward. "For our light and momentary troubles are achieving for us an eternal glory that far outweighs them all" (2 Corinthians 4:17).

Think It Through
••••

Exactly how do hard times produce character in your life? Do you turn to Christ when the pressures rise in your life? In your most recent stressful situation, how good an example were you to others? Do you really believe God gives future glory for those who patiently endure present difficulties?

Work It Out
••••

If you find yourself in a stressful situation right now, quit focusing on your negative circumstances. Ask God to show you the positive possibilities instead.

Memorize one of the verses cited in today's "Look It Up" section. Quote that verse to yourself every time you're tempted to forget that God is in control of the stresses in your life.

Nail It Down
••••

Read the promise in Romans 8:28.

Turn to pages 546, 778, 1058 and 1280 for other readings on stress.
Turn to page 1220 for Friday's reading.

Topic
••••

ARE YOU BECOMING LIKE CHRIST?

Terrance would like to become a millionaire.
Albert wants to become a famous singer.
Nerine's hero is the president of the United States.
Julia admires a favorite female talk show mediator and wants to be just like her someday.
Kenitra has a different goal: to become like Jesus Christ.

Look It Up
••••

The apostle Paul understood that God's desire is to make us like his Son. And so Paul wrote his purpose, his goal:
"I want to know Christ and the power of his resurrection and the fellowship of sharing in his sufferings, becoming like him in his death, and so, somehow, to attain to the resurrection from the dead.
"Not that I have already obtained all this, or have already been made perfect, but I press on to take hold of that for which Christ Jesus took hold of me. Brothers, I do not consider myself yet to have taken hold of it. But one thing I do: Forgetting what is behind and straining toward what is ahead, I press on toward the goal to win the prize for which God has called me heavenward in Christ Jesus" (Philippians 3:10–14).

Think It Through
••••

God gives us different abilities and desires, and he calls us into different arenas of service. Whether you sing, go into business, run for office, preach—whatever you do—don't forget his ultimate purpose: to make you like his Son.
Are you like clay (which can be molded into something new) or like hardened pottery (which has to be broken to be changed)?

Work It Out
••••

Pick one of these projects and go for it.
1. Find out how some of your friends see you. Ask them, "Based on how I live, what would you say is my purpose in life?"
2. Look up the word *purpose* in the dictionary.
3. Spend five minutes imagining what your life would be like if you were more like Christ. What specific changes would you see?
4. Discuss with some friends what 1 John 3:2 means.
5. Think of a loving act that Christ might do if he were in your shoes. Do it in the power of the Holy Spirit.

Nail It Down
••••

Read and consider the message of Romans 8:29.

Turn to pages 502, 1102 and 1158 for other readings on purpose.
Turn to page 1222 for the weekend reading.

Topic
••••

PURPOSE

gave him up for us all — how will he not also, along with him, graciously give us all things? [33]Who will bring any charge against those whom God has chosen? It is God who justifies. [34]Who is he that condemns? Christ Jesus, who died — more than that, who was raised to life — is at the right hand of God and is also interceding for us. [35]Who shall separate us from the love of Christ? Shall trouble or hardship or persecution or famine or nakedness or danger or sword? [36]As it is written:

> "For your sake we face death all day long;
> we are considered as sheep to be slaughtered."[a]

[37]No, in all these things we are more than conquerors through him who loved us. [38]For I am convinced that neither death nor life, neither angels nor demons,[b] neither the present nor the future, nor any powers, [39]neither height nor depth, nor anything else in all creation, will be able to separate us from the love of God that is in Christ Jesus our Lord.

God's Sovereign Choice

9 I speak the truth in Christ — I am not lying, my conscience confirms it in the Holy Spirit — [2]I have great sorrow and unceasing anguish in my heart. [3]For I could wish that I myself were cursed and cut off from Christ for the sake of my brothers, those of my own race, [4]the people of Israel. Theirs is the adoption as sons; theirs the divine glory, the covenants, the receiving of the law, the temple worship and the promises. [5]Theirs are the patriarchs, and from them is traced the human ancestry of Christ, who is God over all, forever praised![c] Amen.

[6]It is not as though God's word had failed. For not all who are descended from Israel are Israel. [7]Nor because they are his descendants are they all Abraham's children. On the contrary, "It is through Isaac that your offspring will be reckoned."[d] [8]In other words, it is not the natural children who are God's children, but it is the children of the promise who are regarded as Abraham's offspring. [9]For this was how the promise was stated: "At the appointed time I will return, and Sarah will have a son."[e]

[10]Not only that, but Rebekah's children had one and the same father, our father Isaac. [11]Yet, before the twins were born or had done anything good or bad — in order that God's purpose in election might stand: [12]not by works but by him who calls — she was told, "The older will serve the younger."[f] [13]Just as it is written: "Jacob I loved, but Esau I hated."[g]

[14]What then shall we say? Is God unjust? Not at all! [15]For he says to Moses,

> "I will have mercy on whom I have mercy,
> and I will have compassion on whom I have compassion."[h]

[16]It does not, therefore, depend on man's desire or effort, but on God's mercy. [17]For the Scripture says to Pharaoh: "I raised you up for this very purpose, that I might display my power in you and that my name might be proclaimed in all the earth."[i] [18]Therefore God has mercy on whom he wants to have mercy, and he hardens whom he wants to harden.

[19]One of you will say to me: "Then why does God still blame us? For who resists his will?" [20]But who are you, O man, to talk back to God? "Shall what is formed say to him who formed it, 'Why did you make me like this?'"[j] [21]Does not the potter have the right to make out of the same lump of clay some pottery for noble purposes and some for common use?

[22]What if God, choosing to show his wrath and make his power known, bore with great patience the objects of his wrath — prepared for destruction? [23]What if he did this to make the riches of his glory known to the objects of his mercy, whom he prepared in advance for glory — [24]even us, whom he also called, not only from the Jews but also from the Gentiles? [25]As he says in Hosea:

> "I will call them 'my people' who are not my people;
> and I will call her 'my loved one' who is not my loved one,"[k]

[26]and,

> "It will happen that in the very place where it was said to them,
> 'You are not my people,'
> they will be called 'sons of the living God.' "[l]

---

[a]36 Psalm 44:22   [b]38 Or *nor heavenly rulers*   [c]5 Or *Christ, who is over all. God be forever praised!* Or *Christ. God who is over all be forever praised!*   [d]7 Gen. 21:12   [e]9 Gen. 18:10,14   [f]12 Gen. 25:23   [g]13 Mal. 1:2,3   [h]15 Exodus 33:19   [i]17 Exodus 9:16   [j]20 Isaiah 29:16; 45:9   [k]25 Hosea 2:23   [l]26 Hosea 1:10

A LESSON ON LONELINESS

• •

**Work It
Out**
• • • •

Have you ever been in a huge crowd of people—perhaps at a concert or a sporting event or with a bunch of friends at the mall—and suddenly felt isolated? All alone? Terribly lonely?

Everyone struggles with loneliness at one time or another. Some people constantly fight feelings of loneliness; others only occasionally feel alone.

Whenever you feel lonely, remember the words of Romans 8:38–39. Even when you feel deserted by friends and family, even when teachers and pastors and co-workers have let you down, God is there. Nothing will ever separate you from him. So whenever you feel desperately alone, go to God, your first and your ultimate cure for loneliness.

**Nail It
Down**
• • • •

Read the promise in Romans 8:38–39.

• •

**Think It
Through**
• • • •

Don't feel guilty about feeling alone. It's part of living in a sinful world. Do something about it instead. Here are a few suggestions to help reduce the lonely feelings in your life:

• Tell God about it. He already has a good idea how you feel, but telling him will help relieve the hurt inside you.

• Get to know God better. Read his Word and pray. He has enough love and compassion for you to deal with any loneliness you might experience.

• Fill your life with good activities. Form relationships with other Christians, people who are kind and fun to be with. Reach out and help someone who has a need. Get involved in energetic physical activity.

• If you still feel lonely, seek out a pastor or counselor to help you.

**Nail It
Down**
• • • •

Memorize Romans 8:38–39. For further insight read Psalm 68:5–6.

**Turn to pages 5, 816 and 1047 for other readings on loneliness.
Turn to page 1225 for Monday's reading.**

Topic
• • • •

LONELINESS

27Isaiah cries out concerning Israel:

"Though the number of the Israelites be
    like the sand by the sea,
only the remnant will be saved.
28For the Lord will carry out
    his sentence on earth with speed and
    finality."*a*

29It is just as Isaiah said previously:

"Unless the Lord Almighty
    had left us descendants,
we would have become like Sodom,
    we would have been like
    Gomorrah."*b*

Israel's Unbelief

30What then shall we say? That the Gentiles, who did not pursue righteousness, have obtained it, a righteousness that is by faith; **31**but Israel, who pursued a law of righteousness, has not attained it. **32**Why not? Because they pursued it not by faith but as if it were by works. They stumbled over the "stumbling stone." **33**As it is written:

"See, I lay in Zion a stone that causes
    men to stumble
and a rock that makes them fall,
and the one who trusts in him will
    never be put to shame."*c*

10 Brothers, my heart's desire and prayer to God for the Israelites is that they may be saved. **2**For I can testify about them that they are zealous for God, but their zeal is not based on knowledge. **3**Since they did not know the righteousness that comes from God and sought to establish their own, they did not submit to God's righteousness. **4**Christ is the end of the law so that there may be righteousness for everyone who believes.

5Moses describes in this way the righteousness that is by the law: "The man who does these things will live by them."*d* **6**But the righteousness that is by faith says: "Do not say in your heart, 'Who will ascend into heaven?'*e*" (that is, to bring Christ down) **7**"or 'Who will descend into the deep?'*f*" (that is, to bring Christ up from the dead). **8**But what does it say? "The word is near you; it is in your mouth and in your heart,"*g* that is, the word of faith we are proclaiming: **9**That if you confess with your mouth, "Jesus is Lord," and believe in your heart that God raised him from the dead, you will be saved.

10For it is with your heart that you believe and are justified, and it is with your mouth that you confess and are saved. **11**As the Scripture says, "Anyone who trusts in him will never be put to shame."*h* **12**For there is no difference between Jew and Gentile—the same Lord is Lord of all and richly blesses all who call on him, **13**for, "Everyone who calls on the name of the Lord will be saved."*i*

14How, then, can they call on the one they have not believed in? And how can they believe in the one of whom they have not heard? And how can they hear without someone preaching to them? **15**And how can they preach unless they are sent? As it is written, "How beautiful are the feet of those who bring good news!"*j*

16But not all the Israelites accepted the good news. For Isaiah says, "Lord, who has believed our message?"*k* **17**Consequently, faith comes from hearing the message, and the message is heard through the word of Christ. **18**But I ask: Did they not hear? Of course they did:

"Their voice has gone out into all the
    earth,
their words to the ends of the
    world."*l*

19Again I ask: Did Israel not understand? First, Moses says,

"I will make you envious by those who
    are not a nation;
I will make you angry by a nation that
    has no understanding."*m*

20And Isaiah boldly says,

"I was found by those who did not seek
    me;
I revealed myself to those who did
    not ask for me."*n*

21But concerning Israel he says,

"All day long I have held out my hands
    to a disobedient and obstinate
    people."*o*

The Remnant of Israel

11 I ask then: Did God reject his people? By no means! I am an Israelite myself, a descendant of Abraham, from the tribe of Benjamin. **2**God did not reject his people, whom he foreknew. Don't you know what the Scripture says in the passage about

a28 Isaiah 10:22,23 *b29* Isaiah 1:9 *c33* Isaiah 8:14; 28:16 *d5* Lev. 18:5 *e6* Deut. 30:12
f7 Deut. 30:13 *g8* Deut. 30:14 *h11* Isaiah 28:16 *i13* Joel 2:32 *j15* Isaiah 52:7 *k16* Isaiah 53:1
l18 Psalm 19:4 *m19* Deut. 32:21 *n20* Isaiah 65:1 *o21* Isaiah 65:2

Elijah—how he appealed to God against Israel: [3]"Lord, they have killed your prophets and torn down your altars; I am the only one left, and they are trying to kill me"[a]? [4]And what was God's answer to him? "I have reserved for myself seven thousand who have not bowed the knee to Baal."[b] [5]So too, at the present time there is a remnant chosen by grace. [6]And if by grace, then it is no longer by works; if it were, grace would no longer be grace.[c]

[7]What then? What Israel sought so earnestly it did not obtain, but the elect did. The others were hardened, [8]as it is written:

"God gave them a spirit of stupor,
    eyes so that they could not see
    and ears so that they could not hear,
to this very day."[d]

[9]And David says:

"May their table become a snare and a
    trap,
    a stumbling block and a retribution
        for them.
[10]May their eyes be darkened so they
        cannot see,
    and their backs be bent forever."[e]

Ingrafted Branches

[11]Again I ask: Did they stumble so as to fall beyond recovery? Not at all! Rather, because of their transgression, salvation has come to the Gentiles to make Israel envious. [12]But if their transgression means riches for the world, and their loss means riches for the Gentiles, how much greater riches will their fullness bring!

[13]I am talking to you Gentiles. Inasmuch as I am the apostle to the Gentiles, I make much of my ministry [14]in the hope that I may somehow arouse my own people to envy and save some of them. [15]For if their rejection is the reconciliation of the world, what will their acceptance be but life from the dead? [16]If the part of the dough offered as firstfruits is holy, then the whole batch is holy; if the root is holy, so are the branches.

[17]If some of the branches have been broken off, and you, though a wild olive shoot, have been grafted in among the others and now share in the nourishing sap from the olive root, [18]do not boast over those branches. If you do, consider this: You do not support the root, but the root supports

you. [19]You will say then, "Branches were broken off so that I could be grafted in." [20]Granted. But they were broken off because of unbelief, and you stand by faith. Do not be arrogant, but be afraid. [21]For if God did not spare the natural branches, he will not spare you either.

[22]Consider therefore the kindness and sternness of God: sternness to those who fell, but kindness to you, provided that you continue in his kindness. Otherwise, you also will be cut off. [23]And if they do not persist in unbelief, they will be grafted in, for God is able to graft them in again. [24]After all, if you were cut out of an olive tree that is wild by nature, and contrary to nature were grafted into a cultivated olive tree, how much more readily will these, the natural branches, be grafted into their own olive tree!

All Israel Will Be Saved

[25]I do not want you to be ignorant of this mystery, brothers, so that you may not be conceited: Israel has experienced a hardening in part until the full number of the Gentiles has come in. [26]And so all Israel will be saved, as it is written:

"The deliverer will come from Zion;
    he will turn godlessness away from
        Jacob.
[27]And this is[f] my covenant with them
    when I take away their sins."[g]

[28]As far as the gospel is concerned, they are enemies on your account; but as far as election is concerned, they are loved on account of the patriarchs, [29]for God's gifts and his call are irrevocable. [30]Just as you who were at one time disobedient to God have now received mercy as a result of their disobedience, [31]so they too have now become disobedient in order that they too may now[h] receive mercy as a result of God's mercy to you. [32]For God has bound all men over to disobedience so that he may have mercy on them all.

Doxology

[33]Oh, the depth of the riches of the
        wisdom and[i] knowledge of God!
    How unsearchable his judgments,
        and his paths beyond tracing out!
[34]"Who has known the mind of the Lord?

---

[a]3 1 Kings 19:10,14   [b]4 1 Kings 19:18   [c]6 Some manuscripts by grace. But if by works, then it is no longer grace; if it were, work would no longer be work.   [d]8 Deut. 29:4; Isaiah 29:10   [e]10 Psalm 69:22,23   [f]27 Or will be   [g]27 Isaiah 59:20,21; 27:9; Jer. 31:33,34   [h]31 Some manuscripts do not have now.   [i]33 Or riches and the wisdom and the

EATING DISORDER DISCUSSION

On Saturday night six friends are eating together at McMurphy's, a very popular restaurant. What's going through the minds of two of the girls as they look at the menu?

Anorexic Caroline (all ninety-seven pounds of her) is thinking, "I really shouldn't eat. I'm just too fat."

Bulimic Rita (while feeling for the laxatives in her purse) is thinking that no matter what she eats, she can always get rid of it.

Look It Up
••••

Eating disorders are usually the result of:

Deception: In a shallow society that stresses outer appearance and says, "Without a beautiful body, you are worthless," we so easily forget that God stresses inner character (1 Samuel 16:7) and says, "Because you are specially created and deeply loved, you are priceless" (Psalm 139:13–16; 1 John 3:1).

Rejection: Some who fail to find acceptance (Romans 15:7) use eating disorders to try to gain approval, to get back at parents or to establish control over at least one part of their lives.

Obsession: Many young people with even mild eating disorders think constantly of food, food, food. To them the Bible says, "Life is more than food" (Luke 12:23). Often those with eating disorders think constantly about *self*. To them the Bible reminds, "Nobody should seek his own good, but the good of others" (1 Corinthians 10:24).

Think It Through
••••

Do you ever starve yourself because you think you're too fat (even though you're actually underweight)? Do you "binge and purge" (that is, overeat and then make yourself vomit what you've eaten)? Are you obsessed with weighing yourself and/or counting calories? Do you feel the need to exercise excessively?

Work It Out
••••

If you answered yes to any of those questions:

1. Share your secret today with a mature Christian whom you trust. Ask him or her to help you find the help you need. That brave step could be a major turning point and the first step toward a healthier, happier life.

2. With a Christian friend, list some Bible verses that will help transform your thinking regarding food, looks and your self-worth.

3. Memorize one of the verses from your list each night before going to sleep.

Nail It Down
••••

Read what God says about how you should view your body in Romans 12:1–2.

Turn to pages 146 and 188 for other readings on food.
Turn to page 1227 for Tuesday's reading.

Topic
••••

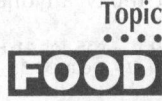
FOOD

Or who has been his counselor?"*a*
35"Who has ever given to God,
    that God should repay him?"*b*
36For from him and through him and to
    him are all things.
To him be the glory forever! Amen.

Living Sacrifices

12 Therefore, I urge you, brothers, in
view of God's mercy, to offer your
bodies as living sacrifices, holy and pleasing
to God—this is your spiritual*c* act of worship. 2Do not conform any longer to the pattern of this world, but be transformed by the
renewing of your mind. Then you will be
able to test and approve what God's will is—
his good, pleasing and perfect will.

3For by the grace given me I say to every
one of you: Do not think of yourself more
highly than you ought, but rather think of
yourself with sober judgment, in accordance with the measure of faith God has giv-
en you. 4Just as each of us has one body
with many members, and these members
do not all have the same function, 5so in
Christ we who are many form one body, and
each member belongs to all the others. 6We
have different gifts, according to the grace
given us. If a man's gift is prophesying, let
him use it in proportion to his*d* faith. 7If it
is serving, let him serve; if it is teaching, let
him teach; 8if it is encouraging, let him encourage; if it is contributing to the needs of
others, let him give generously; if it is leadership, let him govern diligently; if it is
showing mercy, let him do it cheerfully.

Love

9Love must be sincere. Hate what is evil;
cling to what is good. 10Be devoted to one
another in brotherly love. Honor one another above yourselves. 11Never be lacking in
zeal, but keep your spiritual fervor, serving
the Lord. 12Be joyful in hope, patient in affliction, faithful in prayer. 13Share with
God's people who are in need. Practice hospitality.

14Bless those who persecute you; bless
and do not curse. 15Rejoice with those who
rejoice; mourn with those who mourn.
16Live in harmony with one another. Do not
be proud, but be willing to associate with
people of low position.*e* Do not be conceited.

17Do not repay anyone evil for evil. Be

careful to do what is right in the eyes of everybody. 18If it is possible, as far as it depends on you, live at peace with everyone.
19Do not take revenge, my friends, but leave
room for God's wrath, for it is written: "It is
mine to avenge; I will repay,"*f* says the
Lord. 20On the contrary:

"If your enemy is hungry, feed him;
    if he is thirsty, give him something to
    drink.
In doing this, you will heap burning
    coals on his head."*g*

21Do not be overcome by evil, but overcome
evil with good.

Submission to the Authorities

13 Everyone must submit himself to
the governing authorities, for there
is no authority except that which God has
established. The authorities that exist have
been established by God. 2Consequently, he
who rebels against the authority is rebelling
against what God has instituted, and those
who do so will bring judgment on themselves. 3For rulers hold no terror for those
who do right, but for those who do wrong.
Do you want to be free from fear of the one
in authority? Then do what is right and he
will commend you. 4For he is God's servant
to do you good. But if you do wrong, be
afraid, for he does not bear the sword for
nothing. He is God's servant, an agent of
wrath to bring punishment on the wrongdoer. 5Therefore, it is necessary to submit to
the authorities, not only because of possible
punishment but also because of conscience.

6This is also why you pay taxes, for the
authorities are God's servants, who give
their full time to governing. 7Give everyone
what you owe him: If you owe taxes, pay
taxes; if revenue, then revenue; if respect,
then respect; if honor, then honor.

Love, for the Day Is Near

8Let no debt remain outstanding, except
the continuing debt to love one another, for
he who loves his fellowman has fulfilled the
law. 9The commandments, "Do not commit
adultery," "Do not murder," "Do not steal,"
"Do not covet,"*h* and whatever other commandment there may be, are summed up in
this one rule: "Love your neighbor as yourself."*i* 10Love does no harm to its neighbor.
Therefore love is the fulfillment of the law.

---

*a*34 Isaiah 40:13   *b*35 Job 41:11   *c*1 Or *reasonable
menial work*   *f*19 Deut. 32:35   *g*20 Prov. 25:21,22
*i*9 Lev. 19:18

*d*6 Or *in agreement with the*   *e*16 Or *willing to do*
*h*9 Exodus 20:13-15,17; Deut. 5:17-19,21

PEOPLE AND PROBLEMS PERFECT YOUR PATIENCE ☐ TUESDAY

●●

Friends can't believe how easygoing and laid-back fifteen-year-old Randall is.

He lives in a cramped apartment with three family members—his mom, his little brother and his grandfather (who suffers from Alzheimer's disease).

Because of the family's situation, Randall has to be at home much of the time. But he seldom complains.

"Man," says one classmate, "I'd go nuts in his situation—having to baby-sit all the time."

"I know," says another, "but the guy never seems to lose his cool. He's always smiling."

Look It Up ●●●●

Some Scriptural reminders for those who need to be:

Patient in trying times—"Consider it pure joy, my brothers, whenever you face trials of many kinds, because you know that the testing of your faith develops perseverance. Perseverance must finish its work so that you may be mature and complete, not lacking anything" (James 1:2–4).

Patient with trying people—"And we urge you, brothers, warn those who are idle, encourage the timid, help the weak, be patient with everyone" (1 Thessalonians 5:14).

Think It Through ●●●●

Look at it this way: For the rest of your life you will have to deal with irritating people. And for the rest of your life you will encounter frustrating situations beyond your control.

So you have a choice. You can ask God for a patient attitude and make the best of life's negative situations. Or you can get ticked and increase your anxiety level.

What's better—turmoil outside and inside? Or turmoil outside and peace inside?

Work It Out ●●●●

Make a list of the tough situations you currently face. Make a second list of the trying people with whom you must interact on a regular basis. Get a Christian friend to make similar lists. Then bat around these questions and statements:

1. What is God trying to teach me?
2. My current reaction to these situations/people is _____.
3. A better response would be to _____.
4. How can I make the most of each situation?

Nail It Down ●●●●

Read the wise advice in Romans 12:12.

Turn to pages 12, 58 and 85 for other readings on patience.
Turn to page 1228 for Wednesday's reading.

Topic
●●●●
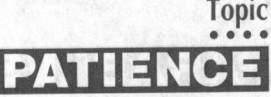

THE MARK OF A CHRISTIAN

Mark and Bill are at a big Memorial Day parade and celebration when they bump into a group of girls from school. One of the girls, Carla, is totally drunk and about to be sick. Gail asks the guys for help in getting Carla home.

Mark whispers to Bill, "Tell her to forget it. It's their own fault for getting drunk. Besides, we'll miss all the fun."

Bill can't believe it. "C'mon, Mark! Can't you see they need our help?"

Look It Up

Jesus told the story of the Good Samaritan when an expert in the Jewish law pretended not to understand the command to love your neighbor. "Who is my neighbor?" the man asked.

Jesus told about a Jew who was beaten and robbed while on a journey. Two Jewish leaders passed the wounded man and ignored him. Finally, a Samaritan traveler (Jews despised Samaritans because of their mixed ancestry) stopped and ministered to the man's needs.

After telling the story, Jesus asked the lawyer, " 'Which of these three do you think was a neighbor to the man who fell into the hands of robbers?'

"The expert in the law replied, 'The one who had mercy on him.'

"Jesus told him, 'Go and do likewise.' " (Luke 10:36–37).

Think It Through

Jesus was not teaching that good works make you right with God. He was saying that good works—such as being compassionate to those in need—result from being right with God. That's what a neighbor is—anyone with a need that another person sees and is able to meet.

Why are Christians often less compassionate and caring than non-Christians? What are some ways you could have been a neighbor yesterday?

Work It Out

There are all kinds of ways you can be a neighbor today. Get homework assignments for a sick friend who is absent from school. Hug or play with a little brother or sister who feels ignored. Assist someone whose car is stalled in traffic. Provide taxi service for an elderly person with no transportation. Donate blood for a person who is undergoing surgery. Take some canned goods and old clothes down to the Salvation Army.

And the ultimate way to be a neighbor? Show a non-Christian friend how he or she can know Christ and find love, forgiveness and a meaningful life.

Nail It Down

Read Romans 13:9–10 for a summary of what being a good neighbor means.

Turn to pages 932, 1098 and 1108 for other readings on parables.
Turn to page 1230 for Thursday's reading.

Topic

PARABLES

[11]And do this, understanding the present time. The hour has come for you to wake up from your slumber, because our salvation is nearer now than when we first believed. [12]The night is nearly over; the day is almost here. So let us put aside the deeds of darkness and put on the armor of light. [13]Let us behave decently, as in the daytime, not in orgies and drunkenness, not in sexual immorality and debauchery, not in dissension and jealousy. [14]Rather, clothe yourselves with the Lord Jesus Christ, and do not think about how to gratify the desires of the sinful nature.[a]

The Weak and the Strong

14 Accept him whose faith is weak, without passing judgment on disputable matters. [2]One man's faith allows him to eat everything, but another man, whose faith is weak, eats only vegetables. [3]The man who eats everything must not look down on him who does not, and the man who does not eat everything must not condemn the man who does, for God has accepted him. [4]Who are you to judge someone else's servant? To his own master he stands or falls. And he will stand, for the Lord is able to make him stand.

[5]One man considers one day more sacred than another; another man considers every day alike. Each one should be fully convinced in his own mind. [6]He who regards one day as special, does so to the Lord. He who eats meat, eats to the Lord, for he gives thanks to God; and he who abstains, does so to the Lord and gives thanks to God. [7]For none of us lives to himself alone and none of us dies to himself alone. [8]If we live, we live to the Lord; and if we die, we die to the Lord. So, whether we live or die, we belong to the Lord.

[9]For this very reason, Christ died and returned to life so that he might be the Lord of both the dead and the living. [10]You, then, why do you judge your brother? Or why do you look down on your brother? For we will all stand before God's judgment seat. [11]It is written:

" 'As surely as I live,' says the Lord,
'every knee will bow before me;
    every tongue will confess to God.' "[b]

[12]So then, each of us will give an account of himself to God.

[13]Therefore let us stop passing judgment on one another. Instead, make up your mind not to put any stumbling block or obstacle in your brother's way. [14]As one who is in the Lord Jesus, I am fully convinced that no food[c] is unclean in itself. But if anyone regards something as unclean, then for him it is unclean. [15]If your brother is distressed because of what you eat, you are no longer acting in love. Do not by your eating destroy your brother for whom Christ died. [16]Do not allow what you consider good to be spoken of as evil. [17]For the kingdom of God is not a matter of eating and drinking, but of righteousness, peace and joy in the Holy Spirit, [18]because anyone who serves Christ in this way is pleasing to God and approved by men.

[19]Let us therefore make every effort to do what leads to peace and to mutual edification. [20]Do not destroy the work of God for the sake of food. All food is clean, but it is wrong for a man to eat anything that causes someone else to stumble. [21]It is better not to eat meat or drink wine or to do anything else that will cause your brother to fall.

[22]So whatever you believe about these things keep between yourself and God. Blessed is the man who does not condemn himself by what he approves. [23]But the man who has doubts is condemned if he eats, because his eating is not from faith; and everything that does not come from faith is sin.

15 We who are strong ought to bear with the failings of the weak and not to please ourselves. [2]Each of us should please his neighbor for his good, to build him up. [3]For even Christ did not please himself but, as it is written: "The insults of those who insult you have fallen on me."[d] [4]For everything that was written in the past was written to teach us, so that through endurance and the encouragement of the Scriptures we might have hope.

[5]May the God who gives endurance and encouragement give you a spirit of unity among yourselves as you follow Christ Jesus, [6]so that with one heart and mouth you may glorify the God and Father of our Lord Jesus Christ.

[7]Accept one another, then, just as Christ accepted you, in order to bring praise to God. [8]For I tell you that Christ has become a servant of the Jews[e] on behalf of God's truth, to confirm the promises made to the patriarchs [9]so that the Gentiles may glorify God for his mercy, as it is written:

---

[a]14 Or *the flesh*   [b]11 Isaiah 45:23   [c]14 Or *that nothing*   [d]3 Psalm 69:9   [e]8 Greek *circumcision*

BUT WE'RE ON THE SAME TEAM

THURSDAY ☐

Church A and church B are not only in the same neighborhood, they're also part of the same religious denomination. You might expect them to work together on projects.

Well, think again. The truth is that the two churches act as if they're mortal enemies! If A launches a new ministry, B follows suit. If the youth group at B plans an event, the staff at A schedules something even bigger!

Look It Up

Hey, Christians! You are not in competition with each other. And you never have been.

"For when one says, 'I follow Paul,' and another, 'I follow Apollos,' are you not mere men?

"What, after all, is Apollos? And what is Paul? Only servants, through whom you came to believe—as the Lord has assigned to each his task. I planted the seed, Apollos watered it, but God made it grow. So neither he who plants nor he who waters is anything, but only God, who makes things grow . . . . For we are God's fellow workers" (1 Corinthians 3:4-7,9).

Think It Through

Think for a minute about what would happen to your body if its parts suddenly quit working together. A nerve decides, "Enough of this cooperation. I want all the attention on me!" Suddenly your whole body is screaming with pain.

Then your heart turns to your eyes and says, "I bet I can beat faster than you can blink." And off they go!

With every individual part doing its own thing, your body is soon in total chaos! You're incapable of functioning.

The same thing happens when members of the body of Christ compete instead of cooperate.

Work It Out

Work to create a spirit of cooperation among your Christian friends:
• Pray for unity (John 17:22-23).
• Reject the temptation to bad-mouth other believers or churches (1 Timothy 5:13).
• Reread Paul's words in 1 Corinthians 3, and note that the focus and goal of all Christians should be the same—bringing glory to God, not self.

Nail It Down

Notice that in Romans 13:13 dissension and jealousy are included in a list of very undesirable behaviors.

**Turn to pages 18, 43 and 1360 for other readings on competition.
Turn to page 1235 for Friday's reading.**

Topic

COMPETITION

"Therefore I will praise you among the
Gentiles;
I will sing hymns to your name."[a]

[10]Again, it says,

"Rejoice, O Gentiles, with his people."[b]

[11]And again,

"Praise the Lord, all you Gentiles,
and sing praises to him, all you
peoples."[c]

[12]And again, Isaiah says,

"The Root of Jesse will spring up,
one who will arise to rule over the
nations;
the Gentiles will hope in him."[d]

[13]May the God of hope fill you with all joy
and peace as you trust in him, so that you
may overflow with hope by the power of the
Holy Spirit.

Paul the Minister to the Gentiles

[14]I myself am convinced, my brothers,
that you yourselves are full of goodness,
complete in knowledge and competent to
instruct one another. [15]I have written you
quite boldly on some points, as if to remind
you of them again, because of the grace God
gave me [16]to be a minister of Christ Jesus to
the Gentiles with the priestly duty of proclaiming the gospel of God, so that the Gentiles might become an offering acceptable to
God, sanctified by the Holy Spirit.

[17]Therefore I glory in Christ Jesus in my
service to God. [18]I will not venture to speak
of anything except what Christ has accomplished through me in leading the Gentiles
to obey God by what I have said and done—
[19]by the power of signs and miracles,
through the power of the Spirit. So from Jerusalem all the way around to Illyricum, I
have fully proclaimed the gospel of Christ.
[20]It has always been my ambition to preach
the gospel where Christ was not known, so
that I would not be building on someone
else's foundation. [21]Rather, as it is written:

"Those who were not told about him
will see,
and those who have not heard will
understand."[e]

[22]This is why I have often been hindered
from coming to you.

Paul's Plan to Visit Rome

[23]But now that there is no more place for
me to work in these regions, and since I
have been longing for many years to see
you, [24]I plan to do so when I go to Spain. I
hope to visit you while passing through and
to have you assist me on my journey there,
after I have enjoyed your company for a
while. [25]Now, however, I am on my way to
Jerusalem in the service of the saints there.
[26]For Macedonia and Achaia were pleased
to make a contribution for the poor among
the saints in Jerusalem. [27]They were
pleased to do it, and indeed they owe it to
them. For if the Gentiles have shared in the
Jews' spiritual blessings, they owe it to the
Jews to share with them their material blessings. [28]So after I have completed this task
and have made sure that they have received
this fruit, I will go to Spain and visit you on
the way. [29]I know that when I come to you,
I will come in the full measure of the blessing of Christ.

[30]I urge you, brothers, by our Lord Jesus
Christ and by the love of the Spirit, to join
me in my struggle by praying to God for me.
[31]Pray that I may be rescued from the unbelievers in Judea and that my service in Jerusalem may be acceptable to the saints there,
[32]so that by God's will I may come to you
with joy and together with you be refreshed.
[33]The God of peace be with you all. Amen.

Personal Greetings

16 I commend to you our sister Phoe-
be, a servant[f] of the church in Cenchrea. [2]I ask you to receive her in the Lord
in a way worthy of the saints and to give her
any help she may need from you, for she
has been a great help to many people, including me.

[3]Greet Priscilla[g] and Aquila, my fellow
workers in Christ Jesus. [4]They risked
their lives for me. Not only I but all the
churches of the Gentiles are grateful to
them.
[5]Greet also the church that meets at their
house.
Greet my dear friend Epenetus, who was
the first convert to Christ in the province of Asia.
[6]Greet Mary, who worked very hard for
you.
[7]Greet Andronicus and Junias, my relatives
who have been in prison with me. They

---

[a]9 2 Samuel 22:50; Psalm 18:49   [b]10 Deut. 32:43   [c]11 Psalm 117:1   [d]12 Isaiah 11:10   [e]21 Isaiah 52:15
[f]1 Or deaconess   [g]3 Greek Prisca, a variant of Priscilla

are outstanding among the apostles, and they were in Christ before I was. [8]Greet Ampliatus, whom I love in the Lord. [9]Greet Urbanus, our fellow worker in Christ, and my dear friend Stachys. [10]Greet Apelles, tested and approved in Christ.

Greet those who belong to the household of Aristobulus. [11]Greet Herodion, my relative.

Greet those in the household of Narcissus who are in the Lord. [12]Greet Tryphena and Tryphosa, those women who work hard in the Lord.

Greet my dear friend Persis, another woman who has worked very hard in the Lord. [13]Greet Rufus, chosen in the Lord, and his mother, who has been a mother to me, too. [14]Greet Asyncritus, Phlegon, Hermes, Patrobas, Hermas and the brothers with them. [15]Greet Philologus, Julia, Nereus and his sister, and Olympas and all the saints with them. [16]Greet one another with a holy kiss.

All the churches of Christ send greetings.

[17]I urge you, brothers, to watch out for those who cause divisions and put obstacles in your way that are contrary to the teaching you have learned. Keep away from them. [18]For such people are not serving our Lord Christ, but their own appetites. By smooth talk and flattery they deceive the minds of naive people. [19]Everyone has heard about your obedience, so I am full of joy over you; but I want you to be wise about what is good, and innocent about what is evil.

[20]The God of peace will soon crush Satan under your feet.

The grace of our Lord Jesus be with you. [21]Timothy, my fellow worker, sends his greetings to you, as do Lucius, Jason and Sosipater, my relatives.

[22]I, Tertius, who wrote down this letter, greet you in the Lord.

[23]Gaius, whose hospitality I and the whole church here enjoy, sends you his greetings.

Erastus, who is the city's director of public works, and our brother Quartus send you their greetings.[a]

[25]Now to him who is able to establish you by my gospel and the proclamation of Jesus Christ, according to the revelation of the mystery hidden for long ages past, [26]but now revealed and made known through the prophetic writings by the command of the eternal God, so that all nations might believe and obey him— [27]to the only wise God be glory forever through Jesus Christ! Amen.

---

[a]23 Some manuscripts *their greetings.* [24]*May the grace of our Lord Jesus Christ be with all of you. Amen.*

1 CORINTHIANS

CORINTH is known as a center for commerce, as well as a center for sin. There is a church in Corinth, but there is a lot of Corinth in the church. In fact, the believers there severely compromise their witness through immorality. In this letter Paul addresses these problems and answers some other questions. He places a high priority on being obedient to Christ and striving for unity, humility and love in the church. As you read, resolve to seek the Lord's will in everything you do, to love others, and to become one in fellowship with other believers.

Outline of Contents

1 Paul, called to be an apostle of Christ Jesus by the will of God, and our brother Sosthenes,

2To the church of God in Corinth, to those sanctified in Christ Jesus and called to be holy, together with all those everywhere who call on the name of our Lord Jesus Christ — their Lord and ours:

3Grace and peace to you from God our Father and the Lord Jesus Christ.

Thanksgiving

4I always thank God for you because of his grace given you in Christ Jesus. 5For in him you have been enriched in every way — in all your speaking and in all your knowledge — 6because our testimony about Christ was confirmed in you. 7Therefore you do not lack any spiritual gift as you eagerly wait for our Lord Jesus Christ to be revealed. 8He will keep you strong to the end, so that you will be blameless on the day of our Lord Jesus Christ. 9God, who has called you into fellowship with his Son Jesus Christ our Lord, is faithful.

Divisions in the Church

10I appeal to you, brothers, in the name of our Lord Jesus Christ, that all of you agree with one another so that there may be no divisions among you and that you may be perfectly united in mind and thought. **11**My brothers, some from Chloe's household have informed me that there are quarrels among you. **12**What I mean is this: One of you says, "I follow Paul"; another, "I follow Apollos"; another, "I follow Cephas*a*"; still another, "I follow Christ."

13Is Christ divided? Was Paul crucified for you? Were you baptized into*b* the name of Paul? **14**I am thankful that I did not baptize any of you except Crispus and Gaius, **15**so no one can say that you were baptized into my name. **16**(Yes, I also baptized the household of Stephanas; beyond that, I don't remember if I baptized anyone else.) **17**For Christ did not send me to baptize, but to preach the gospel—not with words of human wisdom, lest the cross of Christ be emptied of its power.

Christ the Wisdom and Power of God

18For the message of the cross is foolishness to those who are perishing, but to us who are being saved it is the power of God. **19**For it is written:

"I will destroy the wisdom of the wise;
    the intelligence of the intelligent I will
        frustrate."*c*

20Where is the wise man? Where is the scholar? Where is the philosopher of this age? Has not God made foolish the wisdom of the world? **21**For since in the wisdom of God the world through its wisdom did not know him, God was pleased through the foolishness of what was preached to save those who believe. **22**Jews demand miraculous signs and Greeks look for wisdom, **23**but we preach Christ crucified: a stumbling block to Jews and foolishness to Gentiles, **24**but to those whom God has called, both Jews and Greeks, Christ the power of God and the wisdom of God. **25**For the foolishness of God is wiser than man's wisdom, and the weakness of God is stronger than man's strength.

26Brothers, think of what you were when you were called. Not many of you were wise by human standards; not many were influential; not many were of noble birth. **27**But God chose the foolish things of the world to shame the wise; God chose the weak things of the world to shame the strong. **28**He chose the lowly things of this world and the despised things—and the things that are not—to nullify the things that are, **29**so that no one may boast before him. **30**It is because of him that you are in Christ Jesus, who has become for us wisdom from God—that is, our righteousness, holiness and redemption. **31**Therefore, as it is written: "Let him who boasts boast in the Lord."*d*

2 When I came to you, brothers, I did not come with eloquence or superior wisdom as I proclaimed to you the testimony about God.*e* **2**For I resolved to know nothing while I was with you except Jesus Christ and him crucified. **3**I came to you in weakness and fear, and with much trembling. **4**My message and my preaching were not with wise and persuasive words, but with a demonstration of the Spirit's power, **5**so that your faith might not rest on men's wisdom, but on God's power.

Wisdom From the Spirit

6We do, however, speak a message of wisdom among the mature, but not the wisdom of this age or of the rulers of this age, who are coming to nothing. **7**No, we speak of God's secret wisdom, a wisdom that has been hidden and that God destined for our glory before time began. **8**None of the rulers of this age understood it, for if they had, they would not have crucified the Lord of glory. **9**However, as it is written:

"No eye has seen,
    no ear has heard,
    no mind has conceived
        what God has prepared for those who
            love him"*f*—

10but God has revealed it to us by his Spirit.

The Spirit searches all things, even the deep things of God. **11**For who among men knows the thoughts of a man except the man's spirit within him? In the same way no one knows the thoughts of God except the Spirit of God. **12**We have not received the spirit of the world but the Spirit who is from God, that we may understand what God has freely given us. **13**This is what we speak, not in words taught us by human wisdom but in words taught by the Spirit, expressing spiritual truths in spiritual words.*g* **14**The man

*a*12 That is, Peter   *b*13 Or *in*; also in verse 15   *c*19 Isaiah 29:14   *d*31 Jer. 9:24   *e*1 Some manuscripts
as I proclaimed to you God's mystery   *f*9 Isaiah 64:4   *g*13 Or *Spirit, interpreting spiritual truths to spiritual*
men

GOD THE FATHER KNOWS BEST

Andy: "I don't get it. You get to the age of, say fourteen or fifteen, where you start having strong feelings for someone and then your parents quote you the Bible and say, 'Now, son, we know you like Leslie a lot, but you have to wait till you're married to have a sexual relationship. God's plan is that sex is only for marriage.' Hey, I won't get married for another ten years! That's ridiculous! God doesn't really expect me to wait that long, does he?"

Look It Up
••••

The real issue here isn't sex, it's God's wisdom. Wisdom is the unusual ability to understand situations and people and how to deal with them. Does God have such understanding?

"To God belong wisdom and power; counsel and understanding are his" (Job 12:13).

"He made the earth by his power; he founded the world by his wisdom and stretched out the heavens by his understanding" (Jeremiah 51:15).

Hundreds of verses repeat this great truth: God created the universe; therefore he knows what he's talking about.

Think It Through
••••

Every new VCR comes with an owner's manual. This crucial booklet describes how the VCR is put together, how to hook it up, how to get the most enjoyment out of it and what to do if you have problems with it. Most people don't read their owner's manual. They bury it in some drawer and then wonder six months later why their VCR keeps eating their tapes!

You could do the same thing with God. Having made you, he knows what's best for you and how you can have the most satisfying life possible. He's provided an "owner's manual" for you—the Bible—so that you can maximize your performance for him. But probably sometimes you begin to think that you know better than God what's best for you. And by ignoring his wisdom, you can end up like a trashed videotape.

Work It Out
••••

On one side of a sheet of paper write: "God—100 percent wisdom (Job 12:13)." This represents God's total wisdom in every area of life. On the other side write your name and an estimate of how much of all the wisdom in the world you possess. Rejoice that you serve a wise God who is willing to share his wisdom with his unwise children (Ephesians 1:17).

Nail It Down
••••

Read Paul's description of the wisdom of the world compared to God's wisdom in 1 Corinthians 3:18–23.

Turn to pages 599, 980, 998, 1126 and 1330 for other readings on knowing God.
Turn to page 1237 for the weekend reading.

Topic
••••

KNOWING GOD

without the Spirit does not accept the things that come from the Spirit of God, for they are foolishness to him, and he cannot understand them, because they are spiritually discerned. **15**The spiritual man makes judgments about all things, but he himself is not subject to any man's judgment:

16"For who has known the mind of the Lord
    that he may instruct him?"*a*

But we have the mind of Christ.

On Divisions in the Church

3 Brothers, I could not address you as spiritual but as worldly — mere infants in Christ. **2**I gave you milk, not solid food, for you were not yet ready for it. Indeed, you are still not ready. **3**You are still worldly. For since there is jealousy and quarreling among you, are you not worldly? Are you not acting like mere men? **4**For when one says, "I follow Paul," and another, "I follow Apollos," are you not mere men?

5What, after all, is Apollos? And what is Paul? Only servants, through whom you came to believe — as the Lord has assigned to each his task. **6**I planted the seed, Apollos watered it, but God made it grow. **7**So neither he who plants nor he who waters is anything, but only God, who makes things grow. **8**The man who plants and the man who waters have one purpose, and each will be rewarded according to his own labor. **9**For we are God's fellow workers; you are God's field, God's building.

10By the grace God has given me, I laid a foundation as an expert builder, and someone else is building on it. But each one should be careful how he builds. **11**For no one can lay any foundation other than the one already laid, which is Jesus Christ. **12**If any man builds on this foundation using gold, silver, costly stones, wood, hay or straw, **13**his work will be shown for what it is, because the Day will bring it to light. It will be revealed with fire, and the fire will test the quality of each man's work. **14**If what he has built survives, he will receive his reward. **15**If it is burned up, he will suffer loss; he himself will be saved, but only as one escaping through the flames.

16Don't you know that you yourselves are God's temple and that God's Spirit lives in you? **17**If anyone destroys God's temple, God will destroy him; for God's temple is sacred, and you are that temple.

18Do not deceive yourselves. If any one of you thinks he is wise by the standards of this age, he should become a "fool" so that he may become wise. **19**For the wisdom of this world is foolishness in God's sight. As it is written: "He catches the wise in their craftiness"*b*; **20**and again, "The Lord knows that the thoughts of the wise are futile."*c* **21**So then, no more boasting about men! All things are yours, **22**whether Paul or Apollos or Cephas*d* or the world or life or death or the present or the future — all are yours, **23**and you are of Christ, and Christ is of God.

Apostles of Christ

4 So then, men ought to regard us as servants of Christ and as those entrusted with the secret things of God. **2**Now it is required that those who have been given a trust must prove faithful. **3**I care very little if I am judged by you or by any human court; indeed, I do not even judge myself. **4**My conscience is clear, but that does not make me innocent. It is the Lord who judges me. **5**Therefore judge nothing before the appointed time; wait till the Lord comes. He will bring to light what is hidden in darkness and will expose the motives of men's hearts. At that time each will receive his praise from God.

6Now, brothers, I have applied these things to myself and Apollos for your benefit, so that you may learn from us the meaning of the saying, "Do not go beyond what is written." Then you will not take pride in one man over against another. **7**For who makes you different from anyone else? What do you have that you did not receive? And if you did receive it, why do you boast as though you did not?

8Already you have all you want! Already you have become rich! You have become kings — and that without us! How I wish that you really had become kings so that we might be kings with you! **9**For it seems to me that God has put us apostles on display at the end of the procession, like men condemned to die in the arena. We have been made a spectacle to the whole universe, to angels as well as to men. **10**We are fools for Christ, but you are so wise in Christ! We are weak, but you are strong! You are honored, we are dishonored! **11**To this very hour we go hungry and thirsty, we are in rags, we are brutally treated, we are homeless. **12**We work hard with our own hands. When we are cursed, we bless; when we are persecut-

a16 Isaiah 40:13   *b19* Job 5:13   *c20* Psalm 94:11   *d22* That is, Peter

GOD'S DESIGN FOR SEX

Work It Out
••••

How many of the following statements express how you honestly feel about sex before marriage?

• I think sex was created by God as a way for two *married* people to express their love for each other.

• I think sex before marriage is wrong.

• I will stay sexually pure before marriage by taking a firm stand for sexual purity, by not getting myself into situations where I might be tempted, and by dating only those who agree with me.

Could you sign such a statement? If not, you're a prime candidate for getting sexually involved before marriage. This isn't a decision your parents can make for you, and you can't decide to just "wait and see." The pressure society exerts on you to become sexually active demands that you decide how you'll respond before you are faced with sexual temptation.

If you think you can't sign a statement like this because you've already been sexually active, think again. You can start fresh—right now—to be sexually pure before marriage.

Nail It Down
••••

Read the warning in 1 Corinthians 6:9–11.

Think It Through
••••

Being sexually involved before marriage is dangerous. It should never be taken lightly. The dangers involve the obvious possibilities of pregnancy, sexually transmitted diseases, the damage to the relationship between the two people involved, the hurt such activity will cause a future marriage partner, and last—but far, far from least—the separation from God that sin always brings.

God has made it clear that he designed sex for marriage. He's hurt when we put our desires for physical pleasure above his will for our lives. What's more important to you? Your own desires, your own way, or God's perfect plan for your life? The choice is up to you.

Nail It Down
••••

Reread 1 Corinthians 6:9–11. For further insight read Proverbs 6:20–29.

Turn to pages 124, 654 and 705 for other readings on sex.
Turn to page 1239 for Monday's reading.

Topic
••••
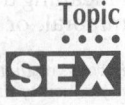
SEX

ed, we endure it; [13]when we are slandered, we answer kindly. Up to this moment we have become the scum of the earth, the refuse of the world.

[14]I am not writing this to shame you, but to warn you, as my dear children. [15]Even though you have ten thousand guardians in Christ, you do not have many fathers, for in Christ Jesus I became your father through the gospel. [16]Therefore I urge you to imitate me. [17]For this reason I am sending to you Timothy, my son whom I love, who is faithful in the Lord. He will remind you of my way of life in Christ Jesus, which agrees with what I teach everywhere in every church.

[18]Some of you have become arrogant, as if I were not coming to you. [19]But I will come to you very soon, if the Lord is willing, and then I will find out not only how these arrogant people are talking, but what power they have. [20]For the kingdom of God is not a matter of talk but of power. [21]What do you prefer? Shall I come to you with a whip, or in love and with a gentle spirit?

Expel the Immoral Brother!

5 It is actually reported that there is sexual immorality among you, and of a kind that does not occur even among pagans: A man has his father's wife. [2]And you are proud! Shouldn't you rather have been filled with grief and have put out of your fellowship the man who did this? [3]Even though I am not physically present, I am with you in spirit. And I have already passed judgment on the one who did this, just as if I were present. [4]When you are assembled in the name of our Lord Jesus and I am with you in spirit, and the power of our Lord Jesus is present, [5]hand this man over to Satan, so that the sinful nature[a] may be destroyed and his spirit saved on the day of the Lord.

[6]Your boasting is not good. Don't you know that a little yeast works through the whole batch of dough? [7]Get rid of the old yeast that you may be a new batch without yeast—as you really are. For Christ, our Passover lamb, has been sacrificed. [8]Therefore let us keep the Festival, not with the old yeast, the yeast of malice and wickedness, but with bread without yeast, the bread of sincerity and truth.

[9]I have written you in my letter not to associate with sexually immoral people—[10]not at all meaning the people of this world who are immoral, or the greedy and swin-

dlers, or idolaters. In that case you would have to leave this world. [11]But now I am writing you that you must not associate with anyone who calls himself a brother but is sexually immoral or greedy, an idolater or a slanderer, a drunkard or a swindler. With such a man do not even eat.

[12]What business is it of mine to judge those outside the church? Are you not to judge those inside? [13]God will judge those outside. "Expel the wicked man from among you."[b]

Lawsuits Among Believers

6 If any of you has a dispute with another, dare he take it before the ungodly for judgment instead of before the saints? [2]Do you not know that the saints will judge the world? And if you are to judge the world, are you not competent to judge trivial cases? [3]Do you not know that we will judge angels? How much more the things of this life! [4]Therefore, if you have disputes about such matters, appoint as judges even men of little account in the church![c] [5]I say this to shame you. Is it possible that there is nobody among you wise enough to judge a dispute between believers? [6]But instead, one brother goes to law against another—and this in front of unbelievers!

[7]The very fact that you have lawsuits among you means you have been completely defeated already. Why not rather be wronged? Why not rather be cheated? [8]Instead, you yourselves cheat and do wrong, and you do this to your brothers.

[9]Do you not know that the wicked will not inherit the kingdom of God? Do not be deceived: Neither the sexually immoral nor idolaters nor adulterers nor male prostitutes nor homosexual offenders [10]nor thieves nor the greedy nor drunkards nor slanderers nor swindlers will inherit the kingdom of God. [11]And that is what some of you were. But you were washed, you were sanctified, you were justified in the name of the Lord Jesus Christ and by the Spirit of our God.

Sexual Immorality

[12]"Everything is permissible for me"—but not everything is beneficial. "Everything is permissible for me"—but I will not be mastered by anything. [13]"Food for the stomach and the stomach for food"—but God will destroy them both. The body is not meant for sexual immorality, but for the Lord, and the

---

[a]5 Or *that his body*; or *that the flesh*   [b]13 Deut. 17:7; 19:19; 21:21; 22:21,24; 24:7   [c]4 Or *matters, do you appoint as judges men of little account in the church?*

THE HIGH COST OF A CHEAP THRILL

□ MONDAY

If their skin, bones and muscle tissue were transparent, the drug users at Devlin High just might change their ways.

Terry would be able to see the serious damage he's inflicting on his brain from his recreational drug use.

Jennifer wouldn't believe the sight of her diseased liver and kidneys. Too much glue sniffing, Jen.

Rob would enjoy a double thrill—by seeing how much harm marijuana smoking has done to his lungs, he might also get to watch his heart stop beating!

Look It Up
••••

One of the clearest Scriptural principles against abusing our bodies with drugs can be found in 2 Corinthians 6:16: "For we are the temple of the living God."

Get the message? God lives within you. He owns you. You're just a tenant. You're supposed to honor him by taking care of what is his property.

Since drugs damage the property, the issue is settled: You must avoid every kind of substance abuse.

Think It Through
••••

God has created you and by his Spirit makes you his temple. A temple is a holy and beautiful place. It is your responsibility to keep God's temple clean and healthy.

Work It Out
••••

If drugs are a problem at your school, expose their dangers by:
• Writing an article for the school newspaper.
• Tackling the topic as a speech class assignment.
• Getting your teachers to invite outside speakers (medical doctors or drug counselors) into the classroom to discuss the problem.
• Starting an antidrug organization.

Nail It Down
••••

Another clear passage of Scripture against abusing our bodies can be found in 1 Corinthians 6:19–20.

Turn to pages 1115, 1151 and 1350 for other readings on drugs.
Turn to page 1241 for Tuesday's reading.

Topic
••••

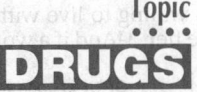

DRUGS

Lord for the body. **14**By his power God raised the Lord from the dead, and he will raise us also. **15**Do you not know that your bodies are members of Christ himself? Shall I then take the members of Christ and unite them with a prostitute? Never! **16**Do you not know that he who unites himself with a prostitute is one with her in body? For it is said, "The two will become one flesh."*a* **17**But he who unites himself with the Lord is one with him in spirit.

18Flee from sexual immorality. All other sins a man commits are outside his body, but he who sins sexually sins against his own body. **19**Do you not know that your body is a temple of the Holy Spirit, who is in you, whom you have received from God? You are not your own; **20**you were bought at a price. Therefore honor God with your body.

Marriage

7 Now for the matters you wrote about: It is good for a man not to marry.*b* **2**But since there is so much immorality, each man should have his own wife, and each woman her own husband. **3**The husband should fulfill his marital duty to his wife, and likewise the wife to her husband. **4**The wife's body does not belong to her alone but also to her husband. In the same way, the husband's body does not belong to him alone but also to his wife. **5**Do not deprive each other except by mutual consent and for a time, so that you may devote yourselves to prayer. Then come together again so that Satan will not tempt you because of your lack of self-control. **6**I say this as a concession, not as a command. **7**I wish that all men were as I am. But each man has his own gift from God; one has this gift, another has that.

8Now to the unmarried and the widows I say: It is good for them to stay unmarried, as I am. **9**But if they cannot control themselves, they should marry, for it is better to marry than to burn with passion.

10To the married I give this command (not I, but the Lord): A wife must not separate from her husband. **11**But if she does, she must remain unmarried or else be reconciled to her husband. And a husband must not divorce his wife.

12To the rest I say this (I, not the Lord): If any brother has a wife who is not a believer and she is willing to live with him, he must not divorce her. **13**And if a woman has a husband who is not a believer and he is willing to live with her, she must not divorce him. **14**For the unbelieving husband has been sanctified through his wife, and the unbelieving wife has been sanctified through her believing husband. Otherwise your children would be unclean, but as it is, they are holy.

15But if the unbeliever leaves, let him do so. A believing man or woman is not bound in such circumstances; God has called us to live in peace. **16**How do you know, wife, whether you will save your husband? Or, how do you know, husband, whether you will save your wife?

17Nevertheless, each one should retain the place in life that the Lord assigned to him and to which God has called him. This is the rule I lay down in all the churches. **18**Was a man already circumcised when he was called? He should not become uncircumcised. Was a man uncircumcised when he was called? He should not be circumcised. **19**Circumcision is nothing and uncircumcision is nothing. Keeping God's commands is what counts. **20**Each one should remain in the situation which he was in when God called him. **21**Were you a slave when you were called? Don't let it trouble you—although if you can gain your freedom, do so. **22**For he who was a slave when he was called by the Lord is the Lord's freedman; similarly, he who was a free man when he was called is Christ's slave. **23**You were bought at a price; do not become slaves of men. **24**Brothers, each man, as responsible to God, should remain in the situation God called him to.

25Now about virgins: I have no command from the Lord, but I give a judgment as one who by the Lord's mercy is trustworthy. **26**Because of the present crisis, I think that it is good for you to remain as you are. **27**Are you married? Do not seek a divorce. Are you unmarried? Do not look for a wife. **28**But if you do marry, you have not sinned; and if a virgin marries, she has not sinned. But those who marry will face many troubles in this life, and I want to spare you this.

29What I mean, brothers, is that the time is short. From now on those who have wives should live as if they had none; **30**those who mourn, as if they did not; those who are happy, as if they were not; those who buy something, as if it were not theirs to keep; **31**those who use the things of the world, as if not engrossed in them. For this world in its present form is passing away.

a16 Gen. 2:24   *b1* Or "It is good for a man not to have sexual relations with a woman."

IN THE WORLD BUT NOT OF THE WORLD
☐ TUESDAY

Had any brushes with the world lately?

• Christy innocently told her new friends that she plans to remain a virgin until marriage. They laughed in her face.

• Lynn's father was fired last week because he refused to go along with an unethical business decision his company was making.

• Kim's friends told her she was crazy when they found out that she had participated in a pro-life rally.

Look It Up

In a prayer just before his arrest and crucifixion, Jesus summed up our mission to be in the world, but not of it.

"I have given them your word and the world has hated them, for they are not of the world any more than I am of the world. My prayer is not that you take them out of the world but that you protect them from the evil one. They are not of the world, even as I am not of it . . . . As you sent me into the world, I have sent them into the world" (John 17:14–16,18).

Think It Through

In the New Testament, *world* almost always refers to the universal system of wrong values and non-Christian people. It is inspired and energized by the unseen forces of evil, and it is antagonistic to God and his plan. This invisible entity isn't listed in the phone book, it doesn't have an office building, and its adherents don't carry membership cards. Still, it is very real.

As a Christian, you're called to live right in the middle of that world. More than that you're called to help the captives of that world find true freedom.

Work It Out

While thinking about the verses you just read, make four mental lists.

1. List the ways the world has "hated" you this past week.

2. List some of the ways you've seen the "evil one" oppose the plan of God this past week.

3. List the parts of the world into which the Lord has sent you.

4. List the people trapped in the world system that you'd most like to see rescued. (Begin praying for these individuals and for a chance to show them the light!)

Nail It Down

Read 1 Corinthians 7:31 to discover the destiny of the present world and all its values.

Turn to pages 1060 and 1393 for other readings on worldliness.
Turn to page 1243 for Wednesday's reading.

Topic

WORLDLINESS

32I would like you to be free from concern. An unmarried man is concerned about the Lord's affairs — how he can please the Lord. **33**But a married man is concerned about the affairs of this world — how he can please his wife — **34**and his interests are divided. An unmarried woman or virgin is concerned about the Lord's affairs: Her aim is to be devoted to the Lord in both body and spirit. But a married woman is concerned about the affairs of this world — how she can please her husband. **35**I am saying this for your own good, not to restrict you, but that you may live in a right way in undivided devotion to the Lord.

36If anyone thinks he is acting improperly toward the virgin he is engaged to, and if she is getting along in years and he feels he ought to marry, he should do as he wants. He is not sinning. They should get married. **37**But the man who has settled the matter in his own mind, who is under no compulsion but has control over his own will, and who has made up his mind not to marry the virgin — this man also does the right thing. **38**So then, he who marries the virgin does right, but he who does not marry her does even better.[a]

39A woman is bound to her husband as long as he lives. But if her husband dies, she is free to marry anyone she wishes, but he must belong to the Lord. **40**In my judgment, she is happier if she stays as she is — and I think that I too have the Spirit of God.

Food Sacrificed to Idols

8 Now about food sacrificed to idols: We know that we all possess knowledge.[b] Knowledge puffs up, but love builds up. **2**The man who thinks he knows something does not yet know as he ought to know. **3**But the man who loves God is known by God.

4So then, about eating food sacrificed to idols: We know that an idol is nothing at all in the world and that there is no God but one. **5**For even if there are so-called gods, whether in heaven or on earth (as indeed there are many "gods" and many "lords"), **6**yet for us there is but one God, the Father, from whom all things came and for whom we live; and there is but one Lord, Jesus Christ, through whom all things came and through whom we live.

7But not everyone knows this. Some people are still so accustomed to idols that when they eat such food they think of it as having been sacrificed to an idol, and since their conscience is weak, it is defiled. **8**But food does not bring us near to God; we are no worse if we do not eat, and no better if we do.

9Be careful, however, that the exercise of your freedom does not become a stumbling block to the weak. **10**For if anyone with a weak conscience sees you who have this knowledge eating in an idol's temple, won't he be emboldened to eat what has been sacrificed to idols? **11**So this weak brother, for whom Christ died, is destroyed by your knowledge. **12**When you sin against your brothers in this way and wound their weak conscience, you sin against Christ. **13**Therefore, if what I eat causes my brother to fall into sin, I will never eat meat again, so that I will not cause him to fall.

The Rights of an Apostle

9 Am I not free? Am I not an apostle? Have I not seen Jesus our Lord? Are you not the result of my work in the Lord? **2**Even though I may not be an apostle to others, surely I am to you! For you are the seal of my apostleship in the Lord.

3This is my defense to those who sit in judgment on me. **4**Don't we have the right to food and drink? **5**Don't we have the right to take a believing wife along with us, as do the other apostles and the Lord's brothers and Cephas[c]? **6**Or is it only I and Barnabas who must work for a living?

7Who serves as a soldier at his own expense? Who plants a vineyard and does not eat of its grapes? Who tends a flock and does not drink of the milk? **8**Do I say this merely from a human point of view? Doesn't the Law say the same thing? **9**For it is written in the Law of Moses: "Do not muzzle an ox while it is treading out the grain."[d] Is it about oxen that God is concerned? **10**Surely he says this for us, doesn't he? Yes, this was written for us, because when the plowman plows and the thresher threshes, they ought to do so in the hope of sharing in the har-

---

a36-38 Or 36If anyone thinks he is not treating his daughter properly, and if she is getting along in years, and he feels she ought to marry, he should do as he wants. He is not sinning. He should let her get married. 37But the man who has settled the matter in his own mind, who is under no compulsion but has control over his own will, and who has made up his mind to keep the virgin unmarried — this man also does the right thing. 38So then, he who gives his virgin in marriage does right, but he who does not give her in marriage does even better. b1 Or "We all possess knowledge," as you say c5 That is, Peter d9 Deut. 25:4

OUR PERFECT FATHER

In each home on Oakwood Drive the story is just a little bit different.

Clarissa's dad is abusive. He yells a lot, and when he gets really angry, he hits anyone who happens to be within his reach. (He hits hard too.)

Because his parents are divorced, David only sees his dad on holidays. And when David does see him, his dad seems distant and cold. It hurts David to feel that his father doesn't care.

Amy's father is really nice when she makes good grades or gets any kind of award, but watch out if she makes the slightest mistake! When that happens, her dad becomes critical and gives her a look that says: "You're a total loser. Get lost!"

Look It Up

Isn't it great to know that even if your earthly dad fails you, you have a perfect Father in God? It's true!

"Yet, O LORD, you are our Father" (Isaiah 64:8).

"For you did not receive a spirit that makes you a slave again to fear, but you received the Spirit of sonship. And by him we cry, 'Abba, Father' " (Romans 8:15).

"There is . . . one God and Father of all, who is over all and through all and in all" (Ephesians 4:4,6).

Think It Through

Many Christians believe that the way you view your earthly father has a big effect on how you view God. For instance, if your dad is absent, strict, mean, unfair or quick-tempered, you might wrongly think God is the same way. But of course he isn't any of those things! He is always with us, always totally kind and loving, always completely patient and fair.

Do you see this principle at work in your own life? That is, have you begun to see God as a heavenly version of your earthly dad? In what ways?

Work It Out

List the qualities of the ideal dad. Then across the top of the list write: "God, my perfect, heavenly Father." End your time with God by thanking him for being a loving and caring Father for you.

Nail It Down

Read Paul's statement about God as Father in 1 Corinthians 8:6.

Turn to pages 619, 761, 1208 and 1210 for other readings on God.
Turn to page 1246 for Thursday's reading.

Topic

vest. [11]If we have sown spiritual seed among you, is it too much if we reap a material harvest from you? [12]If others have this right of support from you, shouldn't we have it all the more?

But we did not use this right. On the contrary, we put up with anything rather than hinder the gospel of Christ. [13]Don't you know that those who work in the temple get their food from the temple, and those who serve at the altar share in what is offered on the altar? [14]In the same way, the Lord has commanded that those who preach the gospel should receive their living from the gospel.

[15]But I have not used any of these rights. And I am not writing this in the hope that you will do such things for me. I would rather die than have anyone deprive me of this boast. [16]Yet when I preach the gospel, I cannot boast, for I am compelled to preach. Woe to me if I do not preach the gospel! [17]If I preach voluntarily, I have a reward; if not voluntarily, I am simply discharging the trust committed to me. [18]What then is my reward? Just this: that in preaching the gospel I may offer it free of charge, and so not make use of my rights in preaching it.

[19]Though I am free and belong to no man, I make myself a slave to everyone, to win as many as possible. [20]To the Jews I became like a Jew, to win the Jews. To those under the law I became like one under the law (though I myself am not under the law), so as to win those under the law. [21]To those not having the law I became like one not having the law (though I am not free from God's law but am under Christ's law), so as to win those not having the law. [22]To the weak I became weak, to win the weak. I have become all things to all men so that by all possible means I might save some. [23]I do all this for the sake of the gospel, that I may share in its blessings.

[24]Do you not know that in a race all the runners run, but only one gets the prize? Run in such a way as to get the prize. [25]Everyone who competes in the games goes into strict training. They do it to get a crown that will not last; but we do it to get a crown that will last forever. [26]Therefore I do not run like a man running aimlessly; I do not fight like a man beating the air. [27]No, I beat my body and make it my slave so that after I have preached to others, I myself will not be disqualified for the prize.

Warnings From Israel's History

10 For I do not want you to be ignorant of the fact, brothers, that our forefathers were all under the cloud and that they all passed through the sea. [2]They were all baptized into Moses in the cloud and in the sea. [3]They all ate the same spiritual food [4]and drank the same spiritual drink; for they drank from the spiritual rock that accompanied them, and that rock was Christ. [5]Nevertheless, God was not pleased with most of them; their bodies were scattered over the desert.

[6]Now these things occurred as examples[a] to keep us from setting our hearts on evil things as they did. [7]Do not be idolaters, as some of them were; as it is written: "The people sat down to eat and drink and got up to indulge in pagan revelry."[b] [8]We should not commit sexual immorality, as some of them did—and in one day twenty-three thousand of them died. [9]We should not test the Lord, as some of them did—and were killed by snakes. [10]And do not grumble, as some of them did—and were killed by the destroying angel.

[11]These things happened to them as examples and were written down as warnings for us, on whom the fulfillment of the ages has come. [12]So, if you think you are standing firm, be careful that you don't fall! [13]No temptation has seized you except what is common to man. And God is faithful; he will not let you be tempted beyond what you can bear. But when you are tempted, he will also provide a way out so that you can stand up under it.

Idol Feasts and the Lord's Supper

[14]Therefore, my dear friends, flee from idolatry. [15]I speak to sensible people; judge for yourselves what I say. [16]Is not the cup of thanksgiving for which we give thanks a participation in the blood of Christ? And is not the bread that we break a participation in the body of Christ? [17]Because there is one loaf, we, who are many, are one body, for we all partake of the one loaf.

[18]Consider the people of Israel: Do not those who eat the sacrifices participate in the altar? [19]Do I mean then that a sacrifice offered to an idol is anything, or that an idol is anything? [20]No, but the sacrifices of pagans are offered to demons, not to God, and I do not want you to be participants with demons. [21]You cannot drink the cup of the

---

[a]6 Or *types*; also in verse 11   [b]7 Exodus 32:6

Lord and the cup of demons too; you cannot have a part in both the Lord's table and the table of demons. **22**Are we trying to arouse the Lord's jealousy? Are we stronger than he?

The Believer's Freedom

23"Everything is permissible"—but not everything is beneficial. "Everything is permissible"—but not everything is constructive. **24**Nobody should seek his own good, but the good of others.

25Eat anything sold in the meat market without raising questions of conscience, **26**for, "The earth is the Lord's, and everything in it."*a*

27If some unbeliever invites you to a meal and you want to go, eat whatever is put before you without raising questions of conscience. **28**But if anyone says to you, "This has been offered in sacrifice," then do not eat it, both for the sake of the man who told you and for conscience' sake*b*— **29**the other man's conscience, I mean, not yours. For why should my freedom be judged by another's conscience? **30**If I take part in the meal with thankfulness, why am I denounced because of something I thank God for?

31So whether you eat or drink or whatever you do, do it all for the glory of God. **32**Do not cause anyone to stumble, whether Jews, Greeks or the church of God— **33**even as I try to please everybody in every way. For I am not seeking my own good but the good of many, so that they may be saved. **11 1**Follow my example, as I follow the example of Christ.

Propriety in Worship

2I praise you for remembering me in everything and for holding to the teachings,*c* just as I passed them on to you. **3**Now I want you to realize that the head of every man is Christ, and the head of the woman is man, and the head of Christ is God. **4**Every man who prays or prophesies with his head covered dishonors his head. **5**And every woman who prays or prophesies with her head uncovered dishonors her head—it is just as though her head were shaved. **6**If a woman does not cover her head, she should have her hair cut off; and

if it is a disgrace for a woman to have her hair cut or shaved off, she should cover her head. **7**A man ought not to cover his head,*d* since he is the image and glory of God; but the woman is the glory of man. **8**For man did not come from woman, but woman from man; **9**neither was man created for woman, but woman for man. **10**For this reason, and because of the angels, the woman ought to have a sign of authority on her head.

11In the Lord, however, woman is not independent of man, nor is man independent of woman. **12**For as woman came from man, so also man is born of woman. But everything comes from God. **13**Judge for yourselves: Is it proper for a woman to pray to God with her head uncovered? **14**Does not the very nature of things teach you that if a man has long hair, it is a disgrace to him, **15**but that if a woman has long hair, it is her glory? For long hair is given to her as a covering. **16**If anyone wants to be contentious about this, we have no other practice—nor do the churches of God.

The Lord's Supper

17In the following directives I have no praise for you, for your meetings do more harm than good. **18**In the first place, I hear that when you come together as a church, there are divisions among you, and to some extent I believe it. **19**No doubt there have to be differences among you to show which of you have God's approval. **20**When you come together, it is not the Lord's Supper you eat, **21**for as you eat, each of you goes ahead without waiting for anybody else. One remains hungry, another gets drunk. **22**Don't you have homes to eat and drink in? Or do you despise the church of God and humiliate those who have nothing? What shall I say to you? Shall I praise you for this? Certainly not!

23For I received from the Lord what I also passed on to you: The Lord Jesus, on the night he was betrayed, took bread, **24**and when he had given thanks, he broke it and said, "This is my body, which is for you; do this in remembrance of me." **25**In the same way, after supper he took the cup, saying, "This cup is the new covenant in my blood; do this, whenever you drink it, in remembrance of me." **26**For whenever you eat this

---

a26 Psalm 24:1   *b28* Some manuscripts *conscience' sake, for "the earth is the Lord's and everything in it"*
c2 Or *traditions*   *d4-7* Or *4Every man who prays or prophesies with long hair dishonors his head. 5And every woman who prays or prophesies with no covering [of hair] on her head dishonors her head—she is just like one of the "shorn women." 6If a woman has no covering, let her be for now with short hair, but since it is a disgrace for a woman to have her hair shorn or shaved, she should grow it again. 7A man ought not to have long hair*

A CHECKLIST FOR CHOOSING

Andy is facing a really tough decision.

During the same week that the youth group has scheduled to host back-to-back Christmas parties for an orphanage and a nursing home, a non-Christian friend has invited Andy to go snow skiing.

As a leader of his group, Andy feels responsible to be at the youth functions.

And yet, he remembers how much fun he had the only other time he went skiing. "Not only would I get to spend some time with Randy, but if I skied a whole week, I could really improve!"

Look It Up
●●●●

The apostle Paul's letter to the Corinthian Christians gives you some practical advice for choosing wisely. Your decisions should result in actions that:

• Spiritually benefit yourself and others: " 'Everything is permissible for me'—but not everything is beneficial" (1 Corinthians 6:12);

• Help spread the gospel (1 Corinthians 9:19–22);

• Cause you to excel for Christ (1 Corinthians 9:25).

On the other hand, your choices should never:

• Lead you into enslaving habits (1 Corinthians 6:12);

• Encourage another Christian to sin: "Therefore, if what I eat causes my brother to fall into sin, I will never eat meat again, so that I will not cause him to fall" (1 Corinthians 8:13);

• Be selfish: "Nobody should seek his own good, but the good of others" (1 Corinthians 10:24).

Think It Through
●●●●

Put yourself in Andy's shoes. How do you think you might feel? What do you think you'd actually decide to do? Why?

Can you think of any other Biblical criteria for making wise choices in life's gray areas?

Work It Out
●●●●

Here are some other practical suggestions for making good decisions when the Bible doesn't spell out what you should do:

1. Pray, confidently expecting God to give you guidance (James 1:5–8).

2. Get wise advice from several trustworthy Christian friends (Proverbs 20:5,18).

3. Explore God's Word for timeless principles that might apply to your specific situation.

Nail It Down
●●●●

Read about the ultimate criterion for any choice you face: 1 Corinthians 10:31.

**Turn to pages 246, 257 and 1005 for other readings on decisions.
Turn to page 1248 for Friday's reading.**

Topic
●●●●

bread and drink this cup, you proclaim the Lord's death until he comes.

27Therefore, whoever eats the bread or drinks the cup of the Lord in an unworthy manner will be guilty of sinning against the body and blood of the Lord. **28**A man ought to examine himself before he eats of the bread and drinks of the cup. **29**For anyone who eats and drinks without recognizing the body of the Lord eats and drinks judgment on himself. **30**That is why many among you are weak and sick, and a number of you have fallen asleep. **31**But if we judged ourselves, we would not come under judgment. **32**When we are judged by the Lord, we are being disciplined so that we will not be condemned with the world.

33So then, my brothers, when you come together to eat, wait for each other. **34**If anyone is hungry, he should eat at home, so that when you meet together it may not result in judgment.

And when I come I will give further directions.

Spiritual Gifts

12 Now about spiritual gifts, brothers, I do not want you to be ignorant. **2**You know that when you were pagans, somehow or other you were influenced and led astray to mute idols. **3**Therefore I tell you that no one who is speaking by the Spirit of God says, "Jesus be cursed," and no one can say, "Jesus is Lord," except by the Holy Spirit.

4There are different kinds of gifts, but the same Spirit. **5**There are different kinds of service, but the same Lord. **6**There are different kinds of working, but the same God works all of them in all men.

7Now to each one the manifestation of the Spirit is given for the common good. **8**To one there is given through the Spirit the message of wisdom, to another the message of knowledge by means of the same Spirit, **9**to another faith by the same Spirit, to another gifts of healing by that one Spirit, **10**to another miraculous powers, to another prophecy, to another distinguishing between spirits, to another speaking in different kinds of tongues,*a* and to still another the interpretation of tongues.*a* **11**All these are the work of one and the same Spirit, and he gives them to each one, just as he determines.

One Body, Many Parts

12The body is a unit, though it is made up of many parts; and though all its parts are many, they form one body. So it is with Christ. **13**For we were all baptized by*b* one Spirit into one body—whether Jews or Greeks, slave or free—and we were all given the one Spirit to drink.

14Now the body is not made up of one part but of many. **15**If the foot should say, "Because I am not a hand, I do not belong to the body," it would not for that reason cease to be part of the body. **16**And if the ear should say, "Because I am not an eye, I do not belong to the body," it would not for that reason cease to be part of the body. **17**If the whole body were an eye, where would the sense of hearing be? If the whole body were an ear, where would the sense of smell be? **18**But in fact God has arranged the parts in the body, every one of them, just as he wanted them to be. **19**If they were all one part, where would the body be? **20**As it is, there are many parts, but one body.

21The eye cannot say to the hand, "I don't need you!" And the head cannot say to the feet, "I don't need you!" **22**On the contrary, those parts of the body that seem to be weaker are indispensable, **23**and the parts that we think are less honorable we treat with special honor. And the parts that are unpresentable are treated with special modesty, **24**while our presentable parts need no special treatment. But God has combined the members of the body and has given greater honor to the parts that lacked it, **25**so that there should be no division in the body, but that its parts should have equal concern for each other. **26**If one part suffers, every part suffers with it; if one part is honored, every part rejoices with it.

27Now you are the body of Christ, and each one of you is a part of it. **28**And in the church God has appointed first of all apostles, second prophets, third teachers, then workers of miracles, also those having gifts of healing, those able to help others, those with gifts of administration, and those speaking in different kinds of tongues. **29**Are all apostles? Are all prophets? Are all teachers? Do all work miracles? **30**Do all have gifts of healing? Do all speak in tongues*c*? Do all interpret? **31**But eagerly desire*d* the greater gifts.

Love

And now I will show you the most excellent way.

*a*10 Or *languages*; also in verse 28   *b*13 Or *with*; or in *eagerly desiring*   *c*30 Or *other languages*   *d*31 Or *But you are*

THE POTHOLE OF COMPARISON

•••

Shay has overcome some big-time obstacles so far in his trip down the narrow road:

Through diligent study (and lots of prayer), he has brought his algebra average up eleven points!

Mr. Aswell, the principal, let Shay have a classroom for his Bible study and twelve students came to the first one!

Rather than being influenced by Stephanie, Shay is having an influence on his non-Christian friend.

Yet, all of a sudden, Shay finds himself jarred by constant comparisons to a senior named Len—a very talented, handsome and committed Christian.

Look It Up
••••

Comparisons are like potholes. They can really throw you off course. Sometimes you may even go so far as to *copy* those you respect. Remember when David was preparing to fight Goliath?

"Saul dressed David in his own tunic. He put a coat of armor on him and a bronze helmet on his head. David fastened on his sword over the tunic and tried walking around, because he was not used to them.

" 'I cannot go in these,' he said . . . . So he took them off" (1 Samuel 17:38–39).

Wisely, David understood the danger in comparisons. He realized, "This isn't me! I'm trying to be Saul, and God doesn't expect that. He wants me to fight this battle with the gifts he has given *me*."

Think It Through
••••

Do you find that you are often comparing yourself with other people? What qualities about them do you admire or wish you had?

What might have happened if scrawny little David had tried to use the heavy armor of the much larger Saul? What finally happened in the David-Goliath duel?

Work It Out
••••

Make a list of the unique abilities and attributes God has given you. (If you need help, ask your mom. Most moms are great when it comes to pointing out strong points.)

Spend a few minutes thanking God for the talents and skills he has given you. Then pray: "Lord, keep me from comparing myself to others. Remind me that you want me to be me, not someone else. Amen."

That kind of proper alignment will keep you cruising down the narrow road!

Nail It Down
••••

Read 1 Corinthians 12:7–26 for information on how God works with each of you as individuals.

Turn to pages 486, 1056, 1087 and 1367 for other readings on obstacles.
Turn to page 1250 for the weekend reading.

Topic
••••

OBSTACLES

13 If I speak in the tongues[a] of men and of angels, but have not love, I am only a resounding gong or a clanging cymbal. [2]If I have the gift of prophecy and can fathom all mysteries and all knowledge, and if I have a faith that can move mountains, but have not love, I am nothing. [3]If I give all I possess to the poor and surrender my body to the flames,[b] but have not love, I gain nothing.

[4]Love is patient, love is kind. It does not envy, it does not boast, it is not proud. [5]It is not rude, it is not self-seeking, it is not easily angered, it keeps no record of wrongs. [6]Love does not delight in evil but rejoices with the truth. [7]It always protects, always trusts, always hopes, always perseveres.

[8]Love never fails. But where there are prophecies, they will cease; where there are tongues, they will be stilled; where there is knowledge, it will pass away. [9]For we know in part and we prophesy in part, [10]but when perfection comes, the imperfect disappears. [11]When I was a child, I talked like a child, I thought like a child, I reasoned like a child. When I became a man, I put childish ways behind me. [12]Now we see but a poor reflection as in a mirror; then we shall see face to face. Now I know in part; then I shall know fully, even as I am fully known.

[13]And now these three remain: faith, hope and love. But the greatest of these is love.

Gifts of Prophecy and Tongues

14 Follow the way of love and eagerly desire spiritual gifts, especially the gift of prophecy. [2]For anyone who speaks in a tongue[c] does not speak to men but to God. Indeed, no one understands him; he utters mysteries with his spirit.[d] [3]But everyone who prophesies speaks to men for their strengthening, encouragement and comfort. [4]He who speaks in a tongue edifies himself, but he who prophesies edifies the church. [5]I would like every one of you to speak in tongues,[e] but I would rather have you prophesy. He who prophesies is greater than one who speaks in tongues,[e] unless he interprets, so that the church may be edified.

[6]Now, brothers, if I come to you and speak in tongues, what good will I be to you, unless I bring you some revelation or knowledge or prophecy or word of instruction? [7]Even in the case of lifeless things that make sounds, such as the flute or harp, how will anyone know what tune is being played unless there is a distinction in the notes? [8]Again, if the trumpet does not sound a clear call, who will get ready for battle? [9]So it is with you. Unless you speak intelligible words with your tongue, how will anyone know what you are saying? You will just be speaking into the air. [10]Undoubtedly there are all sorts of languages in the world, yet none of them is without meaning. [11]If then I do not grasp the meaning of what someone is saying, I am a foreigner to the speaker, and he is a foreigner to me. [12]So it is with you. Since you are eager to have spiritual gifts, try to excel in gifts that build up the church.

[13]For this reason anyone who speaks in a tongue should pray that he may interpret what he says. [14]For if I pray in a tongue, my spirit prays, but my mind is unfruitful. [15]So what shall I do? I will pray with my spirit, but I will also pray with my mind; I will sing with my spirit, but I will also sing with my mind. [16]If you are praising God with your spirit, how can one who finds himself among those who do not understand[f] say "Amen" to your thanksgiving, since he does not know what you are saying? [17]You may be giving thanks well enough, but the other man is not edified.

[18]I thank God that I speak in tongues more than all of you. [19]But in the church I would rather speak five intelligible words to instruct others than ten thousand words in a tongue.

[20]Brothers, stop thinking like children. In regard to evil be infants, but in your thinking be adults. [21]In the Law it is written:

"Through men of strange tongues
    and through the lips of foreigners
I will speak to this people,
    but even then they will not listen to
        me,"[g]
says the Lord.

[22]Tongues, then, are a sign, not for believers but for unbelievers; prophecy, however, is for believers, not for unbelievers. [23]So if the whole church comes together and everyone speaks in tongues, and some who do not understand[h] or some unbelievers come in, will they not say that you are out of your mind? [24]But if an unbeliever or someone who does not understand[i] comes in while

---

a1 Or *languages*   *b3* Some early manuscripts *body that I may boast*   *c2* Or *another language*; also in verses 4, 13, 14, 19, 26 and 27   *d2* Or *by the Spirit*   *e5* Or *other languages*; also in verses 6, 18, 22, 23 and 39   *f16* Or *among the inquirers*   *g21* Isaiah 28:11,12   *h23* Or *some inquirers*   *i24* Or *or some inquirer*

WHAT LOVE IS

Work It Out
••••

Make a written list of six things you think love is. Begin each one with: Love is . . .

Perhaps you'll write that love is doing the dishes when your mom is tired (and so are you). Or love is letting your sister borrow your new sweater (the one you haven't even worn yet). Or love is listening (again) when your friend calls to complain about his girl troubles (at least he has a girl!). Or love is helping your younger brother with his science project (when you've got hours of your own homework to do yet).

Whatever you write, by the time you're finished, you'll probably have figured out what love *isn't*. Love isn't always easy. But it is important. Without love this life would be a pretty lonely and worthless existence. Thank God for love!

Nail It Down
••••

Read the famous love chapter in 1 Corinthians 13.

Think It Through
••••

Read verses 4–6 again in 1 Corinthians 13. In your family life, how do you measure up? If you examine yourself in the light of this definition, how loving are you? If each of your words and actions at home were on a meter, would the arm point toward love all, most, or only some of the time?

As sad as it seems, often the hardest place to be loving is at home. We treat our friends and even acquaintances better than our own family. Family members of all ages, young children, teens, adults, parents, all have been guilty of not being as loving as they could be or as loving as God would have them be.

Make a commitment to be more loving to the people you live with every day.

Nail It Down
••••

Reread 1 Corinthians 13. For further insight read Proverbs 3:1–4.

Turn to pages 1153, 1215 and 1313 for other readings on love.
Turn to page 1253 for Monday's reading.

Topic
••••
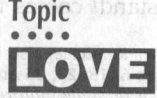

everybody is prophesying, he will be convinced by all that he is a sinner and will be judged by all, 25and the secrets of his heart will be laid bare. So he will fall down and worship God, exclaiming, "God is really among you!"

Orderly Worship

26What then shall we say, brothers? When you come together, everyone has a hymn, or a word of instruction, a revelation, a tongue or an interpretation. All of these must be done for the strengthening of the church. 27If anyone speaks in a tongue, two—or at the most three—should speak, one at a time, and someone must interpret. 28If there is no interpreter, the speaker should keep quiet in the church and speak to himself and God.

29Two or three prophets should speak, and the others should weigh carefully what is said. 30And if a revelation comes to someone who is sitting down, the first speaker should stop. 31For you can all prophesy in turn so that everyone may be instructed and encouraged. 32The spirits of prophets are subject to the control of prophets. 33For God is not a God of disorder but of peace.

As in all the congregations of the saints, 34women should remain silent in the churches. They are not allowed to speak, but must be in submission, as the Law says. 35If they want to inquire about something, they should ask their own husbands at home; for it is disgraceful for a woman to speak in the church.

36Did the word of God originate with you? Or are you the only people it has reached? 37If anybody thinks he is a prophet or spiritually gifted, let him acknowledge that what I am writing to you is the Lord's command. 38If he ignores this, he himself will be ignored.a

39Therefore, my brothers, be eager to prophesy, and do not forbid speaking in tongues. 40But everything should be done in a fitting and orderly way.

The Resurrection of Christ

15 Now, brothers, I want to remind you of the gospel I preached to you, which you received and on which you have taken your stand. 2By this gospel you are saved, if you hold firmly to the word I preached to you. Otherwise, you have believed in vain.

3For what I received I passed on to you as of first importanceb: that Christ died for our sins according to the Scriptures, 4that he was buried, that he was raised on the third day according to the Scriptures, 5and that he appeared to Peter,c and then to the Twelve. 6After that, he appeared to more than five hundred of the brothers at the same time, most of whom are still living, though some have fallen asleep. 7Then he appeared to James, then to all the apostles, 8and last of all he appeared to me also, as to one abnormally born.

9For I am the least of the apostles and do not even deserve to be called an apostle, because I persecuted the church of God. 10But by the grace of God I am what I am, and his grace to me was not without effect. No, I worked harder than all of them—yet not I, but the grace of God that was with me. 11Whether, then, it was I or they, this is what we preach, and this is what you believed.

The Resurrection of the Dead

12But if it is preached that Christ has been raised from the dead, how can some of you say that there is no resurrection of the dead? 13If there is no resurrection of the dead, then not even Christ has been raised. 14And if Christ has not been raised, our preaching is useless and so is your faith. 15More than that, we are then found to be false witnesses about God, for we have testified about God that he raised Christ from the dead. But he did not raise him if in fact the dead are not raised. 16For if the dead are not raised, then Christ has not been raised either. 17And if Christ has not been raised, your faith is futile; you are still in your sins. 18Then those also who have fallen asleep in Christ are lost. 19If only for this life we have hope in Christ, we are to be pitied more than all men.

20But Christ has indeed been raised from the dead, the firstfruits of those who have fallen asleep. 21For since death came through a man, the resurrection of the dead comes also through a man. 22For as in Adam all die, so in Christ all will be made alive. 23But each in his own turn: Christ, the firstfruits; then, when he comes, those who belong to him. 24Then the end will come, when he hands over the kingdom to God the Father after he has destroyed all dominion, authority and power. 25For he must reign until he has put all his enemies under his feet.

a38 Some manuscripts *If he is ignorant of this, let him be ignorant*   b3 Or *you at the first*   c5 Greek *Cephas*

26The last enemy to be destroyed is death. 27For he "has put everything under his feet."a Now when it says that "everything" has been put under him, it is clear that this does not include God himself, who put everything under Christ. 28When he has done this, then the Son himself will be made subject to him who put everything under him, so that God may be all in all.

29Now if there is no resurrection, what will those do who are baptized for the dead? If the dead are not raised at all, why are people baptized for them? 30And as for us, why do we endanger ourselves every hour? 31I die every day—I mean that, brothers—just as surely as I glory over you in Christ Jesus our Lord. 32If I fought wild beasts in Ephesus for merely human reasons, what have I gained? If the dead are not raised,

"Let us eat and drink,
    for tomorrow we die."b

33Do not be misled: "Bad company corrupts good character." 34Come back to your senses as you ought, and stop sinning; for there are some who are ignorant of God—I say this to your shame.

The Resurrection Body

35But someone may ask, "How are the dead raised? With what kind of body will they come?" 36How foolish! What you sow does not come to life unless it dies. 37When you sow, you do not plant the body that will be, but just a seed, perhaps of wheat or of something else. 38But God gives it a body as he has determined, and to each kind of seed he gives its own body. 39All flesh is not the same: Men have one kind of flesh, animals have another, birds another and fish another. 40There are also heavenly bodies and there are earthly bodies; but the splendor of the heavenly bodies is one kind, and the splendor of the earthly bodies is another. 41The sun has one kind of splendor, the moon another and the stars another; and star differs from star in splendor.

42So will it be with the resurrection of the dead. The body that is sown is perishable, it is raised imperishable; 43it is sown in dishonor, it is raised in glory; it is sown in weakness, it is raised in power; 44it is sown a natural body, it is raised a spiritual body.

If there is a natural body, there is also a spiritual body. 45So it is written: "The first man Adam became a living being"c; the last

Adam, a life-giving spirit. 46The spiritual did not come first, but the natural, and after that the spiritual. 47The first man was of the dust of the earth, the second man from heaven. 48As was the earthly man, so are those who are of the earth; and as is the man from heaven, so also are those who are of heaven. 49And just as we have borne the likeness of the earthly man, so shall wed bear the likeness of the man from heaven.

50I declare to you, brothers, that flesh and blood cannot inherit the kingdom of God, nor does the perishable inherit the imperishable. 51Listen, I tell you a mystery: We will not all sleep, but we will all be changed— 52in a flash, in the twinkling of an eye, at the last trumpet. For the trumpet will sound, the dead will be raised imperishable, and we will be changed. 53For the perishable must clothe itself with the imperishable, and the mortal with immortality. 54When the perishable has been clothed with the imperishable, and the mortal with immortality, then the saying that is written will come true: "Death has been swallowed up in victory."e

55"Where, O death, is your victory?
    Where, O death, is your sting?"f

56The sting of death is sin, and the power of sin is the law. 57But thanks be to God! He gives us the victory through our Lord Jesus Christ.

58Therefore, my dear brothers, stand firm. Let nothing move you. Always give yourselves fully to the work of the Lord, because you know that your labor in the Lord is not in vain.

The Collection for God's People

16 Now about the collection for God's people: Do what I told the Galatian churches to do. 2On the first day of every week, each one of you should set aside a sum of money in keeping with his income, saving it up, so that when I come no collections will have to be made. 3Then, when I arrive, I will give letters of introduction to the men you approve and send them with your gift to Jerusalem. 4If it seems advisable for me to go also, they will accompany me.

Personal Requests

5After I go through Macedonia, I will come to you—for I will be going through Macedonia. 6Perhaps I will stay with you awhile, or

a27 Psalm 8:6   b32 Isaiah 22:13   c45 Gen. 2:7   d49 Some early manuscripts so let us   e54 Isaiah 25:8
f55 Hosea 13:14

IT DOESN'T AFFECT ME!

On Wednesday, David is still ticked that his dad wouldn't let him see the rock group Sal Monella and the Disease in concert. (Dave's friend Sam told him how awesome the concert was: Sal barfed on all the people in the first two rows!) Not surprisingly, a youth group discussion of rock music causes David's anger to surface:

"Why does everyone over twenty get so upset about music? I listen to the radio all the time . . . and it doesn't affect me. Why can't I listen to rock music if I don't pay attention to the lyrics?"

Look It Up

A lot of folks in the Bible felt just like David.

Lot thought he could hang out with sinners and not be affected, but "that righteous man, living among them day after day, was tormented in his righteous soul by the lawless deeds he saw and heard" (2 Peter 2:8).

Solomon thought he could have a huge harem of pagan women and not be affected, but "as Solomon grew old, his wives turned his heart after other gods, and his heart was not fully devoted to the LORD his God" (1 Kings 11:4).

The Christians at Corinth thought that immorality in the church wouldn't affect them, but they were wrong (1 Corinthians 5).

Think It Through

In a very real way, music is like food for the soul. One girl's regular "diet" is a smorgasbord of songs that promote immorality, rebellion, hopelessness and violence. Another girl fills her mind with positive songs that fit the requirements of Philippians 4:8.

Which girl will be more healthy emotionally and spiritually? Which girl will have better information in her head when it comes time to make choices involving values and morality?

Work It Out

Are you compromising in the area of music? "I can listen and still be a strong Christian. It won't affect me!" Oh yeah? How do you know? How much stronger might you be if you cut out the negative influence of certain groups?

Evaluate your musical diet. Sit down with one or two Christian friends and compare the lyrics of your favorite tunes to the standard of Philippians 4:8.

Nail It Down

Read what 1 Corinthians 15:33–34 has to say about bad company.

Turn to pages 1323 and 1338 for other readings on music.
Turn to page 1256 for Tuesday's reading.

Topic

MUSIC

even spend the winter, so that you can help me on my journey, wherever I go. **7**I do not want to see you now and make only a passing visit; I hope to spend some time with you, if the Lord permits. **8**But I will stay on at Ephesus until Pentecost, **9**because a great door for effective work has opened to me, and there are many who oppose me.

10If Timothy comes, see to it that he has nothing to fear while he is with you, for he is carrying on the work of the Lord, just as I am. **11**No one, then, should refuse to accept him. Send him on his way in peace so that he may return to me. I am expecting him along with the brothers.

12Now about our brother Apollos: I strongly urged him to go to you with the brothers. He was quite unwilling to go now, but he will go when he has the opportunity.

13Be on your guard; stand firm in the faith; be men of courage; be strong. **14**Do everything in love.

15You know that the household of Stephanas were the first converts in Achaia, and they have devoted themselves to the service of the saints. I urge you, brothers, **16**to submit to such as these and to everyone who joins in the work, and labors at it. **17**I was glad when Stephanas, Fortunatus and Achaicus arrived, because they have supplied what was lacking from you. **18**For they refreshed my spirit and yours also. Such men deserve recognition.

Final Greetings

19The churches in the province of Asia send you greetings. Aquila and Priscilla*a* greet you warmly in the Lord, and so does the church that meets at their house. **20**All the brothers here send you greetings. Greet one another with a holy kiss.

21I, Paul, write this greeting in my own hand.

22If anyone does not love the Lord—a curse be on him. Come, O Lord*b*!

23The grace of the Lord Jesus be with you.

24My love to all of you in Christ Jesus. Amen.*c*

---

*a*19 Greek *Prisca*, a variant of *Priscilla*   *b*22 In Aramaic the expression *Come, O Lord* is *Marana tha.*
*c*24 Some manuscripts do not have *Amen.*

2 CORINTHIANS

WHEW! Talk about problems. After the church in Corinth receives Paul's first letter, some of the believers attack the apostle's motives, character and even his teaching. Paul responds by writing 2 Corinthians in which he defends his apostolic credentials, detailing a lot of his own experiences. As you read this letter, remember that the Bible was written by men who wrote under God's authority. You can always trust that Paul and the other Bible writers wrote the truth.

1 Paul, an apostle of Christ Jesus by the will of God, and Timothy our brother,

To the church of God in Corinth, together with all the saints throughout Achaia:

²Grace and peace to you from God our Father and the Lord Jesus Christ.

The God of All Comfort

³Praise be to the God and Father of our Lord Jesus Christ, the Father of compassion and the God of all comfort, ⁴who comforts us in all our troubles, so that we can comfort those in any trouble with the comfort we ourselves have received from God. ⁵For just as the sufferings of Christ flow over into our lives, so also through Christ our comfort overflows. ⁶If we are distressed, it is for your comfort and salvation; if we are comforted, it is for your comfort, which produces in you patient endurance of the same sufferings we suffer. ⁷And our hope for you is firm, because we know that just as you share in our sufferings, so also you share in our comfort.

⁸We do not want you to be uninformed, brothers, about the hardships we suffered in the province of Asia. We were under great pressure, far beyond our ability to endure, so that we despaired even of life. ⁹Indeed, in our hearts we felt the sentence of death. But this happened that we might not rely on ourselves but on God, who raises the dead. ¹⁰He has delivered us from such a deadly peril, and he will deliver us. On him we have set our hope that he will continue to deliver us, ¹¹as you help us by your prayers. Then

THE HIDDEN BLESSING IN ALL THAT'S DEPRESSING

TUESDAY ☐

For a long time, Rebecca's depression wasn't getting any better. In fact, she began to lose hope that things would ever change. She couldn't seem to stop her downward spiral. On three occasions, she seriously contemplated suicide.

Last night, however, while flipping through the channels on cable, Rebecca came across a call-in show that featured two Christian counselors who seemed to be really caring and really wise.

Rebecca got excited and called. "Maybe this is what I need."

Look It Up

Paul considered emotional weakness to be a blessing in disguise.

"But he [the Lord] said to me, 'My grace is sufficient for you, for my power is made perfect in weakness.' Therefore I will boast all the more gladly about my weaknesses, so that Christ's power may rest on me. That is why, for Christ's sake, I delight in weaknesses, in insults, in hardships, in persecutions, in difficulties. For when I am weak, then I am strong" (2 Corinthians 12:9–10).

Though he doesn't mention depression by name, his point is clear: Hard times are good if they cause you to turn to God and depend on his strength.

Think It Through

Do you know that it's okay to cry? In fact, it may be good for you! Some researchers believe that crying helps correct the chemical imbalances found in many depressed individuals. A good cry also releases stress that might otherwise lead to ulcers.

When was the last time you cried?

When was the last time you thanked God for a depressing situation?

Work It Out

If, for you, life is currently depressing, start looking for a blessing!

1. Use your current experience with depression to examine your own life—what's okay and what needs changing.

2. Let your pain drive you close to God.

3. Take the lessons you learn and use them to build friendships with others who are hurting. (Record your feelings in a journal, so that when your depression is behind you, you will be able to remember just how low you felt.)

4. Draw strength from the promise in Isaiah 43:2.

Nail It Down

Read about Paul's hard times and what he learned from them in 2 Corinthians 1:8–11.

Turn to pages 360, 527, 601 and 1197 for other readings on depression.
Turn to page 1259 for Wednesday's reading.

Topic

DEPRESSION

many will give thanks on our[a] behalf for the gracious favor granted us in answer to the prayers of many.

Paul's Change of Plans

12Now this is our boast: Our conscience testifies that we have conducted ourselves in the world, and especially in our relations with you, in the holiness and sincerity that are from God. We have done so not according to worldly wisdom but according to God's grace. **13**For we do not write you anything you cannot read or understand. And I hope that, **14**as you have understood us in part, you will come to understand fully that you can boast of us just as we will boast of you in the day of the Lord Jesus.

15Because I was confident of this, I planned to visit you first so that you might benefit twice. **16**I planned to visit you on my way to Macedonia and to come back to you from Macedonia, and then to have you send me on my way to Judea. **17**When I planned this, did I do it lightly? Or do I make my plans in a worldly manner so that in the same breath I say, "Yes, yes" and "No, no"?

18But as surely as God is faithful, our message to you is not "Yes" and "No." **19**For the Son of God, Jesus Christ, who was preached among you by me and Silas[b] and Timothy, was not "Yes" and "No," but in him it has always been "Yes." **20**For no matter how many promises God has made, they are "Yes" in Christ. And so through him the "Amen" is spoken by us to the glory of God. **21**Now it is God who makes both us and you stand firm in Christ. He anointed us, **22**set his seal of ownership on us, and put his Spirit in our hearts as a deposit, guaranteeing what is to come.

23I call God as my witness that it was in order to spare you that I did not return to Corinth. **24**Not that we lord it over your faith, but we work with you for your joy, because it is by faith you stand firm. **2** **1**So I made up my mind that I would not make another painful visit to you. **2**For if I grieve you, who is left to make me glad but you whom I have grieved? **3**I wrote as I did so that when I came I should not be distressed by those who ought to make me rejoice. I had confidence in all of you, that you would all share my joy. **4**For I wrote you out of great distress and anguish of heart and with many tears, not to grieve you but to let you know the depth of my love for you.

Forgiveness for the Sinner

5If anyone has caused grief, he has not so much grieved me as he has grieved all of you, to some extent—not to put it too severely. **6**The punishment inflicted on him by the majority is sufficient for him. **7**Now instead, you ought to forgive and comfort him, so that he will not be overwhelmed by excessive sorrow. **8**I urge you, therefore, to reaffirm your love for him. **9**The reason I wrote you was to see if you would stand the test and be obedient in everything. **10**If you forgive anyone, I also forgive him. And what I have forgiven—if there was anything to forgive—I have forgiven in the sight of Christ for your sake, **11**in order that Satan might not outwit us. For we are not unaware of his schemes.

Ministers of the New Covenant

12Now when I went to Troas to preach the gospel of Christ and found that the Lord had opened a door for me, **13**I still had no peace of mind, because I did not find my brother Titus there. So I said good-by to them and went on to Macedonia.

14But thanks be to God, who always leads us in triumphal procession in Christ and through us spreads everywhere the fragrance of the knowledge of him. **15**For we are to God the aroma of Christ among those who are being saved and those who are perishing. **16**To the one we are the smell of death; to the other, the fragrance of life. And who is equal to such a task? **17**Unlike so many, we do not peddle the word of God for profit. On the contrary, in Christ we speak before God with sincerity, like men sent from God.

3 Are we beginning to commend ourselves again? Or do we need, like some people, letters of recommendation to you or from you? **2**You yourselves are our letter, written on our hearts, known and read by everybody. **3**You show that you are a letter from Christ, the result of our ministry, written not with ink but with the Spirit of the living God, not on tablets of stone but on tablets of human hearts.

4Such confidence as this is ours through Christ before God. **5**Not that we are competent in ourselves to claim anything for ourselves, but our competence comes from God. **6**He has made us competent as ministers of a new covenant—not of the letter but

---

a11 Many manuscripts *your*   *b19* Greek *Silvanus*, a variant of *Silas* of the Spirit; for the letter kills, but the Spirit gives life.

The Glory of the New Covenant

7Now if the ministry that brought death, which was engraved in letters on stone, came with glory, so that the Israelites could not look steadily at the face of Moses because of its glory, fading though it was, **8**will not the ministry of the Spirit be even more glorious? **9**If the ministry that condemns men is glorious, how much more glorious is the ministry that brings righteousness! **10**For what was glorious has no glory now in comparison with the surpassing glory. **11**And if what was fading away came with glory, how much greater is the glory of that which lasts!

12Therefore, since we have such a hope, we are very bold. **13**We are not like Moses, who would put a veil over his face to keep the Israelites from gazing at it while the radiance was fading away. **14**But their minds were made dull, for to this day the same veil remains when the old covenant is read. It has not been removed, because only in Christ is it taken away. **15**Even to this day when Moses is read, a veil covers their hearts. **16**But whenever anyone turns to the Lord, the veil is taken away. **17**Now the Lord is the Spirit, and where the Spirit of the Lord is, there is freedom. **18**And we, who with unveiled faces all reflect*a* the Lord's glory, are being transformed into his likeness with ever-increasing glory, which comes from the Lord, who is the Spirit.

Treasures in Jars of Clay

4 Therefore, since through God's mercy we have this ministry, we do not lose heart. **2**Rather, we have renounced secret and shameful ways; we do not use deception, nor do we distort the word of God. On the contrary, by setting forth the truth plainly we commend ourselves to every man's conscience in the sight of God. **3**And even if our gospel is veiled, it is veiled to those who are perishing. **4**The god of this age has blinded the minds of unbelievers, so that they cannot see the light of the gospel of the glory of Christ, who is the image of God. **5**For we do not preach ourselves, but Jesus Christ as Lord, and ourselves as your servants for Jesus' sake. **6**For God, who said, "Let light shine out of darkness,"*b* made his light shine in our hearts to give us the light of the knowledge of the glory of God in the face of Christ.

7But we have this treasure in jars of clay to show that this all-surpassing power is from God and not from us. **8**We are hard pressed on every side, but not crushed; perplexed, but not in despair; **9**persecuted, but not abandoned; struck down, but not destroyed. **10**We always carry around in our body the death of Jesus, so that the life of Jesus may also be revealed in our body. **11**For we who are alive are always being given over to death for Jesus' sake, so that his life may be revealed in our mortal body. **12**So then, death is at work in us, but life is at work in you.

13It is written: "I believed; therefore I have spoken."*c* With that same spirit of faith we also believe and therefore speak, **14**because we know that the one who raised the Lord Jesus from the dead will also raise us with Jesus and present us with you in his presence. **15**All this is for your benefit, so that the grace that is reaching more and more people may cause thanksgiving to overflow to the glory of God.

16Therefore we do not lose heart. Though outwardly we are wasting away, yet inwardly we are being renewed day by day. **17**For our light and momentary troubles are achieving for us an eternal glory that far outweighs them all. **18**So we fix our eyes not on what is seen, but on what is unseen. For what is seen is temporary, but what is unseen is eternal.

Our Heavenly Dwelling

5 Now we know that if the earthly tent we live in is destroyed, we have a building from God, an eternal house in heaven, not built by human hands. **2**Meanwhile we groan, longing to be clothed with our heavenly dwelling, **3**because when we are clothed, we will not be found naked. **4**For while we are in this tent, we groan and are burdened, because we do not wish to be unclothed but to be clothed with our heavenly dwelling, so that what is mortal may be swallowed up by life. **5**Now it is God who has made us for this very purpose and has given us the Spirit as a deposit, guaranteeing what is to come.

6Therefore we are always confident and know that as long as we are at home in the body we are away from the Lord. **7**We live by faith, not by sight. **8**We are confident, I say, and would prefer to be away from the body and at home with the Lord. **9**So we make it our goal to please him, whether we are at

---

a 18 Or contemplate   b6 Gen. 1:3   c13 Psalm 116:10

WHERE DO WE GET OUR VALUES?

Mrs. Huff questions her sociology class, "Where do we get our values?"

"I think a person's family plays a big part."

"Yeah. And your friends too."

"I say it's the media. I mean, I'm always watching TV and movies, reading magazines and books, listening to music. I'm sure all that affects me."

"Well, I get my values from my religion."

Look It Up

Is there an ultimate source for all the values people have? Consider this:

The New Testament repeatedly encourages believers to establish godly values: "Do not conform any longer to the pattern of this world, but be transformed by the renewing of your mind. Then you will be able to test and approve what God's will is—his good, pleasing and perfect will" (Romans 12:2).

Meanwhile, Satan is working to establish false values in order to keep individuals from seeing what is really true. At the same time, God is working by his Spirit, through his Word and through his church to communicate the true values that lead to eternal life: "For God . . . made his light shine in our hearts to give us the light of the knowledge of the glory of God in the face of Christ" (2 Corinthians 4:6).

Think It Through

Are we suggesting that every newscaster or teacher or parent who isn't a Christian is pro-Satan? No! In fact, most people don't think in those terms. Most people aren't even aware that there is a struggle taking place between God and Satan.

What we are saying is that spiritual warfare is real. And that the fiercest fighting is taking place in the realm of values. The enemy knows that if he can get people to adopt the wrong principles, he has a good chance of keeping them in his camp forever!

Work It Out

Take a few minutes to make a list of your present values. Be honest. What are your convictions when it comes to: Family? Money? Sex? Friendships? Work? Church?

Examine each principle closely, asking yourself two questions: (1) What is the ultimate source of this value? and (2) Is it possible that this ideal is really a subtle trap by Satan to get me to focus on the wrong things?

Talk with a Christian friend about your values.

Nail It Down

Read the warning in 2 Corinthians 4:4.

Turn to pages 716, 1000 and 1192 for other readings on values.
Turn to page 1261 for Thursday's reading.

Topic

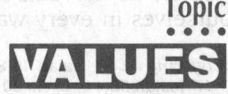

VALUES

home in the body or away from it. [10]For we must all appear before the judgment seat of Christ, that each one may receive what is due him for the things done while in the body, whether good or bad.

The Ministry of Reconciliation

[11]Since, then, we know what it is to fear the Lord, we try to persuade men. What we are is plain to God, and I hope it is also plain to your conscience. [12]We are not trying to commend ourselves to you again, but are giving you an opportunity to take pride in us, so that you can answer those who take pride in what is seen rather than in what is in the heart. [13]If we are out of our mind, it is for the sake of God; if we are in our right mind, it is for you. [14]For Christ's love compels us, because we are convinced that one died for all, and therefore all died. [15]And he died for all, that those who live should no longer live for themselves but for him who died for them and was raised again.

[16]So from now on we regard no one from a worldly point of view. Though we once regarded Christ in this way, we do so no longer. [17]Therefore, if anyone is in Christ, he is a new creation; the old has gone, the new has come! [18]All this is from God, who reconciled us to himself through Christ and gave us the ministry of reconciliation: [19]that God was reconciling the world to himself in Christ, not counting men's sins against them. And he has committed to us the message of reconciliation. [20]We are therefore Christ's ambassadors, as though God were making his appeal through us. We implore you on Christ's behalf: Be reconciled to God. [21]God made him who had no sin to be sin[a] for us, so that in him we might become the righteousness of God.

6 As God's fellow workers we urge you not to receive God's grace in vain. [2]For he says,

"In the time of my favor I heard you,
    and in the day of salvation I helped
        you."[b]

I tell you, now is the time of God's favor, now is the day of salvation.

Paul's Hardships

[3]We put no stumbling block in anyone's path, so that our ministry will not be discredited. [4]Rather, as servants of God we commend ourselves in every way: in great endurance; in troubles, hardships and distresses; [5]in beatings, imprisonments and riots; in hard work, sleepless nights and hunger; [6]in purity, understanding, patience and kindness; in the Holy Spirit and in sincere love; [7]in truthful speech and in the power of God; with weapons of righteousness in the right hand and in the left; [8]through glory and dishonor, bad report and good report; genuine, yet regarded as impostors; [9]known, yet regarded as unknown; dying, and yet we live on; beaten, and yet not killed; [10]sorrowful, yet always rejoicing; poor, yet making many rich; having nothing, and yet possessing everything.

[11]We have spoken freely to you, Corinthians, and opened wide our hearts to you. [12]We are not withholding our affection from you, but you are withholding yours from us. [13]As a fair exchange—I speak as to my children—open wide your hearts also.

Do Not Be Yoked With Unbelievers

[14]Do not be yoked together with unbelievers. For what do righteousness and wickedness have in common? Or what fellowship can light have with darkness? [15]What harmony is there between Christ and Belial[c]? What does a believer have in common with an unbeliever? [16]What agreement is there between the temple of God and idols? For we are the temple of the living God. As God has said: "I will live with them and walk among them, and I will be their God, and they will be my people."[d]

[17]"Therefore come out from them
    and be separate,
                    says the Lord.
Touch no unclean thing,
    and I will receive you."[e]
[18]"I will be a Father to you,
    and you will be my sons and
        daughters,
                says the Lord Almighty."[f]

7 Since we have these promises, dear friends, let us purify ourselves from everything that contaminates body and spirit, perfecting holiness out of reverence for God.

Paul's Joy

[2]Make room for us in your hearts. We have wronged no one, we have corrupted no one, we have exploited no one. [3]I do not say this to condemn you; I have said before that you have such a place in our hearts that we

[a]21 Or be a sin offering   [b]2 Isaiah 49:8   [c]15 Greek Beliar, a variant of Belial   [d]16 Lev. 26:12; Jer. 32:38; Ezek. 37:27   [e]17 Isaiah 52:11; Ezek. 20:34,41   [f]18 2 Samuel 7:14; 7:8

CHOOSING PAIN OVER PLEASURE

C hristopher could have had a dream summer—sleeping late every day and working the coveted afternoon lifeguard shift (excellent rays, lots of girl watching, and decent pay). But he surprised everyone when he said no to the pool job and yes to a missions project in Haiti.

Instead of a pleasure-filled summer of sun and fun, Christopher did back-breaking labor in the most primitive conditions . . . and he wants to go back!

A lot of people think Christopher is weird. But maybe he's on to something.

Look It Up
••••

The life of Moses can teach you about tough choices:

"By faith Moses, when he had grown up, refused to be known as the son of Pharaoh's daughter. He chose to be mistreated along with the people of God rather than to enjoy the pleasures of sin for a short time. He regarded disgrace for the sake of Christ as of greater value than the treasures of Egypt, because he was looking ahead to his reward" (Hebrews 11:24–26).

Think It Through
••••

Most people look at all their options and then take the path of least resistance (or the road to the most pleasure). Situations that look difficult or that might result in hardship and discomfort are avoided at all costs! How many people do you know who are willing to choose a path of pain?

Could you make the tough choice that Christopher made? Had you been in Moses' situation, do you think you could have willingly traded a life of ease for a life of suffering? Why or why not?

Work It Out
••••

Make a list of the decisions you'll face in the next few weeks. Chances are good that in at least some of those instances you'll be able to choose either an easy road of pleasure or a tough road of pain. Some of your options might even include suffering for being a Christian.

Make one decision for Christ today that will shake up your comfortable lifestyle—and that possibly could result in discomfort.

Nail It Down
••••

Read about Paul's hardships in 2 Corinthians 6:4–10.

Turn to pages 518, 525, 1309 and 1369 for other readings on suffering.
Turn to page 1262 for Friday's reading.

Topic
••••

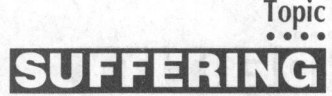

YOU ARE GOD'S CONTAINER

For several weeks this past spring, Kent and his girlfriend Lois began to get out of control in their physical relationship. Soon Kent noticed that he was often getting depressed. And then he started thinking, "If I really am a Christian, would I be acting like this?"

While on a spring retreat a couple of weeks later, Kent realized that God demands (not suggests) obedience. So, he got down on his knees and said, "Lord, I am truly sorry. Forgive me for my foolishness."

That was the end of Kent and Lois's late night "couch wrestling."

Look It Up
••••

What Kent realized is this truth: God does not bless someone involved in willful disobedience.

"In a large house there are articles not only of gold and silver, but also of wood and clay; some are for noble purposes and some for ignoble. If a man cleanses himself from the latter, he will be an instrument for noble purposes, made holy, useful to the Master and prepared to do any good work" (2 Timothy 2:20–21).

In this passage, Paul urged his young friend Timothy to guard against outer corruption (at the hands of false teachers) and to develop inner purity.

Think It Through
••••

The Greek word translated "articles" in the passage above is translated elsewhere in the New Testament as "jar" (Luke 8:16) and "pottery" (Revelation 2:27). In other words, Paul is talking about various household containers.

Would you want to drink out of a cup that had old coffee grounds and mold growing in it? Would you want to prepare a green salad in the family garbage can?

If God isn't using you right now, could it be that there is some filth in your life that needs cleaning up?

Work It Out
••••

Do you want to be useful to God? Do you want to be prepared for whatever situation he might bring your way? Then clean up your act on a daily basis. Here's how:

Ask him to show you any sin in your life that needs to be dealt with (Psalm 139:23).

Admit your failures, turning away from them and back to God (1 John 1:9).

Ask God to use you to accomplish his work (2 Timothy 2:21).

Nail It Down
••••

Read 2 Corinthians 7:1 for what Paul had to say about keeping pure.

Turn to pages 397, 1145 and 1377 for other readings on identity.
Turn to page 1264 for the weekend reading.

Topic
••••

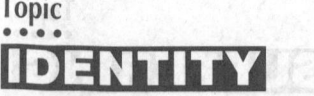

would live or die with you. **4**I have great confidence in you; I take great pride in you. I am greatly encouraged; in all our troubles my joy knows no bounds.

5For when we came into Macedonia, this body of ours had no rest, but we were harassed at every turn—conflicts on the outside, fears within. **6**But God, who comforts the downcast, comforted us by the coming of Titus, **7**and not only by his coming but also by the comfort you had given him. He told us about your longing for me, your deep sorrow, your ardent concern for me, so that my joy was greater than ever.

8Even if I caused you sorrow by my letter, I do not regret it. Though I did regret it—I see that my letter hurt you, but only for a little while— **9**yet now I am happy, not because you were made sorry, but because your sorrow led you to repentance. For you became sorrowful as God intended and so were not harmed in any way by us. **10**Godly sorrow brings repentance that leads to salvation and leaves no regret, but worldly sorrow brings death. **11**See what this godly sorrow has produced in you: what earnestness, what eagerness to clear yourselves, what indignation, what alarm, what longing, what concern, what readiness to see justice done. At every point you have proved yourselves to be innocent in this matter. **12**So even though I wrote to you, it was not on account of the one who did the wrong or of the injured party, but rather that before God you could see for yourselves how devoted to us you are. **13**By all this we are encouraged.

In addition to our own encouragement, we were especially delighted to see how happy Titus was, because his spirit has been refreshed by all of you. **14**I had boasted to him about you, and you have not embarrassed me. But just as everything we said to you was true, so our boasting about you to Titus has proved to be true as well. **15**And his affection for you is all the greater when he remembers that you were all obedient, receiving him with fear and trembling. **16**I am glad I can have complete confidence in you.

Generosity Encouraged

8 And now, brothers, we want you to know about the grace that God has given the Macedonian churches. **2**Out of the most severe trial, their overflowing joy and their extreme poverty welled up in rich generosity. **3**For I testify that they gave as much as they were able, and even beyond their ability. Entirely on their own, **4**they urgently pleaded with us for the privilege of sharing in this service to the saints. **5**And they did not do as we expected, but they gave themselves first to the Lord and then to us in keeping with God's will. **6**So we urged Titus, since he had earlier made a beginning, to bring also to completion this act of grace on your part. **7**But just as you excel in everything—in faith, in speech, in knowledge, in complete earnestness and in your love for us*a*—see that you also excel in this grace of giving.

8I am not commanding you, but I want to test the sincerity of your love by comparing it with the earnestness of others. **9**For you know the grace of our Lord Jesus Christ, that though he was rich, yet for your sakes he became poor, so that you through his poverty might become rich.

10And here is my advice about what is best for you in this matter: Last year you were the first not only to give but also to have the desire to do so. **11**Now finish the work, so that your eager willingness to do it may be matched by your completion of it, according to your means. **12**For if the willingness is there, the gift is acceptable according to what one has, not according to what he does not have.

13Our desire is not that others might be relieved while you are hard pressed, but that there might be equality. **14**At the present time your plenty will supply what they need, so that in turn their plenty will supply what you need. Then there will be equality, **15**as it is written: "He who gathered much did not have too much, and he who gathered little did not have too little."*b*

Titus Sent to Corinth

16I thank God, who put into the heart of Titus the same concern I have for you. **17**For Titus not only welcomed our appeal, but he is coming to you with much enthusiasm and on his own initiative. **18**And we are sending along with him the brother who is praised by all the churches for his service to the gospel. **19**What is more, he was chosen by the churches to accompany us as we carry the offering, which we administer in order to honor the Lord himself and to show our eagerness to help. **20**We want to avoid any criticism of the way we administer this liberal gift. **21**For we are taking pains to do what is right, not only in the eyes of the Lord but also in the eyes of men.

a7 Some manuscripts in our love for you   b15 Exodus 16:18

GROWING UP

Work It Out
••••

How mature are you? Take this maturity fitness test to find out. Just answer with a simple yes or no.

1. When my parents aren't looking, I pinch my brother's arm and then say I don't know why he's crying.

2. When my teacher leaves the room, I immediately start to goof around.

3. When my parents aren't home, I bend and break the rules simply because they aren't there to see.

4. I think it's okay to swear as long as no one hears me.

5. When my youth pastor isn't watching, I distract the other kids in my youth group by being silly and not listening.

6. I think it's okay to go places my parents don't approve of as long as they don't find out.

Get the picture? Maturity is doing what's right and what's good no matter who sees, no matter who knows or doesn't know. How mature are you?

Nail It Down
••••

Four words in 2 Corinthians 8:3–4 describe the maturity of the Macedonians. Can you identify them?

Think It Through
••••

The four words from 2 Corinthians 8:3–4 that describe the maturity of the Macedonians are, "entirely on their own." The Macedonian church gave a gift to the poor believers in Jerusalem. They gave much more than Paul expected them to give, and their giving was entirely their own idea. They didn't need a set of rules to tell them when to give. They didn't need directions or a command from Paul to give. They were mature. They knew the Christians in Jerusalem were in need, so they took a collection and gave.

That's maturity: When you follow the rules—no matter who's watching—simply because *on your own* you've decided it's the right thing to do. When you do what's right simply because *on your own* you've decided that it's a good thing to do. Are you mature? Or do you need to do a little growing up *on your own*?

Nail It Down
••••

Reread 2 Corinthians 8:3–4. For further insight read Proverbs 2:1–8.

Turn to pages 272, 1266 and 1284 for other readings on maturity.
Turn to page 1266 for Monday's reading.

Topic
••••

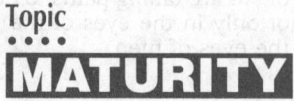
MATURITY

²²In addition, we are sending with them our brother who has often proved to us in many ways that he is zealous, and now even more so because of his great confidence in you. ²³As for Titus, he is my partner and fellow worker among you; as for our brothers, they are representatives of the churches and an honor to Christ. ²⁴Therefore show these men the proof of your love and the reason for our pride in you, so that the churches can see it.

9 There is no need for me to write to you about this service to the saints. ²For I know your eagerness to help, and I have been boasting about it to the Macedonians, telling them that since last year you in Achaia were ready to give; and your enthusiasm has stirred most of them to action. ³But I am sending the brothers in order that our boasting about you in this matter should not prove hollow, but that you may be ready, as I said you would be. ⁴For if any Macedonians come with me and find you unprepared, we — not to say anything about you — would be ashamed of having been so confident. ⁵So I thought it necessary to urge the brothers to visit you in advance and finish the arrangements for the generous gift you had promised. Then it will be ready as a generous gift, not as one grudgingly given.

Sowing Generously

⁶Remember this: Whoever sows sparingly will also reap sparingly, and whoever sows generously will also reap generously. ⁷Each man should give what he has decided in his heart to give, not reluctantly or under compulsion, for God loves a cheerful giver. ⁸And God is able to make all grace abound to you, so that in all things at all times, having all that you need, you will abound in every good work. ⁹As it is written:

> "He has scattered abroad his gifts to the poor;
> his righteousness endures forever."ᵃ

¹⁰Now he who supplies seed to the sower and bread for food will also supply and increase your store of seed and will enlarge the harvest of your righteousness. ¹¹You will be made rich in every way so that you can be generous on every occasion, and through us your generosity will result in thanksgiving to God.

¹²This service that you perform is not only supplying the needs of God's people but is also overflowing in many expressions of thanks to God. ¹³Because of the service by which you have proved yourselves, men will praise God for the obedience that accompanies your confession of the gospel of Christ, and for your generosity in sharing with them and with everyone else. ¹⁴And in their prayers for you their hearts will go out to you, because of the surpassing grace God has given you. ¹⁵Thanks be to God for his indescribable gift!

Paul's Defense of His Ministry

10 By the meekness and gentleness of Christ, I appeal to you — I, Paul, who am "timid" when face to face with you, but "bold" when away! ²I beg you that when I come I may not have to be as bold as I expect to be toward some people who think that we live by the standards of this world. ³For though we live in the world, we do not wage war as the world does. ⁴The weapons we fight with are not the weapons of the world. On the contrary, they have divine power to demolish strongholds. ⁵We demolish arguments and every pretension that sets itself up against the knowledge of God, and we take captive every thought to make it obedient to Christ. ⁶And we will be ready to punish every act of disobedience, once your obedience is complete.

⁷You are looking only on the surface of things.ᵇ If anyone is confident that he belongs to Christ, he should consider again that we belong to Christ just as much as he. ⁸For even if I boast somewhat freely about the authority the Lord gave us for building you up rather than pulling you down, I will not be ashamed of it. ⁹I do not want to seem to be trying to frighten you with my letters. ¹⁰For some say, "His letters are weighty and forceful, but in person he is unimpressive and his speaking amounts to nothing." ¹¹Such people should realize that what we are in our letters when we are absent, we will be in our actions when we are present.

¹²We do not dare to classify or compare ourselves with some who commend themselves. When they measure themselves by themselves and compare themselves with themselves, they are not wise. ¹³We, however, will not boast beyond proper limits, but will confine our boasting to the field God has assigned to us, a field that reaches even to you. ¹⁴We are not going too far in our boasting, as would be the case if we had not come to you, for we did get as far as you with the gospel of Christ. ¹⁵Neither do we go beyond

ᵃ9 Psalm 112:9   ᵇ7 Or *Look at the obvious facts*

MATURITY BEGINS IN YOUR MIND

D uring a wintry week in which the McKays are snowbound, Gordon is abusing his five-year-old little brother with a series of mental games:

"How about if I trade you this nice shiny penny for that ugly, dirty quarter?"

"Yes means no and no means yes. Do you want me to give you a wedgie?"

"I'll pay your way out of jail if you give me Boardwalk and Park Place. I wouldn't offer such a good deal to anyone else. It's only because I like you so much."

Look It Up
••••

Being tricked in a game is not such a big deal. But being fooled in life can have serious consequences. And since Satan is the master deceiver, the apostle Paul warned, "Brothers, stop thinking like children. In regard to evil be infants, but in your thinking be adults" (1 Corinthians 14:20).

Why is it so important to grow up in the way that we think? Because "then we will no longer be infants, tossed back and forth by the waves, and blown here and there by every wind of teaching and by the cunning and craftiness of men in their deceitful scheming" (Ephesians 4:14).

Think It Through
••••

Why is it so easy to fool little kids? Because they don't know how to reason. They have not yet developed a sense of logic or the ability to discern between a good thing and a bad one.

Why does the devil fool so many Christians, getting them involved in cults and weird philosophies? Because many of them don't think critically in the spiritual realm (either because of immaturity or laziness).

Work It Out
••••

Right thinking is necessary for right behavior. So start thinking like a spiritual adult.

First, cut back on the world's input in your life. If all you put into your head are wrong thoughts and ideas, then when you come to a point where you need to make a tough decision, you'll only have bad information to work with!

Second, increase the amount of spiritual input in your life. Listen to Christian music, start going to a weekly Bible study, read through the Proverbs this month (a chapter a day), memorize a Scripture verse each week, purchase and read a Christian book that will give you deeper understanding of a particular problem in your life.

Nail It Down
••••

Read what Paul says about right thinking in 2 Corinthians 10:5.

Turn to pages 272, 1264 and 1284 for other readings on maturity.
Turn to page 1270 for Tuesday's reading.

Topic
••••

MATURITY

our limits by boasting of work done by others.*a* Our hope is that, as your faith continues to grow, our area of activity among you will greatly expand, **16**so that we can preach the gospel in the regions beyond you. For we do not want to boast about work already done in another man's territory. **17**But, "Let him who boasts boast in the Lord."*b* **18**For it is not the one who commends himself who is approved, but the one whom the Lord commends.

Paul and the False Apostles

11 I hope you will put up with a little of my foolishness; but you are already doing that. **2**I am jealous for you with a godly jealousy. I promised you to one husband, to Christ, so that I might present you as a pure virgin to him. **3**But I am afraid that just as Eve was deceived by the serpent's cunning, your minds may somehow be led astray from your sincere and pure devotion to Christ. **4**For if someone comes to you and preaches a Jesus other than the Jesus we preached, or if you receive a different spirit from the one you received, or a different gospel from the one you accepted, you put up with it easily enough. **5**But I do not think I am in the least inferior to those "super-apostles." **6**I may not be a trained speaker, but I do have knowledge. We have made this perfectly clear to you in every way.

7Was it a sin for me to lower myself in order to elevate you by preaching the gospel of God to you free of charge? **8**I robbed other churches by receiving support from them so as to serve you. **9**And when I was with you and needed something, I was not a burden to anyone, for the brothers who came from Macedonia supplied what I needed. I have kept myself from being a burden to you in any way, and will continue to do so. **10**As surely as the truth of Christ is in me, nobody in the regions of Achaia will stop this boasting of mine. **11**Why? Because I do not love you? God knows I do! **12**And I will keep on doing what I am doing in order to cut the ground from under those who want an opportunity to be considered equal with us in the things they boast about.

13For such men are false apostles, deceitful workmen, masquerading as apostles of Christ. **14**And no wonder, for Satan himself masquerades as an angel of light. **15**It is not surprising, then, if his servants masquerade as servants of righteousness. Their end will be what their actions deserve.

Paul Boasts About His Sufferings

16I repeat: Let no one take me for a fool. But if you do, then receive me just as you would a fool, so that I may do a little boasting. **17**In this self-confident boasting I am not talking as the Lord would, but as a fool. **18**Since many are boasting in the way the world does, I too will boast. **19**You gladly put up with fools since you are so wise! **20**In fact, you even put up with anyone who enslaves you or exploits you or takes advantage of you or pushes himself forward or slaps you in the face. **21**To my shame I admit that we were too weak for that!

What anyone else dares to boast about—I am speaking as a fool—I also dare to boast about. **22**Are they Hebrews? So am I. Are they Israelites? So am I. Are they Abraham's descendants? So am I. **23**Are they servants of Christ? (I am out of my mind to talk like this.) I am more. I have worked much harder, been in prison more frequently, been flogged more severely, and been exposed to death again and again. **24**Five times I received from the Jews the forty lashes minus one. **25**Three times I was beaten with rods, once I was stoned, three times I was shipwrecked, I spent a night and a day in the open sea, **26**I have been constantly on the move. I have been in danger from rivers, in danger from bandits, in danger from my own countrymen, in danger from Gentiles; in danger in the city, in danger in the country, in danger at sea; and in danger from false brothers. **27**I have labored and toiled and have often gone without sleep; I have known hunger and thirst and have often gone without food; I have been cold and naked. **28**Besides everything else, I face daily the pressure of my concern for all the churches. **29**Who is weak, and I do not feel weak? Who is led into sin, and I do not inwardly burn?

30If I must boast, I will boast of the things that show my weakness. **31**The God and Father of the Lord Jesus, who is to be praised forever, knows that I am not lying. **32**In Damascus the governor under King Aretas had the city of the Damascenes guarded in order to arrest me. **33**But I was lowered in a basket

a13-15 Or 13We, however, will not boast about things that cannot be measured, but we will boast according to the standard of measurement that the God of measure has assigned us—a measurement that relates even to you. 14 .... 15Neither do we boast about things that cannot be measured in regard to the work done by others.
b17 Jer. 9:24

from a window in the wall and slipped through his hands.

Paul's Vision and His Thorn

12 I must go on boasting. Although there is nothing to be gained, I will go on to visions and revelations from the Lord. ²I know a man in Christ who fourteen years ago was caught up to the third heaven. Whether it was in the body or out of the body I do not know—God knows. ³And I know that this man—whether in the body or apart from the body I do not know, but God knows— ⁴was caught up to paradise. He heard inexpressible things, things that man is not permitted to tell. ⁵I will boast about a man like that, but I will not boast about myself, except about my weaknesses. ⁶Even if I should choose to boast, I would not be a fool, because I would be speaking the truth. But I refrain, so no one will think more of me than is warranted by what I do or say.

⁷To keep me from becoming conceited because of these surpassingly great revelations, there was given me a thorn in my flesh, a messenger of Satan, to torment me. ⁸Three times I pleaded with the Lord to take it away from me. ⁹But he said to me, "My grace is sufficient for you, for my power is made perfect in weakness." Therefore I will boast all the more gladly about my weaknesses, so that Christ's power may rest on me. ¹⁰That is why, for Christ's sake, I delight in weaknesses, in insults, in hardships, in persecutions, in difficulties. For when I am weak, then I am strong.

Paul's Concern for the Corinthians

¹¹I have made a fool of myself, but you drove me to it. I ought to have been commended by you, for I am not in the least inferior to the "super-apostles," even though I am nothing. ¹²The things that mark an apostle—signs, wonders and miracles—were done among you with great perseverance. ¹³How were you inferior to the other churches, except that I was never a burden to you? Forgive me this wrong!

¹⁴Now I am ready to visit you for the third time, and I will not be a burden to you, because what I want is not your possessions but you. After all, children should not have to save up for their parents, but parents for their children. ¹⁵So I will very gladly spend for you everything I have and expend myself as well. If I love you more, will you love me

less? ¹⁶Be that as it may, I have not been a burden to you. Yet, crafty fellow that I am, I caught you by trickery! ¹⁷Did I exploit you through any of the men I sent you? ¹⁸I urged Titus to go to you and I sent our brother with him. Titus did not exploit you, did he? Did we not act in the same spirit and follow the same course?

¹⁹Have you been thinking all along that we have been defending ourselves to you? We have been speaking in the sight of God as those in Christ; and everything we do, dear friends, is for your strengthening. ²⁰For I am afraid that when I come I may not find you as I want you to be, and you may not find me as you want me to be. I fear that there may be quarreling, jealousy, outbursts of anger, factions, slander, gossip, arrogance and disorder. ²¹I am afraid that when I come again my God will humble me before you, and I will be grieved over many who have sinned earlier and have not repented of the impurity, sexual sin and debauchery in which they have indulged.

Final Warnings

13 This will be my third visit to you. "Every matter must be established by the testimony of two or three witnesses."[a] ²I already gave you a warning when I was with you the second time. I now repeat it while absent: On my return I will not spare those who sinned earlier or any of the others, ³since you are demanding proof that Christ is speaking through me. He is not weak in dealing with you, but is powerful among you. ⁴For to be sure, he was crucified in weakness, yet he lives by God's power. Likewise, we are weak in him, yet by God's power we will live with him to serve you.

⁵Examine yourselves to see whether you are in the faith; test yourselves. Do you not realize that Christ Jesus is in you—unless, of course, you fail the test? ⁶And I trust that you will discover that we have not failed the test. ⁷Now we pray to God that you will not do anything wrong. Not that people will see that we have stood the test but that you will do what is right even though we may seem to have failed. ⁸For we cannot do anything against the truth, but only for the truth. ⁹We are glad whenever we are weak but you are strong; and our prayer is for your perfection. ¹⁰This is why I write these things when I am absent, that when I come I may not have to be harsh in my use of authority—the au-

---

a 1 Deut. 19:15

thority the Lord gave me for building you up, not for tearing you down.

Final Greetings

11Finally, brothers, good-by. Aim for perfection, listen to my appeal, be of one mind, live in peace. And the God of love and peace will be with you.

12Greet one another with a holy kiss. **13**All the saints send their greetings.

14May the grace of the Lord Jesus Christ, and the love of God, and the fellowship of the Holy Spirit be with you all.

PEACE TREATIES WITH OTHER PEOPLE

Let's all pay a visit to the Stewart home. Trudy and Jeremy have both just gotten home from school:

"Hey, Trudy, do you think you could sit any closer to the TV? Sheesh! You're gonna get cancer all over your face."

A look of death. "Face cancer would only improve your looks, Jeremy."

"Shut up, you fat little freshman!"

A magazine flies in one direction. A fist in the other. Guess it's time to excuse ourselves.

Look It Up
• • • •

Knowing Christ means that you have the ability (and the obligation!) to relate to others in a peaceful way:

"If it is possible, as far as it depends on you, live at peace with everyone" (Romans 12:18).

"Let us therefore make every effort to do what leads to peace and to mutual edification" (Romans 14:19).

"Let the peace of Christ rule in your hearts, since as members of one body you were called to peace" (Colossians 3:15).

Think It Through
• • • •

Take a look at the actions/comments listed below. Which ones do you think would promote peace? Which ones would only generate conflict?

1. "Keep your fat face out of my business!"
2. Shoving your brother's head into the family aquarium.
3. Writing a note of apology.
4. "Hey, thanks, I really appreciate that."
5. Borrowing clothes without asking.
6. "I'm sorry. Will you forgive me?"

Pretty obvious, isn't it?

Work It Out
• • • •

Harmonious interaction with friends and family members doesn't just happen. Without real efforts to both maintain peace and restore it when it's been broken, relationships can degenerate into small-scale wars.

In your head, replay the scene from the opening story. What kind of words and actions from either Trudy or Jeremy might have caused that scene to turn out better?

Which one of the items mentioned above do you need to do or say today? Work to keep peace in at least one relationship and to establish peace in another. Peacekeeping and peacemaking are hard work, but they're always worth the effort.

Nail It Down
• • • •

Read Paul's final greeting to the Corinthians in 2 Corinthians 13:11.

Turn to pages 724, 736 and 991 for other readings on peace.
Turn to page 1272 for Wednesday's reading.

Topic
• • • •
PEACE

GALATIANS

EMERGENCY! The Galatian believers are in trouble. They are fooled into thinking that salvation is by grace plus works. Not so, writes Paul. No one can be saved by relying on the ceremonies of the law, which merely picture the coming Messiah. On the cross, Jesus sets us free from the law's ceremonies. Christians who rely on keeping the law to get right with God are like freed slaves returning to their former master. As you read, remember that Christ set you free to live by the power of the Holy Spirit.

1 Paul, an apostle—sent not from men nor by man, but by Jesus Christ and God the Father, who raised him from the dead— ²and all the brothers with me,

To the churches in Galatia:

³Grace and peace to you from God our Father and the Lord Jesus Christ, ⁴who gave himself for our sins to rescue us from the present evil age, according to the will of our God and Father, ⁵to whom be glory for ever and ever. Amen.

No Other Gospel

⁶I am astonished that you are so quickly deserting the one who called you by the grace of Christ and are turning to a different gospel— ⁷which is really no gospel at all. Evidently some people are throwing you into confusion and are trying to pervert the gospel of Christ. ⁸But even if we or an angel from heaven should preach a gospel other than the one we preached to you, let him be eternally condemned! ⁹As we have already said, so now I say again: If anybody is preaching to you a gospel other than what you accepted, let him be eternally condemned!

¹⁰Am I now trying to win the approval of men, or of God? Or am I trying to please men? If I were still trying to please men, I would not be a servant of Christ.

Paul Called by God

¹¹I want you to know, brothers, that the gospel I preached is not something that man

CUTTING OFF A HEAD TO SAVE A FACE

L arry (a Christian) is waiting in line with four of his friends (all non-Christians) at the theater when up walks Dion (a slightly mentally disabled kid who goes to Larry's church).

"Hey, Larry! Going to the movie?"

The guys snicker. Larry's face flushes. Rolling his eyes, he mumbles, "What does it look like I'm doing, Dion?"

"Can I sit with you?"

Everyone stares at Larry. Finally he shakes his head. "Look, Dion, I just want to be with my friends tonight, okay?"

Dion hangs his head and walks away.

Look It Up
••••

Have you heard the expression, "He cut off his nose to spite his face"? Well, here's the story of a man who cut off another man's head to save his own face!

"On Herod's birthday the daughter of Herodias danced for them and pleased Herod so much that he promised with an oath to give her whatever she asked. Prompted by her mother, she said, 'Give me here on a platter the head of John the Baptist.' The king was distressed, but because of his oaths and his dinner guests, he ordered that her request be granted" (Matthew 14:6–9).

Think It Through
••••

Larry's not a bad guy, and he didn't want to hurt poor Dion. But because he let his embarrassment control him, he ended up doing the wrong thing.

Have you ever been in a situation similar to the one Larry faced? If Larry had been at church and Dion had asked to sit with him, do you think Larry would have responded differently? Why or why not?

Work It Out
••••

Decide right now that you will do the right thing, no matter how embarrassing it may be, no matter who happens to be watching.
• Be kind (no matter what!) to that kid who's different.
• Get out of a car where alcohol is being consumed.
• Walk out of a movie that is filled with violence.
• Bow out of the conversation when the talk gets dirty.

And the wisest move of all? Don't even get into situations where you know you'll be made to feel embarrassed for doing what is right.

Nail It Down
••••

Read Galatians 2:11–14 for how even the apostle Peter let embarrassment control what he did.

Turn to pages 52 and 1063 for other readings on embarrassment.
Turn to page 1274 for Thursday's reading.

Topic
••••

EMBARRASSMENT

made up. [12]I did not receive it from any man, nor was I taught it; rather, I received it by revelation from Jesus Christ.

[13]For you have heard of my previous way of life in Judaism, how intensely I persecuted the church of God and tried to destroy it. [14]I was advancing in Judaism beyond many Jews of my own age and was extremely zealous for the traditions of my fathers. [15]But when God, who set me apart from birth[a] and called me by his grace, was pleased [16]to reveal his Son in me so that I might preach him among the Gentiles, I did not consult any man, [17]nor did I go up to Jerusalem to see those who were apostles before I was, but I went immediately into Arabia and later returned to Damascus.

[18]Then after three years, I went up to Jerusalem to get acquainted with Peter[b] and stayed with him fifteen days. [19]I saw none of the other apostles—only James, the Lord's brother. [20]I assure you before God that what I am writing you is no lie. [21]Later I went to Syria and Cilicia. [22]I was personally unknown to the churches of Judea that are in Christ. [23]They only heard the report: "The man who formerly persecuted us is now preaching the faith he once tried to destroy." [24]And they praised God because of me.

Paul Accepted by the Apostles

2 Fourteen years later I went up again to Jerusalem, this time with Barnabas. I took Titus along also. [2]I went in response to a revelation and set before them the gospel that I preach among the Gentiles. But I did this privately to those who seemed to be leaders, for fear that I was running or had run my race in vain. [3]Yet not even Titus, who was with me, was compelled to be circumcised, even though he was a Greek. [4]This matter arose, because some false brothers had infiltrated our ranks to spy on the freedom we have in Christ Jesus and to make us slaves. [5]We did not give in to them for a moment, so that the truth of the gospel might remain with you.

[6]As for those who seemed to be important—whatever they were makes no difference to me; God does not judge by external appearance—those men added nothing to my message. [7]On the contrary, they saw that I had been entrusted with the task of preaching the gospel to the Gentiles,[c] just as Peter had been to the Jews.[d] [8]For God,

who was at work in the ministry of Peter as an apostle to the Jews, was also at work in my ministry as an apostle to the Gentiles. [9]James, Peter[e] and John, those reputed to be pillars, gave me and Barnabas the right hand of fellowship when they recognized the grace given to me. They agreed that we should go to the Gentiles, and they to the Jews. [10]All they asked was that we should continue to remember the poor, the very thing I was eager to do.

Paul Opposes Peter

[11]When Peter came to Antioch, I opposed him to his face, because he was clearly in the wrong. [12]Before certain men came from James, he used to eat with the Gentiles. But when they arrived, he began to draw back and separate himself from the Gentiles because he was afraid of those who belonged to the circumcision group. [13]The other Jews joined him in his hypocrisy, so that by their hypocrisy even Barnabas was led astray.

[14]When I saw that they were not acting in line with the truth of the gospel, I said to Peter in front of them all, "You are a Jew, yet you live like a Gentile and not like a Jew. How is it, then, that you force Gentiles to follow Jewish customs?

[15]"We who are Jews by birth and not 'Gentile sinners' [16]know that a man is not justified by observing the law, but by faith in Jesus Christ. So we, too, have put our faith in Christ Jesus that we may be justified by faith in Christ and not by observing the law, because by observing the law no one will be justified.

[17]"If, while we seek to be justified in Christ, it becomes evident that we ourselves are sinners, does that mean that Christ promotes sin? Absolutely not! [18]If I rebuild what I destroyed, I prove that I am a lawbreaker. [19]For through the law I died to the law so that I might live for God. [20]I have been crucified with Christ and I no longer live, but Christ lives in me. The life I live in the body, I live by faith in the Son of God, who loved me and gave himself for me. [21]I do not set aside the grace of God, for if righteousness could be gained through the law, Christ died for nothing!"[f]

Faith or Observance of the Law

3 You foolish Galatians! Who has bewitched you? Before your very eyes

---

a15 Or from my mother's womb   *b18 Greek Cephas*   *c7 Greek uncircumcised*   *d7 Greek circumcised; also* in verses 8 and 9   *e9 Greek Cephas; also in verses 11 and 14*   *f21 Some interpreters end the quotation* after verse 14.

LABELS: CONVENIENT, EASY... AND WRONG!

Lewis and Leonard laugh about their first meeting.

Lewis: "I thought he was a dumb jock. I didn't want to have anything to do with him!"

Leonard: "I remember thinking, 'Oh, great! I'm going to be living next door to a freak!' His hair was kind of long, and he had—shall we say—different musical tastes."

It's a good thing the guys didn't stick with their first impressions. Over the last year they have become extremely close friends.

Look It Up

We are masters at labeling. We see someone. We quickly examine his or her appearance and/or behavior. We make a snap judgment, assign a label and then—if it's a category that's threatening or different—we dismiss the person. How easy . . . how convenient . . . how wrong!

Such intolerance almost kept Nathanael from meeting Christ!

"Philip found Nathanael and told him, 'We have found the one Moses wrote about in the Law, and about whom the prophets also wrote—Jesus of Nazareth, the son of Joseph.'

" 'Nazareth! Can anything good come from there?' Nathanael asked.

" 'Come and see,' said Philip (John 1:45–46).

Fortunately, Nathanael went beyond labeling. Because he did, he found a friend—and a Savior (John 1:49)—in Jesus Christ.

Think It Through

The world says, "First impressions are everything!" God says that you must get beyond the surface (1 Samuel 16:7) in order to appreciate the uniqueness of each individual.

Are you missing out on a potentially great friendship because you have labeled someone?

Work It Out

Think of all the categories you use to label people at your school and in your church. What labels do you think people attach to you?

Reach out today to someone you would ordinarily ignore. Look beyond the surface impression that he or she is odd, a jock, a brain, whatever. Strike up a conversation and try to get to know the real person behind the label you've given.

Nail It Down

Read what Galatians 3:26–28 has to say about labeling others.

Turn to pages 1089, 1132 and 1182 for other readings on intolerance.
Turn to page 1276 for Friday's reading.

Topic

INTOLERANCE

Jesus Christ was clearly portrayed as crucified. [2]I would like to learn just one thing from you: Did you receive the Spirit by observing the law, or by believing what you heard? [3]Are you so foolish? After beginning with the Spirit, are you now trying to attain your goal by human effort? [4]Have you suffered so much for nothing—if it really was for nothing? [5]Does God give you his Spirit and work miracles among you because you observe the law, or because you believe what you heard?

[6]Consider Abraham: "He believed God, and it was credited to him as righteousness."[a] [7]Understand, then, that those who believe are children of Abraham. [8]The Scripture foresaw that God would justify the Gentiles by faith, and announced the gospel in advance to Abraham: "All nations will be blessed through you."[b] [9]So those who have faith are blessed along with Abraham, the man of faith.

[10]All who rely on observing the law are under a curse, for it is written: "Cursed is everyone who does not continue to do everything written in the Book of the Law."[c] [11]Clearly no one is justified before God by the law, because, "The righteous will live by faith."[d] [12]The law is not based on faith; on the contrary, "The man who does these things will live by them."[e] [13]Christ redeemed us from the curse of the law by becoming a curse for us, for it is written: "Cursed is everyone who is hung on a tree."[f] [14]He redeemed us in order that the blessing given to Abraham might come to the Gentiles through Christ Jesus, so that by faith we might receive the promise of the Spirit.

The Law and the Promise

[15]Brothers, let me take an example from everyday life. Just as no one can set aside or add to a human covenant that has been duly established, so it is in this case. [16]The promises were spoken to Abraham and to his seed. The Scripture does not say "and to seeds," meaning many people, but "and to your seed,"[g] meaning one person, who is Christ. [17]What I mean is this: The law, introduced 430 years later, does not set aside the covenant previously established by God and thus do away with the promise. [18]For if the inheritance depends on the law, then it no longer depends on a promise; but God in his grace gave it to Abraham through a promise.

[19]What, then, was the purpose of the law? It was added because of transgressions until the Seed to whom the promise referred had come. The law was put into effect through angels by a mediator. [20]A mediator, however, does not represent just one party; but God is one.

[21]Is the law, therefore, opposed to the promises of God? Absolutely not! For if a law had been given that could impart life, then righteousness would certainly have come by the law. [22]But the Scripture declares that the whole world is a prisoner of sin, so that what was promised, being given through faith in Jesus Christ, might be given to those who believe.

[23]Before this faith came, we were held prisoners by the law, locked up until faith should be revealed. [24]So the law was put in charge to lead us to Christ[h] that we might be justified by faith. [25]Now that faith has come, we are no longer under the supervision of the law.

Sons of God

[26]You are all sons of God through faith in Christ Jesus, [27]for all of you who were baptized into Christ have clothed yourselves with Christ. [28]There is neither Jew nor Greek, slave nor free, male nor female, for you are all one in Christ Jesus. [29]If you belong to Christ, then you are Abraham's seed, and heirs according to the promise.

4 What I am saying is that as long as the heir is a child, he is no different from a slave, although he owns the whole estate. [2]He is subject to guardians and trustees until the time set by his father. [3]So also, when we were children, we were in slavery under the basic principles of the world. [4]But when the time had fully come, God sent his Son, born of a woman, born under law, [5]to redeem those under law, that we might receive the full rights of sons. [6]Because you are sons, God sent the Spirit of his Son into our hearts, the Spirit who calls out, "Abba,[i] Father." [7]So you are no longer a slave, but a son; and since you are a son, God has made you also an heir.

Paul's Concern for the Galatians

[8]Formerly, when you did not know God, you were slaves to those who by nature are not gods. [9]But now that you know God—or rather are known by God—how is it that you are turning back to those weak and misera-

a6 Gen. 15:6   b8 Gen. 12:3; 18:18; 22:18   c10 Deut. 27:26   d11 Hab. 2:4   e12 Lev. 18:5   f13 Deut. 21:23   g16 Gen. 12:7; 13:15; 24:7   h24 Or charge until Christ came   i6 Aramaic for Father

RAMPAGING HORMONES

• •

Friday, 11:15 P.M., overlooking Lake Wiley, in a 1988 Mustang: (There's no dialogue in this scene—just a lot of heavy breathing. And since the car's windows are fogged up, we're unable to describe the action for you. Let's just say that from here it doesn't look like Doug and Suzanne are discussing yesterday's algebra test!)

Look It Up
• • • •

Having self-control over your sexual desires is difficult. Not impossible by any means, but difficult. Maybe that's why God's Word has so many warnings on this subject. For example:

"Live by the Spirit, and you will not gratify the desires of the sinful nature. For the sinful nature desires what is contrary to the Spirit, and the Spirit what is contrary to the sinful nature. . . . The acts of the sinful nature are obvious: sexual immorality, impurity and debauchery. . . . But the fruit of the Spirit is . . . self-control. . . . Those who belong to Christ Jesus have crucified the sinful nature with its passions and desires. Since we live by the Spirit, let us keep in step with the Spirit" (Galatians 5:16–25).

Think It Through
• • • •

Take your pick. You can either: (1) listen to your sinful nature, "go for it" sexually, and end up a slave of your passions; or (2) live according to God's Word and experience the freedom of self-control.

But before you make your decision, remember that choice number one angers God, produces guilt and frustration, and ruins relationships. Choice number two pleases God, produces character and respect and strengthens relationships.

Work It Out
• • • •

Some couples get alone in a dark place, start kissing and caressing each other, and then want to know why they can't stop. Forget it! Self-control begins by avoiding dangerous situations altogether.

If you're having trouble exercising self-control in your dating life, pray this prayer: "Lord, I need you. I've sinned by getting too physical in my relationships. I know that's wrong, and I want to come back to what's right. Forgive and cleanse me. Give me your strength so that I can say no to my sinful nature. I want to live by the Spirit. Give me the wisdom to avoid tempting situations in the future. Through Christ, my Lord. Amen."

Nail It Down
• • • •

Read Galatians 5:16 for instruction on how to live a pure life.

Turn to pages 550 and 665 for other readings on self-control.
Turn to page 1278 for the weekend reading.

Topic
• • • •

SELF-CONTROL

ble principles? Do you wish to be enslaved by them all over again? **10**You are observing special days and months and seasons and years! **11**I fear for you, that somehow I have wasted my efforts on you.

12I plead with you, brothers, become like me, for I became like you. You have done me no wrong. **13**As you know, it was because of an illness that I first preached the gospel to you. **14**Even though my illness was a trial to you, you did not treat me with contempt or scorn. Instead, you welcomed me as if I were an angel of God, as if I were Christ Jesus himself. **15**What has happened to all your joy? I can testify that, if you could have done so, you would have torn out your eyes and given them to me. **16**Have I now become your enemy by telling you the truth?

17Those people are zealous to win you over, but for no good. What they want is to alienate you ⸤from us⸥, so that you may be zealous for them. **18**It is fine to be zealous, provided the purpose is good, and to be so always and not just when I am with you. **19**My dear children, for whom I am again in the pains of childbirth until Christ is formed in you, **20**how I wish I could be with you now and change my tone, because I am perplexed about you!

Hagar and Sarah

21Tell me, you who want to be under the law, are you not aware of what the law says? **22**For it is written that Abraham had two sons, one by the slave woman and the other by the free woman. **23**His son by the slave woman was born in the ordinary way; but his son by the free woman was born as the result of a promise.

24These things may be taken figuratively, for the women represent two covenants. One covenant is from Mount Sinai and bears children who are to be slaves: This is Hagar. **25**Now Hagar stands for Mount Sinai in Arabia and corresponds to the present city of Jerusalem, because she is in slavery with her children. **26**But the Jerusalem that is above is free, and she is our mother. **27**For it is written:

> "Be glad, O barren woman,
>   who bears no children;
> break forth and cry aloud,
>   you who have no labor pains;
> because more are the children of the
>   desolate woman
>   than of her who has a husband."[a]

28Now you, brothers, like Isaac, are children of promise. **29**At that time the son born in the ordinary way persecuted the son born by the power of the Spirit. It is the same now. **30**But what does the Scripture say? "Get rid of the slave woman and her son, for the slave woman's son will never share in the inheritance with the free woman's son."[b] **31**Therefore, brothers, we are not children of the slave woman, but of the free woman.

Freedom in Christ

5 It is for freedom that Christ has set us free. Stand firm, then, and do not let yourselves be burdened again by a yoke of slavery.

2Mark my words! I, Paul, tell you that if you let yourselves be circumcised, Christ will be of no value to you at all. **3**Again I declare to every man who lets himself be circumcised that he is obligated to obey the whole law. **4**You who are trying to be justified by law have been alienated from Christ; you have fallen away from grace. **5**But by faith we eagerly await through the Spirit the righteousness for which we hope. **6**For in Christ Jesus neither circumcision nor uncircumcision has any value. The only thing that counts is faith expressing itself through love.

7You were running a good race. Who cut in on you and kept you from obeying the truth? **8**That kind of persuasion does not come from the one who calls you. **9**"A little yeast works through the whole batch of dough." **10**I am confident in the Lord that you will take no other view. The one who is throwing you into confusion will pay the penalty, whoever he may be. **11**Brothers, if I am still preaching circumcision, why am I still being persecuted? In that case the offense of the cross has been abolished. **12**As for those agitators, I wish they would go the whole way and emasculate themselves!

13You, my brothers, were called to be free. But do not use your freedom to indulge the sinful nature[c]; rather, serve one another in love. **14**The entire law is summed up in a single command: "Love your neighbor as yourself."[d] **15**If you keep on biting and devouring each other, watch out or you will be destroyed by each other.

Life by the Spirit

16So I say, live by the Spirit, and you will not gratify the desires of the sinful nature.

---

a27 Isaiah 54:1　　*b30* Gen. 21:10　　*c13* Or *the flesh*; also in verses 16, 17, 19 and 24　　*d14* Lev. 19:18

DEFINING CONCEIT

Work It Out
••••

Look up the word *conceited* in the dictionary. What does it say? Conceit is a personality trait, a characteristic. And not a very positive one. A conceited person is someone with an exaggerated opinion of his or her own importance.

Conceited is thinking you're better simply because you wear the "right" jeans. Conceited is thinking you're more important because you're on the student council. Conceited is thinking you're one step higher than others because you go to church and youth group. Conceited is treating others as if they're not terribly important to you or anyone else for that matter.

Conceit should not be a characteristic of your life as a Christian. Do you have work to do on your character?

Nail It Down

Read Paul's words on conceit in Galatians 5:25–26.

Think It Through
••••

Think about it. And be honest. Do you ever look down on someone at school simply because they wear not-so-stylish clothes? Do you ever treat those around you as if they don't matter? Do you ever look down your nose at your neighbors who don't go to church?

Being conceited is totally out of character for the Christian. Paul says those parts of your sinful nature were crucified with Christ. But those negative characteristics have a funny way of turning up just when you think you've got them conquered.

Be on the alert, looking for any sign of conceit in your life. If you find it, get rid of it . . . fast.

Nail It Down
••••

Reread Paul's words in Galatians 5:25–26. For further insight read Proverbs 3:27–35.

Turn to pages 678, 751, 853 and 1325 for other readings on character.
Turn to page 1280 for Monday's reading.

Topic
••••

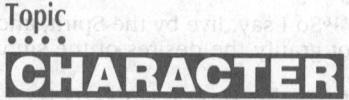

CHARACTER

17For the sinful nature desires what is contrary to the Spirit, and the Spirit what is contrary to the sinful nature. They are in conflict with each other, so that you do not do what you want. **18**But if you are led by the Spirit, you are not under law.

19The acts of the sinful nature are obvious: sexual immorality, impurity and debauchery; **20**idolatry and witchcraft; hatred, discord, jealousy, fits of rage, selfish ambition, dissensions, factions **21**and envy; drunkenness, orgies, and the like. I warn you, as I did before, that those who live like this will not inherit the kingdom of God.

22But the fruit of the Spirit is love, joy, peace, patience, kindness, goodness, faithfulness, **23**gentleness and self-control. Against such things there is no law. **24**Those who belong to Christ Jesus have crucified the sinful nature with its passions and desires. **25**Since we live by the Spirit, let us keep in step with the Spirit. **26**Let us not become conceited, provoking and envying each other.

Doing Good to All

6 Brothers, if someone is caught in a sin, you who are spiritual should restore him gently. But watch yourself, or you also may be tempted. **2**Carry each other's burdens, and in this way you will fulfill the law of Christ. **3**If anyone thinks he is something when he is nothing, he deceives himself. **4**Each one should test his own actions. Then he can take pride in himself, without comparing himself to somebody else, **5**for each one should carry his own load.

6Anyone who receives instruction in the word must share all good things with his instructor.

7Do not be deceived: God cannot be mocked. A man reaps what he sows. **8**The one who sows to please his sinful nature, from that nature*ᵃ* will reap destruction; the one who sows to please the Spirit, from the Spirit will reap eternal life. **9**Let us not become weary in doing good, for at the proper time we will reap a harvest if we do not give up. **10**Therefore, as we have opportunity, let us do good to all people, especially to those who belong to the family of believers.

Not Circumcision but a New Creation

11See what large letters I use as I write to you with my own hand!

12Those who want to make a good impression outwardly are trying to compel you to be circumcised. The only reason they do this is to avoid being persecuted for the cross of Christ. **13**Not even those who are circumcised obey the law, yet they want you to be circumcised that they may boast about your flesh. **14**May I never boast except in the cross of our Lord Jesus Christ, through which*ᵇ* the world has been crucified to me, and I to the world. **15**Neither circumcision nor uncircumcision means anything; what counts is a new creation. **16**Peace and mercy to all who follow this rule, even to the Israel of God.

17Finally, let no one cause me trouble, for I bear on my body the marks of Jesus.

18The grace of our Lord Jesus Christ be with your spirit, brothers. Amen.

ᵃ8 Or *his flesh, from the flesh*   *ᵇ14* Or *whom*

1280

LEARNING TO SHARE THE LOAD

Seventeen-year-old Adrian is on the verge of losing it. Last year her mother suddenly left and is now living with some guy in Idaho. Now, on top of studies, a part-time job, and involvement in a couple of groups at school and church, Adrian has the added pressure of being a stand-in mom to her little sister while her dad works an extra job.

Yesterday, when she got an English paper back with a big red D on it, she dissolved in tears.

"Adrian, get a grip! It's just one paper," urged Judi.

"You don't understand!" Adrian sobbed.

Look It Up ••••

You don't have to live in a broken home to feel the pressure of too much responsibility. That kind of stress is everywhere! Consider the advice Moses got when he was worn out from settling the disputes of the people:

"What you are doing is not good . . . . The work is too heavy for you; you cannot handle it alone" (Exodus 18:17–18).

The speaker was Jethro, Moses' father-in-law. He urged the exhausted leader of Israel to find some helpers. "That will make your load lighter, because they will share it with you. If you do this and God so commands, you will be able to stand the strain" (Exodus 18:22–23).

Think It Through ••••

How can you tell when the stress levels in your life are too high? Any of the following may be warning signals: nervousness, depression, irritability, sleeping difficulty, loss of appetite (or binge eating), headaches, fatigue, frequent crying, inability to concentrate, skin problems, apathy.

Work It Out ••••

Stressed out? Seek out others who can help lighten your load.
• Find a prayer partner during especially stressful periods.
• Look for a study buddy in your hardest class.
• Confide in a close friend during painful times.
• Pour out your heart to a parent or youth leader when you feel weary.
• Ask a brother or sister for help in completing tough tasks.

Why try to carry burdens that are too heavy for one person? The body of Christ is there to help you. But you first have to ask for help!

Nail It Down ••••

Memorize Galatians 6:2.

Turn to pages 546, 778, 1058 and 1219 for other readings on stress.
Turn to page 1282 for Tuesday's reading.

Topic
••••

EPHESIANS

WHAT you believe affects how you behave. If you are a believer in Christ you have unlimited spiritual wealth at your disposal, so live that way! In the first half of his letter to the Ephesians, Paul explains God's plan to redeem the world through Christ, showing what a spiritual treasure that great truth is. In the second half Paul shows believers how to apply those resources in their earthly walk. As you read Ephesians, examine your life. Make sure that you translate your belief about God into actions and attitudes that honor God.

Outline of Contents

1 Paul, an apostle of Christ Jesus by the will of God,

To the saints in Ephesus,*a* the faithful*b* in Christ Jesus:

2Grace and peace to you from God our Father and the Lord Jesus Christ.

Spiritual Blessings in Christ

3Praise be to the God and Father of our Lord Jesus Christ, who has blessed us in the heavenly realms with every spiritual blessing in Christ. **4**For he chose us in him before the creation of the world to be holy and blameless in his sight. In love **5**he*c* predes-tined us to be adopted as his sons through Jesus Christ, in accordance with his pleasure and will— **6**to the praise of his glorious grace, which he has freely given us in the One he loves. **7**In him we have redemption through his blood, the forgiveness of sins, in accordance with the riches of God's grace **8**that he lavished on us with all wisdom and understanding. **9**And he*d* made known to us the mystery of his will according to his good pleasure, which he purposed in Christ, **10**to be put into effect when the times will have reached their fulfillment—to bring all things in heaven and on earth together under one head, even Christ.

---

a1 Some early manuscripts do not have *in Ephesus.*   *b1* Or *believers who are*   *c4,5* Or *sight in love.* *5He*
d8,9 Or *us. With all wisdom and understanding,* *9he*

MYTH: HUMANS ARE ALL ALONE

Kim fell asleep before she could finish reading *The Stranger* by Albert Camus. So she got up early to finish the last chapter and review her notes for the quiz.

In the dim, early light of dawn, she thought to herself, "How depressing!"

Bingo! *The Stranger* is about a man who lives in a world of despair, where God is absent and where people are alienated from each other. But depressing as that point of view sounds, it's commonly believed today. It's exactly how many people feel.

Look It Up
••••

Another famous book, the Bible, states that humans are *not* alone in the universe. The Bible begins with these magnificent words: "In the beginning God . . ." (Genesis 1:1). In other words, God exists!

The Bible ends with these exciting words: "Now the dwelling of God is with men, and he will live with them. They will be his people, and God himself will be with them and be their God. He will wipe every tear from their eyes. There will be no more death or mourning or crying or pain, for the old order of things has passed away" (Revelation 21:3–4).

In other words, you do not have to despair or live in alienation. You can know the God who exists, and you can live with him forever!

Think It Through
••••

Many people throughout history have struggled with the same feelings of despair that Camus felt. After all, if God doesn't exist, there is no meaningful origin or meaningful destiny. Anything goes, nothing matters, life is a cosmic mistake.

Work It Out
••••

What's the alternative? Turn to your Creator and find meaning and security in this world. Trust Christ and know that you aren't alone in a strange universe. Here's a prayer for today:

"God, I want to gain a better understanding of human nature. But more than that, I want to know you. Thank you that I am not alone in the universe. Open my eyes and change my life as I spend time in your Word. Amen."

Nail It Down
••••

Think about Ephesians 2:8–19 and how it should affect the way you live.

Turn to pages 439, 768 and 1311 for other readings on human nature.
Turn to page 1284 for Wednesday's reading.

Topic
••••

HUMAN NATURE

11In him we were also chosen,*a* having been predestined according to the plan of him who works out everything in conformity with the purpose of his will, **12**in order that we, who were the first to hope in Christ, might be for the praise of his glory. **13**And you also were included in Christ when you heard the word of truth, the gospel of your salvation. Having believed, you were marked in him with a seal, the promised Holy Spirit, **14**who is a deposit guaranteeing our inheritance until the redemption of those who are God's possession—to the praise of his glory.

Thanksgiving and Prayer

15For this reason, ever since I heard about your faith in the Lord Jesus and your love for all the saints, **16**I have not stopped giving thanks for you, remembering you in my prayers. **17**I keep asking that the God of our Lord Jesus Christ, the glorious Father, may give you the Spirit*b* of wisdom and revelation, so that you may know him better. **18**I pray also that the eyes of your heart may be enlightened in order that you may know the hope to which he has called you, the riches of his glorious inheritance in the saints, **19**and his incomparably great power for us who believe. That power is like the working of his mighty strength, **20**which he exerted in Christ when he raised him from the dead and seated him at his right hand in the heavenly realms, **21**far above all rule and authority, power and dominion, and every title that can be given, not only in the present age but also in the one to come. **22**And God placed all things under his feet and appointed him to be head over everything for the church, **23**which is his body, the fullness of him who fills everything in every way.

Made Alive in Christ

2 As for you, you were dead in your transgressions and sins, **2**in which you used to live when you followed the ways of this world and of the ruler of the kingdom of the air, the spirit who is now at work in those who are disobedient. **3**All of us also lived among them at one time, gratifying the cravings of our sinful nature*c* and following its desires and thoughts. Like the rest, we were by nature objects of wrath. **4**But because of his great love for us, God, who is rich in mercy, **5**made us alive with Christ even when we were dead in transgressions—it is by grace you have been saved. **6**And God raised us up

with Christ and seated us with him in the heavenly realms in Christ Jesus, **7**in order that in the coming ages he might show the incomparable riches of his grace, expressed in his kindness to us in Christ Jesus. **8**For it is by grace you have been saved, through faith—and this not from yourselves, it is the gift of God— **9**not by works, so that no one can boast. **10**For we are God's workmanship, created in Christ Jesus to do good works, which God prepared in advance for us to do.

One in Christ

11Therefore, remember that formerly you who are Gentiles by birth and called "uncircumcised" by those who call themselves "the circumcision" (that done in the body by the hands of men)— **12**remember that at that time you were separate from Christ, excluded from citizenship in Israel and foreigners to the covenants of the promise, without hope and without God in the world. **13**But now in Christ Jesus you who once were far away have been brought near through the blood of Christ.

14For he himself is our peace, who has made the two one and has destroyed the barrier, the dividing wall of hostility, **15**by abolishing in his flesh the law with its commandments and regulations. His purpose was to create in himself one new man out of the two, thus making peace, **16**and in this one body to reconcile both of them to God through the cross, by which he put to death their hostility. **17**He came and preached peace to you who were far away and peace to those who were near. **18**For through him we both have access to the Father by one Spirit.

19Consequently, you are no longer foreigners and aliens, but fellow citizens with God's people and members of God's household, **20**built on the foundation of the apostles and prophets, with Christ Jesus himself as the chief cornerstone. **21**In him the whole building is joined together and rises to become a holy temple in the Lord. **22**And in him you too are being built together to become a dwelling in which God lives by his Spirit.

Paul the Preacher to the Gentiles

3 For this reason I, Paul, the prisoner of Christ Jesus for the sake of you Gentiles—

2Surely you have heard about the administration of God's grace that was given to me

a11 Or were made heirs   b17 Or a spirit   c3 Or our flesh

THE GOAL OF SPIRITUAL GROWTH

Kevin is baby-sitting for the "terrible Turners." After rescuing the hamster from the trash compactor, he manages to get the baby to sleep. He then focuses his attention on removing part of a peanut butter sandwich from the VCR. As he works, the following exchange takes place:

Melissa yells, "I'm gonna be a doctor when I grow up!" Without looking up, Kevin mumbles, "You keep it up, kid, and you won't live that long."

"I'm gonna be a fighter!" shouts six-year-old Timmy as he body slams Melissa into the couch.

Look It Up
••••

A major concern of little kids is that they grow up physically to be like someone they idolize. A major concern of God is that we grow up spiritually to become like Jesus Christ.

"For those God foreknew he also predestined to be conformed to the likeness of his Son" (Romans 8:29).

"And we, who . . . all reflect the Lord's glory, are being transformed into his likeness with ever-increasing glory" (2 Corinthians 3:18).

"Dear friends, now we are children of God, and what we will be has not yet been made known. But we know that when he appears, we shall be like him, for we shall see him as he is" (1 John 3:2).

Think It Through
••••

As a kid, Kevin was unsure about what he wanted to be. He changed his mind about a thousand times. In high school he narrowed his choices. Now in college he has a single objective: a degree in engineering. That's a sign of maturity: being able to choose, pursue and reach a single goal.

Is your top spiritual priority to become like Christ? Are you shooting for that important goal?

Work It Out
••••

Spiritual maturity is impossible without the right goal—the commitment to become like Jesus Christ. You can begin your spiritual journey with this prayer:

"Father, just as I'm developing physically, emotionally and intellectually, I know I also need to grow spiritually. Teach me this week how to do that. I want to become more like you."

Then sit down and write down some specific things you could begin doing today to become more like Christ. Before the day is over, do at least one of those things.

Nail It Down
••••

Read Ephesians 4:11–13 for Paul's encouragement to grow spiritually.

Turn to pages 272, 1264 and 1266 for other readings on maturity.
Turn to page 1286 for Thursday's reading.

Topic
••••
MATURITY

for you, ³that is, the mystery made known to me by revelation, as I have already written briefly. ⁴In reading this, then, you will be able to understand my insight into the mystery of Christ, ⁵which was not made known to men in other generations as it has now been revealed by the Spirit to God's holy apostles and prophets. ⁶This mystery is that through the gospel the Gentiles are heirs together with Israel, members together of one body, and sharers together in the promise in Christ Jesus.

⁷I became a servant of this gospel by the gift of God's grace given me through the working of his power. ⁸Although I am less than the least of all God's people, this grace was given me: to preach to the Gentiles the unsearchable riches of Christ, ⁹and to make plain to everyone the administration of this mystery, which for ages past was kept hidden in God, who created all things. ¹⁰His intent was that now, through the church, the manifold wisdom of God should be made known to the rulers and authorities in the heavenly realms, ¹¹according to his eternal purpose which he accomplished in Christ Jesus our Lord. ¹²In him and through faith in him we may approach God with freedom and confidence. ¹³I ask you, therefore, not to be discouraged because of my sufferings for you, which are your glory.

A Prayer for the Ephesians

¹⁴For this reason I kneel before the Father, ¹⁵from whom his whole family[a] in heaven and on earth derives its name. ¹⁶I pray that out of his glorious riches he may strengthen you with power through his Spirit in your inner being, ¹⁷so that Christ may dwell in your hearts through faith. And I pray that you, being rooted and established in love, ¹⁸may have power, together with all the saints, to grasp how wide and long and high and deep is the love of Christ, ¹⁹and to know this love that surpasses knowledge — that you may be filled to the measure of all the fullness of God.

²⁰Now to him who is able to do immeasurably more than all we ask or imagine, according to his power that is at work within us, ²¹to him be glory in the church and in Christ Jesus throughout all generations, for ever and ever! Amen.

Unity in the Body of Christ

4 As a prisoner for the Lord, then, I urge you to live a life worthy of the calling you have received. ²Be completely humble and gentle; be patient, bearing with one another in love. ³Make every effort to keep the unity of the Spirit through the bond of peace. ⁴There is one body and one Spirit — just as you were called to one hope when you were called — ⁵one Lord, one faith, one baptism; ⁶one God and Father of all, who is over all and through all and in all.

⁷But to each one of us grace has been given as Christ apportioned it. ⁸This is why it[b] says:

"When he ascended on high,
  he led captives in his train
  and gave gifts to men."[c]

⁹(What does "he ascended" mean except that he also descended to the lower, earthly regions[d]? ¹⁰He who descended is the very one who ascended higher than all the heavens, in order to fill the whole universe.) ¹¹It was he who gave some to be apostles, some to be prophets, some to be evangelists, and some to be pastors and teachers, ¹²to prepare God's people for works of service, so that the body of Christ may be built up ¹³until we all reach unity in the faith and in the knowledge of the Son of God and become mature, attaining to the whole measure of the fullness of Christ.

¹⁴Then we will no longer be infants, tossed back and forth by the waves, and blown here and there by every wind of teaching and by the cunning and craftiness of men in their deceitful scheming. ¹⁵Instead, speaking the truth in love, we will in all things grow up into him who is the Head, that is, Christ. ¹⁶From him the whole body, joined and held together by every supporting ligament, grows and builds itself up in love, as each part does its work.

Living as Children of Light

¹⁷So I tell you this, and insist on it in the Lord, that you must no longer live as the Gentiles do, in the futility of their thinking. ¹⁸They are darkened in their understanding and separated from the life of God because of the ignorance that is in them due to the hardening of their hearts. ¹⁹Having lost all sensitivity, they have given themselves over to sensuality so as to indulge in every kind of impurity, with a continual lust for more.

²⁰You, however, did not come to know Christ that way. ²¹Surely you heard of him and were taught in him in accordance with the truth that is in Jesus. ²²You were taught,

---

a15 Or *whom all fatherhood*   *b8* Or *God*   *c8* Psalm 68:18   *d9* Or *the depths of the earth*

INNER C'S FOR INNER PEACE

Stan has been accepted at two different schools—Freedom University and Einstein College. He has good friends going to each place. He likes certain things about each school. What should he do?

Should Angela take a job at the clothing store or the dry cleaners? The pay is about the same.

Curt can either play baseball or be in the spring play, but not both. He's both a good athlete and a gifted actor.

Look It Up
••••

Here are three C's to find the will of God:

1. *Common Sense*. Christianity is a rational faith. God is a logical God. You can use your Biblically informed reason to make decisions. Paul often used common sense (Acts 15:38).

2. *Compulsion*. Often God will give inner impressions to follow or not to follow a certain course. This was Paul's experience: "And now, compelled by the Spirit, I am going to Jerusalem" (Acts 20:22). God will use such methods to lead you as well. "Those who are led by the Spirit of God are sons of God" (Romans 8:14). Remember, if you feel led, it's probably God. If you feel pressured, it's probably not.

3. *Contentment*. Being in God's will should result in an inner peace in your life (Colossians 3:15).

Think It Through
••••

In light of the following facts, what would your counsel be? Stan found out that he doesn't have the money for Einstein College. Plus it doesn't offer the major he wants. Angela has been praying a lot and has a gut feeling that she ought to work at the clothing store. Curt, even though he's a good actor, doesn't enjoy drama nearly as much as baseball.

Of course, be careful not to make decisions solely on these factors. Sometimes God asks his people to do things that seem illogical (Hosea 3:1). Sometimes inner impressions can mislead us. Sometimes his will isn't pleasant (Jonah 1:1–2). Always evaluate these C's in light of God's Word.

Work It Out
••••

Even with all these criteria, sometimes it's still hard to know what's right. But if we're really open to God and willing to do whatever he wants, we can be confident that he will direct our steps.

Since we've barely scratched the surface of figuring out what the Father wants, ask your youth pastor to recommend a book on knowing God's will.

Meanwhile, try to begin putting these introductory suggestions into practice. Start today.

Nail It Down
••••

Read and memorize the warning in Ephesians 5:17.

Turn to pages 78, 644 and 1298 for other readings on God's will.
Turn to page 1288 for Friday's reading.

Topic
••••

GOD'S WILL

with regard to your former way of life, to put off your old self, which is being corrupted by its deceitful desires; **23**to be made new in the attitude of your minds; **24**and to put on the new self, created to be like God in true righteousness and holiness.

25Therefore each of you must put off falsehood and speak truthfully to his neighbor, for we are all members of one body. **26**"In your anger do not sin"*a*: Do not let the sun go down while you are still angry, **27**and do not give the devil a foothold. **28**He who has been stealing must steal no longer, but must work, doing something useful with his own hands, that he may have something to share with those in need.

29Do not let any unwholesome talk come out of your mouths, but only what is helpful for building others up according to their needs, that it may benefit those who listen. **30**And do not grieve the Holy Spirit of God, with whom you were sealed for the day of redemption. **31**Get rid of all bitterness, rage and anger, brawling and slander, along with every form of malice. **32**Be kind and compassionate to one another, forgiving each other, just as in Christ God forgave you.

5 Be imitators of God, therefore, as dearly loved children **2**and live a life of love, just as Christ loved us and gave himself up for us as a fragrant offering and sacrifice to God.

3But among you there must not be even a hint of sexual immorality, or of any kind of impurity, or of greed, because these are improper for God's holy people. **4**Nor should there be obscenity, foolish talk or coarse joking, which are out of place, but rather thanksgiving. **5**For of this you can be sure: No immoral, impure or greedy person— such a man is an idolater—has any inheritance in the kingdom of Christ and of God.*b* **6**Let no one deceive you with empty words, for because of such things God's wrath comes on those who are disobedient. **7**Therefore do not be partners with them.

8For you were once darkness, but now you are light in the Lord. Live as children of light **9**(for the fruit of the light consists in all goodness, righteousness and truth) **10**and find out what pleases the Lord. **11**Have nothing to do with the fruitless deeds of darkness, but rather expose them. **12**For it is shameful even to mention what the disobedient do in secret. **13**But everything exposed by the light becomes visible, **14**for it is light

that makes everything visible. This is why it is said:

"Wake up, O sleeper,
　rise from the dead,
and Christ will shine on you."

15Be very careful, then, how you live—not as unwise but as wise, **16**making the most of every opportunity, because the days are evil. **17**Therefore do not be foolish, but understand what the Lord's will is. **18**Do not get drunk on wine, which leads to debauchery. Instead, be filled with the Spirit. **19**Speak to one another with psalms, hymns and spiritual songs. Sing and make music in your heart to the Lord, **20**always giving thanks to God the Father for everything, in the name of our Lord Jesus Christ.

21Submit to one another out of reverence for Christ.

Wives and Husbands

22Wives, submit to your husbands as to the Lord. **23**For the husband is the head of the wife as Christ is the head of the church, his body, of which he is the Savior. **24**Now as the church submits to Christ, so also wives should submit to their husbands in everything.

25Husbands, love your wives, just as Christ loved the church and gave himself up for her **26**to make her holy, cleansing*c* her by the washing with water through the word, **27**and to present her to himself as a radiant church, without stain or wrinkle or any other blemish, but holy and blameless. **28**In this same way, husbands ought to love their wives as their own bodies. He who loves his wife loves himself. **29**After all, no one ever hated his own body, but he feeds and cares for it, just as Christ does the church— **30**for we are members of his body. **31**"For this reason a man will leave his father and mother and be united to his wife, and the two will become one flesh."*d* **32**This is a profound mystery—but I am talking about Christ and the church. **33**However, each one of you also must love his wife as he loves himself, and the wife must respect her husband.

Children and Parents

6 Children, obey your parents in the Lord, for this is right. **2**"Honor your father and mother"—which is the first commandment with a promise— **3**"that it may

---

a26 Psalm 4:4　　*b5* Or *kingdom of the Christ and God*　　*c26* Or *having cleansed*　　*d31* Gen. 2:24

1288

THE HOME IS UNDER ATTACK!

Consider the home situations of the four students riding the school bus to McKenzie Estates:

Tad's parents are in the middle of a messy divorce.

Roberta's mom is physically abusive to Roberta and her younger brother.

Derrick's dad keeps a huge box of pornographic magazines and videos in his closet.

Melissa's family is rarely together. When they are, they just sit around and watch TV.

Look It Up

There's no doubt about it—the home is under attack. The mastermind behind this evil assault? The devil himself!

From without, he inspires evil governments to inflict harm on the family unit (Exodus 1:15–22). He also creates havoc within homes by leading individuals into violence and murder (Genesis 4:8), incest (Genesis 19:30–38), divorce (Matthew 19:4–6) and adultery (Matthew 5:27–28).

No wonder the apostle Peter gave this warning:

"Be self-controlled and alert. Your enemy the devil prowls around like a roaring lion looking for someone to devour. Resist him" (1 Peter 5:9).

Think It Through

How is the institution of the home affected by:
• The growing pornography industry?
• Violent films? Movies that mock authority?
• Legalized abortion?
• Quick divorces?
• Court rulings that give family status to homosexual or unmarried couples?
• Poverty and homelessness?
• Incest?
• Television?

Work It Out

Pray for your home today. If things are good, thank God for his grace and protection. If the situation there is not so good, ask God to use you to make a positive difference.

Think about your own conduct at home. Are there things that you are presently doing that make it easier for the enemy to cause problems in your family?

A long-term project: Watch for decisions by your government officials that have a negative effect on the home. Whenever possible, write your elected officials and ask them to sponsor pro-family legislation.

Nail It Down

Read more about Satan's attack on the home in Ephesians 6.

Turn to pages 391 and 1304 for other readings on home.
Turn to page 1290 for the weekend reading.

Topic

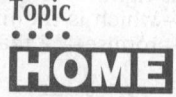

go well with you and that you may enjoy long life on the earth."[a]

[4]Fathers, do not exasperate your children; instead, bring them up in the training and instruction of the Lord.

Slaves and Masters

[5]Slaves, obey your earthly masters with respect and fear, and with sincerity of heart, just as you would obey Christ. [6]Obey them not only to win their favor when their eye is on you, but like slaves of Christ, doing the will of God from your heart. [7]Serve wholeheartedly, as if you were serving the Lord, not men, [8]because you know that the Lord will reward everyone for whatever good he does, whether he is slave or free.

[9]And masters, treat your slaves in the same way. Do not threaten them, since you know that he who is both their Master and yours is in heaven, and there is no favoritism with him.

The Armor of God

[10]Finally, be strong in the Lord and in his mighty power. [11]Put on the full armor of God so that you can take your stand against the devil's schemes. [12]For our struggle is not against flesh and blood, but against the rulers, against the authorities, against the powers of this dark world and against the spiritual forces of evil in the heavenly realms. [13]Therefore put on the full armor of God, so that when the day of evil comes, you may be able to stand your ground, and after you have done everything, to stand. [14]Stand firm then, with the belt of truth buckled around your waist, with the breastplate of righteousness in place, [15]and with your feet fitted with the readiness that comes from the gospel of peace. [16]In addition to all this, take up the shield of faith, with which you can extinguish all the flaming arrows of the evil one. [17]Take the helmet of salvation and the sword of the Spirit, which is the word of God. [18]And pray in the Spirit on all occasions with all kinds of prayers and requests. With this in mind, be alert and always keep on praying for all the saints.

[19]Pray also for me, that whenever I open my mouth, words may be given me so that I will fearlessly make known the mystery of the gospel, [20]for which I am an ambassador in chains. Pray that I may declare it fearlessly, as I should.

Final Greetings

[21]Tychicus, the dear brother and faithful servant in the Lord, will tell you everything, so that you also may know how I am and what I am doing. [22]I am sending him to you for this very purpose, that you may know how we are, and that he may encourage you.

[23]Peace to the brothers, and love with faith from God the Father and the Lord Jesus Christ. [24]Grace to all who love our Lord Jesus Christ with an undying love.

[a]3 Deut. 5:16

DRESSING FOR THE OCCASION

Work It Out
••••

Picture in your mind what you would wear for each of the following occasions:

- a job interview at an office
- school
- a funeral
- a wedding
- prom night
- a game of beach volleyball
- watching TV at home

Each different occasion requires different clothes. You wouldn't wear the same thing to play softball and to go to a wedding. The special clothes you would wear to the prom are different from the clothes you'd wear while watching TV at home.

There's one other occasion for which you'll need a special outfit: the battle of life. You'll need armor, the full armor of God. This armor, of course, isn't the heavy metal type worn by medieval knights. It's a spiritual armor that will protect you from Satan and help you remain true to Jesus Christ. Are you dressed for the occasion?

Nail It Down
••••

Read the description of your armor in Ephesians 6:10–18.

Think It Through
••••

Putting on the armor of God involves more than just dabbling in religion. It involves more than just putting on one or two pieces and thinking that will be good enough.

In order to be really "strong in the Lord," you'll need a full set of armor, a total commitment to God and an unswerving desire to live for him and follow him. That's the only way to fight off the "devil's schemes."

Get spiritually dressed for the occasion of life. Dress for warfare against the devil. Put on God's full armor.

Nail It Down
••••

Reread the description of your armor in Ephesians 6:10–18. For further insight read Psalm 1.

Turn to pages 420, 658, 1315, 1341 and 1356 for other readings on temptation.
Turn to page 1292 for Monday's reading.

Topic
••••

TEMPTATION

PHILIPPIANS

PAUL writes to the believers in Philippi: "Rejoice! Thank God! Don't be anxious!" Sounds like a celebration, so life must be going great. Well, not quite. Paul is a prisoner in Rome, but God is using his imprisonment to accomplish great things for the gospel. Paul reminds the Philippians that Jesus willingly humbled himself to accomplish something great: our salvation, and he is sufficient for every need. Like Paul and Jesus, we can rejoice even in the middle of tough times. As you read, remember to rejoice and be content, regardless of your situation.

Outline of Contents

1 Paul and Timothy, servants of Christ Jesus,

To all the saints in Christ Jesus at Philippi, together with the overseers[a] and deacons:

²Grace and peace to you from God our Father and the Lord Jesus Christ.

Thanksgiving and Prayer

³I thank my God every time I remember you. ⁴In all my prayers for all of you, I always pray with joy ⁵because of your partnership in the gospel from the first day until now, ⁶being confident of this, that he who began a good work in you will carry it on to completion until the day of Christ Jesus.

⁷It is right for me to feel this way about all of you, since I have you in my heart; for whether I am in chains or defending and confirming the gospel, all of you share in God's grace with me. ⁸God can testify how I long for all of you with the affection of Christ Jesus.

⁹And this is my prayer: that your love may abound more and more in knowledge and depth of insight, ¹⁰so that you may be able to discern what is best and may be pure and blameless until the day of Christ, ¹¹filled with the fruit of righteousness that comes

---

a1 Traditionally *bishops*

BE A GIVER NOT A TAKER!

Early Saturday morning, Marcia calls Mark. "Hey, Mark! Did I wake you up?"

"Yeah."

"Oh, I'm sorry! Say, listen, I know you said the other day that you couldn't come help us with our service project down in the inner city . . . but since you're already up, why don't you reconsider? It really will be fun. Besides, we could sure use another guy."

Long pause. "Are we gonna get paid for this?"

"Paid? Mark, it's a service project!"

Longer pause. "Um . . . look, I really have a lot of things I need to do. Maybe another time, okay?"

Look It Up
••••

If anyone has ever lived with perfect priorities, it is Jesus Christ. Consider what he said about serving and giving:

"Whoever wants to become great among you must be your servant, and whoever wants to be first must be slave of all. For even the Son of Man did not come to be served, but to serve, and to give his life as a ransom for many" (Mark 10:43–45).

"It is more blessed to give than to receive" (Acts 20:35).

As you read the Gospels, you realize that these weren't just empty words to Christ—he lived them!

Think It Through
••••

Most people are interested primarily in what they can get and how they can be served. (They hate the idea of having to serve someone else!) If asked, "What is your top priority—your number one concern?" most individuals (if they're honest) would have to answer, "Me!"

What about you? Is your goal in life to be served and to get? Or is it to serve and to give?

Work It Out
••••

Take some steps today to begin to develop the right priorities in the areas of giving and serving.

1. Do a task around the house without being asked.

2. Take the money that you were planning to spend on yourself this weekend and give it to someone who is needy.

3. Volunteer to help out at church—stuffing envelopes, making photocopies, stapling, whatever.

4. Instead of sitting around with your friends and complaining, "There's nothing to do," find someone who needs help and lend a hand.

Nail It Down
••••

Think hard about the priorities of Christ that are reflected in Philippians 2:5–11.

Turn to pages 432, 796, 1015 and 1142 for other readings on priorities.
Turn to page 1294 for Tuesday's reading.

Topic
••••

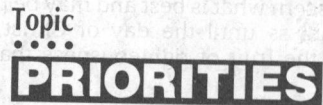

through Jesus Christ—to the glory and praise of God.

Paul's Chains Advance the Gospel

12Now I want you to know, brothers, that what has happened to me has really served to advance the gospel. 13As a result, it has become clear throughout the whole palace guard[a] and to everyone else that I am in chains for Christ. 14Because of my chains, most of the brothers in the Lord have been encouraged to speak the word of God more courageously and fearlessly.

15It is true that some preach Christ out of envy and rivalry, but others out of goodwill. 16The latter do so in love, knowing that I am put here for the defense of the gospel. 17The former preach Christ out of selfish ambition, not sincerely, supposing that they can stir up trouble for me while I am in chains.[b] 18But what does it matter? The important thing is that in every way, whether from false motives or true, Christ is preached. And because of this I rejoice.

Yes, and I will continue to rejoice, 19for I know that through your prayers and the help given by the Spirit of Jesus Christ, what has happened to me will turn out for my deliverance.[c] 20I eagerly expect and hope that I will in no way be ashamed, but will have sufficient courage so that now as always Christ will be exalted in my body, whether by life or by death. 21For to me, to live is Christ and to die is gain. 22If I am to go on living in the body, this will mean fruitful labor for me. Yet what shall I choose? I do not know! 23I am torn between the two: I desire to depart and be with Christ, which is better by far; 24but it is more necessary for you that I remain in the body. 25Convinced of this, I know that I will remain, and I will continue with all of you for your progress and joy in the faith, 26so that through my being with you again your joy in Christ Jesus will overflow on account of me.

27Whatever happens, conduct yourselves in a manner worthy of the gospel of Christ. Then, whether I come and see you or only hear about you in my absence, I will know that you stand firm in one spirit, contending as one man for the faith of the gospel 28without being frightened in any way by those who oppose you. This is a sign to them that they will be destroyed, but that you will be saved—and that by God. 29For it has been granted to you on behalf of Christ not only to believe on him, but also to suffer for him, 30since you are going through the same struggle you saw I had, and now hear that I still have.

Imitating Christ's Humility

2 If you have any encouragement from being united with Christ, if any comfort from his love, if any fellowship with the Spirit, if any tenderness and compassion, 2then make my joy complete by being like-minded, having the same love, being one in spirit and purpose. 3Do nothing out of selfish ambition or vain conceit, but in humility consider others better than yourselves. 4Each of you should look not only to your own interests, but also to the interests of others.

5Your attitude should be the same as that of Christ Jesus:

6Who, being in very nature[d] God,
    did not consider equality with God
        something to be grasped,
7but made himself nothing,
    taking the very nature[e] of a servant,
    being made in human likeness.
8And being found in appearance as a
        man,
    he humbled himself
    and became obedient to death—
        even death on a cross!
9Therefore God exalted him to the
        highest place
    and gave him the name that is above
        every name,
10that at the name of Jesus every knee
        should bow,
    in heaven and on earth and under the
        earth,
11and every tongue confess that Jesus
        Christ is Lord,
    to the glory of God the Father.

Shining as Stars

12Therefore, my dear friends, as you have always obeyed—not only in my presence, but now much more in my absence—continue to work out your salvation with fear and trembling, 13for it is God who works in you to will and to act according to his good purpose.

14Do everything without complaining or arguing, 15so that you may become blameless and pure, children of God without fault in a crooked and depraved generation, in which you shine like stars in the universe

---

[a]13 Or *whole palace*   [b]16,17 Some late manuscripts have verses 16 and 17 in reverse order.   [c]19 Or *salvation*   [d]6 Or *in the form of*   [e]7 Or *the form*

STUMBLING BEGINS WITH GRUMBLING

It's 6:30 A.M. in Centerville. That means the grumbling is just beginning.

Fourteen-year-old Simone takes a quick inventory of the clothes hanging in her closet. Then, dejectedly, she flops backward across her bed. "My clothes are the worst in the history of the world!" she sighs.

As fifteen-year-old Wendell stubs his toe on his little brother's bed, he mutters, "&%$#*, I want my own room!"

Blake, sixteen, looks with disgust at his physique in the mirror. "That does it! I'm joining the health club today!"

Look It Up
••••

One of the quickest ways to find out if you've contracted the disease of dissatisfaction is to listen to what comes out of your mouth. If complaining and grumbling are part of your regular conversation, look out!

Despite deliverance from Egyptian slavery and miraculous provision from above, the Israelites constantly complained. They were never content! Over and over again they whined (Numbers 11; 14:2–4; 16:11,41; 20:2–5; 21:4–7). Finally God said, "How long will this wicked community grumble against me? . . . They will meet their end in this desert; here they will die" (Numbers 14:27,35).

Think It Through
••••

Listen carefully: It is not wrong to have nice clothes, your own room or a good physique. It's not even wrong—up to a point—to want these things. The problems begin when you forget all that you *do* have and focus with discontent on what you *don't* have.

Have you been grumbling a lot lately? What are the areas in your life where you find the most dissatisfaction?

Work It Out
••••

You can begin today to be more content by doing these five things:

1. Tell God you're sorry for the times you complained *last* week.
2. Ask him to help you change your focus *this* week.
3. Invite a friend to study the topic of contentment with you.
4. Memorize 1 Timothy 6:6.
5. Look around your room and thank God for some of the things you do possess.

Nail It Down
••••

Read and begin to try to follow the command in Philippians 2:14.

Turn to pages 696, 1321 and 1354 for other readings on contentment.
Turn to page 1296 for Wednesday's reading.

Topic
••••

CONTENTMENT

16as you hold out*a* the word of life—in order that I may boast on the day of Christ that I did not run or labor for nothing. **17**But even if I am being poured out like a drink offering on the sacrifice and service coming from your faith, I am glad and rejoice with all of you. **18**So you too should be glad and rejoice with me.

Timothy and Epaphroditus

19I hope in the Lord Jesus to send Timothy to you soon, that I also may be cheered when I receive news about you. **20**I have no one else like him, who takes a genuine interest in your welfare. **21**For everyone looks out for his own interests, not those of Jesus Christ. **22**But you know that Timothy has proved himself, because as a son with his father he has served with me in the work of the gospel. **23**I hope, therefore, to send him as soon as I see how things go with me. **24**And I am confident in the Lord that I myself will come soon.

25But I think it is necessary to send back to you Epaphroditus, my brother, fellow worker and fellow soldier, who is also your messenger, whom you sent to take care of my needs. **26**For he longs for all of you and is distressed because you heard he was ill. **27**Indeed he was ill, and almost died. But God had mercy on him, and not on him only but also on me, to spare me sorrow upon sorrow. **28**Therefore I am all the more eager to send him, so that when you see him again you may be glad and I may have less anxiety. **29**Welcome him in the Lord with great joy, and honor men like him, **30**because he almost died for the work of Christ, risking his life to make up for the help you could not give me.

No Confidence in the Flesh

3 Finally, my brothers, rejoice in the Lord! It is no trouble for me to write the same things to you again, and it is a safeguard for you.

2Watch out for those dogs, those men who do evil, those mutilators of the flesh. **3**For it is we who are the circumcision, we who worship by the Spirit of God, who glory in Christ Jesus, and who put no confidence in the flesh— **4**though I myself have reasons for such confidence.

If anyone else thinks he has reasons to put confidence in the flesh, I have more: **5**circumcised on the eighth day, of the people of Israel, of the tribe of Benjamin, a He-

brew of Hebrews; in regard to the law, a Pharisee; **6**as for zeal, persecuting the church; as for legalistic righteousness, faultless.

7But whatever was to my profit I now consider loss for the sake of Christ. **8**What is more, I consider everything a loss compared to the surpassing greatness of knowing Christ Jesus my Lord, for whose sake I have lost all things. I consider them rubbish, that I may gain Christ **9**and be found in him, not having a righteousness of my own that comes from the law, but that which is through faith in Christ—the righteousness that comes from God and is by faith. **10**I want to know Christ and the power of his resurrection and the fellowship of sharing in his sufferings, becoming like him in his death, **11**and so, somehow, to attain to the resurrection from the dead.

Pressing on Toward the Goal

12Not that I have already obtained all this, or have already been made perfect, but I press on to take hold of that for which Christ Jesus took hold of me. **13**Brothers, I do not consider myself yet to have taken hold of it. But one thing I do: Forgetting what is behind and straining toward what is ahead, **14**I press on toward the goal to win the prize for which God has called me heavenward in Christ Jesus.

15All of us who are mature should take such a view of things. And if on some point you think differently, that too God will make clear to you. **16**Only let us live up to what we have already attained.

17Join with others in following my example, brothers, and take note of those who live according to the pattern we gave you. **18**For, as I have often told you before and now say again even with tears, many live as enemies of the cross of Christ. **19**Their destiny is destruction, their god is their stomach, and their glory is in their shame. Their mind is on earthly things. **20**But our citizenship is in heaven. And we eagerly await a Savior from there, the Lord Jesus Christ, **21**who, by the power that enables him to bring everything under his control, will transform our lowly bodies so that they will be like his glorious body.

4 Therefore, my brothers, you whom I love and long for, my joy and crown, that is how you should stand firm in the Lord, dear friends!

*a*16 Or *hold on to*

THE ARCHENEMY OF EXCELLENCE

Carl, fifteen, lives a very average, very unspectacular life.
At school, he settles for C's when he could be making B's.

At work, he does just enough to keep the boss off his back.

At band practice, he goofs off and seems unwilling to make the effort to improve his trombone playing.

Carl's spiritual life consists of once-a-week church attendance and an occasional prayer when in trouble. Ask him if he's following after God, and he responds, "Huh?"

Look It Up
••••

The philosophies "I'll do just enough to get by" and "Don't take anything too seriously!" were foreign to the apostle Paul. Listen to his counsel.

1. Be a winner! "Do you not know that in a race all the runners run, but only one gets the prize? Run in such a way as to get the prize." (1 Corinthians 9:24).

2. Do your best! "Do your best to present yourself to God as one approved, a workman who does not need to be ashamed and who correctly handles the word of truth" (2 Timothy 2:15).

Think It Through
••••

The word *mediocre* originally meant "in the middle of the mountain." Perhaps the image is that of a mountain climber who, halfway to the summit, decides to quit. He settles for less than the top. He's mediocre.

That's like a professional athlete saying, "Oh, I don't really care if we win today. My goal is just to go through the motions and pick up my paycheck. If I have just an average performance, I'll be happy." What would you think if you heard that? Would you pay to watch someone with that kind of attitude?

Work It Out
••••

Take ten minutes to examine your own life. Think back on your attitudes and actions of the last month. Have you been "doing your best" and "being a winner"? Or have you been acting more like Carl?

Pray this prayer: "Lord, use your Word and these devotions to shake me up. I don't want to be mediocre. I want to be excellent in every way . . . for you. In Jesus' name I pray. Amen."

Nail It Down
••••

Read Paul's encouragement to us to be more than mediocre in Philippians 3:13–14.

Turn to pages 93, 212, 1332 and 1334 for other readings on excellence.
Turn to page 1298 for Thursday's reading.

Topic
••••

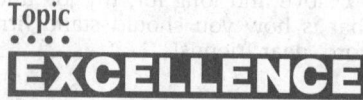
EXCELLENCE

Exhortations

2I plead with Euodia and I plead with Syntyche to agree with each other in the Lord. **3**Yes, and I ask you, loyal yokefellow,[a] help these women who have contended at my side in the cause of the gospel, along with Clement and the rest of my fellow workers, whose names are in the book of life.

4Rejoice in the Lord always. I will say it again: Rejoice! **5**Let your gentleness be evident to all. The Lord is near. **6**Do not be anxious about anything, but in everything, by prayer and petition, with thanksgiving, present your requests to God. **7**And the peace of God, which transcends all understanding, will guard your hearts and your minds in Christ Jesus.

8Finally, brothers, whatever is true, whatever is noble, whatever is right, whatever is pure, whatever is lovely, whatever is admirable — if anything is excellent or praiseworthy — think about such things. **9**Whatever you have learned or received or heard from me, or seen in me — put it into practice. And the God of peace will be with you.

Thanks for Their Gifts

10I rejoice greatly in the Lord that at last you have renewed your concern for me. Indeed, you have been concerned, but you had no opportunity to show it. **11**I am not saying this because I am in need, for I have learned to be content whatever the circumstances. **12**I know what it is to be in need, and I know what it is to have plenty. I have learned the secret of being content in any and every situation, whether well fed or hungry, whether living in plenty or in want. **13**I can do everything through him who gives me strength.

14Yet it was good of you to share in my troubles. **15**Moreover, as you Philippians know, in the early days of your acquaintance with the gospel, when I set out from Macedonia, not one church shared with me in the matter of giving and receiving, except you only; **16**for even when I was in Thessalonica, you sent me aid again and again when I was in need. **17**Not that I am looking for a gift, but I am looking for what may be credited to your account. **18**I have received full payment and even more; I am amply supplied, now that I have received from Epaphroditus the gifts you sent. They are a fragrant offering, an acceptable sacrifice, pleasing to God. **19**And my God will meet all your needs according to his glorious riches in Christ Jesus.

20To our God and Father be glory for ever and ever. Amen.

Final Greetings

21Greet all the saints in Christ Jesus. The brothers who are with me send greetings. **22**All the saints send you greetings, especially those who belong to Caesar's household.

23The grace of the Lord Jesus Christ be with your spirit. Amen.[b]

---

a3 Or loyal Syzygus   b23 Some manuscripts do not have Amen.

GETTING GUIDANCE FROM GOD

A group of Blaine's friends from Southside High are taking a senior trip to Florida. Blaine is pretty sure it's going to be a wild trip—in fact by the end of the week, almost the whole graduating class will be there. A couple of the guys going are Christian friends from church, but most of them aren't.

Blaine feels torn. He wants to be with his friends. But at the same time, he doesn't want to go down there, get in a bunch of tempting situations and blow his witness.

How can he figure out what's best?

**Look
It Up**
••••

Christians often overlook one of the best ways to discover God's will—simply talking to God in prayer.

When the Israelites entered Canaan, they were commanded to defeat and destroy all the inhabitants of the land. After a couple of victories, they encountered a group of people from nearby Gibeon who pretended to be from a faraway land. The Gibeonites' deception worked perfectly because "the men of Israel . . . did not inquire of the LORD. Then Joshua made a treaty of peace with [the Gibeonites] to let them live" (Joshua 9:14–15).

The point is this: by not seeking God's wisdom in complicated situations, we're asking for trouble.

**Think It
Through**
••••

Thousands of people write every day to advice columnists, asking for advice. Often the counsel they get is superficial. Why do so many Christians fail to ask God for help in making decisions?

Do you think Christians are sometimes unwilling to talk to God about what to do because deep down they already know what's best? Is it possible that this is how Blaine is feeling?

**Work It
Out**
••••

If you're facing a tough decision, you can't afford not to get God's wisdom. You need to talk things over with him . . . right now.

There's nothing magical or mysterious about prayer. It's simply talking with God, honestly pouring out your heart just like you would with a best friend. God is a great listener.

Present your situation to him, and ask him to reveal the best thing to do. Sooner or later, you'll get the answer you need (maybe not what you want, and maybe not the way you expect, but definitely what you need).

**Nail It
Down**
••••

For reassurance read Philippians 4:6–7.

Turn to pages 78, 644 and 1286 for other readings on God's will.
Turn to page 1300 for Friday's reading.

Topic
••••

GOD'S WILL

COLOSSIANS

THE church at Colosse is facing a deadly heresy. Paul's solution is to remind the Colossian Christians that Jesus Christ is the supreme Lord of all the universe, sufficient for all of life. Believers don't need to look elsewhere for salvation, worship, or guidance in holy living. As you read this book, keep in mind that since Christ is all and in all, then he ought to be in all you do, say and think.

Outline of Contents

1 Paul, an apostle of Christ Jesus by the will of God, and Timothy our brother,

2To the holy and faithful^a brothers in Christ at Colosse:

Grace and peace to you from God our Father.^b

Thanksgiving and Prayer

3We always thank God, the Father of our Lord Jesus Christ, when we pray for you, 4because we have heard of your faith in Christ Jesus and of the love you have for all the saints— 5the faith and love that spring from the hope that is stored up for you in heaven and that you have already heard about in the word of truth, the gospel 6that has come to you. All over the world this gospel is bearing fruit and growing, just as it has been doing among you since the day you heard it and understood God's grace in all its truth. 7You learned it from Epaphras, our dear fellow servant, who is a faithful minister of Christ on our^c behalf, 8and who also told us of your love in the Spirit.

9For this reason, since the day we heard about you, we have not stopped praying for you and asking God to fill you with the knowledge of his will through all spiritual wisdom and understanding. 10And we pray this in order that you may live a life worthy of the Lord and may please him in every way: bearing fruit in every good work,

---

a2 Or believing   b2 Some manuscripts Father and the Lord Jesus Christ   c7 Some manuscripts your

APPEARANCES CAN BE DECEIVING

Debbie goes to a Christian school. She also attends church and youth group faithfully.

That's not all. Debbie works in a Christian bookstore, has a regular quiet time and listens only to Christian music. Moreover, she has vowed to date only Christian guys.

If outer conduct was all that mattered to God, Debbie would have it made in the shade. No one acts more religious.

But God cares most about a person's inner condition. And Debbie's heart is full of pride, jealousy and selfishness.

Look It Up
••••

Do you recall the harsh words Jesus spoke to the religious people of his day?

"Woe to you, teachers of the law and Pharisees, you hypocrites! You clean the outside of the cup and dish, but inside they are full of greed and self-indulgence. Blind Pharisee! First clean the inside of the cup and dish, and then the outside also will be clean.

"Woe to you, teachers of the law and Pharisees, you hypocrites! You are like whitewashed tombs, which look beautiful on the outside but on the inside are full of dead men's bones and everything unclean. In the same way, on the outside you appear to people as righteous but on the inside you are full of hypocrisy and wickedness" (Matthew 23:25–28).

Think It Through
••••

Based on what Jesus told the Pharisees, is a person who is doing right things automatically right with God?

Are you living like a Pharisee?

Work It Out
••••

Evaluate your own spiritual conduct. Are you mechanically "going through the motions"? Is your primary motive "to be seen by others and to be thought of as a neat person"? If so:
- Confess your wrong attitudes (1 John 1:9).
- Return to your first love (Revelation 2:4). Make Jesus—not appearances—your top priority.
- Quit seeking the praise of men (John 12:43).
- Make a renewed effort to practice Christianity in secret as well as in public (Matthew 6:1–8).

Nail It Down
••••

Read Colossians 2:20–23 for insight into some Colossians who had their focus in the wrong place.

Turn to pages 488, 560 and 1358 for other readings on appearance.
Turn to page 1302 for the weekend reading.

Topic
••••

APPEARANCE

growing in the knowledge of God, **11**being strengthened with all power according to his glorious might so that you may have great endurance and patience, and joyfully **12**giving thanks to the Father, who has qualified you*a* to share in the inheritance of the saints in the kingdom of light. **13**For he has rescued us from the dominion of darkness and brought us into the kingdom of the Son he loves, **14**in whom we have redemption,*b* the forgiveness of sins.

The Supremacy of Christ

15He is the image of the invisible God, the firstborn over all creation. **16**For by him all things were created: things in heaven and on earth, visible and invisible, whether thrones or powers or rulers or authorities; all things were created by him and for him. **17**He is before all things, and in him all things hold together. **18**And he is the head of the body, the church; he is the beginning and the firstborn from among the dead, so that in everything he might have the supremacy. **19**For God was pleased to have all his fullness dwell in him, **20**and through him to reconcile to himself all things, whether things on earth or things in heaven, by making peace through his blood, shed on the cross.

21Once you were alienated from God and were enemies in your minds because of*c* your evil behavior. **22**But now he has reconciled you by Christ's physical body through death to present you holy in his sight, without blemish and free from accusation — **23**if you continue in your faith, established and firm, not moved from the hope held out in the gospel. This is the gospel that you heard and that has been proclaimed to every creature under heaven, and of which I, Paul, have become a servant.

Paul's Labor for the Church

24Now I rejoice in what was suffered for you, and I fill up in my flesh what is still lacking in regard to Christ's afflictions, for the sake of his body, which is the church. **25**I have become its servant by the commission God gave me to present to you the word of God in its fullness — **26**the mystery that has been kept hidden for ages and generations, but is now disclosed to the saints. **27**To them God has chosen to make known among the Gentiles the glorious riches of this mys-

tery, which is Christ in you, the hope of glory. **28**We proclaim him, admonishing and teaching everyone with all wisdom, so that we may present everyone perfect in Christ. **29**To this end I labor, struggling with all his energy, which so powerfully works in me.

2 I want you to know how much I am struggling for you and for those at Laodicea, and for all who have not met me personally. **2**My purpose is that they may be encouraged in heart and united in love, so that they may have the full riches of complete understanding, in order that they may know the mystery of God, namely, Christ, **3**in whom are hidden all the treasures of wisdom and knowledge. **4**I tell you this so that no one may deceive you by fine-sounding arguments. **5**For though I am absent from you in body, I am present with you in spirit and delight to see how orderly you are and how firm your faith in Christ is.

Freedom From Human Regulations Through Life With Christ

6So then, just as you received Christ Jesus as Lord, continue to live in him, **7**rooted and built up in him, strengthened in the faith as you were taught, and overflowing with thankfulness.

8See to it that no one takes you captive through hollow and deceptive philosophy, which depends on human tradition and the basic principles of this world rather than on Christ.

9For in Christ all the fullness of the Deity lives in bodily form, **10**and you have been given fullness in Christ, who is the head over every power and authority. **11**In him you were also circumcised, in the putting off of the sinful nature,*d* not with a circumcision done by the hands of men but with the circumcision done by Christ, **12**having been buried with him in baptism and raised with him through your faith in the power of God, who raised him from the dead. **13**When you were dead in your sins and in the uncircumcision of your sinful nature,*e* God made you*a* alive with Christ. He forgave us all our sins, **14**having canceled the written code, with its regulations, that was against us and that stood opposed to us; he took it away, nailing it to the cross. **15**And having disarmed the powers and authorities, he made a public spectacle of them, triumphing over them by the cross.*f*

---

a12, 13 Some manuscripts *us*   *b14* A few late manuscripts *redemption through his blood*   *c21* Or *minds, as shown by*   *d11* Or *the flesh*   *e13* Or *your flesh*   *f15* Or *them in him*

THE HARD WORK OF FORGIVING

Work It Out
••••

Think over all the things that have happened in your life in the last year. Was there a time when you had to forgive someone for something he or she had done to you? Was forgiving easy?

Perhaps you had to forgive classmates for spreading untrue rumors about you. Perhaps you had to forgive a former boyfriend or girlfriend for how he or she treated you. Perhaps you had to forgive your parents for how they handled a particular situation. Perhaps you had to forgive a friend for ignoring you when you were feeling down.

Forgiving others doesn't usually come easy. You're hurt, you're angry, you're upset, but you know you should forgive. It's the only way to heal the relationship and move forward in life. But it's hard. Very hard.

Is there someone you need to forgive even now? Are you having trouble getting above the hurt and anger so that you can forgive? Pray. God will give you the strength and the desire to do what you know is right.

Nail It Down
••••

Read Paul's command to forgive in Colossians 3:13.

Think It Through
••••

If you need help in forgiving others, remember how much God has forgiven you. It's a lot easier to forgive someone who has wronged you if you remember where to keep your focus. Instead of focusing on the wrong, focus on how much you've been forgiven by others and by God.

A change in focus makes everything look different, doesn't it? The one sin committed against you seems pretty insignificant when you compare it with the many sins you've committed against God. And he freely and lovingly offers you forgiveness. Can you do the same to others?

Nail It Down
••••

Memorize Colossians 3:13. For further insight read Psalm 25:11.

Turn to pages 580, 771, 809, 966, 1068 and 1352 for other readings on forgiveness.
Turn to page 1304 for Monday's reading.

Topic
••••

FORGIVENESS

[16]Therefore do not let anyone judge you by what you eat or drink, or with regard to a religious festival, a New Moon celebration or a Sabbath day. [17]These are a shadow of the things that were to come; the reality, however, is found in Christ. [18]Do not let anyone who delights in false humility and the worship of angels disqualify you for the prize. Such a person goes into great detail about what he has seen, and his unspiritual mind puffs him up with idle notions. [19]He has lost connection with the Head, from whom the whole body, supported and held together by its ligaments and sinews, grows as God causes it to grow.

[20]Since you died with Christ to the basic principles of this world, why, as though you still belonged to it, do you submit to its rules: [21]"Do not handle! Do not taste! Do not touch!"? [22]These are all destined to perish with use, because they are based on human commands and teachings. [23]Such regulations indeed have an appearance of wisdom, with their self-imposed worship, their false humility and their harsh treatment of the body, but they lack any value in restraining sensual indulgence.

Rules for Holy Living

3 Since, then, you have been raised with Christ, set your hearts on things above, where Christ is seated at the right hand of God. [2]Set your minds on things above, not on earthly things. [3]For you died, and your life is now hidden with Christ in God. [4]When Christ, who is your[a] life, appears, then you also will appear with him in glory.

[5]Put to death, therefore, whatever belongs to your earthly nature: sexual immorality, impurity, lust, evil desires and greed, which is idolatry. [6]Because of these, the wrath of God is coming.[b] [7]You used to walk in these ways, in the life you once lived. [8]But now you must rid yourselves of all such things as these: anger, rage, malice, slander, and filthy language from your lips. [9]Do not lie to each other, since you have taken off your old self with its practices [10]and have put on the new self, which is being renewed in knowledge in the image of its Creator. [11]Here there is no Greek or Jew, circumcised or uncircumcised, barbarian, Scythian, slave or free, but Christ is all, and is in all.

[12]Therefore, as God's chosen people, holy and dearly loved, clothe yourselves with compassion, kindness, humility, gentleness and patience. [13]Bear with each other and forgive whatever grievances you may have against one another. Forgive as the Lord forgave you. [14]And over all these virtues put on love, which binds them all together in perfect unity.

[15]Let the peace of Christ rule in your hearts, since as members of one body you were called to peace. And be thankful. [16]Let the word of Christ dwell in you richly as you teach and admonish one another with all wisdom, and as you sing psalms, hymns and spiritual songs with gratitude in your hearts to God. [17]And whatever you do, whether in word or deed, do it all in the name of the Lord Jesus, giving thanks to God the Father through him.

Rules for Christian Households

[18]Wives, submit to your husbands, as is fitting in the Lord.

[19]Husbands, love your wives and do not be harsh with them.

[20]Children, obey your parents in everything, for this pleases the Lord.

[21]Fathers, do not embitter your children, or they will become discouraged.

[22]Slaves, obey your earthly masters in everything; and do it, not only when their eye is on you and to win their favor, but with sincerity of heart and reverence for the Lord. [23]Whatever you do, work at it with all your heart, as working for the Lord, not for men, [24]since you know that you will receive an inheritance from the Lord as a reward. It is the Lord Christ you are serving. [25]Anyone who does wrong will be repaid for his wrong, and there is no favoritism.

4 Masters, provide your slaves with what is right and fair, because you know that you also have a Master in heaven.

Further Instructions

[2]Devote yourselves to prayer, being watchful and thankful. [3]And pray for us, too, that God may open a door for our message, so that we may proclaim the mystery of Christ, for which I am in chains. [4]Pray that I may proclaim it clearly, as I should. [5]Be wise in the way you act toward outsiders; make the most of every opportunity. [6]Let your conversation be always full of grace, seasoned with salt, so that you may know how to answer everyone.

Final Greetings

[7]Tychicus will tell you all the news about me. He is a dear brother, a faithful minister

---

[a]4 Some manuscripts *our*   [b]6 Some early manuscripts *coming on those who are disobedient*

MAKING PEACE WITH YOUR PARENTS

• •

As Nicole walks into her house with her friend Bess, her mother snaps, "Upstairs, now! You left your room a wreck!"

"I'm sorry, Mom. I'll clean it up right away."

Upstairs Bess is in shock. "Sheesh, what's with your mom? And how in the world did you keep from yelling at her? Hey, if my mom snapped at me like that, I'd have let her have it right back."

"Bess, why should I get mad at her? What good would that do? Besides, she was right; and I can tell she's had a really rough day."

Look It Up
• • • •

Here's how to make your home a battlefield and guarantee a miserable life for yourself: Declare war on your parents!

• Ignore the Biblical command to submit to their wishes. "Children, obey your parents in everything " (Colossians 3:20).

• Respond to their kind acts and generosity by being rude and ungrateful. "If a man pays back evil for good, evil will never leave his house" (Proverbs 17:13).

• Refuse to show respect. " 'Cursed is the man who dishonors his father or his mother.' Then all the people shall say, 'Amen!' " (Deuteronomy 27:16).

• Steal from them (Proverbs 28:24).

Think It Through
• • • •

Right beliefs must translate into right behavior. And right behavior at home is one of the best tests for assessing how mature you are in the Lord.

Someone has said that if a person's faith doesn't work at home, then that individual's faith isn't worth very much. Do you agree with that statement?

How is your faith at home?

Work It Out
• • • •

Make peace with your parents. Decide right now to do everything within your power to resolve present conflicts (and avoid future fights) at home.

Do what your folks ask with no back talk. Show appreciation for the sacrifices they have made (and still make) for you. Treat them like you want to be treated.

Even if your parents are far less than you would like them to be, you are still required by God to honor them. Let God deal with their wrong behavior. You deal with your own.

Nail It Down
• • • •

Read Colossians 3:20 to find out what pleases God.

Turn to pages 391 and 1288 for other readings on home.
Turn to page 1306 for Tuesday's reading.

Topic
• • • •

HOME

and fellow servant in the Lord. [8]I am sending him to you for the express purpose that you may know about our[a] circumstances and that he may encourage your hearts. [9]He is coming with Onesimus, our faithful and dear brother, who is one of you. They will tell you everything that is happening here.

[10]My fellow prisoner Aristarchus sends you his greetings, as does Mark, the cousin of Barnabas. (You have received instructions about him; if he comes to you, welcome him.) [11]Jesus, who is called Justus, also sends greetings. These are the only Jews among my fellow workers for the kingdom of God, and they have proved a comfort to me. [12]Epaphras, who is one of you and a servant of Christ Jesus, sends greetings. He is always wrestling in prayer for you, that you may stand firm in all the will of God, mature and fully assured. [13]I vouch for him that he is working hard for you and for those at Laodicea and Hierapolis. [14]Our dear friend Luke, the doctor, and Demas send greetings. [15]Give my greetings to the brothers at Laodicea, and to Nympha and the church in her house.

[16]After this letter has been read to you, see that it is also read in the church of the Laodiceans and that you in turn read the letter from Laodicea.

[17]Tell Archippus: "See to it that you complete the work you have received in the Lord."

[18]I, Paul, write this greeting in my own hand. Remember my chains. Grace be with you.

---

[a]8 Some manuscripts *that he may know about your*

GUARDING YOUR OWN GOOD STANDING

Sarah, Miss Average American High School Student, has a great reputation at school, not only with her close friends but also with other kids at school and with her teachers. What does Sarah do—if anything—to maintain such a good reputation?

Well, she attends a weekly Bible study for youth at her church. Plus she's careful to spend time reading the Bible and praying on her own every morning. Most important, she not only reads what the Bible says—she also does it.

As her dad has told her many times, "Sarah, you just keep yourself straight with the Lord, and everything else will fall into place."

Look It Up
••••

Moses taught the Israelites this same principle as they prepared to go into the promised land.

"See, I have taught you decrees and laws as the LORD my God commanded me, so that you may follow them in the land you are entering to take possession of it. Observe them carefully, for this will show your wisdom and understanding to the nations, who will hear about all these decrees and say, 'Surely this great nation is a wise and understanding people'" (Deuteronomy 4:5–6).

The lesson simply stated? Obedience to the Lord usually results in a good reputation.

Think It Through
••••

Sarah's motive for reading the Bible and going to youth group is not to make others think she's super spiritual. She does those things solely because she wants to please God. Her number one goal is to be right with him. Her good reputation is just a by-product of doing those good things.

Do you work at keeping a good reputation or do you work at keeping yourself right with God? Is it possible to have a good reputation and not be right with God? Is it possible to have a bad reputation and be right with God?

Work It Out
••••

Sit down with a good Christian friend today and discuss your reputations. Each of you can pick one thing to do (or quit doing) that will lead to a closer walk with God. Hold each other accountable for the rest of the month. Then see if your reputation has improved as a result of your improved walk.

Nail It Down
••••

Read about the importance of a good reputation among unbelievers in Colossians 4:5.

Turn to pages 150, 674, 1074 and 1078 for other readings on reputation.
Turn to page 1309 for Wednesday's reading.

Topic
••••

REPUTATION

1 THESSALONIANS

THE church in Thessalonica is bringing Paul a lot of joy. Their fellowship is dynamic. Their work for the gospel is filled with love. But they are being persecuted. So Paul writes to the Thessalonians: Continue to persevere; continue to resist the sexual temptations all around you. And be encouraged: you will one day be with the Lord. As you read this book, find comfort that when you die, you will still be under God's care and will "be with the Lord forever" (1 Thessalonians 4:17).

1 Paul, Silas[a] and Timothy,

To the church of the Thessalonians in God the Father and the Lord Jesus Christ:

Grace and peace to you.[b]

Thanksgiving for the Thessalonians' Faith

²We always thank God for all of you, mentioning you in our prayers. ³We continually remember before our God and Father your work produced by faith, your labor prompted by love, and your endurance inspired by hope in our Lord Jesus Christ.

⁴For we know, brothers loved by God, that he has chosen you, ⁵because our gospel came to you not simply with words, but also with power, with the Holy Spirit and with deep conviction. You know how we lived among you for your sake. ⁶You became imitators of us and of the Lord; in spite of severe suffering, you welcomed the message with the joy given by the Holy Spirit. ⁷And so you became a model to all the believers in Macedonia and Achaia. ⁸The Lord's message rang out from you not only in Macedonia and Achaia—your faith in God has become known everywhere. Therefore we do not need to say anything about it, ⁹for they themselves report what kind of reception you gave us. They tell how you turned to God from idols to serve the living and true God, ¹⁰and to wait for his Son from heaven,

---

a1 Greek *Silvanus*, a variant of *Silas*   *b1* Some early manuscripts *you from God our Father and the Lord Jesus Christ* whom he raised from the dead—Jesus, who rescues us from the coming wrath.

Paul's Ministry in Thessalonica

2 You know, brothers, that our visit to you was not a failure. [2]We had previously suffered and been insulted in Philippi, as you know, but with the help of our God we dared to tell you his gospel in spite of strong opposition. [3]For the appeal we make does not spring from error or impure motives, nor are we trying to trick you. [4]On the contrary, we speak as men approved by God to be entrusted with the gospel. We are not trying to please men but God, who tests our hearts. [5]You know we never used flattery, nor did we put on a mask to cover up greed—God is our witness. [6]We were not looking for praise from men, not from you or anyone else.

As apostles of Christ we could have been a burden to you, [7]but we were gentle among you, like a mother caring for her little children. [8]We loved you so much that we were delighted to share with you not only the gospel of God but our lives as well, because you had become so dear to us. [9]Surely you remember, brothers, our toil and hardship; we worked night and day in order not to be a burden to anyone while we preached the gospel of God to you.

[10]You are witnesses, and so is God, of how holy, righteous and blameless we were among you who believed. [11]For you know that we dealt with each of you as a father deals with his own children, [12]encouraging, comforting and urging you to live lives worthy of God, who calls you into his kingdom and glory.

[13]And we also thank God continually because, when you received the word of God, which you heard from us, you accepted it not as the word of men, but as it actually is, the word of God, which is at work in you who believe. [14]For you, brothers, became imitators of God's churches in Judea, which are in Christ Jesus: You suffered from your own countrymen the same things those churches suffered from the Jews, [15]who killed the Lord Jesus and the prophets and also drove us out. They displease God and are hostile to all men [16]in their effort to keep us from speaking to the Gentiles so that they may be saved. In this way they always heap up their sins to the limit. The wrath of God has come upon them at last. [a]

Paul's Longing to See the Thessalonians

[17]But, brothers, when we were torn away from you for a short time (in person, not in thought), out of our intense longing we made every effort to see you. [18]For we wanted to come to you—certainly I, Paul, did, again and again—but Satan stopped us. [19]For what is our hope, our joy, or the crown in which we will glory in the presence of our Lord Jesus when he comes? Is it not you? [20]Indeed, you are our glory and joy.

3 So when we could stand it no longer, we thought it best to be left by ourselves in Athens. [2]We sent Timothy, who is our brother and God's fellow worker[b] in spreading the gospel of Christ, to strengthen and encourage you in your faith, [3]so that no one would be unsettled by these trials. You know quite well that we were destined for them. [4]In fact, when we were with you, we kept telling you that we would be persecuted. And it turned out that way, as you well know. [5]For this reason, when I could stand it no longer, I sent to find out about your faith. I was afraid that in some way the tempter might have tempted you and our efforts might have been useless.

Timothy's Encouraging Report

[6]But Timothy has just now come to us from you and has brought good news about your faith and love. He has told us that you always have pleasant memories of us and that you long to see us, just as we also long to see you. [7]Therefore, brothers, in all our distress and persecution we were encouraged about you because of your faith. [8]For now we really live, since you are standing firm in the Lord. [9]How can we thank God enough for you in return for all the joy we have in the presence of our God because of you? [10]Night and day we pray most earnestly that we may see you again and supply what is lacking in your faith.

[11]Now may our God and Father himself and our Lord Jesus clear the way for us to come to you. [12]May the Lord make your love increase and overflow for each other and for everyone else, just as ours does for you. [13]May he strengthen your hearts so that you will be blameless and holy in the presence of our God and Father when our Lord Jesus comes with all his holy ones.

---

a 16 Or *them fully*   *b 2* Some manuscripts *brother and fellow worker*; other manuscripts *brother and God's servant*

ALL OVER THE WORLD, ALL THE TIME

☐ WEDNESDAY

• •

O n a sunny August day, Sherri lies on a towel beside the pool, soaking up rays, listening to the new portable CD player she got for her birthday and thinking about last night: Keith told her he loves her! Things couldn't be better!

Meanwhile, the lives of other teens in the same city are filled with pain.

Paul's parents are in the middle of a nasty divorce.

Mike's mom has cancer.

Jan's year-old nephew died last Thursday.

Beth's father keeps molesting her.

Tim faces major reconstructive surgery after injuring his knee at football practice.

Look It Up
• • • •

The Bible states that as long as sinful people continue to live in this fallen world, suffering will be a fact of life. In the Old Testament we are told, "Yet man is born to trouble as surely as sparks fly upward" (Job 5:7).

In the New Testament, Jesus asserted, "In this world you will have trouble" (John 16:33).

Think It Through
• • • •

The question really isn't "Will I suffer?" but "When will I suffer?" Things are going great for Sherri right now, but circumstances can change suddenly. (How is she going to feel on September 7 when Keith dumps her for Missy?)

Which statement best describes your feelings right now?

1. "Suffering is too unpleasant to even think about."
2. "I'm going to pray that I never suffer in my whole life."
3. "I know serious pain and trouble will come my way at some point, so I want to learn how to respond in the right way."

Work It Out
• • • •

Get today's newspaper or watch a news program on TV. Make a list of all the types of suffering that are reported. Make other lists of the suffering you are aware of in your own neighborhood, church and family.

Then pray, "God, the issue of suffering is an ancient puzzle. I know I won't find all the answers, but please at least teach me one or two things that will help me cope, and that will also help me to be a comfort to others who are in pain. Amen."

Nail It Down
• • • •

Read what Paul had to say about the inevitability of suffering in 1 Thessalonians 3:2–4.

Turn to pages 518, 525, 1261 and 1369 for other readings on suffering.
Turn to page 1311 for Thursday's reading.

Topic
• • • •

SUFFERING

Living to Please God

4 Finally, brothers, we instructed you how to live in order to please God, as in fact you are living. Now we ask you and urge you in the Lord Jesus to do this more and more. **2**For you know what instructions we gave you by the authority of the Lord Jesus.

3It is God's will that you should be sanctified: that you should avoid sexual immorality; **4**that each of you should learn to control his own body*a* in a way that is holy and honorable, **5**not in passionate lust like the heathen, who do not know God; **6**and that in this matter no one should wrong his brother or take advantage of him. The Lord will punish men for all such sins, as we have already told you and warned you. **7**For God did not call us to be impure, but to live a holy life. **8**Therefore, he who rejects this instruction does not reject man but God, who gives you his Holy Spirit.

9Now about brotherly love we do not need to write to you, for you yourselves have been taught by God to love each other. **10**And in fact, you do love all the brothers throughout Macedonia. Yet we urge you, brothers, to do so more and more.

11Make it your ambition to lead a quiet life, to mind your own business and to work with your hands, just as we told you, **12**so that your daily life may win the respect of outsiders and so that you will not be dependent on anybody.

The Coming of the Lord

13Brothers, we do not want you to be ignorant about those who fall asleep, or to grieve like the rest of men, who have no hope. **14**We believe that Jesus died and rose again and so we believe that God will bring with Jesus those who have fallen asleep in him. **15**According to the Lord's own word, we tell you that we who are still alive, who are left till the coming of the Lord, will certainly not precede those who have fallen asleep. **16**For the Lord himself will come down from heaven, with a loud command, with the voice of the archangel and with the trumpet call of God, and the dead in Christ will rise first. **17**After that, we who are still alive and are left will be caught up together with them in the clouds to meet the Lord in the air. And so we will be with the Lord forever. **18**Therefore encourage each other with these words.

5 Now, brothers, about times and dates we do not need to write to you, **2**for you know very well that the day of the Lord will come like a thief in the night. **3**While people are saying, "Peace and safety," destruction will come on them suddenly, as labor pains on a pregnant woman, and they will not escape.

4But you, brothers, are not in darkness so that this day should surprise you like a thief. **5**You are all sons of the light and sons of the day. We do not belong to the night or to the darkness. **6**So then, let us not be like others, who are asleep, but let us be alert and self-controlled. **7**For those who sleep, sleep at night, and those who get drunk, get drunk at night. **8**But since we belong to the day, let us be self-controlled, putting on faith and love as a breastplate, and the hope of salvation as a helmet. **9**For God did not appoint us to suffer wrath but to receive salvation through our Lord Jesus Christ. **10**He died for us so that, whether we are awake or asleep, we may live together with him. **11**Therefore encourage one another and build each other up, just as in fact you are doing.

Final Instructions

12Now we ask you, brothers, to respect those who work hard among you, who are over you in the Lord and who admonish you. **13**Hold them in the highest regard in love because of their work. Live in peace with each other. **14**And we urge you, brothers, warn those who are idle, encourage the timid, help the weak, be patient with everyone. **15**Make sure that nobody pays back wrong for wrong, but always try to be kind to each other and to everyone else.

16Be joyful always; **17**pray continually; **18**give thanks in all circumstances, for this is God's will for you in Christ Jesus.

19Do not put out the Spirit's fire; **20**do not treat prophecies with contempt. **21**Test everything. Hold on to the good. **22**Avoid every kind of evil.

23May God himself, the God of peace, sanctify you through and through. May your whole spirit, soul and body be kept blameless at the coming of our Lord Jesus Christ. **24**The one who calls you is faithful and he will do it.

25Brothers, pray for us. **26**Greet all the brothers with a holy kiss. **27**I charge you before the Lord to have this letter read to all the brothers.

28The grace of our Lord Jesus Christ be with you.

---

*a*4 Or *learn to live with his own wife; or learn to acquire a wife*

MYTH: HUMANS ARE PURELY PHYSICAL

In psychology class, Kim and her classmates are studying about B.F. Skinner, the famous behaviorist.

"Skinner believed," the teacher droned, "that man is purely a 'biological system.' In other words, man doesn't have a nonphysical side. There's no soul or consciousness. These concepts are outdated, primitive religious beliefs. Skinner focused on the behavior of the complex machine known as man."

Everyone nodded sleepily.

Look It Up ••••

Dr. Skinner and God disagree. Scripture uses several terms for the nonphysical aspect of people:

1. Soul (Deuteronomy 4:29): includes the emotional aspect.

2. Spirit: "The lamp of the LORD searches the spirit of a man; it searches out his inmost being" (Proverbs 20:27).

3. Heart (1 Timothy 1:5): supplies the control center of a person's life.

4. Conscience (Hebrews 13:18): provides the inner moral voice.

5. Mind (Romans 1:28; 12:2): perceives, understands, judges and determines.

6. Will (1 Corinthians 7:37): chooses.

Think It Through ••••

Christianity isn't at odds with science. In fact, early scientists such as Bacon, Copernicus, Kepler and Newton were creationists. They believed that since God made and ordered the universe, they could count on its regular behavior, the basis for scientific investigation.

But Christianity is at odds with scientism. Scientism begins with this assumption: The natural world is all that exists. Any explanation of observed facts that appeals to a supernatural entity—for example, explaining love as something more than mere chemistry—is ruled out from the start, regardless of the evidence.

Work It Out ••••

If scientism is being forced on you in school, don't be afraid! Ask God to protect your faith. Read up on what intelligent Christian writers have to say about creation and science. Christianity in the twentieth century doesn't lack convincing proofs of its claims. It just needs young Christians to learn and boldly share them!

Nail It Down ••••

Read the warning in 1 Thessalonians 5:23.

Turn to pages 439, 768 and 1282 for other readings on human nature.
Turn to page 1313 for Friday's reading.

Topic ••••

HUMAN NATURE

2 THESSALONIANS

THE day of the Lord has already come! So say some Thessalonian believers who misunderstand Paul's first letter. As a result of their faulty understanding of Paul's teaching, many of these people quit their jobs and were depending on help from more productive Christians. Get back to work! Paul writes. Why? Because certain things must happen before the Lord returns. Paul's instruction is just as valuable today: Don't just sit around. Work while you wait for Christ's return.

Outline of Contents

1 Paul, Silas[a] and Timothy,

To the church of the Thessalonians in God our Father and the Lord Jesus Christ:

[2] Grace and peace to you from God the Father and the Lord Jesus Christ.

Thanksgiving and Prayer

[3] We ought always to thank God for you, brothers, and rightly so, because your faith is growing more and more, and the love every one of you has for each other is increasing. [4] Therefore, among God's churches we boast about your perseverance and faith in all the persecutions and trials you are enduring.

[5] All this is evidence that God's judgment is right, and as a result you will be counted worthy of the kingdom of God, for which you are suffering. [6] God is just: He will pay back trouble to those who trouble you [7] and give relief to you who are troubled, and to us as well. This will happen when the Lord Jesus is revealed from heaven in blazing fire with his powerful angels. [8] He will punish those who do not know God and do not obey the gospel of our Lord Jesus. [9] They will be punished with everlasting destruction and shut out from the presence of the Lord and from the majesty of his power [10] on the day he comes to be glorified in his holy people and to be marveled at among all those who have believed. This includes you, because you believed our testimony to you.

[11] With this in mind, we constantly pray for you, that our God may count you worthy

THE LABORATORY OF LOVE

J ulie is a student at Love U. She recently signed up for course 777, The Laboratory of Love, because the title sounded so interesting.

Boy, was she surprised! She's no longer studying theories of love. Now Julie has to actually love several very unlovable people! Whether or not she gets her "Master's" degree depends on how well she does.

The professor, Dr. H. Spirit, assigned her to love three people: her stepfather ("I can't stand him!"), her chemistry lab partner ("What a weirdo!"), and the little kid next door ("He's a brat!"). Professor Spirit assured her he would help her, but Julie's not too thrilled.

Look It Up
••••

Jesus pointed out in the Sermon on the Mount that it's no big deal to love the people in your life who treat you right. The hard part comes when you're commanded to love those who aren't so nice.

"You have heard that it was said, 'Love your neighbor and hate your enemy.' But I tell you: Love your enemies and pray for those who persecute you, that you may be sons of your Father in heaven" (Matthew 5:43–45).

Think It Through
••••

Jesus commands you to love your enemies. But how can you know if what you're doing is truly loving?

The apostle John had a clear answer: "And this is love: that we walk in obedience to his commands" (2 John 6).

Work It Out
••••

John says that love is defined by God's commands. Given John's definition of love, how can you love people you don't really feel good about?

If they're your parents (or others in authority over you), honor them with obedience and respect.

If they're your peers, show respect for their lives by, for example, driving safely and refusing to pick fights; show respect for their purity by refusing to tempt them to sexual sin; deal with them honestly and fairly, refusing to steal; tell them the truth; rejoice in their good fortune without envy or greed.

Those ideas aren't new; they're ancient. You'll find every one of them in the Ten Commandments, which are, according to John, the definition of love.

Nail It Down
••••

Read about the love that the Thessalonians had for each other in 2 Thessalonians 1:3.

Turn to pages 1153, 1215 and 1250 for other readings on love.
Turn to page 1315 for the weekend reading.

Topic
••••
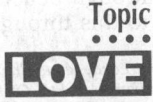

of his calling, and that by his power he may fulfill every good purpose of yours and every act prompted by your faith. **12**We pray this so that the name of our Lord Jesus may be glorified in you, and you in him, according to the grace of our God and the Lord Jesus Christ.*a*

The Man of Lawlessness

2 Concerning the coming of our Lord Jesus Christ and our being gathered to him, we ask you, brothers, **2**not to become easily unsettled or alarmed by some prophecy, report or letter supposed to have come from us, saying that the day of the Lord has already come. **3**Don't let anyone deceive you in any way, for ˌthat day will not comeˌ until the rebellion occurs and the man of lawlessness*b* is revealed, the man doomed to destruction. **4**He will oppose and will exalt himself over everything that is called God or is worshiped, so that he sets himself up in God's temple, proclaiming himself to be God.

5Don't you remember that when I was with you I used to tell you these things? **6**And now you know what is holding him back, so that he may be revealed at the proper time. **7**For the secret power of lawlessness is already at work; but the one who now holds it back will continue to do so till he is taken out of the way. **8**And then the lawless one will be revealed, whom the Lord Jesus will overthrow with the breath of his mouth and destroy by the splendor of his coming. **9**The coming of the lawless one will be in accordance with the work of Satan displayed in all kinds of counterfeit miracles, signs and wonders, **10**and in every sort of evil that deceives those who are perishing. They perish because they refused to love the truth and so be saved. **11**For this reason God sends them a powerful delusion so that they will believe the lie **12**and so that all will be condemned who have not believed the truth but have delighted in wickedness.

Stand Firm

13But we ought always to thank God for you, brothers loved by the Lord, because from the beginning God chose you*c* to be saved through the sanctifying work of the Spirit and through belief in the truth. **14**He called you to this through our gospel, that you might share in the glory of our Lord Jesus Christ. **15**So then, brothers, stand firm and hold to the teachings*d* we passed on to you, whether by word of mouth or by letter.

16May our Lord Jesus Christ himself and God our Father, who loved us and by his grace gave us eternal encouragement and good hope, **17**encourage your hearts and strengthen you in every good deed and word.

Request for Prayer

3 Finally, brothers, pray for us that the message of the Lord may spread rapidly and be honored, just as it was with you. **2**And pray that we may be delivered from wicked and evil men, for not everyone has faith. **3**But the Lord is faithful, and he will strengthen and protect you from the evil one. **4**We have confidence in the Lord that you are doing and will continue to do the things we command. **5**May the Lord direct your hearts into God's love and Christ's perseverance.

Warning Against Idleness

6In the name of the Lord Jesus Christ, we command you, brothers, to keep away from every brother who is idle and does not live according to the teaching*e* you received from us. **7**For you yourselves know how you ought to follow our example. We were not idle when we were with you, **8**nor did we eat anyone's food without paying for it. On the contrary, we worked night and day, laboring and toiling so that we would not be a burden to any of you. **9**We did this, not because we do not have the right to such help, but in order to make ourselves a model for you to follow. **10**For even when we were with you, we gave you this rule: "If a man will not work, he shall not eat."

11We hear that some among you are idle. They are not busy; they are busybodies. **12**Such people we command and urge in the Lord Jesus Christ to settle down and earn the bread they eat. **13**And as for you, brothers, never tire of doing what is right.

14If anyone does not obey our instruction in this letter, take special note of him. Do not associate with him, in order that he may feel ashamed. **15**Yet do not regard him as an enemy, but warn him as a brother.

---

a12 Or *God and Lord, Jesus Christ*   *b3* Some manuscripts *sin*   *c13* Some manuscripts *because God chose you as his firstfruits*   *d15* Or *traditions*   *e6* Or *tradition*

STANDING FIRM

**Work It
Out**
••••

Have you ever stood right on the edge of a steep cliff or deep gorge? The closer you get to the edge the more dangerous it is. And yet the temptation is to stand on the very edge, close to where the ground drops away and the footing isn't firm. There's danger, obviously, but also a thrill.

Many Christians treat sin in the same way. Instead of "standing firm," as Paul is urging here, instead of staying far away from sin, they get as close to the edge as they possibly can without actually falling off. But the danger is there. The closer they get, the more likely they will eventually fall into some sin or other.

The best defense against sin is to stay away from it, as far away as possible. Are you standing firm? Or are you standing on the edge?

**Nail It
Down**
••••

Read Paul's words about standing firm in 2 Thessalonians 2:15.

**Think It
Through**
••••

Every day of your life you will face the unavoidable pressure to sin. You live in a society that approves of many activities God has labeled "sin." The influences aren't always easy to recognize, but they are there nonetheless.

Some of the temptations to sin cannot be avoided. So why not at least stay away from those that *can* be avoided. Choose activities, friends, attitudes, radio stations, TV programs that encourage you to do and be good rather than those that only tempt you to sin.

Living on the edge of the cliff, close to sin, may be exciting, but it's dangerous. Move back a bit and "stand firm."

Reread 2 Thessalonians 2:15. For further insight read Psalm 119:9–16.

Turn to pages 420, 658, 1290, 1341 and 1356 for other readings on temptation.
Turn to page 1319 for Monday's reading.

Topic
••••

TEMPTATION

Final Greetings

16Now may the Lord of peace himself give you peace at all times and in every way. The Lord be with all of you.

17I, Paul, write this greeting in my own hand, which is the distinguishing mark in all my letters. This is how I write.

18The grace of our Lord Jesus Christ be with you all.

1 TIMOTHY

IS the church an organism or an organization? The answer is . . . yes. Yes, the church is the body of Christ—a living organism. And yes, as a living organism, the church is highly organized. It needs qualified leaders. Paul's first letter to Timothy, the overseer of the church at Ephesus, is somewhat of a leadership manual. As you read, keep this in mind: If you ever want to lead a church, a business, a family, or anything else, here's a gold mine of leadership principles direct from God himself.

1 Paul, an apostle of Christ Jesus by the command of God our Savior and of Christ Jesus our hope,

²To Timothy my true son in the faith:

Grace, mercy and peace from God the Father and Christ Jesus our Lord.

Warning Against False Teachers of the Law

³As I urged you when I went into Macedonia, stay there in Ephesus so that you may command certain men not to teach false doctrines any longer ⁴nor to devote themselves to myths and endless genealogies. These promote controversies rather than God's work—which is by faith. ⁵The goal of this command is love, which comes from a pure heart and a good conscience and a sin-

cere faith. ⁶Some have wandered away from these and turned to meaningless talk. ⁷They want to be teachers of the law, but they do not know what they are talking about or what they so confidently affirm.

⁸We know that the law is good if one uses it properly. ⁹We also know that law[a] is made not for the righteous but for lawbreakers and rebels, the ungodly and sinful, the unholy and irreligious; for those who kill their fathers or mothers, for murderers, ¹⁰for adulterers and perverts, for slave traders and liars and perjurers — and for whatever else is contrary to the sound doctrine ¹¹that conforms to the glorious gospel of the blessed God, which he entrusted to me.

The Lord's Grace to Paul

¹²I thank Christ Jesus our Lord, who has

a9 Or that the law

given me strength, that he considered me faithful, appointing me to his service. [13]Even though I was once a blasphemer and a persecutor and a violent man, I was shown mercy because I acted in ignorance and unbelief. [14]The grace of our Lord was poured out on me abundantly, along with the faith and love that are in Christ Jesus.

[15]Here is a trustworthy saying that deserves full acceptance: Christ Jesus came into the world to save sinners — of whom I am the worst. [16]But for that very reason I was shown mercy so that in me, the worst of sinners, Christ Jesus might display his unlimited patience as an example for those who would believe on him and receive eternal life. [17]Now to the King eternal, immortal, invisible, the only God, be honor and glory for ever and ever. Amen.

[18]Timothy, my son, I give you this instruction in keeping with the prophecies once made about you, so that by following them you may fight the good fight, [19]holding on to faith and a good conscience. Some have rejected these and so have shipwrecked their faith. [20]Among them are Hymenaeus and Alexander, whom I have handed over to Satan to be taught not to blaspheme.

Instructions on Worship

2 I urge, then, first of all, that requests, prayers, intercession and thanksgiving be made for everyone — [2]for kings and all those in authority, that we may live peaceful and quiet lives in all godliness and holiness. [3]This is good, and pleases God our Savior, [4]who wants all men to be saved and to come to a knowledge of the truth. [5]For there is one God and one mediator between God and men, the man Christ Jesus, [6]who gave himself as a ransom for all men — the testimony given in its proper time. [7]And for this purpose I was appointed a herald and an apostle — I am telling the truth, I am not lying — and a teacher of the true faith to the Gentiles.

[8]I want men everywhere to lift up holy hands in prayer, without anger or disputing.

[9]I also want women to dress modestly, with decency and propriety, not with braided hair or gold or pearls or expensive clothes, [10]but with good deeds, appropriate for women who profess to worship God.

[11]A woman should learn in quietness and full submission. [12]I do not permit a woman to teach or to have authority over a man; she must be silent. [13]For Adam was formed first, then Eve. [14]And Adam was not the one deceived; it was the woman who was deceived and became a sinner. [15]But women[a] will be saved[b] through childbearing — if they continue in faith, love and holiness with propriety.

Overseers and Deacons

3 Here is a trustworthy saying: If anyone sets his heart on being an overseer,[c] he desires a noble task. [2]Now the overseer must be above reproach, the husband of but one wife, temperate, self-controlled, respectable, hospitable, able to teach, [3]not given to drunkenness, not violent but gentle, not quarrelsome, not a lover of money. [4]He must manage his own family well and see that his children obey him with proper respect. [5](If anyone does not know how to manage his own family, how can he take care of God's church?) [6]He must not be a recent convert, or he may become conceited and fall under the same judgment as the devil. [7]He must also have a good reputation with outsiders, so that he will not fall into disgrace and into the devil's trap.

[8]Deacons, likewise, are to be men worthy of respect, sincere, not indulging in much wine, and not pursuing dishonest gain. [9]They must keep hold of the deep truths of the faith with a clear conscience. [10]They must first be tested; and then if there is nothing against them, let them serve as deacons.

[11]In the same way, their wives[d] are to be women worthy of respect, not malicious talkers but temperate and trustworthy in everything.

[12]A deacon must be the husband of but one wife and must manage his children and his household well. [13]Those who have served well gain an excellent standing and great assurance in their faith in Christ Jesus.

[14]Although I hope to come to you soon, I am writing you these instructions so that, [15]if I am delayed, you will know how people ought to conduct themselves in God's household, which is the church of the living God, the pillar and foundation of the truth. [16]Beyond all question, the mystery of godliness is great:

> He[e] appeared in a body,[f]
>   was vindicated by the Spirit,
>   was seen by angels,

---

[a]15 Greek *she*   [b]15 Or *restored*   [c]1 Traditionally *bishop*; also in verse 2   [d]11 Or *way, deaconesses*
[e]16 Some manuscripts *God*   [f]16 Or *in the flesh*

CAN YOU TELL ME THE WAY TO LIFE?

••

Suppose Kurt, one of the most popular guys in school, was in your chemistry class. And suppose Kurt stopped you after school one day. And suppose this conversation took place:

"Hey, can I talk to you for a minute?"

"Sure," you reply, a bit surprised that the "most excellent" guy in school would speak to you.

"Look," Kurt says (he's a little bit embarrassed), "this might sound strange, but I've noticed that no matter what happens to you, you handle it. You really have it together.

"I don't get it," he continues. "You don't party a lot. And I know you're kind of religious. But it seems like you have more fun than anyone else. What's your secret?"

Look It Up
••••

What Kurt is really after is life, fulfillment, meaning. He senses you've got it, and now he's asking, "How can I have what you've got?"

What would you tell him is the way to life?

How about taking him to a statement made by Jesus Christ, the source of life.

"Whoever believes in the Son has eternal life, but whoever rejects the Son will not see life, for God's wrath remains on him" (John 3:36).

The way to life? Believing in Jesus Christ.

That means trusting him to forgive your sins and direct you in the right path.

Think It Through
••••

The Gospel of John is clear. In Christ there is life and light (John 1:4). Apart from Christ there is death and darkness (John 3:19; 5:24). So, if you want life, you have to come to him.

But if Jesus is the only way to life, what about all the people who are counting on false religion or good works? And what about all the people who never even stop to think about the source of life or the way to life? Do you think God will bend the rules for them?

Work It Out
••••

If you're depending on anything or anyone other than Jesus Christ to give you real life and ultimate fulfillment, you're wasting your time. He's the only way.

Trust him right now for forgiveness and life through simple prayer: "Lord, I'm dead and in darkness apart from you. I trust you to save me and give me life. Amen."

If you're already a Christian, obey Christ. That way, people like Kurt will see what having real life looks like.

Nail It Down
••••

Read Paul's statement on the way to life in 1 Timothy 1:16.

**Turn to pages 951, 1160, 1164, 1167 and 1217 for other readings on real life.
Turn to page 1321 for Tuesday's reading.**

Topic
••••

REAL LIFE

was preached among the nations,
was believed on in the world,
    was taken up in glory.

Instructions to Timothy

4 The Spirit clearly says that in later times some will abandon the faith and follow deceiving spirits and things taught by demons. ²Such teachings come through hypocritical liars, whose consciences have been seared as with a hot iron. ³They forbid people to marry and order them to abstain from certain foods, which God created to be received with thanksgiving by those who believe and who know the truth. ⁴For everything God created is good, and nothing is to be rejected if it is received with thanksgiving, ⁵because it is consecrated by the word of God and prayer.

⁶If you point these things out to the brothers, you will be a good minister of Christ Jesus, brought up in the truths of the faith and of the good teaching that you have followed. ⁷Have nothing to do with godless myths and old wives' tales; rather, train yourself to be godly. ⁸For physical training is of some value, but godliness has value for all things, holding promise for both the present life and the life to come.

⁹This is a trustworthy saying that deserves full acceptance ¹⁰(and for this we labor and strive), that we have put our hope in the living God, who is the Savior of all men, and especially of those who believe.

¹¹Command and teach these things. ¹²Don't let anyone look down on you because you are young, but set an example for the believers in speech, in life, in love, in faith and in purity. ¹³Until I come, devote yourself to the public reading of Scripture, to preaching and to teaching. ¹⁴Do not neglect your gift, which was given you through a prophetic message when the body of elders laid their hands on you.

¹⁵Be diligent in these matters; give yourself wholly to them, so that everyone may see your progress. ¹⁶Watch your life and doctrine closely. Persevere in them, because if you do, you will save both yourself and your hearers.

Advice About Widows, Elders and Slaves

5 Do not rebuke an older man harshly, but exhort him as if he were your father. Treat younger men as brothers, ²older women as mothers, and younger women as sisters, with absolute purity.

³Give proper recognition to those widows who are really in need. ⁴But if a widow has children or grandchildren, these should learn first of all to put their religion into practice by caring for their own family and so repaying their parents and grandparents, for this is pleasing to God. ⁵The widow who is really in need and left all alone puts her hope in God and continues night and day to pray and to ask God for help. ⁶But the widow who lives for pleasure is dead even while she lives. ⁷Give the people these instructions, too, so that no one may be open to blame. ⁸If anyone does not provide for his relatives, and especially for his immediate family, he has denied the faith and is worse than an unbeliever.

⁹No widow may be put on the list of widows unless she is over sixty, has been faithful to her husband,ᵃ ¹⁰and is well known for her good deeds, such as bringing up children, showing hospitality, washing the feet of the saints, helping those in trouble and devoting herself to all kinds of good deeds.

¹¹As for younger widows, do not put them on such a list. For when their sensual desires overcome their dedication to Christ, they want to marry. ¹²Thus they bring judgment on themselves, because they have broken their first pledge. ¹³Besides, they get into the habit of being idle and going about from house to house. And not only do they become idlers, but also gossips and busybodies, saying things they ought not to. ¹⁴So I counsel younger widows to marry, to have children, to manage their homes and to give the enemy no opportunity for slander. ¹⁵Some have in fact already turned away to follow Satan.

¹⁶If any woman who is a believer has widows in her family, she should help them and not let the church be burdened with them, so that the church can help those widows who are really in need.

¹⁷The elders who direct the affairs of the church well are worthy of double honor, especially those whose work is preaching and teaching. ¹⁸For the Scripture says, "Do not muzzle the ox while it is treading out the grain,"ᵇ and "The worker deserves his wages."ᶜ ¹⁹Do not entertain an accusation against an elder unless it is brought by two or three witnesses. ²⁰Those who sin are to be rebuked publicly, so that the others may take warning.

ᵃ9 Or *has had but one husband*   ᵇ18 Deut. 25:4   ᶜ18 Luke 10:7

UNHAPPY WITH THE WAY YOU LOOK?

• •

Take a look at Blake. He's searching the mirror frantically for signs of muscle and dejectedly vowing to take up body-building.

Granted, the guy's no body-building champion, but let's be objective—he's no poster child for world hunger either. At 5'10" and 160 pounds, Blake looks pretty decent. He's not overweight, and he's well proportioned.

The truth is, there are a lot of guys who would gladly trade their physique for Blake's.

Look It Up
• • • •

There has never been a time in history when a culture has been as obsessed with physical fitness and appearance as ours is right now.

Liposuction is now the number one type of cosmetic surgery. The number of gyms and spas is mushrooming. Home exercise equipment sales are exploding. What does all this mean? People are dissatisfied with the way they look, and they're willing to do almost anything to change their appearance.

Consequently, these words are appropriate:

"The LORD does not look at the things man looks at. Man looks at the outward appearance, but the LORD looks at the heart" (1 Samuel 16:7)

Think It Through
• • • •

It isn't wrong to be on an exercise program or to take good care of your body. But it *is* wrong to become obsessed with your appearance—to never be content with the way you look.

Remember four things:
• God made you.
• Perfect looks are impossible to attain.
• Good looks are hard to keep.
• Physical fitness/outer appearance has only limited value.

Work It Out
• • • •

Now, do these four things:
1. Evaluate how much emphasis you place on looks.
2. Evaluate on a scale of one to ten how contented you are with your looks (ten being very contented; one being very *dis*contented).
3. Ask God to give you his perspective on the importance of physical appearance.
4. Look at yourself in a mirror and point out the good features you do have.

Nail It Down
• • • •

Consider the message of 1 Timothy 4:8.

Turn to pages 696, 1294 and 1354 for other readings on contentment.
Turn to page 1323 for Wednesday's reading.

Topic
• • • •

CONTENTMENT

²¹I charge you, in the sight of God and Christ Jesus and the elect angels, to keep these instructions without partiality, and to do nothing out of favoritism.

²²Do not be hasty in the laying on of hands, and do not share in the sins of others. Keep yourself pure.

²³Stop drinking only water, and use a little wine because of your stomach and your frequent illnesses.

²⁴The sins of some men are obvious, reaching the place of judgment ahead of them; the sins of others trail behind them. ²⁵In the same way, good deeds are obvious, and even those that are not cannot be hidden.

6 All who are under the yoke of slavery should consider their masters worthy of full respect, so that God's name and our teaching may not be slandered. ²Those who have believing masters are not to show less respect for them because they are brothers. Instead, they are to serve them even better, because those who benefit from their service are believers, and dear to them. These are the things you are to teach and urge on them.

Love of Money

³If anyone teaches false doctrines and does not agree to the sound instruction of our Lord Jesus Christ and to godly teaching, ⁴he is conceited and understands nothing. He has an unhealthy interest in controversies and quarrels about words that result in envy, strife, malicious talk, evil suspicions ⁵and constant friction between men of corrupt mind, who have been robbed of the truth and who think that godliness is a means to financial gain.

⁶But godliness with contentment is great gain. ⁷For we brought nothing into the world, and we can take nothing out of it. ⁸But if we have food and clothing, we will be content with that. ⁹People who want to get rich fall into temptation and a trap and into many foolish and harmful desires that plunge men into ruin and destruction. ¹⁰For the love of money is a root of all kinds of evil. Some people, eager for money, have wandered from the faith and pierced themselves with many griefs.

Paul's Charge to Timothy

¹¹But you, man of God, flee from all this, and pursue righteousness, godliness, faith, love, endurance and gentleness. ¹²Fight the good fight of the faith. Take hold of the eternal life to which you were called when you made your good confession in the presence of many witnesses. ¹³In the sight of God, who gives life to everything, and of Christ Jesus, who while testifying before Pontius Pilate made the good confession, I charge you ¹⁴to keep this command without spot or blame until the appearing of our Lord Jesus Christ, ¹⁵which God will bring about in his own time—God, the blessed and only Ruler, the King of kings and Lord of lords, ¹⁶who alone is immortal and who lives in unapproachable light, whom no one has seen or can see. To him be honor and might forever. Amen.

¹⁷Command those who are rich in this present world not to be arrogant nor to put their hope in wealth, which is so uncertain, but to put their hope in God, who richly provides us with everything for our enjoyment. ¹⁸Command them to do good, to be rich in good deeds, and to be generous and willing to share. ¹⁹In this way they will lay up treasure for themselves as a firm foundation for the coming age, so that they may take hold of the life that is truly life.

²⁰Timothy, guard what has been entrusted to your care. Turn away from godless chatter and the opposing ideas of what is falsely called knowledge, ²¹which some have professed and in so doing have wandered from the faith.

Grace be with you.

THEN WHAT CAN I LISTEN TO?

D avid is trying to tell Sam about a great new Christian music group. David is just beginning to realize the great Christian music he could be listening to instead of a lot of the secular stuff that has been dragging him down.

"Aw, man, you're not turning fanatic, are you?" responds Sam. "I never thought I'd hear you saying this kind of thing."

"Sam, be honest. Do you really believe that most of the stuff we've been listening to is helping us grow as Christians?"

"Okay, 'Reverend Dave,' then what *can* I listen to?"

Look It Up ● ● ● ●

The Bible gives us some excellent listening guidelines:
1. Avoid immorality. "Flee from sexual immorality" (1 Corinthians 6:18).
2. Avoid violence (Proverbs 24:1–2).
3. Avoid rebelliousness (2 Timothy 3:1–5).
4. Avoid the negative (Philippians 4:8).
5. Avoid untruthfulness. "No one who practices deceit will dwell in my house; no one who speaks falsely will stand in my presence" (Psalm 101:7).

In your musical listening habits, do you avoid these things. . . or seek them out?

Think It Through ● ● ● ●

The point isn't to single out mainstream rock for attack. (Wrong philosophies and shallow ideas are communicated through every musical style: country and western, R&B, heavy metal, middle of the road, punk/New Wave, urban/rap—sometimes even Christian music!)

Nor is the point to make a blanket statement that all secular music is evil.

No, the point is simply to say that music does shape our attitudes. That's why we must be extremely careful about what we allow to come into our minds.

Work It Out ● ● ● ●

Join a Christian friend in making the tough commitment to quit listening to music that spreads false values. Use the principles above to evaluate what you hear. Turn off every song that contains wrong thoughts.

Nail It Down ● ● ● ●

Read Paul's instructions to Timothy in 1 Timothy 6:20–21.

Turn to pages 1253 and 1338 for other readings on music.
Turn to page 1325 for Thursday's reading.

Topic
● ● ● ●

2 TIMOTHY

IMAGINE knowing your life is drawing to a close. And imagine that you're watching your life's work attacked from all sides. That's Paul's situation when he writes this letter to his "dear son," Timothy. Times are tough, and Paul wants Timothy to toughen up. As you read this book, remember that Christianity has been a difficult way of life since the time of Christ himself. Strengthen your relationship with God through daily times in his Word, and he will strengthen your resolve to persevere through life's tough times.

Outline of Contents

Greeting (1:1–2)
Encouragement to be faithful (1:3–2:13)
The false and the true way (2:14–3:9)
Paul's charge to Timothy (3:10–4:8)
Conclusion (4:9–22)

---

1 Paul, an apostle of Christ Jesus by the will of God, according to the promise of life that is in Christ Jesus,

²To Timothy, my dear son:

Grace, mercy and peace from God the Father and Christ Jesus our Lord.

Encouragement to Be Faithful

³I thank God, whom I serve, as my forefathers did, with a clear conscience, as night and day I constantly remember you in my prayers. ⁴Recalling your tears, I long to see you, so that I may be filled with joy. ⁵I have been reminded of your sincere faith, which first lived in your grandmother Lois and in your mother Eunice and, I am persuaded, now lives in you also. ⁶For this reason I re-

mind you to fan into flame the gift of God, which is in you through the laying on of my hands. ⁷For God did not give us a spirit of timidity, but a spirit of power, of love and of self-discipline.

⁸So do not be ashamed to testify about our Lord, or ashamed of me his prisoner. But join with me in suffering for the gospel, by the power of God, ⁹who has saved us and called us to a holy life—not because of anything we have done but because of his own purpose and grace. This grace was given us in Christ Jesus before the beginning of time, ¹⁰but it has now been revealed through the appearing of our Savior, Christ Jesus, who has destroyed death and has brought life and immortality to light through the gospel. ¹¹And of this gospel I was appointed a her-

WELCOME TO THE MR./MISS INITIATIVE CONTEST! □ THURSDAY

Imagine flipping on the TV and seeing what you think is some sort of beauty pageant. Soon you realize it has nothing to do with beautiful bodies, swimsuits or evening gowns. It's an initiative contest . . . and it includes girls and guys!

"What!?" you exclaim. About that time the TV blares: "And the winner is Ed of Mayberry, North Carolina! Ed, you're our Mr. Initiative for today!"

You watch in disbelief as this diligent kid from North Carolina carries home a ton of prizes (including a huge scholarship)!

Look It Up

Today our society places a much greater value on beauty than on initiative. And most likely things won't change in your lifetime. Initiative is pretty much a forgotten trait. But God's Word says:

> Go to the ant, you sluggard;
>   consider its ways and be wise!
> It has no commander,
>   no overseer or ruler,
> yet it stores its provisions in summer
>   and gathers its food at harvest (Proverbs 6:6–8).

It's true! Ants don't sit around waiting for a command to get with it. They're always busy—always accomplishing what needs to be done!

Think It Through

Initiative is simply doing the right things without having to be pushed and nagged.

Do you have this valuable quality? Do you see needs and then work to meet those needs without being asked? Why or why not?

Work It Out

Take steps today to begin making the important trait of initiative a part of your life. Here are some suggestions:

Do a job around the house before your parents ask you.

Get a big school project done two weeks in advance.

Find a need that isn't being met at school and offer to do it. (For example: Start a welcoming committee for new students. Sponsor a teacher appreciation day.)

Take it on yourself to greet at least one new person at church each week.

Whatever you choose, remember this: It takes initiative to develop initiative! Ask God for his strength.

Nail It Down

Read about the initiative shown by Onesiphorus in 2 Timothy 1:16–18.

Turn to pages 678, 751, 853 and 1278 for other readings on character.
Turn to page 1327 for Friday's reading.

Topic
CHARACTER

ald and an apostle and a teacher. **12**That is why I am suffering as I am. Yet I am not ashamed, because I know whom I have believed, and am convinced that he is able to guard what I have entrusted to him for that day.

13What you heard from me, keep as the pattern of sound teaching, with faith and love in Christ Jesus. **14**Guard the good deposit that was entrusted to you — guard it with the help of the Holy Spirit who lives in us.

15You know that everyone in the province of Asia has deserted me, including Phygelus and Hermogenes.

16May the Lord show mercy to the household of Onesiphorus, because he often refreshed me and was not ashamed of my chains. **17**On the contrary, when he was in Rome, he searched hard for me until he found me. **18**May the Lord grant that he will find mercy from the Lord on that day! You know very well in how many ways he helped me in Ephesus.

2 You then, my son, be strong in the grace that is in Christ Jesus. **2**And the things you have heard me say in the presence of many witnesses entrust to reliable men who will also be qualified to teach others. **3**Endure hardship with us like a good soldier of Christ Jesus. **4**No one serving as a soldier gets involved in civilian affairs — he wants to please his commanding officer. **5**Similarly, if anyone competes as an athlete, he does not receive the victor's crown unless he competes according to the rules. **6**The hardworking farmer should be the first to receive a share of the crops. **7**Reflect on what I am saying, for the Lord will give you insight into all this.

8Remember Jesus Christ, raised from the dead, descended from David. This is my gospel, **9**for which I am suffering even to the point of being chained like a criminal. But God's word is not chained. **10**Therefore I endure everything for the sake of the elect, that they too may obtain the salvation that is in Christ Jesus, with eternal glory.

11Here is a trustworthy saying:

If we died with him,
   we will also live with him;
12if we endure,
   we will also reign with him.
If we disown him,
   he will also disown us;
13if we are faithless,

he will remain faithful,
   for he cannot disown himself.

A Workman Approved by God

14Keep reminding them of these things. Warn them before God against quarreling about words; it is of no value, and only ruins those who listen. **15**Do your best to present yourself to God as one approved, a workman who does not need to be ashamed and who correctly handles the word of truth. **16**Avoid godless chatter, because those who indulge in it will become more and more ungodly. **17**Their teaching will spread like gangrene. Among them are Hymenaeus and Philetus, **18**who have wandered away from the truth. They say that the resurrection has already taken place, and they destroy the faith of some. **19**Nevertheless, God's solid foundation stands firm, sealed with this inscription: "The Lord knows those who are his,"*a* and, "Everyone who confesses the name of the Lord must turn away from wickedness."

20In a large house there are articles not only of gold and silver, but also of wood and clay; some are for noble purposes and some for ignoble. **21**If a man cleanses himself from the latter, he will be an instrument for noble purposes, made holy, useful to the Master and prepared to do any good work.

22Flee the evil desires of youth, and pursue righteousness, faith, love and peace, along with those who call on the Lord out of a pure heart. **23**Don't have anything to do with foolish and stupid arguments, because you know they produce quarrels. **24**And the Lord's servant must not quarrel; instead, he must be kind to everyone, able to teach, not resentful. **25**Those who oppose him he must gently instruct, in the hope that God will grant them repentance leading them to a knowledge of the truth, **26**and that they will come to their senses and escape from the trap of the devil, who has taken them captive to do his will.

Godlessness in the Last Days

3 But mark this: There will be terrible times in the last days. **2**People will be lovers of themselves, lovers of money, boastful, proud, abusive, disobedient to their parents, ungrateful, unholy, **3**without love, unforgiving, slanderous, without self-control, brutal, not lovers of the good, **4**treacherous, rash, conceited, lovers of pleasure rather than lovers of God — **5**hav-

---

a19 Num. 16:5 (see Septuagint)

STEERING CLEAR OF CONFRONTATION

Yesterday Darrell had three prime opportunities to either get into or cause conflicts. First, a friend made a really rude remark about Darrell in front of Hannah. Darrell started to reply. Then he just bit his tongue and walked away. Second, someone asked Darrell about a juicy rumor involving Hal that was floating around the school. Darrell replied, "Why don't you ask Hal?" Third, Darrell's sister charged into the living room and demanded to watch her favorite TV program. Darrell gave her the remote control and went upstairs.

Not long ago, any one of those situations would have resulted in some serious conflicts. What a difference a month makes!

Look It Up
••••

Not only is it possible to clear up conflict . . . it's possible to steer clear of it. Can you avoid some squabbles altogether? Yes!

1. Learn to keep your mouth shut. "Starting a quarrel is like breaching a dam; so drop the matter before a dispute breaks out" (Proverbs 17:14).

2. Mind your own business. "Like one who seizes a dog by the ears is a passer-by who meddles in a quarrel not his own" (Proverbs 26:17).

3. Give up your rights (Genesis 13:5–11).

Think It Through
••••

Conflict isn't always destructive. It can serve a very constructive purpose. God can use it in your life to help you grow (Proverbs 27:17). And often he uses it to accomplish a larger purpose (Acts 15:36–41).

Your goal should be threefold: to resolve the conflicts you now face, to avoid unnecessary fights, and to manage wisely those disagreements where neither party is clearly right or wrong.

Is that your goal today?

Work It Out
••••

At least once today do each of the following:

1. Refuse to say a hurtful remark that could start a conflict.

2. Refuse to spread the latest tidbit of gossip.

3. Refuse to squabble over petty matters. (If someone wants your seat, your parking space, the last piece of food or the right to the TV or telephone, quietly submit. It's hard and it hurts a little, but it's a whole lot less trouble than a fight!)

Nail It Down
••••

Read what Paul has to say to Timothy about conflict in 2 Timothy 2:23–24.

Turn to pages 15 and 178 for other readings on conflict.
Turn to page 1330 for the weekend reading.

Topic
••••

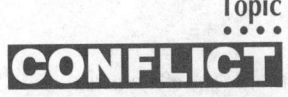

ing a form of godliness but denying its power. Have nothing to do with them.

[6]They are the kind who worm their way into homes and gain control over weak-willed women, who are loaded down with sins and are swayed by all kinds of evil desires, [7]always learning but never able to acknowledge the truth. [8]Just as Jannes and Jambres opposed Moses, so also these men oppose the truth—men of depraved minds, who, as far as the faith is concerned, are rejected. [9]But they will not get very far because, as in the case of those men, their folly will be clear to everyone.

Paul's Charge to Timothy

[10]You, however, know all about my teaching, my way of life, my purpose, faith, patience, love, endurance, [11]persecutions, sufferings—what kinds of things happened to me in Antioch, Iconium and Lystra, the persecutions I endured. Yet the Lord rescued me from all of them. [12]In fact, everyone who wants to live a godly life in Christ Jesus will be persecuted, [13]while evil men and impostors will go from bad to worse, deceiving and being deceived. [14]But as for you, continue in what you have learned and have become convinced of, because you know those from whom you learned it, [15]and how from infancy you have known the holy Scriptures, which are able to make you wise for salvation through faith in Christ Jesus. [16]All Scripture is God-breathed and is useful for teaching, rebuking, correcting and training in righteousness, [17]so that the man of God may be thoroughly equipped for every good work.

4 In the presence of God and of Christ Jesus, who will judge the living and the dead, and in view of his appearing and his kingdom, I give you this charge: [2]Preach the Word; be prepared in season and out of season; correct, rebuke and encourage—with great patience and careful instruction. [3]For the time will come when men will not put up with sound doctrine. Instead, to suit their own desires, they will gather around them a great number of teachers to say what their itching ears want to hear. [4]They will turn their ears away from the truth and turn aside to myths. [5]But you, keep your head in all situations, endure hardship, do the work of an evangelist, discharge all the duties of your ministry.

[6]For I am already being poured out like a drink offering, and the time has come for my departure. [7]I have fought the good fight, I have finished the race, I have kept the faith. [8]Now there is in store for me the crown of righteousness, which the Lord, the righteous Judge, will award to me on that day—and not only to me, but also to all who have longed for his appearing.

Personal Remarks

[9]Do your best to come to me quickly, [10]for Demas, because he loved this world, has deserted me and has gone to Thessalonica. Crescens has gone to Galatia, and Titus to Dalmatia. [11]Only Luke is with me. Get Mark and bring him with you, because he is helpful to me in my ministry. [12]I sent Tychicus to Ephesus. [13]When you come, bring the cloak that I left with Carpus at Troas, and my scrolls, especially the parchments.

[14]Alexander the metalworker did me a great deal of harm. The Lord will repay him for what he has done. [15]You too should be on your guard against him, because he strongly opposed our message.

[16]At my first defense, no one came to my support, but everyone deserted me. May it not be held against them. [17]But the Lord stood at my side and gave me strength, so that through me the message might be fully proclaimed and all the Gentiles might hear it. And I was delivered from the lion's mouth. [18]The Lord will rescue me from every evil attack and will bring me safely to his heavenly kingdom. To him be glory for ever and ever. Amen.

Final Greetings

[19]Greet Priscilla[a] and Aquila and the household of Onesiphorus. [20]Erastus stayed in Corinth, and I left Trophimus sick in Miletus. [21]Do your best to get here before winter. Eubulus greets you, and so do Pudens, Linus, Claudia and all the brothers.

[22]The Lord be with your spirit. Grace be with you.

---

[a]19 Greek *Prisca*, a variant of *Priscilla*

TITUS

LIARS. Brutes. Gluttons. The people of Crete have a bad reputation. Titus is to oversee the growth of the church there—a tough assignment indeed. To help Titus in his task, Paul writes this letter instructing him about how to appoint and train qualified spiritual leaders, how to discern and resist false teachers, and how to help the people live godly lives. As you read Titus, don't miss God's concern for holy living and proper order in the church.

Outline of Contents

1 Paul, a servant of God and an apostle of Jesus Christ for the faith of God's elect and the knowledge of the truth that leads to godliness— ²a faith and knowledge resting on the hope of eternal life, which God, who does not lie, promised before the beginning of time, ³and at his appointed season he brought his word to light through the preaching entrusted to me by the command of God our Savior,

⁴To Titus, my true son in our common faith:

Grace and peace from God the Father and Christ Jesus our Savior.

Titus' Task on Crete

⁵The reason I left you in Crete was that you might straighten out what was left unfinished and appoint*a* elders in every town, as I directed you. ⁶An elder must be blameless, the husband of but one wife, a man whose children believe and are not open to the charge of being wild and disobedient. ⁷Since an overseer*b* is entrusted with God's work, he must be blameless—not overbearing, not quick-tempered, not given to drunkenness, not violent, not pursuing dishonest gain. ⁸Rather he must be hospitable, one who loves what is good, who is self-controlled, upright, holy and disciplined. ⁹He must hold firmly to the trustworthy message as it has been taught, so that he can encourage others by sound doctrine and refute those who oppose it.

¹⁰For there are many rebellious people,

*a*5 Or *ordain*   *b*7 Traditionally *bishop*

DO-GOODERS

**Work It
Out**
• • • •

Picture this scene in your mind:
A well-known Christian musician is giving a free concert. Thousands of people have lined up outside, waiting to get into the concert hall. The line snakes back and forth in front of the doors, and those in line sing praise songs together while they wait.

Suddenly, the doors to the hall open. Many of the people who were just singing together turn to push and shove and force their way ahead of others through the doors.

The two actions just don't mix in the Christian life, do they? Singing songs of praise and then pushing others out of the way in order to be first gives a mixed message.

Many people say they believe in God; they say they're Christians. But are they really? We won't know in this life. But their actions speak volumes.

Keep that in mind whatever you're doing. More than anything you could ever say in words, your actions tell others what you truly believe.

**Nail It
Down**
• • • •

Read about the do-gooders in Titus 1:16.

**Think It
Through**
• • • •

People who give lip service to Christianity—those who go to church at least occasionally, live a moral life, keep their yard clean and neat—are not necessarily good. Nor are they necessarily Christian.

True goodness comes only from knowing God. You can't claim to know God and then do whatever pleases you on Friday night—or when the doors to a concert open.

True goodness comes from the heart and expresses itself in right actions. Do-gooders do good things only when others are watching, only when they will get benefit. The heart is not involved.

How involved is your heart in your actions? Do you claim to know God but then deny him by your actions? Or do you claim to know God and then express that knowledge in a lifestyle that brings honor to him?

**Nail It
Down**
• • • •

Reread Titus 1:16. For further insight read Proverbs 29:6–7.

Turn to pages 599, 980, 998, 1126 and 1235 for other readings on knowing God.
Turn to page 1332 for Monday's reading.

Topic
• • • •

KNOWING GOD

mere talkers and deceivers, especially those of the circumcision group. **11**They must be silenced, because they are ruining whole households by teaching things they ought not to teach — and that for the sake of dishonest gain. **12**Even one of their own prophets has said, "Cretans are always liars, evil brutes, lazy gluttons." **13**This testimony is true. Therefore, rebuke them sharply, so that they will be sound in the faith **14**and will pay no attention to Jewish myths or to the commands of those who reject the truth. **15**To the pure, all things are pure, but to those who are corrupted and do not believe, nothing is pure. In fact, both their minds and consciences are corrupted. **16**They claim to know God, but by their actions they deny him. They are detestable, disobedient and unfit for doing anything good.

What Must Be Taught to Various Groups

2 You must teach what is in accord with sound doctrine. **2**Teach the older men to be temperate, worthy of respect, self-controlled, and sound in faith, in love and in endurance.

3Likewise, teach the older women to be reverent in the way they live, not to be slanderers or addicted to much wine, but to teach what is good. **4**Then they can train the younger women to love their husbands and children, **5**to be self-controlled and pure, to be busy at home, to be kind, and to be subject to their husbands, so that no one will malign the word of God.

6Similarly, encourage the young men to be self-controlled. **7**In everything set them an example by doing what is good. In your teaching show integrity, seriousness **8**and soundness of speech that cannot be condemned, so that those who oppose you may be ashamed because they have nothing bad to say about us.

9Teach slaves to be subject to their masters in everything, to try to please them, not to talk back to them, **10**and not to steal from them, but to show that they can be fully trusted, so that in every way they will make the teaching about God our Savior attractive.

11For the grace of God that brings salvation has appeared to all men. **12**It teaches us to say "No" to ungodliness and worldly passions, and to live self-controlled, upright and godly lives in this present age, **13**while we wait for the blessed hope — the glorious appearing of our great God and Savior, Jesus Christ, **14**who gave himself for us to redeem us from all wickedness and to purify for himself a people that are his very own, eager to do what is good.

15These, then, are the things you should teach. Encourage and rebuke with all authority. Do not let anyone despise you.

Doing What Is Good

3 Remind the people to be subject to rulers and authorities, to be obedient, to be ready to do whatever is good, **2**to slander no one, to be peaceable and considerate, and to show true humility toward all men.

3At one time we too were foolish, disobedient, deceived and enslaved by all kinds of passions and pleasures. We lived in malice and envy, being hated and hating one another. **4**But when the kindness and love of God our Savior appeared, **5**he saved us, not because of righteous things we had done, but because of his mercy. He saved us through the washing of rebirth and renewal by the Holy Spirit, **6**whom he poured out on us generously through Jesus Christ our Savior, **7**so that, having been justified by his grace, we might become heirs having the hope of eternal life. **8**This is a trustworthy saying. And I want you to stress these things, so that those who have trusted in God may be careful to devote themselves to doing what is good. These things are excellent and profitable for everyone.

9But avoid foolish controversies and genealogies and arguments and quarrels about the law, because these are unprofitable and useless. **10**Warn a divisive person once, and then warn him a second time. After that, have nothing to do with him. **11**You may be sure that such a man is warped and sinful; he is self-condemned.

Final Remarks

12As soon as I send Artemas or Tychicus to you, do your best to come to me at Nicopolis, because I have decided to winter there. **13**Do everything you can to help Zenas the lawyer and Apollos on their way and see that they have everything they need. **14**Our people must learn to devote themselves to doing what is good, in order that they may provide for daily necessities and not live unproductive lives.

15Everyone with me sends you greetings. Greet those who love us in the faith.

Grace be with you all.

A FIRST-CLASS, FAITH-FILLED LIFE

Is it possible for people to change?
You'd better believe it!

Ho-hum Carl, whose life is mediocre in every area, including spiritual, recently went to a spring retreat. There he was challenged to be excellent for Christ's sake. So . . . he has declared war on mediocrity. And now:

- He's making the honor roll.
- He has a new attitude at work . . . and his employer is noticing!
- He's much improved on the trombone. (Though he still can't hit a D flat, treble clef!)
- His devotional times are getting very exciting.

Look It Up

God's Word says that we should strive for excellence in every way.

"But just as you excel in everything—in faith, in speech, in knowledge, in complete earnestness and in your love for us—see that you also excel in this grace of giving" (2 Corinthians 8:7).

And as we *are* excellent, we will become *known* for excellence: "Those who have served well gain an excellent standing and great assurance in their faith in Christ Jesus" (1 Timothy 3:13).

Think It Through

If you don't think excellent thoughts, if you refuse to live an excellent life, if you fail to share the excellent message of the gospel, what excuse do you plan to use when you stand before your excellent God?

Are you tired of being mediocre? Would you like your faith to be first-class? If so, read on.

Work It Out

Here are some tips for becoming a person of excellence.

1. Get to know God. (Don't settle for the five minutes it takes to read this devotion. Talk to him all day today and every day. Read his Word morning, noon and night.)

2. Hang around excellent people. (Ask each to help you become better in a certain area of life.)

3. Resist the temptation to compare yourself to others. (Godly excellence is not so much being better than everyone else, but— read this carefully—it is walking in the power of the Holy Spirit to be the best you can be wherever it is that God has placed you.)

4. Examine your life carefully at least once a week.

Nail It Down

Read an excellent reminder in Titus 3:1–8.

Turn to pages 93, 212, 1296 and 1334 for other readings on excellence.
Turn to page 1334 for Tuesday's reading.

Topic

EXCELLENCE

PHILEMON

WHILE the Bible doesn't explicitly forbid slavery, books like Philemon laid the foundation for slavery's ultimate demise. Onesimus, a slave of Philemon, escapes. In his flight, he eventually meets Paul who leads him to Christ. Paul writes to ask Philemon, who is also a Christian, to welcome Onesimus back—as a brother, not a slave. As you read this very short letter, remember that Christ freed you from sin and made you his brother. Just as he forgave you, be willing to forgive others, no matter what they do to you.

---

[1]Paul, a prisoner of Christ Jesus, and Timothy our brother,

To Philemon our dear friend and fellow worker, [2]to Apphia our sister, to Archippus our fellow soldier and to the church that meets in your home:

[3]Grace to you and peace from God our Father and the Lord Jesus Christ.

Thanksgiving and Prayer

[4]I always thank my God as I remember you in my prayers, [5]because I hear about your faith in the Lord Jesus and your love for all the saints. [6]I pray that you may be active in sharing your faith, so that you will have a full understanding of every good thing we have in Christ. [7]Your love has given me great joy and encouragement, because you, brother, have refreshed the hearts of the saints.

Paul's Plea for Onesimus

[8]Therefore, although in Christ I could be bold and order you to do what you ought to do, [9]yet I appeal to you on the basis of love. I then, as Paul—an old man and now also a prisoner of Christ Jesus — [10]I appeal to you for my son Onesimus,[a] who became my son while I was in chains. [11]Formerly he was useless to you, but now he has become useful both to you and to me.

[12]I am sending him—who is my very heart—back to you. [13]I would have liked to keep him with me so that he could take your place in helping me while I am in chains for

---

[a] 10 *Onesimus* means *useful*.

A MESSAGE WELL WORTH SHARING

Andrea likes to talk. (Or as her enemies might put it, "She has a big mouth!")

Politics, fashion, world problems, who is dating whom, school activities—you start a conversation, and Andrea turns into a magpie.

Except with one topic.

Andrea is reluctant to discuss her relationship with Jesus Christ.

"Why do you clam up when it comes to spiritual matters, Andrea?"

"I don't know. I guess I feel like people might ask me some hard question that I wouldn't know how to answer."

Look It Up

How sad that many Christians are reluctant to talk about the most excellent topic of all—the gospel of Jesus Christ. Why do we say the message of Christ is excellent? Because:

• It is true (2 Timothy 2:15).

• It offers hope to a hopeless world. "Continue in your faith, established and firm, not moved from the hope held out in the gospel" (Colossians 1:23).

• It brings salvation. "I am not ashamed of the gospel, because it is the power of God for the salvation of everyone who believes: first for the Jew, then for the Gentile" (Romans 1:16).

• It changes lives. "All over the world this gospel is bearing fruit and growing" (Colossians 1:6).

No wonder *gospel* means "good news"!

Think It Through

How would you counsel Andrea to be more vocal about her faith in Christ?

Can you think of any other reasons the gospel message is excellent?

When was the last time you talked to a non-Christian friend about spiritual matters?

Work It Out

Here are some helpful ideas for talking about your faith.

1. Pray for natural opportunities to arise (and wisdom and boldness when they do).

2. Practice sharing your own testimony—how you came to know Christ and how he has made a difference in your life. (Keep it brief—three minutes or so—and sincere.)

3. Memorize Bible verses dealing with salvation (John 1:12; Romans 3:23; 5:8; 6:23; 1 John 5:11–12).

4. Ask God to fill you with his Holy Spirit so that you might be an effective witness (Acts 1:8).

Nail It Down

Read what Paul heard about Philemon in Philemon 4–5.

Turn to pages 93, 212, 1296 and 1332 for other readings on excellence.
Turn to page 1338 for Wednesday's reading.

Topic

EXCELLENCE

the gospel. **14**But I did not want to do anything without your consent, so that any favor you do will be spontaneous and not forced. **15**Perhaps the reason he was separated from you for a little while was that you might have him back for good — **16**no longer as a slave, but better than a slave, as a dear brother. He is very dear to me but even dearer to you, both as a man and as a brother in the Lord.

17So if you consider me a partner, welcome him as you would welcome me. **18**If he has done you any wrong or owes you anything, charge it to me. **19**I, Paul, am writing this with my own hand. I will pay it back — not to mention that you owe me your very

self. **20**I do wish, brother, that I may have some benefit from you in the Lord; refresh my heart in Christ. **21**Confident of your obedience, I write to you, knowing that you will do even more than I ask.

22And one thing more: Prepare a guest room for me, because I hope to be restored to you in answer to your prayers.

23Epaphras, my fellow prisoner in Christ Jesus, sends you greetings. **24**And so do Mark, Aristarchus, Demas and Luke, my fellow workers.

25The grace of the Lord Jesus Christ be with your spirit.

HEBREWS

SUPPOSE you order something you really want from a catalog. After a long wait, it finally comes. You tear open the box, set the item aside, and stare at the picture some more, right? Of course not! But some early Christians wanted to go back to the Old Testament priestly system that only pictured Christ. Hebrews instructs these believers that Christ is the full expression of God's revelation, better than anything in the Old Testament. As you read this book, commit yourself to grow daily in your Christian faith and to depend on Christ alone.

Outline of Contents

The Son Superior to Angels

1 In the past God spoke to our forefathers through the prophets at many times and in various ways, ²but in these last days he has spoken to us by his Son, whom he appointed heir of all things, and through whom he made the universe. ³The Son is the radiance of God's glory and the exact representation of his being, sustaining all things by his powerful word. After he had provided purification for sins, he sat down at the right hand of the Majesty in heaven. ⁴So he became as much superior to the angels as the name he has inherited is superior to theirs.

⁵For to which of the angels did God ever say,

"You are my Son;
    today I have become your
        Father*ᵃ*"ᵇ?

Or again,

ᵃ5 Or *have begotten you*   ᵇ5 Psalm 2:7

"I will be his Father,
and he will be my Son"[a]?

[6]And again, when God brings his firstborn into the world, he says,

"Let all God's angels worship him."[b]

[7]In speaking of the angels he says,

"He makes his angels winds,
his servants flames of fire."[c]

[8]But about the Son he says,

"Your throne, O God, will last for ever and ever,
and righteousness will be the scepter of your kingdom.
[9]You have loved righteousness and hated wickedness;
therefore God, your God, has set you above your companions
by anointing you with the oil of joy."[d]

[10]He also says,

"In the beginning, O Lord, you laid the foundations of the earth,
and the heavens are the work of your hands.
[11]They will perish, but you remain;
they will all wear out like a garment.
[12]You will roll them up like a robe;
like a garment they will be changed.
But you remain the same,
and your years will never end."[e]

[13]To which of the angels did God ever say,

"Sit at my right hand
until I make your enemies
a footstool for your feet"[f]?

[14]Are not all angels ministering spirits sent to serve those who will inherit salvation?

Warning to Pay Attention

2 We must pay more careful attention, therefore, to what we have heard, so that we do not drift away. [2]For if the message spoken by angels was binding, and every violation and disobedience received its just punishment, [3]how shall we escape if we ignore such a great salvation? This salvation, which was first announced by the Lord, was confirmed to us by those who heard him. [4]God also testified to it by signs, wonders and various miracles, and gifts of the Holy Spirit distributed according to his will.

Jesus Made Like His Brothers

[5]It is not to angels that he has subjected the world to come, about which we are speaking. [6]But there is a place where someone has testified:

"What is man that you are mindful of him,
the son of man that you care for him?
[7]You made him a little[g] lower than the angels;
you crowned him with glory and honor
[8] and put everything under his feet."[h]

In putting everything under him, God left nothing that is not subject to him. Yet at present we do not see everything subject to him. [9]But we see Jesus, who was made a little lower than the angels, now crowned with glory and honor because he suffered death, so that by the grace of God he might taste death for everyone.

[10]In bringing many sons to glory, it was fitting that God, for whom and through whom everything exists, should make the author of their salvation perfect through suffering. [11]Both the one who makes men holy and those who are made holy are of the same family. So Jesus is not ashamed to call them brothers. [12]He says,

"I will declare your name to my brothers;
in the presence of the congregation I will sing your praises."[i]

[13]And again,

"I will put my trust in him."[j]

And again he says,

"Here am I, and the children God has given me."[k]

[14]Since the children have flesh and blood, he too shared in their humanity so that by his death he might destroy him who holds the power of death—that is, the devil—[15]and free those who all their lives were held in slavery by their fear of death. [16]For surely it is not angels he helps, but Abraham's descendants. [17]For this reason he had to be made like his brothers in every way, in order that he might become a merciful and faithful high priest in service to God, and that he

[a]5 2 Samuel 7:14; 1 Chron. 17:13   [b]6 Deut. 32:43 (see Dead Sea Scrolls and Septuagint)   [c]7 Psalm 104:4
[d]9 Psalm 45:6,7   [e]12 Psalm 102:25-27   [f]13 Psalm 110:1   [g]7 Or him for a little while; also in verse 9
[h]8 Psalm 8:4-6   [i]12 Psalm 22:22   [j]13 Isaiah 8:17   [k]13 Isaiah 8:18

IT'S JUST HARMLESS ENTERTAINMENT!

"Hey, Dad, Sam just called. He's got an extra ticket to the concert tonight. Can I go?"

"What concert is that?"

(Mumbling) "Uh . . . it's a new group called Sal Monella and the Disease."

"David, isn't that the group that prances around in their underwear, drinks sour milk and swings cats around by their tails?!"

"Dad! They did that one time! C'mon, they're not that wild. It's just harmless entertainment."

"No way! You might as well get that idea out of your head right now, young man."

Look It Up
● ● ● ●

Just entertainment? No. Every band also has a philosophy. Some are into hedonism ("Get loaded, have sex and party!"); others preach politics ("Overthrow the system!"); still others promote pessimism and despair ("Life is meaningless!"). But behind all the bright lights and costumes there is always a message. No wonder Scripture warns:

"Above all else, guard your heart, for it is the wellspring of life" (Proverbs 4:23).

"Guard what has been entrusted to your care. Turn away from . . . the opposing ideas of what is falsely called knowledge, which some have professed and in so doing have wandered from the faith" (1 Timothy 6:20–21).

Think It Through
● ● ● ●

Bands entertain (and rake in the cash!), but they also philosophize through their songs. Music and its message reaches deep into our conscious and unconscious minds. That's why it's so important to know exactly what the group and their songs are saying.

How would you summarize the philosophy of your favorite secular group? Is their value system Biblical?

Work It Out
● ● ● ●

The subject of music generates intense conflict because, by its very nature, music touches emotions.

As you examine the music to which you listen and your reactions to it, try not to get defensive. Read this and other articles on music as (Biblical) food for thought. What you decide about music is between you and the Lord.

Ask the Holy Spirit to open your heart to what he wants to show you.

Nail It Down
● ● ● ●

Read Hebrews 3:1 to find the best place to fix your thoughts.

Turn to pages 1253 and 1323 for other readings on music.
Turn to page 1341 for Thursday's reading.

Topic
● ● ● ●

might make atonement for[a] the sins of the people. [18]Because he himself suffered when he was tempted, he is able to help those who are being tempted.

Jesus Greater Than Moses

3 Therefore, holy brothers, who share in the heavenly calling, fix your thoughts on Jesus, the apostle and high priest whom we confess. [2]He was faithful to the one who appointed him, just as Moses was faithful in all God's house. [3]Jesus has been found worthy of greater honor than Moses, just as the builder of a house has greater honor than the house itself. [4]For every house is built by someone, but God is the builder of everything. [5]Moses was faithful as a servant in all God's house, testifying to what would be said in the future. [6]But Christ is faithful as a son over God's house. And we are his house, if we hold on to our courage and the hope of which we boast.

Warning Against Unbelief

[7]So, as the Holy Spirit says:

"Today, if you hear his voice,
[8] do not harden your hearts
as you did in the rebellion,
during the time of testing in the desert,
[9]where your fathers tested and tried me
and for forty years saw what I did.
[10]That is why I was angry with that generation,
and I said, 'Their hearts are always going astray,
and they have not known my ways.'
[11]So I declared on oath in my anger,
'They shall never enter my rest.' "[b]

[12]See to it, brothers, that none of you has a sinful, unbelieving heart that turns away from the living God. [13]But encourage one another daily, as long as it is called Today, so that none of you may be hardened by sin's deceitfulness. [14]We have come to share in Christ if we hold firmly till the end the confidence we had at first. [15]As has just been said:

"Today, if you hear his voice,
do not harden your hearts
as you did in the rebellion."[c]

[16]Who were they who heard and rebelled? Were they not all those Moses led

out of Egypt? [17]And with whom was he angry for forty years? Was it not with those who sinned, whose bodies fell in the desert? [18]And to whom did God swear that they would never enter his rest if not to those who disobeyed[d]? [19]So we see that they were not able to enter, because of their unbelief.

A Sabbath-Rest for the People of God

4 Therefore, since the promise of entering his rest still stands, let us be careful that none of you be found to have fallen short of it. [2]For we also have had the gospel preached to us, just as they did; but the message they heard was of no value to them, because those who heard did not combine it with faith.[e] [3]Now we who have believed enter that rest, just as God has said,

"So I declared on oath in my anger,
'They shall never enter my rest.' "[f]

And yet his work has been finished since the creation of the world. [4]For somewhere he has spoken about the seventh day in these words: "And on the seventh day God rested from all his work."[g] [5]And again in the passage above he says, "They shall never enter my rest."

[6]It still remains that some will enter that rest, and those who formerly had the gospel preached to them did not go in, because of their disobedience. [7]Therefore God again set a certain day, calling it Today, when a long time later he spoke through David, as was said before:

"Today, if you hear his voice,
do not harden your hearts."[c]

[8]For if Joshua had given them rest, God would not have spoken later about another day. [9]There remains, then, a Sabbath-rest for the people of God; [10]for anyone who enters God's rest also rests from his own work, just as God did from his. [11]Let us, therefore, make every effort to enter that rest, so that no one will fall by following their example of disobedience.

[12]For the word of God is living and active. Sharper than any double-edged sword, it penetrates even to dividing soul and spirit, joints and marrow; it judges the thoughts and attitudes of the heart. [13]Nothing in all creation is hidden from God's sight. Everything is uncovered and laid bare before

---

[a]17 Or and that he might turn aside God's wrath, taking away   [b]11 Psalm 95:7-11   [c]15,7 Psalm 95:7,8
[d]18 Or disbelieved   [e]2 Many manuscripts because they did not share in the faith of those who obeyed
[f]3 Psalm 95:11; also in verse 5   [g]4 Gen. 2:2

the eyes of him to whom we must give account.

Jesus the Great High Priest

¹⁴Therefore, since we have a great high priest who has gone through the heavens,ᵃ Jesus the Son of God, let us hold firmly to the faith we profess. ¹⁵For we do not have a high priest who is unable to sympathize with our weaknesses, but we have one who has been tempted in every way, just as we are—yet was without sin. ¹⁶Let us then approach the throne of grace with confidence, so that we may receive mercy and find grace to help us in our time of need.

5 Every high priest is selected from among men and is appointed to represent them in matters related to God, to offer gifts and sacrifices for sins. ²He is able to deal gently with those who are ignorant and are going astray, since he himself is subject to weakness. ³This is why he has to offer sacrifices for his own sins, as well as for the sins of the people.

⁴No one takes this honor upon himself; he must be called by God, just as Aaron was. ⁵So Christ also did not take upon himself the glory of becoming a high priest. But God said to him,

"You are my Son;
    today I have become your
        Father.ᵇ"ᶜ

⁶And he says in another place,

"You are a priest forever,
    in the order of Melchizedek."ᵈ

⁷During the days of Jesus' life on earth, he offered up prayers and petitions with loud cries and tears to the one who could save him from death, and he was heard because of his reverent submission. ⁸Although he was a son, he learned obedience from what he suffered ⁹and, once made perfect, he became the source of eternal salvation for all who obey him ¹⁰and was designated by God to be high priest in the order of Melchizedek.

Warning Against Falling Away

¹¹We have much to say about this, but it is hard to explain because you are slow to learn. ¹²In fact, though by this time you ought to be teachers, you need someone to teach you the elementary truths of God's word all over again. You need milk, not solid food! ¹³Anyone who lives on milk, being still

an infant, is not acquainted with the teaching about righteousness. ¹⁴But solid food is for the mature, who by constant use have trained themselves to distinguish good from evil.

6 Therefore let us leave the elementary teachings about Christ and go on to maturity, not laying again the foundation of repentance from acts that lead to death,ᵉ and of faith in God, ²instruction about baptisms, the laying on of hands, the resurrection of the dead, and eternal judgment. ³And God permitting, we will do so.

⁴It is impossible for those who have once been enlightened, who have tasted the heavenly gift, who have shared in the Holy Spirit, ⁵who have tasted the goodness of the word of God and the powers of the coming age, ⁶if they fall away, to be brought back to repentance, becauseᶠ to their loss they are crucifying the Son of God all over again and subjecting him to public disgrace.

⁷Land that drinks in the rain often falling on it and that produces a crop useful to those for whom it is farmed receives the blessing of God. ⁸But land that produces thorns and thistles is worthless and is in danger of being cursed. In the end it will be burned.

⁹Even though we speak like this, dear friends, we are confident of better things in your case—things that accompany salvation. ¹⁰God is not unjust; he will not forget your work and the love you have shown him as you have helped his people and continue to help them. ¹¹We want each of you to show this same diligence to the very end, in order to make your hope sure. ¹²We do not want you to become lazy, but to imitate those who through faith and patience inherit what has been promised.

The Certainty of God's Promise

¹³When God made his promise to Abraham, since there was no one greater for him to swear by, he swore by himself, ¹⁴saying, "I will surely bless you and give you many descendants."ᵍ ¹⁵And so after waiting patiently, Abraham received what was promised.

¹⁶Men swear by someone greater than themselves, and the oath confirms what is said and puts an end to all argument. ¹⁷Because God wanted to make the unchanging nature of his purpose very clear to the heirs of what was promised, he confirmed it with

---

ᵃ14 Or gone into heaven   ᵇ5 Or have begotten you   ᶜ5 Psalm 2:7   ᵈ6 Psalm 110:4   ᵉ1 Or from useless rituals   ᶠ6 Or repentance while   ᵍ14 Gen. 22:17

BECOMING AN OVERCOMER!

J anie's idea of heaven would be a sunny place with plenty of open road where she could put on her shades, pop the top on her very own convertible, crank up the stereo and drive to her heart's content. More than anything, she loves to drive.

Problem is, Janie's only fourteen. So, how does she know how much fun driving is? Answer: She sneaks the car out when her parents are gone! The minute they leave, the tempter shows up: "Go for it, Janie! Now's your chance!"

Janie seems powerless to say no.

Look It Up

How can Janie (or anyone) become an overcomer when temptation strikes?

1. By remembering the command of God: "Do not offer the parts of your body to sin, as instruments of wickedness, but rather offer yourselves to God, as those who have been brought from death to life; and offer the parts of your body to him as instruments of righteousness" (Romans 6:13).

2. By remembering the promise of God: "No temptation has seized you except what is common to man. And God is faithful; he will not let you be tempted beyond what you can bear. But when you are tempted, he will also provide a way out so that you can stand up under it" (1 Corinthians 10:13).

Think It Through

How would you advise Janie?

Is there a particular area in your life where, like Janie, you seem to be especially susceptible to temptation?

What advice would you give to someone who is facing a problem exactly like yours?

(Why not take your own advice?)

Work It Out

Today when temptation strikes (and it will, unless you're dead!), remember:

• Others are facing similar temptations. (Band together and draw strength from each other!)

• God won't let the temptation become unbearable. (No matter how you feel, you *can* resist!)

• God will provide a way out. (Look for an escape hatch!)

Nail It Down

Read Hebrews 4:15–16 for instructions on how to become an overcomer.

Turn to pages 420, 658, 1290, 1315 and 1356 for other readings on temptation.
Turn to page 1342 for Friday's reading.

Topic
••••

BUT LOOK AT THE RISKS!

Hey, guys, jump in the truck. I need you to help me take some boxes of clothes and toys to the family shelter downtown."

Dwight and Derek, who are spending their summer on a service team at their church, stare at each other. They've heard the stories. The shelter is located in the absolute worst part of town. It's surrounded by drug dealers, beggars, pimps and prostitutes.

Sitting in the truck waiting for Reverend Moore, they talk in hushed tones.

"What if we get mugged?"

"What if we catch some kind of disease?!"

Look It Up • • • •

Is it risky to be a servant? Without a doubt!

1. Servants face major problems. Listen to the apostle Paul's testimony: "We are hard pressed on every side, but not crushed; perplexed, but not in despair; persecuted, but not abandoned; struck down, but not destroyed" (2 Corinthians 4:8–9).

2. Most servants get little or no recognition. In the list of the seven deacons chosen in Acts 6:5, only the actions of Stephen and Philip are described. Procorus, Nicanor, Timon, Parmenas and Nicolas labored in obscurity!

3. Servants are targeted by Satan for special attack (Luke 22:25–32).

Think It Through • • • •

Have you ever felt used or unappreciated? Has something you've done for someone else ever been ignored, not even acknowledged? Such a reaction hurts, doesn't it?

How must Jesus have felt as he lived and died for a human race that either ignored or else rejected him?

Work It Out • • • •

No doubt about it, there are certain risks involved in giving your life away for others. So you have a choice. You can either: (a) refuse to step out of your comfort zone and settle for a dull, selfish life; or (b) step out in faith, trusting that God will care for you, his servant.

Pick one of the following "risky" projects and be a servant today:

• Spend an evening working in your city's family shelter.
• Do hospital visitation with your pastor or youth director.
• Volunteer to work one night a week at a nursing home.
• Donate blood to your local hospital.

Nail It Down • • • •

Read the promise found in Hebrews 6:10.

Turn to pages 312, 718, 1008, 1019 and 1034 for other readings on serving.
Turn to page 1346 for the weekend reading.

Topic • • • •

SERVING

an oath. **18**God did this so that, by two unchangeable things in which it is impossible for God to lie, we who have fled to take hold of the hope offered to us may be greatly encouraged. **19**We have this hope as an anchor for the soul, firm and secure. It enters the inner sanctuary behind the curtain, **20**where Jesus, who went before us, has entered on our behalf. He has become a high priest forever, in the order of Melchizedek.

Melchizedek the Priest

7 This Melchizedek was king of Salem and priest of God Most High. He met Abraham returning from the defeat of the kings and blessed him, **2**and Abraham gave him a tenth of everything. First, his name means "king of righteousness"; then also, "king of Salem" means "king of peace." **3**Without father or mother, without genealogy, without beginning of days or end of life, like the Son of God he remains a priest forever.

4Just think how great he was: Even the patriarch Abraham gave him a tenth of the plunder! **5**Now the law requires the descendants of Levi who become priests to collect a tenth from the people — that is, their brothers — even though their brothers are descended from Abraham. **6**This man, however, did not trace his descent from Levi, yet he collected a tenth from Abraham and blessed him who had the promises. **7**And without doubt the lesser person is blessed by the greater. **8**In the one case, the tenth is collected by men who die; but in the other case, by him who is declared to be living. **9**One might even say that Levi, who collects the tenth, paid the tenth through Abraham, **10**because when Melchizedek met Abraham, Levi was still in the body of his ancestor.

Jesus Like Melchizedek

11If perfection could have been attained through the Levitical priesthood (for on the basis of it the law was given to the people), why was there still need for another priest to come — one in the order of Melchizedek, not in the order of Aaron? **12**For when there is a change of the priesthood, there must also be a change of the law. **13**He of whom these things are said belonged to a different tribe, and no one from that tribe has ever served at the altar. **14**For it is clear that our Lord descended from Judah, and in regard to that tribe Moses said nothing about

priests. **15**And what we have said is even more clear if another priest like Melchizedek appears, **16**one who has become a priest not on the basis of a regulation as to his ancestry but on the basis of the power of an indestructible life. **17**For it is declared:

"You are a priest forever,
    in the order of Melchizedek."[a]

18The former regulation is set aside because it was weak and useless **19**(for the law made nothing perfect), and a better hope is introduced, by which we draw near to God.

20And it was not without an oath! Others became priests without any oath, **21**but he became a priest with an oath when God said to him:

"The Lord has sworn
    and will not change his mind:
'You are a priest forever.' "[a]

22Because of this oath, Jesus has become the guarantee of a better covenant.

23Now there have been many of those priests, since death prevented them from continuing in office; **24**but because Jesus lives forever, he has a permanent priesthood. **25**Therefore he is able to save completely[b] those who come to God through him, because he always lives to intercede for them.

26Such a high priest meets our need — one who is holy, blameless, pure, set apart from sinners, exalted above the heavens. **27**Unlike the other high priests, he does not need to offer sacrifices day after day, first for his own sins, and then for the sins of the people. He sacrificed for their sins once for all when he offered himself. **28**For the law appoints as high priests men who are weak; but the oath, which came after the law, appointed the Son, who has been made perfect forever.

The High Priest of a New Covenant

8 The point of what we are saying is this: We do have such a high priest, who sat down at the right hand of the throne of the Majesty in heaven, **2**and who serves in the sanctuary, the true tabernacle set up by the Lord, not by man.

3Every high priest is appointed to offer both gifts and sacrifices, and so it was necessary for this one also to have something to offer. **4**If he were on earth, he would not be a priest, for there are already men who offer the gifts prescribed by the law. **5**They serve

a 17,21 Psalm 110:4   *b 25* Or *forever*

at a sanctuary that is a copy and shadow of what is in heaven. This is why Moses was warned when he was about to build the tabernacle: "See to it that you make everything according to the pattern shown you on the mountain."[a] [6]But the ministry Jesus has received is as superior to theirs as the covenant of which he is mediator is superior to the old one, and it is founded on better promises.

[7]For if there had been nothing wrong with that first covenant, no place would have been sought for another. [8]But God found fault with the people and said[b]:

"The time is coming, declares the Lord,
    when I will make a new covenant
with the house of Israel
    and with the house of Judah.
[9]It will not be like the covenant
    I made with their forefathers
when I took them by the hand
    to lead them out of Egypt,
because they did not remain faithful to
    my covenant,
and I turned away from them,
                declares the Lord.
[10]This is the covenant I will make with
        the house of Israel
    after that time, declares the Lord.
I will put my laws in their minds
    and write them on their hearts.
I will be their God,
    and they will be my people.
[11]No longer will a man teach his
        neighbor,
    or a man his brother, saying, 'Know
        the Lord,'
because they will all know me,
    from the least of them to the greatest.
[12]For I will forgive their wickedness
    and will remember their sins no
        more."[c]

[13]By calling this covenant "new," he has made the first one obsolete; and what is obsolete and aging will soon disappear.

Worship in the Earthly Tabernacle

9 Now the first covenant had regulations for worship and also an earthly sanctuary. [2]A tabernacle was set up. In its first room were the lampstand, the table and the consecrated bread; this was called the Holy Place. [3]Behind the second curtain was a room called the Most Holy Place, [4]which had the golden altar of incense and the gold-covered ark of the covenant. This ark contained the gold jar of manna, Aaron's staff that had budded, and the stone tablets of the covenant. [5]Above the ark were the cherubim of the Glory, overshadowing the atonement cover.[d] But we cannot discuss these things in detail now.

[6]When everything had been arranged like this, the priests entered regularly into the outer room to carry on their ministry. [7]But only the high priest entered the inner room, and that only once a year, and never without blood, which he offered for himself and for the sins the people had committed in ignorance. [8]The Holy Spirit was showing by this that the way into the Most Holy Place had not yet been disclosed as long as the first tabernacle was still standing. [9]This is an illustration for the present time, indicating that the gifts and sacrifices being offered were not able to clear the conscience of the worshiper. [10]They are only a matter of food and drink and various ceremonial washings—external regulations applying until the time of the new order.

The Blood of Christ

[11]When Christ came as high priest of the good things that are already here,[e] he went through the greater and more perfect tabernacle that is not man-made, that is to say, not a part of this creation. [12]He did not enter by means of the blood of goats and calves; but he entered the Most Holy Place once for all by his own blood, having obtained eternal redemption. [13]The blood of goats and bulls and the ashes of a heifer sprinkled on those who are ceremonially unclean sanctify them so that they are outwardly clean. [14]How much more, then, will the blood of Christ, who through the eternal Spirit offered himself unblemished to God, cleanse our consciences from acts that lead to death,[f] so that we may serve the living God!

[15]For this reason Christ is the mediator of a new covenant, that those who are called may receive the promised eternal inheritance—now that he has died as a ransom to set them free from the sins committed under the first covenant.

[16]In the case of a will,[g] it is necessary to prove the death of the one who made it,

---

[a]5 Exodus 25:40   [b]8 Some manuscripts may be translated *fault and said to the people.*   [c]12 Jer. 31:31-34
[d]5 Traditionally *the mercy seat*   [e]11 Some early manuscripts *are to come*   [f]14 Or *from useless rituals*
[g]16 Same Greek word as *covenant*; also in verse 17

17because a will is in force only when somebody has died; it never takes effect while the one who made it is living. **18**This is why even the first covenant was not put into effect without blood. **19**When Moses had proclaimed every commandment of the law to all the people, he took the blood of calves, together with water, scarlet wool and branches of hyssop, and sprinkled the scroll and all the people. **20**He said, "This is the blood of the covenant, which God has commanded you to keep."*a* **21**In the same way, he sprinkled with the blood both the tabernacle and everything used in its ceremonies. **22**In fact, the law requires that nearly everything be cleansed with blood, and without the shedding of blood there is no forgiveness.

23It was necessary, then, for the copies of the heavenly things to be purified with these sacrifices, but the heavenly things themselves with better sacrifices than these. **24**For Christ did not enter a man-made sanctuary that was only a copy of the true one; he entered heaven itself, now to appear for us in God's presence. **25**Nor did he enter heaven to offer himself again and again, the way the high priest enters the Most Holy Place every year with blood that is not his own. **26**Then Christ would have had to suffer many times since the creation of the world. But now he has appeared once for all at the end of the ages to do away with sin by the sacrifice of himself. **27**Just as man is destined to die once, and after that to face judgment, **28**so Christ was sacrificed once to take away the sins of many people; and he will appear a second time, not to bear sin, but to bring salvation to those who are waiting for him.

Christ's Sacrifice Once for All

10 The law is only a shadow of the good things that are coming — not the realities themselves. For this reason it can never, by the same sacrifices repeated endlessly year after year, make perfect those who draw near to worship. **2**If it could, would they not have stopped being offered? For the worshipers would have been cleansed once for all, and would no longer have felt guilty for their sins. **3**But those sacrifices are an annual reminder of sins, **4**because it is impossible for the blood of bulls and goats to take away sins. **5**Therefore, when Christ came into the world, he said:

"Sacrifice and offering you did not
    desire,
    but a body you prepared for me;
6with burnt offerings and sin offerings
    you were not pleased.
7Then I said, 'Here I am — it is written
    about me in the scroll —
    I have come to do your will,
        O God.' "*b*

8First he said, "Sacrifices and offerings, burnt offerings and sin offerings you did not desire, nor were you pleased with them" (although the law required them to be made). **9**Then he said, "Here I am, I have come to do your will." He sets aside the first to establish the second. **10**And by that will, we have been made holy through the sacrifice of the body of Jesus Christ once for all.

11Day after day every priest stands and performs his religious duties; again and again he offers the same sacrifices, which can never take away sins. **12**But when this priest had offered for all time one sacrifice for sins, he sat down at the right hand of God. **13**Since that time he waits for his enemies to be made his footstool, **14**because by one sacrifice he has made perfect forever those who are being made holy.

15The Holy Spirit also testifies to us about this. First he says:

16"This is the covenant I will make with
        them
    after that time, says the Lord.
    I will put my laws in their hearts,
    and I will write them on their
        minds."*c*

17Then he adds:

"Their sins and lawless acts
    I will remember no more."*d*

18And where these have been forgiven, there is no longer any sacrifice for sin.

A Call to Persevere

19Therefore, brothers, since we have confidence to enter the Most Holy Place by the blood of Jesus, **20**by a new and living way opened for us through the curtain, that is, his body, **21**and since we have a great priest over the house of God, **22**let us draw near to God with a sincere heart in full assurance of faith, having our hearts sprinkled to cleanse us from a guilty conscience and having our bodies washed with pure water. **23**Let us hold unswervingly to the hope we profess,

a20 Exodus 24:8   *b7* Psalm 40:6-8 (see Septuagint)   *c16* Jer. 31:33   *d17* Jer. 31:34

ON YOUR OWN

SATURDAY ☐

●●

Work It Out
●●●●

Suppose your family was moving to a remote mountain cabin, miles from anywhere. Just you, your parents and your brother(s) and sister(s) will be living together, wilderness family style.

How does it sound? Wonderful? Okay? Just awful? You love your family, but does living alone with them sound like it would take some getting used to? Do you have friends you'd miss? After a while do you think you just might miss going to school? How about church? Would you miss church?

The writer to the Hebrews wants you to know that the Christian life wasn't meant to be lived in isolation. You need other believers in your life. Other believers will help you through the rough times, give you support in trouble, and rejoice with you when things are great.

Nail It Down
●●●●

Read Hebrews 10:24–25.

SUNDAY ☐

●●

Think It Through
●●●●

Now let's take a look at the other side of the coin. Just as you need others in your Christian life, they need you.

When fellow believers face a difficult decision, perhaps you can be the one to help them decide. When they are facing a hard situation, a death or loss of some sort, you can be there to support them. When life seems meaningless or boring to them, you can be the one to add a spark of life.

Christians need each other. There's no getting around it. So don't "give up meeting together," and always look for ways to "encourage one another."

Nail It Down
●●●●

Reread Hebrews 10:24–25. For further insight read Proverbs 27:5–10.

Turn to pages 195, 291, 509 and 670 for other readings on friendship.
Turn to page 1348 for Monday's reading.

Topic
●●●●

FRIENDSHIP

for he who promised is faithful. **24**And let us consider how we may spur one another on toward love and good deeds. **25**Let us not give up meeting together, as some are in the habit of doing, but let us encourage one another—and all the more as you see the Day approaching.

26If we deliberately keep on sinning after we have received the knowledge of the truth, no sacrifice for sins is left, **27**but only a fearful expectation of judgment and of raging fire that will consume the enemies of God. **28**Anyone who rejected the law of Moses died without mercy on the testimony of two or three witnesses. **29**How much more severely do you think a man deserves to be punished who has trampled the Son of God under foot, who has treated as an unholy thing the blood of the covenant that sanctified him, and who has insulted the Spirit of grace? **30**For we know him who said, "It is mine to avenge; I will repay,"*a* and again, "The Lord will judge his people."*b* **31**It is a dreadful thing to fall into the hands of the living God.

32Remember those earlier days after you had received the light, when you stood your ground in a great contest in the face of suffering. **33**Sometimes you were publicly exposed to insult and persecution; at other times you stood side by side with those who were so treated. **34**You sympathized with those in prison and joyfully accepted the confiscation of your property, because you knew that you yourselves had better and lasting possessions.

35So do not throw away your confidence; it will be richly rewarded. **36**You need to persevere so that when you have done the will of God, you will receive what he has promised. **37**For in just a very little while,

"He who is coming will come and will
    not delay.
38   But my righteous one*c* will live by
        faith.
And if he shrinks back,
    I will not be pleased with him."*d*

39But we are not of those who shrink back and are destroyed, but of those who believe and are saved.

By Faith

11 Now faith is being sure of what we hope for and certain of what we do not see. **2**This is what the ancients were commended for.

3By faith we understand that the universe was formed at God's command, so that what is seen was not made out of what is visible.

4By faith Abel offered God a better sacrifice than Cain did. By faith he was commended as a righteous man, when God spoke well of his offerings. And by faith he still speaks, even though he is dead. **5**By faith Enoch was taken from this life, so that he did not experience death; he could not be found, because God had taken him away. For before he was taken, he was commended as one who pleased God. **6**And without faith it is impossible to please God, because anyone who comes to him must believe that he exists and that he rewards those who earnestly seek him.

7By faith Noah, when warned about things not yet seen, in holy fear built an ark to save his family. By his faith he condemned the world and became heir of the righteousness that comes by faith.

8By faith Abraham, when called to go to a place he would later receive as his inheritance, obeyed and went, even though he did not know where he was going. **9**By faith he made his home in the promised land like a stranger in a foreign country; he lived in tents, as did Isaac and Jacob, who were heirs with him of the same promise. **10**For he was looking forward to the city with foundations, whose architect and builder is God.

11By faith Abraham, even though he was past age—and Sarah herself was barren—was enabled to become a father because he*e* considered him faithful who had made the promise. **12**And so from this one man, and he as good as dead, came descendants as numerous as the stars in the sky and as countless as the sand on the seashore.

13All these people were still living by faith when they died. They did not receive the things promised; they only saw them and welcomed them from a distance. And they admitted that they were aliens and strangers on earth. **14**People who say such things show that they are looking for a country of their own. **15**If they had been thinking of the country they had left, they would have had opportunity to return. **16**Instead, they were longing for a better country—a heavenly one. Therefore God is not ashamed to be

---

*a*30 Deut. 32:35   *b*30 Deut. 32:36; Psalm 135:14   *c*38 One early manuscript *But the righteous*   *d*38 Hab. 2:3,4   *e*11 Or *By faith even Sarah, who was past age, was enabled to bear children because she*

A HORSE OF A DIFFERENT COLOR

To prove the theory of evolution, Alene's science teacher Mrs. Turner uses words like *alleles, amino acids, homology,* and *paleobiochemistry.* She concludes, "I think the evidence is pretty clear—every species has evolved from a single living cell that mysteriously formed billions of years ago."

Alene's head is spinning!

Look It Up
• • • •

The Bible is not against micro-evolution—the idea that certain species undergo change. What the Bible disputes is macro-evolution—the theory that one species can produce an entirely different one:

"And God said, 'Let the land produce living creatures according to their kinds: livestock, creatures that move along the ground, and wild animals, each according to its kind' " (Genesis 1:24; see also 1:11,21).

"Each according to its kind." In other words, two horses might produce a horse of a different color, but they will never produce anything but horses!

Think It Through
• • • •

Skeptics scoff at the Biblical idea of God speaking the universe into being. "That's absurd! No one can create something from nothing." Yet many of these same individuals say that the universe just happened. In other words, they believe nothing created something out of nothing!

And isn't it odd that many intelligent scientists spend their lifetimes in laboratories trying to produce life . . . in order to prove that no intelligent being created the first life forms?

Work It Out
• • • •

The best approach to the creation/evolution controversy is not to ignore it or run away from it. Meet the issue head on. Get with a friend and study both views of origins. You may be surprised to find that the "fact" of evolution is constantly undergoing modification and is actually facing serious challenges from within the scientific community.

To help you in your study, check out of the library several books with varying points of view on creation and on evolution.

Nail It Down
• • • •

Read Hebrews 11:3 to find out about the true origin of life.

Turn to pages 2, 529, 621 and 1188 for other readings on origins.
Turn to page 1350 for Tuesday's reading.

Topic
• • • •

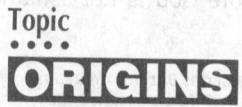
ORIGINS

called their God, for he has prepared a city for them.

[17]By faith Abraham, when God tested him, offered Isaac as a sacrifice. He who had received the promises was about to sacrifice his one and only son, [18]even though God had said to him, "It is through Isaac that your offspring[a] will be reckoned."[b] [19]Abraham reasoned that God could raise the dead, and figuratively speaking, he did receive Isaac back from death.

[20]By faith Isaac blessed Jacob and Esau in regard to their future.

[21]By faith Jacob, when he was dying, blessed each of Joseph's sons, and worshiped as he leaned on the top of his staff.

[22]By faith Joseph, when his end was near, spoke about the exodus of the Israelites from Egypt and gave instructions about his bones.

[23]By faith Moses' parents hid him for three months after he was born, because they saw he was no ordinary child, and they were not afraid of the king's edict.

[24]By faith Moses, when he had grown up, refused to be known as the son of Pharaoh's daughter. [25]He chose to be mistreated along with the people of God rather than to enjoy the pleasures of sin for a short time. [26]He regarded disgrace for the sake of Christ as of greater value than the treasures of Egypt, because he was looking ahead to his reward. [27]By faith he left Egypt, not fearing the king's anger; he persevered because he saw him who is invisible. [28]By faith he kept the Passover and the sprinkling of blood, so that the destroyer of the firstborn would not touch the firstborn of Israel.

[29]By faith the people passed through the Red Sea[c] as on dry land; but when the Egyptians tried to do so, they were drowned.

[30]By faith the walls of Jericho fell, after the people had marched around them for seven days.

[31]By faith the prostitute Rahab, because she welcomed the spies, was not killed with those who were disobedient.[d]

[32]And what more shall I say? I do not have time to tell about Gideon, Barak, Samson, Jephthah, David, Samuel and the prophets, [33]who through faith conquered kingdoms, administered justice, and gained what was promised; who shut the mouths of lions, [34]quenched the fury of the flames, and escaped the edge of the sword; whose weakness was turned to strength; and who became powerful in battle and routed foreign armies. [35]Women received back their dead, raised to life again. Others were tortured and refused to be released, so that they might gain a better resurrection. [36]Some faced jeers and flogging, while still others were chained and put in prison. [37]They were stoned[e]; they were sawed in two; they were put to death by the sword. They went about in sheepskins and goatskins, destitute, persecuted and mistreated— [38]the world was not worthy of them. They wandered in deserts and mountains, and in caves and holes in the ground.

[39]These were all commended for their faith, yet none of them received what had been promised. [40]God had planned something better for us so that only together with us would they be made perfect.

God Disciplines His Sons

12 Therefore, since we are surrounded by such a great cloud of witnesses, let us throw off everything that hinders and the sin that so easily entangles, and let us run with perseverance the race marked out for us. [2]Let us fix our eyes on Jesus, the author and perfecter of our faith, who for the joy set before him endured the cross, scorning its shame, and sat down at the right hand of the throne of God. [3]Consider him who endured such opposition from sinful men, so that you will not grow weary and lose heart.

[4]In your struggle against sin, you have not yet resisted to the point of shedding your blood. [5]And you have forgotten that word of encouragement that addresses you as sons:

"My son, do not make light of the Lord's discipline,
　and do not lose heart when he rebukes you,
[6]because the Lord disciplines those he loves,
　and he punishes everyone he accepts as a son."[f]

[7]Endure hardship as discipline; God is treating you as sons. For what son is not disciplined by his father? [8]If you are not disciplined (and everyone undergoes discipline), then you are illegitimate children and not true sons. [9]Moreover, we have all had human fathers who disciplined us and we respected them for it. How much more should we submit to the Father of our spirits and

---

[a]18 Greek seed　[b]18 Gen. 21:12　[c]29 That is, Sea of Reeds　[d]31 Or unbelieving　[e]37 Some early manuscripts stoned; they were put to the test;　[f]6 Prov. 3:11,12

THE "WHY" FOR GETTING HIGH

When some of the drug users at Devlin High were asked, "Why do you get high?" here's what they said:

Ken: "It's a form of amusement. Drugs make me feel good. They're enjoyable."

Gina: "Drugs cover up the pain. They take away the depression . . . except that after you do them awhile, you have to keep using them just to feel normal."

Michelle: "There's too much pressure. You've got your friends telling you, 'C'mon, be cool!' and your parents and teachers telling you, 'Study, study, study!' It's just a way to cope. It's no different from my dad having a couple of drinks after work or my mom taking tranquilizers to deal with her stress."

Look It Up
••••

Are those good reasons to do drugs? So we can feel good, escape, or cope with pressure? Not really. Consider:
• Moses' tough decision—"He chose to be mistreated along with the people of God rather than to enjoy the pleasures of sin for a short time" (Hebrews 11:25).
• King David's response to hard times—"Why are you downcast, O my soul? Why so disturbed within me? Put your hope in God, for I will yet praise him, my Savior and my God" (Psalm 42:5–6).
• Jesus' method of handling stress—(Mark 1:32–35).

Think It Through
••••

Ken's statement that drugs are a form of amusement is interesting. The word *amusement* literally means "without thinking." In other words, "shut down your brain."

While God is not against us enjoying life, he is against the notion that we turn off our minds (2 Corinthians 10:5). He is also against the practice of pursuing pleasure through sin.

Work It Out
••••

Can you think of ways other than drug abuse that people could use to find amusement or cope with the pressures of life?
Jot down how you would react to the pressure if:
1. Your best friend died.
2. Your boyfriend/girlfriend dropped you for someone else.
3. You were paralyzed in an accident.
4. Your parents got a divorce.
5. You discovered you had cancer.

Nail It Down
••••

Read Hebrews 11:26–27 for the factors that helped Moses choose long-term obedience rather than a lifestyle of temporary pleasure.

Turn to pages 1115, 1151 and 1239 for other readings on drugs.
Turn to page 1352 for Wednesday's reading.

Topic
••••
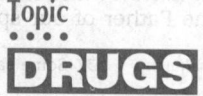

live! [10]Our fathers disciplined us for a little while as they thought best; but God disciplines us for our good, that we may share in his holiness. [11]No discipline seems pleasant at the time, but painful. Later on, however, it produces a harvest of righteousness and peace for those who have been trained by it.

[12]Therefore, strengthen your feeble arms and weak knees. [13]"Make level paths for your feet,"[a] so that the lame may not be disabled, but rather healed.

Warning Against Refusing God

[14]Make every effort to live in peace with all men and to be holy; without holiness no one will see the Lord. [15]See to it that no one misses the grace of God and that no bitter root grows up to cause trouble and defile many. [16]See that no one is sexually immoral, or is godless like Esau, who for a single meal sold his inheritance rights as the oldest son. [17]Afterward, as you know, when he wanted to inherit this blessing, he was rejected. He could bring about no change of mind, though he sought the blessing with tears.

[18]You have not come to a mountain that can be touched and that is burning with fire; to darkness, gloom and storm; [19]to a trumpet blast or to such a voice speaking words that those who heard it begged that no further word be spoken to them, [20]because they could not bear what was commanded: "If even an animal touches the mountain, it must be stoned."[b] [21]The sight was so terrifying that Moses said, "I am trembling with fear."[c]

[22]But you have come to Mount Zion, to the heavenly Jerusalem, the city of the living God. You have come to thousands upon thousands of angels in joyful assembly, [23]to the church of the firstborn, whose names are written in heaven. You have come to God, the judge of all men, to the spirits of righteous men made perfect, [24]to Jesus the mediator of a new covenant, and to the sprinkled blood that speaks a better word than the blood of Abel.

[25]See to it that you do not refuse him who speaks. If they did not escape when they refused him who warned them on earth, how much less will we, if we turn away from him who warns us from heaven? [26]At that time his voice shook the earth, but now he has promised, "Once more I will shake not only the earth but also the heavens."[d] [27]The words "once more" indicate the removing of what can be shaken—that is, created things—so that what cannot be shaken may remain.

[28]Therefore, since we are receiving a kingdom that cannot be shaken, let us be thankful, and so worship God acceptably with reverence and awe, [29]for our "God is a consuming fire."[e]

Concluding Exhortations

13 Keep on loving each other as brothers. [2]Do not forget to entertain strangers, for by so doing some people have entertained angels without knowing it. [3]Remember those in prison as if you were their fellow prisoners, and those who are mistreated as if you yourselves were suffering.

[4]Marriage should be honored by all, and the marriage bed kept pure, for God will judge the adulterer and all the sexually immoral. [5]Keep your lives free from the love of money and be content with what you have, because God has said,

"Never will I leave you;
    never will I forsake you."[f]

[6]So we say with confidence,

"The Lord is my helper; I will not be
    afraid.
What can man do to me?"[g]

[7]Remember your leaders, who spoke the word of God to you. Consider the outcome of their way of life and imitate their faith. [8]Jesus Christ is the same yesterday and today and forever.

[9]Do not be carried away by all kinds of strange teachings. It is good for our hearts to be strengthened by grace, not by ceremonial foods, which are of no value to those who eat them. [10]We have an altar from which those who minister at the tabernacle have no right to eat.

[11]The high priest carries the blood of animals into the Most Holy Place as a sin offering, but the bodies are burned outside the camp. [12]And so Jesus also suffered outside the city gate to make the people holy through his own blood. [13]Let us, then, go to him outside the camp, bearing the disgrace he bore. [14]For here we do not have an enduring city, but we are looking for the city that is to come.

[15]Through Jesus, therefore, let us continually offer to God a sacrifice of praise—the

WHAT HAPPENS IF I REFUSE TO FORGIVE?

Yesterday, Judy rode home from church with a new girl named Jean Marie. Eventually the small talk turned into a serious conversation about forgiveness.

"That was really good, that stuff you said about forgiving others," the newcomer mumbled. "I guess I should feel that way too . . . but there's no way." After a long pause, Jean Marie's eyes filled with tears. "I can never forgive my stepfather for all the wrong things he's done to me." She burst out crying, "I hate him so much! I pray every night that he'll die!"

Look It Up
••••

Bitterness hurts us far more than it will ever harm anyone else. The story of Saul is a sober reminder of this fact. He became bitter because the people praised David more than they did him: "As they danced, they sang:

> 'Saul has slain his thousands,
> and David his tens of thousands.'

"Saul was very angry; this refrain galled him. . . . And from that time on Saul kept a jealous eye on David" (1 Samuel 18:7–9).

From that point, Saul's life was all downhill. He became insecure, violent and irrational. Because he never dealt with his bitterness, his life ended in ruin and disgrace.

Think It Through
••••

One pastor has summed up the danger of an unforgiving spirit like this: "It is like a hot coal. The longer and tighter it is held, the deeper the burn. Like a hot coal, bitterness will leave a scar that even time cannot erase."

Work It Out
••••

If you are having trouble forgiving someone, if you are becoming angry and bitter, there is a way out:

First, list all the ways you feel you have been wronged. Second, remember that God has forgiven you and that he expects you to forgive others. Third, confess your bitter attitude as sin (others can't make you bitter; bitterness is a choice). Fourth, when appropriate, talk with the individual(s) involved, confess your bitter attitude and ask them to forgive you. These four steps may seem too hard, too difficult; but they are the only way to be rid of a bitter spirit. It's that simple.

Nail It Down
••••

Read what the writer to the Hebrews has to say about bitterness in Hebrews 12:15.

Turn to pages 580, 771, 809, 966, 1068 and 1302 for other readings on forgiveness.
Turn to page 1354 for Thursday's reading.

Topic
••••

FORGIVENESS

fruit of lips that confess his name. [16]And do not forget to do good and to share with others, for with such sacrifices God is pleased.

[17]Obey your leaders and submit to their authority. They keep watch over you as men who must give an account. Obey them so that their work will be a joy, not a burden, for that would be of no advantage to you.

[18]Pray for us. We are sure that we have a clear conscience and desire to live honorably in every way. [19]I particularly urge you to pray so that I may be restored to you soon.

[20]May the God of peace, who through the blood of the eternal covenant brought back from the dead our Lord Jesus, that great Shepherd of the sheep, [21]equip you with everything good for doing his will, and may he work in us what is pleasing to him, through Jesus Christ, to whom be glory for ever and ever. Amen.

[22]Brothers, I urge you to bear with my word of exhortation, for I have written you only a short letter.

[23]I want you to know that our brother Timothy has been released. If he arrives soon, I will come with him to see you.

[24]Greet all your leaders and all God's people. Those from Italy send you their greetings.

[25]Grace be with you all.

A BAD CASE OF THE "I WANTS"

Yesterday Simone was lamenting the sad state of her wardrobe. As we catch up with her today, she's in the mall—and her mood is deteriorating rapidly!

"This is so ridiculous! All my friends have nice clothes, and I have to dress like some kind of street person. Then I come to the mall to try to find something decent that won't cost a fortune, and I can't find anything for under $50!

"Why doesn't my family have more money? I don't want a lot of clothes, just a few nice outfits."

Look It Up
●●●●

Some people, like Simone, want more clothes. For others the wish list includes a nicer car (or even just a car, period), a better stereo or just some extra cash. Whatever the want, we all need to remember this fact:

"For we brought nothing into the world, and we can take nothing out of it" (1 Timothy 6:7).

We also need to adopt the writer's (the apostle Paul's) attitude:

"But if we have food and clothing, we will be content with that" (1 Timothy 6:8).

Think It Through
●●●●

Question: How do manufacturers and merchants get you to buy their products or services? Answer: They spend billions of dollars each year on advertising. Each ad is carefully designed to make you feel discontented: "My car is a bomb; I need a new one" or "My clothes are the worst; time to go shopping" or "My body is a wreck; I'll join the health club."

Advertisers know that feeding your dissatisfaction works like a charm!

Work It Out
●●●●

See if this helps:

1. Make a list of all the material things that you wish you had. Don't hold back—write everything down.

2. Pray this: "Father, as my list indicates, I have a bad case of the 'I wants.' Instead of seeking your kingdom first [Matthew 6:33], I guess I've been seeking *things* first. Change me, Lord. Help me to become less attracted to stuff and more devoted to you. Right now I lay all my desires before you. Do what you think is best. Amen."

Nail It Down
●●●●

Read what Hebrews 13:5 has to say about contentment.

Turn to pages 696, 1294 and 1321 for other readings on contentment.
Turn to page 1356 for Friday's reading.

Topic
●●●●

CONTENTMENT

JAMES

FAITH. It's not a feeling; it's not an action. True faith is a change of heart that produces action. To make that point, James (a brother of Jesus) urges Christians to express true faith in daily living. False faith merely hears God's Word; true faith does what God's Word says. True faith endures trials, says no to prejudice, gets a grip on the tongue, and stops the devil in his tracks. As you read James, ask yourself if you have true faith. Can others see by what you do and say that you believe in Jesus?

Outline of Contents

1 James, a servant of God and of the Lord Jesus Christ,

To the twelve tribes scattered among the nations:

Greetings.

Trials and Temptations

2Consider it pure joy, my brothers, whenever you face trials of many kinds, 3because you know that the testing of your faith develops perseverance. 4Perseverance must finish its work so that you may be mature and complete, not lacking anything. 5If any of you lacks wisdom, he should ask God, who gives generously to all without finding fault, and it will be given to him. 6But when he asks, he must believe and not doubt, because he who doubts is like a wave of the sea, blown and tossed by the wind. 7That man should not think he will receive anything from the Lord; 8he is a double-minded man, unstable in all he does.

9The brother in humble circumstances ought to take pride in his high position. 10But the one who is rich should take pride in his low position, because he will pass away like a wild flower. 11For the sun rises with scorching heat and withers the plant; its blossom falls and its beauty is destroyed. In the same way, the rich man will fade away even while he goes about his business.

12Blessed is the man who perseveres under trial, because when he has stood the test, he will receive the crown of life that God has promised to those who love him. 13When tempted, no one should say, "God is tempting me." For God cannot be tempted by evil, nor does he tempt anyone; 14but

ANATOMY OF A SEDUCTION

Innocent incidents or potential problems?
- Standing by a magazine rack in a convenience store, Carlos yells to Gene, "Hey, come check this out!"
- "Come on, it'll be great! My parents are out of town until tomorrow!"
- "Class, I have to step out of the room for two minutes. Keep your eyes on your own test paper!"
- "Look, I promise we'll stop as soon as things start getting out of hand!"

Look It Up
•••

For a classic picture of how temptation works, we need look no further than King David's downward slide into adultery and murder.

"In the spring, at the time when kings go off to war, David sent Joab out with . . . the whole Israelite army. . . . But David remained in Jerusalem.

"One evening David got up from his bed and walked around on the roof of the palace. From the roof he saw a woman bathing. The woman was very beautiful, and David sent someone to find out about her" (2 Samuel 11:1–3).

The next verse records that "David sent messengers to get her. She came to him, and he slept with her" (2 Samuel 11:4).

Maybe you know the rest of the story. The woman, Bathsheba, ended up pregnant, and David had her husband killed to cover his sin.

Think It Through
••••

Do you think David consciously thought: "I know what! I'll spend tonight with somebody else's wife! For a few hours of pleasure, I'll ruin my life. Yep, that's what I want to accomplish today!"?

Of course not! No one purposely plans to wreck his or her life!

But think about it: If a godly person like David could so easily yield to temptation, what does that say to you and me?

Work It Out
••••

Here are a few things you can learn from David's mistakes:

1. Be where you're supposed to be! (If David had been with his troops, the sad story recorded in 2 Samuel 11 would not have happened.)

2. Don't be idle! (By lazing around with nothing to do, David was a prime candidate for a big fall.)

3. At the first sign of trouble, run! (David stopped and stared.)

4. Don't entertain thoughts of sin! (As soon as David inquired about Bathsheba, he was hooked. The only thing left was to send for her.)

Nail It Down
••••

Read James' description of how temptation works in James 1:14–15.

Turn to pages 420, 658, 1290, 1315, and 1341 for other readings on temptation.
Turn to page 1358 for the weekend reading.

Topic
••••

TEMPTATION

each one is tempted when, by his own evil desire, he is dragged away and enticed. ¹⁵Then, after desire has conceived, it gives birth to sin; and sin, when it is full-grown, gives birth to death.

¹⁶Don't be deceived, my dear brothers. ¹⁷Every good and perfect gift is from above, coming down from the Father of the heavenly lights, who does not change like shifting shadows. ¹⁸He chose to give us birth through the word of truth, that we might be a kind of firstfruits of all he created.

Listening and Doing

¹⁹My dear brothers, take note of this: Everyone should be quick to listen, slow to speak and slow to become angry, ²⁰for man's anger does not bring about the righteous life that God desires. ²¹Therefore, get rid of all moral filth and the evil that is so prevalent and humbly accept the word planted in you, which can save you.

²²Do not merely listen to the word, and so deceive yourselves. Do what it says. ²³Anyone who listens to the word but does not do what it says is like a man who looks at his face in a mirror ²⁴and, after looking at himself, goes away and immediately forgets what he looks like. ²⁵But the man who looks intently into the perfect law that gives freedom, and continues to do this, not forgetting what he has heard, but doing it — he will be blessed in what he does.

²⁶If anyone considers himself religious and yet does not keep a tight rein on his tongue, he deceives himself and his religion is worthless. ²⁷Religion that God our Father accepts as pure and faultless is this: to look after orphans and widows in their distress and to keep oneself from being polluted by the world.

Favoritism Forbidden

2 My brothers, as believers in our glorious Lord Jesus Christ, don't show favoritism. ²Suppose a man comes into your meeting wearing a gold ring and fine clothes, and a poor man in shabby clothes also comes in. ³If you show special attention to the man wearing fine clothes and say, "Here's a good seat for you," but say to the poor man, "You stand there" or "Sit on the floor by my feet," ⁴have you not discriminated among yourselves and become judges with evil thoughts?

⁵Listen, my dear brothers: Has not God chosen those who are poor in the eyes of the world to be rich in faith and to inherit the kingdom he promised those who love him? ⁶But you have insulted the poor. Is it not the rich who are exploiting you? Are they not the ones who are dragging you into court? ⁷Are they not the ones who are slandering the noble name of him to whom you belong?

⁸If you really keep the royal law found in Scripture, "Love your neighbor as yourself,"ᵃ you are doing right. ⁹But if you show favoritism, you sin and are convicted by the law as lawbreakers. ¹⁰For whoever keeps the whole law and yet stumbles at just one point is guilty of breaking all of it. ¹¹For he who said, "Do not commit adultery,"ᵇ also said, "Do not murder."ᶜ If you do not commit adultery but do commit murder, you have become a lawbreaker.

¹²Speak and act as those who are going to be judged by the law that gives freedom, ¹³because judgment without mercy will be shown to anyone who has not been merciful. Mercy triumphs over judgment!

Faith and Deeds

¹⁴What good is it, my brothers, if a man claims to have faith but has no deeds? Can such faith save him? ¹⁵Suppose a brother or sister is without clothes and daily food. ¹⁶If one of you says to him, "Go, I wish you well; keep warm and well fed," but does nothing about his physical needs, what good is it? ¹⁷In the same way, faith by itself, if it is not accompanied by action, is dead.

¹⁸But someone will say, "You have faith; I have deeds."

Show me your faith without deeds, and I will show you my faith by what I do. ¹⁹You believe that there is one God. Good! Even the demons believe that — and shudder.

²⁰You foolish man, do you want evidence that faith without deeds is uselessᵈ? ²¹Was not our ancestor Abraham considered righteous for what he did when he offered his son Isaac on the altar? ²²You see that his faith and his actions were working together, and his faith was made complete by what he did. ²³And the scripture was fulfilled that says, "Abraham believed God, and it was credited to him as righteousness,"ᵉ and he was called God's friend. ²⁴You see that a person is justified by what he does and not by faith alone.

ᵃ8 Lev. 19:18   ᵇ11 Exodus 20:14; Deut. 5:18   ᶜ11 Exodus 20:13; Deut. 5:17   ᵈ20 Some early manuscripts *dead*   ᵉ23 Gen. 15:6

1358

JUDGING BY APPEARANCES

SATURDAY ☐

Work It Out
••••

Two people enter your church just before the morning worship service begins. Both are attending your church for the first time. Both stop just inside the door and look around. One is dressed in the latest and most expensive fashions. The other is wearing old, shabby, cast-off clothing.

Who will be greeted first in your church? Will the well-to-do person be welcomed and the shabby person snubbed? Or will both be equally welcome?

The writer of the book of James is pretty clear that we should never judge by appearances. He says that those who do "become judges with evil thoughts." Those are pretty strong words, words that most of us need to take more seriously. We so easily reject those who don't quite fit in, those who don't quite measure up in our eyes. And we do it almost without thinking.

Jesus, our perfect example, lovingly accepted the rich and the poor, the healthy and the sick, the ruler and the beggar, the accepted and the unacceptable. Follow his example, and stop judging by appearances.

Nail It Down
••••

Read James's warning against judging by appearances in James 2:1–4.

SUNDAY ☐

Think It Through
••••

There are many reasons why you shouldn't judge by appearances. Here are just a few:
• It hurts those who are rejected.
• It evaluates people's worth by how they look or dress rather than by who they are.
• It isn't loving, and as Christians we are commanded to be loving.
• It reveals pride within the one doing the judging.
• It is sin.

Nail It Down
••••

Reread James 2:1–4. For further insight read Isaiah 11:1–5.

Turn to pages 488, 560 and 1300 for other readings on appearance.
Turn to page 1360 for Monday's reading.

Topic
••••

APPEARANCE

25In the same way, was not even Rahab the prostitute considered righteous for what she did when she gave lodging to the spies and sent them off in a different direction? 26As the body without the spirit is dead, so faith without deeds is dead.

Taming the Tongue

3 Not many of you should presume to be teachers, my brothers, because you know that we who teach will be judged more strictly. 2We all stumble in many ways. If anyone is never at fault in what he says, he is a perfect man, able to keep his whole body in check.

3When we put bits into the mouths of horses to make them obey us, we can turn the whole animal. 4Or take ships as an example. Although they are so large and are driven by strong winds, they are steered by a very small rudder wherever the pilot wants to go. 5Likewise the tongue is a small part of the body, but it makes great boasts. Consider what a great forest is set on fire by a small spark. 6The tongue also is a fire, a world of evil among the parts of the body. It corrupts the whole person, sets the whole course of his life on fire, and is itself set on fire by hell.

7All kinds of animals, birds, reptiles and creatures of the sea are being tamed and have been tamed by man, 8but no man can tame the tongue. It is a restless evil, full of deadly poison.

9With the tongue we praise our Lord and Father, and with it we curse men, who have been made in God's likeness. 10Out of the same mouth come praise and cursing. My brothers, this should not be. 11Can both fresh water and salt*a* water flow from the same spring? 12My brothers, can a fig tree bear olives, or a grapevine bear figs? Neither can a salt spring produce fresh water.

Two Kinds of Wisdom

13Who is wise and understanding among you? Let him show it by his good life, by deeds done in the humility that comes from wisdom. 14But if you harbor bitter envy and selfish ambition in your hearts, do not boast about it or deny the truth. 15Such "wisdom" does not come down from heaven but is earthly, unspiritual, of the devil. 16For where you have envy and selfish ambition, there you find disorder and every evil practice.

17But the wisdom that comes from heaven is first of all pure; then peace-loving, considerate, submissive, full of mercy and good fruit, impartial and sincere. 18Peacemakers who sow in peace raise a harvest of righteousness.

Submit Yourselves to God

4 What causes fights and quarrels among you? Don't they come from your desires that battle within you? 2You want something but don't get it. You kill and covet, but you cannot have what you want. You quarrel and fight. You do not have, because you do not ask God. 3When you ask, you do not receive, because you ask with wrong motives, that you may spend what you get on your pleasures.

4You adulterous people, don't you know that friendship with the world is hatred toward God? Anyone who chooses to be a friend of the world becomes an enemy of God. 5Or do you think Scripture says without reason that the spirit he caused to live in us envies intensely?*b* 6But he gives us more grace. That is why Scripture says:

"God opposes the proud
    but gives grace to the humble."*c*

7Submit yourselves, then, to God. Resist the devil, and he will flee from you. 8Come near to God and he will come near to you. Wash your hands, you sinners, and purify your hearts, you double-minded. 9Grieve, mourn and wail. Change your laughter to mourning and your joy to gloom. 10Humble yourselves before the Lord, and he will lift you up.

11Brothers, do not slander one another. Anyone who speaks against his brother or judges him speaks against the law and judges it. When you judge the law, you are not keeping it, but sitting in judgment on it. 12There is only one Lawgiver and Judge, the one who is able to save and destroy. But you—who are you to judge your neighbor?

Boasting About Tomorrow

13Now listen, you who say, "Today or tomorrow we will go to this or that city, spend a year there, carry on business and make money." 14Why, you do not even know what will happen tomorrow. What is your life? You are a mist that appears for a little while and then vanishes. 15Instead, you ought to say, "If it is the Lord's will, we will live and do this or that." 16As it is, you boast and

---

a11 Greek *bitter* (see also verse 14)   *b5* Or *that God jealously longs for the spirit that he made to live in us;* or *that the Spirit he caused to live in us longs jealously*   *c6* Prov. 3:34

CRUNCH TIME IN THE CLASSROOM

Marianne makes straight A's. She's intelligent, she knows it, and she lets everyone else know it! Her goal is to be the valedictorian of the senior class.

Trouble is, David is equally smart. And he is also determined to graduate number one.

What a fierce competition! The two students keeping track of each other's GPAs . . . going crazy over every missed bonus question . . . rejoicing over each slip by the "enemy."

Look It Up
••••

It has nothing to do with grades, but this Biblical reference to Satan illustrates that pride is often the motivation behind the desire to be number one:

"You said in your heart, 'I will ascend to heaven; I will raise my throne above the stars of God; I will sit enthroned on the mount of assembly, on the utmost heights of the sacred mountain. I will ascend above the tops of the clouds; I will make myself like the Most High' " (Isaiah 14:13–14).

Essentially, Satan was competing with God!

Think It Through
••••

The basic cause behind all competition is pride. You feel a need or desire to be better or have more than the next person. You find pleasure in having something only if you have more of it than those around you.

Do you have trouble with pride when it comes to grades? How about athletics? Or looks? Or in other areas of life?

Work It Out
••••

First, pray that God will change your attitude from "I have to be the best" to "I want to do my best."

Second, try to avoid finding out the grades—or salaries or test scores—others receive. (What's the point? If you do better, you'll be prideful; if you do worse, you'll feel inferior!)

Third, let your goal in school be learning, not grades.

Nail It Down
••••

Read James 4:6 to find out how God deals with the pride.

Turn to pages 18, 43 and 1230 for other readings on competition.
Turn to page 1362 for Tuesday's reading.

Topic
••••

COMPETITION

brag. All such boasting is evil. [17]Anyone, then, who knows the good he ought to do and doesn't do it, sins.

Warning to Rich Oppressors

5 Now listen, you rich people, weep and wail because of the misery that is coming upon you. [2]Your wealth has rotted, and moths have eaten your clothes. [3]Your gold and silver are corroded. Their corrosion will testify against you and eat your flesh like fire. You have hoarded wealth in the last days. [4]Look! The wages you failed to pay the workmen who mowed your fields are crying out against you. The cries of the harvesters have reached the ears of the Lord Almighty. [5]You have lived on earth in luxury and self-indulgence. You have fattened yourselves in the day of slaughter.[a] [6]You have condemned and murdered innocent men, who were not opposing you.

Patience in Suffering

[7]Be patient, then, brothers, until the Lord's coming. See how the farmer waits for the land to yield its valuable crop and how patient he is for the autumn and spring rains. [8]You too, be patient and stand firm, because the Lord's coming is near. [9]Don't grumble against each other, brothers, or you will be judged. The Judge is standing at the door! [10]Brothers, as an example of patience in the face of suffering, take the prophets who spoke in the name of the Lord. [11]As you know, we consider blessed those who have persevered. You have heard of Job's perseverance and have seen what the Lord finally brought about. The Lord is full of compassion and mercy.

[12]Above all, my brothers, do not swear—not by heaven or by earth or by anything else. Let your "Yes" be yes, and your "No," no, or you will be condemned.

The Prayer of Faith

[13]Is any one of you in trouble? He should pray. Is anyone happy? Let him sing songs of praise. [14]Is any one of you sick? He should call the elders of the church to pray over him and anoint him with oil in the name of the Lord. [15]And the prayer offered in faith will make the sick person well; the Lord will raise him up. If he has sinned, he will be forgiven. [16]Therefore confess your sins to each other and pray for each other so that you may be healed. The prayer of a righteous man is powerful and effective.

[17]Elijah was a man just like us. He prayed earnestly that it would not rain, and it did not rain on the land for three and a half years. [18]Again he prayed, and the heavens gave rain, and the earth produced its crops.

[19]My brothers, if one of you should wander from the truth and someone should bring him back, [20]remember this: Whoever turns a sinner from the error of his way will save him from death and cover over a multitude of sins.

[a]5 Or yourselves as in a day of feasting

"ME!"–THE SIGN OF OUR TIMES

Is it just our imagination, or are more and more people becoming more and more self-centered?

Marty and Dave, rushing to get to a movie at the mall, speed past a distraught elderly lady whose car has stalled in rush-hour traffic.

Sharon was all set to join the youth group this Saturday. She assumed they were going to a nearby amusement park. However, when a last-minute minor emergency turned the group's fun outing into a service project, Sharon changed her plans.

Bart gladly spent $45 for the latest style in hair cuts, but he wouldn't donate a cent during a recent church drive to feed the homeless.

Look It Up
• • • •

People have always been selfish (Genesis 13:10–11; Luke 10:30–32), but perhaps the human preoccupation with self is growing in our time: "But mark this: There will be terrible times in the last days. People will be lovers of themselves" (2 Timothy 3:1–2).

Elsewhere, the apostle Paul cites selfishness as a trait of someone who is not controlled by the Holy Spirit: "The acts of the sinful nature are obvious: . . . selfish ambition . . . and the like. I warn you, as I did before, that those who live like this will not inherit the kingdom of God" (Galatians 5:19–21).

Think It Through
• • • •

Do you think you are a self-centered person? Here's a quick test: How do you react when you see a mirror?

For more insight into yourself, select the response that best describes you: I get concerned about the misfortunes of other people: (a) a lot; (b) sometimes; (c) especially if their problems happen to affect me; (d) rarely—I'm too busy with my own problems; (e) what other people?

Work It Out
• • • •

Thumb through a daily newspaper or a news magazine. What evidences do you see of the selfishness of the human race?

Pray this: "Dear Lord, open my heart this week to understand your Word. Show me where and how I am being selfish. And please begin to make me an unselfish person. Amen."

Nail It Down
• • • •

Read James' warning to the selfish of his day in James 5:1–6.

Turn to pages 1095 and 1106 for other readings on selfishness.
Turn to page 1365 for Wednesday's reading.

Topic
• • • •

SELFISHNESS

1 PETER

HELP! cry the believers scattered throughout the Roman Empire. They are being persecuted for their faith. Rejoice! writes Peter in response. Through trials, our character is refined and improved. We become more like Christ, who suffered for us. But the message of 1 Peter isn't just "grin and bear it." Peter reminds believers that Jesus suffered and that he gives us hope for a glorious future. As you read, decide to live a holy life—in spite of any suffering you might experience. Do that, and God will give you help.

Outline of Contents

1 Peter, an apostle of Jesus Christ,

To God's elect, strangers in the world, scattered throughout Pontus, Galatia, Cappadocia, Asia and Bithynia, 2who have been chosen according to the foreknowledge of God the Father, through the sanctifying work of the Spirit, for obedience to Jesus Christ and sprinkling by his blood:

Grace and peace be yours in abundance.

Praise to God for a Living Hope

3Praise be to the God and Father of our Lord Jesus Christ! In his great mercy he has given us new birth into a living hope through the resurrection of Jesus Christ from the dead, 4and into an inheritance that can never perish, spoil or fade—kept in heaven for you, 5who through faith are shielded by God's power until the coming of the salvation that is ready to be revealed in the last time. 6In this you greatly rejoice, though now for a little while you may have had to suffer grief in all kinds of trials. 7These have come so that your faith—of greater worth than gold, which perishes even though refined by fire—may be proved genuine and may result in praise, glory and honor when Jesus Christ is revealed. 8Though you have not seen him, you love him; and even though you do not see him now, you believe in him and are filled with an inexpressible and glorious joy, 9for you are receiving the goal of your faith, the salvation of your souls.

[10]Concerning this salvation, the prophets, who spoke of the grace that was to come to you, searched intently and with the greatest care, [11]trying to find out the time and circumstances to which the Spirit of Christ in them was pointing when he predicted the sufferings of Christ and the glories that would follow. [12]It was revealed to them that they were not serving themselves but you, when they spoke of the things that have now been told you by those who have preached the gospel to you by the Holy Spirit sent from heaven. Even angels long to look into these things.

Be Holy

[13]Therefore, prepare your minds for action; be self-controlled; set your hope fully on the grace to be given you when Jesus Christ is revealed. [14]As obedient children, do not conform to the evil desires you had when you lived in ignorance. [15]But just as he who called you is holy, so be holy in all you do; [16]for it is written: "Be holy, because I am holy."[a]

[17]Since you call on a Father who judges each man's work impartially, live your lives as strangers here in reverent fear. [18]For you know that it was not with perishable things such as silver or gold that you were redeemed from the empty way of life handed down to you from your forefathers, [19]but with the precious blood of Christ, a lamb without blemish or defect. [20]He was chosen before the creation of the world, but was revealed in these last times for your sake. [21]Through him you believe in God, who raised him from the dead and glorified him, and so your faith and hope are in God.

[22]Now that you have purified yourselves by obeying the truth so that you have sincere love for your brothers, love one another deeply, from the heart.[b] [23]For you have been born again, not of perishable seed, but of imperishable, through the living and enduring word of God. [24]For,

"All men are like grass,
    and all their glory is like the flowers
        of the field;
the grass withers and the flowers fall,
25   but the word of the Lord stands
        forever."[c]

And this is the word that was preached to you.

2 Therefore, rid yourselves of all malice and all deceit, hypocrisy, envy, and slander of every kind. [2]Like newborn babies, crave pure spiritual milk, so that by it you may grow up in your salvation, [3]now that you have tasted that the Lord is good.

The Living Stone and a Chosen People

[4]As you come to him, the living Stone—rejected by men but chosen by God and precious to him—[5]you also, like living stones, are being built into a spiritual house to be a holy priesthood, offering spiritual sacrifices acceptable to God through Jesus Christ. [6]For in Scripture it says:

"See, I lay a stone in Zion,
    a chosen and precious cornerstone,
and the one who trusts in him
    will never be put to shame."[d]

[7]Now to you who believe, this stone is precious. But to those who do not believe,

"The stone the builders rejected
    has become the capstone,[e]"[f]

[8]and,

"A stone that causes men to stumble
    and a rock that makes them fall."[g]

They stumble because they disobey the message—which is also what they were destined for.

[9]But you are a chosen people, a royal priesthood, a holy nation, a people belonging to God, that you may declare the praises of him who called you out of darkness into his wonderful light. [10]Once you were not a people, but now you are the people of God; once you had not received mercy, but now you have received mercy.

[11]Dear friends, I urge you, as aliens and strangers in the world, to abstain from sinful desires, which war against your soul. [12]Live such good lives among the pagans that, though they accuse you of doing wrong, they may see your good deeds and glorify God on the day he visits us.

Submission to Rulers and Masters

[13]Submit yourselves for the Lord's sake to every authority instituted among men: whether to the king, as the supreme authority, [14]or to governors, who are sent by him to punish those who do wrong and to commend those who do right. [15]For it is God's

---

[a]16 Lev. 11:44,45; 19:2; 20:7   [b]22 Some early manuscripts *from a pure heart*   [c]25 Isaiah 40:6-8
[d]6 Isaiah 28:16   [e]7 Or *cornerstone*   [f]7 Psalm 118:22   [g]8 Isaiah 8:14

I JUST DON'T FEEL LIKE THINKING

L ast year, Collin's main form of amusement was to flick on the TV or put on the stereo headphones and put his brain in neutral. Occasionally he would completely ignore his homework, his friends and his family, renting and watching up to six movies in a weekend.

As a Christian whose worst vice was being a couch potato, and as a respected student with a "nice guy/doesn't party" reputation, Collin should have felt good about his life, shouldn't he?

So why did he decide last month to make some big changes in his entertainment habits?

Look It Up
••••

One of Satan's most effective strategies for attacking believers is to get them into a frame of mind where they just don't feel like thinking or being responsible. That attack probably sidelines more Christians than anything else. No wonder the apostles Paul and Peter issued these sober warnings:

"Let us not be like others, who are asleep, but let us be alert and self-controlled" (1 Thessalonians 5:6).

"Be clear minded and self-controlled so that you can pray" (1 Peter 4:7).

"Be self-controlled and alert" (1 Peter 5:8).

Notice that the Bible never says, "Turn off your mind and escape."

Think It Through
••••

Now Collin realizes what was going on: "For me, all the TV watching, the music, the movie marathons—they were really just ways to escape. It was like hitting the pause button on my life. I could forget my pressures and responsibilities for a little while. Before long, even though I looked like this great Christian, I was turning into a slob."

What about you? Do you use the media to escape?

Work It Out
••••

Today, honestly examine your activities—especially your use of TV, movies and music. In each case ask two questions: (1) "Am I doing this to escape or avoid a responsibility?" and (2) "If I turn off my mind here, will I be vulnerable to Satan's bad ideas?"

If you have to answer yes to either question, don't do that activity. Be clear minded and alert, not empty-headed and inactive!

Nail It Down
••••

Read Peter's counsel in 1 Peter 1:13.

Turn to pages 867, 1021 and 1390 for other readings on escape.
Turn to page 1367 for Thursday's reading.

Topic
••••

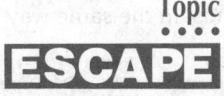
ESCAPE

will that by doing good you should silence the ignorant talk of foolish men. **16**Live as free men, but do not use your freedom as a cover-up for evil; live as servants of God. **17**Show proper respect to everyone: Love the brotherhood of believers, fear God, honor the king.

18Slaves, submit yourselves to your masters with all respect, not only to those who are good and considerate, but also to those who are harsh. **19**For it is commendable if a man bears up under the pain of unjust suffering because he is conscious of God. **20**But how is it to your credit if you receive a beating for doing wrong and endure it? But if you suffer for doing good and you endure it, this is commendable before God. **21**To this you were called, because Christ suffered for you, leaving you an example, that you should follow in his steps.

22"He committed no sin,
    and no deceit was found in his
      mouth."[a]

23When they hurled their insults at him, he did not retaliate; when he suffered, he made no threats. Instead, he entrusted himself to him who judges justly. **24**He himself bore our sins in his body on the tree, so that we might die to sins and live for righteousness; by his wounds you have been healed. **25**For you were like sheep going astray, but now you have returned to the Shepherd and Overseer of your souls.

Wives and Husbands

3 Wives, in the same way be submissive to your husbands so that, if any of them do not believe the word, they may be won over without words by the behavior of their wives, **2**when they see the purity and reverence of your lives. **3**Your beauty should not come from outward adornment, such as braided hair and the wearing of gold jewelry and fine clothes. **4**Instead, it should be that of your inner self, the unfading beauty of a gentle and quiet spirit, which is of great worth in God's sight. **5**For this is the way the holy women of the past who put their hope in God used to make themselves beautiful. They were submissive to their own husbands, **6**like Sarah, who obeyed Abraham and called him her master. You are her daughters if you do what is right and do not give way to fear.

7Husbands, in the same way be consider-ate as you live with your wives, and treat them with respect as the weaker partner and as heirs with you of the gracious gift of life, so that nothing will hinder your prayers.

Suffering for Doing Good

8Finally, all of you, live in harmony with one another; be sympathetic, love as brothers, be compassionate and humble. **9**Do not repay evil with evil or insult with insult, but with blessing, because to this you were called so that you may inherit a blessing. **10**For,

"Whoever would love life
    and see good days
must keep his tongue from evil
    and his lips from deceitful speech.
11He must turn from evil and do good;
    he must seek peace and pursue it.
12For the eyes of the Lord are on the
      righteous
    and his ears are attentive to their
      prayer,
but the face of the Lord is against those
    who do evil."[b]

13Who is going to harm you if you are eager to do good? **14**But even if you should suffer for what is right, you are blessed. "Do not fear what they fear[c]; do not be frightened."[d] **15**But in your hearts set apart Christ as Lord. Always be prepared to give an answer to everyone who asks you to give the reason for the hope that you have. But do this with gentleness and respect, **16**keeping a clear conscience, so that those who speak maliciously against your good behavior in Christ may be ashamed of their slander. **17**It is better, if it is God's will, to suffer for doing good than for doing evil. **18**For Christ died for sins once for all, the righteous for the unrighteous, to bring you to God. He was put to death in the body but made alive by the Spirit, **19**through whom[e] also he went and preached to the spirits in prison **20**who disobeyed long ago when God waited patiently in the days of Noah while the ark was being built. In it only a few people, eight in all, were saved through water, **21**and this water symbolizes baptism that now saves you also — not the removal of dirt from the body but the pledge[f] of a good conscience toward God. It saves you by the resurrection of Jesus Christ, **22**who has gone into heaven and is at God's right hand — with angels, authorities and powers in submission to him.

THE TEMPTING DETOUR OF SIN

• •

Shay started this school year with one goal: a deep desire to live for Christ. He'll never forget singing "I Have Decided to Follow Jesus" that last night of summer camp. Shay meant every word with all his heart.

You might say Shay is cruising, racing even, straight down the middle of the narrow road. But there are some dangerous detours up ahead.

Be careful, Shay. Use your road map. And don't get off track!

Look It Up
• • • •

The most common obstacles along the journey of faith are the frequent detours of sin.

No wonder the Bible warns, "Let us throw off everything that hinders and the sin that so easily entangles, and let us run with perseverance the race marked out for us. Let us fix our eyes on Jesus, the author and perfecter of our faith" (Hebrews 12:1–2).

And if we ignore the warning? Our trips into sin will cost us dearly (1 Corinthians 9:24–27).

Think It Through
• • • •

Temptation is like a deceptive billboard. "Enjoy delicious homestyle cooking at Mom's Family Restaurant, three miles ahead on your left." Starving, you endure three agonizingly long miles, your mouth watering and your stomach rumbling. You're all set for an inexpensive and scrumptious feast. But what you end up with is a bad, not to mention overpriced, case of indigestion.

Isn't that just like sin? You never quite get what you were hoping for. It always costs more than it's worth.

Work It Out
• • • •

If you've left the straight and narrow road for a sightseeing tour through Sinville, it's time to make a U-turn—pronto. Confess your sin, get back in the race and ask God to keep you moving in the right direction.

For the next week, take an extra fifteen minutes each day to read and study your road map (the Bible). That's the only way you'll be able to recognize the dangerous detours that lurk ahead.

Remember, it's never too late to start doing the right thing. Get back on track and keep your eyes not on the road but on Christ!

Nail It Down
• • • •

Read 1 Peter 2:11 for what Peter is urging you to do.

Turn to pages 486, 1056, 1087 and 1248 for other readings on obstacles.
Turn to page 1369 for Friday's reading.

Topic
• • • •

OBSTACLES

Living for God

4 Therefore, since Christ suffered in his body, arm yourselves also with the same attitude, because he who has suffered in his body is done with sin. ²As a result, he does not live the rest of his earthly life for evil human desires, but rather for the will of God. ³For you have spent enough time in the past doing what pagans choose to do—living in debauchery, lust, drunkenness, orgies, carousing and detestable idolatry. ⁴They think it strange that you do not plunge with them into the same flood of dissipation, and they heap abuse on you. ⁵But they will have to give account to him who is ready to judge the living and the dead. ⁶For this is the reason the gospel was preached even to those who are now dead, so that they might be judged according to men in regard to the body, but live according to God in regard to the spirit.

⁷The end of all things is near. Therefore be clear minded and self-controlled so that you can pray. ⁸Above all, love each other deeply, because love covers over a multitude of sins. ⁹Offer hospitality to one another without grumbling. ¹⁰Each one should use whatever gift he has received to serve others, faithfully administering God's grace in its various forms. ¹¹If anyone speaks, he should do it as one speaking the very words of God. If anyone serves, he should do it with the strength God provides, so that in all things God may be praised through Jesus Christ. To him be the glory and the power for ever and ever. Amen.

Suffering for Being a Christian

¹²Dear friends, do not be surprised at the painful trial you are suffering, as though something strange were happening to you. ¹³But rejoice that you participate in the sufferings of Christ, so that you may be overjoyed when his glory is revealed. ¹⁴If you are insulted because of the name of Christ, you are blessed, for the Spirit of glory and of God rests on you. ¹⁵If you suffer, it should not be as a murderer or thief or any other kind of criminal, or even as a meddler. ¹⁶However, if you suffer as a Christian, do not be ashamed, but praise God that you bear that name. ¹⁷For it is time for judgment to begin with the family of God; and if it begins with us, what will the outcome be for those who do not obey the gospel of God? ¹⁸And,

"If it is hard for the righteous to be saved,
    what will become of the ungodly and the sinner?"ᵃ

¹⁹So then, those who suffer according to God's will should commit themselves to their faithful Creator and continue to do good.

To Elders and Young Men

5 To the elders among you, I appeal as a fellow elder, a witness of Christ's sufferings and one who also will share in the glory to be revealed: ²Be shepherds of God's flock that is under your care, serving as overseers—not because you must, but because you are willing, as God wants you to be; not greedy for money, but eager to serve; ³not lording it over those entrusted to you, but being examples to the flock. ⁴And when the Chief Shepherd appears, you will receive the crown of glory that will never fade away.

⁵Young men, in the same way be submissive to those who are older. All of you, clothe yourselves with humility toward one another, because,

"God opposes the proud
    but gives grace to the humble."ᵇ

⁶Humble yourselves, therefore, under God's mighty hand, that he may lift you up in due time. ⁷Cast all your anxiety on him because he cares for you.

⁸Be self-controlled and alert. Your enemy the devil prowls around like a roaring lion looking for someone to devour. ⁹Resist him, standing firm in the faith, because you know that your brothers throughout the world are undergoing the same kind of sufferings.

¹⁰And the God of all grace, who called you to his eternal glory in Christ, after you have suffered a little while, will himself restore you and make you strong, firm and steadfast. ¹¹To him be the power for ever and ever. Amen.

Final Greetings

¹²With the help of Silas,ᶜ whom I regard as a faithful brother, I have written to you briefly, encouraging you and testifying that this is the true grace of God. Stand fast in it.

¹³She who is in Babylon, chosen together with you, sends you her greetings, and so does my son Mark. ¹⁴Greet one another with a kiss of love.

Peace to all of you who are in Christ.

ᵃ18 Prov. 11:31   ᵇ5 Prov. 3:34   ᶜ12 Greek *Silvanus*, a variant of *Silas*

THE GOD WHO SUFFERS WITH US

Maria's father, a policeman, was killed recently during a drug bust. Listen as she describes her feelings:

"I know I'm supposed to believe that the Lord is in control and that he loves me. But I feel totally abandoned—like he couldn't care less. When I pray, I feel like I'm just wasting my time. It's like my prayers bounce off the ceiling. And when I try to explain it all to my friends, they just can't understand what I'm feeling.

"You tell me—how is my family going to make it? What are we going to do?"

Look It Up
• • • •

Notice how God responded when his chosen people were suffering as slaves in Egypt:

"I have indeed seen the misery of my people in Egypt. I have heard them crying out because of their slave drivers, and I am concerned about their suffering. So I have come down to rescue them from the hand of the Egyptians and to bring them up out of that land into a good and spacious land, a land flowing with milk and honey" (Exodus 3:7–8).

Exodus goes on to show how God used his servant Moses to deliver the people.

Think It Through
• • • •

That passage says a lot. It tells you that when God's people are hurting: (1) he sees; (2) he hears; (3) he cares; and (4) he acts.

If you are suffering, be comforted by the message of Exodus. If you know someone who is suffering, be challenged by Exodus 3 to be a Moses in that person's life.

How could God use you to help bring comfort to someone who is hurting?

Work It Out
• • • •

Soothe some suffering hearts this week:

• Make personal visits. Telephone calls are okay. Notes are nice. But your physical presence means much more.

• Don't feel the need to offer profound reasons or to glibly spout off a bunch of familiar Bible verses. A shoulder to cry on and a listening ear offer more comfort than a wagging tongue.

• Don't make people feel guilty for feeling down. If they are sad, be sad with them (Romans 12:15).

Nail It Down
• • • •

Read about the sufferings of the Son of God in 1 Peter 4:1.

Turn to pages 518, 525, 1261 and 1309 for other readings on suffering.
Turn to page 1370 for the weekend reading.

Topic
• • • •

SUFFERING

IS THERE HELP FOR HASSLES?

● ●

Work It Out
● ● ● ●

Have you ever had a day when:
Your hair looked like something the dog dragged in?
Your car decided it wanted to stay in the garage for the day?
Your teachers all turned into slave drivers?
Your parents decided to make a prisoner of you?
Your shoestring decided it wanted to be in two pieces instead of one?
Your friends all decided at once that you weren't worth knowing?
Your TV decided one station was enough for any TV to broadcast and it had to be the station that only shows old cartoons?

Hey! Everyone has a bad day now and again, when more seems to go wrong than right. But what you do with that day is up to you. You can let it conquer you, or you can hand it all over to the one who cares about you and your hassles: Jesus.

Nail It Down
● ● ● ●

Read the promise in 1 Peter 5:7.

● ●

Think It Through
● ● ● ●

Days when things just don't go right are all part of real life. You can't expect everything to always go your way. You can't expect everything to always be sweet and perfect. Real life in a sinful world just isn't like that.

But you can expect help. This verse in Peter's letter is a promise that God will help you deal with all the little and large hassles of life because he cares for you. Don't expect the hassles to go away and never reappear. But go to the ultimate source of help for hassles: Jesus.

Nail It Down
● ● ● ●

Memorize 1 Peter 5:7. For further insight read Psalm 55:22.

Turn to pages 633, 1136 and 1172 for other readings on tough questions.
Turn to page 1372 for Monday's reading.

Topic
● ● ● ●

TOUGH QUESTIONS

2 PETER

FALSE teachers are seeking to destroy the church. They are enticing the people to immorality and denying that Christ will return. Peter writes this second letter to remind believers that they can oppose false teachers through the knowledge of God's Word. Therefore they must increase their knowledge of God's Word. Peter also writes that Christ is coming back. When that happens, those who have denied him will die; those who have been faithful to him will live in a new, righteous world. Ask the Lord to guide you as you learn more of his Word.

Outline of Contents

1 Simon Peter, a servant and apostle of Jesus Christ,

To those who through the righteousness of our God and Savior Jesus Christ have received a faith as precious as ours:

²Grace and peace be yours in abundance through the knowledge of God and of Jesus our Lord.

Making One's Calling and Election Sure

³His divine power has given us everything we need for life and godliness through our knowledge of him who called us by his own glory and goodness. ⁴Through these he has given us his very great and precious promises, so that through them you may participate in the divine nature and escape the cor-ruption in the world caused by evil desires.

⁵For this very reason, make every effort to add to your faith goodness; and to goodness, knowledge; ⁶and to knowledge, self-control; and to self-control, perseverance; and to perseverance, godliness; ⁷and to godliness, brotherly kindness; and to brotherly kindness, love. ⁸For if you possess these qualities in increasing measure, they will keep you from being ineffective and unproductive in your knowledge of our Lord Jesus Christ. ⁹But if anyone does not have them, he is nearsighted and blind, and has forgotten that he has been cleansed from his past sins.

¹⁰Therefore, my brothers, be all the more eager to make your calling and election sure. For if you do these things, you will never fall, ¹¹and you will receive a rich welcome

YOU'VE GOT WHAT IT TAKES!

Dave's family has traveled miles to be at their Uncle Pete's funeral, and Dave is fuming. For about thirty minutes Judy lets her brother Dave vent all his frustrations. Afterward he's able to be more rational.

"I don't know what to think. I mean, I feel bad for Mom. Uncle Pete was her older brother. I guess I should want to be here for her, but I'd really rather be back home with all my friends. Is that selfish?"

Judy shrugs, "I don't know what to tell you."

"I guess it sorta is. Maybe if I was 'godly' like about fifty people have told me Uncle Pete was, I wouldn't feel this way. But I guess I just don't have what it takes to be like that."

Look It Up
••••

Dave needs to know two important facts:

1. The Bible tells everyone to live a godly life. "For the grace of God that brings salvation has appeared to all men. It teaches us to say 'No' to ungodliness and worldly passions, and to live self-controlled, upright and godly lives in this present age" (Titus 2:11–12).

2. The Bible says that, with discipline, anyone can reach that goal: "Have nothing to do with godless myths and old wives' tales; rather, train yourself to be godly" (1 Timothy 4:7).

Think It Through
••••

It's common to think that only a few "super-saints"—people like Billy Graham, Mother Teresa and Uncle Pete—have what it takes to be godly. It's easy to think, "I'll never be like them, so what's the use?"

The problem with this type of thinking is that the Bible clearly commands you to live a godly life. Question: Would God ask you to do something that is impossible?

Work It Out
••••

Train yourself to be godly. Here are some practical ideas:

• Set aside twenty minutes each day (morning, noon or night—it doesn't really matter when) for the next few days to spend a few extra minutes with God.

• Use spare time during the day (driving, standing in line, waiting in traffic, taking a break at work) to pray, sing little praise songs to God or memorize Scripture.

• Find a training buddy who will get serious with you.

• Cut out one activity that is hurting your walk with God.

Nail It Down
••••

Read 2 Peter 1:3 to find out that God has given you everything you need in order to live a godly life.

Turn to pages 9 and 864 for other readings on godliness.
Turn to page 1374 for Tuesday's reading.

Topic
••••

GODLINESS

into the eternal kingdom of our Lord and Savior Jesus Christ.

Prophecy of Scripture

12So I will always remind you of these things, even though you know them and are firmly established in the truth you now have. **13**I think it is right to refresh your memory as long as I live in the tent of this body, **14**because I know that I will soon put it aside, as our Lord Jesus Christ has made clear to me. **15**And I will make every effort to see that after my departure you will always be able to remember these things.

16We did not follow cleverly invented stories when we told you about the power and coming of our Lord Jesus Christ, but we were eyewitnesses of his majesty. **17**For he received honor and glory from God the Father when the voice came to him from the Majestic Glory, saying, "This is my Son, whom I love; with him I am well pleased."*a* **18**We ourselves heard this voice that came from heaven when we were with him on the sacred mountain.

19And we have the word of the prophets made more certain, and you will do well to pay attention to it, as to a light shining in a dark place, until the day dawns and the morning star rises in your hearts. **20**Above all, you must understand that no prophecy of Scripture came about by the prophet's own interpretation. **21**For prophecy never had its origin in the will of man, but men spoke from God as they were carried along by the Holy Spirit.

False Teachers and Their Destruction

2 But there were also false prophets among the people, just as there will be false teachers among you. They will secretly introduce destructive heresies, even denying the sovereign Lord who bought them — bringing swift destruction on themselves. **2**Many will follow their shameful ways and will bring the way of truth into disrepute. **3**In their greed these teachers will exploit you with stories they have made up. Their condemnation has long been hanging over them, and their destruction has not been sleeping.

4For if God did not spare angels when they sinned, but sent them to hell,*b* putting them into gloomy dungeons*c* to be held for judgment; **5**if he did not spare the ancient world when he brought the flood on its ungodly people, but protected Noah, a preacher of righteousness, and seven others; **6**if he condemned the cities of Sodom and Gomorrah by burning them to ashes, and made them an example of what is going to happen to the ungodly; **7**and if he rescued Lot, a righteous man, who was distressed by the filthy lives of lawless men **8**(for that righteous man, living among them day after day, was tormented in his righteous soul by the lawless deeds he saw and heard) — **9**if this is so, then the Lord knows how to rescue godly men from trials and to hold the unrighteous for the day of judgment, while continuing their punishment.*d* **10**This is especially true of those who follow the corrupt desire of the sinful nature*e* and despise authority.

Bold and arrogant, these men are not afraid to slander celestial beings; **11**yet even angels, although they are stronger and more powerful, do not bring slanderous accusations against such beings in the presence of the Lord. **12**But these men blaspheme in matters they do not understand. They are like brute beasts, creatures of instinct, born only to be caught and destroyed, and like beasts they too will perish.

13They will be paid back with harm for the harm they have done. Their idea of pleasure is to carouse in broad daylight. They are blots and blemishes, reveling in their pleasures while they feast with you.*f* **14**With eyes full of adultery, they never stop sinning; they seduce the unstable; they are experts in greed — an accursed brood! **15**They have left the straight way and wandered off to follow the way of Balaam son of Beor, who loved the wages of wickedness. **16**But he was rebuked for his wrongdoing by a donkey — a beast without speech — who spoke with a man's voice and restrained the prophet's madness.

17These men are springs without water and mists driven by a storm. Blackest darkness is reserved for them. **18**For they mouth empty, boastful words and, by appealing to the lustful desires of sinful human nature, they entice people who are just escaping from those who live in error. **19**They promise them freedom, while they themselves are slaves of depravity — for a man is a slave to whatever has mastered him. **20**If they have escaped the corruption of the world by

---

a17 Matt. 17:5; Mark 9:7; Luke 9:35   *b4* Greek *Tartarus*   *c4* Some manuscripts *into chains of darkness*   *d9* Or *unrighteous for punishment until the day of judgment*   *e10* Or *the flesh*   *f13* Some manuscripts *in their love feasts*

THE OBSCENITY OF GREED

Even though Constance got three new sweaters for her birthday last week, she went back to the mall today and bought two more. She explains, "They were on sale, and besides, this fall sweaters will be very in."

On the way home in her year-old sports car, she saw a woman in a brand new luxury model and said, "Oh, it's beautiful! I've got to have it."

When she got home, she almost broke her neck on the mountain of toys her little sister Whitney had left on the living room floor. Kicking Barbie, Ken and their pink Corvette behind the couch, Constance yelled, "Good night, Whitney! You've got enough dolls here to start your own city!"

She's right.

Look It Up
••••
Maybe you're not as wealthy as Constance, but so what? The issue isn't how much you've got, but how much you want. Like a tapeworm of the soul, greed has a voracious appetite. It can never get enough wealth to satisfy. No wonder Paul wrote:

"People who want to get rich fall into temptation and a trap and into many foolish and harmful desires that plunge men into ruin and destruction. For the love of money is a root of all kinds of evil. Some people, eager for money, have wandered from the faith and pierced themselves with many griefs" (1 Timothy 6:9–10).

Think It Through
••••
What a paradox! The world says that striving for wealth can set you free and put you on top of the world. The Word says just the opposite—that excess devotion to riches can trap you, causing you to fall and to plunge into activities that will wreck your faith.

What about you? Are you caught up in money and things, and in wanting even more?

Work It Out
••••
Get a concordance and look up some of the verses in the Bible that have the word *greed* or *greedy* in them. Is it portrayed as a good thing, a bad thing or something that's no big deal?

Fight greed today. Give away something you really care about; spend your allowance on a gift for a friend; use the material things in your care in a way that benefits someone else. That's how you can say no to the power of money—by giving it away (which is to say, investing it in others). Giving is the antidote to greed.

Nail It Down
••••
Read 2 Peter 2:18–19 for Peter's warning against the world's variety of "freedom."

Turn to pages 441, 1110 and 1396 for other readings on wealth.
Turn to page 1377 for Wednesday's reading.

Topic
••••

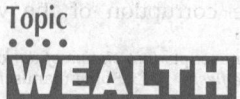
WEALTH

knowing our Lord and Savior Jesus Christ and are again entangled in it and overcome, they are worse off at the end than they were at the beginning. [21]It would have been better for them not to have known the way of righteousness, than to have known it and then to turn their backs on the sacred command that was passed on to them. [22]Of them the proverbs are true: "A dog returns to its vomit,"[a] and, "A sow that is washed goes back to her wallowing in the mud."

The Day of the Lord

3 Dear friends, this is now my second letter to you. I have written both of them as reminders to stimulate you to wholesome thinking. [2]I want you to recall the words spoken in the past by the holy prophets and the command given by our Lord and Savior through your apostles.

[3]First of all, you must understand that in the last days scoffers will come, scoffing and following their own evil desires. [4]They will say, "Where is this 'coming' he promised? Ever since our fathers died, everything goes on as it has since the beginning of creation." [5]But they deliberately forget that long ago by God's word the heavens existed and the earth was formed out of water and by water. [6]By these waters also the world of that time was deluged and destroyed. [7]By the same word the present heavens and earth are reserved for fire, being kept for the day of judgment and destruction of ungodly men.

[8]But do not forget this one thing, dear friends: With the Lord a day is like a thousand years, and a thousand years are like a day. [9]The Lord is not slow in keeping his promise, as some understand slowness. He is patient with you, not wanting anyone to perish, but everyone to come to repentance.

[10]But the day of the Lord will come like a thief. The heavens will disappear with a roar; the elements will be destroyed by fire, and the earth and everything in it will be laid bare.[b]

[11]Since everything will be destroyed in this way, what kind of people ought you to be? You ought to live holy and godly lives [12]as you look forward to the day of God and speed its coming.[c] That day will bring about the destruction of the heavens by fire, and the elements will melt in the heat. [13]But in keeping with his promise we are looking forward to a new heaven and a new earth, the home of righteousness.

[14]So then, dear friends, since you are looking forward to this, make every effort to be found spotless, blameless and at peace with him. [15]Bear in mind that our Lord's patience means salvation, just as our dear brother Paul also wrote you with the wisdom that God gave him. [16]He writes the same way in all his letters, speaking in them of these matters. His letters contain some things that are hard to understand, which ignorant and unstable people distort, as they do the other Scriptures, to their own destruction.

[17]Therefore, dear friends, since you already know this, be on your guard so that you may not be carried away by the error of lawless men and fall from your secure position. [18]But grow in the grace and knowledge of our Lord and Savior Jesus Christ. To him be glory both now and forever! Amen.

---

[a]22 Prov. 26:11   [b]10 Some manuscripts *be burned up*   [c]12 Or *as you wait eagerly for the day of God to come*

WHEN a storm is approaching, the air pressure changes. And you can measure that change on a barometer. First John is like a spiritual barometer that measures your spiritual condition. Do you believe in Jesus? Do you obey his commands? Do you walk in the light? Do you walk as Jesus walked? Do these things, writes John, and you can know you have eternal life. Keep in mind as you read that if you live according to John's barometer, you'll avoid spiritual storms.

Outline of Contents

The Word of Life

1 That which was from the beginning, which we have heard, which we have seen with our eyes, which we have looked at and our hands have touched—this we proclaim concerning the Word of life. ²The life appeared; we have seen it and testify to it, and we proclaim to you the eternal life, which was with the Father and has appeared to us. ³We proclaim to you what we have seen and heard, so that you also may have fellowship with us. And our fellowship is with the Father and with his Son, Jesus Christ. ⁴We write this to make our*ᵃ* joy complete.

Walking in the Light

⁵This is the message we have heard from him and declare to you: God is light; in him there is no darkness at all. ⁶If we claim to have fellowship with him yet walk in the darkness, we lie and do not live by the truth. ⁷But if we walk in the light, as he is in the light, we have fellowship with one another, and the blood of Jesus, his Son, purifies us from all*ᵇ* sin.

⁸If we claim to be without sin, we deceive ourselves and the truth is not in us. ⁹If we confess our sins, he is faithful and just and will forgive us our sins and purify us from all unrighteousness. ¹⁰If we claim we have not

ᵃ4 Some manuscripts *your*   *ᵇ7* Or *every*

YOU ARE THE LIGHT OF THE WORLD

Kent hadn't been working on the school paper very long when two amazing things happened.

First, during an editorial meeting the members of the staff got into a big discussion about religion. Kent was surprised: No one else claimed to be a Christian, but several people seemed interested in spiritual matters.

Second, at a statewide, overnight high school newspaper workshop, Kent found out he'd be rooming with Carl, the paper's editor, one of the guys most interested in God.

As they lugged their bags up to the tenth floor of the hotel, Kent thought, "Lord, I want to be a light for you this weekend."

Look It Up
• • • •

Kent prayed that prayer because he remembered these words of Christ:

"You are the light of the world. A city on a hill cannot be hidden. Neither do people light a lamp and put it under a bowl. Instead they put it on its stand, and it gives light to everyone in the house. In the same way, let your light shine before men, that they may see your good deeds and praise your Father in heaven" (Matthew 5:14–16).

Think It Through
• • • •

Think of pitching a tent at night without the aid of a lantern or walking down a dark trail without a flashlight. You'd be stumbling, fumbling and completely lost without some sort of light to show you the way! Light reveals, guides and provides comfort.

In the same way, Christians are lights in a dark world. By shining for Christ and letting his life and love radiate through your life, you point lost people to the proper path.

Work It Out
• • • •

How do you shine for God in a dark world? By doing what Jesus called "good deeds." Everything you say and do should reflect your love for God and your care for others. Here are some specific and practical good deeds you can do today:

Run an errand for someone who's sick.

Take some toys and old clothes to the Salvation Army or Goodwill.

Contribute your allowance to a local crisis pregnancy organization.

Get your youth group to sponsor an after-school program for kids with working mothers.

Pick one of these projects and start shining!

Nail It Down
• • • •

Read 1 John 1:5–7 for a description of walking in the light.

Turn to pages 397, 1145 and 1262 for other readings on identity.
Turn to page 1379 for Thursday's reading.

Topic
• • • •

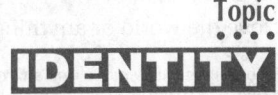

sinned, we make him out to be a liar and his word has no place in our lives.

2 My dear children, I write this to you so that you will not sin. But if anybody does sin, we have one who speaks to the Father in our defense — Jesus Christ, the Righteous One. **2**He is the atoning sacrifice for our sins, and not only for ours but also for*a* the sins of the whole world.

3We know that we have come to know him if we obey his commands. **4**The man who says, "I know him," but does not do what he commands is a liar, and the truth is not in him. **5**But if anyone obeys his word, God's love*b* is truly made complete in him. This is how we know we are in him: **6**Whoever claims to live in him must walk as Jesus did.

7Dear friends, I am not writing you a new command but an old one, which you have had since the beginning. This old command is the message you have heard. **8**Yet I am writing you a new command; its truth is seen in him and you, because the darkness is passing and the true light is already shining.

9Anyone who claims to be in the light but hates his brother is still in the darkness. **10**Whoever loves his brother lives in the light, and there is nothing in him*c* to make him stumble. **11**But whoever hates his brother is in the darkness and walks around in the darkness; he does not know where he is going, because the darkness has blinded him.

12I write to you, dear children,
  because your sins have been forgiven
    on account of his name.
13I write to you, fathers,
  because you have known him who is
    from the beginning.
I write to you, young men,
  because you have overcome the evil
    one.
I write to you, dear children,
  because you have known the Father.
14I write to you, fathers,
  because you have known him who is
    from the beginning.
I write to you, young men,
  because you are strong,
  and the word of God lives in you,
  and you have overcome the evil one.

Do Not Love the World

15Do not love the world or anything in the world. If anyone loves the world, the love of the Father is not in him. **16**For everything in the world — the cravings of sinful man, the lust of his eyes and the boasting of what he has and does — comes not from the Father but from the world. **17**The world and its desires pass away, but the man who does the will of God lives forever.

Warning Against Antichrists

18Dear children, this is the last hour; and as you have heard that the antichrist is coming, even now many antichrists have come. This is how we know it is the last hour. **19**They went out from us, but they did not really belong to us. For if they had belonged to us, they would have remained with us; but their going showed that none of them belonged to us.

20But you have an anointing from the Holy One, and all of you know the truth.*d* **21**I do not write to you because you do not know the truth, but because you do know it and because no lie comes from the truth. **22**Who is the liar? It is the man who denies that Jesus is the Christ. Such a man is the antichrist — he denies the Father and the Son. **23**No one who denies the Son has the Father; whoever acknowledges the Son has the Father also.

24See that what you have heard from the beginning remains in you. If it does, you also will remain in the Son and in the Father. **25**And this is what he promised us — even eternal life.

26I am writing these things to you about those who are trying to lead you astray. **27**As for you, the anointing you received from him remains in you, and you do not need anyone to teach you. But as his anointing teaches you about all things and as that anointing is real, not counterfeit — just as it has taught you, remain in him.

Children of God

28And now, dear children, continue in him, so that when he appears we may be confident and unashamed before him at his coming.

29If you know that he is righteous, you know that everyone who does what is right has been born of him.

3 How great is the love the Father has lavished on us, that we should be called children of God! And that is what we are! The reason the world does not know us is

---

a2 Or *He is the one who turns aside God's wrath, taking away our sins, and not only ours but also*   *b5* Or *word, love for God*   *c10* Or *it*   *d20* Some manuscripts *and you know all things*

THE GREATEST LOVE OF ALL

Marcy fidgets nervously as the counselor begins. "Marcy, your parents are really worried about you. They say you won't talk to them. I've heard their side of the story. Now I want to hear what you're thinking. What's going on inside? Tell me how you feel."

At first, Marcy makes small talk. Finally, it's like a dam breaking. The tears come rushing out as she sobs uncontrollably. "I just want them to love me! Is that asking too much? I don't want all the stuff—the cars and clothes. I just want to feel like they accept me!"

Look It Up
••••

Our deepest desire? To feel completely loved. Yet with imperfect parents, sweethearts and friends, we often feel more rejected than accepted. And that's devastating to our self-esteem! But look: "How great is the love the Father has lavished on us, that we should be called the children of God! And that is what we are!" (1 John 3:1).

Wow! In God we find the total acceptance we're craving. He doesn't just like us a little. He doesn't just love us sometimes. He "lavishes" (that is, pours out an overabundance) his love on us!

Think It Through
••••

Like Marcy, do you have parents who give you everything but love? Because of a divorce or the breakup of a romance, you may feel like no one loves you. Or perhaps you're new in town and you feel like people don't accept you. Or maybe you feel just plain worthless.

What does 1 John 3:1 say? In what ways has God poured out his love on you?

Work It Out
••••

Proper self-esteem is possible when you:
1. Quit focusing on feelings. Don't deny your feelings; feelings are real and need to be confronted. Just don't let your feelings control you. Why? Because they don't always reflect the truth. For example, you may feel unloved, but the fact is that God says he loves you unconditionally!
2. Focus on the facts of God's Word. Get together with a friend and look up all the verses you can that mention how much God loves and accepts his children. Pray together that you would base your self-image on these facts and not on feelings of rejection.

Nail It Down
••••

Memorize 1 John 3:1.

Turn to pages 584, 641, 1029 and 1100 for other readings on self-esteem.
Turn to page 1382 for Friday's reading.

Topic
••••

SELF-ESTEEM

that it did not know him. ²Dear friends, now we are children of God, and what we will be has not yet been made known. But we know that when he appears,ᵃ we shall be like him, for we shall see him as he is. ³Everyone who has this hope in him purifies himself, just as he is pure.

⁴Everyone who sins breaks the law; in fact, sin is lawlessness. ⁵But you know that he appeared so that he might take away our sins. And in him is no sin. ⁶No one who lives in him keeps on sinning. No one who continues to sin has either seen him or known him.

⁷Dear children, do not let anyone lead you astray. He who does what is right is righteous, just as he is righteous. ⁸He who does what is sinful is of the devil, because the devil has been sinning from the beginning. The reason the Son of God appeared was to destroy the devil's work. ⁹No one who is born of God will continue to sin, because God's seed remains in him; he cannot go on sinning, because he has been born of God. ¹⁰This is how we know who the children of God are and who the children of the devil are: Anyone who does not do what is right is not a child of God; nor is anyone who does not love his brother.

Love One Another

¹¹This is the message you heard from the beginning: We should love one another. ¹²Do not be like Cain, who belonged to the evil one and murdered his brother. And why did he murder him? Because his own actions were evil and his brother's were righteous. ¹³Do not be surprised, my brothers, if the world hates you. ¹⁴We know that we have passed from death to life, because we love our brothers. Anyone who does not love remains in death. ¹⁵Anyone who hates his brother is a murderer, and you know that no murderer has eternal life in him.

¹⁶This is how we know what love is: Jesus Christ laid down his life for us. And we ought to lay down our lives for our brothers. ¹⁷If anyone has material possessions and sees his brother in need but has no pity on him, how can the love of God be in him? ¹⁸Dear children, let us not love with words or tongue but with actions and in truth. ¹⁹This then is how we know that we belong to the truth, and how we set our hearts at rest in his presence ²⁰whenever our hearts con-

demn us. For God is greater than our hearts, and he knows everything.

²¹Dear friends, if our hearts do not condemn us, we have confidence before God ²²and receive from him anything we ask, because we obey his commands and do what pleases him. ²³And this is his command: to believe in the name of his Son, Jesus Christ, and to love one another as he commanded us. ²⁴Those who obey his commands live in him, and he in them. And this is how we know that he lives in us: We know it by the Spirit he gave us.

Test the Spirits

4 Dear friends, do not believe every spirit, but test the spirits to see whether they are from God, because many false prophets have gone out into the world. ²This is how you can recognize the Spirit of God: Every spirit that acknowledges that Jesus Christ has come in the flesh is from God, ³but every spirit that does not acknowledge Jesus is not from God. This is the spirit of the antichrist, which you have heard is coming and even now is already in the world.

⁴You, dear children, are from God and have overcome them, because the one who is in you is greater than the one who is in the world. ⁵They are from the world and therefore speak from the viewpoint of the world, and the world listens to them. ⁶We are from God, and whoever knows God listens to us; but whoever is not from God does not listen to us. This is how we recognize the Spiritᵇ of truth and the spirit of falsehood.

God's Love and Ours

⁷Dear friends, let us love one another, for love comes from God. Everyone who loves has been born of God and knows God. ⁸Whoever does not love does not know God, because God is love. ⁹This is how God showed his love among us: He sent his one and only Sonᶜ into the world that we might live through him. ¹⁰This is love: not that we loved God, but that he loved us and sent his Son as an atoning sacrifice forᵈ our sins. ¹¹Dear friends, since God so loved us, we also ought to love one another. ¹²No one has ever seen God; but if we love one another, God lives in us and his love is made complete in us.

¹³We know that we live in him and he in us, because he has given us of his Spirit. ¹⁴And we have seen and testify that the Fa-

---

ᵃ2 Or *when it is made known*   ᵇ6 Or *spirit*   ᶜ9 Or *his only begotten Son*   ᵈ10 Or *as the one who would turn aside his wrath, taking away* ther has sent his Son to be the Savior of the world. ¹⁵If anyone acknowledges that Jesus is the Son of God, God lives in him and he in God. ¹⁶And so we know and rely on the love God has for us.

God is love. Whoever lives in love lives in God, and God in him. ¹⁷In this way, love is made complete among us so that we will have confidence on the day of judgment, because in this world we are like him. ¹⁸There is no fear in love. But perfect love drives out fear, because fear has to do with punishment. The one who fears is not made perfect in love.

¹⁹We love because he first loved us. ²⁰If anyone says, "I love God," yet hates his brother, he is a liar. For anyone who does not love his brother, whom he has seen, cannot love God, whom he has not seen. ²¹And he has given us this command: Whoever loves God must also love his brother.

Faith in the Son of God

5 Everyone who believes that Jesus is the Christ is born of God, and everyone who loves the father loves his child as well. ²This is how we know that we love the children of God: by loving God and carrying out his commands. ³This is love for God: to obey his commands. And his commands are not burdensome, ⁴for everyone born of God overcomes the world. This is the victory that has overcome the world, even our faith. ⁵Who is it that overcomes the world? Only he who believes that Jesus is the Son of God.

⁶This is the one who came by water and blood—Jesus Christ. He did not come by water only, but by water and blood. And it is the Spirit who testifies, because the Spirit is the truth. ⁷For there are three that testify: ⁸the^a Spirit, the water and the blood; and the three are in agreement. ⁹We accept man's testimony, but God's testimony is greater because it is the testimony of God, which he has given about his Son. ¹⁰Anyone who believes in the Son of God has this testimony in his heart. Anyone who does not believe God has made him out to be a liar, because he has not believed the testimony God has given about his Son. ¹¹And this is the testimony: God has given us eternal life, and this life is in his Son. ¹²He who has the Son has life; he who does not have the Son of God does not have life.

Concluding Remarks

¹³I write these things to you who believe in the name of the Son of God so that you may know that you have eternal life. ¹⁴This is the confidence we have in approaching God: that if we ask anything according to his will, he hears us. ¹⁵And if we know that he hears us—whatever we ask—we know that we have what we asked of him.

¹⁶If anyone sees his brother commit a sin that does not lead to death, he should pray and God will give him life. I refer to those whose sin does not lead to death. There is a sin that leads to death. I am not saying that he should pray about that. ¹⁷All wrongdoing is sin, and there is sin that does not lead to death.

¹⁸We know that anyone born of God does not continue to sin; the one who was born of God keeps him safe, and the evil one cannot harm him. ¹⁹We know that we are children of God, and that the whole world is under the control of the evil one. ²⁰We know also that the Son of God has come and has given us understanding, so that we may know him who is true. And we are in him who is true—even in his Son Jesus Christ. He is the true God and eternal life.

²¹Dear children, keep yourselves from idols.

---

^a7,8 Late manuscripts of the Vulgate *testify in heaven: the Father, the Word and the Holy Spirit, and these three are one.* ⁸*And there are three that testify on earth: the* (not found in any Greek manuscript before the sixteenth century)

DO YOU KNOW WHERE YOU'RE GOING?

Shawn went with a friend on a church youth retreat last weekend. She had fun, but something the speaker said Sunday morning is really bugging her five days later.

He asked the question, "If you died today, do you know for sure where you would spend eternity?"

All week Shawn has been wrestling with that question. She wants to get the issue settled in her mind, but she doesn't know where to find the answer.

Look It Up
••••

Talking about this issue of personal destiny, Jesus said:

• "Whoever believes in him [the Son of God] is not condemned, but whoever does not believe stands condemned already" (John 3:18).

• "I tell you the truth, whoever hears my word and believes him who sent me has eternal life and will not be condemned; he has crossed over from death to life" (John 5:24).

Paul said, "The gift of God is eternal life in Christ Jesus our Lord" (Romans 6:23).

Notice that, according to Jesus, "whoever believes" will receive this gift of eternal life.

Think It Through
••••

Every person on this planet will spend eternity somewhere. Either hell: a horrible place where unbelievers will end up. Or heaven: a magnificent place where God lives and believers will enter. In heaven believers will actively serve and worship God and reign with him forever.

Having said all that, the big question is, "Do you know your destiny?"

Work It Out
••••

You can know for sure where you will spend eternity. If you have truly trusted Jesus Christ to forgive your sins, God's Word guarantees you eternal life with God in heaven (John 3:16). Your response now is to live under the lordship of Christ and allow him to work in and through you to help others obtain the same destiny.

If you have never trusted Christ, you need to do so now. Talk to God in prayer and tell him that you know you are a sinner— you've broken his law. Admit to him that you cannot save yourself. Tell him that you want Christ's death on the cross to pay for your sin. Then ask him to change your life.

That's a request he *will* answer!

Nail It Down
••••

Read John's assurances that believers have eternal life in 1 John 5:11–13.

Turn to pages 1042, 1080, 1403 and 1407 for other readings on destiny.
Turn to page 1384 for the weekend reading.

Topic
••••

YOU wouldn't open your door to just anyone, would you? Of course not. But sometimes believers open their minds to anybody's teachings, regardless of how deceptive they may be. Don't do that, John writes. Instead, reject anyone who comes with a teaching other than that of Christ. As you read this book, remember that there are deceivers roaming around—even in the church. It's good to open your mind; it's not good to let down your guard.

Outline of Contents

¹The elder,

To the chosen lady and her children, whom I love in the truth—and not I only, but also all who know the truth— ²because of the truth, which lives in us and will be with us forever:

³Grace, mercy and peace from God the Father and from Jesus Christ, the Father's Son, will be with us in truth and love.

⁴It has given me great joy to find some of your children walking in the truth, just as the Father commanded us. ⁵And now, dear lady, I am not writing you a new command but one we have had from the beginning. I ask that we love one another. ⁶And this is love: that we walk in obedience to his commands. As you have heard from the beginning, his command is that you walk in love.

⁷Many deceivers, who do not acknowledge Jesus Christ as coming in the flesh, have gone out into the world. Any such person is the deceiver and the antichrist. ⁸Watch out that you do not lose what you have worked for, but that you may be rewarded fully. ⁹Anyone who runs ahead and does not continue in the teaching of Christ does not have God; whoever continues in the teaching has both the Father and the Son. ¹⁰If anyone comes to you and does not bring this teaching, do not take him into your house or welcome him. ¹¹Anyone who welcomes him shares in his wicked work.

¹²I have much to write to you, but I do not want to use paper and ink. Instead, I hope to visit you and talk with you face to face, so that our joy may be complete.

¹³The children of your chosen sister send their greetings.

SATURDAY ☐

Work It Out
• • • •

There are many people in your life whom you love. Family, relatives, friends, your dog (you almost think of him as a person, don't you?). For today, however, let's focus in on the love you have for your parents.

Get out a piece of paper and a pencil and write a love letter to your parents. You may have your differences with them, you may not agree on certain issues, but deep down you love them. Tell them, okay?

You don't have to get mushy. Just state the facts. Be honest about your differences. Ask them to forgive you for the times you mess up. Tell them you forgive them for the times they don't handle a situation well. And then make sure they know you love them.

Nail It Down
• • • •

Read John's message on love in 2 John 5–6.

SUNDAY ☐

Think It Through
• • • •

Love is Christianity's most basic ingredient. It holds together all that Christianity teaches. Love is also the most basic ingredient in family living. It's the glue that holds families together.

When John talks about walking in love, he means an arm-in-arm attitude of holding each other up and holding each other together. That means that you'll provide support when situations are difficult. It means you won't jump in and cause unnecessary conflict or trouble. It means you don't ignore your family or treat them as though they don't exist.

Start today to walk with your family, in love. You *and* your family will be glad you did.

Nail It Down
• • • •

Reread 2 John 5–6. For further insight read Psalm 68:4–6.

Turn to pages 62, 122 and 680 for other readings on parents.
Turn to page 1386 for Monday's reading.

Topic
• • • •

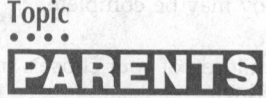
PARENTS

3 JOHN

DO close the door to God's enemies, John writes in 2 John. Do not close the door to God's people, he writes in 3 John. Gaius and Demetrius are examples of Christians who open their doors to other believers. But Diotrephes' pride has replaced love in his life, and he persecutes those who live differently. Everything Gaius is, Diotrephes is not. As you read this book, keep in mind that God wants you to be hospitable and charitable, not proud and selfish. Godly character and loyalty to the truth earn God's richest commendation.

Outline of Contents

¹The elder,

To my dear friend Gaius, whom I love in the truth.

²Dear friend, I pray that you may enjoy good health and that all may go well with you, even as your soul is getting along well. ³It gave me great joy to have some brothers come and tell about your faithfulness to the truth and how you continue to walk in the truth. ⁴I have no greater joy than to hear that my children are walking in the truth.

⁵Dear friend, you are faithful in what you are doing for the brothers, even though they are strangers to you. ⁶They have told the church about your love. You will do well to send them on their way in a manner worthy of God. ⁷It was for the sake of the Name that they went out, receiving no help from the pagans. ⁸We ought therefore to show hospitality to such men so that we may work together for the truth.

⁹I wrote to the church, but Diotrephes, who loves to be first, will have nothing to do with us. ¹⁰So if I come, I will call attention to what he is doing, gossiping maliciously about us. Not satisfied with that, he refuses to welcome the brothers. He also stops those who want to do so and puts them out of the church.

¹¹Dear friend, do not imitate what is evil but what is good. Anyone who does what is good is from God. Anyone who does what is evil has not seen God. ¹²Demetrius is well spoken of by everyone—and even by the

FINDING A FEW FAITHFUL FRIENDS

A fter being grounded for three weeks for breaking his curfew by more than two hours, Matt is determined not to get in major trouble like that again. He knew that if he'd have listened to what his own mind was telling him rather than what his friends were saying about a late-night cruise into the city, he wouldn't have gotten into this trouble.

Yesterday, he ate lunch with Peggy, a girl from his youth group. She told him about "Prime Time."

"What's that?"

"It's like a Bible study before school every Tuesday. This guy named Greg leads it. A lot of juniors go. And a few freshmen."

"Do you go?"

"I did this morning."

"Is it any good?"

"I think it's great!"

Look It Up
•••

Peggy is smart to seek out some Christian friends. Why?

1. If you hang around with non-Christians all the time, you may eventually yield to their negative influence.

"Do not set foot on the path of the wicked or walk in the way of evil men" (Proverbs 4:14).

"Do not envy wicked men, do not desire their company" (Proverbs 24:1).

2. On the other hand, Christian friends can surround you with positive peer pressure. "He who walks with the wise grows wise, but a companion of fools suffers harm" (Proverbs 13:20).

Think It Through
•••

Negative peer pressure can be compared to a huge, floating vacuum cleaner that sucks up weak individuals. Positive peer pressure, however, is like a strong surge of gravity! In stormy times, positive influences can keep you standing strong . . . right where you need to be!

Work It Out
•••

What can you do to find some committed Christian friends?

Become more involved in your church's youth programs.

Attend the meetings of Christian groups that minister on your school campus.

Try to get permission to start a before-school or after-school Bible study. With approval, pass out some flyers and tape up a few posters. You might be surprised at what happens. A bunch of new Christian friends? A chance to minister to an interested non-Christian or two? Go for it!

Nail It Down
•••

Read 3 John 11 for what we should imitate.

Turn to pages 163, 683 and 1174 for other readings on peer pressure.
Turn to page 1390 for Tuesday's reading.

Topic
••••
PEER PRESSURE

truth itself. We also speak well of him, and you know that our testimony is true.

13 I have much to write you, but I do not want to do so with pen and ink. 14 I hope to see you soon, and we will talk face to face.

Peace to you. The friends here send their greetings. Greet the friends there by name.

ACCORDING to Jude, (a brother of Jesus and James) the church is in a fight for the faith. And it's a fight to the finish between true believers and false teachers—those who deny the deity of Christ and use God's grace as an excuse for immorality. But there's a happy ending: God will win that struggle, and he will protect his people from harm. Jude tells his readers to do two things: keep themselves from sin and rescue others heading toward it. As you read this short letter, commit yourself to doing just that.

Outline of Contents

¹Jude, a servant of Jesus Christ and a brother of James,

To those who have been called, who are loved by God the Father and kept by^a Jesus Christ:

²Mercy, peace and love be yours in abundance.

The Sin and Doom of Godless Men

³Dear friends, although I was very eager to write to you about the salvation we share, I felt I had to write and urge you to contend for the faith that was once for all entrusted to the saints. ⁴For certain men whose condemnation was written about^b long ago have secretly slipped in among you. They are godless men, who change the grace of our God into a license for immorality and deny Jesus Christ our only Sovereign and Lord.

⁵Though you already know all this, I want to remind you that the Lord^c delivered his people out of Egypt, but later destroyed those who did not believe. ⁶And the angels who did not keep their positions of authority but abandoned their own home—these he has kept in darkness, bound with everlasting chains for judgment on the great Day. ⁷In a similar way, Sodom and Gomorrah and the surrounding towns gave themselves up to sexual immorality and perversion. They serve as an example of those who suffer the punishment of eternal fire.

⁸In the very same way, these dreamers pollute their own bodies, reject authority and slander celestial beings. ⁹But even the archangel Michael, when he was disputing

^a*1 Or for; or in* ^b*4 Or men who were marked out for condemnation* ^c*5 Some early manuscripts Jesus*

with the devil about the body of Moses, did not dare to bring a slanderous accusation against him, but said, "The Lord rebuke you!" [10]Yet these men speak abusively against whatever they do not understand; and what things they do understand by instinct, like unreasoning animals — these are the very things that destroy them.

[11]Woe to them! They have taken the way of Cain; they have rushed for profit into Balaam's error; they have been destroyed in Korah's rebellion.

[12]These men are blemishes at your love feasts, eating with you without the slightest qualm — shepherds who feed only themselves. They are clouds without rain, blown along by the wind; autumn trees, without fruit and uprooted — twice dead. [13]They are wild waves of the sea, foaming up their shame; wandering stars, for whom blackest darkness has been reserved forever.

[14]Enoch, the seventh from Adam, prophesied about these men: "See, the Lord is coming with thousands upon thousands of his holy ones [15]to judge everyone, and to convict all the ungodly of all the ungodly acts they have done in the ungodly way, and of all the harsh words ungodly sinners have spoken against him." [16]These men are grumblers and faultfinders; they follow their own evil desires; they boast about themselves and flatter others for their own advantage.

A Call to Persevere

[17]But, dear friends, remember what the apostles of our Lord Jesus Christ foretold. [18]They said to you, "In the last times there will be scoffers who will follow their own ungodly desires." [19]These are the men who divide you, who follow mere natural instincts and do not have the Spirit.

[20]But you, dear friends, build yourselves up in your most holy faith and pray in the Holy Spirit. [21]Keep yourselves in God's love as you wait for the mercy of our Lord Jesus Christ to bring you to eternal life.

[22]Be merciful to those who doubt; [23]snatch others from the fire and save them; to others show mercy, mixed with fear — hating even the clothing stained by corrupted flesh.

Doxology

[24]To him who is able to keep you from falling and to present you before his glorious presence without fault and with great joy — [25]to the only God our Savior be glory, majesty, power and authority, through Jesus Christ our Lord, before all ages, now and forevermore! Amen.

MAKE THE EMPTY FEELING GO AWAY

At a party this past week, seventeen-year-old Theresa hit rock bottom. She got drunk and had sex with a guy she had never even seen before.

Kris took Theresa home and stayed with her. The more Theresa sobered up, the harder she sobbed. "I feel so dirty inside. What am I gonna do?"

Kris didn't know what to say, so she hugged her friend, and after a while the crying stopped. Later, Kris inquired, "Why do you get yourself into these kinds of situations?"

"I don't know. It's like I feel so empty inside. And I guess I think that if I can get guys to like me, I can make the empty feelings go away."

Look It Up
••••

Before you try to end your emptiness through the escape of sex, consider the prophet Isaiah's recipe for satisfaction:

> Come, all you who are thirsty,
>   come to the waters;
> and you who have no money,
>   come, buy and eat!
> Come, buy wine and milk
>   without money and without cost.
> Why spend money on what is not bread,
>   and your labor on what does not satisfy?
> Listen, listen to me, and eat what is good,
>   and your soul will delight in the richest of fare
>   (Isaiah 55:1–2).

In poetic language, Isaiah was saying that the only escape that can ever fulfill your deepest desire to be loved is escaping to God.

Think It Through
••••

Let's say you're incredibly thirsty. Would it make sense to go eat some crackers? No! Crackers are good at the right time, but they're not what you need when you're thirsty. (In fact they'll only increase your thirst!)

In the same way, sex is good at the right time (marriage), but it's not what you need when you feel empty inside. (In fact, it may only make you feel more empty!) Your real need is Christ.

Work It Out
••••

If you've never accepted God's free gift of eternal life, tell him right now that's what you want. Ask him to satisfy you with his great love. He'll fill you up like nothing else in the world ever can.

If you already know Christ, share that message with a friend so that he or she won't make the same mistake Theresa made.

Nail It Down
••••

Read Jude 20–23 for a prescription for emptiness and an admonition to help others like Theresa escape their emptiness.

Turn to pages 867, 1021 and 1365 for other readings on escape.
Turn to page 1393 for Wednesday's reading.

Topic
••••

ESCAPE

REVELATION

IMPRESONMENT. Exile. Execution. First-century Christians endure these and other terrible troubles, and the apostle John, himself banished to the island of Patmos, writes to comfort them. Through visions of God in control of both the present and the future, he declares victory. Jesus is King of kings, and he is coming back to defeat Satan and all God's enemies. As you read this book, rejoice in the awesome power of Christ, and remember that regardless of what happens now or in the future, nothing can ever separate you from God's love.

Outline of Contents

Prologue

1 The revelation of Jesus Christ, which God gave him to show his servants what must soon take place. He made it known by sending his angel to his servant John, ²who testifies to everything he saw—that is, the word of God and the testimony of Jesus Christ. ³Blessed is the one who reads the words of this prophecy, and blessed are those who hear it and take to heart what is written in it, because the time is near.

Greetings and Doxology

⁴John,

To the seven churches in the province of Asia:

Grace and peace to you from him who is, and who was, and who is to come, and from the seven spirits*a* before his throne, ⁵and from Jesus Christ, who is the faithful witness, the firstborn from the dead, and the ruler of the kings of the earth.

a4 Or the sevenfold Spirit

To him who loves us and has freed us from our sins by his blood, **6**and has made us to be a kingdom and priests to serve his God and Father — to him be glory and power for ever and ever! Amen.

7Look, he is coming with the clouds,
   and every eye will see him,
even those who pierced him;
   and all the peoples of the earth will
      mourn because of him.
               So shall it be! Amen.

8"I am the Alpha and the Omega," says the Lord God, "who is, and who was, and who is to come, the Almighty."

One Like a Son of Man

9I, John, your brother and companion in the suffering and kingdom and patient endurance that are ours in Jesus, was on the island of Patmos because of the word of God and the testimony of Jesus. **10**On the Lord's Day I was in the Spirit, and I heard behind me a loud voice like a trumpet, **11**which said: "Write on a scroll what you see and send it to the seven churches: to Ephesus, Smyrna, Pergamum, Thyatira, Sardis, Philadelphia and Laodicea."

12I turned around to see the voice that was speaking to me. And when I turned I saw seven golden lampstands, **13**and among the lampstands was someone "like a son of man,"*a* dressed in a robe reaching down to his feet and with a golden sash around his chest. **14**His head and hair were white like wool, as white as snow, and his eyes were like blazing fire. **15**His feet were like bronze glowing in a furnace, and his voice was like the sound of rushing waters. **16**In his right hand he held seven stars, and out of his mouth came a sharp double-edged sword. His face was like the sun shining in all its brilliance.

17When I saw him, I fell at his feet as though dead. Then he placed his right hand on me and said: "Do not be afraid. I am the First and the Last. **18**I am the Living One; I was dead, and behold I am alive for ever and ever! And I hold the keys of death and Hades.

19"Write, therefore, what you have seen, what is now and what will take place later. **20**The mystery of the seven stars that you saw in my right hand and of the seven golden lampstands is this: The seven stars are the angels*b* of the seven churches, and the seven lampstands are the seven churches.

To the Church in Ephesus

2 "To the angel*c* of the church in Ephesus write:

These are the words of him who holds the seven stars in his right hand and walks among the seven golden lampstands: **2**I know your deeds, your hard work and your perseverance. I know that you cannot tolerate wicked men, that you have tested those who claim to be apostles but are not, and have found them false. **3**You have persevered and have endured hardships for my name, and have not grown weary.

4Yet I hold this against you: You have forsaken your first love. **5**Remember the height from which you have fallen! Repent and do the things you did at first. If you do not repent, I will come to you and remove your lampstand from its place. **6**But you have this in your favor: You hate the practices of the Nicolaitans, which I also hate.

7He who has an ear, let him hear what the Spirit says to the churches. To him who overcomes, I will give the right to eat from the tree of life, which is in the paradise of God.

To the Church in Smyrna

8"To the angel of the church in Smyrna write:

These are the words of him who is the First and the Last, who died and came to life again. **9**I know your afflictions and your poverty — yet you are rich! I know the slander of those who say they are Jews and are not, but are a synagogue of Satan. **10**Do not be afraid of what you are about to suffer. I tell you, the devil will put some of you in prison to test you, and you will suffer persecution for ten days. Be faithful, even to the point of death, and I will give you the crown of life.

11He who has an ear, let him hear what the Spirit says to the churches. He who overcomes will not be hurt at all by the second death.

To the Church in Pergamum

12"To the angel of the church in Pergamum write:

These are the words of him who has

---

a13 Daniel 7:13   *b20* Or *messengers*   *c1* Or *messenger*; also in verses 8, 12 and 18

THE STORY OF THE FLIRTY FIANCÉE

All the girls in the youth group were sad yesterday morning when they heard the news: Luke, their popular hunk of a youth director, is planning to marry Fawn, a girl he met on a ski vacation last Christmas.

"I don't like her," declared thirteen-year-old Ashley. "She's not good enough for Luke!"

"I know what you mean," agreed Bess.

Imagine the girls' shock last night when they spotted Fawn holding hands and acting romantic in the mall—with some other guy!

Look It Up • • • •

The New Testament uses marriage terminology to describe the relationship between Christians and Jesus Christ.

The church is engaged to be married to Christ. "I promised you to one husband, to Christ, so that I might present you as a pure virgin to him" (2 Corinthians 11:2).

The wedding ceremony will take place in heaven. "The wedding of the Lamb has come, and his bride has made herself ready" (Revelation 19:7).

This mysterious arrangement that is described in Ephesians 5:32 explains why Christians (individually and collectively) need to be faithful in their love to Christ and why they must stop flirting with the world.

Think It Through • • • •

How would you feel if you were engaged (and deeply in love) and you found out that your future spouse was messing around with someone else? Would you feel angry or hurt? Would you feel both emotions?

How do you think Jesus feels when he sees us, part of his church, his future bride, "romantically" involved with the things of this world?

Work It Out • • • •

Don't be unfaithful. As a member of the church, you're engaged! You're part of the bride of Christ!

If you are flirting with the things of the world (that is, if you are desiring them more than you desire Christ), then:

1. Repent. Ask Christ to forgive your unfaithfulness (1 John 1:9).
2. Reaffirm your commitment to the Lord (Romans 12:1).
3. Remember that you don't have to love the world or be friends with the world (James 4:4) to live in it and reach others.

Nail It Down • • • •

Read Revelation 2:4–5 for the warning given to those who "flirt."

Turn to pages 1060 and 1241 for other readings on worldliness.
Turn to page 1396 for Thursday's reading.

Topic
• • • •

WORLDLINESS

the sharp, double-edged sword. [13]I know where you live — where Satan has his throne. Yet you remain true to my name. You did not renounce your faith in me, even in the days of Antipas, my faithful witness, who was put to death in your city — where Satan lives.

[14]Nevertheless, I have a few things against you: You have people there who hold to the teaching of Balaam, who taught Balak to entice the Israelites to sin by eating food sacrificed to idols and by committing sexual immorality. [15]Likewise you also have those who hold to the teaching of the Nicolaitans. [16]Repent therefore! Otherwise, I will soon come to you and will fight against them with the sword of my mouth.

[17]He who has an ear, let him hear what the Spirit says to the churches. To him who overcomes, I will give some of the hidden manna. I will also give him a white stone with a new name written on it, known only to him who receives it.

To the Church in Thyatira

[18]"To the angel of the church in Thyatira write:

These are the words of the Son of God, whose eyes are like blazing fire and whose feet are like burnished bronze. [19]I know your deeds, your love and faith, your service and perseverance, and that you are now doing more than you did at first.

[20]Nevertheless, I have this against you: You tolerate that woman Jezebel, who calls herself a prophetess. By her teaching she misleads my servants into sexual immorality and the eating of food sacrificed to idols. [21]I have given her time to repent of her immorality, but she is unwilling. [22]So I will cast her on a bed of suffering, and I will make those who commit adultery with her suffer intensely, unless they repent of her ways. [23]I will strike her children dead. Then all the churches will know that I am he who searches hearts and minds, and I will repay each of you according to your deeds. [24]Now I say to the rest of you in Thyatira, to you who do not hold to her teaching and have not learned Satan's so-called deep secrets (I will not impose any other bur-

den on you): [25]Only hold on to what you have until I come.

[26]To him who overcomes and does my will to the end, I will give authority over the nations —

[27]'He will rule them with an iron scepter;
    he will dash them to pieces like pottery'[a] —

just as I have received authority from my Father. [28]I will also give him the morning star. [29]He who has an ear, let him hear what the Spirit says to the churches.

To the Church in Sardis

3 "To the angel[b] of the church in Sardis write:

These are the words of him who holds the seven spirits[c] of God and the seven stars. I know your deeds; you have a reputation of being alive, but you are dead. [2]Wake up! Strengthen what remains and is about to die, for I have not found your deeds complete in the sight of my God. [3]Remember, therefore, what you have received and heard; obey it, and repent. But if you do not wake up, I will come like a thief, and you will not know at what time I will come to you.

[4]Yet you have a few people in Sardis who have not soiled their clothes. They will walk with me, dressed in white, for they are worthy. [5]He who overcomes will, like them, be dressed in white. I will never blot out his name from the book of life, but will acknowledge his name before my Father and his angels. [6]He who has an ear, let him hear what the Spirit says to the churches.

To the Church in Philadelphia

[7]"To the angel of the church in Philadelphia write:

These are the words of him who is holy and true, who holds the key of David. What he opens no one can shut, and what he shuts no one can open. [8]I know your deeds. See, I have placed before you an open door that no one can shut. I know that you have little strength, yet you have kept my word

---

[a]27 Psalm 2:9   [b]1 Or *messenger*; also in verses 7 and 14   [c]1 Or *the sevenfold Spirit*

and have not denied my name. **9**I will make those who are of the synagogue of Satan, who claim to be Jews though they are not, but are liars — I will make them come and fall down at your feet and acknowledge that I have loved you. **10**Since you have kept my command to endure patiently, I will also keep you from the hour of trial that is going to come upon the whole world to test those who live on the earth.

11I am coming soon. Hold on to what you have, so that no one will take your crown. **12**Him who overcomes I will make a pillar in the temple of my God. Never again will he leave it. I will write on him the name of my God and the name of the city of my God, the new Jerusalem, which is coming down out of heaven from my God; and I will also write on him my new name. **13**He who has an ear, let him hear what the Spirit says to the churches.

To the Church in Laodicea

14"To the angel of the church in Laodicea write:

These are the words of the Amen, the faithful and true witness, the ruler of God's creation. **15**I know your deeds, that you are neither cold nor hot. I wish you were either one or the other! **16**So, because you are lukewarm — neither hot nor cold — I am about to spit you out of my mouth. **17**You say, 'I am rich; I have acquired wealth and do not need a thing.' But you do not realize that you are wretched, pitiful, poor, blind and naked. **18**I counsel you to buy from me gold refined in the fire, so you can become rich; and white clothes to wear, so you can cover your shameful nakedness; and salve to put on your eyes, so you can see.

19Those whom I love I rebuke and discipline. So be earnest, and repent. **20**Here I am! I stand at the door and knock. If anyone hears my voice and opens the door, I will come in and eat with him, and he with me.

21To him who overcomes, I will give the right to sit with me on my throne, just as I overcame and sat down with my Father on his throne. **22**He who has an ear, let him hear what the Spirit says to the churches."

The Throne in Heaven

4 After this I looked, and there before me was a door standing open in heaven. And the voice I had first heard speaking to me like a trumpet said, "Come up here, and I will show you what must take place after this." **2**At once I was in the Spirit, and there before me was a throne in heaven with someone sitting on it. **3**And the one who sat there had the appearance of jasper and carnelian. A rainbow, resembling an emerald, encircled the throne. **4**Surrounding the throne were twenty-four other thrones, and seated on them were twenty-four elders. They were dressed in white and had crowns of gold on their heads. **5**From the throne came flashes of lightning, rumblings and peals of thunder. Before the throne, seven lamps were blazing. These are the seven spirits*a* of God. **6**Also before the throne there was what looked like a sea of glass, clear as crystal.

In the center, around the throne, were four living creatures, and they were covered with eyes, in front and in back. **7**The first living creature was like a lion, the second was like an ox, the third had a face like a man, the fourth was like a flying eagle. **8**Each of the four living creatures had six wings and was covered with eyes all around, even under his wings. Day and night they never stop saying:

> "Holy, holy, holy
> is the Lord God Almighty,
> who was, and is, and is to come."

9Whenever the living creatures give glory, honor and thanks to him who sits on the throne and who lives for ever and ever, **10**the twenty-four elders fall down before him who sits on the throne, and worship him who lives for ever and ever. They lay their crowns before the throne and say:

> **11**"You are worthy, our Lord and God,
> to receive glory and honor and power,
> for you created all things,
> and by your will they were created
> and have their being."

The Scroll and the Lamb

5 Then I saw in the right hand of him who sat on the throne a scroll with writing on both sides and sealed with seven seals. **2**And I saw a mighty angel proclaiming in a loud voice, "Who is worthy to break the

a5 Or *the sevenfold Spirit*

THE TEMPTING TRAP OF AFFLUENCE

During their mission trip to Tennessee, the thirty-eight members of the Eastside youth group were split into two groups. One group spent a week working with the poor people of Appalachia to renovate their homes. The response was incredible—more than twenty decisions for Christ!

The other group stayed at an affluent church in a nearby city doing door-to-door visitation in a ritzy neighborhood. The attitude of the people there was one of rudeness and indifference. Ken, one of the participants, counted over one hundred doors slammed in his face.

Look It Up
••••

Jesus had a stern warning to those whose wealth crowds God out of their lives:

"No one can serve two masters. . . . You cannot serve both God and Money" (Matthew 6:24). Jesus states here that wealth is a dangerous rival to God and a trap that can capture a person's devotion.

"Again I tell you, it is easier for a camel to go through the eye of a needle than for a rich man to enter the kingdom of God" (Matthew 19:24). In this instance Jesus was demonstrating that wealth often succeeds in ruling over individuals, keeping them from knowing the truth of the gospel.

Wealth can be dangerous. It can become a god, effectively blinding its devotees to their need for Christ.

Think It Through
••••

Suppose you take the message of Christ's life, love and forgiveness to two different people. One is a street person who has nothing. She is dirty and unloved, dying a slow death. The other is a wealthy, healthy woman who has many friends at the club, innumerable clothes in the closet, and who lives the good life in a $350,000 home.

Do you think one is more likely to be receptive to your message than another?

Work It Out
••••

Make a list of ten good things that would happen to you if you had millions of dollars. Now just to keep it all in perspective, make a list of ten negative things that might result from being super wealthy.

Make this your prayer for the week: "Dear God, compared to most people in the world, I am super wealthy. You have given me so many more things than I really need. Help me this week to understand your perspective on worldly wealth. And help me to use for your kingdom the material things you have given me. Amen."

Nail It Down
••••

Read what Revelation has to say about wealth in Revelation 3:17.

Turn to pages 441, 1110 and 1374 for other readings on wealth.
Turn to page 1403 for Friday's reading.

Topic
••••

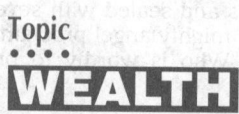

seals and open the scroll?" **3**But no one in heaven or on earth or under the earth could open the scroll or even look inside it. **4**I wept and wept because no one was found who was worthy to open the scroll or look inside. **5**Then one of the elders said to me, "Do not weep! See, the Lion of the tribe of Judah, the Root of David, has triumphed. He is able to open the scroll and its seven seals."

6Then I saw a Lamb, looking as if it had been slain, standing in the center of the throne, encircled by the four living creatures and the elders. He had seven horns and seven eyes, which are the seven spirits*a* of God sent out into all the earth. **7**He came and took the scroll from the right hand of him who sat on the throne. **8**And when he had taken it, the four living creatures and the twenty-four elders fell down before the Lamb. Each one had a harp and they were holding golden bowls full of incense, which are the prayers of the saints. **9**And they sang a new song:

"You are worthy to take the scroll
    and to open its seals,
    because you were slain,
        and with your blood you purchased
            men for God
        from every tribe and language and
            people and nation.
10You have made them to be a kingdom
        and priests to serve our God,
    and they will reign on the earth."

11Then I looked and heard the voice of many angels, numbering thousands upon thousands, and ten thousand times ten thousand. They encircled the throne and the living creatures and the elders. **12**In a loud voice they sang:

"Worthy is the Lamb, who was slain,
to receive power and wealth and
        wisdom and strength
and honor and glory and praise!"

13Then I heard every creature in heaven and on earth and under the earth and on the sea, and all that is in them, singing:

"To him who sits on the throne and to
        the Lamb
be praise and honor and glory and
        power,
            for ever and ever!"

14The four living creatures said, "Amen," and the elders fell down and worshiped.

The Seals

6 I watched as the Lamb opened the first of the seven seals. Then I heard one of the four living creatures say in a voice like thunder, "Come!" **2**I looked, and there before me was a white horse! Its rider held a bow, and he was given a crown, and he rode out as a conqueror bent on conquest.

3When the Lamb opened the second seal, I heard the second living creature say, "Come!" **4**Then another horse came out, a fiery red one. Its rider was given power to take peace from the earth and to make men slay each other. To him was given a large sword.

5When the Lamb opened the third seal, I heard the third living creature say, "Come!" I looked, and there before me was a black horse! Its rider was holding a pair of scales in his hand. **6**Then I heard what sounded like a voice among the four living creatures, saying, "A quart*b* of wheat for a day's wages,*c* and three quarts of barley for a day's wages,*c* and do not damage the oil and the wine!"

7When the Lamb opened the fourth seal, I heard the voice of the fourth living creature say, "Come!" **8**I looked, and there before me was a pale horse! Its rider was named Death, and Hades was following close behind him. They were given power over a fourth of the earth to kill by sword, famine and plague, and by the wild beasts of the earth.

9When he opened the fifth seal, I saw under the altar the souls of those who had been slain because of the word of God and the testimony they had maintained. **10**They called out in a loud voice, "How long, Sovereign Lord, holy and true, until you judge the inhabitants of the earth and avenge our blood?" **11**Then each of them was given a white robe, and they were told to wait a little longer, until the number of their fellow servants and brothers who were to be killed as they had been was completed.

12I watched as he opened the sixth seal. There was a great earthquake. The sun turned black like sackcloth made of goat hair, the whole moon turned blood red, **13**and the stars in the sky fell to earth, as late figs drop from a fig tree when shaken by a strong wind. **14**The sky receded like a scroll, rolling up, and every mountain and island was removed from its place. **15**Then the kings of the earth, the princes, the generals, the rich, the mighty, and every

---

*a*6 Or *the sevenfold Spirit*   *b*6 Greek *a choinix* (probably about a liter)   *c*6 Greek *a denarius* slave and every free man hid in caves and among the rocks of the mountains. **16**They called to the mountains and the rocks, "Fall on us and hide us from the face of him who sits on the throne and from the wrath of the Lamb! **17**For the great day of their wrath has come, and who can stand?"

144,000 Sealed

7 After this I saw four angels standing at the four corners of the earth, holding back the four winds of the earth to prevent any wind from blowing on the land or on the sea or on any tree. **2**Then I saw another angel coming up from the east, having the seal of the living God. He called out in a loud voice to the four angels who had been given power to harm the land and the sea: **3**"Do not harm the land or the sea or the trees until we put a seal on the foreheads of the servants of our God." **4**Then I heard the number of those who were sealed: 144,000 from all the tribes of Israel.

5From the tribe of Judah 12,000 were sealed,
from the tribe of Reuben 12,000,
from the tribe of Gad 12,000,
6from the tribe of Asher 12,000,
from the tribe of Naphtali 12,000,
from the tribe of Manasseh 12,000,
7from the tribe of Simeon 12,000,
from the tribe of Levi 12,000,
from the tribe of Issachar 12,000,
8from the tribe of Zebulun 12,000,
from the tribe of Joseph 12,000,
from the tribe of Benjamin 12,000.

The Great Multitude in White Robes

9After this I looked and there before me was a great multitude that no one could count, from every nation, tribe, people and language, standing before the throne and in front of the Lamb. They were wearing white robes and were holding palm branches in their hands. **10**And they cried out in a loud voice:

"Salvation belongs to our God,
who sits on the throne,
and to the Lamb."

11All the angels were standing around the throne and around the elders and the four living creatures. They fell down on their faces before the throne and worshiped God, **12**saying:

"Amen!
Praise and glory
and wisdom and thanks and honor

and power and strength
be to our God for ever and ever.
Amen!"

13Then one of the elders asked me, "These in white robes—who are they, and where did they come from?"

14I answered, "Sir, you know."

And he said, "These are they who have come out of the great tribulation; they have washed their robes and made them white in the blood of the Lamb. **15**Therefore,

"they are before the throne of God
and serve him day and night in his
temple;
and he who sits on the throne will
spread his tent over them.
16Never again will they hunger;
never again will they thirst.
The sun will not beat upon them,
nor any scorching heat.
17For the Lamb at the center of the
throne will be their shepherd;
he will lead them to springs of living
water.
And God will wipe away every tear from
their eyes."

The Seventh Seal and the Golden Censer

8 When he opened the seventh seal, there was silence in heaven for about half an hour.

2And I saw the seven angels who stand before God, and to them were given seven trumpets.

3Another angel, who had a golden censer, came and stood at the altar. He was given much incense to offer, with the prayers of all the saints, on the golden altar before the throne. **4**The smoke of the incense, together with the prayers of the saints, went up before God from the angel's hand. **5**Then the angel took the censer, filled it with fire from the altar, and hurled it on the earth; and there came peals of thunder, rumblings, flashes of lightning and an earthquake.

The Trumpets

6Then the seven angels who had the seven trumpets prepared to sound them.

7The first angel sounded his trumpet, and there came hail and fire mixed with blood, and it was hurled down upon the earth. A third of the earth was burned up, a third of the trees were burned up, and all the green grass was burned up.

8The second angel sounded his trumpet, and something like a huge mountain, all ablaze, was thrown into the sea. A third of the sea turned into blood, **9**a third of the living creatures in the sea died, and a third of the ships were destroyed.

10The third angel sounded his trumpet, and a great star, blazing like a torch, fell from the sky on a third of the rivers and on the springs of water — **11**the name of the star is Wormwood.*a* A third of the waters turned bitter, and many people died from the waters that had become bitter.

12The fourth angel sounded his trumpet, and a third of the sun was struck, a third of the moon, and a third of the stars, so that a third of them turned dark. A third of the day was without light, and also a third of the night.

13As I watched, I heard an eagle that was flying in midair call out in a loud voice: "Woe! Woe! Woe to the inhabitants of the earth, because of the trumpet blasts about to be sounded by the other three angels!"

9 The fifth angel sounded his trumpet, and I saw a star that had fallen from the sky to the earth. The star was given the key to the shaft of the Abyss. **2**When he opened the Abyss, smoke rose from it like the smoke from a gigantic furnace. The sun and sky were darkened by the smoke from the Abyss. **3**And out of the smoke locusts came down upon the earth and were given power like that of scorpions of the earth. **4**They were told not to harm the grass of the earth or any plant or tree, but only those people who did not have the seal of God on their foreheads. **5**They were not given power to kill them, but only to torture them for five months. And the agony they suffered was like that of the sting of a scorpion when it strikes a man. **6**During those days men will seek death, but will not find it; they will long to die, but death will elude them.

7The locusts looked like horses prepared for battle. On their heads they wore something like crowns of gold, and their faces resembled human faces. **8**Their hair was like women's hair, and their teeth were like lions' teeth. **9**They had breastplates like breastplates of iron, and the sound of their wings was like the thundering of many horses and chariots rushing into battle. **10**They had tails and stings like scorpions, and in their tails they had power to torment people for five months. **11**They had as king over them the angel of the Abyss, whose name in Hebrew is Abaddon, and in Greek, Apollyon.*b*

12The first woe is past; two other woes are yet to come.

13The sixth angel sounded his trumpet, and I heard a voice coming from the horns*c* of the golden altar that is before God. **14**It said to the sixth angel who had the trumpet, "Release the four angels who are bound at the great river Euphrates." **15**And the four angels who had been kept ready for this very hour and day and month and year were released to kill a third of mankind. **16**The number of the mounted troops was two hundred million. I heard their number.

17The horses and riders I saw in my vision looked like this: Their breastplates were fiery red, dark blue, and yellow as sulfur. The heads of the horses resembled the heads of lions, and out of their mouths came fire, smoke and sulfur. **18**A third of mankind was killed by the three plagues of fire, smoke and sulfur that came out of their mouths. **19**The power of the horses was in their mouths and in their tails; for their tails were like snakes, having heads with which they inflict injury.

20The rest of mankind that were not killed by these plagues still did not repent of the work of their hands; they did not stop worshiping demons, and idols of gold, silver, bronze, stone and wood — idols that cannot see or hear or walk. **21**Nor did they repent of their murders, their magic arts, their sexual immorality or their thefts.

The Angel and the Little Scroll

10 Then I saw another mighty angel coming down from heaven. He was robed in a cloud, with a rainbow above his head; his face was like the sun, and his legs were like fiery pillars. **2**He was holding a little scroll, which lay open in his hand. He planted his right foot on the sea and his left foot on the land, **3**and he gave a loud shout like the roar of a lion. When he shouted, the voices of the seven thunders spoke. **4**And when the seven thunders spoke, I was about to write; but I heard a voice from heaven say, "Seal up what the seven thunders have said and do not write it down."

5Then the angel I had seen standing on the sea and on the land raised his right hand to heaven. **6**And he swore by him who lives for ever and ever, who created the heavens and all that is in them, the earth and all that is in it, and the sea and all that is in it, and said, "There will be no more delay! **7**But in the days when the seventh angel is about to

---

*a*11 That is, Bitterness   *b*11 *Abaddon* and *Apollyon* mean *Destroyer.*   *c*13 That is, projections sound his trumpet, the mystery of God will be accomplished, just as he announced to his servants the prophets."

⁸Then the voice that I had heard from heaven spoke to me once more: "Go, take the scroll that lies open in the hand of the angel who is standing on the sea and on the land."

⁹So I went to the angel and asked him to give me the little scroll. He said to me, "Take it and eat it. It will turn your stomach sour, but in your mouth it will be as sweet as honey." ¹⁰I took the little scroll from the angel's hand and ate it. It tasted as sweet as honey in my mouth, but when I had eaten it, my stomach turned sour. ¹¹Then I was told, "You must prophesy again about many peoples, nations, languages and kings."

The Two Witnesses

11 I was given a reed like a measuring rod and was told, "Go and measure the temple of God and the altar, and count the worshipers there. ²But exclude the outer court; do not measure it, because it has been given to the Gentiles. They will trample on the holy city for 42 months. ³And I will give power to my two witnesses, and they will prophesy for 1,260 days, clothed in sackcloth." ⁴These are the two olive trees and the two lampstands that stand before the Lord of the earth. ⁵If anyone tries to harm them, fire comes from their mouths and devours their enemies. This is how anyone who wants to harm them must die. ⁶These men have power to shut up the sky so that it will not rain during the time they are prophesying; and they have power to turn the waters into blood and to strike the earth with every kind of plague as often as they want.

⁷Now when they have finished their testimony, the beast that comes up from the Abyss will attack them, and overpower and kill them. ⁸Their bodies will lie in the street of the great city, which is figuratively called Sodom and Egypt, where also their Lord was crucified. ⁹For three and a half days men from every people, tribe, language and nation will gaze on their bodies and refuse them burial. ¹⁰The inhabitants of the earth will gloat over them and will celebrate by sending each other gifts, because these two prophets had tormented those who live on the earth.

¹¹But after the three and a half days a breath of life from God entered them, and they stood on their feet, and terror struck those who saw them. ¹²Then they heard a loud voice from heaven saying to them, "Come up here." And they went up to heaven in a cloud, while their enemies looked on.

¹³At that very hour there was a severe earthquake and a tenth of the city collapsed. Seven thousand people were killed in the earthquake, and the survivors were terrified and gave glory to the God of heaven.

¹⁴The second woe has passed; the third woe is coming soon.

The Seventh Trumpet

¹⁵The seventh angel sounded his trumpet, and there were loud voices in heaven, which said:

"The kingdom of the world has become
> the kingdom of our Lord and of
> his Christ,
and he will reign for ever and ever."

¹⁶And the twenty-four elders, who were seated on their thrones before God, fell on their faces and worshiped God, ¹⁷saying:

"We give thanks to you, Lord God
> Almighty,
the One who is and who was,
because you have taken your great
> power
and have begun to reign.
¹⁸The nations were angry;
> and your wrath has come.
The time has come for judging the
> dead,
> and for rewarding your servants the
> prophets
and your saints and those who
> reverence your name,
> both small and great—
and for destroying those who destroy
> the earth."

¹⁹Then God's temple in heaven was opened, and within his temple was seen the ark of his covenant. And there came flashes of lightning, rumblings, peals of thunder, an earthquake and a great hailstorm.

The Woman and the Dragon

12 A great and wondrous sign appeared in heaven: a woman clothed with the sun, with the moon under her feet and a crown of twelve stars on her head. ²She was pregnant and cried out in pain as she was about to give birth. ³Then another sign appeared in heaven: an enormous red dragon with seven heads and ten horns and seven crowns on his heads. ⁴His tail swept a third of the stars out of the sky and flung them to the earth. The dragon stood in front of the woman who was about to give birth, so that he might devour her child the moment it was born. **5**She gave birth to a son, a male child, who will rule all the nations with an iron scepter. And her child was snatched up to God and to his throne. **6**The woman fled into the desert to a place prepared for her by God, where she might be taken care of for 1,260 days.

7And there was war in heaven. Michael and his angels fought against the dragon, and the dragon and his angels fought back. **8**But he was not strong enough, and they lost their place in heaven. **9**The great dragon was hurled down — that ancient serpent called the devil, or Satan, who leads the whole world astray. He was hurled to the earth, and his angels with him.

10Then I heard a loud voice in heaven say:

"Now have come the salvation and the
        power and the kingdom of our
        God,
    and the authority of his Christ.
For the accuser of our brothers,
    who accuses them before our God
        day and night,
    has been hurled down.
11They overcame him
    by the blood of the Lamb
    and by the word of their testimony;
they did not love their lives so much
    as to shrink from death.
12Therefore rejoice, you heavens
    and you who dwell in them!
But woe to the earth and the sea,
    because the devil has gone down to
        you!
He is filled with fury,
    because he knows that his time is
        short."

13When the dragon saw that he had been hurled to the earth, he pursued the woman who had given birth to the male child. **14**The woman was given the two wings of a great eagle, so that she might fly to the place prepared for her in the desert, where she would be taken care of for a time, times and half a time, out of the serpent's reach. **15**Then from his mouth the serpent spewed water like a river, to overtake the woman and sweep her away with the torrent. **16**But the earth helped the woman by opening its mouth and swallowing the river that the dragon had spewed out of his mouth.

17Then the dragon was enraged at the woman and went off to make war against the rest of her offspring — those who obey God's commandments and hold to the testimony of Jesus. **1**And the dragon[a] stood on the shore of the sea.

13

The Beast out of the Sea

And I saw a beast coming out of the sea. He had ten horns and seven heads, with ten crowns on his horns, and on each head a blasphemous name. **2**The beast I saw resembled a leopard, but had feet like those of a bear and a mouth like that of a lion. The dragon gave the beast his power and his throne and great authority. **3**One of the heads of the beast seemed to have had a fatal wound, but the fatal wound had been healed. The whole world was astonished and followed the beast. **4**Men worshiped the dragon because he had given authority to the beast, and they also worshiped the beast and asked, "Who is like the beast? Who can make war against him?"

5The beast was given a mouth to utter proud words and blasphemies and to exercise his authority for forty-two months. **6**He opened his mouth to blaspheme God, and to slander his name and his dwelling place and those who live in heaven. **7**He was given power to make war against the saints and to conquer them. And he was given authority over every tribe, people, language and nation. **8**All inhabitants of the earth will worship the beast — all whose names have not been written in the book of life belonging to the Lamb that was slain from the creation of the world.[b]

9He who has an ear, let him hear.

10If anyone is to go into captivity,
    into captivity he will go.
If anyone is to be killed[c] with the
        sword,
    with the sword he will be killed.

This calls for patient endurance and faithfulness on the part of the saints.

The Beast out of the Earth

11Then I saw another beast, coming out of the earth. He had two horns like a lamb, but he spoke like a dragon. **12**He exercised all the authority of the first beast on his behalf, and made the earth and its inhabitants worship the first beast, whose fatal wound had been healed. **13**And he performed great and

---

_a1_ Some late manuscripts _And I_   _b8_ Or _written from the creation of the world in the book of life belonging to the Lamb that was slain_   _c10_ Some manuscripts _anyone kills_ miraculous signs, even causing fire to come down from heaven to earth in full view of men. [14]Because of the signs he was given power to do on behalf of the first beast, he deceived the inhabitants of the earth. He ordered them to set up an image in honor of the beast who was wounded by the sword and yet lived. [15]He was given power to give breath to the image of the first beast, so that it could speak and cause all who refused to worship the image to be killed. [16]He also forced everyone, small and great, rich and poor, free and slave, to receive a mark on his right hand or on his forehead, [17]so that no one could buy or sell unless he had the mark, which is the name of the beast or the number of his name.

[18]This calls for wisdom. If anyone has insight, let him calculate the number of the beast, for it is man's number. His number is 666.

The Lamb and the 144,000

14 Then I looked, and there before me was the Lamb, standing on Mount Zion, and with him 144,000 who had his name and his Father's name written on their foreheads. [2]And I heard a sound from heaven like the roar of rushing waters and like a loud peal of thunder. The sound I heard was like that of harpists playing their harps. [3]And they sang a new song before the throne and before the four living creatures and the elders. No one could learn the song except the 144,000 who had been redeemed from the earth. [4]These are those who did not defile themselves with women, for they kept themselves pure. They follow the Lamb wherever he goes. They were purchased from among men and offered as firstfruits to God and the Lamb. [5]No lie was found in their mouths; they are blameless.

The Three Angels

[6]Then I saw another angel flying in midair, and he had the eternal gospel to proclaim to those who live on the earth—to every nation, tribe, language and people. [7]He said in a loud voice, "Fear God and give him glory, because the hour of his judgment has come. Worship him who made the heavens, the earth, the sea and the springs of water."

[8]A second angel followed and said, "Fallen! Fallen is Babylon the Great, which made all the nations drink the maddening wine of her adulteries."

[9]A third angel followed them and said in a loud voice: "If anyone worships the beast and his image and receives his mark on the forehead or on the hand, [10]he, too, will drink of the wine of God's fury, which has been poured full strength into the cup of his wrath. He will be tormented with burning sulfur in the presence of the holy angels and of the Lamb. [11]And the smoke of their torment rises for ever and ever. There is no rest day or night for those who worship the beast and his image, or for anyone who receives the mark of his name." [12]This calls for patient endurance on the part of the saints who obey God's commandments and remain faithful to Jesus.

[13]Then I heard a voice from heaven say, "Write: Blessed are the dead who die in the Lord from now on."

"Yes," says the Spirit, "they will rest from their labor, for their deeds will follow them."

The Harvest of the Earth

[14]I looked, and there before me was a white cloud, and seated on the cloud was one "like a son of man"[a] with a crown of gold on his head and a sharp sickle in his hand. [15]Then another angel came out of the temple and called in a loud voice to him who was sitting on the cloud, "Take your sickle and reap, because the time to reap has come, for the harvest of the earth is ripe." [16]So he who was seated on the cloud swung his sickle over the earth, and the earth was harvested.

[17]Another angel came out of the temple in heaven, and he too had a sharp sickle. [18]Still another angel, who had charge of the fire, came from the altar and called in a loud voice to him who had the sharp sickle, "Take your sharp sickle and gather the clusters of grapes from the earth's vine, because its grapes are ripe." [19]The angel swung his sickle on the earth, gathered its grapes and threw them into the great winepress of God's wrath. [20]They were trampled in the winepress outside the city, and blood flowed out of the press, rising as high as the horses' bridles for a distance of 1,600 stadia.[b]

Seven Angels With Seven Plagues

15 I saw in heaven another great and marvelous sign: seven angels with the seven last plagues—last, because with them God's wrath is completed. [2]And I saw what looked like a sea of glass mixed with fire and, standing beside the sea, those who

---

[a]14 Daniel 7:13   [b]20 That is, about 180 miles (about 300 kilometers)

BUT WHAT WILL WE DO IN HEAVEN?

Jenny asks the question that everyone else is thinking:
"Heaven sounds, well, um—don't get mad at me for saying this,
but—heaven sounds boring. I mean, I know it'll probably be
beautiful and everything—diamonds and gold and stuff. But what
are we going to *do* there? If all you do is sit around and sing, then
that sounds to me like going to church for eternity. And church
isn't always that fun. And heaven is supposed to be a place where
we'll be happy, right?"

**Look
It Up**
••••

Good question, Jenny. What are we going to do in heaven? Well,
according to the Bible we will:
Fellowship with other believers (Revelation 19:7–9).
Know God perfectly (Revelation 21:3; 22:4).
Worship God (Revelation 19:1–8).
Serve God (Revelation 22:3).
Reign with God (Revelation 22:5).

**Think It
Through**
••••

Have you ever met someone and thought, "Yuck!" only to find out
later that you had been totally wrong about that person? Perhaps
he or she even turned out to be a best friend or a great date!
   It's that way with God sometimes. He gets a lot of bad press.
For thousands of years now, people have been spreading rumors
that he's mean, boring and not someone with whom you want to
get too involved.
   Wrong! Knowing God (when you find out what he's really like)
is the greatest joy in life. And living with him in heaven will be
the ultimate excitement!

**Work It
Out**
••••

It's not clear how believers will serve God and reign with him for
all eternity. Will you zoom around the universe in a glorified,
resurrected body (Philippians 3:21)? Will you govern other planets
in the new heaven and new earth (Revelation 21:1)? Only God
knows.
   What is clear is that your actions now determine your heavenly
role later! Think about that. If you faithfully serve God here, he'll
give you greater responsibilities and honor there (Matthew 25:14–
30). With that in mind, get back to basics today: In every situation
you face, ask God, "What do you want me to do?" Then do it—
out of love for God and others.

**Nail It
Down**
••••

Read about the ultimate rest in heaven in Revelation 14:13.

Turn to pages 1042, 1080, 1382 and 1407 for other readings on destiny.
Turn to page 1407 for the weekend reading.

Topic
••••

had been victorious over the beast and his image and over the number of his name. They held harps given them by God ³and sang the song of Moses the servant of God and the song of the Lamb:

"Great and marvelous are your deeds,
  Lord God Almighty.
Just and true are your ways,
  King of the ages.
⁴Who will not fear you, O Lord,
  and bring glory to your name?
For you alone are holy.
All nations will come
  and worship before you,
for your righteous acts have been
  revealed."

⁵After this I looked and in heaven the temple, that is, the tabernacle of the Testimony, was opened. ⁶Out of the temple came the seven angels with the seven plagues. They were dressed in clean, shining linen and wore golden sashes around their chests. ⁷Then one of the four living creatures gave to the seven angels seven golden bowls filled with the wrath of God, who lives for ever and ever. ⁸And the temple was filled with smoke from the glory of God and from his power, and no one could enter the temple until the seven plagues of the seven angels were completed.

The Seven Bowls of God's Wrath

16 Then I heard a loud voice from the temple saying to the seven angels, "Go, pour out the seven bowls of God's wrath on the earth."

²The first angel went and poured out his bowl on the land, and ugly and painful sores broke out on the people who had the mark of the beast and worshiped his image.

³The second angel poured out his bowl on the sea, and it turned into blood like that of a dead man, and every living thing in the sea died.

⁴The third angel poured out his bowl on the rivers and springs of water, and they became blood. ⁵Then I heard the angel in charge of the waters say:

"You are just in these judgments,
  you who are and who were, the Holy
    One,
  because you have so judged;
⁶for they have shed the blood of your
    saints and prophets,

and you have given them blood to
  drink as they deserve."

⁷And I heard the altar respond:

"Yes, Lord God Almighty,
  true and just are your judgments."

⁸The fourth angel poured out his bowl on the sun, and the sun was given power to scorch people with fire. ⁹They were seared by the intense heat and they cursed the name of God, who had control over these plagues, but they refused to repent and glorify him.

¹⁰The fifth angel poured out his bowl on the throne of the beast, and his kingdom was plunged into darkness. Men gnawed their tongues in agony ¹¹and cursed the God of heaven because of their pains and their sores, but they refused to repent of what they had done.

¹²The sixth angel poured out his bowl on the great river Euphrates, and its water was dried up to prepare the way for the kings from the East. ¹³Then I saw three evil*a* spirits that looked like frogs; they came out of the mouth of the dragon, out of the mouth of the beast and out of the mouth of the false prophet. ¹⁴They are spirits of demons performing miraculous signs, and they go out to the kings of the whole world, to gather them for the battle on the great day of God Almighty.

¹⁵"Behold, I come like a thief! Blessed is he who stays awake and keeps his clothes with him, so that he may not go naked and be shamefully exposed."

¹⁶Then they gathered the kings together to the place that in Hebrew is called Armageddon.

¹⁷The seventh angel poured out his bowl into the air, and out of the temple came a loud voice from the throne, saying, "It is done!" ¹⁸Then there came flashes of lightning, rumblings, peals of thunder and a severe earthquake. No earthquake like it has ever occurred since man has been on earth, so tremendous was the quake. ¹⁹The great city split into three parts, and the cities of the nations collapsed. God remembered Babylon the Great and gave her the cup filled with the wine of the fury of his wrath. ²⁰Every island fled away and the mountains could not be found. ²¹From the sky huge hailstones of about a hundred pounds each fell upon men. And they cursed God on ac-

a 13 Greek unclean

count of the plague of hail, because the plague was so terrible.

The Woman on the Beast

17 One of the seven angels who had the seven bowls came and said to me, "Come, I will show you the punishment of the great prostitute, who sits on many waters. ²With her the kings of the earth committed adultery and the inhabitants of the earth were intoxicated with the wine of her adulteries."

³Then the angel carried me away in the Spirit into a desert. There I saw a woman sitting on a scarlet beast that was covered with blasphemous names and had seven heads and ten horns. ⁴The woman was dressed in purple and scarlet, and was glittering with gold, precious stones and pearls. She held a golden cup in her hand, filled with abominable things and the filth of her adulteries. ⁵This title was written on her forehead:

MYSTERY
BABYLON THE GREAT
THE MOTHER OF PROSTITUTES
AND OF THE ABOMINATIONS OF THE EARTH.

⁶I saw that the woman was drunk with the blood of the saints, the blood of those who bore testimony to Jesus.

When I saw her, I was greatly astonished. ⁷Then the angel said to me: "Why are you astonished? I will explain to you the mystery of the woman and of the beast she rides, which has the seven heads and ten horns. ⁸The beast, which you saw, once was, now is not, and will come up out of the Abyss and go to his destruction. The inhabitants of the earth whose names have not been written in the book of life from the creation of the world will be astonished when they see the beast, because he once was, now is not, and yet will come.

⁹"This calls for a mind with wisdom. The seven heads are seven hills on which the woman sits. ¹⁰They are also seven kings. Five have fallen, one is, the other has not yet come; but when he does come, he must remain for a little while. ¹¹The beast who once was, and now is not, is an eighth king. He belongs to the seven and is going to his destruction.

¹²"The ten horns you saw are ten kings who have not yet received a kingdom, but who for one hour will receive authority as kings along with the beast. ¹³They have one

purpose and will give their power and authority to the beast. ¹⁴They will make war against the Lamb, but the Lamb will overcome them because he is Lord of lords and King of kings—and with him will be his called, chosen and faithful followers."

¹⁵Then the angel said to me, "The waters you saw, where the prostitute sits, are peoples, multitudes, nations and languages. ¹⁶The beast and the ten horns you saw will hate the prostitute. They will bring her to ruin and leave her naked; they will eat her flesh and burn her with fire. ¹⁷For God has put it into their hearts to accomplish his purpose by agreeing to give the beast their power to rule, until God's words are fulfilled. ¹⁸The woman you saw is the great city that rules over the kings of the earth."

The Fall of Babylon

18 After this I saw another angel coming down from heaven. He had great authority, and the earth was illuminated by his splendor. ²With a mighty voice he shouted:

"Fallen! Fallen is Babylon the Great!
    She has become a home for demons
and a haunt for every evil*ᵃ* spirit,
    a haunt for every unclean and
        detestable bird.
³For all the nations have drunk
    the maddening wine of her adulteries.
The kings of the earth committed
        adultery with her,
    and the merchants of the earth grew
        rich from her excessive luxuries."

⁴Then I heard another voice from heaven say:

"Come out of her, my people,
    so that you will not share in her sins,
    so that you will not receive any of her
        plagues;
⁵for her sins are piled up to heaven,
    and God has remembered her crimes.
⁶Give back to her as she has given;
    pay her back double for what she has
        done.
    Mix her a double portion from her
        own cup.
⁷Give her as much torture and grief
    as the glory and luxury she gave
        herself.
In her heart she boasts,
    'I sit as queen; I am not a widow,
    and I will never mourn.'

ᵃ2 Greek unclean

[8]Therefore in one day her plagues will
overtake her:
death, mourning and famine.
She will be consumed by fire,
for mighty is the Lord God who judges
her.

[9]"When the kings of the earth who committed adultery with her and shared her luxury see the smoke of her burning, they will
weep and mourn over her. [10]Terrified at her
torment, they will stand far off and cry:

" 'Woe! Woe, O great city,
O Babylon, city of power!
In one hour your doom has come!'

[11]"The merchants of the earth will weep
and mourn over her because no one buys
their cargoes any more — [12]cargoes of gold,
silver, precious stones and pearls; fine lin-
en, purple, silk and scarlet cloth; every sort
of citron wood, and articles of every kind
made of ivory, costly wood, bronze, iron and
marble; [13]cargoes of cinnamon and spice, of
incense, myrrh and frankincense, of wine
and olive oil, of fine flour and wheat; cattle
and sheep; horses and carriages; and bodies and souls of men.

[14]"They will say, 'The fruit you longed for
is gone from you. All your riches and splendor have vanished, never to be recovered.'
[15]The merchants who sold these things and
gained their wealth from her will stand far
off, terrified at her torment. They will weep
and mourn [16]and cry out:

" 'Woe! Woe, O great city,
dressed in fine linen, purple and
scarlet,
and glittering with gold, precious
stones and pearls!
[17]In one hour such great wealth has been
brought to ruin!'

"Every sea captain, and all who travel by
ship, the sailors, and all who earn their living from the sea, will stand far off. [18]When
they see the smoke of her burning, they will
exclaim, 'Was there ever a city like this great
city?' [19]They will throw dust on their heads,
and with weeping and mourning cry out:

" 'Woe! Woe, O great city,
where all who had ships on the sea
became rich through her wealth!
In one hour she has been brought to
ruin!
[20]Rejoice over her, O heaven!
Rejoice, saints and apostles and
prophets!

God has judged her for the way she
treated you.' "

[21]Then a mighty angel picked up a boulder the size of a large millstone and threw
it into the sea, and said:

"With such violence
the great city of Babylon will be
thrown down,
never to be found again.
[22]The music of harpists and musicians,
flute players and trumpeters,
will never be heard in you again.
No workman of any trade
will ever be found in you again.
The sound of a millstone
will never be heard in you again.
[23]The light of a lamp
will never shine in you again.
The voice of bridegroom and bride
will never be heard in you again.
Your merchants were the world's great
men.
By your magic spell all the nations
were led astray.
[24]In her was found the blood of prophets
and of the saints,
and of all who have been killed on
the earth."

Hallelujah!

19 After this I heard what sounded like
the roar of a great multitude in heav-
en shouting:

"Hallelujah!
Salvation and glory and power belong to
our God,
[2]   for true and just are his judgments.
He has condemned the great prostitute
who corrupted the earth by her
adulteries.
He has avenged on her the blood of his
servants."

[3]And again they shouted:

"Hallelujah!
The smoke from her goes up for ever
and ever."

[4]The twenty-four elders and the four living creatures fell down and worshiped God,
who was seated on the throne. And they
cried:

"Amen, Hallelujah!"

[5]Then a voice came from the throne, saying:

"Praise our God,

THE FINAL WORSHIP SERVICE

☐ SATURDAY

Work It Out
••••

Have you ever been to a really super Christian concert? What was it like? Do you remember how you felt? The music was beautiful, and it surrounded you with its sound. The words of the songs were a response of praise to God from your heart. You knew God was very near and very great, and you wanted to praise him. You felt absolutely, positively, totally WONDERFUL!

Then you went home and the exhilarating feelings faded all too quickly.

Do you want to experience those feelings again? Would you like to feel that way all the time? Then be sure you make it to heaven. When you get to heaven it will be like an awesome Christian concert where the praise and the singing and the great feelings never end.

Wanna go?

Nail It Down
••••

Read the description of a heavenly worship service in Revelation 19:1–10.

☐ SUNDAY

Think It Through
••••

As you rush through life, it's easy to forget that the final day on earth is coming. That day is as sure as the fact that your heart is beating and your lungs are taking in air. It's also easy to forget that the final day is closer than it has ever been before. It gets closer day by day, minute by minute, second by second.

That final day will bring judgment to those who have lived their lives separated from God. It will be a terrible day for them. But for those who have followed Jesus, that day will bring a future beyond their wildest imagination.

Does the thought of that final day fill you with hope or with dread? If it fills you with hope, praise God! If it fills you with dread, turn to God today. He's waiting to forgive you. And he offers you an abundant life here on earth and a marvelous future in heaven.

Nail It Down
••••

Reread Revelation 19:1–10. For further insight read Psalm 16:11.

Turn to pages 1042, 1080, 1382 and 1403 for other readings on destiny.
Turn to page 2 for Monday's reading.

Topic
••••

all you his servants,
you who fear him,
  both small and great!"

6Then I heard what sounded like a great multitude, like the roar of rushing waters and like loud peals of thunder, shouting:

"Hallelujah!
  For our Lord God Almighty reigns.
7Let us rejoice and be glad
  and give him glory!
For the wedding of the Lamb has come,
  and his bride has made herself ready.
8Fine linen, bright and clean,
  was given her to wear."
(Fine linen stands for the righteous acts of the saints.)

9Then the angel said to me, "Write: 'Blessed are those who are invited to the wedding supper of the Lamb!' " And he added, "These are the true words of God." .

10At this I fell at his feet to worship him. But he said to me, "Do not do it! I am a fellow servant with you and with your brothers who hold to the testimony of Jesus. Worship God! For the testimony of Jesus is the spirit of prophecy."

The Rider on the White Horse

11I saw heaven standing open and there before me was a white horse, whose rider is called Faithful and True. With justice he judges and makes war. **12**His eyes are like blazing fire, and on his head are many crowns. He has a name written on him that no one knows but he himself. **13**He is dressed in a robe dipped in blood, and his name is the Word of God. **14**The armies of heaven were following him, riding on white horses and dressed in fine linen, white and clean. **15**Out of his mouth comes a sharp sword with which to strike down the nations. "He will rule them with an iron scepter."*a* He treads the winepress of the fury of the wrath of God Almighty. **16**On his robe and on his thigh he has this name written:

KING OF KINGS AND LORD OF LORDS.

17And I saw an angel standing in the sun, who cried in a loud voice to all the birds flying in midair, "Come, gather together for the great supper of God, **18**so that you may eat the flesh of kings, generals, and mighty men, of horses and their riders, and the flesh of all people, free and slave, small and great."

19Then I saw the beast and the kings of the earth and their armies gathered together to make war against the rider on the horse and his army. **20**But the beast was captured, and with him the false prophet who had performed the miraculous signs on his behalf. With these signs he had deluded those who had received the mark of the beast and worshiped his image. The two of them were thrown alive into the fiery lake of burning sulfur. **21**The rest of them were killed with the sword that came out of the mouth of the rider on the horse, and all the birds gorged themselves on their flesh.

The Thousand Years

20 And I saw an angel coming down out of heaven, having the key to the Abyss and holding in his hand a great chain. **2**He seized the dragon, that ancient serpent, who is the devil, or Satan, and bound him for a thousand years. **3**He threw him into the Abyss, and locked and sealed it over him, to keep him from deceiving the nations anymore until the thousand years were ended. After that, he must be set free for a short time.

4I saw thrones on which were seated those who had been given authority to judge. And I saw the souls of those who had been beheaded because of their testimony for Jesus and because of the word of God. They had not worshiped the beast or his image and had not received his mark on their foreheads or their hands. They came to life and reigned with Christ a thousand years. **5**(The rest of the dead did not come to life until the thousand years were ended.) This is the first resurrection. **6**Blessed and holy are those who have part in the first resurrection. The second death has no power over them, but they will be priests of God and of Christ and will reign with him for a thousand years.

Satan's Doom

7When the thousand years are over, Satan will be released from his prison **8**and will go out to deceive the nations in the four corners of the earth—Gog and Magog—to gather them for battle. In number they are like the sand on the seashore. **9**They marched across the breadth of the earth and surrounded the camp of God's people, the city he loves. But fire came down from heaven and devoured them. **10**And the devil, who deceived them, was thrown into the lake of

a15 Psalm 2:9

burning sulfur, where the beast and the false prophet had been thrown. They will be tormented day and night for ever and ever.

The Dead Are Judged

[11]Then I saw a great white throne and him who was seated on it. Earth and sky fled from his presence, and there was no place for them. [12]And I saw the dead, great and small, standing before the throne, and books were opened. Another book was opened, which is the book of life. The dead were judged according to what they had done as recorded in the books. [13]The sea gave up the dead that were in it, and death and Hades gave up the dead that were in them, and each person was judged according to what he had done. [14]Then death and Hades were thrown into the lake of fire. The lake of fire is the second death. [15]If anyone's name was not found written in the book of life, he was thrown into the lake of fire.

The New Jerusalem

21 Then I saw a new heaven and a new earth, for the first heaven and the first earth had passed away, and there was no longer any sea. [2]I saw the Holy City, the new Jerusalem, coming down out of heaven from God, prepared as a bride beautifully dressed for her husband. [3]And I heard a loud voice from the throne saying, "Now the dwelling of God is with men, and he will live with them. They will be his people, and God himself will be with them and be their God. [4]He will wipe every tear from their eyes. There will be no more death or mourning or crying or pain, for the old order of things has passed away."

[5]He who was seated on the throne said, "I am making everything new!" Then he said, "Write this down, for these words are trustworthy and true."

[6]He said to me: "It is done. I am the Alpha and the Omega, the Beginning and the End. To him who is thirsty I will give to drink without cost from the spring of the water of life. [7]He who overcomes will inherit all this, and I will be his God and he will be my son. [8]But the cowardly, the unbelieving, the vile, the murderers, the sexually immoral, those who practice magic arts, the idolaters and all liars — their place will be in the fiery lake of burning sulfur. This is the second death."

[9]One of the seven angels who had the seven bowls full of the seven last plagues came and said to me, "Come, I will show you the bride, the wife of the Lamb." [10]And he carried me away in the Spirit to a mountain great and high, and showed me the Holy City, Jerusalem, coming down out of heaven from God. [11]It shone with the glory of God, and its brilliance was like that of a very precious jewel, like a jasper, clear as crystal. [12]It had a great, high wall with twelve gates, and with twelve angels at the gates. On the gates were written the names of the twelve tribes of Israel. [13]There were three gates on the east, three on the north, three on the south and three on the west. [14]The wall of the city had twelve foundations, and on them were the names of the twelve apostles of the Lamb.

[15]The angel who talked with me had a measuring rod of gold to measure the city, its gates and its walls. [16]The city was laid out like a square, as long as it was wide. He measured the city with the rod and found it to be 12,000 stadia[a] in length, and as wide and high as it is long. [17]He measured its wall and it was 144 cubits[b] thick,[c] by man's measurement, which the angel was using. [18]The wall was made of jasper, and the city of pure gold, as pure as glass. [19]The foundations of the city walls were decorated with every kind of precious stone. The first foundation was jasper, the second sapphire, the third chalcedony, the fourth emerald, [20]the fifth sardonyx, the sixth carnelian, the seventh chrysolite, the eighth beryl, the ninth topaz, the tenth chrysoprase, the eleventh jacinth, and the twelfth amethyst.[d] [21]The twelve gates were twelve pearls, each gate made of a single pearl. The great street of the city was of pure gold, like transparent glass.

[22]I did not see a temple in the city, because the Lord God Almighty and the Lamb are its temple. [23]The city does not need the sun or the moon to shine on it, for the glory of God gives it light, and the Lamb is its lamp. [24]The nations will walk by its light, and the kings of the earth will bring their splendor into it. [25]On no day will its gates ever be shut, for there will be no night there. [26]The glory and honor of the nations will be brought into it. [27]Nothing impure will ever enter it, nor will anyone who does what is shameful or deceitful, but only those whose names are written in the Lamb's book of life.

---

[a]16 That is, about 1,400 miles (about 2,200 kilometers)   [b]17 That is, about 200 feet (about 65 meters)
[c]17 Or high   [d]20 The precise identification of some of these precious stones is uncertain.

The River of Life

22 Then the angel showed me the river of the water of life, as clear as crystal, flowing from the throne of God and of the Lamb ²down the middle of the great street of the city. On each side of the river stood the tree of life, bearing twelve crops of fruit, yielding its fruit every month. And the leaves of the tree are for the healing of the nations. ³No longer will there be any curse. The throne of God and of the Lamb will be in the city, and his servants will serve him. ⁴They will see his face, and his name will be on their foreheads. ⁵There will be no more night. They will not need the light of a lamp or the light of the sun, for the Lord God will give them light. And they will reign for ever and ever.

⁶The angel said to me, "These words are trustworthy and true. The Lord, the God of the spirits of the prophets, sent his angel to show his servants the things that must soon take place."

Jesus Is Coming

⁷"Behold, I am coming soon! Blessed is he who keeps the words of the prophecy in this book."

⁸I, John, am the one who heard and saw these things. And when I had heard and seen them, I fell down to worship at the feet of the angel who had been showing them to me. ⁹But he said to me, "Do not do it! I am a fellow servant with you and with your brothers the prophets and of all who keep the words of this book. Worship God!"

¹⁰Then he told me, "Do not seal up the words of the prophecy of this book, because the time is near. ¹¹Let him who does wrong continue to do wrong; let him who is vile continue to be vile; let him who does right continue to do right; and let him who is holy continue to be holy."

¹²"Behold, I am coming soon! My reward is with me, and I will give to everyone according to what he has done. ¹³I am the Alpha and the Omega, the First and the Last, the Beginning and the End.

¹⁴"Blessed are those who wash their robes, that they may have the right to the tree of life and may go through the gates into the city. ¹⁵Outside are the dogs, those who practice magic arts, the sexually immoral, the murderers, the idolaters and everyone who loves and practices falsehood.

¹⁶"I, Jesus, have sent my angel to give you[a] this testimony for the churches. I am the Root and the Offspring of David, and the bright Morning Star."

¹⁷The Spirit and the bride say, "Come!" And let him who hears say, "Come!" Whoever is thirsty, let him come; and whoever wishes, let him take the free gift of the water of life.

¹⁸I warn everyone who hears the words of the prophecy of this book: If anyone adds anything to them, God will add to him the plagues described in this book. ¹⁹And if anyone takes words away from this book of prophecy, God will take away from him his share in the tree of life and in the holy city, which are described in this book.

²⁰He who testifies to these things says, "Yes, I am coming soon."

Amen. Come, Lord Jesus.

²¹The grace of the Lord Jesus be with God's people. Amen.

a16 The Greek is plural.

WEIGHTS & MEASURES
READING PLANS
SUBJECT INDEX

WEIGHTS & MEASURES

The figures of the table are calculated on the basis of a shekel equaling 11.5 grams, a cubit equaling 18 inches and an ephah equaling 22 liters. The quart referred to is either a dry quart (slightly larger than a liter) or a liquid quart (slightly smaller than a liter), whichever is applicable. The ton referred to in the footnotes is the American ton of 2,000 pounds.

This table is based upon the best available information, but it is not intended to be mathematically precise; like the measurement equivalents in the footnotes, it merely gives the approximate amounts and distances. Weights and measures differed somewhat at various times and places in the ancient world. There is uncertainty particularly about the ephah and the bath; further discoveries may give more light on these units of capacity.

	BIBLICAL UNIT		APPROXIMATE AMERICAN EQUIVALENT	APPROXIMATE METRIC EQUIVALENT
WEIGHTS	talent	*(60 minas)*	75 pounds	34 kilograms
	mina	*(50 shekels)*	1 1/4 pounds	0.6 kilogram
	shekel	*(2 bekas)*	2/5 ounce	11.5 grams
	pim	*(2/3 shekel)*	1/3 ounce	7.6 grams
	beka	*(10 gerahs)*	1/5 ounce	5.5 grams
	gerah		1/50 ounce	0.6 gram
LENGTH	cubit		18 inches	0.5 meter
	span		9 inches	23 centimeters
	handbreadth		3 inches	8 centimeters
CAPACITY **Dry Measure**	cor [homer]	*(10 ephahs)*	6 bushels	220 liters
	lethek	*(5 ephahs)*	3 bushels	110 liters
	ephah	*(10 omers)*	3/5 bushel	22 liters
	seah	*(1/3 ephah)*	7 quarts	7.3 liters
	omer	*(1/10 ephah)*	2 quarts	2 liters
	cab	*(1/18 ephah)*	1 quart	1 liter
Liquid Measure	bath	*(1 ephah)*	6 gallons	22 liters
	hin	*(1/6 bath)*	4 quarts	4 liters
	log	*(1/72 bath)*	1/3 quart	0.3 liter

READING PLANS

God's Word is his personal message of love to you today. The best way to grow as a Christian and get to know God in a more personal way is to spend time in his Word. Here are three ways for you to read the Bible in a disciplined manner.

1. If you are reading the Bible for the first time:
   - Begin by reading the Gospel of Mark or the Gospel of John in the New Testament.
   - After reading one of these gospels, read the book of Acts or the book of Romans.
   - After reading Acts or Romans, pick an Old Testament book like Genesis or perhaps Psalms.

2. If you want to read through the entire Bible in one year:
   - Read three chapters each day, Monday through Saturday, and five chapters on Sunday.

3. If you want to read through the entire Bible in two years:
   - Read two chapters each day, Sunday through Saturday.

The following chart covers every book and chapter of the Bible. To keep track of what you have read, mark off each chapter as you complete it.

GENESIS ☐ 1 ☐ 2 ☐ 3 ☐ 4 ☐ 5 ☐ 6 ☐ 7
☐ 8 ☐ 9 ☐ 10 ☐ 11 ☐ 12 ☐ 13 ☐ 14 ☐ 15
☐ 16 ☐ 17 ☐ 18 ☐ 19 ☐ 20 ☐ 21 ☐ 22
☐ 23 ☐ 24 ☐ 25 ☐ 26 ☐ 27 ☐ 28 ☐ 29
☐ 30 ☐ 31 ☐ 32 ☐ 33 ☐ 34 ☐ 35 ☐ 36
☐ 37 ☐ 38 ☐ 39 ☐ 40 ☐ 41 ☐ 42 ☐ 43
☐ 44 ☐ 45 ☐ 46 ☐ 47 ☐ 48 ☐ 49 ☐ 50

EXODUS ☐ 1 ☐ 2 ☐ 3 ☐ 4 ☐ 5 ☐ 6 ☐ 7
☐ 8 ☐ 9 ☐ 10 ☐ 11 ☐ 12 ☐ 13 ☐ 14 ☐ 15
☐ 16 ☐ 17 ☐ 18 ☐ 19 ☐ 20 ☐ 21 ☐ 22
☐ 23 ☐ 24 ☐ 25 ☐ 26 ☐ 27 ☐ 28 ☐ 29
☐ 30 ☐ 31 ☐ 32 ☐ 33 ☐ 34 ☐ 35 ☐ 36
☐ 37 ☐ 38 ☐ 39 ☐ 40

LEVITICUS ☐ 1 ☐ 2 ☐ 3 ☐ 4 ☐ 5 ☐ 6 ☐ 7
☐ 8 ☐ 9 ☐ 10 ☐ 11 ☐ 12 ☐ 13 ☐ 14 ☐ 15
☐ 16 ☐ 17 ☐ 18 ☐ 19 ☐ 20 ☐ 21 ☐ 22
☐ 23 ☐ 24 ☐ 25 ☐ 26 ☐ 27

NUMBERS ☐ 1 ☐ 2 ☐ 3 ☐ 4 ☐ 5 ☐ 6 ☐ 7
☐ 8 ☐ 9 ☐ 10 ☐ 11 ☐ 12 ☐ 13 ☐ 14
☐ 15 ☐ 16 ☐ 17 ☐ 18 ☐ 19 ☐ 20 ☐ 21
☐ 22 ☐ 23 ☐ 24 ☐ 25 ☐ 26 ☐ 27 ☐ 28
☐ 29 ☐ 30 ☐ 31 ☐ 32 ☐ 33 ☐ 34 ☐ 35
☐ 36

DEUTERONOMY ☐ 1 ☐ 2 ☐ 3 ☐ 4 ☐ 5
☐ 6 ☐ 7 ☐ 8 ☐ 9 ☐ 10 ☐ 11 ☐ 12 ☐ 13
☐ 14 ☐ 15 ☐ 16 ☐ 17 ☐ 18 ☐ 19 ☐ 20
☐ 21 ☐ 22 ☐ 23 ☐ 24 ☐ 25 ☐ 26 ☐ 27
☐ 28 ☐ 29 ☐ 30 ☐ 31 ☐ 32 ☐ 33 ☐ 34

JOSHUA ☐ 1 ☐ 2 ☐ 3 ☐ 4 ☐ 5 ☐ 6 ☐ 7
☐ 8 ☐ 9 ☐ 10 ☐ 11 ☐ 12 ☐ 13 ☐ 14 ☐ 15
☐ 16 ☐ 17 ☐ 18 ☐ 19 ☐ 20 ☐ 21 ☐ 22
☐ 23 ☐ 24

JUDGES ☐ 1 ☐ 2 ☐ 3 ☐ 4 ☐ 5 ☐ 6 ☐ 7
☐ 8 ☐ 9 ☐ 10 ☐ 11 ☐ 12 ☐ 13 ☐ 14
☐ 15 ☐ 16 ☐ 17 ☐ 18 ☐ 19 ☐ 20 ☐ 21

RUTH ☐ 1 ☐ 2 ☐ 3 ☐ 4

1 SAMUEL ☐ 1 ☐ 2 ☐ 3 ☐ 4 ☐ 5 ☐ 6 ☐ 7
☐ 8 ☐ 9 ☐ 10 ☐ 11 ☐ 12 ☐ 13 ☐ 14
☐ 15 ☐ 16 ☐ 17 ☐ 18 ☐ 19 ☐ 20 ☐ 21
☐ 22 ☐ 23 ☐ 24 ☐ 25 ☐ 26 ☐ 27 ☐ 28
☐ 29 ☐ 30 ☐ 31

2 SAMUEL ☐ 1 ☐ 2 ☐ 3 ☐ 4 ☐ 5 ☐ 6 ☐ 7
☐ 8 ☐ 9 ☐ 10 ☐ 11 ☐ 12 ☐ 13 ☐ 14
☐ 15 ☐ 16 ☐ 17 ☐ 18 ☐ 19 ☐ 20 ☐ 21
☐ 22 ☐ 23 ☐ 24

1 KINGS ☐ 1 ☐ 2 ☐ 3 ☐ 4 ☐ 5 ☐ 6 ☐ 7 ☐ 8
☐ 9 ☐ 10 ☐ 11 ☐ 12 ☐ 13 ☐ 14 ☐ 15
☐ 16 ☐ 17 ☐ 18 ☐ 19 ☐ 20 ☐ 21
☐ 22

2 KINGS □ 1 □ 2 □ 3 □ 4 □ 5 □ 6 □ 7 □ 8 □ 9 □ 10 □ 11 □ 12 □ 13 □ 14 □ 15 □ 16 □ 17 □ 18 □ 19 □ 20 □ 21 □ 22 □ 23 □ 24 □ 25

1 CHRONICLES □ 1 □ 2 □ 3 □ 4 □ 5 □ 6 □ 7 □ 8 □ 9 □ 10 □ 11 □ 12 □ 13 □ 14 □ 15 □ 16 □ 17 □ 18 □ 19 □ 20 □ 21 □ 22 □ 23 □ 24 □ 25 □ 26 □ 27 □ 28 □ 29

2 CHRONICLES □ 1 □ 2 □ 3 □ 4 □ 5 □ 6 □ 7 □ 8 □ 9 □ 10 □ 11 □ 12 □ 13 □ 14 □ 15 □ 16 □ 17 □ 18 □ 19 □ 20 □ 21 □ 22 □ 23 □ 24 □ 25 □ 26 □ 27 □ 28 □ 29 □ 30 □ 31 □ 32 □ 33 □ 34 □ 35 □ 36

EZRA □ 1 □ 2 □ 3 □ 4 □ 5 □ 6 □ 7 □ 8 □ 9 □ 10

NEHEMIAH □ 1 □ 2 □ 3 □ 4 □ 5 □ 6 □ 7 □ 8 □ 9 □ 10 □ 11 □ 12 □ 13

ESTHER □ 1 □ 2 □ 3 □ 4 □ 5 □ 6 □ 7 □ 8 □ 9 □ 10

JOB □ 1 □ 2 □ 3 □ 4 □ 5 □ 6 □ 7 □ 8 □ 9 □ 10 □ 11 □ 12 □ 13 □ 14 □ 15 □ 16 □ 17 □ 18 □ 19 □ 20 □ 21 □ 22 □ 23 □ 24 □ 25 □ 26 □ 27 □ 28 □ 29 □ 30 □ 31 □ 32 □ 33 □ 34 □ 35 □ 36 □ 37 □ 38 □ 39 □ 40 □ 41 □ 42

PSALMS □ 1 □ 2 □ 3 □ 4 □ 5 □ 6 □ 7 □ 8 □ 9 □ 10 □ 11 □ 12 □ 13 □ 14 □ 15 □ 16 □ 17 □ 18 □ 19 □ 20 □ 21 □ 22 □ 23 □ 24 □ 25 □ 26 □ 27 □ 28 □ 29 □ 30 □ 31 □ 32 □ 33 □ 34 □ 35 □ 36 □ 37 □ 38 □ 39 □ 40 □ 41 □ 42 □ 43 □ 44 □ 45 □ 46 □ 47 □ 48 □ 49 □ 50 □ 51 □ 52 □ 53 □ 54 □ 55 □ 56 □ 57 □ 58 □ 59 □ 60 □ 61 □ 62 □ 63 □ 64 □ 65 □ 66 □ 67 □ 68 □ 69 □ 70 □ 71 □ 72 □ 73 □ 74 □ 75 □ 76 □ 77 □ 78 □ 79 □ 80 □ 81 □ 82 □ 83 □ 84 □ 85 □ 86 □ 87 □ 88 □ 89 □ 90 □ 91 □ 92 □ 93 □ 94 □ 95 □ 96 □ 97 □ 98 □ 99 □ 100 □ 101 □ 102 □ 103 □ 104 □ 105 □ 106 □ 107 □ 108 □ 109 □ 110 □ 111 □ 112 □ 113 □ 114 □ 115 □ 116 □ 117 □ 118 □ 119 □ 120 □ 121 □ 122 □ 123 □ 124 □ 125 □ 126 □ 127 □ 128 □ 129 □ 130 □ 131 □ 132 □ 133 □ 134 □ 135 □ 136 □ 137 □ 138 □ 139 □ 140 □ 141 □ 142 □ 143 □ 144 □ 145 □ 146 □ 147 □ 148 □ 149 □ 150

PROVERBS □ 1 □ 2 □ 3 □ 4 □ 5 □ 6 □ 7 □ 8 □ 9 □ 10 □ 11 □ 12 □ 13 □ 14 □ 15 □ 16 □ 17 □ 18 □ 19 □ 20 □ 21 □ 22 □ 23 □ 24 □ 25 □ 26 □ 27 □ 28 □ 29 □ 30 □ 31

ECCLESIASTES □ 1 □ 2 □ 3 □ 4 □ 5 □ 6 □ 7 □ 8 □ 9 □ 10 □ 11 □ 12

SONG OF SONGS □ 1 □ 2 □ 3 □ 4 □ 5 □ 6 □ 7 □ 8

ISAIAH □ 1 □ 2 □ 3 □ 4 □ 5 □ 6 □ 7 □ 8 □ 9 □ 10 □ 11 □ 12 □ 13 □ 14 □ 15 □ 16 □ 17 □ 18 □ 19 □ 20 □ 21 □ 22 □ 23 □ 24 □ 25 □ 26 □ 27 □ 28 □ 29 □ 30 □ 31 □ 32 □ 33 □ 34 □ 35 □ 36 □ 37 □ 38 □ 39 □ 40 □ 41 □ 42 □ 43 □ 44 □ 45 □ 46 □ 47 □ 48 □ 49 □ 50 □ 51 □ 52 □ 53 □ 54 □ 55 □ 56 □ 57 □ 58 □ 59 □ 60 □ 61 □ 62 □ 63 □ 64 □ 65 □ 66

JEREMIAH □ 1 □ 2 □ 3 □ 4 □ 5 □ 6 □ 7 □ 8 □ 9 □ 10 □ 11 □ 12 □ 13 □ 14 □ 15 □ 16 □ 17 □ 18 □ 19 □ 20 □ 21 □ 22 □ 23 □ 24 □ 25 □ 26 □ 27 □ 28 □ 29 □ 30 □ 31 □ 32 □ 33 □ 34 □ 35 □ 36 □ 37 □ 38 □ 39 □ 40 □ 41 □ 42 □ 43 □ 44 □ 45 □ 46 □ 47 □ 48 □ 49 □ 50 □ 51 □ 52

LAMENTATIONS □ 1 □ 2 □ 3 □ 4 □ 5

EZEKIEL □ 1 □ 2 □ 3 □ 4 □ 5 □ 6 □ 7 □ 8 □ 9 □ 10 □ 11 □ 12 □ 13 □ 14 □ 15 □ 16 □ 17 □ 18 □ 19 □ 20 □ 21 □ 22 □ 23 □ 24 □ 25 □ 26 □ 27 □ 28 □ 29 □ 30 □ 31 □ 32 □ 33 □ 34 □ 35 □ 36 □ 37 □ 38 □ 39 □ 40 □ 41 □ 42 □ 43 □ 44 □ 45 □ 46 □ 47 □ 48

DANIEL □ 1 □ 2 □ 3 □ 4 □ 5 □ 6 □ 7 □ 8 □ 9 □ 10 □ 11 □ 12

HOSEA □ 1 □ 2 □ 3 □ 4 □ 5 □ 6 □ 7 □ 8 □ 9 □ 10 □ 11 □ 12 □ 13 □ 14

JOEL □ 1 □ 2 □ 3

AMOS □ 1 □ 2 □ 3 □ 4 □ 5 □ 6 □ 7 □ 8 □ 9

OBADIAH □ Obadiah

JONAH □ 1 □ 2 □ 3 □ 4

MICAH □ 1 □ 2 □ 3 □ 4 □ 5 □ 6 □ 7

NAHUM □ 1 □ 2 □ 3

HABAKKUK □ 1 □ 2 □ 3

ZEPHANIAH □ 1 □ 2 □ 3

HAGGAI □ 1 □ 2

ZECHARIAH □ 1 □ 2 □ 3 □ 4 □ 5 □ 6 □ 7 □ 8 □ 9 □ 10 □ 11 □ 12 □ 13 □ 14

MALACHI □ 1 □ 2 □ 3 □ 4

MATTHEW □ 1 □ 2 □ 3 □ 4 □ 5 □ 6 □ 7 □ 8 □ 9 □ 10 □ 11 □ 12 □ 13 □ 14 □ 15 □ 16 □ 17 □ 18 □ 19 □ 20 □ 21 □ 22 □ 23 □ 24 □ 25 □ 26 □ 27 □ 28

MARK □ 1 □ 2 □ 3 □ 4 □ 5 □ 6 □ 7 □ 8 □ 9 □ 10 □ 11 □ 12 □ 13 □ 14 □ 15 □ 16

LUKE □ 1 □ 2 □ 3 □ 4 □ 5 □ 6 □ 7 □ 8 □ 9 □ 10 □ 11 □ 12 □ 13 □ 14 □ 15 □ 16 □ 17 □ 18 □ 19 □ 20 □ 21 □ 22 □ 23 □ 24

JOHN ☐ 1 ☐ 2 ☐ 3 ☐ 4 ☐ 5 ☐ 6 ☐ 7 ☐ 8
☐ 9 ☐ 10 ☐ 11 ☐ 12 ☐ 13 ☐ 14 ☐ 15
☐ 16 ☐ 17 ☐ 18 ☐ 19 ☐ 20 ☐ 21

ACTS ☐ 1 ☐ 2 ☐ 3 ☐ 4 ☐ 5 ☐ 6 ☐ 7 ☐ 8
☐ 9 ☐ 10 ☐ 11 ☐ 12 ☐ 13 ☐ 14 ☐ 15
☐ 16 ☐ 17 ☐ 18 ☐ 19 ☐ 20 ☐ 21 ☐ 22
☐ 23 ☐ 24 ☐ 25 ☐ 26 ☐ 27 ☐ 28

ROMANS ☐ 1 ☐ 2 ☐ 3 ☐ 4 ☐ 5 ☐ 6 ☐ 7
☐ 8 ☐ 9 ☐ 10 ☐ 11 ☐ 12 ☐ 13 ☐ 14
☐ 15 ☐ 16

1 CORINTHIANS ☐ 1 ☐ 2 ☐ 3 ☐ 4 ☐ 5
☐ 6 ☐ 7 ☐ 8 ☐ 9 ☐ 10 ☐ 11 ☐ 12 ☐ 13
☐ 14 ☐ 15 ☐ 16

2 CORINTHIANS ☐ 1 ☐ 2 ☐ 3 ☐ 4 ☐ 5
☐ 6 ☐ 7 ☐ 8 ☐ 9 ☐ 10 ☐ 11 ☐ 12 ☐ 13

GALATIANS ☐ 1 ☐ 2 ☐ 3 ☐ 4 ☐ 5 ☐ 6

EPHESIANS ☐ 1 ☐ 2 ☐ 3 ☐ 4 ☐ 5 ☐ 6

PHILIPPIANS ☐ 1 ☐ 2 ☐ 3 ☐ 4

COLOSSIANS ☐ 1 ☐ 2 ☐ 3 ☐ 4

1 THESSALONIANS ☐ 1 ☐ 2 ☐ 3 ☐ 4 ☐ 5

2 THESSALONIANS ☐ 1 ☐ 2 ☐ 3

1 TIMOTHY ☐ 1 ☐ 2 ☐ 3 ☐ 4 ☐ 5 ☐ 6

2 TIMOTHY ☐ 1 ☐ 2 ☐ 3 ☐ 4

TITUS ☐ 1 ☐ 2 ☐ 3

PHILEMON ☐ Philemon

HEBREWS ☐ 1 ☐ 2 ☐ 3 ☐ 4 ☐ 5 ☐ 6 ☐ 7
☐ 8 ☐ 9 ☐ 10 ☐ 11 ☐ 12 ☐ 13

JAMES ☐ 1 ☐ 2 ☐ 3 ☐ 4 ☐ 5

1 PETER ☐ 1 ☐ 2 ☐ 3 ☐ 4 ☐ 5

2 PETER ☐ 1 ☐ 2 ☐ 3

1 JOHN ☐ 1 ☐ 2 ☐ 3 ☐ 4 ☐ 5

2 JOHN ☐ 2 John

3 JOHN ☐ 3 John

JUDE ☐ Jude

REVELATION ☐ 1 ☐ 2 ☐ 3 ☐ 4 ☐ 5 ☐ 6
☐ 7 ☐ 8 ☐ 9 ☐ 10 ☐ 11 ☐ 12 ☐ 13
☐ 14 ☐ 15 ☐ 16 ☐ 17 ☐ 18 ☐ 19 ☐ 20
☐ 21 ☐ 22

INDEX

When faced with a difficult or confusing situation, many people ask, "What would Jesus do?" in order to find answers. You'll find just those sorts of answers in this topical index. Look up a situation or topic and you'll be directed to devotions, hot topics and Scripture passages that give you answers.

A TO C

E TO G

LAZINESS
See the devotions on pages 257, 692, 1296.
See Proverbs 6:6–11; 2 Thessalonians 3:6–13;
Hebrews 6:10–12.

LEADERSHIP
See the devotions on pages 784, 910, 913, 1174, 1272.
See Numbers 14:13–25; 1 Timothy 5:17–18.

LEISURE
See the devotions on pages 81, 339, 553, 609, 692.
See Mark 7:24.
For other related material, look under Relaxation, Vacations.

LONELINESS
See the devotions on pages 5, 694, 816, 1047, 1174, 1222.
See 1 Kings 19:10–18; Mark 15:33–37;
2 Timothy 4:9–17.

LOVE
See the devotions on pages 153, 1215, 1250, 1313, 1384.
See 1 Corinthians 13; 1 John 4:17–21.

LOVE FOR ENEMIES
See the devotions on pages 724, 1313.
See 1 Samuel 24:3–7; Matthew 5:43–48; Acts 7:59–60.

LYING
See Deceiving.

MARRIAGE
See the devotions on pages 315, 478, 819, 996.
See the hot topic "Divorce."
See Ephesians 5:22–33.

MATERIALISM
See the devotions on pages 696, 713, 1015, 1354, 1396.
See the hot topic "Materialism."
For other related material, look under Values, Wealth.

MATURITY
See the devotions on pages 85, 272, 649, 1264, 1266, 1284, 1327.
See Ephesians 4:11–16; James 1:2–5; 1 Peter 2:1–5.

MEANING OF LIFE
See the devotions on pages 584, 1151, 1167, 1282, 1319.
For other related material, look under Purpose.

MERCY
See the devotion on page 1089.
See Luke 10:25–37; 1 Timothy 1:16; James 2:12–13.
For other related material, look under Forgiveness.

MORAL STANDARDS
See the devotions on pages 315, 654, 705, 816, 949, 1237.
See the hot topics "Abortion," "AIDS,"
"Date Rape," "Homosexuality."
See 1 Corinthians 6:18–20; Ephesians 5:3–7; 1 Thessalonians 4:3–8.

MOVING
See the devotions on pages 984, 998, 1047, 1219.
See Genesis 12:1–5; Psalm 139:7–10;
Daniel 1.
For other related material, look under Change.

MUSIC
See the devotions on pages 1253, 1323, 1338.
See 2 Samuel 6:12–21; Psalm 92:1–4

NATURE
See the devotions on pages 594, 1208.
See Job 38—41.
For other related material, look under Creation.

OBEDIENCE
See the devotions on pages 159, 281, 892, 1013, 1082, 1156, 1341.
See Hebrews 13:17.

OBEYING GOD
See the devotions on pages 192, 229, 336, 502, 1262, 1290, 1306.
See 1 Samuel 15:22; 1 John 2:3–6.

OBSESSION
See the devotions on pages 348, 705.
For other related material, look under Idols.

OBSTACLES
See the devotions on pages 486, 976, 1056, 1087, 1248, 1367.
See Romans 16:17.

OCCUPATION
See Vocation.

ORIGINS
See the devotions on pages 2, 529, 621, 1188, 1311, 1348.
For other related material, look under Creation, Evolution.

PARABLES
See the devotions on pages 932, 1098, 1108, 1228.
See Luke 8:9–10.

PARENTS
See the devotions on pages 15, 62, 122, 391, 680, 1243, 1304, 1384.
For other related material, look under Family Life, Home.

Hot Topic

Do you ever secretly pig out and then force yourself to throw up everything you just ate? Do you ever starve yourself for days or even weeks because you think you're too fat?

If you answered yes to either of these questions (or if you have a friend who does these things), here are some facts you need to know:

Uncommon Names for Common Problems

If you participate in the "munch a bunch—lose your lunch" routine known as bulimia or the voluntary act of self-starvation called anorexia nervosa, you are not alone. Eating disorders usually strike during the teen years and affect millions. While the majority of the victims are female, about 10 percent are male.

Bulimia can involve the eating and vomiting process, the chewing and then spitting out of food, or binge eating followed by the excessive use of laxatives. Anorexia nervosa on the other hand involves voluntary self-starvation and rigid dieting habits. While eating disorders may seem harmless, they are very serious. They cause an alarming number of deaths each year.

The Frightening Fear of Fat

Why do people become victims of eating disorders? Among the probable causes are low self-esteem, misconceptions about appearance, perfectionism, and a distorted view of sexuality. If the media says that "thin is in," it must mean that "fat is failure." Consequently, thousands of young people are literally dying to be thin. While society has declared that a person's outward appearance dictates his or her worth, the Bible declares that God looks at the heart (1 Samuel 16:7). God is far more concerned with your inner character than he is with your outer appearance (1 Peter 3:3-4).

Overcoming the Obsession With Obesity

If you are struggling with an eating disorder, you need to seek both God's help and the help of others. Consulting with your family doctor will ensure your *physical safety*. Seeking out another person—someone who will help you discover the reasons behind your eating problems—will provide the *emotional support* you need.

Eating Disorders

Hot Topic

Here Are the Chilling Facts:

One out of every three American teenagers has contemplated suicide. The number of teenage suicides has more than tripled in the last ten years.

Suicide is the second leading cause of death among young people. Only accidents cause more deaths. Some experts believe that it is really the *leading* cause—with many teen suicides incorrectly reported as accidents.

Christians are not immune. Regretfully, believers *do* commit suicide.

Why?

Those who have attempted suicide cited many reasons, among them: 1) pressure to succeed and excel; 2) confusing complexities of modern society; 3) breakdown of the family; 4) significant loss of another person; 5) drug and alcohol abuse; 6) sexual and verbal abuse; 7) isolation and loneliness; 8) depression.

Most said they felt an overwhelming sense of helplessness or hopelessness and a desire to escape the tensions of life. Others attempted suicide in order to gain someone's attention or to manipulate or punish another person.

What About Others?

If you have a friend or relative who is extremely withdrawn and depressed, here are a few suggestions to help:

• Don't ignore the problem. Talk to them openly and willingly.

• Listen more than you talk.

• Don't judge. Give support.

• Don't argue.

• Do get help.

What About Yourself?

If you are contemplating suicide or if thoughts of killing yourself are in your mind constantly, *get help*. Suicide is a very permanent answer to what is probably a temporary problem. Your negative feelings may not seem temporary, but hang on. Help is available so that you can face your problems and go forward to enjoy life.

Suicide

Hot Topic

An Easy Solution to a Difficult Problem?

In many states a girl under the age of seventeen or eighteen must have her parents' permission to go on a school-sponsored class trip, donate blood or have her teeth pulled. But in those same states she may have an abortion without her parents' consent or knowledge. The U.S. courts have declared that any female—regardless of age, with or without her parents' consent and sometimes even without their knowledge—has the legal right to an abortion.

The Fetus: Valuable Person or Disposable Tissue?

More than 26 million times women have chosen abortion as a way to terminate a pregnancy since the landmark 1973 U.S. Supreme Court Roe v. Wade. Many people make the pregnant woman's rights the only rights to be considered in the abortion controversy. But the rights of the fetus must also be considered. The crucial question remains: Is a fetus a human being to be protected or simply a piece of tissue that can be discarded? While opinions are mixed and heated on the issue, both scientific and Biblical facts indicate that the unborn child is a person, not just a piece of tissue.

The Scientific Argument

Genetic studies indicate that even though unborn children are dependent on the women carrying them, they actually are separate and unique entities. At the moment of conception, the characteristics of a new individual are fixed. This tiny being is not an extension of a woman's body but is a unique biological unit within her womb.

The Biblical Argument

In Scripture the same Greek and Hebrew words refer to fetus, infant or young child. The Bible states that humans are knit together by God while yet in their mothers' wombs (Psalm 139:13), and unborn children share in the sinful nature of the human race (Psalm 51:5). In many instances the Bible refers to God's protection in the development of the unborn child: Job 31:15; Psalm 22:10; Isaiah 44:2,24; Jeremiah 1:5.

The Verdict?

While it may appear to be a convenient way to avoid the consequences of an unwanted pregnancy, abortion is actually the ending of an innocent human life. If you or one of your friends is considering an abortion, please think again. Abortion may be legal, and it may appear to be the easy way out. But it is *not* the right choice.

Abortion

Hot Topic

It has infected people from all walks of life. Teachers. Factory workers. Movie stars. Teenagers. Basketball stars. Even newborn babies. It eventually kills 100 percent of those infected. It is a deadly epidemic that is sweeping the globe. It is AIDS, auto-immune deficiency syndrome.

Prevention

Researchers agree that by far the majority of AIDS infections are caused by engaging in promiscuous sex (whether homosexual or heterosexual) or by sharing a dirty needle when using drugs. A small percentage of victims have been infected by receiving contaminated blood or by being the spouse or child of an infected person. Therefore, most doctors now agree that by abstaining from premarital sex and remaining faithful after marriage, one can radically reduce the chances of contracting the AIDS virus.

Education

Often today's AIDS education promotes what is called "safe sex." But there is really no such thing. The failure rate of condoms, the most commonly mentioned form of protection, is alarmingly high . . . and far from safe. Also, the argument for "safe sex" ignores a critical point: The only truly safe sex is sex according to God's standard—to one sexual partner (of the opposite sex) for life in marriage. God's pattern for sexual expression has been beautifully proven to be best by millions of faithful married couples, non-Christian as well as Christian. Sexual purity is what God's Word has always commanded (1 Corinthians 6:9,18; Colossians 3:5).

Compassion

AIDS victims don't deserve to be treated like modern-day lepers. As God's people we know the love and compassion and forgiveness of Christ. We must show that same love and compassion and forgiveness to these desperate and dying individuals. We must pray for and reach out to those who have nowhere else to turn. We must pray for a cure. If we Christians are callous and insensitive toward those with AIDS, we are no better than the self-righteous Pharisees of Jesus' day, who looked with contempt on society's sick and wretched. (See John 8:1-11, Mark 1:40-42, and Mark 2:13-17 for examples of how Jesus treated the helpless and hopeless.).

Hot Topic

Once upon a time divorce was a dirty word. Today some people change marriage partners like they change clothes. In fact, recent statistics show that one divorce occurs for every two marriages. Even Christian couples are breaking up. What in the world is happening?

Not God's Ideal:

The Bible condemns divorce in the strongest possible terms: "'I hate divorce,' says the LORD God of Israel" (Malachi 2:16).

It has always been God's plan for married couples to stay together until death. Marriage binds a couple together in a unique way (Genesis 2:24). Jesus noted this and added, "What God has joined together, let man not separate" (Matthew 19:6).

Different Views:

Christians are divided over the divorce issue. Some, citing Jesus' words above, believe that divorce is wrong in all cases (Matthew 19:6). Others argue that divorce is allowable only when sexual immorality is involved (Matthew 19:9). Still others offer less strict interpretations. And the argument goes on.

Steps to Take:

Divorce is a complicated and painful issue. Perhaps you live in a home that has experienced a failed marriage. Maybe you have friends in that situation. Whatever the case, there are several things you can do.

Study what God has to say: Matthew 5:32; 1 Corinthians 7:10-15; Ephesians 5:22-23. Pray that he will help you determine if divorce is ever acceptable for a Christian.

Be reminded of God's faithfulness and love during painful family times (Psalm 30).

Do some reading about how to deal with conflict, what to look for in a partner, and how to build strong relationships. Begin to pray today for your future partner. In a world that has forgotten what it means to be committed, ask God for his amazing grace, so that you and your future partner will stay married for life.

$ Hot Topic

We live in a material world where we are constantly confronted with new items and are told, "You've got to have this." Deep down we think, "If only I could drive this car [wear those clothes, have that gadget, live in such-and-such a house—take your pick], then I'd be happy." We think and act as though material goods will bring us the satisfaction we desire.

Is this the way believers in Christ should live? What does God say about material possessions?

Material Wealth in the Bible

By scanning the pages of Scripture, we find that many of the people used by God were wealthy (Abraham, David, Job). The Bible also acknowledges God as the source of wealth. He owns everything (Psalm 24:1), he gives wealth (Genesis 26:12-13; Deuteronomy 8:16-18), and he decides who will be rich and poor (1 Samuel 2:7). However, Paul *carefully* pointed out that "we brought nothing into the world, and we can take nothing out of it" (1 Timothy 6:7). So, no matter how many possessions we might accumulate, we can't take them with us when we die.

Jesus and Materialism

Jesus told his followers to store up treasures in heaven rather than treasures on earth. His reasoning was clear—worldly wealth is only temporary, while heavenly treasure is eternal (Matthew 6:19-21) and can never be lost.

Jesus understood that what we value in life will determine our direction in life. When we value earthly things and invest in them, our focus is on the material world. On the other hand, when we concentrate our time, energy and resources on eternal investments, we are more concerned with the things of God.

As a follower of Christ:

- What possessions matter most to you?

- How would you react if you lost those possessions?

- Are you investing in what can be *lost* or in what will always *last*?

- "For where your treasure is, there your heart will be also" (Matthew 6:21).

Materialism

Hot Topic

Date and Rape

The terms just shouldn't go together. And yet, alarming numbers of people are going out on "friendly" dates and coming home as rape victims. Date rape is a huge problem that stems from two perversions:

A Perverted Purpose in Life

For many, "having sex" has replaced "having relationships." Make no mistake: The Bible says that sex is important (Hebrews 13:4), but it is to take place in the context of marriage and love, not lust and violence.

A Perverted View of Others

The date rapist sees the date as a sexual object, someone to be used to satisfy physical desires without any real concern for the other person involved. Rape is a violent act of total selfishness.

When surveyed, an alarming number of young teens (over half) thought it would be acceptable for a person to force a date to have sex if they had been going together for more than six months. Contrast this with how God views men and women— made in his image (Genesis 1:27) and deserving of respect (Philippians 2:3-4).

Rape Versus Love

Forced sex has nothing to do with real love. In 2 Samuel 13 the Bible tells of a time when Amnon attempted to seduce his half-sister Tamar. When she refused, he raped her. What happened next is all too familiar in cases of forced sex. "Then Amnon hated her with intense hatred. In fact, he hated her more than he had loved her" (2 Samuel 13:15).

Getting Help

If you have been violated sexually on a date, please . . . talk to a trusted Christian adult—a parent, pastor or counselor. He or she will help determine what steps to take in regard to your attacker as well as find the help you need to deal with your pain.

If you have ever forced a date to have sex with you, you have committed date rape. Rape is a sin and a crime; it leaves long-lasting scars. Until you acknowledge what you have done, you stand guilty before God. Don't delay a minute. Go to God and ask for his forgiveness. He will cast your sins to the bottom of the sea (Micah 7:19). Then ask forgiveness from the person you violated. And last but not least, seek help. A counselor can help you discover why you feel this temptation, and God will give you the strength to overcome in the future (Philippians 4:13).

Hot Topic

In the last decade homosexuality has come out of the "closet." Homosexuals have their own communities, their own magazines and newspapers, even their own churches. But if you think that it hasn't as yet touched your church, you're probably wrong. If you attend a church that has more than fifty members, chances are someone in your church is struggling with homosexuality. This issue is one that we as Christians need to face in a compassionate and straightforward manner.

The Facts

Opinions vary greatly on the causes behind homosexuality. Some people say it's purely a matter of genetic orientation. Others say it is purely a matter of choice. The past experiences of homosexuals do, however, reveal several consistent patterns. Most homosexuals had difficulty bonding with their parent of the same sex. Many experienced some form of sexual abuse in the past. Rejection by their peers also impacted many homosexuals, especially being labeled by their peers as "queer" or "faggot" or "dyke."

God's Word speaks plainly on the issue of homosexual behavior. It condemns it in strong language: "Do not be deceived: Neither the sexually immoral nor idolaters . . . nor homosexual offenders . . . will inherit the kingdom of God" (1 Corinthians 6:9-10; see also Leviticus 18:22; Romans 1:26-27).

The Hope

God's Word may condemn homosexual behavior as sin, but it doesn't leave the homosexual in that sin with no hope. Paul condemns homosexual behavior, as well as many other sinful acts, in 1 Corinthians 6:9-10. But then in verse 11 he moves on to say: "And that is what some of you were." Did you catch that? The writer Paul knew that some of the members of the Corinthian church were former homosexuals! But they were also "washed . . . sanctified . . . justified in the name of the Lord Jesus Christ and by the Spirit of our God."

Conclusion

If you or someone you know is struggling with homosexual tendencies, don't give up. There is hope. God has promised "hope and a future" (Jeremiah 29:11) to every Christian. You can contact Exodus International, PO Box 77652, Seattle, WA 98177 (206) 784-7799 for information and help.

Homo Sexuality